One-Stop Internet Resources

Log on to tav.glencoe.com

ONLINE STUDY TOOLS

- Chapter Overviews
- Interactive Tutor
- Self-Check Quizzes
- E-Flashcards

ONLINE RESEARCH

- Student Web Activities
- Web Resources
- Current Events
- State Resources
- Beyond the Textbook Features

ONLINE STUDENT EDITION

- Complete Interactive Student Edition
- Textbook Updates

FOR TEACHERS

- Teacher Forum
- Web Activity Lesson Plans
- Literature Connections

Honoring America

For Americans, the flag has always had a special meaning. It is a symbol of our nation's freedom and democracy.

Flag Etiquette

Over the years, Americans have developed rules and customs concerning the use and display of the flag. One of the most important things every American should remember is to treat the flag with respect.

- The flag should be raised and lowered by hand and displayed only from sunrise to sunset. On special occasions, the flag may be displayed at night, but it should be illuminated.

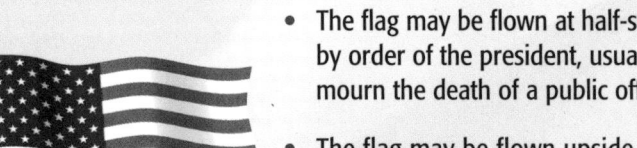

- The flag may be displayed on all days, weather permitting, particularly on national and state holidays and on historic and special occasions.

- No flag may be flown above the American flag or to the right of it at the same height.

- The flag should never touch the ground or floor beneath it.

- The flag may be flown at half-staff by order of the president, usually to mourn the death of a public official.

- The flag may be flown upside down only to signal distress.

- The flag should never be carried flat or horizontally, but always carried aloft and free.

- When the flag becomes old and tattered, it should be destroyed by burning. According to an approved custom, the Union (stars on blue field) is first cut from the flag; then the two pieces, which no longer form a flag, are burned.

The American's Creed

I believe in the United States of America as a Government of the people, by the people, for the people, whose just powers are derived from the consent of the governed; a democracy in a republic; a sovereign Nation of many sovereign States; a perfect union, one and inseparable; established upon those principles of freedom, equality, justice, and humanity for which American patriots sacrificed their lives and fortunes.

I therefore believe it is my duty to my Country to love it; to support its Constitution; to obey its laws; to respect its flag, and to defend it against all enemies.

The Pledge of Allegiance

I pledge allegiance to the Flag of the United States of America and to the Republic for which it stands, one Nation under God, indivisible, with liberty and justice for all.

New York
Edition

The American Vision

Joyce Appleby, Ph.D.

Alan Brinkley, Ph.D.

Albert S. Broussard, Ph.D.

James M. McPherson, Ph.D.

Donald A. Ritchie, Ph.D.

NATIONAL
GEOGRAPHIC

Mc Graw Hill **Glencoe**

New York, New York   Columbus, Ohio   Chicago, Illinois   Peoria, Illinois   Woodland Hills, California

Joyce Appleby, Ph.D., is Professor of History at UCLA. Dr. Appleby's published works include *Inheriting the Revolution: The First Generation of Americans; Capitalism and a New Social Order: The Jeffersonian Vision of the 1790s;* and *Ideology and Economic Thought in Seventeenth-Century England,* which won the Berkshire Prize. She served as president of both the Organization of American Historians and the American Historical Association, and chaired the Council of the Institute of Early American History and Culture at Williamsburg. Dr. Appleby has been elected to the American Philosophical Society and the American Academy of Arts and Sciences, and is a Corresponding Fellow of the British Academy.

Alan Brinkley, Ph.D., is Allan Nevins Professor of American History at Columbia University. His published works include *Voices of Protest: Huey Long, Father Coughlin, and the Great Depression,* which won the 1983 National Book Award; *The End of Reform: New Deal Liberalism in Recession and War; The Unfinished Nation: A Concise History of the American People;* and *Liberalism and its Discontents.* He received the Levenson Memorial Teaching Prize at Harvard University.

Albert S. Broussard, Ph.D., is Professor of History and Graduate Coordinator at Texas A&M University. Before joining the Texas A&M faculty, Dr. Broussard was Assistant Professor of History and Director of the African American Studies Program at Southern Methodist University. Among his publications are the books *Black San Francisco: The Struggle for Racial Equality in the West, 1900–1954* and *African American Odyssey: The Stewarts, 1853–1963.* Dr. Broussard has also served as president of the Oral History Association.

James M. McPherson, Ph.D., is George Henry Davis Professor of American History at Princeton University. Dr. McPherson is the author of 11 books about the Civil War era. These include *Battle Cry of Freedom: The Civil War Era,* for which he won the Pulitzer Prize in 1989, and *For Cause and Comrades: Why Men Fought in the Civil War,* for which he won the 1998 Lincoln Prize. He is a member of many professional historical associations, including the Civil War Preservation Trust.

Donald A. Ritchie, Ph.D., is Associate Historian of the United States Senate Historical Office. Dr. Ritchie received his doctorate in American history from the University of Maryland after service in the U.S. Marine Corps. He has taught American history at various levels, from high school to university. He edits the Historical Series of the Senate Foreign Relations Committee and is the author of several books, including *Doing Oral History, The Oxford Guide to the United States Government,* and *Press Gallery: Congress and the Washington Correspondents,* which received the Organization of American Historians Richard W. Leopold Prize. Dr. Ritchie has served as president of the Oral History Association and as a council member of the American Historical Association.

The National Geographic Society, founded in 1888 for the increase and diffusion of geographic knowledge, is the world's largest nonprofit scientific and educational organization. Since its earliest days, the Society has used sophisticated communication technologies, from color photography to holography, to convey knowledge to its worldwide membership. The School Publishing Division supports the Society's mission by developing innovative educational programs—ranging from traditional print materials to multimedia programs including CD-ROMs, videodiscs, and software. "National Geographic Geography & History," featured in each unit of this textbook, and "National Geographic Moment in Time," featured in chapters 8–29 of this textbook, were designed and developed by the National Geographic Society's School Publishing Division.

About the Cover See page 1135 for a complete explanation of the cover images.

Glencoe

The McGraw·Hill Companies

National Geographic Geography & History and Moment in History © 2006 by the National Geographic Society. The name "National Geographic Society" and the "Yellow Border Rectangle" are trademarks of the Society, and their use without prior written permission is strictly prohibited.

TIME Notebook © by TIME, Inc. Prepared by TIME School Publishing in collaboration with Glencoe/McGraw-Hill.

Send all inquiries to: Glencoe/McGraw-Hill, 8787 Orion Place, Columbus, OH 43240-4027

ISBN 0-07-873459-2 (Student Edition), ISBN 0-07-868695-4 (Teacher Wraparound Edition)

Printed in the United States of America.

1 2 3 4 5 6 027/055 09 08 07 06 05

New York Advisory Board

Contributors

Robert Dytell
President
New York State Council for Social Studies
Jericho, New York

Barbara Rosenberg
Consultant
Westchester Teaching Consultants
Millwood, New York

Reviewers

Levi Anthony
Social Studies Teacher
Information Technology High School
New York City, New York

Charles R. Coon
Adjunct Professor of American History
SUNY College at Cortland
Cortland, New York
Social Studies Teacher (Retired)
Baker High School
Baldwinsville, New York

Robbin DeHollander
Social Studies Teacher
Monroe High School
Rochester, New York

Alice Grant
Educational Consultant
Social Studies Chairperson (Retired)
Pelham Memorial High School
Pelham, New York

Virginia Mancini
K–12 Social Studies Chairperson
Pleasantville School District
Pleasantville, New York

Carol Maurer
Social Studies Department Chairperson
Rye Neck High School
Mamaroneck, New York

Joy M. Miller
Social Studies Teacher
Fairport High School
Fairport, New York

Patricia H. Ponzi
Social Studies Teacher
Bay Shore Schools
Bay Shore, New York
Adjunct Professor of Education
Dowling College
Oakdale, New York

Stuart Rubin
Social Studies Chairperson (Retired)
W.C. Mepham High School
Bellmore, New York

Mr. Steve Schockow
Social Studies Contact Teacher
Dake Junior High School
West Irondequoit Schools
Rochester, New York

Academic Consultants

Richard G. Boehm
Professor of Geography
Southwest Texas State University
San Marcos, Texas

Gloria Contreras
Professor, Department of Teacher Education
and Administration
University of North Texas
Denton, Texas

Frank de Varona
Visiting Associate Professor
Department of Curriculum and Instruction
Florida International University
Miami, Florida

Larry Elowitz
Carl Vinson Professor of Political Science
Georgia College and State University
Milledgeville, Georgia

Susan Hartmann
Professor of American Women's History
The Ohio State University
Columbus, Ohio

Cole C. Kingseed
Professor of Military History
United States Military Academy
at West Point
West Point, New York

David E. Maas
Professor of History
Wheaton College
Wheaton, Illinois

William E. Nelson, Jr.
Research Professor of Black Studies and Professor of
Political Science
The Ohio State University
Columbus, Ohio

Bernard Reich
Professor of Political Science and
International Affairs
George Washington University
Washington, D.C.

Calbert A. Seciwa
Director, American Indian Institute
Arizona State University
Tempe, Arizona

Athan Theoharis
Professor of History
Marquette University
Milwaukee, Wisconsin

Mark Van Ells
Professor of History
Queensborough Community College
New York, New York

Teacher Reviewers

Ann T. Ackerman
Teacher
Nashua High School
Nashua, New Hampshire

Susan Andrew
Teacher
Gadsden High School
Gadsden, Alabama

Jack Bovee
Coordinator, K–12 Social Studies
Collier County School District
Naples, Florida

Edward Brickner
Social Studies Teacher
Woodbury High School
Prescott, Wisconsin

P. Nathan Collins
Social Studies Teacher
Buffalo Gap High School
Swoope, Virginia

Carmen Crosse
Teacher and Department Head
Socorro High School
Socorro Independent School
District
El Paso, Texas

John R. Doyle
Administrative Director, Division of Social Sciences
Miami-Dade County Public Schools
Miami, Florida

Bruce L. Eddy
Teacher, History and Social Science Department
Evanston Township High School
Evanston, Illinois

Debra B. Elarbee
Social Studies Chairperson/ Teacher
Central High School
Carrollton, Georgia

George W. Henry, Jr.
History Teacher
Rowland Hall St. Mark's School
Salt Lake City, Utah

Tom S. Hodge
Teacher
Clay-Chalkville High School
Pinson, Alabama

Marjorie B. Hollowell
Social Studies Teacher
John A. Holmes High School
Edenton, North Carolina

Merle Knight
Emeritus Social Studies Teacher and
Coordinator of Social Studies
Department
Lewis S. Mills High School
Torrington, Connecticut

Tom Laichas
History Teacher
Crossroads School
Santa Monica, California

Denny Shillings
Social Studies Teacher
Homewood Flossmoor High School
Flossmoor, Illinois

Julia Ann Stodghill
Social Studies Teacher
Troup County Comprehensive
High School
Lagrange, Georgia

Steve Swett
History Teacher
Hingham High School
Hingham, Massachusetts

James Wolfe
History Teacher and Department Chair
Suitland High School
Forrestville, Maryland

A Note From the Authors

Welcome to United States History and *The American Vision*. We have written this text with several goals in mind. First, we want you to succeed in this course. We also want you to succeed on the New York Regents Examination. To help you, we have provided the New York Core Curriculum for United States History and Government, which tells you what you are expected to learn throughout the school year. As you study American history, pay attention to the curriculum and be prepared to become a successful student!

This section of your book contains the following:

New York Core Curriculum for
U.S. History and Government **NY6**

How Does *The American Vision*
Help Me Learn the Curriculum? **NY29**

Keys to Succeeding on the
Regents Exam **NY30**

How Does *The American Vision* Help Me
Succeed on the Regents Exam? **NY33**

Countdown to the New York
Regents Exam **NY62**

A Guide to Students and Parents

How do I succeed in United States History?

Welcome to United States History Studies and to Glencoe's *The American Vision.* The content of this course focuses on the political, economic, and social events that have shaped the United States. You will be viewing and interpreting periods in U.S. history from various perspectives, including historical, geographic, political, economic, and cultural. Together, these perspectives can help you to understand how the past has led to our present and to appreciate your role in shaping our future.

Your textbook includes a variety of tools designed to help you be successful as you study U.S. history. One of the most valuable of these is a list of the objectives that you will be expected to master by the end of the school year. This list is called the New York Core Curriculum and you can find it on pages NY8–NY28 of this book.

Knowing what you are expected to learn from the very beginning of the year will help focus your study of U.S. history. It will also help you and your parents or caregivers see when you might need extra help in mastering the concepts of a particular unit of study. Such extra help will ensure that your study of U.S. history will be both enjoyable and successful.

Image 100 Ltd.

What is the New York Core Curriculum for Social Studies?

The New York State Education Department developed the New York State Social Studies Core Curriculum to help measure your achievement of the learning standards for social studies. In high school, an important part of your course work in social studies will be the study of United States history and government. The purpose of the curriculum is to provide you, the student, with expectations for achievement in New York. These standards represent the knowledge and skills you will need to be successful on the Regents Exam.

Why does the New York Core Curriculum matter to me?

The New York Core Curriculum is a list of things you should learn and be able to do as you take the course. Your teachers base their lessons and tests on the Core Curriculum.

So, to be successful in this course, you may want to read over the curriculum with your parents or caregivers (see the list on pages NY8–NY28).

Although some of the material may not be familiar to you at first, you and your family can outline some steps to take to achieve proficiency. As you take this course, review the curriculum from time to time to help the things you are learning fall into place.

What is included on the following pages?

New York Core Curriculum for U.S. History and Government

- Pages NY8–NY28 include a listing of the New York Core Curriculum for this course.

- Turn to page NY29 to see how Glencoe's *The American Vision* will help you learn the curriculum and be successful in this course.

Keys to succeeding on the Regents Exam

- Page NY30 includes an explanation of the Regents Examination that you will take when you complete your course work.

- Turn to page NY33 to see how Glencoe's *The American Vision* will help you succeed on the Regents Exam.

▼ **The Statue of Liberty at Sunset**

Photodisc

UNIT ONE: INTRODUCTION

I. Geography

A. The physical/cultural setting in the Americas

1. Size and location
2. Major zones/areas
3. Factors that shaped the identity of the United States
4. Barriers to expansion/development

B. Role/influence of geography on historical/cultural development

1. Influences on early Native American Indians
2. Influence on colonization patterns and colonial development
3. Territorial expansion
4. Impact during wartime
5. Effect of location on United States foreign policy

C. Geographic issues today

1. Waste disposal
2. Water/air pollution
3. Shifting populations
4. Energy usage
5. Urban problems/challenges

D. Demographics

1. Characteristics
2. Immigration
3. Migration
4. Population relationships/trends since 1865
5. Current issues

▼ **New York City from the Empire State building**

UNIT TWO: CONSTITUTIONAL FOUNDATIONS FOR THE UNITED STATES DEMOCRATIC REPUBLIC

I. *The Constitution: The Foundation of American Society*

A. Historical foundations

1. 17th- and 18th-century Enlightenment thought
2. The peoples and peopling of the American colonies (voluntary and involuntary)
3. Colonial experience: political rights and mercantile relationships
4. The Revolutionary War and the Declaration of Independence
5. New York State Constitution based on republican principles
6. Articles of Confederation
7. Northwest Ordinance

B. Constitutional Convention

1. Representation and process
2. Conflict and compromise: seeking effective institutions
3. The document: structure of government
4. Ratification

C. The Bill of Rights

D. Basic structure and function: three branches and their operation

E. Basic constitutional principles

Photodisc

F. Implementing the new constitutional principles

1. Creating domestic stability through sound financial policies: Hamilton's financial plans

2. Development of unwritten constitutional government under Washington, Adams, and Jefferson: cabinet, political parties, judicial review, executive and Congressional interpretation, lobbying; the Marshall Court

3. Establishing a stable political system

4. Neutrality and national security, Washington through Monroe: foreign affairs, establishing boundaries

II. The Constitution Tested: Nationalism and Sectionalism

A. Factors unifying the United States, 1789–1861

1. The first and second two-party systems

2. The market economy and interstate commerce

3. The Marshall Court

B. Constitutional stress and crisis

1. Developing sectional differences and philosophies of government
2. Equal rights and justice: expansion of franchise; search for minority rights; expansion of slavery; abolitionist movement; the underground railroad; denial of Native American Indian rights and land ownership
3. The great constitutional debates: states' rights versus federal supremacy (nullification); efforts to address slavery issue (Missouri Compromise, Compromise of 1850, fugitive slave law, *Dred Scott* v. *Sanford*, 1857); preservation of the Union

C. Territorial expansion through diplomacy, migration, annexation, and war; Manifest Destiny

1. The Louisiana Purchase
2. Exploring and settling the West (explorers, Lewis and Clark expedition, naturalists, trappers and traders, trailblazers, missionaries, pioneers, the Mormon Church)
3. The Spanish, Mexican, and Native American West
4. Motives for and implications of expansion and western settlement
5. Politics of western expansion (Manifest Destiny, the Texas and Oregon questions, the Mexican War)
6. Impact of western expansion upon Mexicans and Native Americans

▼ **Harbor in Buffalo, New York**

© Royalty-Free/CORBIS

D. The Constitution in jeopardy: The American Civil War

1. United States society divided
2. Wartime actions

UNIT THREE: INDUSTRIALIZATION OF THE UNITED STATES

I. The Reconstructed Nation

A. Reconstruction plans

1. Lincoln's plan
2. Congressional Reconstruction
3. Post-Civil War amendments (13th, 14th, and 15th)
4. Impeachment of Andrew Johnson
5. The reconstructed nation and shifting relationships between the federal government, state governments, and individual citizens

B. The North

1. Economic and technological impacts of the Civil War
2. Expanding world markets
3. Developing labor needs

C. The New South

1. Agriculture: land and labor (sharecropping and tenant farming)
2. Status of freedmen
3. Struggle for political control in the New South
4. Supreme Court interpretations of the 13th and 14th amendments (*Civil Rights Cases*, 1883)
5. The emerging debate over "proper" role of African-Americans

D. End of Reconstruction

1. Disputed election of 1876
2. End of military occupation
3. Restoration of white control in the South (1870s and 1880s) and abridgment of rights of freed African-Americans
4. *Plessy* v. *Ferguson*, 1896: "separate but equal"

E. The Impact of the Civil War and Reconstruction: Summary

1. On political alignments
2. On the nature of citizenship
3. On federal-state relations
4. On the development of the North as an industrial power
5. On American society

II. The Rise of American Business, Industry, and Labor, 1865–1920

A. Economic transformation and the "search for order"

1. Business response to change: organize and rationalize
2. Organizational responses

B. Major areas of growth in business and industry

1. Transportation: railroads and automobiles; urban transportation
2. Building materials: steel
3. Energy sources: coal, oil, electricity
4. Communications: telegraph, telephone

C. Representative entrepreneurs: Case studies in concentrated wealth and effort

1. John D. Rockefeller: oil; Andrew Carnegie: steel; Ford: auto
2. Work ethic: Cotton Mather to Horatio Alger
3. Conflict between public good and private gain, e.g., use of resources

▼ **Field and mountains**

Photodisc

D. New business and government practices: Popular and government responses

1. Laissez-faire and government support; interpretation of 14th Amendment by Supreme Court

2. Railroad "pooling": rate inequities (*Wabash, St. Louis, and Pacific Railway* v. *Illinois*, 1886); railroad regulation: state and national ICC

3. Competition and absorption; mergers and trusts; Sherman Antitrust Act, 1890 (*United States* v. *E.C. Knight*, 1895)

E. Labor's response to economic change: Organize

1. Efforts at national labor unions: Knights of Labor (1869); AF of L (1881–1886); ILGWU (1900)

2. Struggle and conflict

F. Agrarian response to economic change: Organize and protest

▼ **Midtown Manhattan skyline, New York City**

Comstock Images

III. *Adjusting Society to Industrialism: American People and Places*

A. Impact of industrialization

1. Urban growth
2. Work and workers
3. Women, families, and work
4. The growing middle class (consumerism and its material benefits and effects)
5. Art and literature (Mark Twain and penny dailies)

B. Immigration, 1850–1924

1. New sources: eastern/southern Europe; Asia—the "new ethnicity"
2. The impulses abroad
3. The attractions here: labor shortages, liberty, and freedoms
4. Urbanization: ghettos
5. "Americanization" process
6. Impacts on family, religion, education, and politics
7. Contributions to American society

▼ **Niagara Falls**

© Royalty-Free/CORBIS

C. Reactions to the "new" immigration

1. Cultural pluralism: assimilation (Americanization), acculturation ("melting pot" or cultural pluralism), or both
2. Nativist reactions: stereotyping and prejudice
3. Impact on African-Americans and other established minorities
4. "Yellow Peril," West Coast restrictions
5. Literacy testing, 1917
6. The Red Scare
7. Quota acts of 1921 and 1924

D. The frontier (1850–1890)

1. Land west of the Mississippi
2. The impact of industrialization
3. Native American Indians

▼ Taxi in Times Square, New York City

© Royalty-Free/CORBIS

UNIT FOUR: THE PROGRESSIVE MOVEMENT: RESPONSES TO THE CHALLENGES BROUGHT ABOUT BY INDUSTRIALIZATION AND URBANIZATION

I. Reform in America

A. Pressures for reform

1. Progressives supported the use of government power for different reform purposes
2. Effects of developing technologies and their social, ethical, and moral impacts
3. Struggle of fair standards of business operation and working conditions (*Lochner* v. *New York*, 1905; *Muller* v. *Oregon*, 1908)
4. Increasing inequities between wealth and poverty
5. Rising power and influence of the middle class

B. Progress: Social and economic reform and consumer protection

1. The "Muckrakers" and reform
2. Other areas of concern

©Royalty-Free/CORBIS

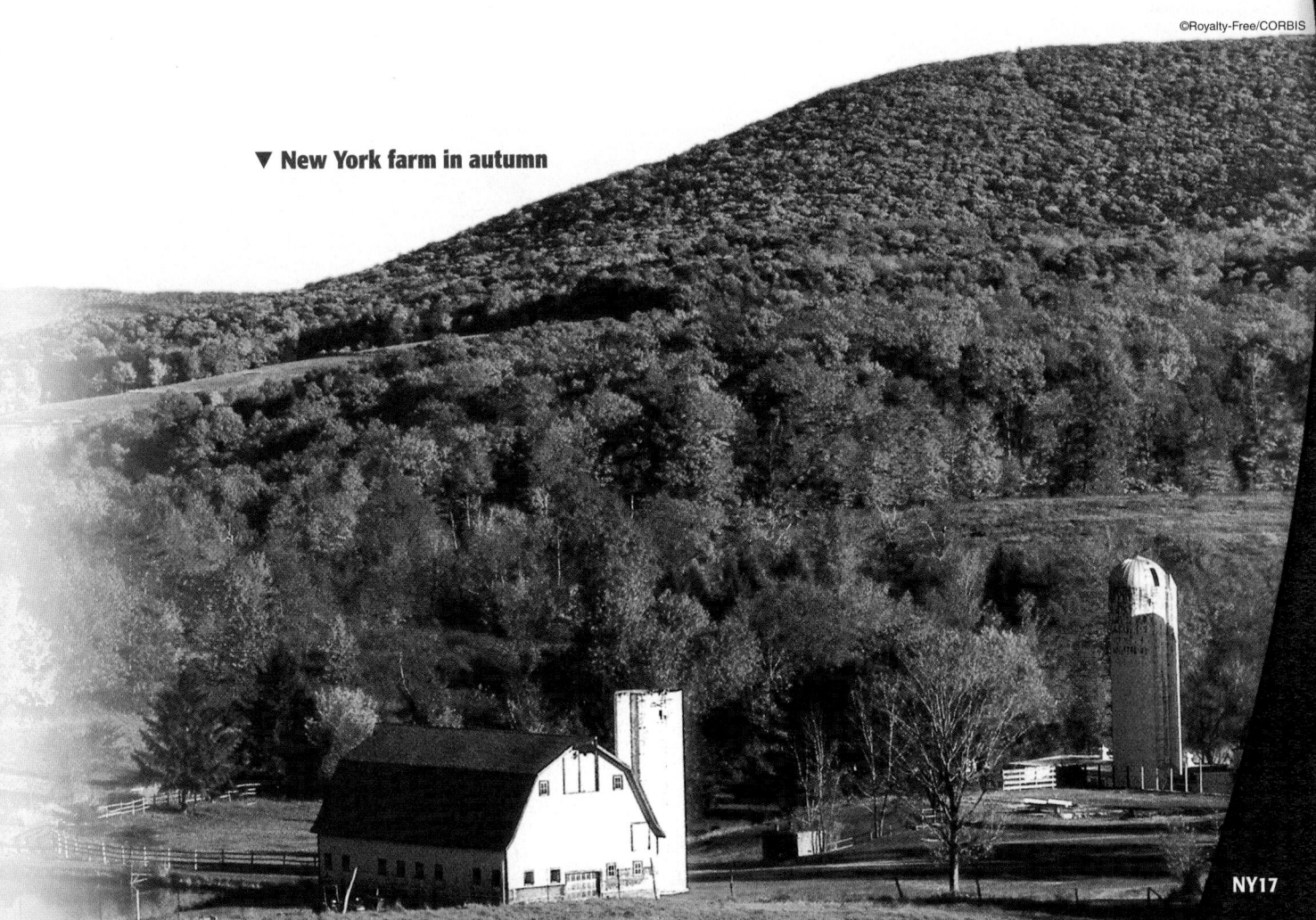

▼ New York farm in autumn

C. Progressivism and government action

1. Emerging Progressive movement: political reform
2. Theodore Roosevelt and the Square Deal
3. Conservation
4. Woodrow Wilson and the New Freedom
5. World War I: effect on domestic reform

II. The Rise of American Power

A. An emerging global involvement

1. From old diplomacy to new, 1865–1900
2. Other Pacific overtures
3. Imperialism: the Spanish-American War
4. Latin American affairs

B. Restraint and involvement: 1914–1920

1. United States involvement

▼ **Trees by Hunn's Lake in winter**

© Royalty-Free/CORBIS

C. Wartime constitutional issues

1. War opposition and patriotism: the draft issue
2. Espionage and Sedition acts
3. *Schenck* v. *United States,* 1919; clear and present danger doctrine
4. Red Scare, 1918–1919

D. The search for peace and arms control: 1914–1930

1. The peace movement: Women's International League for Peace and Freedom
2. War aims: The Fourteen Points
3. Treaty of Versailles: Wilson's role

▼ **Buildings in New York City's Chinatown**

Photodisc

4. League of Nations: Henry Cabot Lodge and the United States Senate rejection

5. Washington Naval Disarmament Conference (1920s)

6. Reparations and war debts (United States as a world banker)

7. Kellogg-Briand Pact (1928)

8. Establishment of the World Court

UNIT FIVE: AT HOME AND ABROAD: PROSPERITY AND DEPRESSION, 1917–1940

I. War and Prosperity: 1917–1929

A. Impact of war

1. War's effects on gender roles, on African-Americans, and other minority groups

2. Case study: Movement of African-Americans from the South to northern cities

3. Return to "normalcy": 1918–1921

▼ Ellis Island Immigra[tion] Museum, New York

B. The twenties: Business boom or false prosperity?

1. Post-World War I recession
2. Avarice and scandal: Teapot Dome
3. Coolidge prosperity; not for everyone
4. Problems on the farm
5. Speculative boom: the "big bull market"

C. Mass consumption and the clash of cultural values

1. Mass consumption
2. Constitutional and legal issues
3. Shifting cultural values

II. The Great Depression

A. Onset of the Depression

1. Weakness in the economy
2. The stock market crash
3. The Hoover response
4. Unemployment, the Bonus Army, Hoovervilles; impact on women and minorities

B. Franklin D. Roosevelt and the New Deal: Relief, recovery, and reform programs

1. Relief of human suffering
2. Recovery of the United States economy
3. Search for effective reform (program examples)
4. Labor's response: Formation of CIO
5. Controversial aspects of the New Deal
6. The human factor
7. Culture of the Depression
8. Opposition to the New Deal: Al Smith, Norman Thomas, Huey Long, Father Coughlin, Dr. Townsend

UNIT SIX: THE UNITED STATES IN AN AGE OF GLOBAL CRISIS: RESPONSIBILITY AND COOPERATION

I. Peace in Peril: 1933–1950

A. Isolation and neutrality
1. Causes of disillusion and pacifism
2. Neutrality Acts of 1935–37
3. Spanish Civil War: testing war technology and ideology
4. FDR's "quarantine" speech (1937)

B. Failure of peace; triumph of aggression
1. Aggressions of Japan, Germany, Italy: 1932–1940
2. Appeasement: The Munich Conference (1938)
3. German attack on Poland; start of World War II in Europe
4. Gradual United States involvement

C. The United States in World War II
1. Pearl Harbor
2. The human dimensions of the war
3. Allied strategy and leadership
4. The atomic bomb
5. The war's impact on minorities
6. Demobilization

▼ Tenement apartments, New York City

© Royalty-Free/CORBIS

II. Peace with Problems: 1945–1960

A. International peace efforts

1. Formation of the United Nations
2. United Nations Universal Declaration of Human Rights
3. Displaced persons: refugee efforts

B. Expansion and containment: Europe

1. Summitry: Yalta and Potsdam, establishing "spheres of influence"
2. The Iron Curtain: Winston Churchill
3. Postwar uses for United States power

C. Containment in Asia, Africa, and Latin America

1. The United States and Japan
2. The United States and China
3. USSR tests an A-bomb (1949)
4. The "hot war" in Asia: Korean War
5. Point four aid: Africa, Asia, Latin America

D. The Cold War at home

1. Truman and government loyalty checks

   Case studies: The Smith Act and the House Un-American Activities Committee (*Watkins* v. *United States*, 1957); the Alger Hiss case (1950); the Rosenberg trial (1950)

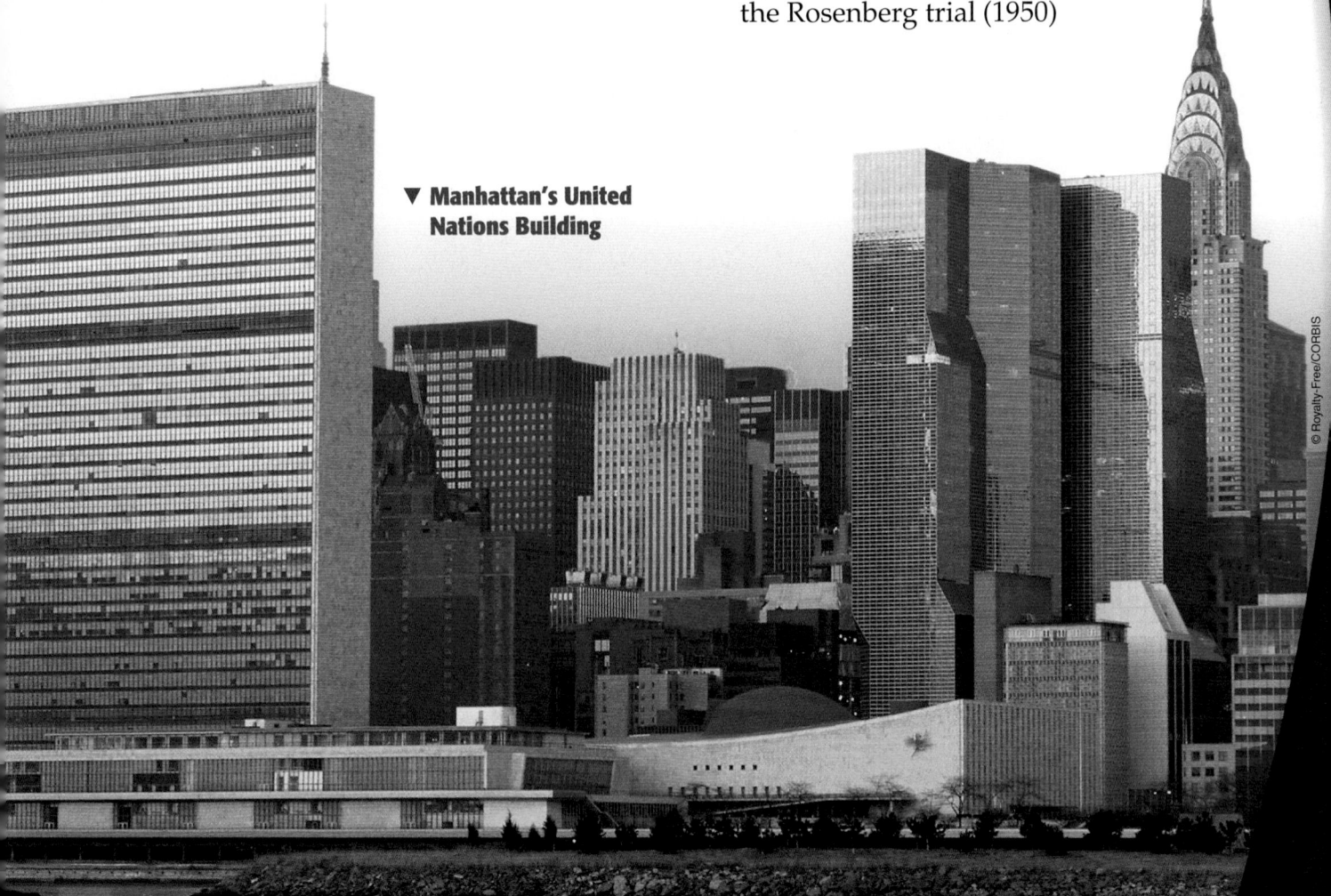

▼ **Manhattan's United Nations Building**

© Royalty-Free/CORBIS

2. Loyalty and dissent: the case of Robert Oppenheimer
3. McCarthyism
4. Politics of the Cold War

UNIT SEVEN: WORLD IN UNCERTAIN TIMES: 1950–PRESENT

I. Toward a Postindustrial World: Living in a Global Age

A. Changes within the United States

1. Energy sources (nuclear power)
2. Materials (plastics, light metals)
3. Technology (computers)
4. Corporate structures (multinational corporations)
5. Nature of employment (agriculture to industry to service)
6. Problems (waste disposal, air/water pollution, growing energy usage, depleting resources, e.g., domestic oil supply)

II. Containment and Consensus: 1945–1960

A. Review postwar events

1. Emerging power relationships: East/West; North/South; (haves/have-nots; developed/developing nations)

B. Eisenhower foreign policies

1. The end of the Korean War
2. John Foster Dulles, the domino theory and massive retaliation; brinkmanship posture
3. The H-bomb; atoms for peace
4. Summits and U-2s
5. Establishment of SEATO
6. Controversy: Aswan Dam and Suez Canal
7. Polish and Hungarian uprisings
8. Eisenhower Doctrine: intervention in Lebanon
9. Sputnik: initiating the space race

C. Domestic politics and constitutional issues

1. The Eisenhower peace
2. Civil rights

D. The people

1. Prosperity and conservatism
2. Migration and immigration

III. Decade of Change: 1960s

A. The Kennedy years

1. The New Frontier: dreams and promises
2. Foreign policy and Cold War crises
3. Movement for rights of disabled citizens
4. Assassination in Dallas

▼ Lake George and fall colors, Adirondack Mountains

Digital Vision

B. Johnson and the Great Society

1. Expanding on the Kennedy social programs
2. The Moon landing: the challenge of space exploration
3. Continued demands for equality: civil rights movement
4. Demands for equality: women
5. Rising consciousness of Hispanic-Americans
6. Demands for equality: American Indian Movement (AIM) and other protests
7. Rights of the accused
8. Legislative reapportionment: *Baker* v. *Carr*, 1962

IV. The Limits of Power: Turmoil at Home and Abroad, 1965–1972

A. Vietnam: sacrifice and turmoil

1. The French-Indochinese War: early United States involvement; Truman, Eisenhower, and Kennedy policies (review how foreign policy is formulated)
2. United States and the spread of communism; domino theory; credibility of other United States commitments
3. Civil war in South Vietnam; concept of guerrilla warfare
4. LBJ and the Americanization of the war
5. Student protests at home
6. 1968: A year of turmoil

© Royalty-Free/CORBIS

V. The Trend Toward Conservatism, 1972–1985

A. Nixon as President, 1969–1974

1. Domestic policies and events
2. Nixon's internationalism
3. The Presidency in crisis

B. The Ford and Carter Presidencies

1. The appointive Presidency: Ford and Rockefeller (the constitutional aspects)
2. Domestic policy issues
3. Foreign policy issues: the United States after Vietnam

C. Reagan and Bush, the "new" federalism and growth of conservatism

1. Supply-side economics
2. Tax policy and deficits
3. Environmental and civil rights policies
4. Effects on minorities
5. The Supreme Court and the schools

D. New approaches to old problems

1. Feast and famine: the farmer's dilemma
2. The problems of poverty in an affluent society—"the underclass"
3. The "new" immigrants; (Immigration Reform and Control Act of 1986)
4. Changing demographic patterns (growing numbers of elderly)

▼ Aerial view of Central Park

E. Renewed United States power image

1. Central America and the Caribbean: debt and stability; Sandinistas, Contras, El Salvadorians
2. Middle East: war and hostages

F. Trade imbalance and divesting

1. Japan: trade imbalance
2. United States and South Africa

G. United States–Soviet relations

1. Gorbachev and Soviet relations
2. "Star Wars" and arms limitation efforts
3. Cuts in defense spending and the fall of the Soviet Union

VI. Approaching the Next Century, 1986–1999

A. The Bush Presidency

1. Case study: The election of 1988
2. Domestic issues
3. Foreign policy issues

B. The Clinton Presidency

1. Domestic issues
2. Foreign policy issues

▼ **Sailboat Pond in Central Park, New York City**

© Royalty-Free/CORBIS

How Does *The American Vision* Help Me Learn the Curriculum?

Glencoe's *The American Vision* has been carefully organized to ensure that the textbook's content, features, maps, and activities provide comprehensive coverage of the New York Core Curriculum for U.S. History and Government (commencement level). To further help you, Glencoe has reproduced the New York Core Curriculum on the previous pages to help you relate the major concepts that you should know to the textbook as you read and study. For example, below are objectives from Unit Five:

UNIT FIVE: AT HOME AND ABROAD: PROSPERITY AND DEPRESSION, 1917–1940

I. War and Prosperity: 1917–1929

A. Impact of war

1. War's effects on gender roles, on African-Americans, and other minority groups
2. Case study: Movement of African-Americans from the South to northern cities
3. Return to "normalcy": 1918–1921

Each unit begins by identifying the broad historical time period and subject matter. For example, this unit is concerned with the period of U.S. history from 1917 to 1940, and item I is concerned with the specific period from 1917 to 1929. By understanding that, you know in which chapters of the textbook you will find relevant information. The list (item A, 1–3) helps you learn more detail about the historical context being discussed.

How should you use the core curriculum? Try the following strategies:

- Read through the objectives before you begin your study of each chapter. Based on the content of that chapter, decide which objectives relate to the material you are about to read.

- Keep these objectives in mind as you read the chapter and take notes on the relevant information you find.

- Review these objectives after you complete the chapter to see if you have indeed learned what you need to know.

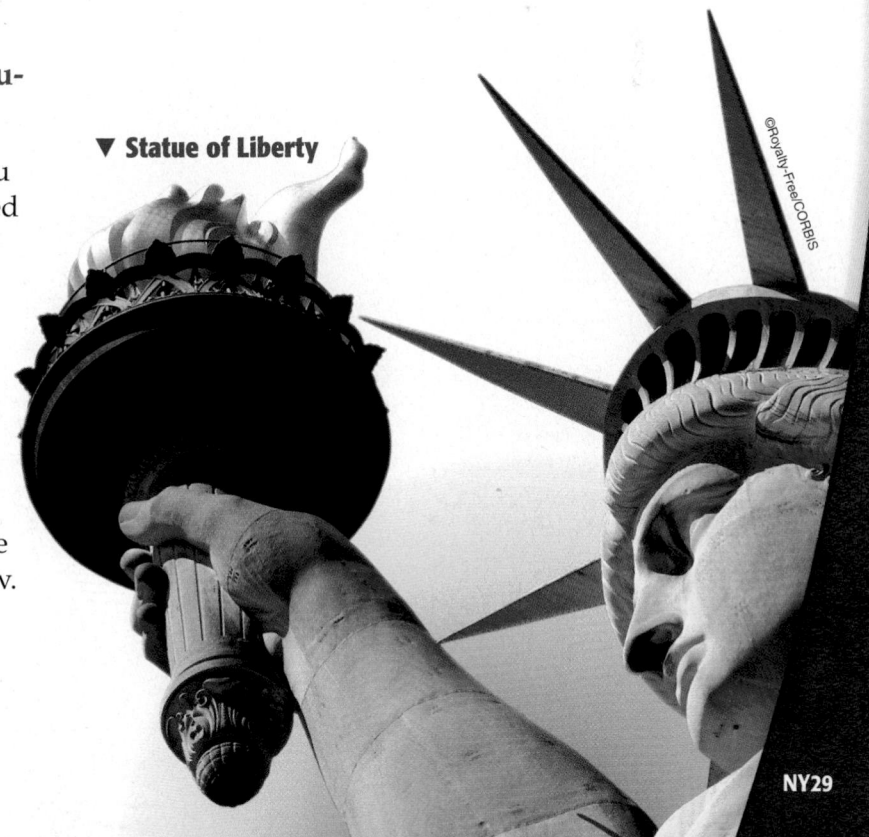

▼ **Statue of Liberty**

©Royalty-Free/CORBIS

What is the Regents Examination?

The Regents Examination for United States History and Government is given to all New York students at commencement level (high school). It is intended to measure your achievement of the skills and content in your study of United States history and government. Students are allowed up to three hours to complete the exam. The exam consists of three parts. Part I consists of multiple-choice questions; part II is a thematic essay; and part III consists of open-ended and document-based questions.

Why Does the Regents Examination Matter to Me?

All public schools in the state are required to administer the New York State Regents Examination for U.S. History and Government. The exam is based on New York State's Social Studies Core Curriculum. The test is used to evaluate your progress in achieving mastery of the five New York State Learning Standards in Social Studies at the commencement level: History of the United States and New York; World History; Geography; Economics; and Civics, Citizenship, and Government. These learning standards describe the facts that you need to know and the expected level of thinking and problem-solving skills you should achieve. Success on the exam helps to ensure that you have the skills you need to be successful upon graduation.

▼ Flags in Ellis Island Immigration Museum Hall

What Is a Document-Based Question?

A document-based question (DBQ) assesses your ability to understand, interpret, and analyze historical documents. You will be presented with a series of documents. These documents could appear in various forms. For example, they could be text excerpts, cartoons, or pictures. The exam will present a historical context and a task to help put the documents in perspective. The questions you answer about each document will help you write your essay in the second part of the question.

For the DBQ, you are asked to:

1. Answer specific short-answer questions about each document.

2. Write an essay drawing upon your understanding of a group of the documents.

The following example is based on a DBQ from the January 2005 Regents Exam for U.S. History and Government. The following represents only a *partial* example of the number of documents you will see on the exam.

DOCUMENT-BASED QUESTION

As you read the following documents, note the source of each document as well as its point of view. Commenting on the author's background or background of the document in your essay makes your essay stronger and more analytical.

Historical Context: During the late 1800s and early 1900s, Progressive reformers worked to improve American society. Their goals included **protecting consumers, regulating child labor, improving working conditions,** and **expanding democracy.**

Task: Answer the questions that follow each document in Part A. Your answers to the questions will help you write an essay in Part B.

Part A Short-Answer Questions
Directions: Analyze the documents and answer the short-answer questions.

Document 1a

> . . . During the same winter three boys from a Hull-House club were injured at one machine in a neighboring factory for lack of a guard which would have cost but a few dollars. . . .
>   . . . Florence Kelley . . . suggested to the Illinois State Bureau of Labor that they investigate the sweating system [sweatshops] in Chicago with its attendant [use of] child labor. . . . When the report was presented to the Illinois Legislature, a special committee was appointed to look into the Chicago conditions. . . .
>
> Source: Jane Addams, *Twenty Years at Hull-House with Autobiographical Notes*, MacMillan, 1912

1a Based on this document, identify *one* social problem Jane Addams wanted to reform.

_____

Document 1b

First Factory Law of Illinois

FACTORIES AND WORKSHOPS

. . . 4. Children under 14 years of age prohibited from being employed in any manufacturing establishment, factory or work shop in the state. Register of children under 16 years shall be kept. The employment of children between ages of 14 and 16 years prohibited unless an affidavit by the parent or guardian shall first be filed in which shall be stated the age date and place of birth. Certificates of physical health may be demanded by the inspectors. . . .

Source: "Factories and Workshops," *Laws of the State of Illinois,* Thirty-Eighth General Assembly, 1893

1b Based on this document, state one provision of the Illinois factory law.

_____

_____

Part B Essay

Directions: Using information from the documents and your knowledge of United States history, write an essay in which you choose *three* goals mentioned in the historical context and for *each*

• Discuss the conditions that led Progressive reformers to address the goal.
• Discuss the extent to which the goal was achieved.

▼ **New York State Capitol and Rose Garden, Albany, New York**

© Royalty-Free/CORBIS

How Does *The American Vision* Help Me Succeed on the Regents Exam?

When you study United States history with Glencoe's *The American Vision* textbook, you are also preparing yourself for the New York State Regents Exam in U.S. History and Government. By mastering the content in the textbook, you are taking the most important step in preparing for the Regents Exam. In addition to the narrative, however, there are other elements of the textbook to make your test preparations easier.

- Glencoe's *The American Vision* provides a Countdown to the Regents Exam on pages NY64–NY87. These practice questions are just like those on the Regents Exam. By working through this Countdown throughout the school year, you can prepare for the actual test.

- You will find many graphs, tables, and maps in *The American Vision*, each of them with questions based on the content of the visual. The Regents Exam also asks questions based on maps and other visuals, so your textbook helps you prepare for these questions.

- Each section and chapter of your textbook features assessments with questions based on graphic organizers. Chapter assessments also include questions asking you to interpret maps, graphs, or charts.

- Each chapter assessment features a Standardized Test Practice question. The style of these multiple-choice questions is the same as that for the questions in the Regents Exam. Completing these questions as you review each chapter will help you prepare for the Regents Exam.

Contents

Previewing Your Textbook NY52
Scavenger Hunt NY57
Reading for Information NY58
How Do I Study History? NY60
Countdown to the New York
    Regents Exam NY62
Thematic Essay NY88
Reading Skills Handbook RH1

NATIONAL GEOGRAPHIC Reference Atlas

United States Political RA2
United States Physical RA4
United States Congressional Reapportionment RA6
United States Territorial Growth RA8
Middle America Physical/Political RA10
Canada Physical/Political RA12
Middle East Physical/Political RA14
World Political RA16

United States Facts RA18

NATIONAL GEOGRAPHIC Geography Handbook

Introduction RA20
Globes and Maps 1
Using Maps 2
The Elements of Geography 4
Geographic Dictionary 6

UNIT 1

Three Worlds Meet   8
Beginnings to 1763

CHAPTER 1
Converging Cultures,
    Prehistory to 1520 10
    1 The Migration to America 12
    2 Native American Cultures 20
    3 African Cultures 26
    4 European Cultures 32
    5 Europe Encounters America 38

CHAPTER 2
Colonizing America, 1519–1733 48
    1 The Spanish and French Build Empires 50
    2 English Colonies in America 58
    3 New England 66
    4 The Middle and Southern Colonies 72

CHAPTER 3
Colonial Ways of Life, 1607–1763 82
    1 The Southern Colonies 84
    2 New England and the Middle Colonies 91
    3 The Imperial System 98
    4 A Diverse Society 104

UNIT 2

Creating a Nation   112
1754–1816

CHAPTER 4
The American Revolution,
    1754–1783 114
    1 The Colonies Fight for Their Rights 116
    2 The Revolution Begins 126

    The Text of the Declaration
    of Independence 134

    3 The War for Independence 138
    4 The War Changes American Society 147

CHAPTER 5
Creating a Constitution,
    1781–1789 156
    1 The Confederation 158
    2 A New Constitution 164
    3 Ratification 172

    The Constitution Handbook 178
    The Constitution of the United States 188

CHAPTER 6
Federalists and Republicans,
    1789–1816 208
    1 Washington and Congress 210
    2 Partisan Politics 215
    3 Jefferson in Office 221
    4 The War of 1812 228

UNIT 3

The Young Republic 236
1789–1850

CHAPTER 7
Growth and Division, 1816–1832......**238**
- **1** American Nationalism 240
- **2** Early Industry 245
- **3** The Land of Cotton 251
- **4** Growing Sectionalism 257

CHAPTER 8
The Spirit of Reform, 1828–1845......**264**
- **1** Jacksonian America 266
- **2** A Changing Culture 273
- **3** Reforming Society 278
- **4** The Abolitionist Movement 284

CHAPTER 9
Manifest Destiny, 1835–1848.........**292**
- **1** The Western Pioneers 294
- **2** Independence for Texas 300
- **3** The War With Mexico 306

UNIT 4

The Crisis of Union 316
1848–1877

CHAPTER 10
**Sectional Conflict Intensifies,
  1848–1860** **318**
- **1** Slavery and Western Expansion 320
- **2** Mounting Violence 326
- **3** The Crisis Deepens 332
- **4** The Union Dissolves 340

CHAPTER 11
The Civil War, 1861–1865 ....**348**
- **1** The Opposing Sides 350
- **2** The Early Stages 357
- **3** Life During the War 364
- **4** The Turning Point 369
- **5** The War Ends 376

CHAPTER 12
Reconstruction, 1865–1877 ....**384**
- **1** Reconstruction Plans 386
- **2** Congressional Reconstruction 391
- **3** Republican Rule 398
- **4** Reconstruction Collapses 403

UNIT 5

The Birth of Modern America 410
1865–1900

CHAPTER 13
Settling the West, 1865–1900.........**412**
- **1** Miners and Ranchers 414
- **2** Farming the Plains 420
- **3** Native Americans 425

CHAPTER 14
Industrialization, 1865–1901 ....**434**
- **1** The Rise of Industry 436
- **2** The Railroads 442
- **3** Big Business 447
- **4** Unions 454

CHAPTER 15
Urban America, 1865–1896...........**462**
- **1** Immigration 464
- **2** Urbanization 469
- **3** The Gilded Age 476
- **4** The Rebirth of Reform 481

CHAPTER 16
Politics and Reform, 1877–1896......**490**
- **1** Stalemate in Washington 492
- **2** Populism 500
- **3** The Rise of Segregation 508

Contents

UNIT 6

Imperialism and Progressivism
1890–1919   516

CHAPTER 17
Becoming a World Power,
1872–1912 . . . . **518**
 1 The Imperialist Vision 520
 2 The Spanish-American War 527
 3 New American Diplomacy 536

CHAPTER 18
The Progressive Movement,
1890–1919 . . . . **544**
 1 The Roots of Progressivism 546
 2 Roosevelt in Office 555
 3 The Taft Administration 562
 4 The Wilson Years 566

CHAPTER 19
World War I and Its Aftermath,
1914–1920 . . . . **574**
 1 The United States Enters World War I 576
 2 The Home Front 584
 3 A Bloody Conflict 592
 4 The War's Impact 599

UNIT 7

Boom and Bust   606
1920–1941

CHAPTER 20
The Jazz Age, 1921–1929 . . . . **608**
 1 A Clash of Values 610
 2 Cultural Innovations 620
 3 African American Culture 626

CHAPTER 21
Normalcy and Good Times,
1921–1929 . . . . **634**
 1 Presidential Politics 636
 2 A Growing Economy 640
 3 The Policies of Prosperity 647

CHAPTER 22
The Great Depression Begins,
1929–1932 . . . . **654**
 1 Causes of the Depression 656
 2 Life During the Depression 661
 3 Hoover Responds 668

CHAPTER 23
Roosevelt and the New Deal,
1933–1939 . . . . **676**
 1 Roosevelt Takes Office 678
 2 The First New Deal 682
 3 The Second New Deal 689
 4 The New Deal Coalition 695

UNIT 8

Global Struggles   704
1931–1960

CHAPTER 24
A World in Flames, 1931–1941 . . . . **706**
 1 America and the World 708
 2 World War II Begins 713
 3 The Holocaust 719
 4 America Enters the War 725

CHAPTER 25
America and World War II,
1941–1945 . . . . **734**
 1 Mobilizing for War 736
 2 The Early Battles 742
 3 Life on the Home Front 749
 4 Pushing the Axis Back 755
 5 The War Ends 764

CHAPTER 26
The Cold War Begins, 1945–1960 776
1 Origins of the Cold War 778
2 The Early Cold War Years 783
3 The Cold War and American Society 790
4 Eisenhower's Policies 797

CHAPTER 27
Postwar America, 1945–1960 806
1 Truman and Eisenhower 808
2 The Affluent Society 814
3 Popular Culture of the 1950s 820
4 The Other Side of American Life 828

UNIT 9

A Time of Upheaval 836
1954–1980

CHAPTER 28
**The New Frontier and the
Great Society, 1961–1968** 838
1 The New Frontier 840
2 JFK and the Cold War 846
3 The Great Society 854

CHAPTER 29
**The Civil Rights Movement,
1954–1968** 864
1 The Movement Begins 866
2 Challenging Segregation 873
3 New Issues 881

CHAPTER 30
The Vietnam War, 1954–1975 890
1 The United States Focuses on Vietnam 892
2 Going to War in Vietnam 896
3 Vietnam Divides the Nation 904
4 The War Winds Down 910

CHAPTER 31
**The Politics of Protest,
1960–1980** 918
1 The Student Movement and the Counterculture 920
2 The Feminist Movement 926
3 New Approaches to Civil Rights 932
4 Saving the Earth 939

UNIT 10

A Changing Society 948
1968–Present

CHAPTER 32
**Politics and Economics,
1971–1980** 950
1 The Nixon Administration 952
2 The Watergate Scandal 958
3 Ford and Carter 963
4 The "Me" Decade: Life in the 1970s 970

CHAPTER 33
**Resurgence of Conservatism,
1980–1992** 978
1 The New Conservatism 980
2 The Reagan Years 985
3 Life in the 1980s 994
4 The End of the Cold War 1001

CHAPTER 34
**Into a New Century,
1992–present** 1010
1 The Technological Revolution 1012
2 The Clinton Years 1016
3 An Interdependent World 1022
4 America Enters a New Century 1026
5 The War on Terrorism 1031

Appendix

Presidents of the United States 1041

Primary Sources Library 1046

Documents of American History 1058

Supreme Court Case Summaries 1080

Flag Etiquette 1084

Glossary 1085

Spanish Glossary 1095

Index 1107

Acknowledgments and Photo Credits 1135

Features

Primary Sources Library

Letter of Don Antonio de Otermin on
Popé's Revolt in 1680 1048
Patrick Henry's "Give Me Liberty or
Give Me Death" 1049
John O'Sullivan on Manifest Destiny 1050
"Battle Cry of Freedom" 1051
Willa Cather's *My Ántonia* 1052
Andrew Carnegie's "Gospel of Wealth" 1053
John Steinbeck's *The Grapes of Wrath* 1054
Georgia O'Keeffe's *Oriental Poppies* 1055
Audie Murphy's "Alone and Far Removed" 1055
"Letter from a Birmingham Jail"
by Martin Luther King, Jr. 1056
Elva Trevino Hart's *Barefoot Heart* 1057

Documents of American History

The Magna Carta, 1215 1060
The Mayflower Compact, 1620 1061
The Fundamental Orders of Connecticut, 1639 ... 1062
The English Bill of Rights, 1689 1063
Second Treatise of Government, 1690 1064
The Virginia Statute for Religious
Freedom, 1786 1065
The Federalist No. 10, 1787 1066
The Federalist No. 51, 1788 1067
The Federalist No. 59, 1788 1067
Washington's Farewell Address, 1796 1068
The Kentucky Resolution, 1799 1069
"The Star-Spangled Banner," 1814 1069
The Monroe Doctrine, 1823 1070
The Seneca Falls Declaration, 1848 1070
The Emancipation Proclamation, 1863 1071
The Gettysburg Address, 1863 1072
The Pledge of Allegiance, 1892 1072
President Harrison on Hawaiian
Annexation, 1893 1073
The American's Creed, 1918 1073
The Fourteen Points, 1918 1074
The Four Freedoms, 1941 1075
The Truman Doctrine, 1947 1076
Brown v. *Board of Education,* 1954 1077
"I Have a Dream," 1963 1078
The Gulf of Tonkin Resolution, 1964 1079
President George W. Bush's Address to Joint Session
of Congress, September 20, 2001 1079

American LITERATURE

The Constitution of the Five Nations 25
The American Crisis, Number 1,
by Thomas Paine 153
Walden, by Henry David Thoreau 283
Narrative of the Life of Frederick Douglass,
by Frederick Douglass 339
An Indian Teacher Among Indians,
by Gertrude Simmons Bonnin 431
The Jungle, by Upton Sinclair 571
Selected Poems by Langston Hughes 631
Farewell to Manzanar, by Jeanne Wakatsuki
Houston and James D. Houston 773
The Yellow Wallpaper,
by Charlotte Perkins Gilman 931
Hunger of Memory, by Richard Rodriguez 1007

What If...

The Declaration of Independence Had
Condemned Slavery? 132
Lee Had Not Followed Virginia in Secession? 355
English Spelling Reform Had Been Accepted? 484
Operation Overlord Had Failed? 758

TECHNOLOGY & History

The Caravel 36
The Cotton Gin 252
The Telegraph 365
The Mining Sluice 415
Modern Battleships 524
The Assembly Line 641
The Hydrogen Bomb 798
Solar Energy 942
Magnetic Resonance Imaging 1014

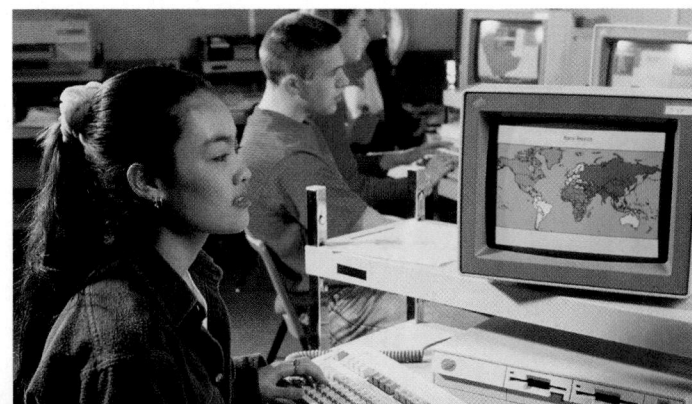

Linking Past & Present

Refugee Migration to America 56
Popular Protest 121
Advances in Transportation 249
The Income Tax 352
Virginia City 416
The NAACP 569
Roosevelt Dime 680
The Incredible Shrinking Computer 817

Different Viewpoints

The Spanish in Mexico 52
Should the Majority Rule? 174
Did Manifest Destiny Violate American Ideals? 308
Carpetbaggers: Corrupt or Well-Intentioned? 401
Two Views of Immigration 466
Abrams v. United States, 1919 588
What Should the Government's Role in the
    Economy Be? 669
Dropping the Atomic Bomb: Was It the
    Right Decision? 770
Should the War in Korea Be Expanded? 788
The Vietnam War 898
Carter and Reagan on Government 986

NATIONAL GEOGRAPHIC Geography & History

Land Bridge to America 18
Westward to the Pacific 226
Spanish Missions 312
Gettysburg: The Final Day 374
Immigrants Arrive in Chicago 474
The Story of Yosemite 560
Hoover Dam 666
A Day for Heroes 762
Global Cars 944
Urban America on the Move 992

NATIONAL GEOGRAPHIC MOMENT in HISTORY

Rush to the Colors 344
Campaigning in Virginia 377
Winds of Change 388
The End of a Way of Life 426
Labor Savers 450
Teeming Tenements 472
Hard Life on the Plains 505
Feisty Leader for a New Century 531
Youthful Protest 552
Hero's Homecoming 600
Entertainment for a New Era 622
On the Road 642
Image of an Era 662
Brief Respite for FDR 691
Never Give In 717
Behind Barbed Wire 752
Aid for War's Youngest Victims 780
The King of Rock 823
Youth's Helping Hand 859
American Segregation 867
America's Longest War 900
Woodstock Nation 924
Hostage to Terror 968
A City Reunited 1003
Terrorism in the Heartland 1024

World History Connection

The Compass 37
Gunpowder 373
The Trans-Siberian Railroad 444
The Suez Canal 540
Jazz's Global Roots 629

World Geography Connection

The Spread of American Democracy 148
The Cowboys of Argentina 419
Global War 597
Geography and War 730
The War's Refugees 914
The Islamic State 969

Features

Profiles IN HISTORY

Christopher Columbus, 1451–1506 41
Bartolomé de Las Casas, 1474–1566 55
Pocahontas, 1596–1617 62
Anne Bradstreet, c. 1612–1672 101
John Peter Zenger, 1697–1746 106
Sam Adams, 1722–1803 122
Bernardo de Gálvez, 1746–1786 143
Elizabeth Freeman (Mumbet), c. 1742–1829 149
James Madison, 1751–1836 165
Roger Sherman, 1721–1793 167
Tecumseh, c. 1768–1813 230
Henry Clay, 1777–1852 241
John C. Calhoun, 1782–1850 241
Nat Turner, 1800–1831 256
Margaret Fuller, 1810–1850 276
Prudence Crandall, 1803–1890 286
Lorenzo de Zavala, 1788–1836 302
Sam Houston, 1793–1863 302
Harriet Tubman, c. 1820–1913 328
John Brown, 1800–1859 338
Federico Cavada, 1832–1871 361
Ulysses S. Grant, 1822–1885 372
Robert E. Lee, 1807–1870 372
Hiram Revels, 1822–1901 399
Joseph Rainey, 1832–1887 399
Sitting Bull, 1831–1890 429
Mother Jones, 1830–1930 456
Booker T. Washington, 1856–1915 485
George Washington Carver, 1864–1943 485
Mary Ellen Lease, 1853–1933 504
Mary Church Terrell, 1863–1954 510
Susan B. Anthony, 1820–1906 550
Jeannette Rankin, 1880–1973 580
Bessie Coleman, c. 1892–1926 643
Amelia Earhart, 1897–1937 643
Dorothea Lange, 1895–1965 665
Mary McLeod Bethune, 1875–1955 696
Frances Perkins, 1882–1965 696
Albert Einstein, 1879–1955 720
Chester W. Nimitz, 1885–1966 746
Isoroku Yamamoto, 1884–1943 746
The Navajo Code Talkers 750
Jonas Salk, 1914–1995 819
Esther Peterson, 1906–1997 860
Thurgood Marshall, 1908–1993 870
Roy P. Benavidez, 1935– 912
Shirley Chisholm, 1924–2005 929

Dolores Huerta, 1930– 936
José Angel Gutiérrez, 1944– 936
Romana Acosta Bañuelos, 1925– 954
Sandra Day O'Connor, 1930– 989
Franklin R. Chang-Diaz, 1950– 998
Jerry Yang, 1968– 1015

SKILLBUILDER

Social Studies
Reading a Time Line 45
Understanding the Parts of a Map 65
Reading a Bar Graph 103
Reading a Flowchart 233
Reading a Line Graph 261
Understanding Latitude and Longitude 305
Interpreting Political Cartoons 390
Interpreting Statistics 424
Reading a Thematic Map 748
Conducting an Interview 915
Reading a Cartogram 1030

Critical Thinking
Understanding Cause and Effect 146
Making Comparisons 163
Predicting Consequences 325
Making Inferences 441
Hypothesizing 487
Interpreting Points of View 513
Analyzing Information 598
Synthesizing Information 617
Distinguishing Fact From Opinion 651
Making Generalizations 731
Making Decisions 803
Problem Solving 861
Analyzing Primary Sources 938
Analyzing Secondary Sources 975
Analyzing News Media 1000

Study & Writing
Taking Notes 554
Outlining 701
Writing a Journal 833
Preparing a Bibliography 887

Technology
Developing a Multimedia Presentation 289
Evaluating a Web Site 381
Using an Electronic Spreadsheet 526
Building a Database 673

Why It Matters

The Columbian Exchange 42
The Northwest Ordinance 160
The 1828 Election 268
The Fourteenth Amendment 392
Land-Grant Colleges 422
The Panama Canal 538
The TVA 684
Interstate Highways 812
The Space Program 848
Strait of Hormuz 1004

What Life Was Like...

Old-Fashioned School Days 280
Flappers 614
1930s Entertainment 698
Disco 972

You're the Historian

Comparing Accounts of the Boston Massacre 124
Investigating Standard Oil 452
Who Sank the *Maine?* 534
The Sacco-Vanzetti Case 618
Incident in the Gulf of Tonkin 902

TIME NOTEBOOK

Colonizing America: 1519–1732 78
Forging a Nation: 1781–1789 170
Moving West: 1816–1850 298
Rebuilding the Nation: 1865–1877 396
The Gilded Age: 1865–1896 498
A War to End All Wars: 1914–1918 590
The Jazz Age: 1920–1929 624
An Age of Prosperity: 1945–1960 826
New Frontiers: 1961–1968 852

Fact Fiction Folklore

Pass the Popcorn 24
Spain, 1492 44
Flag of New France 57
John Locke 102
English Flag 108
America's Flags 145
The Preamble 169
The Star-Spangled Banner, 1779–1818 229
Invasion of the Velocipedes 250
Abolitionist Songs 285
Dangers on the Western Trails 307
"Born in a Log Cabin" 334
Same Battles, Different Names 358
Expanding the Nation 395
Buffalo Bill's Wild West Show 427
The New York Stock Exchange 451
The Seventh-Inning Stretch 479
The Teddy Bear 558
New Words 615
Cartoon Symbols 638
The Tomb of the Unknown Soldier 650
Hobo Signs 664
The Battle of Dunkirk 716
Family Sacrifices 771
Cold War Words 796
Quick and Easy Eats 822
Camelot 843
The Peace Symbol 907
New 1960s Words 923
The Day the Pitcher Refused to Play 933
"Ping-Pong Diplomacy" 955
Put on a Happy Face 974
Food and Fashion 995

Causes and Effects

Causes and Effects of European Exploration 35
Causes and Effects of Tensions with Britain 120
Causes and Effects of the American Revolution 129
Causes and Effects of the Civil War 345
Effects of World War I on the United States 601
Causes of the Great Depression 658
Causes and Effects of the Cold War 784

Primary Source Quotes

A variety of quotations and excerpts throughout the text express the thoughts, feelings, and life experiences of people, past and present.

CHAPTER 1 • Converging Cultures, Prehistory to 1520

Frank H.H. Roberts, Jr., adapted from *The First American: A Story of North American Archaeology* 12

Anonymous Natchez man, quoted in *America in 1492* 20

Mahmoud Kati, adapted from *Wonders of the African World* 26

Abu Hamid al-Andalusi, quoted in *African Kingdoms* 28

Leo Africanus, quoted in *African Kingdoms* 29

Pope Urban II, quoted in *The Discoverers* 32

Anonymous English monk, quoted in *Colloquy* 33

Christopher Columbus, adapted from *The Log of Christopher Columbus* 38

Christopher Columbus, quoted in *500 Nations* 40

Christopher Columbus, quoted in *The Voyage of Christopher Columbus* 40

CHAPTER 2 • Colonizing America: 1519–1733

Anonymous Aztec, quoted in *The Broken Spears: The Aztec Account of the Conquest of Mexico* 50

Anonymous Aztec, quoted in *The Broken Spears: The Aztec Account of the Conquest of Mexico* 52

Hernán Cortés, quoted in *Five Letters of Cortés to the Emperor* 52

Anonymous Aztec, quoted in *The Broken Spears: The Aztec Account of the Conquest of Mexico* 53

Sir George Yeardley, adapted from *Jamestown, 1544–1699* 58

Ralph Hamor, quoted in *Colonial America* 63

Pilgrim's agreement, adapted from *Basic Documents in American History* 66

John Winthrop, from "A Model of Christian Charity" 68

Dutch citizens, adapted from *A New World* and *Colonial New York* 72

CHAPTER 3 • Colonial Ways of Life, 1607–1763

William Byrd II, quoted in *The Growth of the American Republic* 84

Olaudah Equiano, from *The Interesting Narrative of the Life of Olaudah Equiano, or Gustavus Vassa the African* 89

Francis Higginson, from "On the Riches of New England," *The Annals of America* 91

Benjamin Franklin and the *Boston Gazette*, adapted from *The Rise of American Civilization* 98

Jonathan Mayhew, quoted in *The Making of American Democracy* 102

Benjamin Franklin, adapted from *Colonial Pennsylvania: A History* 104

Cotton Mather, quoted in *The Colonial Image* 105

CHAPTER 4 • The American Revolution, 1754–1783

John Hughes, adapted from *What They Didn't Teach You About the American Revolution* 116

John Adams, quoted in *America's History* 120

Wife of a pro-British merchant, quoted in *Eyewitness Accounts of the American Revolution* 121

George Hewes, quoted in *The Spirit of 'Seventy-Six* . . .126

Thomas Paine, from *Common Sense* 133

Henry Beckman Livingston, adapted from *A Salute to Courage* 138

Thomas Paine, from *The American Crisis* 141

William Cushing, adapted from *Founding the Republic* 147

Thomas Jefferson, in the *Virginia Statute for Religious Freedom* 149

CHAPTER 5 • Creating a Constitution, 1781–1789

George Washington, adapted from *The Forging of the Union* 158

Benjamin Franklin, quoted in *An Outline of American History* 164

Benjamin Franklin, quoted in *Benjamin Franklin: A Biography* 167

Patrick Henry, quoted in *Patrick Henry: A Biography* . . .172

Amos Singletary, quoted in the *Massachusetts Gazette* . .173

James Madison, from *The Federalist No. 10* 174

Thomas Jefferson, letter to Madison, December 20, 1787 174

Jedidiah Morse, quoted in *Readings in American History* 177

CHAPTER 6 • Federalists and Republicans, 1789–1816

George Washington, adapted from *Washington: The Indispensable Man* 210

Alexander Hamilton, quoted in *America, A Narrative History* 212

John Marshall, adapted from *The Flavor of the Past* . .215

George Washington, from Washington's Farewell Address 218

Anonymous Washington, D.C. resident, quoted in *The Life of Thomas Jefferson* 221

Philip Barton Key, quoted in *The American Spirit* 225

Francis Scott Key, from "The Star-Spangled Banner" 228

Primary Source Quotes

James Madison, from Madison's *War Message to Congress* 230
Massachusetts residents, quoted in the *Columbian Centinel,* July 20, 1812 234

CHAPTER 7 • Growth and Division, 1816–1832
James Monroe, from James Monroe's Inaugural Address, March 1817 240
Seminole leader Kinache, quoted in *The Seminoles of Florida* 243
Anonymous Erie Canal investor, quoted in *The Artificial River* 245
Lucy Larcom, quoted in *Ordinary Americans* 249
Reporter, from *A History of the United States* 250
Solomon Northup, quoted in *Twelve Years a Slave* ... 251
Mark Twain, from *Huckleberry Finn* 253
Frederick Douglass, from *Narrative of the Life of Frederick Douglass* 254
Samuel Ringgold Ward, quoted in *Long Memory: The Black Experience in America* 255
Thomas Jefferson, quoted in *The Annals of America* 257
Andrew Jackson Donelson, quoted in *Henry Clay* 259
John Marshall, from *McCulloch* v. *Maryland,* 1819 262

CHAPTER 8 • The Spirit of Reform, 1828–1845
Margaret Bayard Smith, adapted from *First Forty Years of Washington Society* 266
Daniel Webster, quoted in *The Writings and Speeches of Daniel Webster* 269
Daniel Guiney, quoted in *Out of Ireland* 273
August Blümmer, quoted in *News from the Land of Freedom* 274
Dorothea Dix, adapted from *Old South Leaflets* 278
Horace Mann, from "Report of the Massachusetts Board of Education," 1848 280
William Lloyd Garrison, quoted in *Witness to America* 284
William Lloyd Garrison, from the *Liberator* 286
Editorial from the *Raleigh Register,* November 9, 1829 290

CHAPTER 9 • Manifest Destiny, 1835–1848
Mary Richardson Walker, quoted in *Women of the West* 294
Elizabeth Geer, quoted in *Women's Diaries of the Westward Journey* 296
Stephen F. Austin, quoted in *Stephen F. Austin: Empresario of Texas* 300
William B. Travis, quoted in *History of Texas* 302

Napoleon Dana, adapted from *Monterrey is Ours!* 306
Albert Gallatin, quoted in *The Mission of the United States* 308
John L. O'Sullivan, quoted in *Annexation* 309
Anonymous army officer, from *Memoirs of a Maryland Volunteer* 309
Charles Sumner, quoted in *Readings in American History* 315

CHAPTER 10 • Sectional Conflict Intensifies, 1848–1860
Daniel Webster, from the *Congressional Globe,* 31st Congress 324
Isabella Beecher and Harriet Beecher Stowe, adapted from *Harriet Beecher Stowe: A Life* 326
Levi Coffin, quoted in *The Underground Railroad* 328
Abraham Lincoln, quoted in *Abraham Lincoln* 332
Roger B. Taney, from *Dred Scott* v. *Sandford* 335
Robert Purvis, quoted in *Witness for Freedom* 335
Abraham Lincoln, quoted in *The Civil War: An Illustrated History* 336
Abraham Lincoln, quoted in *The Civil War: Opposing Viewpoints* 337
John Brown, quoted in *John Brown, 1800–1859* 338
Mary Chesnut, adapted from *Mary Chesnut's Civil War* 340
Abraham Lincoln, from Lincoln's Inaugural Address, March 4, 1861 343
Edward A. Pollard, from *The Lost Cause* 346

CHAPTER 11 • The Civil War, 1861–1865
Theodore Upson, adapted from *With Sherman to the Sea* 350
Charles Coffin, quoted in *Voices of the Civil War* 357
George Julian, quoted in *Battle Cry of Freedom* 363
Robert Stiles, quoted in *Voices of the Civil War* 364
Frederick Douglass, quoted in *Battle Cry of Freedom* 366
The *New York Tribune,* from *Like Men of War* 366
Carl Schurz, quoted in *The Civil War* 367
Kate Cumming, quoted in *Battle Cry of Freedom* 368
Samuel Wilkeson, quoted in *Eyewitness to History* 369
Jesse Bowman Young, quoted in *Voices of the Civil War* 371
Abraham Lincoln, from the Gettysburg Address 372
Abraham Lincoln and guest, adapted from *The Civil War* 376
Robert E. Lee, from *Personal Reminiscences, Anecdotes, and Letters of General Robert E. Lee* ... 383

CHAPTER 12 • Reconstruction, 1865–1877
Houston Holloway, quoted in *A Short History of Reconstruction* 386

Henry Wilson 388
Charles Sumner, quoted in *Charles Sumner* 391
Essic Harris, adapted from *The Fiery Cross* 398
Oliver Morton, quoted in *Reconstruction:*
    Opposing Viewpoints 401
William Manning Lowe, quoted in
    Reconstruction: Opposing Viewpoints 401
Anonymous African American organization,
    from *Records of the U.S. Senate, 42nd Congress* . . . 402
Rutherford B. Hayes, quoted in
    Rutherford B. Hayes 406

CHAPTER 13 • Settling the West,
    1865–1900
John Waldorf, adapted from *A Kid*
    on the Comstock 414
Nat Love, quoted in *Life and Adventures*
    of Nat Love 418
Charley O'Kieffe, adapted from *Western Story:*
    Recollections of Charley O'Kieffe 420
William Allen White, from the *Emporia Gazette* 423
Ten Bears, adapted from *Tribes of the*
    Southern Plains 425
Chief Joseph, quoted in *Bury My Heart*
    at Wounded Knee 429
Satanta, quoted in *Bury My Heart at*
    Wounded Knee 432

CHAPTER 14 • Industrialization,
    1865–1901
Thomas Alva Edison, quoted in
    Eyewitness to America 436
Grenville Dodge, quoted in *Mine Eyes Have Seen* 442
Grenville Dodge, quoted in *The Growth of the*
    American Republic 443
Ida Tarbell, quoted in *All in the Day's Work* 447
Andrew Carnegie, quoted in *The Growth of the*
    American Republic 449
John Siney, quoted in *Labor's Untold Story* 454
William Sylvis, quoted in *Industrialism and the*
    American Worker 456
Ida Tarbell, quoted in *Readings in*
    American History 460

CHAPTER 15 • Urban America, 1865–1896
Mary Hayye, adapted from *Witnessing America* 464
Edward Steiner, quoted in *World of Our Fathers* 465
Lee Chew, quoted in *A Sunday Between Wars* 467
Frank Lloyd Wright, quoted in *Eyewitness*
    to America 469
Anonymous professor's wife, quoted in
    A Sunday Between Wars 471
Zalmen Yoffeh, quoted in *How We Lived* 471

George Plunkitt, quoted in
    In Search of America 473
William Lyon Phelps, adapted from
    Social Darwinism in American Thought 476
Edward Atkinson, quoted in *America's History* 477
Andrew Carnegie, quoted in *Voices*
    from America's Past 478
Lillian Wald, quoted in *The House on*
    Henry Street 481
Henry George, from *Progress and Poverty* 482
Anonymous editorial, from *the Commercial*
    and Financial Chronicle 488

CHAPTER 16 • Politics and Reform,
    1877–1896
Charles Guiteau, quoted in *Garfield* 492
Leonidas L. Polk, quoted in *Democratic Promise:*
    The Populist Movement in America 500
William Jennings Bryan, quoted in *America in*
    the Gilded Age 506
Tom Watson, adapted from *Tom Watson:*
    Agrarian Rebel 508
Henry King, quoted in *Eyewitness: The Negro*
    in History 509
Booker T. Washington, adapted from *Up*
    from Slavery 512
Washington Gladden, quoted in *Forum* 514

CHAPTER 17 • Becoming a World Power,
    1872–1912
John L. Stevens, adapted from *A History of*
    the American People 520
John Fiske, quoted in *Expansionists of 1898* 521
Clara Barton, adapted from *The Spanish War* 527
William McKinley, quoted in *A Diplomatic*
    History of the American People 532
Theodore Roosevelt, quoted in *The Growth of*
    the United States 541
Carl Schurz, quoted in *The Policy of*
    Imperialism 542

CHAPTER 18 • The Progressive Movement,
    1890–1919
Rose Winslow, quoted in *Jailed for Freedom* 546
Theodore Roosevelt, presidential speech,
    Washington, D.C., April 14, 1906 547
Lincoln Steffens, quoted in *Theodore*
    Roosevelt, A Life 555
Upton Sinclair, from *The Jungle* 558
Theodore Roosevelt, Nellie Taft, and William Howard
    Taft, adapted from *The American*
    Heritage Pictorial History of the Presidents
    of the United States 562

William Howard Taft, quoted in *The American Heritage Pictorial History of the Presidents of the United States* 563

Woodrow Wilson, adapted from *Wilson: The Road to the White House* 566

Ida Husted Harper, quoted in *The Independent,* 1901 573

CHAPTER 19 • World War I and Its Aftermath, 1914–1920

Edith O'Shaughnessy, adapted from *A Diplomat's Wife In Mexico* 576

Woodrow Wilson, quoted in the *Congressional Record,* 1917 583

Eugene Debs, adapted from *Echoes of Distant Thunder* 584

John H. Clarke, majority opinion from *Abrams* v. *United States,* 1919 588

Oliver Wendell Holmes, Jr., dissenting opinion from *Abrams* v. *United States,* 1919 588

Newton Baker, quoted in *Echoes of Distant Thunder* 589

John J. Pershing, quoted in *The Yanks Are Coming* ... 592

Anonymous American soldier, quoted in *The American Spirit* 593

Henry Cabot Lodge, from "On the League of Nations" speech 598

Mary Harris Jones, quoted in *Labor in Crisis* 599

Warren G. Harding, quoted in *Portrait of a Nation* ... 603

Eugene V. Debs, quoted in *Echoes of Distant Thunder* ... 604

CHAPTER 20 • The Jazz Age, 1921–1929

Alfred Levitt, quoted in *Centenarians: The Story of the Twentieth Century by the Americans Who Lived It* 610

Henry Curran, quoted in *Ellis Island: Echoes from a Nation's Past* 612

F. Scott Fitzgerald, quoted in *Echoes of the Jazz Age* 620

Brooks Atkinson, from *New York's Greenwich Village* 621

Edna St. Vincent Millay, "First Fig" 621

Louis Armstrong, quoted in *The African American Family Album* 626

W.E.B. DuBois, from *When Harlem Was in Vogue* 629

Arna Bontemps, from "A Black Man Talks of Reaping" 633

CHAPTER 21 • Normalcy and Good Times, 1921–1929

Calvin Coolidge and Charles Hopkinson, adapted from *Flappers, Bootleggers, "Typhoid Mary" and the Bomb* 636

Alice Roosevelt Longworth, quoted in *The Perils of Prosperity, 1914–1932* 637

Henry Ford, adapted from *The Fords: An American Epic* 640

Lena Stanley, quoted in *Centenarians: The Story of the Twentieth Century by the Americans Who Lived It* 643

Harry Daugherty, adapted from *Mellon's Millions* 647

Calvin Coolidge, from President Coolidge's Annual Message to Congress, December 4, 1928 652

CHAPTER 22 • The Great Depression Begins, 1929–1932

Annetta Gibson, quoted in *Centenarians: The Story of the Twentieth Century by the Americans Who Lived It* 656

Arthur Marx, quoted in *The Year of the Great Crash* 658

Dynamite Garland, adapted from *Hard Times* 661

Peggy Terry, quoted in *Hard Times* 662

John Steinbeck, from *The Grapes of Wrath* 665

Joseph Heffernan, adapted from *The Great Depression* 668

Herbert Hoover, from his Madison Square Garden Address, 1928 669

Franklin Roosevelt, from Roosevelt's Inaugural Address, 1933 669

E.Y. Harburg, from "Brother, Can You Spare a Dime?" 674

CHAPTER 23 • Roosevelt and the New Deal, 1933–1939

Louis Howe, adapted from *The Crisis of the Old Order* 678

Franklin Roosevelt, quoted in *The Public Papers and Addresses of Franklin D. Roosevelt* 679

Harold Clurman, quoted in *Franklin Roosevelt and the New Deal* 680

Will Rogers, adapted from *Will Rogers: A Biography* .. 682

Harry Hopkins, adapted from *The Politics of Upheaval* 689

Bruce Bliven, quoted in *The Great Depression* 693

Robert Vann, adapted from *The Politics of Upheaval* 695

Franklin Roosevelt, quoted in *Public Papers and Addresses of Franklin D. Roosevelt* 698

CHAPTER 24 • A World in Flames, 1931–1941

Dorothy Thompson, quoted in *The Women Who Wrote the War* 708

Franklin Roosevelt, quoted in *Freedom from Fear* 712

Sumner Welles, quoted in *Roosevelt and Churchill* ... 713

Primary Source Quotes

Winston Churchill, quoted in *Freedom from Fear* 717
Mira Ryczke, quoted in *Echoes from the Holocaust* 719
Frederick Morton, quoted in *Facing History
and Ourselves* 721
Leon Bass, quoted in *Facing History and Ourselves* 723
Daniel Inouye, quoted in *Eyewitness to America* 725
Franklin Roosevelt, quoted in *Franklin D.
Roosevelt: A Rendezvous with Destiny* 730
Charles Lindbergh, from his speech to
the America First Committee 733

CHAPTER 25 • America and World War II, 1941–1945
Franklin and Eleanor Roosevelt and Frank Knox,
adapted from *No Ordinary Time* 736
George C. Marshall, quoted in *Miracle of
World War II* 738
Saunders Redding, quoted in *America at War* 740
James Thach, quoted in *The Pacific War
Remembered* 742
Leon Beck, quoted in *Death March: The Survivors
of Bataan* 743
Laura Briggs, quoted in *Wartime America:
The World War II Home Front* 749
Inez Sauer, quoted in *Eyewitness to World War II* 750
John Bentz Carroll, quoted in *D-Day: Piercing
the Atlantic Wall* 755
Robert Sherrod, from *Tarawa:
The Story of a Battle* 759
Luther Fletcher, quoted in *World War II: From the
Battle Front to the Home Front* 764
Anonymous survivor of Tokyo firebombing,
quoted in *New History of World War II* 768
Nozaki Kiyoshi, quoted in *Senso: The Japanese
Remember the Pacific War* 770
Gar Alperovitz, quoted in *The Decision to Use
the Atomic Bomb, and the Architecture of
an American Myth* 770
Herbert Feis, quoted in *Japan Subdued: The Atomic
Bomb and the End of the War in the Pacific* 771
Alexander Allen, quoted in *Wartime America* 774

CHAPTER 26 • The Cold War Begins, 1945–1960
Harry S Truman and Vyacheslav Molotov, adapted
from *The Cold War: A History* 778
Winston Churchill, quoted in *The United States
and the Origins of the Cold War, 1941–1947* 782
George C. Marshall, quoted in
Marshall: A Hero for Our Times 785
Harry S Truman defends limited war 788
Douglas MacArthur, address to Congress,
April 19, 1951 788

Ruth Goldberg, adapted from *Red Scare* 790
Joseph R. McCarthy, quoted in *The Fifties* 793
Francis Gary Powers, adapted from *May-Day:
The U-2 Affair* 797
John Foster Dulles, quoted in *Rise to Globalism* 799
Margaret Chase Smith, from "Declaration of
Conscience" 805

CHAPTER 27 • Postwar America, 1945–1960
Robert Eubanks, adapted from *When Dreams
Came True* 808
Harry S Truman, quoted in *The Growth of the
American Republic* 809
Kemmons Wilson, adapted from *The Fifties* 814
Milton Bracker, quoted in *Voices from
America's Past* 819
Sidney Poitier, quoted in *The Fifties: The Way
We Really Were* 822
Elvis Presley, quoted in *God's Country: America
in the Fifties* 824
Lorraine Hansberry, adapted from *To Be Young,
Gifted, and Black* 828
Michael Harrington, from *The Other America* 829
Benjamin Reifel, quoted in *The Earth Shall Weep* 831
George Gallup, quoted in *Vital Speeches
of the Day* 834

CHAPTER 28 • The New Frontier and the Great Society, 1961–1968
Anonymous citizens, adapted from
The Great Debate 840
Pierre Salinger, quoted in *With Kennedy* 842
Tami Gold, quoted in *Collective Memories of
the Cuban Missile Crisis* 846
John F. Kennedy, quoted in *Let the
Word Go Forth* 847
John Rath, quoted in *Division Street: America* 854
Lyndon B. Johnson, quoted in *Lyndon Johnson
and the American Dream* 855
Anonymous writer, from *Lyndon Johnson:
The Exercise of Power* 855

CHAPTER 29 • The Civil Rights Movement, 1954–1968
Rosa Parks, E.D. Nixon, and J.P. Blake, adapted from
Parting the Waters: America in the King Years 866
Martin Luther King, Jr., quoted in *Parting the
Waters: America in the King Years* 870
The Greensboro Four, adapted from *Civilities
and Civil Rights* 873
John F. Kennedy, from Kennedy's White House
Address, June 11, 1963 877

Martin Luther King, Jr., quoted in *Freedom Bound:*
A History of America's Civil Rights Movement 878
Anonymous, adapted from *Anyplace But Here* 881
Stokely Carmichael, from the *New York Review*
of Books, September 1966 884

CHAPTER 30 • The Vietnam War, 1954–1975

Joe Marm, quoted in *The Soldiers' Story* 892
Archimedes Patti, quoted in *The Perfect War* 894
Dwight D. Eisenhower, quoted in *America*
in Vietnam 894
Marlene Kramel, adapted from *The Living and*
the Dead 896
George W. Ball, from an address in January 1966 898
George F. Kennan, speaking before the
Senate Foreign Relations Committee 899
McGeorge Bundy, quoted in *The Best and*
the Brightest 899
Ronald J. Glasser, quoted in *Vietnam, A History* 900
Martin Jezer, quoted in *The Vietnam War:*
Opposing Viewpoints 904
Martin Luther King, Jr., quoted in
A Testament of Hope 906
Frank Snepp, quoted in *Decent Interval* 910
Jan Barry, quoted in *Who Spoke Up?* 911
Doug Johnson, quoted in *Touched*
by the Dragon 913
Anonymous soldier, quoted in *Nam* 916

CHAPTER 31 • The Politics of Protest, 1960–1980

Mario Savio, quoted in *Decade of Shocks* 920
Todd Gitlin, from *The Sixties* 921
Herma Snider, quoted in *The Female Experience:*
An American Documentary 926
Betty Friedan, from *The Feminine Mystique* 928
Vernon Bellecourt, quoted in
Native American Testimony 932
Ruth Baston, quoted in *Freedom Bound* 934
Victor Yannacone, quoted in *Since Silent Spring* 939
Rachel Carson, from *Silent Spring* 940
Ralph Nader, from *Unsafe at Any Speed* 943

CHAPTER 32 • Politics and Economics, 1971–1980

G.L. Halbert, quoted in *Newsweek,*
September 16, 1968 952
Richard Nixon, quoted in *The Limits of Power* 956
Maurice Stans, quoted in *Nixon:*
An Oral History of His Presidency 957
Bob Woodward, quoted in *Nixon:*
An Oral History of His Presidency 962

Ellen Griffith and Robert Everson, adapted from the
New York Times, February 3, 1977 963
Hamilton Jordan, quoted in *Crisis: The Last*
Year of the Carter Presidency 969
Stoyan Christowe, quoted in *Newsweek,*
July 4, 1976 970
Kathy Smith, quoted in *The Century* 971
Gus Rodriguez, quoted in *The Century* 973
Unknown author, from article in *U.S. News &*
World Report, December 3, 1973 976

CHAPTER 33 • Resurgence of Conservatism, 1980–1992

Midge Decter, quoted in *Commentary,*
September 1977 980
Ronald Reagan, quoted in
Where's the Rest of Me? 985
Jimmy Carter, from his acceptance speech at
the Democratic National Convention,
August 14, 1980 986
Ronald Reagan, from his acceptance speech
at the Republican National Convention,
July 17, 1980 986
Ronald Reagan, from Reagan's First
Inaugural Address 987
Ronald Reagan, quoted in *Ronald Reagan* 989
Julie Katzman, from *Sleepwalking*
Through History 994
Ronald Reagan, from *Speaking My Mind* 998
George Bush and advisers, adapted from
Triumph Without Victory and *PBS Frontline*
Gulf War Interviews 1001
Ronald Reagan, from *Speaking My Mind* 1008

CHAPTER 34 • Into a New Century, 1992–present

Michael Kinsley, from "*Slate* Goes Free,"
Slate, February 13, 1999 1012
George Stephanopoulos, quoted in
All Too Human 1016
Madeleine Albright, quoted in *Madeleine*
Albright and the New American Diplomacy 1022
May Akabogu-Collins, quoted in *Time,*
December 11, 2000 1026
George W. Bush, from his televised statement,
December 13, 2000 1029
George W. Bush, from his Address to the Joint
Session of Congress, September 20, 2001 1034
George W. Bush, from his Address to the Nation,
October 7, 2001 1036
Tim Radford, from *World Press Review,*
February 2001 1038

NATIONAL GEOGRAPHIC Maps

Reference Atlas

United States Political RA2
United States Physical RA4
United States Congressional Reapportionment RA6
United States Territorial Growth RA8
Middle America Physical/Political RA10
Canada Physical/Political RA12
Middle East Physical/Political RA14
World Political RA16

Geography Handbook

Winkel Tripel Projection 2
Robinson Projection 3
Goode's Interrupted Equal-Area Projection 3
Mercator Projection 3

Unit 1

Mesoamerica, B.C. 500–1500 A.D. 13
North American Cultures, A.D. 1300 22
Empires of West and Central Africa, c. 1100–1525 30
Europe in the Age of Exploration, c. 1100–1400 34
The Columbian Exchange, c. 1500s 43
The Crusades, 1095–1204 47
European Explorations and Settlements, 1497–1682 59
The Thirteen Colonies, 1750 65
The Great Migration, 1620–1646 68
New England Colonies 70
The Middle Colonies, c. 1700 75
The Southern Colonies, c. 1733 76
Settlement of the Colonies, 1587–1700 81
Southern Agriculture, 1750 85
Economy of the Northern and Middle Colonies, 1750 92
Sudbury, Massachusetts, c. late 1600s 93
Colonial Trade Network, 1750 96
Ethnic Diversity in Colonial America, 1760 107
Colonization and Exports in the Americas, 1750 111

Unit 2

The Proclamation of 1763 119
Battles of Lexington and Concord, April 1775 130
War for Independence, 1775–1777 140
War for Independence, 1778–1781 144
Emancipation After Independence, 1780–1804 150
Land Claims in North America, 1783 155
Northwest Territory, 1780s 161
Western Land Claims of the Original States, 1787 177
The Election of 1800 220
The War of 1812 231
Treaty of Greenville, 1795 235

Unit 3

Adams-Onis Treaty Line 244
Roads, Canals, and Railroads, 1820–1840 246
The Missouri Compromise, 1820 258
The United States in 1824 263
Election of 1828 269

NATIONAL GEOGRAPHIC — Route of the Freedom Riders, 1961

Native American Removal, 1832–1841 270
African American Populations, 1820 and 1860 287
Overland Trails West, 1840–1860 296
Texas War for Independence, 1835–1836 303
Oregon Country, 1840 305
The War With Mexico, 1846–1848 310
Spanish Missions, 1776 312
Treaty of Guadalupe Hidalgo, 1848 315

Unit 4

Slavery and the Underground Railroad, 1830–1860 329
"Bleeding Kansas," 1856 330
The Election of 1860 341
Seceding States, 1860–1861 347
First Battle of Bull Run, 1861 358
War in the West, 1862–1863 360
War in the East, 1862–1863 362
Final Campaigns of the Civil War, 1864–1865 379
Peninsula Campaign, April–May 1862 383
Military Districts, 1867 394
The Election of 1876 405

Unit 5

Mining Country and Cattle Trails, 1848–1890 417
Native American Battles and Reservations, late 1800s 428
Major Industries, c. 1900 437
Railroads, 1870 and 1890 445
Strikes and Labor Unrest, 1870–1890 457
"Old" and "New" Immigrants, 1870–1900 465
The Election of 1884 494

Unit 6

Spanish-American War in the Philippines and
   the Caribbean, 1898 530
The Panama Canal, 1990s 539
U.S. Possessions in the Pacific, 1899 543
Woman Suffrage, 1869–1920 551
Early National Parks 560

NATIONAL GEOGRAPHIC **Major Terrorist Attacks Affecting Americans, 1970–2002**

1 1970 Terrorists hijack airplanes to Jordan

2 1979 Fifty-two Americans held hostage in Iran for more than a year

3 1983 Bombing of U.S. Marine barracks in Beirut, Lebanon, kills 241

4 1985 TWA flight 847 hijacked; hostages held for 17 days in Beirut, Lebanon

5 1986 Bombing at West Berlin dance club; kills 3, injures 150

6 1988 Bomb on Pan Am flight 103 kills 270 in Lockerbie, Scotland

7 1993 Bomb at World Trade Center kills 6

8 1995 Truck bomb destroys a federal building in Oklahoma City; kills 168, injures more than 500

9 1996 Bomb at U.S. complex in Dharan, Saudi Arabia, kills 19 American soldiers

10 1998 Bombing at U.S. embassies in Kenya and Tanzania kills more than 200

11 2000 Bomb kills 17 American sailors and injures 39 aboard USS *Cole*

12 2001 Hijacked airliners crash into the World Trade Center, the Pentagon, and a field in Pennsylvania, killing thousands

13 2002 Bombing at nightclub in Bali, Indonesia, kills 202

The Federal Reserve System. 568
The Progressive Movement and State Governments, 1889–1912 . . 573
European Alliances, 1914. 579
Battles of World War I, 1914–1918 594
Western Front, 1914–1918. 595
Europe After World War I, 1920 605

Unit 7
European Immigration Totals, 1890–1920 613
Dust Bowl, 1930s 663
The TVA, 1940. 684

Unit 8
Axis Expansion, 1935–1941 715
Jewish Losses, 1939–1945 724
Pearl Harbor, Hawaii, December 7, 1941 728
Nazi Concentration and Extermination Camps,1933–1945. . 733
Battle of Midway, 1942. 744
Bataan and Corregidor, December 1941–May 1942 748
Migration in the United States, 1940–1950. 751
Island-Hopping in the Pacific, 1942–1945. 760
World War II in Europe and Africa, 1939–1945 766
Rise and Fall of Axis Powers. 767
Battle of the Bulge, December 1944–January 1945. 775

Divided Europe, 1948. 782
Korean War, 1950–1953 787
NATO and the Warsaw Pact, 1955. 800
The Occupation of Berlin After World War II, 1945 805
The Election of 1948. 811
The Interstate System, 2000. 812

Unit 9
The Election of 1960. 863
Route of the Freedom Riders, 1961. 889
Indochina, 1959 893
The Tet Offensive, 1968 908
The Vietnam War 917
ERA Ratification, 1972–1982 947

Unit 10
The Election of 1968. 953
Rise of the Sunbelt, 1950–1980. 983
Revolution in Eastern Europe, 1989–1993 1002
War in the Persian Gulf, 1991 1005
The Election of 1992. 1009
The Election of 2000. 1028
Major Terrorist Attacks Affecting Americans, 1970–2002 . . 1034

Unit 1

American Civilizations 14
Comparing European Colonies in the
      Americas, c. 1700 77
Tobacco Imported by England, 1705–1775 85
Major Navigation Acts 100
Population of Six English Colonies, 1700 103
Major Cities, c. 1760 107

Unit 2

The Opposing Sides 139
Some Weaknesses of the Articles of Confederation ... 162
The Articles of Confederation and
      the United States Constitution 163
The Federal System 180
Checks and Balances 181
The Bill of Rights: The First Ten Amendments 182
How a Bill Becomes a Law 183
The Amendment Process 184
The Federal Court System 185
Competing National Visions 214
Presidential Election, 1800 220
Circumstances Leading to the
      Louisiana Purchase 233

Unit 3

Major Supreme Court Decisions, 1803–1824 242
The Transportation Revolution 246

Urban and Rural Populations in the United States,
      1810–1870 261
U.S. Patents Issued 1810–1840 263
Increased Voter Participation 268
Major American Political Parties Since 1789 272
Voter Participation, 1824–1840 291

Unit 4

The Compromise of 1850 324
Events of the 1840s: Results and Reactions 325
Political Parties of the Era 333
Presidential Election, 1860 341
Resources of the Union and of the Confederacy...... 354
The Anaconda Plan 356
Casualties of the Civil War, 1861–1865 378
American War Deaths 378
The Costs of War 378
Presidential Election, 1876 405
Agricultural Production in the South, 1860–1900 409

Unit 5

The Railroad and Native American Population 424
Native American Population 433
American Inventions 438
Miles of Track, 1870–1890 445
Vertical Integration, Horizontal Integration 449
Steel Production, 1865–1900 461

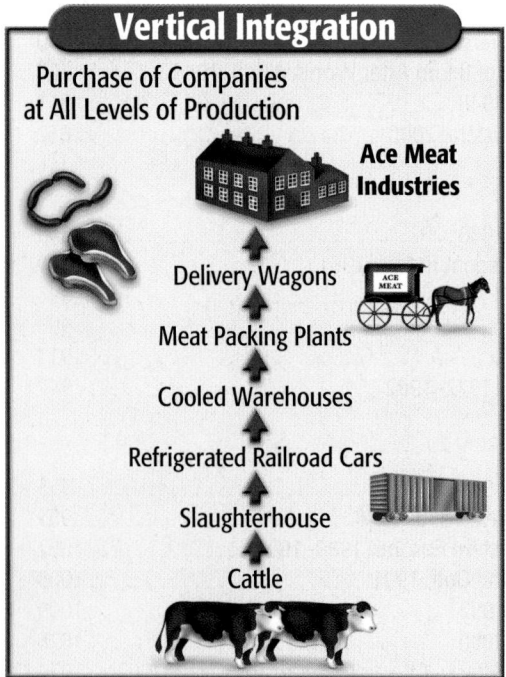

Vertical Integration

Purchase of Companies
at All Levels of Production

Ace Meat Industries

Delivery Wagons

Meat Packing Plants

Cooled Warehouses

Refrigerated Railroad Cars

Slaughterhouse

Cattle

Horizontal Integration

Purchase of Competing
Companies in Same Industry

U.S. Oil Company

Independent Oil Refineries

Charts & Graphs

Immigration, 1870–1900 465
Death Rates for Specific Causes 482
High School Graduation Rates 482
Life Expectancy. 482
Immigration's Contribution to Population Growth,
    1860–1900 489
Presidential Election, 1884 494
Farm Prices, 1860–1900 515

Unit 6
U.S. Foreign Investments at the Turn of
    the Century 521
U.S. Deaths in the Spanish-American War 530
U.S. Exports, 1890–1910 537
Mayor-Council Form 549
Commission Form 549
Council-Manager Form 549
Federal Mobilization Agencies 587
World War I Military Deaths 595

Unit 7
Women's Status in the 1920s 617
U.S. Immigration, 1921 and 1925. 633
Percentage of National Income Generated by
    Industry, 1919–1928 645
Farm Wages 645
The Washington Conference, November 1921–
    February 1922 649
Cost of a Model T, 1908–1924 653
The Great Depression: Cyclical Effect. 658
Stock Prices, 1920–1932 658
The Great Depression: Causes 658
Crop Prices, 1910–1935 675
The First New Deal, 1933–1935 687
The Second New Deal, 1935. 692
Union Membership, 1933–1943. 693
Unemployment, 1933–1940 703

Unit 8
Automobile Production, 1941–1945 738
Tank Production, 1941–1945 739
Military and Civilian Deaths in World War II 767
Percent of Military and Civilian Deaths in
    World War I and World War II 767
Presidential Election, 1948 811

Immigration's Contribution to Population Growth, 1860–1900

Source: *Historical Statistics of the United States: Colonial Times to 1970.*

The Baby Boom 816
American Scene, 1950–1960 827
Suburban Dwellers, 1910–1980 835

Unit 9
Major Decisions of the Warren Court, 1954–1967 844
Major Great Society Programs 858
Vietnam War Deaths, 1965–1972 901
Opposition to the Vietnam War 909
U.S. Hispanic Population Growth Since 1980 935

Unit 10
Presidential Election, 1968 953
Inflation, 1960–1992 977
Military Spending and the Deficit, 1980–1992 990
Estimated World Oil Production in 2000
    (by region) 1004
Presidential Election, 1992 1009
The Florida Election, 2000. 1027
Presidential Election, 2000 1028
Population Density by Region in the U.S., 1996 1030
American Diversity, 2000 1039

Previewing Your Textbook

Your textbook has been organized to help you learn about the significant events and people that make up American history. Before you start reading, though, here is a road map to help you understand what you will encounter in the pages of this textbook. Follow this road map before you read so that you can understand how this textbook works.

Units

Your textbook is divided into 10 units. Each unit begins with two pages of information to help you start your study of the topics.

WHY IT MATTERS

Each unit begins with *Why It Matters*. This is a short summary about the important topics and what you will study in the unit.

QUOTATION

A short quotation gives a glimpse of the ideas of a key figure from the unit's era.

UNIT

1 Three Worlds Meet

Beginnings to 1763

Why It Matters

The interactions among Native Americans, Europeans, and Africans shaped the history of the Americas. Native Americans struggled to live alongside Europeans and their ever-growing settlements and colonies. Africans tried to adapt to the new continent to which they were brought involuntarily. Studying these early cultural interactions will help you understand the centuries of history that followed. The following resources offer more information about this period in American history.

Primary Sources Library
See pages 1048–1049 for primary source readings to accompany Unit 1.

Use the **American History Primary Source Document Library** **CD-ROM** to find additional primary sources about the meeting of Native Americans, Europeans, and Africans.

8

Pre-Cherokee necklace, c. 1300

Cherokee Settlement by Felix Marie Ferdinand Storelli

"*Long before they had heard the word Spaniard, they [Native Americans] had properly organized states, wisely ordered by excellent laws, religion, and custom.*"

—Bartolomé de Las Casas, 1550

PRIMARY SOURCES LIBRARY

This tells you where to find the *Primary Sources Library* readings that accompany the unit.

VISUALS

A photograph or painting shows you what life was like during the time period of the unit.

Chapters

Each unit in *The American Vision* is made up of chapters. Each chapter starts by providing you with background information to help you get the most out of the chapter.

CHAPTER TITLE

The chapter title tells you the main topic you will be reading about.

WHY IT MATTERS

Why It Matters tells you why the events you will study are important.

THE IMPACT TODAY

The Impact Today explains how these events changed the way we live today.

CHAPTER

1 Converging Cultures

Prehistory to 1520

Why It Matters

Before 1492, the cultures that arose in the Americas had almost no contact with the rest of the world. Then, in the late 1300s, momentous events began taking place that would bring the cultures of Europe and Africa into direct contact with the Americas. This contact had profound effects on the future of the world's civilization.

The Impact Today

The convergence of the world's cultures in the 1400s launched an era of change that still affects our lives today.
- Many of our foods, customs, and traditions were originally introduced in the Americas as a result of this cultural contact.
- Contact among the cultures of the three continents profoundly changed the society of each.
- American society today includes elements of Native American, European, and African cultures.

The American Vision Video The Chapter 1 video, "America Before the Americans," examines the early Americas.

The Landing of Columbus in San Salvador by Albert Bierstadt, 1893

The Americas

- **c. 28,000–13,000 B.C.**
  · First humans migrate to North America from Asia
- **c. 1200 B.C.**
  · Early Mesoamerican civilizations arise
- **c. A.D. 200**
  · Mayan culture arises in Central America
- **A.D. 300**
  · Hohokam culture arises in North America
- **c. 1130**
  · Drought strikes Native American cliff dwellings at Chaco Canyon
- **c. 1300**
  · Cahokia civilization collapses
- **1492**
  · Christopher Columbus lands in America
- **1500s**
  · Navajo arrive in Southwest of North America

28,000 B.C.   1200 B.C.   A.D. 250   500   1100   1200   1300   1400   1500

World

- **c. 3000 B.C.**
  · Sumerians create cuneiform writing
- **1750 B.C.**
  · Death of Hammurabi in the Middle East
- **A.D. 400**
  · Ghana civilization develops in West Africa
- **c. 610**
  · Muhammed begins teaching ideas of Islam
- **1240**
  · Mali empire expands in West Africa
- **1420s**
  · Portugal begins exploring African coast
- **c. 1450**
  · Songhai empire expands in West Africa

HISTORY Online
Chapter Overview
Visit the *American Vision* Web site at tav.glencoe.com and click on *Chapter Overviews—Chapter 1* to preview chapter information.

10   11

TIME LINE

The time line shows you when and where events happened during the period of time covered in the chapter.

VISUALS

A photograph or painting depicts a scene from the chapter's era.

WEB SITE

History Online directs you to the Internet, where you can find activities, quizzes, and additional information about the chapter's topic.

Previewing Your Textbook

Sections

A section is a division, or part, of the chapter. The first page of the section, the section opener, helps you set a purpose for reading.

READING STRATEGY

Completing the *Reading Strategy* activity will help you organize information as you read the section.

READING OBJECTIVES

Keep the *Reading Objectives* statements in mind as you read the section.

SECTION THEMES

Your textbook organizes the events of your nation's past and present around themes. You can read about the themes on pages NY60–NY61.

MAIN IDEA

The *Main Idea* of this section is introduced here. Below it are important terms you will encounter as you read.

TIME LINE

The time line identifies important events you will study in the section.

AN AMERICAN STORY

Think of *An American Story* as a moment in time. It introduces you to an important event that you will read about.

SECTION 1 **The Migration to America**

Guide to Reading

Main Idea
Native Americans are descended from Asians who probably began migrating to North America approximately 15,000 to 30,000 years ago.

Key Terms and Names
radiocarbon dating, Ice Age, glacier, Beringia, nomad, agricultural revolution, maize, civilization, obsidian, Aztec, Chaco Canyon, kiva, pueblo, Cahokia

Reading Strategy
Categorizing As you read about the first people to live in North America, complete a graphic organizer similar to the one below by filling in the names of Native American groups who settled in various regions.

Region	Native American Groups
Mesoamerica	
North American Southwest	
North American Midwest	

Reading Objectives
• **Explain** why scientists believe that the earliest Americans migrated from Asia.
• **Describe** the early civilizations of Mesoamerica and the early cultures of North America.

Section Theme
Geography and History Scientists theorize that Asian hunters migrated to North America across a land bridge exposed during the last Ice Age.

Preview of Events

♦30,000 B.C.	♦15,000 B.C.	♦0	♦A.D. 1500

c. 28,000–13,000 B.C.
First humans migrate to North America

c. 8000–7000 B.C.
Agriculture begins

c. 1200 B.C.
Early Mesoamerican civilizations arise

c. A.D. 200
Maya culture arises

c. A.D. 1300
Cahokia collapses

★ *An American Story* ★

In 1925 an African American cowboy named George McJunkin was riding along a gully near the town of Folsom, New Mexico, when he noticed something gleaming in the dirt. He began digging and found a bone and a flint arrowhead. J.D. Figgins of the Colorado Museum of Natural History knew the bone belonged to a type of bison that had been extinct for 10,000 years. The arrowhead's proximity to the bones implied that human beings had been in America at least 10,000 years, which no one had believed at that time.

The following year, Figgins found another arrowhead embedded in similar bones. In 1927 he led a group of scientists to the find. Anthropologist Frank H.H. Roberts, Jr., wrote, "There was no question but that here was the evidence. . . . The point was still embedded . . . between two of the ribs of the animal skeleton." Further digs turned up more arrowheads, now called Folsom points. Roberts later noted: "The Folsom find was accepted as a reliable indication that man was present in the Southwest at an earlier period than was previously supposed."

—adapted from *The First American: A Story of North American Archaeology*

The Asian Migration to America

No one can say for certain when the first people arrived in America. The Folsom discoveries proved that people were here at least 10,000 years ago, but more recent research suggests that humans arrived much earlier. Presently, scientific speculation points to a

12 CHAPTER 1 Converging Cultures

Reading Roadmap

You will get more out of your textbook if you recognize the different elements that help you understand what you read.

MAPS

Easy-to-read maps provide a link between geography and history. Questions test your understanding of the map's information.

PHOTOGRAPHS

Photographs show you important people, places, and events of the time. Questions help you interpret the photographs and relate them to content.

READING CHECKS

Reading Checks allow you to stop and check your understanding of the main ideas.

OUTLINE

Think of the headings as forming an outline. The blue titles are the main headings. The red titles that follow are the subheadings.

VOCABULARY

The words in blue are the section's key terms. They are defined within the text.

SECTION ASSESSMENT

The *Section Assessment* is the last item in every section. Completing the assessment can help you evaluate your comprehension of section material.

(Sample textbook pages shown, including:)

NATIONAL GEOGRAPHIC — War in the East, 1862–1863

PENNSYLVANIA

Gettysburg July 1–3, 1863

Antietam Sept. 17, 1862

MARYLAND

Frederick

Baltimore

WEST VIRGINIA (1863)

Washington

Manassas Junction

Bull Run (Second Battle) Aug. 29–30, 1862

Chancellorsville May 1–3, 1863

Fredericksburg Dec. 13, 1862

VIRGINIA

Richmond

Seven Days June 25–July 1, 1862

- Union forces
- Confederate forces
- Union Victory
- Confederate Victory

50 miles
50 kilometers
Albers Conic Equal-Area projection

Monitor & Virginia Mar. 9, 1862

Geography Skills

1. **Interpreting Maps** Which battles shown took place outside of Virginia's borders?
2. **Applying Geography Skills** How far apart are the capital cities of Richmond and Washington, D.C.?

army, inflicting heavy casualties. After Johns... wounded in the battle, General Robert E. ... placed in command.

In late June of 1862, Lee began a series of a... McClellan's army that became known colled... the **Seven Days' Battle.** Although Lee was ... decisively defeat the Union army, he inflict... casualties and forced McClellan to retreat to ... River. Together the two sides suffered over 30... alties. Despite McClellan's protests, Lincol... him to withdraw from the peninsula and ... troops back to Washington.

362 CHAPTER 11 The Civil War

Picturing History

African American Soldiers Battery A of the 2nd U.S. Colored Light Artillery was only one of many groups of African Americans who fought for their own freedom. Why did Frederick Douglass favor African American enlistment?

African Americans in the Military

The Emancipation Proclamation officially permitted African Americans to enlist in the Union army and navy. Almost immediately, thousands of African Americans, including Frederick Douglass's two sons, Charles and Lewis, rushed to join the military. Douglass approved of his sons' decision. He believed that serving in the military would help African Americans overcome discrimination:

> Once let the black man get upon his person the brass letters U.S.; let him get an eagle on his button, and a musket on his shoulder and bullets in his pocket, and there is no power on earth which can deny that he has earned the right to citizenship.

— quoted in *Battle Cry of Freedom*

About 180,000 African Americans served in the Union army during the Civil War, roughly 9 percent of the army's total soldiers. Another 10,000 to 15,000 served in the Union navy, making up about 10 to 12 percent of the navy's sailors.

Among the first African American regiments officially organized in the North was the **54th Massachusetts.** The regiment fought valiantly at Fort Wagner near Charleston Harbor in July 1863, losing nearly half of its members in the battle. "Men all around me fell and roll down the slope into the ditch," remembered Lewis Douglass. "Swept down like chaff, still our men went on and on."

At the end of the war, the *New York Tribune* declared that the heroism of the 54th Massachusetts

366 CHAPTER 11 The Civil War

---

regiment forever answered the question of whether African Americans could make good soldiers:

> It is not too much to say that if this Massachusetts Fifty-Fourth had faltered when its trial came, two hundred thousand [African Americans] for whom it was a pioneer would never have been put into the field. . . . But it did not falter. It made Fort Wagner such a name to [African Americans] as Bunker Hill has been for ninety years to white Yankees.

— from *Like Men of War*

✓ **Reading Check** Analyzing Why do you think African Americans were so willing to volunteer to fight during the Civil War?

Military Life

Early in the war, General Irwin McDowell's troops stopped to pick berries and foolishly wasted water from their canteens to wash them. "They were not used to denying themselves much; they were not u... to journeys on foot," the Union commander later reflected. Self-denial and long marches would prove to be only one of the harsh lessons of the war.

The Soldiers in the Field Union and Confederate soldiers suffered many hardships during the long days and weeks between battles. Some Southern soldiers had to sleep without blankets and tramp the roads shoeless. Union soldier Elisha Rhodes wrote home that "all that we have to eat is the cattle killed by the way. No bread or salt in the Regiment and I am most starved."

Soldiers learned to gulp down tasteless food. For the Union soldier, meals often consisted of hardtack (a hard biscuit made of wheat flour), potatoes, and beans, flavored at times with dried salt pork (pork fat cured in salty brine). Confederate soldiers had little coffee, and their bread was usually made of cornmeal. Whenever possible, soldiers on both sides supplemented their diet with fruit or vegetables seized or purchased from farms they passed.

Battlefield Medicine When Americans went to war in 1861, most were not prepared for the horrors of battle. "The sights and smells that assailed us were simply indescribable," wrote one Southern soldier. "Corpses were swollen to twice their size, some actually burst asunder. . . . The odors were so deadly that in a short time we all sickened [and] . . . most of us [were] vomiting profusely."

---

mockery of our sufferings and sacrifices, if slavery

SECTION 2 ASSESSMENT

Checking for Understanding

1. **Define:** bounty, blockade runner.
2. **Identify:** "Stonewall" Jackson, Irwin McDowell, David G. Farragut, Ulysses S. Grant, George B. McClellan, Emancipation Proclamation.
3. **Summarize** why David G. Farragut was considered a hero in the North.

Reviewing Themes

4. **Geography and History** Why was seizing control of the Mississippi River an important strategy of the Union navy?

Critical Thinking

5. **Forming an Opinion** Do you think the draft for military service during the Civil War violated civil liberties, or was the need for defense more important? Explain your answer.
6. **Organizing** Use a graphic organizer to explain President Lincoln's reasons for issuing the Emancipation Proclamation and the effects it had on the war.

Reasons for → Emancipation Proclamation → Effect on War

Analyzing Visuals

7. **Examining Art** Examine the painting of the battle between the *Monitor* and the *Virginia* on page 359. What made these vessels superior to regular warships used by the Union and the Confederacy?

Writing About History

8. **Persuasive Writing** Imagine that you are asked to advise President Lincoln about issuing the Emancipation Proclamation. Write a short paper in which you explain the reasons for the advice you give him.

CHAPTER 11 The Civil War **363**

Special Features

A variety of special features will help you as you study *The American Vision.*

PROFILES IN HISTORY

Profiles in History tell you the stories of individuals who have influenced American history.

SKILLBUILDERS

Skillbuilders teach valuable skills that will be useful throughout the book.

DIFFERENT VIEWPOINTS

Different Viewpoints compare the opposing viewpoints of two historic figures on a particular issue.

AMERICAN LITERATURE

American Literature analyzes poems and excerpts from biographies, American fiction, and other writings, and describes the excerpts' historical lessons.

Tecumseh's flight to British-held Canada seemed to prove that the British were supporting and arming the Native Americans. Many Western farmers believed that war with Britain would enable the United States to seize Canada and end Native American attacks.

In early June 1812, President Madison gave in to the pressure and asked Congress to declare war. His war message spoke about national honor and emphasized the abuse Americans had suffered at the hands of the British:

"Thousands of American citi-

Profiles IN HISTORY

Tecumseh
c. 1768–1813

Tecumseh was a Shawnee chief born near present-day Springfield, Ohio. The Shawnee had taken part in many wars in the Northwest Territory. After the Treaty of Greenville in 1795, Tecumseh and many other Shawnee moved to the Indiana territory to escape American settlers.

Tecumseh urged all Native Americans to unite. They were all one people, he said, and should cooperate in a confederacy to control their destiny. He was furious when the Delaware ... commander, he met his end at the

---

Social Studies SKILLBUILDER

Reading a Thematic Map

Why Learn This Skill?

In your study of American history, you will often encounter thematic, or special-purpose, maps. Knowing how to read a thematic map will help you get more out of it.

Learning the Skill

NATIONAL GEOGRAPHIC Bataan
Decem

Camp
O'Donnell
April 15

ZAMBALES

---

it killed civilians indiscriminately. He believed that an economic blockade and conventional bombing would convince Japan to surrender. Secretary of War Henry Stimson wanted to warn the Japanese about the bomb while at the same time telling them that they could keep the emperor if they surrendered. Secretary of State James Byrnes, however, wanted to drop the bomb without any warning to shock Japan into surrendering.

President Truman later wrote that he "regarded the bomb as a military weapon and never had any doubts that it should be used." His advisers had warned him to expect massive casualties if the United States invaded Japan. Truman believed it was his duty as president to use every weapon available to save American lives.

The Allies threatened Japan with "prompt and utter destruction" if the nation did not surrender unconditionally, but the Japanese did not reply. Truman then ordered the military to drop the bomb. On August 6, 1945, a B-29 bomber named the *Enola Gay* dropped an atomic bomb, code-named "Little

Boy," on Hiroshima, an ... bomb was dropped at 8 ... later, it exploded. Heat, ... shock wave slammed in ...

The bomb destroyed ... percent of the city. Som ... 120,000 people died in ... died later from bur ... Everywhere, as witne ... were "horrific scenes":

"The center of the c ... like live charcoal. Roof ... numerous war dead w ... We found five or six h ... Inside were piles of c ... smoke. . . . A young ... tucked under her bre ... wax dolls than huma ...

Different Viewpoints

Dropping the Atomic Bomb: Was It the Right Decision?

More than half a century later, people continue to debate what some historians have called the most important event of the twentieth century—President Truman's order to drop the atomic bomb on Japan. Did his momentous decision shorten the war and save lives on both sides, or was it prompted by Truman's fear that the Soviet Union, poised to invade, would gain control of Japan after the war?

A historian opposes Truman'...

Historian Gar Alperovitz ma ... alternatives to the atomic bom ... in order to force Japan's surre ... could mount an invasion and s ... territory.

"Quite simply, it is not true ... because it was the only way to ... sands' or 'millions' of lives as ... readily available options were ... and/or await the shock of the ...

Perhaps it is ... confront our ow ... questions—for ... most inflated e ... atomic bomb, ... of violent dest ... tions of noncombatants.

—quoted in *The Decision to Use the Atomic Bomb, and the Architecture of an American Myth*

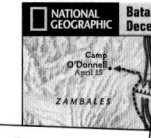
Hiroshima in the aftermath of the atomic bomb

America LITERATU...

from *The American Cris... Number 1*
by Thomas Paine

The call to arms during the Revolution was heard not only on the fields of battle but off, echoed by the leading writers of the day. Some of the most inspiring words that rang out against British tyranny were those of **Thomas Paine**, a sometime teacher, sailor, and grocer who became a journalist in his late thirties. The first essay from Paine's collection *The American Crisis*, issued in December 1776, was read by General George Washington to boost the spirits of his beleaguered troops.

Read to Discover

What language does Paine use to encourage support for the American revolutionary cause?

Reader's Dictionary
tyranny: absolute power wielded unjustly

consolation: comfort

esteem: value

impious: not respectful

These are the times that try men's souls. The summer soldier and the sunshine patriot will in this crisis, shrink from the service of his country; but he that stands it NOW deserves the love and thanks of man and woman. Tyranny, like hell, is not easily conquered; yet we have this consolation with us, that the harder the conflict, the more glorious the triumph. What we obtain too cheap, we esteem too lightly; 'tis dearness only that gives everything its value. Heaven knows how to put a proper price upon its goods and it would be strange indeed, if so celestial an article as FREEDOM should not be highly rated. Britain, with an army to enforce her tyranny, has declared that she has a right (not only to TAX) but "to BIND us in ALL CASES WHATSOEVER," and if being bound in that manner, is not slavery, then is there not such a thing as slavery upon earth. Even the expression is impious, for so unlimited a power can belong only to God. . . .

. . . Let it be told to the future world that in the depth of winter, when nothing but hope and virtue could survive, that the city and the

country, alarmed at one c ... danger, came forth to meet ... repulse it. . . . I love the m ...

> "These are the times that try men's souls."

... can sm ... trouble, th ... gather st ... from di ... and grow ... by reflecti ... is the business of little min ... shrink; but he whose heart is ... and whose conscience approve ... conduct, will pursue his princ ... unto death.

Analyzing Literatu...

1. **Recall and Interpret** What does ... Paine mean by the phrase "the sum ... mer soldier and the sunshine patric ...

2. **Evaluate and Connect** What purpo ... do you think essays such as this one ... serve in times of war and crisis?

Interdisciplinary Activity
Language Arts The language in Paine's ... essay may seem outdated now, but the ... emotions and ideas he expresses are still ... common. Rewrite the first paragraph of ... the essay, using words that a modern ... politician might use in a speech. Try to ... think of current phrases that would make ... sense—for example, what might we say ... today instead of the "summer soldier"?

2. Using the internet or other resources, find an account of the bombing from the point of a Japanese citizen. How does it differ from the accounts above, and why?

Scavenger Hunt

The American Vision contains a wealth of information. The trick is to know where to look to access all the information in the book. If you go through this scavenger hunt, either alone or with your teacher or parents, you will quickly learn how the textbook is organized and how to get the most out of your reading and study time. Let's get started!

1. How many units and chapters are in the book?

2. What is the difference between the glossary and the index?

3. Most sections of a chapter open with a primary source—a document or other testimony dating from the period. Where else can you find primary sources in the textbook?

4. In what special feature can you find the definition of a physical map, a political map, and a special-purpose map?

5. If you want to quickly find all the maps, charts, and graphs about World War II, where in the front do you look?

6. How can you find information about William Penn's colonization of Pennsylvania?

7. Where can you find a graphic organizer that summarizes the major events of the Civil War discussed in Chapter 11?

8. What are the key terms and names for Chapter 8, Section 3, and how are they highlighted in the text?

9. The Web site for the book is listed three times in Chapter 16. After finding all three, list how the Web site can help you.

10. Which of the book's main features will provide you with strategies for improving your studying and writing skills?

Reading for Information

Think of your textbook as a tool that helps you learn more about the world around you. It is an example of nonfiction writing—it describes real-life events, people, ideas, and places. Here is a menu of reading strategies that will help you become a better textbook reader. As you come to passages in your textbook that you don't understand, refer to these reading strategies for help.

✔ Before You Read

Set a purpose
- Why are you reading the textbook?
- How does the subject relate to your life?
- How might you be able to use what you learn in your own life?

Preview
- Read the chapter title to find what the topic will be.
- Read the subtitles to see what you will learn about the topic.
- Skim the photos, charts, graphs, or maps. How do they support the topic?
- Look for vocabulary words that are boldfaced. What are their definitions?

Draw From Your Own Background
- What have you read or heard concerning new information on the topic?
- How is the new information different from what you already know?
- How will the information that you already know help you understand the new information?

Question

What is the main idea?

How do the photos, charts, graphs, and maps support the main idea?

Connect

Think about people, places, and events in your own life. Are there any similarities with those in your textbook?

Can you relate the textbook information to other areas of your life?

Predict

Predict events or outcomes by using clues and information that you already know.

Change your predictions as you read and gather new information.

Visualize

Pay careful attention to details and descriptions.

Create graphic organizers to show relationships that you find in the information.

Look For Clues As You Read

Comparison and Contrast Sentences

■ Look for clue words and phrases that signal comparison, such as *similarly, just as, both, in common, also,* and *too.*

■ Look for clue words and phrases that signal contrast, such as *on the other hand, in contrast to, however, different, instead of, rather than, but,* and *unlike.*

Cause-and-Effect Sentences

■ Look for clue words and phrases such as *because, as a result, therefore, that is why, since, so, for this reason,* and *consequently.*

Chronological Sentences

■ Look for clue words and phrases such as *after, before, first, next, last, during, finally, earlier, later, since,* and *then.*

✓ After You Read

Summarize

■ Describe the main idea and how the details support it.

■ Use your own words to explain what you have read.

Assess

■ What was the main idea?

■ Did the text clearly support the main idea?

■ Did you learn anything new from the material?

■ Can you use this new information in other school subjects or at home?

■ What other sources could you use to find more information about the topic?

How Do I Study History?

As you read *The American Vision*, you will be given help in sorting out all the information you encounter. This textbook organizes the events of your nation's past and present around 10 themes. A theme is a concept, or main idea that happens again and again throughout history. By recognizing these themes, you will better understand events of the past and how they affect you today.

Themes in *The American Vision*

Culture and Traditions
Being aware of cultural differences helps us understand ourselves and others. People from around the world for generations have sung of the "land of the Pilgrims' pride, land where our fathers died," even though their ancestors arrived on these shores long after these events occurred.

Continuity and Change
Recognizing our historic roots helps us understand why things are the way they are today. This theme includes political, social, religious, and economic changes that have influenced the way Americans think and act.

Geography and History
Understanding geography helps us understand how humans interact with their environment. The United States succeeded in part because of its rich natural resources and its vast open spaces. In many regions, the people changed the natural landscape to fulfill their wants and needs.

Individual Action

Responsible individuals have often stepped forward to help lead the nation. Americans' strong values helped create such individuals. These values spring in part from earlier times when the home was the center of many activities, including work, education, and spending time with one's family.

Groups and Institutions

Identifying how political and social groups and institutions operate helps us work together. From the beginning, Americans formed groups and institutions to act in support of their economic, political, social, and religious beliefs.

Government and Democracy

Understanding the workings of government helps us become better citizens. Abraham Lincoln explained the meaning of democracy as "government of the people, by the people, for the people." Democracy, at its best, is "among" the people.

Science and Technology

Americans have always been quick to adopt innovations. The nation was settled and built by people who gave up old ways in favor of new. Americans' lives are deeply influenced by technology, the use of science, and machines. Perhaps no machine has so shaped modern life as the automobile. Understanding the role of science and technology helps us see their impact on our society and the roles they will play in the future.

Economic Factors

The free enterprise economy of the United States is consistent with the nation's history of rights and freedoms. Freedom of choice in economic decisions supports other freedoms. Understanding the concept of free enterprise is basic to studying American history.

Global Connections

Being aware of global interdependence helps us make decisions and deal with the difficult issues we will encounter.

Civic Rights and Responsibilities

For a democratic system to survive, its citizens must take an active role in government. The foundation of democracy is the right of every person to take part in government and to voice one's views on issues. An appreciation for the struggle to preserve these freedoms is vital to the understanding of democracy.

Using the Themes

You will find Section Themes at the beginning of every section of your text. You are asked questions that help you put it all together to better understand how ideas and themes are connected across time—and to see why history is important to you today.

WHAT IS THE REGENTS EXAM?

The New York Regents Exam for United States History and Government is administered in all New York public schools to measure student achievement. The test is directly aligned with the Core Curriculum for U.S. History and Government.

HOW CAN I PREPARE FOR THE EXAM?

Pages NY64–NY87 of this text include a section called Countdown to the Regents Exam. Each page contains 5 questions that are just like those on the Regents Exam for United States History and Government. You should plan to complete one page each week to help you prepare for the test.

Plan to spend a few minutes each day working on the exam question for that day unless your teacher asks you to do otherwise. While all questions are multiple-choice questions, some also include visuals such as documents, maps, charts, and graphs that need to be interpreted in order to answer the questions. If you have difficulty with any question, you can refer to the section in your textbook referenced in parentheses in the top part of the question. For example, if you see *Sections 1.3 and 1.4,* you can find more information by looking in Chapter 1, Sections 3 and 4.

You can find a printable worksheet to record your work and your answers for each week at <u>tav.glencoe.com</u>. When you get to the Web site, click on New York on the map that appears and select the worksheet. At the end of the week, your teacher may want you to turn in this answer sheet.

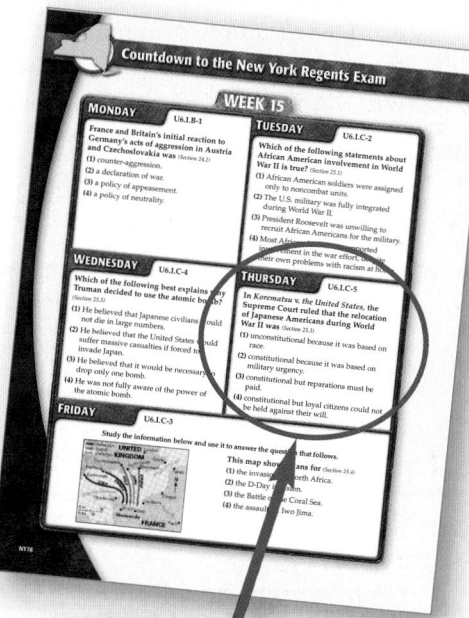

THURSDAY   U6.I.C-5

In *Korematsu* v. *the United States,* the Supreme Court ruled that the relocation of Japanese Americans during World War II was *(Section 25.3)*

(1) unconstitutional because it was based on race.

(2) constitutional because it was based on military urgency.

(3) constitutional but reparations must be paid.

(4) constitutional but loyal citizens could not be held against their will.

HOW DOES MY TEXTBOOK HELP ME PREPARE FOR THE EXAM?

Your textbook contains many opportunities for you to get ready for the exam every day. Take advantage of these so you don't need to cram before the exam.

- The **sections** contain many maps and charts, Skillbuilders, and other features with corresponding questions that allow you to practice interpreting text and visuals.

- The **section assessments** at the end of each section allow for further practice in evaluating, analyzing, and interpreting information and visuals.

- The **chapter assessments** provide additional opportunities to practice your skills.

- The **Standardized Test Practice** questions at the end of each chapter assessment help you prepare for the multiple-choice format of the exam.

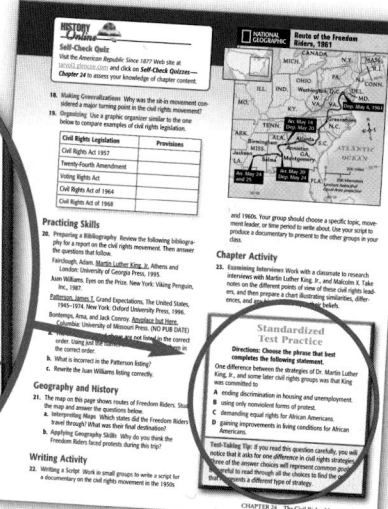

TEST-TAKING TIPS

- Go to bed early the night before the test.
- Read each question carefully and think about ways to solve it before you try to answer the question.
- Relax. Most people get nervous when taking a test. It's natural. Just do your best.
- Answer questions you are sure about first. If you do not know the answer, skip it and go back to that question later.
- Make sure to look at any visuals that are part of the question before you select your answer.

TEST PRACTICE WORKBOOK

The New York Regents Review Series for United States History and Government is a printed workbook that will help you prepare for the Regents Exam. The workbook includes the same kinds of questions you will find in the exam along with strategies, instructions, and tips. There is an outline and commentary that is based on your textbook, *The American Vision*, to be used for reviewing the content. Each unit is followed by Regents questions for practice. The workbook concludes with three complete Regents Exams to provide complete test practice.

Countdown to the New York Regents Exam

WEEK 1

MONDAY — U1.I.B-1

The Tlingit and Chinook peoples were able to dwell in permanent settlements **because** *(Section 1.2)*

(1) they practiced agriculture.

(2) the region's coastal waters and rivers teemed with fish.

(3) they used lumber from the forests to create totem poles.

(4) they were warriors.

TUESDAY — U1.I.A-4

Which of the following was a hardship faced by settlers on the Great Plains? *(Section 13.2)*

(1) forest fires

(2) tropical storms

(3) constant flooding

(4) grasshopper infestations

WEDNESDAY — U1.I.D-1

What religious group, in their attempt to escape persecution, settled the Great Salt Lake area in present-day Utah? *(Section 9.1)*

(1) Quakers

(2) Mormons

(3) Catholics

(4) Calvinists

THURSDAY — U1.I.D-4

The area to which large numbers of Americans began moving during World War II to take jobs in war factories, a trend that continued after the war, is **known as** *(Section 33.1)*

(1) the Northwest.

(2) the Southwest.

(3) the Rust Belt.

(4) the Sunbelt.

FRIDAY — U1.I.A-1

Study the information below and use it to answer the question that follows.

The Beringia Land Bridge

According to the map, the Beringia land bridge once connected Siberia and *(Section 1.1)*

(1) Alaska.

(2) the Arctic Circle.

(3) the Arctic Ocean.

(4) the Bering Sea.

WEEK 2

MONDAY U2.I.B-4

The primary reason that most Antifederalists opposed the Constitution was their belief that *(Section 5.3)*

(1) it took too much power from the states.

(2) it allowed wealthy creditors to get rid of paper money and foreclose on others' lands.

(3) it did not provide for a separation of powers.

(4) it did not provide for adequate checks and balances.

TUESDAY U2.I.C

The Tenth Amendment in the Bill of Rights states that *(Section 6.1)*

(1) the people have other rights that are not listed.

(2) the people have the right to bear arms.

(3) powers not given to the federal government are reserved for the states.

(4) the people have the right to life, liberty, and the pursuit of happiness.

WEDNESDAY U2.I.D

The ability of the president to veto an act of Congress is an example of *(Section 5.2)*

(1) popular sovereignty.

(2) separation of powers.

(3) federalism.

(4) checks and balances.

THURSDAY U2.I.F-1

Madison's argument against Hamilton's plan for a national bank was that *(Section 6.1)*

(1) it was not among the federal government's enumerated powers.

(2) the paper money issued by the bank would soon become worthless.

(3) Southern planters would own most of the stock because only they could afford it.

(4) the Constitution expressly forbade the federal government from creating a bank.

FRIDAY U2.I.A-4

Study the information below and use it to answer the question that follows.

We hold these truths to be self-evident, that all men are created equal, that they are endowed by their Creator with certain unalienable Rights, that among these are Life, Liberty, and the pursuit of Happiness.

That to secure these rights, Governments are instituted among Men, deriving their just powers from the consent of the governed.

This quote from the Declaration of Independence demonstrated the influence of *(Section 4.2)*

(1) Thomas Paine's *Common Sense.*

(2) John Locke's *Two Treatises of Government.*

(3) Baron Montesquieu's *Spirit of the Laws.*

(4) James Madison's *The Federalist.*

Countdown to the New York Regents Exam

WEEK 3

MONDAY   U2.II.A-1

Which of the following statements about the first American political parties is true? *(Section 6.1)*

(1) Hamilton's supporters called themselves Democratic-Republicans.

(2) Madison and Jefferson were leaders of the Federalists.

(3) Federalists opposed a strong national government.

(4) The rural South and West tended to support the Democratic-Republicans.

TUESDAY   U2.II.B-3

In the Compromise of 1850, which of the following provisions was a clear victory for the South? *(Section 10.1)*

(1) California was admitted to the Union as a free state.

(2) Popular sovereignty was allowed to determine the slavery issue in the Utah and New Mexico territories.

(3) The slave trade, but not slavery itself, was abolished in the District of Columbia.

(4) Congress passed the Fugitive Slave Act.

WEDNESDAY   U2.II.C-5

Which of the following was a result of the war with Mexico? *(Section 9.3)*

(1) Texas was annexed by the United States.

(2) Mexico ceded land that is now California, Utah, and Nevada to the United States.

(3) Slavery was outlawed in the American Southwest.

(4) The Nueces River became the southwest border of Texas.

THURSDAY   U2.II.D-1

The Supreme Court decision in the *Dred Scott* case *(Section 10.3)*

(1) removed the issue of slavery in the territories from politics.

(2) upheld the ban on slavery in territory north of Missouri's southern border.

(3) stated that the federal government could not prohibit slavery in the territories.

(4) was cheered by Republicans.

FRIDAY   U2.II.A-2

Study the information below and use it to answer the question that follows.

Freight Costs in 1844

According to the graph, which transportation method resulted in the cheapest way to ship freight in 1844? *(Section 7.2)*

(1) wagon

(2) railroad

(3) river

(4) canal

WEEK 4

MONDAY — U2.I.A-3

What proposal was made by the Albany Plan of Union? *(Section 4.1)*

(1) that the colonies negotiate an alliance with the Iroquois

(2) that the colonies unite to form a federal government

(3) that the Ohio River valley area be given to the French

(4) that the British grant independence to the colonies

TUESDAY — U2.I.A-7

According to the Northwest Ordinance of 1787, when could a territory apply to become a state? *(Section 5.1)*

(1) when 5,000 adult male citizens had settled there

(2) when a governor, secretary, and three judges for the territory were chosen

(3) when the population reached 60,000

(4) when the territory agreed to ban slavery

WEDNESDAY — U2.I.F-4

What prompted the declaration known as the Monroe Doctrine? *(Section 7.1)*

(1) Most of the Spanish colonies in the Americas had tried unsuccessfully to gain their independence.

(2) President Monroe was concerned that Spain and Russia intended to expand their empires in the Western hemisphere.

(3) Great Britain issued a statement supporting Spain's right to regain control of its overseas colonies.

(4) President Monroe was concerned because Spain had regained control of Florida.

THURSDAY — U2.II.D-2

Why was the Battle of Antietam considered a crucial victory for the North? *(Section 11.2)*

(1) The Union victory convinced Britain to recognize the Union.

(2) McClellan broke through Lee's lines and forced a rapid retreat of the Southern forces.

(3) It was the bloodiest battle in the war.

(4) The British delayed plans to recognize the Confederacy.

FRIDAY — U2.II.B-2

Study the information below and use it to answer the question that follows.

We hold these truths to be self-evident: that all men and women are created equal; that they are endowed by their Creator with certain inalienable rights . . .

— The Seneca Falls Declaration, 1848

This declaration is most associated with which reform movement? *(Section 8.3)*

(1) abolition

(2) temperance

(3) women's rights

(4) prison reform

WEEK 5

MONDAY   U3.I.A-1

To receive a pardon under Lincoln's Reconstruction plan, Southerners had to accept the abolition of slavery and *(Section 12.1)*

(1) promise never to secede again.

(2) pay damages to the North.

(3) take an oath of loyalty to the United States.

(4) set up schools for former enslaved workers.

TUESDAY   U3.I.A-3

What did the Thirteenth, Fourteenth, and Fifteenth Amendments have in common? *(Sections 11.5 and 12.2)*

(1) They were all passed after the end of the Civil War.

(2) They guaranteed freedoms or rights to African Americans.

(3) They were popular in the Southern states.

(4) They had the support of President Andrew Johnson.

WEDNESDAY   U3.I.C-2

Study the information below and use it to answer the question that follows.

The Freedmen's Bureau
Helped former slaves find work on plantations.
Negotiated labor contracts with planters, including amount of pay and hours worked.
Established special courts to deal with grievances between workers and planters.
Worked with charities to provide education for former slaves.
Provided housing for schools, paid teachers, and helped establish colleges to train African American teachers.

According to the chart, the Freedmen's Bureau attempted to help former slaves in regard to *(Section 12.1)*

(1) religion.

(2) negotiation of contracts with planters.

(3) special grievances against slave owners.

(4) becoming owners of plantations.

THURSDAY   U3.I.D-2

Which event brought about the end of Reconstruction? *(Section 12.4)*

(1) The Democrats regained control of all Southern state legislatures.

(2) The Democrats used intimidation and fraud to force federal troops out of the South.

(3) With the economic depression following the Panic of 1873, the federal government could no longer afford Reconstruction policies.

(4) After the Compromise of 1877 assured his presidency, Rutherford Hayes pulled federal troops out of the South.

FRIDAY   U3.I.E-5

With the collapse of Reconstruction, many African Americans returned to plantations owned by whites, where they became tenant farmers and eventually *(Section 12.4)*

(1) landowners.

(2) sharecroppers.

(3) furnishing merchants.

(4) overseers.

Countdown to the New York Regents Exam

WEEK 6

MONDAY — U3.II.A-2

When a single company achieves control of an entire market, it is called a *(Section 14.3)*

(1) corporation.

(2) trust.

(3) holding company.

(4) monopoly.

TUESDAY — U3.II.C-1

Which entrepreneur decided to concentrate his investments in the steel industry after meeting Sir Henry Bessemer? *(Section 14.3)*

(1) Andrew Carnegie

(2) Thomas Edison

(3) Henry Ford

(4) John D. Rockefeller

WEDNESDAY — U3.II.B-2

Study the information below and use it to answer the question that follows.

Steel Production, 1865–1900

Source: *Historical Statistics of the United States: Colonial Times to 1970.*

According to the graph, when did steel production begin to rise significantly within the United States? *(Section 14.1)*

(1) between 1865 and 1873

(2) between 1875 and 1885

(3) between 1885 and 1895

(4) between 1870 and 1875

THURSDAY — U3.II.D-1

Which of the following measures was favored by supporters of laissez-faire? *(Section 14.1)*

(1) high taxes

(2) high tariffs

(3) federal subsidies

(4) low government debt

FRIDAY — U3.II.E-1

Samuel Gompers, who called his approach to labor relations unionism, led the *(Section 14.4)*

(1) Knights of Labor.

(2) American Federation of Labor.

(3) American Railway Union.

(4) Congress of Industrial Organizations.

Countdown to the New York Regents Exam

WEEK 7

MONDAY
U3.I.A-4

What event caused the impeachment of Andrew Johnson? *(Section 12.2)*

(1) He violated the Tenure of Office Act by firing Secretary of War Stanton.

(2) He issued a Proclamation of Amnesty that pardoned all former Confederate citizens who took an oath of loyalty to the Union.

(3) He vetoed the Military Reconstruction Act of 1867.

(4) He initiated the purchase of Alaska without Congressional approval.

TUESDAY
U3.I.D-4

In *Plessy* v. *Ferguson*, the Supreme Court *(Section 16.3)*

(1) endorsed separate but equal facilities for African Americans.

(2) ended slavery in the territories.

(3) demanded racial equality.

(4) made discrimination illegal.

WEDNESDAY
U3.II.D-3

The Sherman Antitrust Act *(Section 16.1)*

(1) created the Interstate Commerce Commission.

(2) declared illegal any combination that resulted in restraint of trade or commerce among states.

(3) allowed the president to decide which federal jobs would be filled.

(4) put the federal government in charge of regulating interstate commerce.

THURSDAY
U3.II.E-2

The Pullman strike occurred after the company *(Section 14.4)*

(1) increased wages.

(2) hired immigrants.

(3) cut wages.

(4) demanded overtime.

FRIDAY
U3.II.F

Study the information below and use it to answer the question that follows.

. . . from New York to the Golden Gate, the farmers have risen up and inaugurated . . . a revolution of thought. . . . The farmer of North Carolina, Georgia, Texas, South Carolina is your brother. . . . Some people have stirred up sectional feelings and have kept us apart for twenty-five years. . . . Congress could give us a bill in forty-eight hours to relieve us, but Wall Street says nay. . . . I believe that both of the parties are afraid of Wall Street.

—Democratic Promise:
The Populist Movement in America

From this quote, what can you determine that the Populists support? *(Section 16.2)*

(1) a march on Washington, D.C., in 48 hours

(2) farmers uniting across the nation to shape economic policy

(3) a revolt against the government similar to Shays's Rebellion

(4) an economic policy similar to that used during the past 25 years

Countdown to the New York Regents Exam

WEEK 8

MONDAY — U3.III.A-1

"Survival of the fittest" became the catchphrase of which philosophy? *(Section 15.3)*

(1) Gospel of Wealth

(2) Social Darwinism

(3) realism

(4) philanthropy

TUESDAY — U3.III.B-5

Asian immigrants were most likely to arrive in the United States at *(Section 15.1)*

(1) Ellis Island.

(2) Alcatraz Island.

(3) Angel Island.

(4) Golden Gate Island.

WEDNESDAY — U3.III.C-4

The Chinese Exclusion Act reflected nativism because it *(Section 15.1)*

(1) welcomed Asian immigrants.

(2) granted citizenship to Chinese immigrants.

(3) attempted to stop Asian immigration.

(4) encouraged Asian families to settle here.

THURSDAY — U3.III.D-1

The government passed the Homestead Act to encourage *(Section 13.2)*

(1) settlement of the Great Plains.

(2) increased railroad building.

(3) the growth of large-scale farms.

(4) Native American settlement.

FRIDAY — U3.III.B-1

Study the information below and use it to answer the question that follows.

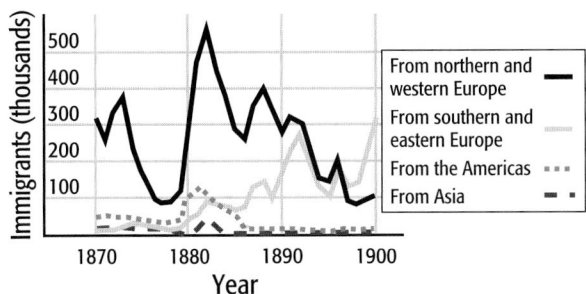

Which of the following best explains the changes in immigration shown in the graph? *(Section 15.1)*

(1) The need for workers on the railroads caused a dramatic increase in immigration from Asia in the late 1800s.

(2) A lack of jobs in western Europe after 1890 motivated many people to immigrate to the United States.

(3) Religious persecution in Poland and Russia in the late 1800s caused many Jews to flee to the United States.

(4) Labor unions opposed immigration, because many immigrants would work for lower wages than American-born workers.

MONDAY — U4.I.B-1

In *The Jungle*, author Upton Sinclair exposed the dangers and horrors of *(Section 18.2)*

(1) organized industrial labor unions.

(2) the meatpacking industry.

(3) the patent medicine industry.

(4) conditions in the nation's coal mines.

TUESDAY — U4.I.B-2

Jane Addams, who opened Hull House in Chicago, inspired other settlement houses including the Henry Street Settlement in New York run by *(Section 15.4)*

(1) Lillian Wald.

(2) Dwight L. Moody.

(3) George Washington Carver.

(4) Susan B. Anthony.

WEDNESDAY — U4.I.A-1

Study the information below and use it to answer the question that follows.

Beliefs of Progressives
People can improve society by relying on science and knowledge.
Industrialism and urbanization cause problems.
Government should fix problems.
Government itself should be reformed in order to achieve reform.

According to the chart, what did Progressives believe would solve the problems of U.S. society? *(Section 18.1)*

(1) urbanization patterns

(2) legislative action

(3) industrial development

(4) scientific discoveries

THURSDAY — U4.I.C-1

An idea inspired by Governor La Follette's reforms in Wisconsin, the initiative allowed *(Section 18.1)*

(1) party members to vote for a candidate to run in the general election.

(2) a group of citizens to introduce legislation and required the legislature to vote on it.

(3) proposed legislation to be submitted to the voters for approval.

(4) voters to demand a special election to remove an elected official from office.

FRIDAY — U4.I.C-4

In 1913, the Democrat-controlled Congress passed the Underwood Tariff that *(Section 18.4)*

(1) protected high tariffs on imported goods.

(2) had no effect on existing tariffs.

(3) reduced the average tariff on imported goods.

(4) made it illegal to levy an income tax on individuals.

MONDAY — U4.II.A-1

Which of the following is the main economic reason that many Americans in the late 1800s began to support imperialism and an expansion of American power overseas? *(Section 17.1)*

(1) the need to develop new overseas markets for American products

(2) the Social Darwinist idea that nations competed with each other and only the strongest would ultimately survive

(3) the belief that it was part of Manifest Destiny to expand overseas

(4) the belief that they had an obligation to spread Christianity to other nations

TUESDAY

What was the most significant result of the Spanish-American War for the United States? *(Section 17.2)*

(1) We quickly left Cuba and let the country govern itself independently.

(2) We decided to return the Philippines to Spain.

(3) We became an imperial power with overseas possessions.

(4) We annexed Hawaii.

WEDNESDAY — U4.II.B-1

Study the information below and use it to answer the question that follows.

. . . Property can be paid for; the lives of innocent and peaceful people cannot. The present German submarine warfare against commerce is a warfare against mankind.

—A Declaration of War

According to the excerpt, why is the United States declaring war against Germany? *(Section 19.1)*

(1) Property had been wrongly seized.

(2) German submarine attacks have killed innocent people.

(3) German submarines have stopped all trade routes.

(4) Innocent people have been killed in their homes.

THURSDAY — U4.II.C-3

In *Schenck v. the United States*, the Supreme Court ruled that an individual's freedom of speech could be curbed when the words uttered *(Section 19.2)*

(1) are false.

(2) are accusations against the U.S. president.

(3) constitute a clear and present danger.

(4) are meant to incite rioting.

FRIDAY — U4.II.D-3

Which provision of the Treaty of Versailles of 1919 demonstrates the influence of Woodrow Wilson? *(Section 19.3)*

(1) the establishment of the new country of Poland

(2) the requirement that Germany acknowledge guilt for the outbreak of the war

(3) the dissolution of the Ottoman Empire

(4) the creation of the League of Nations

WEEK 11

MONDAY — U4.I.C-2

In *Northern Securities* v. *the United States*, the Supreme Court ruled that Northern Securities had violated the *(Section 18.2)*

(1) Clayton Antitrust Act.

(2) Sherman Antitrust Act.

(3) Hepburn Act.

(4) Payne-Aldrich Tariff Act.

TUESDAY — U4.II.A-2

Because Queen Liliuokalani disliked American influence in Hawaii, she *(Section 17.1)*

(1) introduced tariffs on American goods coming into Hawaii.

(2) exiled planters who came from the United States.

(3) negotiated a trade treaty to ease tensions.

(4) opposed efforts to annex Hawaii to the United States.

WEDNESDAY — U4.II.A-4

The Hay-Pauncefote Treaty between the United States and Great Britain cleared the way for the United States to *(Section 17.3)*

(1) annex Hawaii.

(2) bring economic and political stability to Latin America.

(3) build the Panama Canal.

(4) increase trade with Japan.

THURSDAY — U4.II.D-7

Signing nations of the Kellogg-Briand Pact agreed to *(Section 21.3)*

(1) abandon war and settle disputes by peaceful means.

(2) a 10-year moratorium on constructing warships.

(3) accept less in reparations from Germany.

(4) respect the others' territory in the Pacific.

FRIDAY — U4.I.B-2

Study the information below and use it to answer the question that follows.

The wisest among my race understand that . . . the enjoyment of all the privileges that will come to us must be the result of severe and constant struggle rather than of artificial forcing. . . . It is important and right that all privileges of the law be ours, but it is vastly more important that we be prepared for the exercise of these privileges.

—Up from Slavery

According to this quotation by Booker T. Washington, how will privileges be gained? *(Section 16.3)*

(1) through education

(2) through continuing struggles

(3) through legislative changes

(4) through societal change

WEEK 12

MONDAY U5.I.A-2

American soldiers returning from World War I in Europe found that they were competing for jobs and housing with African Americans resulting in *(Section 19.4)*

(1) new industries.

(2) racial harmony.

(3) race riots.

(4) new zoning laws.

TUESDAY U5.I.B-4

The "quiet depression" of the 1920s refers to the *(Section 21.2)*

(1) decline in prices paid for U.S. farm products.

(2) damage done to U.S. manufacturers by high U.S. tariffs.

(3) decrease in real wages among U.S. workers.

(4) lack of well-paying jobs for African Americans.

WEDNESDAY U5.I.C-2

Which of the following was an unintended result of Prohibition in the 1920s? *(Section 20.1)*

(1) an increase in the unemployment rate

(2) an increase in domestic violence

(3) an increase in poverty

(4) an increase in organized crime

THURSDAY U5.I.C-3

The growth of African American artistic, social, cultural, and political expression after World War I was known as *(Section 20.3)*

(1) the Great Migration.

(2) the Cotton Club.

(3) the Harlem Renaissance.

(4) the Second Great Awakening.

FRIDAY U5.I.C-1

Study the information below and use it to answer the question that follows.

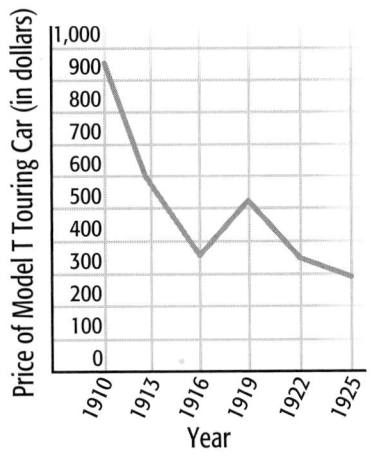

What industrial development best explains the price trend shown in this chart? *(Section 21.2)*

(1) the open shop

(2) welfare capitalism

(3) the assembly line

(4) the eight-hour workday

WEEK 13

MONDAY U5.II.A-4

Another name for shantytowns—communities where the newly homeless put up shacks on unused or public lands—was *(Section 22.2)*

(1) Depressionvilles.

(2) Hobotowns.

(3) Hoovervilles.

(4) Herbertowns.

TUESDAY U5.II.B-3

The Social Security Act of 1935 originally provided benefits for *(Section 23.3)*

(1) retired workers only.

(2) unemployed workers only.

(3) both retired workers and unemployed workers.

(4) neither retired workers nor unemployed workers.

WEDNESDAY U5.II.B-4

The Committee for Industrial Organization became *(Section 23.3)*

(1) the nation's first trade union.

(2) the first nationwide labor union.

(3) the first union to use strikes to achieve its goals.

(4) the first union to organize all workers in a particular industry.

THURSDAY U5.II.B-6

How did the Dust Bowl add to the nation's problems during the Great Depression? *(Section 22.2)*

(1) Farmers stopped cultivating their land and thus lowered food supplies.

(2) The loss of arable land worsened a food supply problem the whole nation experienced at that time.

(3) Farmers now had no money to spend and could not help in improving the nation's economy.

(4) Many families lost their farms and became homeless and impoverished.

FRIDAY U5.II.A-2

Study the information below and use it to answer the question that follows.

Stock Prices, 1920–1932

Price per Share

— Annual high
— Annual low

$350
$300
$250
$200
$150
$100
$50
0

1920 1922 1924 1926 1928 1930 1932
Dow-Jones Industrial Averages
Source: Standard and Poor's *Security Price Index Record.*

In what year, according to the graph, was the gap between the annual high and annual low in the stock market the largest? *(Section 22.1)*

(1) 1928

(2) 1929

(3) 1930

(4) 1931

WEEK 14

MONDAY U5.I.B-2

In the Teapot Dome scandal, Harding's secretary of the interior accepted bribes for *(Section 21.1)*

(1) allowing private interests to drill for oil in a national park.

(2) allowing lumber companies to cut trees in national forests.

(3) allowing private interests to lease lands containing U.S. Navy oil reserves.

(4) allowing immunity for business owners who overcharged the U.S. Navy.

TUESDAY U5.I.C-1

In the 1920s, radio, movies, newspapers, and magazines helped to *(Section 20.2)*

(1) foster local ties.

(2) create informed consumers.

(3) unify the nation and spread new ideas and attitudes.

(4) encourage minority rights.

WEDNESDAY U5.I.C-2

As strikes erupted across the United States in 1919, the fear that Communists might seize power led to a nationwide panic known as the *(Section 19.4)*

(1) Communist Scare.

(2) Red Scare.

(3) Russian Scare.

(4) Socialist Scare.

THURSDAY U5.II.B-8

Democratic Senator Huey Long gained a following due to his belief that the government should *(Section 23.3)*

(1) balance the budget.

(2) share the wealth of the rich.

(3) pay citizens over age 60 a monthly pension.

(4) not interfere with business.

FRIDAY U5.II.B-3

Study the information below and use it to answer the question that follows.

The second step we have taken in the restoration of normal business enterprise has been to clean up thoroughly unwholesome conditions in the field of investment. . . . I sincerely hope that as a result people will be discouraged in unhappy efforts to get rich quick by speculating. . . .

—Franklin D. Roosevelt, fireside chat, 1934

In this fireside chat, President Roosevelt was referring to *(Section 23.2)*

(1) the Home Owners' Loan Corporation.

(2) the Securities and Exchange Commission.

(3) Social Security.

(4) the National Industrial Administration.

Countdown to the New York Regents Exam

WEEK 15

MONDAY
U6.I.B-1

France and Britain's initial reaction to Germany's acts of aggression in Austria and Czechoslovakia was *(Section 24.2)*

(1) counter-aggression.

(2) a declaration of war.

(3) a policy of appeasement.

(4) a policy of neutrality.

TUESDAY
U6.I.C-2

Which of the following statements about African American involvement in World War II is true? *(Section 25.1)*

(1) African American soldiers were assigned only to noncombat units.

(2) The U.S. military was fully integrated during World War II.

(3) President Roosevelt was unwilling to recruit African Americans for the military.

(4) Most African Americans supported involvement in the war effort, despite their own problems with racism at home.

WEDNESDAY
U6.I.C-4

Which of the following best explains why Truman decided to use the atomic bomb? *(Section 25.5)*

(1) He believed that Japanese civilians would not die in large numbers.

(2) He believed that the United States would suffer massive casualties if forced to invade Japan.

(3) He believed that it would be necessary to drop only one bomb.

(4) He was not fully aware of the power of the atomic bomb.

THURSDAY
U6.I.C-5

In *Korematsu* v. *the United States,* the Supreme Court ruled that the relocation of Japanese Americans during World War II was *(Section 25.3)*

(1) unconstitutional because it was based on race.

(2) constitutional because it was based on military urgency.

(3) constitutional but reparations must be paid.

(4) constitutional but loyal citizens could not be held against their will.

FRIDAY
U6.I.C-3

Study the information below and use it to answer the question that follows.

This map shows plans for *(Section 25.4)*

(1) the invasion of North Africa.

(2) the D-Day invasion.

(3) the Battle of the Coral Sea.

(4) the assault on Iwo Jima.

WEEK 16

MONDAY   U6.II.A-1

Unlike the League of Nations, U.S. participation in the United Nations was assured because *(Section 25.5)*

(1) the new organization received its charter in San Francisco.

(2) each member nation would have one vote in the General Assembly.

(3) the United States would have veto power as a permanent member of the Security Council.

(4) the General Assembly was responsible for international peace and security.

TUESDAY   U6.II.B-1

At the Yalta Conference of 1945, Roosevelt, Churchill, and Stalin *(Section 26.1)*

(1) settled the issue of German reparations payments to the Soviet Union.

(2) decided to divide Germany into two zones—one controlled by the Soviet Union, the other by the allies.

(3) agreed to turn Poland into a buffer zone under Soviet control.

(4) issued the Declaration of Liberated Europe, giving people the right to choose the form of government under which they would live.

WEDNESDAY   U6.II.D-3

The term "McCarthyism" was coined from Senator McCarthy's *(Section 26.3)*

(1) requirement that all his employees sign a loyalty oath.

(2) tactic of bringing witches to trial.

(3) insistence that all Communists be deported.

(4) tactic of damaging reputations with unsubstantiated charges.

THURSDAY   U6.II.C-4

When North Korea invaded South Korea in 1950, President Truman *(Section 26.2)*

(1) sent American troops from Japan to the Korean peninsula.

(2) ordered an attack across the Yalu River.

(3) fired General McArthur for insubordination.

(4) ordered a blockade of Chinese ports.

FRIDAY   U6.II.B-2

Study the information below and use it to answer the question that follows.

From Stettin in the Baltic to Trieste in the Adriatic, an iron curtain has descended across the continent. . . .

—Winston Churchill

What was the "iron curtain" to which Churchill referred in this quote? *(Section 26.1)*

(1) the wall separating East and West Berlin

(2) the political and military barrier that separated the Communist nations of Eastern Europe from the West

(3) the division of Germany agreed upon at the Yalta Conference

(4) the railroad system in Eastern Europe

Countdown to the New York Regents Exam

WEEK 17

MONDAY — U6.I.A-2

The Neutrality Act of 1935 *(Section 24.1)*

(1) required warring countries to buy supplies from the United States on a "cash-and-carry" basis.

(2) prohibited Congress from declaring war on any country.

(3) made oaths of loyalty illegal.

(4) prohibited Americans from selling arms to any country at war.

TUESDAY — U6.I.C-2

Limiting the availability of products to individuals to ensure that enough is available for military use is known as *(Section 25.3)*

(1) wage and price controls.

(2) relocating.

(3) savings.

(4) rationing.

WEDNESDAY — U6.I.C-6

Which of these Fair Deal proposals by President Truman was enacted? *(Section 27.1)*

(1) national health insurance

(2) federal aid to schools

(3) an increase in the minimum wage

(4) farm subsidies

THURSDAY — U6.II.D-1

As part of President Truman's loyalty review program in 1948, *(Section 26.3)*

(1) Whittaker Chambers was convicted of perjury.

(2) Alger Hiss was accused of being a Communist.

(3) J. Edgar Hoover was accused of subversion.

(4) the FBI fired over 2,000 people.

FRIDAY — U6.II.B-3

Study the information below and use it to answer the question that follows.

Cold War Initiatives from 1947	
Policy	**Objective**
Marshall Plan	to give European nations American aid to rebuild their economies
Truman Doctrine	to aid "free peoples who are resisting attempted subjugation by armed minorities or by outside pressures"

The goal of both the Truman Doctrine and the Marshall Plan was to *(Section 26.2)*

(1) offer aid only to Western European nations.

(2) provide military rather than economic aid to anti-Communist nations.

(3) ensure freedom for sovereign nations.

(4) provide aid to war-ravaged China.

WEEK 18

MONDAY U7.I.A-1

Which energy source did supporters hail as cleaner and less expensive than fossil fuels, while opponents raised the concern of risks such as radiation? *(Section 31.4)*

(1) nuclear

(2) solar

(3) coal

(4) hydroelectric

TUESDAY U7.I.A-3

Which technological development allowed many Americans to work more quickly and efficiently? *(Section 27.2)*

(1) the jet airplane

(2) the computer

(3) the space satellite

(4) the polio vaccine

WEDNESDAY U7.I.A-4

Large corporations that expand overseas are called *(Section 27.2)*

(1) franchises.

(2) mega chains.

(3) conglomerates.

(4) multinational corporations.

THURSDAY U7.I.A-5

By the late 1950s, mechanization in farms and factories had led to an increase in *(Section 27.2)*

(1) blue-collar workers.

(2) white-collar workers.

(3) agricultural workers.

(4) unemployment.

FRIDAY U7.I.A-6

Study the information below and use it to answer the question that follows.

Urban Renewal Programs	
Problem	**Poverty**
Government's Solution	Tear down slums and build new high-rise buildings
New Problem	Increase in violence due to crowded, anonymous living conditions

According to this chart, urban renewal programs sometimes *(Section 27.4)*

(1) resolved overcrowding issues.

(2) reduced poverty.

(3) generated undesirable and unforeseen results.

(4) renovated older buildings.

Countdown to the New York Regents Exam

WEEK 19

MONDAY — U7.II.A-1

To prevent Communist uprisings in other countries, Eisenhower had the CIA conduct covert operations that were primarily carried out in *(Section 26.4)*

(1) industrial nations.

(2) developing nations.

(3) the Soviet Union.

(4) Europe.

TUESDAY — U7.II.C-2

What Supreme Court case overturned the doctrine of "separate but equal" and opened the way to desegregation? *(Section 29.1)*

(1) *Plessy* v. *Ferguson*

(2) *Norris* v. *Alabama*

(3) *Brown* v. *Board of Education*

(4) *Sweatt* v. *Painter*

WEDNESDAY — U7.II.C-1

The Warren Court's requirement of state legislatures to reapportion electoral districts so that all citizens' votes would have equal weight *(Section 28.1)*

(1) shifted political power to urban, more liberal areas.

(2) shifted political power to rural, more conservative areas.

(3) equalized political power between rural and urban areas.

(4) lessened the political power of African Americans and Hispanics.

THURSDAY — U7.II.B-2

President Eisenhower used the domino theory to justify *(Section 30.1)*

(1) U.S. support of the French military campaign in Vietnam.

(2) the withdrawal of U.S. troops from South Korea.

(3) the development of intercontinental ballistic missiles.

(4) cuts in federal spending.

FRIDAY — U7.II.D-1

Study the information below and use it to answer the question that follows.

Which of the following statements best explains the trend in birthrates shown in this graph? *(Section 27.2)*

(1) There was a surge in immigration to the United States following World War II.

(2) More married women entered the workforce in the 1950s.

(3) Young couples who had delayed marriage during World War II and the Korean War married and began their families.

(4) The population in the suburbs doubled in the 1950s.

WEEK 20

MONDAY U7.III.A-2

To end the Cuban Missile Crisis of 1962, (Section 28.2)

(1) Khrushchev agreed to remove Soviet missiles from Cuba, and Kennedy agreed to remove U.S. missiles from Turkey.

(2) Khrushchev and Kennedy agreed to a test-ban treaty for nuclear weapons.

(3) Kennedy agreed not to invade Cuba, and Khrushchev agreed to remove Fidel Castro from power.

(4) Khrushchev agreed to remove Soviet missiles from Cuba, and Kennedy agreed to withdraw troops from West Berlin.

TUESDAY U7.III.B-3

The Voting Rights Act of 1965 (Section 29.2)

(1) overturned many advancements in civil rights.

(2) suspended African Americans' voting rights

(3) created social equality for African Americans.

(4) allowed federal examiners to register qualified voters.

WEDNESDAY U7.III.A-1

Study the information below and use it to answer the question that follows.

One may . . . ask: "How can you advocate breaking some laws and obeying others?" The answer lies in the fact that there are two types of laws: just and unjust. . . . One has not only a legal but a moral responsibility to obey just laws. Conversely, one has a moral responsibility to disobey unjust laws. . . .

–Martin Luther King, Jr.,
Letter from a Birmingham Jail

This quote illustrates King's belief in (Section 29.2)

(1) a moral duty to obey all laws.

(2) a moral duty to obey unjust laws.

(3) a moral duty to disobey unjust laws.

(4) a moral duty to disobey all laws.

THURSDAY U7.III.B-4

Which of the following represented an advancement for women in the workplace? (Section 31.2)

(1) Civil Rights Act of 1964

(2) *Roe* v. *Wade* decision

(3) Title IX

(4) publication of *The Feminine Mystique*

FRIDAY U7.III.B-5

Which leader organized a boycott of grapes in order to obtain better wages and better benefits for farmworkers? (Section 31.3)

(1) Jesse Jackson

(2) Dolores Huerta

(3) José Angel Gutiérrez

(4) César Chávez

Countdown to the New York Regents Exam

WEEK 21

MONDAY   U7.II.B-6

Strong pressure exerted by the United States during the Suez Canal crisis resulted in *(Section 26.4)*

(1) Egyptian troops seizing the Suez Canal.

(2) British and French troops invading Egypt.

(3) the British and French calling off the invasion of Egypt.

(4) the Soviet Union threatening rocket attacks on the United States.

TUESDAY   U7.II.D-2

What is a reason people began moving to the suburbs after World War II? *(Section 27.2)*

(1) because homes were more affordable in city neighborhoods.

(2) because most suburban houses looked identical.

(3) because of the declining birthrate after World War II.

(4) so they could have a better life for their families.

WEDNESDAY   U7.III.B-3

What organization, which would play a key role in desegregating public facilities and would send volunteers into rural areas of the South to register African Americans, was established by students? *(Section 29.2)*

(1) SCLC

(2) NAACP

(3) SNCC

(4) CORE

THURSDAY   U7.III.A-4

The assassination of President Kennedy in 1963 was investigated by *(Section 28.2)*

(1) the Alliance for Progress.

(2) the Warren Commission.

(3) the Peace Corps.

(4) the Oswald Commission.

FRIDAY   U7.III.B-1

Study the information below and use it to answer the question that follows.

Major Great Society Programs		
Health and Welfare	**Education**	**War on Poverty**
Medicare	The Elementary and Secondary Education Act	The Office of Economic Opportunity
Medicaid	Higher Education Act	Housing and Urban Development Act
Child Nutrition Act	Project Head Start	Demonstration Cities and Metropolitan Development Act

The most accurate assessment of the Great Society based on the items in the chart and your knowledge is that *(Section 28.3)*

(1) most Great Society programs were easy to manage and evaluate.

(2) the Great Society had the same aims as the New Deal.

(3) the Great Society focused mainly on economic reforms.

(4) the Great Society created massive growth in the federal government.

WEEK 22

MONDAY — U7.IV.A-1

The United States supported France in the French-Indochinese War because officials *(Section 30.1)*

(1) thought France should control Vietnam.

(2) did not want Vietnam to be Communist.

(3) did not want Vietnam to be part of Indochina.

(4) supported colonialism.

TUESDAY — U7.IV.A-3

After the defeat of Japan in 1945, Ho Chi Minh announced that *(Section 30.1)*

(1) Thailand was part of Vietnam.

(2) Vietnam was an independent nation.

(3) the Soviet Union should stay out of Vietnam.

(4) the United States should stay out of Vietnam.

WEDNESDAY — U7.IV.A-4

In 1968, the Tet offensive by the Vietcong and North Vietnamese resulted in *(Section 30.3)*

(1) a military victory for the Communists.

(2) a political victory for the Communists.

(3) a political victory for the South Vietnamese.

(4) a high approval rating for the U.S. president.

THURSDAY — U7.IV.A-5

The event that sparked a deadly student protest at Kent State University was *(Section 30.4)*

(1) the publication of the Pentagon Papers.

(2) President Nixon's announcement of the invasion of Cambodia.

(3) news reports about the My Lai massacre.

(4) the new policy of Vietnamization.

FRIDAY — U7.IV.A-6

Study the information below and use it to answer the question that follows.

Vietnam War's Impact on the United States
Passage of War Powers Act: required the president to inform Congress of any commitment of troops within 48 hours and to withdraw them in 60 to 90 days unless Congress approved the troop commitment
Increased American cynicism in their government, as many felt they had been misled about the war
Shook the nation's confidence and morale
Led to a spirit of isolationism amongst Americans

After the Vietnam War, Americans were more likely to *(Section 30.4)*

(1) support sending troops abroad.

(2) have confidence in their leaders.

(3) be more supportive of government.

(4) be wary of their leaders.

Countdown to the New York Regents Exam

WEEK 23

MONDAY — U7.V.A-3

The legislative effect of Watergate was *(Section 32.2)*

(1) proposed legislation to eliminate the executive branch.

(2) an amendment to the Constitution redefining impeachment.

(3) Congress's increased control and oversight of the FBI.

(4) a series of laws intending to limit the power of the executive branch.

TUESDAY — U7.V.B-3

In 1978 President Carter helped negotiate a peace treaty, known as the Camp David Accords, between Israel and *(Section 32.3)*

(1) the Palestine Liberation Organization.

(2) Egypt.

(3) Syria.

(4) Lebanon.

WEDNESDAY — U7.V.A-2

Study the information below and use it to answer the question that follows.

We must understand that détente is not a love fest. It is an understanding between nations that have opposite purposes, but which share common interests, including the avoidance of a nuclear war.

—Richard Nixon

Nixon recommended this policy of détente to improve U.S. relations with *(Section 32.1)*

(1) China.

(2) the Soviet Union.

(3) both China and the Soviet Union.

(4) Europe.

THURSDAY — U7.V.C-3

During the 1980s, environmentalists objected to government plans to *(Section 33.2)*

(1) increase safety checks on pesticides.

(2) declare groups such as the Sierra Club illegal.

(3) increase the amount of land opened for drilling, mining, and logging.

(4) ignore the problems caused by chemicals called chlorofluorocarbons (CFCs).

FRIDAY — U7.V.G-2

The signing of the Intermediate-Range Nuclear Forces (INF) treaty helped lead to the *(Section 33.2)*

(1) Strategic Defense Initiative (SDI), or "Star Wars".

(2) end of the Cold War.

(3) Iran-Contra scandal.

(4) buildup of the U.S. military.

Countdown to the New York Regents Exam

WEEK 24

MONDAY U7.VI.A-2

Hundreds of savings and loans institutions collapsed in the early 1990s due to *(Section 33.4)*

(1) downsizing of major corporations.

(2) the capital gains tax hurting investors.

(3) increased competition following deregulation.

(4) failed risky and dishonest investments made possible after deregulation.

TUESDAY U7.VI.A-3

The Iraqi invasion of Kuwait resulted in *(Section 33.4)*

(1) Operation Desert Storm.

(2) the Iran-Iraq War.

(3) the fall of the government of Saddam Hussein.

(4) the ousting of the Taliban from Afghanistan.

WEDNESDAY U7.VI.B-1

During his first term, President Clinton appointed a task force headed by his wife to *(Section 34.2)*

(1) encourage the passage of new gun-control laws.

(2) spearhead the deregulation of major industries.

(3) look into ways to improve public education.

(4) develop a plan for health insurance reform.

THURSDAY U7.VI.B-2

In 1994 the United States joined Mexico in the North American Free Trade Agreement (NAFTA) in order to *(Section 34.3)*

(1) prevent the establishment of the European Union (EU).

(2) export jobs to Mexico.

(3) reduce its trade surplus.

(4) keep Canada from interfering with U.S.-Mexican trade.

FRIDAY U7.VI.A-3

Study the information below and use it to answer the question that follows.

| 1989 | 1990 | 1991 | 1992 |

May, 1989 — Tiananmen Square protests begin

November, 1989 — Berlin Wall falls

August, 1990 — Iraq invades Kuwait

January, 1991 — Persian Gulf War begins

December, 1991 — Soviet Union collapses

Which event on the time line is most associated with the end of the Cold War?
(Section 33.4)

(1) Tiananmen Square protests

(2) fall of Berlin Wall

(3) invasion of Kuwait

(4) Persian Gulf War

Thematic Essay

Introduction

The thematic essay portion of the Regents Exam requires you to write a well-developed essay based upon a specific theme/concept that is found in the New York State Education Department Core Curriculum. This part of the examination is worth approximately 15 percent of your total score of 100 (it can vary somewhat from examination to examination based upon how the exam is scored). The specific theme/concept will change from examination to examination.

The thematic essay is different than the essay you will write for the document-based question (see page NY31). With the document-based question, you are given a set of documents to be used in developing the essay. The thematic essay is a more challenging task; you have nothing in front of you other than the concept and a question based upon that concept.

What should you do as a student to prepare for this portion of the examination? It is very important that you create a list of the themes/concepts that were covered in your class during the course. After you identify the themes/concepts, you should be able to develop a working definition for as many of them as possible. Your teacher should have provided you with this material during the course of the school year.

What Are Themes/Concepts?

You should be familiar with the major themes that might be tested in the Regents Exam for the United States History and Government Core Curriculum. Concepts/themes are found in the *Social Studies Resource Guide with Core Curriculum* document from the New York State Education Department. Your teacher can provide you with this *Resource Guide,* or you can download it from the Internet at www.nysed.gov.

The *Resource Guide* includes a listing of concepts and themes for United States History and Government. You should realize that many of these concepts and themes are very general and can fit into U.S. history in different eras and in a variety of places.

How do you know which concept/theme goes with certain content? At any point in the *Resource Guide* you should look at the concepts/themes column and also the content column. The thematic essay is created from a common theme that recurs across time and place in history. Your essay should be developed from the content with which you are most familiar, based upon what you have been taught and what you have read and know about.

A Sample Thematic Essay

Following is the thematic essay question that appeared on the January, 2005 United States History and Government Regents Examination.

THEMATIC ESSAY QUESTION

Directions: Write a well-organized essay that includes an introduction, several paragraphs addressing the task below, and a conclusion.

Theme: Foreign Policy

> Since 1900, United States foreign policy actions have often been based on national self-interest. These actions have had immediate and long-term results.

Task:

> Identify **two** important United States foreign policy actions **since 1900** and for **each**
> • Discuss the historical circumstances surrounding the action
> • Discuss *one* immediate **or** *one* long-term result of the action
> • Evaluate the extent to which the action promoted the nation's self-interest

You may use any important foreign policy action since 1900 from your study of United States history. Some suggestions you might wish to consider include Theodore Roosevelt's Corollary to the Monroe Doctrine (1904), Woodrow Wilson's Fourteen Points (1918), the Lend-Lease Act (1941), the Marshall Plan (1947), the blockade of Cuba (1962), the Strategic Arms Limitation Talks (SALT) agreements (1972), and the Persian Gulf War (1991).

You are *not* limited to these suggestions.

Guidelines:

In your essay, be sure to:
• Develop all aspects of the task
• Support the theme with relevant facts, examples, and details
• Use a logical and clear plan of organization, including an introduction and a conclusion that are beyond a restatement of the theme

Breaking Down the Question

The first thing that you should do as the test taker is to read the thematic essay question carefully so you can fully understand what the question requires you to answer.

Using the sample on the previous page, let us analyze the question.

- What is the theme in this essay? *The theme is foreign policy.*

- What is the task or question to be answered? *You must select two U.S. foreign policy actions since 1900. For each action, discuss the historical circumstances and one immediate or one long-term result. Also evaluate the extent to which each action promoted the nation's self-interest.*

- What foreign policy actions should you avoid writing about in your essay? *You SHOULD NOT write about any foreign policy action before 1900.*

- What foreign policy actions may you write about in your essay? *You may choose to write about any foreign policy action since 1900 that you studied in class or about which you read a great deal. You are not limited to the list of suggestions.*

- You now have broken down the question into its separate components.

Outlining Your Answer to the Thematic Essay

Before you begin to write your answer to the thematic essay, it is generally wise to outline what you are going to include. Remember, you have three hours to finish the Regents examination and you certainly have the time to plan what you are going to write. Remember that an essay in social studies is really a composition with a specific content focus.

Following is a simple, skeletal outline that you could use to answer the sample essay. Each bullet represents a potential paragraph.

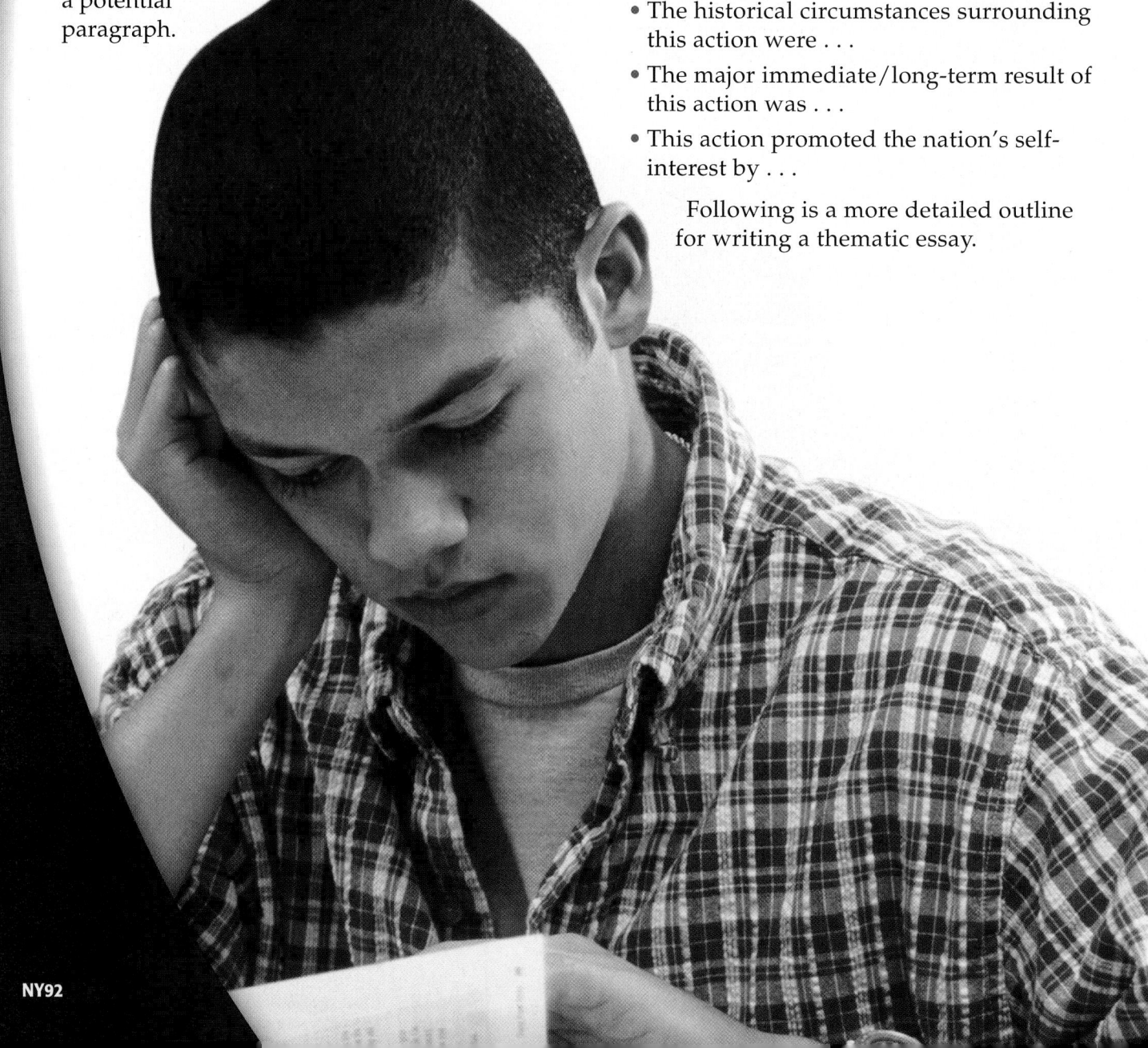

- A foreign policy action since 1900 that was based on national self-interest was . . .

  - The historical circumstances surrounding this action were . . .

  - The major immediate/long-term result of this action was . . .

  - This action promoted the nation's self-interest by . . .

- Another foreign policy action since 1900 that was based on national self-interest was . . .

  - The historical circumstances surrounding this action were . . .

  - The major immediate/long-term result of this action was . . .

  - This action promoted the nation's self-interest by . . .

    Following is a more detailed outline for writing a thematic essay.

Paragraph 1: Introductory Paragraph

Look at the statement of the theme and then try to rewrite the theme in your own words. You should establish a framework that is beyond a simple restatement of the task. You also should name the two foreign policies that you are going to write about, and you should specify whether you are discussing their immediate or long-term results. You also should include a discussion of how the actions you have chosen were designed to promote national self-interest. An example follows:

> Throughout United States history, the national self-interest often motivated U.S. foreign policy actions. I will write about the Marshall Plan and the blockade of Cuba because . . .

Paragraph 2: the Marshall Plan*

The historical circumstances surrounding this policy action were that

- World War II had left Europe in economic and political chaos.

- Many Europeans were starving.

- Soviet influence was spreading in the world.

One important immediate result was that the plan pumped billions of dollars worth of supplies, machinery, and food into Western Europe, helping the region recover.

The plan promoted the nation's self-interest by weakening the appeal of communism and opening new markets for U.S. trade.

Paragraph 3: the Blockade of Cuba*

The historical circumstances surrounding this policy action were that

- Cold War tensions were high between the United States and the Soviet Union.

- Fidel Castro, a Communist dictator with ties to the Soviet Union, had seized power in Cuba.

- American spy planes confirmed that the Soviets had placed long-range nuclear missiles in Cuba, a country within missile range of the United States.

- President John F. Kennedy ordered a naval blockade of Cuba to stop the Soviets from delivering more missiles.

- President Kennedy demanded that the Soviets dismantle the existing missile sites and warned that if any weapons were launched against the United States, he would respond fully against the Soviet Union.

One important immediate result was that Soviet leader Nikita Khrushchev backed down and removed the missiles, avoiding nuclear holocaust.

The plan promoted the nation's self-interest by removing the serious threat to national security of nuclear weapons in the hands of a hostile nation on America's doorstep.

Paragraph 4: Conclusion to the Essay

The final paragraph should restate the main ideas developed in your essay and then conclude with a summation of the theme or problem.

---

*This content could be expanded into more than one paragraph.

Scoring the Thematic Essay

The thematic essay is worth approximately 15 percent of your total examination grade. However, based upon a conversion chart for the specific examination, this can vary from 12 to 18 percent of your final grade. Your grade for the thematic essay is generated from a generic scoring rubric that has been developed by the New York State Education Department. On the rubric, the highest score is a five and the lowest score is a zero. Ask your teacher how to access the generic scoring rubric from the New York State Education Department Web site.

Now, let us look at the key elements of the thematic essay rubric. A 5 (the highest score) must fulfill certain criteria. The most critical criteria are italicized.

What constitutes a 5 essay?

- *Thoroughly* develops *all* aspects of the task *evenly* and *in depth*

- Is more *analytical* than *descriptive*, showing an ability to *analyze, evaluate, compare and/or contrast* issues and events and create information

- Richly supports the theme with many *relevant facts*, *examples*, and *details*

- Demonstrates *a logical and clear plan of organization*; includes an *introduction* and a *conclusion* that are *beyond* a restatement of the theme

Analysis of a 5 Essay

Let us take a look at the italicized words from the bulleted list above to understand the criteria that are needed for a superior thematic essay.

- The word "thorough" means complete. If the essay demonstrates only a "good" and not a "thorough" understanding, it is scored a 4. All aspects of the task must be addressed for a 4 or a 5.

- An analysis, evaluation, comparison, and/or contrasting of issues and events must be done in depth for a 4 or a 5. Remember, a 5 is more analytical than descriptive.

- A rich inclusion of supporting facts, examples, and details distinguishes a 5 from a 4 essay.

- A logical and clear plan of organization is utilized consistently in a 5 essay. A framework for the task that is beyond just a simple restatement is required for either a 4 or a 5. You need to be able to write your essay with an introduction and a conclusion that is developed in the overall context of the significance of the theme in your study of U.S. History and Government.

Analysis of a 2 Essay

For comparison purposes, let us look at a 2 essay in the rubric.

- *Minimally* develops all aspects of the task or develops some aspects of the task in some depth

- Is primarily descriptive; may include *faulty*, *weak*, or *isolated* application or analysis

- Includes *few relevant facts*, *examples*, and *details*; may include some *inaccuracies*

- Demonstrates a general plan of organization; may *lack focus*; may *contain digressions*; may not clearly identify which aspect of the task is being addressed; may *lack an introduction and/or a conclusion*

How to Practice for the Thematic Essay

It should be obvious to you that there are vast differences between an excellent essay and one that does not reach the level of being satisfactory. It is most important that you familiarize yourself with the generic rubric. Please note that the scoring is on a continuum from 5 to 0. A zero is a blank or illegible paper. Most of the answers to the thematic essay are somewhere in between.

You can take action to help ensure that you earn a satisfactory grade. For example, you can practice writing an outline for the thematic essay. You can then practice writing a thematic essay based on your outline. The outline that you use should be logical and sequential. Make certain that you always have an introduction and a conclusion to your essay.

READING TO LEARN

This handbook focuses on skills and strategies that can help you understand the words you read. The strategies you use to understand whole texts depend on the kind of text you are reading. In other words, you don't read a textbook the way you read a novel. You read a textbook mainly for information; you read a novel mainly for fun. To get the most out of your reading, you need to choose the right strategy to fit the reason you're reading.

USE THIS HANDBOOK TO HELP YOU LEARN

- how to identify new words and build your vocabulary
- how to adjust the way you read to fit your reason for reading
- how to use specific reading strategies to better understand what you read
- how to use critical thinking strategies to think more deeply about what you read

You will also learn about

- text structures
- reading for research

TABLE OF CONTENTS

Identifying Words and
  Building Vocabulary RH1

Reading for a Reason RH3

Understanding What You Read RH4

Thinking About Your Reading RH6

Understanding Text Structure RH7

Reading for Research RH9

Identifying Words and Building Vocabulary

What do you do when you come across a word you do not know as you read? Do you skip over the word and keep reading? If you are reading for fun or entertainment, you might. But if you are reading for information, an unfamiliar word may get in the way of your understanding. When that happens, try the following strategies to figure out how to say the word and what the word means.

Reading Unfamiliar Words

Sounding out the word One way to figure out how to say a new word is to sound it out, syllable by syllable. Look carefully at the word's beginning, middle, and ending. Inside the word, do you see a word you already know how to pronounce? What vowels are in the syllables? Use the following tips when sounding out new words.

- **Roots and base words** The main part of a word is called its root. When the root is a complete word, it may be called the base word. When you come across a new word, check whether you recognize its root or base word. It can help you pronounce the word and figure out the word's meaning.

ASK YOURSELF

- What letters make up the beginning sound or beginning syllable of the word?

  Example: In the word *coagulate, co* rhymes with *so*.

- What sounds do the letters in the middle part of the word make?

  Example: In the word *coagulate*, the syllable *ag* has the same sound as the

  ag in *bag*, and the syllable *u* is pronounced like the letter *u*.

- What letters make up the ending sound or syllable?

  Example: In the word *coagulate, late* is a familiar word you already know how to pronounce.

- Now try pronouncing the whole word:

  co ag u late.

- **Prefixes** A prefix is a word part that can be added to the beginning of a root or base word. For example, the prefix *pre-* means "before," so *prehistory* means "before history." Prefixes can change, or even reverse, the meaning of a word. For example, *un-* means "not," so *unconstitutional* means "not constitutional."

- **Suffixes** A suffix is a word part that can be added to the end of a root or base word to change the word's meaning. Adding a suffix to a word can also change that word from one part of speech to another. For example, the word *joy,* which is a noun, becomes an adjective when the suffix *-ful* (meaning "full of") is added. *Joyful* means "full of joy."

Determining a Word's Meaning

Using syntax Like all languages, the English language has rules and patterns for the way words are arranged in sentences. The way a sentence is organized is called the **syntax** of the sentence. If English is your first language, you have known this pattern since you started talking in sentences. If you're learning English now, you may find the syntax is different from the patterns you know in your first language.

In a simple sentence in English, someone or something (the *subject*) does something (the *predicate* or *verb*) to or with another person or thing (the *object*): The *soldiers attacked* the *enemy*.

Sometimes adjectives, adverbs, and phrases are added to add details to the sentence: The *courageous young* soldiers *fearlessly* attacked the *well-entrenched* enemy *shortly after dawn*.

CHECK IT OUT

Knowing about syntax can help you figure out the meaning of an unfamiliar word. Just look at how syntax can help you figure out the following nonsense sentence.

The blizzy kwarkles sminched the flerky fleans.

Your experience with English syntax tells you that the action word, or verb, in this sentence is *sminched*. Who did the *sminching?* The *kwarkles*. What kind of kwarkles were they? *Blizzy.* Whom did they *sminch?* The fleans. What kind of fleans were they? *Flerky.* Even though you don't know the meaning of the words in the nonsense sentence, you can make some sense of the entire sentence by studying its syntax.

Using context clues You can often figure out the meaning of an unfamiliar word by looking at its context, the words and sentences that surround it. To learn new words as you read, follow these steps for using context clues.

1. Look before and after the unfamiliar word for:
  • a definition or a synonym, another word that means the same as the unfamiliar word.
  • a general topic associated with the word.
  • a clue to what the word is similar to or different from.
  • an action or a description that has something to do with the word.
2. Connect what you already know with what the author has written.
3. Predict a possible meaning.
4. Use the meaning in the sentence.
5. Try again if your guess does not make sense.

Using reference materials Dictionaries and other reference sources can help you learn new words. Check out these reference sources:

• A **dictionary** gives the pronunciation and the meaning or meanings of words. Some dictionaries also give other forms of words, their parts of speech, and synonyms. You might also find the historical background of a word, such as its Greek, Latin, or Anglo-Saxon origins.

• A **glossary** is a word list that appears at the end—or Appendix—of a book or other written work and includes only words that are in that work. Like dictionaries, glossaries have the pronunciation and definitions of words.

• A **thesaurus** lists groups of words that have the same, or almost the same, meaning. Words with similar meanings are called *synonyms.* Seeing the synonyms of words can help you build your vocabulary.

Recognizing Word Meanings Across Subjects

Have you ever learned a new word in one class and then noticed it in your reading for other subjects? The word probably will not mean exactly the same thing in each class. But you can use what you know about the word's meaning to help you understand what it means in a different subject area.

CHECK IT OUT

Look at the following example from three subjects:

Social studies: One major **product** manufactured in the South is cotton cloth.

Math: After you multiply those two numbers, explain how you arrived at the **product.**

Science: One **product** of photosynthesis is oxygen.

Reading for a Reason

Why are you reading that paperback mystery? What do you hope to get from your geography textbook? And are you going to read either of these books in the same way that you read a restaurant menu? The point is, you read for different reasons. The reason you are reading something helps you decide on the reading strategies you use with a text. In other words, how you read will depend on **why** you're reading.

Knowing Your Reason for Reading

In school and in life, you will have many reasons for reading, and those reasons will lead you to a wide range of materials. For example,

- **to learn and understand new information,** you might read news magazines, textbooks, news on the Internet, books about your favorite pastime, encyclopedia articles, primary and secondary sources for a school report, instructions on how to use a calling card, or directions for a standardized test.

- **to find specific information,** you might look at the sports section for the score of last night's game, a notice on where to register for a field trip, weather reports, bank statements, or television listings.

- **to be entertained,** you might read your favorite magazine, e-mails or letters from friends, the Sunday comics, or even novels, short stories, plays, or poems!

Adjusting How Fast You Read

How quickly or how carefully you should read a text depends on your purpose for reading it. Because there are many reasons and ways to read, think about your purpose and choose a strategy that works best. Try out these strategies:

- **Scanning** means quickly running your eyes over the material, looking for *key words or phrases* that point to the information you're looking for. Scan when you need to find a particular piece or type of information. For example, you might scan a newspaper for movie show times.

- **Skimming** means quickly reading a piece of writing *to find its main idea* or to *get a general overview* of it. For example, you might skim the sports section of the daily newspaper to find out how your favorite teams are doing. Or you might skim a chapter in your textbook to prepare for a test.

- **Careful reading** involves *reading slowly and paying attention* with a purpose in mind. Read carefully when you're learning new concepts, following complicated directions, or preparing to explain information to someone else.

Understanding What You Read

Reading without understanding is like trying to drive a car on an empty gas tank. Fortunately, there are techniques you can use to help you concentrate on and understand what you read. Skilled readers adopt a number of strategies before, during, and after reading to make sure they understand what they read.

Previewing

If you were making a preview for a movie, you would want to let your audience know what the movie is like. When you preview a piece of writing, you are trying to get an idea about that piece of writing. If you know what to expect before reading, you will have an easier time understanding ideas and relationships. Follow these steps to preview your reading assignments.

DO IT!

1. Look at the title and any illustrations that are included.
2. Read the headings, subheadings, and anything in bold letters.
3. Skim over the passage to see how it is organized. Is it divided into many parts?

Is it a long poem or short story? Don't forget to look at the graphics—pictures, maps, or diagrams.

4. Set a purpose for your reading. Are you reading to learn something new? Are you reading to find specific information?

Using What You Know

Believe it or not, you already know quite a bit about what you are going to read. You bring knowledge and personal experience to a selection. Drawing on your own background is called *activating prior knowledge,* and it can help you create meaning in what you read. Ask yourself, *What do I already know about this topic?*

Predicting

You do not need any special knowledge to make *predictions* when you read. The predictions do not even have to be accurate. Take educated guesses before and during your reading about what might happen in the story or article you are reading.

Visualizing

Creating pictures in your mind as you read—called *visualizing*—is a powerful aid to understanding. As you read, set up a movie theater in your imagination. Picture the setting—city streets, the desert, or the surface of the moon. If you can visualize what you read, selections will be more vivid, and you will recall them better later on.

Identifying Sequence

When you discover the logical order of events or ideas, you are identifying *sequence.* Do you need to understand step-by-step directions? Are you reading a persuasive speech with the reasons listed in order of importance? Look for clues and signal words that will help you find the way information is organized.

Determining the Main Idea

When you look for the *main idea* of a selection, you look for the most important idea. The examples, reasons, and details that further explain the main idea are called *supporting details.* Some main ideas are clearly stated within a passage— often in the first sentence of a paragraph, or sometimes in the last sentence of a passage. Other times, an author does not directly state the main idea but provides details that help readers figure out what the main idea is.

ASK YOURSELF

- **What is each sentence about?**
- **Is there one sentence that tells about the whole passage or that is more important**

than any of the other sentences?
- **What main idea do the supporting details point out?**

Questioning

Keep up a conversation with yourself as you read by *asking questions* about the text. Ask about the importance of the information you are reading. Ask how one event relates to another. Ask yourself if you understand what you just read. As you answer your questions, you are making sure that you understand what is going on.

Clarifying

Clear up, or *clarify,* confusing or difficult passages as you read. When you realize you do not understand something, try these techniques to help you clarify the ideas.
- *Reread* the confusing parts slowly and carefully.
- *Look up* unfamiliar words.
- Simply *"talk out"* the part to yourself.
Reread the passage. The second time is often easier and more informative.

Reviewing

You probably *review* in school what you learned the day before so the ideas are firm in your mind. Reviewing when you read does the same thing. Take time now and then to pause and review what you have read. Think about the main ideas and reorganize them for yourself so you can recall them later. Filling in study aids such as graphic organizers, notes, or outlines can help you review.

Monitoring Your Comprehension

As you read, check your understanding by using the following strategies.

- **Summarize** what you read by pausing from time to time and telling yourself the main ideas of what you have just read. Answer the questions *Who? What?*

Where? When? Why? and *How?* Summarizing tests your comprehension by encouraging you to clarify key points in your own words.

- **Paraphrase** Sometimes you read something that you "sort of" understand, but not quite. Use paraphrasing as a test to see whether you really got the point. *Paraphrasing* is retelling something in your own words. So shut the book and try putting what you have just read into your own words. If you cannot explain it clearly, you should probably have another look at the text.

Thinking About Your Reading

Sometimes it is important to think more deeply about what you have read so you can get the most out of what the author says. These critical thinking skills will help you go beyond what the words say and get at the important messages of your reading.

Interpreting

When you listen to your best friend talk, you do not just hear the words he or she says. You also watch your friend, listen to the tone of voice, and use what you already know about that person to put meaning to the words. In doing so, you are interpreting what your friend says. Readers do the same thing when they interpret as they read. *Interpreting* is asking yourself, *What is the writer really saying here?* and then using what you know about the world to help answer that question.

Inferring

You may not realize it, but you infer, or make inferences, every day. Here is an example: You run to the bus stop a little later than usual. There is no one there. "I have missed the bus," you say to yourself. You may be wrong, but that is the way our minds work. You look at the evidence (you are late; no one is there) and come to a conclusion (you have missed the bus).

When you read, you go though exactly the same process because writers don't always directly state what they want you to understand. By providing clues and interesting details, they suggest certain information. Whenever you combine those clues with your own background and knowledge, you are making an inference.

An *inference* involves using your thinking and experience to come up with an idea based on what an author implies or suggests. In reading, you *infer* when you use context clues and your own knowledge to figure out the author's meaning.

Drawing Conclusions

Skillful readers are always *drawing conclusions,* or figuring out much more than an author says directly. The process is like a detective solving a mystery. You combine information and evidence that the author provides to come up with a statement about the topic. Drawing conclusions helps you find connections between ideas and events and gives you a better understanding of what you are reading.

Analyzing

Analyzing, or looking at separate parts of something to understand the entire piece, is a way to think critically about written work.

- In analyzing persuasive *nonfiction,* you might look at the writer's reasons to see if they actually support the main point of the argument.

- In analyzing *informational text,* you might look at how the ideas are organized to see what is most important.

Distinguishing Fact From Opinion

Distinguishing between fact and opinion is one of the most important reading skills you can learn. A *fact* is a statement that can be proved with supporting information. An *opinion,* on the other hand, is what a writer believes, on the basis of his or her personal viewpoint. Writers can support their opinions with facts, but an opinion is something that cannot be proved.

FOR EXAMPLE

Look at the following examples of fact and opinion.

Fact: George III was the British king during the American Revolution.

Opinion: King George III was an evil despot.

You could prove that George III was king during that period. It's a fact. However, not everyone might see that King George III was a despot. That's someone's opinion.

As you examine information, always ask yourself, "Is this a fact or an opinion?" Don't think that opinions are always bad. Very often they are just what you want. You read editorials and essays for their authors' opinions. Reviews of books, movies, plays, and CDs can help you decide whether to spend your time and money on something. It's when opinions are based on faulty reasoning or prejudice or when they are stated as facts that they become troublesome.

Evaluating

When you form an opinion or make a judgment about something you are reading, you are *evaluating.* If you are reading informational texts or something on the Internet, it is important to evaluate how qualified the author is to be writing about the topic and how reliable the information is that is presented. Ask yourself whether the author seems biased, whether the information is one-sided, and whether the argument presented is logical.

Synthesizing

When you *synthesize,* you combine ideas (maybe even from different sources) to come up with something new. It may be a new understanding of an important idea or a new way of combining and presenting information. For example, you might read a manual on coaching soccer, combine that information with your own experiences playing soccer, and come up with a winning plan for coaching your sister's team this spring.

Understanding Text Structure

Good writers do not just put together sentences and paragraphs in any order. They structure each piece of their writing in a specific way for a specific purpose. That pattern of organization is called *text structure.* When you know the text structure of a selection, you will find it easier to locate and recall an author's ideas. Here are four ways that writers organize text.

Comparison and Contrast

Comparison-and-contrast structure shows the similarities and differences between people, things, and ideas. Maybe you have overheard someone at school say something like "He is better at throwing the football, but I can run faster than he can." This student is using comparison-and-contrast structure. When writers use comparison-and-contrast structure, often they want to show you *how things that seem alike are different, or how things that seem different are alike.*

- **Signal words and phrases:** *similarly, on the one hand, on the other hand, in contrast to, but, however*

Cause and Effect

Just about everything that happens in life is the cause or the effect of some other event or action. Sometimes what happens is pretty minor: You do not look when you are pouring milk *(cause)*; you spill milk on the table *(effect)*. Sometimes it is a little more serious: You do not look at your math book before the big test *(cause)*; you mess up on the test *(effect)*.

Writers use cause-and-effect structure to explore the reasons for something happening and to examine the results of previous events. This structure helps answer the question that everybody is always asking: *Why?* A historian might tell us why an empire rose and fell. Cause-and-effect structure is all about explaining things.

- **Signal words and phrases:** *so, because, as a result, therefore, for the following reasons*

Problem and Solution

How did scientists overcome the difficulty of getting a person to the moon? How will I brush my teeth when I have forgotten my toothpaste? These questions may be very different in importance, but they have one thing in common: Each identifies a problem and asks how to solve it. *Problems* and *solutions* are part of what makes life interesting. Problems and solutions also occur in fiction and nonfiction writing.

- **Signal words and phrases:** *how, help, problem, obstruction, difficulty, need, attempt, have to, must*

Sequence

Take a look at three common forms of sequencing, *the order in which thoughts are arranged.*

- **Chronological order** refers to the order in which events take place. First you wake up; next you have breakfast; then you go to school. Those events don't make much sense in any other order.

    Signal words: *first, next, then, later,* and *finally.*

- **Spatial order** tells you the order in which to look at objects. For example, take a look at this description of an ice cream sundae: *At the bottom of the dish are two scoops of vanilla. The scoops are covered with fudge and topped with whipped cream and a cherry.* Your eyes follow the sundae from the bottom to the top. Spatial order is important in descriptive writing because it helps you as a reader to see an image the way the author does.

Signal words: *above*, *below*, *behind*, and *next to*.

- **Order of importance** is going from most important to least important or the other way around. For example, a typical news article has a most-to-least-important structure.

   Signal words: *principal*, *central*, *important*, and *fundamental*.

CHECK IT OUT

- **Tables of contents** Look at the table of contents first to see whether a resource offers information you need.
- **Indexes** An index is an alphabetical listing of significant topics covered in a book. It is found in the back of a book.
- **Headings and subheadings** Headings often tell you what information is going to follow in the text you're reading. Subheadings allow you to narrow your search for information even further.
- **Graphic features** Photos, diagrams, maps, charts, graphs, and other graphic features can communicate large amounts of information at a glance.

Reading for Research

An important part of doing research is knowing how to get information from a wide variety of sources. The following skills will help you when you have a research assignment for a class or when you want information about a topic outside of school.

Reading Text Features

Researching a topic is not only about asking questions; it is about finding answers. Textbooks, references, magazines, and other sources provide a variety of text features to help you find those answers quickly and efficiently.

Organizing Information

When researching a topic, you have to make sense of that information, organize it, and put it all together in ways that will help you explain it to someone else. Here are some ways of doing just that.

- **Record** information from your research and keep track of your resources on note cards.

- **Interpret graphic aids** carefully. These could include charts, graphs, maps and photographs.

- **Summarize** information before you write it on a note card. That way you will have the main ideas in your own words.

- **Outline** ideas so you can see how subtopics and supporting information will fit under the main ideas.

- **Make a table or graph** to compare items or categories of information.

REFERENCE ATLAS

NATIONAL GEOGRAPHIC

United States Political RA2

United States Physical RA4

United States 2000 Congressional
   Reapportionment RA6

United States Territorial Growth RA8

Middle America
   Physical/Political RA10

Canada Physical/Political RA12

Middle East Physical/Political RA14

World Political RA16

ATLAS KEY

Tundra
Evergreen forest
Mixed forest
Mountains
Grassland
Ice cap
Oceans
Seas
Desert

SYMBOL KEY

⊥⊥⊥⊥ Canal	∘ Depression	⬭ Below sea level	⬳ Lava
············ Claimed boundary	+ Elevation	⬭ Dry salt lake	⬳ Sand
International boundary	⊛ National capital	⬭ Lake	⌁ Swamp
	• • • Towns	� Rivers	

UNITED STATES
PHYSICAL

0 mi   300
0 km   300
ALBERS CONIC EQUAL-AREA PROJECTION

NATIONAL GEOGRAPHIC

C A N A D A

A

Lake of the Woods

Isle Royale
Lake Superior

Upper Peninsula

Minneapolis

Mississippi

Lower Peninsula

Lake Michigan

Lake Huron

Milwaukee

Chicago

C E N T R A L

L O W L A N D

Detroit

Lake Erie

Cleveland

Ohio

Pittsburgh

Indianapolis

St. Louis

Wabash

lint
ills

Ozark Plateau

Boston Mts.

Memphis

Tennessee

Ouachita Mts.

Cumberland

Cumberland Plateau

Appalachian Plateau
Allegheny Mts.

Blue Ridge

Appalachian Plateau

A P P A L A C H I A N   M O U N T A I N S

Lake Champlain

Adirondack Mts.

Green Mts.

White Mts.

Gulf of Maine

Connecticut

Boston

Cape Cod

Lake Ontario

Niagara Falls

Hudson

Long Island

New York City

Philadelphia

Baltimore

Delaware Bay

Washington

A T L A N T I C

O C E A N

Chesapeake Bay

Cape Hatteras

Mt. Mitchell
6,684 ft
2,037 m

P

Atlanta

Savannah

Piedmont

P L A I N

Black Belt

C O A S T A L

Mississippi

Red

A

Houston

New Orleans

*Mississippi
River Delta*

Jacksonville

Cape Canaveral

Lake Okeechobee

The Everglades

Miami

Gulf of Mexico

Florida Keys
Straits of Florida
TROPIC OF CANCER

C U B A

PRINCIPAL HAWAIIAN ISLANDS

Niihau   *Kauai*

Honolulu

Oahu

Molokai

Lanai

Kahoolawe

Maui — 21°N

Hawaii

Mauna Kea
13,796 ft
4,205 m

*P A C I F I C
O C E A N*

0 mi   100
0 km   100

95°W

90°W

95°W   90°W   85°W   80°W   75°W   70°W   65°W

50°N
75°N

45°N

40°N

65°W

35°N

30°N

70°W

20°N

75°W

159°W   156°W

A New Nation, 1787

BRITISH NORTH AMERICA

Claimed by U.S. and Great Britain

Claimed by U.S. and Great Britain

Claimed by N.H. and N.Y.

Part of Mass.

NEW HAMPSHIRE

Awarded to Pa. from Conn. 1782

Ceded by Mass. to N.Y. 1786

MASSACHUSETTS

RHODE ISLAND

CONNECTICUT

Ceded by Mass. to U.S. 1785

NORTHWEST TERRITORY

Ceded by Va. to U.S. 1784

New York City (1787-1790)

Mississippi

PA.

NEW JERSEY

MD.

DELAWARE

Ceded by Conn. to U.S. 1786 & 1800

Missouri

SPANISH

SPANISH LOUISIANA

Arkansas

Wabash

Ohio

UNITED

VIRGINIA

NORTH

STATES

Ceded by New York to U.S. 1782

Claimed by Virginia

NORTH CAROLINA

Colorado

AMERICA

Claimed by North Carolina

ALTA CALIFORNIA

Gila

Ceded by S.C. to Ga. 1787

Claimed by Georgia

SOUTH CAROLINA

GEORGIA

Original 13 states

Land still claimed by states 1787

U.S. territory

British territory

Spanish territory

Disputed boundary

BAJA CALIFORNIA

WESTERN INTERIOR PROVINCES

Rio Grande

Claimed by Ga., Spain and U.S.

SPANISH FLORIDA

EASTERN INTERIOR PROVINCES

Coming of Age, 1821

Columbia

U.S.–British treaty line of 1818

BRITISH NORTH AMERICA

Claimed by U.S. and Great Britain

OREGON COUNTRY

U.S.–British agreement to joint occupation in 1818

RED RIVER BASIN To U.S. 1818

MAINE

1820

Snake

Adams–Onis Treaty line of 1819

Mississippi

MICHIGAN TERRITORY

UNORGANIZED

TERRITORY

Missouri

INDIANA

1816

Washington

ALTA CALIFORNIA

ILLINOIS

1818

Ohio

Wabash

Arkansas

MISSOURI

1821

MEXICO

ARKANSAS TERRITORY

Red

MISSISSIPPI

1817

ALABAMA

1819

Rio Grande

TEXAS

LOUISIANA

1812

FLORIDA To U.S. 1819

UNITED STATES

TERRITORIAL GROWTH

NATIONAL GEOGRAPHIC

Expanding West of the Mississippi, 1803

BRITISH NORTH AMERICA

Claimed by U.S. and Great Britain

OREGON COUNTRY
Claimed by Great Britain, Russia, Spain, and United States

Claimed by U.S. and Great Britain

VERMONT 1791

INDIANA

NEW SPAIN (SPANISH MEXICO)

LOUISIANA PURCHASE
Purchased by U.S. in 1803 from France

Mississippi

Missouri

Arkansas

TERRITORY

OHIO 1803

Ohio

Wabash

⊕ **Philadelphia** (1790-1800)
⊕ **Washington** (new capital 1800)

KENTUCKY 1792

Red

TENNESSEE 1796

BAJA CALIFORNIA

Rio Grande

Claimed by U.S. and Spain

Ceded by Georgia to U.S. 1802

MISSISSIPPI TERR.

SPANISH FLORIDA

Claimed by U.S. and Spain

▢	States previously in the Union
▢	States newly admitted

Coast to Coast, 1850 and beyond

BRITISH NORTH AMERICA

Treaty line of 1846

Treaty line of 1842

Treaty line of 1842

WASHINGTON 1889

MONTANA 1889

NORTH DAKOTA 1889

MINNESOTA 1858

OREGON TERRITORY
Added to U.S. in 1846

MICHIGAN 1837

OREGON 1859

IDAHO 1890

Snake

MINNESOTA TERRITORY

WISCONSIN 1848

WYOMING 1890

SOUTH DAKOTA 1889

NEVADA 1864

UNORGANIZED

Missouri

IOWA 1846

⊕ **Washington**

W. VA. 1863

UTAH TERRITORY

TERRITORY

NEBRASKA 1867

Wabash

Ohio

CALIFORNIA 1850

UTAH 1896

COLORADO 1876

KANSAS 1861

Arkansas

ARIZONA 1912

Colorado

Gila

NEW MEXICO TERRITORY

OKLAHOMA 1907

Red

ARKANSAS 1836

GADSDEN PURCHASE
To U.S. 1853

NEW MEXICO 1912

Mississippi

Rio Grande

TEXAS 1845

RUSSIA

ALASKA 1959
Purchased by U.S. 1867

MEXICO

FLORIDA 1845

HAWAII 1959
Annexed by U.S. 1898

⋯⋯ States admitted after 1850

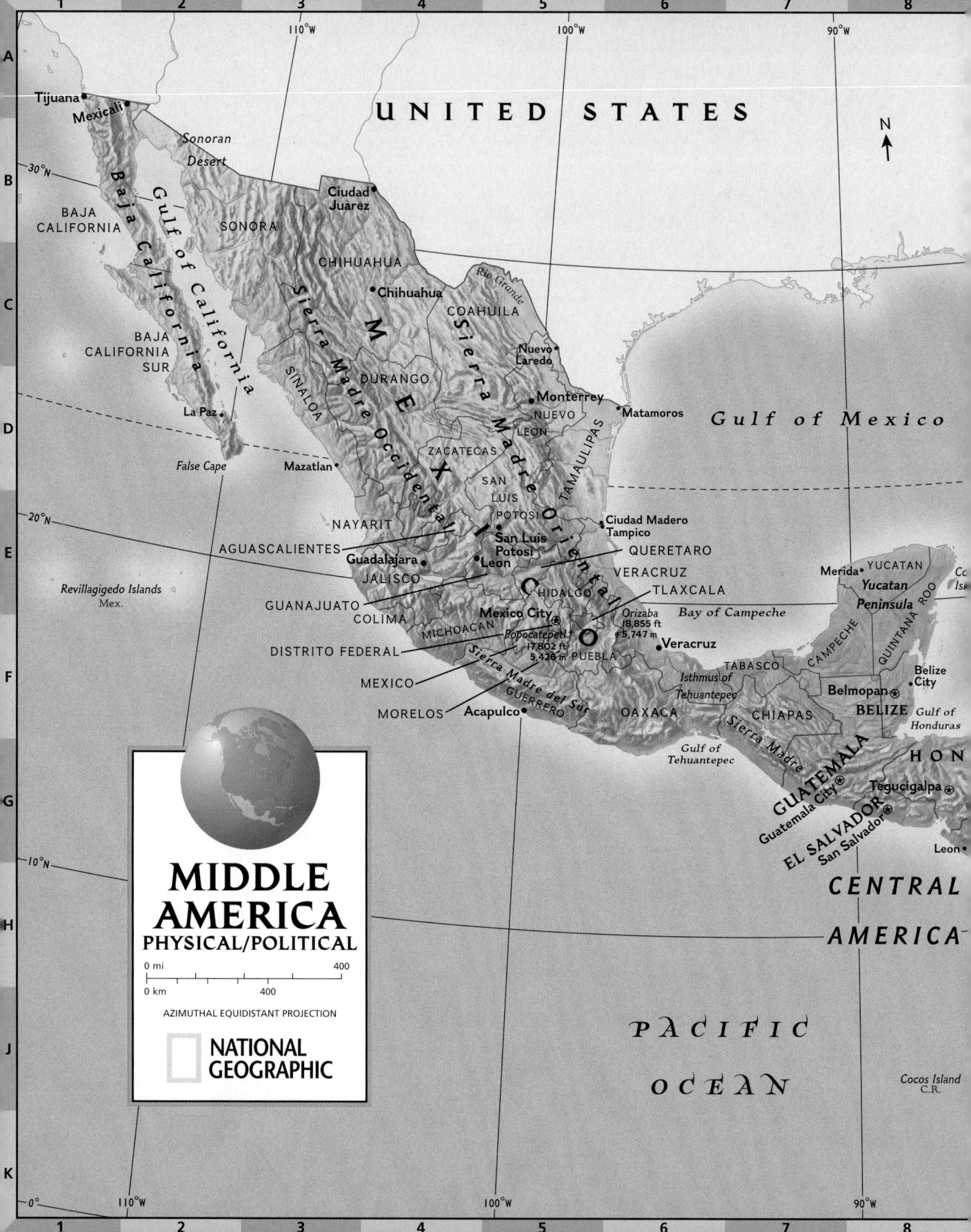

UNITED STATES

N

Tijuana
Mexicali

Sonoran Desert

30°N

BAJA CALIFORNIA

SONORA

Ciudad Juarez

Gulf of California

CHIHUAHUA

Rio Grande

COAHUILA

Chihuahua

BAJA CALIFORNIA SUR

Baja California

La Paz

M

Sierra Madre Occidental

DURANGO

Nuevo Laredo

NUEVO LEON

Monterrey

Matamoros

Gulf of Mexico

20°N

False Cape

SINALOA

ZACATECAS

E

Mazatlan

SAN LUIS POTOSI

X

Sierra Madre Oriental

TAMAULIPAS

NAYARIT

AGUASCALIENTES

Guadalajara

Ciudad Madero
Tampico

QUERETARO

VERACRUZ

Merida

YUCATAN

Cc Isl

Revillagigedo Islands
Mex.

San Luis Potosi
Leon

I

TLAXCALA

Yucatan
Peninsula

GUANAJUATO

JALISCO

COLIMA

MICHOACAN

C

HIDALGO

Bay of Campeche

CAMPECHE

QUINTANA ROO

DISTRITO FEDERAL

Mexico City

Popocatepetl
17,802 ft
5,426 m

PUEBLA

Orizaba
18,855 ft
5,747 m

Veracruz

Belize City

MEXICO

Sierra Madre del Sur

TABASCO

Isthmus of Tehuantepec

Belmopan

BELIZE

Gulf of Honduras

MORELOS

Acapulco

GUERRERO

OAXACA

CHIAPAS

Sierra Madre

Gulf of Tehuantepec

10°N

MIDDLE AMERICA

PHYSICAL/POLITICAL

GUATEMALA

Guatemala City

EL SALVADOR

Tegucigalpa

HON

Leon

H

0 mi   400

0 km   400

AZIMUTHAL EQUIDISTANT PROJECTION

NATIONAL GEOGRAPHIC

San Salvador

CENTRAL

AMERICA

PACIFIC

J

OCEAN

Cocos Island
C.R.

0°

110°W

100°W

90°W

ATLANTIC OCEAN

TROPIC OF CANCER

30°N
20°N

•Freeport

B A H A M A S

⊛ Nassau

Straits of Florida

Andros Island

Turks & Caicos Islands U.K.

ST. KITTS & NEVIS

W E S T

I N D I E S

ANTIGUA & BARBUDA

⊛ Havana

CUBA

•Camaguey

•Holguin

•Santiago de Cuba

Santiago

San Juan ⊛

Virgin Islands U.S. & U.K.

Isle of Youth

Hispaniola

Santo Domingo

Puerto Rico U.S.

Guadeloupe Fr.

Cayman Islands U.K.

HAITI

DOMINICAN REPUBLIC

DOMINICA

G

Port-au-Prince

Bird I. Venez.

Martinique Fr.

Montego Bay

r e a t e r

A n t i l l e s

ST. LUCIA

BARBADOS

JAMAICA

⊛ Kingston

ST. VINCENT & THE GRENADINES

L e s s e r   A n t i l l e s

GRENADA

C

C a r i b b e a n   S e a

Neth.

Curacao Bonaire

TRINIDAD & TOBAGO

Tobago

Port-of-Spain ⊛

10°N
60°W

Aruba Neth.

Lesser Antilles

Trinidad

U R A S

Coco

Mosquito Coast

NICARAGUA

⊛ Managua

Lake Nicaragua

COSTA

Puerto •Limon

Gulf of Mosquitos

Isthmus of Panama

SOUTH

San Jose ⊛

RICA

⊛ Panama City

AMERICA

•David

P A N A M A

Gulf of Panama

0°

EQUATOR

80°W

70°W

Map labels (reading order):

1	2	3	4	5	6	7	8

A

RUSSIA

170°W · 70°N · 160°W · 150°W · 80°N

ARCTIC OCEAN

Queen

B

170°W

ARCTIC CIRCLE

130°W

120°W
North Magnetic Pole +

Elizabeth

Prince Patrick I.

Melville Island

Bathurst Island

Island

ALASKA
U.S.

Beaufort Sea

Banks Island

160°W

Somers· Islar

Prince of Wales I.

C

· Inuvik

Victoria Island

Booth Penins·

YUKON
TERRITORY

Mt. Logan
19,551 ft
+ 5,959 m

Yukon Plateau

Mackenzie Mts.

Mackenzie

Great Bear Lake

D

· Whitehorse

**NORTHWEST
TERRITORIES**

N
U
N

50°N

150°W

· Virginia Falls

◎ Yellowknife

Great Slave Lake

C
A
N
A
D
I

E

Slave

Peace

Lake Athabasca

Churchill

F

PACIFIC

Queen Charlotte Islands

**BRITISH
COLUMBIA**

Fraser Plateau

· Prince George

Athabasca

ALBERTA

Athabasca

G R E A T

Saskatchewan

MANITOBA

Nelson

Churchill

G

140°W

Coast Mountains

Fraser

Columbia Mts.

◎ Edmonton

SASKATCHEWAN

· Saskatoon

Lake Winnipegosis

Lake Winnipeg

OCEAN

ROCKY MOUNTAINS

· Calgary

P L A I N S

H

Vancouver Island

Vancouver ·
Victoria ◎

· Regina

Winnipeg ◎

Lake of the Woods

40°N

J

130°W · 120°W

UNITED STATES

110°W · 100°W

K

1 2 3 4 5 6 7 8

CANADA
PHYSICAL/POLITICAL

0 mi   400
0 km   400

AZIMUTHAL EQUIDISTANT PROJECTION

NATIONAL GEOGRAPHIC

MIDDLE EAST

PHYSICAL / POLITICAL

0 mi — 500

0 km — 500

AZIMUTHAL EQUIDISTANT PROJECTION

NATIONAL GEOGRAPHIC

WORLD POLITICAL

0 mi 2000

0 km 2000

WINKEL TRIPEL PROJECTION

NATIONAL GEOGRAPHIC

Labels visible on map:

ARCTIC

150°W 120°W 90°W 60°W 30°W 0°

Queen Elizabeth Islands

GREENLAND (KALAALLIT NUNAAT) Den.

Chukchi Sea

Beaufort Sea

Baffin Bay

Greenland Sea

RUSSIA

Yukon

ALASKA U.S.

60°N

Anchorage

Great Bear Lake

Baffin Island

Nuuk

ARCTIC CIRCLE

Reykjavik ICELAND

Bering Sea

Gulf of Alaska

Great Slave Lake

Mackenzie

CANADA

Hudson Bay

Labrador Sea

Aleutian Islands

UNITED KINGDOM

Dublin IRELAND

London

Vancouver

Seattle

Calgary

Missouri

Island of Newfoundland

NORTH

Toronto Ottawa

Chicago New York City

Washington

ATLANTIC

Madrid PORTUGAL SPAIN

NORTH PACIFIC OCEAN

San Francisco

UNITED STATES

Ohio

Azores Port.

30°N

Los Angeles

Houston

Atlanta

Mississippi

OCEAN

Madeira Is. Port.

Rabat MOROCCO

TROPIC OF CANCER

Gulf of Mexico

Canary Is. Sp.

Morocco

WESTERN SAHARA

Hawaiian Islands U.S.

MEXICO

Havana CUBA

BAHAMAS

DOMINICAN REP.

Santo Domingo

PUERTO RICO U.S.

MAURITANIA

Guadalajara

BELIZE

HAITI

ST. KITTS & NEVIS

ANTIGUA & BARBUDA

CAPE VERDE

Mexico City

JAMAICA

Caribbean Sea

DOMINICA

SENEGAL

GUATEMALA

HONDURAS

ST. LUCIA

BARBADOS

GAMBIA

GUINEA

Guatemala City

NICARAGUA

GRENADA

ST. VINCENT & THE GRENADINES

GUINEA-BISSAU

EL SALVADOR

TRINIDAD & TOBAGO

BURKINA FASO

COSTA RICA

Caracas

SIERRA LEONE

LIBERIA

CÔTE D'IVOIRE

GHANA

PANAMA

VENEZUELA

FRENCH GUIANA Fr.

Christmas Island Kiribati

Medellin

Bogota

GUYANA

EQUATOR

COLOMBIA

SURINAME

0°

Quito

Galapagos Islands Ecua.

ECUADOR

Manaus

Negro

Amazon

Madeira

Marquesas Islands Fr.

PERU

Recife

BRAZIL

Lima

Salvador (Bahia)

São Francisco

SAMOA

AMERICAN SAMOA U.S.

La Paz

BOLIVIA

Brasilia

SOUTH

FRENCH POLYNESIA Fr.

Sucre

Rio de Janeiro

TONGA

TROPIC OF CAPRICORN

PARAGUAY

São Paulo

ATLANTIC

Asuncion

Paraguay

Cordoba

Porto Alegre

OCEAN

30°S

Santiago

URUGUAY

Buenos Aires

Montevideo

SOUTH PACIFIC OCEAN

CHILE

ARGENTINA

Falkland Islands U.K.

Tierra del Fuego

South Georgia U.K.

Strait of Magellan

MERIDIAN OF GREENWICH (LONDON)

Drake Passage

60°S

Antarctic Peninsula

ANTARCTIC CIRCLE

Weddell Sea

Ross Sea

Berkner Island

United States Facts

Washington, D.C.
Population: 572,059
Land area: 61 sq. mi.

U.S. Territories

Puerto Rico
Population: 3,808,610
Land area: 3,425 sq. mi.

Guam
Population: 155,000 (est.)
Land area: 209 sq. mi.

U.S. Virgin Islands
Population: 121,000 (est.)
Land area: 134 sq. mi.

American Samoa
Population: 65,000 (est.)
Land area: 77 sq. mi.

The states are listed in the order they were admitted to the Union.

Population figures are based on U.S. Bureau of the Census for 2000. House of Representatives figures are from the Clerk of the House of Representatives. States are not drawn to scale.

1 Delaware
Year Admitted: 1787
Population: 783,600
Land area: 1,955 sq. mi.
Representatives: 1
★ Dover

2 Pennsylvania
Year Admitted: 1787
Population: 12,281,054
Land area: 44,820 sq. mi.
Representatives: 19
Harrisburg ★

3 New Jersey
Year Admitted: 1787
Population: 8,414,350
Land area: 7,419 sq. mi.
Representatives: 13
Trenton ★

9 New Hampshire
Year Admitted: 1788
Population: 1,235,786
Land area: 8,969 sq. mi.
Representatives: 2
Concord ★

10 Virginia
Year Admitted: 1788
Population: 7,078,515
Land area: 39,598 sq. mi.
Representatives: 11
Richmond ★

11 New York
Year Admitted: 1788
Population: 18,976,457
Land area: 47,224 sq. mi.
Representatives: 29
★ Albany

17 Ohio
Year Admitted: 1803
Population: 11,353,140
Land area: 40,953 sq. mi.
Representatives: 18
★ Columbus

18 Louisiana
Year Admitted: 1812
Population: 4,468,976
Land area: 43,566 sq. mi.
Representatives: 7
Baton Rouge ★

19 Indiana
Year Admitted: 1816
Population: 6,080,485
Land area: 35,870 sq. mi.
Representatives: 9
Indianapolis ★

25 Arkansas
Year Admitted: 1836
Population: 2,673,400
Land area: 52,075 sq. mi.
Representatives: 4
Little Rock ★

26 Michigan
Year Admitted: 1837
Population: 9,938,444
Land area: 56,809 sq. mi.
Representatives: 15
Lansing ★

27 Florida
Year Admitted: 1845
Population: 15,982,378
Land area: 53,997 sq. mi.
Representatives: 25
★ Tallahassee

33 Oregon
Year Admitted: 1859
Population: 3,421,399
Land area: 96,003 sq. mi.
Representatives: 5
★ Salem

34 Kansas
Year Admitted: 1861
Population: 2,688,418
Land area: 81,823 sq. mi.
Representatives: 4
Topeka ★

35 West Virginia
Year Admitted: 1863
Population: 1,808,344
Land area: 24,087 sq. mi.
Representatives: 3
★ Charleston

36 Nevada
Year Admitted: 1864
Population: 1,998,257
Land area: 109,806 sq. mi.
Representatives: 3
★ Carson City

42 Washington
Year Admitted: 1889
Population: 5,894,121
Land area: 66,582 sq. mi.
Representatives: 9
★ Olympia

43 Idaho
Year Admitted: 1890
Population: 1,293,953
Land area: 82,751 sq. mi.
Representatives: 2
★ Boise

44 Wyoming
Year Admitted: 1890
Population: 493,782
Land area: 97,105 sq. mi.
Representatives: 1
Cheyenne ★

45 Utah
Year Admitted: 1896
Population: 2,233,169
Land area: 82,168 sq. mi.
Representatives: 3
★ Salt Lake City

4 Georgia
Year Admitted: 1788
Population: 8,186,453
Land area: 57,919 sq. mi.
Representatives: 13

★ Atlanta

5 Connecticut
Year Admitted: 1788
Population: 3,405,565
Land area: 4,845 sq. mi.
Representatives: 5

★ Hartford

6 Massachusetts
Year Admitted: 1788
Population: 6,349,097
Land area: 7,838 sq. mi.
Representatives: 10

Boston ★

7 Maryland
Year Admitted: 1788
Population: 5,296,486
Land area: 9,775 sq. mi.
Representatives: 8

Annapolis ★

8 South Carolina
Year Admitted: 1788
Population: 4,012,012
Land area: 30,111 sq. mi.
Representatives: 6

Columbia ★

12 North Carolina
Year Admitted: 1789
Population: 8,049,313
Land area: 48,718 sq. mi.
Representatives: 13

Raleigh ★

13 Rhode Island
Year Admitted: 1790
Population: 1,048,319
Land area: 1,045 sq. mi.
Representatives: 2

★ Providence

14 Vermont
Year Admitted: 1791
Population: 608,827
Land area: 9,249 sq. mi.
Representatives: 1

★ Montpelier

15 Kentucky
Year Admitted: 1792
Population: 4,041,769
Land area: 39,732 sq. mi.
Representatives: 6

Frankfort ★

16 Tennessee
Year Admitted: 1796
Population: 5,689,283
Land area: 41,220 sq. mi.
Representatives: 9

★ Nashville

20 Mississippi
Year Admitted: 1817
Population: 2,844,658
Land area: 46,914 sq. mi.
Representatives: 4

★ Jackson

21 Illinois
Year Admitted: 1818
Population: 12,419,293
Land area: 55,593 sq. mi.
Representatives: 19

★ Springfield

22 Alabama
Year Admitted: 1819
Population: 4,447,100
Land area: 50,750 sq. mi.
Representatives: 7

Montgomery ★

23 Maine
Year Admitted: 1820
Population: 1,274,923
Land area: 30,865 sq. mi.
Representatives: 2

★ Augusta

24 Missouri
Year Admitted: 1821
Population: 5,595,211
Land area: 68,898 sq. mi.
Representatives: 9

Jefferson City ★

28 Texas
Year Admitted: 1845
Population: 20,851,820
Land area: 261,914 sq. mi.
Representatives: 32

Austin ★

29 Iowa
Year Admitted: 1846
Population: 2,926,324
Land area: 55,875 sq. mi.
Representatives: 5

Des Moines ★

30 Wisconsin
Year Admitted: 1848
Population: 5,363,675
Land area: 54,314 sq. mi.
Representatives: 8

Madison ★

31 California
Year Admitted: 1850
Population: 33,871,648
Land area: 155,973 sq. mi.
Representatives: 53

★ Sacramento

32 Minnesota
Year Admitted: 1858
Population: 4,919,479
Land area: 79,617 sq. mi.
Representatives: 8

Saint Paul ★

37 Nebraska
Year Admitted: 1867
Population: 1,711,263
Land area: 76,878 sq. mi.
Representatives: 3

Lincoln ★

38 Colorado
Year Admitted: 1876
Population: 4,301,261
Land area: 103,730 sq. mi.
Representatives: 7

Denver ★

39 North Dakota
Year Admitted: 1889
Population: 642,200
Land area: 68,994 sq. mi.
Representatives: 1

Bismarck ★

40 South Dakota
Year Admitted: 1889
Population: 754,844
Land area: 75,898 sq. mi.
Representatives: 1

Pierre ★

41 Montana
Year Admitted: 1889
Population: 902,195
Land area: 145,556 sq. mi.
Representatives: 1

★ Helena

46 Oklahoma
Year Admitted: 1907
Population: 3,450,654
Land area: 68,679 sq. mi.
Representatives: 5

Oklahoma City ★

47 New Mexico
Year Admitted: 1912
Population: 1,819,046
Land area: 121,365 sq. mi.
Representatives: 3

Santa Fe ★

48 Arizona
Year Admitted: 1912
Population: 5,130,632
Land area: 113,642 sq. mi.
Representatives: 8

Phoenix ★

49 Alaska
Year Admitted: 1959
Population: 626,932
Land area: 570,374 sq. mi.
Representatives: 1

Juneau ★

50 Hawaii
Year Admitted: 1959
Population: 1,211,537
Land area: 6,432 sq. mi.
Representatives: 2

Honolulu ★

NATIONAL GEOGRAPHIC

Geography Handbook

The story of the United States begins with geography—the study of the earth in all of its variety. Geography describes the earth's land, water, and plant and animal life. It is the study of places and the complex relationships between people and their environments.

The United States is a land of startling physical differences. Within the borders of the United States is a rich variety of landscapes—dense forests, hot deserts, rolling grasslands, and snow-capped mountains. It is also a nation of diverse groups of people. With a total land area of 3,537,441 square miles (9,161,930 sq. km)—the United States is the world's fourth largest country in size. Only Russia, Canada, and China are larger. Because of its size and diversity, the United States has offered people from Europe, Africa, Asia, and other parts of the Americas many opportunities. Today more than 287 million people make the United States their home.

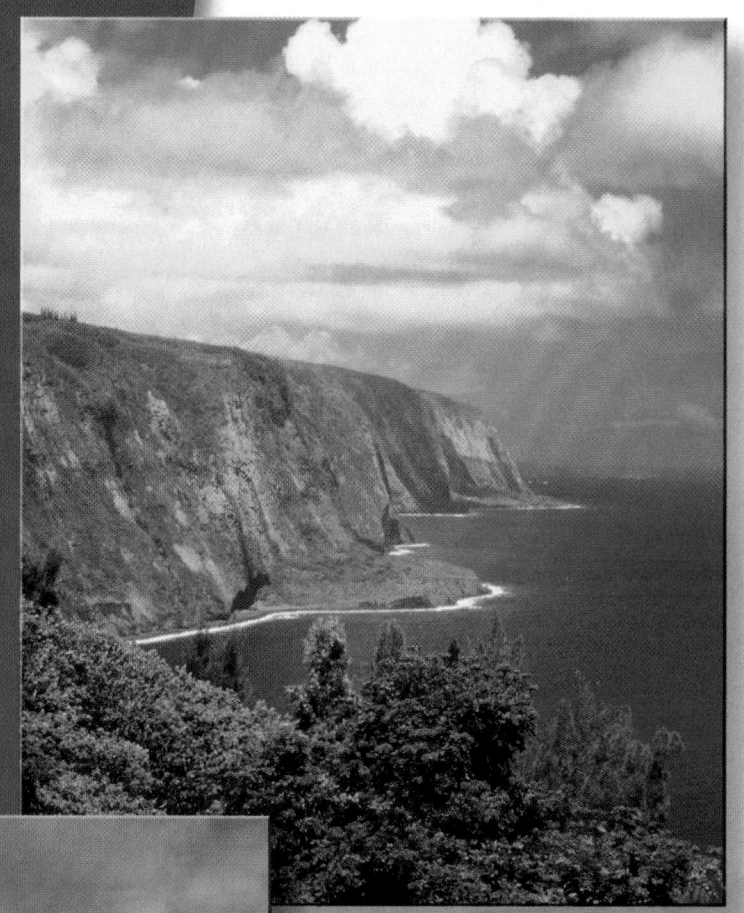

▲ Makapuu Point, Hawaii

◀ Mount Hood, Oregon

Globes and Maps

Globes

Photographs from space show the earth in its true form—a great ball spinning around the sun. The most accurate way to depict the earth is as a globe, or a round form. A globe gives a true picture of the earth's relative size and the shape of its landmasses and bodies of water. Globes are proportionally correct, thus showing the true distances and directions between places.

Maps

A map is a flat drawing of the earth's surface. People use maps to locate places, plot routes, and judge distances. Maps can also display useful information about the nation's peoples, such as political boundaries, population densities, or even voting results by city and state.

What advantages does a map have over a globe? Unlike a globe, a map allows you to see all areas of the world at the same time. Maps also show much more detail and can be folded and more easily carried.

Types of Maps

This text uses many different kinds of maps to help you see the connection between geography and the history of the United States.

General-Purpose Maps Maps that show a wide range of general information about a particular area are called **general-purpose maps.** Two of the most common general-purpose maps are physical maps and political maps. **Physical maps** show the location and the shape, or **topography,** of the earth's physical features. **Political maps** show the boundaries between different countries.

Special-Purpose Maps Special-purpose maps, also called **thematic maps,** show information on specific topics, such as climate, land use, or vegetation. Human activities, such as exploration routes, territorial expansion, or battle sites, also appear on special-purpose maps. Colors and map key symbols are very important on these maps.

LANDSAT and GIS Maps LANDSAT maps are made from photos taken from satellites in space. LANDSAT images allow scientists to study whole mountain ranges, oceans, and geographic regions and to track changes to the earth's environment. Graphic information systems (GIS) use computer software to combine and display a wide range of information about an area. Data can include satellite photos, rainfall amounts, or the location of houses. Layers of data can be switched on and off for different purposes.

◀ Special-purpose map

▲ LANDSAT map

Using Maps

Map Projections Maps, however, do have their limitations. As you can imagine, drawing a round object on a flat surface is very difficult. **Cartographers,** or mapmakers, have drawn many projections, or kinds of maps. Each map projection is a different way of showing the round earth on a flat map. Different map projections include the Winkel Tripel, Robinson, Goode's Interrupted Equal-Area, and Mercator projections. It is impossible to accurately represent the round earth on a flat surface without distorting some part of the earth. Thus, map projections typically distort distance, direction, shape, or area.

Winkel Tripel Projection

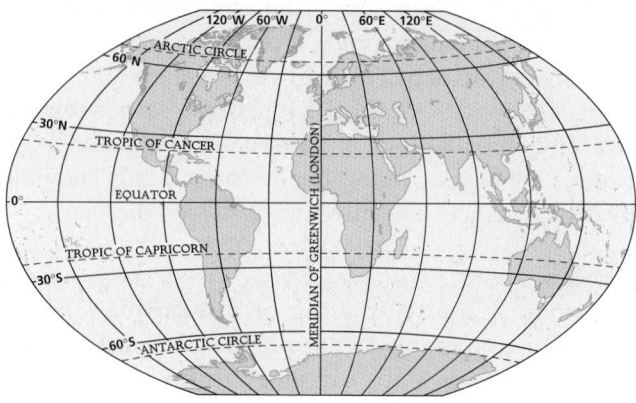

▲ Most general reference maps use the Winkel Tripel projection. Adopted by the National Geographic Society in 1998, this projection provides a better balance between the size and shape of land areas as they are shown on the map.

Reading a Map

Maps include several important tools to help you interpret the information contained on a particular map. Learning to use these map tools will help you read the symbolic language of maps more easily.

Compass Rose A compass rose is a marker that indicates directions. The four cardinal directions—north, south, east, and west—are usually indicated with arrows or points of a star. Sometimes a compass rose may indicate only one direction, because the other directions can be determined in relation to the one given. The compass rose on this map indicates all four cardinal directions.

Key Cartographers use a variety of symbols to represent map information. Because these symbols are graphic and commonly used, most maps can be read and understood by people around the world. To be sure that the symbols are clear, however, every map contains a key—a list that explains what the symbols represent. This key shows symbols used for a battle map in this text. It indicates troop movements, supply lines, and U.S. bases.

Robinson Projection

▲ The Robinson projection has minor distortions. The sizes and shapes near the eastern and western edges of the map are accurate, and the outlines of the continents appear much as they do on the globe. The shapes of the polar areas, however, are somewhat flat.

Goode's Interrupted Equal-Area Projection

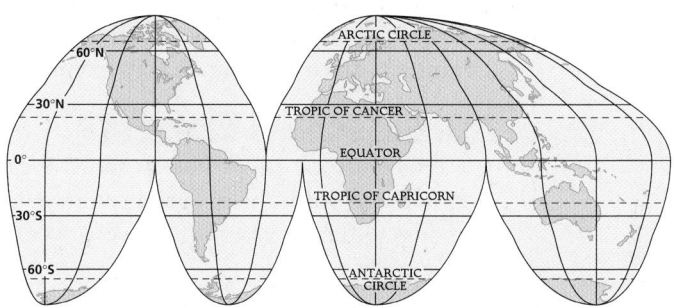

▲ An interrupted projection looks something like a globe that has been cut apart and laid flat. Goode's Interrupted Equal-Area projection shows the true size and shape of the earth's landmasses, but distances are distorted.

Relative Location Relative location is the location of one place in relation to another, while absolute location indicates the exact position of a place on the earth's surface. On this map, the relative location of where the Vietnam War took place is given in relation to the rest of Asia.

Cities and Capitals Cities are symbolized by a solid circle. Sometimes the relative sizes of cities are shown with circles of different sizes. Capitals are represented by a star within a circle.

Boundary Lines On political maps of large areas, boundary lines highlight the borders between different countries, states, or counties.

Scale Bar Every map is a representation of a part of the earth. The scale bar shows the relationship between map measurements and actual distance. Scale can be measured with a ruler to calculate actual distances in standard or metric measurements. On this map, 5/8 inch represents 150 miles (241 km).

Mercator Projection

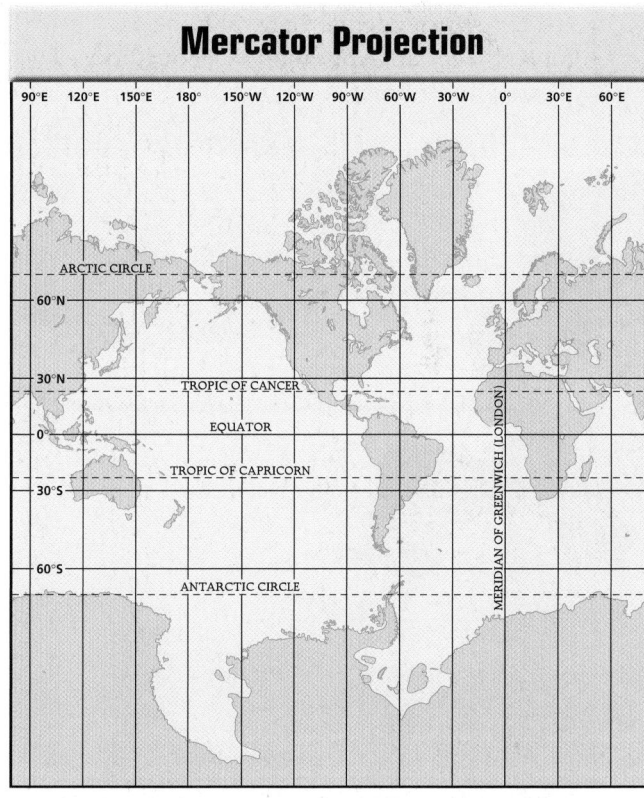

▲ The Mercator projection increasingly distorts size and distance as it moves away from the Equator. However, Mercator projections accurately show true directions and the shapes of the landmasses.

The Elements of Geography

To understand how our world is connected, some geographers have broken down the study of geography into five themes. The **Five Themes of Geography** are (1) location, (2) place, (3) human/environment interaction, (4) movement, and (5) regions.

Six Essential Elements

Recently, as suggested in the **Geography Skills for Life,** geographers have broken down the study of geography into **Six Essential Elements.** Being aware of these elements will help you sort out what you are learning about geography.

Element 1

The World in Spatial Terms Geographers first look at where a place is located. **Location** serves as a starting point by asking, "Where is it?" Knowing the location of places helps you develop an awareness of the world around you. For example, the surrender of Confederate General Robert E. Lee took place at Appomattox Courthouse, located in Virginia.

Element 2

Place and Regions **Place** has a special meaning in geography. It means more than where an area is located. It also describes what features a place includes. These features may be physical characteristics, such as landforms, climate, and plant or animal life. They may also be human characteristics, including language and way of life. For example, the English settlement of Jamestown was located in a swampy area with mosquitoes and high humidity. This made the way of life difficult for the new settlers.

To help them organize their study, geographers often group places into regions. **Regions** are united by one or more common characteristics. The original thirteen colonies, for instance, were divided into three regions—New England Colonies, Middle Colonies, and Southern Colonies.

Element 3

Physical Systems When studying places and regions, geographers analyze the ways in which **physical systems**—such as hurricanes, volcanoes, and glaciers—shape the earth's surface. They also look at communities of plants and animals that depend upon one another and their surroundings for survival. Glaciers are an example of a physical system. Near the end of the Ice Age, glaciers melted, raising ocean levels and covering a land bridge that once connected Asia and North America.

Element 4

Human Systems Geographers also examine an area's **human systems,** or how people have shaped our world. They look at how boundary lines are determined and analyze why people settle in certain places and not in others. A key theme in geography is the continual **movement** of people, ideas, and goods. An example of such movement occurred in the 1820s, when Stephen F. Austin organized a group of Americans to settle in the Mexican territory of Texas.

Element 5

Environment and Society "How does the relationship between people and their natural surroundings influence the way people live?" This is one of the questions that the geographic element of **environment and society** answers. This element also shows how people use the environment and how their actions affect it. One example was when some people in the South established large plantations to take advantage of the warm climate and fertile soil.

Element 6

The Uses of Geography Knowledge of geography helps people understand the relationships between people, places, and environment over time. Understanding geography and knowing how to use the tools and technology available to study it prepares you for life in our modern society. Early European explorers, for example, relied on their knowledge of geography to discover lands never seen before by Europeans.

Geographic Dictionary

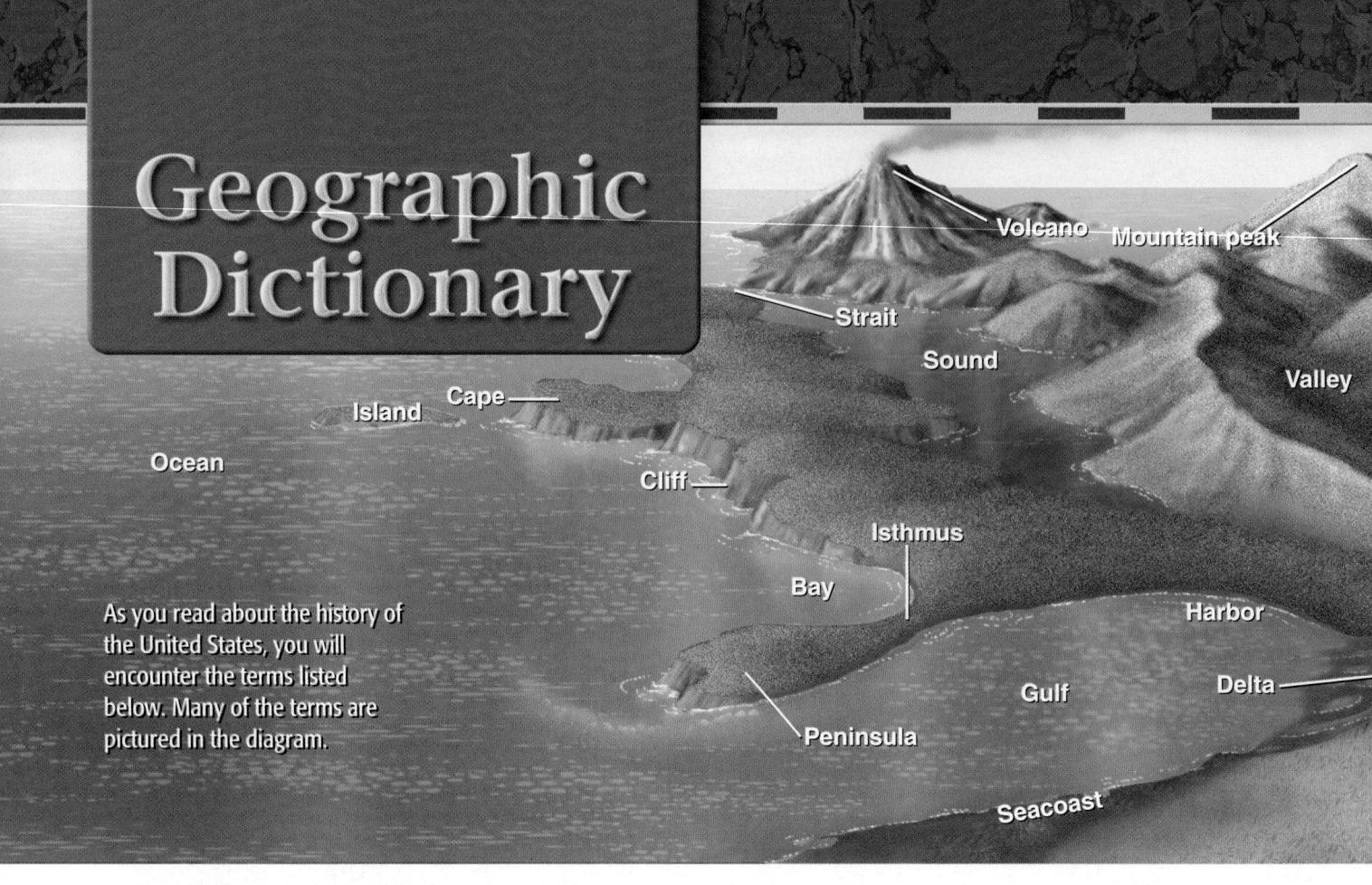

As you read about the history of the United States, you will encounter the terms listed below. Many of the terms are pictured in the diagram.

Labels in diagram: Volcano, Mountain peak, Strait, Sound, Valley, Cape, Island, Ocean, Cliff, Isthmus, Bay, Harbor, Peninsula, Gulf, Delta, Seacoast

absolute location exact location of a place on the earth described by global coordinates

basin area of land drained by a given river and its branches; area of land surrounded by lands of higher elevations

bay part of a large body of water that extends into a shoreline, generally smaller than a gulf

canyon deep and narrow valley with steep walls

cape point of land that extends into a river, lake, or ocean

channel wide strait or waterway between two landmasses that lie close to each other; deep part of a river or other waterway

cliff steep, high wall of rock, earth, or ice

continent one of the seven large landmasses on the earth

cultural feature characteristic that humans have created in a place, such as language, religion, housing, and settlement pattern

delta flat, low-lying land built up from soil carried downstream by a river and deposited at its mouth

divide stretch of high land that separates river systems

downstream direction in which a river or stream flows from its source to its mouth

elevation height of land above sea level

Equator imaginary line that runs around the earth halfway between the North and South Poles; used as the starting point to measure degrees of north and south latitude

glacier large, thick body of slowly moving ice

gulf part of a large body of water that extends into a shoreline, generally larger and more deeply indented than a bay

harbor a sheltered place along a shoreline where ships can anchor safely

highland elevated land area such as a hill, mountain, or plateau

hill elevated land with sloping sides and rounded summit; generally smaller than a mountain

island land area, smaller than a continent, completely surrounded by water

isthmus narrow stretch of land connecting two larger land areas

lake a large inland body of water

latitude distance north or south of the Equator, measured in degrees

longitude distance east or west of the Prime Meridian, measured in degrees

lowland land, usually level, at a low elevation

map drawing of the earth shown on a flat surface

meridian one of many lines on the global grid running from the North Pole to the South Pole; used to measure degrees of longitude

mesa broad, flat-topped landform with steep sides; smaller than a plateau

mountain land with steep sides that rises sharply (1,000 feet or more) from surrounding land; generally larger and more rugged than a hill

mountain peak pointed top of a mountain

mountain range a series of connected mountains

mouth (of a river) place where a stream or river flows into a larger body of water

ocean one of the four major bodies of salt water that surround the continents

ocean current stream of either cold or warm water that moves in a definite direction through an ocean

parallel one of many lines on the global grid that circle the earth north or south of the Equator; used to measure degrees of latitude

peninsula body of land jutting into a lake or ocean, surrounded on three sides by water

physical feature characteristic of a place occurring naturally, such as a landform, body of water, climate pattern, or resource

plain area of level land, usually at a low elevation and often covered with grasses

plateau large area of flat or rolling land at a high elevation, about 300–3,000 feet high

Prime Meridian line of the global grid running from the North Pole to the South Pole at Greenwich, England; starting point for measuring degrees of east and west longitude

relief changes in elevation over a given area of land

river large natural stream of water that runs through the land

sea large body of water completely or partly surrounded by land

seacoast land lying next to a sea or ocean

sea level position on land level with surface of nearby ocean or sea

sound body of water between a coastline and one or more islands off the coast

source (of a river) place where a river or stream begins, often in highlands

strait narrow stretch of water joining two larger bodies of water

tributary small river or stream that flows into a larger river or stream; a branch of the river

upstream direction opposite the flow of a river; toward the source of a river or stream

valley area of low land between hills or mountains

volcano mountain created as ash or liquid rock erupts from inside the earth

UNIT
1 Three Worlds Meet

Beginnings to 1763

Why It Matters

The interactions among Native Americans,
Europeans, and Africans shaped the
history of the Americas. Native Americans
struggled to live alongside Europeans
and their ever-growing settlements and
colonies. Africans tried to adapt to the
new continent to which they were brought
involuntarily. Studying these early cultural
interactions will help you understand the
centuries of history that followed. The following resources offer more information
about this period in American history.

Primary Sources Library

See pages 1048–1049 for primary source
readings to accompany Unit 1.

Use the **American History
Primary Source Document Library
CD-ROM** to find additional primary
sources about the meeting of Native
Americans, Europeans, and Africans.

Pre-Cherokee
necklace, c. 1300

Cherokee Settlement by
Felix Marie Ferdinand Storelli

"*Long before they had heard the word Spaniard, they [Native Americans] had properly organized states, wisely ordered by excellent laws, religion, and custom.*"

—Bartolomé de Las Casas, 1550

CHAPTER

1 Converging Cultures

Prehistory to 1520

Why It Matters

Before 1492, the cultures that arose in the Americas had almost no contact with the rest of the world. Then, in the late 1300s, momentous events began taking place that would bring the cultures of Europe and Africa into direct contact with the Americas. This contact had profound effects on the future of the world's civilizations.

The Impact Today

The convergence of the world's cultures in the 1400s launched an era of change that still affects our lives today.
- *Many of our foods, customs, and traditions were originally introduced in the Americas as a result of this cultural contact.*
- *Contact among the cultures of the three continents profoundly changed the society of each.*
- *American society today includes elements of Native American, European, and African cultures.*

 The American Vision Video *The Chapter 1 video, "America Before the Americans," examines the early Americas.*

The Americas

c. 28,000–13,000 B.C.
- First humans migrate to North America from Asia

c. 1200 B.C.
- Early Mesoamerican civilizations arise

c. A.D. 200
- Mayan culture arises in Central America

A.D. 300
- Hohokam culture arises in North America

| 28,000 B.C. | 1200 B.C. | A.D. 250 | 500 |

World

c. 3000 B.C.
- Sumerians create cuneiform writing

1750 B.C.
- Death of Hammurabi in the Middle East

A.D. 400
- Ghana civilization develops in West Africa

The Landing of Columbus in San Salvador by Albert Bierstadt, 1893

c. 1130
• Drought strikes Native American cliff dwellings at Chaco Canyon

c. 1300
• Cahokia civilization collapses

1492
• Christopher Columbus lands in America

1500s
• Navajo arrive in Southwest of North America

| 1100 | 1200 | 1300 | 1400 | 1500 |

c. 610
• Muhammed begins teaching ideas of Islam

1240
• Mali empire expands in West Africa

1420s
• Portugal begins exploring African coast

c. 1450
• Songhai empire expands in West Africa

HISTORY Online
Chapter Overview
Visit the *American Vision* Web site at tav.glencoe.com and click on **Chapter Overviews—Chapter 1** to preview chapter information.

The Migration to America

Guide to Reading

Main Idea

Native Americans are descended from Asians who probably began migrating to North America approximately 15,000 to 30,000 years ago.

Key Terms and Names

radiocarbon dating, Ice Age, glacier, Beringia, nomad, agricultural revolution, maize, civilization, obsidian, Aztec, Chaco Canyon, kiva, pueblo, Cahokia

Reading Strategy

Categorizing As you read about the first people to live in North America, complete a graphic organizer similar to the one below by filling in the names of Native American groups who settled in various regions.

Region	Native American Groups
Mesoamerica	
North American Southwest	
North American Midwest	

Reading Objectives

• **Explain** why scientists believe that the earliest Americans migrated from Asia.
• **Describe** the early civilizations of Mesoamerica and the early cultures of North America.

Section Theme

Geography and History Scientists theorize that Asian hunters migrated to North America across a land bridge exposed during the last Ice Age.

Preview of Events

| ◆30,000 B.C. | ◆15,000 B.C. | ◆0 | ◆A.D. 1500 |

c. 28,000–13,000 B.C.
First humans migrate to North America

c. 8000–7000 B.C.
Agriculture begins

c. 1200 B.C.
Early Mesoamerican civilizations arise

c. A.D. 200
Maya culture arises

c. A.D. 1300
Cahokia collapses

★ *An American Story* ★

In 1925 an African American cowboy named George McJunkin was riding along a gully near the town of Folsom, New Mexico, when he noticed something gleaming in the dirt. He began digging and found a bone and a flint arrowhead. J.D. Figgins of the Colorado Museum of Natural History knew the bone belonged to a type of bison that had been extinct for 10,000 years. The arrowhead's proximity to the bones implied that human beings had been in America at least 10,000 years, which no one had believed at that time.

The following year, Figgins found another arrowhead embedded in similar bones. In 1927 he led a group of scientists to the find. Anthropologist Frank H.H. Roberts, Jr., wrote, "There was no question but that here was the evidence. . . . The point was still embedded . . . between two of the ribs of the animal skeleton." Further digs turned up more arrowheads, now called Folsom points. Roberts later noted: "The Folsom find was accepted as a reliable indication that man was present in the Southwest at an earlier period than was previously supposed."

—**adapted from** *The First American: A Story of North American Archaeology*

The Asian Migration to America

No one can say for certain when the first people arrived in America. The Folsom discoveries proved that people were here at least 10,000 years ago, but more recent research suggests that humans arrived much earlier. Presently, scientific speculation points to a period between 15,000 and 30,000 years ago—much earlier than what scientists believed at the time of George McJunkin's discovery.

How long ago the first Americans appeared remains a hotly debated question. Scientists can state much more confidently, however, who these earliest people were, how they arrived in America, and what their lives were like.

To learn the origins of ancient peoples, scientists study their skulls, bones, and teeth. In recent years they have been able to examine DNA—which stands for **d**eoxyribo**n**ucleic **a**cid—a molecule described as the basic building material of all life on Earth. DNA recovered from the bones of people who died many thousands of years ago enables scientists to trace their ethnic, and thus their geographic, origins. From DNA and other evidence, researchers have concluded that the earliest Americans probably came from Asia.

To determine how old objects are, scientists rely on radiocarbon dating. With this method, they measure the radioactivity left in a special type of carbon called carbon 14, which can be taken from fragments of wood and bone. Radiocarbon dating works because all living things absorb carbon. Knowing the rate at which carbon 14 loses its radioactivity, experts can calculate the age of the objects the carbon came from.

Studies of the earth's history offer other important clues. About 100,000 years ago, the earth began to cool gradually, entering what scientists call a period of glaciation. Such periods are often called Ice Ages. Much of the earth's water froze into huge ice sheets, or glaciers. As ocean levels dropped, they eventually exposed an area of dry land that connected Asia with the part of North America that is now Alaska. The land was named **Beringia,** after Vitus Bering, a later explorer of the region. Scientists think that about 15,000 years ago, people from Asia began trekking eastward across this new land bridge to America in search of food. Others may also have come by boat even earlier, hugging the shoreline of Beringia.

These early arrivals were probably nomads, people who continually moved from place to place. In this case, the people were hunters who stalked herds of animals across Beringia. They hunted such massive prey as the wooly mammoth, as well as antelope, caribou, bison, musk ox, and wild sheep. Wild plants, birds, and fish probably made up an important part of their diet, too. These early peoples did not come all at once. Their migrations probably continued until rising seawater once again submerged the land bridge about 10,000 years ago, creating a waterway that today is called the Bering Strait.

Scientists believe that as the last Ice Age ended, the nomads' favorite prey, the wooly mammoth, began to die out, either from too much hunting or because of the changing environment. Faced with a dwindling food supply, early Americans began to make use of other types of food, including fish, shellfish, nuts, and small game.

✓ **Reading Check** **Explaining** How do scientists determine the origins of ancient peoples?

Early Civilizations of Mesoamerica

As time passed, early Americans learned how to plant and raise crops. This agricultural revolution occurred between 9,000 and 10,000 years ago in Mesoamerica—*meso* coming from the Greek word for middle. This region includes what is today central and southern Mexico and Central America.

The first crops grown in America included pumpkins, peppers, squashes, gourds, and beans. The most

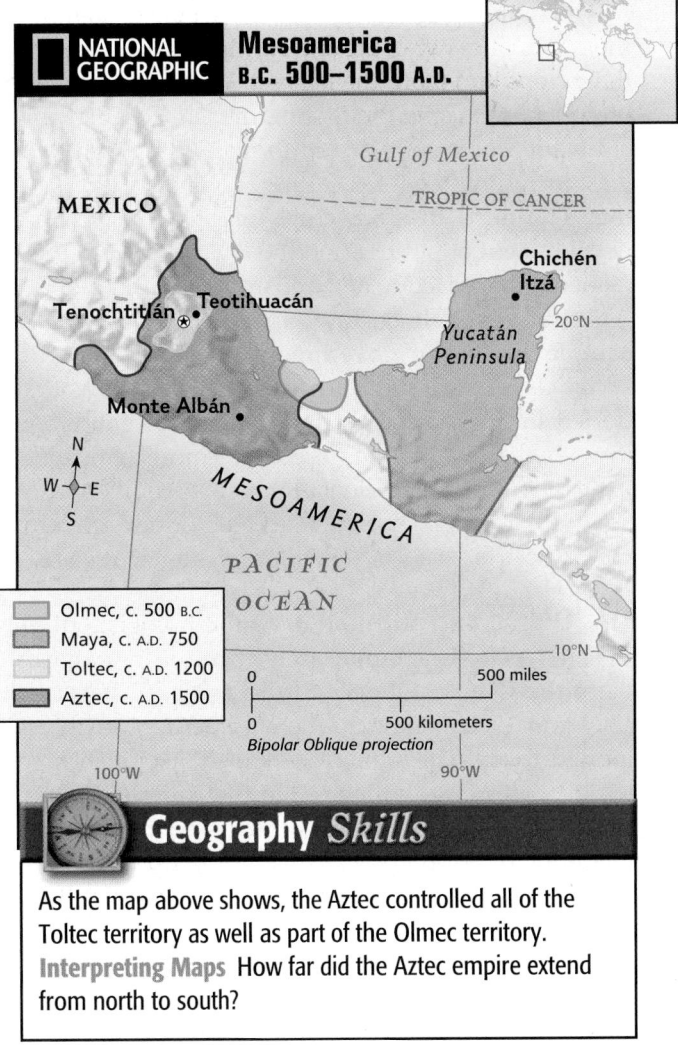

NATIONAL GEOGRAPHIC

Mesoamerica B.C. 500–1500 A.D.

Gulf of Mexico

TROPIC OF CANCER

MEXICO

Chichén Itzá

Tenochtitlán · Teotihuacán

Yucatán Peninsula

20°N

Monte Albán ·

MESOAMERICA

PACIFIC OCEAN

☐ Olmec, c. 500 B.C.
☐ Maya, c. A.D. 750
☐ Toltec, c. A.D. 1200
☐ Aztec, c. A.D. 1500

0   500 miles
0   500 kilometers
Bipolar Oblique projection

10°N

100°W   90°W

Geography Skills

As the map above shows, the Aztec controlled all of the Toltec territory as well as part of the Olmec territory. **Interpreting Maps** How far did the Aztec empire extend from north to south?

c. 28,000 B.C.
Asians begin migrating to North America across the Bering Strait

c. 8000 B.C.
Agricultural societies begin to cultivate crops in Mesoamerica

c. 200 B.C.
Hopewell culture rises in North America

1500 B.C.   *1000 B.C.*   *500 B.C.*

c. 9000 B.C.
Human populations reach the tip of South America

c. 1500 B.C.
Olmec civilization develops in Mesoamerica

c. 1000 B.C.
Adena culture thrives in North America

Olmec stone mask

important crop of all was a large-seeded grass called maize, which is known today as corn. Maize was important because it could be ground into flour to make bread and could be dried and stored for long periods of time.

The shift to agriculture allowed people to abandon their nomadic way of life and stay in one place to tend their crops and store the harvest. With the discovery of agriculture came the first permanent villages. The cultivation of crops also led to many new technologies, including tools for cutting, digging, and grinding. The need to store crops probably led to the development of pottery, and the development of permanent villages led to new construction technologies.

As more people began to live in one place, more complex forms of government developed, as did social classes. People learned specialized skills and traded their products for food and other goods. As these village societies became more complex, America's first civilizations emerged. A civilization is a highly organized society marked by trade, government, the arts, science, and, often, written language.

The Olmec and the Maya Anthropologists think the first people to build a civilization in America were the Olmec. Olmec culture emerged between 1500 and 1200 B.C., near where Veracruz, Mexico, is located today. The Olmec developed a sophisticated society with large villages, temple complexes, and pyramids. They also sculpted imposing monuments, including 8-foot-high heads weighing up to 20 tons, from a hard rock known as basalt. Olmec culture lasted until about 300 B.C.

Olmec ideas spread throughout Mesoamerica, influencing other peoples. One of these peoples constructed the first large city in America, called

Teotihuacán (TAY·oh·TEE·wah·KAHN), about 30 miles northeast of where Mexico City is located today. The city was built near a volcano, where there were large deposits of obsidian, or volcanic glass. Obsidian was very valuable. Its sharp, strong edges were perfect for tools and weapons. Teotihuacán built up an elaborate trade network and greatly influenced the development of Mesoamerica. The city lasted from about 300 B.C. to about A.D. 650.

Around A.D. 200, as Teotihuacán's influence spread, the Mayan culture emerged in the Yucatán peninsula and expanded into what is now Central America and southern Mexico. The Maya had a talent for engineering and mathematics. They developed complex and accurate calendars linked to the positions of the stars. They also built great temple pyramids. These pyramids formed the centerpieces of Mayan cities, such as Tikal and Chichén Itzá. Marvels of engineering, some pyramids were 200 feet (61 m) high. Topping each pyramid was a temple where elaborately dressed priests performed ceremonies dedicated to the many Mayan gods.

Although trade and a common culture linked the Mayan people, they were not unified. Each city-state controlled its own territory. Because of the fragmented nature of Mayan society, the different cities frequently went to war.

The Toltec and the Aztec Despite their frequent wars, the Mayan people continued to thrive until the A.D. 900s, when their cities in the Yucatán were abandoned for unknown reasons. Some anthropologists believe Mayan farmers may have exhausted the region's soil. This in turn would have led to famine, riots, and the collapse of the cities. Others believe that invaders from the north devastated the region.

Mayan pyramid

Toltec statues

C. A.D. 1200 — Population of Cahokia reaches 16,000

C. A.D. 1325 Aztec build Tenochtitlán

♦ A.D. 500　　　　♦ A.D. 1000　　　　♦ A.D. 1500

C. A.D. 200 — Mayan culture emerges in Mesoamerica

C. A.D. 300 — Hohokam build irrigation systems in southwestern North America

C. A.D. 800 — Toltec conquer Teotihuacán and dominate Mesoamerica

C. A.D. 1100 — Anasazi communities form at Chaco Canyon and Mesa Verde

C. A.D. 1400–1500 — Incan empire reaches its peak in South America

Mayan cities in the highlands of what is today Guatemala flourished for several more centuries, although by the 1500s, they too were in decline.

In the meantime, people known as the Toltec began building a city called Tula. The Toltec were master architects. They built large pyramids and huge palaces with pillared halls. They were among the first Native Americans to use gold and copper for art and jewelry.

About A.D. 1200, Tula fell to invaders from the north, known as the Chichimec. One group of Chichimec, called the Mexica, established the city of Tenochtitlán (tay·NAWCH·teet·LAHN) in 1325 on the site of what is today Mexico City. The Mexica took the name **Aztec** for themselves, from the name of their original homeland, Aztlán. Aztlán is thought to have been located somewhere in the American Southwest.

The Aztec created a mighty empire by conquering neighboring cities. Using their military power, the Aztec controlled trade in the region and demanded tribute, or payment, from the cities they conquered. They also brought some of the people they conquered to Tenochtitlán to serve as human sacrifices in their religious ceremonies. When the Europeans arrived in the 1500s, an estimated five million people were living under Aztec rule.

✔ **Reading Check**　**Examining** How did the shift to agriculture allow early peoples to advance beyond mere survival?

North American Cultures

North of Mesoamerica, other peoples developed their own cultures and civilizations. Many anthropologists think that the agricultural technology of Mesoamerica spread north into the American Southwest and up the Mississippi River. There it transformed many of the scattered hunter-gatherers of North America into farmers.

The Hohokam　Beginning in A.D. 300 in what is now south-central Arizona, a group called the Hohokam created a civilization that featured a very elaborate system of irrigation canals. The Hohokam used the Gila and Salt Rivers as their water supply. Their canals carried water hundreds of miles to their farms.

The Hohokam grew large crops of corn, cotton, beans, and squash. They also made decorative red-on-buff pottery and turquoise pendants, and they created the world's first etchings by using cactus juice to etch shells. Hohokam culture flourished for more than 1,000 years. In the 1300s, they began to abandon their irrigation systems, most likely due to floods. Increased competition for farmland probably led to wars and emigration. By 1500 the Hohokam had vanished from history.

The Anasazi　Between A.D. 700 and 900, the people living in villages in the Four Corners area, where Utah, Colorado, Arizona, and New Mexico now meet, came together to create a civilization. We know these people only by the name the Navajo gave them—*Anasazi*, or "ancient ones."

In the harsh desert environment of the American Southwest, the Anasazi accumulated water for their crops by building networks of basins and ditches to channel rain into stone-lined depressions with high earthen banks.

Between A.D. 850 and 1100, the Anasazi living in **Chaco Canyon** in what is now northwest New Mexico began constructing large, multi-story buildings of adobe and cut stone with connecting passageways and circular ceremonial rooms called kivas. Early Spanish explorers called these structures pueblos, the Spanish word for villages. The Anasazi built these pueblos at junctions where streams of rainwater, draining from the canyon, ran together. One particular pueblo in Chaco Canyon, called Pueblo Bonito, covered more than three acres. Its 600 rooms probably housed at least 1,000 people. Later, at Mesa Verde in what is today southwestern Colorado, the Anasazi built equally impressive cliff dwellings.

Beginning around A.D. 1130, Chaco Canyon experienced a devastating drought that lasted at least 50 years. This probably caused the Anasazi to abandon their pueblos. The Mesa Verde pueblos lasted for another 200 years, but when another drought struck in the 1270s, they too were abandoned. Some anthropologists think that epidemics or attacks by hunter-gatherers may have caused the Anasazi civilization to collapse.

The Adena and Hopewell Cultures
About the same time that the Olmec people began to build a civilization in Mesoamerica, the people living in North America's eastern woodlands were developing their own unique cultures. The people of the eastern woodlands developed woodworking tools, including stone axes and gouges. They built dugout canoes and made nets to snare birds. They also made clay pots by stacking up coils of clay.

Beginning about 1000 B.C., the people of the region began burying their dead under massive dome-shaped mounds of earth. The most important early mound-building culture was the Adena culture, which lasted from 1000 B.C. to about A.D. 200. The Adena culture originated in the Ohio River valley and spread east into what is now New York and New England.

As the people of the Ohio valley began to plant crops and build permanent settlements between 200 and 100 B.C., another new civilization known as the Hopewell culture rose to prominence. It featured huge, geometric earthworks to serve as ceremonial centers, observatories, and burial places. The Hopewell culture mysteriously began to decline after A.D. 400.

The Mississippian Culture
Between A.D. 700 and 900, as agricultural technology and improved strains of maize and beans spread north from Mexico and up the Mississippi River, another new culture—the **Mississippian**—emerged. It began in the Mississippi River valley, where the rich soil of the flood plains

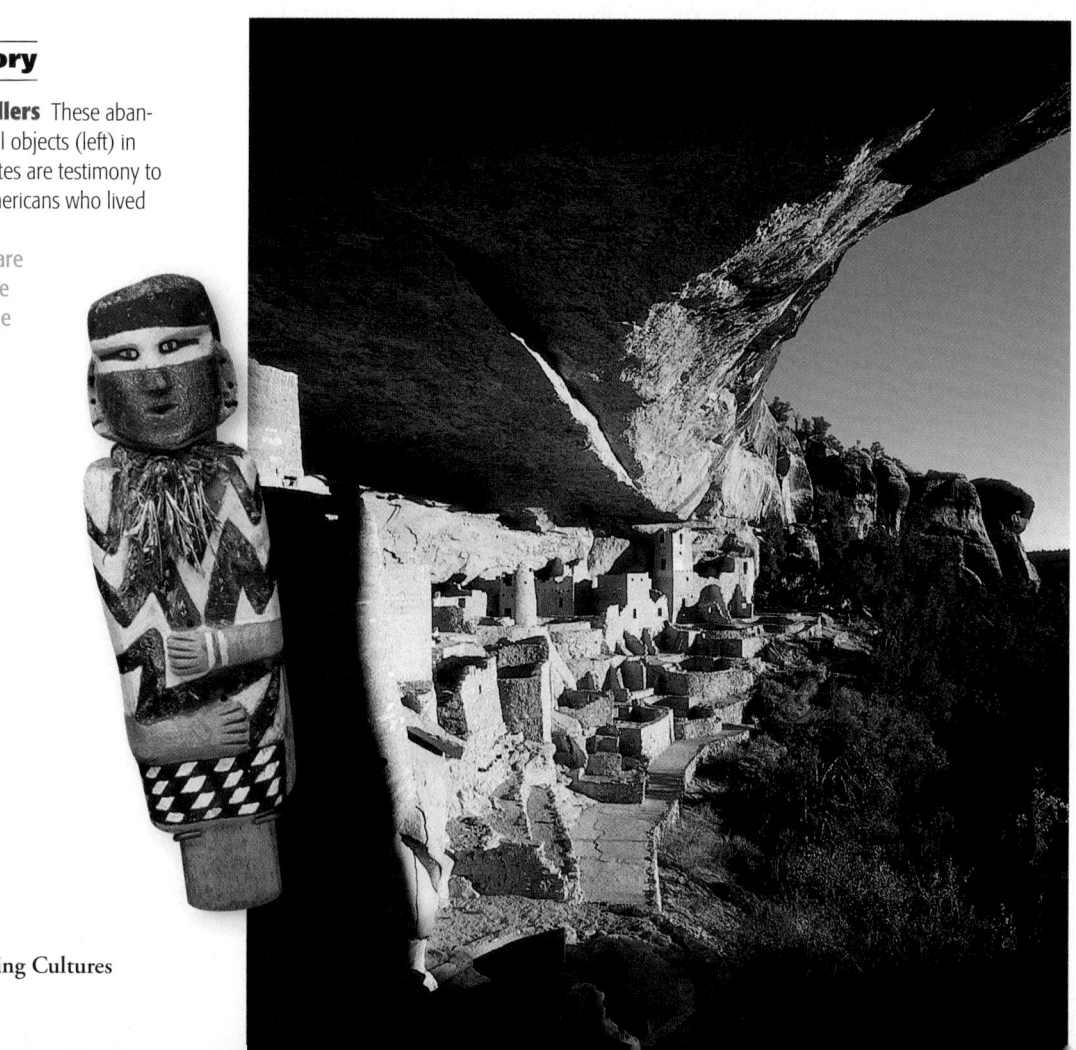

Picturing History

Southwestern Cliff Dwellers These abandoned ruins (right) and ritual objects (left) in the southwestern United States are testimony to the civilizations of Native Americans who lived on the continent before the arrival of Europeans. What are some reasons scientists give for the disappearance of the Anasazi civilization?

was perfectly suited to the intensive cultivation of maize and beans.

The Mississippians were great builders. Eight miles from what is now St. Louis, near Collinsville, Illinois, lie the remains of one of their largest cities, which anthropologists named **Cahokia.** At its peak between about A.D. 1050 and 1250, Cahokia covered 5 square miles (13 sq km), contained over 100 flat-topped pyramids and mounds, and was home to an estimated 16,000 people. Most of the people lived in pole-and-thatch houses that spread out over 2,000 acres (810 ha). The largest pyramid, named Monks Mound, was 100 feet (30.5 m) high, had four levels, and covered 16 acres (6.5 ha). The base of Monks Mound was larger than that of any pyramid in Egypt or Mexico. A log wall with watchtowers and gates surrounded the central plaza and larger pyramids.

From the Mississippi valley, Mississippian culture spread widely, following the Missouri, Ohio, Red, and Arkansas Rivers. Expanding east across the American South, Mississippian culture led to the rise of at least three other large cities with flat-topped mounds—at present-day Spiro, Oklahoma; Moundville, Alabama; and Etowah, Georgia.

Cahokia itself collapsed around A.D. 1300. An attack by other Native Americans may have caused its destruction, or the population may simply have become too large to feed, resulting in famine and emigration. Another possibility is that an epidemic

Adena and Hopewell Culture The Great Serpent Mound in southern Ohio (above) is an example of the earthen mounds built by the Adena culture. The copper falcon (right) is a Hopewell design. These artifacts help scientists learn more about the culture of ancient civilizations. For what did Native Americans use their earthen mounds?

may have devastated the population. Although Cahokia came to an end, many aspects of Mississippian culture survived in the Southeast until the Europeans arrived in America.

✓ **Reading Check** **Explaining** By what route did agricultural technology spread from Mesoamerica into North America?

SECTION 1 ASSESSMENT

Checking for Understanding

1. **Define:** radiocarbon dating, Ice Age, glacier, nomad, agricultural revolution, maize, civilization, obsidian, kiva, pueblo.
2. **Identify:** Beringia, Aztec, Chaco Canyon, Cahokia.
3. **Explain** how the agricultural revolution led to the establishment of permanent settlements.

Reviewing Themes

4. **Geography and History** How did Asians migrate to America?

Critical Thinking

5. **Evaluating** Choose an early culture group in Mesoamerica or North America. What kind of civilization did this group develop?
6. **Categorizing** Use a graphic organizer like the one below to list the advances of early culture groups in North America.

Culture Groups	Advances

Analyzing Visuals

7. **Picturing History** Study the photographs on this page and on page 16. How did the Native Americans in each region adapt to their environments?

Writing About History

8. **Expository Writing** Using library or Internet resources, find more information on one of the culture groups discussed in this section. Use the information to write an in-depth report about the culture group.

Geography&History

Cut marks on this bone from a mammoth found in Blue Fish Cave indicate that pieces have been intentionally flaked off. The bone is part of mounting evidence suggesting that people may have lived in Beringia more than 23,000 years ago.

LAURENTIDE ICE SHEET

Route between melting ice sheets 14,000 years ago

Land bridge the

CORDILLERA ICE SHEET

Old Crow
Bluefish Cave

Gallagher
Flint Station

Mesa   Putu

B E R I N G I A

Driftwood
Creek

Onion
Portage

Batza   Fairbanks
Tena

Healy Lake
Broken Mammoth

S I B E R I A

Dry
Creek   Tangle
Lakes

Ground
Hog Bay

Hidden Falls

49-PET-408

Trail
Creek

Coastal ro

Early American Sites

	Animal remains and artifacts	Human remains and artifacts
More than 13,500 years ago	◼	●
10,900 to 13,500 years ago	◼	●
7,000 to 10,900 years ago	◻	○
Extent of present-day ice cap	﹏﹏﹏	

Vegetation and glaciation as of 21,000 years ago is shown on map

| 0 | 250 | 500 miles |
| 0 | 250 | 500 kilometers |

Ugashik

When glaciers formed during the last Ice Age, sea levels fell to expose new shorelines (below, left). As the Ice Age ended, melting glaciers reversed the process, raising sea levels and creating the present-day island shoreline (below, right).

Anangula

MODERN ISLAND
SHORELINE

ICE AGE ISLAND
SHORELINE

GLACIER

Ancient stone points and blades—some made 20,000 years ago—have helped archaeologists develop new theories about the first Americans and when they arrived.

Lindsay

Carter/Kerr-McGee

Horner

Vermilion Lake

Shoup

Cooper's Ferry

Marmes

Buhl

ken

ose

Kennewick

Roaring Springs Cave

Leonard

Fishbone Cave

ory

Borax Lake

Mostin

Land Bridge to America

During the last Ice Age, the Bering Strait that now separates Alaska and Siberia was dry land. Across this so-called land bridge, bands of fur-clad hunter-gatherers from Asia trekked to the northwestern corner of America (purple arrows at left). As they followed herds of woolly mammoths and other big game animals, they slowly spread east through a corridor between two glaciers and then pushed south into the interior of the continent.

These intrepid travelers have been held up as the original Americans. They flourished on the Great Plains and the Southwest of the present-day United States. In less than a thousand years, their descendants had settled most of the hemisphere, from the Arctic Circle to the tip of South America.

The intercontinental land bridge that made this amazing journey possible was up to 1,000 miles (1,609 km) wide. Known as Beringia, it emerged when vast ice sheets absorbed the water, dropping the sea level about 300 feet (91 km) to reveal the floor of the Bering Sea. Many scientists

agree that the Beringia migration began between 14,000 and 15,000 years ago. Recently, however archaeologists have found artifacts that suggest people were in America even before the land corridor had opened. The new evidence has led to theories suggesting other possible routes to the Americas.

One theory proposes that people crossed from northeast Asia in skin-covered boats, skirting the shore and landing occasionally to hunt for food and water (red arrows at left). Continuing south along the coast, they would have reached South America quicker than by any land route (see inset map below). The Pacific crossing theory suggests that migrants from Southeast Asia went south to Australia and across the Pacific Ocean, hopping from island to island until they reached South America. Yet a third theory, the Atlantic crossing theory, suggests that America's earliest inhabitants were from southwestern Europe (modern-day southern France and Spain). Hugging the edge of the glaciers of the North Atlantic, they may have sailed from Iceland and Greenland down to North America. A skull found in Brazil has also prompted some people to consider the possibility of an early migration from Africa.

The peopling of the Americas was probably a more complex process than migration across the Bering land bridge alone. Settlers may have arrived in many waves of migration and by a number of routes. As shown in the map at left, they may have traveled from Europe or Australia as well as from Asia.

Area enlarged

ASIA   Land bridge theory

Bering Sea

Coastal route theory

NORTH AMERICA

Kennewick

(Clovis) Blackwater Draw

Cactus Hill

Greenland

Iceland

Atlantic crossing theory

Atlantic Ocean

EUROPE

AFRICA

Pacific Ocean

Quebrada Tacahuay

SOUTH AMERICA

AUSTRALIA   Pacific crossing theory

Monte Verde

Extent of ice cap during the Ice Age

Fells Cave

LEARNING FROM GEOGRAPHY

1. What geographical event made the sea level drop to reveal the land bridge between Asia and America?

2. What other ways may settlers have made their way to the Americas?

Native American Cultures

Guide to Reading

Main Idea

The Native Americans of what is today the United States had diverse social structures and religions.

Key Terms and Names

kachina, Algonquian, Iroquoian, slash-and-burn agriculture, longhouse, wigwam, kinship group, Dekanawidah, Hiawatha

Reading Strategy

Categorizing As you read about Native Americans, complete a chart like the one below by filling in the names of the Native American groups who lived in each region.

Region	Groups
West	
Far North	
Eastern Woodlands	

Reading Objectives

• **Describe** the cultures of Native American groups of the West, the Far North, and the Eastern Woodlands.
• **Describe** the agricultural techniques of the Woodlands Native Americans.

Section Theme

Culture and Traditions The cultural differences between Native American groups can be explained by studying the geography where each group lived.

Preview of Events

1300	1400	1500		1600

c. 1300
Fighting erupts among the Iroquois

c. 1492
Europeans arrive in the Americas

c. 1500
People of the western Great Plains become nomadic

1500s
Navajo arrive in the Southwest

c. 1570
Iroquois League created

★ An American Story ★

Did the Natchez people of the southeastern United States descend from the Toltec of Mesoamerica? A Natchez man told this story to a European explorer in the mid-1700s:

❝Before we came into this land we lived yonder under the sun (pointing with his finger nearly south-west, by which I understood that he meant Mexico). . . . There our Suns [Mexican rulers were called Suns] had their abode and our nation maintained itself for a long time. . . . Our nation extended itself along the great water [Gulf of Mexico] where this large river [the Mississippi] loses itself; but as our enemies were become very numerous . . . our Suns sent some of their subjects who lived near this river, to examine whether we could return into the country through which it flowed. The country on the east side of the river being found extremely pleasant, the Great Sun, upon the return of those who had examined it, ordered all his subjects who lived in the plains, and who still defended themselves against the ancients of the country, to remove into this land, here to build a temple. . . .❞

—quoted in *America in 1492*

The West

Although Mesoamerican civilization may have shaped Natchez society, the culture of most Native Americans developed in response to their environments. By the time the first Europeans arrived, Native Americans were fragmented into many small groups that had adapted to the different regions of North America. Fragmentation in the American West was especially severe because of the great variations in the region's climate and geography.

The Southwest

The descendants of the Anasazi and Hohokam lived in small groups in the arid Southwest. These groups included the Zuni, Hopi, and other Pueblo peoples. The people of the Southwest depended on corn to survive. Farmers cultivated several species of corn whose seeds could withstand the dry soil. With a long taproot, the corn grew deep, reaching moisture far below the surface. The farmers also grew squash and beans.

Among these groups, when a man married, he joined the household of his bride's mother. Within the family, men's and women's work was separate. Men farmed and herded sheep. They also performed most ceremonies, made moccasins, and wove clothing and blankets. It was women's work to take care of the house. In addition, women crafted pottery and baskets and hauled water. The women also helped the men in two occupations—farming and constructing houses.

When boys turned six, they joined the kachina cult. A kachina was a good spirit. The Pueblo people believed kachinas visited their town each year with messages from the gods. Members of the kachina cult would wear masks symbolizing the spirits, and they would dance to bring the spirits to the town.

Sometime around the 1500s, two other peoples—the Apache and the Navajo—came to the region from the far northwest of North America. Although many of the Apache remained primarily nomadic hunters, the Navajo learned farming from the Pueblo people and lived in widely dispersed settlements, where they grew corn, beans, and squash.

The Pacific Coast

Many different groups, including the Tlingit, Haida, Kwakiutls, Nootkas, Chinook, and Salish peoples, lived in the lands bordering the Pacific Ocean from what is now southeastern Alaska to Washington state. Although they did not practice agriculture, these groups dwelt in permanent settlements. They looked to the dense coastal forests for lumber, which they used not only to build homes and to fashion canoes, but also to create elaborate works of art, ceremonial masks, and totem poles. They were able to stay in one place because the region's coastal waters and many rivers teemed with fish, particularly salmon. Farther inland, between the Cascade Range and the Rocky Mountains, the Nez Perce, Yakima, and other groups fished, hunted deer, and gathered roots and berries.

South of the Nez Perce's territory, between the Sierra Nevada and Rocky Mountains, the climate was much drier. There, groups such as the Ute and Shoshone lived a nomadic life. Because the land was too arid for farming, they roamed widely in search of food that was often scarce.

West of the Ute lands in what is today central California, several groups enjoyed abundant wildlife and a mild climate. The Pomo, for example, gathered acorns, caught fish in nets and traps, and snared small game and birds. Pomo hunters, working together, would drive deer toward a spot where the village's best archer waited, hidden and disguised in a deer-head mask. Sometimes, the hunters stampeded game into a corral, where the animals could be easily killed. When game was scarce, however, the Pomo relied upon the acorn, which they had learned to convert from a hard, bitter nut into an edible flour.

The Great Plains

When Europeans arrived in America, the people of the Great Plains were nomads. Before this, up until about 1500, people living on the Great Plains practiced agriculture. Influenced by the Hopewell and Mississippian cultures, these peoples lived near the Missouri and other rivers, where they could plant corn and find wood to build their homes.

Around 1500 the peoples of the western plains abandoned their villages and became nomads, possibly because of war or drought. Those in the east—including the Pawnee, Kansas, and Iowa peoples—continued to farm as well as hunt. Peoples of the western plains, such as the Sioux, followed migrating buffalo herds on foot and lived in cone-shaped tents called tepees.

Life for the Sioux and others on the Great Plains changed dramatically after they began taming horses. The Spanish had brought horses to North America in the 1500s. Over the next few centuries, as horses either escaped or were stolen, the animals spread northward, eventually reaching the Great Plains. There the Sioux encountered and mastered them, and in the process became some of the world's greatest mounted hunters and warriors.

Sioux men achieved fame in the community through bravery in both hunting and war. Sioux warriors would take the scalps of enemies they had killed, but they could gain even greater glory through

Pacific coast totem pole

the dangerous but nonviolent act of "counting *coup*," from the French word meaning "blow" or "touch." A warrior would charge into a group of the enemy and simply touch one of them with a stick—as a means of humiliating the enemy—then gallop away.

✓ **Reading Check** **Contrasting** How did Native Americans respond to the different climates of the American West?

The Far North

Two different Native American groups made the Far North their home. The most northern and widespread were the Inuit, whose territory stretched across the Arctic from present-day Alaska to Greenland. The Aleut settled Alaska's Aleutian Islands.

The Inuit and Aleut depended heavily upon hunting for their livelihood. They hunted seals, walruses, whales, polar bears, caribou, musk oxen, and smaller game. Over time, they invented a wide variety of devices to cope with the harsh environment, including the harpoon, the kayak, the dogsled, boots with ivory spikes for walking on ice, and special goggles to prevent snow blindness. They also were the only Native Americans to develop lamps. They used whale oil and blubber for fuel. Occupying a harsh and unforgiving land, they lived in groups—from a single family to a few hundred people—spaced widely apart.

✓ **Reading Check** **Identifying** What technologies did the Native Americans of the Far North develop?

NATIONAL GEOGRAPHIC

North American Cultures, c. A.D. 1300

Agriculture
Fishing
Hunting
Hunting-Gathering
Uninhabited

Southwest pueblo

Northeastern longhouse

1,000 miles

1,000 kilometers
Lambert Azimuthal Equal-Area projection

Geography *Skills*

1. **Interpreting Maps** What was the main food source for the Northwest?
2. **Applying Geography Skills** Why were Great Plains peoples nomadic?

Eastern Woodlands Native Americans hunted the abundant deer in the East by disguising themselves in cleaned deerskins and sneaking very close to their target. French artist Jacques Le Moyne created this illustration in 1591 depicting the practice. What other food sources did Eastern Woodlands peoples have?

The Eastern Woodlands

East of the Mississippi River and south of the Great Lakes lay almost a million square miles of woodlands. This landscape supported an amazing range of plant and animal life. Almost all of the Native Americans in the Eastern Woodlands provided for themselves by combining hunting and fishing with farming. Deer were plentiful in the region, and deer meat regularly supplemented the corn, beans, and squash the people planted. Deer hide was also used for clothing.

The Peoples of the Northeast
Most of the peoples of the Northeast were divided into two major language groups—those who spoke **Algonquian** (al·GAHN·kwee·UHN) languages and those who spoke **Iroquoian** (IHR·uh·KWOY·uhn) languages. The Algonquian-speaking peoples included most of the groups living in what later became known as New England. Among these peoples were the Wampanoag in Massachusetts, the Narragansett in Rhode Island, and the Pequot in Connecticut. Farther south in what is today Virginia lived the Algonquian-speaking peoples of the Powhatan Confederacy. Native Americans in New England and Virginia were among the first to encounter English settlers.

Other Algonquian-speaking peoples included the Delaware who lived near the Delaware River and the Shawnee who lived in the Ohio River valley. Words from the Algonquian language used in English today include *succotash, hominy, moccasin,* and *papoose.*

Stretching west from the Hudson River across what is today New York and southern Ontario and north to Georgian Bay were the Iroquoian-speaking peoples. They included the Huron, Neutral, Erie, Wenro,

Seneca, Cayuga, Onondaga, Oneida, and Mohawk.

Many peoples in the Northeast, including the Algonquians of New England and the Iroquoians of New York, practiced slash-and-burn agriculture. By cutting down parts of forests and then burning the cleared land, they were left with nitrogen-rich ashes, which they then worked into the soil, making it more fertile.

The early peoples of the Northeast used several types of houses. Many villages, enclosed by wooden stockades, had large rectangular longhouses with barrel-shaped roofs covered in bark. Others built wigwams. These dwellings were either conical or dome-shaped and were made using bent poles covered with hides or bark.

The Iroquoian and Algonquian peoples shared some traits. Both made beads of white and purple shells that they arranged on strings and wove into belts called wampum. The designs on the wampum recorded important events and agreements. Both groups also viewed land as a resource for a group of people to use, and not for one person to buy or sell.

GOVERNMENT

The Iroquois League
All of the Iroquoian peoples had similar cultures. They lived in longhouses in large towns, which they protected by building stockades. The people lived in large kinship groups, or extended families, headed by the elder women of each clan. Iroquois women occupied positions of power and importance in their communities. They were responsible for the planting and harvesting of crops. Up to 10 related families lived together in each longhouse.

HISTORY Online

Student Web Activity Visit the *American Vision* Web site at tav.glencoe.com and click on *Student Web Activities— Chapter 1* for an activity on America's prehistory.

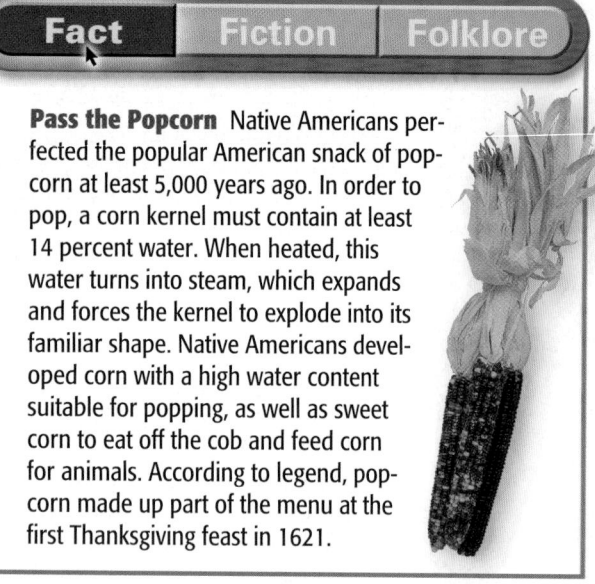

Pass the Popcorn Native Americans perfected the popular American snack of popcorn at least 5,000 years ago. In order to pop, a corn kernel must contain at least 14 percent water. When heated, this water turns into steam, which expands and forces the kernel to explode into its familiar shape. Native Americans developed corn with a high water content suitable for popping, as well as sweet corn to eat off the cob and feed corn for animals. According to legend, popcorn made up part of the menu at the first Thanksgiving feast in 1621.

Despite their similar cultures, war often erupted among the Iroquoian groups. In the late 1500s, five of the nations in western New York—the Seneca, Cayuga, Onondaga, Oneida, and Mohawk—formed an alliance to maintain peace. This alliance was later called the **Iroquois League** or Iroquois Confederacy. Europeans called these five nations the Iroquois, even though other nations spoke Iroquoian as well.

According to Iroquois tradition, **Dekanawidah** (DEK·uh·nuh·WEE·duh), a shaman or tribal elder, and **Hiawatha,** a chief of the Mohawk, founded the League. They were worried that war was tearing the five nations apart at a time when the more powerful Huron people threatened them all. The five nations agreed to the Great Binding Law, a constitution that defined how the confederacy worked.

Although the 50 chiefs who made up the ruling council of the Iroquois League were all men, the women who headed the kinship groups selected them. Council members were appointed for life, but the women could also get rid of an appointee if they disagreed with his actions. In this way, Iroquois women enjoyed considerable political influence.

The Peoples of the Southeast Almost all of the people in the Southeast lived in towns. Women did most of the farming, while the men hunted deer, bear, wildfowl, and even alligator. The Mississippian culture influenced many of the people in the Southeast. The town buildings were arranged around a central plaza. Stockades usually surrounded the towns, although moats and earthen walls were also used. The houses were built out of poles and covered with grass, mud, or thatch.

The Cherokee were the largest group in the Southeast. They lived in what is today western North Carolina and eastern Tennessee. About 20,000 Cherokee lived in some 60 towns when the Europeans arrived. The Cherokee and a nearby group of people called the Tuscarora were Iroquoian speakers. Other people in the Southeast included the Choctaw, Chickasaw, Natchez, and Creek. The Creek were a large group living in what is today Georgia and Alabama. They lived in about 50 villages that were divided into War Towns, where the war leaders lived and men trained for war, and Peace Towns, where the political leaders lived.

By the 1500s, Native Americans had created a wide array of cultures and languages. They had also developed economies and lifestyles well suited to the geography and climate in their particular corners of North America.

✓ **Reading Check** **Analyzing** How did some Woodlands Native Americans increase their crop yield?

SECTION 2 ASSESSMENT

Checking for Understanding

1. **Define:** kachina, slash-and-burn agriculture, longhouse, wigwam, kinship group.
2. **Identify:** Algonquian, Iroquoian, Dekanawidah, Hiawatha.
3. **Explain** why five Native American groups formed the Iroquois League.

Reviewing Themes

4. **Culture and Traditions** How did geography and climate affect the customs and traditions of Native American groups?

Critical Thinking

5. **Analyzing** Why were some Native American groups more nomadic than others?
6. **Categorizing** Use a graphic organizer like the one below to list North American regions and the ways Native Americans living in these regions obtained food.

Region	Ways of Getting Food

Analyzing Visuals

7. **Analyzing Maps** Examine the map of North American cultures on page 22. Which method of acquiring food was used over the largest geographical area of North America?

Writing About History

8. **Descriptive Writing** Take on the role of a Sioux teenager living in North America around 1500. Write a journal entry describing a typical day in your life. Be sure to discuss where you live and how your family obtains food.

American LITERATURE

Among the Native American groups with the richest oral literary traditions are the Iroquois. The Iroquois lived in what is today New York state. For a long time, they were a mighty and warlike people given to fighting amongst themselves. During the 1500s a shaman, or tribal elder, named Dekanawidah urged the Iroquois to stop fighting and unite to protect themselves from their common enemies. Dekanawidah's ideas led to the formation of the Iroquois Confederation of the Five Nations, commonly known as the Iroquois League.

Read to Discover
How did the Iroquois Confederation organize the Confederate Council?

Reader's Dictionary
foundation: basis

unanimous: in complete agreement

render: make; provide

from *The Constitution of the Five Nations*

I am Dekanawidah and with the Five Nations' Confederate Lords I plant the Tree of Great Peace. . . .

The Mohawk Lords are the foundation of the Great Peace and it shall, therefore, be against the Great Binding Law [the constitution] to pass measures in the Confederate Council after the Mohawk Lords have protested against them.

All the business of the Five Nations Confederate Council shall be conducted by the two combined bodies of Confederate Lords. . . . In all cases the procedure must be as follows: when the Mohawk and Seneca Lords have unanimously agreed upon a question, they shall report their decision to the Cayuga and Oneida Lords who shall deliberate upon the question and report a unanimous decision to the Mohawk Lords. The Mohawk Lords will then report the standing of the case to the Firekeepers [the Onondaga], who shall render a decision as they see fit in case of a disagreement by the two bodies. . . .

There shall be one War Chief for each Nation and their duties shall be to carry messages for their Lords and to take up the arms of war in case of emergency. They shall not participate in . . . the Confederate Council.

Whenever a very important matter or a great emergency is presented

before the Confederate Council [that] affects the entire body of the Five Nations . . . the Lords of the Confederacy must submit the matter to the decision of their people and the decision of the people shall affect the decision of the Confederate Council.

Analyzing Literature
1. **Recall and Interpret** Which of the Five Nations settles disputes within the Confederate Council?
2. **Evaluate and Connect** Which Nation seems to have the most individual power?

Interdisciplinary Activity
Government Imagine that you and several classmates are leaders of five small nations that are going to join together as one. In small groups, develop a new constitution under which all members of the new nation will live.

Guide to Reading

Main Idea
Peoples in West, Central, and Southern Africa developed diverse governments and lifestyles.

Key Terms and Names
Sahara, savannah, Islam, Muslim, Soninke, mosque, Malinke, Sorko, Yoruba, matrilineal

Reading Strategy
Organizing As you read about the civilizations and peoples of West, Central, and Southern Africa, complete a graphic organizer similar to the one below by filling in the names of several groups from each region.

West Africa	Central and Southern Africa

Reading Objectives
• **Describe** the culture of early West African kingdoms.
• **Describe** the lifestyles of early Central and Southern African peoples.

Section Theme
Global Connections The interaction of West African and European civilizations created changes in both cultures.

Preview of Events

A.D. 400 — 750 — 1100 — 1450

A.D. 400
West Africa's first empire, Ghana, arises

A.D. 610
Muhammad begins teaching ideas of Islam

1009
First Songhai state established

1240
Mali expands its power

1450
Songhai empire expands in West Africa

★ *An African Story* ★

In 1324 Mansa Musa, ruler of the Mali empire, made a pilgrimage to the Arabian city of Makkah (Mecca), a place holy to his religion, Islam.

Musa had encouraged scholarship and trade in his realm, establishing his empire's leading city, Timbuktu, as a great center of learning. A man named Mahmoud Kati, a native of the city, wrote a book praising Timbuktu for "the solidity of its institutions, its political liberties, the purity of its morals, the security of persons, its consideration and compassion towards foreigners, its courtesy toward students and men of learning and the financial assistance which it provided for the latter. . . ."

Musa was not the first African king to visit Makkah, but no one there or along his route had ever seen anything as dazzling as his traveling party. With him came 60,000 men, 12,000 of them personal servants he had enslaved. All were lavishly dressed. His vast caravan included 80 camels carrying 300 pounds of gold each.

Along the route, Musa's generous spending brought prosperity to the towns he passed and made his name famous. More importantly, the unmistakable wealth of his empire opened the eyes of North Africans, Arabs, and Europeans to the greatness of the Mali civilization.

—adapted from *Wonders of the African World*

West Africa

Between the 400s and 1500s, three great empires—Ghana, Mali, and Songhai—rose and fell in West Africa. These realms grew and prospered in large measure by trading in two precious commodities—gold and salt.

The Lay of the Land

Africa's geography helped determine where these empires arose. West Africa is an immense bulge of territory bordered on the north by the Mediterranean Sea and on the west and south by the Atlantic Ocean. Its northern and southern perimeters are well watered and fertile, but between them lies the vast expanse of the **Sahara,** whose name comes from an ancient Arabic word meaning *desert*. At the edges of the Sahara, regions of scrub forest and a kind of rolling grassland called savannah make for a more hospitable landscape.

From the western tip of the continent, where the Atlantic coast curves eastward to form West Africa's southern edge, a tropical rain forest grows. Civilizations both large and small arose in the rain forest and in the savannah along the Niger River, which cuts through West Africa and long served as its major path for east-west migration and trade.

Other important trade routes in West Africa crossed the vast Sahara. Early merchants bravely trekked through the desert using oxen, donkeys, and horses to carry their wares. Although pack oxen could travel a few days without water, long distance trade was rare and risky. For centuries most trade across the Sahara remained local. People living on the edge of the Sahara would exchange food for salt mined in the desert.

When Arab merchants introduced camels to the region between the third and fifth centuries A.D., they revolutionized trans-Saharan trade. Camels could carry more weight than oxen or horses, and they could walk for a much longer period each day. Most importantly, camels could go for over a week without water and could easily withstand the desert's scorching days and cold nights.

Although crossing the Sahara was still risky, camels enabled merchants to open up long-distance trade routes across the desert. Gold, ivory, ostrich feathers, and furs from south of the Sahara soon became more available to North Africa and Europe. As the demand for West African products increased, large trading settlements developed at the northern and southern boundaries of the Sahara.

Islam and West African Civilizations

Ideas as well as goods traveled along these African trade routes. Among the most significant of these were the religious ideas of **Islam.**

In the early A.D. 600s, Islam began winning converts outside of its native Arabia. By 711 Islam, whose followers are called **Muslims,** had spread all the way across northern Africa to the Atlantic Ocean. Through both armed conquest and the sense of religious solidarity that Islam promoted, this new creed won wide acceptance.

By the 900s, the nomadic peoples who controlled the trade caravans in the Sahara had become Muslim as well. They in turn carried Islam across the Sahara into the heart of West Africa, where many people living in the region's cities and market towns would eventually embrace it.

The Lure of Gold

West Africa prospered primarily because of the gold trade. The Muslim conquest of North Africa greatly increased the demand for gold in the 800s and 900s because the new Muslim states of the region used gold coins.

Later, in the 1200s, trade between Europe and North Africa experienced an economic revival as the rulers of Europe shifted from silver and copper coins to gold coins. By the 1300s, as much as two-thirds of the gold in Europe and North Africa had come from trade with West Africa.

Reading Check **Explaining** Why were camels better than horses or oxen for traveling in the desert?

The Empires of West Africa

The African peoples who lived on the southern edge of the Sahara were perfectly positioned to benefit from the growing trade in gold. Being in the middle of the trade, they had access both to the gold from the south and the salt and other goods coming from the north. Their ability to control this trade increased their wealth and power and enabled them to build large empires.

Ghana

The earliest empire to emerge was Ghana in the A.D. 400s. Located between the gold mines of Bambuk (just east of present-day Senegal) and the salt mines of Taghaza in the Sahara, the **Soninke,** as the people of Ghana were called, controlled the region's trade and built West Africa's first empire. A visitor from Spain, Abu Hamid al-Andalusi, wrote of Ghana:

Gourd drum from Africa's west coast

> ❝In the sands of that country is gold, treasure inexpressible. . . . Merchants trade with salt for it, taking the salt on camels from the salt mines. They . . . travel in the desert as it were upon the sea, having guides to pilot them by the stars or rocks. . . . They take provisions for six months, and when they reach Ghana they weigh their salt and sell it against a certain unit of weight of gold. . . .❞
>
> —quoted in *African Kingdoms*

After the Muslim conquest of North Africa and the Sahara in the 600s and 700s, Ghana's merchants grew wealthy from the gold and salt trade. Muslim traders from the north found a warm welcome in Ghana's capital of Kumbi-Saleh, where the ruler even permitted them to build their own mosques—Muslim places of worship. Ghana's ruler taxed the trade and became very wealthy as well. Most of Ghana's people, however, were farmers and herders who did not profit from the trade.

Despite this success, Ghana's empire had collapsed by the early 1200s. Although Ghana had become a Muslim kingdom in the 1100s, it was hurt by frequent wars with the Muslims of the Sahara. Equally contributing to Ghana's collapse was a change in the environment. Ghana's land was exhausted, and its farmers could no longer feed its people.

At the same time that these factors were combining to weaken Ghana, new gold mines opened in Bure (located in what is today northeast Guinea). Trade routes to these mines bypassed Ghana to the east, depriving Ghana's rulers of the wealth they needed to keep their empire together.

Mali East of Ghana, the **Malinke** people controlled the upper Niger Valley. This enabled them to direct the gold trade from Bure. With their new wealth and power, the Malinke conquered the Soninke of Ghana and built the empire of Mali.

By the mid-1300s, the empire of Mali had spread east down the Niger River past Timbuktu and west down the Senegal and Gambia Rivers to the Atlantic Ocean. The ruler of Mali was called the *mansa*. The government of Mali was similar to that of Ghana. In both empires, a bureaucracy of scribes and treasurers lived in the capital city with the emperor.

In outlying towns, traditional rulers stayed in power and managed local affairs. To stay in power, local leaders had to collect tribute from the farmers and send a portion to the capital. To enforce the system, the *mansa* kept a large army ready and made army leaders important officials in his government. Although the rulers and traders of Mali adopted Islam, many of the people—especially the farmers—clung to their traditional belief in "spirits of the land," whom they thought ensured the growth of their crops.

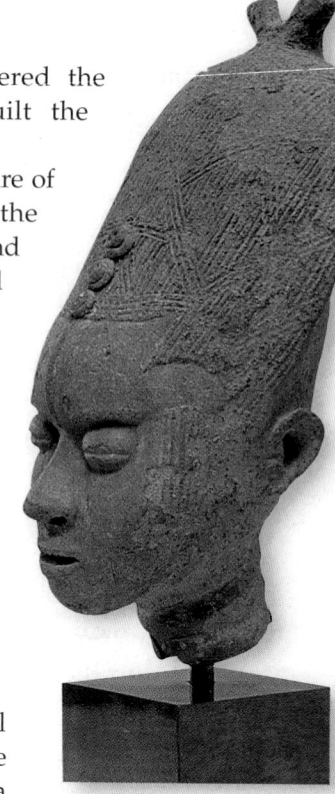

Akan memorial head

The empire of Mali reached its peak in the 1300s under the leadership of **Mansa Musa** and his brother Mansa Sulayman. By that time, new gold mines had opened in the Akan region (located in what is today Ghana), shifting the trade routes farther east and leading to the rise of Timbuktu as a great center of trade and Muslim scholarship.

Songhai The **Sorko** people who lived along the middle Niger, east of Mali, built the Songhai empire. The Sorko fashioned canoes and fished for a living. They also used their canoes to control the river and trade with peoples to the north and south, gaining both wealth and power. By the 800s they had created the kingdom of Songhai. Although Songhai had contact with Mali, most of its territory never came under Mali's control.

When Mali began to decline, the ruler of Songhai, **Sonni Ali,** used a powerful army of cavalry backed by a fleet of war canoes to seize Timbuktu in 1468. Until his death in 1492, Ali led his cavalry and war canoes in a series of wars of conquest. After taking Timbuktu, Ali pushed northward into the Sahara to

Wooden stool from Ghana

the Taghazi salt mines, and then he expanded southward down the Niger about 200 miles (322 km) to capture the town of Jenne. According to legend, Sonni Ali's army never lost a battle.

Sonni Ali's son and successor proved to be an ineffectual ruler, and within a year a Songhai general named **Askiya Muhammad** seized the throne. Askiya Muhammad, a devout Muslim, revived Timbuktu as a great center of learning, encouraged more trade across the Sahara, and centralized power in the Songhai capital, Gao. Visiting Gao in 1513, a young Moroccan named Leo Africanus wrote:

> 66Its inhabitants are rich merchants who travel constantly about the region with their wares. A great many Blacks come to the city bringing quantities of gold with which to purchase goods imported from the Berber country [North Africa] and from Europe, but they never find enough goods on which to spend all their gold and always take half or two-thirds of it home.99
>
> —quoted in *African Kingdoms*

Songhai remained a powerful and wealthy empire until 1591, when Moroccan troops, armed

Picturing History

West African Empire This turreted mosque in Djenné, Mali, dates back to the 1300s. It still provides a vital worship center in the Sahara, much as it did during the days of the West African empires. Why did so many empires arise in West Africa?

with guns and cannon, defeated Songhai's armies. After the battle shattered its army, the Songhai empire began to decline.

✓ **Reading Check** **Describing** Why did the empire of Ghana begin to decline?

The Forest Kingdoms of Guinea

Ghana, Mali, and Songhai arose on the wide vistas of West Africa's savannah, an open landscape that made it easier to control large territories. The situation differed in the dense, almost impenetrable forests of West Africa's southern coast, an area called Guinea. There, smaller states and kingdoms, such as Ife and Benin, developed.

Both the **Yoruba** people of Ife and the **Edo** people of Benin were a mixture of hunters, farmers, and traders living in small village communities. The rich farmlands and tropical climate enabled the people of the forest kingdoms to produce surplus food that was then used to support rulers, government officials, artisans, and artists. Surplus food was also traded for copper and salt from the Sahara. Ife artists produced some of the most impressive art in West Africa. They carved wood and ivory, made terra-cotta sculptures, and cast metal.

To the south and east of Ife, the Edo people developed the city-state of Benin in the eleventh or twelfth century. By 1400, Benin was a large, walled city measuring several miles across. The ruler of Benin was called the *oba*. In the mid-1400s, **Oba Ewuare** assembled a

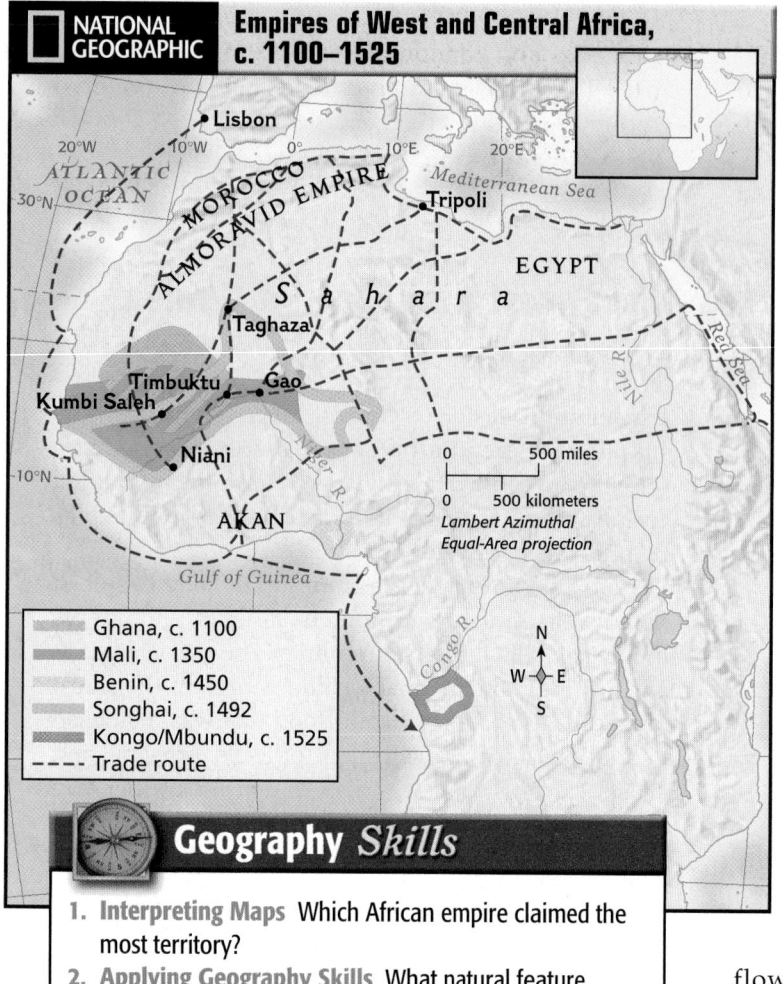

Empires of West and Central Africa, c. 1100–1525

Ghana, c. 1100
Mali, c. 1350
Benin, c. 1450
Songhai, c. 1492
Kongo/Mbundu, c. 1525
---- Trade route

Geography *Skills*

1. **Interpreting Maps** Which African empire claimed the most territory?
2. **Applying Geography Skills** What natural feature determined the location of these empires?

difficult. Many Central African villages, located on rivers, gained a living from fishing but also grew wheat and raised livestock. The villagers had complex family structures and maintained close links to their communities. Other Central Africans lived nomadic lives and subsisted by hunting and gathering.

Like the Iroquois in America, many Central African societies were **matrilineal.** People traced their lineage, or descent, through their mothers rather than through their fathers. Upon marriage a man became a member of his bride's family.

Though women took responsibility for child rearing and cooking, they also played a major role in trade. In many places the women farmed while the men hunted, fished, and raised livestock. Tribal chiefs were almost always male, but a chief's son could not expect to succeed his father. Instead, the son of the chief's eldest sister inherited the post. Thus, Central and Southern African women of the time enjoyed far more influence and authority than women in many other parts of the world.

The Central African kingdom of Kongo originated around 1400 in a group of prosperous villages along the Zaire River, which flows southwestward through the region to the Atlantic. Fertile soil and abundant rainfall allowed the farmers who lived in these villages to produce food surpluses. By the early 1500s, the Kongo king ruled over a large region from the Atlantic to the Kwango River. South of Kongo, another large kingdom arose among the Mbundu-speaking people in the region that is now Angola.

Reading Check **Analyzing** Why were the peoples of the Kongo able to produce food surpluses?

powerful army and built Benin into an empire that stretched from the Niger delta west to where the city of Lagos, Nigeria, is located today.

After establishing his empire, Ewuare appointed district chiefs to replace the local rulers he had conquered. Benin's leaders also began trading enslaved people they had captured in war to the Portuguese in exchange for Portuguese goods. They then sold the Portuguese ivory, pepper, gum, and cotton. Later, when Benin collapsed into civil war in the 1700s, many Benin citizens were themselves enslaved and traded to the Portuguese.

Reading Check **Examining** Why were the states and kingdoms smaller in Guinea than in West Africa's savannah area?

Central and Southern Africa

To the southeast of Benin lay the impenetrable reaches of the rain forests. There, the dense vegetation made the movement of people and goods

Slavery

As in other parts of the world, slavery existed in African society. Most of the people enslaved in African societies had been captured in war. A few were convicted criminals who had been enslaved as punishment. Before the Arabs and Europeans began purchasing enslaved Africans, most African societies would either ransom captives back to their people or absorb them into their own society. With hard work and good luck, enslaved Africans had a chance to improve their difficult position. In rare instances, they could purchase their freedom by selling produce they had grown or marry into their captor's society and improve their social status.

African slavery began to change with the arrival of Islam. Muslims in the Middle East were permitted to enslave non-Muslims. Arab traders began to trade horses, cotton, and other goods in exchange for enslaved Africans captured in war.

The Gold Trade The gold trade also changed slavery in West Africa. In the early 1400s, the Akan people began mining gold and trading it to the Mali empire. To increase their production, they acquired enslaved Africans from Mali traders for use in clearing the land and mining the gold.

In the 1420s, the Portuguese began exploring the west coast of Africa and trading with West African merchants. They traded European goods for African gold, ivory, pepper, and palm oil. When Portuguese merchants arrived on the coast south of the Akan region, they began to supply the Akan people with enslaved Africans in exchange for gold. They also purchased enslaved Africans to work on Portuguese sugar plantations.

Sugar and Slavery Europeans learned about the cultivation and processing of sugarcane from the Muslims during the 1100s. The introduction of sugar changed the diet of Europeans, who had formerly used honey and fruit juices to sweeten their foods. Demand for sugar began to rise steadily. Eventually about 20 percent of all calories consumed in Europe came from sugar.

Europeans set up sugar plantations on the Mediterranean islands of Cyprus and Sicily. These locations, unlike most of Europe, provided the specific climate and type of soil sugarcane needs to grow well.

Sugarcane cultivation requires heavy manual labor. The cane is tough and thick and has to be chopped down using heavy knives. A huge amount of sugarcane has to be cut to produce a pound of sugar. Consequently, plantation owners needed a large labor force. To get people to do the work, they either had to pay very high wages or find a way to force people to do the work without paying them. As a result, the introduction of sugarcane farming encouraged Europeans to use enslaved workers and to enter into the slave trade.

The first enslaved workers used by the Europeans on sugar farms were captured Muslims and Slavic peoples. Rising demand for sugar in the 1400s led Spain and Portugal to establish sugarcane plantations on the Canary and Madeira Islands off the west coast of Africa. They then brought in enslaved Africans to work the fields. The limited amount of land available to Europeans to plant sugarcane kept their participation in the slave trade limited during the 1400s. This would change dramatically after Europeans introduced sugarcane to America.

As the European demand for slave labor rose following the colonization of America, slavery in Africa completely changed. Traders took enslaved Africans from their homes and sent them across the Atlantic. For the most part, enslaved Africans shipped to America had little chance of winning their freedom. Torn from their own cultures, they had to learn a completely new way of life amid often horrifying conditions.

✓ **Reading Check** **Analyzing** Why did Europeans want slaves?

SECTION 3 ASSESSMENT

Checking for Understanding
1. **Define:** savannah, mosque, matrilineal.
2. **Identify:** Sahara, Islam, Muslim, Soninke, Malinke, Sorko, Yoruba.
3. **Explain** why Songhai became a great empire.

Reviewing Themes
4. **Global Connections** How did the concept of slavery change as trade between Africa and Europe flourished in the 1500s?

Critical Thinking
5. **Comparing** How were Central and Southern African societies different from each other?
6. **Categorizing** Use a graphic organizer similar to the one below to list ways of making a living in African cultures.

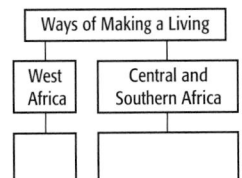

Ways of Making a Living

West Africa

Central and Southern Africa

Analyzing Visuals
7. **Examining Artifacts** Study the West African artifacts on pages 27 and 28. The skillful handiwork of these items indicates a society able to devote time to artistic pursuits in addition to necessary tasks. What two commodities were essential to the prosperity of West Africa?

Writing About History
8. **Descriptive Writing** Imagine you are a Portuguese explorer in West Africa. Write a journal entry describing a West African civilization.

Guide to Reading

Main Idea

The fall of Rome fragmented Europe. Between 1100 and 1400, several developments helped reunify parts of Europe and encouraged new explorations.

Key Terms and Names

Crusades, Roman Empire, feudalism, manorialism, serf, Renaissance, astrolabe, lateen sail, caravel, Henry the Navigator, Bartolomeu Dias, Vasco da Gama

Reading Strategy

Organizing As you read about European life in the Middle Ages, complete a graphic organizer similar to the one below by filling in the key events that brought Europe out of its long isolation.

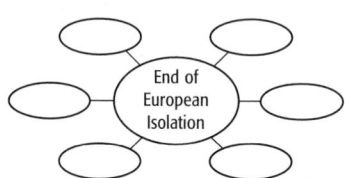

End of European Isolation

Reading Objectives

- **Discuss** the impact of the Crusades on Europe's contact with the Middle East.
- **Analyze** the impact of the Renaissance on European exploration.

Section Theme

Science and Technology The Renaissance helped start a scientific revolution that enabled Europeans to explore the world.

Preview of Events

♦1095   ♦1230   ♦1365   ♦1500

1095
Pope Urban II launches the Crusades

1200s
Mongol empire established

1300s
Renaissance begins in Italy

1420s
Portugal begins exploring the African coast

1497
Vasco da Gama reaches India

★ *A European Story* ★

In 1095 Pope Urban II, the head of the Roman Catholic Church, was a worried man. The Holy Land, the birthplace of Christianity, was in the hands of Muslims, who, Urban feared, would no longer allow Christians access to holy religious sites. To meet this threat, Urban organized a great meeting of Christians in Clermont, France. On November 18, before a huge outdoor crowd of bishops, knights, and common people, Urban made an impassioned speech, calling on Europeans to seize control of Christianity's holiest sites by armed conquest. A cleric known as Robert the Monk recorded the Pope's speech in these words:

❝Jerusalem is the navel of the world. . . . This is the land which the Redeemer of mankind illuminated by his coming, adorned by his life, consecrated by his passion, redeemed by his death, and sealed by his burial. This royal city, situated in the middle of the world, is now held captive by his enemies. . . . It looks for help from you, especially, because God has bestowed glory in arms upon you more than on any other nation. Undertake this journey, therefore, for the remission of your sins, with the assurance of 'glory which cannot fade' in the kingdom of heaven.❞

—quoted in *The Discoverers*

European Society

Pope Urban II's call to arms launched nearly two centuries of armed struggle to regain the Holy Land. These expeditions were called the **Crusades,** from the Latin word *crux,* meaning "cross." The Crusades helped pry western Europe out of centuries of isolation and triggered a series of events that revolutionized European society and encouraged a new desire for exploration.

For centuries, the **Roman Empire** had dominated much of Europe, imposing a stable social and political order. By A.D. 500, however, the Roman political and economic system had collapsed, isolating western Europe from the rest of the world. Trade declined. Cities, bridges, and roads fell into disrepair. Law and order vanished, and money was no longer used. For most people, life did not extend beyond the tiny villages where they were born, lived, and died. This period, lasting roughly from 500 to 1400, is known as the **Middle Ages.**

Feudalism With the weakening of central government, a new political system known as feudalism developed in western Europe. Under this system, a king would give estates to nobles in exchange for their loyalty and military support. Eventually, the nobles owning the estates became strong enough to assume many of the powers usually held by government. They raised their own armies, dispensed justice, and even minted coins. In return, the nobles swore an oath of loyalty and promised to provide knights, or mounted warriors, for the royal army.

By 1100 feudalism had spread throughout much of Europe. Because the system lacked a strong central government, warfare occurred frequently in feudal society. As a result, most nobles built castles, or fortified manor houses, for defense.

The Manorial System The wealth of a feudal lord came from the labor of the peasants who lived on his land. Since the fall of the Roman Empire, many peasants had worked for large landowners, in part because they could not obtain their own land and in part for protection.

A lord's manor, or estate, varied in size from several hundred to several hundred thousand acres. Each manor included the lord's house, pastures for livestock, fields for crops, forest, and a peasant village. While feudalism describes the political relationships between nobles, manorialism describes the economic ties between nobles and peasants.

In return for protection, peasants provided various services for the lord. Chief among these were farming the lord's land and making various payments of goods. Warfare and bandits made trade difficult, so the manor had to produce nearly everything its residents needed.

History *Through Art*

The Middle Ages This Bayeaux tapestry and a prayer book show art styles in Europe in the Middle Ages. What aspect of life in the Middle Ages does the tapestry depict?

Peasants rarely left the manor. Most were serfs, people who were bound to the manor and could not leave it without permission. Serfs were not considered enslaved, however, since they could not be sold from the land where they lived and worked. Serfs typically lived in tiny, one-room houses with dirt floors, a hole in the roof for a chimney, and one or two crude pieces of furniture. Coarse bread, a few vegetables, and grain for porridge made up their usual diet. They spent most of their waking hours working. Here, an English monk describes a serf's account of his day:

> 66 I work very hard. I go out at dawn, driving the oxen to the field, and I yoke them to the plough; however hard the winter I dare not stay home for fear of my master; but, having yoked the oxen and made the ploughshare and coulter fast to the plough, every day I have to plough a whole acre or more. 99
>
> —quoted in *Colloquy*

An Improving Economy The economy of western Europe, devastated since the fall of Rome, began to improve around 1000. The invention of a better plow allowed farmers to produce more food, as did the invention of the horse collar, which allowed farmers to use horses instead of oxen. Horses could pull a plow faster than an ox, enabling farmers to plant more crops each year.

The ability of many villages to produce a surplus of food helped to revive trade in Europe and encouraged the growth of towns. Some European rulers succeeded in building strong central governments. Warfare and raids by bandits decreased, and roads were soon filled with traders carrying goods to market. The number of towns in western Europe grew tremendously between 1000 and 1200.

The Church The Roman Catholic Church struggled mightily against the social and political fragmentation of Europe that followed the fall of Rome. In the face of civil chaos and personal insecurity, it promoted stability and order. It had its own laws and courts that dealt with cases related to the clergy, doctrine, marriage, and morals.

Disobedience to Church laws resulted in severe penalties for common persons and rulers alike—including excommunication for those who committed grave offenses. Excommunication barred people from participating in Church rites. They also lost political and legal rights.

✓ **Reading Check** **Describing** What was the social order in Europe during the Middle Ages?

Expanding Horizons

Pope Urban II's call for Christians to free their religion's holy places from the Muslims launched a period of profound change in Europe. The Crusades

NATIONAL GEOGRAPHIC **Europe in the Age of Exploration, c. 1100–1400**

- • Major commercial centers
- ◀--- Major trade routes

Geography *Skills*

1. **Interpreting Maps** Which city was Europe's overland gateway to India?
2. **Applying Geography Skills** Which Eastern empire was crucial for organizing the movement of goods between Europe and China?

helped change western European society by bringing western Europeans into contact with the Muslim and Byzantine civilizations of eastern Europe and the Middle East. The western European presence in this region heightened demand at home for Eastern luxury goods: spices, sugar, melons, tapestries, silk, and other items. Trade increased in the eastern Mediterranean area and especially benefited Italian cities such as Venice, Pisa, and Genoa.

By 1200 Italian and Arab merchants controlled much of the trade in the eastern Mediterranean. Chinese and Indian traders sold silk, spices, and other goods to Arab merchants, who then moved the goods overland to the Mediterranean coast, where they reaped huge profits selling the goods to Italian merchants.

As trade increased, merchants found that many Arab traders would only accept money in payment. European merchants therefore needed a common medium of exchange, and this led to the rise of an economy based on money. The increasing demand for gold from Africa to make gold coins during the 1200s was a direct result of Europe's expanding trade with Asia.

The rise of the Mongol empire in the 1200s helped to increase the flow of goods from China and other parts of Asia. Mongol horsemen swept out of central Asia in the early part of the century and built one of largest empires in world history. The Mongol conquest integrated much of Asia's economy. It broke down trade barriers, opened borders, and secured the roads against bandits, encouraging even more trade between Asia and Europe.

By the 1300s Europe was importing vast quantities of spices, silks, and other goods from Asia. To the frustration of European merchants, however, the Mongol empire collapsed in the 1300s, and Asia again separated into dozens of independent kingdoms and empires. The flow of goods from Asia declined, and the price of spices, already very high, rose even more. Increasingly European merchants and rulers began to look for a route to Asia that bypassed the Muslim kingdoms. If they could not reach China by land, they thought, perhaps they could reach it by sea.

✓ **Reading Check** **Summarizing** Describe the effects of the Crusades on Europe.

New States, New Technology

The wealth that could be earned by trading directly with Asia had given Europeans a compelling motive to begin exploring the world. Before the 1300s, however, western European rulers and merchants did not have the ability to look for a direct sea route to Asia.

Causes and Effects of European Exploration

Causes

- The Crusades broadened European horizons and stimulated interest in luxury goods.
- Monarchs of new states wanted to acquire gold to strengthen their rule.
- The Renaissance promoted a scientific and practical view of the world.
- New technology like the compass and astrolabe made exploration possible.

Effects

- An exchange of goods and ideas between Europe and the Americas began.
- European diseases devastated Native American populations; American diseases spread to Europe.
- Europeans became increasingly involved in the West African slave trade.

Graphic Organizer → Skills

European explorations brought profound cultural changes to many parts of the world.

Evaluating How did technology play a role in exploration?

Feudalism had created a society so fragmented and torn by war that no western European kingdom had the wealth to finance exploration and overseas trade. Western Europeans also lacked the technology to even attempt to reach China by sea. Beginning in the 1300s, however, a number of major changes took place in Europe that enabled the Europeans to begin sending ships into the Atlantic Ocean in search of a water route to China.

GOVERNMENT

Strong States Emerge Western Europeans began exploring the world in the 1400s and 1500s for several reasons. First of all, feudalism was in decline. Both the Crusades and trade with Asia had helped to weaken this system. The rise of towns and merchants had provided kings and queens with a new source of wealth they could tax. They could now use their armed forces to open up and protect trade routes and to enforce uniform trade laws and a common currency

Caravel

The caravel was typical of Spanish and Portuguese ship design during the early years of European world exploration. Ranging in length from 75 to 90 feet (23 to 27 m), caravels were suited for sailing along shallow coastlines. They were not, however, well suited for very long voyages, as they could not carry enough crew and supplies. Caravels were usually rigged with three or four masts, employing both square and triangular sails. *How did the caravel's lateen sails help sailors?*

1 The triangular **lateen sail** caught wind that blew perpendicular to the ship, providing more manueverability.

2 **Ballast stones** were placed in the hull of the ship to provide better balance.

3 A **bilge pump**, operated from the main deck, removed water from storage areas.

lateen sail

bilge pump

ballast stones

within their kingdoms. Merchants, who stood to benefit as well from increased trade, loaned money to monarchs to further finance their operations.

The revenue from trade meant that European rulers did not have to rely as much upon the nobility for support. Increasingly, western European monarchs asserted their power over the nobles. They began to unify their kingdoms and create strong central governments. By the mid-1400s, four strong states—Portugal, Spain, England, and France—had emerged in western Europe. Starting with Portugal in the early 1400s, all four began financing voyages of exploration in the hope of expanding their trade and national power.

The Renaissance Spurs Discoveries The political and economic changes that encouraged western Europeans to begin exploring the world would not have mattered had they not had the technology necessary to launch their expeditions. Fortunately, at about the same time that new unified kingdoms were emerging in western Europe, an intellectual revolution known as the Renaissance began as well. This period began around A.D. 1350 and lasted until around 1600.

Renaissance is a French word that means "rebirth." In this case, it referred to a rebirth of interest in the culture of ancient Greece and Rome. European scholars rediscovered the works of Greek and Roman philosophers, geographers, and mathematicians. They also began to read works by Arab scholars. The Renaissance started with a renewed interest in the past, but it quickly became much more. The Renaissance not only produced spectacular works of art, it also marked a renewed commitment to learning and helped to trigger a scientific revolution.

New Technology If western Europeans were going to find a water route to Asia, they needed navigational instruments that would enable sailors to travel out of sight of land and still find their way home. They also required ships capable of long-distance travel across the ocean. By the early 1400s, Europeans had acquired these technologies.

By studying Arab texts, western Europeans learned about the astrolabe, a device invented by the ancient Greeks and refined by Arab navigators. An astrolabe uses the position of the sun to determine direction, latitude, and local time. Europeans also acquired the compass from Arab traders. Invented in China, this device reliably showed the direction of magnetic north.

Navigational tools were important to exploration, but not as essential as ships capable of long-distance travel. Late in the 1400s, European shipwrights began to outfit ships with triangle-shaped **lateen sails** perfected by Arab traders. These sails made it possible for ships to sail against the wind. Shipwrights also began using multiple masts with several smaller sails hoisted one above the other, which made ships travel much faster. Also, moving the rudder from the side to the stern made ships easier to steer.

In the 1400s a Portuguese ship called the caravel incorporated all these improvements. A caravel was a small vessel capable of carrying about 130 tons (118 t) of cargo. Because a caravel needed little water to sail, it allowed explorers to venture up shallow inlets and to beach the ships to make repairs. Caravels and ships with similar technology finally enabled Europe to explore the world.

☑ **Reading Check** **Examining** What political and technological developments made it possible for Europeans to begin exploring the world?

Portuguese Exploration

Sailing their caravels, Portuguese explorers became the first Europeans to find a sea route to Asia. In 1419 Prince Henry of Portugal, known as **Henry the Navigator,** set up a center for astronomical and geographical studies at Sagres on Portugal's southwestern tip. He invited mapmakers, astronomers, and shipbuilders from throughout the Mediterranean world to come there to study and plan voyages of exploration.

World History Connection

The Compass
While the Europeans made numerous advances in navigation, it was the Chinese who invented one of the more important seafaring tools: the compass. Evidence of this fact includes a Chinese document from 1086 that talks of sea captains relying on a "south-pointing needle" to help them find their way in foggy weather. The date on the document is more than 100 years earlier than the first recorded use of the compass in Europe. *What other inventions aided European exploration?*

Early compasses

Beginning in 1420, Portuguese explorers began mapping Africa's west coast. In 1488 a Portuguese ship commanded by **Bartolomeu Dias** reached the southern tip of Africa, later named the Cape of Good Hope. Nine years later, four ships commanded by **Vasco da Gama** sailed from Portugal, rounded Africa, and then headed across to India and landed on India's southwest coast. A water route to eastern Asia had been found.

☑ **Reading Check** **Describing** How did Henry the Navigator help encourage exploration?

SECTION 4 ASSESSMENT

Checking for Understanding
1. **Define:** feudalism, manorialism, serf, Renaissance, astrolabe, caravel.
2. **Identify:** Crusades, Roman Empire, lateen sail, Henry the Navigator, Bartolomeu Dias, Vasco da Gama.
3. **Describe** how feudalism brought about social and political order during the Middle Ages.

Reviewing Themes
4. **Science and Technology** How did scientific advancements affect geographical knowledge?

Critical Thinking
5. **Synthesizing** How did the Renaissance lead to European exploration?
6. **Organizing** Use a graphic organizer similar to the one below to list the effects of the Crusades.

Crusades ⟨

7. **Analyzing** If you had been a merchant in Europe during the 1400s, would you have supported attempts to find new routes to Asia? Why or why not?

Analyzing Visuals
8. **Examining Maps** Study the map of European exploration on page 34. How do you think the Crusades assisted the development of the trade routes throughout the European and Asian continents?

Writing About History
9. **Descriptive Writing** Imagine you are a serf living in Europe in the year 1100. Write a letter to a relative describing your daily life.

SECTION 5 Europe Encounters America

Guide to Reading

Main Idea

Columbus sought a sea route to Asia. Instead, he landed in the Americas.

Key Terms and Names

Vikings, Christopher Columbus, Claudius Ptolemy, San Salvador Island, Santo Domingo, Pope Alexander VI, line of demarcation, Amerigo Vespucci, Florida, circumnavigate, Columbian Exchange

Reading Strategy

Organizing As you read about European exploration of the Americas, complete a chart like the one below by filling in the outcome of each exploration listed in the chart.

Exploration	Outcome
Vikings	
Columbus	
Vespucci	
Balboa	
Magellan	

Reading Objectives

• **Describe** Viking and Spanish explorations of North America.
• **Summarize** Columbus's journeys and their impact on Native Americans and Europeans.

Section Theme

Global Connections Material exchanges between Europe and the Americas yielded both positive and negative results.

Preview of Events

| ♦1000 | ♦1475 | ♦1500 | ♦1525 |

C. A.D. 1001
Vikings reach North America

1475
Ptolemy's *Geography* revolutionizes mapmaking

1492
Christopher Columbus lands in America

1494
Treaty of Tordesillas

1522
Magellan's expedition circumnavigates the earth

★ *An American Story* ★

In 1492 Christopher Columbus led 90 sailors on a voyage into the unknown. On September 9 Columbus noted in his log: "This day we completely lost sight of land, and many men sighed and wept for fear they would not see it again for a long time." As the voyage dragged on, the sailors grew nervous and began plotting mutiny. Columbus wrote:

❝All day long and all night long those who are awake and able to get together never cease to talk to each other in circles, complaining that they will never be able to return home. . . . I am told . . . that if I persist in going onward, the best course of action will be to throw me into the sea some night.❞

Then, on the morning of October 12, the *Pinta's* lookout, Rodrigo de Triana, let out a joyous cry— "Tierra! Tierra!" ("Land! Land!"). At dawn a relieved and triumphant Columbus went ashore. He believed he had arrived in the Indies—islands located southeast of China.

—adapted from *The Log of Christopher Columbus*

The Vikings Arrive in America

Although his historic journey set the stage for permanent European settlement in the Americas, Christopher Columbus was not the first European to arrive there. Strong archaeological evidence credits that accomplishment to the Norse, or **Vikings,** a people who came from Scandinavia.

Beginning in the late A.D. 700s, Viking ships, called **longboats,** began to venture outward from their homeland. Most headed south, some to trade with the wealthier peoples to the south and others to raid their settlements. Still others braved the violent North Atlantic Ocean and headed west.

Sometime around A.D. 1000, **Leif Ericsson** and 35 Vikings explored the coast of Labrador and may have stayed the winter in Newfoundland. Although the Vikings later tried to set up colonies in the region, their attempts failed, in large part because the Native Americans opposed them. Unlike later European colonists, the Vikings did not have better weapons than those of the Native Americans, who outnumbered them. It would take a new series of European expeditions, embarking in the 1400s and 1500s from points much farther south, to establish a permanent European presence in the Americas.

✓ **Reading Check** **Examining** How do we know that Columbus was not the first European in the Americas?

Spain Sends Columbus West

For more than 400 years after the Vikings abandoned their settlements in North America, there is no convincing evidence that Europeans traveled to the Americas. In the mid-1400s, the Renaissance renewed European interest in the world's geography. With many European states eager to find a sea route to Asia, a few persons, including an Italian navigator named **Christopher Columbus,** became interested in sailing west across the Atlantic.

A New Geography By the 1400s most educated Europeans knew that the world was round. On the most accurate European maps of the time, however, only the Mediterranean, Europe, the Middle East, and Africa's northern coast showed any detail. Then a book appeared that revolutionized European exploration.

Twelve centuries earlier, a Greek-educated Egyptian geographer and astronomer named **Claudius Ptolemy** had drawn maps of a round world, complete with 360 lines of longitude, one degree apart, projected onto a flat surface. Ptolemy's *Geography* was rediscovered in 1406 and printed in 1475. It became very influential, and its basic system of lines of latitude and longitude is still used today.

European mariners also consulted the work of a twelfth century Arab geographer named **al-Idrisi,** who had traveled widely in the Middle East. In 1154 al-Idrisi published a geographical survey of as much

of the world as was then known to Europeans and Muslims. By studying the maps of Ptolemy and al-Idrisi, Western mariners finally obtained a reliable idea of the geography of the eastern African coast and the Indian Ocean.

Columbus's Plan Despite its usefulness, Ptolemy's *Geography* had seriously underestimated the distance that each degree of longitude represented, making the earth seem much smaller than it actually was. Basing his own calculations on Ptolemy's, Christopher Columbus predicted with wild optimism that "the end of Spain and the beginning of India are not far apart . . . and it is known that this sea is navigable in a few days' time with favoring wind."

Columbus sought Portuguese financial backing to make a voyage across the Atlantic to Asia. In 1484 he applied to the king of Portugal, who referred him to a committee of experts in navigation. Basing their decision on sources other than Ptolemy's maps, the scholars reasoned correctly that Columbus had greatly underestimated the distance to Asia. Furthermore, when news arrived in 1488 that Bartolomeu Dias had successfully rounded the southern tip of Africa, the Portuguese lost all interest in supporting Columbus.

History *Through Art*

Archaeological Evidence This carving of a European figure (left) and Viking calendar (above) prove that the Vikings arrived in North America before Columbus. Why were Vikings unable to colonize successfully?

Exploration New technology such as the caravel and improved mapmaking made world exploration easier. What publication helped improve mapmaking?

For the next few years, Columbus tried to win backing from other rulers. His brother Bartholomew, a respected mapmaker in Europe, tried and failed to secure financing for Columbus's expedition from the rulers of England and France. Having no success with them, he spent six years trying to persuade King Ferdinand and Queen Isabella of Spain that his scheme would bring them wealth, empire, and converts to Catholicism. Finally, in 1492, after it became clear that Portugal was about to reach Asia by going east around Africa, Ferdinand agreed.

TURNING POINT

The First Voyage Columbus and his three ships—the *Niña,* the *Pinta,* and the *Santa Maria*—finally left Spain in August 1492. First he sailed south to the Canary Islands to take on fresh supplies. Then he embarked on the harrowing voyage westward across the mysterious and frightening Atlantic until, unaware of where he was, he reached the Caribbean and landed in the Bahamas, probably on what is today **San Salvador Island.** There, for the first time, he encountered the Taino people, a part of the Arawak. He called the people *Indians* because he thought he had reached the fabled Indies. Columbus noticed that some of the local people had a small piece of gold "hanging from a hole which they have in their nose." After several attempts to ask where the gold had come from, he learned that "there was a king who had large vessels of it, and possessed much gold. . . ." Columbus then headed deeper into the Caribbean, determined to find this gold he had heard about. He found the island of Cuba, and he also found Hispaniola, which today is divided into the countries of Haiti and the Dominican Republic. Columbus mistakenly concluded that Cuba was the coast of China and that Hispaniola was Japan.

Columbus and his sailors felt equal parts admiration and curiosity toward the Native Americans that they encountered in the Bahamas and Hispaniola. Columbus wrote the following of the Arawak:

> ❝[They are] artless and generous with what they have, to such a degree as no one would believe but he who had seen it. Of anything they have, if it be asked for, they never say no, but do rather invite the person to accept it, and show as much lovingness as though they would give their hearts.❞
>
> —quoted in *500 Nations*

For their part, the Arawak must have been equally curious about the white-skinned, bearded Spanish. Columbus recorded his interpretation of their reaction to him and his men:

> ❝The people kept coming down to the beach, calling to us and giving thanks to God. Some brought us water, some food; others, seeing that I did not wish to go ashore, swam out to us. . . . One old man climbed into the boat, and the others, men and women, kept shouting, 'Come and see the men who have come from Heaven; bring them food and drink.'❞
>
> —quoted in *The Voyage of Christopher Columbus*

Like other Native Americans, the Arawak had an intense spiritual life. To Columbus, however, they appeared to have no religion. He predicted that "they would become Christians very easily."

On Christmas Eve Columbus's flagship, the *Santa Maria*, struck a reef off Hispaniola and broke apart. He built a small fort called La Navidad on the island and left 40 crew members to search for gold while he headed home with his remaining ships.

In March 1493 Columbus made a triumphant return to the Spanish court with gold, parrots, spices, and Native Americans he had brought back. The king and queen awarded him the titles "Admiral of the Ocean Sea" and "Viceroy and Governor of the Indies." Ferdinand and Isabella listened closely as Columbus promised "as much gold as they want if their Highnesses will render me a little help. . . ."

Columbus's Later Voyages Less than six months after Columbus returned to Spain, he headed back across the Atlantic, this time with 17 ships and over 1,200 Spanish colonists. In November 1493 he anchored off the coast of Hispaniola, only to learn that the men he had left behind had been killed and their fort destroyed. Abandoning the ruins, Columbus founded a new colony, called Isabella.

Many of the colonists were Spanish nobles. They had come expecting to get rich, and they refused to plant crops or do other manual labor. They accused Columbus of misleading them with false promises of gold, and many of them headed back to Spain to complain to the government.

Hoping to find more gold and save his reputation, Columbus began exploring the interior of Hispaniola. There he discovered enough loose gold to make mining worthwhile. He then decided to enslave the local Taino and force them to work for the Spanish, mining gold and planting crops.

In 1496 Columbus headed back to Spain. In the meantime, his brother Bartholomew founded a new town named **Santo Domingo** on the south coast of Hispaniola closer to the gold mines. Santo Domingo became the first capital of Spain's empire in America.

Columbus made a third voyage to America in 1498. After arriving on the northern coast of South America and studying the volume of fresh water at the mouth of the Orinoco River, he wrote in his journal, "I believe that this is a very great continent, which until today has been unknown." Columbus

made one final voyage in 1502. He mapped the American coastline from Guatemala to Panama before turning back.

Reading Check **Describing** Describe the results of Columbus's voyages.

Spain Claims America

After Columbus had shown the way, Spanish explorers and settlers flocked to the Caribbean hoping to become wealthy through conquest and trade. By the early 1500s, the Spanish had explored the major Caribbean islands, established colonies on Hispaniola, Cuba, Jamaica, and Puerto Rico, and begun exploring the American mainland.

The Treaty of Tordesillas Before colonization could begin, however, Ferdinand and Isabella had to establish their claim to the new lands. Portugal had claimed the right to control the Atlantic route to Asia. To resolve the issue peacefully, they appealed to the pope for a decision.

Profiles IN HISTORY

Christopher Columbus
1451–1506

Christopher Columbus was born in Genoa, Italy. Growing up in a bustling seaport gave Columbus a glimpse of the wider world. Although he was the eldest son, he decided to leave his family's wool-weaving business and go to sea at the age of 14. After sailing for more than 10 years, Columbus settled in Lisbon, Portugal. His brother Bartholomew soon joined him, and the two brothers worked together as mapmakers—although Columbus continued to sail as well.

In 1479 Columbus married the sister of the governor of Porto Santo in the Madeira Islands and moved to the island to live. There he witnessed the use of enslaved Africans as forced labor on the sugar plantations. He would later introduce similar practices to America.

In the 1480s Columbus served on several Portuguese expeditions to Africa, where he schooled himself in

Atlantic currents and wind patterns. In the process, he developed his theory that the easiest way to reach Asia was to sail west across the Atlantic.

Despite his achievements, Columbus remained unhappy. A devout Christian, he believed God had destined him to find the western route to Asia and spread the Christian faith. He died in 1506, frustrated that he had not found Asia nor been given the honors and recognition that he felt he deserved.

In 1493, to prevent a war between the two rival Catholic nations, **Pope Alexander VI** established a line of demarcation, an imaginary north-to-south line running down the middle of the Atlantic. This line granted Spain control of everything west of the line and Portugal control of everything east. King John II of Portugal accepted the idea of division, but he asked for the line to be moved farther west.

The following year the two countries resolved their differences over the dividing line in the **Treaty of Tordesillas,** named for a town northwest of the Spanish capital, Madrid. The treaty moved the line almost 1,000 miles (1,609 km) to the west.

The Treaty of Tordesillas did two things. It confirmed Portugal's right to control the route around Africa to India, and it also confirmed Spain's claim to the new lands of America. Unknowingly, however, the line had been drawn so far west that it cut through part of South America, giving much of the land that is now Brazil to Portugal.

Naming America Interestingly enough, Columbus did not give his name to the new land he had encountered while trying to reach Asia. In 1499 an Italian named **Amerigo Vespucci,** sailing under the Spanish flag, repeated Columbus's initial attempt to sail west to Asia. Exploring part of the coast of South America, Vespucci, like Columbus, assumed that he had reached Asia.

Vespucci made his next voyage in 1501, this time commissioned by Portugal. He sailed far south along the coast of South America, and he eventually came to the conclusion that this large land mass could not be part of Asia. Vespucci's descriptions of America were published and widely read in Europe. In 1507 a German scholar named Martin Waldseemüller published a study in which he proposed that the new continent be named America for "Amerigo the discoverer."

Continuing Spanish Expeditions Even though Europe now knew that the Americas were not a part of Asia, explorers continued to chart the region. In 1513 the Spanish governor of Puerto Rico, **Juan Ponce de Leon,** sailed north. According to a traditional story, he was searching for a wondrous fountain that was said to magically restore youth, although historians have disputed whether or not

Why It Matters

The Columbian Exchange

European contact with the Americas marked the start of an extensive exchange of plants and animals between the two areas of the world. Dramatic changes resulted from the exchange of plant life, leading to a revolution in the diets of peoples in both hemispheres.

Maize (corn), potatoes, many kinds of beans, tomatoes, and pumpkins were among the products the Eastern Hemisphere received from the Americas. Meanwhile, the Eastern Hemisphere introduced rice, wheat, barley, oats, melons, coffee, bananas, and many other plants to the Western Hemisphere.

▲ **Animals**
The Spanish reintroduced horses to the Americas. Horses native to the Americas had died out during the Ice Age. Their reintroduction transformed Native American societies.

◄ **Plants**
By about 1600, American maize and sweet potatoes were staple crops in China. They contributed to a worldwide population explosion beginning in this period.

this was really his motivation. In any event, De Leon did discover a land full of blooming wildflowers and fragrant plants. Before leaving, he gave it the name **Florida,** which means "land of flowers."

Spanish explorers continued to search for a passage to China and India by sailing west. In 1510 **Vasco de Balboa,** a planter from Hispaniola trying to escape his creditors, stowed away on a ship heading to the American mainland. There he founded a colony on the Isthmus of Panama. After hearing tales from Native Americans of a "south sea" that led to an empire of gold, Balboa hacked his way across steamy, disease-ridden jungles and swamps until he reached the opposite coast. There, in 1513, Balboa became the first European to reach the Pacific coast of America.

In 1520 **Ferdinand Magellan,** a Portuguese mariner working for Spain, discovered the strait later named for him at the southernmost tip of South America. After navigating its stormy narrows, he sailed into the ocean Balboa had seen. Its waters seemed so peaceful, or *pacific,* that Magellan gave the new ocean that name. Although Magellan died in the Philippine Islands, his crew continued west, arriving in Spain in 1522. They became the first known people to circumnavigate, or sail around, the globe.

✔ **Reading Check** **Analyzing** Why was the Treaty of Tordesillas important?

The Columbian Exchange

The arrival of European colonists in the Americas set in motion a series of complex interactions between peoples and environments. These interactions, called the Columbian Exchange, permanently altered the world's ecosystems and changed nearly every culture around the world.

From America to Europe Native Americans taught the Europeans local farming methods and introduced them to new crops. Corn, which colonists soon adopted as a basic food, traveled back to Spain on Columbus's very first journey and then spread to the rest of Europe. Other American foods, such as squash, pumpkins, beans, sweet potatoes, tomatoes, chili peppers, peanuts, chocolate, and potatoes also made their way to Europe, as did tobacco and chewing gum.

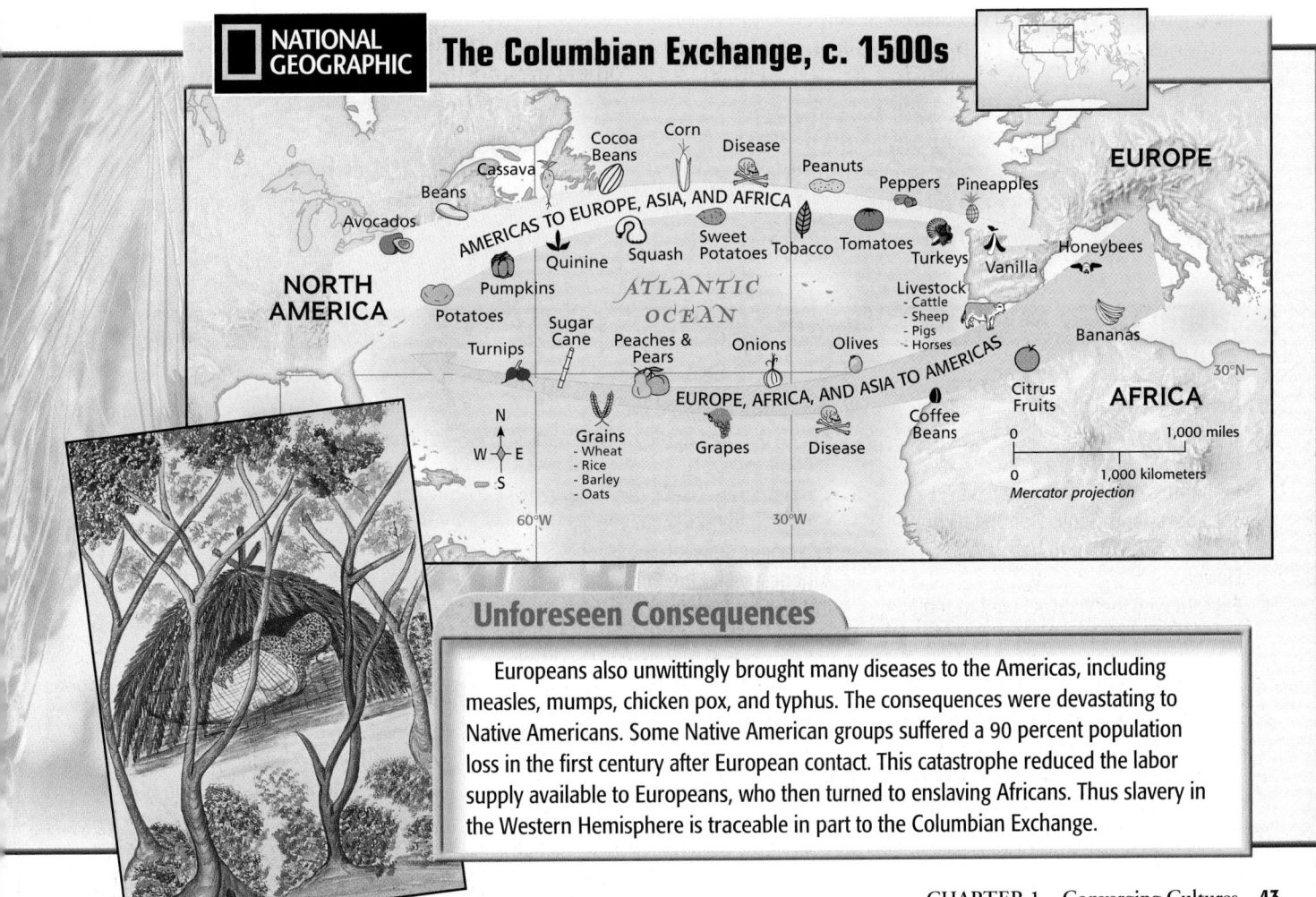

NATIONAL GEOGRAPHIC **The Columbian Exchange, c. 1500s**

Unforeseen Consequences

Europeans also unwittingly brought many diseases to the Americas, including measles, mumps, chicken pox, and typhus. The consequences were devastating to Native Americans. Some Native American groups suffered a 90 percent population loss in the first century after European contact. This catastrophe reduced the labor supply available to Europeans, who then turned to enslaving Africans. Thus slavery in the Western Hemisphere is traceable in part to the Columbian Exchange.

Spain, 1492 Christopher Columbus proudly carried the Spanish banner of Castile and Leon to the shores of the Bahamas. The flag's castle represented Queen Isabella. The lion symbolized her husband, King Ferdinand.

Perhaps the most important discovery for Europeans was the potato. European farmers learned that if they planted potatoes instead of rye, about four times as many people could live off the same amount of land. Europeans also adopted many devices invented by Native Americans, including the canoe, the snowshoe, the hammock, the poncho, the toboggan, and the parka.

From Europe to America The Europeans introduced Native Americans to wheat, oats, barley, rye, rice, coffee, dandelions, onions, bananas, and oranges and other new citrus fruits, none of which existed in America. Europeans also brought over domestic livestock such as chickens, cattle, pigs, sheep, and horses. In addition, they introduced Native Americans to a range of technologies, including new types of metalworking, new techniques of shipbuilding, and new forms of weapons, including firearms.

No beneficial European import, however, could ever offset the dreadful effects of an invisible one—the bacteria and viruses that caused such diseases as influenza, measles, chicken pox, mumps, typhus, and smallpox. Native Americans had never experienced these diseases and had no immunity. Exposure led to catastrophic epidemics in which millions of Native Americans died.

The movement of disease, however, was not one-way. Native American illnesses made their way to Europe as well, where they infected millions of people. Unlike European diseases, Native American illnesses did not lead to a catastrophic collapse of the European population.

No one in Columbus's time could have imagined the course of events in the Americas that have led to the present day. Some people feel that the tragic epidemics and military conquests that devastated the Native Americans and the subsequent introduction of slavery overshadow the positive effects of the exchange Columbus initiated. The human drama that unfolded over the next few centuries, however, also led ultimately to the founding of the United States. Despite tragic events along the way, the people of the United States managed to build a nation that honors the worth of the individual and protects the rights and freedoms of its citizens and others around the globe. This too is one of the legacies of Christopher Columbus.

✓ **Reading Check** **Describing** Why did millions of Native Americans die as a result of contact with Europeans?

SECTION 5 ASSESSMENT

Checking for Understanding

1. **Define:** line of demarcation, circumnavigate, Columbian Exchange.
2. **Identify:** Vikings, Christopher Columbus, Claudius Ptolemy, San Salvador Island, Santo Domingo, Pope Alexander VI, Amerigo Vespucci, Florida.
3. **Explain** why the Vikings failed to settle in Newfoundland.

Reviewing Themes

4. **Global Connections** How did the maps drawn by Ptolemy and al-Idrisi revolutionize European sea exploration?

Critical Thinking

5. **Analyzing** Why did the king and queen of Spain agree to Columbus's second voyage?
6. **Categorizing** Use a graphic organizer similar to the one below to list the exchanges between the Native Americans and the Europeans in the Columbian Exchange.

Columbian Exchange

Europeans Received	Native Americans Received

Analyzing Visuals

7. **Examining Images** Study the images on pages 42 and 43 illustrating the importance of the Columbian Exchange. Do you think the positive effects of the exchange outweigh the negative effects? Explain your answer.

Writing About History

8. **Descriptive Writing** Take on the role of a sailor on Columbus's first voyage to the Americas. Write a journal entry about the Caribbean islands you encounter.

Social Studies SKILLBUILDER

Reading a Time Line

c. 1000
Vikings arrive

1270s
Drought forces Anasazi to abandon pueblos

c. 1300
Cahokia collapses; fighting breaks out among Iroquois

1492
Columbus arrives

The Americas

1000–1100s | 1200s | 1300s | 1400s

The World

1095
Pope Urban II launches Crusades

1271
Marco Polo journeys to China

1324
Mansa Musa makes pilgrimage to Makkah

1475
Ptolemy's *Geography* is republished

Why Learn This Skill?

When you read a time line, you see not only when an event took place but also what events took place before and after it. A time line can help you develop the skill of **chronological thinking.** Developing a strong sense of chronology—when events took place and in what order they took place—will help you examine relationships among the events. It will also help you understand what events caused or were the result of other events.

Learning the Skill

A time line is a chart that lists events that occurred between specific dates. The number of years between dates is the **time span.** A time line that begins in 1490 and ends in 1500 has a 10-year time span. Some time lines are divided into centuries. The twentieth century includes the 1900s, the nineteenth century includes the 1800s, and so on.

Time lines are usually divided into smaller segments, or **time intervals.** If you look at the two time lines below, you will see that the first time line has a 30-year time span divided into 10-year time intervals, and the second time line has a 6-year time span divided into 2-year time intervals.

1400   1410   1420   1430

1490   1492   1494   1496

Practicing the Skill

Sometimes a time line shows events that occurred during the same time period but in two different parts of the world. The time line above shows some events in the Americas and in the rest of the world during the same time span. Study the time line, and then answer the questions.

❶ What time span and intervals appear on this time line?

❷ What two important events took place around A.D. 1300 in North America?

❸ About how many years before Ptolemy's *Geography* was republished did the Vikings reach North America?

❹ When did Pope Urban II begin the Crusades?

Skills Assessment

Complete the Practicing Skills questions on page 47 and the Chapter 1 Skill Reinforcement Activity to assess your mastery of this skill.

Applying the Skill

Reading a Time Line Extend the time line on this page to include at least five additional events that took place in North America between A.D. 500 and 1000.

Glencoe's **Skillbuilder Interactive Workbook CD-ROM, Level 2,** provides instruction and practice in key social studies skills.

Reviewing Key Terms

On a sheet of paper, use each of these terms in a sentence.

1. radiocarbon dating
2. Ice Age
3. glacier
4. nomad
5. agricultural revolution
6. maize
7. civilization
8. obsidian
9. kiva
10. pueblo
11. kachina
12. slash-and-burn agriculture
13. longhouse
14. wigwam
15. kinship group
16. savannah
17. mosque
18. matrilineal
19. feudalism
20. manorialism
21. serf
22. Renaissance
23. astrolabe
24. caravel
25. line of demarcation
26. circumnavigate
27. Columbian Exchange

Reviewing Key Facts

28. **Identify:** Dekanawidah, Hiawatha, Henry the Navigator, Bartolomeu Dias, Vasco da Gama, Christopher Columbus, Claudius Ptolemy, Pope Alexander VI, Amerigo Vespucci.

29. How and why did Asians migrate to the Americas during the Ice Age?

30. How do scientists determine the age of ancient artifacts?

31. Why did some Native American groups settle in villages while other Native Americans groups were nomads?

32. How and why did the arrival of camels affect the trans-Saharan trade in West Africa?

33. How did the religion of Islam spread throughout West Africa?

34. What were four major factors that encouraged European exploration in the 1400s and 1500s?

35. Why were Europeans searching for a sea route to Asia?

36. What new inventions increased agricultural yields in Europe in the Middle Ages?

Chapter Summary

Europe

- **A.D. 1095–late 1400s:** The Crusades, the emergence of strong states, the Renaissance, and new technology lead to European exploration of Africa and North America.
- **1400s:** European explorers discover gold and sugarcane, which leads to the first enslavement of African peoples by Europeans.
- **Late 1400s:** Europeans encounter the Americas and later colonize the area, leading to the expansion of the slave trade.

North America

- **About 30,000 years ago:** Asians begin migrating to North America.
- **Between 9,000 and 10,000 years ago:** Agricultural revolution begins.
- **A.D. 200–late 1500s:** Various Native American culture groups shaped by the environment develop.
- **1500s:** Native American groups begin to be affected by European diseases and military conquests.
- **1565–early 1600s:** Spanish and French establish towns in St. Augustine, Quebec, and Santa Fe.

Africa

- **A.D. 400–1450:** Various African groups with different cultures shaped by the environment developed in West, Central, and Southern Africa.
- **1300s and 1400s:** The arrival of Arabs and Europeans leads to the beginning of the slave trade; many cultures are destroyed by the demand for enslaved Africans.

HISTORY Online

Self-Check Quiz

Visit the *American Vision* Web site at tav.glencoe.com and click on **Self-Check Quizzes—Chapter 1** to assess your knowledge of chapter content.

Critical Thinking

37. Analyzing Themes: Cultures and Traditions How did environment, climate, and food supplies influence the lifestyles of early peoples in the Americas?

38. Forming an Opinion If you had been King Ferdinand or Queen Isabella, would you have agreed to support Christopher Columbus on his voyages to the Americas? Why or why not?

39. Sequencing Use a graphic organizer similar to the one below to list some major events in the early history of the Americas.

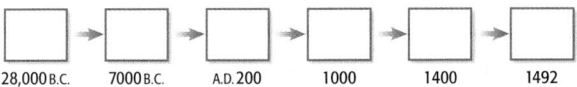

28,000 B.C. → 7000 B.C. → A.D. 200 → 1000 → 1400 → 1492

Practicing Skills

40. Reading a Time Line Refer to the time line on page 45. Then answer the following questions.

   a. Interpreting Time Lines What is the time span on this time line?

   b. Synthesizing Information How much time elapsed between the publication of Ptolemy's *Geography* and Columbus's landing in America?

Chapter Activities

41. Technology Activity: Using a Database Search a library or the Internet to find information about the early civilizations in the Americas and in Africa that were discussed in this chapter. Build a database collecting information about the cultures of these early civilizations. Include information about religious customs and traditions, ways of making a living, government, and housing. Include a map showing the locations of these civilizations.

42. American History Primary Source Document Library CD-ROM Read "Letter From Christopher Columbus" under *Exploring the Americas.* Work with a few of your classmates to describe how Columbus mapped the region he visited.

Writing Activity

43. Portfolio Writing Choose an early civilization described in the chapter and write a script for a scene in a documentary about it. Describe the location of the scene, what the scene would be like, and what the people in the scene would be doing. Place the script in your portfolio.

NATIONAL GEOGRAPHIC

The Crusades, 1095–1204

Christian world
Islamic world
1st Crusade
2nd Crusade
3rd Crusade
4th Crusade

Geography and History

44. The map above shows the routes of the Crusades. Study the map and answer the questions below.

   a. Interpreting Maps Which Crusade ended at Constantinople?

   b. Applying Geography Skills Which Crusade traveled almost exclusively by land?

Standardized Test Practice

Directions: Choose the best answer to the following question.

As part of the Columbian Exchange, Spanish explorers brought such things as chocolate and tobacco from the Americas to Europe. What is one thing they brought from Europe to the Americas?

A Hieroglyphic writing

B Democratic government

C Horses

D Corn

Test-Taking Tip: Eliminate answers that don't make sense. For instance, the Spanish had a monarchy, not a democracy. Therefore, it would be illogical for them to bring democratic government to the Americas.

2 Colonizing America *1519–1733*

Why It Matters

Spanish, French, and English colonists came to North America. The colonies they founded often reflected the values and traditions of their homelands. These values and traditions helped shape core beliefs that most Americans share today.

The Impact Today

Several developments of the early colonial period are evident in the nation today.
- *The language and culture of the southwestern United States reflect the influence of the early Spanish settlers.*
- *Religious conflicts convinced the colonists of the importance of toleration and freedom of religion, values important to Americans today.*
- *The democratic traditions and institutions of the modern United States originated during colonial times.*

The* American Vision *Video *The Chapter 2 video, "Early Explorers," chronicles the voyages of some of the early European explorers.*

1519
- Cortés arrives on the Mexican coast

1526
- Pizarro encounters the Inca in Peru

1609–1610
- Santa Fe founded

1608
- Champlain founds Quebec

The Americas

1500   *1550*   *1600*

World

1517
- Protestant Reformation begins

1527
- Henry VIII breaks with Catholic Church

1588
- English defeat Spanish Armada

1600
- Tokugawa period of feudal rule begins in Japan

This 1638 painting by Dutch artist Adam Willaerts
is believed to depict the Plymouth colony.

1619
• First meeting of
Virginia House of
Burgesses

1680
• Popé leads Native American
rebellion in New Mexico

1630
• Massachusetts Bay
Colony established

1681
• William Penn's charter
for Pennsylvania granted

1650

1700

1642
• English Civil
War begins

1688
• Glorious Revolution establishes
limited monarchy in England

HISTORY
Online

Chapter Overview
Visit the *American Vision*
Web site at tav.glencoe.com
and click on ***Chapter
Overviews—Chapter 2*** to
preview chapter information.

The Spanish and French Build Empires

Guide to Reading

Main Idea
The Spanish and French colonies in America reflected the values of European society and the geography of the regions in which they settled.

Key Terms and Names
conquistador, Francisco Pizarro, presidio, Popé, *hidalgo, encomienda,* hacienda, vaquero, Northwest Passage, coureur de bois

Reading Strategy
Taking Notes As you read about the Spanish and French colonies in America, use the section headings to create an outline similar to the one below.

The Spanish and French Build Empires
I.   The Conquest of Mexico
     A.
     B.
II.
     A.
     B.
     C.

Reading Objectives
- **Explain** the early Spanish settlement of North America.
- **Describe** the colonial society in New France.

Section Theme
Global Connections European colonizers shaped the new cultures of North America.

Preview of Events

♦1500   ♦1550   ♦1600   ♦1650

1519
Cortés lands on Mexican coast

1532
Pizarro invades Incan empire

1565
St. Augustine, Florida, established

1608
City of Quebec founded

1609–1610
Santa Fe, New Mexico, founded

★ An American Story ★

In the spring of 1519, a courier arrived in Tenochtitlán, capital of the Aztec empire. He had news for the emperor, Montezuma II. Bearded white men bearing crosses were encamped on the eastern shores of the emperor's realm.

Montezuma was worried. For several years he had heard reports of strange men with "very light skin" operating in the Caribbean. His subjects had also seen "towers or small mountains floating on the waves of the sea." Now these strange white men had come to his lands, and Montezuma did not know what to do.

The men on the coast were Spanish soldiers. As they watched the soldiers, the people of eastern Mexico felt both fear and awe. One Aztec later recalled:

❝They came in battle array, as conquerors . . . their spears glinted in the sun, and their pennons fluttered like bats. They made a loud clamor as they marched, for their coats of mail and their weapons clashed and rattled. . . . They terrified everyone who saw them.❞

—quoted in *The Broken Spears: The Aztec Account of the Conquest of Mexico*

The Conquest of Mexico

Leading the Spanish march into the Aztec empire was a 34-year-old Spaniard named **Hernán Cortés.** At age 19, Cortés had boarded a ship bound for the Spanish Indies determined to make his fortune. He had no idea then that 15 years later he would overturn a civilization and change the lives of millions of people.

The Spanish Encounter the Aztec

In 1511 Spanish troops, led by **Diego Velázquez,** conquered Cuba. Cortés took part in the invasion, and his courage impressed Velázquez. He rewarded Cortés by giving him control of several Native American villages.

Six years later, smallpox swept across Cuba, killing thousands of Native Americans. Without Native American labor, the farms and mines the Spanish had built in Cuba could not function. Velázquez asked Cortés to lead an expedition to the Yucatán Peninsula to find new peoples who could be forced to work for the Spanish. He also wanted to investigate reports of a wealthy civilization there. On February 18, 1519, Cortés set sail for Mexico. He had 11 ships, 550 men, and 16 horses.

The Invasion Begins

After crossing the Gulf of Mexico, Cortés landed in the Yucatán Peninsula. There he found a shipwrecked sailor—Jerónimo de Aguilar—who spoke the local language and could act as translator. Despite this advantage, Cortés could not prevent an attack by thousands of warriors from a nearby city. The battle showed that the Spanish had a technological advantage over the local people. Spanish swords, crossbows, guns, and cannons quickly killed more than 200 warriors. As a peace offering, the leaders of the city gave Cortés 20 young women. Cortés then continued up the coast.

The people farther up the coast spoke a language Aguilar did not know, but among the 20 women traveling with the Spanish was **Malinche,** a woman who knew the language. She translated for Aguilar and he translated the words into Spanish for Cortés. Malinche impressed Cortés. He had her baptized, giving her the name Marina. He called her Doña Marina, and she became one of his closest advisers.

From his talks with local rulers, Cortés learned that the Aztec had conquered many peoples in the region and were at war with others, including the powerful Tlaxcalan people. He realized that if he acted carefully, he might convince the Tlaxcalan to join him against the Aztec.

As Cortés marched inland to Tlaxcala, his army's physical appearance helped him gain allies. The local people had never seen horses before. Their foaming muzzles and the glistening armor they wore were astonishing and terrifying, and when they charged it seemed to one Aztec chronicler "as if stones were raining on the earth." Equally terrifying were the "shooting sparks" of the Spanish cannons. After several encounters that displayed Spanish power, the Tlaxcalan agreed to join with Cortés.

Two hundred miles away, Montezuma had to decide how to respond to the Spanish. He believed in a prophecy that said that the god **Quetzalcoatl**—a fair-skinned, bearded deity—would someday return from the east to conquer the Aztec. Montezuma did not know if Cortés was Quetzalcoatl, but he did not want to attack him until he knew for sure.

When he learned Cortés was negotiating with the Tlaxcalan, Montezuma sent envoys to meet the Spanish leader. The envoys promised Cortés that Montezuma would pay a yearly tribute to the king of Spain if Cortés halted his advance. To further appease the Spanish, the envoys sacrificed several captives and gave their blood to the Spanish to drink. The act horrified the Spanish and alarmed Montezuma, since he knew that Quetzalcoatl also hated human sacrifice.

With a joint Spanish-Tlaxcalan force heading toward him, Montezuma decided to ambush Cortés at the city of Cholula. Warned of the ambush by Doña Marina, the Spanish attacked first, killing over 6,000 Cholulans. Montezuma now believed Cortés could not be stopped. On November 8, 1519, Spanish troops peacefully entered the Aztec capital of Tenochtitlán.

TURNING POINT

Cortés Defeats the Aztec

Sitting on an island in the center of a lake, the city of Tenochtitlán astonished the Spanish. It was larger than most European cities. The central plaza had a huge double pyramid, and canoes carried people along stone canals around the city.

Spanish suit of armor, helmet, and pistols

Different Viewpoints

The Spanish in Mexico

Historians are still not sure exactly what took place when Hernán Cortés arrived in Tenochtitlán in 1519. The Aztec version of events was recorded in artists' sketches and passed down verbally for centuries, while Cortés and others, seeking to justify what they had done, wrote the original Spanish reports. To determine what actually took place, historians must compare the stories and other evidence and draw their own conclusions.

The battle in Tenochtitlán

Cortés describes events to Spanish Emperor Charles V:

"I asked [Montezuma] to send some of his own men, to whom I would add an equal number of Spaniards, to the estates and houses of those nobles who had publicly offered themselves as vassals of your Majesty, asking them to do your Majesty some service with what riches they might possess. . . . With my men he sent his own, ordering them to visit the rulers of those cities and to require each one of them in my name a certain measure of gold. And so it came about that each one of those lords to whom he sent gave very freely when he was asked, whether jewels, small bars and plates of gold and silver, or other valuables which he possessed; of all this treasure gathered together the fifth due to your Majesty amounted to over two thousand four hundred *pesos* of gold. . . ."

Conquistador's sword

—quoted in *Five Letters of Cortés to the Emperor*

Some of what the Spanish saw here horrified them as well. The central plaza, for example, contained the *tzompantli*—a huge rack displaying thousands of human skulls—and the Aztec priests wore their long hair matted down with dried human blood.

Surrounded by thousands of Aztec, Cortés decided to take Montezuma hostage. Montezuma, resigned to his fate, did not resist. Under instructions from Cortés, he stopped all human sacrifice and ordered the statues of the gods to be replaced with Christian crosses and images of the Virgin Mary.

Enraged at their loss of power, the Aztec priests organized a rebellion in the spring of 1520. The battle raged for days. Spanish cannons and crossbows killed thousands of Aztec. While trying to stop the fighting, Montezuma was hit by stones and later died. Realizing they would soon be overrun, the Spanish fought their way out of the city. Over 450 Spaniards died in the battle, as did more than 4,000 Aztec, in what became known as *Noche Triste*—the "Sad Night."

Although he had been driven from the city, Cortés refused to give up. He and his men took refuge with the Tlaxcalan and began building boats to attack the Aztec capital by water. At the same time, smallpox erupted in the region. Tens of thousands of Native Americans died. As one Aztec recorded, the disease devastated the defenders of Tenochtitlán:

> 66While the Spaniards were in Tlaxcala, a great plague broke out here in Tenochtitlán. . . . Sores erupted on our faces, our breasts, our bellies; we were covered with agonizing sores from head to foot. The illness was so dreadful that no one could walk or move. . . . If they did move their bodies, they screamed with pain.99

—quoted in *The Broken Spears: The Aztec Account of the Conquest of Mexico*

Finally, in May 1521, Cortés launched his attack against the greatly weakened Aztec forces. His fleet sank the Aztec canoes and landed troops in the city. By August 1521, Cortés had won.

✔ **Reading Check** **Examining** What was the purpose of Hernán Cortés's expedition to Mexico?

New Spain Expands

After defeating the Aztec, Cortés ordered a new city to be built on the ruins of Tenochtitlán. The city, named Mexico, became the capital of the new

The Aztec view of the Spanish actions:

"When the Spaniards were installed in the palace, they asked Motecuhzoma [Montezuma] about the city's resources and reserves. . . . They questioned him closely and then demanded gold. Motecuhzoma guided them to it. . . . When they arrived at the treasure house called Teucalco, the riches of gold and feathers were brought out to them. . . . Next they went to Motecuhzoma's storehouse, in the place called Totocalco [Palace of the Birds], where his personal treasures were kept. The Spaniards grinned like little beasts and patted each other with delight. When they entered the hall of treasures, it was as if they had arrived in Paradise. They searched everywhere and coveted everything; they were slaves to their own greed. . . . They seized these treasures as if they were their own, as if this plunder were merely a stroke of good luck."

Aztec war club

—quoted in *The Broken Spears: The Aztec Account of the Conquest of Mexico*

Learning From History

1. How would you describe the different tones and attitudes in each account?
2. What factors should you consider when evaluating why these passages present different versions of the same events?

Spanish colony of **New Spain.** Cortés then sent several expeditions to conquer the rest of the region. The men who led these expeditions became known as conquistadors, or "conquerors."

Pizarro Conquers the Inca

While the Spanish were fighting for control of Central America, a Spanish army captain named **Francisco Pizarro** began exploring South America's west coast. In 1526 he landed in Peru and encountered the Inca empire. After the Spanish king granted him permission to conquer the Inca, Pizarro returned to Peru in 1531 with a small force. When he later marched inland in the spring of 1532, he learned that a powerful emperor named Atahualpa governed the Inca. After reaching the Incan town of Cajamarca, Pizarro sent his brother to find Atahualpa and invite him to Cajamarca.

While waiting for the emperor to arrive, Pizarro hid cavalry and cannons around the town square. If Atahualpa refused to submit to Spain, Pizarro intended to kidnap him. When Atahualpa arrived, he entered the square backed by some 6,000 of his followers. Pizarro sent a priest to meet Atahualpa first. When the priest gave a Bible to Atahualpa, the emperor

threw it to the ground. This rejection of Christianity was enough for Pizarro, who ordered the cannons to fire and the cavalry to charge. He and 20 soldiers then rushed the emperor and took him prisoner.

Pizarro tried to rule Peru by keeping Atahualpa as a hostage. Less than a year later, however, he executed the Incan emperor and installed a series of figurehead emperors who ruled in name only and had to follow his orders. Although many people accepted the new system created by Pizarro, others fled to the mountains and continued to fight the Spanish conquistadors until 1572.

Searching for Cities of Gold

Pizarro's success in finding Peru fueled rumors of other wealthy cities. In 1528, Pánfilo de Narváez searched northern Florida for a fabled city of gold. Finding nothing and having lost contact with his ships, Narváez and his men built rafts and tried to sail to Mexico by following the coastline. They made it to what is today Texas, although most of the men, including Narváez, died in the attempt. The survivors, led by **Álvar Núñez Cabeza de Vaca** and an enslaved man named Estéban, wandered across Texas and New Mexico before reaching New Spain in 1536.

Many conquistadors had also heard tales of the Seven Golden Cities of Cibola rumored to exist north of New Spain. Hoping to find Cibola, the Spanish sent a large expedition northward in 1540 under the command of **Francisco Vásquez de Coronado.** For several months Coronado wandered through the southwestern area of what is today the United States. Members of his expedition traveled west to the Colorado River and east into territory that today belongs to Kansas. Finding nothing but wind-swept plains and strange "shaggy cows" (buffalo), Coronado returned to Mexico.

While Coronado explored the southwestern region of North America, **Hernando de Soto** took a large expedition into the region north of Florida. De Soto's expedition explored parts of what are today North Carolina, Tennessee, Alabama, Arkansas, and Texas. As they crisscrossed the region, the Spanish killed many Native Americans and raided their villages for supplies. After more than four years of wandering, the expedition returned to New Spain, but without De Soto, who had become sick and died. His men buried him in the Mississippi River.

The Spanish Settle the Southwest

The failure of explorers to find gold or other wealth north of New Spain slowed Spanish settlement of the region. It was not until 1598 that settlers, led by Juan de Oñate, migrated north of the Rio Grande. Oñate's expedition almost perished while crossing northern Mexico. When they finally reached the Rio Grande, the survivors organized a feast to give thanks. This "Spanish Thanksgiving" is celebrated each April in El Paso, Texas.

The Spanish gave the name **New Mexico** to the territory north of New Spain. Pedro de Peralta, the first governor of New Mexico, founded the capital city of Santa Fe in 1609 or 1610. The Spanish also built forts called presidios throughout the region to protect settlers and to serve as trading posts. Despite these efforts, few Spaniards migrated to the harsh region. Instead, the Catholic Church became the primary force for colonizing the Southwest.

Throughout the seventeenth and eighteenth centuries, Spanish priests built missions and spread the Christian faith among the Navaho and Pueblo peoples of New Mexico. Beginning in 1769, Spanish missionaries led by the Franciscan priest **Junipero Serra** took control of California by establishing a chain of missions from San Diego to San Francisco. A road called **El Camino Real**—or the Royal Highway—linked the missions together.

The priests and missionaries in California and those in New Mexico took different approaches to their work. In California, they forced the mostly nomadic Native Americans to live in villages near the missions. In New Mexico, on the other hand, the priests and missionaries adapted their efforts to fit into the lifestyle of the Pueblo people. They built churches near where the Pueblo people lived and farmed, and tried to teach them Catholic ideas and European culture.

Picturing History

Mission Life The oldest surviving mission in Santa Fe, the Chapel of San Miguel, is a reminder of Spanish colonial rule. What role did missions play in Spanish rule?

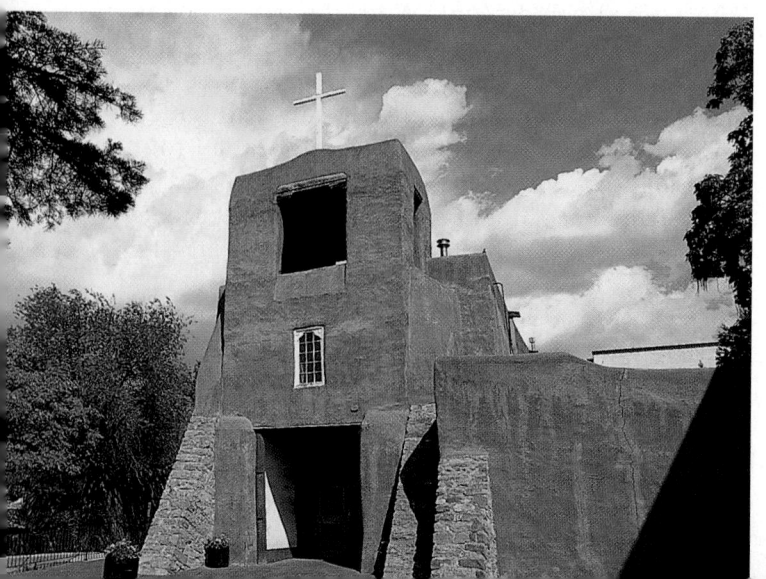

The Spanish priests tried to end traditional Pueblo religious practices that conflicted with Catholic beliefs. Some priests beat and whipped Native Americans who defied them. In response, a Native American religious leader named **Popé** organized an uprising against the Spanish in 1680. Some 17,000 warriors destroyed most of the missions in New Mexico. It took the Spanish more than a decade to regain control of the region.

Reading Check **Identifying** Where did most people who colonized the southwest part of North America come from?

Spanish American Society

The society that developed in New Spain was a product of the Spanish conquest. The conquistadors were adventurers. Most were low-ranking nobles, called hidalgos, or working-class tradespeople. They had come to the colonies in America in search of wealth and prestige. The society they built in America reflected those goals.

The *Encomienda* System After defeating the Aztec, Cortés rewarded his men by giving each of them control over some of the towns in the Aztec empire. This was called the encomienda system. Each Spaniard deserving a reward was made an encomendero, or commissioner, and was given control over a group of Native American villages. The villagers had to pay their encomendero a share of the products they harvested or produced.

Under this system, the encomendero had obligations too. He was supposed to protect the Native Americans and work to convert them to Christianity. Unfortunately, many encomenderos abused their power. Native Americans were frequently overworked, and many died.

A Society Based on Class The people of Spain's colonies in the Americas formed a highly structured society. Birth, income, and education determined a person's position. At the top were *peninsulares*—people who had been born in Spain and who were appointed to most of the higher government and church positions. Below the *peninsulares* were *criollos* (kree·OH·yohs)—those born in the colonies of Spanish parents. Many *criollos* were wealthy, but high colonial positions were reserved only for *peninsulares*.

Mestizos made up the next level of society. They were of mixed Spanish and Native American parentage. Since many Spanish immigrants married Native

Americans, there were many *mestizos*, and their social status varied greatly. A few were accepted at the top of society. Others worked as artisans, merchants, and shopkeepers. Most, however, were poor and lived at the lowest level of society. The lowest level also included Native Americans, Africans, and people of mixed Spanish and African or African and Native American ancestry. These people provided most of the labor for New Spain's farms, mines, and ranches.

To govern this vast, diverse empire in America, the Spanish king created the **Council of the Indies.** The Council advised the king and watched over all colonial activities. To manage local affairs, the king created a special court in Mexico known as the *audiencia*. The *audiencia's* members were not only judges but also administrators and lawmakers. To ensure that his interests were represented, the king divided his American empire into regions called viceroyalties. He then appointed a viceroy to rule each region as his representative.

Mining and Ranching When the Spanish realized that most Native American cities did not have much gold, they set up mines and used Native American labor to extract minerals from the ground. Ultimately, however, it was not gold that enriched Spain, but silver. The Spanish discovered huge deposits of silver ore in the 1540s and set up mining camps all across northern Mexico, transforming the economy. The work in the dark, damp mineshafts was very difficult. Many miners were killed by explosions and cave-ins. Others died from exhaustion.

Many of the silver mines were located in the arid lands of the north. The land could not grow crops, but it could feed vast herds of cattle and sheep. To feed the miners, Spaniards created large cattle ranches in northern Mexico. These huge ranches covering thousands of acres were called haciendas. The men who herded the cattle were called vaqueros, and cowhands in the United States later adopted their lifestyle. The words *lasso* and *corral* are Spanish words that originated with the vaqueros.

✓ **Reading Check** **Describing** Why did the Spaniards set up mines and cattle ranches in northern Mexico?

The French Empire in America

In 1524, three years after Cortés conquered the Aztec, King Francis I of France sent **Giovanni da Verrazano** to map North America's coastline. Francis wanted to find the Northwest Passage—the northern route through North America to the Pacific Ocean. Verrazano mapped the coastline from North Carolina to Newfoundland, but he found no sign of a passage through the continent. Ten years later, as he watched Spain's powerful empire grow stronger, Francis sent another explorer named **Jacques Cartier** to North America.

France Explores America On his first two trips to North America, Cartier discovered and mapped the St. Lawrence River. He then returned a third time in 1541 intending to found a colony, but the harsh winter convinced him to return to France. In the decades after Cartier's last voyage, fighting between Catholics and Protestants tore apart France. For the next 60 years, the French government made no further attempt to colonize North America. In the early 1600s, however, the French government's interest revived.

New France Is Founded In the 1500s, the French began to fish near North America. The fishing crews often went ashore to trade their goods for furs from the Native Americans. By 1600 fur—particularly beaver fur—had become very fashionable in Europe. As the demand for fur increased, French merchants became interested in expanding the fur trade. In 1602 King Henry IV of France authorized a group of French merchants to create colonies in North America.

The merchants hired the royal geographer, **Samuel de Champlain,** to help them colonize North America. In 1605 Champlain helped establish a French colony in Acadia, what is today Nova Scotia. The site was attractive because of the many rivers that flowed to Acadia's eastern seaboard. In 1608 he founded Quebec, which became the capital of the new colony of **New France.**

Linking Past & Present

Refugee Migration to America

Past: The Huguenots
French Protestants, known as Huguenots, migrated to America in large numbers during the late 1600s. Violent persecutions under King Louis XIV caused around one million people to leave France. Many settled in South Carolina, while others found sanctuary in Rhode Island, New York, and Virginia.

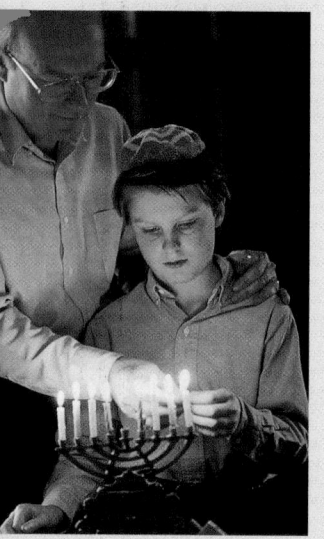

Present: Jewish Immigration
Following the tragic events of World War II, thousands of homeless European Jews came to the United States. Many Eastern Jews, particularly from Iran and Syria, soon followed. With the collapse of the Soviet Union in 1991, many Russian Jews migrated to America. Unlike the Russian immigrants of the 1800s, these Jews had little opportunity to maintain Jewish customs or to study Hebrew.

Life in New France The company that founded New France wanted to make money from the fur trade, and so they did not need settlers to clear the land and build farms. As a result the colony grew slowly, and by 1666 it had just over 3,000 people. Most of the fur traders did not even live in the colony. Known as coureurs de bois (ku·RUHR·duh·BWAH), or "runners of the woods," the fur traders lived among the Native Americans with whom they traded. They learned their languages and customs and often married Native American women.

The fur traders were not the only ones who traveled into the woods to live with the Native Americans. Soon after the founding of Quebec, Jesuit missionaries arrived intending to convert the Native Americans to Christianity. Known as "black robes" to the Native Americans, the Jesuits tried to live among the local people and teach them the Catholic faith.

✓ **Reading Check** **Explaining** Why did King Francis I of France send Verrazano and Cartier to America?

New France Expands

The slow growth of New France worried the French as they watched the Spanish and English build prosperous colonies farther south. Finally, in 1663, France's king Louis XIV seized control of New France and made it a royal colony. His government then launched a series of projects to expand the colony's population.

The French government began by shipping over 4,000 immigrants to New France. It then sent over 900 young women to provide wives for the many single men in the colony. If a woman under 16 or a man under 20 married, they received a royal wedding gift. Parents who had more than 10 children received financial bonuses. Fathers whose children did not get married early were fined. By the 1670s the population was nearly 7,000, and by 1760 it was over 60,000.

Exploring the Mississippi In addition to promoting immigration to New France, the French government began exploring North America. In 1673 a fur trader named **Louis Joliet** and a Jesuit priest named **Jacques Marquette** set off in search of a waterway the Algonquian people called the "big river"—the Mississippi. Canoeing along inland lakes and rivers, the two men finally found the Mississippi River and followed it as far south as the Arkansas River. In 1682 **René-Robert Cavelier de La Salle** (known as Lord La Salle) followed the Mississippi all the way to the Gulf of Mexico, becoming the first European to do so.

La Salle then claimed the region for France, and he named the entire territory Louisiana in honor of King Louis XIV.

GEOGRAPHY

Settling Louisiana **Count Frontenac,** the governor of New France, hoped to ship furs to France by way of the Mississippi River and the Gulf of Mexico. Unfortunately, settling the lower Mississippi proved to be very difficult. The coastline had no good harbors, and shifting sandbars made navigation dangerous. The oppressive heat caused food to spoil quickly. The swamps were breeding grounds for mosquitoes that spread yellow fever and malaria.

The French did not permanently settle the region until 1698, when Lord d'Iberville founded Biloxi, in what is today Mississippi. Over the next few decades, more French settlements appeared in Louisiana, including Mobile and New Orleans. Farther upriver, the French built several forts, including Fort St. Louis and Fort Detroit, to ensure control of the Mississippi River.

The French settlers in southern Louisiana realized that the crops that could be grown there, such as sugar, rice, tobacco, and indigo, required hard manual labor. Few settlers were willing to do that kind of labor unless they were paid extremely well. Enslaved people, on the other hand, could be compelled to do the work. By 1721 the French in Louisiana had imported over 1,800 enslaved Africans to work on their plantations.

Rivalry With Spain The Spanish had always been concerned about the French colonies in North America. Indeed, they had founded the town of St. Augustine, Florida, in 1565 to protect their claim

Fact **Fiction** **Folklore**

Flag of New France Settlers in New France often flew this flag of the French Royal Navy. They also flew the French Royal Banner, which was blue instead of white.

to the region after the French had tried to settle what is today the Carolinas. St. Augustine prospered and became the first permanent town established by Europeans in what is today the United States. The arrival of the French at the mouth of the Mississippi spurred the Spanish into action once again. In 1690 they established their first mission in what is today eastern Texas. In 1716 the first Spanish settlers arrived in eastern Texas to secure the Spanish claim and to block French expansion into the region. The French and Spanish empires in North America now bordered each other. Neither empire, however, posed a serious threat to the other's position in North America. The real challenge to French and Spanish domination of North America would come from another quarter. While Spain focused its colonies primarily in the Southwest and France along the Mississippi River, England began settling numerous colonies along a narrow strip of the Atlantic coast.

✓ **Reading Check** **Explaining** Why did the French establish forts and settlements along the Mississippi?

SECTION 1 ASSESSMENT

Checking for Understanding

1. **Define:** conquistador, presidio, *hidalgo, encomienda,* hacienda, vaquero, Northwest Passage, coureur de bois.
2. **Identify:** Francisco Pizarro, Popé.
3. **Explain** how the fur trade contributed to the slow growth of New France.

Reviewing Themes

4. **Global Connections** The king of Spain created a scheme to oversee his empire in America. What system did he use to govern the distant colonies?

Critical Thinking

5. **Synthesizing** Why did the various groups of Spaniards come to North America?
6. **Analyzing** Were the French or Spanish colonies more successful? Why?
7. **Categorizing** Use a graphic organizer similar to the one below to list the social classes that developed in New Spain.

Highest _____
_____
_____
Lowest _____

Analyzing Visuals

8. **Analyzing Photographs** Study the photograph of the Chapel of San Miguel on page 54. How did the Catholic Church contribute to the Spanish settlement of the New Mexico territory?

Writing About History

9. **Persuasive Writing** Imagine you are an officeholder for the French king and want to support his policies. Write an advertisement for a French newspaper to encourage people to settle in New France.

English Colonies in America

Main Idea

Religious, economic, and political changes in England led the English to establish colonies along the eastern coast of North America.

Key Terms and Names

John Cabot, Puritan, joint-stock company, privateer, Walter Raleigh, Powhatan Confederacy, burgesses, headright, proprietary colony

Reading Strategy

Organizing As you read about the early troubles of the Jamestown colony, complete a graphic organizer similar to the one below by listing the problems that faced the colonists.

Jamestown's Troubles

Reading Objectives

• **Explain** the religious and economic reasons why England became interested in America.

• **Describe** the founding of Jamestown and explain why it succeeded.

Section Theme

Geography and History The headright system provided settlers with new ways to acquire more land.

Preview of Events

♦1500	♦1550	♦1600	♦1650

1497
John Cabot explores North America's coastline for England

1587
Roanoke colony founded

1607
Jamestown founded

1619
House of Burgesses meets for the first time

1634
Maryland founded

★ An American Story ★

On July 30, 1619, the first elected assembly in the English colonies met in Jamestown, Virginia. Two delegates from each of the 10 Virginia settlements, along with the governor and his 6 councilors, met in the choir of the Jamestown church. This governing body became known as the House of Burgesses.

When Governor Sir George Yeardley had arrived in Jamestown in April 1619, he carried instructions to call an assembly so that the settlers could "make and ordain whatsoever laws and orders should by them be thought good and profitable." The House of Burgesses met for five days, "sweating and stewing, and battling flies and mosquitoes." It passed strict laws against swearing, gambling, drunkenness, and excess in dress. It also made church attendance compulsory and passed laws against injuring the Native Americans.

The House of Burgesses meeting marked the first time colonists had been given a voice in their colonial government. They believed that right was now irrevocable.

—adapted from Jamestown, 1544–1699

England Takes Interest in America

The Jamestown colony was England's first permanent settlement in North America, but it was established more than 100 years after the first English explorers arrived. In May 1497, **John Cabot** headed west across the Atlantic. King Henry VII of England had sent Cabot to "discover and find, whatsoever isles, countries, regions or provinces . . . which before this time have been unknown to all Christians." Cabot, an Italian navigator, had long hoped to find a western route to Asia. He wanted, he said, to reach "the lands from which Oriental caravans brought their goods. . . ."

Cabot landed somewhere near Nova Scotia, then sailed southward along the "barren shores" and "wooded coasts" of America. While he did not see any people, he did see "notched trees, snares for game, and needles for making nets." Back in England, King Henry granted Cabot a pension and bonus for finding what the king called the "new found land."

The next year, Cabot sailed west on a second expedition to America. He was never seen again.

Although John Cabot arrived in America less than five years after Columbus, the English did not try to colonize America for the next 80 years. The English government had little money, and Cabot had found no gold or other wealth. There was also no compelling reason for anyone in England to migrate to America. Furthermore, the Spanish had already claimed America, and their claim had been upheld by the pope. In 1497 Spain and England were both Catholic countries and allies against France. Any English attempt to settle America would have

NATIONAL GEOGRAPHIC

European Explorations and Settlements, 1497–1682

Legend:
- English exploration
- French exploration
- Spanish exploration
- Dutch exploration

Geography Skills

1. **Interpreting Maps** According to the map, what nation first explored North America in 1497?
2. **Applying Geographic Skills** In what areas did French explorers Champlain and Cartier concentrate their efforts?

angered the Spanish and upset the alliance. During the late 1500s, however, a series of dramatic religious, economic, and political changes occurred that led to the founding of the first English colonies in America.

TURNING POINT

The Reformation Divides Europe

At the time Cabot sailed to America, virtually all of western Europe was Catholic. This unity began to break apart in 1517, when a German monk named **Martin Luther** published an attack on the Church, accusing it of corruption. Luther's attack marked the beginning of the **Protestant Reformation.** In 1520 Luther was expelled from the Catholic Church, but his ideas continued to spread rapidly across western Europe. Luther himself went on to found the German Protestant Church, now called the Lutheran Church.

As the Reformation spread, an important development occurred in Switzerland when **John Calvin** suggested that neither kings nor bishops should control the Church. Calvin argued that congregations should choose their own elders and ministers to run the Church for them. Calvin's ideas had a profound impact on England, and ultimately America, because many of the first English settlers in America shared Calvin's ideas.

The Reformation Changes England

In contrast to the theological debate sweeping Europe, the Reformation in England began with a simple disagreement between the king and the pope. In 1527 King Henry VIII asked the pope to annul his marriage to Catherine of Aragon. It was not unusual for the pope to grant a divorce to a king, but in this case the pope hesitated. Catherine was the king of Spain's aunt, and the pope did not want to anger the Spanish king.

The pope's delay infuriated Henry. He broke with the Catholic Church, declared that he was now the head of England's church, and arranged for the divorce himself. The Catholic Church in England became the **Anglican Church,** but because Henry agreed with Catholic doctrine, the Anglican Church kept the organization and most of the rituals of the Catholic Church.

Following Henry's break with the Catholic Church, those who wanted to keep the Catholic organization of the Anglican Church began to struggle with those who wanted to "purify" it of all Catholic elements. People who wanted to purify the Church became known as Puritans.

Under the reign of Henry's daughter, **Queen Elizabeth I,** many Puritan ideas such as the supreme authority of the Bible gained acceptance within the Anglican Church. Still, many Catholic rituals remained unchanged. Although the Puritans objected to the Catholic rituals, the most important issue was who controlled the Church. John Calvin's ideas had influenced many Puritan leaders. They argued that every congregation should elect its own ministers and elders to control the Church instead of having bishops and archbishops appointed by the monarch.

The Puritan cause suffered a serious setback in 1603, when James I became king. Although King James was Protestant, he refused to tolerate any changes in the structure of the Anglican Church. Since the king headed the Church and appointed its leaders, the Puritan idea of electing ministers was a direct challenge to royal authority. James's refusal to reform the Church made many Puritans willing to leave England. Ultimately, many would choose America as their refuge.

Economic Changes in England

At the same time that the Reformation was transforming the English Church, a revolution in trade and agriculture was changing English society. At the beginning of the 1500s, much of England's land was divided into large estates. The nobles who owned these estates rented their land to tenant farmers. In the 1500s, Europeans

History *Through Art*

Warring Empires In 1588 the Spanish Armada, depicted in this painting, set out with a huge fleet to settle scores with England. Spain was defeated, but if it had won, England might have become Catholic again. Why did England become more strongly Protestant after this event?

began to buy large quantities of English wool. As the demand for wool increased, many English landowners realized they could make more money by raising sheep than by renting their land.

The landowners converted their estates into sheep farms by enclosing their land and evicting the tenants. This became known as the **enclosure movement.** It created thousands of poor, unemployed beggars who wandered from town to town looking for work. For these people, leaving England for a chance at a better life in America was appealing.

By 1550 England was producing more wool than Europeans would buy, and the price fell. England's merchants needed to find new markets to sell their surplus wool, and they began organizing joint-stock companies to find those new markets.

Joint-stock companies pooled the money of many investors. This enabled the company to raise large amounts of money for big projects. The development of joint-stock companies meant that English merchants could afford to trade with, and colonize, other parts of the world without government financing.

Reading Check **Explaining** Why did many Puritans become willing to leave England?

England Returns to America

The need to find new markets for their wool convinced English merchants to begin searching for a northern water route through North America to Asia.

In 1576 an Englishman named Martin Frobisher took three ships to America to search for a northwest passage. He made two more trips by 1578, but he did not find the passage. Although he failed, Frobisher's voyages were important. For the first time in several decades, the English had returned to America.

England's new interest in America contributed to its growing rivalry with Spain. The Reformation had changed Europe's balance of power. England had become the leading Protestant power, while Spain remained a staunch defender of Catholicism. The former allies were now enemies.

After the Reformation, England not only had new enemies, it had new allies as well. By the 1560s, most Dutch people had become Protestant despite being part of the Spanish empire. When the Spanish tried to suppress Protestantism in the Netherlands, the Dutch rebelled. To help the Dutch revolt, Queen Elizabeth allowed English privateers to attack Spanish ships. Privateers are privately owned ships licensed by the government to attack ships of other countries.

Gilbert and Raleigh English privateers found it difficult to attack Spanish ships in the Caribbean because England had no bases in the region. This led many of Queen Elizabeth's advisers to recommend that England establish outposts in America to support naval operations against Spain.

The first attempts at colonization were not promising. In 1578 Sir Humphrey Gilbert, a well-known English soldier, received a charter from Queen Elizabeth to create a colony in America. Gilbert made two attempts to colonize America. Both failed, and Gilbert himself died at sea.

Gilbert's half-brother, **Walter Raleigh,** persuaded Queen Elizabeth to renew Gilbert's charter in his own name. He then sent two ships to scout the American coastline. The ships passed through the Outer Banks along what is today North Carolina and landed on an island the Native Americans called **Roanoke.** Impressed by the discovery, Queen Elizabeth knighted Raleigh, and he in turn named the land Virginia—in honor of Elizabeth, who was known as "the Virgin Queen."

The Lost Colony of Roanoke In 1585 Raleigh sent about 100 men to settle on Roanoke. After a hard winter, the unhappy colonists returned to England.

Raleigh tried again in 1587. He sent 91 men, 17 women, and 9 children to Roanoke. A month later Roanoke's governor, John White, headed back to England for more supplies. War erupted between

England and Spain while White was in England, and he was not able to return until 1590. When he finally returned, the colony was gone. There were no bodies, only empty houses and the letters "CRO" carved on a post, possibly referring to the Croatoan—a Native American group who lived nearby. No one knows what happened, and the fate of the "Lost Colony" of Roanoke remains a mystery today.

✓ **Reading Check** **Summarizing** Why did England want to establish outposts in America?

Jamestown Is Founded

Shortly after the war with Spain ended in 1604, a group of English investors petitioned the new king of England, James I, for a charter to plant colonies in Virginia. In 1606 James granted the charter. Their new company was named the **Virginia Company.**

On December 20, 1606, the Virginia Company sent three small ships—the *Susan Constant,* the *Godspeed,* and the *Discovery*—and 144 men to Virginia. After a difficult trip, the ships arrived off the coast of North America, and the colonists founded a settlement on the banks of a river. In honor of their king, they named the river the James River and their settlement **Jamestown.** Unfortunately, the colonists' site turned out to be too close to the sea. The land they selected was swampy and swarming with malaria-carrying mosquitoes. The location was just the beginning of Jamestown's problems.

Early Troubles Most of Jamestown's colonists were townspeople. They knew little about living in the woods and could not make use of the abundant fish and game around them. Even worse, none of the colonists knew how to raise livestock or cultivate crops. Additional problems occurred when the upperclass "gentlemen" among the colonists refused to do manual labor. Making matters worse, Jamestown's governing council argued constantly and could not make decisions. The results of all of these problems were nearly catastrophic. Lawlessness, sickness, and food shortages all took their toll. Although about 200 new settlers arrived in 1608, only 53 colonists were still alive by the end of the year. All of the remaining colonists may have died as well, in fact, had it not been for two men— Captain **John Smith** and Chief **Powhatan.**

Captain John Smith, a member of the colony's governing council, emerged as Jamestown's only strong leader. Born into a poor family, Smith had left home as a young man to become a soldier of fortune. In late 1607, with winter approaching and the colony short of food, Smith explored the region around Jamestown and began trading with the local Native Americans—a group called the **Powhatan Confederacy,** led by Chief Powhatan. It was this trade that helped the colony get through its first two winters.

Frustrated by events in Jamestown, the Virginia Company appointed a new governor with absolute authority, Thomas West, Lord De La Warr. To entice settlers, the company offered land

Profiles IN HISTORY

Pocahontas *1596–1617*

In 1623 Captain John Smith told a remarkable tale to a British commission investigating the Virginia Company. In 1607 Native Americans had captured him and prepared, as he said, to "beate out his braines." Just then, Pocahontas, the 11-year-old daughter of Chief Powhatan, "got his head in her armes, and laid her owne upon his to save him from death."

Although her father watched the English with concern, Pocahontas continued to interact with the people in the Jamestown settlement. Unfortunately, her friendliness and curiosity were not kindly repaid. While visiting a nearby Native American settlement in 1613, Pocahontas was abducted by Captain Samuel Argall, a Jamestown resident. Pocahontas was supposedly being held as ransom for the lives of English prisoners and for arms, tools, and food. After the Native Americans gave what they could, however, the English still refused to return Pocahontas.

The following year, a battle seemed imminent when the two sides met, but two of Pocahontas's brothers were so excited to see her that they agreed to work out a truce. Soon thereafter, a member of the Virginia Company

named John Rolfe announced to the colonial administrator that he and Pocahontas had fallen in love, and he asked to marry her.

After hearing the proposal, Chief Powhatan gave his consent, and the couple soon married. Eventually, Pocahontas bore one son, whom they named Thomas. In 1616 Pocahontas traveled with her husband and son to England to search for investors for the Virginia Company. Unfortunately, Pocahontas grew ill in 1617, just before the family was due to return to America, and she died of pneumonia or smallpox.

to anyone who worked for the colony for seven years. The offer produced results. In August 1609, 400 new settlers arrived in Jamestown.

The arrival of so many settlers late in the summer created a crisis. There was not enough food, nor could enough be grown before winter. Governor De La Warr had not arrived yet, and John Smith had suffered a gunpowder burn and returned to England. Without strong leadership, the colony rapidly deteriorated. As winter neared, the settlers began to steal food from the Native Americans. In response, Native American warriors attacked the settlers.

The winter of 1609 and 1610 became known as the "starving time." The colonists at Jamestown ate "dogs, rats, snakes, toadstools, [and] horsehides," and a few settlers even engaged in cannibalism, digging up corpses from graves and eating them.

By the spring of 1610, only 60 settlers were still alive. They abandoned Jamestown and headed downriver. On the way, they met three English ships heading for the colony. On board were supplies, 150 more settlers, and the colony's governor, Lord De La Warr. De La Warr convinced the settlers to stay. Instead of returning to Jamestown, however, many decided to establish other towns along the James River. By 1618 there were several towns in Virginia.

De La Warr's deputy, Thomas Dale, then drafted a harsh code of laws for Jamestown. Settlers were organized into work gangs and required to work at least six hours per day. Dale's discipline saved the colony, but Jamestown still did not thrive. In 1614 Dale decided to permit private cultivation. Settlers could acquire three acres of land if they gave the colony one month of work and 2½ barrels of corn. Whatever else they produced, they could keep. According to one colonist, Ralph Hamor, the new system dramatically increased production:

> ❝When our people were fed out of the common store and labored jointly . . . glad was the man that could slip from his labor . . . presuming that howsoever the harvest prospered, the general store must maintain them, by which means we reaped not so much corn for the labors of 30 men, as three men have done for themselves.❞
>
> —quoted in *Colonial America*

The new policy ensured Jamestown's survival, but the colony still had to find a product to sell for profit

Critical Leadership Captain John Smith (left) helped save early Jamestown by trading with the local Native Americans. Sidney King painted Jamestown's fort as it must have appeared around 1607. *Why do you think the fort was set up with only three sides?*

in England. The solution was a product King James had already condemned as a "vile weed [of] black stinking fumes [that were] baleful to the nose, harmful to the brain, and dangerous to the lungs"—tobacco.

Tobacco Saves the Colony Well before the founding of Jamestown, the Spanish began shipping tobacco from their Caribbean colonies to Europe. Smoking tobacco became very popular in Europe in the early 1600s. The Jamestown settlers had tried growing tobacco, but the local variety was too bitter.

One colonist named **John Rolfe** continued to experiment, using seeds imported from Trinidad. He developed a new curing method, and in 1614 he shipped about 2,600 pounds (1,180 kg) to England. Rolfe's tobacco was not as good as Spanish tobacco, but it sold for a good price, and the settlers soon began planting large quantities of it.

The First Assembly In 1618 the new head of the Virginia Company in London, Edwin Sandys, introduced major reforms to attract settlers. The first reform gave the colony the right to elect its own assembly to propose laws. The first general assembly met in the Jamestown church on July 30, 1619. The new Virginia government included a governor, 6 councilors, and 20 representatives, 2 from each of the colony's 10 towns. The representatives were called burgesses, and the assembly was called the House of Burgesses.

Headrights Lure Settlers To entice new settlers to Virginia, the company also introduced the system of headrights, in which new settlers who bought a share in the company or paid for their passage were granted 50 acres of land. They were given 50 more acres for each family member over 15 years of age and for each servant they transported to Virginia.

Up to that point, Jamestown had been a colony made up mostly of men. In 1619 the Virginia Company sent about 90 women to the colony. The first Africans also arrived in 1619 when a slave ship stopped to trade. The settlers purchased 20 Africans as "Christian servants," not enslaved people. The Africans had been baptized, and at that time English law said that Christians could not be enslaved.

Virginia Becomes a Royal Colony The new policies triggered a wave of immigration. By 1622 more than 4,500 settlers had arrived in Virginia. The dramatic increase in settlers alarmed the Native Americans. In March 1622, they attacked Jamestown, burning homes and killing nearly 350 settlers. The settlers eventually put an end to the uprising, but the colony was devastated. The uprising was the final straw for King James. An English court revoked the company's charter, and Virginia became a royal colony run by a governor appointed by the king.

✓ **Reading Check** **Describing** How did Captain John Smith and the Powhatan Confederacy save Jamestown?

Maryland Is Founded

A joint-stock company had founded Virginia, but the colony north of it resulted from the aspirations of one man, George Calvert, **Lord Baltimore.** Lord Baltimore had been a member of the English Parliament until he converted to Catholicism. This decision ruined his career, but he remained a good friend of King James I and his son, Charles I.

Catholics were opposed in England for much the same reason as Puritans. Catholics did not accept the king as head of the Church, nor did they accept the authority of Anglican bishops and priests. They were viewed as potential traitors who might help Catholic countries overthrow the English king. Consequently, they were forbidden to practice law or teach school.

As he watched the persecution of his fellow Catholics, Lord Baltimore decided to found a colony where Catholics could practice their religion. In 1632 King Charles granted him a large area of land northeast of Virginia. Baltimore named the new colony Maryland.

Baltimore owned Maryland, making it England's first proprietary colony. The proprietor, or owner, could govern the colony any way he wished. He could appoint officials, coin money, impose taxes, establish courts, grant lands, and create towns. In most respects, he had a king's powers.

Lord Baltimore died shortly before settlers arrived in his colony. In 1634, 20 gentlemen, mostly Catholic, and 200 servants and artisans, mostly Protestant, arrived in Maryland. Despite Baltimore's hope that Maryland would become a Catholic refuge, most of its settlers were Protestant, although the government officials and most large estate owners were Catholic. The friction between the two groups plagued the colony for many years.

✓ **Reading Check** **Analyzing** Why did Lord Baltimore found Maryland?

SECTION 2 ASSESSMENT

Checking for Understanding

1. **Define:** Puritan, joint-stock company, privateer, burgesses, headright, proprietary colony.
2. **Identify:** John Cabot, Walter Raleigh, Powhatan Confederacy.
3. **Explain** how tobacco saved Jamestown.

Reviewing Themes

4. **Geography and History** How did the enclosure movement change England's society?

Critical Thinking

5. **Interpreting** What caused friction in the Maryland colony?
6. **Categorizing** Use a graphic organizer similar to the one below to list three ways the Virginia Company tried to attract settlers to the Jamestown colony.

Ways to Attract Settlers

Analyzing Visuals

7. **Analyzing Art** Examine the painting on pages 60 and 61. What factors contributed to the growing rivalry between Spain and England?

Writing About History

8. **Persuasive Writing** Take on the role of Captain John Smith of Jamestown. Write a town circular explaining to your fellow colonists why trading with the Powhatan Confederacy is a good survival strategy.

SKILLBUILDER

Understanding the Parts of a Map

Why Learn This Skill?

Maps can direct you down the street or around the world. There are as many different kinds of maps as there are uses for them. Being able to read a map begins with learning about its parts.

Learning the Skill

Maps usually include a key, a compass rose, and a scale bar. The map key explains the meaning of special colors, symbols, and lines used on the map. On a road map, for example, the key tells what map lines stand for paved roads, dirt roads, and interstate highways.

After reading the map key, look for the compass rose. It is the direction marker that shows the cardinal directions of north, south, east, and west. A measuring line, often called a scale bar, helps you estimate distance on a map. The map's scale tells you what distance on the earth is represented by the measurement on the scale bar. For example, 1 inch (2.54 cm) on the map may represent 100 miles (160.9 km) on the earth. Knowing the scale allows you to visualize the extent of an area and to measure distances.

Practicing the Skill

The map on this page shows the early English colonization of the eastern coast of North America. Look at the parts of the map, and then answer the questions.

❶ What information is given in the key?

❷ What body of water serves as the eastern border for the colonies?

❸ What color represents the Middle Colonies?

❹ What is the approximate distance, in miles, between the settlements of Charles Town and Jamestown?

❺ What is the approximate distance, in kilometers, between the northernmost and southernmost settlements?

NATIONAL GEOGRAPHIC **The Thirteen Colonies, 1750**

Key:
- Town or City
- New England Colonies
- Middle Colonies
- Southern Colonies

Skills Assessment

Complete the Practicing Skills questions on page 81 and the Chapter 2 Skill Reinforcement Activity to assess your mastery of this skill.

Applying the Skill

Understanding the Parts of a Map Study the map of European Explorations and Settlements on page 59. Use the map to answer the following questions.

1. When did Marquette and Joliet explore the Mississippi River?

2. What English explorer arrived in North America at the end of the 1400s?

3. Which explorer traveled the farthest north?

 GO TO

Glencoe's **Skillbuilder Interactive Workbook CD-ROM, Level 2,** provides instruction and practice in key social studies skills.

New England

Main Idea

In the 1600s, English Puritans fleeing religious persecution and economic difficulties founded several colonies in New England.

Key Terms and Names

Separatist, Pilgrim, William Bradford, Squanto, John Winthrop, Massachusetts Bay Company, Great Migration, heretic, Roger Williams, Anne Hutchinson

Reading Strategy

Organizing As you read about the founding of colonies in New England, complete a graphic organizer similar to the one below by listing the causes of King Philip's War.

Causes of King Philip's War

Reading Objectives

- **Discuss** why John Winthrop founded Massachusetts and describe the kind of society the Puritans built there.
- **Describe** why Roger Williams and Anne Hutchinson left the Massachusetts colony.

Section Theme

Culture and Traditions Puritan religious beliefs shaped the cultural history of New England.

Preview of Events

♦1620   ♦1640   ♦1660   ♦1680

1620
Pilgrims arrive in Massachusetts

1630
Massachusetts Bay Colony established

1636
Roger Williams founds Providence

1639
Fundamental Orders of Connecticut introduced

1675
King Philip's War begins

★ An American Story ★

On a bleak November day in 1620, a tiny three-masted English ship named the *Mayflower* dropped anchor off the coast of Cape Cod. The eyes of all those aboard, 101 English men, women, and children, focused on the low strip of land before them. They were not where they were supposed to be. They had a patent for land in Virginia, but the land on the horizon was clearly not Virginia. If they went ashore, they would be on land to which they had no title in a territory where no English government existed.

On November 11, 1620, 41 adult men met in the ship's cabin to sign a document later known as the Mayflower Compact. In it they declared their intention to create a government and obey its laws. They agreed to "solemnly and mutually in the presence of God and one of another, covenant and combine ourselves together in a civil body politic, for our better ordering and preservation," and to "frame such just and equal laws, ordinances, acts, constitutions and officers, from time to time, as shall be thought most meet and convenient for the general good of the Colony, unto which we promise all due submission and obedience."

—adapted from *Basic Documents in American History*

The Pilgrims Land at Plymouth

The events that led to the arrival of the *Mayflower* off the coast of New England began several years earlier in England. A group of Puritans, called Separatists, broke away from the Anglican Church to form their own congregations. King James I viewed this action as a challenge to his authority, and he imprisoned Separatist leaders. To escape this persecution, one group fled to Holland in 1608. These Separatists, who came to be known as the Pilgrims, found it difficult to live in Holland. They also worried that their children were losing their English heritage. In early 1617, the congregation decided to sail to America.

The *Mayflower* Arrives in America Before setting sail for America, the Pilgrims first returned to England, where they joined another group of Separatists aboard the *Mayflower*. In September 1620, 102 passengers set off on the journey across the Atlantic. The trip took 65 days. Most of the food ran out, many passengers became ill, and one died. Making matters worse, a severe storm blew the small ship off course. Finally, in early November, the Pilgrims sighted Cape Cod and tried to follow the coastline south. After encountering rough weather, they turned back.

Although they were not where they expected, the Pilgrims were not completely lost. In 1614 the Virginia Company had hired Captain John Smith to explore the region. The Pilgrims had a copy of Smith's "Map of New England," and they decided to move across Massachusetts Bay to the area Smith had labeled "Plymouth" on his map. *(See page 1061 for an excerpt from the Mayflower Compact.)*

Plymouth Colony According to **William Bradford,** one of the colony's leaders, the Pilgrims went to work as soon as they arrived at Plymouth. After constructing a "common house," the settlers built modest homes of frame construction and thatched roofs. Soon, however, a plague swept through the colony, sparing only 50 settlers.

Even the surviving Pilgrims might have perished were it not for the help of **Squanto,** a Native American man who taught them about their new environment. Bradford wrote that Squanto "directed them how to set their corn, where to take fish and [how] to procure other commodities." Squanto also helped the Pilgrims negotiate a peace treaty with the Wampanoag people who lived nearby. The following autumn, the Pilgrims joined the Wampanoag in a three-day festival to celebrate the harvest and give thanks to God for their good fortune. This celebration later became the basis for the Thanksgiving holiday.

Reading Check **Summarizing** How did Squanto help the Pilgrims?

The Puritans Found Massachusetts

Although many Puritans in England shared the frustrations that had driven the Pilgrims to leave the country, most worked for reform within the Anglican Church. After King Charles took the throne in 1625, opposition to the Puritans began to increase, and many Puritans became willing to leave England.

A City on a Hill At about this time, a depression struck England's wool industry, which caused high unemployment, particularly in England's southeastern counties where many Puritans lived. As he watched his fellow Puritans suffering religious and economic hardship, **John Winthrop,** a wealthy attorney, wrote despairingly to his wife: "I am verily persuaded God will bring some heavy affliction upon this land, and that speedily."

Winthrop and several other wealthy Puritans were stockholders in the **Massachusetts Bay Company.** The company had already received a royal charter in March 1629 to create a colony in New England. Convinced that there was no future for Puritans in England, Winthrop decided to change what had been merely a business investment into a refuge for Puritans in America. Other Puritans embraced the idea, and in March 1630, eleven ships carrying about 900 settlers set sail. As they headed to America, John Winthrop delivered a sermon entitled "A Model of

 History *Through Art*

Solemn Signing Tompkins Matteson, a nineteenth-century artist, painted his vision of the signing of the Mayflower Compact. By signing this document, the Pilgrims wanted to set up a legal basis for their new colony. How did the artist try to suggest the seriousness of the occasion in this painting?

NATIONAL GEOGRAPHIC

The Great Migration, 1620–1646

To New England, 20,000

To Chesapeake Colonies, 5,000

To West Indian Islands, 20,000

NEW ENGLAND 1620
MARYLAND 1645
VIRGINIA 1635
BERMUDA 1642
BAHAMAS 1646
ST. CROIX, 1625
ST. KITTS, 1623
NEVIS, 1628
BARBADOS, 1625

ENGLAND

ATLANTIC OCEAN

TROPIC OF CANCER

← Immigration Route

0   1,000 miles
0   1,000 kilometers
Mercator projection

The Puritan *by Augustus Saint-Gaudens*

Geography *Skills*

1. **Interpreting Maps** How many settlers immigrated to the Chesapeake Colonies as compared to New England?
2. **Applying Geography Skills** Approximately how many miles was the migration route from England to the New England Colonies?

Christian Charity." The new colony, Winthrop told his fellow Puritans, would be an example to the world:

> ❝The Lord will make our name a praise and glory, so that men shall say of succeeding plantations: 'The Lord make it like that of New England.' For we must consider that we shall be like a City upon a Hill; the eyes of all people are on us.❞

By the end of the year, 17 ships had brought another 1,000 settlers, and Massachusetts rapidly expanded. Several towns were founded, including Boston, which became the colony's capital. As conditions in England grew worse, many people began to leave the country in what was later called the **Great Migration.** By 1643 an estimated 20,000 settlers had arrived in New England.

Church and State The charter of the Massachusetts Bay Company defined the colony's government. People who owned stock in the company were called "freemen." All of the freemen together were called the **General Court.** The General Court made the laws and elected the governor.

John Winthrop had been chosen to be the first governor. To ensure that the colony became the kind of society he wanted, Winthrop ignored the charter and told the settlers that only the governor and his assistants could make laws for the colony. No one knew that these rules were not in the charter because Winthrop kept the charter locked in a chest.

Winthrop managed to restrict the freemen's power for four years, but eventually the settlers grew frustrated with how little voice they had in governing the colony. In 1634 town representatives demanded to see the charter, and Winthrop had no basis to refuse the request. As they read the charter, the representatives realized that the General Court was supposed to make the laws. When the General Court assembled in May 1634, they reorganized the government. The General Court became a representative assembly. They decided that elections would be held each year, and the freemen of each town would elect up to three deputies to send to the General Court.

John Winthrop believed that each congregation should control its own church, but he also believed that the government should help the church. Laws were passed requiring everyone to attend church. The government collected taxes to support the church and also regulated behavior. Gambling,

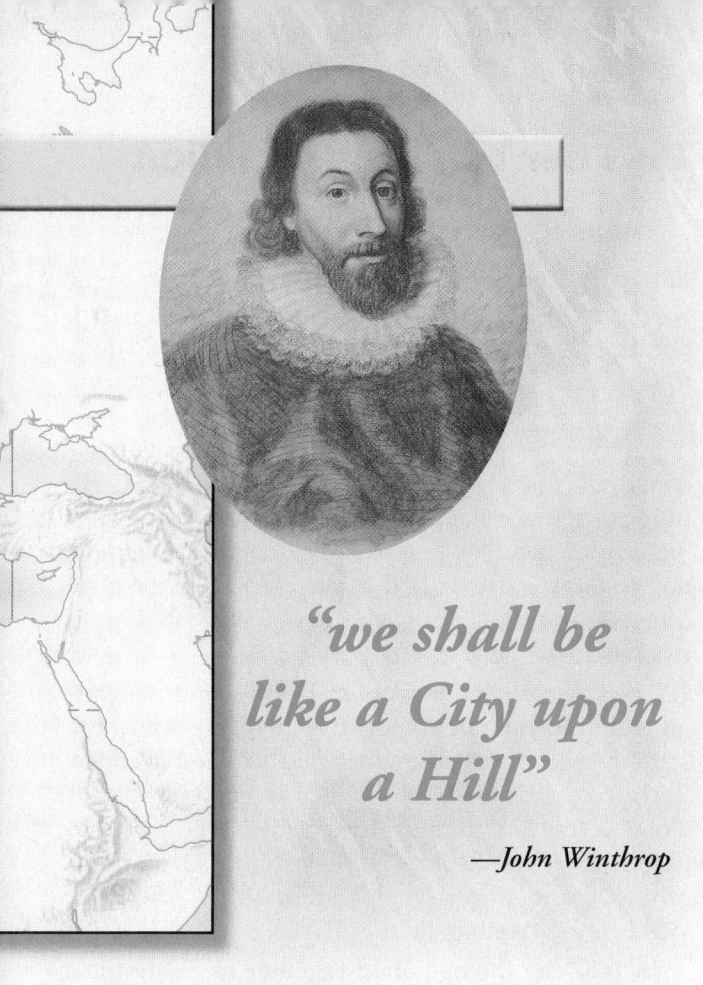

"we shall be like a City upon a Hill"

—John Winthrop

blasphemy, adultery, and drunkenness were all illegal and punished severely, often by flogging.

The leaders of the Massachusetts Bay Colony tried to prevent religious ideas that differed from Puritan beliefs. If settlers publicly challenged Puritan ideas, they could be charged with heresy and banished from the colony. Heretics—people whose religious beliefs differ from those accepted by the majority— were considered a threat to the community.

✓ **Reading Check** **Analyzing** How did John Winthrop's religious beliefs affect the way the Massachusetts Bay Colony was governed?

Rhode Island and Religious Dissent

Puritan efforts to suppress other religious beliefs inevitably led to conflict with those who disagreed with them. Eventually, just as Anglican intolerance of the Puritans led to the founding of Massachusetts, Puritan intolerance led to the founding of other colonies in New England.

Roger Williams Founds Providence In 1631 a young minister named **Roger Williams** arrived in Boston. When the Boston congregation offered him a teaching position, Williams refused, saying he

"[would] not officiate to an unseparated people." Williams was a strict Separatist. He believed Puritans corrupted themselves by remaining as part of the Anglican Church.

Williams became a teacher in Salem, where Separatist ideas were more accepted, but his continuing condemnation of the Puritan churches angered many people. As pressure against him mounted, Williams decided to move to Plymouth Colony. While in Plymouth, he declared that the land belonged to the Native Americans and that the king did not have the right to give it away.

Williams's ideas greatly alarmed John Winthrop. If the king heard that Puritans in Massachusetts were denying the king's authority, he might revoke the charter and impose a royal government. Winthrop feared that if that happened, the Puritans would lose control of their churches.

When Williams returned to Massachusetts in 1633, he continued to challenge Puritan authority. In October 1635, the General Court ordered him to leave the colony. Williams then headed south to found his own colony. He purchased land from the Narragansett people and founded the town of Providence. In Providence, the government had no authority in religious matters. Different religious beliefs were tolerated rather than suppressed.

Anne Hutchinson Is Banished
In the midst of the uproar over Roger Williams, a woman named **Anne Hutchinson** arrived in Boston. Hutchinson was intelligent, charismatic, and widely admired. A devout Puritan, Hutchinson began to hold prayer meetings in her home. Her groups discussed sermons and compared ministers.

As Hutchinson's following grew, she began to claim to know which ministers had salvation from God and which did not. This created a problem for Puritan leaders. Hutchinson was attacking the authority of ministers. If people believed her, they would stop listening to the ministers she had condemned. In late 1637, the General Court called Hutchinson before them to answer to charges of heresy.

When questioned by the court, Hutchinson did not confess or repent. She said that God "hath let me see which was the clear [correct] ministry and which the wrong. . . ." When asked how God let her know, she replied that God spoke to her "by an immediate revelation." By claiming God spoke to her directly, Hutchinson contradicted the Puritan belief that God only spoke through the Bible. The General Court immediately banished her for heresy. Hutchinson and

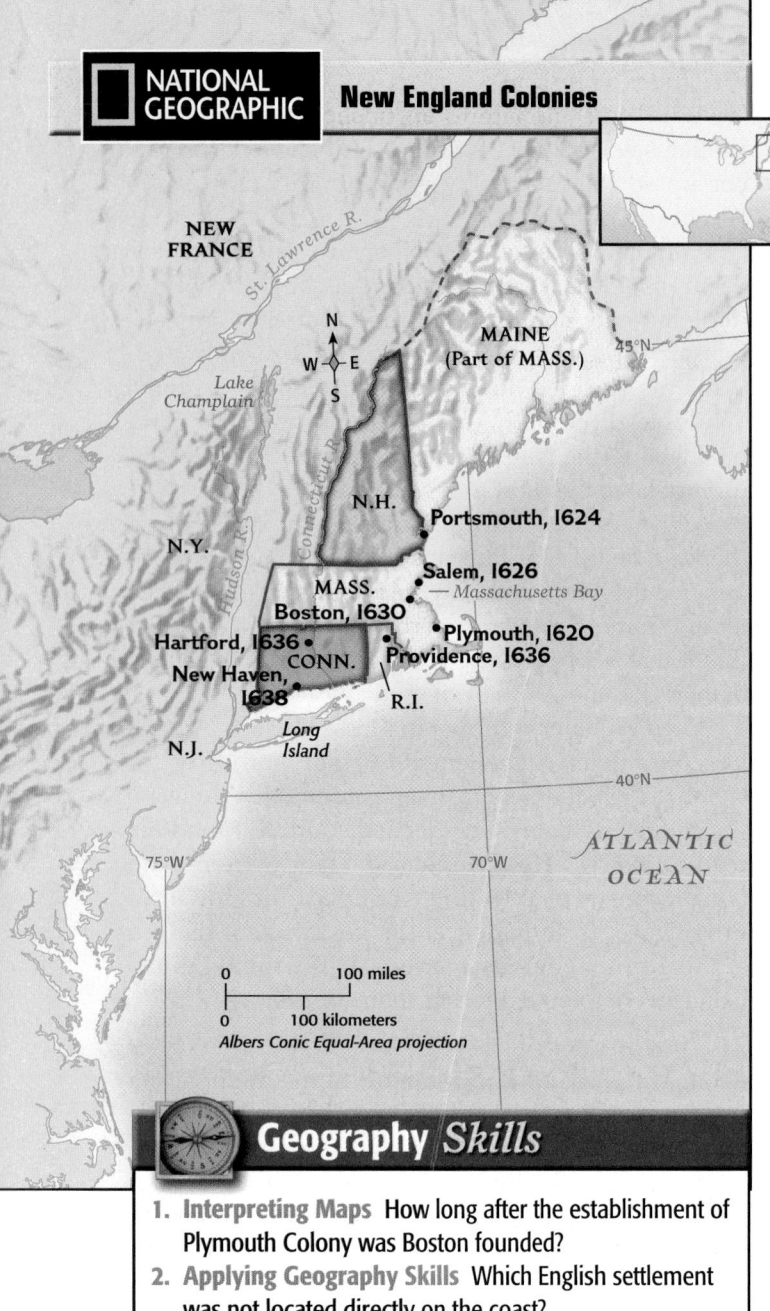

NEW
FRANCE

St. Lawrence R.

Lake
Champlain

MAINE
(Part of MASS.)

45°N

N.Y.

Connecticut R.

Hudson R.

N.H.

Portsmouth, 1624

Salem, 1626
MASS. —*Massachusetts Bay*
Boston, 1630

Hartford, 1636 •
New Haven,
1638

Plymouth, 1620
CONN. • Providence, 1636

R.I.

N.J.

Long
Island

40°N

*ATLANTIC
OCEAN*

75°W

70°W

| 0 | 100 miles |
| 0 | 100 kilometers |

Albers Conic Equal-Area projection

Geography *Skills*

1. **Interpreting Maps** How long after the establishment of Plymouth Colony was Boston founded?
2. **Applying Geography Skills** Which English settlement was not located directly on the coast?

several of her followers headed south. They settled on an island and founded the town of Pocasset, later known as Portsmouth.

The Colony of Rhode Island Over the next few years, Massachusetts banished other dissenting Puritans. They too headed south and founded two more towns—Newport in 1639 and Warwick in 1643. In 1644 these two towns joined together with Portsmouth and Providence to become the colony of Rhode Island and Providence Plantations. Religious freedom, with a total separation of church and state, was a key part of the colony's charter.

✓ **Reading Check** **Explaining** Why were Roger Williams and Anne Hutchinson banished from Massachusetts?

The River Towns of Connecticut

In 1636 the Reverend **Thomas Hooker** asked the General Court of Massachusetts for permission to move his entire congregation to the Connecticut River valley. His congregation wanted to migrate because they did not have enough land near their town to raise cattle. Hooker also had his own reasons for leaving. Unlike Roger Williams, Hooker was an orthodox Puritan, but like Williams, he was frustrated by the Massachusetts political system. He thought that everyone should be allowed to vote, not just church members. Hooker argued that "the foundation of authority is laid in the consent of the governed," and that "the choice of the magistrate belongs to the people."

The General Court allowed Hooker and his congregation to migrate. A few months later, some 100 settlers headed to the Connecticut River and founded the town of Hartford. Hooker's congregation was not alone in the Connecticut River valley. Trading posts had been established in the region in 1633, and two other congregations had founded the towns of Windsor and Wethersfield in 1634.

In 1637 the towns joined together to create their own General Court. Two years later they adopted a constitution known as the **Fundamental Orders of Connecticut**—the first written constitution of the American colonies. Their government was similar to that of Massachusetts, but it had one major exception: it allowed all adult men, not just church members, to elect the governor and the General Court. 📖 *(See page 1062 for the text of the Fundamental Orders of Connecticut.)*

East of the Connecticut River lived the Pequot people, who considered the valley part of their territory. The Pequot chief Sassacus, who ruled both the Pequot and the Mohegan peoples, tolerated the English settlers at first because he needed allies against the Narraganset in Rhode Island. In 1636, however, two Massachusetts traders were killed in Pequot territory. When Massachusetts sent troops to retaliate, the Pequot War erupted. The Pequot began raiding towns along the Connecticut River. In April 1637, they surprised the town of Wethersfield and killed nine people. Furious, the Connecticut settlers assembled an army under the command of Captain John Mason. Seizing the opportunity to free themselves, the Mohegan rebelled against the Pequot and sent warriors to fight alongside Mason's troops. The Narraganset, bitter rivals of the Pequot, also joined in the attack.

Mason's troops and their Native American allies set fire to the main Pequot fort near Mystic Harbor.

When the Pequot tried to surrender, the troops opened fire, killing about 400 people, including women and children. The Connecticut General Court then put a bounty on the surviving Pequot. Many were captured and sold into slavery, while others were given to the Narraganset and Mohegan as war prizes. The Pequot were treated so poorly by the other Native Americans that in 1655, the Connecticut government resettled the survivors in two villages near the Mystic River.

✓ **Reading Check** **Contrasting** How did the Connecticut and Massachusetts constitutions differ?

New Hampshire and Maine

Not all of the settlers who left Massachusetts headed for Rhode Island or Connecticut. Although Anne Hutchinson had moved south, 36 of her followers headed north and founded the town of Exeter. During the 1640s, several other towns were also established north of Massachusetts. Many of the settlers in these towns were fishers and fur traders.

Much of the territory north of Massachusetts had been granted to two men, Sir Fernando Gorges and Captain John Mason who split the grant in half. Mason took the southern part and named it New Hampshire, while Gorges's territory in the north came to be called Maine. The government of Massachusetts claimed both New Hampshire and Maine and challenged the claims of Mason and Gorges in court. In 1677 an English court ruled against Massachusetts. Two years later, New Hampshire became a royal colony. Massachusetts, however, bought Maine from Gorges's heirs, and Maine remained part of Massachusetts until 1820.

✓ **Reading Check** **Identifying** What two colonies were established north of Massachusetts?

TURNING POINT
King Philip's War

For almost 40 years after the Pequot War, the New England settlers and Native Americans had good relations. The fur trade, in particular, facilitated peace. It enabled Native Americans to acquire tools, guns, metal, and other European products in exchange for furs. By the 1670s, however, the fur trade was in decline. At the same time, colonial governments began to demand that Native Americans follow English laws and customs. Such demands angered Native Americans, who felt that the English were trying to destroy their way of life.

Tensions peaked in 1675 when Plymouth Colony arrested, tried, and executed three Wampanoag for a murder. Angry and frustrated, Wampanoag warriors attacked the town of Swansea. This marked the beginning of what came to be called **King Philip's War,** after the Wampanoag leader **Metacomet,** whom the settlers called King Philip. Metacomet was killed in 1676, but fighting continued in Maine and New Hampshire. The war, which the settlers won in 1678, was a turning point. Afterward, few Native Americans remained in New England, and those who survived were scattered. New England now belonged to the English settlers.

✓ **Reading Check** **Analyzing** In what way was King Philip's War a turning point for Native Americans and settlers in New England?

SECTION 3 ASSESSMENT

Checking for Understanding

1. **Define:** Separatist, Pilgrim, heretic.
2. **Identify:** William Bradford, Squanto, John Winthrop, Massachusetts Bay Company, Great Migration, Roger Williams, Anne Hutchinson.
3. **Explain** Why was John Winthrop concerned about the ideas of Roger Williams?

Reviewing Themes

4. **Culture and Traditions** How did Thomas Hooker's beliefs promote the idea of separation of church and state?

Critical Thinking

5. **Comparing** In what ways were the causes and effects of the Pequot War and King Philip's War similar?
6. **Categorizing** Use a graphic organizer similar to the one below to list the New England Colonies and the reasons for their founding.

Colony	Reasons Founded

Analyzing Visuals

7. **Analyzing Art** Study the painting of the signing of the Mayflower Compact on page 67. Why did the Pilgrims feel it was necessary to create their own government?

Writing About History

8. **Descriptive Writing** Imagine you are a Pilgrim in Plymouth Colony. Write a letter to your friends in Europe describing your first few weeks in the new land. Explain what you hope your life will be like here.

The Middle and Southern Colonies

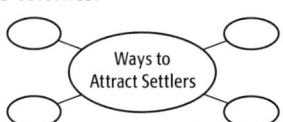
Preview of Events

♦1650	♦1675	♦1700	♦1725

1642
English Civil War begins

1660
English monarchy restored

1664
English capture New Amsterdam

1681
William Penn receives charter for Pennsylvania

1733
First English settlers arrive in Georgia

★ An American Story ★

On August 26, 1664, an English fleet arrived near the Dutch town of New Amsterdam. Its commander sent a note to Governor Peter Stuyvesant of New Netherland, demanding that the town surrender. Stuyvesant bellowed that he would rather "be carried out dead in his coffin." Badly outnumbered, however, leading Dutch citizens petitioned the governor to surrender:

❝We, your sorrowful community and subjects, [believe] that we cannot conscientiously foresee that anything else is to be expected . . . than misery, sorrow, conflagration, the dishonor of women . . . and, in a word, the absolute ruin and destruction of about fifteen hundred innocent souls, only two hundred and fifty of whom are capable of bearing arms. . . .❞

Two days later, Stuyvesant watched two English warships approach. Beside him stood a gunner, ready to fire. The minister at New Amsterdam talked urgently to the governor, then led him away. On September 8, the Dutch surrendered, and New Amsterdam became New York.

—adapted from *A New World* and *Colonial New York*

The English Civil War and the Colonies

The fall of New Amsterdam and the founding of New York in 1664 marked the beginning of a new wave of English colonization. For more than 20 years, no new English colonies had been founded in America because the struggle between the Puritans and the English king had finally led to war.

The **English Civil War** began in 1642, when King Charles I sent troops into the English Parliament to arrest several Puritan leaders. Parliament, which was dominated by Puritans, responded by organizing its own army, and a civil war began. In 1646 Parliament's army defeated the king's troops and captured King Charles. Two and a half years later, a Parliamentary court tried King Charles and condemned him to death. **Oliver Cromwell,** the commander of Parliament's army, then dissolved Parliament and seized power, giving himself the title "Lord Protector of England."

The Colonies Choose Sides Once the English Civil War began, England's colonies had to decide whether to support the king or Parliament. In Virginia, the governor and the House of Burgesses supported the king until 1652, when a fleet sent by Parliament forced them to change sides.

Across Chesapeake Bay from Virginia, Maryland experienced its own civil war. Lord Baltimore, Maryland's proprietor, had supported the king against Parliament, as had Maryland's governor. In 1644 Protestants in Maryland rebelled. To calm things down, Lord Baltimore appointed a Protestant as governor and introduced the **Maryland Toleration Act** in 1649. The act granted religious toleration to all Christians in Maryland and was intended to protect the Catholic minority from the Protestants.

In New England, the English Civil War was a time for rejoicing. The Puritan colonies backed Parliament, and their populations fell as settlers headed home to fight in the war.

Colonization Resumes After nearly 20 years of turmoil, England's leaders longed for stability. When Cromwell died in 1658, no strong leader stepped forward to replace him. England's leaders decided to restore the monarchy that had been abruptly ended with the execution of King Charles I. In the spring of 1660, Parliament invited Charles's son, Charles II, to take the throne. This became known as the **Restoration.**

With the king back on the throne, a new round of colonization began in America. From this point forward, the English government took the lead in promoting colonization. Colonies were no longer seen as risky business ventures. English leaders now viewed them as vital sources of raw materials and as markets for manufactured goods.

Reading Check **Examining** What started the English Civil War?

Picturing **History**

Puritan General Oliver Cromwell directed Parliament's troops in the English Civil War. What in his appearance suggests that he was a Puritan?

New Netherland Becomes New York

As King Charles II and his advisers studied the situation in North America, two regions attracted their interest. The first region was south of Virginia, and the second was located between Maryland and Connecticut. Taking control of the latter area would link Virginia and Maryland to New England. Unfortunately, the Dutch had already claimed much of that land. If the English wanted the region, they would have to take it from the Dutch.

The History of New Netherland In 1609 the Dutch East India Company hired an English navigator named **Henry Hudson** to find a route through North America to the Pacific. Hudson found a wide river, today known as the Hudson River. His report convinced many Dutch merchants that the Hudson River valley was rich in fur-bearing animals. They claimed the region, calling it New Netherland, and they established fur-trading posts there in 1614.

The Dutch located their major settlement, New Amsterdam, on Manhattan Island. According to tradition, the Dutch bought Manhattan Island from the local people for 60 florins (about 24 dollars) worth of goods. As in New France, the emphasis on the fur trade kept the Dutch colony from growing quickly. As late as 1646, New Netherland had only 1,500 people, compared to 25,000 in New England.

To increase the colony's size, the Dutch allowed anyone to buy land in the colony. Soon settlers from many countries began to move to New Netherland. By 1664 the colony had over 10,000 people. Settlers came from France, Germany, Poland, Spain, Italy, and other parts of Europe. A group of Portuguese Jews moved to New Amsterdam and founded one of the first synagogues in North America.

The need for labor brought unwilling immigrants to the colony as well, when Dutch merchants entered the slave trade. The first enslaved Africans arrived in New Netherland in the 1620s. By 1664 Africans made up 10 percent of the population.

New York and New Jersey By the time King Charles II took the throne in 1660, the Dutch controlled a large portion of the fur trade. They also had begun helping English colonists smuggle tobacco to Europe and illegally import European products. In 1664 King Charles decided that the time had come to seize New Netherland. In March, Charles granted all the land from Delaware Bay to the Connecticut River to his brother James, the Duke of York. James was lord high admiral for the king, and he quickly dispatched four warships to seize New Netherland from the Dutch.

After seizing New Netherland, now named New York, James granted a large portion of his land to two of the king's closest advisers, Sir George Carteret and Lord John Berkeley. James named the new colony New Jersey, in honor of Sir George Carteret, who was from the island of Jersey. To attract settlers, the proprietors offered generous land grants, religious freedom, and the right to elect a legislative assembly. These terms convinced a large number of settlers, many of them Puritans, to head to New Jersey.

Reading Check **Summarizing** Why did King Charles II want to seize New Netherland from the Dutch?

Pennsylvania and Delaware

Admiral William Penn was another close friend of King Charles. Penn had loaned ships and money to King Charles but died before the king could pay back the money he owed him.

Admiral Penn's son, who was also named **William Penn,** inherited his father's estate, including the

History *Through Art*

The Beginnings of Pennsylvania William Penn began his colony by signing a treaty with Native Americans who lived in the region. Penn also granted parts of his land to other settlers, as seen in this formal land deed (right). In the painting, what are the colonists giving the Native Americans in return for their land?

money the king owed his father. In 1680 William Penn petitioned the king for a grant of land between New York and Maryland to settle the debt. The request put the king in a dilemma. Although granting a colony was a cheap way to pay off the debt, the young man belonged to a religious group Charles had banned and persecuted. William Penn was a Quaker.

The Quakers Quakers believed that everyone had their own "inner light" from God. There was no need for a church or ministers. Even the Bible had less authority than a person's inner light. Quakers objected to all political and religious authority, including forcing people to pay taxes or serve in the military. They advocated pacifism—opposition to war or violence as a means to settle disputes.

Quaker beliefs put them into conflict with the government as well as other religions. To escape opposition, many Quakers fled to America, but they were persecuted in almost every colony. This convinced the Quakers that they needed their own colony, but they probably would never have been granted one had it not been for William Penn.

The "Holy Experiment" William Penn was one of the few wealthy Quakers and a good friend of King Charles. Penn became involved in Quaker attempts to create a colony in the 1670s, when he and other Quakers bought New Jersey from Berkeley and Carteret. Many Quakers moved to New Jersey, but Penn did not think it was the best solution since the Puritan settlers there were hostile to Quakers. In 1680 Penn asked King Charles for his own colony across the Delaware River from New Jersey. Charles agreed but insisted that the new colony be called Pennsylvania (or Penn's Woods) in honor of William Penn's father.

Penn regarded Pennsylvania as a "holy experiment" where complete political and religious freedom would be practiced. He also believed that Native Americans had been treated unjustly in other colonies, and he resolved to win the friendship of those who lived in Pennsylvania.

In late 1682, Penn made good on his word when he signed the Treaty of Shackamaxon, in which the Lenni Lenape, a Native American group, ceded land to the colonists. The treaty marked the beginning of over 70 years of peace in Pennsylvania between the European settlers and the Native Americans. On the land ceded by the Lenni Lenape, Penn built the capital of his new colony and named it Philadelphia, or "the city of brotherly love."

Penn also prepared a constitution, or "frame of government," for his colony. His initial constitution

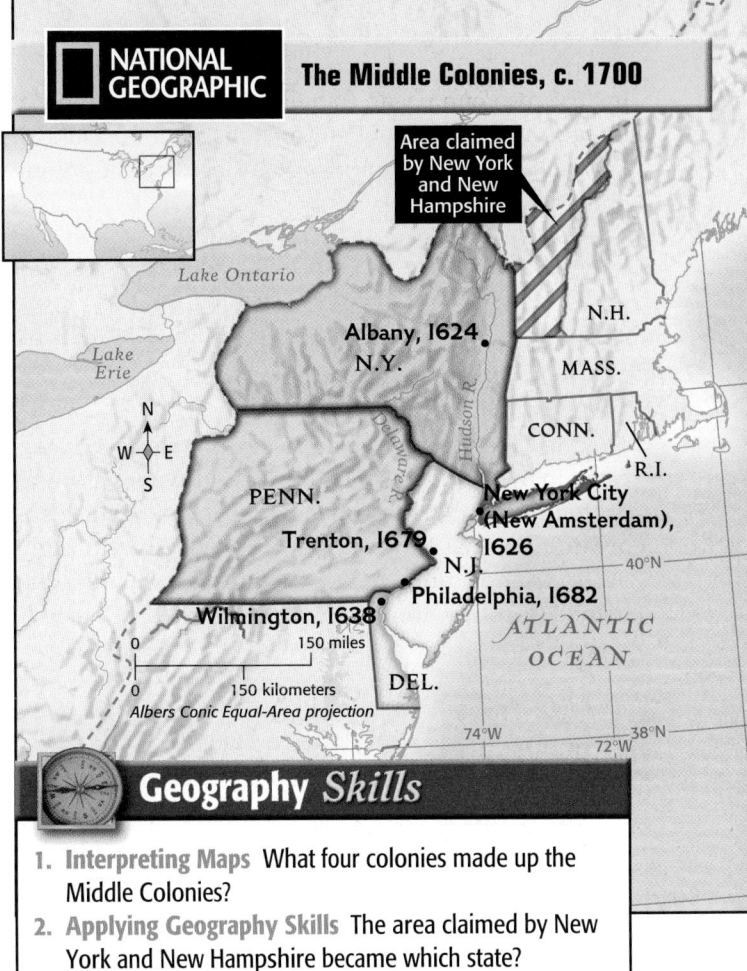

NATIONAL GEOGRAPHIC **The Middle Colonies, c. 1700**

Area claimed by New York and New Hampshire

Lake Ontario
Lake Erie
Albany, 1624
N.Y.
N.H.
MASS.
CONN.
R.I.
PENN.
New York City (New Amsterdam), 1626
Trenton, 1679
N.J.
Philadelphia, 1682
Wilmington, 1638
ATLANTIC OCEAN
DEL.
150 miles
150 kilometers
Albers Conic Equal-Area projection
40°N
74°W
72°W
38°N

Geography Skills

1. **Interpreting Maps** What four colonies made up the Middle Colonies?
2. **Applying Geography Skills** The area claimed by New York and New Hampshire became which state?

allowed anyone who owned land or paid taxes to vote, but it was confusing in structure. After several confrontations with settlers over the government's structure, Penn issued a new charter establishing a legislative assembly elected directly by the voters. The proprietor appointed the governor. The charter gave the right to vote to all colonists who owned 50 acres of land and professed a faith in Jesus Christ. Despite this example of discrimination against non-Christians, the charter guaranteed all Pennsylvanians the right to practice their religion without interference.

Penn also made land readily available to settlers, a practice that attracted thousands of colonists. Many were English Quakers, but large numbers of Germans and Scots-Irish migrated to the colony as well. By 1684 Pennsylvania had over 7,000 colonists, and by 1700 Philadelphia rivaled Boston and New York City as a center for trade and commerce.

HISTORY Online

Student Web Activity Visit the *American Vision* Web site at tav.glencoe.com and click on **Student Web Activities— Chapter 2** for an activity on the founding of Pennsylvania.

In 1682, as Penn began to build his colony, he bought three counties south of Pennsylvania from the Duke of York. These "lower counties" later became the colony of Delaware.

✓ **Reading Check** **Evaluating** Why did William Penn regard Pennsylvania as a "holy experiment"?

New Southern Colonies

King Charles and his advisers were very interested in the land south of Virginia. The year before he granted New York to his brother James, Charles II awarded a vast territory south of Virginia to eight other friends and political allies. The land was named Carolina, from the Latin version of "Charles."

NATIONAL GEOGRAPHIC **The Southern Colonies, c. 1733**

Geography *Skills*

1. **Interpreting Maps** What five colonies made up the Southern Colonies?
2. **Applying Geography Skills** What natural barrier served as the western border of the Southern Colonies?

North Carolina From the beginning, Carolina developed as two separate regions. North Carolina was home to a small and scattered population. Most of the settlers were farmers who began drifting into the region from Virginia in the 1650s.

North Carolina did not have a good harbor, and the coastline, protected by the Outer Banks, was very hard for ships to reach. As a result, the colony grew very slowly, and by 1700 only 3,000 people lived in the region. Eventually North Carolina farmers began growing tobacco. They also began to export naval supplies such as tar, pitch, and turpentine.

South Carolina The proprietors who had been granted Carolina were never interested in the northern part of the colony. South Carolina, on the other hand, was believed to be suitable for growing sugarcane. The first settlers arrived in South Carolina in 1670. They named their settlement Charles Town (today called Charleston), after King Charles.

Sugarcane, it turned out, did not grow well in this region. The first product South Carolina exported in large quantity was deerskin, which had become popular for leather in England. The colony also began to capture Native Americans and ship them to the Caribbean, where the demand for enslaved workers was high.

The Georgia Experiment In the 1720s, General **James Oglethorpe,** a wealthy member of Parliament, was appalled to find that many people in England were in prison simply because they could not pay their debts. He asked King George II for a colony south of Carolina where the poor could start over.

The English government saw advantages to a new southern colony. It might help England's poor, and it would provide a strategic buffer between South Carolina and Spanish Florida. King George granted Oglethorpe and 19 other trustees permission in 1732 to settle a region between the Savannah and Altamaha Rivers. The new colony was named Georgia, in honor of the king. Oglethorpe led the first settlers to the mouth of the Savannah River in 1733.

The Georgia trustees banned slavery, rum, and brandy in the new colony and limited land grants to 500 acres. The colony attracted settlers from all over Europe, including Scots, Welsh, Germans, Swiss, Italians, and a few Portuguese Jews.

Increasingly the settlers objected to the colony's rules. In the 1740s, the trustees lifted restrictions on brandy, rum, and slavery; in 1750 they granted the settlers an elected assembly. In 1751 Georgia became a royal colony.

Comparing European Colonies in the Americas, c. 1700

Colony	Early Settlement	Population	Areas Where Concentrated	Political and Economic Organization	Economic Focus
Spanish					
	1490s–early 1500s	Between 5–7 million (including conquered Native Americans)	Mexico, Florida, Texas, Central America, the Caribbean, California, New Mexico, north and west coast of South America	Governors with strong links to Spain; large bureaucracy; *encomiendas* and haciendas	Gold, silver mining; ranching
English					
	1490s–early explorers; early 1600s–permanent settlements	250,000	Eastern seaboard of North America	Governors with weak links to English Crown; elected assemblies; small farms; plantations; private merchants	Trade and farming
French					
	1535–early explorers; 1670s–permanent settlements	15,000	St. Lawrence River; Louisiana territory; outposts on Great Lakes and Mississippi River	Strong governors; large estates	Exporting furs

Chart Skills

1. **Interpreting Charts** Which set of colonies had the narrowest economic focus? Explain.
2. **Making Inferences** Which set of colonies seemed best equipped to settle the Americas most effectively?

England's American Colonies By 1775 England's colonies in North America were home to a growing population of roughly 2.5 million people. Despite the stumbling start in Jamestown, the English had succeeded in building a large and prosperous society on the east coast of North America. England's success, however, proved to be its own undoing. The English government had permitted new patterns of land ownership, new types of worship, and new kinds of government in its colonies. Once established, however, these practices became fixed principles. The colonists became used to self-government and gradually came to think of it as their right. Inadvertently, the English government had planted the seeds of rebellion and laid the foundation for what would eventually become the United States of America.

Reading Check **Explaining** Why were South Carolina and Georgia settled?

SECTION 4 ASSESSMENT

Checking for Understanding
1. **Define:** pacifism.
2. **Identify:** English Civil War, Maryland Toleration Act, Restoration, William Penn, James Oglethorpe.

Reviewing Themes
3. **Global Connections** After the Restoration, why did the English government openly work to promote additional colonization in North America?

Critical Thinking
4. **Analyzing** How did the English Civil War affect the English colonies in America?
5. **Categorizing** Use a graphic organizer similar to the one below to list the reasons the colonies discussed in this section were founded.

Colony	Reasons Founded
New York	
New Jersey	
Pennsylvania	

Analyzing Visuals
6. **Analyzing Art** Study the painting of Oliver Cromwell on page 73. What events led to Cromwell's rise to power in England?

Writing About History
7. **Persuasive Writing** Imagine that you have been hired by the proprietors of New Jersey to persuade settlers to come there. Write an editorial for a newspaper in England to convince people to settle in New Jersey.

BROWN BROTHERS

Profile

JOHN WHITE, *leader of the English settlers at Roanoke Island, returned to England for supplies in the colony's first year, leaving his family behind. With the war against Spain being fought at home, it was three years before he found passage back to Virginia. His ship was caught in a Nor'easter trying to reach the shore.*

At daybreak, we landed and we . . . proceeded to walk along the shore, rounding the northern part of the island, until we came to the place where we left our colony in the year 1586. . . . As we went inshore up the sandy bank we saw a tree on the brow of a cliff curiously carved with the clear Roman letters *CRO.*

We knew at once that these letters indicated the place to which the planters had gone. Before I left them we had agreed on a secret token. They were to write or carve on trees or doorposts the name of the place where they had settled. . . .

The weather grew fouler and fouler. Our food supply was diminishing, and we had lost our cask of fresh water. We therefore decided to go . . . visit our countrymen in Virginia on the return trip.

IT'S THE LAW

JAMESTOWN, 1619. All colonists are required to attend two divine services every Sunday, and they must bring along "their pieces, swords, powder and shot."

PLYMOUTH, MASSACHUSETTS, 1639. The General Court of Massachusetts prohibits the drinking of toasts. "The common custom of drinking to one another is a mere useless ceremony and draweth on the abominable practice of drinking healths."

NEW AMSTERDAM, 1658. Governor Peter Stuyvesant has prohibited tennis during the time of divine services.

Banned in Boston

Among the crimes for which colonists were punished in 1655 and 1656 were:

eavesdropping

scolding

neglect of work

meddling

pushing one's wife

pulling hair

profane dancing

uncharitableness

bad grinding at a mill

drinking

tobacco smoking

playing cards

delivering naughty speeches

Milestones

FORMED, 1570. THE IROQUOIS LEAGUE, an alliance among the Cayuga, Oneida, Seneca, Mohawk, and Onandage tribes. The goal is to avoid war by settling differences in tribal councils. *Ohwichiras*, women heads of families, choose male delegates to the League.

INTRODUCED, 1630. THE FORK, by John Winthrop, who brought the utensil to America in a leather case with a bodkin (dagger) and knife. Queen Elizabeth made use of the fork popular in England despite the condemnation of the practice by many clergy.

MISSING, 1687. THE CONNECTICUT CHARTER, a document establishing greater self-governance for the colony. Its principles are opposed by Sir Edmund Andros, governor of the Dominion of New England, who demanded the charter be surrendered. When the Connecticut assembly reluctantly displayed the document, the candles mysteriously blew out, and the charter vanished. Informed sources hint it may be found in the hollow of an oak tree.

BETTMANN/CORBIS

SET SAIL, 1715. FIRST WHALING EXPEDITION from Nantucket, Massachusetts. Spurred on by the capture of the first sperm whale in 1711, the six sloops returned home with cargo yielding 600 barrels of oil and 11,000 pounds of bone.

CONSECRATED, 1730. FIRST JEWISH SYNAGOGUE, in New York. A group of Sephardic Jews who had fled the Inquisition in Portuguese Brazil established the congregation in New Amsterdam in 1655.

NUMBERS

10 million
Subjects of Montezuma II, the Aztec ruler in 1519

100 Rooms in Montezuma's palace

100 Baths in Montezuma's palace

200,000
Soldiers in Montezuma's army

550 Soldiers in the army of Hernán Cortés

1 year
Elapsed time between Cortés's arrival in Mexico and his conquest of the Aztec

25.2 million
Estimated population of Mexico in 1518

NORTH WIND PICTURES

Montezuma

2 ASSESSMENT and ACTIVITIES

Reviewing Key Terms

On a sheet of paper, use each of these terms in a sentence.

1. conquistador
2. presidio
3. *hidalgo*
4. *encomienda*
5. hacienda
6. vaquero
7. Northwest Passage
8. coureurs de bois
9. Puritan
10. joint-stock company
11. privateer
12. burgesses
13. headright
14. proprietary colony
15. Separatist
16. Pilgrim
17. heretic
18. pacifism

Reviewing Key Facts

19. **Identify:** Francisco Pizarro, John Cabot, Walter Raleigh, William Bradford, Squanto, John Winthrop, Roger Williams, Anne Hutchinson, Oliver Cromwell, Henry Hudson, William Penn, James Oglethorpe.
20. Why were the Spanish able to defeat the Aztec and the Inca?

21. What factors determined social class in the Spanish colonies?
22. What was the purpose of the Council of the Indies?
23. What role did Bartolomé de Las Casas play in reforming Spain's policies toward Native Americans?
24. How did the French treat the Native Americans?
25. How did joint-stock companies help colonize North America?
26. How did tobacco save the Jamestown colony?
27. What caused Roger Williams to leave Massachusetts and found the town of Providence?
28. Why was Georgia founded?

Critical Thinking

29. **Analyzing Themes: Cultures and Traditions** How did the relationships between Native Americans and the Spanish differ from those between Native Americans and the French?
30. **Evaluating** How were England's royal colonies and proprietary colonies governed?
31. **Identifying Cause and Effect** How did the English Civil War affect the English colonies in North America?

Chapter Summary

French Colonies

- Established to expand fur trade
- Colonization effort grew slowly
- Population of New France increased by promotion of immigration
- Enslaved Africans imported to work plantations in Louisiana

British Colonies

- Established as places to earn profits and to practice religion freely
- Provided a place for the poor to start a new life
- Offered right to elect legislative assembly
- Used as sources of raw materials and markets for British goods

Spanish Colonies

- Established to gain wealth and spread Christianity and European culture
- Structured society based on birth, income, and education
- Economy dominated by mining and ranching

Dutch Colonies

- Founded to make money in fur trade
- Settlers from many countries populated New Netherland
- Need for laborers led to Dutch involvement in slave trade
- Territory eventually surrendered to Britain

Mercator projection

Self-Check Quiz

Visit the *American Vision* Web site at tav.glencoe.com and click on **Self-Check Quizzes—Chapter 2** to assess your knowledge of chapter content.

32. Categorizing Use a graphic organizer like this one to list the reasons for English colonization in North America.

Reasons for Colonization

Practicing Skills

33. Understanding the Parts of a Map Study the map of the Great Migration on page 68. Then use the skills described on that page to answer the following questions.
a. In what directions did English Puritans travel when they migrated to New England and to the Bahamas?

b. Using the map labels, estimate the total number of Puritan immigrants to the New World between the 1620s and the 1640s.

Chapter Activity

34. American History Primary Source Document Library CD-ROM Read "The German Settlements in Pennsylvania" by Francis D. Pastorius, under *Colonial America.* Work with a small group of your classmates to draw a plan of Germantown based on Pastorius's description.

Writing Activity

35. Descriptive Writing The English colonies were founded for various reasons. New governments in each of these colonies offered incentives to new settlers. Pretend you have decided to move from England to America. Write a letter to your family and friends explaining why you have chosen to settle in a particular colony.

Geography and History

36. The map on this page shows English colonial settlements. Study the map and answer the questions below.
a. Interpreting Maps Which colonies had the most territory by 1660?

b. Applying Geography Skills Along which natural features had most of the colonies settled by 1700?

NATIONAL GEOGRAPHIC
Settlement of the Colonies, 1587–1700

ME. (Part of MASS.)
NEW ENGLAND
N.H. • Portsmouth
N.Y.
Boston
MASS. • Plymouth
• Providence
Hartford • R.I.
CONN.
New Haven
MIDDLE COLONIES N.J. New Amsterdam
PA.
Philadelphia
Baltimore • — DEL.
MD. ATLANTIC OCEAN
VA. Williamsburg
Jamestown
SOUTHERN COLONIES
N.C.
S.C.
Charles Town
GA.
Savannah

Lake Ontario
Lake Erie
St. Lawrence R.
APPALACHIAN MOUNTAINS
40°N
70°W
80°W

N W E S

• City
— Regional Boundary
Settled by 1660
Settled by 1700

0   200 miles
0   200 kilometers
Albers Conic Equal-Area Projection

CHAPTER 3

Colonial Ways of Life
1607–1763

Why It Matters

An agricultural society developed in the American colonies. In the South, a large number of Africans were enslaved for plantation labor. In the North, commerce took hold, and England's trade policies proved cause for concern. High birth rates and immigration expanded the population as American society began to take shape.

The Impact Today

Key developments in this period have influenced American society.
- *The northern United States is still more urban than much of the South.*
- *The United States remains a nation made up of immigrants from many countries.*

The American Vision *Video* *The Chapter 3 video, "The Middle Passage," chronicles the journey enslaved Africans endured when they were forcibly brought to the colonies.*

1676
- Nathaniel Bacon leads popular revolt in Jamestown, Virginia

1607
- Jamestown founded in Virginia

1638
- Maryland is first English colony to legally recognize slavery

1619
- First Africans arrive in North America via Dutch traders

1683
- Mennonites found Germantown, Pennsylvania

The Americas

1605

1645

1685

World

1642
- English Civil War begins

1651
- English Parliament introduces stronger Navigation Act

1660
- Several small kingdoms established on Africa's upper Niger River
- Louis XIV, the Sun King, rules France

Colonial Wedding by Edward Lamson Henry, 1911

1686
• Dominion of New England established

1692
• Salem witchcraft trials begin

1705
• Virginia's slave code formally regulates slavery

1727
• Coffee first planted in Brazil

1734
• Libel trial of newspaper publisher John Peter Zenger helps establish free press tradition

1763
• French and Indian War ends in North America

1725

1765

1688
• Power of English king restricted as Parliament awards William and Mary the throne in Glorious Revolution

1725
• Russian czar Peter the Great dies

1707
• Act of Union creates United Kingdom

1742
• Handel's "Messiah" debuts in Dublin, Ireland

HISTORY
Online

Chapter Overview
Visit the *American Vision* Web site at tav.glencoe.com and click on **Chapter Overviews—Chapter 3** to preview chapter information.

The Southern Colonies

★ An American Story ★

William Byrd II, a wealthy eighteenth-century Virginia planter, played a central role in his colony's government. In addition to serving as colonel of the county militia and as a member of the House of Burgesses, Byrd founded the city of Richmond and experimented with a variety of crops on his plantation. His wealth gave him the leisure to pursue cultural interests, and he amassed over 4,000 books—the biggest private library in the colonies. He left behind several diaries detailing life on Southern plantations. On January 27, 1711, he noted:

❝I rose at 5 o'clock and read two chapters in Hebrew and some Greek in Lucian. I said my prayers and ate boiled milk for breakfast. . . . I settled several accounts; then I read some English which gave me great light into the nature of spirit. . . . In the afternoon my wife and I took a little walk and then danced together. Then I read some more English. At night I read some Italian and then played at piquet [a card game] with my wife. . . . I said my prayers and had good health, good thoughts, and good humor, thank God Almighty.❞

—quoted in *The Growth of the American Republic*

The Southern Economy

The wealth of Westover, Byrd's plantation, was built in large part on the labor of enslaved Africans. In Byrd's Virginia, a class of wealthy planters stood on society's top rung, while enslaved Africans were at the bottom. In between were many farmers who owned small farms and held few or no slaves.

From the earliest days of settlement, the Southern Colonies developed an economy based on commercial agriculture. A few years after the founding of Jamestown, tobacco became the South's first successful cash crop, or crop grown primarily for market. Tobacco became the main cash crop grown in Virginia and Maryland and, to a lesser extent, North Carolina. Rice and indigo became the main cash crops in South Carolina. These cash crops needed the right kind of climate and techniques to be cultivated. These requirements led to the rise of plantations, or large commercial estates where many laborers lived on the land and cultivated the crops for the landowner.

GEOGRAPHY

Tobacco and the Chesapeake
Between 1620 and 1660, the demand for tobacco in Europe was greater than the supply. This kept the price high, ensuring that most tobacco planters could make money even if they grew only a small amount. Those who could grow and harvest a large quantity of tobacco could become wealthy.

Growing tobacco required intensive manual labor. Each plant had to be carefully nurtured before being cut and hung up to cure. After curing, the leaves were packed into hogsheads—huge wooden barrels—that, once filled and sealed, often weighed close to 1,000 pounds (454 kg). The amount of labor needed to grow tobacco meant that to become wealthy, a tobacco farmer needed a large work force to cultivate a large crop.

The geography of the Chesapeake Bay region was perfectly suited to tobacco farming. The bay acted like a wide road. Numerous inlets and navigable rivers connected to the bay. If tobacco farmers located their farms next to a river, they could ship their crop from their own wharves. The colonists built very few roads or towns because they had no need to move goods overland. Instead, merchant ships made their way up the rivers from farm to farm, picking up tobacco and selling supplies.

NATIONAL GEOGRAPHIC

Southern Agriculture, 1750

Rice
Indigo
Tobacco
Proclamation Line

Tobacco Imported by England, 1705–1775

= 1,000 pounds

Pounds (in thousands)

Year

Source: *Historical Statistics of the United States: Colonial Times to 1970.*

Geography *Skills*

1. **Interpreting Maps** Why were tobacco and rice farms located next to rivers?
2. **Interpreting Charts** Approximately how many pounds of tobacco did England import in 1735?

The Ideal Plantation This painting depicts the well-structured plantation as a world unto itself. Centered around the family home, the plantation's fields, support houses, and merchant ships unite to serve the needs of the plantation. Why did plantations develop in the South?

Indentured Servants

In the early days of Virginia and Maryland, there was plenty of land for tobacco farmers but not enough labor to work it. England had the opposite problem. Many poor tenant farmers had been forced off the land during the enclosure movement, creating high unemployment and a large number of people willing to sell their labor for a chance to come to America and acquire their own land. To pay for their passage, these people agreed to become indentured servants.

In this system, colonists in America agreed to pay the cost of transporting the servants to the colonies and promised to provide food, clothing, and shelter to them until their indentures, or labor contracts, expired. In exchange, the servants agreed to work for the owner of their contract for a specific number of years. These contracts usually specified four years, but some were for seven years or even more if the indentured servant arrived as a child.

For much of the 1600s, indentured servitude was a very good system for tobacco planters. Indentured servants could produce five times the price of their contracts in tobacco in the first year alone. Under the headright system, every indentured servant transported to America also earned the landowner another 50 acres of land. As large numbers of indentured servants arrived in Virginia and Maryland, tobacco production rose steadily.

Rice and Indigo in South Carolina

South of Virginia, the proprietors of South Carolina had hoped their colony's warm climate would permit the cultivation of sugarcane as a cash crop. When sugarcane failed, the settlers also tried and failed to cultivate rice. This venture also failed, because the settlers did not know how to properly harvest rice. In addition, the extreme humidity, swamps, mosquitoes, and muddy fields of the lowlands where rice had to be planted discouraged cultivation.

In the 1690s, a new type of rice was introduced, and the planters—many of whom had come from Barbados and Jamaica where slavery was common—decided to import enslaved Africans to cultivate it. West Africans had cultivated rice for centuries. Although their techniques were very labor-intensive, they knew how to harvest rice and remove the hull. Rice rapidly became a major cash crop in South Carolina and, to a lesser extent, in Georgia.

In the early 1740s, South Carolina began to develop another cash crop called indigo. Indigo was used to make blue dye for cloth—a dye much in demand in Europe. Previously, planters in South Carolina had tried to grow indigo without much success. Then, in the early 1740s, 17-year-old **Eliza Lucas,** began experimenting with the plant. Lucas discovered that indigo needed high ground and sandy soil, not the wetlands that suited rice.

Indigo was a good second crop for the rice plantations. It could be grown on land unsuitable for rice, and it required care and harvesting only in seasons when the enslaved workers were not busy with rice.

Reading Check **Describing** Why did attempts to grow rice in South Carolina fail at first?

Southern Society

Although many immigrants to the Southern Colonies hoped to become wealthy, very few did. The nature of the plantation system tended to create a society with distinct social classes. Planters who could afford to bring in many slaves or indentured servants received much larger land grants. With their large labor force and land area, they could produce a much larger crop. The money they earned enabled them to acquire still more workers and to extend their estates up and down the rivers of a region. The result was a society where a wealthy elite controlled most of the land and relied upon the labor of others to work it for them.

The Planter Elite

The wealthy landowners, sometimes referred to as the Southern gentry or the planter elite, enjoyed enormous economic and political influence. They represented their communities in the governing councils and assemblies, commanded the local militias, and served as county judges.

With few towns or roads in the region, the plantations of the Southern gentry had to function as self-contained communities. The residents lived near each other in a group of buildings, including the planter's great house, stables and barns, and the workers' cabins. Plantations often had other facilities such as schools and chapels, and workshops for blacksmiths, carpenters, weavers, coopers (barrel makers), and leather workers.

In the 1600s, most plantations were small, rough estates. In many cases, they were little more than stump-filled clearings where the planters and their indentured servants worked side-by-side under very difficult conditions. Many became sick and died. Even in the late 1600s, plantation workforces rarely exceeded 30 people. The great houses on most of these early plantations were small, with only four to seven rooms.

In the early 1700s, as wealthier planters in Virginia and Maryland switched from indentured to slave labor, the size of their plantations began to grow. As their wealth and property increased, the gentry began to build large brick mansions with imposing steps and doorways and elaborate gardens. They also tried to copy the fashions and lifestyle of England's upper class. No longer did they labor in the fields with their workers. Instead, the gentry hired overseers to manage the enslaved Africans, while they looked after accounts and other business matters on the plantation.

As the wealth of the planter elite increased, so too did their leisure time. The gentry often amused themselves by hunting and fishing, and by gambling on horse races, cards, and dice. Some, like William Byrd, enjoyed intellectual pursuits such as reading or practicing music.

Backcountry Farmers Close to half the indentured servants who came to the Chesapeake region in the 1600s died before gaining their freedom. Of those who became free, less than half acquired their own land. Although land itself was very easy to acquire, settlers had to pay for the deed and land survey and also had to pay for tools, seeds, and livestock. Many could not afford these costs, and instead they became tenant farmers, working lands that they rented from the planter elite.

Despite such difficulties, some former indentured servants did acquire their own land. Although wealthy planters owned most of the land along the rivers, most landowners in the colonial South were actually small farmers living in the "backcountry" farther inland. These farmers are sometimes referred to as **yeomen,** to distinguish them from the gentry.

The backcountry farmers worked small plots of land and lived in tiny one- or two-room houses with few furnishings. Although these farmers grew some tobacco, they also practiced subsistence farming, or farming only enough crops to feed their own families. Subsistence crops included corn, beans, potatoes, barley, and rye. Hogs and other livestock were allowed to run wild until needed for meat.

By the 1670s, the colonial South was a sharply divided society, with a small group of wealthy planters at the top and many poor backcountry farmers, landless tenant farmers, servants, and enslaved Africans at the bottom. Eventually, this uneven distribution of wealth and power led to rebellion.

 Reading Check **Discussing** What led to the rise of the planter elite in colonial Southern society?

Bacon's Rebellion

By the 1660s, wealthy planters led by the governor, **Sir William Berkeley,** dominated Virginia's society. Berkeley controlled the legislature through his

Picturing History

Bacon's Rebellion This uprising pitted backcountry farmers against Virginia's ruling gentry. Was Nathaniel Bacon a backcountry farmer? How would you describe his depiction in this engraving?

appointments to the colony's governing council and gifts of land to members of the House of Burgesses.

Once Governor Berkeley had assembled a majority of supporters in the House of Burgesses, he exempted himself and his councilors from taxation. Convinced that voting should be reserved for the wealthy, Berkeley also arranged for the House of Burgesses to restrict the vote to people who owned property, cutting the number of voters in Virginia in half. All of these developments angered the backcountry and tenant farmers. Ultimately, however, it was the governor's Native American policies that sparked a revolt.

Crisis Over Land

The most important issue for most colonists was to acquire land. Many indentured servants and tenant farmers wanted to own farms eventually. Backcountry farmers wanted to expand their holdings. By the 1670s, most remaining land was in areas claimed by Native Americans in the Piedmont, the region of rolling hills between the coastal plains and the Appalachians.

Most wealthy planters lived near the coast in the region known as the **Tidewater.** They had no interest in the backcountry and did not want to endanger their plantations by risking war with the Native Americans. Therefore, they opposed expanding the colony into Native American lands. This stand angered the backcountry farmers.

In 1675 war erupted between backcountry settlers and the Susquehannock people of the region. Governor Berkeley tried to calm things down. He refused to sanction any further military action against the Native Americans. Instead he asked the House of Burgesses for money to build new forts along the frontier—the westernmost point of colonial settlement.

Nathaniel Bacon Leads a Revolt

In April 1676, a group of backcountry farmers met to discuss the situation. At the meeting was a well-to-do planter named Nathaniel Bacon, who had recently purchased a large tract of land near the frontier. Although he was a member of the governor's council, Bacon took up the cause of the backcountry farmers. Native Americans had recently attacked his plantation, and he wanted to do something.

Bacon organized his own militia and attacked the Native Americans. Governor Berkeley decided to call new elections. He needed an assembly supported by the voters to calm the situation. The newly elected House of Burgesses authorized Bacon to raise a force

African Culture Crosses the Ocean: A Woman's Song

On a steamy March day in 1997, in the tiny town of Senehun Ngola in Sierra Leone, West Africa, Mary Moran, an African American from Georgia, first met Baindu Jabati, a Sierra Leonean. The two women had something amazing in common: a song each woman had known all her life.

In an emotional meeting, Moran and Jabati shared the song that the female ancestors of each of them had passed down for more than 200 years. Although the melody of the American version had changed, the words of this song in the Mende language of Sierra Leone probably came to America's South on the slave ships that sailed from West Africa in the 1700s.

The women in Mary Moran's family had passed the song down through the generations. Over time, the true origin of the song was lost. Although she had sung the song all her life, Moran never knew what its words meant. She imagined that it was an old African song.

Wanting to trace her family's history, Moran consulted with ethnomusicologists, who study folk music. Moran discovered that her family's song came from southern Sierra Leone and that it was traditionally sung at funerals. Jabati, who had inherited the traditional duty to sing at funerals, said that meeting Moran would have been better only if her ancestors could have been there also for the joyous occasion.

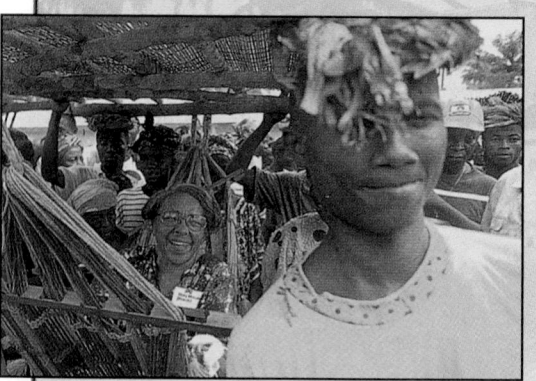

Mary Moran (center) at a Sierra Leone market

of 1,000 troops to attack the Native Americans. The assembly then restored the vote to all free men and took away the tax exemptions Berkeley had granted to his supporters.

Despite these reforms, Bacon was not satisfied. In July 1676 he returned to Jamestown with several hundred armed men and seized power, charging Berkeley with corruption. Berkeley fled Jamestown and raised his own army. The two sides battled until October 1676, when Bacon, hiding in a swamp, became sick and died. Without his leadership, his army rapidly disintegrated.

Slavery Increases in Virginia Bacon's Rebellion convinced many wealthy planters that the best way to keep Virginian society stable was to have land available for the backcountry farmers. From the 1680s onward, Virginia's government generally supported expanding the colony westward, regardless of the impact on Native Americans.

Bacon's Rebellion also accelerated an existing trend in Virginia—the use of enslaved Africans instead of indentured servants to work the fields. In the 1680s, after the rebellion, the number of Africans brought to the colony increased dramatically.

Planters began to switch to enslaved Africans for several reasons. Enslaved workers, unlike indentured servants, did not have to be freed and therefore would never need their own land. In addition, when

cheap land became available in the 1680s in the new colony of Pennsylvania, fewer English settlers were willing to become indentured servants.

At the same time, the English government adopted policies that encouraged slavery. English law limited trade between the English colonies and other countries. Before the 1670s, if settlers wanted to acquire enslaved Africans, they had to buy them from the Dutch or Portuguese, which was difficult to arrange. In 1672, however, King Charles II granted a charter to the **Royal African Company** to engage in the slave trade. With an English company in the slave trade, it became much easier to acquire enslaved people.

✔ **Reading Check** **Examining** What government policies caused some backcountry farmers to rebel?

Slavery in the Colonies

For enslaved Africans, the voyage to America usually began with a march to a European fort on the West African coast. Tied together with ropes around their necks and hands, they were traded to Europeans, branded, and forced aboard a ship. Historians estimate that between 10 and 12 million Africans were forcibly transported to the Americas between 1450 and 1870. Of those 10 to 12 million, roughly 2 million died at sea.

Olaudah Equiano, also known as Gustavus Vassa, was kidnapped from his West African home by other Africans in the 1760s. He was then traded to Europeans and shipped to America. Years later, after winning his freedom, he wrote a memoir. In it, he described the terrible journey across the Atlantic, known to Europeans as the Middle Passage:

Elmire Castle, a Portuguese-built fort on the coast of Ghana, was a holding area for slaves who would soon travel across the Atlantic Ocean in the hold of crowded slave ships (depicted below).

❝At last, when the ship we were in had got in all her cargo, . . . we were all put under deck. . . . The closeness of the place, and heat of the climate, added to the number in the ship, which was so crowded that each had scarcely room to turn himself, almost suffocated us. . . . [This] brought on a sickness among the slaves, of which many died. . . . The shrieks of the women, and the groans of the dying, rendered the whole a scene of horror almost inconceivable. . . .❞

—from *The Interesting Narrative of the Life of Olaudah Equiano, or Gustavus Vassa the African*

Chained and crammed into the ships' filthy holds for more than a month, prisoners like Equiano could hardly sit or stand and were given minimal food and drink. Africans who died or became sick were thrown overboard. Those who refused to eat were whipped.

Olaudah Equiano Fortunate to eventually win his own freedom, Equiano still suffered the brutal journey to the American colonies and years of slavery. *How did Equiano end up on a slave ship bound for the United States?*

Of the 8 to 10 million Africans who reached the Americas, approximately 3.5 million went to Brazil, and another 1.5 million went to the Spanish colonies. The British, French, and Dutch colonies in the Caribbean imported nearly 4 million others to work on their sugar plantations. Approximately 500,000 Africans were transported to North America before the slave trade ended in the 1800s.

When the first Africans arrived in Virginia in 1619, English law did not recognize chattel slavery, where one human being is said to be owned by another. As a result, slavery developed slowly in the Chesapeake colonies. The first Africans brought to Virginia and Maryland were treated in a manner similar to indentured servants, and children born to Africans were not always considered enslaved.

Some of the first enslaved Africans obtained their freedom by converting to Christianity. To many English settlers in the early 1600s, enslaving Africans was acceptable not because of their race, but because they were not Christians. As the number of Africans increased in Virginia and Maryland, their status changed. In 1638 Maryland became the first British colony to formally recognize slavery when it denied Africans the same rights as English citizens. Beginning in the 1660s, new laws in Virginia and Maryland gradually lowered the status of all Africans, regardless of their religion, and changed slavery into a hereditary system based on race.

Finally, in 1705, Virginia pulled all of these different laws together into a slave code—a set of laws that formally regulated slavery and defined the relationship between enslaved Africans and free people. Other colonies created their own slave codes. Over time slave codes became increasingly strict. Africans were denied the right to own property or to testify against a white person in court. Their movements were regulated, and they were often forbidden to assemble in large numbers. By the early 1700s, slavery had become a recognized and generally accepted institution in colonial society, particularly in the Southern Colonies, where the labor of hundreds of thousands of enslaved Africans played a vital role in the growth of the plantation economy.

Reading Check **Explaining** How did the concept of slavery in the Southern Colonies change over time?

SECTION 1 ASSESSMENT

Checking for Understanding

1. **Define:** cash crop, plantation, indentured servant, gentry, subsistence farming, Middle Passage, slave code.
2. **Identify:** Eliza Lucas, William Berkeley, Royal African Company.
3. **Explain** why South Carolina began producing indigo.

Reviewing Themes

4. **Geography and History** How did the geography of the Chesapeake region affect its economic development?

Critical Thinking

5. **Contrasting** How did the economies of the Chesapeake region and South Carolina differ?
6. **Analyzing** How did the slave trade develop in the Americas?
7. **Categorizing** Use a graphic organizer similar to the one below to list the causes of Bacon's Rebellion.

Causes

Bacon's Rebellion

Analyzing Visuals

8. **Analyzing Art** Study the painting on page 87 depicting Bacon's Rebellion. What motivated Nathaniel Bacon to lead his rebellion against the Virginia gentry?

Writing About History

9. **Descriptive Writing** Imagine you are a backcountry farmer in Virginia. Write a letter to your local newspaper describing how you feel about Sir William Berkeley and the policies he instituted.

New England and the Middle Colonies

Guide to Reading

Main Idea

In New England and the Middle Colonies, a diverse economy supported many large port cities.

Key Terms and Names

Grand Banks, fall line, town meeting, selectmen, meetinghouse, bill of exchange, triangular trade, artisan, entrepreneur, capitalist

Reading Strategy

Categorizing As you read about New England and the Middle Colonies, complete a chart similar to the one below describing how resources affected economic development.

Resources	Industries
Sea	

Reading Objectives

- **List** the geographical conditions that determined the economy of the New England Colonies.
- **Summarize** how life in the Middle Colonies differed from life in the New England Colonies.

Section Theme

Culture and Traditions The culture of the New England Colonies developed differently from that of the Southern Colonies.

Preview of Events

♦1630   ♦1650   ♦1670   ♦1690

1630
Massachusetts Bay Colony is founded

1635
First New England sawmill built

1681
City of Philadelphia first laid out by William Markham

1692
Salem witchcraft trials take place in Massachusetts

★ An American Story ★

New England's soil was thin and rocky, and from the earliest days, many settlers knew they would have to depend on the sea for their livelihood. Although some people back in England believed New England offered only a meager existence, the Reverend Francis Higginson learned otherwise. One of New England's earliest settlers, Higginson here describes the rich fishing off the coast of New England:

❝I saw great store of whales and grampuses, and such abundance of mackerels that it would astonish one to behold. . . . There is a fish called a bass, a most sweet and wholesome fish as ever I did eat. . . . Of this fish our fishers may take many hundreds together, which I have seen lying on the shore, to my admiration. Yea, their nets ordinarily take more than they are able to haul to land. . . . And besides bass, we take plenty of skate and thornback, and abundance of lobsters; and the least boy in the plantation may both catch and eat what he will of them.❞

—from "On the Riches of New England," *The Annals of America*

New England's Economy

Although the fishing industry made few New Englanders rich, it did provide a living for many settlers who built ships or engaged in foreign trade. Farther inland, numerous small farms, sawmills, and other industries helped to create a very diverse economy in New England.

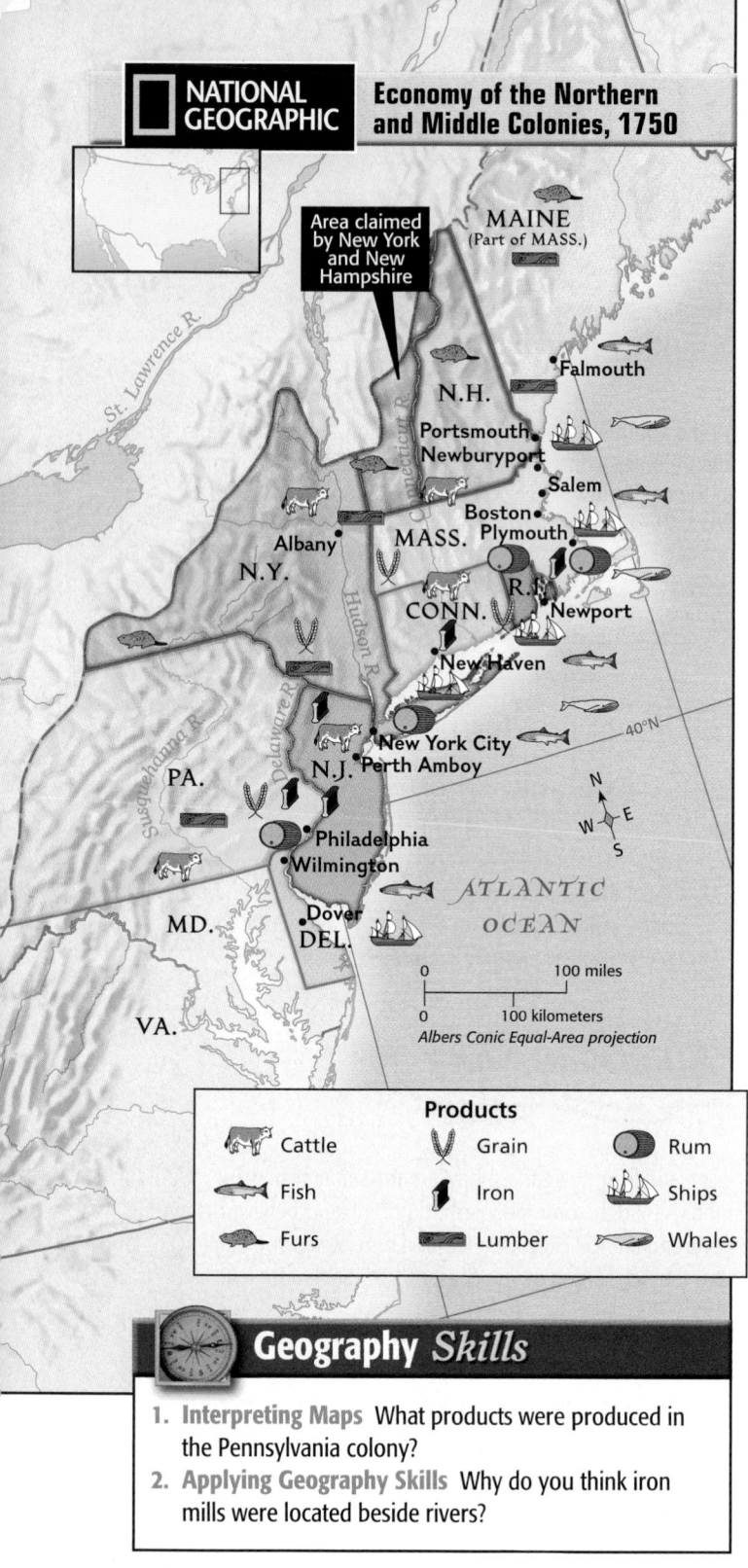

Economy of the Northern and Middle Colonies, 1750

Area claimed by New York and New Hampshire

MAINE (Part of MASS.)

Falmouth

N.H.

Portsmouth
Newburyport

Salem

Boston
Plymouth

Albany

MASS.

N.Y.

R.I.

CONN.

Newport

New Haven

New York City
Perth Amboy

PA.

N.J.

Philadelphia
Wilmington

Dover
DEL.

MD.

VA.

ATLANTIC OCEAN

40°N

N
W E
S

0   100 miles
0   100 kilometers
Albers Conic Equal-Area projection

St. Lawrence R.
Connecticut R.
Hudson R.
Susquehanna R.
Delaware R.

Products

Cattle	Grain	Rum
Fish	Iron	Ships
Furs	Lumber	Whales

Geography Skills

1. **Interpreting Maps** What products were produced in the Pennsylvania colony?
2. **Applying Geography Skills** Why do you think iron mills were located beside rivers?

None of the crops that could be grown in New England were in great demand elsewhere. The region's unsuitability for cash crops prevented the development of large plantations. Instead, on small farms that dotted the New England landscape from Connecticut to Maine, New England farmers practiced subsistence farming, using nearly everything they produced.

Although New England farmers tried to grow wheat, in most places the soil was too poor, and the presence of a fungus called black rust prevented any real success during the colonial era. As a result, the main crop grown in colonial New England was corn.

Corn had a short growing season, and its long taproot allowed it to grow well even in New England's rocky soil. As New England became more settled, farmers began to grow barley, oats, and rye, as well as many types of vegetables, including beans, peas, pumpkins, squash, and turnips. Most farms also included orchards. Apple trees were common because apples could be used for cider or dried to feed livestock in the winter. Farmers also made use of berries, particularly cranberries, blackberries, and strawberries, which grew wild throughout New England.

New England farmers also raised livestock. They used oxen to pull plows and wagons and used horses for travel. Dairy cattle provided milk for butter and cheese, and sheep provided wool. Pigs supplied meat, and salted pork was a common source of protein during the long winter months.

GEOGRAPHY

Fishing and Whaling The geography of New England almost guaranteed that fishing would become a major industry in the region. Northeast of New England lay the **Grand Banks,** a shallow region in the Atlantic Ocean where the mixing of the warm Gulf Stream and the cold North Atlantic produced an environment favorable to plankton—an important food supply for many types of fish and whales. In the colonial era the Grand Banks teemed with fish, including cod, mackerel, halibut, and herring.

At the same time, New England's coastline had many good harbors and plenty of timber for building fishing boats. There was a great demand for fish, as it was an important source of nutrition in the colonies, southern Europe, and the Caribbean. Fishing, more than any other industry, brought prosperity to New England. Nearly every coastal town had a fishing fleet. In the early 1700s, an estimated 4,000 to 5,000 people in New England made their living by fishing.

Whaling also played a major role in New England's economy, especially for people living on Nantucket Island and in Provincetown at the end of Cape Cod. Whalers sought their prey for its blubber, used for making candles and lamp oil; ambergris, a waxy intestinal substance used to make perfume; and bones, used for buttons and combs and as supports in women's clothing.

Sudbury, Massachusetts, c. late 1600s

Common Swamp

GENERAL FIELD ⑤

Sudbury R.

Cranberry Swamp

③

②

①

NORTH FIELD

GENERAL FIELD

C O M M O N

④

Mill

SOUTH FIELD

① Near the common was the church, called the "meetinghouse" by Puritans.

② Each household received a three- to five-acre home lot where they built a house, a storage building, and pens for livestock.

③ Town proprietors distributed farmland based on each family's size, wealth, and status.

④ Most families, such as John Goodnow's, received several strips of land.

⑤ Around the town were common fields; town members jointly agreed on crops grown there, and cows grazed on the common land.

Commonly held land
Privately held lots
John Goodnow's holdings
▪ Residences
⚑ Meetinghouse

Source: *American History.*

Sudbury, Massachusetts The town was the basic unit of community life in New England in the 1600s. Houses were laid out around a central pasture called a common. In this map, the holdings of one man, John Goodnow, are highlighted in purple to show the way each person's land holdings could be scattered about the town. Who decided how much land each person received?

Lumbering and Shipbuilding

Dense forest covered much of North America's eastern coastline in the 1600s. Although settlers relied on wood from these forests in every colony, New England's geography—particularly in Maine and New Hampshire—provided the conditions necessary for the development of a lumber industry.

In New England the **fall line**—the area where rivers descend from a high elevation to a lower one, causing waterfalls—is near the coast. Waterfalls were used to power sawmills. The first sawmill in the colonies was probably built in New Hampshire in 1635. Others soon followed. Lumber cut at these sawmills could easily be transported downriver to the coast and shipped to other colonies or to England.

Every colony needed lumber. Colonists wanted walnut, maple, and sycamore wood for furniture. They used cedar for doorframes and windowsills. Maple was made into spinning wheels. Oak and pine provided materials for boards, shingles, and barrel staves. Barrel making was a very important industry in the colonies because barrels were used to store and ship almost everything. Coopers in the colonial era made between 300,000 and 400,000 barrels per year. The lumber industry also made possible another important industry in New England—shipbuilding.

With forests and sawmills close to the coast, ships could be built quickly and cheaply. The large fishing industry and the growing trade between New England and the other colonies created a steady demand for ships. English merchants purchased many ships from the colonies because the ships could be built for 30 to 50 percent less in America than in England. By the 1770s, one out of every three English ships had been built in America.

Reading Check **Summarizing** How did geography shape New England's industries?

Life in New England's Towns

If self-sufficient plantations defined the social organization in the South, Puritan New England's social life centered on the town. Puritans believed that God had entered into a covenant—or solemn contract—with human beings that enabled them to obtain salvation. As a result they also believed that groups of Christians should come together to form church covenants—voluntary agreements to worship together.

The commitment to church covenants encouraged the development of towns. Instead of granting land to individuals, the general courts in the New

England Colonies granted land to groups of people, who then became the town proprietors. The town proprietors were usually prominent members of a congregation that wanted to establish a new community. The town became the heart of New England society. It determined how the land was settled and how the people were governed.

GOVERNMENT

Town Meetings Town residents met to discuss local problems and issues. Free men in the towns elected leaders and chose deputies to go to the General Court of their colony. These town meetings developed into the local town government. Although anyone in the town could attend a town meeting and express an opinion, voting was limited to men who had been granted land by the town. As town meetings became more frequent, the men began to pass laws for the town and to elect officials.

The men chosen to manage the town's affairs were called selectmen, and they were elected annually. The selectmen appointed any other officials the town needed, such as clerks, constables, and justices of the peace. Town meetings were very important. Unlike farmers in England, the settlers in New England were allowed to directly participate in their own local government. They developed a strong belief that they had the right to govern themselves. Town meetings helped set the stage for the American Revolution and the emergence of democratic government.

Puritan Society The Puritans' houses were located close to the church, or **meetinghouse,** and so they could never claim distance as an excuse to miss Sunday worship, sermons, and Thursday night religious lectures. These sermons and lectures reinforced the Puritans' obedience to strict rules regulating most activities of daily life. Puritan law banned "Those infamous Games of Cards and Dice because of the lottery which is in them." Puritans also frowned upon "Stage-Players and Mixed Dancing."

Puritans also felt a sense of responsibility for the moral welfare of their neighbors. Watching over their neighbors' behavior was elevated to a religious duty, which Puritans termed "Holy Watching," or "doing the Lord's work."

Although the Puritans have acquired a reputation for being intolerant and rigidly moral, they were not opposed to everything that was fun and pleasurable. Puritans drank rum, enjoyed music, and liked to wear brightly colored clothing that indicated their wealth and social position. They worked hard, and Puritan artisans and architects produced beautiful and elegant works. In the Puritan view, God had made the world, and the things in it were to be enjoyed by people. As one colonist wrote at the time, "In New England . . . the farmers live in the midst of a

The Salem witchcraft trials (below) led to several executions (right).

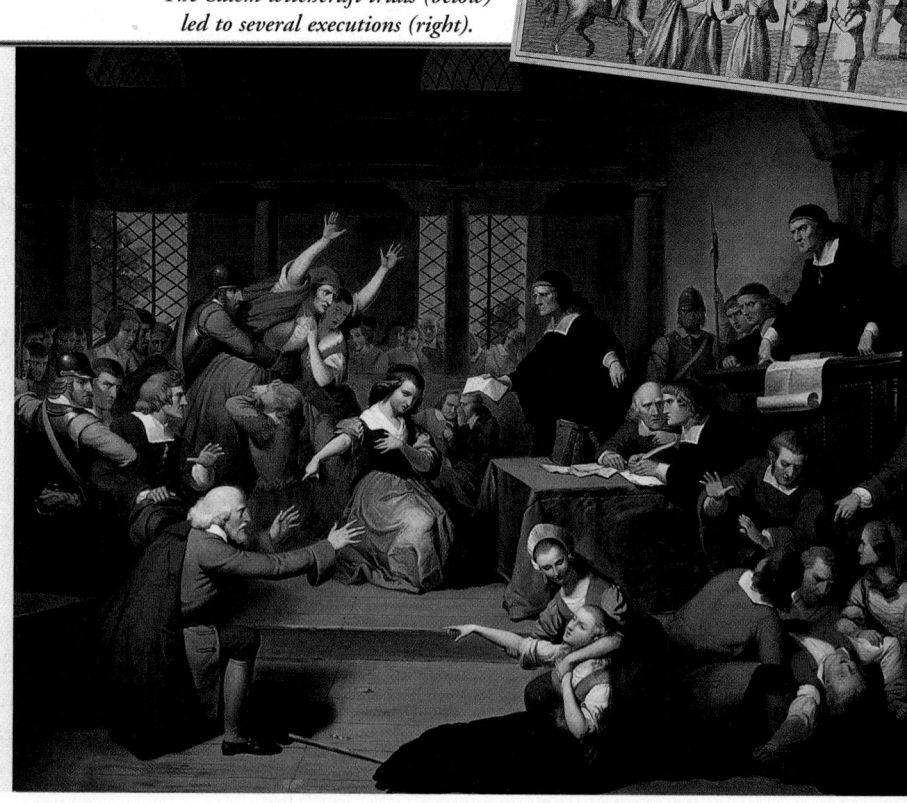

Salem and Witchcraft

Devout Puritans in the late 1600s firmly believed that Satan used witches to work evil in the world. In 1692 accusations of witchcraft resulted in the execution of 20 residents of Salem, Massachusetts.

Salem's witch trials began when a group of teenage girls accused an African servant of being a witch. Their accusations soon grew to include others, including some prominent people in town. Accused witches were often spared if they confessed, especially if they pointed a finger at other community members.

Some people who denied being witches were hanged. Only after the Salem witchcraft trials ended in 1692 did the original accusers admit that they had made up the entire story. The incident may have reflected community strains and resentments. The accusers tended to be less successful people who clung to Salem's agricultural roots. Many of those accused of witchcraft were prosperous and associated with the town's seaport.

plenty of the necessaries of life; they do not acquire wealth, but they have comforts in abundance."

✓ **Reading Check** **Synthesizing** How did New England town meetings prepare the colonists for the future?

Trade and the Rise of Cities

In the early colonial era, New England produced few goods or crops that England wanted, but England produced many items that settlers wanted. Such items included hardware and various mechanical instruments, as well as fine cloth, linens, ceramic plates, and other luxury items. This situation, combined with New England's shipbuilding industry and good ports, encouraged some settlers to become merchants. The growth of trade in New England, in turn, led to the rise of cities along the coast.

Triangular Trade The only way colonial merchants could acquire the English goods that settlers wanted was to sell New England's products somewhere else in exchange for goods that England wanted. Fortunately, the sugar plantations in the Caribbean wanted to buy New England's fish, lumber, and meat.

To pay for the food and lumber from New England, Caribbean sugar planters would either trade raw sugar to the New England merchants or give them bills of exchange. Bills of exchange were credit slips English merchants gave the planters in exchange for their sugar. These bills worked as a kind of money. New England merchants would take the bills, as well as any sugar they had acquired, back home to New England and use them to buy English manufactured goods.

New England's trade with the sugar plantations of the Caribbean made many merchants very wealthy and led to new industries in New England. Using their new wealth, merchants in Northern cities built factories to refine raw sugar and distilleries to turn molasses into rum. Merchants also began trading with the Southern Colonies, exchanging Northern fish, rum, and grain for Southern rice, tobacco, and indigo.

The three-way trade New England merchants established with the Caribbean colonies and England is an example of triangular trade. Other three-way trade systems also existed. For example, New England merchants would trade rum to British merchants in exchange for British goods. British merchants then traded the rum to West Africans in exchange for enslaved Africans, who were then transported across the Atlantic to the Caribbean and traded for sugar.

A New Urban Society The rise of trade in the colonies caused several ports to grow rapidly into colonial America's first cities. By 1760 Philadelphia had over 23,000 people, making it the largest colonial city. Charles Town, South Carolina, with 8,000 people, was the largest city in the South. Within these cities and others, a new society developed with distinct social classes.

At the top of society were a small group of wealthy merchants who controlled the city's trade. The merchants in the coastal cities, in many ways similar to the planter elite in the South, patterned themselves after the British upper class. They wore elegant imported clothing, built luxurious mansions surrounded by gardens and maintained by servants, and rode through the crowded city streets in fancy carriages.

Although the merchants were the wealthiest people living in colonial cities, they were only a tiny minority. Artisans and their families made up nearly half of the urban population in colonial America. Artisans were skilled workers who knew how to manufacture various goods. They included carpenters, masons, coopers, iron and silversmiths, glassmakers, bakers, seamstresses, shoemakers, and many other tradespeople. Some artisans owned their own tools and shops, but most were employed in shops other people owned. Equal to the artisans in social status were innkeepers and retailers who owned their own places of business.

At the bottom of urban colonial society were the people without skills or property. Many of these people were employed at the harbor, where they loaded and serviced ships. Others worked as servants, washing clothes, grooming horses, cleaning houses, hauling garbage, and sweeping streets. These people made up about 30 percent of urban society during the colonial period. Below them in status were indentured servants and enslaved Africans. Enslaved Africans composed between 10 and 20 percent of the urban population. They too served as manual laborers and servants for the city's wealthier inhabitants.

The rapid development of cities created many problems, including overcrowding, crime, pollution, and epidemics. To deal with these problems, city governments established specific departments and offices. Constables' offices provided residents with some protection from crime. Charities began to address the problems of the urban poor, whose numbers swelled whenever a recession caused trade to decline.

✓ **Reading Check** **Examining** What new social classes developed in the Northern Colonies, and what contributed to their development?

Colonial Trade Network, 1750

Legend:
- Colonial Exports
- British Exports
- Imports from West Indies
- Middle Passage

From Northern Colonies to Britain:
Furs, fish, fruit
From Britain to Northern Colonies:
Manufactured goods

Furs, fish, fruit

Manufactured goods

Rice, indigo, tobacco, naval stores

Fish, fruit, meat

BRITAIN

EUROPE

Boston
New York City
Philadelphia
Norfolk
Charles Town
Savannah

Flour, fish, meat, lumber, manufactured goods

Sugar, molasses

Sugar, molasses

ATLANTIC OCEAN

Rum

From Northern Colonies to Europe:
Fish, fruit, meat
From Southern Colonies to Britain:
Rice, indigo, tobacco,
naval stores (pitch, tar, masts)
From Britain to Southern Colonies:
Manufactured goods

From Northern Colonies
to West Africa: Rum

From West Indies to Northern Colonies
and Britain: Sugar, molasses
From Northern Colonies to West Indies:
Flour, fish, meat, lumber,
manufactured goods

0   500 miles
0   500 kilometers
Azimuthal Equidistant projection

N
W E
S

Enslaved persons, gold dust

From West Africa to West Indies:
Enslaved persons, gold dust

WEST
AFRICA

Geography Skills

1. **Interpreting Maps** What commodity was shipped from the colonies to West Africa?
2. **Applying Geography Skills** In what sequence was rum produced and shipped to markets?

Society in the Middle Colonies

The Middle Colonies—Pennsylvania, New York, New Jersey, and Delaware—contained some of the most fertile farmland in North America. Unlike the subsistence farmers in New England, most farmers in the Middle Colonies were able to produce a surplus that they could sell. The rich soil of the region crumbled easily under their plows, and the longer growing season enabled them to bring forth bumper crops of rye, oats, barley, and potatoes. The most important crop, however, was wheat, which quickly became the region's main cash crop.

The Growth of the Middle Colonies

Merchants based in the Middle Colonies rapidly duplicated the success of the New England merchants and began selling wheat and flour to the colonies in the Caribbean. The Middle Colonies also benefited from their geography. Unlike New England, the Middle Colonies had three wide rivers—the Hudson, the Delaware, and the Susquehanna—that ran deep into the interior. These rivers made it easy for farmers

to move their goods to the coast for shipping to markets elsewhere in America and Europe.

Hundreds of small ships sailed up and down the region's rivers, exchanging European goods for barrels of wheat and flour. At the same time, thousands of wagons moved goods overland from interior farms to river towns, where they could be loaded on ships and moved downriver. As might be expected, towns located where the rivers emptied into the Atlantic Ocean rapidly grew into major cities. The prosperity of the Middle Colonies enabled New York City and Philadelphia to become the two largest cities in the British colonies.

The Wheat Boom

In the early 1700s, Europe's climate began to get warmer just as the diseases there began to decline. The result was a population explosion and a flood of new immigrants into

America—particularly into the Middle Colonies, where land was still available. At the same time, this population explosion created a huge demand for wheat to feed the soaring number of people in Europe. Between 1720 and 1770, wheat prices more than doubled in the colonies. This brought a surge of prosperity to the Middle Colonies.

The rapid rise of the wheat trade and the arrival of so many new settlers changed the society of the Middle Colonies. Some farmers became very wealthy by hiring poor immigrants to work on their farms for wages. This enabled them to raise large amounts of wheat for sale. Other colonists became wealthy as entrepreneurs, or businesspeople who risked their money by buying land, equipment, and supplies and then selling them to the new immigrants for a profit.

One of the reasons the American colonies had few industries and had to import so many manufactured goods from England was that the British government limited manufacturing in the colonies. Money to invest in factories was also scarce. The wheat boom created a new group of capitalists, people who had money to invest in new businesses. Industry did not develop on a large scale during the colonial era, but these early capitalists did build large gristmills near New York and Philadelphia that produced tens of thousands of barrels of flour for export. Other early entrepreneurs in the Middle Colonies established glass and pottery works.

Although many farmers prospered from growing wheat, very few became wealthy, primarily because of the limited technology of the time. There were no mechanical harvesters, so all of the wheat had to be cut by hand using a sickle. Threshing, or separating the grain from the chaff, also had to be done by hand

Bethlehem, Pennsylvania This painting of a town in the Middle Colonies represents a typical layout of that region of colonial America. *What was the main cash crop in the Middle Colonies?*

by beating the grain with a wooden flail. Using sickles, most farm families could harvest no more than 15 acres of wheat in a season. This was enough to produce a small surplus, but not enough to make most farmers rich. Only those farmers who were able to hire workers or who had extra land that they could rent to tenant farmers became wealthy.

As a result, distinct classes developed in the Middle Colonies, as they did in the other regions. At the top were wealthy entrepreneurs who owned large farms and other businesses. In the middle were many farmers who owned only a few acres and could generate a small surplus from their land. At the bottom of society were landless workers, who either rented land from large landowners or worked for wages.

Reading Check **Explaining** Why did the colonies experience a population boom in the early 1700s?

SECTION 2 ASSESSMENT

Checking for Understanding

1. **Define:** town meeting, selectmen, bill of exchange, triangular trade, artisan, entrepreneur, capitalist.
2. **Identify:** Grand Banks, fall line, meetinghouse.
3. **Describe** the different social classes in New England and the Middle Colonies.

Reviewing Themes

4. **Culture and Traditions** How did Puritanism affect the development of New England society and government?

Critical Thinking

5. **Understanding Cause and Effect** How did the geography of the New England and Middle Colonies contribute to their economic development?
6. **Categorizing** Use a graphic organizer similar to the one below to show the effects of wheat farming on the Middle Colonies.

Effects

Wheat Farming

Analyzing Visuals

7. **Examining Maps** Study the map of a New England town on page 93. Would the practice of "Holy Watching" have been easy to do in this town? Why or why not?

Writing About History

8. **Descriptive Writing** Imagine that you are barrel maker in the New England Colonies. Write a letter to a government official stating the problems you have that you want the government to address.

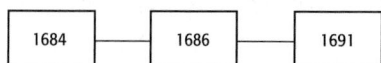
Guide to Reading

Main Idea
During the 1600s, England adopted several measures to make its trade with the American colonies more profitable.

Key Terms and Names
mercantilism, Charles II, James II, Dominion of New England, Glorious Revolution, natural rights

Reading Strategy
Sequencing As you read about England's trade relationship with the American colonies, complete a graphic organizer similar to the one below by describing English attempts at various times to control the colonies.

1684 — 1686 — 1691

Reading Objectives
• **Describe** mercantilism and its effect on the relationship between the colonies and England.
• **Explain** how the Glorious Revolution in England affected the colonies.

Section Theme
Individual Action Individual colonists reacted differently to the political turmoil in England.

Preview of Events

♦1684 ♦1687 ♦1690

1685
James II succeeds Charles II as English monarch

1686
Dominion of New England established

1688
Glorious Revolution in England

1690
John Locke publishes *Two Treatises of Government*

★ An American Story ★

In the later 1600s and early 1700s, Parliament passed a series of laws that restricted and controlled colonial manufacturing. One of these laws affected the hat industry, and another affected the iron industry. These laws annoyed many colonists, including Benjamin Franklin, who argued:

❝The hatters of England have prevailed to obtain an act in their own favor restraining that manufacture in America. . . . In the same manner have a few nail makers and a still smaller body of steelmakers (perhaps there are not half a dozen of these in England) prevailed totally to forbid by an act of Parliament the erecting of slitting mills or steel furnaces in America; that Americans may be obliged to take all their nails for their buildings and steel for their tools from these artificers [craft workers].❞

An article in the *Boston Gazette* also complained:

❝A colonist cannot make a button, a horseshoe, nor a hobnail, but some sooty ironmonger or respectable buttonmaker of Britain shall bawl and squall that his honor's worship is . . . maltreated, injured, cheated, and robbed by the rascally American republicans.❞

—adapted from *The Rise of American Civilization*

Mercantilism

Mercantilism is a set of ideas about the world economy and how it works. These ideas were popular in the 1600s and 1700s. Mercantilists believed that to become wealthy and powerful, a country had to accumulate gold and silver. A country could do this by selling more goods to other countries than it bought from them, causing more gold and silver to flow into the country than what was flowing out to pay for products from other countries.

Mercantilists also argued that a country should be self-sufficient in raw materials. If it had to buy raw materials from another country, gold and silver would flow out to pay for those materials. In order to be self-sufficient, a country should establish colonies where raw materials were available. The home country would then buy the raw materials from its colonies and, in turn, sell them manufactured goods.

Mercantilism did provide some benefits to colonies. It gave them a reliable market for some of their raw materials and an eager supplier of the manufactured goods they needed. This system also had drawbacks, however. It prevented colonies from selling goods to other nations, even if they could get a better price. Also, if a colony produced nothing the home country needed, the colony could not acquire gold or silver to buy manufactured goods. This was a serious problem in New England, and it explains in part why New England merchants turned to triangular trade and smuggling. These methods were the only way for the colonies to get the gold and silver they needed.

The Navigation Acts During the first half of the 1600s, England's mercantilist policy was very simple. The government tried to encourage exports and restrict imports. Other than some attempts to regulate the tobacco trade from Virginia, little attention was paid to the colonies and how they fit into England's economic system.

When **Charles II** assumed the throne in 1660, however, he and his advisers were determined to generate wealth for England by regulating trade and expanding the colonies in America. In 1660 Charles asked Parliament to pass a navigation act. The act required all goods imported or exported from the colonies to be carried on English ships, and stated that at least three-fourths of the crew on each ship had to be English. The act also listed specific raw materials that could be sold only to England or other English colonies. The list included sugar, tobacco, lumber, cotton, wool, and indigo—the major products that earned money for the colonies. Many colonists, especially tobacco planters, complained about the

act. They argued that it forced them to deal with English merchants who charged such high prices for shipping that the planters were robbed of their profit.

Three years later, in 1663, Parliament passed another navigation act called the **Staple Act.** This act required everything the colonies imported to come through England. All merchants bringing European goods to the colonies had to stop in England, pay taxes, and then ship the goods out again on English ships. This generated money for England but also increased the price of goods in the colonies.

Frustration with these acts encouraged colonial merchants to break the new laws. To enforce the acts in the colonies Parliament authorized the appointment of customs inspectors, who would report directly to the English government. As a colonial power, England had the authority to enact and enforce the Navigation Acts. Problems arose, however, when it tried to do so.

Problems With Enforcement In 1675 King Charles II appointed a committee called the Lords Commissioners of Trade and Plantations to oversee colonial trade and advise him about problems. It was soon discovered that Dutch and other foreign ships crowded Boston Harbor and that the merchants of Massachusetts routinely ignored the Navigation Acts and smuggled goods to Europe, the Caribbean, and Africa. Massachusetts's governor, John Laverett, wasted no time in informing England that

Picturing **History**

Port of Boston As one of the main points of entry for goods entering and leaving the colonies, Boston was sensitive to the effects of the Navigation Acts. *What was the main goal of the Navigation Acts?*

Massachusetts was not required to obey laws made by Parliament unless it was in the interest of Massachusetts to do so.

For the next few years, Massachusetts refused to answer the charges that had been brought against it. Finally, in 1684, King Charles II responded to this defiance by depriving Massachusetts of its charter and declaring it to be a royal colony.

The Dominion of New England James II, who succeeded his brother Charles to the English throne in 1685, went even further in asserting royal authority and punishing the merchants of New England for their defiance. In 1686 the English government merged Massachusetts, Plymouth, and Rhode Island together to create a new royal province called the **Dominion of New England.** The following year Connecticut and New Jersey were forced to join the Dominion, and by the spring of 1688, New York had been added as well.

The Dominion was to be run by a governor-general and councilors appointed directly by the king. All colonial assemblies were abolished. The governor-general and his council would have the power to make laws, impose taxes, administer justice, and confirm or deny all existing land grants.

King James II appointed **Sir Edmund Andros** to be the first governor-general. Andros, a former soldier and governor of New York, was loyal to the king. His contempt for the Puritan religion and his determination to overturn the systems of government in the colonies heightened tensions there.

Andros declared all deeds and land titles issued under the Massachusetts charter to be worthless, and he insisted that anyone who wanted a new deed would have to pay an annual tax to the government.

Working closely with English soldiers and the Royal Navy, he also rigorously enforced the Navigation Acts.

Equally disturbing to Puritans were the governor-general's efforts to undermine the Puritan Church. Andros declared that only marriages performed in Anglican churches were legal, and he demanded that Puritan meeting halls be made available for Anglican services every other Sunday. He also declared that no one was to teach school, a traditional function of Church leaders in New England, without permission.

Andros had managed to anger nearly everyone in New England society—landowners, church leaders, and merchants. Fortunately, just as tensions were peaking in New England, a peaceful revolution took place back in England, preempting violence in the colonies.

✓ **Reading Check** **Examining** In what ways did the Navigation Acts affect trade in the colonies?

The Glorious Revolution of 1688

While the colonists in New England raged at the actions of Governor-General Andros, the people of England were growing suspicious of their new king, James II. James insisted upon his divine right to rule, and he frequently rejected the advice of Parliament. He had revoked the charters of many English towns and corporations and offended many English people by openly practicing Catholicism. He had also prosecuted Anglican bishops for defying his wishes concerning appointments in the Anglican Church. Many members of Parliament worried that if James continued to act in this manner, he might lead the country into another civil war.

Major Navigation Acts

Year	Act
1651	Colonial trade was to be carried in English ships
1660	Tightened earlier restrictions; certain items, including tobacco, to be sold only to England or its colonies
1663	Colonial goods sold to Europe had to pass through English ports first to be taxed
1673	Duties imposed on trade *between* American colonies
1696	Gave customs officials the power to use general search warrants; Board of Trade created to oversee colonial economic activity

Chart *Skills*

1. **Evaluating** Why did the colonists resent the Navigation Acts?
2. **Determining Cause and Effect** What effect did the 1651 act have on colonial shipping?

A Bloodless Revolution Most of the English people and members of Parliament were willing to tolerate James because they expected his Protestant daughter Mary and her Dutch husband, William of Orange, to succeed James to the throne. These hopes were shattered in June 1688, when James's second wife gave birth to a son. The son was now the heir to the throne and would be raised Catholic.

News of the birth triggered protests. Unwilling to risk a Catholic dynasty on the throne of England, Parliament invited William and Mary to take the throne of England. When William arrived, James fled, and William became the new king of England. This bloodless change of power became known as the **Glorious Revolution.**

Before assuming the throne, William and Mary were required to swear that they would obey the laws of Parliament. In 1689 Parliament read a bill of rights to William and Mary, outlining what would be required of them. The **English Bill of Rights** abolished the king's absolute power to suspend laws and create his own courts. It also made it illegal for the king to impose taxes or raise an army without the consent of Parliament. The Bill of Rights also guaranteed freedom of speech within Parliament and banned excessive bail and cruel and unusual punishments. Every English subject was guaranteed the right to petition the king and the right to a fair and impartial jury in legal cases. Later that same year, Parliament passed the **Toleration Act,** granting freedom of worship to nearly all Protestants but not to Catholics and Jews.

📖 *(See page 1063 for an excerpt from the English Bill of Rights).*

The changes the Glorious Revolution brought to England contributed significantly to the colonists' ideas of government. Eventually the ideas found in the English Bill of Rights and the Toleration Act would be expanded and incorporated into the American Bill of Rights. At the time, however, England's Glorious Revolution offered colonists a justification to revolt against Governor-General Andros.

The Glorious Revolution in America
As soon as word reached Massachusetts that Parliament had dethroned James II, an uprising occurred in Boston. Andros and his councilors were seized and imprisoned. They were later returned to England. Although

Profiles IN HISTORY

Anne Bradstreet
c. 1612–1672

Anne Dudley was born about 1612 in Northampton, England. At the age of 16 she married Simon Bradstreet, and two years later she accompanied her husband on board the *Arabella* to America. The Bradstreets, traveling with John Winthrop's party, were among the first settlers of the Massachusetts Bay Colony.

In America Anne Bradstreet faced the difficult task of building a home in the wilderness. Despite the hard work of raising eight children, she found time to write poetry. In 1650 the first edition of her poetry was published in England as *The Tenth Muse Lately Sprung Up in America.* Bradstreet had not anticipated this recognition. Her brother-in-law had secretly taken a copy of her manuscript to a London publisher.

Anne Bradstreet was a devoted supporter of her husband, who became a leading political figure in Massachusetts, serving two terms as governor. During the period of the Dominion of New England, he spoke out against the harsh rule of Edmund Andros. In a poem, *To My Dear Loving Husband,* published after her death, Anne described their relationship:

If ever two were one, then surely we.
If ever man were loved by wife, then thee;
If ever wife was happy in a man,
Compare with me ye women if you can.

William and Mary let the hated Dominion of New England die quietly, they did not completely restore the old system. They permitted Rhode Island and Connecticut to resume their previous forms of government, but they were unwilling to surrender all control over Massachusetts. Instead they issued a new charter in 1691. The new charter combined the Massachusetts Bay Colony, Plymouth colony, and Maine into the royal colony of Massachusetts.

Under the new charter, the people of Massachusetts were given the right to elect an assembly. The assembly, in turn, was given the right to elect the governor's councilors, but King William insisted that the governor had to be appointed by the king. The new charter also changed who could vote. Under the new system, voters had to own property, but they did not have to be members of a Puritan congregation. The new charter also granted freedom of worship to Anglicans living in Massachusetts.

GOVERNMENT

The Legacy of John Locke
The Glorious Revolution of 1688 also set a very important precedent. It showed that there were times when revolution against the king was justified. During this turmoil, a political philosopher named John Locke wrote a book entitled *Two Treatises of Government,* in which he

Fact | Fiction | Folklore

John Locke John Locke is best known for his writings on the philosophy of government. He did, however, have other talents. Though he never completed a degree in medicine, Locke was known as "Dr. Locke" in some circles. In 1666 he successfully performed an operation on the Earl of Shaftsbury to clean out an abscess in the chest. In return the earl allowed Locke to live at his home and devote his time to philosophical writings.

explained the basis of political obligation and justified revolution. 📖 *(See page 1064 for an excerpt of Locke's Two Treatises of Government.)*

Locke argued that a monarch's right to rule came from the people. He asserted that all people were born with certain natural rights, including the right to life, liberty, and property. Before governments were created, Locke said, people lived in a "state of nature" where their rights were not safe. To protect their rights, people had come together and mutually agreed to create a government. In effect the people had formed a contract. They had agreed to obey the government's laws, and the government agreed to uphold their rights in return. Locke claimed that monarchs were parties to this contract, and if they violated the people's rights, the people were justified in overthrowing the monarch and changing their system of government.

Locke's ideas had a profound influence on American colonists. The colonists understood Locke's "natural rights" to be the specific rights of English citizens that had developed over the centuries in England and were referred to in documents such as the Magna Carta and the English Bill of Rights. Furthermore, Locke seemed to be describing the colonial experience. Settlers had arrived in America in a state of nature and then built governments based on contractual arrangements. The Mayflower Compact, the Fundamental Orders of Connecticut, and the various colonial charters were all agreements between the people and their government.

Others in England and America reinforced Locke's ideas in the decades that followed the Glorious Revolution. In January 1750, for example, Pastor Jonathan Mayhew of Boston's West Church preached:

❝If we calmly consider the nature of the thing itself, nothing can well be imagined more directly contrary to common sense than to suppose that millions of people should be subjected to the arbitrary, precarious pleasure of one single man—who has naturally no superiority over them in point of authority. . . . What unprejudiced man can think that God made *all* to be thus subservient to the lawless pleasure and fancy of one so that it shall always be a sin to resist him?❞

—quoted in *The Making of American Democracy*

Only a few years later, the American colonies would put these ideas into practice when they launched their own revolution against Britain.

✔ **Reading Check** **Summarizing** What actions did William and Mary take upon becoming the English monarchs?

SECTION 3 ASSESSMENT

Checking for Understanding

1. **Define:** mercantilism, natural rights.
2. **Identify:** Charles II, James II, Dominion of New England, Glorious Revolution.
3. **Discuss** how England's Glorious Revolution influenced the American colonies.

Reviewing Themes

4. **Individual Action** How did Governor-General Andros's attempt to weaken colonial resolve increase colonists' anger towards England?

Critical Thinking

5. **Predicting Consequences** How did the ideas of the philosopher John Locke contribute to revolutionary ideas in the American colonies?
6. **Categorizing** Use a graphic organizer similar to the one below to fill in the benefits of mercantilism.

Benefits for England ⟩

Benefits for American Colonies ⟩

Analyzing Visuals

7. **Examining Art** Study the picture of Boston on page 99. Why do you think colonial merchant shippers were angry about the Navigation Acts?

Writing About History

8. **Expository Writing** Take on the role of a colonial merchant. Write a letter to a relative in England explaining how the Navigation Acts have affected your business.

SKILLBUILDER

Reading a Bar Graph

Why Learn This Skill?

Graphs are a way of displaying numbers or statistics in a clear, easy-to-read way. Learning to read graphs will help you understand and compare statistical data. One type of graph often used to compare statistics is a bar graph.

Learning the Skill

A bar graph provides information along two sides, or axes, of a graph. The **horizontal axis** is the line across the bottom of the graph. The **vertical axis** is the line along the side. Both have labels to tell you what kind of information they are showing. Bars on the graph run horizontally or vertically along these axes. A double bar graph, such as the one on this page, shows a comparison of information. A key tells you what each bar represents.

Practicing the Skill

The bar graph above shows the population of six English colonies in 1700. Study the graph and then answer the questions.

❶ What two kinds of populations are shown on this graph?

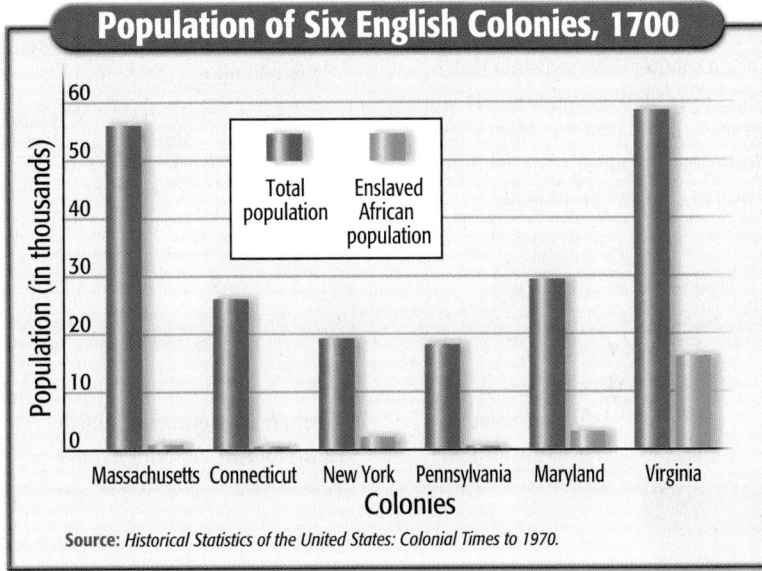

Population of Six English Colonies, 1700

Total population · Enslaved African population

Population (in thousands)

Massachusetts · Connecticut · New York · Pennsylvania · Maryland · Virginia

Colonies

Source: *Historical Statistics of the United States: Colonial Times to 1970.*

❷ Which colony had the highest total population in 1700? The lowest?

❸ Which colony had the largest enslaved African population? The lowest? How do you account for the difference?

❹ Approximately what percentage of Maryland's total population was enslaved Africans?

Skills Assessment

Complete the Practicing Skills questions on page 111 and the Chapter 3 Skill Reinforcement Activity to assess your mastery of this skill.

1750 tapestry of Beacon Hill and Boston Common

Applying the Skill

Reading a Bar Graph Gather information about the number of students in each of your classes. Create a bar graph comparing the total number of students with the number involved in after-school clubs or sports. Be sure to include a title for your graph.

 GO TO Glencoe's **Skillbuilder Interactive Workbook CD-ROM, Level 2,** provides instruction and practice in key social studies skills.

Guide to Reading

Main Idea

America in the 1700s matured into a rich and diverse society.

Key Terms and Names

Cotton Mather, Pennsylvania Dutch, Stono Rebellion, Enlightenment, Great Awakening, rationalism, John Locke, Montesquieu, pietism, revival, Jonathan Edwards, George Whitefield

Reading Strategy

Categorizing As you read about colonial society in the 1700s, complete a graphic organizer similar to the one below by identifying why immigrants settled in the colonies.

Group	Where They Settled	Reasons for Immigrating
Germans		
Scotch-Irish		
Jews		

Reading Objectives

- **Summarize** the plight of enslaved Africans and explain their methods of resistance.
- **Explain** how the Enlightenment and the Great Awakening affected the colonies.

Section Theme

Global Connections Immigrants to the American colonies in the 1700s came from all across Europe or were brought by force from Africa.

Preview of Events

♦1650   ♦1680   ♦1710   ♦1740

1654
Jews arrive in New Amsterdam

1683
German immigrants establish Germantown in Pennsylvania

1734
John Peter Zenger goes on trial

1739
Stono Rebellion

★ *An American Story* ★

Early on Sunday morning, October 6, 1723, a 16-year-old boy from Boston stepped off a boat onto Philadelphia's Market Street wharf. Within just a few years, Benjamin Franklin would stride into American history. That day, however, he simply wanted to find breakfast:

❝I was in my working dress, my best clothes being to come round by sea. I was dirty from my journey . . . and I knew no soul nor where to look for lodging. I was fatigued with traveling, rowing, and want of rest; I was very hungry; and my whole stock of cash consisted of a Dutch dollar and about a shilling in copper.❞

With some of his money Franklin bought "three great puffy rolls . . . and, having no room in my pockets, walked off with a roll under each arm, and eating the other . . . I made . . . a most awkward, ridiculous appearance."

Franklin's passion for books and writing led him to Philadelphia, where he achieved success as a printer, writer, scientist, and philosopher. By the time he was 42, the man who popularized the proverb "Time is money" could afford to retire and devote himself to public life.

—adapted from *Colonial Pennsylvania: A History*

Family Life in Colonial America

Benjamin Franklin's meteoric rise from poverty to riches was extraordinary. However, his huge family—Franklin was 1 of 17 children—was not unusual in America in the 1700s. The population of the American colonies was in a period of explosive growth, partly because people were having large families, and partly because immigrants—some willing, some forced—were flooding into the colonies from Europe and Africa.

Population Growth The birthrate in the American colonies was high in the 1700s. Most women married in their early twenties, typically to men in their early to mid-twenties. On average, colonial women gave birth to seven children, although giving birth to twice that number of children was not uncommon.

Between 1640 and 1700, the population of the American colonies increased from 25,000 to more than 250,000. In the 1700s, the population more than doubled every 25 years. More than 1 million colonists lived in America in the 1750s, and by the time of the American Revolution, the population had reached roughly 2.5 million people.

Women in Colonial Society In the American colonies, as in Europe, law and custom gave men greater authority and importance than women—in politics and in the household. In the early colonial era, married women had no legal status. A married woman could not own anything, and all of the property she brought into the marriage became her husband's. In most colonies, a married woman could not make a contract, be party to a lawsuit, or make a will. Husbands were the sole guardians of the children and were allowed to physically discipline both their wives and their children. Single women and widows, on the other hand, had considerably more rights. They could own and manage property, file lawsuits, and run businesses.

In the 1700s, the status of married women improved considerably. In most colonies, for example, husbands could not sell or mortgage their land without their wife's signature on the contract. Also, in several colonies, married women began engaging in business as well. Despite the legal limitations, many colonial women worked outside of their homes. Women operated taverns and shops, managed plantations, ran print shops, and published newspapers.

Health and Disease Improvements in housing and sanitation helped American colonists resist some diseases. Still, they frequently suffered from typhoid fever, tuberculosis, cholera, diphtheria, "fluxes" (diarrhea), "malignant fever" (influenza), typhus, and scarlet fever.

These diseases ravaged residents in colonial cities. When an epidemic of deadly smallpox swept through Boston in 1721, the scientific interests

Pennsylvania Dutch decorated pie dish

of a minister and the knowledge of enslaved Africans combined to save hundreds of lives. Reverend **Cotton Mather,** a Puritan leader, had read that the Turks had successfully developed an inoculation for smallpox. Making inquiries among enslaved Africans, Mather discovered that they also knew this technique. At Mather's urging, Dr. Zabdiel Boylston, a Boston physician and friend, inoculated willing Bostonians against the disease. Despite furious opposition, Mather and Boylston persisted in their experiment. In July 1721, Mather wrote:

> ❝I have instructed our Physicians in the new Method used by the Africans and Asiaticks, to prevent and abate the Dangers of the Small-Pox, and infallibly to save the Lives of those that have it wisely managed upon them. The Destroyer, being enraged at the Proposal of any Thing, that may rescue the Lives of our poor People from him, has taken a strange Possession of the People on this Occasion. They rave, they rail, they blaspheme; they talk not only like Ideots but also like Franticks, . . . I also am an Object of their Fury. . . .❞

—quoted in *The Colonial Image*

The daring experiment proved to be a great success. Of the 6,000 people who were not inoculated and caught smallpox, about 900, or 15 percent, died. In stark contrast, only 6 of the 241 inoculated people, or less than 3 percent, died of the disease.

☑ **Reading Check** **Summarizing** What rights did colonial law deny women?

Immigrants in Colonial America

The American colonies grew rapidly due to immigration and a high birthrate. Hundreds of thousands of free white immigrants arrived between 1700 and 1775, settling throughout the colonies. At the same time, traders brought large numbers of enslaved Africans to America, mostly to the Southern Colonies.

German Immigrants Arrive in Pennsylvania
America's first large group of German immigrants came to Pennsylvania looking for religious freedom. First to arrive were a group of Mennonites who founded Germantown in 1683. Large-scale

German immigration to Pennsylvania started in the early 1700s. By 1775, more than 100,000 Germans had arrived in the colony, where they made up about one-third of the population. Known as the **Pennsylvania Dutch** (from their own word *Deutsche,* meaning "German"), these settlers became some of the colony's most prosperous farmers. They introduced the Conestoga wagon, which later generations would adapt for use in crossing the country. As early as the 1720s, many Germans also headed south along the Great Philadelphia Wagon Road to the Shenandoah River valley of Virginia. From there they spread throughout the backcountry of Virginia and the Carolinas.

The Scotch-Irish Head West

The Scotch-Irish were descendants of the Scots who had helped England claim control of Northern Ireland. Beginning in 1717, rising taxes, poor harvests, and religious discrimination convinced many Scotch-Irish to flee Ireland. An estimated 150,000 Scotch-Irish immigrated to the American colonies between 1717 and 1776.

Although the Scotch-Irish settled in many colonies, most headed to Pennsylvania. Unwilling and often unable to purchase land, many migrated west to the frontier, where they occupied vacant land. Many Scotch-Irish also followed the Great Philadelphia Wagon Road south into the backcountry of the Southern Colonies.

Colonial America's Jewish Community

A small group of Jews, fleeing from the Portuguese in Brazil and seeking an opportunity to practice their religion, first arrived in the colonies in New Amsterdam (later called New York City) in 1654. By 1776 approximately 1,500 Jews lived in the colonies. Most lived in the cities of New York, Philadelphia, Charles Town, Savannah, and Newport, where they were allowed to worship as they pleased. They made their living as artisans and merchants. Unlike in western Europe, where Jews could not own property or participate in professions, colonial Jews lived and worked alongside Christians.

Reading Check **Explaining** Why did many Germans immigrate to Pennsylvania in the 1700s?

Africans in Colonial America

Africans arrived in the colonies from many different regions of West Africa. In the colonies, they tried to maintain their specific languages and traditions even though white planters intentionally bought slaves from different regions who spoke different languages to make it difficult for them to plot rebellion.

Africans Build a New Culture

In South Carolina, where rice cultivation required a large, coordinated workforce, Africans worked and lived in larger groups than in other Southern Colonies. Their isolation from the white planters resulted in a more independent African culture, which developed its own language called Gullah. Gullah combined English and African words, and it allowed Africans from a variety of homelands to converse. In the Chesapeake region, where more of the enslaved population had been born in America, Africans spoke English.

Using a common language helped Africans from diverse backgrounds develop a new culture in America. African traditional religious beliefs became mixed with the practices of the Christian faith. African rhythms became a part of new musical forms. The fear of being sold and separated

Profiles IN HISTORY

John Peter Zenger *1697–1746*

In 1710 Britain had paid for German families to immigrate to the American colonies. In time, one of these immigrants, 13-year-old John Peter Zenger, would help change colonial society.

By 1726 Zenger was running a failing printing business in New York. His only successful venture to this point had been to print the colonies' first arithmetic text.

In 1732 Zenger's luck changed when an unpopular royal governor dismissed New York's chief justice from office. The chief justice hired Zenger to publish an anti-government newspaper. In 1734 Zenger's paper called the royal governor's supporters "the dregs and scandal of human nature."

Zenger was arrested and charged for printing libel, or slanderous information. Indeed, according to British law, criticizing the royal governor—even if the criticisms were true—was a grave offense. For the eight months he spent in prison, a defiant Zenger continued to edit his newspaper through a hole in his cell door.

Zenger's attorney, Andrew Hamilton, the colonies' most famous lawyer, called Zenger's cause "the cause of liberty." Only a press free to criticize the government could prevent that government from abusing its power, Hamilton argued. The jury took only a few minutes to reach its verdict. They found Zenger not guilty. Zenger's trial helped establish the American commitment to freedom of the press.

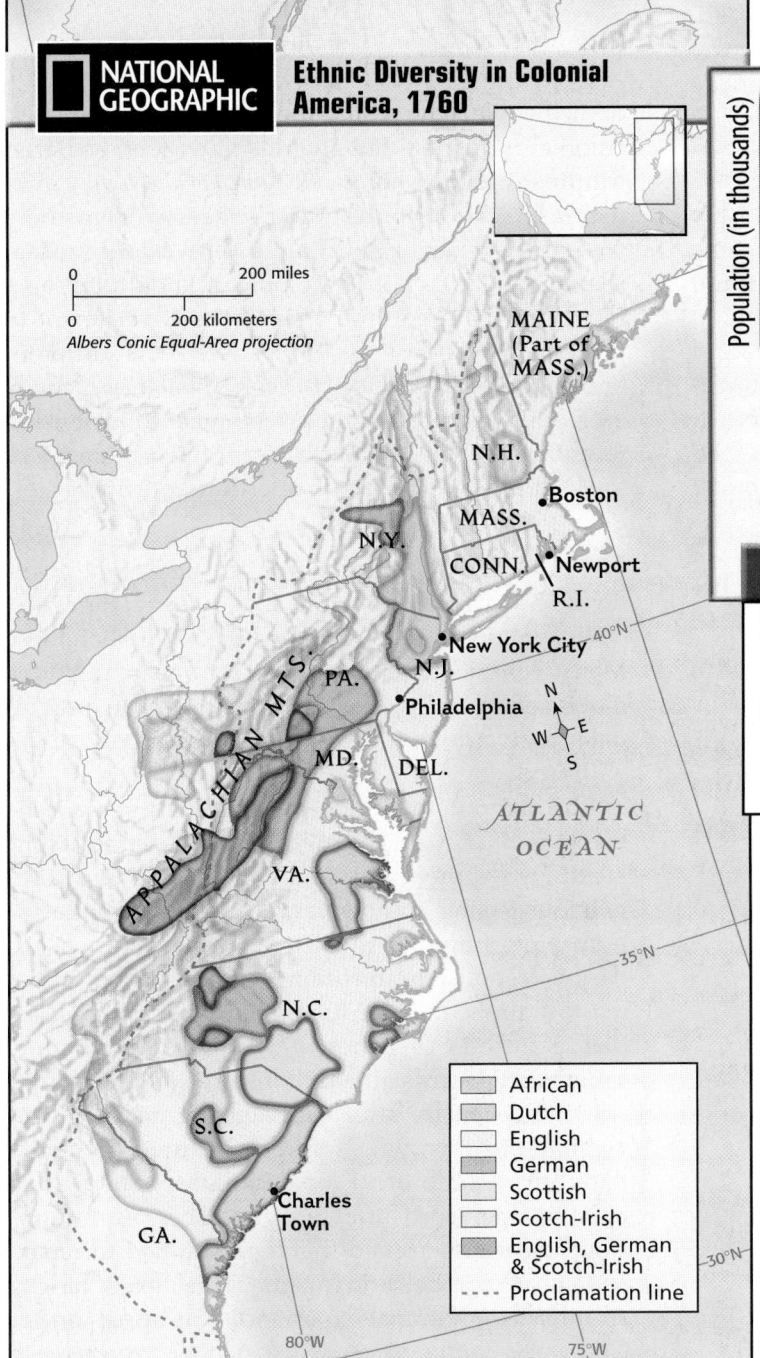

National Geographic

Ethnic Diversity in Colonial America, 1760

0 — 200 miles
0 — 200 kilometers
Albers Conic Equal-Area projection

MAINE (Part of MASS.)

N.H.

MASS. • Boston

N.Y.

CONN. • Newport
R.I.

• New York City 40°N

PA. N.J.

• Philadelphia

APPALACHIAN MTS.

MD. DEL.

ATLANTIC OCEAN

VA.

35°N

N.C.

S.C.

Charles Town

GA.

80°W   75°W   30°N

Legend:
- African
- Dutch
- English
- German
- Scottish
- Scotch-Irish
- English, German & Scotch-Irish
- --- Proclamation line

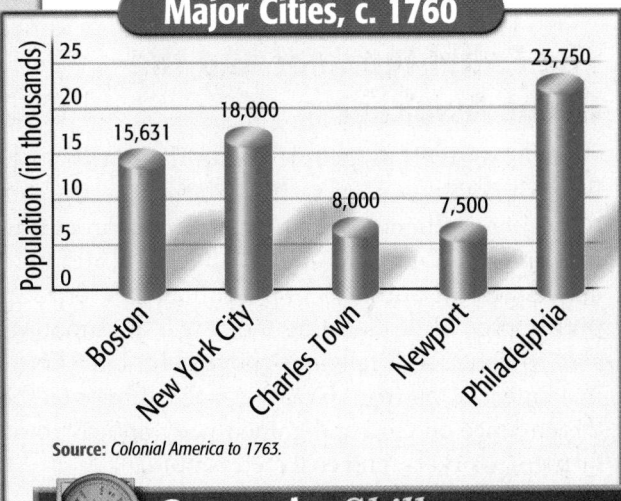

Major Cities, c. 1760

Population (in thousands)

City	Population
Boston	15,631
New York City	18,000
Charles Town	8,000
Newport	7,500
Philadelphia	23,750

Source: *Colonial America to 1763.*

Geography *Skills*

1. **Interpreting Maps** Where were the majority of Dutch settlers located in colonial America?
2. **Interpreting Graphs** According to the map, which of the cities listed on the graph had a predominantly African population?

In Virginia the enslaved population was smaller in relation to the white population, and the work was less tiring. While planters still used harsh methods to force obedience, they also applied persuasion. They might promise enslaved workers extra food or days off for completing a particular task.

While slaveholders tried to force enslaved Africans to obey, Africans themselves developed different ways to fight slavery. Some used passive resistance; that is, they would stage deliberate work slowdowns, lose or break tools, or simply refuse to work hard. A few even managed to gain freedom by escaping. Others purchased their liberty with money earned on their own or were set free by their slaveholders. By the mid-1700s, in fact, there were a few thousand free Africans living in the colonies.

Occasionally groups of slaves banded together to resist the slaveholders. In the late 1730s, the governor of Spanish Florida, in an attempt to weaken South Carolina, promised freedom and land to any enslaved Africans who fled south to Florida. In 1739, 75 Africans gathered near the Stono River, attacked their white overseers, stole their guns, and raced south toward Florida, attacking whites as they traveled. The local militia eventually ended the **Stono Rebellion,** killing between 30 and 40 of the Africans.

from one's family, however, was always present. Despite these conditions, many Africans managed to pass on their family names and cultural traditions.

Oppression and Resistance In South Carolina, where often as few as 5 whites would oversee roughly 100 enslaved Africans, authority was maintained through harsh means. Whippings and beatings were common. Disobedient workers were branded, and some planters would slit noses or amputate fingers and toes as punishment and to terrify other workers into obeying orders. Africans in South Carolina needed passes to leave their plantations, and planters organized regular night patrols to watch for rebellion and runaways.

✓ **Reading Check** **Summarizing** In what ways did Africans resist their enslavement?

The Enlightenment and the Great Awakening

Ideas as well as people made their way to the English colonies. During the 1700s, America came under the influence of two great European cultural movements. One movement, the Enlightenment, challenged the authority of the church in science and philosophy while elevating the power of human reason. In contrast, a religious movement, later known in America as the Great Awakening, stressed dependence on God and gained wide appeal among farmers, workers, and enslaved people.

The Enlightenment Enlightenment thinkers believed that natural laws applied to social, political, and economic relationships, and that people could figure out these natural laws if they employed reason. This emphasis on logic and reasoning was known as rationalism.

One of the earliest and most influential Enlightenment writers was **John Locke.** His contract theory of government and natural rights is a good example of the way Enlightenment thinkers attempted to use reason to discover natural laws that applied to politics and society.

Even more significant in some ways was Locke's *Essay on Human Understanding.* In this work, Locke argued that contrary to what the Church taught, people were not born sinful. Instead their minds were blank slates that could be shaped by society and education, making people better. These ideas that all people have rights and that society can be improved became core beliefs in American society.

French thinker Jean Jacques Rousseau carried these ideas further. In *The Social Contract,* he argued that a government should be formed by the consent of the people, who would then make their own laws. Another influential Enlightenment writer was **Baron Montesquieu.** In his work *Spirit of the Laws,* published in 1748, Montesquieu suggested that there were three types of political power—executive, legislative, and judicial. These powers should be separated into different branches of the government to protect the liberty of the people. The different branches would provide checks and balances against each other and prevent the government from abusing its authority. Montesquieu's idea influenced many of the leaders who wrote the American Constitution.

The Great Awakening While some Americans turned away from a religious worldview in the 1700s, others enthusiastically renewed their Christian faith. Many Americans embraced a European religious movement called pietism, which stressed an individual's piety (devoutness) and an emotional union with God.

Throughout the colonies, ministers spread the message of pietism through revivals—large public meetings for preaching and prayer. This revival of religious feeling is known as the Great Awakening.

In New England the Great Awakening was, in part, a response to declining religious fervor and a reaction to the ideas of the Enlightenment. In 1734 a Massachusetts preacher and philosopher named **Jonathan Edwards** aimed to restore New England's spiritual intensity after experiencing his own conversion. His terrifying sermons pictured humanity dangling on the brink of damnation, suspended only by the "forbearance of an incensed [angry] God." Edwards argued that a person had to repent and convert, to be "born again." This idea of having an internal emotional experience that brings one to God was a central idea of the Great Awakening.

The Great Awakening began in earnest when the Anglican minister **George Whitefield** arrived in Philadelphia in 1739. The ideas of John Wesley, the founder of Methodism, influenced Whitefield, and both had an impact on America. Whitefield was a powerful, emotional speaker, and he attracted large crowds everywhere he preached.

Whitefield also warned of the dangers of listening to ministers who had not been born again. This challenge to the authority of other ministers created tensions within colonial congregations. During the Great Awakening, nearly all New England churches split into factions called the New Lights and the Old Lights, or the New Side and the Old Side. Many ministers found themselves dismissed by their congregations depending on which side they took. Those

| Fact | Fiction | Folklore |

English Flag This flag flew over the English settlements throughout the colonial period. First used in 1606, the flag displays the red cross of England (cross of St. George) superimposed on the white cross of Scotland (cross of St. Andrew), on the blue background field of Scotland. This "Union Flag," as it was called, remained in use until January 1, 1801.

churches that embraced the new ideas—including the Baptists, some Presbyterians and Congregationalists, and the new group called the Methodists—experienced a surge in membership, while other churches' memberships declined.

The Great Awakening also had a profound effect in the South, where the emotion and energy of Baptist preaching won converts among poor tenant and backcountry farmers. Baptists also welcomed enslaved Africans at their revivals and condemned the brutality of slavery. Hundreds of Africans joined Baptist congregations and listened to sermons that taught that all people were equal before God.

The Baptist effort to preach to the enslaved Africans provoked a violent response from the planters, who feared losing control of their workforce. Sheriffs and justices of the peace organized armed groups of planters to break up Baptist meetings by force. Despite the violence, by 1775, 20 percent of Virginia's whites and thousands of enslaved Africans had joined Baptist congregations. Within the enslaved community, converts spread the word even further, creating a separate African Christian culture on the plantations.

The Great Awakening was one of the last major cultural developments in America before the American Revolution. Like the Enlightenment, it implanted ideas that are still a very powerful part of American society.

The Enlightenment and the Great Awakening had different origins and directions. Both movements, however, served to emphasize an individualism that supported America's political independence. The

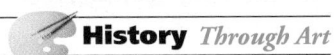
History *Through Art*

The Great Awakening George Whitefield was one of the most famous ministers of this period of intense religious revival in the colonies. How did Whitefield's emphasis on being "born again" affect churches?

Enlightenment provided arguments against British rule. The Great Awakening undermined allegiance to traditional authority.

Reading Check **Describing** How did the Great Awakening affect New England churches?

SECTION 4 ASSESSMENT

Checking for Understanding

1. **Define:** Enlightenment, Great Awakening, rationalism, pietism, revival.
2. **Identify:** Cotton Mather, Pennsylvania Dutch, Stono Rebellion, John Locke, Montesquieu, Jonathan Edwards, George Whitefield.
3. **Explain** how the Enlightenment and the Great Awakening influenced the American colonies.

Reviewing Themes

4. **Global Connections** What factors and motivations drove immigration to the American colonies in the 1700s?

Critical Thinking

5. **Making Comparisons** In what ways did enslaved Africans develop their own culture in the American colonies?
6. **Organizing** Use a graphic organizer similar to the one below to explain the reasons for the population increase in the colonies in the 1700s.

Factors Contributing to Colonial Population Increase

Analyzing Visuals

7. **Studying Paintings** Examine the painting of George Whitefield on this page. How does the imagery of the painting suggest the emotionalism that Whitefield was known for during the Great Awakening?

Writing About History

8. **Persuasive Writing** Imagine that you are a German immigrant to the colonies in 1725. Write a letter to your relatives explaining what your life in the colonies is like and encouraging them to join you in America.

Reviewing Key Terms

On a sheet of paper, use the following terms in a sentence.

1. cash crop
2. plantation
3. indentured servant
4. gentry
5. subsistence farming
6. Middle Passage
7. slave code
8. town meeting
9. selectmen
10. bill of exchange
11. triangular trade
12. artisan
13. entrepreneur
14. capitalist
15. mercantilism
16. natural rights
17. Enlightenment
18. Great Awakening
19. rationalism
20. pietism
21. revival

Reviewing Key Facts

22. **Identify:** William Berkeley, Royal African Company, Charles II, James II, Pennsylvania Dutch, John Locke, Montesquieu, Jonathan Edwards, George Whitefield.
23. What crops did the economy of the Southern Colonies depend on?
24. Why did Southern planters come to rely on enslaved labor?
25. How did trade affect the economy of the New England Colonies?
26. Why did England pass the Navigation Acts?
27. Why was the creation of the Dominion of New England unpopular in the English Colonies?
28. Why did Africans in South Carolina develop a more independent slave culture than Africans in other Southern Colonies?
29. How did the Great Awakening influence the American colonies?

Chapter Summary

The American Colonies

Region	Geography	Economy	People and Society
New England Colonies	Coastal areas with good natural harbors; inland areas with dense forests; poor rocky soil and short growing season	Small farms, lumber mills, fishing, shipbuilding, and trade flourished; cities developed along coast.	Most people organized as congregations lived on farms; in the cities merchants controlled trade, artisans made goods, unskilled workers and enslaved Africans provided labor.
Middle Colonies	Fertile soil and long growing season; rivers ran into backcountry	Colonies grew large amounts of rye, oats, barley, potatoes, and wheat as cash crops to sell; cities developed on the coast.	Wealthiest people owned large farms and other businesses. Most farmers produced a small surplus. Tenant farmers rented land from large landowners or worked for wages.
Southern Colonies	Favorable climate and soil for agriculture; wide rivers made cities unnecessary	Tobacco, rice, and indigo grown on large plantations emerged as cash crops.	Wealthy elite controlled most of the land. Cash crops required a large amount of labor, which was supplied on large farms by indentured servants and enslaved Africans.

HISTORY Online

Self-Check Quiz
Visit the *American Vision* Web site at tav.glencoe.com and click on **Self-Check Quizzes—Chapter 3** to assess your knowledge of chapter content.

Critical Thinking

30. **Analyzing Themes: Global Connections** Draw your own mental map of the triangular trade, then explain how Caribbean merchants paid for products from New England.

31. **Evaluating** Do you think Nathaniel Bacon was justified in staging a revolt against Virginia's government?

32. **Forming an Opinion** Do you think slavery would have become entrenched in the South if the region's economy had not depended on cash crops and a large labor force? Why or why not?

33. **Categorizing** Use a graphic organizer similar to the one below to compare the economies of the New England, Middle, and Southern Colonies.

New England Colonies	Middle Colonies	Southern Colonies

Practicing Skills

34. **Reading a Bar Graph** Study the graph of tobacco imports on page 85. Then use the steps you learned about reading a bar graph on page 103 to answer the following questions.
    a. **Interpreting Graphs** In which year did imports reach the highest level?
    b. **Synthesizing Information** Which region would benefit most by the rise in tobacco imports from 1725 to 1735?

Geography and History

35. The map on this page shows colonization and exports in the Americas in 1750. Study the map and answer the following questions.
    a. **Interpreting Maps** Which region produced diamonds?
    b. **Applying Geography Skills** Which European country controlled the most territory in the Americas? Which controlled the least?

Writing Activity

36. **Writing a Magazine Article** Find out about slavery throughout history in various cultural and geographic areas of the world. Choose one area and compare slavery there with the slavery of Africans in the American colonies. Present your findings in a magazine article and place it in your portfolio.

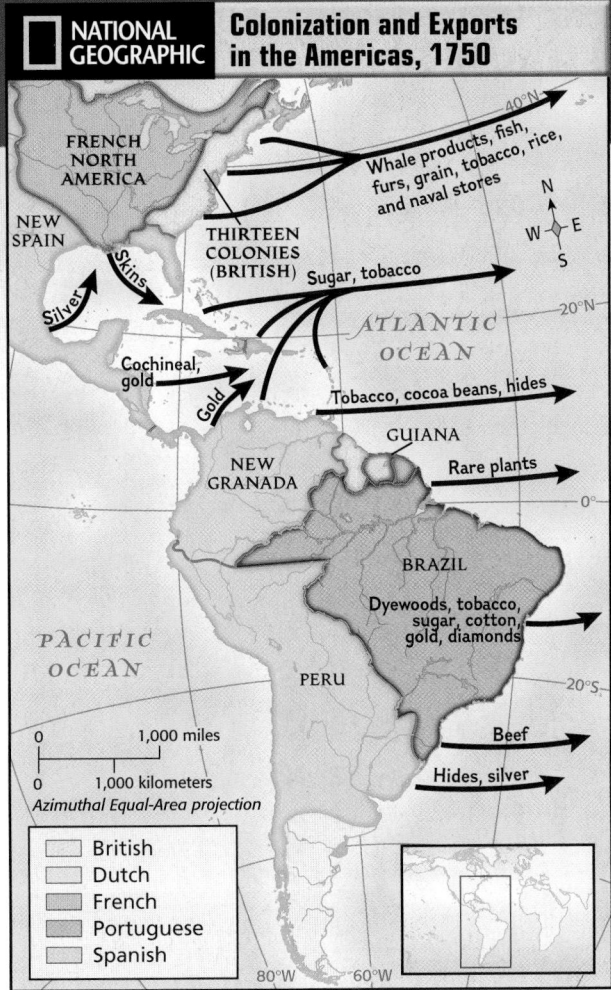

NATIONAL GEOGRAPHIC
Colonization and Exports in the Americas, 1750

Chapter Activity

37. **Technology Activity: Using the Internet** Search the Internet for sites that describe what life was like for colonists in America in the 1700s. Create a travel brochure titled "Visit Colonial America."

Standardized Test Practice

Directions: Choose the best answer to the following question.

All of the following are examples of strong community life in New England colonies EXCEPT

A plantations.

B schools.

C town meetings.

D churches.

Test-Taking Tip: Think about New England's geography and society. Which of the answers does not describe New England's society?

Creating a Nation

1754–1816

Why It Matters

The British colonies grew to dominate the American coastline, especially after defeating their major rivals—the French—in the French and Indian War. As Britain's position in America became secure, however, the colonists challenged the authority of a distant British government. Discontent grew to rebellion, and the United States of America emerged from the Revolutionary War with unique visions of government. Understanding the events of the early history of the United States will help you understand the government's design and the nation's ideals. The following resources offer more information about this period in American history.

Bible used to swear in
President Washington

Primary Sources Library

See pages 1048–1049 for primary source readings to accompany Unit 2.

Use the **American History Primary Source Document Library CD-ROM** to find additional primary sources about the early history of the United States.

Washington's Inauguration at Independence Hall, 1793 by Jean Leon Gérôme Ferris

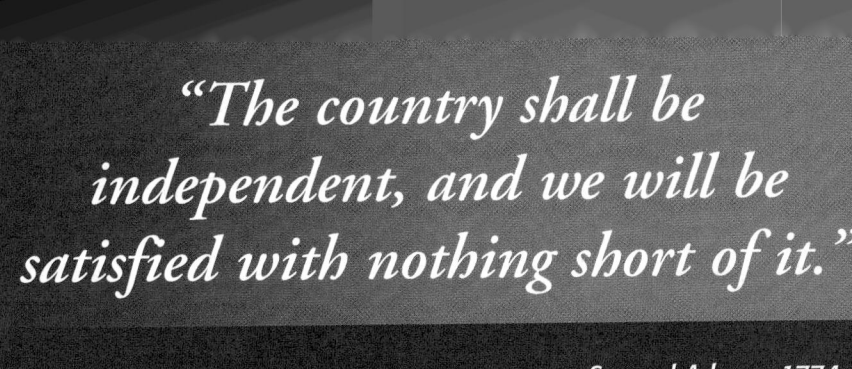

"*The country shall be independent, and we will be satisfied with nothing short of it.*"

—Samuel Adams, 1774

4 The American Revolution *1754–1783*

Why It Matters

In the early colonial period, the colonies grew accustomed to running their own affairs. When Britain tried to reestablish control, tensions mounted over taxes and basic rights. In 1775 these tensions led to battle, and in 1776 the colonists declared their independence from Britain. With the help of France and Spain, the colonists defeated the British in 1781. The Treaty of Paris in 1783 formally ended the war.

The Impact Today

The Revolutionary War experience had important results.
• *Common political traditions of our nation were born under the pressures of war.*
• *Americans value and protect local liberties and the right to representation in government.*

 The American Vision *Video* *The Chapter 4 video, "Women of the Revolution," chronicles the lives of women during the Revolutionary era.*

1754
• French and Indian War begins

1765
• Parliament passes the Stamp Act, triggering protests throughout the colonies

North America

1745   1755   1765

World

1748
• Montesquieu's *Spirit of the Laws* published

1751
• Chinese invade Tibet and control succession to the throne

1755
• Samuel Johnson's *Dictionary of the English Language* published

Washington Crossing the Delaware by Emanuel Gottlieb Leutze, 1851

1775
• First shots of the Revolutionary War fired at Lexington and Concord in Massachusetts

1770
• Bristish troops fire on colonists in Boston Massacre

1781
• Cornwallis surrenders at Yorktown, marking the end of the Revolutionary War

1783
• Treaty of Paris signed to officially end Revolutionary War and recognize the independence of the United States

1776
• Declaration of Independence signed

1775

1785

HISTORY Online
Chapter Overview
Visit the *American Vision* Web site at tav.glencoe.com and click on *Chapter Overviews—Chapter 4* to preview chapter information.

1770s
• Catherine the Great's effort to abolish Russian serfdom fails

1769
• Steam engine patented by James Watt

1776
• Adam Smith's treatise on mercantilism, *Wealth of Nations,* published

1780
• Empress Maria Theresa of Austria-Hungary dies

The Colonies Fight for Their Rights

Guide to Reading

Main Idea
Tensions between Britain and its American colonies grew as British leaders sought greater control over their North American empire.

Key Terms and Names
Albany Plan of Union, French and Indian War, Treaty of Paris, customs duty, inflation, Quartering Act, nonimportation agreement, writ of assistance

Reading Strategy
Organizing As you read about the growing tensions between Britain and the American colonies, complete a graphic organizer like the one below by listing the causes of the French and Indian War.

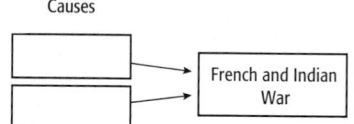

Causes

French and Indian War

Reading Objectives
- **Summarize** events that fueled colonial discontent.
- **Explain** how the Stamp Act affected the relationship between Britain and the colonies.

Section Theme
Civic Rights and Responsibilities The colonies used economic protest to fight Parliamentary power.

Preview of Events

♦1754	♦1758	♦1762	♦1766

1754
French and Indian War begins; Albany Conference meets

1763
Treaty of Paris ends French and Indian War

1764
Sugar Act passed

1765
Stamp Act passed

1767
Townshend Acts passed

★ An American Story ★

At first, Pennsylvania colonist John Hughes was delighted when his friend Ben Franklin helped him to get the position of stamp tax collector. By September 1765, however, he feared his job might cost him his life. Anti-tax protests had grown so strong that Hughes barricaded himself inside his house to avoid being attacked. He wrote frantically to Franklin in London:

❝You are now from Letter to Letter to suppose each may be the last you will receive from your old Friend, as the Spirit of . . . Rebellion is to a high Pitch. . . . Madness has got hold of the people. . . . I fancy some Lives will be lost before this Fire is put out. . . .❞

Just a few years earlier, British soldiers and American colonists had fought side by side in a successful war against France. After the war ended, tensions between Britain and its colonies grew. Britain wanted the colonies to help pay for the war, while the colonists questioned Britain's authority to make them do so. Misunderstanding and distrust slowly turned many colonists against the British, creating situations that would eventually lead to revolution.

—adapted from *What They Didn't Teach You About the American Revolution*

The French and Indian War

The French and English had been vying for dominance in Europe since the late 1600s, fighting three major wars between 1689 and 1748. Although most of the fighting took place in Europe, the conflict eventually spilled over into America. Whenever

France and England were at war, their colonies went to war as well. In 1754 a fourth struggle began.

The First Skirmish In the 1740s, the British and French both became interested in the Ohio River valley. The French had discovered that they could cross from Lake Ontario to the Ohio River in western Pennsylvania and follow the river south to the Mississippi. This allowed the French to travel from New France to Louisiana easily. At the same time, British fur traders entered the region, and land speculators—people who bought empty land hoping to sell it to settlers for a profit—became interested in the Ohio River valley.

To block British claims in the region, New France's governor, the Marquis Duquesne, ordered a chain of French forts to be built from Lake Ontario to the Ohio River. Duquesne's actions prompted Robert Dinwiddie, the governor of Virginia, to order a British fort built in western Pennsylvania. Before the British fort was completed, the French seized it and built Fort Duquesne at the site. Dinwiddie then asked George Washington, a young officer in the Virginia militia, to raise a force and expel the French.

As Washington's troops marched toward the Ohio River in the spring of 1754, they encountered a small French force near Great Meadows. After a brief battle, Washington retreated and built a stockade named Fort Necessity. A little over a month later, a large French force arrived and forced Washington to surrender. After being released, Washington returned to Virginia, leaving the French in control of the Ohio River valley. As the fighting between France and Britain expanded into a world war, the 22-year-old Washington became a hero in the colonies for his courageous attempt to resist the French.

The Albany Conference Even before fighting started in the Ohio River valley, the British government urged its colonies to work together to prepare for the coming war. The government also suggested that the colonies negotiate an alliance with the Iroquois. The Iroquois controlled western New York—territory the French had to pass through to reach the Ohio River. In response, 7 colonies sent representatives to meet with 150 Iroquois leaders at Albany, New York, in June 1754. This meeting became known as the Albany Conference.

The Albany Conference achieved several things. Although the Iroquois refused an alliance with the British, they did agree to

remain neutral. The colonies also agreed that Britain should appoint one supreme commander of all British troops in the colonies. Finally, the conference issued the **Albany Plan of Union,** a scheme developed by a committee led by Benjamin Franklin. The Plan of Union proposed that the colonies unite to form a federal government. Although the colonies rejected the Plan of Union, the effort showed that many colonial leaders had begun to think about joining their colonies together for their common defense.

The British Triumph In 1755 the new British commander in chief, General Edward Braddock, arrived in Virginia with 1,400 British troops. He linked up with 450 local militia troops and appointed Lieutenant Colonel George Washington to serve as his aide. Braddock then headed west intending to attack Fort Duquesne. The general was not worried about being ambushed by the Huron and other Native American allies of the French. "These savages may indeed be a formidable enemy to your raw American militia," he told Benjamin Franklin. "Upon the King's regular and disciplined troops, it is impossible they should make any impression."

Seven miles from Fort Duquesne, French and Native American forces did ambush Braddock's troops. Braddock was shot and later died. His inexperienced troops panicked. Only George Washington's leadership saved the British from disaster. As shots whizzed past him—four holes were later found in his

Analyzing *Political Cartoons*

Appeal for Unity In 1754, as French and Native American forces were threatening the colonies, Ben Franklin drew this cartoon urging colonists to stand together. A popular legend at the time said a snake could put itself back together and live if it did so before sunset. Why did Franklin's use of the serpent legend make his appeal for unity seem urgent?

hat and clothes—Washington rallied the troops and organized a retreat. The ambush had further consequences. Having seen that the British could be beaten, the Delaware people of western Pennsylvania began attacking British settlers in their territory.

For the next two years, the **French and Indian War** raged along the frontier, as both sides raided each other's territory. Then, in 1756, the fighting between Britain and France spread to Europe, where it later became known as the Seven Years' War. While Britain's allies fought the French in Europe, British Prime Minister William Pitt decided to send most of Britain's troops and fleet to North America and India to attack the French and seize their empire.

The British fleet quickly cut off the flow of supplies and reinforcements France had been sending to North America. In the meantime, the Iroquois, realizing the tide had turned in favor of the British, pressured the Delaware to end their attacks. With their Native American allies giving up the battle, the French found themselves badly outnumbered.

In 1758 General John Forbes, the new British commander in the colonies, sent troops to attack Fort Duquesne. Realizing they were outnumbered, the French burned the fort and retreated. The British built Fort Pitt, named after the prime minister, on the same site. Fort Pitt eventually became the city of Pittsburgh.

In 1759 a British fleet commanded by General James Wolfe sailed up the St. Lawrence River to Quebec City. Wolfe discovered a path from the river up the steep cliffs that protected the city. On September 12, 1759, as his troops marched onto the Plains of Abraham near the city, the French under General Louis Joseph Montcalm attacked. Both Wolfe and Montcalm were killed, and the British won the battle. Fighting continued elsewhere in the world until 1763, but the British victory at Quebec was the turning point in North America.

After Spain entered the war in 1761 on the side of France, Britain seized Spain's colonies in Cuba and the Philippines. The **Treaty of Paris** finally ended the war in 1763. Except for a few offshore islands, the treaty eliminated French power in North America. New France became part of the British Empire, as did all of Louisiana east of the Mississippi except for

History *Through Art*

Fatal Meeting The Battle of Quebec in 1759 was one of Britain's most dramatic victories over the French during the French and Indian War. Both commanding generals, the French Montcalm and the British Wolfe, were killed on the Plains of Abraham, the bluffs above the St. Lawrence River. **What did the Treaty of Paris stipulate about the status of New France?**

New Orleans. To get Cuba and the Philippines back, Spain gave Florida to Britain. To compensate Spain for its losses, the French signed a separate treaty giving Spain control of New Orleans and all of Louisiana west of the Mississippi.

Reading Check **Examining** Why were the French and the British interested in the Ohio River valley?

The Colonies Grow Discontented

To achieve its victory in 1763, the British government had borrowed an enormous amount of money to pay for the war and was now deeply in debt. Many British officials thought that the colonies should pay for part of the war, especially the cost of stationing British troops in the colonies. The policies Britain adopted to solve its financial problems angered the colonists and set the two sides on a course to confrontation.

The Proclamation Act of 1763 In the spring of 1763, a Native American religious leader known as the Delaware Prophet convinced **Pontiac,** chief of the Ottawa people, to go to war against the British. After uniting several Native American groups, including the Ottawa, Delaware, Shawnee, and Seneca peoples, Pontiac's forces attacked forts along the frontier and burned down several towns before British troops stopped them.

Pontiac's war did not surprise British officials. They had been expecting trouble since 1758, when reports first indicated that settlers were moving into western Pennsylvania in defiance of the colony's treaty with the region's Native Americans. British officials did not want to bear the cost of another war. Many officials also owned shares in fur trading companies operating in the region and did not want to disrupt the fur trade. They decided that the best solution was to limit western settlement until new treaties could be negotiated.

In early October, King George issued the **Royal Proclamation of 1763.** The Proclamation drew a line from north to south along the Appalachian Mountains and declared that colonists could not settle west of the line without the British government's permission. This enraged many farmers and land speculators, who wanted access to the land.

Customs Reform At the same time the Royal Proclamation Act was angering western farmers, new British tax policies were disturbing eastern merchants. In 1763 **George Grenville** became prime minister and

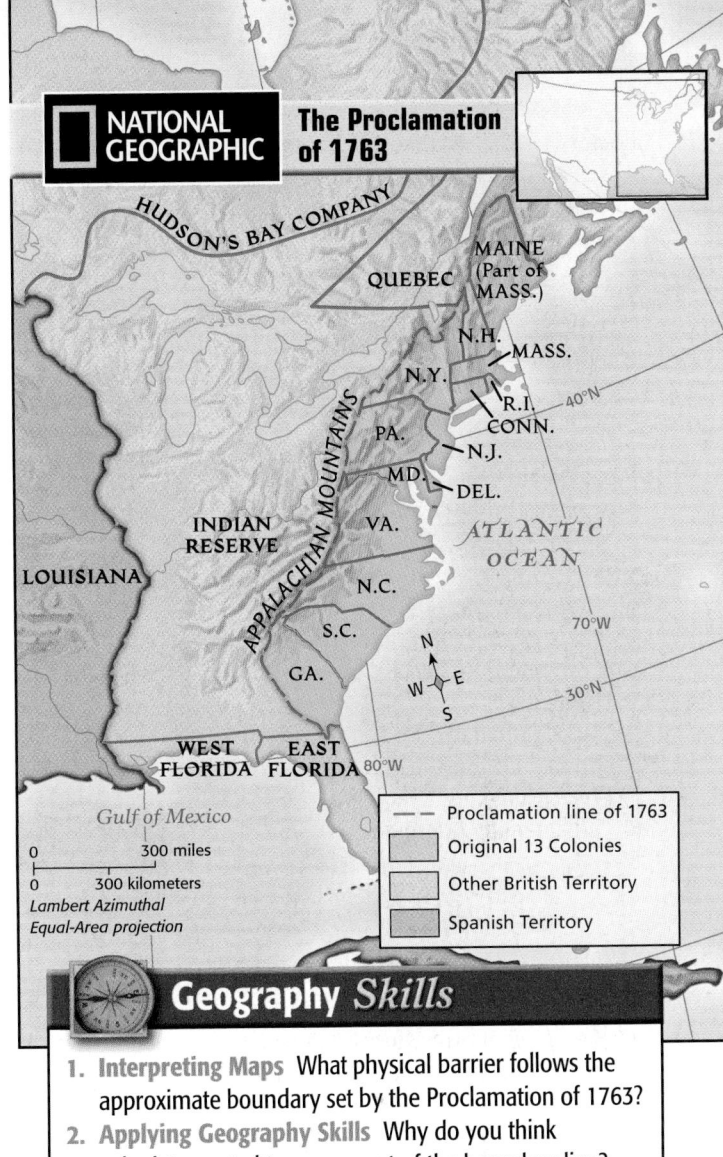

NATIONAL GEOGRAPHIC **The Proclamation of 1763**

HUDSON'S BAY COMPANY

QUEBEC — MAINE (Part of MASS.)

N.H. — MASS. — N.Y. — R.I. — CONN. — PA. — N.J. — MD. — DEL.

APPALACHIAN MOUNTAINS

INDIAN RESERVE

LOUISIANA — VA. — N.C. — S.C. — GA.

ATLANTIC OCEAN

40°N — 70°W — 30°N — 80°W

WEST FLORIDA — EAST FLORIDA

Gulf of Mexico

0 ——— 300 miles
0 ——— 300 kilometers
Lambert Azimuthal
Equal-Area projection

- - - Proclamation line of 1763
Original 13 Colonies
Other British Territory
Spanish Territory

Geography *Skills*

1. **Interpreting Maps** What physical barrier follows the approximate boundary set by the Proclamation of 1763?
2. **Applying Geography Skills** Why do you think colonists wanted to move west of the boundary line?

first lord of the Treasury. Grenville had to find a way to reduce Britain's debt and pay for the 10,000 British troops now stationed in North America. New tax policies emerged from his efforts.

Grenville discovered that British customs agents in America were collecting very little money. Obviously, merchants were smuggling goods into and out of the colonies without paying customs duties—taxes on imports and exports. Grenville convinced Parliament to pass a law allowing customs agents to send smugglers to a new vice-admiralty court in Halifax, Nova Scotia. Unlike colonial courts, where the juries were often sympathetic to smugglers, vice-admiralty courts were run by naval officers. These courts had no juries and did not follow British common law, a violation of the traditional English right to a jury of one's peers. Transporting colonists to distant Nova Scotia also violated their right to a speedy trial.

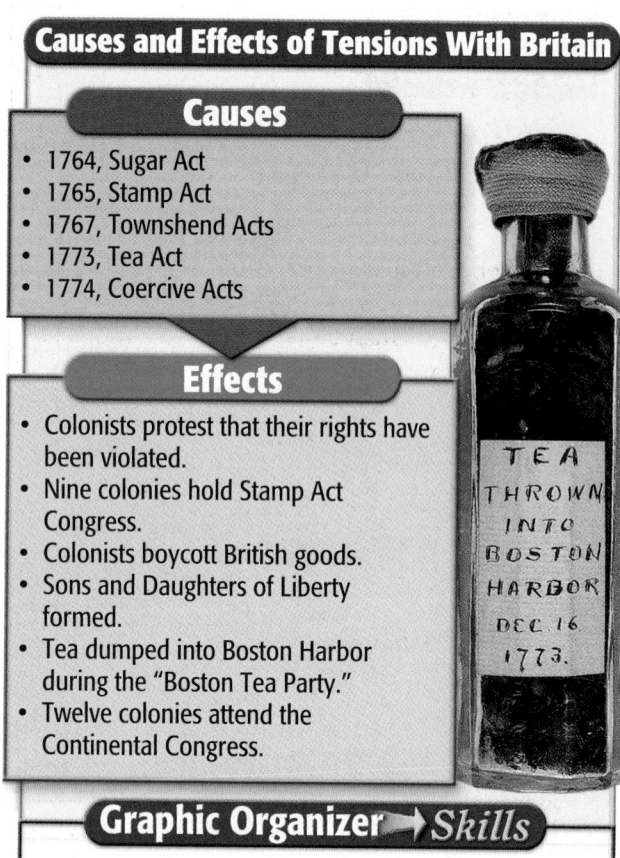

Causes and Effects of Tensions With Britain

Causes

- 1764, Sugar Act
- 1765, Stamp Act
- 1767, Townshend Acts
- 1773, Tea Act
- 1774, Coercive Acts

Effects

- Colonists protest that their rights have been violated.
- Nine colonies hold Stamp Act Congress.
- Colonists boycott British goods.
- Sons and Daughters of Liberty formed.
- Tea dumped into Boston Harbor during the "Boston Tea Party."
- Twelve colonies attend the Continental Congress.

TEA THROWN INTO BOSTON HARBOR DEC 16 1773.

Graphic Organizer → Skills

Parliament's efforts to tax the colonists led to growing protests in the colonies.

Analyzing Information If you had been a colonist, how would you have reacted to these taxes? Why?

Among those arrested for smuggling and tried by the vice-admiralty court was **John Hancock.** Hancock had made a fortune in the sugar trade, smuggling molasses from French colonies in the Caribbean. Defending Hancock was a young lawyer named **John Adams.** Adams argued that the use of vice-admiralty courts denied colonists their rights as British citizens:

❝Here is the contrast that stares us in the face. The Parliament in one clause guarding the people of the realm, and securing to them the benefit of tryal by the law of the land, and by the next clause depriving all Americans of that privilege. . . . Is there not in this clause a brand of infamy, or degradation or disgrace, fixed upon every American?❞

—quoted in *America's History*

The Sugar Act In addition to strictly enforcing customs duties, Grenville also introduced the American Revenue Act of 1764, better known as the **Sugar Act.**

The act changed the tax rates levied on raw sugar and molasses imported from foreign colonies. It also placed new taxes on silk, wine, coffee, pimento, and indigo.

Merchants throughout the colonies complained to Parliament that the Sugar Act hurt trade. Many were also furious that the act violated several traditional English rights. The act specified that merchants accused of smuggling were presumed guilty until proven innocent. The Sugar Act also allowed British officials to seize goods without **due process,** or proper court procedures, in some circumstances, and prevented lawsuits by merchants whose goods had been improperly seized. Parliament, however, ignored the protests of the merchants.

In many colonial cities, pamphlets soon circulated condemning the Sugar Act. One pamphlet, written by **James Otis,** argued that because the colonists had no representatives in Parliament, they could not be taxed for the purpose of raising money. Parliament had the right to control trade, but taxing Americans to pay for British programs was different. Otis's arguments gave rise to the popular expression, "No taxation without representation."

Despite the protests, the Sugar Act remained in force, and Grenville pressed ahead with other new policies. To slow inflation, which happens when money loses its value over time, Parliament passed the **Currency Act of 1764.** This act banned the use of paper money in the colonies, because it tended to lose its value very quickly. The act angered colonial farmers and artisans. They liked paper money precisely because it lost value quickly. They could use paper money to pay back loans, and since the money was not worth as much as when they borrowed it, the loans were easier to pay back.

✓ **Reading Check** **Summarizing** How did the British government hope to solve its financial problems caused by the cost of the French and Indian War?

The Stamp Act Crisis

Although the Sugar Act began to bring in money for Britain, Grenville did not believe it would raise enough to pay all of the government's expenses in America. To raise more money, he asked Parliament to introduce a stamp tax in the American colonies. The **Stamp Act** passed Parliament in March 1765.

The Stamp Act required stamps to be placed on most printed materials, including newspapers, pamphlets, posters, wills, mortgages, deeds, licenses, and even diplomas, dice, and playing cards. The stamp tax was different from other taxes the colonies had paid to Britain. Parliament had imposed many taxes on trade, but the stamp tax was the first direct tax Britain had ever placed on the colonists.

With the Stamp Act set to take effect on November 1, 1765, Parliament passed one more law. The **Quartering Act** forced the colonies to pay more for their own defense. If the colonies did not provide barracks for British troops, the act stated that troops could stay in taverns, inns, vacant buildings, and barns, and the colonies had to pay the rent.

As word of the Stamp Act spread through the colonies in the spring of 1765, a huge debate began. A flood of editorials, pamphlets, speeches, and resolutions against the tax swept through the colonies. In Virginia, the House of Burgesses passed a series of resolutions declaring that Virginians were entitled to the rights of British people and could only be taxed by their own representatives. Other colonial assemblies passed similar statements.

By the summer of 1765, huge mass meetings and demonstrations were taking place. In Connecticut, a merchant named Isaac Sears organized a group called the **Sons of Liberty.** The organization grew quickly throughout the colonies. The Sons of Liberty organized outdoor meetings and demonstrations. They also intimidated stamp distributors. In August 1765, for example, a Boston mob hung an effigy of the city's new stamp distributor from a tree, then pulled his house apart and burned the wood. In Newport, Rhode Island, the wife of a pro-British merchant described a similar protest:

> 66 In the morning . . . a mob assembled and erected a gallows near the town house and then dispers'd, and about ten a clock reassembled and took the effigy's of [several] men and the Stamp Master . . . to said gallows where they was hung up by the neck. . . . And about five a clock in the afternoon they made a fire under the gallows which consumed the effigy's, gallows and all. . . . About dusk they all muster'd out again, and . . . broke every window in his house, frames and all, likewise chairs, tables, pictures and everything they cou'd come across. 99
>
> —quoted in *Eyewitness Accounts of the American Revolution*

In October 1765, representatives from nine colonies met for what became known as the **Stamp Act Congress.** Together they issued the Declaration of Rights and Grievances. Drafted by a wealthy farmer from Pennsylvania named John Dickinson,

the declaration argued that only the colonists' political representatives and not Parliament had the right to tax them. The congress then sent a petition to King George asking for relief and to the British Parliament asking for the repeal of the Stamp Act.

On November 1 the Stamp Act took effect, but the colonists ignored it. Throughout the colonies, a movement began to boycott all British goods. People substituted sage and sassafras for imported tea. They stopped buying British cloth. In New York, 200 merchants signed a nonimportation agreement, pledging not to buy any British goods until Parliament repealed the Stamp Act.

The boycott had a very powerful effect on Britain. Thousands of workers lost their jobs as orders from the colonies were cancelled. British merchants could not collect money the colonies owed them. "The avenues of trade are all shut up," complained one merchant. "We have no remittances and are at our wits end for want of money. . . ."

Popular Protest

Past: Colonial Protests
In the 1770s, colonial women entered into the spirit of protest, too. They stopped drinking British tea and substituted chocolate or coffee. Sometimes they even gave up buying the ribbons they used to trim their bonnets. The British cartoon above made fun of women protesters in Edenton, North Carolina.

Present: World Trade
In late 1999, protesters gathered in Seattle, Washington, to protest the World Trade Organization meeting. Established in 1995, the WTO handles trade disputes and enforces agreements on international trade. Protesters objected that large corporations had too much influence in the WTO. They also objected to WTO meetings being held in closed session. Farmers, environmentalists, and labor groups were among the protesters.

Sam Adams
1722–1803

A passionate defender of colonial rights, Boston's Sam Adams was either a saint or a scoundrel—depending on who was describing him. His second cousin, John Adams, who would become the nation's second president, portrayed Sam as a "plain, simple, decent citizen of middling stature, dress, and manners." Sam's enemies, however, saw him quite differently. The royal governor of the colony called him "the most dangerous man in Massachusetts." Adams enjoyed his reputation as a fiery agitator. "Where there is a spark of patriotic fire," he once declared, "we will enkindle it."

Born in Boston, Adams graduated from Harvard College in 1740. He briefly studied law, worked as a clerk and merchant, and managed a brewery before being elected tax collector for Boston. As tensions with Great Britain increased, Adams, who had a passion for political issues, discovered his true talents: speaking out against British tax laws and organizing resistance against them. He helped organize the Boston

chapter of the Sons of Liberty and wrote several political pamphlets that encouraged Americans to rebel against the Bristish.

Adams showed particular skill in uniting Bostonians of different social classes. He forged an anti-British alliance of merchants, lawyers, and other members of the social elite with artisans, shopkeepers, and common laborers, all of whom worked together to protest British tax policies.

---

paper, paint, and tea imported into the colonies. Violators of the Revenue Act had to face trial in vice-admiralty courts, where they were presumed guilty unless they could prove their innocence. The Townshend Acts, like the Sugar Act, allowed officials to seize private property under certain circumstances without following due process.

To assist customs officers in arresting smugglers, the Revenue Act legalized the use of writs of assistance. The writs were general search warrants that enabled customs officers to enter any location to look for evidence of smuggling. Writs had been used before, but in 1760 James Otis had argued in court that they were "instruments of slavery" that violated people's rights. The issue remained unresolved until the Revenue Act of 1767 declared writs of assistance to be legal.

Action and Reaction Not surprisingly, the Townshend Acts infuriated many colonists. During the winter of 1767 and 1768, John Dickinson published a series of essays entitled *Letters From a Pennsylvania Farmer.* In these essays, Dickinson reasserted that only assemblies elected by the colonists had the right to tax them. In addition, he called on the colonies to become "firmly bound together" to "form one body politic" to resist the Townshend Acts.

Less than a month after Dickinson's first letter appeared, the Massachusetts assembly began organizing resistance against Britain. Among the leaders of this resistance was **Sam Adams,** cousin of John Adams. In February 1768, Sam Adams, with the help of James Otis, drafted a "circular letter" for the Massachusetts assembly to pass and circulate to other colonies. In the letter, the men pointed out that Townshend's taxes would be used to pay the salaries of government officials, a power the colonial assemblies then held. By taking this power away, the Townshend Acts would weaken the assemblies, which the colonists elected to control officials appointed by the king.

British officials ordered the Massachusetts assembly to withdraw the letter. The assembly refused. Furious, the British government ordered the Massachusetts assembly dissolved. In August 1768, the merchants of Boston and New York responded by signing nonimportation agreements, promising not to

---

With protests against the Stamp Act mounting in both Britain and America, British lawmakers repealed the act in 1766. To demonstrate its authority over the colonies, however, Parliament also passed the **Declaratory Act.** This act asserted that Parliament had the power to make laws for the colonies.

Reading Check **Evaluating** How was the Stamp Act different from other taxes Britain imposed on the colonies?

The Townshend Acts

During the Stamp Act crisis, the financial problems facing the British government had worsened. Protests in Britain had forced Parliament to lower property taxes there, which caused a further drop in revenue. As a result, **Charles Townshend,** the new Chancellor of the Exchequer, introduced a series of new regulations and taxes in 1767. These came to be called the **Townshend Acts.**

One of the Townshend Acts was the **Revenue Act of 1767.** This act put new customs duties on glass, lead, import any goods from Britain. Philadelphia's merchants joined the boycott in March 1769.

In May 1769, Virginia's House of Burgesses passed the **Virginia Resolves,** stating that only the House had the right to tax Virginians. Under orders from Britain, Virginia's governor dissolved the House of Burgesses. In response, the leaders of the House of Burgesses—including George Washington, Patrick Henry, and Thomas Jefferson—immediately called the members to a convention. This convention then passed a nonimportation law, blocking the sale of British goods in Virginia.

As the boycott spread through the colonies, Americans again stopped drinking British tea or buying British cloth. Women's groups, calling themselves the **Daughters of Liberty,** began spinning their own rough cloth, called "homespun." Wearing homespun became a sign of patriotism. Throughout the colonies, the Sons of Liberty encouraged people to support the boycotts. In 1769 colonial imports from Britain declined sharply from what they had been in 1768.

The Boston Massacre In the fall of 1768, as violence against customs officers in Boston increased, Britain dispatched roughly 1,000 troops to the city to maintain order. Bostonians referred to the British troops stationed there as "lobster backs" due to the red coats they wore. Crowds constantly heckled and harassed the troops. On March 5, 1770, a crowd of colonists began taunting and throwing snowballs at a British soldier guarding a customs house. His call for help brought Captain Thomas Preston and a squad of soldiers.

In the midst of the tumult, the troops began firing into the crowd. According to accounts, the first colonist to die was a man of African and Native

History *Through Art*

American Mockery In this cartoon, a funeral procession mourns the repeal of the Stamp Act. Third in line is "Mr. George Stamp, full of grief and despair," carrying a coffin of his "favorite child, Miss America Stamp," who "died hard in 1766." Who do you think George Stamp is supposed to represent?

American descent known as both Michael Johnson and Crispus Attucks. When the smoke cleared, three people lay dead, two more would die later, and six others were wounded. The shootings became known as the **Boston Massacre.** Colonial newspapers portrayed the British as tyrants who were willing to kill people who stood up for their rights.

News of the Boston Massacre raced like lightning across the colonies. It might have set off a revolution then and there, but only a few weeks later, news arrived that the British had repealed almost all of the Townshend Acts. Parliament kept one tax—a tax on tea—to uphold its right to tax the colonies. The repeal of the Townshend Acts again brought peace and stability to the colonies, but only temporarily.

Reading Check **Examining** What was stated in the Virginia Resolves passed by Virginia's House of Burgesses?

SECTION 1 ASSESSMENT

Checking for Understanding

1. **Define:** customs duty, inflation, nonimportation agreement, writ of assistance.

2. **Identify:** Albany Plan of Union, French and Indian War, Treaty of Paris, Quartering Act.

Reviewing Themes

3. **Civic Rights and Responsibilities** What argument did the Stamp Act Congress make in protest against the British taxes?

Critical Thinking

4. **Evaluating** Why do you think the British were so willing to pass new taxes in the face of colonial opposition?

5. **Classifying** Use a graphic organizer similar to the one below to list the acts passed by the British Parliament and the colonists' reactions to the acts.

Act	Colonists' Reactions
———→	———
———→	———
———→	———
———→	———
———→	———

Analyzing Visuals

6. **Examining Art** Study the painting of the Battle of the Plains of Abraham on page 118. How were the British able to move their troops up the steep cliffs near the city?

Writing About History

7. **Persuasive Writing** Imagine that you are a member of the Sons of Liberty or the Daughters of Liberty. Write a pamphlet explaining what your group does and urging colonists to join.

Comparing Accounts of the Boston Massacre

The Bloody Massacre,
engraving by Paul Revere, 1770

On the night of March 5, 1770, Captain Thomas Preston sent British troops to protect the Customs House in Boston from a group of colonists who had gathered nearby. Twenty minutes later, the troops had killed or wounded 11 people. The tragedy became known as the Boston Massacre. What happened that night? You're the historian.

Read the two accounts of the Boston Massacre below. One is Captain Preston's report of the event. The other is a colonist's account that quotes eyewitness Samuel Drowne. After reading the accounts, answer the questions and complete the activities that follow.

From Captain Thomas Preston's account

On Monday night . . . about 9 some of the guards came to and informed me the town inhabitants were assembling to attack the troops. . . . In a few minutes after I reached the guard, about 100 people passed it and went towards the custom house where the king's money is lodged. They immediately surrounded the sentry posted there, and with clubs and other weapons threatened to execute their vengeance on him. . . .

I immediately sent a noncommissioned officer and 12 men to protect both the sentry and the king's money, and very soon followed myself to prevent, if possible, all disorder, fearing lest the officer and soldiers, by the insults and provocations of the rioters, should be thrown off their guard and commit some rash act. . . .

Nay, so far was I from intending the death of any person that I suffered the troops to go . . . without any loading in their [guns]; nor did I ever give orders for loading them. . . .

The mob still increased and were more outrageous, striking their clubs or bludgeons one against another, and calling out come on you rascals, you bloody backs, you lobster scoundrels, fire if you dare. . . .

At this time I was between the soldiers and the mob . . . endeavoring all in my power to persuade them to retire peaceably, but to no purpose. They advanced to the points of the bayonets, [and] struck some of them. . . . A general attack was made on the men by a great number of heavy clubs and snowballs being thrown at them, by which

all our lives were in imminent danger, some persons at the same time from behind calling out, damn you bloods—why don't you fire. Instantly three or four of the soldiers fired, one after another, and directly after three more in the same confusion and hurry. . . .

The whole of the melancholy affair was transacted in almost twenty minutes. On my asking the soldiers why they fired without orders, they said that they heard the word fire and supposed it came from me. This might be the case as many of the mob called out fire, fire, but I assured the men that I gave no such order; that my words were, don't fire, stop your firing. In short, it was scarcely possible for the soldiers to know who said fire, or don't fire, or stop your firing.

Crispus Attucks, the first colonist to die in the Boston Massacre

From the colonist's account

Samuel Drowne [a witness] declares that, about nine o'clock of the evening of the fifth of March current, standing at his own door in Cornhill, he saw about fourteen or fifteen soldiers. . . . [The soldiers] came upon the inhabitants of the town, then standing or walking in Cornhill, and abused some, and violently assaulted others as they met them; most of them were without so much of a stick in their hand to defend themselves, as he clearly could discern, it being moonlight, and himself being one of the assaulted persons.

All or most of the said soldiers he saw go into King Street (some of them through Royal Exchange Land), and there followed them, and soon discovered them to be quarreling and fighting with the people whom they saw there, which he thinks were not more than a dozen. . . .

The outrageous behavior and the threats of the said party occasioned the ringing of the meeting house bell . . . which bell . . . presently brought out a number of the inhabitants, who . . . were naturally led to King Street, where [the British] had made a stop but a little while before, and where their stopping had drawn together a number of boys, round the sentry at the Custom House. . . .

There was much foul language between them, and some of them, in consequence of his pushing at them with his bayonet, threw snowballs at him, which occasioned him to knock hastily at the door of the Custom House. . . .

The officer on guard was Captain Preston, who with seven or eight soldiers, with firearms and charged bayonets, issued from the guardhouse, and in great haste posted himself and his soldiers in front of the Custom House, near the corner aforesaid. In passing to this station the soldiers pushed several persons with their bayonets, driving through the people in . . . disturbance. This occasioned some snowballs to be thrown at them, which seems to be the only provocation that was given. . . .

Captain Preston is said to have ordered them to fire, and to have repeated the order. One gun was fired first; then others in succession, and with deliberation, till ten or a dozen guns were fired; or till that number of discharges were made from the guns that were fired. By which means eleven persons were killed and wounded.

The site of the Boston Massacre in present-day Boston

Understanding the Issue

1. On what events of the night of March 5, 1770, do the two accounts excerpted here agree?

2. On what descriptions of the events do the two accounts differ?

3. As the historian, how do you assess the credibility of the two accounts?

Activities

1. **Investigate** What happened to Captain Preston after March 5? What were the immediate results of the Boston Massacre? Check other sources, including the Internet.

2. **Mock Trial** Assign class members roles in a mock trial of the Boston Massacre. Include other witnesses, a prosecutor, a defense attorney, a judge, and a jury.

The Revolution Begins

Main Idea

After years of escalating tensions and out-breaks of fighting, the colonists declared their independence from Britain on July 4, 1776.

Key Terms and Names

committee of correspondence, Boston Tea Party, Intolerable Acts, minuteman, Loyalist, Patriot, Battle of Bunker Hill, Declaration of Independence

Reading Strategy

Taking Notes As you read about the rising tensions between the colonies and Britain, use the major headings of the section to create an outline similar to the one below.

The Revolution Begins
I. Massachusetts Defies Britain
   A.
   B.
   C.
   D.
II.

Reading Objectives

• **Describe** ways in which Massachusetts continued to defy Britain after the repeal of the Townshend Acts.

• **Summarize** the first battles between Britain and the colonies.

Section Theme

Government and Democracy The First Continental Congress acted as a government during the Revolutionary crisis.

Preview of Events

♦1773	♦1774	♦1775	♦1776
1773 Boston Tea Party	**1774** First Continental Congress	**1775** Battles of Lexington and Concord; Second Continental Congress	**1776** Declaration of Independence drafted and signed

★ An American Story ★

On the night of December 17, 1773, a group of men secretly assembled along a Boston dock to strike a blow against Britain. One of the men was George Hewes, a struggling Boston shoemaker, who had grown to despise the British. Initially, Hewes had taken offense when British soldiers stopped and questioned him on the street and when they refused to pay him for shoes. After the Boston Massacre, which Hewes witnessed, his hatred grew deeper and more political.

So, after he "daubed his face and hands with coal dust, in the shop of a blacksmith," he gladly joined the other volunteers on that cold December night as they prepared to sneak aboard several British ships anchored in Boston Harbor and destroy the tea stored on board:

❝When we arrived at the wharf . . . they divided us into three parties for the purpose of boarding the three ships which contained the tea. . . . We then were ordered by our commander to open the hatches and take out all the chests of tea and throw them overboard, and we immediately proceeded to execute his orders, first cutting and splitting the chests with our tomahawks, so as thoroughly to expose them to the effects of the water. . . . In about three hours . . . we had thus broken and thrown over board every tea chest . . . in the ship.❞

—quoted in *The Spirit of 'Seventy-Six*

Massachusetts Defies Britain

Despite the tragedy of the Boston Massacre, the British decision to repeal the Townshend Acts had ended another crisis in colonial relations. For more than two years the situation remained calm. Then, in the spring of 1772, a new crisis began. Britain introduced several new policies that again ignited the flames of rebellion in the American colonies.

The *Gaspee* Affair

To intercept smugglers, the British sent customs ships to patrol North American waters. One such ship was the *Gaspee*, stationed off the coast of Rhode Island. Many Rhode Islanders hated the commander of the *Gaspee* because he often searched ships without a warrant and sent his crew ashore to seize food without paying for it. In June 1772, when the *Gaspee* ran aground, some 150 colonists seized and burned the ship.

This incident outraged the British. They sent a commission to investigate and gave it authority to take suspects to England for trial. This angered the colonists, who believed it violated their right to a trial by a jury of their peers. Rhode Island's assembly then sent a letter to the other colonies asking for help.

In March 1773, Thomas Jefferson suggested that each colony create a committee of correspondence to communicate with the other colonies about British activities. The committees of correspondence helped unify the colonies and shape public opinion. They also helped colonial leaders coordinate their plans for resisting the British.

The Boston Tea Party

With tensions simmering in the colonies, England's new prime minister, Lord North, made a serious mistake. In May 1773, he decided to help the **British East India Company,** which was almost bankrupt. Corrupt management and costly wars in India had put the company deeply in debt, while British taxes on tea had encouraged colonial merchants to smuggle in cheaper Dutch tea. As a result, the company had over 17 million pounds of tea in its warehouses.

To help the company sell its tea, Parliament passed the **Tea Act** of 1773. The Tea Act refunded four-fifths of the taxes the company had to pay to ship tea to the colonies, leaving only the Townshend tax. East India Company tea could now be sold at lower prices than smuggled Dutch tea. The act also allowed the East India Company to sell directly to shopkeepers, bypassing American merchants who normally distributed the tea. The Tea Act enraged the colonial merchants, who feared it was the first step by the British to squeeze them out of business.

In October 1773, the East India Company shipped 1,253 chests of tea to Boston, New York, Charles Town, and Philadelphia. The committees of correspondence rapidly alerted the colonies that the tea was on the way. The committees decided that the tea must not be allowed to land. When the first shipments arrived in New York and Philadelphia, the colonists forced the agents for the East India Company to return home with the tea. In Charles Town, customs officers seized the tea and stored it in a local warehouse.

The most dramatic showdown occurred in December 1773, when the tea ships arrived in Boston Harbor. On the night before customs officials planned to bring the tea ashore, approximately 150 men boarded the ships. Several thousand people on shore cheered as the men dumped 342 chests of tea into the harbor. The raid came to be called the **Boston Tea Party.**

The Coercive Acts

The Boston Tea Party was the last straw for the British. King George III informed Lord North that "concessions have made matters worse.

Picturing History

Tea Tantrum In December 1773, colonists in Boston took matters into their own hands and dumped hated imported tea into Boston Harbor. Why did Boston tea merchants hate the Tea Act so much?

Analyzing *Political Cartoons*

Paying the Tea Tax This cartoon by a British artist shows Bostonians forcing tea down the throat of a tarred and feathered customs official. In the background, colonists dump tea in Boston Harbor. Why do you think the words "Stamp Act" are hung upside down on the Liberty Tree?

The time has come for compulsion." In the spring of 1774, Parliament passed four new laws that came to be known as the **Coercive Acts.** These laws were intended to punish Massachusetts and end colonial challenges to British authority.

The first act shut down Boston's port until the city paid for the tea that had been destroyed. The second act required all council members, judges, and sheriffs in Massachusetts to be appointed by the governor instead of being elected. This act also banned most town meetings. The third act allowed the governor to transfer trials of British soldiers and officials to England to protect them from American juries. The final act required local officials to provide lodging for British soldiers at the scene of a disturbance, in private homes if necessary. To enforce the acts, the British moved 2,000 troops to New England and appointed General Thomas Gage as the new governor of Massachusetts.

Taken together, the Coercive Acts violated several traditional English rights, including the right to trial by a jury of one's peers and the right not to have troops quartered in one's home. The king was also not supposed to maintain a standing army in peacetime

without the consent of Parliament. Although the British Parliament had authorized the troops, colonists believed their own local assemblies should have had to give their consent as well.

In July 1774, a month after the last Coercive Act had become law, the British introduced the **Quebec Act.** This law had nothing to do with events in the American colonies, but it angered the colonists nonetheless. The Quebec Act stated that a governor and council appointed by the king would run Quebec. The act also gave more territory to Quebec, including much of what is today Ohio, Illinois, Michigan, Indiana, and Wisconsin. If colonists moved west, they would have to live in territory where they had no elected assembly.

The Quebec Act, coming so soon after the Coercive Acts, seemed to imply that the British were trying to seize control of the colonial governments. In the colonies, the Coercive Acts and the Quebec Act together became known as the **Intolerable Acts.**

The First Continental Congress In May 1774, the Virginia House of Burgesses called for a day of fasting and prayer to protest the arrival of British troops in Boston. When Virginia's governor dissolved the House, the burgesses went to a nearby tavern. In a resolution, they urged the colonies to suspend trade with Britain and to send delegates to a colonial congress to discuss more action. At least one burgess, Patrick Henry, was ready for war: "I know not what course others may take, but as for me, give me liberty or give me death!"

In New York and Rhode Island, similar calls for a congress had already been made. The committees of correspondence rapidly coordinated the different proposals, and on September 5, 1774, the **First Continental Congress** met in Philadelphia.

The 55 delegates to the Congress represented 12 of Britain's North American colonies. Florida, Georgia, Nova Scotia, and Quebec did not attend. They also represented a wide range of opinion. Although opposed to the Intolerable Acts, moderate delegates believed a compromise was possible. Other more radical delegates believed the time had come to fight.

Shortly after the Congress began, the moderates, led by Joseph Galloway of Pennsylvania, put forward a compromise. Galloway's plan proposed a federal government for the colonies similar to the one outlined in the Albany Plan of Union. After the radicals argued that the plan would not protect American rights, the colonies voted to put off its consideration.

When the Congress learned that the British had suspended the Massachusetts assembly, they responded with the **Declaration of Rights and Grievances.** The declaration expressed loyalty to the king but condemned the Coercive Acts. It also announced that the colonies were forming a nonimportation association. Several days later, the delegates approved the Continental Association, a plan for every county and town to form committees to enforce a boycott of British goods. The delegates then agreed to hold a second Continental Congress in May 1775 if the crisis had not been resolved.

✓ **Reading Check** **Examining** How did the British react to the Boston Tea Party?

The Revolution Begins

In October 1774, while the Continental Congress was still meeting, the Massachusetts assembly defied General Gage and organized the Massachusetts Provincial Congress. They then formed the Committee of Safety and chose John Hancock to lead it, giving him the power to call up the militia. In effect, the Provincial Congress had made Hancock a rival governor to General Gage.

A full-scale rebellion was now underway. Militias began to drill and practice shooting. The town of Concord created a special unit of men trained and ready to "stand at a minute's warning in case of alarm." These were the famous minutemen. All through the summer and fall of 1774, British control of the colonies weakened as colonists created provincial congresses and militias raided military depots for ammunition and gunpowder. These rebellious acts infuriated British officials.

Loyalists and Patriots British officials were not alone in their anger. Although many colonists did not agree with Parliament's policies, some still felt a strong sense of loyalty to the king and believed British law should be upheld. Americans who backed Britain came to be known as Loyalists, or Tories.

Loyalists came from all parts of American society. Many were government officials or Anglican ministers. Others were prominent merchants and landowners. Quite a few backcountry farmers on the frontier remained loyal as well, because they regarded the king as their protector against the planters and merchants who controlled the local governments.

On the other side were those who believed the British had become tyrants. These people were known as Patriots, or Whigs. Patriots also represented a wide cross section of society. They were artisans, farmers, merchants, planters, lawyers, and urban workers.

The Patriots were strong in New England and Virginia, while most of the Loyalists lived in Georgia, the Carolinas, and New York. Political differences divided communities and even split families. The American Revolution was not simply a war between the Americans and the British. It was also a civil war between Patriots and Loyalists.

Even before the Revolution, Patriot groups brutally enforced the boycott of British goods. They tarred and feathered Loyalists, and broke up Loyalist gatherings. Loyalists fought back, but they were outnumbered and not as well organized. Caught between the two groups were many Americans, possibly a majority, who did not favor either side and would support whomever won.

Causes and Effects of the American Revolution

Causes	**Effects**
• Colonists' tradition of self-government • Americans' sense of a separate identity from Britain • Proclamation of 1763 • British policies toward the colonies after 1763	• United States declares independence • A long war with Great Britain • World recognition of American independence

Graphic Organizer → *Skills*

The conflict between Britain and America grew worse after the passage of the Intolerable Acts of 1774.

Analyzing Information Why do you think the tradition of self-government played a role in the colonists' decision to declare independence?

Lexington and Concord In April 1775, the British government ordered General Gage to arrest the Massachusetts Provincial Congress, even if it meant risking armed conflict. Gage did not know where the Congress was located, so he decided to seize the militia's supply depot at Concord instead. On April 18, about 700 British troops set out for Concord on a road that took them past the town of Lexington.

Patriot leaders heard about the plan and sent **Paul Revere** and **William Dawes** to spread the alarm. Revere reached Lexington by midnight and warned the people there that the British were coming. He and Dawes and a third man, **Dr. Samuel Prescott,** then set out for Concord. A British patrol stopped Revere and Dawes, but Prescott got through in time to warn Concord.

On April 19, British troops arrived in Lexington and spotted some 70 minutemen lined up on the village green. The British marched onto the field and ordered them to disperse. The minutemen had begun to back away when a shot was fired; no one is sure by whom. The British soldiers, already nervous, fired at the minutemen, killing 8 and wounding 10.

The British then headed to Concord, but when they arrived, they found that most of the military supplies had been removed. When they tried to cross the North Bridge on the far side of town, they ran into some 400 colonial militia. A fight broke out, forcing the British to retreat.

Having completed their mission, the British decided to return to Boston. Along the way, militia and farmers fired at them from behind trees, stone walls, barns, and houses. By the time the British reached Boston, they had lost 99 men, and another 174 were wounded. The colonial forces had lost 49 militia, and another 46 were wounded.

News of the fighting spread across the colonies. Militia from all over New England raced to the area to help fight the British. By May 1775, militia troops had surrounded Boston, trapping the British inside.

The Second Continental Congress Three weeks after the battles at Lexington and Concord, the Second Continental Congress met in Philadelphia. The first issue was defense. The Congress voted to "adopt" the militia army surrounding Boston, and they named it the Continental Army. On June 15, 1775, the Congress appointed George Washington as general and commander in chief of the new army.

NATIONAL GEOGRAPHIC

Battles of Lexington and Concord, April 1775

❸ Colonial militia inflict 14 casualties on British at Concord's North Bridge.

❹ In retreat to Boston, British suffer over 250 casualties and Americans suffer 95.

Minutemen
Prescott
Minutemen
North Bridge
Concord April 19, 1775
Gage
Lexington April 19, 1775
Mystic River
Medford

❷ Revere captured; Dawes turned back.

Menotomy (Arlington)
Revere

❶ April 19, 1775, fighting begins on Lexington Common: eight Americans die, 10 wounded.

Cambridge
Charlestown
Dawes
Boston
Boston Harbor

Sudbury River
Charles River
DORCHESTER HEIGHTS

MASSACHUSETTS

N W E S

← Colonial troops
← Colonial messengers
← British troops
✦ American victory
✦ British victory

0   5 miles
0   5 kilometers
Lambert Equal-Area projection

Geography *Skills*

1. **Interpreting Maps** Which side suffered the most casualties at Lexington and Concord?
2. **Applying Geography Skills** About how far was Lexington from Boston?

Before Washington could get to his new command, however, the British landed reinforcements in Boston. Determined to gain control of the area, the British decided to seize the hills north of the city. Warned in advance, the militia acted first. On June 16, 1775, they dug in on Breed's Hill near Bunker Hill and began building a fort at the top.

The following day, General Gage sent 2,200 of his troops to take the hill. His soldiers, wearing heavy packs and woolen uniforms, launched an uphill, frontal attack in blistering heat. According to legend, an American commander named William Prescott told his troops, "Don't fire until you see the whites of their eyes." When the British closed to within 50 yards, the Americans took aim and fired. They turned back two British advances and were forced to retreat only after running out of ammunition.

The **Battle of Bunker Hill,** as it came to be called, helped to build American confidence. It showed that the colonial militia could stand up to one of the world's most feared armies. The British suffered more than 1,000 casualties in the fighting. Shortly afterward, General Gage resigned and was replaced by General William Howe. The situation then returned to a stalemate, with the British trapped in Boston surrounded by militia.

Reading Check **Interpreting** Why was the Battle of Bunker Hill important to the Americans?

The Decision for Independence

Despite the onset of fighting, many colonists in the summer of 1775 were not prepared to break away from Great Britain. Most members of the Second Continental Congress wanted the right to govern themselves, but they did not want to break with the British Empire. By 1776, however, opinion had changed. Frustrated by Britain's refusal to compromise, many Patriot leaders began to call for independence.

Efforts at Peace In July 1775, as the siege of Boston continued, the Continental Congress sent a document known as the **Olive Branch Petition** to the king. John Dickinson wrote the petition. It stated that the colonies were still loyal to the king and asked George III to call off hostilities until the situation could be worked out peacefully.

In the meantime, the radical delegates of the Congress convinced the body to order an attack on the British troops based in Quebec. They hoped the attack would convince the French in Quebec to rebel

History *Through Art*

Colonial Confidence Alonzo Chappel painted *The Battle of Bunker Hill.* The battle showed the colonists they could win against the British. How does the artist portray the colonists' courage?

and join the Americans in fighting the British. The American forces captured the city of Montreal, but the French did not rebel.

The attack on Quebec convinced British officials that there was no hope of reconciliation. When the Olive Branch Petition arrived in England, King George refused to look at it. On August 22, 1775, he issued the Proclamation for Suppressing Rebellion and Sedition, stating that the colonies were now "open and avowed enemies."

With no compromise likely, the Continental Congress increasingly began to act like an independent government. It sent people to negotiate with the Native Americans, and it established a postal system and a Continental Navy and Marine Corps. It also authorized privateering. By March 1776, the Continental Navy had raided the Bahamas and begun seizing British merchant ships.

The Fighting Spreads As the revolution began, Governor Dunmore of Virginia organized two Loyalist armies to assist the British troops in

What If...

The Declaration of Independence Had Condemned Slavery?

In 1776 the Continental Congress chose a committee to draft the Declaration of Independence. The committee included Thomas Jefferson, John Adams, Roger Sherman, Benjamin Franklin, and Robert Livingston. Jefferson later recalled the following in his memoirs: "[The committee members] unanimously pressed on myself alone to undertake the draught. I consented; I drew it; but before I reported it to the committee I communicated it separately to Dr. Franklin and Mr. Adams requesting their corrections. . . ."

Franklin and Adams urged Jefferson to delete his condemnation of King George's support of slavery. The two realized that the revolution needed support from all the colonies to succeed, and condemning slavery would certainly alienate pro-slavery colonists and force them to support the king. Jefferson modified the draft accordingly. If the Declaration of Independence had included Jefferson's condemnation of slavery, which is excerpted below, the history of the United States might have been very different.

❝He [King George] has waged cruel war against human nature itself, violating its most sacred rights of life and liberty in the persons of a distant people who never offended him, captivating and carrying them into slavery in another hemisphere, or to incur miserable death in their transportation thither. . . . He has [stopped] every legislative attempt to prohibit or to restrain this execrable commerce determining to keep open a market where [people] should be bought and sold. . . .❞

Virginia, one composed of white Loyalists, the other of enslaved Africans. Dunmore proclaimed that Africans enslaved by rebels would be freed if they fought for the Loyalists. The announcement convinced many Southern planters to support independence. Otherwise, they might lose their lands and labor force. They also increased their efforts to raise a large Patriot army. In December 1775, the Patriot troops attacked and defeated Dunmore's forces near Norfolk, Virginia. The British then pulled their soldiers out of Virginia, leaving the Patriots in control.

In North Carolina, Patriot troops dispersed Loyalists at the Battle of Moore's Creek in February 1776. The British then decided to seize Charles Town, South Carolina, but the Charles Town militia thwarted the British plans.

While fighting raged in the South, Washington ordered his troops to capture the hills south of Boston. He intended to place cannons on the hills to bombard the British. After the Americans seized the hills, however, the British Navy evacuated the British troops from Boston, leaving the Patriots in control.

Despite their defeats, it was clear that the British were not backing down. In December 1775, the king issued the Prohibitory Act, shutting down trade with the colonies and ordering a naval blockade. The British also began expanding their army by recruiting mercenaries, or soldiers for hire, from Germany. By the spring of 1776, the British had hired 30,000 German mercenaries, mostly Hessians from the region of Hesse.

***Common Sense* and Independence** As the war dragged on, more and more Patriots began to think the time had come to declare independence, although they feared that most colonists were still loyal to the king. In January 1776, however, public opinion began to change when Thomas Paine published a lively and persuasive pamphlet called

HISTORY Online

Student Web Activity Visit the *American Vision* Web site at tav.glencoe.com and click on **Student Web Activities—Chapter 4** for an activity on the American Revolution.

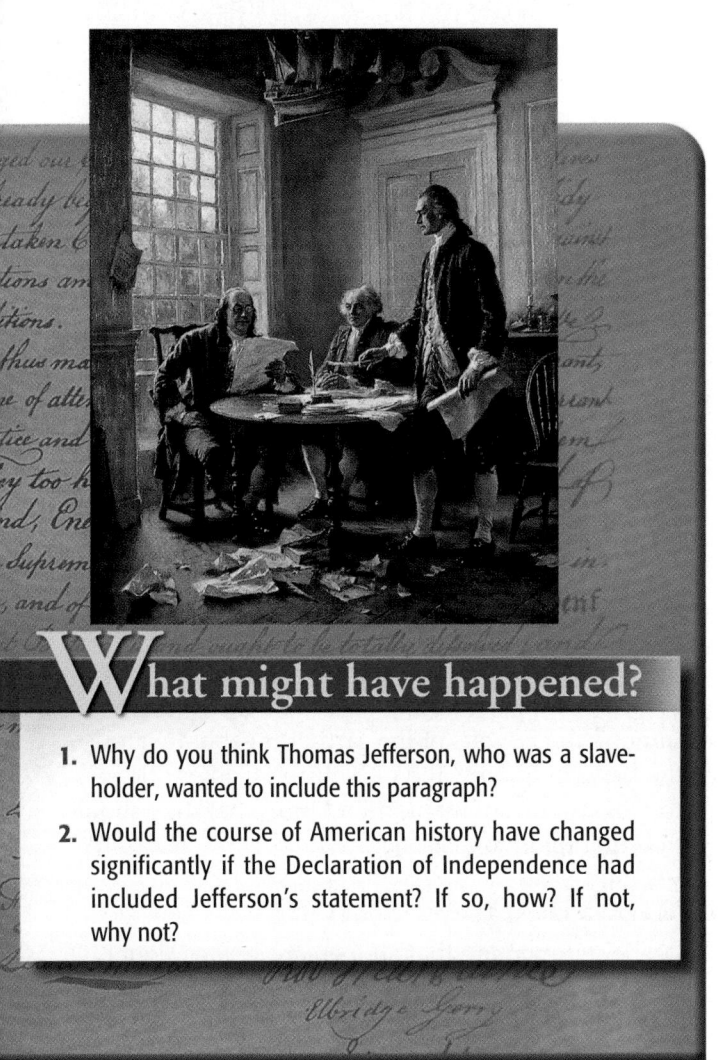

What might have happened?

1. Why do you think Thomas Jefferson, who was a slaveholder, wanted to include this paragraph?

2. Would the course of American history have changed significantly if the Declaration of Independence had included Jefferson's statement? If so, how? If not, why not?

Common Sense. Until *Common Sense* appeared, nearly everyone viewed Parliament as the enemy, not the king. In *Common Sense,* Paine attacked King George III. Parliament, he wrote, did nothing without the king's support. Paine argued that monarchies had been set up by seizing power from the people. George III was a tyrant, and it was time to declare independence:

> 66 Everything that is right or reasonable pleads for separation. The blood of the slain, the weeping voice of nature cries, 'Tis Time To Part. . . . Every spot of the old world is overrun with oppression. Freedom hath been hunted round the globe . . . [and] England hath given her warning to depart. Oh! Receive the fugitive, and prepare in time an asylum for mankind. 99

—from *Common Sense*

Within three months, *Common Sense* had sold 100,000 copies. George Washington wrote, "*Common Sense* is working a powerful change in the minds of men." Increasingly, many colonists were ready to declare independence. One by one the provincial congresses and assemblies told their representatives at the Continental Congress to vote for independence.

In early July a committee composed of John Adams, Benjamin Franklin, Roger Sherman, Robert Livingston, and Thomas Jefferson submitted a document Jefferson had drafted on independence. On July 4, 1776, the Continental Congress issued this **Declaration of Independence,** declaring themselves the United States of America. The American Revolution had begun.

Reading Check **Analyzing** How did Thomas Paine help persuade colonists to declare independence?

SECTION 2 ASSESSMENT

Checking for Understanding

1. **Define:** committee of correspondence, minuteman, Loyalist, Patriot.

2. **Identify:** Boston Tea Party, Intolerable Acts, Second Continental Congress, Battle of Bunker Hill, Declaration of Independence.

Reviewing Themes

3. **Government and Democracy** After King George III refused to consider the Olive Branch Petition, in what ways did the Continental Congress begin to act like an independent government?

Critical Thinking

4. **Synthesizing** What role did the committees of correspondence play in the colonists' move toward independence?

5. **Organizing** Use a graphic organizer similar to the one below to indicate ways in which colonists defied Britain after the repeal of the Townshend Acts.

Colonists Acts of Defiance

Analyzing Visuals

6. **Examining Maps** Study the map on page 130. Why do you think Paul Revere and William Dawes took different routes on the first leg of their journey?

Writing About History

7. **Descriptive Writing** Imagine that you were a participant in the Boston Tea Party. Write a diary entry describing the event.

The Declaration of Independence

In Congress, July 4, 1776. The unanimous Declaration of the thirteen united States of America,

[Preamble]

When in the Course of human events, it becomes necessary for one people to dissolve the political bands which have connected them with another, and to assume among the Powers of the earth, the separate and equal station to which the Laws of Nature and of Nature's God entitle them, a decent respect to the opinions of mankind requires that they should declare the causes which **impel** them to the separation.

[Declaration of Natural Rights]

We hold these truths to be self-evident, that all men are created equal, that they are **endowed** by their Creator with certain unalienable Rights, that among these are Life, Liberty, and the pursuit of Happiness.

That to secure these rights, Governments are instituted among Men, deriving their just powers from the consent of the governed,

That whenever any Form of Government becomes destructive of these ends, it is the Right of the People to alter or to abolish it, and to institute new Government, laying its foundation on such principles and organizing its powers in such form, as to them shall seem most likely to effect their Safety and Happiness. Prudence, indeed, will dictate that Governments long established should not be changed for light and transient causes; and accordingly all experience hath shown, that mankind are more disposed to suffer, while evils are sufferable, than to right themselves by abolishing the forms to which they are accustomed. But when a long train of abuses and usurpations, pursuing invariably the same Object evinces a design to reduce them under absolute **Despotism,** it is their right, it is their duty, to throw off such Government, and to provide new Guards for their future security.

[List of Grievances]

Such has been the patient sufferance of these Colonies; and such is now the necessity which constrains them to alter their former Systems of Government. The history of the present King of Great Britain is a history of repeated injuries and **usurpations,** all having in direct object the establishment of an absolute Tyranny over these States. To prove this, let Facts be submitted to a candid world.

He has refused his Assent to Laws, the most wholesome and necessary for the public good.

What It Means

The Preamble The Declaration of Independence has four parts. The Preamble explains why the Continental Congress drew up the Declaration.

impel *force*

What It Means

Natural Rights The second part, the Declaration of Natural Rights, states that people have certain basic rights and that government should protect those rights. John Locke's ideas strongly influenced this part. In 1690 Locke wrote that government was based on the consent of the people and that people had the right to rebel if the government did not uphold their right to life, liberty, and property.

endowed *provided*

despotism *unlimited power*

What It Means

List of Grievances The third part of the Declaration lists the colonists' complaints against the British government. Notice that King George III is singled out for blame.

usurpations *unjust uses of power*

He has forbidden his Governors to pass Laws of immediate and pressing importance, unless suspended in their operation till his Assent should be obtained; and when so suspended, he has utterly neglected to attend to them.

He has refused to pass other Laws for the accommodation of large districts of people, unless those people would **relinquish** the right of Representation in the Legislature, a right **inestimable** to them and formidable to tyrants only.

He has called together legislative bodies at places unusual, uncomfortable, and distant from the depository of their Public Records, for the sole purpose of fatiguing them into compliance with his measures.

He has dissolved Representative Houses repeatedly, for opposing with manly firmness his invasions on the rights of the people.

He has refused for a long time, after such dissolutions, to cause others to be elected; whereby the Legislative Powers, incapable of **Annihilation,** have returned to the People at large for their exercise; the State remaining in the mean time exposed to all the dangers of invasion from without, and **convulsions** within.

He has endeavoured to prevent the population of these States; for that purpose obstructing the Laws for **Naturalization of Foreigners;** refusing to pass others to encourage their migrations hither, and raising the conditions of new Appropriations of Lands.

He has obstructed the Administration of Justice, by refusing his Assent to Laws for establishing Judiciary Powers.

He has made Judges dependent on his Will alone, for the **tenure** of their offices, and the amount and payment of their salaries.

He has erected a multitude of New Offices, and sent hither swarms of Officers to harass our people, and eat out their substance.

relinquish *give up*
inestimable *priceless*

annihilation *destruction*

convulsions *violent disturbances*

Naturalization of Foreigners *process by which foreign-born persons become citizens*

tenure *term*

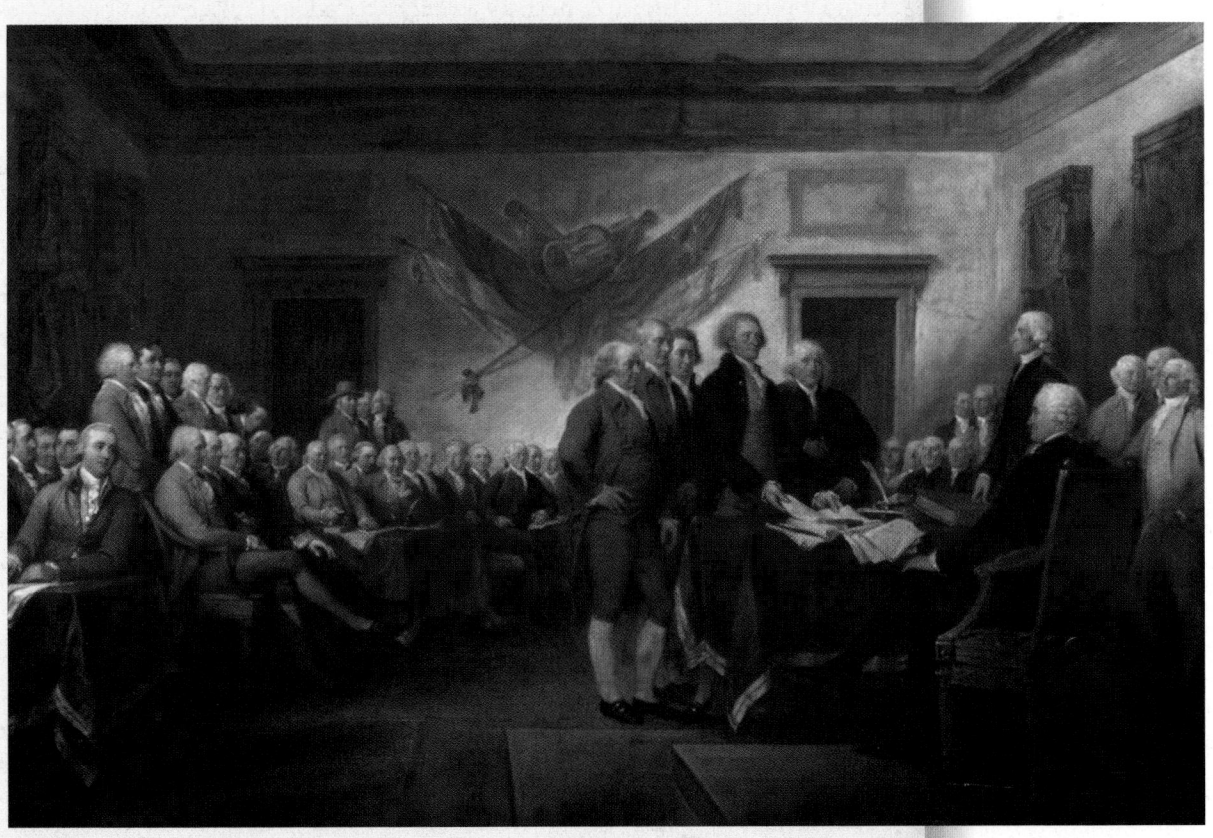

The Declaration of Independence **135**

He has kept among us, in times of peace, Standing Armies without the Consent of our legislature.

He has affected to render the Military independent of and superior to the Civil Power.

He has combined with others to subject us to a jurisdiction foreign to our constitution, and unacknowledged by our laws; giving his Assent to their acts of pretended legislation:

For **quartering** large bodies of troops among us:

For protecting them, by a mock Trial, from Punishment for any Murders which they should commit on the Inhabitants of these States:

For cutting off our Trade with all parts of the world:

For imposing taxes on us without our Consent:

For depriving us in many cases, of the benefits of Trial by Jury:

For transporting us beyond Seas to be tried for pretended offences:

For abolishing the free System of English Laws in a neighbouring Province, establishing therein an Arbitrary government, and enlarging its Boundaries so as to **render** it at once an example and fit instrument for introducing the same absolute rule into these Colonies:

For taking away our Charters, abolishing our most valuable Laws, and altering fundamentally the Forms of our Governments:

For suspending our own Legislature, and declaring themselves invested with Power to legislate for us in all cases whatsoever.

He has **abdicated** Government here, by declaring us out of his Protection and waging War against us.

He has plundered our seas, ravaged our Coasts, burnt our towns, and destroyed the lives of our people.

He is at this time transporting large armies of foreign mercenaries to compleat the works of death, desolation and tyranny, already begun with circumstances of Cruelty & **perfidy** scarcely paralleled in the most barbarous ages, and totally unworthy the Head of a civilized nation.

He has constrained our fellow Citizens taken Captive on the high Seas to bear Arms against their Country, to become the executioners of their friends and Brethren, or to fall themselves by their Hands.

He has excited domestic **insurrections** amongst us, and has endeavoured to bring on the inhabitants of our frontiers, the merciless Indian Savages, whose known rule of warfare, is an undistinguished destruction of all ages, sexes and conditions.

In every stage of these Oppressions We have **Petitioned for Redress** in the most humble terms: Our repeated Petitions have been answered only by repeated injury. A Prince, whose character is thus marked by every act which may define a Tyrant, is unfit to be the ruler of a free People.

Nor have We been wanting in attention to our British brethren. We have warned them from time to time of attempts by their legislature to extend an **unwarrantable jurisdiction** over us. We have reminded them of the circumstances of our emigration and settlement here. We have appealed to their native justice and magnanimity, and we have conjured them by the ties of our common kindred to disavow these usurpations, which, would inevitably interrupt our connections and correspondence. They too have been deaf to the voice of justice and of **consanguinity**. We must, therefore, acquiesce in the necessity, which denounces our Separation, and hold them, as we hold the rest of mankind, Enemies in War, in Peace Friends.

quartering *lodging*

render *make*

abdicated *given up*

perfidy *violation of trust*

insurrections *rebellions*

petitioned for redress *asked formally for a correction of wrongs*

unwarrantable jurisdiction *unjustified authority*

consanguinity *originating from the same ancestor*

[Resolution of Independence by the United States]

We, therefore, the Representatives of the united States of America, in General Congress, Assembled, appealing to the Supreme Judge of the world for the **rectitude** of our intentions, do, in the Name, and by Authority of the good People of these Colonies, solemnly publish and declare, That these United Colonies are, and of Right ought to be Free and Independent States; that they are Absolved from all Allegiance to the British Crown, and that all political connection between them and the State of Great Britain, is and ought to be totally dissolved; and that as Free and Independent States, they have full Power to levy War, conclude Peace, contract Alliances, establish Commerce, and to do all other Acts and Things which Independent States may of right do.

And for the support of this Declaration, with a firm reliance on the Protection of Divine Providence, we mutually pledge to each other our Lives, our Fortunes and our sacred Honor.

John Hancock
    President from
    Massachusetts

Georgia
Button Gwinnett
Lyman Hall
George Walton

North Carolina
William Hooper
Joseph Hewes
John Penn

South Carolina
Edward Rutledge
Thomas Heyward, Jr.
Thomas Lynch, Jr.
Arthur Middleton

Maryland
Samuel Chase
William Paca
Thomas Stone
Charles Carroll
    of Carrollton

Virginia
George Wythe
Richard Henry Lee
Thomas Jefferson
Benjamin Harrison
Thomas Nelson, Jr.
Francis Lightfoot Lee
Carter Braxton

Pennsylvania
Robert Morris
Benjamin Rush
Benjamin Franklin
John Morton
George Clymer
James Smith
George Taylor
James Wilson
George Ross

Delaware
Caesar Rodney
George Read
Thomas McKean

New York
William Floyd
Philip Livingston
Francis Lewis
Lewis Morris

New Jersey
Richard Stockton
John Witherspoon
Francis Hopkinson
John Hart
Abraham Clark

New Hampshire
Josiah Bartlett
William Whipple
Matthew Thornton

Massachusetts
Samuel Adams
John Adams
Robert Treat Paine
Elbridge Gerry

Rhode Island
Stephen Hopkins
William Ellery

Connecticut
Samuel Huntington
William Williams
Oliver Wolcott
Roger Sherman

What It Means
Resolution of Independence The Final section declares that the colonies are "Free and Independent States" with the full power to make war, to form alliances, and to trade with other countries.

rectitude *rightness*

What It Means
Signers of the Declaration The signers, as representatives of the American people, declared the colonies independent from Great Britain. Most members signed the document on August 2, 1776.

The War for Independence

Main Idea

After a war lasting several years, the colonists finally won their independence from Great Britain.

Key Terms and Names

William Howe, guerrilla warfare, Nathan Hale, Valley Forge, Marquis de Lafayette, Saratoga, letters of marque, John Paul Jones, Charles Cornwallis, Battle of Kings Mountain

Reading Strategy

Sequencing As you read about the war for independence, complete a time line similar to the one below to record the major battles and their outcomes.

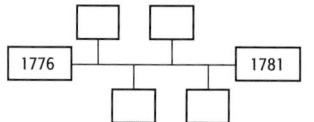

Reading Objectives

• **Describe** the strategies behind the Northern Campaign.
• **Summarize** the scope of the war at sea.

Section Theme

Global Connections Hostility between the French and British caused France to support the colonies.

Preview of Events

♦1775   ♦1778   ♦1781   ♦1784

1776
Battle of Trenton

1777
The British surrender at Saratoga

1777–1778
Washington camps at Valley Forge for the winter

1781
Cornwallis surrenders at Yorktown

1783
Treaty of Paris signed

★ An American Story ★

Colonel Henry Beckman Livingston could only watch helplessly the suffering around him. A veteran of several military campaigns, Livingston huddled with the rest of George Washington's army at its winter quarters at Valley Forge, Pennsylvania. The winter of 1777 to 1778 was brutally cold, and the army lacked food, clothing, and other supplies. Huddled in small huts, soldiers wrapped themselves in blankets and survived on the smallest of rations. Livingston described the army's plight in a letter to his brother, Robert:

❝Our troops are in general almost naked and very often in a starveing condition. All my men except 18 are unfit for duty for want of shoes, stockings, and shirts. . . . Poor Jack has been necessitated to make up his blanket into a vest and breeches. If I did not fear starveing with cold I should be tempted to do the same.❞

—adapted from *A Salute to Courage*

The Opposing Sides

The struggle at Valley Forge was a dark hour for the patriots. No one knew if they were strong enough to defeat the powerful British Empire. On the same day that the Continental Congress voted for independence, the British began landing troops in New York. By mid-August, they had assembled an estimated 32,000 men under the command of General **William Howe.** British officials did not expect the rebellion to last long. The British troops, called "redcoats" because of their uniforms, were disciplined, well trained, and well equipped.

Compared to the British troops, the Continental Army was inexperienced and poorly equipped. Throughout the war, it struggled to keep its recruits and pay their wages. Although over 230,000 men served in the Continental Army, they rarely numbered more than 20,000 at any one time. Many soldiers deserted or refused to reenlist when their term was up. Others left their posts and returned to their farms at planting or harvest time.

Paying for the war was equally difficult. Lacking the power to tax, the Continental Congress issued paper money. These "Continentals" were not backed by gold or silver and became almost worthless very quickly. Fortunately **Robert Morris,** a wealthy Pennsylvania merchant and banker, personally pledged large amounts of money for the war effort. Morris also set up an efficient method of buying rations and uniforms, arranged for foreign loans, and convinced the Congress to create the Bank of North America to finance the military.

The Continental Army was not the only force the British had to worry about. They also had to fight the local militias. The militias were poorly trained, but they fought differently. They did not always line up for battle. They hid among trees and behind walls and ambushed British troops and supply wagons, then disappeared. This kind of fighting is called guerrilla warfare, and it is very difficult to defeat.

Another problem for the British was that they were not united at home. Many merchants and members of Parliament opposed the war. The British had to win quickly and cheaply; otherwise, opinions in Parliament would shift against the war. The United States did not have to defeat Britain—it simply had to survive until the British became tired of paying for the war.

The European balance of power also hampered the British. The French, Dutch, and Spanish were all eager to exploit Britain's problems. As a result, Britain had to station much of its military elsewhere in the world to defend its empire. The European balance of power also meant that the Patriots might be able to find allies against the British.

✓ **Reading Check** **Identifying** What three major disadvantages did the British face in the American Revolution?

The Northern Campaign

The British knew that to end the war quickly, they not only had to win several battles but also had to convince the American people that their cause was hopeless. At the same time, the British had to make it safe to surrender. If the Patriots thought they would be hanged for treason, they would never surrender.

General Howe's strategy had two parts. The first part was military. He began a massive buildup in New York, hoping to intimidate the Americans and capture New York City. This would separate New

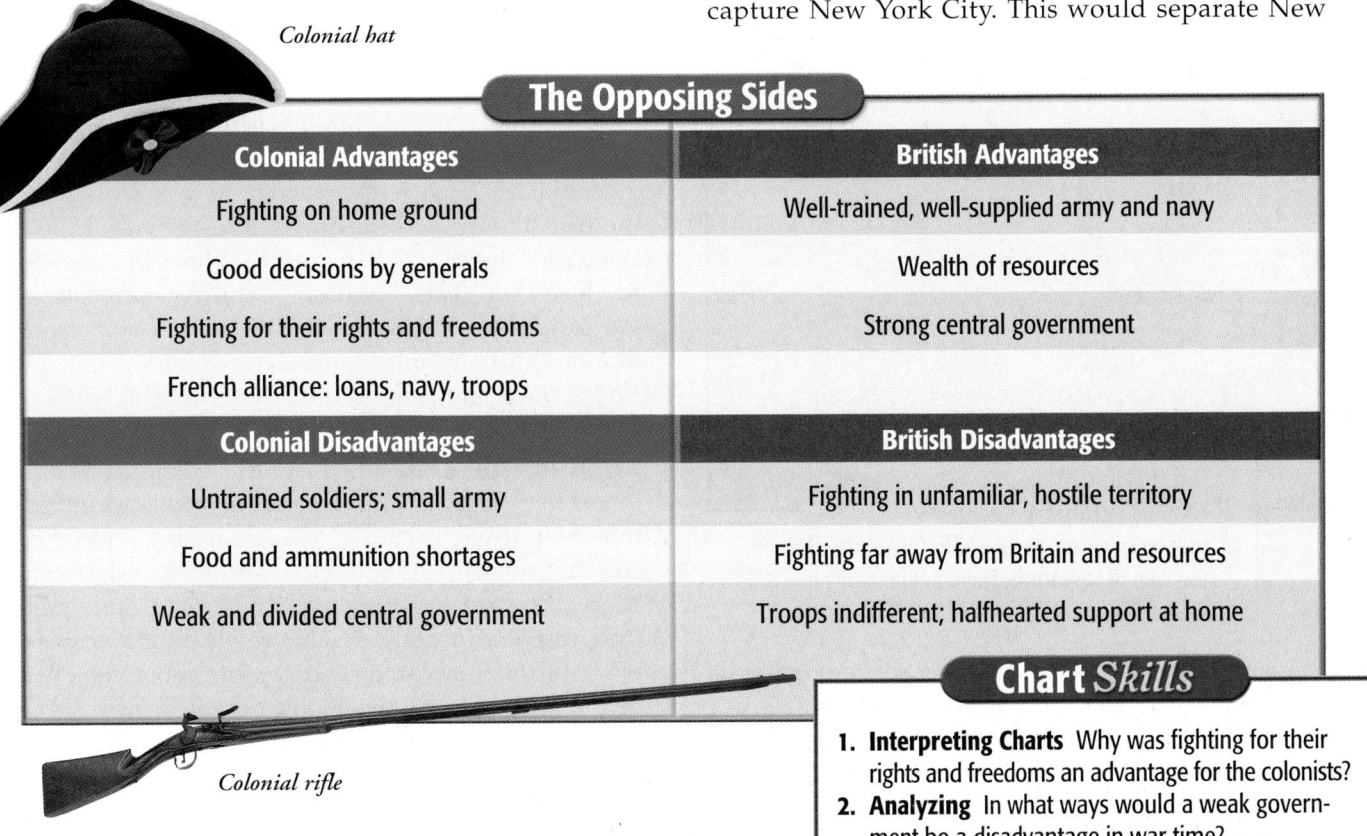

Colonial hat

Colonial rifle

The Opposing Sides

Colonial Advantages	British Advantages
Fighting on home ground	Well-trained, well-supplied army and navy
Good decisions by generals	Wealth of resources
Fighting for their rights and freedoms	Strong central government
French alliance: loans, navy, troops	
Colonial Disadvantages	**British Disadvantages**
Untrained soldiers; small army	Fighting in unfamiliar, hostile territory
Food and ammunition shortages	Fighting far away from Britain and resources
Weak and divided central government	Troops indifferent; halfhearted support at home

Chart *Skills*

1. **Interpreting Charts** Why was fighting for their rights and freedoms an advantage for the colonists?
2. **Analyzing** In what ways would a weak government be a disadvantage in war time?

War for Independence, 1775–1777

Legend:
- American forces
- British forces
- American victory
- British victory
- Fort

0   100 miles
0   100 kilometers
Albers Conic Equal-Area projection

QUEBEC

St. Lawrence R.

MAINE
(Part of MASS.)

45°N

Burgoyne, 1777

Montreal

St. Leger, 1777

Ft. Ticonderoga
July 6, 1777

❹ Burgoyne surrenders
at Saratoga,
Oct. 17, 1777

N.H.

Saratoga

Bennington
Aug. 15, 1777

General Howe
March 17, 1776

Oriskany
Aug. 6, 1777

Albany

MASS. Boston

Bemis Heights
Oct. 7, 1777

N.Y.

Kingston

CONN. R.I.

40°N

Ft. Montgomery

❶ British capture
New York City, 1776

New York City

Brooklyn Heights
Aug. 27, 1776

PA.

N.J.

Princeton

Germantown
Oct. 4, 1777

General Howe, July 1776

70°W

Brandywine Creek
Sept. 11, 1777

Trenton

Philadelphia

❷ Americans attack British
at Trenton, Dec. 1776,
and Princeton, Jan. 1777

❸ Howe captures
Philadelphia, 1777

DEL.

General Howe, 1777

MD.

VA.

ATLANTIC
OCEAN

N
W E
S

Chesapeake
Bay

35°N

NOVA
SCOTIA

Geography Skills

1. **Interpreting Maps** Name two sites of colonial victories in New Jersey.
2. **Applying Geography Skills** What was the role of the British Navy in the war?

Benjamin Franklin, John Adams, and Edward Rutledge. Howe told them that anyone who put down their arms and swore loyalty to the king would be pardoned. The Americans quickly realized that Howe had no authority to negotiate a compromise and was only interested in talking them into surrendering. They refused to talk further, and the stage was set for the first major battle.

Opening Moves Despite the size of the British forces preparing to seize New York City, the Continental Congress asked Washington to defend the city. Congressional leaders feared that if New York fell without a fight, it would hurt American morale. Washington agreed with this assessment, and he moved much of his army to Long Island and Manhattan Island.

The inexperience of Washington's troops became obvious when British troops landed on Long Island in the summer of 1776. Many American soldiers fled, and another 1,500 became casualties. Fortunately, the British did not move quickly after their victory, and the surviving American troops escaped to Manhattan Island where they joined the remainder of Washington's army defending New York City.

Using their ships, the British could have landed troops north of New York City and surrounded the American positions, but again, they moved too slowly. Washington abandoned the city and headed to the northern end of Manhattan. The British then captured New York and used it as their headquarters for the rest of the war.

About this time, Washington sent Captain **Nathan Hale** to spy on the British. Although Hale was disguised as a Dutch schoolteacher, he was caught by the British and hanged. Brave until the end, Hale's last words were: "I only regret that I have but one life to lose for my country." Shortly afterward, Washington moved most of his troops from Manhattan to White Plains, New York, where the British once again engaged the Americans in battle.

Crossing the Delaware At the Battle of White Plains in October 1776, the British forced Washington to retreat again. Then they surprised him. Instead of coming after the Continental Army, the British troops headed toward Philadelphia, where the Continental Congress was meeting. Washington's troops received word of this new plan. They had to move fast, but they managed to get there ahead of the British.

While this march was taking place, Thomas Paine wrote another pamphlet to help boost American morale. In *The American Crisis*, he

England from the Southern states and demonstrate to Americans that they could not win.

The second part of Howe's strategy was diplomatic. He invited delegates from the Continental Congress to a peace conference. The Congress sent reminded his fellow Americans that "the harder the conflict, the more glorious the triumph":

> 66These are the times that try men's souls. The summer soldier and the sunshine patriot will in this crisis shrink from the service of their country; but he that stands it now deserves the love and thanks of man and woman.99
>
> —from *The American Crisis*

By the time Washington reached Pennsylvania, winter had begun. The British stopped their advance and dispersed into winter quarters in New Jersey. In the 1700s, armies did not usually fight in the winter because of the weather and scarce food supplies.

At this point, Washington tried something daring and unexpected—a winter attack. On December 25, 1776, he led approximately 2,400 men across the icy Delaware River. The army then attacked a group of Hessians at Trenton in the middle of a sleet storm. They killed or captured almost 1,000 men. Several days later, at Princeton, Washington's forces scattered three British regiments. Having achieved two small victories, Washington headed into the hills of northern New Jersey for the winter.

Philadelphia Falls

In March 1777, King George III approved a plan developed by General John Burgoyne to isolate New England from the other American states. Burgoyne proposed a three-pronged attack on New York. He would take a large force south into New York from Montreal. Another force would move from Montreal up the St. Lawrence River to Lake Ontario then head east into New York. A third force, led by General Howe, would march north from New York City up the Hudson River valley. The three forces would meet near Albany, then march east into New England.

Unfortunately for the British, they did not coordinate the plan. By spring 1777, General Howe had made his own plans. He loaded about 13,000 men onto ships and moved them to Maryland. From there he attacked Philadelphia from the south. Howe believed that capturing Philadelphia and the Continental Congress would cripple the Revolution.

Howe's operation was a military success but a political failure. On September 11, 1777, he defeated Washington at the Battle of Brandywine Creek and captured Philadelphia. To Howe's frustration, however, the Continental Congress escaped. Howe failed to destroy the Continental Army, which soon took up winter quarters at **Valley Forge.** There, the bitter cold and food shortages killed nearly 2,500 men.

Even amidst the harsh conditions of Valley Forge, Washington managed to secure training for his army. Joining him at Valley Forge were two European military officers, the **Marquis de Lafayette** from France and Baron Friedrich von Steuben from Prussia. These officers helped Washington improve discipline and boost morale among the weary troops.

France Enters the War

General Burgoyne did not know Howe had gone south to attack Philadelphia. In June 1777, he and an estimated 8,000 troops marched south from Quebec into New York. From the eastern end of Lake Ontario, another 900 troops and over 1,000 Iroquois warriors headed east toward Albany. The Iroquois had allied with the British hoping to keep American settlers off Iroquois lands.

Despite some early victories, Burgoyne's forces were not able to defeat the Americans defending upper New York. The British troops and Iroquois marching east from Lake Ontario were ambushed by militia and then driven back by American troops under General **Benedict Arnold.** Meanwhile, Burgoyne's own troops could not drive off the militia. With his supplies dwindling, Burgoyne surrendered at Saratoga, New York. The American victory at **Saratoga** was a turning point

History *Through Art*

A Savage Winter William B.T. Trego painted *The March to Valley Forge,* depicting the difficult conditions soldiers faced during the winter of 1777 to 1778. What hardships did the troops face at Valley Forge?

in the war. It improved American morale and also convinced France to commit troops to the American cause.

Both Spain and France had been secretly sending arms and supplies to the United States well before Saratoga. The Congress appreciated the supplies but wanted the French to send troops too. In September 1776, the Congress sent Benjamin Franklin, Arthur Lee, and Silas Deane to France to ask for troops. The French, however, were not willing to risk war until they believed the Americans could win, and the victory at Saratoga assured them. Shortly afterward, they began negotiations with the United States to create an alliance against Britain.

On February 6, 1778, the United States signed its first two treaties. In the first treaty, France became the first country to recognize the United States as an independent nation. The second treaty was an alliance between the United States and France. By June 1778, Britain and France were at war. In 1779 the Spanish entered the war as well, as an ally of France but not of the United States.

✓ **Reading Check** **Summarizing** What was General Howe's two-part strategy for winning the war?

The War in the West

Not all of the fighting in the Revolutionary War took place in the East. In 1778, Patriot **George Rogers Clark** took 175 troops down the Ohio River and captured several towns. By February 1779, the British had surrendered, giving the Americans control of the region.

While Clark fought the British in the West, Chief Joseph Brant, also known as Thayendanegea, convinced four Iroquois nations to join the British. In July 1778, British troops and Iroquois warriors attacked western Pennsylvania, burning towns and killing over 200 militia. The following summer, American troops defeated the British and Iroquois in western New York. These battles destroyed the power of the Iroquois people.

Farther south, the Cherokee people suffered a similar fate. After the Revolution began, a delegation of Shawnee, Delaware, and Mohawk convinced the Cherokee that the time had come to drive American settlers off Cherokee lands. The Cherokee attacked settlers in Virginia and North Carolina, but the American militia units were too strong. By 1780 militia units had burned down hundreds of Cherokee towns.

✓ **Reading Check** **Describing** What was the effect of the war on the western frontier of the United States?

The War at Sea

Americans fought the British at sea as well as on land. Instead of attacking the British fleet directly, American warships attacked British merchant ships. To further disrupt British trade, the Congress began issuing letters of marque, or licenses, to private ship owners, authorizing them to attack British merchant ships. By the end of the war, millions of dollars of cargo had been seized, seriously harming Britain's trade and economy.

Perhaps the most famous naval battle of the war involved the American naval officer, **John Paul Jones.**

The Turning Point: Saratoga

General John Burgoyne's plan to capture upper New York and seal off New England from the rest of the United States began well. His troops easily seized Fort Ticonderoga with its large store of gunpowder and supplies. In response, the Continental Congress sent in a new commander, General Horatio Gates.

After this early victory, Burgoyne's march slowed to a crawl. The Americans felled trees in front of his army and removed crops and cattle from the region to deprive his troops of food. Militia forces staged ambushes and hit-and-run raids. These tactics exasperated Burgoyne. In desperation, he retreated to Saratoga. An American army nearly three times the size of his own quickly surrounded his troops. On October 17, 1777, Burgoyne surrendered to General Gates.

Jones commanded a ship named the *Bonhomme Richard.* While sailing near Britain in September 1779, Jones encountered a group of British merchant ships protected by the warships *Serapis* and *Countess of Scarborough.* Jones attacked the *Serapis,* but the heavier guns of the British ship nearly sank the *Bonhomme Richard.* With the American ship in distress, the British commander called on Jones to surrender. Jones replied, "I have not yet begun to fight." He lashed his ship to the *Serapis* so it could not sink, then boarded the British ship. The battle lasted more than three hours before the British surrendered.

✓ Reading Check Summarizing

What was the American strategy for attacking the British at sea?

The Southern Campaign

After the British defeat at Saratoga, General Howe resigned and was replaced by Sir Henry Clinton. British officials told Clinton to begin a campaign in the southern states where the British believed they had the strongest Loyalist support. The southern states were also valuable because they produced tobacco and rice. The British hoped they could keep the South, even if they lost the northern states.

The Fall of Savannah and Charles Town
In December 1778, 3,500 British troops captured Savannah, Georgia. They seized control of Georgia's backcountry and returned the British royal governor to power.

After defeating the American and French troops trying to take Savannah, General Clinton attacked Charles Town, South Carolina. Nearly 14,000 British troops surrounded the city, trapping the American forces. On May 12, 1780, the Americans surrendered. Nearly 5,500 American troops were taken prisoner, the greatest American defeat in the war. Clinton returned to New York, leaving General **Charles Cornwallis** in command. The Continental Congress then sent General Horatio Gates, the hero of Saratoga, to defend the South Carolina backcountry. Gates attempted to destroy a British supply base at Camden, South Carolina, but failed.

TURNING POINT
The Patriots Rally After the battle of Camden, the British began subduing the Carolina backcountry. At first, everything went well for them. Many of the settlers were Loyalists and agreed to fight for Britain. Two British cavalry officers, Banastre Tarleton and Patrick Ferguson, led many of the Loyalist forces in the region. These troops became known for their brutality.

Ferguson finally went too far when he tried to subdue the people living in the Appalachian Mountains. Enraged at his tactics, the "overmountain" men, as they were known, put together a militia force. They intercepted Ferguson at Kings Mountain on October 7, 1780, and destroyed his army. The **Battle of Kings Mountain** was a turning point in the South. Southern farmers, furious with British treatment, began organizing their own forces.

The new American commander in the region, General Nathaniel Greene, hoped to wear down the British in battle while militia destroyed their supplies. Greene organized the militia into small units to carry out hit-and-run raids against British camps and supply wagons. **Francis Marion,** who was known as the "Swamp Fox," led the most famous of these units. Greene's strategy worked. By late 1781, the British

❸ Washington and Rochambeau rush toward Virginia, August 1781

❺ Cornwallis is trapped; the British surrender at Yorktown, 1781

❹ French Admiral De Grasse keeps British ships away

❷ British capture Charles Town and Camden, but are defeated at Kings Mountain in 1780 and at Cowpens in 1781

❶ British capture Savannah, 1778

	American and/or allied forces
	British forces
	American victory
	British victory
•	Fort

ME.
(Part of MASS.)

N.H.

N.Y.
West Point

MASS.

R.I.
CONN.

New York City

N.J.

PA.
Valley Forge

Fort Detroit

Fort Miami

Fort Pitt

HAMILTON

Vincennes (Feb. 1779)

Cahokia (1778)

CLARK

Kaskaskia (July 1778)

Ohio River

Mississippi River

MD.
DEL.

VA.
CORNWALLIS

Yorktown

BRITISH FLEET, 1781

DE GRASSE

N.C.
Wilmington

GREENE

Kings M

Cowpens

CORNWALLIS

MARION

Camden

Charles Town

S.C.

BRITISH FLEET, 1780

ATLANTIC OCEAN

GA.
Savannah

BRITISH FLEET, 1778

Lake Superior

Lake Michigan

Lake Huron

Lake Erie

0   200 miles
0   200 kilometers
Albers Conic Equal-Area projection

N W E S

45°N
40°N
70°W
35°N
30°N
80°W   75°W

Geography *Skills*

1. **Interpreting Maps** How did the French help American forces?
2. **Applying Geography Skills** Where did the final battle of the war occur?

controlled very little territory in the South except for Savannah, Charles Town, and Wilmington.

✓ **Reading Check** **Explaining** Why was the Battle of Kings Mountain a turning point of the war in the South?

The War Is Won

In the spring of 1781, General Cornwallis decided to invade Virginia. As long as the Americans controlled Virginia, he believed, new troops and supplies could keep coming south. With more French troops on the way to America, the British knew they had very little time left to win the war. They had to secure Virginia.

The Battle of Yorktown In late April 1781, Cornwallis marched into Virginia, where he linked up with forces under the command of Benedict Arnold. Arnold had been an American commander early in the war but had later sold military information to the British. When his treason was discovered, Arnold fled to British-controlled New York City. There he was given command of British troops and ordered to begin raiding American positions in Virginia.

After Arnold's forces joined those of Cornwallis, the British began to conquer Virginia. Their combined forces encountered very little resistance until June 1781, when a large American force led by General **Anthony Wayne** arrived in Virginia. Outnumbered and too far inland, Cornwallis retreated to the coastal town of Yorktown to protect his supplies and to maintain communications by sea.

Cornwallis's retreat created an opportunity for the Americans and their French allies. The previous year, 6,000 French troops had arrived in New England. With this support, Washington decided to march on New York City. As the troops headed to New York, the French general Rochambeau learned that a French fleet commanded by Admiral Francois de Grasse was on its way north from the Caribbean.

When he learned of the French fleet, Washington canceled the attack on New York. Instead, he and Rochambeau led their forces to Yorktown. As the American and French troops raced south, Admiral de Grasse moved into Chesapeake Bay near Yorktown. With the French fleet nearby, Cornwallis could not escape by sea or receive supplies.

On September 28, 1781, American and French forces surrounded Yorktown and began to bombard it. On October 14, Washington's aide, Alexander Hamilton, led an attack that captured key British defenses. Three days later, Cornwallis began negotiations to surrender, and on October 19, 1781, approximately 8,000 British troops marched out of Yorktown and laid down their weapons. During the surrender, a British military band played a popular nursery tune, "The World Turn'd Upside Down."

Fact | Fiction | Folklore

America's Flags On June 14, 1777, the Continental Congress declared the first Stars and Stripes the official flag. The Congress determined that "the Flag of the United States be 13 stripes, alternate red and white; that the Union be 13 stars, white in a blue field representing a new constellation." For Americans past and present, the color red symbolizes courage; white, purity of ideals; and blue, strength and unity of the states.

The Treaty of Paris When Lord North, the British prime minister, learned of the surrender at Yorktown, he knew the war was over. In March 1782, Parliament voted to begin peace negotiations. John Adams, Benjamin Franklin, and John Jay conducted most of the negotiations for the United States.

The final settlement, known as the **Treaty of Paris,** was signed on September 3, 1783. In this treaty, Britain recognized the United States of America as a new nation with the Mississippi River as its western border. Britain also gave Florida back to Spain. France received colonies in Africa and the Caribbean that the British had seized from them in 1763. On November 24, 1783, the last British troops left New York City. The Revolutionary War was over. The creation of a new nation was about to begin.

Reading Check **Describing** How was the war won at Yorktown?

SECTION 3 ASSESSMENT

Checking for Understanding

1. **Define:** guerrilla warfare, letters of marque.
2. **Identify:** William Howe, Nathan Hale, Valley Forge, Marquis de Lafayette, Saratoga, John Paul Jones, Charles Cornwallis, Battle of Kings Mountain.

Reviewing Themes

3. **Global Connections** Why were the French at first reluctant to sign an alliance with the colonies?

Critical Thinking

4. **Evaluating** How did European countries aid the Americans in the war for independence?
5. **Categorizing** Use a graphic organizer similar to the one below to list the provisions of the Treaty of Paris.

Provisions of
Treaty of Paris, 1783

Analyzing Visuals

6. **Examining Art** Study the painting on page 141. How has the artist portrayed the condition of Washington's army?

Writing About History

7. **Persuasive Writing** Imagine that you are a colonist during the Revolutionary War. Write a letter to convince European nations to support the Americans in the war.

Critical Thinking SKILLBUILDER

Understanding Cause and Effect

Why Learn This Skill?

To understand past events, you should look for why or how an event or a chain of events took place. This process is using the skill of understanding causes and effects.

Learning the Skill

The French and Indian War left Britain in debt. To raise money Britain introduced a stamp tax in the American colonies. The war was the *cause* that led to Britain's need for more money. The tax on the colonies was the *effect*, or result. The chart below shows how one event—the **cause**—led to another—the **effect**.

Cause and Effect

Cause
- Britain passes Stamp Act

Effect
- Colonists boycott British goods

You can often identify cause-and-effect relationships in sentences from clue words such as the following:

because	therefore	produced
due to	thus	in order to
so that	led to	as a result

In a chain of events, an effect often becomes the cause of other events. The next chart shows the chain of events in the colonial rebellion.

Practicing the Skill

Make a chart showing which events are causes and which are effects in the sentences listed in column 2.

CAUSE	Britain needs money

EFFECT / CAUSE	Britain passes Stamp Act

EFFECT / CAUSE	Colonies rebel against Stamp Act

EFFECT	Britain repeals Stamp Act but replaces it with Townshend Acts

❶ The Treaty of Paris, which ended the French and Indian War in 1763, eliminated French power in North America.

❷ Thousands of British workers lost their jobs after the colonies cancelled orders for British goods.

❸ The British failure to listen to colonial grievances led to armed conflict.

❹ The French decided to send aid to the Americans after Burgoyne surrendered at Saratoga.

Skills Assessment

Complete the Practicing Skills questions on page 155 and the Chapter 4 Skill Reinforcement Activity to assess your mastery of this skill.

Applying the Skill

Understanding Cause and Effect Read an account of a recent event in your community in a local newspaper. Determine at least one cause and one effect of that event. Show the chain of events in a chart.

 GO TO Glencoe's **Skillbuilder Interactive Workbook CD-ROM, Level 2,** provides instruction and practice in key social studies skills.

The War Changes American Society

Guide to Reading

Main Idea
The American Revolution changed American society in a variety of ways.

Key Terms and Names
republic, Virginia Statute for Religious Freedom, Molly Pitcher, emancipation, manumission, John Trumbull, Charles Willson Peale

Reading Strategy
Organizing As you read about changes in American society after the American Revolution, complete a graphic organizer like the one below by listing the features of the U.S. political system set up after the war.

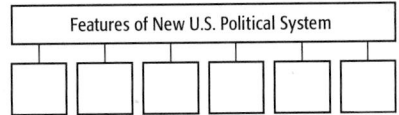

Features of New U.S. Political System

Reading Objectives
• **Describe** the features of the political system of the United States set up after the Revolutionary War.
• **Explain** the position of women and African Americans in the new political system.

Section Theme
Culture and Traditions A uniquely American culture arose as the Revolutionary War ended.

Preview of Events

♦1775　　　♦1779　　　♦1783　　　♦1787

1776
Virginia passes Declaration of Rights

1779
Judith Sargent Murray writes "On the Equality of the Sexes"

1780
New Massachusetts constitution introduced

1786
Virginia's Statute for Religious Freedom passed

★ An American Story ★

In 1781 an enslaved Massachusetts man named Quock Walker took an extraordinary step: He took legal action against a white man who had assaulted him. Given the times, this was a bold step, but Walker believed he had the law on his side. Massachusetts's new constitution referred to the "inherent liberty" of all men. The judge, William Cushing, agreed:

❝Our Constitution [of Massachusetts] sets out with declaring that all men are born free and equal—and that every subject is entitled to liberty, and to have guarded by the laws, as well as life and property—and in short is totally repugnant to the idea of being born slaves. This being the case, I think the idea of slavery is inconsistent with our own conduct and Constitution.❞

While the Quock Walker case did not abolish slavery, it demonstrated that the Massachusetts courts would not support the institution. As a result of this ruling and various antislavery efforts, slavery ceased to exist in Massachusetts by 1790.

—adapted from *Founding the Republic*

New Political Ideas

When American leaders declared independence and founded the United States of America, they were very much aware that they were creating something new. By severing their ties to the king, they had established a republic. A republic is a form of government where power resides with a body of citizens entitled to vote. Elected representatives who are responsible to the citizens and who must govern according to laws or a constitution exercise power.

While many Europeans viewed a republic as radical and dangerous, Americans believed that a republican society could be better than other societies. In an ideal republic, all citizens are equal under the law, regardless of their wealth or social class. Americans also believed that in a republic, the government derives its authority from the people.

Such ideas conflicted with many traditional beliefs, including ideas about slavery, the idea that women should not be allowed to vote or own property, and the idea that wealthy people were "better" than others. Despite these contradictions, republican ideas helped to change American society and government in the years following the war.

New State Constitutions Events before the Revolution led many Americans to believe that each state's constitution should be written down and that it should limit the government's power over the people. The Revolutionary War and new republican ideas convinced Americans that the best form of government was a constitutional republic.

At the same time, many American leaders, including John Adams, worried that democracy could endanger a republican government. Adams argued that government needed "checks and balances" to prevent any group in society from becoming strong enough to take away the rights of the minority.

A true democracy, Adams argued, would lead to a tyranny by the majority. Minority groups would not have their rights protected. For example, the poor might vote to take everything away from the rich and undermine the right to property. Instead, Adams argued, the best government was a "mixed government" with a separation of powers. The executive, legislative, and judicial branches should be separate.

Adams also argued that the legislature should have two houses: a senate to represent people of property and an assembly to protect the rights of the common people. Adams's ideas influenced several state constitutions. Virginia's constitution of 1776 and Massachusetts's constitution of 1780 established an elected governor, senate, and assembly. By the 1790s, most of the other states had created similar constitutions.

In addition to writing new constitutions, many new states began to attach a list of rights to their constitutions. This began in 1776, when George Mason drafted Virginia's Declaration of Rights. These rights guaranteed to all Virginians freedom of speech, freedom of religion, the right to bear arms, and the right to trial by jury. The declaration also proclaimed that the state could not search someone's home without a warrant, nor could it take away property without proper court proceedings. Other states followed Virginia's example and incorporated a bill of rights into their constitutions as well.

Voting Rights Expand The Revolution not only increased support for constitutional government, it also led to an expansion of voting rights. The experience of fighting side by side with people from every social class and region increased people's belief in equality, especially for white men. Everyone was fighting for the same cause and risking death for the same ideas. If everyone was equal, then everyone deserved the right to vote.

The war also weakened feelings of deference toward people in the upper classes. The Revolution had showed many farmers and artisans that they were equal to the rich planters and merchants they fought beside. While sitting in a tavern with farmers who were spitting and pulling off their muddy boots, one wealthy Virginian noted: "Every one who bore arms esteems himself upon an equal footing with his neighbors. . . . Each of these men considers himself, in every respect, my equal."

The Revolution enabled the lower classes to demand a greater role in choosing their leaders. In almost every state, the new constitutions made it easier to gain the right to vote. Many states allowed any

World Geography Connection

The Spread of American Democracy
While the Revolutionary War certainly transformed North America, it had a great impact on other parts of the world as well. American ideals of democracy inspired independence movements around the globe—especially in the colonies of Latin America, which overthrew their European rulers one after the other throughout the early 1800s. In Venezuela, for example, colonists developed their own "declaration of independence," in which they, like the Americans, listed their grievances with their colonial rulers, declared their desire to live free, and pledged their lives to the effort. *What may have happened to American ideals of democracy if the colonists had lost the war?*

white male who paid taxes to vote, whether or not he owned property.

Although voting rights expanded, people still had to own a certain amount of property to hold elective office, although usually much less than before the Revolution. The practice of paying veterans with land grants for their services during the war also increased the number of people eligible to hold office. In the North, before the Revolution, over 80 percent of the people elected were from the upper class. Ten years after the war, only a little over one-third of officeholders were wealthy. In the South, higher property qualifications kept the wealthy planters in power. Before the Revolution, almost 90 percent of people elected to office were wealthy. Afterward, the figure dropped by about 20 percent, indicating small farmers had gained some ground.

Freedom of Religion The new concern with rights led to changes in the relationship between the church and the state. Many of the Revolution's leaders opposed "ecclesiastical tyranny"—the power of a church, backed by the government, to make people worship in a certain way. After the war, the idea that government should not aid churches became more accepted.

The new push to end state funding of churches began in Virginia, where Baptists led a movement to abolish taxes collected to support the Anglican Church. In 1786 Governor Thomas Jefferson pushed the legislature to pass the **Virginia Statute for Religious Freedom.** The statute declared that Virginia no longer had an official church and that the state could not collect taxes for churches. Written by Jefferson, the statute declared:

66[O]ur civil rights have no dependence on our religious opinions, any more than our opinions in physics or geometry; . . . therefore . . . proscribing any citizen as unworthy the public confidence . . . unless he profess or renounce this or that religious opinion, is depriving him injuriously of those privileges and advantages to which in common with his fellow citizens he has a natural right.99

Profiles IN HISTORY

Elizabeth Freeman (Mumbet) *c. 1742–1829*

Elizabeth Freeman was born about 1742 to enslaved African American parents. At the age of six months she was acquired, along with her sister, by John Ashley, a wealthy Massachusetts slaveholder. She became known as "Mumbet" or "Mum Bett."

For nearly 40 years Mumbet served the Ashley family. One day, Ashley's wife tried to strike Mumbet's sister with a shovel. Mumbet intervened and took the blow instead. Furious, she stormed out of the house and refused to come back. When the Ashleys tried to make her return, Mumbet contacted a lawyer, Theodore Sedgwick. With his help, Mumbet sued for her freedom.

While serving the Ashleys, Mumbet had listened to many discussions of the new Massachusetts constitution. If the constitution said that all people were free and equal, then she thought it should apply to her. A jury agreed, and Mumbet won her freedom—the first enslaved person in Massachusetts to do so under the new constitution.

Oddly enough, after the trial, the Ashleys asked Mumbet to come back and work for them as a paid employee. She declined and instead went to work for Sedgwick. Mumbet died in 1829, but her legacy lived on in her many descendants. One of her great-grandchildren was W.E.B. DuBois, one of the founders of the NAACP, and a prominent writer and spokesperson for African American civil rights in the late 1800s and early 1900s.

Mumbet's tombstone still stands in the Massachusetts cemetery where she was buried. It reads, in part: "She was born a slave and remained a slave for nearly thirty years. She could neither read nor write, yet in her own sphere she had no superior or equal."

The idea of denying tax support to churches spread slowly throughout the newly independent nation. Massachusetts permitted Quakers and Baptists to assign their tax money to their church instead of to the congregational churches—the successors to the Puritan churches—but it did not abolish religious taxes entirely until 1833. *(See page 1065 for the text of the Virginia Statute for Religious Freedom.)*

✓ **Reading Check** **Examining** Which freedoms did Virginia's constitution guarantee in its bill of rights?

The War and American Society

The postwar notions of greater equality and liberty, as noble as they were, applied mainly to white men. For most women and African Americans, these ideals were still out of reach. Both groups participated in the Revolutionary War, and the Revolution's ideals led to some changes in the

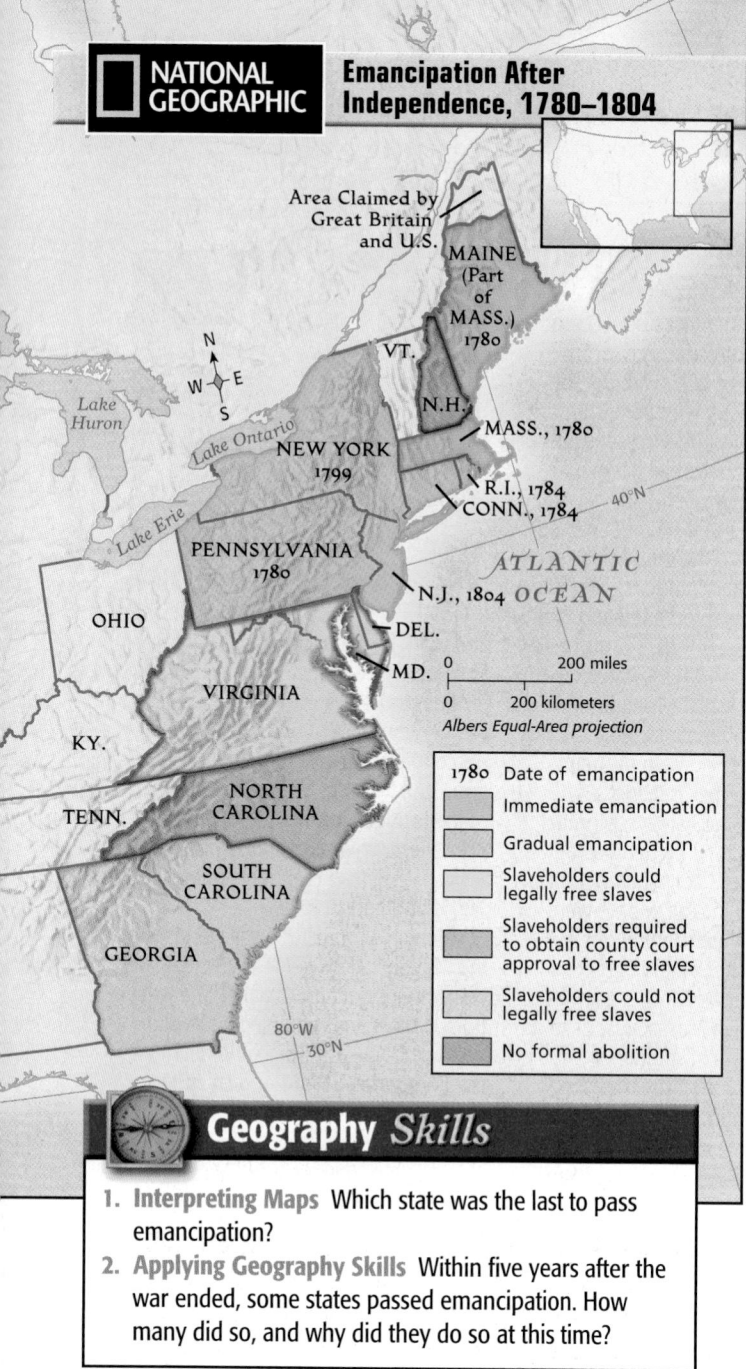

Emancipation After Independence, 1780–1804

Area Claimed by Great Britain and U.S.

MAINE (Part of MASS.) 1780

VT.

N.H.

NEW YORK 1799

MASS., 1780

R.I., 1784
CONN., 1784

Lake Huron

Lake Ontario

Lake Erie

PENNSYLVANIA 1780

ATLANTIC OCEAN

40°N

N.J., 1804

OHIO

DEL.

MD.

VIRGINIA

KY.

NORTH CAROLINA

TENN.

SOUTH CAROLINA

GEORGIA

80°W
30°N

0   200 miles
0   200 kilometers
Albers Equal-Area projection

1780 Date of emancipation
Immediate emancipation
Gradual emancipation
Slaveholders could legally free slaves
Slaveholders required to obtain county court approval to free slaves
Slaveholders could not legally free slaves
No formal abolition

Geography Skills

1. **Interpreting Maps** Which state was the last to pass emancipation?
2. **Applying Geography Skills** Within five years after the war ended, some states passed emancipation. How many did so, and why did they do so at this time?

status of both women and African Americans in the years following the end of the conflict.

Women at War

Women played a vital role in the Revolutionary War, contributing on both the home front and the battlefront. With their husbands and sons at war, some women took over running the family farm. Others traveled with the army—cooking, washing, and nursing the wounded. Women also served as spies and couriers, and a few even joined the fighting. Mary Ludwig Hays, known as **Molly Pitcher,** carried water to Patriot gunners during the Battle of Monmouth. Margaret Corbin accompanied her husband to battle, and after his death she took his place at his cannon and held the position until the battle ended.

After the war, as Americans began to think about what their revolutionary ideals implied, women made some advances. They could more easily obtain a divorce, and they gained greater access to education. In 1779 Judith Sargent Murray wrote an essay entitled "On the Equality of the Sexes." The essay argued that women were as intelligent as men but lacked the education needed to achieve more in life. After the Revolution, many schools for girls were founded, and the number of women able to read increased.

African Americans Thousands of enslaved African Americans obtained their freedom during the Revolution. In an effort to undermine the colonial economy and hurt the rebellion in the South, the British Army freed thousands of enslaved people. British officials, however, also seized thousands of African Americans and shipped them to British plantations in the Caribbean.

Many planters promised to free their slaves if the slaves fought against the British. General Washington, in order to counter the British offer to free enslaved people who joined the British, permitted African Americans to join the Continental Army. He also urged state militias to admit African Americans and to offer freedom to all who served. About 5,000 African Americans fought in the militias and the Continental Army during the Revolutionary War.

After the Revolution, more enslaved Africans gained their freedom. Many American leaders realized that enslaving people did not fit in with the new language of liberty and equality. Opposition to slavery had been growing steadily even before the Revolution, especially in the northern and middle states.

After the war began, emancipation, or freedom from enslavement, became a major issue. Many Northern states took steps to end slavery. Vermont banned slavery in 1777. In 1780 Pennsylvania freed all children born enslaved when they reached age 28. Rhode Island decreed in 1784 that enslaved men born thereafter would be free when they turned 21 and women when they turned 18. In 1799 New York freed enslaved men born that year or later when they reached age 28 and women when they reached age 25. The ending of slavery in the North was thus a gradual process that took several decades.

Discrimination did not disappear with the increase in African American freedom. While enslaved, some African Americans worked in skilled positions, such as blacksmithing. Northern whites did not want free African Americans taking these jobs from them. African Americans often were unable to get more than menial jobs—digging, carrying, loading, or sweeping. Free African Americans also faced voting restrictions, segregation, and possible kidnapping and transportation into the South, where they would again be enslaved.

Despite the hardships, freedom offered choices. Once free, African Americans typically moved to the cities to find employment. Some found opportunities in previously barred occupations, such as artists or ministers. Often, they discarded their former names or worked for several years to purchase the freedom of friends or family members.

A small group of African Americans achieved some wealth and social status. The discrimination of Northern whites encouraged them to focus on building their own distinct culture. Religion was a strong element of that emerging culture. Now free to enter the ministry, African Americans created their own style of worship. In 1816 African American church leaders formed the first independent African American denomination, the African Methodist Episcopal (AME) Church.

The story was quite different in the South. The South relied heavily on enslaved labor to sustain its agricultural economy. As a result, Southern leaders—most of whom were slaveholders themselves—showed little interest in abolishing slavery. Only Virginia took steps toward ending the institution. In 1782 the state passed a law encouraging manumission, or the voluntary freeing of enslaved persons, especially for those who had fought in the Revolution. Through this law, about 10,000 slaves obtained their freedom, but the vast majority remained in bondage.

The Loyalists Flee Many women and African Americans found their lives little changed as a result of the Revolution, but for many Loyalists, the end of the war changed everything. Because of their support for the British, Loyalists often found themselves shunned by former friends, and state governments sometimes seized their property.

Unwilling to live under the new government and often afraid for their lives, approximately 100,000 Loyalists fled the United States after the war. Some went to England or the British West Indies, but most moved to British North America, particularly to Nova Scotia, New Brunswick, and the region near Niagara Falls. This region was part of Quebec at the time, but in 1791, Britain made it a separate colony called Upper Canada. Today it is the province of Ontario.

Americans grappled with what to do with the property and assets of Loyalists. In North Carolina, Patriots confiscated Loyalist lands outright. Officials in New York also seized Loyalist lands and goods, claiming the "sovereignty of the people of this state in respect to all property." Other public officials opposed such actions. The Massachusetts Constitution of 1780, for example, extended the rights of "life, liberty, and property" to Loyalists, and gave much of the land seized from departing Loyalists to their agents or relatives who had remained behind.

 Reading Check **Summarizing** How did life change for women, African Americans, and Loyalists after the Revolutionary War?

An American Culture Emerges

In the United States, victory over the British united Americans and created powerful nationalist feelings. The Revolutionary War helped this process in two ways. First, Americans in all of the states had a common enemy. Soldiers from all over the country fought side by side in each other's states. Second, the

---

✎ **History** *Through Art*

Joseph Brant Gilbert Stuart painted this portrait of Joseph Brant, leader of the Mohawks, who sided with the Loyalists during the Revolution. After the Treaty of Paris, Brant led a large group of Iroquois north into British Canada. Why did Brant and other Loyalists leave the United States?

History *Through Art*

Family Scene Charles Willson Peale painted *The Peale Family,* showing his own family in an everyday pose. American artists favored informal scenes over the more formal European styles. What aspects of daily life does the artist show?

Revolution gave rise to many patriotic symbols and a common folklore. Stories of the Revolution and its heroes helped Americans to think of themselves as all belonging to the same group.

American Painters The Revolution sparked the creativity of American painters, including **John Trumbull** and **Charles Willson Peale.** Their work and that of other artists helped to build an American identity. Both men portrayed the heroic deeds and leaders of the Revolution. Trumbull served in the Continental Army as an aide to Washington. He is best known for his depiction of battles and important events in the Revolution. Peale fought at Trenton and Princeton and survived the winter at Valley Forge. He is best known for his portraits of Washington and other Patriot leaders.

Changes in Education As they started a new nation, American leaders considered an educated public to be critical to the republic's success. Jefferson called it the "keystone of our arch of government." Several state constitutions provided for government-funded universities. In 1795 the University of North Carolina became the first state university in the nation. At the same time, elementary education began to institute an American-centered style of teaching. Tossing out British textbooks, schools taught republican ideas and the history of the struggle for independence.

As the American people began to build a national identity, leaders of the United States turned their attention to the creation of a government that could hold the new nation together and promote the ideals and beliefs that the colonists had fought so hard to secure.

✓ **Reading Check** **Identifying** In what ways did the Revolutionary War help create powerful nationalist feelings in the United States?

SECTION 4 ASSESSMENT

Checking for Understanding
1. **Define:** republic, emancipation, manumission.
2. **Identify:** Virginia Statute for Religious Freedom, Molly Pitcher, John Trumbull, Charles Willson Peale.
3. **List** three features of the political system of the United States set up after the Revolutionary War.

Reviewing Themes
4. **Culture and Traditions** What new aspects of American culture emerged after the Revolutionary War?

Critical Thinking
5. **Synthesizing** Why did nationalist feelings emerge in the United States after the American Revolution?
6. **Categorizing** Use a graphic organizer similar to the one below to list the position of women, African Americans, and Loyalists in American society after the Revolution.

	Position in American Society
Women	
African Americans	
Loyalists	

Analyzing Visuals
7. **Examining Art** Study the painting by Charles Willson Peale shown above. How does this painting reveal the republican ideas of the time?

Writing About History
8. **Expository Writing** Imagine you are on a committee to write a new state constitution. List the freedoms you want attached to your state's constitution, and explain why you feel it is important to guarantee these rights.

American LITERATURE

The call to arms during the Revolution was heard not only on the fields of battle but off, echoed by the leading writers of the day. Some of the most inspiring words that rang out against British tyranny were those of **Thomas Paine,** a sometime teacher, sailor, and grocer who became a journalist in his late thirties. The first essay from Paine's collection *The American Crisis,* issued in December 1776, was read by General George Washington to boost the spirits of his beleaguered troops.

Read to Discover
What language does Paine use to encourage support for the American revolutionary cause?

Reader's Dictionary
tyranny: absolute power wielded unjustly

consolation: comfort

esteem: value

impious: not respectful

from *The American Crisis, Number 1*
by Thomas Paine

These are the times that try men's souls. The summer soldier and the sunshine patriot will in this crisis, shrink from the service of his country; but he that stands it NOW deserves the love and thanks of man and woman. Tyranny, like hell, is not easily conquered; yet we have this consolation with us, that the harder the conflict, the more glorious the triumph. What we obtain too cheap, we esteem too lightly; 'tis dearness only that gives everything its value. Heaven knows how to put a proper price upon its goods and it would be strange indeed, if so celestial an article as FREEDOM should not be highly rated. Britain, with an army to enforce her tyranny, has declared that she has a right (*not only to* TAX) but "to BIND *us in* ALL CASES WHATSOEVER," and if being *bound in that manner,* is not slavery, then is there not such a thing as slavery upon earth. Even the expression is impious, for so unlimited a power can belong only to God. . . .

. . . Let it be told to the future world that in the depth of winter, when nothing but hope and virtue could survive, that the city and the country, alarmed at one common danger, came forth to meet and to repulse it. . . . I love the man that can smile in trouble, that can gather strength from distress, and grow brave by reflection. It is the business of little minds to shrink; but he whose heart is firm, and whose conscience approves his conduct, will pursue his principles unto death.

> **"These are the times that try men's souls."**

Analyzing Literature
1. **Recall and Interpret** What does Paine mean by the phrase "the summer soldier and the sunshine patriot"?

2. **Evaluate and Connect** What purpose do you think essays such as this one serve in times of war and crisis?

Interdisciplinary Activity
Language Arts The language in Paine's essay may seem outdated now, but the emotions and ideas he expresses are still common. Rewrite the first paragraph of the essay, using words that a modern politician might use in a speech. Try to think of current phrases that would make sense—for example, what might we say today instead of "the summer soldier"?

Reviewing Key Terms

On a sheet of paper, use each of these terms in a sentence.

1. customs duty
2. inflation
3. nonimportation agreement
4. writ of assistance
5. committee of correspondence
6. minuteman
7. Loyalist
8. Patriot
9. guerrilla warfare
10. letters of marque
11. republic
12. emancipation
13. manumission

Reviewing Key Facts

14. **Identify:** French and Indian War, Boston Tea Party, Intolerable Acts, Battle of Bunker Hill, Declaration of Independence.
15. Why did King George III issue the Proclamation of 1763?
16. What were the effects of the Boston Tea Party?
17. Why was the Battle of Saratoga a turning point in the Revolutionary War?
18. What were the terms of the Treaty of Paris?
19. Why did a new American culture emerge after the war?

Critical Thinking

20. **Analyzing Themes: Civic Rights and Responsibilities** What rights did the colonists want from Britain?
21. **Evaluating** During the war, how did *The American Crisis, No. 1,* by Thomas Paine influence the morale of Washington's troops?
22. **Comparing and Contrasting** After the American Revolution, a new culture emerged in the United States. Compare and contrast American culture before and after the war in these areas: government, society, the arts, and education.
23. **Categorizing** Use a graphic organizer similar to the one below to list the events that led to the American Revolution.

Events That Led to the American Revolution

24. **Interpreting Primary Sources** In 1766 Benjamin Franklin testified before Parliament about the colonists' reactions to the Stamp Act. Read the excerpt from his testimony and answer the questions that follow.

   Q. What is your name, and place of abode?
   A. Franklin, of Philadelphia.
   Q. Are not the colonies . . . very able to pay the stamp [tax]?
   A. In my opinion there is not enough in the colonies to pay the stamp duty for one year.
   Q. Don't you know that the money arising from the stamps was all to be laid out in America?
   A. I know it is appropriated by the act to the American service; but it will be spent in the conquered colonies where the soldiers are, not in the colonies that pay it. . . .
   Q. Do you think it right that America should be protected by this country and pay no part of the expense?

Chapter Summary

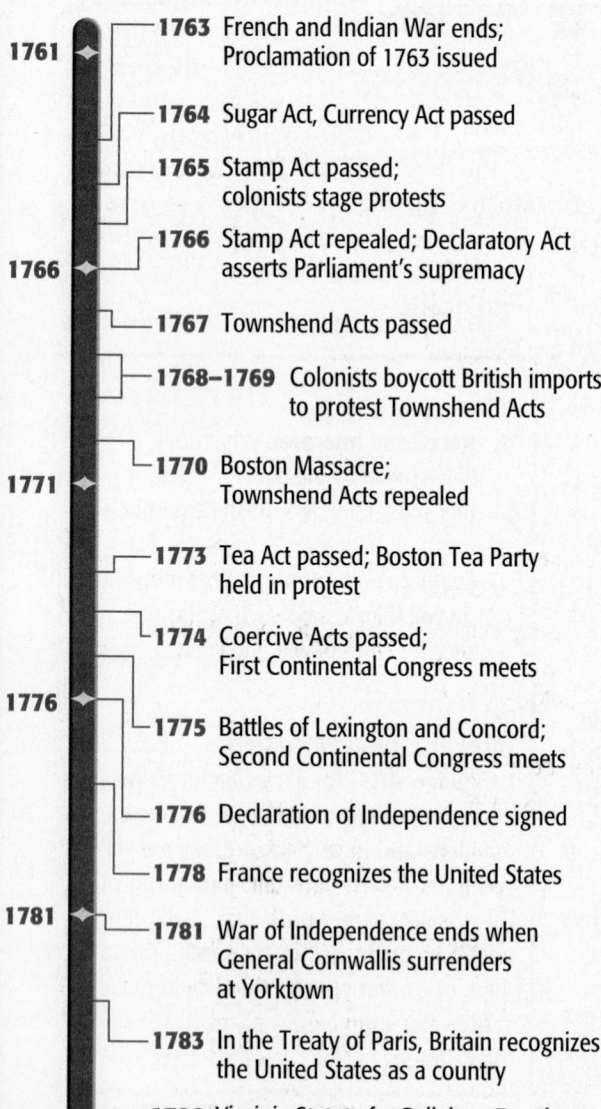

1761

1763 French and Indian War ends; Proclamation of 1763 issued

1764 Sugar Act, Currency Act passed

1765 Stamp Act passed; colonists stage protests

1766 Stamp Act repealed; Declaratory Act asserts Parliament's supremacy

1766

1767 Townshend Acts passed

1768–1769 Colonists boycott British imports to protest Townshend Acts

1770 Boston Massacre; Townshend Acts repealed

1771

1773 Tea Act passed; Boston Tea Party held in protest

1774 Coercive Acts passed; First Continental Congress meets

1776

1775 Battles of Lexington and Concord; Second Continental Congress meets

1776 Declaration of Independence signed

1778 France recognizes the United States

1781

1781 War of Independence ends when General Cornwallis surrenders at Yorktown

1783 In the Treaty of Paris, Britain recognizes the United States as a country

1786

1786 Virginia Statute for Religious Freedom introduced

A. That is not the case. The colonies raised, clothed, and paid, during the last war, near 25,000 men and spent many millions.

Q. Were you not reimbursed by Parliament?

A. We were only reimbursed what, in your opinion, we had advanced beyond our proportion, or beyond what might reasonably be expected from us; and it was a very small part of what we spent. Pennsylvania, in particular, disbursed about 500,000 pounds, and the reimbursements, in the whole, did not exceed 60,000 pounds. . . .

    a. Where does Franklin say that the British will spend the money they collect from the stamp tax?

    b. Why does Franklin say that the stamp taxes are unfair?

Practicing Skills

25. Examining Cause and Effect Study the chart on page 129. Then answer the questions below.
    a. What are the four causes of the colonies' declaring independence?
    b. On page 146, the Skillbuilder lists clue words that often appear in cause-and-effect discussions. Using those clue words, write three sentences about the effects of the colonial rebellion.

Chapter Activities

26. Research Project Research some popular American painters after the Revolutionary War, such as John Trumbull and Charles Willson Peale. Write a report that explains how the themes of their paintings helped build an American identity.

27. American History Primary Source Document Library CD-ROM Read "On Liberty" by John Adams. Assuming the role of a Patriot or a Loyalist, write a letter to the editor of the *Boston Gazette* in reaction to the article.

Writing Activity

28. Descriptive Writing Imagine that you are a resident of Charles Town in 1780. The city has had to surrender, and you must face British troops wherever you go. Then you hear about Francis Marion, the "Swamp Fox," who is making hit-and-run attacks on the British. Write to a friend in New York City describing your experiences and your hopes for victory over the British.

NATIONAL GEOGRAPHIC Land Claims in North America, 1783

Geography and History

29. The map above shows the land claims in North America as a result of the 1783 Treaty of Paris. Study the map and answer the questions below.
    a. Interpreting Maps After the Revolutionary War, what were the borders for the United States on the north? On the south? On the west?
    b. Applying Geography Skills Which countries shared a border with the United States?

Standardized Test Practice

Directions: Choose the best answer to the following question.

The colonists complained about having to pay British taxes while not being allowed to vote for members of the British Parliament. Which of the following quotations best expresses their complaint?

A "Give me liberty or give me death."

B "Taxation without representation is tyranny."

C "These are the times that try men's souls."

D "Don't fire until you see the whites of their eyes."

Test-Taking Tip: Use the process of elimination to rule out any answers that you know are wrong. For example, two of the answers suggest that the colonists and the British may already be at war, while only one answer mentions the main issue.

CHAPTER 5 Creating a Constitution

1781–1789

Why It Matters

After the American Revolution, the new nation struggled to draw up a plan for government. Americans wanted to make sure the government did not have too much power. Eventually they came up with a way to balance federal and state power and to divide federal power into three branches. Promising to add a bill of rights helped win approval for the Constitution.

The Impact Today

The Constitution is central to American life and ideals.
- *The Constitution continually defines the rights of citizens and the limits of governmental power.*
- *The Constitution remains a model for representative government.*

The American Vision *Video* *The Chapter 5 video, "The Power of the Constitution," discusses one of the nation's most important documents.*

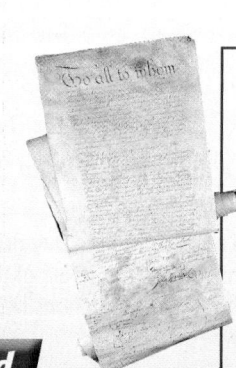

1781
- The United States's first formal constitution, the Articles of Confederation, ratified by the states

1786
- Shays's Rebellion begins in western Massachusetts

1787
- Constitutional Convention in Philadelphia writes the Constitution of the United States

1789
- George Washington elected president of the United States

Washington 1789–1797

United States PRESIDENTS

1780   *1785*   *1790*

World

1778
- James Cook lands on Hawaii

1783
- Latin American soldier and statesman Simón Bolívar born

1787
- Sierra Leone founded by freed Africans

1789
- French Revolution begins

1790
- Lavoisier's *Table of Thirty-One Chemical Elements* published

"Ship of State" float parading through New York City during
the 1788 ratification celebration

1791
• Bill of Rights added
  to Constitution

1798
• Eli Whitney introduces
  idea of interchangeable
  parts in manufacturing

J. Adams
1797–1801

1795   *1800*

1798
• Thomas Malthus publishes
  essay on population explosion

HISTORY
Online

Chapter Overview
Visit the *American Vision*
Web site at tav.glencoe.com
and click on *Chapter
Overviews— Chapter 5* to
preview chapter information.

The Confederation

Main Idea

The 13 states ratified the Articles of Confederation, which created a national government for the new nation.

Key Terms and Names

Articles of Confederation and Perpetual Union, Northwest Ordinance, duty, recession, Shays's Rebellion

Reading Strategy

Organizing As you read about the new government created by the Articles of Confederation, complete a graphic organizer similar to the one below by listing the achievements of the Confederation Congress.

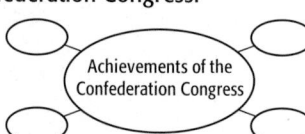

Achievements of the Confederation Congress

Reading Objectives

- **List** the achievements of the newly formed Confederation Congress.
- **Summarize** the weaknesses of the Confederation Congress.

Section Theme

Government and Democracy The Articles of Confederation provided a workable but faulty national government.

Preview of Events

◆1781   ◆1783   ◆1785   ◆1787

1781
Articles of Confederation ratified

1783
Newburgh conspiracy

1784
Postwar economic recession begins

1786–1787
Shays's Rebellion

1787
Northwest Ordinance becomes law

★ An American Story ★

On March 15, 1783, General George Washington arrived in Newburgh, New York. He had come to convince his officers—members of the so-called Newburgh conspiracy—not to rebel against the government.

Many officers were deeply in debt and angry with Congress for not giving them their back pay and pensions. Several had sent an angry letter to other officers arguing that the time had come to take action. When Washington read a copy of the letter, he called a meeting of all high-ranking officers at Newburgh and criticized their "insidious purposes" that threatened the separation between "military and civil" affairs.

Washington then said that he wished to read a different letter, and he pulled out a pair of reading glasses. No one had ever seen him wear them before. "Gentlemen," Washington began, "you must pardon me. I have grown gray in the service of my country and now feel myself growing blind." This simple statement drained the tension from the room. Some officers wept. Shortly afterward, the officers pledged their loyalty to Congress. Washington's integrity had preserved a basic principle—that the army should not interfere in politics.

—**adapted from** *The Forging of the Union*

The Achievements of the Confederation Congress

Even before independence was declared, Patriot leaders at the Continental Congress realized that the colonies needed to be united under some type of central government. In November 1777, the Continental Congress adopted the **Articles of Confederation and Perpetual Union**—a plan for a loose union of the states under the authority of the Congress.

The Articles of Confederation The Articles of Confederation established a very weak central government. The states had spent several years fighting for independence from Britain. They did not want to give up that independence to a new central government that might become tyrannical.

Under the Articles, once a year, each state would select a delegation to send to the capital city. This group, generally referred to as the Confederation Congress, was the entire government. There were no separate executive and judicial branches.

The Confederation Congress had the right to declare war, raise armies, and sign treaties. Although these powers were significant, the Congress was not given the power to impose taxes, and it was explicitly denied the power to regulate trade.

GEOGRAPHY

Western Policies Lacking the power to tax or regulate trade, the only way for the Confederation Congress to raise money to pay its debts and finance its operations was to sell the land it controlled west of the Appalachian Mountains. To get people to buy the land and settle in the region, the Congress had to establish an orderly system for dividing and selling the land and governing the new settlements. The Land Ordinance of 1785 established a method for surveying the western lands. It arranged the land into townships six miles square. Each township was divided into 36 sections, one mile square.

Two years later, the Congress passed the **Northwest Ordinance,** which provided the basis for governing much of the western territory. The law created a new territory north of the Ohio River and east of the Mississippi, which could eventually be divided into three to five states. Initially the Congress would choose a governor, a secretary, and three judges for the territory. When 5,000 adult male citizens had settled in a territory, they could elect a territorial legislature. When the population of a territory reached 60,000, the territory could apply to become a state "on an equal footing with the original states."

The Northwest Ordinance also guaranteed certain rights to people living in the territory. This included freedom of religion, property rights, and the right to trial by jury. The ordinance also stated that "there [would] be neither slavery nor involuntary servitude in the said territory." The exclusion of slavery from the Northwest Territory meant that as the United States expanded in future years, it would be divided between Southern slaveholding states and Northern free states.

Success in Trade In addition to organizing western settlement, the Confederation Congress tried to promote trade with other nations. After the Revolutionary War ended, the British government imposed sharp restrictions on American access to British markets. The British insisted that American goods sold to British colonies in the Caribbean had to be carried on British ships. American ships could still carry goods to Britain, but only goods from their respective states. A ship from Massachusetts, for example, could not carry goods from New York.

To overcome these problems, representatives from the Congress negotiated several trade treaties with other countries, including Holland, Prussia, and Sweden. A previous commercial treaty with France also permitted American merchants to sell goods to French colonies in the Caribbean. By 1790 the trade of the United States was greater than the trade of the American colonies before the Revolution.

Reading Check **Describing** What were the provisions of the Northwest Ordinance of 1787?

The Congress Falters

The Confederation Congress's commercial treaties and its system of settling the west were two of its major achievements. Other problems facing the new nation were not so easily solved.

Problems With Trade During the boycotts of the 1760s and the Revolutionary War, American artisans and manufacturers had prospered by making goods that people had previously bought from the British. After the war ended, British merchants flooded the United States with inexpensive British goods, driving many American artisans out of business.

The problems facing artisans and merchants convinced many American states to fight back by restricting British imports. Unfortunately, the states did not all impose the same duties, or taxes on imported goods. The British would then land their goods at the states that had the lowest taxes or fewest restrictions. Once the British goods were in the United States, they moved overland into the states that had tried to keep them out.

Because the Confederation Congress was not allowed to regulate commerce, the states began setting up customs posts on their borders to prevent the British from exploiting the different trade laws. They also levied taxes on each other's goods to raise revenue. New York, for example, taxed firewood from Connecticut and cabbage from New Jersey.

New Jersey retaliated by charging New York for a harbor lighthouse on the New Jersey side of the Hudson River. Each state was beginning to act as an independent country, and this behavior threatened the unity of the new United States.

Problems With Diplomacy The Confederation Congress also had problems in other areas of foreign policy. The first problems surfaced immediately after the Treaty of Paris, which ended the Revolutionary War, was signed.

Before the war, many American merchants and planters had borrowed money from British lenders. In the peace treaty, the United States had agreed that the states should allow these lenders to recover their prewar debts by suing in American courts. The Congress had no power to compel the states to do this, however, and many states restricted Britain's ability to collect its debts. The United States also had agreed that the states should return the property that had been confiscated from Loyalists during the war. Again, the Congress could not compel the states to do this, which further angered the British.

In retaliation, the British refused to evacuate American soil as specified in the treaty. They continued to occupy a string of frontier posts south of the Great Lakes inside American territory. Congress had no way to resolve these problems. It did not have the power to impose taxes, so it could not raise the money to pay a financial settlement to Britain for the debts and Loyalist property. Since it could not regulate trade, it also had no way to pressure the British into a settlement.

American dealings with Spain also showed the weaknesses of the Confederation Congress. The major dispute with Spain involved the border between Spanish territory and the state of Georgia. The Spanish stopped Americans from depositing their goods on Spanish territory at the mouth of the Mississippi River. This effectively closed the river to American farmers who used it to ship their goods to market.

Again, the Confederation Congress had no leverage to pressure the Spanish, and the dispute over Georgia's border and navigation on the Mississippi remained unresolved. Once more, the limited powers of the Confederation Congress had prevented any diplomatic solution from being worked out.

The Economic Crisis While the Confederation Congress struggled with diplomatic issues, many other Americans were struggling economically. The end of the Revolutionary War and the reining in of economic activity with Britain plunged the new United States into a severe recession, or economic slowdown.

Farmers were among those most affected by the recession. Although they were not earning as much money as they once did, they had to keep borrowing to get their next crop in the ground. Many also had mortgages to pay. At the same time, the Revolutionary War had left both the Confederation Congress and many states in debt. To pay for the war, many states had issued bonds as a way to borrow money from wealthy merchants and planters. With the war over, the people holding those bonds wanted to redeem them for gold or silver.

To pay off their debts, the states could raise taxes, but farmers and other people in debt urged the state governments to issue paper money instead. They also wanted the states to make the paper money available to farmers through government loans on farm mortgages.

Since paper money would not be backed up by gold and silver, and people would not trust it, inflation—a decline in the value of money—would begin. Debtors would be able to pay their debts using paper money that was worth less than the value printed on it. This would let them pay off their debts more easily. Lenders, on the other hand, including many merchants

Why It Matters

The Northwest Ordinance

One of the major challenges facing the Confederation Congress was formulating a plan for dealing with the territory west of the Appalachian Mountains. Formerly claimed by individual states, these vast lands were now the territory of the entire United States. The Northwest Ordinance that the Congress adopted stands as one of the few successes of the Confederation.

The Ordinance provided for the survey of land west of the Appalachian Mountains, including the present-day states of Ohio, Illinois, Wisconsin, Michigan, and Indiana. It also set up a clear and orderly process by which new states were admitted on an equal basis to the Union.

and importers, strongly opposed paper money because they would not be receiving the true amount they were owed. Beginning in 1785, seven states began issuing paper money.

In Rhode Island, the paper money eventually became so worthless that merchants refused to accept it in payment for debts. After an angry mob rioted against the merchants, Rhode Island's assembly passed a law forcing people to accept paper money at its stated value. Those who refused could be arrested and fined.

To people with property, this signaled danger. If states were passing such laws, it was because poorer, debt-ridden citizens controlled them. With the spread of democratic ideals and a lowering of property qualifications for voting, many states had begun electing such citizens to office.

Shays's Rebellion The property owners' fears seemed justified when a full-scale rebellion, known as **Shays's Rebellion,** erupted in Massachusetts in 1786. The rebellion started when the government of Massachusetts decided to raise taxes instead of issuing paper money to pay off its debts. The taxes fell most heavily on farmers, particularly poor farmers in the western part of the state. As the recession grew worse, many found it impossible to pay their taxes as well as their mortgages and other debts. Those who could not pay often faced the loss of their farms.

Angry at the legislature's indifference to their plight, in late August 1786, farmers in western Massachusetts rebelled. They closed down several county courthouses to prevent farm foreclosures,

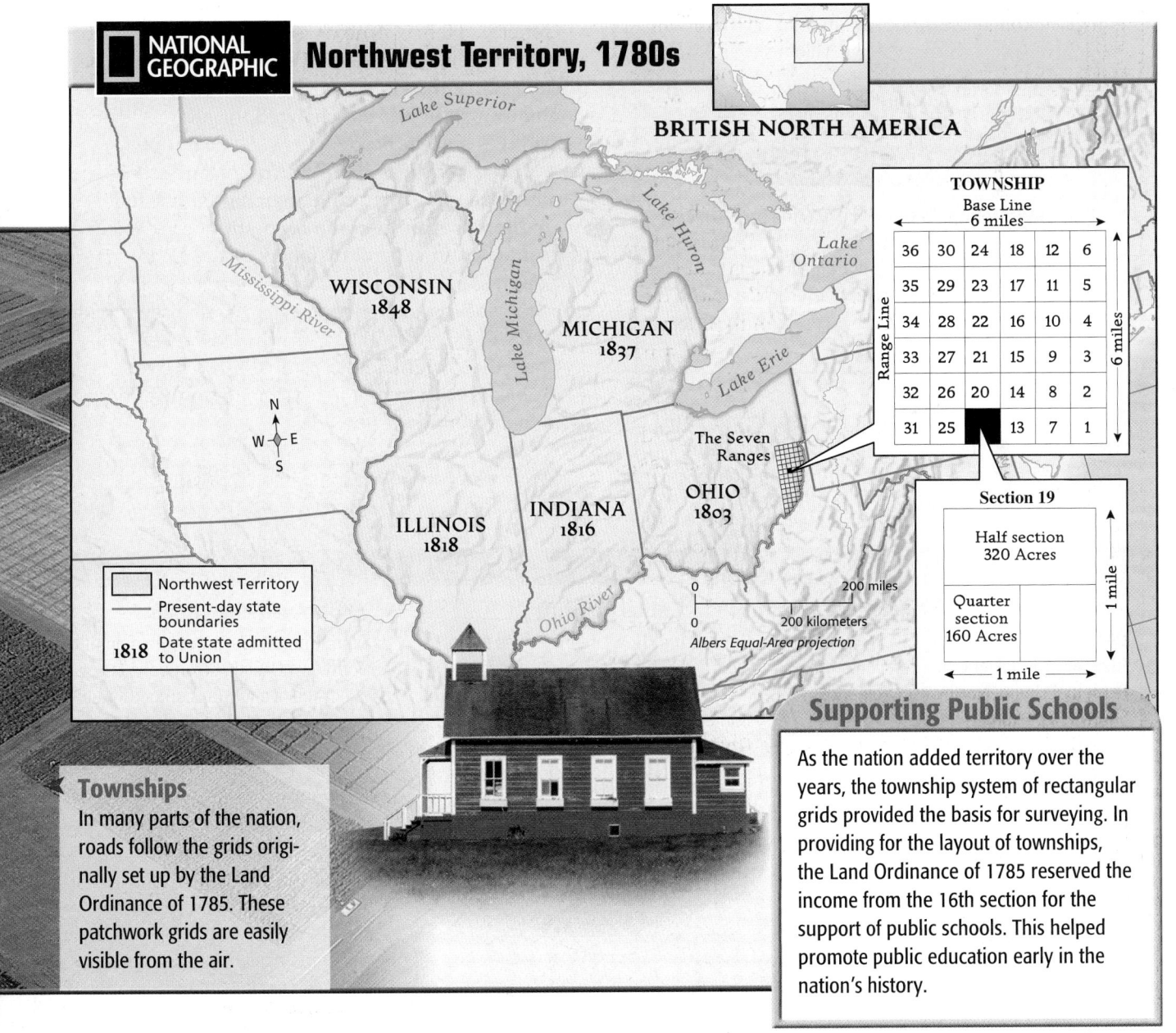

NATIONAL GEOGRAPHIC
Northwest Territory, 1780s

BRITISH NORTH AMERICA

Lake Superior

Lake Huron

Lake Michigan

Lake Ontario

Lake Erie

Mississippi River

WISCONSIN
1848

MICHIGAN
1837

The Seven Ranges

OHIO
1803

ILLINOIS
1818

INDIANA
1816

Ohio River

TOWNSHIP

Base Line
6 miles

Range Line

6 miles

36	30	24	18	12	6
35	29	23	17	11	5
34	28	22	16	10	4
33	27	21	15	9	3
32	26	20	14	8	2
31	25		13	7	1

Section 19

Half section
320 Acres

Quarter section
160 Acres

1 mile

1 mile

Northwest Territory
Present-day state boundaries
1818 Date state admitted to Union

0   200 miles
0   200 kilometers
Albers Equal-Area projection

Townships
In many parts of the nation, roads follow the grids originally set up by the Land Ordinance of 1785. These patchwork grids are easily visible from the air.

Supporting Public Schools
As the nation added territory over the years, the township system of rectangular grids provided the basis for surveying. In providing for the layout of townships, the Land Ordinance of 1785 reserved the income from the 16th section for the support of public schools. This helped promote public education early in the nation's history.

Some Weaknesses of the Articles of Confederation

Provision	Problem Created
Congress has no power to tax	Weak currency and growing debt
	Inability to pay army leads to threats of mutiny
Congress has no power to enforce treaties	Foreign countries angry when treaties are not honored; for example, Britain keeps troops on American soil
Every state, despite size, has one vote	Populous states not equally represented
Congress has no power to regulate commerce	Trade hindered by states imposing high tariffs on each other
Amendment requires unanimous vote of states	Difficult to adapt articles to changing needs

Chart Skills

1. **Interpreting Charts** What was the problem with requiring a unanimous vote of the states to create changes in the Articles of Confederation?
2. **Understanding Cause and Effect** Why do you think the states approved a government with so many weaknesses?

and then marched on the state supreme court. At this point, Daniel Shays, a former captain in the Continental Army who was now a bankrupt farmer, emerged as one of the rebellion's leaders.

In January 1787, Shays and about 1,200 farmers headed to a state arsenal intending to seize weapons before marching on Boston. In response, the governor sent more than 4,000 volunteers under the command of General Benjamin Lincoln to defend the arsenal. Before they arrived, Shays attacked, and the militia defending the arsenal opened fire. Four farmers died in the fighting. The rest scattered. The next day Lincoln's troops arrived and ended the rebellion. The fears the rebellion had raised, however, were harder to disperse.

A Call for Change People with greater income and social status tended to see the rebellion, as well as inflation and an unstable currency, as signs that the republic itself was at risk. They feared that as state legislatures became more democratic and responsive to poor people, they would weaken property rights and vote to take property from the wealthy. As General Henry Knox, a close aide to George Washington, concluded: "What is to afford our security against the violence of lawless men? Our government must be braced, changed, or altered to secure our lives and property."

These concerns were an important reason why many people, including merchants, artisans, and creditors, began to argue for a stronger central government, and several members of the Confederation Congress called on the states to correct "such defects as may be discovered to exist" in the present government. The Confederation's failure to deal with conditions that might lead to rebellion, as well as the problems with trade and diplomacy, only added fuel to their argument.

Reading Check **Explaining** What caused Shays's Rebellion?

SECTION 1 ASSESSMENT

Checking for Understanding

1. **Define:** duty, recession.
2. **Identify:** Articles of Confederation and Perpetual Union, Northwest Ordinance, Shays's Rebellion.
3. **Describe** the conditions that led to Shays's Rebellion.

Reviewing Themes

4. **Government and Democracy** What do you think was the most serious flaw of the Articles of Confederation? Why do you think so?

Critical Thinking

5. **Comparing** How are the issues faced by the federal government today similar to those that were faced by the Confederation Congress?
6. **Organizing** Use a graphic organizer similar to the one below to list the weaknesses of the Confederation Congress.

Weaknesses of the Confederation Congress

Analyzing Visuals

7. **Examining Maps** Study the map of the Northwest Ordinance on page 161. What significant provision of this law would contribute to dividing the nation into competing regions?

Writing About History

8. **Persuasive Writing** Take on the role of a journalist during the time of the Confederation Congress. Write an editorial expressing your opinion of Shays's Rebellion, and suggest how the government might handle such situations better in the future.

Making Comparisons

Why Learn This Skill?

Suppose you want to buy a portable compact disc (CD) player, and you must choose among three models. You would probably compare characteristics of the three models, such as price, sound quality, and size to figure out which model is best for you. In the study of American history, you often compare people or events from one time period with those from a different time period.

Learning the Skill

When making comparisons, you examine two or more groups, situations, events, or documents. Then you identify any similarities and differences. For example, the chart on this page compares two documents with regard to the powers they gave the central government. The Articles of Confederation were passed and implemented before the United States Constitution, which took their place. The chart includes a check mark in each column that applies. For example, the entry *Protect copyrights* does not have a check under *Articles of Confederation.* This shows that the government under the Articles lacked that power. The entry is checked under *United States Constitution,* showing that the government under the Constitution does have that power.

When making comparisons, you first decide what items will be compared and determine which characteristics you will use to compare them. Then you identify similarities and differences in these characteristics.

Practicing the Skill

Analyze the information on the chart on this page. Then answer the questions.

❶ What items are being compared? How are they being compared?

❷ What are the similarities and differences of the documents?

❸ Which document had the most power regarding legal matters? How can you tell?

The Articles of Confederation and the United States Constitution

Powers of the Central Government	Articles of Confederation	United States Constitution
Declare war; make peace	✔	✔
Coin money	✔	✔
Manage foreign affairs	✔	✔
Establish a postal system	✔	✔
Impose taxes		✔
Regulate trade		✔
Organize a court system		✔
Call state militia for service		✔
Protect copyrights		✔
Take other necessary actions to run the federal government		✔

❹ Which document had the most power in dealing with other nations? How can you tell?

Skills Assessment

Complete the Practicing Skills questions on page 177 and the Chapter 5 Skill Reinforcement Activity to assess your mastery of this skill.

Applying the Skill

Making Comparisons On the editorial page of your local newspaper, read two columns that express different viewpoints on the same issue. Identify the similarities and differences between the two points of view.

 Glencoe's **Skillbuilder Interactive Workbook CD-ROM, Level 2,** provides instruction and practice in key social studies skills.

A New Constitution

Guide to Reading

Main Idea
In 1787 the Constitutional Convention set up a new government.

Key Terms and Names
Virginia Plan, New Jersey Plan, Great Compromise, Three-Fifths Compromise, popular sovereignty, federalism, separation of powers, legislative branch, executive branch, judicial branch, checks and balances, veto, impeach, amendment

Reading Strategy
Taking Notes As you read about the new government that the Constitution created, use the major headings of the section to fill in an outline similar to the one below.

A New Constitution
I. The Constitutional Convention
   A.
   B.
II.
   A.
   B.

Reading Objectives
- **Describe** the issues at stake during the Constitutional Convention.
- **Discuss** the compromises reached during the convention.

Section Theme
Culture and Traditions The new Constitution tried to uphold the principle of state authority while providing needed national authority.

Preview of Events

♦April 1787   ♦June 1787   ♦August 1787   ♦October 1787

May 14
Constitutional Convention opens in Philadelphia

May 29
Virginia Plan introduced

June 15
New Jersey Plan introduced

July 2
Ben Franklin's committee begins seeking a compromise

September 17
Final draft of Constitution signed

★ *An American Story* ★

As Benjamin Franklin arrived at the Pennsylvania statehouse on September 17, 1787, he rejoiced with his colleagues about the freshness of the morning air. For 16 weeks, the 81-year-old Franklin had made the short journey from his home just off Market Street to the statehouse. There, delegates to the Constitutional Convention had exhaustively debated the future of the nation. Today, they would have a chance to sign a draft plan for the nation's new constitution.

When it came Franklin's turn to sign, the elderly leader had to be helped forward in order to write his name on the parchment. Tears streamed down his face as he signed. When the remaining delegates had finished signing, a solemn silence enveloped the hall. Franklin relieved the tension with a few well-chosen words. Pointing to the half-sun painted in gold on the back of George Washington's chair, he observed:

❝I have often . . . looked at that [sun] behind the President [of the Convention] without being able to tell whether it was rising or setting; but now, at length, I have the happiness to know it is a rising, and not a setting, Sun.❞

—quoted in *An Outline of American History*

The Constitutional Convention

The weakness of the Confederation Congress worried many American leaders, who believed that the United States would not survive without a strong central government. People who supported a stronger central government became known as "nationalists."

Prominent nationalists included George Washington, John Adams, Benjamin Franklin, Alexander Hamilton, and the financier Robert Morris.

One of the most influential nationalists was **James Madison,** a member of the Virginia Assembly and head of its commerce committee. As head of the commerce committee, Madison was well aware of Virginia's trade problems with the other American states and with Britain. He firmly believed that a stronger national government was needed.

In 1786 Madison convinced Virginia's assembly to call a convention of all the states to discuss trade and taxation problems. Representatives from the states were to meet in Annapolis, Maryland, but when the convention began, delegates from only five states were present, too few to reach a final decision on the problems facing the states. Many of the delegates did discuss the weakness of the Articles of Confederation and expressed interest in modifying them.

New York delegate **Alexander Hamilton** recommended that the Congress itself call for another convention to be held in Philadelphia in May 1787. At first, the Congress was divided over whether or not to call a convention. News of Shays's Rebellion, however, and reports of unrest elsewhere convinced the Congress to call for a convention of the states "for the sole purpose of revising the Articles of Confederation."

Every state except Rhode Island sent delegates to what became known as the Constitutional Convention. In May 1787 the delegates took their places in the Pennsylvania statehouse in Philadelphia. They knew they faced a daunting task: to balance the rights and aspirations of the states with the need for a stronger national government.

The Founders The 55 delegates who attended the convention in Philadelphia included some of the shrewdest and most distinguished leaders in the United States. The majority were lawyers, and most of the others were planters and merchants. Most had experience in colonial, state, or national government. Seven had served as state governors. Thirty-nine had been members of the Confederation Congress. Eight had signed the Declaration of Independence. In the words of Thomas Jefferson, who was unable to attend the convention because he was serving as American minister to France, the convention in Philadelphia was no less than "an assembly of demigods."

The delegates chose stern and proper George Washington of Virginia, hero of the American Revolution, as presiding officer. Benjamin Franklin was a delegate from Pennsylvania. Now 81 years old, he tired easily and had other state delegates read his speeches for him. He provided assistance to many of his younger colleagues, and his experience and good humor helped smooth the debates.

Other notable delegates included New York's Alexander Hamilton and Connecticut's Roger Sherman. Virginia sent a well-prepared delegation, including the scholarly James Madison, who kept a record of the debates. Madison's records provide the best source of information about what went on in the sessions. The meetings were closed to the public to help ensure honest and open discussion free from outside political pressures.

Profiles IN HISTORY

James Madison
1751–1836

Although many individuals contributed to the framing of the United States Constitution, the master builder was James Madison. An avid reader, the 36-year-old Virginia planter spent the better part of the year preceding the Philadelphia Convention with his nose in books. Madison read volume after volume on governments throughout history. He scoured the records of ancient Greece and Rome and delved into the administrations of Italian city-states such as Florence and Venice. He even looked at the systems used by federal alliances like Switzerland and the Netherlands. "From a spirit of industry and application," said one colleague, Madison was "the best-informed man on any point in debate."

Bringing together his research and his experience in helping to draft Virginia's constitution, Madison created the Virginia Plan. His proposal strongly influenced the final document. Perhaps Madison's greatest achievement was in defining the true source of political power. He argued that all power, at all levels of government, flowed ultimately from the people.

At the Constitutional Convention, Madison served his nation well. The ordeal, he later said, "almost killed" him. In the years to come, though, the nation would call on him again. In 1801 he became President Thomas Jefferson's secretary of state. In 1808 he was elected the fourth president of the United States.

The Virginia and New Jersey Plans The Virginia delegation arrived at the convention with a detailed plan—mostly the work of James Madison—for a new national government. A few days after the proceedings began, the governor of Virginia, **Edmund Randolph,** introduced the plan. "A national government," declared Randolph, "ought to be established, consisting of a supreme Legislative, Executive, and Judiciary." The **Virginia Plan,** as it came to be called, proposed scrapping the Articles of Confederation entirely and creating a new national government with the power to make laws binding upon the states and to raise its own money through taxes.

The Virginia Plan proposed that the legislature be divided into two houses. The voters in each state would elect members of the first house. Members of the second house would be nominated by the state governments but actually elected by the first house. In both houses, the number of representatives for each state would reflect that state's population. The Virginia Plan, therefore, would benefit large states like Virginia, New York, and Massachusetts, which had more votes than the smaller states.

The Virginia Plan drew sharp reactions. The delegates accepted the idea of dividing the government into executive, legislative, and judicial branches, but the smaller states strongly opposed any changes that would decrease their influence by basing representation on population. They feared that the larger states would outvote them. **William Paterson,** a delegate from New Jersey, offered a counterproposal that came to be called the **New Jersey Plan.**

The New Jersey Plan did not abandon the Articles of Confederation. Instead it modified them to make the central government stronger. Under the plan, Congress would have a single house in which each state was equally represented, but it would also have the power to raise taxes and regulate trade.

If progress was to be made, the delegates had to choose one plan for further negotiation. After debating on June 19, the convention voted to proceed with the Virginia Plan. With this vote, the convention delegates decided to go beyond their original purpose of revising the Articles of Confederation. Instead, they began work on a new constitution for the United States.

✓ **Reading Check** **Explaining** Why did small states oppose the Virginia Plan?

History *Through Art*

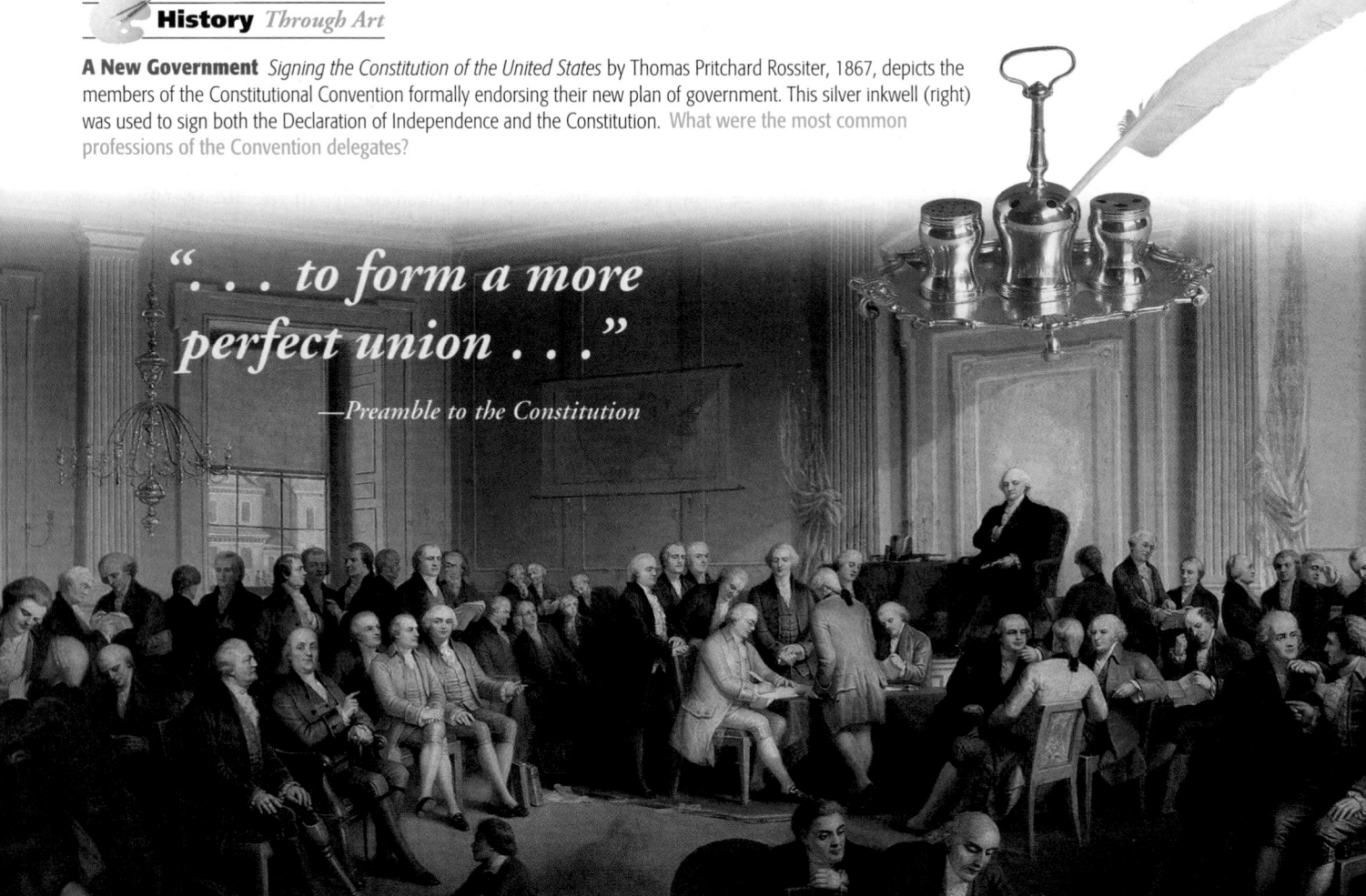

A New Government *Signing the Constitution of the United States* by Thomas Pritchard Rossiter, 1867, depicts the members of the Constitutional Convention formally endorsing their new plan of government. This silver inkwell (right) was used to sign both the Declaration of Independence and the Constitution. What were the most common professions of the Convention delegates?

" . . . to form a more perfect union . . . "

—*Preamble to the Constitution*

A Union Built on Compromise

As the convention hammered out the details of the new constitution, the delegates found themselves divided geographically. The small states demanded changes that would protect them against the voting power of the big states. At the same time, Northern and Southern states were divided over how to treat slavery in the new constitution. The only way to resolve these differences was through compromise.

TURNING POINT

The Connecticut Compromise After the convention voted to proceed with the Virginia Plan, tempers flared as delegates from the small states insisted that each state had to have an equal vote in Congress. The hot Philadelphia summer offered no relief, and angry delegates from the larger states threatened to walk out. By early July 1787, the convention had reached a turning point. As a delegate from North Carolina warned, "If we do not concede on both sides, our business must soon end."

In an attempt to find a solution, the convention appointed a special committee to resolve the differences between the large and small states. Delegates who were strongly committed to one side or the other were left off the committee, leaving only those who were undecided or willing to change their minds. Ben Franklin was chosen to chair the proceedings.

Throughout the proceedings, Franklin remained a calm voice of conciliation. Here, he warns the delegates about what would happen if they failed to agree:

> 66 [You will] become a reproach and by-word down to future ages. And what is worse, mankind may hereafter, from this unfortunate instance, despair of establishing governments by human wisdom, and leave it to chance, war, and conquest. 99
>
> —quoted in *Benjamin Franklin: A Biography*

The compromise that the committee worked out was based on an idea Roger Sherman of Connecticut proposed, which is why it is sometimes known as the **Connecticut Compromise.** Other historians refer to it as the **Great Compromise.**

Franklin's committee proposed that in one house of Congress—the House of Representatives—the states would be represented according to the size of their populations. In the other house—the Senate—each state would have equal representation. The eligible voters in each state would elect the House of Representatives, but the state legislatures would choose senators.

Compromise Over Slavery Franklin's committee also proposed that each state could elect one member to the House of Representatives for every 40,000 people in the state. This proposal caused a split between Northern and Southern delegates. Southern delegates wanted to count enslaved people when determining how many representatives they could elect. Northern delegates objected, pointing out that enslaved people could not vote.

Northern delegates also suggested that if slaves were going to be counted for representation, they should be counted for purposes of taxation as well. In the end, a solution, referred to as the **Three-Fifths Compromise,** was worked out. Every five enslaved people in a state would count as three free persons for determining both representation and taxes.

The dispute over how to count enslaved people was not the only issue dividing the delegates. Southerners feared that a strong national government with the power to regulate trade might impose taxes on the export of farm products or ban the import of enslaved Africans. These Southern delegates insisted that the new constitution forbid interference with the slave trade and limit Congress's power to regulate trade. Northern delegates, on the other hand, knew that Northern merchants and artisans needed a government capable of controlling foreign imports into the United States.

Eventually, another compromise was worked out. The delegates agreed that the new Congress could not tax exports. They also agreed that it could not ban the slave trade until 1808 or impose high taxes on the import of enslaved persons.

The Great Compromise and the compromises between Northern and Southern delegates ended most of the major disputes between the state delegations. This enabled the convention to focus on the details of how the new government would operate.

By mid-September, the delegates had completed their task. Although everyone had had to compromise, the 39 delegates who signed the new Constitution believed it was a vast improvement over the Articles of Confederation. On September 20, they sent it to the Confederation Congress for approval. Eight days later, the Congress

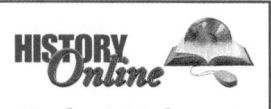

Student Web Activity Visit the *American Vision* Web site at tav.glencoe.com and click on *Student Web Activities— Chapter 5* for an activity about the Constitution.

voted to submit the Constitution to the states for approval. The struggle for the Constitution now moved into a new phase. Nine of the thirteen states had to ratify the Constitution for it to take effect.

Reading Check **Describing** How did the South want to count enslaved persons when counting the population of the states?

A Framework for Limited Government

The new constitution that the states were considering was based on the principle of popular sovereignty, (SAH·vuhrn·tee) or rule by the people. Rather than a direct democracy, it created a representative system of government in which elected officials represented the voice of the people. The Constitution also created a system of government known as federalism. It divided government power between the federal, or national, government and the state governments.

The Constitution provided for a separation of powers among the three branches of the federal government. The two houses of Congress made up the legislative branch of the government. They would make the laws. The executive branch, headed by a president, would implement and enforce the laws passed by Congress. The judicial branch—a system of federal courts—would interpret federal laws and render judgment in cases involving those laws. No one serving in one branch could serve in either of the other branches at the same time.

Checks and Balances In addition to separating the powers of the government into three branches, the delegates to the convention created a system of checks and balances to prevent any one of the three branches from becoming too powerful. Within this system, each branch of government had the ability to limit the power of the other branches.

Under the Constitution, the president—as head of the executive branch—was given far-reaching powers. The president could propose legislation, appoint judges, put down rebellions, and veto, or reject, acts of Congress. The president would also be the commander in chief of the armed forces. According to one delegate in Philadelphia, these powers might not have been so great "had not many of the members cast their eyes towards George Washington as president."

Although the president could veto acts of Congress, the legislature could override the veto with a two-thirds vote in both houses. The Senate also had to approve or reject presidential appointments to the executive branch as well as any treaties the president negotiated. Furthermore, Congress could, if necessary, impeach, or formally accuse of misconduct, and then remove the president or any other high official in the executive or judicial branch.

Members of the judicial branch of government could hear all cases arising under federal law and the Constitution. The powers of the judiciary were balanced by the other two branches. The president could nominate members of the judiciary, but the Senate had to confirm or reject such nominations. Once appointed, however, federal judges would serve for life, thus ensuring their independence from both the executive and the legislative branches.

Amending the Constitution The delegates in Philadelphia recognized that the Constitution they wrote in the summer of 1787 might need to be

amended, or changed over time. To ensure this could happen, they created a clear system for making amendments, or changes to the Constitution. To prevent the government from being changed constantly, they made it difficult for amendments to be adopted.

The delegates established a two-step process for amending the Constitution—proposal and ratification. An amendment could be proposed by a vote of two-thirds of the members of both houses of Congress. Alternatively, two-thirds of the states could call a constitutional convention to propose new amendments. To become effective, the proposed amendment then had to be ratified by three-fourths of the state legislatures or by conventions in three-fourths of the states.

The success of the Philadelphia Convention in creating a government that reflected the country's many different viewpoints was, in Washington's words, "little short of a miracle." The convention, John Adams declared, was "the single greatest effort of national deliberation that the world has ever seen."

✓ **Reading Check** Explaining How is power divided under the system of federalism?

SECTION 2 ASSESSMENT

Checking for Understanding

1. **Define:** popular sovereignty, federalism, separation of powers, legislative branch, executive branch, judicial branch, checks and balances, veto, impeach, amendment.

2. **Identify:** Virginia Plan, New Jersey Plan, Great Compromise, Three-Fifths Compromise.

Reviewing Themes

3. **Culture and Traditions** Were the delegates to the Constitutional Convention representative of the American public? Why or why not?

Critical Thinking

4. **Analyzing** Do you think the Founders were right in making the amendment process difficult? Why or why not?

5. **Organizing** Use a graphic organizer similar to the one below to list the compromises that the Founders reached in creating the new Constitution.

Compromises Reached

Analyzing Visuals

6. **Examining Art** Study the painting of the members of the Constitutional Convention on page 166. Why did the delegates choose to conduct the convention behind closed doors?

Writing About History

7. **Descriptive Writing** Take on the role of an observer at the Constitutional Convention. Write a journal entry describing what you witnessed. Be sure to record the arguments you heard from each side of the issues discussed, and relate your own opinion on the issues.

Profile

GEORGE WASHINGTON *At the age of 16, George Washington carefully transcribed in his own hand the* Rules of Civility and Decent Behaviour in Company and Conversation. *Among the rules our first president lived by:*

- Every action done in company ought to be with some sign of respect to those that are present.

- When in company, put not your hands to any part of the body, not usually [un]covered.

- Put not off your clothes in the presence of others, nor go out your chamber half dressed.

- Sleep not when others speak.

- Spit not in the fire, nor stoop low before it. Neither put your hands into the flames to warm them, nor set your feet upon the fire, especially if there is meat before it.

- Shake not the head, feet or legs. Roll not the eyes. Lift not one eyebrow higher than the other. Wry not the mouth, and bedew no man's face with your spittle, by approaching too near him when you speak.

- Show not yourself glad at the misfortune of another though he were your enemy.

- Be not hasty to believe flying reports to the disparagement of any.

- Think before you speak.

- Cleanse not your teeth with the Table Cloth.

VERBATIM
WAR'S END

❝I hope you will not consider yourself as commander-in-chief of your own house, but be convinced, that there is such a thing as equal command.❞

LUCY FLUCKER KNOX,
to her husband Henry Knox, upon his return as a hero from the Revolutionary War

❝The American war is over, but this is far from being the case with the American Revolution. Nothing but the first act of the drama is closed.❞

BENJAMIN RUSH,
signer of the Declaration of Independence and member of the Constitutional Convention

❝You could not have found a person to whom your schemes were more disagreeable.❞

GEORGE WASHINGTON,
to Colonel Lewis Nicola, in response to his letter urging Washington to seize power and proclaim himself king

❝It appears to me, then, little short of a miracle that the delegates from so many states . . . should unite in forming a system of national government.❞

GEORGE WASHINGTON,
in a letter to the Marquis de Lafayette at the close of the Constitutional Convention

❝It astonishes me to find this system approaching to near perfection as it does; and I think it will astonish our enemies.❞

BENJAMIN FRANKLIN,
remarking on the structure of the new United States government

whether it should be ratified. The debate took place in state legislatures, in mass meetings, in the columns of newspapers, and in everyday conversations.

Federalists and Antifederalists Supporters of the Constitution called themselves Federalists. The name was chosen with care. It emphasized that the Constitution would create a federal system. Power would be divided between a central government and regional governments. They hoped the name would remind those Americans who feared a central government that the states would retain many of their powers.

Supporters of the Federalists and the new Constitution included large landowners who wanted the property protection a strong central government could provide. Supporters also included merchants and artisans living in large coastal cities. The inability of the Confederation Congress to regulate trade had hit these citizens hard. They believed that an effective federal government that could impose taxes on foreign goods would help their businesses.

Many farmers who lived near the coast or along rivers that led to the coast also supported the Constitution, as did farmers who shipped goods across state borders. These farmers depended on trade for their livelihood and had been frustrated by the different tariffs and duties the states imposed. They wanted a strong central government that could regulate trade consistently.

Opponents to the Constitution were called Antifederalists, a somewhat misleading name, as they were not truly against federalism. They accepted the need for a national government. The real issue, as far as they were concerned, was whether the national government or the state governments would be supreme. Prominent Antifederalists included **John Hancock, Patrick Henry,** Richard Henry Lee of Virginia, and George Clinton, governor of New York. Two members of the Constitutional Convention, Edmund Randolph and George Mason, became Antifederalists because they believed the new Constitution should have included a bill of rights. Sam Adams agreed. He opposed the Constitution because he believed it endangered the independence of the states.

Many Antifederalists were western farmers living far from the coast. These people considered themselves self-sufficient and were suspicious of the wealthy and powerful. Many of them were also deeply in debt and suspected that the new Constitution was simply a way for wealthy creditors to get rid of paper money and foreclose on their farms. One farmer named Amos Singletary wrote to the *Massachusetts Gazette* expressing views that many western farmers shared:

> 66These lawyers and men of learning, and moneyed men, that talk so finely, and gloss over matters so smoothly, to make us poor, illiterate people swallow down the pill, expect to get into Congress themselves; they expect to be managers of this Constitution, and get all the power and all the money into their own hands, and then they will swallow up all us little folks, like the great Leviathan, Mr. President; yes, just like the whale swallowed up Jonah.99

GOVERNMENT

The Federalist Although many influential American leaders opposed the new Constitution, several factors worked against the Antifederalists. First of all, their campaign was a negative one. The Federalists presented a definite program to meet the nation's problems. Although the Antifederalists

Analyzing *Political Cartoons*

Support for Ratification A pro-Federalist cartoon celebrates New Hampshire becoming the ninth state to ratify the Constitution in 1788. Based on the imagery of the cartoon, which state was the first to ratify the Constitution?

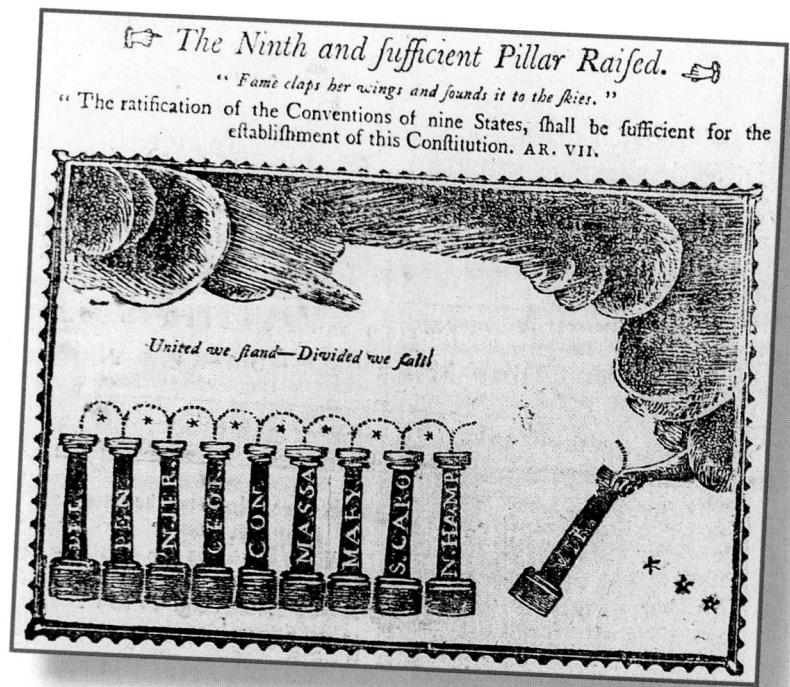

Different Viewpoints

Should the Majority Rule?

James Madison argued persuasively for the Constitution's ratification. In *The Federalist #10,* Madison explained that the Constitution would prevent the effects of *faction*—the self-seeking party spirit of a democracy. In contrast, Thomas Jefferson argued that the will of the majority would thwart the tyranny of oppressive government.

James Madison opposes majority rule:

"When a majority is included in a faction, the form of popular government . . . enables it to sacrifice to its ruling passion or interest both the public good and the rights of other citizens.

. . . [A] pure democracy . . . can admit of no cure for the mischiefs of faction [and has always] been found incompatible with personal security or the rights of property. . . .

A republic, by which I mean a government in which the scheme of representation takes place . . . promises the cure for which we are seeking. . . . The effect of [a republic] is, on the one hand, to refine and enlarge the public views, by passing them through the medium of a chosen body of citizens, whose wisdom may best discern the true interest of their country, and whose patriotism and love of justice will be least likely to sacrifice it to temporary or partial considerations."

Thomas Jefferson defends majority rule:

"I own I am not a friend to a very energetic government. It is always oppressive. The late rebellion in Massachusetts has given more alarm than I think it should have done. Calculate that one rebellion in 13 states in the course of 11 years, is but one for each state in a century & a half. No country should be so long without one.

. . . After all, it is my principle that the will of the Majority should always prevail. If they approve the proposed [Constitution] in all its parts, I shall concur in it chearfully, in hopes that they will amend it whenever they shall find it works wrong. . . . Above all things I hope the education of the common people will be attended to; convinced that on their good sense we may rely with the most security for the preservation of a due degree of liberty."

Learning From History

1. What were the "mischiefs" that Madison believed republican government could prevent?
2. Was Jefferson correct in believing the voice of the common people would preserve liberty? Explain.

---

complained that the Constitution failed to protect basic rights, they had nothing to offer in its place.

The Federalists were also better organized than their opponents. Most of the nation's newspapers supported them. The Federalists were able to present a very convincing case in their speeches, pamphlets, and debates in state conventions.

The Federalists' arguments for ratification were summarized in *The Federalist*—a collection of 85 essays written by James Madison, Alexander Hamilton, and John Jay. Under the joint pen name of Publius, the three men published most of the essays in New York newspapers in late 1787 and early 1788 before collecting them in *The Federalist.* 📖 *(See pages 1066–1067 for examples of Federalist writings.)*

The essays explained how the new Constitution worked and why it was needed. They were very influential. Even today, judges, lawyers, legislators, and historians rely upon *The Federalist* to help them interpret the Constitution and understand what the original framers intended.

Reading Check **Summarizing** Which groups of people tended to support the new Constitution?

The Fight for Ratification

As the ratifying conventions began to gather, the Federalists knew that they had clear majorities in some states but that the vote was going to be much closer in others, including the large and important states of Massachusetts, Virginia, and New York.

The first state conventions took place in December 1787 and January 1788. Although Delaware,

Pennsylvania, New Jersey, Georgia, and Connecticut all quickly ratified the Constitution, the most important battles still lay ahead.

Ratification in Massachusetts

In Massachusetts, opponents of the Constitution held a clear majority when the convention met in January 1788. They included the great patriot Samuel Adams. Federalists moved quickly to meet Adams's objections to the Constitution.

They promised to attach a bill of rights to the Constitution once it was ratified. They also agreed to support an amendment that would reserve for the states all powers not specifically granted to the federal government. These concessions, combined with most artisans siding with the Federalists, persuaded Adams to vote for ratification. In the final vote, 187 members of the convention voted in favor of the Constitution while 168 voted against it.

By the end of June 1788, Maryland, South Carolina, and New Hampshire had ratified the Constitution. The Federalists had reached the minimum number of states required to put the new Constitution into effect, but Virginia and New York still had not ratified. Without the support of these two large states, many feared the new government would not succeed.

Virginia and New York

George Washington and James Madison presented arguments for ratification to the Virginia convention. Patrick Henry, Richard Henry Lee, and other Antifederalists made arguments against it. In the end, Madison's promise to add a bill of rights won the day for the Federalists.

In New York, two-thirds of the members elected to the state convention, including Governor George Clinton, were Antifederalists. The Federalists, led by Alexander Hamilton and John Jay, managed to delay the final vote until news arrived that New Hampshire and Virginia had both ratified the Constitution and that the new federal government was now in effect. If New York refused to ratify, it would be in a very awkward position. It would have to operate independently of all of the surrounding states. This argument convinced enough Antifederalists to change sides. The vote was very close, 30 to 27, but the Federalists won.

By July 1788, all the states except Rhode Island and North Carolina had ratified the Constitution. Because ratification by nine states was all that the Constitution required, the new government could be launched without them. In mid-September 1788, the Confederation Congress established a timetable for the election of the new government. It chose March 4, 1789, as the date for the first meeting of the new Congress.

The two states that had held out finally ratified the Constitution after the new government was in place. North Carolina waited until a bill of rights had actually been proposed, then voted to ratify the Constitution in November 1789. Rhode Island, still nervous about losing its independence, did not ratify the Constitution until May 1790, and even then the vote was very close—34 to 32.

The United States now had a new government, but no one knew if the new Constitution would work any better than the Articles of Confederation. With both anticipation and nervousness, the American people waited for their new government to begin. Many expressed great confidence, because George Washington had been chosen to become the first president under the new Constitution.

Reading Check **Examining** Why was it important for Virginia and New York to ratify the Constitution, even after the required nine states had done so?

SECTION 3 ASSESSMENT

Checking for Understanding
1. **Define:** Federalist, Antifederalist.
2. **Identify:** John Hancock, Patrick Henry.
3. **List** the groups of people who opposed ratification of the Constitution.
4. **Explain** why the Federalists had an advantage over the Antifederalists.

Reviewing Themes
5. **Government and Democracy** Do you think it was important for all the states to ratify the Constitution? Why or why not?

Critical Thinking
6. **Analyzing** How did the Federalists attempt to assure ratification of the Constitution?
7. **Organizing** Use a graphic organizer similar to the one below to list the factors that worked against the Antifederalists.

Factors Working
Against Antifederalists

Analyzing Visuals
8. **Studying Cartoons** Examine the cartoon on page 173. Why was New Hampshire's ratification of the Constitution important?

Writing About History
9. **Persuasive Writing** Take on the role of a Federalist or an Antifederalist at a state ratifying convention. Write a speech in which you try to convince your audience to either accept or reject the new Constitution.

Reviewing Key Terms

On a sheet of paper, use each of these terms in a sentence.

1. duty
2. recession
3. popular sovereignty
4. federalism
5. separation of powers
6. legislative branch
7. executive branch
8. judicial branch
9. checks and balances
10. veto
11. impeach
12. amendment
13. Federalist
14. Antifederalist

Reviewing Key Facts

15. **Identify:** Northwest Ordinance, Shays's Rebellion, Three-Fifths Compromise, John Hancock, Patrick Henry.

16. How did Shays's Rebellion indicate the need for a stronger national government?

17. How did the Founders provide for a separation of powers in the federal government?

18. Why did large landowners and merchants support the Constitution?

19. What was the purpose of *The Federalist*?

Critical Thinking

20. **Analyzing Themes: Government and Democracy** What do you think was the most serious flaw of the Articles of Confederation? Why do you think so?

21. **Organizing** Use a graphic organizer similar to the one below to indicate what details the Founders included in the Constitution to provide for a limited government.

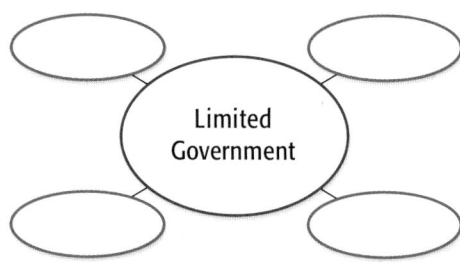

Limited Government

22. **Interpreting Primary Sources** In his 1789 textbook *The American Geography,* Reverend Jedidiah Morse discusses the defects of the Articles of Confederation. Read the excerpt and answer the questions that follow.

Chapter Summary

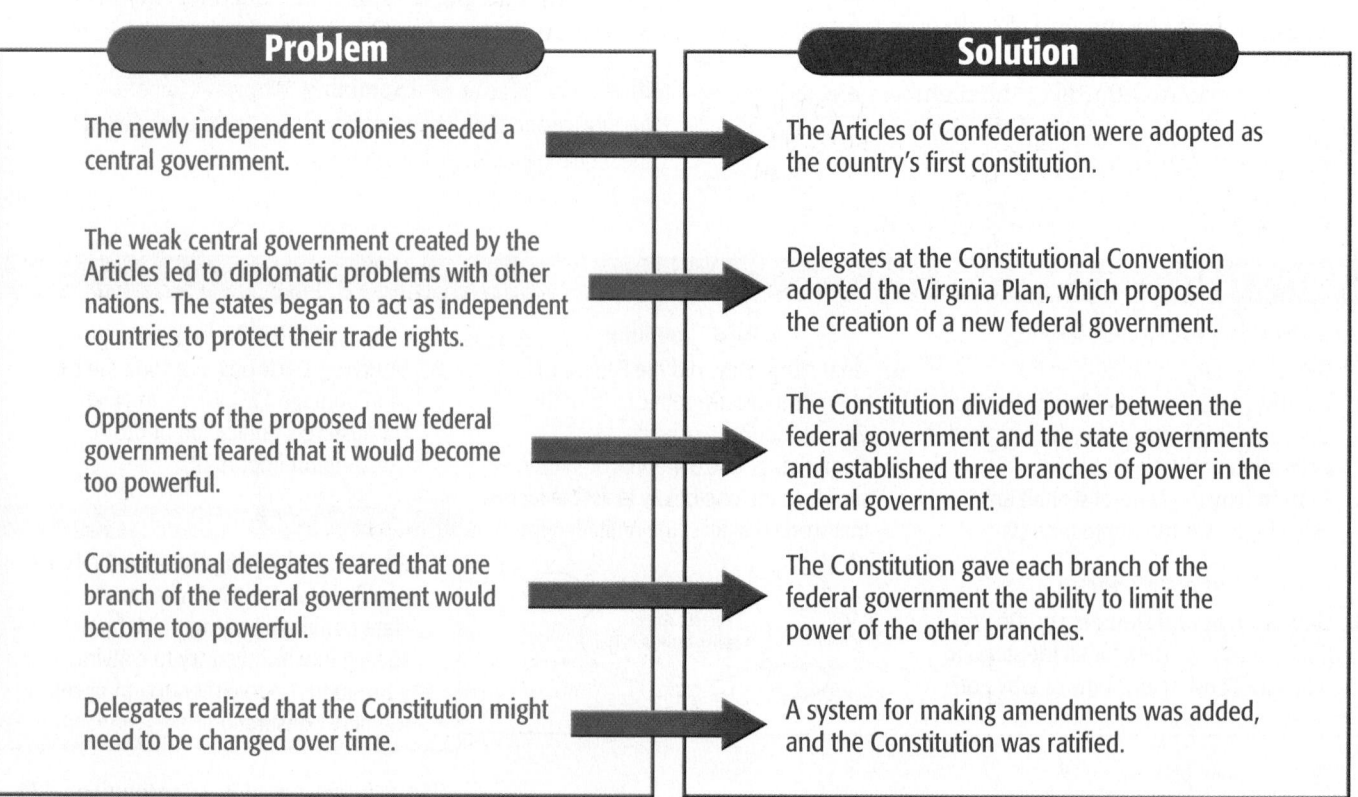

Problem	Solution
The newly independent colonies needed a central government.	The Articles of Confederation were adopted as the country's first constitution.
The weak central government created by the Articles led to diplomatic problems with other nations. The states began to act as independent countries to protect their trade rights.	Delegates at the Constitutional Convention adopted the Virginia Plan, which proposed the creation of a new federal government.
Opponents of the proposed new federal government feared that it would become too powerful.	The Constitution divided power between the federal government and the state governments and established three branches of power in the federal government.
Constitutional delegates feared that one branch of the federal government would become too powerful.	The Constitution gave each branch of the federal government the ability to limit the power of the other branches.
Delegates realized that the Constitution might need to be changed over time.	A system for making amendments was added, and the Constitution was ratified.

Self-Check Quiz

Visit the *American Vision* Web site at tav.glencoe.com and click on *Self-Check Quizzes—Chapter 5* to assess your knowledge of chapter content.

66[The Articles of Confederation] were framed during the rage of war, when a principle of common safety supplied the place of a coercive power in government. . . .

When resolutions were passed in Congress, there was no power to compel obedience. . . . Had one state been invaded by its neighbour, the union was not constitutionally bound to assist in repelling the invasion. . . .99

— quoted in *Readings in American History*

a. What defects in the Articles does Morse see?

b. Why does Morse think the Articles were effective during the American Revolution but not afterward?

Practicing Skills

23. **Making Comparisons** Reread the passage about the Virginia and New Jersey Plans from Chapter 5, Section 2, on page 166. Then answer the following questions.
    a. Which plan gave more power to the states?

    b. What new power did the New Jersey plan grant to Congress?

Writing Activity

24. **Portfolio Writing** Take on the role of an American living during the Constitution's ratification. Write a letter to a friend in Britain describing the form of the new government. Tell why you support or oppose ratification and what you think life will be like under the new government.

Chapter Activity

25. **Technology Activity: Sending an E-Mail** Use the Internet to find the latest bills that are pending in Congress. Choose one of these bills or choose an issue that is important to you and your community. Send an e-mail to your senator or representative, persuading him or her how to vote on the issue. Provide reasons for your position.

Geography and History

26. The map on this page shows the western land claims of the original states. Study the map and answer these questions.
    a. **Interpreting Maps** Which state had the largest land claims in the West?

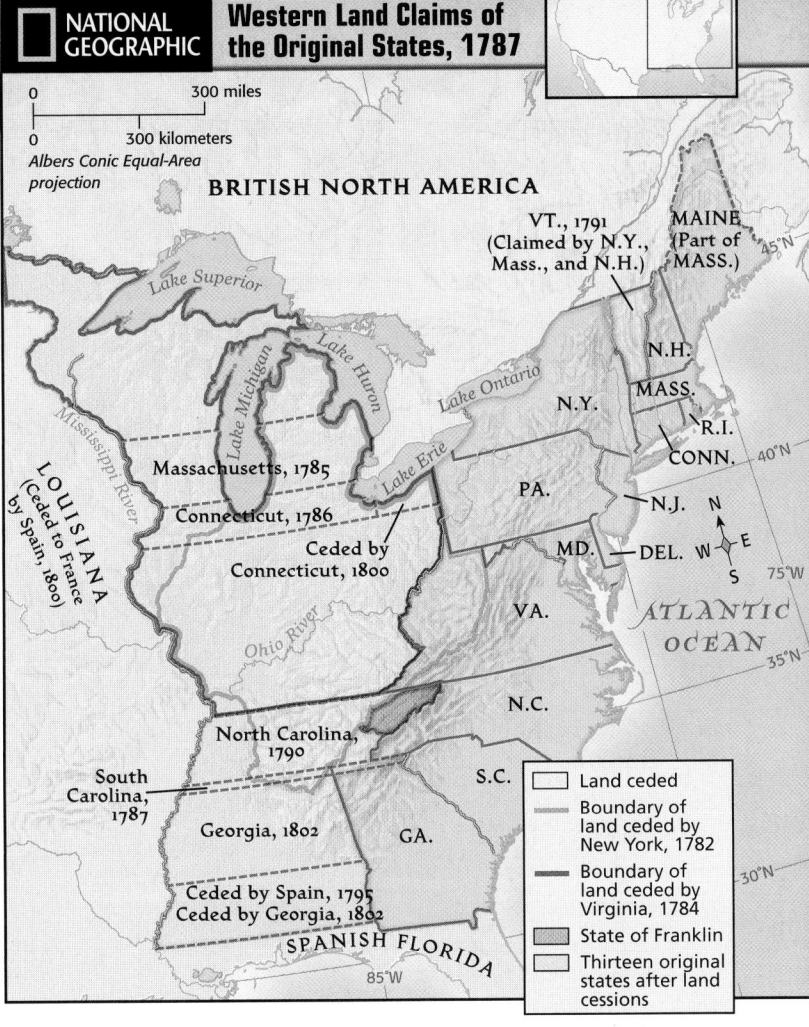

NATIONAL GEOGRAPHIC

Western Land Claims of the Original States, 1787

b. **Applying Geography Skills** Why do you think the states eventually agreed to surrender their land claims to the Confederation Congress?

Standardized Test Practice

Directions: Choose the best answer to the following question.

Which of the following is an *opinion* about the Constitution?

F By 1790 all states had ratified the Constitution.

G A major concern in writing the Constitution was how many representatives each state would have.

H Under the Constitution, the federal government could raise money to operate the government.

J Because of the Constitution, the United States has a better democracy than other countries.

Test-Taking Tip: An *opinion* is not a proven fact (such as answer F). Opinions often contain subjective words, like *best*.

The Constitution Handbook

★ ★

Main Idea
The Constitution was designed to provide the United States with a stronger national government while remaining flexible enough to meet the changing circumstances of the growing nation.

Key Terms and Names
popular sovereignty, federalism, enumerated powers, reserved powers, concurrent powers, override, appropriate, impeach, constituent, bill, standing committee, select committee, joint committee, conference committee, cabinet, judicial review, due process

Reading Strategy
Taking Notes As you read about the Constitution, use the major headings of the handbook to fill in an outline similar to the one below.

I. Major Principles
   A.
   B.
   C.
   D.
   E.
   F.
   G.
II.

Reading Objectives:
- **Identify** the branches of the federal government and their separate areas of power.
- **Understand** and describe the responsibilities that American citizens share.

Section Theme
Civic Rights and Responsibilities The success of the American system of government depends on citizens being informed. An understanding of the Constitution is key to understanding how the American government operates.

Preview of Events

| ♦1786 | ♦1787 | ♦1788 | ♦1789 | ♦1790 | ♦1791 | ♦1792 |

September 1786
Annapolis Convention begins

May 1787
Constitutional Convention begins

September 1787
Constitution signed and Convention adjourns

June 1788
New Hampshire ratifies Constitution, making it the new form of government

December 1791
The Bill of Rights becomes part of the Constitution

★ *An American Story* ★

In 1987 the United States began a four-year celebration commemorating the Constitution's bicentennial. In a series of ceremonies that lasted to 1991, the nation reflected on the writing and ratifying of the document providing the country's foundation of government. Proclaiming the creation of Citizenship Day and Constitution Week in August 1990, President George Bush quoted the words of Daniel Webster:

❝'We may be tossed upon an ocean where we can see no land—nor, perhaps, the sun or stars. But there is a chart and a compass for us to study, to consult, and to obey. That chart is the Constitution.'❞

Serving as the framework of national government and the source of American citizens' basic rights, the Constitution is the United States's most important document. As President Bush reminded the nation in his proclamation: "[I]f we are to continue to enjoy the blessings of freedom and self-government, each of us must understand our rights and responsibilities as citizens."

—adapted from *Proclamation of Citizenship Day* and *Constitution Week*

Major Principles

The principles outlined in the Constitution were the Framers' solution to the complex problems of a representative government. The Constitution rests on seven major principles of government: (1) popular sovereignty, (2) republicanism, (3) limited government, (4) federalism, (5) separation of powers, (6) checks and balances, and (7) individual rights.

Popular Sovereignty

The opening words of the Constitution, "We the people," reinforce the idea of popular sovereignty, or "authority of the people." In the Constitution, the people consent to be governed and specify the powers and rules by which they shall be governed.

The Articles of Confederation form of government had few powers, and it was unable to cope with the many challenges facing the nation. The new constitutional government had greater powers and influence, but it also had specific limitations. A system of interlocking responsibilities kept any one branch of government from becoming too powerful.

Republicanism

Voters hold sovereign power in a republican system. The people elect representatives and give them the responsibility to make laws and conduct government. For most Americans today, the terms *republic* and *representative democracy* mean the same thing: a system of limited government where the people are the final source of authority.

Limited Government

Although the Framers agreed that the nation needed a stronger central authority, they feared misuse of power. They wanted to prevent the government from using its power to give one group special advantages or to deprive another group of its rights. By creating a limited government, they restricted the government's authority to specific powers granted by the people.

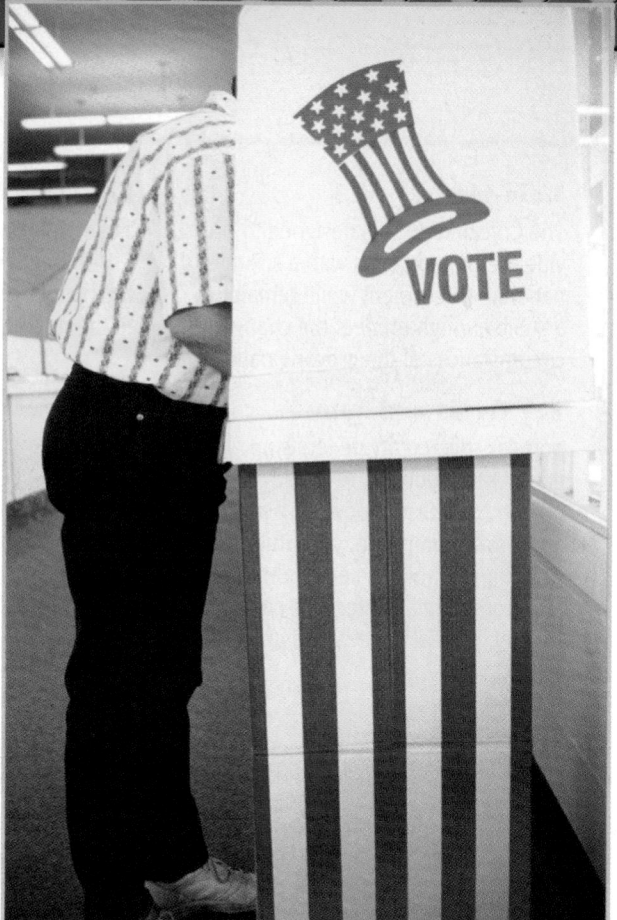

The Right to Vote The voting booth is a symbol of one of the Constitution's major principles—popular sovereignty. What does popular sovereignty mean?

The members of the Constitutional Convention wished to list the range of powers granted to the new government as specifically as possible. Their decision to write down the governmental outline also served as a clear record of what they intended. Article I of the Constitution states the powers that the government has and does not have. Other limits on government appear in the Bill of Rights, which guarantees certain rights and liberties to the people.

Federalism

In establishing a strong central government, the Framers did not deprive states of all authority. The states would give up some powers to the national government while retaining others. States could no longer print their own money or tax items imported from other states, but mostly, each state continued to govern itself much as it had in the past.

This principle of shared power is federalism. Our federal government allows the people of each state to deal with their needs in their own way. At the same time, it lets the states act together to deal with matters that affect all Americans.

The Constitution defines three types of government powers. Certain powers belong only to the

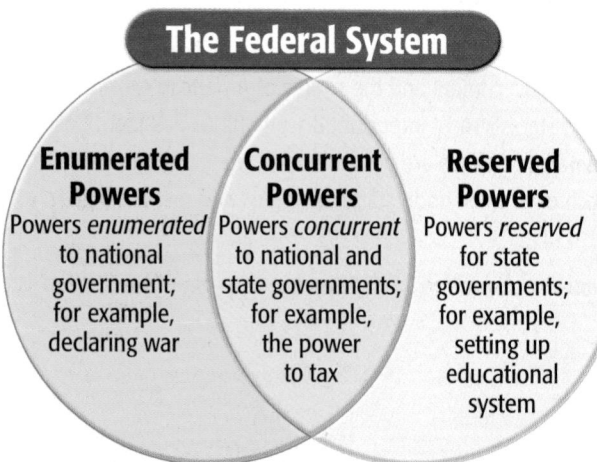

The Federal System

Enumerated Powers	Concurrent Powers	Reserved Powers
Powers *enumerated* to national government; for example, declaring war	Powers *concurrent* to national and state governments; for example, the power to tax	Powers *reserved* for state governments; for example, setting up educational system

Checks and Balances

Legislative Branch
• **Congress Makes the Law**

Judicial Branch
• **Supreme Court Interprets the Law**

Checks on the Legislative Branch:
• Can declare acts of Congress unconstitutional

Checks on the Executive Branch:
• Can declare executive actions unconstitutional

Checks on the Judicial Branch:
• Creates lower federal courts
• Can impeach and remove judges
• Can propose amendments to overrule judicial decisions
• Approves appointments of federal judges

Checks on the Executive Branch:
• Can override presidential veto
• Confirms executive appointments
• Ratifies treaties
• Can declare war
• Appropriates money
• Can impeach and remove president

Checks on the Legislative Branch:
• Can propose laws
• Can veto laws
• Can call special sessions of Congress
• Makes appointments to federal posts
• Negotiates foreign treaties

Executive Branch
• **President Carries Out the Law**

Checks on the Judicial Branch:
• Appoints federal judges
• Can pardon federal offenders

Chart *Skills*

Each branch can limit the others' power.

Analyzing Information How can the president help control the judiciary?

federal government. These enumerated powers include the power to coin money, regulate interstate and foreign trade, maintain the armed forces, and create federal courts (Article I, Section 8).

The second kind of powers are those retained by the states, known as reserved powers, including the power to establish schools, pass marriage and divorce laws, and regulate trade within a state. Although specific reserved powers are not listed in the Constitution, the Tenth Amendment says that all powers not specifically granted to the federal government "are reserved to the States."

The third set of powers defined by the Constitution are concurrent powers—powers the state and federal governments share. They include the right to raise taxes, borrow money, provide for public welfare, and administer criminal justice.

Conflicts between state law and federal law must be settled in a federal court. The Constitution declares that it is "the supreme Law of the Land."

Separation of Powers

To prevent any single group or institution in government from gaining too much authority, the Framers divided the federal government into three branches: legislative, executive, and judicial. Each branch has its own functions and powers. The legislative branch, Congress, makes the laws. The executive branch, headed by the president, carries out the laws. The judicial branch, consisting of the Supreme Court and other federal courts, interprets and applies the laws.

In addition to giving separate responsibility to separate branches, the membership of each branch is chosen in different ways. The president nominates federal judges and the Senate confirms the appointments. People vote for members of Congress. Voters cast ballots for president, but the method of election is indirect. On Election Day the votes in each state are counted. Whatever candidate receives a majority receives that state's electoral votes, which total the number of senators and representatives the state has in Congress. Electors from all states meet in December after the November election to formally elect a president. A candidate must receive at least 270 of 538 electoral votes to win.

Checks and Balances

The Framers also established a system of checks and balances in which each branch of government can check, or limit, the

The Bill of Rights: The First Ten Amendments

Amendment 1	Guarantees freedom of religion, of speech, and of the press, and the right to assemble peaceably and to petition the government
Amendment 2	Guarantees the right to organize state militias and bear arms
Amendment 3	Prohibits quartering soldiers in private homes in peacetime and limits it in time of war
Amendment 4	Prohibits the unreasonable search and seizure of persons and property without a valid warrant
Amendment 5	Requires a grand jury for serious criminal charges; prohibits double jeopardy; prohibits forcing accused persons to testify against themselves; guarantees that no one may be deprived of life, liberty, or property, without due process of law; prohibits government taking private property for public use without just compensation
Amendment 6	Guarantees suspects the right to a speedy trial by jury in criminal cases; to know all charges; to question and obtain witnesses; and to have counsel
Amendment 7	Guarantees a jury trial in most civil cases
Amendment 8	Prohibits excessive bail and fines and cruel and unusual punishment
Amendment 9	Assures people that they may have other basic rights in addition to those mentioned in the Constitution
Amendment 10	Guarantees that rights not given to the federal government, nor denied to the states, are reserved to the states or to the people

Chart *Skills*

Antifederalists demanded a specific list of individual rights and freedoms.

Analyzing Information Why did the Framers include Amendment 4, prohibiting unreasonable searches?

power of the other branches. This system helps balance the power of the three branches. For example, imagine that Congress passes a law. Then the president can reject the law by vetoing it. However, Congress can override, or reverse, the president's veto if two-thirds of the members of both the Senate and the House of Representatives vote again to approve the law.

Individual Rights The Bill of Rights became part of the Constitution in 1791. These first 10 amendments protect basic liberties and rights that some Americans may take for granted—including freedom of speech, freedom of the press, freedom of assembly, freedom of religion, and the right to a trial by jury.

The 17 amendments that follow the Bill of Rights expand the rights of Americans and adjust certain provisions of the Constitution. Included among them are amendments that abolish slavery, define citizenship, guarantee voting rights, authorize an income tax, and set a two-term limit on the presidency.

The Legislative Branch

The legislative branch includes the two houses of Congress: the House of Representatives and the Senate. Congress's two primary roles are to make the nation's laws and to control federal spending.

The Role of Congress The government cannot spend any money unless Congress appropriates, or sets aside, funds. All tax and spending bills must originate in the House of Representatives and gain approval in both the House and the Senate before moving on to the president for signature.

Congress also monitors the executive branch and investigates possible abuses of power. The House of Representatives can impeach, or bring formal charges against, any federal official it suspects of wrongdoing or misconduct. If an official is impeached, the Senate acts as a court and tries the accused official. Officials who are found guilty may be removed from office.

The Senate also holds certain special powers. Only the Senate can ratify treaties made by the president and confirm presidential appointments of federal officials such as department heads, ambassadors, and federal judges.

All members of Congress have the responsibility of representing their constituents, the people of their home states and districts. As a constituent, you can expect your senators and representative to promote national and state interests.

Congress at Work Thousands of bills—proposed laws—are introduced in Congress every year. Because individual members of Congress cannot possibly study all these bills carefully, both houses use committees of selected members to evaluate proposed legislation.

Standing committees are permanent committees in both the House and the Senate that specialize in a particular topic, such as agriculture, commerce, or veterans' affairs. These committees are usually divided into subcommittees that focus on a particular aspect of an issue.

The House and the Senate sometimes form temporary select committees to deal with issues requiring special attention. These committees meet only until they complete their task.

Occasionally the House and the Senate form joint committees with members from both houses. These committees meet to consider specific issues, such as the system of federal taxation. One type of joint committee, a conference committee, has a special function. If the House and the Senate pass different versions of the same bill, a conference committee tries to work out a compromise bill acceptable to both houses.

Once a committee in either house of Congress approves a bill, it is sent to the full Senate or House for debate. After debate the bill may be passed, rejected, or returned to the committee for further changes.

When both houses pass a bill, it goes to the president. If the president approves the bill and signs it, the bill becomes law. If the president vetoes the bill, it does not become law unless Congress overrides the veto.

The Executive Branch

The executive branch of government includes the president, the vice president, and various executive offices, departments, and agencies. The executive branch carries out the laws that Congress passes. The president plays a number of different roles in government, each of which has specific powers and responsibilities. These roles include the nation's

How a Bill Becomes Law

1. A legislator introduces a bill in the House or Senate, where it is referred to a committee for review.

2. After review, the committee decides whether to shelve it or to send it back to the House or Senate with or without revisions.

3. The House or Senate then debates the bill, making revisions if desired. If the bill is passed, it is sent to the other house.

4. If the House and Senate pass different versions of the bill, the houses must meet in a conference committee to decide on a compromise version.

5. The compromise bill is then sent to both houses.

6. If both houses pass the bill, it is sent to the president to sign.

7. If the president signs the bill, it becomes law.

8. The president may veto the bill, but if two-thirds of the House and Senate vote to approve it, it becomes law without the president's approval.

Chart Skills

The legislative process is complex.

Analyzing Information What is the role of a conference committee?

The Amendment Process

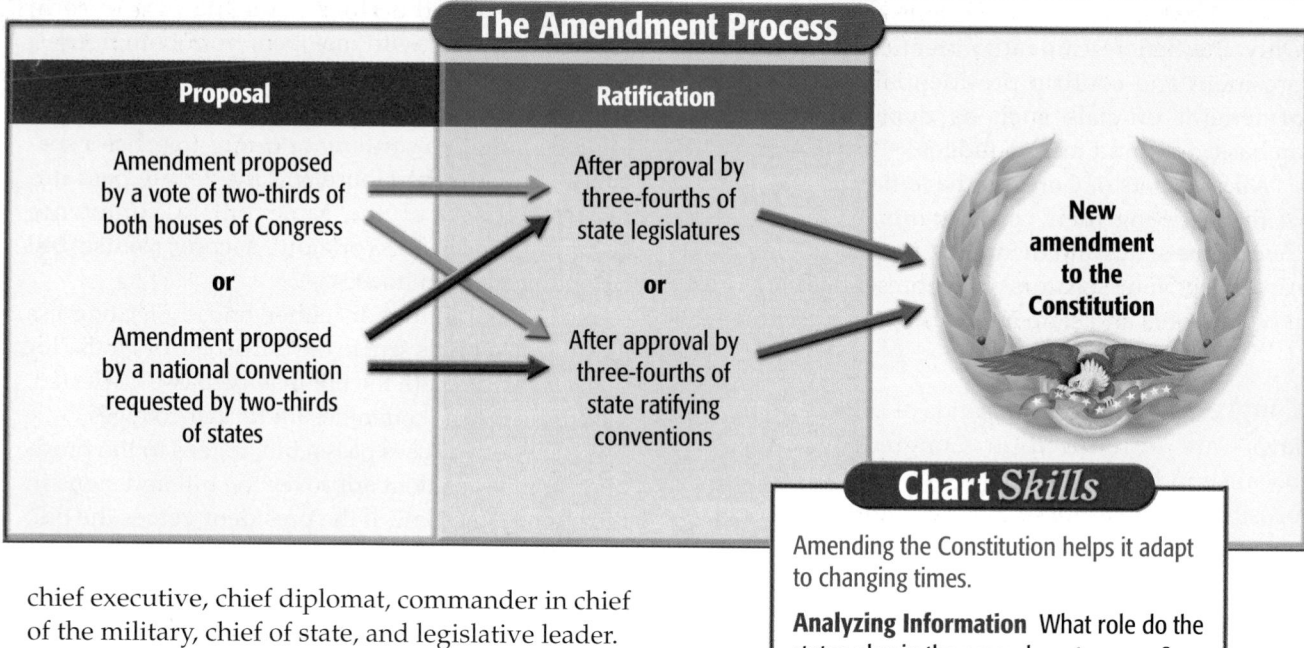

Proposal	Ratification
Amendment proposed by a vote of two-thirds of both houses of Congress	After approval by three-fourths of state legislatures
or	**or**
Amendment proposed by a national convention requested by two-thirds of states	After approval by three-fourths of state ratifying conventions

New amendment to the Constitution

Chart *Skills*

Amending the Constitution helps it adapt to changing times.

Analyzing Information What role do the states play in the amendment process?

chief executive, chief diplomat, commander in chief of the military, chief of state, and legislative leader.

The President's Roles

- **Chief Executive and Chief Diplomat** As chief executive, the president is responsible for carrying out the nation's laws. As chief diplomat, the president directs foreign policy, appoints ambassadors, and negotiates treaties with other nations.
- **Commander in Chief** As commander in chief of the armed forces, the president can use the military to intervene or offer assistance in crises at home and around the world. The president cannot declare war; only Congress holds this power. The president can send troops to other parts of the world for up to 60 days but must notify Congress when doing so. The troops may remain longer only if Congress gives its approval or declares war.
- **Chief of State** As chief of state, the president serves a symbolic role as the representative of all Americans. The president fulfills this role when receiving foreign ambassadors or heads of state, visiting foreign nations, or honoring Americans.
- **Legislative Leader** The president serves as a legislative leader by proposing laws to Congress and working to see that they are passed. In the annual State of the Union address, the president presents goals for legislation.

The Executive Branch at Work

Many executive offices, departments, and independent agencies help the president carry out and enforce the nation's laws. The Executive Office of the President (EOP) is made up of individuals and agencies that directly assist the president. Presidents rely heavily on the EOP for advice and for gathering information needed for decision making.

The executive branch also includes 15 executive departments, each responsible for a different area of government. For example, the Department of State plans and carries out foreign policy, and the Department of the Interior manages and protects the nation's public lands and natural resources. The heads of these departments, who have the title of secretary, are members of the president's cabinet. This group helps the president make decisions and set government policy.

The Judicial Branch

Article III of the Constitution calls for the creation of a Supreme Court and "such inferior [lower] courts as Congress may from time to time ordain and establish." Today the judicial branch consists of three main categories of courts, including:

- **District Courts** United States district courts are the lowest level of the federal court system. These courts consider criminal and civil cases that come under federal authority, including such criminal offenses as kidnapping and federal tax evasion. Civil cases cover claims against the federal government and cases involving constitutional rights, such as free speech. There are 91 district courts, with at least one in every state.
- **Appellate Courts** The appellate courts, or appeals courts, consider district court decisions in which the losing side has asked for a review of the

verdict. If an appeals court disagrees with the lower court's decision, it can either overturn the verdict or order a retrial. There are 14 appeals courts in the United States, one for each of the 12 federal districts, a military appeals court, and an appellate court for the federal circuit.

- **The Supreme Court** The Supreme Court, the final authority in the federal court system, consists of a chief justice and eight associate justices. Most of the Supreme Court's cases come from appeals of lower court decisions. Only cases involving foreign ambassadors or disputes between states can begin in the Supreme Court.

Supreme Court Independence The Supreme Court is the least public of the government's branches. The president appoints the Court's justices for life, and the Senate confirms the appointments. The public has no input. The Framers hoped that because judges were appointed rather than elected, they would be free to evaluate the law with no consideration of pleasing a group of electors.

Judicial Review The role of the judicial branch is not described in very much detail in the Constitution, but the role of the courts has grown as powers implied in the Constitution have been put into practice. In 1803 Chief Justice John Marshall expanded the powers of the Supreme Court by striking down an act of Congress in the case of *Marbury* v. *Madison*. Although not mentioned in the Constitution, judicial review has become a major power of the judicial branch. Judicial review gives the Supreme Court the ultimate authority to interpret the meaning of constitutional provisions and explain how the words of this 200-year-old document apply to our modern nation. *(See page 1081 for more information on* Marbury v. Madison.*)*

The Rights of American Citizens

The rights of Americans fall into three broad categories: the right to be protected from unfair actions of the government, to receive equal treatment under the law, and to retain basic freedoms.

Protection from Unfair Actions Parts of the Constitution and the Bill of Rights protect all Americans from unfair treatment by the government or the law. Among these rights are the right to a lawyer when accused of a crime and the right to trial by jury when charged with a crime. In addition, the Fourth Amendment protects us from unreasonable searches and seizures. This provision requires police to have a court order before searching a person's home for criminal evidence. To obtain this, the police must have a very strong reason to suspect the person of committing a crime.

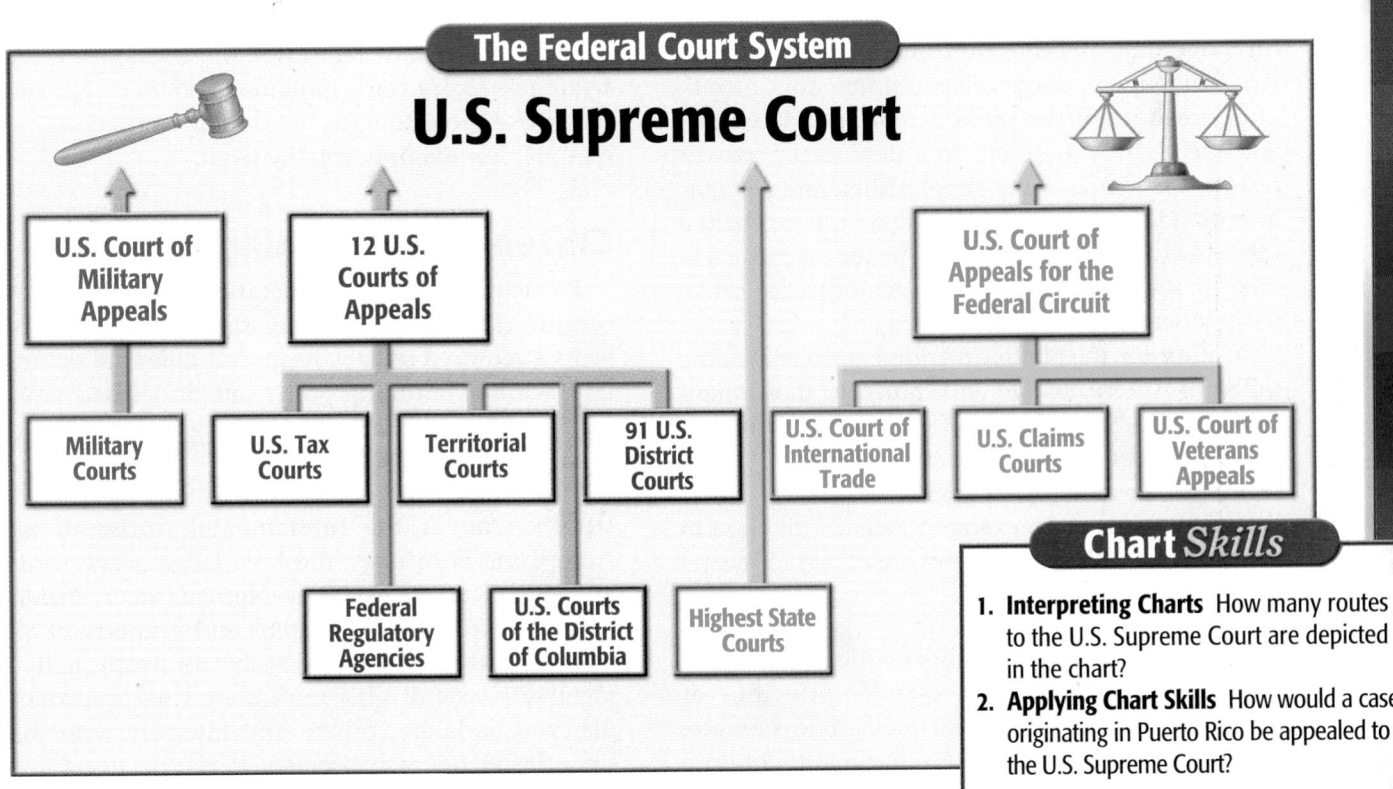

The Federal Court System

U.S. Supreme Court

- U.S. Court of Military Appeals
- 12 U.S. Courts of Appeals
- U.S. Court of Appeals for the Federal Circuit

- Military Courts
- U.S. Tax Courts
- Territorial Courts
- 91 U.S. District Courts
- U.S. Court of International Trade
- U.S. Claims Courts
- U.S. Court of Veterans Appeals

- Federal Regulatory Agencies
- U.S. Courts of the District of Columbia
- Highest State Courts

Chart *Skills*

1. **Interpreting Charts** How many routes to the U.S. Supreme Court are depicted in the chart?
2. **Applying Chart Skills** How would a case originating in Puerto Rico be appealed to the U.S. Supreme Court?

Democracy in Action Town meetings in New England give local residents the chance to express their views. It is a responsibility of American citizens to remain informed about the actions of their local, state, and national government.

Equal Treatment All Americans, regardless of race, religion, or political beliefs, have the right to be treated the same under the law. The Fifth Amendment states that no person shall "be deprived of life, liberty, or property, without due process of law." Due process means that the government must follow procedures established by law and guaranteed by the Constitution, treating all people equally. The Fourteenth Amendment requires every state to grant its citizens "equal protection of the laws."

Basic Freedoms The basic freedoms involve the fundamental liberties outlined in the First Amendment—freedom of speech, freedom of religion, freedom of the press, freedom of assembly, and the right to petition. In a democracy, power rests in the hands of the people. Therefore, citizens in a democratic society must be able to exchange ideas freely. The First Amendment allows citizens to criticize the government, in speech or in the press, without fear of punishment.

In addition, the Ninth Amendment states that the rights of Americans are not limited to those mentioned in the Constitution. This has allowed basic freedoms to expand over the years through the passage of other amendments and laws. The Twenty-sixth Amendment, for example, extends the right to vote to American citizens who are at least 18 years of age.

Limits on Rights The rights of Americans have certain limitations, based on the principle of respecting everyone's rights equally. For example, many cities and towns require groups to obtain a permit to march on city streets. While such a law does limit free speech, it also protects the community by allowing the police to make provisions so that the march will not disturb the lives of other people. However, a law banning all marches would be unreasonable and would violate the First Amendment rights of free speech and assembly. Similarly, a law preventing only certain groups from marching would be unfair because it would not apply equally to everyone.

In this and other cases, the government balances an individual's rights, the rights of others, and the community's health and safety. Most Americans are willing to accept some limitations on their rights to gain these protections as long as the restrictions are reasonable and apply equally to all.

Citizens' Responsibilities

Participation in a democratic society involves certain duties and responsibilities. Duties are actions required by law. Responsibilities are voluntary actions. Fulfilling both your duties and your responsibilities helps ensure good government and protects your rights.

Duties One of the fundamental duties of all Americans is to obey the law. Laws serve three important functions. They help maintain order; they protect the health, safety, and property of all citizens; and they make it possible for people to live together peacefully. If you disobey laws, for example, you endanger others and interfere with the smooth functioning of society. If you believe a law needs to be changed, you can work through your electoral representatives to improve it.

Americans also have a duty to pay taxes. The government uses tax money to defend the nation, provide health insurance for people over 65, and build roads and bridges. Americans benefit from services provided by the government.

Another duty of citizens is to defend the nation. All males aged 18 and older must register with the government in case the nation needs to call on them for military service. Military service is not automatic, but a war could make it necessary.

The Constitution guarantees all Americans the right to a trial by a jury of their equals. For this reason, you should be prepared for jury duty when you become eligible at the age of 18. Having a large group of jurors on hand is necessary to guarantee the right to a fair and speedy trial. You also have a duty to serve as a trial witness if called to do so.

Most states require you to attend school until a certain age. School is where you gain the knowledge and skills needed to be a good citizen. In school you learn to think more clearly, to express your opinions more accurately, and to analyze the statements and ideas of others. These skills will help you make informed choices when you vote.

Responsibilities The responsibilities of citizens are not as clear-cut as their duties. Responsibilities are as important as duties, however, because they help maintain the quality of government and society.

One important responsibility is to become well informed. You need to know what is happening in your community, your state, your country, and the world. Knowing what your government representatives are doing and expressing your feelings about their actions can help keep the government responsive to the wishes of the people.

You also need to be informed about your rights and to exercise them when necessary. Knowing your rights helps preserve them. Other responsibilities include respecting diversity, accepting responsibility for your actions, and supporting your family.

Vote, Vote, Vote! Perhaps your most important responsibility as an American citizen will be to vote when you reach the age of 18. Voting allows you to participate in government and guide its direction. When you vote for people to represent you in government, you will be exercising your right of self-government. If you disapprove of the job your representatives are doing, it will be your responsibility to help elect other people in the next election. You can also let your representatives know how you feel about issues through letters, telephone calls, and petitions and by taking part in public meetings or political rallies.

To enjoy your rights to the fullest, you must be prepared to respect the rights of others. Respecting the rights of others also means respecting the rights of people with whom you disagree. Respecting and accepting others regardless of race, religion, beliefs, or other differences is essential in a democracy.

Constitution Handbook Assessment

Checking for Understanding

1. **Define:** popular sovereignty, federalism, enumerated powers, reserved powers, concurrent powers, override, appropriate, impeach, constituent, bill, standing committee, select committee, joint committee, conference committee, cabinet, judicial review, due process.
2. **Summarize** the provisions of the First Amendment.

Reviewing Themes

3. **Civic Rights and Responsibilities** What is the difference between a duty and a responsibility?

Critical Thinking

4. **Comparing** Some people want a limit on the number of terms one can serve in the legislature. What are some of the advantages of the present system, which does not limit the number of terms? What are some of the disadvantages? How would one make term limits an official part of the Constitution?
5. **Organizing** Use a graphic organizer like the one below to list reasons why the Framers of the Constitution provided for separation of powers.

Separation of Powers

Analyzing Visuals

6. **Analyzing Photographs** Study the photograph on page 122. How does the democratic voting process reflect our national identity?

Writing About History

7. **History and Government** Working with a partner, choose one of the constitutional rights listed below. Write a report that traces the right's historical development, from the time the Constitution was ratified to the present.
   suffrage
   freedom of speech
   freedom of religion
   equal protection of law

The Constitution of the United States

The Constitution of the United States is a truly remarkable document. It was one of the first written constitutions in modern history. The entire text of the Constitution and its amendments follow. For easier study, those passages that have been set aside or changed by the adoption of amendments are printed in blue. Also included are explanatory notes that will help clarify the meaning of important ideas presented in the Constitution.

A burst of fireworks celebrating the 200-year anniversary of the Constitution highlights Independence Hall in Philadelphia.

Preamble

We the People of the United States, in Order to form a more perfect Union, establish Justice, insure domestic Tranquility, provide for the common defence, promote the general Welfare, and secure the Blessings of Liberty to ourselves and our Posterity, do ordain and establish this Constitution for the United States of America.

Article I

Section 1

All legislative Powers herein granted shall be vested in a Congress of the United States, which shall consist of a Senate and House of Representatives.

Section 2

[1.] The House of Representatives shall be composed of Members chosen every second Year by the People of the several States, and the Electors in each State shall have the Qualifications requisite for Electors of the most numerous Branch of the State Legislature.

[2.] No person shall be a Representative who shall not have attained to the Age of twenty five Years, and been seven Years a Citizen of the United States, and who shall not, when elected, be an Inhabitant of that State in which he shall be chosen.

[3.] Representatives and direct Taxes shall be apportioned among the several States which may be included within this Union, according to their respective Numbers, which shall be determined by adding to the whole Number of free Persons, including those bound to Service for a Term of Years, and excluding Indians not taxed, three fifths of all other Persons. The actual Enumeration shall be made within three Years after the first Meeting of the Congress of the United States, and within every subsequent Term of ten Years, in such Manner as they shall by Law direct. The Number of Representatives shall not exceed one for every thirty Thousand, but each State shall have at Least one Representative; and until such enumeration shall be made, the State of New Hampshire shall be entitled to chuse three; Massachusetts eight, Rhode-Island and Providence Plantations one, Connecticut five, New-York six, New Jersey four, Pennsylvania eight, Delaware one, Maryland six, Virginia ten, North Carolina five, South Carolina five, and Georgia three.

[4.] When vacancies happen in the Representation from any State, the Executive Authority thereof shall issue Writs of Election to fill such Vacancies.

[5.] The House of Representatives shall chuse their Speaker and other Officers; and shall have the sole Power of Impeachment.

The Preamble introduces the Constitution and sets forth the general purposes for which the government was established. The Preamble also declares that the power of the government comes from the people.

The printed text of the document shows the spelling and punctuation of the parchment original.

Article I. The Legislative Branch

The Constitution contains seven divisions called articles. Each article covers a general topic. For example, Articles I, II, and III create the three branches of the national government—the legislative, executive, and judicial branches. Most of the articles are divided into sections.

Section 1. Congress

Lawmaking The power to make laws is given to a Congress made up of two chambers to represent different interests: the Senate to represent the states and the House to be more responsive to the people's will.

Section 2. House of Representatives

Division of Representatives Among the States The number of representatives from each state is based on the size of the state's population. Each state is entitled to at least one representative. The Constitution states that each state may specify who can vote, but the Fifteenth, Nineteenth, Twenty-fourth, and Twenty-sixth Amendments have established guidelines that all states must follow regarding the right to vote. *What are the qualifications for members of the House of Representatives?*

Vocabulary

preamble: *introduction*
constitution: *principles and laws of a nation*
enumeration: *census or population count*
impeachment: *bringing charges against an official*

Section 3. The Senate
Voting Procedure Originally, senators were chosen by the legislators of their own states. The Seventeenth Amendment changed this, so that senators are now elected by their state's people. There are 100 senators, 2 from each state.

What Might Have Been
Electing Senators South Carolina delegate Charles Pinckney suggested during the Convention that the members of the Senate come from four equally proportioned districts within the United States and that the legislature elect the executive every seven years.

Section 3. The Senate
Trial of Impeachments One of Congress's powers is the power to impeach—to accuse government officials of wrongdoing, put them on trial, and, if necessary, remove them from office. The House decides if the offense is impeachable. The Senate acts as a jury, and when the president is impeached, the Chief Justice of the United States serves as the judge. A two-thirds vote of the members present is needed to convict impeached officials. *What punishment can the Senate give if an impeached official is convicted?*

Vocabulary
president pro tempore: *presiding officer of Senate who serves when the vice president is absent*
quorum: *minimum number of members that must be present to conduct sessions*

Section 3
[1.] The Senate of the United States shall be composed of two Senators from each State, chosen by the Legislature thereof, for six Years; and each Senator shall have one Vote.

[2.] Immediately after they shall be assembled in Consequence of the first Election, they shall be divided as equally as may be into three Classes. The Seats of the Senators of the first Class shall be vacated at the Expiration of the second Year, of the second Class at the Expiration of the fourth Year, and of the third Class at the Expiration of the sixth Year, so that one third may be chosen every second Year; and if Vacancies happen by Resignation, or otherwise, during the Recess of the Legislature of any State, the Executive thereof may make temporary Appointments until the next Meeting of the Legislature, which shall then fill such Vacancies.

[3.] No Person shall be a Senator who shall not have attained to the Age of thirty Years, and been nine Years a Citizen of the United States, and who shall not, when elected, be an Inhabitant of that State for which he shall be chosen.

[4.] The Vice President of the United States shall be President of the Senate, but shall have no Vote, unless they be equally divided.

[5.] The Senate shall chuse their other Officers, and also a President pro tempore, in the Absence of the Vice-President, or when he shall exercise the Office of the President of the United States.

[6.] The Senate shall have the sole Power to try all Impeachments. When sitting for that Purpose, they shall be on Oath or Affirmation. When the President of the United States is tried, the Chief Justice shall preside: And no Person shall be convicted without the Concurrence of two thirds of the Members present.

[7.] Judgment in Cases of Impeachment shall not extend further than to removal from Office, and disqualification to hold and enjoy any Office of honor, Trust or Profit under the United States: but the Party convicted shall nevertheless be liable and subject to Indictment, Trial, Judgment and Punishment, according to Law.

Section 4
[1.] The Times, Places and Manner of holding Elections for Senators and Representatives, shall be prescribed in each State by the Legislature thereof; but the Congress may at any time by Law make or alter such Regulations, except as to the Places of chusing Senators.

[2.] The Congress shall assemble at least once in every Year, and such Meeting shall be on the first Monday in December, unless they shall by Law appoint a different Day.

Section 5
[1.] Each House shall be the Judge of the Elections, Returns and Qualifications of its own Members, and a Majority of each shall constitute a Quorum to do

Business; but a smaller Number may adjourn from day to day, and may be authorized to compel the Attendance of absent Members, in such Manner, and under such Penalties as each House may provide.

[2.] Each House may determine the Rules of its Proceedings, punish its Members for disorderly Behaviour, and, with the Concurrence of two thirds, expel a Member.

[3.] Each House shall keep a Journal of its Proceedings, and from time to time publish the same, excepting such Parts as may in their Judgment require Secrecy; and the Yeas and Nays of the Members of either House on any question shall, at the Desire of one fifth of those Present, be entered on the Journal.

[4.] Neither House, during the Session of Congress, shall, without the Consent of the other, adjourn for more than three days, nor to any other Place than that in which the two Houses shall be sitting.

Section 6

[1.] The Senators and Representatives shall receive a Compensation for their Services, to be ascertained by Law, and paid out of the Treasury of the United States. They shall in all Cases, except Treason, Felony and Breach of the Peace, be privileged from Arrest during their Attendance at the Session of their respective Houses, and in going to and returning from the same; and for any Speech or Debate in either House, they shall not be questioned in any other Place.

[2.] No Senator or Representative shall, during the Time for which he was elected, be appointed to any civil Office under the Authority of the United States, which shall have been created, or the Emoluments whereof shall have been encreased during such time; and no Person holding any Office under the United States, shall be a Member of either House during his Continuance in Office.

Section 7

[1.] All Bills for raising Revenue shall originate in the House of Representatives; but the Senate may propose or concur with Amendments as on other Bills.

[2.] Every Bill which shall have passed the House of Representatives and the Senate, shall, before it become a Law, be presented to the President of the United States; If he approve he shall sign it, but if not he shall return it, with his Objections to that House in which it shall have originated, who shall enter the Objections at large on their Journal, and proceed to reconsider it. If after such Reconsideration two thirds of that House shall agree to pass the Bill, it shall be sent, together with the Objections, to the other House, by which it shall likewise be reconsidered, and if approved by two thirds of that House, it shall become a Law. But in all such Cases the Votes of both Houses shall be determined by yeas and Nays, and the Names of the Persons voting for and against the Bill shall be entered on the Journal of each House respectively. If any Bill shall not be returned by the President within ten Days (Sundays excepted) after it

Vocabulary

adjourn: *to suspend a session*
concurrence: *agreement*
emoluments: *salaries*
revenue: *income raised by government*
bill: *draft of a proposed law*

Section 6. Privileges and Restrictions

Pay and Privileges To strengthen the federal government, the Founders set congressional salaries to be paid by the United States Treasury rather than by members' respective states. Originally, members were paid $6 per day. In 2002, all members of Congress received a base salary of $150,000.

Section 7. Passing Laws

Revenue Bill All tax laws must originate in the House of Representatives. This ensures that the branch of Congress that is elected by the people every two years has the major role in determining taxes.

Section 7. Passing Laws

How Bills Become Laws A bill may become a law only by passing both houses of Congress and by being signed by the president. The president can check Congress by rejecting—vetoing—its legislation. *How can Congress override the president's veto?*

shall have been presented to him, the Same shall be a Law, in like Manner as if he had signed it, unless the Congress by their Adjournment prevent its Return, in which Case it shall not be a Law.

[3.] Every Order, Resolution, or Vote to which the Concurrence of the Senate and House of Representatives may be necessary (except on a question of Adjournment) shall be presented to the President of the United States; and before the Same shall take Effect, shall be approved by him, or being disapproved by him, shall be repassed by two thirds of the Senate and House of Representatives, according to the Rules and Limitations prescribed in the Case of a Bill.

Section 8

[1.] The Congress shall have the Power to lay and collect Taxes, Duties, Imposts and Excises, to pay the Debts and provide for the common Defence and general Welfare of the United States; but all Duties, Imposts and Excises shall be uniform throughout the United States;

[2.] To borrow Money on the credit of the United States;

[3.] To regulate Commerce with foreign Nations, and among the several States, and with the Indian Tribes;

[4.] To establish an uniform Rule of Naturalization, and uniform Laws on the subject of Bankruptcies throughout the United States;

[5.] To coin Money, regulate the Value thereof, and of foreign Coin, and fix the Standard of Weights and Measures;

[6.] To provide for the Punishment of counterfeiting the Securities and current Coin of the United States;

[7.] To establish Post Offices and post Roads;

[8.] To promote the Progress of Science and useful Arts, by securing for limited Times to Authors and Inventors the exclusive Right to their respective Writings and Discoveries;

[9.] To constitute Tribunals inferior to the supreme Court;

[10.] To define and punish Piracies and Felonies committed on the high Seas, and Offences against the Law of Nations;

[11.] To declare War, grant Letters of Marque and Reprisal, and make Rules concerning Captures on Land and Water;

[12.] To raise and support Armies, but no Appropriation of Money to that Use shall be for a longer Term than two Years;

[13.] To provide and maintain a Navy;

[14.] To make Rules for the Government and Regulation of the land and naval Forces;

[15.] To provide for calling forth the Militia to execute the Laws of the Union, suppress Insurrections and repel Invasions;

[16.] To provide for organizing, arming, and disciplining, the Militia, and for governing such Part of them as may be employed in the Service of the United States, reserving to the States respectively, the Appointment of the Officers, and the Authority of training the Militia according to the discipline prescribed by Congress;

Section 8.
Powers Granted to Congress

Expressed Powers Expressed powers are those powers directly stated in the Constitution. Most of the expressed powers of Congress are itemized in Article I, Section 8. These powers are also called enumerated powers because they are numbered 1 to 18. *Which clause gives Congress the power to declare war?*

Though Congress has many specific powers, the people have the right of protest.

Vocabulary

resolution: *legislature's formal expression of opinion*

naturalization: *procedure by which a citizen of a foreign nation becomes a citizen of the United States.*

[17.] To exercise exclusive Legislation in all Cases whatsoever, over such District (not exceeding ten Miles square) as may, by Cession of particular States, and the Acceptance of Congress, become the Seat of Government of the United States, and to exercise like Authority over all Places purchased by the Consent of the Legislature of the State in which the Same shall be, for the Erection of Forts, Magazines, Arsenals, dock-Yards, and other needful Buildings; And

[18.] To make all Laws which shall be necessary and proper for carrying into Execution the foregoing Powers, and all other Powers vested by this Constitution in the Government of the United States, or in any Department or Officer thereof.

Section 9

[1.] The Migration or Importation of such Persons as any of the States now existing shall think proper to admit, shall not be prohibited by the Congress prior to the Year one thousand eight hundred and eight, but a Tax or duty may be imposed on such Importation, not exceeding ten dollars for each Person.

[2.] The Privilege of the Writ of Habeas Corpus shall not be suspended, unless when in Cases of Rebellion or Invasion the public Safety may require it.

[3.] No Bill of Attainder or ex post facto Law shall be passed.

[4.] No Capitation, or other direct, Tax shall be laid, unless in Proportion to the Census or Enumeration herein before directed to be taken.

[5.] No Tax or Duty shall be laid on Articles exported from any State.

[6.] No Preference shall be given by any Regulation of Commerce or Revenue to the Ports of one State over those of another: nor shall Vessels bound to, or from, one State, be obliged to enter, clear, or pay Duties in another.

[7.] No Money shall be drawn from the Treasury, but in Consequence of Appropriations made by Law; and a regular Statement and Account of the Receipts and Expenditures of all public Money shall be published from time to time.

[8.] No Title of Nobility shall be granted by the United States: And no Person holding any Office of Profit or Trust under them, shall, without the Consent of the Congress, accept of any present, Emolument, Office, or Title, of any kind whatever, from any King, Prince, or foreign State.

Section 10

[1.] No State shall enter into any Treaty, Alliance, or Confederation; grant Letters of Marque and Reprisal; coin Money; emit Bills of Credit; make any Thing but gold and silver Coin a Tender in Payment of Debts; pass any Bill of Attainder, ex post facto Law, or Law impairing the Obligation of Contracts, or grant any Title of Nobility.

[2.] No State shall, without the Consent of the Congress, lay any Imposts or Duties on Imports or Exports, except

Section 8.
Powers Granted to Congress

Elastic Clause The final enumerated power is often called the "elastic clause." This clause gives Congress the right to make all laws "necessary and proper" to carry out the powers expressed in the other clauses of Article I. It is called the elastic clause because it lets Congress "stretch" its powers to meet situations the Founders could not have anticipated.

What does the phrase "necessary and proper" in the elastic clause mean? It was a subject of dispute from the beginning. The issue was whether a strict or a broad interpretation of the Constitution should be applied. The dispute was first addressed in 1819, in the case of *McCulloch v. Maryland,* when the Supreme Court ruled in favor of a broad interpretation. The Court stated that the elastic clause allowed Congress to use its powers in any way that was not specifically prohibited by the Constitution.

Section 9. Powers Denied to the Federal Government

Original Rights A writ of habeas corpus issued by a judge requires a law official to bring a prisoner to court and show cause for holding the prisoner. A bill of attainder is a bill that punishes a person without a jury trial. An "ex post facto" law is one that makes an act a crime after the act has been committed. *What does the Constitution say about bills of attainder?*

Section 10.
Powers Denied to the States

Limitations on Powers Section 10 lists limits on the states. These restrictions were designed, in part, to prevent an overlapping in functions and authority with the federal government.

Article II. The Executive Branch

Article II creates an executive branch to carry out laws passed by Congress. Article II lists the powers and duties of the president, describes qualifications for office and procedures for electing the president, and provides for a vice president.

What Might Have Been

Term of Office Alexander Hamilton also provided his own governmental outline at the Constitutional Convention. Some of its most distinctive elements were that both the executive and the members of the Senate were "elected to serve during good behaviour," meaning there was no specified limit on their time in office.

Section 1.
President and Vice President

Former Method of Election In the election of 1800, the top two candidates received the same number of electoral votes, making it necessary for the House of Representatives to decide the election. To eliminate this problem, the Twelfth Amendment, added in 1804, changed the method of electing the president stated in Article II, Section 3. The Twelfth Amendment requires that the electors cast separate ballots for president and vice president.

what may be absolutely necessary for executing it's inspection Laws: and the net Produce of all Duties and Imposts, laid by any State on Imports and Exports, shall be for the Use of the Treasury of the United States; and all such Laws shall be subject to the Revision and Controul of the Congress.

[3.] No State shall, without the Consent of Congress, lay any Duty of Tonnage, keep Troops, or Ships of War in time of Peace, enter into any Agreement or Compact with another State, or with a foreign Power, or engage in War, unless actually invaded, or in such imminent Danger as will not admit of delay.

Article II

Section 1

[1.] The executive Power shall be vested in a President of the United States of America. He shall hold his Office during the Term of four Years, and, together with the Vice-President, chosen for the same Term, be elected, as follows

[2.] Each State shall appoint, in such Manner as the Legislature thereof may direct, a Number of Electors, equal to the whole Number of Senators and Representatives to which the State may be entitled in the Congress: but no Senator or Representative, or Person holding an Office of Trust or Profit under the United States, shall be appointed an Elector.

[3.] The Electors shall meet in their respective States, and vote by Ballot for two Persons, of whom one at least shall not be an Inhabitant of the same State with themselves. And they shall make a List of all the Persons voted for, and of the Number of Votes for each; which List they shall sign and certify, and transmit sealed to the Seat of the Government of the United States, directed to the President of the Senate. The President of the Senate shall, in the Presence of the Senate and House of Representatives, open all the Certificates, and the Votes shall then be counted. The Person having the greatest Number of Votes shall be the President, if such Number be a Majority of the whole Number of Electors appointed; and if there be more than one who have such Majority, and have an equal Number of Votes, then the House of Representatives shall immediately chuse by Ballot one of them for President; and if no person have a Majority, then from the five highest on the List the said House shall in like Manner chuse the president. But in chusing the President, the Votes shall be taken by States, the Representation from each State having one Vote; A quorum for this Purpose shall consist of a Member or Members from two thirds of the States, and a Majority of all the States shall be necessary to a Choice. In every Case, after the Choice of the President, the Person having the greatest Number of Votes of the Electors shall be the Vice-President. But if there should remain two or more who have equal Votes, the Senate shall chuse from them by Ballot the Vice President.

[4.] The Congress may determine the Time of chusing the Electors, and the Day on which they shall give their Votes; which Day shall be the same throughout the United States.

[5.] No Person except a natural born Citizen, or a Citizen of the United States, at the time of the Adoption of this Constitution, shall be eligible to the Office of President; neither shall any Person be eligible to that Office who shall not have attained to the Age of thirty five Years, and been fourteen Years a Resident within the United States.

[6.] In Case of the Removal of the President from Office, or of his Death, Resignation, or Inability to discharge the Powers and Duties of the said Office, the Same shall devolve on the Vice-President, and the Congress may by Law provide for the Case of Removal, Death, Resignation or Inability, both of the President and Vice-President, declaring what Officer shall then act as President, and such Officer shall act accordingly, until the Disability be removed, or a President shall be elected.

[7.] The President shall, at stated Times, receive for his Services, a Compensation, which shall neither be encreased nor diminished during the Period for which he shall have been elected, and he shall not receive within that Period any other Emolument from the United States, or any of them.

[8.] Before he enter on the Execution of his Office, he shall take the following Oath or Affirmation—"I do solemnly swear (or affirm) that I will faithfully execute the Office of President of the United States, and will to the best of my Ability, preserve, protect and defend the Constitution of the United States."

Section 2

[1.] The President shall be Commander in Chief of the Army and Navy of the United States, and of the Militia of the several States, when called into the actual Service of the United States; he may require the Opinion, in writing, of the principal Officer in each of the executive Departments, upon any Subject relating to the Duties of their respective Offices, and he shall have Power to grant Reprieves and Pardons for Offences against the United States, except in Cases of Impeachment.

[2.] He shall have Power, by and with the Advice and Consent of the Senate, to make Treaties, provided two thirds of the Senators present concur; and he shall nominate, and by and with the Advice and Consent of the Senate, shall appoint Ambassadors, other public Ministers and Consuls, Judges of the supreme Court, and all other Officers of the United States, whose Appointments are not herein otherwise provided for, and which shall be established by Law: but the Congress may by Law vest the Appointment of such inferior Officers, as they think proper, in the President alone, in the Courts of Law, or in the Heads of Departments.

Section 1.
President and Vice President
Qualifications The president must be a citizen of the United States by birth, at least 35 years of age, and a resident of the United States for 14 years.

What Might Have Been
Qualifications At the Constitutional Convention, the New Jersey Amendments, sponsored by the smaller states, raised the possibility of making the executive a committee of people rather than a single individual. Also, executives were not allowed to run for a second term of office under this plan.

Section 1.
President and Vice President
Vacancies If the president dies, resigns, is removed from office by impeachment, or is unable to carry out the duties of the office, the vice president becomes president.

Section 1.
President and Vice President
Salary Originally, the president's salary was $25,000 per year. The president's current salary is $400,000 plus a $50,000 nontaxable expense account per year. The president also receives living accommodations in two residences—the White House and Camp David.

Section 2.
Powers of the President
Cabinet Mention of "the principal officer in each of the executive departments" is the only suggestion of the president's cabinet to be found in the Constitution. The cabinet is an advisory body, and its power depends on the president. Section 2, Clause 1 also makes the president the head of the armed forces. This established the principle of civilian control of the military.

Section 2.
Powers of the President
Treaties With Foreign Nations The president is responsible for the conduct of relations with foreign countries. *What role does the Senate have in approving treaties?*

Section 3.
Duties of the President

Executive Orders An important presidential power is the ability to issue executive orders. An executive order is a rule or command the president issues that has the force of law. Only Congress can make laws under the Constitution, but executive orders are considered part of the president's duty to "take care that the laws be faithfully executed." This power is often used during emergencies. During the Civil War, for example, President Lincoln issued an order suspending writs of habeas corpus. Over time the scope of executive orders has expanded, increasing the president's power. Decisions by federal agencies and departments are also considered to be executive orders.

Section 4. Impeachment

Reasons for Removal From Office This section states the reasons for which the president and vice president may be impeached and removed from office. Only Andrew Johnson and Bill Clinton have been impeached by the House. Richard Nixon resigned before the House could vote on possible impeachment.

Article III. The Judicial Branch

The term *judicial* refers to courts. The Constitution set up only the Supreme Court but provided for the establishment of other federal courts. The judiciary of the United States has two different systems of courts. One system consists of the federal courts, whose powers derive from the Constitution and federal laws. The other includes the courts of each of the 50 states, whose powers derive from state constitutions and laws.

Section 2. Jurisdiction

General Jurisdiction Federal courts deal mostly with "statute law," or laws passed by Congress, treaties, and cases involving the Constitution itself.

Vocabulary

original jurisdiction: *authority to be the first court to hear a case*

appellate jurisdiction: *authority to hear cases that have been appealed from lower courts*

Section 2. Jurisdiction

The Supreme Court A court with "original jurisdiction" has the authority to be the first court to hear a case. The Supreme Court generally has "appellate jurisdiction" in that it mostly hears cases appealed from lower courts.

[3.] The President shall have Power to fill up all Vacancies that may happen during the Recess of the Senate, by granting Commissions which shall expire at the End of their next Session.

Section 3

He shall from time to time give to the Congress Information of the State of the Union, and recommend to their Consideration such Measures as he shall judge necessary and expedient; he may, on extraordinary Occasions, convene both Houses, or either of them, and in Case of Disagreement between them, with Respect to the Time of Adjournment, he may adjourn them to such Time as he shall think proper; he shall receive Ambassadors and other public Ministers; he shall take Care that the Laws be faithfully executed, and shall Commission all the Officers of the United States.

Section 4

The President, Vice-President and all civil Officers of the United States, shall be removed from Office on Impeachment for, and Conviction of, Treason, Bribery, or other high Crimes and Misdemeanors.

Article III
Section 1

The judicial Power of the United States, shall be vested in one supreme Court, and in such inferior Courts as the Congress may from time to time ordain and establish. The Judges, both of the supreme and inferior Courts, shall hold their Offices during good Behaviour, and shall, at stated Times, receive for their Services, a Compensation, which shall not be diminished during their Continuance in Office.

Section 2

[1.] The judicial Power shall extend to all Cases, in Law and Equity, arising under this Constitution, the Laws of the United States, and Treaties made, or which shall be made, under their Authority;—to all Cases affecting Ambassadors, other public Ministers and Consuls;—to all Cases of admiralty and maritime Jurisdiction;—to Controversies to which the United States shall be a Party;—to Controversies between two or more States; —between a State and Citizens of another State;— between Citizens of different States,—between Citizens of the same State claiming Lands under Grants of different States, and between a State, or the Citizens thereof, and foreign States, Citizens or Subjects.

[2.] In all Cases affecting Ambassadors, other public Ministers and Consuls, and those in which a State shall be Party, the supreme Court shall have original Jurisdiction. In all the other Cases before mentioned, the supreme Court shall have appellate Jurisdiction, both as to Law and Fact, with such Exceptions, and under such Regulations as the Congress shall make.

[3.] The Trial of all Crimes, except in Cases of Impeachment, shall be by Jury; and such Trial shall be held in the State where the said Crimes shall have been committed; but when not committed within any State, the Trial shall be at such Place or Places as the Congress may by Law have directed.

Section 3

[1.] Treason against the United States, shall consist only in levying War against them, or in adhering to their Enemies, giving them Aid and Comfort. No Person shall be convicted of Treason unless on the Testimony of two Witnesses to the same overt Act, or on Confession in open Court.

[2.] The Congress shall have Power to declare the Punishment of Treason, but no Attainder of Treason shall work Corruption of Blood, or Forfeiture except during the Life of the Person attainted.

Article IV

Section 1

Full Faith and Credit shall be given in each State to the public Acts, Records, and judicial Proceedings of every other State. And the Congress may by general Laws prescribe the Manner in which such Acts, Records and Proceedings shall be proved, and the Effect thereof.

Section 2

[1.] The Citizens of each State shall be entitled to all Privileges and Immunities of Citizens in the several States.

[2.] A Person charged in any State with Treason, Felony, or other Crime, who shall flee from Justice, and be found in another State, shall on Demand of the executive Authority of the State from which he fled, be delivered up, to be removed to the State having Jurisdiction of the Crime.

[3.] No Person held to Service of Labour in one State, under the Laws thereof, escaping into another, shall, in Consequence of any Law or Regulation therein, be discharged from such Service or Labour, but shall be delivered up on Claim of the Party to whom such Service or Labour may be due.

Section 3

[1.] New States may be admitted by the Congress into this Union; but no new State shall be formed or erected within the Jurisdiction of any other State; nor any State be formed by the Junction of two or more States, or Parts of States, without the Consent of the Legislatures of the States concerned as well as of the Congress.

[2.] The Congress shall have Power to dispose of and make all needful Rules and Regulations respecting the Territory or other Property belonging to the United States; and nothing in this Constitution shall be so construed as to Prejudice any Claims of the United States, or of any particular State.

Section 2. Jurisdiction
Jury Trial Except in cases of impeachment, anyone accused of a crime has the right to a trial by jury. The trial must be held in the state where the crime was committed. Jury trial guarantees were strengthened in the Sixth, Seventh, Eighth, and Ninth Amendments.

Article IV. Relations Among the States

Article IV explains the relationship of the states to one another and to the national government. This article requires each state to give citizens of other states the same rights as its own citizens, addresses the admission of new states, and guarantees that the national government will protect the states.

Section 1. Official Acts
Recognition by States This provision ensures that each state recognizes the laws, court decisions, and records of all other states. For example, a marriage license issued by one state must be accepted by all states.

Vocabulary

treason: *violation of the allegiance owed by a person to his or her own country, for example, by aiding an enemy*

Section 3.
New States and Territories
New States Congress has the power to admit new states. It also determines the basic guidelines for applying for statehood. Two states, Maine and West Virginia, were created within the boundaries of another state. In the case of West Virginia, President Lincoln recognized the West Virginia government as the legal government of Virginia during the Civil War. This allowed West Virginia to secede from Virginia without obtaining approval from the Virginia legislature.

Vocabulary

amendment: *a change to the Constitution*
ratification: *process by which an amendment is approved*

Article V. The Amendment Process

Article V explains how the Constitution can be amended, or changed. All of the 27 amendments were proposed by a two-thirds vote of both houses of Congress. Only the Twenty-first Amendment was ratified by constitutional conventions of the states. All other amendments have been ratified by state legislatures. *What is an amendment?*

Article VI. Constitutional Supremacy

Article VI contains the "supremacy clause." This clause establishes that the Constitution, laws passed by Congress, and treaties of the United States "shall be the supreme Law of the Land." The "supremacy clause" recognizes the Constitution and federal laws as supreme when in conflict with those of the states.

Article VII. Ratification

Article VII addresses ratification and states that, unlike the Articles of Confederation, which required approval of all thirteen states for adoption, the Constitution would take effect after it was ratified by nine states.

Section 4

The United States shall guarantee to every State in this Union a Republican Form of Government, and shall protect each of them against Invasion; and on Application of the Legislature, or of the Executive (when the Legislature cannot be convened) against domestic Violence.

Article V

The Congress, whenever two thirds of both Houses shall deem it necessary, shall propose Amendments to this Constitution, or, on the Application of the Legislatures of two thirds of the several States, shall call a Convention for proposing Amendments, which, in either Case, shall be valid to all Intents and Purposes, as Part of this Constitution, when ratified by the Legislatures of three fourths of the several States, or by Conventions in three fourths thereof, as the one or the other Mode of Ratification may be proposed by the Congress; Provided that no Amendment which may be made prior to the Year One thousand eight hundred and eight shall in any Manner affect the first and fourth Clauses in the Ninth Section of the first Article; and that no State, without its Consent, shall be deprived of its equal Suffrage in the Senate.

Article VI

[1.] All Debts contracted and Engagements entered into, before the Adoption of this Constitution, shall be as valid against the United States under this Constitution, as under the Confederation.
[2.] This Constitution, and the Laws of the United States which shall be made in Pursuance thereof; and all Treaties made, or which shall be made, under the Authority of the United States, shall be the supreme Law of the Land; and the Judges in every State shall be bound thereby, any Thing in the Constitution or Laws of any State to the Contrary notwithstanding.
[3.] The Senators and Representatives before mentioned, and the Members of the several State Legislatures, and all executive and judicial Officers, both of the United States and of the several States, shall be bound by Oath or Affirmation, to support this Constitution; but no religious Test shall ever be required as a Qualification to any Office or public Trust under the United States.

Article VII

The Ratification of the Conventions of nine States, shall be sufficient for the Establishment of this Constitution between the States so ratifying the same.

Done in Convention by the Unanimous Consent of the States present the Seventeenth Day of September in the Year of our Lord one thousand seven hundred and Eighty seven and of the Independence of the United States of America the Twelfth. In witness whereof We have hereunto subscribed our Names,

Signers

George Washington,
President and Deputy
from Virginia

New Hampshire
John Langdon
Nicholas Gilman

Massachusetts
Nathaniel Gorham
Rufus King

Connecticut
William Samuel Johnson
Roger Sherman

New York
Alexander Hamilton

New Jersey
William Livingston
David Brearley
William Paterson
Jonathan Dayton

Pennsylvania
Benjamin Franklin
Thomas Mifflin
Robert Morris
George Clymer
Thomas FitzSimons
Jared Ingersoll
James Wilson
Gouverneur Morris

Delaware
George Read
Gunning Bedford, Jr.
John Dickinson
Richard Bassett
Jacob Broom

Maryland
James McHenry
Daniel of St. Thomas
Jenifer
Daniel Carroll

Virginia
John Blair
James Madison, Jr.

North Carolina
William Blount
Richard Dobbs Spaight
Hugh Williamson

South Carolina
John Rutledge
Charles Cotesworth
Pinckney
Charles Pinckney
Pierce Butler

Georgia
William Few
Abraham Baldwin

Attest:
William Jackson,
Secretary

Amendment I

Congress shall make no law respecting an establishment of religion, or prohibiting the free exercise thereof; or abridging the freedom of speech, or of the press; or the right of the people peaceably to assemble, and to petition the Government for a redress of grievances.

Amendment II

A well regulated Militia, being necessary to the security of a free State, the right of the people to keep and bear Arms, shall not be infringed.

Amendment III

No Soldier shall, in time of peace be quartered in any house, without the consent of the Owner, nor in time of war, but in a manner to be prescribed by law.

Amendment IV

The right of the people to be secure in their persons, houses, papers, and effects, against unreasonable searches and seizures, shall not be violated, and no Warrants shall issue, but upon probable cause, supported by Oath or affirmation, and particularly describing the place to be searched, and the persons or things to be seized.

Amendment V

No person shall be held to answer for a capital, or otherwise infamous crime, unless on a presentment or indictment of a Grand Jury, except in cases arising in the

The Amendments

This part of the Constitution consists of changes and additions. The Constitution has been amended 27 times throughout the nation's history.

The Bill of Rights

The first 10 amendments are known as the Bill of Rights (1791). These amendments limit the powers of the federal government. The First Amendment protects the civil liberties of individuals in the United States. The amendment freedoms are not absolute, however. They are limited by the rights of other individuals. *What freedoms does the First Amendment protect?*

Vocabulary

quarter: *to provide living accommodations*
warrant: *document that gives police particular rights or powers*
probable cause: *police must have a reasonable basis to believe a person is linked to a crime*

Amendment 5

Rights of the Accused This amendment contains important protections for people accused of crimes. One of the protections is that government may not deprive any person of life, liberty, or property without due process of law. This means that the government must follow proper constitutional procedures in trials and in other actions it takes against individuals. *According to Amendment V, what is the function of a grand jury?*

Amendment 6

Right to Speedy and Fair Trial A basic protection is the right to a speedy, public trial. The jury must hear witnesses and evidence on both sides before deciding the guilt or innocence of a person charged with a crime. This amendment also provides that legal counsel must be provided to a defendant. In 1963, in *Gideon* v. *Wainwright,* the Supreme Court ruled that if a defendant cannot afford a lawyer, the government must provide one to defend him or her. *Why is the right to a "speedy" trial important?*

Vocabulary

common law: *law established by previous court decisions*

bail: *money that an accused person provides to the court as a guarantee that he or she will be present for a trial*

Amendment 9

Powers Reserved to the People This amendment prevents government from claiming that the only rights people have are those listed in the Bill of Rights.

Amendment 10

Powers Reserved to the States This amendment protects the states and the people from the federal government. It establishes that powers not given to the national government and not denied to the states by the Constitution belong to the states or to the people. These are checks on the "necessary and proper" power of the federal government, which is provided for in Article I, Section 8, Clause 18.

Amendment 11

Suits Against States The Eleventh Amendment (1795) provides that a lawsuit brought by a citizen of the United States or a foreign nation against a state must be tried in a state court, not in a federal court. The Supreme Court had ruled in *Chisholm* v. *Georgia* (1793) that a federal court could try a lawsuit brought by citizens of South Carolina against a citizen of Georgia.

land or naval forces, or in the Militia, when in actual service in time of War or public danger; nor shall any person be subject for the same offence to be twice put in jeopardy of life or limb; nor shall be compelled in any criminal case to be a witness against himself, nor be deprived of life, liberty, or property, without due process of law; nor shall private property be taken for public use without just compensation.

Amendment VI

In all criminal prosecutions, the accused shall enjoy the right to a speedy and public trial, by an impartial jury of the State and district wherein the crime shall have been committed, which district shall have been previously ascertained by law, and to be informed of the nature and cause of the accusation; to be confronted with the witnesses against him; to have compulsory process for obtaining Witnesses in his favor, and to have the assistance of counsel for his defence.

Amendment VII

In Suits at common law, where the value in controversy shall exceed twenty dollars, the right of trial by jury shall be preserved, and no fact tried by a jury, shall be otherwise reexamined in any Court of the United States, than according to the rules of common law.

Amendment VIII

Excessive bail shall not be required, nor excessive fines imposed, nor cruel and unusual punishments inflicted.

Amendment IX

The enumeration in the Constitution, of certain rights, shall not be construed to deny or disparage others retained by the people.

Amendment X

The powers not delegated to the United States by the Constitution, nor prohibited by it to the States, are reserved to the States respectively, or to the people.

Amendment XI

The Judicial power of the United States shall not be construed to extend to any suit in law or equity, commenced or prosecuted against one of the United States by Citizens of another State, or by Citizens or Subjects of any Foreign State.

Amendment XII

The electors shall meet in their respective states and vote by ballot for President and Vice-President, one of whom, at least, shall not be an inhabitant of the same state with themselves; they shall name in their ballots the person voted for as President, and in distinct ballots the person voted for as Vice-President, and they shall make distinct lists of all persons voted for as President, and of all persons voted for as Vice-President, and of the number of votes for each, which lists they shall sign and certify, and transmit sealed to the seat of the government of the United States, directed to the President of the Senate;—The President of the Senate shall, in the presence of the Senate and House of Representatives, open all the certificates and the votes shall then be counted;—The person having the greatest number of votes for President, shall be the President, if such number be a majority of the whole number of Electors appointed; and if no person have such majority, then from the persons having the highest numbers not exceeding three on the list of those voted for as President, the House of Representatives shall choose immediately, by ballot, the President. But in choosing the President, the votes shall be taken by states, the representation from each state having one vote; a quorum for this purpose shall consist of a member or members from two-thirds of the states, and a majority of all the states shall be necessary to a choice. And if the House of Representatives shall not choose a President whenever the right of choice shall devolve upon them, before the fourth day of March next following, then the Vice-President shall act as President, as in the case of the death or other constitutional disability of the President. The person having the greatest number of votes as Vice-President, shall be the Vice-President, if such number be a majority of the whole number of Electors appointed, and if no person have a majority, then from the two highest numbers on the list, the Senate shall choose the Vice-President; a quorum for the purpose shall consist of two-thirds of the whole number of Senators, and a majority of the whole number shall be necessary to a choice. But no person constitutionally ineligible to the office of President shall be eligible to that of Vice-President of the United States.

Amendment 12
Election of President and Vice President The Twelfth Amendment (1804) corrects a problem that had arisen in the method of electing the president and vice president, which is described in Article II, Section 1, Clause 3. This amendment provides for the Electoral College to use separate ballots in voting for president and vice president. *If no candidate receives a majority of the electoral votes, who elects the president?*

Vocabulary

majority: *more than half*

Amendment XIII

Section 1

Neither slavery nor involuntary servitude, except as a punishment for crime whereof the party shall have been duly convicted, shall exist within the United States, or any place subject to their jurisdiction.

Amendment 13
Abolition of Slavery Amendments Thirteen (1865), Fourteen, and Fifteen often are called the Civil War amendments because they grew out of that conflict. The Thirteenth Amendment outlaws slavery.

Section 2
Congress shall have power to enforce this article by appropriate legislation.

Amendment 14
Rights of Citizens The Fourteenth Amendment (1868) originally was intended to protect the legal rights of the freed slaves. Its interpretation has been extended to protect the rights of citizenship in general by prohibiting a state from depriving any person of life, liberty, or property without "due process of law." In addition, it states that all citizens have the right to equal protection of the laws in all states.

Amendment 14. Section 2
Representation in Congress This section reduced the number of members a state had in the House of Representatives if it denied its citizens the right to vote. Later civil rights laws and the Twenty-fourth Amendment guaranteed the vote to African Americans.

Vocabulary
abridge: *to reduce*
insurrection: *rebellion against the government*

Amendment 14. Section 3
Penalty for Engaging in Insurrection The leaders of the Confederacy were barred from state or federal offices unless Congress agreed to remove this ban. By the end of Reconstruction, all but a few Confederate leaders were allowed to return to public service.

Amendment 14. Section 4
Public Debt The public debt acquired by the federal government during the Civil War was valid and could not be questioned by the South. However, the debts of the Confederacy were declared to be illegal. *Could former slaveholders collect payment for the loss of their slaves?*

Amendment XIV

Section 1
All persons born or naturalized in the United States, and subject to the jurisdiction thereof, are citizens of the United States and of the State wherein they reside. No State shall make or enforce any law which shall abridge the privileges or immunities of citizens of the United States; nor shall any State deprive any person of life, liberty, or property, without due process of law; nor deny to any person within its jurisdiction the equal protection of the laws.

Section 2
Representatives shall be apportioned among the several States according to their respective numbers, counting the whole number of persons in each State, excluding Indians not taxed. But when the right to vote at any election for the choice of electors for President and Vice-President of the United States, Representatives in Congress, the Executive and Judicial officers of a State, or the members of the Legislature thereof, is denied to any of the male inhabitants of such State, being twenty-one years of age, and citizens of the United States, or in any way abridged, except for participation in rebellion, or other crime, the basis of representation therein shall be reduced in the proportion which the number of such male citizens shall bear to the whole number of male citizens twenty-one years of age in such State.

Section 3
No person shall be a Senator or Representative in Congress, or elector of President and Vice-President, or hold any office, civil or military, under the United States, or under any State, who, having previously taken an oath, as a member of Congress, or as an officer of the United States, or as a member of any State legislature, or as an executive or judicial officer of any State, to support the Constitution of the United States, shall have engaged in insurrection or rebellion against the same, or given aid or comfort to the enemies thereof. But Congress may by a vote of two-thirds of each House, remove such disability.

Section 4
The validity of the public debt of the United States, authorized by law, including debts incurred for payment of pensions and bounties for service, in suppressing insurrection or rebellion, shall not be questioned. But neither the United States nor any State shall assume or pay any debt or obligation incurred in aid of insurrection or rebellion against the United States, or any

claim for the loss or emancipation of any slave; but all such debts, obligations and claims shall be held illegal and void.

Section 5
The Congress shall have power to enforce, by appropriate legislation, the provisions of this article.

Amendment XV

Section 1
The right of citizens of the United States to vote shall not be denied or abridged by the United States or by any State on account of race, color, or previous condition of servitude.

Section 2
The Congress shall have power to enforce this article by appropriate legislation.

Amendment XVI

The Congress shall have power to lay and collect taxes on incomes, from whatever source derived, without apportionment among the several States and without regard to any census or enumeration.

Amendment XVII

Section 1
The Senate of the United States shall be composed of two Senators from each State, elected by the people thereof, for six years; and each Senator shall have one vote. The electors in each State shall have the qualifications requisite for electors of the most numerous branch of the State legislatures.

Section 2
When vacancies happen in the representation of any State in the Senate, the executive authority of such State shall issue writs of election to fill such vacancies: *Provided*, That the legislature of any State may empower the executive thereof to make temporary appointments until the people fill the vacancies by election as the legislature may direct.

Section 3
This amendment shall not be so construed as to affect the election or term of any Senator chosen before it becomes valid as part of the Constitution.

Amendment XVIII

Section 1
After one year from ratification of this article, the manufacture, sale, or transportation of intoxicating liquors within, the importation thereof into, or the

Amendment 15
Voting Rights The Fifteenth Amendment (1870) prohibits the government from denying a person's right to vote on the basis of race. Despite the law, many states denied African Americans the right to vote by such means as poll taxes, literacy tests, and white primaries.

Amendment 16
Income Tax The origins of the Sixteenth Amendment (1913) date back to 1895, when the Supreme Court declared a federal income tax unconstitutional. To overturn this decision, this amendment authorizes an income tax that is levied on a direct basis.

Amendment 17
Direct Election of Senators The Seventeenth Amendment (1913) states that the people, instead of state legislatures, elect United States senators. *How many years are in a Senate term?*

Vocabulary
apportionment: *distribution of seats in House based on population*
vacancy: *an office or position that is unfilled or unoccupied*

Amendment 18
Prohibition The Eighteenth Amendment (1919) prohibited the production, sale, or transportation of alcoholic beverages in the United States. Prohibition proved to be difficult to enforce. This amendment was later repealed by the Twenty-first Amendment.

exportation thereof from the United States and all territory subject to the jurisdiction thereof for beverage purposes is hereby prohibited.

Section 2

The Congress and the several States shall have concurrent power to enforce this article by appropriate legislation.

Section 3

This article shall be inoperative unless it shall have been ratified as an amendment to the Constitution by the legislatures of the several States, as provided in the Constitution, within seven years from the date of the submission hereof to the States by the Congress.

Amendment XIX

Section 1

The right of citizens of the United States to vote shall not be denied or abridged by the United States or by any state on account of sex.

Section 2

Congress shall have power by appropriate legislation to enforce the provisions of this article.

Amendment XX

Section 1

The terms of the President and Vice President shall end at noon on the 20th day of January, and the terms of the Senators and Representatives at noon on the 3rd day of January, of the years in which such terms would have ended if this article had not been ratified; and the terms of their successors shall then begin.

Section 2

The Congress shall assemble at least once in every year, and such meeting shall begin at noon on the 3rd day of January, unless they shall by law appoint a different day.

Section 3

If, at the time fixed for the beginning of the term of the President, the President elect shall have died, the Vice President elect shall become President. If a President shall not have been chosen before the time fixed for the beginning of his term, or if the President elect shall have failed to qualify, then the Vice President elect shall act as President until a President shall have qualified; and the Congress may by law provide for the case wherein neither a President elect nor a Vice President elect shall have qualified, declaring who shall then act as President, or the manner in which one who is to act shall be selected, and such person shall act accordingly until a President or Vice President shall have qualified.

Amendment 19

Woman Suffrage The Nineteenth Amendment (1920) guaranteed women the right to vote. By then women had already won the right to vote in many state elections, but the amendment made their right to vote in all state and national elections constitutional.

Amendment 20

"Lame Duck" The Twentieth Amendment (1933) sets new dates for Congress to begin its term and for the inauguration of the president and vice president. Under the original Constitution, elected officials who retired or who had been defeated remained in office for several months. For the outgoing president, this period ran from November until March. Such outgoing officials, referred to as "lame ducks," could accomplish little. *What date was fixed as Inauguration Day?*

Amendment 20. Section 3

Succession of President and Vice President This section provides that if the president-elect dies before taking office, the vice president-elect becomes president.

Vocabulary

president-elect: *individual who is elected president but has not yet begun serving his or her term*

Section 4

The Congress may by law provide for the case of the death of any of the persons from whom the House of Representatives may choose a President whenever the right of choice shall have devolved upon them, and for the case of the death of any of the persons from whom the Senate may choose a Vice President whenever the right of choice shall have devolved upon them.

Section 5

Sections 1 and 2 shall take effect on the 15th day of October following the ratification of this article.

Section 6

This article shall be inoperative unless it shall have been ratified as an amendment to the Constitution by the legislatures of three-fourths of the several States within seven years from the date of its submission.

Amendment XXI

Section 1

The eighteenth article of amendment to the Constitution of the United States is hereby repealed.

Section 2

The transportation or importation into any State, Territory, or possession of the United States for delivery or use therein of intoxicating liquors, in violation of the laws thereof, is hereby prohibited.

Section 3

This article shall be inoperative unless it shall have been ratified as an amendment to the Constitution by conventions in the several States, as provided in the Constitution, within seven years from the date of the submission hereof to the States by the Congress.

Amendment XXII

Section 1

No person shall be elected to the office of the President more than twice, and no person who had held the office of President, or acted as President, for more than two years of a term to which some other person was elected President shall be elected to the office of the President more than once. But this Article shall not apply to any person holding the office of President when this Article was proposed by the Congress, and shall not prevent any person who may be holding the office of President, or acting as President, during the term within which this Article becomes operative from holding the office of President or acting as President during the remainder of such term.

Amendment 21

Repeal of Prohibition The Twenty-first Amendment (1933) repeals the Eighteenth Amendment. It is the only amendment ever passed to overturn an earlier amendment. It is also the only amendment ratified by special state conventions instead of state legislatures.

Amendment 22

Presidential Term Limit The Twenty-second Amendment (1951) limits presidents to a maximum of two elected terms. The amendment wrote into the Constitution a custom started by George Washington. It was passed largely as a reaction to Franklin D. Roosevelt's election to four terms between 1933 and 1945. It also provides that anyone who succeeds to the presidency and serves for more than two years of the term may not be elected more than one more time.

Vocabulary

District of Columbia: *site of nation's capital occupying an area between Maryland and Virginia*

Amendment 23

D.C. Electors The Twenty-third Amendment (1961) allows citizens living in Washington, D.C., to vote for president and vice president, a right previously denied residents of the nation's capital. The District of Columbia now has three presidential electors, the number to which it would be entitled if it were a state.

Amendment 24

Abolition of the Poll Tax The Twenty-fourth Amendment (1964) prohibits poll taxes in federal elections. Prior to the passage of this amendment, some states had used such taxes to keep low-income African Americans from voting. In 1966 the Supreme Court banned poll taxes in state elections as well.

Amendment 25

Presidential Disability and Succession The Twenty-fifth Amendment (1967) established a process for the vice president to take over leadership of the nation when a president is disabled. It also set procedures for filling a vacancy in the office of vice president.

This amendment was used in 1973, when Vice President Spiro Agnew resigned from office after being charged with accepting bribes. President Richard Nixon then appointed Gerald R. Ford as vice president in accordance with the provisions of the Twenty-fifth Amendment. A year later, President Nixon resigned during the Watergate scandal, and Ford became president. President Ford then had to fill the vice presidency, which he had left vacant upon assuming the presidency. He named Nelson A. Rockefeller as vice president. Thus individuals who had not been elected held both the presidency and the vice presidency. *Who does the president inform if he or she cannot carry out the duties of the office?*

Section 2

This article shall be inoperative unless it shall have been ratified as an amendment to the Constitution by the legislatures of three-fourths of the several States within seven years from the date of its submission to the States by the Congress.

Amendment XXIII

Section 1

The District constituting the seat of Government of the United States shall appoint in such manner as the Congress may direct:

A number of electors of President and Vice President equal to the whole number of Senators and Representatives in Congress to which the District would be entitled if it were a State, but in no event more than the least populous State; they shall be in addition to those appointed by the States, but they shall be considered, for the purposes of the election of President and Vice President, to be electors appointed by a State; and they shall meet in the District and perform such duties as provided by the twelfth article of amendment.

Section 2

The Congress shall have power to enforce this article by appropriate legislation.

Amendment XXIV

Section 1

The right of citizens of the United States to vote in any primary or other election for President or Vice President, for electors for President or Vice President, or for Senator or Representative in Congress, shall not be denied or abridged by the United States or any State by reason of failure to pay any poll tax or other tax.

Section 2

The Congress shall have power to enforce this article by appropriate legislation.

Amendment XXV

Section 1

In case of the removal of the President from office or his death or resignation, the Vice President shall become President.

Section 2

Whenever there is a vacancy in the office of the Vice President, the President shall nominate a Vice President who shall take the office upon confirmation by a majority vote of both Houses of Congress.

Section 3

Whenever the President transmits to the President pro tempore of the Senate and the Speaker of the House of

Representatives his written declaration that he is unable to discharge the powers and duties of his office, and until he transmits to them a written declaration to the contrary, such powers and duties shall be discharged by the Vice President as Acting President.

Section 4

Whenever the Vice President and a majority of either the principal officers of the executive departments or of such other body as Congress may by law provide, transmit to the President pro tempore of the Senate and the Speaker of the House of Representatives their written declaration that the President is unable to discharge the powers and duties of his office, the Vice President shall immediately assume the power and duties of the office of Acting President.

Thereafter, when the President transmits to the President pro tempore of the Senate and the Speaker of the House of Representatives his written declaration that no inability exists, he shall resume the powers and duties of his office unless the Vice President and a majority of either the principal officers of the executive department or of such other body as Congress may by law provide, transmit within four days to the President pro tempore of the Senate and the Speaker of the House of Representatives their written declaration that the President is unable to discharge the powers and duties of his office. Thereupon Congress shall decide the issue, assembling within forty-eight hours for that purpose if not in session. If the Congress, within twenty-one days after receipt of the latter written declaration, or, if Congress is not in session, within twenty-one days after Congress is required to assemble, determines by two-thirds vote of both Houses that the President is unable to discharge the powers and duties of his office, the Vice President shall continue to discharge the same as Acting President; otherwise, the President shall resume the power and duties of his office.

Amendment XXVI

Section 1

The right of citizens of the United States, who are eighteen years of age or older, to vote shall not be denied or abridged by the United States or by any State on account of age.

Section 2

The Congress shall have power to enforce this article by appropriate legislation.

Amendment XXVII

No law, varying the compensation for the services of Senators and Representatives, shall take effect, until an election of representatives shall have intervened.

Amendment 26
Voting Age of 18 The Twenty-sixth Amendment (1971) lowered the voting age in both federal and state elections to 18.

Amendment 27
Congressional Salary Restraints The Twenty-seventh Amendment (1992) makes congressional pay raises effective during the term following their passage. James Madison offered the amendment in 1789, but it was never adopted. In 1982 Gregory Watson, then a student at the University of Texas, discovered the forgotten amendment while doing research for a school paper. Watson made the amendment's passage his crusade.

6 Federalists and Republicans *1789–1816*

Why It Matters

In the first government under the Constitution, important new institutions included the cabinet, a system of federal courts, and a national bank. Political parties gradually developed from the different views of citizens in the Northeast, West, and South. The new government faced special challenges in foreign affairs, including the War of 1812 with Great Britain.

The Impact Today

During this period, fundamental policies of American government came into being.
- *Politicians set important precedents for the national government and for relations between the federal and state governments. For example, the idea of a presidential cabinet originated with George Washington and has been followed by every president since that time*
- *President Washington's caution against foreign involvement powerfully influenced American foreign policy.*

*The American Vision **Video*** *The Chapter 6 video, "The Battle of New Orleans," focuses on this important event of the War of 1812.*

1789
- Washington elected president

Washington 1789–1797

1794
- Jay's Treaty signed

1798
- Alien and Sedition Acts introduced

J. Adams 1797–1801

1803
- Louisiana Purchase doubles size of the nation

1804
- Lewis and Clark begin to explore and map Louisiana Territory

Jefferson 1801–1809

United States
PRESIDENTS

1790

1797

1804

World

1793
- Louis XVI guillotined during French Revolution

1794
- Polish rebellion suppressed by Russians

1800
- Beethoven's Symphony no. 1 written

1805
- British navy wins Battle of Trafalgar

Painter and President by J.L.G. Ferris

1807
- Embargo Act blocks American trade with Britain and France

Madison 1809–1817

1811
- Battle of Tippecanoe fought against Tecumseh and his confederacy

1812
- United States declares war on Britain

1814
- Hartford Convention meets
- Treaty of Ghent signed

1811   *1818*

1808
- Source of the Ganges River discovered

1812
- Napoleon's invasion and retreat from Russia

1816
- Argentina declares independence

HISTORY Online

Chapter Overview
Visit the *American Vision* Web site at tav.glencoe.com and click on **Chapter Overviews—Chapter 6** to preview chapter information.

Washington and Congress

Guide to Reading

Main Idea

With the adoption of the new Constitution, Americans and their leaders had to establish a central government to deal effectively with the challenges facing the new nation.

Key Terms and Names

cabinet, Tariff of 1789, bond, speculator, enumerated powers, implied powers, Bank of the United States, Whiskey Rebellion, agrarianism

Reading Strategy

Organizing As you read about how the leaders of the United States established a central government, complete a graphic organizer similar to the one below by indicating the tasks completed by Congress.

```
            ( )        ( )
               \      /
        ( )----Tasks of----( )
               Congress
               /      \
            ( )        ( )
```

Reading Objectives

- **Explain** Alexander Hamilton's economic initiatives.
- **Discuss** the growing tensions between the nation's political parties.

Section Theme

Culture and Traditions George Washington helped define the office of the American presidency.

Preview of Events

◆1789   ◆1791   ◆1793   ◆1795

1789
George Washington elected president

1791
First Bank of the United States chartered

1792
Washington reelected president

1794
Whiskey Rebellion quelled in western Pennsylvania

★ An American Story ★

On April 6, 1789, the ballots of the presidential electors were officially counted in the new United States Senate. As expected, George Washington became the first president of the United States under the new Constitution. Americans everywhere greeted the news with great joy, but Washington remained unexcited. Calling his election "the event which I have long dreaded," Washington described his feelings as "not unlike those of a culprit who is going to the place of his execution."

Although Washington had high hopes for the new Constitution, he did not know if it would work as intended. "I am . . . [bringing] the voice of the people and a good name of my own on this voyage; but what returns will be made of them, Heaven alone can foretell." Despite his doubts and frustrations with the "ten thousand embarrassments, perplexities and troubles of the presidency," the new president retained his faith in the American people. He explained that "nothing but harmony, honesty, industry and frugality are necessary to make us a great and happy people. . . . We are surrounded by the blessings of nature."

—adapted from *Washington: The Indispensable Man*

Creating a New Government

The Philadelphia Convention had given the nation a new Constitution. Washington's task, and the task facing the newly elected Congress, was to take the words of the Constitution and turn them into an effective government for the United States.

Institutions of Power

One of the first tasks of the new government was to provide the president with a bureaucracy to handle different responsibilities. In 1789 Congress created the Department of State, the Department of the Treasury, the Department of War, and the Office of the Attorney General.

To manage these departments, Washington wanted individuals who were "disposed to measure matters on a Continental Scale" instead of thinking only of their own states. He chose Thomas Jefferson as secretary of state, Alexander Hamilton for the Treasury Department, and General Henry Knox as secretary of war. For attorney general, Washington selected Edmund Randolph, the former governor of Virginia. Washington regularly met with these men to ask for their advice. The department heads came to be known as the cabinet, a group of advisers to the president.

Congress also organized the judicial branch. In the Judiciary Act of 1789, Congress established 13 district courts, 3 courts of appeal, and the Supreme Court. With the Senate's consent, Washington chose the federal judges, including John Jay as the first chief justice of the United States.

The Bill of Rights

One of the most important acts of Congress was the introduction of the Bill of Rights. During the campaign to ratify the Constitution, the Federalists had promised to add such a bill. James Madison, one of the leaders in Congress, made the passage of a Bill of Rights top priority. He hoped it would demonstrate the good faith of federal leaders and build support for the new government.

In drafting the Bill of Rights, Madison relied heavily on the Virginia Declaration of Rights that George Mason had prepared in 1776 and the Virginia Statute for Religious Freedom that Thomas Jefferson had written in 1786. In late September 1789, after many debates, Congress agreed on 12 constitutional amendments. They were then sent to the states for ratification, but only 10 were approved. These 10 went into effect in 1791. They are generally referred to as the Bill of Rights, although only the first 8 protect the rights of individuals against actions of the federal government. The Ninth Amendment states that the people have other rights not listed. The Tenth Amendment states that any powers not specifically given to the federal government are reserved for the states.

Reading Check **Identifying** What executive departments did Congress establish?

Financing the Government

By the end of 1789, the new federal government was up and running. The government's most pressing need now was a source of revenue. Without money, the government could not operate. James Madison and Alexander Hamilton responded to this need with different plans for financing the government.

The Tariff of 1789

James Madison suggested that the federal government raise most of its money by taxing imports from other countries. After much discussion, Congress passed the **Tariff of 1789.** This law required importers to pay a percentage of the value of their cargo when they landed it in the United States. Shippers also had to pay tonnage—a tax based on how much their ships carried.

The tariffs and tonnage rates angered many Southern planters. High tonnage rates meant they would be charged higher rates to ship their rice and

History *Through Art*

First Cabinet Depicted with the president (far right) are, from left, Henry Knox, Thomas Jefferson, Edmund Randolph, and Alexander Hamilton. What departments did these four cabinet members head?

tobacco to Europe. The new duty meant higher prices for the many goods they imported. Many Southerners began to suspect that the new federal government was opposed to their region's interests.

ECONOMICS

Hamilton's Financial Program Hamilton supported the Tariff of 1789, but he believed the government also needed the ability to borrow money. In 1790, he asked Congress to accept the debts of the Continental Congress at their full value. To fund the Revolutionary War, the Confederation Congress had issued bonds—paper notes promising to repay money after a certain length of time with interest. By 1789, the United States owed roughly $40 million to American citizens and another $11.7 million to France, Spain, and the Netherlands. Few believed the bonds would be repaid in full, and they had fallen in value to as little as 10 cents on the dollar.

History *Through Art*

First Capital Washington took his oath of office on the balcony of Federal Hall in New York City, the nation's first capital. This Amos Doolittle engraving was made from a famous painting. Why is Federal Hall identified as "the seat of Congress"?

Hamilton believed that by accepting these debts at their full value, the wealthy creditors, bankers, and merchants who owned the bonds would have a stake in the federal government's success and enough confidence in its financial stability to loan it money in the future. Hamilton had described the importance of debt several years earlier:

> ❝A national debt, if it is not excessive, will be to us a national blessing; it will be a powerful cement of our new union. It will also create a necessity for keeping up taxation . . . which without being oppressive, will be a spur to industry. . . .❞
>
> —quoted in *America, A Narrative History*

Opposition to Hamilton's Plan Led by Madison, critics argued that Hamilton's plan was unfair to the original purchasers of the bonds, many of whom were farmers and Revolutionary War veterans and their widows. These people, fearing they would never be paid, had sold their bonds at a discount to speculators—people willing to take a risk in hopes of a future financial gain. Madison was outraged that speculators who had paid as little as $10 for a $100 bond would now receive full value.

Madison and other Southerners were also upset because Northerners owned most of the bonds, while much of the tax money that would be used to pay off the bonds would come from the South. Madison also worried that creditors would eventually dominate American society and endanger liberty.

The congressional debate over Hamilton's proposals raged for months. Finally, in July 1790, Hamilton, Madison, and Jefferson struck a deal. Madison and Jefferson would use their influence to convince Southerners in Congress to vote for Hamilton's plan. In return, the capital of the United States would be moved from New York to a section of land along the Potomac River to be called the District of Columbia. Southerners believed that having the capital in the South would help to offset the strength of the Northern states in Congress.

The Bank of the United States With his system of public credit finally in place, Hamilton asked Congress to create a national bank. He argued that the government needed the bank to manage its debts and interest payments. The bank would also issue bank notes—paper money. The notes also would provide a national currency that would promote trade, encourage investment, and stimulate economic growth.

Southerners opposed the plan. They pointed out that Northern merchants would own most of the bank's stock. Madison argued that Congress could not establish a bank because it was not among the federal government's *enumerated powers,* or powers specifically mentioned in the Constitution.

Despite Madison's objections, Congress passed the bank bill. Washington realized that his decision to sign the bill or to veto it would set an important precedent. Attorney General Randolph and Secretary of State Jefferson argued that the Constitution did not give the federal government the power to create a bank. Hamilton disagreed, pointing out that Article I, Section 8, of the Constitution gave the federal government the power "to make all laws which shall be necessary and proper" to execute its responsibilities. The "necessary and proper" clause created *implied powers*— powers not explicitly listed in the Constitution but necessary for the government to do its job.

A national bank, Hamilton argued, was necessary to collect taxes, regulate trade, and provide for the common defense. Jefferson agreed that implied powers existed, but he believed "necessary and proper" meant absolutely necessary, not simply convenient. After studying Hamilton's response, Washington agreed to sign the bill. In 1791 the **Bank of the United States** was established for a 20-year period.

The Whiskey Rebellion Hamilton believed the federal government also had to establish its right to impose direct taxes on the people. In 1791, at Hamilton's urging, Congress imposed a tax on the manufacture of whiskey. The new tax enraged Western farmers. In the Western regions of the United States, where bank notes and coins were not available in large quantities, whiskey was used as a medium of exchange. Because the Spanish had closed the Mississippi, distilling whiskey was also the easiest way for Western farmers to move their grain to Eastern markets.

Although complaints against the whiskey tax began in 1791, it was not until the summer of

Commander in chief reviewing the troops

1794 that a rebellion erupted. In western Pennsylvania, farmers terrorized tax collectors, stopped court proceedings, robbed the mail, and destroyed the whiskey-making stills of those who paid the tax.

Hamilton wanted to establish firmly the authority of the federal government. He urged President Washington to put down the rebellion. In August 1794 Washington sent nearly 15,000 troops to crush the **Whiskey Rebellion.** The huge army caused the rebels to disperse without a fight. The federal government's willingness to use troops against its own citizens, however, worried many people.

☑ **Reading Check** **Explaining** Why did Madison object to Hamilton's plan for a national bank?

The Rise of Political Parties

During Washington's first term in office, the debate over Hamilton's financial program split Congress into factions. These factions became the nation's first political parties. Hamilton's supporters called themselves **Federalists.** Hamilton's opponents, led by Madison and Jefferson, took the name Democratic-Republicans, although most people at the time referred to them as **Republicans.** In the 1800s, the party became known as the Democrats. Today's Republican Party is a different party.

Student Web Activity Visit the *American Vision* Web site at tav.glencoe.com and click on *Student Web Activities— Chapter 6* for an activity on early political parties.

Competing National Visions

Hamilton and the Federalists	Jefferson and the Democratic-Republicans
National government supreme	State governments supreme
Ruling power given to wealthy, educated	Ruling power given to *all* landowners
Government should promote manufacturing	Government should promote agriculture
Loose interpretation of the Constitution	Strict interpretation of the Constitution
Protective tariffs protect domestic industries	Protective tariffs burden farmers

Chart Skills

1. **Interpreting Charts** Which party favored tariffs, and why?
2. **Drawing Conclusions** Which party do you think distrusted national government more?

Hamilton and the Federalists Hamilton favored a strong national government. He believed that democracy was dangerous to liberty and stated that "the people are turbulent and changing; they seldom judge or determine right." This distrust led him to favor putting government into the hands of the "rich, well born, and able."

Hamilton also believed that manufacturing and trade were the basis of national wealth and power. He favored policies that would support these areas of the economy. Supporters of the Federalist Party often included artisans, merchants, manufacturers, and bankers. The party also attracted urban workers and Eastern farmers who benefited from trade.

Jefferson and the Republicans Although James Madison led the opposition to Hamilton's program in Congress, Thomas Jefferson emerged as the leader of the Democratic-Republicans. Jefferson believed that the strength of the United States was its independent farmers. His ideas are sometimes referred to as agrarianism. Jefferson argued that owning land enabled people to be independent. As long as most people owned their own land, they would fight to preserve the Republic.

Jefferson feared that too much of an emphasis on commerce would lead to a society divided between the rich who owned everything and the poor who worked for wages. He also believed that the wealthy would corrupt the government and threaten the rights and liberties of ordinary people. In general, Democratic-Republicans supported agriculture over commerce and trade. They also expressed concern that Hamilton's policies tended to favor the North. Over time, the Democratic-Republicans became the party that stood for the rights of states against the power of the federal government.

The development of America's first two political parties divided the country regionally. The rural South and West tended to support the Republicans, while the more urban Northeast tended to support the Federalists. Although these parties emerged during the dispute over Hamilton's programs, events in Europe would deepen the divisions between them and create new crises for the young Republic.

✓ **Reading Check** **Classifying** What were the nation's first two political parties, and what issues did they favor?

SECTION 1 ASSESSMENT

Checking for Understanding

1. **Define:** cabinet, bond, speculator, enumerated powers, implied powers, agrarianism.
2. **Identify:** Tariff of 1789, Bank of the United States, Whiskey Rebellion.
3. **Describe** the intended purpose of the national bank.

Reviewing Themes

4. **Culture and Traditions** What precedent did George Washington set as president of the United States?

Critical Thinking

5. **Synthesizing** Why did Hamilton think it was important to pay the national debt, the domestic debt, and the state debts?
6. **Categorizing** Use a graphic organizer similar to the one below to list the first political parties, who their supporters were, and what issues they supported.

Political Party	Supporters	Issues Supported

Analyzing Visuals

7. **Studying Art** Examine the painting on page 211 of President Washington's first cabinet. What was the function of this group, and who served as its first members?

Writing About History

8. **Expository Writing** Imagine you are James Madison. Write a speech explaining why you are against Alexander Hamilton's financial program.

Partisan Politics

Guide to Reading

Main Idea
The United States faced difficult foreign policy challenges during the presidencies of Washington and Adams.

Key Terms and Names
Jay's Treaty, most-favored nation, Pinckney's Treaty, Washington's Farewell Address, Quasi-War, Alien and Sedition Acts, alien, sedition, interposition, nullification

Reading Strategy
Categorizing As you read about the foreign policy challenges of the Washington and Adams presidencies, complete a graphic organizer similar to the one below by filling in the provisions of treaties made by the United States.

Treaty	Provisions
Jay's Treaty	
Pinckney's Treaty	
Convention of 1800	

Reading Objectives
- **Discuss** the rising tensions between Western settlers and Native Americans.
- **Explain** the importance of Washington's Farewell Address.

Section Theme
Civic Rights and Responsibilities Disagreements between political parties threatened citizens' rights.

Preview of Events

♦1795   ♦1797   ♦1799   ♦1801

1794
Jay's Treaty signed with Britain

1795
Pinckney's Treaty signed with Spain; Treaty of Greenville signed with 12 Native American nations

1798
Alien and Sedition Acts introduced

1801
House of Representatives chooses Jefferson to be president

★ An American Story ★

In 1797 Americans John Marshall, Charles Pinckney, and Elbridge Gerry went to Paris to hold talks with the French government about improving relations between the two countries. After weeks of waiting, three agents representing Charles Maurice de Talleyrand, the French minister of foreign affairs, approached the Americans. They asked for a bribe of $250,000 just to initiate talks, and they also sought an American loan of $12 million. In his journal, Marshall recounts an exchange between Pinckney and one of the agents (a "Mr. H."):

❝Mr. H. again returned to the subject of money. Said he Gentlemen you do not speak to the point— it is money—it is expected that you will offer money—Genl. Pinckney said we had spoken to that point very explicitly. . . . No said he, you have not. What is your answer? Genl. Pinckney replied it is no, no, not a sixpence.❞

When President John Adams informed Congress of the incident, he referred to the French agents as X, Y, and Z, inspiring newspapers to refer to the incident as the XYZ Affair. Newspaper writers turned Pinckney's response into the stirring Federalist slogan, "Millions for defense, but not one cent for tribute."

—adapted from *The Flavor of the Past*

Washington's Foreign Policy

Shortly after George Washington was inaugurated in 1789, the French Revolution began in Europe. At first, most Americans sympathized with the revolutionaries, who seemed to be fighting for the same rights Americans had won a few years earlier. By the

A Fiery Protest Antifederalists burned at the stake a figure representing John Jay after Jay's Treaty with England was signed in 1794. What parts of the treaty angered people such as those shown here?

On April 22, 1793, Washington issued a proclamation declaring the United States to be "friendly and impartial" toward both warring powers.

Jay's Treaty Despite Washington's declaration, the British navy began intercepting all neutral ships carrying goods to French ports, including hundreds of American ships. At the same time, reports appeared that the British, operating out of forts they still occupied on American territory, were inciting Native Americans to attack western settlers. These reports, combined with British seizures of American ships, pushed Congress to the brink of war in 1794.

Desperately hoping to avoid war, Washington sent John Jay to Britain to seek a solution. The British were busy fighting France. They did not want to fight the United States, but they also knew that the United States depended on trade with Britain. They agreed to sign **Jay's Treaty,** but they drove a hard bargain.

Jay was forced to agree that Britain had the right to seize cargoes bound for French ports. He also failed to get compensation for American merchants whose goods had been seized. The British did agree, however, to submit the issue to international arbitration—a hearing by neutral third countries. In return, the British gave the United States most-favored nation status. This meant that American merchants would not be discriminated against when they traded with Britain. Britain also allowed limited American trade with its Caribbean colonies.

When Jay's Treaty was sent to the Senate for ratification, the senators were shocked by its terms and tried to keep them secret. Although they eventually ratified the treaty, news of its terms leaked to the public. The Republicans immediately attacked the treaty, accusing the Federalists of being pro-British. Across much of the country, public meetings were held condemning the treaty. After prolonged deliberation, Washington agreed to implement the treaty. The decision prevented war with Great Britain and protected the fragile American economy.

spring of 1793, however, a new group of French radicals had seized control. They stripped aristocrats of their property and executed thousands of people, including the king and queen.

The radicals soon executed the French king and declared war on Britain. Since both Britain and France traded with the United States, Americans quickly found themselves embroiled in the European conflict.

The American Response Americans were divided over the French Revolution. Many Federalists, horrified by the violence and chaos, opposed it. Despite the bloodshed, many Republicans supported it, admiring the fight for liberty.

The war between Britain and France put Washington in a difficult position. The Treaty of 1778 with France required the United States to help defend France's colonies in the Caribbean. Fulfilling this agreement might mean war with Great Britain.

Pinckney's Treaty Jay's Treaty also helped the United States win concessions from Spain, which still controlled Florida and territory west of the Mississippi River. In 1795 Spain joined France in its struggle against Britain. The signing of Jay's Treaty raised fears in Spain that the British and Americans might now join forces to seize Spain's North American holdings. Spain quickly offered to negotiate all outstanding issues with the United States. Washington sent **Thomas Pinckney** from South Carolina to negotiate with Spain.

In 1795 the Spanish signed the Treaty of San Lorenzo—better known as **Pinckney's Treaty.** The treaty granted the United States the right to navigate the Mississippi and to deposit goods at the port of New Orleans. The treaty won broad acceptance, especially among western farmers who wanted to use the Mississippi to get crops to market.

> ✓ **Reading Check** **Summarizing** Why did President Washington choose neutrality in the war between Britain and France?

GEOGRAPHY
Westward Expansion

By 1790 the area between the Appalachian Mountains and the Mississippi River had become the most rapidly growing region in the United States. Drawn by abundant land, fertile soil, wide rivers, and a wide variety of fish and game, Americans flocked to the region. In less than a decade, Kentucky had grown from a few hundred settlers to over 70,000, and in 1792, it became a state. Four years later, Tennessee became a state as well. In the meantime, other settlers were moving steadily west from Pennsylvania and Virginia into the Northwest Territory. The rise in white settlement led to confrontations with Native Americans in the region.

In the Northwest Territory, a chief of the Miami people named **Little Turtle** had formed a confederacy of the Miami, Shawnee, Delaware, and other groups. The confederacy sought to defend its land against white settlement. In the fall of 1790, Little Turtle's warriors defeated American troops led by General Josiah Harmar. In November 1791, they ambushed another American force led by General Arthur St. Clair, killing nearly half his men.

After these disasters, Washington sent General Anthony Wayne to put down Native American resistance. In August 1794, a large force made up of Shawnee, Ottawa, Chippewa, and Potawatomi warriors, led by the Shawnee chief Blue Jacket, attacked Wayne's troops at the Battle of Fallen Timbers, near where Toledo, Ohio, is located today. This time the American troops inflicted heavy losses on the Native Americans.

Wayne's victory dealt a decisive blow to Native American resistance in the Northwest Territory. In August 1795, 12 Native American nations signed the Treaty of Greenville. (See map on page 235.) They agreed to give up part of what is today southern Ohio and Indiana in exchange for a yearly payment of $10,000 from the federal government. They also gave up land near where Chicago, Detroit, and Vincennes, Indiana, are located today. After the treaty signing, the flow of Americans into the region rapidly increased. By 1803 Ohio had enough settlers to become a state.

> ✓ **Reading Check** **Examining** Why did Little Turtle form a confederacy?

Washington Leaves Office

By the end of his second term in office, George Washington had grown exasperated by party politics and the attacks on his character. He decided to retire.

The Farewell Address Before leaving office, the president wrote a letter to the American people. Widely reprinted, **Washington's Farewell Address** warned Americans against sectionalism—to avoid

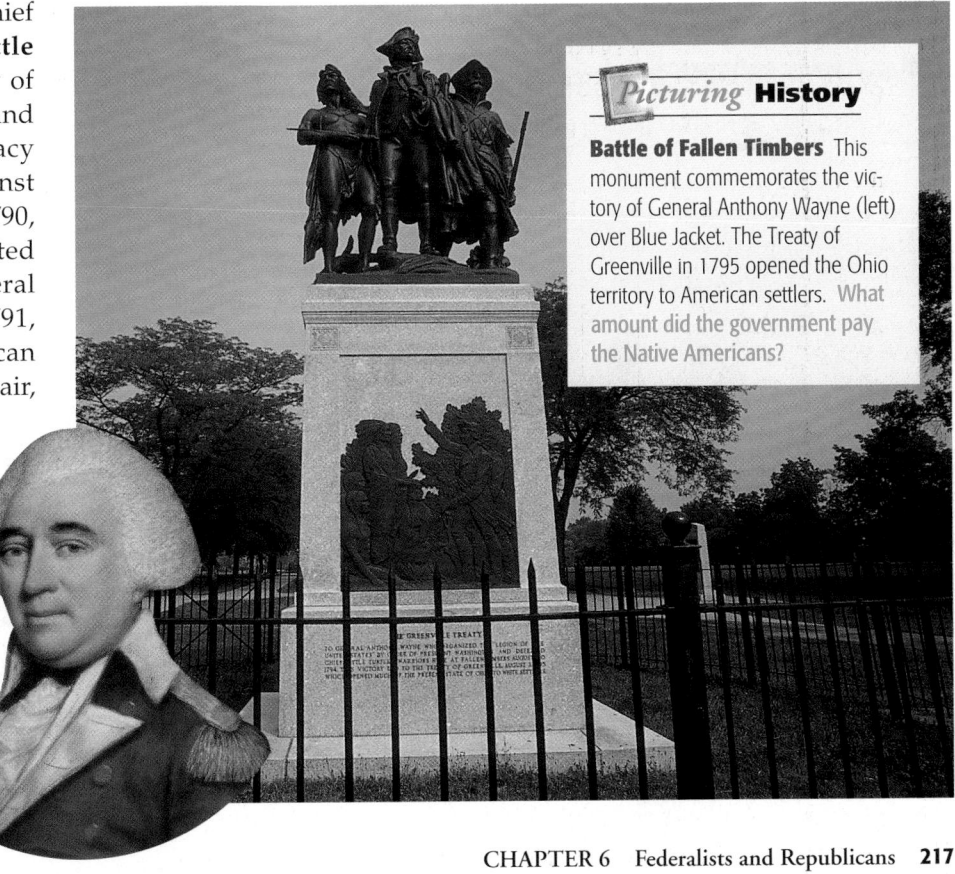

Picturing **History**

Battle of Fallen Timbers This monument commemorates the victory of General Anthony Wayne (left) over Blue Jacket. The Treaty of Greenville in 1795 opened the Ohio territory to American settlers. *What amount did the government pay the Native Americans?*

dividing the country into North against South or East against West. Washington also cautioned Americans about political parties:

> **❝** Let me now . . . warn you in the most solemn manner against the baneful effects of the spirit of party. . . . The disorders and miseries, which result, gradually incline the minds of men to seek security and repose in the absolute power of an individual. **❞**

Washington also warned against Americans becoming too attached to any foreign nation:

> **❝** The great rule of conduct for us, in regard to foreign nations is in extending our commercial relations to have with them as little *political* connection as possible. . . . 'Tis our true policy to steer clear of permanent alliances with any portion of the foreign world. **❞**
>
> —from Washington's Farewell Address

📖 *(See page 1068 for a longer excerpt from Washington's Farewell Address.)*

The Election of 1796 With Washington stepping down, the United States held its first openly contested election. The Federalists rallied around John Adams for president, while the Republicans nominated Thomas Jefferson. Anger over Jay's Treaty made the election close, but when the electoral votes were tallied, John Adams edged out Jefferson 71 to 68 and became the second president of the United States.

✓ **Reading Check** **Describing** What advice did Washington give about political parties and alliances?

The Quasi-War With France

President Adams faced troubled times at home and abroad. Enraged by Jay's Treaty, the French had begun stopping American ships and seizing their goods if they were going to Britain. France's actions led many Federalists to call for war against France. Although critical of the French, Adams, like Washington, was reluctant to involve the United States in a major war. Instead he sent Charles Pinckney, Elbridge Gerry, and John Marshall to negotiate with France. Americans called the French effort to get bribes before beginning negotiations the XYZ Affair (described on page 215).

Irate Americans, who had been angry with Britain a few years earlier, now called for war against France. Resolutions, mass meetings, and patriotic songs further aroused the public. In June 1798, Congress suspended trade with France and directed the navy to capture armed French ships. The two nations were soon fighting an undeclared war at sea that came to be known as the **Quasi-War.**

In the fall of 1798, France proposed new negotiations. In September 1800, the two countries signed the Convention of 1800. In this agreement, the United State gave up all claims against France for damages to American shipping. In return, France released the United States from the treaty of 1778. With the signing of the Convention of 1800, the Quasi-War came to an end.

✓ **Reading Check** **Explaining** What caused the Quasi-War?

Analyzing *Political Cartoons*

French Bribes Americans took a dim view of the French after the XYZ Affair. Here French leaders harass a woman who stands for the United States. On a hill in the distance, the British watch while other nations gossip over the affair. What nation was France at war with at this time?

The War Between the Parties

The Quasi-War also affected domestic politics in the United States. Many Federalists resented the harsh criticisms printed in Republican newspapers. They remembered the angry Republican crowds that had protested Jay's Treaty. Now, the Quasi-War had reversed the situation, and Federalists in Congress decided to strike back at the Republicans.

The Alien and Sedition Acts

At the height of public anger at France in 1798, the Federalists pushed four laws through Congress. These laws became known as the **Alien and Sedition Acts.**

The first three laws were aimed at aliens—people living in the country who were not citizens. The Federalists knew that many recent immigrants had come from France and Ireland. These immigrants were often anti-British and tended to vote for the Republican Party once they became citizens. The first law required immigrants to wait 14 years before becoming citizens, thus weakening Republican support. The next two laws gave the president the power to deport without trial any alien deemed dangerous to the United States.

The fourth law was aimed at preventing sedition, or incitement to rebellion. This law made it a federal crime to utter or print anything "false, scandalous, and malicious" against the federal government or any officer of the government. In short, the act deprived citizens of their right to criticize public officials. The government indicted 15 people under this act, including several Republican newspaper editors and politicians.

The Virginia and Kentucky Resolutions

In 1798 and 1799, the Republican-controlled legislatures of Kentucky and Virginia passed resolutions, secretly written by Jefferson and Madison, criticizing the Alien and Sedition Acts. Both resolutions argued that since the states had created the Constitution, they could declare federal laws unconstitutional.

The Virginia Resolutions introduced the theory of interposition. They argued that if the federal government did something unconstitutional, the state could interpose between the federal government and the people and stop the illegal action. The Kentucky Resolutions advanced the theory of nullification. According to this theory, if the federal government passed an unconstitutional law, the states had the right to nullify the law, or declare it invalid. Although these resolutions had little effect in 1800, states used these ideas in later decades to defend their regional interests.

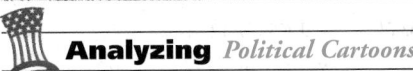

Analyzing *Political Cartoons*

War Between the Parties This cartoon reveals the emotions of American politics in the 1790s. Republican Matthew Lyon and Federalist Roger Griswold are shown fighting in the House of Representatives. How did Federalists respond to Republican attacks?

TURNING POINT

The Election of 1800

Although John Adams hoped to win reelection in 1800, he faced an uphill battle. The Alien and Sedition Acts had angered many people, as had a new tax the Federalists had introduced on houses, land, and enslaved Africans. The Republican nominees, Thomas Jefferson for president and Aaron Burr for vice president, campaigned against the new taxes and the national bank. They accused the Federalists of favoring monarchy and of discouraging political participation.

The election was closely contested and had an unexpected outcome, one that revealed a flaw in the system for selecting the president. The Constitution does not let citizens vote directly for the chief executive. Instead each state chooses electors—the same number as it has senators and representatives. This group, known as the Electoral College, then votes for the president.

The Constitution called for each elector in the Electoral College to vote for two people. The normal practice was for an elector to cast one vote for his party's presidential candidate and another for the vice presidential candidate. To avoid a tie between Jefferson and Burr, the Republicans had intended for one elector to refrain from voting for Burr, but the plan went awry. When the votes were counted, Jefferson and Burr each had 73. Since no candidate had a majority, the Federalist-controlled House of Representatives had to choose a president.

Many Federalists despised Jefferson and wanted to select Burr, but Alexander Hamilton preferred Jefferson. Hamilton urged his followers to support Jefferson, leading to a tie in the House of Representatives.

Presidential Election, 1800			
Candidate	Popular Vote	Electoral Vote	Political Party
Jefferson	Unknown	73	Democratic Republican
Adams	Unknown	65	Federalist
Burr	Unknown	73	Democratic Republican
Pinckney	Unknown	64	Federalist
Jay	Unknown	1	Federalist

N.H. 6
VT. 4
TERR. N.W. OF OHIO R.
MASS. 16
N.Y. 12
R.I. 4
PA. 8
CONN. 7
INDIANA TERR.
N.J. 9
VA. 21
DEL. 3
KY. 4
N.C. 4
MD. 5
TENN. 3
MD. 5
TERR. SOUTH OF OHIO R.
S.C. 8
GA. 4
MISS. TERR.

Geography *Skills*

1. **Interpreting Maps** Which states split their electoral votes between Jefferson and Adams?
2. **Applying Geography Skills** Where were the Federalists strong? What policies did they favor that would account for their strength there?

*According to the Constitution, each elector in the Electoral College voted for two people in a presidential election. The person receiving the most votes became president, and the person receiving the second-highest number of votes became vice president. Under this system a tie was possible, as happened in the case of the tie between Thomas Jefferson and Aaron Burr in 1800. The House of Representatives then elected Jefferson after 35 rounds of voting in which there was no clear winner. To prevent such confusion in the future, the Twelfth Amendment was added to the Constitution in 1804. The amendment stipulates that electoral votes for president and vice president are counted and listed separately.

Finally, in February 1801, Jefferson let Federalist James Bayard know that if elected, Jefferson would not fire all the Federalists in the government, nor dismantle Hamilton's financial system. These assurances convinced Bayard to cast a blank ballot, ensuring that Jefferson would receive more votes than Burr. Jefferson became the new president.

The election of 1800 was an important turning point in American history. At the time, the Federalists controlled the army, the presidency, and the Congress. They could have refused to step down and overthrown the Constitution. Instead, they respected the people's right to choose the president. The election of 1800 demonstrated that power in the United States could be peacefully transferred despite strong disagreements between the parties.

Reading Check **Analyzing** What was the purpose of the Alien and Sedition Acts?

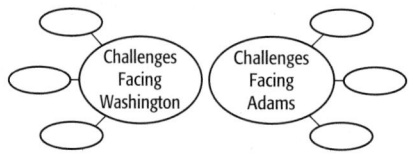

SECTION 2 ASSESSMENT

Checking for Understanding

1. **Define:** most-favored nation, alien, sedition, interposition, nullification.
2. **Identify:** Jay's Treaty, Pinckney's Treaty, Washington's Farewell Address, Quasi-War, Alien and Sedition Acts.

Reviewing Themes

3. **Civic Rights and Responsibilities** How did the Alien and Sedition Acts interfere with the lives of people living in the United States?

Critical Thinking

4. **Synthesizing** How did France and Great Britain test American neutrality?
5. **Organizing** Use a graphic organizer similar to the one below to list the foreign policy challenges that Washington and Adams faced during their presidencies.

Challenges Facing Washington
Challenges Facing Adams

Analyzing Visuals

6. **Analyzing Political Cartoons** Study the cartoon pictured on page 219. Why do you think the political situation of the 1790s led to fights among members of Congress?

Writing About History

7. **Expository Writing** Write an editorial that responds to George Washington's Farewell Address. Explain whether or not you think Washington was correct in warning Americans against political parties and alliances.

Guide to Reading

Main Idea

As president, Jefferson worked to limit the scope of the federal government, obtain the Louisiana Territory, and keep the United States out of European wars.

Key Terms and Names

John Marshall, judicial review, Louisiana Purchase, Meriwether Lewis, William Clark, Sacagawea, Zebulon Pike, impressment, embargo

Reading Strategy

Sequencing As you read about Thomas Jefferson's administration, complete a time line similar to the one below to record the major events of Jefferson's presidency.

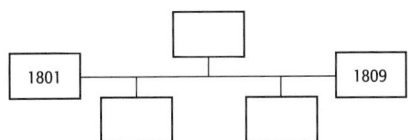

Reading Objectives

• **Evaluate** the changing role of the Supreme Court.
• **Discuss** the events leading to the Louisiana Purchase.

Section Theme

Government and Democracy An important Supreme Court decision asserted that the Court had the power to decide whether laws passed by Congress were constitutional.

Preview of Events

♦1800 ♦1803 ♦1806 ♦1809

1801
Thomas Jefferson takes office

1803
Marbury v. *Madison* case decided; Louisiana Purchase expands nation

1804
Lewis and Clark head west

1807
Embargo Act passed

★ An American Story ★

March 4, 1801, was Inauguration Day in Washington, D.C. The still unfinished capital of the United States was only a tiny village. Stumps and mud holes filled Pennsylvania Avenue, and a swampy wilderness separated Capitol Hill from the president's mansion. A Washington resident described the modest inauguration ceremony:

66The sun shone bright on that morning. . . . Mr. Jefferson had not yet arrived. He was seen walking from his lodgings, which were not far distant, attended by five or six gentlemen who were his fellow lodgers. Soon afterwards he entered . . . and bowing to the Senate, who arose to receive him, he approached a table on which the Bible lay and took the oath which was administered to him by the Chief Justice. . . . The new President walked home with two or three of the gentlemen who lodged in the same house. At dinner . . . a gentleman from Baltimore, . . . asked permission to wish him joy. 'I would advise you,' answered Mr. Jefferson smiling, 'to follow my example on nuptial occasions when I always tell the bridegroom I will wait till the end of the year before offering my congratulations.' And this was the only and solitary instance of any notice taken of the event of the morning.99

—quoted in *The Life of Thomas Jefferson*

Thomas Jefferson Takes Office

Thomas Jefferson privately referred to his election as the "Revolution of 1800." He believed that Washington and Adams had acted too much like royalty, and he tried to create a less formal style for the presidency. He rode horseback rather than traveling in carriages. In place of formal receptions, he entertained at more intimate dinners around a circular table so that, as he said, "When brought together in society, all are perfectly equal." Although Jefferson set a new style for the presidency, he did not overturn all of the Federalists' policies. Instead he sought to integrate Republican ideas into the policies that the Federalists had already put in place.

A strong believer in small government, Jefferson hoped to limit the scope of federal power. He began paying off the federal debt, cut government spending, and did away with the hated whiskey tax. Instead of a standing army, he planned to rely on local militia.

Jefferson's economic ideas had worried many Federalists, who expected the new president to dismantle the national bank. Jefferson's choice of Albert Gallatin as secretary of the treasury reassured them. Gallatin was a skilled financier who supported Hamilton's system.

✓ **Reading Check** **Summarizing** What was new about Jefferson's approach to the presidency?

The Rise of the Supreme Court

Before their term expired, the Federalist majority in Congress passed the Judiciary Act of 1801. This act created 16 new federal judges. Before leaving office,

President Adams appointed Federalists to these positions. These judges were nicknamed "midnight judges" because Adams supposedly signed appointments until midnight on his last day in office.

Impeaching Judges Neither Jefferson nor the Republicans in Congress were pleased that the Federalists controlled the courts. One of the first acts of Congress after Jefferson took office was to repeal the Judiciary Act of 1801, thereby doing away with the "midnight judges" by abolishing their offices.

The Republicans then tried to remove other Federalists from the judiciary by impeachment. Republican leaders believed that the impeachment power was one of the checks and balances in the Constitution. Congress could impeach and remove judges for arbitrary or unfair decisions, not just for criminal behavior.

In 1804, the House impeached Supreme Court Justice Samuel Chase. During one trial, Chase had ordered "any of those persons or creatures called democrats" removed from the jury. He had also denounced Jefferson while addressing another jury. Although these actions may have been unfair, the Senate did not convict Chase. Many senators did not think he was guilty of "treason, bribery, or other high

Birth of a Capital

To plan the new national capital, President Washington chose Pierre Charles L'Enfant. One of L'Enfant's first decisions was to place the future "Congress House" (what would become the Capitol) on high ground with a commanding view of the Potomac River. Congress House was to be the central point in a square grid of streets slashed by avenues that radiated from Capitol Hill like spokes on a wheel. L'Enfant's plan called for circular intersections to join three or more avenues at strategic spots.

After a series of disputes with the local landowners, L'Enfant was removed from the project, and he took his plans with him. Fortunately one of the surveyors, an African American named Benjamin Banneker, was able to draw the plans from memory, thus enabling the project to continue. Modern Washington, D.C., still retains many of the elements of this plan.

The clothes President Jefferson wore at his inauguration in the new capital

crimes and misdemeanors" that the Constitution required for his removal. The impeachment of Justice Chase established that judges could only be removed for criminal behavior, not simply because Congress disagreed with their decisions.

Marbury v. Madison

The most important judicial appointment President Adams made before leaving office was to choose **John Marshall** as Chief Justice of the United States. Marshall served as Chief Justice for 34 years. He was more responsible than any other justice for making the Supreme Court into a powerful, independent branch of the federal government.

Initially, the Supreme Court was a very minor body, but its role began to change in 1803 with the case of *Marbury* v. *Madison*. William Marbury was a Federalist who had been appointed justice of the peace in Washington, D.C., shortly before Adams left office. Although Adams had signed Marbury's appointment, the documents were not delivered before Adams left office. The new Secretary of State, James Madison, was supposed to deliver the documents, but Jefferson told him to hold them, hoping Marbury would quit and allow Jefferson to appoint a Republican to the job.

Instead, Marbury asked the Supreme Court to issue a court order telling Madison to deliver the documents. Marbury based this request on the Judiciary Act of 1789, which stipulated that requests for federal court orders go directly to the Supreme Court. In *Marbury* v. *Madison*, the Supreme Court unanimously agreed with Chief Justice Marshall that the Court could not issue the order.

Marshall explained that the Court could not issue the order because it had no jurisdiction. The Constitution, Marshall pointed out, was very specific about the kind of cases that could be taken directly to the Supreme Court. A request for a court order was not one of those cases, making that section of the Judiciary Act of 1789 unconstitutional and invalid. The decision strengthened the Supreme Court because it asserted the Court's right of judicial review, the power to decide whether laws passed by Congress were constitutional and to strike down those laws that were not.

(*See page 1081 for more information on* Marbury v. Madison.)

Reading Check **Explaining** Why did Congress repeal the Judiciary Act of 1801?

The United States Expands West

One of Jefferson's strongest beliefs was that a republic could only survive if most of the people owned land. This belief led him to support the idea of expanding the country farther west.

The Louisiana Purchase

In 1800 French leader Napoleon Bonaparte convinced Spain to give Louisiana back to France in exchange for helping Spain take control of part of Italy. Napoleon's deal worried Jefferson, because it gave France control of the lower Mississippi. Jefferson believed that having France back in North America would force the United States into an alliance with the British, whom Jefferson despised.

Jefferson ordered his ambassador to France, **Robert Livingston,** to try to block the deal or gain concessions for the United States. Livingston arrived in Paris in the spring of 1801, but his negotiations accomplished little until 1803.

By 1803 Napoleon had begun making plans to conquer Europe. If France resumed its war against Britain, the last thing the French wanted was an alliance between the United States and Great Britain. Furthermore, France's government was short on funds. In 1803, therefore, Napoleon offered to sell all of the Louisiana Territory, as well as New Orleans, to the United States. Livingston immediately accepted.

Souvenir handkerchief showing the layout of Washington, D.C.

Medallion honoring Pierre L'Enfant

Picturing **History**

Mountain Explorer Besides giving his name to Colorado's Pikes Peak, army officer Zebulon Pike led an expedition to find the Mississippi's headwaters. What skills might army officers have that would aid them in such an assignment?

On April 30, 1803, the United States bought Louisiana from France for $11.25 million. It also agreed to take on French debts owed to American citizens. These debts were worth about $3.75 million, making the total cost about $15 million. The Senate overwhelmingly ratified the **Louisiana Purchase.** As a result of the deal, the United States more than doubled its size and gained control of the entire Mississippi River.

The Lewis and Clark Expedition

Even before Louisiana became a part of the United States, Jefferson asked Congress to fund a secret expedition into the Louisiana Territory to trace the Missouri River and find a route to the Pacific Ocean. After Congress approved the expedition, Jefferson chose **Meriwether Lewis,** his private secretary, and **William Clark,** the younger brother of Revolutionary War hero George Rogers Clark, to lead the expedition.

In May 1804 the "Corps of Discovery," as the expedition was called, headed west up the Missouri River. Along the way they met **Sacagawea,** a Shoshone woman who joined the expedition as a guide and interpreter. The expedition found a path through the Rocky Mountains and eventually traced the Columbia River to the Pacific Ocean. The expedition greatly increased American knowledge of the Louisiana Territory and also gave the United States a claim to the Oregon territory along the coast.

The Pike Expedition

Lewis and Clark's expedition was not the only one exploring the Louisiana Purchase. In 1805 **Zebulon Pike** mapped much of the upper Mississippi, and in 1806 he headed west to find the headwaters of the Arkansas River. Pike traveled to Colorado, where he charted the mountain now known as Pikes Peak. He later mapped part of the Rio Grande and traveled across northern Mexico and what is now southern Texas. Pike's account of this trip gave Americans their first detailed description of the Great Plains and the Rocky Mountains.

The Essex Junto

The Louisiana Purchase alarmed New England Federalists. It meant that eventually their region would lose its influence in national affairs while the South and West gained political strength through new states. In Massachusetts, a small group of Federalists known as the **Essex Junto** drafted a plan to take New England out of the Union.

Hoping to expand their movement, they persuaded Vice President Aaron Burr to run for governor of New York in 1804. During the campaign, Alexander Hamilton called Burr "a dangerous man, and one who ought not be trusted with the reins of government." An offended Burr challenged Hamilton to a duel. When the two met on July 11, 1804, though, Hamilton refused to fire. Burr shot and killed his foe. In 1807 Burr was accused of plotting to create a new country in the western United States. He was charged with treason but found not guilty.

✓ **Reading Check** **Describing** Why did Thomas Jefferson want to purchase the Louisiana Territory?

Rising International Tensions

Burr's schemes were only a minor annoyance to President Jefferson. During his second term in office, the president was much more concerned with keeping the United States out of the war between Britain and France. A fragile peace between France and England had fallen apart in mid-1803, when Napoleon's armies surged out of France and headed east.

Economic Warfare At first, the war actually benefited American merchants. As the British seized French ships, American merchants began trading with French colonies in the Caribbean. The British left the American ships alone because the United States had proclaimed neutrality.

In 1806 Britain issued regulations known as the Orders in Council. These declared that all ships going to Europe needed British licenses and would be searched for contraband. In response, Napoleon declared that merchants who obeyed the British system would have their goods confiscated when they reached Europe. Americans were caught in the middle. No matter whom they obeyed, they were going to lose their goods.

Impressment Although British and French trade restrictions upset Americans, the British practice of stopping American ships to seize sailors angered them even more. The British navy was short of recruits because of its low pay and terrible shipboard conditions. British sailors often deserted for American vessels. Britain solved this problem by impressment, a legalized form of kidnapping that forced people into military service. Britain claimed the right to stop American ships and search for deserters. On many occasions they impressed American citizens into service as well.

In June 1807, these tensions reached the boiling point when the British warship *Leopard* stopped the American warship *Chesapeake* to search for British deserters. When the captain of the *Chesapeake* refused to comply, the *Leopard* opened fire, killing three Americans. After the Americans surrendered, the British went aboard and seized four sailors.

Economic Diplomacy Fails The attack on the *Chesapeake* enraged the public, and American newspapers clamored for war. Like Washington and Adams before him, however, President Jefferson did not want to entangle the United States in the affairs of Europe. Instead of going to war, he asked Congress to pass the Embargo Act of 1807, halting all trade between the United States and Europe.

The embargo, a government ban on trade with other countries, wound up hurting the United States more than France or Britain. In the Northeast, once-lucrative shipping businesses came to a standstill, while farmers in the South and West saw the demand for their crops plummet. In Congress, Maryland's Philip Barton Key railed against the embargo:

> ❝It has paralyzed industry. . . . Our most fertile lands are reduced to sterility. It will drive our seamen into foreign employ, and our fishermen to foreign sandbanks. . . . It has dried up our revenue.❞
> —quoted in *The American Spirit*

Realizing that the embargo was not working and that it was costing the Republican Party political support, Congress repealed it in March 1809, shortly before Jefferson left office.

After his second term, President Jefferson gladly retired to his estate, Monticello, in Virginia. While the embargo made Jefferson unpopular, his administration had reversed the Federalist course by limiting the power of the federal government. It had also acquired a vast new territory in the West.

✓ **Reading Check** **Examining** Why did Jefferson have Congress pass the Embargo Act of 1807?

SECTION 3 ASSESSMENT

Checking for Understanding

1. **Define:** judicial review, impressment, embargo.
2. **Identify:** John Marshall, Louisiana Purchase, Meriwether Lewis, William Clark, Sacagawea, Zebulon Pike.

Reviewing Themes

3. **Government and Democracy** How did the Supreme Court decision in *Marbury* v. *Madison* strengthen the federal judiciary?

Critical Thinking

4. **Comparing and Contrasting** How was Jefferson's presidency similar to and different from those of Washington and Adams in political style, goals, and foreign policy?
5. **Organizing** Use a graphic organizer similar to the one below to list the causes and effects of the Embargo Act of 1807.

Causes   Effects

Embargo Act of 1807

Analyzing Visuals

6. **Examining Maps** Study the sketch of Washington, D.C., on page 223. Why do you think Pierre L'Enfant designed the city with wide avenues and circular intersections?

Writing About History

7. **Descriptive Writing** Imagine you are a member of the Zebulon Pike expedition in the Colorado territory. Write a journal entry describing what you have seen on the trip.

BITTERROOT RANGE

Lolo Pass
5,233 ft. (1595 m)

Ajax Peak
10,030 ft. (3057 m)

Lost Trail Pass
7,014 ft. (2138 m)

Bitterroot River

TRAVELER'S REST
September 9, 1805

BEAVERHEAD MOUNTAINS

Anaconda Range

SAPPHIRE MOUNTAINS

Lemhi Pass
7,373 ft. (2247 m)

Baldy Mt.
10,568 ft. (3221 m)

Mt. Evans
10,640 ft. (3243 m)

Flint Creek Range

Clark Fork River

Red M
9,409 ft. (28

CAMP FORTUNATE
August 17, 1805

Beaverhead River

The Journey West

⬤ ⬤ ⬤ Route west

- - - Continental Divide

△ Camp

Scale of map varies in this perspective

Jefferson River

Crow Peak
9,413 ft. (2869 m)

GATES OF THE ROCKY MOUNTA.

ROUTE OF THE CORPS OF DISCOVERY

Missouri River

Madison River

△ **THREE FORKS**
July 27, 1805

Mt. Edith
9,504 ft. (2897 m)

BIG BELT MOUNTAINS

Smith

Area enlarged

British Territory

Claimed by Britain, Spain, and Russia

LOUISIANA PURCHASE 1803

St. Louis

UNITED STATES and Territories

Spanish Territory

Pacific Ocean

Atlantic Ocean

Gulf of Mexico

This locator map shows Lewis and Clark's route from St. Louis to the Pacific Ocean. The expedition collected valuable information about the people, plants, animals, and geography of the West. Americans soon followed in the footsteps of the intrepid explorers to open up the American West.

Westward to the Pacific

In May 1804, the Corps of Discovery—Meriwether Lewis, William Clark, and about 40 others—set sail up the Missouri River from their camp outside of St. Louis. Their mission was to find the so-called Northwest Passage—a water route across the continent to the Pacific Ocean. However, after crossing the Great Plains, they discovered the enormous obstacle between them and the Pacific: the Rocky Mountains. Tackling those "terrible mountains," wrote Lewis, proved "the most perilous and difficult part of our voyage" (see map at left).

One of their first challenges was to get beyond the Great Falls of the Missouri. It took them nearly a month to move their boats and supplies almost 18 miles (29 km) around the falls to a more navigable part of the river. Clear of the falls, they pressed on, up through a deep canyon known as the Gates of the Rocky Mountains —"the most remarkable cliffs that we have yet seen," recalled Lewis. From here, the Missouri River ran fast, and its current was strong. In late July 1805, the expedition arrived at Three Forks. After trekking up each fork of the river, Lewis and Clark opted for the western branch, which they named for President Thomas Jefferson. From here, progress slowed. The men often had to wade through the increasingly shallow water, drag-ging their boats behind them. Soon they would have to abandon the boats altogether; but first they needed horses to carry their supplies over the mountains.

Lewis and three men went on ahead. On August 12 they crossed the Continental Divide at Lemhi Pass, becoming the first explorers from the United States to do so. As Lewis and his party descended the steep mountains, they encountered a band of Shoshone. Lewis convinced Cameahwait, their leader, to go back to meet the others. To everyone's astonishment, the Shoshone recognized their Native American guide, Sacagawea, as a member of their band who had been kidnapped long ago. Sacagawea suddenly realized Chief Cameahwait was her brother, and she joyfully embraced him.

With Sacagawea's help, Lewis convinced the Shoshone to sell them horses and provide a guide. The Corps crossed into the Bitterroot Range around Lost Trail Pass. After a pause at Traveler's Rest, the expedition headed over the massive peaks. They climbed the snow-covered slopes and struggled around the fallen trees, watching in horror as their horses slipped and rolled down. Game was so scarce that the famished explorers were forced to kill and eat three of their colts. Despite the hardships, the weary party trudged on until they arrived at a village of the Nez Perce, who provided food and water. The explorers finally reached a tributary of the Columbia River, built dugout boats, abandoned their horses, and floated west all the way to the Pacific Ocean.

An accomplished geographer and cartographer, William Clark compiled this detailed map of the expedition's route around the Great Falls of the Missouri River.

Area of Clark's map in log book shown above

Sun River

W S N E

GREAT FALLS
June 13, 1805

Camp above the falls

Camp below the falls

On May 26, 1805, from a bluff above the Missouri River, Meriwether Lewis "beheld the Rocky Mountains for the first time."

LEARNING FROM GEOGRAPHY

1. Why were Lewis and Clark unable to complete their mission?

2. Imagine that you are a member of the expedition. Write a letter home detailing some of the sights you have seen.

SECTION 4 The War of 1812

Guide to Reading

Main Idea

While the War of 1812 produced no clear winner, it gave Americans a strong sense of national pride.

Key Terms and Names

Non-Intercourse Act, War Hawks, Tecumseh, William Henry Harrison, Oliver Perry, Hartford Convention, nationalism, Treaty of Ghent

Reading Strategy

Organizing As you read about the War of 1812, complete a graphic organizer similar to the one below by listing the causes of the war.

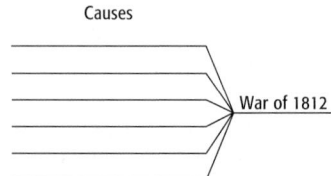

Causes → War of 1812

Reading Objectives

• **Describe** why the United States declared war on Britain, and discuss the major campaigns of the war.
• **List** the results of the Treaty of Ghent.

Section Theme

Individual Action Military leaders, including William Henry Harrison, Tecumseh, Oliver Perry, and Andrew Jackson, helped decide the outcome of the War of 1812.

Preview of Events

◆1809   ◆1811   ◆1813   ◆1815

1809
Embargo Act repealed

1811
Battle of Tippecanoe

1812
United States declares war on Britain

1814
British troops burn Washington, D.C.

1815
Battle of New Orleans

★ An American Story ★

On the night of September 13, 1814, Francis Scott Key, a young Maryland lawyer, stood on the deck of a British ship in Baltimore Harbor and watched the British bombard Fort McHenry. The shelling continued into the morning hours. Explosions lit up the night, and shells with trailing fuses streaked towards the fort. Rockets arced across the sky, as a huge American flag waved over the fort.

As the sun rose, Key strained to see if the flag still waved. To his great joy, it did. He took a letter from his pocket and began scribbling these words for a poem on the back:

> ❝Oh, say can you see, by the dawn's early light,
> What so proudly we hailed at the twilight's last gleaming?
> Whose broad stripes and bright stars, through the perilous fight,
> O'er the ramparts we watched, were so gallantly streaming?
> And the rockets' red glare, the bombs bursting in air,
> Gave proof through the night that our flag was still there.
> Oh, say does that star spangled banner yet wave,
> O'er the land of the free and the home of the brave?❞

—from "The Star-Spangled Banner"

The Decision for War

After Thomas Jefferson announced that he would not run again for president in 1808, the Republican Party nominated James Madison. The Federalists nominated Charles Pinckney. Despite some lingering anger about the Embargo of 1807, Madison won the election easily.

Madison assumed office in the midst of an international crisis. Tensions between the United States and Britain were rising, and it would fall to Madison to decide whether or not to lead the United States into its first full-scale war since the Revolution.

Economic Pressures Like Jefferson, Madison wanted to avoid war. To force the British to stop seizing American ships, he asked Congress to pass the **Non-Intercourse Act.** This act forbade trade with France and Britain while authorizing the president to reopen trade with whichever country removed its trade restrictions first. The idea was to play France and Britain against each other, but the plan failed.

In May 1810, Congress took a different approach with a plan drafted by Nathaniel Macon of North Carolina. The plan, called Macon's Bill Number Two, reopened trade with both Britain and France, but it stated that if either nation agreed to drop its restrictions on trade, the United States would stop importing goods from the other nation.

Soon afterward, Napoleon announced that France would no longer restrict American trade, although his statement still allowed for the seizure of American ships. Madison accepted Napoleon's statement, despite its conditions, hoping to pressure the British into dropping their trade restrictions. When the British refused, Congress passed a non-importation act against Britain in early 1811.

Madison's strategy eventually worked. By early 1812 the refusal of the United States to buy British goods had begun to hurt the British economy. British merchants and manufacturers began to pressure their government to repeal its restrictions on trade. Finally, in June 1812, Britain ended all restrictions on American trade, but it was too late. Two days later, the British learned that the United States Congress had declared war on Great Britain.

The War Hawks Although it appeared that Britain's actions against the United States had hurt mainly Eastern merchants, most members of Congress who voted for war came from the South and West. They were led by Henry Clay of Kentucky, John C. Calhoun of South Carolina, and Felix Grundy of Tennessee. Their opponents nicknamed them the War Hawks.

Americans in the South and West wanted war for two reasons. British trade restrictions hurt Southern planters and Western farmers, who earned much of their income by shipping tobacco, rice, wheat, and cotton overseas. Eastern merchants could make a profit despite British restrictions because they passed the cost of losing ships and goods onto the farmers.

Western farmers also blamed the British for clashes with Native Americans along the frontier. In the early 1800s, settlers had begun moving past the line established by the Treaty of Greenville. As clashes with Native Americans increased, many settlers accused the British in Canada of arming the Native Americans and encouraging them to attack American settlements.

Tecumseh and Tippecanoe Although Western settlers blamed the British for their problems with the Native Americans, it was the increasing demands of speculators and settlers that sparked Native American resistance. **Tecumseh,** a Shawnee leader, believed that Native Americans needed to unite to protect their lands.

While Tecumseh worked for political union, his brother Tenskwatawa (known as "the Prophet") called for a spiritual rebirth of Native American cultures. His followers lived in Prophetstown on the Tippecanoe River in Indiana, where they tried to practice traditional Native American ways of living.

Aware that Tecumseh's movement was becoming more militant, **William Henry Harrison,** governor of the Indiana territory, prepared to stamp it out. In November 1811, Harrison gathered a force and marched towards Prophetstown. Tenskwatawa decided to strike first, sending fighters to attack Harrison and his troops near the Tippecanoe River. The bloody Battle of Tippecanoe left about one-fourth of Harrison's troops dead or wounded, but its impact on the Native Americans was far greater. The clash shattered Native American confidence in the Prophet's leadership. Many, including Tecumseh, fled to Canada.

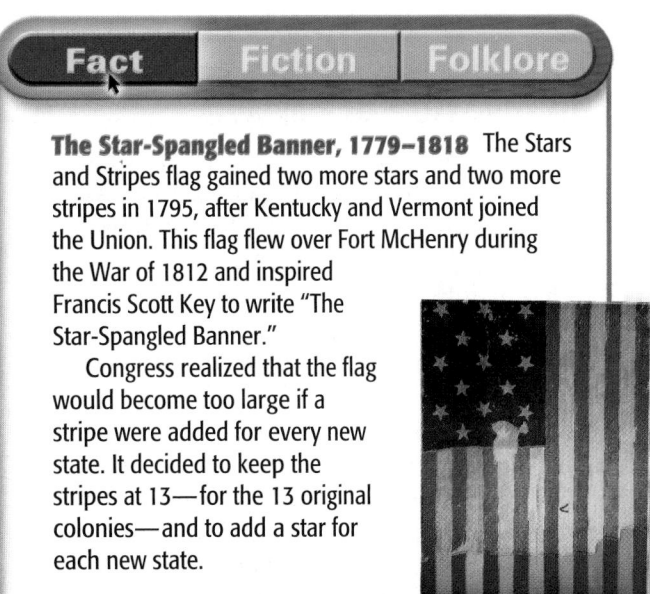

Fact Fiction Folklore

The Star-Spangled Banner, 1779–1818 The Stars and Stripes flag gained two more stars and two more stripes in 1795, after Kentucky and Vermont joined the Union. This flag flew over Fort McHenry during the War of 1812 and inspired Francis Scott Key to write "The Star-Spangled Banner."

Congress realized that the flag would become too large if a stripe were added for every new state. It decided to keep the stripes at 13—for the 13 original colonies—and to add a star for each new state.

Tecumseh's flight to British-held Canada seemed to prove that the British were supporting and arming the Native Americans. Many Western farmers argued that war with Britain would enable the United States to seize Canada and end Native American attacks.

In early June 1812, President Madison gave in to the pressure and asked Congress to declare war. His war message spoke about national honor and emphasized the abuse Americans had suffered at the hands of the British:

66Thousands of American citizens, under the safeguard of public law and of their national flag, have been torn from . . . everything dear to them; have been dragged on board ships of a foreign nation . . . to be exiled to the most distant and deadly climes to risk their lives in battles of their oppressors.99

—from Madison's
War Message to Congress

In Congress, the vote split along regional lines. The South and West generally voted for war, while the Northeast did not.

Reading Check **Examining** Why did Americans in the South and West favor war with Great Britain?

The Invasion of Canada

Although the Republican-led Congress had called for war, the nation was not ready to fight. The army had fewer than 7,000 troops and little equipment. The navy had only 16 ships. Also, Americans were deeply divided over the war. Many people in New York and New England called it "Mr. Madison's War," implying that it was a private fight that did not deserve the nation's support.

Paying for the war also posed a problem. The year before the war, Republicans had shut down the Bank of the United States by refusing to renew its charter. This made it difficult for the government to borrow money because most private bankers were located in the Northeast. They opposed the war and would not

Profiles IN HISTORY

Tecumseh
c. 1768–1813

Tecumseh was a Shawnee chief born near present-day Springfield, Ohio. The Shawnee had taken part in many wars in the Northwest Territory. After the Treaty of Greenville in 1795, Tecumseh and many other Shawnee moved to the Indiana territory to escape American settlers.

Tecumseh urged all Native Americans to unite. They were all one people, he said, and should cooperate in a confederacy to control their destiny. He was furious when the Delaware and Potawatomi agreed to cede about 3 million acres (1.2 million ha) to the United States. The land belonged to all Native Americans, Tecumseh argued. How could one group give it up?

In the end, Tecumseh saw no choice but to fight: "The hunting grounds are fast disappearing and they are driving the red man farther and farther to the west." Ominously, he warned, "Surely [this] will be the fate of all tribes if the power of the whites is not forever crushed. . . ."

During the War of 1812, Tecumseh allied himself with the British. A superb

commander, he met his end at the Battle of the Thames River, fought near Chatham, Ontario, in October 1813. There, 400 British troops commanded by General Henry Proctor and about 1,000 Native Americans led by Tecumseh fought some 3,000 American troops led by General William Henry Harrison. During the battle, the British broke ranks and fled, leaving Tecumseh's men to face the American forces alone. After Tecumseh's death, his confederacy collapsed, leaving the United States in firm control of the Northwest Territory.

loan money to the government. Despite the nation's military and financial weakness, President Madison ordered the military to invade Canada.

Three Strikes Against Canada American military leaders planned to attack Canada from three directions—from Detroit, from Niagara Falls, and up the Hudson River valley toward Montreal. All three attacks failed. The British navy on Lake Erie rapidly shuttled troops to Detroit and forced the American commander, General William Hull, to surrender.

Next, the British shifted their troops to Niagara Falls, where they took up positions on Queenston Heights. From there, they easily drove off some 600 American troops who had landed on the Canadian side of the Niagara River. The American force would have been larger, except that the New York militia, many of whom opposed the war, refused to cross the river. They argued that the terms of their military service did not require them to leave the country.

The third American attack fared no better than the first two. General Henry Dearborn, marching up the Hudson River toward Montreal, called off the attack after the militia accompanying his troops refused to cross the border.

Perry's Victory on Lake Erie The following year, the United States had more success after Commodore **Oliver Perry** secretly arranged for the construction of a fleet on the coast of Lake Erie in Ohio. On September 10, 1813, Perry's fleet attacked the British fleet on Lake Erie near Put-in-Bay. When his own ship was no longer able to fight, Perry rowed to another vessel. After a grueling four-hour battle, the British surrendered.

Perry's victory gave the Americans control of Lake Erie. It also enabled General Harrison to recover Detroit and march into Canada, where he defeated a combined force of British troops and Native Americans at the Battle of the Thames River.

Harrison's attack from the west was supposed to meet up with American troops from Niagara Falls in the east. British troops and Canadian militia, however, stopped the American attack from the east at the Battle of Stony Creek. When Harrison learned of the defeat, he retreated to Detroit. By the end of 1813, the United States still had not conquered any territory in Canada.

✔ **Reading Check**

Explaining Why was conquering Canada an important American goal in the War of 1812?

The War Ends

In 1814, Napoleon's empire collapsed. With the war against France over, the British were able to send much of their navy and many more troops to deal with the United States. The British strategy for the war had three parts. First, the British navy would raid American cities along the coast. Second, they would march south into New York from Montreal, cutting New

England off from the rest of the country. Third, they would seize New Orleans and close the Mississippi River to western farmers. The British believed this strategy would force the United States to make peace.

Raids on Washington, D.C., and Baltimore With attention focused on Canada, in August 1814 a British fleet sailed into Chesapeake Bay and landed troops within marching distance of Washington, D.C. The British easily dispersed the poorly trained militia defending the capital and entered the city unopposed. Madison and other government officials hastily fled. The British set fire to both the White House and the Capitol. They then prepared to attack Baltimore.

Unlike Washington, D.C., Baltimore was ready for the British. The city militia inflicted heavy casualties on the British troops that went ashore. After bombarding Fort McHenry throughout the night of September 13, the British abandoned their attack on the city.

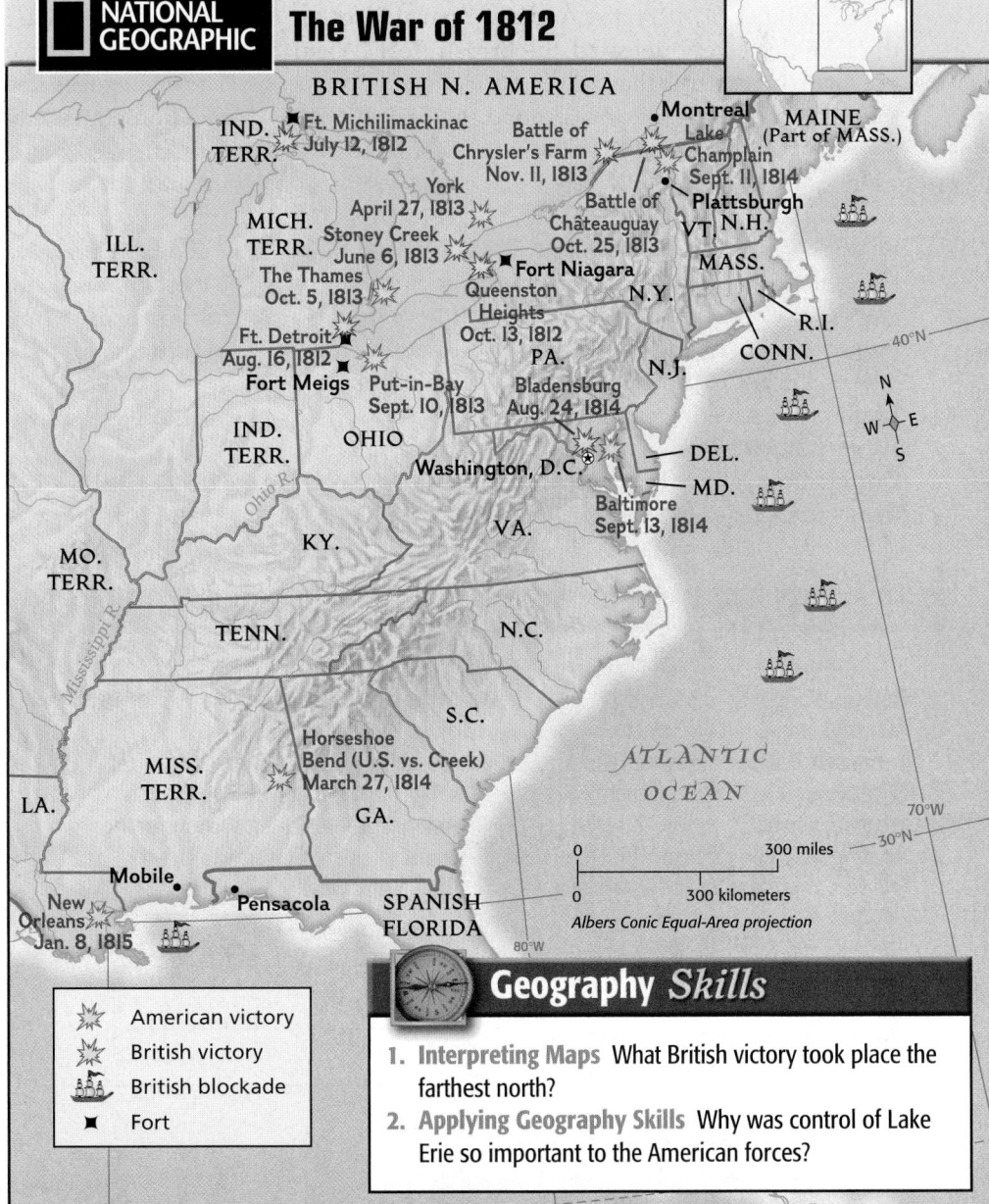

NATIONAL GEOGRAPHIC

The War of 1812

BRITISH N. AMERICA

IND. TERR.
■ Ft. Michilimackinac
July 12, 1812

Battle of Chrysler's Farm
Nov. 11, 1813

Montreal
Lake Champlain
Sept. 11, 1814

MAINE (Part of MASS.)

York
April 27, 1813

Battle of Châteauguay
Oct. 25, 1813

Plattsburgh
N.H.
VT.

MICH. TERR.
Stoney Creek
June 6, 1813
The Thames
Oct. 5, 1813

ILL. TERR.

■ Fort Niagara

MASS.

Queenston Heights
Oct. 13, 1812

N.Y.

R.I.

Ft. Detroit
Aug. 16, 1812 ■

PA.

CONN.

40°N

Fort Meigs

Put-in-Bay
Sept. 10, 1813

Bladensburg
Aug. 24, 1814

N.J.

IND. TERR.

OHIO

DEL.

Washington, D.C. ☆

MD.

Baltimore
Sept. 13, 1814

MO. TERR.

Ohio R.

KY.

VA.

TENN.

N.C.

Mississippi R.

S.C.

Horseshoe Bend (U.S. vs. Creek)
March 27, 1814

ATLANTIC OCEAN

MISS. TERR.

LA.

GA.

70°W
30°N

0   300 miles
0   300 kilometers
Albers Conic Equal-Area projection

Mobile

New Orleans
Jan. 8, 1815

Pensacola

SPANISH FLORIDA

80°W

✺ American victory
✺ British victory
⚓ British blockade
■ Fort

Geography Skills

1. **Interpreting Maps** What British victory took place the farthest north?
2. **Applying Geography Skills** Why was control of Lake Erie so important to the American forces?

Battle of New Orleans This John Landis engraving depicts the triumph of Andrew Jackson (on horseback at right) over the British during the War of 1812. What was unusual about the timing of the battle?

The Battle of Lake Champlain That same month, about 15,000 well-trained British soldiers advanced southward from Montreal into New York. The key to the British advance was control of Lake Champlain. On September 11, 1814, the American naval force on the lake decisively defeated the British fleet. When the British realized that the Americans could use their control of the lake to surround the British, they abandoned the attack and retreated to Montreal.

The Hartford Convention The British offensive increased New England's opposition to the war. In December 1814, Federalists from the region met in Hartford, Connecticut, to discuss what they could do independently of the United States. Although members of the Essex Junto at the convention urged New England to secede, moderate delegates refused to support such extreme action. Instead, the **Hartford Convention** called for several constitutional amendments to increase the region's political power.

The Battle of New Orleans Less than a month after the Hartford Convention began, an American victory in the South put a stop to Federalist complaints. In January 1815, a British fleet with some 7,500 men landed near New Orleans. The American commander, General Andrew Jackson, quickly improvised a defense using cotton bales. The thick bales absorbed the British bullets, while the British advancing in the open provided easy targets for the American troops. The fighting ended in a decisive American victory.

The **Battle of New Orleans** made Andrew Jackson a national hero. It also helped to destroy the Federalist Party. As nationalism, or feelings of strong patriotism, surged, the Federalists at the Hartford Convention appeared divisive and unpatriotic. They never recovered politically, and within a few years the party ceased to exist.

The Treaty of Ghent Peace negotiations began in the European city of Ghent even before the major battles of 1814. On December 24, 1814, the negotiators signed the **Treaty of Ghent,** ending the War of 1812. The treaty restored prewar boundaries but did not mention neutral rights or impressment, and no territory changed hands. Still, the War of 1812 increased the nation's prestige overseas and generated a new spirit of patriotism and national unity.

Four years later in the Convention of 1818, the United States and Great Britain set the U.S.-Canadian border from what is now Minnesota to the Rocky Mountains at 49° north latitude. The countries also agreed to claim jointly for the next ten years a region farther west known as the Oregon Country.

Reading Check **Examining** What were the effects of the Battle of New Orleans?

SECTION 4 ASSESSMENT

Checking for Understanding
1. **Define:** War Hawks, nationalism.
2. **Identify:** Non-Intercourse Act, Tecumseh, William Henry Harrison, Oliver Perry, Hartford Convention, Treaty of Ghent.
3. **Analyze** why Perry's victory on Lake Erie was important for the Americans.

Reviewing Themes
4. **Individual Action** What did Tecumseh's death signify for Native Americans of the Northwest Territory?

Critical Thinking
5. **Synthesizing** How did the War of 1812 affect the United States?
6. **Classifying** Use a graphic organizer similar to the one below to list how Americans in different sections of the country felt about war with Great Britain and why.

Section of U.S.	Position on War	Reason for War Position
West		
South		
North		

Analyzing Visuals
7. **Studying Art** Look carefully at the painting of the Battle of New Orleans pictured above. What advantage did the American forces have that helped them win the battle?

Writing About History
8. **Descriptive Writing** Think of an event that made you feel patriotic about the United States. Write a paragraph explaining why the event made you feel this way.

Reading a Flowchart

Why Learn This Skill?

Sometimes, determining a sequence of events can be confusing, particularly when many events are occurring at the same time. Reading a flowchart can help you understand how events are related and how one event leads to others.

Learning the Skill

Flowcharts show the steps in a process or a sequence of events. A flowchart could be used to show the movement of goods through a factory, of people through a training program, or of a bill through Congress. The following steps explain how to read a flowchart:

- Read the title or caption of the flowchart to find out what you are studying.
- Read all of the labels or sentences on the flowchart.
- Look for numbers indicating sequence or arrows showing the direction of movement.
- Evaluate the information in the flowchart.

Practicing the Skill

The flowchart on this page shows a sequence of events that led to the expansion of territory within the United States. Analyze the information in the flowchart and then answer the questions.

❶ What does the flowchart show?

❷ How do you know in what sequence the events took place?

❸ What inspired Napoleon to acquire the Louisiana Territory from Spain?

❹ How did the United States react to France's acquisition of the Louisiana Territory?

❺ What additional information from the chapter could you add to the flowchart to show a further sequence of events?

Circumstances Leading to the Louisiana Purchase

French leader Napoleon plans to rebuild France's empire in North America.

Napoleon convinces Spain to give the Louisiana Territory back to France.

President Jefferson sends ambassador Robert Livingston to France to try to block the deal.

Napoleon later wants to conquer Europe, but he needs funds to carry out his plans.

President Jefferson agrees to purchase Louisiana Territory.

Skills Assessment

Complete the Practicing Skills questions on page 235 and the Chapter 6 Skill Reinforcement Activity to assess your mastery of this skill.

Applying the Skill

Making a Flowchart Gather information about the steps necessary to apply to college. Then make up a flowchart outlining the steps. Present your flowchart to the class.

 GO TO

Glencoe's **Skillbuilder Interactive Workbook CD-ROM, Level 2,** provides instruction and practice in key social studies skills.

Reviewing Key Terms

On a sheet of paper, use each of these terms in a sentence.

1. cabinet
2. bond
3. speculator
4. enumerated powers
5. implied powers
6. agrarianism
7. most-favored nation
8. alien
9. sedition
10. interposition
11. nullification
12. judicial review
13. impressment
14. embargo
15. War Hawks
16. nationalism

Reviewing Key Facts

17. **Identify:** Bank of the United States, Whiskey Rebellion, Alien and Sedition Acts, John Marshall, Meriwether Lewis, William Clark, Sacagawea, Tecumseh, Treaty of Ghent.
18. What was the main focus of the first eight amendments in the Bill of Rights?
19. Why did James Madison oppose the establishment of a national bank?
20. Why did tensions between western settlers and Native Americans increase during Washington's presidency?
21. What events led to the purchase of the Louisiana Territory?
22. What events caused the United States to declare war on Great Britain in 1812?

Critical Thinking

23. **Analyzing Themes: Government and Democracy** What was the most important task for Congress after the U.S. Constitution was ratified? Explain why you think this task was important.
24. **Identifying Effects** What were the effects of the War of 1812 on the United States?
25. **Forming an Opinion** Do you think the Alien and Sedition Acts were unconstitutional? Why or why not?
26. **Classifying** Use a graphic organizer similar to the one below to list the differences between the first political parties in the United States.

Federalists	Republicans
Favored:	Favored:

27. **Interpreting Primary Sources** Many people in New England did not support the War of 1812. At a town meeting in Brewster, Massachusetts, on July 20, 1812, the residents wrote a petition to President Madison. In this petition, they stated the reasons that they opposed the war. Read the excerpt and answer the questions that follow.

66In attending to the *reasons* for the present state of warfare as exhibited to our view by public documents, we lament that they do not furnish to our minds satisfactory evidence of its prosperity. . . .

Chapter Summary

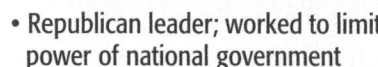
George Washington

- Established legitimacy of the new government
- Created executive departments
- Favored neutrality
- Used troops to stop Native American resistance in the West

Thomas Jefferson

- Republican leader; worked to limit power of national government
- Favored land ownership for all people
- Supported farmers over commerce and trade
- Negotiated purchase of the Louisiana Territory

John Adams

- Federalist leader in favor of strong national government
- Supported commerce and trade
- Favored neutrality; negotiated treaties with Britain and France to avoid war
- Angered farmer and landowners with taxes; angered political opponents with Alien and Sedition Acts

James Madison

- Republican who favored neutrality
- Asked Congress to declare war on Britain to protect trade interest in the East and farmers and settlers in the West
- Under his administration, the War of 1812 generated feelings of nationalism, and the Treaty of Ghent established fishing rights and boundaries with Canada

Self-Check Quiz

Visit the *American Vision* Web site at tav.glencoe.com and click on *Self-Check Quizzes—Chapter 6* to assess your knowledge of chapter content.

> We ask leave in conclusion to state that about three fourths of our townsmen depend on the sea for means of subsistence for themselves and families. By the recent declaration of war more than one half of that proportion is liable to fall into the hands of the enemy with a large proportion of their property, and many of their wives and children may thereby be reduced to extreme poverty. We would be permitted further to remark that out of this large proportion of [sailors] belonging to this town, we have but *four* detained by foreign nations. . . .

—quoted in the *Columbian Centinel,* July 20, 1812

a. What reasons do the residents give for opposing the war?

b. According to the petition, were the residents of Brewster worried more about losing townsmen and property to impressment by foreign nations or to fighting the British in the war? What reasoning do the residents use?

Practicing Skills

28. **Making a Flowchart** Reread the passage titled *Westward Expansion* on page 217. Then create a flowchart documenting events leading up to the end of Native American resistance in the Northwest Territory. Use the following events as the first and last items in your flowchart. Find at least four events to fit in between these first and last entries.

    First event: White settlers move from Pennsylvania and Virginia into the Northwest Territory.

    Last event: Treaty of Greenville is signed by 12 Native American nations in August 1795.

Writing Activity

29. **Expository Writing** Imagine that you are a political editor for a newspaper in 1817. Write an article on the high and low points of the presidencies of George Washington, John Adams, Thomas Jefferson, and James Madison. Use evidence to support your ideas.

Chapter Activity

30. **American History Primary Source Document Library CD-ROM** Under *A New Nation,* read the "Farewell Address" by George Washington and the "First Inaugural Address" by Thomas Jefferson. Work with classmates to hold a debate about the effectiveness of today's political parties, using the opinions about parties presented by Washington and Jefferson in these primary sources.

NATIONAL GEOGRAPHIC

Treaty of Greenville, 1795

Land ceded by Native Americans in Treaty of Greenville, 1795

■ Fort

Geography and History

31. The map above shows land ceded by Native Americans in the Treaty of Greenville. Study the map and answer the questions below.

    a. **Interpreting Maps** The Native Americans gave up most of which present-day state in the Treaty of Greenville?

    b. **Applying Geography Skills** Why was the land the Native Americans gave up valuable to white settlers?

Standardized Test Practice

Directions: Choose the best answer to the following question.

President Jefferson wanted to limit the power of the Federal government. Which of the following was an action he took to achieve this goal?

F   He increased the size of the army.

G   He proposed renewing the Alien and Sedition Acts.

H   He dissolved the Republican Party to eliminate political conflict.

J   He cut the federal budget.

Test-Taking Tip: Think about the word *limit.* It means to reduce or restrict. Therefore, you can eliminate answer G—it gave the government more power. You can also eliminate H because dissolving a party would not reduce governmental power.

UNIT

3 The Young Republic

1789–1850

Why It Matters

The United States faced many challenges in its early years. Internal improvements and industrial development began to reshape the nation, but this reshaping also highlighted the growing differences between North and South. Westward expansion generated new conflicts with Native Americans and also with Great Britain in the Northwest and Mexico in the Southwest. The push for social reforms intensified, addressing issues of education, temperance, women's rights, and slavery. Understanding these developments will help you comprehend the crises that would soon engulf the nation. The following resources offer more information about this period in American history.

Nineteenth-century water keg

Primary Sources Library

See pages 1050–1051 for primary source readings to accompany Unit 3.

💿 *Use the **American History Primary Source Document Library CD-ROM** to find additional primary sources about the young Republic.*

New York and the Erie Canal by William Coventry Wall, 1862

"*The happy Union of these States is a wonder; their Constitution a miracle; their example the hope of Liberty throughout the world.*"

—James Madison, 1829

CHAPTER
7 Growth and Division *1816–1832*

Why It Matters

After the War of 1812, a new spirit of nationalism took hold in American society. A new national bank was chartered, and Supreme Court decisions strengthened the federal government. New roads and canals helped connect the country. Industry prospered in the North, while an agricultural economy dependent on slavery grew strong in the South. Regional differences began to define political life.

The Impact Today

Many developments of this period shaped our lives today.
* *Many Americans have a strong sense of national loyalty.*
* *Federal authority over interstate commerce helped create a truly national economy.*

The American Vision *Video* *The Chapter 7 video, "Young People of the North," describes the lifestyle of Americans in the 1800s.*

1820
* Henry Clay guides the Missouri Compromise through Congress

1819
* Spain cedes Florida to the United States
* *McCulloch v. Maryland*

1816
* Congress establishes Second Bank of the United States

1825
* Erie Canal opens

1823
* Monroe Doctrine declared

United States PRESIDENTS

Madison 1809–1817 | Monroe 1817–1825 | J.Q. Adams 1825–1829

1815   1820   1825

 World

1815
* Napoleon defeated at Battle of Waterloo

1817
* Exploration of Australia's interior begins

1821
* Mexican independence proclaimed

1822
* Greek independence proclaimed

1825
* Decembrist revolt in Russia

Election Day in Philadelphia by John L. Krimmel, 1815

1828
• Jackson defeats Adams's re-election bid

1831
• Nat Turner slave rebellion

Jackson 1829–1837

1830

1835

1829
• Slavery abolished in Mexico

1830
• French seize control of Algiers

1832
• Male voting rights expanded in England

HISTORY Online

Chapter Overview
Visit the *American Vision* Web site at tav.glencoe.com and click on *Chapter Overviews—Chapter 7* to preview chapter information.

Guide to Reading

Main Idea
Americans developed powerful feelings of patriotism and national unity after the War of 1812.

Key Terms and Names
Era of Good Feelings, John C. Calhoun, revenue tariff, protective tariff, John Marshall, Kinache, Adams-Onís Treaty, Quadruple Alliance

Reading Strategy
Organizing As you read about the United States after the War of 1812, complete a graphic organizer similar to the one below by listing actions that strengthened the federal government.

Reading Objectives
- **Analyze** how John Marshall strengthened the Supreme Court.
- **Evaluate** how nationalism affected the nation's foreign policy after the War of 1812.

Section Theme
Continuity and Change Increased national pride marked the years immediately following the War of 1812.

Preview of Events

♦1816   ♦1819   ♦1822   ♦1825

1816
Second Bank of the United States established

1819
Spain cedes Florida to United States; *McCulloch* v. *Maryland*

1823
Monroe Doctrine introduced

1824
Gibbons v. *Ogden*

★ *An American Story* ★

On a March day in 1817, a dignified group of Americans gathered in Washington, D.C., to witness the inauguration of the fifth president of the United States. The audience was full of hope and optimism as James Monroe delivered his inaugural address.

❝Never did a government commence under auspices so favorable. . . . If we look to the history of other nations, ancient or modern, we find no example of a growth so rapid, so gigantic, of a people so prosperous and happy. In contemplating what we have still to perform, the heart of every citizen must expand with joy when he reflects how near our Government has approached to perfection. . . . If we persevere in the career in which we have advanced so far and in the path already traced, we can not fail, under the favor of a gracious Providence, to attain the high destiny which seems to await us.❞

—from James Monroe's Inaugural Address, March 1817

The Era of Good Feelings

President Monroe's words emphasized the sense of national pride that swept the United States after the War of 1812. For a time, Americans' loyalty to the United States overrode their historical identity with state or region. The *Columbian Centinal,* a Boston newspaper, declared this time to be an **Era of Good Feelings.** The phrase has since been used to describe the Monroe presidency.

Harmony in national politics had reached a new high mostly because only one major political party—the Republicans—had any power. The Federalist Party had lost political influence and popularity, in part because of the public's disapproval of their actions at the Hartford Convention. At the same time, the War of 1812 had taught a new generation of Republican leaders that a stronger federal government was advantageous.

Reading Check **Examining** Why is the Monroe presidency known as the Era of Good Feelings?

Economic Nationalism

American leaders prepared an ambitious program to bind the nation together. The program included creating a new national bank, protecting American manufacturers from foreign competition, and building canals and roads to improve transportation and link the country together.

ECONOMICS

The Second Bank Republicans traditionally had opposed the idea of a national bank. They had blocked the rechartering of the First Bank of the United States in 1811 and offered nothing in its place. The results were disastrous. State chartered banks and other private banks greatly expanded their lending with bank notes that were used as money. Without the regulatory presence of the national bank, prices rose rapidly during the War of 1812. When the government borrowed money to pay for the war, it had to pay high interest rates on its loans.

Because of these problems, many Republicans changed their minds after the war. In 1816 Representative **John C. Calhoun** of South Carolina introduced a bill proposing the Second Bank of the United States. With the support of **Henry Clay** of Kentucky and **Daniel Webster** of Massachusetts, the bill passed in 1816. This legislation gave the Bank power to issue notes that would serve as a national currency and to control state banks.

Tariffs and Transportation Protection of manufacturers was another example of the Republican plan. Because an embargo had prevented Americans from buying British goods during the War of 1812, American industries had increased their output to meet the demand. Once the war was over, British goods flowed into the United States at such low prices they threatened to put American companies out of business.

Congress responded with the Tariff of 1816. Unlike earlier revenue tariffs, which provided income for the federal government, this was a protective tariff, designed to nurture American manufacturers by taxing imports to drive up their prices. New England shippers and Southern farmers opposed the tariff and the higher prices it caused, but they could not block its passage.

The Republicans also wanted to improve the nation's transportation system. In 1816 Calhoun sponsored a federal internal improvement plan, but

Profiles IN HISTORY

Henry Clay
1777–1852

Henry Clay was known as the Great Compromiser for his role in working out various agreements between leaders of the North and South. He served as a Kentucky state legislator, speaker of the U.S. House of Representatives, U.S. senator, and secretary of state. Although a slaveholder himself, Clay supported the gradual emancipation of enslaved persons. He later abandoned the idea, however, when it proved unpopular with his fellow Kentuckians.

Clay was a consistent champion of nationalism and devoted his career to strengthening the Union. Although a five-time presidential candidate, the popularity of his opponents and the weakness of his political party, the Whigs, kept him from achieving his lifelong goal of winning the presidency.

John C. Calhoun
1782–1850

John C. Calhoun of South Carolina was an influential member of Congress and, at least for a time, a close friend of Henry Clay. Calhoun was a War Hawk—one who urged war with Great Britain in 1812. He was also an ardent nationalist in his early career. After the War of 1812, Calhoun helped introduce congressional bills for a new Bank of the United States, a permanent road system to connect the nation, and a tariff to protect the nation's industries.

In the 1830s Calhoun abandoned his nationalist stance in favor of states' rights and sectional interests. Fearing that the North intended to dominate the South, Calhoun spent the rest of his career trying to prevent the federal government from weakening states' rights and from interfering with the Southern way of life.

President Madison vetoed it, arguing that spending money to improve transportation was not expressly granted in the Constitution. Nevertheless, road and canal construction soon began, with private businesses and state and local governments funding much of the work.

✓ **Reading Check** **Summarizing** What were three examples of economic nationalism after the War of 1812?

Judicial Nationalism

The judicial philosophy of the Chief Justice of the United States, **John Marshall,** provided another boost to the forces helping unify the nation after the war. Between 1816 and 1824, Marshall ruled in three important cases that established the dominance of the nation over the states and shaped the future of American government.

Martin v. *Hunter's Lessee*

In 1816 the Court decided in *Martin* v. *Hunter's Lessee* that it had the authority to hear all appeals of state court decisions in cases involving federal statutes and treaties. In this case, Denny Martin, a British subject, tried to sell Virginia land inherited from his uncle, Lord Fairfax, a British Loyalist during the war. At that time, Virginia law stated that no "enemy" could inherit land. The Supreme Court upheld Martin's case, ruling that Virginia's law

John Marshall

conflicted with the 1783 Treaty of Paris, which recommended that the states restore confiscated property to Loyalists. This historic decision helped establish the Supreme Court as the nation's court of final appeal.

McCulloch v. *Maryland*

This 1819 case concerned Maryland's attempt to tax the Second Bank of the United States. Before addressing Maryland's right to tax the national bank, the Supreme Court ruled on the federal government's right to create a national bank in the first place. In the Court's opinion, written by Marshall, the bank was constitutional, even though the Constitution did not specifically give Congress the power to create one.

Marshall observed that the Constitution gave the federal government the power to collect taxes, to borrow money, to regulate commerce, and to raise armies and navies. He noted that the national bank helped the federal government exercise these powers. He concluded that the Constitution's "necessary and proper" clause allowed the federal government to create a bank.

Opponents argued that the "necessary and proper" clause meant the government could only do things absolutely necessary, but Marshall rejected that idea. Instead, he held that "necessary and proper" meant the government could use any method that was convenient for carrying out its powers as long as the method was not expressly forbidden.

Marshall then argued that the federal government was "supreme in its own sphere of action." This meant that a state government could not interfere

Major Supreme Court Decisions, 1801–1824

Marbury v. *Madison* (1803)	Declared congressional act unconstitutional; Court asserts power of judicial review
Fletcher v. *Peck* (1810)	Protected contracts from legislative interference; Court could overturn state laws that opposed specific provisions of Constitution
Martin v. *Hunter's Lessee* (1816)	Court can accept appeals of state court decisions and review state decisions that involve federal statutes or treaties; asserted the Supreme Court's sovereignty over state courts
McCulloch v. *Maryland* (1819)	Upheld constitutionality of the Bank of the United States; doctrine of "implied powers" provided Congress more flexibility to enact legislation
Cohens v. *Virginia* (1821)	Reasserted federal judicial authority over state courts; argued that when states ratified Constitution, they gave up some sovereignty to federal courts
Gibbons v. *Ogden* (1824)	Revoked an existing state monopoly; Court gave Congress the right to regulate interstate commerce

Source: *The Oxford Companion to the Supreme Court of the United States*

Chart *Skills*

1. **Interpreting Charts** In which case did Chief Justice Marshall assert the Court's right of judicial review?
2. **Analyzing** Was Marshall a strict interpreter of the Constitution? How can you tell?

with an agency of the federal government exercising its specific constitutional powers within a state's borders. Taxing the national bank was a form of interference and therefore unconstitutional.

Gibbons* v. *Ogden This 1824 case involved a company that had a state-granted monopoly over steamboat traffic in New York waters. When the company tried to expand its monopoly to include traffic crossing the Hudson River to New Jersey, the matter went to court.

The Supreme Court declared this monopoly unconstitutional. In the Court's opinion, Marshall stated that the state legislature had overstepped its power in granting the original monopoly. The Constitution granted the federal government control over interstate commerce, which the court interpreted to include all trade along the coast or on waterways dividing the states. The state could, however, regulate commerce within its own borders.

In writing the Supreme Court's decision, Marshall defined interstate commerce in a way that went far beyond the mere exchange of goods between states. By ruling that anything crossing state boundaries came under federal control, Marshall ensured that federal law would take precedence over state law in interstate transportation.

In these cases, Marshall's nationalism strengthened the power of the federal government at the expense of the states. Although defenders of states' rights bitterly attacked Marshall's decisions, his views helped make the "necessary and proper" clause and the interstate commerce clause major vehicles for expanding federal power. 📖 *(See page 1081 for more information on* Martin v. *Hunter's Lessee,* McCulloch v. *Maryland, and* Gibbons v. *Ogden.)*

✓ **Reading Check** **Identifying** How did the Supreme Court establish and expand the power of the federal government over the states?

Nationalist Diplomacy

The wave of nationalism within Congress and among voters influenced the nation's foreign affairs as well. Feeling proud and confident, the United States under President Monroe expanded its borders and asserted itself on the world stage.

Jackson Invades Florida
Throughout the early 1800s, Spanish-held Florida was a source of anger and frustration for Southerners. Many runaway slaves fled there, knowing that Americans could not cross the border into Spanish territory. Similarly,

Picturing **History**

Seminole Resistance Perhaps the most famous Seminole leader was Osceola, who helped lead the resistance against U.S. attempts to relocate the Seminoles to the West. He was captured by treachery while bearing a flag of truce. *From which Native American group did the Seminoles originate?*

many of the Creek people had retreated to Florida as American settlers seized their lands. These people took a new name for themselves—**Seminole,** meaning "runaway" or "separatist." The Seminoles used Florida as a base to stage raids against American settlements in Georgia. Spain was unable to control the border, causing many Americans to clamor for the United States to step in. As tensions heightened in the region, the Seminole leader **Kinache** warned a U.S. general to stay out of Florida:

    ❝You charge me with killing your people, stealing your cattle and burning your houses; it is I that have cause to complain of the Americans. . . . I shall use force to stop any armed Americans from passing my towns or my lands.❞

      —quoted in *The Seminoles of Florida*

The warning fell on deaf ears. Former representative Calhoun, now secretary of war, authorized action against the Seminoles. In 1818 he sent U.S. troops under the command of General **Andrew Jackson** into Florida. After destroying several Seminole villages, Jackson disobeyed orders and seized the Spanish settlements of St. Marks and Pensacola. He then removed the Spanish governor of Florida from power.

Furious Spanish officials demanded that Jackson be punished, and President Monroe sided initially with Spain. Secretary of State **John Quincy Adams** defended Jackson and argued that the true cause of the dispute lay in Spain's failure to keep order in Florida. Adams used this

Florida turmoil to put pressure on Spain in ongoing border negotiations. Occupied with problems throughout its Latin American empire, Spain gave in and ceded all of Florida to the United States in the **Adams-Onís Treaty** of 1819. The treaty also finalized the western border of the Louisiana Purchase along Texas's Sabine and Red Rivers, west along the Arkansas River, and then north to the 42nd Parallel before turning west to the Pacific Ocean.

The Monroe Doctrine In 1809 rebellions began to erupt in Spain's colonies. By 1824 all of Spain's colonies on the American mainland had declared independence. Spain's once vast empire had been reduced to three islands: Cuba, Puerto Rico, and Santo Domingo.

Meanwhile a group of European countries—Great Britain, Austria, Prussia, and Russia (later joined by France)—formed the **Quadruple Alliance** in an effort to suppress movements against monarchies in Europe. Over Britain's objection, the alliance raised the possibility of helping Spain regain control of its overseas colonies in 1822.

Great Britain and the United States were not pleased. Both nations enjoyed profitable trade with Latin America and would not welcome a return of Spanish rule. In August 1823, British officials suggested that the two nations issue a joint statement supporting the independence of the new Latin American countries. Britain also wished to limit future American expansion in the hemisphere.

Russia's increasing influence on North America's Pacific Coast also worried members of President Monroe's administration. Russia already claimed Alaska, and in 1821 it announced that its empire extended south into the Oregon country between Russian Alaska and the western United States.

Secretary Adams urged Monroe to avoid working with the British when dealing with Spain and Russia. He believed it would be "more dignified to avow our principles explicitly" than to allow the United States to be looked upon as Great Britain's junior partner. Acting without the British, Monroe declared in 1823 that the American continents were "henceforth not to be considered as subjects for future colonization by any European powers."

The president's proclamation, later called the **Monroe Doctrine,** was a bold act, because the United States might not have been able to back up its new policy if challenged. The Monroe Doctrine marked the beginning of a long-term American policy of preventing other great powers from interfering in Latin American political affairs. At the same time, by keeping the European powers out of the Americas, the Monroe Doctrine upheld Washington's policy of avoiding entanglements in European power struggles.

✓ **Reading Check** **Examining** In what ways did U.S. foreign policy become more assertive in the early 1800s?

SECTION 1 ASSESSMENT

Checking for Understanding

1. **Define:** revenue tariff, protective tariff.
2. **Identify:** Era of Good Feelings, John C. Calhoun, John Marshall, Kinache, Adam-Onís Treaty, Quadruple Alliance.
3. **Summarize** how the Supreme Court rulings in *McCulloch* v. *Maryland* and *Gibbons* v. *Ogden* strengthened the federal government.

Reviewing Themes

4. **Continuity and Change** How did the Monroe Doctrine reinforce President Washington's foreign policy goals?

Critical Thinking

5. **Explaining** How did nationalism affect the foreign affairs of the United States?
6. **Organizing** Use a graphic organizer similar to the one below to list examples of nationalism in the United States after the War of 1812.

Examples of Nationalism		
Economic	Judicial	Diplomatic

Analyzing Visuals

7. **Examining Art** Study the painting of Osceola on page 243. What elements of this picture indicate that he was very accustomed to European culture?

Writing About History

8. **Expository Writing** Imagine you are an editor of a newspaper in Spanish-held Florida. Write an editorial in which you either attack or defend the actions of Andrew Jackson and his militia in seizing Spanish settlements in Florida.

Early Industry

Guide to Reading

Main Idea
Beginning in the early 1800s, revolutions in transportation and industry brought great changes to the North.

Key Terms and Names
National Road, Robert Fulton, Industrial Revolution, Francis C. Lowell, Eli Whitney, interchangeable parts, Samuel F.B. Morse, labor union, strike

Reading Strategy
Categorizing As you read about changes that occurred in the United States in the early 1800s, complete a graphic organizer similar to the one below by filling in milestones in transportation and industrialization.

Transportation	Industrialization

Reading Objectives
- **Examine** the changes that took place in transportation in the early 1800s.
- **Discuss** how the Industrial Revolution changed methods of production.

Section Theme
Science and Technology New manufacturing techniques reshaped the organization of the American workforce.

Preview of Events

◆1800　　　　◆1815　　　　◆1830　　　　◆1845

1807
Fulton's steamboat launched

1825
Erie Canal opens

1830
Tom Thumb carries first railroad passengers

1844
First inter-city telegraph message transmitted from Baltimore to Washington

---

★ An American Story ★

In the summer of 1817, explosions suddenly began disturbing the peace and quiet of rural upstate New York. What had started was not a war but a great engineering challenge: a canal, 40 feet (12.2 m) wide and 4 feet (1.2 m) deep, to be built from the Hudson River at Albany to Lake Erie at Buffalo. The longest canal in the nation at that time ran almost 28 miles (45 km) . The new canal would be a colossal 363 miles (584.1 km) long.

Building the canal was difficult and dangerous. Canal beds collapsed, burying diggers. Blasting accidents killed other workers. In 1819 alone more than 1,000 men were stricken with diseases contracted in the swamps through which they dug. Here, one investor coldly complains that the number of deaths is raising costs:

❝In consequence of the sickness that prevailed in this section and its vicinity, we were under the necessity of raising wages from twelve to fourteen and some as high as seventeen dollars per month for common Labourers, and pay Physicians for atten[d]ing to the sick, purchase Coffins and grave clothes, and attend with Hands to bury the Dead.❞

—quoted in *The Artificial River*

A Revolution in Transportation

Despite the dangers they faced, the canal workers pressed on and completed the immense project in 1825. The **Erie Canal** was a striking example of a revolution in transportation that swept through the Northern states in the early 1800s. This revolution led to dramatic social and economic changes.

NATIONAL GEOGRAPHIC

Roads, Canals, and Railroads, 1820–1840

Canal
Railroad
Road

BRITISH NORTH AMERICA

The Transportation Revolution

Wagon rates
Railroad rates
Upstream river rates
Canal rates
Downstream river rates

Cents per Ton-Mile

40
30
20
10
8
6
4
2

1804   1814   1824   1834   1844

Year

Sources: *Making America; America's History; National Geographic Magazine* (Nov. 1990).

View of Lockport, New York, on the Erie Canal

Geography Skills

1. **Interpreting Maps** Which Southern state had the most miles of railroad track?
2. **Interpreting Graphs** Which transportation rate dropped most rapidly?

Roads and Turnpikes As early as 1806, the nation took the first steps toward a transportation revolution when Congress funded the building of a major east–west highway, the **National Road.** In 1811 laborers started cutting the roadbed westward from the Potomac River at Cumberland, Maryland. By 1818 the roadway had reached Wheeling, Virginia (now West Virginia) on the Ohio River. Conestoga wagons drawn by teams of oxen or mules carried migrating pioneers west on this road, while livestock and wagonloads of farm produce traveled the opposite way, toward the markets of the East.

Rather than marking the start of a federal campaign to improve transportation, the National Road turned out to be the only great federally funded transportation project of its time. Jefferson and his successors believed in a strict interpretation of the Constitution and doubted that the federal government had the power to fund roads and other "internal improvements."

Instead, states, localities, and private businesses took the initiative. Private companies laid down hundreds of miles of toll roads. By 1821, some 4,000 miles (6,400 km) of toll roads had been built, mainly to connect eastern cities, where heavy traffic made the roads extremely profitable. Even so, major roads west had also been built, connecting Pittsburgh, Pennsylvania, and Buffalo, New York, to eastern markets.

Steamboats and Canals Rivers offered a far faster, more efficient, and cheaper way to move goods than did roads, which were often little more than wide paths. A barge could hold many wagonloads of grain or coal. Loaded boats and barges, however, could usually travel only downstream, as moving against the current with heavy cargoes proved difficult.

The steamboat changed all that. In 1807 **Robert Fulton** and Robert R. Livingston stunned the nation when the *Clermont* chugged 150 miles up the Hudson River from New York City to Albany in just 32 hours. The steamboat made river travel more reliable and upstream travel easier. By 1850 over 700 steamboats, also called riverboats, traveled along the nation's waterways.

The growth of river travel—and the success of the Erie Canal—spurred a wave of canal building throughout the country. By 1840 more than 3,300 miles of canals snaked through the nation, increasing trade and stimulating new economic growth.

The "Iron Horse" Another mode of transportation—railroads—also appeared in the early 1800s. A wealthy, self-educated industrialist named **Peter Cooper** built an American engine based on the ones developed in Great Britain. In 1830 Cooper's tiny but powerful locomotive *Tom Thumb* pulled the nation's first load of train passengers. Forty adventuresome men and women travelled at the then incredible speed of 10 miles per hour along 13 miles of track between Baltimore and Ellicott City, Maryland. The railroad era had dawned.

The new machines did not win universal favor. Some said they were not only dangerous and uncomfortable but dirty and ugly as well. "It is the Devil's own invention," declared one critic, "compounded of fire, smoke, soot, and dirt, spreading its infernal poison throughout the fair countryside."

Others responded to the train's awesome presence. "When I hear the iron horse make the hills echo with his snort like thunder, shaking the earth with his feet, and breathing fire and smoke from his nostrils," wrote the poet Henry David Thoreau, "it seems as if the earth had got a race now worthy to inhabit it."

The advantages of train travel soon became apparent to almost everyone. Trains traveled much faster than stagecoaches or wagons, and unlike steamboats, they could go nearly anywhere track was laid. Perhaps more than any other kind of transportation, trains helped settle the West and expand trade between the nation's different regions.

As railroads expanded, they created national markets for many goods by making transportation cheaper. They increased the demand for iron and coal even more directly. Between 1830 and 1861, the United States built more than 30,000 miles of railroads—so it needed 60,000 miles of iron rail. Since mills used coal to make iron, the need for rails added to the increasing demand for coal. Coal production shot up from 50,000 tons in 1820 to 14 million tons in 1860.

HISTORY Online

Student Web Activity Visit the *American Vision* Web site at tav.glencoe.com and click on **Student Web Activities— Chapter 7** for an activity on the Erie Canal.

Reading Check **Evaluating** What were two advantages of trains over other kinds of transportation in the 1800s?

A New System of Production

Along with dramatic changes in transportation, a revolution occurred in business and industry. The **Industrial Revolution,** which began in Britain in the middle 1700s, consisted of several basic developments. Manufacturing shifted from hand tools to large, complex machines. Skilled artisans gave way to workers, organized by specific tasks, and often unskilled. Factories, some housing hundreds of machines and workers, replaced home-based workshops. Manufacturers sold their wares nationwide or abroad instead of just locally.

Peter Cooper's *Tom Thumb* races a horse.

Picturing History

Young Mill Worker Girls like this one often worked in the textile factories that were being built in the northeastern United States during the Industrial Revolution. *Why was industry initially concentrated in the Northeast?*

ECONOMICS

Industrialization Sweeps the North
Industry developed quickly in the United States in the early 1800s for several reasons. Perhaps the most important factor was the American system of free enterprise based on private property rights. Individuals could acquire capital and make their own choices about how to use it, without strict government controls.

The free enterprise system also encouraged industrialization because companies in competition with each other were always willing to experiment with new technologies to make goods cheaper and to transport them faster. The era's low taxes also meant that entrepreneurs had more money to invest.

Beginning in the 1830s, many states encouraged industrialization by passing general incorporation laws. These laws allowed companies to become corporations and to raise money by issuing stock without having to obtain a charter from the state legislature. These laws also limited liability. If a person bought stock in a company and it went bankrupt, the person risked losing his or her investment

but was not responsible for the company's debts. By limiting liability, the new state laws encouraged people to invest money, spurring economic growth.

Industrialization began in the Northeast, where many swift-flowing streams provided factories with waterpower. The region was also home to many entrepreneurs and merchants who were willing to invest in British industrial techniques.

At first, importing British technology was not easy. Britain had passed strict laws with harsh penalties for anyone passing on its industrial know-how to foreigners. A young English textile worker named Samuel Slater was willing to take the risk. In 1789 he moved to Rhode Island, where he reconstructed the British water frame from memory. The frame stretched and spun raw cotton fiber into cotton thread.

Taking matters a key step further was **Francis C. Lowell,** who opened a series of mills in northeastern Massachusetts beginning in 1814. Using machinery he built after touring British textile mills, Lowell introduced mass production of cotton cloth to the United States. His Boston Manufacturing Company built residences for workers in a new town named after Lowell. The company employed thousands of workers—mostly women and children, who would work for lower wages than men.

By 1840, scores of textile factories had been built in the Northeast. Industrialists soon applied factory techniques to the production of lumber, shoes, leather, wagons, and other products.

Technological Advances
A wave of inventions and technological innovations spurred the nation's industrial growth. An ingenious young New Englander named **Eli Whitney** popularized the concept of interchangeable parts, transforming gunmaking from a one-by-one process into a factory process. Using this process, machines turned out large quantities of identical pieces that workers assembled into finished weapons.

Communications improved as well. American inventor **Samuel F.B. Morse** began work on the telegraph in 1832 and developed the Morse code for sending messages. In 1844 the first long-distance telegraph line connected Washington, D.C., and Baltimore. Morse publicly demonstrated the device, tapping out in code the words "What hath God wrought?" From Baltimore came a return message: "What is the news from Washington?"

Journalists saw the telegraph as a tool for speedy transmission of the news. In 1848 a group of newspapers pooled their resources to collect and share news over the wires. This organization was the Associated

Press. Spurred by journalists and other users of the telegraph, more than 50,000 miles of telegraph wire connected most parts of the country by 1860.

✓ **Reading Check** **Summarizing** Name two reasons the factory system began in the Northeast.

The Rise of Large Cities

The industrialization of the United States drew thousands of people from farms and villages to towns in search of factory jobs with higher wages. Many city populations doubled or tripled. In 1820 only one American city boasted more than 100,000 residents. By 1860, eight cities had reached that size.

The growing cities provided opportunities for many different kinds of occupations. One group was printers and publishers, who shared the goal of keeping the public informed. America had always claimed a high literacy rate, and by 1840, over 75 percent of the total population and over 90 percent of the white population could read. The publishing industry arose to satisfy the growing demand for reading materials.

Many of the early writers, editors, and teachers were educated women. Sarah Buell Hale and Lydia Howard Huntley Sigourney were leading editors and literary figures of their day. Unlike women who worked in factories, women in publishing generally came from the young Republic's growing middle class.

✓ **Reading Check** **Describing** How did industrialization affect cities?

Workers Begin to Organize

The industrial boom created a new kind of laborer, the factory worker, whose ranks swelled to 1.3 million by 1860. While early factory mills stressed a paternalistic concern for their workers, the relationship between management and labor became more strained when prices slumped and wages dropped.

Eleven-year-old Lucy Larcom went to work at the Lowell Mills after her father's death left her family in financial hardship. Although at first she felt excited by the change from farm life, she soon came to dread the drudgery of her work:

❝I know that sometimes the confinement of the mill became very wearisome to me. In the sweet June weather I would lean far out of the window, and try not to hear the unceasing clash of the sound inside. Looking away to the hills, my whole stifled being would cry out, 'Oh, that I had wings!'❞

—quoted in *Ordinary Americans*

Hoping to help improve working conditions, some workers began to join together in labor unions. During the late 1820s and early 1830s about 300,000 men and women belonged to some form of union. Most of the organizations were local and focused on a single trade, such as printing or shoemaking. Although these unions worked separately, they began pushing for similar changes, such as higher wages or a shorter 10-hour workday.

During this time, unions had little success. Most employers refused to recognize or bargain with them. Unions also had little power or money to support strikes, or work stoppages, to achieve their goals.

The courts often ruled against early unions, seeing them as unlawful conspiracies that limited free enterprise. "Competition is the life of trade," a New York court declared in an 1835 case involving a union's demand that its workers be paid at least one dollar to make a pair of shoes. "If the defendants cannot make

Linking Past & Present

Advances in Transportation

Past: The Steamboat
John Fitch demonstrated the first working steamboat in 1787, but his passenger and freight service from Philadelphia to New Jersey was not profitable. Robert Fulton's *Clermont* was more successful. Early steamboats were not very powerful and worked best on calm waters.

Present: The Hovercraft
Sir Christopher Cockerell invented the hovercraft, which rides above the water on a cushion of air trapped in a flexible skirt. Not used commercially until the 1950s and 1960s, hovercrafts are often seen today ferrying automobile drivers across rivers and small bodies of water.

Invasion of the Velocipedes Invented in France in the 1790s and later improved by Germans, bicycles—known back then as "velocipedes," or swift walkers—were introduced in the United States in 1819. The two-wheeled contraptions did not win immediate universal popularity. In August 1819, the New York City council passed a law "to prevent the use of velocipedes in the public places and on the sidewalks of the city of New York."

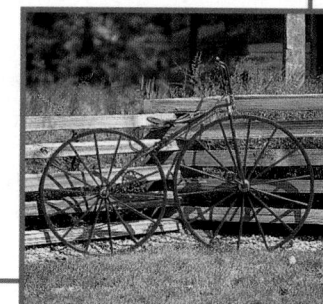

coarse boots for less than one dollar per pair, let them refuse to do so: but let them not directly or indirectly undertake to say that others shall not do the same work for less price."

Unions did make some gains, however. In 1840 President Martin Van Buren showed his gratitude for labor's political support by reducing the workday for federal employees to 10 hours. Two years later, in *Commonwealth* v. *Hunt,* the Massachusetts Supreme Court ruled that union strikes were legal. Still, decades would pass before organized labor achieved real influence.

✓ **Reading Check** Explaining What was life like for a factory worker in the early 1820s?

The Family Farm

Even though industry and cities expanded in the Northeast during the early 1800s, agriculture remained the country's leading economic activity. Until late in the century, farming employed more people and produced more wealth than any other kind of work.

Northern farmers produced enough to sell their surplus in eastern cities and towns. The profit was often used to buy machinery and other items. Thus, their labor not only helped feed the population but nourished the region's economy as well.

In the first half of the century, the North had more than a million farms. Northern farmers and their families worked long, hard days raising livestock and crops for the nation's growing population. A reporter traveling through Ohio in 1841 described a scene that resembled much of the North at that time:

❝As far as the eye can stretch in the distance nothing but corn and wheat fields are to be seen; and on some points in the Scioto Valley as high as a thousand acres of corn may be seen in adjoining fields, belonging to some eight or ten different proprietors.❞

—from *A History of the United States*

Farming was even more important in the South, which had few cities and less industry. As parts of the North began concentrating on manufacturing, the South continued to tie its fortunes to agriculture—and to the institution of slavery.

✓ **Reading Check** Comparing Why was farming more important in the South than in the North?

SECTION 2 ASSESSMENT

Checking for Understanding

1. **Define:** interchangeable parts, labor union, strike.
2. **Identify:** National Road, Robert Fulton, Industrial Revolution, Francis C. Lowell, Eli Whitney, Samuel F.B. Morse.
3. **List** the changes that occurred as a result of the Industrial Revolution.
4. **Describe** advances that were made in transportation during this period.

Reviewing Themes

5. **Science and Technology** How did interchangeable parts revolutionize the manufacturing process?

Critical Thinking

6. **Synthesizing** Why did early labor unions have little success?
7. **Organizing** Use a graphic organizer similar to the one below to list the effects of some of the technological advances of the early 1800s.

Technological Advances	Effects
Steamboat →	
Railroad →	

Analyzing Visuals

8. **Analyzing Art** Study the painting of the steamboat on page 249. Why were steamboats so much more efficient than other shipping methods of the time?

Writing About History

9. **Descriptive Writing** Imagine you are a teenager working in a textile factory in the early 1800s. Write a letter to your family describing your way of life as a factory worker.

The Land of Cotton

Guide to Reading

Main Idea
The South developed a social structure based largely on agriculture and the institution of slavery.

Key Terms and Names
cotton gin, planter, yeoman farmer, task system, gang system, driver, Frederick Douglass, slave code, Denmark Vesey, Nat Turner

Reading Strategy
Organizing As you read about how the South developed, complete a graphic organizer similar to the one below by listing the main categories of Southern society.

Southern Society

Highest _____

_____

_____

Lowest _____

Reading Objectives
- **Explain** why cotton dominated the Southern economy.
- **Describe** the social classes in the South.

Section Theme
Continuity and Change The invention of the cotton gin made cotton a key part of the South's economy. Cotton farming ensured that slavery continued to shape the South's society and culture.

Preview of Events

1790	1805	1820	1835

1793
Eli Whitney invents the cotton gin

1808
Congress bans international slave trade

1822
Denmark Vesey executed

1831
Nat Turner rebellion

★ An American Story ★

Solomon Northup was born free in Minerva, New York, about 1808. His parents were successful farmers. Northup, his wife, and three children also prospered in agriculture, although he supplemented his income as a violinist. In March 1841, two white men offered Northup a job as a musician in their circus. Northup accepted the job and left for Washington, D.C. Two days after arriving in the nation's capital, he was drugged, robbed of his money and papers, chained, and sold to slave traders.

For the next 12 years, Northup lived in bondage in the sugarcane and cotton regions of Louisiana. His first slaveholder, William Ford, treated him well, but Northup never stopped dreaming of freedom. In 1852 he was finally able to obtain documentation proving he was a free man.

Reflecting on his experience, Northup cut to the central cruelty of the institution of slavery:

66There may be humane masters, as there certainly are inhumane ones; there may be slaves well-clothed, well-fed, and happy, as there surely are those half-clad, half-starved and miserable; nevertheless, the institution that tolerates such wrong and inhumanity . . . is a cruel, unjust, and barbarous one.99

—quoted in *Twelve Years a Slave*

The Southern Economy

The South thrived on the production of several major cash crops. In the upper Southern states—Maryland, Virginia, Kentucky, and Tennessee—farmers grew tobacco. Rice paddies dominated the coastal regions of South Carolina and Georgia. In Louisiana and parts of eastern Texas, fields of sugarcane stretched for miles. No crop, however, played a greater role in the South's fortunes than cotton. This crop was grown in a wide belt stretching from inland South Carolina, west through Georgia, Alabama, and Mississippi, and into eastern Texas.

TURNING POINT

Cotton Becomes King During a visit to the South in 1793, Eli Whitney, the inventive young New Englander, noticed that removing cotton seeds by hand from the fluffy bolls was so tedious that it took a worker an entire day to separate a pound of cotton lint. An acquaintance knew of Whitney's mechanical ingenuity and suggested that he try building a machine to pick out the seeds. In only 10 days Whitney built a simple cotton gin—"gin" being short for engine—that quickly and efficiently combed the seeds out of cotton bolls.

The invention of the cotton gin happened at the same time that textile mills were expanding in Europe. Mills in England and France clamored for all the cotton they could get. In 1792, the year before Whitney invented his cotton gin, the South produced about 6,000 bales of cotton. By 1801, annual production reached 100,000 bales.

Cotton soon dominated the region. By the late 1840s Southerners were producing more than two million bales of cotton annually, and in 1860 production reached almost four million bales. That year, Southern cotton sold for a total of $191 million in European markets—nearly two-thirds of the total export trade of the United States. Southerners began saying, rightly, "Cotton is King."

"The whole interior of the Southern states was languishing," said one Southern official in describing the region before the cotton gin. After Whitney's invention, he added, "Individuals who were depressed with poverty, and sunk with idleness, have suddenly risen to wealth and respectability. Our debts have been paid off, our capitals increased; and our lands are treble [triple] in value."

While the cotton gin made some Southern planters rich, it also strengthened the institution of slavery. The spread of cotton plantations all over the Deep

TECHNOLOGY & History

The Cotton Gin

While visiting Catherine Greene's Georgia plantation in 1793, Eli Whitney had an inspiration. He built a device that removed the seeds of the "green-seed" cotton variety that grew in abundance throughout the South. Whitney devised a "gin" (short for *engine*) that combed the seeds out of the cotton. This simple cotton gin was easy to mass produce, and it increased cotton's profitability for many Southern farmers. *How did the invention of the cotton gin affect slavery in the South?*

1 Cotton bolls are dumped into the **hopper.**

2 A **crank** turns the **cylinder** with wire teeth. The teeth pull the cotton past a grate.

3 Slots in the **grate** allow the cotton, but not its seeds, to pass through.

4 A second cylinder with **brushes** pulls the cotton off the toothed cylinder and sends it out of the gin.

crank · grate · hopper · brushes · cylinder

South made the demand for slave labor skyrocket. Congress had outlawed the foreign slave trade in 1808, but a high birthrate among enslaved women—encouraged by slaveholders eager to sell new laborers at high prices—kept the enslaved population growing. Between 1820 and 1850, the number of enslaved people in the South rose from about 1.5 million to nearly 4 million.

Industry Lags Although the South became prosperous from agriculture, it did not industrialize as quickly as the North. For the most part, the South remained a region of rural villages and plantations, with only three large cities: Baltimore, Charleston, and New Orleans.

The South did have some industry. Coal, iron, salt, and copper mines, as well as ironworks and textile mills, could be found there. The region still relied heavily on imported goods, however, which worried some people. As one Southerner noted, "For what have we not looked to our Northern friends? From them we get not only our clothes, carriages, saddles, hats, shoes, flour, potatoes, but even our onions and horn buttons." At this time, in 1860, manufacturing in the South accounted for only 16 percent of the nation's manufacturing total. Most Southerners were content to rely on agriculture.

✓ **Reading Check** **Synthesizing** What effect did the cotton gin have on slavery in the South?

Society in the South

Social attitudes shaped Southern life and produced a definite class structure for the region. At the top were the planters, who owned the region's larger plantations. The 1850 census showed that in a Southern white population of just over 6 million, a total of 347,725 families were slaveholders. Of this number, around 37,000 were planters, defined as those who held 20 or more enslaved people. Less than 8,000 of these planters held 50 or more people in slavery, and only 11 held 500 or more.

A very small percentage of Southern slaveholders lived a life of gentility in grand mansions. Many planter mansions were little more than cottages with newly built facades. The boom in cotton production allowed some smaller-scale planters to rapidly ascend the social ladder, quickly adopting refined habits as they expanded their property. Although the wealthy planters made up a tiny group—representing less than half of one percent of white Southern families and slightly over two percent of

slaveholding families—they dominated the region's economy as well as its political and legal systems.

Ordinary farmers—who were often called yeoman farmers—and their families made up the vast majority of the white population. They may have held four or fewer enslaved persons, though most held none at all, and they worked on the land themselves. Here, writer Mark Twain gives his impressions of a typical small Southern farm in his book *Huckleberry Finn*:

> ❝A rail fence around a two-acre yard . . . big double log house for the white folks—hewed logs, with the chinks stopped up with mud or mortar . . . outside of the fence a garden; . . . then the cotton fields begin; and after the fields, the woods.❞
> —from *Huckleberry Finn*

Near the bottom of the social ladder stood the rural poor. This group, made up mostly of families living on land too barren for successful farming, scratched a meager existence from hunting and fishing, vegetable gardening, and raising a few half-wild hogs and chickens. They made up less than 10 percent of the white population.

At the bottom of society were African Americans, 93 percent of them enslaved. In 1850 nearly 3.6 million African Americans lived in the South—about 37 percent of the total Southern population.

Rounding out Southern society was a small urban class of lawyers, doctors, merchants, and other professionals. Agriculture's influence was so great that even many of these city dwellers invested in or owned farms. As one observer noted, "No matter how one might begin, as lawyer, physician, clergyman, mechanic, or merchant, he ended, if prosperous, as proprietor of a rice or cotton plantation."

✓ **Reading Check** **Identifying** What classes made up the South's social structure?

Slavery

The rice and cotton plantations depended on enslaved labor for their existence. The overwhelming majority of enslaved African Americans toiled in the South's fields. Some, however, worked in the South's few industrial plants or as skilled workers, such as blacksmiths, carpenters, and coopers. Others became house servants.

Enslaved African Americans working in the fields were organized using two basic labor systems. On farms and small plantations that held few enslaved

Plantation Life *The Wedding* by E.L. Henry depicts Southern gentry and their sometimes lavish lifestyle. Wealthy planters depended upon enslaved labor to work their fields, and they purchased such labor at auctions advertised in local newspapers (left). Why did such a small number of elite Southern planters have so much influence in the South?

people, the **task system** was used. Under this system workers were given a specific set of jobs to accomplish every day and worked until these were complete. After completing their tasks, the individuals were allowed to spend the remainder of the day on their own. Some enslaved people earned money through their skill as artisans. Others cultivated personal gardens or hunted for extra food.

In the 1800s, as cotton production became more common and slavery more widespread, slaveholders who owned large plantations adopted the **gang system** of labor. Under this system, enslaved persons were organized into work gangs that labored from sunup to sundown—plowing, planting, cultivating, or picking, depending on the season.

A **driver** acted as the director of a work gang. Often these individuals were enslaved people themselves, chosen for their loyalty or willingness to cooperate. They supervised the progress of the gangs, ensuring that the workers continued laboring throughout the entire day.

No matter which labor system was used, slavery was a degrading experience. **Frederick Douglass,** who rose from slavery to become a prominent leader of the anti-slavery movement, recalled how life as an enslaved person affected him:

❝My natural elasticity was crushed; my intellect languished; the disposition to read departed; the cheerful spark that lingered about my eye died out; the dark night of slavery closed in upon me, and behold a man transformed to a brute.❞

—from *Narrative of the Life of Frederick Douglass*

African Americans' Legal Status In addition to enduring a lifetime of bondage, enslaved persons had few legal rights. State slave codes forbade enslaved men and women from owning property or leaving a slaveholder's premises without permission. They could not possess firearms or testify in court against a white person. Furthermore, laws banned them from learning to read and write. Society viewed enslaved persons as property and treated them that way.

Free African Americans Although most African Americans of the time lived in slavery, some did not. By 1850 some 225,000 free African Americans resided in the South. Most lived in the towns and cities of the upper Southern states, especially Maryland and Virginia. A few were descended from Africans brought to the United States as indentured servants in the 1700s before the slave system became universal. Some had earned their freedom fighting in the American Revolution, and still others were the half-white children of slaveholders, who had granted them freedom. There were also some former enslaved persons who had managed to purchase freedom for themselves and their families or whose slaveholders had freed them.

Free African Americans occupied an ambiguous position in Southern society. In cities like Charleston and New Orleans, some were successful enough to become slaveholders themselves. One such African American was Cecee McCarty, who amassed a fortune in New Orleans by retailing imported dry goods. McCarty dispatched a sales force of 32 enslaved Africans around the state to merchandise her highly prized wares. Still, the experiences of freed African Americans differed from state to state. In some states they had to obtain special licenses to preach or to own firearms. Like those in slavery, they always had to remember how dangerous it was to act any way but humble and subservient when dealing with white people.

Another 196,000 free African Americans lived in the North, where slavery had been outlawed, but they were not embraced there either. Samuel Ringgold Ward, who was African American, lamented that racial prejudice was "ever at my elbow":

> 66As a servant, it denied me a seat at the table with my white fellow servants . . . along the streets it ever pursued, ever ridiculed, ever abused me. If I sought redress, the very complexion I wore was pointed out as the best reason for my seeking it in vain; if I desired to turn to account a little learning, in the way of earning a living by it, the idea of employing a black clerk was preposterous—too absurd to be seriously entertained. . . .99
>
> —quoted in *Long Memory: The Black Experience in America*

Still, free African Americans could organize their own churches and voluntary associations, plus earn money from the jobs they held.

An African American who not only kept his wages but also multiplied them many times over was James Forten of Philadelphia. He went to sea in his teens as a powder monkey—the person on board a warship who handled explosives—on a Revolutionary privateer. Privateers were private ships licensed to attack enemy ships. Later, he worked as a maker of sails. By the age of 32, he owned a thriving sail factory employing 40 African American and white workers. He devoted much of his wealth to the cause of abolishing slavery.

✓ **Reading Check** **Summarizing** What were some basic rights denied to enslaved persons?

Coping With Enslavement

African Americans dealt with the horrors of slavery in a variety of ways. From language to music to religion, they developed a culture that provided them with a sense of unity, pride, and mutual support.

African American Culture Songs were important to many enslaved people. Field workers often used songs to pass the long workday and to help them enjoy their scant leisure time in the evening. Some songs were more provocative than most plantation owners knew, using subtle language and secret meanings to lament the singers' bondage and express a continuing hope for freedom.

Songs also played a key role in one of the most important parts of African American culture: religion. By the early 1800s, large numbers of African Americans were Christians, though their Christianity sometimes incorporated religious traditions from Africa. The religious services enslaved persons held often centered around praying about their particular concern—their dreams of freedom or a better life in the next world.

"the dark night of slavery closed in upon me"

—*Frederick Douglass*

Profiles IN HISTORY

Nat Turner 1800–1831

The man who led perhaps the nation's best-known slave revolt believed from an early age—through his mother's encouragement—that he was divinely inspired. "I was intended for some great purpose," he once declared.

Although many considered Nat Turner a religious fanatic—he claimed to take his directions from mysterious voices and the movements of heavenly bodies—others knew him to have a sharp mind. "He certainly never had the advantages of education," said the man later appointed to be his lawyer, "but he can read and write . . . and for natural intelligence and quickness of apprehension is surpassed by few men I have ever seen."

As he awaited execution, Turner reportedly showed little remorse for his deeds, certain that he had acted in the name of God to free his people. "I am here loaded with chains and willing to suffer the fate that awaits me," he said.

Turner's lack of remorse chilled those around him, including his lawyer, who described the calm, deliberate composure with which Turner spoke of what he had done. "I looked on him," the lawyer wrote, "and my blood curdled in my veins."

Turner's revolt sent a wave of terror through the South and heightened fears of future uprisings. As a result, many states adopted even harsher restrictions on both enslaved and free African Americans.

Resistance and Rebellion Many enslaved men and women found ways to oppose the dreadful lifestyle forced on them. Some quietly staged work slowdowns. Others broke tools or set fire to houses and barns. Still others risked beatings or mutilations to run away.

Some enslaved persons turned to more violent means of rebellion. Despite the awful consequences they faced for doing so, some African Americans turned on their slaveholders and killed them.

On occasion, enslaved persons plotted uprisings. In 1822, for example, **Denmark Vesey,** a free African American who operated a woodworking shop in Charleston, South Carolina, was accused of planning an armed revolt to free the region's slaves. Whether or not Vesey actually planned an uprising is not known. The Charleston authorities claimed to have learned of the plot from an informer, and in 1822 Vesey was tried, convicted, and hanged.

A group of African Americans in Virginia did carry out an armed uprising during the early hours of August 22, 1831. Leading the attack was **Nat Turner,** an enslaved minister who believed God had chosen him to bring his people out of bondage. Turner and his followers killed more than 50 white men, women, and children before state and local troops put down the uprising. A court then tried Turner and sentenced him to hang.

 Reading Check **Describing** What was life like for African Americans in the 1800s?

SECTION 3 ASSESSMENT

Checking for Understanding

1. **Define:** cotton gin, planter, yeoman farmer, slave code.

2. **Identify:** task system, gang system, driver, Frederick Douglass, Denmark Vesey, Nat Turner.

3. **Explain** why industry lagged in the South compared to the North.

Reviewing Themes

4. **Continuity and Change** How did cotton farming change the South? What aspects of Southern life stayed the same?

Critical Thinking

5. **Synthesizing** Why was song an important part of the enslaved African American culture?

6. **Organizing** Use a graphic organizer similar to the one below to list the provisions of some slave codes for enslaved African Americans.

Slave Codes

Analyzing Visuals

7. **Examining Art** Study the painting of the Southern wedding on page 254. What elements of the painting suggest a wealthy lifestyle? Did all Southern planters live in such a lavish manner?

Writing About History

8. **Expository Writing** Imagine you are a European visitor to the South in 1830. Write a letter home explaining your impressions of life in this part of the nation.

Guide to Reading

Main Idea
Sectional disputes eroded the spirit of nationalism that swept the country after the War of 1812.

Key Terms and Names
Missouri Compromise, Henry Clay, "favorite son," William Crawford, American System, "corrupt bargain," Democratic-Republican, mudslinging

Reading Strategy
Organizing As you read about growing sectionalism, complete a graphic organizer similar to the one below by filling in the divisive issues of the 1820s.

Divisive Issues of the 1820s

Reading Objectives
• **List** the major parts of the Missouri Compromise.
• **Describe** why the election of 1824 was controversial.

Section Theme
Groups and Institutions The rise of a new political party represented a disagreement between those who wanted to expand federal power and those who wanted to limit it.

Preview of Events

| ♦1820 | ♦1823 | ♦1825 | ♦1828 |

1820
Missouri Compromise enacted

1824
Presidential election fails to produce a clear winner

1825
House of Representatives names John Quincy Adams president

1828
Jackson defeats Adams's re-election bid

★ *An American Story* ★

As May approached in 1820, Thomas Jefferson should have been enjoying his retirement from public life. Instead, a bitter political controversy had him feeling deeply troubled. After more than a year of debate, Congress finally had crafted a plan to allow the Missouri Territory to enter the Union as a slave state while Maine came in as a free state. This arrangement preserved the delicate balance in the number of free and slave states. The arrangement, known as the Missouri Compromise, highlighted the growing dispute over slavery's expansion into the Western territories—a dispute that Jefferson feared could tear the nation apart:

66This momentous question, like a firebell in the night, awakened and filled me with terror. I considered it at once as the knell [funeral bell] of the Union. It is hushed, indeed, for the moment. But this is a reprieve only, not a final sentence.99

—quoted in *The Annals of America*

The Missouri Compromise

The Monroe administration's Era of Good Feelings could not ward off the nation's growing sectional disputes and the passionately differing opinions over slavery. Tensions rose to the boiling point in 1819, when Missouri's application for statehood stirred up the country's most divisive issue: whether slavery should expand westward.

In 1819 the Union consisted of 11 free and 11 slave states. While the House of Representatives already had a majority of Northerners, admitting any new state, either slave or free, would upset the balance in the Senate and touch off a bitter struggle over political power.

NATIONAL GEOGRAPHIC **The Missouri Compromise, 1820**

OREGON COUNTRY

UNORGANIZED TERRITORY

MICHIGAN TERRITORY

Claimed by U.S. and Great Britain

MAINE

VT.

N.H.

N.Y.

MASS.

R.I.

PA.

CONN.

MEXICO

OHIO

IND.

ILL.

N.J.

DEL.

MD.

VA.

MO.

KY.

36°30′N
Missouri Compromise Line

TENN.

N.C.

ARK. TERR.

MISS. ALA.

S.C.

GA.

LA.

FLORIDA TERRITORY

☒ States admitted under conditions of the Missouri Compromise

☐ States and territories closed to slavery

☐ States and territories open to slavery

Geography *Skills*

1. **Interpreting Maps** The Missouri Compromise allowed which two states to enter the Union?
2. **Applying Geography Skills** Why did the South readily agree to making slavery illegal in the unorganized Louisiana Territory?

Missouri's territorial government requested admission into the Union as a slave state in 1819. Acting for slavery's opponents, Congressman James Tallmadge, Jr., of New York proposed a resolution that prohibited slaveholders from bringing new slaves into Missouri. The resolution also called for all enslaved children currently living in Missouri to be freed at age 25. The House accepted the proposal, but the Senate rejected it. Most Senators and members of the House of Representatives from the South voted against the ban, while most from the North voted in favor of it.

Finally, a solution emerged when Maine, which for decades had been part of Massachusetts, requested admission to the Union as a separate state. The Senate decided to combine Maine's request with Missouri's, and it voted to admit Maine as a free state and Missouri as a slave state. This solution preserved the balance in the Senate. Senator Jesse Thomas of Illinois then proposed an amendment that would prohibit slavery in the Louisiana Purchase territory north of Missouri's southern border. This would allow slavery to expand into

Arkansas territory south of Missouri, but it would keep it out of the rest of the Louisiana Purchase.

Since many people at the time thought the Great Plains area north of Missouri was not suitable for farming, it appeared that this **Missouri Compromise** benefited the South. By a very close vote, carefully managed by **Henry Clay** of Kentucky, the House of Representatives voted to accept the Compromise. The Compromise held out the hope that pairing the admission of free and slave states together would quiet the dispute over the expansion of slavery.

Once the issue was settled, however, a new problem developed. Pro-slavery members of the Missouri constitutional convention added a clause to the proposed state constitution prohibiting free African Americans from entering the state. This new controversy threatened final approval of Missouri's admission to the Union. Clay again engineered a solution by getting the Missouri legislature to state that they would not honor the spirit of the clause's wording.

Despite Clay's efforts, many leaders feared that the Missouri Compromise was only a temporary solution. "I take it for granted," John Quincy Adams wrote, "that the present question is a mere preamble—a title page to a great tragic volume."

✓ **Reading Check** **Examining** Why was the Missouri Compromise proposed?

The Election of 1824

Politics reflected the sectional tensions of the day. Although the Republicans had supporters throughout the nation, sectional differences over beliefs and policies were growing obvious. The presidential campaign of 1824 showed how splintered the party was becoming.

GOVERNMENT

A Battle of Favorite Sons Four candidates ran for president in 1824. All belonged to the Republican Party and all were "favorite sons," men who enjoyed the support of leaders from their own state and region. Two candidates, Henry Clay of Kentucky and Andrew Jackson of Tennessee, represented the West. John Quincy Adams, a Massachusetts man then serving as President Monroe's secretary of state, was New England's favorite son. **William Crawford** of Georgia represented the South.

Crawford ran on the original principles of Jefferson's party—states' rights and strict interpretation of the Constitution. Clay favored the national bank, the protective tariff, and nationwide internal improvements—collectively known as the **American System.** Adams was also in favor of internal improvements, but he was less enthusiastic about tariffs. Jackson steered clear of specific issues. His campaign focused on his personal heroism at the Battle of New Orleans.

On Election Day Jackson won the most popular votes, but no candidate won a majority in the Electoral College. Following constitutional procedure, the election went to the House of Representatives, whose members would select the president from the three candidates who received the highest number of electoral votes. Clay, who had placed fourth, was eliminated.

As the Speaker of the House, Henry Clay enjoyed tremendous influence there, and few doubted which candidate he would support. Clay and Jackson had been rivals for political leadership of the West and disliked each other intensely. Clay once described Jackson as "ignorant, passionate, hypocritical, [and] corrupt." Jackson referred to Clay as the "meanest scoundrel that ever disgraced the image of his god."

On a snowy February 9, 1825, the representatives met to make their choice. As expected, Clay threw his political weight behind Adams and helped him win the House election easily. Adams received 13 votes, while Jackson won 7 and Crawford won 4.

The Corrupt Bargain The hard feelings of the election campaign only intensified with Adams's victory. Andrew Jackson Donelson, Jackson's nephew, joined others in accusing Clay of arranging votes for Adams in return for a cabinet post:

> ❝It is rumored and believed by every body here that Mr. Clay will be made Secretary of State. . . . What a farce! That Mr. Adams should swear to support the constitution of the [United] States which he has purchased from Representatives who betrayed the constitution, and which he must distribute among them as rewards for the iniquity.❞
>
> —quoted in *Henry Clay*

Upon taking office, the new president did indeed name Clay as his secretary of state, and Jackson's supporters cried foul. They accused Adams and Clay of striking a "corrupt bargain."

Adams and Clay denied any wrongdoing, and no evidence of a deal ever emerged. Still, Jackson's outraged supporters came together in opposition to the Adams presidency. They took the name **Democratic-Republicans** to stress their differences with the party of John Quincy Adams—now called the **National Republicans.** Eventually the pro-Jackson party shortened the name to Democrats.

Reading Check **Summarizing** How did John Quincy Adams win the election of 1824?

The Presidency of John Quincy Adams

John Quincy Adams, son of the second president, had earned a reputation as the greatest secretary of state in the nation's brief history. A highly intelligent and hardworking man, he intended to leave his mark on the presidency.

In his first message to Congress, Adams announced an ambitious program of nationalist legislation that exceeded even Clay's American System. Alongside standard internal improvements, Adams

John Quincy Adams

urged that federal revenue also be used to build a national university and astronomical observatories, and to fund scientific research. To bar the federal government from these activities, he wrote, "would be to hide in the earth the talent committed to our change."

Adams's proposals, however, struck many legislators as a renewal of his father's Federalist principles. His opponents received the president's initiatives with scorn. It would be extravagant, they believed, to spend the taxpayers' money on such projects.

In the end, Congress granted the president funds for improving rivers and harbors and for extending the National Road westward, but this was far less than he had wanted. The repeated rebuffs he suffered in Congress set the stage for Adams's defeat in his 1828 reelection attempt.

Reading Check **Identifying** What did John Quincy Adams hope to accomplish during his presidency?

The Election of 1828

The presidential election of 1828 pitted John Quincy Adams against Andrew Jackson. The two men waged a bitter campaign, as Jackson fought to achieve a victory that his supporters believed had been unjustly denied him four years earlier.

The campaign descended into mudslinging, in which candidates criticized each other's personalities and morals. Adams called his opponent "incompetent both by his ignorance and by the fury of his passions." Jackson portrayed himself as the candidate of the common man and attacked Adams as an out-of-touch aristocrat. Jackson's supporters also called Adams a gambler for purchasing a billiard table and chess set for the White House. Jackson also revived the

Stumping for Old Hickory This campaign poster for the 1828 presidential election reminds voters of Jackson's heroic military reputation and of the 1824 election. What elements in the poster refer to the "corrupt bargain"?

alleged "corrupt bargain" between Adams and Clay as evidence that the president was untrustworthy.

When the results came in, Jackson had 56 percent of the popular vote and 178 of the 261 electoral votes, a clear victory. Many of the voters who supported Jackson were from the West and South, rural and small-town men who saw Jackson as the candidate most likely to represent their interests. The man whose fiery personality had earned him the nickname "Old Hickory," after a tough, hard wood found on the frontier, finally had reached the White House.

Reading Check **Summarizing** How did Adams and Jackson portray each other during the 1828 campaign?

SECTION 4 ASSESSMENT

Checking for Understanding

1. **Define:** "favorite son," "corrupt bargain," mudslinging.
2. **Identify:** Missouri Compromise, Henry Clay, William Crawford, American System, Democratic-Republican.
3. **Compare** the different campaign strategies of the candidates in the 1824 election.

Reviewing Themes

4. **Groups and Institutions** Why was the Democratic-Republican Party formed after the election of 1824?

Critical Thinking

5. **Synthesizing** Why do you think the candidates in the 1828 election focused on mudslinging instead of issues?
6. **Organizing** Use a graphic organizer similar to the one below to list the terms of the Missouri Compromise.

Missouri Compromise

Analyzing Visuals

7. **Examining Photographs** Study the early daguerreotype of John Quincy Adams on page 259. What characteristics of Adams shown in the image give clues as to the kind of person he was?

Writing About History

8. **Expository Writing** Imagine you are a voter in the election of 1828. Write a letter to a family member explaining which presidential candidate you will vote for and why.

Social Studies
SKILLBUILDER

Reading a Line Graph

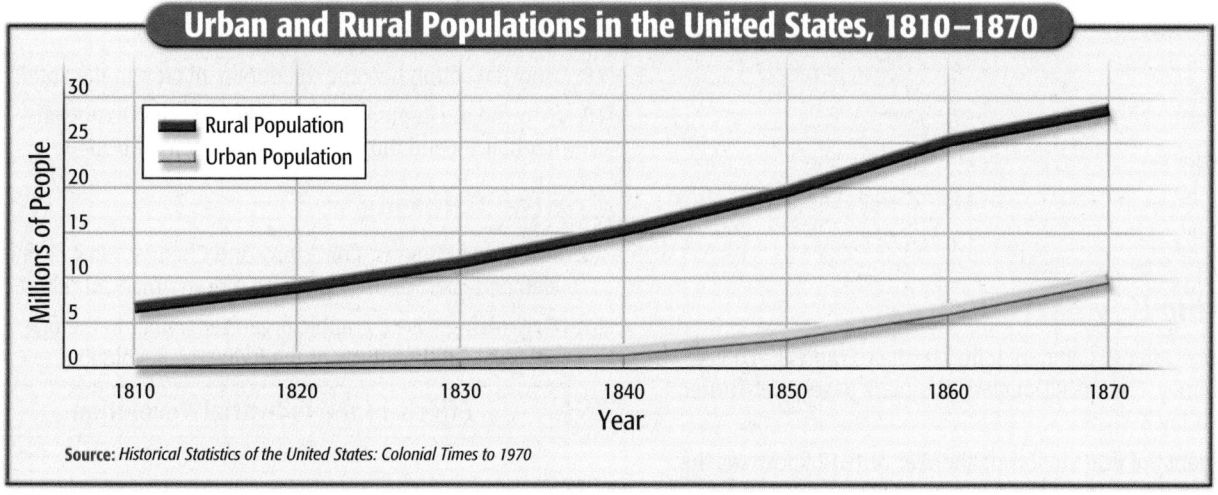

Urban and Rural Populations in the United States, 1810–1870

Source: Historical Statistics of the United States: Colonial Times to 1970

Why Learn This Skill?

Line graphs are a way of showing numbers visually, making them easier to read and understand. Learning to read line graphs will help you compare changes over time or differences between places, groups of people, or related events.

Learning the Skill

Line graphs are often used to show changes in number or quantity over time. They show information in two dimensions. The horizontal axis (or x-axis) is the line along the bottom of the graph. If the graph shows information over time, this axis usually shows the time period. The vertical axis (or y-axis) is the line that runs up the side of the graph. This axis usually displays the quantity, or amount, of whatever is being measured.

A double-line graph shows more than one line, recording related quantities. For instance, you and a friend might both record your running speeds for races over a period of time on one graph, using a line of a different color for each of you. Before trying to understand any graph, be sure to read the labels on both axes and the key for each line.

Practicing the Skill

Study the line graph and answer the following questions.

❶ What kind of information does the graph compare?

❷ What are the time intervals on the horizontal axis?

❸ What quantity is measured on the vertical axis?

❹ What trend does the graph seem to show?

❺ What two phenomena from the chapter explain the changes in the population?

Skills Assessment

Complete the Practicing Skills questions on page 263 and the Chapter 7 Skill Reinforcement Activity to assess your mastery of this skill.

Applying the Skill

Reading a Line Graph Create a line graph comparing the urban and rural population figures from 1910 to 1970. Compare your graph with the one on this page and write a summary of the differences you notice between the two.

Glencoe's **Skillbuilder Interactive Workbook CD-ROM, Level 2,** provides instruction and practice in key social studies skills.

Reviewing Key Terms

On a sheet of paper, use each of these terms in a sentence.

1. revenue tariff
2. protective tariff
3. interchangeable parts
4. labor union
5. strike
6. cotton gin
7. planter
8. yeoman farmer
9. slave code
10. "favorite son"
11. "corrupt bargain"
12. mudslinging

Reviewing Key Facts

13. **Identify:** John C. Calhoun, John Marshall, Francis C. Lowell, Eli Whitney, Frederick Douglass, Denmark Vesey, Nat Turner, Henry Clay.
14. Why were the years following the War of 1812 known as the Era of Good Feelings?
15. What were three actions that strengthened the federal government after the War of 1812?

Chapter Summary

Nationalism in Government

- War of 1812 sparks national pride
- Second Bank of the United States and protective tariffs set up to promote nation's economy
- Supreme Court rulings give federal government power over states
- Spain cedes Florida
- Monroe Doctrine establishes foreign policy

Nationalism in Society

- Steamboats and railroads link the nation's regions
- Telegraph establishes fast, long-distance communication
- Rural farmers and immigrants come together in Northern cities to find work

Sectionalism Emerges

- South's agricultural economy relies on slavery
- Northern leaders view slavery as morally wrong
- Missouri Compromise pits Northern leaders against Southern leaders
- Disputed election of 1824 leads to return to two-party political system
- Congress votes almost strictly along sectional lines

16. What prompted the American declaration known as the Monroe Doctrine?
17. Why was agriculture, and not industry, the leading economic activity in the United States in the early 1800s?
18. How did cotton become the dominant crop in the South?
19. Why did the Republican Party split into the Democratic-Republican and the National Republican Parties?

Critical Thinking

20. **Analyzing Themes: Continuity and Change** What distinctive elements characterized enslaved African American culture?
21. **Organizing** Use a graphic organizer similar to the one below to list the effects of the Industrial Revolution.

Effects of the Industrial Revolution

22. **Interpreting Primary Sources** In *McCulloch* v. *Maryland,* the Supreme Court decided whether Congress had the power to set up the Bank of the United States. The following excerpt is from Chief Justice John Marshall's ruling. Read the excerpt and answer the questions that follow.

66 The government of the United States . . . though limited in its powers, is supreme; . . . Among the enumerated powers, we do not find establishing a bank or creating a corporation. But there is no phrase [which] requires that everything granted shall be expressly and minutely described. . . . Among the enumerated powers of government . . . we find the great powers to lay and collect taxes . . . to declare war and conduct a war; . . . A government entrusted with such ample powers . . . must also be entrusted with ample means for their execution. . . . All means which are appropriate, which are plainly adapted to that end, which are not prohibited, but consist with the letter and spirit of the constitution, are constitutional. . . . 99

—from *McCulloch* v. *Maryland,* 1819

a. What was Marshall's opinion about the power of the government of the United States?
b. Why do you think Marshall's ruling helped strengthen nationalist feelings in the United States?

HISTORY Online

Self-Check Quiz

Visit the *American Vision* Web site at tav.glencoe.com and click on *Self-Check Quizzes—Chapter 7* to assess your knowledge of chapter content.

Geography and History

23. The map on the right shows the United States in 1824. Study the map and answer the questions below.
    a. **Interpreting Maps** What international boundary was in dispute in 1824?
    b. **Applying Geography Skills** What geographic features determined the southern boundary of the Louisiana Purchase?

Practicing Skills

24. **Reading a Line Graph** The line graph below plots the number of patents issued between 1810 and 1840. Use the graph to answer the questions below.
    a. When did the number of patents issued drop sharply?

    b. During what time span did the number of patents issued increase the most?

U.S. Patents Issued 1810–1840

Source: *Historical Statistics of the United States: Colonial Times to 1970*

Writing Activity

25. **Reporting on Primary Sources** Search the Internet for a primary source (speech, letter, song, political cartoon, etc.) that describes heightened feelings of nationalism after the War of 1812. Write a brief explanation of the primary source and present your report to the class.

Chapter Activity

26. **Research Project** Research one of the technological advances made during the early 1800s. Write a description of the technological advance you have researched and create a diagram showing how it works. Place the description and the diagram in your portfolio.

NATIONAL GEOGRAPHIC

Legend:
- British Territory
- Mexico
- - - Louisiana Purchase
- United States

Standardized Test Practice

Directions: Read the excerpt below, taken from the Monroe Doctrine, and answer the question that follows.

The American continents, by the free and independent condition which they have assured and maintain, are hence forth not to be considered as subjects for future colonization by any European powers.

We should consider any attempt on their part to extend their system to any portion of this hemisphere as dangerous to our peace and safety.

The Monroe Doctrine sent a clear message to European powers from the United States. The Doctrine was designed to

A preserve the United States's trade routes with Europe.

B prohibit European nations from colonizing any lands in the Western Hemisphere.

C prevent Central American countries from declaring war against the United States.

D protect the United States from invasion by Central American nations.

Test-Taking Tip: Look *in the passage* to find clues to support your answer. Try not to get confused by the long sentences or old-fashioned language in this passage. Ask yourself what the *main idea* is. Then look for an answer that matches the main idea.

CHAPTER

8 The Spirit of Reform *1828–1845*

Why It Matters

Reform was a key theme of the 1830s and 1840s. Political reform came with the growth of popular democracy. President Jackson's election symbolized the new power of common citizens. For many Americans, social or religious reform was a goal. Some wanted to end slavery. Others wanted to expand education or women's rights. Throughout this period, sectional rivalries grew more bitter.

The Impact Today

Social and political ideals born in this period became important American values.
- *Many Americans value education highly and believe that anyone, regardless of background, might rise to a high political office if they have a good education.*
- *The desire to help others inspires many Americans.*

 The American Vision *Video* *The Chapter 8 video, "The Spirit of Reform," chronicles important reform campaigns of this era.*

1830
- Mormon religion officially organizes

1832
- Democrats hold their first presidential nominating convention

1828
- North-South rift develops over tariff

1833
- American Antislavery Society founded by William Lloyd Garriso

Jackson 1829–1837

 United States
PRESIDENTS

1825   1830   1835

World

1829
- Slavery abolished in Mexico

1835
- Fairy tales of Hans Christian Andersen published

1836
- First botany textbook published

264

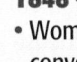

The Verdict of the People by George Caleb Bingham, 1855

Van Buren
1837–1841

W. Harrison
1841

Tyler
1841–1845

1838
• Cherokee are driven from Georgia and embark on the Trail of Tears

1848
• Women's rights convention held at Seneca Falls, New York

1840

1845

1837
• Queen Victoria ascends to English throne

1842
• China opened by force to foreign trade

1845
• Irish potato famine begins

HISTORY
Online

Chapter Overview
Visit the *American Vision* Web site at tav.glencoe.com and click on **Chapter Overviews—Chapter 8** to preview chapter information.

SECTION 1 Jacksonian America

Guide to Reading

Main Idea
The election of Andrew Jackson ushered in a new era of American politics.

Key Terms and Names
spoils system, caucus system, Tariff of Abominations, secede, John C. Calhoun, nullification, Daniel Webster, Force Bill, Indian Removal Act, Trail of Tears, Panic of 1837

Reading Strategy
Organizing As you read about Andrew Jackson's administration, complete a graphic organizer similar to the one below by listing the positions of Jackson and Calhoun during the nullification crisis.

Nullification	
Jackson's Position	Calhoun's Position

Reading Objectives
- **Explain** how Jackson's background influenced his ideas of democratic government.
- **Describe** how the nullification crisis sparked debate over states' rights.

Section Theme
Groups and Institutions The American political system became more democratic during the Jacksonian era.

Preview of Events

◆1825　　　　　◆1830　　　　　◆1835　　　　　◆1840

1828
Andrew Jackson elected president

1830
Webster-Hayne debate held in Senate

1836
Martin Van Buren elected president

1838
United States drives the Cherokee out of Georgia

★ An American Story ★

Margaret Bayard Smith was one of the thousands of Americans who attended the presidential inauguration of Andrew Jackson in 1829. She later wrote to a friend about how much the atmosphere in Washington, D.C., impressed her. "Thousands and thousands of people, without distinction of rank, collected in an immense mass around the Capitol, silent, orderly and tranquil," she explained.

On that day, President Jackson broke a long tradition by inviting the public to his reception. When Smith later attended the White House gala, however, she quickly formed a different opinion about the crowd she had so admired just hours before. "The majesty of the people had disappeared, and a rabble, a mob, of boys, . . . women, children—[were] scrambling, fighting romping," she wrote. "The President, after having been *literally* nearly pressed to death and almost suffocated and torn to pieces by the people in their eagerness to shake hands with Old Hickory, had retreated through the back way. . . . Cut glass and china to the amount of several thousand dollars had been broken in the struggle to get refreshments. . . . Ladies and gentlemen only had been expected at this levee, not the people *en masse.* But it was the people's day, and the people's President, and the people would rule."

—**adapted from** *First Forty Years of Washington Society*

A New Era in Politics

The citizens who had turned the normally dignified inauguration reception into a boisterous affair represented a new class of American voters and a new era in American politics. Beginning in the early 1800s and continuing through the presidency of

Andrew Jackson, the nation's political system became more democratic. During this time, government became more inclusive and ordinary citizens became a greater political force.

States Expand Voting Rights

In the early 1800s, hundreds of thousands of Americans, mostly white men, gained the right to vote. This was largely because many states lowered or eliminated property ownership as a voting qualification. In addition, as cities and towns grew, the percentage of working people who did not own property increased. These people paid taxes and had an interest in the political affairs of their communities—and they too wanted a greater voice in electing those who represented them.

The expansion of voting rights was very much in evidence in the presidential election of 1828. In 1824 about 355,000 Americans had voted for president. Four years later, more than 1.1 million citizens cast a ballot in the presidential election. The expansion of suffrage continued, and by 1840, more than 2.4 million Americans voted in the presidential election.

The People's President

In 1828, it was Andrew Jackson who won the support of these new voters, many of whom resided on the frontiers of the West and South. Many of the citizens who voted for the first time in 1828 saw in Jackson a man they truly could admire. Orphaned at the age of 14, Jackson received little formal education. His achievements were due to his diligence, hard work, and innate intelligence. Jackson was elected Tennessee's first representative to Congress before the age of 30. In the War of 1812, he won fame leading his troops to victory at the Battle of New Orleans. In 1818, forces under his command invaded and captured Spanish Florida. Jackson's most obvious trait was his force of will, a characteristic that became evident when someone tried to defy him.

Jackson's early life was notable for violent personal quarrels. He took part in five duels, once killing his opponent. As Jackson grew older, his temper and actions became milder. By the time he entered the White House, he had become a person of dignity and courtesy.

The Spoils System

As president, Andrew Jackson returned the common people's admiration of him. He had a great belief in the capability and intelligence of average Americans. More than earlier presidents, Jackson felt that the majority should rule in a democracy and that ordinary citizens should play a more prominent role in government.

Toward that end, Jackson strongly supported the spoils system, the practice of appointing people to government jobs on the basis of party loyalty and support. Rewarding supporters with government jobs had long been part of American politics, but Jackson was the first president to force out large numbers of government employees in order to appoint his own followers. A shocked John Quincy Adams charged that the president's actions made government "a perpetual . . . scramble for office."

Jackson considered the spoils system to be democratic. By getting rid of a permanent office-holding class, he opened up government to more ordinary citizens. He felt that since government jobs were "so plain and simple," they should be rotated at will and given to supporters.

History *Through Art*

Jackson's Popularity Andrew Jackson attracted large crowds on his trip to Washington, D.C., in 1829 to take office. His determined character can be seen in the portrait on the right by famous painter Asher Durand. In what ways was Jackson different from previous presidents?

Why It Matters

The 1828 Election

The election of 1828, which put Andrew Jackson in office, was one of the most significant in American history. It showed the increasing strength of the West, the power of sectionalism, and the impact of a more democratic process.

Increased Voter Participation

Did not Vote 73.1%	Voted 26.9%

1824

Did not Vote 42.4%	Voted 57.6%

1828

Source: *Historical Statistics of the United States: Colonial Times to 1970*

The percentage of eligible voters who actually cast a ballot increased dramatically in the election of 1828. So did the absolute number: three times as many people voted for president in 1828 than in 1824. This was mainly because many states had lowered or eliminated property ownership as a voting qualification. In Jacksonian terms, it was a new era, the era of the "common man."

◄ At a public reception open to all, crowds flocked to the White House to celebrate Jackson's inauguration. In the confusion, people trampled over one another, soiling the carpets and ruining furniture as they rushed to meet the president. "It was a proud day for the people," wrote a friend of the president. "General Jackson is their own President." Other observers were horrified. Joseph Story, a Supreme Court justice, remarked with disgust, "The reign of King 'Mob' seems triumphant."

A More Open Electoral System In addition to these measures aimed at strengthening democracy, Jackson's supporters moved to make the political system—specifically, the way in which presidential candidates were chosen—more democratic. At that time, political parties used the caucus system to select presidential candidates. The members of the party who served in Congress, known as the party caucus, would meet to choose the nominee for president. Jackson's supporters believed that such a method restricted access to office mainly to the elite and well connected.

The Jacksonians replaced the caucus with the **national nominating convention.** At nominating conventions, delegates from the states gathered to decide on the party's presidential nominee. Through the convention, proponents believed, political power would come from the people rather than from elite political institutions. In 1832 the Democrats held a nominating convention to renominate Andrew Jackson for president.

✓ **Reading Check** **Examining** In what ways did the United States become more democratic in the early 1800s?

The Nullification Crisis

Jackson had not been in office long before he had to focus on a national crisis. It centered on South Carolina, but it also highlighted the growing rift between the nation's Northern and Southern regions.

The Debate Over Nullification Throughout the early 1800s, South Carolina's economy had been weakening. Many of the state's residents blamed this situation on the nation's tariffs. Because it had few industries, South Carolina purchased many of its manufactured goods, such as cooking utensils and tools, from England, but tariffs made them extremely expensive. When Congress levied yet another new tariff in 1828—which critics called the **Tariff of Abominations**—many South Carolinians threatened to secede, or withdraw, from the Union.

The growing turmoil troubled one politician in particular: **John C. Calhoun,** the nation's vice president and a resident of South Carolina. Calhoun felt torn between upholding the country's policies and helping his fellow South Carolinians. Rather than support secession, Calhoun put forth the idea of nullification

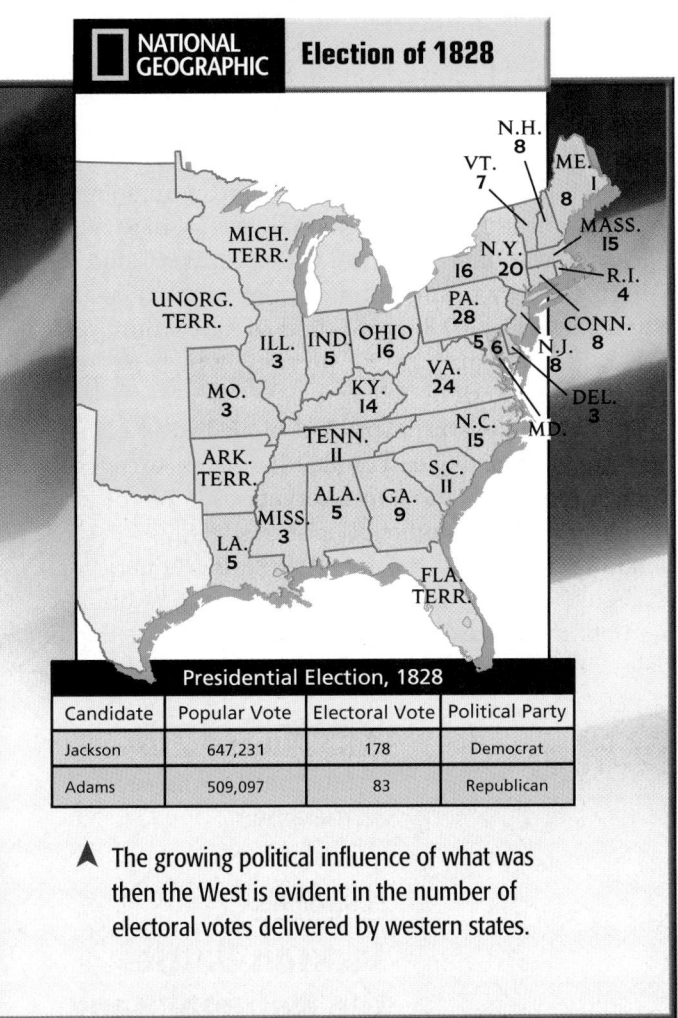

Presidential Election, 1828			
Candidate	Popular Vote	Electoral Vote	Political Party
Jackson	647,231	178	Democrat
Adams	509,097	83	Republican

▲ The growing political influence of what was then the West is evident in the number of electoral votes delivered by western states.

to defuse the situation. He explained this idea in an anonymously published work, *The South Carolina Exposition and Protest,* which argued that states had the right to declare a federal law null, or not valid. Calhoun theorized that the states had this right since they had created the federal Union.

The issue continued to simmer beneath the surface until January 1830, when **Robert Hayne** of South Carolina and **Daniel Webster** of Massachusetts confronted each other on the floor of the Senate. Webster, perhaps the greatest orator of his day, was a ferocious defender of the Union. Hayne was an eloquent champion of the right of states to chart their own course.

Hayne asserted that the Union was no more than a voluntary association of states and advocated the motto, "Liberty first and Union afterward." Webster countered that neither liberty nor the Union could survive without binding federal laws:

66I have not allowed myself, sir, to look beyond the Union, to see what might lie hidden in the dark recess behind. I have not coolly weighed the chances of preserving liberty when the bonds that unite us together shall be broken asunder. I have not

accustomed myself to hang over the precipice of disunion, to see whether, with my short sight, I can fathom the depth of the abyss below. . . . Liberty *and* Union, now and for ever, one and inseparable!99

—quoted in *The Writings and Speeches of Daniel Webster*

Jackson Defends the Union Several months after the Webster-Hayne debate, President Jackson let everyone know where he stood on the issue. During a political dinner, Jackson stood to make a toast. Looking directly at John Calhoun, he said, "Our federal Union—it must be preserved." Calhoun's hand shook, and he spilled wine as he rose to counter Jackson with, "The Union—next to our liberty, most dear."

The war of words erupted into a full confrontation in 1832, when Congress passed yet another tariff law. At President Jackson's request, the new law cut tariffs significantly, but South Carolinians were not satisfied. The state legislature asked South Carolina voters to elect a special state convention. In November 1832, the convention adopted an ordinance of nullification declaring the tariffs of 1828 and 1832 to be unconstitutional.

Jackson considered the nullification an act of treason, and he sent a warship to Charleston. In 1833 Congress passed the **Force Bill,** authorizing the president to use the military to enforce acts of Congress. As tensions rose, Senator Henry Clay pushed through Congress a bill that would lower the nation's tariffs gradually until 1842. In response, South Carolina repealed its nullification of the tariff law. Both sides claimed victory, and the issue was laid to rest—at least temporarily.

✓ **Reading Check** **Summarizing** What caused the nullification crisis?

Policies Toward Native Americans

Andrew Jackson's commitment to extending democracy did not benefit everyone. His attitude toward Native Americans reflected the views of many westerners at that time. Jackson had fought the Creek and Seminole people in Georgia and Florida, and in his inaugural address he declared his intention to move all Native Americans to the Great Plains.

This idea had been gaining support in the United States since the Louisiana Purchase. John C. Calhoun had formally proposed it in 1823 when he was secretary of war. Many Americans believed that the

Great Plains was a wasteland that would never be settled. They thought that if they moved Native Americans to that region, the nation's conflict with them would be over. In 1830, Jackson pushed through Congress the **Indian Removal Act,** which provided money for relocating Native Americans.

Most Native Americans eventually gave in and resettled in the West, but not the Cherokee of Georgia. Over the years, this Native American group had adopted aspects of white culture, and they hired lawyers to sue the state of Georgia. Their case, *Worcester* v. *Georgia*, eventually reached the Supreme Court. In 1832 Chief Justice John Marshall ordered state officials to honor Cherokee property rights. Jackson refused to support the decision. "Marshall has made his opinion," the president reportedly said, "now let him enforce it." (See page 1083 for information on *Worcester v. Georgia.)*

Until 1838 most of the Cherokee resisted the government's offers of western land. Jackson's successor, Martin Van Buren, eventually sent in the army to resolve the conflict. The army forced the remaining people out of their homes and marched them to what is now Oklahoma. About 2,000 Cherokee died in camps while waiting for the migration to begin. Approximately 2,000 more died of starvation, disease, and exposure on the journey, which became known as the **Trail of Tears.**

By 1838, the government had moved most Native Americans still living east of the Mississippi, except for the Seminole of Florida, to reservations. Most people supported these removal policies. Only a few denounced the harsh treatment of Native Americans. Non-supporters included some of the National Republicans and a few religious denominations, especially the Quakers and Methodists.

Reading Check

Interpreting What was the Trail of Tears?

NATIONAL GEOGRAPHIC — **Native American Removal, 1832–1841**

In 1832 Sauk and Fox warriors led by Chief Black Hawk fought to reclaim territory east of the Mississippi River, but were defeated.

The Cherokee took their refusal to move to the Supreme Court—and won. Federal troops forced them to leave in 1838.

Chief Osceola led the Seminole in rebellion.

Legend:
- Ceded by Native Americans
- Ceded to Native Americans
- Multi-Group Removal Route
- Single Group Removal Route
- Trail of Tears
- Fort
- 1840 border

0   200 miles
0   200 kilometers
Albers Conic Equal-Area projection

Geography Skills

1. **Interpreting Maps** Name two Native American groups in the northern half of the United States that were forced to move.
2. **Applying Geography Skills** Where did the Trail of Tears end?

ECONOMICS

Jackson Battles the National Bank

One of the most contentious developments of Jackson's presidency was his campaign against the Second Bank of the United States. Like most Westerners and many working people, President Jackson was suspicious of the Bank. He regarded it as a monopoly that benefited the wealthy elite.

Despite its reputation, the Bank played an important role in keeping the money supply of the United States stable. At the time, most American paper money consisted of bank notes issued by private state banks. State banks issued bank notes with the promise that the notes could always be turned in for "hard" money—gold or silver coins.

The state banks, however, would often issue more paper money than they could redeem in gold or silver. This let them make more loans at lower interest rates, but it created the danger of inflation. To prevent the state banks from loaning too much money, the Bank of the United States regularly collected bank notes and asked state banks to redeem them for gold and silver. This action forced state banks to be careful about how much money they loaned, and it also limited inflation.

The Bank had done a good job stabilizing the money supply and interest rates, but many western settlers, who needed easy credit to run their farms, were unhappy with the Bank's lending policies. President Jackson also believed the Bank was unconstitutional, despite the Supreme Court's ruling in *McCulloch* v. *Maryland*. He did not believe that as president he had to accept this Supreme Court ruling.

To make the Bank an issue in the 1832 presidential campaign, Jackson's congressional opponents introduced a bill extending the Bank's charter for another 20 years. Congress passed the bill, but Jackson vetoed it. When the election was over, it was clear that most Americans supported Jackson. He easily won a second term.

Jackson took his re-election as a directive from the people to destroy the Bank at once, even though its charter did not run out until 1836. He removed the government's deposits from the Bank and placed them in state banks. The removal of the deposits forced the Bank to call in its loans and stop lending.

By putting an end to the Bank of the United States, Jackson had won a considerable political victory. Later, however, critics would charge that the end of the Bank contributed significantly to the financial woes that plagued the country in the years ahead.

Reading Check **Examining** Why was President Jackson against the Second Bank of the United States?

A New Party Emerges

Andrew Jackson's forceful style had earned him plenty of detractors, and by the mid-1830s a new party emerged to oppose him. The group named itself the Whigs after the party in England that had worked to limit the king's power. The Whigs advocated a larger federal government, industrial and commercial development, and a centralized economy. Jackson's Democrats, on the other hand, favored a limited federal government, and they distrusted eastern merchants and business leaders.

Analyzing *Political Cartoons*

Kingly Rule? Jackson's strong-willed leadership attracted many critics. Here the cartoonist portrays Jackson as an absolute monarch. What does Jackson appear to be trampling underfoot?

The Presidency of Martin Van Buren The Whigs were united in opposing Jackson, but they were unable to settle on a leader. During the 1836 presidential election, Jackson's popularity and the nation's continuing prosperity helped Democrat Martin Van Buren defeat the Whigs, who had three candidates for president.

The new president had little time to savor his victory. Shortly after Van Buren took office, a crippling economic crisis hit the nation. During this **Panic of 1837,** as the crisis was called, many banks and businesses failed. Thousands of farmers lost their land, and unemployment soared among eastern factory workers. Van Buren, a firm believer in his party's philosophy of a limited federal government, did little to ease the crisis.

"Tippecanoe and Tyler Too" With the nation experiencing hard times, the Whigs looked forward to ousting the Democrats in the presidential election of 1840. They nominated General William Henry Harrison, who was regarded as a hero for his role in

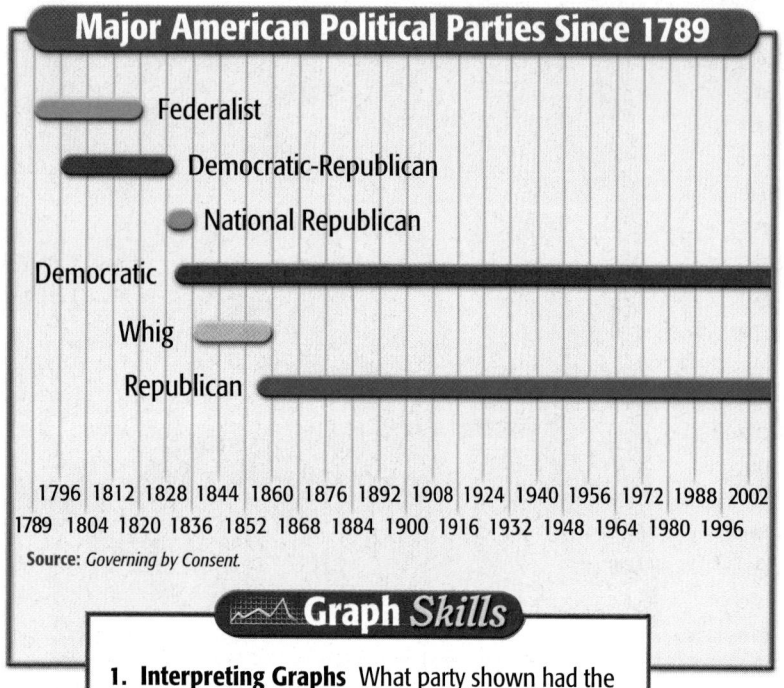

Major American Political Parties Since 1789

Federalist

Democratic-Republican

National Republican

Democratic

Whig

Republican

1796 1812 1828 1844 1860 1876 1892 1908 1924 1940 1956 1972 1988 2002
1789 1804 1820 1836 1852 1868 1884 1900 1916 1932 1948 1964 1980 1996

Source: *Governing by Consent.*

Graph Skills

1. **Interpreting Graphs** What party shown had the shortest life span?
2. **Comparing** How long have Republicans and Democrats been major political rivals?

the Battle of Tippecanoe and in the War of 1812. John Tyler, a Southerner and former Democrat who had left his party in protest over the nullification issue, joined the ticket as the vice presidential candidate. Adopting the campaign slogan "Tippecanoe and Tyler too," the Whigs blamed Van Buren for the economic depression. To attract western voters, they presented Harrison, a man born to wealth and privilege, as a simple frontiersman.

The strategy worked. Harrison won a decisive victory—234 electoral votes to 60, although the popular vote was much closer. On March 4, 1841, Harrison delivered his inauguration speech. The weather that day was bitterly cold, but Harrison insisted on delivering his nearly two-hour address without a hat or coat. He came down with pneumonia and died 32 days later, thereby serving the shortest term of any American president. Vice President John Tyler then succeeded to the presidency.

The Tyler Years Tyler's rise to the presidency shocked Whig leaders. Tyler actually opposed many Whig policies, and party leaders had placed him on the ticket mainly to attract Southern voters. Congress and the press mockingly called Tyler, "His Accidency." The Whigs in Congress tried to push through their agenda anyway, including a Third Bank of the United States and a higher tariff, but Tyler sided with the Democrats on these key issues.

Foreign relations occupied the country's attention during much of Tyler's administration, especially relations with Great Britain. Disputes over the Maine-Canadian border and other issues resulted in the 1842 **Webster-Ashburton Treaty**, which established a firm boundary between the United States and Canada from Maine to Minnesota.

By the middle of the 1800s, a wave of social change was sweeping across the nation. Americans began examining numerous aspects of their culture. A social transformation soon began, which eventually led to the shaping of a uniquely American society.

Reading Check **Identifying** What new political party won the presidential election of 1840?

SECTION 1 ASSESSMENT

Checking for Understanding

1. **Define:** spoils system, caucus system, secede, nullification.
2. **Identify:** Tariff of Abominations, John C. Calhoun, Daniel Webster, Force Bill, Indian Removal Act, Trail of Tears, Panic of 1837.

Reviewing Themes

3. **Groups and Institutions** In what ways did the United States become more democratic during Jackson's presidency?

Critical Thinking

4. **Determining Cause and Effect** What effect did the Panic of 1837 have on the presidential election of 1840?

5. **Categorizing** Use a graphic organizer similar to the one below to list the policies of the Whigs and Jackson's Democrats.

Party	Policies
Whigs	
Democrats	

Analyzing Visuals

6. **Examining Art** Study the artwork on page 267. Some wealthy Americans claimed that President Jackson's supporters were a "mob" element in the nation. How does the artist portray Jackson's supporters? Why do you think so?

Writing About History

7. **Persuasive Writing** Imagine you are a Native American living in the United States during Andrew Jackson's presidency. Write a letter to President Jackson giving your opinion of the Indian Removal Act.

A Changing Culture

Main Idea

The United States underwent dramatic social and cultural changes during the early and mid-1800s.

Key Terms and Names

nativism, Know-Nothings, Second Great Awakening, Charles Grandison Finney, Joseph Smith, romanticism, transcendentalism, utopia

Reading Strategy

Categorizing Complete a graphic organizer similar to the one below by listing beliefs of various religious groups of the Second Great Awakening.

Religious Groups	Beliefs

Reading Objectives

- **Explain** the goals of the different groups active in the Second Great Awakening.
- **Identify** the key ideas of romanticism and two important romantic thinkers or writers.

Section Theme

Groups and Institutions The Second Great Awakening increased support for many religious groups in the United States.

Preview of Events

♦1830　　　　♦1838　　　　♦1846　　　　♦1854

1830
Mormon religion officially organizes

1845
Potato famine strikes Ireland

1850
Hawthorne's *Scarlet Letter* published

1854
American Party forms

★ *An American Story* ★

By June of 1850, Daniel Guiney had made up his mind. He was going to leave his impoverished town in Ireland and move to the United States. The enthusiastic letters he had received from friends convinced him that life had to be better in the United States. Ireland was suffering a devastating famine. Tens of thousands of citizens were dying of starvation, while many more were fleeing the country.

By August 1850, Guiney and a group from his neighborhood had moved to Buffalo, New York. After settling in, Guiney wrote back home about the wondrous new land where they now resided.

❝We mean to let you know our situation at present. . . . We arrived here about five o'clock in the afternoon of yesterday, fourteen of us together, where we were received with the greatest kindness of respectability. . . . When we came to the house we could not state to you how we were treated. We had potatoes, meat, butter, bread, and tea for dinner. . . . If you were to see Denis Reen when Daniel Danihy dressed him with clothes suitable for this country, you would think him to be a boss or steward, so that we have scarcely words to state to you how happy we felt at present.❞

—quoted in *Out of Ireland*

The New Wave of Immigrants

Daniel Guiney was just one of the millions of immigrants who came to the United States in search of a better life in the mid-1800s. The arrival of these newcomers coincided with a time when Americans were blazing new paths in a host of cultural

The Bay and Harbor of New York Immigrants arrive in New York City. Castle Garden, the building in the distant left, served as a processing facility for immigrants beginning in 1855. Many immigrants saw posters such as this one (left) advertising passage between Liverpool and Boston. **What two nationalities made up the majority of immigrants to America during the mid-1800s?**

areas, including religion, art, and literature. Together, these events helped bring great changes to American society in the years before the Civil War.

Between 1815 and 1860, the United States experienced a massive influx of immigrants. Over 5 million foreigners arrived on its shores. Many had fled violence and political turmoil at home, while others sought to escape starvation and poverty. Most of these newcomers found opportunity and a fresh start, but some also found discrimination and prejudice.

Newcomers From Ireland and Germany The

largest wave of immigrants, almost 2 million, came from Ireland. The driving force behind the massive exodus was the onset of widespread famine in 1845, when a fungus destroyed much of the nation's crop of potatoes, a mainstay of the Irish diet. Most Irish immigrants arrived in the United States with no money and few marketable skills. They generally settled in the industrialized cities of the Northeast, where many worked as unskilled laborers and servants.

Between 1815 and 1860, Germans represented the second largest group of immigrants. By 1860 over 1.5 million Germans had arrived in the United States. Most had enough money to move beyond the large

eastern cities and settle in the Midwest. There they became farmers or went into business. Like most other immigrants, Germans reveled in their newfound sense of freedom and liberty. German immigrant August Blümmer expressed this sentiment in a letter he wrote in 1838:

❝Over there [Germany] common sense and free speech lie in shackles. . . . I invite you to come over here, should you want to obtain a clear notion of genuine public life, freedom of people and a sense of being a nation. . . . I have never regretted that I came here, and never! never! again shall I bow my head under the yoke of despotism and folly.❞

—quoted in *News from the Land of Freedom*

Nativism While immigrants often found a new

sense of freedom in the United States, some encountered discrimination. The presence of people from different cultures, with different languages and different religions, produced feelings of nativism, or hostility toward foreigners.

In the 1800s, many Americans were strongly anti-Catholic. Many prominent ministers preached anti-Catholic sermons. Occasionally, anti-Catholic riots erupted. The arrival of millions of predominantly Catholic Irish and German immigrants led to the rise of several nativist groups, such as the Supreme Order of the Star Spangled Banner, founded in 1849. These groups pledged never to vote for a Catholic and pushed for laws banning immigrants and Catholics from holding public office. In July 1854, delegates from these groups formed the American Party. Membership in the party was secret, and those questioned were obliged to answer, "I know nothing." The **Know-Nothings,** as the party was nicknamed, built a large following in the 1850s.

Reading Check **Analyzing** Why did nativism become so strong in the mid-1800s?

A Religious Revival

As immigrants added to the diversity of society, Americans were transforming the society in which they lived. One important change came in American religious life, where traditional Protestantism experienced a dramatic revival, and new forms of worship became prominent.

The Second Great Awakening By the end of the 1700s, many church leaders sensed that Americans' commitment to organized religion was weakening. This deterioration was due in large part to the growth of scientific knowledge and rationalism, notions that challenged the doctrine of faith. In the early 1800s, religious leaders organized to revive Americans' commitment to religion. The resulting movement came to be called the **Second Great Awakening.** It began in Kentucky, among frontier farmers, and quickly spread to the rest of the country. Leaders of the various Protestant denominations—most often Methodists, Baptists, and Presbyterians—held camp meetings that attracted thousands of followers for days of song, prayer, and emotional outpourings of faith.

The basic message of the Second Great Awakening was that individuals must readmit God and Christ into their daily lives. The new revivalism rejected the traditional Calvinist idea that only a chosen few were predestined for salvation. Instead, ministers preached that all people could attain grace through faith.

One of the most prominent advocates of this new message was a Presbyterian minister named **Charles Grandison Finney.** Finney preached that each person contained within himself or herself the capacity for spiritual rebirth and salvation. Finney helped found modern revivalism. His camp meetings were carefully planned and rehearsed to create as much emotion as possible. He compared his methods to those used by politicians and salespeople, and he used emotion to focus people's attention on his message. Finney began preaching in upstate New York, where he launched a series of revivals in towns along the Erie Canal. He then took his message to the cities of the Northeast.

Finney also served as president of Oberlin College in Ohio, the first college in the United States to admit women and African Americans. Although Oberlin became a center for social reform movements in the United States, Finney warned against using politics to change society. He believed that if Christian ideas reformed people from within, society would become better, but if people remained selfish and immoral, political reforms would not make any difference.

New Religious Groups Emerge A number of other religious groups also flourished during this period. The Unitarians and Universalists broke away from the New England Congregational Church. Unitarians reject the idea that Jesus was the son of God, arguing instead that he was a great teacher. Their name comes from the belief that God is a unity, not a trinity of Father, Son, and Holy Spirit. Universalists believe in the universal salvation of souls. They reject the idea of hell and believe God intends to save everyone.

History *Through Art*

Religious Zeal J. Maze Burban's *Religious Camp Meeting* dramatizes religious revivalism, showing a charismatic preacher reaching many in the audience. From studying the image, can you suggest other reasons people might want to attend?

Margaret Fuller
1810–1850

As a young woman, Margaret Fuller was a member of a group of prominent New England writers and philosophers who developed transcendentalism. In 1840, with the help of Ralph Waldo Emerson, she founded the magazine *The Dial,* which published poetry and essays of the transcendentalist movement.

Fuller also organized groups of Boston women to promote their education and intellectual development. These meetings convinced her to write the book *Women in the Nineteenth Century,* in which she argued that women deserved equal political rights.

Fuller's success in editing *The Dial* caught the eye of Horace Greeley, the famous editor of the *New York Tribune.* In 1844 Greeley hired Fuller to be the *Tribune's* literary critic. In 1846 he sent Fuller to Europe to cover European reform efforts. While visiting Italy, Fuller met and married Giovanni Angelo Ossoli, a revolutionary fighting to unite Italy into one country.

Fuller sent home reports about the Italian revolution of 1848, becoming the first American woman foreign war correspondent. In 1850, as the revolution fell apart, Fuller, Ossoli, and their young son set sail for the United States. Tragedy struck when their ship sank near Long Island, New York, and all three drowned.

Another religious group that emerged during this period was the Church of Jesus Christ of Latter-day Saints, whose followers are commonly known as Mormons. **Joseph Smith,** a New Englander living in western New York, began preaching Mormon ideas in 1830 after claiming to have been called to restore the Christian church to its original form. Smith published *The Book of Mormon* that year, saying it was a translation of words inscribed on golden plates that he had received from an angel. The text told of the coming of God and the need to build a kingdom on Earth to receive him.

After enduring continuous harassment in Ohio, Missouri, and elsewhere, Mormons from around the Midwest moved to Commerce, Illinois, in the spring of 1839. They bought the town, renamed it Nauvoo, and began building a self-contained community. The group prospered in the Midwest, with Nauvoo numbering about 15,000 in 1844. Persecution continued, however, and that same year local residents murdered Smith. After Smith's death, Brigham Young became the leader of the Church. The Mormons then left Illinois and trekked westward to the Utah territory, where they put down permanant roots.

✓ **Reading Check** **Summarizing** What was the basic message of the Second Great Awakening?

A Literary Renaissance

The optimism of the Second Great Awakening about human nature also influenced philosophers and writers. Many leading thinkers of the day adopted the tenets of romanticism, a movement that began in Europe in the 1800s. Romanticism advocated feeling over reason, inner spirituality over external rules, the individual above society, and nature over environments created by humans.

One notable expression of American romanticism came from New England writers and philosophers who were known as the transcendentalists. Transcendentalism urged people to transcend, or overcome, the limits of their minds and let their souls reach out to embrace the beauty of the universe.

American Writers Emerge The most influential transcendentalist was **Ralph Waldo Emerson.** In his 1836 essay *Nature,* Emerson wrote that those who wanted fulfillment should work for communion with the natural world. Emerson influenced other writers, including **Margaret Fuller** and **Henry David Thoreau.** Thoreau believed that individuals must fight the pressure to conform. "If a man does not keep pace with his companions, perhaps it is because he hears a different drummer," he wrote. "Let him step to the music which he hears, however measured or far away."

Emerson and Thoreau were only two of many writers who set out to create uniquely American works. Washington Irving, famous for his "Legend of Sleepy Hollow" (1819), became one of the first prominent American writers. **James Fenimore Cooper** romanticized Native Americans and frontier explorers in his Leatherstocking Tales, the most famous being *The Last of the Mohicans* (1826). **Nathaniel Hawthorne,** a New England customs official, wrote over 100 tales and novels. His novel *The Scarlet Letter* (1850), with its Puritan setting, explored the persecution and psychological suffering that results from sin. **Herman Melville,** another New Englander, wrote the great *Moby Dick* (1851). **Edgar Allan Poe,** a poet and short story writer, achieved fame as a writer of terror and mystery. Perhaps the most important poet of the era was **Walt Whitman,** who published a volume of poetry in 1855 called *Leaves of Grass.* Whitman loved nature, the common people, and American democracy, and his famous work reflects these passions. The best-remembered female poet of the era was **Emily Dickinson,** who wrote simple, personal, deeply emotional poetry.

The Penny Press Another important development of the early 1800s was the rise of the mass newspaper. Before the 1800s, most newspapers catered to well-educated readers. They were typically published once a week and cost around six cents, which was far beyond the reach of the average worker.

As more Americans learned to read and gained the right to vote, publishers began producing inexpensive newspapers, known as **penny papers,** which provided the kind of news most people liked. Reports of fires, crimes, marriages, gossip, politics, and local news made the papers an instant success.

General interest magazines that catered to a more specialized readership also emerged around this time. In 1830 Louis A. Godey founded *Godey's Lady's Book,* the first American magazine for women. The poet James Russell Lowell launched *Atlantic Monthly,* another magazine for the well-educated, in 1857, while *Harper's Weekly* covered everything from book reviews to news reports.

✓ **Reading Check** **Evaluating** What were the main themes of American writers in the early 1800s?

Utopian Communities

The ideas that drove the religious and artistic movements of the United States in the mid-1800s—optimism about human nature and a belief in people's ability to redefine their lives—also spurred the establishment of new communities. The people who formed these communities believed that society tended to corrupt human nature. They thought that the way to a better life was to separate themselves from society and form their own utopia, or ideal society. Cooperative living and the absence of private property characterized these communities, and dozens of them sprang up and flourished during the Jacksonian Era.

In New England, near West Roxbury, Massachusetts, transcendentalist George Ripley established a utopian community known as **Brook Farm** in 1841. The farm offered its members the chance to engage in intellectual activity while cooperatively running a farm. Ultimately, Brook Farm collapsed after a large fire left the group with huge debts.

The religious group known as the **Shakers** established small utopian communities from Maine to Kentucky. The group got its name from a ritual "shaking" dance that members performed. The Shakers reached their peak in the mid-1800s with some 6,000 members. Since they did not believe in marrying or having children, the group could only expand by making converts.

In the end, the number of Americans who chose to live in utopian communities was relatively small. Many more, inspired by a strong faith in human goodness, attempted not to escape society but to reform it.

✓ **Reading Check** **Interpreting** What spurred the establishment of utopian societies?

SECTION 2 ASSESSMENT

Checking for Understanding

1. **Define:** nativism, romanticism, transcendentalism, utopia.
2. **Identify:** Know-Nothings, Second Great Awakening, Charles Grandison Finney, Joseph Smith.
3. **Summarize** the goals of the Know-Nothings.

Reviewing Themes

4. **Groups and Institutions** What religious denominations increased their influence in the United States during the Second Great Awakening?

Critical Thinking

5. **Interpreting** How did the writers of the early to mid-1800s reflect American life?
6. **Organizing** Use a graphic organizer similar to the one below to list American cultural movements in the mid-1800s.

Movements in American Culture in the Mid-1800s

Analyzing Visuals

7. **Examining Art** Study the painting on page 275 of the camp meeting. What elements of the image suggest that the revival attracted many working-class people?

Writing About History

8. **Expository Writing** Imagine you are an Irish or German immigrant in the mid-1800s. Write an essay contrasting the United States with your homeland. Describe your new life in the United States and how you are treated.

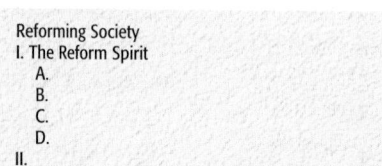
Main Idea

Spurred on by a revival of religion and a heightened belief in the power of individuals, Americans engaged in reform efforts in the early and mid-1800s.

Key Terms and Names

Dorothea Dix, Lyman Beecher, benevolent society, temperance, penitentiary, Horace Mann, Elizabeth Cady Stanton

Reading Strategy

Taking Notes As you read about American reform efforts in the early and mid-1800s, use the section's major headings to create an outline like the one below.

> Reforming Society
> I. The Reform Spirit
>   A.
>   B.
>   C.
>   D.
> II.

Reading Objectives

- **Analyze** the connection between religious and social reform.
- **List** major areas of society that reformers set out to improve.

Section Theme

Continuity and Change Reform movements sought to change American society, but in ways that upheld American values and ideals.

Preview of Events

♦1843	♦1847	♦1851	♦1855

1843
Dorothea Dix calls for reforming care of mentally ill

1848
Seneca Falls Convention

1851
Maine passes first state law prohibiting alcohol

1852
Massachusetts passes first mandatory school attendance law

★ *An American Story* ★

By 1841 Dorothea Dix had been a schoolteacher in Massachusetts for many years. That year, a clergyman asked her to lead a Sunday school class at a local prison. What Dix saw there appalled her. Mentally ill persons lay neglected in dirty, unheated rooms. Putting aside her teaching career, she began a crusade to improve prison conditions for the mentally ill and to provide them with the treatment they needed.

In 1843 Dix composed a letter to the Massachusetts legislature calling for such reforms. She pointed to the example of one local woman as evidence that more humane treatment might help many of the mentally ill. "Some may say these things cannot be remedied," she wrote. "I *know* they can. . . . A young woman, a pauper . . . was for years a raging maniac. A cage, chains, and the whip were the agents for controlling her, united with harsh tones and profane language." Dix explained that a local couple took the woman in and treated her with care and respect. "They are careful of her diet. They keep her very clean. She calls them 'father' and 'mother.' Go there now, and you will find her 'clothed,' and though not perfectly in her 'right mind,' so far restored as to be a safe and comfortable inmate."

—adapted from *Old South Leaflets*

The Reform Spirit

Largely through the efforts of **Dorothea Dix,** more than a dozen states enacted sweeping prison reforms and created special institutions for the mentally ill. As influential as she was, Dix was just one of many citizens who worked to reform various aspects of American society in the mid 1800s.

The reform movements of the mid-1800s stemmed in large part from the revival of religious fervor. Revivalists preached the power of individuals to improve themselves and the world. **Lyman Beecher,** a prominent minister, insisted that it was the nation's citizenry more than its government that should take charge of building a better society. True reform, he said, could take place only through "the voluntary energies of the nation itself."

Under the guidance of Beecher and other religious leaders, associations known as benevolent societies sprang up in cities and towns across the country. At first, they focused on spreading the word of God and attempting to convert nonbelievers. Soon, however, they sought to combat a number of social problems.

One striking feature of the reform effort was the overwhelming presence of women. Young women in particular had joined the revivalist movement in much larger numbers than men. One reason was that many unmarried women with uncertain futures discovered in religion a foundation on which to build their lives. As more women turned to the church, many also joined religious-based reform groups. These reform groups targeted aspects of American society they considered in dire need of change. Among these issues were excessive drinking, prisons, and education.

The Temperance Movement

A number of reformers argued that no social vice caused more crime, disorder, and poverty than the excessive use of alcohol. Men who drank excessively, they argued, spent their money on liquor rather than food and other family necessities, and they sometimes abused their wives and children. While some may have disagreed with this assessment, no one could dispute the fact that alcoholism was widespread during the early 1800s. In small towns throughout the West, citizens drank to ease the isolation and loneliness of rural life, while in the pubs and saloons in eastern cities, drinking was the main leisure activity for many workers.

Although advocates of temperance, or moderation in the consumption of alcohol, had been active since the late 1700s, the new reformers energized the campaign and greatly increased its influence. Temperance groups formed across the country, preaching the evils of alcohol and persuading heavy drinkers to give up liquor. In 1833 several of these groups joined together to form the **American Temperance Union.**

Temperance societies also pushed for laws to prohibit the sale of liquor. In 1851 Maine passed the first state prohibition law, an example followed by a dozen other states by 1855. Other states passed "local option" laws, which allowed towns and villages to prohibit liquor sales within their boundaries.

Prison Reform

The spirit of reform also prompted Americans to consider ways to improve the prison system. Inmates of all kinds, from violent offenders to debtors and the mentally ill, often were indiscriminately crowded together in jails and prisons, which were literally holes in the ground in some cases. One jail in Connecticut, for example, was an abandoned mineshaft. Beginning around 1816, many states began building new facilities to provide a better environment for inmates.

History *Through Art*

Drunkard's Progress In 1846 Nathaniel Currier made this lithograph (left), or print made by engraving on stone. It clearly lays out the path to degradation that begins in Step 1, a glass of alcohol with a friend. Some innkeepers advertised their temperance principles with a sign such as the one above. From looking at the lithograph, how can you tell that women were often temperance supporters?

What *Life* Was Like...

Old-Fashioned School Days

Public schools in the early to mid-1800s were rough-and-ready affairs. Students came in all ages and sizes, teachers often had little training, and books and supplies were hard to obtain.

One-Room Schoolhouse
The painting *New England School* by Charles Frederick Bosworth tells the tale of teachers' challenges in early public schools. With a mixed-aged class, the teacher had to teach a few students at a time, leaving the others to their own education—or entertainment.

School ink jar

School lunch pail

Underlying the prison reform movement was a belief in rehabilitating prisoners rather than merely locking them up. Officials designed forms of rigid discipline to rid criminals of the "laxness" that had led them astray. Solitary confinement and the imposition of silence on work crews were meant to give prisoners the chance to meditate and think about their wrongdoing. Even the name of these new prisons, penitentiaries, highlighted the notion that they were places where individuals would work to achieve penitence, or remorse.

Educational Reform In the early 1800s, many reformers began to push for a system of public education—government-funded schools open to all citizens. The increase in the number of voters in the 1820s and 1830s and the arrival of millions of new immigrants convinced many people of the need for public education. Most American leaders and social reformers believed that a democratic republic could only survive if the electorate was well educated and informed.

One of the leaders of the public education movement was Massachusetts legislator **Horace Mann.** As president of the Massachusetts Senate, Mann pressed for more public education and backed a bill in 1837 creating a state board of education in Massachusetts.

He then stepped down from his elective office to serve as secretary of the new board. During his 12 years in that post he doubled teachers' salaries, opened 50 new high schools, and established schools for teacher training called "normal schools." Massachusetts quickly became the model for all other northern states. Mann's driving conviction was that a nation without an educated populace would have to struggle just to survive, much less prosper:

> ❝The establishment of a republican government, without well-appointed and efficient means for the universal education of the people, is the most rash and foolhardy experiment ever tried by man. . . . It may be an easy thing to make a republic, but it is a very laborious thing to make republicans; and woe to the republic that rests upon no better foundations than ignorance, selfishness and passion!❞
>
> —from "Report of the Massachusetts Board of Education," 1848

In 1852 Massachusetts passed the first mandatory school attendance law; New York passed a similar measure the next year. In the years before the Civil War, reformers campaigned for district, or common,

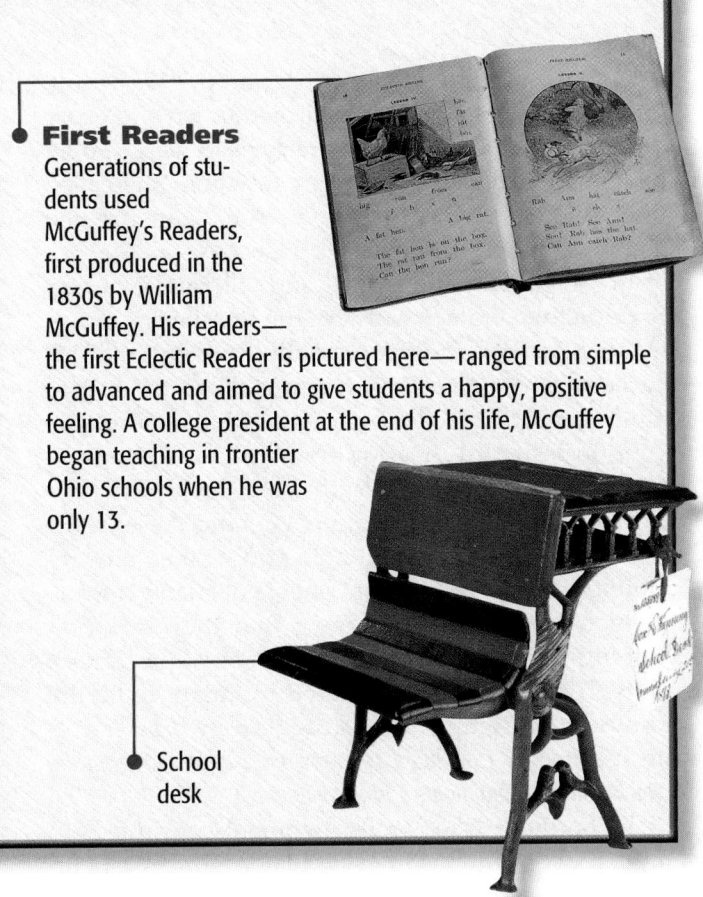

First Readers Generations of students used McGuffey's Readers, first produced in the 1830s by William McGuffey. His readers—the first Eclectic Reader is pictured here—ranged from simple to advanced and aimed to give students a happy, positive feeling. A college president at the end of his life, McGuffey began teaching in frontier Ohio schools when he was only 13.

School desk

schools at the primary level. Reformers believed that such schools could teach all children the basics of reading, writing, and arithmetic, as well as instill a work ethic. District schools were open to all and were supported by district taxes, state funds, and tuition paid by parents.

By the 1850s, tax-supported elementary schools had gained widespread support in the northeastern states and had begun to spread to the rest of the country. Rural areas responded more slowly because children were needed to help with planting and harvesting.

In the South, a reformer named **Calvin Wiley** played a similar role in North Carolina to that of Horace Mann in Massachusetts. In 1839 North Carolina began providing support to local communities that established taxpayer-funded schools. Wiley traveled throughout the state, building support for public education. By 1860, about two-thirds of North Carolina's white children attended school part of the year. The South as a whole responded less quickly, and only about one-third of southern white children were enrolled in public schools by 1860. African American children were excluded almost entirely.

Women's Education When officials talked about educating voters, they had men in mind—women were still not allowed to cast a ballot in the 1800s. Nonetheless, a number of women took advantage

of the reform movement to create more educational opportunities for girls and women.

Emma Willard, who founded a girls' boarding school in Vermont in 1814, was an early educational pioneer. Her school covered the usual subjects for young women, such as cooking and etiquette, but it also included academic subjects like history, math, and literature, which were rarely taught to women. In 1837 another educator, **Mary Lyon,** opened the Mount Holyoke Female Seminary in South Hadley, Massachusetts, the first institution of higher education for women only.

Also in the 1800s, **Elizabeth Blackwell** became the first woman to earn a medical degree in the United States or Europe. In 1857 she founded the New York Infirmary for Women and Children, which was staffed entirely by women.

✓ **Reading Check** **Identifying** What three areas of social reform did reformers target?

The Early Women's Movement

In the early 1800s, the Industrial Revolution began to change the economic roles of men and women. In the 1700s, most economic activity took place in or near the home because most Americans lived and worked in a rural farm setting. Although husbands and wives had distinct chores, maintaining the farm was the focus of their efforts. By the mid-1800s, these circumstances had started to change, especially in the northeastern states. The development of factories and other work centers separated the home from the workplace. Men now often left home to go to work, while women tended the house and children. In time, this development led to the emergence of the first women's movement.

"True Womanhood" As the nature of work changed, many Americans began to divide life into two spheres of activity—the home and the workplace. Many believed the home to be the proper sphere for women, partly because the outside world was seen as corrupt and dangerous, and partly because of popular ideas about the family.

The Christian revivalism of the 1820s and 1830s greatly influenced the American family. For many

HISTORY Online

Student Web Activity Visit the *American Vision* Web site at tav.glencoe.com and click on *Student Web Activities—Chapter 8* for an activity on reform movements.

parents, raising children was treated as a solemn responsibility because it prepared young people for a disciplined Christian life. Women often were viewed as more moral and charitable than men, and they were expected to be models of piety and virtue to their children and husbands.

The idea that women should be homemakers and should take responsibility for developing their children's characters evolved into a set of ideas known as "true womanhood." Magazine articles and novels aimed at women reinforced the value of their role at home. In 1841 **Catherine Beecher,** a daughter of minister and reformer Lyman Beecher, wrote a book called *A Treatise on Domestic Economy*. The popular volume argued that women could find fulfillment at home and gave instruction on childcare, cooking, and health matters.

Women Seek Greater Rights Many women did not feel the ideas of true womanhood were limiting. Instead, the new ideas implied that wives were now partners with their husbands and in some ways were morally superior to them. Women were held up as the conscience of the home and society.

The idea that women had an important role to play in building a virtuous home was soon extended to making society more virtuous. As women became involved in the great moral crusades of the era, some began to argue that they needed greater political rights to promote their ideas.

An advocate of this idea was Margaret Fuller. Fuller argued that every woman had her own relationship with God and needed "as a soul to live freely and unimpeded." She declared, "We would have every arbitrary barrier thrown down and every path laid open to women as freely as to men." Fuller believed that if men and women, whom she called the "two sides" of human nature, were treated equally, it would end injustice in society.

In 1848 **Lucretia Mott** and **Elizabeth Cady Stanton,** two women active in the antislavery movement, organized the **Seneca Falls Convention.** This gathering of women reformers marked the beginning of an organized women's movement. The convention issued a "Declaration of Sentiments and Resolutions" that began with words expanding the Declaration of Independence: "We hold these truths to be self-evident: that all men and women are created equal. . . ." Stanton shocked many of the women present by proposing that they focus on gaining the right to vote. Nevertheless, the Seneca Falls Convention is considered by many to be the unofficial beginning of the struggle for women's voting rights. 📖 *(See page 1070 for more information on the "Declaration of Sentiments and Resolutions.")*

Throughout the 1850s, women continued to organize conventions to gain greater rights for themselves. The conventions did meet with some success. By 1860, for example, reformers had convinced 15 states to pass laws permitting married women to retain their property if their husbands died. Above all, these conventions drew attention to their cause and paved the way for a stronger movement to emerge after the Civil War.

✓ **Reading Check** **Examining** What events of the mid-1800s sparked the first women's movement?

SECTION 3 ASSESSMENT

Checking for Understanding
1. **Define:** benevolent society, temperance, penitentiary.
2. **Identify:** Dorothea Dix, Lyman Beecher, Horace Mann, Elizabeth Cady Stanton.
3. **State** the main goal of the early women's movement.

Reviewing Themes
4. **Continuity and Change** How did the Second Great Awakening affect the reform movements of the mid-1800s?

Critical Thinking
5. **Evaluating** In what ways did the new penitentiaries change the prison system?
6. **Organizing** Use a graphic organizer similar to the one below to list the major reform areas.

Analyzing Visuals
7. **Examining Art** Study the painting of the New England school on page 280. How was the room heated? What kinds of supplies did the students have?

Writing About History
8. **Expository Writing** Think of reforms you believe are needed today in the United States. Write a letter to your legislator expressing why you believe the reforms are needed. Give examples of problems in your community as evidence.

American LITERATURE

from Walden
by Henry David Thoreau

Henry David Thoreau was part of the Transcendentalist movement that started as a reform movement within the Unitarian Church. Transcendentalism stressed the connection of the soul of the individual to the soul of the world. Simply put, the Transcendentalists believed that God resided in each person. None of the works of poetry and prose during this period more fully embodied Transcendental ideals than Thoreau's *Walden*. Part journal, part social commentary, and part sermon, the work summarizes and expands Thoreau's experiences at Walden Pond, near Concord, Massachusetts, where he built a cabin and lived in relative solitude for two years.

Read to Discover
What does Thoreau say we must do to live in society?

Reader's Dictionary
swath: path

sublime: supreme; awesome

perturbation: annoyance; irritation

I went to the woods because I wished to live deliberately, to front only the essential facts of life, and see if I could not learn what it had to teach, and not, when I came to die, discover that I had not lived. I did not wish to live what was not life, living is so dear; nor did I wish to practice resignation, unless it was quite necessary. I wanted to live deep and suck out all the marrow of life, to live so sturdily and Spartan-like as to put to rout all that was not life, to cut a broad swath and shave close, to drive life into a corner, and reduce it to its lowest terms, and, if it proved to be mean, why then to get the whole and genuine meanness of it, and publish its meanness to the world; or if it were sublime, to know it by experience. . . . For most men, it appears to me, are in a strange uncertainty about it, whether it is of the devil or of God, and have *somewhat hastily* concluded that it is the chief end of man here to "glorify God and enjoy him forever."

Still we live meanly, like ants. . . . Our life is frittered away by detail. An honest man has hardly need to count more than his ten fingers. . . . Simplicity, simplicity, simplicity! I say, let your affairs be as two or three, and not a hundred or a thousand; instead of a million count half a dozen, and keep your accounts on your thumbnail. . . .

Let us spend one day as deliberately as Nature, and not be thrown off the track by every nutshell and mosquito's wing that falls on the rails. . . . Why should we knock under and go with the stream?

Analyzing Literature
1. **Recall** What motivated Thoreau to go and live alone in the wilderness?

2. **Interpret** What do you think the phrase "every nutshell and mosquito's wing" means?

3. **Evaluate and Connect** Do you think you could live alone in the woods for two years as Thoreau did? Explain.

Interdisciplinary Activity
Language Arts Imagine you are Thoreau at the end of your first year at Walden. Write a diary entry describing your feelings looking back on the first year and ahead to the year to come.

The Abolitionist Movement

Main Idea

In the midst of the nation's reform movement, a number of citizens embarked on a crusade known as abolitionism to end slavery in the United States.

Key Terms and Names

gradualism, American Colonization Society, abolition, William Lloyd Garrison, emancipation, American Antislavery Society, Frederick Douglass

Reading Strategy

Sequencing As you read about the beginning of the abolitionist movement, complete a time line similar to the one below to record early events of this movement.

Reading Objectives

- **List** groups involved in the early abolitionist movement.
- **Analyze** how Northerners and Southerners viewed abolitionism.

Section Theme

Individual Action Abolitionist reformers challenged the morality and legality of slavery in the United States.

Preview of Events

♦1830   ♦1832   ♦1834   ♦1836

1831
William Lloyd Garrison begins publishing the *Liberator*

1833
Prudence Crandall arrested; American Antislavery Society founded

1834
Mob attacks William Lloyd Garrison

1836
House of Representatives adopts gag rule on abolitionist petitions

---

★ *An American Story* ★

In 1831 William Lloyd Garrison began publishing a fiery antislavery newspaper in Boston. One day in 1834, a large group gathered outside Garrison's office to express its disapproval of his views. An onlooker, Thomas Low Nichols, described what followed:

❝I was in the editorial office of Mr. Garrison when the crowd began to gather in the street below. . . . There were hundreds—then thousands. It was a mob of people dressed in black broadcloth, a mob of gentlemen—capitalists, merchants, bankers, a mob of the Stock Exchange and of the first people in Boston, which considered itself the nicest of cities, and intellectually the 'hub of the universe'. . . . There was a great howl of rage; but, a moment after, it became a yell of triumph. Garrison had been seen to go from the building into a narrow lane behind it. Pursued, he took refuge in a carpenter's shop, only to be dragged out and carried into the midst of the mob. . . . I saw him, his hat off, his bald head shining, his scanty locks flying, his face pale. . . .❞

—quoted in *Witness to America*

Early Opposition to Slavery

By the 1830s, a growing number of Americans had begun to demand an immediate end to slavery in the South. Of all the reform movements that began in the early 1800s, the movement to end slavery was the most divisive. By pitting North against South, it polarized the nation and helped bring about the Civil War.

Gradualism From the earliest days of the Republic, many Americans had opposed slavery. Many of the country's founders knew that a nation based on the principles of liberty and equality would have difficulty remaining true to its ideals if it continued to enslave human beings. Quakers and Baptists in both the North and South had long argued that slavery was a sin. After the Revolution, Baptists in Virginia called for "every legal measure to [wipe out] this horrid evil from the land."

Early antislavery societies generally supported an approach known as gradualism, or the belief that slavery had to be ended gradually. First they would stop new slaves from being brought into the country. Then they would phase out slavery in the North and the Upper South before finally ending slavery in the Lower South. Slaveholders would also be compensated for their loss. Supporters of gradualism believed it would give the South's economy time to adjust to the loss of enslaved labor.

Colonization The first antislavery societies also believed that ending slavery would not end racism in the United States. Many thought that the best solution was to send African Americans back to their ancestral homelands in Africa. In December 1816, antislavery reformers founded the **American Colonization Society** (ACS) to move African Americans to Africa. The society had the support of many prominent Americans, including James Madison, James Monroe, Henry Clay, Daniel Webster, and John Marshall.

By 1821 the ACS had acquired land in West Africa. The following year, free African Americans began boarding ships chartered by the society to take them to Africa. There they established a colony that eventually became the country of Liberia. It declared its independence as a republic in 1847 and adopted a constitution designed after the U.S. Constitution. The capital, Monrovia, was named for President Monroe.

Colonization was never a realistic solution to slavery and racism, however. The cost of transporting African Americans was high, and the ACS had to depend on donations. Moving the roughly 1.5 million African Americans who lived in the United States in 1820 to Africa was nearly impossible. Furthermore, most African Americans regarded the United States as their home and were not prepared to migrate to another continent. Only an estimated 12,000 African Americans moved to Africa between 1821 and 1860.

Reading Check **Identifying** What two religious groups were among the first to oppose slavery?

Fact Fiction Folklore

Abolitionist Songs Abolitionists used songs to stir up enthusiasm for their cause. To make songs easier to learn, they often wrote new words for old tunes. Here is a stanza William Lloyd Garrison wrote to the tune of "Auld Lang Syne":

I am an abolitionist!
I glory in the name;
Though now by Slavery's minions hiss'd,
And covered o'er with shame;
It is a spell of light and power—
The watchword of the free:—
Who spurns it in this trial-hour,
A craven soul is he!

Banner celebrating Garrison's abolitionist newspaper, the Liberator

The New Abolitionists

Gradualism and colonization remained the main goals of antislavery groups until the 1830s, when a new idea, abolition, began to gain ground. Abolitionists argued that enslaved African Americans should be freed immediately, without gradual measures or compensation to former slaveholders.

TURNING POINT

Garrison Stirs a New Movement Abolitionism began to gain support in the 1830s for several reasons. As with other reform movements of the era, it drew its strength from the Second Great Awakening, with its focus on sin and repentance. In the eyes of abolitionists, slavery was an enormous evil of which the country needed to repent.

The first well-known advocate of abolition was a free African American from North Carolina named **David Walker,** who published *Appeal to the Colored Citizens of the World.* In this pamphlet, Walker advocated violence and rebellion as the only way to end slavery. Although Walker's ideas were influential, the rapid development of a large national abolitionist movement in the 1830s was largely due to the efforts of **William Lloyd Garrison.**

In 1829 Garrison became assistant to Benjamin Lundy, the Quaker publisher of the Baltimore antislavery newspaper, *Genius of Universal Emancipation.* Garrison admired Lundy but grew impatient with his gradualist approach. In 1831 Garrison left his mentor and, with fellow abolitionist Isaac Knapp, founded Boston's antislavery newspaper, the *Liberator.*

Prudence Crandall
1803–1890

In 1831 Prudence Crandall was running a successful school for girls in Canterbury, Connecticut, when Sarah Harris, the daughter of a prominent African American farmer, sought admission. When Crandall agreed to let her in, local parents objected, and many withdrew their children from the school.

Rather than reverse her decision, Crandall announced that she was reorganizing her school as a teacher-training institution for African American women. The citizens of Canterbury erupted in protest. To combat Crandall's effort, the state legislature passed the "Black Law," which forbade Connecticut schools from admitting out-of-state African American students and severely limited the type of schools that in-state African Americans could attend. Crandall ignored the law and was arrested in August 1833.

In a highly publicized case, prosecutors convicted her, but her conviction was overturned on appeal. In the wake of the trial, residents terrorized the school, dirtying its well, refusing it supplies, and creating other hardships. In 1834, Crandall closed her school.

Upon her death nearly 60 years later, a friend recalled her willingness to fight for what she believed in. "She had deep convictions of right. . . . Neither death, life, angels, principalities, things present, things to come, heights, depths, nor any other creature could keep her from following her convictions."

mind, the situation was very clear: Slavery was immoral and slaveholders were evil. The only option was immediate and complete emancipation, or the freeing of all enslaved people.

Garrison soon attracted enough followers in the North to enable him to found the New England Antislavery Society in 1832 and the **American Antislavery Society** in 1833. Membership in both organizations grew quickly. By the mid-1830s, there were hundreds of society chapters, and in 1838, there were more than 1,350 chapters with over 250,000 members.

Other Abolitionists at Work As the antislavery movement gained momentum, new leaders emerged from Garrison's shadow and carried on the effort. Theodore Weld, a disciple of the evangelist Charles Grandison Finney, was one of the most effective leaders, recruiting and training many abolitionists for the American Antislavery Society. Arthur and Lewis Tappan, two devout and wealthy brothers from New York City, also emerged as leaders.

The orator Wendell Phillips, the poet John Greenleaf Whittier, and many others became active in the cause as well. Many women also gave their efforts to the abolitionist movement. Prudence Crandall worked as a teacher and abolitionist in Connecticut, and Lucretia Mott often spoke out in favor of abolitionism. Some Southern women also joined the crusade. Among the earliest were Sarah and Angelina Grimké, South Carolina sisters who moved north to work openly against slavery.

African American Abolitionists Not surprisingly, free African Americans took a prominent role in the abolitionist movement. African Americans in the North, who numbered over 190,000 by 1850, endured much prejudice, but they cherished their freedom nonetheless. When Garrison launched his newspaper, African Americans rushed to his support, not only buying the paper but also helping to sell it. Many began writing and speaking out against slavery and taking part in protests and demonstrations.

One of the most prominent African American figures in the movement was **Frederick Douglass,** who had escaped from slavery in Maryland. Douglass was a brilliant thinker and an electrifying speaker. "I appear before the immense assembly this evening as a thief and a robber," he told one Massachusetts

The paper's style was anything but moderate, as Garrison wrote caustic attacks on slavery and called for an immediate end to it. To those who objected to his fiery language, he responded that the time for moderation was over:

> ❝I am aware that many object to the severity of my language; but is there not cause for severity? I will be as harsh as truth and as uncompromising as justice. On this subject I do not wish to think, or speak, or write with moderation. No! No! Tell a man whose house is on fire to give a moderate alarm; tell him to moderately rescue his wife from the hands of the ravisher; tell the mother to gradually [remove] her babe from the fire into which it has fallen—but urge me not to use moderation in a cause like the present. I am in earnest; I will not equivocate; I will not excuse; I will not retreat a single inch—AND I WILL BE HEARD.❞

—from the *Liberator*

With his balding head, his steel-rimmed glasses, and his plain black suits, Garrison was as mild-looking as his words were strong. Inside this soft-spoken man, however, an intense passion burned. In his group in 1842. "I stole this head, these limbs, this body from my master, and ran off with them." Douglass published his own antislavery newspaper, the *North Star,* and wrote an autobiography, *Narrative of the Life of Frederick Douglass,* which quickly sold 4,500 copies after its publication in 1845.

Another important African American abolitionist was **Sojourner Truth.** She gained freedom in 1827 when New York freed all remaining enslaved people in the state. In the 1840s her antislavery speeches—eloquent, joyous, and deeply religious—drew huge crowds. Though lacking a formal education, Truth enthralled listeners with her folksy wit, engaging stories, contagious singing, and strong message.

✓ **Reading Check** **Summarizing** How did William Lloyd Garrison work to end slavery?

The Response to Abolitionism

Abolitionism was a powerful force, and it provoked a powerful public response. In the North, citizens looked upon the abolitionist movement with views ranging from support to indifference to opposition. In the South, many residents feared that their entire way of life was under attack. They rushed to defend the institution of slavery, which they saw as the key to the region's economy.

Reaction in the North While many Northerners disapproved of slavery, some opposed extreme abolitionism even more. They viewed the movement as a dangerous threat to the existing social system. Some whites, including many prominent businesspeople, warned it would produce a destructive war between the North and the South. Others feared it might lead to a great influx of freed African Americans to the North, overwhelming the labor and housing markets. Many in the North also had no desire to see the South's economy crumble. If that happened, they might lose the huge sums of money Southern planters owed to Northern banks, as well as the Southern cotton that fed Northern textile mills.

Given such attitudes, the attack on Garrison in Boston was not surprising. In fact, it was one of many such assaults. In 1837 in Illinois, for example,

NATIONAL GEOGRAPHIC
African American Populations, 1820 and 1860

African American Percentage of Total Population

10.0 1820   10.0 1860

* 1830 data (Florida)
** Includes present-day West Virginia (Virginia)
*** No data for 1820 (Texas)

MO. 16.4 10.1
KY. 22.9 20.4
MD. 36.1 24.9
VA.** 49.6 45.0
N.C. 34.4 36.5
TENN. 19.6 25.5
ARK. 14.3 25.5
S.C. 52.7 58.5
MISS. 44.0 55.2
ALA. 32.8 45.4
GA. 44.3 44.1
TEX.*** 30.3
LA. 52.3 49.4
FLA.* 45.7 45.0

ATLANTIC OCEAN
Gulf of Mexico

0   200 miles
0   200 kilometers
Albers Conic Equal-Area projection

35°N
30°N
95°W   90°W   85°W   80°W

Geography *Skills*

1. **Interpreting Maps** What two states had the highest percentage of African American population in 1820?

2. **Applying Geography Skills** Why do you think support for gradualism and colonization was stronger in Virginia than in South Carolina?

Fredrick Douglass (seated at left) at an abolitionist rally in Cazenovia, New York, in 1850

abolitionist publisher Reverend Elijah P. Lovejoy was killed trying to protect his printing press from a mob. Yet Northerners also resented Southern slave-catchers, who kidnapped African American runaways in the North and hauled them back to the South. In response, several states in the North passed personal liberty laws restricting slave recapture.

Reaction in the South To most Southerners, slavery was a "peculiar institution," one that was distinctive and vital to the Southern way of life. While the North was building cities and factories, the South remained mostly agricultural, becoming increasingly tied to cotton and the enslaved people who planted and picked it. Southerners responded to the growing

attacks against slavery by strongly defending the institution. South Carolina's governor called it a "national benefit," while Thomas Dew, a leading Southern academic, claimed that most slaves had no desire for freedom, because they enjoyed a close and beneficial relationship with their slaveholders. "We have no hesitation in affirming," he declared, "that, throughout the whole slaveholding country, the slaves of good [slaveholders] are his warmest, most constant, and most devoted friends."

Less than eight months after Garrison printed his first shocking words in the *Liberator* in 1831, **Nat Turner,** an enslaved preacher, led an uprising that killed over 50 Virginians. Many Southerners believed that papers like the *Liberator* sparked this rebellion. Although Garrison's paper did not even circulate in the South, furious Southerners demanded the suppression of abolitionist material as a condition for remaining in the Union. Southern postal workers refused to deliver abolitionist newspapers. In 1836, under Southern pressure the House of Representatives passed a gag rule providing that all abolitionist petitions be shelved without debate.

For all the uproar it caused, the abolitionist movement remained relatively small. Very few people before the Civil War ever accepted the idea that slavery must be immediately eliminated. The crusade that William Lloyd Garrison had started, however, and that thousands of men and women struggled to keep alive, became a constant and powerful reminder of how much slavery was dividing the nation.

✓ **Reading Check** **Evaluating** How did Northerners and Southerners view abolitionism?

SECTION 4 ASSESSMENT

Checking for Understanding

1. **Define:** gradualism, abolition, emancipation.
2. **Identify:** American Colonization Society, William Lloyd Garrison, American Antislavery Society, Frederick Douglass.
3. **Describe** how free African Americans worked to end slavery.

Reviewing Themes

4. **Individual Action** Which individuals helped build support for abolition, and what did they do to win that support?

Critical Thinking

5. **Interpreting** Why is William Lloyd Garrison's publication of the *Liberator* considered a turning point in the abolitionist movement?
6. **Organizing** Use a graphic organizer similar to the one below to list the reasons why many Northerners opposed extreme abolitionism.

> Reasons Northerners Opposed Extreme Abolitionism

Analyzing Visuals

7. **Analyzing Maps** Study the map on page 287. In which states did the percentage of African American population decrease by at least 5 percent between 1820 and 1860?

Writing About History

8. **Descriptive Writing** Imagine that you are working for the *Liberator* in the 1830s. Write a letter to a friend describing what you hope to accomplish as a member of the staff of an abolitionist newspaper. Be sure to explain why you accepted the job.

SKILLBUILDER

Developing a Multimedia Presentation

Why Learn This Skill?

You want to present a research report on some aspect of the Second Great Awakening to your classmates, and you want to hold their attention. How do you do it? You might try using a variety of media. Using a variety of media in your presentations makes them more interesting and engaging for your audience.

Learning the Skill

A basic multimedia presentation involves using several types of media. Suppose you wanted to present a report on the American literary renaissance. To introduce the important writers of the era, you might show photographs of them. You also could play a voice recording of a story written by one of the writers or present a video showing a screenplay based on one of their books.

You can also develop a multimedia presentation on a computer. Multimedia, as it relates to computer technology, is the combination of text, video, audio, and animation in an interactive program.

To create multimedia presentations on a computer, you need to have certain tools. These may include traditional computer graphics tools, draw programs, animation programs that make images move, and authoring systems that tie everything together. Your computer manual will tell you which tools your computer can support.

Practicing the Skill

Ask yourself the following questions when developing a multimedia presentation:

❶ Which forms of media do I want to include? Video? Sound? Animation? Photographs? Graphics?

❷ Which of these media forms does my computer support?

❸ What kind of software programs or systems do I need? A paint program? A draw program? An animation program? A program to create interactive, or two-way, communication? An authoring system that will allow me to change images, sound, and motion?

❹ Is there a "do-it-all" program I can use to develop the kind of presentation I want?

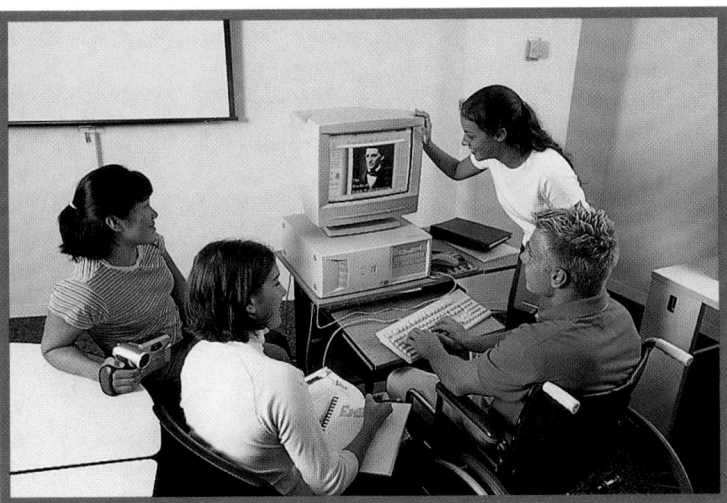

Skills Assessment

Complete the Practicing Skills questions on page 291 and the Chapter 8 Skill Reinforcement Activity to assess your mastery of this skill.

Applying the Skill

Developing a Multimedia Presentation Using your answers to the questions under "Practicing the Skill" as guidelines, write a plan describing a multimedia presentation on writers of the American literary renaissance or romanticism. Indicate what tools you will need and what you must do for a successful presentation.

 Glencoe's **Skillbuilder Interactive Workbook CD-ROM, Level 2,** provides instruction and practice in key social studies skills.

Reviewing Key Terms

On a sheet of paper, use each of these terms in a sentence.

1. spoils system
2. caucus system
3. secede
4. nullification
5. nativism
6. romanticism
7. transcendentalism
8. utopia
9. benevolent society
10. temperance
11. penitentiary
12. gradualism
13. abolition
14. emancipation

Chapter Summary

Democracy Expanded for Some

- Nominating convention replaced caucus system of choosing presidential candidates.
- Voting rights were expanded for white males.
- Jackson's spoils system favored common people.

Change Was Limited for Others

- Women's movement gained attention but accomplished little else.
- Native Americans were driven out of the South.
- Nativism led to discrimination against immigrants.

The Second Great Awakening Inspired Reform

- Commitment to religion swelled church congregations.
- New religions were established.
- American literature blossomed; romanticism and transcendentalism influenced art.
- Prison reform movement resulted in better facilities.
- Access to education was expanded.
- Abolitionist and temperance movements grew steadily.

Reform Efforts Led to Further Division

- Members of newly established religions were persecuted.
- Many Northerners opposed slavery but saw abolition as a threat to the existing social system.
- Some publishers of abolitionist literature were attacked.
- Southerners defended slavery as an economic necessity.
- House of Representatives was pressured to impose a gag rule limiting debate on abolitionist petitions.

Reviewing Key Facts

15. **Identify:** Tariff of Abominations, Daniel Webster, Trail of Tears, Second Great Awakening, Joseph Smith, Lyman Beecher, Horace Mann, William Lloyd Garrison.

16. In what two ways did President Andrew Jackson expand democracy?

17. What were two factors that led to President Jackson's decision to sign the Indian Removal Act?

18. What main ideas did American romanticists and transcendentalists believe?

19. How did reformers improve the public education system in the early to mid-1800s?

20. Name four groups of people involved in the abolitionist movement, and list what each did to try to end slavery.

Critical Thinking

21. **Analyzing Themes: Groups and Institutions** Which group or groups of Americans did not benefit from the reforms of the early to mid-1800s? Explain.

22. **Synthesizing** What were the main themes of American writers, philosophers, and artists during the Second Great Awakening? Do you think their writings and works of art influenced the reform movements in the United States during the early to mid-1800s? Explain your answer.

23. **Organizing** Use a graphic organizer similar to the one below to list the areas of life that people in the United States tried to improve during the early to mid-1800s.

Reform Movements

24. **Interpreting Primary Sources** Some people did not support free public education in the early 1800s. The excerpt below was an editorial written to the members of the legislature. It appeared in the *Raleigh Register* of November 9, 1829. Read the excerpt and answer the questions that follow.

❝Common schools indeed! Money is very scarce, and the times are unusually hard. . . . Gentlemen, it appears to me that schools are sufficiently plenty, and that the people have no desire they should be increased. Those now in operation are not all filled, and it is very doubtful if they are productive or of much real benefit. Would it not redound as much to the advantage of young persons, and to the honour of the State, if they should pass their days in the cotton patch, or at the plow, or in the cornfield, instead of being [confined] in a school house, where they are earning nothing?**"**

—from the *Raleigh Register,* November 9, 1829

a. What reasons does the author give for opposing free public education?

b. Are the author's reasons valid? Explain your answer.

Practicing Skills

25. Developing a Multimedia Presentation Develop a plan for a presentation on the social and cultural changes in the United States discussed in this chapter. Consider the following points to help guide you.
a. What specific examples would you use to show the different social and cultural changes taking place in the country?
b. What form of media would you use for each example?

Writing Activity

26. Portfolio Writing You read in a Boston newspaper that the Massachusetts legislature is going to hear statements from citizens concerning the care of the mentally ill. Prepare and write a paper that you can read to the committee members on this subject. In the paper, explain your ideas on caring for the mentally ill and whether or not you feel society has an obligation to do so. Save the paper in your portfolio.

Chapter Activities

27. Research Project Conduct research to learn more about one reformer discussed in the chapter. Role-play the person by introducing yourself to the class and describing your background, what you want to reform, and how you will go about making these improvements.

28. American History Primary Source Document Library CD-ROM Read "Women's Rights" by Sojourner Truth, under *The Growing Nation.* Imagine that you are a reporter for a newspaper and your assignment is to cover the Ohio Women's Convention. Write an article in which you review Truth's speech. In your article, explain her arguments for women's rights and describe how members of the convention reacted to her speech.

Voter Participation, 1824–1840

Source: *Historical Statistics of the United States: Colonial Times to 1970.*

Geography and History

29. The graph above shows voter participation from 1824 to 1840. Study the graph, and then answer the questions below.
a. Interpreting Graphs In which presidential election year did voter participation increase the most from the previous presidential election year?

b. Applying Graph Skills What do you think accounted for the increase in voter participation?

Standardized Test Practice

Directions: Read the passage below and answer the question that follows.

Susan B. Anthony, who was raised as a Quaker, was a powerful organizer in the women's rights movement. A dedicated reformer, she joined the temperance movement and worked for the American Antislavery Society.

Sojourner Truth, a former enslaved person, spoke out against slavery and in defense of women's rights. Truth often attended women's rights conventions to remind women that their African American sisters had a place in the movement.

Susan B. Anthony and Sojourner Truth both worked for which of the following reforms?

A Abolitionism and education

B Education and temperance

C Temperance and women's rights

D Women's rights and abolitionism

Test-Taking Tip: The important word in this question is *both.* Several reform movements are mentioned, but the question asks about the reforms *both* women supported.

CHAPTER 9
Manifest Destiny *1835–1848*

Why It Matters

In this period, Americans strove to expand the nation's boundaries. Many believed they had a "manifest destiny" to spread democratic ideals. Others simply wanted to go west to find a new and better life. In Texas, settlers came into conflict with Mexico, while those going west on the Oregon Trail came into conflict with Native Americans.

The Impact Today

Developments of the era have left a legacy for Americans.
- *The nation now stretches from the Atlantic to the Pacific Oceans.*
- *Americans remain a restless people, ready to move to pursue economic opportunity.*
- *Many Americans continue to view themselves as destined to succeed and prosper.*

 The American Vision *Video* *The Chapter 9 video, "Manifest Destiny," chronicles the war between Texas and Mexico from the Mexican point of view.*

1836
- Texas war for independence
- Battle of the Alamo
- Texas wins independence from Mexico

1841
- President Harrison dies of pneumonia, becoming first president to die in office

United States
PRESIDENTS

Van Buren 1837–1841

W. Harrison 1841

Tyler 1841–1845

1836   *1839*   *1842*

 World

1839
- First pedal-propelled bicycle designed by Kirkpatrick MacMillan of Scotland

1842
- China cedes Hong Kong to Britain

The Emigrant Train Bedding Down for the Night by Kenneth John Myers, 1867

1845
- Congress votes to annex Republic of Texas

1846
- Great Britain and U.S. agree to divide Oregon Territory at 49th parallel
- United States begins war with Mexico

1848
- Treaty of Guadalupe Hidalgo ends war with Mexico

Polk
1845–1849

1845

1848

1843
- Charles Dickens's *A Christmas Carol* published

1845
- Irish potato famine begins

1848
- Karl Marx and Frederick Engels publish *The Communist Manifesto*
- Numerous revolutions sweep Europe

HISTORY
Online

Chapter Overview
Visit the *American Vision* Web site at tav.glencoe.com and click on *Chapter Overviews—Chapter 9* to preview chapter information.

The Western Pioneers

Guide to Reading

Main Idea

In the 1840s, Americans headed west to the frontier states of the Midwest and the rich lands of California and Oregon.

Key Terms and Names

John Louis O'Sullivan, Manifest Destiny, squatter, Jethro Wood, John Deere, Cyrus McCormick, John Sutter, Kit Carson, Jim Bridger, overlander, Donner Party, Brigham Young

Reading Strategy

Organizing As you read about the westward movement of emigrants in the 1840s, complete a graphic organizer similar to the one below by filling in the names of the main trails they used.

Trails to the West

Reading Objectives

- **Discuss** the inventions that made it easier to farm the plains.
- **Analyze** why Americans were willing to give up their lives in the East to move to the West.

Section Theme

Science and Technology Several inventions of this period helped make settling the West possible.

Preview of Events

♦1835	♦1840	♦1845	♦1850
1834 McCormick reaper patented	**1841** Preemption Act passed	**1847** The Mormons arrive at the Great Salt Lake	**1851** Treaty of Fort Laramie signed

★ An American Story ★

Mary Richardson Walker, a young woman from the East with a strong religious faith, wanted to serve God as a missionary to Native Americans. In April 1838 she and her husband started out from Missouri, bound for Oregon. After a 129-day trek along the Oregon Trail, they established a mission at Tshimakain near what is now Spokane, Washington, and began their efforts to convert the Nez Perce people to Christianity. She wrote in her diary of some of her experiences:

❝January 21, 1839. The Indians have covered our house with grass & boughs & chinked it so that we are very comfortable.

August 5, 1839. I have just been exercising some [Nez Perce] boys in adding numbers. I never could make white children understand half as quick. . . .

December 9, 1847. We were hoping to have Dr. Whitman to supper with us tonight. But about sunset, Old Solomon arrived bringing the sad intelligence that Dr. & Mrs. Whitman . . . & others have been murdered by the Indians. . . . I do not see why I should expect to be preserved when more faithful servants are cut off.❞

—quoted in *Women of the West*

Americans Head West

In 1800 only around 387,000 white settlers lived west of the Appalachian Mountains. By 1820 that number had grown to more than 2.4 million people, and the numbers continued to rise rapidly. By the time the Civil War began, more Americans lived west of the Appalachians than lived in states along the Atlantic coast.

Some Americans headed west for religious reasons. Others were lured by the chance to own their own farms. While most settled east of the Mississippi River, more than 250,000 Americans headed farther west, across the Great Plains and Rocky Mountains to California and the Pacific Northwest.

In 1845 a magazine editor named **John Louis O'Sullivan** declared that it was the "manifest destiny" of Americans "to overspread the continent allotted by Providence. . . ." Many Americans believed in this concept of Manifest Destiny—the idea that God had given the continent to Americans and wanted them to settle western land.

Farming the New Lands Early settlers marked out farms on the rich river bottom land. Others occupied fertile woodland soil. These pioneers became known as squatters, because they settled on lands they did not own. The federal government intended to survey the land and then sell large parcels to real estate companies, but squatters wanted to buy the land they occupied directly from the government.

Bowing to public pressure, Congress passed the Preemption Act of 1830, a renewable law made permanent in 1841. This law protected squatters by guaranteeing them the right to claim land before it was surveyed and the right to buy up to 160 acres for the government's minimum price of $1.25 per acre.

Plows and Reapers A few decades earlier, farmers had only wooden plows to break the grass cover and roots of Midwestern sod. **Jethro Wood** patented an iron-bladed plow in 1819, and in 1837, **John Deere** engineered a plow with sharp-edged steel blades that cut cleanly through the sod. This reduced by half the labor needed to prepare an acre for farming.

Midwestern agriculture also received a boost from the mechanical reaper, which **Cyrus McCormick** patented in 1834. For centuries farmers had cut grain by hand using a sickle or a scythe—time-consuming and exhausting work. Switching from a sickle to a McCormick reaper pulled by horses or mules, farmers could harvest far more grain with far less effort.

✓ **Reading Check** **Explaining** How did Congress help squatters attain land in the West?

Settling the Pacific Coast

Latecomers to the Midwest set their sights on California and Oregon. This push to the Pacific Ocean happened partly because emigrants assumed that the treeless expanse of the Great Plains, which lay just beyond the frontier, contained poor land for farming.

Dividing Oregon Other nations, as well as Native Americans, had already laid claim to parts of Oregon and California. In the case of Oregon, the United States and Great Britain competed for possession, though they had agreed in 1818 to occupy the land jointly and settle their disputes later. In the late 1830s, American missionaries began arriving in Oregon, hoping to convert Native Americans. It was these missionaries who first spread the word about Oregon, persuading many Easterners to come to the lush Willamette Valley.

Populating California In 1821, after a bloody struggle, Mexico gained its independence from Spain. The new nation controlled a vast territory, including California, but that territory lay far from the central government in Mexico City. The local California government often relied on foreign settlers because it could not attract enough emigrants from Mexico. In 1839, hoping to attract more settlers, Juan Bautista Alvarado, governor of California, granted 50,000 acres (20,250 ha) in the Sacramento Valley to **John Sutter,** a German immigrant. There Sutter built a trading post and cattle ranch. Sutter's Fort—as it was called—was often the first stopping point for Americans reaching California. By 1845 more than 200 Americans had settled in California.

GEOGRAPHY

The Trails West Much of the terrain between the frontier jumping-off points and the Pacific was difficult. A small number of trailblazers—mountain men like **Kit Carson** and **Jim Bridger**—made their living by trapping beaver and selling the furs to traders. At the same time they gained a thorough knowledge of the territory and the local Native Americans.

By the 1840s the mountain men had carved out several east-to-west passages that played a vital role in western settlement. The most popular route was the **Oregon Trail.** Others included the California Trail and the Santa Fe Trail.

Wagon Train Life Emigrants made the journey in trains of covered wagons. Before starting out, the trains

HISTORY *Online*

Student Web Activity Visit the *American Vision* Web site at tav.glencoe.com and click on *Student Web Activities— Chapter 9* for an activity on westward expansion.

Overland Trails West, 1840–1860

NATIONAL GEOGRAPHIC

Conestoga wagon storage box

BRITISH NORTH AMERICA

Columbia R.

WASHINGTON TERR.

Portland

Ft. Walla Walla

OREG.

Snake R.

Ft. Boise

OREGON TRAIL

Missouri R.

NEBRASKA TERR.

UNORG. TERR.

MINN.

WIS.

MICH.

N.Y.

MASS.

R.I.

CONN.

South Pass

40°N

CALIFORNIA TRAIL

Donner Pass

Great Salt Lake

Ft. Bridger

Ft. Laramie

Platte R.

MORMON TRAIL

IOWA

Council Bluffs

PA.

N.J.

Sacramento

PONY EXPRESS

Salt Lake City

UTAH TERR.

Ft. Kearny

Nauvoo

ILL.

IND.

OH.

DEL.

MD.

San Francisco

OLD SPANISH TRAIL

Denver

SANTA FE TRAIL

St. Joseph

Independence

VA.

CALIF.

Colorado R.

Bent's Fort

KANSAS TERR.

St. Louis

MO.

KY.

N.C.

Los Angeles

Santa Fe

NEW MEXICO TERR.

CIMARRON CUTOFF

UNORG. TERR.

Arkansas R.

TENN.

S.C.

Red R.

Fort Smith

ARK.

MISS.

Conestoga wagon

30°N

Tucson

El Paso

Rio Grande

BUTTERFIELD OVERLAND MAIL

TEX.

LA.

Mississippi R.

PACIFIC OCEAN

MEXICO

Gulf of Mexico

0 500 miles

0 500 kilometers

Lambert Azimuthal Equal-Area projection

- - - Continental Divide

)(Pass

★ Fort

—— 1860 border

110°W

Geography *Skills*

1. **Interpreting Maps** Name two Missouri cities that served as starting points for western emigrants.
2. **Applying Geography Skills** Why did emigrants bypass the open territory of the Great Plains for a grueling journey to the Far West?

assembled at staging areas outside a frontier town. There, families exchanged information about routes, bought supplies, trained oxen, and practiced steering the cumbersome wagons, which new drivers were apt to tip over.

The first wagon trains hired mountain men to guide them. Once the trails became well worn, most of the travelers—known as overlanders—found their own way with the help of guidebooks written by earlier emigrants.

Sometimes the guidebooks were wrong, leading to tragedy. In 1846 a group of 87 overlanders, known as the **Donner Party** after the two brothers who led them, were trapped by winter snows high up in the Sierra Nevada. After 41 died of starvation, those still alive faced the choice of death or cannibalism. Many, in desperation, did resort to cannibalism in order to survive.

The typical trip west took five to six months, the wagon trains progressing about 15 miles (24 km) per day. Generally, men drove the wagons, hunted game, and bedded down the animals at night, while women looked after the children, cooked their families' food,

cleaned the camp, and laundered the clothes. As Elizabeth Geer recalls here, the journey west was exhausting and difficult:

❝I carry my babe and lead, or rather carry, another through snow, mud, and water, almost to my knees. It is the worst road. . . . [T]here was not one dry thread on one of us—not even my babe. . . . I have not told you half we suffered. I am not adequate to the task.❞

—quoted in *Women's Diaries of the Westward Journey*

Native Americans Early travelers feared attacks by Native American warriors, but such encounters were rare. By one estimate 362 emigrants died due to Native American attacks between 1840 and 1860. The same estimate calculates that emigrants killed

Wagon interior

Wagon wheel

Mormons heading west

tools, and countless other necessities of everyday life. Now they feared that the increasing flow of American settlers across their hunting grounds would disrupt the age-old wanderings of the buffalo herds.

Hoping to ensure peace, the federal government negotiated the **Treaty of Fort Laramie** in 1851. Eight Native American groups agreed to specific geographic boundaries, while the United States promised that these territories would belong to the Native Americans forever.

✓ **Reading Check** **Describing** What were the difficulties facing Western settlers?

The Mormon Migration

Unlike those bound for the West Coast in search of land, the Mormons followed a deeply rooted American tradition—the quest for religious freedom. The Mormons, however, sought that freedom by leaving the United States.

In 1844, after a mob murdered Joseph Smith, the Church's new leader **Brigham Young** took his people west to escape further persecution. Several thousand Mormons forged their way along a path that became known as the **Mormon Trail.** Along with the Oregon Trail, it served as a valuable route into the western United States. In 1847 the Mormons stopped at the Great Salt Lake in what is now Utah. Young declared that here the Mormons would build a new settlement. Undeterred by the wildness of the area, they staked a claim on the land they called "Deseret."

✓ **Reading Check** **Examining** Why did the Mormons emigrate to the West?

426 Native Americans. In fact, Native Americans often gave emigrants gifts of food as well as helpful information about routes, edible plants, and sources of water. They often traded fresh horses for items such as cotton clothing and ammunition.

As the overland traffic increased, Native Americans on the Great Plains became concerned and angry over the threat immigration posed to their way of life. The Sioux, Cheyenne, Arapaho, and other groups relied on the buffalo for food, shelter, clothing,

---

SECTION 1 ASSESSMENT

Checking for Understanding

1. **Define:** Manifest Destiny, squatter, overlander.
2. **Identify:** John Louis O'Sullivan, Jethro Wood, John Deere, Cyrus McCormick, John Sutter, Kit Carson, Jim Bridger, Donner Party, Brigham Young.
3. **Evaluate** how mountain men helped settle the West.

Reviewing Themes

4. **Science and Technology** What two inventions made it easier to farm the frontier?

Critical Thinking

5. **Synthesizing** How did the United States settle its land disputes with Great Britain and the Plains Indians?
6. **Organizing** Use a graphic organizer similar to the one below to list the reasons why Americans emigrated to the West.

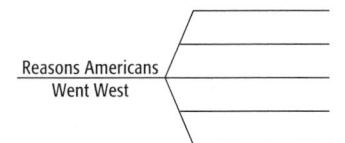

Reasons Americans Went West

Analyzing Visuals

7. **Examining Artifacts** Examine the feature about western migration on pages 296 and 297, especially the photo of a wagon's interior. Why would people need all of the items shown as they traveled west?

Writing About History

8. **Descriptive Writing** Imagine that you emigrated from the East and are living on a frontier farm in the West. Write a letter to a friend in the East describing your daily life.

Eulogy

EDWARD S. CURTIS/CORBIS

CHIEF JOSEPH (above), a leader of the Nez Perce of the Wallowa Valley in eastern Oregon, remembers his father, Old Joseph. The Nez Perce were forced to leave the Wallowa Valley less than a decade after Old Joseph's death.

My father sent for me. I saw he was dying. I took his hand in mine. He said, "My son, my body is returning to my mother earth, and my spirit is going very soon to see the Great Spirit Chief. When I am gone, think of your country. You are the chief of these people. They look to you to guide them. Always remember that your father never sold his country. You must stop your ears whenever you are asked to sign a treaty selling your home. A few years more, and white men will be all around you. They have their eyes on this land. My son, never forget my dying words. This country holds your father's body. Never sell the bones of your father and your mother."

I pressed my father's hand and told him I would protect his grave with my life. My father smiled and passed to the spirit land.

I buried him in that beautiful valley of winding rivers. I love that land more than all the rest of the world. A man who would not love his father's grave is worse than a wild animal.

Baseball for Beginners

Thinking of taking up the new game of baseball? Watch out! The rules keep changing!

1845
- Canvas bases will be set 90 feet apart in a diamond shape.
- Only nine men will play on each side.
- Pitches are to be thrown underhanded.
- A ball caught on the first bounce is an out.

1846
- At first base, a fielder can tag the bag before the runner reaches it and so make an out.

1847
- Players may no longer throw the ball at a runner to put him out.

These changes may be coming:
- A poor pitch is a ball; nine balls gives the runner first base, a walk.
- A ball caught on the first bounce is no longer an out.

O. PIERRE HAVENS/CORBIS

The New York baseball team

WESTERN WORD PLAY

Word Watch

Can you talk Western? Match the word to its meaning.

1. maverick
2. Hangtown fry
3. grubstake
4. bonanza
5. palo alto
6. pard or rawwheel

a. gold rush favorite, made of eggs, bacon, and oysters

b. inexperienced '49er, Eastern type not used to wearing boots

c. a lucky discovery of gold; a source of sudden wealth

d. a style of hat worn by gold rush miners

e. a lone dissenter who takes an independent stand, from the name of a Texas cattleman who left his herd unbranded

f. food provided by an investor to a gold prospector in exchange for a share of whatever gold he finds

answers: 1.e; 2.a; 3.f; 4.c; 5.d; 6.b

Milestones

SETTLED, 1847. THE VALLEY OF THE GREAT SALT LAKE, by Brigham Young, leader of the Mormons, and a party of 143, to escape hostility toward their group in Illinois. Young plans to return to Council Bluffs, Iowa, and lead the rest of the members of his faith to a permanent home in Utah.

MOVED, 1845. HENRY DAVID THOREAU, writer, to Walden Pond, Concord, Massachusetts. Thoreau intends to build his own house on the shore of the pond and earn his living by the labor of his hands only. "Many of the so-called comforts of life," writes Thoreau, "are not only not indispensable, but positive hindrances to the elevation of mankind."

AILING, 1847. EDGAR ALLAN POE, in Baltimore, following the death of his wife, Virginia. Other than a poem on death, Poe has written little this year, devoting his dwindling energies to plagiarism suits against other authors.

Frederick Douglass

LIBRARY OF CONGRESS/CORBIS

EMIGRATED, 1845. FREDERICK DOUGLASS, former slave, author, and abolitionist leader, to England to escape the danger of re-enslavement in reaction to his autobiography, *Narrative of the Life of Frederick Douglass*. On his 1845 trip across the Atlantic, Douglass was not permitted cabin accommodations. After a lecture during the crossing, some passengers threatened to throw him overboard.

DISCOVERED, 1846. THE PLANET NEPTUNE, by German astronomer Johann Galle.

NUMBERS

18,000 Miles from New York to California by sea route around Cape Horn

90,000 People arriving in California in 1849, half by sea, half by overland route

Panning for gold

BETTMANN/CORBIS

$20 Average earned per day by California gold miners in 1849

$18 Average expenses per day for California gold miners in 1849

$390 Value of miners' average daily earnings in 2001 dollars

50 Number of years after the signing of the Declaration of Independence that Thomas Jefferson and John Adams die—within hours of each other.

17,069,453 U.S. population in 1840

55,000 Number of emigrants moving west along the Oregon Trail in 1850

Independence for Texas

Guide to Reading

Main Idea

Settlers emigrated from the United States to Texas and fought Mexico to gain independence.

Key Terms and Names

Tejano, empresario, National Colonization Act, Washington-on-the-Brazos, Antonio López de Santa Anna, Sam Houston, Alamo, William B. Travis, annexation

Reading Strategy

Categorizing As you read about Americans settling in Texas and gaining independence, complete a graphic organizer similar to the one below by filling in the major battles of the Texas revolution and the outcome of each.

Major Battle	Outcome

Reading Objectives

• **Chronicle** the opening of Texas to American settlers.

• **Discuss** the major battles of the war against Mexico.

Section Theme

Groups and Institutions Texans hoped to transplant American institutions to their new homes.

Preview of Events

◆*January, 1836*   ◆*February, 1836*   ◆*March, 1836*   ◆*April, 1836*

February 23, 1836
Santa Anna's troops begin arriving at San Antonio

March 2, 1836
Texas declares independence

March 6, 1836
Siege at the Alamo ends

April 21, 1836
Santa Anna's army defeated at the Battle of San Jacinto

★ An American Story ★

In July 1821, Stephen F. Austin set off from Louisiana for the Texas territory in the northeastern corner of Mexico. The Spanish government had promised to give his father, Moses, a huge tract of Texas land if the elder Austin settled 300 American families there. Moses died before he could fulfill his end of the deal. On his deathbed, he asked Stephen to take his place in Texas. Austin was favorably impressed with the region. As he surveyed the land grant between the Brazos and Colorado Rivers, he noted its natural abundance:

❝The Prairie comes bluff to the river . . . and affords a most beautiful situation for a Town or settlement. . . . The country . . . is as good in every respect as man could wish for, Land all first rate, plenty of timber, fine water, beautifully rolling.❞

—**quoted in** *Stephen F. Austin: Empresario of Texas*

Opening Texas to Americans

When Austin settled in Texas, it was not a wild and empty land. Long a part of Spain's Mexican colony, the area was under Mexican control after the country achieved independence from Spain in 1821. The Spanish-speaking inhabitants of the area, called *Tejanos,* had established such settlements as San Antonio de Bexar and Hidalgo in the southern portion of the region. Few *Tejanos* lived north of these settlements. That area was the territory of the Apache, Comanche, and other Native American groups.

Unable to persuade its own citizens to move closer to the Native American groups, Mexico decided to continue Spanish policy and invite Americans and other foreigners to settle there. Between 1823 and 1825 Mexico passed three colonization laws, which offered cheap land to nearly anyone willing to come. The last law granted new immigrants a 10-year exemption from paying taxes but required that they become Mexican citizens, live under Mexican law, and convert to Roman Catholicism.

Empresarios and Settlers Although some American emigrants headed to Texas on their own, most came at the encouragement of *empresarios,* a Spanish word meaning "agents" or "contractors." Under the **National Colonization Act,** Mexico gave 26 *empresarios* large grants of Texas land. In exchange, the *empresarios* promised to fill it with a certain number of settlers. The *empresarios* assigned a plot to each family and governed the colonies they established.

Stephen Austin was not only the first but also by far the most successful *empresario.* He founded the town of **Washington-on-the-Brazos** and, by the mid-1830s, had persuaded some 1,500 American families to immigrate.

Americanizing Texas The Americans who emigrated to Texas initially accepted Mexican citizenship as required. The government assumed they would also adopt Mexican customs and come to see Mexico as their own country, but for various reasons few did. The Spanish Catholic Church was alien to the traditions of most American settlers, and only a few bothered to learn Spanish.

Many Mexicans, in turn, distrusted the new settlers because of their American lifestyle and dismissal of Mexican ways. The Mexicans' unease increased in 1826, when *empresario* Haden Edwards's brother Benjamin led a rebellion against Mexican authority. Angry over disagreements about whether the Mexican government or the *empresario* controlled the region, Edwards declared that the settlements of Americans in Texas now constituted the independent nation of **Fredonia.** He gained few followers, however, and Stephen Austin led a contingent of troops that helped Mexico crush the revolt.

Although nearly all of the settlers ignored Edwards's call for revolution, the Mexican government feared that it signaled an American plot to acquire Texas. In 1830 Mexico closed its borders to further immigration by Americans and banned the import of enslaved labor as well. Mexico also placed taxes on goods imported from foreign countries, hoping to discourage trade with the United States.

These new laws infuriated the settlers. Without immigration their settlements could not grow. The import tax meant higher prices for goods they were accustomed to purchasing from the United States. Perhaps worst of all, the Mexican government was telling them what they could and could not do. They saw no reason to follow the orders of a government they hardly considered their own.

 Reading Check **Examining** What did Mexico's colonization laws offer people willing to settle in northern Texas, and what did the laws require of these settlers?

Texas Goes to War

With tensions simmering, settlers met at two conventions in the Texas town of San Felipe in 1832 and 1833. They chose Stephen Austin as president of the first convention. The convention asked Mexico to reopen Texas to American immigrants and to loosen the taxes on imports. The second convention in 1833 was more aggressive. At that time, Texas was part of the Mexican state of Coahuila. The convention recommended separating Texas from Coahuila and creating a new Mexican state. The convention also created a constitution for the new state and designated Austin to travel to Mexico City to negotiate with the Mexican government. In the fall of 1833, the negotiations stalled, and an irritated Austin sent a letter to *Tejano* leaders in San Antonio that suggested

Picturing **History**

Land in Texas This April 1836 poster from New Orleans sought volunteers during the Texas war for independence. The offer of land also drew settlers to Texas before the war. Why do you think the sponsors offered more land to settlers who stayed longer?

TEXAS!!

Emigrants who are desirous of assisting Texas at this important crisis of her affairs may have a free passage and equipments, by applying at the

NEW-YORK and PHILADELPHIA HOTEL,

On the Old Levee, near the Blue Stores.

Now is the time to ensure a fortune in Land: To all who remain in Texas during the War will be allowed 1280 Acres.

To all who remain Six Months, 640 Acres.

To all who remain Three Months, 320 Acres.

And as Colonists, 4600 Acres for a family and 1470 Acres for a Single Man.

New Orleans, April 23d, 1836.

Profiles IN HISTORY

Lorenzo de Zavala
1788–1836

Lorenzo de Zavala demonstrated his fierce support of democratic principles both in his native Mexico and as a citizen of the Republic of Texas.

Born in the Yucatán peninsula, Zavala was jailed in his youth for advocating Mexican independence from Spain. Soon after Mexico gained independence in 1821, Zavala was elected to the new national congress. Battles for political power in early Mexico were intense. Zavala was forced into exile but granted a huge tract of land in southeastern Texas.

Politics in Texas proved no less intense than in Mexico. Most Mexicans in Texas were loyal to Mexico, but Zavala's disapproval of Santa Anna's policies led him to support Texan independence. As a speaker of both Spanish and English, he helped draft the new republic's constitution and design its flag. He also served as vice president of the Republic-in-Arms until ill health forced him to resign.

Sam Houston
1793–1863

Standing over six feet tall, Sam Houston seemed larger than life. A military hero in the Creek wars, he had a brief political career in Tennessee before heading to Texas in 1832. He soon revived his military career and led the army of the Republic of Texas to victory over Mexico at the Battle of San Jacinto. Texans elected him president of the Republic and later, when Texas joined the Union, Houston served as a U.S. senator.

Despite being a slaveholder himself, Houston voted with the antislavery faction because he believed a compromise was necessary to save the Union. When the Civil War broke out, Houston refused to take an oath of loyalty to the new Southern government, and he was removed from office. In his farewell address, he declared, "Oh my fellow countrymen, the fearful conflict will fill our land with untold suffering, misfortune, and disaster." He died in July 1863 at the height of the Civil War.

Texas should start peacefully organizing its own state government. Mexican officials intercepted the letter.

After sending the letter, Austin managed to persuade President **Antonio López de Santa Anna** to agree to several demands, including lifting the hated immigration ban. On January 3, 1834, as Austin was returning home, officials arrested him for treason on the basis of the intercepted letter. The Mexican officials took Austin back to Mexico City and threw him in jail, where he languished without trial until he was released in July 1835.

Shortly after Austin was imprisoned, in April 1834, President Santa Anna abruptly denounced Mexico's Constitution of 1824 and made himself dictator. Even Austin, finally released from prison, now saw that negotiation with Santa Anna was impossible. In September 1835, he concluded that war was inevitable. He urged Texans to organize an army, which they quickly did.

The Early Battles

The Texan army faced a Mexican army with serious problems. Continuing political instability in Mexico City had denied the army sound leadership, training, and support. Against this handicapped force the Texan army enjoyed its first taste of victory at the military post of **Gonzales,** about 75 miles east of San Antonio. There, Mexican soldiers ordered the Texans to surrender their arms. In response, the rebels pointed a cannon at the Mexican force and held up a cloth sign painted with the taunt,

"Come and Take It." Having no orders to attack, the Mexicans retreated to San Antonio, and the Texans followed them. The rebels, numbering only about 350, drove the much larger Mexican force out of San Antonio in December 1835.

Despite these early successes, the Texans faced tremendous difficulties of their own. Few of the men had any military training, and no one could agree at first on who should lead them. Finally a former governor of Tennessee and proven military leader named **Sam Houston** took command. In the meantime, Santa Anna organized a force of about 6,000 troops to put down the rebellion.

The Alamo

When Santa Anna's forces arrived at San Antonio in February 1836, they found over 180 rebels holed up in an abandoned Spanish Catholic mission called the **Alamo.** Under the command of Lieutenant Colonel **William B. Travis,** the small force sought to delay Santa Anna and give Houston's army more time to prepare. From within the mission Travis dispatched a courier through Mexican lines with a plea to fellow Texans and U.S. citizens for help:

> ❝I call on you, in the name of liberty, of patriotism, and everything dear to American character, to come to our aid with all dispatch. . . . Though this call may be neglected, I am determined to sustain myself as long as possible, and die like a soldier. . . . Victory or death!❞
>
> —quoted in *History of Texas*

The call for reinforcements went almost unanswered. Only 32 settlers from Gonzales, deciding on their own to join the fight, made it into the Alamo. Running low on ammunition and gunpowder, the Texans held off Santa Anna's besieging army for 13 days. During the standoff the new Texas government met at Washington-on-the-Brazos and formally declared independence from Mexico.

On March 6, 1836, Santa Anna's army stormed the Alamo. The Texans fought off the attackers for six hours, killing or wounding about 600 before being overrun. Although the defenders of the Alamo had been defeated, they had bought Houston's army nearly two extra weeks to organize.

Goliad Two weeks later the Mexican army overwhelmed Texan troops led by James W. Fannin at Goliad, a town southeast of San Antonio near the Gulf Coast. Fannin and his men surrendered, hoping the Mexicans would disarm them and expel them from Texas. Though the Mexican field general at Goliad wrote to Santa Anna requesting clemency, Santa Anna demanded execution. At dawn on March 27, a firing squad executed more than 300 men. The losses at the Alamo and Goliad devastated Texans but also united them behind their new country.

TURNING POINT

The Battle of San Jacinto
With the Texan army in disarray, Sam Houston desperately needed time to recruit fresh volunteers and to train the soldiers who remained. Rather than fight, he chose to retreat, heading east toward Louisiana.

Houston was biding his time. Up against a larger, more disciplined army, he decided to wait for Santa Anna to make a mistake. Such a mistake occurred on April 21, when both armies were encamped along the San Jacinto River near what is now the city of Houston. Santa Anna no longer saw Houston's army as a threat, so he allowed his men to sleep in the afternoon, confident that Houston would wait until the next day to launch an attack.

Eager for a fight, Houston's soldiers convinced the officers to launch an afternoon assault. Shielded from sight by a hill, Houston's troops crept up on Santa Anna's sleeping soldiers and charged. The surprise attack threw the Mexicans into a panic.

The Battle of San Jacinto lasted less than 20 minutes, but the killing continued for hours. Yelling "Remember the Alamo" and "Remember Goliad," Houston's men attacked the Mexican troops with guns, knives, and clubs. In addition to hundreds killed, over 700

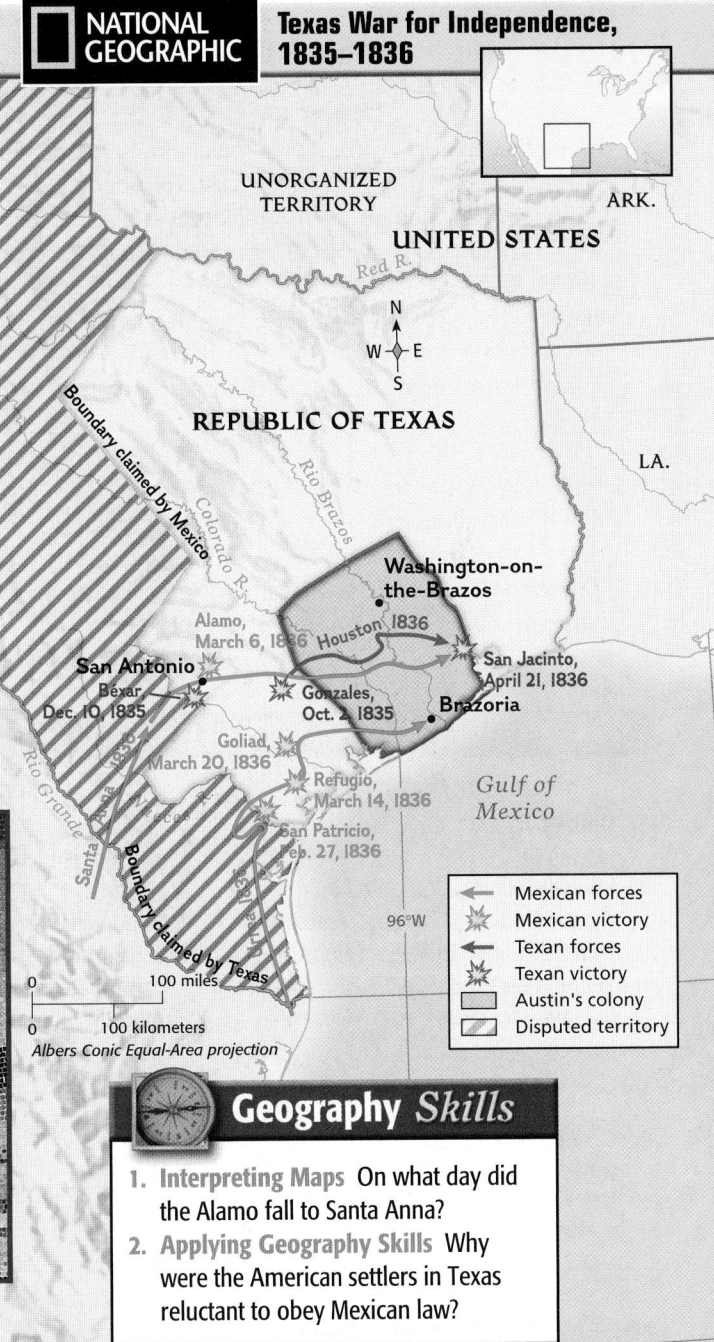

Mosaic of the Gonzales cannon

NATIONAL GEOGRAPHIC

Texas War for Independence, 1835–1836

Geography *Skills*

1. **Interpreting Maps** On what day did the Alamo fall to Santa Anna?
2. **Applying Geography Skills** Why were the American settlers in Texas reluctant to obey Mexican law?

History *Through Art*

Battle of San Jacinto H.A. McArdle's painting (above) and this monument (at right) commemorate the pivotal battle of the war between Texas and Mexico. *Why were Santa Anna and his troops surprised by Houston's attack?*

members of Santa Anna's force were taken captive. The Texans suffered only 9 killed and 34 wounded.

Among the captured troops was Santa Anna himself. Houston forced Santa Anna to order his army out of Texas and sign a treaty recognizing independence for the Republic of Texas. The Mexican Congress refused to accept the treaty, but it was unwilling to launch another military campaign. Texas had won the war.

The Republic of Texas In September 1836 the newly independent republic called its citizens to the polls. They elected Sam Houston as their first president and voted 3,277 to 91 in favor of annexation, or becoming part of the United States.

Given that Americans had enthusiastically supported the war, most Texans assumed the United States would want to annex the republic. Many Northern members of Congress, however, opposed admitting Texas as a slave state.

President Andrew Jackson did not want to increase North-South tensions or risk a costly war with Mexico, which continued to claim ownership of Texas. Jackson made no move toward annexation, though on his last day in office he did sign a resolution officially recognizing Texas as an independent nation.

✓ **Reading Check** **Summarizing** What difficulties did the Texans face in their war against Mexico?

SECTION 2 ASSESSMENT

Checking for Understanding

1. **Define:** *Tejano, empresario, annexation.*
2. **Identify:** National Colonization Act, Washington-on-the Brazos, Antonio López de Santa Anna, Sam Houston, Alamo, William B. Travis.
3. **Explain** why Texas declared war on Mexico.

Reviewing Themes

4. **Groups and Institutions** Why did some Northern leaders oppose admitting Texas to the United States?

Critical Thinking

5. **Synthesizing** How did the Texan defeats at the Alamo and Goliad affect Texans?
6. **Categorizing** Use a graphic organizer similar to the one below to list the reasons that Texans did not wish to become Mexican citizens.

Reasons Texans Opposed Mexican Citizenship

Analyzing Visuals

7. **Examining Art** Examine the poster on page 301 advertising land to Texas settlers. How were permanent settlers and soldiers for hire rewarded differently?
8. **Examining Art** Study the painting on this page. Why do you think the artist painted the clearing blue sky in the top right of the work?

Writing About History

9. **Persuasive Writing** Imagine that you are living in Texas in the late 1830s. Write a letter to the U.S. Congress arguing why members should or should not vote to annex Texas.

Social Studies
SKILLBUILDER

Understanding Latitude and Longitude

Why Learn This Skill?

Mapmakers use lines of latitude and longitude to pinpoint locations on maps and globes. Understanding these lines and what they signify will help you locate any place on a map—around the corner or around the world.

Learning the Skill

The imaginary horizontal lines that circle the globe from east to west are called lines of **latitude.** Because the distance between the lines of latitude is always the same, they are also called *parallels.* The imaginary vertical lines that intersect the parallels are lines of **longitude,** also called *meridians.*

Parallels and meridians are numbered in degrees. The **Equator,** located halfway between the North and South Poles, is at 0°. Moving north or south of the Equator, the number of degrees increases until reaching 90°N or 90°S latitude at the poles.

The **Prime Meridian** is at 0° longitude. Moving east or west of the Prime Meridian, the number of degrees east or west increases up to 180°. The 180° line of longitude is located on the opposite side of the globe from the Prime Meridian and is called the *International Date Line.*

The point at which parallels and meridians intersect is the grid address, or coordinates, of an exact location. The coordinates for Salt Lake City, for example, are 41°N latitude and 112°W longitude.

Practicing the Skill

Analyze the information on the map on this page, and then answer the questions.

❶ What are the approximate coordinates of Fort Victoria?

❷ At what line of latitude was the Oregon country divided between the United States and Britain? How many degrees south would you need to go from there to reach the South Pole?

❸ What geographic feature lies at about 42°N and 109°W?

NATIONAL GEOGRAPHIC — Oregon Country, 1840

❹ The United States originally wanted Oregon's northern border to be between 54° and 55°N. Does the 1846 Boundary lie north or south of this boundary? By approximately how many degrees?

Skills Assessment

Complete the Practicing Skills questions on page 315 and the Chapter 9 Skill Reinforcement Activity to assess your mastery of this skill.

Applying the Skill

Understanding Latitude and Longitude Study the map of western trails on page 296. Use the map to answer the following questions.

1. St. Joseph is closest to which parallel?

2. Which fort is located north of 40°N latitude and east of 100°W longitude?

 Glencoe's **Skillbuilder Interactive Workbook CD-ROM, Level 2** provides instruction and practice in key social studies skills.

Guide to Reading

Main Idea
The United States clashed with Mexico in an attempt to gain new territory.

Key Terms and Names
John Tyler, James K. Polk, "Fifty-four Forty or Fight," envoy, Zachary Taylor, John C. Frémont, Bear Flag Republic, Winfield Scott, Treaty of Guadalupe Hidalgo, cede

Reading Strategy
Taking Notes As you read about the war with Mexico, use the major headings of the section to complete the outline started below.

The War With Mexico
I. The Lingering Question of Texas
II.
   A.
   B.
   C.

Reading Objectives
• **Describe** the circumstances under which Texas and Oregon were admitted to the Union.
• **Discuss** the major events of the war with Mexico.

Section Theme
Continuity and Change The war with Mexico brought new territories under the control of the United States.

Preview of Events

| ♦1845 | ♦1846 | ♦1847 | ♦1848 |

February 1845
Congress votes to annex Texas

May 13, 1846
Congress declares war on Mexico

June 18, 1846
Oregon boundary dispute settled

September 14, 1847
U.S. troops storm Mexico City

February 2, 1848
Treaty of Guadalupe Hidalgo signed

★ *An American Story* ★

"Monterrey is ours," wrote U.S. Army lieutenant Napoleon Dana to his wife Sue in September 1846. "I can hardly describe to you with my pen what difficulties, dangers, and labors we have gone through to gain it." Lieutenant Dana had just survived four days of intense fighting as American troops captured the Mexican city of Monterrey.

❝The enemy fought very obstinately here, and we had to fight them by inches and advance upon them from house to house. . . . Soon after dark our mortar began to fire. . . . The shells all burst beautifully right in the plaza, scattering death and devastation.❞

Dana and other American troops remained in the city for two months, taking over the houses of wealthy residents. The army assigned Dana to the home of "one Don Manuel Somebody." He wrote Sue of beautiful palace grounds "such as you may have seen in pictures of Italian gardens in older times." In mid-December, the night before leaving Monterrey, he paid a farewell visit to Don Manuel, whom he now regarded as a "right good old fellow." As the elderly Mexican said goodbye, he made "a long and affecting speech . . . while his eyes filled. . . . He said that if the war continued, he foresaw nothing but the ruin of his native land."

—**adapted from** *Monterrey Is Ours!*

The Lingering Question of Texas

The stage had been set for war with Mexico years before. Territorial disputes between the United States and its southern neighbor began as far back as 1803, when the United States claimed Texas as part of the Louisiana Purchase. The United States renounced that claim in the Adams-Onís Treaty of 1819, but the idea of Manifest Destiny and of acquiring Mexican territory had strong popular support.

Tensions grew during the administration of **John Tyler,** who hoped to bring Texas into the Union. Because Texas already possessed a significant population of Southerners who had taken enslaved African Americans into Texas, it was certain to support the cause of slavery. Antislavery leaders in Congress therefore opposed annexation. Moreover, Mexico had never recognized the independence of Texas and still considered it Mexican territory.

✓ **Reading Check** **Analyzing** Why did antislavery members of Congress oppose admitting Texas to the Union?

Texas and Oregon Enter the Union

In early 1844, after spearheading a publicity campaign in favor of annexation, President Tyler brought the matter before the Senate. He blundered, however, by including in the supporting documents a letter written by Secretary of State John C. Calhoun that contained a fierce defense of slavery. Outraged Northerners pointed to the letter as evidence that annexation was nothing but a pro-slavery plot, and by a count of 35 to 16, the Senate voted against annexation. The maneuver that Tyler believed would win him a second term instead destroyed his chances of retaining the presidency.

The Election of 1844 As the presidential race began later that year, the front-runners for the nomination were Whig senator **Henry Clay** and former Democratic president Martin Van Buren. Although politicians on both sides of the annexation issue pressed the candidates to state their positions, both responded cautiously to avoid losing supporters.

Van Buren's indecision cost him the Democratic nomination. His party instead chose **James K. Polk,** a former

Congressman and governor of Tennessee. Polk promised to annex not only Texas but also the contested Oregon territory in the Northwest. In addition, he vowed to buy California from Mexico. The ambitious platform appealed to both Northerners and Southerners because it expanded the country while promising to maintain the delicate balance between free and slave states.

The Democrats' unity on annexation caused Clay to backpedal. Reversing a statement made in the

 History

Tensions Grow With Mexico From the time of the Louisiana Purchase in 1803, territorial tensions between the United States and Mexico threatened the possibility of war. In the late 1840s, war began between the two nations. This rare daguerreotype shows American soldiers patrolling Mexican territory. How did Texas's annexation contribute to the start of the war?

Different Viewpoints

Did Manifest Destiny Violate American Ideals?

In the 1800s, many Americans believed the United States was destined to reach from the Atlantic Ocean to the Pacific Ocean. This national mission also implied that Americans were superior to their neighbors who also controlled territory in North America. Did this belief in American superiority contradict the spirit of equality important to so many Americans?

Public servant Albert Gallatin opposes Manifest Destiny:

At the age of 86, after a distinguished career in public service, Albert Gallatin became president of the New York Historical Society. The war against Mexico revived his interest in politics, and he wrote:

"It is said that the people of the United States have a hereditary superiority of race over the Mexicans, which gives them the right to subjugate and keep in bondage the inferior nation. . . .

Is it compatible with the principle of democracy, which rejects every hereditary claim of individuals, to admit a hereditary superiority of races? . . . Can you for a moment suppose that a very doubtful descent from men who lived 1,000 years ago has transmitted to you a superiority over your fellow men?

. . . At this time the claim is but a pretext for covering and justifying unjust usurpation and unbounded ambition.

. . . Among ourselves the most ignorant, the most inferior, either in physical or mental faculties, is recognized as having equal rights, and he has an equal vote with anyone, however superior to him in all those respects. This is founded on the immutable principle that no one man is born with the right to governing another man."

—quoted in *The Mission of the United States*

spring of 1844 against immediate annexation, Clay now supported annexation of Texas as long as it was done without causing war with Mexico. This so angered antislavery Whigs in his party that they threw their support to the Liberty Party—a small third party that supported abolition. With the Whig vote split, Polk won the election.

The Oregon Question In public, Polk took a strong stance on Oregon. Despite British claims on the region, he said that the United States had a "clear and unquestionable" right to it. His supporters cried **"Fifty-four Forty or Fight,"** declaring that they wanted all of Oregon to the line of 54° 40' north latitude.

In private, however, Polk agreed to split the territory. In June 1846 Great Britain and the United States resolved the dispute. The United States received all of Oregon south of 49° north latitude, except for the southern tip of Vancouver Island.

The Annexation of Texas Even before Polk took office, outgoing president Tyler pushed an annexation resolution through Congress in February 1845.

The resolution succeeded because it needed only a simple majority of both houses rather than the two-thirds majority needed to ratify a treaty. Texas joined the Union in 1845. Mexico was outraged and broke diplomatic relations with the U.S. government. Matters worsened when the two countries disputed the location of Texas's southwestern border. Mexico said it was the Nueces River. Texans, and then the United States, claimed the Rio Grande, about 150 miles (240 km) farther west and south, as the boundary. The Texas-United States claim covered far more territory than the Mexican claim, including some of what is now eastern New Mexico.

Polk's intentions in California added to the growing strife. In November 1845 he sent **John Slidell** as special envoy, or representative, to Mexico City to try to purchase the territory. Mexico's new president, José Joaquín Herrera, refused even to meet with Slidell.

✓ **Reading Check** **Examining** What did James Polk promise to do if he was elected president?

Learning From History

1. What does Albert Gallatin think is the real motivation underlying the idea of Manifest Destiny?
2. Can you find other instances in American history when Americans believed their nation had a special destiny?

The War With Mexico

Herrera's snub ended any realistic chance of a diplomatic solution. Polk ordered troops led by General **Zachary Taylor** to cross the Nueces River—in Mexico's view, an invasion of its territory. Polk wanted Mexican soldiers to fire the first shot. If he could say Mexico was the aggressor, he could more easily win popular support for a war.

Finally, on May 9, 1846, news reached him that a force of Mexicans had attacked Taylor's men. In an address to Congress, Polk declared that the United States was at war "by the act of Mexico herself." Hoping to incite the public's indignation, he added that "American blood has been shed on American soil!"

Many Whigs opposed the war as yet another plot to extend slavery. Most Washington politicians, though, recognized that however questionable Polk's

actions, the United States was committed to war. On May 13 the Senate voted 40 to 2 and the House 174 to 14 in favor of the war.

Calling All Volunteers Polk and his advisers developed a three-pronged military strategy. Taylor's troops would continue to move south, crossing the Rio Grande near the Gulf of Mexico. A separate force to the northwest would capture Santa Fe, an important trading center in what is now New Mexico, and then march west to take control of California with the help of the American navy. Finally, U.S. forces would advance to Mexico City and force Mexico to surrender.

To implement the ambitious plan, the United States needed to expand the army. Congress authorized the president to call for 50,000 volunteers, and men from all over the country rushed to enlist. Almost 73,000 answered the call.

Undisciplined and unruly, the volunteers proved to be less than ideal soldiers. As one officer observed, "They will do well enough to defend their own firesides, but they can not endure the fatigue incident to an invading army." Another bemoaned in a half-comical way their constant demands on his attention:

❝[O]ne wanted me to read a letter he had just received; another wanted me to write one for him; another wanted me to send his money home; another wanted me to keep it for him. . . . [O]ne complained that his uniform was too large, another that his was too small.❞

—from *Memoirs of a Maryland Volunteer*

The Fighting Begins In early May, several days before Polk signed the declaration of war, Taylor's troops defeated Mexican forces, first at Palo Alto and

Picturing **History**

General Zachary Taylor
President Polk's desire to provoke Mexico resulted in Zachary Taylor leading American soldiers south of the Nueces River into disputed territory. What geographical feature did the United States claim was the boundary between the United States and Mexico?

then at Resaca de la Palma. Taylor then moved south, overcoming more enemy forces at Matamoros. By late September he had marched about 200 miles (322 km) west from the Gulf Coast and captured Monterrey.

In the meantime, Colonel Stephen W. Kearny led troops from Fort Leavenworth, west of Missouri, toward Santa Fe. The march through the dry countryside was brutal, but when Kearny's men reached the city in August, the Mexican force there had already fled. With Santa Fe secured, a small U.S. force headed on to California.

Before Kearny's force arrived and even before war with Mexico was officially declared, settlers in northern California, led by American general **John C. Frémont,** had begun an uprising. The official Mexican presence in the territory had never been strong, and the settlers had little trouble overcoming

it. On June 14, 1846, they declared California independent of Mexico and renamed the region the **Bear Flag Republic.** A few weeks later, the Bear Flag Republic came to an end when naval forces of the United States occupied San Francisco and San Diego and took possession of California for the United States.

To Mexico City The war had proceeded just as President Polk had hoped, but despite having lost vast territories, Mexico's leaders refused to surrender. Polk decided to force things to a conclusion with the third phase of his battle plan. He sent soldiers on ships to the Mexican port of Veracruz, from where they would march west and capture the Mexican capital, Mexico City.

Polk, seeing Taylor as a potential rival in the 1848 election, eased him out of the war by placing General

NATIONAL GEOGRAPHIC

The War With Mexico, 1846–1848

General Winfield Scott

Legend:
- → American troops
- ✸ American victory
- → Mexican troops
- ✸ Mexican victory
- ⚓ U.S. naval blockade

0 — 300 miles
0 — 300 kilometers
Albers Conic Equal-Area projection

Geography *Skills*

1. **Interpreting Maps** Which American officer assisted Frémont's attacks in northern California?

2. **Applying Geography Skills** What land did the United States get from the Treaty of Guadalupe Hidalgo?

Winfield Scott, a member of the Whig Party, in command of this campaign. In March 1847 Scott's force landed at Veracruz. The troops headed for Mexico City, battling the enemy along the way. On September 14, after a hard fight, they finally captured the capital.

The Peace Treaty After the fall of Mexico City, Mexico's leaders could no longer hold out. On February 2, 1848, they signed the **Treaty of Guadalupe Hidalgo.** In the agreement, Mexico ceded, or gave up, more than 500,000 square miles (1,295,000 sq. km) of territory to the United States. This land is now the states of California, Utah, and Nevada, as well as parts of New Mexico, Arizona, Colorado, and Wyoming. Mexico also accepted the Rio Grande as the southern border of Texas. In exchange, the United States paid Mexico $15 million and agreed to take over $3.25 million in debts Mexico owed to American citizens.

With Oregon and the former Mexican territories now under the American flag, the dream of Manifest Destiny was finally realized: the United States now stretched from ocean to ocean. Valuable ports on the west coast opened up new avenues to the Pacific nations of Asia. The question of whether the new lands should allow slavery, however, would soon lead the country into another bloody conflict. The experience that

 History *Through Art*

General Scott's Entrance Into Mexico This 1851 painting by Carl Nebel re-creates the scene of General Scott leading troops into Mexico City in the final phase of the war with Mexico. How do the Mexican people seem to be reacting to the arrival of the American troops?

such men as Robert E. Lee and Ulysses S. Grant gained during the war would soon be used to lead Americans against each other.

Reading Check **Summarizing** What was President Polk's military strategy in the war with Mexico?

SECTION 3 ASSESSMENT

Checking for Understanding
1. **Define:** envoy, cede.
2. **Identify:** John Tyler, James K. Polk, "Fifty-four Forty or Fight," Zachary Taylor, John C. Frémont, Bear Flag Republic, Winfield Scott, Treaty of Guadalupe Hidalgo.
3. **Summarize** the controversy between Mexico and the United States over Texas.

Reviewing Themes
4. **Continuity and Change** The idea of Manifest Destiny was realized as a result of the war with Mexico. What new problems did this increase in land cause for the United States?

Critical Thinking
5. **Evaluating** What was the military strategy of the United States during the war with Mexico? Evaluate the success of this strategy.
6. **Organizing** Use a graphic organizer similar to the one below to list the provisions of the Treaty of Guadalupe Hidalgo.

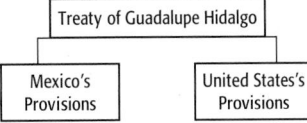

Treaty of Guadalupe Hidalgo

Mexico's Provisions — United States's Provisions

Analyzing Visuals
7. **Examining Art** Study the portrait of General Winfield Scott on page 310. Why did President Taylor place Scott in charge of the invasion of Mexico City?
8. **Examining Art** Study the painting *American Progress* by John Gast on page 308. What symbols of progress are shown trailing the spirit figure heading westward?

Writing About History
9. **Expository Writing** Pretend you are James K. Polk, the Democratic candidate for president in the 1844 election. Write a speech in which you explain your platform.

Spanish Missions

The Spanish settlers who came to the American Southwest had two aims: to claim the land and to convert the Native Americans to Catholicism. To achieve these aims, the Spaniards set up fortified religious settlements known as missions.

The missions reflected both the culture of Spain and the demands of life in an arid land. By the late eighteenth century, the missions were thriving, self-contained communities.

Arranged in a quadrangle around a central courtyard, the complex was a bustling world of workshops, storage areas, gardens, and living quarters. Its location was often determined by the availability of wood, water, and fields for raising crops and grazing the livestock that the Spanish brought to the Americas. The form of the mission was dictated by the building materials available. The thick walls of the one-story buildings were usually made of stone or sun-dried mud bricks known as adobe.

For security, most of the mission's residences were connected, and all windows faced inward. The entrances were locked at night. A covered arcade, or outdoor hallway, ran along the inner walls of the residences. The complex was usually dominated by a large church. Thousands of Native Americans were lured to the missions by gifts and by the prospect of finding safety and food. They were instructed in Catholicism and Spanish and put to work. Women wove cloth and cooked; men labored at handicrafts or in the fields. In addition to the native beans and corn, the converts planted crops introduced by the Spaniards such as wheat, oats, oranges, olives, and grapes.

Some of the missions would not allow the Native Americans to leave without permission once they had entered the community. Making this transition to a regimented life was difficult, and escapes were common. To enforce order and hunt down runaways, many missions had a small detachment of soldiers. The soldiers rode on horses, which the Spaniards brought to the Southwest.

The Spaniards also brought measles and smallpox—devastating diseases against which the Native Americans had no natural immunity. Mission cemeteries often held the bones of thousands of Native Americans who died of these European diseases.

Crops

Priests' quarters

Soldiers' barracks

Stable

Watering trough

LEARNING FROM GEOGRAPHY

1. What factors determined the selection of a mission site?

2. Why did the Spanish station troops at missions?

San Francisco

San Juan

SanLuis Obispo

Santa Fe

San Juan Capistrano

San Diego

Tomé

Socorro

Tucson

Tubac

El Paso

Fronteras

San Antonio

Horcasitas

San José y San Miguel de Aguayo

Loreto

Monterrey

Spanish Missions, 1776

✝	Mission	......	Present–day boundary
✞	Mission & Presidio		Road
■	Presidio		Migration

0   200 miles
0   200 kilometers

The Virgin of Guadalupe adorns the church at the mission of San José y San Miguel de Aguayo.

Fruit trees

Living quarters

Gate

Oven

Workshop

Well

Pottery makers

Nut trees

Livestock corral

Garden

Catholic church

Fruit trees

Cemetery and garden

Granary

Tannery and workshops

Entrance

Soldiers

Years before the English unfurled their flag at Jamestown, Spanish missionaries and colonists from New Spain, as Mexico was known, were settling in the Southwest. The map shows their major migration routes into present-day New Mexico, Texas, and California, as well as the location of their missions and presidios, or garrisoned forts.

The Spanish built the church of San José y San Miguel de Aguayo in San Antonio, Texas, in the 1720s. Such churches were only part of much larger mission complexes. The art above shows the layout of a typical mission.

Reviewing Key Terms

On a sheet of paper, use each of these terms in a sentence.

1. Manifest Destiny
2. squatter
3. overlander
4. *Tejano*
5. *empresario*
6. annexation
7. envoy
8. cede

Reviewing Key Facts

9. **Identify:** John Louis O'Sullivan, John Sutter, Brigham Young, Antonio López de Santa Anna, Sam Houston, William B. Travis, John Tyler, James K. Polk, Zachary Taylor, Winfield Scott.
10. Why were many Americans willing to give up their lives in the East and move to the West?
11. What were five trails that Americans followed as they emigrated west?
12. Why did the Mexican government encourage Americans to settle in northern Texas?
13. What caused settlers in Texas to declare independence from Mexico?
14. What did the United States gain from the Treaty of Guadalupe Hidalgo?

Critical Thinking

15. **Analyzing Themes: Science and Technology** How did the inventions of Deere's steel plow and McCormick's reaper encourage the settlement of the western plains?
16. **Identifying Points of View** Why was James Polk's platform in the presidential election of 1844 popular with both Northerners and Southerners?
17. **Categorizing** Use a graphic organizer similar to the one below to list the causes and the effects of westward movement by Americans.

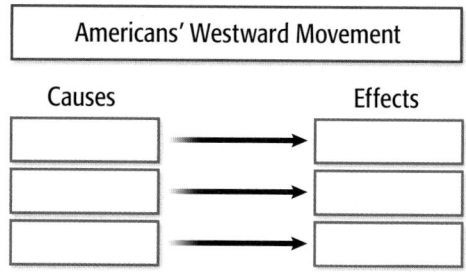

Americans' Westward Movement

Causes → Effects

18. **Interpreting Primary Sources** In April of 1847, Charles Sumner presented his views on the causes of the war with Mexico in his "Report on the War with Mexico" to the Commonwealth of Massachusetts. Read the excerpt and answer the questions that follow.

Chapter Summary

Oregon

- Great Britain and the United States claimed parts of Oregon.
- The area was almost completely British until American missionaries arrived in the 1830s.
- Large numbers of Americans sought farmland in southern Oregon in 1840.
- The two countries divided the territory without conflict.

California

- The territory was part of Mexico, although Americans still settled there.
- The local California government invited foreign settlers but was suspicious of them.
- The United States tried to purchase California from Mexico, but Mexico refused.
- An uprising overthrew the California government, and troops secured the territory during the war with Mexico.

The Midwest

- In the early 1800s, squatters settled land that they did not own in Ohio, Indiana, Illinois, Michigan, and Wisconsin.
- The Preemption Act allowed squatters to buy up to 160 acres of land.

Texas and the Southwest

- Mexico invited Americans and others to populate Texas.
- Mexico passed strict laws against American immigrants, which led to Texas's war for independence.
- Congress voted to annex Texas in 1845, and Texas also voted for annexation.
- Boundary disputes in Texas, along with the American attempt to purchase the California territory, led to the start of the war with Mexico.
- The United States won the war and gained Texas, California, and much of the territory that is now the West and Southwest.

Self-Check Quiz

Visit the *American Vision* Web site at tav.glencoe.com and click on *Self-Check Quizzes—Chapter 9* to assess your knowledge of chapter content.

❝It can no longer be doubted that this is a war of conquest. . . . In a letter to Commodore Sloat, . . . the Secretary [of War] says, 'You will take such measures as will render that vast region [California] a desirable place of residence for emigrants from our soil.' In a letter to Colonel Kearny . . . he says: 'Should you conquer and take possession of New Mexico and Upper California, you will establish civil governments therein. You may assure the people of these provinces that it is the wish of the United States to provide for them a free government with the least possible delay. . . .❞

—quoted in *Readings in American History*

a. According to Charles Sumner, why did the United States become involved in the war with Mexico?

b. What evidence does Sumner provide to show that this was the U.S. government's intention?

Practicing Skills

19. **Understanding Latitude and Longitude** Study the map of western trails on page 296. Then use the steps you learned on page 305 to answer the following questions.

    a. The Continental Divide lies between what two lines of longitude?

    b. About how many degrees of latitude are there between Salt Lake City and Los Angeles?

Writing Activity

20. **Interviewing** You and a group of your classmates should take on these roles of people in North America in the early to mid-1800s: a journalist, a British settler and an American settler in the Oregon Country, a Native American of the Great Plains, a pioneer, a Mexican official, and a farmer in the East. The journalist then interviews the people about their attitudes toward Manifest Destiny. Write summaries of each interview and place them in your portfolio.

Chapter Activity

21. **Technology Activity: Using an Electronic Card Catalog** Search your library's card catalog for books containing information about western settlement in the 1800s. Use this information to make an alphabetical directory of western trails and historic sites that tourists might like to visit. Your

NATIONAL GEOGRAPHIC | **Treaty of Guadalupe Hidalgo, 1848**

☐ Area gained by the United States as a result of the Treaty of Guadalupe Hidalgo, 1848

list might include cities along the trails, pioneer museums, mountain passes, and other places of interest.

Geography and History

22. The map above shows land acquired after the war with Mexico. Study the map and answer the questions below.

    a. **Interpreting Maps** What seven U.S. states now hold territory acquired in the Treaty of Guadalupe Hidalgo?

    b. **Applying Geography Skills** What group of immigrants who had moved outside the United States was brought back under American jurisdiction as a result of the treaty?

Standardized Test Practice

Directions: Choose the best answer to the following question.

Which of the following is NOT a condition set by Mexico for American settlers coming to live in Texas?

A They received a ten-year exemption from paying taxes.

B They could never return to live in the United States.

C They were required to become Mexican citizens.

D They were required to convert to the Roman Catholic faith.

Test-Taking Tip: Be careful—overlooking the words NOT or EXCEPT in a question is a common error. Look for the answer choice that does NOT fit the question. For example, since a tax exemption *was* a benefit for Texas newcomers, you can eliminate answer A.

UNIT
4 The Crisis of Union

1848–1877

Why It Matters

The growing sectional crisis in the 1800s led to the Civil War, the most wrenching war in American history. The peace that was forged after four years of internal conflict reunited the nation and ended slavery. It did not, however, end the problems of racial inequality. Understanding the war and the Reconstruction period that followed will help you understand the challenges of a multicultural society that our nation still faces today. The following resources offer more information about this period in American history.

Cap of a Confederate soldier

Primary Sources Library

See pages 1050–1051 for primary source readings to accompany Unit 4.

Use the **American History Primary Source Document Library CD-ROM** to find additional primary sources about the Civil War.

Union flag flown at Fort Sumter before surrender to the Confederates

Why It Matters

When the nation gained new territory, the slavery controversy intensified. Would new states be slave or free? Who would decide? States that allowed slavery were determined to prevent free states from gaining a majority in the Senate. Political compromise broke down by 1860, and when Lincoln was elected president, many Southern states decided to secede.

The Impact Today

The political and social debates of this period continue to have influence.
- *Older sectional loyalties still define some regions of the country.*
- *The modern Republican Party grew in part from opposition to slavery.*

 The American Vision *Video* *The Chapter 10 video, "Tales From the Underground Railroad," features a dramatization of enslaved African Americans using the Underground Railroad to reach freedom.*

1850
- Compromise of 1850 adopted in an attempt to ease sectional tensions

1849
- California Gold Rush begins

1854
- Republican Party founded

United States PRESIDENTS

| Polk 1845–1849 | Taylor 1849–1850 | Fillmore 1850–1853 | Pierce 1853–1857 |

1846   *1850*   *1854*

World

1847
- Working hours limited in Britain

1848
- Serfdom abolished in Austrian Empire

1852
- Livingstone explores Africa's Zambezi River

1853
- Crimean War pitting Russia against Great Britain and Turkey begins

View of Harpers Ferry by Ferdinand Richardt, 1858, depicts the peaceful town a year before a raid on the federal arsenal there triggered a crisis for the Union.

1858
- Lincoln-Douglas debates take place during the Illinois Senate campaign

1856
- Conflict between pro-slavery and antislavery forces causes riots in Lawrence, Kansas

1859
- John Brown raids the federal arsenal at Harpers Ferry, Virginia

1860
- South Carolina secedes from the Union

1861
- Fort Sumter bombarded by Confederate forces; the Civil War begins

Buchanan 1857–1861

Lincoln 1861–1865

CHARLESTON
MERCURY
EXTRA.

THE
UNION
IS
DISSOLVED!

1858

1862

1859
- Darwin's *Origin of Species* published

HISTORY Online

Chapter Overview
Visit the *American Vision* Web site at tav.glencoe.com and click on **Chapter Overviews—Chapter 10** to preview chapter information.

Slavery and Western Expansion

Guide to Reading

Main Idea
The question of whether to admit new states to the Union led to new tensions between the North and South over slavery.

Key Terms and Names
Wilmot Proviso, Lewis Cass, popular sovereignty, Conscience Whigs, Cotton Whigs, Free-Soil Party, "Forty-Niners," secession

Reading Strategy
Categorizing As you read about the political aftermath of the war with Mexico, complete a graphic organizer like the one below by pairing the presidential candidates of 1848 with their positions on slavery in the West.

Candidate	Position

Reading Objectives
- **Explain** how the government dealt with slavery in the territories acquired after the war with Mexico.
- **List** the major features of the Compromise of 1850.

Section Theme
Geography and History The acquisition of new lands heightened sectional tensions over slavery.

Preview of Events

♦1847   ♦1848   ♦1849   ♦1850

August 1846
Wilmot Proviso presented

March 1848
Treaty of Guadalupe Hidalgo signed

August 1848
Free-Soil Party formed

1849
California Gold Rush begins

September 1850
Compromise of 1850 adopted

★ An American Story ★

Early one cold morning in January 1847, Mrs. Crosswait woke to the sound of pistol shots. Without a word she rushed to her sleeping children, while her husband ran downstairs to bolt the door. The Crosswaits knew instantly the danger they were facing. Kidnappers had come to snatch them from their Michigan home and drag them back to Kentucky—and slavery.

The family had fled north after learning, to their horror, that the man who held them in slavery planned to sell them away from each other. They ended up in Marshall, Michigan. Home to a strong community of Quakers, Marshall welcomed them warmly.

Now, clutching her children, Mrs. Crosswait peeked fearfully from an upper window as three strangers fired bullet after bullet into their front door and demanded that the family surrender. She heard her husband pushing furniture against the door.

Then over the din came the voice of a neighbor, urging people to aid the family. Soon, friends came running. Shouting threats at the intruders, the townspeople intimidated them into leaving, thereby saving the family.

—adapted from *Black Pioneers: An Untold Story*

The Impact of the War With Mexico

The Crosswaits' struggle with kidnappers was not unique. Although many people escaped from slavery and headed north into free territory, they were not safe. Southerners believed that Article 4, Section 2, of the Constitution gave them the right to retrieve an enslaved person who fled across state lines. Some Northerners, however, held strong beliefs to the contrary and acted on those beliefs by sheltering runaways and helping them escape.

The Mexican War only heightened these opposing viewpoints and led to increasingly divisive sectional tensions. The war opened vast new lands to American settlers. This territorial expansion once again raised the divisive issue of whether slavery should be allowed to spread westward. As part of the debate over the new western territories, Southerners also demanded new laws to help them retrieve African Americans who escaped to free territory.

President Polk Sees Trouble Ahead James K. Polk, a Southern Democrat and a slaveholder, believed any argument about slavery in the new territories acquired from Mexico was "an abstract question." No one would take enslaved African Americans to the Southwest, Polk thought, because the dry climate would not support the kinds of farming that made slavery profitable.

As an angry debate broke out in Congress, however, Polk realized that the issue of slavery in the territories was not something he could brush aside. His diary reflected his fear that the question "cannot fail to destroy the Democratic Party, if it does not ultimately threaten the Union itself."

GOVERNMENT

The Wilmot Proviso In August 1846, Representative David Wilmot, a Democrat from Pennsylvania, proposed an addition to a war appropriations bill. His amendment, known as the **Wilmot Proviso,** proposed that in any territory the United States gained from Mexico "neither slavery nor involuntary servitude shall ever exist."

Wilmot was one of a group of Northern Democrats who believed the president was "pro-Southern." Polk had supported a new tariff that helped the South at the expense of Northern manufacturers. He had then compromised with the British on Oregon, a territory where slavery was likely to be banned, but had gone to war against Mexico for land that Southerners would occupy.

Wilmot's proposal outraged Southerners. They believed that any antislavery decision about the territories would threaten slavery everywhere. Despite fierce Southern opposition, a coalition of Northern Democrats and Whigs passed the Wilmot Proviso in the House of Representatives. The Senate, however, refused to vote on it.

During the debate, Senator John C. Calhoun of South Carolina, although weak from tuberculosis, prepared a series of resolutions to counter the Wilmot Proviso. The Calhoun Resolutions never came to a vote—moderates in the Senate were unwilling to consider them—but they demonstrated the growing anger of many Southerners.

In the resolutions, Calhoun argued that the states owned the territories of the United States in common, and that Congress had no right to ban slavery in the territories. Calhoun warned somberly that "political revolution, anarchy, [and] civil war" would surely erupt if the North failed to heed Southern concerns.

Popular Sovereignty The Wilmot Proviso had stirred passions on both sides in Congress. The issue of slavery's expansion had divided the country along sectional lines, North against South. Many moderates began searching for a solution that would spare Congress from having to wrestle with the issue of slavery in the territories.

Senator **Lewis Cass** of Michigan proposed one solution. Cass suggested that the citizens of each new territory should be allowed to decide for themselves if they wanted to permit slavery or not. This idea came to be called popular sovereignty.

Popular sovereignty appealed strongly to many members of Congress because it removed the slavery issue from national politics. It also appeared

Poster calling for antislavery meeting

democratic since the settlers themselves would make the decision. Abolitionists argued that it still denied African Americans their right not to be enslaved, but many Northerners, especially in the Midwest, supported the idea because they believed Northern settlers would occupy most of the new territory and would ban slavery from their states.

The Free-Soil Party Emerges

With the 1848 election approaching, the Whigs chose Zachary Taylor, hero of the war with Mexico, to run for president. The Whig Party in the North was split. Many Northern Whigs, known as **Conscience Whigs,** opposed slavery. They also opposed Taylor because they believed he wanted to expand slavery westward. Other Northern Whigs supported Taylor and voted with the Southern Whigs to nominate him. These Northern Whigs were known as **Cotton Whigs** because many of them were linked to Northern cloth manufacturers who needed Southern cotton.

The decision to nominate Taylor convinced many Conscience Whigs to quit the party. They then joined with antislavery Democrats from New York who were frustrated that their party had nominated Lewis Cass instead of Martin Van Buren. These two groups joined with members of the abolitionist Liberty Party to form the **Free-Soil Party,** which opposed slavery in the "free soil" of western territories.

Although some Free Soilers condemned slavery as immoral, most simply wanted to preserve the western territories for white farmers. They felt that allowing slavery to expand would make it difficult for free men to find work. The Free-Soil Party's slogan summed up their views: "Free soil, free speech, free labor, and free men."

The 1848 Election Candidates from three parties campaigned for the presidency in 1848. Democrat Lewis Cass of Michigan supported popular sovereignty, although this support was not mentioned in the South. His promise to veto the Wilmot Proviso, should Congress pass it, however, was often reported. Former president Martin Van Buren led the Free-Soil Party, which took a strong position against slavery in the territories and backed the Wilmot Proviso. General Zachary Taylor, the Whig candidate, avoided the whole issue.

On Election Day, support for the Free-Soilers split the Whig vote in Ohio, giving the state to Cass. More importantly, it also split the Democratic vote in New York, giving the state to Taylor. When the votes were counted, Taylor had won the election.

✓ **Reading Check** **Evaluating** How did the war with Mexico affect the slavery debate?

The Search for Compromise

Within a year of President Taylor's inauguration, the issue of slavery once again took center stage. The discovery of gold in California had quickly led to that territory's application for statehood. The decision had to be made about whether California would enter the Union as a free state or a slave state.

The 1848 discovery of gold brought thousands to California. By the end of 1849, more than 80,000 **"Forty-Niners"** had arrived to look for gold. Mining towns sprang up overnight, and the frenzy for gold led to chaos and violence. Needing a strong government to maintain order, Californians began to organize for statehood.

Forty-Niners Rush for Gold

In January 1848, carpenter James Marshall found traces of gold in a stream near a sawmill he was building in Sacramento. Though Marshall tried to keep his discovery a secret, word leaked out by spring, and San Franciscans rushed to the mountains in search of gold. During the summer, news of the find swept all the way to the East Coast and beyond, and the California Gold Rush was on.

Gold nuggets and $50 gold coin

Forty-niners at slush box in California

Daniel Webster

Henry Clay

John C. Calhoun

Before leaving office, President Polk had urged Congress to create territorial governments for California and New Mexico. Congress, bitterly divided along sectional lines, had not been able to agree on whether to allow slavery in these territories.

Although Zachary Taylor was from the South and a slaveholder, he did not think slavery's survival depended on its expansion westward. He believed that the way to avoid a fight in Congress was to have the people in California make their own decisions about slavery. California now had enough people to skip the territorial stage and come directly into the Union as a state.

With Taylor's encouragement, California applied in December 1849 for admission to the Union as a free state. Thus, the Gold Rush had forced the nation once again to confront the divisive issue of slavery.

The Great Debate Begins If California entered the Union as a free state, the slaveholding states would become a minority in the Senate. Southerners dreaded losing power in national politics, fearing it would lead to limits on slavery and states' rights. A few Southern politicians began to talk openly of secession—of taking their states out of the Union.

In early 1850, one of the most senior and influential leaders in the Senate, Henry Clay of Kentucky, tried to find a compromise that would enable California to join the Union. Clay, nicknamed "The Great Compromiser" because of his role in promoting the Missouri Compromise in 1820 and solving the nullification crisis in 1833, proposed eight resolutions to solve the crisis.

Clay grouped the resolutions in pairs, offering concessions to both sides. The first pair allowed California to come in as a free state but organized the rest of the Mexican cession without any restrictions on slavery. The second pair settled the border between New Mexico and Texas in favor of New Mexico but compensated Texas by having the federal government take on its debts. This would win Southern votes for the compromise because many Southerners held Texas bonds.

Clay's third pair of resolutions outlawed the slave trade in the District of Columbia but did not outlaw slavery itself. The final two resolutions were concessions to the South. Congress would be prohibited from interfering with the domestic slave trade and would pass a new fugitive slave act to help Southerners recover enslaved African Americans who had fled north. These concessions were necessary to assure the South that after California joined the Union, the North would not use its control of the Senate to abolish slavery.

Clay's proposal triggered a massive debate. Any such compromise would need the approval of Senator Calhoun, the great defender of the South's rights. Calhoun was too ill to address the Senate. He composed a speech in reply to Clay's proposal and then sat, hollow-eyed and shrouded in flannel blankets, as another senator read it aloud.

Calhoun's address was brutally frank. It asserted flatly that Northern agitation against slavery threatened to destroy the South. He did not think Clay's compromise would save the Union. The South needed an acceptance of its rights, the return of fugitive slaves, and a guarantee of balance between the sections. If the Southern states could not live in safety within the Union, Calhoun darkly predicted, secession was the only honorable solution.

Three days later, Senator **Daniel Webster** of Massachusetts rose to respond to Calhoun's talk of

The Compromise of 1850

Legislative Item	Victory for?
• California admitted to the Union as free state	Clear victory for the North
• Popular sovereignty to determine slavery issue in Utah and New Mexico territories	Moderate victory for both sides
• Texas border dispute with New Mexico resolved • Texas receives $10 million	Moderate Southern victories
• Slave trade, but not slavery itself, abolished in the District of Columbia	Moderate Northern victory
• Strong federal enforcement of new Fugitive Slave Act	Clear victory for the South

Chart *Skills*

1. **Interpreting Charts** Did the new Fugitive Slave Act appeal to the North or the South?
2. **Generalizing** Which side, North or South, achieved more of its goals in the Compromise of 1850?

66I wish to speak to-day, not as a Massachusetts man, nor as a Northern man, but as an American. . . . I speak today for the preservation of the Union. Hear me for my cause. . . . There can be no such thing as a peaceable secession. Peaceable secession is an utter impossibility. . . . I see as plainly as I see the sun in heaven what that disruption itself must produce; I see that it must produce war, and such a war as I will not describe. . . .99

—from the *Congressional Globe,* 31st Congress

The Compromise of 1850 In the end, Congress did not pass Clay's bill, in part because President Taylor opposed it. Then, unexpectedly, Taylor died in office that summer. Vice President Millard Fillmore succeeded him, and he quickly threw his support behind the compromise.

By the end of summer, Calhoun was dead, Webster had accepted the position of secretary of state, and Clay was exhausted, leaving leadership of the Senate to younger men. Thirty-seven-year-old Stephen A. Douglas of Illinois divided the large compromise initiative into several smaller bills. This allowed his colleagues from different sections to abstain or vote against whatever parts they disliked while supporting the rest. By fall, Congress had passed all the parts of the original proposal as Clay had envisioned it, and President Fillmore had signed them into law.

For a short time, the **Compromise of 1850** eased the tensions over slavery. In the next few years, however, the hope of a permanent solution through compromise would begin to fade.

✓ **Reading Check** **Summarizing** How did the Gold Rush affect the issue of slavery?

secession. Calling on the Senate to put national unity above sectional loyalties, Webster voiced his support for Clay's plan, claiming that it was the only hope for preserving the Union. Although he sought conciliation, Senator Webster did not back away from speaking bluntly—and with chilling foresight:

SECTION 1 ASSESSMENT

Checking for Understanding

1. **Define:** popular sovereignty, secession.
2. **Identify:** Wilmot Proviso, Lewis Cass, Conscience Whigs, Cotton Whigs, Free-Soil Party, "Forty-Niners."
3. **Summarize** how Americans responded to the idea of popular sovereignty.

Reviewing Themes

4. **Geography and History** How did the war with Mexico and the Gold Rush affect the slavery issue in the United States?

Critical Thinking

5. **Explaining** Why did Zachary Taylor win the election of 1848?
6. **Organizing** Use a graphic organizer similar to the one below to list the main elements of the Compromise of 1850.

Analyzing Visuals

7. **Examining Art** Study the painting of the debate between Clay and Calhoun on page 323. What elements of the painting suggest the seriousness of the slavery issue being debated?

Writing About History

8. **Persuasive Writing** Imagine you are Henry Clay. Write a speech to present to the Senate. In your speech, try to persuade Congress to pass your compromise.

Critical Thinking SKILLBUILDER

Predicting Consequences

Why Learn This Skill?

Did you ever wish you could see into the future? Although predicting future events is very difficult, you can develop skills that will help you identify the logical consequences of decisions or actions.

Learning the Skill

Follow these steps to help you accurately predict consequences:

- Review what you already know about a situation by listing facts, events, and people's responses. The list will help you recall events and how they affected people.

- Analyze patterns. Try to determine what the patterns show.

- Use your knowledge and observations of similar situations. In other words, ask yourself, "What were the consequences of a similar decision or action that occurred in the past?"

- Analyze each of the potential consequences by asking, "How likely is it that this will occur?"

- Make a prediction.

Practicing the Skill

Candidates for public office often make campaign promises based on how they think voters will respond. Use the information in the chart on this page to help you predict what type of candidate would be elected president in 1848. Then answer the questions that follow.

❶ What event initially forced candidates to address the issue of slavery in new territories?

❷ Review the facts and events listed on the chart. Do you notice any patterns? What do the facts tell you about the 1840s?

❸ What kind of president do you think Northerners would want? Southerners?

Events of the 1840s	Results and Reactions
Victory in war with Mexico creates new territory in Southwest.	➡ Americans torn over whether area should be free or slave territory.
Wilmot Proviso proposes ban on slavery in any area taken from Mexico.	➡ Southerners are outraged.
Members of Congress try to avoid issue of slavery in territories.	➡ Northerners and Southerners continue to angrily debate the issue.
Popular sovereignty lets settlers decide whether territories should be free or not.	➡ Abolitionists argue against popular sovereignty; most Northerners support it.
Whig Party nomination of Zachary Taylor angers some party members.	➡ Many Northern Whigs split and join with others to create the Free-Soil Party.

Skills Assessment

Complete the Practicing Skills questions on page 347 and the Chapter 10 Skill Reinforcement Activity to assess your mastery of this skill.

Applying the Skill

Predicting Consequences Read several newspaper articles about an event affecting your community today. Make an educated prediction about what will happen, and explain your reasoning. Write a letter to the editor, summarizing your prediction. You may want to check back at a later time to see if your prediction came true.

 GO TO

Glencoe's **Skillbuilder Interactive Workbook CD-ROM, Level 2,** provides instruction and practice in key social studies skills.

Guide to Reading

Main Idea

Resentment over the Compromise of 1850 led to a further increase in sectional tensions.

Key Terms and Names

Uncle Tom's Cabin, Fugitive Slave Act, Underground Railroad, Harriet Tubman, transcontinental railroad, Gadsden Purchase, Kansas-Nebraska Act, Charles Sumner

Reading Strategy

Organizing As you read about the growing sectional conflict over slavery in the West, complete a graphic organizer similar to the one below by listing the sequence of key events leading from debate to violence.

Key Events From Debate to Violence

Reading Objectives

• **Evaluate** how both the Fugitive Slave Act and the transcontinental railroad heightened sectional tensions.

• **Summarize** the effects of the Kansas-Nebraska Act.

Section Theme

Civic Rights and Responsibilities As sectional tensions rose, some Americans openly defied laws they thought were unjust.

Preview of Events

♦1851 ♦1853 ♦1855 ♦1857

March 1852
Uncle Tom's Cabin published

May 1854
Kansas-Nebraska Act adopted

November 1855
"Bleeding Kansas" conflict begins

May 1856
Charles Sumner assaulted in the Senate

★ An American Story ★

One evening in 1851, the comfortable, well-educated, deeply religious Stowe family sat in their parlor in Brunswick, Maine, listening to a letter being read aloud. The letter was from Harriet Beecher Stowe's sister, Isabella, in Boston.

The new Fugitive Slave Act, part of the Compromise of 1850, had gone into effect, Isabella reported, and slave-catchers prowled the streets. They pounced on African Americans without warning, breaking into their houses, destroying their shops, and carrying them off.

Isabella described daily attacks. She also told of outraged Bostonians, white and African American alike, who rallied to resist the kidnappers.

Stowe listened with growing despair. She had lived for many years in Cincinnati, across the Ohio River from the slave state of Kentucky. There she had met many runaways from slavery and heard their tragic tales. She had also visited Kentucky and witnessed slavery firsthand.

As the reading of her sister's letter continued, Stowe, who was an accomplished author, received a challenge. "Now Hattie," Isabella wrote, "if I could use a pen as you can, I would write something that would make this whole nation feel what an accursed thing slavery is." Stowe suddenly rose from her chair and announced, "I will write something. I will if I live." That year, she began writing sketches for a book called *Uncle Tom's Cabin.*

—adapted from *Harriet Beecher Stowe: A Life*

Uncle Tom's Cabin

After running as a serial in an antislavery newspaper, **Uncle Tom's Cabin** came out in book form in 1852 and sold 300,000 copies in its first year—astounding numbers for the time. Today the writing may seem overly sentimental, but to Stowe's original readers, mostly Northerners, it was powerful. Her depiction of the enslaved hero, Tom, and the villainous overseer, Simon Legree, changed Northern perceptions of African Americans and slavery.

Stowe presented African Americans as real people imprisoned in dreadful circumstances. Because she saw herself as a painter of slavery's horrors rather than an abstract debater, Stowe was able to evoke pity and outrage even in readers who were unmoved by rational arguments.

Southerners tried unsuccessfully to have the novel banned and strongly attacked its portrayal of slavery, accusing Stowe of writing "distortions" and "falsehoods." One Southern editor told a writer he wanted a review of *Uncle Tom's Cabin* to be "as hot as hellfire, blasting and searing the reputation of the vile wretch in petticoats."

Despite Southern outrage, the book eventually sold millions of copies. It had such a dramatic impact on public opinion that many historians consider it one of the causes of the Civil War.

✓ **Reading Check** **Evaluating** Why was *Uncle Tom's Cabin* so controversial?

The Fugitive Slave Act

Motivating Harriet Beecher Stowe to write *Uncle Tom's Cabin* was not the only unintended consequence of the **Fugitive Slave Act.** Although Henry Clay had conceived the law as a benefit to slaveholders, it actually hurt the Southern cause by creating active hostility toward slavery among Northerners who had previously seemed indifferent.

The Act's Inflammatory Effects Under the Fugitive Slave Act of 1850, a person claiming that an African American had escaped from slavery had only to point out that person as a runaway to take him or her into custody. The accused then would be brought before a federal commissioner. A sworn statement asserting that the captive had escaped from a slaveholder or testimony by white witnesses was all a court needed to order the person sent south. African Americans accused of being fugitives had no right to a trial and were not allowed to testify in court.

The law also included a financial incentive for the federal commissioners to find in favor of the slaveholder. The commissioner received $10 if he decided for the slaveholder but only $5 if the decision went the other way. The law also required federal marshals to help slaveholders capture African American fugitives and authorized marshals to deputize citizens on the spot to help them capture a fugitive. Any Northerner could be compelled to help catch African Americans. A person who refused to cooperate could be jailed.

Newspaper accounts of the seizure of African Americans and descriptions of the law's injustice fueled Northern indignation. In New York, Henry Long was waiting tables at the Pacific Hotel when kidnappers seized him. Although Long had been living in New York several months before his supposed escape from a Virginia plantation, he was forced to return to the South and into slavery. The New York *Independent* publicized Long's kidnapping, noting that "almost no colored man is safe in our streets."

Northern Resistance Grows As outraged as Northerners were over such incidents, the law's requirement that ordinary citizens help capture runaways was what drove many into active defiance. Frederick Douglass emphasized this part of the law over and over again in his speeches. A powerful orator, Douglass would paint an emotional picture of an African American fleeing kidnappers. Then he would ask his audience whether they would give the runaway over to the "pursuing bloodhounds." "No!" the crowd would roar.

Antislavery activists often used the words of writer Henry David Thoreau to justify defying the Fugitive Slave Act. In his 1849 essay "Civil Disobedience," Thoreau advocated disobeying laws on moral grounds. "Unjust laws exist," he wrote. "Shall we be content to obey them, or shall we endeavor to amend them, and obey them until we have succeeded, or shall we transgress them at once?" For many Northerners the answer was to disobey them without delay.

Northern resistance became frequent, public, and sometimes violent. The violence was justified, some believed, by the violence and cruelty of the slaveholders and their hirelings. In a pamphlet, Douglass proposed "The True Remedy for the Fugitive Slave Law—A good revolver, a steady hand, and a determination to shoot down any man attempting to kidnap."

The Underground Railroad Although the Fugitive Slave Act included heavy fines and prison terms for helping a runaway, whites and free African Americans continued their work with the Underground Railroad. This informal but well-organized system that was legendary during the 1830s helped thousands of enslaved persons escape. Members, called "conductors," transported runaways north in secret, gave them shelter and food along the way, and saw them to freedom in the Northern states or Canada with some money for a fresh start.

Dedicated people, many of them African Americans, made dangerous trips into the South to guide enslaved persons along the Underground Railroad to freedom. The most famous of these conductors was **Harriet Tubman,** herself a runaway. She risked many trips to the South.

In Des Moines, Iowa, Isaac Brandt used secret signals to communicate with conductors on the Underground Railroad—a hand lifted palm outwards, for example, or a certain kind of tug at the ear. "I do not know how these signs or signals originated," he later remembered, "but they had become well understood. Without them the operation of the system of running slaves into free territory would not have been possible."

Levi Coffin, a Quaker born in North Carolina, allowed escaped African Americans to stay at his home in Indiana, where three Underground Railroad routes from the South converged.

> ❝We knew not what night or what hour of the night we would be roused from slumber by a gentle rap at the door. . . . Outside in the cold or rain, there would be a two-horse wagon loaded with fugitives, perhaps the greater part of them women and children. I would invite them, in a low tone, to come in, and they would follow me into the darkened house without a word, for we knew not who might be watching and listening.❞
>
> —quoted in *The Underground Railroad*

An estimated 2,000 African Americans stopped at Coffin's red brick house on their way to freedom. Coffin later moved to Cincinnati, Ohio, where he assisted another 1,300 African Americans who had crossed the river from Kentucky to freedom. A thorn in the side to slaveholders, the Underground Railroad deepened Southern mistrust of Northern intentions.

✓ **Reading Check** **Examining** What was an unintended consequence of the Fugitive Slave Act?

The Transcontinental Railroad

Sectional disagreements did not fade away when settlers left their old homes and headed west into new territories. The settlers firmly retained their identities as Northerners or Southerners. By the early 1850s, many settlers and land speculators had become interested in the fertile lands west of Missouri and Iowa. Unfortunately for the settlers, the territory was unorganized. Until the federal government organized it as a territory, it could not be surveyed and settled.

At the same time, the opening of Oregon and the admission of California to the Union had convinced Americans that a transcontinental railroad should be built to connect the West Coast to the rest of the country.

In the 1850s, getting to the West Coast of the United States required many grueling weeks of travel overland or a long sea voyage around the tip of South America. A transcontinental railroad would reduce the journey to four relatively easy days while promoting further settlement and growth in the territories along the route.

The transcontinental railroad had broad appeal, but the choice of its eastern starting point became a new element in the sectional conflict. Many Southerners preferred a southern route from New Orleans, but the geography of the Southwest required the railroad to pass through northern Mexico. Secretary of War Jefferson Davis, a strong supporter of the South's interests, sent James Gadsden,

---

Profiles IN HISTORY

Harriet Tubman
c. 1820–1913

Known as "Moses" for her courage in leading enslaved persons to freedom, Harriet Tubman was a heroine of the antislavery movement. Tubman was born into slavery in Maryland and struggled early against the system's brutality. At age 13, when she tried to save another enslaved person from punishment, an overseer struck her savagely and fractured her skull. Miraculously, she recovered from the injury, but she suffered from occasional blackouts for the rest of her life.

Tubman escaped to freedom in 1849 when she was 29 years old. Upon crossing into Pennsylvania, she later wrote, "I looked at my hands to see if I was the same person. There was such a glory over everything. The sun came up like gold through the trees, and I felt like I was in Heaven."

Her joy inspired her to help others. After Congress passed the Fugitive Slave Act, Tubman returned to the South 19 times to guide enslaved persons along the Underground Railroad to freedom.

Tubman became notorious in the eyes of slaveholders, but despite a large reward offered for her capture, no one ever betrayed her whereabouts. Furthermore, in all her rescues on the Underground Railroad, she never lost a single "passenger." Tubman's bravery and determination made her one of the most important figures in the antislavery movement.

NATIONAL GEOGRAPHIC

Slavery and the Underground Railroad, 1830–1860

The Underground Railroad existed as early as the 1780s, but its spread throughout most of the North occurred after 1830.

Battle Creek, MICH.–burial site of abolitionist Sojourner Truth

Ashtabula, OHIO–site of Hubbard House, one of the end points on the route north

Thousands of African Americans escaped slavery through the Underground Railroad between 1830 and 1860.

Doll of runaway child

Legend:
- More than 50% of people enslaved
- 10–50%
- Less than 10%
- No enslaved or data
- ← Underground RR routes
- — 1860 border

Geography Skills

1. **Interpreting Maps** How far north did many underground routes reach?
2. **Applying Geography Skills** How many states had areas where more than 50 percent of the people were enslaved?

a South Carolina politician and railroad promoter, to buy land from Mexico. The Mexican leader, Santa Anna, agreed to sell a 30,000-square-mile strip of land that today is part of southern Arizona and New Mexico and includes the city of Tucson. In 1853 Mexico accepted $10 million for the territory, known as the **Gadsden Purchase.**

Meanwhile in Congress, the head of the Senate committee on territories, Democratic Senator Stephen A. Douglas, had his own ideas for a transcontinental railroad. Douglas was from Illinois. He wanted the eastern terminus to be in Chicago, but he knew that any route from the north required Congress to organize the territory west of Missouri and Iowa.

In 1853 Douglas prepared a bill to organize the region into a new territory to be called Nebraska. Although the House of Representatives passed the bill quickly, Southern senators who controlled key committees refused to go along, and they prevented

the bill from coming to a vote. These senators made it clear to Douglas that if he wanted Nebraska organized, he needed to repeal the Missouri Compromise and allow slavery in the new territory.

Reading Check **Summarizing** Why did the United States make the Gadsden Purchase?

The Kansas-Nebraska Act

Stephen Douglas knew that any attempt to repeal the Missouri Compromise would divide the country. Nevertheless, he wanted to open the northern Great Plains to settlement. Douglas also believed that if he skillfully maneuvered his bill through Congress, he could split the Whig Party and quiet the slavery issue. Unfortunately, Douglas had badly misjudged the depth of antislavery feelings in the North. By persisting, he inadvertently set the country on the road to war.

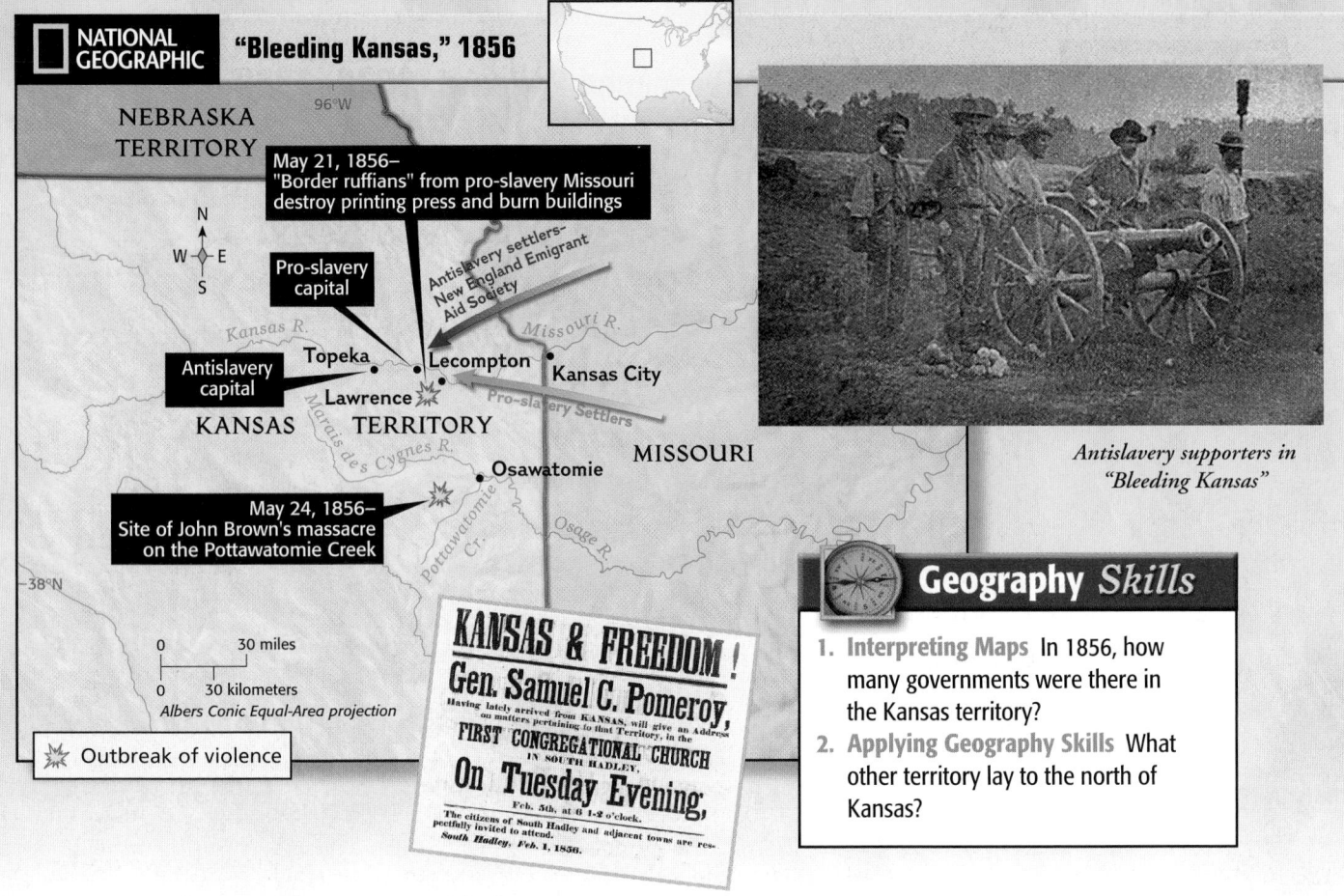

NATIONAL GEOGRAPHIC "Bleeding Kansas," 1856

NEBRASKA TERRITORY
96°W

May 21, 1856–
"Border ruffians" from pro-slavery Missouri destroy printing press and burn buildings

Antislavery settlers-New England Emigrant Aid Society

Pro-slavery capital

Kansas R.

Missouri R.

Topeka
Antislavery capital
Lecompton
Kansas City

Lawrence
Pro-slavery Settlers

KANSAS TERRITORY
MISSOURI

Marais des Cygnes R.

Osawatomie

May 24, 1856–
Site of John Brown's massacre on the Pottawatomie Creek

Pottawatomie Cr.
Osage R.

38°N

0   30 miles
0   30 kilometers
Albers Conic Equal-Area projection

Outbreak of violence

Antislavery supporters in "Bleeding Kansas"

KANSAS & FREEDOM!
Gen. Samuel C. Pomeroy,
Having lately arrived from KANSAS, will give an Address on matters pertaining to that Territory, in the
FIRST CONGREGATIONAL CHURCH
IN SOUTH HADLEY,
On Tuesday Evening,
Feb. 5th, at 6 1-2 o'clock.
The citizens of South Hadley and adjacent towns are respectfully invited to attend.
South Hadley, Feb. 1, 1856.

Geography *Skills*

1. **Interpreting Maps** In 1856, how many governments were there in the Kansas territory?
2. **Applying Geography Skills** What other territory lay to the north of Kansas?

Two New Territories At first, Douglas tried to dodge the issue and gain Southern support for his bill by saying that any states organized in the new Nebraska territory would be allowed to exercise popular sovereignty on slavery.

Southern leaders in the Senate were not fooled. If the Missouri Compromise remained in place while the region was settled, slaveholders would not move there. As a result, the states formed in the region would naturally become free states. Determined to get the territory organized, Douglas went a fateful step further. In his next version of the bill, he proposed to undo the Missouri Compromise and allow slavery in the region. He also proposed dividing the region into two territories. Nebraska would be on the north, adjacent to the free state of Iowa, and Kansas would be on the south, west of the slave state of Missouri. This looked like Nebraska was intended to be free territory, while Kansas was intended for slavery.

Douglas's bill outraged Northern Democrats and Whigs. Free-Soilers and antislavery Democrats called the act an "atrocious plot." They charged that abandoning the Missouri Compromise broke a solemn promise to limit the spread of slavery. Despite this opposition, the leaders of the Democrats in Congress won enough support to pass the **Kansas-Nebraska Act** in May 1854.

Bleeding Kansas Kansas became the first battleground between those favoring the extension of slavery and those opposing it. Since eastern Kansas offered the same climate and rich soil as the slave state of Missouri, settlers moving there from Missouri were likely to bring enslaved persons with them and claim Kansas for the South. Northerners responded by hurrying into the territory themselves, intent on creating an antislavery majority. Northern settlers could count on the support of the New England Emigrant Aid Society, an abolitionist group founded to recruit and outfit antislavery settlers bound for Kansas. Carrying supplies and rifles, hordes of Northerners headed for the new territory.

Pro-slavery senator David Atchison of Missouri responded by calling on men from his state to storm into Kansas. In the spring of 1855, thousands of armed Missourians—called "border ruffians" in the press—voted illegally in Kansas, helping elect a pro-slavery legislature. Furious antislavery settlers countered by holding a convention in Topeka and drafting their own constitution that excluded slavery. By March 1856, Kansas had two governments.

On May 21, 1856, border ruffians, worked up by the arrival of more Northerners, attacked the town of Lawrence, a stronghold of antislavery settlers. The attackers wrecked newspaper presses, plundered shops and homes, and burned a hotel and the home of the elected free-state governor.

"Bleeding Kansas," as newspapers dubbed the territory, became the scene of a territorial civil war between pro-slavery and antislavery settlers. By the end of 1856, 200 people had died in the fighting and two million dollars' worth of property had been destroyed.

The Caning of Charles Sumner
While bullets flew and blood ran in Kansas, the Senate hotly debated the future of the Western territories. In mid-May 1856, Senator **Charles Sumner** of Massachusetts, a fiery abolitionist, delivered a speech accusing pro-slavery senators of forcing Kansas into the ranks of slave states. He singled out Senator **Andrew P. Butler** of South Carolina, saying Butler had "chosen a mistress . . . the harlot, Slavery."

Several days later, on May 22, Butler's second cousin, Representative Preston Brooks, approached Sumner at his desk in the Senate chamber. Brooks shouted that Sumner's speech had been "a libel on South Carolina, and Mr. Butler, who is a relative of mine." Before Sumner could respond, Brooks raised a gold-handled cane and beat him savagely, leaving the senator severely injured and bleeding on the floor. The growing violence over slavery had come to the very center of government.

Many Southerners considered Brooks to be a hero. Some Southerners even sent him canes

SOUTHERN CHIVALRY — ARGUMENT versus CLUB'S.

Analyzing *Political Cartoons*

Violence in the Senate Representative Preston Brooks beat Senator Charles Sumner savagely for criticizing Brooks's cousin, Senator Andrew Butler. Many Southerners voiced their approval by sending Brooks canes like the one shown here. What emotions did the event stir up in the North and South?

inscribed "Hit Him Again." Shocked by the attack and outraged by the flood of Southern support for Brooks, Northerners strengthened their determination to resist the "barbarism of slavery." One New York clergyman confided in his journal that "no way is left for the North, but to strike back, or be slaves."

Reading Check **Describing** Why did Stephen Douglas propose repealing the Missouri Compromise?

SECTION 2 ASSESSMENT

Checking for Understanding
1. **Define:** Underground Railroad, transcontinental railroad.
2. **Identify:** *Uncle Tom's Cabin,* Fugitive Slave Act, Harriet Tubman, Gadsden Purchase, Kansas-Nebraska Act, Charles Sumner.
3. **Explain** how the transcontinental railroad intensified the slavery issue.

Reviewing Themes
4. **Civic Rights and Responsibilities** How did antislavery activists justify disobeying the Fugitive Slave Act?

Critical Thinking
5. **Synthesizing** What events led to "Bleeding Kansas"?
6. **Categorizing** Use a graphic organizer similar to the one below to list the effects of the Fugitive Slave Act.

Effects

Fugitive Slave Act

Analyzing Visuals
7. **Interpreting Maps** Study the map of the Underground Railroad on page 329. Consider the entire expanse of the United States and its territories in the 1850s. If slavery failed to expand, what effect would this have on the South's influence on national policy?

Writing About History
8. **Expository Writing** Imagine you are a reporter for a Southern or Northern newspaper in the 1850s. Write an article on public reaction to *Uncle Tom's Cabin.*

The Crisis Deepens

Main Idea

The slavery controversy accelerated both the breakdown of the major political parties and the growth of hostility between North and South.

Key Terms and Names

Republican Party, Know-Nothings, Dred Scott, referendum, Lecompton constitution, Freeport Doctrine, insurrection

Reading Strategy

Categorizing As you read about the North-South split, complete a graphic organizer like the one below to group events as executive, legislative, judicial, or nongovernmental.

Executive	
Legislative	
Judicial	
Nongovernmental	

Reading Objectives

• **Analyze** the events that increased sectional tensions in the late 1850s.
• **Describe** the Lincoln-Douglas Senate campaign of 1858.

Section Theme

Groups and Institutions Due to differing opinions within established parties, Americans forged new political alliances in the 1850s.

Preview of Events

♦1854	♦1856	♦1858	♦1860

July 1854
Republican Party founded

March 1857
Supreme Court announces *Dred Scott* decision

1857
Lecompton constitution drafted in Kansas

1858
Lincoln-Douglas debates

October 1859
John Brown and followers raid Harpers Ferry

★ *An American Story* ★

By the 1850s, feelings were running high among Northerners and Southerners over whether slavery should be allowed in new territories. These strong feelings also tore old political parties apart and created new ones. Soon after Lincoln was defeated in his race for senator from Illinois, he wrote to a Springfield friend:

❝I think I am a Whig; but others say there are not Whigs, and that I am an abolitionist. . . . I now do no more than oppose the extension of slavery. I am not a Know-Nothing. . . . How could I be? How can any one who abhors the oppression of negroes, be in favor of degrading classes of white people? . . . As a nation, we began by declaring 'all men are created equal.' We now practically read it 'all men are created equal except negroes.' When the Know-Nothings get control, it will read 'all men are created equal, except negroes, and foreigners, and catholics.' When it comes to this I should prefer emigrating to some country where they make no pretence of loving liberty—to Russia for instance. . . .❞

—quoted in *Abraham Lincoln*

Birth of the Republican Party

When the Kansas-Nebraska Act repealed the Missouri Compromise, it enraged many people who opposed the extension of slavery. A few of these people resorted to violence, but the effect was just as dramatic on political parties—both the Whigs and the Democrats were split. In the Whig Party, pro-slavery Southern Whigs and antislavery Northern Whigs had long battled for control of their party. With passage of the Kansas-Nebraska

Political Parties of the Era

Party	Characteristics	Major Leaders
Whig (1834–1854)	Party strongly divided into sectional factions; united only in opposition to Democratic Party	Daniel Webster, Henry Clay
Democrat (1828–present)	Largely controlled federal government from 1828 to 1860 but increasingly dominated by Southern Democrats after 1840	John C. Calhoun
Liberty (1839–c. 1844)	Promoted abolition of slavery; after Liberty Party's failure, members supported Free-Soil and Republican Parties	James Birney
Free-Soil (1848–1854)	Composed of Liberty Party members, antislavery Whigs, and antislavery New York Democrats	Martin Van Buren, Charles Francis Adams
Republican (c. 1854–present)	Composed of Northern Whigs and Free-Soilers; opposed further expansion of slavery	Abraham Lincoln
American Party (Know-Nothings) (1849–c. 1860)	Anti-immigrant and anti-Catholic	Millard Fillmore (former Whig)

Source: *Encarta Encyclopedia*

Chart *Skills*

1. **Interpreting Charts** Which party had the shortest life span?
2. **Drawing Conclusions** Does any party listed not have an obvious connection to the slavery issue?

Act, disaster was complete. Every Northern Whig in Congress had voted against the bill, while most Southern Whigs had supported it. "We Whigs of the North," wrote one member from Connecticut, "are unalterably determined never to have even the slightest political correspondence or connexion" with the Southern Whigs.

Anger over the Kansas-Nebraska Act convinced former Whigs, members of the Free-Soil Party, and a few antislavery Democrats to work together during the congressional elections of 1854. These coalitions took many different names, including the Anti-Nebraska Party, the Fusion Party, the People's Party, and the Independent Party. The most popular name for the new coalition was the **Republican Party.**

Republicans Organize At a convention in Michigan in July 1854, the Republican Party was officially organized. In choosing the same name as Jefferson's original party, the Republicans declared their intention to revive the spirit of the American Revolution. Just as Jefferson had chosen the name because he wanted to prevent the United States from becoming a monarchy, the new Republicans chose their name because they feared that the Southern planters were becoming an aristocracy that controlled the federal government.

Republicans did not agree on whether slavery should be abolished in the Southern states, but they did agree that it had to be kept out of the territories. A large majority of Northern voters seemed to agree, enabling the Republicans and the other antislavery parties to make great strides in the elections of 1854.

The Know-Nothings At the same time, public anger against the Northern Democrats also enabled the American Party—better known as the **Know-Nothings**—to make great gains as well, particularly in the Northeast. The American Party was an anti-Catholic and nativist party. It opposed immigration, particularly Catholic immigration, into the United States. Prejudice and fear that immigrants would take away jobs enabled the Know-Nothings to win many seats in Congress and the state legislatures in 1854.

Soon after the election, the Know-Nothings suffered the same fate as the Whigs. Many Know-Nothings had been elected from the Upper South, particularly Maryland, Tennessee, and Kentucky. They quickly split with Know-Nothings from the North over their support for the Kansas-Nebraska

Act. Furthermore, the violence in Kansas and the beating of Charles Sumner made slavery a far more important issue to most Americans than immigration. Eventually, the Republican Party absorbed the Northern Know-Nothings.

✓ **Reading Check** **Examining** What events led to the founding of the Republican Party?

The Election of 1856

To gain the widest possible support in the 1856 campaign, the Republicans nominated **John C. Frémont,** a famous Western explorer nicknamed "The Pathfinder." Frémont had spoken in favor of Kansas becoming a free state. He had little political experience but also no embarrassing record to defend.

The Democrats nominated **James Buchanan.** Buchanan had served in Congress for 20 years and had been the American ambassador to Russia and then to Great Britain. He had been in Great Britain during the debate over the Kansas-Nebraska Act and had not taken a stand on the issue, but his record in Congress showed that he believed the best way to save the Union was to make concessions to the South.

The American Party tried to reunite its Northern and Southern members at its convention, but most of

the Northern delegates walked out when the party refused to call for the repeal of the Kansas-Nebraska Act. The rest of the convention then chose former president Millard Fillmore to represent the American Party, hoping to attract the vote of former Whigs.

The campaign was really two separate contests: Buchanan against Frémont in the North, and Buchanan against Fillmore in the South. Buchanan had solid support in the South and only needed his home state of Pennsylvania and one other to win the presidency. Democrats campaigned on the idea that only Buchanan could save the Union and that the election of Frémont would cause the South to secede. When the votes were counted, Buchanan had won.

✓ **Reading Check** **Identifying** What political party and candidate won the presidency in 1856?

Sectional Divisions Grow

Despite Buchanan's determination to adopt policies that would calm the growing sectional strife in the country, a series of events helped drive Americans in the North and South even further apart.

The *Dred Scott* Decision In his March 1857 inaugural address, James Buchanan suggested that the nation let the Supreme Court decide the question of slavery in the territories. Most people who listened to the address did not know that Buchanan had contacted members of the Supreme Court and therefore knew that a decision was imminent.

Many Southern members of Congress had quietly pressured the Supreme Court justices to issue a ruling on slavery in the territories. They expected the Southern majority on the court to rule in favor of the South. They were not disappointed. Two days after the inauguration, the Court released its opinion in the case of *Dred Scott* v. *Sandford.* 📖 *(See page 1080 for more information on* Dred Scott *v. Sandford.)*

Dred Scott was an enslaved man whose Missouri slaveholder had taken him to live in free territory before returning to Missouri. Assisted by abolitionists, Scott sued to end his slavery, arguing that the time he had spent in free territory meant he was free. The case went all the way to the Supreme Court.

On March 6, 1857, Chief Justice Roger B. Taney delivered the majority opinion in the case. Taney ruled against Scott because, he claimed, African Americans were not citizens and therefore could not sue in the courts. Taney then addressed the Missouri Compromise's ban on slavery in territory north of Missouri's southern border:

Fact | Fiction | Folklore

"Born in a Log Cabin" The image of a "common man" president was appealing to campaign managers in the 1800s. As voting rights spread beyond landowners, the candidate with humble roots was a potent political image. Although many nineteenth-century candidates sought to appeal to the masses, only five presidents were actually born in a log home: Andrew Jackson, James K. Polk, James Buchanan, Abraham Lincoln, and James Garfield. Of these five, Jackson, Lincoln, Buchanan, and Garfield actually experienced serious poverty in childhood. William Henry Harrison campaigned with images of a log cabin childhood, but he was actually born into an elite Virginia family that was acquainted with George Washington.

> **66**It is the opinion of the court that the Act of Congress which prohibited a citizen from holding and owning [enslaved persons] in the territory of the United States north of the line therein mentioned is not warranted by the Constitution and is therefore void.**99**
>
> —from *Dred Scott* v. *Sandford*

Instead of removing the issue of slavery in the territories from politics, the *Dred Scott* decision itself became a political issue that further intensified the sectional conflict. The Supreme Court had said that the federal government could not prohibit slavery in the territories. Free soil, one of the basic ideas uniting Republicans, was unconstitutional.

Democrats cheered the decision, but Republicans condemned it and claimed it was not binding. Instead they argued that it was an **obiter dictum,** an incidental opinion not called for by the circumstances of the case. Southerners, on the other hand, called on Northerners to obey the decision if they wanted the South to remain in the Union.

Many African Americans, among them Philadelphia activist Robert Purvis, publicly declared contempt for any government that could produce such an edict:

> **66**Mr. Chairman, look at the facts— here, in a country with a sublimity of impudence that knows no parallel, setting itself up before the world as a *free country,* a *land of liberty!,* 'the *land of the free,* and the *home of the brave,*' the *'freest country in all the world'* . . . and yet here are millions of men and women . . . bought and sold, whipped, manacled, killed all the day long.**99**
>
> —quoted in *Witness for Freedom*

Kansas's Lecompton Constitution
Frustration with the government also fueled the conflict between antislavery and pro-slavery forces in "Bleeding Kansas." Hoping to end the troubles there, President Buchanan urged the territory to apply for statehood. The pro-slavery legislature scheduled an election for delegates to a constitutional convention, but antislavery Kansans boycotted it, claiming it was rigged. The resulting constitution, drafted in the town of Lecompton in 1857, legalized slavery in the territory.

Each side then held its own referendum, or popular vote, on the constitution. Antislavery forces voted down the constitution; pro-slavery forces approved it. Buchanan accepted the pro-slavery vote and asked

Front-Page News Chief Justice Roger B. Taney delivered the Supreme Court's ruling in the *Dred Scott* case. The decision made Scott a topic for the nation's press. What impression of Scott's family do you get from the engravings shown here?

Congress to admit Kansas as a slave state. The Senate quickly voted to accept the **Lecompton constitution,** but the House of Representatives blocked it. Many members of Congress became so angry during the debates that fistfights broke out. Southern leaders were stunned when even Stephen Douglas of Illinois refused to support them. Many had hoped that Douglas, a Northern leader and possible future president, understood the South's concerns and would make the compromise necessary to keep the South in the Union.

Finally, to get the votes they needed, President Buchanan and Southern leaders in Congress agreed to allow another referendum in Kansas on the constitution. Southern leaders expected to win this referendum. If the settlers in Kansas rejected the Lecompton constitution, they would delay statehood for Kansas for at least two more years.

Despite these conditions, the settlers in Kansas voted overwhelmingly in 1858 to reject the Lecompton constitution. They did not want slavery in their state. As a result, Kansas did not become a state until 1861.

✓ **Reading Check** **Summarizing** Why did Dred Scott sue the slaveholder who held him?

Lincoln and Douglas

In 1858 Illinois Republicans chose a relative unknown named Abraham Lincoln to run for the Senate against the Democratic incumbent, Stephen A. Douglas. Lincoln launched his campaign in June with a memorable speech, in which he declared:

> ❝A house divided against itself cannot stand. I believe this Government cannot endure, permanently half *slave* and half *free.* I do not expect the Union to be *dissolved*—I do not expect the house to *fall*—but I do expect it will cease to be divided. It will become *all* one thing or *all* the other.❞
>
> —quoted in *The Civil War: An Illustrated History*

The nationally prominent Douglas, a short, stocky man nicknamed "The Little Giant," regularly drew large crowds on the campaign trail. Seeking to overcome Douglas's fame, Lincoln proposed a series of debates between the candidates, which would expose him to larger audiences than he could attract on his own. Douglas confidently accepted.

Born on the Kentucky frontier and raised in Indiana, Lincoln had experienced little more than small-town life. A storekeeper, mill hand, and rail-splitter during his youth, he went on to study and practice law. Later he served in the Illinois state legislature and, for a single term, in the U.S. House of Representatives as a member of the Whig Party. Despite this modest background, Lincoln proved himself a gifted debater. Both witty and logical, he regularly illuminated his points with quotations from scripture or appealing homespun stories from everyday life.

Although not an abolitionist, Lincoln believed slavery to be morally wrong and opposed its spread into western territories. Douglas, by contrast, supported popular sovereignty. During a debate in Freeport, Lincoln asked Douglas if the people of a territory could legally exclude slavery before achieving statehood? If Douglas said yes, he would appear to be supporting popular sovereignty and opposing the *Dred Scott* ruling, which would cost him Southern support. If he said no, it would make it seem as if he had abandoned popular sovereignty, the principle on which he had built his national following.

Douglas tried to avoid the dilemma, formulating an answer that became known as the **Freeport Doctrine.** He replied that he accepted the *Dred Scott* ruling, but he argued that people could still keep slavery out by refusing to pass the laws needed to

"The right of the people to make a slave Territory or a free Territory is perfect and complete."

—*Stephen Douglas*

regulate and enforce it. "Slavery cannot exist . . . anywhere," said Douglas, "unless it is supported by local police regulations." Douglas's response pleased Illinois voters but angered Southerners.

Lincoln also attacked Douglas's claim that he "cared not" whether Kansans voted for or against slavery. Denouncing "the modern Democratic idea that slavery is as good as freedom," Lincoln called on voters to elect Republicans, "whose hearts are in the work, who *do care* for the result":

❝Has any thing ever threatened the existence of this Union save and except this very institution of slavery? What is it that we hold most dear amongst us? Our own liberty and prosperity. What has ever threatened our liberty and prosperity save and except this institution of slavery? If this is true, how do you propose to improve the condition of things by enlarging slavery—by spreading it out and making it bigger? You may have a wen [sore] or cancer upon your person and not be able to cut it out lest you bleed to death; but surely it is no way to cure it, to engraft it and spread it over your whole body. That is no proper way of treating what you regard a wrong.❞

—quoted in *The Civil War: Opposing Viewpoints*

History *Through Art*

Charleston Confrontation Lincoln and Douglas matched wits seven times during the 1858 senatorial campaign. This painting by Robert Root shows them in Charleston, Illinois. How did the debates help Lincoln?

Douglas won the election, but Lincoln did not come away empty-handed. He had seized the opportunity in the debates to make clear the principles of the Republican Party. He had also established a national reputation for himself as a man of clear, insightful thinking who could argue with force and eloquence. Within a year, however, national attention shifted to another figure, a man who opposed slavery not with well-crafted phrases, but with a gun.

✓ **Reading Check** **Examining** What were the positions of Stephen Douglas and Abraham Lincoln on slavery?

John Brown's Raid

John Brown was a fervent abolitionist who believed, as one minister who knew him in Kansas said, "that God had raised him up on purpose to break the jaws of the wicked." In 1859, he developed a plan to seize the federal arsenal at Harpers Ferry, Virginia (today in West Virginia), free and arm the enslaved people of the neighborhood, and begin an insurrection, or rebellion, against slaveholders.

On the night of October 16, 1859, Brown and 18 followers seized the arsenal. To the terrified night watchman, he announced, "I have possession now of the United States armory, and if the citizens interfere with me I must only burn the town and have blood."

Soon, however, Brown was facing a contingent of U.S. Marines, rushed to Harpers Ferry from Washington, D.C., under the command of Colonel Robert E. Lee. Just 36 hours after it had begun, Brown's attempt to start a slave insurrection ended with his capture. A Virginia court tried and

"Has any thing ever threatened the existence of this Union save and except this very institution of slavery?"

—*Abraham Lincoln*

John Brown
1800–1859

John Brown, who believed he was acting with God's approval, helped to bring about the Civil War. A dedicated abolitionist, Brown initially worked with the Underground Railroad in Pennsylvania. When conflict between pro-slavery and free-soil settlers in Kansas became violent, Brown moved to Kansas to help six of his sons and other free-soil settlers in their struggle against slavery.

After pro-slavery forces from Missouri sacked the town of Lawrence, Kansas, on May 21, 1856, Brown vowed revenge. The following day, he learned of the caning of Charles Sumner in the Senate and, in the words of one witness, he "went crazy—*crazy.*" Two days later, he abducted and murdered five pro-slavery settlers living near Pottawatomie Creek. Later he said of the deaths, "I believe that I did God service in having them killed."

Brown was never arrested for the Pottawatomie Massacre, and for some Northern abolitionists he became a hero for his willingness to fight back. Three years later, he launched his raid on Harpers Ferry. Although the raid ended in disaster and Brown himself was hanged, his desperate act terrified Southerners and brought the nation another step closer to disunion and civil war.

if it is deemed necessary that I should forfeit my life for the furtherance of the ends of justice and mingle my blood . . . with the blood of millions in this slave country whose rights are disregarded by wicked, cruel and unjust enactments, I say, let it be done!"

—quoted in *John Brown, 1800–1859*

On December 2, the day of his execution, Brown handed one of his jailers a prophetic note: "I, John Brown, am now quite *certain* that the crimes of this *guilty land* will never be purged *away* but with Blood. I had *as I now think vainly* flattered myself that without *very much* bloodshed it might be done."

Many Northerners viewed Brown as a martyr in a noble cause. The execution, Henry David Thoreau predicted, would strengthen abolitionist feeling in the North. "He is not old Brown any longer," Thoreau declared, "he is an angel of light."

For most Southerners, however, Brown's raid offered all the proof they needed that Northerners were actively plotting the murder of slaveholders. "Defend yourselves!" cried Georgia senator Robert Toombs. "The enemy is at your door!"

convicted him and sentenced him to death. In his last words to the court, Brown, repenting nothing, declared:

"I believe that to have interfered as I have done, as I have always freely admitted I have done in behalf of [God's] despised poor, I did no wrong, but right. Now

Reading Check **Evaluating** In what ways might a Northerner and a Southerner view John Brown's action differently?

SECTION 3 ASSESSMENT

Checking for Understanding
1. **Define:** referendum, insurrection.
2. **Identify:** Republican Party, Know-Nothings, Dred Scott, Lecompton constitution, Freeport Doctrine.
3. **List** the two rulings in *Dred Scott* v. *Sandford* that increased sectional divisiveness.

Reviewing Themes
4. **Groups and Institutions** What were the main goals of the Republican and American Parties?

Critical Thinking
5. **Synthesizing** How did Americans react to John Brown's raid?
6. **Categorizing** Use a graphic organizer similar to the one below to list causes of the growing tensions between North and South.

Causes

Growing Tensions

Analyzing Visuals
7. **Studying Charts** Examine the chart on page 333. Did any parties besides the Republican and Democratic survive after 1865? How does this support the idea that the 1850s and 1860s were an important transition era in the nation's history?

Writing About History
8. **Expository Writing** Imagine you have just read the Supreme Court's ruling in the *Dred Scott* case. Write a letter to the editor explaining your reaction to the decision.

American LITERATURE

Frederick Douglass was born into slavery in Maryland in 1818. During the course of his incredible life, he escaped from slavery and eventually became renowned for eloquent lectures and writings for the causes of abolition and liberty. One of his most famous works is his autobiography about growing up under the shadow of slavery. In the following excerpt, Douglass is around eight years old, and Mrs. Auld, the wife of his slaveholder, has begun to teach him to read. Mr. Auld discovers what his wife has been doing, and his reaction causes young Frederick to decide to learn to read on his own, no matter what.

Read to Discover

Why did some slaveholders not want enslaved people to learn to read?

Reader's Dictionary

sentiments: feelings

revelation: discovery

conscious: aware

diligently: with great effort

from Narrative of the Life of Frederick Douglass
by Frederick Douglass

"Now," said [Mr. Auld], "if you teach that [boy] how to read, there would be no keeping him. It would forever unfit him to be a slave. He would at once become unmanageable, and of no value to his master. As to himself, it could do him no good, but a great deal of harm. It would make him discontented and unhappy." These words sank deep into my heart, stirred up sentiments within that lay slumbering, and called into existence an entirely new train of thought. It was a new and special revelation, explaining dark and mysterious things, with which my youthful understanding had struggled, but struggled in vain. . . . From that moment, I understood the pathway from slavery to freedom. It was just what I wanted, and I got it at a time when I least expected it. Whilst I was saddened by the thought of losing the aid of my kind mistress, I was gladdened by the invaluable instruction which, by the merest accident, I had gained from my master. Though conscious of the difficulty of learning without a teacher, I set out with high hope, and a fixed purpose, at whatever cost of trouble, to learn to read. . . . That which to [Mr. Auld] was a great evil, to be carefully shunned, was to me a great good, to be dili-

gently sought; and the argument which he so warmly urged, against my learning to read, only served to inspire me with a desire and determination to learn. In learning to read, I owe almost as much to the bitter opposition of my master, as to the kindly aid of my mistress. I acknowledge the benefit of both.

Analyzing Literature

1. **Recall** Why did Mr. Auld oppose the idea of Douglass learning to read?

2. **Interpret** What do you think Douglass means when he speaks of "a revelation, explaining dark and mysterious things"?

3. **Evaluate and Connect** How would you feel if someone had forbidden you to learn to read?

Interdisciplinary Activity

Art Design a poster promoting literacy. Include reasons why everyone should learn to read and write and get an education.

The Union Dissolves

Guide to Reading

Main Idea
Many events pushed the nation into civil war.

Key Terms and Names
John C. Breckinridge, John Bell, Crittenden's Compromise, Confederacy, Jefferson Davis, martial law

Reading Strategy
Taking Notes As you read about the downward spiral toward civil war in the United States, use the major headings of the section to create an outline similar to the one below.

The Union Dissolves
I. The Election of 1860
   A.
   B.
   C.
II.

Reading Objectives
• **Describe** the various attempts to find a compromise between the demands of the North and the South.
• **Explain** how and why the Civil War began.

Section Theme
Civic Rights and Responsibilities After Lincoln's election, many Southerners placed state loyalty above loyalty to the Republic.

Preview of Events

◆January 1861   ◆March 1861   ◆May 1861

December 20, 1860
South Carolina secedes from the Union

February 8
The Confederate States of America is formed

March 4
Lincoln inaugurated

April 12
Fort Sumter bombarded

April 17
Virginia secedes

★ An American Story ★

"I do not pretend to sleep," wrote Mary Chesnut of the night of April 12, 1861. "How can I?"

Hours earlier her husband, former South Carolina senator James Chesnut, had gone by rowboat to Fort Sumter, in Charleston Harbor. He was delivering an ultimatum to U.S. Army Major Robert Anderson to surrender the fort by four o'clock in the morning or be fired upon by the South Carolina militia.

Through the long night Mary Chesnut lay awake, until she heard chimes from a local church ring four times. The hour of surrender had arrived, and, she confessed, "I beg[a]n to hope." Her hopes of a peaceful outcome faded when, a half-hour later, she heard the cannons begin to boom. "I sprang out of bed. And on my knees . . . I prayed as I never prayed before."

She ran to the roof, where others had gathered to watch the bombardment of Fort Sumter. Mary Chesnut shivered and felt the first terrifying evidence of the horrors to come.

"The regular roar of the cannon—there it was. And who could tell what each volley accomplished of death and destruction."

—adapted from *Mary Chesnut's Civil War*

The Election of 1860

John Brown's raid on Harpers Ferry was a turning point for the South. The possibility of an African American uprising had long haunted many Southerners, but they were frightened and angered by the idea that Northerners would deliberately try to arm enslaved people and encourage them to rebel.

Although the Republican leaders quickly denounced Brown's raid, many Southerners blamed Republicans. To them, the key point was that both the Republicans and John Brown opposed slavery. As one Atlanta newspaper noted: "We regard every man who does not boldly declare that he believes African slavery to be a social, moral, and political blessing as an enemy to the institutions of the South."

In the Senate, Robert Toombs of Georgia warned that the South would "never permit this Federal government to pass into the traitorous hands of the Black Republican party." In April 1860, with the South in an uproar, Democrats headed to Charleston, South Carolina, to choose their nominee for president.

The Democrats Split In 1860 the debate over slavery in the western territories finally tore the Democratic Party apart. Their first presidential nominating convention ended in dispute. Northern delegates wanted to support popular sovereignty, while Southern delegates wanted the party to uphold the *Dred Scott* decision and endorse a federal slave code for the territories. Stephen Douglas was not able to get the votes needed to be nominated for president, but neither could anyone else.

In June 1860, the Democrats met again, this time in Baltimore, to select their candidate. Douglas's supporters in the South had organized rival delegations to ensure Douglas's endorsement. The original Southern delegations objected to these rival delegates and again walked out. The remaining Democrats then chose Douglas as their candidate for president.

The Southern Democrats who had walked out organized their own convention and nominated the current vice president, **John C. Breckinridge** of Kentucky, for president. Breckinridge supported the *Dred Scott* decision and agreed to endorse the idea of a federal slave code for the western territories.

The split in the Democratic Party greatly improved Republican prospects, which was what some of the more radical Southern delegates had intended all along. They hoped that a Republican victory would be the final straw that would convince the Southern states to secede.

Other people, including many former Whigs, were greatly alarmed at the danger to the Union.

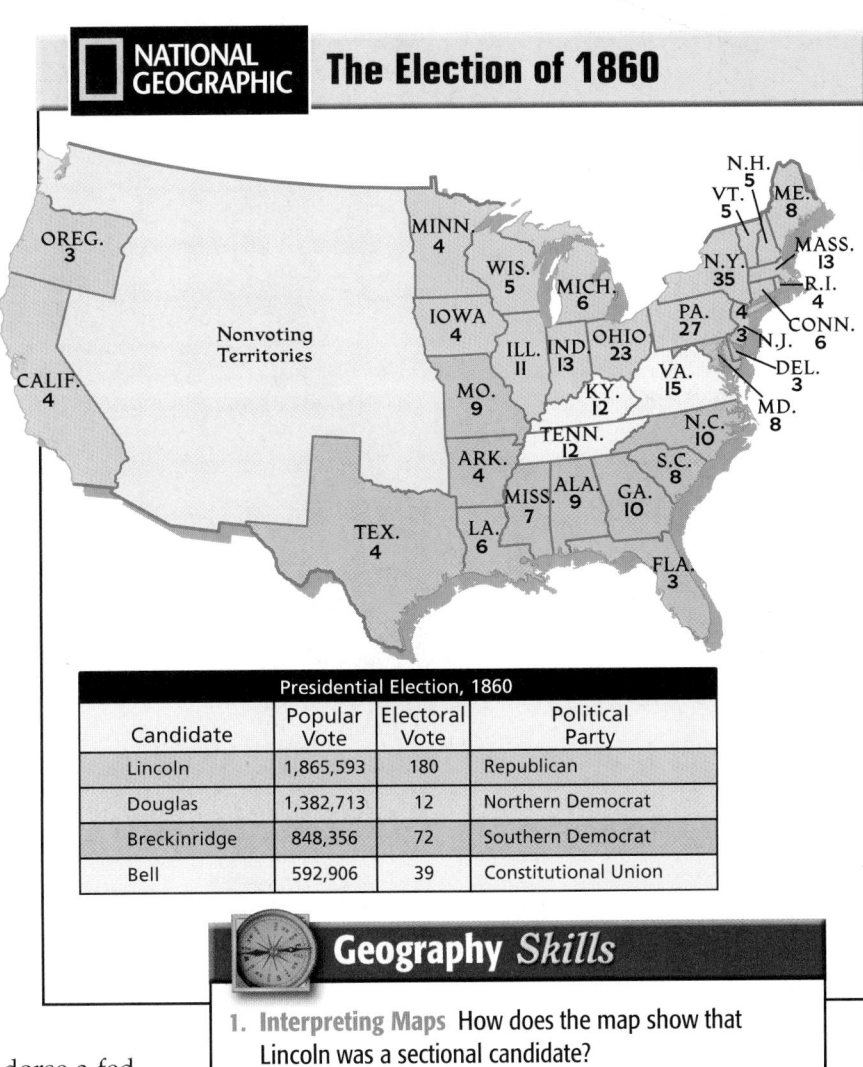

NATIONAL GEOGRAPHIC The Election of 1860

Presidential Election, 1860			
Candidate	Popular Vote	Electoral Vote	Political Party
Lincoln	1,865,593	180	Republican
Douglas	1,382,713	12	Northern Democrat
Breckinridge	848,356	72	Southern Democrat
Bell	592,906	39	Constitutional Union

Geography *Skills*

1. **Interpreting Maps** How does the map show that Lincoln was a sectional candidate?
2. **Applying Geography Skills** What explains the fact that Stephen Douglas won only one state, Missouri?

They created another new party, the Constitutional Union Party, and chose former Tennessee senator **John Bell** as their candidate. The Constitutional Unionists campaigned on a position of upholding both the Constitution and the Union.

TURNING POINT

Lincoln Is Elected With no possibility of winning electoral votes in the South, the Republicans needed a candidate who could sweep the North. Delegates at the Republicans' Chicago convention did not think their first choice, William Seward, had a wide enough appeal. Instead they nominated Lincoln, whose debates with Douglas had made him very popular in the North.

During the campaign, the Republicans tried to persuade voters they were more than just an antislavery party. They denounced John Brown's raid and reaffirmed the right of the Southern states to preserve

THE NATIONAL GAME. THREE "OUTS" AND ONE "RUN".
ABRAHAM WINNING THE BALL.

Analyzing *Political Cartoons*

Baseball and Politics In this cartoon, baseball language is used to explain Lincoln's 1860 victory. John Bell is sad that the opponents struck out. Stephen Douglas claims Lincoln had the advantage of his "rail," and John Breckinridge admits they were "skunk'd." Why is Lincoln pictured with a rail?

slavery within their borders. They also supported higher tariffs, a new homestead law for western settlers, and a transcontinental railroad.

The Republican proposals greatly angered many Southerners. Nevertheless, with Democratic votes split between Douglas and Breckinridge, Lincoln won the election without Southern support. For the South, the election of a Republican president represented the victory of the abolitionists. The survival of Southern society and culture seemed to be at stake. For many, there was now no choice but to secede.

Secession The dissolution of the Union began with South Carolina, where anti-Northern secessionist sentiment had long been intense. Shortly after Lincoln's election, the state legislature called for a convention. Amid a frenzy of fireworks and drills, the convention unanimously voted for the Ordinance of Secession. By February 1, 1861, six more states in the Lower South—Mississippi, Florida, Alabama, Georgia, Louisiana, and Texas— had voted to secede. Many Southerners felt

secession was in the Revolutionary tradition and that they were fighting for American rights.

Reading Check **Identifying** What main event triggered the secession of Southern states?

Compromise Fails

As the states of the Lower South seceded one after another, Congress tried to find a compromise to save the Union. Ignoring Congress's efforts, the secessionists seized all federal property in their states, including arsenals and forts. Only the island strongholds of Fort Sumter in Charleston Harbor and Fort Pickens in Pensacola Harbor, as well as a few other islands off the coast of Florida, remained out of Southern hands.

Although the confiscation of property horrified Northern members of Congress, they were willing to compromise. To that end, Kentucky senator John J. Crittenden proposed several amendments to the Constitution. One would guarantee slavery where it already existed. Another would also reinstate the

Missouri Compromise line, extending it to the California border. Slavery would be prohibited north of the line and protected south of it.

Lincoln, however, asked congressional Republicans to stand firm, and **Crittenden's Compromise** did not pass.

A Last Attempt at Peace

Finally, Virginia—a slave state but still in the Union—proposed a peace conference in a last-ditch effort at peace. Delegates from 21 states attended the conference in Washington, D.C. The majority came from Northern and border states. None came from the secessionist states. The delegates met for three weeks but came up with little more than a modified version of Crittenden's Compromise. When presented to Congress, the plan went down in defeat.

Founding the Confederacy

On the same day the peace conference met, delegates from the seceding states met in Montgomery, Alabama. There, in early February, they declared themselves to be a new nation—the Confederate States of America—or the Confederacy, as it became known.

Their convention drafted a constitution based largely on the U.S. Constitution but with some important changes. It declared that each state was independent and guaranteed the existence of slavery in Confederate territory. It also banned protective tariffs and limited the presidency to a single six-year term.

The convention then chose former Mississippi senator **Jefferson Davis** as president of the Confederacy. In his inaugural address, Davis declared, "The time for compromise has now passed. The South is determined to . . . make all who oppose her smell Southern powder and feel Southern steel."

✓ **Reading Check** **Summarizing** What did Virginia do to try to reverse secession?

The Civil War Begins

In the months before Lincoln took office, he had watched the nation fall apart. Preparing for his inauguration, he faced a splintered Union, a newly declared nation to the south, and the possibility that other states would soon secede.

Lincoln Takes Office In his inaugural speech on March 4, 1861, Lincoln addressed the seceding states directly. He repeated his commitment not to interfere with slavery where it existed but insisted that "the Union of these States is perpetual." Lincoln did not threaten the seceded states, but he said he intended to "hold, occupy, and possess" federal property in those states. Lincoln also encouraged reconciliation:

> ❝In *your* hands, my dissatisfied countrymen, and not in *mine* is the momentous issue of civil war. The government will not assail *you.* You can have no conflict, without yourselves being the aggressors. . . . We are not enemies, but friends. We must not be enemies. Though passion may have strained, it must not break our bonds of affection.❞
>
> —from Lincoln's Inaugural Address, March 4, 1861

TURNING POINT

Fort Sumter Falls In April Lincoln announced that he intended to resupply Fort Sumter. President Jefferson Davis of the Confederacy now faced a dilemma. To tolerate federal troops in the South's most vital harbor seemed unacceptable for a sovereign

"The time for compromise has now passed."
— *Jefferson Davis*

Picturing History

Southern Leader A former soldier, representative, and senator, Jefferson Davis became the first president of the Confederacy. Why did Davis give up on compromise?

nation, as the South now saw itself. After Lincoln's warning, however, firing on the supply ship would undoubtedly lead to war with the United States.

Davis decided to take Fort Sumter before the supply ship arrived. If he was successful, peace might be preserved. Confederate leaders then delivered a note to Major Robert Anderson demanding Fort Sumter's surrender by the morning of April 12, 1861.

Anderson stood fast. The fateful hour came and went, and cannon fire suddenly shook the air. Confederate forces bombarded Fort Sumter for 33 relentless hours, wrecking the fort but killing no one, until Anderson and his exhausted men finally surrendered. The Civil War had begun.

The Upper South Secedes
After the fall of Fort Sumter, President Lincoln called for 75,000 volunteers to serve in the military for 90 days. The call for troops created a crisis in the Upper South. Many people there did not want to secede, but faced with the prospect of civil war, they believed they had no choice but to leave the Union. Virginia acted first,

passing an Ordinance of Secession on April 17, 1861. The Confederate Congress responded by moving the capital of the Confederacy to Richmond, Virginia. By early June of 1861, Arkansas, North Carolina, and Tennessee had also seceded.

GEOGRAPHY

Hanging on to the Border States
With the Upper South gone, Lincoln was determined to keep the slaveholding border states from seceding. Delaware seemed safe, but Lincoln worried about Kentucky, Missouri, and Maryland. Virginia's secession had placed a Confederate state across the Potomac River from the nation's capital. If Maryland seceded, Washington would be surrounded by Confederate territory.

To prevent Maryland's secession, Lincoln imposed martial law in Baltimore, where angry mobs had already attacked federal troops. Under martial law, the military takes control of an area and replaces civilian authorities, and it suspends

NATIONAL GEOGRAPHIC
MOMENT in HISTORY

RUSH TO THE COLORS
In the turbulent days following the bombardment of Fort Sumter in April 1861, tens of thousands of young men in the North and South hastened to join their states' volunteer regiments. Most had no idea of the horrors that awaited them. Many saw the war as an escape from the boredom of the family farm or the misery of city tenements. Their only fear was that the fighting might end before they could take part. Here, members of the First Virginia Militia, the "Richmond Grays," pose for the camera before their first taste of battle.

certain civil rights. Anyone supporting secession could be arrested and held without trial. Union Army officers imprisoned dozens of suspected secessionist leaders.

Lincoln knew that Kentucky was divided over whether to secede and that its control of the Ohio River's south bank was strategically important. When Kentucky declared itself neutral, Lincoln promised to leave the state alone so long as the Confederacy did the same.

Kentucky's neutrality lasted until September 1861, when Confederate forces occupied the southwest corner of the state, prompting Union troops to move in as well. The Confederate invasion angered many in the Kentucky legislature, who now voted to go to war against the Confederacy. This decision led other Kentuckians who supported the Confederacy to create a rival government and secede.

The third border state Lincoln worried about was Missouri. Although many people in the state sympathized strongly with the Confederacy, its convention voted almost unanimously against secession. A struggle then broke out between the convention and pro-secession forces led by Governor Claiborne F. Jackson. In the end, Missouri was held to the Union's cause with the support of federal forces.

From the very beginning of the Civil War, Lincoln had been willing to take political, even constitutional, risks to preserve the Union. The issue of its preservation now shifted to the battlefield.

✓ **Reading Check** **Describing** Why were the border states of Maryland and Kentucky important to the Union?

Causes and Effects of the Civil War

Causes
- Disagreement over the legality, morality, and politics of slavery
- Kansas-Nebraska Act sparked violence in Kansas.
- *Dred Scott* ruling voided any limitations on expansion of slavery.
- John Brown's raid on Harpers Ferry polarized North and South.
- Southern states seceded from the Union.
- Confederates attacked Fort Sumter in South Carolina.

Effects
- Slavery was outlawed in the United States.
- Southern states rebuilt their economy.
- African Americans gained citizenship and voting rights.
- The first U.S. civil rights laws were passed.

Graphic Organizer → Skills

Mounting sectional tensions erupted into open warfare in 1861.

Analyzing What do you think was the most important cause of the Civil War? Why?

SECTION 4 ASSESSMENT

Checking for Understanding
1. **Define:** Confederacy, martial law.
2. **Identify:** John C. Breckinridge, John Bell, Crittenden's Compromise, Jefferson Davis.
3. **List** two provisions of Crittenden's Compromise.

Reviewing Themes
4. **Civic Rights and Responsibilities** How did Lincoln prevent Kentucky, Missouri, and Maryland from seceding? Was Lincoln justified in his actions? Why or why not?

Critical Thinking
5. **Analyzing** Why did Virginia's secession surprise Northerners?
6. **Categorizing** Use a graphic organizer similar to the one below to list the various parties' candidates and political positions in the 1860 election.

Party	Candidate	Position
Northern Democrat		
Southern Democrat		
Constitutional Unionist		
Republican		

Analyzing Visuals
7. **Analyzing Political Cartoons** Study the cartoon on page 342 about the presidential election of 1860. What does the use of a baseball comparison imply about politics?

Writing About History
8. **Persuasive Writing** Imagine you are an adviser to President Lincoln, and you have just heard about the firing on Fort Sumter. Write a brief report for the president, advising him on what steps to take next.

Reviewing Key Terms

On a sheet of paper, use each of these terms in a sentence.

1. popular sovereignty
2. secession
3. Underground Railroad
4. transcontinental railroad
5. referendum
6. insurrection
7. Confederacy
8. martial law

Chapter Summary

Key Events of the 1850s:

- California entered Union as a free state, giving free states a Senate majority
- Fugitive Slave Act passed to help Southerners recover enslaved people who escaped to North; act caused outrage in North
- *Uncle Tom's Cabin* published, angered many Southerners
- Kansas-Nebraska Act passed

Kansas-Nebraska Act heightened tensions:

- Angered Northerners by repealing Missouri Compromise
- Popular sovereignty regarding slavery issue led to violence in "Bleeding Kansas"
- Republican Party formed by former Whigs and members of Free-Soil Party
- *Dred Scott* decision by Southern-dominated Supreme Court angered Northerners
- Debates in Senate over Kansas led to caning of Charles Sumner
- Events in Kansas angered John Brown, who then raided Harpers Ferry

Election of 1860:

- Democratic Party split between North and South
- Republicans nominated eventual winner Abraham Lincoln
- Southern states established Confederacy in February 1861
- Fort Sumter fired upon in April 1861, starting the Civil War

Reviewing Key Facts

9. **Identify:** Wilmot Proviso, Fugitive Slave Act, Harriet Tubman, Kansas-Nebraska Act, Charles Sumner, Dred Scott, John C. Breckinridge, John Bell.
10. What were the main elements of the Compromise of 1850?
11. Why did Southern politicians begin talking about secession?
12. Why did Northerners resist the Fugitive Slave Act?
13. How did the Republican Party try to gain Southern voters in the presidential election of 1860?
14. Why is John Brown's Harpers Ferry raid considered a turning point on the road to war?
15. What efforts were made to prevent the outbreak of war?
16. What border states did Lincoln try to keep in the Union?

Critical Thinking

17. **Analyzing Themes: Civic Rights and Responsibilities** How did the Fugitive Slave Act and the *Dred Scott* decision affect formerly enslaved African Americans living in the North?
18. **Evaluating** Why did many members of Congress support popular sovereignty?
19. **Forming an Opinion** John Brown's goal in seizing the arsenal at Harpers Ferry was to begin a rebellion against slaveholders. Do you think John Brown should have been executed for this action? Why or why not?
20. **Organizing** Use a graphic organizer similar to the one below to list the main events that pushed the nation into civil war.

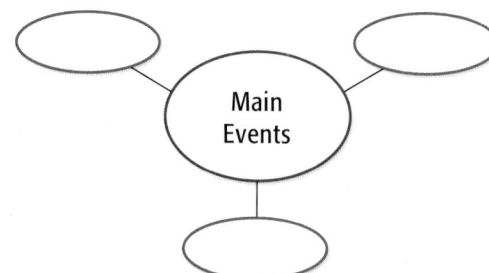

21. **Interpreting Primary Sources** Many people have written essays on the causes of the Civil War. Edward A. Pollard of Virginia was the editor of the *Daily Richmond Examiner* during the Civil War. He wrote a book, *The Lost Cause,* about the Civil War from a Southern point of view. In the book, Pollard includes his view of the causes of the Civil War. Read the excerpt and answer the questions that follow.

❝In the ante-revolutionary period, the differences between the populations of the Northern and Southern colonies had already been strongly developed. The

NATIONAL GEOGRAPHIC — Seceding States, 1860–1861

W. VA. separated from VA. in 1861 and was admitted to the Union in 1863.

On February 8, 1861, delegates from several Southern states created the Confederacy.

S.C. was the first state to secede from the Union.

- ☐ Union free state
- ☐ Union slave state
- ☐ Slave state seceding before Fort Sumter, April 1861
- ▨ Slave state seceding after Fort Sumter, April 1861
- ☐ Territory
- — Union-Confederate border

0   400 miles
0   400 kilometers
Lambert Equal-Area projection

early colonists did not bear with them from the mother-country to the shores of the New World any greater degree of congeniality than existed among them at home. They had come not only from different stocks of population, but from different feuds in religion and politics. There could be no congeniality between . . . New England, and the . . . South. . . .**"**

—from *The Lost Cause*

a. According to Pollard, when did the differences between the North and South begin?

b. What did he believe caused the differences between the people of the North and the South?

Practicing Skills

22. **Predicting Consequences** Review the skill on predicting consequences on page 325. Then read the following statements and predict three consequences for each. Rank the three consequences in order of the one most likely to occur to the one least likely to occur.
    a. A person elected to a political office does not support the issues he or she claimed to represent while campaigning.
    b. Engineers develop an effective, efficient automobile powered by solar energy.

Writing Activity

23. **American History Primary Source Document Library CD-ROM** Read the decision in *Dred Scott* v. *Sandford* by Roger B. Taney, under *Civil War and Reconstruction.* Work with your classmates to outline the major points. Then prepare a counter-decision, addressing each major point and explaining why it could or should be overturned.

Chapter Activity

24. **Research Project: Mental Mapping** Mental maps are the images people have in their minds of places they know or imagine. Based on what you have read in the chapter and additional research, sketch a possible escape route on the Underground Railroad as an enslaved person in the South might have drawn it. Make sure to include important geographic features. Share your findings with your class.

Geography and History

25. The map above shows states that seceded from 1860 to 1861. Study the map and answer the questions below.
    a. **Interpreting Maps** Which slave states remained in the Union after the Fort Sumter attack?
    b. **Applying Geography Skills** Which states did not secede until after the Fort Sumter attack?

Standardized Test Practice

Directions: Choose the best answer to the following questions.

Several events in the 1850s caused anger in both North and South, making war more likely. Which of the following was not a cause of increasing tension?

A The Fugitive Slave Act

B The publication of *Uncle Tom's Cabin*

C John Brown's Harpers Ferry raid

D Crittenden's Compromise

Test-Taking Tip: Be careful—overlooking the words *not* or *except* on a question is a common error. Also, answer D refers to a compromise, which does not suggest a cause of anger.

CHAPTER 11

The Civil War
1861–1865

Why It Matters

The Civil War was a milestone in American history. The four-year-long struggle determined the nation's future. With the North's victory, slavery was abolished. During the war, the Northern economy grew stronger, while the Southern economy stagnated. Military innovations, including the expanded use of railroads and the telegraph, coupled with a general conscription, made the Civil War the first "modern" war.

The Impact Today

The outcome of this bloody war permanently changed the nation.
- *The Thirteenth Amendment abolished slavery.*
- *The power of the federal government was strengthened.*

The American Vision Video *The Chapter 11 video, "Lincoln and the Civil War," describes the hardships and struggles that Abraham Lincoln experienced as he led the nation in this time of crisis.*

1862
- Confederate loss at Battle of Antietam halts Lee's first invasion of the North

1861
- Fort Sumter fired upon
- First Battle of Bull Run

1863
- Lincoln presents Emancipation Proclamation
- Battle of Gettysburg

1859
- John Brown leads raid on federal arsenal at Harpers Ferry, Virginia

United States
PRESIDENTS

Lincoln 1861–1865

1859   *1861*   *1863*

World

1861
- Russian serfs emancipated by Czar Alexander II

1862
- Source of the Nile River confirmed by John Hanning Speke and James A. Grant

1863
- French troops occupy Mexico City

1859
- Work on the Suez Canal begins in Egypt

Charge by Don Troiani, 1990, depicts the advance of the
Eighth Pennsylvania Cavalry during the Battle of Chancellorsville.

1865
- Lee surrenders to Grant at Appomattox Courthouse
- Abraham Lincoln assassinated by John Wilkes Booth

1864
- Fall of Atlanta
- Sherman marches to the sea

A. Johnson 1865–1869

1865

1867

1864
- Karl Marx founds First International Workingmen's Association to promote socialism

1866
- Gregor Mendel publishes theory on genetic heredity

1867
- Swedish chemist Alfred Nobel invents dynamite

HISTORY *Online*

Chapter Overview
Visit the *American Vision* Web site at tav.glencoe.com and click on **Chapter Overviews—Chapter 11** to preview chapter information.

Main Idea

The North and the South each had distinct advantages and disadvantages at the beginning of the Civil War.

Key Terms and Names

Robert E. Lee, greenback, Copperheads, conscription, habeas corpus, James Mason, John Slidell, *Trent* Affair, attrition, Anaconda Plan

Reading Strategy

Taking Notes As you read about the North and South's advantages and disadvantages at the start of the Civil War, use the major headings of the section to create an outline similar to the one below.

> I. Choosing Sides
> II.
>   A.
>   B.
> III.
> IV.

Reading Objectives

- **Assess** the strengths and weaknesses of each region's economy.
- **Contrast** the political situations of the Union and the Confederacy.

Section Theme

Groups and Institutions The Confederacy's weak central government had difficulty coordinating the war effort.

Preview of Events

| ♦April 1861 | ♦October 1861 | ♦April 1862 |

April 1861
Robert E. Lee resigns from the U.S. Army

November 1861
Trent Affair

February 1862
Congress passes Legal Tender Act

April 1862
Confederate Congress passes conscription law

★ An American Story ★

While husking corn on his family's Indiana farm in April 1861, 16-year-old Theodore Upson heard a neighbor tell his father Jonathan that "the Rebels have fired upon and taken Fort Sumter."

"Father said little," Upson remembered. However, when the family sat down for dinner later, the boy saw that his father "looked ten years older."

Upson later recalled, "We sat down to the table. Grandma wanted to know what was the trouble. Father told her and she began to cry. 'Oh, my poor children in the South. Now they will suffer!'"

Upson's father offered to let their Southern relatives come and stay at the farm. "No, they will not do that," the grandmother replied. "There is their home. There they will stay. Oh, to think that I should have lived to see the day when Brother should rise against Brother."

—adapted from *With Sherman to the Sea*

Choosing Sides

On the same day that he learned his home state of Virginia had voted to secede from the Union, **Robert E. Lee**—one of the best senior officers in the United States Army—received an offer from General Winfield Scott to command the Union's troops. Although Lee had spoken against secession and considered slavery "a moral and political evil," he wrote, "I cannot raise my hand against my birthplace, my home, my children." Instead, he resigned from the army and offered his services to the Confederacy.

Lee was only one of hundreds of military officers who had to choose whether to support the Union or the Confederacy. Eventually 313 officers, or about one-third of the total, resigned to join the Confederacy. These officers enabled the South to organize an effective fighting force quickly, as did the strong military tradition in the South. In 1860 the United States had eight military colleges, but seven of them were in the South. These colleges provided the South with a large number of trained officers to lead its armies.

Just as the South had a strong military tradition, the North had a strong naval tradition. More than three-quarters of the United States Navy's officers came from the North. At the same time, the crews of American merchant ships were almost entirely from the North. They provided a large pool of trained sailors for the Union navy as it expanded. Perhaps even more important, most of the navy's warships and all but one of the country's shipyards remained under Union control as well.

☑ **Reading Check** **Explaining** What advantage did the Southern army have as the war began?

Advantages and Disadvantages

Although the South had many experienced officers to lead its troops in battle, the North had several economic advantages. In 1860 the population of the North was about 22 million, while the South had about 9 million people. The North's larger population gave it a great advantage in raising an army and in supporting the war effort. Because of the smaller population in the South, about one-third of whom were enslaved, a larger percentage of its men had to fight if Southern armies were to match the Union armies in size. As a result, the South had fewer people working to support the war effort.

ECONOMICS

Industry and Agriculture The North's industries gave the region an important economic advantage over the South. In 1860 roughly 80 percent of the nation's factories were in the North. These Northern factories produced more than 90 percent of the country's clothing, boots, and shoes, and 93 percent of its pig iron (unrefined iron), essential for manufacturing weapons and equipment. Almost all of the country's firearms were manufactured in the North, and the Du Pont factories in Delaware made most of the nation's gunpowder. In contrast, the South had only one factory capable of producing cannons, the **Tredegar Iron Works** in Richmond, Virginia, and no major facilities for making gunpowder.

To remedy these deficiencies, the Confederacy's Ordnance Bureau set up armories and foundries in several Southern states, and it created a huge gunpowder mill in Augusta, Georgia. By the summer of

Picturing **History**

Brother Against Brother The Civil War divided the nation, but it also divided families. Even the First Lady, Mary Todd Lincoln, a Kentuckian, had half-brothers who fought for the Confederacy. As the nation divided, why was the Confederacy able to organize an effective army so quickly?

1862, the South was producing enough weapons, gunpowder, and ammunition to meet its needs.

The South also was capable of producing its own food. Although much of the South's fertile land was used for the production of cash crops such as cotton and tobacco, Southern farmers also grew rice and great quantities of corn. The problem facing the South was not its ability to produce food, but its ability to distribute it once the war began and Union troops invaded Southern soil.

The South had only half as many miles of railroad track as the North and had only one line—from Memphis to Chattanooga—connecting the western states of the Confederacy to the east. This made it much easier for Northern troops to disrupt the Southern rail system and prevent the movement of food and troops.

Financing the War Both the North and the South had to act quickly to raise money for the war. The North enjoyed several financial advantages. In addition to controlling the national treasury, the Union could expect continued revenue from tariffs. Many Northern banks also held large reserves of cash, which they loaned the government by purchasing bonds.

Concern about the North's ability to win the war caused many people to withdraw gold and silver from the banks. Without gold and silver, the banks could not buy government bonds, and without the gold and silver from the sale of bonds, the government could not pay its suppliers and troops. To solve this problem, Congress passed the **Legal Tender Act** in February 1862. This act created a national currency and allowed the government to issue paper money. The paper money came to be known as greenbacks, because of its color.

In contrast to the Union, the Confederacy's financial situation was not good, and it became worse over time. Most Southern planters were in debt and unable to buy bonds. At the same time, Southern banks were small and had few cash reserves. They too could not buy many bonds.

The best hope for the South to raise money was by taxing trade. Shortly after the war began, however, the Union Navy blockaded Southern ports, which reduced trade and revenues. The Confederacy then resorted to direct taxation of its own people. It imposed new taxes on property and farm products, but many Southerners resented the taxes and refused to pay.

Lacking sufficient money from taxes or bonds, the Confederacy was also forced to print paper money to pay its bills. This caused rapid inflation in the South. Confederate paper money became almost worthless. By the end of the war, the South had experienced 9,000 percent inflation, compared to only 80 percent in the North.

Reading Check **Examining** How was having a larger population than the South an advantage for the North?

The Income Tax

Past: Funding the War
On July 1, 1862, a new tax law gave the United States a comprehensive federal income tax. A temporary way of funding the war debt, the tax was repealed in 1872. Another income tax passed in 1894 was challenged in court, and the Supreme Court ruled that the idea of an income tax was unconstitutional. The Sixteenth Amendment (1913) again made the income tax legal.

$5 greenback

Present: The IRS Today
Today the income tax is the biggest source of federal government funding. The Internal Revenue Service (IRS) administers the tax, receiving and processing about 200 million returns every year.

Party Politics in the North

As the Civil War began, President Lincoln had to contend with divisions within his own party. Many members of the Republican Party were abolitionists. Lincoln's goal, however, was to preserve the Union, even if it meant allowing slavery to continue.

The president also had to contend with Democrats who challenged his policies. Northern Democrats were themselves sharply divided. One faction, called **War Democrats,** strongly supported the conflict and hoped to restore the Union to the way it was before the war. This group also opposed ending slavery.

Another faction of Northern Democrats were known as the Peace Democrats. This group opposed the war and called for reuniting the states through negotiation rather than force. Their support of this unlikely possibility angered Republicans, who saw any opposition to the war as treason. Republicans referred to Peace Democrats as **Copperheads,** after the venomous snake.

One major disagreement between Republicans and Democrats concerned civil liberties. In the summer of 1862, Congress introduced a militia law that required states to use conscription—or forcing people into military service—if this was necessary to fill their regiments. Many Democrats opposed the law, and riots erupted in several strongly Democratic districts in Indiana, Ohio, Pennsylvania, and Wisconsin.

To enforce the militia law, Lincoln suspended writs of habeas corpus. Habeas corpus refers to a person's right not to be imprisoned unless charged with a crime and given a trial. A writ of habeas corpus is a court order that requires the government to either charge an imprisoned person with a crime or let the person go free. When writs of habeas corpus are suspended, a person can be imprisoned indefinitely without trial. In this case, President Lincoln suspended the writ for anyone who openly supported the rebels or encouraged others to resist the militia draft.

Criticized for his suspension of writs of habeas corpus, Lincoln justified his actions: "Must I shoot a simple-minded soldier boy who deserts," the president asked, "while I must not touch a hair of a wily agitator who induces him to desert?"

Reading Check **Summarizing** How were Northern Democrats divided over the Civil War?

Weak Southern Government

Although the South had no organized opposition party, President Jefferson Davis still faced many political problems. The Confederate constitution emphasized states' rights and limited the central government's power. This commitment to states' rights often interfered with Davis's ability to conduct the war.

Analyzing *Political Cartoons*

Political Disagreements Northern Democrats who favored peace were mockingly called "Copperheads," after the poisonous snake, by their political opponents. How did President Lincoln deal with political criticism during the Civil War?

Although many Southern leaders supported the war, some opposed Jefferson Davis when he supported conscription and established martial law in the spring of 1862. Leaders from North Carolina and Georgia, including Davis's vice president, **Alexander Stephens,** were among those who dissented. They objected to the Confederacy forcing people to join the army and opposed Davis's decision to suspend writs of habeas corpus. The new taxes the Confederacy had imposed were another complaint.

Reading Check **Summarizing** What problems did Jefferson Davis face in governing the Confederacy?

The Diplomatic Challenge

The outbreak of the Civil War put the major governments of Europe in a difficult situation. The United States did not want the Europeans interfering in the war. In particular, it did not want the Europeans to recognize the Confederate States of America as an independent country. It also wanted the Europeans to respect the Union navy's blockade of the South.

Confederate leaders wanted the exact opposite. They wanted the Europeans, particularly the British, to recognize the South, declare the Union blockade illegal, and then use the British navy to assist the South in

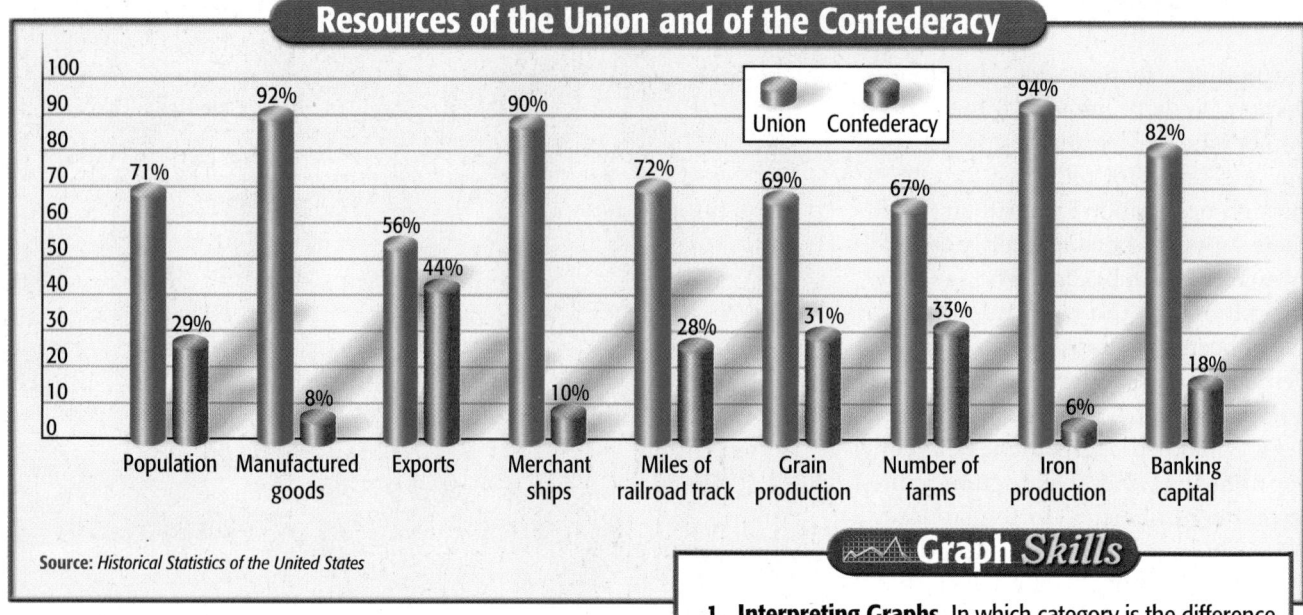

Resources of the Union and of the Confederacy

Category	Union	Confederacy
Population	71%	29%
Manufactured goods	92%	8%
Exports	56%	44%
Merchant ships	90%	10%
Miles of railroad track	72%	28%
Grain production	69%	31%
Number of farms	67%	33%
Iron production	94%	6%
Banking capital	82%	18%

Source: *Historical Statistics of the United States*

Graph Skills

1. **Interpreting Graphs** In which category is the difference between the resources of Union and the Confederacy the greatest?
2. **Making Inferences** What additional factors are not considered when comparing population percentages between the Union and the Confederacy?

its struggle with the North. Southern leaders knew that European textile factories, particularly in Britain and France, depended on Southern cotton. To pressure the British and French, many Southern planters voluntarily agreed not to sell their cotton in these markets until the Europeans recognized the Confederacy.

The British and French met informally with Confederate representatives in May 1861. The French promised to recognize the Confederacy if the British would do so as well. British leaders, however, did not want to risk war with the United States unless absolutely necessary. They also were not willing to recognize the Confederacy until decisive victories on the battlefield proved the South could survive and eventually win the war.

At one point, Britain and the United States did come close to war. In the autumn of 1861, the Confederacy decided to send permanent ministers to Britain and France to represent its interests. **James Mason** of Virginia was to go to Britain, and **John Slidell** of Louisiana was to go to France. Mason and Slidell slipped past the Union blockade on a Southern ship and traveled to Havana, Cuba, where they boarded the *Trent*, a British ship. When the ship left Havana, Charles Wilkes, captain of the Union warship *San Jacinto*, intercepted the *Trent* and arrested the two men.

Northerners applauded Wilkes's action. The British, however, were furious over the interference with their ship. They sent an ultimatum to the United States, demanding the release of the two Confederates. Britain sent troops to Canada to strengthen the Atlantic fleet, and war seemed imminent. After a few tense weeks, Lincoln freed Mason and Slidell, commenting, "One war at a time."

After being freed, the diplomats continued on their journey to seek Confederate allies. Although the arrest of Mason and Slidell in the so-called *Trent* Affair had excited interest worldwide, their diplomatic mission failed to gain the support the South wanted.

Reading Check **Explaining** Why did the Confederate States want Britain and France to recognize them?

The First "Modern" War

The economic and political situation in the North and South was very important to the outcome of the war because, in many respects, the Civil War was the first "modern" war. Unlike most of the wars fought in Europe during the previous two centuries, the Civil War was not fought by small disciplined armies with limited goals. It involved huge armies made up mostly of civilian volunteers that required vast amounts of supplies and equipment.

Military Technology and Tactics Many of the top officers who led the Union and Confederate troops had studied the campaigns of Napoleon and had themselves fought in the war with Mexico in the 1840s. They believed that the best way to win a battle was to organize the troops into tight columns and go on the offensive. Troops would march toward the enemy, firing in massed volleys. When they got close enough, they would charge the enemy and attack with **bayonets**—long knives attached to the front of their guns. These tactics were necessary earlier in the century because soldiers used smoothbore muskets loaded with round metal balls. These muskets were very inaccurate except at close range.

By the 1850s, French and American inventors had developed a new inexpensive conoidal—or cone-shaped—bullet for rifles. Rifles firing conoidal bullets were accurate at much greater ranges. This meant that troops would be fired upon several more times while charging enemy lines.

At the same time, instead of standing in a line, troops defending positions in the Civil War began to use trenches and barricades to protect themselves. The combination of rifles and trenches created a deadly situation where the attacking force often suffered very high casualties.

High casualties meant that armies had to keep replacing their soldiers. Attrition—the wearing down of one side by the other through exhaustion of soldiers and resources—played a critical role as the war dragged on. The North, with its large population, could draw on new troops for replacements, but the South had fewer men to replace soldiers who died or were wounded in battle.

Conoidal bullets

The South's Strategy Early in the war, Jefferson Davis imagined a struggle similar to the American war for independence against Britain. Like George Washington, his generals would pick their battles carefully, attacking and retreating when necessary and avoiding large battles that might risk heavy losses. In this manner, the South would wage a

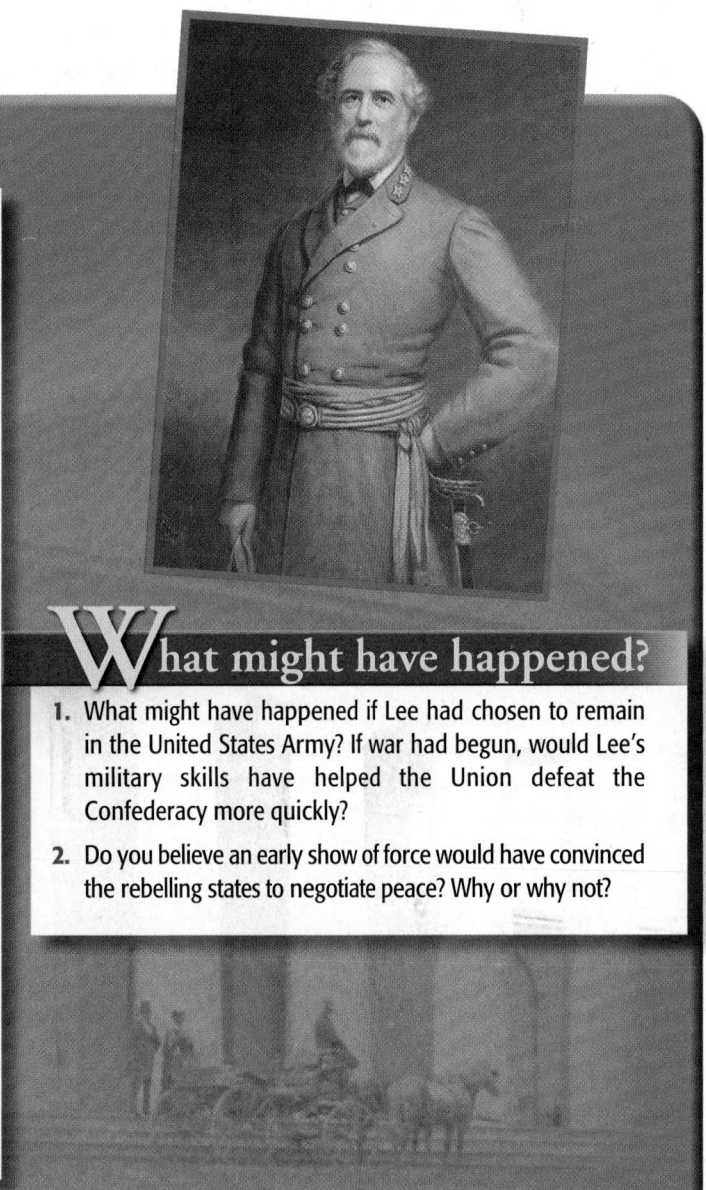

What If...

Lee Had Not Followed Virginia in Secession?

General Robert E. Lee was one of the most famous Confederate officers. The troops and the Southern population trusted his leadership and military judgment. Lee's tactical skill allowed his army to achieve many battlefield successes against difficult odds. What if, however, Lee had remained loyal to the U.S. Army at the start of the war?

U.S. General Winfield Scott met with Lee on the day after Virginia voted to break ties with the United States. Scott offered Lee the opportunity to lead the Union army into the South, hoping that a strong display of force would forestall actual warfare. The *Alexandria Gazette* also speculated about what Lee would do:

❝It is probable that the secession of Virginia will cause an immediate resignation of many officers of the Army and Navy from this State. . . . [If Lee] should resign his present position in the Army of the United States, we call the immediate attention of our State to him. . . . There is no man who would command more of the confidence of the people of Virginia, than this distinguished officer; and no one under whom the volunteers and militia would more gladly rally.❞

—from *Almost America*

What might have happened?

1. What might have happened if Lee had chosen to remain in the United States Army? If war had begun, would Lee's military skills have helped the Union defeat the Confederacy more quickly?

2. Do you believe an early show of force would have convinced the rebelling states to negotiate peace? Why or why not?

The Anaconda Plan

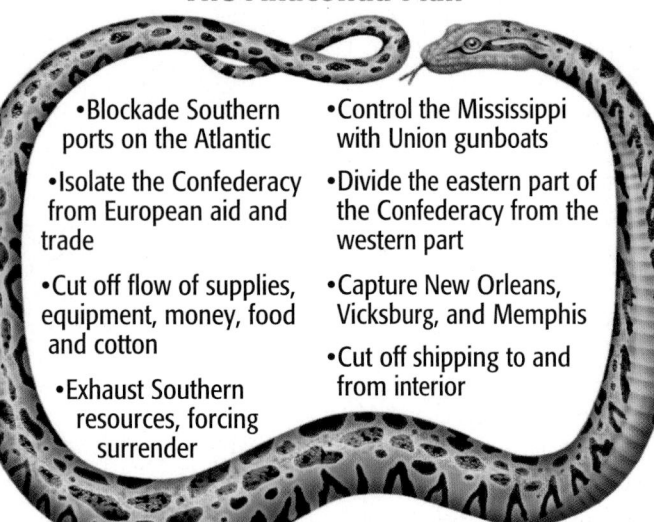

- Blockade Southern ports on the Atlantic
- Isolate the Confederacy from European aid and trade
- Cut off flow of supplies, equipment, money, food and cotton
- Exhaust Southern resources, forcing surrender
- Control the Mississippi with Union gunboats
- Divide the eastern part of the Confederacy from the western part
- Capture New Orleans, Vicksburg, and Memphis
- Cut off shipping to and from interior

Chart Skills

1. **Interpreting Charts** How would a naval blockade accomplish several elements of the Anaconda Plan at once?
2. **Analyzing** Why was General Winfield Scott in favor of this plan?

defensive war of attrition, Davis believed, forcing the Union to spend its resources until it became tired of the war and agreed to negotiate.

The idea of a defensive war of attrition, however, outraged many Southerners. Believing themselves superior fighters, they scorned the idea of defensive warfare. "The idea of waiting for blows, instead of inflicting them, is altogether unsuited to the genius of our people," declared the *Richmond Examiner* in 1861.

The Southern disdain for remaining on the defensive meant that when battles occurred, Southern troops often went on the offensive, charging enemy lines and suffering enormous casualties. In 1862 and 1863, Confederate armies fought nine large battles. In six of those battles they went on the offensive, and they suffered 20,000 more casualties than the Union. These were losses the South could not afford.

The Union's Anaconda Plan Early in the war, the general in chief of the United States, **Winfield Scott,** proposed a strategy for defeating the South. Scott suggested that the Union blockade Confederate ports and send gunboats down the Mississippi to divide the Confederacy. The South, thus separated, would gradually run out of resources and surrender. The plan would take time, Scott admitted, but it would defeat the South with the least amount of bloodshed.

Many Northerners rejected the plan as too slow and indirect for certain victory, favoring instead a strong, quick invasion of the South. Northern newspapers scorned this strategy, which they called the **Anaconda Plan,** after the snake that slowly strangles its prey to death. Although Lincoln eventually agreed to implement Scott's suggestions and imposed a blockade of Southern ports, he hoped that a quick victory by Northern troops over the Southern forces massing in Virginia might discredit the secessionists and bring about a negotiated end to the crisis. Ultimately, he and other Union leaders realized that only a long war that focused on destroying the South's armies had any chance of success.

Reading Check **Describing** What war strategy did Jefferson Davis develop for the South?

SECTION 1 ASSESSMENT

Checking for Understanding

1. **Define:** greenback, conscription, habeas corpus, attrition.
2. **Identify:** Robert E. Lee, Copperheads, James Mason, John Slidell, *Trent* Affair, Anaconda Plan.
3. **Explain** why the South had difficulty getting supplies from foreign nations.

Reviewing Themes

4. **Groups and Institutions** How did a belief in states' rights hamper the South during the war?

Critical Thinking

5. **Comparing** Why did the North have an economic advantage over the South?
6. **Analyzing** Why did the South resort to using paper money during the war?
7. **Organizing** Using a graphic organizer similar to the one below, list the military innovations of the Civil War era.

Military Innovations

Analyzing Visuals

8. **Examining Artifacts** Examine the conoidal bullets shown on page 355. How did conoidal bullets affect the war effort? What other innovations made the Civil War the first "modern" war?

Writing About History

9. **Descriptive Writing** Imagine that you are living in one of the border states at the beginning of the Civil War. Write a letter to a relative explaining why you are planning on joining either the Union or Confederate army.

SECTION 2 The Early Stages

Guide to Reading

Main Idea
Union forces suffered defeat in Virginia, advanced down the Mississippi, and stopped the South's invasion of Maryland.

Key Terms and Names
"Stonewall" Jackson, Irwin McDowell, bounty, blockade runner, David G. Farragut, Ulysses S. Grant, George B. McClellan, Emancipation Proclamation

Reading Strategy
Categorizing As you read about the early battles of the war, complete a chart like the one below by filling in the results of each battle listed.

Battle	Results
First Battle of Bull Run	
Battle of Shiloh	
Battle of Murfreesboro	
Seven Days' Battle	
Second Battle of Bull Run	

Reading Objectives
- **Describe** the progress of war in the West.
- **Compare** the eastern campaigns to those in the West.

Section Theme
Geography and History The Union hoped to seize the Mississippi Valley and cut the Confederacy in two.

Preview of Events

| ♦1861 | ♦1862 | ♦1863 |

1861
Confederates defeat Union forces at First Battle of Bull Run

1862
20,000 casualties at the Battle of Shiloh

1862
23,000 casualties at the Battle of Antietam

1863
The Emancipation Proclamation takes effect

★ An American Story ★

On July 21, 1861—a hot, sultry Sunday perfect for family outings—hundreds of people from Washington, D.C., picnicked along Bull Run near Manassas Junction, Virginia. They had gathered to watch the first battle between the Union and Confederate forces.

"The spectators were all excited," wrote one reporter, "and a lady with an opera glass who was near me was quite beside herself when an unusually heavy discharge roused the current of her blood: 'That is splendid! Oh, my! Is not that first-rate?'"

The spectators who came to Bull Run expected a short, exciting fight and a quick surrender by the rebel troops. Unexpectedly, the Confederates routed the Union army. A reporter with the Boston *Journal*, Charles Coffin, described the chaos:

❝Men fall. . . . They are bleeding, torn, and mangled. . . . The trees are splintered, crushed, and broken, as if smitten by thunderbolts. . . . There is smoke, dust, wild talking, shouting; hissings, howlings, explosions. It is a new, strange, unanticipated experience to the soldiers of both armies, far different from what they thought it would be.❞

—quoted in *Voices of the Civil War*

Mobilizing the Troops

In the first months of the Civil War, President Lincoln was under great pressure to strike quickly against the South. Confederate troops, led by General **P.G.T. Beauregard,** were gathering 25 miles (40 km) south of Washington, D.C., near Manassas Junction, an important railroad center in northern Virginia. Lincoln approved an assault on these forces, hoping that a Union victory would lead to a quick end to the conflict.

NATIONAL GEOGRAPHIC **First Battle of Bull Run, 1861**

Legend:
- ← Confederate advance
- ← Union advance
- ←-- Union retreat
- —— Turnpike
- +++++ Railroad
- ✳ Battle

MARYLAND

Potomac River

DISTRICT OF COLUMBIA

VIRGINIA

LOUDOUN & HAMPSHIRE RAILROAD

LITTLE RIVER TURNPIKE

Bull Run

WARRENTON TURNPIKE

Washington, D.C.
Arlington

Bull Run

Centreville
McDowell

Johnston

ORANGE & ALEXANDRIA RAILROAD

Alexandria

Manassas Junction

Occoquan Creek

0   4 miles
0   4 kilometers
Lambert Equal-Area projection

Geography Skills

1. **Interpreting Maps** Who led the Confederate forces at the First Battle of Bull Run?
2. **Applying Geography Skills** How many miles from Washington, D.C., was the battlefield?

At first, the attack went well for the Union. Its forces slowly pushed the Confederates back from their positions behind a stream called Bull Run. During the fighting, Southern reinforcements from Virginia, led by Thomas J. Jackson moved into the line. As Confederate troops retreated past Jackson, their commander yelled: "There is Jackson standing like a stone wall! Rally behind the Virginians!" Afterward, Jackson became known as **"Stonewall" Jackson,** and he went on to become one of the most effective commanders in the Confederate army.

As Confederate reinforcements arrived, Union commander General **Irwin McDowell** decided to fall back. The retreat quickly turned into a panic, although the exhausted Confederate troops did not pursue the Union forces very far.

The Union defeat at the First Battle of Bull Run made it clear that the North would need a large, well-trained army to defeat the South. Lincoln had originally called for 75,000 men to serve for three months. The day after Bull Run, he signed another bill for the enlistment of 500,000 men for three years.

At first, excitement about the war inspired many Northern and Southern men to enlist, swamping recruitment offices and training camps. As the war

dragged on and casualties rose, however, fewer young men volunteered, forcing both governments to resort to conscription. The South introduced conscription in April 1862 for all white men between the ages of 18 and 35. Exemptions were provided for key government workers, for teachers, and for planters who held at least 20 enslaved African Americans.

The North at first tried to encourage voluntary enlistment by offering a **bounty**—a sum of money given as a bonus—to individuals who promised three years of military service. Congress also passed the **Militia Act** in July 1862, giving Lincoln the authority to call state militias, which included drafted troops, into federal service. Finally, in 1863, Congress introduced a national draft to raise the necessary troops.

✓ Reading Check **Summarizing** What was the significance of the First Battle of Bull Run?

The Naval War

While the Union and Confederacy mobilized their armies, the Union navy began operations against the South. In April 1861, President Lincoln proclaimed a blockade of all Confederate ports. By the spring of 1862, the Union navy had sealed off every major Southern harbor along the Atlantic coast, except for Charleston, South Carolina and Wilmington, North Carolina. Lincoln intended to

Fact | Fiction | Folklore

Same Battles, Different Names Many Civil War battles have two names. The Union usually named battles after the nearest body of water, while the Confederacy usually named them after the nearest settlement. Therefore, the battle known as the Battle of Bull Run (a creek) in the North was known as the Battle of Manassas (a town) in the South. Likewise, the Battle of Antietam was remembered in the South as the Battle of Sharpsburg.

put as much pressure on the South's economy as possible by cutting its trade with the world.

The Blockade Although the Union blockade became increasingly effective as the war dragged on, Union vessels were thinly spread and found it difficult to stop all of the blockade runners—small, fast vessels the South used to smuggle goods past the blockade, usually under cover of night. By using blockade runners, the South could ship at least some of its cotton to Europe in exchange for shoes, rifles, and other supplies. The amount of material that made it through the blockade, however, was much less than the amount that had been shipped before the war.

At the same time, Confederate ships operating out of foreign ports attacked Northern merchant ships at sea. Two of the most famous Confederate raiders were the warships *Alabama* and *Florida*, both of which the Confederacy had built in Britain. The *Alabama* captured 64 ships before a Union warship sank it off the coast of France in 1864. The *Florida* destroyed 38 merchant ships before being captured at a harbor in Brazil.

The damage done by these two ships strained relations between the United States and Great Britain. Union officials did not think Great Britain should have allowed the ships to be built, and they demanded Britain pay damages for the losses the Union suffered.

Farragut Captures New Orleans While the Union navy fought to seal off the Confederacy's Atlantic ports, it also began preparations to seize New Orleans and gain control of the lower Mississippi River. In February 1862, **David G. Farragut** took command of a Union force composed of 42 warships and 15,000 soldiers led by General Benjamin Butler.

At the time, Farragut was 60 years old. He had gone to sea at age 9 and was a veteran of the War of 1812 and the war with Mexico. His father had moved to the United States from Spain in 1776 and had fought in the Revolutionary War and served as governor of the Mississippi Territory. Although born in the South, Farragut was a staunch supporter of the Union.

Farragut's actions at the battle for New Orleans made him a hero in the North. In early April, his fleet began bombarding Confederate forts defending the lower Mississippi River. When the attack failed to destroy the forts, Farragut made a daring decision. At 2:00 A.M. on April 24, 1862, his ships headed upriver past the forts in single file, exposing themselves to attack. The forts opened fire with more than 80 guns, while Confederate gunboats tried to ram the fleet and tugboats placed flaming rafts in front of the Union ships. Remarkably, all but four of Farragut's ships survived the battle and continued upriver.

Ironclads Clash at Sea, March 9, 1862

Southerners hoped to break the Union blockade with a secret weapon—an iron-plated ship built by covering the hull of the wooden ship *Merrimack,* a captured Union warship, with iron. The armored vessel, renamed the *Virginia,* could easily withstand Union cannon fire.

On March 8, 1862, the *Virginia* sank two Union ships guarding the James River at Hampton Roads, Virginia. On the worst day of the war for the Union navy, 240 sailors died. The next day, the Union's own ironclad ship, the newly completed *Monitor,* challenged the *Virginia.* The two ships fought for hours, but neither could deliver a decisive blow. Although the vessels never fought again, the *Monitor's* presence kept the *Virginia* from breaking the Northern blockade.

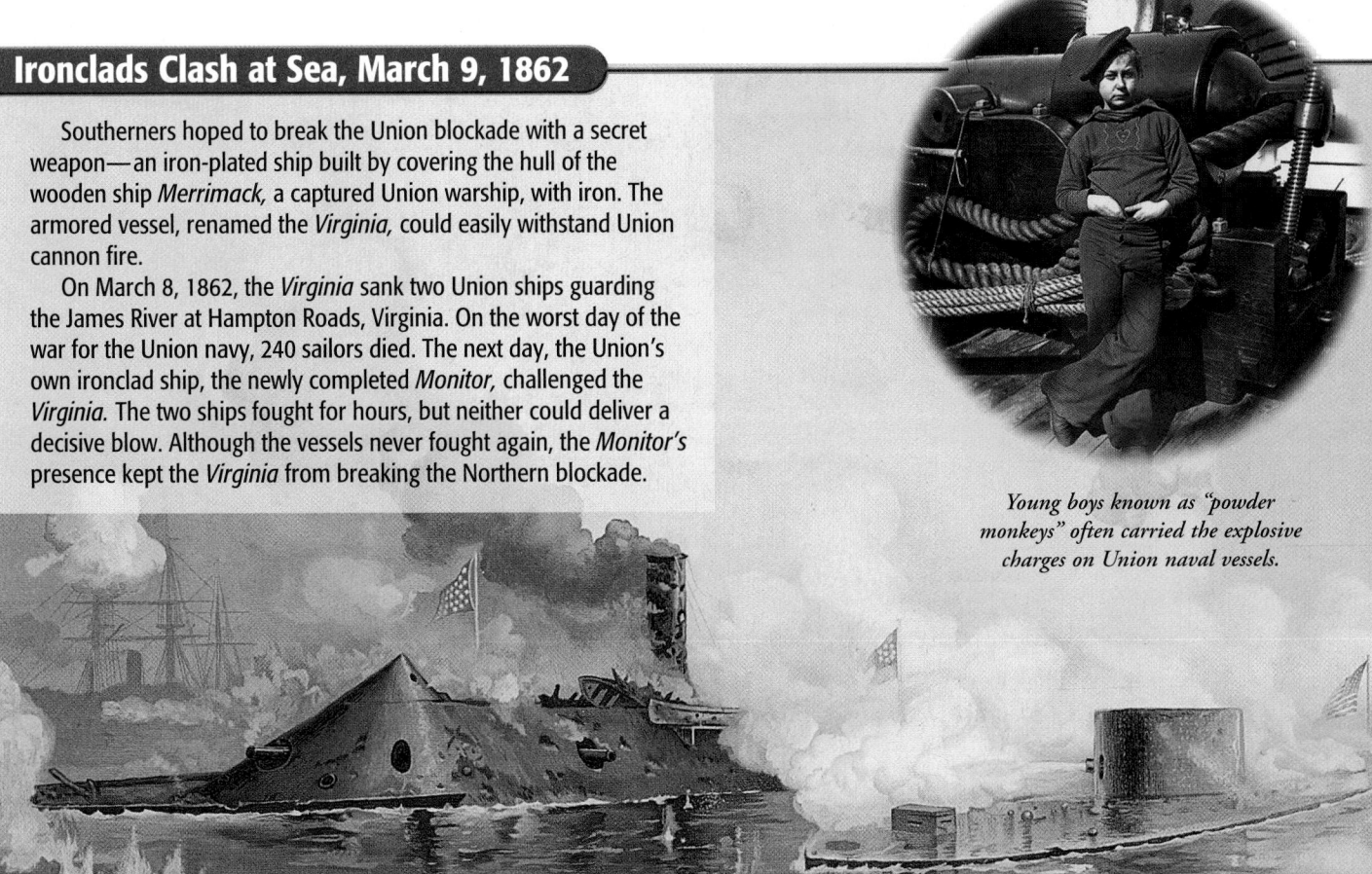

Young boys known as "powder monkeys" often carried the explosive charges on Union naval vessels.

On April 25, 1862, Farragut arrived at New Orleans. Six days later, General Butler's troops took control of the city. The South's largest city, and a center of the cotton trade, was now in Union hands.

✓ **Reading Check** **Explaining** How did the Confederates try to break the Union blockade?

The War in the West

In February 1862, as Farragut prepared for his attack on New Orleans, Union general **Ulysses S. Grant** began a campaign to seize control of two rivers: the Cumberland River, which flowed west past Nashville through Tennessee, and the Tennessee River, which flowed through northern Alabama and western Tennessee. Control of these rivers would cut Tennessee in two and provide the Union with a river route deep into Confederate territory.

Backed by armored gunboats, Grant first seized Fort Henry, the Confederacy's main fort on the Tennessee River. He then marched his troops east and surrounded Fort Donelson on the Cumberland River. With the fall of Fort Donelson and Fort Henry, all of Kentucky and most of western Tennessee came under Union military control.

Shiloh After Grant's victories at Fort Donelson and Fort Henry, his troops headed up the Tennessee River to attack Corinth, Mississippi. Seizing Corinth would cut the Confederacy's only rail line connecting Mississippi and western Tennessee to the east.

Early on April 6, 1862, Confederate forces launched a surprise attack on Grant's troops, who were camped about 20 miles (32 km) north of Corinth near a small church named Shiloh. Hearing the attack, Grant raced from his headquarters to the battle. Although the Union troops were forced back, Grant rushed around the battlefield and managed to assemble a defensive line that held off repeated Southern attacks.

When the first day of the battle ended, several of Grant's commanders advised him to retreat.

NATIONAL GEOGRAPHIC

War in the West, 1862–1863

The "Hornet's Nest" at the Battle of Shiloh

ILL.   IND.   W.VA. 1863

Missouri River   Mississippi River   Ohio River

MO.   KY.

Perryville Oct. 7, 1862

Ft. Donelson Feb. 16, 1862

Ft. Henry Feb. 6, 1862

Murfreesboro

Pea Ridge Mar. 6–8, 1862   Shiloh Apr. 6, 1862   Chattanooga Nov. 23–25, 1863

TENN.

Memphis   Decatur   Chickamauga Sep. 19–20, 1863

Little Rock   Red River

ARK.   Corinth Oct. 4, 1862   GA.

MISS.   ALA.

Dallas   Vicksburg June 26–28, 1862   Montgomery

TEX.   Jackson May 14, 1863

LA.   Mobile

Austin   Sabine Pass Sep. 24–25, 1862   Port Hudson May 21– July 9, 1863   New Orleans   FLA.

Houston

San Antonio   Galveston Oct. 4, 1862   Gulf of Mexico

Laredo

	Union states
	Confederate states
←	Union forces
←	Confederate forces
✸	Union victory
✸	Confederate victory

0   300 miles

0   300 kilometers
Albers Conic Equal-Area projection

90°W   85°W

Geography Skills

1. **Interpreting Maps** Which of the battles listed on the map is the farthest west?

2. **Applying Geography Skills** Most of the battles of this period took place in which state?

Knowing reinforcements were on the way, Grant replied: "Retreat? No. I propose to attack at daylight and whip them." Grant went on the offensive the next morning, surprising the Confederates and forcing General Beauregard, their commander, to order a retreat.

The Battle of Shiloh stunned people in both the North and the South. Twenty thousand troops had been killed or wounded, more than in any other battle up to that point. When newspapers demanded Grant be fired because of the high casualties, Lincoln refused, saying, "I can't spare this man; he fights."

Murfreesboro Grant's victory at Shiloh cheered Lincoln, but it was clear that the fighting was not over. Confederate troops evacuated Corinth and quickly shifted east by railroad to Chattanooga, Tennessee, where they were placed under the command of General **Braxton Bragg.**

Bragg took his troops north into Kentucky, hoping the Union armies would follow. He also hoped that his invasion of Kentucky would lead to an uprising of pro-Confederate supporters in the state. Bragg's invasion failed. Union troops led by General **Don Carlos Buell** stopped Bragg's forces at the battle of Perryville.

After Bragg retreated, General Buell was ordered to seize Chattanooga and cut the railroad lines that passed through the city. Lincoln knew that eastern Tennessee was home to many Union sympathizers, and he wanted the region under Union control. He also knew that by cutting the region's rail lines, he would deprive the Confederacy of "hogs and hominy"—vital supplies of meat and corn that the South needed.

Buell's slow advance across Tennessee frustrated Lincoln, who fired him and replaced him with General **William S. Rosecrans.** As Rosecrans's forces headed south, Bragg's forces attacked them west of the Stones River near Murfreesboro. Although the Union lines fell back before the onslaught, they did not break, and the battle ended inconclusively. Four days later, with Union reinforcements arriving from Nashville, Bragg decided to retreat.

> **Reading Check** **Evaluating** What was the significance of the Battle of Shiloh?

The War in the East

While Union and Confederate troops were struggling for control of Tennessee and the Mississippi River, another major campaign was being waged in the east to capture Richmond, Virginia. After General McDowell's failure at the First Battle of Bull Run, President Lincoln ordered General **George B. McClellan** to lead the Union army in the east.

McClellan's Peninsula Campaign After taking several months to prepare his forces, McClellan began transporting his troops by ship to the mouth of the James River, southeast of Yorktown, Virginia. From there he intended to march up the peninsula formed by the James and York Rivers toward Richmond, only 70 miles (113 km) away.

Although popular with the troops, McClellan proved overly cautious and unwilling to attack unless he had overwhelming strength. He took 30 days to capture Yorktown, giving the Confederates time to move their troops into position near Richmond.

As McClellan advanced toward Richmond, he made another mistake. He allowed his forces to become divided by the Chickahominy River. Seizing this opportunity, the Confederate commander, General **Joseph E. Johnston,** attacked McClellan's

PENNSYLVANIA

76°W

Antietam
Sept. 17, 1862

Gettysburg
July 1–3, 1863

MARYLAND

Frederick

Baltimore

NEW JERSEY

WEST VIRGINIA (1863)

Bull Run

Washington, D.C.

Manassas Junction

DELAWARE

Chesapeake Bay

Bull Run (Second Battle)
Aug. 29–30, 1862

VIRGINIA

Chancellorsville
May 1–3, 1863

Fredericksburg
Dec. 13, 1862

Potomac R.

Rappahannock R.

38°N

N
W—E
S

Richmond
Seven Days
June 25–July 1, 1862

ATLANTIC OCEAN

→ Union forces
→ Confederate forces
✸ Union Victory
✸ Confederate Victory

0   50 miles
0   50 kilometers
Albers Conic Equal-Area projection

Monitor & Virginia
Mar. 9, 1862   Norfolk

Geography Skills

1. **Interpreting Maps** Which battles shown took place outside of Virginia's borders?
2. **Applying Geography Skills** How far apart are the two capital cities of Richmond and Washington, D.C.?

army, inflicting heavy casualties. After Johnston was wounded in the battle, General Robert E. Lee was placed in command.

In late June of 1862, Lee began a series of attacks on McClellan's army that became known collectively as the **Seven Days' Battle.** Although Lee was unable to decisively defeat the Union army, he inflicted heavy casualties and forced McClellan to retreat to the James River. Together the two sides suffered over 30,000 casualties. Despite McClellan's protests, Lincoln ordered him to withdraw from the peninsula and bring his troops back to Washington.

The Second Battle of Bull Run

As McClellan's troops withdrew, Lee decided to attack the Union forces defending Washington. The maneuvers by the two sides led to another battle at Bull Run, near Manassas Junction—the site of the first major battle of the war. Again, the South forced the North to retreat, leaving the Confederate forces only 20 miles (32 km) from Washington. Soon after, word arrived that Lee's forces had crossed into Maryland and begun an invasion of the North.

TURNING POINT

The Battle of Antietam Lee decided to invade Maryland for several reasons. Both he and Jefferson Davis believed that only an invasion would convince the North to accept the South's independence. They also thought that a victory on Northern soil might help the South win recognition from the British and help the Peace Democrats gain control of Congress in the upcoming midterm elections. By heading north, Lee could also feed his troops from Northern farms and draw Union troops out of Virginia during harvest season.

When he learned that McClellan had been sent after him, Lee ordered his troops to congregate near Sharpsburg, Maryland. Meanwhile, McClellan's troops took positions along Antietam (an·TEE·tuhm) Creek, east of Lee. On September 17, 1862, McClellan ordered his troops to attack.

The Battle of Antietam, the bloodiest one-day battle in the war and in American history, ended with over 6,000 men killed and another 16,000 wounded. Although McClellan did not break Lee's lines, he inflicted so many casualties that Lee decided to retreat to Virginia.

The Battle of Antietam was a crucial victory for the Union. The British government had been ready to intervene in the war as a mediator if Lee's invasion had succeeded. It had also begun making plans to recognize the Confederacy in the event the North rejected mediation. Lee's defeat at Antietam changed everything. The British decided once again to wait and see how the war progressed, and with this decision the South lost its best chance at gaining international recognition and support. The South's defeat at Antietam had an even greater political impact in the United States. It convinced Lincoln that the time had come to end slavery in the South.

✓ **Reading Check** **Explaining** Why did President Lincoln choose General George B. McClellan after the Union's failure at the First Battle of Bull Run?

The Emancipation Proclamation

Although most Democrats opposed any move to end slavery, Republicans were divided on the issue. Many Republicans were strong abolitionists, but others, like Lincoln, did not want to endanger the loyalty of the slaveholding border states that had chosen to remain in the Union. The war's primary purpose, in their opinion, was to save the Union.

With Northern casualties rising to staggering levels, however, many Northerners began to agree that slavery had to end, in part to punish the South and in part to make the soldiers' sacrifices worthwhile. George Julian, a Republican from Indiana, summed up the argument for freeing the slaves in an important speech delivered early in 1862:

❝When I say that this rebellion has its source and life in slavery, I only repeat a simple truism. . . . The mere suppression of the rebellion will be an empty mockery of our sufferings and sacrifices, if slavery shall be spared to canker the heart of the nation anew, and repeat its diabolical misdeeds.❞

—quoted in *Battle Cry of Freedom*

As Lee's forces marched toward Antietam, Lincoln said that if the Union could drive those forces from Northern soil, he would issue a proclamation ending slavery.

On September 22, 1862, encouraged by the Union victory at Antietam, Lincoln publicly announced that he would issue the **Emancipation Proclamation**—a decree freeing all enslaved persons in states still in rebellion after January 1, 1863. Because the Proclamation freed enslaved African Americans only in states at war with the Union, it did not address slavery in the border states. Short of a constitutional amendment, however, Lincoln could not end slavery in the border states, nor did he want to endanger their loyalty. 📖 *(See page 1071 for the text of the Emancipation Proclamation.)*

The Proclamation, by its very existence, transformed the conflict over preserving the Union into a war of liberation. "We shout for joy that we live to record this righteous decree," exulted Frederick Douglass. Abolitionists rejoiced at the president's announcement, and they looked forward to new energy among Union forces. "We were no longer merely the soldiers of a political controversy," recalled Union officer Regis de Trobiand. "We were now the missionaries of a great work of redemption, the armed liberators of millions."

✓ **Reading Check** **Examining** Why did Lincoln issue the Emancipation Proclamation?

SECTION 2 ASSESSMENT

Checking for Understanding
1. **Define:** bounty, blockade runner.
2. **Identify:** "Stonewall" Jackson, Irwin McDowell, David G. Farragut, Ulysses S. Grant, George B. McClellan, Emancipation Proclamation.
3. **Summarize** why David G. Farragut was considered a hero in the North.

Reviewing Themes
4. **Geography and History** Why was seizing control of the Mississippi River an important strategy of the Union navy?

Critical Thinking
5. **Forming an Opinion** Do you think the draft for military service during the Civil War violated civil liberties, or was the need for defense more important? Explain your answer.
6. **Organizing** Use a graphic organizer to explain President Lincoln's reasons for issuing the Emancipation Proclamation and the effects it had on the war.

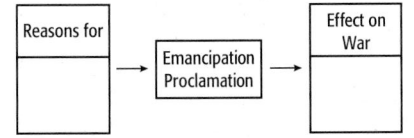

Analyzing Visuals
7. **Examining Art** Examine the painting of the battle between the *Monitor* and the *Virginia* on page 359. What made these vessels superior to regular warships used by the Union and the Confederacy?

Writing About History
8. **Persuasive Writing** Imagine that you are asked to advise President Lincoln about issuing the Emancipation Proclamation. Write a short paper in which you explain the reasons for the advice you give him.

Life During the War

★ *An American Story* ★

In December 1862, as Union and Confederate forces prepared for battle near the Virginia town of Fredericksburg, the civilian residents fled in haste. Confederate artillery operator Robert Stiles remembers seeing women and children evacuating their homes:

❝I never saw a more pitiful procession than they made trudging through the deep snow . . . little children tugging along with their doll babies . . . women so old and feeble that they could carry nothing and could barely hobble themselves. There were women carrying a baby in one arm, and its bottle, its clothes, and its covering in the other. Some had a Bible and a toothbrush in one hand, a picked chicken and a bag of flour in the other.

Most of them had to cross a creek swollen with winter rains, and deadly cold with winter ice and snow. We took the battery horses down and ferried them over, taking one child in front and two behind, and sometimes a woman or a girl on either side with her feet in stirrups, holding on by our shoulders. Where they were going we could not tell, and I doubt if they could.❞

—**quoted in** *Voices of the Civil War*

The Wartime Economies

Pressed by the costs of the war, both North and South struggled to keep their economies working. The South, with few financial resources and little industry, suffered more from wartime inflation and critical shortages. The North, supported by banks and developing industries, responded quickly to the changes brought about by the war.

Southern Shortages, Falling Morale By the end of 1862, the South's economy had begun to suffer from the war. Although many farms had converted from cotton to food crops, the collapse of the South's transportation system and the presence of Union troops in several important agricultural regions led to severe food shortages during the winter of 1862.

The food shortages hurt Southern morale, and people began to question the sacrifices they were being called upon to make—or to demand of others. Hearing of the hardships, many Confederate soldiers deserted and returned home to help their families.

In the spring of 1863, the food shortages led to riots. In several communities, mobs of women armed with knives and guns marched into shops to seize food. In Richmond, several hundred women broke into shops, yelling, "Bread, bread," and then began to loot the stores for food, clothing, shoes, and other goods. The riot finally ended when Jefferson Davis confronted the mob with a company of militia troops and ordered the rioters to disperse.

The Union's War Boom In contrast, the North experienced an economic boom because of the war. Its growing industries supplied the troops at the front with clothes, munitions, and other necessities, while innovations in agriculture helped minimize the loss of labor as men left to fight.

The expanded use of mechanized reapers and mowers made farming possible with fewer workers, many of whom were women. One traveler in Iowa in late 1862 commented that he "met more women driving teams on the road and saw more at work in the fields than men."

Women also filled labor shortages in various industries, particularly in clothing and shoemaking factories. New sewing machines greatly increased the productivity of seamstresses. As women entered the textile industry, the North produced an abundance of clothes for its soldiers, and the industry profited from government contracts.

✓ **Reading Check** **Explaining** What were the effects of food shortages on the South?

TECHNOLOGY & History

The Telegraph

Invented by Samuel Morse in 1837, the telegraph was indispensable during the Civil War. It was used to send battle orders and to verify the locations of troops. With no telegraph in the White House, President Lincoln often visited the War Department's telegraph room to receive current information. Telegraph operators sent messages by pressing a key in a pattern of short and long clicks, following Morse's alphabetic code. *In what other areas of life was the telegraph useful?*

1 The telegraph operator pressed a switch, called the **key**, breaking an electric current.

2 The electric current activated a **sounder**, an electromagnet consisting of coiled wire wrapped around an iron core. The changing electric current created a clicking sound.

3 Skilled operators were able to send up to 60 **messages** each hour, keying a message with one hand while translating incoming messages with the other hand.

4 **Telegraph wires** allowed the clicking codes to be transmitted geographically.

sounder

key

African American Soldiers Battery A of the 2nd U.S. Colored Light Artillery was only one of many groups of African Americans who fought for their own freedom. *Why did Frederick Douglass favor African American enlistment?*

African Americans in the Military

The Emancipation Proclamation officially permitted African Americans to enlist in the Union army and navy. Almost immediately, thousands of African Americans, including Frederick Douglass's two sons, Charles and Lewis, rushed to join the military. Douglass approved of his sons' decision. He believed that serving in the military would help African Americans overcome discrimination:

> ❝Once let the black man get upon his person the brass letters U.S.; let him get an eagle on his button, and a musket on his shoulder and bullets in his pocket, and there is no power on earth which can deny that he has earned the right to citizenship.❞
>
> —quoted in *Battle Cry of Freedom*

About 180,000 African Americans served in the Union army during the Civil War, roughly 9 percent of the army's total soldiers. Another 10,000 to 15,000 served in the Union navy, making up about 10 to 12 percent of the navy's sailors.

Among the first African American regiments officially organized in the North was the **54th Massachusetts.** The regiment fought valiantly at Fort Wagner near Charleston Harbor in July 1863, losing nearly half of its soldiers in the battle. "Men all around me would fall and roll down the slope into the ditch," remembered Lewis Douglass. "Swept down like chaff, still our men went on and on."

At the end of the war, the *New York Tribune* declared that the heroism of the 54th Massachusetts

regiment forever answered the question of whether African Americans could make good soldiers:

> ❝It is not too much to say that if this Massachusetts Fifty-Fourth had faltered when its trial came, two hundred thousand [African Americans] for whom it was a pioneer would never have been put into the field. . . . But it did not falter. It made Fort Wagner such a name to [African Americans] as Bunker Hill has been for ninety years to white Yankees.❞
>
> —from *Like Men of War*

✓ **Reading Check** **Analyzing** Why do you think African Americans were so willing to volunteer to fight during the Civil War?

Military Life

Early in the war, General Irwin McDowell's troops stopped to pick berries and foolishly wasted water from their canteens to wash them. "They were not used to denying themselves much; they were not used to journeys on foot," the Union commander later reflected. Self-denial and long marches would prove to be only one of the harsh lessons of the war.

The Soldiers in the Field Union and Confederate soldiers suffered many hardships during the long days and weeks between battles. Some Southern soldiers had to sleep without blankets and tramp the roads shoeless. Union soldier Elisha Rhodes wrote home that "all that we have to eat is the cattle killed by the way. No bread or salt in the Regiment and I am most starved."

Soldiers learned to gulp down tasteless food. For the Union soldier, meals often consisted of hardtack (a hard biscuit made of wheat flour), potatoes, and beans, flavored at times with dried salt pork (pork fat cured in salty brine). Confederate soldiers had little coffee, and their bread was usually made of cornmeal. Whenever possible, soldiers on both sides supplemented their diet with fruit or vegetables seized or purchased from farms they passed.

Battlefield Medicine When Americans went to war in 1861, most were not prepared for the horrors of battle. "The sights and smells that assailed us were simply indescribable," wrote one Southern soldier. "Corpses were swollen to twice their size, some actually burst asunder. . . . The odors were so deadly that in a short time we all sickened [and] . . . most of us [were] vomiting profusely."

The Civil War produced huge numbers of casualties, and doctors struggled to tend to the wounded. In the mid-1800s, doctors had little understanding of infectious germs. They used the same unsterilized instruments on patient after patient, and, as a result, infection spread quickly in the field hospitals.

Disease was one of the greatest threats facing Civil War soldiers. In many cases, regiments lost half their men to illness before ever going into battle. Crowded together in army camps, drinking from unsanitary water supplies, many soldiers became sick. Smallpox, when it erupted, could be deadly, as could dysentery, typhoid, and pneumonia.

Battlefield physicians also used extreme measures in treating casualties. Faced with appalling wounds, doctors often amputated arms and legs to prevent gangrene and other infections from spreading to other parts of the body. As one military officer, General Carl Schurz, commented:

> 66As a wounded man was lifted on the table, often shrieking with pain . . . the surgeon quickly examined the wound and resolved upon cutting off the wounded limb. Some ether was administered. . . . The surgeon snatched the knife from between his teeth, where it had been while his hands were busy, wiped it rapidly once or twice across his blood-stained apron, and the cutting began. The operation accomplished, the surgeon would look around with a deep sigh, and then—'Next!'99
>
> —quoted in *The Civil War*

The Role of Women in the War

Women helped the war effort at home by managing family farms and businesses. On the battlefield, women made dramatic contributions to the Civil War by serving as nurses to the wounded. Before the Civil War, most army nurses were men. Inspired by the famous British nurse **Florence Nightingale,** American women took on many of the nursing tasks in army hospitals.

In 1861 **Elizabeth Blackwell,** the first female physician in the United States, started the nation's first training program for nurses. Her work led to the creation of the **United States Sanitary Commission,** an organization that provided medical assistance and supplies to army camps and hospitals. Tens of thousands of women volunteered to work for the Commission, raising money to send bandages, medicine, clothing, and food to army camps.

Not all women helping at the front lines were members of the Sanitary Commission. On her own, **Clara Barton** decided to leave her job in a patent office to nurse soldiers on the battlefield. With her face sometimes bluish with gunpowder, Barton fed the sick, bandaged the wounded, and even dug out bullets with her own small knife.

Although Southern women were encouraged to stay at home and support the troops by making bandages and other supplies, many founded small hospitals or braved the horrors of the battlefield. Kate Cumming of Mobile, Alabama, served as a nurse following the Battle of Shiloh. In her diary she vividly described a makeshift hospital:

Picturing **History**

Battlefield Medicine The greatest impact women had on the battlefield was through serving as nurses. Even with their help, disease and infection claimed many thousands of soldiers. What woman laid the groundwork for the United States Sanitary Commission?

Picturing **History**

Female Volunteers Soldiers were not the only ones who experienced the Civil War. Wives, mothers, and sisters protected their homes from bands of soldiers. How else did Southern women experience the effects of the war?

66Nothing that I had ever heard or read had given me the faintest idea of the horrors witnessed here. . . . The men are lying all over the house. . . . The foul air from this mass of human beings at first made me giddy and sick, but I soon got over it. . . .99

—quoted in *Battle Cry of Freedom*

The Civil War was a turning point for the nursing profession in the United States. The courage and energy shown by women also helped to break down the belief that women were weaker than men.

Military Prisons The horrors of the battlefield and danger of disease were not the only hardships endured by soldiers during the Civil War. Prisoners of war—soldiers captured by the enemy in battle—also suffered terribly during the conflict.

Early in the war, the United States and the Confederacy held formal prisoner exchanges. After Lincoln issued the Emancipation Proclamation, however, the Confederacy announced that it would not exchange freed African Americans for Southern white prisoners. Instead, it would either re-enslave or execute all African American troops captured in battle.

In response to the South's treatment of African American troops, Lincoln stopped all prisoner exchanges. As a result, both the North and the South found themselves with large and growing numbers of prisoners of war. Taking care of them proved difficult, especially in the South. While conditions were bad in Northern prisons, the South was not even able to adequately feed their prisoners because of food shortages.

The most infamous prison in the South, **Andersonville** in southwest Georgia, was an open camp with no shade or shelter for its huge population. Exposure, overcrowding, lack of food, and disease killed more than 100 men per day during the sweltering summer of 1864. In all, 13,000 of the 45,000 prisoners sent to Andersonville died in the camp. After the war, **Henry Wirz,** the commandant at Andersonville, became the only person executed for war crimes during the Civil War.

Life in the Union and Confederate armed forces during the Civil War was brutally hard. Both sides, however, were strongly committed to their cause and prepared to endure whatever hardships were necessary to achieve victory.

Reading Check **Summarizing** What medical problems did Union and Confederate soldiers face?

SECTION 3 ASSESSMENT

Checking for Understanding
1. **Define:** hardtack.
2. **Identify:** 54th Massachusetts, Elizabeth Blackwell, United States Sanitary Commission, Clara Barton, Henry Wirz.
3. **State** the two factors that contributed to a food shortage in the South during the Civil War.

Reviewing Themes
4. **Groups and Institutions** How did the Emancipation Proclamation affect African Americans in the military?

Critical Thinking
5. **Analyzing** In what ways do you think the Civil War changed people's opinions about women's capabilities?
6. **Organizing** Complete a graphic organizer like the one below listing the contributions of women during the Civil War.

Women's Contributions to the Civil War

Analyzing Visuals
7. **Examing Photographs** Examine the photographs of battlefield hospitals on page 367. Why did infections spread so easily in hospitals, resulting in numerous deaths?

Writing About History
8. **Descriptive Writing** Imagine that you are a nurse on one of the battlefields during the Civil War. Write a journal entry describing the conditions of the soldiers and your reaction to the situation.

The Turning Point

Main Idea

The tide of the war turned after the North won pivotal battles in the west at Vicksburg and in the east at Gettysburg.

Key Terms and Names

Benjamin Grierson, forage, siege, Ambrose Burnside, Joseph Hooker, George Meade, Pickett's Charge, William Tecumseh Sherman

Reading Strategy

Categorizing As you read about Civil War battles that shaped the war, complete a graphic organizer listing the results of the following battles.

Battle	Results
Vicksburg	
Chancellorsville	
Gettysburg	
Chickamauga Creek	
Missionary Ridge	

Reading Objectives

- **Evaluate** the importance of events at Vicksburg and Gettysburg.
- **Describe** how battles in Tennessee helped turn the war increasingly in favor of the Union.

Section Theme

Geography and History The Union victory at Vicksburg cut the Confederacy into two parts.

Preview of Events

| ♦July 1863 | ♦November 1863 | ♦February 1864 |

July 1–3, 1863
Battle of Gettysburg

July 4, 1863
Vicksburg falls to Grant's soldiers

November 19, 1863
Lincoln delivers Gettysburg Address

November 24–25, 1863
Battle of Chattanooga

February 1864
Grant named general in chief

★ An American Story ★

At Gettysburg, Pennsylvania, in early July of 1863, Samuel Wilkeson, a reporter, sat to write his account of the battle that had raged for three days near the town. As he composed his dispatch, the body of Lieutenant Bayard Wilkeson—his son—lay dead beside him.

Wilkeson recorded the events that destroyed the peace of the Gettysburg countryside. He recalled "the singing of a bird, which had a nest in a peach tree within the tiny yard of the whitewashed cottage" that served as the Union army headquarters:

❝In the midst of its warbling a shell screamed over the house, instantly followed by another and another, and in a moment the air was full of the most complete artillery prelude to an infantry battle that was ever exhibited. Every size and form of shell known to British and to American gunnery shrieked, moaned, whirled, whistled, and wrathfully fluttered over our ground.❞

—quoted in *Eyewitness to History*

Vicksburg Falls

Gettysburg was only one of a series of horrific encounters in 1863. The first battle took place farther west, where a vital part of the Union strategy involved gaining control of the Mississippi River. In April 1862, Admiral David Farragut had captured New Orleans and secured Union control of the Mississippi River delta. Later that year, Grant seized control of the river as far south as Memphis after his victory at Shiloh. If the Union could capture Vicksburg, Mississippi, the last major Confederate stronghold on the river, the North could cut the South in two.

Grierson's Raid The city of Vicksburg was located on the east bank of the Mississippi River. At first Grant tried to approach the city from the north, but the land was too swampy, and the rivers in the area were covered with vegetation and blocked by trees. To get at Vicksburg, Grant decided to move his troops across the Mississippi to the west bank and then march south. Once he was past the city, he intended to cross back to the east bank of the river and attack the city from the south.

To distract the Confederates while he carried out this difficult maneuver, Grant ordered **Benjamin Grierson** to take 1,700 troops on a cavalry raid through Mississippi. Grierson's forces traveled 600 miles (965 km) in two weeks, tearing up railroads, burning depots, and fighting skirmishes. His raid distracted the Confederate forces defending Vicksburg and enabled Grant to move his troops south of the city.

The Siege of Vicksburg After returning to the east bank of the Mississippi, Grant embarked on a daring march east, ordering his troops to live off the country. Foraging— or searching and raiding for food—as they marched, Grant's troops headed east into Mississippi. They captured the town of Jackson before turning back west toward Vicksburg. Grant's troops marched an astonishing 180 miles (290 km) in 17 days, fought 5 battles, and inflicted 7,200 casualties on the Confederates. The march ended by driving the Confederate forces back into their defenses at Vicksburg.

In May 1863, Grant launched two assaults on Vicksburg, but the city's defenders repulsed both attacks and inflicted high casualties. Grant decided that the only way to take the city was to put it under siege—to cut off its food and supplies and bombard the city until its defenders gave up. On July 4, 1863, with his troops starving, the Confederate commander at Vicksburg surrendered. The Union victory had cut the Confederacy in two.

✓ **Reading Check** **Explaining** Why did President Lincoln want the Union army to capture Vicksburg?

The Road to Gettysburg

Shortly after McClellan's victory at Antietam, Lincoln became frustrated with the general. At Antietam, McClellan could have destroyed Lee's army, but he let the Confederates slip away. He then moved so slowly after the battle that Lee was able to recover from his defeat at Antietam and block McClellan's advance on Richmond. On November 7, 1862, Lincoln fired McClellan and gave command of the army to General **Ambrose Burnside.**

Lincoln wanted a general who was not intimidated by Lee's reputation. He urged Burnside to push south into Virginia and destroy Lee's army. Lincoln did not know that the turning point in the east would come not in Virginia, but far to the north in Pennsylvania.

Fredericksburg and Chancellorsville On December 13, 1862, Burnside ordered a series of bloody assaults against Lee's troops entrenched in the hills south of Fredericksburg, Virginia. The Union troops suffered more than 12,000 casualties, more than twice as many as the Confederates. Distressed by the defeat and faced with complaints about Burnside from other officers, Lincoln replaced him with General **Joseph Hooker.**

Hooker devised a plan to get at Lee's troops on the hills near Fredericksburg. First, he left a large part of his army at Fredericksburg to keep Lee's troops from moving. He then took the rest of the army

Picturing **History**

Vicksburg Besieged Union troops used this house as a headquarters during the siege of Vicksburg. Nearby are Union trenches and the opening to a tunnel being dug under Confederate lines. For how long was the city of Vicksburg under siege by Grant's Union forces?

west to circle around behind Lee's troops and attack them from the rear. Realizing what was going on, Lee also divided his forces. He too left a small force at Fredericksburg and headed west with most of his troops to stop Hooker.

On May 2, 1863, Lee's troops attacked Hooker's forces in dense woods known as the Wilderness near the town of Chancellorsville, Virginia. Although outnumbered two to one, Lee aggressively divided his forces and repeatedly defeated the Union troops. On May 5, Hooker decided to retreat.

TURNING POINT

The Battle of Gettysburg Having weakened Union forces at Chancellorsville, Lee wanted to launch another invasion of the North. In June 1863 Lee marched into Pennsylvania, where his troops seized livestock, food, and clothing. After Hooker failed to stop Lee, Lincoln removed him from command and appointed General **George Meade** as his replacement. Meade immediately headed north to intercept Lee.

At the end of June, as Lee's army foraged in the Pennsylvania countryside, some of his troops headed into the town of Gettysburg, hoping to seize a supply of shoes. When they arrived near the town, they encountered Union cavalry. On July 1, 1863, the Confederates pushed the Union troops out of the town into the hills to the south. At the same time, the main forces of both armies hurried to the scene of the fighting. (See pages 374–375.)

On July 2 Lee attacked, but the Union troops held their ground. The following day, Lee ordered nearly 15,000 men under the command of General George E. Pickett and General A.P. Hill to make a massive assault. The attack became known as **Pickett's Charge.** As the mile-wide line of Confederate troops marched across open farmland toward Cemetery Ridge where Union forces stood, Union cannons and guns opened fire, inflicting 7,000 casualties in a less than half an hour of fighting. Soldiers like Lieutenant Jesse Bowman Young, who survived Gettysburg, later recalled the deafening gunfire and horrifying bloodshed of the final assault:

> ❝The caisson [ammunition chest] was set on fire, and in a moment with all its stock of ammunition, it exploded. . . . [T]here flashed for a single instant against the sky the sight of wheels, limbs of horses and of men, pieces of timber, and scores of exploding shells, all inextricably interwoven into a spectacle of horror. . . . Then the smoke covered the scene. . . .❞
> —quoted in *Voices of the Civil War*

Bridging the Rappahannock Union troops build a pontoon bridge across the river in preparation for the assault on Confederate forces at Fredericksburg. The battle was a decisive Southern victory.

Aftermath of the Battle Less than 5,000 Confederate troops made it up the ridge, and Union troops overwhelmed those who did. Lee quickly rallied his troops, withdrew from Gettysburg on a rainy July 4, and retreated to Virginia. At Gettysburg the Union suffered 23,000 casualties, but the South lost an estimated 28,000 troops, over one-third of Lee's entire force.

The disaster at Gettysburg proved to be the turning point of the war. The Union's victory strengthened the Republicans politically and ensured that the British would not recognize the Confederacy. For the rest of the war, Lee's forces remained on the defensive, slowly giving ground to the Union army.

The Gettysburg Address In November 1863, Lincoln came to Gettysburg to dedicate a portion of the battlefield as a military cemetery. His speech—the Gettysburg Address—became one of the best-known orations in American history. Lincoln reminded his listeners that the nation was "conceived in liberty, and dedicated to the proposition that all men are created equal." He explained that the war was not a battle between regions but a fight for freedom:

HISTORY Online

Student Web Activity Visit the *American Vision* Web site at tav.glencoe.com and click on *Student Web Activities— Chapter 11* for an activity on the Civil War.

Profiles IN HISTORY

Ulysses S. Grant
1822–1885

Before his victories in Kentucky and Tennessee, Ulysses S. Grant had been a mediocre West Point cadet, a failed businessperson, and an undistinguished army officer. More than any other Union commander, however, Grant changed the strategy—and the outcome—of the Civil War. Grant's restless urge for offensive fighting and his insistence on "unconditional surrender" at Fort Donelson convinced Lincoln to place the general in command of all the Union troops in 1864. Lincoln's confidence was not misplaced. Despite mounting casualties and accusations that he was a "butcher," Grant pushed relentlessly until he finally accepted Lee's surrender at Appomattox, Virginia.

The Union's enthusiasm for its victorious general made Grant a two-term president after the war, although scandals in his administration marred his reputation. The Civil War had been the high point of Grant's life, the challenge that brought out his best qualities. More than any monument or memorial—including Grant's Tomb, in New York City—Lincoln's defense of his embattled general during the war sums up Grant's character and achievement: "I can't spare this man; he fights."

Robert E. Lee
1807–1870

The son of a distinguished—though not wealthy—Virginia family, Robert E. Lee was raised in the socially exclusive world of the aristocratic South. From the beginning, he seemed marked by fate for brilliant success. At West Point he excelled in both his studies and his social life, impressing teachers and fellow cadets with his talent and good nature. As an army officer in the war with Mexico, he performed with brilliance and courage.

Offered command of the Union troops at the beginning of the Civil War, Lee refused, unable to oppose his fellow Virginians. He later commanded the army of Northern Virginia.

A hero to Southerners during the war, Lee felt a responsibility to set an example of Southern honor in defeat. His swearing of renewed allegiance to the United States after the war inspired thousands of former Confederate soldiers to follow his example. As president of Washington College in Virginia (later renamed Washington and Lee), Lee encouraged his students to put the war behind them and to behave as responsible citizens.

Lee died at age 63. In his last moments, he seemed to give orders to his troops, and then at last called out, "Strike the tent!"

❝It is . . . for us to be here dedicated to the great task remaining before us—that from these honored dead we take increased devotion to that cause for which they gave the last full measure of devotion; that we here highly resolve that these dead shall not have died in vain; that this nation, under God, shall have a new birth of freedom; and that the government of the people, by the people, and for the people, shall not perish from the earth.❞

—from the Gettysburg Address

📖 *(See page 1072 for more information on the Gettysburg Address.)*

✓ **Reading Check** **Summarizing** What was the result of Pickett's Charge?

Grant Secures Tennessee

After the Union's major victories at Vicksburg and Gettysburg, fierce fighting erupted in Tennessee near Chattanooga. Chattanooga was a vital railroad junction. Both sides knew that if the Union forces captured Chattanooga, they would control a major railroad running south to Atlanta. The way would be open for a Union advance into Georgia.

Chickamauga During the summer of 1863, Union general William Rosecrans outmaneuvered General Braxton Bragg. In early September, he forced the Confederates to evacuate Chattanooga without a fight. Bragg did not retreat far, however. When Rosecrans advanced into Georgia, Bragg launched an assault against him at Chickamauga Creek on September 19, 1863. Bragg soon smashed through part of the Union defenses, and Rosecrans ordered his troops to fall back to Chattanooga, where he found himself almost completely surrounded by Bragg's forces.

The Battle of Chattanooga In an effort to save the Union forces in Chattanooga, Lincoln decided to send some of Meade's forces to help Rosecrans. Dozens of trains were assembled, and 11 days later, 20,000 men with their artillery, horses, and equipment arrived near Chattanooga after travelling more than 1,200 miles (1,930 km).

Lincoln also decided to reorganize the military leadership in the west, and he placed Grant in overall command. Grant then hurried to Chattanooga to take charge of the coming battle. In late November, he ordered his troops to attack Confederate positions on Lookout Mountain. Charging uphill through swirling fog, the Union forces quickly drove the Southern troops off the mountain.

Confederates retreating from Lookout Mountain hurried to join the Southern forces at Missionary Ridge east of Chattanooga. The Confederates were outnumbered, but they awaited a Union attack, secure on a high rugged position just as the Union troops had been at Cemetery Ridge near Gettysburg.

Grant did not intend to storm Missionary Ridge. He believed an all-out assault would be suicidal. Instead he ordered General **William Tecumseh Sherman** to attack Confederate positions on the north end of the ridge. When Sherman failed to break through, Grant ordered 23,000 men under General George Thomas to launch a limited attack against the Confederates in front of Missionary Ridge as a diversion.

To Grant's astonishment, Thomas's troops overran the Confederate trenches and charged up the steep slope of Missionary Ridge itself. "They shouted 'Chickamauga,'" one Confederate remembered, "as though the word itself were a weapon." The rapid charge scattered the surprised Confederates, who retreated in panic, leaving Missionary Ridge—and Chattanooga—to the Union army.

Grant Becomes General in Chief By the spring of 1864, Grant had accomplished two crucial objectives for the Union. His capture of Vicksburg had given the Union control of the Mississippi River, while his

World History Connection

Gunpowder

The cannon and rifle fire that echoed throughout the valleys of Tennessee during Grant's campaign had become a familiar sound on the battlefields of the United States and the rest of the world by the mid-1800s. The key ingredient in these powerful weapons was gunpowder. Scholars believe that the Chinese invented this explosive mixture and were using it in fireworks and signals as early as the 900s. In 1304 the Arabs used the powder to develop the first gun. In the centuries that followed, numerous nations would develop and improve on the gun—which made all other weapons before it obsolete. *For what peaceful purposes can gunpowder be used?*

victory at Chattanooga had secured eastern Tennessee and cleared the way for an invasion of Georgia. Lincoln rewarded Grant by appointing him general in chief of the Union forces and promoting him to lieutenant general, a rank no one had held since George Washington. When the president met Grant in March 1864, he told him, "I wish to express my satisfaction with what you have done. . . . The particulars of your plan I neither know nor seek to know." The president had finally found a general he trusted to win the war.

✓ **Reading Check** **Examining** Why was capturing Chattanooga important for the Union?

SECTION 4 ASSESSMENT

Checking for Understanding

1. **Define:** forage, siege.
2. **Identify:** Benjamin Grierson, Ambrose Burnside, Joseph Hooker, George Meade, Pickett's Charge, William Tecumseh Sherman.
3. **Explain** why the Union victory at Gettysburg was so important.

Reviewing Themes

4. **Geography and History** Why was capturing Vicksburg important for the Union?

Critical Thinking

5. **Analyzing** What do you think might have been the outcome of the war if the Confederates had won the Battle of Gettysburg? Why do you think so?
6. **Organizing** Using a graphic organizer similar to the one below, list the results of the Battle of Gettysburg. Make sure you consider both the Union and the Confederacy.

Battle of Gettysburg

Analyzing Visuals

7. **Examining Photographs** Examine the photograph on page 370 of Vicksburg, Mississippi. From looking at the picture, what do you think life was like for troops during a siege? Why do you think the troops were trying to tunnel under Confederate lines?

Writing About History

8. **Descriptive Writing** Take on the role of a Confederate soldier at the Battle of Gettysburg. Write a journal entry describing the battle and your feelings about the result of the battle.

Geography&History

Map labels:

Hanover Road
York Pike
Benner's Hill
Wolf Hill
Johnson
Rock Creek
Culp's Hill
Early
Town of GETTYSBURG
Cemetery Hill
12th Corps SLOCUM 8,700
Army of the Potomac General George G. Meade
Baltimore P
Power's Hill
11th Corps HOWARD 5,800
2nd Corps EWELL 15,000
Cemetery
2nd Corps GIBBON 6,800
Taneytown Road
Ridge
1st Corps NEWTON 6,000
3rd Co BIRN 6,40
Rodes
Pickett's Charge
12,500 3 pm
Plum Run
Seminary Ridge
Pettigrew
Garnett
Anderson
Kemper
Armistead
Lang
Wilcox
Emmitsburg Road
Peach Orchard
3rd Corps HILL 15,200
Trimble
Pickett
Army of Northern Virginia General Robert E. Lee
N E S W
McLaws
1st Corps LONGSTREET 15,500

INVADING THE NORTH

Map labels (inset):
PENNSYLVANIA
Harrisburg
Carlisle
Chambersburg
Gettysburg
York
Frederick
Baltimore
MARYLAND
Washington, D.C.
Winchester
Front Royal
VIRGINIA
Chancellorsville
Fredericksburg

After their victory at Chancellorsville in May 1863, the Confederates invaded the North (red arrow). Using the Blue Ridge Mountains to screen their movements, the Confederates advanced down the Shenandoah Valley, crossed the Potomac River, and pushed into Pennsylvania. The Federal army (purple arrow) placed itself between the Confederates and Washington, D.C. On July 1, the two armies met at the crossroads town of Gettysburg, Pennsylvania.

A nurse poses with wounded soldiers outside one of the 400 tents set up as a temporary hospital at Gettysburg. During the battle, the Union army suffered 23,000 casualties, the Confederates 28,000.

CANNON BOMBARDMENT
Pickett's Charge was preceded by a massive artillery bombardment. However, much of the Confederate artillery overshot the Federal positions on Cemetery Ridge, landing well to the rear of the frontline troops.

11th AC Hospital

Artillery Reserves

5th Corps SYKES 9,500

6th Corps SEDGWICK 13,600

Gettysburg Forces

Union troops

Confederate troops

3rd Corps Corp
HILL Commander
15,200 Number of troops (as of noon, July 3rd)

Scale of map varies in this perspective (distance from Gettysburg to Big Round Top 3 miles)

Little Round Top

Big Round Top

Vheat Field

Devil's Den

Hood

Hood

"It's all my fault. It is I who have lost this fight," Lee told the survivors as they struggled back after Pickett's Charge.

Gettysburg: The Final Day

The Confederate invasion of Union territory in the summer of 1863 was a bold stroke. By moving north, the Confederate commander of the Army of Northern Virginia, General Robert E. Lee, had relieved pressure on battle-ravaged Virginia. He had threatened the Federal capital of Washington, D.C., and gained access to the rich farms and other resources of Pennsylvania. Indeed, it was the prospect of finding shoes and other army supplies that lured the Confederates to Gettysburg.

By the morning of July 3, however, Lee was lamenting lost opportunities. When his troops arrived in Gettysburg on July 1, they had driven the Federals out of the town. Quickly grasping the advantages of defending the high ground, Major General George Meade had ordered his Federal Army of the Potomac to take up positions in the hills south of town. The Federal line stretched from Culp's Hill and Cemetery Hill south along Cemetery Ridge to another hill called Little Round Top. The Confederates had taken up a position along a roughly parallel ridge to the west known as Seminary Ridge. Between the two positions stretched pastureland and fields of wheat. On July 2, Lee's troops had attacked Federal positions on Culp's Hill, Cemetery Hill, and Little Round Top, but they were pushed back. Now, on the morning of July 3, Lee was determined to punch a hole in the Federal line. Among the officers preparing to attack was Major General George Pickett, who would give his name to the day's infantry charge.

At about 3:00 P.M., more than 12,000 Confederates set out from Seminary Ridge. Three-fourths of a mile away, the Federals waited atop Cemetery Ridge. Federal artillery ripped holes in the Confederate line as it advanced. When the Confederates were 200 yards from the crest of Cemetery Ridge, the Federals unleashed volley after volley. Still the Confederates pressed on. Hundreds made it all the way up the slope of the ridge, but as they did, Federal reinforcements rushed in. Firing at point-blank range, stabbing with bayonets, and striking with the ends of rifles, the Federals drove the Confederates back down the slope. Pickett's Charge had been repulsed. Lee retreated to Virginia, and the tide of war turned in favor of the North.

LEARNING FROM GEOGRAPHY

1. How did the Confederate army use the mountains of Virginia in its invasion of the North?

2. Why was the Federal army in such a strong position at Gettysburg?

The War Ends

Main Idea

After four long years of fighting, the Civil War ended in 1865 in victory for the Union.

Key Terms and Names

Philip Sheridan, "Sherman neckties," March to the Sea, pillage, mandate, Thirteenth Amendment, Appomattox Courthouse, John Wilkes Booth

Reading Strategy

Sequencing As your read about the final battles of the war, complete a time line similar to the one below to record the final battles of the Civil War and their results.

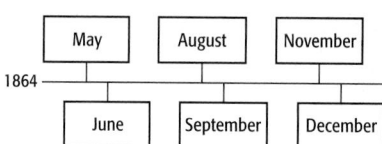

1864 — May | August | November
June | September | December

Reading Objectives

- **Explain** the importance of Union victories in Virginia and the Deep South.
- **Discuss** Lee's surrender and the events of the war's aftermath.

Section Theme

Individual Action In the final year of the Civil War, General Ulysses S. Grant refused to take the pressure off of Lee's weary troops.

Preview of Events

| ♦September 1864 | ♦November 1864 | ♦January 1865 | ♦April 1865 |

September 1864
Fall of Atlanta

November 1864
Lincoln reelected

January 1865
Thirteenth Amendment goes to states for ratification

April 9, 1865
Lee surrenders at Appomattox

April 14, 1865
Lincoln assassinated at Ford's Theater

★ An American Story ★

"Why, here is General Grant," Lincoln called out at a White House reception in March 1864. "Well, this is a great pleasure, I assure you!" As guests applauded, the president reached over and shook Grant's hand. The crowd, as eager for a look at the victorious general as they were to see the president, pressed in on the pair.

At last Grant climbed up on a couch to greet the crowd, who clamored to see him. For an hour, he balanced there, exchanging greetings with his well-wishers. "For once at least," a guest recalled, "the President of the United States was not the chief figure in the picture. The little, scared-looking man who stood on a crimson-covered sofa was the idol of the hour."

—adapted from *The Civil War*

Grant Versus Lee

In the spring of 1864, the most successful general of the Union army faced the most renowned Confederate commander. Grant put his most trusted subordinate, William Sherman, in charge of Union operations in the west, then headed to Washington, D.C., to take command of the Union troops facing Lee.

From the Wilderness to Cold Harbor "Whatever happens, there will be no turning back," Grant promised Lincoln. He was determined to march southward, attacking Lee's forces relentlessly, until the South surrendered.

The first battle of Grant's campaign erupted in the Wilderness, a densely forested area near Fredericksburg, Virginia. The battle lasted two days, continuing even after the woods caught fire, blinding and choking the combatants. Despite suffering heavy casualties,

Grant did not pause. He headed southeast toward Spotsylvania Courthouse. First in terrible heat and then in pouring rain, the two armies battled near Spotsylvania for 11 days, often in bloody hand-to-hand combat that left many traumatized.

Unlike past campaigns in which several weeks of reinforcing and resupplying followed battles, warfare now continued without pause. Savage combat, advances and retreats, and the digging of defensive trenches filled most days and nights. One Union officer noted that the men "had grown thin and haggard. The experience . . . seemed to have added twenty years to their age."

Unable to break Lee's lines at Spotsylvania, Grant headed toward Cold Harbor, a strategic crossroads northeast of Richmond. Convinced that his relentless attacks had weakened and demoralized Lee's troops, Grant decided to launch an all-out assault on Lee's forces at Cold Harbor. The attack cost his army 7,000 casualties, compared to 1,500 for the South. Grant conceded, "I regret this assault more than any one I have ever ordered."

The Siege of Petersburg Stopped by Lee at Cold Harbor, Grant tried another plan similar to the one he had used near Vicksburg. He ordered General **Philip Sheridan** to stage a cavalry raid north and west of Richmond. While Sheridan's troops distracted Lee, Grant headed southeast, crossed the James River, and then turned west toward Petersburg. Capturing Petersburg would cut the only rail line into Richmond.

When the first Union troops reached the outskirts of Petersburg, they paused. The city was defended by miles of barricades 20 feet (7 m) thick. In front of the Confederate trenches were ditches up to 15 feet (4.6 m) deep to slow down attackers. Carefully positioned cannons supported the Confederate lines.

The strength of the defenses the Confederates had erected at Petersburg intimidated the Union troops, who were already exhausted. Realizing a full-scale frontal assault would be suicidal, Grant ordered his troops to put the city under siege.

✓ **Reading Check** **Summarizing** Why did General Grant decide to capture Petersburg?

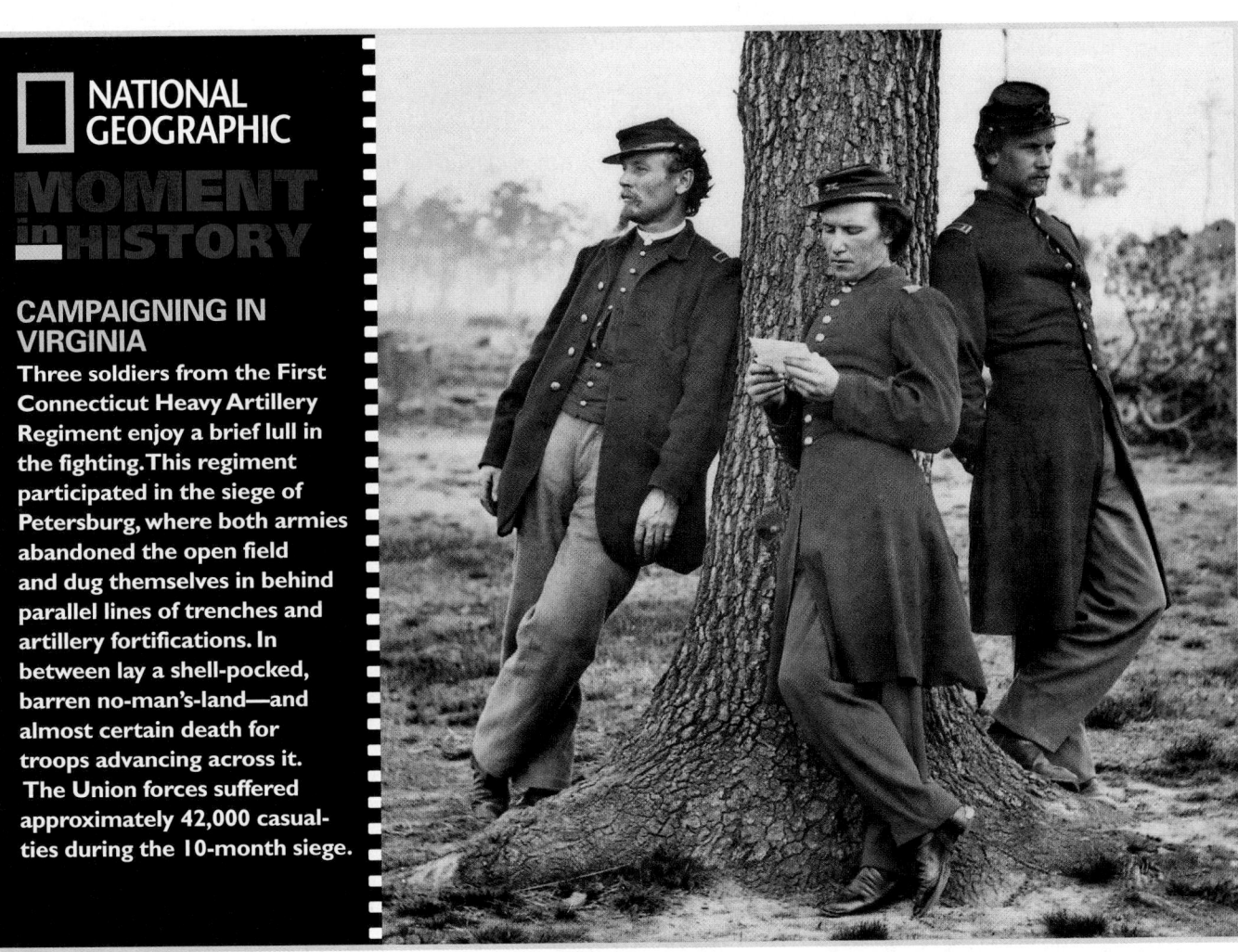

NATIONAL GEOGRAPHIC
MOMENT IN HISTORY

CAMPAIGNING IN VIRGINIA

Three soldiers from the First Connecticut Heavy Artillery Regiment enjoy a brief lull in the fighting. This regiment participated in the siege of Petersburg, where both armies abandoned the open field and dug themselves in behind parallel lines of trenches and artillery fortifications. In between lay a shell-pocked, barren no-man's-land—and almost certain death for troops advancing across it. The Union forces suffered approximately 42,000 casualties during the 10-month siege.

Union Victories in the South

While Grant battled Lee in Virginia, General Sherman marched his army from Chattanooga toward Atlanta. Meanwhile, the Union navy launched an operation to close the port of Mobile, Alabama, the last major Confederate port on the Gulf of Mexico east of the Mississippi.

Farragut Attacks Mobile On August 5, 1864, David Farragut took 18 ships past the three Confederate forts defending Mobile Bay. As the fleet headed into the bay, a mine—which in the 1860s was called a torpedo—blew up a Union ship. The explosion brought the fleet to a halt, right in front of a fort's guns. "Damn the torpedoes! Full speed ahead!" cried Farragut, whose ship led the way through the minefield.

After getting past the Confederate forts, Farragut's ships destroyed a Confederate fleet defending Mobile Bay. Although Farragut did not capture Mobile, he did seal off the bay. Blockade runners moving goods in and out of the Deep South east of the Mississippi could no longer use any port on the Gulf of Mexico.

The Fall of Atlanta While Farragut had been preparing for his attack on Mobile Bay, Sherman's army pushed toward Atlanta. In late August 1864, Sherman sent his troops south around Atlanta to cut the roads and railways leading into the city. His troops destroyed the rail lines by heating the rails and twisting them into snarls of steel nicknamed **"Sherman neckties."** To avoid being trapped in the city, Confederate General John B. Hood evacuated Atlanta on September 1.

NATIONAL GEOGRAPHIC — Final Campaigns of the Civil War, 1864–1865

Casualties of the Civil War, 1861–1865

Troops (in thousands)

North   South

Total Deaths | Battle-Related Deaths | Non-Battle Deaths

Source: *For the Common Defense.*

Burned-out Atlanta railyard after the departure of Sherman's troops

The Costs of War

- Physical destruction of much of the South's rails, roads, farms, and industrial plants
- $6.2 billion spent by the North
- $2.1 billion spent by the South
- Massive inflation: 80% rate in the North; 9,000% rate in the South

American War Deaths
(approximate figures)

Revolutionary War 25,000
War with Mexico 13,000
Korean War 36,500
Other major wars 5,000
Vietnam War 58,000
World War I 107,000
World War II 407,000
Civil War 620,000

Source: United States Civil War Center; *For the Common Defense*

Sherman's March to the Sea After occupying Atlanta, Sherman proposed to march across Georgia. "I could cut a swath to the sea," he explained, "and divide the Confederacy in two." The march would be "a demonstration to the world . . . that we have a power that Davis cannot resist. I can make the march, and make Georgia howl!"

Sherman ordered all civilians to leave Atlanta. He explained to the city's mayor that he was "not only fighting hostile armies, but a hostile people." To end the war, he believed, he had no choice but to "make old and young, rich and poor, feel the hard hand of war." Sherman then ordered his troops to destroy everything in the city of military value, including railroads, warehouses, mills, factories, and machine shops. Sherman's troops set fires to destroy these structures, but the fires quickly spread, burning down more than one-third of the city.

On November 15, 1864, Sherman began his **March to the Sea.** His troops cut a path of destruction through Georgia that was in places 60 miles (97 km) wide. They ransacked houses, burned crops, and killed cattle. By December 21, 1864, they had reached the coast and seized the city of Savannah.

After reaching the sea, Sherman turned north and headed into South Carolina—the state that many people believed had started the Civil War. "The whole army," Sherman wrote, "is burning with an insatiable desire to wreak vengeance upon South Carolina." As one of Sherman's soldiers declared about South Carolina, "Here is where treason began and . . . here is where it shall end."

The troops burned and pillaged, or looted, nearly everything in front of them. At least 12 towns were set on fire, including Columbia, the state capital. The march demoralized Southerners. As one South Carolinian wrote, "All is gloom, despondency and inactivity. Our army is demoralized and the people panic stricken . . . to fight longer seems madness."

✓ **Reading Check** **Examining** Why did General Sherman march his army through Georgia?

The South Surrenders

When Sherman and Grant began their campaigns in the spring of 1864, Lincoln knew that his own reelection depended on their success. By summer, sensing the public's anger over the costly war, Lincoln confided to an army officer, "I am going to be beaten." He did not know that the war was rapidly approaching its conclusion. Only a few months later, the Confederacy was on the verge of collapse.

The Election of 1864 To oppose Lincoln in the 1864 election, the Democrats nominated General George McClellan, whose popularity had remained high despite his dismissal earlier in the war. Playing to the country's growing war weariness, McClellan promised to stop the hostilities and open negotiations with the South to restore the Union peaceably.

The capture of Atlanta came just in time to revitalize Northern support for the war and for Lincoln himself. The president won reelection with 55 percent of the popular vote.

Lincoln interpreted his reelection as a mandate, or clear sign from the voters, to end slavery permanently by amending the Constitution. To get the amendment through Congress, Republicans appealed to Democrats who were against slavery to help them. On January 31, 1865, the **Thirteenth Amendment** to the

Geography *Skills*

1. **Interpreting Maps** How long did the siege of Petersburg last?
2. **Applying Geography Skills** Why did Sherman conduct his march through the South?

Constitution, banning slavery in the United States, narrowly passed the House of Representatives and was sent to the states for ratification.

Surrender Meanwhile, in the trenches near Petersburg, Lee knew that time was running out. On April 1, 1865, Union troops led by Phil Sheridan cut the last rail line into Petersburg at the Battle of Five Forks. The following night, Lee's troops withdrew from their positions near the city and raced west.

Lee's desperate attempt to escape Grant's forces failed when Sheridan's cavalry got ahead of Lee's troops and blocked the road at **Appomattox Courthouse.** When his troops failed to break through, Lee sadly observed, "There is nothing left for me to do but go and see General Grant, and I would rather die a thousand deaths." With his ragged and battered troops surrounded and outnumbered, Lee surrendered to Grant on April 9, 1865.

Grant's generous terms of surrender guaranteed that the United States would not prosecute Confederate soldiers for treason. When Grant agreed to let Confederates take their horses home "to put in a crop to carry themselves and their families through the next winter," Lee thanked him, adding that the kindness would "do much toward conciliating our people." As Lee left, he shook hands with Ely Parker, a Senecan who served as Grant's secretary. "I am glad to see a real American here," Lee told the Native American. Parker replied, "We are all Americans."

Lincoln's Assassination With the war over, Lincoln described his plan to restore the Southern states to the Union, and in the speech he mentioned including African Americans in Southern state governments. One listener, the actor **John Wilkes Booth,** sneered to a friend, "That is the last speech he will ever make."

The president's advisers repeatedly warned him not to appear unescorted in public. Nevertheless, Lincoln went to Ford's Theater with his wife on the evening of April 14, 1865, to see a play. During the third act, Booth slipped quietly behind him and shot the president in the back of the head.

Lincoln's death shocked the nation. Once viewed as a rustic, unsophisticated man not suited for the presidency, Lincoln had become the Union's greatest champion. The usually stern General Grant wept openly as Lincoln's body lay in state at the White House. Tens of thousands of men, women, and children lined railroad tracks across the nation as Lincoln's body was transported back to Springfield, Illinois.

Aftermath of the Civil War The North's victory in the Civil War strengthened the power of the federal government over the states. It also transformed American society by finally ending the enslavement of millions of African Americans. At the same time, it left the South socially and economically devastated.

Following the war, many questions remained unresolved. No one yet knew how to bring the Southern states back into the Union, nor what the status of African Americans would be in Southern society. Americans from the North and the South tried to answer these questions in the years following the Civil War—an era known as Reconstruction.

✔ **Reading Check** **Explaining** Why did President Lincoln doubt he could win the 1864 election?

SECTION 5 ASSESSMENT

Checking for Understanding
1. **Define:** pillage, mandate.
2. **Identify:** Philip Sheridan, "Sherman neckties," March to the Sea, Thirteenth Amendment, Appomattox Courthouse, John Wilkes Booth.
3. **Describe** how General Grant conducted the Confederate surrender.

Reviewing Themes
4. **Individual Action** How did Northern military strategy change after General Ulysses S. Grant took command of the Union army?

Critical Thinking
5. **Evaluating** What was the effect of Farragut's blockade of Mobile Bay?
6. **Organizing** Complete a graphic organizer similar to the one below by listing the purpose for the Union march on Atlanta and the effects of the city's capture on the North and South.

Purpose → Union March on Atlanta → Effects

Analyzing Visuals
7. **Examining Charts** Examine the charts of war deaths on page 378. What would account for the thousands of non-battle deaths listed in one of the charts?

Writing About History
8. **Descriptive Writing** Take on the role of a reporter living in Georgia during General Sherman's March to the Sea. Write a brief article describing the Union's actions and their effects on the people living there.

Technology SKILLBUILDER

Evaluating a Web Site

Why Learn This Skill?

The Internet has become a valuable research tool. It is convenient to use, and the information contained on the Internet is plentiful. However, some Web site information is not necessarily accurate or reliable. When using the Internet as a research tool, you will need to distinguish between quality information and inaccurate or incomplete information.

Learning the Skill

There are a number of issues to consider when evaluating a Web site. Most important is to check the accuracy of the source and content. The author and publisher or sponsor of the site should be clearly indicated, and the user must also determine the usefulness of the site. The information on the site should be current, and the design and organization of the site should be appealing and easy to navigate.

To evaluate a Web site, ask yourself the following questions:

- Are the facts on the site documented?
- Is more than one source used for background information within the site?
- Are the links within the site appropriate and up-to-date?
- Is the author clearly identified?
- Does the site contain links to other useful resources?
- Is the information easy to access? Is it properly labeled?
- Is the design appealing?

Practicing the Skill

Visit the following Web site and answer the questions that follow.

http://sunsite.utk.edu/civil-war/

❶ Who is the author or sponsor of the Web site?

❷ What links does the site contain? Are they appropriate to the topic?

❸ What sources were used for the information contained on the site?

❹ Is the design of the site appealing? Why or why not?

❺ How is the home page organized?

Skills Assessment

Complete the Practicing Skills questions on page 383 and the Chapter 11 Skill Reinforcement Activity to assess your mastery of this skill.

Applying the Skill

Comparing Web Sites Locate two other Web sites about the Civil War. Evaluate them for accuracy and usefulness, and then compare them to the site featured above. Be certain to go through the various links that the site includes so that you can do a thorough evaluation of the site. Share your findings with the class.

GO TO

Glencoe's **Skillbuilder Interactive Workbook, CD-ROM Level 2,** provides instruction and practice in key social studies skills.

Reviewing Key Terms

On a sheet of paper, use each of these terms in a sentence.

1. greenback
2. conscription
3. habeas corpus
4. attrition
5. bounty
6. blockade runner
7. hardtack
8. forage
9. siege
10. pillage
11. mandate

Reviewing Key Facts

12. **Identify:** Robert E. Lee, Copperheads, *Trent* Affair, "Stonewall" Jackson, Ulysses S. Grant, George B. McClellan, Emancipation Proclamation, 54th Massachusetts, Henry Wirz, George Meade, William Tecumseh Sherman, Thirteenth Amendment, John Wilkes Booth.

13. What were the military advantages of the North and South at the start of the Civil War?

14. What effects did the Emancipation Proclamation have on the war?

15. How did the Civil War affect the economies of the North and the South?

Critical Thinking

16. **Analyzing Themes: Civic Rights and Responsibilities** President Lincoln suspended writs of habeas corpus to prevent interference with the draft. Do you think suspending civil liberties is justified in some situations? Why or why not?

17. **Interpreting Primary Sources** At the beginning of the Civil War, Robert E. Lee wrote to his sister, Mrs. Anne Marshall, of his decision to resign from the U.S. Army. Read the excerpt and answer the questions that follow.

Chapter Summary

	1861	1862	1863	1864	1865
Military Campaigns	**July** • The Battle of Bull Run (Manassas) demonstrates that the war will not be over quickly. **September** • Grant leads troops into Kentucky and Missouri.	**March** • Two ironclad ships, the *Monitor* and the *Virginia*, battle to a draw. **April** • The Battle of Shiloh makes General Grant well known. **May** • Union forces capture New Orleans. **September** • The Battle of Antietam marks the bloodiest one-day battle in U.S. history.	**July** • The Battle of Gettysburg turns the tide of war in favor of the Union.	**May** • Grant and Lee battle in the Wilderness and at Spotsylvania. **June** • Grant and Lee battle at Cold Harbor. • The siege of Petersburg begins. **September** • Atlanta falls. **November** • William Sherman begins his destructive March to the Sea.	**April** • Lee surrenders to Grant at Appomattox Courthouse.
Domestic and Foreign Affairs	**April** • Elizabeth Blackwell starts the nation's first training program for nurses. • President Lincoln orders a blockade of all Confederate ports. **November** • The *Trent* Affair increases tension between Great Britain and the United States.	**April** • The South introduces conscription for military service.	**January** • Lincoln's Emancipation Proclamation goes into effect. **April** • Food shortages in the South lead to rioting. **November** • Lincoln delivers the Gettysburg Address.	**March** • Lincoln promotes Ulysses S. Grant to general-in-chief of the Union army. **November** • Lincoln is reelected.	**January** • The Thirteenth Amendment to the Constitution, banning slavery in the United States, passes the House of Representatives. **April** • John Wilkes Booth assassinates Lincoln.

HISTORY Online

Self-Check Quiz

Visit the *American Vision* Web site at tav.glencoe.com and click on *Self-Check Quizzes—Chapter 11* to assess your knowledge of chapter content.

❝My Dear Sister:

. . . With all my devotion to the Union and the feeling of loyalty and duty of an American citizen, I have not been able to make up my mind to raise my hand against my relatives, my children, my home. I have, therefore, resigned my commission in the Army, and, save in defense of my native state . . . I hope I may never be called on to draw my sword. I know you will blame me; but you must think as kindly of me as you can. . . .❞

—from *Personal Reminiscences, Anecdotes, and Letters of General Robert E. Lee*

a. What were Robert E. Lee's feelings about the war?

b. Why did he feel it necessary to resign from the Union army and become commander of the Virginia army?

18. Organizing Complete a graphic organizer similar to the one below by explaining the results of the Civil War on the nation.

Results of Civil War

Practicing Skills

19. Evaluating a Web Site Go through the steps described on page 381 for evaluating a Web site. Then search for Web sites about prisoners of war during the Civil War. Write a report describing the best and worst sites.

Writing Activity

20. Portfolio Writing Write a newspaper article about the surrender of General Robert E. Lee. Write from the perspective of either a Southern or Northern reporter.

Chapter Activity

21. Technology Imagine that you are a travel agent preparing a vacation for a family interested in visiting battle sites of the Civil War and Civil War museums in the United States. Search the Internet to find such sites. Using this information, prepare a brochure on the sites.

NATIONAL GEOGRAPHIC Peninsula Campaign, April–May 1862

— Confederate positions — Union positions
◄‑ ‑ Confederate retreat ◄— Union movements
+++++ Railroad ✳ Union victories

Geography and History

22. The map above shows the Peninsula Campaign of 1862. Study the map and answer the questions below.

a. Interpreting Maps How did McClellan move his troops to the southern end of the peninsula?

b. Applying Geography Skills What disadvantages did both armies face while fighting on the peninsula?

Standardized Test Practice

Directions: Choose the phrase that best completes the statement below.

One advantage the Southern states held during the Civil War was that

F they received military and financial support from the British and the French.

G many battles occurred on lands with which Southerners were more familiar.

H the largest weapons factories were located in the South.

J most people in the country agreed with the position of Southern states.

Test-Taking Tip: When you are not sure of an answer, it can be helpful to use the process of elimination. For example, you probably remember (from Section 1) that the North had a greater population than the South. Therefore, you can eliminate answer J.

CHAPTER 12 Reconstruction
1865–1877

Why It Matters

The nation faced difficult problems after the Civil War. The first issue was how to bring the South back into the Union. Lincoln had wanted to make reunion relatively easy. After he died, Congress designed a plan that focused on punishing the South and ensuring that African Americans had the right to vote. These policies increased hostility between the regions. Pressures on the South to reform eased with the Compromise of 1877.

The Impact Today

The Reconstruction era has permanently affected American society.
- *The Fourteenth and Fifteenth Amendments provide constitutional protections for all Americans.*
- *The Radical Republicans' rule so antagonized the South that the region remained solidly Democratic for nearly a century.*

 The American Vision *Video* The Chapter 12 video, "The Aftermath of War," chronicles the struggles of the nation to heal itself after the Civil War.

1863
- Lincoln's Proclamation of Amnesty and Reconstruction issued

1865
- Freedmen's Bureau founded
- President Lincoln assassinated

1867
- Congress passes the Military Reconstruction Act

1868
- House impeaches President Johnson in February
- Senate acquits the president in May

1870
- Fifteenth Amendment ratified

United States PRESIDENTS

Lincoln 1861–1865

A. Johnson 1865–1869

Grant 1869–1877

1860

1865

1870

World

1866
- Completion of transatlantic cable

1868
- Meiji Restoration begins Japanese modernization

1869
- First ships pass through Suez Canal

Upland Cotton by Winslow Homer shows that even after emancipation, many African Americans continued working long hours in the cotton fields.

1877
• Compromise of 1877 ends Reconstruction efforts

1875
• "Whiskey Ring" scandal breaks

Hayes
1877–1881

1875   *1880*

1871
• Unification of Germany completed; German Empire proclaimed

1874
• First Impressionist art exhibit opens in Paris

HISTORY
Online
Chapter Overview
Visit the *American Vision* Web site at tav.glencoe.com and click on **Chapter Overviews—Chapter 12** to preview chapter information.

Reconstruction Plans

Guide to Reading

Main Idea

In the months after the Civil War, the nation began the effort to rebuild and reunite.

Key Terms and Names

Reconstruction, amnesty, Thaddeus Stevens, Radical Republicans, Wade-Davis Bill, pocket veto, freedmen, Freedmen's Bureau

Reading Strategy

Organizing As you read, complete a graphic organizer similar to the one below to compare plans for readmitting Southern states to the Union.

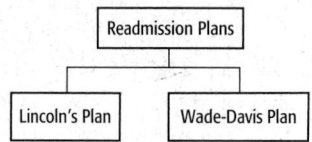

Readmission Plans

Lincoln's Plan   Wade-Davis Plan

Reading Objectives

• **Contrast** Lincoln's plan to reunite the nation with that of the Radical Republicans
• **Discuss** life in the South immediately after the war.

Section Theme

Groups and Institutions Northerners disagreed on which policies would best rebuild the South and safeguard the rights of African Americans.

Preview of Events

♦1863   ♦1864   ♦1865   ♦1866

1863
Lincoln issues Proclamation of Amnesty and Reconstruction

1864
Congress passes Wade-Davis Bill

March 1865
Freedmen's Bureau founded

April 1865
Lincoln assassinated

1866
Congress passes Fourteenth Amendment

★ **An American Story** ★

Houston Holloway was ready for freedom. By 1865 the 20-year-old enslaved man had toiled under three different slaveholders. President Lincoln's Emancipation Proclamation, delivered in 1863, had freed him—but only in theory. The proclamation freed enslaved persons in the Confederacy, but because the Union could not enforce its laws in Confederate territory, many African Americans in the South continued to endure a life of bondage. Holloway knew that his only hope was a Northern victory in the Civil War.

Freedom finally came in the spring of 1865 when Union troops overran his community in Georgia. Holloway rejoiced upon being freed:

❝I felt like a bird out of a cage. Amen. Amen. Amen. I could hardly ask to feel better than I did that day. . . . The week passed off in a blaze of glory.❞

—quoted in *A Short History of Reconstruction*

The Reconstruction Battle Begins

Houston Holloway and millions like him faced freedom in a devastated South. By 1865 large areas of the former Confederacy lay in ruins. A traveler on a railroad journey through the South described the region as a "desolated land," adding, "Every village and station we stopped at presented an array of ruined walls and chimneys standing useless and solitary."

Union troops and cannons had left few Southern cities untouched. Describing Columbia, the capital of South Carolina, a Northern reporter noted, "Two-thirds of the buildings in the place were burned, including . . . everything in the business portion. Not a store, office, or shop escaped."

The devastation had left the South's economy in a state of collapse. The value of land had fallen significantly. Confederate money was worthless. Roughly two-thirds of the transportation system lay in ruins, with dozens of bridges destroyed and miles of railroad twisted and rendered useless.

Most dramatically of all, the emancipation of African Americans had thrown the agricultural system into chaos. Until the South developed a new system to replace enslaved labor, it could not maintain its agricultural output.

The president and Congress grappled with the difficult task of Reconstruction, or rebuilding after the war. They had to decide under what terms and conditions the former Confederate states would rejoin the Union.

Lincoln's Plan

The problem of how to bring the Southern states back into the Union began shortly after the Civil War started. As Union forces advanced into Tennessee, Arkansas, and Louisiana in 1862, President Lincoln appointed military governors for the regions under Union control. He also began developing a plan for restoring a regular government in those states.

Lincoln wanted a moderate policy that would reconcile the South with the Union instead of punishing it for treason. In December 1863, he set forth his plan in the Proclamation of Amnesty and Reconstruction. He offered a general amnesty, or pardon, to all Southerners who took an oath of loyalty to the United States and accepted the Union's proclamations concerning slavery. When 10 percent of a state's voters in the 1860 presidential election had taken this oath, they could organize a new state government.

Thaddeus Stevens

The Radical Republicans

Resistance to Lincoln's plan surfaced at once among the more radical Republicans in Congress. Led by Representative **Thaddeus Stevens** of Pennsylvania and Senator Charles Sumner of Massachusetts, the radicals did not want to reconcile with the South. They wanted, in Stevens's words, to "revolutionize Southern institutions, habits, and manners."

The **Radical Republicans** had three main goals. First, they wanted to prevent the leaders of the Confederacy from returning to power after the war. Second, they wanted the Republican Party to become a powerful institution in the South. Third, they wanted the federal government to help African Americans achieve political equality by guaranteeing their right to vote in the South.

Congressional Republicans knew that once the South was restored to the Union, it would gain about 15 seats in the House of Representatives. Before the Civil War, the number of Southern seats in the House was based on the Three-Fifths Compromise in the Constitution. According to this compromise, each enslaved person counted as only three-fifths of a free person. The abolition of slavery entitled the South to more seats in the House of

Picturing History

War-Shattered City The Civil War wreaked terrible devastation on Richmond, Virginia. Why do you think the women pictured here are dressed in black?

NATIONAL GEOGRAPHIC

MOMENT in HISTORY

WINDS OF CHANGE
Two formerly enslaved women in the rural, postwar South share a treasure that was once forbidden to them—a book. Before the Civil War, it was illegal in some states to teach an enslaved person to read and write. Despite the well-intentioned efforts of some federal officials during Reconstruction, the education of African Americans continued to be an issue after the war. In 1865 only about 10 percent of African Americans could read. By 1880 more than 25 percent were considered literate and around 40 percent of African American children were enrolled in school.

Representatives. This would endanger Republican control of Congress, unless Republicans could find a way to protect African Americans' voting rights.

Although Radical Republicans knew that giving African Americans in the South the right to vote would help their party win elections, most were not acting cynically. Many had been abolitionists before the Civil War and had pushed Lincoln into making emancipation a goal of the war. They believed in a right to political equality for all Americans, regardless of their race. Senator Henry Wilson of Massachusetts summarized their position by saying:

> ❝[Congress] must see to it that the man made free by the Constitution is a freeman indeed; that he can go where he pleases, work when and for whom he pleases . . . go into schools and educate himself and his children; that the rights and guarantees of the common law are his, and that he walks the earth proud and erect in the conscious dignity of a free man. ❞

The Wade-Davis Bill Caught between Lincoln and the Radical Republicans was a large number of moderate Republicans. The moderates thought Lincoln was being too lenient, but they also thought the radicals were going too far in their support for African Americans.

By the summer of 1864, the moderates and radicals had come up with a Reconstruction plan that they could both support as an alternative to Lincoln's and introduced it in Congress as the **Wade-Davis Bill.** This bill required the majority of the adult white men in a former Confederate state to take an oath of allegiance to the Union. The state could then hold a constitutional convention to create a new state government. Each state's convention would then have to abolish slavery, reject all debts the state had acquired as part of the Confederacy, and deprive all former Confederate government officials and military officers of the right to vote or hold office.

Although Congress passed the Wade-Davis Bill, Lincoln blocked it with a pocket veto, that is, he let the session of Congress expire without signing the legislation. Although Lincoln sympathized with some of the radical goals, he felt that imposing a harsh peace would be counterproductive. The president wanted "no persecution, no bloody work."

✓ **Reading Check** **Summarizing** Why did President Lincoln favor a generous policy toward the South after the end of the Civil War?

The Freedmen's Bureau

Lincoln realized that harsh Reconstruction terms would only alienate many whites in the South. Also, the South was already in chaos. The devastation of the war and the collapse of the economy left hundreds of thousands of people unemployed, homeless, and hungry. At the same time, the victorious Union armies had to contend with the large numbers of African Americans who flocked to Union lines as the war progressed. As Sherman marched through Georgia and South Carolina, thousands of freed African Americans—now known as freedmen—began following his troops seeking food and shelter.

To help the freed people feed themselves, Sherman reserved all abandoned plantation land within 30 miles of the coast from Charleston, South Carolina, to Jacksonville, Florida, for use by freed African Americans. Over the next few months, Union troops settled more than 40,000 African Americans on roughly half a million acres of land in South Carolina and Georgia.

The refugee crisis prompted Congress to establish the Bureau of Refugees, Freedmen, and Abandoned Lands—better known as the **Freedmen's Bureau.**

The Bureau was given the task of feeding and clothing war refugees in the South using surplus army supplies. Beginning in September 1865, the Bureau issued nearly 30,000 rations a day for the next year. It helped prevent mass starvation in the South.

The Bureau also helped formerly enslaved people find work on plantations. It negotiated labor contracts with planters, specifying the amount of pay workers would receive and the number of hours they had to work. It also established special courts to deal with grievances between workers and planters.

Although many Northerners backed the Bureau, some argued that those who were formerly enslaved should be given "forty acres and a mule" to support themselves. These people urged the federal government to seize Confederate land and distribute it to emancipated African Americans. To others, however, taking land from plantation owners violated individual property rights. Ultimately, Congress rejected land confiscation.

The Freedmen's Bureau made a lasting and important contribution in the field of education. The Bureau worked closely with Northern charities to educate formerly enslaved African Americans. It also provided housing for schools, paid teachers, and helped to establish colleges for training African American teachers.

Many freed African Americans served in the U.S. Cavalry in units formed after 1866. Most were stationed in the southwestern United States, where they become known as "buffalo soldiers."

✓ **Reading Check** **Explaining** What were the purposes of the Freedmen's Bureau?

SECTION 1 ASSESSMENT

Checking for Understanding

1. **Define:** Reconstruction, amnesty, pocket veto, freedmen.
2. **Identify:** Thaddeus Stevens, Radical Republicans, Wade-Davis Bill, Freedmen's Bureau.
3. **Explain** why the efforts to provide African Americans with their own land failed.

Reviewing Themes

4. **Groups and Institutions** What services did the Freedmen's Bureau provide to Southern refugees and to newly freed people?

Critical Thinking

5. **Analyzing** What are the benefits of a compromise such as the Wade-Davis Bill to a government? What are the drawbacks?
6. **Categorizing** Use a graphic organizer similar to the one below to list the effects of the Civil War on the South.

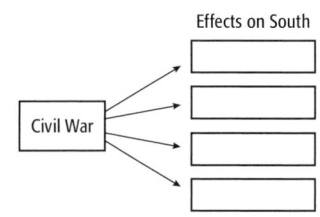

Effects on South

Civil War

Analyzing Visuals

7. **Examining Photographs** Study the National Geographic photograph of formerly enslaved women on the previous page. How would you describe the women's environment? Do you think there were other books in the house?

Writing About History

8. **Descriptive Writing** Take on the role of a Southerner after the Civil War. Write a journal entry describing the postwar South and what you hope the future will hold for the South.

Interpreting Political Cartoons

Why Learn This Skill?

Do you enjoy reading the comics section in the newspaper? Many people enjoy reading comic strips. Cartoons also appear on the editorial page. These cartoons express opinions on political issues. Political cartoons are good sources of historical information because they reflect opinions on current events.

Learning the Skill

Political cartoonists rely mostly on images to communicate a message. By using *caricatures* and *symbols,* political cartoonists help readers see relationships and draw conclusions about events. A caricature exaggerates a detail, such as a subject's features, in a drawing. Cartoonists use caricature to create a positive or negative impression of a subject. For example, if a cartoon shows one figure three times larger than another, it implies that the larger figure is more powerful than the smaller one or perhaps is a bully.

A symbol is an image or object that represents something else. For example, a cartoonist may use a crown to represent a monarch. Symbols often represent nations or political parties. The bald eagle and Uncle Sam are common symbols for the United States, a bear often stands for Russia, and a dragon might be used to represent China.

To analyze a political cartoon, first identify the topic and main characters. Then read labels and messages and note relationships between the figures and symbols. Review your knowledge of the cartoon's topic to determine the cartoonist's viewpoint and message.

Practicing the Skill

The political cartoon on this page, published in an 1872 newspaper, makes a statement about the Reconstruction years. After the Civil War, Southerners gave the nickname "carpetbaggers" to Northerners who moved South. Southerners claimed Northerners came with nothing but a small bag made from carpet fabric, ready to gain wealth at Southerners' expense. Study the cartoon, and then answer the following questions.

❶ The figure at the top is President Ulysses S. Grant. What symbols are surrounding him? What do these symbols represent? Why do you think Grant is placed among them?

❷ In what symbol is Grant sitting? What might this object represent?

❸ What symbols depict the North? How are they shown? What does this imply about the North's feelings about Reconstruction?

❹ Summarize the cartoonist's opinion of Reconstruction and explain why you agree or disagree with this point of view.

Skills Assessment

Complete the Practicing Skills questions on page 409 and the Chapter 12 Skill Reinforcement Activity to assess your mastery of this skill.

Applying the Skill

Interpreting Political Cartoons Find a political cartoon in a newspaper or magazine. If an editorial appears with the cartoon, read that as well. Write a summary of the cartoon's message and explain whether or not you agree with this message.

Glencoe's **Skillbuilder Interactive Workbook CD-ROM, Level 2,** provides instruction and practice in key social studies skills.

Congressional Reconstruction

Guide to Reading

Main Idea
Dissatisfied with the president's lenient policies toward the South, Congress seized control of Reconstruction.

Key Terms and Names
black codes, Civil Rights Act, Fourteenth Amendment, Military Reconstruction Act, Tenure of Office Act, impeach

Reading Strategy
Categorizing As you read about Reconstruction, complete a graphic organizer like the one below to show how each piece of legislation listed affected African Americans.

Legislation	Effect
black codes	
Civil Rights Act of 1866	
Fourteenth Amendment	
Fifteenth Amendment	

Reading Objectives
- **Analyze** the Reconstruction dispute between President Johnson and Congress.
- **Describe** the major features of congressional Reconstruction.

Section Theme
Civic Rights and Responsibilities Congressional Reconstruction promoted civil rights for formerly enslaved persons.

Preview of Events

♦1866   ♦1868   ♦1870

1866
Congress passes Fourteenth Amendment

1867
Congress passes Reconstruction Act

1868
House impeaches President Johnson; Senate acquits Johnson

1870
States ratify Fifteenth Amendment

★ An American Story ★

Tensions ran high in the nation's capital as Congress reconvened in December 1865. President Andrew Johnson had implemented his Reconstruction plan, which was lenient toward the South, despite strong opposition by many members of Congress. One of the more vocal critics was Massachusetts senator Charles Sumner. Sumner advocated greater rights for formerly enslaved people and stronger punishment for the South. Just days before Christmas, Sumner expressed his distrust of the former Confederate states:

❝They will continue to assert the inferiority of the African, and they would today, if possible, precipitate the United States into a foreign war, believing that they could then reassert and obtain their independence. . . . On the whole, looking at the affair from all sides, it amounts to just this: If the Northern people are content to be ruled over by the Southerners, they will continue in the Union, if not, the first chance they get they will rise again.❞

—quoted in *Charles Sumner*

Johnson Takes Office

Lincoln's assassination dramatically changed the politics of Reconstruction. Lincoln's vice president, Andrew Johnson, now became president. Johnson had been a Democrat living in Tennessee before the Civil War. He had served as a mayor and state legislator before being elected to the United States Senate. When Tennessee seceded from the

Why It Matters

The Fourteenth Amendment

Key provisions of the Fourteenth Amendment (1868) made all persons born in the United States citizens of both the nation and the state where they resided. States were prohibited from abridging the rights of citizenship or depriving persons of due process and equal protection of the law. The Supreme Court has often cited the Fourteenth Amendment when reviewing whether state or federal laws and actions violate the Constitution. The Court continues to do so today.

1954
In *Brown* v. *Board of Education,* the Court found that segregated education denied minority school-children like Linda Brown (far left) the equal protection of the laws provided by the Fourteenth Amendment. This decision partially reversed *Plessy* v. *Ferguson.*

Testing the Fourteenth Amendment

◆ *1896*   ◆ *1954*

1896
In *Plessy* v. *Ferguson,* the Supreme Court decided that Jim Crow laws—state-mandated segregation of public facilities such as railroad cars—did not violate the Fourteenth Amendment. The Court ruled that separate facilities could be equal and allowed segregation to continue.

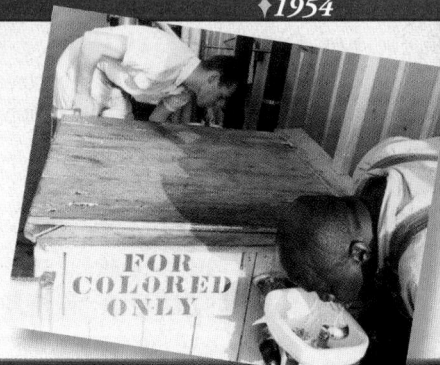

Union, Johnson remained loyal and stayed in the Senate, making him a hero in the North.

As Union troops advanced into Tennessee in 1862, Lincoln appointed Johnson military governor of the state. The president then approved Johnson's nomination as vice president in 1864, hoping to convince some Democrats to vote for the Republicans. Johnson was hot-tempered and stubborn at times, but, like Lincoln, he believed that a moderate policy was needed to bring the South back into the Union and to win Southern loyalty.

Johnson's Plan In the summer of 1865, with Congress in recess, Johnson began to implement what he called his restoration program, which closely resembled Lincoln's plan. In late May 1865, he issued a new Proclamation of Amnesty to supplement the one Lincoln had issued earlier. Johnson offered to pardon all former citizens of the Confederacy who took an oath of loyalty to the Union and to return their property. He excluded from the pardon former Confederate officers and officials as well as all former Confederates who owned property worth more than $20,000. These were the people—the rich planter elite—who Johnson believed had caused the Civil War. Those who were excluded could apply to the president individually for a pardon for their acts during the war.

On the same day he issued the Proclamation of Amnesty, Johnson issued another proclamation for North Carolina. This became a model of how he wanted to restore the South to the Union. Under it, each former Confederate state had to call a constitutional convention to revoke its ordinance of secession and ratify the Thirteenth Amendment. The conventions also had to reject all Civil War debts.

The former Confederate states, for the most part, met Johnson's conditions. While the Southern states organized their new governments and elected people to Congress, Johnson began granting pardons to thousands of Southerners.

By the time Congress gathered for its next session in December 1865, Johnson's plan was well underway. Many members of Congress were astonished and angered when they realized that Southern voters had elected to Congress many former Confederate officers and political leaders, including Alexander Stephens, the former vice president of the Confederacy. Many Radical and moderate Republicans found this unacceptable and voted to reject the new Southern members of Congress.

Black Codes The election of former Confederates to Congress was not the only development that angered congressional Republicans. The new Southern state legislatures also passed a series of

1963

In *Gideon* v. *Wainright,* the Supreme Court ruled that the state of Florida had violated the due process clause when it refused to appoint a lawyer to represent Clarence Gideon (right). The ruling extended the Bill of Rights to state courts.

♦1963   ♦2000

2000

In the disputed presidential race between George W. Bush and Al Gore, the Supreme Court decided a crucial case based on the Fourteenth Amendment. Justices argued that a lack of uniform standards for hand recounts of ballots in Florida would violate the equal protection of all the state's voters. The decision allowed Bush to claim a controversial victory.

laws known as black codes, which severely limited African Americans' rights in the South.

The black codes varied from state to state, but they all seemed intended to keep African Americans in a condition similar to slavery. African Americans were generally required to enter into annual labor contracts. African American children had to accept apprenticeships in some states and could be whipped or beaten while serving in these apprenticeships. Several state codes set specific work hours for African Americans and required them to get licenses to work in nonagricultural jobs.

The black codes enraged many Northerners. Gideon Welles, the secretary of the navy, warned, "The entire South seem to be stupid and vindictive, know not their friends, and are pursuing just the course which their opponents, the Radicals, desire."

Reading Check **Summarizing** Who did President Johnson blame for the Civil War?

Radical Republicans Take Control

The election of former Confederates to office and the introduction of the black codes convinced many moderate Republicans to join the Radicals in opposing Johnson's Reconstruction policies. In late 1865, House and Senate Republicans created the Joint Committee on Reconstruction. Their goal was to develop their own program for rebuilding the Union.

The Fourteenth Amendment In March 1866, in an effort to override the black codes, Congress passed the **Civil Rights Act** of 1866. The act granted citizenship to all persons born in the United States except Native Americans. It allowed African Americans to own property and stated that they were to be treated equally in court. It also gave the federal government the power to sue people who violated those rights.

Fearing that the Civil Rights Act might be overturned in court, the Republicans introduced the **Fourteenth Amendment** to the Constitution. This amendment granted citizenship to all persons born or naturalized in the United States and declared that no state could deprive any person of life, liberty, or property "without due process of law." It also declared that no state could deny any person "equal protection of the laws."

Increasing violence in the South convinced moderate Republicans to support the amendment. The most dramatic incident occurred in Memphis, Tennessee, in May 1866. White mobs killed 46 African Americans, and burned hundreds of black homes, churches, and schools. Congress passed the amendment in June 1866 and sent it to the states for ratification.

The Election of 1866 President Johnson attacked the Fourteenth Amendment and made it the major issue of the 1866 congressional elections. He hoped Northern voters would turn against the Radical Republicans and elect a new majority in Congress that would support his plan for Reconstruction.

As the election campaign got under way, more violence erupted in the South. In July 1866, a white mob attacked delegates to a convention in New Orleans supporting voting rights for African Americans. As Johnson attacked Radical Republicans, Republicans responded by accusing Democrats of being traitors and starting the Civil War. When the votes were counted, the Republicans achieved an overwhelming victory, winning an approximate three-to-one majority in Congress.

HISTORY Online

Student Web Activity Visit the *American Vision* Web site at tav.glencoe.com and click on *Student Web Activities— Chapter 12* for an activity on Reconstruction.

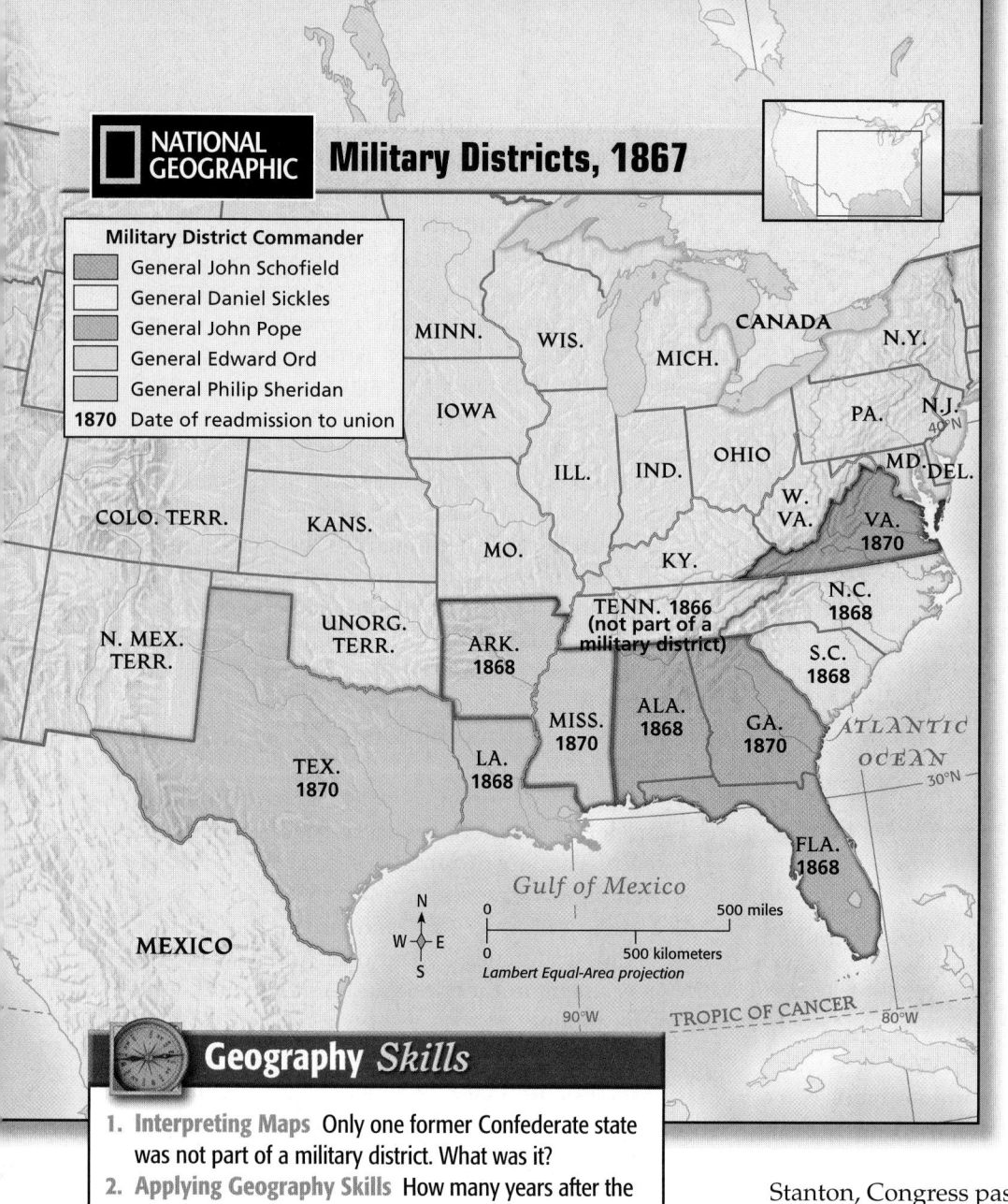

NATIONAL GEOGRAPHIC Military Districts, 1867

Military District Commander

- General John Schofield
- General Daniel Sickles
- General John Pope
- General Edward Ord
- General Philip Sheridan

1870 Date of readmission to union

CANADA

MINN. WIS. MICH. N.Y.

IOWA PA. N.J. 40°N

ILL. IND. OHIO MD. DEL.

COLO. TERR. KANS. W. VA. VA. **1870**

MO. KY.

N. MEX. TERR. UNORG. TERR. ARK. **1868** TENN. 1866 (not part of a military district) N.C. **1868**

S.C. **1868**

MISS. **1870** ALA. **1868** GA. **1870** ATLANTIC OCEAN 30°N

TEX. **1870** LA. **1868**

FLA. **1868**

MEXICO

Gulf of Mexico

N W E S

0   500 miles
0   500 kilometers
Lambert Equal-Area projection

90°W TROPIC OF CANCER 80°W

Geography *Skills*

1. **Interpreting Maps** Only one former Confederate state was not part of a military district. What was it?
2. **Applying Geography Skills** How many years after the war was the last Southern state readmitted to the Union?

Military Reconstruction In March 1867, Congressional Republicans passed the **Military Reconstruction Act,** which essentially wiped out Johnson's programs. The act divided the former Confederacy, except for Tennessee—which had ratified the Fourteenth Amendment in 1866—into five military districts. A Union general was placed in charge of each district.

In the meantime, each former Confederate state had to hold another constitutional convention to design a constitution acceptable to Congress. The new state constitutions had to give the right to vote to all adult male citizens, regardless of their race. After a state had ratified its new constitution, it had to ratify the Fourteenth Amendment before it would be allowed to elect people to Congress.

With military officers supervising the registration of voters, the Southern states began holding elections and organizing constitutional conventions. By the end of 1868, six former Confederate states—North Carolina, South Carolina, Florida, Alabama, Louisiana, and Arkansas—had met all of the requirements and were readmitted to the Union.

Impeachment The Republicans knew they had the votes to override any veto of their policies, but they also knew that President Johnson could still interfere with their plans by refusing to enforce the laws they passed. Although they distrusted Johnson, Republicans in Congress knew that Secretary of War Edwin M. Stanton agreed with their program and would enforce it. They also trusted General Ulysses S. Grant, the head of the army, to support the policies of Congress.

To prevent Johnson from bypassing Grant or firing Stanton, Congress passed the Command of the Army Act and the **Tenure of Office Act.** The Command of the Army Act required all orders from the president to go through the headquarters of the general of the army—Grant's headquarters. The Tenure of Office Act required the Senate to approve the removal of any government official, including Stanton, whose appointment had required the Senate's consent.

Determined to challenge the Tenure of Office Act, Johnson fired Stanton on February 21, 1868. Stanton barricaded himself inside his office and refused to leave. Three days later, the House of Representatives voted to impeach Johnson, meaning that they charged him with "high crimes and misdemeanors" in office. The main charge against Johnson was that he had broken the law by refusing to uphold the Tenure of Office Act. Also, because Johnson had removed four commanders in the Southern military districts who supported the Republicans, the House charged him with attempting to undermine the Reconstruction program.

As provided in the Constitution, the Senate then put the president on trial. If two-thirds of the senators found the president guilty, he would be removed from office. For more than two months the Senate debated the president's fate. On May 16, 1868, the Senate voted 35 to 19 that Johnson was guilty of high crimes and misdemeanors—just one vote short of what was needed for conviction. Seven Republican senators joined with the Democrats in refusing to convict Johnson. These senators believed that it would set a dangerous precedent to impeach a president simply because he did not agree with congressional policies.

The Election of 1868 Although Johnson remained in office, the impeachment stripped him of what little power he had left. Demoralized, he finished his term quietly and did not run for election in 1868. The logical candidate for the Republicans was General Grant, the most popular war hero in the North. In 1868 the Republican convention unanimously nominated Grant to run for president.

During the campaign, ongoing violence in the South convinced many Northern voters that the South could not be trusted to reorganize its state governments without military supervision. At the same time, the presence of Union troops in the South enabled African Americans to vote in large numbers. As a result, Grant won six Southern states and most of the Northern states. The Republicans retained large majorities in both houses of Congress.

The Fifteenth Amendment With their majority securely established and a trusted president in office, congressional Republicans moved rapidly to continue

| Fact | Fiction | Folklore |

Expanding the Nation An important diplomatic achievement during President Andrew Johnson's administration was the purchase of Alaska in 1867. Secretary of State William H. Seward orchestrated the deal, buying the vast expanse of wilderness from Russia for $7.2 million. Initially, the public ridiculed the purchase. Critics labeled the newly acquired territory "Seward's Icebox." Eventually, Americans recognized the value of the region, which turned out to be rich in such resources as oil and gold.

their Reconstruction program. Recognizing the importance of African American suffrage, the Republican-led Congress passed the **Fifteenth Amendment** to the Constitution. This amendment declared that the right to vote "shall not be denied . . . on account of race, color, or previous condition of servitude." By March 1870, enough states had ratified the amendment to make it part of the Constitution.

Radical Reconstruction had a dramatic impact on the South, particularly in the short term. It changed Southern politics by bringing hundreds of thousands of African Americans into the political process for the first time. It also began to change Southern society. As it did so, it angered many white Southerners, who began to fight back against the federal government's policies.

Reading Check **Identifying** What two laws did the Radical Republicans pass to reduce presidential power?

SECTION 2 ASSESSMENT

Checking for Understanding

1. **Define:** black codes, impeach.
2. **Identify:** Civil Rights Act, Fourteenth Amendment, Military Reconstruction Act, Tenure of Office Act.
3. **Evaluate** why the congressional election of 1866 was significant to the Radical Republicans.

Reviewing Themes

4. **Civic Rights and Responsibilities** What actions by the Radical Republicans were intended to protect the civil rights of African Americans?

Critical Thinking

5. **Evaluating** Do you think Presidents Lincoln and Johnson were wise in not seeking harsh treatment of the Southern states? Why or why not?
6. **Taking Notes** Use an outline similar to the one below to list the major events of congressional Reconstruction.

   I. Johnson Takes Office
      A.
      B.
      C.
   II.
      A.
      B.
      C.

Analyzing Visuals

7. **Analyzing Maps** Study the map of Military Districts on page 394. Then list the Confederate states that were readmitted to the Union in 1868, the earliest year for any such state to gain readmission.

Writing About History

8. **Persuasive Writing** Imagine that you are a citizen during Andrew Johnson's administration. Write a letter to a member of Congress urging him to vote either for or against Johnson's impeachment. Include reasons for your position.

Eyewitness

WILLIAM H. CROOKE *served as a bodyguard for President Andrew Johnson and witnessed the decisive vote by Edmund Ross during the impeachment trial in the Senate on Saturday, May 16, 1868. Here, Crooke recalls the scene:*

The tension grew. There was a weary number of names before that of Ross was reached. When the clerk called it, and Ross [senator from Kansas] stood forth, the crowd held its breath.

'Not guilty,' called the senator from Kansas. It was like the babbling [sic] over of a caldron. The Radical Senators, who had been laboring with Ross only a short time before, turned to him in rage; all over the house people began to stir. The rest of the roll-call was listened to with lessened interest. . . . When it was over, and the result—35 to 19—was announced, there was a wild outburst, chiefly groans of anger and disappointment, for the friends of the president were in the minority.

It was all over in a moment, and Mr. Johnson was ordering some whiskey from the cellar. [President Johnson was not convicted.]

VERBATIM

"If the South is ever to be made a safe Republic, let her lands be cultivated by the toil of the owners, or the free labor of intelligent citizens."
THADDEUS STEVENS,
arguing for land redistribution in the South during Reconstruction

"In the South, the [Civil] war is what A.D. is elsewhere; they date from it."
MARK TWAIN,
from Life on the Mississippi

"For we colored people did not know how to be free and the white people did not know how to have a free colored person about them."
HOUSTON HARTSFIELD HOLLOWAY,
freedman, on the problem of Reconstruction

"As in the war, freedom was the keynote of victory, so now is universal suffrage the keynote of Reconstruction."
ELIZABETH CADY STANTON,
arguing for universal suffrage, 1867

"We thought we was goin' to be richer than the white folks, 'cause we was stronger and knowed how to work, and the whites didn't and they didn't have us to work for them anymore. But it didn't turn out that way. We soon found out that freedom could make folks proud but it didn't make 'em rich."
FELIX HAYWOOD,
former slave

PRESIDENTIAL SUPERLATIVES

Andrew Johnson

While he was neither "first in war, first in peace" nor "first in the hearts of his countrymen," President Andrew Johnson left his mark on history:

- First to have never attended school
- First to be impeached
- First to be elected to the Senate both before and after being president
- First to host a queen at the White House

- First tailor/president who made his own clothes
- Last not to attend successor's inauguration
- Most vetoes overridden
- Father of the Homestead Act

(Re)inventing America

Patents awarded to African American inventors during the Reconstruction period:

ALEXANDER ASHBOURNE biscuit cutter

LANDROW BELL locomotive smokestack

LEWIS HOWARD LATIMER water closets (toilets) for railway cars, electric lamp with cotton filament, dough kneader

THOMAS ELKINS refrigerator with cooling coils

THOMAS J. MARTIN fire extinguisher

ELIJAH McCOY automatic oil cup and 57 other devices and machine parts, including an ironing board and lawn sprinkler

Refrigerators keep foods cool.

Milestones

REEXAMINED. THE ROMANTIC STORY OF POCAHONTAS, based on the written account of Captain John Smith. The *London Spectator*, reporting on the work of Mr. E. Neils, debunks Smith's tale of the young Pocahontas flinging herself between him and her father's club. The young girl was captured and held prisoner on board a British ship and then forcibly married to Mr. John Rolfe. Comments *Appleton's Journal* in 1870: "All that is heroic, picturesque, or romantic in history seems to be rapidly disappearing under the microscopic scrutiny of modern critics."

FOUNDED, 1877. NICODEMUS, KANSAS, by six African American and two white Kansans. On the high, arid plains of Graham County, the founders hope to establish a community of homesteading former slaves.

TOPPED, 1875. THE ONE MILLION MARK FOR POPULATION, by New York City. New York is the ninth city in the history of the world to achieve a population level of more than one million. The first was Rome in 133 B.C.

Pocahontas

EXTINGUISHED, 1871. THE PESHTIGO FOREST FIRE in Wisconsin. The conflagration caused 2,682 deaths. The Peshtigo tragedy has been overshadowed by the Great Chicago Fire of the same year, which killed 300.

PUBLISHED, 1865. *DRUM TAPS,* by Walt Whitman. Based on his experiences as a hospital volunteer, Whitman's new poems chronicle the horrors of the Civil War.

THROWN, 1867. FIRST CURVEBALL, by William A. "Candy" Cummings of the Brooklyn Excelsiors. In a game against Harvard, pitcher Cummings put a spin on the ball to make it swerve downward. Most spectators thought the ball's curved path was an illusion.

NUMBERS

$7,200,000 Purchase price paid by U.S. to Russia for Alaska in 1867

2¢ Price paid per acre for Alaska

$30 Boarding and tuition, per quarter, at Saint Frances Academy, boarding school for African American girls in Baltimore, Maryland. Students come from states as distant as Florida and Missouri for an education "productive of the happiest effects among individuals and in society."

$5 Extra charge for instruction in embroidery

$25 Extra charge for instruction in making wax fruit

$3 Tuition, per quarter, for local "day scholars"

5,407 Number of pupils in Mississippi Freedmen's schools in 1866

50 Number of schools established for freed African Americans in Mississippi in 1866

20% Percentage of state income of Mississippi spent on artificial arms and legs for war veterans in 1866

Freedmen's classroom

SECTION 3 Republican Rule

Guide to Reading

Main Idea
Under Republican rule, the South began to rebuild. African Americans gained new opportunities, and some Southerners organized to resist the Republicans.

Key Terms and Names
carpetbagger, scalawag, Joseph Rainey, Hiram Revels, graft, Ku Klux Klan Act

Reading Strategy
Organizing As you read about Southern attempts to rebuild, complete a graphic organizer to identify how African Americans helped govern the Reconstruction South.

[African Americans' Political Roles]

Reading Objectives
- **Discuss** Republican rule in the South during Reconstruction.
- **Describe** how African Americans worked to improve their lives.

Section Theme
Groups and Institutions Despite opposition, African Americans took active roles in politics during Reconstruction.

Preview of Events

♦1866   ♦1868   ♦1870   ♦1872

1866
Ku Klux Klan formed; Fisk School, later Fisk University, founded in Tennessee

1870
First Enforcement Act passed; first African Americans elected to Congress

1871
Ku Klux Klan Act passed

★ An American Story ★

On a moonlit December night in the late 1860s, Essic Harris, a formerly enslaved man, woke suddenly after hearing loud noises outside his small home in Chatham County, North Carolina. He peered out his bedroom window and a wave of terror rushed over him. Thirty men in white robes and hoods stood around the house. Many held shotguns. They were members of the Ku Klux Klan, an organization that used violence and intimidation to force African Americans and white Republicans out of Southern politics. They had come to harass Harris, who was active in local politics.

As Klan members began firing shotgun blasts at his home, Harris pushed his family into a corner and grabbed his own shotgun. He rushed to the front door and fired back, then shouted to one of his childen, "Boy, bring my five-shooter!" Harris had no such gun, but his bluff worked. The Klan members cursed Harris and rode off, but they would return. They continued harassing Harris until he abandoned his home and moved to another county.

—adapted from *The Fiery Cross*

Republican Rule in the South

By late 1870, all of the former Confederate states had rejoined the Union under the congressional Reconstruction plan. Throughout the South, the Republican Party took power and introduced several major reforms. Most white Southerners scorned the Republicans, however, partly because the party included Northerners and African Americans. Southerners also believed the Union army had forced the new Republican governments on them.

Carpetbaggers and Scalawags As Reconstruction began many Northerners moved to the South. Quite a few were eventually elected or appointed to positions in the South's new state governments. Southerners, particularly Democratic Party supporters, referred to these newcomers as carpetbaggers because some arrived with suitcases made of carpet fabric. Many local residents viewed the Northerners as intruders seeking to exploit the South.

Some carpetbaggers did seek to take advantage of the war-torn region. Others, however, hoped to find more opportunities than existed for them in the North and West. Some simply wanted to help. Many Northern schoolteachers, for example, moved south to help educate whites and African Americans.

Carpetbag

While many Southerners despised carpetbaggers, they also disliked white Southerners who worked with the Republicans and supported Reconstruction. They called these people scalawags—an old Scotch-Irish term for weak, underfed, worthless animals.

The scalawags were a diverse group. Some were former Whigs who had grudgingly joined the Democratic Party before the war. Many were owners of small farms who did not want the wealthy planters to regain power. Still others were business people who favored Republican plans for developing the South's economy.

African Americans Enter Politics Thousands of formerly enslaved people also took part in governing the South. Having gained the right to vote, African Americans quickly began organizing politically. "You never saw a people more excited on the subject of politics than are the [African Americans] of the South," wrote one plantation manager.

At first, African American leaders in the South came from those who had been educated before the war. These included artisans, shopkeepers, and ministers. Many had lived in the North and fought in the Union army. Helped by the Republican Party, these African Americans delivered speeches to former plantation workers, drawing them into politics.

Within a few remarkable years, African Americans went from enslaved workers to legislators and administrators on nearly all levels of government. Hundreds of formerly enslaved people served as delegates to state constitutional conventions. They also won election to numerous local offices, from mayor to police chief to school commissioner. Dozens of

Profiles IN HISTORY

Hiram Revels 1822–1901

For a man reluctant to enter politics, Hiram Revels went a long way— becoming the first African American in the United States Senate. Revels was born to free parents in Fayetteville, North Carolina. In 1845 he became a minister in the African Methodist Church. Soon after, Revels settled in Baltimore, where he worked as a church pastor and as the principal of an African American school.

After the Civil War, Revels settled in Natchez, Mississippi, where he continued his religious work. At first, Revels expressed reluctance to wade too deeply into politics, but he overcame this concern and won the respect of both whites and African Americans. In 1870 Revels was elected to the Senate. The first African American senator, he served in a subdued manner, speaking much less than other African American members of Congress. Upon his retirement from the Senate, Revels served twice as president of Alcorn University, an African American college in Mississippi.

Joseph Rainey 1832–1887

At the outbreak of the Civil War, Joseph Rainey was working as a barber in Georgetown, South Carolina. Less than 10 years later, he became the first African American elected to the U.S. House of Representatives.

Rainey was born to enslaved parents who bought their freedom in the 1840s. They opened a barbershop, where Rainey worked until the war broke out. After the war, Rainey entered politics, and in 1870 he was elected to the House of Representatives, serving in Congress until 1879.

As the body's first African American, Rainey found himself the object of intense scrutiny. During this time, he showed considerable knowledge of politics and made impressive speeches in favor of legislation to enforce the Fourteenth Amendment and the Ku Klux Klan Act. Throughout his tenure in Congress, Rainey worked tirelessly—both in and out of the House chamber—to advance African American civil rights.

African Americans served in Southern state legislatures, while 14 were elected to the House of Representatives and 2 to the Senate.

With formerly enslaved people making such political gains, many Southerners claimed that "Black Republicanism" ruled the South. Such claims, however, were greatly exaggerated. No African American was ever elected governor. In South Carolina, where African Americans made up a majority of the population, they did achieve a majority in the legislature, but it lasted for only one legislative term. African Americans participated in government, but they did not control it.

The Republican Party took power in the South because it also had the support of a large number of white Southerners. Poor white farmers, who resented the planters and the Democratic Party that dominated the South before the Civil War, often joined with African American voters to elect Republicans.

Republican Reforms in the South
The newly elected Republican governments in the South quickly instituted a number of reforms. They repealed the black codes and made many more state offices elective. They established state hospitals and institutions for orphans, the hearing and visually impaired, and the mentally ill. They rebuilt roads, railways, and bridges and provided funds for the construction of new railroads and industries in the South. They also established a system of public schools.

The Republican reforms did not come without cost. Many state governments were forced to borrow money and to impose high property taxes to pay for the repairs and new programs. Many property owners, unable to pay these new taxes, lost their land.

Although many Republicans wanted to help the South, others were corrupt. One Republican governor admitted accepting more than $40,000 in bribes. Graft, or gaining money illegally through politics, was common in the South, just as it was in the North at the time, but it gave Southern Democrats another issue that would help them regain power in the 1870s.

Reading Check **Summarizing** What three groups helped elect Republicans in the South during Reconstruction?

African American Communities

In addition to their efforts on the political stage, African Americans worked to improve their lives in other ways during Reconstruction. Many sought to gain an education and establish their own thriving communities.

A Desire to Learn Once they were freed, many African Americans wanted to get an education. In the first years of Reconstruction, the Freedmen's Bureau, with the help of Northern charities, established schools for African Americans across the South. By 1870 some 4,000 schools and 9,000 teachers—half of them African American—taught 200,000 formerly enslaved people of all ages. In the 1870s, Reconstruction governments built a comprehensive public school system in the South, and by 1876 about 40 percent of all African American children (roughly 600,000 students) attended school in the region.

Several African American academies offering advanced education also began operating in the South. These academies grew into an important network of African American colleges and universities, including Fisk University in Tennessee and Atlanta University and Morehouse College in Georgia.

Churches and Social Organizations With the same determination they showed in pursuing an education, formerly enslaved people across the South worked to

Schools for African Americans O.O. Howard, head of the Freedmen's Bureau, is pictured here (seated, far right) with the students of a Freedmen's school.

Different Viewpoints

Carpetbaggers: Corrupt or Well-Intentioned?

According to Southerners, many carpetbaggers were corrupt Northerners who came south to get rich or to get elected. Films like *Gone with the Wind* influenced many generations to accept this view. The opposing interpretation argues that Northerners were not necessarily corrupt but often simply wanted to make new lives or aid African Americans.

In 1871 Oliver Morton, a Radical Republican senator from Indiana, defended Northerners who relocated to the South, claiming they were beneficial to that region:

"When the war ended many men who had been in the Union army remained in the South, intending to make it their home. . . . Others emigrated from the North, taking with them large capital, believing that the South presented fine prospects for business. . . . It so happened, and was, in fact, necessary, that many of these men should be elected to office. This was their right and the natural result of the circumstances by which they were surrounded. . . . Emigration is a part of the genius of the American people. . . . it is an odious and anti-American doctrine that a man has no right to be elected to an office in a State because he was not born in it. . . . What the South needs is emigrants with carpet bags well filled with capital to revive industry. . . . "

—quoted in *Reconstruction: Opposing Viewpoints*

In an 1871 question-and-answer session before Congress, William Manning Lowe, a former Confederate colonel and Alabama lawyer, criticized his state's U.S. senators, Willard Warner and George Spencer. Both were originally from Northern states:

"[A] carpet-bagger is generally understood to be a man who comes here for office sake, of an ignorant or bad character, and who seeks to array the Negroes against the whites . . . in order to get office through them. . . . (The term) does not apply to all northern men who come here. . . . We regard any republican or any man as a man of bad character, whether he is native or foreign born, who seeks to obtain office from the Negroes by exciting their passions and prejudices against the whites. We think that a very great evil—very great. We are intimately associated with the Negro race; we have a large number in the country, and we think it essential that we shall live in peace together. . . . No, sir; the term is never applied to a democrat under any circumstances. . . ."

—quoted in *Reconstruction: Opposing Viewpoints*

Learning From History

1. **Evaluating** Which of these two viewpoints most accurately describes carpetbaggers? Why?

2. **Analyzing** Choose one of the viewpoints above. Write three questions you would like to ask your chosen speaker.

---

establish their own churches. Religion had long played a central role in the lives of many African Americans, and with the shackles of slavery now gone, the building of churches quickly began.

Churches served as the center of many African American communities, as they housed schools and hosted social events and political gatherings. In rural areas, church picnics, festivals, and other activities provided residents with many of their recreational and social opportunities. In many communities, churches often acted as unofficial courts by promoting social values, settling disputes among residents, and disciplining individuals for improper behavior.

African Americans also established thousands of other organizations to help and support each other. These organizations ranged from burial societies and debating clubs to drama societies and trade associations.

✓ **Reading Check** **Examining** How did education for African Americans change during Reconstruction?

Southern Resistance

At the same time these changes were taking place, African Americans faced intense resentment from many Southern whites. Many Southerners also despised the "Black Republican" governments, which they believed vindictive Northerners had forced upon them.

The Ku Klux Klan Unable to strike openly at the Republicans running their states, some Southerners organized secret societies. The largest of these groups was the Ku Klux Klan. Started in 1866 by former Confederate soldiers in Pulaski, Tennessee, the Klan spread rapidly throughout the South. Its goal was to drive out the Union troops and carpetbaggers and regain control of the South for the Democratic Party.

Hooded, white-robed Klan members rode in bands at night terrorizing supporters of the Republican governments. They broke up Republican meetings, drove Freedmen's Bureau officials out of their communities, burned African American homes, schools, and churches, and attempted to keep African Americans and white Republicans from voting.

Republicans and African Americans formed their own militia groups and fought back. As the violence perpetrated by both sides increased, one African American organization sent a report to the federal government asking for help:

❝We believe you are not familiar with the description of the Ku Klux Klan's riding nightly over the country, going from county to county, and in the county towns spreading terror wherever they go by robbing, whipping, ravishing, and killing our people without provocation. . . . We pray you will take some steps to remedy these evils.❞
—from the Records of the U.S. Senate, 42nd Congress

Picturing **History**

Enforcement Efforts In 1871 President Grant signed an anti–Ku Klux Klan Bill. What actions did the Klan take to interfere with African American voting rights?

The Enforcement Acts The Ku Klux Klan's activities outraged President Grant and congressional Republicans. In 1870 and 1871, Congress passed three Enforcement Acts to combat the violence in the South. The first act made it a federal crime to interfere with a citizen's right to vote. The second put federal elections under the supervision of federal marshals. The third act, also known as the **Ku Klux Klan Act,** outlawed the activities of the Klan. Local authorities and federal agents, acting under the Enforcement Acts, arrested more than 3,000 Klan members throughout the South. Southern juries, however, convicted only about 600, and fewer still served any time in prison.

✓ **Reading Check** **Describing** Why did Congress pass the Enforcement Acts?

SECTION 3 ASSESSMENT

Checking for Understanding
1. **Define:** carpetbagger, scalawag, graft.
2. **Identify:** Joseph Rainey, Hiram Revels, Ku Klux Klan Act.
3. **Describe** how some white Southerners reacted to the Republican Party gaining power in the South.

Reviewing Themes
4. **Groups and Institutions** How did the establishment of schools, churches, and social organizations benefit African Americans during Reconstruction?

Critical Thinking
5. **Analyzing** Why did white Southerners resent both carpetbaggers and scalawags?
6. **Categorizing** Use a graphic organizer similar to the one below to identify both the negative and positive aspects of carpetbag rule.

Carpetbag Rule	
Positives	Negatives

Analyzing Visuals
7. **Analyzing Photographs** Study the photograph of the Freedmen's school on page 400. By 1876, around how many children attended schools such as the one pictured here?

Writing About History
8. **Descriptive Writing** Imagine you are living in the postwar South. You are either a Northerner who has recently moved there or a longtime Southern resident. Write a friend and describe Southern life as you see it.

Reconstruction Collapses

Main Idea

After a little more than a decade, Reconstruction ended shortly after the election of 1876.

Key Terms and Names

"sin tax," Horace Greeley, "Whiskey Ring," Panic of 1873, Compromise of 1877, tenant farmer, sharecropper, furnishing merchant, crop lien, debt peonage

Reading Strategy

Taking Notes As you read about the Grant administration and the end of Reconstruction, use the major headings of the section to create an outline similar to the one below.

I. The Grant Administration
    A.
    B.
    C.
II.
    A.
    B.

Reading Objectives

- **Discuss** the policies and problems of Grant's administration.
- **Explain** how Reconstruction ended, and contrast the New South and the Old South.

Section Theme

Economic Factors After Reconstruction the South tried to build a new economy, but many problems remained.

Preview of Events

♦1872   ♦1874   ♦1876   ♦1878

1872
Grant reelected

1873
Jay Cooke and Company declares bankruptcy

1875
"Whiskey Ring" scandal breaks

1877
Hayes named president

★ *An American Story* ★

Ethelbert Barksdale could hardly contain his excitement as the 1875 election campaign in Mississippi wound down. For the past several years, Democrats had steadily regained power throughout the South, winning back various local and state offices from Republicans through political organizing and through intimidation and harassment of African Americans and other Republican supporters.

Barksdale, the editor of the *Weekly Clarion*, a Democratic Mississippi newspaper, now watched with joy and anticipation as Democrats prepared to recapture numerous political offices in his state. To Barksdale and many other white Southerners, the efforts by the Democrats to regain political control was nothing less than a revolution to free the South from despised Republican rule. "When a government is oppressed with very bad rulers, and national affairs are tending toward corruption, the people . . . bear these grievances for a long time hoping that a reformation may come," he wrote on the eve of Election Day.

—adapted from *Reconstruction and Redemption in the South*

The Grant Administration

As commander of the Union forces, Ulysses S. Grant had led the North to victory in the Civil War. His reputation had then carried him into the White House in the election of 1868. Unfortunately, Grant had little experience in politics. He believed that the

I BEG TO REPEAT THAT THESE FRAUDS ON THE GOVERNMENT SHALL BE PROBED TO THE VERY BOTTOM.

TAMMANY RING. CANAL RING. WHISKEY RING. INDIAN RING. PRESS RING. STATE RING. COUNTY RING. TOWN RING. WARD RING. BELKNAP. FRAUD CLAIMS. BACK PAY GRAB. WHISKEY FRAUDS. BRIBERY.

Analyzing *Political Cartoons*

Political Corruption A cartoonist shows the Grant administration looking for those guilty of fraud in a whiskey barrel—symbol of the "Whiskey Ring." How far does the cartoonist believe the corruption goes?

president's role was to carry out the laws and leave the development of policy to Congress. This approach pleased the Radical Republicans in Congress, but it left the president weak and ineffective when dealing with other issues. Eventually, Grant's lack of political experience helped to divide the Republican Party and to undermine public support for Reconstruction.

The Republicans Split

During Grant's first term in office, the Republican-controlled Congress continued to enforce Reconstruction. At the same time, Congress expanded the programs it had introduced during the Civil War to promote commerce and industry. It kept tariffs high, tightened banking regulations, promised to repay its debts with gold and not paper money, and increased federal spending on railroads, port facilities, and the national postal system.

The Republican Congress also kept in place the taxes on alcohol and tobacco that had been introduced as emergency measures during the war. These taxes, nicknamed "sin taxes," helped the government pay off the bonds that had been issued to pay for the Civil War.

Democrats attacked these Republican economic policies, arguing they benefited the wealthy, such as government bondholders, at the expense of the poor,

who paid most of the sin taxes. They argued that wealthy Americans were gaining too much influence in Grant's administration.

Some Republicans, known as Liberal Republicans, agreed with the Democrats. They were concerned that men who were in office to make money and sell influence were beginning to dominate the Republican Party. The Liberal Republicans tried to prevent Grant from being nominated for a second term. When that failed, they left the Republican Party in 1872 and nominated their own candidate, **Horace Greeley,** the influential newspaper publisher.

To attract Southern support, the Liberal Republicans promised to pardon nearly all former Confederates and to remove Union troops from the South. As a result, the Democratic Party, believing that only a united effort would defeat Grant, also nominated Greeley. Despite the split in his own party, Grant won the election easily.

Scandals Mar Grant's Second Term

During Grant's second term, a series of scandals badly hurt his administration's reputation. In one scandal, Grant's secretary of war, **William Belknap,** was found to have accepted bribes from merchants operating at army posts in the West. He was impeached but resigned before the Senate could try him. Then, in 1875, the **"Whiskey Ring"** scandal broke. A group of government officials and distillers in St. Louis cheated the government out of millions of dollars by filing false tax reports. It was reported that Orville E. Babcock, Grant's private secretary, was in this group, although the charges were never proven.

The Panic of 1873

In addition to dealing with political scandals, Grant and the nation endured a severe economic crisis that began during Grant's second term. The turmoil started in 1873 when a series of bad railroad investments forced the powerful banking firm of Jay Cooke and Company to declare bankruptcy. A wave of fear known as the **Panic of 1873** quickly spread though the nation's financial community. The panic prompted scores of smaller banks to close and the stock market to plummet. Thousands of businesses shut down, and tens of thousands of Americans were thrown out of work.

The scandals in the Grant administration and the deepening economic depression hurt the Republicans politically. In the 1874 midterm elections, the Democrats won control of the House of Representatives and made gains in the Senate. These newly elected Democrats immediately launched investigations into the scandals, further embarrassing Grant and the Republicans.

Reading Check **Explaining** Why did the Liberal Republicans oppose President Grant?

Reconstruction Ends

The rising power of the Democrats in Congress meant that enforcing Reconstruction policies became more difficult. At the same time, many Northerners were weary of the decade-long struggle to impose a new society on the South. They were more concerned with their own economic problems than with the political situation in the South.

Democrats "Redeem" the South Throughout the 1870s, Southern Democrats had worked to regain control of their state and local governments from Republicans. Southern militia groups intimidated African American and white Republican voters, while some Democrats resorted to various forms of election fraud, such as stuffing ballot boxes, bribing vote counters, and stealing ballot boxes in Republican precincts. Southern Democrats also called on all whites to help "redeem"—or save—the South from "Black Republican" rule.

By appealing to white racism and defining the elections as a struggle between whites and African Americans, Democrats were able to win back the support of white owners of small farms who had supported the Republicans. By 1876 the Democrats had taken control of all Southern state legislatures except those of Louisiana, South Carolina, and Florida. In those states, the large number of African American voters, protected by Union troops, were able to keep the Republicans in power.

TURNING POINT

The Compromise of 1877

With Grant's reputation damaged by scandals, the Republicans decided not to nominate him for a third term in 1876. Instead, they nominated **Rutherford B. Hayes,** a former governor of Ohio. Many Americans regarded Hayes as a moral man untainted by scandal or corruption. Hayes wanted to end Radical Reconstruction.

The Democrats responded by nominating **Samuel Tilden,** a wealthy corporate lawyer and former governor of New York who had tried to end the corruption in New York City's government. On Election Day, Tilden clearly won 184 electoral votes, 1 short of a majority. Hayes clearly won 165 electoral votes, leaving 20 votes in dispute. Nineteen of the votes were in the three Southern states Republicans still controlled: Louisiana, South Carolina, and Florida. There had been so much election fraud on both sides that no one could tell who had won.

To resolve the situation, Congress appointed a commission of 15 persons made up equally of members of the House, Senate, and Supreme Court. The commission had 8 Republicans and 7 Democrats and eventually voted along party lines—voting 8 to 7 to give the electoral votes to Hayes. The commission's recommendations, however, were not binding if both houses of Congress rejected them.

After much debate, several Southern Democrats joined with Republicans in the Democrat-controlled House of Representatives and voted to accept the commission's findings, giving the election to Hayes,

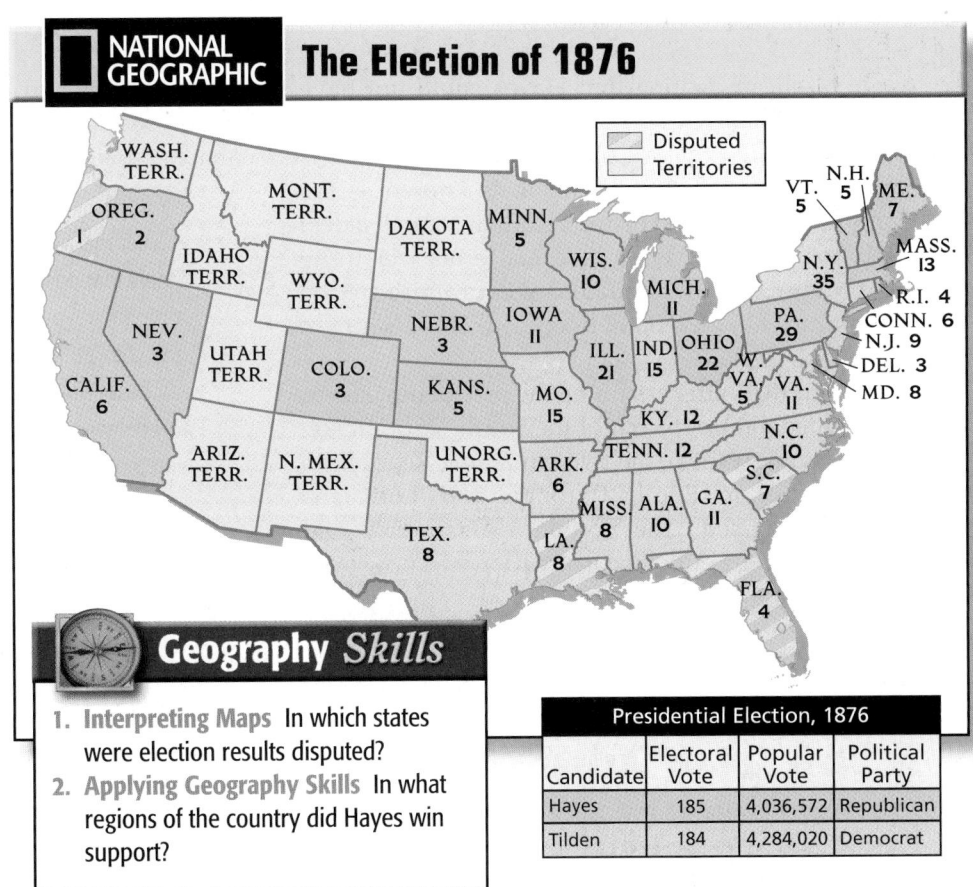

NATIONAL GEOGRAPHIC **The Election of 1876**

Legend: Disputed, Territories

Geography *Skills*

1. **Interpreting Maps** In which states were election results disputed?
2. **Applying Geography Skills** In what regions of the country did Hayes win support?

Presidential Election, 1876			
Candidate	Electoral Vote	Popular Vote	Political Party
Hayes	185	4,036,572	Republican
Tilden	184	4,284,020	Democrat

History *Through Art*

Atlanta Pride The war devastated Georgia's capital, but this painting by Horace James Bradley portrays the city's revival. Bradley called his painting *Commercial Center of Atlanta.* What elements of the painting show that Atlanta was indeed a commercial center again?

the Republican. Noting that Hayes could not have won without the support of Southern Democrats, many concluded that a deal had been made. This is why the outcome of the election is known as the **Compromise of 1877.** Historians are not sure if a deal really took place or what its exact terms were. The compromise reportedly included a promise by the Republicans to pull federal troops out of the South, if Hayes was elected.

In April 1877, after assuming the presidency, Hayes did pull federal troops out of the South. Without soldiers to support them, the two remaining Republican governments in South Carolina and Louisiana quickly collapsed. The Southern Democrats had "redeemed" the South. Reconstruction was now over.

Reading Check **Explaining** What major issue was settled by the Compromise of 1877?

A "New South" Arises

During his inaugural speech in March 1877, President Hayes expressed his desire to move the country beyond the quarrelsome years of Reconstruction, in part by putting an end to the nation's regional distinctions. He hoped to narrow the divisions of sectionalism that had long plagued the nation:

> ❝Let me assure my countrymen of the Southern States that it is my earnest desire to regard and promote their truest interests—the interests of the white and colored people both equally—and to put forth my best efforts in behalf of a civil policy which will forever wipe out . . . the distinction between North and South, . . . that we may have not merely a united North or a united South, but a united country.❞
>
> —quoted in *Rutherford B. Hayes*

Many Southern leaders realized the South could never return to the pre–Civil War agricultural economy dominated by the planter elite. Instead, these Southerners called for the creation of a **"New South"**—a phrase coined by Henry Grady, editor of the *Atlanta Constitution.* They were convinced that the region had to develop a strong industrial economy.

New Industries An alliance between powerful white Southerners and Northern financiers brought great economic changes to some parts of the South. Northern capital helped to build railroads, and by 1890, almost 40,000 miles of railroad track criss-crossed the South—nearly four times the amount there in 1860. Southern industry also grew. A thriving iron and steel industry developed around Birmingham, Alabama. In North Carolina, tobacco processing became big business, and cotton mills appeared in numerous small towns.

In other ways, however, the South changed little. Despite its industrial growth, the region remained largely agrarian. As late as 1900, only 6 percent of the Southern labor force worked in manufacturing. For many African Americans in particular, the end of Reconstruction meant a return to the "Old South," where they had little political power and were forced to labor under difficult and unfair conditions.

Sharecropping The collapse of Reconstruction ended African American hopes of being granted their own land in the South. Instead, many returned to plantations owned by whites, where they either worked for wages or became tenant farmers, paying rent for the land they farmed. Most tenant farmers eventually became sharecroppers. Sharecroppers did not pay their rent in cash. Instead, they paid a share of their crops—often as much as one-half to two-thirds—to cover their rent as well as the cost of the seed, fertilizer, tools, and animals they needed.

Many sharecroppers also needed more seed and other supplies than their landlords could provide. As a result, country stores and local suppliers, known as furnishing merchants, provided sharecroppers with the supplies they needed on credit but at interest rates

Sharecroppers at Work This family of formerly enslaved laborers still faced a difficult existence in the postwar South. Unable to purchase their own farm-land, sharecroppers often amassed large amounts of debt. *To whom did the sharecroppers owe the most money?*

often as high as 40 percent. To make sure sharecroppers paid their debts, laws allowed merchants to put liens on their crops. These crop liens meant that the merchant could take some of the crops to cover the debts.

The crop lien system and high interest rates led many into a financial condition called debt peonage. Debt peonage trapped sharecroppers on the land because they could not make enough money to pay off their debts and leave, nor could they declare bankruptcy. Failure to pay off debts could lead to imprisonment or forced labor. The Civil War had ended slavery, but the failure of Reconstruction left many African Americans trapped in economic circumstances where they lost much of their newly gained freedom.

Reading Check **Summarizing** What alliance brought about an economic rebuilding of the South?

SECTION 4 ASSESSMENT

Checking for Understanding

1. **Define:** "sin tax," tenant farmer, sharecropper, furnishing merchant, crop lien, debt peonage.
2. **Identify:** Horace Greeley, "Whiskey Ring," Panic of 1873, Compromise of 1877.

Reviewing Themes

3. **Economic Factors** What factors contributed to improving the economy of the South after Reconstruction?

Critical Thinking

4. **Analyzing** How did the disputed election of 1876 affect Reconstruction policy?
5. **Organizing** Use a graphic organizer similar to the one below to identify the problems that President Grant's administration faced.

Problems Faced by Grant's Administration

Analyzing Visuals

6. **Interpreting Art** Study the Horace Bradley painting on page 406. What details did the artist include in this painting to suggest dynamic activity?

Writing About History

7. **Expository Writing** Write a short essay explaining what you consider to be the three most important events of the Reconstruction period. Explain why you chose these events.

Reviewing Key Terms

On a sheet of paper, use each of these terms in a sentence.

1. Reconstruction
2. amnesty
3. pocket veto
4. freedmen
5. black codes
6. impeach
7. carpetbagger
8. scalawag
9. graft
10. "sin tax"
11. sharecropper
12. furnishing merchant
13. crop lien
14. debt peonage

Chapter Summary

Needs of the Postwar South

- Land, infrastructure, and economy needed to be rebuilt
- Refugees and freed African Americans needed assistance

Plans

Wade-Davis Bill
- Required majority of adult white men in the South to pledge loyalty to the Union
- Each state's new constitution had to abolish slavery and deprive former Confederate leaders of voting and public service rights
- Killed by Lincoln's pocket veto

Johnson's Plan
- Amnesty for those taking an oath of loyalty to the Union
- Required states to abolish slavery

Congressional Reconstruction
- Passed the Fourteenth and Fifteenth Amendments
- Military Reconstruction Act divided South into five military districts
- New state constitutions had to guarantee voting rights
- Military rule protected voting rights for African Americans
- Empowered African Americans in government and supported their education

Opposition

Southern Reactions to Federal Reconstruction
- Southerners believed Northern Republicans were taking advantage of the weakened South
- Some Southerners were barred from government service; others refused to participate
- Formed secret societies to undermine Republican rule
- Intimidated African American voters

End

Reconstruction Comes to a Close
- Scandals and economic problems weakened Republican Party
- Disputed election of 1876 brought an end to Reconstruction

Reviewing Key Facts

15. **Identify:** Wade-Davis Bill, Freedmen's Bureau, Military Reconstruction Act, Tenure of Office Act, Panic of 1873.
16. What was the main conflict between Presidents Lincoln and Johnson and Congress over Reconstruction?
17. How did the Civil War affect the South's economy?
18. How did the black codes prevent African Americans from achieving equality?
19. How did African Americans seek to improve their lives once they gained their freedom?
20. What supposedly were the provisions of the Compromise of 1877?
21. What motivated Radical Republicans to pass civil rights legislation on behalf of African Americans?
22. Who was Thaddeus Stevens, and what role did he play in Reconstruction?
23. When was the Ku Klux Klan formed, and what was its goal?
24. What did President Johnson do that convinced Congress that he was not carrying out the laws Congress had passed for Reconstruction?
25. What was the goal of the Tenure of Office Act?
26. What constitutional amendments were Southern states asked to ratify before they could reenter the Union?
27. What tactics did Southern Democrats use to try to regain political power?

Critical Thinking

28. **Analyzing Themes: Civic Rights and Responsibilities** Why did the end of slavery not bring about equality for African Americans?
29. **Forming an Opinion** In your opinion, whose approach to Reconstruction was more appropriate—that of Presidents Lincoln and Johnson or that of Congress? Why do you think so?
30. **Synthesizing** Why did African Americans in the 1870s lose some of the political power that they had gained during Reconstruction?
31. **Making Inferences** Who were the "Black Republicans," and what did this name imply?
32. **Evaluating** What were the main features of Lincoln's plan for Reconstruction? Do you think his plan would have worked? Why or why not?
33. **Analyzing** Some leaders, both Northern and Southern, argued that the South should develop a different kind of economy after the Civil War. What kind of economy did they mean?

Self-Check Quiz

Visit the *American Vision* Web site at tav.glencoe.com and click on *Self-Check Quizzes—Chapter 12* to assess your knowledge of chapter content.

34. **Categorizing** Use a graphic organizer similar to the one below to list the positive and negative aspects of Reconstruction.

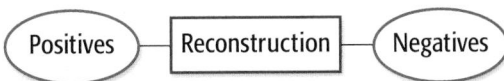

Practicing Skills

35. **Interpreting Political Cartoons** Study the political cartoon on page 404. Then use the steps you learned on page 390 to answer the following questions:

   a. What well-known symbol appears here, and to whom does it refer during this period?

   b. What attitude do you think the cartoonist has about promises of reform? Why do you think so?

Geography and History

36. The graph on this page shows agricultural production in the South from 1860 to 1900. Study the graph and answer the questions below.

   a. **Interpreting Graphs** Which crops surpassed pre–Civil War levels of production by 1890?

   b. **Applying Geography Skills** What factors do you think might have contributed to increased production in the late 1800s?

Writing Activity

37. **Portfolio Writing** Choose one of the events of the Reconstruction period discussed in the chapter. Imagine that the radio had been invented at that time. Write a radio news segment in which you provide information about the event and your view of it. Include the script for the radio segment in your portfolio.

Chapter Activities

38. **Research Project** Use library sources to find examples of political cartoons from the Reconstruction era. Create a display of these cartoons, and write a summary of how they illustrate the major issues of the time period.

39. **Technology Activity: Using the Internet** Search the Internet to find information on an aspect of the Reconstruction era, such as Johnson's impeachment or the role of carpetbaggers. Use the information to write a report to present to your class. In your report, be sure to identify the authors or sources of your Web sites.

Agricultural Production in the South, 1860–1900

Source: *Historical Statistics of the South, 1790–1970*

Standardized Test Practice

Directions: Choose the best answer to the following question.

Which of the following statements about the period of Reconstruction after the Civil War is not true?

A To maintain their strength in Congress, Radical Republicans wanted to be certain African Americans voted.

B Some Northern teachers wanted to help newly emancipated African Americans get education and jobs.

C President Johnson was eager to punish the South and insisted on strict control of the region through the Military Reconstruction Act.

D Southern state legislatures often passed black codes to limit the rights of African Americans in the South.

Test-Taking Tip: Pay careful attention to the wording of the question. This question asks you to select the answer that is NOT true. That means three of the four statements must be true, and you should find the one that is not.

UNIT
5 The Birth of Modern America

Why It Matters

1865–1900

Following the turmoil of the Civil War and Reconstruction, the United States began its transformation from a rural nation to an industrial, urban nation. This change spurred the growth of cities, the development of big business, and the rise of new technologies such as the railroads. New social pressures, including increased immigration, unionization movements, and the Populist movement in politics, characterized the period as well. Understanding this turbulent time will help you understand similar pressures that exist in your life today. The following resources offer more information about this period in American history.

Primary Sources Library

See pages 1052–1053 for primary source readings to accompany Unit 5.

Use the American History Primary Source Document Library CD-ROM to find additional primary sources about the beginnings of the modern United States.

Coat and goggles worn in a horseless carriage

Chicago street scene in 1900

"*The city is the nerve center of our civilization. It is also the storm center.*"

—Josiah Strong, 1885

A BUSY DAY ON
DEARBORN
AND RANDOLPH
STREETS
CHICAGO

GOODFRIEND SHIRTS

SMOKE

Settling the West

1865–1900

Why It Matters

After the Civil War, a dynamic period in American history opened—the settlement of the West. The lives of Western miners, farmers, and ranchers were often filled with great hardships, but the wave of American settlers continued. Railroads hastened this migration. During this period, many Native Americans lost their homelands and their way of life.

The Impact Today

Developments of this period are still evident today.
* *Native American reservations still exist in the United States.*
* *The myth of the Western hero is prominent in popular culture.*

 The American Vision *Video The Chapter 13 video, "Life in the West," chronicles the early days of western settlement in the United States.*

1859
• Comstock Lode of gold and silver discovered in Nevada

1864
• Sand Creek Massacre

1867
• Chisholm Trail cattle drive begins

1881
• President Garfield assassinated

1876
• Battle of the Little Bighorn

| Lincoln 1861–1865 | A. Johnson 1865–1869 | Grant 1869–1877 | Hayes 1877–1881 | Garfield 1881 | Arthur 1881–1885 |

 United States
PRESIDENTS

1860   *1870*   *1880*

World

1867
• Diamonds discovered in South Africa

1868
• Cro-Magnon skeleton discovered in France

1871
• Otto von Bismarck unifies the many German states into modern Germany

1877
• First Wimbledon tennis tournament held

1881
• Japanese emperor Mutsuhito promises to establish national legislature

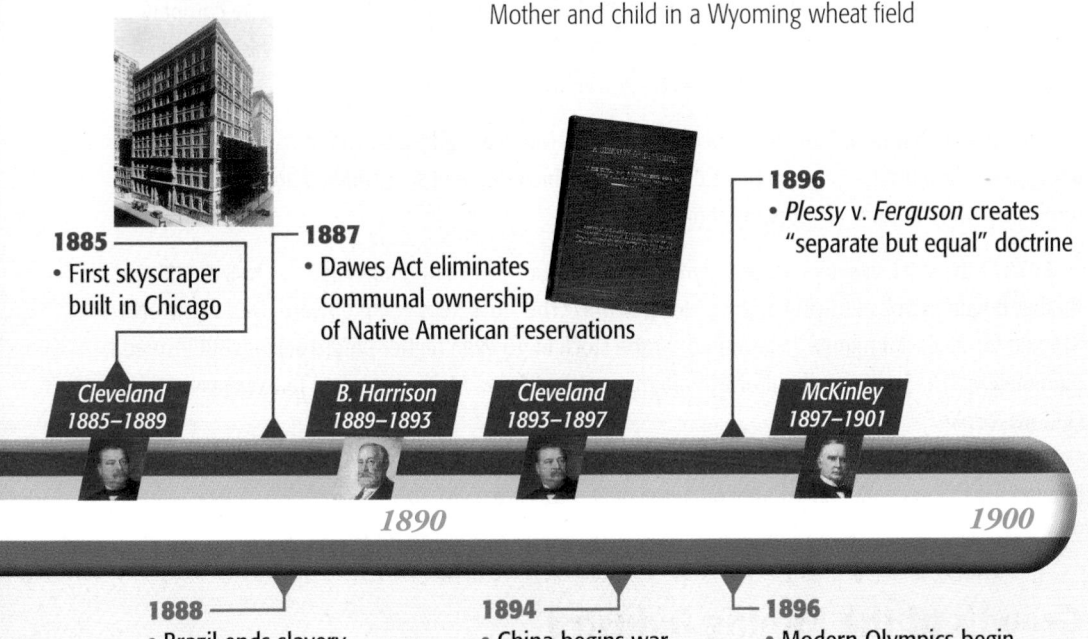

Mother and child in a Wyoming wheat field

1885
• First skyscraper built in Chicago

1887
• Dawes Act eliminates communal ownership of Native American reservations

1896
• *Plessy* v. *Ferguson* creates "separate but equal" doctrine

Cleveland 1885–1889

B. Harrison 1889–1893

Cleveland 1893–1897

McKinley 1897–1901

1890

1900

1888
• Brazil ends slavery

1894
• China begins war against Japan

1896
• Modern Olympics begin in Athens, Greece

HISTORY Online

Chapter Overview
Visit the *American Vision* Web site at tav.glencoe.com and click on **Chapter Overviews—Chapter 13** to preview chapter information.

Miners and Ranchers

Guide to Reading

Main Idea
Miners and ranchers settled large areas of the West.

Key Terms and Names
placer mining, quartz mining, Henry Comstock, vigilance committee, open range, long drive, Chisholm Trail, maverick, barbed wire

Reading Strategy
Organizing As you read about the development of the mining industry, complete a graphic organizer listing the locations of mining booms and the discoveries made there.

Mining Booms & Discoveries

Reading Objectives
• **Trace** the growth of the mining industry in the West.
• **Describe** the ways that new technology changed open-range ranching.

Section Theme
Economic Factors People migrated to the West in search of economic opportunity.

Preview of Events

◆1858	◆1868	◆1878	◆1888

1858
Gold discovered in Colorado

1859
Comstock Lode discovered in Nevada

1867
Cattle drives begin on Chisholm Trail

1875
Gold rush begins in Dakota Territory

1886–1887
Blizzards devastate western ranches

★ An American Story ★

Jacob Waldorf arrived in Virginia City, Nevada, in 1873 to seek his fortune in the fabled silver mines of the Comstock Lode. Like many others, he found work at one of the big mining companies. Seven days a week he toiled in a dangerous mine shaft, earning enough to support his family and buy a little stock in local mining companies. As his son John recalled:

❝The favorite game with our father was stocks. . . . Mother used to say to me, 'Some day we're going back east,' but for years none of the stocks in which Dad invested showed any disposition to furnish us with the price of transportation.❞

In 1877 the stock Waldorf owned skyrocketed in value. "Dad's holdings rose . . . to $10,000 and mother began to talk of buying a farm," John wrote. "The stock kept going upward. Dad was worth $15,000 for at least a minute." He waited for the stock to go even higher before selling, but instead it plummeted: "The bottom fell out of Ophi [a mining stock], and Mother's dream farm fell with it, for Dad was broke."

Jacob Waldorf overcame this financial setback. Earning the respect of his fellow workers, he headed the miners' union in 1880 and later served as a state legislator.

—adapted from *A Kid on the Comstock*

Growth of the Mining Industry

The story of western mining is bigger than the individual stories of fortune seekers like Waldorf. The West's rich deposits of gold, silver, and copper served the needs of growing industries in the East. They also brought the first wave of settlers that populated the mountain states of the West.

News of a mineral strike in an area would start a stampede of prospectors desperately hoping to strike it rich. Early prospectors would extract the shallow deposits of ore largely by hand in a process called placer mining, using simple equipment like picks, shovels, and pans. After these surface deposits dwindled, corporations would move in to begin quartz mining, which dug deep beneath the surface. As those deposits dried up, commercial mining either disappeared or continued on a restricted basis.

ECONOMICS

The Big Strike in Nevada The story of the Comstock Lode is similar to other stories of gold, silver, and copper strikes throughout the West. In 1859 a prospector named **Henry Comstock** staked a claim in Six-Mile Canyon, Nevada. The sticky, blue-gray mud found there turned out to be nearly pure silver ore. News of the Comstock strike brought hordes of miners to Virginia City, Nevada. Almost overnight the town went from a frontier outpost to a boomtown of about 30,000, boasting an opera house, shops with furniture and fashions from Europe, several newspapers, and a six-story hotel with the West's first elevator, called a "rising room." When the silver veins were exhausted several years later, the mines closed. Without the mines, the town's economy collapsed,

and most of the townspeople moved on in search of new opportunities. This cycle of boom and bust—from boomtown to ghost town—was repeated throughout the mountainous West.

During the booms, crime posed a serious problem. Prospectors fought over claims, and thieves haunted the streets and trails. Law enforcers were scarce, and self-appointed volunteers sometimes formed **vigilance committees** to track down and punish wrongdoers. In some cases, they punished the innocent or let the guilty go free, but most people in these communities respected the law and tried to deal firmly but fairly with those accused of crimes.

Mining towns such as Virginia City at first were inhabited mostly by men, but soon they attracted more women. Some women owned property and were influential community leaders. Others worked as cooks or in laundries. Still other women worked at "hurdy-gurdy" houses (named after the mechanical musical instrument), where they danced with men for the price of a drink.

Other Bonanzas Mining also spurred the development of Colorado, the Dakota Territory, and Montana. The discovery of gold near Pikes Peak in 1858 set miners on a frantic rush. Coining the phrase "Pikes Peak

TECHNOLOGY & History

Mining Sluice

Western prospectors used sluices to search riverbeds more quickly than they could with the backbreaking panning method. A sluice diverted the current of a river into earthen or wooden trenches. The water was directed to a box with metal "riffle" bars that disturbed the current, causing heavier minerals to settle to the bottom of the box. A screen at the end of the riffle box prevented the minerals from flowing out. *Why was the sluice more efficient than panning for precious minerals?*

1 Sluices were sometimes simple trenches dug into the ground. Others were made of wood.

2 The riffle box agitated the water flow with metal bars, or sometimes cobble stones or small holes.

3 The box, sometimes called a "tom," had a screen to prevent the separated minerals from escaping with the water and sediment.

screen

sluice

riffle box

or Bust," many panned for gold without success and headed home, complaining of a "Pikes Peak hoax."

In truth, there was plenty of gold and silver in the Colorado mountains, but much of it was hidden beneath the surface and hard to extract. One of the richest strikes occurred in the late 1870s in Leadville, so called for deep deposits of lead that contained large amounts of silver. By the summer of 1879, as many as 1,000 newcomers per week were pouring into Leadville, creating one of the most legendary boomtowns dotting the mining frontier.

Overall, operations at Leadville and other mining towns in Colorado yielded more than $1 billion worth of silver and gold (many billions in today's money). This bonanza spurred the building of railroads through the Rocky Mountains and transformed Denver, the supply point for the mining areas, into the second largest city in the West after San Francisco.

The discovery of gold in the Black Hills of the Dakota Territory and copper in Montana led to rapid development of the northern Great Plains. Miners flooded into the region in the 1870s. After railroads were built in the 1880s, many farmers and ranchers moved to the territory. In 1889, Congress divided the Dakota Territory and admitted North Dakota and South Dakota, as well as Montana, as new states.

Reading Check **Explain** How did the creation of new states change the political boundaries of the Great Plains?

Linking Past & Present

Virginia City

Past: Comstock Boomtown
The wealth of its silver mines turned Virginia City, Nevada, from a leaky-tent mining town into a metropolis with five newspapers and a stock exchange. Express companies carried out silver and brought in supplies for the city's 30,000 people.

Present: Tourist Center
Unlike many mining towns that became ghost towns, Virginia City still exists. The community depends on the tourist industry. Visitors can see the old school building, the opera house, and a mining museum. Virginia City is just a short drive from Carson City and Lake Tahoe.

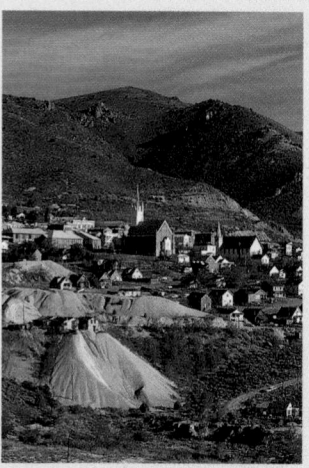

Ranching and Cattle Drives

While many Americans headed to the Rocky Mountains to mine gold and silver after the Civil War, others began building vast cattle ranches on the Great Plains. In the early 1800s, Americans did not think cattle ranches on the Great Plains were practical. Water was scarce, and cattle from the East could not survive on the tough prairie grasses. Farther south, however, in Texas, there existed a breed of cattle adapted to living on the Great Plains.

The Texas longhorn was a breed descended from Spanish cattle that had been brought to Mexico two centuries earlier. Ranchers in Mexico and Texas had allowed their cattle to run wild, and slowly a new breed—the longhorn—had emerged. Lean and rangy, the longhorn could easily survive in the harsh climate of the Plains, and by 1865, as many as 5 million of them roamed the grasslands of Texas.

Mexicans had introduced cattle ranching in New Mexico, California, and Texas before these areas became part of the United States. The industry grew in part because of the open range—a vast area of grassland owned by the government. The open range covered much of the Great Plains and provided land where ranchers could graze their herds free of charge and unrestricted by the boundaries of private farms.

Mexican cowhands developed the tools and techniques for rounding up and driving cattle. These Hispanic herders taught American cowhands their trade and enriched the English vocabulary with words of Spanish origin, including "lariat," "lasso," and "stampede."

NATIONAL GEOGRAPHIC — Mining Country and Cattle Trails, 1848–1890

Helena, Montana in 1865

Legend:
- Gold
- Silver
- 1890 border
- Cattle trails
- Railroads

Cowhands on a cattle drive

Geography *Skills*

1. **Interpreting Maps** What cities were destination points for the Chisholm Trail?
2. **Applying Geography Skills** Why do you think the destination cities at the end of the cattle trails are all located along railroad lines?

Before the Civil War, ranchers had little incentive to round up the longhorns. Beef prices were low, and moving the cattle to eastern markets was not practical. Two developments changed this situation: the Civil War and the construction of the railroads. During the Civil War, eastern cattle were slaughtered in huge numbers to feed the armies of the Union and the Confederacy. After the war, beef prices soared, making it worthwhile to round up the longhorns if a way could be found to move them east.

By the 1860s, railroads had reached the Great Plains. Lines ended at Abilene and Dodge City in Kansas and at Sedalia in Missouri. Ranchers and live-stock dealers realized that if the longhorns were rounded up and driven north several hundred miles to the railroad, they could be sold for a huge profit and shipped east to market.

In 1866 ranchers rounded up cattle and drove about 260,000 of them to Sedalia, Missouri. Although only a fraction of the herds survived this first long drive, the drive overall was a tremendous success, proving that cattle could be driven north to the rail lines and sold for 10 times the price they could get in Texas.

Other trails soon opened. The route to Abilene, Kansas, became the major route north. Between 1867 and 1871, cowboys drove nearly 1.5 million head of cattle up the **Chisholm Trail** to Abilene—a town that, when filled with cowboys at the end of a drive, rivaled the mining towns in terms of rowdi-ness. As the railroads expanded in the West, other trails reached from Texas to more towns in Kansas, Nebraska, Montana, and Wyoming.

The Long Drive A long drive was a spectacular sight. It began with the spring roundup when ranch-ers met with their cowboys to collect cattle from the

Breaking Camp This painting by Charles M. Russell captures the excitement of a long cattle drive. Ranchers hired cowboys to move thousands of cattle north to railroad towns, where the cattle were then shipped east for butchering and sale in the cities. How did the Civil War encourage the start of long cattle drives?

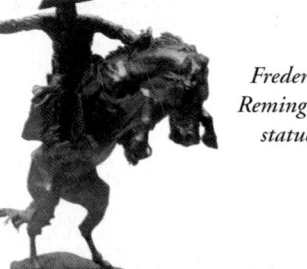

Frederic Remington statue

open range. Stock from many different owners made up these herds. Only their brands showing which rancher owned the cattle distinguished them from one another. Stray calves with no identifying symbols were called **mavericks.** These were divided and branded. The combined herds moving onto the trail could number anywhere from 2,000 to 5,000 cattle.

Cowboys for major ranchers went north with the herds. Most of the cowboys in the early years of the cattle drives were former Confederate army soldiers escaping the harsh life in the South during Reconstruction. A few were Hispanic, and many were African Americans such as Nat Love. Born an enslaved man in Tennessee in 1854, Love was freed at the end of the Civil War. He went west in 1869 and applied for work with a cattle-driving outfit that included several other African American cowhands:

❝After breakfast I asked the camp boss for a job as a cow boy. He asked me if I could ride a wild horse. I said 'yes sir.' He said if you can I will give you a job. So he spoke to one of the colored cow boys called Bronko Jim, and told him to go out and rope old Good Eye, saddle him and put me on his back. Bronko Jim gave me a few pointers and told me to look out for the horse was especially bad. . . . This

proved the worst horse to ride I had ever mounted in my life, but I stayed with him and the cow boys were the most surprised outfit you ever saw, as they had taken me for a tenderfoot, pure and simple. After the horse got tired and I dismounted the boss said he would give me a job and pay me $30.00 per month and more later on.❞

—quoted in *Life and Adventures of Nat Love*

Life for Love and the other cowboys on the trail demanded discipline, endurance, and courage, but those who survived the many dangers collected wages to spend in the towns at the end of the trail. Life in these towns was exciting, but many cowboys told exaggerated tales of daring that often supplied material for what were called "dime novels." These adventure books sold for a dime and helped spread the myths of the "Wild West" in eastern towns and cities.

Ranching Becomes Big Business Cowboys drove millions of cattle north from Texas to Kansas and points beyond. Some of the cattle went straight to slaughterhouses, but many were sold to ranchers who were building up herds and grazing them in Wyoming, Montana, and other territories. When sheep herders moved their flocks onto the range and when farmers settled there, blocking the trails, "range wars" broke out among competing groups. Eventually, and after considerable loss of life, the range was largely fenced off with a new invention—**barbed wire**—which enabled hundreds of square miles to be fenced off cheaply and easily.

At first, ranchers saw barbed wire as more of a threat than an opportunity. They did not want to abandon open grazing and complained when farmers put up barriers that prevented the ranchers' livestock from roaming. Soon, however, ranchers used barbed wire to shut out those competing with them for land and to keep their animals closer to sources of food and water. For cowhands, however, barbed wire ended the excitement of long cattle drives.

The fencing in of the range was not the only reason the long drives ended. Investors from the East and from Britain poured money into the booming cattle business, causing an oversupply of animals on the market. Prices dropped dramatically in the mid-1880s and many ranchers went bankrupt. Then, in the winter of 1886 to 1887, blizzards covered the ground with snow so deep that the cattle could not dig down to the grass. Temperatures fell to more than 40 degrees below zero.

The cattle industry survived this terrible blow, but it was changed forever. The day of the open range had ended. From that point on, herds were raised on fenced-in ranches. New European breeds replaced longhorns, and the cowboy became a ranch hand.

✓ **Reading Check** **Analyzing** How did heavy investment in the cattle industry affect the industry as a whole?

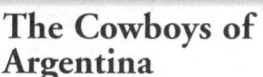

World Geography Connection

The Cowboys of Argentina

While cowboys are often considered a unique part of the American heritage, they also belong to the history of another nation, Argentina. Like the cowboys of the American West, this group of hardy and daring individuals made their living during the 1800s trying to tame the "pampas"—Argentina's frontier grasslands. Known as "gauchos," they rounded up wild cattle and horses on the pampas and sold their hides. Like their counterparts to the north, gauchos wore distinctive clothing—wide-brim hats, ponchos, and loose trousers tucked into low boots—and became highly romanticized and revered figures. They also went the same way as the American cowboy, eventually becoming ranch hands as big business took greater control of the cattle and herding industry. *What were the similarities between the American cowboys and the gauchos?*

lariat

spurs

SECTION 1 ASSESSMENT

Checking for Understanding

1. **Define:** placer mining, quartz mining, open range, long drive, maverick.
2. **Identify:** Henry Comstock, vigilance committee, Chisholm Trail, barbed wire.
3. **List** the factors that contributed to the rise of the cattle industry.
4. **Explain** how cattle ranching shifted from open range to an organized business operation.

Reviewing Themes

5. **Economic Factors** What two developments in the late 1800s led to the decline of the cattle business?

Critical Thinking

6. **Evaluating** How did the mining industry contribute to the development of the West?
7. **Organizing** Use a graphic organizer similar to the one below to list the ways barbed wire was used and the result of using barbed wire on the Great Plains.

Barbed Wire

Purposes

Result

Analyzing Visuals

8. **Examining Maps** Draw a mental map of the western mining country or cattle trails. Then compare your map to the one on page 417, and list the differences between the two maps.

Writing About History

9. **Descriptive Writing** Write a summary for a story line for a Hollywood movie. Your script should realistically portray the lives of either a miner or rancher in the West in the mid- to late 1800s. Be sure to include descriptions of people living in a western settlement.

Farming the Plains

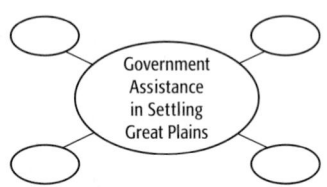
Preview of Events

♦1860	♦1870	♦1880	♦1890
1862 Homestead Act	**1873** Timber Culture Act	**late 1870s** Bonanza farming begins on Great Plains	**late 1880s** Western farmlands hit by drought

★ An American Story ★

On September 15, 1884, the O'Kieffe family left their home in Nebraska and headed west across the state in a covered wagon to start a challenging new life on the open plains. The O'Kieffes faced a new environment that lacked many things that people in the East took for granted, including easy access to water and wood for building a house. Without trees to use as timber, they built their house from chunks of sod, densely packed soil held together by grass roots. To obtain water, the family had to drill a well 134 feet deep and operate the pump by hand. They let nothing go to waste. In summer, they ate the weeds from their garden as well as the vegetables, obeying the rule, "If you can't beat 'em, eat 'em."

There were other settlers in the area, and they would gather to socialize and help each other. When disaster struck, however, each family had to be prepared to face the trouble alone. In January 1888, a three-day blizzard struck without warning. As Charley, the youngest son, reflected: "By the end of the three-day blizzard we were in fine shape to take care of our stock. Many others did not fare so well; but that's life. After all, we said to each other, this was a new country and folks had to learn how to look after themselves."

—adapted from *Western Story: Recollections of Charley O'Kieffe*

Geography of the Plains

The O'Kieffes and their neighbors were early settlers in a region known today as the **Great Plains.** This region extends westward to the Rocky Mountains from around the 100th meridian—an imaginary line running north and south from the central Dakotas through western Texas. Rainfall on the Plains averages less than 20 inches per year, and trees grow naturally only along rivers and streams. For centuries this open country had been home to vast herds of buffalo that grazed on the prairie grasses. Nomadic Native American groups had hunted the buffalo for food and used buffalo hides for clothing and shelter.

Major **Stephen Long,** who explored the region with an army expedition in 1819, called it the "Great American Desert" and concluded that it was "almost wholly unfit for cultivation." He predicted that the scarcity of wood and water would prove to be "an insuperable obstacle in . . . settling the country."

 Reading Check **Examining** What geographic factors created challenges to the settlement of the Great Plains in the late 1800s?

The Beginnings of Settlement

During the late 1800s several factors undermined the belief that the Plains was a "Great American Desert." One important factor was the construction of the railroads, which provided easy access to the Great Plains. Railroad companies sold land along the rail lines at low prices and provided credit to prospective settlers. Railroads opened offices throughout the United States and in major cities in Europe where land was scarce. Posters and pamphlets proclaimed that booking passage to the Plains was a ticket to prosperity.

The catchy slogan "Rain follows the plow," coined by a Nebraskan to sell the idea that cultivating the Plains would increase rainfall, encouraged settlers.

As if to prove the saying correct, the weather cooperated. For more than a decade beginning in the 1870s, rainfall on the Plains was well above average. The lush green of the endless prairies contradicted the popular belief that the region was a desert.

In 1862, the government also supported settlement in the Great Plains region by passing the **Homestead Act.** For a $10 registration fee, an individual could file for a homestead—a tract of public land available for settlement. A homesteader could claim up to 160 acres of public land and could receive title to that land after living there for five years. Later government acts increased the size of the tracts available. The Homestead Act provided a legal method for settlers to acquire clear title to property in the West. With their property rights secured, settlers were more willing to move to the Plains.

When settlers arrived on the Plains, they often found life very difficult. The lack of trees and water forced them to build their first homes from sod cut from the ground and to drill wells up to 300 feet deep. Summer temperatures often soared over 100° Fahrenheit. Prairie fires were a constant danger. Sometimes swarms of grasshoppers swept over farms and destroyed the crops. In winter there were terrible blizzards and extreme cold. Despite these challenges, most homesteaders persisted and learned how to live in the harsh environment.

 Reading Check **Analyzing** What is the relationship between private property rights and the settlement of the Great Plains?

Picturing **History**

Farming the Great Plains Technology made farming the vast open plains of America feasible. Here horse-drawn binders are being used to gather hay in the late 1800s. What other factors encouraged settlement on the Great Plains?

Why It Matters

Land-Grant Colleges

To promote agriculture and manufacturing, the 1862 Morrill Act gave states large tracts of federal lands, with the requirement that part of the land be used to set up and maintain colleges. The colleges were required to offer programs in agriculture and engineering as well as traditional academic subjects. Military training programs were also required at these "land-grant colleges." Most state agricultural and engineering schools were established under the Morrill Act. Today every state, as well as Puerto Rico, has at least one land-grant college.

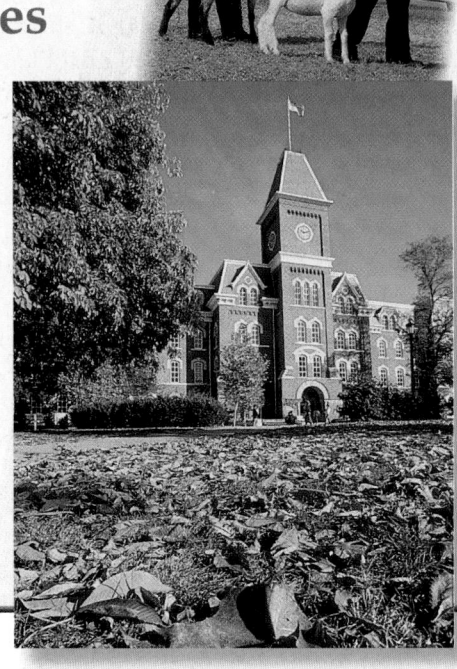

◄ **4-H Programs**
Extension services associated with land-grant colleges coordinate the 4-H programs that help train future farmers. 4-H offers many programs for young people ages 5 to 19.

ROTC ➤
The Reserve Officer Training Corps (ROTC) programs set up at land-grant colleges have been instrumental in providing training for the U.S. military. The program continues to provide scholarships for young Americans around the nation.

The Wheat Belt

For those who had the financial resources, farming could be very profitable on the Plains. Many inventions and new farming methods revolutionized agriculture.

One approach, called dry farming, was to plant seeds deep in the ground where there was enough moisture for them to grow. By the 1860s, farmers on the Plains were employing newly designed steel plows, seed drills, reapers, and threshing machines. The new machines made dry farming possible. Unfortunately, prairie soil often blew away, especially in a dry season. Many sodbusters, as those who plowed the soil on the Plains were called, eventually lost their homesteads through the combined effects of drought, wind erosion, and overuse of the land.

Large landholders faced similar problems, but they were able to make quick profits with the help of mechanical reapers, which speeded the harvest. Mechanical binders tied the stalks into bundles for collection. Threshing machines knocked kernels loose from the stalks. These innovations were well suited for harvesting wheat, which had the advantage of withstanding drought better than corn and some other crops. Wheat became as important to the Great Plains as cotton was to the South.

During the 1880s, many wheat farmers from Minnesota and other Midwestern states moved to the Great Plains to take advantage of the inexpensive land and the new farming technology. This productive new **Wheat Belt** began at the eastern edge of the Great Plains and encompassed much of the Dakotas and the western parts of Nebraska and Kansas.

Commercial Farming The new machines allowed a single family to bring in a substantial harvest on a wheat farm covering several hundred acres. Some wheat farms covered up to 50,000 acres. These were called bonanza farms because they often yielded big profits. Like mine owners, bonanza farmers formed companies, made large investments in property and equipment, and hired laborers as needed.

ECONOMICS

Farmers Fall on Hard Times The bountiful harvests in the Wheat Belt helped the United States become the world's leading exporter of wheat by the 1880s. American wheat growers faced rising competition, however, from other wheat-producing nations. In the 1890s, a glut of wheat on the world market caused prices to drop.

Some farmers tried to make it through lean periods by mortgaging their land—that is, they took bank loans based on the value of their property. If they failed to meet their mortgage payments, they forfeited the land to the bank and had to abandon their farms or work them as tenants for the new owner. By 1900 tenants cultivated about one-third of the farms in the corn and wheat areas.

Beginning in the late 1880s, farmers also faced a prolonged drought that destroyed crops and farms. Kansas newspaper editor William Allen White described a farm family returning from the West:

> ❝These movers . . . had seen it stop raining for months at a time. They had heard the fury of the winter wind as it came whining across the short burned grass. . . . They have tossed through hot nights, wild with worry, and have arisen only to find their worst nightmares grazing in reality on the brown stubble in front of their sun-warped doors.❞

In hard times, some homesteaders gave up and headed home, but others soon took their place.

✓ **Reading Check** **Identifying** What technological innovations helped farmers cultivate the Plains?

Closing the Frontier

On April 22, 1889, the government opened one of the last large territories for settlement, land that later became the state of Oklahoma. Within hours, over 10,000 people raced to stake claims in an event known as the Oklahoma Land Rush.

The next year, the Census Bureau reported that settlement throughout the West had been so rapid "that there can hardly be said to be a frontier line." In reality, much land was still unoccupied, and new settlement continued at a brisk pace into the 1900s. The news that the frontier was closing, however, concerned those who saw it as the end of an era. They believed that unoccupied land at the frontier had provided a "safety-valve of social discontent," the idea that Americans could always make a fresh start.

Most settlers did indeed make a fresh start, adjusting to the often hostile environment of the Plains. Water from their deep wells enabled them to plant trees and gardens. Railroads brought lumber and brick to replace sod as a building material and coal as fuel.

The O'Kieffes, who raised cattle, chickens, and a few crops, were typical of small-scale, self-sustaining homesteaders. They never got rich, but they got by. Those who struggled as the O'Kieffes did to support themselves emerged with a more realistic view of the West. It was not a land of limitless opportunity. As Charley O'Kieffe learned, the real story of the West was not about heroes who rode off into the sunset. It was about ordinary people who settled down and built homes and communities through great effort—"sterling and steady men and women whose lives were spent doing the work as it needed to be done."

✓ **Reading Check** **Examining** Why did some people feel that the closing of the frontier was the end of an era?

HISTORY Online

Student Web Activity Visit the *American Vision* Web site at tav.glencoe.com and click on **Student Web Activities— Chapter 13** for an activity on settling the West.

SECTION 2 ASSESSMENT

Checking for Understanding
1. **Define:** homestead, dry farming, sodbuster, bonanza farm.
2. **Identify:** Great Plains, Stephen Long, Homestead Act, Wheat Belt.
3. **Explain** why the Great Plains was not suitable for homesteading.

Reviewing Themes
4. **Science and Technology** How did the need for new farming techniques on the Great Plains result in technological innovations in agriculture?

Critical Thinking
5. **Analyzing** What factors contributed to the making of the Wheat Belt in the Great Plains and then to troubled times for wheat farmers in the 1890s?
6. **Categorizing** Use a graphic organizer similar to the one below to list the effects of technology on farming in the Great Plains.

Invention	Advantage for Farmers

Analyzing Visuals
7. **Examining Photographs** Study the photograph on page 421 of farmers using binding machines in western Wisconsin. Based on the terrain and the type of work they needed to do, what other types of technology would have helped farmers on the Plains?

Writing About History
8. **Persuasive Writing** Write an advertisement persuading people from the East and from Europe to establish homesteads in the Great Plains.

SKILLBUILDER

Interpreting Statistics

The Railroad and Native American Population					
Year	1860	1870	1880	1890	1900
Approximate miles of railroad track in U.S.:	30,000	53,000	116,000	208,000	259,000
Approximate Native American population:	351,000	323,000	318,000	265,000	248,000

Why Learn This Skill?

Often presented in graphs and tables, statistics are collections of data that are used to support a claim or an opinion. The ability to interpret statistics allows us to understand probable effects and to make predictions.

Learning the Skill

Use the following steps to help you interpret statistical information.

- **Scan** the graph or table, reading the title and labels to get an idea of what is being shown.
- **Examine** the statistics shown, looking for increases and decreases, similarities and differences.
- **Look** for a *correlation* in the statistics. Two sets of data may be related or unrelated. If they are related, we say that there is a correlation between them. In a positive correlation, as one number rises, so does the other number. In a negative correlation, as one number rises, the other number falls. For example, there is a positive correlation between academic achievement and wages, and there is a negative correlation between smoking and life expectancy. Sometimes, statistics may try to show a correlation when none exists. For example, a report that "people who go fishing are less likely to get cancer" may be statistically true but lack any real correlation.
- **Determine** the conclusions you can draw from the statistics.

Practicing the Skill

Study the table above, and then answer the following questions.

❶ What claim does this set of statistics seem to support?

❷ Is there a correlation between miles of railroad tracks and the Native American population? Is the correlation positive or negative? Explain.

Skills Assessment

Complete the Practicing Skills questions on page 433 and the Chapter 13 Skill Reinforcement Activity to assess your mastery of this skill.

Applying the Skill

Interpreting Statistics Create a survey with two questions for which you believe the answers will show a correlation. For example, you might ask, "How many hours of television do you watch per day?" and "How many hours of sleep do you usually get at night?" Organize your statistics in a chart or graph. Then, look for a correlation in your data and evaluate your results. Write a paragraph summarizing your evaluation.

 GO TO

Glencoe's **Skillbuilder Interactive Workbook CD-ROM, Level 2,** provides instruction and practice in key social studies skills.

SECTION 3 · Native Americans

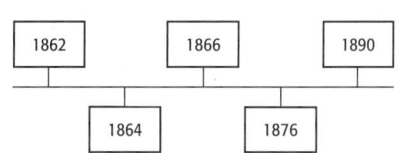

Guide to Reading

Main Idea
The settlement of the West dramatically changed the way of life of the Plains Indians.

Key Terms and Names
nomad, annuity, Little Crow, Indian Peace Commission, George A. Custer, Ghost Dance, assimilate, allotment, Dawes Act

Reading Strategy
Sequencing As you read about the crisis facing Native Americans during the late 1800s, complete a time line to record the battles between Native Americans and the U.S. government and the results of each.

1862		1866		1890
	1864		1876	

Reading Objectives
• **Discuss** conflicts that arose between the Plains Indians and American settlers.
• **Summarize** problems caused by attempts to assimilate Native Americans.

Section Theme
Individual Action Some Native American groups fought the federal government in an attempt to keep their ancestral homelands.

Preview of Events

♦1860   ♦1870   ♦1880   ♦1890

1862
Dakota Sioux uprising

1864
Sand Creek Massacre

1876
Battle of the Little Bighorn

1887
Dawes Act

1890
Wounded Knee Massacre

★ An American Story ★

In October 1867, a Comanche chief named Ten Bears arrived with other Native American leaders and their followers at Medicine Lodge Creek in present-day Kansas to meet with federal treaty-makers and army officers. The federal officials wanted them to sign a treaty agreeing to move to confined areas called reservations and to submit to American authority. In return, the government offered them food, housing, instruction in farming, and other assistance. After listening to the treaty-makers, Ten Bears spoke against moving to a reservation:

❝That which you say we must now live on is too small. The Texans have taken away the places where the grass grew the thickest. . . . The white man has the country which we loved, and we only wish to wander on the prairie until we die.❞

In the end, Ten Bears and the other chiefs had little choice but to sign the treaty. The army's main representative at the council, General William Tecumseh Sherman, told them bluntly that they would have to accept the deal: "You can no more stop this than you can stop the sun or moon; you must submit and do the best you can."

—adapted from *Tribes of the Southern Plains*

Culture of the Plains Indians

For centuries the Great Plains was home to many Native American nations. Some lived in communities as farmers and hunters, but most were nomads who roamed vast distances, following their main source of food—the buffalo.

Despite their differences, the groups of Plains Indians were similar in many ways. They lived in extended family networks and had a close relationship with nature. Plains

Indian nations, sometimes numbering several thousand people, were divided into bands consisting of up to 500 people. A governing council headed each band, but most members participated in making decisions. Gender determined the assignment of tasks. Women generally performed domestic tasks: rearing children, cooking, and preparing hides. Men performed tasks such as hunting, trading, and supervising the military life of the band. Most Plains Indians practiced a religion based on a belief in the spiritual power of the natural world.

✓ **Reading Check** **Comparing** In what ways were different groups of Plains Indians similar?

Cultures Under Pressure

As ranchers, miners, and farmers moved onto the Plains, they deprived Native Americans of their hunting grounds, broke treaties guaranteeing certain lands to the Plains Indians, and often forced them to relocate to new territory. Native Americans resisted by attacking wagon trains, stagecoaches, and ranches. Occasionally an entire group would go to war against nearby settlers and troops. The first major clash on the Plains began in 1862, when the Sioux people in Minnesota launched a major uprising.

The Dakota Sioux Uprising The Dakota Sioux had agreed to live on a small reservation in Minnesota. In exchange for moving to the reservation, the United States government issued annuities, or payments to reservation dwellers, at least once per year. The annuities, however, amounted to only between 5 and 30 cents an acre, and much of that money ended up in the hands of American traders. These traders often made up stories about debts owed to them by the Dakota, and they took the annuities as payments.

Congress made things worse for the Dakota in 1862 by delaying annuities. By August the payments were a month late, and some of the Dakota were starving. Chief **Little Crow** asked traders to provide his people food on credit. "If they are hungry," trader Andrew Myrick replied, "let them eat grass or their

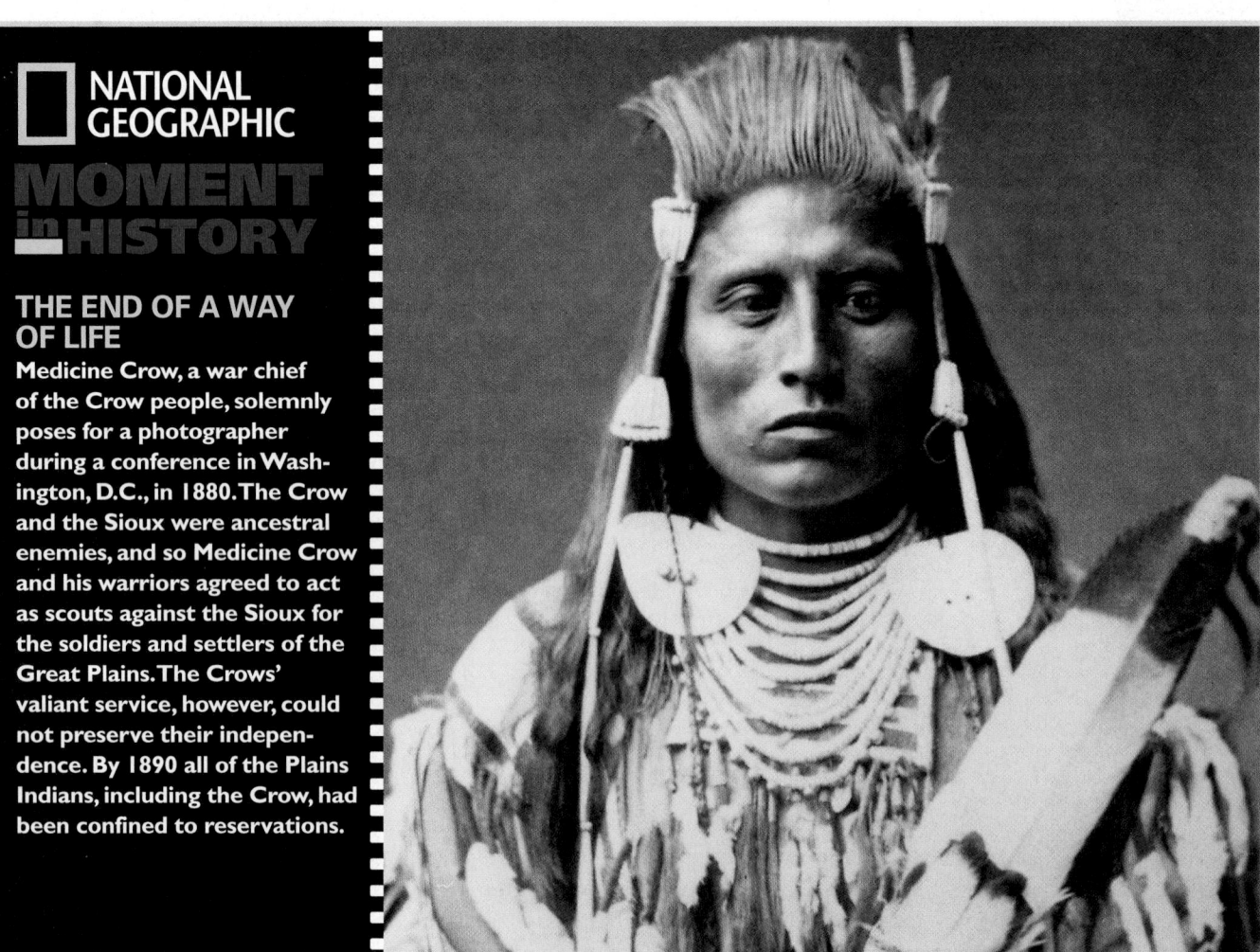

NATIONAL GEOGRAPHIC
MOMENT in HISTORY

THE END OF A WAY OF LIFE

Medicine Crow, a war chief of the Crow people, solemnly poses for a photographer during a conference in Washington, D.C., in 1880. The Crow and the Sioux were ancestral enemies, and so Medicine Crow and his warriors agreed to act as scouts against the Sioux for the soldiers and settlers of the Great Plains. The Crows' valiant service, however, could not preserve their independence. By 1890 all of the Plains Indians, including the Crow, had been confined to reservations.

own dung." Two weeks later, the Dakota rose up in arms, and Myrick was found shot to death with grass stuffed in his mouth.

Little Crow reluctantly agreed to lead this uprising. He wanted to wage war against soldiers, not civilians, but he was unable to keep angry Dakota from slaughtering settlers in the area. Hundreds died before troops arrived from St. Paul and put down the uprising.

A military tribunal sentenced 307 Dakota to death for taking part in the hostilities, but President Lincoln reviewed the evidence and reduced the number executed to 38. Many others who fled the reservation when the troops arrived became exiles in a region that bore their name—the Dakota Territory.

Lakota Sioux Defend Their Territory
Following the Dakota uprising, the army sent patrols far out onto the northern Great Plains to prevent further trouble among the Sioux there. This action did more to stir up hostilities than to prevent them, for it brought troops into contact with another branch of the Sioux—the nomadic Lakota—who had offered refuge to Native Americans from Minnesota. The Lakota fought hard to keep control of their hunting grounds, which extended from the Black Hills westward to the Bighorn Mountains. They had battled rival groups for this country and did not intend to let settlers have it. Leading them were chiefs Red Cloud, Crazy Horse, and Sitting Bull.

The army suffered a stunning defeat at the hands of Red Cloud's forces in Wyoming in December 1866. Army troops were operating a fort on the Bozeman Trail, used by prospectors to reach gold mines in Montana. Crazy Horse, a religious leader as well as a war chief, lured the troops into a deadly trap. He tricked the fort's commander into sending Captain William Fetterman and about 80 soldiers out to pursue what they thought was a small raiding party. Hundreds of warriors were waiting in ambush and wiped out the entire detachment.

Sand Creek
Fetterman's Massacre, as this battle came to be called, was just one example of the growing hostilities between settlers and Native Americans. Another incident, the **Sand Creek Massacre,** took place along Sand Creek in eastern Colorado.

In the 1860s, tensions began to rise between the Cheyenne and Arapaho peoples and the miners who had flocked to Colorado in search of gold and silver. As the number of settlers increased, bands of Native Americans began raiding wagon trains and stealing cattle and horses from ranches. By the summer of 1864, travelers heading to Denver or the mining camps were no longer safe. Trade had come to a

standstill, dozens of ranches had been burned, and an estimated 200 settlers had been killed. The territorial governor, John Evans, ordered the Native Americans to surrender at Fort Lyon, where he said they would be given food and protection. Those who failed to report would be subject to attack.

Although several hundred Native Americans surrendered at the fort, many others did not. In November 1864, Chief Black Kettle brought several hundred Cheyenne to the fort, not to surrender but to negotiate a peace deal. The fort's commander did not have the authority to negotiate, and he told Black Kettle to make camp at Sand Creek while he waited for orders. Shortly afterward, Colonel John Chivington of the Colorado Volunteers was ordered to attack the Cheyenne at Sand Creek.

When Chivington stopped at Fort Lyon, he was told that the Native Americans at Sand Creek were waiting to negotiate. Chivington replied that since the Cheyenne had been attacking settlers, including women and children, there could be no peace.

What actually happened at Sand Creek is unclear. Some witnesses stated afterward that Black Kettle had been flying both an American flag and a white flag of truce, which Chivington ignored. Others reported the American troops fired on the unsuspecting Native Americans, then brutally murdered hundreds of women and children. Still others described a savage battle in which both sides fought ferociously for two days. Fourteen soldiers died, but the number of Native Americans reported killed varied from 69 to 600, with some witnesses stating that very few women or children died. General Nelson Miles later called Chivington's attack "the foulest and most unjustifiable crime in the annals of America," but a Senate committee investigating the incident decided that Chivington should not be charged. The truth of what really happened remains unknown.

GOVERNMENT

A Doomed Plan for Peace Fetterman's Massacre and the Sand Creek Massacre, along with several other incidents, convinced Congress that something had to be done to end the growing conflict with Native Americans on the Great Plains. In 1867 Congress formed an **Indian Peace Commission,** which proposed creating two large reservations on the Plains, one for the Sioux and another for southern Plains Indians. Agents from the federal government's Bureau of Indian Affairs would run the reservations. The army would be given authority to deal with any groups that refused to report or remain there.

This plan was doomed to failure. Pressuring Native American leaders into signing treaties, as negotiators had done at Medicine Lodge Creek in 1867, did not ensure that chiefs or their followers would abide by the terms. Those who did move to reservations faced much the same conditions that drove the Dakota Sioux to violence—poverty, despair, and the corrupt practices of American traders.

Reading Check **Explaining** What proposal did the Indian Peace Commission present to the Plains Indians?

NATIONAL GEOGRAPHIC
Native American Battles and Reservations, late 1800s

FORT LARAMIE TREATIES
1851: Native Americans agree to the construction of roads and forts on their lands.
1868: The Sioux agree to move to a reservation in the Black Hills.

1867 TREATY OF MEDICINE LODGE
Southern Plains Indians agree to move to Indian Territory.

Apache leader Geronimo surrenders at Skeleton Canyon in 1886.

Bear Paw Mountain 1877
Little Bighorn 1876
Rosebud 1876
Wounded Knee 1890
Sand Creek 1864
Ft. Lyon
Ft. Laramie
Medicine Lodge
Canyon de Chelly 1864
Ft. Defiance
Bosque Redondo (1863–1868)
Ft. Sumner

NO MAN'S LAND · CHEROKEE OUTLET · OSAGE
CHEYENNE AND ARAPAHO
CREEK · CHEROKEE
GREER COUNTY (CLAIMED BY TEXAS)
SEMINOLE
CHOCTAW
CHICKASAW
UNASSIGNED LANDS
COMANCHE, KIOWA, AND APACHE

PACIFIC OCEAN · CANADA · WASH. · OREG. · IDAHO · MONT. · N. DAK. · MINN. · WIS. · MICH. · NEV. · WYO. · S. DAK. · IOWA · ILL. · IND. · UTAH TERR. · NEBR. · COLO. · KANS. · MO. · KY. · CALIF. · ARIZ. TERR. · N. MEX. TERR. · TEX. · LA. · MISS. · ALA. · TENN. · ARK. · CASCADE RANGE · ROCKY MOUNTAINS · Black Hills

400 miles
400 kilometers
Lambert Equal-Area projection

Legend:
- ■ Fort
- ✳ Battle
- △ Treaty Site
- —— 1890 border
- ▨ Reservation in 1890
- ◄— Route of the Navajo's Long Walk, 1864
- ◄— Route of Chief Joseph and the Nez Perce, 1877

Geography Skills

1. **Interpreting Maps** Where did Chief Joseph finally give up his flight from the U.S. Army?
2. **Applying Geography Skills** What physical and geographic factors contributed to Native Americans being located to reservations?

The Last Native American Wars

By the 1870s, many Native Americans on the southern Plains had left the reservations in disgust. They preferred hunting buffalo on the open Plains, so they joined others who had also shunned the reservations. Buffalo, however, were rapidly disappearing. Beginning with the Gold Rush, migrants crossing the Plains had killed off thousands of the animals.

Following the Civil War, professional buffalo hunters invaded the area, seeking buffalo hides for markets in the East. Other hunters killed merely for sport, leaving carcasses to rot. Then railroad companies hired sharpshooters to kill large numbers of buffalo that were obstructing rail traffic. The army, determined to force Native Americans onto reservations, encouraged buffalo killing. By 1889 very few of the animals remained.

Battle of the Little Bighorn

In 1876 fortune hunters overran the Lakota Sioux reservation in South Dakota to mine gold in the Black Hills. The Lakota saw no reason why they should abide by a treaty that American settlers were violating, and many left the reservation that spring to hunt near the Bighorn Mountains in southeastern Montana.

The government responded by sending an expedition commanded by General Alfred H. Terry. Lieutenant Colonel **George A. Custer,** commander of the Seventh Cavalry, was with the expedition. An impulsive officer, Custer underestimated the fighting capabilities of the Lakota and Cheyenne.

On June 25, 1876, Custer launched a three-pronged attack in broad daylight on one of the largest groups of Native American warriors ever assembled on the Great Plains. It consisted of about 2,500 Lakota and Cheyenne warriors camped along the Little Bighorn River.

The Native American warriors first repulsed a cavalry charge from the south. Then they turned on Custer and a detachment of 210 soldiers and killed them all. One Lakota warrior recalled the scene afterward: "The soldiers were piled one on top of another, dead, with here and there, an Indian among the soldiers. Horses lay on top of men, and men on top of horses."

Newspapers portrayed Custer as the victim of a massacre. The army stepped up its campaign against the Native Americans. Sitting Bull fled with followers to Canada, but the other Lakota were forced to return to the reservation and give up the Black Hills.

Farther west, members of the Nez Perce, led by Chief Joseph, refused to be moved to a smaller reservation in Idaho in 1877. When the army came to relocate them, they fled their homes and embarked on a flight of more than 1,300 miles. Finally, in October 1877, Chief Joseph surrendered, and his followers were exiled to Oklahoma. His speech summarized the hopelessness of the Native American cause:

> 66Our chiefs are killed. . . . The little children are freezing to death. My people . . . have no blankets, no food. . . . Hear me, my chiefs; I am tired; my heart is sick and sad. From where the sun now stands I will fight no more forever.99
>
> —quoted in *Bury My Heart at Wounded Knee*

Tragedy at Wounded Knee

Native American resistance to federal authority finally came to a tragic end on the Lakota Sioux reservation in 1890. Defying the orders of the government agent, the Lakota continued to perform the **Ghost Dance,** a ritual that celebrated a hoped-for day of reckoning when settlers would disappear, the buffalo would return, and Native Americans would reunite with their deceased ancestors. The government agent blamed the latest defiance on Sitting Bull, who had returned to the reservation from Canada, and he sent police to arrest the chief. Sitting Bull's supporters resisted the police, and the chief himself died in an exchange of gunfire.

The participants of the Ghost Dance then fled the reservation, and U.S. troops went after them. On December 29, 1890, as troops tried to disarm the Native Americans at Wounded Knee Creek, gunfire broke out. A deadly battle ensued, costing the lives of 25 U.S. soldiers and approximately 200 Lakota men, women, and children.

Reading Check **Summarizing** What was the outcome of the battle at the Little Bighorn River?

Assimilation

Some Americans had long opposed the treatment of Native Americans. Author Helen Hunt Jackson described the years of broken promises and assaults on Native Americans in her book, *A Century of Dishonor,* published in 1881. Jackson's descriptions of events such as the massacre at Sand Creek sparked discussions—even in Congress—of better treatment for Native Americans. Some people believed that the situation would improve only if Native Americans could assimilate, or be absorbed,

into American society as landowners and citizens. That meant breaking up reservations into individual allotments, where families could become self-supporting.

This policy became law in 1887 when Congress passed the **Dawes Act.** This act allotted to each head of household 160 acres of reservation land for farming; single adults received 80 acres, and 40 acres were allotted for children. The land that remained after all members had received allotments would be sold to American settlers, with the proceeds going into a trust for Native Americans.

This plan failed to achieve its goals. Some Native Americans succeeded as farmers or ranchers, but many had little training or enthusiasm for either pursuit. Like homesteaders, they often found their allotments too small to be profitable, and so they sold them. Some Native American groups had grown attached to their reservations and hated to see them transformed into homesteads for settlers as well as Native Americans.

In the end, the assimilation policy proved a dismal failure. No legislation could provide a satisfactory solution to the Native American issue, because there was no entirely satisfactory solution to be had. The Plains Indians were doomed because they were dependent on buffalo for food, clothing, fuel, and shelter. When the herds were wiped out, Native Americans on the Plains had no way to sustain their way of life, and few were willing or able to adopt American settlers' lifestyles in place of their traditional cultures.

Reading Check **Cause and Effect** What effect did Helen Hunt Jackson's book *A Century of Dishonor* have?

SECTION 3 ASSESSMENT

Checking for Understanding

1. **Define:** nomad, annuity, assimilate, allotment.
2. **Identify:** Little Crow, Indian Peace Commission, George A. Custer, Ghost Dance, Dawes Act.
3. **Analyze** how Native Americans responded to land lost due to white settlement of the Great Plains.

Reviewing Themes

4. **Individual Action** How did Chief Joseph resist the government's attempts to move the Nez Perce to reservations?

Critical Thinking

5. **Analyzing** Why do you think the government's policy of assimilation of Native Americans was a failure?
6. **Organizing** Use a graphic organizer similar to the one below to list the reasons that the government's plans to move the Plains Indians onto reservations failed.

Analyzing Visuals

7. **Analyzing Maps** Examine the map of battle sites and reservations on page 428. Then, from the point of view of a historian, explain the actions taken against Native Americans within the historical context of the time.

Writing About History

8. **Descriptive Writing** Assume the role of a Plains Indian affected by the assimilation policy of the Dawes Act. Write a journal entry describing how you feel about the policy and how it has affected your life.

American LITERATURE

Gertrude Simmons Bonnin (Zitkala Sa) was a talented and educated Native American woman who spent her life fighting against prejudice toward Native American culture and women. Through her contributions in the fields of literature, music, and politics, Bonnin aimed at creating understanding between the dominant white and Native American cultures. As a woman of mixed white and Native American ancestry, she embodied the need for the two cultures to live cooperatively. In the following excerpt from her essay, *An Indian Teacher Among Indians,* she describes a reunion with her mother after being away from home teaching for several years.

Read to Discover
What evidence do you see of the "generation gap"—the differences between parents and children—in the passage?

Reader's Dictionary
position: job
steadfastly: faithfully
avenge: get even for

from An Indian Teacher Among Indians
by Gertrude Simmons Bonnin

"Mother, why is not your house cemented? Do you have no interest in a more comfortable shelter? . . ."

"You forget, my child, that I am now old, and I do not work with beads any more. Your brother Dawee, too, has lost his position, and we are left without means to buy even a morsel of food," she replied.

Dawee was a government clerk in our reservation when I last heard from him. I was surprised upon hearing what my mother said concerning his lack of employment. Seeing the puzzled expression on my face, she continued: "Dawee! Oh, has he not told you that the Great Father at Washington sent a white son to take your brother's pen from him? Since then Dawee has not been able to make use of the education the Eastern school has given him."

I found no words with which to answer satisfactorily. I found no reason with which to cool my inflamed feelings. . . .

Turning to my mother, I urged her to tell me more about Dawee's trouble, but she only said: "Well, my daughter, this village has been these many winters a refuge for white robbers. The Indian cannot complain to the Great Father in Washington without suffering outrage for it here. . . .

A Native American reservation

"My child, there is only one source of justice, and I have been praying steadfastly to the Great Spirit to avenge our wrongs," she said, seeing I did not move my lips.

My shattered energy was unable to hold longer any faith, and I cried out desperately: "Mother, don't pray again! The Great Spirit does not care if we live or die!"

Analyzing Literature
1. **Recall and Interpret** Why did Bonnin's brother lose his job?
2. **Evaluate and Connect** How does Bonnin's mother react to the injustice of the "Great Father in Washington"? How does Bonnin react?

Interdisciplinary Activity
Drama In small groups, assume the roles of Bonnin, her mother, and her brother, and extend the passage by imagining what might happen when Dawee returns.

Reviewing Key Terms

On a sheet of paper, use each of these terms in a sentence.

1. placer mining
2. quartz mining
3. open range
4. long drive
5. maverick
6. homestead
7. dry farming
8. sodbuster
9. bonanza farm
10. nomad
11. annuity
12. assimilate
13. allotment

Reviewing Key Facts

14. **Identify:** Henry Comstock, Great Plains, Stephen Long, Little Crow, Indian Peace Commission, George A. Custer, Dawes Act.
15. What led to the start of boomtowns, and what caused their decline?
16. What new invention finally brought an end to the open range on the Great Plains?
17. How did the railroads boost the settlement of the West?
18. Why was wheat a suitable crop to grow on the Great Plains?
19. What events brought the way of life of the Plains Indians to an end?

Critical Thinking

20. **Analyzing Themes: Economic Factors** Do you think that people moved to and settled in the West primarily for economic reasons? Why or why not?

21. **Drawing Conclusions** Why do you think that so many people were willing to give up their homes and move to mining towns and homesteads in the West?

22. **Forming an Opinion** How do you think a peaceful settlement might have been reached between the Native Americans and the U.S. government?

23. **Interpreting Primary Sources** In the late 1860s, the U.S. government adopted a policy of forcing Native Americans onto small reservations in the Black Hills of Dakota and barren regions of Oklahoma. The government forced many Native American chiefs to sign treaties and to promise to move onto the reservations. Many Native Americans, however, refused to move and fought to maintain their traditional way of life. In the excerpt that follows, Satanta, a chief of the Kiowa, responds to the government's policy. Read the excerpt and answer the questions that follow:

❝I have heard that you intend to settle us on a reservation near the mountains. I don't want to settle. I love to roam over the prairies. There I feel free and happy, but when we settle down we grow pale and die. I have laid aside my lance, bow, and shield, and yet I feel safe in your presence. I have told you the truth. I have no little lies hid about me, but I don't know how it is with the commissioners. Are they as clear as I am? A long time ago this land belonged to our fathers; but when I go up to the river I see camps of soldiers on its banks. These soldiers cut down my timber; they kill my buffalo;

Chapter Summary

Mining and Ranching

- Discovery of gold, silver, and copper attracted settlers to Colorado, the Dakota Territory, Nevada, and Montana
- Growth of cattle and sheep ranching attracted settlers to Texas, Montana, Wyoming, and other western areas

Farming

- Cheap land of Homestead Act encouraged settlement
- Farming technology and climate moderation made the Great Plains into the Wheat Belt

Native Americans

- Federal government forced Plains Indians off their lands with promise of receiving new land
- White settlers moved into lands promised to Native Americans
- Slaughter of buffalo removed a major part of Native American way of life

Role of Railroads

| Provided easy way to ship sheep and cattle to Eastern markets | Brought scarce timber and coal to the Great Plains; advertised for settlers | Helped displace Native Americans by moving settlers west, taking lands, and promoting buffalo slaughter |

and when I see that, my heart feels like bursting; I feel sorry. . . . Has the white man become a child that he should recklessly kill and not eat? When the red men slay game, they do so that they may live and not starve.99

—quoted in *Bury My Heart at Wounded Knee*

a. What reasons does Satanta give for not wanting to settle on a reservation?

b. How does Satanta view the white settlers' approach to the land and the resources on it?

24. Organizing Use a graphic organizer to list the factors that promoted the settlement of the West.

> Reasons for Settling the West

Practicing Skills

25. Interpreting Statistics Examine the chart on Native American populations displayed on this page. Then use the steps you learned about interpreting statistics to answer the following questions.

a. According to this data, is there a positive or a negative correlation between Native American population and the passage of time?

b. Based on this correlation, what conclusions can you draw about Native American population after 1900?

Writing Activity

26. Portfolio Writing Watch an older movie about the West. Look critically at the movie's depiction of cowhands and Native Americans. Write a movie review in which you assess how accurately the movie portrays the West. Place the review in your portfolio.

Chapter Activity

27. Technology: Using the Internet Search the Internet for sites about old mining towns (ghost towns) in the West. Many of these towns are tourist attractions today. Find out the location and history of a few of these towns, as well as the points of interest. Incorporate the information in a brochure for tourists interested in taking a "ghost town" vacation.

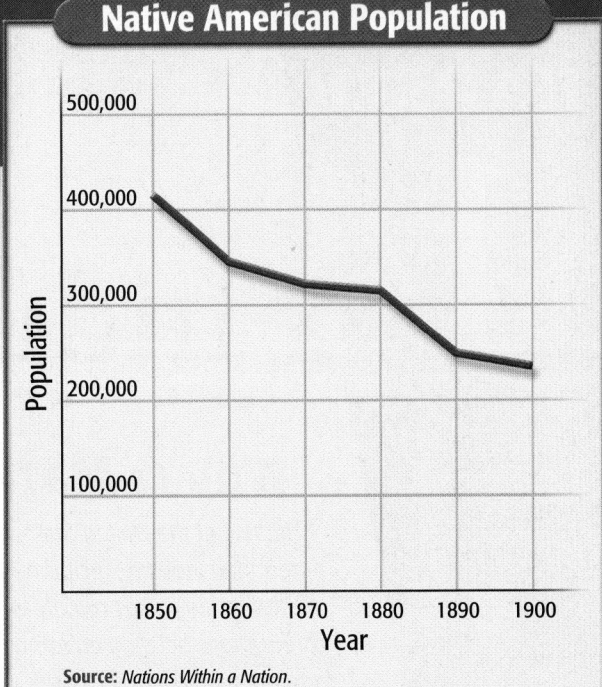

Native American Population

Source: *Nations Within a Nation.*

Geography and History

28. The graph above shows Native American population from 1850 to 1900. Study the graph and answer the questions below.

a. Interpreting Graphs What does the graph indicate about Native American populations between 1850 and 1900?

b. Understanding Cause and Effect What factor caused the Native American populations to decline sharply between 1880 and 1890?

Standardized Test Practice

Directions: Choose the best answer to the following question.

Which of the following did NOT make it easier for settlers to live and farm on the Great Plains?

A Government assistance such as the Homestead Act

B New technology such as the mechanical reaper and the combine

C New farming techniques such as dry farming

D The absence of land speculators

Test-Taking Tip: When you are not sure of an answer, it can be helpful to use the process of elimination. Eliminate the answers that you know are incorrect. For instance, machinery such as the reaper *did* make it easier for farmers to work more land at a quicker pace. Therefore, you can eliminate answer B.

14 Industrialization

1865–1901

Why It Matters

The rise of the United States as an industrial power began after the Civil War. Many factors promoted industry, including cheap labor, new inventions and technology, and plentiful raw materials. Railroads rapidly expanded. Government policies encouraged growth, and large corporations became an important part of the economy. As industry expanded, workers tried to form unions to fight for better wages and working conditions.

The Impact Today

Trends which began in this era can still be seen today.
- *Corporations continue to play an important role.*
- *Technology continues to change American life.*
- *Unions remain powerful in many industries.*

The American Vision *Video* *The Chapter 14 video, "Building America," examines industrial expansion in the United States in the late 1800s.*

1869
- Transcontinental railroad completed

1876
- Alexander Graham Bell invents telephone

1879
- Edison perfects lightbulb

1882
- Standard Oil forms trust

United States PRESIDENTS

A. Johnson 1865–1869 | Grant 1869–1877 | Hayes 1877–1881 | Garfield 1881 | Arthur 1881–1885 | Cleveland 1885–1889

1865   *1875*   *1885*

World

1867
- British colonies unite to form Dominion of Canada

1869
- Chemist Dmitri Mendeleyev creates periodic table of elements

1876
- Korea forced to trade with Japan

1881
- Russian czar Alexander II assassinated

This painting by twentieth-century artist Aaron Bohrod captures the dynamism of an industrializing nation. Bohrod titled his work *The Big Blow: the Bessemer Process.*

1892
• Homestead strike occurs

1894
• Pullman strike begins

1901
• J.P. Morgan forms U.S. Steel

1886
• Haymarket Square riot

1903
• Women's Trade Union League founded

B. Harrison 1889–1893

Cleveland 1893–1897

McKinley 1897–1901

T. Roosevelt 1901–1909

1895

1905

1892
• Rudolf Diesel patents diesel engine

1896
• Athens hosts first modern Olympic games

1900
• Boxer Rebellion begins in China

HISTORY Online

Chapter Overview
Visit the *American Vision* Web site at tav.glencoe.com and click on **Chapter Overviews—Chapter 14** to preview chapter information.

The Rise of Industry

Main Idea

American industry grew rapidly after the Civil War, bringing revolutionary changes to American society.

Key Terms and Names

gross national product, Edwin Drake, laissez-faire, entrepreneur, Morrill Tariff, Alexander Graham Bell, Thomas Alva Edison

Reading Strategy

Organizing As you read about the changes brought about by industrialization, complete a graphic organizer similar to the one below listing the causes of industrialization.

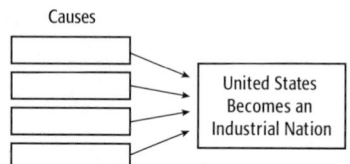

Causes

United States Becomes an Industrial Nation

Reading Objectives

• **Identify** the effects of expanding population on industry.
• **Explain** the effects of technological innovations such as the telephone and telegraph on American development.

Section Theme

Economic Factors The free enterprise system nurtured the growth of American industry.

Preview of Events

◆1860   ◆1870   ◆1880   ◆1890

1859
Edwin Drake drills first oil well

1865
Thaddeus Lowe invents ice machine

1876
Alexander Graham Bell invents telephone

1879
Thomas Edison perfects lightbulb

c. 1893
Northrop automatic loom introduced

★ An American Story ★

On October 21, 1879, Thomas Alva Edison and his team of workers were too excited to sleep. For weeks they had worked to create an electric incandescent lamp, or lightbulb, that would burn for more than a few minutes. For much of the 1800s, inventors had struggled to develop a form of lighting that would be cheaper, safer, and brighter than traditional methods such as candles, whale oil, kerosene, and gas. If Edison and his team could do it, they would change the world. Finally, after weeks of dedicated effort, they turned night into day. Edison later recalled:

❝We sat and looked and the lamp continued to burn and the longer it burned the more fascinated we were. None of us could go to bed and there was no sleep for over 40 hours; we sat and just watched it with anxiety growing into elation. It lasted about 45 hours and then I said, 'If it will burn 40 hours now I know I can make it burn a hundred.'❞

—quoted in *Eyewitness to America*

The United States Industrializes

Although the Industrial Revolution began in the United States in the early 1800s, the nation was still largely a farming country when the Civil War erupted. Out of a population of more than 30 million, only 1.3 million Americans worked in industry in 1860. After the Civil War, industry rapidly expanded, and millions of Americans left their farms to work in mines and factories.

By the early 1900s, Americans had transformed the United States into the world's leading industrial nation. By 1914 the nation's gross national product (GNP)—the total value of all goods and services produced by a country—was eight times greater than it had been when the Civil War ended.

Natural Resources An abundance of raw materials was one reason for the nation's industrial success. The United States contained vast natural resources upon which industry in the 1800s depended, including water, timber, coal, iron, and copper. The presence of these resources meant that American companies could obtain them cheaply and did not have to import them from other countries. Many of the nation's resources were located in the mountains of the American West. The settlement of this region after the Civil War helped to accelerate industrialization, as did the construction of the transcontinental railroad. Railroads brought settlers and miners to the region, and carried the resources back to factories in the East.

At the same time, a new resource, petroleum, began to be exploited. Even before the invention of the automobile, petroleum was in high demand because it could be turned into kerosene. Kerosene was used in lanterns and stoves. The American oil industry was built on the demand for kerosene. It began in western Pennsylvania, where residents had long noticed oil bubbling to the surface of area springs and streams. In 1859 **Edwin Drake** drilled the first oil well near Titusville, Pennsylvania. By 1900 oil fields from Pennsylvania to Texas had been opened. As oil production rose, it fueled economic expansion.

A Large Workforce The human resources available to American industry were as important as natural resources in enabling the nation to industrialize rapidly. Between 1860 and 1910, the population of the United States almost tripled. This population provided industry with a large workforce and also created greater demand for the consumer goods that factories produced.

Population growth stemmed from two causes—large families and a flood of immigrants. American industry began to grow at a time when social and economic conditions in China and eastern Europe convinced many people to leave their nations and move to the United States in search of a better life. Between 1870 and 1910, roughly 20 million immigrants arrived in the United States. These multitudes added to the growing industrial workforce, helping factories increase their production and furthering demand for industrial products.

✓ **Reading Check** **Explaining** How did oil production affect the American economy?

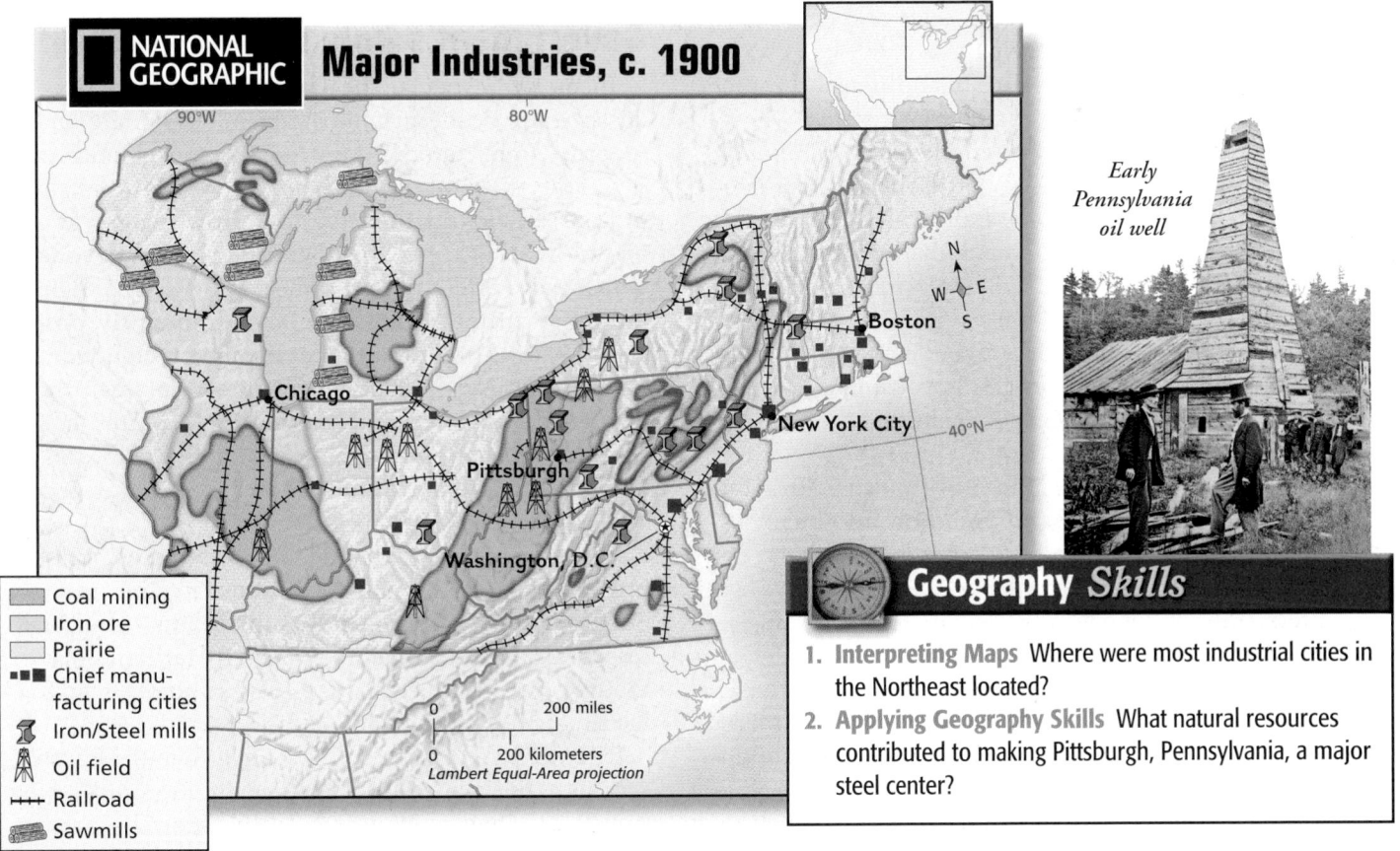

Early Pennsylvania oil well

NATIONAL GEOGRAPHIC

Major Industries, c. 1900

Boston
Chicago
New York City
Pittsburgh
Washington, D.C.

- Coal mining
- Iron ore
- Prairie
- ▪■■ Chief manufacturing cities
- ⚒ Iron/Steel mills
- 🛢 Oil field
- ┼┼┼ Railroad
- Sawmills

0   200 miles
0   200 kilometers
Lambert Equal-Area projection

Geography *Skills*

1. **Interpreting Maps** Where were most industrial cities in the Northeast located?
2. **Applying Geography Skills** What natural resources contributed to making Pittsburgh, Pennsylvania, a major steel center?

American Inventions

1876 Alexander Graham Bell, telephone

1865 Thaddeus Lowe, ice machine

1850

1865

1852 Elisha Otis, elevator brake

1864 George Pullman, rail sleeping car

1874 Stephen Dudley Field, electric streetcar

Free Enterprise

Another important factor that enabled the United States to industrialize rapidly was the free enterprise system. In the late 1800s, many Americans embraced the idea of laissez-faire (leh·say·FAR), literally "let do," a French phrase meaning "let people do as they choose." Supporters of laissez-faire believe the government should not interfere in the economy other than to protect private property rights and maintain peace. These supporters argue that if the government regulates the economy, it increases costs and eventually hurts society more than it helps.

Laissez-faire relies on supply and demand rather than the government to regulate prices and wages. Supporters claim that a free market with competing companies leads to greater efficiency and creates more wealth for everyone. Laissez-faire advocates also support low taxes to ensure that private individuals, not the government, will make most of the decisions about how the nation's wealth is spent. They also believe that the government's debt should be kept limited since money the government borrows from banks is not available to be loaned to individuals for their own uses.

In the United States, the profit motive attracted people of high ability and ambition into business. American entrepreneurs—people who risk their capital in organizing and running a business—appreciated the challenges and rewards of building a business and making profits for themselves.

In the late 1800s, the prospect of making money in manufacturing and transportation attracted many entrepreneurs. The savings that New Englanders accumulated through trade, fishing, whaling, textile mills, and shoe manufacturing helped build hundreds of factories and thousands of miles of railroad track. An equally important source of private capital was Europe, especially Great Britain. Foreign investors saw more opportunity for profit and growth in the United States than at home, and their money also helped to fund the nation's industrial buildup.

Reading Check **Explaining** What does it mean when a government has a laissez-faire economic policy?

Government's Role in Industrialism

In many respects, the United States practiced laissez-faire economics in the late 1800s. State and federal governments kept taxes and spending low and did not impose costly regulations on industry. Nor did they try to control wages and prices. In other ways, the government went beyond laissez-faire and adopted policies intended to help industry, although these policies frequently produced results other than what had been intended.

Since the early 1800s, the struggle between the northeastern states and the southern states had shaped the economic debate in the United States. Northern leaders wanted high tariffs to protect American industry from foreign competition. They also sought federal subsidies for companies building roads, canals, and railroads to the west. Southern leaders opposed subsidizing internal improvements, and they favored low tariffs to promote trade and to keep the cost of imported manufactured goods low.

The Civil War ended this debate. When the South seceded, the Republicans were left in control of Congress. They quickly passed the **Morrill Tariff,**

1877
Thomas Edison, phonograph

1887
Granville T. Woods, electromechanical brake

1893
Charles and J. Frank Duryea, gasoline-powered car

1880

1895

1879
Thomas Edison, incandescent lightbulb

1879
James Ritty, cash register

1883
Jan E. Matzeliger, shoemaking machine

reversing years of declining tariffs. By the end of the Civil War, tariffs had nearly tripled. Congress also gave vast tracts of western land and nearly $65 million in loans to western railroads. The government also sold public lands with mineral resources for much less than their market value. Historians still dispute whether these policies helped to industrialize the country.

Supporters of laissez-faire generally favor free trade and oppose subsidies, believing that tariffs and subsidies drive up prices and protect inefficient companies. They point out that one reason the United States industrialized so rapidly in the 1800s was because it was one of the largest free trade areas in the world. Unlike Europe, which was divided into dozens of states, each with tariffs, the entire United States was open to trade. The Constitution bans states from imposing tariffs, and there were few federal regulations to impede the movement of goods across the country. Similarly, the United States practiced free trade in labor, placing very few restrictions on immigration.

High tariffs, however, contradicted laissez-faire ideas and hurt many Americans. When the United States raised tariffs against foreign goods, other countries raised their tariffs against American goods. This hurt American companies trying to sell goods overseas, and in particular, it hurt farmers who sold their products to Europe. Ironically, the problems farmers faced may have helped speed up industrialization, as many rural Americans decided to leave their farms and take jobs in the new factories.

Despite the problems tariffs created for trade, many business leaders and members of Congress believed they were necessary. Much of Western Europe had already industrialized, and few believed that the new American industries could compete with the large established European factories unless tariffs were put in place to protect them. By the early 1900s, many American industries were large and highly competitive. Business leaders increasingly began to push for free trade because they believed they could compete internationally and win.

Reading Check **Analyzing** Do you think government policies at this time helped or hindered industrialization? Why?

New Inventions

A flood of important inventions helped increase the nation's productive capacity and improved the network of transportation and communications that was vital to the nation's industrial growth. New inventions led to the founding of new corporations, which produced new wealth and new jobs.

TECHNOLOGY

Bell and the Telephone One of the most dramatic inventions in the late 1800s came in the field of communications. In 1874 a young Scottish-American inventor named **Alexander Graham Bell** suggested the idea of a telephone to his assistant, Thomas Watson. Watson recalled, "He had an idea by which he believed it would be possible to talk by telegraph." Bell intended to make an electrical current of varying intensity transmit sound.

Bell worked until 1876 before he succeeded in transmitting his voice. Picking up the crude telephone, he called to the next room, "Come here, Watson, I want you." Watson heard and came. The telephone revolutionized both business and personal communication. In 1877 Bell and others organized the Bell Telephone Company, which eventually became the American Telephone and Telegraph Company (AT&T).

Edison and Electricity

Perhaps the most famous inventor of the late 1800s was **Thomas Alva Edison.** His laboratory at Menlo Park, New Jersey, staffed by skilled assistants, became the forerunner of the modern research laboratory. Edison stood as a symbol for the emerging age of technology.

Edison first achieved international fame in 1877 with the invention of the phonograph. Two years later, he perfected the lightbulb and the electric generator. His laboratory then went on to invent or improve several other major devices, including the battery, the dictaphone, and the motion picture.

In 1882 an Edison company began to transform American society when it started supplying electric power to New York City customers. In 1889 several Edison companies merged to form the Edison General Electric Company, which today is known as GE.

Technology's Impact

As knowledge about technology grew, almost everyone in the United States felt its effects. Shortly after the Civil War, Thaddeus Lowe invented the ice machine, the basis of the refrigerator. In the early 1870s, Gustavus Swift hired an engineer to develop a refrigerated railroad car. In 1877 Swift shipped the first refrigerated load of fresh meat. The widespread use of refrigeration kept food fresh longer and reduced the risk of food poisoning.

The textile industry had long depended on machines to turn fibers into cloth. By the mid-1800s, the introduction of the Northrop automatic loom allowed cloth to be made at an even faster rate. Bobbins, which previously had been changed by hand, were now changed automatically without stopping the loom.

Great changes also took place in the clothing industry. Standard sizes, developed from measurements taken of Union soldiers during the Civil War, were used in the manufacture of ready-made clothes. Power-driven sewing machines and cloth cutters rapidly moved the clothing business from small tailor shops to large factories.

Similar changes took place in shoemaking. Large factories began using new processes and inventions to mass-produce shoes. They could make shoes more efficiently than cobblers and sell them for lower prices. By 1900 local cobblers had nearly disappeared. Prices of many other products also dropped as the United States industrialized.

Technology's impact also included improved connections among people. In 1866 Cyrus Field laid a telegraph cable across the Atlantic Ocean. This transatlantic cable provided instant contact between the United States and Europe. Another innovation was the radio. By the 1920s, radios had become common in American homes, and radio stations sprang up throughout the United States.

Reading Check **Explaining** How did the use of electric power affect the economic development of the United States?

SECTION 1 ASSESSMENT

Checking for Understanding

1. **Define:** gross national product, laissez-faire, entrepreneur.
2. **Identify:** Edwin Drake, Morrill Tariff, Alexander Graham Bell, Thomas Alva Edison.
3. **Explain** how an abundance of natural resources contributed to economic growth in the United States in the late 1800s.

Reviewing Themes

4. **Economic Factors** How did the principles of the free enterprise system, laissez-faire, and profit motive encourage the rise of industry?

Critical Thinking

5. **Synthesizing** What role did the federal government play in increasing industrialization in the United States after the Civil War?
6. **Organizing** Use a graphic organizer similar to the one below to indicate how the inventions listed affected the nature of American work and business.

Invention	Effects
telephone	
lightbulb	
automatic loom	

Analyzing Visuals

7. **Applying Time Lines** Copy the time line on pages 438 and 439 onto a separate sheet of paper. Add other inventions you have learned about to the time line in proper chronological order. Be sure to include the date for each invention.

Writing About History

8. **Descriptive Writing** Imagine you are a young person living in this country in the late 1800s. Choose one of the inventions discussed in the section, and write a journal entry describing its impact on your life. Use standard grammar, spelling, sentence structure, and punctuation.

The Wright Brothers Triumph at Kitty Hawk

Why Learn the Skill?

Just as you are about to leave home to catch your school bus, you hear a radio report. Firefighters are battling a blaze near the bus garage. Your bus is late. Although no one told you, you know that the fire disrupted the bus schedule. You have made an *inference*. From the limited facts available, you formed a conclusion. By combining facts and general knowledge, you inferred that the fire trucks delayed your bus.

Learning the Skill

Learning how to make inferences will help you draw conclusions about particular situations. To make accurate inferences, follow these steps:

- Read or listen carefully for stated facts and ideas.
- Review what you already know about the same topic or situation.
- Use logic and common sense to form a conclusion about the topic.
- If possible, find information that proves or disproves your inference.

Practicing the Skill

Read the following passage about early airplanes, and then answer the questions that follow.

On December 8, 1903, Samuel Langley was ready for his second attempt at flying a manned, self-propelled aircraft. This had never been done before.

Langley used a $50,000 U.S. government grant to build a plane based on unmanned aircraft designs, adding a very powerful engine. The plane broke apart on takeoff and crashed into the Potomac River.

In contrast, Wilbur and Orville Wright used a little more than $1,000 of their personal savings to build their aircraft. The brothers carefully studied the problems with previous planes and designed one with better wings, a more efficient propeller, and a strong but light engine. On December 17, 1903, these intrepid Americans made the first manned, powered flight in history on the sand dunes of Kitty Hawk, North Carolina.

First flight at Kitty Hawk, December 17, 1903

❶ What are the facts regarding Langley's attempt?

❷ What are the facts regarding the Wright brothers' attempt?

❸ What inferences might you draw based on the success of the Wright brothers and failure of Langley?

Skills Assessment

Complete the Practicing Skills questions on page 461 and the Chapter 14 Skill Reinforcement Activity to assess your mastery of this skill.

Applying the Skill

Making Inferences Preview the biography of Mary Harris "Mother" Jones on page 456, and then answer these questions.

1. What kind of work did Jones's husband do before he died?

2. How did Jones travel to West Virginia while working as an organizer for the United Mine Workers?

3. Based on these facts, what inference can you make about Mary Jones? What inference can you make about how the people in the camps felt about her?

 GO TO

Glencoe's **Skillbuilder Interactive Workbook CD-ROM, Level 2,** provides instruction and practice in key social studies skills.

The Railroads

Main Idea

After the Civil War, the rapid construction of railroads accelerated the nation's industrialization and linked the country together.

Key Terms and Names

Pacific Railway Act, Grenville Dodge, Leland Stanford, Cornelius Vanderbilt, time zone, land grant, Jay Gould, Crédit Mobilier, James J. Hill

Reading Strategy

Organizing As you read about the development of a nationwide rail network, complete a graphic organizer similar to the one below listing the effects of this rail network on the nation.

Nationwide Rail Network → Effects

Reading Objectives

- **Discuss** ways in which the railroads spurred industrial growth.
- **Analyze** how the railroads were financed and how they grew.

Section Theme

Individual Action The railroads provided new ways for some Americans to amass wealth.

Preview of Events

♦1870   ♦1875   ♦1880   ♦1885

1869
First transcontinental railroad completed

1872
Crédit Mobilier scandal takes place

1873
First direct rail service between New York and Chicago begins

1883
Time zones instituted

★ An American Story ★

At Promontory Summit, Utah, on May 10, 1869, hundreds of spectators gathered to watch a historic event. Dignitaries from the East and the West met to hammer gold and silver spikes into the final rails that would join two great railroad lines—the Union Pacific and Central Pacific—and span the entire country.

Telegraph offices around the country stood ready to receive news that the last spike had been driven. When the news arrived, bells pealed across the nation, and even the Liberty Bell was rung. In Chicago a seven-mile procession paraded through the streets, and the pealings of church bells resonated throughout the nation's small towns. General Grenville Dodge, who had overseen part of the construction, observed:

66The trains pulled up facing each other, each crowded with workmen who sought advantageous positions to witness the ceremonies. . . . The officers and invited guests formed on each side of the track. . . . Prayer was offered; a number of spikes were driven in the two adjoining rails . . . and thus the two roads were welded into one great trunk line from the Atlantic to the Pacific.99

—quoted in *Mine Eyes Have Seen*

Linking the Nation

In 1865 the United States had about 35,000 miles of railroad track, almost all of it east of the Mississippi River. After the Civil War, railroad construction expanded dramatically, linking the distant regions of the nation in a transportation network. By 1900 the United States, now a booming industrial power, boasted over 200,000 miles of track.

The railroad boom began in 1862 when President Abraham Lincoln signed the **Pacific Railway Act.** This act provided for the construction of a transcontinental railroad by two corporations, the Union Pacific and the Central Pacific railroad companies. To encourage rapid construction, the government offered each company land along its right-of-way. Feverish competition between the two companies developed, as each sought to obtain as much public land and money as possible.

The Union Pacific and Grenville Dodge
Under the direction of engineer **Grenville Dodge,** a former Union general, the Union Pacific began pushing westward from Omaha, Nebraska, in 1865.

The laborers faced blizzards in the mountains, scorching heat in the desert, and sometimes angry Native Americans. Labor, money, and engineering problems plagued the supervisors of the project. As Dodge observed:

> 66At one time we were using at least ten thousand animals, and most of the time from eight to ten thousand laborers. . . . To supply one mile of track with material and supplies required about forty cars. . . . Everything—rails, ties, bridging, fastenings, all

railway supplies, fuel for locomotives and trains, and supplies for men and animals on the entire work— had to be transported from the Missouri River.99
> —quoted in *The Growth of the American Republic*

The railroad workers included Civil War veterans, new immigrants from Ireland recruited especially for the task, frustrated miners and farmers, cooks, adventurers, and ex-convicts. At the height of the project, the Union Pacific employed about 10,000 workers. While most of the laborers camped along the line, about one-fourth of them slept three-deep in bunk beds on rolling boarding cars. Camp life was rough, dirty, and dangerous, with lots of gambling, hard drinking, and fighting.

The Big Four and the Central Pacific
The Central Pacific Railroad began as the dream of engineer Theodore Dehone Judah, who convinced the California legislature to organize a state railroad convention to support his idea. He sold stock in his fledgling Central Pacific Railroad Company to four Sacramento merchants: grocer Leland Stanford, shop owner Charley Crocker, and hardware store owners Mark Hopkins and Collis P. Huntington.

These so-called "Big Four" eventually made huge fortunes from their investment. **Leland Stanford**

Picturing **History**

Engineering Victory The Union Pacific and Central Pacific were joined near Ogden, Utah. The last spike driven was made of gold. It was quickly removed and kept as a symbol. What did the event mean for the nation's commerce?

became governor of California and later served as a United States senator after founding Stanford University in 1885.

Because of a shortage of labor in California, the Central Pacific Railroad hired about 10,000 workers from China. All the equipment—rails, cars, locomotives, and machinery—was shipped from the East, either around Cape Horn at the tip of South America or over the Isthmus of Panama in Central America.

Reading Check **Evaluating** How did the supply difficulties of the Union and Central Railroads differ?

Railroads Spur Growth

The transcontinental railroad was the first of many lines that began to crisscross the nation after the Civil War. This expansion spurred American industrial growth. By linking the nation, railroads helped increase the size of markets for many products. Huge consumers themselves, the railroads also stimulated the economy by spending extraordinary amounts of money on steel, coal, timber, and other necessities.

Linking Other Lines In the early 1800s, most railroads had been built to promote specific cities or to serve local needs. By 1865 hundreds of small unconnected lines existed. The challenge for eastern capitalists was to create a single rail transportation system from this maze of small companies.

Railroad consolidation proceeded rapidly from 1865 to 1900. Large rail lines took over about 400 small railroads, and by 1890 the Pennsylvania Railroad was a consolidation of 73 smaller companies. Eventually seven giant systems with terminals in major cities and scores of branches reaching into the countryside controlled most rail traffic.

One of the most famous and successful railroad consolidators was **Cornelius Vanderbilt,** a former boat captain who had built the largest steamboat fleet in America. By 1869 Vanderbilt had purchased and merged three short New York railroads to form the New York Central, running from New York City to Buffalo. Within four years he had extended his control over lines all the way to Chicago, which enabled him to offer the first direct rail service between New York City and Chicago. In 1871 Vanderbilt began construction of New York's Grand Central terminal.

The Benefits of a National System Before the 1880s each community set its clocks by the sun's position in the sky at high noon. At noon in Chicago, for example, it was 12:50 P.M. in Washington, D.C., 12:09 P.M. in Louisville, Kentucky, and 11:41 A.M. in St. Paul, Minnesota. Local time interfered with train scheduling and at times even threatened passenger safety. When two trains traveled on the same track, collisions could result from scheduling errors caused by variations in time.

To make rail service safer and more reliable, in 1883 the American Railway Association divided the country into four time zones in regions where the same time was kept. The federal government ratified this change in 1918.

Large integrated railroad systems benefited the nation. They were able to shift cars from one section of the country to another according to seasonal needs and in order to speed long-distance transportation. At the same time, new locomotive technology and the introduction of air brakes enabled railroads to put longer and heavier trains on their lines. The new rail systems, along with more powerful locomotives,

HISTORY Online

Student Web Activity Visit the *American Vision* Web site at tav.glencoe.com and click on **Student Web Activities— Chapter 14** for an activity on industrialization.

The Trans-Siberian Railroad

Nearly 50 years after Americans completed their transcontinental railroad, the Russians hammered the final spike into their own cross-country rail line. Begun in 1891 and completed in 1916, the Trans-Siberian Railroad was the longest in the world, running nearly 5,800 miles (9,330 km) from Moscow in the west to Vladivostok on the Sea of Japan in the east. Like the American railroads, the Trans-Siberian line opened up the way for trade and settlement throughout Russia's frontier—an arctic, windswept land known as Siberia.

How might the construction of a railroad affect towns along the line?

NATIONAL GEOGRAPHIC — Railroads, 1870 and 1890

Miles of Track, 1870–1890

Source: *Historical Statistics of the United States: Colonial Times to 1970.*

- ▨ Pacific Time Zone
- ▨ Mountain Time Zone
- ▨ Central Time Zone
- ▨ Eastern Time Zone
- +++ Railroads built by 1870
- +++ Railroads built by 1890
- *Time zones and borders shown as of 1890

Geography *Skills*

1. **Interpreting Maps** What part of the United States saw the greatest expansion in rail lines by 1890?

2. **Applying Geography Skills** In which time zone did the Central Pacific originate?

---

made railroad operation so efficient that the average rate per mile for a ton of freight dropped from two cents in 1860 to three-fourths of a cent in 1900.

The nationwide rail network also helped unite Americans in different regions. Looking back at a quarter century of railroad travel, the *Omaha Daily Republican* observed in 1883 that railroads had "made the people of the country homogeneous, breaking through the peculiarities and provincialisms which marked separate and unmingling sections." This was, perhaps, an overstatement, but it recognized a significant contribution that railroads made to the nation.

☑ Reading Check **Explaining** Why did the American Railway Association divide the country into four time zones?

The Land Grant System

Building and operating railroad lines, especially across the vast unsettled regions of the West, often required more money than most private investors could raise on their own. To encourage railroad construction, the federal government gave land grants to many railroad companies. Railroads would then sell the land to settlers, real estate companies, and other businesses to raise the money they needed to build the railroad.

In the 1850s, the federal government granted individual states over 28 million acres of public lands to give to the railroads. After the Pacific Railway Acts of 1862 and 1864, the government gave the land directly to the railroad companies.

During the 1850s and 1860s, the federal land grant system awarded railroad companies over 120 million acres of land, an area larger than New England, New York, and Pennsylvania combined. Several railroad companies, including the Union Pacific and the Central Pacific, earned enough money from the government's generous land grants to cover much of the cost of building their lines.

☑ Reading Check **Summarizing** How did the government help finance railroads?

Robber Barons

The great wealth many railroad entrepreneurs acquired in the late 1800s led to accusations that they had built their fortunes by swindling investors and taxpayers, bribing government officials, and cheating on their contracts and debts. The person with probably the worst reputation for this kind of activity was **Jay Gould,** who often practiced "insider trading." He used information he received as a railroad owner to manipulate stock prices to his benefit.

Bribery occurred frequently in this era, partly because the state and federal governments were so deeply entangled in funding the railroads. Railroad investors quickly discovered that they could make more money by acquiring government land grants than by operating the railroad. As a result, many investors bribed members of Congress and the state legislatures to vote for more grants.

The Crédit Mobilier Scandal

The corruption in the railroad industry became public in 1872 when the Crédit Mobilier scandal erupted. **Crédit Mobilier** was a construction company set up by several stockholders of the Union Pacific, including Oakes Ames, a member of Congress. Acting for both the Union Pacific and Crédit Mobilier, the investors signed contracts with themselves. Crédit Mobilier greatly overcharged Union Pacific for the work it did, and since the same investors controlled both companies, the railroad agreed to pay the inflated bills.

By the time the Union Pacific railroad was completed, the investors had made several million dollars, but the railroad itself had used up its federal grants and was almost bankrupt. To convince Congress to give the railroad more grants, Ames gave other members of Congress shares in the Union Pacific at a price well below their market value.

During the election campaign of 1872, a disgruntled associate of Ames sent a letter to the *New York Sun* listing the members of Congress who had accepted shares. The scandal led to an investigation that implicated several members of Congress, including Speaker of the House James G. Blaine and James Garfield, who later became president. It also revealed that Vice President Schuyler Colfax had accepted stock from the railroad.

The Great Northern

The Crédit Mobilier scandal provided sensational newspaper headlines. It created the impression that all railroad entrepreneurs were robber barons—people who loot an industry and give nothing back—but the term was not always deserved.

One railroad entrepreneur who was clearly not a robber baron was **James J. Hill.** Hill built and operated the Great Northern Railroad from St. Paul, Minnesota, to Everett, Washington, without any federal land grants or subsidies. He built the Great Northern across good land, carefully planning his route to pass by towns in the region. To increase business, he offered low fares to settlers who homesteaded along his route. He then identified American products that were in demand in China, including cotton, textiles, and flour, and arranged to haul those goods to Washington for shipment to Asia. This enabled the railroad to earn money by hauling goods both east and west, instead of simply sending lumber and farm products east and coming back empty, as many other railroads did. Operating without government subsidies or land grants, the Great Northern became the most successful transcontinental railroad and the only one that was not eventually forced into bankruptcy.

✓ **Reading Check** **Describing** How was the Great Northern different from other railroads of the time?

SECTION 2 ASSESSMENT

Checking for Understanding

1. **Define:** time zone, land grant.
2. **Identify:** Pacific Railway Act, Grenville Dodge, Leland Stanford, Cornelius Vanderbilt, Jay Gould, Crédit Mobilier, James J. Hill.
3. **Explain** the provisions of the Pacific Railway Act.

Reviewing Themes

4. **Individual Action** How did Grenville Dodge contribute to the economic growth of the United States in the late 1800s?

Critical Thinking

5. **Synthesizing** How did railroad expansion in the United States lead to industrial growth?
6. **Organizing** Use a graphic organizer similar to the one below to list the different ways that railroads were financed.

Ways Railroads Were Financed

Analyzing Visuals

7. **Examining Maps and Graphs** Study the map and the graph on page 445. Then make up a quiz of at least five questions based on the information presented.

Writing About History
8. **Persuasive Writing** Take on the role of an employee of a major railroad corporation. Your job assignment is to write an advertisement to recruit workers for your corporation. After writing the advertisement, present it to your class.

Big Business

Main Idea
After the Civil War, big business assumed a more prominent role in American life.

Key Terms and Names
corporation, stockholder, stock, economies of scale, fixed costs, operating costs, pool, Andrew Carnegie, Bessemer process, vertical integration, horizontal integration, monopoly, trust, holding company

Reading Strategy
Organizing As you read about the rise of corporations in the United States, complete a graphic organizer similar to the one below to describe the steps large business owners took to weaken or eliminate competition.

Slashed prices temporarily → ▢ → ▢ → ▢

Reading Objectives
- **Analyze** how large corporations came to dominate American business.
- **Evaluate** how Andrew Carnegie's innovations transformed the steel industry.

Section Theme
Economic Factors Large national corporations formed in the United States in the mid-1800s and contributed to greater production.

Preview of Events

♦1865　　　　♦1875　　　　♦1885　　　　♦1895

1862
John D. Rockefeller buys first oil refinery

1875
Andrew Carnegie opens steel mill in Pittsburgh

1879
Woolworth's chain store opens

1882
Dow Jones & Company founded

1901
J.P. Morgan forms U.S. Steel

★ An American Story ★

In the 1860s, the oil industry in the United States was highly competitive. One highly efficient company was Standard Oil, owned by John D. Rockefeller and his associates. Because his company shipped so much oil, Rockefeller was able to negotiate rebates, or refunds, from railroads that wanted his business. This gave his company an advantage, and he began to pressure other oil companies to sell out to him.

Oil producer Franklin Tarbell pledged never to surrender. Tarbell's daughter Ida later recalled her father's indignation over Rockefeller's maneuvers:

❝It was as if somebody had tried to crowd me off the road. . . . There were rules, you couldn't use the road unless you obeyed those rules. . . . The railroads—so said my father—ran through the valley by the consent of the people; they had given them a right of way. The road on which I trotted was a right of way. One man had the same right as another, but the railroads had given to one something they would not give to another. . . . The strong wrested from the railroads the privilege of preying upon the weak.❞

—quoted in *All in the Day's Work*

The Rise of Big Business

Before the Civil War, the personal wealth of a few people operating in partnership financed most businesses, including many early factories. Most manufacturing enterprises were very small. By 1900 everything had changed. Big businesses dominated the economy, operating vast complexes of factories, warehouses, offices, and distribution facilities.

The Role of Corporations

Big business would not have been possible without the corporation. A corporation is an organization owned by many people but treated by law as though it were a single person. A corporation can own property, pay taxes, make contracts, and sue and be sued. The people who own the corporation are called **stockholders** because they own shares of ownership called **stock.** Issuing stock allows a corporation to raise large amounts of money for big projects while spreading out the financial risk.

Before the 1830s, there were few corporations in the United States because entrepreneurs had to convince a state legislature to issue them a charter. Beginning in the 1830s, however, states began passing general incorporation laws, allowing companies to become corporations and issue stock without charters from the legislature.

Economies of Scale

With the money they raised from the sale of stock, corporations could invest in new technologies, hire a large workforce, and purchase many machines, greatly increasing their efficiency. This enabled them to achieve what is called economies of scale, in which corporations make goods more cheaply because they produce so much so quickly using large manufacturing facilities.

All businesses have two kinds of costs, fixed costs and operating (or variable) costs. Fixed costs are costs a company has to pay, whether or not it is operating. For example, a company would have to pay its loans, mortgages, and taxes, regardless of whether it was operating. Operating costs are costs that occur when running a company, such as paying wages and shipping charges and buying raw materials and other supplies.

The small manufacturing companies that had been typical before the Civil War usually had very low fixed costs but very high operating costs. If sales dropped, it was cheaper to shut down and wait for better economic conditions. By comparison, big companies had very high fixed costs because it took so much money to build and maintain a factory. Compared to their fixed costs, big businesses had low operating costs. Wages and transportation costs were such a small part of a corporation's costs that it made sense to keep operating, even in a recession.

In these circumstances, big corporations had several advantages. They could produce goods more cheaply and efficiently. They could continue to operate in poor economic times by cutting prices to increase sales, rather than shutting down. Many were also able to negotiate rebates from the railroads, thus lowering their operating costs even further.

Small businesses with high operating costs found it difficult to compete against large corporations, and many were forced out of business. At the time, many people criticized corporations for cutting prices and negotiating rebates. They believed the corporations were behaving unethically by using their wealth to drive small companies out of business. In many cases, the changing nature of business organization and the new importance of fixed costs that caused competition to become so severe forced many small companies out of business.

✓ **Reading Check** **Describing** What factors led to the rise of big business in the United States?

The Consolidation of Industry

Many corporate leaders did not like the intense competition that had been forced on them. Although falling prices benefited consumers, they cut into profits. To stop prices from falling, many companies organized pools, or agreements to maintain prices at a certain level.

American courts and legislatures were suspicious of pools because they interfered with competition and property rights. As a result, companies that formed pools had no legal protection and could not enforce their agreements in court. Pools generally did not last long. They broke apart whenever one member cut prices to steal the market share from another, which then allowed competition to resume. By the 1870s, competition had reduced many industries to a few large and highly efficient corporations.

Andrew Carnegie and Steel

The remarkable life of **Andrew Carnegie** illustrates many of the different factors that led to industrialism and the rise of big business in the United States. He was born in Scotland, the son of a poor hand weaver who emigrated to the United States in 1848. At age 12, Carnegie went to work as a bobbin boy in a textile factory earning $1.20 per week. After two years, he became a messenger in a telegraph office, then served as private secretary to Thomas Scott, a superintendent and later president of the Pennsylvania Railroad. Carnegie's energy impressed Scott, and when Scott was promoted, Carnegie succeeded him as superintendent.

As a railroad supervisor, Carnegie knew that he could make a lot of money by investing in companies that served the railroad industry. He bought shares in iron mills and factories that made sleeping cars and

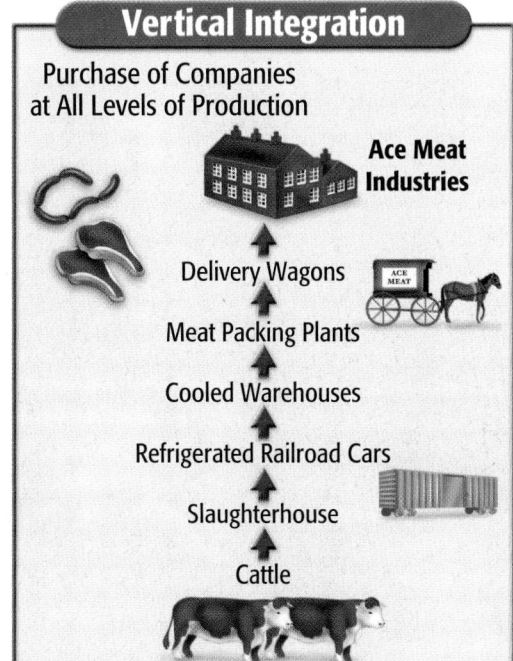

Vertical Integration

Purchase of Companies at All Levels of Production

Ace Meat Industries

↑ Delivery Wagons

↑ Meat Packing Plants

↑ Cooled Warehouses

↑ Refrigerated Railroad Cars

↑ Slaughterhouse

↑ Cattle

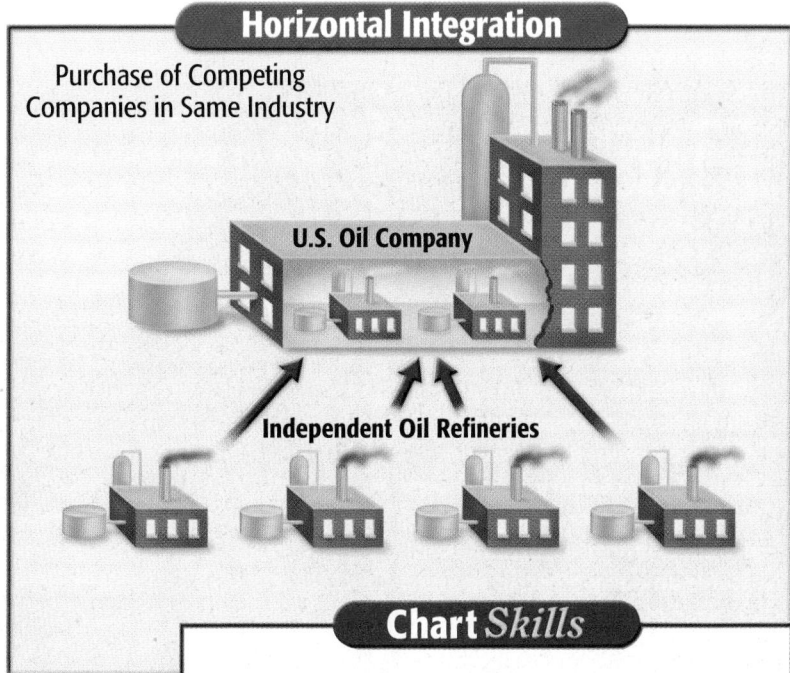

Horizontal Integration

Purchase of Competing Companies in Same Industry

U.S. Oil Company

Independent Oil Refineries

Chart *Skills*

Horizontal and vertical integration were the two most common business combinations in the late 1800s.

Evaluating Which combination do you think would yield the most efficient business? Why?

---

locomotives. He also invested in a company that built railroad bridges. In his early 30s, he was earning $50,000 per year, and he decided to quit his job with the railroad to concentrate on his own business affairs.

As part of his business activities, Carnegie frequently traveled to Europe to sell railroad bonds. On one trip, he met the English inventor, Sir Henry Bessemer, who had invented a new process for making high quality steel efficiently and cheaply. After meeting Bessemer, Carnegie decided to concentrate his investments in the steel industry. He opened a steel company in Pittsburgh in 1875 and quickly adapted his steel mills to use the **Bessemer process.** Carnegie often boasted about how cheaply he could produce steel:

> 66 Two pounds of iron stone mined upon Lake Superior and transported nine hundred miles to Pittsburgh; one pound and one-half of coal mined and manufactured into coke, and transported to Pittsburgh; one-half pound of lime, mined and transported to Pittsburgh; a small amount of manganese ore mined in Virginia and brought to Pittsburgh—and these four pounds of materials manufactured into one pound of steel, for which the consumer pays one cent. 99

> —quoted in *The Growth of the American Republic*

Vertical and Horizontal Integration To increase manufacturing efficiency even further, Carnegie took the next step in building a big business. He did this by beginning the vertical integration of the steel industry. A vertically integrated company owns all of the different businesses on which it depends for its operation. Instead of paying companies for coal, lime, and iron, Carnegie's company bought coal mines, limestone quarries, and iron ore fields. Vertical integration saved companies money while enabling big companies to become even bigger.

Successful business leaders like Carnegie also pushed for horizontal integration, or combining many firms engaged in the same type of business into one large corporation. Horizontal integration took place frequently as companies competed. When a company began to lose market share, it would often sell out to competitors to create a larger organization. By 1880, for example, a series of buyouts had enabled Rockefeller's Standard Oil to gain control of approximately 90 percent of the oil refining industry in the United States. When a single company achieves control of an entire market, it becomes a monopoly. Many Americans feared monopolies because they believed that a company with a monopoly could charge whatever it wanted for its products. Others, however, supported monopolies. They believed that monopolies had to keep prices low because raising prices would encourage competitors to reappear and offer the products for a lower price. In some industries companies had a virtual monopoly in the United States but were competing on a global scale. Standard Oil, for example, came very close to having a monopoly in the United States, but competition with other oil companies throughout the world forced the Standard Oil Company to keep its prices low in the late 1800s and early 1900s.

Trusts By the late 1800s, many Americans had grown suspicious of large corporations and feared the power of monopolies. To preserve competition and prevent horizontal integration, many states made it illegal for one company to own stock in another without specific permission from the state legislature. In 1882 Standard Oil formed the first trust, a new way of merging businesses that did not violate the laws against owning other companies. A trust is a legal concept that allows one person to manage another person's property. The person who manages another person's property is called a trustee.

Instead of buying a company outright, Standard Oil had stockholders give their stocks to a group of Standard Oil trustees. In exchange, the stockholders received shares in the trust, which entitled them to a portion of the trust's profits. Since the trustees did not own the stock but were merely managing it, they were not violating any laws. This arrangement enabled the trustees to control a group of companies as if they were one large merged company.

Holding Companies Beginning in 1889 the state of New Jersey further accelerated the rise of big business with a new general incorporation law. This law allowed corporations chartered in New Jersey to own stock in other businesses without any need for special legislative action. Many companies immediately used the New Jersey law to create a new organization called a holding company. A holding company does not produce anything itself. Instead, it owns the stock of companies that do produce goods. The holding company controls all of the companies it owns, effectively merging them into one large enterprise. By 1904 the United States had 318 holding companies. Together these giant corporations controlled over 5,300 factories and were worth more than $7 billion.

✓ **Reading Check** **Explaining** What techniques did corporations use to consolidate their industries?

Selling the Product

The vast array of products that American industries churned out led retailers to look for new ways to market and sell goods. N.W. Ayer and Son of Philadelphia, for example, developed bold new formats for advertising. Large display ads with illustrations replaced the small-type line ads that had been standard in newspapers. By 1900 retailers were spending over $90 million a year on advertising, approximately 10 times what they had spent in 1865. Advertising attracted readers to the newest retail business, the department store.

In 1877 advertisements billed John Wanamaker's new Philadelphia department store, the Grand Depot, as the "largest space in the world devoted to retail selling on a single floor." When Wanamaker's opened, only a handful of department stores existed in the United States; soon hundreds sprang up. Department stores changed the idea of shopping by bringing a huge array of different products together in a large, elegant building. They created an atmosphere that made shopping seem glamorous and exciting.

Chain stores, a group of similar stores owned by the same company, first appeared in the mid-1800s. In contrast to department stores, which offered many services, chain stores focused on thrift, offering low prices instead of elaborate service and decor. Woolworth's, a chain store that opened in 1879, became one of the most successful retail chains in American history.

To reach the millions of people who lived in rural areas in the late 1800s—far from chain stores or department stores—retailers began issuing mail-order catalogs. Two of the largest mail-order retailers were Montgomery Ward and Sears, Roebuck. Their huge catalogs, widely distributed through the mail, used attractive illustrations and friendly descriptions to advertise thousands of items for sale.

Fact | Fiction | Folklore

The New York Stock Exchange In 1792 businesspeople met in New York City to establish a stock exchange—a marketplace for buying and selling stock in companies. At first, the new stock exchange was located under a buttonwood tree on Wall Street.

The organization took its present name, the New York Stock Exchange, in 1863. Huge amounts of the capital required for the nation's industrialization after the Civil War passed through the New York Stock Exchange.

As stock trading grew, investors across the nation needed financial news. In 1882 Henry Charles Dow and Edward D. Jones founded Dow Jones & Company. This new company sent bulletins on the day's business to Wall Street's financial houses. The day's last delivery contained a news sheet, which became the *Wall Street Journal* in July 1889.

Reading Check **Identifying** What innovations did retailers introduce in the late 1800s to sell goods to consumers?

SECTION 3 ASSESSMENT

Checking for Understanding

1. **Define:** corporation, economies of scale, fixed costs, operating costs, pool, vertical integration, horizontal integration, monopoly, trust, holding company.

2. **Identify:** stockholder, stock, Andrew Carnegie, Bessemer process.

3. **List** the new methods of advertising and selling that helped push consumer goods in the late 1800s.

Reviewing Themes

4. **Economic Factors** What factors allowed corporations to develop in the United States in the late 1800s?

Critical Thinking

5. **Forming an Opinion** Do you think an individual today can rise from "rags to riches" like Andrew Carnegie did? Why or why not?

6. **Organizing** Use a graphic organizer like the one below to list ways business leaders in the late 1800s tried to eliminate competition.

Attempts to Eliminate Competition

Analyzing Visuals

7. **Analyzing Photographs** Study the photograph on page 450 of a woman using an early electric vacuum cleaner. How would you compare this to today's vacuum cleaners? How do you think new mass-produced appliances affected the lives of women in this era?

Writing About History

8. **Expository Writing** Write a newspaper editorial in which you explain why entrepreneurs such as John D. Rockefeller and Andrew Carnegie were a positive or a negative force on the U.S. economy in the late 1800s.

Investigating Standard Oil

By the 1880s, the Standard Oil Company, under the direction of John D. Rockefeller and his associates, had gained control of more than 90 percent of the oil refining business in the United States. Did Standard Oil use unfair tactics? The United States Industrial Commission investigated, calling Rockefeller himself to testify. Rockefeller said his success was due to the efficiency of his company. George Rice, an independent refiner from Marietta, Ohio, told the Industrial Commission that Standard Oil's advantage was criminal collusion with the railroads. Was he right? You're the historian.

Read the following excerpts from the Industrial Commission hearings of 1899. Then complete the questions and activities on the next page.

John D. Rockefeller

Standard Oil stock

From John D. Rockefeller's testimony

Question: To what advantages, or favors, or methods of management do you ascribe chiefly the success of the Standard Oil Company?

Answer [Rockefeller]: I ascribe the success of the Standard to its consistent policy to make the volume of its business large through the merits and cheapness of its products. It has spared no expense in finding, securing, and utilizing the best and cheapest methods of manufacture. It has sought for the best superintendents and workmen and paid the best wages. It has not hesitated to sacrifice old machinery and old plants for new and better ones. It has placed its manufactories at the points where they could supply markets at the least expense. It has not only sought markets for its principal products, but for all possible by-products, sparing no expense in introducing them to the public.

It has not hesitated to invest millions of dollars in methods of cheapening the gathering and distribution of oils by pipe lines, special cars, tank steamers, and tank wagons. . . .

Question: What are, in your judgment, the chief advantages from industrial combinations—(a) financially to stockholders; (b) to the public?

Answer: All the advantages which can be derived from a cooperation of person and aggregation of capital. . . . It is too late to argue about advantages of industrial combinations. They are a necessity. And if Americans are to have the privilege of extending their business in all the States of the Union, and into foreign countries as well, they are a necessity on a large scale, and require the agency of more than one corporation. Their chief advantages are:

1. Command of necessary capital.
2. Extension of limits of business.
3. Increase the number of persons interested in the business.
4. Economy in the business.
5. Improvements and economies which are derived from knowledge of many interested persons of wide experience.
6. Power to give the public improved products at less prices and still make a profit from stockholders.
7. Permanent work and good wages for laborers.

Cartoon criticizing Standard Oil

Oil derricks

From George Rice's testimony

I am a citizen of the United States. . . . Producer of petroleum for more than 30 years, and a refiner of same for 20 years, but my refinery has been shut down during the past 3 years, owing to the powerful and all-prevailing machinations of the Standard Oil Trust, in criminal collusion and conspiracy with the railroads to destroy my business of 20 years of patient industry, toil, and money in building up, wholly by and through unlawful freight discriminations. I have been driven from pillar to post, from one railway line to another, for 20 years, in the absolutely vain endeavor to get equal and just freight rates with the Standard Oil Trust, so as to be able to run my refinery at anything approaching a profit, but which I have been utterly unable to do. I have had to consequently shut down, with my business absolutely ruined and my refinery idle. This has been a very sad, bitter, and ruinous experience for me to endure, but I have endeavored to the best of my circumstances and ability to combat it the utmost I could for many a long waiting year, expecting relief through the honest and proper execution of our laws, which have as yet, however, never come. . . .

Outside of rebates or freight discriminations I had no show with the Standard Oil trust, because of their unlawfully acquired monopoly, by which they could temporarily cut only my customers' prices, and below cost, leaving the balance of the town, nine-tenths, uncut. This they can easily do without any appreciable harm to their general trade, and thus effectually wipe out all competition, as fully set forth. Standard Oil prices generally were so high that I could sell my goods 2 to 3 cents a gallon below their prices and make a nice profit, but these savage attacks and cuts upon my customers' goods, and their consequent loss, plainly showed them their power for evil, and the uselessness to contend against such odds, and they would buy no more of my oil. . . .

Understanding the Issue

1. What potential advantages could companies like Standard Oil offer consumers?
2. What did George Rice believe to be the reason Standard Oil was so successful?
3. How would you assess the credibility of the two accounts?

Activities

1. **Investigate** Today many industries, unions, and special interest groups lobby Congress for favorable legislation. What are the most powerful groups? How do they operate?
2. **Check the News** Are there any companies that recently have been investigated for unfair or monopolistic practices? Collect headlines and news articles and create a bulletin board display.

Unions

Preview of Events

| ♦1875 | ♦1885 | ♦1895 | ♦1905 |

1877
Great Railroad Strike

1886
American Federation of Labor founded

1886
Riot in Chicago's Haymarket Square

1894
Pullman Strike

1903
Women's Trade Union League founded

★ An American Story ★

On September 6, 1869, hundreds of miners' wives and children heard the repeated shrill blasts of the Avondale Mine's whistle, which signaled an accident. The families ran to the mine's entry and beheld a terrifying sight: hot smoke billowing from the mine shaft.

The owners of the Avondale Coal Mine in Luzerne County, Pennsylvania, had not built a second entrance to their mine. Without an escape route, the 179 miners trapped below soon died. Songs to commemorate the disaster later gave voice to the silenced victims:

> ❝And as their souls ascended
> To God who gave them breath
> They plead against the company
> Whose greed had caused their death❞

Following the deaths at Avondale, John Siney, an Irish immigrant and union leader, urged his fellow miners to unionize:

> ❝Men, if you must die with your boots on, die for your families, your homes, your country, but do not longer consent to die like rats in a trap. . . .❞

—quoted in *Labor's Untold Story*

Working in the United States

Life for workers in industrial America was difficult. As machines replaced skilled labor, work became monotonous. Workers had to perform highly specific, repetitive tasks and could take little pride in their work. In addition, working conditions were often unhealthy and dangerous. Workers breathed in lint, dust, and toxic fumes. Heavy machines lacking safety devices caused a high number of injuries.

Despite the difficult working conditions, industrialism brought about a dramatic rise in the standard of living. While only a few entrepreneurs became rich, real wages earned by the average worker rose by about 50 percent between 1860 and 1890.

Despite the rise in the standard of living, the uneven division of income between the wealthy and the working class caused resentment among workers. In 1900 the average industrial worker made 22¢ per hour and worked 59 hours per week.

At the same time, an economic phenomenon of the late 1800s made relations between workers and employers even more difficult. Between 1865 and 1897, the United States experienced deflation, or a rise in the value of money. Throughout the late 1800s, deflation caused prices to fall, which increased the buying power of workers' wages. Although companies cut wages regularly in the late 1800s, prices fell even faster, so that wages were actually still going up in buying power. Workers, however, believed that companies wanted to pay them less money for the same work. Eventually, many workers decided that the only way to improve their working conditions was to organize unions. With a union, they could bargain collectively to negotiate higher wages and better working conditions.

✓ **Reading Check**

Describing What aspects of industrial life caused frustration for workers in the late 1800s?

Early Unions

There were two basic types of industrial workers in the United States in the 1800s—craft workers and common laborers. Craft workers had special skills and training. They included machinists, iron molders, stonecutters, glassblowers, shoemakers, printers, carpenters, and many others. Craft workers generally received higher wages and

had more control over how they organized their time on the shop floor. Common laborers had few skills and received lower wages.

In the 1830s, as industrialism began to spread, craft workers began to form trade unions—unions limited to people with specific skills. By 1873 there were 32 national trade unions in the United States. Among the largest and most successful were the Iron Molders' International Union, the International Typographical Union, and the Knights of St. Crispin—the shoemakers' union.

Industry Opposes Unions Employers were often forced to recognize and negotiate with trade unions because they represented workers whose skills they needed. However, employers generally regarded unions as illegitimate conspiracies that interfered with their property rights. Owners of large corporations particularly opposed industrial unions, which united all craft workers and common laborers in a particular industry.

Companies used several techniques to prevent unions from forming. They required workers to take

 History

Unsafe Working Conditions Workers in the late 1800s often faced unsafe working conditions. Many began to join labor unions in an attempt to improve these conditions. What unsafe conditions does this photograph of a steel mill show?

oaths or sign contracts promising not to join a union, and they hired detectives to go undercover and identify union organizers. Workers who tried to organize a union or strike were fired and placed on a **blacklist**—a list of "troublemakers." Once blacklisted, a laborer could get a job only by changing residence, trade, or even his or her name.

If workers formed a union, companies often used a lockout to break it. They locked workers out of the property and refused to pay them. If the union called a strike, employers would hire replacement workers, or **strikebreakers**, also known as scabs.

Political and Social Opposition

Workers who wanted to organize a union faced several major problems. There were no laws giving workers the right to organize or requiring owners to negotiate with them. Courts frequently ruled that strikes were "conspiracies in restraint of trade," for which labor leaders might be fined or jailed.

Unions also suffered from the perception that they threatened American institutions. In the late 1800s, the ideas of Karl Marx, called Marxism, had become very influential in Europe. Marx argued that the basic force shaping capitalist society was the class struggle between workers and owners. He believed that workers would eventually revolt, seize control of the factories, and overthrow the government.

Marxists claimed that after the revolution, the government would seize all private property and create a socialist society where wealth was evenly divided. Eventually, Marx thought, the state would wither away, leaving a Communist society where classes did not exist. Marxism strongly shaped the thinking of European unions.

While many labor supporters agreed with Marx, a few supported anarchism. Anarchists believe that society does not need any government. At the time, some believed that with only a few acts of violence, they could ignite a revolution to topple the government. In the late 1800s, anarchists assassinated government officials and set off bombs all across Europe, hoping to trigger a revolution.

As Marxist and anarchist ideas spread in Europe, tens of thousands of European immigrants began arriving in the United States. Nativism—anti-immigrant feelings—was already strong in the United States. As people began to associate immigrant workers with revolution and anarchism, they became increasingly suspicious of unions. These fears, as well as the government's duty to maintain law and order, often led officials to use the courts, the police, and even the army to crush strikes and break up unions.

✓ **Reading Check** **Identifying** Why were some Americans suspicious of Unions?

The Struggle to Organize

Although workers attempted on many occasions to create large industrial unions, they rarely succeeded. In many cases the confrontations with owners and the government led to violence and bloodshed. In 1868 William Sylvis, president of the Iron Molders Union and leader of the National Labor Union, wrote to Karl Marx to encourage Marx's work and express his own hopes:

> ❝Our cause is a common one. . . . Go ahead in the good work that you have undertaken, until the most glorious success crowns your efforts . . . monied

Profiles IN HISTORY

Mother Jones *1830–1930*

Mary Harris "Mother" Jones emigrated to the United States from Ireland in 1835 at the age of five. Jones became the nation's most prominent woman union leader after a tragic personal loss. In 1867 her husband George, a union organizer, and their four children died from yellow fever.

Widowed and childless, Jones moved to Chicago and opened a dressmaker's shop. From her shop window, Jones could see the effects of the economic downturn of the 1870s: "poor shivering wretches, jobless and hungry." At night she attended rallies for the Knights of Labor.

By 1890 Jones had become an organizer for the United Mine Workers. In 1897 she traveled to West Virginia. The intrepid labor organizer trudged from camp to camp along railroad tracks or rode atop farm wagons. She slept in a tent.

A journalist who followed Jones on her trip reported that Jones began her speeches slowly, encouraging her listeners to "look on yourselves, and upon each other. Let us consider this together for I am one of you, and I know what it is to suffer." Then Mother Jones would make an impassioned plea for the miners to join the union. "You pity yourselves, but you do not pity your brothers, or you would stand together to help one another."

NATIONAL GEOGRAPHIC

Strikes and Labor Unrest, 1870–1890

Railroad strike
Miners' strike
Other strike or riot
Counties with strike activity, 1881–1894
No strikes reported
— 1890 border

Geography Skills

1. **Interpreting Maps** In what part of the nation did most of the strikes occur?
2. **Applying Geography Skills** Why did most of the labor conflicts take place where they did?

power is fast eating up the substance of the people. We have made war upon it, and we mean to win it. If we can we will win through the ballot box; if not, we will resort to sterner means. A little bloodletting is sometimes necessary in desperate causes. ❞

—quoted in *Industrialism and the American Worker*

The Great Railroad Strike of 1877 In 1873 a severe recession known as the Panic of 1873 struck the American economy and forced many companies to cut wages. In July 1877, as the recession continued, several railroads announced another round of wage cuts. This triggered the first nationwide labor protest. The day after the cuts took effect, railroad workers in Martinsburg, West Virginia, walked off the job and blocked the tracks.

As word spread, railroad workers across the country walked off the job. The strike eventually involved 80,000 railroad workers in 11 states and affected two-thirds of the nation's railways. Angry strikers smashed equipment, tore up tracks, and blocked rail service in New York, Baltimore, Pittsburgh, St. Louis,

and Chicago. The governors of several states called out their militias to stop the violence. In many places, gun battles erupted between the militia and striking workers.

Determined to stop the violence, President Hayes ordered the army to open the railroad between Philadelphia and Pittsburgh. He then sent troops to Chicago, where the strike had paralyzed the entire city. The troops restored order, but by the time the strike ended, more than 100 people lay dead, and millions of dollars of property had been destroyed.

The Knights of Labor The failure of the Great Railroad Strike convinced many labor organizers that workers across the nation needed to be better organized. By the late 1870s, enough workers had joined a new organization, the **Knights of Labor,** to make it the first nationwide industrial union.

The Knights called for an eight-hour workday and a government bureau of labor statistics. They also supported equal pay for women, the abolition of child labor, and the creation of worker-owned factories. The Knights' leaders initially opposed the use of strikes, preferring to use boycotts to pressure employers. They also supported arbitration, a process in which an impartial third party helps workers and management reach an agreement.

In the early 1880s, the Knights began to use strikes, and they achieved great success initially. After striking Knights convinced one of Jay Gould's railroads to reverse wage cuts in 1885, membership in the union leapt from 100,000 to 700,000 in less than a year. The following year, 1886, marked the peak of their success. In the spring of that year, an event known as the **Haymarket Riot** undermined the Knights' reputation, and the union rapidly declined.

The Haymarket Riot In the early 1880s, the movement for an eight-hour workday began to build support. In 1886 organizers called for a nationwide strike on May 1 to show support for the idea. On that date, strikes took place in many cities, including Chicago.

On May 3, a clash between strikers and police in Chicago left one striker dead. The next evening, an anarchist group organized a meeting in Chicago's Haymarket Square to protest the killing. Around 3,000 people gathered to hear the speeches. When police entered the square, someone threw a bomb. The police opened fire, and workers shot back. Seven police officers and four workers were killed.

Police arrested eight people for the bombing. Seven of those arrested were German immigrants and advocates of anarchism. The incident horrified people across the country.

No one knew who threw the bomb. Although the evidence was weak, all eight men were convicted, and four were later executed. Unfortunately for the Knights of Labor, one of the men arrested was a member of the union. The incident badly hurt the Knights' reputation, and they began to lose members rapidly.

The Pullman Strike Although the Haymarket Riot set back the drive to create industrial unions, other labor organizers continued their efforts. In 1893 railroad workers created the American Railway Union (ARU) under the leadership of Eugene V. Debs. One of the companies the ARU unionized was the Pullman Palace Car Company.

The Pullman Company was based in Illinois. It had built a town named Pullman near its factory and required its workers to live in the town and to buy goods from company stores. In 1893 a depression struck the United States, causing the Pullman Company to slash wages. The wage cuts made it difficult for workers to pay their rent or the high prices at the company stores. In May 1894, after Pullman fired three workers who complained, a strike began. In support, the ARU stopped handling Pullman cars all across the United States.

The boycott of Pullman cars tied up railroads and threatened to paralyze the economy. Determined to break the union, railroad managers arranged for U.S. mail cars to be attached to the Pullman cars. If the strikers refused to handle the Pullman cars, they would be interfering with the U.S. mail, a violation of federal law. President Grover Cleveland then sent in troops, claiming it was his responsibility to keep the mail running. When a federal court issued an **injunction,** or formal court order, directing the union to halt the boycott, both the strike at Pullman and the ARU collapsed.

✓ **Reading Check** **Analyzing** Why did industrial unions frequently fail in the late 1800s?

The American Federation of Labor

Although large-scale industrial unions generally failed in the late 1800s, trade unions continued to prosper. In 1886 delegates from over 20 of the nation's trade unions organized the **American Federation of Labor** (AFL). The AFL's first leader was **Samuel Gompers.** His approach to labor relations—which he called "plain and simple" unionism—helped unions to become accepted in American society.

Samuel Gompers

Gompers believed that unions should stay out of politics. He rejected socialist and communist ideas. Rather, he believed that the AFL should fight for small gains—such as higher wages and better working conditions—within the American system. He was willing to use the strike but preferred to negotiate.

Under Gompers's leadership, the AFL had three main goals. First, it tried to convince companies to recognize unions and to agree to collective bargaining. Second, it pushed for closed shops, meaning that companies could only hire union members. Third, it promoted an eight-hour workday.

The AFL grew slowly, but by 1900 it was the biggest union in the country, with over 500,000 members. Still, at that time, the AFL represented less than 15 percent of all non-farm workers. All unions, including railroad unions, represented only 18 percent. As the 1900s began, the vast majority of workers remained unorganized, and unions were relatively weak.

Reading Check **Analyzing** What AFL policies contributed to its growth as a union?

Working Women

Throughout the 1800s, most wage-earning workers in the United States were men. After the Civil War, the number of women wage earners began to increase. By 1900 women made up more than 18 percent of the labor force.

The type of jobs women did outside the home in the late 1800s and early 1900s reflected society's ideas about what constituted "women's work." Roughly one-third of women worked as domestic servants. Another third worked as teachers, nurses, sales clerks, and secretaries. The remaining third were industrial workers, but they were employed in light industrial jobs that people believed appropriate to their gender. Many worked in the garment industry and food processing plants.

Regardless of their employment, women were paid less than men even when they performed the same jobs. It was assumed that a woman had a man helping to support her, either her father or her husband, and that a man needed higher wages to support a family. For this reason, most unions, including the AFL, excluded women.

In 1903 two woman labor organizers, Mary Kenney O'Sullivan and Leonora O'Reilly, decided to establish a separate union for women. With the help

Picturing **History**

Detail Work These women worked in the National Elgin Watch Company's gilding room, where they gilded metal watches with thin layers of gold. *What do you notice about their working conditions?*

of Jane Addams and Lillian Wald—the founders of the settlement house movement—they established the **Women's Trade Union League** (WTUL), the first national association dedicated to promoting women's labor issues. The WTUL pushed for an eight-hour day, the creation of a minimum wage, an end to evening work for women, and the abolition of child labor. The WTUL also collected funds to support women on strike.

Reading Check **Comparing** How were female industrial workers treated differently than male workers in the late 1800s?

SECTION 4 ASSESSMENT

Checking for Understanding

1. **Define:** deflation, trade union, industrial union, lockout, Marxism, arbitration, closed shop.
2. **Identify:** blacklist, Knights of Labor, injunction.
3. **List** the groups of workers represented by the Knights of Labor and the American Federation of Labor.

Reviewing Themes

4. **Individual Action** What political contribution did Mary Harris "Mother" Jones make to American society?

Critical Thinking

5. **Analyzing** Why did early labor unions fail?
6. **Organizing** Use a graphic organizer similar to the one below to list the factors that led to an increase in unions in the late 1800s.

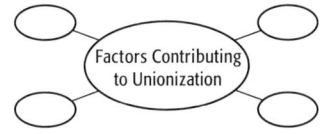

Factors Contributing to Unionization

Analyzing Visuals

7. **Analyzing Photographs** Examine the photograph at the top of this page of workers in a watch factory. Most of the people in the picture are women. What do you think the jobs were of the men in the photograph?

Writing About History

8. **Persuasive Writing** Imagine that you are an American worker living in one of the nation's large cities. Write a letter to a friend explaining why you support or oppose the work of labor unions.

Reviewing Key Terms

On a sheet of paper, use each of these terms in a sentence.

1. gross national product
2. laissez-faire
3. entrepreneur
4. time zone
5. land grant
6. corporation
7. economies of scale
8. fixed costs
9. operating costs
10. pool
11. vertical integration
12. horizontal integration
13. monopoly
14. trust
15. holding company
16. deflation
17. trade union
18. industrial union
19. lockout
20. Marxism
21. arbitration
22. closed shop

Chapter Summary

Factors Behind Industrialization

- Abundant natural resources
- Cheap immigrant labor force
- High tariffs that reduced foreign goods
- National communication and transportation networks

Growth of Business

- Little or no government intervention
- Development of pools, trusts, holding companies, and monopolies
- Small businesses could not compete with economies–of–scale of large businesses
- Practices of some big businesses sometimes limited competition

Changing Workplace

- Rural migration and immigration created large, concentrated workforce
- In large–scale industries, low wages, long hours, and dangerous working conditions were common
- First large unions formed but had little bargaining power against large companies

Reviewing Key Facts

23. **Identify:** Morrill Tariff, Andrew Carnegie.
24. The United States had an advantage in industrializing due to its resources and large workforce. What resources did the nation have? Why was its workforce large?
25. How did inventions contribute to economic growth in the United States in the late 1800s?
26. How did the federal government encourage railroad companies to construct railroads?
27. What new methods of selling products were developed in the late 1800s?
28. Why did workers try to organize labor unions in the United States in the late 1800s?
29. What were the two basic types of workers in American industry at this time?

Critical Thinking

30. **Analyzing Themes: Individual Action** List the names and actions of five people who contributed to American economic growth in the late 1800s.
31. **Organizing** Use a graphic organizer similar to the one below to list the factors that led to making the United States an industrial nation.

Factors Leading to Industrialization

32. **Interpreting Primary Sources** Americans like Ida Tarbell criticized large corporations such as the Standard Oil Company. In the following excerpt from *History of the Standard Oil Company,* she warns of the results of Rockefeller's business practices on the nation's morality. Read the excerpt and answer the questions that follow:

66Very often people who admit the facts, who are willing to see that Mr. Rockefeller has employed force and fraud to secure his ends, justify him by declaring, 'It's business.' That is, 'It's business' has come to be a legitimate excuse for hard dealing, sly tricks, special privileges. It is a common enough thing to hear men arguing that the ordinary laws of morality do not apply in business.

As for the ethical side, there is no cure but in an increasing scorn of unfair play. . . . When the business-man who fights to secure special privileges, to crowd his competitor off the track by other than fair competitive methods, receives the same summary disdainful ostracism by his fellows that the doctor or lawyer who is 'unprofessional,' the athlete who abuses the rules, receives, we shall have gone a long way toward making commerce a fit pursuit for our young men.

—quoted in *Readings in American History*

a. According to Tarbell, what practices had Rockefeller used to establish the Standard Oil Company?

b. In what way did Tarbell believe the attitudes of the American people contributed to Rockefeller's business practices?

33. Analyzing Analyze the impact of technological innovations and industrialization on the American labor movement.

Practicing Skills

34. Making Inferences Reread the passage titled "Working in the United States" from Section 4, page 454. Then answer the following questions.

a. What facts are stated about working conditions in the United States during this time period?

b. Based on your answer to the previous question, what can you infer about the attitude of employers toward their workers during this time?

Writing Activity

35. Portfolio Writing: Persuasive Writing Think of a product that you think is essential to life today. Write an advertisement for this product that would persuade people to purchase it.

Chapter Activity

36. American History Primary Source Document Library CD-ROM Read "Driving the Golden Spike" by Alexander Toponce, under *Reshaping the Nation.* For further background, reread your textbook's coverage of the same subject on page 443. Then prepare a presentation for your classmates. In it, describe what Toponce had to say about the workers during the celebration and what Grenville Dodge

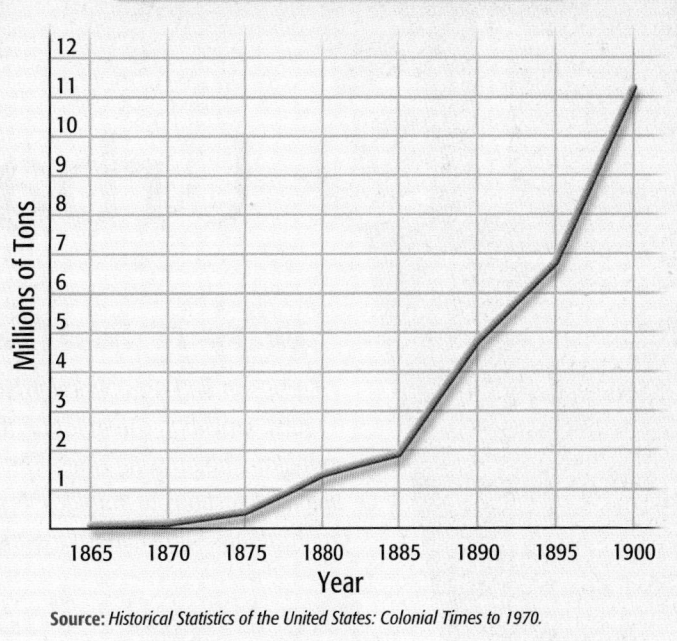

Steel Production, 1865–1900

Millions of Tons / Year

Source: *Historical Statistics of the United States: Colonial Times to 1970.*

had to say about their experience during the project. What attitudes do you think each man had toward the workers?

Economics and History

37. The graph above shows steel production from 1865 to 1900. Study the graph and answer the questions below.

a. Interpreting Graphs Between what years did steel production have the greatest increase?

b. Making Inferences How did increased steel production contribute to American industrialism?

Standardized Test Practice

Directions: Choose the best answer to the following question.

Labor unions were formed for all of these reasons except:

F To improve workers' wages

G To protect factory owners from being sued

H To make factories safer

J To prevent children from working long hours

Test-Taking Tip: If a question uses the word *except,* you need to look for the answer that does not fit. Remember that unions were formed to try to help workers. Which answer is least likely to help workers?

CHAPTER

15 Urban America
1865–1896

Why It Matters

European and Asian immigrants arrived in the United States in great numbers during the late 1800s. Providing cheap labor, they made rapid industrial growth possible. They also helped populate the growing cities. The immigrants' presence affected both urban politics and labor unions. Reactions to immigrants and to an urban society were reflected in new political organizations and in literature and philosophy.

The Impact Today

Industrialization and urbanization permanently influenced American life.
- *The United States continues to be a magnet for immigrants seeking a better way of life.*
- *The cities of the United States continue to draw new residents in search of opportunity.*

The* American Vision *Video *The Chapter 15 video, "Huddled Masses in the City," depicts one of the problems the nation faced during its urbanization period.*

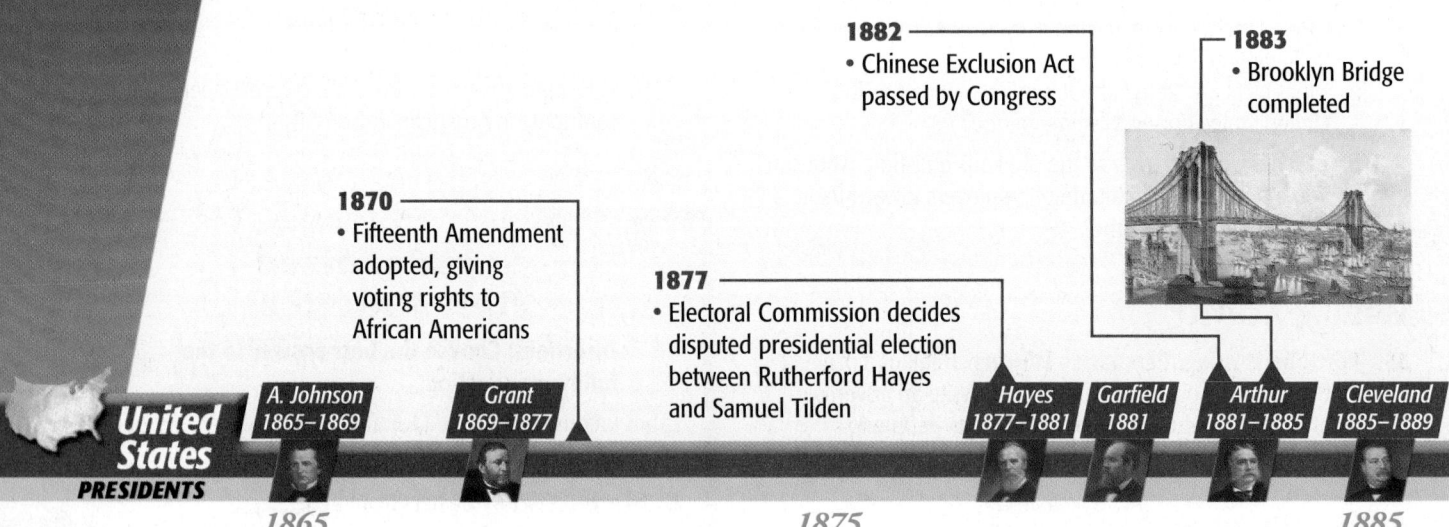

1882
• Chinese Exclusion Act passed by Congress

1883
• Brooklyn Bridge completed

1870
• Fifteenth Amendment adopted, giving voting rights to African Americans

1877
• Electoral Commission decides disputed presidential election between Rutherford Hayes and Samuel Tilden

United States PRESIDENTS

| A. Johnson 1865–1869 | Grant 1869–1877 | Hayes 1877–1881 | Garfield 1881 | Arthur 1881–1885 | Cleveland 1885–1889 |

1865   *1875*   *1885*

World

1873
• Civil war breaks out in Spain

1878
• Independent Serbia recognized

1879
• Chile engages in war with Bolivia and Peru

1885
• Indian National Congress organizes for independence from Great Britain

Immigrants arriving at Ellis Island

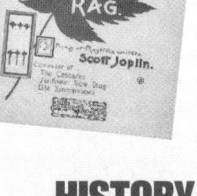

HISTORY *Online*

Chapter Overview
Visit the *American Vision*
Web site at tav.glencoe.com
and click on *Chapter
Overviews—Chapter 15* to
preview chapter information.

1888
• First electric trolley line
opened in Richmond, Virginia

1891
• James Naismith
invents basketball

1896
• National Association of
Colored Women founded

1899
• Scott Joplin's "Maple
Leaf Rag" published

B. Harrison
1889–1893

Cleveland
1893–1897

McKinley
1897–1901

T. Roosevelt
1901–1909

1895   *1905*

1886
• Gold discovered in Transvaal
region of South Africa

1901
• Victorian era ends with death
of Britain's Queen Victoria

★ An American Story ★

In 1894, the day the steamer tickets arrived for the Hayye family, Hannah Hayye became an instant celebrity in her small village in Russian-occupied Poland. Hannah's husband had left for the United States three years earlier to prepare a new home for the Hayye family in Boston. Now that Hannah had received the tickets, she and her four children would finally be able to join him. A stream of curious visitors began to pour into the house. Hannah's daughter Mary, then 13 years old, described the crowd:

❝They wanted to handle the ticket, and mother must read them what is written on it. . . . Were we not all going to have new dresses to travel in? Was it sure that we could get kosher food on the ship? And with the questions poured in suggestions. . . . Mother mustn't carry her money in a pocketbook. She must sew it into the lining of her jacket. . . .❞

Before the family left, they gave away almost all their belongings and spent their last night at an uncle's home. "I did not really sleep," recalled Mary. "Excitement kept me awake, and my aunt snored hideously. In the morning, I was going away from Polotzk, forever and ever. I was going on a wonderful journey. I was going to America. How could I sleep?"

—adapted from *Witnessing America*

Europeans Flood Into the United States

By the 1890s, more than half of all immigrants in the United States were eastern and southern Europeans, including Italians, Greeks, Poles, Slavs, Slovaks, Russians, and Armenians. Like the Hayye family, many of the 14 million immigrants who came to the United States between 1860 and 1900 were eastern European Jews.

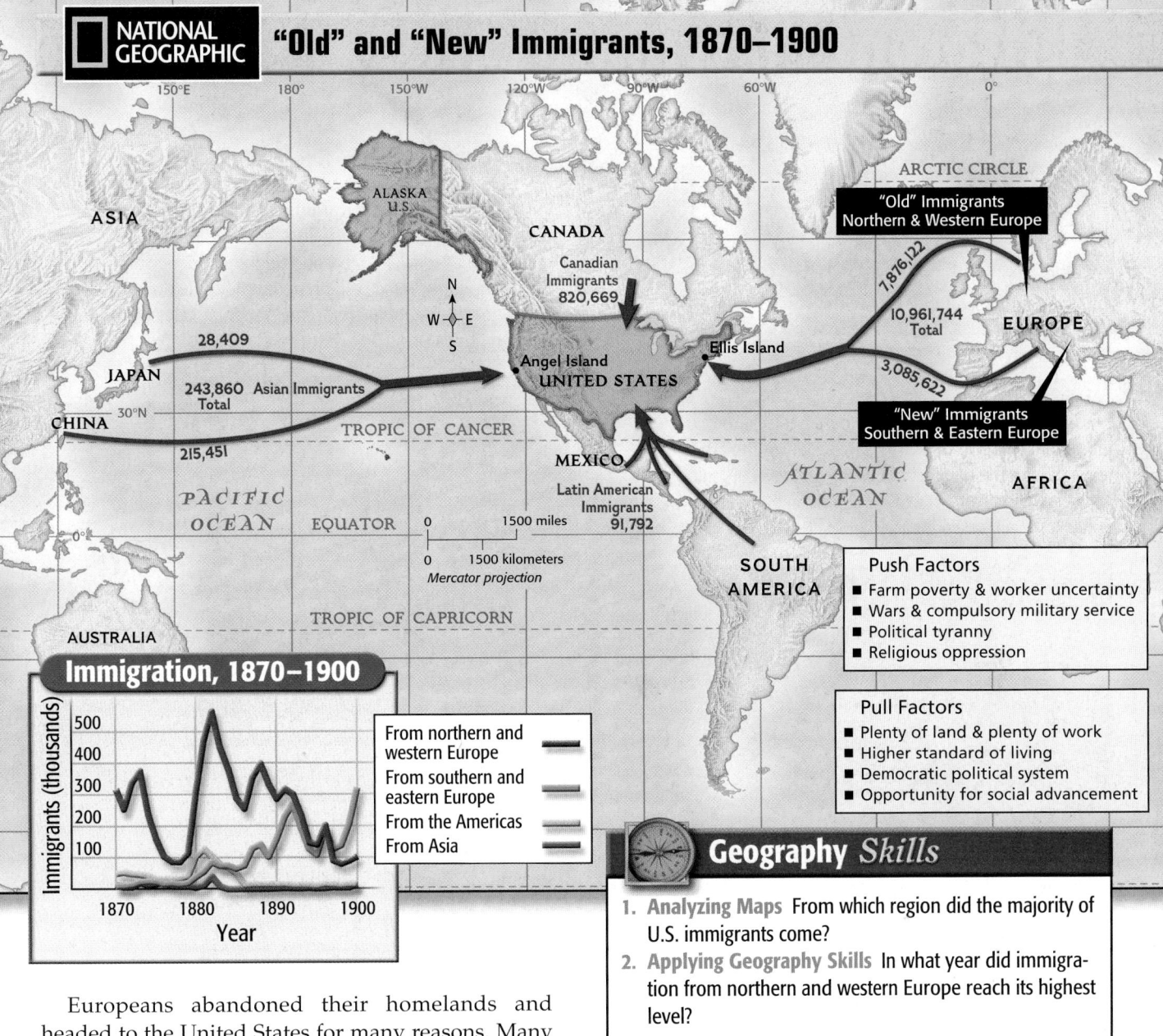

"Old" and "New" Immigrants, 1870–1900

NATIONAL GEOGRAPHIC

"Old" Immigrants
Northern & Western Europe

"New" Immigrants
Southern & Eastern Europe

Canadian Immigrants 820,669

Latin American Immigrants 91,792

Asian Immigrants 243,860 Total

28,409

215,451

7,876,122

10,961,744 Total

3,085,622

Push Factors
- Farm poverty & worker uncertainty
- Wars & compulsory military service
- Political tyranny
- Religious oppression

Pull Factors
- Plenty of land & plenty of work
- Higher standard of living
- Democratic political system
- Opportunity for social advancement

Immigration, 1870–1900

Immigrants (thousands) vs. Year

- From northern and western Europe
- From southern and eastern Europe
- From the Americas
- From Asia

Geography Skills

1. **Analyzing Maps** From which region did the majority of U.S. immigrants come?
2. **Applying Geography Skills** In what year did immigration from northern and western Europe reach its highest level?

Europeans abandoned their homelands and headed to the United States for many reasons. Many poor rural farmers came simply because the United States had plenty of jobs available and few immigration restrictions. Yet Europe in the late 1800s offered plenty of jobs in its booming industrial cities, so economic factors were not the only reason people migrated. Many moved to avoid forced military service, which in some nations could last for many years. Others, especially Jews living in Poland and Russia, fled to avoid religious persecution.

By the late 1800s, most European states had made moving to the United States easy. Immigrants were allowed to take their savings with them, and most countries had repealed old laws that had forced peasants to stay in their villages and had banned skilled workers from leaving the country. At the same time, moving to the United States offered a chance to break away from Europe's class

system and move to a democratic nation where they had a chance to move up the social ladder.

The Atlantic Voyage Getting to the United States was often very difficult. Most immigrants booked passage in steerage, the most basic and cheapest accommodations on a steamship. Edward Steiner, an Iowa clergyman who posed as an immigrant in order to write a book on immigration, described the miserable quarters:

❝Narrow, steep and slippery stairways lead to it. Crowds everywhere, ill smelling bunks, uninviting washrooms—this is steerage. The odors of scattered orange peelings, tobacco, garlic and disinfectants meeting but not blending. No lounge or chairs for

Different Viewpoints

Two Views of Immigration

The history of immigration to the United States has been both celebrated and criticized. Many millions of immigrants arrived in the United States in the late 1800s. The newcomers sought opportunity, enriched American culture, and caused concerns. Here, two political cartoons address the immigration issue.

Pro-Immigration

Uncle Sam plays the role of Noah in this cartoon. As immigrants file two by two into the safety of the ark, they leave behind the dangers of Europe that are darkening the sky. A sign lists some reasons people came to the United States to begin a new life.

Anti-Immigration

"Columbia's Unwelcome Guests" shows another view of immigration. In this 1885 cartoon, the figure of Columbia bars entry to anarchists, Socialists, and Communists who enter from the sewers of Europe's darker society. Some of the inscriptions on the column pedestal beside Columbia read "Anarchy is not liberty," and "When a Man's Rights End, His Neighbor's Begin."

Learning From History

1. According to the cartoons, why were people concerned about immigrants coming to the United States?

2. Which cartoon best expresses your own views on immigration today? Why?

comfort, and a continual babble of tongues—this is steerage. The food, which is miserable, is dealt out of huge kettles into the dinner pails provided by the steamship company. When it is distributed, the stronger push and crowd. . . . "

—quoted in *World of Our Fathers*

At the end of a 14-day journey, the passengers usually disembarked at **Ellis Island,** a tiny island in New York Harbor. There, a huge three-story building served as the processing center for many of the immigrants arriving on the East Coast after 1892.

Ellis Island Most immigrants passed through Ellis Island in about a day. They would not soon forget their hectic introduction to the United States. A medical examiner who worked there later described how "hour after hour, ship load after ship load . . . the stream of human beings with its kaleidoscopic variations was . . . hurried through Ellis Island by the equivalent of 'step lively' in every language of the earth."

In Ellis Island's enormous hall, crowds of immigrants filed past the doctor for an initial inspection. "Whenever a case aroused suspicion," an inspector wrote, "the alien was set aside in a cage apart from the rest . . . and his coat lapel or shirt marked with colored chalk" to indicate the reason for the isolation. About one out of five newcomers was marked with an "H" for heart problems, "K" for hernias, "Sc" for scalp problems, or "X" for mental disability. Newcomers who failed the inspection might be separated from their families and returned to Europe.

GEOGRAPHY

Ethnic Cities Many of those who passed the Ellis Island inspections settled in the nation's cities. By the 1890s, immigrants made up significant percentages of some of the country's largest cities, including New York, Chicago, Milwaukee, and Detroit. **Jacob Riis,** a Danish-born journalist, observed in 1890 that a map of New York City, "colored to designate nationalities, would show more stripes than on the skin of a zebra."

In the cities, immigrants lived in neighborhoods that were often separated into ethnic groups, such as "Little Italy" or the Jewish "Lower East Side" in New York City. There they spoke their native languages and re-created the churches, synagogues, clubs, and newspapers of their homelands.

How well immigrants adjusted depended partly on how quickly they learned English and adapted to American culture. Immigrants also tended to adjust well if they had marketable skills or money, or if they settled among members of their own ethnic group.

As many as one in three immigrants returned to Europe shortly after coming to the United States. Some had never planned to stay and had come simply to make a little money before returning home.

Reading Check **Explaining** How did immigration affect demographic patterns in the United States?

Asian Immigration to America

Many Chinese immigrants began crossing the Pacific to arrive in the United States in the mid-1800s. By that time, China's population had reached about 430 million, and the country was suffering from severe unemployment, poverty, and famine.

The 1848 discovery of gold in California began to lure Chinese immigrants to the United States. Then, in 1850, the Taiping Rebellion erupted in their homeland. This insurrection against the Chinese government took some 20 million lives and caused such suffering that thousands of Chinese left for the United States. In the early 1860s, as the Central Pacific Railroad began construction of its portion of the transcontinental railroad, the demand for railroad workers further increased Chinese immigration.

Chinese immigrants mainly settled in western cities, where they often worked as laborers or servants or in skilled trades. Others worked as merchants. Because native-born Americans kept them out of many businesses, some Chinese immigrants opened their own. To save enough to buy his own laundry, one immigrant, Lee Chew, had to work for two years as a servant:

❝I did not know how to do anything, and I did not understand what the lady said to me, but she showed me how to cook, wash, iron, sweep, dust, make beds, wash dishes, clean windows, paint and brass, polish the knives and forks, etc., by doing the things herself and then overseeing my efforts to imitate her.❞

—quoted in *A Sunday Between Wars*

Another group of Asians, the Japanese, also immigrated to the United States. Until 1900, however, their numbers remained small. Japanese immigration spiraled upward between 1900 and 1910 as Japan began building both an industrial economy and an empire. Both developments disrupted the economy of Japan and caused hardships for its people, thus stimulating emigration.

Until 1910 Asian immigrants arriving in San Francisco first stopped at a two-story shed at the wharf. As many as 500 people at a time were often squeezed into this structure, which Chinese immigrants from Canton called *muk uk*, or "wooden house."

In January 1910, California opened a barracks on **Angel Island** to accommodate the Asian immigrants. Most of the immigrants were young males in their teens or twenties, who nervously awaited the results of their immigration hearings in dormitories packed with double or triple tiers of bunks. This unpleasant delay could last for months. On the walls of the detention barracks, the immigrants wrote anonymous poems in pencil or ink. Some even carved their verse into the wood.

Reading Check **Making Generalizations** Why did Chinese immigrants come to the United States?

HISTORY Online

Student Web Activity Visit the *American Vision* Web site at tav.glencoe.com and click on **Student Web Activities— Chapter 15** for an activity on immigration.

Angel Island Over 200,000 immigrants from Japan and China arrived on the West Coast during the late 1800s.

The Resurgence of Nativism

Eventually the wave of immigration led to increased feelings of nativism on the part of many Americans. Nativism is an extreme dislike for immigrants by native-born people and a desire to limit immigration. It had surfaced earlier in the 1800s during another large wave of immigration. In the 1840s and 1850s, it had focused primarily on Irish immigrants. Now anti-immigrant feelings focused on Asians, Jews, and eastern Europeans.

Nativists opposed immigration for many reasons. Some feared that the influx of Catholics from Ireland and southern and eastern Europe would swamp the mostly Protestant United States, giving the Catholic Church too much power in the American government. Many labor unions also opposed immigration, arguing that immigrants would work for low wages or accept work as strikebreakers, thus undermining American-born workers.

Prejudice Against Newcomers

In the Northeast and Midwest, increased feelings of nativism led to the founding of two major anti-immigrant organizations. One, called the **American Protective Association,** claimed to have 500,000 members in 1887. The organization's founder, Henry Bowers, despised Catholics and foreigners and committed his group to stopping immigration. Membership peaked at about one million but declined rapidly after the economic recession of 1893 ended.

In the West, where sentiment against the Chinese was very strong, widespread racial violence erupted. Denis Kearney, himself an Irish immigrant, organized the **Workingman's Party of California** in the 1870s to fight Chinese immigration. The party won seats in California's legislature and made opposition to Chinese immigration a national issue.

Impact of the Anti-Immigrant Movement

Even though several presidents vetoed other laws that would have stemmed the steady flow of new immigrants, prejudice against immigrants stimulated the passage of a new federal law. Enacted in 1882, the law banned convicts, paupers, and the mentally disabled from immigrating to the United States. The new law also placed a 50¢ head tax on each newcomer.

That same year, Congress passed the **Chinese Exclusion Act**. The law barred Chinese immigration for 10 years and prevented the Chinese already in the country from becoming citizens. The Chinese in the United States did not accept the new law quietly. They protested that white Americans did not oppose immigration by Italians, Irish, or Germans. Some Chinese organized letter-writing campaigns, petitioned the president, and even filed suit in federal court.

These efforts, however, proved fruitless. Congress renewed the Chinese Exclusion Act in 1892 and then made it permanent in 1902. In 1890 the number of Chinese living in the United States totaled 105,000. By 1900 that total had dropped to just above 74,000. In the 40 years after the passage of the act, the Chinese population in the United States continued to decrease. The act was not repealed until 1943.

✓ **Reading Check** **Explaining** Why did the federal government pass the Chinese Exclusion Act?

SECTION 1 ASSESSMENT

Checking for Understanding

1. **Define:** steerage, nativism.
2. **Identify:** Ellis Island, Jacob Riis, Angel Island, Chinese Exclusion Act.
3. **Describe** where most immigrants to the United States settled in the late 1800s.
4. **Explain** why nativist organizations opposed foreign immigrants.

Reviewing Themes

5. **Geography and History** What routes did European and Asian immigrants take to get to the United States?

Critical Thinking

6. **Analyzing** Why did some Americans blame immigrants for the nation's problems?
7. **Organizing** Complete a graphic organizer by listing reasons nativists opposed immigration to the United States.

Reasons Nativists Opposed Immigration

Analyzing Visuals

8. **Analyzing Political Cartoons** Compare the cartoons on page 466. What conclusions can you draw about American views on immigration in the late 1880s? Why do you think various people viewed immigration differently?

Writing About History

9. **Descriptive Writing** Imagine that you are an immigrant who arrived in the 1800s. Write a letter to a relative in your home country describing your feelings during processing at either Ellis Island or Angel Island.

Guide to Reading

Main Idea

During the three decades following the Civil War, the United States transformed rapidly from a rural nation to a more urban one.

Key Terms and Names

skyscraper, Louis Sullivan, tenement, political machine, party boss, George Plunkitt, graft, William M. "Boss" Tweed

Reading Strategy

Organizing As you read about urbanization in the United States in the late 1800s, complete a graphic organizer similar to the one below by filling in the problems the nation's urban areas faced.

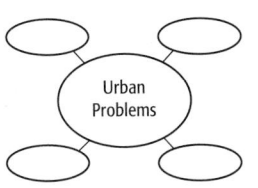

Urban Problems

Reading Objectives

• **Explain** the technological developments that made the growth of cities possible.
• **Evaluate** the role that political machines played in urban politics in the late 1800s.

Section Theme

Government and Democracy Political bosses grew powerful in urban areas by helping immigrants find work and necessities.

Preview of Events

| ◆1875 | ◆1880 | ◆1885 | ◆1890 |

1874
"Boss" Tweed sentenced to prison

1883
Brooklyn Bridge completed

1885
First steel girder construction used in building in Chicago

1888
Nation's first electric trolley line opens in Richmond, Virginia

1890
Jacob Riis publishes *How the Other Half Lives*

★ An American Story ★

With just $3.10 in his pocket, a young man from Wisconsin named Frank Lloyd Wright wandered the streets of Chicago in the late spring of 1887. Sixteen years earlier, almost four square miles of the city had burned in the Chicago Fire of 1871. Now the rebuilt city's towering new buildings beckoned the young visitor who, within a few decades, would become one of the most famous architects in the world.

In Chicago, Wright saw electric lights and cable cars for the first time. What surprised him most about the big city, however, were the signs that seemed to be everywhere:

❝There were glaring signs on the glass shop-fronts against the lights inside, . . . HURRAH signs. STOP signs. COME ON IN signs. HELLO signs set out before the blazing windows on the sidewalks . . . food shops, barber shops, eating houses, saloons, restaurants, groceries, laundries— and [they all] became chaos in a wilderness of Italian, German, Irish, [Polish], Greek, English, Swedish, French, Chinese and Spanish names. . . .❞

—**quoted in *Eyewitness to America***

Americans Migrate to the Cities

During the three decades after the Civil War, the urban population of the United States—those living in towns with a population of 2,500 or more—grew from around 10 million in 1870 to over 30 million in 1900. New York City alone, which had over 800,000 inhabitants in 1860, grew to almost 3.5 million by 1900. Frank Lloyd Wright observed Chicago during an even faster growth period. The Midwestern city swelled from 109,000 residents in 1860 to more than 1.6 million by 1900.

The United States had only 131 cities in 1840; by 1900 that number had risen to over 1,700.

Most of the immigrants who poured into the United States in the late 1800s lacked the money to buy farms and the education to obtain higher-paying jobs. They therefore remained in the nation's growing cities, where they toiled long hours for little pay in the rapidly expanding factories of the United States. Despite the harshness of their new lives, most immigrants found that the move had still improved their standard of living.

Many rural Americans also began moving to the cities at this time. Farmers moved to the cities because urban areas offered more and better-paying jobs than did rural areas. Cities had much to offer, too—bright lights, running water, and modern plumbing, plus many things to do and see, including museums, libraries, and theaters.

Reading Check **Explaining** Why did rural Americans move to the cities in the late 1800s?

The New Urban Environment

As millions of people flooded into the nation's cities, engineers and architects developed new approaches to housing and transporting such a large number of people.

Skyscrapers As city populations grew, demand raised the price of land, giving owners greater incentive to grow upward rather than outward. Soon, tall steel frame buildings called skyscrapers began to appear on American skylines. Chicago's ten-story Home Insurance Building, built in 1885, was the first skyscraper, but other buildings quickly dwarfed it. New York City, with its business district on the narrow island of Manhattan, boasted more skyscrapers than any other city in the world. With limited land, New Yorkers had to build up, not out.

No one contributed more to the design of sky-scrapers than Chicago's **Louis Sullivan,** whose students included Frank Lloyd Wright. "What people are within, the buildings express without," explained Sullivan, whose lofty structures featured simple lines and spacious windows using new durable plate glass.

Mass Transit Various kinds of mass transit developed in the late 1800s to move huge numbers of people around cities quickly. At first, almost all cities relied on the horsecar—a railroad car pulled by horses. In 1890 horsecars moved about 70 percent of urban traffic in the United States.

More than 20 cities, beginning with San Francisco in 1873, installed cable cars, which were pulled along tracks by underground cables. Then, in 1887, engineer **Frank J. Sprague**

The Technology of Urbanization

Before the mid-1800s, few buildings exceeded four or five stories. To make wooden and stone structures taller required enormously thick walls in the lower levels.

By the late 1800s, steel companies were making girders capable of bearing a building's weight. Walls no longer had to support the building—a steel frame skeleton was all that was needed. Meanwhile, Elisha Otis invented the safety elevator in 1852, and by the late 1880s, the first electric elevators had been installed, making tall buildings practical.

Steel also changed the way bridges were built. New technology enabled engineers to suspend bridges from steel towers using cables also made of steel. Using this technique, John A. Roebling, a German American engineer, designed New York's Brooklyn Bridge—the largest suspension bridge in the world at the time it was completed in 1883.

New York City's Flatiron Building

Brooklyn Bridge under construction

developed the electric trolley car. The following year, Richmond, Virginia, opened the country's first electric trolley line.

In the largest cities, congestion became so bad that engineers began looking for ways to move mass transit off the streets. Chicago responded by building an elevated railroad, while Boston, followed by New York, built the first subway systems.

Reading Check **Summarizing** What new technologies helped people in the late 1800s get to and from work?

Separation by Class

In the growing cities, wealthy people and the working class lived in different parts of town. So too did the middle class. The boundaries between neighborhoods were quite definite and can still be seen in many American cities today.

High Society During the last half of the 1800s, the wealthiest families established fashionable districts in the hearts of cities. Americans with enough money could choose to construct a feudal castle, an English manor house, a French château, a Tuscan villa, or a Persian pavilion. In Chicago, merchant and real estate developer Potter Palmer chose a castle. In New York, Cornelius Vanderbilt's grandson commissioned a $3 million French château equipped with a two-story dining room, a gymnasium, and a solid marble bathroom.

Middle-Class Gentility American industrialization not only made the wealth of people like Potter Palmer possible; it also helped create a growing middle class. The nation's rising middle class included doctors, lawyers, engineers, managers, social workers, architects, and teachers. It was typical for many people in the emerging middle class to move away from the central city. Some took advantage of the new commuter rail lines to move to "streetcar suburbs."

During this period, middle-class salaries were about twice that of the average factory worker. In 1905 a college professor earned a middle-class salary of $1,100. That amount, however, still proved insufficient for one turn-of-the-century professor's wife, who complained:

66We pay eighteen dollars a month for this poorly built, eight small-roomed house. . . . With all this straining to live comes a wish from the President and Trustees of the college that we mingle more in town society. . . . Who can afford the evening dress to go? Or the evening's sewing left undone?99

—quoted in *A Sunday Between Wars*

History *Through Art*

The Lesson This painting by John Barnard Whittaker depicts the lifestyle of a wealthy family in the 1870s. What are several elements of this painting that show the family's wealth?

The Working Class The majority of American city dwellers at the turn of the century would have considered an eight-room house an absolute luxury. In New York, three out of four residents squeezed into tenements, dark and crowded multi-family apartments. To supplement the average industrial worker's annual income of $445, many families sent their young children to work in factories or rented precious space to a boarder. Zalmen Yoffeh, a journalist, lived in a New York tenement as a child. He recalled:

66With . . . one dollar a day [our mother] fed and clothed an ever-growing family. She took in boarders. Sometimes this helped; at other times it added to the burden of living. Boarders were often out of work and penniless; how could one turn a hungry man out? She made all our clothes. She walked blocks to reach a place where meat was a penny cheaper, where bread was a half cent less. She collected boxes and old wood to burn in the stove. . . .99

—quoted in *How We Lived*

Reading Check **Explaining** What social class grew as a result of industrialization in the late 1800s?

TEEMING TENEMENTS
The swelling tide of immigration to U.S. cities in the late 1800s led to deplorable living conditions and almost unbearable congestion. By 1890, more than two-thirds of New York's 1.5 million residents lived in overcrowded apartment buildings called tenements. On the Lower East Side, one of the most densely populated areas in the world, people frequented vibrant outdoor markets such as this one on Hester Street for goods from eggs to rugs to pots and pans. Gossip, haggling, and cries of street peddlers—mostly in Yiddish in this Jewish neighborhood—echoed down the street from dawn to dusk.

Urban Problems

City living posed threats such as crime, violence, fire, disease, and pollution, especially for the working poor like Yoffeh and his family. The rapid growth of cities only made these problems worse. Minor criminals, such as pickpockets, swindlers, and thieves, thrived in crowded urban living conditions. Major crimes multiplied as well. From 1880 to 1900, the murder rate jumped sharply from 25 per million people to more than 100 per million people. In comparison, the murder rate in 1999 was 57 per million people.

Native-born Americans often blamed immigrants for the increase in crime and violence. In reality, the crime rate for immigrants was not significantly higher than that for other Americans.

Alcohol did contribute to violent crime, both inside and outside the home. Danish immigrant Jacob Riis, who documented slum life in his 1890 book *How the Other Half Lives*, accused saloons of "breeding poverty," corrupting politics, bringing suffering to the wives and children of drunkards, and fostering "the corruption of the child" by selling beer to minors.

Disease and pollution posed even bigger threats. Improper sewage disposal contaminated city drinking water and triggered epidemics of typhoid fever and cholera. Though flush toilets and sewer systems existed in the 1870s, pollution remained a severe problem as horse waste was left in the streets, smoke belched from chimneys, and soot and ash accumulated from coal and wood fires.

Reading Check **Drawing Conclusions** Why were diseases and pollution big problems in American cities in the late 1800s?

Urban Politics

A new kind of political system developed to meet these urban problems. This system provided essential city services in return for political power.

The Political Machine and the Party Boss The political machine, an informal political group designed to gain and keep power, came about partly because cities had grown much faster than their governments. New city dwellers needed jobs, housing, food, heat, and police protection. In exchange for votes, political machines and the party bosses who ran them eagerly provided these necessities.

George Plunkitt, an Irish immigrant who rose to be one of New York City's most powerful party bosses, explained how the system worked when a fire burned a neighborhood:

> 66 I just get [housing] for them, buy clothes for them if their clothes were burned up, and fix them up till they get things runnin' again. It's philanthropy, but it's politics too—mighty good politics. Who can tell how many votes one of these fires bring me? The poor are the most grateful people in the world, and, let me tell you, they have more friends in their neighborhoods than the rich have in theirs. 99
>
> —quoted in *In Search of America*

As Plunkitt observed, the payoff for party bosses came on Election Day. Urban immigrant groups, which wielded tremendous voting strength, voted in overwhelming numbers for the political machines.

Graft and Fraud The party bosses who ran the political machines also controlled the city's finances. Many machine politicians grew rich as the result of fraud or graft—getting money through dishonest or questionable means. Plunkitt defended what he called "honest graft." For example, a politician might find out in advance where a new park was to be built and buy the land near the site. The politician would then sell the land to the city for a profit. As Plunkitt stated, "I see my opportunity and I take it."

Outright fraud occurred when party bosses accepted bribes from contractors, who were supposed to compete fairly to win contracts to build streets, sewers, and buildings. Corrupt bosses also sold permits to their friends to operate public utilities, such as railroads, waterworks, and power systems.

Tammany Hall Tammany Hall, the New York Democratic political machine for which George Plunkitt performed his labors, was the most famous such organization. **William M. "Boss" Tweed** was its leader during the 1860s and 1870s. Tweed's corruptions led him to prison in 1874.

Other cities' machines controlled all the city services, including the police department. For example, St. Louis's boss never feared arrest when he called out to his supporters at the police-supervised voting booth, "Are there any more repeaters out here that want to vote again?" Based in Kansas City, Missouri, the Pendergast brothers, James and Thomas, ran state and city politics from the 1890s until the 1930s.

Opponents of political machines, such as political cartoonist Thomas Nast, blasted bosses for their corruption. Defenders, though, argued that machines provided necessary services and helped to assimilate the masses of new city dwellers.

✓ **Reading Check** **Evaluating** Why did political machines help city dwellers in the late 1800s?

SECTION 2 ASSESSMENT

Checking for Understanding

1. **Define:** skyscraper, tenement, political machine, party boss, graft.
2. **Identify:** Louis Sullivan, George Plunkitt, William M. "Boss" Tweed.
3. **Explain** what two technologies made the building of skyscrapers possible in the late 1800s.

Reviewing Themes

4. **Government and Democracy** How did political machines respond to the needs of the people?

Critical Thinking

5. **Comparing** Compare the conditions under which the wealthy class, the middle class, and the working class lived in the United States in the late 1800s.
6. **Organizing** Complete a graphic organizer similar to the one below by listing the effects of many Americans moving from rural to urban areas in the late 1800s.

```
                              Effects
  ┌───────────┐              _____
  │ Migration │   ───────▶   _____
  └───────────┘              _____
```

Analyzing Visuals

7. **Examining Photographs** Study the photographs on page 470 of the Brooklyn Bridge and the Flatiron Building. Why was it advantageous to construct taller buildings rather than purchase more land?

Writing About History

8. **Persuasive Writing** Take on the role of an urban planner in a major city in the late 1800s. Write a letter to members of the city government listing specific reasons for the importance of setting aside city land for a park and recreational area.

The Hull House Neighborhood

S. HALSTED STREET

W. 12TH STREET

BUNKER STREET

DE KOVEN STREET

W. TAYLOR STREET

FORQUER STREET

EWING STREET

W. POLK STREET

S. DES PLAINES STREET

S. JEFFERSON STREET

S. CLINTON STREET

HULL HOUSE

- Bohemian
- Chinese
- English speaking
- French Canadian
- French
- German
- Irish
- Italian
- Polish
- Russian
- Scandinavian
- Swiss
- Non-residential

Chicago's apartment buildings, or tenements, were squeezed onto lots that measured 25 by 125 feet (7.6 by 38.1 m). These lots typically held three families and their boarders. Unlike New York City's tenements, most were only two or three stories tall.

Immigrants Arrive In Chicago

A major port and a conduit for the nation's east-west rail travel, Chicago was a booming industrial center for the lumber, grain, meatpacking, and mail-order businesses at the end of the 1800s. Since the early 1870s, more ships had been docking in Chicago than in New York, Baltimore, Philadelphia, Charleston, and San Francisco combined. The city's expansion was phenomenal. In 50 years, it grew from a modest frontier town to the second-largest city in the country.

Immigrants swarmed into Chicago seeking jobs. Poles found work slaughtering livestock; Irish laying railroads; Russian and Polish Jews making clothes; Swedes constructing buildings and Italians forging steel. Women established boardinghouses, took in sewing to do at home, and worked in factories. In most factories, the hours were long and the working conditions difficult: noisy, hot, grimy, and overcrowded. By the beginning of the 1900s, three-fourths of the people in this teeming metropolis were European immigrants and their American-born children.

Ethnic neighborhoods dotted the city, as did blocks of tenements thrown up to house the flood of newcomers. The inset map at left—an enlargement of the highlighted rectangle on the lithograph—shows the Hull House neighborhood in Chicago's West Side in 1893. Hull House was established by social reformer Jane Addams to "investigate and improve the conditions in the industrial districts of Chicago." The neighborhood was one of the city's poorest. Its tenement buildings were disease-ridden and dangerous, crowding about 270 residents into each acre. Jane Addams wrote: "The streets are inexpressibly dirty, the number of schools inadequate, sanitary legislation unenforced, the street lighting bad, the paving miserable and altogether lacking in the alleys."

The neighborhood was also one of the most ethnically diverse. As the inset shows, the bewildered new immigrants tended to settle in enclaves that had already been established by others from their homeland. They banded together as they learned about the ways of the new land. Many immigrants found comfort in social life centered on the church or synagogue. Younger immigrants were more eager to abandon their old customs. Many of them quickly adopted American clothes and manners, learned to speak English, and tried to make American friends.

A visiting nurse puts drops in an infant's eyes. Crowded conditions threatened the health of many of the immigrants in Chicago's tenements.

LEARNING FROM GEOGRAPHY

1. How did the location of Chicago influence its development?

2. Pose and answer five questions about the geographic distributions and patterns shown on this model.

The Gilded Age

Main Idea
Industrialism and urbanization changed American society's ideas and culture in the late 1800s.

Key Terms and Names
Gilded Age, Social Darwinism, Gospel of Wealth, philanthropy, realism, vaudeville, ragtime, Scott Joplin

Reading Strategy
Categorizing Complete a graphic organizer similar to the one below by filling in the main idea of each of the theories and movements listed.

Theory or Movement	Main Idea
Social Darwinism	
Laissez-Faire	
Gospel of Wealth	
Realism	

Reading Objectives
• **Evaluate** the doctrine of Social Darwinism and the impact it had on American industry.
• **Explain** how industrialization promoted leisure time and encouraged new forms of entertainment.

Section Theme
Culture and Traditions The Gilded Age was an era of great cultural change in the United States.

Preview of Events

| 1870 | 1880 | 1890 | 1900 |

1869
The Cincinnati Red Stockings become the first salaried baseball team

1884
Mark Twain publishes
Huckleberry Finn

1891
James Naismith invents basketball

1899
Scott Joplin publishes "The Maple Leaf Rag"

★ An American Story ★

In 1872, at the age of 32, William Graham Sumner became a professor of political and social science at Yale College. Sumner's classes were very popular. One of his students, William Lyon Phelps, illustrated Sumner's tough, no-nonsense approach with this example of a class discussion:

Student: "Professor, don't you believe in any government aid to industries?"
Sumner: "No! It's root, hog, or die."
Student: "Yes, but hasn't the hog got a right to root?"
Sumner: "There are no rights. The world owes nobody a living."
Student: "You believe then, Professor, in only one system, the contract-competitive system?"
Sumner: "That's the only sound economic system. All others are fallacies."
Student: "Well, suppose some professor of political economy came along and took your job away from you. Wouldn't you be sore?"
Sumner: "Any other professor is welcome to try. If he gets my job, it is my fault. My business is to teach the subject so well that no one can take the job away from me."

—adapted from *Social Darwinism in American Thought*

A Changing Culture

In 1873 Mark Twain and Charles Warner wrote a novel together entitled *The Gilded Age*. Historians later adopted the term and applied it to the era in American history that begins about 1870 and ends around 1900.

This era was in many ways a time of marvels. Amazing new inventions led to rapid industrial growth. Cities expanded to sizes never seen before. Masses of workers thronged the streets. Skyscrapers reached to the sky, and electric lights banished the darkness. Newly wealthy entrepreneurs built spectacular mansions.

By calling this era the **Gilded Age,** Twain and Warner were sounding an alarm. Something is gilded if it is covered with gold on the outside but made of cheaper material inside. A gilded age might appear to sparkle, but Twain, Warner, and other writers tried to point out that beneath the surface lay corruption, poverty, crime, and great disparities in wealth between the rich and the poor.

Whether the era was golden or merely gilded, it was certainly a time of great cultural activity. Industrialism and urbanization altered the way Americans looked at themselves and their society, and these changes gave rise to new values, new art, and new forms of entertainment.

The Idea of Individualism One of the strongest beliefs of the era—and one that remains strong today—was the idea of **individualism.** Many Americans firmly believed that no matter how humble their origins, they could rise in society and go as far as their talents and commitment would take them. In 1885 the wealthy cotton manufacturer Edward Atkinson gave a speech to a group of workers at a textile factory in Rhode Island. He told them they had no reason to complain:

> 66There is always plenty of room on the front seats in every profession, every trade, every art, every industry. . . . There are men in this audience who will fill some of those seats, but they won't be boosted into them from behind.99
>
> —quoted in *America's History*

Horatio Alger No one expressed the idea of individualism better than Horatio Alger. A minister from Massachusetts, Alger eventually left the clergy and moved to New York. There he wrote more than 100 "rags-to-riches" novels, in which a poor person goes to the big city and becomes successful. Many young people loved reading these tales. Inspired by Alger's novels they concluded that no matter how many obstacles they faced, success was possible.

✓ **Reading Check** **Describing** What was the main idea behind individualism?

Social Darwinism

Another powerful idea of the era was Social Darwinism, which strongly reinforced the idea of individualism. English philosopher **Herbert Spencer** first proposed this idea. Historian John Fiske, political scientist William Graham Sumner, and the magazine *Popular Science Monthly* all popularized it in the United States.

Herbert Spencer Philosopher Herbert Spencer applied **Charles Darwin's** theory of evolution and natural selection to human society. In his 1859 book, *On the Origin of Species by Means of Natural Selection,* Darwin argued that plant and animal life had evolved over the years by a process he called natural selection. In this process, those species that cannot adapt to the environment in which they live gradually die out, while those that do adapt thrive and live on.

Herbert Spencer

Spencer took this biological theory, intended to explain developments over millions of years, and argued that human society also evolved through competition and natural selection. He argued that society progressed and became better because only the fittest people survived.

Spencer and others who shared his views became known as Social Darwinists, and their ideas were known as **Social Darwinism.** "Survival of the fittest" became the catchphrase of their philosophy. By 1902 over 350,000 copies of Spencer's books had been sold in the United States.

Horatio Alger novel

Social Darwinism also paralleled the economic doctrine of laissez-faire that opposed any government programs that interfered with business. Not surprisingly, industrial leaders like John D. Rockefeller heartily embraced the theory. Rockefeller maintained that survival of the fittest, as demonstrated by the growth of huge businesses like his own Standard Oil, was "merely the working out of the law of nature and the law of God."

Darwinism and the Church Rockefeller may have appreciated Spencer's interpretation of evolution, but Charles Darwin's conclusions about the origin of new species frightened and outraged many devout Christians as well as some leading scientists. They rejected the theory of evolution because they believed it contradicted the Bible's account of creation. Some American scholars and ministers, however, concluded that evolution may have been God's way of creating the world. Henry Ward Beecher of Plymouth Church in Brooklyn called himself a "cordial Christian evolutionist." Beecher accepted Spencer's ideas of Social Darwinism and championed the success of American business.

Carnegie's Gospel of Wealth A wealthy and prominent business leader of the time, Andrew Carnegie believed wholeheartedly in Social Darwinism and laissez-faire. Speaking of the law of unregulated competition, he wrote:

> 66It ensures the survival of the fittest in every department. We accept and welcome, therefore, as conditions to which we must accommodate ourselves, great inequality of environment, the concentration of business, . . . in the hands of a few, and the laws of competition . . . as being not only beneficial, but essential for the future progress of the race.99
>
> —quoted in *Voices from America's Past*

Believing that those who profited from society owed it something in return, Carnegie attempted to extend and soften the harsh philosophy of Social Darwinism with the **Gospel of Wealth.** This philosophy held that wealthy Americans bore the responsibility of engaging in philanthropy—using their great fortunes to further social progress. Carnegie himself, for example, donated millions of dollars as the "trustee and agent for his poorer brethren." Other industrialists also contributed to social causes. 📖 *(See page 1053 for more information on the Gospel of Wealth.)*

✓ **Reading Check**

Summarizing What was the main idea of Social Darwinism?

Realism

Just as Darwin had looked at the natural world scientifically, a new movement in art and literature known as realism attempted to portray people realistically instead of idealizing them as romantic artists had done.

Realism in Art Realist painters rejected the idealistic depictions of the world of the earlier 1800s. One such painter, **Thomas Eakins** of Philadelphia, Pennsylvania, considered no day-to-day

🎨 **History** *Through Art*

Baseball Players Practicing Thomas Eakins painted this work in 1875. A member of the Realist school of art, Eakins tried to depict everyday events in detail. What elements of this painting reflect the Realist movement?

subject beneath his interest and careful observation. On his canvases, with their realistic detail and precise lighting, young men swam, surgeons operated, and scientists experimented. Eakins even dared to paint President Hayes working in shirtsleeves instead of in more traditional formal dress.

Realism in Literature
Writers also attempted to capture the world as they saw it. In several novels, **William Dean Howells** presented realistic descriptions of American life. For example, his 1885 novel *The Rise of Silas Lapham* described the attempts of a self-made businessperson to enter Boston society. Also an influential literary critic, Howells was the first to claim Mark Twain to be an American genius and hailed him as "incomparable, the Lincoln of our literature."

Twain, a Missouri native whose real name was Samuel Clemens, wrote his masterpiece, *Adventures of Huckleberry Finn,* in 1884. In this novel, the title character and his friend Jim, an escaped slave, float down the Mississippi River on a raft. Through their innocent eyes, readers gain a piercing view of American society in the pre–Civil War era. Twain wrote in local dialect with a lively sense of humor. Nevertheless, Howells realized that Twain was more than a humorist. He had written a true American novel, in which the setting, subject matter, characters, and style were unmistakably American.

Howells also recognized talent in the work of a very different writer, **Henry James,** who lived most of his adult life in England. In novels such as *Portrait of a Lady* (1881), James realistically characterized the inner lives of the upper class. Isabel Archer, the lady of the title, reflects one of the prime values of her class—the concern to maintain social position by marrying well. Ultimately Isabel's wealth interferes with her ability to pursue her own happiness.

Edith Wharton, who also concerned herself with the upper class she knew, modeled her realistic writing after those of James. She won a Pulitzer Prize for her novel *The Age of Innocence,* a stark portrait of upper-class New York society in the 1870s.

Reading Check **Explaining** What was the significance of Mark Twain's *Adventures of Huckleberry Finn*?

Popular Culture

Popular culture changed considerably in the late 1800s. Industrialization improved the standard of living for many people, enabling them to spend money on entertainment and recreation. Increasingly, urban Americans, unlike rural people, divided their lives

| Fact | Fiction | Folklore |

The Seventh-Inning Stretch This baseball tradition, where fans often stand up to stretch in the middle of the seventh inning, does not have a completely reliable history. One claim is that in 1869, all the Cincinnati Red Stockings players stood during the seventh inning to seek relief from the hard wooden benches on which they were sitting. Another popular story asserts that in 1910, President William Howard Taft stood to stretch himself; thinking that the president was leaving, fans at the Washington Senators game also stood out of respect.

Moses Fleetwood Walker, early African American baseball player

into separate units—that of work and that of home. Furthermore, people began looking for things to do outside the home and began "going out" to public entertainment.

The Saloon
As Frank Lloyd Wright had noted when he arrived in Chicago, the city's saloons far outnumbered its groceries and meat markets. Functioning like community centers, saloons played a major role in the life of male workers in the 1800s. They also served as political centers. Saloonkeepers often served as key figures in political machines.

Saloons offered free toilets, water for horses, and free newspapers for customers. They even offered the first "free lunch": salty food that made patrons thirsty and eager to drink more. Saloons developed loyal customers. The first workers from the night shift would stream in at 5:00 A.M., and the last would stay until late at night.

Amusement Parks and Sports
While saloons catered mostly to men, working-class families or single adults who sought excitement and escape could go to amusement parks such as New York's **Coney Island.** Amusements there such as water slides and railroad rides cost only a nickel or dime.

Watching professionals box or play baseball also first became popular during the late 1800s. A game much like baseball, known as rounders and derived from the game of cricket, had enjoyed limited popularity in Great Britain in the early 1800s. Versions of the modern game of baseball began to appear in the United States in the early 1800s. As the game grew in popularity, it became a source of profit. The first salaried team, the Cincinnati Red Stockings, was formed in 1869. Other cities soon fielded professional teams, and in 1903 the first modern World Series was played between the Boston Red Sox and the Pittsburgh Pirates.

The second most popular game, football, appealed first to the upper classes, in part because it began in private colleges and universities that the middle and working classes could not afford. By the late 1800s, the game had spread to public universities.

As work became less physically strenuous, many people looked for leisure activities that involved physical exercise. Lawn tennis, golf, and croquet became popular. James Naismith, a Canadian working as an athletic director for a college in Springfield, Massachusetts, invented the game of basketball in 1891.

Vaudeville and Ragtime The many people living in the cities provided large and eager markets for other types of entertainment. Adapted from French theater, vaudeville took on an American flavor in the early 1880s with its hodgepodge of animal acts, acrobats, gymnasts, and dancers. The fast-moving acts, like the tempo of big-city life, went on in continuous shows all day and night.

Ragtime Band This group of African American musicians traveled around the country playing ragtime music at motion picture shows. *What are some of the roots of ragtime music?*

Like vaudeville, ragtime music echoed the hectic pace of city life. Its syncopated rhythms grew out of the music of riverside honky-tonk, saloon pianists, and banjo players, using the patterns of African American music. **Scott Joplin,** one of the most important African American ragtime composers, became known as the "King of Ragtime." He published his signature piece, "The Maple Leaf Rag," in 1899.

✓ **Reading Check** **Describing** What importance did the saloon have in nineteenth-century life?

SECTION 3 ASSESSMENT

Checking for Understanding

1. **Define:** philanthropy, realism, vaudeville, ragtime.
2. **Identify:** Gilded Age, Social Darwinism, Gospel of Wealth, Scott Joplin.
3. **Describe** how changes in art and literature reflected the issues and characteristics of the late nineteenth century.

Reviewing Themes

4. **Culture and Traditions** What were the defining characteristics of the Gilded Age?

Critical Thinking

5. **Synthesizing** Do you think the idea of the Gospel of Wealth is still alive today? Why or why not?
6. **Organizing** Complete a graphic organizer similar to the one below by filling in new forms of entertainment that Americans turned to in the late 1800s.

New Entertainment

Analyzing Visuals

7. **Examining Photographs** Analyze the photograph at the top of this page. How does the clothing the musicians are wearing compare with the clothing worn by musicians today?

Writing About History

8. **Descriptive Writing** Imagine that you are a newspaper editor in the late 1800s. Write an editorial in which you support or oppose the philosophy of Social Darwinism. Include reasons to support your position.

The Rebirth of Reform

Preview of Events

♦1880	♦1885	♦1890	♦1895

1879
Henry George's *Progress and Poverty* published

1881
Booker T. Washington founds Tuskegee Institute

1889
Jane Addams founds Hull House

1893
Stephen Crane's *Maggie: A Girl of the Streets* published

1896
National Association of Colored Women founded

★ An American Story ★

On a drizzly March morning in 1893, a nursing student named Lillian Wald was teaching a public health class to residents of New York's poor Lower East Side. Suddenly a girl broke in, disrupting the lesson. The child's mother desperately needed a nurse. The interruption changed Wald's life. She followed the girl to a squalid tenement, where she found a family of seven sharing their two rooms with boarders. The sick woman lay on a dirty bed. Wald later wrote:

66That morning's experience was a baptism of fire. Deserted were the laboratory and the academic work of the college. I never returned to them. . . . To my inexperience it seemed certain that conditions such as these were allowed because people did not *know,* and for me there was a challenge to know and to tell. . . . If people knew things,—and "things" meant everything implied in the condition of this family,—such horrors would cease to exist. . . .99

—**quoted in *The House on Henry Street***

In 1895 Wald and her friend Mary Brewster established the Henry Street Settlement. The young nurses offered medical care, education, labor organization, and social and cultural programs to the neighborhood residents.

Social Criticism

The tremendous changes brought about by industrialism and urbanization triggered a debate among Americans as to how best to address society's problems. While many Americans embraced the ideas of individualism and Social Darwinism, others disagreed, arguing that society's problems could be fixed only if Americans and their government began to take a more active role in regulating the economy and helping those in need.

Henry George on Progress and Poverty

In 1879 journalist **Henry George** published *Progress and Poverty*. His book quickly became a national bestseller. "The present century has been marked by a prodigious increase in wealth-producing power," George observed, which should have made poverty "a thing of the past." Instead, he argued:

> ❝It becomes no easier for the masses of our people to make a living. On the contrary it becomes harder.... The gulf between the employed and the employer is growing wider; social contrasts are becoming sharper; as liveried carriages appear, so do barefoot children.❞
>
> —from *Progress and Poverty*

Most economists now argue that George's analysis was flawed. Industrialism did make some Americans very wealthy, but it also improved the standard of living for most other Americans as well. At the time, however, in the midst of the poverty, crime, and harsh working conditions, many Americans did not believe things were improving.

George offered a simple solution. Land, he argued, was the basis of wealth, and people could grow wealthy just by waiting for land prices to rise. George proposed a "single tax" on this unearned wealth to replace all other taxes. He believed it would help make society more equal and also provide the government with enough money to help the poor.

Economists have since rejected George's economic theory. His real importance to American history is that he raised questions about American society and led the way in challenging the ideas of Social Darwinism and laissez-faire economics. Many future reform leaders first became interested in reform because of George's book.

Reform Darwinism

Four years after Henry George challenged the ideas of Social Darwinism, **Lester Frank Ward** published *Dynamic Sociology*. Ward took the ideas of Darwinism and used them to reach a very different conclusion than Spencer had. He argued that human beings were different from other animals in nature because they

Social Conditions: Past and Present

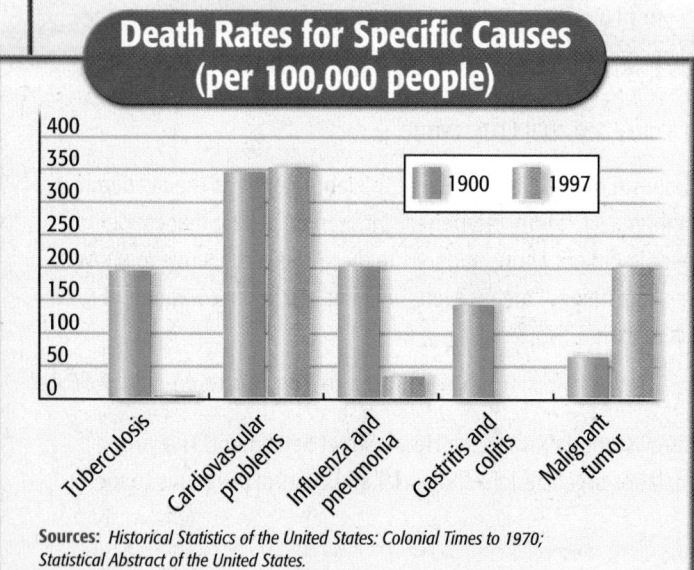

Death Rates for Specific Causes (per 100,000 people)

Legend: 1900, 1997

Categories: Tuberculosis, Cardiovascular problems, Influenza and pneumonia, Gastritis and colitis, Malignant tumor

Sources: *Historical Statistics of the United States: Colonial Times to 1970; Statistical Abstract of the United States.*

High School Graduation Rates

1900: 6.4% Graduated, 93.6% Did Not Graduate

1997: 69% Graduated, 31% Did Not Graduate

Sources: *Historical Statistics of the United States, Colonial Times to 1970; Statistical Abstract of the United States.*

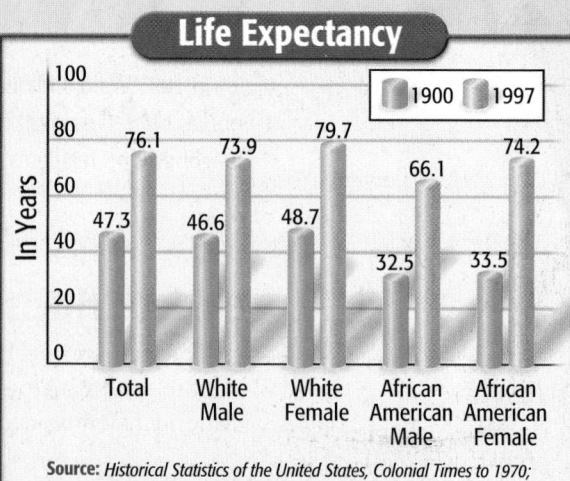

Life Expectancy

Legend: 1900, 1997 (In Years)

	Total	White Male	White Female	African American Male	African American Female
1900	47.3	46.6	48.7	32.5	33.5
1997	76.1	73.9	79.7	66.1	74.2

Source: *Historical Statistics of the United States, Colonial Times to 1970; Statistical Abstract of the United States.*

Graph Skills

1. **Analyzing Graphs** How many people per 100,000 died of tuberculosis in the year 1900?
2. **Understanding Cause and Effect** Collectively, what do these graphs tell you about social conditions as the twentieth century progressed?

had the ability to think ahead and make plans to produce the future outcomes they desired.

Ward's ideas came to be known as Reform Darwinism. People, he insisted, had succeeded in the world not because of their ability to compete but because of their ability to cooperate. Ward believed that competition was wasteful and time consuming. Government, he argued, could regulate the economy, cure poverty, and promote education more efficiently than could competition in the marketplace. While some disagreed with Ward's conclusions, others did think that government should do more to solve society's problems. Among these were the people who became reformers in the late 1800s.

Looking Backward By the late 1880s, some critics of Social Darwinism and laissez-faire economics had moved to the opposite extreme. In 1888 **Edward Bellamy** published *Looking Backward, 2000–1887*, a novel about a young Bostonian who falls asleep in 1887 and awakens in the year 2000 to find that the United States has become a perfect society with no crime, poverty, or politics. In this fictional society, the government owns all industry and shares the wealth equally with all Americans. Bellamy's ideas were essentially a form of socialism. His book quickly became a bestseller, and although few people were willing to go as far as Bellamy suggested, his ideas, like those of George and Ward, helped to shape the thinking of American reformers in the late 1800s.

☑ **Reading Check** **Describing** What were Lester Frank Ward's views on government?

Naturalism in Literature

Criticism of industrial society also appeared in literature in a new style of writing known as naturalism. Social Darwinists and realists argued that people could control their lives and make choices to improve their situation. Naturalists challenged this idea by suggesting that some people failed in life simply because they were caught up in circumstances they could not control. In other words, leaving society and the economy unregulated did not always lead to the best result. Sometimes people's lives were destroyed through no fault of their own.

Among the most prominent naturalist writers were Stephen Crane, Frank Norris, Jack London, and Theodore Dreiser. Stephen Crane's novel, *Maggie, A Girl of the Streets* (1893), told the story of a girl's descent into prostitution and death. Frank Norris's work, *McTeague* (1899), described how a dentist and

Picturing **History**

Urban Poverty The impoverished lifestyle of many Americans like this mother and child in Chicago was a growing concern among social reformers. What organizations were created to help the urban poor?

his wife are driven mad by greed and violence. Jack London's tales of the Alaskan wilderness demonstrated the power of the natural environment over civilization. Theodore Dreiser's stories, such as *Sister Carrie* (1900), painted a world where people sinned without punishment and where the pursuit of wealth and power often destroyed their character.

☑ **Reading Check** **Describing** How did the beliefs of naturalist writers differ from those of Social Darwinists?

Helping the Urban Poor

While naturalist writers expressed pessimism about the individual's life in an industrialized world, some critics of industrial society were working for reform. Their reform efforts gave rise to the Social Gospel movement, the Salvation Army and the YMCA, women's clubs, settlement houses, and temperance movements.

The Social Gospel From about 1870 until 1920, reformers in the Social Gospel movement worked to better conditions in cities according to the biblical ideals of charity and justice. An early advocate of the Social Gospel, **Washington Gladden,** a minister from Columbus, Ohio, tried to apply what he called "Christian law" to social problems. During a coal strike in 1884, for example, Gladden preached about the "right and necessity of labor organizations," despite the fact that his congregation included top officers of the coal company.

Walter Rauschenbusch, a Baptist minister who spent nine years serving in a church in one of New York City's poorest neighborhoods, later led the Social Gospel movement. As he put it, "The Church must either condemn the world and seek to change it, or tolerate the world and conform to it." Unlike Social Darwinists, Rauschenbusch believed that competition was the cause of many social problems, causing good people to behave badly.

The efforts of leaders like Gladden and Rauschenbusch inspired many organized churches to expand their missions. These churches began to take on community functions designed to improve society. Some of their projects included building gyms and providing social programs and day care. Others focused exclusively on helping the poor.

The Salvation Army and the YMCA The combination of religious faith and interest in reform nourished the growth of the Christian Mission, a social welfare organization first organized in England by a minister named William Booth. Adopting a military-style organization, the group became known as the Salvation Army in 1878. It offered practical aid and religious counseling to the urban poor.

Like the Salvation Army, the Young Men's Christian Association (YMCA) also began in England. The YMCA tried to help industrial workers and the urban poor by organizing Bible studies, prayer meetings, citizenship training, and group activities. In the United States, YMCAs, or "Ys," quickly spread from Boston throughout the country. YMCA facilities included libraries, gymnasiums, swimming pools, auditoriums, and low-cost hotel rooms available on a temporary basis to those in need.

Revivalism and Dwight L. Moody One prominent organizer of the American YMCA was **Dwight L. Moody,** who was president of the Chicago YMCA in the late 1860s. A gifted preacher and organizer, Moody founded his own church in Chicago, today known as Moody Memorial Church. By 1867 Moody had begun to organize revival meetings in other

What If...

English Spelling Reform Had Been Accepted?

In 1906 the Simplified Spelling Board suggested a list of 300 words that it thought needed to be simplified. For example, it recommended spelling "axe" without the silent "e." The association also asked for more radical changes, such as replacing the "-ed" at the end of past-tense verbs with a "t." Thus, "kissed" and "missed" would be "kisst" and "misst." "Thoroughly" would be simplified to "thoroly."

Although the reforms were not accepted, they received support from such famous people as Mark Twain and President Theodore Roosevelt. After Roosevelt suggested that the Government Printing Office adopt the new spellings, Mark Twain tried to convince the Associated Press news agency to follow along:

❝If [you] will adopt and use our simplified forms . . . [W]e shall be rid of . . . pneumonia and . . . pterodactyl, and all those other insane words which no man . . . can try to spell. . . . What is the real function . . . of language? Isn't it merely to convey ideas and emotions . . . ? [I]f we can do it with words of fonetic brevity and compactness, why keep the present cumbersome forms?❞

What might have happened?

1. Why do you think these spelling reforms were never accepted?

2. Would English be easier for immigrants to learn and understand if the reforms had been accepted? Why or why not?

Booker T. Washington
1856–1915

Born enslaved on a plantation in Virginia, Booker T. Washington spent his childhood working in the coal mines of West Virginia. At age 16 he heard about the Hampton Institute in Virginia, where African Americans could learn farming or a trade. With little money in his pockets, Washington left home and walked nearly 500 miles to the school, where he was able to work as a janitor to pay for his education.

After Washington completed his degree, Hampton hired him as an instructor in 1879. Two years later, Hampton's founder, Samuel Armstrong, asked Washington to organize an agricultural and industrial school for African Americans in Tuskegee, Alabama. The Tuskegee Institute's beginnings were modest. As Washington recalled, it began with 40 students and a "dilapidated shanty." By 1915 the school had over 100 buildings, about 2,000 students, and an endowment of nearly $2 million. Washington himself became a nationally known spokesperson for the African American community.

George Washington Carver
1864–1943

At about 10 years of age, George Washington Carver left his home in Missouri and began traveling on his own. He worked as a servant, hotel clerk, laundry worker, and farmhand in order to get a formal education. In 1894 he graduated from the Iowa State College of Agriculture and Mechanical Arts. Two years later, he became the director of agricultural research at the Tuskegee Institute, where he began experimenting with various crops.

To help Southern sharecroppers overcome their problems of depleted soil, poverty, and poor nutrition, Carver urged them to plant peanuts and soybeans. These plants restored the soil's nitrogen while providing extra protein in the farmers' diets. To make peanut farming profitable, Carver developed over 300 industrial uses for peanuts, including flour, inks, dyes, wood stains, soap, and cosmetics. By 1940 his research had made the peanut the South's second most lucrative crop after cotton.

American cities. In 1870 Moody met Ira Sankey, a hymn writer and singer. Together they introduced the gospel hymn into worship services in the United States and Great Britain. Moody's preaching and Sankey's hymns drew thousands of people to revival meetings in the 1870s and 1880s.

Moody strongly supported charities that helped the poor, but he rejected both the Social Gospel and Social Darwinism. He believed the way to help the poor was not by providing them with services but by redeeming their souls and reforming their character.

The Settlement House Movement In a way, the settlement house movement was an offshoot of the Social Gospel movement. It attracted idealistic reformers who believed it was their Christian duty to improve living conditions for the poor. During the late 1800s, reformers such as **Jane Addams** established settlement houses in poor neighborhoods. In these establishments, middle-class residents lived and helped poor residents, mostly immigrants.

Addams, who opened the famous Hull House in Chicago in 1889, inspired many more such settlements across the country, including the Henry Street Settlement run by Lillian Wald in New York City. The women who ran settlement houses provided everything from medical care, recreation programs, and English classes to hot lunches for factory workers. Their efforts helped shape the social work profession, in which women came to play a major role.

✓ **Reading Check** **Summarizing** What were the beliefs of Dwight L. Moody?

Public Education

As the United States became increasingly industrialized and urbanized, it needed more workers who were trained and educated. The demand for skilled workers led to a much greater focus on building schools and colleges in the late 1800s.

The Spread of Schools The number of public schools increased quickly after the Civil War. In 1870 around 6,500,000 children attended school. By 1900 that number had risen to over 17,300,000.

Public schools were often crucial to the success of immigrant children. It was there the children usually became knowledgeable about American culture, a process known as Americanization. To assimilate immigrants into American culture, schools taught immigrant children English, American history, and the responsibilities of citizenship. They also tried to instill discipline and a strong work ethic, values considered important to the nation's progress.

Carnegie Library, Shelbyville, Indiana

Americanization could also pose a problem for immigrant children, however, because sometimes parents worried that it would make the children forget their own cultural traditions.

Not everyone had access to school. In the rush to fund education, cities were way ahead of rural areas. Many African Americans, also, did not have equal educational opportunities. To combat this discrimination, some African Americans started their own schools. The leader of this movement was Booker T. Washington, who founded the Tuskegee Institute in Alabama in 1881.

Education for the Workplace
City schools helped immigrants assimilate, and they also helped future workers prepare for the jobs they hoped would lift their families out of poverty. The grammar school system in city schools divided students into eight grades and drilled them in timely attendance, neatness, and efficiency—necessary habits for success in the workplace. At the same time, vocational and technical education in the high schools provided students with skills required in specific trades.

Expanding Higher Education
Colleges also multiplied in the late 1800s, helped by the Morrill Land Grant Act. This Civil War–era law gave federal land grants to states for the purpose of establishing agricultural and mechanical colleges. By 1900 land-grant colleges were established across the Midwest. The number of students enrolled expanded rapidly in this period. In 1870 around 50,000 students attended college, but by 1890 the number had more than tripled to 157,000.

Traditionally, women's educational opportunities lagged behind men's. Around this time, however, things began to change. The opening of private women's colleges such as Vassar, Wellesley, and Smith, along with new women's colleges on the campuses of Harvard and Columbia Universities, served to increase the number of women attending college.

Public Libraries
Like public schools, free libraries also made education available to city dwellers. One of the strongest supporters of the public library movement was industrialist Andrew Carnegie, who believed access to knowledge was the key to getting ahead in life. Carnegie donated millions of dollars toward the construction of libraries all across the United States. These libraries, as well as the various educational and social reform movements that arose in the late 1800s, helped people cope with the harsher aspects of a newly industrialized society.

Reading Check **Explaining** How did the United States try to Americanize immigrants?

SECTION 4 ASSESSMENT

Checking for Understanding
1. **Define:** naturalism, settlement house, Americanization.
2. **Identify:** Henry George, Lester Frank Ward, Edward Bellamy, Jane Addams.
3. **Describe** the way naturalist writers portrayed the fictional characters in their novels.

Reviewing Themes
4. **Individual Action** How did the efforts of Jane Addams and Mary Brewster help poor people in urban areas in the late 1800s?

Critical Thinking
5. **Analyzing** What role do you think the government should play in the economy? Give reasons to support your opinion.
6. **Categorizing** Complete a chart like the one below by listing names and goals of reform movements that arose in the late 1800s to help the urban poor.

Reform Movement	Goals

Analyzing Visuals
7. **Analyzing Graphs** Examine the graphs on page 482, and then develop a quiz with questions based on specific information found in the graphs. Include at least one broad question about a pattern you see. Give the quiz to some of your classmates.

Writing About History
8. **Descriptive Writing** Take on the role of an immigrant in the late 1800s. Write a diary entry in which you describe your feelings about your children becoming Americanized while attending the local public school.

SKILLBUILDER

Hypothesizing

Why Learn This Skill?

When you are reading new material, you may often encounter ideas and events that you do not immediately understand. One way to overcome this difficulty is to make educated guesses about what happened.

Learning the Skill

When you read things that you do not understand, you probably make guesses about what the material means. You may or may not have been able to prove these guesses, but you have taken a step toward deciphering the information. This step is called **hypothesizing.** When you hypothesize, you form one or more hypotheses, which are guesses that offer possible answers to a problem or provide possible explanations for an observation. When hypothesizing, follow these steps.

• Read the material carefully.

• Ask yourself what the material is actually saying. To do this, try to put the material in your own words.

• Determine what you might logically assume from your guesses. Then form one or more hypotheses.

• Test each hypothesis to determine whether or not it is correct. You can usually do this by asking yourself questions that relate to your hypothesis and then researching the answers.

• Based on your research, determine which hypothesis, if any, provides an explanation for the information that you originally read.

Hypotheses are only preliminary explanations. They must be accepted, rejected, or modified as the problem is investigated. Each hypothesis must be tested against the information gathered. Hypotheses that are supported by evidence can be accepted as explanations of the problem.

Practicing the Skill

Using the steps just discussed and what you have read in the chapter, test the following hypotheses and determine if they can be supported.

❶ Most immigrants who came to the United States came in search of work.

❷ Improved transportation led people to move to urban areas from rural areas.

❸ The general laissez-faire approach taken by the government toward growing cities was beneficial to businesses and citizens.

Students collaborating

Skills Assessment

Complete the Practicing Skills questions on page 489 and the Chapter 15 Skill Reinforcement Activity to assess your mastery of this skill.

Applying the Skill

Hypothesizing Reread the passage titled "The Resurgence of Nativism" in Section 1. Using the facts that you are given in these paragraphs, form at least two hypotheses that may explain what is being described. Test each hypothesis, then select the best one. Which hypothesis did you choose? Why?

Glencoe's **Skillbuilder Interactive Workbook CD-ROM, Level 2,** provides instruction and practice in key social studies skills.

Reviewing Key Terms

On a sheet of paper, use each of these terms in a sentence.

1. steerage
2. nativism
3. skyscraper
4. tenement
5. political machine
6. party boss
7. graft
8. philanthropy
9. realism
10. vaudeville
11. ragtime
12. naturalism
13. settlement house
14. Americanization

Reviewing Key Facts

15. **Identify:** Ellis Island, Angel Island, Louis Sullivan, George Plunkitt, William M. ("Boss") Tweed, Gilded Age, Herbert Spencer, Lester Frank Ward, Jane Addams.

16. How did the Chinese in the United States react to the Chinese Exclusion Act of 1882?

17. What attempts did nativist groups make to decrease immigration to the United States in the late 1800s?

18. What problems did cities in the United States face in the late 1800s?

19. What did realist authors such as Mark Twain and Henry James write about?

20. What movements in the late 1800s addressed urban problems?

Critical Thinking

21. **Analyzing Themes: Geography and History** What factors led so many people to immigrate to the United States in the late 1800s?

22. **Analyzing** What methods did political machines use to build support in the late 1800s?

23. **Evaluating** Recall the problems facing city dwellers in the late 1800s. What do you think is the biggest problem facing people living in large cities today? How do you think the problem should be solved?

24. **Interpreting Primary Sources** Reaction in the United States to "old" immigration was generally more favorable than reaction to "new" immigration. Some people, however, still favored all immigration. The following excerpt from an 1882 editorial in the *Commercial and Financial Chronicle* addresses the effects of immigration on the nation.

❝In the very act of coming and traveling to reach his destination, he [the immigrant] adds . . . to the immediate prosperity and success of certain lines of business. . . . Not only do the ocean steamers . . . get very large returns in carrying passengers of this description, but in forwarding them to the places chosen by the immigrants as their future homes the railroad companies also derive great benefit and their passenger traffic is greatly swelled. . . .

Chapter Summary

Immigration and Internal Migration

Rapid Growth of Cities

Urban Problems of Poverty, Crime, and Disease

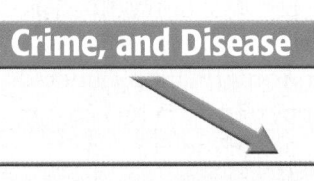

Nativism leads to immigration restrictions and violence against immigrants.

Political machines develop to offer services to city dwellers in exchange for votes.

. . . These immigrants not only produce largely, . . . but, having wants which they cannot supply themselves, create a demand for outside supplies. . . . Thus it is that the Eastern manufacturer finds the call upon him for his wares and goods growing more urgent all the time, thus the consumption of coal keeps on expanding notwithstanding the check to new railroad enterprises, and thus there is a more active and larger interchange of all commodities. . . .✎

a. According to the editorial, what kind of effect did immigration have on the nation's economy?

b. How is the editorial's view of the effects of immigration different from that of the nativists?

25. Organizing Complete a graphic organizer similar to the one below by listing the new technologies that contributed to urban growth in the late 1800s.

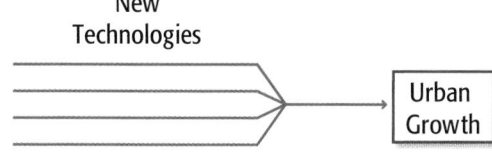

Practicing Skills

26. Hypothesizing Reread the passage titled "The Spread of Schools" from Section 4. Using the information in this passage, form a hypothesis that describes the availability of education to people during this time. Write your hypothesis down and research the topic. Then state whether or not your hypothesis was correct.

Writing Activity

27. Descriptive Writing Find out about an individual in the 1800s who experienced a "rags-to-riches" success story. You might use one of the business leaders or other individuals discussed in the chapter. Write a brief sketch of the person, describing how he or she became a success.

Chapter Activity

28. American History Primary Source Document Library CD-ROM Read the article "The Need for Public Parks" by Frederick Law Olmsted, under *Reshaping the Nation.* Then work with a partner and create a design for a park that you think would meet the recreational needs of people in your community.

Immigration's Contribution to Population Growth, 1860–1900

Source: *Historical Statistics of the United States: Colonial Times to 1970.*

Geography and History

29. The graph above shows how much immigration contributed to population growth in the United States between 1860 and 1900. Study the graph and answer the questions below.

a. Interpreting Graphs By about how much did the population of the United States increase between 1861 and 1900?

b. Understanding Cause and Effect What is the relationship between immigration and population increase?

Standardized Test Practice

Directions: Choose the best answer to the following question.

Which of the following concepts is not associated with both Social Darwinism and the Gospel of Wealth?

A Survival of the fittest

B Laissez-faire

C Unregulated competition

D Philanthropy

Test-Taking Tip: Read the question carefully. From the wording of the question, you can see that Social Darwinism and the Gospel of Wealth DO have three of these concepts in common. Find the one that is part of only ONE of these philosophies.

CHAPTER 16

Politics and Reform *1877–1896*

Why It Matters

During this period, political parties often focused on party competition rather than on important issues. Rural Americans were suffering economically, and they began to organize to obtain relief. Many states passed laws segregating African Americans and limiting their voting rights.

The Impact Today

Events of this period remain significant today.
- *To ensure fair hiring, a federal civil service system was created.*
- *Segregation created problems that Americans are still working to overcome.*

 The* American Vision *Video *The Chapter 16 video, "The 1893 Chicago World's Fair," captures the feeling of this influential age.*

1881
- President Garfield assassinated

1877
- Farmers' Alliance founded in Texas

1883
- Civil Service Act adopted

United States PRESIDENTS

Hayes 1877–1881

Garfield 1881

Arthur 1881–1885

Cleveland 1885–1889

1876

1881

1886

World

1878
- Russians defeat Turks in war over control of Balkans

1880
- France annexes Tahiti

1884
- First subway in London

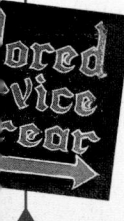

Electioneering in a Country Town by E.L. Henry

1887
- Florida initiates Jim Crow laws
- Interstate Commerce Act adopted

1890
- Sherman Antitrust Act passed

1895
- Booker T. Washington gives Atlanta Compromise speech

1896
- Democrats support free silver

B. Harrison
1889–1893

Cleveland
1893–1897

1891

1896

1893
- France acquires a protectorate over Laos

1894
- Sino-Japanese War breaks out

HISTORY Online

Chapter Overview
Visit the *American Vision* Web site at tav.glencoe.com and click on **Chapter Overviews—Chapter 16** to preview chapter information.

Stalemate in Washington

Guide to Reading

Main Idea

From 1877 to 1896, the Republicans and Democrats were so evenly matched that only a few reforms were possible at the national level.

Key Terms and Names

patronage, Stalwart, Pendleton Act, rebate, Interstate Commerce Commission

Reading Strategy

Organizing As you read about the electoral politics of the 1880s, complete a graphic organizer similar to the one below by filling in the ideals of each Republican Party faction listed.

Stalwarts	Halfbreeds

Reading Objectives

- **Explain** why the Republicans and Democrats were so evenly matched during this period.
- **Cite** the economic problems of the period and the basic viewpoints of each political party.

Section Theme

Continuity and Change Political parties relied on support from different groups and regions of the country.

Preview of Events

♦1881	♦1884	♦1887	♦1890

1881
Garfield assassinated; succeeded by Chester A. Arthur

1883
Civil Service Act adopted

1887
Interstate Commerce Act adopted

1890
Sherman Antitrust Act adopted

★ *An American Story* ★

After the election of President James A. Garfield in 1880, many of his supporters tried to claim the "spoils of office"—the government jobs that follow an election victory. One of these job-seekers was Charles Guiteau. In the spring of 1881, Guiteau made daily trips to the White House or State Department, repeatedly asking for a job. Finally, the night of May 18, he had a crazed inspiration: "[I]f the president was out of the way," he thought, "everything would go better." Unlike Garfield, Guiteau reasoned, Vice President Chester Arthur was comfortable with the old spoils system. Arthur would give him the position he deserved. On July 2, 1881, Guiteau shot President Garfield in a train station near Capitol Hill. In a note left behind, Guiteau stated:

❝The President's tragic death was a sad necessity, but it will unite the Republican party and save the Republic. . . . I had no ill-will toward the President. His death was a political necessity. I am a lawyer, theologian, and politician. I am a Stalwart of the Stalwarts. . . .❞

—quoted in *Garfield*

A Campaign to Clean Up Politics

For many, the assassination of President Garfield highlighted the need to work seriously on reforming politics. Traditionally, under the spoils system, or patronage, government jobs went to supporters of the winning party in an election. Many Americans believed the spoils system prevented government from addressing the nation's issues and corrupted those who worked for the government. By the late 1870s, a movement to reform the civil service had begun to build support.

Stalwarts and Halfbreeds When Rutherford B. Hayes entered the White House in 1877, he attacked the practice of patronage by appointing reformers to his cabinet and replacing officials who owed their jobs to party bosses. His actions infuriated New York senator Roscoe Conkling, who, like other local bosses of Republican political machines, was called a **"Stalwart"** in the newspapers.

The Stalwarts were already angry with Hayes for abandoning Reconstruction, because this abandonment allowed Democrats to regain full control of the South. Conkling labeled the Republican reformers **"Halfbreeds."** He accused them of backing reform simply to create openings for their own supporters. "They are wolves in sheep's clothing," he charged. "Their real object is office and plunder."

As the presidential election of 1880 approached, Hayes announced that he did not intend to run again. The Republicans nominated a mixed ticket—a Halfbreed, James Garfield, for president, and a Stalwart, Chester A. Arthur, for vice president. Despite the party's feud, its ticket managed to win the election. A few months into his presidency, however, Garfield was assassinated.

The Pendleton Act Garfield's assassination further excited public opinion against the spoils system. In 1883 Congress responded by passing the **Pendleton Act.** This law allowed the president to decide which federal jobs would be filled according to rules laid down by a bipartisan Civil Service Commission. Candidates competed for these jobs through examinations, and appointments could be made only from the list of those who took the exams. Once appointed, a civil service official could not be removed for political reasons.

Although President Arthur was a Stalwart, he supported the Pendleton Act. He placed 14,000 jobs (about one-tenth of the total) under the control of the civil service. The federal government had finally begun to shift away from the spoils system.

✓ **Reading Check** **Explaining** Why did Garfield's assassination highlight the need for political reform?

Two Parties, Neck and Neck

Although many people thought corruption prevented the government from addressing the nation's problems, a major reason few new policies were introduced in the 1870s and 1880s was the political system itself. The Republicans held a voting edge in New England and the upper Midwest. As the party that had preserved the Union and established pensions for Civil War veterans, the Republicans had the support of former Union soldiers and Americans who were strongly patriotic. In addition, Republicans had the support of big business and strong support among farmers on the Great Plains. The Republicans were also seen as the party of reform because they supported abolition, temperance, and other reforms. Most Republicans were Protestants who viewed their party as the defender of traditional American morals and values.

While Republicans were sometimes seen as the "party of morality," Democrats portrayed themselves as the "party of personal liberty." The Democrats dominated the South, where white voters remained anti-Republican following the Civil War and Reconstruction. The Democrats also enjoyed strong support in big cities, where large numbers of Catholics and immigrants lived.

From 1877 to 1896, these voting patterns gave the Democrats an edge in the House of Representatives, where voters in each congressional district elected

Picturing **History**

National Tragedy A newspaper artist captured the attack on President Garfield. Why was Charles Guiteau obsessed with the idea of killing the president?

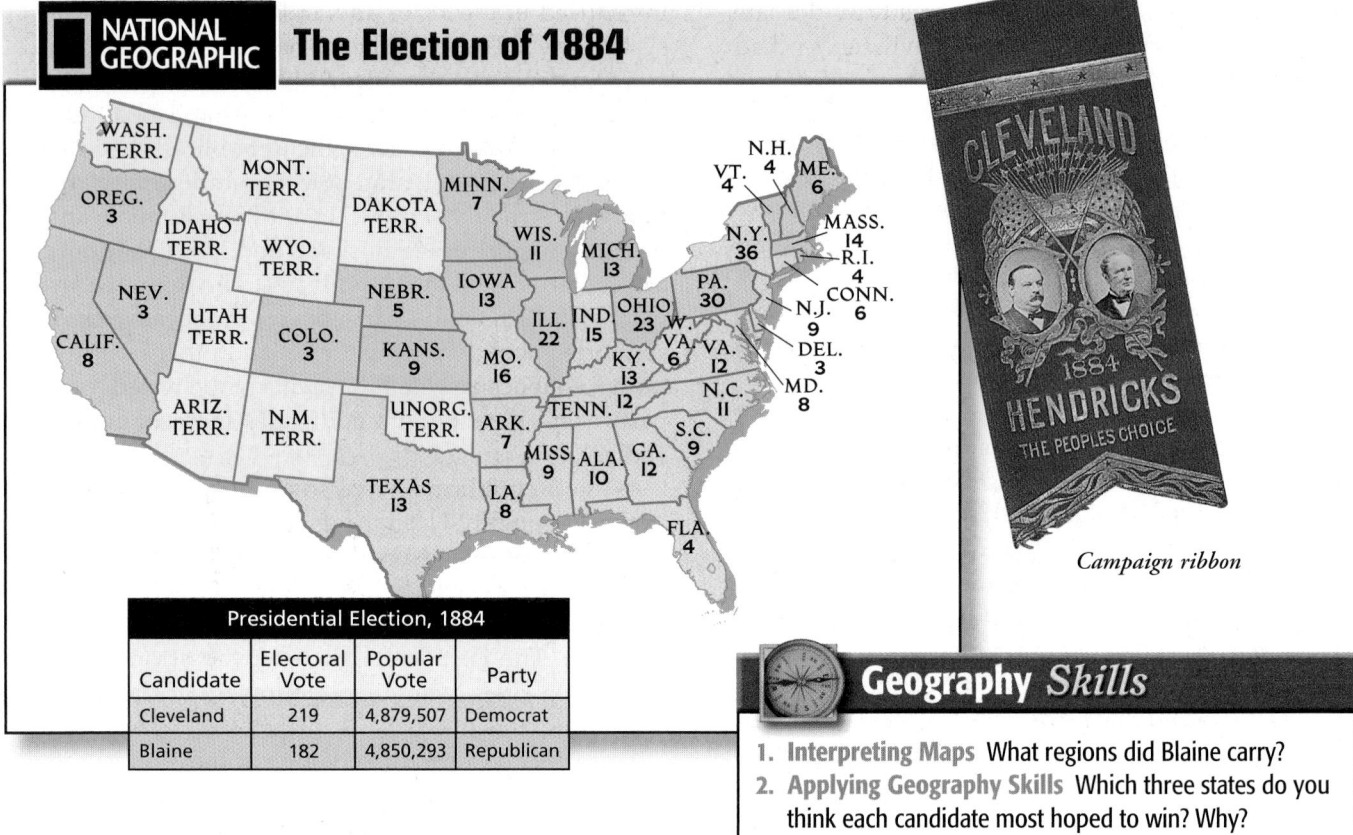

Campaign ribbon

Presidential Election, 1884			
Candidate	Electoral Vote	Popular Vote	Party
Cleveland	219	4,879,507	Democrat
Blaine	182	4,850,293	Republican

Geography *Skills*

1. **Interpreting Maps** What regions did Blaine carry?
2. **Applying Geography Skills** Which three states do you think each candidate most hoped to win? Why?

members directly. The Republicans had the upper hand in the Senate, because state legislatures chose senators and Republicans generally controlled a majority of state governments.

Both parties were well organized to turn out the vote in elections, and narrow margins decided most presidential elections between 1876 and 1896. The elections of 1880 and 1888 came down to the swing states of New York, Ohio, and Pennsylvania, with their big blocks of electoral votes. Twice during this period, in 1876 and 1888, a candidate lost the popular vote but won the election. This happened because even if candidates win several states by slim popular vote margins, they still receive all the electoral votes in those states. These narrow victories then give the candidate an Electoral College majority, regardless of the overall popular vote count.

Although the Republicans won four of the six presidential elections between 1876 and 1896, the president often had to contend with a House controlled by Democrats and a Senate dominated by Republicans who did not always agree with him on the issues. Furthermore, this was an era when local political bosses, not the president, controlled the party. The nearly even division of power produced political deadlock at the federal level.

✓ **Reading Check** **Summarizing** What were the results of most presidential elections between 1876 and 1896?

Democrats Reclaim the White House

As the election of 1884 approached, Democrats saw their best chance to win the White House since before the Civil War. Republicans remained divided over reform, and Democrats went after the votes of pro-reform Republicans by nominating Governor Grover Cleveland of New York. Cleveland was an opponent of **Tammany Hall,** the corrupt Democratic political machine in New York City.

Cleveland's Republican opponent was James G. Blaine, a former speaker of the House of Representatives and chairman of the Maine committee of the Republican Party since 1859. Blaine was wildly popular among party workers. When his name was placed in nomination at the Republican convention in Chicago, delegates launched into a riotous celebration. The cheers "deepened into a roar fully as deafening as the voice of Niagara," a witness reported. "The air quivered, the gas lights trembled and the walls fairly shook."

The campaign was sensational and frenzied. Because so many voters believed corruption was the main problem in American government, they focused their attention on the personal morals of the candidates. The wild show of support for Blaine offended *New York Evening Post* editor Edwin L. Godkin, who called it a "disgrace to decency" and compared the celebration to a "mass meeting of maniacs." Godkin disliked Blaine, who had been accused during the Crédit Mobilier scandal of profiting financially from a political favor he did for the Union Pacific Railroad while serving as Speaker of the House in the 1870s.

Some Republican reformers were so unhappy with Blaine that they abandoned their party and supported Cleveland. These renegade reformers became known as **"Mugwumps,"** from an Algonquian word meaning "great chiefs." They thought of themselves as moral leaders who were more concerned with helping the nation than with helping a particular political party. Mugwumps believed that Blaine was too entrenched in the old system of politics to support their reform issues. Most Mugwumps came from New York and Massachusetts.

Cleveland, a bachelor, also faced moral criticism during the campaign when a newspaper revealed that he had fathered a child 10 years earlier. Aides asked Cleveland how they should respond to reporters seeking to know more about this story, and he replied, "Tell the truth." By admitting to the charge, Cleveland preserved his reputation for honesty and retained the support of many Mugwumps.

Blaine hoped that he could make up for the loss of the Mugwumps by persuading Roman Catholics to defect from the Democratic Party. His mother was an Irish Catholic, and there were half a million Irish Americans in New York state alone at the time. During the campaign, however, Blaine met with a Protestant minister who denounced the Democratic Party for its ties to Catholicism. Because Blaine was slow to denounce the remark, he lost most of the Irish American vote. To make matters worse for Blaine, many pro-temperance Republicans in upstate New York backed the candidate of the Prohibition Party, which was dedicated to banning the sale of alcohol. Cleveland won New York by a margin of about 1,000 votes out of more than 1,000,000 cast, and his victory there decided the election.

Reading Check **Describing** From what sources did Grover Cleveland gain support in the 1884 presidential election?

A President Besieged by Problems

Grover Cleveland was an easy-going man who enjoyed the personal side of politics. Like his predecessors, he was shocked by the crowds that flocked to the White House seeking jobs. "This dreadful . . .

office-seeking hangs over me and surrounds me," he complained, "and makes me feel like resigning."

As the first elected Democratic president since 1856, he faced a horde of supporters who expected him to reward them with jobs. Mugwumps, on the other hand, expected him to multiply the number of positions covered under the merit system. Cleveland chose a middle course and wound up angering both sides. Economic issues, however, soon overshadowed the debate about political reform.

ECONOMICS

The Interstate Commerce Commission With greater industrialization and the growth of the labor movement, unrest among workers was mounting across the country. Many strikes occurred in this period, and police and paid guards sometimes attacked workers with clubs. This period of violence culminated in 1886 when a bomb exploded at a labor demonstration in Haymarket Square in Chicago.

The power of large corporations also concerned Americans. In particular, small businesses and farmers had become angry at the railroads. While large corporations such as Standard Oil were able to negotiate rebates—or partial refunds—and lower rates because of the volume of goods they shipped, others were forced to pay much higher rates. Although the high fixed costs and low operating costs of railroads caused much of this problem, many Americans believed railroads were gouging customers.

Neither Democrats nor Republicans moved quickly at the federal level to address these problems.

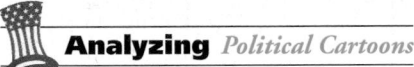
Analyzing *Political Cartoons*

Difficult Passage In Greek mythology, Scylla and Charybdis were sea monsters who threatened the hero Odysseus from opposite sides of a narrow strait. Why do you think the artist chose this image for Grover Cleveland in 1886?

Picturing History

Changing of the Guard Grover Cleveland delivers his inaugural speech in March 1885. His predecessor, Chester Arthur, is seen at left. What were the major issues of this election?

Both parties believed that government should not interfere with corporations' property rights, which courts had held to be the same as those of individuals. Many states had new laws regulating railroad freight rates. In 1886, however, the Supreme Court ruled in the case of *Wabash v. Illinois* that Illinois could not restrict the rates that the Wabash Railroad charged for traffic between states because only the federal government could regulate interstate commerce. 📖 *(See page 1083 for a summary of* Wabash v. Illinois.*)*

Public pressure forced Congress to respond to the *Wabash* ruling. In 1887 Cleveland signed the Interstate Commerce Act creating the **Interstate Commerce Commission** (ICC). This act was the first federal law designed to regulate interstate commerce. The legislation limited railroad rates to what was "reasonable and just," forbade rebates to high-volume users, and made it illegal to charge higher rates for shorter hauls. The commission was not very effective in regulating the industry, however, because it had to rely on the courts to enforce its rulings.

Debating Tariffs Another important economic issue concerned tariffs. Although tariffs had been lowered slightly in the 1870s, they were still much higher than in the years before the Civil War. Many Democrats thought that Congress should cut tariffs

because these taxes had the effect of raising the prices of manufactured goods. While protecting weak domestic manufacturing after the Civil War may have made sense, many questioned the necessity of maintaining high tariffs in the 1880s, when large American companies were fully capable of competing internationally. High tariffs also forced other nations to respond in kind, making it difficult for farmers to export their surpluses.

In December 1887, President Cleveland proposed lowering tariffs. The House, with a Democratic majority, passed moderate tariff reductions, but the Republican-controlled Senate rejected the bill. With Congress deadlocked, tariff reduction became a major issue in the election of 1888.

Reading Check **Examining** Why was the Interstate Commerce Commission unable to carry out its goals effectively?

Republicans Regain Power

The Republicans and their presidential candidate, Benjamin Harrison, received large contributions for the 1888 campaign from industrialists who benefited from tariff protection. Cleveland and the Democrats campaigned against unnecessarily high tariff rates. In one of the closest races in American history,

Harrison lost the popular vote but won the electoral vote with narrow victories in New York and Indiana.

The McKinley Tariff The election of 1888 gave the Republicans control of both houses of Congress as well as the White House. Using this power, the party passed legislation to address points of national concern. One major piece of legislation was McKinley's tariff bill. Representative William McKinley of Ohio pushed through a tariff bill that cut tobacco taxes and tariff rates on raw sugar but greatly increased rates on other goods, such as textiles, to discourage people from buying those imports.

The **McKinley Tariff** lowered federal revenue and transformed the nation's budget surplus into a budget deficit. In 1890, furthermore, Congress passed a new pension law increasing payments to veterans and the number of veterans eligible to receive them. While securing more votes for the Republicans, the new pension plan greatly worsened the federal deficit.

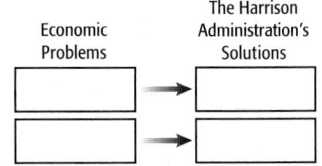
Harrison paper lantern

The Sherman Antitrust Act The Republican-controlled Congress also responded to popular pressure to do something about the power of trusts, large combinations of companies that dominated certain markets. Senator John Sherman of Ohio introduced the **Sherman Antitrust Act** of 1890, which declared illegal any "combination in the form of trust . . . or conspiracy, in restraint of trade or commerce among the several States." The courts were responsible for enforcement, however, and judges saw nothing in this vaguely worded legislation that required them to make big companies change the way they did business. In 1895, for example, the Supreme Court agreed that the American Sugar Refining Company was a trust, enjoying a nearly complete monopoly of sugar manufacturing. Nevertheless, the Court ruled that the company's actions did not violate the Sherman Antitrust Act because manufacturing was not interstate commerce. In the years following passage of the act, businesses formed trusts and combinations at a great rate. In 1899 alone there were over 1,200 recorded mergers in manufacturing and mining firms. Like the ICC, the Sherman Antitrust Act was more important for establishing a precedent than for its immediate impact.

As the midterm congressional election of 1890 approached, some Americans concluded that the two-party system was incapable of solving the nation's problems. That conviction was strongest among farmers, who felt exploited by banks and railroads and neglected by the government. They doubted that either the Democrats or the Republicans would respond to their concerns.

✓ **Reading Check** **Summarizing** What were the results of the McKinley Tariff?

SECTION 1 ASSESSMENT

Checking for Understanding

1. **Define:** patronage, rebate.
2. **Identify:** Stalwart, Halfbreed, Interstate Commerce Commission.
3. **Explain** how the Pendleton Act created civil service reform.
4. **Describe** the events leading to the establishment of the Interstate Commerce Commission.

Reviewing Themes

5. **Continuity and Change** What groups and regions were strongholds for Republicans and Democrats in the 1880s? Where is their support today?

Critical Thinking

6. **Interpreting** Why was the Sherman Antitrust Act ineffective?
7. **Organizing** Use a graphic organizer similar to the one below to list the era's economic problems and the Harrison administration's solutions.

Economic Problems		The Harrison Administration's Solutions
	→	
	→	

Analyzing Visuals

8. **Examining Photographs** Study the photograph on page 496. What similarities do you see between Cleveland's inauguration ceremony and the ones we have today? Do you see any differences between the ceremonies then and now?

Writing About History

9. **Persuasive Writing** Imagine that you are seeking a federal job in the early 1880s. Write a letter to your congressional representatives urging them to support or oppose the Pendleton Act.

Eyewitness

BROWN BROTHERS

In his exposé of urban poverty, How the Other Half Lives *(1890),* **JACOB RIIS** *documented the living conditions in New York City tenements:*

"The statement once made a sensation that between seventy and eighty children had been found in one tenement. It no longer excites even passing attention, when the sanitary police report counting 101 adults and 91 children in a Crosby Street house, one of twins, built together. The children in the others, if I am not mistaken, numbered 89, a total of 180 for two tenements! Or when midnight inspection in Mulberry Street unearths a hundred and fifty "lodgers" sleeping on filthy floors in two buildings. In spite of brown-stone fittings, plate-glass and mosaic vestibule floors, the water does not rise in summer to the second story, while the beer flows unchecked to the all-night picnics on the roof. The saloon with the side-door and the landlord divide the prosperity of the place between them, and the tenant, in sullen submission, foots the bill."

VERBATIM

❝Tell 'em quick, and tell 'em often.❞

WILLIAM WRIGLEY,
soap salesman and promoter of chewing gum,
on his marketing philosophy

❝A pushing, energetic, ingenious person, always awake and trying to get ahead of his neighbors.❞

HENRY ADAMS,
historian, describing the average New Yorker or Chicagoan

❝We cannot all live in cities, yet nearly all seem determined to do so.❞

HORACE GREELEY,
newspaper editor

INDICATORS:
Livin' in the City

Moving off the farm for a factory job? Sharpen your pencil. You'll need to budget carefully to buy all you will need.

Here are the numbers for a Georgia family of four in 1890. The husband is a textile worker, and the wife works at home. There is one child, age 4, and a boarder. They share a two-room, wood-heated, oil-lighted apartment.

INCOME: (annual)

husband's income	$312.00
boarder's rent	10.00
TOTAL INCOME	**$322.00**

EXPENSES: (annual)

medical	$65.00
furniture	46.90
clothing	46.00
rent	21.00
flour/meal	25.00
hog products	17.00
other meat	13.00
vegetables	13.00
lard	6.50
potatoes	6.40
butter	5.00
sugar	4.00
charitable donations	6.10
vacation	3.25
alcohol	3.25
tobacco	3.00
molasses	2.00
other food	27.80
miscellaneous	68.20
TOTAL EXPENSES	**$382.40**

Milestones

ON THE RUN, 1881. THE JESSE JAMES GANG, after robbing a Chicago, Rock Island, and Pacific train near Winston, Missouri, and killing the conductor and a passenger.

OVERTURNED, 1878. By the Supreme Court, a Louisiana court decision that awarded damages to an African American woman who had been refused admission to a steamship stateroom reserved for whites.

PLAGUED BY GRASSHOPPERS, 1874. THE AMERICAN GREAT PLAINS. Insect swarms a mile wide blot out the midday sun. Two inches deep on the ground, they leave "nothing but the mortgage," as one farmer put it.

CELEBRATED IN EUROPE, 1887. ANNIE OAKLEY, star of Buffalo Bill's Wild West Show. Oakley shot a cigarette from the lips of Crown Prince Wilhelm of Germany. Years later, when the U.S. goes to war against Kaiser Wilhelm, Oakley will quip: "I wish I'd missed that day!"

Susan B. Anthony

Jesse James

REMOVED, 1884. IDA B. WELLS, journalist and former slave, from a ladies coach on a train. Wells refused to move to the smoking car where African Americans were to be seated.

ESTABLISHED, 1883. STANDARD TIME. To accommodate the railroad system, noon will no longer be the moment in a given locality when the sun stands highest in the sky but, instead, will be standard across four time zones. Set your watches!

ARRESTED, 1872. SUSAN B. ANTHONY, for casting a ballot in Rochester, New York. Anthony argued that the Fourteenth and Fifteenth Amendments applied to women.

NUMBERS

1 in 12 Americans living in cities of 100,000 or more in 1865

A crowded New York City street

1 in 5 Americans living in cities in 1896

522 Inhabitants in a one-acre area in the Bowery, New York City

$2 Daily wage for a farm laborer, New York, 1869

$4 Daily wage for a plumber, New York City, 1869

50¢ Price of a pair of boy's knee pants, a parasol, button boots, or a necktie (1870s)

$8 Price of a "Fine All-Wool Suit," 1875

$3 Box seat for four at Gilmore's Concert Garden in New York City

4¢ Price for one pound of fancy white rice, 1896

25¢ Admission to "Barnum's American Museum" (featuring the smallest pair of human beings ever seen!), 1896

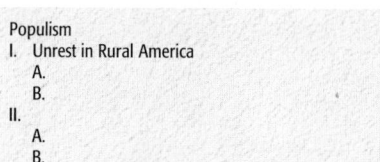

Guide to Reading

Main Idea
In the 1890s an independent political movement called populism emerged to challenge the two major parties.

Key Terms and Names
populism, greenback, inflation, deflation, Grange, cooperative, People's Party, graduated income tax, goldbug, silverite, William Jennings Bryan

Reading Strategy
Taking Notes As you read about the emergence of populism in the 1890s, use the major headings of the section to create an outline similar to the one below.

Populism
I. Unrest in Rural America
    A.
    B.
II.
    A.
    B.

Reading Objectives
• **Explain** why farmers wanted a greenback currency and why the adoption of the gold standard led to the Farmers' Alliance.
• **Describe** who joined the Populist Party and what the party's goals were.

Section Theme
Economic Factors Currency and credit problems led to the rise of the Populist movement.

Preview of Events

◆1865	◆1875	◆1885	◆1895

1867
Grange founded to aid farmers

1873
Congress adopts a gold standard for currency

1877
Farmers' Alliance founded in Texas

1890
People's Party formed in Kansas

1892
National People's Party formed

★ An American Story ★

On July 4, 1890, Leonidas L. Polk took a political gamble. He stepped up to make a speech to a crowd of 6,000 in a small town in Kansas. Polk was a Southerner, a lifelong Democrat, and a former Confederate soldier. He was not in friendly territory.

Polk had come to Kansas because he was now involved in a different kind of battle, one that cut across the lines dividing Northerners from Southerners and Democrats from Republicans. He was calling on farmers from both parties and both regions to unite for their common good. Polk urged the crowd to reject the two-party system and join the emerging movement that became known as populism:

❝I tell you this afternoon that from New York to the Golden Gate, the farmers have risen up and have inaugurated a movement such as the world has never seen. It is a revolution of thought. . . . The farmer of North Carolina, Georgia, Texas, South Carolina is your brother. . . . Some people have stirred up sectional feelings and have kept us apart for twenty-five years. . . . They know that if we get together and shake hands . . . their doom is sealed. . . . Congress could give us a bill in forty-eight hours that would relieve us, but Wall Street says nay. . . . I believe that both of the parties are afraid of Wall Street.❞

—quoted in *Democratic Promise: The Populist Movement in America*

Unrest in Rural America

Populism was the movement to increase farmers' political power and to work for legislation in their interest. The economic crisis that drove farmers to embrace this movement had its origins in the years immediately following the Civil War. A major problem was that farm prices had dropped due to new technology. Farmers were producing more crops, and greater supply tended to lower prices. At the same time, high tariffs increased the cost of manufactured goods farmers needed and made it harder for farmers to sell their goods overseas. Farmers also felt they were victimized by large and faraway entities: the banks from which they obtained loans and the railroads that set their shipping rates. The world that farmers now dealt with was more and more one of big business, and they felt they were losing power and influence.

The Money Supply

One specific problem that greatly concerned farmers was the nation's money supply. To help finance the Union war effort, the United States Treasury had greatly expanded the money supply by issuing millions of dollars in greenbacks—paper currency that could not be exchanged for gold or silver coins. This rapid increase in the money supply without an accompanying increase in goods for sale caused inflation, or a decline in the value of money. As the paper money lost value, the prices of goods soared.

After the Civil War ended, the United States had three types of currency in circulation—greenbacks, gold and silver coins, and national bank notes backed by government bonds. To get inflation under control,

the federal government stopped printing greenbacks and began paying off its bonds. In 1873 Congress also decided to stop making silver into coins.

These decisions meant that the United States did not have a large enough money supply to meet the needs of the country's growing economy. In 1865, for example, there was about $30 in circulation for each American, but by 1895 it had sunk to about $23. As the economy expanded, deflation—or an increase in the value of money and a decrease in the general level of prices—began. As money increased in value, prices began to fall.

Deflation Hurts Farmers

Deflation hit farmers especially hard. Most farmers had to borrow money for seed and other supplies to plant their crops. Because money was in short supply, interest rates began to rise, which increased the amount farmers owed. For those who wanted to expand their farms, rising interest rates also made mortgages more expensive. The falling prices of the period of deflation meant the farmers sold their crops for less. Nevertheless, they still had to make the same mortgage payments to the banks.

Realizing that their problems were due to a shortage of currency, many farmers concluded that Eastern bankers had pressured Congress into reducing the money supply. Some farmers called for the

Picturing **History**

Populist Territory This farm family in Nebraska represents the kind of people who typically supported populism. Why did farmers dislike Eastern bankers?

printing of more greenbacks to expand the money supply. Others, particularly those living in the West where new silver mines had been found, wanted the government to begin minting silver coins. They referred to the decision to stop minting silver as **"The Crime of '73."** Increasingly, farmers realized that if they were going to convince the government to meet their demands, they needed to organize.

The Grange Takes Action In 1866 the United States Department of Agriculture sent Oliver H. Kelley to tour the rural South and report on the condition of the region's farmers. Realizing how isolated the farmers were from each other, the following year, Kelley founded the nation's first national farm organization, the Patrons of Husbandry, better known as the **Grange.**

At first Grangers got together largely for social and educational purposes. Then, in 1873, the nation plunged into a severe recession, and farm income fell sharply. Farmers looking for help joined the Grange in large numbers. By 1874 the Grange had between 800,000 and 1.5 million members.

Grangers responded to the crisis in three ways. Some pressured state legislatures to regulate railroad and warehouse rates, which they believed were too high. Others joined the Independent National Party. This new political party, nicknamed the Greenback Party, wanted the government to print more greenbacks to increase the money supply. Grangers also pooled their resources and tried to create cooperatives—marketing organizations that worked for the benefit of their members.

One of the reasons farmers could not charge higher prices for their crops was that there were so many farmers in competition. If a farmer raised prices, a buyer could always go elsewhere and pay

less. Cooperatives pooled farmers' crops and held them off the market in order to force up prices. Because a cooperative controlled a large quantity of farm products, it could also negotiate better shipping rates with the railroads.

The Grange Fails None of the strategies the Grangers employed improved farmers' economic condition. Several western states passed "Granger laws" setting maximum rates and prohibiting railroads from charging more for short hauls than for long ones. The railroads fought back by cutting services and refusing to lay new track until the laws were repealed. The 1886 Supreme Court ruling in *Wabash v. Illinois* then greatly limited the states' ability to regulate railroads by ruling that states could not regulate commerce that crossed state lines. 📖 *(See pages 496 and 1083 for more information on* Wabash v. Illinois.*)*

Meanwhile the Greenback Party failed to gain much public support. Many Americans were very suspicious of paper money. They did not believe it would hold its value, and they considered the Greenback Party's proposal to print more paper money dangerous for the economy. The Grange's cooperatives also failed, partly because they were too small to have any effect on prices, and partly because Eastern businesses and railroads considered them to be similar to unions—illegitimate conspiracies in restraint of trade—and refused to do business with them. By the late 1870s, membership in the Grange had begun to fall, as farmers moved to other organizations that they hoped would better address their problems.

The Farmers' Alliance

Even as the Grange began to fall apart, a new organization, known as the **Farmers' Alliance,** began to form. The Farmers' Alliance began in Lampasas County, Texas, in 1877. By 1885 it had built a substantial following throughout the state. The following year, Charles W. Macune became the leader of the Alliance. Macune called for the organization to begin recruiting farmers outside of Texas.

The Alliance Grows During the late 1880s, Alliance members traveled across the South and West speaking to farmers and organizing local chapters. By 1890 the Alliance had between 1.5 and 3 million members. Its support was very strong in the South and on the Great Plains, particularly in Kansas, Nebraska, and North and South Dakota.

When Macune became the leader of the Alliance, he also announced a plan to organize very large cooperatives that the Alliance called exchanges.

Farmers' Alliance This small band of farmers met in a cabin in Lampasas County, Texas, to form the Farmers' Alliance.

Hard Labor Southern farmers spent long hours working in their fields. Harvesting cotton (left) and husking corn (right) were family activities that were done by hand with no expensive mechanical equipment. What do you notice about the ages of the group husking corn?

Macune hoped these exchanges would be big enough to force farm prices up and to make loans to farmers at low interest rates. The exchanges had some success. The Texas Exchange successfully marketed cotton at prices slightly higher than those paid to individual farmers, while the Illinois Exchange negotiated slightly better railroad rates for wheat farmers.

The People's Party Despite their temporary success, the large cooperatives failed for several reasons. Many overextended themselves by loaning too much money at low interest rates that was never repaid. In many cases, wholesalers, manufacturers, railroads, and bankers discriminated against them, making it difficult for them to stay in business. The exchanges also failed because they still were too small to dramatically affect world prices for farm products.

By 1890 the failure of the Alliance to fix farmers' problems had started a power struggle within the organization. Some Alliance leaders, particularly in the Western states, wanted to form a new party and push for political reforms. Members of the Kansas Alliance formed the **People's Party,** also known as the Populists, and nominated candidates to run for Congress and the state legislature. Alliances in Nebraska, South Dakota, and Minnesota quickly followed Kansas's example.

The Subtreasury Plan Most Southern leaders of the Alliance, including Charles Macune, opposed the idea of a third party. They did not want to undermine the Democrats' control of the South. Instead, Macune suggested that the Alliance produce a list of demands and promise to vote for candidates who supported those demands. He hoped this strategy would force the Democrats to adopt the Alliance program.

As part of this strategy, Macune introduced the subtreasury plan, which called for the government to set up warehouses called subtreasuries. Farmers would store the crops in the warehouses, and the government would provide low-interest loans to the farmers. Macune believed that the plan would allow farmers to hold their crops off the market in large enough quantities to force prices up. He hoped that the Democrats would adopt the subtreasury plan and thereby win farmers' votes.

✓ **Reading Check** **Explaining** How did the Farmers' Alliance try to help farmers?

The Rise of Populism

In 1890 members of the Farmers' Alliance met in Ocala, Florida, and issued what came to be known as the Ocala Demands. These demands were intended to guide farmers in choosing whom to vote for in 1890. The demands called for the adoption of the sub-treasury plan, the free coinage of silver, an end to protective tariffs and national banks, tighter regulation of the railroads, and direct election of senators by voters instead of by state legislatures.

To prevent farmers from voting for Populists, the Republicans in Congress, led by Senator John Sherman, pushed through the **Sherman Silver Purchase Act of 1890.** This act authorized the United States Treasury to purchase 4.5 million ounces of silver per month. It put more money into circulation and may have reduced the deflation slightly, but it did little to help the farmers.

The midterm elections of 1890 seemed to suggest that both the Southern and Western strategies had worked for the farmers. In the South, four governors, all Democrats, were elected after promising to support the Alliance program. Several Southern legislatures now had pro-Alliance majorities, and over 40 Democrats who supported the Alliance program were elected to Congress. Meanwhile, the new People's Party did equally well in the West. Populists took control of the Kansas and Nebraska legislatures. Populists also held the balance of power in Minnesota and South Dakota. Eight Populists were elected to the U.S. House of Representatives and two to the Senate.

The South Turns to Populism At first Southern members were excited over their success in electing so many pro-Alliance Democrats to Congress and Southern state legislatures, but over the next two years, their excitement turned into frustration.

Despite their promises, few Democrats followed through by supporting the Alliance program, either at the state or the federal level.

In May 1891, Western populists met with some labor and reform groups in Cincinnati. The meeting endorsed the creation of a new national People's Party to run candidates for president. Only a few Southerners attended the convention. By the following year, however, it had become obvious to many Southern members of the Alliance that the Democrats were not going to keep their promises to the Alliance. By early 1892 many Southern farmers had reached the point where they were willing to break with the Democratic Party and join the People's Party.

A Populist for President In July 1892, the People's Party held its first national convention in Omaha, Nebraska. There, members officially organized their party and nominated **James B. Weaver** to run for president. Weaver was a former Union Army General who had run for president before as the candidate of the Greenback Party. The Omaha convention also endorsed a platform, or program, that spelled out the party's positions in strong terms. First of all, the Omaha platform denounced the government's refusal to coin silver as a "vast conspiracy against mankind." To increase the money supply, it called for a return to unlimited coinage of silver at a ratio that gave 16 ounces of silver the same value as 1 ounce of gold. Other platform planks called for federal ownership of railroads and a graduated income tax, one that taxed higher earnings more heavily.

Above all, the Populists wanted to strengthen the hand of government so that it could defend the public against what they saw as greedy and irresponsible private interests. "We believe that the powers of government—in other words, of the people—should be expanded," the platform stated, "as rapidly and as far as the good sense of an intelligent people and the teachings of experience shall justify."

Although the Populists also adopted proposals designed to appeal to organized labor, workers found it hard to identify with the rural Populists. The Populists did have close ties to the Knights of Labor, but that organization was in decline, while the fast-growing American Federation of Labor steered clear of an alliance with them. The Omaha

Profiles IN HISTORY

Mary Ellen Lease
1853–1933

Mary Ellen Lease, a former school-teacher and daughter of an Irish political refugee, earned a law degree while raising four children on the Kansas frontier. She was one of the most passionate speakers for the People's Party in Kansas during the 1890 election campaign. Political opponents nicknamed her "Mary Yellin" and criticized the tall and forceful Lease for acting in an "unfeminine" manner by speaking in public.

Lease's blunt style, however, appealed to Kansas farmers. "Wall Street owns the country," she declared. "It is no longer a government of the people, for the people, by the people, but a government of Wall Street, for Wall Street, and by Wall Street." Lease urged farmers to spend less time raising crops and more time campaigning against the banks and railroads.

HARD LIFE ON THE PLAINS

English-born immigrant farmer David Hilton and his family proudly pose beside their pump organ on their home-stead in Nebraska. The organ, their prized possession, had been rescued from the Hiltons' sod-built dugout after the roof collapsed. Farm families on the sparsely-settled, treeless plains had to cope with isolation as well as a variety of natural haz-ards, including dust storms, tornadoes, erratic rainfall, and the occasional plague of destructive insects that could strip entire fields of crops in a matter of hours.

platform took positions popular with labor, including calling for an eight-hour workday, restricting immigration, and denouncing strikebreaking, but most urban workers still preferred to remain within the Democratic Party.

Democrats retained support in Northern cities by nominating the popular New Yorker, Grover Cleveland, who was seeking to return to the White House after his close defeat in 1888. The South also remained solidly Democratic, despite determined efforts by Populists. When the votes were counted, Cleveland had won a resounding victory in the Electoral College, with 277 votes to 145 for Harrison. The Populist candidate, James Weaver, had done remarkably well, winning four states and splitting two others for a total of 22 electoral votes.

The Panic of 1893

Not long after Cleveland's inauguration in 1893, the nation plunged into the worst economic crisis it had ever experienced. The panic began in March when the Philadelphia and Reading Railroads declared bankruptcy. Many railroads had expanded too rapidly in the period before the panic and now found it hard to repay their loans. The stock market on Wall Street crashed, and banks closed their doors. By 1894 the economy was deep in a depression. About 690,000 workers went on strike that year, and more than 4.6 million more were unemployed, approximately 18 percent of the workforce.

Goldbugs and Silverites

The Panic of 1893 also created a crisis for the United States Treasury. Many American and European investors owned U.S. government bonds, but as the economy worsened, they began cashing in their bonds for gold. This caused gold to drain out of the U.S. Treasury and left the federal government's gold reserves at a dangerously low level.

Although President Cleveland could not stop the flow of gold to redeem bonds, he could protect the government's reserves in another way. Gold was also being lost every time people exchanged silver for gold under the Sherman Silver Purchase Act. Unlike many Democrats, Cleveland believed the United States should use gold as the basis for its currency, not silver or paper money. In June 1893, he summoned Congress into a special session and pushed through the repeal of the Sherman Silver Purchase Act.

Picturing **History**

Campaigns in Contrast In 1896 Democrat William Jennings Bryan (left) ran an energetic campaign for president, traveling far and wide. Republican William McKinley (right) campaigned from the front porch of his Canton, Ohio, home. How did their campaign styles work out?

Cleveland's actions split the Democratic Party into two factions, nicknamed "goldbugs" and "silverites." The goldbugs believed the American currency should be based only on gold, while silverites believed coining silver in unlimited quantities would solve the nation's economic crisis.

> **Reading Check** **Summarizing** What was the main outcome of the Populist campaign in the elections of 1892?

The Election of 1896

As the election of 1896 approached, leaders of the People's Party decided to make the silver issue the focus of their campaign. They also decided to hold their convention after the Republican and Democratic conventions. They believed the Republicans would endorse a gold standard, which they did. They also expected the Democrats to nominate Cleveland again and hoped that when the People's Party strongly endorsed silver, pro-silver Democrats would abandon their party and vote for the Populists in large numbers.

Unfortunately for the Populists, their political strategy failed. The Democrats did not waffle on the silver issue. Instead, they nominated **William Jennings Bryan,** a strong supporter of silver. When the Populists gathered in St. Louis for their own convention, they faced a difficult choice: endorse Bryan and risk undermining their identity as a separate party, or nominate their own candidate and risk splitting the silver vote. They eventually decided to support Bryan.

Bryan's Campaign William Jennings Bryan, a former member of Congress from Nebraska, was only 36 years old when the Democrats and Populists nominated him for president. Bryan had served in Congress for two terms as a representative from Nebraska. He was a powerful speaker, and he won the nomination by delivering an electrifying address in defense of silver, one of the most famous in American political history. He began by telling delegates that he had come to speak "in defense of a cause as holy as the cause of liberty—the cause of humanity." With a few well-chosen words, Bryan transformed the campaign for silver into a crusade:

> ❝Having behind us the producing masses of this nation and the world, supported by the commercial interests, the laboring interests and the toilers everywhere, we will answer their demand for a gold standard by saying to them: You shall not press down upon the brow of labor this crown of thorns; you shall not crucify mankind upon a cross of gold.❞
>
> —quoted in *America in the Gilded Age*

Bryan waged an unusually energetic campaign for the presidency, traveling thousands of miles and making 600 speeches in 14 weeks. Some found his relentless campaigning undignified, however, and his crusade in favor of silver alienated others. Catholic immigrants and other city-dwellers cared little for the silver issue. They did not like Bryan's speaking style either. It reminded them of rural Protestant preachers, who were sometimes anti-Catholic.

Republicans knew that Bryan would be hard to beat in the South and the West. To regain the White House, they would have to sweep the Northeast and the Midwest. They thought that **William McKinley** of Ohio, a former governor and member of Congress, was the candidate who could do it.

The Front Porch Campaign
In sharp contrast to the hectic travels of Bryan, McKinley stayed at his home in Canton, Ohio. He conducted what the newspapers called his "Front-Porch Campaign" by meeting with various delegations that came to visit him. Meanwhile, across the Midwest and Northeast, the Republican Party launched an intensive campaign on McKinley's behalf.

The Republicans campaigned against the Democrats by blaming Cleveland's administration for the depression and promising workers that McKinley would provide a "full dinner pail." This meant a lot more to most urban workers than the issue of silver money. At the same time, most business leaders supported the Republicans, convinced that unlimited silver coinage would ruin the country. They donated huge sums of money to the Republican campaign. Many employers warned their workers that if Bryan won, businesses would fail, unemployment would rise, and wages would be cut.

McKinley's reputation for moderation on labor issues and tolerance toward different ethnic groups helped improve the Republican Party's image with urban workers and immigrants. When the votes were counted, McKinley had won a decisive victory. He captured 51 percent of the popular vote and had a winning margin of 95 electoral votes—hefty numbers in an era of tight elections. As expected, Bryan won the South and most of the West, but few of the states he carried had large populations or delivered many electoral votes. By embracing populism and its rural base, Bryan and the Democrats lost the Northern industrial areas where votes were concentrated.

Populism Declines
Opposition to the gold-based currency dwindled during McKinley's time in office. The depression was over, and prospectors found gold in Canada in 1896 and in Alaska in 1898. That wealth, combined with new gold strikes in South Africa and other parts of the world, increased the money supply without turning to silver. This meant that credit was easier to obtain and farmers were less distressed. In 1900 the United States officially adopted a gold-based currency when Congress passed the Gold Standard Act.

When the silver crusade died out, the Populists lost their momentum. Their efforts to ease the economic hardships of farmers and to regulate big business had not worked. Some of the reforms they favored, however, came about in the next century, including the graduated income tax and some governmental regulation of the economy.

HISTORY Online

Student Web Activity Visit the *American Vision* Web site at tav.glencoe.com and click on **Student Web Activities— Chapter 16** for an activity on political changes in the late 1800s.

✓ **Reading Check** **Evaluating** What were the results of the 1896 presidential election?

SECTION 2 ASSESSMENT

Checking for Understanding

1. **Define:** populism, greenback, inflation, deflation, cooperative, graduated income tax, goldbug, silverite.
2. **Identify:** Grange, People's Party, William Jennings Bryan.
3. **List** the issues that the Democrats endorsed in the 1896 presidential election.

Reviewing Themes

4. **Economic Factors** What economic problems caused farmers to support populism?

Critical Thinking

5. **Analyzing** How did the Farmers' Alliance contribute to the rise of a new political party?
6. **Organizing** Use a graphic organizer similar to the one below to list the factors that contributed to the Panic of 1893 and its effects on the nation.

Factors Contributing to		Effects on Nation
☐		☐
☐	→ Panic of 1893 →	☐
☐		☐

Analyzing Visuals

7. **Analyzing Photographs** Examine the photograph of David Hilton and his family on page 505, showing them with an organ they rescued from a collapsed sod house. Why do you think it was so important for them to rescue the organ?

Writing About History

8. **Persuasive Writing** Imagine you support the Populist Party and that you have been asked to write copy to be used in a campaign poster for your party's candidates. Include a slogan that provides reasons for people to support the Populists.

The Rise of Segregation

Main Idea

In the late 1800s, Southern states passed laws that denied African Americans the right to vote and imposed segregation on them.

Key Terms and Names

sharecropper, poll tax, grandfather clause, segregation, Jim Crow laws, lynching, Ida B. Wells, W.E.B. Du Bois

Reading Strategy

Organizing As you read about the South in the 1890s, complete a web diagram like the one below by listing ways that states disfranchised African Americans and legalized discrimination.

Factors Contributing to Discrimination

Reading Objectives

- **Discuss** how African Americans in the South were disfranchised and how segregation was legalized.
- **Describe** three major African American leaders' responses to discrimination.

Section Theme

Individual Action African Americans stood up to fight against discrimination in the United States.

Preview of Events

| ♦1885 | ♦1890 | ♦1895 | ♦1900 |

1886
Colored Farmers'
National Alliance formed

1887
Florida passes
Jim Crow laws

1890
Mississippi introduces
voting restrictions

1895
Booker T. Washington proposes Atlanta Compromise

★ An American Story ★

In the fall of 1892, H.S. Doyle, a young African American preacher, defied Georgia's power structure—dominated by whites and Democrats—by giving more than 60 speeches on behalf of a white Populist, Tom Watson, who was running for Congress.

Doyle took that risk because Watson was doing something almost unbelievable for a Southern politician. He was urging poor whites and blacks to unite against the wealthy white elite. "You are kept apart that you may be separately fleeced of your earnings," Watson told a racially mixed audience at one gathering. "The accident of color can make no difference in the interests of farmers."

Shortly before the election, Doyle himself received a death threat. Watson offered the preacher refuge in his home and alerted supporters in the area. An estimated 2,000 Populists gathered there with guns in hand. The crowd then marched to the local courthouse, where Watson vowed to protect Doyle and other African American Populists. "We are determined in this free country that the humblest white or black man that wants to talk our doctrine shall do it," he declared, "and the man doesn't live who shall touch a hair of his head, without fighting every man in the People's Party."

—adapted from *Tom Watson: Agrarian Rebel*

Resistance and Repression

For H.S. Doyle and other African Americans, the violence of the election of 1892 was not something they could shrug off. They could see that some Southern leaders were beginning to devise ways to keep them from voting. In the end, even Watson would betray his African

American supporters. He became a political boss in Georgia, cast aside his former ideals, and used crude racist rhetoric to appeal to white voters.

After Reconstruction, many African Americans in the rural South lived in conditions that were little better than slavery. They were technically free, but few escaped from grinding poverty. Most were sharecroppers, landless farmers who had to hand over to the landlord a large portion of their crops to cover the cost of rent, seed, tools, and other supplies. They were always in debt. Many eventually left farming and sought jobs in Southern towns or headed west to claim homesteads.

Exodus to Kansas In 1879, 70-year-old Benjamin "Pap" Singleton, himself formerly enslaved, took action to escape the conditions of the rural South. He organized a mass migration of thousands of African Americans from the rural South to Kansas. The newspapers called it "an Exodus," like the Hebrews' escape from Egyptian bondage. The migrants themselves came to be known as **"Exodusters."** One of them later explained why they went: "The whole South—every State in the South—had got into the hands of the very men that held us as slaves." A journalist named Henry King described the scene when the first group reached Kansas:

> 66One morning in April, 1879, a Missouri steamboat arrived at Wyandotte, Kansas, and discharged a load of negro men, women and children, with . . . barrels, boxes, and bundles of household effects. . . . [T]heir garments were incredibly patched and tattered . . . and there was not probably a dollar in money in the pockets of the entire party. The wind was eager, and they stood upon the wharf shivering. . . . They looked like persons coming out of a dream. And, indeed, such they were . . . for this was the advance guard of the Exodus.99
>
> —quoted in *Eyewitness: The Negro in History*

Forming a Separate Alliance While some African Americans fled the South, others joined with poor white farmers who had created the Farmers' Alliance.

Alliance leaders urged African Americans to form a similar organization. In 1886 African American farmers gathered in Texas at the home of a white minister named R.M. Humphrey and formed the Colored Farmers' National Alliance. By 1890 the organization had an estimated 1.2 million members.

The **Colored Farmers' National Alliance** worked to help its members economically by setting up cooperatives. When the Populist Party formed in 1891, many African American farmers joined the new organization. They hoped that the new People's Party would unite poor whites and poor blacks to challenge the Democratic Party's power in the South.

Crushing the Populist Revolt Populism posed a new challenge to the Democratic Party in the South. If enough poor whites left the party and joined with African American Populists, the coalition might become unbeatable.

To win back the poor white vote, Democratic leaders began appealing to racism, warning whites that support for Populists or joint Republican-Populist parties would return the South to "Black Republican" rule similar to Reconstruction. In addition, although many African Americans in the South were still able to vote as of 1890, election officials began using various methods to make it harder and harder for them to do so. As one Democratic leader in the South told a reporter, "Some of our people, some editors especially, deny that [African Americans] are hindered from voting; but what is the good of lying? They are interfered with, and we are obliged to do it, and we may as well tell the truth."

✓ **Reading Check** **Examining** Who were the Exodusters, and why did they migrate to Kansas in 1879?

Disfranchising African Americans

The Fifteenth Amendment prohibited states from denying citizens the right to vote on the basis of "race, color, or previous condition of servitude." However, it did not bar the governments from requiring that citizens be literate or own property in order to vote. Using this loophole, Southern states began imposing restrictions that barred nearly all African Americans from voting, even though the restrictions seemed on the surface to apply to both races.

Mississippi took this step first in 1890 by requiring that all citizens registering to vote pay a poll tax of $2, a sum beyond the means of most poor African Americans. Mississippi also instituted a literacy test, requiring that prospective voters be able to read or understand the state constitution. More than half of all African Americans who came of age in the South after the Civil War had no school to attend, and those who had grown up under slavery were largely illiterate. Even those who knew how to read often failed the literacy test because local officials deliberately picked complicated passages that few could understand.

Other Southern states later adopted similar restrictions, and the results were devastating. In Louisiana the number of African Americans registered to vote fell from about 130,000 in 1890 to around 5,300 in 1900. In Alabama the number fell from about 181,000 to around 3,700.

Election officials were far less strict in applying the poll tax and literacy requirements to whites, but the number of white voters also fell significantly. Local Democratic Party leaders were not sorry to see poor whites barred from voting, because they had helped fuel the Populist revolt. Some states gave whites a special break, however, by including a so-called grandfather clause in the restrictions. The grandfather clause in Louisiana allowed any man to vote if he had an ancestor on the voting rolls in 1867. The clause made almost all formerly enslaved Louisiana citizens ineligible to vote.

✔ **Reading Check** **Identifying** How did Southern states restrict African American voting in the 1890s?

Legalizing Segregation

Discrimination in the late 1800s was not confined to the South. African Americans in the North had often been barred from many public places used by whites. In the South, segregation, or separation of the races, was different because laws enforced and perpetuated the discrimination. The statutes enforcing segregation were known as Jim Crow laws. The term probably came from the name of a character popularized by a slavery-era blackface minstrel—a white musical stage performer who darkened his face with makeup and crudely imitated supposed African American behavior.

In 1883 the Supreme Court set the stage for legalized segregation by overturning the Civil Rights Act of 1875. That law had prohibited keeping people out of public places on the basis of race, and it also prohibited racial discrimination in selecting jurors. White authorities

Segregation sign from the turn of the century

challenged the law in both the North and the South. The 1883 Supreme Court decision, however, said that the Fourteenth Amendment only provided that "no state" could deny citizens equal protection under the law. Thus, only state actions were subject to challenge. Private organizations and businesses, such as hotels, theaters, and railroads, were free to practice segregation.

Encouraged by the Supreme Court's ruling and by the decline of congressional support for civil rights, Southern states passed a series of laws that enforced segregation in virtually all public places. Southern whites and African Americans could no longer ride together in the same railroad cars, eat in the same dining halls, or even drink from the same water fountains. Restrooms, hotels, and swimming pools were all segregated.

In 1892 an African American named Homer Plessy challenged a Louisiana law that forced him to ride in a separate railroad car from whites. He was arrested for riding in a "whites-only" car and brought to trial before criminal court judge John H. Ferguson. Ferguson rejected Plessy's argument that the law was unconstitutional. In 1896 the Supreme Court, in *Plessy* v. *Ferguson,* upheld the Louisiana law and expressed a new legal doctrine endorsing "separate but equal" facilities for African Americans. 📖 *(See page 1082 for more information on* Plessy v. Ferguson*.)*

The ruling established the legal basis for discrimination in the South for more than 50 years to come. While public facilities for African Americans in the South were always separate, they were far from equal. In many cases, they were inferior.

Racial Violence Even worse than the Jim Crow laws was the brutality leveled against African Americans. In the late 1800s, mob violence increased in the United States, particularly in the South. Between 1890 and 1899, there was an average of 187 lynchings—executions without proper court proceedings—carried out by mobs each year. Over 80 percent of the lynchings occurred in the South, and nearly 70 percent of the victims were African Americans.

✓ **Reading Check** **Summarizing** How did the Supreme Court help to legalize segregation?

The African American Response

In 1892 **Ida B. Wells,** a fiery young African American woman from Tennessee, launched a fearless crusade against lynching. Wells pointed out that

 History

Crusading Journalist Ida B. Wells, seen here with her son, campaigned fiercely against lynching in the 1890s. What two factors did Wells believe to be behind lynchings?

greed, not just racial prejudice, was often behind these brutal acts. Writing in the *Memphis Free Speech* newspaper, she reported that three African American grocers lynched in Memphis had been guilty of nothing more than competing successfully against white grocers.

A mob destroyed the press that printed the *Memphis Free Speech* and drove Wells out of town, but she settled in Chicago and continued her campaign. In 1895 she published a book denouncing mob violence against African Americans and demanding "a fair trial by law for those accused of crime, and punishment by law after honest conviction." Although Congress rejected an anti-lynching bill, the number of lynchings decreased significantly in the 1900s due in great part to the efforts of activists such as Wells.

A Call for Compromise Some African American leaders like Wells chose the path of protest, but others recommended different solutions to discrimination. One such person was the influential educator **Booker T. Washington.** He proposed that African Americans concentrate on achieving economic goals rather than legal or political ones. In 1895

*"color discrimination
is barbarism"*

—*W.E.B. Du Bois*

he summed up his views in a speech before a mostly white audience at the Cotton States and International Exposition in Atlanta. Known as the **Atlanta Compromise,** the address came amid increasing acts of discrimination against African Americans. Washington urged his fellow African Americans to postpone the fight for civil rights and instead concentrate on preparing themselves educationally and vocationally for full equality:

❝The wisest among my race understand that the agitation of questions of social equality is the extremest folly, and that the enjoyment of all the privileges that will come to us must be the result of severe and constant struggle rather than of artificial forcing. . . . It is important and right that all privileges of the law be ours, but it is vastly more important that we be prepared for the exercise of these privileges. The opportunity to earn a dollar in a factory just now is worth infinitely more than the opportunity to spend a dollar in an opera-house.❞

–adapted from *Up From Slavery*

Voice of the Future The Atlanta Compromise speech provoked a strong challenge from **W.E.B. Du Bois,** the leader of a new generation of African American activists born after the Civil War. Du Bois pointed out in his 1903 book *The Souls of Black Folk* that white Southerners continued to strip African Americans of their civil rights. This was true in spite of the progress African Americans were making in education and vocational training. They could regain that lost ground and achieve full equality, Du Bois argued, only by demanding their rights. Du Bois was particularly concerned with protecting and exercising voting rights. "Negroes must insist continually, in season and out of season," he wrote, "that voting is necessary to proper manhood, that color discrimination is barbarism." In the years that followed, many African Americans worked to win the vote and end discrimination. The struggle, however, would prove to be a long one.

✓ **Reading Check** **Describing** How did Ida B. Wells attempt to stop the lynching of African Americans?

SECTION 3 ASSESSMENT

Checking for Understanding

1. **Define:** sharecropper, poll tax, grandfather clause, segregation, Jim Crow laws, lynching.
2. **Identify:** Ida B. Wells, W.E.B. Du Bois.
3. **Explain** what happened to Ida B. Wells after she began campaigning against lynching.

Reviewing Themes

4. **Individual Action** Why did Homer Plessy challenge a Louisiana law in 1892, and what was the significance of his action?

Critical Thinking

5. **Examining** After Reconstruction, why did many African Americans in the South live in conditions that were little better than slavery?
6. **Organizing** Use a graphic organizer similar to the one below to list the responses of some prominent African Americans to racial discrimination.

African American	Response to Discrimination
Ida B. Wells	
Booker T. Washington	
W.E.B. Du Bois	

Analyzing Visuals

7. **Analyzing Photographs** Examine the photograph of an "Exoduster" family on page 509. Pose questions about the photograph to your classmates in a quiz and then have them answer the questions.

Writing About History

8. **Expository Writing** Imagine that you are living in the 1890s. Write a letter to the editor of the local newspaper explaining your view of the Supreme Court ruling in *Plessy* v. *Ferguson.*

Interpreting Points of View

Why Learn This Skill?

Suppose you want to see a new movie, but your friends' opinions range from "terrific" to "boring." People often have different opinions about the same people, events, or issues because they look at them from different points of view.

Learning the Skill

A point of view results from one's own beliefs and values. Many factors affect an individual's point of view, including age, gender, racial or ethnic background, economic class, and religion. To judge the accuracy or the objectivity of an argument, you must first identify the speaker's point of view.

To interpret point of view in written material, gather background information on the author that might reveal his or her point of view. Identify aspects of the topic that the author chooses to emphasize or exclude. Look for emotionally charged words such as *charming, vicious, heartwarming,* and *drastic.* Also notice metaphors and analogies that imply an opinion, such as, "If this budget can work, then pigs can fly."

Practicing the Skill

Read the following excerpts from William Jennings Bryan's "Cross of Gold" speech. Then answer the questions.

The humblest citizen in all the land, when clad in the armor of a righteous cause, is stronger than all the hosts of error. I come to speak to you in defense of a cause as holy as the cause of liberty—the cause of humanity. . . .

When you come before us and tell us that we are about to disturb your business interest, we reply that you have disturbed our business interests by your course. . . . We say not one word against those who live upon the Atlantic coast, but the hardy pioneers who have braved all the dangers of the wilderness, who have made the desert to blossom as the rose . . . it is for these that we speak. . . .

If they ask us why it is that we say more on the money question than we say upon the tariff question, I reply that, if protection has slain its thousands, the gold standard has slain its tens of thousands. . . .

Having behind us the producing masses of this nation and the world, supported by the commercial interest, the laboring interests, and the toilers everywhere, we will answer their demand for a gold standard by saying to them: You shall not press down upon the brow of labor this crown of thorns, you shall not crucify mankind upon a cross of gold.

Cartoon portraying William Jennings Bryan

❶ What subject is Bryan addressing? What group is he speaking for?

❷ What is Bryan's point of view?

❸ What emotionally charged words and phrases does Bryan use in his speech? How do they help reveal his point of view?

Skills Assessment

Complete the Practicing Skills questions on page 515 and the Chapter 16 Skills Reinforcement Activity to assess your mastery of this skill.

Applying the Skill

Interpreting Points of View In a newspaper or magazine, find an editorial or letter to the editor that expresses a point of view on an issue. Write a paragraph analyzing the author's point of view. Compare it to your own and explain why you agree or disagree with the author.

Glencoe's **Skillbuilder Interactive Workbook CD-ROM, Level 2,** provides instruction and practice in key social studies skills.

Reviewing Key Terms

On a sheet of paper, use each of these terms in a sentence.

1. patronage
2. rebate
3. populism
4. greenback
5. inflation
6. deflation
7. cooperative
8. graduated income tax
9. goldbug
10. silverite
11. sharecropper
12. poll tax
13. grandfather clause
14. segregation
15. Jim Crow laws
16. lynching

Reviewing Key Facts

17. **Identify:** Interstate Commerce Commission, Sherman Antitrust Act, Grange, People's Party, William Jennings Bryan, Ida B. Wells, W.E.B. Du Bois

18. What contributed to political deadlock at the federal level between 1876 and 1896?

19. What economic problems did the United States face during the administration of President Cleveland?

20. How did the Grange attempt to solve farmers' problems in the late 1800s?

21. What was the significance of the Supreme Court's ruling in *Plessy* v. *Ferguson?*

Critical Thinking

22. **Analyzing Themes: Economic Factors** Why was the type of currency used in the United States an important issue to farmers in the late 1800s?

23. **Comparing** How did Booker T. Washington's answer to racial discrimination compare to that of W.E.B. Du Bois?

24. **Organizing** Use a graphic organizer similar to the one below to list the major reforms sought by the Populists in the 1892 presidential election.

Populist Reforms

25. **Interpreting Primary Sources** Reform movements in farming led to the organization of the Populist Party in 1891. In the following excerpt from an 1890 article, Washington Gladden, a Congregational minister, discusses the problems facing farmers in the United States.

❝The farmers of the United States are up in arms. . . . They produce the largest share of its wealth; but they are getting, they say, the smallest share for themselves. With the hardest work and with the sharpest economy, the average farmer is unable to make both ends meet;

Chapter Summary

Republican Party

- Popular in North and Midwest; appealed to rural and small town voters
- Party split over civil service reform
- Favored higher tariffs and the gold standard

Populist Party

- Sought government control over business to protect farmers
- Supported national control of railroads, increased money supply, and direct election of U.S. senators
- Support declined when gold crisis was resolved
- Lost presidential elections but inspired reforms that were later adopted

Democratic Party

- Strongly supported by Southerners, immigrants, and urban workers
- Supported civil service reform
- Supported cutting tariffs and regulating interstate commerce
- Party split over silver coinage

Political Inequality for African Americans

- Supreme Court overturned the Civil Rights Act of 1875
- Unfair voting laws disfranchised Southern African Americans
- *Plessy* v. *Ferguson* defended separate but equal public facilities

every year closes with debt, . . . the average annual reward of the farm proprietor [of Connecticut] is $181.31, while the average annual wages of the ordinary hired man is $386.36.

. . . [T]he root of the difficulty is overproduction; that there are too many farms . . . [but] other causes . . . should not be overlooked. The enormous tribute which the farmers of the West are paying to the moneylenders of the East is one source of their poverty. . . .

[Farmers] believe that the miseries under which they are suffering are largely due to political causes and can be cured by legislation. . . . The prime object of the Farmers' Alliance is to better the condition of the farmers of America, mentally, morally, and financially; . . .❞

—quoted in *Forum*

a. According to Gladden, why were farmers up in arms?

b. What was the main purpose of the new Farmers' Alliance?

Practicing Skills

26. **Interpreting Points of View** Study the American Story on page 500 that gives an excerpt of Polk's speech on July 4, 1890. Then answer these questions.

a. How do historians analyze points of view?

b. What emotionally charged words and phrases does Polk use? How do they reveal his point of view?

Writing Activities

27. **Persuasive Writing** Imagine that you are living in 1881 and have just heard about President Garfield's assassination by a disappointed office-seeker. Write to your representatives in Congress, urging them either to pass civil service reform or to keep the current "spoils system" for appointments to federal offices. Explain why you believe your recommendation is rational.

28. **Chronology Quiz** Absolute chronology refers to specific dates, while relative chronology looks at when something occurred with reference to when other things occurred. Memorize the unit titles and time periods in your book, then close your book. Practice relative chronology by writing the unit titles in correct order. Then apply absolute chronology by writing the unit dates.

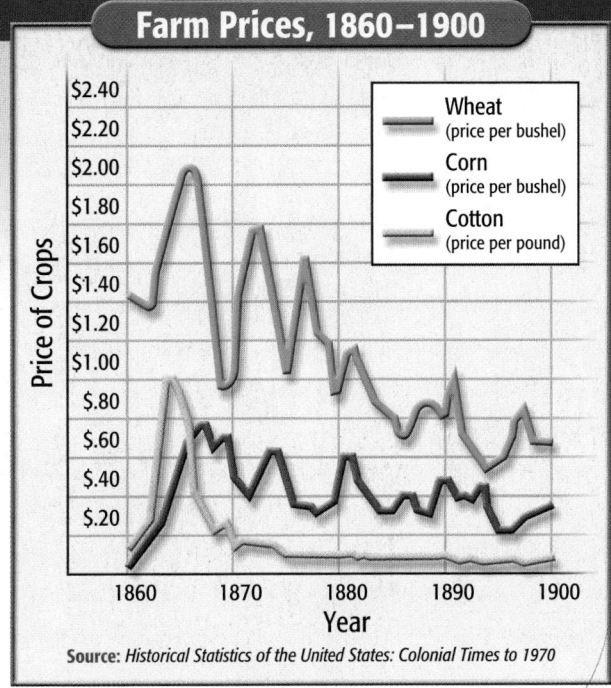

Farm Prices, 1860–1900

Price of Crops

Wheat (price per bushel)
Corn (price per bushel)
Cotton (price per pound)

Year

Source: *Historical Statistics of the United States: Colonial Times to 1970*

Economics and History

29. The graph above shows farm prices in the United States between 1860 and 1900. Study the graph and answer the questions below.

a. **Analyzing Graphs** What happened to prices of crops between 1865 and 1895?

b. **Understanding Cause and Effect** What factors might have contributed to this situation?

Standardized Test Practice

Directions: Choose the best answer to the following question.

The Sherman Antitrust Act of 1890 declared illegal "any combination . . . in restraint of trade or commerce." What *combination* was it originally intended to prevent?

A labor unions

B business mergers

C transcontinental railroads

D Farmers' Alliances

Test-Taking Tip: Make sure your answer reflects the original goal of the Antitrust Act. Only one answer reflects the reason Congress passed the law.

UNIT 6

Imperialism and Progressivism

1890–1919

Why It Matters

As the United States entered the twentieth century, it grew to become a world power. While the nation was expanding its territory into other parts of the world, conditions at home gave rise to a widespread Progressive movement. This movement worked for various reforms in government, business, and society. While Americans focused on their own country, Europe slid into a devastating world war that eventually involved the United States as well. These crucial years of domestic change and foreign conflict provided important foundations for the world you live in today. The following resources offer more information about this period in American history.

Primary Sources Library

See pages 1052–1053 for primary source readings to accompany Unit 6.

Use the **American History Primary Source Document Library CD-ROM** to find additional primary sources about imperialism and progressivism.

World War I pin

American Troops Arriving in Paris July 14, 1918 by J.F. Boucher

"It is hard to fail, but it is worse never to have tried to succeed."

— Theodore Roosevelt, 1899

17 Becoming a World Power

1872–1912

Why It Matters

During this era, economic and military competition from world powers convinced the United States it must be a world power. The United States became an empire when it acquired the Philippines and territory in the Caribbean. American influence in Central and South America grew as the United States took a more active role in Latin American affairs.

The Impact Today

Events of this time continue to influence American politics.
- *The United States continues to use its navy to protect its overseas interests.*
- *The Panama Canal serves as a major route for international commerce.*
- *Puerto Rico remains tied to the United States as a commonwealth.*

The American Vision *Video* *The Chapter 17 video, "Teddy Roosevelt and Yellow Journalism," chronicles the events leading to the United States becoming a world power.*

1881
- President Garfield assassinated by Charles Guiteau

1872
- Victoria Claflin Woodhull becomes first female candidate for U.S. president

1889
- First Pan-American conference

United States PRESIDENTS

| Grant 1869–1877 | Hayes 1877–1881 | Garfield 1881 | Arthur 1881–1885 | Cleveland 1885–1889 |

1870   *1880*   *1890*

World

1874
- Britain annexes Fiji Islands

1876
- Nicholas Otto builds first practical gasoline engine

1880
- John Milne develops the seismograph

1889
- Gustave Eiffel completes tower for Paris World Exhibit

Theodore Roosevelt leads the charge up San Juan Hill.

1893
- Americans overthrow Queen Liliuokalani of Hawaii

1898
- U.S. declares war on Spain

1899
- Hay sends Open Door notes

1901
- President McKinley assassinated

1904
- Panama Canal construction begins
- Roosevelt Corollary to Monroe Doctrine issued

| B. Harrison 1889–1893 | Cleveland 1893–1897 | McKinley 1897–1901 | T. Roosevelt 1901–1909 | Taft 1909–1913 |

1900

1910

1895
- Louis and Auguste Lumière introduce motion pictures

1899
- Boer War begins between Great Britain and South African Republic

1900
- Boxer Rebellion begins in China

1904
- Russo-Japanese War begins

HISTORY Online

Chapter Overview
Visit the *American Vision* Web site at tav.glencoe.com and click on *Chapter Overviews—Chapter 17* to preview chapter information.

Guide to Reading

Main Idea

In the late 1800s, many Americans wanted the United States to expand its military and economic power overseas.

Key Terms and Names

imperialism, protectorate, Anglo-Saxonism, Matthew C. Perry, Queen Liliuokalani, Pan-Americanism, Alfred T. Mahan, Henry Cabot Lodge

Reading Strategy

Organizing As you read about the development of the United States as a world power, use the major headings of the section to create an outline similar to the one below.

The Imperialist Vision
I. Building Support for Imperialism
   A.
   B.
II.
   A.
   B.

Reading Objectives:

• **Analyze** how a desire for more trade and markets led to political change between 1877 and 1898.
• **Cite** the motivations for and methods of American expansion in the Pacific.

Section Theme

Global Connections America's growing trade with the world and rivalry with European nations led to a naval buildup and a search for territory overseas.

Preview of Events

♦1850   ♦1875   ♦1900

1853
Commodore Perry arrives in Japan

1888
Samoan Crisis erupts

1890
Alfred T. Mahan's *Influence of Sea Power Upon History, 1660–1783* published

1893
American settlers overthrow Queen Liliuokalani of Hawaii

★ *An American Story* ★

On January 16, 1893, 162 United States Marines marched off the warship *Boston* and onto the shores of Oahu, one of the Hawaiian Islands. John L. Stevens, the American minister to Hawaii, had ordered the troops ashore. He claimed Hawaii's ruler, Queen Liliuokalani, had created widespread turmoil and endangered American lives and property. Stevens had other motives as well. He wanted to make Hawaii, with its profitable sugarcane plantations, part of the United States.

Stevens ordered the American troops to take up positions near Queen Liliuokalani's palace. Although the marines took no action against the Hawaiian government, their presence intimidated the queen's supporters. Within hours, the American settlers in Hawaii abolished the monarchy and set up a provisional—or temporary—government. On February 1, 1893, at the request of the provisional government, Stevens announced that Hawaii was now under American protection, and he hoisted the American flag over Hawaii's government buildings. Several weeks later, Stevens made his support for annexing Hawaii perfectly clear: "The Hawaiian pear is now fully ripe," he wrote, "and this is the golden hour for the United States to pluck it."

—adapted from *A History of the American People*

Building Support for Imperialism

John Stevens was not alone in his views. Many Americans cheered the events in Hawaii and favored expanding American power elsewhere in the world as well. The American public's enthusiasm, however, was a relatively new phenomenon. In the years immediately following the Civil War, most Americans showed little interest in expanding their nation's territory and international influence. Instead, they focused on reconstructing the South, building up the nation's industries, and settling the West.

Beginning in the 1880s, however, American opinion began to shift. More people wanted to make the United States a world power. Economic and military competition from other nations, as well as a growing feeling of cultural superiority, led to this shift in opinion.

ECONOMICS

A Desire for New Markets Several European nations were already expanding overseas, a development known as the New Imperialism. Imperialism is the economic and political domination of a strong nation over other weaker nations.

Europeans expanded their power overseas for many reasons. Factories depended on raw materials from all over the world. No country had all of the rubber, tin, oil, and other resources its economy needed. In addition, by the late 1800s, most industrialized countries had placed high tariffs against each other. These tariffs were intended to protect a nation's industries from foreign competition. The tariffs reduced trade between industrial countries, forcing companies to look for markets overseas.

At the same time, the growth of investment opportunities in western Europe had slowed. Most of the factories, railroads, and mines that Europe's economy needed had been built. Increasingly, Europeans began looking overseas for places to invest their capital. They began investing in industries in other countries, particularly in Africa and Asia.

To protect their investments, the European nations began exerting control over those territories where they invested their capital and sold their products. Some areas became colonies. Many others became protectorates. In a protectorate, the imperial power allowed the local rulers to stay in control and protected them against rebellions and invasion. In exchange for this protection, the local rulers usually had to accept advice from the Europeans on how to govern their countries.

The expansion of European power overseas did not go unnoticed in the United States. As the United States industrialized, many Americans took interest in the new imperialism. Until the late 1800s, the United States had always been able to expand by settling more territory in North America. Now, with settlers finally filling up the western frontier, many Americans concluded that the nation had to develop new overseas markets to keep its economy strong. "We are raising more than we can consume,"

declared Indiana senator Albert J. Beveridge. "We are making more than we can use. Therefore, we must find new markets for our produce, new occupation for our capital, new work for our labor."

A Feeling of Superiority In addition to economic concerns, certain other key ideas convinced many Americans to encourage their nation's expansion overseas. Many supporters of Social Darwinism argued that nations competed with each other politically, economically, and militarily, and that only the strongest would survive. To them, this idea justified increasing American influence abroad.

Many Americans, such as the well-known writer and historian John Fiske, took this idea even further. Fiske argued that English-speaking nations had superior character, ideas, and systems of government, and were destined to dominate the planet:

> ❝The work which the English race began when it colonized North America is destined to go on until every land . . . that is not already the seat of an old civilization shall become English in its language, in its religion, in political habits and traditions, and to a predominant extent in the blood of its people.❞

> —quoted in *Expansionists of 1898*

This idea, known as **Anglo-Saxonism,** was popular in Britain and the United States. Many Americans saw it as part of the idea of Manifest Destiny. They believed it had been the nation's destiny to expand west to the Pacific Ocean. Now they believed it was

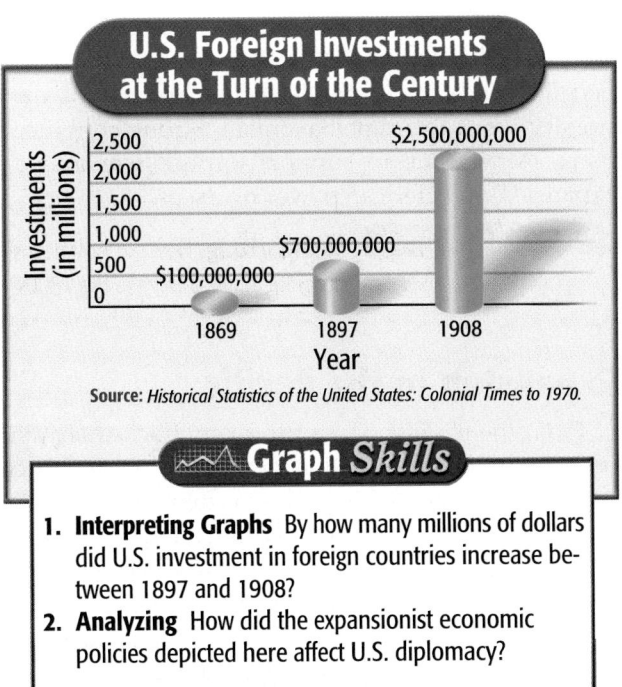

U.S. Foreign Investments at the Turn of the Century

Source: *Historical Statistics of the United States: Colonial Times to 1970.*

Graph Skills

1. **Interpreting Graphs** By how many millions of dollars did U.S. investment in foreign countries increase between 1897 and 1908?
2. **Analyzing** How did the expansionist economic policies depicted here affect U.S. diplomacy?

Matthew C. Perry

the destiny of the United States to expand overseas and spread its civilization to other people.

Another influential advocate of Anglo-Saxonism was **Josiah Strong,** a popular American minister in the late 1800s. Strong linked Anglo-Saxonism to Christian missionary ideas. His ideas influenced many Americans. "The Anglo-Saxon," Strong declared, "[is] divinely commissioned to be, in a peculiar sense, his brother's keeper." By linking missionary work to Anglo-Saxonism, Strong convinced many Americans to support imperialism and an expansion of American power overseas.

✓ **Reading Check** **Summarizing** How did Americans' opinions on overseas expansion begin to change in the 1800s?

Expansion in the Pacific

From the earliest days of the Republic, Americans had expanded their nation by moving west. When Americans began looking overseas for new markets in the 1800s, therefore, they naturally tended to look westward. Even before imperialist ideas became popular, Americans had begun expanding across the Pacific Ocean toward East Asia. By the early 1800s, dozens of ships were making the long trip to China every year.

Perry Opens Japan Many American business leaders believed that the United States would benefit from trade with Japan as well as with China. Japan's rulers, however, believed that excessive contact with the West would destroy their culture and only allowed the Chinese and Dutch to trade with their nation.

In 1852, after receiving several petitions from Congress, President Franklin Pierce decided to force Japan to trade with the United States. He ordered Commodore **Matthew C. Perry** to take a naval expedition to Japan to negotiate a trade treaty.

On July 8, 1853, four American warships under Perry's command entered Yedo Bay (today known as Tokyo Bay). The Japanese had never seen steamships before and were impressed by the display of American technology and firepower. Perry's arrival in Japan forced the Japanese to make changes internally. Realizing that they could not compete against modern Western technology and weapons, the Japanese signed a treaty opening the ports of Simoda and Hakodadi to American trade on March 31, 1854.

The American decision to force Japan to open trade played an important role in Japanese history. Many Japanese leaders concluded that the time had come to remake their society. In 1868, after a long internal power struggle, Japanese leaders began to Westernize their country. They adopted Western technology and launched their own industrial revolution. By the 1890s, the Japanese had built a powerful modern navy, and they set out to build their own empire in Asia.

Annexing Hawaii As trade with China and Japan grew in the 1800s, Americans desired ports in the Pacific Ocean. One of the finest harbors was Pago Pago, one of the Samoan Islands in the South Pacific. American interest in Pago Pago began in the 1830s, and the United States opened its first naval base there in 1878.

More important was Hawaii. Whaling ships and merchant vessels crossing the Pacific stopped there to rest their crews and to take on supplies. In 1819 missionaries from New England settled in Hawaii. American settlers found that sugarcane grew well in Hawaii's climate and soil. By the mid-1800s, many plantations had been established in the islands.

In 1872 a severe recession struck Hawaii. Worried that the economic crisis might force the Hawaiians to turn to the British or French for help, the United States Senate ratified a trade treaty in 1875 that exempted Hawaiian sugar from tariffs. Several years later, when the treaty came up for renewal, the Senate insisted that the Hawaiians grant the United States exclusive rights to a naval base at Pearl Harbor.

The trade treaty led to a boom in the Hawaiian sugar industry and wealth for the planters. In 1887 prominent planters pressured the Hawaiian king into accepting a new constitution that limited the king's authority and increased the planters' power. These developments angered the Hawaiian people, who feared they were losing control of the country.

Tensions between the planters and the Hawaiians mounted. Congress passed the McKinley Tariff in 1890. Although the tariff eliminated all duties on sugar, it also gave subsidies to sugar producers in the United States. Hawaiian sugar was now more expensive than American sugar, despite the lack of tariffs. As sales of Hawaiian sugar declined, the islands' economy went into a tailspin.

In 1891 **Queen Liliuokalani** ascended the Hawaiian throne. Liliuokalani disliked the influence that American settlers had gained in Hawaii. In January 1893, she unsuccessfully attempted to impose a new constitution that would have reasserted her authority as ruler of the Hawaiian people.

Faced with the economic crisis and the queen's actions, the planters backed an attempt to overthrow the monarchy. Supported by the marines from the *Boston*, a group of planters forced the queen to give up power and set up a provisional government. They then requested that the United States annex Hawaii. President Cleveland strongly opposed imperialism. He withdrew the annexation treaty from the Senate and tried to restore Liliuokalani to power. Hawaii's new leaders refused to restore Liliuokalani, and they decided to wait until a new president took office who favored annexation. Five years later, the United States annexed Hawaii. 📖 *(See page 1073 for more text on Hawaiian annexation.)*

(See page 1073 for more text on Hawaiian annexation.)

✓ **Reading Check** **Explaining** How did the desire to expand into new markets help push the United States to become a world power?

Trade and Diplomacy in Latin America

The Pacific was not the only region where the United States sought to increase its influence in the 1800s. It also focused on Latin America. Although the United States bought raw materials from this region, Latin Americans bought most of their manufactured goods from Europe. American business leaders and government officials wanted to increase the sale of American products to the region. They also wanted the Europeans to understand that the United States was the dominant power in the region.

James G. Blaine, who served as secretary of state in two administrations in the 1880s, led early efforts

Hawaiian Queen Liliuokalani

Modern Battleships

In the 1880s, the United States Navy modernized its fleet of warships. Moving away from wooden ships powered solely by the wind, the new navy constructed steel-hulled ships with steam-powered engines as well as sails. Probably the most famous ship of this era was the USS *Maine,* one of the U.S. Navy's first armored battleships (depicted at right). It was one of the first U.S. naval vessels with electrical lighting. It had a top speed of 17 knots and a crew of 392 officers and enlisted men. *Which U.S. naval officer argued for the necessity of a modern navy?*

1 The *Maine* was designed for **sail power** as well as steam, but the sails were never fitted on the ship.

2 It had a maximum **armor** thickness of 12 inches.

3 Eight **steam boilers** powered two engines.

sail power

cowls

torpedo tubes

galley

steam boilers

magazine

armor

4 **Cowls** provided fresh air below decks.

5 Food was prepared in the **galley.**

6 Munitions were stored in the **magazine.**

---

to expand American influence in Latin America. Blaine proposed that the United States invite the Latin American nations to a conference in Washington, D.C. The conference would discuss ways in which the American nations could work together to support peace and to increase trade. The idea that the United States and Latin America should work together came to be called **Pan-Americanism.**

Blaine's idea became reality in 1889 when the Pan-American conference was held in Washington, D.C. Seventeen Latin American nations attended. Blaine had two goals for the conference. He wanted to create a customs union between Latin America and the United States, and he also wanted to create a system for American nations to work out their disputes peacefully.

A customs union would require all of the American nations to reduce their tariffs against each other and to treat each other equally in trade. Blaine hoped that a customs union would turn the Latin Americans away from European products and toward American products. He also hoped that a common system for settling disputes would keep the Europeans from meddling in American affairs.

Although the warm reception they received in the United States impressed the Latin American delegates

to the conference, they rejected both of Blaine's ideas. They did agree, however, to create the Commercial Bureau of the American Republics, an organization that worked to promote cooperation among the nations of the Western Hemisphere. This organization was later known as the Pan-American Union and is today called the **Organization of American States** (OAS).

✓ **Reading Check** **Summarizing** How did Secretary of State Blaine attempt to increase American influence in Latin America?

Building a Modern Navy

As imperialism and Anglo-Saxonism gained support in the late 1800s, the United States became increasingly assertive in foreign affairs. Three international crises illustrated this new approach. In 1888 the country was willing to go to war to prevent Germany from taking control of the Samoa Islands in the South Pacific. Three years later, when a mob in Chile attacked American sailors in the port of Valparaíso, the United States threatened to go to war unless Chile paid reparations for the lives lost. Then, in 1895, the United States backed

Venezuela against Great Britain in a border dispute with the colony of British Guiana. After Britain rejected an American ultimatum to settle the dispute, many newspapers and members of Congress called for war. All three crises were eventually solved peacefully.

As both the American people and their government became more willing to risk war in defense of American interests overseas, support for building a large modern navy began to grow. Supporters argued that if the United States did not build up its navy and acquire bases overseas, it would be shut out of foreign markets by the Europeans.

Captain **Alfred T. Mahan,** an officer in the U.S. Navy who taught at the Naval War College, best expressed this argument. In 1890 Mahan published his lectures in a book called *The Influence of Sea Power Upon History, 1660–1783.* In this book Mahan pointed out that many prosperous peoples in the past, such as the British and Dutch, had built large fleets of merchant ships in order to trade with the world. He then suggested that a nation also needed a large navy to protect its merchant ships and to defend its right to trade with other countries.

After arguing that the United States needed a large navy, Mahan observed that building a modern navy meant that the United States had to acquire territory for naval bases overseas. In the 1890s, navy warships burned coal to power their engines. To operate a navy far from home, a country needed bases and coaling stations in distant regions. This would allow the ships to be resupplied en route to their destination.

Mahan's book became a best-seller, and it helped to build public support for a big navy. In Congress two powerful senators, **Henry Cabot Lodge** and Albert J. Beveridge, pushed for the construction of a new navy. In the executive branch, Benjamin Tracy, secretary of the navy under President Harrison, and John D. Long, secretary of the navy under President McKinley, strongly supported Mahan's ideas—as did future president Theodore Roosevelt, who served as an assistant secretary of the navy in the late 1890s.

By the 1890s, several different ideas had come together in the United States. Business leaders wanted new markets overseas. Anglo-Saxonism had convinced many Americans that they had a destiny to dominate the world. Growing European imperialism threatened America's security. Combined with Mahan's influence, these ideas convinced Congress to authorize the construction of a modern American navy.

By the late 1890s, the United States was well on its way to becoming one of the top naval powers in the world. Although it was not yet an imperial power, it had the power to become one if the opportunity arose. That opportunity was not long in coming. In the spring of 1898, war erupted between Spain and the United States.

Reading Check **Explaining** Why did Alfred T. Mahan and Henry Cabot Lodge call for the building of a strong U.S. navy?

SECTION 1 ASSESSMENT

Checking for Understanding

1. **Define:** imperialism, protectorate.
2. **Identify:** Anglo-Saxonism, Matthew C. Perry, Queen Liliuokalani, Pan-Americanism, Alfred T. Mahan, Henry Cabot Lodge.
3. **Explain** why Secretary of State James G. Blaine convened the Pan-American conference in 1889.

Reviewing Themes

4. **Global Connections** What events in the world convinced Americans to support a large navy?

Critical Thinking

5. **Forming an Opinion** Do you think the United States should have supported the planters in their attempt to overthrow Queen Liliuokalani of Hawaii? Why or why not?
6. **Organizing** Use a graphic organizer to list the factors that led to an imperialist policy in the United States in the 1800s.

Factors Leading to U.S. Imperialist Policy

Analyzing Visuals

7. **Analyzing Art** Study the painting on page 522. How is the U.S. Navy portrayed in relation to the Japanese residents of Yokohama? Do you think the artist shows any bias in this representation? Why or why not?

Writing About History

8. **Persuasive Writing** Imagine that you are living in the United States in the 1890s. Write a letter to the president persuading him to support or oppose an imperialist policy for the United States. Be sure to use standard grammar, spelling, sentence structure, and punctuation.

Technology SKILLBUILDER

Using an Electronic Spreadsheet

Why Learn This Skill?

Electronic spreadsheets can help people manage numbers quickly and easily. Historians use spreadsheets to easily manipulate statistical data. You can use a spreadsheet any time a problem involves numbers that can be arranged in rows and columns.

Learning the Skill

A spreadsheet is an electronic worksheet that follows a basic design of rows and columns. Each *column* (vertical) is assigned a letter or number. Each *row* (horizontal) is assigned a number. Each point where a column and row intersect is called a *cell*. The cell's position on the spreadsheet is labeled according to its column and row. Therefore, Column A, Row 1 is referred to as cell A1; Column B, Row 2 is B2, and so on.

Spreadsheets use standard formulas to calculate numbers. You create a simple mathematical equation that uses these standard formulas, and the computer does the calculations for you.

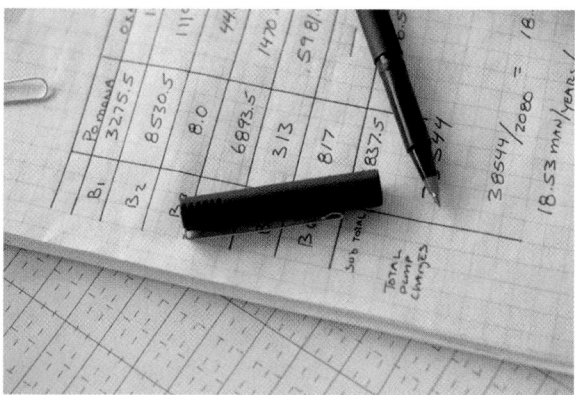

You can also create spreadsheets manually.

A1	B1	C1	D1	E1
A2	B2	C2	D2	E2
A3	B3	C3	D3	E3
A4	B4	C4	D4	E4
A5	B5	C5	D5	E5

Practicing the Skill

Use these steps to create a spreadsheet that will provide the population densities (population per square mile) of the states in the United States in 1900.

❶ In cell A1 type *State;* in cell B1 type *Population;* in cell C1 type *Land area* (*square miles*); in cell D1 type *Population per square mile.*

❷ In cells A2–A46, type each state's name. In cell A47, type the words *Total for the United States.*

❸ In cells B2–B46, enter the population of each of the states listed in cells A2–A46.

❹ In cells C2–C46, enter the land area (square miles) of each state shown in cells A2–A46.

❺ In cell D2, create a formula to calculate the population per square mile. The formula tells what cells (B2 ÷ C2) to divide. Copy this formula into cells D3–D46.

❻ Use the process in step 5 to create and copy a formula to calculate the nation's total population (B2 + B3 + B4 . . .) for cell B47.

❼ Use the process in step 5 to create and copy a formula to calculate the nation's population per square mile (B47 ÷ C47) for cell D47.

Skills Assessment

Complete the Practicing Skills questions on page 543 and the Chapter 17 Skill Reinforcement Activity to assess your mastery of this skill.

Applying the Skill

Using an Electronic Spreadsheet Use a spreadsheet to enter your test scores and homework grades. Following the grading period, create an equation that allows the spreadsheet to calculate your average grade.

 Glencoe's **Skillbuilder Interactive Workbook CD-ROM, Level 2,** provides instruction and practice in key social studies skills.

The Spanish-American War

Main Idea
The United States defeated Spain in a war, acquired new overseas territories, and became an imperial power.

Key Terms and Names
José Martí, William Randolph Hearst, Joseph Pulitzer, yellow journalism, jingoism, Theodore Roosevelt, Platt Amendment

Reading Strategy
Organizing As you read about the Spanish-American War, complete a graphic organizer like the one below by listing the circumstances that contributed to war with Spain.

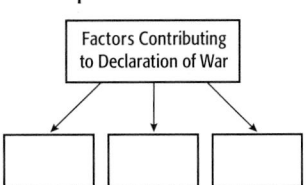

Factors Contributing to Declaration of War

Reading Objectives:
• **Describe** the circumstances that led to war between the United States and Spain in 1898.
• **Explain** how the war made the United States a world power.

Section Theme
Government and Democracy The United States fought Spain to help Cubans gain their independence.

Preview of Events

| ◆January 1898 | ◆May 1898 | ◆September 1898 | ◆December 1898 |

February 1898
U.S.S. *Maine* explodes

April 1898
U.S. declares war on Spain

May 1898
Dewey destroys Spanish fleet in the Philippines

December 1898
Treaty of Paris ends Spanish-American War

★ *An American Story* ★

Clara Barton, the founder and first president of the American National Red Cross, was working late in her villa overlooking the harbor in Havana, Cuba, on the evening of February 15, 1898. As she and an assistant reviewed some paperwork, an enormous blast lit up the sky. She later recalled:

66The deafening roar was such a burst of thunder as perhaps one never heard before. And off to the right, out over the bay, the air filled with a blaze of light, and this in turn filled with black specks like huge specters flying in all directions.99

Barton quickly learned what had happened. The U.S.S. *Maine,* anchored in the Havana harbor, had exploded. Barton rushed to a nearby hospital, where she took a firsthand look at the blast's devastation. The sailors' wounds, she wrote, "were all over them—heads and faces terribly cut, internal wounds, arms, legs, feet and hands burned to the live flesh."

—adapted from *The Spanish War*

The Coming of War

Of the 354 officers and sailors aboard the *Maine* that winter night, 266 died. No one is sure why the *Maine* exploded. The size of the explosion indicates that the ship's ammunition supplies blew up. Some experts think that a fire accidentally ignited the ammunition. Others argue that a mine detonated near the ship set off the ammunition.

History *Through Art*

Cuban Rebellion During the Cuban Revolution in 1895, Spanish general Valeriano Weyler forced much of the Cuban population into guarded camps near military installations. Why were Americans supporting Cuba's fight against Spain?

When the explosion happened, many Americans blamed it on Spain. Cuba was a Spanish colony at the time, but it was in the midst of a revolution. The Cuban people were fighting for independence from Spain. Many Americans regarded the Spanish as tyrants and supported the Cubans in their struggle. These Americans quickly jumped to the conclusion that Spain had blown up the *Maine.* Within a matter of weeks, Spain and the United States were at war. Although the fighting only lasted a few months, the outcome dramatically altered the position of the United States on the world stage.

The Cuban Rebellion Begins

Cuba was one of Spain's oldest colonies in the Americas. Its sugarcane plantations generated considerable wealth for Spain and produced nearly one-third of the world's sugar in the mid-1800s. Until Spain abolished slavery in 1886, about one-third of the Cuban population was enslaved and forced to work for wealthy landowners on the plantations.

In 1868 Cuban rebels declared independence and launched a guerrilla war against Spanish authorities. Lacking internal support, the rebellion collapsed in 1878. Many Cuban rebels then fled to the United States, where they began planning a new revolution.

One of the exiled leaders was **José Martí,** a writer and poet who was passionately committed to the cause of Cuban independence. While living in New York City in the 1880s, Martí brought together different Cuban exile groups living in the United States. The groups raised funds from sympathetic Americans, purchased weapons, and trained their troops in preparation for an invasion of Cuba.

By the early 1890s, the United States and Cuba had become closely linked economically. Cuba exported much of its sugar to the United States, and Americans had invested approximately $50 million in Cuba's mines, railroads, and sugar plantations. These economic ties created a crisis in 1894, when the United States imposed new tariffs—including a tariff on sugar—in an effort to protect its troubled economy from foreign competition. The new tariff wrecked the sale of Cuban sugar in the United States and devastated the island's economy.

With Cuba in an economic crisis, Martí's followers launched a new rebellion in February 1895. Although Martí died in battle shortly after returning to Cuba, the revolutionaries seized control of eastern Cuba, declared independence, and formally established the Republic of Cuba in September 1895.

Americans Support the Cubans

When the uprising in Cuba began, President Grover Cleveland declared the United States neutral. Outside the White House, however, much of the public openly supported the rebels. Some citizens compared the Cubans' struggle to the American Revolution. A few sympathetic Americans even began smuggling guns from Florida to the Cuban rebels.

What led most Americans to support the rebels were the dramatic stories of Spanish atrocities reported in two of the nation's major newspapers, the *New York Journal* and the *New York World.* The *Journal,* owned by **William Randolph Hearst,** and the *World,* owned by **Joseph Pulitzer,** competed with each other to increase their circulation. The *Journal* reported outrageous stories of the Spanish feeding Cuban prisoners to sharks and dogs. Not to be outdone, the *World* described Cuba as a place with "blood on the roadsides, blood in the fields, blood on the doorsteps, blood, blood, blood!" This kind of sensationalist reporting, in which writers often exaggerated or even made up stories to attract readers, became known as yellow journalism.

Although the press invented sensational stories to sell more papers, there is no doubt that the Cuban people indeed suffered horribly. The Spanish dispatched nearly 200,000 troops to the island to put down the rebellion and appointed General Valeriano Weyler to serve as governor. Weyler's harsh policies quickly earned him the nickname *El Carnicero* ("The Butcher").

The Cuban rebels carried out a guerrilla war. They staged hit-and-run raids, burned plantations and sugar mills, tore up railroad tracks, and attacked supply depots. The rebels knew that many American businesses had invested in Cuba's railroads and plantations. They hoped that the destruction of American property would lead to American intervention in the war.

To prevent Cuban villagers from helping the rebels, Weyler herded hundreds of thousands of rural men, women, and children into "reconcentration camps," where tens of thousands died of starvation and disease. News reports of this brutal treatment of civilians enraged Americans and led to renewed calls for American intervention in the war.

Calling Out for War

In 1897 Republican William McKinley became president of the United States. The new president did not want to intervene in the war, believing it would cost too many lives and hurt the economy. In September 1897, he asked the Spanish if the United States could help negotiate an end to the conflict. He made it clear that if the war did not end soon, the United States might have to intervene.

Pressed by McKinley, the Spanish government removed Weyler from power. Spain then offered the Cubans autonomy—the right to their own government—but only if Cuba remained part of the Spanish empire. The Cuban rebels refused to negotiate. They wanted full independence.

Spain's concessions to the rebels enraged many Spanish loyalists in Cuba. In January 1898, the loyalists rioted in Havana. Worried that American citizens in Cuba might be attacked, McKinley made the fateful decision to send the battleship *Maine* to Havana in case the Americans had to be evacuated.

In February 1898, the *New York Journal* printed a private letter written by **Enrique Dupuy de Lôme,** the Spanish ambassador to the United States. A Cuban agent had intercepted the letter and delivered it to the paper. It described McKinley as "weak and a bidder for the admiration of the crowd." The nation erupted in fury over the insult.

Ambassador de Lôme resigned, but before the furor could die down, the *Maine* exploded in the Havana harbor. The press promptly blamed Spain. Rapidly responding to the hysterical anger of the American public, Congress unanimously authorized the president to spend $50 million for war preparations. Shortly afterward, on March 28, 1898, a naval

court of inquiry concluded that a mine had destroyed the *Maine*. Throughout America, people began using the slogan "Remember the *Maine!*" as a rallying cry for war. By early April, President McKinley was under tremendous pressure to go to war. American mobs were demonstrating in the streets against Spain—and against McKinley for refusing to go to war.

Within the Republican Party, jingoism, or an attitude of aggressive nationalism, was very strong, especially among younger members of the party. These members were furious at McKinley for not declaring war. Assistant Secretary of the Navy **Theodore Roosevelt,** for one, raged that McKinley had "no more backbone than a chocolate éclair." Many Democrats were also demanding war, and Republicans feared that if McKinley did not go to war, the Democrats would win the presidency in 1900. Finally, on April 11, 1898, McKinley asked Congress to authorize the use of force to end the conflict in Cuba.

On April 19, Congress declared Cuba independent, demanded that Spain withdraw from the island, and authorized the president to use armed force if necessary. In response, on April 24, Spain declared war on the United States. For the first time in 50 years, the United States was at war with another nation.

Reading Check **Examining** What conditions led to the Cuban rebellion in 1895?

A War on Two Fronts

The Spanish in Cuba were not prepared for war. Tropical diseases and months of hard fighting had weakened their soldiers. Their warships were old and their crews poorly trained. The United States had more battleships, and both sides knew that the war ultimately would be decided at sea. If the United States could defeat Spain's fleet, the Spanish would not be able to get supplies to its troops in Cuba. Eventually, they would have to surrender.

The United States Takes the Philippines

The United States Navy was ready for war with Spain. The navy's North Atlantic Squadron blockaded Cuba, and the American fleet based in British Hong Kong was ordered to attack the Spanish fleet in the Philippines. The Philippines was a Spanish colony, and American naval planners were determined to prevent the fleet there from sailing east to attack the United States.

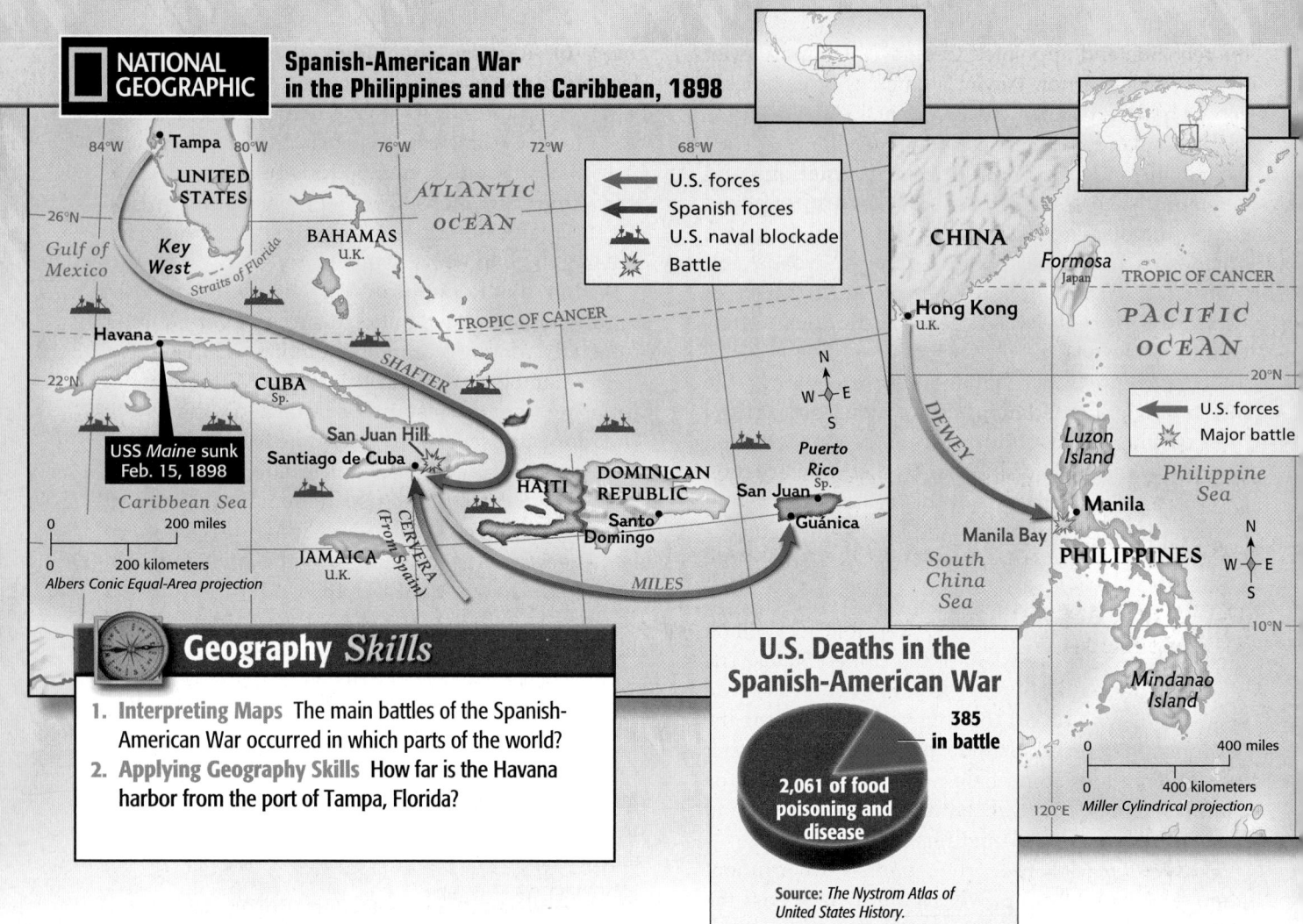

Spanish-American War in the Philippines and the Caribbean, 1898

NATIONAL GEOGRAPHIC

U.S. forces
Spanish forces
U.S. naval blockade
Battle

U.S. forces
Major battle

USS *Maine* sunk Feb. 15, 1898

Geography Skills

1. **Interpreting Maps** The main battles of the Spanish-American War occurred in which parts of the world?
2. **Applying Geography Skills** How far is the Havana harbor from the port of Tampa, Florida?

U.S. Deaths in the Spanish-American War

385 in battle

2,061 of food poisoning and disease

Source: *The Nystrom Atlas of United States History.*

A short time after midnight, on May 1, 1898, Commodore **George Dewey** led his squadron into Manila Bay in the Philippines. As dawn broke, Dewey's fleet opened fire and rapidly destroyed the severely outgunned Spanish warships.

Dewey's quick victory took McKinley and his advisers by surprise. The army was not yet ready to send troops to help Dewey capture the Philippines. Hastily, the army assembled 20,000 troops to sail from San Francisco to the Philippines. On the way to the Philippines, the American troops also seized the island of Guam, another Spanish possession in the Pacific.

While waiting for the American troops to arrive, Dewey contacted **Emilio Aguinaldo,** a Filipino revolutionary leader who had staged an unsuccessful uprising against the Spanish in 1896. Aguinaldo quickly launched a new guerrilla war.

At first, Aguinaldo believed the Americans were his allies, but when American troops arrived in the islands he became suspicious. The Americans quickly seized the Philippine capital of Manila from

the Spanish but refused to allow Aguinaldo's forces into the city. They also refused to recognize his rebel government. Hostility between the Filipinos and the Americans began to grow as both sides waited for the war with Spain to end.

American Forces Battle in Cuba Unlike the mobilization of the navy, which had been very efficient, the mobilization of the American army was very poorly conducted. Although volunteers flooded into army training camps, the army lacked the resources to train and equip them. In many camps, conditions were so unsanitary that epidemics broke out, and hundreds of Americans died. By the end of the war, far more Americans had died in training camps than in actual battle.

Finally, on June 14, 1898, a force of about 17,000 troops landed on the southern coast of Cuba, east of the city of Santiago. A Spanish fleet occupied Santiago Harbor, where it was well protected by powerful shore-based guns. American military planners wanted to capture those guns in order to drive the Spanish fleet out of the harbor and into battle with the American fleet waiting nearby.

Among the American troops advancing toward Santiago was a volunteer cavalry unit from the American West. They were a flamboyant mix of cowboys, miners, and law officers known as the **"Rough Riders."** The commander of the Rough Riders was Colonel **Leonard Wood.** Second in command was Theodore Roosevelt, who had resigned from his post as assistant secretary of the navy to join the fight.

On July 1, American troops attacked the village of El Caney northeast of Santiago. Another force attacked the San Juan Heights, a series of hills overlooking the main road to Santiago. While one group of soldiers attacked San Juan Hill, the Rough Riders—who were on foot, not horseback—attacked Kettle Hill. After seizing Kettle Hill, Roosevelt and his men assisted in the capture of San Juan Hill.

The Rough Riders did not make their attack alone. Accompanying them up Kettle Hill were the all-black 9th and 10th Cavalry Regiments. Many African Americans had responded to the call for volunteers, and roughly one-fourth of the American troops fighting in Cuba were African American.

Four African American soldiers received the Medal of Honor for their bravery during the war.

The Spanish commander in Santiago panicked after the American victories at El Caney and the San Juan Heights. He immediately ordered the Spanish fleet in the harbor to flee. As the Spanish ships raced out of the harbor on July 3, the American warships guarding the entrance attacked them. In the ensuing battle, the American squadron sank or beached every Spanish vessel.

Spanish resistance in Cuba ended with the surrender of Santiago two weeks later. Soon after, American troops occupied the nearby Spanish colony of Puerto Rico. On August 12, 1898, Spain and the United States agreed to a cease-fire.

Reading Check **Describing** How prepared was the U.S. Army to fight a war against Spain?

An American Empire is Born

As American and Spanish leaders met to discuss the terms for a peace treaty, Americans debated what to do about their newly acquired lands. Cuba would

NATIONAL GEOGRAPHIC

MOMENT in HISTORY

FEISTY LEADER FOR A NEW CENTURY

Theodore Roosevelt (center) embodied the spirit of the United States at the turn of the century: full of vitality, brimming with confidence, and convinced that no job was impossible, no challenge insurmountable. Whether hunting big game in Africa, roping cattle from horseback on a Dakota ranch, or leading his "Rough Riders" cavalry (right) up San Juan Hill during the Spanish-American War, Roosevelt never did anything cautiously or quietly. As president, Roosevelt guided the country into its new, unaccustomed role as a world power.

be given its freedom as promised, and Spain had agreed that the United States would annex Guam and Puerto Rico. The big question was what to do with the Philippines. The United States faced a difficult choice—remain true to its republican ideals or become an imperial power.

The Debate Over Annexation

Many supporters of annexing the Philippines emphasized the economic and military benefits of taking the islands. They would provide the United States with a naval base in Asia, a stopover on the way to China, and a large market for American goods.

Other supporters believed America had a duty to teach "less civilized" peoples how to live properly. "Surely this Spanish war has not been a grab for empire," commented a New England minister, "but a heroic effort [to] free the oppressed, and to teach the millions of ignorant, debased human beings thus freed how to live."

Not all Americans supported annexation. Anti-imperialists included industrialist Andrew Carnegie, social worker Jane Addams, writer Samuel Clemens (Mark Twain), and the leader of the American Federation of Labor, Samuel Gompers. Carnegie argued that the cost of an empire far outweighed the economic benefits it provided. Gompers worried that competition from cheap Filipino labor would drive down American wages. Addams, Clemens, and others believed imperialism violated American principles.

President McKinley had to decide what to do with the Philippines. Ultimately, he decided to annex the islands. He later explained his reasoning to a group of ministers:

66And one night late it came to me this way . . . (1) that we could not give them back to Spain—that would be cowardly and dishonorable; (2) that we could not turn them over to France or Germany . . . that would be bad for business and discreditable; (3) that we could not leave them to themselves— they were unfit for self-government . . . and (4) that there was nothing left for us to do but to take them all, and to educate the Filipinos, and uplift and civilize and Christianize them.99

—quoted in *A Diplomatic History of the American People*

On December 10, 1898, the United States and Spain signed the Treaty of Paris. Under the treaty, Cuba became an independent country, and the United States acquired Puerto Rico and Guam and agreed to pay Spain $20 million for the Philippines. After an intense

Building an Empire Two Filipino women nervously converse with American troops in the Philippines. Filipino civilians suffered many hardships while Filipino guerrillas fought American troops. Thousands perished from sickness, starvation, and other indirect effects of war. What American policy contributed to civilian hardships in the Philippines?

debate, the Senate ratified the treaty in February 1899. The United States had become an imperial power.

Rebellion in the Philippines

The United States quickly learned that controlling its new empire would not be easy. Emilio Aguinaldo called the American decision to annex his homeland a "violent and aggressive seizure." He then ordered his troops to attack the American soldiers in the Philippines.

To fight the Filipino guerrillas, General Arthur MacArthur (the father of the future American general Douglas MacArthur) adopted many of the same policies that America had condemned Spain for using in Cuba. MacArthur set up reconcentration camps to separate guerrillas from civilians. The results were also similar to what had happened in Cuba. Thousands of Filipinos died from disease and starvation.

While MacArthur fought the guerrillas, the first U.S. civilian governor of the islands, William Howard Taft, tried to win over the Filipino people by reforming education, transportation, and health care. New railroads, bridges, and telegraph lines strengthened the economy. A public school system was set up, and new health care policies virtually eliminated severe diseases such as cholera and smallpox. These reforms slowly reduced Filipino hostility.

Emilio Aguinaldo

In March 1901, American troops captured Aguinaldo. The following month, Aguinaldo accepted American control of the islands and called on the guerrillas to surrender. By summer 1902, the United States had declared the war over. Eventually the United States allowed the Filipinos a greater role in governing their own country. By the mid-1930s, they were permitted to elect their own congress and president. Finally, in 1946, the United States granted independence to the Philippines.

GOVERNMENT

Governing Puerto Rico Another pressing question facing the United States government was how to govern Puerto Rico. In 1900 Congress passed the **Foraker Act,** making Puerto Rico an unincorporated territory. This meant that Puerto Ricans were not U.S. citizens and had no constitutional rights. The act also stated that Congress could pass whatever laws it wanted for the island.

Congress gradually allowed the inhabitants of Puerto Rico a certain degree of self-government. In 1917 the United States made Puerto Ricans citizens of the United States. In 1947 the island was allowed to elect its own governor. At this time a debate began over whether to grant Puerto Rico statehood, allow it to become an independent country, or continue it as a commonwealth of the United States. This debate over Puerto Rico's status continues today.

Cuba and the Platt Amendment After the war, the United States established a military government in Cuba. Although the United States had promised to grant Cuba its independence, President McKinley took steps to ensure that Cuba would remain tied to the United States. He allowed the Cubans to prepare a new constitution for their country, but he attached conditions. A special amendment that Senator Orville Platt attached to the 1901 army appropriations bill described those conditions.

The **Platt Amendment** specified the following: (1) Cuba could not make any treaty with another nation that would weaken its independence or allow another foreign power to gain territory in Cuba; (2) Cuba had to allow the United States to buy or lease naval stations in Cuba; (3) Cuba's debts had to be kept low to prevent foreign countries from landing troops to enforce payment; and (4) the United States would have the right to intervene to protect Cuban independence and keep order.

Although the Cubans rejected the Platt Amendment at first, they quickly realized that unless they accepted it, the United States would maintain its military government of the island. Reluctantly, they added the amendment to their constitution. The Platt Amendment governed relations between the United States and Cuba until its repeal in 1934. It effectively made Cuba an American protectorate.

HISTORY Online

Student Web Activity Visit the *American Vision* Web site at tav.glencoe.com and click on **Student Web Activities— Chapter 17** for an activity on American imperialism.

☑ **Reading Check** **Explaining** What were the arguments for and against establishing an American empire?

SECTION 2 ASSESSMENT

Checking for Understanding
1. **Define:** yellow journalism, jingoism.
2. **Identify:** José Martí, William Randolph Hearst, Joseph Pulitzer, Theodore Roosevelt, Platt Amendment.
3. **Explain** why many Americans blamed Spain for the explosion of the U.S.S. *Maine.*

Reviewing Themes
4. **Government and Democracy** Why did many Filipinos feel betrayed by the U.S. government after the Spanish-American War?

Critical Thinking
5. **Interpreting** Do you think President McKinley could have taken a different course of action with Spain over Cuba? If so, what kind? If not, why not?
6. **Categorizing** Complete a graphic organizer by summarizing the effects of the United States annexing lands obtained after the Spanish-American War.

Lands Annexed	Effects

Analyzing Visuals
7. **Analyzing Art** Examine the painting on page 519. Considering what you have learned about the Rough Riders and this battle, what is inaccurate about the painting? What kind of bias does this misrepresentation show?

Writing About History
8. **Descriptive Writing** Imagine that you are a Filipino living during the time of the U.S. annexation of the Philippine Islands. Write a journal entry in which you describe your feelings about U.S. control of the islands.

Who Sank the *Maine?*

During Cuba's revolt against Spain, the American battleship *Maine* dropped anchor in the Havana harbor to protect American interests in Cuba. On the night of February 15, 1898, the ship exploded and 266 Americans lost their lives. The United States sent a court of inquiry to Havana on February 21. Despite the lack of evidence concerning the source of the explosion, American newspapers and many public officials claimed that Spain was responsible. Pressured on all sides, President McKinley sent Spain an ultimatum that led to war. Who—or what—really sank the *Maine?*

Read the following excerpts from testimony and evidence. Then answer the questions and complete the activities that follow.

Captain Charles Sigsbee

Newspaper headline

From the commander and an early interview

Telegraph from the commander of the *Maine* to the secretary of the navy, February 15:

"Maine blown up in Havana harbor at nine forty to-night and destroyed. Many wounded and doubtless more killed or drowned. . . . Public opinion should be suspended until further report. . . . Many Spanish officers, including representatives of General Blanco, now with us to express sympathy."

—Captain Charles D. Sigsbee

The court of inquiry was interested in discovering whether the explosion had come from inside or outside the ship. If it came from inside, was it sabotage or an accident? If it came from outside, who or what caused it? Before the court met, the *Washington Evening Star* published a February 18 interview with the U.S. Navy's leading ordnance expert:

"We know of no instances where the explosion of a torpedo or mine under the ship's bottom has exploded the magazine [powder and explosives] within. It has simply torn a great hole in the side or bottom, through which water entered, and in consequence of which the ship sunk. Magazine explosions, on the contrary, produce effects exactly similar to the effects of the explosion on the *Maine.* When it comes to seeking the cause of the explosion of the *Maine's* magazine, we should naturally look not for the improbable or unusual causes. . . . The most common of these is through fires in the bunkers."

—Philip R. Alger

USS Maine

Engraving of the explosion

Mast of the Maine at
Arlington National Cemetery

From the inquiry and later reports

As the court of inquiry concluded its investigation, it considered reports of the divers who examined the *Maine* and evidence that suggested there had been two explosions. On March 11, 1898, Lieutenant Commander Adolph Marix, judge advocate of the court of inquiry, questioned Commander George A. Converse, who was brought in as a technical expert.

Marix: Looking at the plan of the *Maine*'s forward 10-inch and 6-inch magazines, would it be possible for them to have exploded, torn out the ship's side on both sides, and leave that part of the ship forward of frame 18 so water borne as to raise the after portion of that part of the ship, drag it aft, and bring the vertical keel into the condition you see in the sketch?

Converse: It is difficult for me to realize that that effect could have been produced by an explosion of the kind supposed.

Marix: Do you think, then, necessarily, there must have been an underwater mine to produce these explosions?

Converse: Indications are that an underwater explosion produced the conditions there.

In 1911 the U.S. Navy raised the *Maine* from Havana's harbor. The navy's board of inspection reexamined the ship, and its findings were similar to those of 1898. Then, in 1976, Admiral H.G. Rickover and other naval historians gathered a team of experts to examine the official court records of 1898 and 1911. This team's conclusions were very different.

1911 board conclusion:

The board finds that the injuries to the bottom of the *Maine* above described were caused by the explosion of a charge of a low form of explosive exterior to the ship between frames 28 and 31.

H.G. Rickover team conclusion:

The general character of the overall wrecked structure of the *Maine*, with hull sides and whole deck structures peeled back, leaves no doubt that a large internal explosion occurred. . . .

The mines available in 1898 are believed to have been incapable of igniting the *Maine* magazine if they exploded on the harbor bottom or against the ship side. . . . It is most unlikely that the *Maine* explosion was indeed initiated by a mine. . . .

The available evidence is consistent with an internal explosion alone. . . . The most likely source was heat from a fire in the coal bunker adjacent to the 6-inch reserve magazine.

Understanding the Issue

1. Why did the original investigation's conclusion that there was an underwater explosion lead to war with Spain?
2. If there had been an underwater explosion, was it logical to conclude that a Spanish person planted the mine? Why or why not? Is this an example of a biased opinion?
3. Why did the 1976 review conclude that the explosion came from inside the *Maine?*

Activities

1. **Rewriting History** Suppose that the initial court of inquiry had concluded that an internal explosion sank the *Maine.* Write a paragraph describing an alternate course history could have taken in the following year.
2. **Oral Report** Read a biography of one of these key players in the decision of the United States to go to war: Hearst, Roosevelt, or McKinley. Write a short oral presentation on this person's perspective and influence on the war.

New American Diplomacy

Main Idea

Under President Theodore Roosevelt, the United States increased its power on the world stage.

Key Terms and Names

sphere of influence, Open Door policy, Boxer Rebellion, "Great White Fleet," Hay-Pauncefote Treaty, Roosevelt Corollary, dollar diplomacy

Reading Strategy

Organizing As you read about the increasing presence of the United States in the world, complete a graphic organizer like the one below by listing the reasons President Roosevelt gave for wanting a canal in Central America.

Reasons to Build Canal

Reading Objectives:

- **Critique** Theodore Roosevelt's foreign policy as president.
- **Explain** the Open Door policy and its effects on relations between the United States and Asia.

Section Theme

Continuity and Change The commercial interests of the United States spurred its involvement in distant parts of the world, such as China and Latin America.

Preview of Events

♦1898	♦1900	♦1902	♦1904

1899
Secretary of State Hay sends first Open Door note

1900
Boxer Rebellion erupts in China

1901
McKinley assassinated; Theodore Roosevelt becomes president

1904
Construction of Panama Canal begins

★ An American Story ★

Upon arriving in Panama in 1904, Dr. William Crawford Gorgas, a U.S. Army doctor and chief sanitary officer to the Panama Canal project, quickly realized that death awaited American workers. The United States was about to begin constructing the Panama Canal to connect the Atlantic and Pacific Oceans. The task would be daunting because the dense jungles of Panama were home to swarms of mosquitoes that spread the deadly disease of yellow fever.

Gorgas set out to lessen the threat of disease by keeping mosquitoes from breeding. He and his crew drained swamps, gullies, and other sources of stagnant water, a main breeding ground for mosquitoes. On those areas of water they could not drain, they spread kerosene and oil, which killed the mosquito eggs before they hatched. They also fumigated nearly every home in the region and destroyed many buckets, pots, and other outdoor containers that local residents let fill up with rainwater. In two years Gorgas and his crew had wiped out yellow fever in the area.

—adapted from *The Strength to Move a Mountain*

Theodore Roosevelt's Rise to Power

The construction of the Panama Canal might never have taken place had Theodore Roosevelt not become president. "Teddy," as the press called him, gained the presidency largely by accident. Roosevelt's exploits during the Spanish-American War had made him famous and enabled him to win the election for governor of New York in November 1898. In 1900 President McKinley asked Roosevelt to run as his vice president. Less than a year later, a tragic turn of events thrust Roosevelt into the White House.

The Election of 1900 The election of 1900 once again pitted President McKinley against William Jennings Bryan. Bryan, an anti-imperialist, attacked the Republicans for their support of imperialism in Asia. McKinley focused on the country's increased prosperity. Employing the slogan "Four Years More of the Full Dinner Pail," the Republicans promised good times ahead if McKinley was reelected. He did indeed win the election by a wide margin, and Theodore Roosevelt became vice president.

On September 6, 1901, as President McKinley greeted the public during an appearance in Buffalo, New York, a gunman stepped from the crowd. The man was Leon Czolgosz, an avowed anarchist, who opposed all forms of government. Czolgosz fired two shots and hit the president. A few days later, McKinley died from his wounds.

Theodore Roosevelt, just 42 years old at the time, became the youngest person ever to become president. Roosevelt had been chosen as McKinley's running mate because Republican leaders knew his powerful charisma and heroic war record would be a great asset. They also hoped the relatively powerless position of vice president would quiet his reform-minded spirit. Now they cringed at the thought of a headstrong Roosevelt in the White House. Republican senator Mark Hanna exclaimed, "Now look, that . . . cowboy is president of the United States!"

Roosevelt Becomes President Roosevelt brought to the presidency an energy and enthusiasm rarely seen before in the office. Such vigor stemmed in part from his childhood. Born into a wealthy New York family, Roosevelt was a sickly child who endured a host of ailments, including poor eyesight and asthma.

Roosevelt pushed himself to overcome his frailties. He mastered marksmanship and horseback riding and could row up to 20 miles a day. He took up boxing and wrestling in college and continued with both throughout his life, practicing the belief that competition and conflict keep one healthy.

Roosevelt became a strong proponent of increasing American power on the world stage. Just as he refused to sit around idly in life, the president warned Americans not to "sit huddled" and become "an assemblage of well-to-do hucksters who care nothing for what happens beyond." Roosevelt also accepted some of the ideas of Anglo-Saxonism. He believed that the United States had a duty to shape the "less civilized" corners of the earth. The new president intended to make the country a world power.

Reading Check **Summarizing** What was President Roosevelt's opinion on the role of the United States as a world power?

American Diplomacy in Asia

In 1899 the United States was a major power in Asia, with naval bases all across the Pacific. Operating from those bases, the United States Navy—now the third largest in the world—was capable of exerting American power anywhere in East Asia.

The nation's primary interest in Asia, however, was not conquest but commerce. Between 1895 and 1900, American exports to China increased by four times. Although China bought only about two percent of all the goods exported by the United States, the vast Chinese markets excited American business leaders, especially those in the textile, oil, and steel industries.

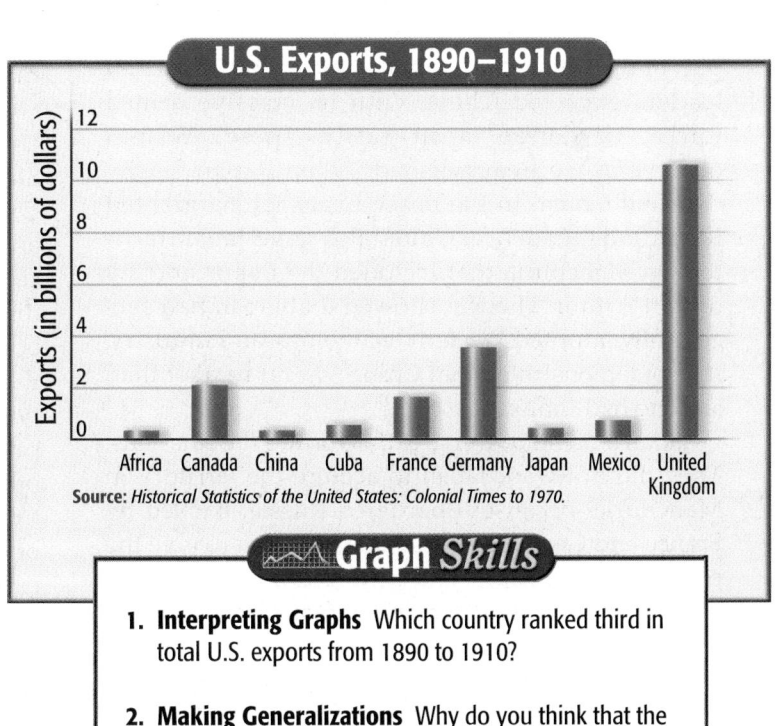

U.S. Exports, 1890–1910

Exports (in billions of dollars)

Africa | Canada | China | Cuba | France | Germany | Japan | Mexico | United Kingdom

Source: *Historical Statistics of the United States: Colonial Times to 1970.*

Graph Skills

1. **Interpreting Graphs** Which country ranked third in total U.S. exports from 1890 to 1910?

2. **Making Generalizations** Why do you think that the vast majority of U.S. exports were going to the United Kingdom?

Why It Matters

The Panama Canal

One of the most impressive feats of engineering in the world, the Panama Canal was built under a 1903 U.S. treaty with Panama. It took 10 years to build, required more than 40,000 laborers, and cost almost $390 million. The canal stretches 50 miles (80 km) across the mountainous regions of Panama. In 1977 a new treaty took effect that gave Panama control of the canal as of December 31, 1999.

A Cartoonist's View ➤

Many people criticized Roosevelt's role in building the Panama Canal. They believed that he was trying to dominate Latin America. The canal was also costly in terms of human life. Accidents and disease claimed the lives of 5,609 people, including about 4,500 Caribbean laborers.

THE MAN WHO CAN MAKE THE DIRT FLY.

▲ **Trade**
Nearly 13,000 oceangoing vessels pass through the canal annually. Roughly 60 percent of the cargo is coming from or going to U.S. ports. The canal's relative share of world cargo has declined somewhat, but its absolute volume has grown with the continued expansion of global trade.

The Open Door Policy

In 1894 war erupted between China and Japan over Korea, which at that time was part of the Chinese empire. European and American leaders expected China, with its massive armed forces, to defeat Japan easily. These Western observers were astonished when Japan easily defeated China. In the peace treaty, China granted Korea independence. China also gave Japan territory in Manchuria that included the important city of Port Arthur. The war showed that Japan had successfully adopted Western technology and industry. It also demonstrated that China was far weaker than anyone had thought.

Japan's rising power greatly worried the Russians. They did not want Japan to acquire the territory in Manchuria, because it bordered Russia. Backed by France and Germany, Russia forced Japan to give the part of Manchuria it had acquired back to China. Then, in 1898, Russia demanded that China lease the territory to Russia instead.

Leasing a territory meant that it would still belong to China, even though a foreign government would maintain overall control. Germany and France demanded leaseholds in China, and Britain insisted on several as well. Each "leasehold" became the center of a country's sphere of influence, an area where a foreign nation controlled economic development such as railroad construction and mining.

These events in northern China greatly worried the United States. President McKinley and Secretary of State John Hay both supported what they called an Open Door policy, in which all countries should be allowed to trade with China. In 1899 Hay sent notes to countries with leaseholds in China asking them not to discriminate against other nations that wanted to do business with the Chinese inside each leasehold. The Europeans and Japanese received the Open Door proposals coolly. Each power claimed to accept them in principle but refused to act on them unless all of the others agreed to do so as well. Hay refused to consider this a rebuff. Once he had received assurances from all of the great powers, he declared that the United States expected the other powers to abide by the plan.

The Boxer Rebellion

While foreign countries debated who should control China, secret Chinese societies were organizing to get rid of foreign control. Westerners referred to one such group as the Boxers. In 1900 the group rose up to wipe out "foreign

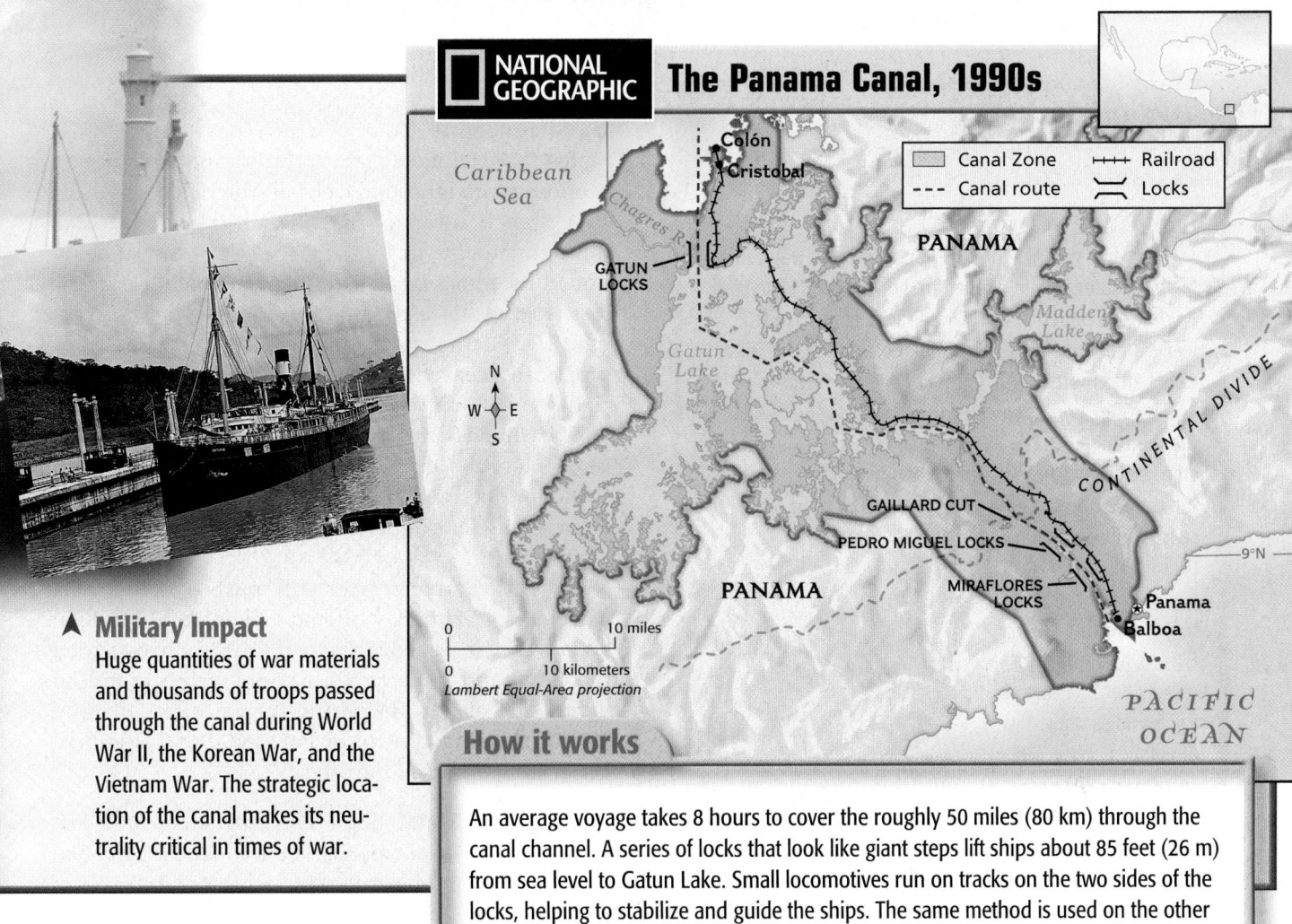

The Panama Canal, 1990s

NATIONAL GEOGRAPHIC

Legend:
- Canal Zone
- Canal route
- Railroad
- Locks

Caribbean Sea

Colón
Cristobal

GATUN LOCKS

Chagres R.

PANAMA

Gatun Lake

Madden Lake

CONTINENTAL DIVIDE

PANAMA

GAILLARD CUT
PEDRO MIGUEL LOCKS
MIRAFLORES LOCKS

Panama
Balboa

PACIFIC OCEAN

9°N

0   10 miles
0   10 kilometers
Lambert Equal-Area projection

How it works

An average voyage takes 8 hours to cover the roughly 50 miles (80 km) through the canal channel. A series of locks that look like giant steps lift ships about 85 feet (26 m) from sea level to Gatun Lake. Small locomotives run on tracks on the two sides of the locks, helping to stabilize and guide the ships. The same method is used on the other side of the lake, where vessels descend through two more locks.

▲ **Military Impact**
Huge quantities of war materials and thousands of troops passed through the canal during World War II, the Korean War, and the Vietnam War. The strategic location of the canal makes its neutrality critical in times of war.

devils" and their Christian converts, whom they believed were corrupting Chinese society. In what became known as the **Boxer Rebellion,** group members besieged foreign embassies in Beijing, killing more than 200 foreigners and taking others prisoner. In August 1900, an international force that included U.S. troops stepped in and quashed the rebellion.

During the crisis, Secretary of State Hay and British leaders worked to persuade European nations not to use the Boxer Rebellion as an excuse to partition China. In a second set of Open Door notes, Hay convinced the participating powers to back away from a full-scale retaliation against China. He urged them instead to accept compensation from China for any damage that the rebellion caused. After some discussion, China was never broken up into colonies. As a result, the United States retained access to China's lucrative trade in tea, spices, and silk and maintained an increasingly larger market for its own goods.

Balancing Power in East Asia As president, Theodore Roosevelt supported the Open Door policy in China and worked to prevent any single nation from monopolizing trade there. This concern prompted Roosevelt to step in to help negotiate peace in a war between Japan and Russia in 1905. At a peace conference in Portsmouth, New Hampshire, Roosevelt convinced the Russians to recognize Japan's territorial gains and persuaded the Japanese to stop fighting and to seek no further territory. For his efforts in ending the war, Roosevelt won the Nobel Peace Prize in 1906.

In the years after the peace treaty, relations between the United States and Japan steadily grew worse. As the two nations vied for greater influence in Asia, they held each other in check through a series of agreements. They agreed to respect each other's territorial possessions, to uphold the Open Door policy, and to support China's independence.

In 1907 President Roosevelt sent 16 battleships of the new United States Navy, known as the **"Great White Fleet,"** on a voyage around the world to showcase the nation's military might. The tour made a stop in Japan to demonstrate that the United States could and would uphold its interests in Asia. This visit did not help ease the growing tensions between the two countries throughout the early 1900s.

✓ **Reading Check** **Explaining** What was the purpose of the Open Door policy?

The Suez Canal

Forty-five years before the Panama Canal was completed, another canal opened that dramatically changed world trade patterns. In 1869 a French company, led by Ferdinand de Lesseps, completed work on the Suez Canal after more than 10 years of construction.

The Suez Canal is located in Egypt. It connects the Mediterranean Sea to the Red Sea, creating a shortcut for ships traveling from Europe to the Indian Ocean. Before the canal's opening, ships had to travel around Africa to reach India and countries in East Asia. The canal greatly reduced travel times between Europe and Asia and rapidly became one of the world's major shipping lanes. *How did the canal change world trade patterns?*

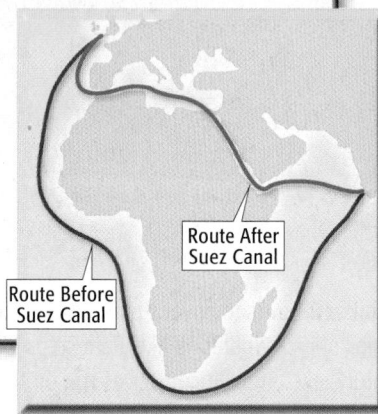

Route After Suez Canal

Route Before Suez Canal

A Growing Presence in the Caribbean

Theodore Roosevelt believed in a strong global military presence. He insisted that displaying American power to the world would make nations think twice about fighting, thus promoting global peace. He often expressed this belief with a West African saying, "Speak softly and carry a big stick." Roosevelt's "big stick" policy was perhaps most evident in the Caribbean.

GEOGRAPHY

The Panama Canal One of Roosevelt's most dramatic actions in the Caribbean was the acquisition of the Panama Canal Zone in 1903. Roosevelt and others viewed the construction of a canal through Central America as vital to American power in the world. A canal would save time and money for both commercial and military shipping.

As early as 1850, the United States and Great Britain had signed a treaty in which each nation had agreed not to build a canal without the other's participation. Because of its strong interest in a canal, however, the United States negotiated a new treaty. In 1901, the United States and Great Britain signed the **Hay-Pauncefote Treaty,** which gave the United States the exclusive right to build and control any proposed canal through Central America.

A French company had begun digging a canal through Panama in 1881. By 1889, however, it abandoned its efforts because of bankruptcy and terrible losses from disease among the workers. The company was reorganized in 1894, but its operations practically ceased and its only hope was to sell its rights to digging the canal.

The United States had long considered two possible canal sites, one through Nicaragua and one through Panama. The French company eased this choice by offering to sell its rights and property in Panama to the United States.

In 1903 Panama was still part of Colombia. Secretary of State Hay offered Colombia $10 million and a yearly rent of $250,000 for the right to construct the canal and to control a narrow strip of land on either side of it. Considering the price too low and afraid of losing control of Panama, the Colombian government refused the offer.

Revolt in Panama Some Panamanians feared losing the commercial benefits of the canal. Panama had opposed Colombian rule since the mid-1800s, and the canal issue added to the tensions. In addition, the French company was still concerned that the United States would build the canal in Nicaragua instead. The French company's agent, Philippe Bunau-Varilla, and Panamanian officials decided that the only way to ensure the canal would be built was to declare independence and make their own deal with the United States. Bunau-Varilla arranged for a small army to stage an uprising in Panama.

On November 3, 1903, Bunau-Varilla's forces revolted. Meanwhile, President Roosevelt sent ships to Panama to prevent Colombian interference. Within a few days, the United States recognized Panama's independence. Less than two weeks later, the two nations signed a treaty allowing the canal to be built.

Protesters in the United States and throughout Latin America condemned Roosevelt's actions as unjustifiable aggression. The president countered that he had advanced "the needs of collective civilization" by building a canal that shortened the distance between the Atlantic and the Pacific by about 8,000 nautical miles (14,816 km).

The Roosevelt Corollary The growing American involvement in foreign affairs caused Roosevelt to expand his "big stick" diplomacy. In an address to Congress in 1904, the president defined what came to be known as the **Roosevelt Corollary** to the Monroe Doctrine. In it, he said that the United States would intervene in Latin American affairs when necessary to maintain economic and political stability in the Western Hemisphere:

❝Chronic wrongdoing . . . may, in America, as elsewhere, ultimately require intervention by some civilized nation, and in the Western Hemisphere the adherence of the United States to the Monroe Doctrine may force the United States, however reluctantly, in flagrant cases of such wrongdoing or impotence, to the exercise of an international police power.❞

—quoted in *The Growth of the United States*

The United States first applied the Roosevelt Corollary in the Dominican Republic, which had fallen behind on its debt payments to European nations. In 1905 the United States assumed the responsibility of collecting customs tariffs in the Dominican Republic, using the United States Marine Corps as its agent.

Latin American nations resented the growing American influence in the region, but Roosevelt's successor, William Howard Taft, continued Roosevelt's policies. Taft placed much less emphasis on military force and more on helping Latin American industry. He believed that if American business leaders supported Latin American and Asian development, everyone would benefit. The United States would increase its trade, American businesses would increase their profits, and countries in Latin America and Asia would rise out of poverty and social disorder. Taft's policy came to be called dollar diplomacy.

Analyzing *Political Cartoons*

American Imperialism This cartoon displays Roosevelt's belief that the United States should "speak softly and carry a big stick" in foreign affairs. In what part of the world did Roosevelt's quote originate?

Although Taft described his brand of diplomacy as "substituting dollars for bullets," in Nicaragua he used both. In 1911 American bankers began making loans to Nicaragua to support its shaky government. The following year, civil unrest forced the Nicaraguan president to appeal for greater assistance. American marines entered the country, replaced the collector of customs with an American agent, and formed a committee of two Americans and one Nicaraguan to control the customs commissions. American troops stayed to support both the government and customs until 1925.

✓ **Reading Check** **Describing** What did the Roosevelt Corollary state?

SECTION 3 ASSESSMENT

Checking for Understanding
1. **Define:** sphere of influence, Open Door policy, dollar diplomacy.
2. **Identify:** Boxer Rebellion, "Great White Fleet," Hay-Pauncefote Treaty, Roosevelt Corollary.

Reviewing Themes
3. **Continuity and Change** Why do you think Latin American nations resented American influence in the region?

Critical Thinking
4. **Analyzing** How did the Open Door policy and dollar diplomacy affect U.S. relations with other countries?
5. **Organizing** Use a graphic organizer to summarize the results of the Open Door policy in China.

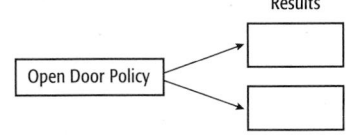

Results

Open Door Policy

Analyzing Visuals
6. **Analyzing Graphs** Examine the graph on page 537. Why do you think such a small number of U.S. exports went to China and Japan?

Writing About History
7. **Persuasive Writing** Imagine you are Theodore Roosevelt, and write a speech justifying the actions that led to the building of the Panama Canal. Be specific.

Reviewing Key Terms

On a sheet of paper, use each of these terms in a sentence.

1. imperialism
2. protectorate
3. yellow journalism
4. jingoism
5. sphere of influence
6. Open Door policy
7. dollar diplomacy

Reviewing Key Facts

8. **Identify:** Matthew C. Perry, Queen Liliuokalani, Alfred T. Mahan, Henry Cabot Lodge, José Martí, Theodore Roosevelt, "Great White Fleet," Roosevelt Corollary.

9. Why did the United States seek to become a world power in the 1890s?

10. How did yellow journalism contribute to American support of the Cuban revolution?

11. What were the provisions of the Treaty of Paris of 1898?

12. Why did President Theodore Roosevelt help negotiate peace between Japan and Russia?

13. What was dollar diplomacy?

Critical Thinking

14. **Analyzing Themes: Government and Democracy** Why did American sugarcane planters in Hawaii revolt against Queen Liliuokalani?

15. **Explaining** What was the significance of the year 1898 as a turning point for the United States?

16. **Evaluating** Do you think the Panama Canal was worth the cost in terms of money spent and lives lost? Analyze the effects of physical and human geographic factors on the building of the canal to determine your answer.

17. **Interpreting Primary Sources** After the Spanish-American War, Carl Schurz, the leader of the liberal wing of the Republican Party, opposed American expansion abroad. In the following excerpt, Schurz attacks the arguments for taking over the Philippine Islands.

❝Taking a general view of the Philippines as a commercial market for us, I need not again argue against the barbarous notion that in order to have a profitable trade with a country we must own it. . . . It is equally needless to show to any well-informed person that the profits of the trade with the islands themselves can never amount to the cost of making and maintaining the conquest of the Philippines.

But there is another point of real importance. Many imperialists admit that our trade with the Philippines themselves will not nearly be worth its cost; but they say that we must have the Philippines as a foothold, a sort of power station, for the expansion of our trade on the Asiatic continent, especially in China. Admitting this, for argument's sake, I ask what kind of a foothold we should really need. Coaling stations and docks for our fleet, and facilities for the establishment of commercial houses and depots. That is all. And now I ask further, whether we could not easily have had these things if we had, instead of making war upon the Filipinos, favored the independence of the islands. Everybody knows that we could. We might have those things now for the mere asking if we stopped the war and came to a friendly understanding with the Filipinos tomorrow. . . .❞

—quoted in *The Policy of Imperialism*

Chapter Summary

U.S. Actions

In the Pacific

- Expanded Chinese and Japanese markets
- Annexed the Midway Islands as refueling depots for expanded navy
- Built coaling stations on Samoan Islands
- American business leaders led successful campaign for Hawaiian annexation
- Victory over Spain gave U.S. control over Guam and the Philippines

In Latin America

- At Pan-American Conference, invited Latin American countries to trade with U.S.
- Supported Cuba's rebellion against Spain, leading to Spanish-American War; victory over Spain gave U.S. control over Cuba, Puerto Rico
- Built the Panama Canal
- Issued the Roosevelt Corollary stating that the U.S. would intervene in Latin America to maintain stability

Self-Check Quiz
Visit the *American Vision* Web site at tav.glencoe.com
and click on *Self-Check Quizzes—Chapter 17* to
assess your knowledge of chapter content.

a. How does Schurz counter the argument that annexation
   of the Philippines was necessary to make the nation a
   commercial market for the United States?

b. What action other than annexation does Schurz suggest
   the United States could have taken to obtain the coaling
   stations, docks, and depots it needed for trade with Asia?

18. **Organizing** Using a graphic organizer similar to the one
    below, list ways that American imperialism affected Hawaii,
    Cuba, and the Philippines.

Practicing Skills

19. **Using an Electronic Spreadsheet** Enter in a spreadsheet
    the land area of the territories that came under U.S. control
    as a result of the Spanish-American War (Puerto Rico, Guam,
    and the Philippines). Enter the current land area of the
    United States in the spreadsheet. Create an equation to cal-
    culate the percentage of land that each territory represents
    compared to the United States land area.

Writing Activity

20. **Portfolio Writing** Imagine that you are Dr. William Gorgas.
    You have just arrived in Havana, where you have been
    assigned to address the problems of workers suffering from
    yellow fever. Write a letter home describing some of the con-
    ditions, problems, and needs facing you as you search for a
    cure. Place the letter in your portfolio.

Chapter Activity

21. **Evaluating the Validity of a Source** Use the library or the
    internet to find writings by people in support of and against
    the Spanish-American War. Evaluate the authors' points
    based on the language and logic they use. Then evaluate the
    authors' backgrounds and experience to determine if they
    are reliable or objective sources.

Geography and History

22. The map on this page shows the expansion of the United
    States in 1900. Study the map and answer the following
    questions.

NATIONAL GEOGRAPHIC | **U.S. Possessions in the Pacific, 1899**

a. **Interpreting Maps** Approximately how far west
   is the island of Guam from the west coast of the
   United States?

b. **Applying Geography Skills** Why did the United States
   acquire so much island territory in the Pacific?

Standardized Test Practice

**Directions: Choose the best answer to the
following question.**

The Platt Amendment specified all of the following conditions EXCEPT:

A Cuba could not allow another foreign power to gain
territory within its borders.

B Cuba must allow the United States to buy or lease naval
stations in the country.

C Cuba would be guaranteed its independence by 1915.

D The United States had the right to intervene to protect
Cuban independence and to keep order.

Test-Taking Tip: Be careful—overlooking the words NOT
or EXCEPT in a question is a common error. Read through
all the answer choices and choose the one that does NOT
fit. Also look for an answer that seems opposed to the
other answers. Which of the answers above is the opposite
of the rest?

CHAPTER 18

The Progressive Movement *1890–1919*

Why It Matters

Industrialization changed American society. Cities were crowded with new immigrants, working conditions were often bad, and the old political system was breaking down. These conditions gave rise to the Progressive movement. Progressives campaigned for both political and social reforms for more than two decades and enjoyed significant successes at the local, state, and national levels.

The Impact Today

Many Progressive-era changes are still alive in the United States today.
- *Political parties hold direct primaries to nominate candidates for office.*
- *The Seventeenth Amendment calls for the direct election of senators.*
- *Federal regulation of food and drugs began in this period.*

The American Vision *Video* *The Chapter 18 video, "The Stockyard Jungle," portrays the horrors of the meatpacking industry first investigated by Upton Sinclair.*

1889
- Hull House opens in Chicago

1890
- Jacob Riis's *How the Other Half Lives* published

1902
- Maryland workers' compensation laws passed

1904
- Ida Tarbell's *History of the Standard Oil Company* published

United States
PRESIDENTS

B. Harrison 1889–1893 | Cleveland 1893–1897 | McKinley 1897–1901 | T. Roosevelt 1901–1909

1890   *1900*

World

1884
- Toynbee Hall, first settlement house, established in London

1900
- Freud's *Interpretation of Dreams* published

1902
- Anglo-Japanese alliance formed

1903
- Russian Bolshevik Party established by Lenin

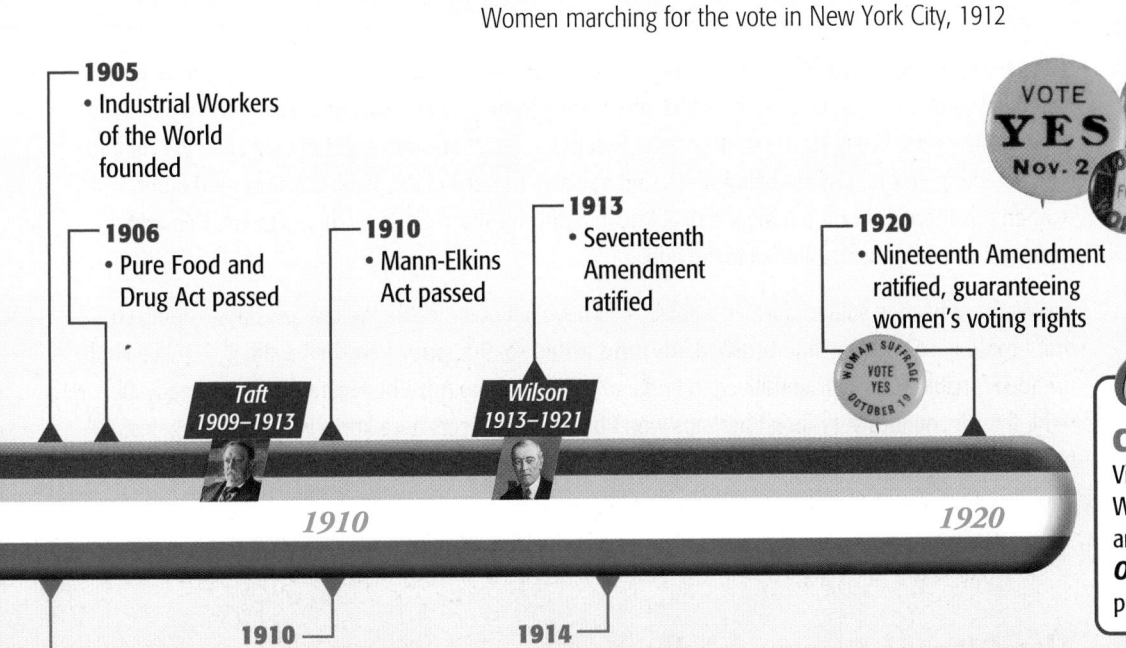

Women marching for the vote in New York City, 1912

1905
- Industrial Workers of the World founded

1906
- Pure Food and Drug Act passed

1910
- Mann-Elkins Act passed

1913
- Seventeenth Amendment ratified

1920
- Nineteenth Amendment ratified, guaranteeing women's voting rights

Taft
1909–1913

Wilson
1913–1921

1910

1920

1910
- Mexican Revolution

1914
- World War I begins in Europe

1905
- Einstein's theory of relativity formulated

VOTE **YES** Nov. 2

VOTE FOR WOMAN SUFFRAGE NOVEMBER 2ND

VOTES FOR WOMEN

WOMAN SUFFRAGE VOTE YES OCTOBER 19

HISTORY
Online

Chapter Overview
Visit the *American Vision* Web site at tav.glencoe.com and click on **Chapter Overviews—Chapter 18** to preview chapter information.

The Roots of Progressivism

Guide to Reading

Main Idea
Progressivism was a diverse response to the problems posed by industrialism and modern life.

Key Terms and Names
progressivism, muckraker, Jacob Riis, commission plan, Robert La Follette, direct primary, initiative, referendum, recall, suffrage, Alice Paul, temperance, prohibition, socialism

Reading Strategy
Organizing As you read about the beginnings of progressivism, complete a graphic organizer similar to the one below by filling in the beliefs of progressives.

Reading Objectives
• **Discuss** the rise of the Progressive movement.
• **Evaluate** the impact of initiative, referendum, and recall, and of the Seventeenth Amendment.

Section Theme
Government and Democracy Progressive reformers focused on political reforms to try to keep the nation true to its democratic ideals.

Preview of Events

♦1890   ♦1900   ♦1910   ♦1920

1890
Jacob Riis's *How the Other Half Lives* published

1901
Galveston, Texas, adopts commission system

1913
Seventeenth Amendment provides for direct election of senators

1920
Nineteenth Amendment gives women the vote

★ *An American Story* ★

In 1917 suffragist Rose Winslow and several other women, including Alice Paul, founder of the National Woman's Party, were arrested for obstructing traffic and blocking sidewalks. The women had been picketing the White House to draw attention to the fact that women did not yet have the right to vote in federal elections. After being sentenced to seven months in jail, Paul, Winslow, and other women prisoners went on a hunger strike. Prison authorities forced the prisoners to eat. Winslow smuggled details of their plight out to the public:

66We have been in solitary for five weeks. . . . I have felt quite feeble the last few days—faint, so that I could hardly get my hair brushed, my arms ached so. But today I am well again. . . . [Alice Paul] dreaded forcible feeding frightfully, and I hate to think how she must be feeling. . . . I am really all right. If this continues very long I perhaps won't be. All the officers here know we are making this hunger strike [so] that women fighting for liberty may be considered political prisoners. . . . [W]e don't want women ever to have to do this over again.99

—quoted in *Jailed for Freedom*

The Rise of Progressivism

The struggle for the right of women to vote was only one of a series of reform efforts that transformed American society in the early 1900s. Historians refer to this era in American history—from about 1890 to 1920—as the Progressive Era.

Who Were the Progressives?

Progressivism was not a tightly organized political movement with a specific set of reforms. Instead, it was a collection of different ideas and activities. Progressives had many different views about how to fix the problems they believed existed in American society.

Progressives generally believed that industrialism and urbanization had created many social problems. Most agreed that the government should take a more active role in solving society's problems. Progressives belonged to both major political parties and usually were urban, educated middle-class Americans. Many leaders of the Progressive movement worked as journalists, social workers, educators, politicians, and members of the clergy.

Beginnings of Progressivism

Progressivism was partly a reaction against laissez-faire economics and its emphasis on an unregulated market. After seeing the poverty of the working class and the filth and crime of urban society, these reformers began to doubt the free market's ability to address those problems. At the same time, they doubted that government in its present form could fix those problems. They concluded that government had to be fixed first before it could be used to fix other problems.

One reason progressives believed people could improve society was because they had a strong faith in science and technology. The application of scientific knowledge had produced the lightbulb, the telephone, the automobile, and the airplane. It had built skyscrapers and railroads. Science and technology had benefited people; thus progressives believed using scientific principles could also produce solutions for society.

The Muckrakers

Among the first people to articulate Progressive ideas was a group of crusading journalists who investigated social conditions and political corruption. These writers became known as muckrakers after a speech by President Theodore Roosevelt:

> ❝Now, it is very necessary that we should not flinch from seeing what is vile and debasing. There is filth on the floor and it must be scraped up with the muck-rake; and there are times and places where this service is the most needed of all the services that can be performed. . . .❞
>
> —Washington, D.C., April 14, 1906

By the early 1900s, American publishers were competing to see who could expose the most corruption and scandal. A group of aggressive 10¢ and 15¢ magazines grew in popularity at this time, including *McClure's*, *Collier's*, and *Munsey's*.

Muckrakers uncovered corruption in many areas. Some concentrated on exposing what they considered to be the unfair practices of large American corporations. In *McClure's*, for example, **Ida Tarbell** published a series of articles critical of the Standard Oil Company. In *Everybody's Magazine*, Charles Edward Russell attacked the beef industry.

Other muckrakers targeted government. David Graham Philips described how money influenced the Senate, while **Lincoln Steffens,** another *McClure's* reporter, reported on vote stealing and other corrupt practices of urban political machines. These were later collected into a book, *The Shame of the Cities.*

Still other muckrakers concentrated on social problems. In his influential book *How the Other Half Lives,* published in 1890, **Jacob Riis** described the poverty, disease, and crime that afflicted many immigrant neighborhoods in New York City. The

HISTORY Online

Student Web Activity Visit the *American Vision* Web site at tav.glencoe.com and click on **Student Web Activities— Chapter 18** for an activity on the Progressive movement.

Picturing **History**

Muckrakers *McClure's* published Ida Tarbell's exposé on Standard Oil. What issues particularly concerned the muckrakers?

muckrakers' articles led to a general public debate on social and economic problems and put pressure on politicians to introduce reforms.

✓ **Reading Check** **Describing** How did the muckrakers help spark the Progressive movement?

Making Government Efficient

There were many different types of progressivism. Different causes led to different approaches, and progressives even took opposing positions on how to solve some problems.

One group of progressives focused on making government more efficient. They believed that many problems in society could be solved if government worked properly. Efficiency progressives took their ideas from business. These progressives believed business had become more efficient by applying the principles of scientific management.

The ideas of scientific management had been developed in the late 1800s and were popularized by Frederick W. Taylor in his book *The Principles of Scientific Management*, published in 1911. Taylor described how a company could become more efficient by managing time, breaking tasks down into small parts, and using standardized tools.

Efficiency progressives argued that managing a modern city required experts, not politicians. They did not want more democracy in government, for they believed that the democratic process led to compromise and corruption. In most American cities, the mayor or city council chose the heads of city departments. Traditionally, these jobs went to political supporters and friends, who often knew little about city services.

Efficiency progressives wanted either a commission plan or a council-manager system. Under the commission plan, a city's government would be divided into several departments, which would each be placed under the control of an expert commissioner. These progressives argued that a board of commissioners or a city manager with expertise in city services should hire the specialists to run city departments. Galveston, Texas, adopted the commission system in 1901. Other cities soon followed.

✓ **Reading Check** **Explaining** Why did progressives want to reorganize city government?

A City and a Storm

On September 8, 1900, a massive hurricane devastated the city of Galveston, Texas. About 6,000 people died. When the political machine that controlled the city government proved incapable of responding to the disaster, local business leaders convinced the state to let them take control. In April 1901, Galveston introduced the commission system of government. Under this system, Galveston chose five commissioners to replace the mayor and city council.

Four commissioners were local business leaders. When the city quickly recovered, reformers in other cities were impressed. Galveston's experience seemed to prove the benefits of running a city like a business by dividing its government into departments and placing each under an expert commissioner. Many other cities soon followed, adopting either the commission plan or the council-manager system.

Democracy and Progressivism

Not all progressives agreed with the efficiency progressives. Many believed that society needed more democracy, not less. They wanted to make elected officials more responsive to voters.

"Laboratory of Democracy" Political reform first came to the state level when Wisconsin voters elected Republican **Robert La Follette** to be governor. La Follette used his office to attack the way political parties ran their conventions. Because party bosses controlled the selection of convention delegates, they also controlled which candidates were chosen to run for office. La Follette pressured the state legislature to require each party to hold a direct primary, in which all party members could vote for a candidate to run in the general election.

La Follette's great reform success gave Wisconsin a reputation as the "laboratory of democracy." La Follette claimed, "Democracy is based upon knowledge. . . . The only way to beat the boss . . . is to keep the people thoroughly informed."

Inspired by La Follette, progressives in other states pushed for similar electoral changes. To force state legislators to respond to voters, three new reforms were introduced in many states. The initiative allowed a group of citizens to introduce legislation and required the legislature to vote on it. The referendum allowed proposed legislation to be submitted to the voters for approval. The recall allowed voters to demand a special election to remove an elected official from office before his or her term had expired.

GOVERNMENT

Direct Election of Senators Another reform the progressives favored affected the federal government—the direct election of senators. As originally written, the United States Constitution directed each state legislature to elect two senators from that state. Political machines or large trusts often influenced the election of senators, who then repaid their supporters with federal contracts and jobs. By the early 1900s, muckraker Charles Edward Russell charged that the Senate had become "only a chamber of butlers for industrialists and financiers."

To counter Senate corruption, progressives called for the direct election of senators by all state voters. In 1912 Congress passed a direct-election amendment. Although the direct election of senators was intended to end corruption, it also removed one of the state legislatures' checks on federal power. In 1913 the amendment was ratified, becoming the Seventeenth Amendment to the Constitution.

Reading Check **Evaluating** What was the impact of the Seventeenth Amendment? What problem was it intended to solve?

The Suffrage Movement

In July 1848, Elizabeth Cady Stanton and Lucretia Mott organized the first women's rights convention in Seneca Falls, New York. Stanton convinced the delegates that their first priority should be getting women the right to vote. The movement for women's voting rights became known as the suffrage movement. Suffrage is the right to vote.

Woman suffrage was an important issue for progressives. Although the suffrage movement began well before progressivism emerged, many progressives joined the movement in the late 1800s and early 1900s.

Mayor-Council Form

Voters → elect

Mayor → actions approved by → City Council

Mayor appoints → Heads of City Departments → carry out policy

Source: *The World Book Encyclopedia.*

Commission Form

Voters → elect → Board of Commissioners

- Police Commissioner
- Fire Commissioner
- Parks Commissioner
- Finance Commissioner
- Public Works Commissioner

Board of Commissioners → pass ordinances; control funds

→ carry out policy

Source: *The World Book Encyclopedia.*

Council-Manager Form

Voters → elect → City Council (makes policy)

City Council hires → City Manager (Chief Administrator)

City Manager appoints → Heads of City Departments → carry out policy

City Council elects → Mayor

Source: *The World Book Encyclopedia.*

Early Problems The suffrage movement got off to a slow start. Women suffragists were accused of being unfeminine and immoral. Several were physically attacked. The movement also remained weak because many of its supporters were abolitionists as well. In the years before the Civil War, they preferred to concentrate on abolishing slavery.

After the Civil War, the Republicans in Congress introduced the Fourteenth and Fifteenth Amendments to the Constitution to protect the voting rights of African Americans. Several leaders of the woman suffrage movement had wanted these amendments worded to give women the right to vote as well. They were bitterly disappointed when Republicans refused.

The debate over the Fourteenth and Fifteenth Amendments split the suffrage movement into two groups: the National Woman Suffrage Association, led by Elizabeth Cady Stanton and Susan B. Anthony, and the American Woman Suffrage Association, led by Lucy Stone and Julia Ward Howe. The first group wanted to focus on passing a constitutional amendment allowing woman suffrage. The second group believed that the best strategy was to convince state governments to give women the right to vote before trying to amend the Constitution.

This split reduced the movement's effectiveness. In 1878 a constitutional amendment granting woman suffrage was introduced in Congress, but it failed to pass. Few state governments granted women the right to vote either. By 1900 only Wyoming, Idaho, Utah, and Colorado had granted women full voting rights.

The Movement Builds Support In 1890 the two groups united to form the **National American Woman Suffrage Association** (NAWSA). The movement still did not make significant gains, however, until about 1910. Part of the problem was convincing women to become politically active. As the Progressive movement began, however, many middle-class women concluded that they needed the vote to promote social reforms they favored. Many working-class women also wanted the vote to ensure passage of labor laws protecting women.

As the suffrage movement grew, members began lobbying lawmakers, organizing marches, and delivering speeches on street corners. By the end of 1912, Washington, Oregon, California, Arizona, and Kansas had granted women full voting rights. On March 3, 1913, the day before President Wilson's inauguration, suffragists marched in Washington, D.C., to draw attention to their cause.

Alice Paul, a Quaker social worker who headed NAWSA's congressional committee, had organized the Washington march. Paul wanted to use protests to force President Wilson to take action on suffrage. Her activities alarmed other members of NAWSA who wanted to negotiate with Wilson. Paul left NAWSA and formed the National Woman's Party. Her supporters picketed the White House, blocked sidewalks, chained themselves to lampposts, and went on hunger strikes if arrested.

In 1915 **Carrie Chapman Catt** became NAWSA's leader. Catt developed what she called her "Winning Plan" to mobilize the suffrage

---

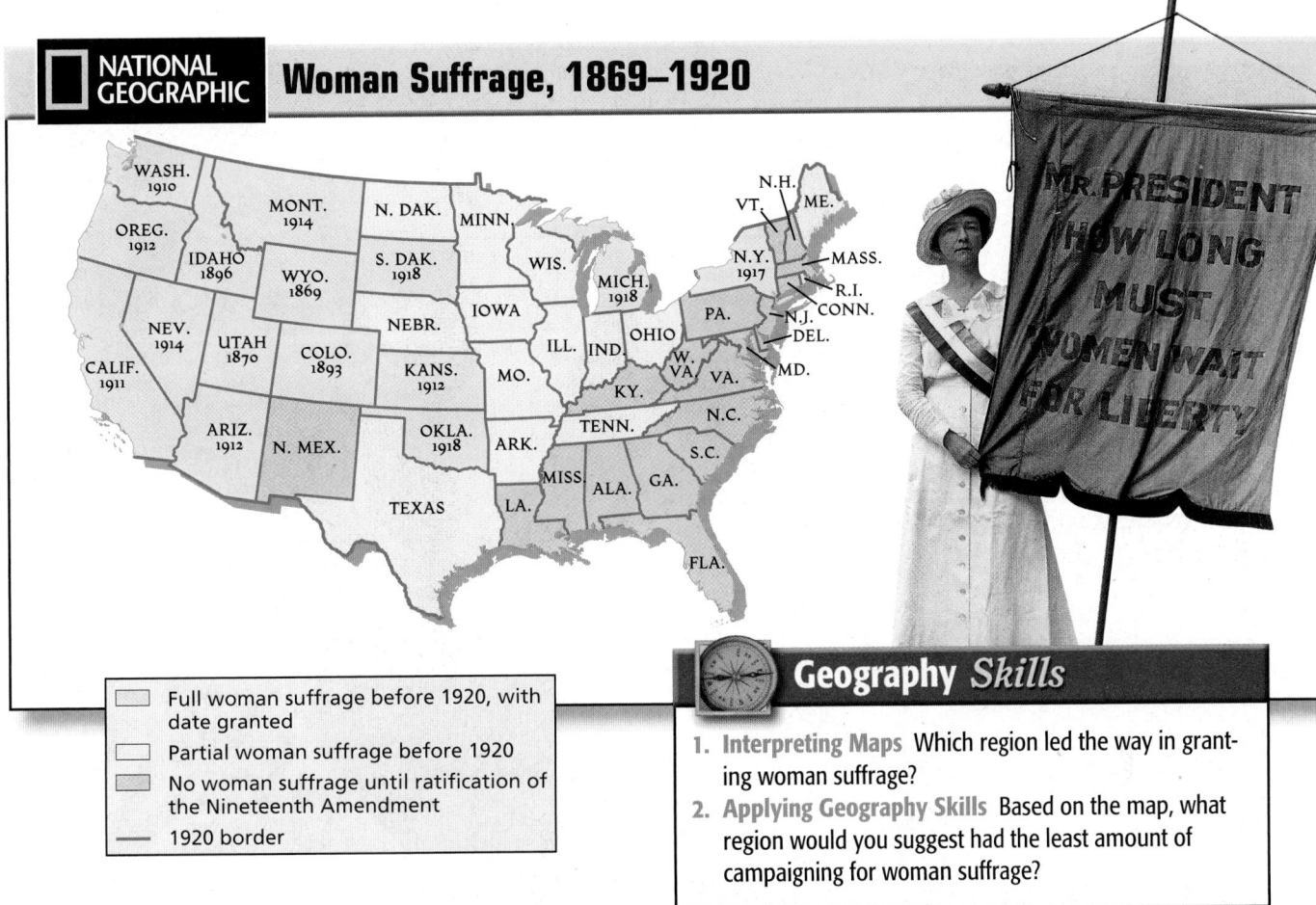

Legend:
- Full woman suffrage before 1920, with date granted
- Partial woman suffrage before 1920
- No woman suffrage until ratification of the Nineteenth Amendment
- 1920 border

Geography Skills

1. **Interpreting Maps** Which region led the way in granting woman suffrage?
2. **Applying Geography Skills** Based on the map, what region would you suggest had the least amount of campaigning for woman suffrage?

movement nation-wide in one final push to gain voting rights. She also threw NAWSA's support behind Wilson in the 1916 election. Although Wilson did not endorse a woman suffrage amendment, he supported the Democratic Party's call for states to give women the vote.

The Nineteenth Amendment As more states granted women the right to vote, Congress began to favor a constitutional amendment. In 1918 the House of Representatives passed a woman suffrage amendment. Wilson then addressed the Senate, asking it to vote for the amendment. Despite his efforts, the amendment failed to pass by two votes.

During the midterm elections of 1918, Catt used NAWSA's resources to defeat two anti-suffrage senators. The following year, in June 1919, the Senate finally passed the Nineteenth Amendment by just more than the two-thirds vote needed. On August 26, 1920, after three-fourths of the states had voted to ratify it, the Nineteenth Amendment guaranteeing women the right to vote went into effect.

✓ **Reading Check** **Evaluating** How successful were women in lobbying to achieve passage of the Nineteenth Amendment?

Social Welfare Progressivism

While many progressives focused on reforming the political system, others focused on social problems, such as crime, illiteracy, alcohol abuse, child labor, and the health and safety of Americans. These social welfare progressives created charities to help the poor and disadvantaged. They also pushed for new laws they hoped would fix social problems.

The Campaign Against Child Labor Probably the most emotional Progressive issue was the campaign against child labor. Children had always worked on family farms, but the factory work that many children performed was monotonous, and the conditions were often unhealthy. In 1900 over 1.7 million children under the age of 16 worked outside the home. Reformers established a National Child Labor Committee in 1904 to work to abolish child labor.

Muckraker John Spargo's 1906 book *The Bitter Cry of the Children* presented detailed evidence on child labor conditions. He told of coal mines where thousands of "breaker boys" were hired at age 9 or 10 to pick slag out of coal and were paid 60¢ for a 10-hour

YOUTHFUL PROTEST
Two young immigrants march in a New York City demonstration against child labor practices in 1907. Both young women wear banners proclaiming the same message—one in English, the other in Yiddish. Such protests helped publicize the exploitation of children in dingy, dangerous "sweatshops" in American cities. At the dawn of the twentieth century, more than a million children—some as young as eight—labored long hours in factories. The weight of popular opinion finally forced state governments to pass laws protecting young workers.

day. He described how the work bent their backs permanently and often crippled their hands. Reports like these convinced states to pass laws that set a minimum age for employment and established other limits on child labor, such as maximum hours children could work. At the same time, many states began passing compulsory education laws, requiring young children to be in school instead of at work.

By the early 1900s, the number of child laborers had begun to decline. For many families, the new wealth generated by industry enabled them to survive without having their children work. For others, the child labor and compulsory education laws meant that wives had to work instead.

Health and Safety Codes Many adult workers also labored in difficult conditions. Factories, coal mines, and railroads were particularly dangerous. For example, in 1911 a terrible fire swept through Triangle Shirtwaist Company in New York City. Nearly 150 women workers died, trapped by doors locked from the outside. Outrage at the deaths caused New York

City to pass strict building codes dealing with fire hazards and unsafe machinery and working conditions.

During the early 1900s, thousands of people died or were injured on the job, but they and their families received little compensation. Progressives joined union leaders to pressure states for workers' compensation laws. These laws established insurance funds financed by employers. Workers injured in industrial accidents received payments from the funds.

Some progressives also favored zoning laws as a method of protecting the public. These laws divided a town or city into zones for commercial, residential, or other development, thereby regulating how land and buildings could be used. Building codes set minimum standards for light, air, room size, and sanitation, and required buildings to have fire escapes. Health codes required restaurants and other facilities to maintain clean environments for their patrons.

The Prohibition Movement Many progressives believed alcohol was responsible for many problems in American life. Settlement house workers hated the effects of drinking on families. Scarce wages were spent on alcohol, and drinking sometimes led to physical abuse and sickness. Many Christians also opposed alcohol.

Some employers believed drinking hurt workers' efficiency, while political reformers viewed the saloon as the informal headquarters of the machine politics they opposed. The temperance movement, which advocated the moderation or elimination of alcohol, emerged from these concerns.

For the most part, women led the temperance movement. In 1874 a group of women formed the **Women's Christian Temperance Union** (WCTU). By 1911 this organization had nearly 250,000 members. In 1893 another organization—the Anti-Saloon League—was formed. When it began, the temperance movement concentrated on reducing alcohol consumption. Later it pressed for prohibition—laws banning the manufacture, sale, and consumption of alcohol.

✓ **Reading Check** **Examining** What actions did progressives take to deal with the issue of child labor?

Progressives Versus Big Business

A fourth group of progressives focused their efforts on regulating big business. Many progressives believed that wealth was concentrated in the hands of too few people. In particular, many became concerned about trusts and holding companies—giant corporations that dominated many industries.

Progressives disagreed, however, over how to go about regulating big business. Some believed that the government should break up big companies to restore competition. This idea led to the Sherman Antitrust Act in 1890. Others argued that big business was the most efficient way to organize the economy. They pushed instead for the creation of government agencies to regulate big companies and prevent them from abusing their power. The Interstate Commerce Commission (ICC), created in 1887, was an early example of this kind of Progressive thinking.

Some progressives went even further and advocated socialism—the idea that the government should own and operate industry for the community as a whole. They wanted the government to buy up large companies, especially industries that affected everyone, such as railroads and utilities.

At its peak, socialism had some national support. **Eugene Debs,** the former American Railway Union leader, won nearly a million votes as the American Socialist Party candidate for president in 1912. Most progressives and most Americans, however, believed in the superiority of the American system of free enterprise.

Efforts to regulate business were focused at the national level. Congress passed a number of proposals to regulate the economy under presidents Theodore Roosevelt, William Taft, and Woodrow Wilson.

✓ **Reading Check** **Evaluating** What was the impact of Eugene Debs and the Socialist Party on the 1912 election?

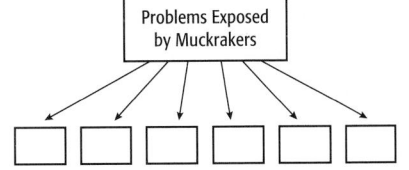

SECTION 1 ASSESSMENT

Checking for Understanding

1. **Define:** progressivism, muckraker, commission plan, direct primary, initiative, referendum, recall, suffrage, temperance, prohibition, socialism.
2. **Identify:** Jacob Riis, Robert La Follette, Alice Paul.
3. **State** what was provided for by the Nineteenth Amendment to the Constitution.

Reviewing Themes

4. **Government and Democracy** How did initiative, referendum, and recall change democracy in the United States?

Critical Thinking

5. **Evaluating** What impact did Susan B. Anthony have on Progressive era reforms?
6. **Organizing** Use a graphic organizer similar to the one below to list the kinds of problems that muckrakers exposed.

Problems Exposed by Muckrakers

Analyzing Visuals

7. **Examining Charts** Study the charts on page 549. Under which system do voters seem to have the most control over department heads? Why do you think so?

Writing About History
8. **Persuasive Writing** Some women in the early 1900s suggested that the Constitution needed an equal rights amendment. Imagine you are living then. Write a letter to the editor of your local paper supporting or opposing such an amendment.

Taking Notes

Why Learn This Skill?

Taking notes is a way of recording the important parts of something you have read. Taking notes also helps you recall information. The guidelines below explain how to get the most out of your notes.

Learning the Skill

One of the best ways to remember something is to write it down. Taking notes involves writing down information in a brief and orderly form. This helps you remember information and makes it easier to study.

There are several styles of taking notes, but all clarify and put information in a logical order. Keep these guidelines in mind when you are taking notes:

- Identify the subject and write it at the top of the page. In your book, for example, look for chapter or section headings.

- Be selective in what information you include in your notes. For example, anything your teacher writes on the chalkboard or shows you from a transparency should be included. If your teacher emphasizes a point or spends a considerable amount of time on a given topic, this is also a clue to its importance. Similarly, if your textbook covers a single topic over several pages, take notes by seeking the topic sentences of paragraphs on the topic. Be certain to write down all words that are in bold or italicized type. Your goal is to listen or read carefully, paying attention to the main ideas or key points. Do not write down every word your teacher says. Your notes should consist of the main ideas and supporting details on the subject.

- Paraphrase the information. Put it in your own words rather than trying to take it down word for word. In order to save time, you might want to develop a personal form of shorthand. For example, eliminating vowels from words saves

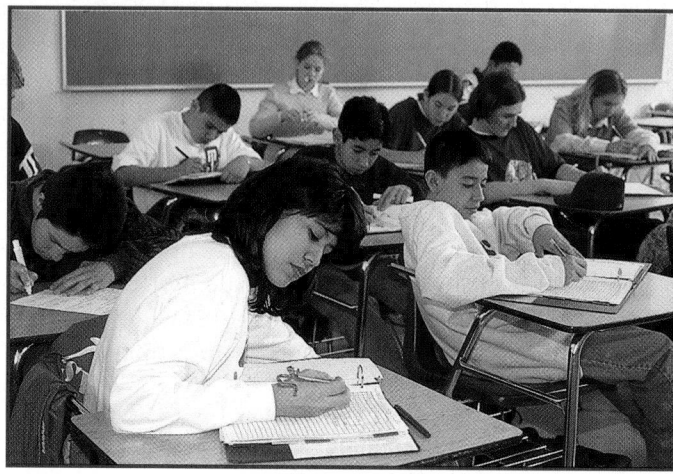

Student success relies on good note-taking.

time: "develop" becomes "dvlp." Use symbols, arrows, or sketches: "&" in place of "and." Use your shorthand whenever you take notes.

- Make sure your notes are neat so you will be able to understand them when you study them later.

Practicing the Skill

After you have carefully read Section 4 of this chapter, follow the general guidelines to taking notes listed above and create notes for the subsection "The Limits of Progressivism."

Skills Assessment

Complete the Practicing Skills questions on page 573 and the Chapter 18 Skill Reinforcement Activity to assess your mastery of this skill.

Applying the Skill

Taking Notes Have a classmate quiz you on the section on which you took notes. How did you do? Did your notes work well? What can be improved about them? What would you change?

Glencoe's **Skillbuilder Interactive Workbook CD-ROM, Level 2,** provides instruction and practice in key social studies skills.

SECTION 2 Roosevelt in Office

★ An American Story ★

William McKinley's assassination brought Teddy Roosevelt to the presidency. Despite the tragic circumstances, he took to the office with great joy. A man who loved the outdoors and physical activity, Roosevelt impressed many people as a new kind of president. One visitor wrote that after spending time with Roosevelt, "you go home and wring the personality out of your clothes."

The famous muckraker, Lincoln Steffens, already knew Roosevelt as a fellow reformer. Steffens went to Washington to see his friend, and this is what he saw:

❝His offices were crowded with people, mostly reformers, all day long. . . . He strode triumphant around among us, talking and shaking hands, dictating and signing letters, and laughing. Washington, the whole country, was in mourning, and no doubt the President felt he should hold himself down; he didn't; he tried to but his joy showed in every word and movement. . . . With his feet, his fists, his face and his free words, he laughed at his luck. . . . And he laughed with glee at the power and place that had come to him.❞

—**quoted in *Theodore Roosevelt, A Life***

Roosevelt Revives the Presidency

Theodore Roosevelt, better known as "Teddy," took office at age 42—the youngest person ever to serve as president. Roosevelt was intensely competitive, strong-willed, and extremely energetic. In international affairs, Roosevelt was a Social Darwinist. He believed the United States was in competition with the other nations of the world and that only the fittest would survive. Domestically, however, Roosevelt was a committed progressive, who firmly believed that government should actively balance the needs of competing groups in American society.

"I shall see to it," Roosevelt declared in 1904, "that every man has a square deal, no less and no more." During his second term, his reform programs became known as the Square Deal. To Roosevelt, it was not inconsistent to believe in Social Darwinism and Progressivism at the same time. He believed the United States needed to adopt progressive reforms in order to maintain an efficient society that could compete successfully against other nations.

Roosevelt Takes on the Trusts Although he admired competition, Roosevelt was also concerned with efficiency. He believed that trusts and other large business organizations were very efficient and part of the reason for America's prosperity. Yet Roosevelt remained concerned that in the pursuit of their private interests, some trusts were hurting the public interest. He wanted to find a way to supervise big business without destroying its economic efficiency. When the *New York Sun* declared that Roosevelt was "bringing wealth to its knees," the president disagreed. "We draw the line against misconduct," he declared, "not against wealth."

During Roosevelt's first year in office, a fight for control of the Burlington Railroad erupted on the New York Stock Exchange. On one side was E.H. Harriman of the Union Pacific Railroad. On the other side were James J. Hill and J.P. Morgan of the Great Northern and Northern Pacific Railroads. The stock battle almost triggered a financial panic that could have plunged the nation into a recession. The three men ultimately compromised by creating a giant new holding company called **Northern Securities.**

The formation of the Northern Securities Company alarmed many Americans, including Roosevelt. The stock battle that led to its creation seemed a classic example of private interests acting in a way that threatened the nation as a whole. Roosevelt decided that the company was in violation of the Sherman Antitrust Act. In early 1902, he ordered his attorney general to file a lawsuit against Northern Securities.

Roosevelt's action pleased many progressives but baffled J.P. Morgan. He immediately traveled to the White House with two supportive senators in tow to present his case. "If we have done anything wrong," he told the president, "send your man to my man and they can fix it up." Unmoved, Roosevelt proceeded with the case. In 1904 in *Northern Securities* v. *the United States,* the Supreme Court ruled that Northern Securities had indeed violated the Sherman Antitrust Act. Roosevelt declared it a great victory. "The most powerful men in the country," he proclaimed, "were held to accountability before the law." Newspapers hailed Roosevelt as a "trustbuster," and his popularity with the American public soared. *(See page 1082 for more information on* Northern Securities *v.* the United States.*)*

Analyzing *Political Cartoons*

Corporate Giants This 1904 cartoon portrays Roosevelt as "Jack the Giant-Killer," but he actually restrained very few trusts. Why do you think the scene is set on Wall Street?

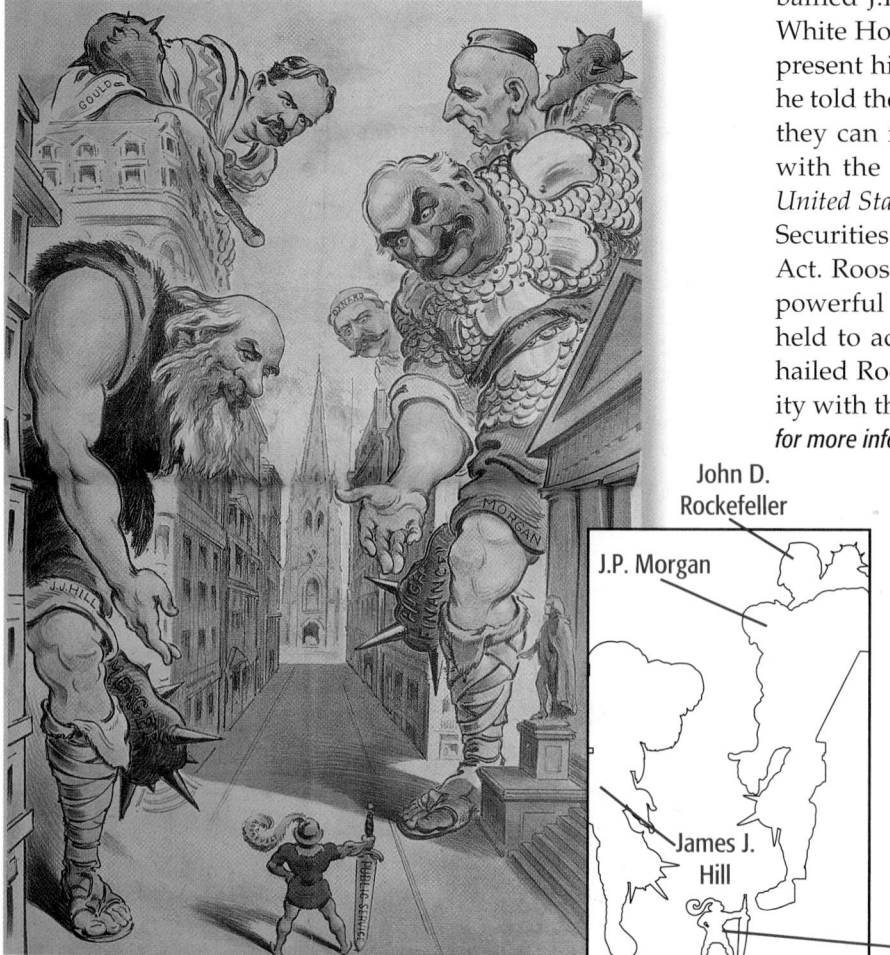

John D. Rockefeller

J.P. Morgan

James J. Hill

T. Roosevelt

The Coal Strike of 1902 As president, Roosevelt regarded himself as the nation's head manager. He believed it was his job to keep society operating efficiently by preventing conflict between the nation's different groups and their interests. In the fall of 1902, he put these beliefs into practice.

The previous spring, the **United Mine Workers** (UMW) union had called a strike of the miners who dug anthracite, or hard coal. Nearly 150,000 workers walked out of eastern Pennsylvania's anthracite mines demanding a pay increase, a reduction in work hours, and recognition for their union.

As the months passed and the strike continued, coal prices began to rise. To Roosevelt it was another example of groups pursuing their private interests at the expense of the nation. If the strike dragged on too long, the country would face a coal shortage that could shut down factories and leave many people's homes cold with winter fast approaching.

Roosevelt urged the union and the owners to accept arbitration—a settlement imposed by an outside party. The union agreed. The mine owners, determined to destroy the UMW, did not. One owner, George Baer, declared, "The rights and interests of the laboring man will be protected and cared for not by the labor agitators, but by the Christian men to whom God in His infinite wisdom has given the control of the property interests of the country."

The mine owners' stubbornness infuriated Roosevelt, as it did much of the public. Roosevelt threatened to order the army to run the mines. Fearful of this, the mine owners finally accepted arbitration. By intervening in the dispute, Roosevelt had taken the first step toward establishing the federal government as an honest broker between powerful groups in society.

The Bureau of Corporations Despite his lawsuit against Northern Securities and his role in the coal strike, Roosevelt was not opposed to big business. He believed most trusts benefited the economy and that breaking them up would do more harm than good. Instead, Roosevelt proposed the creation of a new federal agency to investigate corporations and publicize the results. He believed the most effective way to keep big business from abusing its power was through knowledge and publicity of the facts.

In 1903 Roosevelt convinced Congress to create the Department of Commerce and Labor. Within this department would be a division called the **Bureau of Corporations,** with the authority to investigate corporations and issue reports on their activities.

The following year, the Bureau of Corporations began investigating U.S. Steel, a gigantic holding company that had been created in 1901. Worried about a possible antitrust lawsuit, the company's leaders met privately with Roosevelt and offered a deal. They would open their account books and records to the Bureau of Corporations. In exchange, if the Bureau found anything wrong, the company would be advised privately and allowed to correct the problem without having to go to court.

Miner's Lot In the early 1900s, miners worked under dangerous conditions for little pay. How did Roosevelt respond when they went on strike?

Roosevelt accepted this "gentlemen's agreement," as he called it. Shortly afterward he made similar deals with other companies. These arrangements gave Roosevelt the ability to regulate big business without having to sacrifice economic efficiency by breaking up the trusts.

Congress Follows In addition to creating the Department of Commerce and Labor, Congress passed the Expedition Act, which gave federal antitrust suits precedence on the dockets of circuit courts. Then, in 1906, Roosevelt pushed the **Hepburn Act** through Congress. This act was intended to strengthen the Interstate Commerce Commission (ICC). An early effort to regulate the railroad industry, the ICC had been ineffective because it lacked sufficient authority.

The Hepburn Act tried to strengthen the ICC by giving it the power to set railroad rates. The agency originally was intended to regulate rates to ensure that companies did not compete unfairly. At first, railroad companies were suspicious of the ICC and tied up its decisions by challenging them in court. Eventually, the railroads realized that they could work with the ICC to set rates and regulations that limited competition and prevented new competitors from entering the industry. Over time the ICC became a supporter of the railroads' interests, and by 1920 it had begun setting rates at levels intended to ensure the industry's profits.

✓ **Reading Check** **Comparing** What was the purpose of the Interstate Commerce Commission, and how successful was it?

Social Welfare Action

When Roosevelt took office, he was not greatly concerned about consumer issues, but by 1905 consumer protection had become a national issue. That year, a journalist named Samuel Hopkins Adams published a series of articles in *Collier's* magazine describing the patent medicine business.

Many companies were patenting and marketing potions they claimed would cure a variety of ills. Many patent medicines were little more than alcohol, colored water, and sugar. Others contained caffeine, opium, cocaine, and other dangerous compounds. Consumers had no way to know what they were taking, nor did they receive any assurance that the medicines worked as claimed.

Many Americans were equally concerned about the food they ate. Dr. W.H. Wiley, chief chemist at the United States Department of Agriculture, had issued reports documenting the dangerous preservatives being used in what he called "embalmed meat." Then, in 1906, **Upton Sinclair** published *The Jungle.* Based on Sinclair's close observations of the slaughterhouses of Chicago, the powerful book featured appalling descriptions of conditions in the meatpacking industry:

> 66 There would come all the way back from Europe old sausage that had been rejected, and that was moldy and white—it would be dosed with borax and glycerine, and dumped into the hoppers, and made over again for home consumption. . . . There would be meat stored in great piles in rooms; and the water from leaky roofs would drip over it, and thousands of rats would race about upon it. 99

> —from *The Jungle*

Sinclair's book was a best-seller. It made consumers ill—and angry. Roosevelt and Congress responded with the **Meat Inspection Act.** It required federal inspection of meat sold through interstate commerce and required the Agriculture Department to set standards of cleanliness in meatpacking plants. The **Pure Food and Drug Act,** passed on the same day in 1906, prohibited the manufacture, sale, or shipment of impure or falsely labeled food and drugs.

✓ **Reading Check** **Summarizing** What two pieces of legislation were enacted due to the facts revealed in Upton Sinclair's *The Jungle*?

Conservation

Roosevelt put his stamp on the presidency most clearly in the area of environmental conservation. Realizing that the nation's bountiful natural resources were being used up at an alarming rate, Roosevelt urged Americans to conserve these resources.

An enthusiastic outdoorsman, Roosevelt valued the country's minerals, animals, and rugged terrain. He cautioned against unregulated exploitation of public lands and believed in conservation to manage the nation's resources. As president, Roosevelt eagerly assumed the role of manager. He argued that the government must distinguish "between the man who skins the land and the man who develops the country. I am going to work with, and only with, the man who develops the country."

GEOGRAPHY

Land Development in the West Roosevelt quickly applied his philosophy in the dry Western states, where farmers and city dwellers competed for scarce water. In 1902 Roosevelt supported passage of the **Newlands Reclamation Act,** authorizing the use of

| Fact | Fiction | Folklore |

The Teddy Bear The soft and cuddly teddy bear was named after the gruff and rugged Theodore ("Teddy") Roosevelt. The idea for the toy stemmed from a hunting trip Roosevelt took to Mississippi in 1902. On the trip, the president refused to kill a defenseless bear cub. Cartoonist Clifford Berryman drew a whimsical reenactment of the scene for the *Washington Post,* which in turn inspired Morris Michtom, a toy shop owner in Brooklyn, to create the "teddy bear." The toy became a runaway success in the United States and abroad.

federal funds from public land sales to pay for irrigation and land development projects. Thus it was the federal government that began the large-scale transformation of the West's landscape and economy.

Gifford Pinchot

Roosevelt also backed efforts to save the nation's forests through careful management of the timber resources of the West. He appointed his close friend Gifford Pinchot to head the United States Forest Service. "The natural resources," Pinchot said, "must be developed and preserved for the benefit of the many and not merely for the profit of a few."

As progressives, Roosevelt and Pinchot both believed that trained experts in forestry and resource management should apply the same scientific standards to the landscape that others were applying to the management of cities and industry. They rejected the laissez-faire argument that the best way to preserve public land was to sell it to lumber companies, who would then carefully conserve it because it was the source of their profits. With the president's support, Pinchot's department drew up regulations controlling lumbering on federal lands.

Roosevelt took other steps as well to conserve the nation's resources. He added over 100 million acres to the protected national forests, quadrupling their area, and established 5 new national parks and 51 federal wildlife reservations.

Roosevelt's Legacy

President Roosevelt changed the role of the federal government and the nature of the presidency. Increasingly, Americans began to look to the federal government to solve the nation's economic and social problems. Under Roosevelt, the

 Picturing **History**

Crowd Pleaser Teddy Roosevelt's energetic speaking style captivated audiences across the nation. What impact did he have on the office of the presidency?

executive branch of government had dramatically increased its power. The ICC could set rates, the Agriculture Department could inspect food, the Bureau of Corporations could monitor business, and the attorney general could rapidly bring antitrust lawsuits under the Expedition Act.

✓ **Reading Check** **Examining** How did Roosevelt's policies help the conservation of natural resources?

SECTION 2 ASSESSMENT

Checking for Understanding

1. **Define:** Square Deal, arbitration.
2. **Identify:** Northern Securities, United Mine Workers, Hepburn Act, Upton Sinclair.
3. **Explain** what was provided for in the Hepburn Act.

Reviewing Themes

4. **Individual Action** How did Upton Sinclair contribute to involving the federal government in protecting consumers?

Critical Thinking

5. **Drawing Conclusions** What impact did Roosevelt's use of the Sherman Antitrust Act have on business?
6. **Organizing** Use a graphic organizer similar to the one below to list the results of the Coal Strike of 1902.

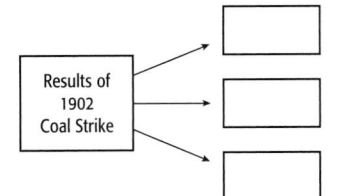

Analyzing Visuals

7. **Analyzing Political Cartoons** Look at the cartoon on page 556. Why are the giants depicted as they are? What do they represent? Roosevelt is called Jack the Giant-Killer. What fairy tale is being referred to?

Writing About History

8. **Descriptive Writing** Imagine you are living in the early 1900s and have just read Sinclair's *The Jungle.* Write a letter to a friend explaining what the novel is about and how it characterizes the Progressive era.

CATHEDRAL RANGE

Clou
9,926 ft

Yosemite
Point

Eagle
Peak

Upper
Yosemite Falls
1,430 ft. (436 m)

El Capitan
7,569 ft. (2,307 m)

Royal Arches

Yosemite Falls
total drop
2,425 ft. (739 m)

Cath
Spi

Yosemite Valley
4,000 ft. (1,219 m)

Cathedral Rocks

Bridalveil Fall
620 ft. (189 m)

Merced River

Early National Parks

● Mount Rainier, 1899

● Sullys Hill, 1904

● Crater Lake, 1902

● Yellowstone, 1872

● Wind Cave, 1903

● Yosemite, 1890
● General Grant (Kings Canyon), 1890
● Sequoia, 1890

● Mesa Verde, 1906

Atlantic
Ocean

Pacific
Ocean

Gulf of Mexico

OUR GROWING HERITAGE

This map of the United States shows 9 of the national parks that existed by the end of President Theodore Roosevelt's administration. Roosevelt established 5 national parks, 4 of which still exist today. He also established 51 wildlife preserves and 150 national forests.

The Story of Yosemite

The image on the left shows the Yosemite Valley landscape with labeled features:

Dome (2,693 m)

Glacier Point 7,214 ft. (2,199 m)

Nevada Falls 594 ft. (181 m)

Sentinel Rock

idalveil Creek

The breathtaking beauty of the Yosemite Valley has always astounded visitors to California's High Sierra. In 1851 volunteer soldiers came upon the valley. One officer felt a "peculiar exalted sensation" as he marveled at his surroundings.

The officer's reaction was a natural one. Carved by glaciers and rivers, the seven-mile-long valley into which he and his men rode lies at an elevation of 4,000 feet (1219 m). Above them rose the near-vertical cliffs and great granite monoliths of El Capitan, Half Dome, and Cathedral Rocks. Down onto the valley floor poured the waters of Bridalveil Fall. A dozen other waterfalls spilled over sheer cliffs elsewhere in the valley, some of them— like Yosemite Falls at 2,425 feet (739 m)—among the highest on Earth. Within five years, horseback parties were coming to gaze at Bridalveil Fall and the face of El Capitan. The tourists had found Yosemite.

To guarantee that the public could continue to enjoy the beauty, in 1864 President Abraham Lincoln granted the valley to California as a wilderness preserve. In so doing, Lincoln laid the foundation for the national park system. (The first official national park, Yellowstone, was not created until eight years later.) By the late 1880s Yosemite was attracting about 5,000 visitors a year. John Muir and other conservationists were anxious to preserve the area. Muir had spent years tramping through the woods and up and down the

President Theodore Roosevelt and John Muir stand atop Glacier Point.

mountains and glaciers of the park. His compelling descriptions swayed many influential people. In 1890 Congress expanded the protected area and made Yosemite an official national park.

In many ways Yosemite established a pattern for our national park system. It started programs to teach visitors about native plants and wildlife and was the first park to build a museum to help visitors understand and enjoy the region.

In 1903 President Theodore Roosevelt visited the park with Muir. The natural beauty of the valley captivated the environmentalist president and stimulated his desire to protect vast areas of the country. "We are not building this country of ours for a day," declared Roosevelt. "It is to last through the ages." During his presidency Roosevelt enlarged Yosemite, established the U.S. Forest Service, and put millions of acres of land under federal protection. In 1916 the National Park Service was established, and today it manages more than 380 areas, including 57 national parks.

Sightseers admire Yosemite Falls as they ride along Glacier Point Trail in 1901. Today some 3.5 million tourists visit the park each year.

LEARNING FROM GEOGRAPHY

1. How was the Yosemite Valley formed?

2. How did the establishment of the national park system help to conserve natural resources?

Main Idea
President Taft continued with Roosevelt's Progressive policies, but he did not live up to the expectations of many progressives.

Key Terms and Names
Joseph G. Cannon, Payne-Aldrich Tariff, Richard Ballinger, syndicate, insubordination

Reading Strategy
Organizing As you read about progressivism in this section, complete a graphic organizer similar to the one below listing Taft's conflicts with the progressives.

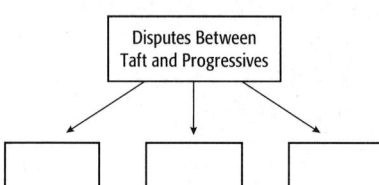

Disputes Between Taft and Progressives

Reading Objectives
• **Explain** how Theodore Roosevelt helped Taft get elected.
• **Discuss** why progressives were disappointed with Taft as president.

Section Theme
Continuity and Change Political differences with Roosevelt caused President Taft to lose Progressive support, even though he supported many Progressive policies.

Preview of Events

1908	1910	1912

1908
Taft elected president

1909
Ballinger-Pinchot controversy

1910
Mann-Elkins Act passed

1911
Antitrust lawsuit filed against U.S. Steel

1912
Roosevelt challenges Taft for Republican nomination

★ An American Story ★

One evening in January 1908, President Theodore Roosevelt sat chatting with Secretary of War William Howard Taft and his wife, Nellie, in the second-floor White House library. The mood was relaxed. Seated comfortably in his easy chair, Roosevelt was talking about a subject he had often discussed with his guests: the future role of Taft. Roosevelt toyed with a couple of options. "At one time it looks like the presidency," he mused, considering a future role for his trusted lieutenant, "then again it looks like the chief justiceship."

The Tafts knew that Roosevelt had the power to bring about either of these options. "Make it the presidency," interrupted Nellie Taft, always ambitious about her husband's career. Taft himself was less convinced that he would make a good chief executive. "Make it the chief justiceship," he uttered.

In the end, Taft bowed to the wishes of his wife and his boss. Following George Washington's example and honoring his own promise of 1904, Roosevelt decided not to seek reelection in 1908. Instead, he endorsed an experienced administrator and moderate progressive to run for president on the Republican ticket: William Howard Taft.

—adapted from *The American Heritage Pictorial History of the Presidents of the United States*

Taft Becomes President

Roosevelt loved "Smiling Bill" Taft like a brother and believed him to be the ideal person to continue his policies. He was, Roosevelt said, a leader who possessed "a scorn of all that is base and mean, a hearty sympathy with the oppressed [and a] kindly generosity of nature which makes him feel that all of his countrymen are in very truth his friends and brothers." Taft had been Roosevelt's most trusted lieutenant. He had served as a judge, as governor of the Philippines, and as Roosevelt's secretary of war. In fact, Taft seemed acceptable to almost everyone. Thanks to Roosevelt's efforts, he easily received his party's nomination. His victory in the general election in November 1908 was a foregone conclusion. The Democratic candidate, twice-defeated William Jennings Bryan, lost once more.

Taft's Approach to Government

"My dear Theodore," Taft wrote to his old friend a couple of weeks after assuming office. "When I am addressed as 'Mr. President,' I turn to see whether you are at my elbow." The comment was telling.

In that same letter, Taft admitted some of his early fears about his presidency:

> ❝I have no doubt that when you return you will find me very much under suspicion. . . . I have not the prestige which you had. . . . I am not attempting quite as much as you did . . . and so I fear that a large part of the public will feel as if I had fallen away from your ideals; but you know me better and will understand that I am still working away on the same old plan.❞
>
> —quoted in *The American Heritage Pictorial History of the Presidents of the United States*

Roosevelt and Taft were very different people. Roosevelt was a dynamic person who loved the spotlight and the rough-and-tumble world of politics. He had grand ideas and schemes but left the details of administering them to others. Taft was the opposite in many ways. He was a skillful administrator and judge. He disliked political maneuvering and preferred to avoid conflict with others. Unlike Roosevelt, who acted quickly and decisively on issues, Taft responded slowly, approaching problems from a legalistic point of view. "I don't like politics," he wrote, "I don't like the limelight." Although committed to many progressive ideas, Taft's personality and approach to politics quickly brought him into conflict with progressives.

Picturing **History**

Presidential Ritual In 1910 President Taft threw out the first baseball of the season at Lincoln Park in Washington, D.C., as his wife Nellie looked on. Why do you think presidents often continue this practice today?

Political Uproar Taft's interior secretary, Richard Ballinger, pictured at left, ignited controversy when he made nearly one million acres of public land available for development. Progressive Gifford Pinchot, at right, leaked the story to the press. How was the controversy resolved?

The Payne-Aldrich Tariff Act Like many progressives, Taft believed high tariffs limited competition, hurt consumers, and protected trusts. Roosevelt had warned him to stay away from tariff reform because it would divide the Republican Party. Taft, however, went ahead and called Congress into special session to lower tariff rates.

To pass a new tariff, Taft needed the help of Speaker of the House **Joseph G. Cannon.** As Speaker, Cannon appointed all committees and decided which bills they handled. By exercising almost total control over debate, Cannon could push some bills through without discussion and see that others never came to a vote. Progressives, however, wanted to unseat Cannon because he often blocked their legislation.

Taft disagreed with the effort to unseat Cannon. He pressured progressive Republicans into stopping their campaign against Cannon. In exchange, Cannon quickly pushed the tariff bill through the House of Representatives. Taft's compromise angered many progressives. The following year, they defied the president by joining with House Democrats and removing Cannon from power.

Taft further alienated progressives when the tariff bill went to the Senate. The powerful head of the Senate Finance Committee, Republican Nelson Aldrich from Rhode Island, wanted to protect high tariffs, as did many other conservative senators. The result was the **Payne-Aldrich Tariff,** which cut tariffs hardly at all and actually raised them on some goods.

After discussions with Aldrich and other senators, however, Taft decided to accept the new tariff.

Progressives felt betrayed and outraged by Taft's decision: "I knew the fire had gone out of [the Progressive movement]," recalled chief forester Gifford Pinchot after Roosevelt left office. "Washington was a dead town. Its leader was gone, and in his place [was] a man whose fundamental desire was to keep out of trouble."

The Ballinger-Pinchot Controversy With Taft's standing among Republican progressives deteriorating, a sensational controversy broke out late in 1909 that helped destroy Taft's popularity with reformers for good. Many progressives had been unhappy when Taft replaced Roosevelt's secretary of the interior, James R. Garfield, an aggressive conservationist, with **Richard A. Ballinger,** a more conservative corporate lawyer. Suspicion of Ballinger grew when he tried to make nearly a million acres of public forests and mineral reserves available for private development.

In the midst of this mounting concern, Gifford Pinchot charged the new secretary with having once plotted to turn over valuable public lands in Alaska to a private syndicate, or business group, for personal profit. Pinchot took the charges to the president. Taft's attorney general investigated the charges and decided they were groundless.

Still not satisfied, Pinchot leaked the story to the press and asked Congress to investigate. Taft fired

Pinchot for insubordination, or disobedience. The congressional committee appointed to study the controversy cleared Ballinger.

By signing the Payne-Aldrich Tariff Act, supporting Ballinger against Pinchot, and backing Cannon, Taft gave the impression that he had "sold the Square Deal down the river." Popular indignation was so great that the congressional elections of 1910 resulted in a sweeping Democratic victory, with Democrats taking the majority in the House and Democrats and Progressive Republicans grabbing control of the Senate from the conservatives.

Reading Check **Summarizing** What problems did President Taft have with progressives on tariff issues?

Taft's Progressive Reforms

Despite his political problems, Taft also had several successes. Although Roosevelt was nicknamed the "trustbuster," Taft was a strong supporter of competition and actually brought twice as many antitrust cases in four years as his predecessor had in seven.

In other areas, too, Taft was at least as strong a progressive as Roosevelt. Taft established the **Children's Bureau,** a federal agency similar to Roosevelt's Bureau of Corporations. The Children's Bureau investigated and publicized problems with child labor. Taft also supported the **Mann-Elkins Act** of 1910, which increased the regulatory powers of the ICC.

The Ballinger-Pinchot controversy aside, Taft was also a dedicated conservationist. His contributions in this area actually equaled or surpassed those of Roosevelt. He set up the Bureau of Mines to monitor the activities of mining companies, expanded the national forests, and protected waterpower sites from private development.

After Taft took office in 1909, Roosevelt left for a big-game hunt in Africa followed by a tour of Europe. He did not return to the United States until June 1910. Although disturbed by stories of Taft's "betrayal" of progressivism, Roosevelt at first refused to criticize the president.

In October 1911, Taft announced an antitrust lawsuit against U.S. Steel, claiming that the company's decision to buy the Tennessee Coal and Iron Company in 1907 had violated the Sherman Antitrust Act. The lawsuit was the final straw for Roosevelt. As president, he had approved U.S. Steel's plan to buy the company.

Roosevelt believed Taft's focus on breaking up trusts was destroying the carefully crafted system of cooperation and regulation that Roosevelt had established with big business through the Bureau of Corporations. In November 1911, Roosevelt publicly criticized Taft's decision. Roosevelt argued that the best way to deal with the trusts was to allow them to exist while at the same time increasing government's ability to regulate them.

Having broken with Taft, it was only a matter of time before progressives convinced Roosevelt to reenter politics. In late February 1912, Roosevelt announced that he would enter the presidential campaign of 1912 and attempt to replace Taft as the Republican nominee for president.

Reading Check **Evaluating** How did President Taft's accomplishments regarding conservation and trustbusting compare to President Roosevelt's?

SECTION 3 ASSESSMENT

Checking for Understanding

1. **Define:** syndicate, insubordination.
2. **Identify:** Joseph G. Cannon, Payne-Aldrich Tariff, Richard Ballinger.
3. **Describe** how Taft helped conservation efforts, alleviated child labor problems, and strengthened the ICC.

Reviewing Themes

4. **Continuity and Change** How did replacing Roosevelt's secretary of the interior cause a dispute between Taft and the progressives?

Critical Thinking

5. **Comparing** What was the difference between Roosevelt and Taft regarding the relationship between the president and Congress?
6. **Organizing** Use a graphic organizer like the one below to list Taft's Progressive reforms.

Taft's Progressive Reforms

Analyzing Visuals

7. **Examining Photographs** Study the photograph on page 563. Note the formal attire of the president and his wife. How would you compare the clothes the people in the photograph are wearing with today's style of dress for leisure activities?

Writing About History

8. **Descriptive Writing** Write a magazine article in which you defend or criticize President Taft's administration in terms of its support of progressivism.

Guide to Reading

Main Idea

Woodrow Wilson pursued a Progressive agenda after his 1912 election victory.

Key Terms and Names

Progressive Party, New Nationalism, New Freedom, income tax, Federal Reserve Act, Federal Trade Commission, unfair trade practices, National Association for the Advancement of Colored People

Reading Strategy

Categorizing As you read about progressivism during the Wilson administration, complete a chart similar to the one below by listing Wilson's Progressive economic and social reforms.

Economic Reforms	Social Reforms

Reading Objectives

• **Describe** Wilson's economic and social reforms.
• **Evaluate** the legacy of the Progressive movement.

Section Theme

Government and Democracy Woodrow Wilson's reforms greatly increased the federal government's role in regulating the nation's economy.

Preview of Events

♦1912	♦1914	♦1916

1912
Woodrow Wilson
elected president

1913
Federal Reserve
Act passed

1914
Federal Trade
Commission Act passed

1916
Keating-Owen Child
Labor Act passed

★ An American Story ★

On September 15, 1910, in the Taylor Opera House in Trenton, New Jersey, a young progressive named Joseph Patrick Tumulty watched as a lean man with iron-gray hair made his way toward the stage. The man was Thomas Woodrow Wilson, the Democratic Party's nominee for governor.

Wilson was the choice of the party bosses. As Tumulty recalled, progressives were "feeling sullen, beaten, and hopelessly impotent." To Tumulty's astonishment, Wilson announced: "I shall enter upon the duties of the office of governor, if elected, with absolutely no pledge of any kind to prevent me from serving the people of the state with singleness of purpose."

Tumulty knew that Wilson was declaring his independence from the New Jersey political machine. It brought the progressives at the convention roaring to their feet. From one came the cry, "Thank God, at last, a leader has come!"

Two years later, Woodrow Wilson was the Democrats' nominee for the presidency, an office they had won only twice since the Civil War. This time they were confident of victory, for Wilson, a committed progressive, faced a Republican Party wracked by division.

—adapted from *Wilson: The Road to the White House*

The Election of 1912

The 1912 presidential campaign featured a current president, a former president, and an academic who had entered politics only two years earlier. The election's outcome determined the path of the Progressive movement and helped shape the nation's path in the 1900s.

The Republican Party Splits Believing that President Taft had failed to live up to Progressive ideals, Theodore Roosevelt informed seven state governors that he was willing to accept the Republican nomination. "My hat is in the ring!" he declared. "The fight is on."

The struggle for control of the Republican Party reached its climax at the national convention in Chicago in June. Conservatives rallied behind Taft. Most of the progressives lined up for Roosevelt. When it became clear that Taft's delegates controlled the nomination, Roosevelt decided to leave the party and campaign as an independent. "We stand at Armageddon," he told his supporters, "and we battle for the Lord."

Declaring himself "fit as a bull moose," Roosevelt became the presidential candidate for the newly formed **Progressive Party,** nicknamed the Bull Moose Party. Because Taft had alienated so many groups, the election of 1912 became a contest between two progressives: the Bull Moose Roosevelt and the Democrat Wilson.

Wilson's Character and Background Woodrow Wilson entered politics as a firm progressive. As governor of New Jersey, he pushed one Progressive reform after another through the statehouse. He revamped election laws, established utility regulatory boards, and allowed cities to change to the commissioner form of government. In less than two years, New Jersey became a model of Progressive reform.

"New Freedom" Versus "New Nationalism" The election of 1912 was a contest between two men who supported progressivism, although they had different approaches to reform. Roosevelt accepted the economic power of the trusts as a fact of life and proposed a more powerful federal government and a strong executive to regulate them. Roosevelt also outlined a complete program of reforms. He favored legislation to protect women and children in the labor force and supported workers' compensation for those injured on the job. He also wanted a federal trade commission to regulate industry in a manner similar to the ICC's authority over railroads. Roosevelt called his program the **New Nationalism.**

Wilson countered with what he called the **New Freedom.** He criticized Roosevelt's program as one that supported "regulated monopoly." Monopolies, he believed, were evils to be destroyed, not regulated. Wilson argued that Roosevelt's approach gave the federal government too much power in the economy

and did nothing to restore competition. Freedom, in Wilson's opinion, was more important than efficiency. "The history of liberty," Wilson declared, "is the history of the limitation of governmental power. . . . If America is not to have free enterprise, then she can have freedom of no sort whatever."

Wilson Is Elected As expected, Roosevelt and Taft split the Republican voters, enabling Wilson to win the Electoral College and the election with 435 votes, even though he received less than 42 percent of the popular vote—less than Roosevelt and Taft combined. For the first time since Grover Cleveland's election in 1892, a Democrat became president of the United States.

✓ **Reading Check** **Summarizing** Who were the three major candidates in the presidential election of 1912?

Regulating the Economy

The new chief executive lost no time in embarking on his program of reform. He immediately took charge of the government. "The president is at liberty, both in law and conscience, to be as big a man as he can,"

Picturing **History**

The New Freedom Woodrow Wilson initially believed that government should break up trusts. Why did Wilson favor economic competition?

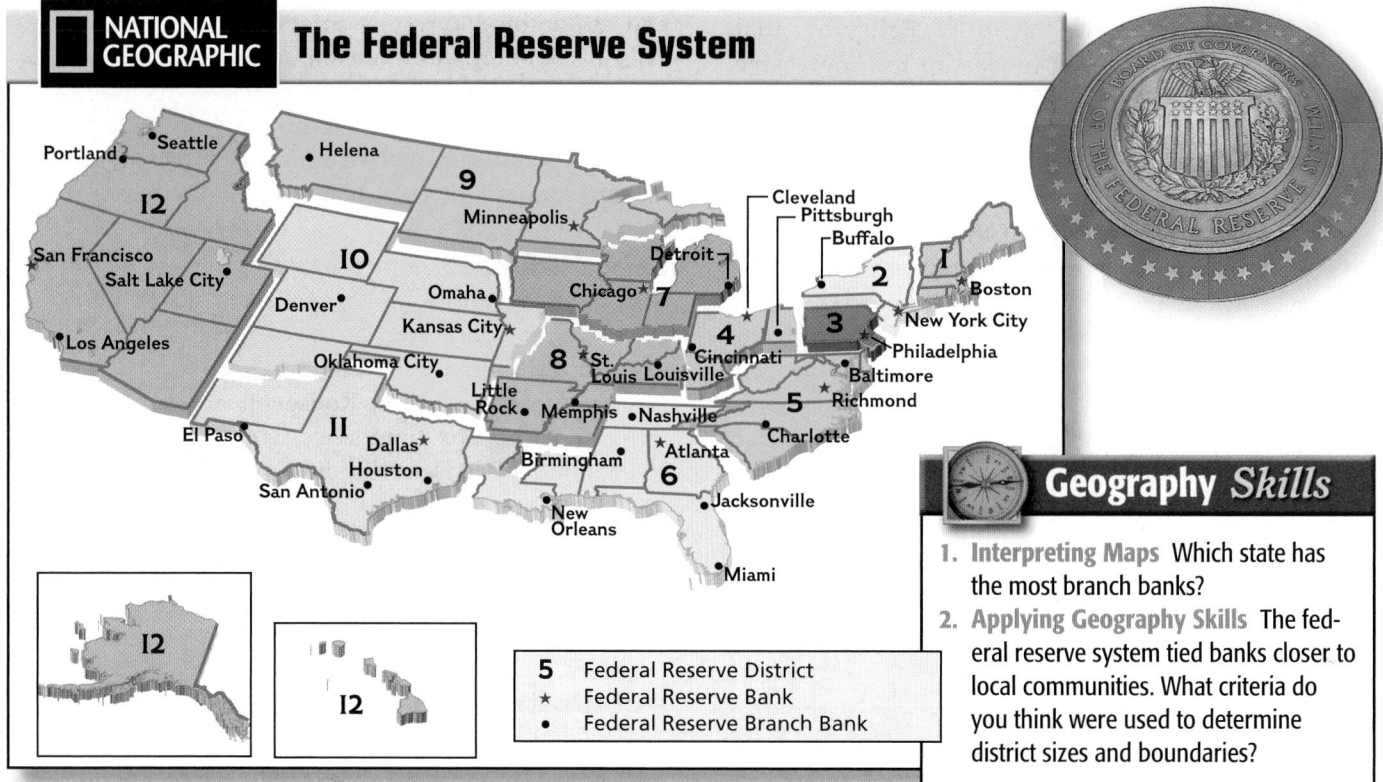

NATIONAL GEOGRAPHIC
The Federal Reserve System

Portland • Seattle
Helena
12
9
Minneapolis ★
San Francisco ★
Salt Lake City
10
Denver •
Omaha •
Chicago ★ 7
Detroit
Cleveland
Pittsburgh
Buffalo
1
2
Boston
Los Angeles •
Kansas City ★
Oklahoma City •
8
St. Louis ★
Louisville
Cincinnati
4
3
New York City
Philadelphia
Baltimore
El Paso •
11
Little Rock •
Memphis •
Nashville •
5
Richmond
Dallas ★
Houston •
Birmingham •
Atlanta ★
Charlotte
San Antonio •
New Orleans •
6
Jacksonville •
Miami •

12 (Alaska)
12 (Hawaii)

5	Federal Reserve District
★	Federal Reserve Bank
•	Federal Reserve Branch Bank

Geography Skills

1. **Interpreting Maps** Which state has the most branch banks?
2. **Applying Geography Skills** The federal reserve system tied banks closer to local communities. What criteria do you think were used to determine district sizes and boundaries?

Wilson had once written. "His capacity will set the limit." During his eight years as president, Wilson demonstrated his power as he crafted reforms affecting tariffs, the banking system, trusts, and workers' rights.

Reforming Tariffs Five weeks after taking office, Wilson appeared before Congress, the first president to do so since John Adams. He had come to present his bill to reduce tariffs.

He personally lobbied members of Congress to support the tariff reduction bill. Not even Roosevelt had taken such an active role in promoting special legislation. In Wilson's message to Congress, he declared that high tariffs had "built up a set of privileges and exemptions from competition behind which it was easy . . . to organize monopoly until . . . nothing is obliged to stand the tests of efficiency and economy."

Wilson believed that the pressure of foreign competition would lead American manufacturers to improve their products and lower their prices. Lower tariff rates, he claimed, would help businesses by putting them under the "constant necessity to be efficient, economical, and enterprising."

In 1913 the Democrat-controlled Congress passed the **Underwood Tariff** and Wilson signed it into law. This piece of legislation reduced the average tariff on imported goods to about 30 percent of the value of the goods, or about half the tariff rate of the 1890s.

An important section of the Underwood Tariff Act was the provision for levying an income tax, or a direct tax on the earnings of individuals and corporations. The Constitution originally prohibited direct taxes unless they were apportioned among the states on the basis of population. In other words, the states would be paying the income tax, not individuals, and states with more people would pay more tax. Passage of the Sixteenth Amendment in 1913, however, made it legal for the federal government to tax the income of individuals directly.

ECONOMY

Reforming the Banks The United States had not had a central bank since the 1830s. During the economic depressions that hit the country periodically after that time, hundreds of small banks collapsed, wiping out the life savings of many of their customers. The most recent of these crises had been in 1907.

To restore public confidence in the banking system, Wilson supported the establishment of a Federal Reserve system. Banks would have to keep a portion of their deposits in a regional reserve bank, which would provide a financial cushion against unanticipated losses.

At the center of the Federal Reserve system would be a Board of Governors, appointed by the president. The Board could set the interest rates the reserve banks charged other banks, thereby indirectly controlling the interest rates of the entire nation and the amount of money in circulation. This gave the Board the ability to fight inflation by raising interest rates and to stimulate the economy during a recession by lowering interest rates. Congress approved the new system at the end of 1913. The **Federal Reserve Act** became one of the most significant pieces of legislation in American history.

Antitrust Action During his campaign, Wilson had promised to restore competition to the economy by breaking up big business monopolies. Roosevelt argued that Wilson's ideas were unrealistic because big business was more efficient and unlikely to be replaced by smaller, more competitive firms. Once in office, Wilson's opinion shifted, and he came to agree with Roosevelt—but progressives in Congress continued to demand action against big business.

In the summer of 1914, at Wilson's request, Congress created the **Federal Trade Commission** (FTC) to monitor American business. The FTC had the power to investigate companies and issue "cease and desist" orders against companies engaging in unfair trade practices, or those which hurt competition. The FTC could be taken to court if a business disagreed with its rulings.

Wilson did not want the FTC to break up big business. Instead, it was to work with business to limit activities that unfairly limited competition. He deliberately appointed conservative business leaders to serve as the FTC's first commissioners.

Wilson's approach did not satisfy progressives in Congress, who responded by passing the **Clayton Antitrust Act.** The act banned tying agreements, which required retailers who bought from one company to stop selling a competitor's products. It also banned price discrimination. Businesses could not charge different customers different prices. Manufacturers could no longer give discounts to chain stores and other retailers who bought a large volume of goods.

Before the act passed, labor unions lobbied Congress to exempt unions from the antitrust laws. The Clayton Antitrust Act specifically declared that unions were not unlawful combinations in restraint of trade. When the bill became law, Samuel Gompers, head of the American Federation of Labor, called the Clayton Antitrust Act the worker's "Magna Carta," because it gave unions the right to exist.

Reading Check **Evaluating** What was the impact of the passage of the Sixteenth Amendment?

Federal Aid and Social Welfare

By the fall of 1914, Wilson believed that his New Freedom program was essentially complete. As a result, he began to retreat from activism.

The congressional elections of 1914, however, shattered the president's complacency. Democrats suffered major losses in the House of Representatives, and voters who had supported the Bull Moose Party in 1912 began returning to the Republicans. Realizing that he would not be able to rely on a divided opposition when he ran for re-election in 1916, Wilson began to support further reforms.

In 1916, for example, Wilson signed the first federal law regulating child labor. The Keating-Owen Child Labor Act prohibited the employment of children under the age of 14 in factories producing goods for interstate commerce. The Supreme Court

The NAACP

Past
Violent race riots broke out in 1908 in Springfield, Illinois, as immigrants and African Americans vied with other residents for scarce jobs. In one riot, a mob killed several African Americans and destroyed much property. Responding to the growing racial violence in the nation, an integrated group of citizens met in New York City to discuss remedies. Out of that meeting, the National Association for the Advancement of Colored People (NAACP) was born.

Present
Today the NAACP works for such causes as school desegregation, fair housing and employment, voter registration, and equal health care and income opportunity. It plays a role in establishing legal precedents to improve the quality of life for African Americans across the nation.

declared the law unconstitutional on the grounds that child labor was not interstate commerce and therefore only states could regulate it. Wilson's effort, however, helped his reputation with progressive voters. Wilson also supported the Adamson Act, which established the eight-hour workday for railroad workers, and the Federal Farm Loan Act, which created 12 Federal Land Banks to provide farmers with long-term loans at low interest rates.

✓ Reading Check **Examining** How did the Adamson Act improve labor conditions in the United States?

The Legacy of Progressivism

During his presidency, Wilson had built upon Roosevelt's foundation. He expanded the role of the federal government and of the president.

A New Kind of Government Progressivism made important changes in the political life of the United States. Before this era, most Americans did not expect the government to pass laws protecting workers or regulating big business. In fact, many courts had previously ruled that it was unconstitutional for the government to do so.

By the end of the Progressive era, however, both legal and public opinion had shifted. Increasingly, Americans expected the government, particularly the federal government, to play a more active role in regulating the economy and solving social problems.

The Limits of Progressivism The most conspicuous limit to progressivism was its failure to address African American reform issues. African Americans themselves, however, were absorbing the reform spirit, which fueled their longstanding desire for advancement.

In 1905 W.E.B. Du Bois and 28 other African American leaders met at Niagara Falls to demand full political rights and responsibilities for African Americans. They met on the Canadian side of the falls because no hotel on the American side would accept them. There they launched what became known as the Niagara Movement. This meeting was one of many steps leading to the founding of the **National Association for the Advancement of Colored People** (NAACP) in 1909. Du Bois and other NAACP founders believed that the vote was essential to bring about an end to lynching and racial discrimination. "The power of the ballot we need in sheer self-defense," Du Bois said, "else what shall save us from a second slavery?"

Despite the failure of most progressives to focus on racial issues, Progressive reform helped change American society in many ways. Although they excluded many groups from their efforts, the progressives expanded democracy and improved the quality of life for millions of men, women, and children. As the country entered World War I, however, Americans soon turned from reforming their own society to a crusade to "make the world safe for democracy."

✓ Reading Check **Evaluating** How did progressivism change American beliefs about the federal government?

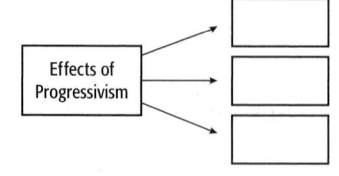

SECTION 4 ASSESSMENT

Checking for Understanding

1. **Define:** income tax, unfair trade practices.
2. **Identify:** Progressive Party, New Nationalism, New Freedom, Federal Reserve Act, Federal Trade Commission, National Association for the Advancement of Colored People.
3. **Explain** why President Wilson proposed the establishment of the Federal Reserve System.

Reviewing Themes

4. **Government and Democracy** What new federal agencies increased the government's power to regulate the economy?

Critical Thinking

5. **Forming an Opinion** Which of Wilson's reforms do you consider most important? Why?
6. **Organizing** Use a graphic organizer similar to the one below to list the effects progressivism had on American society.

```
               ┌──────┐
             ↗ │      │
┌──────────┐   └──────┘
│ Effects of│→ ┌──────┐
│Progressivism│ │      │
└──────────┘   └──────┘
             ↘ ┌──────┐
               │      │
               └──────┘
```

Analyzing Visuals

7. **Analyzing Photographs** Study the photograph on page 571. What details do you see in the image that might have contributed to tainted meat? When do you think the stamp above the photo began to be used?

Writing About History

8. **Expository Writing** Imagine that you are a newspaper editor during President Wilson's administration. Write an article on the shortcomings of the Progressive movement in terms of its attitudes about race. Provide ideas about how the movement might have addressed discrimination and segregation.

American LITERATURE

Born in Maryland in 1878, **Upton Sinclair** spent his life writing about and trying to change what he saw as wrong in the United States. One of his most famous novels, *The Jungle*, deals with working conditions and the rights of immigrants. The novel tells the story of Jurgis Rudkus, a Lithuanian immigrant who comes to the United States with his family in the early 1900s, dreaming of wealth and freedom. What he finds is "Packingtown," the bustling, filthy stockyards of Chicago. In the following excerpt, Sinclair describes the system Jurgis comes to know after gaining his first job in a meatpacking plant.

Read to Discover
What qualities did Sinclair believe a person must have to succeed in Packingtown?

Reader's Dictionary
pitted: set against each other

caldron: a large kettle or pot for boiling

knave: a tricky, deceitful person

from The Jungle
by Upton Sinclair

After Jurgis had been there awhile he would know that the plants were simply honeycombed with rottenness . . . —the bosses grafted off the men, and they grafted off each other; and some day the superintendent would find out about the boss, and then he would graft off the boss. . . . Here was Durham's, for instance, owned by a man who was trying to make as much money out of it as he could, and did not care in the least how he did it; and underneath him . . . were managers and superintendents and foremen, each one driving the man next below him and trying to squeeze out of him as much work as possible. And all the men of the same rank were pitted against each other. . . . So from top to bottom the place was simply a seething caldron of jealousies and hatreds; there was no loyalty or decency anywhere about it, there was no place in it where a man counted for anything against a dollar. . . .

Jurgis would find these things out for himself, if he stayed there long enough; it was the men [like him] who had to do all the dirty jobs. . . . Jurgis had come there, and thought he was going to make himself useful, and rise and become a skilled man; but he would soon find out his error—for nobody rose in Packingtown by doing good work. [I]f you met a man who was

rising in Packingtown, you met a knave. . . . [T]he man who minded his own business and did his work— why, they would (wear) him out, and then . . . throw him into the gutter.

Analyzing Literature
1. According to the passage, what is the plant owner's main goal?

2. What does Sinclair mean when he says, ". . . there was no place in it where a man counted for anything against a dollar. . . ."?

Interdisciplinary Activity
Government When it was published, *The Jungle* was so shocking that it launched a government investigation of the meatpacking industry. The investigation eventually led to laws regulating the industry. Using the Internet, research these laws and read about how they are enforced today. Write a short report on your findings.

Reviewing Key Terms

On a sheet of paper, use each of these terms in a sentence.

1. progressivism
2. muckraker
3. commission plan
4. direct primary
5. initiative
6. referendum
7. recall
8. suffrage
9. temperance
10. prohibition
11. socialism
12. Square Deal
13. arbitration
14. syndicate
15. insubordination
16. income tax
17. unfair trade practices

Reviewing Key Facts

18. **Identify:** Robert La Follette, Alice Paul, Hepburn Act, Upton Sinclair, Payne-Aldrich Tariff, Federal Reserve Act, Federal Trade Commission.
19. What were the characteristics of the Progressive era?
20. How did President Roosevelt influence the outcome of the 1902 coal strike?
21. How did President Wilson attempt to reform the banking industry?

Critical Thinking

22. **Analyzing Themes: Government and Democracy** How did Wisconsin governor Robert La Follette help to expand democracy in the United States?
23. **Analyzing** How did Progressive reforms strengthen the cause of woman suffrage?
24. **Evaluating** What was the impact of reform leaders such as W.E.B. Du Bois and Robert La Follette on American society?
25. **Organizing** Use a graphic organizer similar to the one below to list the economic, political, and social welfare reforms brought about during the Progressive era.

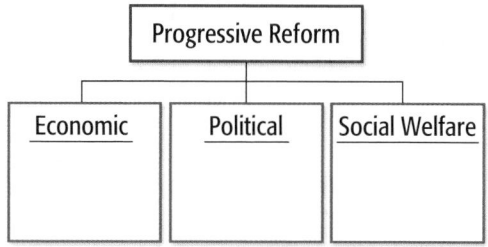

26. **Interpreting Primary Sources** Ida Husted Harper was a social reformer, a newspaper reporter, and a strong supporter of suffrage for women. In the following excerpt, she examines the attitudes of the time toward the kinds of work women should do.

Chapter Summary

Basic Beliefs of Progressives

- People could improve society by relying on science and knowledge.
- Industrialism and urbanization caused problems.
- Government should fix problems.
- To achieve reform, government itself had to be reformed.

Government Reforms

- Commission and city-manager forms of government were adopted.
- Direct primary system let citizens choose office candidates.
- Initiative, referendum, and recall were adopted.
- Seventeenth Amendment gave voters right to elect senators directly.
- Nineteenth Amendment gave women the right to vote.

Business Regulation

- Interstate Commerce Commission was strengthened.
- Consumer protection laws were passed.
- Federal Trade Commission was set up to regulate business.
- Federal Reserve System was set up to control money supply.

Social Reforms

- Zoning laws and building codes improved urban housing.
- Child labor laws were passed.
- Workers' compensation laws were passed.
- Temperance movement worked to ban alcohol.

NATIONAL GEOGRAPHIC **The Progressive Movement and State Governments 1889–1912**

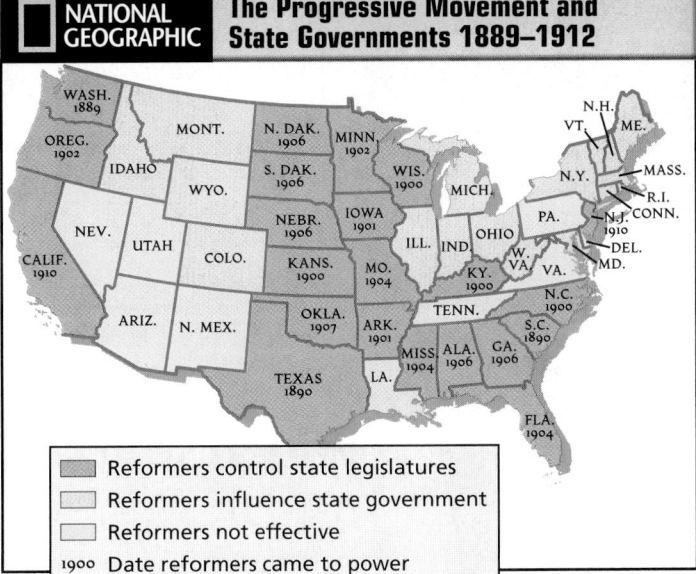

Legend:
- Reformers control state legislatures
- Reformers influence state government
- Reformers not effective
- 1900 Date reformers came to power

66The moment we accept the theory that women must enter wage-earning occupations only when compelled to do so by poverty, that moment we degrade labor and lower the status of all women who are engaged in it. This theory prevailed throughout past ages, and it placed a stigma upon working women which is only beginning to be removed by the present generation. . . .

There is not, there never has been, an effort 'to create a sentiment that home is no place for a girl.' A good home is the one place above all others for a girl, as it is for a boy. It is her rest, her haven, her protection, but this does not necessarily imply that she must not engage in any work outside its limits. . . .

It is wholly impracticable to draw a dividing line between the employments which are suitable and those which are unsuitable for women. They have just as much right as men to decide this question for themselves. . . .

It is not intended to argue that every woman should leave the home and go into business, but only that those who wish to do so shall have the opportunity, and that men shall no longer monopolize the gainful occupations.99

—quoted in *The Independent,* 1901

a. What views does Ida Harper have on the kinds of work women should do?

b. What kinds of work-related issues do women face today?

Practicing Skills

27. **Taking Notes** Reread the subsection titled "The Coal Strike of 1902" on pages 556 and 557. Then use the steps you learned about taking notes on page 554 to take notes on the subsection.

Chapter Activities

28. **Technology** Search the Internet for an article written by a muckraker mentioned in the chapter. Using a word processor, prepare a two-page summary of the article and indicate how its contents may have sparked the demand for reform.

29. **Research Project** Worker safety was an important issue for progressives. Research three worker safety laws in your state, and describe how they benefit workers. Present your findings in a written report.

Writing Activity

30. **Informative Writing** Imagine you are a reporter in 1906, assigned to interview Upton Sinclair. Reread pages 558 and 571, then prepare a list of questions to ask him during the interview.

Geography and History

31. The map above shows the relationship between the Progressive movement and state governments. Study the map and answer the questions below.
    a. **Interpreting Maps** Which three states came under the control of reformers before Wisconsin did?
    b. **Applying Geography Skills** What generalization can you make about progressives in state governments?

Standardized Test Practice

Directions: Choose the best answer to the following question.

In 1920 women won an important victory when the Nineteenth Amendment was ratified. What did this amendment accomplish?

A It required colleges to accept women.

B It guaranteed child care for workers' children.

C It granted women the right to vote.

D It guaranteed equal wages for equal work.

Test-Taking Tip: Some answers can be eliminated by using your own knowledge. For example, you probably know that child care is still an issue for parents today, so it cannot be guaranteed in the Nineteenth Amendment. Therefore, you can eliminate answer B.

CHAPTER 19

World War I and Its Aftermath

1914–1920

Why It Matters

The United States reluctantly entered World War I after German submarines violated American neutrality. After the war ended, President Wilson supported the Treaty of Versailles, believing its terms would prevent another war. The U.S. Senate, however, rejected the treaty. It did not want the country to be tied to European obligations. Instead, Americans turned their attention to the difficult adjustment to peacetime.

The Impact Today

The experience of World War I had a long-term effect on American history.
- The United States continues to be involved in European affairs.
- The horrors of the conflict helped reshape how people view warfare.

The American Vision Video The Chapter 19 video, "Cousins: Royalty and World War I," explains how royal marriages and complex political alliances contributed to the outbreak of war in Europe.

1913
- Woodrow Wilson begins his first presidential term

"The world must be made safe for Democracy!"
—WOODROW WILSON—

1915
- The *Lusitania* is sunk

1917
- U.S. enters war

United States
Wilson 1913–1921
PRESIDENTS

1913   *1915*   *1917*

World

1914
- Archduke Franz Ferdinand assassinated; war begins in Europe

1915
- Italy joins Allies in war
- Japan gains rights in Chinese territory

1916
- British suppress Easter Rebellion in Ireland
- Battle of the Somme begins in July

1917
- Bolshevik Revolution begins in October
- Balfour Declaration favors setting up a Jewish homeland in Palestine

American soldiers in the 23rd Infantry fire on German positions in the Argonne Forest.

1918
- Congress passes Sedition Act
- Battle of Argonne Forest begins in September
- Armistice ends fighting on November 11

1919
- Race riots and strikes take place in Northern cities
- Red Scare and Palmer raids target Communists in the U.S.

Harding 1921–1923

1919

1921

1918
- Treaty of Brest-Litovsk ends Russian-German war

1919
- Treaty of Versailles conference begins

1920
- British government creates the Northern Ireland province

1921
- Irish Free State established by signed treaty

HISTORY Online

Chapter Overview
Visit the *American Vision* Web site at tav.glencoe.com and click on **Chapter Overviews—Chapter 19** to preview chapter information.

The United States Enters World War I

Main Idea

Although the United States tried to remain neutral, events soon pushed the nation into World War I.

Key Terms and Names

Pancho Villa, guerrilla, nationalism, self-determination, Franz Ferdinand, Allies, Central Powers, propaganda, contraband, U-boat, Sussex Pledge, Zimmermann telegram

Reading Strategy

Organizing As you read about the start of World War I, complete a graphic organizer similar to the one below by identifying the factors that contributed to the conflict.

Factors Contributing to World War I

Reading Objectives

- **Discuss** the causes and results of American intervention in Mexico and the Caribbean.
- **Explain** the causes of World War I and why the United States entered the war.

Section Theme

Continuity and Change Ties with the British influenced American leaders to enter World War I on the side of the Allies.

Preview of Events

♦1914   ♦1915   ♦1916   ♦1917

April 1914
U.S. Marines occupy Veracruz, Mexico

June 1914
Assassination of Archduke Franz Ferdinand

July 1914
World War I begins

May 1915
Sinking of the *Lusitania*

April 1917
United States enters the war

★ An American Story ★

Edith O'Shaughnessy could not sleep on the rainy night of April 20, 1914. Living at the American embassy in Mexico City, the wife of diplomat Nelson O'Shaughnessy was well aware of the growing crisis between Mexico and the United States. Earlier that day, President Wilson had asked Congress to authorize the use of force against Mexico. In her diary, O'Shaughnessy described the tensions in the Mexican capital:

❝I can't sleep. National and personal potentialities [possibilities] are surging through my brain. Three stalwart railroad men came to the Embassy this evening. They brought reports of a plan for the massacre of Americans in the street to-night, but, strange and wonderful thing, a heavy rain is falling. . . . Rain is as potent as shell-fire in clearing the streets, and I don't think there will be any trouble.❞

The next day, O'Shaughnessy reported that the conflict had begun: "We are in Mexico, in full intervention! . . . Marines are due to-day in Vera Cruz. . . ."

—**adapted from *A Diplomat's Wife in Mexico***

Woodrow Wilson's Diplomacy

As president, Wilson resolved to "strike a new note in international affairs" and to see that "sheer honesty and even unselfishness . . . should prevail over nationalistic self-seeking in American foreign policy." Wilson strongly opposed imperialism. He also believed that democracy was essential to a nation's stability and prosperity, and that the United States should promote democracy in order to ensure a peaceful world free of revolution and war. During Wilson's presidency, however, other forces at work at home and abroad frustrated his hope to lead the world by moral example. In fact, Wilson's first international crisis was awaiting him when he took office in March 1913.

The Mexican Revolution

From 1884 to 1911, a dictator, Porfirio Díaz, ruled Mexico. Díaz encouraged foreign investment in Mexico to help develop the nation's industry. A few wealthy landowners dominated Mexican society. The majority of the people were poor and landless, and they were increasingly frustrated by their circumstances. In 1911 a revolution erupted, forcing Díaz to flee the country.

Francisco Madero, a reformer who appeared to support democracy, constitutional government, and land reform, replaced Díaz. Madero, however, proved to be an unskilled administrator. Frustrated with Mexico's continued decline, army officers plotted against Madero. Shortly before Wilson took office, General **Victoriano Huerta** seized power in Mexico, and Madero was murdered—presumably on Huerta's orders.

Huerta's brutality repulsed Wilson, who refused to recognize the new government. Wilson was convinced that without the support of the United States, Huerta soon would be overthrown. Wilson therefore tried to prevent weapons from reaching Huerta, and he permitted Americans to arm other political factions within Mexico.

Wilson Sends Troops Into Mexico

In April 1914, American sailors visiting the city of Tampico were arrested after entering a restricted area. Though they were quickly released, their American commander demanded an apology. The Mexicans refused. Wilson used the refusal as an opportunity to overthrow Huerta. He sent marines to seize the Mexican port of Veracruz.

Although the president expected the Mexican people to welcome his action, anti-American riots broke out in Mexico. Wilson then accepted international mediation to settle the dispute. Venustiano Carranza, whose forces had acquired arms from the United States, became Mexico's president.

Mexican forces opposed to Carranza were not appeased, and they conducted raids into the United States hoping to force Wilson to intervene. **Pancho Villa** (VEE·yah) led a group of guerrillas—an

Picturing **History**

Moral Imperialism President Wilson sent General John Pershing (below) to stop Pancho Villa's (right) raids into the United States. *Why was Villa conducting these raids?*

armed band that uses surprise attacks and sabotage rather than open warfare—that burned the town of Columbus, New Mexico, and killed a number of Americans. Wilson responded by sending 6,000 U.S. troops under General **John J. Pershing** across the border to find and capture Villa. The expedition dragged on as Pershing failed to capture the guerrillas. Wilson's growing concern over the war raging in Europe finally caused him to recall Pershing's troops in 1917.

Wilson's Mexican policy damaged U.S. foreign relations. The British ridiculed the president's attempt to "shoot the Mexicans into self-government." Latin Americans regarded his "moral imperialism" as no improvement on Theodore Roosevelt's "big stick" diplomacy. In fact, Wilson followed Roosevelt's example in the Caribbean. During his first term, Wilson sent marines into Nicaragua, Haiti, and the Dominican Republic to preserve order and to set up governments that he hoped would be more stable and democratic than the current regimes.

✓ **Reading Check** **Examining** Why did President Wilson intervene in Mexico?

The Outbreak of World War I

Despite more than 40 years of general peace, tensions among European nations were building in 1914. Throughout the late 1800s and early 1900s, a number of factors created problems among the powers of Europe and set the stage for a monumental war.

The Alliance System

The roots of World War I date back to the 1860s. In 1864, while Americans fought the Civil War, the German kingdom of Prussia launched the first of a series of wars to unite the various German states into one nation. By 1871 Prussia had united Germany and proclaimed the birth of the German Empire. The new German nation rapidly industrialized and quickly became one of the most powerful nations in the world.

The creation of Germany transformed European politics. In 1870, as part of their plan to unify Germany, the Prussians had attacked and defeated France. They then forced the French to give up territory along the German border. From that point forward, France and Germany were enemies. To protect itself, Germany signed alliances with Italy and with Austria-Hungary, a huge empire that controlled much of southeastern Europe. This became known as the **Triple Alliance.**

The new alliance alarmed Russian leaders, who feared that Germany intended to expand eastward into Russia. Russia and Austria-Hungary were also competing for influence in southeastern Europe. Many of the people of southeastern Europe were Slavs—the same ethnic group as the Russians—and the Russians wanted to support them against Austria-Hungary. As a result, Russia and France had a common interest in opposing Germany and Austria-Hungary. In 1894 they signed the Franco-Russian Alliance.

The Naval Race

While the other major powers of Europe divided into competing alliances, Great Britain remained neutral. Then, in 1898, the Germans began to build a navy challenging Great Britain's historical dominance at sea. By the early 1900s, an arms race had begun between Great Britain and Germany, as both sides raced to build warships. The naval race greatly increased tensions between Germany and Britain and convinced the British to establish closer relations with France and Russia. The British refused to sign a formal alliance, so their new relationship with the French and Russians became known as an "entente cordiale"—a friendly understanding. Britain, France, and Russia became known as the **Triple Entente.**

The Balkan Crisis

By the late 1800s, nationalism, or a feeling of intense pride of one's homeland, had become a powerful idea in Europe. Nationalists place

Fateful Couple Archduke Franz Ferdinand and wife Sophia visit Sarajevo the day of the assassination.

primary emphasis on promoting their homeland's culture and interests above those of other countries. Nationalism was one of the reasons for the tensions among the European powers. Each nation viewed the others as competitors, and many people were willing to go to war to expand their nation at the expense of others.

One of the basic ideas of nationalism is the right to self-determination—the idea that people who belong to a nation should have their own country and government. In the 1800s, nationalism led to a crisis in southeastern Europe in the region known as the **Balkans.** Historically, the Ottoman Empire and the Austro-Hungarian Empire had ruled the Balkans. Both of these empires were made up of many different nations. As nationalism became a powerful force in the 1800s, the different national groups within these empires began to press for independence.

Among the groups pushing for independence were the Serbs, Bosnians, Croats, and Slovenes. These people all spoke similar languages and had come to see themselves as one people. They called themselves South Slavs, or Yugoslavs. The first of these people to obtain independence were the Serbs, who formed a nation called Serbia between the Ottoman and Austro-Hungarian empires. Serbs believed their nation's mission was to unite the South Slavs.

Russia supported the Serbs, while Austria-Hungary did what it could to limit Serbia's growth. In 1908 Austria-Hungary annexed Bosnia, which at the time belonged to the Ottoman Empire. The Serbs were furious. They wanted Bosnia to be part of their nation. The annexation demonstrated to the Serbs that Austria-Hungary had no intention of letting the Slavic people in its empire become independent.

A Continent Goes to War

In late June 1914, the heir to the Austro-Hungarian throne, the Archduke **Franz Ferdinand,** visited the Bosnian capital of Sarajevo. As he and his wife rode through the city, a Bosnian revolutionary named Gavrilo Princip rushed their open car and shot the couple to death. The assassin was a member of a Serbian nationalist group nicknamed the "Black Hand." The assassination took place with the knowledge of Serbian officials who hoped to start a war that would bring down the Austro-Hungarian Empire.

The Austro-Hungarian government blamed Serbia for the attack and decided the time had come to crush Serbia in order to prevent Slavic nationalism from undermining its empire. Knowing an

NATIONAL GEOGRAPHIC

European Alliances, 1914

0 ____ 500 miles
0 ____ 500 kilometers
Lambert Azimuthal Equal-Area projection

June 28, 1914
Archduke Franz Ferdinand assassinated by Serb nationalist.

Bulgaria joined the Central Powers in 1915. Romania joined the Allies in 1916.

Italy refused to honor Central Powers alliance and joined Allied Powers on May 23, 1915.

Greece did not enter the war until 1917.

Legend:
- Allied Powers
- Central Powers
- Neutral nations
- → Initial troop movements of Central Powers

Geography *Skills*

1. **Interpreting Maps** Which nations comprised the Central Powers in 1914?
2. **Applying Geography Skills** What was the name of the southeastern European region that sparked the beginning of the war?

June 28
Assassination of Archduke Franz Ferdinand

July 28
Austria-Hungary declares war on Serbia

August 3
Germany declares war on France, begins invasion of Belgium

August 6
Austria-Hungary declares war on Russia

♦ July 1914   *♦ August 1914*

July 30
Russia begins mobilizing troops in defense of Serbia

August 1
Germany declares war on Russia

August 4
Britain declares war on Germany

August 12
France and Great Britain declare war on Austria-Hungary

attack on Serbia might trigger a war with Russia, the Austrians asked their German allies for support. Germany promised to support Austria-Hungary if war erupted.

Austria-Hungary then issued an ultimatum to the Serbian government. The Serbs counted on Russia to back them up, and the Russians, in turn, counted on France. French leaders were worried that they might someday be caught alone in a war with Germany, so they were determined to keep Russia as an ally. They promised to support Russia if war began.

On July 28, Austria declared war on Serbia. Russia immediately mobilized its army, including troops stationed on the German border. On August 1, Germany declared war on Russia. Two days later, it declared war on France. World War I had begun.

Germany's Plan Fails Germany had long been prepared for war against France and Russia. It immediately launched a massive invasion of France, hoping to knock the French out of the war. It would then be able to send its troops east to deal with the Russians.

The German plan had one major problem. It required the German forces to advance through neutral Belgium in order to encircle the French troops. The British had guaranteed Belgium's neutrality. When German troops crossed the Belgian frontier, Britain declared war on Germany.

Those fighting for the Triple Entente were called the **Allies.** France, Russia, and Great Britain formed the backbone of the Allies along with Italy, which joined them in 1915 after the other Allies promised to cede Austro-Hungarian territory to Italy after the war. What remained of the Triple Alliance—Germany and Austria-Hungary—joined with the Ottoman Empire and Bulgaria to form the **Central Powers.**

The German plan seemed to work at first. German troops swept through Belgium and headed into France, driving back the French and British forces. Then, to the great surprise of the Germans, Russian troops invaded Germany. The Germans had not expected Russia to mobilize so quickly. They were forced to pull some of their troops away from the attack on France and send them east to stop the Russians. This weakened the German forces just enough to give the Allies a chance to stop them. The Germans drove to within 30 miles (48 km) of Paris, but stubborn resistance by British and French troops at the Battle of the Marne finally stopped the German advance. Because the swift German attack had failed to defeat the French, both sides became locked in a bloody stalemate along hundreds of miles of trenches that would barely change position for the next three years.

The Central Powers had greater success on the Eastern Front. German and Austrian forces stopped the Russian attack and then went on the offensive. They swept across hundreds of miles of territory and took hundreds of thousands of prisoners. Russia suffered 2 million killed, wounded, or captured in 1915 alone, but it kept fighting.

Reading Check **Explaining** What incident triggered the beginning of World War I?

American Neutrality

When the fighting began, President Wilson declared the United States to be neutral in an attempt to keep the

---

Profiles IN HISTORY

Jeannette Rankin
1880–1973

As he addressed the "Gentlemen of the Congress" on April 2, 1917, President Woodrow Wilson actually misspoke. Sitting in the chamber listening to the president's request for a declaration of war against Germany was Representative Jeannette Rankin—the first woman ever elected to Congress.

Rankin was born in Missoula, Montana, in 1880. She became a social worker and participated in the woman suffrage movement. In 1916 she was elected to the U.S. House of Representatives from Montana—one of the few states at that time that allowed women to vote. As a representative, Rankin sponsored legislation to grant federal voting rights for women and to provide health services for them.

Apart from her title as the first woman in Congress, Rankin is remembered most for her strong pacifism. She was one of 56 legislators who voted against the nation's entry into World War I. "I want to stand by my country," she said, "but I cannot vote for war."

In 1940 Rankin ran again for Congress as a representative from Montana. She ran on an isolationist policy and won. In 1941 she was the only member of Congress to vote against declaring war on Japan and entering World War II.

After leaving Congress in 1943, Rankin continued working for peace. In 1968, at 87 years of age, she led thousands of women in the March on Washington to oppose the Vietnam War.

country from being drawn into a foreign war. "We must be impartial in thought as well as in action," Wilson stated. For many Americans, however, that proved difficult to do.

Americans Take Sides Despite the president's plea, many Americans showed support for one side or the other. This was especially true for recent immigrants from Europe. Many of the 8 million German Americans, for example, supported their homeland. The nation's 4.5 million Irish Americans, whose homeland endured centuries of British rule, also sympathized with the Central Powers.

In general, though, American public opinion favored the Allied cause. Many Americans valued the heritage, language, and political ideals they shared with Britain. Others treasured America's historic links with France, a great friend to America during the Revolutionary War.

Pro-British Sentiment One select group of Americans was decidedly pro-British: President Wilson's cabinet. Only Secretary of State William Jennings Bryan favored neutrality. The other cabinet members, as well as Bryan's chief adviser, Robert Lansing, and Walter Hines Page, the American ambassador to London, argued forcefully on behalf of Britain. American military leaders also backed the British. They believed that an Allied victory was the only way to preserve the international balance of power.

British officials worked diligently to win American support. One method they used was propaganda, or information designed to influence opinion. Both the Allies and the Central Powers used propaganda, but German propaganda was mostly anti-Russian and did not appeal to most Americans. British propaganda, on the other hand, was extremely skillful. Furthermore, Britain cut the transatlantic telegraph cable from Europe to the United States, limiting news about the war mainly to British reports. Stories arrived depicting numerous German war atrocities, including the charge that Germans used corpses from the battlefield to make fertilizer and soap. Although many such reports were questionable, enough Americans believed them to help sway American support in favor of the Allies.

ECONOMICS

Business Links American business interests also leaned toward the Allies. Companies in the United States, particularly on the East Coast, had strong ties with businesses in the Allied countries. As business leader Thomas W. Lamont stated, "Our firm had

never for one moment been neutral: we did not know how to be. From the very start we did everything that we could to contribute to the cause of the Allies."

Many American banks began to invest heavily in an Allied victory. American loans to the cash-hungry Allies skyrocketed. By 1917 such loans would total over $2 billion. Other American banks, particularly in the Midwest, where pro-German feelings were strongest, also lent some $27 million to Germany. Even more might have been lent, but most foreign loans required the approval of William McAdoo, the secretary of the Treasury. McAdoo was strongly pro-British and did what he could to limit loans to Germany. As a result, the country's prosperity was intertwined with the military fortunes of Britain, France, and Russia. If the Allies won, the money would be paid back; if not, the money might be lost forever.

Reading Check **Evaluating** How was American prosperity intertwined with the military fortunes of the Allies?

Moving Toward War

Although most Americans supported the Allies and hoped for their victory, they did not want to join the conflict. However, a series of events gradually eroded American neutrality and drew the nation into the war firmly on the side of the Allies.

The British Blockade Shortly after the war began, the British deployed their navy to blockade Germany and keep it from obtaining supplies. The British planted mines in the North Sea and forced neutral ships into port for inspections in case they were trying to transport valuable materials to Germany or its neutral neighbors. British officials also expanded their definition of contraband, or prohibited materials, to prevent neutral countries from shipping food to Germany.

The Germans knew that the Allies depended on food, equipment, and other supplies from both the United States and their overseas empires. If Germany could strangle that trade, it could starve the British and French

HISTORY Online

Student Web Activity Visit the *American Vision* Web site at tav.glencoe.com and click on *Student Web Activities— Chapter 19* for an activity on World War I.

into surrendering. To get around Britain's blockade, the Germans deployed submarines known as U-boats— from the German word *Unterseeboot* (meaning "underwater boat"). In February 1915, the Germans announced that they would attempt to sink without warning any ship they found in the waters around Britain.

Germany's announcement triggered outrage in the United States and elsewhere. Attacking civilian vessels without warning violated an international treaty stipulating that military vessels must reveal their intentions to merchant ships and make provisions for the safety of the targeted ship's crew and passengers before sinking it. The Germans claimed that many merchant ships were actually warships in disguise and that their U-boats would be placed at great risk if they revealed themselves before firing.

The issue reached a crisis on May 7, 1915. Despite warnings from Germany, the British passenger liner *Lusitania* entered the war zone. A submerged German submarine fired on the ship, killing nearly 1,200 passengers—including 128 Americans. Many Americans were outraged and regarded the attack as an act of terrorism, not war.

Others argued that the passengers traveling on ships of foreign nations did so at their own risk.

Wilson steered a middle course on the issue of the U-boats. He refused to take extreme measures against Germany, saying that the United States was "too proud to fight." Nevertheless, he sent several diplomatic notes to Germany insisting that its government safeguard the lives of noncombatants in the war zones.

Late in March 1916, Wilson's policy was tested when a U-boat torpedoed the French passenger ship *Sussex,* injuring several Americans on board. Although Wilson's closest advisers favored breaking off diplomatic relations with Germany immediately, the president, busy with the crisis in Mexico, chose to issue one last warning. He demanded that the German government abandon its methods of submarine warfare or risk war with the United States.

Germany did not want to strengthen the Allies by drawing the United States into the war. It promised with certain conditions to sink no more merchant ships without warning. The **Sussex Pledge,** as it was called, met the foreign-policy goals of both Germany and President Wilson by keeping the United States out of the war a little longer.

Wilson's efforts to keep American soldiers at home played an important part in his re-election bid in 1916. Campaigning as the "peace" candidate, his campaign slogan, "He kept us out of the war," helped lead Wilson to a narrow victory over the Republican nominee, Charles Evans Hughes.

The United States Declares War Following Wilson's re-election, events quickly brought the country to the brink of war. In January 1917, a German official named Arthur Zimmermann cabled the German ambassador in Mexico, instructing him to make an offer to the Mexican government. Zimmermann proposed that Mexico ally itself with Germany in the event of war between Germany and the United States. In return, Mexico would regain its "lost territory in Texas, New Mexico, and Arizona" after the war. Germany hoped Mexico would tie down the American forces and prevent them from being sent to Europe. British intelligence intercepted the **Zimmermann telegram.** Shortly afterward, it was leaked to American newspapers. Furious, many Americans now concluded war with Germany was necessary.

Then, on February 1, 1917, Germany resumed unrestricted submarine warfare. German military leaders believed that they could starve Britain into

Picturing **History**

The Sinking of the *Lusitania* In May 1915, German U-boats sank the British passenger liner *Lusitania.* Among those who drowned were 128 Americans. Here the *Los Angeles Tribune* reports the attack, and a newspaper advertisement warns ship passengers to travel the Atlantic at their own risk. Why were the Germans sinking passenger liners?

> ## *"The world must be made safe for democracy."*
>
> —*Woodrow Wilson, April 1917*

Picturing History

Americans Go to War Congress voted heavily in favor of entering the European war. Here, excited Americans wave from an Army recruitment truck. What events pushed the United States to finally declare war?

San Francisco Examiner

HOUSE PASSES WAR RESOLUTION, 373 TO 50; 12 INTERNED GERMAN VESSELS SEIZED BY U.S.

submission in four to six months if their U-boats could return to a more aggressive approach of sinking all ships on sight. Although they recognized that their actions might draw the United States into the war, the Germans did not believe that the Americans could raise an army and transport it to Europe in time to prevent the Allies from collapsing.

Between February 3 and March 21, German U-boats sank six American merchant ships without warning. Finally roused to action, President Wilson appeared before a special session of Congress on April 2, 1917, to ask for a declaration of war against Germany.

> ❝It is a fearful thing to lead this great peaceful people into war. . . . But the right is more precious than peace, and we shall fight for the things which we have always carried nearest to our hearts—for democracy, for the right of those who submit to authority to have a voice in their own governments, for the rights and liberties of small nations. . . .❞
>
> —quoted in the Congressional Record, 1917

After a spirited debate, the Senate passed the resolution on April 4 by a vote of 82 to 6. The House concurred 373 to 50 on April 6, and Wilson signed the resolution. America was now at war.

Reading Check **Summarizing** How did Germany's use of unrestricted submarine warfare lead to American entry into World War I?

SECTION 1 ASSESSMENT

Checking for Understanding

1. **Define:** guerrilla, nationalism, self-determination, propaganda, contraband, U-boat.
2. **Identify:** Pancho Villa, Franz Ferdinand, Allies, Central Powers, Sussex Pledge, Zimmermann telegram.
3. **Name** the two alliances that Europe was divided into at the start of World War I.

Reviewing Themes

4. **Continuity and Change** Why did most of President Wilson's cabinet members support the British?

Critical Thinking

5. **Synthesizing** How did European nationalism contribute to the outbreak of World War I?
6. **Organizing** Use a graphic organizer similar to the one below to identify the events that led the United States to enter World War I.

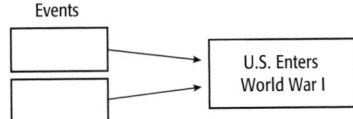

Events → U.S. Enters World War I

Analyzing Visuals

7. **Analyzing Time Lines** Examine the time line on page 579. How does the order in which countries declared war reflect the European alliance system?

Writing About History

8. **Expository Writing** Imagine that you are a Mexican citizen living in Mexico between 1914 and 1917. Write a script for a radio newscast in which you express your feelings about American actions in Mexico. Include reasons for your feelings.

SECTION 2 The Home Front

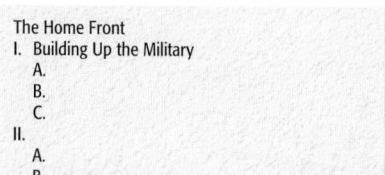

Guide to Reading

Main Idea

To successfully fight the war, the United States had to mobilize the entire nation.

Key Terms and Names

conscription, War Industries Board, Bernard Baruch, victory garden, Liberty Bond, Victory Bond, Committee on Public Information, espionage

Reading Strategy

Taking Notes As you read about how the United States mobilized for war, use the major headings of the section to create an outline similar to the one below.

The Home Front
I. Building Up the Military
   A.
   B.
   C.
II.
   A.
   B.

Reading Objectives
• **Analyze** how the United States raised an army and won support for World War I.
• **Explain** how the economy was controlled to support the war.

Section Theme

Government and Democracy To fight the war, the federal government created new agencies to mobilize the economy, draft soldiers, and build public support.

Preview of Events

◆1917   ◆1918   ◆1919

1917
Selective Service Act and Espionage Act passed

May 1918
Sedition Act passed

September 1918
Eugene Debs imprisoned

1919
Schenck v. *United States*

★ An American Story ★

Even as he began to address the crowd of about 1,200 people, Eugene Debs suspected he was heading for trouble with the authorities. The 62-year-old Socialist leader had traveled to Canton, Ohio, on June 16, 1918, to speak at the state's convention of the Socialist Party. The time had come, Debs decided, to condemn American participation in World War I.

"I realize that in speaking to you this afternoon," he told the crowd, "there are certain limitations placed upon the right of free speech. I must be exceedingly careful, prudent, as to what I say, and even more careful as to how I say it." Laughter came from the crowd, and then applause. "But I am not," Debs continued, "going to say anything that I do not think. I would rather a thousand times be a free soul in jail than to be a . . . coward in the streets!"

When the transcript of Debs' speech arrived at the federal office in Cleveland, a grand jury indicted him for violating the newly passed Espionage Act. The Socialist leader was arrested and imprisoned. Said Debs, "I had a hunch that speech was likely to settle the matter."

—adapted from *Echoes of Distant Thunder*

Building Up the Military

When the United States declared war against Germany in April 1917, progressives controlled the federal government. They did not abandon their ideas simply because a war had begun. Instead, they applied progressive ideas to fighting the war.

Selective Service When the United States entered the war in 1917, the army and National Guard together had slightly more than 300,000 troops. Although many men volunteered after war was declared, many felt more soldiers needed to be drafted.

Many progressives believed that conscription—forced military service—was a violation of democratic and republican principles. Realizing a draft was necessary, however, Congress, with Wilson's support, created a new conscription system called **selective service.** Instead of having the military run the draft from Washington, D.C., the Selective Service Act of 1917 required all men between 21 and 30 to register for the draft. A lottery randomly determined the order they were called before a local draft board in charge of selecting or exempting people from military service.

The thousands of local boards were the heart of the system. The members of the draft boards were civilians from local communities. Progressives believed local people, understanding community needs, would know which men to draft. Eventually about 2.8 million Americans were drafted. Approximately 2 million others volunteered for military service.

African Americans in the War Of the nearly 400,000 African Americans who were drafted, about 42,000 served overseas as combat troops. African American soldiers encountered discrimination and prejudice in the army, where they served in racially segregated units almost always under the supervision of white officers.

Despite these challenges, many African American soldiers fought with distinction in the war. For example, the African American 92nd and 93rd Infantry Divisions fought in bitter battles along the Western Front. Many of them won praise from both the French commander, Marshal Henri Pétain, and the United States commander, General John Pershing. The entire 369th Infantry Division won the highly prized French decoration, the Croix de Guerre ("war cross"), for gallantry in combat.

Women in the Military World War I was the first war in which women officially served in the armed forces, although only in noncombat positions. Women nurses had served in both the army and navy since the early 1900s, but as auxiliaries. Nurses were not assigned ranks, and the women were not technically enlisted in the army or navy.

As the military prepared for war in 1917, it faced a severe shortage of clerical workers because so many men were assigned to active duty. Early in 1917, the navy authorized the enlistment of women to meet its clerical needs. The women wore a standard uniform and were assigned the rank of yeoman. By the end of the war, over 11,000 women had served in the navy. Although most performed clerical duties, others served as radio operators, electricians, pharmacists, photographers, chemists, and torpedo assemblers.

Unlike the navy, the army refused to enlist women. Instead, it began hiring women as temporary employees to fill clerical jobs. The only women to actually serve in the army were in the **Army Nursing Corps.** Army nurses were the only women in the military to be sent overseas during the war. Over 20,000 nurses served in the army during the war, including more than 10,000 overseas.

✓ **Reading Check** **Describing** How did Congress ensure that the United States would have enough troops to serve in World War I?

Organizing Industry

The progressive emphasis on careful planning and scientific management shaped the federal government's approach to mobilizing the American war economy. To efficiently manage the relationship between the federal government and private companies, Congress created special boards to coordinate mobilization of the economy. Instead of having the government control the economy, these boards emphasized cooperation between big business and government. Business executives, professional

Picturing **History**

Women and War Although not allowed in combat, many women served in auxiliary positions, such as nursing. Here, Birmingham, Alabama, women collect money during a Red Cross parade in 1918. In what other capacities did women serve during the war?

managers, and government representatives staffed the boards. Their goal was to ensure the most efficient use of national resources to further the war effort.

The War Industries Board

One of the first agencies established was the **War Industries Board** (WIB). Created in July 1917, the WIB's job was to coordinate the production of war materials. At first, President Wilson was reluctant to give the WIB much authority over the economy, but by March 1918, he decided industrial production needed better coordination. The WIB was reorganized and **Bernard Baruch** was appointed to run it. Under this Wall Street stockbroker's supervision, the WIB told manufacturers what they could and could not produce. It controlled the flow of raw materials, ordered the construction of new factories, and occasionally, with the president's approval, set prices.

Food and Fuel

Perhaps the most successful government agency was the Food Administration, run by Herbert Hoover. This agency was responsible for increasing food production while reducing civilian consumption. Instead of using rationing, Hoover encouraged Americans to save food on their own. Using the slogan "Food Will Win the War—Don't Waste It," the Food Administration encouraged families to "Hooverize" by "serving just enough" and by having Wheatless Mondays, Meatless Tuesdays, and Porkless Thursdays. Hoover also encouraged citizens to plant victory gardens to raise their own vegetables, leaving more for the troops.

While Hoover managed food production, the Fuel Administration, run by Harry Garfield, tried to manage the nation's use of coal and oil. To conserve energy, Garfield introduced **daylight savings time** and shortened workweeks for factories that did not make war materials. He also encouraged Americans to observe Heatless Mondays.

Paying for the War

By the end of World War I, the United States was spending about $44 million a day—leading to a total expenditure of about $32 billion for the entire conflict. To fund the war effort, Congress raised income tax rates. Congress also placed new taxes on corporate profits and an extra tax on the profits of arms factories.

Taxes, however, could not cover the entire cost of the war. To raise the money it needed, the government borrowed more than $20 billion from the American people by selling **Liberty Bonds** and **Victory Bonds.** By buying the bonds, Americans were loaning the government money. The government agreed to repay the money with interest in a specified number of years. Posters, rallies, and "Liberty Loan sermons" encouraged people to buy the bonds as an act of patriotism.

✓ **Reading Check** **Summarizing** What federal agencies helped control American industries during the war?

Picturing **History**

Propaganda Posters George Creel's Committee on Public Information encouraged Americans to do all they could to support the war effort. What is the general theme of these posters? Do you think the posters were effective?

ENLIST
On Which Side of the Window are YOU?

TEAMWORK WIN
UNITED STATES SHIPPING BOARD EMERGENCY FLEET CORPOR

"The world must be made safe for Democracy!"
~ WOODROW WILSON ~

"To the men who run the railways of the country, whether they be managers or operative employees, let me say that the railways are the arteries of the nation's life and that upon them rests the immense responsibility of seeing to it that those arteries suffer no obstruction of any kind, no inefficiency or slackened power."

THE WOMAN'S LAND ARMY of AMERICA
WOMEN *enlist now and help the* FARMER FIGHT THE FOOD FAMINE
APPLY: National Office, 19 West 44th Street New York State Office, 303 Fifth Avenue OR: Nearest U.S. Employment Bureau office

Mobilizing the Workforce

While the WIB and other agencies tried to build cooperation between the government and business, officials knew that they also needed workers to cooperate if mobilization was to succeed. To prevent strikes from disrupting the war effort, the government established the **National War Labor Board** (NWLB) in March 1918. Chaired by William Howard Taft and Frank Walsh, a prominent labor attorney, the NWLB attempted to mediate labor disputes that might otherwise lead to strikes.

The NWLB frequently pressured industry to grant important concessions to workers, including wage increases, an eight-hour workday, and the right of unions to organize and bargain collectively. In exchange, labor leaders agreed not to disrupt war production with strikes or other disturbances. As a result, membership in unions increased by just over one million between 1917 and 1919.

Women Support Industry The war increased work opportunities for women, who filled industrial jobs vacated by men serving in the military. These included factory and manufacturing jobs and various positions in the shipping and railroad industries. War-generated changes in female employment, however, were not permanent. After the war, when the servicemen returned home, most women returned to their previous jobs or stopped working.

The Great Migration Begins With the flow of immigrants from Europe cut off and large numbers of white workers being drafted, the war also opened new doors for African Americans. Wartime job openings and high wages drew thousands of African Americans to factories producing war materials. Encouraged by recruiting agents promising high wages and plentiful work, between 300,000 and 500,000 African Americans left the South to settle in Northern cities. This became known as the "Great Migration." This massive population movement altered the racial makeup of such cities as Chicago, New York, Cleveland, and Detroit.

Mexican Americans Head North African Americans were not the only group to migrate north during the war. Continuing political turmoil in Mexico and the wartime labor shortage in the United States convinced many Mexicans to head north. Between 1917 and 1920, over 100,000 Mexicans migrated into Texas, Arizona, California, and New Mexico, providing labor for the farmers and ranchers of the Southwest.

Federal Mobilization Agencies

Agency	Purpose
War Industries Board	Organized industry to increase efficiency, maximizing production
Railroad Administration	Assumed temporary control of rail lines to modernize equipment and increase operating efficiency
Food Administration	Supervised agricultural production, promoted food conservation and rationing
Fuel Administration	Increased production of coal and oil; maintained conservation of fuel with such innovations as daylight savings time
National War Labor Board	Maintained cooperation between industry management and labor unions; acted as mediator to prevent and quickly settle disputes
Committee on Public Information	Provided propaganda to rally citizen support for all aspects of the war effort

Chart Skills

1. **Interpreting Charts** Which agency worked with manufacturers and labor unions?
2. **Analyzing** How did the Fuel Administration's daylight savings time plan achieve its goal?

Meanwhile, tens of thousands of Mexican Americans headed north to Chicago, St. Louis, Omaha, and other cities to take wartime factory jobs. Many Mexican Americans faced hostility and discrimination when they arrived in American cities. Like other immigrants before them, they tended to settle in their own separate neighborhoods, called **barrios,** where they could support each other.

Reading Check **Evaluating** How permanent were women's advances in the wartime workplace?

Ensuring Public Support

Progressives in the government did not think coordinating business and labor was enough to ensure the success of the war effort. They also believed that the government should take steps to shape public opinion and build support for the war.

Different Viewpoints

Abrams v. United States, 1919

The Espionage Act of 1917 made it a crime to "willfully utter, print, write, or publish any disloyal, profane, scurrilous or abusive language about the government." Although the act limited First Amendment freedoms, many Americans believed winning World War I was more important. ☐ *(See page 1080 for more information on* Abrams v. the United States.*)*

Justice John H. Clarke delivered the majority opinion:

It is argued, somewhat faintly, that the acts charged against the defendants were not unlawful because within the protection of that freedom . . . of speech and of the press . . . and that the entire Espionage Act is unconstitutional. . . .

. . . the plain purpose of their propaganda was to excite, at the supreme crisis of the war, disaffection, sedition, riots, and, as they hoped, revolution, in this country for the purpose of embarrassing, and, if possible, defeating the military plans of the Government in Europe. . . . [T]he language of these circulars was obviously intended to provoke and to encourage resistance to the United States in the war, as the third count runs, and the defendants, in terms, plainly urged and advocated a resort to a general strike of workers in ammunition factories for the purpose of curtailing the production of ordnance and munitions necessary and essential to the prosecution of the war. . . . Thus, it is clear not only that some evidence, but that much persuasive evidence, was before the jury tending to prove that the defendants were guilty as charged. . . .

Justice Oliver Wendell Holmes, Jr., dissenting:

It is only the present danger of immediate evil or an intent to bring it about that warrants Congress in setting a limit to the expression of opinion where private rights are not concerned. Congress certainly cannot forbid all effort to change the mind of the country. Now nobody can suppose that the surreptitious publishing of a silly leaflet by an unknown man, without more, would present any immediate danger that its opinions would hinder the success of the government arms or have any appreciable tendency to do so.

In this case, sentences of twenty years' imprisonment have been imposed for the publishing of two leaflets that I believe the defendants had as much right to publish as the Government has to publish the Constitution of the United States now vainly invoked by them. . . . I regret that I cannot put into more impressive words my belief that, in their conviction upon this indictment, the defendants were deprived of their rights under the Constitution of the United States.

Amendment I

—Congress shall make no law respecting an establishment of religion, or prohibiting the free exercise thereof; or abridging the freedom of speech, or of the press; or the right of the people peaceably to assemble, and to petition the Government for a redress of grievances.

Learning From History

1. What were the charges against the defendants?
2. On what key point did Holmes and Clarke disagree?

Selling the War A new government agency, the **Committee on Public Information,** had the task of "selling" the war to the American people. The head of the CPI was journalist George Creel, who recruited advertising executives, commercial artists, authors, songwriters, entertainers, public speakers, and motion picture companies to help sway public opinion in favor of the war.

The CPI distributed pamphlets and arranged for thousands of short patriotic talks, called "four-minute speeches," to be delivered at movie theaters and public halls and gathering places. The Four-Minute Men urged audiences to support the war in various ways, from buying war bonds to reporting draft dodgers to the proper authorities.

Civil Liberties Curtailed In addition to using propaganda and persuasion, the government also passed legislation to fight antiwar activities or enemies at home. Espionage, or spying to acquire secret government information, was addressed in the Espionage Act of 1917, which established penalties and prison terms for anyone who gave aid to the enemy. This act also penalized disloyalty, giving false reports, or otherwise interfering with the war effort. The Post Office even hired college professors to translate foreign periodicals to find out if they contained antiwar messages.

The Sedition Act of 1918 expanded the meaning of the Espionage Act to make illegal any public expression of opposition to the war. In practice, it allowed officials to prosecute anyone who criticized the president or the government. Combined, these laws generated over 1,500 prosecutions and 1,000 convictions.

A Climate of Suspicion

The fear of spies and emphasis on patriotism quickly led to the mistreatment and persecution of German Americans. To avoid German-sounding names, advertisers began to call sauerkraut "Liberty cabbage" and hamburger "Salisbury steak." Many schools dropped German language classes from their curricula, and orchestras stopped performing the music of Beethoven, Schubert, Wagner, and other German composers. Anti-German feelings sometimes led to violence. Some citizens beat neighbors who were German-born. In Collinsville, Illinois, a mob lynched a German-born man whom they suspected of disloyalty.

German Americans were not the only ones under suspicion. Mobs attacked labor activists, socialists, and pacifists. Newspapers ads urged Americans to monitor the activities of their fellow citizens. Americans even formed private organizations, such as the American Protective League and the Boy Spies of America, to spy on neighbors and coworkers. Secretary of War Newton Baker expressed concern about the growing intolerance:

George Creel

66 There is a growing frenzy of suspicion and hostility toward disloyalty. I am afraid we are going to have a good many instances of people roughly treated on very slight evidence of disloyalty. Already a number of men and some women have been tarred and feathered, and a portion of the press is urging with great vehemence more strenuous efforts at detection and punishment. 99

—quoted in *Echoes of Distant Thunder*

The Supreme Court Limits Free Speech

Despite protests against the government's tactics, however, the courts generally upheld the principle behind them. Although the First Amendment specifically states that "Congress shall make no law . . . abridging the freedom of speech, or of the press," the Supreme Court decided otherwise, departing from a strict literal interpretation of the Constitution.

In the landmark case of *Schenck* v. *the United States* (1919), the Supreme Court ruled that an individual's freedom of speech could be curbed when the words uttered constitute a "clear and present danger." The Court used as an example someone yelling "Fire!" in a crowded theater as a situation in which freedom of speech would be superseded by the theater-goers' right to safety. The Court's majority opinion stated, "When a nation is at war, many things that might be said in times of peace are such a hindrance to its effort that their utterance will not be endured so long as [soldiers] fight. . . ." 📖 *(See page 1083 for more information on* Schenck *v.* the United States.*)*

✔ **Reading Check** **Explaining** Why did Congress pass the Espionage Act in 1917?

SECTION 2 ASSESSMENT

Checking for Understanding

1. **Define:** conscription, victory garden, espionage.
2. **Identify:** War Industries Board, Bernard Baruch, Liberty Bond, Victory Bond, Committee on Public Information.
3. **Describe** the contributions of African Americans during the war.

Reviewing Themes

4. **Government and Democracy** How did government efforts to ensure support for the war conflict with democratic ideals?

Critical Thinking

5. **Analyzing** How did World War I cause the federal government to change its relationship with the business world?
6. **Organizing** Use a graphic organizer similar to the one below to identify the effects of the war on the American workforce.

Effects of War on U.S. Workforce

Analyzing Visuals

7. **Analyzing Posters** Examine the posters on page 586. How do these images encourage support for the war? How effective do you think they would be today?

Writing About History

8. **Persuasive Writing** Imagine that you are working for the Committee on Public Information. Write text for an advertisement or lyrics to a song in which you attempt to sway public opinion in favor of the war.

American soldiers set sail for Europe.

BROWN BROTHERS

World War Firsts

Human ingenuity goes to work in the service of war:

AERIAL COMBAT, 1914. War takes to the air. Two Allied aircraft chase two German planes across Britain.

GAS ATTACKS, 1915. The German High Command admits to using chlorine gas bombs and shells on the field of combat. Deadly mustard gas is used in 1917.

GAS MASKS. Issued to Allied soldiers in 1915.

DONKEY'S EARS. A new trench periscope enables soldiers to observe the battleground from the relative safety of a trench without risking sniper fire.

BIG BERTHA. Enormous howitzer gun bombards Paris. "Big Bertha," named after the wife of its manufacturer, is thought to be located nearly 63 miles behind German lines. Moving at night on railroad tracks, the gun is difficult for the Allies to locate.

BROWN BROTHERS

Color My World

Some bright spots in a dark decade:

- Color newspaper supplements (1914)
- 3-D films (1915)
- Nail polish (1916)
- Three-color traffic lights (1918)
- Color photography introduced by Eastman Kodak (1914)

One of the first color photographs

LEON GIMPLE/SOCIETE FRANCAISE DE PHOTOGRAPHIE/LIFE

How to Make a Doughboy

Take one American infantryman.

BROWN BROTHERS

1. Arm with 107 pieces of fighting equipment, including:
   - rifle
   - rifle cartridges
   - cartridge belt
   - steel helmet
   - clubs
   - knives
   - gas mask
   - wire cutters
   - trench tool
   - bayonet and scabbard
   - grenades

2. Add 50 articles of clothing, including 3 wool blankets and a bedsack.

3. Equip with eating utensils and 11 cooking implements.

4. Train well.

TOTAL COST: $156.30

(not including training and transportation to Europe)

NUMBERS 1915

$1,040 Average annual income for workers in finance, insurance, and real estate

$687 Average income for industrial workers (higher for union workers, lower for nonunion workers)

$510 Average income for retail trade workers

$355 Average income for farm laborers

$342 Average income for domestic servants

$328 Average income for public school teachers

$11.95 Cost of a bicycle

BROWN BROTHERS

$1.15 Cost of a baseball

$1 Average cost of a hotel room

39¢ Cost of one dozen eggs

5¢ Cost of a glass of cola

7¢ Cost of a large roll of toilet paper

Milestones

REPATRIATED, APRIL 10, 1917. VLADIMIR ILYICH LENIN, to Russia, after an 11-year absence. The leader of the leftist Bolshevik party hopes to reorganize his revolutionary group.

CULVER PICTURES

Vladimir Lenin

SHOT DOWN AND KILLED, APRIL 22, 1918. "THE RED BARON," Manfred von Richthofen, Germany's ace pilot. Von Richthofen destroyed more than 80 Allied aircraft. On hearing of the Red Baron's death, English fighter pilot Edward Mannock said, "I hope he roasted all the way down."

BROWN BROTHERS

Jeannette Rankin

ELECTED, NOVEMBER 7, 1916. JEANNETTE RANKIN of Montana, to the U.S. Congress. The first woman congressional representative explained her victory by saying that women "got the vote in Montana because the spirit of pioneer days was still alive."

EXECUTED, OCTOBER 15, 1917. MATA HARI, in France, for espionage. The famous Dutch dancer was sentenced to death for spying for the Germans.

Guide to Reading

Main Idea

After four years of fighting, the war in Europe ended in November 1918.

Key Terms and Names

"no man's land," convoy, Vladimir Lenin, Treaty of Brest-Litovsk, armistice, Fourteen Points, League of Nations, Treaty of Versailles, reparations

Reading Strategy

Organizing As you read about the battles of World War I, complete a graphic organizer similar to the one below by listing the kinds of warfare and technology used in the fighting.

Warfare and Technology Used in World War I

Reading Objectives

• **Discuss** the fighting techniques used in World War I.
• **Characterize** the American response to the Treaty of Versailles.

Section Theme

Individual Action American troops played a major role in helping end the war, while President Wilson played a major role in the peace negotiations.

Preview of Events

♦1915   ♦1917   ♦1919

July 1916
Battle of the Somme begins

November 1917
Communists seize power in Russia

March 1918
Treaty of Brest-Litovsk ends war between Russia and Germany

September 1918
Beginning of Battle of the Argonne Forest

November 1918
Armistice ends war

★ An American Story ★

General John J. Pershing, commander of the American forces in World War I, could not help but feel a sense of pride and excitement as he watched the Second Battalion of the First Division's 16th Infantry march through the streets of Paris on July 4, 1917:

❝. . . The battalion was joined by a great crowd, many women forcing their way into the ranks and swinging along arm in arm with the men. With wreaths about their necks and bouquets in their hats and rifles, the column looked like a moving flower garden. With only a semblance of military formation, the animated throng pushed its way through avenues of people to the martial strains of the French band and the still more thrilling music of cheering voices.❞

—quoted in *The Yanks Are Coming*

While his men marched through Paris, Pershing raced to Picpus Cemetery, the burial place of the Marquis de Lafayette, a French noble who had fought in the American Revolution. One of Pershing's officers, Colonel Charles E. Stanton, raised his hand in salute and acknowledged the continuing American-French relationship by proclaiming, "Lafayette, we are here!"

Combat in World War I

By the spring of 1917, World War I had devastated Europe and claimed millions of lives. Terrible destruction resulted from a combination of old-fashioned strategies and new technologies. Despite the carnage Europeans had experienced, many Americans believed their troops would make a difference and quickly bring the war to an end.

Trench Warfare The early offensives of 1914 quickly demonstrated that the nature of warfare had changed. Troops that dug themselves in and relied upon modern rifles and a new weapon—the rapid-fire machine gun—could easily hold off the attacking forces. On the Western Front, troops dug a network of trenches that stretched from the English Channel to the Swiss border. The space between the opposing trenches was known as **"no man's land,"** a rough, barren landscape pockmarked with craters from artillery fire.

To break through enemy lines, both sides began with massive artillery barrages. Then bayonet-wielding soldiers would scramble out of their trenches, race across no man's land, and hurl grenades into the enemy's trenches. The results were often disastrous. The artillery barrages rarely destroyed the enemy defenses, and troops crossing no man's land were easily stopped by enemy machine guns and rifle fire. These kind of assaults caused staggeringly high casualties. In major battles, both sides often lost several hundred thousand men.

These battles produced horrific scenes of death and destruction, as one American soldier noted in his diary:

> ❝Many dead Germans along the road. One heap on a manure pile . . . Devastation everywhere. Our barrage has rooted up the entire territory like a ploughed field. Dead horses galore, many of them have a hind quarter cut off—the Huns [Germans] need food. Dead men here and there.❞

—quoted in *The American Spirit*

New Technology As it became clear that charging enemy trenches could bring only limited success at great cost, both sides began to develop new technologies to help them break through enemy lines. In April 1915, the Germans first used poison gas in the Second Battle of Ypres. The fumes caused vomiting, blindness, and suffocation. Soon afterward the Allies also began using poison gas, and gas masks became a necessary part of a soldier's equipment.

In 1916 the British introduced the tank into battle. The first tanks were very slow and cumbersome, mechanically unreliable, and fairly easy to destroy. They could roll over barbed wire and trenches, but there were usually not enough of them to make a

An American Hero

Although the brutal trench warfare of World War I led to many acts of astonishing bravery, the heroism of one American, Corporal Alvin York, captured the nation's imagination. Born in 1887, York grew up poor in the mountains of Tennessee, where he learned to shoot by hunting wild game.

On October 8, 1918, during the Battle of the Argonne Forest, York's patrol lost its way and ended up behind enemy lines. When a German machine gun emplacement on a fortified hill fired on the patrol and killed nine men, York took command and charged the machine gun. Although the details of the battle are unclear, when it ended, York had killed between 9 and 25 Germans, captured the machine guns, and taken 132 prisoners. For his actions, he received the Medal of Honor and the French Croix de Guerre. After returning home, he used his fame to raise money for the Alvin York Institute—a school for underprivileged Tennessee children.

Battles of World War I, 1914–1918

difference. While tanks did help troops, they did not revolutionize warfare in World War I.

World War I also saw the first use of airplanes in combat. At first, planes were used mainly to observe enemy activities. Soon, the Allies and Central Powers used them to drop small bombs. As technology advanced, they also attached machine guns to aircraft to engage in deadly air battles known as dogfights.

✓ **Reading Check** **Describing** What new technologies were introduced in World War I?

The Americans and Victory

Wave upon wave of American troops marched into this bloody stalemate—nearly 2 million before the war's end. These **"doughboys,"** a nickname for American soldiers, were largely inexperienced, but they were fresh, so their presence immediately boosted the morale of Allied forces.

Winning the War at Sea No American troopships were sunk on their way to Europe—an accomplishment due largely to the efforts of American Admiral William S. Sims. For most of the war, the British preferred to fight German submarines by sending warships to find them. Meanwhile, merchant ships would race across the Atlantic individually. The British approach had not worked well, and submarines had inflicted heavy losses on British shipping.

Sims proposed that merchant ships and troop transports be gathered into groups, called convoys, and escorted across the Atlantic by warships. If submarines wanted to attack a convoy, they would have to get past the warships protecting it. The convoy system greatly reduced shipping losses and ensured that American troops arrived safely in Europe. They arrived during a pivotal time in late 1917.

Russia Leaves the War In March 1917, riots broke out in Russia over the government's handling of the war and over the scarcity of food and fuel. On March

Western Front, 1914–1918

World War I Military Deaths*

France 1,385,000	Russia 1,700,000
British Empire 908,400	
Italy 650,000	
Romania 335,700	
United States 107,000	
Others 74,200	
Bulgaria 87,500	Germany 1,773,000
Ottoman Empire 325,000	Austria-Hungary 1,200,000

Allies

Central Powers

* Figures are approximate

Geography *Skills*

1. **Interpreting Maps** Where did the majority of World War I battles occur?
2. **Interpreting Charts** Which nation suffered the largest number of military deaths during World War I?

Map legend:
- Allied Powers
- Central Powers
- Neutral nations
- Allied victory
- Central Powers' victory
- Indecisive battle
- Allied offensives
- Central Powers' offensives
- Farthest advance of Central Powers
- Line of trench warfare, 1915–1917
- Armistice Line, 1918

15, Czar Nicholas II, the leader of the Russian Empire, abdicated his throne. Political leadership in Russia passed into the hands of a provisional, or temporary, government, consisting largely of moderate representatives who supported Russia's continued participation in World War I. The government, however, was unable to adequately deal with the major problems, such as food shortages, that were afflicting the nation.

The **Bolsheviks,** a group of Communists, soon competed for power in Russia. In November 1917, **Vladimir Lenin,** the leader of the Bolshevik Party, overthrew the Russian government and established a Communist government.

Germany's military fortunes improved with the Bolshevik takeover of Russia. Lenin's first act after seizing power was to pull Russia out of the war and concentrate on establishing a Communist state. He accomplished this by agreeing to the **Treaty of Brest-Litovsk** with Germany on March 3, 1918. Under this treaty, Russia lost substantial territory,

giving up Ukraine, its Polish and Baltic territories, and Finland. However, the treaty also removed the German army from the remaining Russian lands. With the Eastern Front settled, Germany was now free to concentrate its forces in the west.

The German Offensive Falters

On March 21, 1918, the Germans launched a massive attack along the Western Front, beginning with gas attacks and a bombardment by over 6,000 artillery pieces. German forces, reinforced with troops transferred from the Russian front, pushed deeply into Allied lines. By early June, they were less than 40 miles (64 km) from Paris.

American troops played an important role in containing the German offensive. In late May, as the German offensive continued, the Americans launched their first major attack, quickly capturing the village of Cantigny. On June 1, American and French troops blocked the German drive on Paris at the town of Château-Thierry. On July 15, the

Germans launched one last massive attack in a determined attempt to take Paris, but American and French troops held their ground.

The Battle of the Argonne Forest

With the German drive stalled, French Marshal Ferdinand Foch, supreme commander of the Allied forces, ordered massive counterattacks all along the front. In mid-September, American troops drove back German forces at the battle of Saint-Mihiel. The attack was a prelude to a massive American offensive in the region between the Meuse River and the Argonne Forest. General Pershing assembled over 600,000 American troops, some 40,000 tons of supplies, and roughly 4,000 artillery pieces for the most massive attack in American history.

The attack began on September 26, 1918. Slowly, one German position after another fell to the advancing American troops. The Germans inflicted heavy casualties on the American forces, but by early November, the Americans had shattered the German defenses and opened a hole in the German lines.

The War Ends

While fighting raged along the Western Front, a revolution engulfed Austria-Hungary, and the Ottoman Turks surrendered. Faced with the surrender of their allies and a naval mutiny at Kiel in early November, the people of Berlin rose in rebellion on November 9 and forced the German emperor to step down. At the 11th hour on the 11th day of the 11th month, 1918, the fighting stopped. Germany had finally signed an armistice, or cease-fire, that ended the war.

✓ Reading Check **Explaining** What was Vladimir Lenin's first goal after controlling Russia in 1917?

Picturing **History**

American Artillery This photo shows some of the materials used to fight World War I. Artillery shells are piled at the feet of these American soldiers. What American battle demanded the largest amount of supplies and artillery pieces?

A Flawed Peace

In January 1919, a peace conference began in Paris to try to resolve the complicated issues arising from World War I. The principal figures in the negotiations were the "Big Four," the leaders of the victorious Allied nations: President Wilson of the United States, British prime minister David Lloyd George, French premier Georges Clemenceau, and Italian prime minister Vittorio Orlando. Germany was not invited to participate.

Wilson had presented his plan, known as the **Fourteen Points,** to Congress in January 1918. The Fourteen Points were based on "the principle of justice to all peoples and nationalities." In the first five points, the president proposed to eliminate the general causes of the war through free trade, disarmament, freedom of the seas, impartial adjustment of colonial claims, and open diplomacy instead of secret agreements. The next eight points addressed the right of self-determination. They also required the Central Powers to evacuate all of the countries invaded during the war, including France, Belgium, and Russia. The fourteenth point, perhaps the most important one to Wilson, called for the creation of a "general association of nations" known as the **League of Nations.** The League's member nations would help preserve peace and prevent future wars by pledging to respect and protect each other's territory and political independence. 📖 *(See page 1074 for the text of the* Fourteen Points.*)*

The Treaty of Versailles

As the peace talks progressed in the Palace of Versailles (vehr·SY), it became clear that Wilson's ideas did not coincide with the interests of the other Allied governments. They criticized his plan as too lenient toward Germany.

Despite Wilson's hopes, the terms of peace were harsh. The **Treaty of Versailles,** signed by Germany on June 28, 1919, had weakened or discarded many of Wilson's proposals. Under the treaty, Germany was stripped of its armed forces and was made to pay reparations, or war damages, in the amount of $33 billion to the Allies. This sum was far beyond Germany's financial means. Perhaps most humiliating, the treaty required Germany to acknowledge guilt for the outbreak of World War I and the devastation caused by the war.

The war itself resulted in the dissolution of four empires: the Russian Empire, the Ottoman Empire, which lost territory in the war and fell to revolution in 1922, the German Empire after the abdication of the emperor and loss of territory in the treaty, and

Austria-Hungary, which was split into separate countries. Furthermore, nine new countries were established in Europe, including Yugoslavia, Poland, and Czechoslovakia.

While Wilson expressed disappointment in the treaty, he found consolation in its call for the creation of his cherished League of Nations. He returned home to win approval for the treaty.

The U.S. Senate Rejects the Treaty The Treaty of Versailles, especially the League of Nations, faced immediate opposition from numerous U.S. lawmakers. A key group of senators, nicknamed "the Irreconcilables" in the press, assailed the League as the kind of "entangling alliance" that Washington, Jefferson, and Monroe had warned against. These critics feared that the League might supersede the power of Congress to declare war and thus force the United States to fight in numerous foreign conflicts.

A larger group of senators, known as the "Reservationists," was led by the powerful chairman of the Foreign Relations committee, Henry Cabot Lodge. This group supported the League but would ratify the treaty only with amendments that would preserve the nation's freedom to act independently. Wilson feared such changes would defeat the basic purpose of the League and insisted that the Senate ratify the treaty without changes.

Convinced that he could defeat his opposition by winning public support, Wilson took his case directly to the American people. Starting in Ohio in September 1919, he traveled 8,000 miles and made over 30 major speeches in three weeks. The physical strain of his tour, however, proved too great. Wilson collapsed in Colorado on September 25 and returned to the White

World Geography Connection

Global War

Although World War I was fought mainly in Europe, it touched the lives of peoples throughout the world, including those in Africa and India. By the time the war broke out, both African and Indian society had been turned upside down by European imperialism. While the British controlled much of India, no less than seven European powers had divided up Africa among themselves. In addition to living under the rule of Europeans, Africans and Indians were forced to take part in their great war as well. About one million Indians fought for the British in Europe, while nearly as many Africans served in the French army. The fighting also spread to Africa, as the Allies fought to seize control of Germany's African colonies. *How do you think the average Indian or African felt about World War I?*

House. There, he suffered a stroke and was bedridden for months, isolated from even his closest advisers but determined not to compromise with the Senate.

The Senate voted in November 1919 and again in March 1920, but it refused to ratify the treaty. After Wilson left office in 1921, the United States negotiated separate peace treaties with each of the Central Powers. The League of Nations, the foundation of President Wilson's plan for lasting world peace, took shape without the United States.

✓ **Reading Check** **Examining** What major issues did Wilson's Fourteen Points address?

SECTION 3 ASSESSMENT

Checking for Understanding
1. **Define:** convoy, armistice, reparations.
2. **Identify:** "no man's land," Vladimir Lenin, Treaty of Brest-Litovsk, Fourteen Points, League of Nations, Treaty of Versailles.
3. **List** the four nations that dominated the Paris peace conference in 1919.

Reviewing Themes
4. **Individual Action** Why did President Wilson propose his Fourteen Points?

Critical Thinking
5. **Analyzing** What impact did John J. Pershing and the Battle of the Argonne Forest have on World War I?
6. **Organizing** Use a graphic organizer to list the results of World War I.

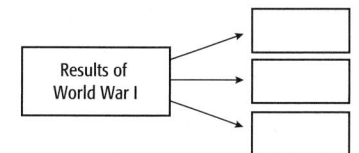

Analyzing Visuals
7. **Analyzing Maps and Charts** Examine the map and graph on page 595. Prepare a quiz with questions based on information from both. Give the quiz to some of your classmates.

Writing About History
8. **Descriptive Writing** Imagine that you are an American soldier fighting in Europe during World War I. Write a letter home describing your situation and how you feel about fighting there.

Analyzing Information

Why Learn This Skill?

The ability to analyze information is important in deciding your position on a subject. For example, you need to analyze a political decision to determine if you should support it. You would also analyze a candidate's position statements to determine if you should vote for him or her.

Learning the Skill

To analyze information, use the following steps:

- Identify the topic that is being discussed.

- Examine how the information is organized. What are the main points?

- Summarize the information in your own words, and then make a statement of your own based on your understanding of the topic and on what you already know.

Practicing the Skill

Read the following information taken from Henry Cabot Lodge's *On the League of Nations* speech. Use the steps listed above to analyze the information and answer the questions that follow.

I am as anxious as any human being can be to have the United States render every possible service to the civilization and the peace of mankind. But I am certain that we can do it best by not putting ourselves in leading strings, or subjecting our policies and our sovereignty to other nations. The independence of the United States is not only more precious to ourselves, but to the world, than any single possession.

I will go as far as anyone in world service that the first step to world service is the maintenance of the United States. You may call me selfish if you will, conservative or reactionary, or use any other harsh adjective you see fit to apply. But an American I was born, an American I've remained all my life. I can never be anything else but an American, and I must think of the United States first. And when I think of the United States first in an argument like this, I am thinking of what is best for the world. For if the United States fails, the best hope of mankind fails with it. I have never had but one allegiance; I cannot divide it now. I have loved but one flag and I cannot share that devotion and give affection to the mongrel banner invented for a league. Internationalism, illustrated by the Bolshevik and by the men to whom all countries are alike, provided they can make money out of them, is to me repulsive. National I must remain and in that way I, like all Americans, can render the amplest service to the world.*

The United States is the world's best hope, but if you fetter her in the interest through quarrels of other nations, if you tangle her in the intrigues of Europe, you will destroy her powerful good, and endanger her very existence.

❶ What topic is being discussed?

❷ What are the main points of this excerpt from Senator Lodge's speech?

❸ Summarize the information in this excerpt, and then provide your analysis based on this information and what you know from the rest of the chapter.

Skills Assessment

Complete the Practicing Skills questions on page 605 and the Chapter 19 Skill Reinforcement Activity to assess your mastery of this skill.

Applying the Skill

Analyzing Information Find a short, informative piece of news, such as a political candidate's position paper, an editorial in a newspaper, or an explanation of a new law that will be enacted soon. Analyze the information and make a statement of your own.

Glencoe's **Skillbuilder Interactive Workbook CD-ROM, Level 2,** provides instruction and practice in key social studies skills.

Guide to Reading

Main Idea

As American society moved from war to peace, turmoil in the economy and fear of communism caused a series of domestic upheavals.

Key Terms and Names

cost of living, general strike, Red Scare, A. Mitchell Palmer, J. Edgar Hoover, deport

Reading Strategy

Organizing As you read about the war's aftermath, complete a graphic organizer similar to the one below to list the effects of the end of World War I on the American economy.

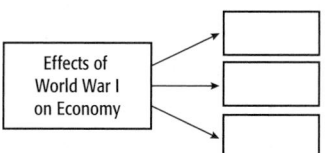

Reading Objectives:
- **Describe** the effects of the postwar recession on the United States.
- **Discuss** the causes of and reaction to the Red Scare.

Section Theme

Continuity and Change The postwar period proved a difficult readjustment period for the United States, in part because of economic turmoil and the fear of communism.

Preview of Events

1917	1918	1919	1920

1917 — Riots erupt in East St. Louis, Illinois

1918 — House approves Nineteenth Amendment giving women the right to vote

1919 — Race riots and strikes erupt in numerous northern cities

1920 — Red Scare and Palmer raids

★ An American Story ★

On August 20, 1919, Mary Harris Jones, also known as "Mother" Jones, was thrown in jail in Homestead, Pennsylvania. The 89-year-old had just finished delivering a fiery, impassioned speech in an attempt to gain support for steel unions. Referring to the owners of the big steel companies, she said:

❝Our Kaisers sit up and smoke seventy-five cent cigars and have lackeys with knee pants bring them champagne while you starve, while you grow old at forty, stoking their furnaces. You pull in your belts while they banquet. They have stomachs two miles long and two miles wide and you fill them. . . . If Gary [chair of U.S. Steel] wants to work twelve hours a day, let him go in the blooming mill and work. What we want is a little leisure, time for music, playgrounds, a decent home, books, and the things that make life worthwhile.❞

—quoted in *Labor in Crisis*

An Economy in Turmoil

The end of World War I brought great upheaval to American society. When the war ended, government agencies removed their controls from the American economy. This released pent-up demand in the economy. People raced to buy goods that had been rationed, while businesses rapidly raised prices they had been forced to keep low during the war. The result was rapid inflation. In 1919 prices rose at an average of more than 15 percent. Inflation greatly increased the cost of living—the cost of food, clothing, shelter, and other essentials that people need to survive.

Inflation Leads to Strikes Many companies had been forced to raise wages during the war, but inflation now threatened to wipe out all the gains workers had made. While workers wanted higher wages to keep up with inflation, companies wanted to hold down wages because inflation was also driving up their operating costs.

During the war, the number of workers in unions had increased dramatically. By the time the war ended, workers were better organized and much more capable of organizing strikes than they had been before. Many business leaders, on the other hand, were determined to break the power of the unions and roll back the gains labor had made. These circumstances led to an enormous wave of strikes in 1919. By the end of the year, more than 3,600 strikes involving more than 4 million workers had taken place.

The Seattle General Strike The first major strike took place in Seattle, when some 35,000 shipyard workers walked off the job demanding higher wages and shorter hours. Soon other unions in Seattle joined the shipyard workers and organized a general strike. A *general strike* is a strike that involves all workers living in a certain location, not just workers in a particular industry. The Seattle general strike involved more than 60,000 people and paralyzed the city for five days. Although the strikers returned to work without making any gains, their actions worried many Americans because the general strike was a common tactic used in Europe by Communists and other radical groups.

The Boston Police Strike Perhaps the most famous strike of 1919 took place in Boston, when roughly 75 percent of the police force walked off the job. Riots and looting soon erupted in the city, forcing the governor of Massachusetts, **Calvin Coolidge,** to send in the National Guard. When the strikers tried to return to work, the police commissioner refused to accept them. He fired the strikers and hired a new police force instead.

Despite protests, Coolidge agreed the men should be fired. He declared, "There is no right to strike

NATIONAL GEOGRAPHIC
MOMENT in HISTORY

HERO'S HOMECOMING
A wounded soldier of the 369th Regiment, the Harlem "Hell-Fighters," accepts congratulations during a victory parade through New York City in 1919. Facing discrimination within their own army, African American soldiers at the front received a warm reception from their French allies. "I have never before experienced what it meant really to be free, to taste real liberty," one soldier wrote home, "in a phrase, 'to be a man.'" Two African American infantry divisions suffered some 6,000 casualties, but at war's end, they still came home to a segregated American society.

Effects of World War I on the United States

Developments in the War

- War-torn economies of Europe
- Russian Revolution
- Industrial demand of wartime
- Sacrifices of wartime; disappointment with Versailles Peace Treaty

Effects on U.S.

- Boom in U.S. economy; emergence of U.S. as world industrial leader
- "Red Scare" in postwar U.S.; suspicion of immigrants
- Internal migration in U.S., especially African American migration to Northern cities
- Failure to join League of Nations

Graphic Organizer → Skills

World War I had profound effects on the United States.

Interpreting Why did the destruction of European economies cause in industrial boom in the United States?

---

against the public safety by anybody, anywhere, anytime." Coolidge's response brought him to national attention and earned him widespread public support. It also convinced the Republicans to make Coolidge their vice presidential candidate in the 1920 election.

The Steel Strike Shortly after the police strike ended, one of the largest strikes in American history began when an estimated 350,000 steelworkers went on strike for higher pay, shorter hours, and recognition of their union. **Elbert H. Gary,** the head of U.S. Steel, refused even to talk to union leaders. Instead, the company set out to break the union by using anti-immigrant feelings to divide the workers.

Many steelworkers were immigrants. The company blamed the strike on foreign radicals and called for loyal Americans to return to work. Meanwhile, the company hired African Americans and Mexicans as replacement workers and managed to keep its steel mills operating despite the strike. Clashes between company guards and strikers were frequent, and in Gary, Indiana, a riot left 18 strikers dead. In early January of 1920, the strike collapsed. The failure of the strike set back the union cause in the steel industry. Steelworkers remained unorganized until 1937.

Reading Check **Explaining** What caused the wave of strikes in 1919?

Racial Unrest

Adding to the nation's economic turmoil was the return of hundreds of thousands of American soldiers from Europe who needed to find employment.

Many African Americans who had moved north during the war were also competing for jobs and housing. Frustration and racism combined to produce violence. In the summer of 1919, over 20 race riots broke out across the nation.

The worst violence occurred in Chicago. On a hot July day, African Americans went to a whites-only beach. Both sides began throwing stones at each other. Whites also threw stones at an African American teenager swimming near the beach to prevent him from coming ashore, and he drowned. A full-scale riot then erupted in the city. Angry African Americans attacked white neighborhoods while whites attacked African American neighborhoods. The riot lasted for almost two weeks. In the end, 38 people died—15 white and 23 black—and over 500 were injured.

Reading Check **Analyzing** Why did the end of the war lead to race riots?

The Red Scare

The wave of strikes in 1919 helped to fuel fears that Communists were conspiring to start a revolution in the United States. Americans had been stunned when Lenin and the Bolsheviks seized power and withdrew Russia from the war. Americans had become very anti-German as the war progressed, and when the Communists withdrew Russia from the war, they seemed to be helping Germany. American anger at Germany quickly expanded into anger at Communists as well. Americans began to associate communism with being unpatriotic and disloyal.

Terror in the Streets After the House of Morgan—a bank in New York City—was damaged by a bomb in 1920, Attorney General A. Mitchell Palmer instituted raids on antigovernment activists and many immigrants, often violating their civil liberties in the process. Whom did Palmer appoint to coordinate these investigations?

Americans had long been suspicious of Communist ideas. Throughout the late 1800s, many Americans had accused immigrants of importing radical socialist and Communist ideas into the United States and blamed them for labor unrest and violence. Now Communists had seized control of an entire nation, and fears surged that they would try to incite revolutions elsewhere. These fears seemed to be confirmed in 1919, when the Soviet Union formed the **Communist International**— an organization for coordinating the activities of Communist parties in other countries.

The Red Scare Begins

As strikes erupted across the United States in 1919, the fear that Communists, or "reds," as they were called, might seize power led to a nationwide panic known as the **Red Scare.** Seattle's mayor, Ole Hanson, spoke for others when he condemned the leaders of the Seattle general strike as revolutionaries who wanted to "take possession of our American government and try to duplicate the anarchy of Russia."

In April the postal service intercepted more than 30 parcels addressed to leading businesspeople and politicians that were triggered to explode when opened. In June eight bombs in eight cities exploded within minutes of one another, suggesting a nationwide conspiracy. One of them damaged the home of United States Attorney General **A. Mitchell Palmer** in Washington, D.C. Most people believed the bombings were the work of Communists or other revolutionaries trying to destroy the American way of life.

The Palmer Raids

Declaring that a "blaze of revolution" was "burning up the foundations of society," Palmer took action. He established a special division within the Justice Department, the General Intelligence Division, headed by **J. Edgar Hoover.** This division eventually became the Federal Bureau of Investigation (FBI). From late 1919 to the spring of 1920, Palmer organized a series of raids on the headquarters of various radical organizations. Although evidence pointed to no single group as the bombers, Palmer's agents focused on foreign residents and immigrants. The authorities detained thousands of suspects and *deported,* or expelled from the country, nearly 600 of them.

Palmer's agents often disregarded the civil liberties of the suspects. Officers entered homes and offices without search warrants. People were mistreated and jailed for indefinite periods of time and were not allowed to talk to their attorneys.

For a while, Palmer was regarded as a national hero. His raids, however, failed to turn up any hard evidence of revolutionary conspiracy. When his dire prediction that violence would rock the nation on May Day 1920—a popular European celebration of workers—proved wrong, Palmer lost much of his credibility and soon faded from prominence.

The Red Scare greatly influenced people's attitudes during the 1920s. Americans often linked radicalism with immigrants, and that attitude led to a call for Congress to limit immigration.

Reading Check **Examining** After World War I, why were Americans suspicious of some union leaders?

An End to Progressivism

Economic problems, labor unrest, and racial tensions, as well as the fresh memories of World War I, all combined to create a general sense of disillusionment in the United States. By 1920 Americans wanted an end to the upheaval. During the 1920 campaign, Ohio Governor James M. Cox and his running mate, Assistant Secretary of the Navy Franklin D. Roosevelt, ran on a platform of keeping alive Woodrow Wilson's progressive ideals. The Republican candidate, Warren G. Harding, called for a return to "normalcy." He urged that what the United States needed was a return to the simpler days before the Progressive Era reforms:

A. Mitchell Palmer and J. Edgar Hoover

❝[Our] present need is not heroics, but healing; not nostrums, but normalcy; not revolution, but restoration; not agitation, but adjustment; not surgery, but serenity; not the dramatic, but the dispassionate; . . . not submergence in internationality, but sustainment in triumphant nationality.❞

—quoted in *Portrait of a Nation*

Harding's sentiments struck a chord with voters, and he won the election by a landslide margin of over 7 million votes. Americans were weary of more crusades to reform society and the world. They hoped to put the country's racial and labor unrest and economic troubles behind them and build a more prosperous and stable society.

Reading Check **Explaining** How was Harding able to win the presidential election of 1920?

SECTION 4 ASSESSMENT

Checking for Understanding

1. **Define:** cost of living, general strike, deport.
2. **Identify:** Red Scare, A. Mitchell Palmer, J. Edgar Hoover.
3. **Describe** the conditions that African Americans faced after the end of World War I.

Reviewing Themes

4. **Continuity and Change** Why did Republican Warren G. Harding win the election of 1920?

Critical Thinking

5. **Analyzing** How did the Palmer raids deprive some citizens of their civil rights?
6. **Organizing** Use a graphic organizer similar to the one below to list the causes of the Red Scare in the United States.

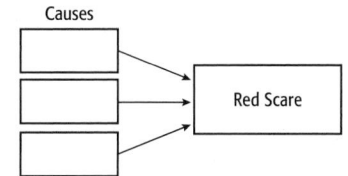

Analyzing Visuals

7. **Analyzing Photographs** Study the photograph on page 600. How might parades such as this one mobilize African Americans to work for an end to discrimination?

Writing About History
8. **Descriptive Writing** Imagine that you are a European immigrant working in a factory in the United States in 1919. Write a letter to a relative in Europe describing the feelings of Americans toward you and other immigrants.

Reviewing Key Terms

On a sheet of paper, use each of these terms in a sentence.

1. guerrilla
2. nationalism
3. self-determination
4. propaganda
5. contraband
6. U-boat
7. conscription
8. victory garden
9. espionage
10. convoy
11. armistice
12. reparations
13. cost of living
14. general strike
15. deport

Reviewing Key Facts

16. **Identify:** Pancho Villa, Franz Ferdinand, Zimmermann telegram, Bernard Baruch, Committee on Public Information, "no man's land," Vladimir Lenin, Fourteen Points, League of Nations, A. Mitchell Palmer, J. Edgar Hoover.

17. What factors contributed to the start of World War I in Europe?

18. What role did American women play in the war effort during World War I?

19. What did the American government do to solve the problem of supplying its troops?

20. What were the provisions of the Treaty of Versailles?

21. What were the Palmer raids?

Critical Thinking

22. **Analyzing Themes: Government and Democracy** Do you think government action to suppress opposition to World War I was justified? Why or why not?

23. **Interpreting Primary Sources** On September 12, 1918, Socialist leader Eugene V. Debs was convicted of violating the Espionage Act. Debs later spoke to the court at his sentencing. Read his speech and answer the questions that follow.

❝I look upon the Espionage laws as a despotic enactment in flagrant conflict with democratic principles and with the spirit of free institutions. . . . I am opposed to the social system in which we live. . . . I believe in fundamental change, but if possible by peaceful and orderly means. . . .

I am thinking this morning of the men in the mills and factories, . . . of the women who for a paltry wage

Chapter Summary

Mobilizing for War

Armed Forces
- Congress passed Selective Service Act which required young men ages 21–30 to register for the draft
- Employed women in noncombat roles

Domestic Front
- War Industries Board controlled war materials and production
- Committee on Public Information created war propaganda
- Government worked with employers and labor to ensure production
- Congress passed Espionage and Sedition Acts to limit opposition to the war
- Congress increased taxes and sold Liberty Bonds to pay for war

Postwar Problems
- Cost of living greatly increased
- Economic problems led to racial violence and widespread strikes
- Fear of communism led to Red Scare and Palmer raids

Self-Check Quiz

Visit the *American Vision* Web site at tav.glencoe.com and click on *Self-Check Quizzes—Chapter 19* to assess your knowledge of chapter content.

are compelled to work out their barren lives; of the little children who in this system are robbed of their childhood and . . . forced into industrial dungeons. . . . In this high noon of our twentieth century Christian civilization, money is still so much more important than the flesh and blood of childhood. In very truth, gold is god. . . . 99

—quoted in *Echoes of Distant Thunder*

a. According to Debs, what were some problems in American society at this time? How did he believe change should be brought about?

b. How did Debs seem to feel about the Espionage Act? Do you agree with him? Why or why not?

24. Organizing Use a table like the one below to list the significant events of each year from 1914 to 1918.

Year	Event	Significance
1914		
1915		
1916		
1917		
1918		

Practicing Skills

25. Analyzing Information Read the subsections titled "The Treaty of Versailles" and "The U.S. Senate Rejects the Treaty" on pages 596 and 597. Using the information on these pages, write an analysis of the effects of the treaty in the form that it was finally accepted.

Geography and History

26. The map on this page shows the geographical changes in Europe after World War I. Study the map and answer the questions below.

a. Interpreting Maps After World War I, what new countries were formed using territory that had belonged to Austria-Hungary?

b. Applying Geography Skills What countries acquired territory from the former Russian Empire?

Writing Activity

27. Persuasive Writing Take on the role of a newspaper editor in 1919. Write an editorial favoring or opposing ratification of the Treaty of Versailles.

NATIONAL GEOGRAPHIC

Europe After World War I, 1920

Chapter Activity

28. Research Project Both the British and the American governments used propaganda to garner support for the war. Use the library and other resources to find examples of these propaganda techniques. Compile your research in an illustrated and captioned poster, and display it in the classroom.

Standardized Test Practice

Directions: Choose the best answer to the following question.

Which of the following was one of the primary causes of World War I?

F A complex set of alliances among European nations

G The exile of Mexican General Victoriano Huerta

H The dissatisfaction of Russian peasants

J The breakup of the Austro-Hungarian Empire

Test-Taking Tip: Eliminate answers you know are incorrect. For example, the breakup of Austria-Hungary took place after World War I, so you can eliminate that answer. Similarly, the exile of Huerta occurred in Mexico, which had little effect on European nations. You also can eliminate that answer.

UNIT
7
Boom and Bust *1920–1941*

Why It Matters

After World War I, the United States enjoyed a time of prosperity and confidence. The decade of the 1920s saw rising stock prices and increased consumer spending. It also witnessed cultural innovations such as jazz music and motion pictures. At the end of the 1920s, however, several economic problems combined to trigger the Great Depression that began in 1929. Understanding the events of these decades will help you understand American society today. The following resources offer more information about this period in American history.

Primary Sources Library

See pages 1054–1055 for primary source readings to accompany Unit 7.

Use the **American History Primary Source Document Library CD-ROM** to find additional primary sources about the Roaring Twenties and the Great Depression.

Hatbox depicting a
New York street scene

Sixth Avenue Elevated at Third St.
by John Sloan, 1928

The Jazz Age
1921–1929

Why It Matters

The 1920s was an era of rapid change and clashing values. Many Americans believed society was losing its traditional values, and they took action to preserve these values. Other Americans embraced new values associated with a freer lifestyle and the pursuit of individual goals. Writers and artists pursued distinctively American themes, and the Harlem Renaissance gave African Americans new pride.

The Impact Today

The 1920s left permanent legacies to American culture.
* *National celebrities in sports and film emerged.*
* *Jazz music became part of American culture.*
* *F. Scott Fitzgerald and Ernest Hemingway wrote classics of American literature.*

The American Vision *Video* *The Chapter 20 video, "The Harlem Renaissance," focuses on Harlem's lively arts and music scene and the movement's contributions to American culture.*

1915
• New Ku Klux Klan founded

1921
• Emergency Quota Act passed, limiting immigration

1922
• Antilynching bill passes in House

1920
• Marcus Garvey leads march through Harlem

United States **PRESIDENTS**

Wilson
1913–1921

Harding
1921–1923

1915

1920

World

1917
• British government's Balfour Declaration supports national home for Jewish people in Palestine

1921
• Ireland becomes an independent country

1922
• Mussolini and Fascists take power in Italy

This photograph of jazz musicians captures the boisterous spirit of the 1920s.

1925
- Scopes trial begins
- F. Scott Fitzgerald's *The Great Gatsby* published

1924
- National Origins Act passed

1926
- Langston Hughes's *The Weary Blues* published

1927
- First feature film with sound debuts
- Lindbergh completes first solo transatlantic flight

Coolidge 1923–1929

Hoover 1929–1933

1925

1930

1924
- Britain recognizes the USSR

1926
- Pavlov's *Conditioned Reflexes* published

1928
- Chiang Kai-shek elected president of China

1923
- Turkish Republic founded

HISTORY Online

Chapter Overview
Visit the *American Vision* Web site at tav.glencoe.com and click on *Chapter Overviews—Chapter 20* to preview chapter information.

A Clash of Values

Main Idea
During the 1920s, clashes between traditional and modern values shook the United States.

Key Terms and Names
anarchist, eugenics, Ku Klux Klan, Emergency Quota Act, flapper, Fundamentalism, evolution, creationism, police powers, speakeasy

Reading Strategy
Organizing As you read about Americans' reactions to immigrants in the 1920s, complete a graphic organizer similar to the one below by filling in the causes and effects of anti-immigrant prejudices.

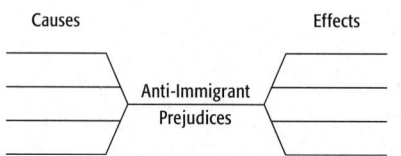

Causes   Effects

Anti-Immigrant Prejudices

Reading Objectives
- **Explain** the rise in racism and nativism in the 1920s.
- **Describe** the clash of values in the 1920s and the changing status of women.

Section Theme
Continuity and Change The rapid changes of the early 1900s challenged Americans who wanted to preserve traditional values.

Preview of Events

♦1919   ♦1924   ♦1929   ♦1934

1919
Eighteenth Amendment ratified

1921
Emergency Quota Act passed

1924
National Origins Act passed

1927
Sacco and Vanzetti executed

1933
Prohibition repealed

★ An American Story ★

In 1911 Alfred Levitt left a small town in Russia to immigrate to New York City. Like many immigrants before and since, he had big ambitions, despite his poor English and lack of education. He wanted to forget his Russian heritage and become a successful American:

❝My conscious drive when I got here was to escape the rigors of poverty, to become somebody of importance. This I don't mean economically, but someone who can justify his presence on the planet. I wonder: Who am I? What am I here for? At seventeen years, the first question for me, though, was: What was I going to do? What will I become? . . . I made up my mind, as young as I was, that I'm going to amount to something in the world, and I'm not going to continue being one of those who starve.❞

—quoted in *Centenarians: The Story of the Twentieth Century by the Americans Who Lived It*

Levitt did indeed "amount to something." A successful artist, he lived the rest of his life in New York City. Twenty of his paintings are part of the permanent collection of the city's Metropolitan Museum of Art.

Nativism Resurges

As the 1920s opened, an economic recession, an influx of immigrants, and racial and cultural tensions combined to create an atmosphere of disillusionment and intolerance. The fear and prejudice many felt toward Germans and Communists expanded to include all immigrants. This triggered a general rise in racism and in nativism, the desire to protect the interests of old-stock Americans against those of immigrants.

During World War I, immigration to the United States had dropped sharply. By 1921, however, it had returned to prewar levels, with the majority of immigrants at this time coming from southern and eastern Europe. Many Americans saw immigrants as a threat to stability and order. The arrival of millions of immigrants also seemed to pose a threat to the four million recently demobilized military men and women searching for work in an economy with soaring unemployment and rising prices.

As the new immigrants, many of whom were unskilled workers, sought to enter the workforce and establish a foothold in American life, many of them encountered ethnic and religious prejudices. The experience of two Italian immigrants, Nicola Sacco and Bartolomeo Vanzetti, exemplified the prejudices and fears of the period.

The Sacco-Vanzetti Case

Shortly after 3:00 P.M. on April 15, 1920, two men shot and killed two employees of the Slater & Morrill Shoe Company in South Braintree, Massachusetts, and robbed the company of its $15,000 payroll. Police subsequently arrested Nicola Sacco, a shoemaker, and Bartolomeo Vanzetti, a fish peddler.

The **Sacco and Vanzetti case** created a furor, as newspapers around the country revealed that the two immigrants were anarchists, or people who oppose all forms of government. They also discovered that Sacco owned a gun similar to the murder weapon and that the bullets used in the murders matched those in Sacco's gun. Although no one at the time knew if Sacco and Vanzetti were guilty, many people leaped to that conclusion because the two men were Italian immigrants and anarchists. Others viewed the case as an example of prejudice against people based on their ethnic origin and political beliefs.

On July 14, 1921, a jury found Sacco and Vanzetti guilty, and the judge sentenced them to death. Many Americans, caught up in the antiforeign fever of the time, applauded the verdict and the penalty. Over the next six years, lawyers filed numerous appeals for a new trial, but all were denied. In April 1927, a special Massachusetts commission studied the case and upheld the verdict. Four months later, on August 23, 1927, Sacco and Vanzetti were executed, proclaiming their innocence all the while. *(See You're the Historian on pages 618–619 for more information on Sacco and Vanzetti.)*

Pseudo-Scientific Racism

Nativist and racist feelings in the 1920s were reinforced by the beliefs of the eugenics movement. Eugenics is a pseudo-science (or false science) that deals with improving hereditary traits. Developed in Europe in the early 1900s, eugenics emphasized that human inequalities were inherited and warned against breeding the "unfit" or "inferior." Eugenics fueled the nativists' argument for the superiority of the "original" American stock—white Protestants of northern European descent. Political, intellectual, and cultural figures like Woodrow Wilson and Henry Cabot Lodge embraced eugenics. By doing so, they lent authority to racist theories, which reinvigorated the nativist argument for strict immigration control.

Return of the Ku Klux Klan

At the forefront of the movement to restrict immigration was the **Ku Klux Klan,** or KKK. The old KKK had flourished in the South after the Civil War and used threats and violence to intimidate newly freed African Americans. The new Klan had other targets as well—Catholics, Jews, immigrants, and other groups believed to represent "un-American" values.

William J. Simmons founded the new Ku Klux Klan in Atlanta, Georgia, in 1915. A former circuit-riding Methodist preacher, Simmons pledged to preserve America's white, Protestant civilization. In the 1920s, Klan publicity claimed that the organization was fighting for "Americanism."

The Klan attracted few members until 1920, when Simmons hired public relations entrepreneurs Edward Young Clarke and Elizabeth Tyler, paying

Analyzing *Political Cartoons*

New Immigrants This cartoon portrays the feelings of many Americans who were opposed to immigration. What comment does the cartoon make about immigrants?

them a commission of $8 of every $10 initiation fee for a new Klan recruit. Clarke and Tyler divided the nation into regions and paid more than 1,000 "salespeople" to promote the Klan. As a result of their strategy, membership in the Ku Klux Klan exploded, reaching nearly 4 million by 1924 as it spread beyond the South and into Northern cities.

The Klan began to decline in the late 1920s, however, largely as a result of scandals and power struggles involving its leaders. Membership shrank, and politicians whom the Klan supported were voted out of office. The sharp reduction in immigrants due to new immigration laws further disabled the Klan, depriving it of a major issue. The Klan never again had a major impact on politics.

✓ **Reading Check** **Explaining** Why did many Americans oppose immigration after World War I?

Controlling Immigration

After World War I, American immigration policies changed in response to the postwar recession and nativist pleas to "Keep America American." Even big business, which previously favored unrestricted immigration as a source of cheap labor, now feared the new immigrants as radicals.

In 1921 President Harding signed the **Emergency Quota Act,** which established a temporary quota system, limiting immigration. According to this act, only three percent of the total number of people in any ethnic group already living in the United States, as indicated in the 1910 census, could be admitted in a single year. This theoretically restricted the number of immigrants from all countries, but in practice it discriminated heavily against people from southern and eastern Europe. Ethnic identity and national origin thus determined admission to the United States.

Henry Curran, the commissioner of Ellis Island from 1922 to 1926, commented on the heartbreak caused by the Emergency Quota Act:

❝The hardest quota cases were those that separated families. When part of the family had been born in a country with a quota still open, while the other part had been born in a country whose quota was exhausted, the law let in the first part and deported the other part. Mothers were torn from children, husbands from wives. The law came down like a sword between them.❞

—quoted in *Ellis Island: Echoes from a Nation's Past*

The National Origins Act of 1924

In 1924 the National Origins Act made immigrant restriction a permanent policy. The law also tightened the quota system, setting quotas at two percent of each national group residing in the country in 1890. By moving back the year to 1890, an even larger proportion of the quotas were allotted to immigrants from northwestern Europe.

A second part of the act, which took effect in 1929, replaced the 1924 quotas with a limit of 150,000 immigrants admitted per year. In addition, the percentage allotted to each nationality would now be based on the 1920 census. This resulted in northwestern European countries accounting for 87 percent of the total immigration quota.

Hispanic Immigration to the United States

The immigration acts of 1921 and 1924 reduced the available labor pool in the United States. While workers and unions rejoiced at the reduction in competition for jobs, employers desperately needed laborers for agriculture, mining, and railroad work. Mexican immigrants helped to fill this need.

The first wave of Mexican immigration to the United States followed the passage of the Newlands Reclamation Act of 1902, which provided funds for irrigation projects in the arid Southwest. Factory farms soon dominated the landscape, and they needed large numbers of agricultural laborers. By 1914 more than 70,000 Mexican immigrants had poured into the United States, many of them fleeing the terror and aftermath of the Mexican Revolution of 1910.

A larger wave of immigration brought more than 600,000 Mexicans to the United States between 1914 and the end of the 1920s. The National Origins Act of 1924 exempted natives of the Western Hemisphere from the quota system. As the demand for cheap farm labor in California and the Southwest steadily increased, Mexican immigrants crossed the border in record numbers.

✓ **Reading Check** **Explaining** How did Hispanic immigrants help shape the national identity of the United States?

The New Morality

Many groups that wanted to restrict immigration also wanted to preserve what they considered to be traditional values. They feared that a "new morality" was taking over the nation. Challenging traditional ways of seeing and thinking, the new morality glorified youth and personal freedom and influenced various aspects of American society.

The New Morality Ideals of the loving family and personal satisfaction—views popularized in magazines and other media—influenced popular views on relationships. As the loving and emotional aspects of marriage grew in importance, the ideas of romance, pleasure, and friendship became linked to successful marriages. Advice books in the 1920s dispensed such hints as, "Have lots of pleasure that both husband and wife enjoy . . . and above all, be good friends."

Women in the workforce also began to define the new morality. Many single, working-class women held jobs simply because they needed the wages for themselves or for their families. For some young, single women, work was a way to break away from parental authority and establish a personal identity. Work also provided the wages that allowed women to participate in the consumer culture.

Women who attended college in the 1920s often found support for their emerging sense of independence. Women's colleges, in particular, encouraged their students to pursue careers and to challenge traditional ideas about the nature of women and their role in society.

The automobile also played a role in encouraging the new morality. The nation's youth loved cars because cars made them more independent and allowed them to escape the careful watch of their parents. Instead of socializing at home with the family, many youths could now use cars to seek new forms of entertainment with their friends and to find privacy.

Women in the 1920s Fashion changed during the 1920s, as women "bobbed," or shortened, their hair, wore flesh-colored silk stockings, and admired the youthful look of movie stars. Though not typical of

European Immigration Totals, 1890–1920

NATIONAL GEOGRAPHIC

Number of People Immigrating to the United States by region, 1890–1920

488,099	2,135,312
672,223	3,060,151
1,130,656	3,695,828
1,195,628	3,859,297

— 1914 border

500 miles
500 kilometers
Lambert Azimuthal Equal-Area projection

Geography *Skills*

1. **Interpreting Maps** Between 1890 and 1920, what European regions sent more than three million immigrants to the United States?

2. **Applying Geography Skills** Why were so many people willing to leave their homelands to come to the United States?

most women, the flapper—a young, dramatic, and stylish woman—personified these changes. She smoked cigarettes, drank prohibited liquor, and dressed in attire considered too revealing by many. Zelda Fitzgerald, wife of writer F. Scott Fitzgerald, symbolized the flapper spirit. She urged women to be "light-hearted [and] unconventional" rather than focused on "a career that calls for hard work."

While flappers pursued social freedoms, other women sought financial independence by entering the workforce, many of them as salesclerks, secretaries, or telephone operators. A few made contributions in science, medicine, law, or literature. In science, Florence Sabin's medical research led to a

What Life Was Like...

Modern Clothing
Women's clothing changed significantly in the 1920s. Hemlines were much shorter and showed more of the body. Stylish new hats also emphasized bold colors and a freer design.

Flappers

Perhaps no other symbol of the 1920s captured the spirit of the time like the flapper. Psychologist G. Stanley Hall wrote his observation of a typical flapper:

❝She wore a knitted hat, with hardly any brim, of a flame or bonfire hue; a henna scarf; two strings of Betty beads, of different colors, twisted together; an open short coat, with ample pockets; a skirt with vertical stripes. . . . Her stockings were woolen and of brilliant hue. But most noticeable of all were her high overshoes, or galoshes. One seemed to be turned down at the top and entirely unbuckled, while the other was fastened below and flapped about her trim ankle in a way that compelled attention.❞

—quoted in *We, the American Women*

New Forms of Expression
Rebelling against older, more formal dancing styles, these Charleston dancers perform steps that one observer described as "knock-kneed and pigeon-toed."

---

dramatic drop in death rates from tuberculosis. In literature, Edith Wharton received the Pulitzer Prize for her novel *The Age of Innocence*. Public health nurse Margaret Sanger, believing that the standard of living could be improved if families limited the number of children they had, founded the American Birth Control League in 1921. This organization became Planned Parenthood in the 1940s. In 1928 **Margaret Mead,** one of the first woman anthropologists, published the highly regarded study, *Coming of Age in Samoa*, which described life in a Pacific island culture.

✓ **Reading Check** **Identifying** What political, social, and economic contributions did women make to American society in the 1920s?

The Fundamentalist Movement

While many Americans embraced the new morality, millions more feared that the country was losing its traditional values. To these Americans, the modern consumer culture, relaxed ethics, and growing urbanism symbolized the nation's moral decline. Many of these people, especially those in small rural

towns, responded by joining a religious movement known as **Fundamentalism**—a name derived from a series of pamphlets titled *The Fundamentals*, published by oil millionaire Lyman Stewart.

Fundamentalist Beliefs Fundamentalists believed that the Bible was literally true and without error. They defended the Protestant faith against ideas that implied that human beings derived their moral behavior from society and nature, not God. In particular, Fundamentalists rejected Charles Darwin's theory of evolution, which said that human beings had developed from lower forms of life over the course of millions of years. Instead, they believed in creationism—the belief that God created the world as described in the Bible.

Two popular evangelical preachers, **Billy Sunday** and **Aimee Semple McPherson,** stirred Fundamentalists' passions by preaching traditional religious and moral values in very nontraditional ways. A former professional baseball player, Sunday drew huge crowds with his rapid-fire sermons and on-stage showmanship. McPherson conducted her revivals and faith healings in Los Angeles in a

Charleston
The Charleston, named after the city of Charleston, South Carolina, was the dance craze of the 1920s. Women who did the Charleston were called flappers, perhaps because of the way they flapped their arms while doing the dance.

flamboyant theatrical style, using stage sets and costumes that expressed the themes of her highly emotional sermons.

The Scopes Trial Evolutionists and creationists eventually clashed in a historic trial. In 1925 Tennessee passed the Butler Act, which outlawed any teaching that denied "the story of the Divine Creation of man as taught in the Bible," and taught instead that "man descended from a lower order of animals." The American Civil Liberties Union (ACLU) advertised for a teacher who would be willing to be arrested for teaching evolution. John T. Scopes, a high school biology teacher in Dayton, Tennessee, volunteered to be the test case. He taught evolution and was subsequently arrested and put on trial.

The trial took place in the summer of 1925. William Jennings Bryan, a three-time Democratic presidential candidate, was the prosecutor and represented the creationists. Clarence Darrow, one of the country's most celebrated trial lawyers, defended Scopes. After eight days of trial, Scopes was found guilty and fined $100, although the conviction was later overturned on a technicality. Parts of the trial had been broadcast over

the radio, and Darrow's blistering cross-examination of Bryan did little for the Fundamentalist cause. Increasingly, Fundamentalists found themselves isolated from mainstream Protestantism, and their commitment to political activism declined.

☑ **Reading Check** **Explaining** What were the major beliefs of Fundamentalists?

Prohibition

The movement to ban alcohol had been building throughout the late 1800s. By the early 1900s, many progressives and traditionalists supported prohibition. Many people believed the prohibition of alcohol would help reduce unemployment, domestic violence, and poverty. Their support helped pass the Eighteenth Amendment, which took effect in January 1920.

To try to enforce the amendment, Congress passed the National Prohibition Act, also known as the **Volstead Act.** Enforcing Prohibition became the responsibility of the U.S. Treasury Department. Treasury agents had enforced federal tax laws for many years, but police powers—a government's power to control people and property in the interest of public safety, health, welfare, and morals—had generally been reserved for the state governments. The Eighteenth Amendment granted federal and state governments the power to enforce Prohibition, marking a dramatic increase in federal police powers.

The Treasury Department's new Prohibition Unit struggled to enforce Prohibition. During the 1920s, treasury agents made more than 540,000 arrests, but Americans persisted in blatantly ignoring the law. People flocked to secret bars called speakeasies, where they could purchase alcohol. In New York City alone, an estimated 32,000 such bars sold liquor illegally. Liquor also was readily available in rural

Fact	Fiction	Folklore

New Words The youth culture of the twenties produced a number of new words and phrases that became a part of their own language. In the mid-1920s, partygoers urged fellow dancers to "Get hot! Get hot!" Young Americans also invented such terms as *beauts, cat's pajamas,* and *cat's whiskers* to describe attractive young women. The terms *lounge lizards, jelly beans,* and *jazzbos* described attractive young men, while the phrase *hard-boiled eggs* described tough guys.

Picturing **History**

Prohibition in Action Federal revenue agents carried out the laws of Prohibition by destroying barrels of alcohol. How successful were their enforcement efforts?

America, where bootlegging—the illegal production and distribution of liquor—was common.

Organized crime specialized in supplying and often running these speakeasies, which popped up all over the country. The huge profits that could be made supplying liquor encouraged some people to become smugglers, bringing liquor into the United States from Canada and the Caribbean. Smuggling and the consumption of liquor by millions helped create an illegal billion-dollar industry for gangsters. More than 70 federal agents were killed while enforcing Prohibition in the 1920s.

Crime became big business, and some gangsters had enough money to corrupt local politicians. Al Capone, one of the most successful and violent gangsters of the era, had many police officers, judges, and other officials on his payroll. Capone dominated organized crime in Chicago, where he ran bootlegging and other criminal rackets. Finally, Eliot Ness, the leader of a special Treasury Department task force, brought Capone to justice.

The battle to repeal Prohibition began almost as soon as the Eighteenth Amendment was ratified. Supporters of repeal associated Prohibition with "priggish fanaticism." The ratification of the Twenty-first Amendment in 1933 repealed the Eighteenth Amendment and ended federally-mandated Prohibition. It was a victory for the forces of modernism and a defeat for the supporters of traditional moral values.

Reading Check **Analyzing** Analyze the reasons for the adoption of the Eighteenth Amendment.

SECTION 1 ASSESSMENT

Checking for Understanding

1. **Define:** anarchist, eugenics, flapper, evolution, creationism, police powers, speakeasy.
2. **Identify:** Ku Klux Klan, Emergency Quota Act, Fundamentalism.
3. **Explain** why the Eighteenth Amendment was repealed.

Reviewing Themes

4. **Continuity and Change** How did the passage of the Eighteenth Amendment and the Volstead Act change the federal government's role?

Critical Thinking

5. **Synthesizing** Why were immigrants from Mexico not included in the quota system set by the immigration acts?
6. **Categorizing** Use a graphic organizer similar to the one below to list the provisions of the immigration acts passed in the 1920s.

Act	Provisions

Analyzing Visuals

7. **Analyzing Photographs** Study the image on this page of the federal agent destroying barrels of alcohol. Why do you think the barrels were destroyed in public with a crowd watching?

Writing About History

8. **Persuasive Writing** Imagine it is the 1920s. Write a letter to your senator to persuade him or her to either continue to support Prohibition or to work for its repeal.

Critical Thinking
SKILLBUILDER

Synthesizing Information

Why Learn This Skill?

The authors of this book gathered information from many sources to present a story of how the United States came about and how the country's people lived. To combine the information into a logical story, the authors used a process called *synthesis*. Being able to synthesize information can be a useful skill for you as a student when you need to gather data from several sources for a report or a presentation.

Learning the Skill

The skill of synthesizing involves combining and analyzing information gathered from separate sources or at different times to make logical connections. Follow these steps to synthesize information:

- Select important and relevant information.
- Analyze the information and build connections.
- Reinforce or modify the connections as you acquire new information.

Suppose you need to write a research paper on the status of women in the 1920s. You would need to synthesize what you learn to inform others. You could begin by detailing the ideas and information you already have about the status of women in the 1920s. A graphic organizer such as the one on this page could help categorize the facts.

Then you could select an article about women in the 1920s, such as the following:

In 1923 the National Woman's Party first proposed an equal rights amendment to the Constitution. This amendment stated that "men and women shall have equal rights throughout the United States and every place subject to its jurisdiction." The National Woman's party pointed out that legislation discriminating against women existed in every state. . . .

Some progressive women reformers, however, opposed the goals of the National Woman's Party. These progressives favored protective legislation, which had brought shorter hours and better working conditions for many women. The efforts of the progressives helped defeat the equal rights amendment.

Women's Status in the 1920s	
Economic:	Many more women worked in factories and other jobs outside the home.
Social:	Women had much more social freedom, including greater choices in clothing styles and public behavior.
Educational:	Many women had a high school education, and more than ever were attending college.

Practicing the Skill

Use the graphic organizer and the passage on this page to answer the following questions.

❶ What information is presented in the table?

❷ What is the main idea of the passage? What information does the passage add to your knowledge of this topic?

❸ By synthesizing the two sources and using what you know from reading Section 1 of this chapter, what conclusions can you draw about the role of women in 1920s society?

Skills Assessment

Complete the Practicing Skills questions on page 633 and the Chapter 20 Skill Reinforcement Activity to assess your mastery of this skill.

Applying the Skill

Synthesizing Information Find two sources of information on the same topic and write a short report. In your report, answer these questions: What kinds of sources did you use—primary or secondary? What are the main ideas in these sources? How does each source add to your understanding of the topic? Do the sources support or contradict each other?

 Glencoe's **Skillbuilder Interactive Workbook CD-ROM, Level 2,** provides instruction and practice in key social studies skills.

The Sacco-Vanzetti Case

On April 15, 1920, in South Braintree, Massachusetts, armed robbers murdered two factory employees during a payroll holdup. Police arrested two Italian immigrants and anarchists—Nicola Sacco and Bartolomeo Vanzetti—as suspects. After a court found the two men guilty, defense attorneys fought for six years for a new trial. The attorneys believed the trial had shown signs of prejudice, intimidation, and dishonesty. Did Sacco and Vanzetti receive a fair trial, or were they victims of the troubled atmosphere in the United States at the time? You're the historian.

Read the following excerpts from testimony and evidence. Then complete the questions and activities that follow.

Painting supporting the accused

From trial testimony

The defense produced several people who supported the defendants' alibis. When arrested, Nicola Sacco had been carrying a pistol. The prosecuting attorney questioned Captain Proctor, a Massachusetts State Police ballistics expert, about the gun.

Q. Captain Proctor, have you an opinion as to whether bullet three was fired from the Colt automatic which is in evidence [Sacco's pistol]?

A. I have.

Q. And what is your opinion?

A. My opinion is that it is consistent with being fired by that pistol.

Defense experts, however, testified that in their judgment, bullet three had not been fired from Sacco's gun. The defense called on Sacco to testify, which gave the prosecution an opportunity to ask Sacco about his political beliefs.

Q. Did you say yesterday you love a free country?

A. Yes, sir.

Q. Did you love this country in the month of May 1917? [At this time, Sacco had gone to Mexico to escape military service.]

A. If you can, Mr. Katzman, if you give me that, —I could explain.

Q. There are two words you can use, Mr. Sacco, yes or no.

A. Yes.

[later]

Q. What did you mean when you said yesterday you loved a free country?

A. . . .When I came to this country I saw there was not what I was thinking before. . . . I could see the best men, intelligent, education, they been arrested and sent to prison and died in prison . . . and Debs, one of the great men in his country, he is in prison . . . because he is a socialist. He wanted the laboring class to have better conditions . . . but they put him in prison. . . . They want the working class to be low all the times.

The jury returned a verdict of guilty. In the sentencing phase, Bartolomeo Vanzetti was asked to explain why he should not be sentenced to death.

I am suffering because I am a radical, and indeed I am a radical. I have suffered because I am an Italian, and indeed I am an Italian. I have suffered more for my family and for my beloved than for myself, but I am so convinced to be right that if you could execute me two times, and if I could be reborn two other times, I would live again to do what I have done already. . . . You know I am innocent. That is the same words I pronounced seven years ago. You condemn two innocent men.

DIED IN CHAIR THIS MORNING

Electrocuted in That Order Soon After Midnight—All Reject Religious
Consolation to the Last—Two Make Statements

Comments on the case

The Sacco-Vanzetti case aroused indignation among intellectuals from the 1920s on. They generally agreed that the two were found guilty because they were Italian radicals, not because there was clear evidence against them. However, two students of the case, Robert Hanson, a local historian, and Francis Russell, who wrote two books on the case, believe Sacco and Vanzetti received a fair trial. Russell cites James Graham, an attorney for Sacco:

We spent considerable time with him [Vanzetti] at the Plymouth County Jail as the case was drawing to a close. . . . Toward the end of the discussion Mr. Vahey said to Vanzetti, in substance, "I can advise you as to what the District Attorney may inquire about the effect of your failure to take the stand, but you are the one who has to make the decision as to whether you will testify or not."

Vanzetti replied,

I don't think I can improve on the alibi which has been established. I had better not take the stand.

Russell also reports that Carlo Tresca, an anarchist who had supported the two Italians, told friends that Sacco was guilty, Vanzetti innocent. Then Russell quotes a letter from labor writer Paul Jacobs:

. . . I had a close friend, Anthony Ramuglia. . . . One day he came to me and said he had a story he wanted me to write. . . . The story was that when he was a young man around the anarchist movement in Boston, he had been approached by one of Sacco's witnesses for his alibi in the restaurant at lunch. My friend Tony agreed, and evidently, was carefully coached in what he was to say, when suddenly he remembered that on the day in question

he had actually been in jail in St. Louis and so might obviously be found out as a perjurer. He told someone about this and was relieved of his responsibilities. . . . I asked Tony whether he thought Sacco and Vanzetti were really guilty, and he replied in much the same way as you quote Tresca. "Sacco could have done it but Vanzetti was never capable of such a thing."

Understanding the Issue

1. Why did the defense attorneys believe that the defendants were not given a fair trial?
2. Why do you think the prosecution questioned Sacco on his political beliefs?
3. After studying the historical context of the case and the frame of reference of the jury, how might a modern historian argue that Sacco and Vanzetti did not receive a fair trial?

Activities

1. **Investigate** Check your local library or the Internet and prepare a report on the latest information on the case.
2. **Create a Simulation** Recreate the trial. Research the testimony and the people involved in the case. Assign roles to class members, including witnesses, jury members, a prosecutor, a defense attorney, and a judge.

Workers showing support for Sacco (right) and Vanzetti (center)

Guide to Reading

Main Idea

An era of exciting and innovative cultural trends, the 1920s witnessed changes in art and literature. This period also saw a dramatic increase in the country's interest in sports and other forms of popular culture.

Key Terms and Names

Bohemian, Carl Sandburg, Eugene O'Neill, Ernest Hemingway, F. Scott Fitzgerald, mass media

Reading Strategy

Organizing As you read about the 1920s, complete a graphic organizer like the one below by filling in the main characteristics of art, literature, and popular culture that reflect the era.

Cultural Movement	Main Characteristics
Art	
Literature	
Popular Culture	

Reading Objectives

- **Describe** the explosion of art and literature and the disillusionment of 1920s artists.
- **Summarize** the effects of sports, movies, radio, and music on popular culture.

Section Theme

Culture and Traditions American culture in the 1920s saw a rise in both the arts and popular entertainment.

Preview of Events

♦1922   ♦1924   ♦1926   ♦1928

1923
Coca-Cola creates the six-pack

1925
F. Scott Fitzgerald's *The Great Gatsby* published

1927
Babe Ruth hits 60 home runs

1927
First feature-length sound motion picture, *The Jazz Singer*

1927
Charles Lindbergh makes solo transatlantic flight

★ An American Story ★

On May 20, 1927, a lanky, sandy-haired young man named Charles Lindbergh took off from an airfield on Long Island, New York, in a small, single-engine plane called the *Spirit of St. Louis* and headed east across the Atlantic Ocean. The next evening—more than 33 hours after Lindbergh left New York—thousands of people waited anxiously at the small Le Bourget airfield outside Paris, France. Attention was riveted on the sky, and the spectators strained their eyes as they watched Lindbergh's small airplane softly slip out of the darkness. When the plane landed, the crowd ecstatically greeted the pilot, who had just completed a historic event—the first solo nonstop flight across the Atlantic Ocean.

In an era when people questioned ideals and heroes, Lindbergh's historic flight symbolized American progress in the modern age, and his solo triumph restored Americans' belief in the courageous, pioneering individual. American writer F. Scott Fitzgerald said of Lindbergh:

❝A young Minnesotan who seemed to have nothing to do with his generation did a heroic thing, and for the moment people set down their glasses in country clubs and speakeasies and thought of their old dreams.❞

—quoted in *Echoes of the Jazz Age*

Art and Literature

The modern age symbolized by Lindbergh's historic transatlantic flight was reflected strongly in American art, literature, and popular culture. During the 1920s, American artists and writers challenged traditional ideas. These artists explored what it meant to be "modern," and they searched for meaning in the emerging challenges of the modern world.

Greenwich Village and the South Side
Many artists, writers, and intellectuals of the era flocked to Manhattan's Greenwich Village and Chicago's South Side. As writer Brooks Atkinson noted in a memoir,

❝The Village was no prude . . . no matter what you did you could hardly be conspicuous. On my street the middle-aged lady in knickers who aired her cat on a pink ribbon twice a day and the rosy-cheeked damsel in overalls who split kindling wood on the side walk . . . were hardly more conspicuous than the formal citizenry. To become conspicuous you would probably have to shoot someone in the street.❞
—from *New York's Greenwich Village*

The artistic and unconventional, or Bohemian, lifestyle of these neighborhoods offered young artists and writers new lifestyles.

Modern American Art
European art movements greatly influenced the modernists of American art. Perhaps most striking was the diverse range of artistic styles, each attempting to express the individual, modern experience.

Taking his cue from the bold and colorful Impressionism of French artist Paul Cézanne, American painter John Marin drew on nature as well as the urban dynamics of New York for inspiration, explaining, "the whole city is alive; buildings, people, all are alive; and the more they move me the more I feel them to be alive." Painter Charles Scheeler applied the influences of photography and the geometric forms of Cubism to urban and rural American landscapes. **Edward Hopper** revived the visual accuracy of Realism in his haunting scenes. His paintings conveyed a modern sense of disenchantment and isolation.

Poets and Writers
Poets and writers of the 1920s varied greatly in their styles and subject matter. Chicago poet **Carl Sandburg** used common speech to glorify the Midwest and the expansive nature of American life. In Greenwich Village, Edna St.

Vincent Millay, in her poem "First Fig," expressed women's freedom and equality and praised a life intensely lived:

❝My candle burns at both ends;
It will not last the night;
But ah, my foes, and oh, my friends—
It gives a lovely light.❞

Several poets of this time had an important impact on the literary culture. Gertrude Stein, for example, was supposed to have been able to make or break a writer's career with a few well-placed remarks. Poets such as Ezra Pound, Amy Lowell, and William Carlos Williams used clear, concise images to express moments in time.

Some poets concentrated on what they considered the negative effects of modernism. In his poem "The Hollow Men," for example, **T.S. Eliot** described a world filled with empty dreams and "hollow men," and he foresaw a world that would end "not with a bang but a whimper."

Among playwrights, one of the most innovative was **Eugene O'Neill.** His plays, filled with bold artistry and modern themes, portrayed realistic characters and situations, offering a vision of life that sometimes touched on the tragic.

Many novelists, affected by the experiences of World War I, wrote about disillusionment and reevaluated the myths of American heroes. They often created characters who were "heroic antiheroes"—flawed individuals who still had heroic qualities of mind and spirit. **Ernest Hemingway,** who served as an ambulance driver in Italy during World War I, was one such writer. His fiction presented a new literary style characterized by direct, simple, and concise prose, as when he wrote about war in such works as *For Whom the Bell Tolls* and *A Farewell to Arms.*

History *Through Art*

Lonely People Like many of his works, Edward Hopper's *Nighthawks* depicts isolated people. How do you think this painting reflects the experience of small-town people who moved to the cities?

John Dos Passos, a critic of America's capitalist culture, experimented with the form of the novel in his innovative trilogy *U.S.A.*, which combined fiction, biography, news headlines, and prose poems. Sinclair Lewis wrote about the absurdities of traditional life in small-town America in his novels *Main Street* and *Babbitt*. **F. Scott Fitzgerald,** perhaps the most famous writer of the era, created colorful, glamorous characters who chased futile dreams in *The Great Gatsby*, a novel that poignantly exposed the emptiness and superficiality of much of modern society.

✓ **Reading Check** **Examining** Why did many artists, writers, and intellectuals flock to New York City's Greenwich Village and Chicago's South Side during the 1920s?

Popular Culture

The economic prosperity of the 1920s provided many Americans with more leisure time and more spending money, which they devoted to making their lives more enjoyable. Millions of Americans eagerly watched and participated in sports and enjoyed music, theater, and other forms of popular entertainment. They also fell in love with radio shows and motion pictures.

Baseball, Boxing, and Other Sports Thanks to radio and motion pictures, sports such as baseball and boxing reached new heights of popularity in the 1920s. Baseball star **Babe Ruth** became a national hero, famous for hitting hundreds of home runs. As one broadcaster later remarked, "He wasn't a baseball player. He was a worldwide celebrity, an international star, the likes of which baseball has never seen since."

Sports fans also idolized boxer Jack Dempsey. Dempsey held the title of world heavyweight champion from 1919 until 1926, when he lost it to Gene Tunney. When Dempsey attempted to win back the title in 1927, fans' enthusiasm for the rematch reached such a frenzy that one store sold $90,000 worth of radios—an incredible sum at that time—in the two weeks before the event.

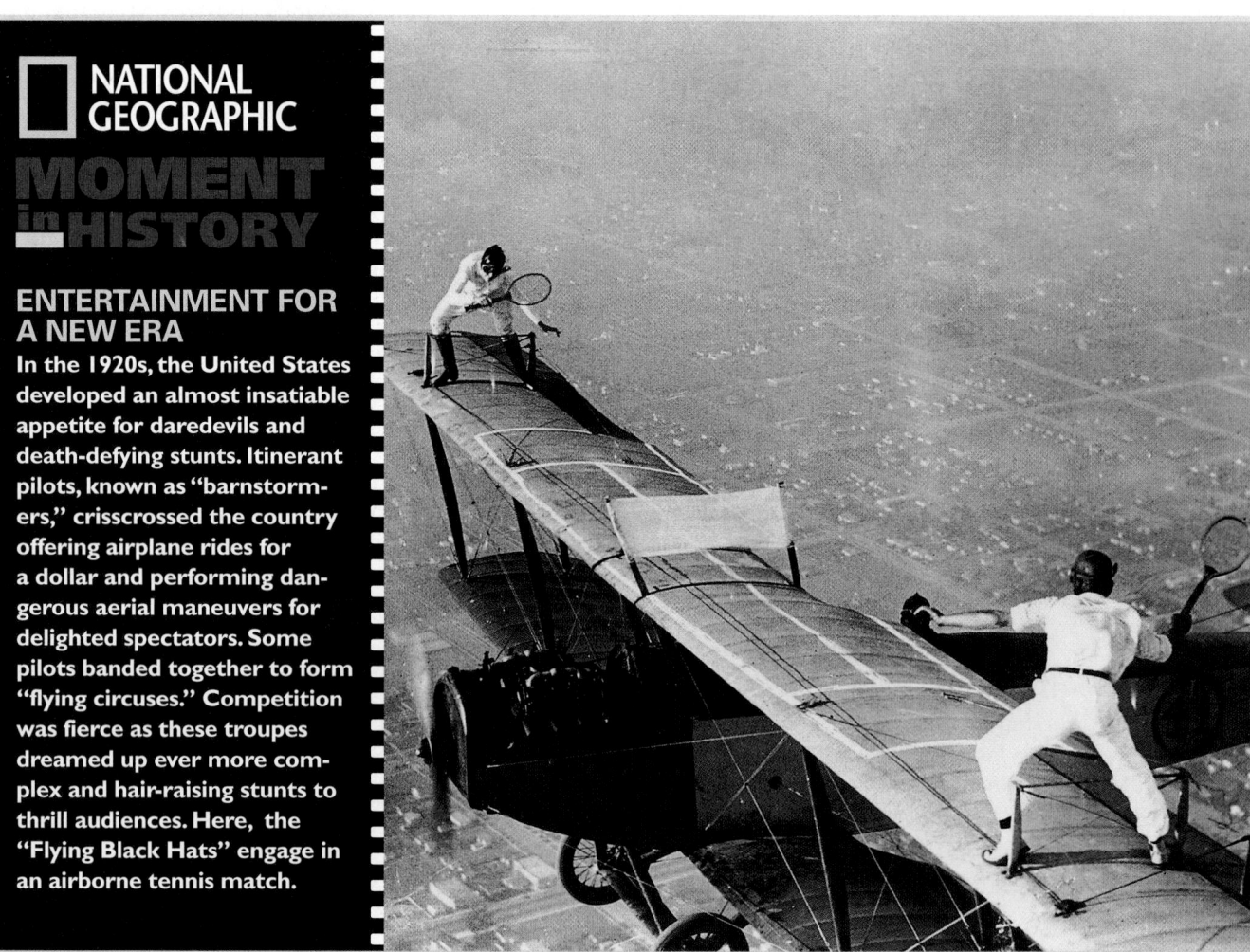

NATIONAL GEOGRAPHIC

MOMENT in HISTORY

ENTERTAINMENT FOR A NEW ERA

In the 1920s, the United States developed an almost insatiable appetite for daredevils and death-defying stunts. Itinerant pilots, known as "barnstormers," crisscrossed the country offering airplane rides for a dollar and performing dangerous aerial maneuvers for delighted spectators. Some pilots banded together to form "flying circuses." Competition was fierce as these troupes dreamed up ever more complex and hair-raising stunts to thrill audiences. Here, the "Flying Black Hats" engage in an airborne tennis match.

Americans eagerly followed other sports and sports figures, too. Newspaper coverage helped generate enthusiasm for college football. One of the most famous players of the 1920s was Red Grange of the University of Illinois. Grange was known as the "Galloping Ghost" because of his speed and ability to evade members of opposing teams.

Millions of sports fans also were thrilled by the achievements of Bobby Jones, the best golfer of the decade, and tennis players Bill Tilden and Helen Wills, who dominated world tennis. In 1926 Jones became the first golfer to win the U.S. Open and the British Open in the same year. In 1927 swimmer Gertrude Ederle enchanted Americans when she shattered records by swimming the English Channel in a little over 14 hours.

The Rise of Hollywood Although sports became increasingly popular in the 1920s, nothing quite matched the allure of motion pictures. Technology had not yet made sound possible in films, so theaters hired piano players to provide music during the feature, while subtitles revealed the plot. Audiences thronged to see such stars as Mary Pickford, Charlie Chaplin, Tom Mix, Douglas Fairbanks, Gloria Swanson, Rudolph Valentino, and Clara Bow. In 1927 the first "talking" picture—*The Jazz Singer*—was produced, and the golden age of Hollywood began.

Popular Radio Shows and Music Radio also enjoyed a large following during the Jazz Age. In 1920, in one of the first commercial radio broadcasts in history, listeners of station KDKA in Pittsburgh learned the news of Warren G. Harding's landslide victory in the presidential election. Within two years, Americans could turn the dial to more than 400 different radio stations around the country.

Most stations in the 1920s played the popular music of the day, such as "Yes! We Have No Bananas" and "Lover Come Back Again." Broadcasts such as *The Eveready Hour* offered everything from classical music to comedy. In one of the most popular radio shows, *Amos 'n' Andy,* the trials and tribulations of two African American characters (portrayed by white actors) captured the nation's attention every evening.

The mass media—radio, movies, newspapers, and magazines aimed at a broad audience—did more than just entertain. Their easy availability to millions helped break down patterns of provincialism, or narrow focus on local interests. They fostered a sense of shared national experience that helped unify the nation and spread the new ideas and attitudes of the time.

Babe Ruth

✓ **Reading Check** **Summarizing** How did the American economy of the 1920s affect popular culture?

SECTION 2 ASSESSMENT

Checking for Understanding
1. **Define:** Bohemian, mass media.
2. **Identify:** Carl Sandburg, Eugene O'Neill, Ernest Hemingway, F. Scott Fitzgerald.
3. **Describe** the main themes of artists and writers during the 1920s.

Reviewing Themes
4. **Culture and Traditions** How did writers, artists, and popular culture of the 1920s affect traditional ideas in the United States?

Critical Thinking
5. **Synthesizing** How did World War I influence the literature written during the 1920s?
6. **Organizing** Use a graphic organizer similar to the one below to list the effects of mass media on American culture.

Effects

Mass Media of 1920s

Analyzing Visuals
7. **Interpreting Art** Study the Edward Hopper painting, *Nighthawks,* on page 621. How do different elements of this piece work to convey a sense of isolation?

Writing About History
8. **Descriptive Writing** Imagine that you have moved to New York's Greenwich Village in the 1920s. Write a letter to a friend describing the atmosphere in your neighborhood.

TIME NOTEBOOK

Appreciation

LOUIS DANIEL ARMSTRONG *Writer Stanley Crouch remembers Louis Armstrong, a Jazz Age great.*

Pops. Sweet Papa Dip. Satchmo. He had perfect pitch and perfect rhythm. His improvised melodies and singing could be as lofty as a moon flight or as low-down as the blood drops of a street thug dying in the gutter. The extent of his influence across jazz and across American music continues to this day.

Not only do we hear Armstrong in trumpet players who represent the present renaissance in jazz, we can also detect his influence in certain rhythms that sweep from country-and-western music to rap.

Louis Daniel Armstrong was born in New Orleans on August 4, 1901. It was at a home for troubled kids that young Louis first put his lips to the mouthpiece of a cornet and later, a trumpet.

In 1922 Armstrong went to Chicago, where he joined King Oliver and his Creole Jazz Band. The band brought out the people and all the musicians, black and white, who wanted to know how it was truly done.

When he first played in New York City in 1924, his improvisations set the city on its head. The stiff rhythms of the time were slashed away by his combination of the percussive and the soaring. He soon returned to Chicago, perfected what he was doing, and made one record after another.

Louis Armstrong was so much, in fact, that every school of jazz since has had to address how he interpreted the basics of the idiom—swing, blues, ballads, and Afro-Hispanic rhythms. His freedom, his wit, and his discipline give his music a perpetual position in the wave of the future that is the station of all great art.

VERBATIM

❝The great creators of the government . . . thought of America as a light to the world, as created to lead the world in the assertion of the right of peoples and the rights of free nations.❞

  WOODROW WILSON,
  in defense of the League of Nations, 1920

❝We seek no part in directing the destinies of the Old World.❞

  WARREN G. HARDING,
  Inaugural Address, 1921

❝Here was a new generation, . . . dedicated more than the last to the fear of poverty and the worship of success; grown up to find . . . all wars fought, all faiths in man shaken.❞

F. Scott Fitzgerald

  F. SCOTT FITZGERALD,
  author, This Side of Paradise

❝There has been a change for the worse during the past year in feminine dress, dancing, manners and general moral standards. [One should] realize the serious ethical consequences of immodesty in girls' dress.❞

  from the **PITTSBURGH OBSERVER**

❝[In New York] I saw 7,000,000 two-legged animals penned in an evil smelling cage, . . . streets as unkempt as a Russian steppe, . . . rubbish, waste paper, cigar butts. . . . One glance and you know no master hand directs.❞

  article in Soviet newspaper **PRAVDA**
  describing New York City in 1925

BROWN BROTHERS

Hide the Hooch

Ingenious Americans are finding unusual places to store their liquor under Prohibition:

- canes
- hot water bottles
- shoe heels
- rolled newspaper
- folds of coats
- perfume bottles

Milestones

EMBARRASSED, 1920. TEXAS SENATOR MORRIS SHEPPARD, a leading proponent of the Eighteenth Amendment, when a large whiskey still is found on his farm.

ERASED, 1922. THE WORD "OBEY," from the Episcopal marriage ceremony, by a vote of American Episcopal bishops.

DIED, 1923. HOMER MOREHOUSE, 27, in the 87th hour of a record-setting 90-hour, 10-minute dance marathon.

EXONERATED, 1921. EIGHT CHICAGO WHITE SOX PLAYERS charged with taking bribes to throw the 1919 World Series. The players were found "not guilty" when grand jury testimony disappeared. Newly appointed commissioner of baseball Kenesaw Mountain Landis banned the "Black Sox" from baseball.

CULVER PICTURES

MAKING A COMEBACK. SANTA CLAUS, after falling into low favor in the last decade. Aiming at children, advertisers are marketing St. Nick heavily.

60,000
Families with radios in 1922

9,000,000
Motor vehicles registered in U.S. in 1920

$2,467,946
Income tax paid by Henry Ford in 1924

500,000
People who wrote to Henry Ford in 1924 begging for money

33.5 Number of hours Charles Lindbergh spent in his nonstop flight from New York to Paris on May 20, 1927

1,800 Tons of ticker tape and shredded paper dropped on Charles Lindbergh in his parade in New York City

$16,000 Cost of cleaning up after the parade

7,000 Job offers received by Lindbergh

3.5 million
Number of letters received by Lindbergh

BROWN BROTHERS

Charles Lindbergh

Invented This Decade

How did we live without . . .

- push-button elevators
- neon signs
- oven thermostats
- electric razors
- tissues
- spiral-bound notebooks
- motels
- dry ice
- zippers
- pop-up toasters
- flavored yogurt
- car radios
- adhesive tape
- food disposals
- water skiing
- automatic potato peeler
- self-winding wristwatch

Beautiful Goodrich ZIPPERS
BROWN BROTHERS

SECTION 3 African American Culture

Guide to Reading

Main Idea
During World War I, the prospect of employment and greater freedoms spurred the "Great Migration" of African Americans from the rural South to industrial cities in the North.

Key Terms and Names
Great Migration, Harlem Renaissance, Claude McKay, Langston Hughes, jazz, Cotton Club, blues, Marcus Garvey

Reading Strategy
Organizing As you read about the African American experience in the 1920s, complete a graphic organizer similar to the one below by filling in the causes and effects of the Harlem Renaissance.

Reading Objectives
- **Describe** the Harlem Renaissance and the rediscovery of African American cultural roots.
- **Explain** the increase in African American political activism.

Section Theme
Groups and Institutions African Americans played stronger political and cultural roles in the 1920s than they had in previous decades.

Preview of Events

♦1922   ♦1924   ♦1926   ♦1928

1922 — Antilynching bill passes in the House but not in the Senate

1924 — The Negro League holds its first world series

1926 — Langston Hughes's *The Weary Blues* published

1928 — Claude McKay's *Home to Harlem* published

★ An American Story ★

On August 8, 1922, a young cornet player named Louis Armstrong took the train from New Orleans to Chicago. His hero, the bandleader Joe "King" Oliver, had sent a telegram to Armstrong offering him a job. Here, Armstrong recalls his trip:

❝When I got to the station in Chicago, I couldn't see Joe Oliver anywhere . . . I'd never seen a city that big. All those tall buildings, I thought they were universities. I said, no, this is the wrong city. I was just fixing to take the next train back home . . . when a red cap [train porter] Joe had left word with came up to me. He took me to the Lincoln Gardens and when I got to the door there and heard Joe and his band wailing so good, I said to myself, 'No, I ain't supposed to be in this band. They're too good.'❞

The next night, near the end of the show, Oliver let Armstrong perform a solo. Armstrong later recalled his feelings: "I had hit the big time. I was up North with the greats. I was playing with my idol, the King, Joe Oliver. My boyhood dream had come true at last."

—quoted in *The African American Family Album*

The Harlem Renaissance

Louis Armstrong's first impressions of Chicago and his desire to fulfill a dream were probably similar to the first impressions and desires of hundreds of thousands of other African Americans who joined in what was called the **Great Migration** from the rural

South to industrial cities in the North. By moving north, African Americans sought to escape the segregated society of the South, to find economic opportunities, and to build better lives. After World War I, black populations swelled in large northern cities. The cities were full of nightclubs and music, particularly in the New York City neighborhood of Harlem—the heart and soul of the African American renaissance. It was there that African Americans created an environment that stimulated artistic development, racial pride, a sense of community, and political organization. The result was a flowering of African American arts that became known as the **Harlem Renaissance.**

The Writers Considered the first important writer of the Harlem Renaissance, **Claude McKay** emigrated from Jamaica to New York. There, he translated the shock of American racism into *Harlem Shadows,* a collection of poetry published in 1922. In such poems as "The Lynching" and "If We Must Die," McKay's eloquent verse expressed a proud defiance and bitter contempt of racism—two striking characteristics of Harlem Renaissance writing.

One of the most prolific, original, and versatile writers of the Harlem Renaissance was **Langston Hughes.** Born in Joplin, Missouri, Hughes became a leading voice of the African American experience in the United States. 📖 *(See American Literature on page 631 for more information on Langston Hughes.)*

Harlem Renaissance authors continue to influence writers today. **Zora Neale Hurston** published her first novels, *Jonah's Gourd Vine* and *Their Eyes Were Watching God*, in the 1930s. These works influenced such contemporary authors as Ralph Ellison and Toni Morrison. Hurston's personal and spirited portrayals of rural African American culture, often set in Florida where she grew up, were also the first major stories featuring African American females as central characters. Other notable writers of the Harlem Renaissance include Countee Cullen, Alain Locke, Dorothy West, and Nella Larsen.

Jazz, Blues, and the Theater Shortly after **Louis Armstrong** arrived in Chicago from New Orleans, he introduced an improvisational, early form of jazz, a style of music influenced by Dixieland music and ragtime, with its ragged rhythms and syncopated melodies.

In 1925, three years after joining Joe "King" Oliver's band, Armstrong awed fellow musicians with a series of recordings made with his group, the "Hot Five." In these recordings, especially in the song "Cornet Chop Suey," Armstrong broke away from the

New Orleans tradition of ensemble or group playing by performing highly imaginative solos. He became the first great cornet and trumpet soloist in jazz music.

Ragtime also influenced the composer, pianist, and bandleader **Duke Ellington,** who listened as a teenager to ragtime piano players in Washington, D.C. In 1923 Ellington formed a small band, moved to New York, and began playing in speakeasies and clubs. He soon created his own sound, a blend of improvisation and orchestration using different combinations of instruments. The Ellington style appeared in such hits as "Mood Indigo" and "Sophisticated Lady."

Like many other African American entertainers, Ellington got his start at the **Cotton Club,** one of the most famous Harlem nightspots. Years later, reflecting on the music of this era, Ellington said, "Everything, and I repeat, *everything* had to swing. And that was just it, those cats really had it; they had that soul. And you know you can't just play some of this music without soul. Soul is very important."

Picturing **History**

Renaissance Writers Claude McKay wrote about his Jamaican homeland, while Zora Neale Hurston celebrated the courage of African Americans in the rural South. How did these writers contribute to African Americans' cultural identity?

Bessie Smith seemed to symbolize soul. Her emotional singing style and commanding voice earned her the title "the Empress of the Blues." Smith sang of unfulfilled love, poverty, and oppression—the classic themes of the blues, a soulful style of music that evolved from African American spirituals. Born in Tennessee, Smith started performing in tent shows, saloons, and small theaters in the South. Discovered by Ma Rainey, one of the first great blues singers, Smith later performed with many of the greatest jazz bands of the era, including those of Louis Armstrong, Fletcher Henderson, and Benny Goodman. Her first recorded song, "Down Hearted Blues," became a major hit in 1923.

While jazz and blues filled the air during the Harlem Renaissance, the theater arts were also flourishing. *Shuffle Along*, the first musical written, produced, and performed by African Americans, made its debut on Broadway in 1921. The show's success helped launch a number of careers, including those of Florence Mills and Paul Robeson.

Paul Robeson, a celebrated singer and actor, received wide acclaim in the title role of a 1924 New York production of *Emperor Jones*, a play by Eugene O'Neill. In 1928 Robeson gained fame for his work in the musical *Show Boat*. He also often appeared at the Apollo Theater, another famous entertainment club in Harlem. Robeson's fame ultimately spread to Europe, where he became well known as a singer and actor.

Perhaps the most daring performer of the era, Josephine Baker transformed a childhood knack for flamboyance into a career as a well-known singer and dancer. Baker performed on Broadway but went to Paris to dance in 1925. Baker took Paris by storm, launching an international career.

The Harlem Renaissance succeeded in bringing international fame to African American arts. It also sparked a political transformation in the United States.

✓ **Reading Check** **Analyzing** Analyze how African Americans helped shape the national identity through the use of music.

Picturing **History**

Harlem Renaissance The growing fame of African American artists, who often performed (but could not be patrons) at Harlem's "Cotton Club," encouraged a flamboyant lifestyle. What conditions encouraged the growth of African American art?

African American Politics

The racial pride that sparked the artistic achievements of the Harlem Renaissance also fueled the political and economic aspirations of many African Americans. The postwar years saw the development of new attitudes among African Americans, who forged new roles in life and in politics. For many, the sight of the 1,300 African American men of the Fifteenth Regiment of New York's National Guard, returning from the war and marching through Manhattan and home to Harlem, symbolized these aspirations. W.E.B. Du Bois, editor of *The Crisis,* captured the new sense of dignity and defiance of African Americans:

> ❝We return.
> We return from fighting.
> We return fighting.
> Make way for democracy! We saved it in France, and by the Great Jehovah, we will save it in the United States of America, or know the reason why.❞
>
> —from *When Harlem Was in Vogue*

The Black Vote in the North

The Great Migration had a significant impact on the political power of African Americans in the North. As their numbers grew in certain city neighborhoods, African Americans became a powerful voting bloc that could sometimes sway the outcome of elections.

At election time, most African American voters in the North cast their votes for Republicans, the party of Abraham Lincoln. In 1928 African American voters in Chicago achieved a significant political breakthrough. Voting as a bloc, they helped elect **Oscar DePriest,** the first African American representative in Congress from a Northern state. During his three terms in Congress, DePriest introduced laws to provide pensions to formerly enslaved African Americans over 75 years old, to declare Lincoln's birthday a public holiday, and to fine and imprison officials who allowed lynchings of prisoners.

The NAACP Battles Lynching

On the legal front, the National Association for the Advancement of Colored People (NAACP) battled valiantly but often unsuccessfully against segregation and discrimination against African Americans. Its efforts focused primarily on lobbying public officials and working through the court system.

From its beginning in 1909, the NAACP lobbied and protested against the horrors of lynching. The NAACP's persistent efforts led to the passage of anti-lynching legislation in the House of

World History Connection

Jazz's Global Roots

Jazz may be an American creation, but its roots stretch across the Atlantic Ocean to Europe and Africa. The music Louis Armstrong and Duke Ellington helped to make famous originated from the spirituals and work songs of African slaves. These songs were a blend of African rhythms and European melodies and harmonies, which African slaves encountered after arriving in North America. This music evolved into ragtime during the late 1800s and early 1900s. By the 1920s, artists had combined aspects of ragtime with the uniquely African American sounds of the blues, and thus jazz was born. *Why do you think music often spreads easily across different cultures?*

Representatives in 1922. The Senate defeated the bill, but the NAACP continued to lobby against lynching throughout the 1920s and 1930s. Its ongoing efforts kept the issue in the news and probably helped to reduce the number of lynchings that took place.

One of the NAACP's greatest political triumphs occurred in 1930 with the defeat of Judge John J. Parker's nomination to the U.S. Supreme Court. The NAACP joined with labor unions to launch a highly organized national campaign against the North Carolina judge, who allegedly was racist and anti-labor. By a narrow margin, the Senate refused to confirm Parker's nomination. His defeat demonstrated that African American voters and lobby groups had finally begun to achieve enough influence to affect national politics and change decisions in Congress.

While some people were fighting for integration and improvement in the economic and political position of African Americans, other groups began to emphasize black nationalism and black pride. Eventually, some began to call for black separation from white society.

Black Nationalism and Marcus Garvey

A dynamic black leader from Jamaica, **Marcus Garvey,** captured the imagination of millions of African Americans with his call for "Negro Nationalism," which glorified the black culture and traditions of the past.

Inspired by Booker T. Washington's call for self-reliance, Garvey founded the Universal Negro Improvement Association (UNIA), an organization aimed at promoting black pride and unity. The central message of Garvey's Harlem-based movement was that African Americans could gain economic and

Black Nationalism Marcus Garvey's Universal Negro Improvement Association advocated African American self-reliance and separation from whites and white society. What eventually happened to Garvey and his movement?

Harlem in a show of support. Garvey told his followers they would never find justice or freedom in America, and he proposed to lead them to Africa.

Garvey's plan to create a settlement in the African country of Liberia alarmed France and Great Britain, which governed surrounding territories. In the United States, the emerging African American middle class and intellectuals distanced themselves from Garvey and his push for racial purity and separation. FBI officials saw UNIA as a dangerous catalyst for black uprisings in urban areas. Garvey also alienated key figures in the Harlem Renaissance by characterizing them as "weak-kneed and cringing . . . [flatterers of] the white man."

Garvey was convicted of mail fraud in 1923 and served time in prison. In 1927 President Coolidge commuted Garvey's sentence and used Garvey's immigrant status to have him deported to Jamaica. Garvey's subsequent attempts to revitalize his movement from abroad failed.

Despite Garvey's failure to keep his movement alive, he inspired millions of African Americans with a sense of pride in their heritage and hope for the future. That sense of pride and hope survived long after Garvey and his "back to Africa" movement was gone. This pride and hope reemerged strongly during the 1950s and played a vital role in the civil rights movement of the 1960s.

political power by educating themselves. Garvey also advocated separation and independence from whites.

In 1920, at the height of his power, Garvey presided over an international conference in the UNIA Liberty Hall in Harlem. After the convention, about 50,000 people, led by Garvey, marched through the streets of

Reading Check **Summarizing** How did World War I change attitudes among African Americans toward themselves and their country?

SECTION 3 ASSESSMENT

Checking for Understanding

1. **Define:** jazz, blues.
2. **Identify:** Great Migration, Harlem Renaissance, Claude McKay, Langston Hughes, Cotton Club, Marcus Garvey.
3. **Explain** how Bessie Smith's blues music conveyed universal themes.
4. **Explain** the importance of the defeat of Judge John Parker's nomination to the U.S. Supreme Court.
5. **Describe** the goals of Marcus Garvey's Universal Negro Improvement Association.

Reviewing Themes

6. **Groups and Institutions** What actions did the NAACP take to expand political rights for African Americans?

Critical Thinking

7. **Synthesizing** How did the Great Migration affect the political power of African Americans in the North?
8. **Analyzing** How did Duke Ellington create a new musical style that grew out of the ragtime tradition?
9. **Organizing** Use a graphic organizer similar to the one below to describe the impact of the Harlem Renaissance on U.S. society.

Impact of Harlem Renaissance

Analyzing Visuals

10. **Examining Photographs** Study the pictures on page 628 of the Cotton Club and African Americans posing by their car. What are some elements of these pictures that show African Americans adopting parts of the 1920s social culture?

Writing About History

11. **Descriptive Writing** Imagine that you witnessed the African American men of the Fifteenth Regiment of New York's National Guard, who had come back from the war, march through Manhattan and home to Harlem. Write a paragraph describing your feelings upon seeing these men.

American LITERATURE

Langston Hughes was born in Joplin, Missouri, in 1902. After high school Hughes went on to Columbia University to study engineering, but he soon dropped out to pursue his first love—poetry. Hughes eventually became known as the "Poet Laureate of Harlem." The following poems are representative of Hughes's work. In "I, Too" he describes the disenfranchisement many African Americans felt in the United States in the 1920s, and their willingness to stand up and take pride in their heritage. In "The Negro Speaks of Rivers," Hughes reveals a profound love of his heritage.

Read to Discover
What is Hughes's perception of the place of African Americans in society at the time he wrote these poems?

Reader's Dictionary
Euphrates: River in the Middle East

Congo and **Nile:** Rivers in Africa

lulled: calmed; soothed

Selected Poems by Langston Hughes

The Negro Speaks of Rivers

I've known rivers:
I've known rivers ancient as the
 world and older than the
flow of human blood in human veins.

My soul has grown deep like the
 rivers.

I bathed in the Euphrates when
 dawns were young.
I built my hut near the Congo and it
 lulled me to sleep.
I looked upon the Nile and raised
 the pyramids above it.
I heard the singing of the Mississippi
 when Abe Lincoln went down to
 New Orleans, and I've seen its
 muddy bosom turn all golden in
 the sunset.

I've known rivers:
Ancient, dusky rivers

My soul has grown deep like the
 rivers.

I, Too

I, too, sing America.

I am the darker brother.
They send me to eat in the kitchen
When company comes,
But I laugh,
And eat well,
And grow strong.

Tomorrow,
I'll be at the table
When company comes.
Nobody'll dare
Say to me,
"Eat in the kitchen,"
Then.

Besides,
They'll see how beautiful I am
And be ashamed—

I, too, am America.

Analyzing Literature

1. **Recall and Interpret** How do you think Hughes's use of punctuation and line breaks helps convey his point?
2. **Evaluate and Connect** Do you think these poems convey a positive message or a negative one? Why?

Interdisciplinary Activity
Response Writing The poem "I, Too" is a response to Walt Whitman's poem, "I Hear America Singing." Using the Internet or other resources, find and read Whitman's poem. In small groups, try to figure out how Hughes's poem ties in to Whitman's. Then write your own response poem to "I Hear America Singing."

Reviewing Key Terms

On a sheet of paper, use each of these terms in a sentence.

1. anarchist
2. eugenics
3. flapper
4. evolution
5. creationism
6. police powers
7. speakeasy
8. Bohemian
9. mass media
10. jazz
11. blues

Chapter Summary

Cultural Changes

- The "new morality" emphasized youth and beauty
- Young people and women gained more independence
- The working class enjoyed more leisure time
- The mass media expanded

African American Renaissance

Harlem Renaissance
- Breakthrough period for African American arts
- Literature revealed racial pride and contempt of racism
- Jazz and blues popularized

Political Renaissance
- Great Migration created strong African American voting blocs in northern cities
- First African American elected to Congress from a northern state
- NAACP battled segregation and discrimination

Revitalized Traditional Values

- Fundamentalists preached traditional religious values
- Emphasis on family and moral values
- Traditionalists supported Prohibition

Nativism

- Nativists used eugenics as a pseudo-scientific basis for ethnic and religious prejudice
- The new Ku Klux Klan targeted African Americans, Jews, Catholics, immigrants, and other groups they considered to be "un-American"
- Congress established immigration quotas

Reviewing Key Facts

12. **Identify:** Emergency Quota Act, Fundamentalism, Carl Sandburg, Eugene O'Neill, Ernest Hemingway, F. Scott Fitzgerald, Great Migration, Harlem Renaissance, Claude McKay, Langston Hughes, Marcus Garvey.
13. Why was there a rise in racism and nativism in the 1920s?
14. What actions did Congress and the president take during the first half of the 1920s to restrict immigration?
15. What national groups were affected most by the new restrictions on immigration?
16. What role did the automobile play in changing the way that young people in the United States lived and socialized?
17. What was the Fundamentalist movement?
18. Why did artists and writers move to Greenwich Village and Chicago's South Side in the 1920s?
19. Why was Harlem the center of the African American renaissance?
20. What were two reasons for the rise in African American political activism?

Critical Thinking

21. **Analyzing Themes: Groups and Institutions** In what ways did the new morality change American family life?
22. **Interpreting** Why was Charles Lindbergh a symbol of modern America?
23. **Determining Cause and Effect** Analyze the causes and effects of the changing role of women in the 1920s.
24. **Identifying** List three works of American art or literature that convey universal themes.
25. **Analyzing** Analyze the impact that Clarence Darrow and William Jennings Bryan had on American society as the lawyers in the Scopes trial.
26. **Categorizing** Use a graphic organizer similar to the one below to list the major organizations and movements of the 1920s and their goals or purposes.

Organizations/Movements	Goals/Purposes

27. **Interpreting Primary Sources** Arna Bontemps was a poet who started his writing career during the Harlem Renaissance. Read the poem and answer the questions that follow.

A Black Man Talks of Reaping

I have sown beside all waters in my day.
I planted deep, within my heart the fear
That wind or fowl would take the grain away.
I planted safe against this stark, lean year.

I scattered seed enough to plant the land
In rows from Canada to Mexico
But for my reaping only what the hand
Can hold at once is all that I can show.

Yet what I sowed and what the orchard yields
My brother's sons are gathering stalk and root,
Small wonder then my children glean in fields
They have not sown, and feed on bitter fruit.

a. What does Bontemps mean by "what the hand can hold at once is all that I can show" and "bitter fruit"?

b. What major theme of Harlem Renaissance writing is evident in this poem?

Practicing Skills

28. Synthesizing Information Read the subsections titled "Nativism Resurges" and "Pseudo-Scientific Racism" at the beginning of Section 1. What information is presented in the first subsection? The second? Synthesize the information in these two subsections and write a short statement that describes American attitudes toward immigrants during the 1920s.

Chapter Activities

29. Research Project Work with another student to research the art of Georgia O'Keeffe of the 1920s. Examine how her efforts reflect the characteristics of the Jazz Age, such as experimentation and innovation. Present your findings to the class.

30. American History Primary Source Document Library CD-ROM Under *The Roaring Twenties,* read "The Movies" by Preston William Slossen. Work with a few of your classmates to write an article that compares and contrasts the motion picture industry in the 1920s with the motion picture industry today.

Writing Activity

31. Persuasive Writing Imagine that you are living during the early 1920s. Marcus Garvey is campaigning to lead African Americans to a new settlement to be founded in Liberia. Write a letter to a newspaper editor in which you take a

U.S. Immigration, 1921 and 1925

1921

Canada and Latin America 15%
Central Europe 22%
Asia 3%
Other countries 2%
Northern and Western Europe 16%
Eastern and Southern Europe 42%

1925

Asia 1%
Canada and Latin America 48%
Other countries 1%
Central Europe 19%
Eastern and Southern Europe 4%
Northern and Western Europe 27%

Source: *Historical Statistics of the United States*

position on the merits of Garvey's plan. In your letter, describe how you think this plan will affect the nation and your own community.

Geography and History

32. The circle graphs above show immigration numbers in the United States in 1921 and 1925. Study the graphs and answer the questions below.

a. Interpreting Graphs What significant changes in immigration do the circle graphs show?

b. Applying Geography Skills Why did these changes in immigration occur between 1921 and 1925?

CHAPTER 21

Normalcy and Good Times
1921–1929

Why It Matters

Prosperity was the theme of the 1920s, and national policy favored business. Although farmers were going through an economic depression, most people remained optimistic about the economy. The middle class bought on credit the many new convenience products available. One of the most popular purchases of the day was the automobile, which had a major impact on how Americans lived.

The Impact Today

Important elements of American life were first seen at this time.
- *The automobile remains central to American transportation.*
- *Credit is a standard means for making purchases.*

 The American Vision Video *The Chapter 21 video, "Tuning in to Radio in the 1920s," describes the growth of a mass media culture in the United States and the importance of the radio.*

1920
- Women vote in national election for the first time

1921
- Washington Conference convenes
- Farm Bloc organized in U.S. Congress

1923
- Teapot Dome scandal erupts
- Ford Motor Company gains 50 percent of the new car market
- President Harding dies

1924
- Dawes Plan negotiated with France, Britain, and Germany
- Calvin Coolidge elected president

United States PRESIDENTS

 Harding 1921–1923

 Coolidge 1923–1929

1921   *1923*   *1925*

World

1923
- Hitler's Munich coup fails

1924
- Leader of Soviet Union, Vladimir Lenin, dies

1925
- Soldier-leader Reza Khan pronounced shah of Iran

Opening Night, Ziegfeld Follies by Howard A. Thain captures the excitement surrounding the opening of a new musical revue in New York City.

1927
• 15 millionth Model T sold

1928
• Kellogg-Briand Pact proposes an end to war

1929
• U.S. radio sales exceed $800 million

Hoover
1929–1933

1927

1929

1926
• British General Strike paralyzes the British economy

1929
• Lateran Treaties with Italy make the Vatican sovereign territory

HISTORY
Online

Chapter Overview
Visit the *American Vision* Web site at tav.glencoe.com and click on *Chapter Overviews—Chapter 21* to preview chapter information.

Presidential Politics

Guide to Reading

Main Idea

Warren Harding's administration suffered from several scandals. His successor, Calvin Coolidge, promised to support business.

Key Terms and Names

normalcy, Ohio Gang, Albert B. Fall, Teapot Dome scandal, immunity, Progressive Party, Robert M. La Follette

Reading Strategy

Taking Notes As you read about Presidents Harding and Coolidge, use the major headings of the section to create an outline similar to the one below.

Presidential Politics
I. The Harding Administration
   A.
   B.
II.
   A.
   B.

Reading Objectives

• **Describe** the corruption that tainted the Harding administration.

• **Explain** how Calvin Coolidge restored public confidence after assuming the presidency.

Section Theme

Government and Democracy The "Ohio Gang" of the Harding administration created scandals and political upheaval.

Preview of Events

♦1920   ♦1922   ♦1924   ♦1926

1920
Women vote in national election for the first time; Warren G. Harding elected president

1923
Teapot Dome scandal; Harding dies; Calvin Coolidge becomes president

1924
Coolidge elected president in his own right

★ *An American Story* ★

In August 1923, Vice President Calvin Coolidge was taking a short vacation at his family's homestead in Plymouth Notch, Vermont. The straitlaced Coolidge went to bed at 9:00 as usual on August 2, but at 2:30 A.M., his father woke him. "I noticed that his voice trembled," Coolidge said later. "I knew that something of the gravest nature had occurred." After learning that President Warren G. Harding was dead, Coolidge dressed hurriedly and went downstairs. Shortly afterward, in a small, sparsely furnished room lit by a flickering kerosene lamp, the elder Coolidge, a farmer and justice of the peace, got out the family Bible and administered the presidential oath of office to his son.

Later, while painting a portrait of the new president, artist Charles Hopkinson asked, "Mr. Coolidge, what was the first thought that came into your mind when you were told that Mr. Harding was dead and the presidency was yours?" Coolidge replied, "I thought I could swing it."

—adapted from *Flappers, Bootleggers, "Typhoid Mary" and the Bomb*

The Harding Administration

Coolidge assumed the presidency during a time when Americans yearned to go back to simpler and steadier times after the carnage of World War I. Coolidge's predecessor, Warren G. Harding, had tailored his presidency to this goal. The oldest of eight children, Harding was born in 1865 in Corsica, Ohio. As an adult, he was active in civic and fraternal organizations, and he also published the *Marion Daily Star*. In 1898 Harding was elected to the Ohio legislature. He fit in comfortably with the powerful Ohio Republican political machine and won election as lieutenant governor in 1903. He failed in his bid for governor in 1910 but was elected to the United States Senate four years later. After serving one term in the Senate, Harding ran for and won the presidency in 1920.

A Self-Doubter in the White House With his silver hair and impressive bearing, Harding looked like a president, but he thought he lacked the intellectual qualifications for the job. "I have such a sure understanding of my own inefficiency," he once said, "that I should really be ashamed to presume myself fitted to reach out for a place of such responsibility."

Despite such doubts, Harding's political philosophy fit in well with the times. He ran on the campaign slogan to return to normalcy, or a return to "normal" life after the war. Harding's charm and genial manner endeared him to the nation. The quiet gloom of President Wilson's last years was replaced by the open, easygoing atmosphere of the first days of the Harding administration. On the day of his election, he went out to play a round of golf—a confident, relaxed gesture.

GOVERNMENT

The Ohio Gang Harding made several distinguished appointments to the cabinet, including former Supreme Court justice Charles Evans Hughes as secretary of state, former Food Administrator Herbert Hoover as secretary of commerce, and business tycoon Andrew Mellon as secretary of the treasury.

Many of Harding's other appointments, however, were disastrous. He gave many cabinet posts and other high-level jobs to friends and political allies from Ohio. Harding named Charles "Doc" Sawyer from Marion, Ohio, as White House physician, a post that came with the rank of brigadier general. Harding made his boyhood friend Daniel Crissinger chairman of the Federal Reserve Board and selected Colonel Charles R. Forbes—another Ohio acquaintance—to head the Veterans Bureau.

Harding felt more comfortable among his old poker-playing friends, known as the **Ohio Gang,** than he did around such sober and serious people as Herbert Hoover. Alice Roosevelt Longworth, the daughter of Theodore Roosevelt, was a keen observer of Washington society. She wrote that it was common to find the Ohio Gang in the White House study, and here she describes a typical scene:

> ❝The air [would be] heavy with tobacco smoke, trays with bottles containing every imaginable brand of whiskey . . . cards and poker chips at hand—a general atmosphere of waistcoat unbuttoned, feet on desk, and spittoons alongside.❞
> —quoted in *The Perils of Prosperity, 1914–1932*

The Ohio Gang did more than drink, smoke, and play poker with the president. Some members used their positions to sell government jobs, pardons, and protection from prosecution. Forbes sold scarce medical supplies from veterans hospitals and kept the money for himself, costing the taxpayers about $250 million. When Harding learned what was going on, he complained privately that he had been betrayed. He said that he had no troubles with his enemies, but his friends were a different story: "They're the ones that keep me walking the floor nights!"

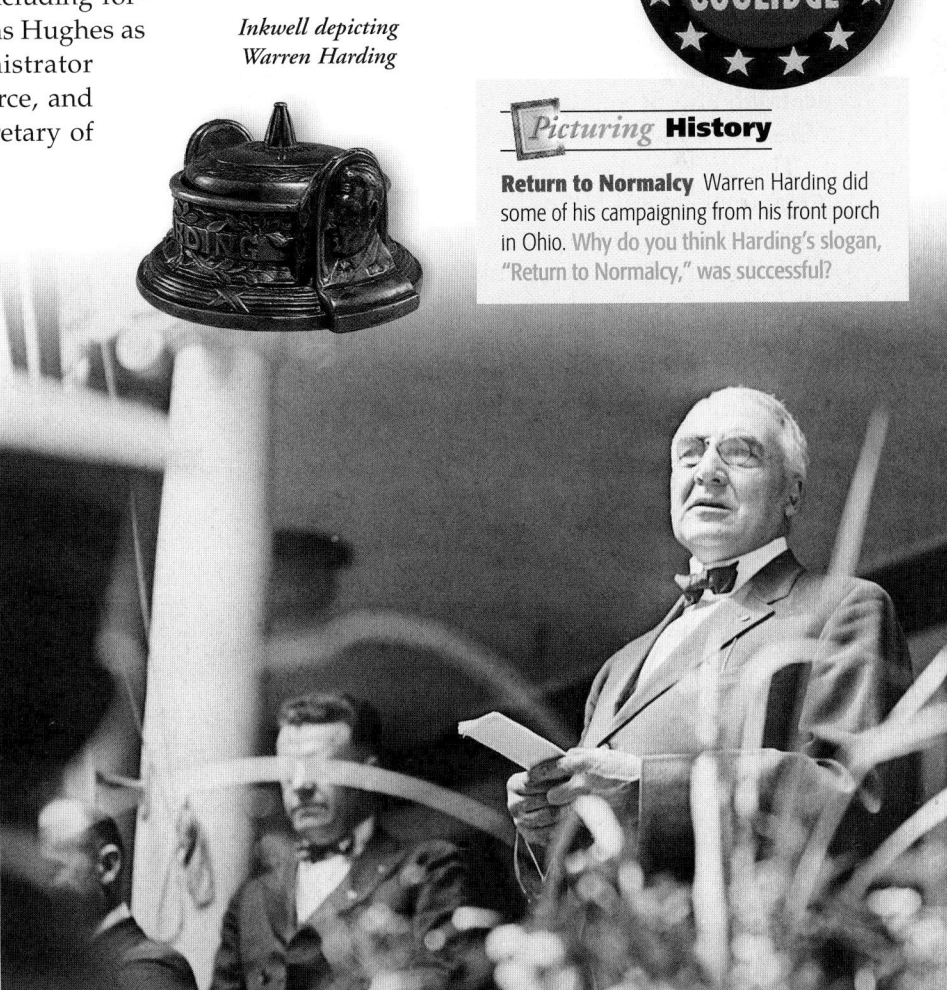

Inkwell depicting Warren Harding

Picturing History

Return to Normalcy Warren Harding did some of his campaigning from his front porch in Ohio. Why do you think Harding's slogan, "Return to Normalcy," was successful?

In June 1923, amid the scandal in the Veterans Bureau and rumors of other unethical behavior, Harding and the First Lady left to tour the West. En route from Alaska to California, he became ill with what was probably a heart attack. He died in San Francisco on August 2, shortly before the news of the Forbes scandal broke.

The Teapot Dome Scandal Other scandals also came to light. Harding's secretary of the interior, **Albert B. Fall,** secretly allowed private interests to lease lands containing U.S. Navy oil reserves at Teapot Dome, Wyoming, and Elk Hills, California. In return, Fall received bribes from these private interests totaling more than $300,000. Eventually the Senate investigated what the newspapers named the **Teapot Dome scandal,** and Secretary Fall became the first cabinet officer in history to go to prison.

The last Harding administration scandal involved Attorney General Harry Daugherty, Harding's former campaign manager. It concerned a German-owned American company that the American government had seized during World War I as enemy property. To acquire the company and its valuable chemical patents, a German agent bribed a "go-between" politician, and a portion of the bribe ended up in an Ohio bank account that Daugherty controlled.

Under investigation by his own Justice Department, Daugherty refused to turn over requested files and bank records. He also refused to testify under oath, claiming immunity, or freedom from prosecution, on the grounds that he had had confidential dealings with the president. Daugherty's actions disgusted the new president, Calvin Coolidge, who demanded his resignation. The tattered reputation of Harding's presidency dissolved in scandal and corruption.

✔ **Reading Check** **Describing** Why was Harding's emphasis on "normalcy" an effective campaign strategy?

The Coolidge Administration

Just as Harding's promise of "normalcy" had appealed to war-weary voters in 1920, the virtue of his successor came as a welcome change from the turmoil of the Harding administration's corruption. Born on July 4, 1872, John Calvin Coolidge grew up on the Vermont farm that his family had worked for five generations. While governor of Massachusetts, Coolidge rose to national prominence for his handling of the Boston police strike in 1919. Shortly afterward, he was asked to run as Harding's vice president.

"Silent Cal" Takes Over Coolidge was very different from Harding. Harding had enjoyed the easy conversation and company of old friends. Coolidge, joked a critic, could be "silent in five languages." With his simple and frugal manner, he contrasted not only with Harding but also with the spirit of the time, the booming, materialistic era of the Roaring Twenties.

Coolidge quickly distanced himself from the Harding administration. He named Harlan Fiske Stone, dean of the Columbia Law School, to replace Daugherty as attorney general. He also asked the most capable cabinet members—Hughes, Mellon, and Hoover—to stay on.

Analyzing *Political Cartoons*

Teapot Dome Scandal In this cartoon, Democrats are enjoying the troubles the Teapot Dome scandal has caused for the GOP elephant. Who is shown being dragged along by the scandal? Why?

© N. Y. "Tribune."

Coolidge's philosophy of government was simple. He believed that prosperity rested on business leadership and that part of his job as president was to make sure that government interfered with business and industry as little as possible. He once said, "Four-fifths of all our troubles in this life would disappear if we would only sit down and keep still."

Calmly and cautiously, Coolidge worked to restore integrity to the presidency. In the year following Harding's death and the revelations of scandals, Coolidge's presidency avoided crises and continued the nation's expanding prosperity. Coolidge easily won the Republican Party's nomination for president in 1924.

The Election of 1924 Even though the scandals of the Harding administration presented the Democrats with a ready-made issue, they lost the chance for victory. Deeply divided between their urban Eastern constituency and their rural following in the South and West, the Democrats had difficulty agreeing on a nominee. They finally compromised on John W. Davis of West Virginia after 103 attempts to find someone acceptable to a majority of the delegates.

The Republicans effectively campaigned on the slogan "Keep Cool with Coolidge," and they urged Americans to retain the party that favored business. In his economic policies, Coolidge aligned himself—and the government—with prosperity and big business.

Not everyone was content to choose between the Republicans and Democrats. Defectors from both parties joined farm, labor, and religious activists to form the new Progressive Party, nominating Wisconsin senator **Robert M. La Follette** as their candidate. Although La Follette captured 16.6

Cool Coolidge President Coolidge believed the nation would run more smoothly if the government was less involved. How did the public react to Coolidge's message on Election Day?

percent of the popular vote, or a total of almost 5 million, he and Davis combined could not keep the Republicans from winning the election. Coolidge won easily with more than half the popular vote and 382 electoral votes.

In a speech to the American Society of Newspaper Editors in 1925, Coolidge said, "The chief business of the American people is business. The man who builds a factory builds a temple. The man who works there worships there." The *Wall Street Journal* joyously exclaimed, "Never before, here or anywhere else, has a government been so completely fused with business." By avoiding war, reform, and scandal, Coolidge promised to give the United States the normalcy Harding had failed to deliver.

Reading Check **Summarizing** How did Calvin Coolidge restore public confidence after becoming president?

SECTION 1 ASSESSMENT

Checking for Understanding

1. **Define:** normalcy, immunity.
2. **Identify:** Ohio Gang, Albert B. Fall, Teapot Dome scandal, Robert M. La Follette.
3. **Evaluate** the effects of the Teapot Dome scandal on citizens' views of the federal government.

Reviewing Themes

4. **Government and Democracy** How did the Ohio Gang tarnish the Harding Administration?

Critical Thinking

5. **Interpreting** How did the Democrats lose the chance for victory in the election of 1924?
6. **Categorizing** Use a graphic organizer similar to the one below to compare and contrast the politics and presidencies of Harding and Coolidge.

	Politics	Presidency
Harding		
Coolidge		

Analyzing Visuals

7. **Analyzing Photographs** Examine the photograph of Calvin Coolidge on this page. How did Coolidge's actions demonstrate effective leadership following the Harding administration?

Writing About History

8. **Expository Writing** Imagine you are a newspaper reporter during President Harding's term. Write an article breaking the news of the Teapot Dome scandal.

Main Idea

The United States experienced stunning economic growth during the 1920s.

Key Terms and Names

mass production, assembly line, Model T, Charles Lindbergh, National Broadcasting Company, Columbia Broadcasting System, welfare capitalism, open shop

Reading Strategy

Organizing As you read about the booming era of the 1920s, complete a graphic organizer to analyze the causes of economic growth and prosperity in the 1920s.

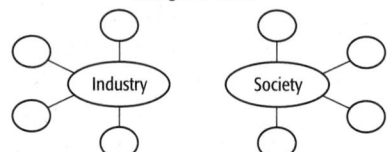

Changes in 1920s

Industry   Society

Reading Objectives

- **Analyze** how the growing importance of the automobile and other new industries improved the U.S. standard of living.
- **Analyze** the growing economic crisis in farming in the 1920s.

Section Theme

Science and Technology New technology such as the automobile and radio helped reshape American lifestyles.

Preview of Events

♦1920   ♦1923   ♦1926   ♦1929

1920
First commercial radio broadcast

1922
Congress passes Fordney-McCumber Act

1923
Ford gains 50 percent of the new car market

1927
The 15-millionth Ford Model T rolls off the assembly line

1929
U.S. radio sales exceed $800 million

★ *An American Story* ★

At around 2:00 A.M. on June 4, 1896, Henry Ford and his friend Jim Bishop readied Ford's "horseless carriage" for a test. The shop doors were too small for the contraption to pass through, so Ford immediately seized a sledgehammer and began knocking out an opening in the brick. Ford later recalled the scene that followed:

❝Mr. Bishop had his bicycle ready to ride ahead and warn drivers of horse-drawn vehicles—if indeed any were to be met with at such an hour. . . . I set the choke and spun the flywheel. As the motor roared and sputtered to life, I climbed aboard and started off. . . .❞

There were many such trips in the following days. Bishop would bicycle ahead, stopping at saloons and stores to warn people that they should come out and hold their horses. Many of the onlookers responded by calling out, "Crazy Henry!" As he climbed out of the car, Ford invariably responded, "Yes, crazy. Crazy like a fox."

—adapted from *The Fords: An American Epic*

The Rise of New Industries

Although neither Ford nor Bishop realized it at the time, "Crazy Henry's" horseless carriage would revolutionize American transportation and with it American society. By the 1920s, the automobile had become an accepted part of American life. In a 1925 survey conducted in Muncie, Indiana, 21 out of 26 families who owned cars did not have bathtubs with running water. Explaining why her family decided a car was more important than indoor plumbing, a farm wife said, "You can't ride to town in a bathtub."

The automobile was just one part of a rising standard of living that Americans experienced in the 1920s. Real per capita earnings soared 22 percent between 1923 and 1929. Meanwhile, as Americans' wages increased, their work hours decreased. In 1923 U.S. Steel cut its daily work shift from 12 hours to 8 hours. In 1926 Henry Ford cut the workweek for his employees from six days to five, and International Harvester, a maker of trucks, tractors, and other farm machinery, instituted an annual two-week paid vacation for employees.

At the same time, the rise of mass production, or large-scale product manufacturing usually done by machinery, created more supply and reduced consumer costs. This formula reshaped the American economy. Within this prosperous and productive atmosphere, innovation thrived and new industries emerged.

TECHNOLOGY

The Assembly Line Another major industrial development enormously increased manufacturing efficiency. First adopted by carmaker Henry Ford, the assembly line divided operations into simple tasks that unskilled workers could do and cut unnecessary

motion to a minimum. In 1913, Ford installed the first moving assembly line at his plant in Highland Park, Michigan. By the following year, workers were building automobiles every 93 minutes. Previously, the task had taken 12 hours. By 1925 a Ford car was rolling off the line every 10 seconds. "The way to make automobiles," Ford said, "is to make one automobile like another . . . to make them come through the factory all alike, just as one pin is like another pin when it comes from the pin factory."

Ford's assembly-line product was the **Model T**— affectionately called the "Tin Lizzie" or "Flivver." In 1908, the Model T's first year, it sold for $850. In 1914 mass production reduced the price to $490. Three years later, improved assembly-line methods and a high volume of sales brought the price down to $360. By 1924 Model Ts were selling for $295, and Ford sold millions of them. His business philosophy was simple: lower the cost per car and thereby increase the volume of sales. "Every time I reduce the charge for our car by one dollar," he boasted, "I get a thousand new buyers." In this way, Ford made the automobile available to millions of American consumers.

Ford also increased his workers' wages in 1914 to an unprecedented $5 a day and reduced the workday

TECHNOLOGY & History

The Assembly Line

The idea of an assembly line had existed before Henry Ford, but he helped popularize its use in manufacturing. Ford combined sub-assembly lines into one continuously moving line, which was positioned at waist level to reduce back strain. Ford's Highland Park factory featured a multistoried assembly line that reduced the construction time of a single Model T from 12 hours, 8 minutes to 1 hour, 33 minutes. *How did Ford's assembly line affect the price of his product?*

1 **Tires** were assembled and delivered downstairs using chutes.

2 **Engines** and gas tanks were assembled at other ends of the factory floor and delivered to the chassis sub-assembly.

3 Automobile **bodies** were assembled and dropped onto the separately assembled chassis with a pully.

In 1914 the Ford Motor Company produced 308,162 automobiles— more than all other auto manufacturers combined.

to eight-hour shifts. Ford took these dramatic steps to build up workers' loyalty and to undercut union organizers.

There were strings attached, however, to the wage increase. Ford created a "Sociological Department," which set requirements workers had to meet. For instance, the common practice of renting living space to nonfamily members was strictly forbidden. Investigators visited employees' homes to verify their eligibility and to see that they spent their wages in approved ways. Workers who transgressed could be disqualified from extra pay, suspended, or even fired.

The low prices made possible by Ford's mass-production methods not only created an immense market for his cars but also spawned imitators. By the mid-1920s, other car manufacturers, notably General Motors and Chrysler, competed successfully with Ford.

The auto industry spurred growth in other industries, such as rubber, plate glass, nickel, and lead. Automaking alone consumed 15 percent of the nation's steel, and the flood of cars stimulated a tremendous expansion of the petroleum industry.

The Social Impact of the Automobile Just as he had revolutionized manufacturing, Henry Ford was the force behind a social revolution related to the automobile. He almost single-handedly changed the auto from a toy of the wealthy to an affordable necessity for the middle class.

Cars revolutionized American life. Although many small businesses declined during the 1920s, the automobile created new small-business opportunities for such enterprises as garages and gas stations.

The automobile eased the isolation of rural life, putting towns within reach of many farmers and the countryside a mere ride away for city dwellers. Cars also enabled more people to live farther from work. An entirely new kind of consumer and worker, the auto commuter, appeared. Commuters lived in growing suburban communities and drove to work in the city.

The Consumer Goods Industry Many other new goods came on the market to take advantage of rising disposable income. Americans bought such innovations as electric razors, disposable facial tissues, frozen foods, and home hair dye.

NATIONAL GEOGRAPHIC
MOMENT in HISTORY

ON THE ROAD
The United States first felt the sweeping impact of the automobile during the 1920s. Mass production, pioneered by Henry Ford with his famous Model T, reduced costs and put practical, reliable cars within the reach of millions of middle-class Americans. Adventurous families—like the one shown here driving an upscale, open touring car through a giant Sequoia tree in Yosemite National Park—set out to explore the country. They used a network of roads that had been little more than rutted wagon trails two decades earlier.

Profiles IN HISTORY

Bessie Coleman c.1892–1926

Bessie Coleman was the first African American woman to receive a pilot's license and the first to become a stunt pilot. She performed in her first air show in September 1922 in Garden City, Long Island.

Coleman was born in Atlanta, Texas, to an African American mother and a Choctaw father. Too poor to attend college for more than one term, she moved to Chicago to become a pilot. No flight school she applied to, however, was willing to admit an African American. With the help of a Chicago publisher, Coleman then went to France to train. Back home, she championed the African American cause through her public statements and impressive flying feats.

Coleman's achievements inspired the founding of Chicago's Coffey School of Aeronautics. Its graduates helped train the U.S. military's first African American pilots, the Tuskegee Airmen, who served with distinction in World War II.

Amelia Earhart 1897–1937

Amelia Earhart, perhaps the world's most celebrated woman pilot, saw her first airplane at the Iowa State Fair when she was 10 years old. She was unimpressed: "It was a thing of rusty wire and wood and not at all interesting. . . ." In her early 20s, however, she attended a California "aerial meet," a fateful decision.

Known for promoting women's flying, Earhart seemed destined for celebrity from early on. By 1932 she was flying solo across the Atlantic.

Earhart's most daring flight was her last. In 1937 she set out to fly around the world with her navigator. Two-thirds of the trip was covered when their plane disappeared. On the trip, she had written her husband, "Please know I am quite aware of the hazards. . . . I want to do it because I want to do it. Women must try to do things as men have tried."

Many of the new products were created for the home. As indoor plumbing became more common, Americans' concern for hygiene spawned the development of numerous household cleaning products. By appealing to people's health concerns, advertisers were able to convince homemakers to buy cleansers to protect their families from disease.

New appliances advertised as labor-savers changed the home. Electric irons, vacuum cleaners, washing machines, and refrigerators, as well as gas stoves and improved glass cookware, changed the way people cleaned their homes and prepared meals.

Another lucrative category of consumer products focused on Americans' concerns with fashion, youthful appearance, and success in personal and business endeavors. Mouthwash, deodorants, cosmetics, and perfumes became popular products in the 1920s.

The Airline Industry Technological advances in aviation during World War I suggested the potential importance of the airplane to the transportation industry. Aviation, however, did not experience the same postwar boom as the automobile industry. In the early 1920s, most Americans still thought of airplanes as dangerous novelties. The only planes they saw were the flimsy craft that barnstorming pilots flew at air shows. Still, the opportunity to go up in the air inspired many Americans, such as Lena Stanley:

❝My first airplane ride was out at Brush Lake. . . . There was an aviator taking riders up; barnstorming, they called it. . . . So we climbed in, just went in and sat down, nothing over us, nothing to hold us down. I didn't know enough to be scared. And that pilot, he flew all around. Oh, it was beautiful, to see down on earth like we seen at that time.❞

—quoted in *Centenarians: The Story of the Twentieth Century by the Americans Who Lived It*

By the 1920s, airplanes were being used for more than just joyrides. President Wilson's postmaster general had introduced the world's first regular airmail service in 1918 by hiring pilots to fly mail between Washington, D.C., and New York. In 1919 the Post Office expanded airmail service across the continent with the aid of railroad connections. The aviation industry received an economic boost in 1925 with the passage of the Kelly Act, which authorized postal officials to contract with private airplane operators to carry mail.

In 1926 the aviation industry received another boost with the passage of the Air Commerce Act, which provided federal aid for building airports. It was the extraordinary transatlantic solo flight of former airmail pilot **Charles Lindbergh** in 1927, however, that demonstrated the possibilities of aviation

Washing machine advertisement

and won popular support for commercial flight. By the end of 1928, 48 airlines were serving 355 American cities.

Advertisers praised the benefits of commercial flying for business executives, as in this 1928 ad for the Ford Motor Company's "Trimotor" plane: "When the occasion comes for your first time up, it will not be to 'joy-ride' in an antiquated and hazardous machine; but far more probably it will be to reach some distant meeting-place in advance of business competition!"

The Radio Industry In 1913 Edwin Armstrong, an American engineer, invented a special circuit that made long-range radio transmission of voice and music practical. The radio industry began a few years later. In November 1920, the Westinghouse Company broadcast the news of Harding's landslide election victory from station KDKA in Pittsburgh— one of the first public broadcasts in history. That success persuaded Westinghouse to open other stations.

In 1926 the **National Broadcasting Company**

HISTORY Online

Student Web Activity Visit the *American Vision* Web site at tav.glencoe.com and click on *Student Web Activities— Chapter 21* for an activity on politics and economics in the 1920s.

(NBC) established a permanent network of stations to distribute daily programs. By 1927 almost 700 stations dotted the country, and the Federal Radio Commission had been established to regulate them. Sales of radio equipment skyrocketed from $12.2 million in 1921 to $842.5 million in 1929, by which time 10 million radio sets were in use in the United States.

In 1928 the **Columbia Broadcasting System** (CBS) assembled a coast-to-coast network of stations to rival NBC. The two networks sold advertising time and hired popular musicians, actors, and comedians from vaudeville, movies, and the nightclub circuit to appear on their shows. In 1928 Americans experienced complete coverage of the first presidential election campaign conducted over the airwaves, when the radio networks sold more than $1 million in advertising time to the Republican and Democratic Parties.

✓ **Reading Check** **Analyzing** How did technological innovations such as the assembly line impact the nature of work?

The Consumer Society

Higher wages and shorter workdays resulted in a decade-long buying spree that kept the economy booming. Shifting from traditional attitudes of thrift and prudence, Americans in the 1920s enthusiastically accepted their new role as consumers.

ECONOMICS

Easy Consumer Credit One notable aspect of the economic boom was the growth of individual borrowing. The prosperity of the 1920s gave many Americans the confidence to go into debt to buy new consumer goods.

Credit had been available before the boom, but most Americans had considered debt to be shameful. Now, however, American attitudes toward debt started changing as people began believing in their ability to pay their debts over time. Many listened to the sales pitch, "Buy now and pay in easy installments," and racked up debts for the family car, radio, furniture, washing machine, and vacuum cleaner. Americans bought 75 percent of their radios and 60 percent of their automobiles on the installment plan. Some started buying on credit at a faster rate than their incomes increased.

Mass Advertising When inventor Otto Rohwedder developed a commercial bread slicer in 1928, he faced a problem common to new inventions: the bread slicer was a device that made a product—sliced bread—that no one knew they needed. To create consumers for their new products, manufacturers turned to advertising, another booming industry in the 1920s.

Advertisers created appealing, persuasive messages that linked their clients' products with qualities associated with the modern era, such as progress, convenience, leisure, success, fashion, and style. In a 1924 magazine advertisement for deodorant, the headline read, "Flappers they may be—but they know the art of feminine appeal!" An advertisement for a prepared spaghetti product told the busy homemaker that heating is the same as cooking: "Just one thing to do and it's ready to serve." Advertisers also preyed on consumers' fears and anxieties, whether they be jarred nerves due to the hectic pace of modern life or insecurities about one's status or weight.

The Managerial Revolution

By the early 1920s, many industries had begun to create modern organizational structures. Companies were divided into divisions with different functions, such as sales, marketing, accounting, and operations. To run these divisions, businesses needed to hire managers. Managers freed executives and owners from the day-to-day business of running their companies and allowed them to develop long-range plans and goals.

The managerial revolution in companies created a new career—the professional manager—and companies began to hire large numbers of people with managerial training from business schools. The large numbers of managers helped to expand the size of the middle class, which in turn added to the nation's prosperity. Similarly, so many companies relied on new technology to drive their business that engineers were also in very high demand. They too joined the ranks of the rapidly growing middle class.

Welfare Capitalism

Middle-class Americans were not the only members of the new consumer society. Industrial workers also prospered in the 1920s, partly due to rising wages and partly because many corporations introduced what came to be called welfare capitalism. Companies allowed workers to buy stock, participate in profit sharing, and receive benefits such as medical care and pensions.

Benefits programs also made unions seem unnecessary to many workers. During the 1920s, unions lost both influence and membership. Employers promoted the open shop—a workplace where employees were not required to join a union.

With benefits covering some of their basic needs, workers were able to spend more of their income. Many eagerly purchased consumer goods they previously could not afford.

✓ **Reading Check** Analyzing Bias How did advertisers try to convince Americans to buy their products?

The Farm Crisis Returns

American farmers did not share in the prosperity of the 1920s. As a group, they earned less than one-third of the average income for workers in the rest of the economy. Technological advances in fertilizers, pesticides, seed varieties, and farm machinery allowed them to produce more, but higher yields without a corresponding increase in demand meant that they received lower prices. Between 1920 and 1921, corn prices dropped almost 19 percent, and

Farm Wages

Monthly Wages (including room and board)

Source: *Historical Statistics of the United States: Colonial Times to 1970.*

Percentage of National Income Generated by Industry, 1919–1928

Finance and Miscellaneous 16.1%
Agriculture 10.5%
Mining 2.5%
Government 9.6%
Manufacturing 21.9%
Services 11.6%
Contract Construction 4.4%
Trade 13.6%
Transportation and Other Public Utilities 9.8%

Source: *Historical Statistics of the United States: Colonial Times to 1970.*

📈 **Graph Skills**

1. **Interpreting Graphs** How far did farm wages fall between 1920 and 1930?
2. **Understanding Cause and Effect** What caused the decline in wages? Do you think farmers could have done anything to prevent this?

Price of Progress With the help of improved technology in the 1920s, farm production went up—and farm prices and farmers' income went down. How do you explain this "quiet depression"?

wheat went from $1.83 a bushel to $1.03. The cost to farmers of the improved technology, meanwhile, continued to increase.

Changing Market Conditions

Many factors contributed to this "quiet depression" in American agriculture. During the war, the government had urged farmers to produce more to meet the great need for food supplies in Europe. Many farmers borrowed heavily to buy new land (at inflated prices) and new machinery in order to raise more crops. Sales were strong, prices were high, and farmers prospered. After the war, however, European farm output rose, and the debt-ridden countries of Europe had little to spend on

American farm products. Congress had unintentionally made matters worse when it passed the Fordney-McCumber Act in 1922. This act raised tariffs dramatically in an effort to protect American industry from foreign competition. By dampening the American market for foreign goods, it provoked a reaction in foreign markets against American agricultural products. Farmers in the United States could no longer sell as much of their output overseas, and prices tumbled.

Helping Farmers Some members of Congress tried to help the farmers sell their surplus. Every year from 1924 to 1928, Senator Charles McNary of Oregon and Representative Gilbert Haugen of Iowa proposed the McNary-Haugen Bill, which called for the federal government to purchase surplus crops and sell them abroad while protecting the American market with a high tariff. McNary and Haugen argued that the plan would immediately raise the domestic price of crops, and it would aid farmers just as the Fordney-McCumber tariffs helped manufacturers.

Congress passed the bill twice, but President Coolidge vetoed it both times. He argued that with money flowing to farmers under this law, the farmers would be encouraged to produce even greater surplus volumes, which the government would be unable to sell in glutted overseas markets. American farmers remained mired in recession throughout the 1920s. Their problems would only grow worse when the Great Depression began in 1929.

✓ **Reading Check** **Synthesizing** What factors led to the growing economic crisis in farming in the 1920s?

SECTION 2 ASSESSMENT

Checking for Understanding
1. **Define:** mass production, assembly line, welfare capitalism, open shop.
2. **Identify:** Model T, Charles Lindbergh, National Broadcasting Company, Columbia Broadcasting System.
3. **Summarize** the factors that led to the new consumer society in the United States during the 1920s.

Reviewing Themes
4. **Science and Technology** How did the automobile impact American society?

Critical Thinking
5. **Identifying Cause and Effect** How did the United States government help spur the growth of the airline industry?

6. **Organizing** Use a graphic organizer similar to the one below to list some of the new industries that grew in importance during the 1920s.

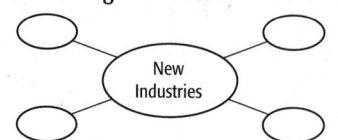

New Industries

Analyzing Visuals
7. **Analyzing Advertisements** Examine the advertisement on page 644. How did the growing consumer culture impact the nation's economy?

Writing About History
8. **Expository Writing** Write an article for a contemporary newspaper analyzing the impact of Charles Lindbergh's transatlantic flight on the development of aviation in the United States and the world.

The Policies of Prosperity

★ An American Story ★

After Election Day 1920, President-elect Harding began searching for qualified Americans for his cabinet. One of the most important posts would be secretary of the treasury. The nation faced a large national debt, and many worried that the country would not easily pull out of its postwar recession.

Harding was considering Andrew W. Mellon, a successful banker and industrialist, but he worried about Mellon's ties to industry and his relative anonymity. Harding's campaign manager, Harry Daugherty, reassured the president with a ringing endorsement of Mellon:

❝A man who can quietly make the millions this modest-looking man has gathered in is little short of a magician. If there is one thing he knows it's money. He will make for you the greatest Secretary of the Treasury since Alexander Hamilton. . . .❞

—adapted from *Mellon's Millions*

Promoting Prosperity

Harry Daugherty's confidence in Andrew Mellon proved to be well founded. Mellon became the chief architect of economic policy in the United States in the 1920s, and he served as secretary of the treasury in three successive Republican administrations. His policies encouraged growth and led to a stock market boom.

History

Harding's Cabinet Some members of Harding's cabinet (posing here with the president, seated center, in 1921) were effective administrators. How did Secretary of the Treasury Andrew Mellon lower the national debt between 1921 and 1929?

ECONOMICS

The Mellon Program
Mellon firmly believed that the government should apply business principles to its operations. In 1921 he convinced Congress to create both the Bureau of the Budget to prepare a unified federal budget and the General Accounting Office to track government spending.

When Mellon took office, he had three major goals—to balance the budget, to reduce the government's debt, and to cut taxes. He was convinced that these policies would promote economic growth and ensure prosperity.

Mellon began by cutting government spending. The federal budget fell from $6.4 billion to less than $3 billion in seven years. One major expense was the interest on the national debt. World War I costs had raised the debt from $5.7 billion in 1917 to almost $26 billion by 1920. Mellon refinanced the debt to lower the interest on it and persuaded the Federal Reserve to lower its interest rates as well. These steps, combined with increased tax revenue from the nation's economic boom, reduced the debt by $7 billion between 1921 and 1929.

In addition to trimming government spending, Mellon focused on reducing tax rates. He believed that high taxes reduced the money available for private investment and prevented business expansion. Mellon further argued that high tax rates actually reduced the amount of tax money the government collected. If taxes were lower, businesses and consumers would spend and invest their extra money, causing the economy to grow. As the economy grew, Americans would earn more money, and the government would actually

collect more taxes at a lower rate than it would if it kept tax rates high. This idea is known today as supply-side economics.

At Mellon's urging, Congress dramatically reduced tax rates. When Mellon took office, most taxpayers paid 4 percent federal income tax, while wealthy Americans in the highest bracket paid 73 percent. By 1928 Congress had reduced the rate most Americans paid to .5 percent and cut the rate for the wealthiest Americans to 25 percent.

Hoover's Cooperative Individualism Mellon's program was only one part of the government's effort to promote economic growth. Secretary of Commerce Herbert Hoover also sought to promote economic stability in various industries. Hoover tried to balance government regulation with his own philosophy of cooperative individualism. This idea involved encouraging manufacturers and distributors to form their own trade associations, which would voluntarily share information with the federal government. Hoover believed this system would reduce costs and promote economic efficiency.

To assist American businesses, Hoover also created several other agencies. He expanded the Bureau of Foreign and Domestic Commerce to find new markets and business opportunities for American companies. He also established the Bureau of Aviation to regulate and support the airline industry and the Federal Radio Commission, which set rules regarding the use of radio frequencies and the power of radio transmitters.

✓ **Reading Check** **Evaluating** What government policies were intended to promote economic growth and improve business efficiency in the 1920s?

Trade and Arms Control

Before World War I the United States had owed billions of dollars more to foreign investors than foreigners owed to Americans. By the end of the war, the situation was reversed. Former wartime allies owed the United States more than $10 billion in war debts incurred for food and armaments. By the 1920s the United States was the dominant economic power in the world—its national income far greater than that of Britain, Germany, France, and Japan combined. This new power presented the United States with a unique diplomatic challenge.

Isolationism In his victory speech after the 1920 election, President Harding declared the issue of American involvement in the League of Nations "deceased." The majority of Americans, tired of being entangled in the baffling, mutually hostile, and dangerous politics of Europe, favored isolationism. They simply wanted to be left alone to pursue prosperity.

The United States, however, was too powerful, too economically interconnected with other countries, and too widely involved in international affairs to retreat into isolationism. American delegations participated in many League conferences. It was United States policy to promote peace through agreements with individual countries rather than doing so through the collective efforts of the League.

The Dawes Plan The United States's former wartime allies had difficulty making the payments on their immense war debts. They claimed that high American tariffs had closed the American market to their products and hampered their economic recovery. If they could not sell their products in the United States, they could not acquire the money they needed to pay off their war debts. They also argued that the United States should be willing to bear more of the financial burden because it had suffered far fewer wartime casualties than its allies.

The United States government took the stance that American taxpayers should not be asked to assume the debts of others. American officials argued further that America's allies had gained new territory as a result of the victory over Germany, while the United

States had gained nothing. These countries also were receiving reparations—huge cash payments Germany was required to make as punishment for starting the war and causing so much destruction. These payments, however, were completely crippling the German economy.

It was vital for the United States that European economies be healthy so that the Europeans could buy American exports and repay their war debts. Thus, in 1924, **Charles G. Dawes,** an American banker and diplomat, negotiated an agreement with France, Britain, and Germany by which American banks would make loans to the Germans that would enable them to meet their reparations payments. At the same time, Britain and France would accept less in reparations and pay more on their war debts.

Although well intended, the Dawes Plan did little to ease Europe's economic problems. Britain, France, and Germany went through the motions of paying what they owed while in fact going deeper into debt to American banks and corporations.

The Washington Conference Despite severe economic hardship, the major powers were involved in a costly postwar naval arms race. To help halt this arms race, the United States invited representatives from eight major countries—Great Britain, France, Italy, China, Japan, Belgium, the Netherlands, and

The Washington Conference, November 1921–February 1922

Treaty	Signers	Terms	Weaknesses
Four-Power Treaty	United States, Great Britain, France, Japan	• All agreed to respect the others' territory in the Pacific • Full and open negotiations in the event of disagreements	• Mutual defense of other co-signers not specified
Five-Power Treaty	United States, Great Britain, France, Japan, Italy	• All agreed to freeze naval production at 1921 levels and halt production of large warships for 10 years • U.S. and Great Britain would not build new naval bases in the western Pacific	• No restrictions on the construction of smaller battle craft such as submarines and naval destroyers • Did not place restrictions on the ground forces
Nine-Power Treaty	United States, Great Britain, France, Japan, Italy, Belgium, China, the Netherlands, Portugal	• All agreed to preserve equal commercial rights to China—a reassertion of the "Open Door Policy"	• No enforcement of the terms of the "Open Door Policy" specified

Chart Skills

1. **Interpreting Charts** Which countries signed the Five-Power Treaty?
2. **Analyzing** Why do you think the terms of the treaties focused on the Pacific region?

The Tomb of the Unknown Soldier On March 4, 1921, Congress approved the burial of an unidentified World War I soldier in Arlington National Cemetery on a hill that overlooks Washington, D.C. This burial site, which was dedicated on November 11, 1921, is called the Tomb of the Unknown Soldier.

In 1958 two unknown soldiers from World War II and the Korean War were buried alongside the original unknown soldier. In 1984 a Vietnam War soldier was added.

On the side of the original tomb are inscribed the words: "Here rests in honored glory an American soldier known but to God." The Tomb is guarded year-round, day and night, regardless of weather.

Portugal—to Washington to discuss disarmament. The Washington Conference opened on November 12, 1921.

In his address to the delegates, Secretary of State **Charles Evans Hughes** proposed a 10-year moratorium—or pause—on the construction of major new warships. He also proposed a list of warships in each country's navy to be destroyed, beginning with some American battleships. The delegates cheered Hughes's speech and then entered into lengthy negotiations.

Their efforts produced three agreements. In the **Five-Power Naval Limitation Treaty,** Britain, France, Italy, Japan, and the United States essentially formalized Hughes's proposal. The **Four-Power Treaty** between the United States, Japan, France, and Britain recognized each country's island possessions in the Pacific. Finally, all the participating countries signed the **Nine-Power Treaty,** which guaranteed China's independence.

As a long-term effort to prevent war, the conference had some serious shortcomings. It did nothing to limit land forces. It also angered the Japanese because it required Japan to maintain a smaller navy than either the United States or Great Britain. It did, however, give Americans cause to look forward to a period of peace, recovery, and prosperity.

Abolishing War The apparent success of the Washington Conference boosted the belief that written agreements could end war altogether. Perhaps the highest expression of that idea occurred when U.S. Secretary of State Frank Kellogg and French Foreign Minister Aristide Briand proposed a treaty to outlaw war. On August 27, 1928, the United States and 14 other nations signed the **Kellogg-Briand Pact.** Eventually 62 nations ratified it.

Though it had no binding force, the pact was hailed as a victory for peace. It stated that all signing nations agreed to abandon war and to settle all disputes by peaceful means. The Kellogg-Briand Pact and the Dawes Plan were perhaps the most notable foreign policy achievements of the Coolidge administration.

✓ **Reading Check**   **Identifying** Why did the Dawes Plan fail to ease Europe's economic problems?

SECTION 3 ASSESSMENT

Checking for Understanding

1. **Define:** supply-side economics, cooperative individualism, isolationism, moratorium.
2. **Identify:** Charles G. Dawes, Charles Evans Hughes, Kellogg-Briand Pact.

Reviewing Themes

3. **Economic Factors** Why did Andrew Mellon work to reduce federal tax rates?

Critical Thinking

4. **Evaluating** What efforts did the United States make to promote permanent peace and worldwide economic recovery? Were these efforts successful? Explain your answer.
5. **Categorizing** Use a graphic organizer like the one below to list the major terms of the treaties resulting from the Washington Conference.

Major Terms of Treaties	

Analyzing Visuals

6. **Analyzing Photographs** Study the photograph on page 648 of President Harding's cabinet of advisers. What differences do you see between politics and the media then and now?

Writing About History

7. **Persuasive Writing** Imagine you are an American business owner or farmer in the 1920s. Write a letter to your representatives in Congress explaining why you think cutting tax rates is a good or bad idea.

Critical Thinking
SKILLBUILDER

Distinguishing Fact From Opinion

Why Learn This Skill?

Imagine that you are watching two candidates for president debate the merits of the college loan program. One candidate says, "In my view, the college loan program must be reformed. Sixty percent of students do not repay their loans on time."

The other candidate responds, "College costs are skyrocketing, but only 30 percent of students default on their loans for more than one year. I believe we should spend more money on this worthy program."

How can you tell who or what to believe? First, you must learn to distinguish a fact from an opinion. Then you will be better prepared to evaluate the statements that other people make.

Learning the Skill

A **fact** is a statement that can be proven. In the example above, the statement "Sixty percent of students do not repay their loans on time" may be a fact. By reviewing statistics on the number of student loan recipients who repay their loans, we can determine whether the statement is true or false. To identify potential facts, look for words and phrases indicating specific people, places, events, dates, amounts, or times.

An **opinion,** on the other hand, expresses a personal belief, viewpoint, or emotion. Because opinions are subjective, we cannot prove or disprove them. In the example above, most statements by the candidates are opinions. To identify opinions, look for qualifying words and phrases such as *I think, I believe, probably, seems to me, may, might, could, ought, should, in my judgment,* and *in my view.* Also, look for expressions of approval or disapproval such as *good, bad, poor,* and *satisfactory.* Be aware of superlatives such as *greatest, worst, finest,* and *best,* and notice words with negative meanings and implications such as *squander, contemptible,* and *disgrace.* Also, identify generalizations such as *none, every, always,* and *never.*

Practicing the Skill

For each pair of statements below, determine which is a fact and which is an opinion. Give a reason for each of your choices.

❶ **a.** President Harding was born in Ohio in 1865.

   b. Harding later became the most scandalous president in United States history.

❷ **a.** Harding's administration suffered numerous public scandals, including the Teapot Dome scandal.

   b. Calvin Coolidge was probably disgusted with Harding's poor performance in the White House.

❸ **a.** Harding stated that the United States needed a return to normalcy, but he did not do anything to help the country.

   b. Coolidge took over the White House after Harding's death and led the nation for the next several years.

❹ **a.** Henry Ford significantly lowered the price of the automobile with his mass production methods.

   b. Ford's Model T was the most significant invention of the 20th century.

Skills Assessment

Complete the Practicing Skills questions on page 653 and the Chapter 21 Skill Reinforcement Activity to assess your mastery of this skill.

Applying the Skill

Distinguishing Fact From Opinion In a newspaper, find a news article and an editorial on the same topic or issue. Identify five facts and five opinions from these sources.

 GO TO

Glencoe's **Skillbuilder Interactive Workbook CD-ROM, Level 2,** provides instruction and practice in key social studies skills.

Reviewing Key Terms

On a sheet of paper, use each of the following terms in a sentence.

1. normalcy
2. immunity
3. mass production
4. assembly line
5. welfare capitalism
6. open shop
7. supply-side economics
8. cooperative individualism
9. isolationism
10. moratorium

Reviewing Key Facts

11. **Identify:** Albert B. Fall, Teapot Dome scandal, Charles Lindbergh, Charles G. Dawes, Charles Evans Hughes, Kellogg-Briand Pact.
12. What was the presidency of Warren G. Harding like?
13. How did President Coolidge restore public confidence?
14. What were four new industries, besides the automobile industry, that grew in importance during the 1920s?
15. How did Henry Ford increase worker loyalty and impact the labor movement?
16. What were Andrew Mellon's strategies for maintaining postwar American prosperity?

Critical Thinking

17. **Analyzing Themes: Culture and Traditions** How did automobiles change the standard of living during the 1920s?

18. **Evaluating** How effective were President Coolidge's attempts to distance himself from the Harding administration? Explain your answer.
19. **Forming an Opinion** The former World War I allies felt that the United States should have borne more of the financial burden after the war. Do you agree or disagree? Explain your answer.
20. **Identifying Cause and Effect** Examine the graph on page 645. What caused the trend illustrated in this graph?
21. **Interpreting Primary Sources** In December 1928, President Coolidge delivered his annual State of the Union message to Congress. Read the excerpt and answer the questions that follow.

66The great wealth created by our enterprise and industry, and saved by our economy, has had the widest distribution among our own people, and has gone out in a steady stream to serve the charity and the business of the world. The requirements of existence have passed beyond the standard of necessity into the region of luxury.... The country can regard the present with satisfaction and anticipate the future with optimism.

The main source of these unexplained blessings lies in the integrity and character of the American people. They have had great faith, which they have supplemented with mighty works.... Yet these remarkable powers would have been exerted almost in vain

Chapter Summary

Government's Role
- Minimal interference with business
- Cut government spending and debt
- Eliminated or reduced taxes
- High tariffs

Business Innovation
- Mass production reduced prices
- Technology such as autos, airplanes, and radios led to new industries
- New consumer goods fueled manufacturing boom

New Consumer Society
- More disposable income
- More leisure time
- Easily available credit
- Mass advertising

Prosperity

without the constant cooperation and careful administration of the Federal Government. . . . 99

> —from President Coolidge's Annual Message to Congress, December 4, 1928

a. According to Coolidge, how should Americans feel about the present economy and the future economy?

b. Whom does Coolidge credit for U.S. prosperity?

22. Organizing Use a graphic organizer like the one below to list the factors that helped create a new consumer society in the United States during the 1920s.

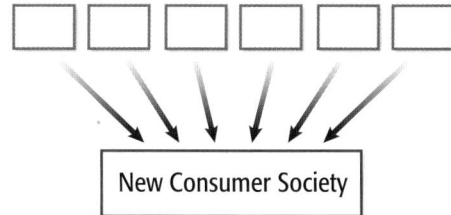

New Consumer Society

Practicing Skills

23. Distinguishing Fact From Opinion Read the following statements. Determine which are facts and which are opinions. Give a reason for each of your choices.

a. American farmers earned less than one-third the average income for workers in the rest of the economy in the 1920s.

b. President Harding's choice to appoint Colonel Charles R. Forbes to head the Veterans Bureau was his worst decision in office.

c. The Kelly Act authorized postal officials to contract with private airplane operators to carry mail.

Chapter Activity

24. American History Primary Source Document Library CD-ROM Under *The Roaring Twenties,* read "Ford and the Model T" by Charles E. Sorenson. Work with a few of your classmates to create a diorama of the first Model T assembly line based on the information in the article.

Writing Activity

25. Persuasive Writing Use the Internet or other resources to research advertisements and products from the 1920s. Then, based on the style of these advertisements, create an ad for a personal-care product that became popular in the 1920s, such as mouthwash or perfume.

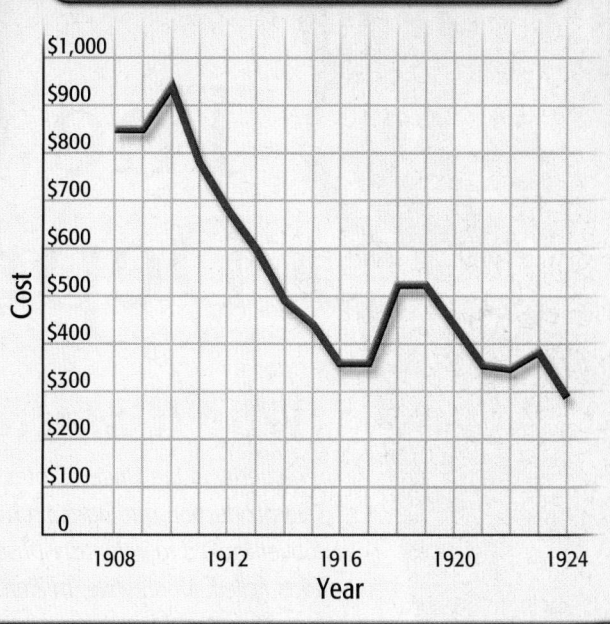

Cost of a Model T, 1908–1924

Economics and History

26. The graph above shows the cost of a new Model T automobile between 1908 and 1924. Study the graph and answer the questions below.

a. Interpreting Graphs By how much did the cost of the Model T drop from 1908 to 1920?

b. Evaluating How was Henry Ford able to lower the price of the Model T?

Standardized Test Practice

Directions: Choose the phrase that best completes the following sentence.

One of the effects of World War I on the American economy was

A a sharp rise in unemployment.

B stronger government control over industry.

C a sharp decrease in taxes.

D the abolition of labor unions, which were seen as unpatriotic.

Test-Taking Tip: This question is asking for a cause-and-effect relationship. Look for an answer that can be *directly related* to the needs of a wartime economy. During the war, it was necessary to produce supplies and munitions for the armed forces (which also needed more personnel), so answer A must be incorrect. In fact, there were more jobs and fewer workers to fill them, so unemployment is not a logical choice.

CHAPTER 22

The Great Depression Begins

1929–1932

Why It Matters

Prosperity in the United States seemed limitless before the Great Depression struck. Overproduction and agricultural problems contributed to the economic catastrophe. President Hoover looked to voluntary business action and limited government relief as solutions, but these efforts failed. Meanwhile, millions of Americans lost their jobs and life savings. Artists and writers depicted this suffering, and many people turned to lighthearted films to escape their difficult lives.

The Impact Today

Events of this period remain important.
- *Hoover's model of business-government cooperation is still influential.*
- *John Steinbeck's novel* The Grapes of Wrath *and Grant Wood's painting* American Gothic *are permanent artistic legacies.*

The **American Vision** *Video The Chapter 22 video, "Brother, Can You Spare a Dime?" chronicles Depression-era life in the United States.*

October 29, 1929
- Stock market crashes on Black Tuesday

1930
- Grant Wood paints *American Gothic*

June 1930
- Hawley-Smoot Tariff passed

United States
PRESIDENTS

Hoover
1929–1933

1929   *1930*   *1931*

World

1929
- Remarque's *All Quiet on the Western Front* published

1930
- Ras Tafari becomes Emperor Haile Selassie of Ethiopia

1931
- Gandhi released from prison in India, ending second passive resistance campaign against British rule

Girls pump for water during a dust storm in Springfield, Colorado.

October 1931
• National Credit Corporation created

1932
• Drought sweeps Great Plains

July 1932
• Bonus Marchers forced out of Washington, D.C.

January 1932
• Reconstruction Finance Corporation created

F. Roosevelt 1933–1945

1932

1933

September 21, 1931
• Britain abandons gold standard

1932
• Salazar becomes premier of Portugal

February 1932
• Japan sets up puppet government in Manchukuo in northern China

HISTORY Online

Chapter Overview
Visit the *American Vision* Web site at tav.glencoe.com and click on *Chapter Overviews—Chapter 22* to preview chapter information.

Causes of the Depression

Guide to Reading

Main Idea

Inflated stock prices, overproduction, high tariffs, and mistakes by the Federal Reserve led to the Great Depression.

Key Terms and Names

Alfred E. Smith, stock market, bull market, margin, margin call, speculation, Black Tuesday, installment, Hawley-Smoot Tariff

Reading Strategy

Categorizing As you read about the election of 1928, complete a graphic organizer similar to the one below comparing the backgrounds and issues of the presidential candidates.

1928 Presidential Campaign		
Candidate	Background	Issues

Reading Objectives

- **Describe** the characteristics of the 1920s stock market.
- **Identify** the causes of the Great Depression.

Section Theme

Economic Factors The Great Depression was caused by a combination of various economic problems and government policies.

Preview of Events

♦November 1928	♦September 1929	♦July 1930

November 1928
Herbert Hoover elected president

October 24, 1929
Stocks fall during Black Thursday

October 29, 1929
Black Tuesday stock market crash

June 1930
Congress passes Hawley-Smoot Tariff

★ An American Story ★

In the years just after the 1929 stock market crash, Annetta Gibson taught English in a Rockford, Illinois, grade school. As a teacher, Gibson was lucky because she was at least able to keep her job, unlike many other American workers.

❝Everyone knew that the teachers' salaries were being held up. . . . The stores charged anything we wanted, and we'd pay them when we got paid, so it wasn't too bad.

The one thing that was bad was that we had worked hard at school to get the children to save. . . . The children would bring, oh, maybe just a few pennies that they would put in their banks. Some of them had nice little bank accounts when the Depression hit, and some of them never got their money back. It wasn't too good a lesson . . . because they thought they might as well spend their money as save it and then have it gone.❞

—quoted in *Centenarians: The Story of the Twentieth Century by the Americans Who Lived It*

The Election of 1928

The economic collapse that began in 1929 had seemed unimaginable only a year earlier. In the election of 1928, the presidential candidates vied with each other to paint a rosy picture of the future. Republican Herbert Hoover declared, "We are nearer to the final triumph over poverty than ever before in the history of any land."

The Candidates When Calvin Coolidge decided not to run for president in 1928, he cleared the way for Herbert Hoover to head the Republican ticket. A successful engineer and former head of the Food Administration during World War I, Hoover had spent eight years as secretary of commerce in the Harding and Coolidge administrations. The Democrats chose **Alfred E. Smith,** four-time governor of New York. Smith was an Irish American from New York's Lower East Side and the first Roman Catholic ever nominated to run for president.

Campaign Issues By 1928 Prohibition had become a major issue among voters. Because he favored the ban on liquor sales, Hoover was considered a "dry" in the popular language of the day. Smith, who disliked the ban, was a "wet."

The candidates' religious differences sparked a smear campaign against Smith. Many Protestants were willing to believe that the Catholic Church financed the Democratic Party and would rule the United States if Smith got into the White House. These slurs embarrassed Hoover, a Quaker, and he tried to quash them, but the charges seriously damaged Smith's candidacy.

Smith's biggest problem, however, was the prosperity of the 1920s, for which the Republicans took full credit. Republican candidates promised to continue the trend with such slogans as "two cars in every garage." Hoover received over 6 million more votes than Smith and won the Electoral College in a landslide, 444 to 87.

On March 4, 1929, an audience of 50,000 stood in the rain to hear Hoover's inaugural speech. Sound movie cameras covered the inauguration for the first time and radios broadcast the address worldwide. "I have no fears for the future of our country," Hoover said. "It is bright with hope."

✓ **Reading Check** **Examining** What campaign issues led to Herbert Hoover's election to the presidency?

The Long Bull Market

The wave of optimism that swept Hoover into the White House also drove stock prices to new highs. The stock market was established as a system for buying and selling shares of companies. Sometimes circumstances in the stock market lead to a long period of rising stock prices, which is known as a bull market. In the late 1920s a prolonged bull market convinced many Americans to invest heavily in stocks. By 1929 between 3 and 4 million Americans, or roughly 10 percent of households, owned stocks.

As the market continued to soar, many investors began buying stocks on margin, meaning they made only a small cash down payment—as low as 10 percent of the price. With $1,000 an investor could buy $10,000 worth of stock. The other $9,000 would come as a loan from a stockbroker, who earned both a commission on the sale and interest on the loan. The broker held the stock as collateral.

As long as stock prices kept rising, buying on margin was safe. For example, an investor who borrowed money to buy $10,000 worth of stocks had to wait only a short time for them to rise to $11,000 in value. The investor could then sell the stock, repay the loan, and make $1,000 in profit. The problem came if the stock price began to fall. To protect the loan, a broker could issue a margin call, demanding the investor repay the loan at once. As a result, many investors were very sensitive to any fall in stock prices. If prices fell, they had to sell quickly, or they might not be able to repay their loans.

Before the late 1920s, the prices investors paid for stocks had generally reflected the stocks' true value. If a company made a profit or had good future sales prospects, its stock price rose, while a drop in earnings or an aging product line could send the price down. In the late 1920s, however, hordes of new investors bid prices up without regard to a company's earnings and profits. Buyers, hoping to make a fortune overnight, engaged in speculation. Instead of investing in the future of the companies whose shares they bought,

Picturing **History**

Herbert Hoover The nation and its new president felt confident about the future in early 1929. Why were Americans so optimistic?

The Great Depression

Causes

- Overproduction and low demand leads to employee layoffs
- Low wages reduce consumer buying power
- High tariffs restrict foreign demand for American goods
- Unemployment reduces buying power further

Cyclical Effect

Automobile sales declined. This loss of demand meant less demand for:

Textiles   Oil

Steel   Rubber

Industry slowed, which caused:

Unemployment

Lower wages

Which helped contribute further to . . .

Stock Prices, 1920–1932

Price per Share

- Annual high
- Annual low

$350
$300
$250
$200
$150
$100
$50
0

1920 1922 1924 1926 1928 1930 1932

Dow-Jones Industrial Averages

Source: Standard and Poor's *Security Price Index Record.*

Graph Skills

1. **Interpreting Graphs** Stock prices peaked in 1929. Before this peak, when did they begin to rise sharply?
2. **Making Generalizations** How did the decline in auto sales affect many other industries?

speculators took risks, betting that the market would continue to climb, thus enabling them to sell the stock and make money quickly.

Reading Check **Summarizing** What was the stock market like in the 1920s?

The Great Crash

The bull market lasted only as long as investors continued putting new money into it. By the latter half of 1929, the market was running out of new customers. In September professional investors sensed danger and began to sell off their holdings. Prices slipped. Other investors sold shares to pay the interest on their brokerage loans. Prices fell further.

TURNING POINT

Crash! On Monday, October 21, Groucho Marx, the comic star of stage and screen, was awakened by a telephone call from his broker. "You'd better get

down here with some cash to cover your margin," the broker said. The stock market had plunged. The dazed comedian had to pay back the money he had borrowed to buy stocks, which were now selling for far less than he had paid.

Other brokers made similar margin calls. Frightened customers put their stocks up for sale at a frenzied pace, driving the market into a tailspin. When Marx arrived at the brokerage, he found ticker tape "knee-deep on the floor." He further recalled, "People were shouting orders to sell and others were frantically scribbling checks in vain efforts to save their original investments."

On October 24, a day that came to be called Black Thursday, the market plummeted further. Marx was wiped out. He had earned a small fortune from plays and films, and now it was gone in the blink of an eye. Like many other investors, he was deeply in debt. Arthur Marx recalled his father's final visit to the brokerage, as Groucho looked around and spotted his broker:

❝He was sitting in front of the now-stilled ticker-tape machine, with his head buried in his hands. Ticker tape was strewn around him on the floor, and the place . . . looked as if it hadn't been swept out in a week. Groucho tapped [him] on the shoulder and said, 'Aren't you the fellow who said nothing could go wrong?' 'I guess I made a mistake,' the broker wearily replied. 'No, I'm the one who made a mistake,' snapped Groucho. 'I listened to you.'99

—quoted in *1929: The Year of the Great Crash*

The following week, on October 29, a day later dubbed **Black Tuesday,** prices took the steepest dive yet. That day stocks lost $10 to $15 billion in value.

By mid-November stock prices had dropped by over one-third. Some $30 billion was lost, a sum roughly equal to the total wages earned by Americans in 1929. The stock market crash was not the major cause of the Great Depression, but it undermined the economy's ability to hold out against its other weaknesses.

Banks in a Tailspin

The market crash severely weakened the nation's banks in two ways. First, many banks had lent money to stock speculators. Second, many banks had invested depositors' money in the stock market, hoping for higher returns than they could get by using the money for conventional loans.

When stock values collapsed, the banks lost money on their investments, and the speculators defaulted on their loans. Having suffered serious losses, many banks cut back drastically on the loans they made. With less credit available, consumers and businesses were unable to borrow as much money as they had previously. This helped to put the economy into a recession.

For some banks, the losses they suffered in the crash were more than they could absorb, and they were forced to close. At that time, the government did not insure bank deposits; therefore, if a bank collapsed, customers lost their savings. The bank failures in 1929 and early 1930 triggered a crisis of confidence in the banking system.

News of bank failures worried many Americans. They began to make runs on the nation's banks, causing the banks to collapse. A bank run takes place when many depositors decide to withdraw their money at one time, usually for fear the bank is going to collapse.

Most banks make a profit by lending money received from depositors and collecting interest on the loans. The bank holds on to only a fraction of the depositors' money to cover everyday business, such as occasional withdrawals. Ordinarily that reserve is enough to meet the bank's needs, but if too many people withdraw their money, the bank will eventually collapse. During the first two years

of the Depression, more than 3,000 banks—over 10 percent of the nation's total—were forced to close.

 Reading Check **Evaluating** How did bank failures contribute to the Great Depression?

The Roots of the Great Depression

The stock market crash helped put the economy into a recession. Yet the crash would not have led to a long-lasting depression if other forces had not been at work. The roots of the Great Depression were deeply entangled in the economy of the 1920s.

The Uneven Distribution of Income Most economists agree that overproduction was a key cause of the Depression. More efficient machinery increased the production capacity of both factories and farms.

Most Americans did not earn enough to buy up the flood of goods they helped produce. While manufacturing output per person-hour rose 32 percent, the average worker's wage increased only 8 percent. In 1929 the top 5 percent of all American households earned 30 percent of the nation's income. By contrast, about two-thirds of families earned less than $2,500 a year, leaving them little expendable income.

Picturing **History**

Wall Street Panic This painting shows the confusion and chaos surrounding the American financial industry in October 1929. How does the artist depict a sense of disorder?

Newspaper headline the day after Black Tuesday

During the 1920s many Americans bought high-cost items, such as refrigerators and cars, on the installment plan, under which they would make a small down payment and pay the rest in monthly installments. Some buyers reached a point where paying off their debts forced them to reduce other purchases. This low consumption then led manufacturers to cut production and lay off employees.

The slowdown in retail manufacturing had repercussions throughout the economy. When radio sales slumped, for example, makers cut back on their orders for copper wire, wood cabinets, and glass radio tubes. Montana copper miners, Minnesota lumberjacks, and Ohio glassworkers, in turn, lost their jobs. Jobless workers had to cut back purchases, further reducing sales. This kind of chain reaction put more and more Americans out of work.

The Loss of Export Sales

Many jobs might have been saved if American manufacturers had sold more goods abroad. As the bull market of the 1920s accelerated, U.S. banks made high-interest loans to stock speculators instead of lending money to foreign companies. Without these loans from U.S. banks, foreign companies purchased fewer products from American manufacturers.

Matters grew worse after June 1930, when Congress passed the **Hawley-Smoot Tariff** raising the average tariff rate to the highest level in American history. Rates went up on more than 900 manufactured items. The Hawley-Smoot Tariff aimed to protect American manufacturers from foreign competition, but it damaged American sales abroad. Because imports now cost much more, Americans bought fewer of them. Foreign countries responded by raising their own tariffs against American products, and this caused fewer American products to be sold overseas. In 1932 U.S. exports fell to about one-fifth of what they had been in 1929, which hurt both American companies and farmers.

Mistakes by the Federal Reserve

Just as consumers were able to buy more goods on credit, access to easy money propelled the stock market. Instead of raising interest rates to curb excessive speculation, the Federal Reserve Board kept its rates very low throughout the 1920s.

The Board's failure to raise interest rates significantly helped cause the Depression in two ways. First, by keeping rates low, it encouraged member banks to make risky loans. Second, its low interest rates led business leaders to think the economy was still expanding. As a result, they borrowed more money to expand production, a serious mistake because it led to overproduction when sales were falling. When the Depression finally hit, companies had to lay off workers to cut costs. Then the Fed made another mistake. It raised interest rates, tightening credit. The economy continued to spiral downward.

✓ **Reading Check** **Examining** How did the decline in worldwide trade contribute to the Depression?

SECTION 1 ASSESSMENT

Checking for Understanding

1. **Define:** stock market, bull market, margin, margin call, speculation, installment.
2. **Identify:** Alfred E. Smith, Black Tuesday, Hawley-Smoot Tariff.
3. **Explain** the significance of the year 1929.

Reviewing Themes

4. **Economic Factors** How did the practices of buying on margin and speculation cause the stock market to rise?

Critical Thinking

5. **Determining Cause and Effect** Why did the stock market crash cause banks to fail?
6. **Organizing** Use a graphic organizer similar to the one below to list the causes of the Great Depression.

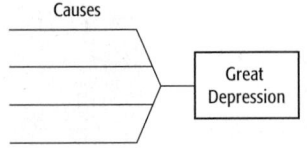

Causes → Great Depression

Analyzing Visuals

7. **Analyzing Graphs** Study the graphs on page 658. Note that decreased demand for automobiles ultimately led to layoffs. These layoffs further decreased the demand for automobiles. What do you think might have ended this cycle?

Writing About History

8. **Expository Writing** Write an article for a financial magazine explaining the rapid decline of the stock market in 1929 and the reasons for the Black Tuesday crash.

SECTION 2 / Life During the Depression

Guide to Reading

Main Idea
Many people were impoverished during the Great Depression, but some found ways to cope with the hard times.

Key Terms and Names
bailiff, shantytown, Hooverville, hobo, Dust Bowl, Walt Disney, soap opera, Grant Wood, John Steinbeck, William Faulkner

Reading Strategy
Taking Notes As you read about life in the United States during the Great Depression, use the major headings of the section to create an outline similar to the one below.

Life During the Depression
I. The Depression Worsens
   A.
   B.
   C.
II.

Reading Objectives
• **Describe** how the Great Depression affected American families.
• **Discuss** how artists portrayed the effects of the Depression.

Section Theme
Culture and Traditions Radio and motion pictures provided ways to escape the worries that plagued people during the Depression's early years.

Preview of Events

1930	1932	1934	1937	1939
Grant Wood paints *American Gothic*	Drought sweeps Great Plains	Dust storms destroy 300 million acres	Walt Disney releases *Snow White and the Seven Dwarfs*	Popular musical *The Wizard of Oz* released

★ An American Story ★

A young girl with the unusual name of Dynamite Garland was living with her family in Cleveland, Ohio, in the 1930s when her father, a railroad worker, lost his job. Unable to afford rent, they gave up their home and moved into a two-car garage.

The hardest aspect of living in a garage was getting through the frigid winters. "We would sleep with rugs and blankets over the top of us," Garland later recalled. "In the morning we'd . . . get some snow and put it on the stove and melt it and wash 'round our faces." When Garland's father found a part-time job in a Chinese restaurant, the family "lived on those fried noodles."

On Sundays the family looked at houses for sale. "That was a recreation during the Depression," said Garland. "You'd go and see where you'd put this and where you could put that, and this is gonna be my room." In this way, the family tried to focus on better times. Movies and radio programs also provided a brief escape from their troubles, but the struggle to survive left little room for pleasure.

—adapted from *Hard Times*

The Depression Worsens

In 1930, 1,352 banks suspended operations across the nation, more than twice the number of bank failures in 1929. The Depression grew steadily worse during Hoover's administration. By 1933 more than 9,000 banks had failed. In 1932 alone some 30,000 companies

NATIONAL GEOGRAPHIC
MOMENT in HISTORY

IMAGE OF AN ERA
Lasting a decade, the Great Depression deprived many Americans of jobs, land, and livelihoods. Plummeting crop prices and farms withering under drought and dust clouds forced many families to take to the road in search of work, often with little success. Dismayed by scenes of destitution and homelessness, photographer Dorothea Lange joined the Resettlement Administration in 1935. In 1936 in rural Nipomo, California, Lange photographed this "Migrant Mother," a 32-year-old woman with seven children. She had just sold her car tires to buy food.

went out of business. By 1933 more than 12 million workers were unemployed—about one-fourth of the workforce. Average family income dropped from $2,300 in 1929 to $1,600 just three years later.

Lining Up at Soup Kitchens
People without jobs often went hungry. Whenever possible they joined **bread lines** to receive a free handout of food or lined up outside **soup kitchens,** which private charities set up to give poor people a meal.

Peggy Terry, a young girl in Oklahoma City during the Depression, later told an interviewer how each day after school, her mother sent her to the soup kitchen:

> ❝If you happened to be one of the first ones in line, you didn't get anything but water that was on top. So we'd ask the guy that was ladling out soup into the buckets—everybody had to bring their own bucket to get the soup—he'd dip the greasy, watery stuff off the top. So we'd ask him to please dip down to get some meat and potatoes from the bottom of the kettle. But he wouldn't do it.❞
>
> —quoted in *Hard Times*

Living in Makeshift Villages
Families or individuals who could not pay their rent or mortgage lost their homes. Some of them, paralyzed by fear and humiliation over their sudden misfortune, simply would not or could not move. Their landlord would then ask the court for an eviction notice. Court officers called bailiffs then ejected the nonpaying tenants, piling their belongings in the street.

Throughout the country, newly homeless people put up shacks on unused or public lands, forming communities called shantytowns. Blaming the president for their plight, people referred to such places as Hoovervilles.

In search of work or a better life, many homeless and unemployed Americans began to wander around the country, walking, hitchhiking, or, most often, "riding the rails." These wanderers, called hobos, would sneak past railroad police to slip into open boxcars on freight trains for a ride to somewhere else. They camped in "hobo jungles," usually situated near rail yards. Hundreds of thousands of people, mostly boys and young men, wandered from place to place in this fashion.

The Dust Bowl Farmers soon faced a new disaster. Since the beginnings of homesteading on the Great Plains, farmers had gambled with nature. Their plows had uprooted the wild grasses that held the soil's moisture. The new settlers then blanketed the region with wheat fields.

When crop prices dropped in the 1920s, however, Midwestern farmers left many of their fields uncultivated. Then, beginning in 1932, a terrible drought struck the Great Plains. With neither grass nor wheat to hold the scant rainfall, the soil dried to dust. From the Dakotas to Texas, America's pastures and wheat fields became a vast "Dust Bowl."

Winds whipped the arid earth, blowing it aloft and blackening the sky for hundreds of miles. When the dust settled, it buried crops and livestock and piled up against farmhouses like snow. No matter how carefully farm families sealed their homes, dust covered everything in the house. As the drought persisted, the number of yearly dust storms grew, from 22 in 1934 to 72 in 1937.

Some Midwestern and Great Plains farmers managed to hold on to their land, but many had no chance. If their withered fields were mortgaged, they had to turn them over to the banks. Then, nearly penniless, many families packed their belongings into old cars or trucks and headed west, hoping for a better life in California. Since many migrants were from Oklahoma, they became known as "Okies." In California, they lived in makeshift roadside camps and remained homeless and impoverished.

Reading Check **Explaining** What chain of events turned the once-fertile Great Plains into the Dust Bowl?

Escaping the Depression

Despite the devastatingly hard times, Americans could escape—if only for an hour or two—through entertainment. Most people could scrape together the money to go to the movies, or they could sit with their families and listen to one of the many radio programs broadcast across the country.

HISTORY *Online*

Student Web Activity Visit the *American Vision* Web site at tav.glencoe.com and click on *Student Web Activities— Chapter 22* for an activity on the Great Depression.

NATIONAL GEOGRAPHIC — The Dust Bowl, 1930s

State with population loss, 1930–1940
Area with severe loss of topsoil
Area with moderate loss of topsoil
Movement of people
Destination of Dust Bowl emigrants

Okies escaping the Dust Bowl

Geography Skills

1. **Interpreting Maps** Which states lost population in the 1930s?
2. **Applying Geography Skills** Why did most of the routes shown on the map lead to cities?

The Hollywood Fantasy Factory Ordinary citizens often went to the movies to see people who were rich, happy, and successful. The 60 to 90 million weekly viewers walked into a fantasy world of thrills and romance. Comical screenplays offered a welcome release from daily worries. Groucho Marx wisecracked while his brothers' antics provoked hilarity in such films as *Animal Crackers.*

Many European actors, writers, and directors, fleeing economic hardship and the threat of dictatorships, went to Hollywood in the 1920s and 1930s. Two European women emerged as superstars. Germany's **Marlene Dietrich** portrayed a range of roles with subtlety. Swedish actress **Greta Garbo** often played a doomed beauty, direct and unhesitating in her speech and actions.

Moviegoers also loved cartoons. **Walt Disney** produced the first feature-length animated film, *Snow White and the Seven Dwarfs,* in 1937. Its box office appeal may have spurred MGM two years later to produce *The Wizard of Oz,* a colorful musical that lifted viewers' spirits.

Even when films focused on serious subjects, they usually contained a note of optimism. In *Mr. Smith Goes to Washington,* James Stewart plays a naïve youth leader who becomes a senator. He dramatically exposes the corruption of some of his colleagues and calls upon his fellow senators to see the American political system as the peak of "what man's carved out for himself after centuries of fighting for something better than just jungle law."

Gone with the Wind, an elaborately costumed film nearly four hours long, topped the Depression-era epics. Its heroine, Scarlett O'Hara, played by British actress Vivien Leigh, struggles to maintain her life on a Georgia plantation during and after the Civil War. Romance enters as Clark Gable, playing the masterful Rhett Butler, woos Scarlett. Audiences found inspiration in Scarlett's unassailable will to survive.

On the Air While movie drama captured the imagination, radio offered entertainment on a more personal level. People listened to the radio every day, gathering around the big wooden box in the living room. It could have been the voice of the president or a newscaster that held their attention. More often it was the comedy of Jack Benny or George Burns and Gracie Allen, or the adventures of a hero like the Green Hornet.

One of the most popular heroes was the Lone Ranger, who fought injustice in the Old West with the help of his "faithful Indian companion," Tonto. The listener needed only to picture the hero with a black mask hiding his identity, as he fired a silver bullet to knock a gun from an outlaw's hand.

Daytime radio dramas carried their stories over from day to day. Programs such as *The Guiding Light* depicted middle-class families confronting illness, conflict, and other problems. These short dramas allowed listeners to escape into a world more exciting than their own. The shows' sponsors were often makers of laundry soaps, so the shows were nicknamed soap operas.

While the Depression tore at the fabric of many towns, radio created a new type of community. Even strangers found common ground in discussing the lives of radio characters.

✓ **Reading Check** **Evaluating** What movies and radio shows entertained Americans during the Depression?

The Depression in Art

Art and literature also flourished in the harsh and emotional 1930s. The homeless and unemployed became the subject of pictures and stories as artists and writers tried to portray life around them.

Thomas Hart Benton and **Grant Wood** led the regionalist school, which emphasized traditional American values, especially those of the rural Midwest and South. Wood's most famous painting,

Fact	Fiction	Folklore

Hobo Signs The hundreds of thousands of hobos who roamed the country developed intricate symbols that they wrote on trees, fences, or buildings to warn or inform other hobos. Many became a part of American folklore.

☋	(a closed eye) This community is indifferent toward hobos.
◠	(an open eye) The authorities here are alert; be careful.
⌸	This is a dangerous neighborhood.
※	Fresh water and a safe campsite.
⊡	This is dangerous drinking water.
⊗	This is a good place for a handout.
⍓	You may sleep in the hayloft here.

Source: *Hobo Signs.*

American Gothic, portrays a stern farmer and his daughter in front of their humble farmhouse. The portrait pays tribute to no-nonsense Midwesterners while at the same time gently making fun of their severity.

Novelists such as **John Steinbeck** added flesh and blood to journalists' reports of poverty and misfortune. Their writing evoked both sympathy for their characters and indignation at social injustice. In *The Grapes of Wrath,* published in 1939, Steinbeck tells the story of an Oklahoma family fleeing the Dust Bowl to find a new life in California. Steinbeck had seen firsthand the plight of migrant farm families uprooted by the Dust Bowl. After visiting camps of these families, he gained a better understanding of their fears. In his novel, he described these "people in flight" along Route 66. Inside one old jalopy sat the members of a family, worrying:

> ❝There goes a gasket. Got to go on. Find a nice place to camp. . . . The food's getting low, the money's getting low. When we can't buy no more gas—what then? Danny in the back seat wants a cup a water. Little fella's thirsty.❞
>
> —from *The Grapes of Wrath*

Other novelists of this time influenced literary style itself. In *The Sound and the Fury,* for example, author **William Faulkner** shows what his characters are thinking and feeling before they speak. Using this stream of consciousness technique, he exposes hidden attitudes of Southern whites and African

Profiles IN HISTORY

Dorothea Lange 1895–1965

Before she had ever used a camera, Dorothea Lange knew she wanted to be a photographer. After finishing high school, she took a photography course in New York, then traveled around the world. Lange earned her keep by taking and selling photos. Her trip ended in San Francisco.

In San Francisco, Lange photographed homeless people and uncovered the desperation of her subjects. One day, while driving through California's Central Valley, Lange noticed a sign: "Pea-Pickers Camp." On impulse, she stopped. She approached a woman and her children gazing listlessly out of a tattered tent. Lange took five pictures while the mother "sat in that lean-to tent with her children huddled around her, and seemed to know that my pictures might help her, and so she helped me."

In the mid-1930s, Lange traveled through the Dust Bowl states, capturing the ravages of dust storms. When the images were reproduced in a best-selling book, *American Exodus,* the state of California created camps to shelter migrant workers.

Americans in a fictional Mississippi county. Another Southern writer, Thomas Wolfe, used the facts of his own life to examine the theme of artistic creation in such powerful novels as *Look Homeward Angel.*

While the written word remained powerful, the printed image was growing in influence. Magazine photographers roamed the nation armed with the new 35-millimeter cameras, seeking new subjects. Photojournalist **Margaret Bourke-White's** striking pictures, displayed in *Fortune* magazine, showed the ravages of drought. In 1936 *Time* magazine publisher Henry Luce introduced *Life,* a weekly photojournalism magazine that enjoyed instant success.

✓ **Reading Check** **Examining** What subjects did artists, photographers, and writers concentrate on during the 1930s?

SECTION 2 ASSESSMENT

Checking for Understanding

1. **Define:** bailiff, shantytown, Hooverville, hobo, Dust Bowl, soap opera.
2. **Identify:** Walt Disney, Grant Wood, John Steinbeck, William Faulkner.
3. **Explain** what caused the Dust Bowl conditions on the Great Plains.

Reviewing Themes

4. **Culture and Traditions** In what ways did people seek to forget about the Depression?

Critical Thinking

5. **Making Inferences** Why do you think *Life* magazine was so popular during the 1930s?
6. **Organizing** Use a graphic organizer to list the effects of the Great Depression.

```
        Effects of the Great Depression
    ┌─────┬─────┬─────┬─────┬─────┐
    │     │     │     │     │     │
    └─────┴─────┴─────┴─────┴─────┘
```

Analyzing Visuals

7. **Analyzing Photos** Study the photograph on page 662. Think of three adjectives that you would use to describe the people in the photograph. Using these adjectives, write a paragraph describing the family pictured.

Writing About History

8. **Descriptive Writing** Imagine that you are living during the Great Depression. Write a journal entry describing a day in your life.

Lake Mohave

EL DORADO MOUNTAINS

95

← to Flagstaff

Power line

NEVADA
ARIZONA

93

Black Canyon

**HOOVER
DAM**

Bo

Fortification Hill
3718 ft. (1133 m)

Boulder
Islands

Sentinel
Island

BLACK MOUNTAINS

LA

ARIZONA
NEVADA

CALIFORNIA

25%
NEVADA

Colorado River

Lake
Powell

Lake
Mead

Las
Vegas   **Hoover Dam**

56%

•Los Angeles

19%
ARIZONA

THE FLOW OF ELECTRICITY

Today Hoover Dam generates more than 4 billion kilowatt-hours
of electricity per year—enough to keep machines humming and
lights burning for over a million people. More than half of that
electricity is sent to California; the remainder goes to Nevada and
Arizona (see inset map).

Hoover Dam

Suspended on ropes, "high scalers" armed with dynamite and jackhammers prepare the walls of Black Canyon to take the concrete of Hoover Dam. Such work was hazardous. Twenty-four workers fell to their deaths during construction of the dam.

American farmers and settlers in the low-lying valleys of southern California and southwestern Arizona have been tapping the waters of the Colorado River for more than a century. Thanks to irrigation canals, the parched desert valleys became year-round gardens that provided fruit and vegetables for the nation. At times, however, the unpredictable river would decrease to a trickle. Other times, it became a raging torrent, destroying all in its path. The federal government decided to dam the Colorado to control it. In 1931 construction began in Black Canyon, whose high rock walls made it an ideal site. Here, on the border between Arizona and Nevada, would rise one of the most ambitious engineering projects the world had ever seen: the Hoover Dam.

Named after President Herbert Hoover, the dam was built in the middle of a forbidding desert. Everything had to be imported, including labor. There was no shortage of candidates. The country was in the grips of the Great Depression; thousands of unemployed workers flocked to the remote canyon. To accommodate them, an entire town was built— Boulder City, Nevada.

The new arrivals faced brutal conditions. Men worked in three shifts around the clock. Summer temperatures climbed higher than 120 degrees in the canyon, and even those who worked at night had to endure temperatures of more than 85 degrees. Still, the project was completed in less than five years. Lake Mead, the 115-mile-long reservoir created by the dam, is large enough to hold two years' worth of the average flow of the Colorado River—enough to cover the entire state of New York with one foot of water. The benefits to the Southwest were immense. Hoover Dam created much-needed employment. It also provided a regular supply of water, irrigating over a million acres of rich agricultural land and producing hydroelectric power, which has allowed Southwestern cities to grow.

Hoover Dam and Environs

- ⋯⋯ State boundary
- – – Aqueduct
- ⌒ Road
- ✳ Power line
- ▬ Urban area

Scale varies in this perspective

Hoover Dam, a major supplier of hydroelectric power, is more than 700 feet (213 m) tall and contains about 4,360,000 cubic yards of concrete— enough for a two-lane highway from Los Angeles to Boston.

LEARNING FROM GEOGRAPHY

1. Why did the federal government decide to dam the Colorado River?

2. Why did engineers choose the Black Canyon site?

SECTION 3 Hoover Responds

Guide to Reading

Main Idea
President Hoover's philosophy of government guided his response to the Depression.

Key Terms and Names
public works, Reconstruction Finance Corporation, relief, foreclose, Bonus Army

Reading Strategy
Categorizing As you read about Hoover's response to the Depression, complete a graphic organizer by listing his major initiatives and their results.

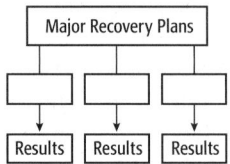

Major Recovery Plans

Results   Results   Results

Reading Objectives
• **Evaluate** President Hoover's attempts to revive the economy.
• **Analyze** the limitations of Hoover's recovery plans.

Section Theme
Groups and Institutions President Hoover began using new government agencies to improve the nation's slumping economy.

Preview of Events

♦1931   ♦1932   ♦1933

October 1931
National Credit Corporation created

January 1932
Congress approves Reconstruction Finance Corporation

July 1932
Congress passes Emergency Relief and Construction Act; soldiers rout the Bonus Marchers

★ *An American Story* ★

In December 1929, Mayor Joseph Heffernan of Youngstown, Ohio, listened impatiently to fellow public officials assembled in the Cleveland Chamber of Commerce hall. He had been called to one of a series of conferences on unemployment that President Hoover had arranged. At the conference, Heffernan grew restless as he listened to the other speakers. He felt that it would take too long to pass their confident proposals for ending unemployment, and by that time, it would be too late to prevent a depression. He asked the other conference members, "Why not tell people the truth?"

Youngstown business leaders criticized Heffernan for trying to tell his constituents how bad the economic outlook was. Heffernan later recalled that one of them said to him, "Don't emphasize hard times and everything will be all right."

The man who rebuked Mayor Heffernan expressed what many, including President Hoover himself, believed in late 1929: The country merely needed to regain its confidence. As the crisis worsened, Hoover took steps to help the economy recover, but only within the limits of his philosophy of government.

—adapted from *The Great Depression*

Promoting Recovery

On Friday, October 25, the day after Black Thursday, President Hoover issued a statement assuring the nation that industry was "on a sound and prosperous basis." In March 1930 he told the public that "the worst effects of the crash . . . will have passed during the next 60 days." Critics derided his optimism as conditions worsened. Hoover, however, hoped to downplay the public's fears. He wanted to avoid more bank runs and layoffs by urging consumers and business leaders to become more rational in their decision making.

Voluntary Efforts and Public Works Despite his soothing words, Hoover was seriously worried about the economy. He organized a series of conferences, bringing together the heads of banks, railroads, and other big businesses, as well as labor and government officials.

He won a pledge from industry to keep factories open and to stop slashing wages. By 1931, however, business leaders had abandoned those pledges. Hoover's next step was to increase public works—government-financed building projects. The resulting construction jobs could replace some of those lost in the private sector. He urged governors and mayors throughout the nation to increase public works spending.

Hoover's actions did spur construction increases, but the effort made up for only a small fraction of the jobs lost in the private sector. The only way the government could create enough new jobs would be to massively increase government spending, which Hoover refused to do.

The problem was that someone had to pay for public works projects. If the government raised taxes to pay for them, it would take money away from consumers and hurt businesses that were already struggling. If the government decided to keep taxes low and run a budget deficit instead—spending more money than it collected in taxes—it would have to borrow the money from banks. If the government did this, less

Different Viewpoints

What Should the Government's Role in the Economy Be?

The government's role in the economy was an important issue in the 1932 presidential election, when the country was in the throes of the Depression. President Herbert Hoover explained, in a 1928 speech why a limited government role was best, while President Franklin Roosevelt argued in his inaugural address in 1933 that an expanded government role was necessary.

from Hoover's Madison Square Garden Address, 1928

"During one hundred and fifty years we have built up a form of self-government and a social system which is peculiarly our own. . . . It is founded upon a particular conception of self-government in which decentralized local responsibility is the very base. . . .

During the war we necessarily turned to the government to solve every difficult economic problem. . . . However justified in time of war, if continued in peacetime it would destroy . . . our progress and freedom. . . . The acceptance of these ideas would have meant the destruction of self-government through centralization of government. It would have meant the undermining of the individual initiative and enterprise through which our people have grown to unparalleled greatness."

from Roosevelt's Inaugural Address, 1933

"Our greatest primary task is to put people to work. This is no unsolvable problem if we face it wisely and courageously. It can be accomplished in part by direct recruiting by the Government itself, treating the task as we would treat the emergency of a war, but at the same time, through this employment, accomplishing greatly needed projects to stimulate and reorganize the use of our natural resources.

. . . The task can be helped . . . by national planning for and supervision of all forms of transportation and of communications and other utilities which have a definitely public character. There are many ways in which it can be helped, but it can never be helped merely by talking about it. We must act and act quickly.

. . . We now realize as we have never realized before our interdependence on each other; . . . that if we are to go forward, we must move as a trained and loyal army willing to sacrifice for the good of a common discipline."

Learning From History

1. **Analyzing Arguments** What did Hoover fear would happen if government programs started during World War I were continued after the war?
2. **Making Inferences** Do you think Roosevelt would have agreed with Hoover's assessment of the government's role during World War I? Why or why not?

money would be available for businesses that wanted to expand and for consumers who wanted mortgages or other loans. Hoover feared that deficit spending would actually delay an economic recovery.

The Midterm Election As the congressional elections of 1930 approached, most Americans felt that worsening unemployment posed a grave threat to their well-being. Citizens blamed the party in power for the stumbling economy. The Republicans lost 49 seats and their majority in the House of Representatives; they held on to the Senate by a single vote.

✓ **Reading Check** **Examining** Why did Hoover oppose deficit spending?

Pumping Money Into the Economy

Hoover soon turned his attention to the problem of money. There was very little in the economy now that so many banks had collapsed. The government, he believed, had to make sure that banks could make loans to corporations so they could expand production and rehire workers.

White Angel Breadline In 1932 a wealthy woman nicknamed the "White Angel" set up a breadline in San Francisco. Dorothea Lange captured the hopelessness of the Depression in this famous photograph of the breadline.

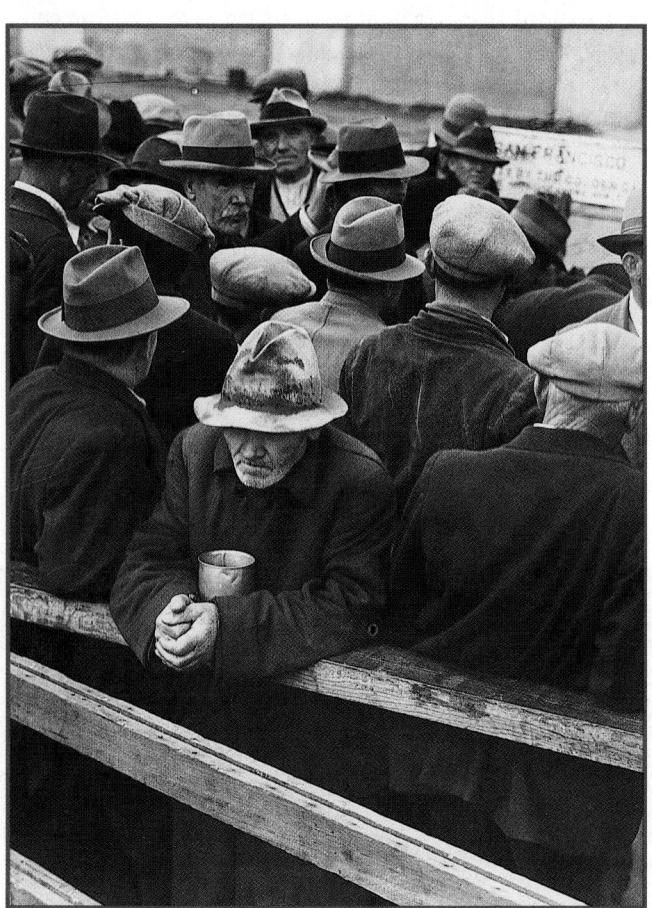

Trying to Rescue the Banks The president asked the Federal Reserve Board to put more currency into circulation, but the Board refused. In an attempt to ease the money shortage, Hoover set up the National Credit Corporation (NCC) in October 1931. The NCC created a pool of money to enable troubled banks to continue lending money in their communities. Hoover then persuaded a number of New York bankers to contribute to the NCC. Their contributions, however, did not meet the nation's needs.

By 1932 Hoover concluded that the only way to provide funding for borrowers was for the government to do the lending. He requested that Congress set up the **Reconstruction Finance Corporation** **(RFC)** to make loans to banks, railroads, and agricultural institutions. By early 1932, the RFC had lent about $238 million to approximately 160 banks, 60 railroads, and 18 building-and-loan organizations. The RFC was overly cautious, however. It failed to increase its loans in sufficient amounts to meet the need, and the economy continued its decline.

Direct Help for Citizens From the start, Hoover strongly opposed the federal government's participation in relief—money that went directly to impoverished families. He believed that only state and city governments should dole out relief. By the spring of 1932, however, they were running out of money.

In 1932 political support was building for a relief measure, and Congress passed the Emergency Relief and Construction Act. Although reluctant, Hoover signed the bill on July 21. The new act called for $1.5 billion for public works and $300 million in loans to the states for direct relief. By this time, however, the new program could not reverse the accelerating collapse.

✓ **Reading Check** **Summarizing** Why did Hoover oppose the federal government's participation in relief programs?

In an Angry Mood

In the months after the Wall Street crash, Americans had seemed resigned to bad economic news. By 1931, however, they were growing increasingly discontented, and open acts of revolt began to occur.

Hunger Marches In January 1931, around 500 men and women in Oklahoma City, shouting angrily about hunger and joblessness, broke into a grocery store and looted it. Crowds began showing

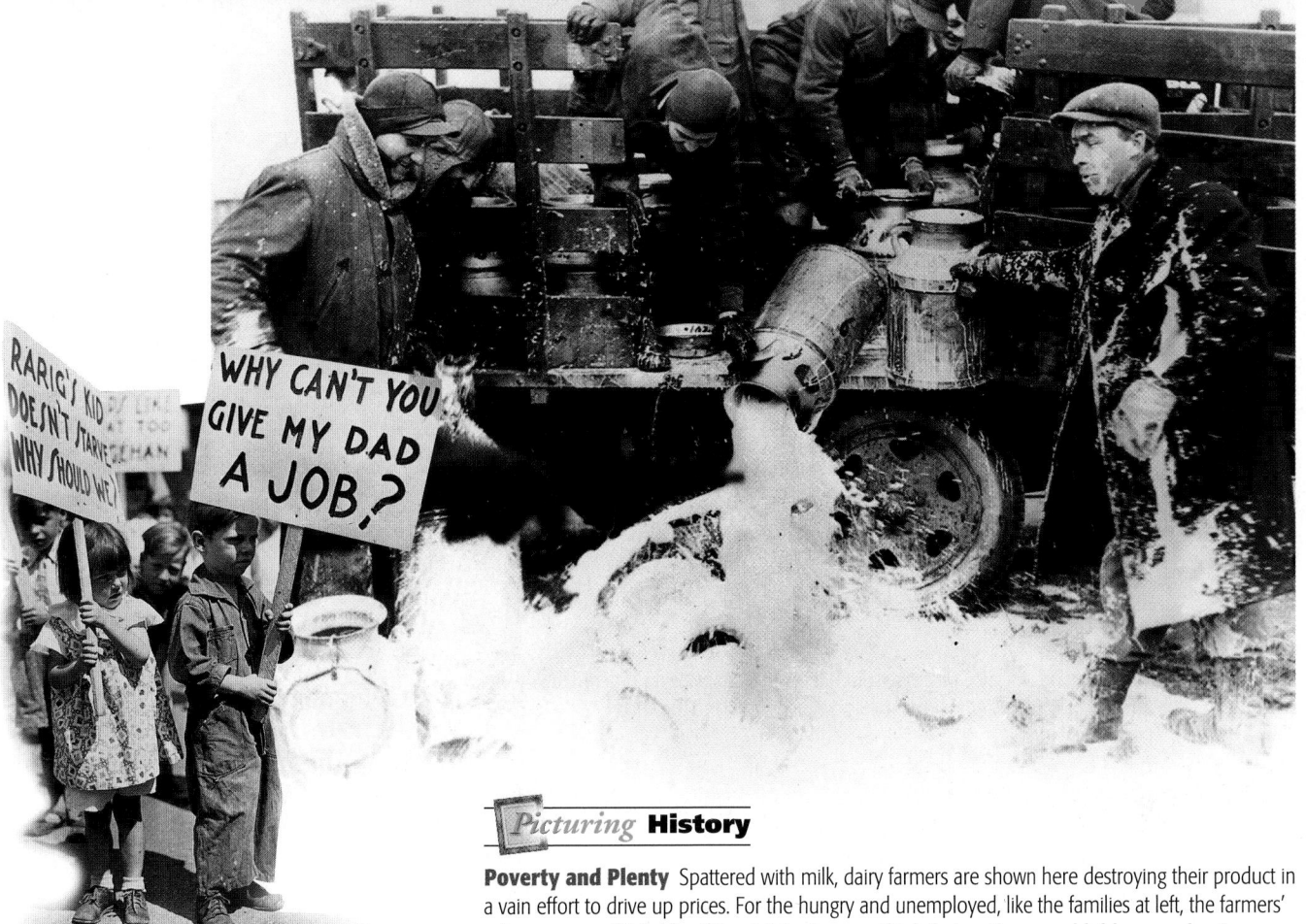

Poverty and Plenty Spattered with milk, dairy farmers are shown here destroying their product in a vain effort to drive up prices. For the hungry and unemployed, like the families at left, the farmers' actions were unthinkable. Why did the farmers think their actions would drive up prices?

up at rallies and "hunger marches" held by the American Communist Party, which was eager to take advantage of national problems to change the American form of government. On December 5, 1932, a freezing day in the nation's capital, around 1,200 hunger marchers assembled and chanted, "Feed the hungry, tax the rich." Police herded them into a blocked-off area, where they had to spend the night sleeping on the sidewalk or in trucks. The police denied them food, water, and medical treatment until some members of Congress insisted on the marchers' right to petition their government. They were then released and permitted to march to Capitol Hill.

Farmers Revolt In the summer of 1932, farmers also took matters into their own hands. Beginning in the boom days of World War I, many farmers had heavily mortgaged their land to pay for seed, feed, and equipment. After the war, prices sank so low that farmers could not even earn back their costs, let alone make a profit. Between 1930 and 1934 creditors foreclosed on nearly one million farms, taking possession of them and evicting the families.

Some farmers began destroying their crops in a desperate attempt to raise crop prices by reducing the supply. In Nebraska grain growers burned corn to heat their homes in the winter. In Iowa food growers forcibly prevented the delivery of vegetables to distributors. Georgia dairy farmers blocked highways and stopped milk trucks, emptying the milk cans into ditches.

The Bonus Marchers In appreciation of the World War I service of American soldiers and sailors, Congress in 1924 had enacted a $1,000 bonus for each veteran, to be distributed in 1945. The economic crisis, however, made the wait more difficult. In 1931 Texas congressman Wright Patman introduced a bill in the House of Representatives that authorized early payment of the veterans' bonuses. The bill later passed the House and moved to the Senate for debate.

In May 1932 several hundred Portland, Oregon, veterans set off on a month-long march to Washington to lobby Congress to pass the legislation. As they moved east, other veterans joined them until they numbered about 1,000. Wearing ragged military uniforms, they trudged along the highways or rode the rails, singing old war songs and reminiscing about army days. The press termed the marchers the **"Bonus Army."**

Once in Washington, the marchers camped in Hoovervilles. As weeks went by, additional veterans joined them, until the Bonus Army swelled to

Picturing History

Clearing Out the Bonus Marchers Fierce battles resulted when President Hoover ordered the Washington, D.C., police to evict the Bonus Army from public buildings and land they had been occupying. How did the public feel when they saw or heard about this event?

ignored Hoover's orders to clear the buildings but to leave the camps alone. He sent cavalry, infantry, and tanks to clear the veterans from the city.

A Federal Trade Commission member, A. Everette McIntyre, watched as the infantry "fixed their bayonets and also fixed their gas masks over their faces. At orders they brought their bayonets at thrust and moved in. The bayonets were used to jab people to make them move." Soon unarmed veterans were on the run with 700 soldiers at their heels. The soldiers tear-gassed stragglers and burned the shacks. Tear gas killed a baby boy.

The nationwide press coverage and newsreel images of veterans under assault by troops presented an ugly picture to the public. The routing of the veterans hounded the president throughout his 1932 re-election campaign.

15,000. President Hoover acknowledged the veterans' petition rights but refused to meet with them.

When the Senate voted the new bonus bill down, veterans waiting outside the Capitol began to grumble, until one of their leaders started them singing "America." Gradually their anger cooled, and many returned home. A significant number of the marchers, however, stayed on since they had no job prospects. Some moved from the camps to unoccupied buildings downtown.

In late July, Hoover ordered the buildings cleared. The police made the first try, but one of them panicked and fired into a crowd, killing two veterans. The Washington, D.C., government then called in the army. Army chief of staff Douglas MacArthur

Hoover failed to resolve the crisis of the Depression, but he did more to expand the economic role of the federal government than any previous president. The Reconstruction Finance Corporation marked the first time the federal government had established a federal agency to stimulate the economy during peacetime. It was the image of the routed Bonus Marchers and the lingering Depression, however, that shaped the public's perception of President Hoover.

✔ **Reading Check** **Evaluating** How did Americans react as the Depression continued?

SECTION 3 ASSESSMENT

Checking for Understanding

1. **Define:** public works, relief, foreclose.
2. **Identify:** Reconstruction Finance Corporation, Bonus Army.
3. **Summarize** three major initiatives taken by Hoover to improve the economy and the results of each.

Reviewing Themes

4. **Groups and Institutions** What did business leaders promise Hoover they would do to help the economy? Did they keep their promises?

Critical Thinking

5. **Interpreting** How did President Hoover's philosophy of government guide his response to the Depression?
6. **Organizing** Use a graphic organizer similar to the one below to list American reactions to the Depression.

American Reactions

Analyzing Visuals

7. **Picturing History** Study the photographs on page 671. The farmers shown would rather dump their milk than sell it. What did they hope to achieve by their actions?

Writing About History

8. **Persuasive Writing** Imagine that you are a veteran of World War I. Write a letter to members of Congress explaining your circumstances and asking them to give you your bonus early.

Technology SKILLBUILDER

Building a Database

Why Learn This Skill?

Do you have a collection of sports cards, CDs, or DVDs? Have you ever kept a list of the names, addresses, and phone numbers of friends and relatives? If you have collected information and kept it in a list or file, then you have created a database.

Learning the Skill

An electronic database is a collection of facts that are stored in a file on a computer. The information is organized in fields.

A database can be organized and reorganized in any way that is useful to you. By using a database management system (DBMS)—special software developed for record keeping—you can easily add, delete, change, or update information. You give commands to the computer that tell it what to do with the information, and it follows these commands. When you want to retrieve information, the computer searches through the file, finds the information, and displays it on the screen.

Practicing the Skill

The Great Depression is a well-known period in American history. Follow these steps to build a database containing the events that led to the Great Depression and its effects on the country.

❶ Determine what facts you want to include in your database.

❷ Follow instructions to set up fields in the DBMS that you are using. Then enter each item of data in its assigned field.

❸ Determine how you want to organize the facts in the database—chronologically by the date of the event, or alphabetically by the name of the event.

❹ Follow the instructions in your computer program to place the information in the order you selected.

Skills Assessment

Complete the Practicing Skills questions on page 675 and the Chapter 22 Skill Reinforcement Activity to assess your mastery of this skill.

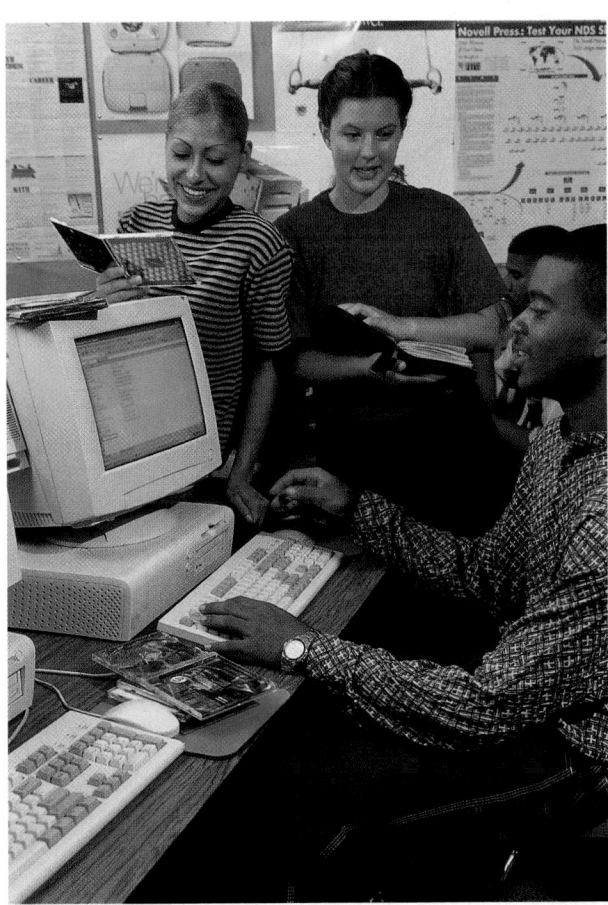

Applying the Skill

Building a Database Bring current newspapers or news magazines to class. Using the steps just described, build a database of current political events in the United States. Include a brief explanation of why the database is organized the way it is and how it might be used in class.

 GO TO

Glencoe's **Skillbuilder Interactive Workbook CD-ROM, Level 2,** provides instruction and practice in key social studies skills.

CHAPTER
22 ASSESSMENT and ACTIVITIES

Reviewing Key Terms

On a sheet of paper, use each of these terms in a sentence.

1. stock market
2. bull market
3. margin
4. margin call
5. speculation
6. installment
7. bailiff
8. shantytown
9. Hooverville
10. hobo
11. Dust Bowl
12. soap opera
13. public works
14. relief
15. foreclose

Reviewing Key Facts

16. **Identify:** Black Tuesday, Hawley-Smoot Tariff, Walt Disney, Grant Wood, John Steinbeck, Reconstruction Finance Corporation, Bonus Army.

17. What was the character of the stock market in the late 1920s, and what caused it to crash?

18. How did artists and writers capture the effects of the Great Depression?

19. Why did "Okies" migrate to California during the Great Depression, and what happened to them once they got there?

20. What three major initiatives did President Hoover take to try to help the economy of the United States?

21. What did World War I veterans do to try to get their service bonuses early?

Critical Thinking

22. **Analyzing Themes: Culture and Traditions** Many people in the United States were impoverished during the Depression, yet 60 to 90 million weekly viewers paid to see movies. Why do you think movies were so popular?

23. **Evaluating** Do you think President Hoover could have done more to end the Great Depression? Why or why not?

24. **Identifying** What approaches were used in literature and photography to highlight social problems during the Depression?

25. **Categorizing** Use a graphic organizer similar to the one below to list the causes and effects of the Great Depression.

Causes	Effects

26. **Interpreting Primary Sources** E.Y. Harburg lived during the Great Depression. After he lost his business, he became a poet and lyricist. He wrote the lyrics to one of the most famous songs of the time, "Brother, Can You Spare a Dime?" Read an excerpt of the lyrics to this song and answer the questions that follow.

❝They used to tell me I was building a dream
With peace and glory ahead—
Why should I be standing on line
Just waiting for bread?

Chapter Summary

Stock Market Helps Trigger Depression
• Bull market encouraged widespread speculation.
• Many investors bought stocks on margin.
• Sharp drop in market prices left investors in debt.
• Bank closings left many in debt.

Underlying Causes of Great Depression
• Overproduction and low interest rates
• Uneven distribution of income, which led to low demand
• Depressed farm sector
• Weak international market with high tariffs

Downward Momentum of the Great Depression

Low Sales → Job Layoffs → Less Income → Fewer Purchases → Lower Sales → More Job Layoffs

Once I built a railroad, made it run,
Made it run against time.
Once I built a railroad,
Now it's done—
Brother, can you spare a dime?

Once I built a tower to the sun.
Brick and rivet and lime,
Once I built a tower,
Now it's done—
Brother, can you spare a dime?**"**

a. How was the narrator's life different before the Great Depression than it was during it?

b. During the 1932 presidential campaign, the Republicans tried to discourage the radio networks from playing this song. Why do you think they did that?

Practicing Skills

27. **Building a Database** Use the business section of your local newspaper to prepare a database that lists the prices of three different stocks for one week. Use the following information in your database:

- Stock symbol
- Date
- Stock price at the end of each day (closing price)

Be sure to follow these steps to build your database:

a. Follow instructions in the DBMS that you are using. Then enter each item in its assigned field.

b. Determine how you want to organize the information in the database.

c. Place the information in the order you choose (by date, alphabetically by symbol, by price, etc.).

d. Check the accuracy of the information. Make necessary changes.

Writing Activity

28. **Creating a Dictionary** Create a dictionary of words and phrases that grew out of the Great Depression. If possible, include pictures or photographs that illustrate the entries.

Chapter Activity

29. **Creating Presentations** Analyze the statistical information you gathered in building the computer database in question 27. Write a short report describing the progress of

Crop Prices, 1910–1935

Source: *Historical Statistics of the United States: Colonial Times to 1970.*

the stocks you followed. Create a chart and a graph as a visual aid to present your findings to the class.

Economics and History

30. The graph above shows changes in crop prices from 1910 to 1935. Study the graph and answer the questions below.

a. **Interpreting Graphs** What trend does this graph show about wheat and corn prices in the 1930s?

b. **Analyzing** Between which 10-year span did the greatest increase and decrease in farm prices occur?

Standardized Test Practice

Directions: Choose the phrase that best completes the following sentence.

A major reason for the collapse of the American economy after 1929 was

A high interest rates.

B decreased farm production.

C low tariffs at home and abroad.

D overproduction of consumer goods.

Test-Taking Tip: If you are not sure of the answer, use the process of elimination. For example, farmers were not prosperous in the 1920s because their huge crops forced down agricultural prices. Therefore, answer B is incorrect.

23 Roosevelt and the New Deal

1933–1939

Why It Matters

Unlike Herbert Hoover, Franklin Delano Roosevelt was willing to employ deficit spending and greater federal regulation to revive the depressed economy. In response to his requests, Congress passed a host of new programs. Millions of people received relief to alleviate their suffering, but the New Deal did not really end the Depression. It did, however, permanently expand the federal government's role in providing basic security for citizens.

The Impact Today

Certain New Deal legislation still carries great importance in American social policy.
- *The Social Security Act still provides retirement benefits, aid to needy groups, and unemployment and disability insurance.*
- *The National Labor Relations Act still protects the right of workers to unionize.*
- *Safeguards were instituted to help prevent another devastating stock market crash.*
- *The Federal Deposit Insurance Corporation still protects bank deposits.*

The American Vision *Video* *The Chapter 23 video, "Franklin Roosevelt and the New Deal," describes the personal and political challenges Franklin Roosevelt faced as president.*

1928
- Franklin Delano Roosevelt elected governor of New York

1931
- The Empire State Building opens for business

1933
- Gold standard abandoned
- Federal Emergency Relief Act and Agricultural Adjustment Act passed

1929
- Great Depression begins

STAGE BROADWAY SCREEN
VARIETY
WALL ST. LAYS AN EGG

Hoover
1929–1933

F. Roosevelt
1933–1945

United States
PRESIDENTS

1928   1931   1934

World

1928
- Alexander Fleming discovers penicillin

1930
- Germany's Nazi Party wins 107 seats in Reichstag

1931
- German unemployment reaches 5.6 million
- Surrealist artist Salvador Dali paints *Persistence of Memory*

1933
- Adolf Hitler appointed German chancellor
- Japan withdraws from League of Nations

In this Ben Shahn mural detail, New Deal planners (at right) design the town of Jersey Homesteads as a home for impoverished immigrants.

1935
- Supreme Court strikes down NIRA
- Social Security Act passed

1937
- Court-packing bill defeated
- "Roosevelt recession" begins

1938
- Fair Labor Standards Act passed

1937   *1940*

1936
- Civil War erupts in Spain

1938
- Hitler annexes Austria

1939
- World War II begins

HISTORY Online

Chapter Overview
Visit the *American Vision* Web site at tav.glencoe.com and click on *Chapter Overviews—Chapter 23* to preview chapter information.

Roosevelt Takes Office

Guide to Reading

Main Idea
Franklin Delano Roosevelt's character and experiences prepared him for the presidency of a nation in crisis.

Key Terms and Names
New Deal, polio, gold standard, bank holiday

Reading Strategy
Organizing As you read about Franklin Roosevelt's background, complete a graphic organizer similar to the one below by listing the early influences and experiences that helped shape Roosevelt as a politician.

Influences and Experiences

Reading Objectives
• **Discuss** Franklin Roosevelt's early political career.
• **Explain** the worsening situation in the U.S. banking system in the early 1930s.

Section Theme
Individual Action Franklin Roosevelt's optimism, determination, and outgoing personality shaped his approach to politics.

Preview of Events

◆1905   ◆1915   ◆1925   ◆1935

1905
Franklin Roosevelt and Eleanor Roosevelt marry

1910
Roosevelt elected to New York State Senate

1921
Roosevelt stricken with polio

1928
Roosevelt elected governor of New York

★ **An American Story** ★

When Louis Howe was a child in Saratoga Springs, New York, a bicycle accident left his face scarred. As an adult and a reporter for his father's newspaper, he cheerfully described himself as "one of the four ugliest men in the state of New York." Howe dressed sloppily, perhaps to demonstrate how little importance he attached to appearance. He worked hard, however, and was respected for his reporting.

In the winter of 1911, Howe traveled to Albany to interview a Democratic state senator, Franklin Delano Roosevelt—or FDR, as he was called. Howe found himself fascinated by the tall, intense young man with the gold-rimmed glasses who paced back and forth in front of him, earnestly answering his questions. He admired the dashing appearance Roosevelt made.

During the interview Roosevelt declared his intention to challenge the party bosses. The usually skeptical Howe found himself believing the young legislator. "I made up my mind," Howe later recalled, "that nothing but an accident could keep him from becoming president."

—adapted from *The Crisis of the Old Order*

Roosevelt's Rise to Power

In mid-June 1932, with the country deep in the Depression, Republicans gathered in Chicago and nominated Herbert Hoover to run for a second term as president. The mood at the convention was somber. Delegates knew the Depression had turned many voters against Hoover.

Later that month, the Democrats also met in Chicago to choose their own candidate for president. It took four ballots and a great deal of negotiating, but the party eventually chose the popular governor of New York, Franklin Delano Roosevelt. When he won the nomination, Roosevelt broke with tradition by flying to Chicago to deliver the first acceptance speech ever made to a nominating convention. Roosevelt's speech set the tone for his campaign:

❝The appearance before a National Convention of its nominee for President . . . is unprecedented and unusual, but these are unprecedented and unusual times. . . . Let it also be symbolic that in so doing I broke traditions. Let it be from now on the task of our Party to break foolish traditions. . . . It is inevitable that the main issue of this campaign should revolve about . . . a depression so deep that it is without precedent. . . . Republican leaders not only have failed in material things, they have failed in national vision, because in disaster they have held out no hope. . . . I pledge you, I pledge myself, to a new deal for the American people.❞

—quoted in *The Public Papers and Addresses of Franklin D. Roosevelt*

The next day, a cartoonist used the words "new deal" to stand for Roosevelt's program. From that point forward, Roosevelt's policies for ending the Depression became known as the **New Deal.** Roosevelt's confidence that he could make things better contrasted sharply with Hoover's apparent failure to do anything effective. On Election Day, Roosevelt won the Electoral College in a landslide, 472 votes to 59, and he received nearly 23 million votes to slightly less than 16 million for Hoover in the general election.

Picturing History

The Young Roosevelts Franklin Roosevelt and Eleanor Roosevelt were married in 1905. They were distantly related through former president Theodore Roosevelt—her uncle and his cousin. *What sort of childhood did Franklin Roosevelt have growing up in Hyde Park, New York?*

Roosevelt's Background

Franklin Roosevelt—a distant cousin of President Theodore Roosevelt—was born in 1882 to a wealthy New York family. Roosevelt grew up on his family's estate at Hyde Park on the Hudson River. There, Roosevelt learned to hunt, fish, ride horses, and sail, and he developed his lifelong commitment to conservation and a love of rural America. Roosevelt was educated at Harvard and Columbia Law School. While at Harvard, he became friends with Theodore Roosevelt's niece, Eleanor. Soon afterward, they were married.

Roosevelt was intensely competitive. He enjoyed winning and liked to be in control. He also liked being around people. His charming personality, deep rich voice, and wide smile expressed confidence and optimism. He could also be very persuasive. Overall, FDR's personality seemed made for a life in politics.

FDR's Early Political Career

Shortly after leaving law school, Roosevelt plunged into politics. In 1910 he won a seat in the New York State Senate, where he earned a reputation as a progressive reformer willing to stand up to the party bosses. Roosevelt strongly supported Woodrow Wilson's presidential campaign in 1912. After winning the election, Wilson rewarded Roosevelt by appointing him assistant secretary of the navy, a position he held through World War I.

In 1920, hoping his name would win votes, the Democrats nominated Roosevelt as their candidate for vice president. After losing the election, Roosevelt temporarily withdrew from politics. The next year he came down with a fever and soon felt numbness in both legs. He had caught the dreaded and paralyzing disease known as **polio.** Although there was no cure, Roosevelt refused to give in. He began a vigorous exercise program to restore muscle control. Eventually, by wearing heavy steel braces on his legs, he was able to appear to walk by leaning on a cane and someone's arm and swinging his legs forward by moving his hips.

While recovering from polio, Roosevelt depended on his wife to keep his name prominent in the New York Democratic Party. Although shy, Eleanor Roosevelt became an effective public speaker. Her efforts during this time kept her husband's political career alive.

Linking Past & Present

Roosevelt Dime

Past: Search for a Cure
In 1921 Franklin Roosevelt contracted polio, a disease that paralyzed his legs. Few people knew of his physical limitations when he became president. His only freedom from braces came when he swam.
After Roosevelt established a foundation for polio victims at Warm Springs, Georgia, entertainer Eddie Cantor suggested that everyone in the country send a dime for polio research to the president. This campaign, which became known as the March of Dimes, produced 150,000 letters a day. In 1945 Congress voted to honor Roosevelt by placing his image on the dime.

Present: A Threat Eliminated
In the early 1950s, Dr. Jonas Salk discovered the polio vaccine. Today polio is no longer the threat to health that it once was.

Governor of New York By the mid-1920s, Roosevelt was again active in the Democratic Party. He became a strong supporter of New York's governor, Alfred E. Smith. When the Democratic Party nominated Smith for president in 1928, Smith urged Roosevelt to run for governor of New York. Roosevelt campaigned hard to demonstrate that his illness had not slowed him down, and he narrowly won the election.

Roosevelt's policies as governor made him very popular. He cut taxes for farmers and worked to reduce the rates charged by public utilities. In 1931, as the Depression worsened, Roosevelt convinced the New York legislature to set up a new state agency to help unemployed New Yorkers. The agency distributed over $25 million in aid that provided relief to about 10 percent of New York's families.

Roosevelt's popularity in New York paved the way for his presidential nomination in 1932. Many Americans applauded his use of the government's power to help people in economic distress. Others believed that his struggle against polio had given him a better understanding of their hardships.

Perhaps most important, Americans saw in Roosevelt an energy and optimism that gave them hope despite the tough economic times. After Roosevelt became president, his serenity and confidence amazed many people. When one aide commented on his attitude, Roosevelt replied, "If you had spent two years in bed, trying to wiggle your big toe, after that anything else would seem easy."

✓ **Reading Check** **Interpreting** What events in Roosevelt's life shaped his ideas and character?

Roosevelt Is Inaugurated

Although Roosevelt won the presidency in November 1932, the country's unemployed and homeless had to endure one more winter as they waited for his inauguration on March 4, 1933. All through the winter, unemployment continued to rise. Theater director Harold Clurman later wrote about the fear:

66Yes, we could smell the depression in the air, that historically cruel winter of 1932–33, which chilled so many of us like a world's end. . . . It was like a raw wind; the very houses we lived in seemed to be shrinking, hopeless of real comfort.99

—quoted in *Franklin Roosevelt and the New Deal*

> ## "... the only thing we have to fear is fear itself ..."
> —*Franklin D. Roosevelt*

Inspiring Words President Roosevelt used his first Inaugural Address of March 1933 to rally the nation's spirits. What problems had made the nation anxious and fearful?

Meanwhile, bank runs greatly increased, further threatening the nation's banking system. Some of the bank runs occurred because people feared Roosevelt would abandon the gold standard and reduce the value of the dollar in order to fight the Depression. Under the gold standard, one ounce of gold equaled a set number of dollars. To reduce the value of the dollar, the United States would have to stop exchanging dollars for gold. Many Americans, and many foreign investors with deposits in American banks, decided to take their money out of the banks and convert it to gold before it lost its value.

Across the nation, people stood in long lines with paper bags and suitcases, waiting to withdraw their money from banks. By March 1933, over 4,000 banks had collapsed, wiping out 9 million savings accounts. In 38 states, governors declared **bank holidays**—closing the remaining banks before bank runs could put them out of business.

By the day of Roosevelt's inauguration, most of the nation's banks were closed. One in four workers was unemployed. The economy seemed paralyzed. Roosevelt knew he had to restore the nation's confidence. "First of all," the president declared in his Inaugural Address, "let me assert my firm belief that the only thing we have to fear is fear itself. . . . This nation asks for action, and action now!"

Reading Check **Summarizing** What was the nation's condition when Roosevelt took office?

SECTION 1 ASSESSMENT

Checking for Understanding

1. **Define:** gold standard.
2. **Identify:** New Deal, polio, bank holiday.
3. **Describe** the ways in which early influences and experiences shaped Roosevelt as a politician.

Reviewing Themes

4. **Individual Action** Why did Roosevelt's election lead to an increase in bank runs?

Critical Thinking

5. **Explaining** How did FDR's experiences as governor of New York prepare him for the presidency?
6. **Organizing** Use a graphic organizer like the one below to list early influences on Roosevelt's political career.

Early Political Influences

Analyzing Visuals

7. **Analyzing Photographs** Study the photograph on this page. What did the president mean when he said "the only thing we have to fear is fear itself"?

Writing About History

8. **Persuasive Writing** Imagine you are living during the Depression. In your hometown, there has been a bank run. Write a letter to the president describing this event. Ask him to take steps to cure the bank crisis.

Guide to Reading

Main Idea

In the first 100 days of Roosevelt's presidency, his team initiated a series of laws that transformed the United States.

Key Terms and Names

Hundred Days, fireside chats, Securities and Exchange Commission, Federal Deposit Insurance Corporation, Agricultural Adjustment Administration, Civilian Conservation Corps

Reading Strategy

Sequencing As you read about President Roosevelt's first three months in office, complete a time line similar to the one below to record the major problems he addressed during this time.

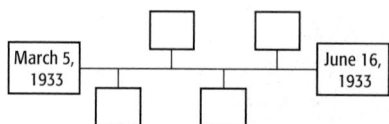

Reading Objectives

• **List** three programs of the First New Deal that provided jobs for the unemployed.

• **Discuss** why New Dealers believed that sometimes the government needs to regulate industry and labor.

Section Theme

Groups and Institutions FDR's attempts to end the Depression resulted in many new government agencies.

Preview of Events

◆March 1933   ◆May 1933   ◆July 1933

March 4, 1933
FDR inaugurated

March 31, 1933
Civilian Conservation Corps created

May 12, 1933
Federal Emergency Relief Act; Agricultural Adjustment Act

June 16, 1933
National Industrial Recovery Act; Glass-Steagall Banking Act; Farm Credit Act

★ An American Story ★

In the 1920s, cowboy and comedian Will Rogers said that his life's work was "to rescue the country from the hands of the politicians." He used his sharp wit to go after these public figures. A friend of presidents and politicians of both parties, Rogers nevertheless satirized them mercilessly in public appearances and on the radio.

With FDR, however, Rogers changed his tune: "President Roosevelt closed the banks before lunch and called Congress into session while he was having dessert. . . . The whole country is with him. . . . Even if he does what is wrong they are with him, just so he does something. . . . If he burned down the Capitol, we would cheer and say, 'Well, we at least got a fire started anyhow.'"

As Roosevelt's New Deal gained momentum, Rogers praised the resulting flurry of legislation: "Mr. Roosevelt just makes out a little list of things every morning that he wants [Congress] to do . . . and the whole country is better off."

—adapted from *Will Rogers: A Biography*

The Hundred Days Begins

Roosevelt and his advisers, sometimes called the Brain Trust, came into office bursting with ideas for recovery from the Depression. Roosevelt had no clear agenda. The previous spring, during his campaign for the presidential nomination, Roosevelt had revealed the approach he would take as president. "The country needs," Roosevelt explained, "bold, persistent experimentation. . . . Above all, try something."

The new president began to send bill after bill to Congress. Between March 9 and June 16, 1933—which came to be called the **Hundred Days**—Congress passed 15 major acts to meet the economic crisis, setting a pace for new legislation that has never been equaled. Together, these programs made up what would later be called the First New Deal.

Origins of the New Deal
The New Deal was not based on a clear strategy shaped by a single philosophy. Roosevelt was not an intellectual, nor did he have a strong political ideology. He was a practical politician. FDR was willing to try a variety of approaches both to see whether they worked and whether they were helping or hurting him politically.

To generate new ideas and programs, Roosevelt sought advice from a wide range of advisers with experience in academia, business, agriculture, government, law, and social work. The president deliberately chose advisers who disagreed with each other. He wanted to hear many different points of view, and by setting his advisers against one another, Roosevelt ensured that he alone made the final decision on what policies to pursue.

A Divided Administration
Roosevelt's advisers were divided roughly into three main groups. Despite their disagreements, most of the advisers had grown up in the Progressive Era, and their approaches reflected progressive ideas. They generally favored some form of government intervention in the economy—although they disagreed over what the government's role should be.

One group that was very influential during the early years of Roosevelt's administration supported the "New Nationalism" of Theodore Roosevelt. These advisers believed that business and government should work together to manage the economy. They had been very impressed by business-government cooperation on the War Industries Board during World War I. They believed that if government agencies worked with businesses to regulate wages, prices, and production, they could lift the economy out of the Depression.

A second group of advisers in the Roosevelt administration went even further. They distrusted big business and blamed business leaders for causing the Depression. These advisers wanted government planners to run key parts of the economy.

A third group in Roosevelt's administration supported the "New Freedom" of Woodrow Wilson. They too blamed large trusts for the Depression, but they believed the government had to restore competition to the economy. These advisers wanted Roosevelt to support "trust busting" by breaking up big companies and allowing competition to set wages, prices, and production levels. They also thought the government should impose regulations on the economy to keep competition fair.

Reading Check **Summarizing** What ideas did Roosevelt's advisers support?

Fixing the Banks and the Stock Market

As the debate over policies and programs swirled around him, President Roosevelt took office with one thing clear in his mind. Very few of the proposed solutions would work as long as the nation's banks remained closed. The first thing he had to do was restore confidence in the banking system.

The Emergency Banking Relief Act
On his very first night in office, Roosevelt told Secretary of the Treasury William H. Woodin he wanted an emergency banking bill ready for Congress in less than five days. The following afternoon, Roosevelt declared a national bank holiday, temporarily closing all banks, and called Congress into a special session scheduled to begin on March 9, 1933.

On the day Congress convened, the House of Representatives unanimously passed the Emergency Banking Relief Act after only 38 minutes of debate.

Picturing **History**

Presidential Assurances President Roosevelt often used radio addresses to calm the public's fears during the Great Depression. At the beginning of his first term, he encouraged Americans to put their money back in federally inspected banks. Why do you think the president declared a bank holiday?

Why It Matters

The TVA

Perhaps no New Deal program produced as many visible benefits as the Tennessee Valley Authority (TVA). This dam-building project was a bold venture to control floods, conserve forestlands, and bring electricity to rural America. The TVA created a comprehensive plan for developing a vast seven-state region drained by the Tennessee and Cumberland Rivers and populated mainly by poor farmers working worn-out land. The TVA erected 20 dams, employing up to 40,000 workers at a time. The agency also reforested millions of acres, built fertilizer factories and power plants, and strung thousands of miles of wire to bring electricity to rural families for the first time.

◄ Recreation
Millions of people each year fish, swim, ski, whitewater raft, or go boating on the reservoirs. Sometimes the reservoir system is referred to as the "Great Lakes of the South."

NATIONAL GEOGRAPHIC

The TVA, 1940

The Senate approved the bill that evening, and Roosevelt signed it into law shortly afterward. The new law required federal examiners to survey the nation's banks and issue Treasury Department licenses to those that were financially sound.

On March 12, President Roosevelt addressed the nation by radio. Sixty million people listened to this first of many "fireside chats," direct talks FDR held with the American people to let them know what he was trying to accomplish. He told the people that their money would now be secure if they put it back into the banks. "I assure you that it is safer to keep your money in a reopened bank than under the mattress." When banks opened the day after the speech, deposits far outweighed withdrawals. The banking crisis was over.

Regulating Banks and Brokers Although President Roosevelt had restored confidence in the banking system, many of his advisers who favored trust-busting and fair competition urged him to go further. They pushed for new regulations for both banks and the stock market. Roosevelt agreed with their ideas and threw his support behind the Securities Act of 1933 and the Glass-Steagall Banking Act.

The Securities Act required companies that sold stocks and bonds to provide complete and truthful information to investors. The following year Congress created an independent agency, the **Securities and Exchange Commission** (SEC), to regulate the stock market and prevent fraud.

The Glass-Steagall Act separated commercial banking from investment banking. Commercial banks handle everyday transactions. They take deposits, pay interest, cash checks, and loan money for mortgages and other business activities. Under the Glass-Steagall Act, these banks were no longer permitted to risk depositors' money by using it to speculate on the stock market.

To further protect depositors, the Glass-Steagall Act also created the **Federal Deposit Insurance Corporation** (FDIC) to provide government insurance

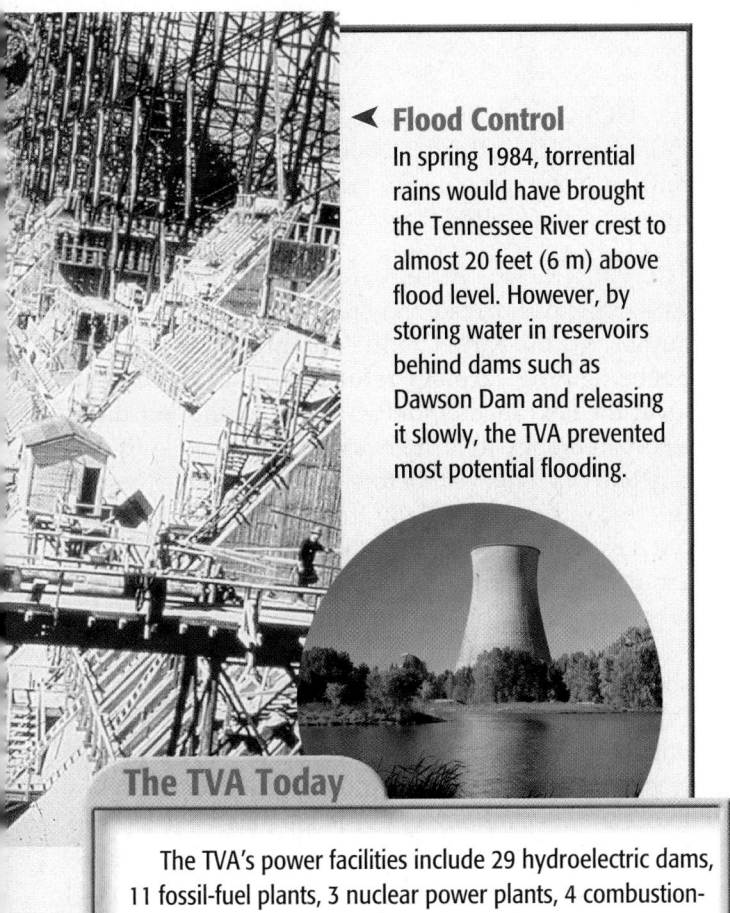

◄ Flood Control

In spring 1984, torrential rains would have brought the Tennessee River crest to almost 20 feet (6 m) above flood level. However, by storing water in reservoirs behind dams such as Dawson Dam and releasing it slowly, the TVA prevented most potential flooding.

The TVA Today

The TVA's power facilities include 29 hydroelectric dams, 11 fossil-fuel plants, 3 nuclear power plants, 4 combustion-turbine plants, a pumped-storage facility, and 17,000 miles of transmission lines. These facilities provide power to nearly 8 million people in the seven-state region.

for bank deposits up to a certain amount. By protecting depositors in this way, the FDIC greatly increased public confidence in the banking system.

✓ **Reading Check** **Explaining** How did the government restore confidence in the banking system?

Managing Farms and Industry

Many of Roosevelt's advisers believed that both farmers and businesses were suffering because prices were too low and production too high. Several advisers believed competition was inefficient and bad for the economy. They wanted business and government to work together and favored the creation of federal agencies to manage the economy.

The Agricultural Adjustment Administration

The nation's farmers had been hit hard by the Depression. One week after calling Congress into special session, Roosevelt announced plans for a new farm program. Working closely with the leaders of the nation's farm organizations, Secretary of Agriculture Henry Wallace raced to complete a new farm bill before planting season began.

The Agricultural Adjustment Act that Roosevelt asked Congress to pass was based on a simple idea—that prices for farm goods were low because farmers grew too much food. Under Roosevelt's program, the government would pay farmers *not* to raise certain livestock, such as hogs, and *not* to grow certain crops, such as cotton, corn, wheat, and tobacco. The farm program was administered by the **Agricultural Adjustment Administration** (AAA).

By the time the AAA was organized, however, farmers had already planted their crops for the year and begun raising the season's livestock. To prevent cotton—which was already at a very low price—from reaching the market, the AAA paid cotton farmers about $100 million to plow under about 25 percent of their crop. Similarly, hog producers slaughtered 6 million piglets instead of fattening them for market.

Over the next two years, farmers withdrew millions of acres from production and received more than $1 billion in support payments. The program accomplished its goal: The farm surplus fell greatly by 1936. Food prices then rose, as did total farm income, which quickly increased by more than 50 percent.

In a nation caught in a Depression, however, raising food prices drew harsh criticism. Furthermore, not all farmers benefited. Large commercial farmers, who concentrated on one crop, profited more than smaller farmers who raised several products. Worse, thousands of poor tenant farmers—many of them African Americans—became homeless and jobless when landlords chose their fields to be taken out of production.

A Blueprint for Industrial Recovery The government turned its attention from farming to manufacturing in June 1933, when Roosevelt and Congress enacted the **National Industrial Recovery Act** (NIRA). The NIRA suspended the antitrust laws and allowed business, labor, and government to cooperate in setting up voluntary rules for each industry.

These rules were known as codes of fair competition. Some codes set prices, established minimum wages, and limited factories to two shifts per day so production could be spread to as many firms as possible. Other codes shortened workers' hours with the goal of creating additional jobs. Another provision in the law guaranteed workers the right to form unions.

Under the leadership of Hugh Johnson, the **National Recovery Administration** (NRA) ran the entire program. Business owners who signed code agreements received signs displaying the NRA's symbol—a blue eagle—and the slogan, "We do our part." Since the NRA had limited power to enforce the codes, it used public opinion to pressure companies into going along. It urged consumers to buy goods only from companies that displayed the blue eagle.

The NRA did produce a revival of a few industries, but the gains proved short-lived. Small companies complained, justifiably, that large corporations wrote the codes to favor themselves. More efficient companies disliked price fixing, which limited competition and made it hard for them to increase their market share by cutting prices. Employers disliked codes that gave workers the right to form unions and bargain collectively over wages and hours. They also argued that paying high minimum wages forced them to charge higher prices to cover their costs.

The codes were also very difficult to administer, and business leaders often ignored them. It became obvious that the NRA was failing when industrial production actually fell after the organization was established. By the time the Supreme Court declared the NRA to be unconstitutional in 1935, it had already lost much of its political support.

✓ **Reading Check** **Examining** What were the provisions of the Agricultural Adjustment Act and the National Industrial Recovery Act?

Providing Debt Relief

While some of Roosevelt's advisers believed low prices had caused the Depression, others believed that debt was the main obstacle to economic recovery. With incomes falling, people had to use most of their money to pay their debts and had little left over to buy goods or pay for services. Many Americans, terrified of losing their homes and farms, deliberately cut back on their spending to make sure they could pay their mortgages. President Roosevelt responded to the crisis by introducing several policies intended to assist Americans with their debts.

The Home Owners' Loan Corporation To help
homeowners pay their mortgages, Roosevelt asked Congress to establish the Home Owners' Loan Corporation (HOLC). The HOLC bought the mortgages of many homeowners who were behind in their payments. It then restructured them with longer terms of repayment and lower interest rates. Roughly 10 percent of the nation's homeowners received HOLC loans.

The HOLC did not help everyone. It only made loans to homeowners who were still employed. When people lost their jobs and could no longer pay their mortgages, the HOLC foreclosed on their property, just as a bank would have done. By 1938

the HOLC had foreclosed on more than 100,000 mortgages. Despite these failures, the HOLC helped refinance one out of every five mortgages on private homes in the United States.

The Farm Credit Administration Three days after
Congress authorized the creation of the HOLC, it authorized the Farm Credit Administration (FCA) to begin helping farmers refinance their mortgages. Over the next seven months, the FCA lent four times as much money to farmers as the entire banking system had done the year before. It was also able to push interest rates substantially lower. "I would be without a roof over my head if it hadn't been for the government loan," wrote one of the millions of farmers who were saved by FCA loans.

Although FCA loans helped many farmers in the short term, their long-term value can be questioned. FCA loans helped less efficient farmers keep their land, but giving loans to poor farmers meant that the money was not available to loan to more efficient businesses in the economy. Although FCA loans may have slowed the overall economic recovery, they did help many desperate and impoverished people hold onto their land.

✓ **Reading Check** **Identifying** What New Deal programs helped farmers and homeowners?

Spending and Relief Programs

While many of Roosevelt's advisers emphasized tinkering with prices and providing debt relief in order to cure the Depression, others maintained that the fundamental cause of the Depression was low consumption. People were simply not buying enough products to keep the economy going. The fastest way out of the Depression, these advisers asserted, was to get money directly into the hands of needy individuals.

Neither President Roosevelt nor his advisers wanted simply to give money to the unemployed. They argued that recipients were more likely to maintain work skills and self-respect if they earned their

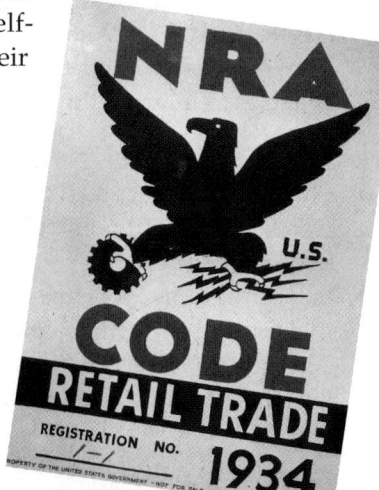

Picturing **History**

The NRA Eagle As a symbol of the National Recovery Administration, this eagle informed consumers about industries that were meeting the standards of the National Industrial Recovery Act. How successful was the NRA?

The First New Deal, 1933–1935

Agency	Established	Function
Civilian Conservation Corps (CCC)	March 1933	Employed single men, ages 18–25, for natural resource conservation
Tennessee Valley Authority (TVA)	May 1933	Built hydroelectric plants and dams aimed at improving seven Southern states and attracting industry to the South
Agricultural Adjustment Act (AAA)	May 1933	Reduced agricultural surplus and raised prices for struggling farmers
Federal Emergency Relief Agency (FERA)	May 1933	Granted federal money to state and local governments to be used to help the unemployed
National Recovery Administration (NRA)	June 1933	Controlled industrial production and prices with industry-created codes of fair competition
Federal Deposit Insurance Corporation (FDIC)	June 1933	Guaranteed bank deposits up to $2,500
Public Works Administration (PWA)	June 1933	Provided employment in construction of airports, parks, schools, and roads
Civil Works Administration (CWA)	November 1933 (cancelled 1934)	
Securities and Exchange Commission (SEC)	June 1934	Regulated the stock market to avoid dishonest practices

Chart Skills

1. **Interpreting Charts** Which of the programs listed was cancelled the year after it was established?
2. **Examining** What steps did the AAA take to ensure its listed function?

money. As a result, Roosevelt urged Congress to establish a series of government agencies that would organize work programs for the unemployed.

The CCC The most highly praised New Deal work relief program was the **Civilian Conservation Corps** (CCC), which combined Roosevelt's love of nature and commitment to conservation with the need to help the unemployed. Beginning in March 1933, the CCC offered unemployed young men 18 to 25 years old the opportunity to work under the direction of the national forestry service planting trees, fighting forest fires, and building reservoirs.

The young men lived in camps near their work areas and earned $30 a month. By midsummer the CCC had created some 1,500 camps. The average CCC worker returned home after six months to a year of service better nourished than before and with greater self-respect. "I weighed about 160 pounds when I went there, and when I left, I was 190," said one. "It made a man of me, all right." By the time it closed down in 1942, the CCC had put 3 million young men to work outdoors.

Public Works and Emergency Relief

A few weeks after authorizing the CCC, Congress established the Federal Emergency Relief Administration (FERA). FERA did not initially create projects for the unemployed. Instead, it channeled money—a half-billion dollars in all—to state and local agencies to fund their relief projects. The leader of FERA was Harry Hopkins, whose nervous energy and sarcastic manner put off many people. Despite his personality, Hopkins became one of the most influential people in Roosevelt's administration.

Half an hour after meeting with Roosevelt to discuss his new job, Hopkins set up a desk in the hallway of his new office. In the next two hours, he spent $5 million on relief projects. When critics charged that some of the projects did not make sense in the long run, Hopkins replied, "People don't eat in the long run—they eat every day."

In June 1933, Congress authorized the creation of another federal relief agency—the **Public Works Administration** (PWA). Roosevelt knew that nearly one-third of the nation's unemployed were in the construction industry. To put them back to work, the PWA began a series of construction projects to build and improve highways, dams, sewer systems, waterworks, schools, and other government facilities.

In most cases, the PWA did not hire workers directly, but instead awarded contracts to construction companies. By insisting that contractors hire African Americans, the agency broke down some of the long-standing racial barriers in the construction trades.

The Civilian Conservation Corps FDR satisfied both the nation's need for employment and his love of nature with the CCC. Workers planted forests, built reservoirs, and received a monthly salary. In what year did the CCC halt operations?

The CWA By the fall of 1933, neither FERA nor the PWA had reduced unemployment significantly. Hopkins realized that unless the federal government acted quickly, a huge number of unemployed would be in severe distress once winter began. After Hopkins explained the situation, President Roosevelt authorized him to set up the **Civil Works Administration** (CWA).

Unlike the PWA, the CWA hired workers directly and put them on the federal government's payroll. That winter the CWA employed 4 million people, 300,000 of them women. Under Hopkins's direction, the agency built or improved 1,000 airports, 500,000 miles of roads, 40,000 school buildings, and 3,500 playgrounds, parks, and playing fields.

The cost of the CWA was huge—the program spent nearly $1 billion in just five months. A former colleague remembered Hopkins as "the kind of guy that seldom wrote a letter. He'd just call and say, 'Send a million dollars to Arkansas, and five million to New York. People are in need.'"

Although the CWA helped many people get through the winter, President Roosevelt was alarmed at how quickly the agency was spending money. He did not want Americans to get used to the federal government providing them with jobs. Warning that the CWA would "become a habit with the country," Roosevelt insisted that it be shut down. "We must not take the position," the president explained, "that we are going to have a permanent depression in this country." By early April 1934, Hopkins had shut down the CWA and fired the 4 million workers the agency had hired.

By the end of his first year in office, President Roosevelt had convinced Congress to pass an astonishing array of programs and policies. The programs passed during the first New Deal did not restore prosperity, but they all reflected Roosevelt's zeal for action, his willingness to experiment, and his openness to new ideas. Perhaps the most important result of the first New Deal was a noticeable change in the spirit of the American people. Roosevelt's actions had inspired hope and optimism, and Americans' faith in their nation had been restored.

Reading Check **Identifying** What three New Deal programs provided work relief to the unemployed?

SECTION 2 ASSESSMENT

Checking for Understanding
1. **Define:** fireside chats.
2. **Identify:** Hundred Days, Securities and Exchange Commission, Federal Deposit Insurance Corporation, Agricultural Adjustment Administration, Civilian Conservation Corps.
3. **Summarize** the different viewpoints of Roosevelt's advisers.

Reviewing Themes
4. **Groups and Institutions** How did the Glass-Steagall Act and the Federal Deposit Insurance Corporation help make the banking industry safer?

Critical Thinking
5. **Interpreting** Did the CCC, CWA, and PWA achieve their goals? Explain your answer.
6. **Organizing** Use a graphic organizer like the one below to list the major agencies of the First New Deal.

Roosevelt's New Agencies

Analyzing Visuals
7. **Analyzing Charts** Examine the chart on page 687. How did the various agencies listed change the historical role of the federal government?

Writing About History

8. **Expository Writing** Research the Agricultural Adjustment Act by rereading the text on page 685. Use library resources and the Internet to complete your research. Then write an article explaining the benefits and drawbacks of this piece of legislation.

The Second New Deal

★ An American Story ★

Harry Hopkins, head of the Federal Emergency Relief Administration, worked long hours in his Washington office, a bare, dingy room with exposed water pipes. He preferred this space to the grandeur of the more conventional offices of high-ranking officials. Here he often defended the New Deal's work relief programs when reporters dropped by, and he lashed out at New Deal critics with headline-making phrases. "Some people just can't stand to see others make a decent living," he said, or, "Hunger is not debatable."

Sometimes Hopkins went on the road to talk about his job. Once, on a trip to his home state of Iowa, Hopkins was extolling New Deal policies to a sympathetic audience when a voice from the crowd shouted, "Who's going to pay for it?" Without a word Hopkins peeled off his jacket, loosened his tie, and rolled up his sleeves. Then his voice ripped through the utter stillness, "You are!"

—adapted from *The Politics of Upheaval*

Challenges to the New Deal

President Roosevelt appreciated Harry Hopkins's feistiness. He needed effective speakers who were willing to contend with his adversaries. Although Roosevelt had been tremendously popular during his first two years in office, opposition to his policies had begun to grow.

The New Deal had been in effect for two years, yet the economy had shown only a slight improvement. Although more than 2 million new jobs had been created, more than 10 million workers remained unemployed, and the nation's total income remained about half of what it had been in 1929. As one of Harry Hopkins's aides reported on a

Critics From the Left Huey Long and Father Charles Coughlin claimed the New Deal did not do enough to help the poor.

visit to Houston, Texas, "Nobody seems to think any more that the thing [the New Deal] is going to work."

Criticism From Left and Right
Hostility toward Roosevelt came from both the right wing and the left wing of the political spectrum. People on the right generally believed the New Deal had imposed too many regulations on business. The right wing also included many Southern Democrats who believed the New Deal had expanded the federal government's power at the expense of states' rights.

The right wing had opposed the New Deal from the beginning, but by late 1934, the opposition began to increase. To pay for his programs, Roosevelt had begun deficit spending. He had abandoned a balanced budget and begun borrowing money to pay for his programs. Many business leaders became greatly alarmed at the government's growing deficit.

In August 1934, business leaders and anti–New Deal politicians from both parties joined together to create the **American Liberty League.** Its purpose was to organize opposition to the New Deal and "teach the necessity of respect for the rights of person and property."

While criticisms from the right threatened to split the Democratic Party and reduce business support for

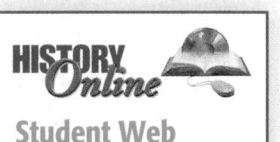
Roosevelt, another serious challenge to the New Deal came from the left. People on the left believed Roosevelt had not gone far enough. They wanted the government to intervene even more dramatically in the economy to shift wealth from the rich to middle-income and poor Americans.

Huey Long
Perhaps the most serious threat from the left came from Democratic senator Huey Long of Louisiana. Long captivated audiences with folksy humor and fiery oratory. As governor of Louisiana, Long had championed the downtrodden. He had improved schools, colleges, and hospitals, and had built roads and bridges. These benefits made Long very popular and enabled him to build a powerful and corrupt political machine.

Long's attacks on the rich gave him a national following, too. His supporters organized some 27,000 "Share Our Wealth" clubs across the country. Pollsters estimated that if he ran against Roosevelt as a third-party candidate in 1936, Long would take 10 percent of Roosevelt's vote—enough, they believed, to ensure a Republican victory.

Father Coughlin
Huey Long's challenge to Roosevelt became even more credible when his supporters were combined with those of Father Charles Coughlin, a Catholic priest in Detroit. Coughlin had a popular radio show that attracted a weekly audience of about 30 to 45 million Americans.

Originally a New Deal supporter, Coughlin had become impatient with its moderate reforms. He called instead for heavy taxes on the wealthy and nationalization of the banking system. In the spring of 1935, Coughlin organized the National Union for Social Justice, which some Democrats feared was the first step to creating a new political party.

The Townsend Plan
A third left-wing challenge to Roosevelt came from Dr. Francis Townsend, a former public health official. Townsend proposed that the federal government pay citizens over age 60 a pension of $200 a month. Recipients would have to retire and spend their entire pension check each month. He believed the plan would increase spending and remove people from the labor force, freeing up jobs for the unemployed.

Townsend's proposal attracted millions of supporters, especially among the elderly, who mobilized as a political force for the first time in American history. Townsend's program was particularly popular in the West. When combined with Long's support in the Midwest and South and Coughlin's support among urban Catholics in the Northeast, there was a real possibility of a coalition that would draw enough votes away from Roosevelt to prevent his re-election in 1936.

✓ **Reading Check** **Examining** What groups of people challenged Roosevelt and the New Deal? What concerns did they have?

Launching the Second New Deal

Although he remained tremendously popular with the American people, Roosevelt realized that his political support could be undermined by the attacks from left and right. He was also disturbed by the failure of the New Deal to generate a rapid economic recovery. In 1935 he launched what came to be called the Second New Deal—another series of programs and reforms that he hoped would speed up the nation's recovery, provide economic security to every American, and ensure his re-election in 1936.

The WPA In January 1935, Roosevelt began by asking Congress for nearly $5 billion "for work relief and to increase employment by providing useful projects." Much of the money would be given to the **Works Progress Administration** (WPA), a new federal agency headed by Harry Hopkins. "The big boss is ready to go places in a big way," Hopkins told a colleague.

Over the next several years, the WPA spent $11 billion. Its 8.5 million workers constructed about 650,000 miles of highways, roads, and streets, 125,000 public buildings, and more than 8,000 parks. It built or improved more than 124,000 bridges and 853 airports.

The WPA's most controversial program was "Federal Number One," a section of the Professional Projects Division that offered work to artists, musicians, theater people, and writers. "They've got to eat just like other people," Hopkins commented to critics of the program. The artists created thousands of murals and sculptural works to beautify the walls and halls of public buildings. Musicians established

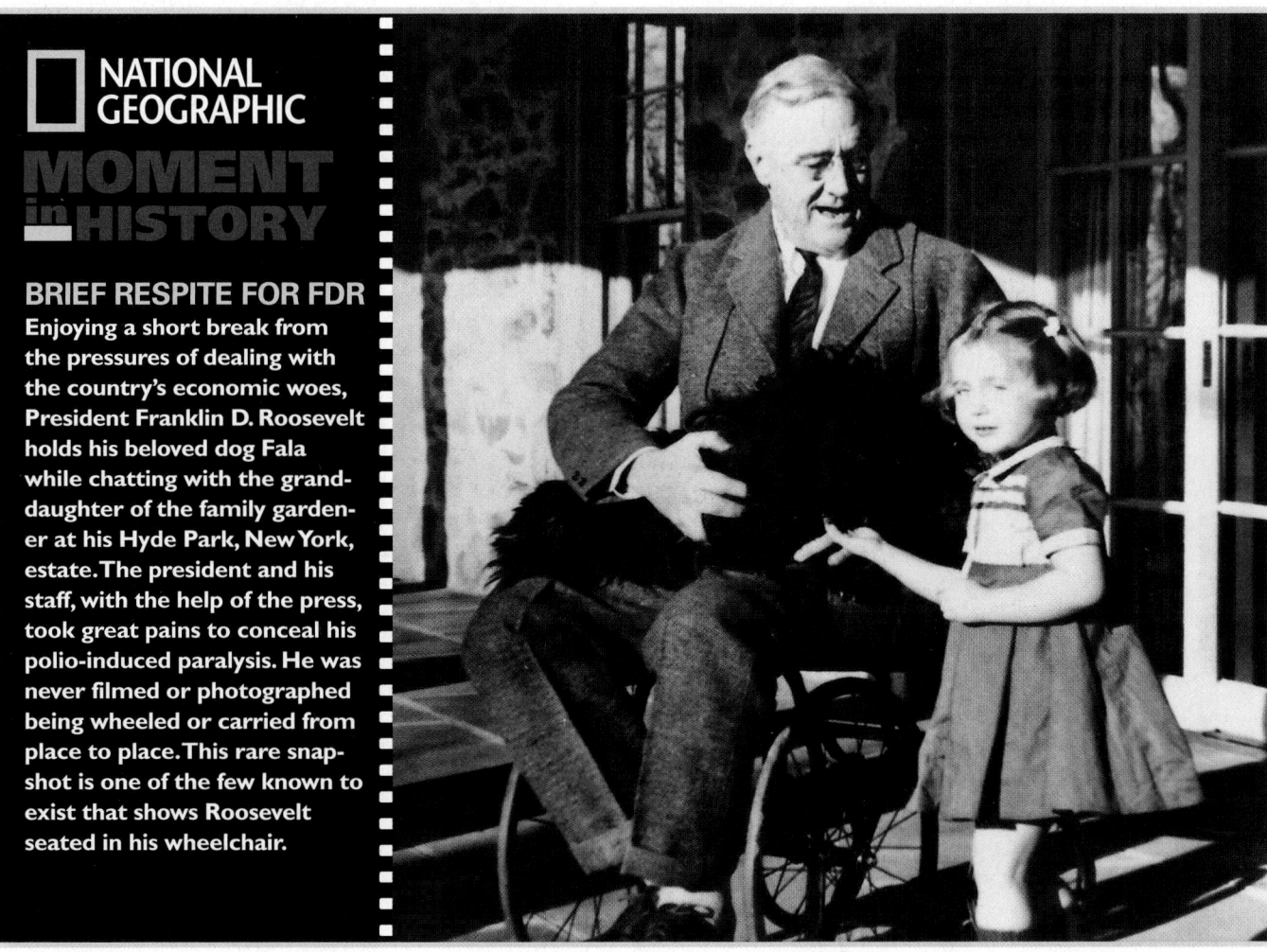

NATIONAL GEOGRAPHIC

MOMENT in HISTORY

BRIEF RESPITE FOR FDR
Enjoying a short break from the pressures of dealing with the country's economic woes, President Franklin D. Roosevelt holds his beloved dog Fala while chatting with the granddaughter of the family gardener at his Hyde Park, New York, estate. The president and his staff, with the help of the press, took great pains to conceal his polio-induced paralysis. He was never filmed or photographed being wheeled or carried from place to place. This rare snapshot is one of the few known to exist that shows Roosevelt seated in his wheelchair.

The Second New Deal, 1935

Agency/Legislation	Function
Works Progress Administration (WPA)	Combated unemployment; created jobs throughout economy
Rural Electrification Administration (REA)	Brought electricity to isolated agricultural areas
Social Security Act	Created unemployment system, disability insurance, old-age pension, and child welfare benefits
Public Utility Holding Company Act	Eliminated unfair practices and abuses of utility companies
Banking Act	Strengthened the Federal Reserve
Resettlement Act	Assisted poor families and sharecroppers in beginning new farms or purchasing land

Chart Skills

1. **Interpreting Charts** What did the Resettlement Act try to accomplish?
2. **Understanding Cause and Effect** How did these acts create a safety net for American citizens?

30 city symphony orchestras, as well as hundreds of smaller musical groups. The Federal Theater Project financed playwrights, actors, and directors. The program also funded historians who interviewed former slaves to document American history.

The Supreme Court's Role When Roosevelt asked Congress to fund the WPA in January 1935, he had expected quick action on the bill. He quickly discovered that opposition to his programs was growing in Congress. The bill creating the WPA did not pass until April 1935. By late May, Congress was preparing to adjourn for the summer, leaving Roosevelt with very few accomplishments.

Suddenly, the political situation shifted. On May 27, 1935, the Supreme Court unanimously struck down the National Industrial Recovery Act in *Schechter* v. *United States.* The Schechter brothers, who had a poultry business in Brooklyn, New York, had been convicted in 1933 of violating the NIRA's Live Poultry Code. They had sold diseased chickens and violated the code's wage-and-hour provisions. *(See page 1082 for more about Schechter v. United States.)*

In what became known as the "sick chicken case," the Court ruled that the Constitution did not allow Congress to delegate its powers to the executive branch. Thus it considered the NIRA codes unconstitutional. The decision worried Roosevelt. The ruling suggested that the Court could soon strike down the rest of the New Deal as well.

Shortly after the Schechter decision, Roosevelt sprang into action. With the Court threatening to strike down the New Deal and with growing challenges from the left and right, the president knew he needed a new series of programs to keep voters' support. He called congressional leaders to a White House conference. Pounding his desk, he thundered that Congress could not go home until it passed his new bills. That summer, Congress began what the press nicknamed the "second hundred days" and worked feverishly to pass Roosevelt's programs.

Reading Check **Examining** How did the Supreme Court's ruling affect the New Deal?

The Rise of Industrial Unions

When the Supreme Court ruled against the NIRA, it also struck down the section of the law that established labor's right to organize. President Roosevelt and the Democrats in Congress knew that the working-class vote was very important in winning re-election in 1936. They also believed that unions could help end the Depression. They thought that high union wages would let workers spend more money, thereby boosting the economy. Opponents disagreed, arguing that high wages forced companies to charge higher prices and to hire fewer people. Despite these concerns, Congress pushed ahead with new labor legislation.

The National Labor Relations Act In July 1935, Congress passed the National Labor Relations Act, also called the Wagner Act after its author, Democratic senator Robert Wagner of New York. The act guaranteed workers the right to organize unions without interference from employers and to bargain collectively. The law set up the **National Labor Relations Board** (NLRB), which organized factory elections by secret ballot to determine whether workers wanted a union. The NLRB then certified the successful unions.

The new law also set up a process whereby dissatisfied union members could take their complaints to binding arbitration, in which a neutral party would listen to both sides and decide the issues. The NLRB was authorized to investigate the actions of employers and had the power to issue "cease and desist" orders against unfair practices.

The CIO The Wagner Act stimulated a burst of labor activity. In the mid-1930s, the United Mine Workers union, led by John L. Lewis, began working with several other unions to organize workers in industries where unions did not yet exist. To coordinate their efforts, they formed the **Committee for Industrial Organization** (CIO) in 1935.

The CIO set out to organize industrial unions, or unions that included all workers in a particular industry, skilled and unskilled. The CIO began by focusing on the automobile and steel industries—two of the largest industries in America where workers were not yet organized into unions.

Sit-Down Strikes In late December 1936, officials at the General Motors auto-body plant in Cleveland, Ohio, demoted two union men. In an unplanned protest, a shift of 135 workers sat down and launched an unprecedented kind of strike. They stopped working but refused to leave the factory. A few days later, the workers at the company's plant in Flint, Michigan, launched their own sit-down strike,

as the press quickly dubbed it. Workers at other plants followed suit or carried out traditional strikes.

Bruce Bliven, editor of *The New Republic* magazine, was among the few journalists allowed into the plant. Regarding the condition of the strike, he reported:

> 66The place was remarkably neat and tidy, at least as clean as it is under normal conditions. Beds were made up on the floor of each car, the seats being removed if necessary. . . . I could not see—and I looked for it carefully—the slightest damage done anywhere to the General Motors Corporation. The nearly completed car bodies, for example, were as clean as they would be in the salesroom, their glass and metal shining.99

—quoted in *The Great Depression*

Violence broke out in Flint when police launched a tear gas assault on one of the smaller plants. The strikers turned back the attack with whatever was at hand—door hinges, bottles, stones, and balls of ice. The police wounded 13 strikers and two bystanders with gunfire, but the strike held. On February 11, 1937, the company gave in and recognized the CIO's

Trying to Improve Working Conditions

Autoworkers stage a sit-down strike in 1937 in Flint, Michigan.

Union Membership, 1933–1943

Year

Source: *Historical Statistics of the United States: Colonial Times to 1970.*

Graph *Skills*

1. **Interpreting Graphs** Approximately how many people were union members in 1936?
2. **Understanding Cause and Effect** Why did union membership increase steadily after 1936?

United Auto Workers (UAW) as its employees' sole bargaining agent. The UAW quickly became one of the most powerful unions in the United States.

The United States Steel Corporation, the nation's largest steel producer, decided it did not want to repeat the General Motors experience. The company recognized the CIO's United Steelworkers of America, which won a 40-hour workweek and a 10-percent pay raise. Smaller steel producers did not initially recognize unions, and strikes broke out around the country. By 1941, however, the steelworkers' union had contracts with the entire industry.

In the late 1930s, workers in other industries also sat down at their jobs to gain union recognition. In only six years, total union membership tripled from roughly 3 million in 1933 to about 9 million in 1939. In 1938 the CIO changed its name to the Congress of Industrial Organizations and became a federation of industrial unions.

✓ **Reading Check** **Examining** What provisions did the National Labor Relations Act establish?

The Social Security Act

After passing the Wagner Act, Congress began work on a bill that ranks as one of the most important pieces of legislation in American history. This was the Social Security Act, which became law in August 1935. Its major goal was to provide some security for the elderly and for unemployed workers.

With the support of Secretary of Labor Frances Perkins, Roosevelt and his team spent months preparing the bill. The framers viewed it primarily as an insurance bill. Workers earned the right to receive benefits because they paid premiums. The legislation also provided modest welfare payments to other needy people, including those with disabilities and poor families with young dependent children.

The core of Social Security was the monthly retirement benefit, which people could collect when they stopped working at age 65. Another important benefit, unemployment insurance, supplied a temporary income to unemployed workers looking for new jobs. Some critics did not like the fact that the money came from payroll taxes imposed on workers and employers, but to Roosevelt these taxes were crucial: "We put those payroll contributions there so as to give the contributors a legal, moral, and political right to collect their pensions and the unemployment benefits."

Since the people receiving benefits had already paid for them, he explained, "no politician can ever scrap my social security program." What Roosevelt did not anticipate was that in the future, Congress would borrow money from the Social Security fund to pay for other programs while failing to raise payroll deductions enough to pay for the benefits.

Social Security helped many people, but initially it left out many of the neediest members of society—farm and domestic workers. Some 65 percent of all African American workers in the 1930s fell into these two categories. Nevertheless, Social Security established the principle that the federal government should be responsible for those who, through no fault of their own, were unable to work.

✓ **Reading Check** **Explaining** How did the Social Security Act protect workers?

SECTION 3 ASSESSMENT

Checking for Understanding

1. **Define:** deficit spending, binding arbitration, sit-down strike, Social Security Act.
2. **Identify:** American Liberty League, Works Progress Administration, National Labor Relations Board.
3. **Contrast** the ideas of Father Charles Coughlin, Senator Huey Long, and Dr. Francis Townsend.

Reviewing Themes

4. **Government and Democracy** How did the New Deal contribute to the growth of industrial unions?

Critical Thinking

5. **Analyzing** Why is the Social Security Act an important piece of legislation?
6. **Organizing** Use a graphic organizer similar to the one below to list the political challenges Roosevelt faced in his first term.

Political Challenges

Analyzing Visuals

7. **Analyzing Graphs** Examine the photo and graph on page 693. How did successful strikes such as the sit-down strike shown in the photograph lead to a rise in union membership?

Writing About History

8. **Descriptive Writing** Imagine you are either a General Motors worker or a member of management during the sit-down strike in Flint, Michigan. Write a letter to your local newspaper describing the strike and explaining your actions during it.

Guide to Reading

Main Idea
Backed by a new coalition of voters, Roosevelt easily won a second term, but the opposition of conservatives weakened his ability to achieve additional reforms.

Key Terms and Names
Frances Perkins, court-packing, Henry Morgenthau, John Maynard Keynes, broker state, safety net

Reading Strategy
Taking Notes As you read about the New Deal coalition, use the major headings of the section to create an outline similar to the one below.

The New Deal Coalition
I. Roosevelt's Second Term
   A.
   B.
   C.
II.
   A.
   B.

Reading Objectives
- **Explain** the achievements and the defeats of Roosevelt's second term.
- **Analyze** how the New Deal affected Americans' sense of security and their attitude toward the role of government.

Section Theme
Groups and Institutions The Democratic Party's victory in 1936 resulted from a new alignment in politics that lasted for several decades.

Preview of Events

◆1936	◆1937	◆1938

1936
FDR reelected

1937
Court-packing bill defeated; Farm Tenant Act; National Housing Act

1937
Roosevelt Recession begins

1938
Fair Labor Standards Act passed

★ An American Story ★

One day in 1932, Emma Guffey Miller, the sister of Democratic senator Joseph Guffey, was having her nails done at a salon in Pittsburgh. Her manicurist mentioned that Robert Vann, publisher of the *Pittsburgh Courier,* a leading African American newspaper, wanted to see the senator. When Senator Guffey met Vann, Vann told him that the Democrats could win most of the 280,000 African American votes in Pennsylvania if they made the effort.

Since the Civil War, most African Americans had voted for the Republicans. Now times had changed. The Depression had hit the African American community very hard, and Republicans had done little to help. In talks to African American voters, Vann often said, "My friends, go home and turn Lincoln's picture to the wall. That debt has been paid in full."

Guffey was impressed. He persuaded party leaders to appoint Vann to lead "the first really effective Negro division a Democratic campaign committee ever had." By 1936 the majority of African American voters had switched their support to the Democratic Party.

—**adapted from *The Politics of Upheaval***

Roosevelt's Second Term

The dramatic shift in party allegiance by African Americans was part of a historic political realignment triggered by FDR's New Deal. As the election of 1936 approached, millions of voters owed their jobs, mortgages, or salvaged bank accounts to the New Deal, and they knew it.

Mary McLeod Bethune
1875–1955

Mary McLeod Bethune was born into a poor South Carolina family, the 15th of 17 children. Although she worked from a young age picking cotton and washing clothes, Bethune was determined to get an education. She won a scholarship to a seminary in North Carolina and later graduated from the Moody Bible Institute in Chicago. Bethune then began teaching at the Haines Institute. In 1904 she founded a school in Florida for the children of African American railroad workers. "I rang doorbells," she later recalled. "I wrote articles . . . distributed leaflets, [and] invaded churches, clubs, lodges, [and] chambers of commerce." Gradually she raised enough money to found the Daytona Normal and Industrial School, later known as Bethune College.

Bethune's efforts gained her a national reputation. In the 1920s, she visited the White House to discuss African American affairs. She also became a good friend of Eleanor Roosevelt. In 1936 FDR appointed her director of the Negro Division of the National Youth Administration (NYA), which provided job training for young people. Bethune also founded the National Council of Negro Women to support civil rights. In later years, she advised Presidents Truman and Eisenhower.

Frances Perkins
1882–1965

From the moment she became FDR's secretary of labor at the age of 50, Frances Perkins confronted the challenge of being the first female cabinet member in the nation's history.

Perkins studied social work at Columbia University. Early in her career, she assisted Jane Addams at Hull House and worked with Florence Kelley of the Consumers' League. From her lobbying efforts there, Perkins learned how to deal with politicians.

Perkins first met Roosevelt when she worked for the New York Committee on Safety, lobbying state legislators to limit the workweek for women to 54 hours. When Roosevelt became governor in 1928, he appointed Perkins state industrial commissioner.

After Roosevelt won the presidency in 1932, he asked Perkins to head the Department of Labor. Upon taking the job, Perkins found many areas that needed improvement: offices that were run down, disorganized files, and lax work schedules, conditions she quickly remedied.

Given her background, it was fitting that one of Perkins's major tasks was to head the team that designed the Social Security program. She also supervised implementation of the Fair Labor Standards Act and built up the Bureau of Labor Statistics.

The white South, which had been the core of the Democratic Party, now became just one part of a new coalition that included farmers, laborers, African Americans, new immigrants, ethnic minorities, women, progressives, and intellectuals. First Lady Eleanor Roosevelt helped bring about the change in the African American and women's vote. She had demonstrated strong sympathies toward these groups, with whom she spoke in her many tours of the country. She recounted her experiences to her husband and persuaded him to address at least some of their problems in his New Deal programs.

African Americans and women made some modest gains during the New Deal. For example, the president appointed a number of African Americans to positions in his administration; informally, they became known as the Black Cabinet. Roosevelt also tried to see that New Deal relief programs did not exclude African Americans.

A similar approach guided New Deal policies toward women. Roosevelt appointed the first woman to a cabinet post, Secretary of Labor **Frances Perkins,** and assigned many women to lower-level jobs in the federal bureaucracy. Even so, the general view was that women did not need federal government action to ensure equal treatment, but rather to provide certain protections for them.

The Election of 1936 To oppose Roosevelt, the Republicans nominated Kansas Governor Alfred Landon. Although Landon favored some New Deal policies, he declared it was time "to unshackle initiative and free the spirit of American enterprise." As the election neared, Landon became more aggressive. The New Deal "violates the basic ideals of the American system," he declared. "If we are to preserve our American form of government, this administration must be defeated."

Despite Landon's attacks, Roosevelt and the New Deal remained overwhelmingly popular with the American people. The challenge from left-wing radicals also proved much weaker than expected—primarily because Huey Long had been assassinated in Louisiana in September of 1935. Long's supporters joined with those of Father Coughlin and Francis Townsend in the summer of 1936 to form a new political movement called the **Union Party,** but without a strong leader, the party had no chance. On Election Day, Roosevelt swept to victory in one of the largest landslides in American history. He won more than 60 percent of the popular vote and carried every state except Maine and Vermont.

The Court-Packing Plan

Although popular opinion supported most of the president's programs, the Supreme Court saw things differently. In January 1936, the Court declared the Agricultural Adjustment Act to be unconstitutional. With cases pending on Social Security and the Wagner Act, it seemed likely the Court would strike down nearly all of the major New Deal programs.

Roosevelt was furious that a handful of jurists, "nine old men" as he called them, were blocking the wishes of a majority of the people. After winning re-election, he decided to try to change the political balance on the Supreme Court. Claiming that the Court was overburdened with work, Roosevelt sent Congress a bill to increase the number of justices: If any justice had served for 10 years and did not retire within six months after reaching the age of 70, the president could appoint an additional justice to the Court. Since four justices were in their 70s and two more were in their late 60s, the bill, if passed, would allow Roosevelt to quickly appoint as many as six new justices.

The **court-packing** plan, as the press called it, was Roosevelt's first serious political mistake as president. Although Congress had the power to change the size of the Court, the scheme created the impression that the president was trying to interfere with the Constitution's separation of powers and undermine the Court's independence.

The issue split the Democratic Party. Many Southern Democrats feared Roosevelt's plan would put justices on the Court who would overturn segregation. At the same time, African American leaders worried that once Roosevelt set the precedent of changing the Court's makeup, a future president might pack the Court with justices opposed to civil rights. Many Americans believed the plan would give the president too much power.

Despite the uproar over the scheme, Roosevelt's actions appeared to force the Supreme Court to back down. In April 1937, the Court upheld the Wagner Act, and in May it declared the Social Security Act to be constitutional. Shortly afterward, one of the more conservative judges resigned, enabling Roosevelt to appoint a supporter of the New Deal to the Court.

In mid-July, the Senate quietly killed the court-packing bill without bringing it to a vote. Although Roosevelt had achieved his goal of changing the Court's view of the New Deal, the fight over the plan had hurt his reputation with the American people and encouraged conservative Democrats in Congress to work with Republicans to oppose further New Deal proposals.

ECONOMICS

The Roosevelt Recession

In late 1937, Roosevelt's reputation suffered another blow when unemployment suddenly surged. Earlier in the year, the economy had seemed to be on the verge of full recovery. Industrial output was almost back to the level it had reached before the Depression began, and many people believed the worst was over.

Although unemployment remained high, Roosevelt decided it was time to balance the budget. Concerned about the dangers of too much debt, Roosevelt ordered the WPA and the PWA to be cut significantly. Unfortunately, Roosevelt cut spending just as the first Social Security payroll taxes removed $2 billion from the economy. Almost immediately the economy plummeted. By the end of 1937, about two million people had been thrown out of work.

The recession of 1937 led to a debate inside Roosevelt's administration over what to do. Treasury Secretary **Henry Morgenthau** favored balancing the

Picturing **History**

Campaigning in 1936 During the 1936 election, FDR's Democratic Party brought together farmers, like this North Dakotan, and many other groups of Americans to form a new coalition of political supporters. This coalition helped give Roosevelt a strong re-election victory. What different groups made up this coalition?

What *Life* Was Like...

1930s Entertainment

During the Depression, people needed entertainment more than ever. Movies topped the list of ways to escape everyday hardship, but music and dance were popular as well. For really cheap entertainment, one could stay at home and play cards or board games.

● **Movie Escapism**
Movies cost less than 25¢ in many places, so children could afford to go, too. These children display door prizes handed out during a matinee in California.

● **Dance Craze**
Dance marathons got their start in the manic 1920s, but they gained wide popularity in the 1930s. Couples might dance hundreds of hours, until they were exhausted. The last couple standing could win substantial prize money.

budget and cutting spending. This would reassure business leaders and encourage them to invest in the economy. Harry Hopkins, head of the WPA, and **Harold Ickes,** head of the PWA, both disagreed with Morgenthau and pushed for more government spending. They pointed to a new theory called "Keynesianism" to support their arguments.

Keynesianism was based on the theories of an influential British economist named **John Maynard Keynes.** In 1936 Keynes published a book that discussed the causes of recessions. He argued that the government should spend heavily during a recession, even if it had to run a deficit, in order to jumpstart the economy.

According to Keynesian economics, Roosevelt had done exactly the wrong thing when he cut back programs in 1937. At first Roosevelt was reluctant to begin deficit spending again. Many critics of his policies had argued that the recession proved the American people were becoming too dependent on government spending, and Roosevelt worried they might be right. Finally, in the spring of 1938, with no recovery in sight, he asked Congress for $3.75 billion for the PWA, the WPA, and other programs.

✓ **Reading Check** **Summarizing** What events weakened Roosevelt's reputation in 1937?

The Last New Deal Reforms

In his second inaugural speech, Roosevelt had pointed out that despite the nation's progress in climbing out of the Depression, many Americans still endured crippling poverty:

> ❝In this nation I see tens of millions of its citizens—a substantial part of its whole population—who at this very moment are denied the greater part of what the very lowest standards of today call the necessities of life. . . . I see one-third of a nation ill-housed, ill-clad, ill-nourished. . . . The test of our progress is not whether we add more to the abundance of those who have much; it is whether we provide enough for those who have too little.❞
>
> —quoted in *Public Papers and Addresses of Franklin D. Roosevelt*

Despite the president's idealistic goals, the fight over the court-packing scheme and the recession of 1937 had weakened Roosevelt politically. Although he pushed ahead with a new series of New Deal programs, his successes were far more limited than they had been in previous years.

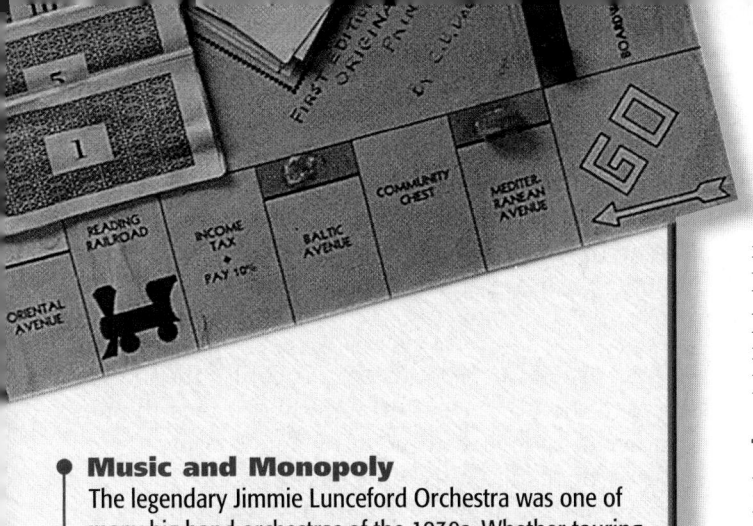

● **Music and Monopoly**

The legendary Jimmie Lunceford Orchestra was one of many big band orchestras of the 1930s. Whether touring the country in one-night gigs or playing on the radio, they drew a huge following. Monopoly was a major 1930s fad. Players of this board game moved pieces around, buying and developing "property" in a race to amass a fortune in fake money.

The National Housing Act

One of the president's goals for his second term was to provide better housing for the nation's poor. The Home Owners Loan Corporation had helped many middle-class citizens, but it had not provided housing for those who could not afford a mortgage. Eleanor Roosevelt, who had toured poverty-stricken regions of Appalachia and the Deep South, was among those urging the president to do something.

Senator Wagner, who shared the First Lady's concerns, prepared a new housing bill with Roosevelt's full support. The 1937 National Housing Act established the United States Housing Authority, which received $500 million to subsidize loans for builders willing to buy blocks of slums and build low-cost housing.

The Farm Security Administration

Before the Supreme Court struck it down, the Agricultural Adjustment Administration had paid many farmers to take land out of production to force food prices to rise. The price-support program raised farm income, but it badly hurt tenant farmers. Landowners often expelled tenants from the land in order to take it out of production. About 150,000 white and 195,000 African American tenants left farming during the 1930s for this reason.

To stop this trend, the Farm Security Administration was created in 1937 to give loans to tenants so they could purchase farms. Over the next four years it extended loans of about $1 billion. Members of Congress, many of whom believed the program made agricultural problems worse by increasing farm production and driving down prices, kept its appropriations at a low level.

The Fair Labor Standards Act In 1938 New Dealers were still trying to reinstate important pro-labor regulations to make up for the Supreme Court's dismantling of the NIRA in 1935. The Fair Labor Standards Act of 1938 provided more protection for workers, abolished child labor, and established a 40-hour workweek for many workers to come into effect within three years.

Congress, however, was beginning to turn against the New Deal. The recession of 1937 enabled the Republicans to win many seats in Congress in the midterm elections of 1938. Together with conservative Southern Democrats, they began blocking further New Deal legislation. Roosevelt, meanwhile, became increasingly preoccupied with the growing international threat posed by Germany and Japan. By 1939 the New Deal era had come to an end.

✓ **Reading Check** **Examining** What groups did Roosevelt's last New Deal programs try to help?

The Legacy of the New Deal

In terms of its main goal of ending the Depression, the New Deal was only a limited success. Unemployment remained high, and economic recovery was not complete until after World War II. Even so, the New Deal gave many Americans a stronger sense of security and stability.

The Broker State As a whole, the New Deal tended to operate so that it balanced competing economic interests. Business leaders, farmers, workers, consumers, homeowners, and others now looked to government to protect their interests.

The federal government's ability to take on this new role was enhanced by two important Supreme Court decisions. In 1937, in *NLRB* v. *Jones and Laughlin Steel,* the Court ruled that the federal government had the constitutional authority, under the interstate commerce clause, to regulate production within a state. In 1942, in *Wickard* v. *Filburn,* the Court used a similar argument to allow the federal government to regulate consumption in the states. These

"Come along. We're going to the Trans-Lux to hiss Roosevelt."

Analyzing *Political Cartoons*

Traitor to His Class By 1936 many wealthy Americans believed that FDR had turned his back on his own upbringing, and they actively worked to prevent his re-election. How did the New Deal change the way many people view government?

decisions increased federal power over the economy and allowed it to mediate between competing groups. 📖 *(See page 1082 and 1083 for more information on these Supreme Court cases.)*

In taking on this mediating role, the New Deal established what some have called the broker state, working out conflicts among different interests. This broker role has continued under the administrations of both parties ever since.

Government's New Role Probably the biggest change the New Deal brought about was the new public attitude toward government. Roosevelt's programs had succeeded in creating something of a safety net for average Americans—safeguards and relief programs that protected them against economic disaster. By the time the Roosevelt years were over, the American people felt that the government had a duty to maintain this safety net even though it required a larger, more expensive federal government than at any time in American history.

Critics continued to argue that the New Deal made the government too powerful. Another legacy of the New Deal, therefore, is a debate that has continued to the present over how much the government should intervene in the economy or support the disadvantaged.

Throughout the hard times of the Depression, most Americans maintained a surprising degree of confidence in the American system. Journalist Dorothy Thompson expressed this feeling in 1940:

66We have behind us eight terrible years of a crisis. . . . Here we are, and our basic institutions are still intact, our people relatively prosperous and most important of all, our society relatively affectionate. . . . No country is so well off.99

✓ **Reading Check** **Summarizing** What was the legacy of Roosevelt's New Deal?

SECTION 4 ASSESSMENT

Checking for Understanding

1. **Define:** broker state, safety net.
2. **Identify:** Frances Perkins, court-packing, Henry Morgenthau, John Maynard Keynes.
3. **Explain** Roosevelt's court-packing plan and how it was received.

Reviewing Themes

4. **Groups and Institutions** What groups made up the New Deal coalition?

Critical Thinking

5. **Interpreting** How did the New Deal change attitudes toward government?
6. **Categorizing** Use a chart like the one below to list the achievements and defeats of Roosevelt's second term.

Achievements	Defeats

Analyzing Visuals

7. **Analyzing Photographs** Study the photograph on page 697. What does it suggest about Roosevelt's method of campaigning?

Writing About History

8. **Persuasive Writing** Write an essay evaluating the effectiveness of New Deal measures in ending the Depression.

Outlining

Why Learn This Skill?

To draw a scene, first you would sketch the rough shape, or outline, of the picture. Then you would fill in this rough shape with details. Outlining written material is a similar process. You begin with the rough shape of the material and gradually fill in the details.

Learning the Skill

When studying written material, outlining helps you identify main ideas and group together related facts. In writing, it helps you put information in a logical order.

There are two kinds of outlines—*formal* and *informal*. An informal outline is similar to taking notes. You write only words and phrases needed to remember ideas. Under the main ideas, jot down related but less important details. This kind of outline is useful for reviewing material before a test.

A formal outline has a standard format. In a formal outline, label main heads with Roman numerals, subheads with capital letters, and details with Arabic numerals. Each level must have at least two entries and should be indented from the previous level. All entries use the same grammatical form. For example, if one entry is a complete sentence, all other entries at that level must also be complete sentences.

When outlining written material, first read the material to identify the main ideas. In textbooks, section heads provide clues to main topics. Next, identify the subheads. List details that support or explain subheads underneath the appropriate subhead.

Practicing the Skill

Study the outline on this page on Roosevelt's New Deal. Then answer the following questions.

❶ Is this an example of a formal or an informal outline?

❷ What are the main headings?

❸ How do the subheads under "Managing Farm and Industry" relate to the main idea?

❹ Give two examples of grammatical inconsistency in this outline:

I. The Hundred Days Begins
  A. Origins of the New Deal
  B. A Divided Administration
    1. Some advisers wanted government and business cooperation.
    2. Others wanted government to run the economy or regulate competition.

II. Fixing the Banks and Stock Market
  A. The Emergency Banking Relief Act
    1. All banks closed temporarily.
    2. The banks reopened and were monitored by federal examiners.
  B. Regulating Banks and Brokers
    1. The Securities Act ensured complete and truthful investment information.
    2. The Glass-Steagall Act separated commercial banking from investment banking.

III. Managing Farms and Industry
  A. The Agricultural Adjustment Administration
    1. Addressed the oversupply of farm products
    2. Increased farm income
  B. A Blueprint for Industrial Recovery
    1. The National Recovery Administration established "fair competition" for industry.
    2. Set minimum wages for employees
    3. The codes were difficult to administer and gains were short-lived.

Skills Assessment

Complete the Practicing Skills questions on page 703 and the Chapter 23 Skill Reinforcement Activity to assess your mastery of this skill.

Applying the Skill

Outlining Write a formal or informal outline for Section 4 of this chapter.

Glencoe's **Skillbuilder Interactive Workbook CD-ROM, Level 2,** provides instruction and practice in key social studies skills.

CHAPTER 23 ASSESSMENT and ACTIVITIES

Reviewing Key Terms

On a sheet of paper, use each of these terms in a sentence.

1. gold standard
2. fireside chats
3. deficit spending
4. binding arbitration
5. sit-down strike
6. Social Security Act
7. broker state
8. safety net

Reviewing Key Facts

9. **Identify:** New Deal, bank holiday, Hundred Days, Securities and Exchange Commission, Federal Deposit Insurance Corporation, Agricultural Adjustment Administration, Works Progress Administration, National Labor Relations Board, Frances Perkins, court-packing, John Maynard Keynes.

10. Why was President Roosevelt reluctant to use deficit spending to help the American economy recover from the Great Depression?

11. Why did the federal government create work programs during the Depression?

12. How did the Supreme Court challenge the New Deal?

13. How did the Wagner Act contribute to the growth of unions?

14. Why did President Roosevelt devise the court-packing plan?

15. What impact did New Deal legislation have on the role of the federal government in state commerce?

Critical Thinking

16. **Analyzing Themes: Economic Factors** What caused the recession in 1937, and how did Keynesian economics explain this recession?

17. **Analyzing** Choose one of the New Deal programs. Describe its goals and evaluate its success.

18. **Forming an Opinion** Which method should be used to settle differences between unions and companies—binding arbitration or sit-down strikes? Explain your answer.

19. **Interpreting Primary Sources** In her autobiography, Eleanor Roosevelt wrote about discussions she had with people across the country. Read the excerpt and answer the questions that follow.

❝This trip to the mining areas was my first contact with the work being done by the Quakers. I liked the idea of trying to put people to work to help themselves. The men were started on projects and taught to use their abilities to develop new skills. The women were encouraged to revive any household arts they might once have known but which they had neglected in the drab life of the mining village.

This was only the first of many trips into the mining districts but it was the one that started the homestead

Chapter Summary

Major New Deal Programs

Financial and Debt
- Emergency Banking Relief Act regulated banks.
- Federal Deposit Insurance Corporation insured bank deposits.
- Farm Credit Administration refinanced farm mortgages.
- Home Owners' Loan Corporation financed homeowners' mortgages.

Work and Relief
- Civilian Conservation Corps created forestry jobs for young men.
- Federal Emergency Relief Administration funded city and state relief programs.
- Public Works Administration created work programs to build public projects, such as roads, bridges, and schools.

Agriculture and Industry
- Agricultural Adjustment Administration paid farmers to limit surplus production.
- National Industrial Recovery Act limited industrial production and set prices.
- National Labor Relations Act gave workers the right to organize unions and bargain collectively.
- Tennessee Valley Authority financed rural electrification and helped develop the economy of a seven-state region.

Social "Safety Net"
- Social Security Act provided:
  – income for elderly, handicapped, and unemployed.
  – monthly retirement benefit for people over 65

idea [placing people in planned communities with homes, farms, and jobs]. . . . It was all experimental work, but it was designed to get people off relief, to put them to work building their own homes and to give them enough land to start growing food.**99**

a. Why did Eleanor Roosevelt like the Quaker project?

b. Based on this excerpt, do you think that Eleanor Roosevelt supported her husband's New Deal programs? Explain your answer.

20. Categorizing Use a graphic organizer like the one below to list groups of people helped by each program.

Practicing Skills

21. Outlining Study the subheads of Section 3, "The Second New Deal," and Section 4, "The New Deal Coalition," to review the sections. Then do the following exercises.

a. Make a formal outline of Section 3. Pay special attention to forming complete sentences.

b. Make an informal outline of Section 4.

Writing Activity

22. Expository Writing Under *Economic Crisis and the New Deal* on the American History Primary Source Document Library CD-ROM, read Roosevelt's First Inaugural Address. Work with another student to write a commentary on the address and then present it as a radio broadcast to the class. Your commentary should include opinions about Roosevelt's economic ideas.

Chapter Activity

23. Technology Activity: Researching the Internet Use the Internet to research two New Deal agencies: the FDIC and

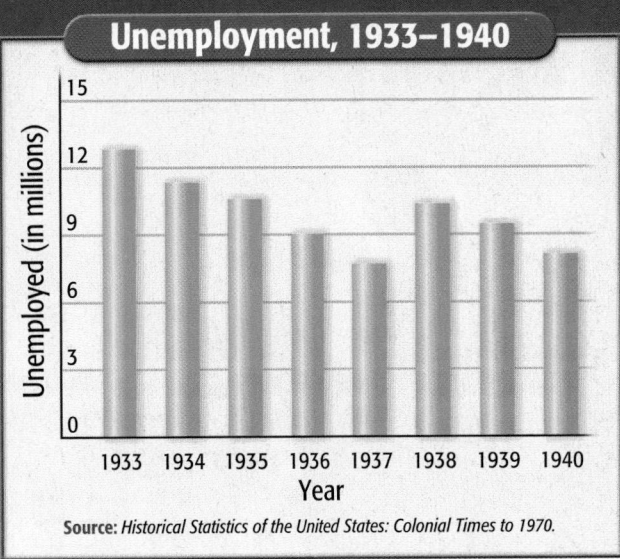

Unemployment, 1933–1940

Source: *Historical Statistics of the United States: Colonial Times to 1970.*

the SEC. Write a short report explaining how they continue to affect the lives of U.S. citizens and the U.S. economy today.

Economics and History

24. Examine the graph above showing unemployment figures, and then answer the questions below.

a. Interpreting Graphs What was the difference in unemployment between 1937 and 1938?

b. Analyzing Why did unemployment decline between 1933 and 1937? Why did it increase in 1938?

Standardized Test Practice

Directions: Choose the best answer to the following question.

Each of the following is true of the bills passed during the first Hundred Days of Roosevelt's presidency EXCEPT:

F They were intended to provide immediate relief to American citizens.

G They were known as the New Deal.

H They were designed as temporary measures to restart the economy.

J They were the subject of divisive and protracted debate in Congress.

Test-Taking Tip: Remember, this question asks for the *exception.* Read through each answer carefully to see if it is true of FDR's first Hundred Days. You are looking for the answer that is false. For example, you probably remember that these bills were intended to combat the effects of the Great Depression. Therefore, answer F is true, so it is not the correct answer.

UNIT
8 Global Struggles

1931–1960

Why It Matters

The rise of dictatorships in the 1930s led to World War II, the most destructive war in the history of the world. After the war, the fragile alliance between the United States and the Soviet Union collapsed into the Cold War—a period of intense political, economic, and military competition. Learning about the events of this crucial period in our nation's history will help you understand the events occurring in the nation and around the world today. The following resources offer more information about this period in American history.

Primary Sources Library

See pages 1054–1055 for primary source readings to accompany Unit 8.

*Use the **American History Primary Source Document Library CD-ROM** to find additional primary sources about global struggles.*

Dog tags

American soldier in World War II

"More than an end to war, we want an end to the beginning of all wars."

—Franklin D. Roosevelt, 1945

CHAPTER
24 A World in Flames
1931–1941

Why It Matters

After World War I, Europe was unstable. Fascists led by Benito Mussolini seized power in Italy, and Adolf Hitler and the Nazis took control of Germany. Meanwhile, Japan expanded its territory in Asia. As the Nazis gained power, they began a campaign of violence against Jews. When Germany attacked Poland, World War II began. The United States clung to neutrality until Japan attacked Pearl Harbor.

The Impact Today

European events of this time serve as lessons for American leaders.
- *The danger of ethnic and religious prejudice is more readily recognized than it was before.*
- *Many American leaders believe that international aggression cannot be ignored.*

 The American Vision *Video* *The Chapter 24 video, "Holocaust Stories," presents firsthand accounts from survivors of the Holocaust.*

1932
- Bonus Army arrives in Washington, D.C.

1931
- Jane Addams awarded Nobel Peace Prize

1933
- Franklin Delano Roosevelt inaugurated

NATIONAL DEFENSE *at Any* EXPENSE
But
KEEP OUR BOYS AT HOME
America First Committee

1935
- First Neutrality Act passed

F. Roosevelt
1933–1945

United States
PRESIDENTS

1930   *1933*   *1936*

World

1931
- Japan invades Manchuria

1933
- Hitler appointed chancellor of Germany

1936
- Hitler reoccupies Rhineland
- Spanish Civil War begins

German chancellor Adolf Hitler reviews a parade of Nazi troops.

1937
• Neutrality Act limits trade with all warring nations

1939
• SS *St. Louis* denied permission to dock in United States

1940
• Roosevelt makes "destroyers-for-bases" deal with Britain

1941
• Roosevelt and Churchill coauthor Atlantic Charter

December 7, 1941
• Japan attacks Pearl Harbor

1939

1942

1938
• Munich Conference appeases Hitler

1939
• World War II begins with Hitler's attack on Poland

1940
• France falls to the Nazis

HISTORY *Online*

Chapter Overview
Visit the *American Vision* Web site at tav.glencoe.com and click on **Chapter Overviews—Chapter 24** to preview chapter information.

America and the World

Main Idea

In the years following World War I, aggressive and expansionist governments took power in both Europe and Asia.

Key Terms and Names

Benito Mussolini, fascism, Vladimir Lenin, Joseph Stalin, Adolf Hitler, Manchuria, Neutrality Act of 1935, internationalism

Reading Strategy

Taking Notes As you read about the events in Europe and Asia after World War I, use the major headings of the section to create an outline similar to the one below.

America and the World
I. The Rise of Dictators
   A.
   B.
   C.
   D.
II.

Reading Objectives

• **Describe** how postwar conditions contributed to the rise of antidemocratic governments in Europe.
• **Explain** why many Americans supported a policy of isolationism in the 1930s.

Section Theme

Global Connections German and Japanese actions in the 1930s led President Roosevelt to work to prevent aggression.

Preview of Events

| ♦1922 | ♦1927 | ♦1932 | ♦1937 |

1922
Fascist Party takes power in Italy; USSR established

1931
Japan takes control of Manchuria

1933
Hitler takes power in Germany

1935
Congress passes first Neutrality Act

1937
Japan attacks China

★ *An American Story* ★

In August 1934, American journalist Dorothy Thompson received an urgent call from the porter at her Berlin hotel. A member of Germany's secret state police wanted to talk to her. Thompson had been reporting on Adolf Hitler's rise to power, and she had written various anti-Nazi articles for the American press. In one she described the beautiful singing she had heard at a Hitler youth camp, where thousands of boys ages 10 to 16 marched and sang. The boys' lovely voices echoing across the hills stirred Thompson, but the words on an enormous banner hanging across one hillside chilled her:

❝It was so prominent that every child could see it many times a day. It was white, and there was a swastika painted on it, and besides that only seven words, seven immense black words: YOU WERE BORN TO DIE FOR GERMANY.❞

When Thompson met with the police, they ordered her to leave Germany immediately. "I, fortunately, am an American," Thompson observed, "so I was merely sent to Paris. Worse things can happen to one."

—quoted in *The Women Who Wrote the War*

The Rise of Dictators

Less than 20 years before the dictatorial German government expelled Dorothy Thompson, the future of democracy in Europe seemed bright. When World War I ended in 1918, President Woodrow Wilson had announced, "Everything for which America fought has been accomplished." Wilson had hoped that the United States could "aid in the establishment of just democracy throughout the world." Instead, the treaty that ended the war, along with the economic depression that followed, contributed to the rise of antidemocratic governments in both Europe and Asia.

Mussolini and Fascism in Italy

One of Europe's first major dictatorships arose in Italy. There, a former schoolmaster and journalist named **Benito Mussolini** returned from World War I convinced that his country needed a strong leader.

In 1919 Mussolini founded Italy's Fascist Party. Fascism was a kind of aggressive nationalism. Fascists believed that the nation was more important than the individual. They argued that individualism made countries weak and that a strong government led by a dictator was needed to impose order on society. Fascists believed a nation became great by expanding its territory and building up its military.

Fascism was also strongly anticommunist. After the Communist revolution in Russia, many Europeans feared that Communists, allied with labor unions, were trying to bring down their governments. Mussolini exploited these fears by portraying fascism as a bulwark against the Communists. Fascism began to stand for the protection of private property and of the middle class. Mussolini also offered the working class full employment and social security. He stressed national prestige, pledging to return Italy to the glories of the Roman Empire.

Backed by the Fascist militia known as the Blackshirts, Mussolini threatened to march on Rome in 1922, claiming he was coming to defend Italy against a Communist revolution. Liberal members of the Italian parliament insisted that the king declare martial law. When he refused, the cabinet resigned. Conservative advisers then persuaded the king to appoint Mussolini as the premier.

Once in office, Mussolini worked quickly to destroy democracy and set up a dictatorship. Weary of strikes and riots, many Italians welcomed Mussolini's leadership. With the support of industrialists, landowners, and the Roman Catholic Church, Mussolini—who took the title of *Il Duce,* or "The Leader"—embarked on an ambitious program of bringing order to Italy.

Stalin Takes Over the USSR

The Communists were a much larger force in Russia than in Italy. After the Russian Revolution began in 1917, the Bolshevik Party, led by **Vladimir Lenin,** established Communist governments throughout the Russian empire. In 1922 they renamed these territories the Union of Soviet Socialist Republics (USSR). They then proceeded to establish control over these territories. To do this, the Communists instituted one-party rule, suppressed individual liberties, and punished opponents. After Lenin died in 1924, a power struggle began. By 1926, **Joseph Stalin** had become the new Soviet dictator. In 1927 Stalin began a massive effort to industrialize his country. Tolerating no opposition, the effort brought about the deaths of 8 to 10 million peasants who resisted the Communist policies.

Hitler and Nazism in Germany

Adolf Hitler was a fervent anticommunist and an admirer of Mussolini. Hitler had fought for Germany in World War I. Germany's surrender and the subsequent Versailles Treaty left him and many other Germans with a smoldering hatred for the victorious Allies and for the German government that had accepted the peace terms.

The political and economic chaos in postwar Germany led to the rise of new political parties. One of these was the National Socialist German Workers' Party, or the **Nazi Party.** The party did not represent the working class, as its name suggested, but was nationalistic and anticommunist. Adolf Hitler was one of the party's first recruits.

In November 1923, the Nazis tried to seize power by marching on city hall in Munich, Germany. Hitler intended to seize power locally

Picturing **History**

Supreme Soviets Joseph Stalin (right) took over control of the Soviet Union after Lenin's death in 1924. He was determined to modernize and industrialize his nation. How many people died while opposing Stalin's leadership?

and then march on Berlin, the German capital, but the plan failed and Hitler was arrested.

While in prison, Hitler wrote his autobiography, titled *Mein Kampf* ("My Struggle"). In the book, Hitler called for the unification of all Germans under one government. He claimed that Germans, particularly blond, blue-eyed Germans, belonged to a "master race" called Aryans. He argued that Germans needed more lebensraum, or living space, and called for Germany to expand east into Poland and Russia. According to Hitler, the Slavic people of Eastern Europe belonged to an inferior race, which Germans should enslave. Hitler's racism was strongest, however, toward Jews. He believed that Jews were responsible for many of the world's problems, especially for Germany's defeat in World War I.

After his release from prison, Hitler changed his tactics. Instead of trying to seize power violently, he focused on getting Nazis elected to the Reichstag, the lower house of the German parliament. When the Great Depression struck Germany, many desperate Germans began to vote for radical parties, including the Nazis and Communists. By 1932 the Nazis were the largest party in the Reichstag.

Many traditional German leaders supported Hitler's nationalism. They believed that if they helped Hitler become leader of Germany legally, they could control him. In 1933 the German president appointed Hitler as chancellor, or prime minister.

After taking office, Hitler called for new elections. He then ordered the police to crack down on the Socialist and Communist Parties. Storm Troopers, as the Nazi paramilitary units were called, began intimidating voters. After the election, the Reichstag, dominated by the Nazis and other right-wing parties, voted to give Hitler dictatorial powers. In 1934 Hitler became president, which gave him control of the army. He then gave himself the new title of führer, or "leader." The following year, he began to rebuild Germany's military, in violation of the Treaty of Versailles.

Militarists Gain Control of Japan In Japan, as in Germany, difficult economic times helped undermine the political system. Japanese industries had to import nearly all of the resources they needed to produce goods. During the 1920s, Japan did not earn enough money from its exports to pay for its imports, which limited economic growth and increased unemployment. When the Depression struck, other countries raised their tariffs. This made the situation even worse.

Many Japanese military officers blamed the country's problems on corrupt politicians. Most officers believed that Japan was destined to dominate East Asia. Many also believed that democracy was "un-Japanese" and bad for the country.

Japanese military leaders and the civilians who supported them argued that the only way for Japan to get needed resources was to seize territory. They targeted the resource-rich province of **Manchuria** in northern China as the perfect place to conquer.

A group of Japanese officers decided to act without the government's permission. In September 1931, the Japanese army invaded Manchuria. After the invasion began, the Japanese government tried to end the war, but when the Japanese prime minister began negotiations, officers assassinated him. From that point forward, the military was effectively in control. Although Japan still had a civilian government, it now supported the nationalist policy of expanding the empire, and it appointed several military officers to serve as prime minister.

Picturing **History**

Meeting of Minds Mussolini and Hitler are shown here meeting in October 1940. What beliefs did they share?

✓ Reading Check

Examining How did postwar conditions contribute to the rise of dictatorships in Europe?

America Turns to Neutrality

The rise of dictatorships and militarism after World War I discouraged many Americans. The sacrifices they had made during the war seemed pointless. Once again, Americans began to support isolationism, or the belief that the United States should avoid international commitments that might drag the nation into another war.

The Nye Committee Isolationist ideas became even stronger in the early 1930s for two reasons. When the Depression began, many European nations found it difficult to repay money they had borrowed during World War I. In June 1934, all of the debtor nations except Finland announced they would no longer repay their war debts.

At about the same time, dozens of books and articles appeared arguing that arms manufacturers had tricked the United States into entering World War I. In 1934 Senator Gerald P. Nye of North Dakota held hearings to investigate the country's involvement in World War I. The **Nye Committee** documented the huge profits that arms factories had made during the war. The report created the impression that these businesses influenced the United States to go to war. The European refusal to repay their loans and the Nye Committee's findings turned even more Americans toward isolationism.

Legislating Neutrality Worried that growing German and Italian aggression might lead to war, Congress passed the **Neutrality Act of 1935.** Based on the belief that arms sales had helped bring the United States into World War I, the act made it illegal for Americans to sell arms to any country at war.

In 1936 a rebellion erupted in Spain after a coalition of Republicans, Socialists, and Communists was elected. General **Francisco Franco** led the rebellion. Franco was backed by the Falangists, or Spanish Fascists, army officers, landowners, and Catholic Church leaders.

The revolt quickly became a civil war and attracted worldwide attention. The Soviet Union provided arms and advisers to the government forces, while Germany and Italy sent tanks, airplanes, and soldiers to help Franco. To keep the United States neutral, Congress passed another neutrality act, banning the sale of arms to either side in a civil war.

Shortly after the **Spanish Civil War** began in 1936, Hitler and Mussolini signed an agreement pledging to cooperate on several international issues. Mussolini referred to this new relationship with Germany as the Rome-Berlin Axis. The following

Picturing History

Anti-Fascist Propaganda Spanish general Francisco Franco led the Fascist rebellion that received support from Hitler and Mussolini. This poster translates to "The claw of the Italian invader intends to make slaves of us." How did the United States respond to these events?

month, Japan aligned itself with Germany and Italy when it signed the **Anti-Comintern Pact** with Germany. The pact required the two countries to exchange information about Communist groups. Together Germany, Italy, and Japan became known as the **Axis Powers,** although they did not formally become allies until September 1940.

With the situation in Europe getting worse, Congress passed the Neutrality Act of 1937. This act continued the ban on selling arms to nations at war, but it also required warring countries to buy nonmilitary supplies from the United States on a "cash-and-carry" basis. If a country at war wanted goods from the United States, it had to send its own ships to pick up the goods, and it had to pay cash. Loans were not allowed. Isolationists knew that attacks on neutral American ships carrying supplies to Europe had helped bring the country into World War I. They were determined to prevent it from happening again.

Roosevelt and Internationalism
When he took office in 1933, President Roosevelt declared that "our international relations, though vastly important, are in point of time and necessity secondary to the establishment of a sound national economy." Roosevelt knew that ending the Depression was his first priority, but he was not an isolationist. He supported internationalism, the idea that trade between nations creates prosperity and helps to prevent war. Internationalists also believed the United States should try to preserve peace in the world.

Roosevelt supported internationalism but knew that the public wanted neutrality. He warned that the neutrality acts "might drag us into war instead of keeping us out," but he did not veto the bills. Isolationism was too strong to resist.

In July 1937, Japanese forces in Manchuria launched a full-scale attack on China. Roosevelt decided to help the Chinese. Since neither China nor Japan had actually declared war, Roosevelt claimed the Neutrality Act of 1937 did not apply, and he authorized the sale of weapons to China. He warned that the nation should not stand by and let an "epidemic of lawlessness" infect the world:

> ❝When an epidemic of physical disease starts to spread, the community . . . joins in a quarantine of the patients in order to protect the health of the community against the spread of the disease. . . . War is a contagion, whether it be declared or undeclared. . . . There is no escape through mere isolation or neutrality. . . .❞
>
> —quoted in *Freedom from Fear*

 Picturing **History**

Imperial Expansion In 1931 Japan occupied the northeast Chinese province of Manchuria. In 1937 the Japanese invaded all of China, prompting FDR to authorize the sale of arms to the Chinese Army. **How did Roosevelt justify his actions in light of the Neutrality Act?**

Despite Roosevelt's words, Americans were still not willing to risk another war to stop aggression overseas. "It is a terrible thing," the president said, "to look over your shoulder when you are trying to lead—and find no one there."

✓ **Reading Check** **Evaluating** Why did many Americans support isolationism?

SECTION 1 ASSESSMENT

Checking for Understanding
1. **Define:** fascism, internationalism.
2. **Identify:** Benito Mussolini, Vladimir Lenin, Joseph Stalin, Adolf Hitler, Manchuria, Neutrality Act of 1935.
3. **Explain** why isolationism was strong in the United States in the early 1930s.

Reviewing Themes
4. **Global Connections** What events caused President Roosevelt to become more of an internationalist?

Critical Thinking
5. **Interpreting** Why did antidemocratic governments rise to power in postwar Europe and Asia?
6. **Categorizing** Use a graphic organizer similar to the one below to compare the antidemocratic governments that arose in Europe and Asia.

Country	Dictator	Ideology

Analyzing Visuals
7. **Analyzing Art** Study the Spanish Civil War era propaganda poster reproduced on page 711. Without being told the phrase, how would you be able to discover the poster's meaning?

Writing About History
8. **Persuasive Writing** Write a newspaper editorial urging fellow citizens to embrace either isolationism or internationalism after World War I. Include reasons your readers should back a specific position.

World War II Begins

Guide to Reading

Main Idea

World War II officially began with the Nazi invasion of Poland and the French and British declaration of war on Germany in September 1939.

Key Terms and Names

Anschluss, appeasement, blitzkrieg, Maginot Line, Winston Churchill, Battle of Britain

Reading Strategy

Sequencing As you read about the events leading up to the beginning of World War II, record them by completing a time line similar to the one below.

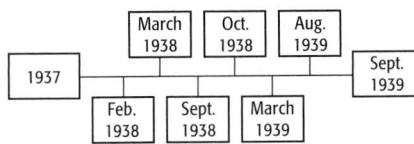

Reading Objectives

- **Explain** why Hitler was able to take over Austria and Czechoslovakia.
- **Describe** the early events of the war and why Britain was able to resist the Nazis.

Section Theme

Continuity and Change The desire of the French and British to avoid another war helped encourage Hitler's aggression in Europe.

Preview of Events

March 1938
Hitler announces German-Austrian unification

August 1939
Hitler and Stalin sign Nazi-Soviet pact

September 1939
World War II begins

June 1940
France surrenders to Germany

August 1940
Battle of Britain begins

★ An American Story ★

In February 1940, President Franklin Roosevelt sent Undersecretary of State Sumner Welles to Europe to report on the political situation. A few months earlier, Germany had invaded Poland, and Roosevelt hoped to negotiate peace before wider hostilities erupted.

In Italy Welles found Mussolini intent on war and judged that "there was not the slightest chance of any successful negotiation." In Paris Welles glumly noted the "sullen apathy" in people's faces and concluded that France had little will to resist a German onslaught. After speaking to Hitler, Welles concluded that a negotiated peace settlement was impossible: "It was only too tragically plain that all decisions had already been made." In London, Welles did not feel the sense of doom he had in Paris. The British, he reported, would "fight to the very last ditch." Welles later reflected on his mission:

66Only one thing could have deflected Hitler from his purpose: the sure knowledge that the power of the United States would be directed against him if he attempted to carry out his intention of conquering the world by force. . . . At that time no representative of this government could have been authorized to intimate any such thing. . . . My mission, therefore, was a forlorn hope.99

—quoted in *Roosevelt and Churchill*

"Peace in Our Time"

Whether or not the United States could have forced Hitler to negotiate is uncertain. By 1940 the German army had been rebuilt, and Hitler was bent on conquest. What is known is that in the years before Welles visited Europe, when the Nazi regime was

Appeasement in Action At Munich in September 1938, Mussolini (second from left), Britain's Neville Chamberlain (left), and Hitler (second from right) were among those deciding Czechoslovakia's fate.

much weaker, European leaders did not try to stop Hitler. Instead, they vainly tried to buy peace by giving in to his demands.

Europe's leaders had several reasons for believing—or wanting to believe—that Hitler could be satisfied and war avoided. First, the shadow of World War I loomed large, making many leaders fearful of another bloody conflict. Second, some thought Hitler's demand that all German-speaking regions of Europe be united with Germany was reasonable. Third, many people assumed that the Nazis would be more interested in peace once they gained more territory.

The Austrian *Anschluss*

Hitler's first demands concerned Austria and Czechoslovakia. In late 1937 Hitler stepped up his call for the unification of all German-speaking people, including those in Austria and Czechoslovakia. Seizing Austria and Czechoslovakia would also gain food supplies, defensible frontiers, and soldiers for Germany. Hitler believed that Germany could only expand its territory by "resort[ing] to force with its attendant risks."

In February 1938 Hitler threatened to invade German-speaking Austria, his native land, unless Austrian Nazis were given important government posts. Austria's chancellor quickly gave in to this demand. Several weeks later, the chancellor tried to put the matter of unification with Germany to a democratic vote. Fearing the outcome, Hitler sent troops into Austria in March and announced the *Anschluss*, or unification, of Austria and Germany.

The Munich Crisis and Appeasement

Shortly after Germany annexed Austria, Hitler announced German claims to the Sudetenland, an area of Czechoslovakia with a large German-speaking population. Since Austrians shared a common culture and language with Germany, many people had accepted the *Anschluss*. In Czechoslovakia, on the other hand, people spoke several different languages. In addition, while Austria had an authoritarian government, Czechoslovakia was a democracy. Furthermore, Austria had no allies to help it defend itself, but Czechoslovakia was allied with France and the Soviet Union.

The Czechs strongly resisted Germany's demands for the Sudetenland. France threatened to fight if Germany attacked, and the Soviet Union also promised assistance. British prime minister **Neville Chamberlain** publicly promised to support France, Britain's ally.

To prevent another war, representatives of Britain, France, Italy, and Germany agreed to meet in Munich to decide Czechoslovakia's fate. At the Munich Conference on September 29, 1938, Britain and France agreed to Hitler's demands, a policy that came to be known as appeasement. Appeasement is the policy of giving concessions in exchange for peace. Supporters of appeasement mistakenly believed that Hitler had a few limited demands. They felt that if they gave Hitler what he wanted, he would be satisfied and war would be avoided. Czechoslovakia was informed that it must give up the Sudetenland or fight Germany on its own.

Chamberlain had gambled that sacrificing part of Czechoslovakia would satisfy Hitler. He also knew that Britain's military was not ready for war, so he was buying time. When Chamberlain returned home he promised "a peace with honor . . . peace in our time," but he also began to speed up British rearmament.

The following March, in brazen violation of the Munich agreement, Germany sent troops into Czechoslovakia and broke up the country. Slovakia became independent in name, but it was actually a satellite state under German control. The Czech lands became a German protectorate.

Danzig and the Polish Corridor

After the Munich conference, Hitler turned his sights on Poland. In October 1938 he demanded the return of Danzig, a Baltic Sea port with strong German roots, to German control. Although Danzig was more than 90 percent German, it had been separated from Germany at the end of World War I to give Poland access to the sea. Hitler also requested a highway and railroad across the Polish Corridor, which separated western Germany from the German state of East Prussia.

Hitler's demands on Poland convinced the British and French that appeasement had failed. On March 31,

1939, the British announced that if Poland went to war to defend its territory, Britain and France would come to its aid. This encouraged the Polish government to refuse Hitler's demands.

In May 1939, Hitler ordered the German army to prepare to invade Poland. He also ordered his foreign minister to begin negotiations with the USSR. If Germany was going to fight Britain and France, Hitler did not want to have to fight the Soviets too.

The Nazi-Soviet Nonaggression Pact When German officials proposed a nonaggression treaty to the Soviets, Stalin agreed. He believed the best way to protect the USSR was to turn the capitalist nations against each other. If the treaty worked, Germany would go to war against Britain and France, and the USSR would be safe.

On August 23, 1939, Germany and the USSR signed the nonaggression pact. The Nazi-Soviet pact shocked the world. Communism and Nazism were supposed to be totally opposed to each other. Leaders in Britain and France understood, however, that Hitler had made the deal to free himself for war against their countries and Poland. What they did not know was that the treaty also contained a secret deal between Germany and the Soviet Union to divide Poland between them.

✓ **Reading Check** **Explaining** What were three reasons European leaders agreed to a policy of appeasement?

The War Begins

On September 1, 1939, Germany invaded Poland from the west, and soon after the Soviets invaded from the east. On September 3, Britain and France declared war on Germany, marking the start of World War II.

Blitzkrieg in Poland Poland bravely resisted Germany's onslaught, but to no avail. The Germans used a new type of warfare called blitzkrieg, or lightning war. Blitzkrieg used large numbers of massed tanks to break through and rapidly encircle enemy

NATIONAL GEOGRAPHIC

Axis Expansion, 1935–1941

2 Germany occupies Rhineland, March 1936

5 Invasion of Poland, Sept. 1, 1939

7 Battle of Britain, Aug. 1940–Oct. 1940

8 Invasion of USSR, June 1941

6 Fall of France, June 1940

4 Annexation of Sudetenland, Sept. 1938

3 Austrian *Anschluss*, 1938

1 Italy invades Ethiopia, Oct. 1935

Legend:
- Axis nations
- Axis satellite states
- Axis conquests
- Allied control
- Neutral countries
- Axis advance
- International boundary, Jan. 1938
- Maginot Line

0   500 miles
0   500 kilometers
Lambert Azimuthal Equal-Area projection

Geography *Skills*

1. **Interpreting Maps** Satellite states were independent in name, but they were under German control. What was the French satellite state called?
2. **Applying Geography Skills** Why was Czechoslovakia physically in danger once the *Anschluss* took place?

positions. Supporting the tanks were waves of aircraft that bombed enemy positions and dropped paratroopers to cut their supply lines. Blitzkrieg depended on radios to coordinate the tanks and aircraft. The Polish army was unable to cope with the German attack. On September 27, the Polish capital of Warsaw fell to the Germans. By October 5, 1939, the Polish army had been defeated.

GEOGRAPHY

The Fall of France In contrast to the war in Poland, western Europe remained eerily quiet. The Germans referred to this situation as the *sitzkrieg,* or sitting war. The British called it the "Bore War," while American newspapers nicknamed it the "Phony War." The British had sent troops to France, but both countries remained on the defensive, waiting for the Germans to attack.

After World War I, the French had built a line of concrete bunkers and fortifications called the **Maginot Line** along the German border. Rather than risk their troops by attacking, the French preferred to wait behind the Maginot Line for the Germans to approach. Unfortunately, this decision allowed Germany to concentrate on Poland first before turning west to face the British and French.

After taking Poland, Hitler and his generals decided to attack Norway and Denmark before invading France. Germany's industry depended on iron ore from Sweden that had to be shipped down Norway's coast part of the year. If the British sent troops to Norway, they could block the iron shipments. On April 9, 1940, the attack began, and within a month, Germany controlled both countries.

With his northern flank secure, Hitler turned his attention to France. Hitler planned to go around the Maginot Line, which protected France's border with Germany but not France's border with Belgium and Luxembourg. To get around the Maginot Line, the Germans would have to invade the Netherlands, Belgium, and Luxembourg first—which is exactly what they did. On May 10, Hitler launched a new blitzkrieg in the west. While German troops parachuted into the Netherlands, an army of tanks rolled into Belgium and Luxembourg.

The British and French had expected the German attack. As soon as it began, British and French forces raced north into Belgium. This was a mistake. Instead of sending their tanks through the open countryside of central Belgium, the Germans sent their main force through the Ardennes Mountains of Luxembourg and eastern Belgium. The French did not think that large numbers of tanks could move through the mountains, and they had left only a few troops to defend that part of the border. The Germans easily smashed through the French lines, then raced west across northern France to the English Channel. The British and French armies were still in Belgium and could not move back into France quickly enough. They were now trapped in Belgium.

The Miracle at Dunkirk After trapping the Allied forces in Belgium, the Germans began to drive them toward the English Channel. The only hope for Britain and France was to evacuate their surviving troops by sea, but the Germans had captured all but one port, **Dunkirk,** a small town in northern France near the Belgian border.

As German forces closed in on Dunkirk, Hitler suddenly ordered them to stop. No one is sure why he gave this order. Historians know that Hitler was nervous about risking his tank forces, and he wanted to wait until more infantry arrived. Hermann Goering, the head of the German air force, was also assuring Hitler that aircraft alone could destroy the trapped soldiers. There is also some evidence that Hitler thought that the British would be more willing to accept peace if the Germans did not humiliate them by destroying their forces at Dunkirk.

Whatever Hitler's reasons, his order provided a three-day delay. This gave the British time to strengthen their lines and begin the evacuation. Some 850 ships of all sizes, from navy warships to small sailboats operated by civilian volunteers, headed to

---

Fact | Fiction | Folklore

The Battle of Dunkirk Hitler's invasion of Poland fueled the fears of Americans who preferred not to become involved in Europe's conflict. In contrast, the evacuation from Dunkirk less than a year later generated very different reactions. For example, soon after the evacuation, the *New York Times* wrote:

> ❝So long as the English tongue survives, the word Dunkirk will be spoken with reverence. For in that harbor, in such a hell as never blazed on earth before, at the end of a lost battle, the rages and blemishes that have hidden the soul of democracy fell away. There, beaten but unconquered, in shining splendor, she faced the enemy.❞

Indeed, the Battle of Dunkirk would soon help to lift the United States out of its isolationism.

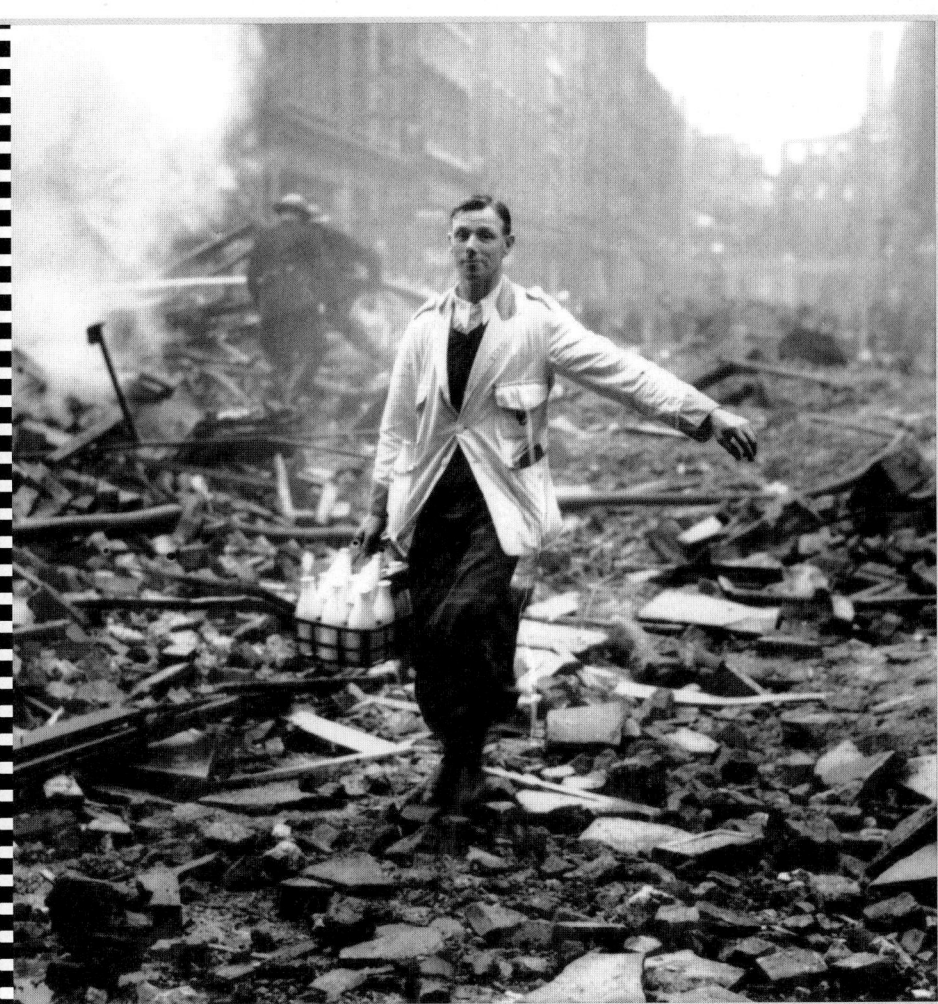

MOMENT in HISTORY

NEVER GIVE IN

Few photographs capture the British resolve to keep a stiff upper lip better than this one. Night after night between September 1940 and May 1941, German warplanes rained bombs on London, Coventry, and other British cities. The attacks were intended to destroy British morale and war production, but Royal Air Force pilots shot down bombers faster than Germany could replace them. Plucky British civilians, like this milkman making his rounds through a debris-strewn London street, remained determined to carry on as usual each morning.

Dunkirk from England. The British had hoped to rescue about 45,000 troops. Instead, when the evacuation ended on June 4, an estimated 338,000 British and French troops had been saved. This stunning success led British newspapers to refer to the evacuation as the "Miracle at Dunkirk."

The evacuation had its price, however. Almost all of the British army's equipment remained at Dunkirk—90,000 rifles, 7,000 tons of ammunition, and 120,000 vehicles. If Hitler invaded Britain, it would be almost impossible to stop him from conquering the country.

Three weeks later, on June 22, 1940, Hitler accepted the French surrender in the same railway car in which the Germans had surrendered at the end of World War I. Germany now occupied much of northern France and its Atlantic coastline. To govern the rest of the country, Germany installed a puppet government at the town of Vichy and made Marshal Philippe Pétain the new government's figurehead leader. Pétain predicted that Britain "will have her neck wrung like a chicken."

✓ **Reading Check** **Summarizing** Why was Germany able to overtake Poland?

Britain Remains Defiant

Neither Pétain nor Adolf Hitler anticipated the bravery of the British people or the spirit of their leader, **Winston Churchill,** who had replaced Neville Chamberlain as prime minister. Hitler fully expected the British to negotiate peace after France surrendered. For Winston Churchill, however, peace was not an option. The war was a fight to defend civilization. On June 4, 1940, Churchill delivered a defiant speech in Parliament, intended not only to rally the British people but to alert the isolationist United States to Britain's plight:

> ❝Even though large tracts of Europe have fallen . . . we shall not flag or fail. . . . We shall defend our island, whatever the cost may be, we shall fight on the beaches, we shall fight on the landing grounds, we shall fight in the fields and in the streets, we shall fight in the hills; we shall never surrender.❞
>
> —quoted in *Freedom from Fear*

When Hitler realized that Britain would not surrender, he ordered his commanders to prepare to invade. Only the choppy waters of the narrow

Picturing **History**

Never Surrender Hitler ordered Nazi aircraft to bomb British cities, intending to weaken the people's will. Though shaken, the British, like the dome of St. Paul's Cathedral (right), stood firm. What technology allowed the outnumbered Royal Air Force to resist the German *Luftwaffe?*

English Channel separated Britain from Germany's powerful army, but getting across the Channel posed a major challenge. Germany had few transport ships, and the British air force would sink them if they tried to land troops in England. To invade, therefore, Germany first had to defeat the British air force.

In June 1940, the German air force, called the *Luftwaffe,* began to attack British shipping in the English Channel. Then, in mid-August, the *Luftwaffe* launched an all-out air battle to destroy the British Royal Air Force. This air battle, which lasted into the fall of 1940, became known as the **Battle of Britain.**

On August 23, German bombers accidentally bombed London, the British capital. This attack on civilians enraged the British, who responded by bombing Berlin the following night. For the first time in the war, bombs fell on the German capital. Infuriated, Hitler ordered the *Luftwaffe* to stop its attacks on British military targets and to concentrate on bombing London.

Hitler's goal now was to terrorize the British people into surrendering. The British people endured, however, hiding out in the city's subway tunnels whenever German bombers appeared.

Although the Royal Air Force was greatly outnumbered, the British had one major advantage. They had developed a new technology called radar. Using radar stations placed along their coast, the British were able to detect incoming German aircraft and direct British fighters to intercept them.

Day after day, the British fighters inflicted more losses on the Germans than they suffered. The skill of a few hundred pilots saved Britain from invasion. Praising the pilots, Churchill told Parliament, "Never in the field of human conflict was so much owed by so many to so few." On October 12, 1940, Hitler cancelled the invasion of Britain.

Reading Check **Evaluating** Why was Britain able to resist Hitler and the Nazis?

SECTION 2 ASSESSMENT

Checking for Understanding

1. **Define:** appeasement, blitzkrieg.
2. **Identify:** *Anschluss,* Maginot Line, Winston Churchill, Battle of Britain.
3. **Explain** why Hitler was able to take over Austria and Czechoslovakia.

Reviewing Themes

4. **Continuity and Change** How did the policy of appeasement affect France and Great Britain?

Critical Thinking

5. **Evaluating** Why were the British able to prevent the Germans from invading their country?
6. **Organizing** Use a graphic organizer similar to the one below to list the early events of the war in Poland and western Europe.

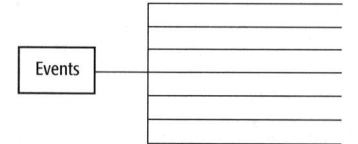

Analyzing Visuals

7. **Analyzing Photographs** Study the photographs on pages 717 and 718. How do they reflect the British resolve to "never surrender"?

Writing About History

8. **Expository Writing** Using library or Internet resources, find more information on the German annexation of Czechoslovakia. Then write a report detailing the events leading up to and including the annexation. Share your report with the class.

★ An American Story ★

Mira Ryczke was born in 1923 to a middle-class Jewish family in Danzig, Poland, a port on the Baltic Sea. After World War II broke out in September 1939, the Nazis expelled Danzig's Jews to Warsaw, where they were forced to live in deplorable conditions in a special area known as the Warsaw ghetto. In 1943 the Nazis emptied the Warsaw ghetto. The Ryczkes had to ride for three days in a suffocating cattle car headed for Auschwitz, the infamous Nazi death camp, and its neighboring camp of Birkenau.

After arriving at the camps, the terrified newcomers learned that a selection was to take place. When 20-year-old Mira asked what the selection was for, an old-time prisoner pointed to chimneys on top of a building and replied, "Selected for the gas chambers to go up in smoke." Mira later wrote:

❝[W]e were told by the old-timers to try to look strong, healthy, and to walk in an upright position when our turn came. . . . Because the women I was with were young, only a few were taken out. Their numbers, tattooed on their left arms, were written down by the SS, and after a few days during roll call, their tattoo numbers were called out and these women were marched to the gas chamber.❞

—quoted in *Echoes from the Holocaust*

Nazi Persecution of the Jews

Mira Ryczke and her family were only a few of the millions of Jews who suffered terrible persecution before and during World War II. During the Holocaust, the catastrophe that ravaged Europe's Jews, the Nazis killed nearly 6 million Jews. The Nazis also killed

Albert Einstein
1879–1955

Among the Jews who left Nazi Germany in the early 1930s was Albert Einstein, whose brilliant scientific theories revolutionized physics. Einstein gained international fame in 1919 when the Royal Society of London announced that calculations had supported his general theory of relativity. Einstein's fame increased after he won the Nobel Prize for Physics in 1921. Lecture invitations poured in from around the world.

Einstein never actively practiced Judaism, but he did proudly identify himself as a Jew. As anti-Semitism took hold in Germany, Einstein's worldwide fame contrasted with the insults he faced in Berlin for practicing "Bolshevism [Communism] in physics." His public support for Zionism, the right of Jews to settle in Palestine (later Israel), aroused further anger among Nazis.

Soon after Hitler became Germany's chancellor in 1933, Einstein renounced his citizenship and left Germany for Belgium. Fears for his life prompted friends to take him secretly by private yacht to England. He later settled in Princeton, New Jersey.

A pacifist who had opposed World War I, Einstein ironically saw his scientific ideas applied to the creation of a powerful and destructive weapon, the atomic bomb. After the United States detonated the first atomic bomb in combat over Hiroshima, Japan, in 1945, Einstein devoted his final years to promoting pacifism. The scientist's greatest legacy, however, would be the revolutionary scientific discoveries he had made in the early 1900s. As Einstein himself had observed, "Politics are for the moment. An equation is for eternity."

---

people were evil no matter what their religion, occupation, or education.

The Nuremberg Laws After the Nazis took power, they quickly moved to deprive German Jews of many rights that all citizens had long taken for granted. In September 1935 the **Nuremberg Laws** took citizenship away from Jewish Germans and banned marriage between Jews and other Germans. Two months later, another decree defined a Jew as a person with at least one Jewish grandparent and prohibited Jews from holding public office or voting. Other laws forbade Jews from employing female German servants under age 35 and compelled Jews with German-sounding names to adopt "Jewish" names. Soon the passports of Jews were marked with a red "J" to clearly identify them as Jewish.

By the summer of 1936, at least half of Germany's Jews were jobless, having lost the right to work as civil servants, journalists, farmers, teachers, and actors. In 1938 the Nazis also banned Jews from practicing law and medicine and from operating businesses. With no source of income, life became very difficult.

Despite worsening conditions, many Jews chose to remain in Germany during the early years of Nazi rule. Well integrated into German society before this time, they were reluctant to leave and give up the lives they had built there. Many also thought that conditions would surely improve after a time. In fact, they soon became worse.

Kristallnacht On November 7, 1938, a young Jewish refugee named Herschel Grynszpan shot and killed a German diplomat in Paris. Grynszpan's father and 10,000 other Jews had been deported from Germany to Poland, and the distraught young man was seeking revenge for this act and for the persecution of the Jews in general.

In retaliation for the killing, an infuriated Hitler ordered his minister of propaganda, Joseph Goebbels, to stage attacks against the Jews that would appear to be a spontaneous popular reaction to news of the murder. On the night of November 9, this plan played out in a spree of destruction.

---

millions of people from other groups they considered inferior. The Hebrew term for the Holocaust is **Shoah,** meaning "catastrophe," but it is often used specifically to refer to the Nazi campaign to exterminate the Jews during World War II.

Nazi Ideology Once the Nazis took power in Germany, they acted swiftly to implement the political racial policies Hitler had outlined in *Mein Kampf.* Although the Nazis persecuted anyone who dared oppose them, as well as the disabled, Gypsies, homosexuals, and Slavic peoples, they reserved their strongest hatred for the Jews. This loathing went far beyond the European anti-Semitism common at the time. Over the centuries, people who were prejudiced against Jews had put down Jewish religious practices and discriminated against Jews in many ways. For example, Jews were sometimes segregated in ghettos or prohibited from owning land. For the Nazis, however, all Jewish

In Vienna a Jewish child named Frederick Morton watched in terror that night as 10 young Nazi Storm Troopers broke into his family's apartment:

> 66 They yanked out every drawer in every one of our chests and cupboards, and tossed each in the air. They let the cutlery jangle across the floor, the clothes scatter, and stepped over the mess to fling the next drawer. . . . 'We might be back,' the leader said. On the way out he threw our mother-of-pearl ashtray over his shoulder, like confetti. We did not speak or move or breathe until we heard their boots against the pavement. 99

—quoted in *Facing History and Ourselves*

The anti-Jewish violence that erupted throughout Germany and Austria that night came to be called *Kristallnacht,* or "night of broken glass," because broken glass littered the streets afterward. When daylight came, more than 90 Jews lay dead, hundreds were badly injured, and thousands more were terrorized. The Nazis had forbidden police to interfere while roving bands of thugs destroyed 7,500 Jewish businesses and wrecked over 180 synagogues.

The lawlessness of *Kristallnacht* did not end with the dawn. Following that night of violence, the **Gestapo,** the government's secret police, arrested at least 20,000 wealthy Jews, releasing them only if they agreed to emigrate and surrender all their possessions. The state also confiscated insurance payments owed to Jewish owners of ruined businesses.

The week after *Kristallnacht,* Nazi interior minister Hermann Goering added insult to injury by fining the Jewish community to pay for the damage. "German Jewry," he proclaimed "shall, as punishment for their abominable crimes . . . have to make a contribution for one billion marks. . . . I would like to say that I would not like to be a Jew in Germany."

Jewish Refugees Try to Flee *Kristallnacht* and its aftermath marked a significant escalation in the Nazi policy of persecution against the Jews. Many Jews, including Frederick Morton's family, decided that it was time to leave and fled to the United States. Between 1933, when Hitler took power, and the start of World War II in 1939, some 350,000 Jews escaped Nazi-controlled Germany. These emigrants included prominent scientists such as Albert Einstein and businesspeople like Otto Frank, who resettled his family in Amsterdam in 1933. Otto's daughter **Anne Frank** would later keep a diary of her family's life in hiding after the Nazis overran the Netherlands.

By 1938 the American consulate in Stuttgart, Germany, had a backlog of over 100,000 visa applications from Jews trying to leave Germany and come to the United States. Following the Nazi *Anschluss,* 3,000 Austrian Jews each day applied for American visas. Many never received visas to the United States

The Final Solution

Before the war, a Jewish family in Germany poses for a photograph during a family outing. Few members of this family would survive the war.

On *Kristallnacht,* roaming bands of thugs destroyed Jewish property and menaced Jewish families throughout Germany.

or to the other countries where they applied. As a result, millions of Jews remained trapped in Nazi-dominated Europe.

Several factors limited Jewish immigration to the United States. First, Nazi orders prohibited Jews from taking more than about four dollars out of Germany. Second, many countries refused to accept Jewish immigrants. In the United States, laws restricted granting a visa to anyone "likely to become a public charge." American customs officials tended to assume that this applied to Jews since Germany had forced them to leave any wealth behind. High unemployment rates in the 1930s also made immigration politically unpopular. Few Americans wanted to raise immigration quotas, even to accommodate European refugees. The existing immigration policy allowed only a total of 150,000 immigrants annually, with a fixed quota from each country. The law permitted no exceptions for refugees or victims of persecution.

At an international conference on refugees in 1938, several European countries, the United States, and Latin America stated their regret that they could not take in more of Germany's Jews without raising their immigration quotas. Meanwhile, Nazi propaganda chief Joseph Goebbels announced that "if there is any country that believes it has not enough Jews, I shall gladly turn over to it all our Jews." Hitler also declared himself "ready to put all these criminals at the disposal of these countries . . . even on luxury ships."

As war loomed in 1939, many ships departed from Germany crammed with Jews desperate to escape. Some of their visas, however, had been forged or sold illegally, and Mexico, Paraguay, Argentina, and Costa Rica all denied access to Jews with such documents. So too did the United States.

On May 27, 1939, the **SS *St. Louis*** entered the harbor in Havana, Cuba, with 930 Jewish refugees on board. Most of these passengers hoped to go to the United States eventually, but they had certificates improperly issued by Cuba's director of immigration giving them permission to land in Cuba. When the ships arrived in Havana, the Cuban government, partly in response to anti-Semitic sentiment stirred up by Nazi propaganda, revoked the certificates and refused to let the refugees come ashore. For several days, the ship's captain steered his ship in circles off the coast of Florida, awaiting official permission to dock at a United States port. Denied such permission, the ship turned back toward Europe on June 6. The forlorn passengers finally disembarked in France, Holland, Belgium, and Great Britain. Within two years, the first three of these countries fell under Nazi domination. Many of the refugees brought to these countries aboard the SS *St. Louis* perished in the Nazis' "final solution."

✓ **Reading Check** **Analyzing** Why did many Jews remain in Germany even though they were persecuted?

The Final Solution

After the war broke out, the Nazis methodically deprived Jews of their rights, confining many to overcrowded ghettos. After weeks of fierce resistance, Jews in the Warsaw ghetto were rounded up for deportation to concentration camps in May 1943.

The Final Solution

On January 20, 1942, 15 Nazi leaders met at the **Wannsee Conference,** held in a Berlin suburb, to determine the "final solution of the Jewish question." Previous "solutions" had included rounding up Jews, Gypsies, and Slavs from conquered areas, shooting them, and piling them into mass graves. Another method required forcing Jews and other "undesirables" into trucks and then piping in exhaust fumes to kill them. These methods, however, had proven too slow and inefficient for the Nazis.

At Wannsee, the Nazis made plans to round up Jews from the vast areas of Nazi-controlled Europe and take them to detention centers known as concentration camps. There, healthy individuals would work as slave laborers until they dropped dead of exhaustion, disease, or malnutrition. Most others, including the elderly, the infirm, and young children, would be sent to extermination camps, attached to many of the concentration camps, to be executed in massive gas chambers.

Concentration Camps

The Nazis had established their first concentration camps in 1933 to jail political opponents. After the war began, the Nazis built concentration camps throughout Europe.

Buchenwald, one of the first and largest concentration camps, was built near the town of Weimar in Germany in 1937. During its operation, over 200,000 prisoners worked 12-hour shifts as slave laborers in nearby factories. Though Buchenwald had no gas chambers, hundreds of prisoners died there every month as a result of exhaustion and the horrible living conditions.

Leon Bass, a young American soldier, described viewing a barracks in Buchenwald at the end of the war. Built to hold 50 people, the room had housed more than 150, with bunks built almost to the ceiling. Bass recalled:

> ❝I looked at a bottom bunk and there I saw one man. He was too weak to get up; he could just barely turn his head. He was skin and bones. He looked like a skeleton; and his eyes were deep set. He didn't utter a sound; he just looked at me with those eyes, and they still haunt me today.❞
>
> —quoted in *Facing History and Ourselves*

Extermination Camps

After the Wannsee Conference, the Nazis built extermination facilities in a number of the concentration camps, mostly in Poland, to kill Jews more efficiently. At these camps, including the infamous Treblinka and Auschwitz, Jews were the Nazis' main victims. **Auschwitz** alone housed about 100,000 people in 300 prison barracks. Its gas chambers, built to kill 2,000 people at a time, sometimes gassed 12,000 people in a day. Of the

By 1943 the Nazis had started implementing their plans to exterminate the Jews. The system of ghettos was abandoned in favor of herding men, women, and children onto cattle cars for transport to death camps.

When the war ended, Allied troops managed to liberate the few surviving inmates of the death camps—many of whom were too shocked to believe they were being freed.

NATIONAL GEOGRAPHIC Jewish Losses, 1939–1945

DENMARK 500

North Sea

NETHERLANDS 105,000

BELGIUM 40,000

Baltic Sea

BALTIC STATES 228,000

RUSSIAN S.S.R. 107,000

BYELORUSSIAN S.S.R. 245,000

GERMANY AND AUSTRIA 210,000

POLAND 3,000,000

CZECHOSLOVAKIA 155,000

FRANCE 90,000

UKRAINIAN S.S.R. 900,000

HUNGARY 450,000

ITALY 8,000

ROMANIA 300,000

YUGOSLAVIA 26,000

Adriatic Sea

Black Sea

BULGARIA 14,000

GREECE 54,000

0   200 miles
0   200 kilometers
Lambert Azimuthal Equal-Area projection

Percentage of Jewish Population Annihilated

83–90	50–60
65–77	11–26

FRANCE 90,000 Number of Jews killed under Nazi racial policies

Geography *Skills*

1. **Interpreting Maps** What country had the highest number of Jews in its population killed?
2. **Applying Geography Skills** A relatively low percentage of Italy's Jewish population died in the Holocaust. From this information, how would you compare Fascists and Nazis in terms of their Jewish policies?

estimated 1,600,000 people who died at Auschwitz, about 1,300,000 were Jews. The other 300,000 were Poles, Soviet prisoners-of-war, and Gypsies.

Upon arrival at Auschwitz, healthy prisoners such as Mira Ryczke were selected for slave labor. Elderly or disabled people, the sick, and mothers and children went immediately to the gas chambers, after which their bodies were burned in giant crematoriums. In her memoirs, Ryczke described "columns of people marching slowly toward the gas chambers" and "the horrible stench in the air—the smell of burning human flesh. I have never forgotten that smell."

In only a few years, Jewish culture, which had existed in Europe for over 1,000 years, had been virtually obliterated by the Nazis in the lands they conquered. Despite exhaustive debate, there is still great controversy about why and how an event so horrifying as the Holocaust could have occurred. No consensus has been reached, but most historians point to a number of factors: the German people's sense of injury after World War I; severe economic problems; Hitler's control over the German nation; the lack of a strong tradition of representative government in Germany; German fear of Hitler's secret police; and a long history of anti-Jewish prejudice and discrimination in Europe.

Reading Check **Summarizing** What methods did Hitler use to try to exterminate Europe's Jewish population?

SECTION 3 ASSESSMENT

Checking for Understanding

1. **Define:** Holocaust, concentration camp, extermination camp.
2. **Identify:** Shoah, Nuremberg Laws, Wannsee Conference.
3. **List** the groups of people who were persecuted by the Nazis.

Reviewing Themes

4. **Civic Rights and Responsibilities** Do you think the German people or other nations could have prevented the Holocaust? Why or why not?

Critical Thinking

5. **Analyzing** What are some factors that attempt to explain the Holocaust?
6. **Organizing** Use a graphic organizer similar to the one below to list the methods used to try to exterminate Europe's Jewish population.

Extermination Methods

Analyzing Visuals

7. **Analyzing Photographs** Study the photographs of the Final Solution on pages 721–723. How do the photographs show the systematic destruction of Jewish life?

Writing About History

8. **Descriptive Writing** Take on the role of a person living in Germany during *Kristallnacht.* Write a diary entry describing that night. Include a description of the events during the days following *Kristallnacht.*

America Enters the War

Main Idea
After World War II began, the United States attempted to continue its prewar policy of neutrality.

Key Terms and Names
America First Committee, Lend-Lease Act, hemispheric defense zone, Atlantic Charter, strategic materials

Reading Strategy
Organizing As you read about the efforts of the United States to stay neutral in the war, complete a graphic organizer similar to the one below by naming two events that shifted American opinion toward helping the Allies.

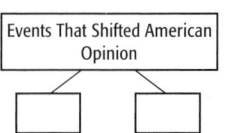

Events That Shifted American Opinion

Reading Objectives
- **Explain** how Roosevelt helped Britain while maintaining official neutrality.
- **Trace** the events that led to increasing tensions, and ultimately war, between the United States and Japan.

Section Theme
Individual Action Even while the United States was officially neutral, President Roosevelt found ways to help the British fight Germany.

Preview of Events

◆September 1940   ◆March 1941   ◆August 1941   ◆December 1941

September 1940
FDR makes destroyers-for-bases deal with Britain

March 1941
Congress passes Lend-Lease Act

August 1941
Roosevelt and Churchill sign Atlantic Charter

October 1941
Germans sink *Reuben James*

December 7, 1941
Japan attacks Pearl Harbor

★ *An American Story* ★

December 7, 1941, dawned like any other Sunday in Hawaii, where teenager Daniel Inouye lived with his family. Like other Americans who lived through the experience, Inouye would never forget what he was doing the moment American isolationism ended:

❝As soon as I finished brushing my teeth and pulled on my trousers, I automatically clicked on the little radio that stood on the shelf above my bed. I remember that I was buttoning my shirt and looking out the window . . . when the hum of the warming set gave way to a frenzied voice. 'This is no test,' the voice cried out. 'Pearl Harbor is being bombed by the Japanese!'❞

The Inouye family ran outside and gazed toward the naval base at Pearl Harbor:

❝And then we saw the planes. They came zooming up out of that sea of gray smoke, flying north toward where we stood and climbing into the bluest part of the sky, and they came in twos and threes, in neat formations, and if it hadn't been for that red ball on their wings, the rising sun of the Japanese Empire, you could easily believe that they were Americans, flying over in precise military salute.❞

—quoted in *Eyewitness to America*

FDR Supports England

The Japanese attack surprised many Americans. Most people had believed that Germany posed the greatest danger. What Americans did not realize was that the causes of the Japanese attack could be traced back more than two years to President Roosevelt's policies for helping Britain against Germany.

Analyzing *Political Cartoons*

Peace Above All Many Americans were willing to help European democracies but did not want to sell them arms. In what ways did the United States assist these nations?

The Neutrality Act of 1939 President Roosevelt officially proclaimed the United States neutral two days after Britain and France declared war on Germany. Despite this declaration, he was determined to do all he could to help the two countries in their struggle against Hitler. Soon after the war began, Roosevelt called Congress into a special session to revise the neutrality laws. He asked Congress to eliminate the ban on arms sales to nations at war. Public opinion strongly supported the president. Congress passed the new law, but isolationists demanded a price for the revision. Under the Neutrality Act of 1939, warring nations could buy weapons from the United States only if they paid cash and carried the arms on their own ships.

Destroyers-for-Bases Deal In the spring of 1940, the United States faced its first test in remaining neutral. In May British Prime Minister Winston Churchill began asking Roosevelt to transfer old American destroyers to Britain. Britain had lost nearly half its destroyers and needed more to protect its cargo ships from German submarines and to block any German attempt to invade Britain.

Determined to give Churchill the destroyers, Roosevelt used a loophole in the provision of the Neutrality Act that required cash for purchases. In exchange for the right to build American bases on British-controlled Newfoundland, Bermuda, and islands in the Caribbean, Roosevelt sent 50 old American destroyers to Britain. Since the deal did not involve an actual sale, the Neutrality Act did not apply. On September 3, 1940, he announced his action to an astonished press.

✓ **Reading Check** **Examining** How were the Neutrality Acts revised?

The Isolationist Debate

Widespread public acceptance of the destroyers-for-bases deal demonstrated a marked change in American public opinion. The shift began after the German invasion of France and the rescue of Allied forces at Dunkirk. By July 1940 most Americans favored offering limited aid to the Allies.

The Range of Opinion American opinion was hardly unanimous. In fact, beginning in the spring of 1940, a spirited debate took place between people who wanted greater American involvement in World War II and those who felt that the United States should remain neutral.

At one extreme was the Fight for Freedom Committee, a group which urged the repeal of all neutrality laws and wanted stronger action against Germany. Closer to the center, the Committee to Defend America by Aiding the Allies, headed by journalist William Allen White, pressed for increased American aid to the Allies but opposed armed intervention.

Roosevelt's destroyers-for-bases deal led to the founding of the **America First Committee,** a staunchly isolationist group that firmly opposed any American intervention or aid to the Allies. The group had many famous members, including aviator Charles Lindbergh, former governor Philip LaFollette, and Senator Gerald Nye.

The Election of 1940 The heated debate over neutrality took place in the midst of the 1940 presidential election campaign. For months Americans had wondered whether President Roosevelt would follow long-standing tradition by retiring at the end of his second term. With the United States in a precarious position, a change of leaders might not be in the country's best interest. Roosevelt decided to run for an unprecedented third term.

During the campaign, FDR steered a careful course between neutrality and intervention. The Republican nominee, Wendell Willkie, did the same, promising that he too would stay out of the war but assist the Allies. The voters re-elected Roosevelt by a wide margin, preferring to stick with a president they knew during this crisis period.

 Reading Check **Analyzing** Why did Roosevelt win an unprecedented third term in office?

Edging Toward War

With the election safely over, Roosevelt expanded the nation's role in the war. Britain was fighting for democracy, he said, and the United States had to help. Speaking to Congress, he listed the "Four Freedoms" for which both the United States and Great Britain stood: freedom of speech, freedom of worship, freedom from want, and freedom from fear. 📖 *(See page 1075 for an excerpt from this speech.)*

The Lend-Lease Act By December 1940, Great Britain had run out of funds to wage its war against Germany. President Roosevelt came up with a way to remove the cash requirement of the Neutrality Act. With the **Lend-Lease Act,** the United States would be able to lend or lease arms to any country considered "vital to the defense of the United States." This act meant that the United States could send weapons to Britain if Britain promised to return or pay rent for them after the war.

The president warned that if Britain fell, an "unholy alliance" of Germany, Japan, and Italy would keep trying to conquer the world, and then "all of us in all the Americas would be living at the point of a gun." The president argued that the United States should become the "great arsenal of democracy" to keep the British fighting and make it unnecessary for Americans to go to war.

The America First Committee disagreed, but Congress passed the Lend-Lease Act by a wide margin. By the time the program ended, the United States had contributed more than $40 billion in weapons, vehicles, and other supplies to the Allied war effort.

While shipments of supplies to Britain began at once, lend-lease aid eventually went to the Soviet Union as well. After calling off the invasion of Britain, Hitler returned to his original goal of carving out lebensraum for Germany in eastern Europe. In June 1941, in violation of the Nazi-Soviet pact, Hitler launched a massive invasion of the Soviet Union. Although Churchill detested communism and

considered Stalin a harsh dictator, he vowed that any person or state "who fights against Nazism will have our aid." Roosevelt, too, supported this policy.

The Hemispheric Defense Zone Congressional approval of the Lend-Lease Act did not solve the problem of how to get American arms and supplies to Britain. German submarines patrolling the Atlantic Ocean were sinking hundreds of thousands of tons of shipping each month, and the British navy simply did not have enough ships in the Atlantic to stop them.

Roosevelt could not simply order the U.S. Navy to protect British cargo ships, since the United States was still technically neutral. Instead, he developed the idea of a hemispheric defense zone. Roosevelt declared that the entire western half of the Atlantic was part of the Western Hemisphere and therefore neutral. He then ordered the U.S. Navy to patrol the western Atlantic and reveal the location of German submarines to the British.

The Atlantic Charter In August 1941 Roosevelt and Churchill met face-to-face on board American and British warships anchored near Newfoundland. During these meetings, the two men agreed on the text of the **Atlantic Charter.** It committed the two

Picturing **History**

Neutrality Debate The America First Committee strongly opposed the increasingly weak neutrality of the United States. Here an American soldier confronts an isolationist marching outside the White House. How did the Lend-Lease Act further weaken the nation's official neutrality?

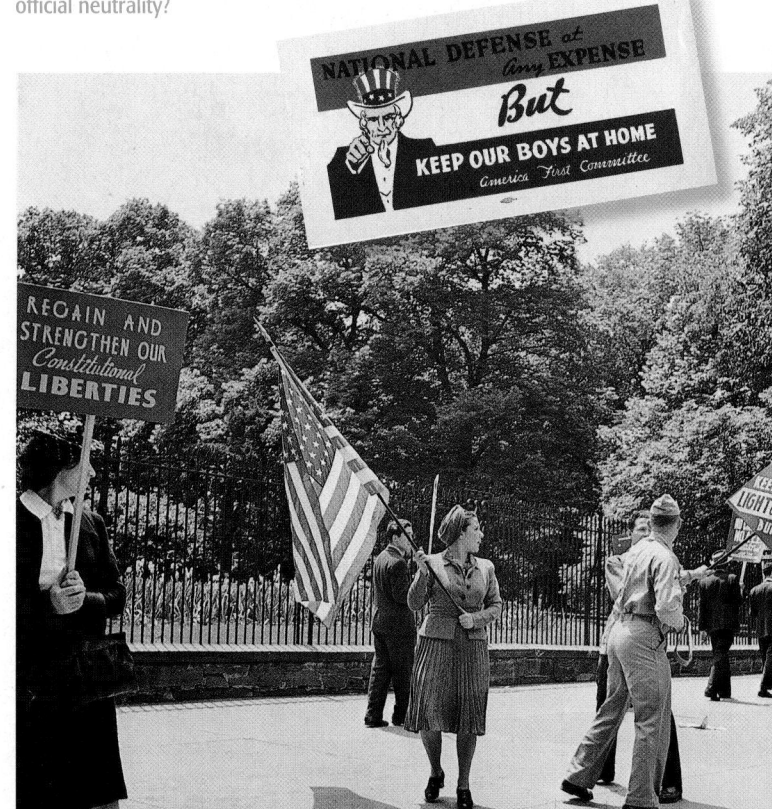

leaders to a postwar world of democracy, non-aggression, free trade, economic advancement, and freedom of the seas. Churchill later said that FDR pledged to "force an 'incident' . . . which would justify him in opening hostilities" with Germany.

An incident quickly presented itself. In early September a German U-boat fired on the American destroyer *Greer*, which had been radioing the U-boat's position to the British. Roosevelt promptly responded by ordering American ships to follow a "shoot-on-sight" policy toward German submarines.

The Germans escalated hostilities the following month, targeting two American destroyers. One of them, the **Reuben James**, broke in two after being torpedoed. It sank into the frigid waters of the North Atlantic, where 115 sailors died. As the end of 1941 grew near, Germany and the United States continued a tense standoff in the North Atlantic.

✓ **Reading Check** **Evaluating** How did the Lend-Lease Act help the Allied war effort?

Japan Attacks the United States

Despite the growing tensions in the Atlantic, the Japanese attack on Pearl Harbor was what finally brought the United States into World War II. Ironically, Japan's decision to attack the United States was a direct result of Roosevelt's efforts to help Britain in its war against Germany.

America Embargoes Japan Between August 1939 and December 1941, Roosevelt's primary goal was to help Britain and its allies defeat Germany. He knew that one of the problems Britain faced was the need to keep much of its navy in Asia to protect British territories there from Japanese attack. As German submarines began sinking British shipping, the British began moving warships from Southeast Asia to the Atlantic, leaving their empire vulnerable. In response, Roosevelt introduced policies to discourage the Japanese from attacking the British Empire.

NATIONAL GEOGRAPHIC **Pearl Harbor, Hawaii, December 7, 1941**

PACIFIC OCEAN

Kaena Point

FIRST WAVE

Kahuku Point

④

Opana radar station

Kahuku

Laie

SECOND WAVE

Waialua

Haleiwa Field

②

Waianae

Wahiawa

Wheeler Field
7:51, 9:10 A.M.

Nanakuli

Ford Island
Naval Air Station
7:55, 9:02 A.M.

Waipahu

Kaneohe
Naval Air Station
7:53, 8:55 A.M.

Ewa Marine Corps
Air Station
7:53, 9:05 A.M.

Pearl City

Pearl Harbor

Kaneohe

Ewa Beach

Hickam Field
7:55, 9:05 A.M.

O A H U

Kailua

③

①

Battleship Row

Honolulu

Bellows Field
8:30, 9:00 A.M.

Diamond Head

Legend:
- First wave of Japanese aircraft
- Second wave of Japanese aircraft
- 7:51 A.M. Time of initial attack (First wave)
- 8:55 A.M. Time of initial attack (Second wave)
- Airfield
- Airfield attacked
- Radar site
- Town

Roosevelt began by putting economic pressure on Japan. Japan depended on the United States for many key materials, including scrap iron, steel, and especially oil. Approximately 80 percent of Japan's oil came from the United States. In July 1940, Congress passed the Export Control Act, giving Roosevelt the power to restrict the sale of strategic materials (materials important for fighting a war) to other nations. Roosevelt immediately blocked the sale of airplane fuel and scrap iron to Japan. Furious, the Japanese signed an alliance with Germany and Italy, formally becoming a member of the Axis.

In 1941 Roosevelt began sending lend-lease aid to China. Japan had invaded China in 1937, and by 1941, it controlled much of the Chinese coast. Roosevelt hoped that lend-lease aid would enable the Chinese to tie down the Japanese and prevent them from attacking elsewhere. The strategy failed. By July 1941, the Japanese had sent troops into southern Indochina, posing a direct threat to the British Empire. Japanese aircraft were now in position to strike British shipping in the Strait of Malacca and bomb Hong Kong and Singapore.

Roosevelt responded very quickly to the Japanese threat. He froze all Japanese assets in the United States, reduced the amount of oil being shipped to Japan, and sent General Douglas MacArthur to the Philippines to build up American defenses there.

Roosevelt made it clear that he would lift the oil embargo only if Japan withdrew from Indochina and made peace with China. With the war against China now in jeopardy because of a lack of oil and other resources, the Japanese military began making plans to attack the resource-rich British and Dutch colonies in Southeast Asia. They also decided to seize the Philippines and to attack the American fleet at Pearl Harbor. They could not risk leaving the United States with a navy in the Pacific to oppose their plans. While the Japanese prepared for war, negotiations with the United States continued, but neither side would back down. On November 26, 1941, six Japanese aircraft carriers, two battleships, and several other warships set sail for Hawaii.

Japan Attacks Pearl Harbor The Japanese government appeared to be continuing negotiations with the United States in good faith. American intelligence, however, had decoded Japanese communications that made it clear that Japan was preparing to go to war against the United States.

On November 27, American commanders at the Pearl Harbor naval base received a war warning from Washington, but Hawaii was not mentioned as a possible target. It was a great distance from Japan to Hawaii, and Washington officials doubted Japan would try to launch such a long-range attack.

The failure to collect sufficient information and the failure of the branches of the U.S. military to share the information available left Pearl Harbor an open target. The result was devastating. Japan's surprise attack on December 7, 1941, sank or damaged 21 ships of the U.S. Pacific Fleet, including 8 battleships, 3 cruisers, 4 destroyers, and

HISTORY Online

Student Web Activity Visit the *American Vision* Web site at tav.glencoe.com and click on *Student Web Activities—Chapter 24* for an activity on Pearl Harbor.

❶ 6:45 A.M.: The destroyer *Ward* sinks a Japanese midget submarine near the entrance to Pearl Harbor.

❷ 7:02 to 7:39 A.M.: Army radar at Opana tracks a cloud of aircraft approaching from the north. An officer at Fort Shafter concludes it is a flight of B-17s due in from California.

❸ 7:49 A.M.: The first wave of 183 Japanese planes is ordered to attack. The force includes 40 torpedo bombers and 49 high-altitude bombers—each armed with a single projectile—bound for Battleship Row. Other bombers and Zero fighters attack airfields.

❹ 8:55 A.M.: The second wave of 167 planes renews the attack on airfields and ships. Oil tanks and most ship-repair facilities are ignored, an omission the Japanese later regret.

"above and beyond the call of duty"

DORIE MILLER
Received the Navy Cross at Pearl Harbor, May 27, 1942

Dorie Miller, World War II's first recognized African American hero, won the Navy Cross for bravery for defending a battleship during the Japanese attack at Pearl Harbor.

World Geography Connection

Geography and War

Throughout history, geography has played a key role in wars. In 1941, for example, Japan attacked Malaya and Indonesia to gain access to oil and rubber. It also wanted control of the Strait of Malacca, an important waterway linking the Indian Ocean with the South China Sea. Geography can also influence a war's outcome, as it did in the Vietnam War. There, miles of dense jungle allowed guerrillas to wage war first against French troops and then against American forces. *Why do you think the Strait of Malacca was so important?*

Malay Peninsula • South China Sea • Strait of Malacca • SINGAPORE • Sumatra

400 miles
400 kilometers   110°E
Miller Cylindrical projection

6 other vessels. The attack also destroyed 188 airplanes and killed 2,403 Americans. Another 1,178 were injured.

On the night of the attack, a gray-faced Roosevelt met with his cabinet to tell them the country now faced the most serious crisis since the outbreak of the Civil War. The next day, the president asked Congress to declare war:

❝Yesterday, December 7, 1941—a date which will live in infamy—the United States of America was suddenly and deliberately attacked by the naval and air forces of Japan. . . . I believe I interpret the will of the Congress and of the people when I assert that we will not only defend ourselves to the uttermost, but we will make very certain that this form of treachery shall never endanger us again. . . . No matter how long it may take us . . . the American people in their righteous might will win through to absolute victory.❞

—quoted in *Franklin D. Roosevelt: A Rendezvous with Destiny*

Following the president's speech, the Senate voted 82 to 0 and the House 388 to 1 to declare war on Japan.

Germany Declares War   Although Japan was now at war with the United States, Hitler did not have to declare war on the Americans. The terms of the alliance with Japan specified that Germany only had to come to Japan's aid if Japan was attacked, not if Japan attacked another country. Hitler, however, had grown frustrated with the American navy's attacks on German submarines, and he believed the time had come to declare war.

Hitler greatly underestimated the strength of the United States, and he expected the Japanese to easily defeat the Americans in the Pacific. He hoped that by helping Japan now, he could count on Japanese support against the Soviet Union once the Americans had been beaten. On December 11, Germany and Italy both declared war on the United States.

✓ **Reading Check**   **Examining** What finally caused the United States to become involved in World War II?

SECTION 4 ASSESSMENT

Checking for Understanding

1. **Define:** hemispheric defense zone, strategic materials.
2. **Identify:** America First Committee, Lend-Lease Act, Atlantic Charter.

Reviewing Themes

3. **Individual Action** After Roosevelt made the destroyers-for-bases deal with Britain, some Americans called him a dictator. Do you think Roosevelt was right or wrong in his actions? Explain your answer.

Critical Thinking

4. **Interpreting** Why was the United States unprepared for Japan's attack on Pearl Harbor?
5. **Organizing** Use a graphic organizer to list how Roosevelt helped Britain while maintaining official neutrality.

Help to Britain

Analyzing Visuals

6. **Analyzing Maps** Study the map on pages 728–729. Based on the geography of Oahu, why was the location of Pearl Harbor perfect for a naval base?

Writing About History

7. **Persuasive Writing** Take on the role of an American in 1940. Write a letter to the editor of your newspaper explaining why you think the United States should either remain neutral or become involved in World War II.

Critical Thinking SKILLBUILDER

Making Generalizations

Why Learn This Skill?

Have you heard statements such as "Only tall people play basketball well," or "Dogs make better pets than cats"? Do you accept these statements at face value, or do you stop and consider whether or not they are valid?

Learning the Skill

The statements listed above are called *generalizations,* which are broad statements about a topic. To be valid, a generalization must be based on accurate information.

Let's examine the generalization, "Only tall people play basketball well." We can find many examples of tall basketball players, but there are also many shorter players who excel at this sport.

In this case, we began with a generalization and looked for facts to support or disprove it. In other cases, you will start with a group of facts about a topic and then make a generalization from these facts. To make a valid generalization, first collect information relevant to the topic. This information must consist of accurate facts, not opinions.

Suppose that you want to make a generalization about the relative danger of airplane travel compared to automobile travel. First, you would collect accident statistics involving airplanes and cars. Your next step would be to classify the information into categories. Then you would look for relationships between these categories. For example, you might put the airplane and automobile statistics in separate categories. You might also categorize the number of accidents and the number of fatalities. Finally, you should make a generalization that is consistent with most of the facts you gathered.

Practicing the Skill

Reread the passage about the Austrian *Anschluss* on page 714, and then answer these questions.

❶ What facts about the *Anschluss* are presented?

❷ Organize these facts into categories.

❸ How does the vote held in Austria relate to the other facts?

❹ What generalization can you make about Austria regarding the *Anschluss?*

Skills Assessment

Complete the Practicing Skills questions on page 733 and the Chapter 24 Skill Reinforcement Activity to assess your mastery of this skill.

Applying the Skill

Making Generalizations Review the information in the chapter about appeasement as it related to the countries of Czechoslovakia, France, and Britain. Write a generalization about Czechoslovakia's role in the appeasement policy. Support your generalization with at least five facts.

Glencoe's **Skillbuilder Interactive Workbook CD-ROM, Level 2,** provides instruction and practice in key social studies skills.

Reviewing Key Terms

On a sheet of paper, use each of these terms in a sentence.

1. fascism
2. internationalism
3. appeasement
4. blitzkrieg
5. Holocaust
6. concentration camp
7. extermination camp
8. hemispheric defense zone
9. strategic materials

Reviewing Key Facts

10. **Identify:** Benito Mussolini, Vladimir Lenin, Adolf Hitler.
11. Where did antidemocratic governments arise in Europe and Asia after World War I?
12. Why was Austria easier for Hitler to annex than Czechoslovakia?
13. What were four ways that Nazis persecuted Jews?
14. In what three ways did Roosevelt help Britain while maintaining an American policy of neutrality?

Critical Thinking

15. **Analyzing Themes: Global Connections** If Roosevelt's internationalist policy had been fully pursued, do you think it could have prevented World War II?
16. **Evaluating** Why were the British able to stop the German invasion of their country?
17. **Determining Cause and Effect** How did the rise of dictatorships and the attack on Pearl Harbor cause the United States to become involved in World War II?
18. **Organizing** Use a graphic organizer similar to the one below to list countries that Hitler and the Nazis seized between 1936 and 1940.

Countries Seized by Hitler and the Nazis

Chapter Summary

Axis

Italy
- Mussolini's Fascist Party believed in supreme power of the state
- Cooperated with Germany from 1936 onward

Germany
- Hitler's Nazi Party believed in all-powerful state, territorial expansion, and ethnic purity
- Invaded Poland in 1939, France in 1940, and the USSR in 1941

Japan
- Military leaders pushed for territorial expansion
- Attacked Manchuria in 1931
- Invaded China in 1937
- Attacked Pearl Harbor in 1941

USSR
- Communists, led by harsh dictator Joseph Stalin, created industrial power
- Signed non-aggression pact with Germany in 1939
- Received U.S. aid; eventually fought with Allies to defeat Germany

Allies

United States
- Passed Neutrality Acts in 1935, 1937, and 1939
- Gave lend-lease aid to Britain, China, and the USSR
- Declared war on Japan in 1941

Great Britain
- Tried to appease Hitler by allowing territorial growth
- Declared war on Germany in 1939
- Resisted German attack in 1940
- Received U.S. aid through lend-lease program and cash-and-carry provision

France
- Along with Great Britain, tried to appease Hitler
- Declared war on Germany in 1939 after Poland was invaded
- Occupied by Nazis in 1940

Self-Check Quiz

Visit the *American Vision* Web site at tav.glencoe.com and click on *Self-Check Quizzes—Chapter 24* to assess your knowledge of chapter content.

19. Interpreting Primary Sources The America First Committee tried to prevent American involvement in World War II. On April 24, 1941, aviator Charles Lindbergh spoke in New York on behalf of this committee. Read the excerpt from his speech and answer the questions that follow.

“War is not inevitable for this country. Such a claim is defeatism in the true sense. No one can make us fight abroad unless we ourselves are willing to do so. No one will attempt to fight us here if we arm ourselves as a great nation should be armed. Over a hundred million people in this nation are opposed to entering the war. If the principles of democracy mean anything at all, that is reason enough for us to stay out. If we are forced into war against the wishes of an overwhelming majority of our people, we will have proved democracy such a failure at home that there will be little use fighting for it abroad.”

—quoted in *Readings In American History*

a. Why did Lindbergh favor isolationism?

b. How do you think Lindbergh might have felt about isolationism after the attack on Pearl Harbor?

Practicing Skills

20. Making Generalizations Read the passage below and answer the questions that follow.

“Hitler and the Nazis believed the Germanic people to be superior to all others. . . . The groups the Nazis held in low regard included homosexuals, the disabled, Gypsies, and Slavic peoples. The Nazis reserved their most virulent hatred for the Jews, however. . . . For the Nazis, all people who were ethnically Jewish were completely evil no matter what their religion, occupation, or education.”

a. What facts are presented about the attitude of Hitler and the Nazis toward Germans and Jews?

b. What generalization can be made from these facts?

Geography and History

21. The map on this page shows Nazi concentration and extermination camps. Study it and answer these questions.

a. Interpreting Maps In which two countries were most of the concentration and extermination camps located?

Nazi Concentration and Extermination Camps, 1933–1945

● Capital city
■ Nazi concentration camp/ death camp

b. Applying Geography Skills What can you conclude about the extent of the Nazis' "final solution"?

Chapter Activity

22. Research Project Research and write a short biography of Winston Churchill. Then describe his career, involvement in World War II, and beliefs to the class.

Writing Activity

23. Descriptive Writing Using the Internet and the library, find firsthand accounts of Holocaust survivors. Create a report on these survivors, and present the report to your classmates.

Standardized Test Practice

Directions: Choose the phrase that best completes the following statement.

When Roosevelt signed the Lend-Lease Act in 1941, he said that the United States must become the "arsenal of democracy" in order to

A end the Depression.

B help the Axis powers.

C remain neutral.

D help Great Britain.

Test-Taking Tip: An *arsenal* is a stockpile or storehouse of weapons. Eliminate any answer that does not relate to using weapons to protect democracy.

CHAPTER
25

America and World War II
1941–1945

Why It Matters

The United States entered World War II unwillingly and largely unprepared. The American people, however, quickly banded together to transform the American economy into the most productive and efficient war-making machine in the world. American forces turned the tide in Europe and the Pacific, and they played a crucial role in the defeat of Germany, Italy, and Japan.

The Impact Today

Many changes that began in World War II are still shaping our lives today.
* *The United Nations was founded.*
* *Nuclear weapons were invented.*
* *The United States became the most powerful nation in the world.*

The American Vision Video *The Chapter 25 video, "Japanese American Internment Camps," chronicles the treatment of Japanese Americans during World War II.*

1943
* Detroit race riots
* Zoot suit riots in Los Angeles

1941
* President Roosevelt forbids racial discrimination in defense industries
* United States enters World War II

1942
* Women's Army Auxiliary Corps established
* Japanese American relocation ordered

United States
F. Roosevelt
1933–1945

PRESIDENTS

1941   *1942*   *1943*

World

1941
* Japan attacks Pearl Harbor and the Philippines

1942 —
* Japan takes Philippines; MacArthur vows: "I shall return."
* Americans turn the tide in the Pacific at the Battle of Midway

1943 —
* Battle of Tarawa
* Germans defeated at Stalingrad
* Allied forces land in Italy

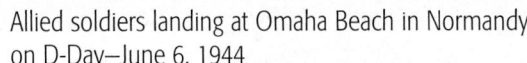

Allied soldiers landing at Omaha Beach in Normandy
on D-Day—June 6, 1944

1944
• Supreme Court rules in
  Korematsu v. *the United States*
  that Japanese American
  relocation is constitutional

1945
• Franklin Roosevelt dies
  in office; Harry S Truman
  becomes president

Truman
1945–1953

1944

1945

1944
• Eisenhower leads D-Day invasion
• Battle of Leyte Gulf

1945
• United States drops atomic bomb on Japan
• World War II ends

HISTORY
Online
Chapter Overview
Visit the *American Vision* Web
site at tav.glencoe.com
and click on *Chapter
Overviews—Chapter 25* to
preview chapter information.

Main Idea

The United States quickly mobilized its economy and armed forces to fight World War II.

Key Terms and Names

cost-plus, Reconstruction Finance Corporation, Liberty ship, War Production Board, Selective Service and Training Act, disfranchise

Reading Strategy

Organizing As you read about American mobilization for World War II, complete a graphic organizer like the one below by filling in the agencies the U.S. government created to mobilize the nation's economy for war.

Government Agencies Created to Mobilize the Economy

Reading Objectives

- **Explain** how the United States mobilized its economy.
- **Describe** the issues involved in raising an American army.

Section Theme

Individual Action The success of the United States in mobilizing for war was due largely to the cooperation of individual American citizens.

Preview of Events

◆1940	◆1941	◆1942	◆1943
1940 Fall of France; Selective Service Act	**December 7, 1941** Japan attacks Pearl Harbor	**1942** Women's Army Auxiliary Corps (WAAC) established	**1943** Office of War Mobilization (OWM) established

★ **An American Story** ★

Shortly after 1:30 P.M. on December 7, 1941, Secretary of the Navy Frank Knox phoned President Roosevelt at the White House. "Mr. President," Knox said, "it looks like the Japanese have attacked Pearl Harbor." A few minutes later, Admiral Harold Stark, chief of naval operations, phoned and confirmed the attack.

As Eleanor Roosevelt passed by the president's study, she knew immediately something very bad had happened:

"All the secretaries were there, two telephones were in use, the senior military aides were on their way with messages." Eleanor also noticed that President Roosevelt remained calm: "His reaction to any event was always to be calm. If it was something that was bad, he just became almost like an iceberg, and there was never the slightest emotion that was allowed to show."

Turning to his wife, President Roosevelt expressed anger at the Japanese: "I never wanted to have to fight this war on two fronts. We haven't got the Navy to fight in both the Atlantic and Pacific. . . . We will have to build up the Navy and the Air Force and that will mean we will have to take a good many defeats before we can have a victory."

—adapted from *No Ordinary Time*

Converting the Economy

Although the difficulties of fighting a global war troubled the president, British Prime Minister Winston Churchill was not worried. Churchill knew that victory in modern war depended on a nation's industrial power. He compared the American economy to a gigantic boiler: "Once the fire is lighted under it there is no limit to the power it can generate."

Churchill was right. The industrial output of the United States during the war astounded the rest of the world. American workers were twice as productive as German workers and five times more productive than Japanese workers. American war production turned the tide in favor of the Allies. In less than four years, the United States achieved what no other nation had ever done—it fought and won a two-front war against two powerful military empires, forcing each to surrender unconditionally.

The United States was able to expand its war production so rapidly after the attack on Pearl Harbor in part because the government had begun to mobilize the economy before the country entered the war. When the German blitzkrieg swept into France in May 1940, President Roosevelt declared a national emergency and announced a plan to build 50,000 warplanes a year. Shocked by the success of the German attack, many Americans were willing to build up the country's defenses.

Roosevelt and his advisers believed that the best way to rapidly mobilize the economy was to give industry an incentive to move quickly. As Henry Stimson, the new secretary of war, wrote in his diary: "If you are going to try and go to war, or to prepare for war, in a capitalist country, you have got to let business make money out of the process or business won't work."

Normally when the government needed military equipment, it would ask companies to bid for the contract, but that system was too slow in wartime. Instead of asking for bids, the government signed cost-plus contracts. The government agreed to pay a company whatever it cost to make a product plus a guaranteed percentage of the costs as profit. Under the cost-plus system, the more a company produced and the faster it did the work, the more money it would make. The system was not cheap, but it did get war materials produced quickly and in quantity.

Although cost-plus convinced many companies to convert to war production, others could not afford to reequip their factories to make military goods. To convince more companies to convert, Congress gave new authority to the **Reconstruction Finance Corporation** (RFC). The RFC, a government agency set up during the Depression, was now permitted to make loans to companies to help them cover the cost of converting to war production.

Reading Check **Analyzing** What government policies helped American industry to produce large quantities of war materials?

American Industry Gets the Job Done

By the fall of 1941, much had already been done to prepare the economy for war, but it was still only partially mobilized. Although many companies were producing military equipment, most still preferred to make consumer goods. The Depression was ending and sales were rising. The Japanese attack on Pearl Harbor, however, changed everything. By the summer of 1942, almost all major industries and some 200,000 companies had converted to war production. Together they made the nation's wartime "miracle" possible.

ECONOMICS

Tanks Replace Cars The automobile industry was uniquely suited to the mass production of military equipment. Automobile factories began to produce trucks, jeeps, and tanks. This was critical in modern warfare because the country that could move troops and supplies most quickly usually

History *Through Art*

WW II Posters War posters were designed to help encourage and inform the American public. How would you have felt to see a poster such as this one?

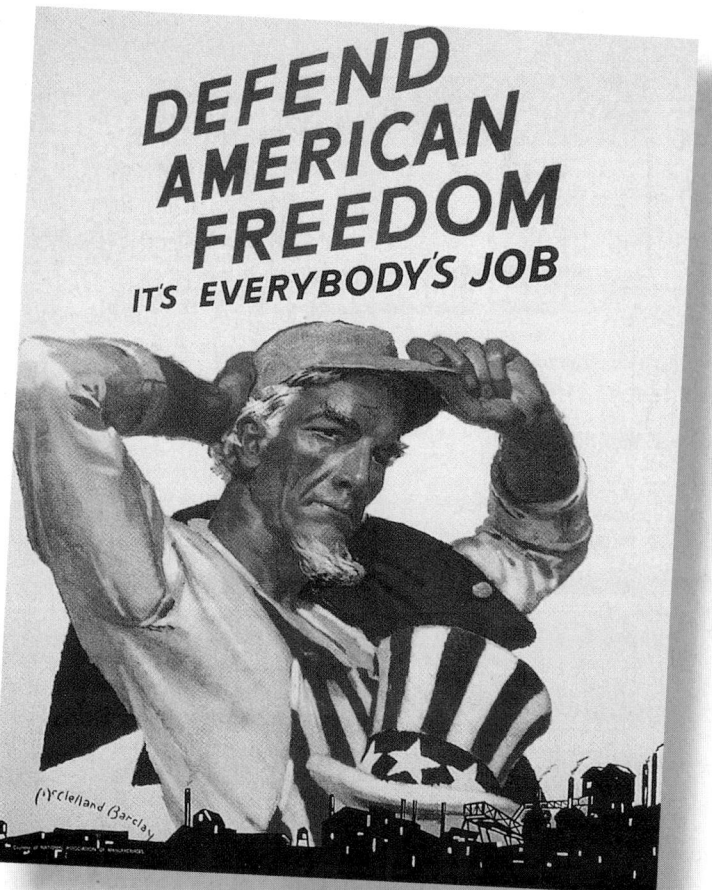

won the battle. As General George C. Marshall, chief of staff for the United States Army, observed:

> 66The greatest advantage the United States enjoyed on the ground in the fighting was . . . the jeep and the two-and-a-half ton truck. These are the instruments that moved and supplied United States troops in battle, while the German army . . . depended on animal transport. . . . The United States, profiting from the mass production achievements of its automotive industry . . . had mobility that completely outclassed the enemy.99
>
> —quoted in *Miracle of World War II*

Automobile factories did not just produce vehicles. They also built artillery, rifles, mines, helmets, pontoon bridges, cooking pots, and dozens of other pieces of military equipment. Henry Ford launched one of the most ambitious projects when he created an assembly line for the enormous B-24 bomber known as "the Liberator" at Willow Run Airport near Detroit. By the end of the war, the factory had built over 8,600 aircraft. Overall, the automobile industry produced nearly one-third of the military equipment manufactured during the war.

Building the Liberty Ships Henry Kaiser's shipyards more than matched Ford's achievement in aircraft production. Kaiser's shipyards built many ships, but they were best known for their production of Liberty ships. The Liberty ship was the basic cargo ship used during the war. Most Liberty ships were welded instead of riveted. Welded ships were cheap, easy to build, and very hard to sink compared to riveted ships.

When a riveted ship was hit, the rivets often came loose, causing the ship to fall apart and sink. A welded ship's hull was fused into one solid piece of steel. A torpedo might blow a hole in it, but the hull would not come apart. A damaged Liberty ship could often get back to port, make repairs, and return to service.

The War Production Board As American companies converted to war production, many business leaders became frustrated with the mobilization process. Government agencies argued constantly about supplies and contracts and whose orders had the highest priority.

After Pearl Harbor, President Roosevelt tried to improve the system by creating the **War Production Board** (WPB). He gave the WPB the authority to set

Switching to Wartime Production

Automobile Production, 1941–1945

Automobiles Produced (in millions)

Year	
1941	3,779,628
1942	222,862
1943	139
1944	610
1945	70,001

Source: *Historical Statistics of the United States: Colonial Times to 1970.*

priorities and production goals and to control the distribution of raw materials and supplies. Almost immediately, the WPB clashed with the military. Military agencies continued to sign contracts without consulting with the WPB. Finally, in 1943, Roosevelt established the **Office of War Mobilization** (OWM) to settle arguments between the different agencies.

✓ **Reading Check** **Explaining** What military need led to the production of Liberty ships?

Building an Army

Converting factories to war production was only part of the mobilization process. If the United States was actually going to fight and win the war, the country also needed to build up its armed forces.

Creating an Army Within days of Germany's attack on Poland, President Roosevelt expanded the army to 227,000 soldiers. After France surrendered to Germany in June 1940, two members of Congress

introduced the **Selective Service and Training Act,** a plan for the first peacetime draft in American history. Before the spring of 1940, college students, labor unions, isolationists, and most members of Congress had opposed a peacetime draft. Opinions changed after Germany defeated France. In September Congress approved the draft by a wide margin.

You're in the Army Now At first the flood of draftees overwhelmed the army's training facilities. Many recruits had to live in tents and use temporary facilities. The army also endured equipment shortages. Troops carried sticks representing guns, threw stones simulating grenades, and practiced maneuvers with trucks carrying signs that read "TANK."

New draftees were initially sent to a reception center, where they were given physical exams and injections against smallpox and typhoid. The draftees were then issued uniforms, boots, and whatever equipment was available. The clothing bore the label "G.I.," meaning "Government Issue," which is why American soldiers were called "GIs."

After taking aptitude tests, recruits were sent to basic training for eight weeks. They learned how to handle weapons, load backpacks, read maps, pitch tents, and dig trenches. Trainees drilled and exercised constantly and learned how to work as a team.

After the war, many veterans complained that basic training had been useless. Soldiers were rushed through too quickly, and the physical training left them too tired to learn the skills they needed. A sergeant in Italy told a reporter for *Yank* magazine that during a recent battle, a new soldier had held up his rifle and yelled, "How do I load this thing?"

Despite its problems, basic training helped to break down barriers between soldiers. Recruits came from all over the country, and training together made them into a unit. Training created a "special sense of kinship," one soldier noted. "The reason you storm the beaches is not patriotism or bravery. It's that sense of not wanting to fail your buddies."

A Segregated Army Although basic training promoted unity, most recruits did not encounter Americans from every part of society. At the start of the war, the U.S. military was completely segregated. White recruits did not train alongside African Americans. African Americans had separate barracks, latrines, mess halls, and recreational facilities.

Tank Production, 1941–1945

Tanks Produced (in thousands)

- 1941: 4,203
- 1942: 23,884
- 1943: 29,497
- 1944: 17,565
- 1945: 11,184

Year

Source: *Historical Statistics of the United States: Colonial Times to 1970.*

Graph Skills

1. **Interpreting Graphs** How does the number of tanks produced relate to the number of automobiles produced in the previous graph?

2. **Making Generalizations** How do these two graphs illustrate the commitment of the United States to winning the war?

Once trained, African Americans were organized into their own military units, but white officers were generally in command of them. Most military leaders also wanted to keep African American soldiers out of combat and assigned them to construction and supply units.

Pushing for "Double V" Some African Americans did not want to support the war. As one student at a black college noted: "The Army Jim Crows us. . . . Employers and labor unions shut us out. Lynchings continue. We are disenfranchised . . . and spat upon. What more could Hitler do to us than that?" By disfranchised, the student meant that African Americans were often denied their right to vote. Despite the bitterness, most African Americans agreed with African American writer Saunders Redding that they should support their country:

> 66There are many things about this war I do not like . . . yet I believe in the war. . . . We know that whatever the mad logic of [Hitler's] New Order there is no hope for us under it. The ethnic theories of the Hitler 'master folk' admit of no chance of freedom. . . . This is a war to keep [people] free. The struggle to broaden and lengthen the road of freedom—our own private and important war to enlarge freedom here in America—will come later. . . . I believe in this war because I believe in America. I believe in what America professes to stand for. . . . 99
>
> —quoted in *America at War*

Picturing **History**

Tuskegee Airmen The Tuskegee Airmen distinguished themselves in combat, yet they were not allowed to serve in integrated units. In what theater of the war did the Tuskegee Airmen serve?

Many African American leaders combined patriotism with protest. In 1941 the National Urban League set two goals for its members: "(1) To promote effective participation of [African Americans] in all phases of the war effort. . . . (2) To formulate plans for building the kind of United States in which we wish to live after the war is over. . . ."

The *Pittsburgh Courier*, a leading African American newspaper, embraced these ideas and launched what it called the **"Double V" campaign.** African Americans, the paper argued, should join the war effort in order to achieve a double victory—a victory over Hitler's racism abroad and a victory over racism at home. If the United States wanted to portray itself as a defender of democracy, Americans might be willing to end discrimination in their own country.

President Roosevelt knew that African American voters had played an important role in his election victories. Under pressure from African American leaders, he ordered the army air force, navy, and marines to begin recruiting African Americans, and he directed the army to put African Americans into combat. He also appointed Colonel **Benjamin O. Davis,** the highest-ranking African American officer in the U.S. Army, to the rank of brigadier general.

African Americans in Combat In response to the president's order, the army air force created the 99th Pursuit Squadron, an African American unit that trained in Tuskegee, Alabama. These African American fighter pilots became known as the **Tuskegee Airmen.** After General Davis urged the military to put African Americans into combat, the 99th Pursuit Squadron was sent to the Mediterranean in April 1943. The squadron played an important role during the Battle of Anzio in Italy.

African Americans also performed well in the army. The all-African American 761st Tank Battalion was commended for its service during the Battle of the Bulge. Fighting in northwest Europe, African Americans in the 614th Tank Destroyer Battalion won 8 Silver Stars for distinguished service, 28 Bronze Stars, and 79 Purple Hearts.

Although the military did not end all segregation during the war, it did integrate military bases in 1943 and steadily expanded the role of African Americans within the armed forces. These successes paved the way for President Truman's decision to fully integrate the military in 1948.

Benjamin O. Davis

Women Join the Armed Forces As in World War I, women joined the armed forces. The army enlisted women for the first time, although they were barred from combat. Instead, as the army's recruiting slogan suggested, women were needed to "release a man for combat." Many jobs in the army were administrative and clerical. By assigning women to these jobs, more men would be available for combat.

Congress first allowed women in the military in May 1942, when it established the **Women's Army Auxiliary Corps** (WAAC) and appointed **Oveta Culp Hobby,** an official with the War Department, to serve as its first director. Although pleased about the establishment of the WAAC, many women were unhappy that it was an auxiliary corps and not part of the regular army. A little over a year later, the army replaced the WAAC with the **Women's Army Corps** (WAC). Director Hobby was assigned the rank of colonel. "You have a debt and a date," Hobby explained to those training to be the nation's first women officers. "A debt to democracy, a date with destiny." The Coast Guard, the navy, and the marines quickly followed the army and set up their own women's units. In addition to serving in these new organizations, another 68,000 women served as nurses in the army and navy.

Americans Go to War The Americans who went to war in 1941 were not well trained. Most of the troops had no previous military experience. Most of the officers had never led men in combat. The armed forces mirrored many of the tensions and prejudices of American society. Despite these challenges, the United States armed forces performed well in battle.

Picturing **History**

Women Pilots General Barney M. Giles inspects the guard of honor of the Women Airforce Service Pilots (WASPS) at Avenger Field in Sweetwater, Texas. Many pilots wore Filfinella patches (right) for good luck. Why do you think the army refused to allow women to fly in combat?

Of all the major powers involved in the war, the United States suffered the fewest casualties in combat.

American troops never adopted the spit-and-polish style of the Europeans. When they arrived at the front, Americans' uniforms were usually a mess, and they rarely marched in step. When one Czechoslovakian was asked what he thought of the sloppy, unprofessional American soldiers, he commented, "They walk like free men."

✓ **Reading Check** **Summarizing** How did the status of women and African Americans in the armed forces change during the war?

SECTION 1 ASSESSMENT

Checking for Understanding

1. **Define:** cost-plus, Liberty ship, disfranchise.
2. **Identify:** Reconstruction Finance Corporation, War Production Board, Selective Service and Training Act.
3. **Describe** the role of the OWM in the war production effort.

Reviewing Themes

4. **Individual Action** Why do you think African Americans were willing to fight in the war even though they suffered discrimination in American society?

Critical Thinking

5. **Evaluating** How effectively did American industry rally behind the war effort? Give examples to support your opinion.
6. **Categorizing** Use a graphic organizer like the one below to list the challenges facing the United States as it mobilized for war.

Challenges to Mobilization

Analyzing Visuals

7. **Analyzing Graphs** Study the graphs of automobile and tank production on pages 738 and 739. Why did automobile production decrease while tank production increased?

Writing About History

8. **Descriptive Writing** Take on the role of a draftee who has just completed the first week of basic training. Write a letter to your parents telling them about basic training and what you hope to accomplish once the training is over.

Guide to Reading

Main Idea
By late 1942, the Allies had stopped the German and Japanese advance.

Key Terms and Names
Chester Nimitz, Douglas MacArthur, James Doolittle, periphery, George Patton, convoy system

Reading Strategy
Sequencing As you read about the military campaigns of 1942, complete a time line similar to the one below to record the major battles discussed and the victor in each.

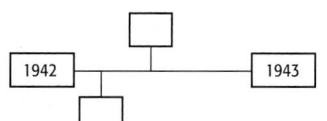

Reading Objectives
• **Analyze** how the Allies were able to fight a war on two fronts and turn the war against the Axis in the Pacific, Russia, and the North Atlantic.
• **Explain** why Stalingrad is considered a major turning point of the war.

Section Theme
Individual Action Many American soldiers made heroic sacrifices in order to turn the tide against the Axis Powers.

Preview of Events

♦1942	♦1943	♦1944

May 1942
Fall of the Philippines; Battle of the Coral Sea

June 1942
Battle of Midway

February 1943
Germans defeated at Stalingrad

May 1943
Germans driven out of North Africa

★ An American Story ★

On June 4, 1942, Lieutenant Commander James Thach climbed into his F4F Wildcat fighter plane. Thach knew that the Japanese Zero fighter planes were better than his Wildcat. To improve his chances against them, he had developed a new tactic he called the "Thach weave." At the Battle of Midway, he had his first chance to try it:

❝So we boarded our planes. All of us were highly excited and admittedly nervous. . . . A very short time after, Zero fighters came down on us—I figured there were twenty. . . . The air was just like a beehive, and I wasn't sure that anything would work. And then my weave began to work! I got a good shot at two Zeros and burned them . . . then Ram, my wingman, radioed: 'There's a Zero on my tail.' . . . I was really angry then. I was mad because my poor little wingman had never been in combat before [and] this Zero was about to chew him to pieces. I probably should have ducked under the Zero, but I lost my temper and decided to keep my fire going into him so he'd pull out. He did, and I just missed him by a few feet. I saw flames coming out of his airplane. This was like playing chicken on the highway with two automobiles headed for each other, except we were shooting at each other as well.❞

—quoted in *The Pacific War Remembered*

Holding the Line Against Japan

While officers like James Thach developed new tactics to fight the Japanese, the commander of the United States Navy in the Pacific, Admiral **Chester Nimitz,** began planning operations against the Japanese navy. Although the Japanese had badly damaged the American fleet at Pearl Harbor, they had missed the American aircraft carriers,

which were at sea on a mission. The United States had several carriers in the Pacific, and Nimitz was determined to use them. In the days just after Pearl Harbor, however, he could do little to stop Japan's advance into Southeast Asia.

The Fall of the Philippines

A few hours after they bombed Pearl Harbor, the Japanese attacked American airfields in the Philippines. Two days later, Japanese troops landed in the islands. The American and Filipino forces defending the Philippines were badly outnumbered. Their commander, General **Douglas MacArthur,** decided to retreat to the Bataan Peninsula. Using the peninsula's rugged terrain, MacArthur's troops held out for more than three months. Gradually, the lack of supplies along with diseases such as malaria, scurvy, and dysentery took their toll. Realizing MacArthur's capture would demoralize the American people, President Roosevelt ordered the general to evacuate to Australia. In Australia MacArthur made a promise: "I came through, and I shall return."

On April 9, 1942, the weary defenders of Bataan finally surrendered. Nearly 78,000 prisoners of war were forced to march—sick, exhausted, and starving—65 miles (105 km) to a Japanese prison camp. Thousands died on this march, which came to be known as the **Bataan Death March.** Here one captured American, Leon Beck, recalls the nightmare:

❝They'd halt us in front of these big artesian wells . . . so we could see the water and they wouldn't let us have any. Anyone who would make a break for water would be shot or bayoneted. Then they were left there. Finally, it got so bad further along the road that you never got away from the stench of death. There were bodies laying all along the road in various degrees of decomposition—swollen, burst open, maggots crawling by the thousands. . . .❞
—quoted in *Death March: The Survivors of Bataan*

Although the troops in the Bataan Peninsula surrendered, a small force held out on the island of **Corregidor** in Manila Bay. Finally, in May 1942, Corregidor surrendered. The Philippines had fallen.

The Doolittle Raid

Even before the fall of the Philippines, President Roosevelt was searching for a way to raise the morale of the American people. He wanted to bomb Tokyo, but American planes could reach Tokyo only if an aircraft carrier brought them close enough. Unfortunately, Japanese ships in the North Pacific prevented carriers from getting close enough to Japan to launch their short-range bombers.

In early 1942, a military planner suggested replacing the carrier's usual short-range bombers with long-range B-25 bombers that could attack from farther away. Although B-25s could take off from a carrier, they could not land on its short deck. After attacking Japan, they would have to land in China.

President Roosevelt put Lieutenant Colonel **James Doolittle** in command of the mission. At the end of March, a crane loaded sixteen B-25s onto the aircraft carrier *Hornet*. The next day the *Hornet* headed west across the Pacific. On April 18, American bombs fell on Japan for the first time.

Striking Back: The Doolittle Raid, April 18, 1942

The plan for the Doolittle raid was to launch B-25 bombers from aircraft carriers between 450 and 650 miles from Japan. The planes would bomb selected targets, and fly another 1,200 miles to airfields in China.

All went well until the Japanese discovered the carriers more than 150 miles from the proposed launch site. Instead of canceling the mission, the bombers took off early. The planes reached Japan and dropped their bombs, but they did not have enough fuel to reach the friendly airfields in China. The crews were forced to bail out or crash-land, and only 71 of the 80 crew members survived. Nevertheless, the raid provided an instant boost to sagging American morale.

Planes arrive in China

Carriers launch B-25s

Tokyo is bombed

Battle of Midway, 1942

Course of *Enterprise* and *Hornet*

Course of *Yorktown*

8 June 4, 5:01 P.M. *Yorktown* fliers join *Enterprise* attack on the *Hiryu*, setting it ablaze.

9 June 6, 1:31 P.M. Japanese submarine *I-168* torpedoes the *Yorktown*, which sinks the next morning.

Hiryu sinks ✕

Course of Japanese fleet

Yorktown sinks

Akagi sinks ✕ *Soryu* sinks ✕
Kaga sinks ✕

6 June 4, 10:22-10:28 A.M. U.S. Dive-bombers score direct hits on *Kaga*, *Akagi*, and *Soryu*.

7 June 4, noon. Planes from the *Hiryu* attack U.S. carriers. *Yorktown* hit. The ship is abandoned but remains afloat.

1 June 4, 4:30 A.M. Japanese carriers launch 108 warplanes to strike U.S. base at Midway.

2 June 4, 6:16 A.M. U.S. fighters clash with attackers.

U.S. Dauntless dive-bomber

5 June 4, 9:17 A.M. Japanese planes return. Fleet turns to engage U.S. carriers.

4 June 4, 7:08 A.M. U.S. fliers from Midway begin attacking Japanese fleet.

Line of U.S. submarines stationed 170 miles from Midway.

Kure Atoll (U.S.)

3 June 4, 6:30 A.M. Japanese begin bombing Midway.

Midway Islands (U.S.)

PACIFIC OCEAN

N W E S

● U.S. actions
● Japanese actions

Geography *Skills*

1. **Interpreting Maps** When did Japan launch the attack on Midway?
2. **Applying Geography Skills** Why were aircraft carriers so vital to the war in the Pacific?

A Change in Japanese Strategy While Americans were overjoyed that the air force had finally struck back, Japanese leaders were aghast. Doolittle's bombs could have killed the emperor. The Doolittle raid convinced Japanese leaders to change their strategy.

Before the raid, the Japanese Navy had been arguing about what to do next. The officers in charge of the navy's planning wanted to cut American supply lines to Australia by capturing the south coast of New Guinea. The commander of the fleet, Admiral Yamamoto, wanted to attack Midway Island—the last American base in the North Pacific west of Hawaii. Yamamoto believed that attacking Midway would lure the American fleet into battle and enable his fleet to destroy it.

After Doolittle's raid, the planners dropped their opposition to Yamamoto's plan. The American fleet had to be destroyed in order to protect Tokyo from bombing. The attack on New Guinea would still go ahead, but only three aircraft carriers were assigned to the mission. All of the other carriers were ordered to prepare for an assault on Midway.

The Battle of the Coral Sea The Japanese believed that they could proceed with two different attacks. They thought the United States was unaware of Japan's activity and would not be able to respond in time. Japan did not know that an American team of code breakers, based in Hawaii, had already broken the Japanese Navy's secret code for conducting operations.

In March 1942, decoded Japanese messages alerted the United States to the Japanese attack on New Guinea. In response, Admiral Nimitz sent two carriers, the *Yorktown* and the *Lexington,* to intercept the Japanese in the Coral Sea. There, in early May, carriers from both sides launched all-out airstrikes against each other. Although the Japanese sank the *Lexington* and badly damaged the *Yorktown,* the American attacks forced the Japanese to call off their landing on the south coast of New Guinea. The American supply lines to Australia stayed open.

JAPANESE FORCES To destroy the U.S. Pacific Fleet, crippled by the 1941 attack on Pearl Harbor, Japan plots an occupation of two Aleutian islands and an invasion of Midway. Strategists believe that the twin actions will lure U.S. carriers to their doom. Two Japanese carriers and 58 other ships sail for the Aleutians. For Midway, Japan commits 4 large carriers, 2 light carriers, 280 planes, 7 battleships, 14 cruisers, 15 submarines, 42 destroyers, and more than 30 supporting ships. These include transports carrying 5,000 troops to take Midway.

U.S. FORCES No battleships guard U.S. carriers sent to Midway to engage the enemy fleet. Into combat go 3 carriers, including battle-damaged Yorktown. Protecting them are 8 cruisers and 16 destroyers. The U.S. has a total of 360 aircraft, including 234 carrier-based fighters and small bombers. Based on Midway are 28 fighters, 46 small bombers, 31 PBY Catalina scout planes, 4 Marauder medium bombers, and 17 Flying Fortresses. Most pilots on Midway have never flown in combat.

TURNING POINT

The Battle of Midway Back at Pearl Harbor, the code-breaking team that had alerted Nimitz to the attack on New Guinea now learned of the plan to attack Midway. With so many ships at sea, Admiral Yamamoto transmitted the plans for the Midway attack by radio, using the same code the Americans had already cracked.

Admiral Nimitz had been waiting for the opportunity to ambush the Japanese fleet. He immediately ordered carriers to take up positions near Midway. Unaware they were heading into an ambush, the Japanese launched their aircraft against Midway on June 4, 1942. The island was ready. The Japanese planes ran into a blizzard of antiaircraft fire, and 38 of them were shot down.

As the Japanese prepared a second wave to attack Midway, aircraft from the American carriers *Hornet, Yorktown,* and *Enterprise* launched a counterattack. The American planes caught the Japanese carriers with fuel, bombs, and aircraft exposed on their flight decks. Within minutes three Japanese carriers were reduced to burning wrecks. A fourth was sunk a few hours later. By nightfall it was apparent that the Americans had

dealt the Japanese navy a deadly blow. Admiral Yamamoto ordered his remaining ships to retreat.

The Battle of Midway was a turning point in the war. The Japanese Navy lost four of its largest carriers—the heart of its fleet. Just six months after Pearl Harbor, the United States had stopped the Japanese advance in the Pacific. As Admiral Ernest King, the commander in chief of the U.S. Navy, later observed, Midway "put an end to the long period of Japanese offensive action." The victory was not without cost, however. The battle killed 362 Americans and 3,057 Japanese. Afterward, one naval officer wrote to his wife: "Let no one tell you or let you believe that this war is anything other than a grim, terrible business."

Reading Check **Explaining** Why was the Battle of Midway considered a turning point?

Turning Back the German Army

In 1942 Allied forces began to win victories in Europe as well. Almost from the moment the United States entered the war, Joseph Stalin, the leader of the Soviet Union, urged President Roosevelt to open a second front in Europe. Stalin appreciated the Lend-Lease supplies that the United States had sent, but the Soviet people were still doing most of the fighting. If British and American troops opened a second front by attacking Germany from the west, it would take pressure off the Soviet Union.

Roosevelt wanted to get American troops into battle in Europe, but Prime Minister Churchill urged caution. He did not believe the United States and Great Britain were ready to launch a full-scale invasion of Europe. Instead Churchill wanted to attack the **periphery,** or edges, of the German empire. Roosevelt agreed, and in July 1942 he ordered the invasion of Morocco and Algeria—two French territories indirectly under German control.

The Struggle for North Africa
Roosevelt decided to invade Morocco and Algeria for two reasons. First, the invasion would give the army some experience without requiring a lot of troops. More importantly, once American troops were in North Africa, they would be able to help British troops fighting the Germans in Egypt.

HISTORY Online

Student Web Activity Visit the *American Vision* Web site at tav.glencoe.com and click on **Student Web Activities— Chapter 25** for an activity on America and World War II.

Fleet Admiral Chester W. Nimitz *1885–1966*

Taking command of the Pacific Fleet after the bombing of Pearl Harbor, Admiral Chester Nimitz did not view the Japanese attack as a complete disaster. The United States still had its aircraft carriers, and base facilities were in good repair. Even though the battle fleet was at the bottom of the harbor, most of the ships could be retrieved and repaired. If the Japanese had attacked the fleet at sea, nothing would have been salvageable.

Nimitz believed that the only way to win the war was to keep constant pressure on the Japanese. He ordered attacks in early 1942 and firmly backed the Doolittle raid. Nimitz planned the American campaigns that turned the tide of war at Midway and Guadalcanal. Nimitz kept the pressure on the Japanese throughout the war, and he signed the Japanese surrender document as the official representative of the United States government in 1945. In less than four years, he had taken a badly damaged fleet and made it victorious throughout the Pacific.

Admiral Isoroku Yamamoto *1884–1943*

The son of a schoolmaster, Isoroku Yamamoto spent his entire adult life in the military. In the 1930s he was one of the few Japanese leaders who opposed war with the United States. Yamamoto did so not because he was a pacifist, but because he feared Japan would lose.

When he realized that Japan's leaders were intent on war, Yamamoto became convinced that Japan's only hope lay in launching a surprise attack that would destroy the American Pacific Fleet. Although some officers opposed his plan, Yamamoto won out, and he planned and implemented the attack on Pearl Harbor. During the first years of the war, he enjoyed tremendous prestige because of Japanese victories he helped engineer.

In April 1943 the admiral took an inspection flight of several islands. Having already broken the Japanese codes, the Americans knew of the flight. On April 18, American fighters shot down Yamamoto's plane in the South Pacific, and the admiral was killed in the attack.

Egypt was very important to Britain because of the Suez Canal. Most of Britain's empire, including India, Hong Kong, Singapore, Malaya, and Australia, used the canal to send supplies to Britain. The German forces in the area, known as the "Afrika Korps," were commanded by General Erwin Rommel—a brilliant leader whose success earned him the nickname "Desert Fox."

The British forced Rommel to retreat at the battle of El Alamein, but his forces remained a serious threat. On November 8, 1942, the American invasion of North Africa began under the command of General Dwight D. Eisenhower. The American forces in Morocco, led by General **George Patton,** quickly captured the city of Casablanca, while those in Algeria seized the cities of Oran and Algiers. The Americans then headed east into Tunisia, while British forces headed west into Libya. The plan was to trap Rommel between the two Allied forces.

When the American troops advanced into the mountains of western Tunisia, they had to fight the German army for the first time. They did not do well. At the **Battle of Kasserine Pass,** the Americans were outmaneuvered and outfought. They suffered roughly 7,000 casualties and lost nearly 200 tanks. Eisenhower fired the general who led the attack and put Patton in

command. Together, the American and British forces finally pushed the Germans back. On May 13, 1943, the last German forces in North Africa surrendered.

The Battle of the Atlantic As American and British troops fought the German army in North Africa, the war against German submarines in the Atlantic Ocean continued to intensify. After Germany declared war on the United States, German submarines entered American coastal waters. They found American cargo ships to be easy targets, especially at night when the glow from the cities in the night sky silhouetted the vessels. To protect the ships, cities on the East Coast dimmed their lights every evening. People also put up special "blackout curtains" and drove with their headlights off.

By August 1942, German submarines had sunk about 360 American ships along the American coast. So many oil tankers were sunk that gasoline and fuel oil had to be rationed. To keep oil flowing, the government built the first long-distance oil pipeline, stretching some 1,250 miles (2,010 km) from the Texas oil fields to Pennsylvania.

The loss of so many ships convinced the U.S. Navy to set up a convoy system. Under this system, cargo ships traveled in groups and were escorted by navy warships. The convoy system improved the

situation dramatically. It made it much harder for a submarine to torpedo a cargo ship and escape without being attacked.

The spring of 1942 marked the high point of the German submarine campaign. In May and June alone, over 1.2 million tons of shipping were sunk. Yet in those same two months, American and British shipyards built over 1.1 million tons of new shipping. From July 1942 onward, American shipyards produced more ships than German submarines managed to sink. At the same time, American airplanes and warships began to use new technology, including radar, sonar, and depth charges, to locate and attack submarines. As the new technology began to take its toll on German submarines, the Battle of the Atlantic slowly turned in favor of the Allies.

TURNING POINT

Stalingrad In the spring of 1942, before the Battle of the Atlantic turned against Germany, Adolf Hitler was very confident he would win the war. Rommel's troops were pushing the British back in Egypt. German submarines were sinking American ships rapidly, and the German army was ready to launch a new offensive to knock the Soviets out of the war.

Hitler was convinced that the only way to defeat the Soviet Union was to destroy its economy. In May 1942, he ordered his army to capture strategic oil fields, industries, and farmlands in southern Russia and Ukraine. The key to the attack was the city of Stalingrad. The city controlled the Volga River and was a major railroad junction. If the German army captured Stalingrad, the Soviets would be cut off from the resources they needed to stay in the war.

When German troops entered Stalingrad in mid-September, Stalin ordered his troops to hold the city

Picturing **History**

Halting the German Advance Soviet troops assault German positions in Stalingrad in November 1942. Why did the Soviet army need to hold on to the city of Stalingrad?

at all cost. Retreat was forbidden. The Germans were forced to fight from house to house, losing thousands of soldiers in the process.

On November 23, Soviet reinforcements arrived and surrounded Stalingrad, trapping almost 250,000 German troops. When the battle ended in February 1943, 91,000 Germans had surrendered, although only 5,000 of them survived the Soviet prison camps and returned home after the war. The Battle of Stalingrad was a major turning point in the war. Just as the Battle of Midway put the Japanese on the defensive for the rest of the war, the Battle of Stalingrad put the Germans on the defensive as well.

Reading Check **Evaluating** What did the Allies do to win the Battle of the Atlantic?

SECTION 2 ASSESSMENT

Checking for Understanding

1. **Define:** periphery, convoy system.
2. **Identify:** Chester Nimitz, Douglas MacArthur, James Doolittle, George Patton.
3. **Explain** the American strategy in North Africa.

Reviewing Themes

4. **Individual Action** How did the Doolittle raid help boost American morale?

Critical Thinking

5. **Analyzing** How did code breakers help stop Japanese advances?
6. **Evaluating** How were the Americans able to win the Battle of the Atlantic?
7. **Organizing** Use a graphic organizer like the one below to list the reasons the Battle of Midway was a major turning point in the war.

Battle of Midway

Analyzing Visuals

8. **Examining Maps** Study the map of Midway on page 744. Why do you think the Japanese forces attacked when they did?

Writing About History

9. **Descriptive Writing** Take on the role of an American soldier fighting in the Pacific in World War II. Write a letter to your family explaining what conditions are like for you and what you hope to accomplish during the war.

Social Studies
SKILLBUILDER

Reading a Thematic Map

Why Learn This Skill?

In your study of American history, you will often encounter thematic, or special-purpose, maps. Knowing how to read a thematic map will help you get more out of it.

Learning the Skill

Military maps use colors, symbols, and arrows to show major battles, troop movements, and defensive positions during a particular battle or over a period of time. When reading a military map, follow these steps:

- **Read the map title.** This will indicate the location and time period covered on the map.

- **Read the map key.** This tells what the symbols on the map represent.

- **Study the map itself.** This will reveal the actual event or sequence of events that took place. Notice the geography of the area, and try to determine how it could affect military strategy.

- **Use the map to draw conclusions.**

Practicing the Skill

The map on this page shows troop movements in the Philippines from December 1941 to May 1942. Analyze the information on the map, then answer the following questions.

❶ What part of the world does the map show?

❷ When did MacArthur leave for Australia? What information on the map shows you this?

❸ Where did the Japanese imprison the survivors of the Bataan Death March?

❹ What geographic features did the Japanese encounter on the Bataan Peninsula?

Skills Assessment

Complete the Practicing Skills questions on page 775 and the Chapter 25 Skill Reinforcement Activity to assess your mastery of this skill.

NATIONAL GEOGRAPHIC

Bataan and Corregidor, December 1941–May 1942

Key:
- ← U.S. retreat to Bataan
- ← Japanese forces
- ←– MacArthur to Australia
- ◄----- "Death March" of U.S. prisoners
- ▲▲▲▲▲ U.S. defensive line at date shown
- ✳ Japanese victory
- ⊛ USAFFE HQ
- ▨ Occupied by Japanese

Applying the Skill

Reading a Thematic Map Study the map of the Battle of Midway on pages 744–745. Use the information on the map to answer the following questions.

1. When was the battle fought?

2. What American aircraft carriers took part in the battle?

3. What was the fate of the *Hiryu?*

 GO TO Glencoe's **Skillbuilder Interactive Workbook CD-ROM, Level 2,** provides instruction and practice in key social studies skills.

SECTION 3 — Life on the Home Front

Guide to Reading

Main Idea

World War II placed tremendous demands on Americans at home and led to new challenges for all Americans.

Key Terms and Names

Rosie the Riveter, A. Philip Randolph, Sunbelt, zoot suit, rationing, victory garden, E bond

Reading Strategy

Categorizing As you read about the challenges facing Americans on the home front, complete a graphic organizer listing opportunities for women and African Americans before and after the war. Also evaluate what progress still needed to be made after the war.

Opportunities

	Before War	After War	Still Needed
Women			
African Americans			

Reading Objectives

- **Describe** how the wartime economy created opportunities for women and minorities.
- **Discuss** how Americans coped with shortages and rapidly rising prices.

Section Theme

Civic Rights and Responsibilities To win the war, American citizens at home made countless changes in work patterns and lifestyles.

Preview of Events

◆1941　◆1942　◆1943　◆1944

June 1941
Executive Order 8802 forbids race discrimination in industries with government contracts

August 1941
Roosevelt creates the Office of Price Administration

February 1942
Japanese American relocation ordered

June 1943
Race riots in Detroit; zoot suit riots in Los Angeles

★ An American Story ★

Laura Briggs was a young woman living on a farm in Idaho when World War II began. As with many other Americans, the war completely changed her outlook on life:

❝When I was growing up, it was very much depression times. . . . As farm prices [during the war] began to get better and better, farm times became good times. . . . We and most other farmers went from a tarpaper shack to a new frame house with indoor plumbing. Now we had an electric stove instead of a wood-burning one, and running water at the sink. . . . The war made many changes in our town. I think the most important is that aspirations changed. People suddenly had the idea, 'Hey I can reach that. I can have that. I can do that. I could even send my kid to college if I wanted to.'❞

—**quoted in *Wartime America: The World War II Home Front***

Women and Minorities Gain Ground

As American troops fought their first battles against the Germans and Japanese, the war began to dramatically change American society at home. In contrast to the devastation the war brought to large parts of Europe and Asia, World War II had a positive effect on American society. The war finally put an end to the Great Depression. Mobilizing the economy created almost 19 million new jobs and nearly doubled the average family's income.

When the war began, American defense factories wanted to hire white men. With so many men in the military, there simply were not enough white men to fill all of the jobs. Under pressure to produce, employers began to recruit women and minorities.

Women in the Defense Plants During the Depression, many people believed married women should not work outside the home, especially if it meant taking jobs away from men trying to support their families. Most women who did work were young, single, and employed in traditional female jobs. The wartime labor shortage, however, forced factories to recruit married women to do industrial jobs that traditionally had been reserved for men.

Although the government hired nearly 4 million women for mostly clerical jobs, it was the women in the factories who captured the public's imagination. The great symbol of the campaign to hire women was **"Rosie the Riveter,"** a character from a popular song by the Four Vagabonds. The lyrics told of Rosie, who worked in a factory while her boyfriend served in the marines. Images of Rosie appeared on posters, in newspapers, and in magazines. Eventually 2.5 million women went to work in shipyards, aircraft factories, and other manufacturing plants. For many older middle-class women like Inez Sauer, working in a factory changed their perspective:

❝I learned that just because you're a woman and have never worked is no reason you can't learn. The job really broadened me. . . . I had always been in a shell; I'd always been protected. But at Boeing I found a freedom and an independence I had never known. After the war I could never go back to playing bridge again, being a clubwoman. . . . when I knew there were things you could use your mind for. The war changed my life completely.❞

—quoted in *Eyewitness to World War II*

Although most women left the factories after the war, their success permanently changed American attitudes about women in the workplace.

African Americans Demand War Work Although factories were hiring women, they resisted hiring African Americans. Frustrated by the situation, **A. Philip Randolph,** the head of the Brotherhood of Sleeping Car Porters—a major union for African American railroad workers—decided to take action.

He informed President Roosevelt that he was organizing "from ten to fifty thousand [African Americans] to march on Washington in the interest of securing jobs . . . in national defense and . . . integration into the military and naval forces."

In response, Roosevelt issued Executive Order 8802, on June 25, 1941. The order declared, "there shall be no discrimination in the employment of workers in defense industries or government because of race, creed, color or national origin." To enforce the order, the president created the Fair Employment Practices Commission—the first civil rights agency established by the federal government since the Reconstruction era.

Mexicans Become Farmworkers The wartime economy needed workers in many different areas. To help farmers in the Southwest overcome the labor shortage, the government introduced the **Bracero Program** in 1942. *Bracero* is Spanish for worker. The federal government arranged for Mexican farmworkers to help in the harvest. Over 200,000 Mexicans came to the United States to help harvest

Profiles IN HISTORY

The Navajo Code Talkers
1942–1945

When American marines stormed an enemy beach, they used radios to communicate. Using radios, however, meant that the Japanese could intercept and translate the messages. In the midst of the battle, however, there was no time to use a code machine. Acting upon the suggestion of Philip Johnston, an engineer who had lived on a Navajo reservation as a child, the marines recruited Navajos to serve as "code talkers."

The Navajo language was a "hidden language"—it had no written alphabet and was known only to the Navajo and a few missionaries and anthropologists. The Navajo recruits developed a code using words from their own language to represent military terms. For example, the Navajo word *jay-sho,* or "buzzard," was code for bomber; *lotso,* or "whale," meant battleship; and *na-ma-si,* or "potatoes," stood for grenades.

Code talkers proved invaluable in combat. They could relay a message in

minutes that would have taken a code machine operator hours to encipher and transmit. At the battle of Iwo Jima, code talkers transmitted more than 800 messages during the first 48 hours as the marines struggled to get ashore under intense bombardment.

Over 400 Navajo served in the marine corps as code talkers. Sworn to secrecy, their mission was not revealed until many years after the war. In 2001 Congress awarded the code talkers the Congressional Gold Medal to recognize their unique contribution to the war effort.

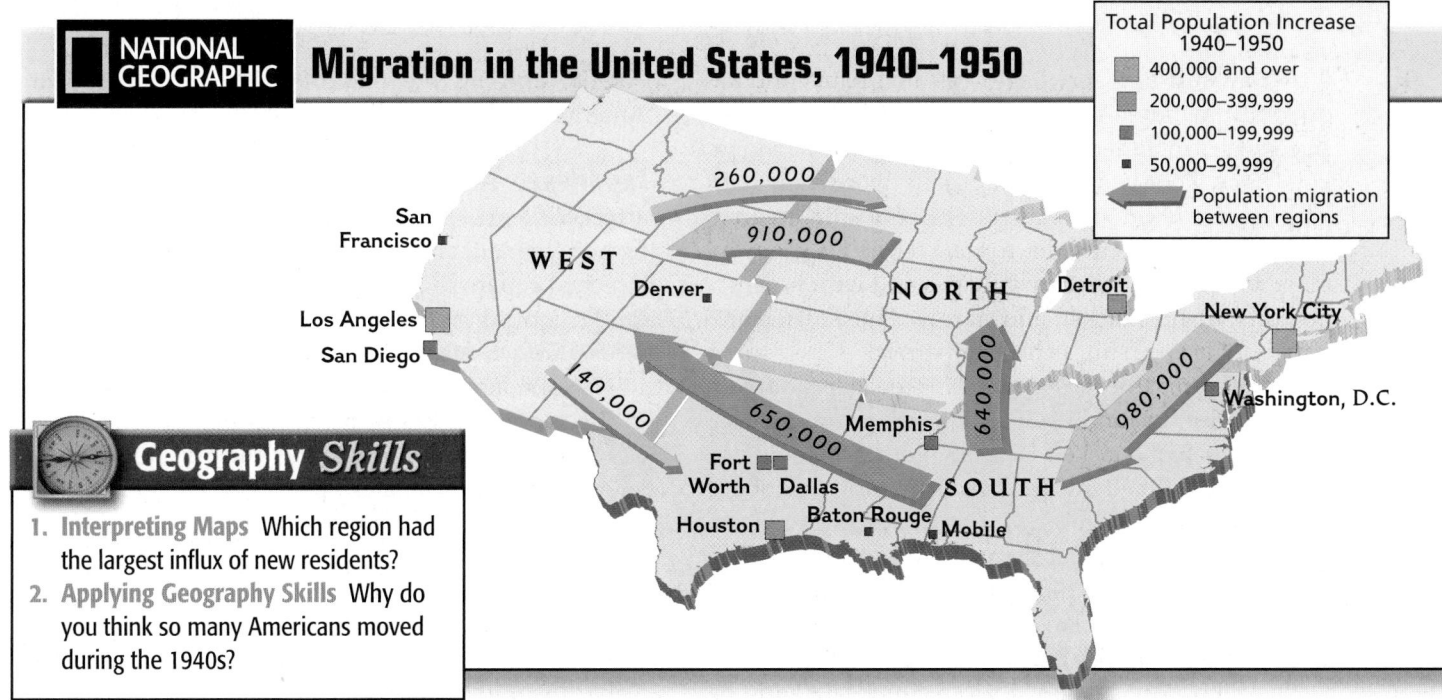

NATIONAL GEOGRAPHIC   **Migration in the United States, 1940–1950**

Total Population Increase
1940–1950
- 400,000 and over
- 200,000–399,999
- 100,000–199,999
- 50,000–99,999

← Population migration between regions

260,000
910,000
140,000
650,000
640,000
980,000

San Francisco
Los Angeles
San Diego
Denver
Memphis
Fort Worth
Dallas
Houston
Baton Rouge
Mobile
Detroit
New York City
Washington, D.C.

WEST
NORTH
SOUTH

Geography Skills

1. **Interpreting Maps** Which region had the largest influx of new residents?
2. **Applying Geography Skills** Why do you think so many Americans moved during the 1940s?

fruit and vegetables in the Southwest. Many also helped to build and maintain railroads. The Bracero Program continued until 1964. Migrant farmworkers became an important part of the Southwest's agricultural system.

Reading Check **Describing** How did mobilizing the economy help end the Depression?

A Nation on the Move

The wartime economy created millions of new jobs, but the Americans who wanted these jobs did not always live nearby. To get to the jobs, 15 million Americans moved during the war. Although the assembly plants of the Midwest and the shipyards of the Northeast attracted many workers, most Americans headed west and south in search of jobs.

Taken together, the growth of southern California and the expansion of cities in the Deep South created a new industrial region—the Sunbelt. For the first time since the Industrial Revolution began in the United States, the South and West led the way in manufacturing and urbanization.

The Housing Crisis Perhaps the most difficult task facing cities with war industries was deciding where to put the thousands of new workers. Many people had to live in tents and tiny trailers. To help solve the housing crisis, the federal government allocated over $1.2 billion to build public housing, schools, and community centers during the war.

Although prefabricated government housing had tiny rooms, thin walls, poor heating, and

almost no privacy, it was better than no housing at all. Nearly two million people lived in government-built housing during the war.

Racism Explodes Into Violence African Americans began to leave the South in great numbers during World War I, but this **"Great Migration,"** as historians refer to it, slowed during the Depression. When jobs in war factories opened up for African Americans during World War II, the Great Migration resumed. When African Americans arrived in the crowded cities of the North and West, however, they were often met with suspicion and intolerance. Sometimes these attitudes led to violence.

The worst racial violence of the war erupted in Detroit on Sunday, June 20, 1943. The weather that day was sweltering. To cool off, nearly 100,000 people crowded into Belle Isle, a park on the Detroit River. Fights erupted between gangs of white and African American teenage girls. These fights triggered others, and a full-scale riot erupted across the city. By the time the violence ended, 25 African Americans and 9 whites had been killed. Despite the appalling violence in Detroit, African American leaders remained committed to their Double V campaign.

The Zoot Suit Riots Wartime prejudice erupted elsewhere as well. In southern California, racial tensions became entangled with juvenile delinquency. Across the nation, crimes committed by young people rose dramatically. In Los Angeles, racism against Mexican Americans and the fear of juvenile crime became linked because of the "zoot suit."

A **zoot suit** had very baggy, pleated pants and an overstuffed, knee-length jacket with wide lapels. Accessories included a wide-brimmed hat and a long key chain. Zoot-suit wearers usually wore their hair long, gathered into a ducktail. The zoot suit angered many Americans. In order to save fabric for the war, most men wore a **"victory suit"**—a suit with no vest, no cuffs, a short jacket, and narrow lapels. By comparison, the zoot suit seemed unpatriotic.

In California, Mexican American teenagers adopted the zoot suit. In June 1943, after hearing rumors that zoot suiters had attacked several sailors, 2,500 soldiers and sailors stormed into Mexican American neighborhoods in Los Angeles. They attacked Mexican American teenagers, cut their hair, and tore off their zoot suits. The police did not intervene, and the violence continued for several days. The city of Los Angeles responded by banning the zoot suit.

Racial hostility against Mexican Americans did not deter them from joining the war effort. Approximately 500,000 Hispanic Americans served in the armed forces during the war. Most—about 400,000—were Mexican American. Another 65,000 were from Puerto Rico. They fought in Europe, North Africa, and the Pacific, and by the end of the war, 17 Mexican Americans had received the Medal of Honor.

Japanese American Relocation When Japan attacked Pearl Harbor, many West Coast Americans turned their anger against Japanese Americans. Mobs attacked Japanese American businesses and homes. Banks would not cash their checks, and grocers refused to sell them food.

Newspapers printed rumors about Japanese spies in the Japanese American community. Members of Congress, mayors, and many business and labor leaders demanded that all people of Japanese ancestry be removed from the West Coast. They did not believe that Japanese Americans would remain loyal to the United States in the face of war with Japan.

On February 19, 1942, President Roosevelt gave in to pressure and signed an order allowing the War Department to declare any part of the United States to be a military zone and to remove anybody they wanted from that zone. Secretary of War Henry Stimson declared most of the West Coast a military zone and ordered all people of Japanese ancestry to evacuate to 10 internment camps.

NATIONAL GEOGRAPHIC
MOMENT in HISTORY

BEHIND BARBED WIRE

As wartime hysteria mounted, the U.S. government rounded up 120,000 people of Japanese ancestry—77,000 of whom were American citizens—and forced them into internment camps in early 1942. Given just days to sell their homes, businesses, and personal property, whole families were marched under military guard to rail depots, then sent to remote, inhospitable sites where they lived in cramped barracks surrounded by barbed wire and watchtowers. By 1945, with the tide of war turned, most had been released, but they did not get an official apology or financial compensation until 1988.

Not all Japanese Americans accepted the relocation without protest. Fred Korematsu argued that his rights had been violated and took his case to the Supreme Court. In December 1944, in *Korematsu* v. *the United States*, the Supreme Court ruled that the relocation was constitutional because it was based not on race, but on "military urgency." Shortly afterward, the Court did rule in *Ex Parte Endo* that loyal American citizens could not be held against their will. In early 1945, therefore, the government began to release the Japanese Americans from the camps. 📖 *(See page 1081 for more information on* Korematsu v. the United States.)

Despite the fears and rumors, no Japanese American was ever tried for espionage or sabotage. Japanese Americans served as translators for the army during the war in the Pacific. The all-Japanese 100th Battalion, later integrated into the **442nd Regimental Combat Team,** was the most highly decorated unit in World War II.

After the war, the **Japanese American Citizens League** (JACL) tried to help Japanese Americans who had lost property during the relocation. In 1988 President Reagan apologized to Japanese Americans on behalf of the U.S. government and signed legislation granting $20,000 to each surviving Japanese American who had been interned.

✓ **Reading Check** **Comparing** Why did racism lead to violence in Detroit and Los Angeles in 1943?

Daily Life in Wartime America

Housing problems and racial tensions were serious difficulties during the war, but mobilization strained society in many other ways as well. Prices rose, materials were in short supply, and the question of how to pay for it all loomed ominously over the entire war effort.

ECONOMICS

Wage and Price Controls As the economy mobilized, the president worried about inflation. Both wages and prices began to rise quickly during the war because of the high demand for workers and raw materials. To stabilize both wages and prices, Roosevelt created the **Office of Price Administration** (OPA) and the Office of Economic Stabilization (OES). The OES regulated wages and the price of farm products. The OPA regulated all other prices. Despite some problems with labor unions, the OPA and OES were able to keep inflation under control.

Picturing **History**

Rationing Products War rationing affected everyone. Women painted seams on their legs to make it appear they were wearing stockings, because silk was needed to make parachutes instead of stockings. *Why was rationing so vital to the war effort?*

While the OPA and OES worked to control inflation, the War Labor Board (WLB) tried to prevent strikes that might endanger the war effort. In support, most American unions issued a "no strike pledge," and instead of striking, asked the WLB to serve as a mediator in wage disputes. By the end of the war, the WLB had helped to settle over 17,000 disputes involving more than 12 million workers.

Blue Points, Red Points The demand for raw materials and supplies created shortages. The OPA began rationing, or limiting the availability of, many products to make sure enough were available for military use. Meat and sugar were rationed to provide enough for the army. To save gasoline and rubber, gasoline was rationed, driving was restricted, and the speed limit was set at 35 miles per hour.

Every month each household would pick up a book of ration coupons. Blue coupons, called blue points, controlled processed foods. Red coupons, or red points, controlled meats, fats, and oils. Other coupons controlled items such as coffee and sugar. When people bought food, they also had to give enough coupon points to cover their purchases.

Illumination for the Shooting Gallery

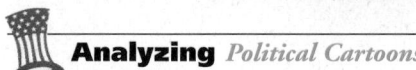

Analyzing *Political Cartoons*

Turning Off the Lights Early in the war, lights from eastern cities silhouetted ships along the east coast, making them easy targets for German submarines. Americans were asked to turn out lights or put up dark curtains. *What point is the cartoon making to Americans?*

Victory Gardens and Scrap Drives Americans also planted gardens to produce more food for the war effort. Any area of land might become a garden—backyards, schoolyards, city parks, and empty lots. The government encouraged victory gardens by praising them in film reels, pamphlets, and official statements.

Certain raw materials were so vital to the war effort that the government organized scrap drives. Americans collected spare rubber, tin, aluminum, and steel. They donated pots, tires, tin cans, car bumpers, broken radiators, and rusting bicycles. Oils and fats were so important to the production of explosives that the WPB set up fat-collecting stations. Americans would exchange bacon grease and meat drippings for extra ration coupons. The scrap drives were very successful and one more reason for the success of American industry during the war.

Paying for the War The United States had to pay for all of the equipment and supplies it needed. The federal government spent more than $300 billion during World War II—more money than it had spent from Washington's administration to the end of Franklin Roosevelt's second term.

To raise money, the government raised taxes. Because most Americans opposed large tax increases, Congress refused to raise taxes as high as Roosevelt requested. As a result, the extra taxes collected covered only 45 percent of the cost of the war.

To raise the rest of the money, the government issued war bonds. When Americans bought bonds, they were loaning money to the government. In exchange for the money, the government promised that the bonds could be cashed in at some future date for the purchase price plus interest. The most common bonds were **E bonds,** which sold for $18.75 and could be redeemed for $25.00 after 10 years. Individual Americans bought nearly $50 billion worth of war bonds. Banks, insurance companies, and other financial institutions bought the rest—over $100 billion worth of bonds.

"V" for Victory Despite the hardships, the overwhelming majority of Americans believed the war had to be fought. Although the war brought many changes to the United States, most Americans remained united behind one goal—winning the war.

✓ **Reading Check** **Evaluating** How did rationing affect daily life in the United States? How did it affect the economy?

SECTION 3 ASSESSMENT

Checking for Understanding

1. **Define:** Sunbelt, rationing, victory garden.
2. **Identify:** Rosie the Riveter, A. Philip Randolph, zoot suit, E bond.
3. **Explain** how the federal government expanded during the war.

Reviewing Themes

4. **Civic Rights and Responsibilities** What changes did American citizens and industry have to make to adapt to the war?

Critical Thinking

5. **Evaluating** If you had been a government official during the war, how would you have proposed paying for the war?
6. **Categorizing** Use a graphic organizer like the one below to list the results of increased racial tensions during the war.

Analyzing Visuals

7. **Examining Maps** Study the map on page 751. Which cities had populations over 400,000?
8. **Analyzing Photographs** Study the photograph on page 752. Why were Japanese Americans interned?

Writing About History

9. **Persuasive Writing** Write a newspaper editorial urging fellow citizens to conserve resources so that these resources can be diverted to the war effort.

Guide to Reading

Main Idea
The Allies slowly pushed back the German and Japanese forces in 1943 and 1944.

Key Terms and Names
Casablanca Conference, Operation Overlord, D-Day, Omar Bradley, amphtrac, Guadalcanal, kamikaze

Reading Strategy
Organizing As you read about the major battles of 1943 and 1944, complete a graphic organizer similar to the one below by filling in the names of the battles fought. Indicate whether each battle was an Allied or an Axis victory.

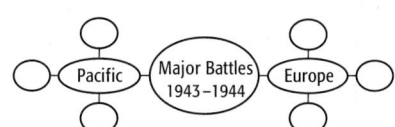

Reading Objectives
- **Describe** the goals of the two major offensives the Allies launched in Europe in 1943.
- **Explain** the American strategy for pushing the Japanese back in the Pacific.

Section Theme
Geography and History The United States fought the war by landing troops in Italy and France and island-hopping across the Pacific toward Japan.

Preview of Events

♦1943		♦1944		♦1945
January 1943 Casablanca Conference	**July 1943** The Allies invade Italy	**November 1943** Roosevelt, Churchill, and Stalin meet at Tehran	**June 6, 1944** D-Day invasion begins	**October 20, 1944** MacArthur returns to the Philippines

★ An American Story ★

On the morning of June 6, 1944, Lieutenant John Bentz Carroll of the 16th Infantry Regiment scrambled down a net ladder from his troop ship to a small landing craft tossing in the waves 30 feet (9 m) below. The invasion of France had begun. Carroll's platoon would be among the first Americans to land in Normandy. Their objective was a beach, code-named "Omaha":

❝Two hundred yards out, we took a direct hit. . . . [A machine gun] was shooting a rat-tat-tat on the front of the boat. Somehow or other, the ramp door opened up . . . and the men in front were being struck by machine gun fire. Everyone started to jump off into the water. They were being hit as they jumped, the machine gun fire was so heavy. . . . The tide was moving us so rapidly. . . . We would grab out on some of those underwater obstructions and mines built on telephone poles and girders, and hang on. We'd take cover, then make a dash through the surf to the next one, fifty feet beyond. The men would line up behind those poles. They'd say, 'You go—you go—you go,' and then it got so bad everyone just had to go anyway, because the waves were hitting with such intensity on these things.❞

—quoted in *D-Day: Piercing the Atlantic Wall*

Striking Back at the Third Reich

As Lieutenant Carroll's experience shows, storming a beach under enemy control can be a terrifying ordeal. There is no cover on a beach, no place to hide, and no way to turn back. Launching an invasion from the sea is very risky. Unfortunately, the Allies had no choice. If they were going to win the war, they had to land their troops in Europe and on islands in the Pacific.

The first large Allied invasion of the war—the attack on North Africa in November 1942—had shown that the Allies could mount a large-scale invasion from the sea. The success of the landings convinced Roosevelt that it was again time to meet with Churchill to plan the next stage of the war. In January 1943, the president headed to Casablanca, Morocco, to meet the prime minister.

At the **Casablanca Conference,** Roosevelt and Churchill agreed to step up the bombing of Germany. The goal of this new campaign was "the progressive destruction of the German military, industrial, and economic system, and the undermining of the morale of the German people." The Allies also agreed to attack the Axis on the island of Sicily. Churchill called Italy the "soft underbelly" of Europe and was convinced that the Italians would quit the war if the Allies invaded their homeland.

Strategic Bombing The Allies had been bombing Germany even before the Casablanca Conference. Britain's Royal Air Force had dropped an average of 2,300 tons (2,093 t) of explosives on Germany every month for over three years. The United States Eighth Army Air Force had joined the campaign in the summer of 1942, and they had dropped an additional 1,500 tons (1,365 t) of bombs by the end of the year.

These numbers were tiny, however, compared to the massive new campaign. Between January 1943 and May 1945, the Royal Air Force and the United States Eighth Army Air Force dropped approximately 53,000 tons (48,230 t) of explosives on Germany every month.

Picturing **History**

Softening the Gustav Line Infantrymen fire an 81-millimeter mortar to soften the German Gustav Line near the Rapido River. Why do you think the Allies decided to attack first in Italy rather than in France?

The bombing campaign did not destroy Germany's economy or undermine German morale, but it did cause a severe oil shortage and wrecked the railroad system. It also destroyed so many aircraft factories that Germany's air force could not replace its combat losses. By the time the Allies landed in France, they had total control of the air, ensuring that their troops would not be bombed.

Striking at the Soft Underbelly As the bombing campaign against Germany intensified, the plan for the invasion of Sicily moved ahead as well. General Dwight D. Eisenhower was placed in overall command of the invasion. General Patton and the British General Bernard Montgomery were put in charge of the actual forces on the ground. The invasion began before dawn on July 10, 1943. Despite bad weather, the Allied troops made it ashore with few casualties. A new vehicle, the **DUKW**—an amphibious truck—proved very effective in bringing supplies and artillery to the soldiers on the beach.

Eight days after the troops came ashore, American tanks led by General Patton smashed through enemy lines and captured the western half of the island. After capturing western Sicily, Patton's troops headed east, staging a series of daring end-runs around the German positions, while the British, under Montgomery, attacked from the south. By August 18, the Germans had evacuated the island.

The attack on Sicily created a crisis within the Italian government. The king of Italy, Victor Emmanuel, and a group of Italian generals decided that it was time to get rid of Mussolini. On July 25, 1943, the king invited the dictator to his palace. "My dear Duce," the king began, "it's no longer any good. Italy has gone to bits. The soldiers don't want to fight anymore. At this moment, you are the most hated man in Italy." The king then placed Mussolini under arrest, and the new Italian government began secretly negotiating with the Allies for Italy's surrender.

On September 8, 1943, the Italian government publicly announced Italy's surrender. The following day, American troops landed at Salerno. Although stunned by the surrender, Hitler was not about to lose Italy to the Allies. German troops went into action at once. They seized control of northern Italy, including Rome, attacked the Americans at Salerno, and put Mussolini back in power.

To stop the Allied advance, the German army took up positions near the heavily

The Big Three Stalin, Roosevelt, and Churchill meet at Tehran.

fortified town of Cassino. The terrain near Cassino was steep, barren, and rocky. Instead of attacking such difficult terrain, the Allies chose to land at Anzio, behind German lines. They hoped the maneuver would force the Germans to retreat. Instead of retreating, however, the Germans surrounded the Allied troops near Anzio.

It took the Allies five months to break through the German lines at **Cassino** and **Anzio.** Finally, in late May 1944, the Germans were forced to retreat. Less than two weeks later, the Allies captured Rome. Fighting in Italy continued, however, until May 2, 1945. The Italian campaign was one of the bloodiest in the war. It cost the Allies more than 300,000 casualties.

Roosevelt Meets Stalin at Tehran
Roosevelt wanted to meet with Stalin before the Allies launched the invasion of France. In late 1943 Stalin agreed, and he proposed that Roosevelt and Churchill meet him in Tehran, Iran.

The leaders reached several agreements. Stalin promised to launch a full-scale offensive against the Germans when the Allies invaded France in 1944. Roosevelt and Stalin then agreed to break up Germany after the war so that it would never again threaten world peace. Stalin also promised that once Germany was beaten, the Soviet Union would help the United States defeat Japan. He also accepted Roosevelt's proposal to create an international organization to help keep the peace after the war.

Reading Check **Explaining** What two major decisions did the Allies make at Casablanca?

Landing in France

After the conference in Tehran, Roosevelt headed to Cairo, Egypt, where he and Churchill continued planning the invasion of France. One major decision still had to be made. The president had to choose the commander for **Operation Overlord**—the code name for the planned invasion. Roosevelt wanted to appoint General George C. Marshall, Chief of Staff for the United States Army, but he depended on Marshall for military advice and did not want to send him to Europe. Instead, the president selected General Eisenhower to command the invasion.

Planning Operation Overlord
Knowing that the Allies would eventually invade France, Hitler had fortified the coast. Although these defenses were formidable, the Allies did have one advantage—the element of surprise. The Germans did not know when or where the Allies would land. They believed that the Allies would land in Pas-de-Calais—the area of France closest to Britain. To convince the Germans they were right, the Allies placed inflated rubber tanks, empty tents, and dummy landing craft along the coast across from Calais. To German spy planes, the decoys looked real, and they succeeded in fooling the Germans. The real target was not Pas-de-Calais, but Normandy.

By the spring of 1944, everything was ready. Over 1.5 million American soldiers, 12,000 airplanes, and more than 5 million tons (4.6 million t) of equipment had been sent to England. Only one thing was left to do—pick the date and give the command to go. The invasion had to begin at night to hide the ships crossing the English Channel. The ships had to arrive at low tide so that they could see the beach obstacles. The low tide had to come at dawn so that gunners bombarding the coast could see their targets. Before the main landing on the beaches, paratroopers would be dropped behind enemy lines. They required a moonlit night in order to see where to land. Perhaps most important of all, the weather had to be good. A storm would ground the airplanes, and high waves would swamp the landing craft.

Given all these conditions, there were only a few days each month when the invasion could begin. The first opportunity would last from June 5 to 7, 1944. Eisenhower's planning staff referred to the day any operation began by the letter D. The date for the invasion, therefore, came to be known as **D-Day.** Heavy cloud cover, strong winds, and high waves made it impossible to land on June 5. A day later the weather briefly improved. The Channel was still rough, but the landing ships and aircraft could operate. It was a difficult decision. Eisenhower's advisers were split on what to do. After looking at weather forecasts one last time, shortly after midnight on June 6, 1944, Eisenhower gave the final order: "OK, we'll go."

The Longest Day Nearly 7,000 ships carrying more than 100,000 soldiers set sail for the coast of Normandy on June 6, 1944. At the same time, 23,000 paratroopers were dropped inland, east and west of the beaches. Allied fighter-bombers raced up and down the coast, hitting bridges, bunkers, and radar sites. As dawn broke, the warships in the Allied fleet let loose with a tremendous barrage of fire. Thousands of shells rained down on the beaches, code-named "Utah," "Omaha," "Gold," "Sword," and "Juno."

The American landing at Utah Beach went very well. The German defenses were weak, and in less than three hours American troops had captured the beach and moved inland, suffering less than 200 casualties in the process. On the eastern flank, the British and Canadian landings also went well. By the end of the day, British and Canadian forces were several miles inland.

Omaha Beach, however, was a different story. Under intense German fire, the American assault almost disintegrated. As General **Omar Bradley,** the commander of the American forces landing at Omaha

What If...

Operation Overlord Had Failed?

In what some historians believe was the most important weather prediction in military history, Group Captain James Stagg, chief meteorologist for the Royal Air Force, predicted gradual clearing for Normandy, France, on June 6, 1944. The prediction was critical for General Dwight D. Eisenhower, Supreme Commander of the Allied Expeditionary Forces. He had already delayed Operation Overlord once. The invasion forces of Operation Overlord were assembled and ready to go at a moment's notice. Everything depended upon a break in the bad weather so that the assault would take the Germans by surprise. Eisenhower trusted the weather prediction and believed in the battle

plan. The day before the invasion, however, he wrote the following note on a small piece of paper—a message he would deliver in the event the invasion failed. He mistakenly jotted "July 5" on the bottom and stuck the note in his wallet.

❝Our landings in the Cherbourg-Havre area have failed to gain a satisfactory foothold and I have withdrawn the troops. My decision to attack at this time and place was based upon the best information available. The troops, the air and the Navy did all that Bravery and devotion to duty could do. If any blame or fault attaches to the attempt it is mine alone.❞

and Utah, grimly watched the carnage, he began making plans to evacuate Omaha. Slowly, however, the American troops began to knock out the German defenses. More landing craft arrived, ramming their way through the obstacles to get to the beach. Nearly 2,500 Americans were either killed or wounded on Omaha, but by early afternoon Bradley received this message: "Troops formerly pinned down on beaches . . . [are] advancing up heights behind beaches." By the end of the day, nearly 35,000 American troops had landed at Omaha, and another 23,000 had landed at Utah. Over 75,000 British and Canadian troops were on shore as well. The invasion had succeeded.

✓ **Reading Check** **Summarizing** What conditions had to be met before Eisenhower could order D-Day to begin?

Driving the Japanese Back

While the buildup for the invasion of France was taking place in Britain, American military leaders were also developing a strategy to defeat Japan. The American plan called for a two-pronged attack. The Pacific Fleet, commanded by Admiral Nimitz, would

What might have happened?

1. What might have happened if the weather had not changed and the troops had landed amidst fog and rain?
2. What if the invasion had been delayed and the element of surprise lost?

advance through the central Pacific by hopping from one island to the next, closer and closer to Japan. Meanwhile, General MacArthur's troops would advance through the Solomon Islands, capture the north coast of New Guinea, and then launch an invasion to retake the Philippines.

GEOGRAPHY

Island-Hopping in the Pacific By the fall of 1943, the navy was ready to launch its island-hopping campaign, but the geography of the central Pacific posed a problem. Many of the islands were coral reef atolls. The water over the coral reef was not always deep enough to allow landing craft to get to the shore. If the landing craft ran aground on the reef, the troops would have to wade to the beach. As some 5,000 United States Marines learned at Tarawa Atoll, wading ashore could cause very high casualties.

Tarawa, part of the Gilbert Islands, was the Navy's first objective in the Pacific. When the landing craft hit the reef, at least 20 ships ran aground. The marines had to plunge into shoulder-high water and wade several hundred yards to the beach. Raked by Japanese fire, only one marine in three made it ashore. Once the marines reached the beach the battle was still far from over. As reporter Robert Sherrod wrote, the marines faced savage hand-to-hand fighting:

> ❝A Marine jumped over the seawall and began throwing blocks of fused TNT into a coconut-log pillbox. . . . Two more Marines scaled the seawall, one of them carrying a twin-cylindered tank strapped to their shoulders, the other holding the nozzle of the flame thrower. As another charge of TNT boomed inside the pillbox, causing smoke and dust to billow out, a khaki-clad figure ran out the side entrance. The flame thrower, waiting for him, caught him in its withering stream of intense fire. As soon as it touched him, the [Japanese soldier] flared up like a piece of celluloid. He was dead instantly . . . charred almost to nothingness.❞

—from *Tarawa: The Story of a Battle*

Over 1,000 marines died on Tarawa. Photos of bodies lying crumpled next to burning landing craft shocked Americans back home. Many people began to wonder how many lives it would cost to defeat Japan.

Although many troops died wading ashore, one vehicle had been able to cross the reef and deliver its troops onto the beaches. The vehicle was the LVT—a boat with tank tracks. Nicknamed the "Alligator," the

NATIONAL GEOGRAPHIC — Island-Hopping in the Pacific, 1942–1945

(Map labels:)

SOVIET UNION
Lake Baikal
MONGOLIA
MANCHURIA
Sea of Okhotsk
Bering Sea
Kiska
Attu May 11–27, 1943
Aleutian Islands
Kuril Islands
Beijing
Sea of Japan
CHINA
Hiroshima Aug. 6, 1945
Nagasaki Aug. 9, 1945
Nanjing
Shanghai
Chongqing
Tokyo
Japan surrenders on battleship *Missouri* Sept. 2, 1945
Okinawa Apr. 1–June 22, 1945
Okinawa
Iwo Jima Feb. 19–March 26, 1945
Midway June 4–7, 1942
PACIFIC OCEAN
Hawaiian Islands
TROPIC OF CANCER
45°N
30°N
INDIA
Lashio
BURMA
Hong Kong U.K.
Manila Luzon March 4, 1945
Philippine Sea
Saipan June 15–July 9, 1944
Guam July 21–Aug. 10, 1944
Wake Is. U.S.
Pearl Harbor
HAWAII U.S.
15°N
SIAM (THAILAND)
Bangkok
South China Sea
PHILIPPINES
Leyte Gulf Oct 23–26, 1944
Guam U.S.
Marshall Islands Feb. 1944
Nimitz Nov. 1943
FRENCH INDOCHINA
Mindanao
Palau Is.
MacArthur
Halsey
Tarawa Nov. 20–23, 1943
EQUATOR
Nauru U.K.
Gilbert Islands
0°
Sumatra
SINGAPORE U.K.
Borneo
Halsey
Batavia
Java
NEW GUINEA
Solomon Is.
Guadalcanal Aug. 7, 1942–Feb. 9, 1943
Ellice Islands
INDIAN OCEAN
Darwin
Coral Sea May 4–8, 1942
Coral Sea
New Hebrides
150°E   165°E   180°

Legend:
- Japanese Empire and conquests
- Farthest extent of Japan's conquests, July 1942
- Allied forces
- Allied victory
- Atomic bombing

0   1,500 miles
0   1,500 kilometers
Miller Cylindrical projection

Geography Skills

1. **Interpreting Maps** Where did the first major battle between the American and Japanese forces in the South Pacific take place?
2. **Applying Geography Skills** Why do you think Americans adopted the policy of island-hopping?

amphibious tractor, or amphtrac, had been invented in the late 1930s to rescue people in Florida swamps. It had never been used in combat, and not until 1941 did the navy decide to buy 200 of them. Had more been available at Tarawa, the number of American casualties probably would have been much lower.

The assault on the next major objective—Kwajalein Atoll in the Marshall Islands—went much more smoothly. This time all of the troops went ashore in amphtracs. Although the Japanese resisted fiercely, the marines captured Kwajalein and nearby Eniwetok with far fewer casualties.

After the Marshall Islands, the navy targeted the Mariana Islands. American military planners wanted to use the Marianas as a base for a new heavy bomber, the B-29 Superfortress. The B-29 could fly farther than any other plane in the world. From airfields in the Marianas, B-29s could bomb Japan. Admiral Nimitz decided to invade three of the Mariana Islands: Saipan, Tinian, and Guam. Despite strong Japanese resistance, American troops captured all three by August 1944. A few months later, B-29 bombers began bombing Japan.

MacArthur Returns to the Philippines As the forces under Admiral Nimitz hopped across the central Pacific, General MacArthur's troops began their own campaign in the southwest Pacific. The campaign began with the invasion of **Guadalcanal** in August 1942. It continued until early 1944, when MacArthur's troops finally captured enough islands to surround Rabaul, the main Japanese base in the region. In response the Japanese withdrew their ships and aircraft from the base, although they left 100,000 troops behind to hold the island.

Worried that the navy's advance across the central Pacific was leaving him behind, MacArthur ordered his forces to leap nearly 600 miles (966 km) past Rabaul to capture the Japanese base at Hollandia on the north coast of New Guinea. Shortly after securing New Guinea, MacArthur's troops seized the island of Morotai—the last stop before the Philippines.

To take back the Philippines, the United States assembled an enormous invasion force. In October 1944, more than 700 ships carrying over 160,000 troops sailed for Leyte Gulf in the Philippines. On October 20, the troops began to land on Leyte, an island on the eastern side of the Philippines. A few hours after the invasion began, MacArthur headed to the beach. Upon reaching the shore, he strode to a radio and spoke into the microphone: "People of the Philippines, I have returned. By the grace of Almighty God, our forces stand again on Philippine soil."

To stop the American invasion, the Japanese sent four aircraft carriers toward the Philippines from the north and secretly dispatched another fleet to the west. Believing the Japanese carriers were leading the main attack, most of the American carriers protecting the invasion left Leyte Gulf and headed north to stop them. Seizing their chance, the Japanese warships to the west raced through the Philippine Islands into Leyte Gulf and ambushed the remaining American ships.

The Battle of Leyte Gulf was the largest naval battle in history. It was also the first time that the Japanese used kamikaze attacks. *Kamikaze* means "divine wind" in Japanese. It refers to the great storm that destroyed the Mongol fleet during its invasion of Japan in the thirteenth century. Kamikaze pilots would deliberately crash their planes into American ships, killing themselves but also inflicting severe damage. Luckily for the Americans, just as their situation was becoming

A Triumphant Return In October 1944, Douglas MacArthur fulfilled his promise and returned to the Philippines.

desperate, the Japanese commander, believing more American ships were on the way, ordered a retreat.

Although the Japanese fleet had retreated, the campaign to recapture the Philippines from the Japanese was long and grueling. Over 80,000 Japanese were killed; less than 1,000 surrendered. MacArthur's troops did not capture Manila until March 1945. The battle left the city in ruins and over 100,000 Filipino civilians dead. The remaining Japanese retreated into the rugged terrain north of Manila, and they were still fighting when word came in August 1945 that Japan had surrendered.

Reading Check **Describing** What strategy did the United States Navy use to advance across the Pacific?

SECTION 4 ASSESSMENT

Checking for Understanding

1. **Define:** amphtrac, kamikaze.
2. **Identify:** Casablanca Conference, Operation Overlord, D-Day, Omar Bradley, Guadalcanal.
3. **Explain** why D-Day's success was so vital to an Allied victory.

Reviewing Themes

4. **Geography and History** How did the geography of the Pacific affect American strategy?

Critical Thinking

5. **Analyzing** What made the invasion of Normandy so important?
6. **Organizing** Use a graphic organizer to explain the significance of each leader listed below.

Leader	Significance
Dwight Eisenhower	
George Patton	
George Marshall	
Omar Bradley	
Douglas MacArthur	

Analyzing Visuals

7. **Examining Photographs** Study the photograph on this page. What effect do you think MacArthur's return had on Philippine morale?

Writing About History

8. **Expository Writing** Using library or Internet resources, find more information on one of the battles discussed in this section. Use the information to write a report detailing the importance of the battle. Share your report with the class.

to BAYEUX

Vaucelles

Cottun

916th

18th

Blay

Mandeville

916th

18th

Trevieres

Flooded plain

Line planned for first-day advance by American forces

MIDNIGHT SECOND DAY

26th

Mosles

18th

115th

Enemy pulling back from this area, midnight, June 8, 1944

726th

MT. CAUVIN

26th

26th

26th

Bellefontaine

Surrain

18th

Ecrammeville

16th

Formigny

18th

Longueville

115th

MT. CAVALIER

MIDNIGHT D-DAY

Extended arrows represent advances on June 8, 1944

Le Grand Hameau

18th

16th

Deux Jumeaux

Montigny

Colleville

16th

18th

18th

26th

Huppain

16th

16th

Port-en-Bessin

26th

Ravine

115th

115th

St. Laurent

116th

Louvieres

Ravine

Ravine

116th

Ravine

Englesqueville

Rocky shore

Ravine

16th

26th

16th

115th

116th

Vierville

Rn.

18th

175th

McCook

16th

116th

Rn.

D E S T R O Y E R   F I R E   S U P P O R T

sunk

G

F

116th

Rn.

Doyle

Carmick

Barton

F I R S T   W A V E   6.30am

Pointe de la Percee
(Pointe de la Percee to Port-en-Bessin 7.75 miles)

Thompson

L

J

FOX GREEN

E

E

F

EASY RED

A

F I R E   S U P P O R T

L I N E   O F   D E P A R T U R E

EASY GREEN

E

DOG RED

F

Frankford

Emmons

Arkansas

E

DOG WHITE

G

DOG GREEN

A

Rn.

Montcalm

Georges Leygues

B O A T   L A N E

Beach landing subsectors

F I R E   S U P P O R T

Glasgow

Texas

Second wave landing craft

Harding

S

E

W

N

American
British
Canadian

UNITED KINGDOM

London

Dover

Strait of Dover

Southampton

Portsmouth

Shoreham

Calais

Portland

Dartmouth

OMAHA

GOLD

JUNO

SWORD

N

UTAH

Dieppe

English Channel

Cherbourg

Le Havre

Seine R.

St.-Lo

Caen

Normandy

Paris

FRANCE

0 mi   50
0 km   50

SLOW GOING

Allied planners had hoped that American forces landing at Omaha early on June 6, 1944, would advance 5 to 10 miles after 24 hours of fighting. Stiff German resistance, however, stopped the invaders cold on the beach. Progress inland was excruciatingly slow and painful. The Americans reached their first-day objective (dotted blue line on map) only after more than two days of bloody fighting. Despite terrible losses, American forces successfully carried out one of the most crucial missions of the war.

A Day for Heroes

The selection of a site for the largest amphibious landing in history was one of the biggest decisions of World War II. Allied planners needed a sheltered location with flat, firm beaches and within range of friendly fighter planes based in England.

There had to be enough roads and paths to move jeeps and trucks off the beaches and to accommodate the hundreds of thousands of American, Canadian, and British troops set to stream ashore following the invasion. An airfield and a seaport that the Allies could use were also needed. Most important was a reasonable expectation of achieving the element of surprise.

Five beaches on the northern coast of Normandy, France, met all the criteria and were chosen as invasion sites. On D-Day the attack on four beaches—Utah in the west and Gold, Juno, and Sword in the east (inset, opposite page)—went according to plan. But at Omaha Beach (map), between Utah and Gold, the bravery and determination of the U.S. 1st Infantry Division was tested in one of the fiercest battles of the war.

Surrounded at both ends by cliffs that rose wall-like from the sea, Omaha was only four miles long. It was the only sand beach in the area, however, and thus the only place for a landing. Unless the Allies were to leave a 20-mile gap between Utah and Gold, they would have to come ashore at Omaha Beach.

Troops crowd into a landing craft to head across the English Channel to Omaha Beach.

To repel the Allies at the water's edge, the Germans built a fortress atop the cliffs at Pointe du Hoc overlooking Omaha from the west. They dug trenches and guns into the 150-foot bluffs lining the beach and along five ravines leading off it (see map).

Wading into the surf, the Americans advanced toward Omaha Beach. Many men were cut down as the doors of their landing craft opened. The survivors had to cross more than 300 yards across a tidal flat strewn with man-made obstacles. Winds and a current pushed landing craft into clumps as the men moved ashore. As a result, soldiers ran onto the beach in groups and became easy targets. Of the more than 9,000 Allied casualties on D-Day, Omaha accounted for about one-third. Although many died, the Americans took control of the beach and fought their way inland. As General Omar Bradley later wrote, **"Every man who set foot on Omaha Beach that day was a hero."**

D-Day Forces

A-L	U.S. Company — 200 men
116th	U.S. Battalion — 900 men
Rn.	U.S. Rangers
916th	German infantry — forces associated with German battalion

German resistance point

German coastal defense

U.S. stronghold

Landing craft

Landing craft — sunk

Battleship

Cruiser

Transport

Hedgerows

Town

Scale varies in this perspective

to ISIGNY

916th — Osmanville

St. Germain du Pert

175th

La Cambe

Cardonville

116th

to MOISY

116th

Rn.

914th

Grandcamp

116th

Rn.

German cannon set up, later removed

Estuary

Pointe du Hoc

Satterlee

Talybont

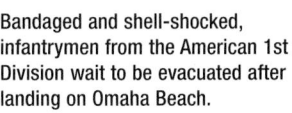

Bandaged and shell-shocked, infantrymen from the American 1st Division wait to be evacuated after landing on Omaha Beach.

LEARNING FROM GEOGRAPHY

1. Why did the Allies choose Normandy as the site of the invasion?

2. Why was the landing at Omaha Beach so much more difficult than U.S. leaders expected?

763

Guide to Reading

The Main Idea
The ferocious military campaigns of 1945 finally convinced the Axis powers to surrender and the Allies to set up organizations to prevent another global war.

Key Terms and Names
hedgerow, Battle of the Bulge, V-E Day, Harry S Truman, Curtis LeMay, napalm, Manhattan Project, V-J Day, United Nations, charter

Reading Strategy
Taking Notes As you read about the end of World War II and the organizations set up to maintain global peace, use the major headings of the section to create an outline similar to the one below.

The War Ends
I. The Third Reich Collapses
    A.
    B.
II.
    A.
    B.

Reading Objectives
• **Explain** the tactics the Allies used to invade Germany and to defeat Japan.
• **Outline** the reasons the Allies created the United Nations and held war crimes trials.

Section Theme
Groups and Institutions Allied leaders forged plans for an international organization to prevent future wars.

Preview of Events

♦1944   ♦1945   ♦1946

December 16, 1944
Battle of the Bulge begins

February 19, 1945
American troops invade Iwo Jima

April 12, 1945
Franklin Roosevelt dies; Harry Truman becomes president

May 7, 1945
Germany surrenders

August 15, 1945
V-J Day, Japan surrenders

★ An American Story ★

In 1945 Captain Luther Fletcher entered the German concentration camp at Buchenwald with a group of Germans who were being forced to see what their country had done. In his diary Fletcher described what they witnessed:

❝They saw blackened skeletons and skulls in the ovens of the crematorium. In the yard outside, they saw a heap of white human ashes and bones. . . . [The] dead were stripped of their clothing and lay naked, many stacked like cordwood waiting to be burned at the crematory. At one time 5,000 had been stacked on the vacant lot next to the crematory. . . . At headquarters of the SS troops who ran the place were lamp shades made from human skin. . . . Often, the guide said, the SS wished to make an example of someone in killing him. . . . They used what I call hay hooks, catching him under the chin and the other in the back of the neck. He hung in this manner until he died.❞

—quoted in *World War II: From the Battle Front to the Home Front*

The Third Reich Collapses

Well before the war ended, President Roosevelt and other Allied leaders were aware that the Nazis were committing atrocities. In 1943 the Allies officially declared that they would punish the Nazis for their crimes after the war. Meanwhile, Roosevelt was convinced that the best way to put an end to the concentration camps was to destroy the Nazi regime. To do that, he believed the Allies had to dedicate their resources to breaking out of Normandy, liberating France, and conquering Germany.

Although D-Day had been a success, it was only the beginning. Surrounding many fields in Normandy were hedgerows—dirt walls, several feet thick, covered in shrubbery. The hedgerows had been built to fence in cattle and crops, but they also enabled the Germans to fiercely defend their positions. The battle of the hedgerows ended on July 25, 1944, when 2,500 American bombers blew a hole in the German lines, enabling American tanks to race through the gap.

As the Allies broke out of Normandy, the French Resistance—French civilians who had secretly organized to resist the German occupation of their country—staged a rebellion in Paris. When the Allied forces liberated Paris on August 25, they found the streets filled with French citizens celebrating their victory. Three weeks later, American troops were within 20 miles (32 km) of the German border.

The Battle of the Bulge
As the Allies closed in on Germany, Hitler decided to stage one last desperate offensive. His goal was to cut off Allied supplies coming through the port of Antwerp, Belgium. The attack began just before dawn on December 16, 1944. Six inches (15 cm) of snow covered the ground, and the weather was bitterly cold. Moving rapidly, the Germans caught the American defenders by surprise. As the German troops raced west, their lines bulged outward, and the attack became known as the **Battle of the Bulge.**

Part of the German plan called for the capture of the town of Bastogne, where several important roads converged. If the Allies held Bastogne, it would greatly delay the German advance. American reinforcements raced to the town, arriving just ahead of the Germans. The Germans then surrounded the town and demanded that the Americans surrender. The American commander sent back a one-word reply: "Nuts!"

Shortly after the Germans surrounded the Americans, Eisenhower ordered General Patton to rescue them. Three days later, faster than anyone expected in the midst of a snowstorm, Patton's troops slammed into the German lines. As the weather cleared, Allied aircraft began hitting German fuel depots. On Christmas Eve, out of fuel and weakened by heavy losses, the German troops driving toward Antwerp were forced to halt. Two days later, Patton's troops broke through to Bastogne.

Although fighting continued for three weeks, the United States had won the Battle of the Bulge. On January 8, the Germans began to withdraw. They had suffered more than 100,000 casualties and lost many tanks and aircraft. They now had very little left to prevent the Allies from entering Germany.

V-E Day: The War Ends in Europe While American and British forces fought to liberate France, the Soviet Union began a massive attack on German troops in Russia. By the time the Battle of the Bulge ended, the Soviets had driven Hitler's forces out of Russia and back across Poland. By February 1945, Soviet troops had reached the Oder River. They were only 35 miles (56 km) from Berlin.

As the Soviets crossed Germany's eastern border, American forces attacked Germany's western border. By the end of February 1945, American troops had fought their way to the Rhine River, Germany's last major line of defense in the west. Then on March 7, American soldiers captured the heights above the town of Remagen. Gazing down at the town, platoon leader Emmet J. Burrows was amazed at what he saw. The Ludendorf Bridge across the Rhine was still intact. The Germans had not blown it up. The American troops raced across the bridge, driving

Picturing **History**

Soldiers and Friends The Americans and the Soviets join forces in a long-awaited meeting. The alliance is symbolized here by Lieutenants William D. Robertson of the U.S. First Army and Alexander Sylvashko of the First Ukrainian Army, in a meeting near Torgau on the Elbe River. What was the Allied strategy during the closing days of the war?

World War II in Europe and Africa, 1939–1945

Legend:
- Major Axis powers
- Greatest extent of Axis control
- Allied or Allied-controlled
- Neutral powers
- Allied advance
- Supply line
- International boundary, Jan. 1938

Supply lines from U.S.

German central armies destroyed May–July, 1944

D-Day June 6, 1944

Aug. 15, 1944

Nov. 8, 1942

July 10, 1943

Oct. 23, 1942

Supply line to Soviet Union from the Middle East

0   500 miles
0   500 kilometers
Lambert Azimuthal Equal-Area projection

back the German defenders. By the end of the day, American tanks were across the Rhine. Hearing the news, General Bradley yelled, "Hot dog . . . this will bust them wide open."

As German defenses crumbled, American troops raced east, closing to within 70 miles (113 km) of Berlin. On April 16, Soviet troops finally smashed through the German defenses on the Oder River. Five days later, they reached the outskirts of Berlin.

Deep in his Berlin bunker, Adolf Hitler knew the end was near. On April 30, 1945, he put a pistol in his mouth and pulled the trigger. His secretary, Martin Bormann, carried Hitler's body outside, doused it in gasoline, and set it on fire. Before killing himself, Hitler chose Grand Admiral Karl Doenitz to be his successor. Doenitz tried to surrender to the

Americans and British while continuing to fight the Soviets, but Eisenhower insisted on unconditional surrender. On May 7, 1945, Germany surrendered unconditionally. The next day—May 8, 1945—was proclaimed **V-E Day,** for "Victory in Europe."

Reading Check   **Explaining**   Why was the Battle of the Bulge such a disastrous defeat for Germany?

Japan Is Defeated

Unfortunately, President Roosevelt did not live to see the defeat of Germany. On April 12, 1945, while vacationing in Warm Springs, Georgia, he suffered a stroke and died. His vice president, **Harry S Truman,** became president during this difficult time.

Rise and Fall of Axis Powers

Axis Expansion The Axis powers included Germany, Italy, Austria, and the Sudetenland.

Axis Control At their height, the Axis controlled almost all of Europe and North Africa.

Axis Collapse The Allies invaded Germany from the east and the west.

Military and Civilian Deaths in World War II		
Country	**Military Deaths**	**Civilian Deaths**
USSR	11,000,000	6,700,000
Germany	3,250,000	2,350,000
Japan	1,740,000	393,000
China	1,400,000	8,000,000
Poland	110,000	5,300,000
United States	405,000	2,000
Great Britain	306,000	61,000
Italy	227,000	60,000
France	122,000	470,000

Source: *World War II: A Statistical Survey.* (Figures are approximate.)

WW I Military 86% Civilian 14%

WW II Military 46% Civilian 54%

War Casualties World War II took more lives than any other war in history. More civilians than soldiers died in the war.

Geography *Skills*

1. **Interpreting Maps** Which European countries remained neutral during the war?
2. **Applying Geography Skills** How did the Soviet Union receive supplies during the war?

The next day, Truman told reporters: "Boys, if you ever pray, pray for me now. . . . When they told me yesterday what had happened, I felt like the moon, the stars, and all the planets had fallen on me." Despite feeling overwhelmed, Truman began at once to make decisions about the war. Although Germany surrendered a few weeks later, the war with Japan continued to intensify, and Truman was forced to make some of the most difficult decisions of the war during his first six months in office.

Uncommon Valor on Iwo Jima On November 24, 1944, bombs fell on Tokyo for the first time since the 1942 Doolittle raid. Above the city flew 80 B-29

Superfortress bombers that had traveled over 1,500 miles (2,414 km) from new American bases in the Mariana Islands.

At first the B-29s did little damage because they kept missing their targets. Japan was simply too far away: By the time the B-29s reached Japan, they did not have enough fuel left to fix their navigational errors or to adjust for high winds. The solution was to capture an island closer to Japan, where the B-29s could refuel. After studying the problem, American military planners decided to invade **Iwo Jima.**

Iwo Jima was perfectly located, roughly halfway between the Marianas and Japan, but its geography was formidable. At its southern tip was Mount Suribachi, a dormant volcano. The terrain was rugged, with rocky cliffs, jagged ravines, and dozens of caves. Volcanic ash covered the ground. Even worse, the Japanese had built a vast network of caves and concrete bunkers connected by miles of tunnels.

On February 19, 1945, 60,000 U.S. Marines landed on Iwo Jima. As the troops leapt from the amphtracs, they sank up to their ankles in the soft ash. Meanwhile, Japanese artillery began to pound the invaders. Robert Sherrod, who had been on Tarawa, was shocked: "[The marines] died with the greatest possible violence. Nowhere in the Pacific have I seen such badly mangled bodies. Many were cut squarely in half. Legs and arms lay 50 feet (15 m) away from any body."

Inch by inch, the marines crawled inland, using flamethrowers and explosives to attack the Japanese bunkers. More than 6,800 marines were killed before the island was captured. Admiral Nimitz later wrote that on Iwo Jima, "uncommon valor was a common virtue."

Firebombing Devastates Japan While American engineers prepared airfields on Iwo Jima, General **Curtis LeMay,** commander of the B-29s based in the Marianas, decided to change strategy. To help the B-29s hit their targets, he ordered them to drop bombs filled with napalm—a kind of a jellied gasoline. The bombs were designed not only to explode but also to start fires. Even if the B-29s missed their targets, the fires they started would spread to the intended targets.

The use of firebombs was very controversial because the fires would also kill civilians; however, LeMay could think of no other way to destroy Japan's war production quickly. Loaded with firebombs, B-29s attacked Tokyo on March 9, 1945. As strong winds fanned the flames, the firestorm grew so intense that it sucked the oxygen out of the air, asphyxiating thousands. As one survivor later recalled:

> ❝The fires were incredible . . . with flames leaping hundreds of feet into the air. . . . Many people were gasping for breath. With every passing moment the air became more foul . . . the noise was a continuing crashing roar. . . . Fire-winds filled with burning particles rushed up and down the streets. I watched people . . . running for their lives. . . . The flames raced after them like living things, striking them down. . . . Wherever I turned my eyes, I saw people . . . seeking air to breathe.❞
>
> —quoted in *New History of World War II*

"uncommon valor was a common virtue"

—*Admiral Chester W. Nimitz*

The Tokyo firebombing killed over 80,000 people and destroyed more than 250,000 buildings. By the end of June 1945, Japan's six most important industrial cities had been firebombed, destroying almost half of their total urban area. By the end of the war, the B-29s had firebombed 67 Japanese cities.

The Invasion of Okinawa
Despite the massive damage the firebombing caused, there were few signs in the spring of 1945 that Japan was ready to quit. Many American officials believed the Japanese would not surrender until Japan had been invaded. To prepare for the invasion, the United States needed a base near Japan to stockpile supplies and build up troops. Iwo Jima was small and still too far away. After much discussion, military planners chose Okinawa—only 350 miles (563 km) from Japan.

American troops landed on Okinawa on April 1, 1945. Instead of defending the beaches, the Japanese troops took up positions in the island's rugged mountains. To dig the Japanese out of their caves and bunkers, the Americans had to fight their way up steep slopes against constant machine gun and artillery fire. More than 12,000 American soldiers, sailors, and marines died during the fighting, but by June 22, 1945, Okinawa had finally been captured.

The Terms for Surrender
Shortly after the United States captured Okinawa, the Japanese emperor urged his government to find a way to end the war. The biggest problem was the American demand for unconditional surrender. Many Japanese leaders were willing to surrender but on one condition—the emperor had to stay in power.

American officials knew that the fate of the emperor was the most important issue for the Japanese. Most Americans, however, blamed the emperor for the war and wanted him removed from power. President Truman was reluctant to go against public opinion. Furthermore, he knew the United States was almost ready to test a new weapon that might force Japan to surrender without any conditions. The new weapon was the atomic bomb.

The Manhattan Project
In 1939 Leo Szilard, one of the world's top physicists, learned that German scientists had split the uranium atom. Szilard had been the first scientist to suggest that splitting the atom might release enormous energy. Worried that the Nazis were working on an atomic bomb, Szilard convinced the world's best-known physicist, Albert

Ship Attacks Kamikaze attacks intensified in 1945, hitting the USS *Bunker Hill* and many other American ships. *Why do you think these Japanese kamikaze pilots were willing to fly suicide missions?*

Einstein, to sign a letter Szilard had drafted and send it to President Roosevelt. In the letter Einstein warned that by using uranium, "extremely powerful bombs of a new type may . . . be constructed."

Roosevelt responded by setting up a scientific committee to study the issue. The committee remained skeptical until 1941, when they met with British scientists who were already working on an atomic bomb. The British research so impressed the Americans that they convinced Roosevelt to begin a program to build an atomic bomb.

The American program to build an atomic bomb was code-named the **Manhattan Project** and was headed by General Leslie R. Groves. The project's first breakthrough came in 1942, when Szilard and Enrico Fermi, another physicist, built the world's first nuclear reactor at the University of Chicago. Groves organized a team of engineers and scientists to build an atomic bomb at a secret laboratory in Los Alamos, New Mexico. J. Robert Oppenheimer led the team. On July 16, 1945, they detonated the world's first atomic bomb near Alamogordo, New Mexico.

The Decision to Drop the Bomb
Even before the bomb was tested, American officials began to debate how to use it. Admiral William Leahy, chairman of the Joint Chiefs of Staff, opposed using the bomb because

it killed civilians indiscriminately. He believed that an economic blockade and conventional bombing would convince Japan to surrender. Secretary of War Henry Stimson wanted to warn the Japanese about the bomb while at the same time telling them that they could keep the emperor if they surrendered. Secretary of State James Byrnes, however, wanted to drop the bomb without any warning to shock Japan into surrendering.

President Truman later wrote that he "regarded the bomb as a military weapon and never had any doubts that it should be used." His advisers had warned him to expect massive casualties if the United States invaded Japan. Truman believed it was his duty as president to use every weapon available to save American lives.

The Allies threatened Japan with "prompt and utter destruction" if the nation did not surrender unconditionally, but the Japanese did not reply. Truman then ordered the military to drop the bomb. On August 6, 1945, a B-29 bomber named the *Enola Gay* dropped an atomic bomb, code-named "Little Boy," on Hiroshima, an important industrial city. The bomb was dropped at 8:15 A.M. Forty-three seconds later, it exploded. Heat, radiation, and an enormous shock wave slammed into Hiroshima.

The bomb destroyed 76,000 buildings—about 63 percent of the city. Somewhere between 80,000 and 120,000 people died instantly, and thousands more died later from burns and radiation sickness. Everywhere, as witness Nozaki Kiyoshi recalled, were "horrific scenes":

> 66The center of the city was still burning bright red, like live charcoal. Roof tiles were popping. We passed numerous war dead who had been carbonized. . . . We found five or six half-burned roofless streetcars. Inside were piles of corpses smoldering under white smoke. . . . A young mother lay face down, her baby tucked under her breast. They looked more like pink wax dolls than human beings.99

—quoted in *Senso: The Japanese Remember the Pacific War*

Different Viewpoints

Dropping the Atomic Bomb: Was It the Right Decision?

More than half a century later, people continue to debate what some historians have called the most important event of the twentieth century—President Truman's order to drop the atomic bomb on Japan. Did his momentous decision shorten the war and save lives on both sides, or was it prompted by Truman's fear that the Soviet Union, poised to invade, would gain control of Japan after the war?

A historian opposes Truman's decision:

Historian Gar Alperovitz maintains that Truman possessed alternatives to the atomic bomb but chose to use the weapon in order to force Japan's surrender before the Soviet Union could mount an invasion and subsequently occupy Japanese territory.

"Quite simply, it is not true that the atomic bomb was used because it was the only way to save the 'hundreds of thousands' or 'millions' of lives as was subsequently claimed. The readily available options were to modify the surrender terms and/or await the shock of the Russian attack.

Perhaps it is here, most poignantly, that we confront our own reluctance to ask the difficult questions—for even if one were to accept the most inflated estimates of lives saved by the atomic bomb, the fact remains that it was an act of violent destruction aimed at large concentrations of noncombatants."

—quoted in *The Decision to Use the Atomic Bomb, and the Architecture of an American Myth*

Hiroshima in the aftermath of the atomic bomb

The bombing stunned the Japanese. Three days later, on August 9, the Soviet Union declared war on Japan. Later that same day, the United States dropped another atomic bomb, code-named "Fat Man," on the city of Nagasaki, killing between 35,000 and 74,000 people.

Faced with such massive destruction and the shock of the Soviets joining the war, the Japanese emperor ordered his government to surrender. On August 15, 1945—**V-J Day**—Japan surrendered. On the other side of the world, Americans celebrated. For American soldiers the news was especially good. As one veteran recalled: "We would not be obliged to run up the beaches near Tokyo assault firing while being mortared and shelled. For all the fake manliness of our facades, we cried with relief and joy. We were going to live. We were going to grow up to adulthood after all." The long war was finally over.

Reading Check **Analyzing** What arguments did Truman consider when deciding whether to use the atomic bomb?

A historian defends Truman's decision:

Historian Herbert Feis argues that Truman's desire to avoid an invasion of Japan, thus saving thousands of lives on both sides, motivated his decision to drop the bomb.

"Our right, legal and historical, to use the bomb may thus well be defended; but those who made the decision to use it were not much concerned over these considerations, taking them for granted. Their thoughts about its employment were governed by one reason which was deemed imperative: that by using the bomb, the agony of war might be ended more quickly.

The primary and sustaining aim from the start of the great exertion to make the bomb was military, and the impelling reason for the decision to use it was military—to end the war victoriously as soon as possible."

—quoted in *Japan Subdued: The Atomic Bomb and the End of the War in the Pacific*

Learning From History

1. Which of the above interpretations do you think is the most valid? Why?

2. Using the internet or other resources, find an account of the bombing from the point of a Japanese citizen. How does it differ from the accounts above, and why?

Fact | Fiction | Folklore

Family Sacrifices Millions of American homes proudly displayed banners such as these during the war. The blue star on the flag indicated that a family member was serving in the military. A gold star proclaimed that an individual had been killed. Many homes displayed banners with several stars, indicating the family had sent many members off to war.

Building a New World

Well before the war ended, President Roosevelt had begun to think about what the world would be like after the war. The president had wanted to ensure that war would never again engulf the world.

Creating the United Nations President Roosevelt believed that a new international political organization could prevent another world war. In 1944, at the Dumbarton Oaks Estate in Washington, D.C., delegates from 39 countries met to discuss the new organization, which was to be called the **United Nations** (UN).

The delegates at the conference agreed that the UN would have a General Assembly, where every member nation in the world would have one vote. The UN would also have a Security Council with 11 members. Five countries would be permanent members of the Security Council: Britain, France, China, the Soviet Union, and the United States—the five big powers that had led the fight against the Axis. These five permanent members would each have veto power.

On April 25, 1945, representatives from 50 countries came to San Francisco to officially organize the United Nations and design its charter, or constitution. The General Assembly was given the power to vote on resolutions, to choose the non-permanent members of the Security Council, and to vote on the UN budget. The Security Council was responsible for international peace and security. It could investigate any international problem and propose settlements to countries that had disputes with each other. It could also take action to preserve the peace, including asking its members to use military force to uphold a UN resolution.

Picturing **History**

V-J Day Photographer Alfred Eisenstaedt captured this image in Times Square during the victory celebration on V-J Day. No one knows the identities of the sailor and the nurse in the photo. Why did this photograph become so famous?

Putting the Enemy on Trial Although the Allies had declared their intention to punish German and Japanese leaders for their war crimes, they did not work out the details until the summer of 1945. In early August, the United States, Britain, France, and the Soviet Union created the **International Military** Tribunal (IMT). At the **Nuremberg trials** in Nuremberg, Germany, the IMT tried German leaders suspected of committing war crimes.

Twenty-two leaders of Nazi Germany were prosecuted at Nuremberg. Three were acquitted and another seven were given prison sentences. The remaining 12 were sentenced to death by hanging. Trials of lower-ranking government officials and military officers continued until April 1949. Those trials led to the execution of 24 more German leaders. Another 107 were given prison sentences.

Similar trials were held in Tokyo for the leaders of wartime Japan. The IMT for the Far East charged 25 Japanese leaders with a variety of war crimes. Significantly, the Allies did not indict the Japanese emperor. They feared that any attempt to put him on trial would lead to an uprising by the Japanese people. Eighteen Japanese defendants were sentenced to prison. The rest were sentenced to death by hanging.

The war crimes trials punished many of the people responsible for World War II and the Holocaust, but they were also part of the American plan for building a better world. As Robert Jackson, chief counsel for the United States at Nuremberg, observed in his opening statement to the court: "The wrongs we seek to condemn and punish have been so calculated, so malignant and so devastating, that civilization cannot tolerate their being ignored because it cannot survive their being repeated."

Reading Check **Describing** How is the United Nations organized?

SECTION 5 ASSESSMENT

Checking for Understanding
1. **Define:** hedgerow, napalm, charter.
2. **Identify:** Battle of the Bulge, V-E Day, Harry S Truman, Curtis LeMay, Manhattan Project, V-J Day, United Nations.
3. **List** the major campaigns on the European and Pacific fronts in 1945.
4. **Explain** how the United States developed the atomic bomb.
5. **Describe** the war crimes trials.

Reviewing Themes
6. **Continuity and Change** Why do you think the goal of world peace has yet to be achieved?

Critical Thinking
7. **Analyzing** If you had been an adviser to President Truman, what advice would you have given him about dropping the atomic bomb? Give reasons why you would have given this advice.
8. **Categorizing** Using a graphic organizer like the one below, fill in the structure of the United Nations.

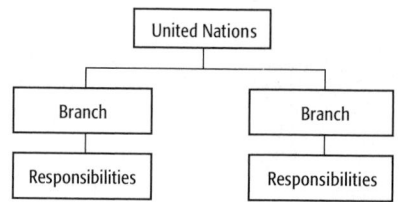

Analyzing Visuals
9. **Examining Photographs** Study the photograph on page 770 of Hiroshima after the atomic bomb was dropped. What effect do you think this photograph may have had on the American public? Why?

Writing About History
10. **Descriptive Writing** Imagine you are on the staff of the International Military Tribunal in Nuremberg after the war. Write a letter to a family member in the United States explaining why the tribunal is conducting trials and what you hope the trials will accomplish.

American LITERATURE

Jeanne Wakatsuki Houston was born in Inglewood, California. In 1942, when she was seven years old, her family was uprooted from their home and sent to live at the Manzanar internment camp in California. The detainees had committed no crimes. They were detained simply because of their heritage.

Farewell to Manzanar is the story of the Wakatsuki family's attempt to survive the indignities of forced detention and living behind barbed wire in the United States.

Read to Discover

How does Jeanne Wakatsuki Houston describe the internment camp that is to be her new home? What does her description remind you of?

Reader's Dictionary

barracks: plain and barren lodgings usually used to house soldiers

milling: wandering

savory: seasoned with spices

from Farewell to Manzanar
by Jeanne Wakatsuki Houston *and* James D. Houston

The following excerpt describes Jeanne Wakatsuki's first impressions as she and her family arrived at the internment camp.

We drove past a barbed-wire fence, through a gate, and into an open space where trunks and sacks and packages had been dumped from the baggage trucks that drove out ahead of us. I could see a few tents set up, the first rows of black barracks, and beyond them . . . rows of barracks that seemed to spread for miles across the plain. People were sitting on cartons or milling around . . . waiting to see which friends or relatives might be on this bus. . . .

We had pulled up just in time for dinner. The mess halls weren't completed yet. . . . They issued us army mess kits, the round metal kind that fold over, and plopped in scoops of canned Vienna sausage, canned string beans, steamed rice that had been cooked too long, and on top of the rice a serving of canned apricots. The caucasian servers were thinking that the fruit poured over rice would make a dessert. Among the Japanese, of course, rice is never eaten with sweet foods, only with salty or savory foods. . . .

After dinner we were taken to Block 16, a cluster of fifteen barracks. . . . The shacks were built of one thickness of pine planking covered with tarpaper. . . . We were assigned two of these for the twelve

people in our family group; and our official family "number" was enlarged by three digits—16 plus the number of this barracks. We were issued steel army cots, two brown army blankets, each, and some mattress covers, which my brothers stuffed with straw.

Analyzing Literature

1. **Recall and Interpret** How did the food served at the camp show a lack of understanding of Japanese culture?

2. **Evaluate and Connect** Why do you think the families in the camps were assigned numbers?

Interdisciplinary Activity

Art and Architecture Draw plans for a community memorial for remembering Japanese Americans who were treated unfairly during World War II.

Reviewing Key Terms

On a sheet of paper, use each of these terms in a sentence.

1. cost-plus
2. Liberty ship
3. disfranchise
4. periphery
5. convoy system
6. Sunbelt
7. rationing
8. victory garden
9. amphtrac
10. kamikaze
11. hedgerow
12. napalm
13. charter

Reviewing Key Facts

14. **Identify:** Selective Service and Training Act, Chester Nimitz, Douglas MacArthur, George Patton, E bond, Casablanca Conference, D-Day, Manhattan Project, United Nations.
15. What was the "Double V" campaign?
16. How did the war change patterns of population movement and settlement in the United States?
17. How did the war effort change employment opportunities for women and African Americans?
18. Why was the Doolittle raid so important to Americans?
19. How did the American government ensure that there were enough necessities to supply the war effort?
20. Why did the United States adopt a policy of island-hopping in the Pacific?
21. What was problematic about the Allied invasion at Omaha Beach?
22. Why were the victories on Iwo Jima and Okinawa so vital to the Allies?
23. What did the Allies do to punish Axis leaders after the war?

Critical Thinking

24. **Interpreting Primary Sources** Many historians believe that the civil rights movement of the 1950s and 1960s had its roots in the Double V campaign and the March on Washington. Alexander Allen, a member of the Urban League during the war, believed that World War II was a turning point for African Americans. Read the excerpt and answer the questions that follow.

❝Up to that point the doors to industrial and economic opportunity were largely closed. Under the pressure of war, the pressures of government policy, the pressures of world opinion, the pressures of blacks themselves and their allies, all this began to change. . . . The war forced the federal government to take a stronger position with reference to discrimination, and things began to change as a result. There was a tremendous attitudinal change that grew out of the war. There had been a new experience for blacks, and many weren't willing to go back to the way it was before. ❞

—quoted in *Wartime America*

a. How did the war change the status of African Americans in American society?

b. Why do you think the war forced the government to take a stronger position on discrimination in the workplace?

25. **Analyzing Themes: Global Connections** How did World War II underscore the importance of an international organization such as the United Nations?

Chapter Summary

	1941	1942	1943	1944	1945
The Pacific	Japan attacks Pearl Harbor on December 7.	The United States defeats Japan in the Battles of the Coral Sea and Midway.	The United States launches its island-hopping campaign.	The United States retakes the Philippines.	The United States drops atomic bombs; Japan surrenders on August 15.
Europe and North Africa		The Allies turn the tide in the Battle of the Atlantic.	The Allies invade Italy; Germans surrender at Stalingrad.	The Allies invade Normandy on June 6.	Germany surrenders unconditionally on May 7.
The Home Front	President Roosevelt forbids race discrimination in defense industries.	WAAC is established; Japanese American relocation is ordered.	OWM is established; Detroit and Zoot Suit Riots occur.	The case of *Korematsu* v. *United States* is decided.	The UN charter is signed.

HISTORY *Online*

Self-Check Quiz

Visit the *American Vision* Web site at <u>tav.glencoe.com</u> and click on *Self-Check Quizzes—Chapter 25* to assess your knowledge of chapter content.

26. **Analyzing Effects** Do you think the opportunities that opened up for women during World War II would have developed if the United States had stayed out of the war? Explain your answer.

27. **Synthesizing** Why do you think the United States was able to successfully fight a war on multiple fronts?

28. **Categorizing** Use a concept web similar to the one below to list the major campaigns in the Pacific and in Europe.

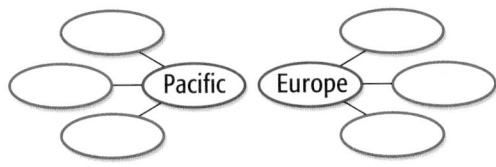

Practicing Skills

29. **Reading a Thematic Map** Study the map of migration patterns on page 751. Then use the steps you learned about reading thematic maps on page 748 to answer the following questions.
    a. **Interpreting Maps** Which regions had a net loss of residents to other regions during this period?

    b. **Synthesizing Information** How were the locations of the four fastest growing cities similar?

Chapter Activities

30. **Research Project** Use library or Internet resources to find information on the United Nations today. Use what you find to design an illustrated brochure highlighting the organization's work.

31. **Analyzing Geographic Patterns and Distributions** Look at the chart on Military and Civilian Deaths in World War II found on page 767. Create a thematic map indicating each country and the deaths that occurred there. Then write a quiz based on the chart about the distribution of casualties around the world and the patterns this suggests.

Writing Activity

32. **Persuasive Writing** Assume the role of an immigrant who fled Fascist Europe in 1933 and who has become a U.S. citizen. You have just read about the proposed United Nations, and you want to write your senator to urge that the United States join the organization or boycott it. Choose which position you support, and write a letter trying to convince the senator to support your position.

NATIONAL GEOGRAPHIC
Battle of the Bulge, December 1944–January 1945

Geography and History

33. The map above shows troop movements at the Battle of the Bulge. Study the map and answer the questions below.
    a. **Interpreting Maps** At what location did the Germans surround American forces on December 25?

    b. **Applying Geography Skills** What geographic features did the Germans encounter as they attacked? What information on the map shows you this?

Standardized Test Practice

Directions: Choose the best answer to the following question.

Why did Britain and France finally declare war in 1939?

A Because Germany annexed part of Czechoslovakia

B Because Germany invaded Poland

C Because Italy invaded France

D Because of the non-aggression pact between Russia and Germany

---

Test-Taking Tip: Use the process of elimination to rule out answers you know are wrong. For example, it is unlikely that a non-aggression pact between Russia and Germany would cause Britain and France to declare war, so this answer can be eliminated.

CHAPTER 26

The Cold War Begins *1945–1960*

Why It Matters

After World War II, an intense rivalry developed between the United States and the Soviet Union—two superpowers with very different political and economic systems. This rivalry, known as the Cold War, led to a massive buildup of military weapons on both sides. The determination of American leaders to contain communism also led to the Korean War, in which over 36,500 Americans died.

The Impact Today

The effects of Cold War events are still evident today.
- *The NATO alliance works to guarantee the security of many democratic countries.*
- *The math and science training important to the space race remains an educational priority.*

 The American Vision *Video* *The Chapter 26 video, "Symbols of the Cold War," examines the era by focusing on the crisis of the Berlin airlift.*

1947
- Truman Doctrine declared

1945
- Yalta conference
- Franklin Roosevelt dies

1948
- Berlin airlift begins

1950
- McCarthy charges that Communists staff the U.S. State Department
- Korean War begins

1949
- NATO established

United States PRESIDENTS

Truman 1945–1953

1945

1950

World

1945
- Italian women gain right to vote

1946
- Orwell's *Animal Farm* published

1949
- People's Republic of China established

1948
- State of Israel created

1952
- Britain produces an atomic bomb

During Nixon's 1959 visit to Moscow, the vice president exchanged angry words with Soviet leader Nikita Khrushchev during the "kitchen" debate at an exhibit at the U.S. Trade and Cultural Fair.

1953
- Rosenbergs executed for treason
- Armistice reached in Korean War

1959
- Khrushchev and Eisenhower hold summit

1960
- U-2 incident

Eisenhower 1953–1961

1955

1960

1953
- Stalin dies

1956
- Suez Canal crisis
- Hungarians rise up against their Communist government

1957
- Soviet Union launches *Sputnik*

HISTORY Online

Chapter Overview
Visit the *American Vision* Web site at tav.glencoe.com and click on **Chapter Overviews—Chapter 26** to preview chapter information.

Preview of Events

♦February 1945 ♦July 1945 ♦December 1945 ♦May 1946

February 1945
Yalta conference held in the USSR

April 1945
President Roosevelt dies

July 1945
Potsdam conference convenes in Germany

March 1946
Churchill delivers "iron curtain" speech

★ An American Story ★

On April 23, 1945, President Harry S Truman welcomed Soviet Foreign Minister Vyacheslav Molotov into the Oval Office of the White House. Truman had been president for less than two weeks, but he was determined to get tough with Molotov.

Truman told the Soviet diplomat how disgusted he was with Moscow's refusal to permit free elections in Poland, expressing his "deep disappointment" that the Soviet Union was not carrying out its agreements. Bluntly, he warned Molotov that Soviet defiance would seriously shake the confidence of the United States and Great Britain in their wartime ally.

Molotov began to explain the Soviet position, but Truman interrupted again and again, repeating his demand that Stalin "carry out that agreement in accordance with his word." Astonished, Molotov blurted out, "I have never been talked to like that in my life!"

"Carry out your agreements," the president snapped back, "and you won't get talked to like that!"

—adapted from *The Cold War: A History*

A Clash of Interests

Even before World War II ended, the wartime alliance between the United States and the Soviet Union had begun to show signs of strain. President Roosevelt had hoped that a victory over the Axis and the creation of the United Nations would lead to a more peaceful world. Instead, the United States and the Soviet Union became increasingly hostile toward each other after the war. This led to an era of confrontation and competition between the United States and the Soviet Union that lasted from about 1946 to 1990. This era became known as the Cold War.

Soviet Security Concerns

Tensions between the United States and the Soviet Union began to increase because the two sides had different goals. As the war ended, Soviet leaders became concerned about security. Germany had invaded Russia twice in less than 30 years. The Soviets wanted to keep Germany weak and make sure that the countries between Germany and the Soviet Union were under Soviet control.

Although security concerns influenced their thinking, Soviet leaders were also Communists. They believed that communism was a superior economic system that would eventually replace capitalism and that the Soviet Union should encourage communism in other nations. Soviet leaders also accepted Lenin's theory that capitalist countries eventually would try to destroy communism. This made Soviet leaders suspicious of capitalist nations.

American Economic Concerns

While Soviet leaders focused on securing their borders, American leaders focused on economic problems. Many American officials believed that the Depression had caused World War II. Without it, Hitler would never have come to power, and Japan would not have wanted to expand its empire.

American advisers also thought the Depression had been overly severe because countries cut back on trade. They believed that when nations seal themselves off economically, it forces them to go to war to get the resources they need. By 1945 President Roosevelt and his advisers were convinced that economic growth was the key to world peace. They wanted to promote economic growth by increasing world trade.

Similar reasoning convinced American leaders to promote democracy and free enterprise. They believed that democratic government with protections for people's rights made countries more stable and peaceful. They also thought that the free enterprise system, with private property rights and limited government intervention in the economy, was the best route to prosperity.

✓ Reading Check

Describing Why did U.S. leaders promote both international trade and free enterprise?

The Yalta Conference

In February 1945, with the war in Europe almost over, Roosevelt, Churchill, and Stalin met at **Yalta**—a Soviet resort on the Black Sea—to plan the postwar world. Although the conference seemed to go well, several agreements reached at Yalta later played an important role in causing the Cold War.

Poland The first issue discussed at Yalta was what to do about Poland. Shortly after the Germans invaded Poland, the Polish government leaders had fled to Britain. In 1944, however, Soviet troops drove back the Germans and entered Poland. As they liberated Poland from German control, the Soviets encouraged Polish Communists to set up a new government. This meant there were now two governments claiming the right to govern Poland, one Communist and one non-Communist.

President Roosevelt and Prime Minister Churchill both argued that the Poles should be free to choose their own government. "This is what we went to war against Germany for," Churchill explained, "that Poland should be free and sovereign."

Stalin quickly responded to Churchill's comments. According to Stalin, the Polish government had to be friendly to the Soviet Union. It was a matter of "life and death." Eventually, the three leaders compromised. Roosevelt and Churchill agreed to recognize the Polish government set up by the Soviets. Stalin agreed that the government would include members

Germany in Ruins World War II devastated many German cities. Here a woman sits among the ruins of Cologne, a northern city on the Rhine River.

of the prewar Polish government and that free elections would be held as soon as possible.

Declaration of Liberated Europe

After reaching a compromise on Poland, Roosevelt, Churchill, and Stalin agreed to issue the **Declaration of Liberated Europe.** The declaration asserted "the right of all people to choose the form of government under which they will live."

The Allies promised that the people of Europe would be allowed "to create democratic institutions of their own choice." They also promised to create temporary governments that represented "all democratic elements" and pledged "the earliest possible establishment through free elections of governments responsive to the will of the people."

Dividing Germany

After agreeing to a set of principles for liberating Europe, the conference focused on Germany. Roosevelt, Churchill, and Stalin agreed to divide Germany into four zones. Great Britain, the United States, the Soviet Union, and France would each control one zone. The same four countries would also divide the city of Berlin, even though it was in the Soviet zone.

Although pleased with the decision to divide Germany, Stalin also wanted to weaken the country economically. He demanded that Germany pay heavy reparations for the war damage it caused. Roosevelt agreed, but he insisted reparations be based on Germany's ability to pay. He also suggested, and Stalin agreed, that Germany pay reparations with trade goods and products instead of cash. The Allies would also be allowed to remove industrial machinery, railroad cars, and other equipment from Germany as reparations.

This decision did not resolve the issue. Over the next few years, arguments about reparations and economic policy in Germany increased tensions between the United States and the Soviet Union. These arguments became one of the major causes of the Cold War.

Tensions Begin to Rise

The Yalta decisions shaped the expectations of the United States. Two weeks after Yalta, the Soviets pressured the King of Romania into

NATIONAL GEOGRAPHIC
MOMENT in HISTORY

AID FOR WAR'S YOUNGEST VICTIMS

The gift of a new pair of shoes from the American Red Cross lights up the face of a young Austrian refugee. Millions of people across Europe were uprooted by almost six years of fighting that seldom distinguished between combatants and civilians. Millions more fled as victorious Soviet troops advanced through Eastern Europe into Germany at the end of World War II. The fate of the refugees became enmeshed in the growing power struggle between the United States and the Soviet Union, which turned the former allies into Cold War enemies.

appointing a Communist government. The United States accused the Soviets of violating the Declaration of Liberated Europe.

Soon afterward, the Soviets refused to allow more than three non-Communist Poles to serve in the 18-member Polish government. There was also no indication that they intended to hold free elections in Poland as promised. On April 1, President Roosevelt informed the Soviets that their actions in Poland were not acceptable. Eleven days later, with Soviet-American relations deteriorating, President Roosevelt died, and Vice President Harry Truman took office.

✓ Reading Check **Identifying** What did the Allies decide at Yalta?

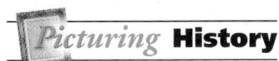 **History**

Potsdam Trio Issues about Germany dominated the Potsdam meeting, which was attended by (from left to right) Britain's Clement Attlee, President Truman, and Soviet leader Joseph Stalin. *What agreement did they reach regarding reparations?*

Truman Takes Control

Although inexperienced in diplomacy, Truman already had his own views about how to deal with the Soviets. Truman was strongly anticommunist and suspicious of Stalin. He believed World War II had begun because Britain had tried to appease Hitler. He was determined not to make the same mistake with Stalin. "We must stand up to the Russians," he told Secretary of State Edward Stettinius, the day after taking office.

Ten days later, Truman did exactly that during his meeting with Soviet Foreign Minister Molotov. Truman immediately brought up the issue of Poland and demanded that Stalin hold free elections as he promised at Yalta. Molotov took the unexpectedly strong message back to Stalin. The meeting marked an important shift in Soviet-American relations and set the stage for further confrontations.

The Potsdam Conference In July 1945, with the war against Japan still raging, Truman finally met Stalin at **Potsdam,** near Berlin. Both men had come to Potsdam primarily to work out a deal on Germany.

Truman was now convinced that German industry was critical. Unless Germany's economy was allowed to revive, the rest of Europe would never recover, and the German people might turn to communism out of desperation.

Stalin and his advisers were equally convinced that they needed reparations from Germany. The war had devastated their economy. Soviet troops had begun stripping their zone in Germany of its machinery and industrial equipment for use back home, but Stalin wanted Germany to pay much more.

At the conference, Truman took a firm stand against heavy reparations. He insisted that Germany's industry had to be allowed to recover. Truman suggested that the Soviets take reparations from their zone, while the Allies allowed industry to revive in the other zones. Stalin opposed this idea since the Soviet zone was mostly agricultural. It could not provide all of the reparations the Soviets wanted.

To get the Soviets to accept the deal, Truman offered Stalin a small amount of German industrial equipment from the other zones but required the Soviets to pay for part of it with food shipments from their zone. He also offered to accept the new German-Polish border the Soviets had established.

Stalin did not like Truman's proposal. At Potsdam, Truman learned that the atomic bomb had been successfully tested, and he told Stalin about the test. Stalin suspected Truman was trying to bully him into a deal and that the Americans were trying to limit reparations to keep the Soviets weak.

Despite his suspicions, Stalin had to accept the deal. American and British troops controlled

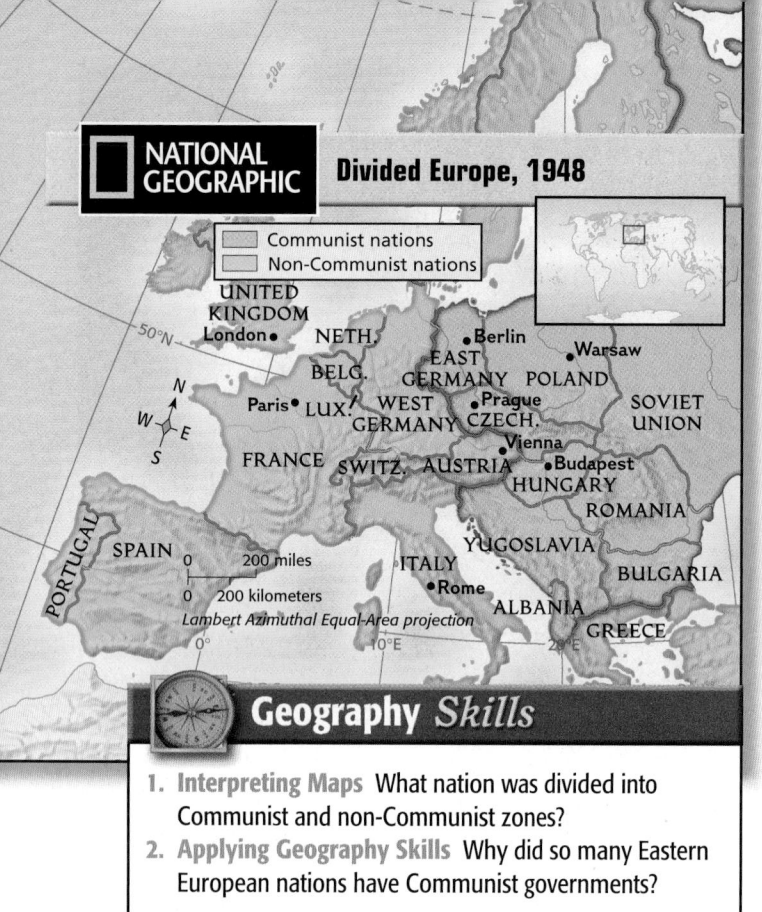

NATIONAL GEOGRAPHIC   **Divided Europe, 1948**

Communist nations
Non-Communist nations

Geography *Skills*

1. **Interpreting Maps** What nation was divided into Communist and non-Communist zones?
2. **Applying Geography Skills** Why did so many Eastern European nations have Communist governments?

Declaration of Liberated Europe. The presence of the Soviet army in Eastern Europe ensured that eventually, pro-Soviet Communist governments would be established in Poland, Romania, Bulgaria, Hungary, and Czechoslovakia. "This war is not as in the past," Stalin commented. "Whoever occupies a territory also imposes his own social system. . . . It cannot be otherwise."

The Communist countries of Eastern Europe came to be called **satellite nations.** Although not under direct Soviet control, they had to remain Communist and friendly to the Soviet Union. They also had to follow policies that the Soviets approved.

As he watched the Communist takeover in Eastern Europe, Winston Churchill coined a phrase to describe what had happened. On March 5, 1946, in a speech delivered in Fulton, Missouri, Churchill said:

> 66From Stettin in the Baltic to Trieste in the Adriatic, an iron curtain has descended across the continent. Behind that line lie all the capitals of the ancient states of central and Eastern Europe. . . . All are subject, in one form or another, not only to Soviet influence, but to a very high and increasing measure of control from Moscow.99
>
> —quoted in *The United States and the Origins of the Cold War, 1941–1947*

With the iron curtain separating the Communist nations of Eastern Europe from the West, the World War II era had come to an end. The Cold War was about to begin.

Reading Check **Explaining** How did the Potsdam conference hurt Soviet-American relations?

Germany's industrial heartland, and there was no way for the Soviets to get any reparations except by cooperating. Nevertheless, the Potsdam conference marked yet another increase in tensions between the Soviets and the Americans, further paving the way for the Cold War.

The Iron Curtain Descends Although Truman had won the argument over reparations, he had less success on other issues at Potsdam. The Soviets refused to make any stronger commitments to uphold the

---

SECTION 1 ASSESSMENT

Checking for Understanding

1. **Define:** Cold War, iron curtain.
2. **Identify:** Potsdam, satellite nation.
3. **Reviewing Facts** Why did tensions grow between the United States and the Soviet Union after World War II?

Reviewing Themes

4. **Global Connections** At Yalta, what agreement did the "Big Three" come to about Germany's future after World War II?

Critical Thinking

5. **Synthesizing** Do you think Roosevelt could have prevented the Cold War? Why or why not?
6. **Organizing** Use a graphic organizer similar to the one below to list events that led to the Cold War.

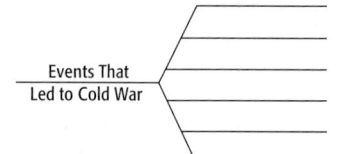

Events That
Led to Cold War

Analyzing Visuals

7. **Analyzing Maps** Study the map on this page. Why did the Soviet Union want the countries on its western border to have strong Communist governments?

Writing About History

8. **Expository Writing** Imagine you are an adviser to President Truman. Write a report explaining your interpretation of Churchill's iron curtain speech.

The Early Cold War Years

Guide to Reading

Main Idea

As the Cold War began, the United States struggled to oppose Communist aggression in Europe and Asia through political, economic, and military measures.

Key Terms and Names

George Kennan, containment, Marshall Plan, NATO, limited war

Reading Strategy

Sequencing As you read about the Cold War, complete a time line similar to the one below by recording the major events involving the Korean War.

Reading Objectives

• **Describe** the American view of the Soviet Union and the policy of containment.
• **Explain** the causes of the Korean War.

Section Theme

Global Connections Beliefs about Soviet goals and actions had a lasting effect on American policies abroad and on the agencies used to carry them out.

Preview of Events

◆1947 ◆1948 ◆1949 ◆1950

March 1947
Truman Doctrine declared

June 1948
Berlin airlift begins

April 1949
NATO forms

October 1949
People's Republic of China established

June 1950
Korean War begins

★ *An American Story* ★

Air Force lieutenant Gail Halvorsen was one of the pilots who airlifted supplies into Berlin in 1948. On one of his days off, he was shooting a home movie outside Berlin's Tempelhof Airport and soon drew a crowd of curious boys and girls. As a wartime pilot, Halvorsen had met children in other cities. They would playfully confront American soldiers, asking, "Any gum, chum?" While digging into his pockets for gum, Halvorsen had an idea. He said that if the children would wait at the end of the runway the next day, he would drop candy from his airplane.

The next day, eager children gathered at the airport. As Halvorsen's plane flew overhead, three small white parachutes floated down with a payload of candy. Halvorsen's "chocolate bombs" became a routine, earning him the nickname *Schokoladenflieger* ("chocolate-flyer"). Other pilots joined in, and by the end of the airlift, American pilots had dropped 250,000 candy parachutes for the children of Berlin.

—adapted from *Berlin in the Balance*

Containing Communism

The early Cold War shaped the politics and economics of many parts of the world, especially Europe. The airlift of supplies to Berlin, like Halvorsen's own candy airlift, reassured Europeans that the United States would help them rebuild their lives, even in the shadow of growing Soviet hostility.

Causes and Effects of the Cold War

Causes

- Soviet Union controls Eastern Europe after World War II.
- Chinese Communists win control of mainland China.
- United States and Soviet Union explode atomic bombs.

Effects

- Marshall Plan provides aid to Western Europe.
- Western nations form NATO; Communist nations respond with Warsaw Pact.
- Korean War erupts.
- American and Soviet arms race begins.
- Red Scare leads to hunt for Communists in the United States.

Graphic Organizer → Skills

The Cold War between the United States and the Soviet Union dominated postwar politics.
Evaluating What do you think was the most important cause of the Cold War? Why?

Despite the growing tensions between the Soviet Union and the United States, many American officials continued to believe cooperation with the Soviets was possible. In late 1945, the foreign ministers of the former wartime Allies met first in London, then in Moscow, to discuss the future of Europe and Asia.

Although Ernest Bevin, the British foreign minister, and James Byrnes, the American secretary of state, pushed the Soviets to hold free elections in Eastern Europe, the Soviets refused to budge. "Our relations with the Russians," Bevin gloomily concluded, "are drifting into the same condition as that in which we had found ourselves with Hitler."

The Long Telegram Increasingly exasperated by the Soviets' refusal to cooperate, officials at the State Department asked the American Embassy in Moscow to explain Soviet behavior. On February 22, 1946, diplomat **George Kennan** responded with what came to be known as the **Long Telegram,** a 5,540-word cable message explaining his views of Soviet goals.

According to Kennan, the Soviets' view of the world came from a traditional "Russian sense of insecurity" and fear of the West, intensified by the Communist ideas of Lenin and Stalin. Because Communists believed that they were in a long-term historical struggle against capitalism, Kennan argued, it was impossible to reach any permanent settlement with them.

Kennan therefore proposed what became the basic American policy throughout the Cold War: "a long-term, patient but firm and vigilant containment of

Russian expansive tendencies." Kennan explained that, in his opinion, the Soviet system had several major economic and political weaknesses. If the United States could keep the Soviets from expanding their power, it was only a matter of time until the Soviet system would fall apart. Communism could be beaten without going to war. The Long Telegram circulated widely in Truman's administration. It gave rise to the policy of containment—keeping communism within its present territory through the use of diplomatic, economic, and military actions.

Crisis in Iran While Truman's administration discussed Kennan's ideas, a series of crises erupted in the spring and summer of 1946. These crises seemed to prove that Kennan was right about the Soviets. The first crisis began in Iran in March 1946.

During World War II, the United States had put troops in southern Iran while Soviet troops occupied northern Iran to secure a supply line from the Persian Gulf. After the war, instead of withdrawing as promised, the Soviet troops remained in northern Iran. Stalin then began demanding access to Iran's oil supplies. To increase the pressure, Soviet troops helped local Communists in northern Iran establish a separate government.

To American officials, these actions signaled a Soviet push into the Middle East. Secretary of State James Byrnes sent Moscow a strong message demanding that they withdraw. At the same time, the battleship USS *Missouri* sailed into the eastern Mediterranean. The pressure seemed to work. Soviet forces withdrew, having been promised a joint Soviet-Iranian oil company. The Iranian parliament later rejected the plan.

The Truman Doctrine Frustrated in Iran, Stalin turned to Turkey. There the straits of the Dardanelles were a vital route from Soviet Black Sea ports to the Mediterranean. For centuries Russia had wanted to control this strategic route. In August 1946, Stalin demanded joint control of the Dardanelles with Turkey. Presidential adviser **Dean Acheson** saw this move as the first step in a Soviet plan to control the Mideast, and he advised Truman to make a show of force. The president declared, "We might as well find out whether the Russians are bent on world conquest." He then ordered the new aircraft carrier *Franklin D. Roosevelt* to join the *Missouri* in protecting Turkey and the eastern Mediterranean.

While the United States supported Turkey, Britain tried to help Greece. In August 1946, Greek Communists launched a guerrilla war against the Greek government. For about six months, British troops helped the Greeks fight the guerrillas. The effort strained Britain's economy, which was still weak from World War II. In February 1947, Britain informed the United States that it could no longer afford to help Greece.

On March 12, 1947, Truman went before Congress to ask for $400 million to fight Communist aggression in Greece and Turkey. His speech outlined a policy which became known as the **Truman Doctrine.** Its goal was to aid "free peoples who are resisting attempted subjugation by armed minorities or by outside pressures." Its immediate effects were to stabilize the Greek government and ease Soviet demands in Turkey. In the long run, it pledged the United States to fight communism worldwide.

📖 *(See page 1076 for more on the Truman Doctrine.)*

ECONOMICS

The Marshall Plan Meanwhile, postwar Western Europe faced grave problems. Economies were in ruin, people were near starvation, and political chaos was at hand. The terrible winter of 1946 made things worse.

In June 1947, Secretary of State George C. Marshall proposed the European Recovery Program, or **Marshall Plan,** which would give European nations American aid to rebuild their economies. Truman saw the Marshall Plan and the Truman Doctrine as "two halves of the same walnut," both essential

George Marshall

for containment. Marshall offered help to all nations planning a recovery program:

> 66 Our policy is not directed against any country or doctrine, but against hunger, poverty, desperation and chaos. Its purpose should be the revival of a working economy in the world so as to permit the emergence of political and social conditions in which free institutions can exist. . . . 99
>
> —quoted in *Marshall: A Hero for Our Times*

The Soviet Union and its satellite nations in Eastern Europe rejected the offer. Instead, the Soviets developed their own economic program. This action further separated Europe into competing regions. The Marshall Plan pumped billions of dollars worth of supplies, machinery, and food into Western Europe. Western Europe's recovery weakened the appeal of communism and opened new markets for trade.

✓ **Reading Check** **Summarizing** What were the goals of the Truman Doctrine and the Marshall Plan?

The Berlin Crisis

The Marshall Plan was only one part of the American strategy for rebuilding Europe. President Truman and his advisers believed that Western Europe's prosperity depended on Germany's recovery. The Soviets, however, still wanted Germany to pay reparations to the Soviet Union. Eventually, the dispute over Germany brought the United States and the Soviet Union to the brink of war.

West Germany Is Founded By early 1948, U.S. officials had concluded that the Soviets were deliberately trying to undermine Germany's economy. In response, the United States, Great Britain, and France announced that they were merging their zones in Germany and allowing the Germans to have their own government. They also agreed to merge their zones in Berlin and to make West Berlin part of the new German republic.

The new nation was officially called the Federal Republic of Germany, but it became known as West Germany. West Germany's economy was completely separate from the Soviet zone, which eventually became known as East Germany. West Germany was not allowed to have a military, but in most respects, it was independent.

Bucking the Blockade The Berlin airlift became a symbol of American determination to resist the Soviet Union's effort to control Berlin. For how many months did American pilots supply Berlin with food and supplies?

Iceland. NATO members agreed to come to the aid of any member who was attacked. For the first time in its history, the United States had committed itself to maintaining peace in Europe. Six years later, NATO allowed West Germany to rearm and join its organization. This decision alarmed Soviet leaders. They responded by organizing a military alliance in Eastern Europe, which became known as the **Warsaw Pact.** The United States also created other regional alliances. The Organization of American States (OAS) started in 1948 and the Southeast Asia Treaty Organization (SEATO) formed in 1954.

✓ **Reading Check** **Evaluating** What triggered the beginning of the Berlin airlift?

The Berlin Airlift The decision to create West Germany convinced the Soviets that they would never get the reparations they wanted. In late June 1948, Soviet troops cut all road and rail traffic to West Berlin. The blockade provoked a crisis. President Truman sent long-range bombers with atomic weapons to bases in Britain. General Lucius Clay, the American commander in Germany, warned of what might happen. "If we mean to hold Europe against communism, then we must not budge," he said.

The challenge was to keep West Berlin alive without provoking war with the Soviets. In June 1948, Truman ordered the **Berlin airlift** to begin. For 11 months, cargo planes supplied Berliners with food, medicine, and coal. The airlift continued through the spring of 1949, bringing in over 2 million tons of supplies. Stalin finally lifted the blockade on May 12. The Berlin airlift symbolized American determination to stand by Berlin.

NATO The Berlin blockade convinced many Americans that the Soviets were bent on conquest. The public began to support a military alliance with Western Europe. By April 1949, an agreement had been reached to create the North Atlantic Treaty Organization (NATO)—a mutual defense alliance.

NATO initially included 12 countries: the United States, Canada, Britain, France, Italy, Belgium, Denmark, Portugal, the Netherlands, Norway, Luxembourg, and

The Cold War Spreads to East Asia

The Cold War eventually spread beyond Europe. Conflicts also emerged in Asia, where events in China and Korea brought about a new attitude toward Japan.

Civil War and Revolution in China In China, Communist forces led by **Mao Zedong** had been struggling against the Nationalist government led by Chiang Kai-shek since the late 1920s. During World War II, the two sides suspended their war to resist Japanese occupation. With the end of World War II, however, civil war broke out again. Although Mao made great gains, neither side could win, and neither would accept a compromise.

To prevent a Communist revolution in Asia, the United States sent the Nationalist government $2 billion in aid beginning in the mid-1940s, but it squandered this advantage with poor military planning and corruption. By 1949 the Communists had captured the Chinese capital of Beijing and moved southward, while support for the Nationalists declined.

In August 1949, the State Department discontinued aid to the Chinese Nationalists. The defeated Nationalists then fled the Chinese mainland for the small island of Taiwan (Formosa). The victorious Communists established the People's Republic of China in October 1949.

After the Fall China's fall to communism shocked Americans. To make matters worse, in September 1949 the Soviet Union announced that it had successfully tested its first atomic weapon. Then, early in 1950, the People's Republic of China and the Soviet Union signed a treaty of friendship and alliance. Many Western leaders feared that China and the Soviet Union would support Communist revolutions in other nations.

The United States kept formal diplomatic relations with only the Nationalists in Taiwan. It used its veto power in the UN Security Council to keep representatives of the new Communist China out of the UN, allowing the Nationalists to retain their seat.

The Chinese revolution brought about a significant change in American policy toward Japan. At the end of World War II, General Douglas MacArthur had taken charge of occupied Japan. His mission was to introduce democracy and keep Japan from threatening war again. Once the United States lost China as its chief ally in Asia, it adopted policies to encourage the rapid recovery of Japan's industrial economy. Just as the United States viewed West Germany as the key to defending all of Europe against communism, it saw Japan as the key to defending Asia.

✓ **Reading Check** **Analyzing** How did the revolution in China affect American foreign policy with Japan?

The Korean War

At the end of World War II, American and Soviet forces entered Korea to disarm the Japanese troops stationed there. The Allies divided Korea at the 38th

NATIONAL GEOGRAPHIC **Korean War, 1950–1953**

June 25, 1950–November 24, 1950
☐ UN-held territory, Sept. 15, 1950
← North Korean advance
← UN counteroffensive
— UN front line, Nov. 24, 1950

SOVIET UNION

CHINA

Yalu River

CHINA

❸ Taken by UN, Oct. 19, 1950
Pyongyang
38th Parallel
NORTH KOREA
Sea of Japan

❷ Liberated by UN, Sept. 28, 1950
Seoul
Inchon

❶ MacArthur lands, Sept. 15, 1950

SOUTH KOREA

Yellow Sea

0   100 miles
0   100 kilometers
Lambert Conformal Conic projection

•Pusan

JAPAN

SOVIET UNION

❹ Chinese counteroffensive, Nov. 26, 1950

CHINA

Yalu River

40°N

NORTH KOREA   Sea of Japan

Pyongyang
38th Parallel

Panmunjom•
Seoul
Inchon•

❺ Armistice line, July 27, 1953

SOUTH KOREA

•Taegu

•Pusan

Yellow Sea

0   100 miles
0   100 kilometers
Lambert Conformal Conic projection

JAPAN

November 24, 1950–July 27, 1953
— UN front line, Nov. 24, 1950
← Chinese counteroffensive, Nov. 25, 1950
— Farthest Chinese advance, Jan. 24, 1951
← UN advance, Jan. 25, 1951

130°E

Geography *Skills*

1. **Interpreting Maps** Along what latitude was Korea divided into two nations after World War II?

2. **Applying Geography Skills** In debates over expanding the Korean War, why do you think Truman opposed MacArthur's request to bomb bridges on the Yalu River?

Different Viewpoints

Should the War in Korea Be Expanded?

A controversy between President Harry S Truman and General Douglas MacArthur began shortly after the outbreak of the Korean War. It reached a climax when the president relieved MacArthur of his command. Truman believed in a limited war in Korea, while MacArthur wanted total victory.

President Harry S Truman defends limited war:

The Kremlin [Soviet Union] is trying, and has been trying for a long time, to drive a wedge between us and the other nations. It wants to see us isolated. It wants to see us distrusted. It wants to see us feared and hated by our allies. Our allies agree with us in the course we are following. They do not believe that we should take the initiative to widen the conflict in the Far East. If the United States were to widen the conflict, we might well have to go it alone.

If we go it alone in Asia, we may destroy the unity of the free nations against aggression. Our European allies are nearer to Russia than we are. They are in far greater danger. . . . Going it alone brought the world to the disaster of World War II. . . .

I do not propose to strip this country of its allies in the face of Soviet danger. The path of collective security is our only sure defense against the dangers that threaten us.

General Douglas MacArthur addresses Congress, April 19, 1951:

History teaches with unmistakable emphasis that appeasement but begets new and bloodier war. . . . Like blackmail, it lays the basis for new and successively greater demands, until, as in blackmail, violence becomes the only other alternative. Why, my soldiers asked of me, surrender military advantage to an enemy in the field? I could not answer.

It was my constant effort to preserve them and end this savage conflict honorably and with the least loss of time and minimum sacrifice of life.

I am closing 52 years of military service. . . . But I still remember the refrain of one of the most popular barrack ballads of that day which proclaimed most proudly that—

"Old soldiers never die, they just fade away." And like the old soldier of that ballad, I now close my military career and just fade away—an old soldier who tried to do his duty as God gave him the light to see that duty. Good-by.

Learning From History

1. **Identifying Central Issues** How did MacArthur view Truman's decision to fight a limited war in Korea? How did Truman see it?
2. **Making Inferences** On the basis of what authority did Truman fire MacArthur?

parallel of latitude. Soviet troops controlled the north, while American troops controlled the south.

As the Cold War began, talks to reunify Korea broke down. A Communist Korean government was organized in the north, while an American-backed government controlled the south. Both governments claimed authority over all of Korea, and border clashes were common. The Soviet Union provided extensive military aid to the North Koreans, who quickly built up a large, well-equipped army. On June 25, 1950, North Korean troops invaded into the south, rapidly driving back the poorly equipped South Korean forces.

The UN Intervenes Truman saw the Communist invasion of South Korea as a test of the containment policy and ordered United States naval and airpower into action. He then called on the United Nations to act. Truman succeeded because the Soviet delegate was boycotting the Security Council over its China policy and was not present to veto the American proposal. With the pledge of UN troops, Truman ordered General MacArthur to send American troops from Japan to the Korean peninsula.

The American and South Korean troops were driven back into a small pocket of territory near the port of Pusan. Inside the "Pusan perimeter," as it came to be called, the troops stubbornly resisted the North Korean onslaught, buying time for MacArthur to organize reinforcements.

On September 15, MacArthur ordered a daring invasion behind enemy lines at the port of Inchon. The Inchon landing took the North Koreans by surprise. Within weeks they were in full retreat back across the 38th parallel. Truman then gave the order to pursue the North Koreans beyond the 38th parallel. MacArthur pushed the North Koreans north to the Yalu River, the border with China.

China Enters the War The Communist Chinese government saw the advancing UN troops as a threat and warned the forces to halt their advance. When those warnings were ignored, China launched a massive attack across the Yalu River in November. Hundreds of thousands of Chinese troops flooded across the border, driving the UN forces back across the 38th parallel.

As his troops fell back, an angry MacArthur demanded approval to expand the war against China. He asked for a blockade of Chinese ports, the use of Chiang Kai-shek's Nationalist forces, and the bombing of Chinese cities with atomic weapons.

Truman Fires MacArthur President Truman refused MacArthur's demands because he did not want to expand the war into China or to use the atomic bomb. MacArthur persisted. He publicly criticized the president, saying, "There is no substitute for victory."

Determined to maintain control of policy and show that the president commanded the military, an exasperated Truman fired MacArthur for insubordination in April 1951. MacArthur, who remained popular despite being fired, returned home to parades and a hero's welcome. Despite criticism, Truman remained committed to limited war—a war fought to achieve a limited objective, such as containing communism.

Changes in Policy Truman chose General Matthew Ridgway to replace MacArthur. By mid-1951, the UN forces had pushed the Chinese and North Korean forces back across the 38th parallel. The war then settled down into a series of relatively small battles over hills and other local objectives. In November 1951, peace negotiations began, but an armistice would not be signed until July 1953. More than 33,600 American soldiers died in action in the Korean War, and more than 2,800 died from accidents or from disease.

The Korean War marked an important turning point in the Cold War. Until 1950 the United States had preferred to use political pressure and economic aid to contain communism. After the Korean War began, the United States embarked on a major military buildup.

The Korean War also helped expand the Cold War to Asia. Before 1950 the United States had focused on Europe as the most important area in which to contain communism. After the Korean War began, the United States became more militarily involved in Asia. Defense agreements were signed with Japan, South Korea, Taiwan, the Philippines, and Australia. American aid also began to flow to the French forces fighting Communist guerrillas in Vietnam.

Reading Check Analyzing How did President Truman view the Communist invasion of South Korea?

HISTORY Online

Student Web Activity Visit the *American Vision* Web site at tav.glencoe.com and click on **Student Web Activities— Chapter 26** for an activity on the Cold War.

SECTION 2 ASSESSMENT

Checking for Understanding

1. **Define:** containment, limited war.
2. **Identify:** George Kennan, Marshall Plan, NATO.
3. **Review Facts** How did the Truman Doctrine and the Marshall Plan address the spread of communism?

Reviewing Themes

4. **Global Connections** What long-term Cold War strategy did the United States follow?

Critical Thinking

5. **Evaluating** How did the Long Telegram influence American policy?
6. **Categorizing** Use a graphic organizer similar to the one below to list early conflicts between the USSR and the U.S.

Conflicts Between the USSR and the U.S.

Analyzing Visuals

7. **Analyzing Maps** Study the maps of the Korean War on page 787. When did the United Nations control the most territory in Korea? When did both sides finally agree upon an armistice line?

Writing About History

8. **Persuasive Writing** Write a letter to the editor of a newspaper explaining whether you agree or disagree with President Truman's firing of General MacArthur.

The Cold War and American Society

Guide to Reading

Main Idea

The Cold War heightened Americans' fears of Communist infiltration and atomic attack.

Key Terms and Names

subversion, loyalty review program, Alger Hiss, perjury, McCarran Act, McCarthyism, censure, fallout, fallout shelter

Reading Strategy

Taking Notes As you read about American reaction to the Cold War, use the major headings of the section to create an outline similar to the one below.

> The Cold War and American Society
> I. A New Red Scare
>   A. The Loyalty Review Program
>   B.
>   C.
>   D.

Reading Objectives

- **Describe** the new Red Scare.
- **Discuss** how American society reflected fears of the nuclear age.

Section Theme

Civic Rights and Responsibilities In the early part of the Cold War, the fear of communism led to a hunt for spies and to intolerance and suspicion of people with radical ideas in the United States.

Preview of Events

♦1947	♦1950	♦1953

March 1947 — Loyalty Review Board established

February 1950 — McCarthy claims to have a list of Communists in the State Department

September 1950 — McCarran Act passed

June 1953 — Rosenbergs executed

★ An American Story ★

In the 1940s, Ruth Goldberg belonged to the Parent-Teacher Association in Queens, New York. In 1947 she agreed to run for PTA president, but the campaign turned nasty. Because Goldberg had associated with people with left-wing interests, a rumor spread through the neighborhood that she was a Communist. Suddenly Goldberg's quiet life became terrifying. Callers threatened her, and the local priest denounced her in his sermons. One afternoon, Goldberg's eight-year-old son came home in tears. A playmate had told him, "You know, your mother's a Red. She should be put up against a wall and shot."

Looking back much later, Goldberg saw the PTA campaign as part of a bigger and more complex pattern of distrust and hatred. "It was a small thing, but it was an indication of what had happened with the Cold War, with this Red specter—that somebody like me could be a danger to a community."

—**adapted from _Red Scare_**

A New Red Scare

During the 1950s, thousands of ordinary people—from teachers to autoworkers to high government officials—shared Ruth Goldberg's disturbing experience. Rumors and accusations of Communists in the United States and of Communist infiltration of the government tapped into fears that the Communists were trying to take over the world.

The Red Scare began in September 1945, when a clerk named Igor Gouzenko walked out of the Soviet Embassy in Ottawa, Canada, and defected. Gouzenko carried documents revealing a massive effort by the Soviet Union to infiltrate organizations and government agencies in Canada and the United States with the specific goal of obtaining information about the atomic bomb.

The Gouzenko case stunned Americans. It implied that spies had infiltrated the American government. Soon, however, the search for spies escalated into a general fear of Communist subversion. Subversion is the effort to secretly weaken a society and overthrow its government. As the Cold War intensified in 1946 and early 1947, Americans began to fear that Communists were secretly working to subvert the American government.

GOVERNMENT

The Loyalty Review Program
In early 1947, just nine days after his powerful speech announcing the Truman Doctrine, the president established a **loyalty review program** to screen all federal employees. Rather than calm public suspicion, Truman's action seemed to confirm fears that Communists had infiltrated the government and helped increase the fear of communism sweeping the nation.

Between 1947 and 1951, over 6 million federal employees were screened for their loyalty—a term difficult to define. A person might become a suspect for reading certain books, belonging to various groups, traveling overseas, or even seeing certain foreign films. About 14,000 employees were subject to intensive scrutiny from the Federal Bureau of Investigation (FBI). Some 2,000 employees quit their jobs during the check, many under pressure. Another 212 were fired for "questionable loyalty," though no actual evidence against them was uncovered.

HUAC Although the FBI helped screen federal employees, FBI Director **J. Edgar Hoover** was not satisfied. In 1947 Hoover went before the House Un-American Activities Committee (HUAC). Formed in 1938 to investigate both Communist and Fascist activities in the United States, HUAC was a relatively minor committee until Hoover catapulted it to prominence.

Hoover urged HUAC to hold public hearings on Communist subversion. The committee, Hoover said, could reveal "the diabolic machinations of sinister figures engaged in un-American activities." Once Communists were identified, he explained, the public would isolate them and end their influence. Hoover's aim was to expose not just Communists but also "Communist sympathizers" and "fellow travelers." Under Hoover's leadership, the FBI sent agents to infiltrate groups suspected of subversion and wiretapped thousands of telephones.

Alger Hiss In 1948 **Whittaker Chambers,** a *Time* magazine editor and former Communist Party member, testified to HUAC that several government officials were also former Communists or spies.

The most prominent government official named by Chambers was **Alger Hiss,** a lawyer and diplomat who had served in Roosevelt's administration, attended the Yalta conference, and taken part in organizing the United Nations. After Hiss sued him for libel, Chambers testified before a grand jury that in 1937 and 1938 Hiss gave him secret documents from the State Department. Hiss denied being either a spy or a member of the Communist Party, and he also denied ever having known Chambers.

The committee was ready to drop the investigation until Representative Richard Nixon of California convinced his colleagues to continue the hearings to determine whether Hiss or Chambers had lied. As the committee continued to question Hiss, he admitted that he had indeed met Chambers in the 1930s. When Chambers continued to claim that Hiss was a Communist, Hiss sued him, claiming that his accusations were unfounded and malicious.

To defend himself, Chambers produced copies of secret documents along with microfilm that he had hidden in a hollow pumpkin on his farm. These "pumpkin papers," Chambers claimed, proved that

Picturing **History**

Convicted of Conspiracy Ethel and Julius Rosenberg were convicted of transmitting atomic secrets to Soviet Russia. What sentence did they receive?

he was telling the truth. A jury agreed and convicted Hiss of perjury, or lying under oath.

The Rosenbergs

Another sensational spy case centered around accusations that American Communists had sold the secrets of the atomic bomb. Many people did not believe that the Soviet Union could have produced an atomic bomb in 1949 without help. This belief intensified the hunt for spies.

In 1950 the hunt led to Klaus Fuchs, a British scientist who admitted sending information to the Soviet Union. His testimony led the FBI to arrest **Julius and Ethel Rosenberg,** a New York couple who were members of the Communist Party. The government charged them with heading a Soviet spy ring.

The Rosenbergs denied the charges but were condemned to death for espionage. Many people believed that they were not leaders or spies, but victims caught up in the wave of anti-Communist frenzy. Appeals, public expressions of support, and pleas for clemency failed, however, and the couple was executed in June 1953.

Project Venona

The American public hotly debated the guilt or innocence of individuals like the Rosenbergs who were accused as spies. There was, however, solid evidence of Soviet espionage, although very few Americans knew it at the time. In 1946 American cryptographers working for a project code-named "Venona" cracked the Soviet spy code of the time, enabling them to read approximately 3,000 messages between Moscow and the United States collected during the Cold War. The messages confirmed extensive Soviet spying and sent federal investigators on a massive hunt. To keep the Soviets from learning how thoroughly the United States had penetrated their codes, authorities chose not to make the intercepted messages public. Not until 1995 did the government reveal **Project Venona's** existence. The Venona documents provided strong evidence that the Rosenbergs were guilty.

The Red Scare Spreads

Following the federal government's example, many state and local governments, universities, businesses, unions, and churches began their own efforts to find Communists. The University of California required its 11,000 faculty members to take loyalty oaths and fired 157 who refused to do so. Many Catholic groups became strongly anticommunist and urged their members to identify Communists within the church.

The Taft-Hartley Act required union leaders to take oaths that they were not Communists, but many union leaders did not object. Instead they launched their own efforts to purge Communists from their organizations. The president of the CIO called Communist sympathizers "skulking cowards" and "apostles of hate." The CIO eventually expelled 11 unions that refused to remove Communist leaders from their organization.

✔ **Reading Check** **Explaining** What was the purpose of the loyalty review boards and HUAC?

Hollywood on Trial

One of HUAC's first hearings focused on the film industry as a powerful cultural force that Communists might use and manipulate. Its interviews routinely began, "Are you now, or have you ever been, a member of the Communist Party?" As fear of Communists in Hollywood spread, producers then drew up a blacklist and agreed not to hire anyone in the film industry who was believed to be a Communist or who refused to cooperate with the committee. The blacklist created an atmosphere of distrust and fear. People could be blacklisted for making chance remarks, criticizing HUAC, or knowing a suspected Communist.

Ronald Reagan, head of the Screen Actors Guild at the time, testified that there were Communists in Hollywood.

Ten screenwriters, known as the "Hollywood Ten" (shown here with their lawyers), used their Fifth Amendment right to protect themselves from self-incrimination and refused to testify before HUAC.

"A Conspiracy So Immense"

In 1949 the Red Scare intensified even further. That year, the Soviet Union successfully tested an atomic bomb, and China fell to communism. To many Americans these events seemed to prove that the United States was losing the Cold War. Deeply concerned, they wanted an explanation as to why their government was failing. As a result, many continued to believe that Communists had infiltrated the government and remained undetected.

In February 1950, soon after Alger Hiss's perjury conviction, a little-known Wisconsin senator gave a political speech to a Republican women's group in West Virginia. Halfway through his speech, Senator **Joseph R. McCarthy** made a surprising statement:

> ❝While I cannot take the time to name all the men in the State Department who have been named as members of the Communist Party and members of a spy ring, I have here in my hand a list of 205 that were known to the Secretary of State as being members of the Communist Party and who nevertheless are still working and shaping the policy of the State Department.❞
>
> —quoted in *The Fifties*

By the next day, the Associated Press had picked up the statement and sent it to papers all over the country. When McCarthy arrived at the Denver airport, reporters crowded around him and asked to see his list of Communists in the state department. McCarthy replied that he would be happy to show them the list, but unfortunately, it was packed in his bag on the plane. In fact, the list never appeared. McCarthy, however, continued to make charges and draw attention.

McCarthy's Charges Born in 1908 near Appleton, Wisconsin, Joseph R. McCarthy studied law and served in World War II before his first run for the Senate. McCarthy's 1946 political campaign sounded the keynote of his career. Without making any specific charges or offering any proof, McCarthy accused his opponent, Robert M. La Follette, Jr., of being "communistically inclined." Fear of communism, plus McCarthy's intense speeches, won him the election.

After becoming a senator, McCarthy continued to proclaim that Communists were a danger both at home and abroad. To some of his audiences, he distributed a booklet called "The Party of Betrayal," which accused Democratic Party leaders of corruption and of protecting Communists. Secretary of State Dean Acheson was a frequent target. According to McCarthy, Acheson was incompetent and a tool of Stalin. He wildly accused George C. Marshall, the former army chief of staff and secretary of state, of disloyalty as a member of "a conspiracy so immense as to dwarf any previous such ventures in the history of man."

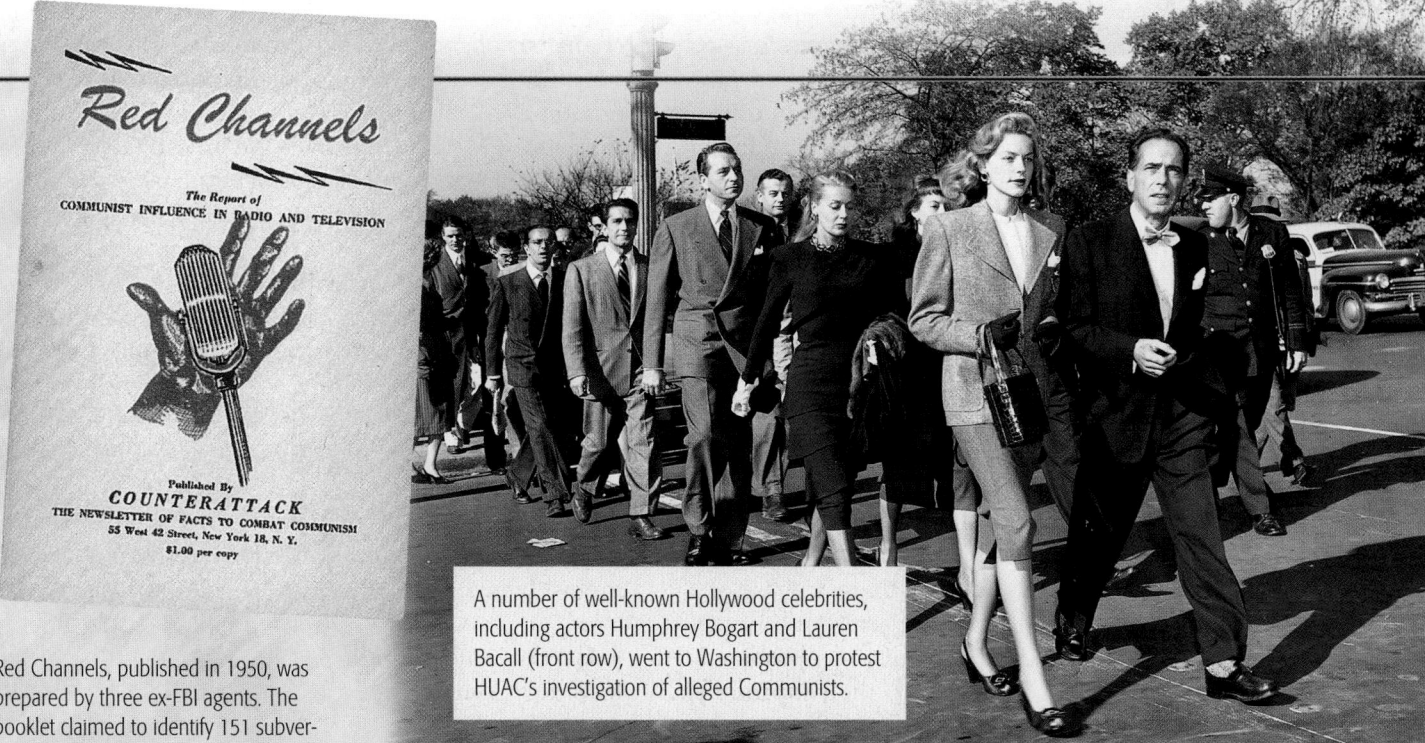

Red Channels, published in 1950, was prepared by three ex-FBI agents. The booklet claimed to identify 151 subversive entertainers in radio and television.

A number of well-known Hollywood celebrities, including actors Humphrey Bogart and Lauren Bacall (front row), went to Washington to protest HUAC's investigation of alleged Communists.

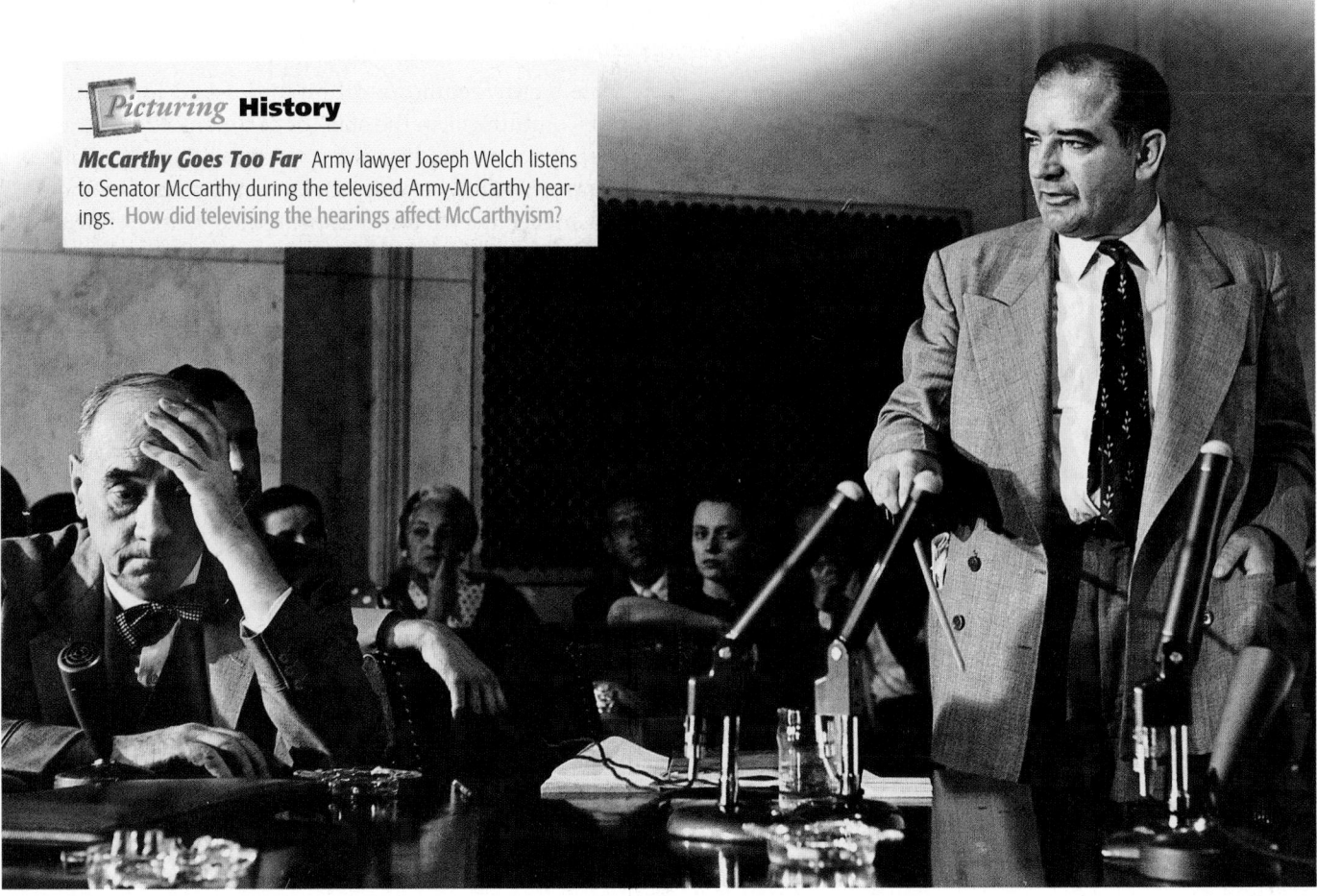

McCarthy Goes Too Far Army lawyer Joseph Welch listens to Senator McCarthy during the televised Army-McCarthy hearings. How did televising the hearings affect McCarthyism?

McCarthy was not alone in making such charges. In the prevailing mood of anxiety about communism, many Americans were ready to believe them.

The McCarran Internal Security Act

In 1950, with the Korean War underway and McCarthy and others arousing fears of Communist spies, Congress passed the Internal Security Act, usually called the **McCarran Act.** Declaring that "world Communism has as its sole purpose the establishment of a totalitarian dictatorship in America," Senator Pat McCarran of Nevada offered a way to fight "treachery, infiltration, sabotage, and terrorism." The act made it illegal to "combine, conspire, or agree with any other person to perform any act which would substantially contribute to . . . the establishment of a totalitarian government." The law required all Communist Party and "Communist-front" organizations to register with the United States attorney general and publish their records. The act also created other restrictions for Communists. For example, they could not get passports to travel abroad.

The McCarran Act did not stop there. In case of a national emergency, it allowed the arrest and detention of Communists and Communist sympathizers. Unwilling to punish people for their opinions, Truman vetoed the bill, but Congress easily passed it

over his veto in 1950. Later Supreme Court cases, however, ensured that the McCarran Act would never be very effective.

McCarthy's Tactics

After the 1952 election gave the Republicans control of Congress, McCarthy became chairman of the Senate subcommittee on investigations. Using the power of his committee to force government officials to testify about alleged Communist influences, McCarthy turned the investigation into a witch hunt—a search for disloyalty based on flimsy evidence and irrational fears. His tactic of damaging reputations with vague and unfounded charges became known as **McCarthyism.**

McCarthy's theatrics and sensational accusations drew the attention of the press, which put him in the headlines and quoted him widely. When he questioned witnesses, McCarthy would badger them and then refuse to accept their answers. His tactics left a cloud of suspicion that McCarthy and others interpreted as guilt. Furthermore, people were afraid to challenge him for fear of becoming targets themselves.

McCarthy's Downfall

In 1954 McCarthy began to look for Soviet spies in the United States Army. Alerted to his intentions, the army conducted its own internal investigation and found no spies or any suspicion of espionage. Furious at the denial, McCarthy took his investigation onto television. He questioned and challenged officers in a harsh voice, harassing them about trivial details and accusing them of misconduct.

During weeks of televised **Army-McCarthy hearings** in the spring of 1954, millions of Americans watched McCarthy bully witnesses. His popular support started to fade. Finally, to strike back at the army lawyer, Joseph Welch, McCarthy brought up the past of a young lawyer in Welch's firm who had been a member of a Communist-front organization during his law school years. Welch, who was fully aware of the young man's past, now exploded at McCarthy for possibly ruining the young man's career: "Until this moment, I think I never really gauged your cruelty or your recklessness. . . . You have done enough. Have you no sense of decency, sir, at long last? Have you left no sense of decency?"

Spectators cheered. Welch had said aloud what many Americans had been thinking. One senator on the committee, Stuart Symington of Missouri, was also repelled: "The American people have had a look at you for six weeks. You are not fooling anyone." McCarthy had lost the power to arouse fear. Newspaper headlines repeated, "Have you no sense of decency?"

Later that year, the Senate passed a vote of censure, or formal disapproval, against McCarthy—one of the most serious criticisms it can level against a member. His influence gone, McCarthy faded from public view. Although he remained in the Senate, he had little influence. He died in 1957, a broken and embittered man.

✓ **Reading Check** **Evaluating** What were the effects of McCarthyism?

Life During the Early Cold War

The Red Scare and the spread of nuclear weapons had a profound impact on life in the 1950s. Fear of communism and of nuclear war dominated life for ordinary Americans as well as for government leaders throughout the era.

Facing the Bomb Already upset by the first Soviet atomic test in 1949, Americans were shocked when the USSR again successfully tested the much more powerful hydrogen bomb, or H-bomb, in 1953. This was less than a year after the United States had tested its own H-bomb.

Americans prepared for a surprise Soviet attack. Schools set aside special areas as bomb shelters. In bomb drills, students learned to duck under their

Picturing **History**

Signs of the Times During the Cold War, the media often gave survival tips for the nuclear holocaust many saw just around the corner. At right, a California resident works on his fallout shelter. How did such fears affect American politics?

Cold War Words The development of nuclear weapons and artificial satellites created not only new anxieties but also new words and expressions.

"*Sputnik,*" the name of the Soviet satellite, started its own language trend, as words gained a *-nik* ending for a foreign-sounding effect. One new word, *beatnik,* described a young person influenced by the style of Beat writers such as Jack Kerouac and Allen Ginsberg. Another word, *peacenik,* was used to describe a peace activist.

The atomic bomb test on Bikini Atoll gave the Nuclear Age two new words: *fallout,* the term for the harmful radiation left over after an atomic blast, and *bikini,* a skimpy swimsuit that French designers promised would produce an "explosion" on the beach.

desks, turn away from the windows, and cover their heads with their hands. These "duck-and-cover" actions were supposed to protect them from a nuclear bomb blast.

"Duck-and-cover" might have made people feel safe, but it would not have protected them from deadly nuclear radiation. According to experts, for every person killed outright by a nuclear blast, four more would die later from fallout, the radiation left over after a blast. To protect themselves, some families built backyard fallout shelters and stocked them with canned food.

Popular Culture in the Cold War
Worries about nuclear war and Communist infiltration filled people's imaginations. Cold War nightmares soon appeared in films and popular fiction.

Matt Cvetic was an FBI undercover informant who secretly infiltrated the Communist Party in Pittsburgh. His story captivated magazine readers in the *Saturday Evening Post* in 1950 and came to the screen the next year as *I Was a Communist for the FBI.* Another suspense film, *Walk East on Beacon* (1951), features the FBI's activities in an espionage case. In 1953 television took up the theme with a series about an undercover FBI counterspy who was also a Communist Party official. Each week, *I Led Three Lives* kept television viewers on edge.

In 1954 author Philip Wylie published *Tomorrow!* This novel describes the horrific effects of nuclear war on an unprepared American city. As an adviser on civil defense, Wylie had failed to convince the federal government to play a strong role in building bomb shelters. Frustrated, he wrote this novel to educate the public about the horrors of atomic war.

At the same time these fears were haunting Americans, the country was enjoying postwar prosperity and optimism. That spirit, combined with McCarthyism, witch hunts, fears of Communist infiltration, and the threat of atomic attack, made the early 1950s a time of contrasts. As the 1952 election approached, Americans were looking for someone or something that would make them feel secure.

✓ **Reading Check** **Describing** How did the Cold War affect life in the 1950s?

SECTION 3 ASSESSMENT

Checking for Understanding

1. **Define:** subversion, perjury, censure, fallout, fallout shelter.
2. **Identify:** loyalty review program, Alger Hiss, McCarran Act, McCarthyism.
3. **Explain** the goals of Project Venona.
4. **Review Facts** What did the McCarran Act propose to do?

Reviewing Themes

5. **Civic Rights and Responsibilities** How did McCarthyism and the Red Scare change American society and government?

Critical Thinking

6. **Interpreting** Why did McCarthy initially receive a lot of support for his efforts to expose Communists?
7. **Organizing** Use a graphic organizer to list the causes and effects of the new Red Scare.

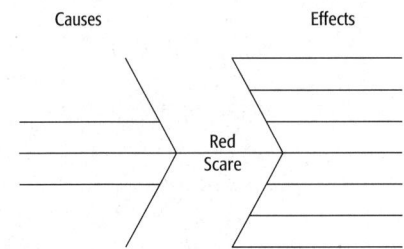

Causes   Effects

Red
Scare

Analyzing Visuals

8. **Analyzing Photographs** Study the photograph on page 794 of the Army-McCarthy hearings. From their postures, how would you describe the attitude of army lawyer Joseph Welch toward Senator Joseph McCarthy? Do you think Welch respects McCarthy's presentation?

Writing About History

9. **Persuasive Writing** Imagine you are a newspaper editor during the McCarthy hearings. Write an editorial supporting or condemning Senator McCarthy. Defend your position.

Eisenhower's Policies

Main Idea

As president, Eisenhower developed plans to reduce world tensions while containing and competing with communism.

Key Terms and Names

massive retaliation, *Sputnik,* brinkmanship, covert, Central Intelligence Agency, developing nation, military-industrial complex

Reading Strategy

Organizing As you read about Eisenhower's presidency, complete a graphic organizer similar to the one below by filling in aspects of Eisenhower's "New Look."

Eisenhower's "New Look"

Reading Objectives

- **Evaluate** Eisenhower's military policy known as the "New Look."
- **Debate** the effectiveness of Eisenhower's foreign policy.

Section Theme

Science and Technology Nuclear technology enabled Eisenhower to change American military policy, while new missile technology marked the beginning of the space age.

Preview of Events

| ◆1952 | ◆1955 | ◆1958 | ◆1961 |

July 1953
Armistice in Korean War

October 1956
Hungarian revolution

October 1956
Suez Canal crisis

October 4, 1957
Soviet Union launches *Sputnik*

May 1960
U-2 incident

★ An American Story ★

On May 1, 1960, CIA pilot Francis Gary Powers sat in the cockpit of his U-2 spy plane, flying at more than 60,000 feet over Afghanistan. His mission was to fly over suspected Soviet missile bases and photograph them.

As Powers passed over the forbidden border into the Soviet Union, he felt a familiar thrill. "There was no abrupt change in topography," he remembered, "yet the moment you crossed the border, you sensed the difference. . . . Knowing there were people who would shoot you down if they could created a strange tension. . . . I wondered how the Russians felt, knowing I was up here, unable to do anything about it. . . . I could imagine their frustration and rage."

Suddenly, Powers heard a dull thump. A surface-to-air missile exploded nearby in a flash of orange. The plane's wings snapped off, leaving the spinning aircraft plummeting down towards the earth. Powers screamed, "I've had it now!"

The downing of Powers's plane set off one of the major confrontations of the Cold War during the presidency of Dwight D. Eisenhower.

—**adapted from** *May-Day: The U-2 Affair*

Eisenhower's "New Look"

By the end of 1952, many Americans were ready for a change in leadership. The Cold War had much to do with that attitude. Many Americans believed that Truman's foreign policy was not working. The Soviet Union had acquired the atomic bomb and consolidated its hold on Eastern Europe. China had fallen to communism, and American troops had been sent across the Pacific to fight in the Korean War.

Tired of the criticism and uncertain he could win, Truman decided not to run again. The Democrats nominated Adlai Stevenson, governor of Illinois. The Republicans chose Dwight D. Eisenhower, the general who had organized the D-Day invasion.

Despite Stevenson's charming personality and skilled speech making, he had no chance against a national hero who had helped win World War II. Americans were looking for someone they could trust to lead the nation in its Cold War struggle against communism. Eisenhower won in a landslide.

"More Bang for the Buck"

The Cold War shaped Eisenhower's thinking from the moment he took office. Eisenhower was convinced that the key to victory in the Cold War was not simply military might but also a strong economy. The United States had to show the world that free enterprise could produce a better and more prosperous society than communism. At the same time, economic prosperity would prevent Communists from gaining support in the United States and protect society from subversion.

As a professional soldier, Eisenhower knew the costs associated with large-scale conventional war. Preparing for that kind of warfare, he believed, would cost far too much money. "We cannot defend the nation in a way which will exhaust our economy," Eisenhower declared. A "New Look" in defense policy was needed. Instead of maintaining a large and expensive army, the nation "must be prepared to use atomic weapons in all forms." Nuclear weapons, he said, gave "more bang for the buck."

Massive Retaliation

The Korean War had convinced Eisenhower that the United States could not contain communism by fighting a series of small wars. Such wars were unpopular and too expensive. Instead, they had to be prevented from happening in the first place. The best way to do that seemed to be to threaten to use nuclear weapons if a Communist state tried to seize territory by force. This policy came to be called massive retaliation.

The new policy enabled Eisenhower to cut military spending from $50 billion to $34 billion. He did this by cutting back the army, which required a lot of money to maintain. At the same time, he increased America's nuclear arsenal from about 1,000 bombs in 1953 to about 18,000 bombs in 1961.

The *Sputnik* Crisis

The New Look's emphasis on nuclear weapons required new technology to deliver them. In 1955 the air force unveiled the huge B-52

TECHNOLOGY & History

The Hydrogen Bomb

The atomic bomb dropped on Hiroshima in 1945 had an explosive force of 20,000 tons of TNT. As devastating as that bomb was, the hydrogen bomb was exponentially more powerful. Designed by Edward Teller and Stanislaw Ulam, the hydrogen test bomb, nicknamed "Mike," was first detonated on November 1, 1952. Its explosive force was equal to 10 million tons of TNT. *How did the two explosive devices combine to create an explosion?*

1 The **plutonium core** provides the radiation from plutonium essential for a fusion reaction.

High explosive charges

Uranium shield

Plutonium 239

2 The **primary device** sets off a smaller atomic explosion that creates x-ray radiation pressure.

3 In the **secondary device**, the fusion process begins when pressure builds inside the bomb casing from the release of radiation.

bomber, which was designed to fly across continents and drop nuclear bombs anywhere in the world. Because bombers could be shot down, Eisenhower also began development of intercontinental ballistic missiles (ICBMs) that could deliver bombs anywhere in the world. He also began a program to build submarines capable of launching nuclear missiles.

As the United States began to develop long-range nuclear missiles, Americans were stunned to discover the Soviet Union had already developed their own. On October 4, 1957, the Soviets launched *Sputnik,* the first artificial satellite to orbit the earth. This technological triumph alarmed Americans, who took it as a sign that the United States was falling behind the Soviet Union in missile technology.

Eisenhower insisted he was not worried just because the Soviets "put one small ball into the air." Members of Congress, on the other hand, feared the nation was falling behind in scientific research. The following year, Congress created the **National Aeronautics and Space Administration** (NASA) to coordinate research in rocket science and space exploration. It also passed the **National Defense Education Act** (NDEA), which provided funds for education and training in science, math, and foreign languages.

✓ **Reading Check** **Summarizing** How did Eisenhower alter the nature of defense spending?

Brinkmanship In Action

President Eisenhower's apparent willingness to threaten nuclear war to maintain the peace worried some people. Secretary of State **John Foster Dulles,** however, the dominant figure in the nation's foreign policy in the 1950s, strongly defended the policy:

❝You have to take chances for peace, just as you must take chances in war. Some say that we were brought to the verge of war. Of course we were brought to the verge of war. The ability to get to the verge without getting into the war is the necessary art. . . . If you try to run away from it, if you are scared to go to the brink, you are lost. We've had to look it square in the face. . . . We walked to the brink and we looked it in the face. We took strong action.❞

—quoted in *Rise to Globalism*

Critics called this brinkmanship—the willingness to go to the brink of war to force the other side to back down—and argued that it was too dangerous.

"So Russia Launched a Satellite, but Has It Made Cars With Fins Yet?"

Analyzing *Political Cartoons*

Cold War Worries The speaker here is comparing American prosperity with the Soviets' launching of *Sputnik.* What is the cartoonist's intent?

Several times, however, President Eisenhower felt compelled to threaten nuclear war during a crisis.

The Korean War Ends During his campaign for the presidency, Eisenhower had said, "I shall go to Korea," promising to end the costly and increasingly unpopular war. On December 4, 1952, just weeks after his election, he kept his promise. Bundled against the freezing Korean winter, the president-elect talked with frontline commanders and their troops.

Eisenhower became convinced that the ongoing battle was costing too many lives and bringing too few victories. "Small attacks on small hills," the former general declared, "[will] not end this war." The president then quietly let the Chinese know that the United States might continue the Korean War "under circumstances of our own choosing"—a hint at nuclear attack.

The threat to go to the brink of nuclear war seemed to work. In July 1953, negotiators signed an armistice. The battle line between the two sides, which was very near the prewar boundary, became the border between North Korea and South Korea. A "demilitarized zone" (DMZ) separated them. There was no victory, but the war had at least stopped the spread of communism in Korea—the goal of containment. American troops are still based in Korea, helping South Korea defend its border.

The Taiwan Crisis Shortly after the war ended, a new crisis erupted in Asia. Although the Chinese Communists had taken power in mainland China, the Chinese Nationalists still controlled Taiwan and several small islands along China's coast.

In the fall of 1954, China threatened to seize two of the islands from the Nationalists. Eisenhower saw Taiwan as part of the "anticommunist barrier" in Asia. When China began shelling the islands and announced that Taiwan would soon be liberated, Eisenhower asked Congress to authorize the use of force to defend Taiwan.

Eisenhower then warned the Chinese that any attempt to invade Taiwan would be resisted by American naval forces stationed nearby. He and Dulles hinted that they would use nuclear weapons to stop an invasion. Soon afterward, China backed down.

The Suez Crisis The year after Eisenhower went to the brink of war with China, a serious crisis erupted in the Middle East. Eisenhower's goal in the Middle East was to prevent Arab nations from aligning with the Soviet Union. To build support among Arabs, Dulles offered to help Egypt finance the construction of a dam on the Nile River. The Egyptians eagerly accepted the American offer.

The deal ran into trouble in Congress, however, because Egypt had bought weapons from Communist Czechoslovakia. Dulles was forced to withdraw the offer. A week later, Egyptian troops seized control of the Suez Canal from the Anglo-French company that had controlled it. The Egyptians intended to use the canal's profits to pay for the dam.

The British and French responded quickly to the Suez Crisis. In October 1956, British and French troops invaded Egypt. Eisenhower was furious with Britain and France. He declared they had made a "complete mess and botch of things." The situation became even more tense when the Soviet Union threatened rocket attacks on Britain and France and offered to send troops to help Egypt. Eisenhower immediately put American nuclear forces on alert, noting, "If those

NATO and the Warsaw Pact, 1955

"Iron Curtain"
Communist nations not in Warsaw Pact
Warsaw Pact countries
Non-Communist nations not in NATO
NATO countries
⊛ Capital

Geography *Skills*

By the mid-1950s, two powerful military alliances, NATO and the Warsaw Pact, were facing each other in Europe. **Applying Geography Skills** How many European nations had Communist governments in 1955?

fellows start something, we may have to hit them—and if necessary, with everything in the bucket."

Under strong American pressure, the British and French called off their invasion. The Soviet Union had won a major diplomatic victory, however, by supporting Egypt. Soon afterward, other Arab nations began accepting Soviet aid as well.

✓ **Reading Check** **Identifying** What was brinkmanship?

Fighting Communism Covertly

President Eisenhower relied on brinkmanship on several occasions, but he knew it could not work in all situations. It could prevent war, but it could not, for example, prevent Communists from staging revolutions within countries. To prevent Communist uprisings in other countries, Eisenhower decided to use covert, or hidden, operations conducted by the **Central Intelligence Agency** (CIA).

Containment in Developing Nations
Many of the CIA's operations took place in developing nations—nations with primarily agricultural economies. Many of these countries blamed European imperialism and American capitalism for their problems. Their leaders looked to the Soviet Union as a model of how to industrialize their countries. They often threatened to nationalize, or put under government control, foreign businesses operating in their countries.

American officials feared that these leaders might align their nations with the Soviet Union or even stage a Communist revolution. One way to stop developing nations from moving into the Communist camp was to provide them with financial aid, as Eisenhower had tried to do in Egypt. In some cases, however, where the threat of communism seemed stronger, the CIA staged covert operations to overthrow anti-American leaders and replace them with pro-American leaders.

Iran and Guatemala
Two examples of covert operations that achieved American objectives took place in Iran and Guatemala. By 1953 Iranian prime minister Mohammed Mossadegh had already nationalized the Anglo-Iranian Oil Company. He seemed ready to make an oil deal with the Soviet Union. In 1953 Mossadegh moved against the pro-American Shah of Iran, who was temporarily forced into exile. Dulles quickly sent agents to organize street riots and arrange a coup that ousted Mossadegh, and the Shah returned to power.

Picturing **History**

Distinguished Brothers John Foster Dulles (right) became secretary of state under Eisenhower; his brother Allen Dulles (center) was director of the CIA in the 1950s. With what policy is John Foster Dulles associated?

The following year, the CIA acted to protect American-owned property in Guatemala. In 1951 Jacobo Arbenz Guzmán won election as president of Guatemala with Communist support. His land reform program took over large estates, including those of the American-owned United Fruit Company. In May 1954, Communist Czechoslovakia delivered arms to Guatemala. The CIA responded by arming the Guatemalan opposition and training them at secret camps in Nicaragua and Honduras. Shortly after these CIA-trained forces invaded Guatemala, Arbenz Guzmán left office.

Uprising in Hungary
Covert operations did not always work as Eisenhower hoped. In 1953 Stalin died, and a power struggle began in the Soviet Union. By 1956 **Nikita Khrushchev** had emerged as the leader of the Soviet Union. That year, Khrushchev delivered a secret speech to Soviet leaders. He attacked Stalin's policies and insisted there were

many ways to build a Communist society. Although the speech was secret, the CIA obtained a copy. With Eisenhower's permission, the CIA arranged for it to be broadcast to Eastern Europe.

Many Eastern Europeans had long been frustrated with Communist rule. Hearing Khrushchev's speech further discredited communism. In June 1956, riots erupted in Eastern Europe. By late October, a full-scale uprising had begun in Hungary. Although Khrushchev was willing to tolerate greater freedom in Eastern Europe, he had never meant to imply that the Soviets would tolerate an end to communism in Eastern Europe. Soon after the uprising began, Soviet tanks rolled into Budapest, the capital of Hungary, and crushed the rebellion.

✓ **Reading Check** **Explaining** Why did Eisenhower use covert operations?

Continuing Tensions

The uprising in Hungary forced Khrushchev to reassert Soviet power and the superiority of communism. Previously, he had supported "peaceful coexistence" with capitalism. Now he accused the "capitalist countries" of starting a "feverish arms race." In 1957, after the launch of Sputnik, Khrushchev boasted, "We will bury capitalism. . . . Your grandchildren will live under communism."

In late 1958 Khrushchev demanded that the United States, Great Britain, and France withdraw their troops from West Berlin. Secretary of State Dulles rejected Khrushchev's demands. If the Soviets threatened Berlin, Dulles announced, NATO would respond, "if need be by military force." Brinkmanship worked again, and Khrushchev backed down.

To try to improve relations, Eisenhower invited Khrushchev to visit the United States in late 1959. The visit went well, and the two leaders agreed to hold a summit in Paris in 1960. A **summit** is a formal face-to-face meeting of leaders from different countries to discuss important issues.

Shortly before the summit was to begin, the Soviet Union shot down the American U-2 spy plane piloted by **Francis Gary Powers.** At first, Eisenhower claimed that the aircraft was a weather plane that had strayed off course. Then Khrushchev dramatically produced the pilot. Eisenhower refused to apologize, saying the flights had protected American security. In response, Khrushchev broke up the summit.

In this climate of heightened tension, President Eisenhower prepared to leave office. In January 1961, he delivered a farewell address to the nation. In the address, he pointed out that a new relationship had developed between the military establishment and the defense industry. He warned Americans to be on guard against the immense influence of this military-industrial complex in a democracy. Although he had avoided war and kept communism contained, Eisenhower admitted to some frustration: "I confess I lay down my official responsibility in this field with a definite sense of disappointment. . . . I wish I could say that a lasting peace is in sight."

✓ **Reading Check** **Evaluating** Why did Eisenhower warn Americans about the military-industrial complex?

SECTION 4 ASSESSMENT

Checking for Understanding

1. **Define:** massive retaliation, brinkmanship, covert, developing nation, military-industrial complex.

2. **Identify:** *Sputnik,* Central Intelligence Agency.

3. **Reviewing Facts** What was the significance of the Soviet Union's launching of *Sputnik* in 1957?

Reviewing Themes

4. **Science and Technology** How did technology shape Eisenhower's military policy?

Critical Thinking

5. **Interpreting** Do you think Eisenhower's foreign policy was successful? Why or why not?

6. **Organizing** Use a graphic organizer similar to the one below to list Eisenhower's strategies for containing Communism.

Analyzing Visuals

7. **Analyzing Maps** Study the map on page 800. How many nations belonged to NATO? How many nations belonged to the Warsaw Pact? Which nations did not belong to either NATO or the Warsaw Pact?

Writing About History

8. **Persuasive Writing** Imagine you are a member of Eisenhower's cabinet. Defend or attack brinkmanship as a foreign policy tactic. Be sure to provide specific reasons for your point of view.

Critical Thinking
SKILLBUILDER

Making Decisions

Why Learn This Skill?

Suppose you have been given the choice of taking an art class or a music class during your free period during school. How will you decide which class to take?

Learning the Skill

When you make a decision, you are making a choice between alternatives. In order to make that choice, you must be informed and aware. There are five key steps you should follow that will help you through the process of making decisions.

- Identify the problem. What are you being asked to choose between?

- Gather information to identify and consider various alternatives that are possible.

- Determine the consequences for each alternative. Identify both positive and negative consequences.

- Evaluate the consequences. Consider both the positive and negative consequences for each alternative.

- Determine which alternative seems to have more positive than negative consequences. Then make your decision.

Practicing the Skill

Decisions throughout history have affected the outcome of events and defined history as we know it today. Identify the alternatives and describe their consequences for each of the following events that occurred after World War II. Each of these events took place as a result of a decision made by a person or a group of people.

❶ Britain and the United States recognize the Soviet-backed government that takes control in Poland.

❷ The United States orchestrates the Berlin airlift to assist residents of West Berlin after Stalin cuts off surface transportation bringing supplies from the West.

President Truman and Dean Acheson

❸ The Marshall Plan for rebuilding war-torn Western Europe is approved.

❹ President Truman relieves General Douglas MacArthur of his command because of insubordination.

Skills Assessment

Complete the Practicing Skills questions on page 805 and the Chapter 26 Skill Reinforcement Activity to assess your mastery of this skill.

Applying the Skill

Making Decisions Use a newspaper or magazine to find a current issue that directly affects your life. Identify the issue, and then review the facts and what you already know about the issue. Identify various alternatives and determine the consequences for each. Use this information to evaluate both positive and negative consequences. Make a sound decision about which alternative would be best for you, and write a paragraph defending your decision.

Glencoe's **Skillbuilder Interactive Workbook CD-ROM, Level 2,** provides instruction and practice in key social studies skills.

Reviewing Key Terms

On a sheet of paper, use each of these terms in a sentence.

1. Cold War
2. iron curtain
3. containment
4. limited war
5. subversion
6. perjury
7. censure
8. fallout
9. fallout shelter
10. massive retaliation
11. brinkmanship
12. covert
13. developing nation
14. military-industrial complex

Reviewing Key Facts

15. **Identify:** Potsdam, Marshall Plan, NATO, McCarthyism.
16. How did Stalin's postwar foreign policy goals add to the growing tensions between the United States and the USSR?
17. Why were NATO and the Warsaw Pact formed?
18. What was the long-term strategy of the United States during the Cold War?
19. What were the effects of the new Red Scare on federal employees?
20. What was President Eisenhower's "new look" for the military?

Critical Thinking

21. **Analyzing Themes: Global Connections** How did the Truman Doctrine and the Marshall Plan cause the United States to change its foreign policy goal of isolationism?

22. **Evaluating** How did the Korean War affect American domestic and international policy?

23. **Organizing** Use a graphic organizer similar to the one below to list the causes of the Cold War.

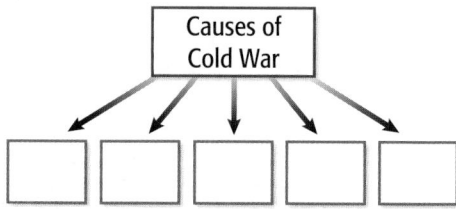

24. **Interpreting Primary Sources** Margaret Chase Smith, a Republican from Maine, was elected to the Senate in 1948. As a newcomer and the only woman in the Senate, she had very little power. Smith was upset by Joseph McCarthy's accusations, but she hoped her senior colleagues would reprimand him. When they failed to do so, Smith made her "Declaration of Conscience" speech. Read the excerpt and answer the questions that follow.

Chapter Summary

The Cold War

Soviet Union		Western Allies
• To create a protective sphere of Communist countries along European border • To promote the spread of communism	**General Goals**	• To contain the spread of communism by supporting capitalist democratic governments
• Occupied Eastern European nations and saw that Communist governments were established	**In Europe**	• Expected free elections to occur in Soviet-controlled Eastern Europe
• Sought access to oil in Iran • Aided Communists in Greece and pressured Turkey for access to the Mediterranean	**In the Middle East**	• Forced Soviet withdrawal from Iran • Pledged aid to halt Soviet threats to Turkey and Greece
• Communists seize power in China in 1949 • China and Soviet Union signed treaty of friendship and alliance • Communist North Korea invaded South Korea to start Korean War • Chinese troops fought for North Korea	**In Asia**	• Aided China's Nationalist government • Dedicated money and troops to establish democratic stronghold in Japan • United Nations troops sent to fight for South Korea in Korean War
• Promoted development of high-technology weapons and surveillance	**At Home**	• Focused on the development of advanced technology weapons

Self-Check Quiz

Visit the *American Vision* Web site at tav.glencoe.com and click on *Self-Check Quizzes—Chapter 26* to assess your knowledge of chapter content.

❝As a United States Senator, I am not proud of the way in which the Senate has been made a publicity platform for irresponsible sensationalism. I am not proud of the reckless abandon in which unproved charges have been hurled from this side of the aisle. I am not proud of the obviously staged, undignified countercharges that have been attempted in retaliation from the other side of the aisle. . . . I am not proud of the way we smear outsiders from the Floor of the Senate and hide behind the cloak of congressional immunity. . . .

As an American, I am shocked at the way Republicans and Democrats alike are playing directly into the Communist design of 'confuse, divide, and conquer'. . . . I want to see our nation recapture the strength and unity it once had when we fought the enemy instead of ourselves.❞

—from *Declaration of Conscience*

a. With whom is Smith angry, and why?

b. According to Smith, who is really dividing the nation?

Practicing Skills

25. Making Decisions Study the text on the Truman Doctrine on page 785. Then use the steps you learned about making decisions on page 803 to identify the alternatives the president had in making a decision to ask for aid to fight Soviet aggression in Turkey and Greece. Create a graphic organizer to list the alternatives.

Chapter Activity

26. Technology Activity: Developing a Multimedia Presentation Use the Internet and other resources to find out more about American popular culture during the Cold War. Then create a multimedia report about popular culture at this time, and present your report to the class. Your report could discuss films, books, and magazine articles.

Writing Activity

27. Persuasive Writing Imagine that you have witnessed the crowds giving General MacArthur a hero's welcome. Write an opinion piece for a magazine justifying his reception or criticizing it because of his disagreement with Truman.

NATIONAL GEOGRAPHIC The Occupation of Berlin After World War II, 1945

Legend:
- ✈ Airports
- American sector
- British sector
- French sector
- Soviet sector

0 — 5 miles
0 — 5 kilometers
Albers Conic Equal-Area projection

Geography and History

28. The map above shows the occupation of Berlin after World War II. Study the map and answer the questions below.

a. Interpreting Maps How was West Berlin's location a disadvantage? How did Stalin use this disadvantage against the Western Allies?

b. Applying Geography Skills What transportation advantage did West Berlin have over East Berlin? How did the United States use this advantage when West Berlin was stranded?

Standardized Test Practice

Directions: Choose the phrase that best completes the following sentence.

One historical lesson from the McCarthy era is the realization that

A loyalty oaths prevent spying.

B communism is influential in prosperous times.

C Communist agents had infiltrated all levels of the U.S. government.

D public fear of traitors can lead to intolerance and discrimination.

Test-Taking Tip: Think about the definition of McCarthyism, the use of unsubstantiated accusations to discredit people. Which of the answers relates best to this definition?

CHAPTER 27

Postwar America
1945–1960

Why It Matters

After World War II, the country enjoyed a period of economic prosperity. Many more Americans could now aspire to a middle-class lifestyle, with a house in the suburbs and more leisure time. Television became a favorite form of entertainment. This general prosperity, however, did not extend to many Hispanics, African Americans, Native Americans, or people in Appalachia.

The Impact Today

The effects of this era can still be seen.
- *The middle class represents a large segment of the American population.*
- *Television is a popular form of entertainment for many Americans.*

The American Vision Video *The Chapter 27 video, "America Takes to the Roads," describes the cultural impact of the automobile and its importance to the growing baby boom generation.*

1946
- Series of work strikes plagues country

1948
- Truman elected president

1947
- Levittown construction begins

1944
- GI Bill enacted

Truman
1945–1953

United States
PRESIDENTS

1944   *1948*   *1952*

World

1946
- Juan Perón elected president of Argentina

1948
- South Africa introduces apartheid

1952
- Scientists led by Edward Teller develop hydrogen bomb

These confident newlyweds capture the prosperous attitude of postwar America.

1953
• Lucille Ball gives birth in real life and on her television show

1955
• Salk polio vaccine becomes widely available

1956
• Elvis Presley appears on *The Ed Sullivan Show*
• Federal Highway Act passed

1957
• Estimated 40 million television sets in use in United States

1958
• Galbraith's *The Affluent Society* published

Eisenhower 1953–1961

1956   *1960*

1954
• Gamal Abdel Nasser takes power in Egypt

1956
• Suez Canal crisis erupts

1957
• USSR launches *Sputnik I* and *Sputnik II* satellites

HISTORY
Online

Chapter Overview
Visit the *American Vision* Web site at tav.glencoe.com and click on **Chapter Overviews—Chapter 27** to preview chapter information.

Truman and Eisenhower

Main Idea

After World War II, the Truman and Eisenhower administrations set out to help the nation adjust to peacetime.

Key Terms and Names

GI Bill, closed shop, right-to-work law, union shop, featherbedding, "Do-Nothing Congress," Fair Deal, dynamic conservatism, Federal Highway Act

Reading Strategy

Categorizing As you read about the Truman and Eisenhower administrations, complete a graphic organizer similar to the one below by listing the characteristics of the postwar economy of the United States.

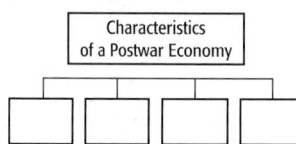

Characteristics of a Postwar Economy

Reading Objectives

- **Explain** the Truman administration's efforts on the domestic front.
- **Describe** President Eisenhower's domestic agenda.

Section Theme

Economic Factors Following World War II, the federal government supported programs that helped the economy make the transition to peacetime production.

Preview of Events

◆1944   ◆1947   ◆1950   ◆1953

1944
Congress passes GI Bill

1946
Strikes take place across the country

1948
Harry S Truman wins presidential election

1952
Dwight D. Eisenhower wins presidential election

★ An American Story ★

As World War II ended, Robert Eubanks was worried as he prepared for his discharge from the army. He had joined the army because, as an African American, it was hard for him to find a job that paid well. Then he heard about something known as the GI Bill, a government program that paid veterans' tuition for college and provided a living allowance.

Eubanks took advantage of the program and enrolled at the Illinois Institute of Technology. He earned three degrees on the GI Bill and eventually became a professor at the University of Illinois.

Years later Eubanks recalled how his life was changed by the bill. "It's very hard to explain how things were during the 1940s," he said. "The restrictions on blacks then were rough. The GI Bill gave me my start on being a professional instead of a stock clerk."

—adapted from *When Dreams Came True*

Return to a Peacetime Economy

After the war many Americans feared the return to a peacetime economy. They worried that after military production halted and millions of former soldiers glutted the labor market, unemployment and recession might sweep the country.

Despite such worries, the economy continued to grow after the war as increased consumer spending helped ward off a recession. After 17 years of economic depression and wartime shortages, Americans rushed out to buy the luxury goods they had long desired.

The Servicemen's Readjustment Act, popularly called the **GI Bill,** further boosted the economy. The act provided generous loans to veterans to help them establish businesses, buy homes, and attend college.

Inflation and Strikes The postwar economy was not without its problems. A greater demand for goods led to higher prices, and this rising inflation soon triggered labor unrest. As the cost of living rose, workers across the country went on strike for better pay. Work stoppages soon affected the automobile, electrical, steel, and mining industries.

Afraid that the nation's energy supply would be drastically reduced because of the striking miners, President Truman forced the miners to return to work after one strike that had lasted over a month. Truman ordered government seizure of the mines while pressuring mine owners to grant the union most of its demands. The president also halted a strike that shut down the nation's railroads by threatening to draft the striking workers into the army.

Republican Victory Labor unrest and high prices prompted many Americans to call for a change. The Republicans seized upon these sentiments during the 1946 congressional elections, winning control of both houses of Congress for the first time since 1930.

Disgusted with the rash of strikes that was crippling the nation, the new conservative Congress quickly set out to curb the power of organized labor. Legislators proposed a measure known as the **Taft-Hartley Act,** which outlawed the closed shop, or the practice of forcing business owners to hire only union members. Under the law, states could pass right-to-work laws, which outlawed union shops (shops in which new workers were required to join the union). The measure also prohibited featherbedding, the practice of limiting work output in order to create more jobs. Furthermore, the bill forbade unions from using their money to support political campaigns. When the bill reached Truman, however, he vetoed it, arguing:

> 66 . . . [It would] reverse the basic direction of our national labor policy, inject the government into private economic affairs on an unprecedented scale, and conflict with important principles of our democratic society. Its provisions would cause more strikes, not fewer. 99
>
> —quoted in *The Growth of the American Republic*

The president's concerns did little to sway Congress, which passed the Taft-Hartley Act in 1947 over Truman's veto. Its supporters claimed the law held irresponsible unions in check just as the Wagner Act of 1935 had restrained antiunion activities and employers. Labor leaders called the act a "slave labor" law and insisted that it erased many of the gains that unions had made since 1933.

✓ **Reading Check**

Explaining Why did Truman veto the Taft-Hartley Act?

HISTORY Online

Student Web Activity Visit the *American Vision* Web site at tav.glencoe.com and click on *Student Web Activities— Chapter 27* for an activity on postwar America.

Truman's Domestic Program

The Democratic Party's loss of members in the 1946 elections did not dampen President Truman's spirits or his plans. Shortly after taking office, Truman had proposed a series of domestic measures that sought to continue the work done as part of Franklin Roosevelt's New Deal. During his tenure in office, Truman worked to push this agenda through Congress.

Truman's Legislative Agenda Truman's proposals included the expansion of Social Security benefits; the raising of the legal minimum wage from 40¢ to 75¢ an hour; a program to ensure full employment through aggressive use of federal spending and investment; public housing and slum clearance; long-range environmental and public works planning; and a system of national health insurance.

Truman also boldly asked Congress in February 1948 to pass a broad civil rights bill that would

The GI Bill African American soldiers review the benefits of the GI Bill, which included loans to attend college and to buy homes.

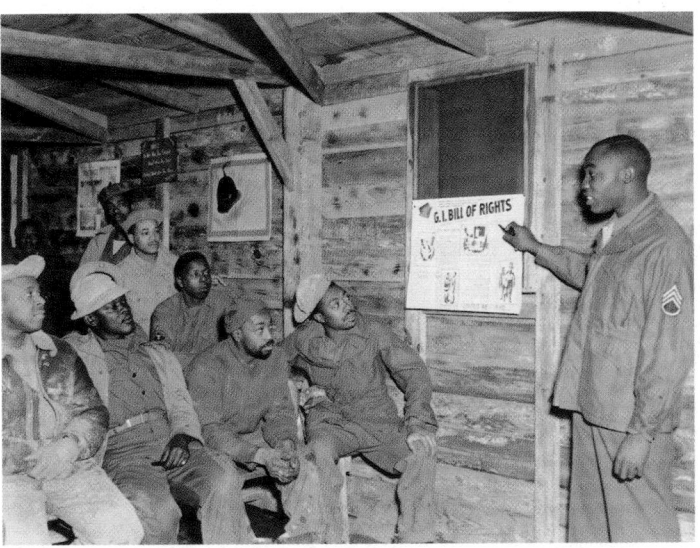

protect African Americans' right to vote, abolish poll taxes, and make lynching a federal crime. He also issued an executive order barring discrimination in federal employment, and he ended segregation in the armed forces.

Most of Truman's legislative efforts, however, met with little success, as a coalition of Republicans and conservative Southern Democrats defeated many of his proposals. While these defeats angered Truman, the president soon had to worry about other matters.

The Election of 1948 As the presidential election of 1948 approached, most observers gave Truman little chance of winning. Some Americans still believed that he lacked the stature for the job, and they viewed his administration as weak and inept.

Divisions within the Democratic Party also seemed to spell disaster for Truman. At the Democratic Convention that summer, two factions abandoned the party altogether. Reacting angrily to Truman's support of civil rights, a group of Southern Democrats formed the States' Rights, or Dixiecrat, Party and nominated South Carolina governor **Strom Thurmond** for president. At the same time, the party's more liberal members were frustrated by Truman's ineffective domestic policies and critical of his anti-Soviet foreign policy. They formed a new Progressive Party, with Henry A. Wallace as their presidential candidate. In addition, the president's Republican opponent was New York governor Thomas Dewey, a dignified and popular candidate who seemed unbeatable. After polling 50 political writers, *Newsweek* magazine declared three weeks before the election, "The landslide for Dewey will sweep the country."

Picturing **History**

African Americans Rally for Truman During the 1948 election, President Truman spoke at many rallies similar to this one in New York City. What legislative proposals by President Truman built African American political support?

Perhaps the only one who gave Truman a chance to win was Truman himself. "I know every one of those 50 fellows," he declared about the writers polled in *Newsweek*. "There isn't one of them has enough sense to pound sand in a rat hole." Ignoring the polls, the feisty president poured his efforts into an energetic campaign. He traveled more than 20,000 miles by train and made more than 350 speeches. Along the way, Truman attacked the majority Republican Congress as "do-nothing, good-for-nothing" for refusing to enact his legislative agenda.

Truman's attacks on the **"Do-Nothing Congress"** did not mention that both he and Congress had been very busy dealing with foreign policy matters. Congress had passed the Truman Doctrine's aid program to Greece and Turkey, as well as the Marshall Plan. It had also created the Department of Defense and the CIA and established the Joint Chiefs of Staff as a permanent organization. The 80th Congress, therefore, did not "do nothing" as Truman charged, but its accomplishments were in areas that did not affect most Americans directly. As a result, Truman's charges began to stick, and to the surprise of almost everyone, his efforts paid off.

With a great deal of support from laborers, African Americans, and farmers, Truman won a narrow but stunning victory over Dewey. Perhaps just as remarkable as the president's victory was the resurgence of the Democratic Party. When the dust had cleared after Election Day, Democrats had regained control of both houses of Congress.

GOVERNMENT

The Fair Deal Truman's State of the Union message to the new Congress repeated the domestic agenda he had put forth previously. "Every segment of our population and every individual," he declared, "has a right to expect from . . . government a fair deal." Whether intentional or not, the president had coined a name—the **Fair Deal**—to set his program apart from the New Deal.

The 81st Congress did not completely embrace Truman's Fair Deal. Legislators did raise the legal minimum wage to 75¢ an hour. They also approved an important expansion of the Social Security system, increasing benefits by 75 percent and extending them to 10 million additional people. Congress also passed the National Housing Act of 1949, which provided for the construction of more than 800,000 units of low-income housing, accompanied by long-term rent subsidies.

Congress refused, however, to pass national health insurance or to provide subsidies for farmers or

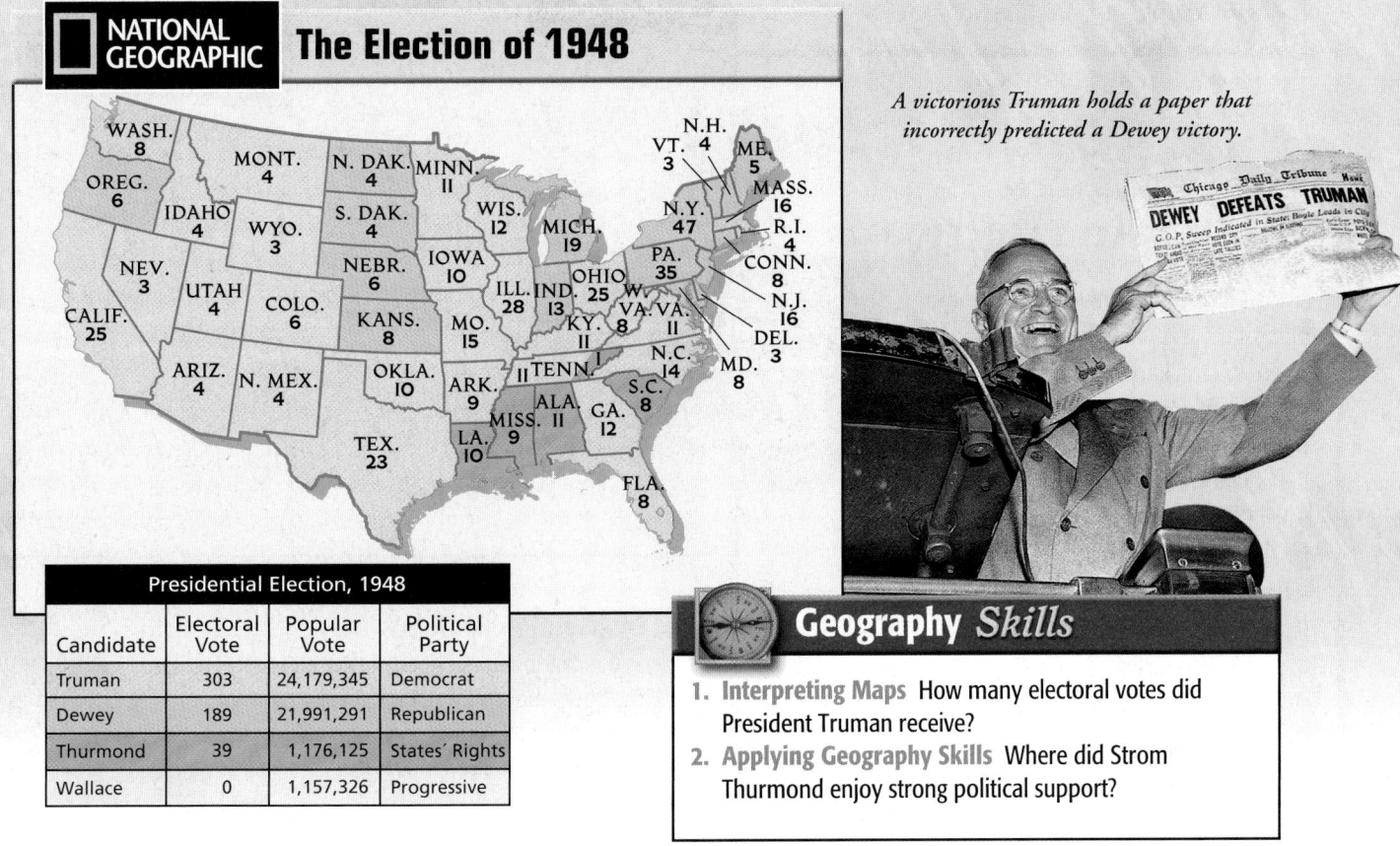

federal aid for schools. In addition, legislators opposed Truman's efforts to enact civil rights legislation.

✔ **Reading Check** **Summarizing** What was the outcome of Truman's proposed legislative agenda?

The Eisenhower Years

In 1950 the United States went to war in Korea. The war consumed the nation's attention and resources and basically ended Truman's Fair Deal. By 1952, with the war a bloody stalemate and his approval rating dropping quickly, Truman declined to run again for the presidency. With no Democratic incumbent to face, Republicans pinned their hopes of regaining the White House on a popular World War II hero.

The Election of 1952 Dwight Eisenhower decided to run as the Republican nominee for president in 1952. His running mate was a young California senator, Richard Nixon. The Democrats nominated Illinois governor Adlai Stevenson, a witty and eloquent speaker who had the support of leading liberals and organized labor.

The Republicans adopted the slogan: "It's time for a change!" The warm and friendly Eisenhower, known as "Ike," promised to end the war in Korea. "I like Ike" became the Republican rallying cry.

Eisenhower's campaign soon came under fire as reports surfaced that Richard Nixon had received gifts from California business leaders totaling $18,000 while he was a senator. For a while, it looked as if Nixon might be dropped from the ticket. In a nationwide speech broadcast on radio and television, Nixon insisted the funds had been used for legitimate political purposes. He did admit that his family had kept one gift, a cocker spaniel puppy named "Checkers." He declared, "The kids love the dog, [and] regardless about what they say about it, we're going to keep it." This so-called "Checkers speech" won praise from much of the public and kept Nixon on the ticket.

Eisenhower won the election by a landslide, carrying the Electoral College 442 votes to 89. The Republicans also gained an eight-seat majority in the House, while the Senate became evenly divided between Democrats and Republicans.

Ike as President President Eisenhower had two favorite phrases. "Middle of the road" described his political beliefs, which fell midway between conservative and liberal. He also referred to the notion of "dynamic conservatism," which meant balancing economic conservatism with some activism.

Why It Matters

Interstate Highways

As Cold War tensions rose, American officials realized that the ability to move troops and military equipment across the country quickly and efficiently could very well determine whether the nation could survive attack. Since the haphazard system of two-lane highways that crisscrossed America could not handle such a task, the Eisenhower administration proposed a 41,000-mile network of multi-lane interstate highways. The interstate system changed American life in several significant ways.

NATIONAL GEOGRAPHIC The Interstate System, 2000

CANADA

ATLANTIC OCEAN

HAWAII

MEXICO

Gulf of Mexico

TROPIC OF CANCER

Albers Conic Equal-Area projection

Interstate highway
Interstate highway

More Efficient Distribution of Goods ➤

The interstates made the distribution of goods faster and more efficient. In the 1990s, trucks moved more than 6 billion tons of goods each year, nearly half of all commercial transports in the United States. Most of these trucks used interstates.

Eisenhower wasted little time in showing his conservative side. The new president's cabinet appointments included several business leaders. Under their guidance, Eisenhower ended government price and rent controls, which many conservatives had viewed as unnecessary federal control over the business community. The Eisenhower administration viewed business growth as vital to the nation. The president's secretary of defense, formerly the president of General Motors, declared to the Senate that "what is good for our country is good for General Motors, and vice versa."

Eisenhower's conservatism showed itself in other ways as well. In an attempt to curb the federal budget, the president vetoed a school construction bill and agreed to slash government aid to public housing. Along with these cuts, he supported some modest tax reductions.

Eisenhower also targeted the federal government's continuing aid to businesses, or what he termed "creeping socialism." Shortly after taking office, the president abolished the Reconstruction Finance Corporation (RFC), which since 1932 had lent money to banks, railroads, and other large institutions in financial trouble. Another Depression-era agency, the Tennessee Valley Authority (TVA), also came under Eisenhower's economic scrutiny.

During his presidency, appropriations for the TVA fell from $185 million to $12 million.

In some areas, President Eisenhower took an activist role. For example, he advocated the passage of two large government projects. During the 1950s, as the number of Americans who owned cars increased, so too did the need for greater and more efficient travel routes. In 1956 Congress responded to this growing need by passing the **Federal Highway Act,** the largest public works program in American history. The act appropriated $25 billion for a 10-year effort to construct more than 40,000 miles (64,400 km) of interstate highways. Congress also authorized construction of the Great Lakes-St. Lawrence Seaway to connect the Great Lakes with the Atlantic Ocean through a series of locks on the St. Lawrence River. Three previous presidents had been unable to reach agreements with Canada to build this waterway to aid international shipping. Through Eisenhower's efforts, the two nations finally agreed on a plan to complete the project.

Extending the New Deal Although President Eisenhower cut federal spending and worked to limit the federal government's role in the nation's economy, he also agreed to extend the Social Security system to an additional 10 million people. He also extended unemployment compensation to an

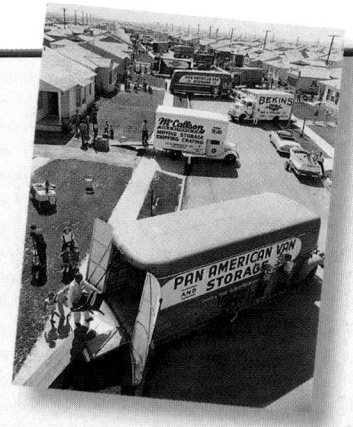

◀ Suburbanization and Urban Sprawl
The interstate system contributed to the growth of suburban communities and the eventual geographic spread of center-less cities. Using the interstates, suburbanites could commute to their jobs miles away.

A New Road Culture ▶
The interstates created an automobile society. In 1997, $687 billion were spent on private automobiles compared to $22.8 billion for public transit. Additionally, chains of fast food restaurants and motels replaced independent operators across the country.

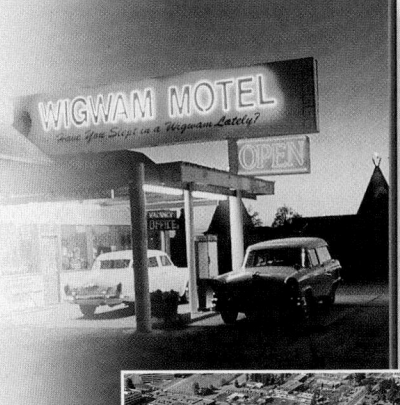

Speed of Travel

The interstate highways drastically decreased the time it took to travel across the continent. In 1919 a young Dwight D. Eisenhower joined 294 other members of the army to travel the 2,800 miles from Washington, D.C., to San Francisco. They made the trip in 62 days, averaging 5 miles per hour. During World War II, General Eisenhower was impressed with the modern design of Germany's freeway system, the Autobahn. "The old convoy," he said, "had started me thinking about good, two-lane highways, but Germany had made me see the wisdom of broader ribbons across the land." Wide lanes and controlled entrance and exit points allowed cars to travel at much higher speeds. Using the interstate highways, Eisenhower's trip would now take 4½ days.

Travel Times: Washington, D.C., to San Francisco

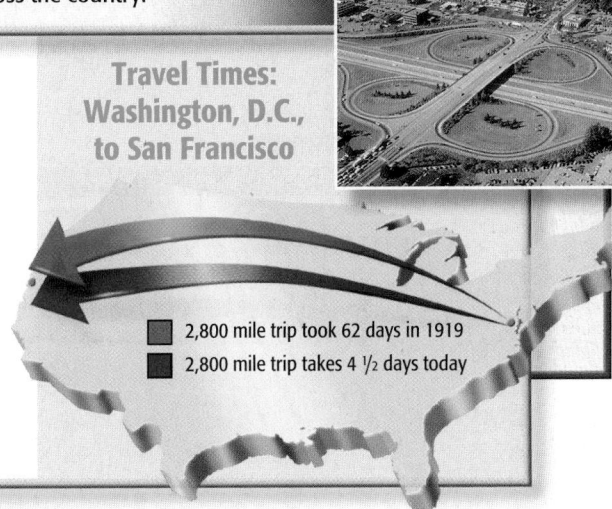

- ■ 2,800 mile trip took 62 days in 1919
- ■ 2,800 mile trip takes 4 ½ days today

additional 4 million citizens and agreed to increase the minimum hourly wage from 75¢ to $1 and to continue to provide some government aid to farmers.

By the time Eisenhower ran for a second term in 1956—a race he won easily—the nation had successfully completed the transition from a wartime to a peacetime economy. The battles between liberals and conservatives over whether to continue New Deal policies would continue. In the meantime, however, most Americans focused their energy on enjoying what had become a decade of tremendous prosperity.

✓ **Reading Check** **Evaluating** What conservative and activist measures did Eisenhower take during his administration?

SECTION 1 ASSESSMENT

Checking for Understanding
1. **Define:** closed shop, right-to-work law, union shop, featherbedding, dynamic conservatism.
2. **Identify:** GI Bill, "Do-Nothing Congress," Fair Deal, Federal Highway Act.

Reviewing Themes
3. **Economic Factors** How did President Eisenhower aid international shipping during his administration?

Critical Thinking
4. **Interpreting** In what ways did the Taft-Hartley Act hurt labor unions?
5. **Categorizing** Use a graphic organizer to compare the agendas of the Truman and Eisenhower administrations.

```
        Agendas

  Truman     Eisenhower

  [    ]       [    ]
```

Analyzing Visuals
6. **Analyzing Maps** Study the map on page 811. Which parts of the country did Dewey win? Why do you think he did so well in these areas?

Writing About History
7. **Persuasive Writing** Take on the role of a member of Congress during the Truman administration. Write a speech in which you try to persuade the 81st Congress to either pass or defeat Truman's Fair Deal measures.

SECTION 2 The Affluent Society

Guide to Reading

Main Idea

The postwar economic boom brought great changes to society, including the ways many Americans worked and lived.

Key Terms and Names

John Kenneth Galbraith, white-collar, blue-collar, multinational corporation, franchise, David Riesman, Levittown, baby boom, Jonas Salk

Reading Strategy

Sequencing As you read about American society in the 1950s, complete a time line similar to the one below by recording the scientific and technological breakthroughs of the time.

Reading Objectives

• **Explain** the reasons for and the effects of the nation's economic boom.
• **Describe** changes to the American family that took place during the 1950s.

Section Theme

Continuity and Change Americans became avid consumers in the atmosphere of postwar abundance.

Preview of Events

♦1946   ♦1950   ♦1954   ♦1958

1947
Construction of Levittown begins

1950
David Riesman's *The Lonely Crowd* published

1955
Salk polio vaccine becomes widely available

1958
John Kenneth Galbraith's *The Affluent Society* published

★ An American Story ★

In the summer of 1951, Kemmons Wilson traveled with his family from Memphis, Tennessee, to Washington, D.C. He noticed that some of the motels they stayed in were terrible. Each added a $2 charge per child to the standard room price, and many were located far from restaurants, forcing travelers back into their cars to search for meals.

Frustrated, Wilson decided to build a motel chain that would provide interstate travelers with comfortable lodgings. They would be located near good family restaurants and allow kids to stay free. Together with a group of investors, Wilson began building the Holiday Inn motel chain. Families loved his motels, and soon Holiday Inns were sprouting up all over the country.

Wilson said he never doubted the success of his endeavor. "I like to think that I'm so . . . normal that anything I like, everybody else is going to like too," he said. "The idea that my instincts are out of line just doesn't occur to me." His prosperity mirrored a growing affluence in the nation. This time of prosperity made the shortages of the Great Depression and World War II a distant memory.

—adapted from *The Fifties*

American Abundance

Wilson's motel chain proved successful largely because the 1950s was a decade of incredible prosperity. In 1958 economist **John Kenneth Galbraith** published *The Affluent Society,* in which he claimed that the nation's postwar prosperity was a new phenomenon. In the past, Galbraith said, all societies had an "economy of scarcity," meaning that a lack of resources and overpopulation had limited economic productivity. Now, the United States and a few other industrialized nations had created what Galbraith called an "economy of abundance." New business techniques and improved technology enabled these nations to produce an abundance of goods and services for their people—all of which allowed many of them to enjoy a standard of living never before thought possible.

The Spread of Wealth Some critics accused Galbraith of overstating the situation, but the facts and figures seemed to support his theory. Between 1940 and 1955, the average income of American families roughly tripled. Americans in all income brackets—poor, middle-class, and wealthy—experienced this rapid rise in income. The dramatic rise in home ownership also showed that the income of average families had risen significantly. Between 1940 and 1960, the number of Americans owning their own homes rose from about 41 to about 61 percent.

Accompanying the country's economic growth were dramatic changes in work environments. Mechanization in farms and factories meant that fewer farmers and laborers were needed to provide the public with food and goods. As a result, more Americans began working in what are called white-collar jobs, such as those in sales and management. In 1956, for the first time, white-collar workers outnumbered blue-collar workers, or people who perform physical labor in industry.

Multinationals and Franchises Many white-collar employees worked for large corporations. As these businesses competed with each other, some expanded overseas. These multinational corporations located themselves closer to important raw materials and benefited from a cheaper labor pool, which made them more competitive.

The 1950s also witnessed the rise of franchises, in which a person owns and runs one or several stores of a chain operation. Because many business leaders believed that consumers valued dependability and familiarity, the owners of chain operations often demanded that their franchises present a uniform look and style.

The Organization Man Like franchise owners, many corporate leaders also expected their employees to conform to company standards. In general, corporations did not desire free-thinking individuals or people who might speak out or criticize the company.

Some social observers recognized this phenomenon and disapproved of it. In his 1950 book, *The Lonely Crowd*, sociologist **David Riesman** argued that this conformity was changing people. Formerly, he claimed, people were "inner-directed," judging themselves on the basis of their own values and the esteem of their families. Now, however, people were becoming "other-directed," concerning themselves with winning the approval of the corporation or community.

In his 1956 book *The Organization Man*, writer **William H. Whyte, Jr.,** assailed the similarity many business organizations cultivated in order to keep any individual from dominating. "In group doctrine," Whyte wrote, "the strong personality is viewed with overwhelming suspicion," and the person with ideas is considered "a threat."

The New Consumerism The conformity of the 1950s included people's desires to own the same new products as their neighbors. With more disposable income, Americans bought more luxury items, such as refrigerators, washing machines, vacuum cleaners, and air conditioners. Americans also bought a variety of labor-saving machines. As *House and Garden* magazine boasted in a 1954 article, coffeemakers, blenders, and lawn trimmers "[replaced] the talents of caretaker, gardener, cook, [and] maid."

"He never wastes a minute, J.P.—that's his lunch."

Analyzing *Political Cartoons*

The Organization Man In the 1950s, more and more people worked in white-collar corporate jobs. Some social critics worried that this development emphasized conformity. In what other ways did society encourage people to conform?

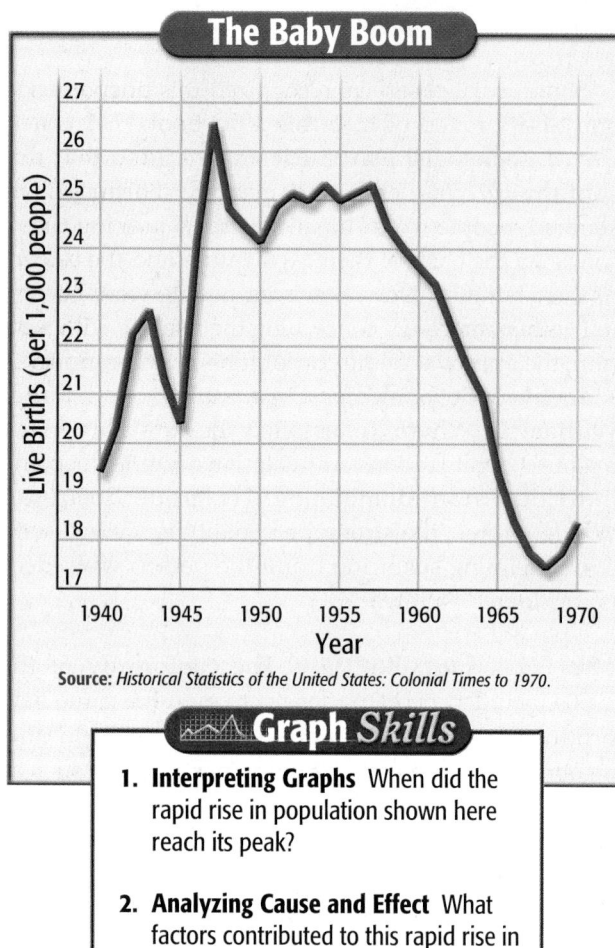

The Baby Boom

Live Births (per 1,000 people)

Year

Source: *Historical Statistics of the United States: Colonial Times to 1970.*

Graph Skills

1. **Interpreting Graphs** When did the rapid rise in population shown here reach its peak?

2. **Analyzing Cause and Effect** What factors contributed to this rapid rise in births?

Accompanying the nation's spending spree was the growth of more sophisticated advertising. Advertising became the fastest-growing industry in the United States, as manufacturers employed new marketing techniques to sell their products. These techniques were carefully planned to whet the consumer's appetite. The purpose of these advertisers was to influence choices among brands of goods that were essentially the same. According to the elaborate advertising campaigns of the time, a freezer became a promise of plenty, a second car became a symbol of status, and a mouthwash became the key to immediate success.

The Growth of Suburbia Advertisers targeted their ads to consumers who had money to spend. Many of these consumers lived in the nation's growing suburbs that grew up around cities.

Levittown, New York, was one of the earliest of the new suburbs. The driving force behind this planned residential community was Bill Levitt, who mass-produced hundreds of simple and similar-looking homes in a potato field 10 miles east of New York City. Between 1947 and 1951, thousands of families rushed to buy the inexpensive homes, and

soon other communities similar to Levittown sprang up throughout the United States.

Suburbs became increasingly popular throughout the 1950s, accounting for about 85 percent of new home construction. The number of suburban dwellers doubled, while the population of cities themselves rose only 10 percent. Reasons for the rapid growth of suburbia varied. Some people wanted to escape the crime and congestion of city neighborhoods. Others viewed life in the suburbs as a move up to a better life for themselves and their children. In contrast to city life, suburbia offered a more picturesque environment. As developers in earlier periods had done, the developers of the 1950s attracted home buyers with promises of fresh air, green lawns, and trees.

Affordability became a key factor in attracting home buyers to the suburbs. Because the GI Bill offered low-interest loans, new housing was more affordable during the postwar period than at any other time in American history. Equally attractive was the government's offer of income tax deductions for home mortgage interest payments and property taxes. For millions of Americans, the suburbs came to symbolize the American dream. They owned their homes, sent their children to good schools, lived in safe communities, and enjoyed economic security.

Nevertheless, some observers viewed the growth of such plain and identical-looking communities as another sign of Americans' tendency toward conformity. "You too can find a box of your own," one sarcastic critic wrote about Levittown, "inhabited by people whose age, income, number of children, problems, habits, conversations, dress, possessions, perhaps even blood types are almost precisely like yours."

Reading Check **Interpreting** What were two causes and effects of the economic boom of the 1950s?

The 1950s Family

In addition to all the other transformations taking place in the nation during the 1950s, the American family also was changing. Across the country, many families grew larger, and more married women entered the workforce.

The Baby Boom The American birthrate exploded after World War II. From 1945 to 1961, a period known as the baby boom, more than 65 million children were born in the United States. At the height of the baby boom, a child was born every seven seconds.

Several factors contributed to the baby boom. First, young couples who had delayed marriage during

World War II and the Korean War could now marry, buy homes, and begin their families. In addition, the government encouraged the growth of families by offering generous GI benefits for home purchases. Finally, on television and in magazines, popular culture celebrated pregnancy, parenthood, and large families.

Women in the Fifties Many women focused on their traditional role of homemaker during the 1950s. Even though 8 million American women had gone to work during the war, the new postwar emphasis on having babies and establishing families now discouraged women from seeking employment. Many Americans assumed that a good mother should stay home to take care of her children.

"Let's face it, girls," declared one female writer in *Better Homes and Gardens* in April 1955, "that wonderful guy in your house—and in mine—is building your house, your happiness and the opportunities that will come to your children." The magazine advised stay-at-home wives to "set their sights on a happy home, a host of friends and a bright future through success in HIS job."

Despite the popular emphasis on homemaking, however, the number of women who held jobs outside the home actually increased during the 1950s. Most women who went to work did so in order to help their families maintain their comfortable lifestyles. By 1960 nearly one-third of all married women were part of the paid workforce.

Reading Check **Evaluating** What were three factors that contributed to the baby boom?

Technological Breakthroughs

As the United States underwent many social changes during the postwar era, the nation also witnessed several important scientific advances. In medicine, space exploration, and electronics, American scientists broke new ground during the 1950s.

Advances in Electronics The electronics industry made rapid advances after World War II. In 1947 three American physicists—John Bardeen, Walter H. Brattain, and William Shockley—developed the transistor, a tiny device that generated electric signals and made it possible to miniaturize radios and calculators.

The age of computers also dawned in the postwar era. In 1946 scientists working under a U.S. Army contract developed one of the nation's earliest

computers—known as ENIAC (Electronic Numerical Integrator and Computer)—to make military calculations. Several years later, a newer model called UNIVAC (Universal Automatic Computer) would handle business data and launch the computer revolution. The computer, along with changes and improvements in communication and transportation systems, allowed many Americans to work more quickly and efficiently. As a result, families in the 1950s had more free time, and new forms of leisure activity became popular.

Medical Miracles The medical breakthroughs of the 1950s included the development of powerful antibiotics to fight infection; the introduction of new drugs to combat arthritis, diabetes, cancer, and heart

The Incredible Shrinking Computer

Past: The First Computer
ENIAC (Electronic Numerical Integrator and Computer) was the first large-scale digital computer. Operating from 1946 to 1955, its primary function was to provide data for the military. It weighed more than 30 tons and took up 1,800 square feet—more than some houses!

Present: Modern Marvels
Modern computers are very small and very fast. Many personal computers now fit easily in a briefcase or backpack. They are also more efficient. While the ENIAC could perform approximately 5,000 calculations per second, the typical home computer performs about 70 million calculations per second—14,000 times faster!

Picturing History

Polio Epidemic In the 1940s and 1950s, Americans were very concerned about the wave of polio cases that struck so many young children. Here, devices known as iron lungs help polio patients breathe. How did people try to safeguard against the spread of the disease?

disease; and groundbreaking advances in surgical techniques. Polio, however, continued to baffle the medical profession.

Periodic polio epidemics had been occurring in the United States since 1916. The disease had even struck the young Franklin Roosevelt and forced him to use a wheelchair. In the 1940s and 1950s, however, polio struck the nation in epidemic proportions. Officially known as infantile paralysis because it generally targeted the young, the disease brought a wave of terror to the country. No one knew where or when polio would strike, but an epidemic broke out in some area of the country each summer, crippling and killing its victims. People watched helplessly while neighbors fell sick. Many died, and those who did not were often confined to iron lungs—large metal tanks with pumps that helped patients breathe. If they eventually recovered, they were often paralyzed for the rest of their lives.

Because no one knew what caused the disease, parents searched for ways to safeguard their families each summer. Some sent their children to the country to avoid excessive contact with others. Public swimming pools and beaches were closed. Parks and playgrounds across the country stood deserted. Nevertheless, the disease continued to strike. In 1952 a record 58,000 new cases were reported.

Finally, a research scientist named **Jonas Salk** developed an injectable vaccine that prevented polio. Salk first tested the vaccine on himself, his wife, and his three sons. It was then tested on 2 million schoolchildren. In 1955 the vaccine was declared safe and effective and became available to the general public. The results were spectacular. New cases of polio fell to 5,700 in 1958 and then to 3,277 in 1960. American scientist Albert Sabin then developed an oral vaccine for polio. Because it was safer and more convenient than Salk's injection vaccine, the Sabin vaccine became the most common form of treatment against the disease. In the years to come, the threat of polio would almost completely disappear.

Conquering Space After the Soviet Union launched *Sputnik*, the world's first space satellite, in October 1957, the United States hastened to catch up with its

Cold War rival. Less than four months later, on January 31, 1958, the United States launched its own satellite from Cape Canaveral, Florida. Reporter Milton Bracker described the jubilant scene:

❝As the firing command neared, a deadly silence fell on those who were watching. In the glare of the search-lights, a stream of liquid oxygen could be seen venting like a lavender cloud from the side of the seventy-foot rocket. . . . At fourteen and one-half seconds after time zero . . . the main stage engine came to life with an immeasurable thrust of flame in all directions. . . . With thousands of eyes following it, the rocket dug into the night and accelerated as its sound loudened. Spectators on near-by beaches pointed and craned their necks and cried, 'There it is!' and began to cheer.❞

—quoted in *Voices from America's Past*

Meanwhile, engineers were building smoother and faster commercial planes. Poet Carl Sandburg wrote about taking the first American jet flight from New York to Los Angeles. The trip took only five and a half hours. "You search for words to describe the speed of this flight," wrote an amazed Sandburg.

Profiles IN HISTORY

Dr. Jonas Salk
1914–1995

The man who developed the vaccine for one of the nation's most feared diseases almost did not go into medicine. Jonas Salk enrolled in college as a pre-law student but soon changed his mind. "My mother didn't think I would make a very good lawyer," Salk said, "probably because I could never win an argument with her." Salk switched his major to premed and went on to become a research scientist.

Salk initially directed the search for a cure to the dreaded ailment of polio at the University of Pittsburgh's Virus Research Laboratory. Every so often, Salk would make rounds in the over-crowded polio wards of nearby Municipal Hospital, where nurses described their feelings of pity and helpless rage as paralyzed children cried for water. As one nurse said, "I can remember how the staff used to kid Dr. Salk—kidding in earnest—telling him to hurry up and do something."

Salk became famous for his break-through vaccine. The shy doctor, however, did not desire fame. About his becoming a celebrity, Salk observed that it was "a transitory thing and you wait till it blows over. Eventually people will start thinking, 'That poor guy,' and leave me alone. Then I'll be able to get back to my laboratory."

"You are whisked . . . from an ocean on one side of the continent to an ocean on the opposite side in less time than it takes the sun to trace a 90-degree arc across the sky."

✔ **Reading Check** **Examining** What medical and technological advances met specific needs in the late 1940s and 1950s?

SECTION 2 ASSESSMENT

Checking for Understanding
1. **Define:** white-collar, blue-collar, multi-national corporation, franchise, baby boom.
2. **Identify:** John Kenneth Galbraith, David Riesman, Levittown, Jonas Salk.
3. **Describe** how and why the suburbs became popular places to live.

Reviewing Themes
4. **Continuity and Change** How was the affluent society of the United States in the 1950s different from previous decades?

Critical Thinking
5. **Interpreting** What caused the advertising industry boom in the 1950s?
6. **Organizing** Use a graphic organizer similar to the one below to list the causes and effects of the economic boom of the 1950s.

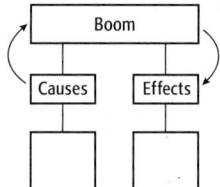

Analyzing Visuals
7. **Analyzing Photographs** Study the photograph on page 818 of children suffering from polio. What do you think it was like to live in such an environment? Do Americans today face similar medical fears?

Writing About History
8. **Descriptive Writing** Write an article for a magazine such as *Better Homes and Gardens* describing changes the American family underwent during the 1950s.

Popular Culture of the 1950s

Guide to Reading

Main Idea
During the carefree and prosperous 1950s, Americans turned to television, new forms of music, cinema, and literature to entertain themselves.

Key Terms and Names
Ed Sullivan, Alan Freed, Elvis Presley, generation gap, Jack Kerouac, Little Richard

Reading Strategy
Categorizing As you read about the popular culture of the 1950s, complete a graphic organizer similar to the one below comparing new forms of mass media during the 1950s.

New Forms of Mass Media	Description

Reading Objectives
- **Explain** the characteristics of the new youth culture.
- **Discuss** the contributions of African Americans to 1950s culture.

Section Theme
Culture and Traditions The 1950s added such elements as rock 'n' roll music and sitcom television to modern culture.

Preview of Events

♦1955   ♦1956   ♦1957   ♦1958

1955 — The quiz show *The $64,000 Question* debuts

1956 — Elvis Presley appears on the *Ed Sullivan Show;* Allen Ginsberg's "Howl" published

1957 — 40 million television sets in use in the United States

1958 — TV quiz show scandals begin to surface

★ An American Story ★

In 1953 Lucille Ball and her real-life husband, Desi Arnaz, were starring in one of the most popular shows on American television, *I Love Lucy.* In January, Ball had a baby—both in real life and on her show. Her pregnancy and the birth of her baby became a national event that captivated her audience. A pre-filmed segment of the show showed Lucy and her husband going to the hospital to have the baby, and the show was broadcast only a few hours after the real birth. More than two-thirds of the nation's television sets tuned in, an audience of around 44 million viewers. Far fewer people watched the next day when television broadcast a presidential inauguration.

I Love Lucy was so popular that some people actually set up their work schedules around the show. Marshall Field's, which had previously held sales on the same night the show was on, eventually switched its sales to a different night. A sign on its shop window explained, "We love Lucy too, so we're closing on Monday nights." A relatively new medium, television had swept the nation by the mid-1950s.

—adapted from *Watching TV: Four Decades of American Television*

The New Mass Media

Although regular television broadcasts had begun in the early 1940s, there were few stations, and sets were expensive. By the end of the 1950s, however, the small, black-and-white-screened sets sat in living rooms across the country. Television's popularity forced the other forms of mass media—namely motion pictures and radio—to innovate in order to keep their audiences.

The Rise of Television Popularity

During World War II, televisions became more affordable for consumers. In 1946 it is estimated there were between 7,000 and 8,000 sets in the entire United States. By 1957 there were 40 million television sets in use. Over 80 percent of families had televisions.

By the late 1950s, television news had become an important vehicle for information. Television advertising spawned a growing market for many new products. Advertising, after all, provided television with the money that allowed it to flourish. As one critic concluded, "Programs on television are simply a device to keep the advertisements and commercials from bumping loudly together." Televised athletic events gradually made professional and college sports one of the most prominent sources of entertainment.

Comedy, Action, and Games

Early television programs fell into several main categories including comedy, action and adventure, and variety-style entertainment. Laughter proved popular in other formats besides the half-hour situation comedy. Many of the early television comedy shows, such as those starring Bob Hope and Jack Benny, were adapted from popular old radio shows. Benny enjoyed considerable television success with his routines of bad violin playing and stingy behavior.

Television watchers in the 1950s also relished action shows. Westerns such as *Hopalong Cassidy, The Lone Ranger,* and *Gunsmoke* grew quickly in popularity. Viewers also enjoyed police programs such as *Dragnet,* a hugely successful show featuring Joe Friday and his partner hunting down a new criminal each week.

Variety shows such as **Ed Sullivan's** *Toast of the Town* provided a mix of comedy, opera, popular song, dance, acrobatics, and juggling. Quiz shows attracted large audiences, too, after the 1955 debut of *The $64,000 Question.* In this show and its many imitators, two contestants tried to answer questions from separate glass-encased booths. The questions, stored between shows in a bank vault, arrived at the studio at airtime in the hands of a stern-faced bank executive flanked by two armed guards. The contestants competed head-to-head, with the winner returning the following week to face a new challenger.

TV Nation

Television programming depicted a narrow view of American culture in the 1950s. Most television shows during these years centered around a common image of American life—an image that was predominantly white, middle-class, and suburban, epitomized by the popular situation comedy *The Adventures of Ozzie and Harriet.* Such shows also reinforced traditional gender roles, showing fathers working and mothers staying home to raise children and take care of the house.

Westerns were also popular at the time, especially *The Lone Ranger,* in which a mysterious masked man helped people in distress. *The Howdy Doody Show,* which featured Buffalo Bob and his freckle-faced marionette, was the first network kids' show to run five days a week, the first television show ever broadcast in color, and the first show ever to air more than 1,000 continuous episodes.

Howdy Doody

Ozzie and Harriet

Tonto and the Lone Ranger

In 1956 the quiz show *Twenty-One* caused an uproar across the nation after **Charles Van Doren,** a young assistant professor with a modest income, won $129,000 during his weeks on the program. The viewing public soon learned, however, that Van Doren and many of the other contestants had received the answers to the questions in advance. Before a congressional committee in 1959, Van Doren admitted his role in the scandal and apologized to his many fans, saying, "I was involved, deeply involved, in a deception." In the wake of the *Twenty-One* fraud, many quiz shows went off the air.

Hollywood Adapts to the Times As the popularity of television grew, movies lost viewers. "Hollywood's like Egypt," lamented producer David Selznick in 1951. "Full of crumbling pyramids." While the film business may not have been collapsing, it certainly did suffer after the war. Attendance dropped from 82 million in 1946 to 36 million by 1950. By 1960, when some 50 million Americans owned a television, one-fifth of the nation's movie theaters had closed.

Throughout the decade, Hollywood struggled mightily to recapture its audience. "Don't be a 'Living Room Captive,'" one industry ad pleaded. "Step out and see a great movie!" When contests, door prizes, and an advertising campaign announcing that "Movies Are Better Than Ever" failed to lure people out of their homes, Hollywood began to try to make films more exciting. Between 1952 and 1954, audiences of 3-D films received special

glasses that gave the impression that a monster or a knife was lunging directly at them from off the screen. Viewers, however, soon tired of both the glasses and the often ridiculous plots of 3-D movies.

Cinemascope, movies shown on large, panoramic screens, finally gave Hollywood a reliable lure. Wide-screen spectacles like *The Robe, The Ten Commandments,* and *Around the World in 80 Days* cost a great deal of money to produce. These blockbusters, however, made up for their cost by attracting huge audiences and netting large profits. The movie industry also made progress by taking the "if you can't beat 'em, join 'em" approach. Hollywood eventually began to film programs especially for television and also sold old movies, which could be rebroadcast cheaply, to the networks.

Like television, the films of the fifties for the most part adhered to the conformity of the times. Roles for single women who did not want families were few and far between. For example, each of Marilyn Monroe's film roles featured the blond movie star as married, soon to be married, or unhappy that she was not married.

Movies with African Americans routinely portrayed them in stereotypical roles, such as maids, servants, or sidekicks for white heroes. Even when African Americans took leading roles, they were often one-dimensional characters who rarely showed human emotions or characteristics. African American actor Sidney Poitier resented having to play such parts:

> 66 The black characters usually come out on the screen as saints, as the other-cheek-turners, as people who are not really people: who are so nice and good. . . . As a matter of fact, I'm just dying to play villains. 99
>
> —quoted in *The Fifties: The Way We Really Were*

Radio Draws Them In Television also lured away radio listeners and forced the radio industry, like Hollywood, to develop new ways to win back audiences. After television took over many of radio's concepts of comedies, dramas, and soap operas, for example, many radio stations began to specialize in presenting recorded music, news, talk shows, weather, public-service programming, and shows for specific audiences.

As a result of this targeted programming, radio stations survived and even flourished. Their numbers more than doubled between 1948, when 1,680 stations were broadcasting to the nation, and 1957, when more than 3,600 stations filled the airwaves.

✓ **Reading Check** **Identifying** How did the television industry affect the U.S. economy?

The New Youth Culture

While Americans of all ages embraced the new mass media, some of the nation's youth rebelled against such a message. During the 1950s, a number of young Americans turned their backs on the conformist ideals adult society promoted. Although these youths were a small minority, their actions brought them widespread attention. In general, these young people longed for greater excitement and freedom, and they found an outlet for such feelings of restlessness in new and controversial styles of music and literature.

Rock 'n' Roll In the early 1950s, rock 'n' roll emerged as the distinctive music of the new generation. In 1951 at a record store in downtown Cleveland,

Ohio, radio disc jockey **Alan Freed** noticed white teenagers buying African American rhythm and blues records and dancing to the music in the store. A week later, Freed won permission from his station manager to play the music on the air. Just as the disc jockey had suspected, the listeners went crazy for it. Soon, white artists began making music that stemmed from these African American rhythms and sounds, and a new form of music, **rock 'n' roll,** had been born.

With a loud and heavy beat that made it ideal for dancing along with lyrics about romance, cars, and other themes that spoke to young people, rock 'n' roll grew wildly popular among the nation's teens. Before long boys and girls around the country were rushing out to buy the latest hits from such artists as Buddy Holly, Chuck Berry, and Bill Haley and the Comets. In 1956 teenagers found their first rock 'n' roll hero in **Elvis Presley.** Presley, who had been born in rural Mississippi and grown up poor in Memphis, Tennessee, eventually claimed the title of "King of Rock 'n' Roll."

While in high school, Presley had learned to play guitar and sing by imitating the rhythm and blues

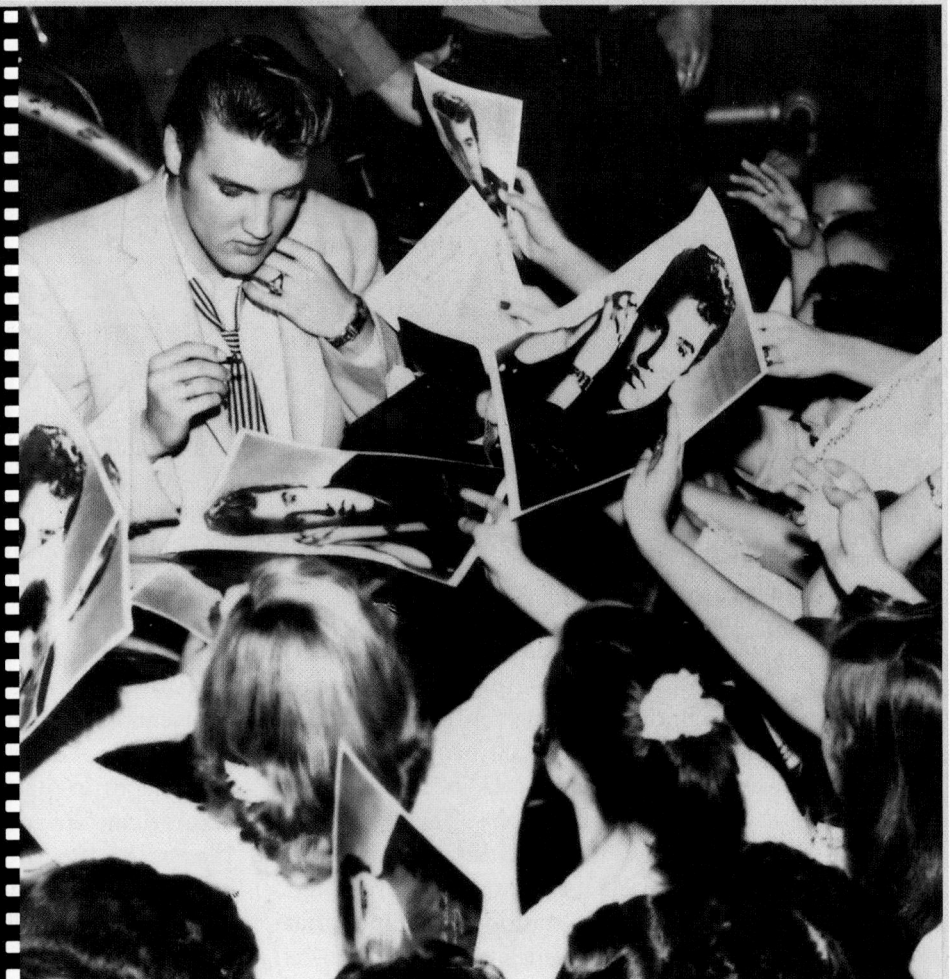

NATIONAL GEOGRAPHIC
MOMENT in HISTORY

THE KING OF ROCK
Elvis Presley, shown here signing autographs after a performance in Houston, took American youth in the 1950s by storm. Parents, on the other hand, were less than thrilled with his music—a blend of African American-inspired rhythm and blues and early rock 'n' roll—and his hip-swiveling gyrations on stage. For Presley's first appearance on The Ed Sullivan Show, the host insisted that cameras show him only from the waist up. Elvis added to his fame by starring in a string of films that audiences loved but critics panned.

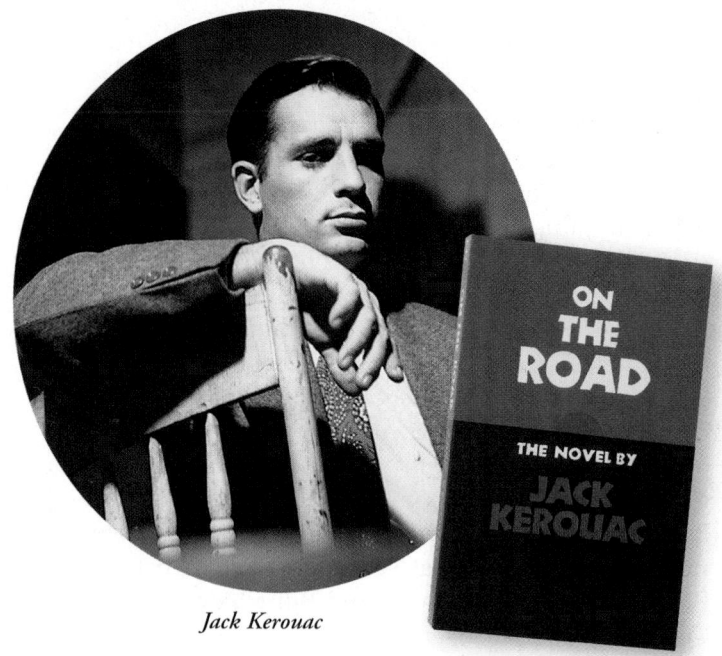

Jack Kerouac

music he heard on the radio. By 1956 Elvis had a record deal with RCA Victor, a movie contract, and public appearances on several television shows. At first the popular television variety show host Ed Sullivan refused to invite Presley on, insisting that the rock 'n' roll music was not fit for a family-oriented show. When a competing show featuring Presley upset his own high ratings, however, Sullivan relented. He ended up paying Presley $50,000 per performance for three appearances, more than triple the amount he had paid any other performer.

The dark-haired and handsome Presley owed his wild popularity as much to his moves as to his music. During his performances he would gyrate his hips and dance in other suggestive ways that shocked many in the audience. Presley himself admitted the importance of this part of his act:

> ❝I'm not kidding myself. My voice alone is just an ordinary voice. What people come to see is how I use it. If I stand still while I'm singing, I'm dead, man. I might as well go back to driving a truck.❞
>
> —quoted in *God's Country: America in the Fifties*

Not surprisingly, parents—many of whom listened to Frank Sinatra and other more mellow and mainstream artists—condemned rock 'n' roll as loud, mindless, and dangerous. The city council of San Antonio, Texas, actually banned rock 'n' roll from the jukeboxes at public swimming pools. The music, the council declared, "attracted undesirable elements given to practicing their gyrations in abbreviated bathing suits." A minister in Boston complained that "rock and roll inflames and excites youth."

The rock 'n' roll hits that teens bought in record numbers united them in a world their parents did not share. Thus in the 1950s rock 'n' roll helped to create what became known as the generation gap, or the cultural separation between children and their parents.

The Beat Movement If rock 'n' roll helped to create a generation gap, a group of mostly white artists who called themselves **beats,** or beatniks, highlighted a values gap in the 1950s United States. The term *beat* may have come from the feeling among group members of being "beaten down" by American culture, or from jazz musicians who would say, "I'm beat right down to my socks."

The beats sought to live unconventional lives as fugitives from a culture they despised. Beat poets, writers, and artists harshly criticized what they considered the sterility and conformity of American life, the meaninglessness of American politics, and the emptiness of popular culture.

In 1956, 29-year-old beat poet **Allen Ginsberg** published a long poem called "Howl," which blasted modern American life. Another beat member, **Jack Kerouac,** published *On the Road* in 1957. Although Kerouac's book about his freewheeling adventures with a car thief and con artist shocked some readers, the book went on to become a classic in modern American literature.

☑ **Reading Check** **Summarizing** How did rock 'n' roll help create the generation gap?

African American Entertainers

While artists such as Jack Kerouac rejected American culture, African American entertainers struggled to find acceptance in a country that often treated them as second-class citizens. With a few notable exceptions, television tended to shut out African Americans. In 1956, NBC gave a popular African American singer named Nat King Cole his own 15-minute musical variety show. In 1958, after 64 episodes, NBC canceled the show after failing to secure a national sponsor for a show hosted by an African American.

African American rock 'n' roll singers had more luck gaining acceptance. The talented African American singers and groups who recorded hit songs in the fifties included **Chuck Berry, Ray Charles, Little Richard,** and the **Drifters.** The latter years of the 1950s also saw the rise of several African American women's groups, including the

Little Richard

Fats Domino

Picturing History

African American Entertainers Rhythm and blues music provided the roots of the 1950s rock 'n' roll sound. Did African American rock 'n' roll artists experience the same acceptance as artists like Elvis Presley? Why or why not?

Crystals, the **Chiffons,** the **Shirelles,** and the **Ronettes.** With their catchy, popular sound, these groups became the musical ancestors of the famous late 1960s groups **Martha and the Vandellas** and the **Supremes.**

Over time, the music of the early rock 'n' roll artists had a profound influence on music throughout the world. Little Richard and Chuck Berry, for example, provided inspiration for the Beatles, whose music swept Britain and the world in the 1960s. Elvis's music transformed generations of rock 'n' roll bands that were to follow him and other pioneers of rock.

Despite the innovations in music and the economic boom of the 1950s, not all Americans were part of the affluent society. For much of the country's minorities and rural poor, the American dream remained well out of reach.

Reading Check **Evaluating** What impact did American rock 'n' roll artists have on the rest of the world?

SECTION 3 ASSESSMENT

Checking for Understanding

1. **Define:** generation gap.
2. **Identify:** Ed Sullivan, Alan Freed, Elvis Presley, Jack Kerouac, Little Richard.
3. **Explain** what happened to motion pictures and radio when television became popular.

Reviewing Themes

4. **Culture and Traditions** What roles did African Americans play in television and rock 'n' roll?

Critical Thinking

5. **Comparing** How did the themes of television shows of the 1950s differ from the themes of the literature of the beat movement?
6. **Organizing** Use a graphic organizer similar to the one below to list the styles of music and literature that made up the new youth culture of the 1950s.

New Youth Culture

Analyzing Visuals

7. **Analyzing Photographs** Study the photographs on pages 820 and 821. Many people have criticized these television programs for presenting a one-sided view of American life. Do you agree with this criticism? Why or why not?

Writing About History

8. **Expository Writing** Imagine you are a beat writer in the 1950s. Explain to your readers how the themes you write about are universal themes that could apply to everyone.

TIME NOTEBOOK

BETTMANN/CORBIS

Profile

JAMES DEAN *had a brief but spectacular career as a film star. His role in* Rebel Without a Cause *made him an icon for American youth in the mid-50s. In 1955 Dean was killed in a car crash. He was 24.*

"I guess I have as good an insight into this rising generation as any other young man my age. Therefore, when I do play a youth, I try to imitate life. *Rebel Without a Cause* deals with the problems of modern youth. . . . If you want the kids to come and see the picture, you've got to try to reach them on their own grounds. If a picture is psychologically motivated, if there is truth in the relationships in it, then I think that picture will do good."

—*from an interview for* Rebel Without a Cause

VERBATIM

"It will make a wonderful place for the children to play in, and it will be a good storehouse, too."
> **MRS. RUTH CALHOUN,**
> *mother of three, on her backyard fallout shelter, 1951*

"Riddle: What's college? That's where girls who are above cooking and sewing go to meet a man they can spend their lives cooking and sewing for."
> *ad for Gimbel's department store campus clothes, 1952*

"Radioactive poisoning of the atmosphere and hence annihilation of any life on Earth has been brought within the range of technical possibilities."
> **ALBERT EINSTEIN,**
> *physicist, 1950*

"If the television craze continues with the present level of programs, we are destined to have a nation of morons."
> **DANIEL MARSH,**
> *President of Boston University, 1950*

"Every time the Russians throw an American in jail, the House Un-American Activities Committee throws an American in jail to get even."
> **MORT SAHL,**
> *comedian, 1950s*

WINNERS & LOSERS

ARCHIVE PHOTOS

POODLE CUTS
Short, curly hairstyle gains wide popularity and acceptance

TV GUIDE
New weekly magazine achieves circulation of 6.5 million by 1959

PALMER PAINT COMPANY OF DETROIT
Sells 12 million paint-by-number kits ranging from simple landscapes and portraits to Leonardo da Vinci's *The Last Supper*

Poodle Cut

THE DUCKTAIL
Banned in several Massachusetts schools in 1957

COLLIER'S
The respected magazine loses circulation, publishes its final edition on January 4, 1957

LEONARDO DA VINCI'S *THE LAST SUPPER*
Now everyone can paint their own copy to hang in their homes

The Ducktail

SUPER STOCK

1950s WORD PLAY
Translation, Please!

Match the word to its meaning.

Teen-Age Lingo

1. cool
2. hang loose
3. hairy
4. yo-yo

a. a dull person, an outsider
b. worthy of approval
c. formidable
d. don't worry

answers: 1. b; 2. d; 3. c; 4. a

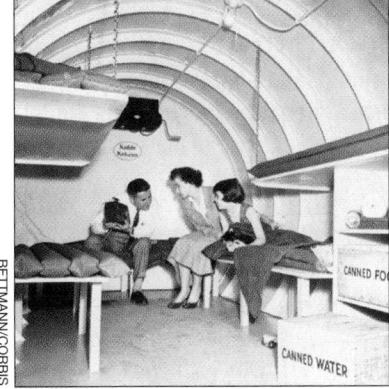

BETTMANN/CORBIS

Bomb Shelter

Be Prepared

"Know the Bomb's True Dangers. Know the Steps You Can Take to Escape Them!—You Can Survive."
Government pamphlet, 1950

DIGGING YOUR OWN BOMB SHELTER? Better go shopping. Below is a list of items included with the $3,000 Mark I Kidde Kokoon, designed to accommodate a family of five for a three- to five-day underground stay.

- air blower
- radiation detector
- protective apparel suit
- face respirator
- radiation charts (4)
- hand shovel combination (for digging out after the blast)
- gasoline driven generator
- gasoline (10 gallons)

- chemical toilet
- toilet chemicals (2 gallons)
- bunks (5)
- mattresses and blankets (5)
- air pump (for blowing up mattresses)
- incandescent bulbs (2) 40 watts
- fuses (2) 5 amperes
- clock—non-electric

- first aid kit
- waterless hand cleaner
- sterno stove
- canned water (10 gallons)
- canned food (meat, powdered milk, cereal, sugar, etc.)
- paper products

NUMBERS 1957

3¢ Cost of first-class postage stamp

19¢ Cost of loaf of bread

25¢ Cost of issue of *Sports Illustrated*

35¢ Cost of movie ticket

50¢ Cost of gallon of milk (delivered)

$2.05 Average hourly wage

$2,845 Cost of new car

POPPERFOTO/ARCHIVE PHOTO

$5,234 Median income for a family of four

$19,500 Median price to buy a home

American Scene, 1950–1960
(MILLIONS)

24.3 / 35.5
1950 / 1960
Children 5–14

1.8 / 4.0
1950 / 1960
Girl Scouts & Brownies

2.0 / 3.8
1950 / 1960
Bicycle Production

1.5 / 6.6
1950 / 1960
National Forest Campers

2.8 / 5.8
1950 / 1960
Outboard Motors in Use

The Other Side of American Life

Guide to Reading

Main Idea
Not everyone in the United States prospered during the nation's postwar boom, as millions of minorities and rural whites struggled daily with poverty.

Key Terms and Names
poverty line, Michael Harrington, urban renewal, Bracero program, termination policy, juvenile delinquency

Reading Strategy
Taking Notes As you read about social problems in the United States in the 1950s, use the major headings of the section to create an outline similar to the one below.

The Other Side of American Life
I. Poverty Amidst Prosperity
   A.
   B.
   C.
   D.
   E.
II.

Reading Objectives
• **Identify** those groups that found themselves left out of the American economic boom following World War II.
• **Explain** the factors that contributed to the poverty among various groups.

Section Theme
Continuity and Change For some groups, poverty continued during the apparent abundance of the 1950s.

Preview of Events

| ♦1953 | ♦1956 | ♦1959 | ♦1962 |

1953
Federal government institutes termination policy directed at Native Americans

1955
Rudolf Flesch's *Why Johnny Can't Read* published

1959
A Raisin in the Sun opens on Broadway

1962
Michael Harrington's *The Other America* published

★ An American Story ★

In 1959 Lorraine Hansberry's play, *A Raisin in the Sun,* opened on Broadway. The play told the story of a working-class African American family struggling against poverty and racism. The title referred to a Langston Hughes poem that wonders what happens to an unrealized dream: "Does it dry up like a raisin in the sun?" Hansberry's play won the New York Drama Critics Circle Award for the best play of the year. Reflecting later upon the play's theme, she wrote:

66Vulgarity, blind conformity, and mass lethargy need not triumph in the land of Lincoln and Frederick Douglass. . . . There is simply no reason why dreams should dry up like raisins or prunes or anything else in the United States. . . . I believe that we can impose beauty on our future.99

Postwar prosperity had bypassed many segments of the population. Minorities and the poor wondered when they could seize their own piece of the American dream.

—**adapted from *To Be Young, Gifted, and Black***

Poverty Amidst Prosperity

Although the 1950s saw a tremendous expansion of the middle class, at least 1 in 5 Americans, or about 30 million people, lived below the poverty line, a figure the government set to reflect the minimum income required to support a family. Such poverty remained invisible to most Americans, who assumed that the country's general prosperity had provided everyone with a comfortable existence. The writer **Michael Harrington,** however, made no such assumptions. During the 1950s, Harrington set out to chronicle poverty in the United States. In his book, *The Other America*, published in 1962, he alerted those in the mainstream to what he saw in the run-down and hidden communities of the country:

> 66Tens of millions of Americans are, at this very moment, maimed in body and spirit, existing at levels beneath those necessary for human decency. If these people are not starving, they are hungry, and some-times fat with hunger, for that is what cheap foods do. They are without adequate housing and educa-tion and medical care.99

—from *The Other America*

The poor included single mothers and the elderly; minority immigrants such as Puerto Ricans and Mexicans; rural Americans, black and white; and inner city residents, who remained stuck in crowded slums as wealthier citizens fled to the suburbs. Poverty also gripped many Americans in the nation's Appalachian region, which stretches from Pennsylvania to Georgia, as well as Native Americans, many of whom endured grinding poverty whether they stayed on reservations or migrated to cities.

ECONOMICS

The Decline of the Inner City

The poverty in the 1950s was most apparent in the nation's urban centers. As white families moved to the suburbs, many inner cities became home to poorer, less educated minority groups. The centers of many cities deteriorated, because as the middle class moved out, their tax money went with them. This deprived inner cities of the tax dollars necessary to provide adequate public transportation, housing, and other services.

When government tried to help inner city residents, it often made matters worse. During the 1950s, for example, urban renewal programs tried to eliminate poverty by tearing down slums and erecting new high-rise buildings for poor residents. The crowded, anonymous conditions of these high-rise projects, however, often created an atmosphere of violence. The government also unwittingly encouraged the residents of public housing to remain poor by evicting them as soon as they began to earn any money.

In the end, urban renewal programs actually destroyed more housing space than they created. Too often in the name of urban improvement, the wrecking ball destroyed poor people's homes to make way for roadways, parks, universities, tree-lined boulevards, or shopping centers.

African Americans Many of the citizens left behind in the cities as families fled to the suburbs were African American. The large number of African American inner city residents resulted largely from the migration of more than 3 million African Americans from the South to the North between 1940 and 1960.

Many African Americans had migrated in the hopes of finding greater economic opportunity and escaping violence and racial intimidation. For many of these migrants, however, life proved to be little better in Northern cities. Fewer and fewer jobs were available as numerous factories and mills left the cities for suburbs and smaller towns in order to cut their costs. Long-standing patterns of racial discrimination in schools, housing, hiring, and salaries in the North kept inner-city African Americans poor. The last hired and the first fired for good jobs, they often remained stuck in the worst-paying occupations. In 1958 African American salaries, on average, equaled only 51 percent of what whites earned.

Picturing **History**

Inner-City Poverty This young African American girl in Chicago's inner city struggles to fill a bowl with water that has frozen due to lack of heat. Why did the numbers of poor in the country's inner cities grow in the 1950s?

Poverty and racial discrimination also deprived many African Americans of other benefits, such as decent medical care. Responding to a correspondent who had seen *A Raisin in the Sun*, Lorraine Hansberry wrote, "The ghettos are killing us; not only our dreams . . . but our very bodies. It is not an abstraction to us that the average [African American] has a life expectancy of five to ten years less than the average white." Several African American groups, such as the NAACP and the Congress of Racial Equality (CORE), pressed for greater economic opportunity for African Americans. In general, however, these organizations met with little success.

Hispanics African Americans were not the only minority group that struggled with poverty. Much of the nation's Hispanic population faced the same problems. During the 1950s and early 1960s, the **Bracero program** brought nearly 5 million Mexicans to the United States to work on farms and ranches in the Southwest. The Braceros were temporary contract workers, and many later returned home. Some came with their families, however, and about 350,000 settled permanently in the United States.

These laborers, who worked on large farms throughout the country, lived a life of extreme poverty and hardship. They toiled long hours for little pay in conditions that were often unbearable. As Michael Harrington noted, "[The nation's migrant laborers] work ten-eleven-twelve hour days in temperatures over one hundred degrees. Sometimes there is no drinking water. . . . Women and children work on ladders and with hazardous machinery. Babies are brought to the field and are placed in 'cradles' of wood boxes."

Away from the fields, many Mexican families lived in small, crudely built shacks, while some did not even have a roof over their heads. "They sleep where they can, some in the open," Harrington noted about one group of migrant workers. "They eat when they can (and sometimes what they can)." The nation would pay little attention to the plight of Mexican farm laborers until the 1960s, when the workers began to organize for greater rights.

Native Americans Native Americans also faced challenges throughout the postwar era of prosperity. By the middle of the 1900s, Native Americans—who made up less than one percent of the population—were the poorest group in the nation. Average annual family income for Native American families, for example, was $1,000 less than that for African Americans.

After World War II, during which many Native American soldiers had served with distinction, the U.S. government launched a program to bring Native Americans into mainstream society—whether they wanted to assimilate or not. Under the plan, which became known as the termination policy, the federal government withdrew all official recognition of the Native American groups as legal entities and made them subject to the same laws as white citizens. At the same time, the government encouraged Native Americans to blend in to larger society by helping them move off the reservations to cities such as Minneapolis, Minnesota.

Although the idea of integrating Native Americans into mainstream society began with good intentions, some of its supporters had more selfish goals. Speculators and developers sometimes gained rich farmland at the expense of destitute Native American groups.

Most Native Americans found termination a disastrous policy that only deepened their poverty. In the mid-1950s, for example, the Welfare Council of Minneapolis described Native American living conditions in that city as miserable. "One Indian family of five or six, living in two rooms, will take in relatives and friends who come from the reservations seeking jobs until perhaps fifteen people will be crowded into the space," the council reported. During the 1950s, Native Americans in Minneapolis could expect to live only 37 years, compared to 46

Picturing **History**

Vocational Training Native American Franklin Beaver learns to become a stone mason at this vocational school sponsored by the U.S. Indian Bureau. Why was the government trying to bring Native Americans into mainstream society?

Poverty in Appalachia This mining family lived in the kind of extreme poverty that was often overlooked in the 1950s. Eight people lived in this three-room house lined with newspaper. Why was infant mortality so high in Appalachia?

years for all Minnesota Native Americans and 68 years for other Minneapolis residents. Benjamin Reifel, a Sioux, described the widespread despair that the termination policy produced:

> 66 The Indians believed that when the dark clouds of war passed from the skies overhead, their rising tide of expectations, though temporarily stalled, would again reappear. Instead they were threatened by termination. . . . Soaring expectations began to plunge. Termination took on the connotation of extermination for many. 99

—quoted in *The Earth Shall Weep*

Appalachia The nation's minorities were not the only people dealing with poverty. The picturesque streams and mountains of Appalachia hid the ruined mines, scarred hills, and abandoned farms of impoverished families who had dwelled in these hills for generations.

During the 1950s, 1.5 million people abandoned Appalachia to seek a better life in the nation's cities. They left behind elderly and other less mobile residents. "Whole counties," wrote one reporter who visited the region, "are precariously held together by a

flour-and-dried-milk paste of surplus foods. . . . The men who are no longer needed in the mines and the farmers who cannot compete . . . have themselves become surplus commodities in the mountains."

A host of statistics spoke to Appalachia's misery. Studies revealed high rates of nutritional deficiency and infant mortality. Appalachia had fewer doctors per thousand people than the rest of the country, and the doctors it did have were older than their counterparts in other areas. In addition, schooling in the region was considered even worse than in inner city slums.

Reading Check **Identifying** Which groups of people were left out of the country's economic boom of the 1950s?

Juvenile Delinquency

During the 1950s, many middle-class white Americans found it easy to ignore the poverty and racism that afflicted many of the nation's minorities, since they themselves were removed from it. Some social problems, however, became impossible to ignore.

One problem at this time was a rise in, or at least a rise in the reporting of, juvenile delinquency—antisocial or criminal behavior of young people. Between 1948 and 1953, the United States saw a 45 percent rise in juvenile crime rates. A popular 1954 book titled *1,000,000 Delinquents* correctly calculated that in the following year, about 1 million young people would get into some kind of criminal trouble. Car thefts topped the list of juvenile crimes, but people were

Rebelling Against Conformity This biker, one of the Louisville "Outlaws," fits the stereotype of the 1950s juvenile delinquent.

also alarmed at the behavior of young people who belonged to street gangs and committed muggings, rape, and even murder.

Americans could not agree on what had triggered the rise in delinquency. Experts blamed it on a host of reasons, including poverty, lack of religion, television, movies, comic books, racism, busy parents, a rising divorce rate, and anxiety over the military draft. Some cultural critics claimed that young people were rebelling against the hypocrisy and conformity of their parents. Conservative commentators pinned the blame on a lack of discipline. Doting parents, complained Bishop Fulton J. Sheen, had raised bored children who sought new thrills, such as "alcohol, marijuana, even murder." Liberal observers preferred to pinpoint social causes, blaming teen violence on poverty and feelings of hopelessness among underprivileged youths. Delinquency in the 1950s, however, cut across class and racial lines—the majority of car thieves, for example, had grown up in middle-class homes.

Most teens, of course, steered clear of gangs, drugs, and crime. Nonetheless, the public tended to stereotype young people as juvenile delinquents, especially those teens who favored unconventional clothing, long hair, or street slang.

Many parents were also growing concerned over the nation's educational system. As baby boomers began entering the school system, they ignited a spurt in school construction. During the 1950s, school enrollments increased by 13 million. School districts struggled to erect new buildings and hire new teachers. Nevertheless, shortages sprang up in both buildings and the people to staff them.

Americans' education worries only intensified in 1957 after the Soviet Union launched the world's first space satellites, *Sputnik I* and *Sputnik II*. Many Americans felt they had fallen behind their Cold War enemy and blamed what they felt was a lack of technical education in the nation's schools. *Life* magazine proclaimed a "Crisis in Education," and offered a grim warning: "What has long been an ignored national problem, *Sputnik* has made a recognized crisis." In the wake of the *Sputnik* launches, efforts began to improve math and science education in the schools. Profound fears about the country's young people, it seemed, dominated the end of a decade that had brought great progress for many Americans.

✓ Reading Check **Evaluating** How did many Americans feel about the education system of the 1950s?

SECTION 4 ASSESSMENT

Checking for Understanding

1. **Define:** poverty line, urban renewal, termination policy, juvenile delinquency.
2. **Identify:** Michael Harrington, Bracero program.
3. **Evaluate** how the federal government's termination policy affected Native Americans.

Reviewing Themes

4. **Continuity and Change** Why did urban renewal fail the poor of the inner cities?

Critical Thinking

5. **Interpreting** What were some possible reasons for a dramatic rise in juvenile delinquency in the 1950s?
6. **Organizing** Use a graphic organizer similar to the one below to list the groups of Americans who were left out of the country's postwar economic boom.

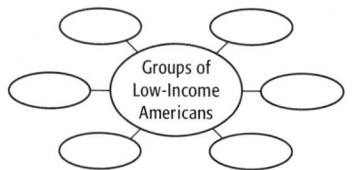

Groups of Low-Income Americans

Analyzing Visuals

7. **Analyzing Photographs** Study the photograph on this page. What in the photograph might attract young people to this type of life? Why would others oppose such a life?

Writing About History

8. **Expository Writing** Using library or Internet resources, find information about juvenile delinquency in the United States today to write a report. Compare today's problems with those of the 1950s. Share your report with the class.

Writing a Journal

Why Learn This Skill?

Journal writing is personal writing with a casual style. The style in which you write is not as important as what you write about—your experiences, interests, and feelings. Journal writing can help you generate new ideas, and it can also give you a clearer picture of your thoughts and help you put them in order.

Learning the Skill

A journal is a written account that records what you have learned or experienced. In a journal you can express your feelings about a subject, summarize key topics, describe difficulties or successes in solving particular problems, and draw maps or other visuals. To help you get started writing in your journal, follow these steps.

- Jot down notes or questions about a specific topic or event as you read your textbook. Then look for details and answers about it as you continue reading.

- Describe your feelings as you read a selection or look at a photograph. Are you angry, happy, frustrated, or sad? Explain why you are reacting in this way.

- Ask yourself if drawing a map or flowchart would help you understand an event better. If so, draw in your journal.

Practicing the Skill

The following excerpt is a journal entry describing the launching of the nation's first satellite in 1958. Read the excerpt, and then use the following questions to help you write entries in your own journal.

"As the firing command neared, a deadly silence fell on those who were watching. . . . At fourteen and one-half seconds after time zero, after the priming fuel had ignited almost invisibly, the main stage engine came to life with an immeasurable thrust of flame in all directions. . . . With thousands of eyes following it, the rocket dug into the night and accelerated as its sound loudened. Spectators on nearby beaches pointed and craned their necks and cried, 'There it is!' and began to cheer."

❶ What is particularly interesting about this description?

❷ What are your feelings as you read the excerpt?

❸ Note the descriptive phrases and details that make the event come to life. Try to use similar techniques when writing in your journal.

❹ Draw a map or other visual to help you understand the situation described here.

Cover from a World War II journal

Skills Assessment

Complete the Practicing Skills questions on page 835 and the Chapter 27 Skill Reinforcement Activity to assess your mastery of this skill.

Applying the Skill

Writing a Journal Imagine that you have had the chance to take part in a great adventure—for instance, serving in the armed forces during a war overseas or participating in a spaceflight. Make notes for a journal entry describing what you have done and seen.

Glencoe's **Skillbuilder Interactive Workbook CD-ROM, Level 2,** provides instruction and practice in key social studies skills.

Reviewing Key Terms

On a sheet of paper, use each of these terms in a sentence.

1. closed shop
2. right-to-work law
3. union shop
4. featherbedding
5. dynamic conservatism
6. white-collar
7. blue-collar
8. multinational corporation
9. franchise
10. baby boom
11. generation gap
12. poverty line
13. urban renewal
14. termination policy
15. juvenile delinquency

Reviewing Key Facts

16. **Identify:** GI Bill, Fair Deal, John Kenneth Galbraith, David Riesman, Ed Sullivan, Alan Freed, Elvis Presley, Jack Kerouac, Michael Harrington.
17. What were three characteristics of the economy of the United States after World War II?
18. What were two reasons for the economic boom of the 1950s?
19. What caused many Americans to move to the suburbs in the 1950s?
20. How did the scientific discovery of the transistor affect communications?
21. Which groups of Americans found themselves left out of the postwar economic boom?

Critical Thinking

22. **Analyzing Themes: Continuity and Change** How has mass media changed since the 1950s?
23. **Evaluating** What factors led to a rise in juvenile delinquency in the United States during the 1950s?
24. **Comparing and Contrasting** Harry S Truman was a Democrat, and Dwight D. Eisenhower was a Republican. How were the domestic agendas of these two presidents different? How were they similar?
25. **Interpreting Primary Sources** George Gallup, one of the nation's first pollsters, spoke at the University of Iowa in 1953 about the importance of mass media in the United States. Read the excerpt and answer the questions that follow.

❝One of the real threats to America's future place in the world is a citizenry which duly elects to be entertained and not informed. From the time the typical citizen arises and looks at his morning newspaper until he turns off his radio or television set before going to bed,

Chapter Summary

	Signs of Prosperity	**Signs of Inequality**
Economy	• The GI Bill provided loans to millions of war veterans. • Consumer spending increased rapidly. • More Americans owned homes than ever before.	• Workers went on strike for higher wages. • Truman's civil rights bill did not pass. • Eisenhower cut back New Deal programs.
Population Patterns	• The U.S. population grew dramatically. • The number of working women increased.	• Financially able people moved from crowded cities to new suburbs. • Many poor people remained in cities that now faced major economic and social problems.
Science, Technology, and Medicine	• Medical breakthroughs included the polio vaccine, antibiotics, and treatments for heart disease, arthritis, cancer, and diabetes. • Improvements in communication, transportation, and electronics allowed Americans to work more efficiently.	• Many poor people in inner cities and rural areas had limited access to health care.
Popular Culture	• Popular culture included new forms of music, radio, cinema, and literature. • Television replaced radio as the nation's newest form of mass media.	• African Americans and other minorities were, for the most part, not depicted on television. • Many television programs promoted stereotypical gender roles.

he has unwittingly cast his vote a hundred times for entertainment or for education. Without his knowing it, he has helped to determine the very character of our three most important media of communication—the press, radio, and television. . . .❞

—quoted in *Vital Speeches of the Day*

a. According to Gallup, what is a threat to the future of the United States in the world?

b. How do American citizens determine what is read, seen, and heard in the mass media?

26. **Organizing** Use a graphic organizer similar to the one below to list the changes to the American family during the 1950s.

Changes to American Family

Practicing Skills

27. **Writing a Journal** Imagine that you are Dr. Jonas Salk, and you realize that you have just discovered the world's first successful polio vaccine. Write a journal entry that describes how you feel about this accomplishment and what impact it will have on the world.

Writing Activity

28. **Writing a Book Report** Read one of the books about American society in the 1950s, such as *Why Johnny Can't Read* or *The Other America.* Write a book report explaining the main concepts of the book and whether or not the issues are similar to or different from the main issues in American society today.

Chapter Activities

29. **American History Primary Source Document Library CD-ROM** Read the speech "On Television" by Newton Minow, under *The Postwar World.* Working with a few of your classmates, evaluate whether television has improved since Minow's critical assessment. Has television content changed since the 1950s? If so, how? Present your findings and comparisons to your class.

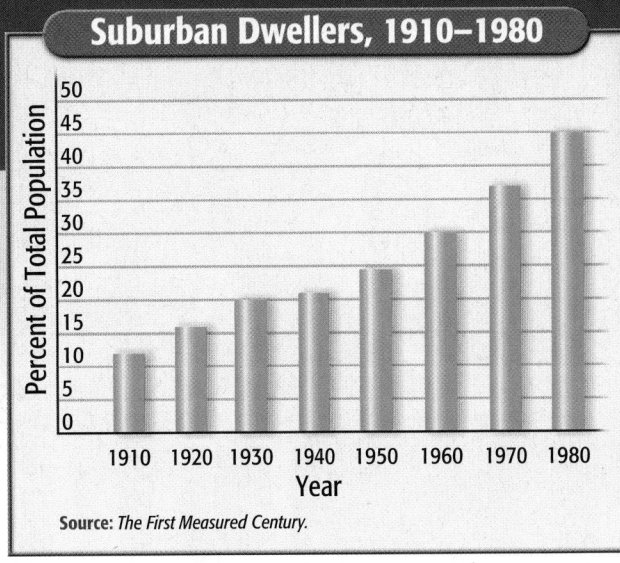

Suburban Dwellers, 1910–1980

Percent of Total Population (y-axis: 0, 5, 10, 15, 20, 25, 30, 35, 40, 45, 50)

Year (x-axis: 1910, 1920, 1930, 1940, 1950, 1960, 1970, 1980)

Source: *The First Measured Century.*

30. **Research Project** Work with a small group to research advertisements from the 1950s. Write a report comparing and contrasting advertisements from that decade with advertisements today. Present one or more of the advertisements along with your comparisons to your class.

Geography and History

31. The graph above shows the number of suburban dwellers in the United States as a percentage of the total population. Study the data displayed in the graph and answer the questions below.

a. **Interpreting Graphs** What trend in the percentage of suburban dwellers does this graph show?

b. **Understanding Cause and Effect** How might the trend of suburban dwellers shown on this graph have affected life in suburbs and cities?

Standardized Test Practice

Directions: Choose the phrase that best completes the following statement.

The Eisenhower administration worked to achieve all of the following EXCEPT

F   ending wage and price controls.

G   winning passage for the Federal Highway Act.

H   repealing right-to-work laws.

J   extending the Social Security system.

Test-Taking Tip: Pay careful attention to the wording of the question. Note here that *EXCEPT* means that three of the four choices were part of Eisenhower's programs.

UNIT
9
A Time of Upheaval
1954–1980

Mural on building in Davenport, Iowa

Why It Matters

From a presidential assassination to massive governmental programs, from the Vietnam War to the civil rights movement, the post–World War II decades immensely affected the lives of Americans. The nation struggled to put its social and political ideals into practice while fighting military wars overseas and social wars at home. Understanding how these events unfolded provides a window to the world you live in today. The following resources offer more information about this period in American history.

Primary Sources Library

See pages 1056–1057 to find additional primary source readings to accompany Unit 9.

Use the **American History Primary Source Document Library CD-ROM** to find additional primary sources about this eventful era.

MARCH ON WASHINGTON FOR JOBS AND FREEDOM AUGUST 28, 1963

We Shall

Overcome

Poster from the March on Washington

"What we won when all of our people united . . . must not now be lost in suspicion, distrust, selfishness, and politics. . . ."

—Lyndon Johnson, 1968

We must learn to live together as brothers or perish together as fools.

True Peace is not merely the absence of tension, it is the presence of Justice.

A sound mind has no specific color in which to be heard from bu carries out an emphatic message of every human race. Sherwin Q. Robinson S

NELSON MANDELA

CHAPTER 28

The New Frontier and the Great Society

1961–1968

Why It Matters

President John F. Kennedy urged Americans to work for progress and to stand firm against the Soviets. Cold War tensions and the threat of nuclear war peaked during the Cuban missile crisis. Kennedy's assassination changed the nation's mood, but President Lyndon Johnson embraced ambitious goals, including working toward the passage of major civil rights legislation and eradicating poverty.

The Impact Today

Initiatives introduced in this era remain a part of American society.
- *Medicaid and Medicare legislation provides major health benefits for elderly and low-income people.*
- *The Head Start program provides early educational opportunities for disadvantaged children.*

The American Vision Video *The Chapter 28 video, "A New Frontier: The Space Race," explores the dramatic history of the American space program.*

November 1963
- Kennedy assassinated; Lyndon Johnson becomes president

April 1961
- Bay of Pigs invasion

December 1961
- Presidential Commission on the Status of Women created

June 1963
- Kennedy visits Berlin Wall

October 1962
- Cuban missile crisis

Kennedy 1961–1963

L. Johnson 1963–1969

United States PRESIDENTS

1960

1962

1964

World

1959
- Cuban revolution brings Castro to power

April 1961
- Eichmann goes on trial for crimes against Jews

August 1961
- Construction of Berlin Wall begins

1964
- South Africa's Nelson Mandela sentenced to life in prison

President John F. Kennedy at his inaugural ball in 1961

July 1965
• Congress establishes Medicare and Medicaid programs

October 1966
• Fair Packaging and Labeling Act passed

March 1968
• Lyndon Johnson announces that he will not run for re-election

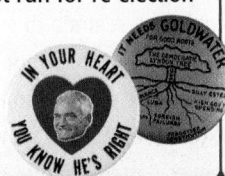

1966

1968

1966
• Indira Gandhi becomes prime minister of India

1968
• Student riots paralyze France

HISTORY Online

Chapter Overview
Visit the *American Vision* Web site at <u>tav.glencoe.com</u> and click on **Chapter Overviews— Chapter 28** to preview chapter information.

SECTION 1 The New Frontier

Guide to Reading

Main Idea
John F. Kennedy encountered both success and setbacks on the domestic front.

Key Terms and Names
missile gap, New Frontier, Earl Warren, reapportionment, due process

Reading Strategy
Categorizing As you read about the presidency of John F. Kennedy, complete a graphic organizer similar to the one below by filling in the domestic successes and setbacks of Kennedy's administration.

Successes	Setbacks

Reading Objectives
• **Summarize** Kennedy's economic policies.
• **Explain** why Congress often did not support Kennedy's proposals.

Section Theme
Civic Rights and Responsibilities The Supreme Court made decisions that protected individual rights, including the "one man, one vote" decision.

Preview of Events

♦1960   ♦1961   ♦1962   ♦1963

1960
John Kennedy defeats Richard Nixon for the presidency

1961
Kennedy creates Presidential Commission on the Status of Women

1962
Supreme Court issues *Baker* v. *Carr* ruling

1963
Kennedy signs Equal Pay Act for women

★ An American Story ★

On September 26, 1960, at 9:30 P.M. eastern standard time, streets all across the United States grew strangely still. An estimated 75 million people sat indoors, focused on their television sets, where they saw two men standing behind lecterns. One was John F. Kennedy, and the other was Richard M. Nixon.

For the first time, thanks to the wonders of television, two presidential candidates were coming right into the nation's living rooms to debate. Americans were enthralled: "You hear each man directly," observed one. "There's nothing between you and what he says," added another. "You can see which man gets rattled easily."

The man who seemed to get rattled easily was Nixon. Kennedy, the Democratic nominee, looked healthy, strong, and confident. Nixon, the Republicans' choice, came across as tired and frazzled. "He appeared ill," one viewer commented. In fact, Nixon had been ill recently. Kennedy had a glowing tan, while Nixon's face was pale and drawn, shadowed by the stubble of a beard. As one observer noted, "Nixon's eyes darted around, perspiration was clearly noticeable on his chin, and with the tight shots . . . these things were more obvious."

—**adapted from *The Great Debate***

The Election of 1960

The television debates of the 1960 presidential election had enormous impact. Following the first debate, the media focused more strongly on the appearance of the candidates. Suddenly the whole country seemed to have become experts on makeup and television lighting. One Republican leader even wondered if the Democrats had supplied Nixon's makeup.

With that debate, the era of television politics had begun. Though television had been used in campaigns as early as 1948, it was not until the 1960 election that a large majority of voters used the medium as a voting tool. The nation itself seemed on the brink of a new age. Having lived through a decade of unprecedented prosperity and the onset of the Cold War and the atomic age, Americans looked to the future with excitement and anxiety.

Both candidates shared the desire to lead the nation through the challenges of a new decade, but they differed in many ways. Kennedy, a Catholic, came from a wealthy and influential Massachusetts family. Nixon, a Quaker, was a Californian from a financially struggling family. Kennedy seemed outgoing and relaxed, while Nixon struck many as formal and even stiff in manner.

A New Kind of Campaign Compared to earlier campaigns, the 1960 presidential race made new use of television, with both major parties spending substantial amounts of money on television ads. The Democrats spent over $6 million in television and radio spots, while the Republicans spent more than $7.5 million.

Not everyone was happy with this new emphasis on image. Television news commentator Eric Sevareid complained that the candidates had become "packaged products," and he stated that "the Processed Politician has finally arrived."

The Main Issues The campaign centered on the economy and the Cold War. Although the candidates presented different styles, they differed little on these two issues. Both promised to boost the economy, and both portrayed themselves as "Cold Warriors" determined to stop the forces of communism.

Kennedy argued that the nation faced serious threats from the Soviets. In Cuba, Fidel Castro was allying himself with the Soviet Union. At home, many people lived in fear of a Soviet nuclear attack. Kennedy voiced his concern about a suspected "missile gap," in which the United States lagged behind the Soviets in weaponry. (Decades later, Americans learned that, in fact, the only area where the Soviet Union was briefly ahead was in rocketry). The nation, Kennedy argued, had grown complacent and aimless. "It is time to get this country moving again."

Nixon countered that the United States was on the right track under the current administration. "I'm tired of hearing our opponents downgrade the United States," the vice president said. Nixon also warned that the Democrats' fiscal policies would boost inflation, and that only he had the necessary foreign policy experience to guide the nation.

Kennedy came under scrutiny about his religion. The United States had never had a Catholic president, and many Protestants had concerns about Kennedy. Kennedy decided to confront this issue openly in a speech. "I believe in an America where the separation of the church and state is absolute," he said, "where no Catholic prelate would tell the president, should he be a Catholic, how to act."

The four televised debates strongly influenced the outcome of the election, one of the closest in American history. Kennedy won the popular vote by 119,000 out of 68 million votes cast and the Electoral College by 303 votes to 219. In several states only a few thousand votes could have swung the Electoral College numbers the other way.

✓ **Reading Check** **Identifying** What were two main issues of the 1960 presidential election?

The Kennedy Mystique

Despite his narrow victory, John F. Kennedy, commonly referred to as JFK, captured the imagination of the American public as few presidents before him had. During the campaign, many had been taken with Kennedy's youth and optimism. The new president strongly reinforced this impression when he gave his Inaugural Address.

Inauguration Day, January 20, 1961, was crisp and cold in Washington, D.C. At the site of the ceremony, a crowd gathered, wrapped in coats and blankets. As Kennedy rose to take the oath of office, he wore neither a coat nor a hat. During his speech, the new president declared, "The torch has been passed to a new generation," and he called on his fellow citizens to take a more active role in making the United States a better place. "My fellow Americans," he exclaimed, "ask not what your country can do for you—ask what you can do for your country."

Kennedy, his wife Jacqueline, their children Caroline and John, and their large extended family seemed to have been created for media coverage. Reporters followed the family everywhere.

Kennedy tie clasp (left) and Nixon pendant from 1960 presidential campaign

The Kennedy White House Jacqueline Kennedy (center right) brought youthful elegance and style to the White House. Why do you think the media scrutinized the First Family so much?

Kennedy himself was a master of the media, particularly television. He was the first to broadcast his press conferences live on television.

The Kennedy charisma inspired many of his staff members. His press secretary, Pierre Salinger, put this feeling into words:

> ❝None of us will ever have a better job as long as we live. . . . The big *plus*—the fringe benefit that made it all worthwhile—was JFK himself. . . . Our faith in him and in what he was trying to do was absolute, and he could impart to our work together a sense of challenge and adventure—a feeling that he was moving, and the world with him, toward a better time.❞

—quoted in *With Kennedy*

Reading Check **Summarizing** In what ways did John F. Kennedy inspire the nation?

Success and Setback on the Domestic Front

Not everyone in the nation fell for the Kennedy mystique. His high culture, elite Northeast upbringing, and Catholicism irritated some Americans. Congress also was less than taken with the new president. Upon entering office, President Kennedy set out to implement a legislative agenda, which became known as the **New Frontier.** He hoped to increase aid to education, provide health insurance to the elderly, create a Department of Urban Affairs, and help migrant workers. He would soon find that transforming lofty ideals into real legislation was no easy task on Capitol Hill.

Kennedy Struggles With Congress Although the Democratic Party enjoyed large majorities in both houses of Congress, Kennedy was unable to push through many of his domestic programs. Kennedy had trailed Nixon in many Democratic districts and had not helped many Democrats get elected. Those who did win, therefore, did not feel they owed him anything. As one Democrat in Congress told *U.S. News & World Report*, "A good many [congressional representatives] were elected in 1960 in spite of his presence on the ticket rather than because his name was there." As a result, legislators found it easy to follow their own interests rather than those of the president.

In addition, Republicans as well as conservative Southern Democrats—who were responsible for holding the Democratic majority in Congress—viewed the New Frontier as too big and too costly. Senator Everett Dirksen, Republican minority leader from Illinois, claimed that Kennedy's efforts to increase the power and reach of the federal government would push the nation down an ominous path.

In the end, Congress defeated a number of JFK's proposals, including health insurance for the elderly, a Department of Urban Affairs, and federal aid to education. The president often resisted calls to push harder for his agenda. He decided not to fight every battle on Capitol Hill and preferred to reserve his bargaining power for issues that were both truly important and winnable.

ECONOMICS

Strengthening the Economy Kennedy did achieve some victories in Congress, particularly in his efforts to improve the nation's economy. The American economy, which had soared through much of the 1950s, had slowed by the end of the decade. From 1960 to 1961, the growth rate of the gross national product was only 2 percent, while the unemployment rate hovered near 7 percent of the workforce, the second-highest figure since World War II.

In an effort to increase growth and create more jobs, Kennedy advocated the New Deal strategy of deficit spending, first implemented during Franklin Roosevelt's presidency. The new president convinced Congress to invest more funds in defense and in space exploration. Such spending did indeed create more jobs and stimulate economic growth. Reluctant to rely too heavily on deficit spending, which tends to cause inflation, Kennedy also sought to boost the economy by increasing business production and efficiency. In addition, his administration asked businesses to hold down prices and labor leaders to hold down pay increases.

Prodded by Secretary of Labor Arthur Goldberg, labor unions in the steel industry agreed to reduce their demands for higher wages. In 1962, however, several steel companies raised prices sharply.

The president threatened to have the Department of Defense buy cheaper steel from foreign companies and instructed the Justice Department to investigate whether the steel industry was guilty of price-fixing. In response to Kennedy's tactics, the steel companies backed down and cut their prices. To achieve this victory, however, the president had strained his relations with the nation's business community.

In an effort to get the economy moving, Kennedy also adopted supply-side ideas and pushed for a cut in tax rates. When opponents argued that a tax cut would only help the wealthy, Kennedy asserted that lower taxes meant businesses would have more money to expand, which would create new jobs and benefit everybody. "A rising tide lifts all boats," Kennedy explained, as a way to illustrate how tax cuts would stimulate the economy and help all Americans.

Congress refused to pass the tax cut because many members feared it would cause inflation. However, they did support Kennedy's request to raise the minimum wage and his proposal for an Area Redevelopment Act and a Housing Act. These two programs provided funds to poor areas. They helped to clear slums, create jobs, and build low-income housing.

Women's Rights
Kennedy also helped women make strides during the 1960s. Although Kennedy never appointed a woman to his cabinet, a number of women worked in prominent positions in his administration, including **Esther Peterson,** assistant secretary of labor and director of the Women's Bureau of the Department of Labor.

Kennedy advanced women's rights in other ways as well. In 1961 he created the **Presidential Commission on the Status of Women.** The commission called for federal action against gender discrimination and affirmed the right of women to equally paid employment. Kennedy responded by issuing an executive order ending gender discrimination in the federal civil service, and in 1963 he signed the Equal Pay Act for women. The commission also sparked the creation of similar groups on the state level and inspired many women to work together to further their interests.

Reading Check **Evaluating** Why did Kennedy have difficulty getting his New Frontier legislation passed?

Warren Court Reforms
During the Kennedy years, the Supreme Court also took an active role in social issues. In 1953 President Eisenhower had nominated **Earl Warren,** the popular Republican governor of California, to become Chief Justice of the United States. More so than previous courts, the Warren Court took an activist stance, helping to shape national policy by taking a forceful stand on a number of key issues of the day.

GOVERNMENT

"One Man, One Vote" One of the Warren Court's more notable decisions had a powerful impact on who would hold political power in the United States. This decision concerned reapportionment, or the way in which states draw up political districts based on changes in population. By 1960 many more Americans resided in cities and suburbs than in rural areas. Yet many states had failed to restructure their electoral districts to reflect that change.

In Tennessee, for example, a rural county with only 2,340 voters had 1 representative in the state assembly, while an urban county with 133 times more voters had only 7. The vote of a city dweller counted for less than the vote of a rural resident. Some Tennessee voters took the matter to court.

The *Baker* v. *Carr* case reached the Supreme Court after a federal court ruled that the issue should be

Fact	Fiction	Folklore

Camelot In December 1960, *Camelot,* a musical starring Richard Burton and Julie Andrews, opened on Broadway in New York City. The Kennedys attended the show, which told the legend of the heroism of King Arthur and the Knights of the Round Table, and so enjoyed it that they listened to the music often. The president's favorite song included the lines: "Don't let it be forgot, that once there was a spot, for one brief shining moment that was known as Camelot."

In later years, the Kennedy presidency became known as "Camelot," largely because of Mrs. Kennedy. Shortly after the president's death in 1963, she told a journalist that all she could think about was the president's favorite line. She went on to say: "There'll be great presidents again, . . . but there'll never be another Camelot again." Journalist Theodore H. White later wrote that "all she could repeat was, 'Tell people there will never be that Camelot again.'"

Major Decisions of the Warren Court, 1954—1967

Civil Rights

Brown v. *Board of Education* (1954)	Segregation in public schools unconstitutional
Baker v. *Carr* (1962)	Established that federal courts can hear lawsuits seeking to force state authorities to redraw electoral districts
Reynolds v. *Sims* (1964)	State legislative districts should be equal in population
Heart of Atlanta Motel v. *United States* (1964)	Desegregation of public accommodations established in the Civil Rights Act of 1964 is legal
Loving v. *Virginia* (1967)	States may not ban interracial marriage

Due Process

Mapp v. *Ohio* (1961)	Unlawfully seized evidence is inadmissible at trial
Gideon v. *Wainwright* (1963)	Suspects are entitled to court-appointed attorney if unable to afford one on their own
Escobedo v. *Illinois* (1964)	Accused has the right to an attorney during police questioning
Miranda v. *Arizona* (1966)	Police must inform suspects of their rights during the arrest process

Freedom of Religion and Freedom of Speech

Engel v. *Vitale* (1962)	State-mandated prayer in school banned
Abington School District v. *Schempp* (1963)	State-mandated Bible readings in school banned
New York Times v. *Sullivan* (1964)	Celebrities may sue the media for libel only in certain circumstances

Chart *Skills*

1. **Interpreting Charts** Analyze the effects *Brown* v. *Board of Education* and *Reynolds* v. *Sims* had on the nation.
2. **Summarizing** What three major areas of policy did the Warren Court's decisions affect?

solved by legislation. The Fourteenth Amendment specifically gives Congress authority to enforce voting rights. In 1962 the Supreme Court ruled that the federal courts did have jurisdiction and sent the matter back to the lower courts. 📖 *(See page 1080 for more information on* Baker v. Carr.*)*

Two years later, in June 1964, the Supreme Court ruled in *Reynolds* v. *Sims* that the current apportionment system in most states was indeed unconstitutional. In a decision that helped to promote the principle of "one man, one vote," the Warren Court required state legislatures to reapportion electoral districts so that all citizens' votes would have equal weight. The Court's decision was a momentous one, for it shifted political power throughout the country from rural and often conservative areas to urban areas, where more liberal voters resided. The Court's decision also boosted the political power of African Americans and Hispanics, who typically lived in cities. 📖 *(See page 1082 for more information on* Reynolds v. Sims.*)*

Extending Due Process In a series of historic rulings in the 1960s, the U.S. Supreme Court began to use the Fourteenth Amendment to apply the Bill of Rights to the states. Originally, the Bill of Rights applied only to the federal government. Many states had their own bill of rights, but some federal rights did not exist at the state level. The Fourteenth Amendment specifically stated that "no state shall . . . deprive any person of life, liberty, or property without due process of law." Due process means that the law may not treat individuals unfairly, arbitrarily, or unreasonably, and that courts must follow proper procedures and rules when trying cases. Due process ensures that all people are treated the same by the court system. In the 1960s, the Supreme Court ruled in several cases that upholding due process meant applying the federal bill of rights to the states.

In 1961 the Supreme Court ruled in *Mapp* v. *Ohio* that state courts could not consider evidence obtained in violation of the federal Constitution. In *Gideon* v. *Wainwright* (1963), the Court ruled that a defendant in a state court had the right to a lawyer, regardless of his or her ability to pay. The following year, in *Escobedo* v. *Illinois,* the justices ruled that a suspect must be allowed access to a lawyer and must be informed of his or her right to remain silent before being questioned by the police. *Miranda* v. *Arizona* (1966) went even further, requiring that authorities immediately give suspects a fourfold warning. The warning consisted of informing suspects that they have the right to remain silent, that anything they say can and will be used against them in court, that they have a right to a lawyer while being questioned, and that if they cannot afford a lawyer, the court will appoint one for them. Today these warnings are known as the Miranda rights. 📖 *(See pages 1081–1082 for more information on* Mapp *v.* Ohio, Gideon *v.* Wainwright, Escobedo *v.* Illinois, *and* Miranda *v.* Arizona.*)*

Many citizens and police departments and even some of the Supreme Court justices accused the Warren Court of favoring criminals. Others cheered the decisions, seeing them as promoting the rights of all citizens, even the less privileged.

Prayer and Privacy The Supreme Court also handed down decisions that reaffirmed the separation of church and state. The Court applied the First Amendment to the states in *Engel* v. *Vitale* (1962). In this ruling, the Court decided that states could not compose official prayers and require those prayers to be recited in state public schools. The following year, in *Abington School District* v. *Schempp,* it ruled against state-mandated Bible readings in public schools. Weighing in on another controversial issue, the Court ruled in *Griswold* v. *Connecticut* (1965) that prohibiting the sale and use of birth control devices violated citizens' constitutional right to privacy. 📖 *(See pages 1080–1081 for more information on these Supreme Court cases.)*

Activist Court The Warren Court poses for its official portrait in 1962, with Chief Justice Earl Warren front and center.

As with most rulings of the Warren Court, these decisions delighted some and deeply disturbed others. What most people did agree upon, however, was the Court's pivotal role in shaping national policy. The Warren Court, wrote *New York Times* columnist Anthony Lewis, "has brought about more social change than most Congresses and most Presidents."

From the political arena to the legal system to people's everyday lives, the Warren Court indeed left its imprint on the nation. Meanwhile, away from the domestic arena, President Kennedy worked to make his mark on the country's foreign affairs during a time of rising Cold War tensions.

✓ **Reading Check** **Examining** What was the significance of the Warren Court's "One Man, One Vote" ruling?

SECTION 1 ASSESSMENT

Checking for Understanding

1. **Define:** missile gap, reapportionment, due process.
2. **Identify:** New Frontier, Earl Warren.
3. **Summarize** the progress made for women's rights during Kennedy's administration.

Reviewing Themes

4. **Civic Rights and Responsibilities** Name three decisions of the Warren Court that protected civil rights.

Critical Thinking

5. **Interpreting** In what way was the 1960 presidential election a turning point in campaign history?
6. **Organizing** Use a graphic organizer similar to the one below to list the economic policies of the Kennedy administration.

Economic Policies	

Analyzing Visuals

7. **Analyzing Charts** Study the chart of Warren Court decisions on page 844. How did the Court expand the rights of the accused? Were these sound decisions? Why or why not?

Writing About History

8. **Expository Writing** In his Inaugural Address, President Kennedy asked his fellow Americans to "Ask what you can do for your country." Respond to this statement in an essay.

JFK and the Cold War

Main Idea

As president, John F. Kennedy had to confront the challenges and fears of the Cold War.

Key Terms and Names

flexible response, Peace Corps, space race, Berlin Wall, Warren Commission

Reading Strategy

Sequencing As you read about the crises of the Cold War, complete a time line similar to the one below to record the major events of the Cold War in the late 1950s and early 1960s.

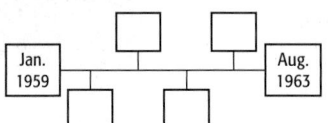

Reading Objectives

- **Describe** Kennedy's plan for the armed forces.
- **Explain** how the Cold War influenced foreign aid and the space program.

Section Theme

Science and Technology During the Cold War, the nation devoted much of its scientific and technological resources to competing with the Soviet Union, especially in getting to the moon.

Preview of Events

♦1961   ♦1962   ♦1963   ♦1964

April 1961 — Bay of Pigs invasion

May 1961 — Kennedy informs Congress of moon expedition goal

October 1962 — Cuban missile crisis

September 1963 — Senate ratifies Limited Test Ban Treaty

November 22, 1963 — Kennedy assassinated

★ *An American Story* ★

Like millions of other Americans in late October 1962, Tami Gold was having trouble concentrating on anything. For several tension-filled days that fall, the world seemed headed for nuclear destruction. U.S. officials had discovered that the Soviet Union had placed missiles in Cuba—a mere 90 miles (145 km) from the shores of the United States. When the Soviets refused to remove the weapons, a bitter weeklong standoff ensued in which the two superpowers hurled threats and warnings at each other and moved to the brink of nuclear war. Gold, then a seventh-grade student in Long Island, New York, recalled the events of one particular day:

❝I remember I was in the bathroom of the school . . . when they had said over the loud speaker . . . that everyone had to return to their homerooms immediately and get instruction from their homeroom teacher. And it was probably one of the scariest moments of my life, it was like the sensation that our country could go to war and I didn't understand at all what it was about, but the fact that the country could go to war at any moment was really really present. . . . It was chilling, it was scary, it was really nauseating. . . .❞

—quoted in *Collective Memories of the Cuban Missile Crisis*

Kennedy Confronts Global Challenges

The Cuban missile crisis, as the standoff came to be called, may have been the most dramatic foreign policy episode Kennedy faced. It was not the only one, however. As Kennedy entered the White House, the nation's dangerous rivalry with the Soviet Union continued to intensify. As a result, the new president had to devote much of his energy in foreign policy matters to guiding the nation through the deepening Cold War.

Kennedy appeared ready to stand up to the Soviets. Upon taking the oath of office, the new president devoted much of his Inaugural Address to the role of the United States in a divided world:

> 66Let the word go forth from this time and place . . . that the torch has been passed to a new generation of Americans—born in this century, tempered by war, disciplined by a hard and bitter peace, proud of our ancient heritage—and unwilling to witness or permit the slow undoing of those human rights to which this nation has always been committed. . . . Let every nation know, whether it wishes us well or ill, that we shall pay any price, bear any burden, meet any hardship, support any friend, oppose any foe, to assure the survival and the success of liberty.99
>
> —quoted in *Let the Word Go Forth*

Kennedy attempted to reduce the threat of nuclear war and to stop the spread of communism with a range of programs. These included a conventional weaponry program, economic aid, and the Peace Corps.

A More Flexible Response

Kennedy took office at a time of growing global instability. Nationalism was exploding throughout the developing world, and the Soviet Union actively supported "wars of national liberation." *Newsweek* magazine wrote that the "greatest single problem that faces John Kennedy is how to meet the aggressive power of the Communist bloc."

Kennedy felt that Eisenhower had relied too heavily on nuclear weapons, which could only be used in extreme situations. To allow for a "flexible response" if nations needed help against Communist movements, the president pushed for a buildup of conventional troops and weapons. Although costly, a flexible response plan would allow the United States to fight a limited style of warfare.

In adopting this plan, Kennedy supported the Special Forces, a small army unit created in the 1950s to wage guerrilla warfare in limited conflicts. Kennedy expanded it and allowed the soldiers to wear their distinctive "Green Beret" headgear.

Aid to Other Countries

One area of the world where Kennedy wanted to renew diplomatic focus was Latin America. Conditions in much of Latin American society were not good: Governments were often in the hands of the wealthy few and many of their citizens lived in extreme poverty. In some Latin American countries, these conditions spurred the growth of left-wing movements aimed at overthrowing their governments. When the United States was involved in Latin America, it was usually to help existing governments stay in power in order to prevent Communist movements from flourishing. Poor Latin Americans resented this intrusion, just as they resented American corporations that had business operations in their countries, a presence that was seen as a kind of imperialism.

To improve relations between the United States and Latin America, President Kennedy proposed an **Alliance for Progress,** a series of cooperative aid projects with Latin American governments. The alliance was designed to create a "free and prosperous Latin America" that would be less likely to support Communist-inspired revolutions.

Over a 10-year period, the United States pledged $20 billion to help Latin American countries establish better schools, housing, health care, and fairer land distribution. The results were mixed. In some countries—notably Chile, Colombia, Venezuela, and the Central American republics—the alliance did promote real reform. In others, governing rulers used the money to keep themselves in power.

The Peace Corps Another program aimed at helping less developed nations fight poverty was the **Peace Corps,** an organization that sent young Americans to perform humanitarian services in these countries.

After rigorous training, volunteers spent two years in countries that had requested assistance. They laid out sewage systems in Bolivia and trained medical technicians in Chad. Others taught English or helped to build roads. By late 1963 thousands of Peace Corps volunteers were serving in over 30 countries. Today, the Peace Corps is still active and remains one of Kennedy's most enduring legacies.

TECHNOLOGY

The Cold War Moves Into Space

President Kennedy sought to increase the country's presence not only around the world but also in space. With Cold War tensions continuing to rise, the United States and the Soviet Union engaged in a space race—vying for dominance of the heavens to enhance their competitive positions on Earth.

HISTORY Online

Student Web Activity Visit the *American Vision* Web site at tav.glencoe.com and click on **Student Web Activities— Chapter 28** for an activity on the New Frontier.

Why It Matters

The Space Program

The space program expanded significantly when President Kennedy announced his determination to beat the Soviets to the moon. By the time Neil Armstrong and Edwin ("Buzz") Aldrin walked on the moon in 1969, the National Aeronautics and Space Administration (NASA) had spent over $33 billion. Since that time, NASA expenditures have affected far more than space missions. NASA research findings have advanced knowledge of the nature of the universe, and people have applied them to many technical fields and manufacturing processes.

▼ Moon boot material developed for the space program is used in many running shoes. It has improved shock absorption and provides superior stability and motion control.

Kennedy was determined that the first humans to reach the moon would be Americans, not Russians. In 1961 he recommended to Congress that "this nation should commit itself to achieving the goal, before this decade is out, of landing a man on the moon." Kennedy's dream was realized in July 1969, during Richard Nixon's first administration, when astronaut Neil Armstrong became the first person to set foot on the moon.

✓ **Reading Check** **Examining** What global challenges did Kennedy face during his presidency?

Crises of the Cold War

President Kennedy's efforts to combat Communist influence in other countries led to some of the most intense crises of the Cold War. At times these crises left Americans and people in many other nations wondering whether the world would survive.

The Bay of Pigs The first crisis occurred in Cuba, only 90 miles (145 km) from American shores. There, Fidel Castro had overthrown the corrupt Cuban dictator Fulgencio Batista in 1959. Almost

immediately, Castro established ties with the Soviet Union, instituted drastic land reforms, and seized foreign-owned businesses, many of them American. Cuba's alliance with the Soviets worried many Americans. The Communists were now too close for comfort, and Soviet Premier Nikita Khrushchev was also expressing his intent to strengthen Cuba militarily.

Fearing that the Soviets would use Cuba as a base from which to spread revolution throughout the Western Hemisphere, President Eisenhower had authorized the Central Intelligence Agency (CIA) to secretly train and arm Cuban exiles, known as La Brigada, to invade the island. The invasion was intended to touch off a popular uprising against Castro.

When Kennedy became president, his advisers approved the plan. In office fewer than three months and trusting his experts, Kennedy agreed to the operation with some changes. On April 17, 1961, 1,400 armed Cuban exiles landed at the **Bay of Pigs** on the south coast of Cuba. The invasion was a disaster. La Brigada's boats ran aground on coral reefs, Kennedy cancelled their air support to keep United States involvement a secret, and the

▼ Assistance for People With Disabilities

The NASA tele-operator and robot technology was used to develop a voice-controlled wheelchair and manipulator. Using a minicomputer, the wheelchair responds to 35 single-word voice commands, helping physically challenged people perform tasks like picking up packages, opening doors, and turning on appliances.

Increased Safety ➤

Remote-controlled robots reduce human injury levels because they can perform hazardous tasks men and women used to carry out. Robots can also perform operations no human being ever could, such as volcano research on the Puna Ridge of Kilauea, Hawaii.

Communication Advances

A communications satellite now in development will provide better telephone, television, and data service between western Europe, the Americas, and Africa. Another communications satellite has improved ship-to-shore communications, which used to be interrupted frequently by bad weather.

---

expected popular uprising never happened. Within two days, Castro's forces killed or captured almost all the members of La Brigada.

The Bay of Pigs was a dark moment for the Kennedy administration. The action exposed an American plot to overthrow a neighbor's government, and the outcome made the United States look weak and disorganized.

The Berlin Wall Goes Up Still reeling from the Bay of Pigs fiasco, Kennedy faced another foreign policy challenge beginning in June 1961 when he met with Khrushchev in Vienna, Austria. The Soviet leader was determined to test the resolve of the young president. Khrushchev also wanted to stop the flood of Germans pouring out of Communist East Germany into West Berlin. He demanded that the Western powers recognize East Germany and that the United States, Great Britain, and France withdraw from Berlin, a city lying completely within East Germany. Kennedy refused and reaffirmed the West's commitment to West Berlin.

Khrushchev retaliated by building a wall through Berlin, blocking movement between the Soviet sector and the rest of the city. Guards posted along the wall shot at many of those attempting to escape from the East. For nearly 30 years afterward, the **Berlin Wall** stood as a visible symbol of the Cold War division between East and West.

The Cuban Missile Crisis By far the most terrifying crisis of the Kennedy era occurred the next year. Once again, the crisis dealt with Cuba. Over the summer of 1962, American intelligence agencies learned that Soviet technicians and equipment had arrived in Cuba and that military construction was in progress. Then, on October 22, President Kennedy announced on television that American spy planes had taken aerial photographs showing that the Soviet Union had placed long-range missiles in Cuba. Enemy missiles stationed so close to the United States posed a dangerous threat.

Kennedy ordered a naval blockade to stop the Soviets from delivering more missiles, demanded that they dismantle existing missile sites, and warned that if any weapons were launched against the United States, he would respond fully against the Soviet Union. Still, work on the missile sites continued. Nuclear holocaust seemed imminent.

Then, after a flurry of secret negotiations, the Soviet Union offered a deal. It would remove the missiles if the United States promised not to invade Cuba and to remove its missiles from Turkey near the Soviet border. As American officials considered the offer, letters and cables flew between the two leaders and their chief advisers.

The reality was that neither Kennedy nor Khrushchev wanted nuclear war. "Only lunatics . . . who themselves want to perish and before they die destroy the world, could do this," wrote the Soviet leader. Still, the dangerous standoff persisted. On October 28, the leaders reached an agreement. Kennedy publicly agreed not to invade Cuba and privately agreed to remove the Turkish missiles; the Soviets agreed to remove their missiles from Cuba. The world could breathe again.

The Impact of the Cuban Missile Crisis

The Cuban missile crisis brought the world closer to nuclear war than at any time since World War II. Both the United States and the Soviet Union had been forced to consider the consequences of such a war. In the following months, each country seemed ready to work to lessen world tensions. In August 1963, the United States and the Soviet Union concluded years of negotiation by agreeing to a treaty to ban the testing of nuclear weapons in the atmosphere—the first step toward mutual arms reduction since the beginning of the Cold War.

In the long run, however, the missile crisis had ominous consequences. The humiliating retreat the United States forced upon the Soviet leadership undermined the position of Nikita Khrushchev and contributed to his fall from power a year later. The new leadership was less interested in reaching agreements with the West. Perhaps more important, the crisis gave the Soviets evidence of their military inferiority and helped produce a dramatic Soviet arms buildup over the next two decades. This buildup contributed to a comparable military increase in the United States in the early 1980s. For a time, the arms race undermined American support for negotiating with the Soviets.

Reading Check **Summarizing** How was the Cuban missile crisis resolved?

The Death of a President

Soon after the Senate ratified the test ban treaty, John F. Kennedy's presidency came to a shocking and tragic end. On November 22, 1963, Kennedy and his wife traveled to Texas with Vice President Lyndon Johnson for a series of political appearances. As the presidential motorcade rode slowly through the

MISSILE ERECTOR

THEODOLITE STATION

5 TRUCKS UNDER CAMOUFLAGE NETTING

CABLE

5 TRUCKS UNDER CAMOUFLAGE NETTING

MISSILE SHELTER TENTS

Picturing **History**

Cold War Peak Fears of communism peaked during the Cuban missile crisis. Routine reconnaissance flights over Cuba revealed the construction of missile sites, fueling facilities, and launch pads. What steps did Kennedy take to deal with the crisis?

crowded streets of Dallas, gunfire rang out. Someone had shot the president twice—once in the throat and once in the head. Horrified government officials sped Kennedy to a nearby hospital, where he was pronounced dead moments later.

Lee Harvey Oswald, the man accused of killing Kennedy, appeared to be a confused and embittered Marxist who had spent time in the Soviet Union. He himself was shot to death while in police custody two days after the assassination. The bizarre situation led some to speculate that the second gunman, local nightclub owner Jack Ruby, killed Oswald to protect others involved in the crime. In 1964 a national commission headed by Chief Justice Warren concluded that Oswald was the lone assassin. The report of the **Warren Commission** left some questions unanswered, and theories about a conspiracy to kill the president have persisted, though none has gained wide acceptance.

In the wake of the assassination, the United States and the world went into mourning. Americans across the land sobbed in public. Thousands traveled to Washington, D.C., and waited in a line that stretched for several miles outside the Capitol in order to walk silently past the president's flag-draped casket. Millions of others spent hours in front of their televisions, simply watching people file past the casket. In Rome, Italy, people brought flowers to the American embassy. In the streets of New Delhi, India, crowds wept. In Africa, the president of Guinea said, "I have lost my only true friend in the outside world."

John F. Kennedy served as president for little more than 1,000 days. Yet his powerful personality and active approach to the presidency made a profound impression on most Americans. Aided by the tidal

Picturing **History**

A Final Salute John F. Kennedy, Jr. (right) bravely salutes his father's coffin during the state funeral. How did people around the world react to JFK's assassination?

wave of emotion that followed the president's death, his successor, Lyndon Baines Johnson, would set out to promote many of the programs that Kennedy left behind.

Reading Check **Evaluating** How did Kennedy's presidency end?

SECTION 2 ASSESSMENT

Checking for Understanding

1. **Define:** flexible response, space race.
2. **Identify:** Peace Corps, Berlin Wall, Warren Commission.
3. **Explain** the goals of the Alliance for Progress.

Reviewing Themes

4. **Science and Technology** What was Kennedy's goal for the United States in the space race?

Critical Thinking

5. **Interpreting** What was the role of foreign aid in the relations between the United States and Latin America?
6. **Organizing** Use a graphic organizer similar to the one below to list the programs that Kennedy used to reduce the threat of nuclear war and to try to stem communism.

Analyzing Visuals

7. **Analyzing Photographs** Study the photographs on pages 848–849. Explain how space exploration has led to other innovations that have affected our daily lives and standard of living.

Writing About History
8. **Descriptive Writing** Take on the role of an American citizen during the Cuban missile crisis. Write a journal entry describing the mood of the country during that time.

BETTMANN/CORBIS

Eyewitness

On May 22, 1964, **PRESIDENT LYNDON JOHNSON** *delivered a speech in Ann Arbor, Michigan, outlining his domestic agenda that would become known as "The Great Society." Speechwriter and policy adviser Richard Goodwin watched the speech on videotape the next morning back in Washington. He recalls his reaction:*

Then, with the cheers, at first muted as if the audience were surprised at their own response, then mounting toward unrestrained, accepting delight, Johnson concluded: "There are those timid souls who say . . . we are condemned to a soulless wealth. I do not agree. We have the power to shape civilization. . . . But we need your will, your labor, your hearts. . . . So let us from this moment begin our work, so that in the future men will look back and say: It was then, after a long and weary way, that man turned the exploits of his genius to the full enrichment of his life."

Watching the film in the White House basement, almost involuntarily I added my applause to the tumultuous acclaim coming from the sound track. . . . I clapped for the President, and for our country.

WHAT IS A PIP, ANYWAY?

Match these rock 'n' roll headliners with their supporting acts.

1. Paul Revere and	**a.** the Union Gap
2. Martha and	**b.** the Supremes
3. Gary Puckett and	**c.** the Miracles
4. Gladys Knight and	**d.** the Vandellas
5. Smokey Robinson and	**e.** the Raiders
6. Diana Ross and	**f.** the Pips

answers: 1. e ; 2. d ; 3. a ; 4. f ; 5. c ; 6. b

Space Race

Want to capture some of the glamour and excitement of space exploration? Create a new nickname for your city. You won't be the first.

CITY	NICKNAME
Danbury, CT	Space Age City
Muscle Shoals, AL	Space Age City
Houston, TX	Space City, USA
Galveston, TX	Space Port, USA
Cape Kennedy, FL	Spaceport, USA
Blacksburg, VA	Space Age Community
Huntsville, AL	~~Rocket City, USA~~
	~~Space City, USA~~
	~~Space Capital of the Nation~~
	Space Capital of the World

RALPH MORSE/TIMEPIX

John Glenn, first American to orbit Earth

Milestones

PERFORMED IN ENGLISH, 1962. THE CATHOLIC MASS, following Pope John XXIII's Second Vatican Council. "Vatican II" allows the Latin mass to be translated into local languages around the world.

ENROLLED, 1962. JAMES MEREDITH, at the University of Mississippi, following a Supreme Court ruling that ordered his admission to the previously segregated school. Rioting and a showdown with state officials who wished to bar his enrollment preceded Meredith's entrance to classes.

BROKEN, 1965. 25-DAY FAST BY CÉSAR CHÁVEZ, labor organizer. His protest convinced others to join his nonviolent strike against the grape growers; shoppers boycotted table grapes in sympathy.

STRIPPED, 1967. MUHAMMAD ALI, of his heavyweight champion title, after refusing induction into the army following a rejection of his application for conscientious objector status. The boxer was arrested, given a five-year sentence, and fined $10,000.

PICKETED, 1968. The Miss America Pageant in Atlantic City, by protesters who believe the contest's emphasis on women's physical beauty is degrading and minimizes the importance of women's intellect.

AP

REMOVED, 1968. TOY GUNS, from the Sears, Roebuck Christmas catalog after the assassinations of Martin Luther King, Jr., and Robert Kennedy.

NUMBERS

7% of African American adults registered to vote in Mississippi in 1964 before passage of the Voting Rights Act of 1965

67% of African American adults in Mississippi registered to vote in 1969

70% of white adults registered to vote in 1964, nationwide

90% of white adults registered to vote nationwide in 1969

57 Number of days senators filibustered to hold up passage of the Civil Rights Bill in 1964

14½ Hours duration of all-night speech delivered by Senator Robert Byrd before a cloture vote stopped the filibuster

72% of elementary and high school teachers approve of corporal punishment as a disciplinary measure in 1961

HULTON-DEUTSCH COLLECTION/CORBIS

$80–90 Weekly pay for a clerk/typist in New York in 1965

$200 Rent for a two-bedroom apartment at Broadway and 72nd Street on New York City's Upper West Side in 1965

Guide to Reading

Main Idea
Lyndon Johnson succeeded John F. Kennedy as president and greatly expanded Kennedy's agenda with far-reaching programs in many areas.

Key Terms and Names
consensus, war on poverty, VISTA, Great Society, Medicare, Medicaid, Head Start, Robert Weaver

Reading Strategy
Organizing As you read about Lyndon Johnson's presidency, complete a graphic organizer similar to the one below to list the social and economic programs started during his administration.

Johnson's Programs

Reading Objectives
• **Explain** what inspired Johnson's Great Society programs.
• **Identify** several specific health and employment programs of the Johnson administration.

Section Theme
Government and Democracy In a time of prosperity, President Johnson won support for extending government aid to the poor and elderly.

Preview of Events

♦November 1963	♦June 1964	♦January 1965	♦August 1965

November 1963
Johnson becomes president upon Kennedy's death

August 1964
Congress enacts Economic Opportunity Act

November 1964
Johnson wins election as president

July 1965
Congress passes Medical Care Act, establishing Medicare and Medicaid

★ An American Story ★

In 1961, 61-year-old John Rath lived in a sparsely furnished room in Chicago. In the room sat a stove, a sink, a package of cereal, and a tiny icebox. The plaster on the wall was crumbling, the ceiling was cracked, and the window shades were smudged. Telling his story to an interviewer, Rath said:

❝I come home to an empty room. I don't even have a dog. No, this is not the kind of life I would choose. If a man had a little piece of land or something, a farm, or well . . . anyway, you've got to have something. You sit down in a place like this, you grit your teeth, you follow me? So many of them are doing that, they sit down, they don't know what to do, they go out. I see 'em in the middle of the night, they take a walk. Don't know what to do. Have no home environment, don't have a dog, don't have nothing . . . just a big zero.❞

—quoted in *Division Street: America*

Johnson Takes the Reins

John Rath's life was not the image that many Americans had of their country in the mid-1960s. The United States that President Lyndon Johnson inherited from John F. Kennedy appeared to be a booming, bustling place. From new shopping malls to new roads with new cars to fill them, everything in the country seemed to shout prosperity.

Away from the nation's affluent suburbs, however, was another country, one inhabited by the poor, the ill-fed, the ill-housed, and the ill-educated. Writer Michael Harrington examined the nation's impoverished areas in his 1962 book, *The Other America*. Harrington claimed that while the truly poor numbered almost 50 million, they remained largely hidden in city slums, in rural areas, in the Deep South, and on Native American reservations.

Harrington's book moved many Americans and inspired both President Kennedy and his successor, Lyndon Johnson, to make the elimination of poverty a major policy goal. The nation was prosperous, and many leaders had come to believe that the economy could be managed so that prosperity would be permanent. They believed the federal government could afford to fund a new antipoverty program.

Lyndon Johnson decided to continue with Kennedy's plan soon after taking office. Immediately after President Kennedy was pronounced dead, officials whisked Johnson to the airport. At 2:38 P.M. on November 22, 1963, he stood in the cabin of Air Force One, the president's plane, with Jacqueline Kennedy on one side of him and his wife, Lady Bird, on the other. Johnson raised his right hand, placed his left hand on a Bible, and took the oath of office.

Johnson knew that he had to assure a stunned public that he could hold the nation together, that he was a leader. He later recalled the urgency with which he had to act:

66A nation stunned, shaken to its very heart, had to be reassured that the government was not in a state of paralysis . . . that the business of the United States would proceed. I knew that not only the nation but the whole world would be anxiously following every move I made—watching, judging, weighing, balancing. . . . It was imperative that I grasp the reins of power and do so without delay. Any hesitation or wavering, any false step, any sign of self-doubt, could have been disastrous.99

—quoted in *Lyndon Johnson and the American Dream*

Days after the assassination, Johnson appeared before Congress and urged the nation to move on. "The ideas and ideals which [Kennedy] so nobly represented must and will be translated into effective action," he stated. "John Kennedy's death commands what his life conveyed—that America must move forward."

Johnson's Leadership Style

Lyndon Baines Johnson was born and raised in the "hill country" of central Texas, near the banks of the Pedernales River. He remained a Texan in his heart and in his life.

Johnson's style posed a striking contrast with Kennedy's. He was a man of impressive stature who spoke directly, convincingly, and even roughly at times. His style was more that of a persuasive and personable politician than of the elegant society man. Finding it difficult to gain acceptance from the Eastern establishment in the nation's capital, he often reveled in his rough image.

Johnson had honed his style in long years of public service. By the time he became president at age 55, he already had 26 years of congressional experience behind him. He had been a congressional staffer, a member of the U.S. House of Representatives, a U.S. senator, Senate majority leader, and vice president.

As he moved up the political ladder, Johnson developed a reputation as a man who got things done. He did favors, twisted arms, bargained, flattered, and threatened. The tactics he used to persuade others became known throughout Washington as the "Johnson treatment." Several writers described this often overpowering and intimidating style:

66The Treatment could last ten minutes or four hours. . . . Its tone could be supplication, accusation, cajolery, exuberance, scorn, tears, complaint, the hint of threat. It was all these together. . . . Interjections from the target were rare. Johnson anticipated them

Picturing History

Home on the Range Born and raised in Texas, President Johnson loved to get back to his ranch in the Texas hill country. How does this image contrast with those of his predecessors?

before they could be spoken. He moved in close, his face a scant millimeter from his target, his eyes widening and narrowing, his eyebrows rising and falling. From his pocket poured clippings, memos, statistics. Mimicry, humor, and the genius of analogy made The Treatment an almost hypnotic experience and rendered the target stunned and helpless. **"**

—from *Lyndon Johnson: The Exercise of Power*

With every technique he could think of, Johnson sought to find consensus, or general agreement. His ability to build coalitions had made him one of the most effective and powerful leaders in the Senate's history.

A War on Poverty As president, Johnson used his considerable talents to push through a number of Kennedy's initiatives. Before the end of 1964, he won passage of a tax cut, a major civil rights bill, and a significant anti-poverty program.

Why was this powerful man so concerned about poor people? Johnson liked to exaggerate the poor conditions of his childhood for dramatic effect, but he had in fact known hard times. He had also seen extreme poverty firsthand in a brief career as a teacher in a low-income area. Johnson understood suffering, and he believed deeply in social action. He felt that a wealthy, powerful government could and should try to improve the lives of its citizens. Kennedy himself had said of Johnson, "He really cares about this nation." Finally, there was Johnson's ambition. He wanted to achieve great things so that history would record him as a great president. Attacking poverty was a good place to begin.

Plans for an anti-poverty program were already in place when Johnson took office, and he knew that he would be able to command strong support for any program that could be linked to Kennedy. In his State of the Union address to Congress in 1964, barely seven weeks after taking office, President Johnson told his audience: "Unfortunately, many Americans live on the outskirts of hope, some because of their poverty and some because of their color and all too many because of both." Johnson concluded his speech by announcing that his administration was declaring an "unconditional war on poverty in America."

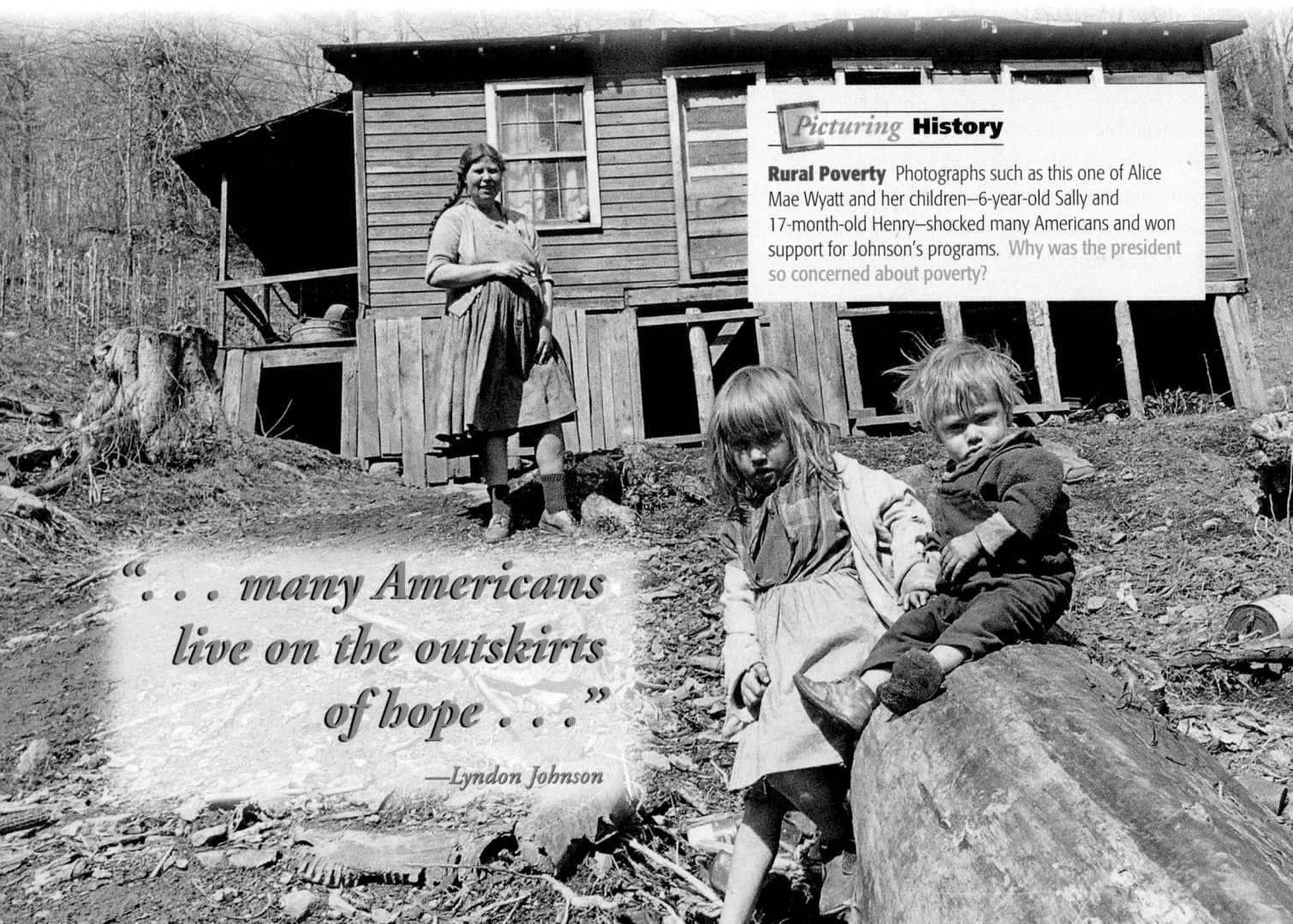

Picturing **History**

Rural Poverty Photographs such as this one of Alice Mae Wyatt and her children—6-year-old Sally and 17-month-old Henry—shocked many Americans and won support for Johnson's programs. **Why was the president so concerned about poverty?**

" . . . many Americans live on the outskirts of hope . . . "

—*Lyndon Johnson*

By the summer of 1964, Johnson had convinced Congress to pass the Economic Opportunity Act. The act established a wide range of programs aimed at creating jobs and fighting poverty. It also created a new government agency, the Office of Economic Opportunity (OEO) to coordinate the new programs. Many of the new programs were directed at young Americans living in the inner city. The Neighborhood Youth Corps provided work-study programs to help underprivileged young men and women earn a high school diploma or college degree. The Job Corps tried to help young unemployed people find jobs. One of the more dramatic programs introduced was **VISTA** (Volunteers in Service to America), which was essentially a domestic Peace Corps. VISTA put young people with skills and community-minded ideals to work in poor neighborhoods and rural areas to help people overcome poverty.

The Election of 1964 As early as April 1964, *Fortune* magazine declared, "Lyndon Johnson has achieved a breadth of public approval few observers would have believed possible when he took office." Johnson had little time to enjoy such praise, for he was soon to run for the office he had first gained through a tragic event.

Johnson's Republican opponent in the 1964 presidential election was **Barry Goldwater** of Arizona, a senator known for his outspoken conservatism. He set the tone for his campaign when he accepted his party's nomination, declaring, "Extremism in the defense of liberty is no vice! And let me remind you also that moderation in the pursuit of justice is no virtue!"

Few Americans were ready to embrace Goldwater's message, which was too aggressive for a nation nervous about nuclear war. On Election Day, Johnson won in a landslide, winning all but five southern states and Arizona. "For the first time in my life," he said later, "I truly felt loved by the American people."

Reading Check **Examining** What inspired the war on poverty?

The Great Society

After his election, Johnson began working with Congress to create the "Great Society" he had promised during his campaign. In this same period, major goals of the civil rights movement were achieved with the passage of the Civil Rights Act of 1964, which barred discrimination of many kinds, and the Voting Rights Act of 1965, which ensured African Americans' right to vote.

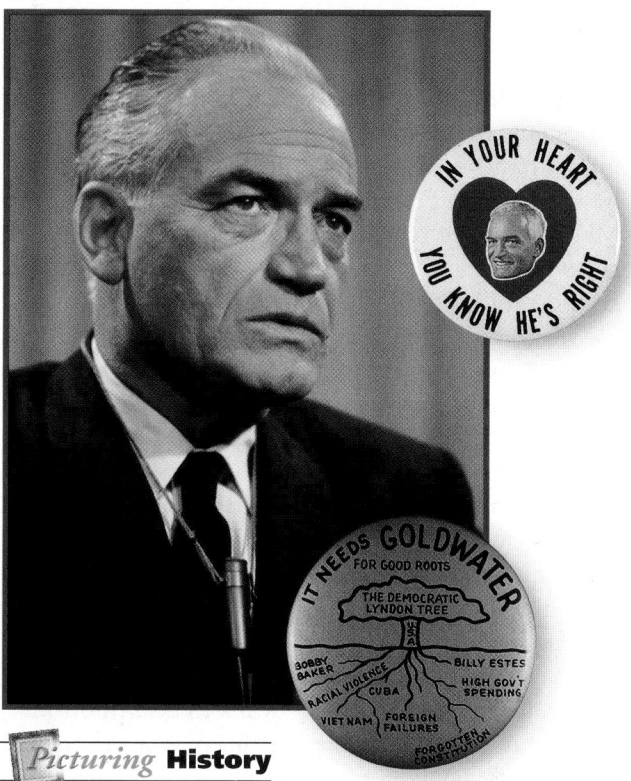

Picturing **History**

Conservative Stance The extreme language of Senator Barry Goldwater's campaign posed little challenge to President Johnson. How many states did Goldwater win?

The **Great Society** was Johnson's vision of the more perfect and equitable society the United States could and should become. According to Bill Moyers, who served as Johnson's press secretary, Johnson admired Franklin Roosevelt and wanted to fulfill FDR's mission. To do that would require a program that would be on the same large scale as the New Deal.

Johnson's goals were consistent with the times for several reasons. The civil rights movement had brought the grievances of African Americans to the forefront, reminding many that greater equality of opportunity had yet to be realized. Economics also supported Johnson's goal. The economy was strong, and many believed it would remain so indefinitely. There was no reason, therefore, that poverty could not be significantly reduced—especially when some had so much and others had so little.

Johnson first elaborated on the goals of the Great Society during a speech at the University of Michigan. It was clear that the president did not intend only to expand relief to the poor or to confine government efforts to material things. The president wanted, he said, to build a better society for all, a society "where leisure is a welcome chance to build and reflect, . . . where the city of man serves not only the needs of the body and the demands of commerce but the desire for beauty and the hunger for community. . . ."

This ambitious vision encompassed a multitude of programs. In the three years between 1965 and 1968, more than 60 programs were passed. Among the most significant programs were **Medicare** and **Medicaid.** Health care reform had been a major issue since the days of Harry Truman. By the 1960s, public support for better health care benefits had solidified. Medicare had especially strong support since it was directed at the entire elderly population—in 1965, around half of those over the age of 65 had no health insurance.

Johnson convinced Congress to set up Medicare as a health insurance program funded through the Social Security system. Medicare's twin program, Medicaid, financed health care for welfare recipients, those who were living below the poverty line. Like the New Deal's Social Security program, both programs created what have been called "entitlements," that is, they entitle certain categories of Americans to benefits. Today, the cost of these programs has become a permanent part of the U.S. budget.

Great Society programs also strongly supported education. For Johnson, who had taught school when he was a young man, education was a personal passion. Vice President Hubert Humphrey once said that Johnson "was a nut on education. . . . [He] believed in it, just like some people believe in miracle cures."

The Elementary and Secondary Education Act of 1965 granted millions of dollars to public and private schools for textbooks, library materials, and special education programs. Efforts to improve education also extended to preschoolers, where Project **Head Start,** administered by the Office of Economic Opportunity, was directed at disadvantaged children who had "never looked at a picture book or scribbled with a crayon." Another program, Upward Bound, was designed to provide college preparation for low-income teenagers.

Improvements in health and education were only the beginning of the Great Society programs. Because of the deterioration of inner cities, Johnson told Congress that "America's cities are in crisis." Conditions in the cities—poor schools, crime, slum housing, poverty, and pollution—blighted the lives of those who lived there. Johnson urged Congress to act on several pieces of legislation addressing this issue.

Major Great Society Programs

Health and Welfare	Education	The "War on Poverty"	Consumer and Environmental Protection
Medicare (1965) established a comprehensive health insurance program for all elderly people; financed through the Social Security system.	**The Elementary and Secondary Education Act** (1965) targeted aid to students and funded related activities such as adult education and education counseling.	**The Office of Economic Opportunity** (1964) oversaw many programs to improve life in inner cities, including Job Corps, an education and job training program for at-risk youth.	**The Water Quality Act and Clean Air Acts** (1965) supported development of standards and goals for water and air quality.
Medicaid (1965) funded by federal and state governments, provided health and medical assistance to low-income families.	**Higher Education Act** (1965) supported college tuition scholarships, student loans, and work-study programs for low- and middle-income students.	**Housing and Urban Development Act** (1965) established new housing subsidy programs and made federal loans and public housing grants easier to obtain.	**The Highway Safety Act** (1966) supported highway safety by improving federal, state, and local coordination and by creating training standards for emergency medical technicians.
Child Nutrition Act (1966) established a school breakfast program and expanded the school lunch program and milk program to improve poor children's nutrition.	**Project Head Start** (1965) funded a preschool program for the disadvantaged.	**Demonstration Cities and Metropolitan Development Act** (1966) helped revitalize urban areas through a variety of social and economic programs.	**The Fair Packaging and Labeling Act** (1966) required all consumer products to have true and informative labels.

Chart Skills

1. **Interpreting Charts** What was the purpose of the Office of Economic Opportunity?
2. **Evaluating** Which Great Society program do you think had the most impact on American society? Why?

YOUTH'S HELPING HAND

In 1965 VISTA (Volunteers in Service to America) was created as part of President Johnson's war on poverty. Roused by the social consciousness of the early 1960s, thousands of students and young people focused their energy into working with local agencies in low-income communities around the nation. One of VISTA's basic themes was to help local communities mobilize their own resources. Since 1993 VISTA has been a part of the AmeriCorps network of service programs.

One created a new cabinet agency, the Department of Housing and Urban Development, in 1965. Its first secretary, **Robert Weaver,** was the first African American to serve in a cabinet. A broad-based program informally called "Model Cities" authorized federal subsidies to many cities nationwide. The funds, matched by local and state contributions, supported an array of programs, including transportation, health care, housing, and policing. Since many depressed urban areas lacked sufficient or affordable housing, legislation also authorized about $8 billion to build houses for low- and middle-income people.

One notable Great Society measure changed the composition of the American population: the Immigration Reform Act of 1965. For a brief time, this act maintained a strict limit on the number of immigrants admitted to the United States each year: 170,000 from the Eastern Hemisphere and 120,000 from the Western Hemisphere. It did, however, eliminate the national origins system established in the 1920s, which had given preference to northern European immigrants. The new measure opened wider the door of

the United States to newcomers from all parts of Europe, as well as from Asia and Africa.

✔ **Reading Check** **Summarizing** What were the Great Society programs?

Legacy of the Great Society

The Great Society programs touched nearly every aspect of American life and improved thousands if not millions of lives. In the years since President Johnson left office, however, debate has continued over whether or not the Great Society was truly a success.

In many ways, the impact of the Great Society was limited. In his rush to get as much done as he could, Johnson did not calculate exactly how his programs might work. As a result, some of them did not work as well as people had hoped. Furthermore, the programs grew so quickly they were often unmanageable and difficult to evaluate.

Cities, states, and groups eligible for aid began to expect immediate and life-changing benefits. These

Esther Peterson
1906–1997

In the 1930s, Boston employers asked women who sewed aprons for them to switch from square pockets to a more difficult heart-shaped pocket, but they did not offer any increase in pay. Esther Peterson, a local teacher and outspoken advocate for women's rights, led the workers in a strike for more money. The women won their pay raise. For 60 years, Esther Peterson continued to use her tact and will to fight for women's rights, trade unions, and consumers.

Born in Provo, Utah, as Esther Eggertsen, Peterson became a teacher in the 1930s. She taught milliners, telephone operators, and garment workers at the innovative Bryn Mawr Summer School for Women Workers in Industry. In 1961 President Kennedy selected her to serve as Assistant Secretary of Labor and Director of the Women's Bureau.

Peterson then encouraged Kennedy to create a Presidential Commission on the Status of Women to focus attention on working women.

Under President Johnson, Peterson served as Special Assistant for Consumer Affairs, where she worked on consumer concerns. Lynda Johnson Robb, daughter of President Johnson, described Peterson this way: "She had a velvet hammer and talked people into doing what was right, even if we didn't know it at the time." Peterson continued to use her "velvet hammer" for the public good throughout her long life. At the time of her death at the age of 91, she was actively promoting senior citizens' health issues.

expectations often left many feeling frustrated and angry. Other Americans opposed the massive growth of federal programs and criticized the Great Society for intruding too much into their lives.

A lack of funds also hurt the effectiveness of Great Society programs. The programs themselves were expensive enough. When Johnson attempted to fund both his grand domestic agenda and the increasingly costly war in Vietnam, the Great Society eventually suffered. Some Great Society initiatives have survived to the present, however. These include Medicare and Medicaid, two cabinet agencies—the Department of Transportation and the Department of Housing and Urban Development (HUD)—and Project Head Start. Overall, the programs provided some important benefits to poorer communities and gave political and administrative experience to minority groups.

An important legacy of the Great Society was the questions it produced, questions Americans continue to consider. How can the federal government help its disadvantaged citizens? How much government help can a society have without weakening the private sector? How much help can its people receive without losing motivation to fight against hardships on their own?

Lyndon Johnson came into office determined to change the United States in a way few other presidents had attempted. If he fell short, it was perhaps that the goals he set were so high. In evaluating the administration's efforts, the *New York Times* wrote, "The walls of the ghettos are not going to topple overnight, nor is it possible to wipe out the heritage of generations of social, economic, and educational deprivation by the stroke of a Presidential pen."

✔ **Reading Check** **Evaluating** What was the impact of the Great Society?

SECTION 3 ASSESSMENT

Checking for Understanding

1. **Define:** consensus, war on poverty.
2. **Identify:** VISTA, Great Society, Medicare, Medicaid, Head Start, Robert Weaver.
3. **Describe** how the Great Society programs were inspired.

Reviewing Themes

4. **Government and Democracy** How did Johnson's war on poverty strive to ensure greater fairness in American society?

Critical Thinking

5. **Interpreting** What were three legacies of the Great Society?
6. **Organizing** Use a graphic organizer similar to the one below to list five of the Great Society initiatives that have survived to the present.

Great Society Initiatives

Analyzing Visuals

7. **Photographs** Study the photograph on page 856. Why do you think pictures such as this one would help build support for the war on poverty?

Writing About History

8. **Descriptive Writing** Take on the role of a biographer. Write a chapter in a biography of Lyndon Johnson in which you compare and contrast his leadership style to that of John Kennedy.

Critical Thinking SKILLBUILDER

Problem Solving

Why Learn This Skill?

Imagine you have just done poorly on a chemistry exam. You wonder why you cannot do better since you always go to class, take notes, and study for exams. In order to improve your grades, you need to identify the specific problem and then take actions to solve it.

Learning the Skill

There are six key steps you should follow that will help you through the problem-solving process.

- Identify the problem. In the case listed above, you know that you are not doing well on chemistry exams.

- Gather information. You know that you always go to class and take notes. You study by yourself for about two hours each day for two or three days before the exam. You also know that you sometimes forget details or get confused about things as you are taking the exam.

- List and consider possible solutions. For example, instead of studying by yourself, you might try studying with a friend or a group. You might also study for shorter timespans to avoid overloading yourself with information.

- Consider the advantages and disadvantages of each solution.

- Now that you have listed and considered the possible options, you need to choose the best solution to your problem. Choose what you think is the right solution, and carry it out.

- Evaluate the effectiveness of the solution. This will help you determine if you have solved the problem. If you earn better scores on the next few chemistry tests, you will know that you have solved your problem.

Practicing the Skill

Reread the material in Section 1 on page 842 under the heading "Kennedy Struggles with

Congress." Use that information and the steps listed on this page to answer the following questions.

❶ What problem did Kennedy encounter as he tried to pass domestic policy legislation through Congress?

❷ What options were available to the president in facing this opposition? What were the advantages and disadvantages?

❸ Explain the solution Kennedy implemented to solve his problem.

❹ Evaluate the effectiveness of Kennedy's solution. Was it successful? How do you determine this?

Skills Assessment

Complete the Practicing Skills questions on page 863 and the Chapter 28 Skill Reinforcement Activity to assess your mastery of this skill.

Applying the Skill

Problem Solving The conservation club at your school has no money to continue its recycling project. The school district allocated money to the club at the beginning of the year, but that money has been spent. As a member of the club, you have been asked to join a committee to save the conservation club and its projects. Write an essay describing the problem, the list of options and their advantages and disadvantages, a solution, and an evaluation of the chosen solution.

Glencoe's **Skillbuilder Interactive Workbook CD-ROM, Level 2,** provides instruction and practice in key social studies skills.

Reviewing Key Terms

On a sheet of paper, use each of these terms in a sentence.

1. missile gap
2. reapportionment
3. due process
4. flexible response
5. space race
6. consensus
7. war on poverty

Reviewing Key Facts

8. **Identify:** New Frontier, Earl Warren, Peace Corps, Warren Commission, Great Society, Head Start.

9. How was the 1960 presidential election a new kind of campaign?

10. What main issues did Nixon and Kennedy discuss in their televised debate?

11. How close was the outcome of the 1960 presidential election between Nixon and Kennedy?

12. What was Kennedy's response to the steel industry's decision to raise prices sharply?

13. What were three measures Kennedy took to strengthen the economy?

14. What were three programs set up by Kennedy to reduce the threat of nuclear war and to try to stem communism?

15. What inspired President Johnson's war on poverty?

16. What was the purpose of Medicare, passed during Johnson's administration?

17. Which Great Society initiatives are still in effect today?

Critical Thinking

18. **Analyzing Themes: Government and Democracy** Why were Medicare and Medicaid landmark pieces of legislation in American history?

19. **Evaluating** In the 1960 presidential debate, most radio listeners thought Nixon had won, while most television viewers thought Kennedy had. Why do you think this was so?

20. **Drawing Conclusions** How did Kennedy help prevent Communist movements from flourishing in Latin America?

21. **Analyzing** President Kennedy was unable to pass civil rights legislation. What were some of the factors that allowed President Johnson to push civil rights forward after Kennedy's assassination?

22. **Organizing** Use a graphic organizer similar to the one below to list the crises of the Cold War during the Kennedy administration.

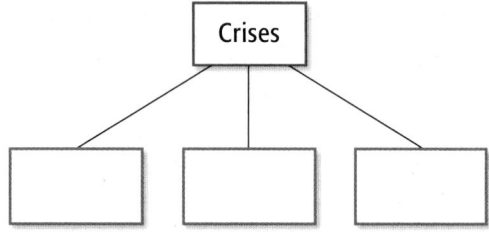

23. **Evaluating** How did the Warren Court decisions in *Baker* v. *Carr* and *Reynolds* v. *Sims* affect voting power in the nation?

24. **Interpreting Primary Sources** Although the standard of living for most Americans rose dramatically throughout the

Chapter Summary

The New Frontier and the Great Society

Domestic Programs

- Office of Economic Opportunity fights illiteracy, unemployment, and disease.
- Civil Rights Act of 1964 prohibits race discrimination and social segregation.
- Voting Rights Act protects the right to vote.
- Medicare and Medicaid Acts provide federal medical aid to the elderly and poor.
- Elementary and Secondary Education Act increases aid for public schools.

Foreign Policy

- "Flexible response" policy maintains opposition to communism.
- U.S. pledges aid to struggling Latin American nations.
- Peace Corps offers humanitarian aid in poor countries.
- Nuclear Test Ban Treaty with the Soviet Union eases Cold War tensions.

Supreme Court Cases

- *Reynolds* v. *Sims* boosts voting power of urban dwellers, including many minorities.
- Extension of due process gives more protection to people accused of crimes.
- Court rules that states could not require prayer and Bible readings in public schools.

Self-Check Quiz

Visit the *American Vision* Web site at tav.glencoe.com and click on *Self-Check Quizzes—Chapter 28* to assess your knowledge of chapter content.

1960s, some Americans remained mired in poverty. Reread the excerpt on page 854 in which John Rath discusses his personal experiences with coping with poverty in his sparsely furnished room in Chicago. Then answer the following questions.

a. What does Rath think might help him to have some purpose in his life?

b. What does Rath mean when he says: "You sit down in a place like this, you grit your teeth. . . ."?

Practicing Skills

25. **Problem Solving** Reread the passage on pages 849–850 titled "The Cuban Missile Crisis." Use that information to answer the following questions.

a. What problem did Kennedy encounter in Cuba?

b. What options were available to the president in this situation? What were the advantages and disadvantages of each option?

c. Explain the solution Kennedy used to resolve the Cuban missile crisis.

d. Was Kennedy's solution successful? Why or why not?

Chapter Activity

26. **Technology Activity: Using the Internet** Search the Internet to check the status of Great Society programs today. Find out how these programs have changed since they were initiated. Make a chart showing the provisions of the programs in the 1960s compared to the provisions of the programs today.

Writing Activity

27. **Expository Writing** Assume the role of a historian. Evaluate the effectiveness of Kennedy's New Frontier and Johnson's Great Society programs. Write an article for a historical journal explaining the successes and setbacks of each president's policy agendas.

Geography and History

28. The map on this page shows the results of the presidential election of 1960. Study the map and answer the questions below.

a. **Interpreting Maps** Which regions of the country supported Kennedy? Which regions supported Nixon?

b. **Applying Geography Skills** What would have happened if Kennedy had lost New York to Nixon?

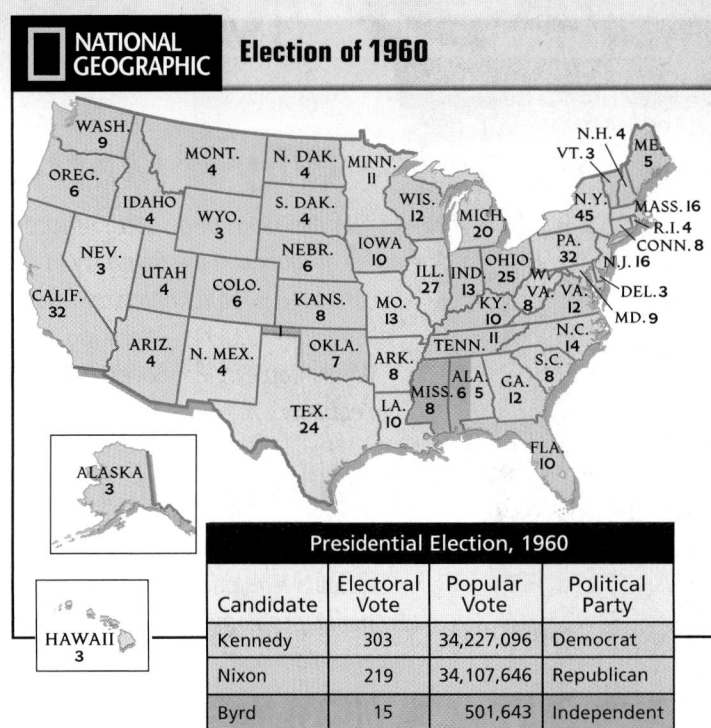

NATIONAL GEOGRAPHIC Election of 1960

Presidential Election, 1960			
Candidate	Electoral Vote	Popular Vote	Political Party
Kennedy	303	34,227,096	Democrat
Nixon	219	34,107,646	Republican
Byrd	15	501,643	Independent

Standardized Test Practice

Directions: Choose the best answer to the following question.

All of the following were effects of rulings by the Warren Court EXCEPT:

A Involved federal courts in the reapportionment of state election districts

B Extended rights for people accused of crimes

C Protected religious minorities through greater separation of church and state

D Increased state authority at the expense of federal authority

Test-Taking Tip: This question calls for an answer that does NOT accurately complete the statement. The Warren Court expanded individual civil liberties and the power of the judicial branch. Eliminate answers that had either of those effects.

The Civil Rights Movement *1954–1968*

Why It Matters

In the 1950s and 1960s, African Americans made major strides. They began by challenging segregation in the South. With the Montgomery bus boycott, Martin Luther King, Jr., achieved national and worldwide recognition. His peaceful resistance inspired many, especially students. After King's assassination, the civil rights movement shifted focus. Many people in the movement began to see economic opportunity as the key to equality.

The Impact Today

Changes brought about by the civil rights movement are still with us.
* *Civil rights legislation provides protection against discrimination for all citizens.*
* *Economic programs for inner-city residents by government and social service agencies continue.*

The American Vision *Video* *The Chapter 29 video, "The Civil Rights Movement," chronicles the milestones of the movement to win rights for African Americans.*

1957
* Eisenhower sends troops to a Little Rock, Arkansas, high school to ensure integration

1955
* Rosa Parks refuses to give up bus seat; Montgomery bus boycott begins in Alabama

1960
* Sit-in protests begin

1954
* *Brown* v. *Board of Education* ruling issued by Supreme Court

LITTLE ROCK CENTRAL

United States
PRESIDENTS

Eisenhower
1953–1961

Kennedy
1961–1963

1953

1957

1961

World

1955
* West Germany admitted to NATO

1958
* Pasternak's *Dr. Zhivago* awarded Nobel Prize for Literature

1960
* France successfully tests nuclear weapons

1959
* Mary Leakey discovers 1.7 million-year-old hominid skull fragment in Tanzania

Americans march from Selma, Alabama, to Montgomery in support of the civil rights movement.

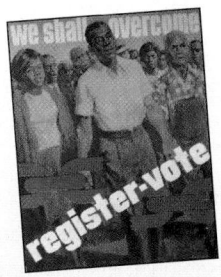

1963
- Over 200,000 civil rights supporters march on Washington, D.C.

1965
- Malcolm X assassinated
- Race riots erupt in Los Angeles neighborhood of Watts

1968
- Civil Rights Act of 1968 passed
- Martin Luther King, Jr., assassinated

Johnson
1963–1969

1965

1969

1963
- Organization of African Unity formed
- Kenya becomes an independent nation

1965
- China's Cultural Revolution begins

1967
- Arab-Israeli War brings many Palestinians under Israeli rule

HISTORY
Online
Chapter Overview
Visit the *American Vision* Web site at tav.glencoe.com and click on **Chapter Overviews—Chapter 29** to preview chapter information.

Guide to Reading

Main Idea
After World War II, African Americans and other supporters of civil rights challenged segregation in the United States.

Key Terms and Names
separate-but-equal, de facto segregation, NAACP, sit-in, Thurgood Marshall, Linda Brown, Dr. Martin Luther King, Jr., Southern Christian Leadership Conference

Reading Strategy
Organizing As you read about the birth of the civil rights movement, complete a graphic organizer similar to the one below by filling in the causes of the civil rights movement.

Reading Objectives
- **Explain** the origin of the Southern Christian Leadership Conference.
- **Discuss** the changing role of the federal government in civil rights enforcement.

Section Theme
Government and Democracy In the 1950s, African Americans began a movement to win greater social equality.

Preview of Events

| 1954 | 1955 | 1956 | 1957 |

1954
Brown v. *Board of Education of Topeka, Kansas,* decision

1955
Rosa Parks refuses to give up bus seat in Montgomery, Alabama

1956
Group of 101 Southern members of Congress sign Southern Manifesto

1957
Southern Christian Leadership Conference formed

★ An American Story ★

On December 1, 1955, Rosa Parks left her job as a seamstress in Montgomery, Alabama, and boarded a bus to go home. In 1955 buses in Montgomery reserved seats in the front for whites and seats in the rear for African Americans. Seats in the middle were open to African Americans, but only if there were few whites on the bus.

Rosa Parks took a seat just behind the white section. Soon all of the seats on the bus were filled. When the bus driver noticed a white man standing at the front of the bus, he told Parks and three other African Americans in her row to get up and let the white man sit down. Nobody moved. The driver cautioned, "You better make it light on yourselves and let me have those seats." The other three African Americans rose, but Rosa Parks did not. The driver then called the Montgomery police, who took Parks into custody.

News of the arrest soon reached E.D. Nixon, a former president of the local chapter of the National Association for the Advancement of Colored People (NAACP). Nixon wanted to challenge bus segregation in court, and he told Parks, "With your permission we can break down segregation on the bus with your case." Parks told Nixon, "If you think it will mean something to Montgomery and do some good, I'll be happy to go along with it."

—adapted from *Parting the Waters: America in the King Years*

The Origins of the Movement

When Rosa Parks agreed to challenge segregation in court, she did not know that her decision would launch the modern civil rights movement. Within days of her arrest, African Americans in Montgomery had organized a boycott of the bus system. Mass protests began across the nation. After decades of segregation and inequality, many African Americans had decided the time had come to demand equal rights.

The struggle would not be easy. The Supreme Court had declared segregation to be constitutional in *Plessy* v. *Ferguson* in 1896. The ruling had established the "separate-but-equal" doctrine. Laws segregating African Americans were permitted as long as equal facilities were provided for them.

After the *Plessy* decision, laws segregating African Americans and whites spread quickly. These laws, nicknamed "Jim Crow" laws, segregated buses and trains, schools, restaurants, swimming pools, parks, and other public facilities. Jim Crow laws were common throughout the South, but segregation existed in other states as well. Often it was left up to each local community to decide whether to pass segregation laws. Areas without laws requiring segregation often had de facto segregation—segregation by custom and tradition. 📖 *(See page 1082 for more information on* Plessy v. Ferguson.*)*

Court Challenges Begin

The civil rights movement had been building for a long time. Since 1909, the **National Association for the Advancement of Colored People** (NAACP) had supported court cases intended to overturn segregation. Over the years, the NAACP achieved some victories. In 1935, for example, the Supreme Court ruled in *Norris* v. *Alabama* that Alabama's exclusion of African Americans from juries violated their right to equal protection under the law. In 1946 the Court ruled in *Morgan* v. *Virginia* that segregation on interstate buses was unconstitutional. In 1950 it ruled in *Sweatt* v. *Painter* that state law schools had to admit qualified African American applicants, even if parallel black law schools existed. 📖 *(See pages 1082–1083 for more information on these cases.)*

HISTORY Online

Student Web Activity Visit the *American Vision* Web site at tav.glencoe.com and click on *Student Web Activities—Chapter 29* for an activity on the civil rights movement.

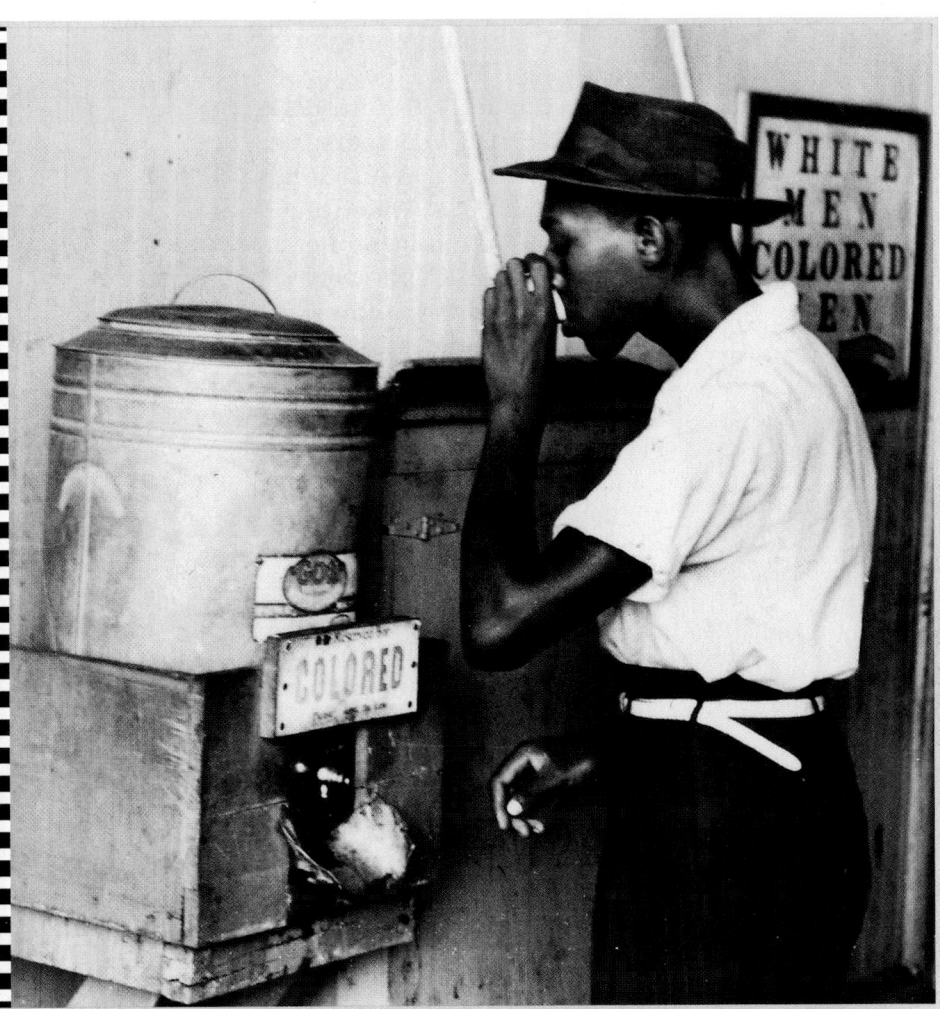

NATIONAL GEOGRAPHIC

MOMENT in HISTORY

AMERICAN SEGREGATION

In an Oklahoma City streetcar station in 1939, a man takes a drink from a water cooler labeled "COLORED." Racially segregated facilities—waiting rooms, railroad cars, lavatories, and drinking fountains—were prevalent all across the South. Under the so-called Jim Crow system, African Americans were legally entitled to "separate-but-equal" education, housing, and social services. In practice, however, only a small percentage of public funds earmarked for schools, streets, police, and other expenses found its way to African American neighborhoods.

New Political Power In addition to a string of court victories, African Americans enjoyed increased political power. Before World War I, most African Americans lived in the South, where they were largely excluded from voting. During the Great Migration, many moved to Northern cities, where they were allowed to vote. Increasingly, Northern politicians sought their votes and listened to their concerns.

During the 1930s, many African Americans benefited from FDR's New Deal programs. Thus they began supporting the Democratic Party, giving it new strength in the North. This wing of the party was now able to counter Southern Democrats, who often supported segregation.

The Push for Desegregation During World War II, African American leaders began to use their new political power to demand more rights. Their efforts helped end discrimination in factories that held government contracts and increased opportunities for African Americans in the military.

In Chicago in 1942, James Farmer and George Houser founded the **Congress of Racial Equality** (CORE). CORE began using sit-ins, a form of protest first used by union workers in the 1930s. In 1943 CORE attempted to desegregate restaurants that refused to serve African Americans. Using the sit-in strategy, members of CORE went to segregated restaurants. If they were denied service, they sat down and refused to leave. The sit-ins were intended to shame restaurant managers into integrating their restaurants. Using these protests, CORE successfully integrated many restaurants, theaters, and other public facilities in Chicago, Detroit, Denver, and Syracuse.

✓ **Reading Check**

Examining How had the ruling in *Plessy* v. *Ferguson* contributed to segregation?

Separate but Unequal Linda Brown's court case ended decades of official segregation in the South.

The Civil Rights Movement Begins

When World War II ended, many African American soldiers returned home optimistic that their country would appreciate their loyalty and sacrifice. In the 1950s, when change did not come as quickly as hoped, their determination to change prejudices in the United States led to protests and marches—and to the emergence of the civil rights movement.

Brown v. Board of Education After World War II, the NAACP continued to challenge segregation in the courts. From 1939 to 1961, the NAACP's chief counsel and director of its Legal Defense and Education Fund was the brilliant African American attorney **Thurgood Marshall.** After World War II, Marshall focused his efforts on ending segregation in public schools.

In 1954 the Supreme Court decided to combine several different cases and issue a general ruling on segregation in schools. One of the cases involved a young African American girl named **Linda Brown,** who was denied admission to her neighborhood school in Topeka, Kansas, because of her race. She was told to attend an all-black school across town. With the help of the NAACP, her parents then sued the Topeka school board.

On May 17, 1954, the Supreme Court ruled unanimously in the case of *Brown* v. *Board of Education of Topeka, Kansas,* that segregation in public schools was unconstitutional and violated the equal protection clause of the Fourteenth Amendment. Chief Justice Earl Warren summed up the Court's decision when he wrote: "In the field of public education, the doctrine of separate but equal has no place. Separate educational facilities are inherently unequal." 📖 *(See pages 1077 and 1080 for information on* Brown v. Board of Education.*)*

The Southern Manifesto The Brown decision marked a dramatic reversal of the ideas expressed in the *Plessy* v. *Ferguson* case. *Brown* v. *Board of Education* applied only to public schools, but the ruling threatened the entire system of segregation. Although it convinced many African Americans that the time had come to challenge other forms of segregation, it also angered many white Southerners, who became even more determined to defend segregation, regardless of what the Supreme Court ruled.

Although some school districts in border states integrated their schools in compliance with the Court's ruling, anger and opposition was a far more common reaction. In Washington, D.C., Senator Harry F. Byrd of Virginia called on Southerners to

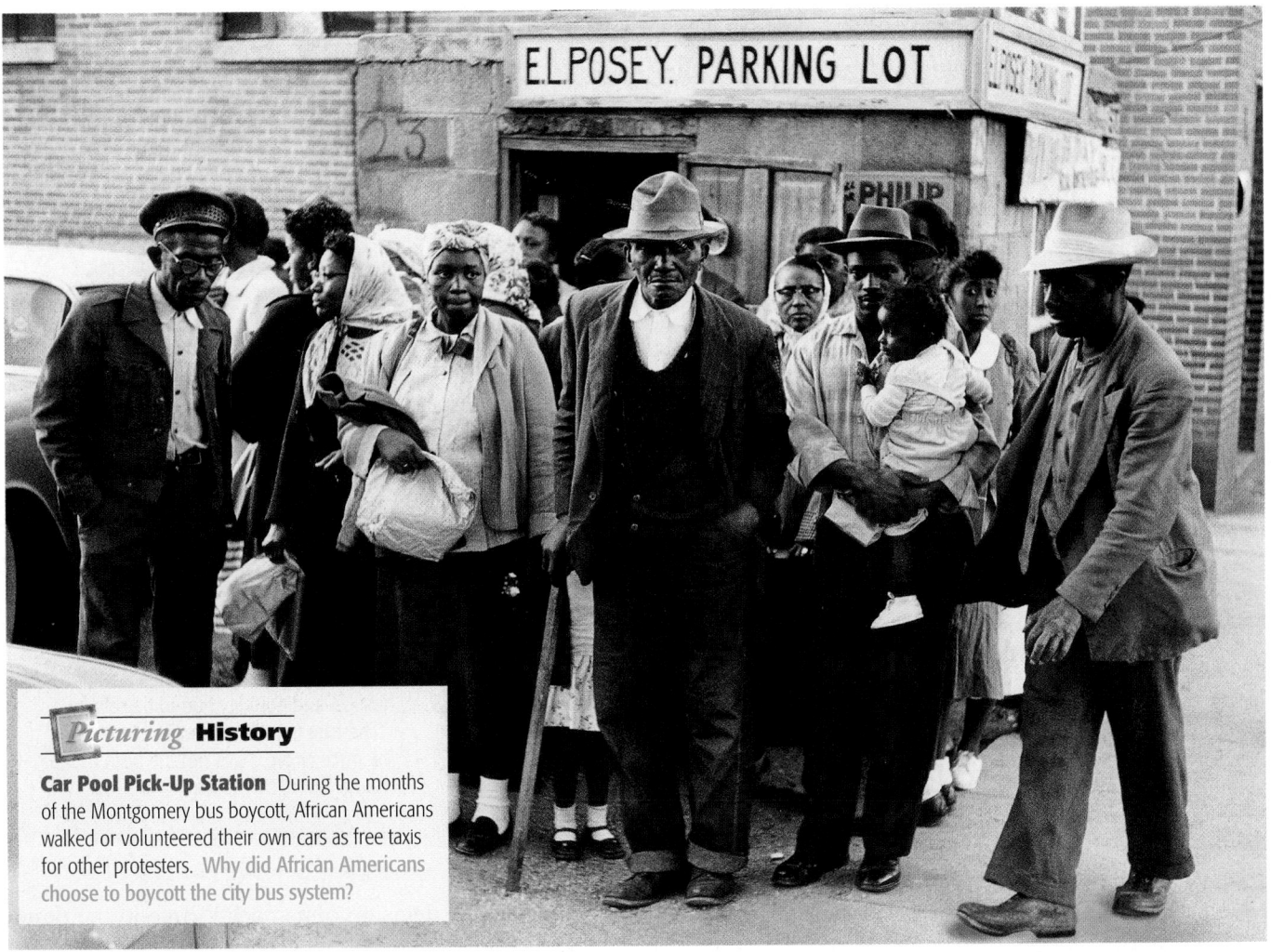

Car Pool Pick-Up Station During the months of the Montgomery bus boycott, African Americans walked or volunteered their own cars as free taxis for other protesters. Why did African Americans choose to boycott the city bus system?

adopt "massive resistance" against the ruling. Across the South, hundreds of thousands of white Americans joined citizens' councils to pressure their local governments and school boards into defying the Supreme Court. Many states adopted pupil assignment laws. These laws created an elaborate set of requirements other than race that schools could use to prevent African Americans from attending white schools.

The Supreme Court inadvertently encouraged white resistance when it followed up its decision in *Brown* v. *Board* a year later. The Court ordered school districts to proceed "with all deliberate speed" to end school segregation. The wording was vague enough that many districts were able to keep their schools segregated for many more years.

Massive resistance also appeared in the halls of Congress. In 1956 a group of 101 Southern members of Congress signed the **Southern Manifesto,** which denounced the Supreme Court's ruling as "a clear abuse of judicial power" and pledged to use "all lawful means" to reverse the decision. Although the Southern

Manifesto had no legal standing, the statement encouraged white Southerners to defy the Supreme Court.

The Montgomery Bus Boycott In the midst of the uproar over the *Brown* v. *Board of Education* case, Rosa Parks made her decision to challenge segregation of public transportation. Outraged by Parks's arrest, Jo Ann Robinson, head of a local organization called the Women's Political Council, called on African Americans to boycott Montgomery's buses on the day Rosa Parks appeared in court.

The boycott was a dramatic success. That afternoon, several African American leaders formed the Montgomery Improvement Association to run the boycott and to negotiate with city leaders for an end to segregation. They elected a 26-year-old pastor named **Martin Luther King, Jr.,** to lead them.

On the evening of December 5, 1955, a meeting was held at Dexter Avenue Baptist Church, where Dr. King was pastor. In the deep, resonant tones and powerful phrases that characterized his speaking style, King encouraged the people to continue their protest. "There comes a time, my friends," he said, "when people get tired of being thrown into the abyss of humiliation, where they experience the bleakness of nagging despair." He explained, however, that the protest had to be peaceful:

❝Now let us say that we are not advocating violence. . . . The only weapon we have in our hands this evening is the weapon of protest. If we were incarcerated behind the iron curtains of a communistic nation—we couldn't do this. If we were trapped in the dungeon of a totalitarian regime—we couldn't do this. But the great glory of American democracy is the right to protest for right!❞

—quoted in *Parting the Waters: America in the King Years*

King had earned a Ph.D. in theology from Boston University. He believed that the only moral way to end segregation and racism was through nonviolent passive resistance. He told his followers, "We must use the weapon of love. We must realize that so many people are taught to hate us that they are not totally responsible for their hate." African Americans, he urged, must say to racists and segregationists: "We will soon wear you down by our capacity to suffer, and in winning our freedom we will so appeal to your heart and conscience that we will win you in the process."

King drew upon the philosophy and techniques of Indian leader Mohandas Gandhi, who had used nonviolent resistance effectively against British rule in India. Like Gandhi, King encouraged his followers to disobey unjust laws. Believing in people's ability to transform themselves, King was certain that public opinion would eventually force the government to end segregation.

Stirred by King's powerful words, African Americans in Montgomery continued their boycott for over a year. Instead of riding the bus, they organized car pools or walked to work. They refused to be intimidated, yet they avoided violence. Meanwhile Rosa Parks's legal challenge to bus segregation worked its way through the courts. Finally, in December 1956, the Supreme Court

Profiles IN HISTORY

Thurgood Marshall
1908–1993

Over his long lifetime, Thurgood Marshall made many contributions to the civil rights movement. Perhaps his most famous accomplishment was representing the NAACP in the *Brown* v. *Board of Education* case.

Marshall's speaking style was both simple and direct. During the *Brown* case, Justice Frankfurter asked Marshall for a definition of equal. "Equal means getting the same thing, at the same time and in the same place," Marshall answered.

Born into a middle-class Baltimore family in 1908, Marshall earned a law degree from Howard University Law School. The school's dean, Charles Hamilton Houston, enlisted Marshall to work for the NAACP. Together the two laid out the legal strategy for challenging discrimination in many arenas of American life.

Marshall became the first African American on the Supreme Court when President Lyndon Johnson appointed him in 1967. On the Court, he remained a voice for civil rights. In his view, the Constitution was not perfect because it had accepted slavery. Its ideas of liberty, justice, and equality had to be refined. "The true miracle of the Constitution," he once wrote, "was not the birth of the Constitution, but its life."

affirmed the decision of a special three-judge panel declaring Alabama's laws requiring segregation on buses to be unconstitutional.

✓ **Reading Check** **Describing** What was the ruling in *Brown* v. *Board of Education*?

African American Churches

Martin Luther King, Jr., was not the only prominent minister in the bus boycott. Many of the other leaders were African American ministers. The boycott could not have succeeded without the support of the African American churches in the city. As the civil rights movement gained momentum, African American churches continued to play a critical role. They served as forums for many of the protests and planning meetings, and they also mobilized many of the volunteers for specific civil rights campaigns.

After the Montgomery bus boycott demonstrated that nonviolent protest could be successful, African American ministers led by King established the **Southern Christian Leadership Conference** (SCLC) in 1957. The SCLC set out to eliminate segregation from American society and to encourage

African Americans to register to vote. Dr. King served as the SCLC's first president. Under his leadership, the organization challenged segregation at the voting booths and in public transportation, housing, and public accommodations.

Reading Check **Summarizing** What role did African American churches play in the civil rights movement?

Eisenhower and Civil Rights

President Eisenhower sympathized with the goals of the civil rights movement, and he personally disagreed with segregation. Following the precedent set by President Truman, he ordered navy shipyards and veterans' hospitals to be desegregated.

At the same time, however, Eisenhower disagreed with those who wanted to roll back segregation through protests and court rulings. He believed that people had to allow segregation and racism to end gradually as values changed. With the nation in the midst of the Cold War, he worried that challenging white Southerners on segregation might divide the nation and lead to violence at a time when the country

had to pull together. Publicly, he refused to endorse the *Brown* v. *Board of Education* decision. Privately, he remarked, "I don't believe you can change the hearts of men with laws or decisions."

Despite his belief that the *Brown* v. *Board of Education* decision was wrong, Eisenhower felt he had to uphold the authority of the federal government, including its court system. As a result, he became the first president since Reconstruction to send federal troops into the South to protect the constitutional rights of African Americans.

Crisis in Little Rock In September 1957, the school board in Little Rock, Arkansas, won a court order to admit nine African American students to Central High, a school with 2,000 white students. Little Rock was a racially moderate Southern city, as was most of the state of Arkansas. A number of Arkansas communities, as well as the state university, had already begun to desegregate their schools.

The governor of Arkansas, Orval Faubus, was believed to be a moderate on racial issues, unlike many other Southern politicians. Faubus was determined to win re-election, however, and so he began to campaign

Picturing **History**

Crisis in Little Rock Fifteen-year-old Elizabeth Eckford (in sunglasses at right) braves an angry crowd of Central High School students in Arkansas. How did Governor Orval Faubus react to attempts to integrate the high school?

as a defender of white supremacy. He ordered troops from the Arkansas National Guard to prevent the nine African American students from entering the school. The next day, as the National Guard troops surrounded the school, an angry white mob joined the troops to protest the integration plan and to intimidate the African American students trying to register.

Television coverage of this episode placed Little Rock at the center of national attention. Faubus had used the armed forces of a state to oppose the authority of the federal government—the first such challenge to the Constitution since the Civil War. Eisenhower knew that he could not allow Faubus to defy the federal government. After a conference between Eisenhower and Faubus proved fruitless, the district court ordered the governor to remove the troops. Instead of ending the crisis, however, Faubus simply left the school to the mob. After the African American students entered the school, angry whites beat at least two African American reporters and broke many of the school's windows. The police had to take the terrified African American students away to safety.

The mob violence finally pushed President Eisenhower's patience to the breaking point. Federal authority had to be upheld. He immediately ordered the U.S. Army to send troops to Little Rock. In addition, he federalized the Arkansas National Guard. By nightfall 1,000 soldiers of the elite 101st Airborne Division had arrived. By 5:00 A.M. the troops had encircled the school, bayonets ready. A few hours later, the nine African American students arrived in an army station wagon, and they walked into the high school. The law had been upheld, but the troops were forced to remain in Little Rock for the rest of the school year.

New Civil Rights Legislation The same year that the Little Rock crisis began, Congress passed the first civil rights law since Reconstruction. The **Civil Rights Act of 1957** was intended to protect the right of African Americans to vote. Eisenhower believed firmly in the right to vote, and he viewed it as his responsibility to protect voting rights. He also knew that if he sent a civil rights bill to Congress, conservative Southern Democrats would try to block the legislation. In 1956 he did send the bill to Congress, hoping not only to split the Democratic Party but also to convince more African Americans to vote Republican.

Several Southern senators did try to stop the Civil Rights Act of 1957, but the Senate majority leader, Democrat Lyndon Johnson, put together a compromise that enabled the act to pass. Although its final form was much weaker than originally intended, the act still brought the power of the federal government into the civil rights debate. The act created a civil rights division within the Department of Justice and gave it the authority to seek court injunctions against anyone interfering with the right to vote. It also created the United States Commission on Civil Rights to investigate allegations of denial of voting rights. After the bill passed, the SCLC announced a campaign to register 2 million new African American voters.

✔ **Reading Check** **Explaining** Why did President Eisenhower intervene in the civil rights controversy?

SECTION 1 ASSESSMENT

Checking for Understanding

1. **Define:** separate-but-equal, de facto segregation, sit-in.
2. **Identify:** NAACP, Thurgood Marshall, Linda Brown, Martin Luther King, Jr., Southern Christian Leadership Conference.
3. **State** the outcome of the *Brown* v. *Board of Education* case.

Reviewing Themes

4. **Government and Democracy** Why did the role of the federal government in civil rights enforcement change?

Critical Thinking

5. **Interpreting** Do you think the civil rights movement would have been successful in gaining civil rights for African Americans without the help of the NAACP and the SCLC? Explain.
6. **Organizing** Use a graphic organizer similar to the one below to list the efforts made to end segregation.

Efforts to End Segregation

Analyzing Visuals

7. **Examining Photographs** Study the photograph of Central High School students on page 871. How would you describe Elizabeth Eckford's demeanor compared to those around her? What might this tell you about her character?

Writing About History

8. **Expository Writing** Take on the role of an African American soldier returning to the U.S. after fighting in World War II. Write a letter to the editor of your local newspaper describing your expectations of civil rights as an American citizen.

Challenging Segregation

Main Idea

African American citizens and white supporters created organizations that directed protests, targeted specific inequalities, and attracted the attention of the mass media and the government.

Key Terms and Names

Jesse Jackson, Ella Baker, Freedom Riders, filibuster, cloture, Civil Rights Act of 1964, poll tax

Reading Strategy

Organizing As you read about challenges to segregation in the South, complete a cause/effect chart like the one below.

Cause	Effect
Sit-In Movement	
Freedom Riders	
	African American support of Kennedy
	African American voter registration

Reading Objectives

- **Evaluate** the Civil Rights Act of 1964.
- **Summarize** the efforts to establish voting rights for African Americans.

Section Theme

Science and Technology The civil rights movement gained momentum in the early 1960s due to national television coverage.

Preview of Events

♦1960	♦1962	♦1964	♦1966

May 1961
Freedom Riders attempt to desegregate interstate buses in the South

Spring 1963
Martin Luther King, Jr., jailed in Birmingham

August 28, 1963
March on Washington

July 1964
President Johnson signs Civil Rights Act of 1964

1965
Voting Rights Act passed

★ An American Story ★

In the fall of 1959, four young African Americans—Joseph McNeil, Ezell Blair, Jr., David Richmond, and Franklin McCain—enrolled at North Carolina Agricultural and Technical College in Greensboro. The four freshmen became close friends and spent evenings talking about the civil rights movement. In January 1960, McNeil told his friends that he thought the time had come to take action, and he suggested a sit-in at the whites-only lunch counter in the nearby Woolworth's department store.

"All of us were afraid," Richmond later recalled, "but we went and did it." On February 1, 1960, the four friends entered the Woolworth's. They purchased school supplies and then sat at the lunch counter and ordered coffee. When they were refused service, Blair said, "I beg your pardon, but you just served us at [the checkout] counter. Why can't we be served at the counter here?" The students stayed at the counter until it closed, then announced that they would sit at the counter every day until they were given the same service as white customers.

As they left the store, the four were excited. McNeil recalled, "I just felt I had powers within me, a superhuman strength that would come forward." McCain was also energized, saying, "I probably felt better that day than I've ever felt in my life."

—adapted from *Civilities and Civil Rights*

The Sit-In Movement

News of the daring sit-in at the Woolworth's store spread quickly across Greensboro. The following day, 29 African American students arrived at Woolworth's determined to sit at the counter until served. By the end of the week, over 300 students were taking part.

Starting with just four students, a new mass movement for civil rights had begun. Within two months, sit-ins had spread to 54 cities in 9 states. Sit-ins were staged at segregated stores, restaurants, hotels, movie theaters, and swimming pools. By 1961 sit-ins had been held in more than 100 cities.

The sit-in movement brought large numbers of idealistic and energized college students into the civil rights struggle. Many African American students had become discouraged by the slow pace of desegregation. Students like **Jesse Jackson,** a student leader at North Carolina Agricultural and Technical College, wanted to see things change. The sit-in offered them a way to take matters into their own hands.

At first the leaders of the NAACP and the SCLC were nervous about the sit-in movement. They feared that students did not have the discipline to remain nonviolent if they were provoked enough. For the most part, the students proved them wrong. Those conducting sit-ins were heckled by bystanders, punched, kicked, beaten with clubs, and burned with cigarettes, hot coffee, and acid—but most did not fight back. They remained peaceful, and their heroic behavior grabbed the nation's attention.

✓ Reading Check **Examining** What were the effects of the sit-in movement?

SNCC

As the sit-ins spread, student leaders in different states realized that they needed to coordinate their efforts. The person who brought them together was **Ella Baker,** the 55-year-old executive director of the SCLC. In April 1960, Baker invited student leaders to

Picturing **History**

Sit-Ins Fight Segregation African American students challenged Southern segregation laws by demanding equal service at lunch counters. How did the NAACP initially feel about the sit-in movement?

attend a convention at Shaw University in Raleigh, North Carolina. At the convention, Baker urged students to create their own organization instead of joining the NAACP or the SCLC. Students, she said, had "the right to direct their own affairs and even make their own mistakes."

The students agreed with Baker and established the **Student Nonviolent Coordinating Committee** (SNCC). Among SNCC's early leaders were **Marion Barry,** who later served as mayor of Washington, D.C., and John Lewis, who later became a member of Congress. African American college students from all across the South made up the majority of SNCC's members, although many whites also joined.

Between 1960 and 1965, SNCC played a key role in desegregating public facilities in dozens of Southern communities. SNCC also began sending volunteers into rural areas of the Deep South to register African Americans to vote. The idea for what came to be called the Voter Education Project began with Robert Moses, an SNCC volunteer from New York. Moses pointed out that the civil rights movement tended to focus on urban areas. He urged SNCC to fill in the gap by helping rural African Americans. Moses himself went to rural Mississippi, where African Americans who tried to register to vote frequently met with violence.

Despite the danger, many SNCC volunteers headed to Mississippi and other parts of the Deep South. Several had their lives threatened, and others were beaten. In 1964 local officials in Mississippi brutally murdered three SNCC workers as the workers attempted to register African American voters.

One SNCC organizer, a former sharecropper named **Fannie Lou Hamer,** had been evicted from her farm after registering to vote. She was then arrested in Mississippi for urging other African Americans to register, and she was severely beaten by the police while in jail. She then helped organize the Mississippi Freedom Democratic Party, and she challenged the legality of the segregated Democratic Party at the 1964 Democratic National Convention.

✓ Reading Check **Explaining** What role did Ella Baker play in forming SNCC?

The Freedom Riders

Despite rulings outlawing segregation in interstate bus service, bus travel remained segregated in much of the South. In 1961 CORE leader James Farmer asked teams of African Americans and whites to travel into the South to draw attention to the South's refusal to integrate bus terminals. The teams became known as the **Freedom Riders.**

In early May 1961, the first Freedom Riders boarded several southbound interstate buses. When the buses carrying them arrived in Anniston, Birmingham, and Montgomery, Alabama, angry white mobs attacked them. The mobs slit the bus tires and threw rocks at the windows. In Anniston, someone threw a firebomb into one bus, although fortunately no one was killed.

In Birmingham the riders emerged from a bus to face a gang of young men armed with baseball bats, chains, and lead pipes. They beat the riders viciously. One witness later reported, "You couldn't see their faces through the blood." The head of the police in Birmingham, Public Safety Commissioner Theophilus Eugene ("Bull") Connor, explained that there had been no police at the bus station because it was Mother's Day, and he had given many of his officers the day off. FBI evidence later showed that Connor had contacted the local Ku Klux Klan and told them he wanted the Freedom Riders beaten until "it looked like a bulldog got a hold of them."

The violence in Alabama made national news, shocking many Americans. The attack on the Freedom Riders came less than four months after President John F. Kennedy took office. The new president felt compelled to do something to get the violence under control.

Picturing **History**

Riding Into Danger On May 14, 1961, Freedom Riders were driven from their bus outside of Anniston, Alabama, when angry townspeople set the bus on fire. Which civil rights protest organization coordinated the Freedom Riders?

✓ **Reading Check** **Summarizing** What was the goal of the Freedom Riders?

John F. Kennedy and Civil Rights

While campaigning for the presidency in 1960, John F. Kennedy promised to actively support the civil rights movement if elected. His brother, Robert F. Kennedy, had used his influence to get Dr. King released from jail after a demonstration in Georgia. African Americans responded by voting overwhelmingly for Kennedy. Their votes helped him narrowly win several key states, including Illinois, which Kennedy carried by only 9,000 votes. Once in office, however, Kennedy at first seemed as cautious as Eisenhower on civil rights, which disappointed many African Americans. Kennedy knew that he needed the support of many Southern senators to get

other programs he wanted through Congress, and that any attempt to push through new civil rights legislation would anger them.

Kennedy did, however, name approximately 40 African Americans to high-level positions in the federal government. He also appointed Thurgood Marshall to a judgeship on the Second Circuit Appeals Court in New York—one level below the Supreme Court and the highest judicial position an African American had attained to that point. Kennedy also created the **Committee on Equal Employment Opportunity** (CEEO) to stop the federal bureaucracy from discriminating against African Americans when hiring and promoting people.

The Justice Department Takes Action Although President Kennedy was unwilling to challenge Southern Democrats in Congress, he allowed the Justice Department, run by his brother Robert, to actively support the civil rights movement. Robert Kennedy tried to help African Americans register to vote by having the civil rights division of the Justice Department file lawsuits throughout the South.

When violence erupted against the Freedom Riders, the Kennedys came to their aid as well, although not at first. At the time the Freedom Riders took action, President Kennedy was preparing for a meeting with Nikita Khrushchev, the leader of the Soviet Union. Kennedy did not want violence in the South to disrupt the meeting by giving the impression that his country was weak and divided.

After the Freedom Riders were attacked in Montgomery, the Kennedys publicly urged them to stop the rides and give everybody a "cooling off" period. James Farmer replied that African Americans "have been cooling off now for 350 years. If we cool off anymore, we'll be in a deep freeze." Instead he announced that the Freedom Riders planned to head into Mississippi on their next trip.

To stop the violence, President Kennedy made a deal with Senator James Eastland of Mississippi, a strong supporter of segregation. If Eastland would use his influence in Mississippi to prevent violence, Kennedy would not object if the Mississippi police arrested the Freedom Riders. Eastland kept the deal. No violence occurred when the buses arrived in Jackson, Mississippi, but the riders were arrested.

The cost of bailing the Freedom Riders out of jail used up most of CORE's funds, which meant that the rides would have to end unless more money could be found. When Thurgood Marshall learned of the situation, he offered James Farmer the use of the NAACP's Legal Defense Fund's huge bail bond account to keep the rides going.

When President Kennedy returned from his meeting with Khrushchev and found that the Freedom Riders were still active, he changed his position and ordered the Interstate Commerce Commission to tighten its regulations against segregated bus terminals. In the meantime, Robert Kennedy ordered the Justice Department to take legal action against Southern cities that were maintaining segregated bus terminals. The continuing pressure of CORE and the actions of the ICC and the Justice Department finally produced results. By late 1962, segregation in interstate travel had come to an end.

James Meredith

As the Freedom Riders were trying to desegregate bus terminals, efforts continued to integrate Southern schools. On the very day John F. Kennedy was inaugurated, an African American air force veteran named **James Meredith** applied for a transfer to the University of Mississippi. Up to that point, the university had avoided complying with the Supreme Court ruling ending segregated education.

In September 1962, Meredith tried to register at the university's admissions office, only to find Ross Barnett, the governor of Mississippi, blocking his path. Although Meredith had a court order directing the university to register him, Governor Barnett stated emphatically, "Never! We will never surrender to the evil and illegal forces of tyranny."

Frustrated, President Kennedy dispatched 500 federal marshals to escort Meredith to the campus. Shortly after Meredith and the marshals arrived, an

angry white mob attacked the campus, and a full-scale riot erupted. The mob hurled rocks, bottles, bricks, and acid at the marshals. Some people fired shotguns at them. The marshals responded with tear gas, but they were under orders not to fire.

The fighting continued all night. By morning, 160 marshals had been wounded. Reluctantly Kennedy ordered the army to send several thousand troops to the campus. For the rest of the year, Meredith attended classes at the University of Mississippi under federal guard. He graduated the following August.

Violence in Birmingham

The events in Mississippi frustrated Martin Luther King, Jr., and other civil rights leaders. Although they were pleased that Kennedy had intervened to protect Meredith's rights, they were disappointed that the president had not seized the moment to push for a new civil rights law. When the Cuban missile crisis began the following month, civil rights issues dropped out of the news, and for the next several months, foreign policy became the main priority at the White House.

Reflecting on the problem, Dr. King came to a difficult decision. It seemed to him that only when violence and disorder got out of hand would the federal government intervene. "We've got to have a crisis to bargain with," one of his advisers observed. King agreed. In the spring of 1963, he decided to launch demonstrations in Birmingham, Alabama, knowing they would probably provoke a violent response. He believed it was the only way to get President Kennedy to actively support civil rights.

The situation in Birmingham was volatile. Public Safety Commissioner Bull Connor, who had arranged for the attack on the Freedom Riders, was now running for mayor. Eight days after the protests began, King was arrested and held for a time in solitary confinement. While in prison, King began writing on scraps of paper that had been smuggled into his cell. The "Letter From a Birmingham Jail" that he produced is one of the most eloquent defenses of nonviolent protest ever written.

In his letter, King explained that although the protesters were breaking the law, they were following a higher moral law based on divine justice. To the charge that the protests created racial tensions, King argued that the protests "merely bring to the surface the hidden tension that is already alive." Injustice, he insisted, had to be exposed "to the light of human conscience and the air of national opinion before it can be cured." 📖 *(See page 1056 for more on "Letter From a Birmingham Jail.")*

After King was released, the protests, which had been dwindling, began to grow again. Bull Connor responded with force, ordering the police to use clubs, police dogs, and high-pressure fire hoses on the demonstrators. Millions of people across the nation watched the graphic violence on television. Outraged by the brutality and worried that the government was losing control, Kennedy ordered his aides to prepare a new civil rights bill.

 Reading Check **Evaluating** How did President Kennedy help the civil rights movement?

The Civil Rights Act of 1964

Determined to introduce a civil rights bill, Kennedy now waited for a dramatic opportunity to address the nation on the issue. Alabama's governor, George Wallace, soon gave the president his chance. Wallace was committed to segregation. At his inauguration, he had stated, "I draw a line in the dust . . . and I say, Segregation now! Segregation tomorrow! Segregation forever!" On June 11, 1963, Wallace personally stood in front of the University of Alabama's admissions office to block the enrollment of two African Americans. He stayed until federal marshals ordered him to move. The following day a white segregationist murdered Medger Evers, a civil rights activist in Mississippi.

President Kennedy seized the moment to announce his civil rights bill. That evening, he went on television to speak to the American people about a "moral issue . . . as old as the scriptures and as clear as the American Constitution":

66The heart of the question is whether . . . we are going to treat our fellow Americans as we want to be treated. If an American, because his skin is dark, cannot eat lunch in a restaurant open to the public, if he cannot send his children to the best public school available, if he cannot vote for the public officials who will represent him . . . then who among us would be content to have the color of his skin changed and stand in his place?

One hundred years of delay have passed since President Lincoln freed the slaves, yet their heirs, their grandsons, are not fully free. . . . And this nation, for all its hopes and all its boasts, will not be fully free until all its citizens are free. . . . Now the time has come for this nation to fulfill its promise.99

—from Kennedy's White House Address, June 11, 1963

TURNING POINT

The March on Washington Dr. King realized that Kennedy would have a very difficult time pushing his civil rights bill through Congress. Therefore, he searched for a way to lobby Congress and to build more public support. When A. Philip Randolph suggested a march on Washington, King agreed.

On August 28, 1963, more than 200,000 demonstrators of all races flocked to the nation's capital. The audience heard speeches and sang hymns and songs as they gathered peacefully near the Lincoln Memorial. Dr. King then delivered a powerful speech outlining his dream of freedom and equality for all Americans:

Picturing **History**

Forcing Change Birmingham police used high-pressure hoses to force civil rights protesters to stop their marches. Why did King's followers offer no resistance?

Picturing History

A Dream Deferred The 1963 March on Washington was the emotional high point of the civil rights movement. Its nonviolent atmosphere and Dr. King's eloquent speech made it one of the most momentous American events of the twentieth century. *What significant legislation resulted from the March on Washington?*

❝I have a dream that one day this nation will rise up and live out the true meaning of its creed . . . that all men are created equal. . . . I have a dream that one day . . . the sons of former slaves and the sons of former slave owners will be able to sit together at the table of brotherhood. . . . I have a dream that my four little children will one day live in a nation where they will not be judged by the color of their skin but by the content of their character. I have a dream . . . when all of God's children, black men and white men, Jews and Gentiles, Protestants and Catholics, will be able to join hands and sing . . . 'Free at last, Free at last, Thank God Almighty, we are free at last.'❞

—quoted in *Freedom Bound: A History of America's Civil Rights Movement*

King's speech and the peacefulness and dignity of the March on Washington had built momentum for the civil rights bill. Opponents in Congress, however, continued to do what they could to slow the bill down, dragging out their committee investigations and using procedural rules to delay votes. *(See page 1078 for an excerpt from Dr. King's "I Have a Dream" speech.)*

The Civil Rights Bill Becomes Law

Although the civil rights bill was likely to pass the House of Representatives, where a majority of Republicans and Northern Democrats supported the measure, it faced a much more difficult time in the Senate. There, a small group of determined senators would try to block the bill indefinitely.

In the U.S. Senate, senators are allowed to speak for as long as they like when a bill is being debated. The Senate cannot vote on a bill until all senators have finished speaking. A filibuster occurs when a small group of senators take turns speaking and refuse to stop the debate and allow a bill to come to a vote. Today a filibuster can be stopped if at least 60 senators vote for cloture, a motion which cuts off debate and forces a vote. In the 1960s, however, 67 senators had to vote for cloture to stop a filibuster. This meant that a minority of senators opposed to civil rights could easily prevent the majority from enacting new civil rights laws.

Worried the bill would never pass, many African Americans became even more disheartened. Then President Kennedy was assassinated in Dallas, Texas, on November 22, 1963, and his vice president, Lyndon Johnson, became president. Johnson was from Texas and had been the leader of the Senate Democrats before becoming vice president. Although he had helped push the Civil Rights Acts of 1957 and 1960 through the Senate, he had done so by weakening their provisions and by compromising with other Southern senators.

To the surprise of the civil rights movement, Johnson committed himself wholeheartedly to getting Kennedy's program, including the civil rights bill, through Congress. Unlike Kennedy, Johnson was very familiar with how Congress operated, having served there for many years. He knew how to build public support, how to put pressure on members of Congress, and how to use the rules and procedures to get what he wanted.

In February 1964, President Johnson's leadership began to produce results. The civil rights bill passed the House of Representatives by a majority of 290 to 130. The debate then moved to the Senate. In June, after 87 days of filibuster, the Senate finally voted to end debate by a margin of 71 to 29—four votes over the two-thirds needed for cloture. On July 2, 1964, President Johnson signed the **Civil Rights Act of 1964** into law.

The Civil Rights Act of 1964 was the most comprehensive civil rights law Congress had ever enacted. It gave the federal government broad power to prevent racial discrimination in a number of areas. The law made segregation illegal in most places of public accommodation, and it gave citizens of all races and nationalities equal access to such facilities as restaurants, parks, libraries, and theaters. The law gave the attorney general more power to bring lawsuits to force school desegregation, and it required private employers to end discrimination in the workplace. It also established the **Equal Employment Opportunity Commission** (EEOC) as a permanent agency in the federal government. This commission monitors the ban on job discrimination by race, religion, gender, and national origin.

Reading Check **Examining** How did Dr. King lobby Congress to expand the right to participate in the democratic process?

The Struggle for Voting Rights

Even after the Civil Rights Act of 1964 was passed, voting rights were far from secure. The act had focused on segregation and job discrimination, and it did little to address voting issues. The Twenty-fourth Amendment, ratified in 1964, helped somewhat by eliminating poll taxes, or fees paid in order to vote, in federal (but not state) elections. African Americans still faced hurdles, however, when they tried to vote. As the SCLC and SNCC stepped up their voter registration efforts in the South, their members were often attacked and beaten, and several were murdered.

Across the South, bombs exploded in African American businesses and churches. Between June and October 1964, arson and bombs destroyed 24 African American churches in Mississippi alone. Convinced that a new law was needed to protect African American voting rights, Dr. King decided to stage another dramatic protest.

The Selma March In January 1965, the SCLC and Dr. King selected Selma, Alabama, as the focal point for their campaign for voting rights. Although African Americans made up a majority of Selma's

Voting Rights In the early 1960s, African Americans focused on increasing their political power.

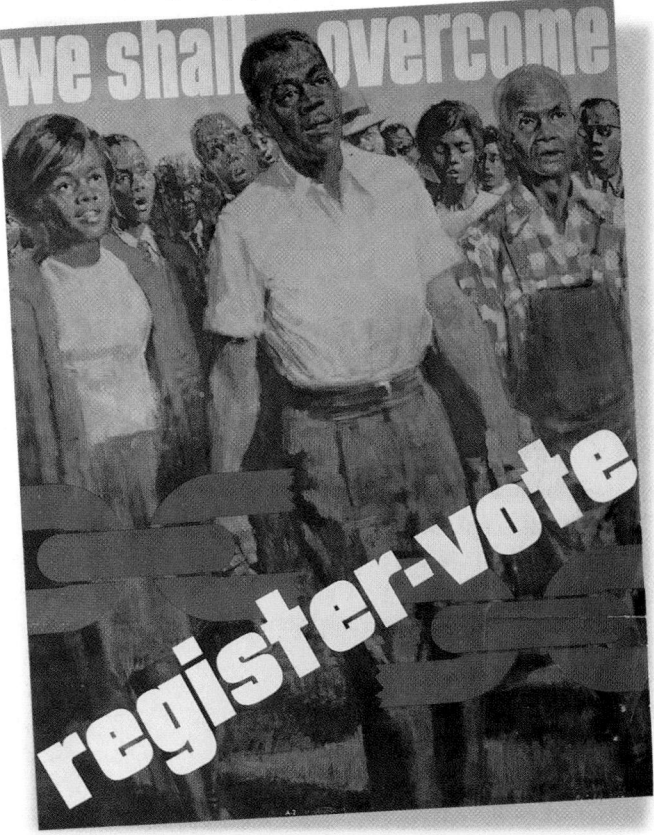

population, they comprised only 3 percent of registered voters. To prevent African Americans from registering to vote, Sheriff Jim Clark had deputized and armed dozens of white citizens. His posse terrorized African Americans and frequently attacked demonstrators with clubs and electric cattle prods.

Just weeks after receiving the Nobel Peace Prize in Oslo, Norway, for his work in the civil rights movement, Dr. King stated, "We are not asking, we are demanding the ballot." King's demonstrations in Selma led to approximately 2,000 African Americans, including schoolchildren, being arrested by Sheriff Clark. Clark's men attacked and beat many of the demonstrators, and Selma quickly became a major story in the national news.

To keep pressure on the president and Congress to act, Dr. King joined with SNCC activists and organized a "march for freedom" from Selma to the state capitol in Montgomery, a distance of about 50 miles (80 km). On Sunday, March 7, 1965, the march began. The SCLC's Hosea Williams and SNCC's John Lewis led 500 protesters toward U.S. Highway 80, the route that marchers had planned to follow to Montgomery.

As the protesters approached the Edmund Pettus Bridge, which led out of Selma, Sheriff Clark ordered them to disperse. While the marchers kneeled in prayer, more than 200 state troopers and deputized citizens rushed the demonstrators. Many were beaten in full view of television cameras. This brutal attack, known later as "Bloody Sunday," left 70 African Americans hospitalized and many more injured.

The nation was stunned as it viewed the shocking footage of law enforcement officers beating peaceful demonstrators. Watching the events from the White House, President Johnson became furious. Eight days later, he appeared before a nationally televised joint session of the legislature to propose a new voting rights law.

The Voting Rights Act of 1965
On August 3, 1965, the House of Representatives passed the voting rights bill by a wide margin. The following day, the Senate also passed the bill. The **Voting Rights Act of 1965** authorized the attorney general to send federal examiners to register qualified voters, bypassing local officials who often refused to register African Americans. The law also suspended discriminatory devices such as literacy tests in counties where less than half of all adults had been allowed to vote.

The results were dramatic. By the end of the year, almost 250,000 African Americans had registered as new voters. The number of African American elected officials in the South also increased, from about 100 in 1965 to more than 5,000 in 1990.

The passage of the Voting Rights Act of 1965 marked a turning point in the civil rights movement. The movement had now achieved its two major legislative goals. Segregation had been outlawed, and new federal laws were in place to prevent discrimination and protect voting rights.

After 1965 the movement began to shift its focus. It began to pay more attention to the problem of achieving full social and economic equality for African Americans. As part of that effort, the movement turned its attention to the problems of African Americans trapped in poverty and living in ghettos in many of the nation's major cities.

Reading Check **Summarizing** How did the Twenty-fourth Amendment affect African American voting rights?

SECTION 2 ASSESSMENT

Checking for Understanding
1. **Define:** Freedom Riders, filibuster, cloture, poll tax.
2. **Identify:** Jesse Jackson, Ella Baker, Civil Rights Act of 1964.
3. **Describe** the provisions of the Civil Rights Act of 1964 aimed at ending segregation and racial discrimination.

Reviewing Themes
4. **Science and Technology** How did television help the civil rights movement?

Critical Thinking
5. **Evaluating** How did protesting and lobbying lead to the passage of the Voting Rights Act of 1965?
6. **Sequencing** Use a time line like the one below to show relative chronology of events in the civil rights movement.

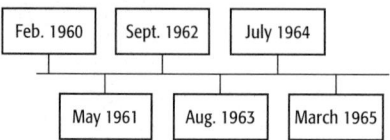

Feb. 1960 | Sept. 1962 | July 1964

May 1961 | Aug. 1963 | March 1965

Analyzing Visuals
7. **Examining Photographs** Study the photographs in this section. What elements of the photographs show the sacrifices African Americans made in the civil rights movement?

Writing About History
8. **Descriptive Writing** Take on the role of a journalist for the student newspaper of a college in 1960. Write an article for the newspaper describing the sit-in movement taking place across the country.

New Issues

Guide to Reading

Main Idea

In the mid-1960s, civil rights leaders began to understand that merely winning political rights for African Americans would not address the problem of African Americans' economic status.

Key Terms and Names

racism, Chicago Movement, Richard Daley, black power, Stokely Carmichael, Malcolm X, Black Panthers

Reading Strategy

Organizing As you read about the changing focus of the civil rights movement, complete a chart similar to the one below. Fill in five major violent events and their results.

Event	Result

Reading Objectives

- **Describe** the division between Dr. Martin Luther King, Jr., and the black power movement.
- **Discuss** the direction and progress of the civil rights movement after 1968.

Section Theme

Civic Rights and Responsibilities In the late 1960s, the civil rights movement tried to address the persistent economic inequality of African Americans.

Preview of Events

◆1965	◆1966	◆1967	◆1968

1965
Watts riots break out in Los Angeles; Malcolm X assassinated

1966
Chicago Movement fails

1967
Kerner Commission studies problems of inner cities

1968
Dr. Martin Luther King, Jr., assassinated

★ An American Story ★

Thursday, July 12, 1965, was hot and humid in Chicago. That evening Dessie Mae Williams, a 23-year-old African American woman, stood on the corner near the firehouse at 4000 West Wilcox Street. A firetruck sped out of the firehouse, and the driver lost control. The truck smashed into a stop sign near Williams, and the sign struck and killed her.

African Americans had already picketed this firehouse because it was not integrated. Hearing of Williams's death, 200 neighborhood young people streamed into the street, surrounding the firehouse. For two nights, rioting and disorder reigned. Angry youths threw bricks and bottles at the firehouse and nearby windows. Shouting gangs pelted police with rocks and accosted whites and beat them. Approximately 75 people were injured.

African American detectives, clergy, and National Guard members eventually restored order. Mayor Richard Daley then summoned both white and black leaders to discuss the area's problems. An 18-year-old man who had been in the riot admitted that he had lost his head. "We're sorry about the bricks and bottles," he said, "but when you get pushed, you shove back. Man, you don't like to stand on a corner and be told to get off it when you got nowhere else to go."

—adapted from *Anyplace But Here*

Problems Facing Urban African Americans

Civil rights leaders had made great progress in the decade following the Montgomery bus boycott, but full equality still eluded many African Americans. Until 1965 the civil rights movement had focused on ending segregation and restoring the voting rights of

African Americans in the South. These were goals that could be achieved through court decisions and by convincing Congress to pass new laws.

Despite the passage of several civil rights laws in the 1950s and 1960s, racism—prejudice or discrimination toward someone because of his or her race—was still common in American society. Changing the law could not change people's attitudes immediately, nor could it help those African Americans trapped in poverty in the nation's big cities.

In 1965 nearly 70 percent of African Americans lived in large cities. Many had moved from the South to the big cities of the North and West during the Great Migration of the 1920s and 1940s. There, they often found the same prejudice and discrimination that had plagued them in the South. Many whites refused to live with African Americans in the same neighborhood. When African Americans moved into a neighborhood, whites often moved out. Real estate agents and landlords in white neighborhoods refused to rent or sell to African Americans, who often found it difficult to arrange for mortgages at local banks.

Even if African Americans had been allowed to move into white neighborhoods, poverty trapped many of them in inner cities while whites moved to the suburbs. Many African Americans found themselves channeled into low-paying jobs. They served as custodians and maids, porters and dock workers, with little chance of advancement. Those who did better typically found employment as blue-collar workers in factories, but very few advanced beyond that. In 1965 only 15 percent of African Americans held professional, managerial, or clerical jobs, compared to 44 percent of whites. Almost half of all African American families lived in poverty, and the median income of an African American family was only 55 percent of that of the average white family. African American unemployment was typically twice that of whites.

Poor neighborhoods in the nation's major cities were overcrowded and dirty, leading to higher rates of illness and infant mortality. At the same time, the crime rate increased in the 1960s, particularly in low-income neighborhoods. Incidents of juvenile delinquency rose, as did the rate of young people dropping out of school. Complicating matters even more was a rise in the number of single-parent households. All poor neighborhoods suffered from these problems, but because more African Americans lived in poverty, their communities were disproportionately affected.

Many African Americans living in urban poverty knew the civil rights movement had made enormous gains, but when they looked at their own circumstances, nothing seemed to be changing. The movement had raised their hopes, but their everyday problems were economic and social, and therefore harder to address. As a result, their anger and frustration began to rise—until it finally erupted.

The Watts Riot Just five days after President Johnson signed the Voting Rights Act, a race riot broke out in Watts, an African American neighborhood in Los Angeles. Allegations of police brutality had served as the catalyst of this uprising, which lasted for six days and required over 14,000 members of the National Guard and 1,500 law officers to restore order. Rioters burned and looted entire neighborhoods and destroyed about $45 million in property. They killed 34 people, and about 900 suffered injuries.

More rioting was yet to come. Race riots broke out in dozens of American cities between 1965 and 1968. It seemed that they could explode at any place and at any time. The worst riot took place in Detroit in 1967. Burning, looting, and skirmishes with police and National Guard members resulted in 43 deaths and over 1,000 wounded. Eventually the U.S. Army sent in tanks and soldiers armed with machine guns to get control of the situation. Nearly 4,000 fires destroyed

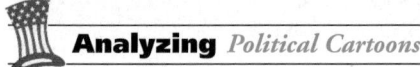

Analyzing *Political Cartoons*

"Perilous Going" This political cartoon highlights the problems that American cities were experiencing in the mid-1960s. Why did riots break out in the Los Angeles neighborhood of Watts?

1,300 buildings, and the damage in property loss was estimated at $250 million. The governor of Michigan, who viewed the smoldering city from a helicopter, remarked that Detroit looked like "a city that had been bombed."

GOVERNMENT

The Kerner Commission In 1967 President Johnson appointed the National Advisory Commission on Civil Disorders, headed by Governor Otto Kerner of Illinois, to study the causes of the urban riots and to make recommendations to prevent them from happening again in the future. The **Kerner Commission,** as it became known, conducted a detailed study of the problem. The commission blamed white society and white racism for the majority of the problems in the inner city. "Our nation is moving toward two societies, one black, one white—separate and unequal," it concluded.

The commission recommended the creation of 2 million new jobs in the inner city, the construction of 6 million new units of public housing, and a renewed federal commitment to fight de facto segregation. President Johnson's war on poverty, however, which addressed some of the same concerns for inner-city jobs and housing, was already underway. Saddled with massive spending for the Vietnam War, however, President Johnson never endorsed the recommendations of the commission.

✓ **Reading Check** **Explaining** What was the federal government's response to the race riots in Los Angeles and Detroit?

The Shift to Economic Rights

By the mid-1960s, a number of African American leaders were becoming increasingly critical of Martin Luther King's nonviolent strategy. They felt it had failed to improve the economic position of African Americans. What good was the right to dine at restaurants or stay at hotels if most African Americans could not afford these services anyway? Dr. King became sensitive to this criticism, and in 1965 he began to focus on economic issues.

In 1965 Albert Raby, president of a council of community organizations that worked to

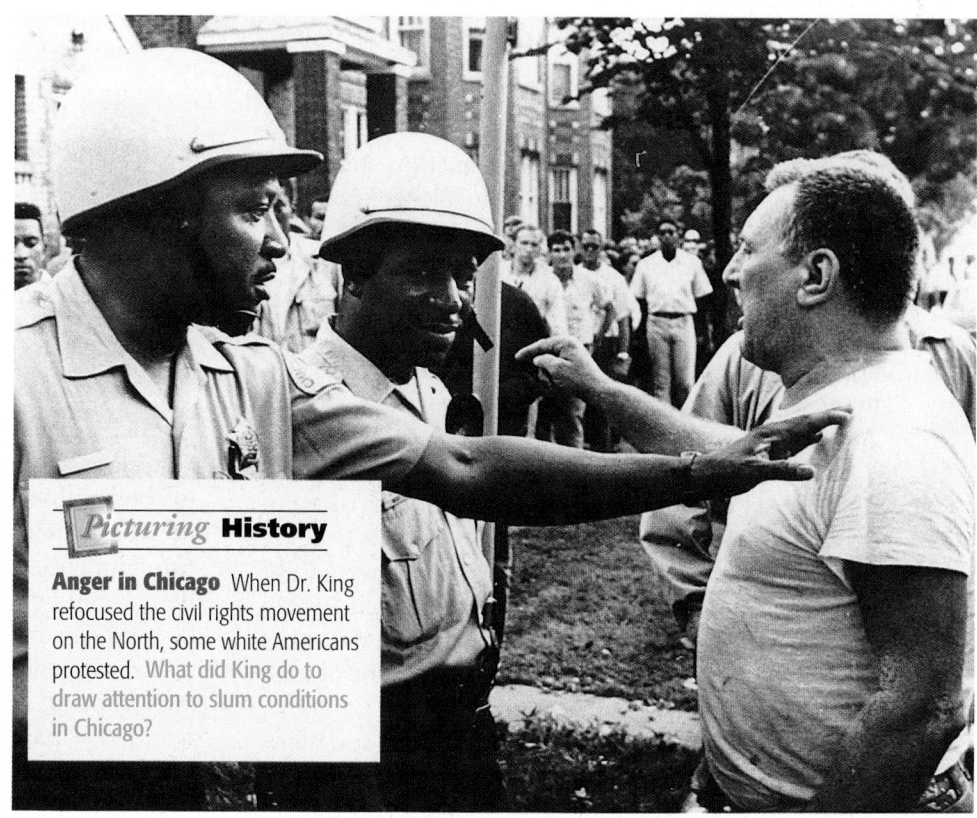

Picturing **History**

Anger in Chicago When Dr. King refocused the civil rights movement on the North, some white Americans protested. What did King do to draw attention to slum conditions in Chicago?

improve conditions for Chicago's poor, invited Dr. King to visit the city. Dr. King and his staff had never conducted a civil rights campaign in the North. By focusing on the problems that African Americans faced in Chicago, Dr. King believed he could call greater attention to poverty and other racial problems that lay beneath the urban race riots.

To call attention to the deplorable housing conditions that many African American families faced, Dr. King and his wife Coretta moved into a slum apartment in an African American neighborhood in Chicago. Dr. King and the SCLC hoped to work with local leaders to improve the economic status of African Americans in Chicago's poor neighborhoods.

The **Chicago Movement,** however, made little headway. When Dr. King led a march through the all-white suburb of Marquette Park to demonstrate the need for open housing, he was met by angry white mobs similar to those in Birmingham and Selma. Mayor **Richard Daley** ordered the Chicago police to protect the marchers, but he wanted to avoid any repeat of the violence. He met with Dr. King and proposed a new program to clean up the slums. Associations of realtors and bankers also agreed to promote open housing. In theory, mortgages and rental property would be available to everyone, regardless of race. In practice, very little changed.

✓ **Reading Check** **Describing** How did Dr. King and SCLC leaders hope to address economic concerns?

Black Power

Dr. King's failure in Chicago seemed to show that nonviolent protests could do little to change economic problems. After 1965 many African Americans, especially young people living in cities, began to turn away from King. Some leaders called for more aggressive forms of protest. Their new strategies ranged from armed self-defense to the suggestion that the government set aside a number of states where African Americans could live free from the presence of whites.

As African Americans became more assertive, they placed less emphasis on cooperation with sympathetic whites in the civil rights movement. Some African American organizations, including CORE and SNCC, voted to expel all whites from leadership positions within their organizations, believing that African Americans alone should determine the course and direction of their struggle.

Many young African Americans called for black power, a term that had many different meanings. A few interpreted black power to mean that physical self-defense and even violence were acceptable in defense of one's freedom—a clear rejection of Dr. King's philosophy. To most, including **Stokely Carmichael,** the leader of SNCC in 1966, the term meant that African Americans should control the social, political, and economic direction of their struggle:

❝This is the significance of black power as a slogan. For once, black people are going to use the words they want to use—not just the words whites want to hear. . . . The need for psychological equality is the reason why SNCC today believes that blacks must organize in the black community. Only black people can . . . create in the community an aroused and continuing black consciousness. . . . Black people must do things for themselves; they must get . . . money they will control and spend themselves; they must conduct tutorial programs themselves so that black children can identify with black people.❞

—from the *New York Review of Books,*
September 1966

Black power also stressed pride in the African American cultural group. It emphasized racial distinctiveness rather than **cultural assimilation**—the process by which minority groups adapt to the dominant culture in a society. African Americans showed pride in their racial heritage by adopting new Afro hairstyles and African-style clothing. Many also took on African names. In universities, students demanded that African and African American Studies courses be adopted as part of the standard school curriculum. Dr. King and some other leaders criticized black power as a philosophy of hopelessness and despair. The idea was very popular, however, in the poor urban neighborhoods where many African Americans resided.

Malcolm X and the Nation of Islam By the early 1960s, a man named **Malcolm X** had become a symbol of the black power movement that was sweeping the nation. Born Malcolm Little in Omaha, Nebraska, he experienced a difficult childhood and adolescence. He drifted into a life of crime, and in 1946, he was convicted of burglary and sent to prison for six years.

Prison transformed Malcolm. He began to educate himself, and he played an active role in the prison debate society. Eventually he joined the **Nation of Islam,** commonly known as the Black Muslims, who were led by Elijah Muhammad. Despite their name, the Black Muslims do not hold the same beliefs as mainstream Muslims. The Nation of Islam preached black nationalism. Like Marcus Garvey in the 1920s, Black Muslims believed that African Americans should separate themselves from whites and form their own self-governing communities.

Shortly after joining the Nation of Islam, Malcolm Little changed his name to Malcolm X. The "X" stood as a symbol for the family name of his African ancestors who had been enslaved. Malcolm argued that his true family name had been stolen from him by slavery, and he did not intend to use the name white society had given him.

The Black Muslims viewed themselves as their own nation and attempted to make themselves as economically self-sufficient as possible. They ran their own businesses, organized their own schools, established

Picturing **History**

Malcolm X Makes His Point Once the most visible spokesperson for the Nation of Islam, Malcolm X originally disagreed with Dr. King's passive protest tactics. What did the "X" in his name symbolize?

their own weekly newspaper (*Muhammad Speaks*), and encouraged their members to respect each other and to strengthen their families. Although the Black Muslims did not advocate violence, they did advocate self-defense. Malcolm X was a powerful and charismatic speaker, and his criticisms of white society and the mainstream civil rights movement gained national attention for the Nation of Islam.

By 1964 Malcolm X had broken with the Black Muslims. Discouraged by scandals involving the Nation of Islam's leader, he went to the Muslim holy city of Makkah (also called Mecca) in Saudi Arabia. After seeing Muslims from many different races worshipping together, he concluded that an integrated society was possible. In a revealing letter describing his pilgrimage to Makkah, he stated that many whites that he met during the pilgrimage displayed a spirit of brotherhood that gave him a new, positive insight into race relations.

After Malcolm X broke with the Nation of Islam, he continued to criticize the organization and its leader, Elijah Muhammad. Because of this, three organization members shot and killed him in February 1965 while he was giving a speech in New York. Although Malcolm X left the Nation of Islam before his death, his speeches and ideas from those years with the Black Muslims are those for which he is most remembered. In Malcolm's view, African Americans may have been victims in the past, but they did not have to allow racism to victimize them in the present. His ideas have influenced African Americans to take pride in their own culture and to believe in their ability to make their way in the world.

The Black Panthers Malcolm X's ideas influenced a new generation of militant African American leaders who also preached black power, black nationalism, and economic self-sufficiency. In 1966 in Oakland, California, Huey Newton, Bobby Seale, and Eldridge Cleaver organized the Black Panther Party for Self-Defense, or the **Black Panthers,** as they were known. They considered themselves the heirs of Malcolm X, and they recruited most of their members from poor urban communities across the nation.

The Black Panthers believed that a revolution was necessary in the United States, and they urged African Americans to arm themselves and confront white society in order to force whites to grant them equal rights. Black Panther leaders adopted a "Ten-Point Program," which called for black empowerment, an end to racial oppression, and control of major institutions and services in the African American community, such as schools, law enforcement, housing, and medical

Picturing History

Black Power U.S. athletes Tommie Smith and John Carlos give the black power salute during the medal ceremony at the 1968 Olympic Games in Mexico City. How did black power supporters demonstrate their belief in the movement?

facilities. **Eldridge Cleaver,** who served as the minister of culture, articulated many of the organization's objectives in his 1967 best-selling book, *Soul on Ice.*

Reading Check **Describing** What caused a division between Dr. Martin Luther King, Jr., and the black power movement?

The Assassination of Martin Luther King, Jr.

By the late 1960s, the civil rights movement had fragmented into dozens of competing organizations with philosophies for reaching equality. At the same time, the emergence of black power and the call by some African Americans for violent action angered many white civil rights supporters. This made further legislation to help blacks economically less likely.

In this atmosphere, Dr. King went to Memphis, Tennessee, to support a strike of African American sanitation workers in March 1968. At the time, the SCLC had been planning a national "Poor People's Campaign" to promote economic advancement for

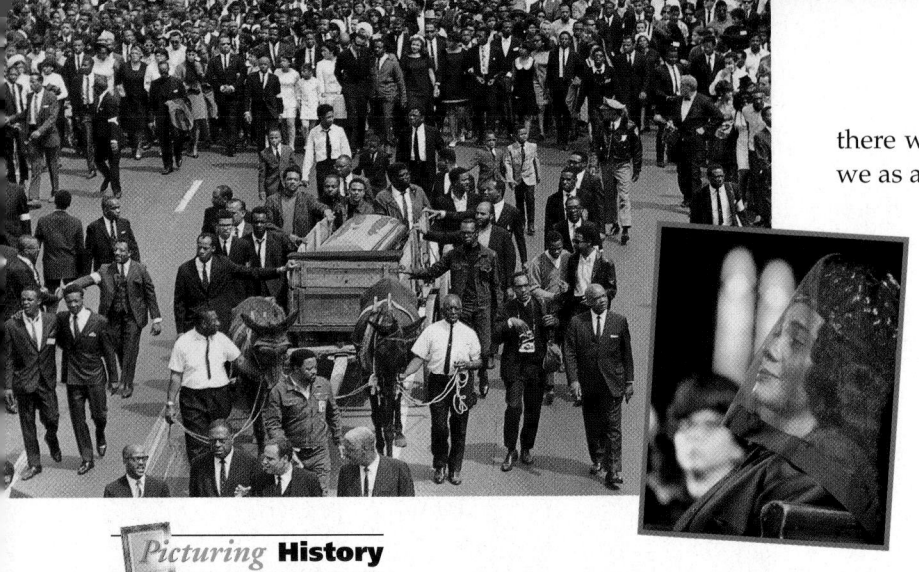

Picturing History

Atlanta Mourns Martin Luther King, Jr. The nation joined Coretta Scott King (right) in sorrow following the assassination of her husband in 1968. Why was King in Memphis at the time of his death?

all impoverished Americans. The purpose of this campaign, the most ambitious one that Dr. King would ever lead, was to lobby the federal government to commit billions of dollars to end poverty and unemployment in the United States. People of all races and nationalities were to converge on the nation's capital, as they had in 1963 during the March on Washington, where they would camp out until both Congress and President Johnson agreed to pass the requested legislation to fund the proposal.

On the evening of April 4, 1968, as he stood on his hotel balcony in Memphis, Dr. King was assassinated by a sniper. Ironically, he had told a gathering at a local African American church just the previous night, "I've been to the mountaintop. . . . I've looked over and I've seen the Promised Land. I may not get there with you, but I want you to know tonight that we as a people will get to the Promised Land."

Dr. King's assassination touched off both national mourning and riots in more than 100 cities, including Washington, D.C. The Reverend **Ralph Abernathy,** who had served as a trusted assistant to Dr. King for many years, led the Poor People's Campaign in King's absence. The demonstration, however, did not achieve any of the major objectives that either King or the SCLC had hoped it would.

In the wake of Dr. King's death, Congress passed the Civil Rights Act of 1968. The act contained a fair housing provision outlawing discrimination in housing sales and rentals and gave the Justice Department authority to bring suits against such discrimination.

Dr. King's death marked the end of an era in American history. Although the civil rights movement continued, it lacked the unity of purpose and vision that Dr. King had given it. Under his leadership, and with the help of tens of thousands of dedicated African Americans, many of whom were students, the civil rights movement transformed American society. Although many problems remain to be resolved, the achievements of the civil rights movement in the 1950s and 1960s dramatically improved life for African Americans, creating new opportunities where none had existed before.

✓ **Reading Check** **Summarizing** What were the goals of the Poor People's Campaign?

SECTION 3 ASSESSMENT

Checking for Understanding
1. **Define:** racism, black power.
2. **Identify:** Chicago Movement, Richard Daley, Stokely Carmichael, Malcolm X, Black Panthers.
3. **Explain** the goals of the Nation of Islam in the 1960s.
4. **Summarize** the findings of the Kerner Commission.

Reviewing Themes
5. **Civic Rights and Responsibilities** How was the Civil Rights Act of 1968 designed to help end discrimination?

Critical Thinking
6. **Identifying Cause and Effect** What were the effects of the assassination of Dr. Martin Luther King, Jr.?
7. **Categorizing** Using a graphic organizer like the one below, list the main views of the three leaders listed.

Leader	Views
Dr. Martin Luther King, Jr.	
Malcolm X	
Eldridge Cleaver	

Analyzing Visuals
8. **Analyzing Political Cartoons** The cartoon on page 882 suggests that the violence of the mid-1960s was as bad as the violence of the Vietnam War going on at the same time. What images does the cartoonist use to compare violence at home with the violence of the war?

Writing About History
9. **Expository Writing** Take on the role of a reporter in the late 1960s. Imagine you have interviewed a follower of Dr. King and a Black Panther member. Write out a transcript of each interview.

Preparing a Bibliography

Why Learn This Skill?

When you write research reports, you should include a list of the sources used to find your information. This list, called a *bibliography*, allows you to credit the sources you cited and supports the report's accuracy.

Learning the Skill

A bibliography is a list of sources used in a research report. These sources include books; articles from newspapers, magazines, and journals; interviews; and other sources.

There are two main reasons to write a bibliography. First, those who read your report may want to learn more about the topic. Second, a bibliography supports the reliability of your report.

A bibliography follows an established format. The entry for each source contains all the information needed to find that source, including the author, title, page numbers, publisher information, and publication date. You should document this information as you carry out your research. If you neglect this step early in your research, you must locate your sources again in order to credit them in your report.

You should arrange bibliographic entries alphabetically by the author's last name. The following are acceptable formats, followed by sample entries. Note that all lines after the first line are indented.

Books:

Author's last name, first name. *Full Title*. Place of publication: publisher, copyright date.

Hay, Peter. *Ordinary Heroes: The Life and Death of Chana Szenes, Israel's National Heroine*. New York: Paragon House, 1986.

Articles:

Author's last name, first name. "Title of Article." *Name of Periodical* in which article appears, volume number (date of issue): page numbers.

Watson, Bruce. "The New Peace Corps in the New Kazakhstan." *Smithsonian*, Vol. 25 (August 1994): pp. 26–35.

Other Sources:

For other kinds of sources, adapt the format for book entries as needed.

Practicing the Skill

Review the sample bibliography below from a report on Martin Luther King, Jr. Then answer the questions that follow.

Patrick, Diane. *Martin Luther King, Jr.* New York: Franklin Watts, 1990.

Franklin, John H. "Jim Crow Goes to School: The Genesis of Legal Segregation in Southern Schools." *South Atlantic Quarterly*, 57 (1956): pp. 225–235.

Washington, James Melvin, ed. *A Testament of Hope: The Essential Writings of Martin Luther King, Jr.* San Francisco: Harper & Row.

King, Jr., Martin Luther. Time for Freedom has Come. *New York Times Magazine* (Sept. 10, 1961).

❶ Are the bibliography entries in the correct order? Why or why not?

❷ What is missing from the second book listing?

❸ What features are missing from the second article listing?

Skills Assessment

Complete the Practicing Skills questions on page 889 and the Chapter 29 Skill Reinforcement Activity to assess your mastery of this skill.

Applying the Skill

Preparing a Bibliography Put together a bibliography of at least five sources that you could use for a report on the civil rights movement. Include books, periodicals, and any other sources you wish.

Glencoe's **Skillbuilder Interactive Workbook CD-ROM, Level 2,** provides instruction and practice in key social studies skills.

Reviewing Key Terms

On a sheet of paper, use each of these terms in a sentence.

1. separate-but-equal
2. de facto segregation
3. sit-in
4. Freedom Riders
5. filibuster
6. cloture
7. poll tax
8. racism
9. black power

Reviewing Key Facts

10. **Identify:** NAACP, Thurgood Marshall, Linda Brown, Martin Luther King, Jr., Southern Christian Leadership Conference, Jesse Jackson, Chicago Movement, Stokely Carmichael, Malcolm X.

11. What event led to the bus boycott in Montgomery, Alabama?

12. Why was the decision in *Brown* v. *Board of Education* a significant step toward ending segregation?

13. What was the role of SNCC in the civil rights movement?

14. How did the government react to race riots in cities such as Los Angeles and Detroit?

15. What were two changes in the focus of the civil rights movement in the mid-1960s?

Critical Thinking

16. **Analyzing Themes: Civic Rights and Responsibilities** Do you agree with the viewpoint of Dr. Martin Luther King, Jr., or with that of the Black Panthers concerning the civil rights movement? Explain your answer.

17. **Evaluating** Why did the civil rights movement make fewer gains after 1968?

Chapter Summary

Major Events in Civil Rights Movement

1954
- *Brown* v. *Board of Education* attacks school segregation.
- Separate-but-equal doctrine is ruled unconstitutional.

1955
- Rosa Parks inspires Montgomery bus boycott.

1957
- SCLC is formed to fight segregation and encourage African Americans to vote.
- Eisenhower sends army troops to Little Rock, Arkansas.

1960
- Sit-ins begin and spread to over 100 cities.
- SNCC is formed and leads fight against segregated public facilities.

1961
- Freedom Rides begin.

1963
- Birmingham demonstrations and the March on Washington help build support for the civil rights movement.

1964
- Twenty-fourth Amendment abolishes poll tax.
- Civil Rights Act of 1964 outlaws discrimination based on race, gender, religion, or national origin, and gives equal access to public facilities.

1965
- Voting Rights Act ensures African Americans of the right to vote.
- Watts riot sparks a five-year period of urban racial violence.
- Splinter groups within the civil rights movement advocate more aggressive means of gaining racial equality.

1968
- Dr. Martin Luther King, Jr. assassinated.
- Civil Rights Act of 1968 outlaws discrimination in the sale and rental of housing.

◆ 1954   ◆ 1961   ◆ 1968

18. **Making Generalizations** Why was the sit-in movement considered a major turning point in the civil rights movement?

19. **Organizing** Use a graphic organizer similar to the one below to compare examples of civil rights legislation.

Civil Rights Legislation	Provisions
Civil Rights Act 1957	
Twenty-Fourth Amendment	
Voting Rights Act	
Civil Rights Act of 1964	
Civil Rights Act of 1968	

Practicing Skills

20. **Preparing a Bibliography** Review the following bibliography for a report on the civil rights movement. Then answer the questions that follow.

Fairclough, Adam. <u>Martin Luther King, Jr.</u> Athens and London: University of Georgia Press, 1995.

Juan Williams. Eyes on the Prize. New York: Viking Penguin, Inc., 1987.

<u>Patterson, James T.</u> Grand Expectations, The United States, 1945–1974. New York: Oxford University Press, 1996.

Bontemps, Arna, and Jack Conroy. <u>Anyplace but Here.</u> Columbia: University of Missouri Press. (NO PUB DATE)

a. The entries presented above are not listed in the correct order. Using just the names of the authors, put them in the correct order.

b. What is incorrect in the Patterson listing?

c. Rewrite the Juan Williams listing correctly.

Geography and History

21. The map on this page shows routes of Freedom Riders. Study the map and answer the questions below.

a. Interpreting Maps Which states did the Freedom Riders travel through? What was their final destination?

b. Applying Geography Skills Why do you think the Freedom Riders faced protests during this trip?

Writing Activity

22. **Writing a Script** Work in small groups to write a script for a documentary on the civil rights movement in the 1950s and

NATIONAL GEOGRAPHIC
Route of the Freedom Riders, 1961

1960s. Your group should choose a specific topic, movement leader, or time period to write about. Use your script to produce a documentary to present to the other groups in your class.

Chapter Activity

23. **Examining Interviews** Work with a classmate to research interviews with Martin Luther King, Jr., and Malcolm X. Take notes on the different points of view of these civil rights leaders, and then prepare a chart illustrating similarities, differences, and any bias which shapes their beliefs.

Standardized Test Practice

Directions: Choose the phrase that best completes the following statement.

One difference between the strategies of Dr. Martin Luther King, Jr., and some later civil rights groups was that King was committed to

A ending discrimination in housing and unemployment.

B using only nonviolent forms of protest.

C demanding equal rights for African Americans.

D gaining improvements in living conditions for African Americans.

Test-Taking Tip: If you read this question carefully, you will notice that it asks for one *difference* in civil rights strategies. Three of the answer choices will represent *common goals*. Be careful to read through all the choices to find the one that represents a *different* type of strategy.

CHAPTER 30
The Vietnam War

1954–1975

Why It Matters

The Vietnam War created very bitter divisions within the United States. Supporters argued that patriotism demanded that communism be halted. Opponents argued that intervening in Vietnam was immoral. Many young people protested or resisted the draft. Victory was not achieved, although more than 58,000 American soldiers died. After the war, the nation had many wounds to heal.

The Impact Today

Changes brought about by the war are still evident in the United States today.
• The nation is reluctant to commit troops overseas.
• The War Powers Act limits a president's power to involve the nation in war.

The American Vision Video The Chapter 30 video, "Vietnam: A Different War," explores the causes and the impact of this longest war in American history.

1954
• Vietminh defeat French
• Geneva Accords signed

1964
• Congress passes Gulf of Tonkin Resolution

1965
• U.S. combat troops arrive in Vietnam

United States PRESIDENTS

Eisenhower 1953–1961

Kennedy 1961–1963

L. Johnson 1963–1969

1955

1960

1965

World

1955
• Khrushchev is dominant leader in USSR

1958
• De Gaulle heads France's Fifth Republic

1964
• Japan introduces first high-speed passenger train

The dedication ceremony for the Vietnam Veterans Memorial in Washington, D.C., November 13, 1982

1967
• March on the Pentagon takes place

1968
• Tet offensive
• Students protest at Democratic National Convention in Chicago

Nixon 1969–1974

1970
• National Guard troops kill students at Kent State University

1973
• Cease-fire signed with North Vietnam

Ford 1974–1977

1975
• Evacuation of last Americans from Vietnam

1970

1975

1967
• First heart transplant performed

1968
• Soviets repress Czechoslovakia's rebellion

1971
• Pakistani civil war leads to independent Bangladesh

1975
• Civil war breaks out in Angola

HISTORY
Online
Chapter Overview
Visit the *American Vision* Web site at tav.glencoe.com and click on **Chapter Overviews—Chapter 30** to preview chapter information.

The United States Focuses on Vietnam

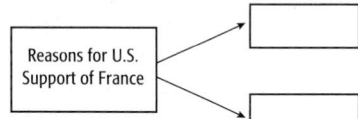

Guide to Reading

Main Idea
American efforts to stop the spread of communism led to U.S. involvement in the affairs of Vietnam.

Key Terms and Names
Ho Chi Minh, domino theory, guerrilla, Dien Bien Phu, Ngo Dinh Diem

Reading Strategy
Organizing As you read about the increasing involvement of the United States in Vietnam, complete a graphic organizer similar to the one below by providing reasons that the United States aided France in Vietnam.

Reasons for U.S. Support of France

Reading Objectives
• **Describe** the nationalist motives of Vietnamese leader Ho Chi Minh.
• **Explain** the origins of American involvement in Vietnam during the 1950s.

Section Theme
Government and Democracy American involvement in Vietnam was a reflection of Cold War strategy.

Preview of Events

♦1946   ♦1950   ♦1954   ♦1958

1946
French-Vietminh War begins

1950
The United States supplies military aid to France

1954
Vietminh defeat French at Dien Bien Phu; Geneva Accords signed in Paris

1956
Ngo Dinh Diem refuses to participate in nationwide elections in Vietnam

★ An American Story ★

In 1965 the first major battle between American and North Vietnamese soldiers took place in the Ia Drang Valley in South Vietnam. During the battle, a platoon of American soldiers was cut off and surrounded. Lieutenant Joe Marm's platoon was among those sent to rescue the trapped Americans. When his men came under heavy fire, Marm acted quickly: "I told the men to hold their fire. . . . Then I ran forward. . . . That's the principle we use in the infantry, 'Lead by your own example.'" Marm raced across open ground and hurled grenades at the enemy, and although he was shot in the jaw, he managed to kill the troops firing at his men. For his extraordinary bravery, Lieutenant Marm received the Medal of Honor:

❝I feel I'm the recipient of the medal for the many, many brave soldiers whose deeds go unsung. . . [T]he medal is as much theirs as it is mine. It's always tough to get men to go into battle, but we were a tight unit, and there were Americans out there that we were trying to get to. We're all in it together, and we were fighting for each other and for our guys. . . . I had the best soldiers. . . . They were fearless, and they were just great Americans and they're going to go down in history.❞

—quoted in *The Soldiers' Story*

Early American Involvement in Vietnam

In the late 1940s and early 1950s, most Americans knew little about Vietnam. During this time, however, American officials came to view the nation as increasingly important in the campaign to halt the spread of communism.

The Growth of Vietnamese Nationalism When the Japanese seized power in Vietnam during World War II, it was one more example of foreigners ruling the Vietnamese people. China had controlled the region off and on for hundreds of years. From the late 1800s until World War II, France ruled Vietnam and neighboring Laos and Cambodia—a region known collectively as French Indochina.

By the early 1900s, nationalism had become a powerful force in Vietnam. The Vietnamese formed several political parties to push for independence or reform of the French colonial government. One of the leaders of the nationalist movement was Nguyen Tat Thanh—better known by his alias, **Ho Chi Minh,** or "Bringer of Light." He was born in 1890 in central Vietnam. As a young man, Ho Chi Minh taught at a village school. At the age of 21, he sailed for Europe on a French freighter, paying his passage by working in the galley. During his travels abroad, including a stay in the Soviet Union, Ho Chi Minh became an advocate of communism. In 1930 he returned to Southeast Asia, where he helped found the Indochinese Communist Party and worked to overthrow French rule.

Ho Chi Minh's activities made him a wanted man. He fled Indochina and spent several years in exile in the Soviet Union and China. In 1941 he returned to Vietnam. By then Japan had seized control of the country. Ho Chi Minh organized a nationalist group called the **Vietminh.** The group united both Communists and non-Communists in the struggle to expel the Japanese forces. Soon afterward, the United States began sending military aid to the Vietminh.

The United States Supports the French With the Allies' victory over Japan in August 1945, the Japanese surrendered control of Indochina. Ho Chi Minh and his forces quickly announced that Vietnam was an independent nation. He even crafted a Vietnam Declaration of Independence. Archimedes Patti, an American officer stationed in Vietnam at the time, helped the rebel leader write the document. When a translator read aloud the opening—"All men are created equal; they are endowed by their Creator with certain inalienable rights; among these are liberty, life, and the pursuit of happiness"—Patti suddenly sat up, startled, recognizing the words as very similar to the American Declaration of Independence.

Picturing **History**

Rural Economy Most of Vietnam's people live in the country's low-lying fertile lands near the Red River delta in the north and the Mekong River delta in the south. What does the image below suggest about the use of human labor in the country's agricultural economy?

NATIONAL GEOGRAPHIC

Indochina, 1959

CHINA

BURMA 1948

NORTH VIETNAM 1954 Hanoi

LAOS 1954

Vientiane

Rangoon

THAILAND Never a European colony

Bangkok

CAMBODIA 1954

Phnom Penh

SOUTH VIETNAM 1954 Saigon

Gulf of Tonkin

Gulf of Thailand

South China Sea

0   200 miles
0   200 kilometers
Miller Cylindrical projection

1954 Date of independence

Geography *Skills*

1. **Interpreting Maps** What three countries border North and South Vietnam?
2. **Applying Geography Skills** A mountain chain extends nearly 800 miles (1,290 km) from North to South Vietnam. How do you think this terrain aided the Vietnamese guerrillas who were fighting U.S. troops?

66I stopped him and turned to Ho in amazement and asked if he really intended to use it in his declaration. . . . Ho sat back in his chair, his palms together with fingertips touching his lips ever so lightly, as though meditating. Then, with a gentle smile he asked softly, 'Should I not use it?' I felt sheepish and embarrassed. Of course, I answered, why should he not?99

—quoted in *The Perfect War*

France, however, had no intention of seeing Vietnam become independent. Seeking to regain their colonial empire in Southeast Asia, French troops returned to Vietnam in 1946 and drove the Vietminh forces into hiding in the countryside. By 1949 French officials had set up a new government in Vietnam.

The Vietminh fought back against the French-dominated regime and slowly increased their control over large areas of the countryside. As fighting between the two sides escalated, France appealed to the United States for help.

The request put American officials in a difficult position. The United States opposed colonialism. It had pressured the Dutch to give up their empire in Indonesia, and it supported the British decision to give India independence in 1947. In Vietnam, however, the independence movement had become entangled with the Communist movement. American officials did not think France should control Vietnam, but they did not want Vietnam to be Communist either.

Picturing **History**

Nationalist Leader Ho Chi Minh was already involved in fighting for Vietnam's independence when this photograph was taken in 1946. What foreign country was he opposing at that time?

Two events convinced the Truman administration to help France—the fall of China to communism, and the outbreak of the Korean War. Korea, in particular, convinced American officials that the Soviet Union had begun a major push to impose communism on East Asia. Shortly after the Korean War began, Truman authorized a massive program of military aid to French forces fighting in Vietnam.

On taking office in 1953, President Eisenhower continued to support the French military campaign against the Vietminh. By 1954 the United States was paying roughly three-fourths of France's war costs. During a news conference that year, Eisenhower defended United States policy in Vietnam by stressing what became known as the domino theory—the belief that if Vietnam fell to communism, so too would the other nations of Southeast Asia:

66You have a row of dominoes set up, you knock over the first one, and what will happen to the last one is the certainty that it will go over very quickly. . . . Asia, after all, has already lost 450 million of its peoples to the Communist dictatorship, and we simply can't afford greater losses. . . .99

—quoted in *America in Vietnam*

✓ **Reading Check** **Summarizing** Why did Ho Chi Minh lead a resistance movement against France?

The Vietminh Drive Out the French

Despite significant amounts of aid from the United States, the French struggled against the Vietminh, who consistently frustrated the French with hit-and-run and ambush tactics. These are the tactics of guerrillas, irregular troops who usually blend into the civilian population and are often difficult for regular armies to fight. The mounting casualties and the inability of the French to defeat the Vietminh made the war very unpopular in France. Finally, in 1954, the struggle reached a turning point.

TURNING POINT

Defeat at Dien Bien Phu In 1954 the French commander ordered his forces to occupy the mountain town of **Dien Bien Phu.** Seizing the town would interfere with the Vietminh's supply lines and force them into open battle.

Soon afterward, a huge Vietminh force surrounded Dien Bien Phu and began bombarding the town. "Shells rained down on us without stopping like a hailstorm on a fall evening," recalled one

French soldier. "Bunker after bunker, trench after trench collapsed, burying under them men and weapons." On May 7, 1954, the French force at Dien Bien Phu fell to the Vietminh. The defeat convinced the French to make peace and withdraw from Indochina.

Geneva Accords Negotiations to end the conflict were held in Geneva, Switzerland. The **Geneva Accords** temporarily divided Vietnam along the 17th parallel, with Ho Chi Minh and the Vietminh in control of North Vietnam and a pro-Western regime in control of the South. In 1956 elections were to be held to reunite the country under a single government. The Geneva Accords also recognized Cambodia's independence. (Laos had gained independence the previous year.)

Shortly after the Geneva Accords partitioned Vietnam, the French finally left. The United States almost immediately stepped in and became the principal protector of the new government in the South, led by a nationalist leader named **Ngo Dinh Diem** (NOH DIHN deh·EHM). Like Ho Chi Minh, Diem had been educated abroad, but unlike the North Vietnamese leader, Diem was pro-Western and fiercely anti-Communist. A Catholic, he welcomed the roughly one million North Vietnamese Catholics who migrated south to escape Ho Chi Minh's rule.

When the time came in 1956 to hold countrywide elections, as called for by the Geneva Accords, Diem refused. He knew that the Communist-controlled north would not allow genuinely free elections, and that Ho Chi Minh would almost certainly have won as a result. Eisenhower supported Diem and increased American military and economic aid to South Vietnam. In the wake of Diem's actions, tensions between the North and South intensified. The nation seemed headed toward civil war, with the United States caught in the middle of it.

Picturing **History**

Last Stand French troops assemble a tank near the Dien Bien Phu airfield shortly before their defeat by the Vietminh. How did this defeat influence French policy in Indochina?

✓ **Reading Check** **Examining** What was the effect of the French defeat at Dien Bien Phu?

SECTION 1 ASSESSMENT

Checking for Understanding

1. **Define:** domino theory, guerrilla.
2. **Identify:** Ho Chi Minh, Dien Bien Phu, Ngo Dinh Diem.
3. **Explain** the goals of the Vietminh.

Reviewing Themes

4. **Government and Democracy** Why did Ngo Dinh Diem refuse to hold country-wide elections in Vietnam in 1956?

Critical Thinking

5. **Interpreting** Why do you think the United States supported the government of Ngo Dinh Diem?
6. **Organizing** Use a graphic organizer like the one below to list provisions of the Geneva Accords.

Geneva Accords Provisions

Analyzing Visuals

7. **Analyzing Photographs** Study the Vietnam scene on page 893. How would you describe the contrast between American and Vietnamese societies? How do you think this contrast influenced American thinking toward the war?

Writing About History

8. **Descriptive Writing** Take on the role of a Vietnamese peasant in the 1940s. Write a journal entry on your feelings toward the French.

Going to War in Vietnam

Guide to Reading

Main Idea
After providing South Vietnam with much aid and support, the United States finally sent in troops to fight as well.

Key Terms and Names
Vietcong, Gulf of Tonkin Resolution, napalm, Agent Orange, Ho Chi Minh trail

Reading Strategy
Taking Notes As you read about the beginnings of the Vietnam War, use the major headings of the section to create an outline similar to the one below.

Going to War in Vietnam
I. American Involvement Deepens
   A.
   B.
II.
   A.
   B.

Reading Objectives
- **Describe** how President Johnson deepened American involvement in Vietnam.
- **Discuss** how the Vietcong and the North Vietnamese were able to frustrate the American military.

Section Theme
Science and Technology American military procedures differed significantly from those of the Vietcong troops.

Preview of Events

| ◆1963 | ◆1964 | ◆1965 | ◆1966 |

1963
Number of American military advisers in South Vietnam reaches around 15,000

1964
Congress passes Gulf of Tonkin Resolution

1965
The United States begins bombing North Vietnam; first American combat troops arrive in Vietnam

★ An American Story ★

Marlene Kramel joined the Army Nurse Corps in 1965 when she was 21, and she went to Vietnam the following year. She was working in a makeshift hospital on what was a particularly quiet night. Most of the patients who filled the beds that evening were suffering from malaria.

Suddenly, a row of helicopters roared in from over the horizon, carrying wounded from a nearby battle. As the casualties came in on stretchers, the hospital turned chaotic. Doctors ran about the facility screaming orders and frantically trying to treat patients.

The only nurse on duty at the time, Kramel felt overwhelmed by the confusion. "Every one of the doctors is yelling for me," she recalled. "I didn't know what to do next. 'Start this. Do that.' Everybody's yelling at me. I couldn't do enough." Things happened so quickly that night, she insisted, that she could not remember most of it. "I can't remember blood, even. I can only remember, 'What am I going to do?' And the doctors moving at tremendous speed. And I'm there. And I'm not able to move fast enough. . . . That's all I remember."

—adapted from *The Living and the Dead*

American Involvement Deepens

The steps that led to the chaos and casualties Marlene Kramel experienced in 1966 began in the mid-1950s when American officials decided to support the government of South Vietnam in its struggle against North Vietnam. After Ngo Dinh Diem refused to hold national elections, Ho Chi Minh and his followers began an armed struggle to reunify the nation. They organized a new guerrilla army, which became known as the Vietcong. As fighting began between the Vietcong and South Vietnam's forces, President Eisenhower increased American aid, and sent hundreds of military advisers to train South Vietnam's army.

Despite the American assistance, the Vietcong continued to grow more powerful, in part because many Vietnamese opposed Diem's government, and in part because of the Vietcong's use of terror. By 1961 the Vietcong had assassinated thousands of government officials and established control over much of the countryside. In response Diem looked increasingly to the United States to keep South Vietnam from collapsing.

Kennedy Takes Over On taking office in 1961, President Kennedy continued the nation's policy of support for South Vietnam. Like presidents Truman and Eisenhower before him, Kennedy saw the Southeast Asian country as vitally important in the battle against communism.

In political terms, Kennedy needed to appear tough on communism, since Republicans often accused Democrats of having lost China to communism during the Truman administration. Kennedy's administration sharply increased military aid and sent more advisers to Vietnam. From 1961 to late 1963, the number of American military personnel in South Vietnam jumped from about 2,000 to around 15,000.

American officials believed the Vietcong continued to grow because Diem's government was unpopular and corrupt. They urged him to create a more democratic government and to introduce reforms to help Vietnam's peasants. Diem introduced some limited reforms, but they had little effect.

One program Diem introduced, at the urging of American advisers, made the situation worse. The South Vietnamese created special fortified villages, known as **strategic hamlets.** These villages were protected by machine guns, bunkers, trenches, and barbed wire. Vietnamese officials then moved villagers to the

Picturing History

Self-Immolation On June 11, 1963, flames erupted around a Buddhist monk as he set himself on fire to protest government religious policies. What policies did Ngo Dinh Diem take toward Buddhism?

strategic hamlets, partly to protect them from the Vietcong, and partly to prevent them from giving aid to the Vietcong. The program proved to be extremely unpopular. Many peasants resented being uprooted from their villages, where they had worked to build farms and where many of their ancestors lay buried.

The Overthrow of Diem Diem made himself even more unpopular by discriminating against Buddhism, one of the country's most widely practiced religions. In the spring of 1963, Diem, a Catholic, banned the traditional religious flags for Buddha's birthday. When Buddhists took to the streets in protest, Diem's police killed 9 people and injured 14 others. In the demonstrations that followed, a Buddhist monk set himself on fire, the first of several to do so. The photograph of his self-destruction appeared on television and on the front pages of newspapers around the world. It was a stark symbol of the opposition to Diem.

In August 1963, American ambassador Henry Cabot Lodge arrived in Vietnam. He quickly learned that Diem's unpopularity had so alarmed several Vietnamese generals that they were plotting to overthrow him. When Lodge expressed American sympathy for their cause, the generals launched a military coup. They seized power on November 1, 1963, and executed Diem shortly afterward.

Diem's overthrow only made matters worse. Despite his unpopularity with some Vietnamese, Diem had been a respected nationalist and a capable administrator. After his death, South Vietnam's government grew increasingly weak and unstable. The United States became even more deeply involved in order to prop up the weak South Vietnamese government. Coincidentally, three weeks after Diem's death, President Kennedy was also assassinated. The presidency, as well as the growing problem of Vietnam, now belonged to Kennedy's vice president, Lyndon Johnson.

Reading Check **Examining** What was the main goal of the Vietcong?

Johnson and Vietnam

Initially President Johnson exercised caution and restraint regarding the conflict in Vietnam. "We seek no wider war," he repeatedly promised. At the same time, Johnson was determined to prevent South Vietnam from becoming Communist. "The battle against communism," he declared shortly before becoming president, "must be joined . . . with strength and determination."

Politics also played a role in Johnson's Vietnam policy. Like Kennedy, Johnson remembered that many Republicans blamed the Truman administration for the fall of China to communism in 1949. Should the Democrats also "lose" Vietnam, Johnson feared, it might cause a "mean and destructive debate that would shatter my Presidency, kill my administration, and damage our democracy."

TURNING POINT

The Gulf of Tonkin Resolution On August 2, 1964, President Johnson announced that North Vietnamese torpedo boats had fired on two American destroyers in the Gulf of Tonkin. Two days later, the president reported that another similar attack had taken place. Johnson was campaigning for the presidency and was very sensitive to accusations of being soft on communism. He insisted that North Vietnam's attacks were unprovoked and immediately ordered American aircraft to attack North Vietnamese ships and naval facilities. Johnson

Different Viewpoints

The Vietnam War

As the war in Vietnam dragged on, a clear division of American opinion emerged. In January 1966, George W. Ball, undersecretary of state to President Johnson, delivered an address to indicate "how we got [to Vietnam] and why we must stay." George F. Kennan, former ambassador to Russia, testified before the Senate Foreign Relations Committee that same year, arguing that American involvement in Vietnam was "something we would not choose deliberately if the choice were ours to make all over again today."

George W. Ball:

"[T]he conflict in Vietnam is a product of the great shifts and changes triggered by the Second World War. Out of the war, two continent-wide powers emerged—the United States and the Soviet Union. The colonial systems through which the nations of Western Europe had governed more than a third of the people of the world were, one by one, dismantled.

. . . [E]ven while the new national boundaries were still being marked on the map, the Soviet Union under Stalin exploited the confusion to push out the perimeter of its power and influence in an effort to extend the outer limits of Communist domination by force or the threat of force.

The bloody encounters in [Vietnam] are thus in a real sense battles and skirmishes in a continuing war to prevent one Communist power after another from violating internationally recognized boundary lines fixing the outer limits of Communist dominion.

. . . The evidence shows clearly enough that, at the time of French withdrawal . . . the Communist regime in Hanoi never intended that South Vietnam should develop in freedom.

. . . In the long run our hopes for the people of South Vietnam reflect our hopes for people everywhere. What we seek is a world living in peace and freedom."

did not reveal that the American warships had been helping the South Vietnamese conduct electronic spying and commando raids against North Vietnam.

Johnson then asked Congress to authorize the use of force to defend American forces. Congress agreed to Johnson's request with little debate. Most members of Congress agreed with Republican Representative Ross Adair of Indiana, who defiantly declared, "The American flag has been fired upon. We will not and cannot tolerate such things."

On August 7, 1964, the Senate and House passed the **Gulf of Tonkin Resolution,** authorizing the president to "take all necessary measures to repel any armed attack against the forces of the United States and to prevent further aggression." With only two dissenting votes, Congress had, in effect, handed its war powers over to the president. 📖 *(See page 1079 for more on the Gulf of Tonkin Resolution.)*

The United States Sends in Troops Shortly after Congress passed the Gulf of Tonkin Resolution, the Vietcong began to attack bases where American advisers were stationed in South Vietnam. The attacks began in the fall of 1964 and continued to escalate. After a Vietcong attack on a base at Pleiku in February 1965 left 7 Americans dead and more than 100 wounded, President Johnson decided to respond. Less than 14 hours after the attack, American aircraft assaulted North Vietnam.

After the airstrikes, one poll showed that Johnson's approval rating on his handling of Vietnam jumped from 41 percent to 60 percent. The president's actions also met with strong approval from his closest advisers, including Secretary of Defense **Robert McNamara** and National Security Adviser **McGeorge Bundy.**

There were some dissenters in the White House, chief among them Undersecretary of State George Ball, a long-time critic of U.S. policy in Vietnam. He warned that if the United States got too deeply involved in Vietnam, it might become difficult to get out. "Once on the tiger's back," he warned, "we cannot be sure of picking the place to dismount."

Most of the advisers who surrounded Johnson, however, firmly believed the nation had a duty to halt communism in Vietnam, both to maintain stability in Southeast Asia and to ensure the United States's continuing power and prestige in the world. In a memo to the president, Bundy argued:

> ❝The stakes in Vietnam are extremely high. The American investment is very large, and American responsibility is a fact of life which is palpable in the atmosphere of Asia, and even elsewhere. The international prestige of the U.S. and a substantial part of our influence are directly at risk in Vietnam.❞
>
> —quoted in *The Best and the Brightest*

In March 1965, Johnson expanded American involvement by shifting his policy to a sustained bombing campaign against North Vietnam. The campaign was named **Operation Rolling Thunder.** That month the president also ordered the first combat troops into Vietnam. American soldiers were now fighting alongside the South Vietnamese troops against the Vietcong.

✓ **Reading Check** **Describing** How did politics play a role in President Johnson's Vietnam policy?

A Bloody Stalemate Emerges

By the end of 1965, more than 180,000 American combat troops were fighting in Vietnam. In 1966 that number doubled. Since the American military was

---

George F. Kennan:

"Vietnam is not a region of major military and industrial importance. It is difficult to believe that any decisive developments of the world situation would be determined in normal circumstances by what happens on that territory. . . . Even a situation in which South Vietnam was controlled exclusively by the Vietcong, while regrettable . . . would not, in my opinion, present dangers great enough to justify our direct military intervention.

. . . To attempt to crush North Vietnamese strength to a point where [it] could no longer give any support for Vietcong political activity in the South, would . . . have the effect of bringing in Chinese forces at some point.

. . . Our motives are widely misinterpreted, and the spectacle emphasized and reproduced in thousands of press photographs and stories . . . produces reactions among millions of people throughout the world profoundly detrimental to the image we would like them to hold of this country."

Learning From History

1. **Recognizing Ideologies** How do the two speakers assess the value of Vietnam and its people to the United States?
2. **Making Inferences** Why does George Kennan believe that the United States government got involved in Vietnam when it did? How does he feel about this involvement?

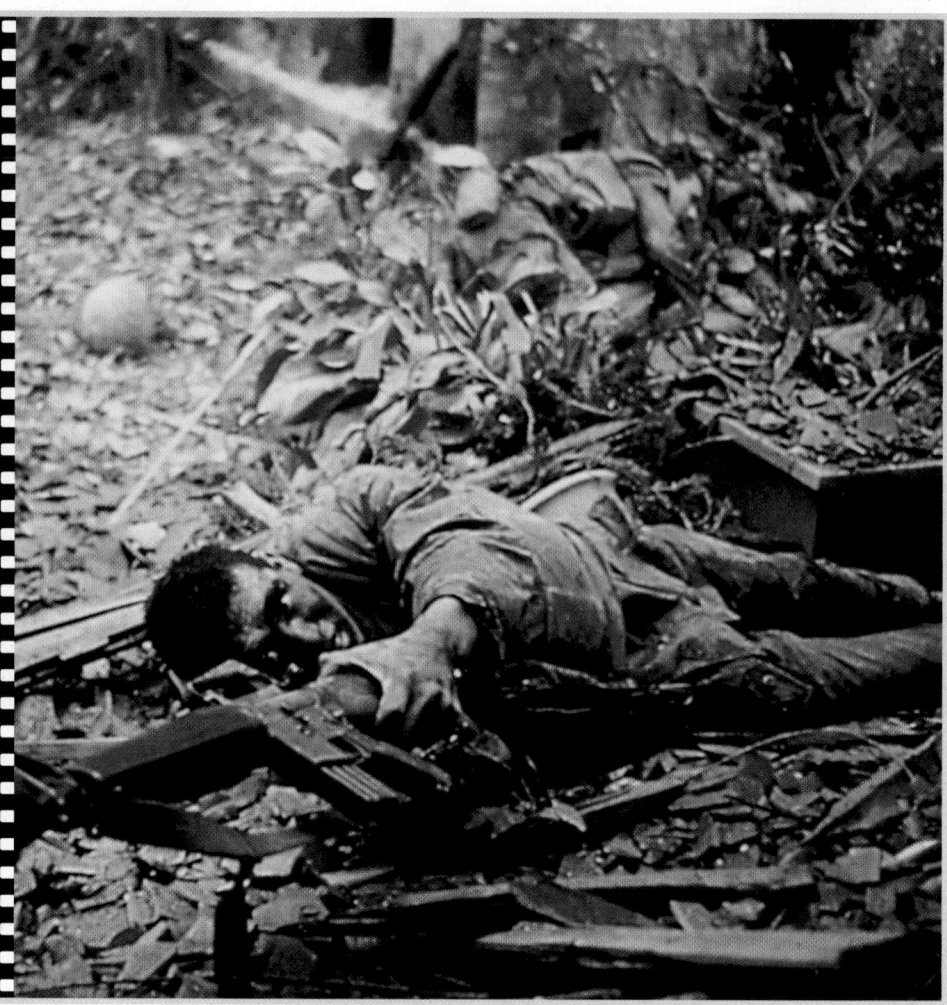

extremely strong, it marched into Vietnam with great confidence. "America seemed omnipotent then," said Philip Caputo, one of the first marines to arrive. "We saw ourselves as the champions of a 'cause that was destined to triumph.'"

Frustrating Warfare Lacking the firepower of the Americans, the Vietcong used ambushes, booby traps, and guerrilla tactics. Ronald J. Glasser, an American army doctor, described the devastating effects of one booby trap:

> 66 Three quarters of the way through the tangle, a trooper brushed against a two-inch vine, and a grenade slung at chest high went off, shattering the right side of his head and body. . . . Nearby troopers took hold of the unconscious soldier and, half carrying, half dragging him, pulled him the rest of the way through the tangle. 99
>
> —quoted in *Vietnam, A History*

The Vietcong also frustrated American troops by blending in with the general population in the cities and the countryside and then quickly vanishing. "It was a sheer physical impossibility to keep the enemy from slipping away whenever he wished," one American general said. Journalist Linda Martin noted, "It's a war where nothing is ever quite certain and nowhere is ever quite safe."

To counter the Vietcong's tactics, American troops went on "search and destroy" missions. They tried to find enemy troops, bomb their positions, destroy their supply lines, and force them out into the open for combat.

American forces also sought to take away the Vietcong's ability to hide in the thick jungles by literally destroying the landscape. American planes dropped napalm, a jellied gasoline that explodes on contact. They also used **Agent Orange,** a chemical that strips leaves from trees and shrubs, turning farmland and forest into wasteland.

A Determined Enemy United States military leaders underestimated the Vietcong's strength. They also misjudged the enemy's stamina. American generals believed that continuously bombing and killing large numbers of Vietcong would destroy the enemy's morale and force them to give up. The guerrillas, however, had no intention of surrendering, and they were willing to accept huge losses in human lives.

In the Vietcong's war effort, North Vietnamese support was a major factor. Although the Vietcong forces were made up of many South Vietnamese, North Vietnam provided arms, advisers, and significant leadership. Later in the war, as Vietcong casualties mounted, North Vietnam began sending regular North Vietnamese Army units to fight in South Vietnam.

North Vietnam sent arms and supplies south by way of a network of jungle paths known as the **Ho Chi Minh trail.** The trail wound through the countries of Cambodia and Laos, bypassing the border between North and South Vietnam. Because the trail passed through countries not directly involved in the war, President Johnson refused to allow a full-scale attack on the trail to shut it down.

North Vietnam itself received military weapons and other support from the Soviet Union and China. One of the main reasons President Johnson refused to order a full-scale invasion of North Vietnam was his fear that such an attack would bring China into the war, as had happened in Korea. By placing limits on the war, however, Johnson made it very difficult to win. Instead of conquering enemy territory, American troops were forced to fight a war of attrition—a strategy of defeating the enemy forces by slowly wearing them down. This strategy led troops to conduct grisly body counts after battles to determine how many enemy soldiers had been killed.

Bombing from American planes killed as many as 220,000 Vietnamese between 1965 and 1967. Nevertheless, the Vietcong and North Vietnamese troops showed no sign of surrendering. Meanwhile, American

casualties continued to mount. By the end of 1966, more than 6,700 American soldiers had been killed.

As the number of Americans killed and wounded continued to grow, the notion of a quick and decisive victory grew increasingly remote. As a result, many citizens back home began to question the nation's involvement in the war.

Reading Check **Describing** What tactics did the United States adopt to fight the Vietcong?

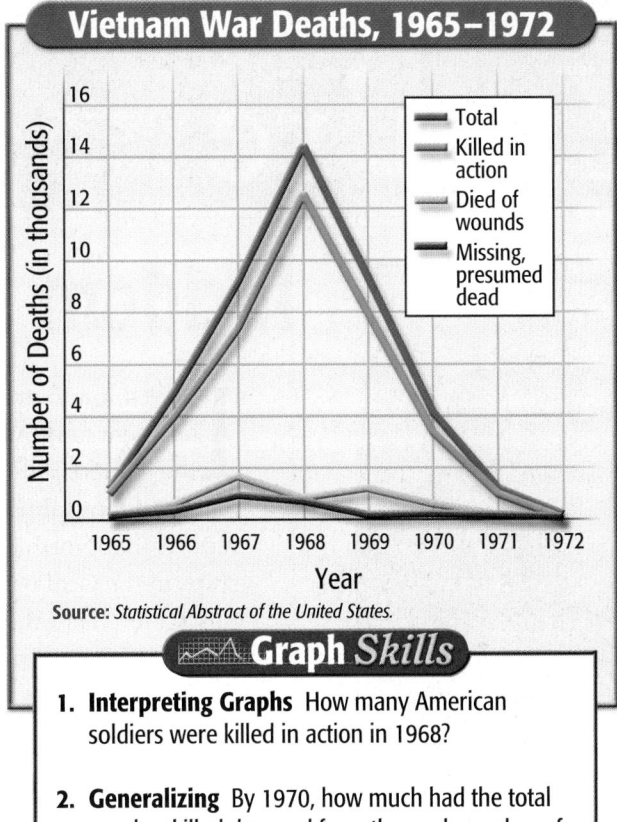

Vietnam War Deaths, 1965–1972

Number of Deaths (in thousands) vs. Year (1965–1972)

Legend:
- Total
- Killed in action
- Died of wounds
- Missing, presumed dead

Source: *Statistical Abstract of the United States.*

Graph *Skills*

1. **Interpreting Graphs** How many American soldiers were killed in action in 1968?

2. **Generalizing** By 1970, how much had the total number killed dropped from the peak number of deaths in 1968?

SECTION 2 ASSESSMENT

Checking for Understanding

1. **Define:** Vietcong, napalm.
2. **Identify:** Gulf of Tonkin Resolution, Agent Orange, Ho Chi Minh trail.
3. **Explain** how the Gulf of Tonkin Resolution affected the powers of Congress and the presidency.

Reviewing Themes

4. **Science and Technology** Why did the United States use napalm and Agent Orange in its fight against the Vietcong?

Critical Thinking

5. **Analyzing** Why did fighting in Vietnam turn into a stalemate by the mid-1960s?
6. **Sequencing** Complete a time line similar to the one below to fill in events leading to American involvement in Vietnam.

August 1963 — November 1, 1963 — August 2, 1964

August 7, 1964 — February 1965 — March 1965

Analyzing Visuals

7. **Analyzing Photographs** Look closely at the photograph on page 897 of Buddhist monk Reverend Quang Duc. What in it suggests that this event was planned by Buddhists to protest their treatment in South Vietnam?

Writing About History

8. **Persuasive Writing** Imagine that you are a member of Congress in August 1964. Write a statement supporting or opposing the Gulf of Tonkin Resolution.

Incident in the Gulf of Tonkin

President Lyndon Johnson

I n 1964 the Vietcong in South Vietnam were trying to topple the government and unite the country under communism. To prevent this, the United States had already committed money, supplies, and advisers. President Johnson asked Congress to authorize using force after reports that North Vietnam had made unprovoked attacks on U.S. warships in the Gulf of Tonkin. Congress responded with the Gulf of Tonkin Resolution. Had the warship USS *Maddox* provoked the attack? Was Johnson fully informed of events in the Gulf? You're the historian.

Read the following excerpts, then answer the questions and complete the activities that follow.

From accounts of an unprovoked attack

The sources advising President Johnson on the Gulf of Tonkin incident included the navy and the Defense Department. These excerpts suggest how difficult it was to know what had happened—and also how tension influenced the American interpretation.

U.S. Navy Commander John Herrick of the USS *Maddox:*
I am being approached by high-speed craft with apparent intention of torpedo attack. I intend to open fire in self-defense if necessary.

—from a cable of August 2, 1964

U.S. Defense Department:
While on routine patrol in international waters . . . the U.S. destroyer *Maddox* underwent an unprovoked attack by three PT-type boats in . . . the Tonkin Gulf.

The attacking boats launched three torpedoes and used 37-millimeter gunfire. The *Maddox* answered

with 5-inch gunfire. . . . The PT boats were driven off, with one seen to be badly damaged and not moving. . . .

No casualties or damage were sustained by the *Maddox* or the aircraft.

—from a press release of August 2, 1964

National Security Council Meeting:
Secretary McNamara: The North Vietnamese PT boats have continued their attacks on the two U.S. destroyers in international waters in the Gulf of Tonkin. . . .

Secretary Rusk: An immediate and direct action by us is necessary. The unprovoked attack on the high seas is an act of war for all practical purposes. . . .

CIA Director McCone: The proposed U.S. reprisals will result in sharp North Vietnamese military action, but such actions would not represent a deliberate

decision to provoke or accept a major escalation of the Vietnamese war.

President Johnson: Do they want a war by attacking our ships in the middle of the Gulf of Tonkin?

U.S. Intelligence Agency Director Rowan: Do we know for a fact that the North Vietnamese provocation took place?

Secretary McNamara: We will know definitely in the morning.

—August 2, 1964

Secretary Rusk:
We believe that present OPLAN 34-A activities are beginning to rattle Hanoi [capital of North Vietnam], and the *Maddox* incident is directly related to their effort to resist these activities. We have no intention of yielding to pressure.

—from a top secret telegram to Ambassador Maxwell Taylor (South Vietnam), August 3, 1964

From accounts of a possible mistake

Two days after the alleged attack, the Turner Joy *joined the* Maddox *in the Gulf. On the night of August 4, 1964, the two destroyers experienced a series of events they interpreted as a second attack. However, Commander Herrick later revised this report. President Johnson referred to the "repeated" attacks later when he asked Congress for war powers.*

Commander Herrick:

Review of action makes many contacts and torpedoes fired appear doubtful. Freak weather effects on radar and overeager sonarmen may have accounted for many reports. No actual visual sightings by *Maddox*. Suggest complete evaluation before any further action. . . .

Turner Joy also reports no actual visual sightings or wake. . . . Entire action leaves many doubts except for apparent attempt to ambush at beginning.

—from two cables of August 4, 1964

President Johnson:

The initial attack on the destroyer *Maddox*, on August 2, was repeated today by a number of hostile vessels attacking two U.S. destroyers with torpedoes. The destroyers and supporting aircraft acted at once on the orders I gave after the initial act of aggression. . . . Repeated acts of violence against the Armed Forces of the United States must be met not only with alert defense, but with positive reply.

—in a television and radio address, August 4, 1964

In 1968 Senator William Fulbright opened an investigation into the 1964 Gulf of Tonkin incident. The following exchange took place between Senator Fulbright and Secretary McNamara.

Secretary McNamara: I don't believe Commander Herrick in his cable stated that he had doubt that the attack took place. He questioned certain details of the attack. . . . Secondly, his doubts were resolved that afternoon before the retaliatory action was taken.

Senator Fulbright: I think he went further than that. He advised you not to do anything until it had been reevaluated. . . . It is a very strong statement.

Secretary McNamara: Nothing was done until it was reevaluated.

Senator Fulbright: He says "Suggest complete reevaluation before any further action." Now that is a very strong recommendation from a man on the scene in charge of the operation. . . . Both committees, except for the Senator from Oregon [Morse], unanimously accepted your testimony then as the whole story, and I must say this raises very serious questions about how you make decisions to go to war.

Understanding the Issue

1. What statement by Rusk suggests the United States may have provoked the attack on the *Maddox?*
2. Do you think President Johnson was misled by his advisers? Explain.
3. How soon after the alleged attacks did the president address the American people? Did the United States rush to judgment in this case? Explain.

Activities

1. **Investigate** What were the conclusions of the Fulbright investigations into the Gulf of Tonkin incident? Check sources, including the Internet.
2. **Discuss** Research and review American decisions to go to war in 1898, 1917, and 1941. What were the concerns? Do you think the nation made the right decisions?

Vietcong guerrillas

Vietnam Divides the Nation

Main Idea

The experience of Vietnam produced sharp divisions between Americans who supported the war and those who did not.

Key Terms and Names

William Westmoreland, credibility gap, teach-in, dove, hawk, Tet offensive

Reading Strategy

Organizing As you read about Americans' reactions to the Vietnam War, complete a graphic organizer like the one below to list the reasons for opposition to the war.

Reasons for Opposition to Vietnam War

Reading Objective

• **Analyze** why support for the war began to weaken.
• **Describe** the motives of those in the antiwar movement.

Section Theme

Civic Rights and Responsibilities Many Americans protested their country's involvement in the Vietnam War.

Preview of Events

♦1965 ♦1966 ♦1967 ♦1968

1965
Teach-ins on college campuses begin

1966
Senate Foreign Relations Committee begins Vietnam hearings

1967
March on the Pentagon

January 1968
Tet offensive

★ An American Story ★

Martin Jezer, a 27-year-old copywriter living in New York City, had never considered himself a radical. "I campaigned for Lyndon Johnson in 1964," he recalled. As his opposition to the war in Vietnam grew, however, Jezer decided to stage a public protest.

On April 15, 1967, he and dozens of other young men gathered with their military draft cards in New York's Central Park. Before an audience of reporters, photographers, FBI officials, and citizens, the men pulled out matches and lighters and burned the cards.

❝We began singing freedom songs and chanting, 'Resist! Resist!' and 'Burn Draft Cards, Not People'. . . . People in the audience were applauding us, shouting encouragement. Then some guys began to come out of the audience with draft cards in hand. They burned them. Alone, in pairs, by threes they came. Each flaming draft card brought renewed cheering and more people out of the crowd. . . . Some of the draft card burners were girls, wives, or girlfriends of male card burners. . . . It lasted this way for about half an hour.❞

—**quoted in *The Vietnam War: Opposing Viewpoints***

A Growing Credibility Gap

Jezer's protest was just one of many, as American opposition to the Vietnam War grew in the late 1960s. When American troops first entered the Vietnam War in the spring of 1965, many Americans had supported the military effort. A Gallup poll published around that time showed that 66 percent of Americans approved of the policy in Vietnam. As the war dragged on, however, public support began to drop. Suspicion of the government's truthfulness about the war was a significant reason. Throughout the early years of the war, the American commander in South Vietnam, General **William Westmoreland,** reported that the enemy was on the brink of defeat. In 1967 he confidently declared that the "enemy's hopes are bankrupt" and added, "we have reached an important point where the end begins to come into view."

Contradicting such reports were less optimistic media accounts, especially on television. Vietnam was the first "television war," with footage of combat appearing nightly on the evening news. Day after day, millions of people saw images of wounded and dead Americans and began to doubt government reports. In the view of many, a credibility gap had developed, meaning it was hard to believe what the Johnson administration said about the war.

Congress, which had given the president a nearly free hand in Vietnam, soon grew uncertain about the war. Beginning in February 1966, the Senate Foreign Relations Committee held "educational" hearings on Vietnam, calling in Secretary of State **Dean Rusk** and other policy makers to explain the administration's war program. The committee also listened to critics such as American diplomat George Kennan. Although Kennan had helped create the policy of containment, he argued that Vietnam was not strategically important to the United States.

Reading Check **Explaining** Why was the Vietnam War the first "television war"?

An Antiwar Movement Emerges

As casualties mounted in Vietnam, many people began to protest publicly against the war and to demand that the United States pull out. Although many other Americans supported the war, opponents of the conflict received the most attention.

Teach-Ins Begin In March 1965, a group of faculty members and students at the University of Michigan abandoned their classes and joined together in a teach-in. Here, they informally discussed the issues surrounding the war and reaffirmed their reasons for opposing it. The gathering inspired teach-ins at many campuses. In May 1965, 122 colleges held a "National Teach-In" by radio for more than 100,000 antiwar demonstrators.

People who opposed the war did so for different reasons. Some saw the conflict as a civil war in which the United States had no business. Others viewed South Vietnam as a corrupt dictatorship and insisted that defending that country was immoral and unjust.

Anger at the Draft Young protesters especially focused on what they saw as an unfair draft system. At the beginning of the war, a college student was often able to defer military service until after graduation. By contrast, young people from low-income families were more likely to be sent to Vietnam because they were unable to afford college. This meant minorities, particularly African Americans, made up a disproportionately large number of the soldiers in Vietnam. By 1967, for example, African Americans accounted for about 20 percent of American combat deaths—about twice their proportion of the population within the United States. That number would decline to roughly match their population proportion by the war's end.

 Analyzing *Political Cartoons*

Dark Passage One particular phrase came to represent the government's claims that it was on the verge of ending the Vietnam War: "the light at the end of the tunnel." Why did many people become skeptical about such government claims?

Picturing **History**

Flower Power Student antiwar protests ranged from violent confrontation to this peaceful but dramatic demonstration near the Pentagon in Washington, D.C. What were some reasons many people opposed the war?

The high number of African Americans and poor Americans dying in Vietnam angered African American leaders, including Dr. Martin Luther King, Jr. Early on, King had refrained from speaking out against the war for fear that it would draw attention from the civil rights movement. In April 1967, however, he broke his silence and publicly condemned the conflict:

66Somehow this madness must cease. I speak as a child of God and brother to the suffering poor of Vietnam and the poor of America who are paying the double price of smashed hopes at home and death and corruption in Vietnam. I speak as a citizen of the world, for the world as it stands aghast at the path we have taken. I speak as an American to the leader of my own nation. The great initiative in this war is ours. The initiative to stop must be ours.99

—quoted in *A Testament of Hope*

As the war escalated, American officials increased the draft call, putting many college students at risk. An estimated 500,000 draftees refused to go. Many publicly burned their draft cards or simply did not

report when called for induction. Some fled the country, moving to Canada, Sweden, or other nations. Others stayed and went to prison rather than fight in a war they opposed.

Between 1965 and 1968, officials prosecuted more than 3,300 Americans for refusing to serve. The draft became less of an issue in 1969 when the government introduced a lottery system, in which only those with low lottery numbers were subject to the draft.

Protests against the war were not confined to college campuses. Demonstrators held public rallies and marches in towns across the country. In April 1965, Students for a Democratic Society (SDS), a left-wing student organization, organized a march on Washington, D.C., that drew more than 20,000 participants. Two years later, in October 1967, a rally at Washington's Lincoln Memorial drew tens of thousands of protesters as well.

Anger over the draft also fueled discussions of voting age. Many draftees argued that if they were old enough to fight, they were old enough to vote. In 1971 the Twenty-sixth Amendment to the Constitution was ratified, giving all citizens age 18 and older the right to vote in all state and federal elections.

Hawks and Doves In the face of growing opposition to the war, President Johnson remained determined to continue fighting. He assailed his critics in Congress as "selfish men who want to advance their own interests." As for the college protesters, Johnson viewed them as naive and unable to appreciate the importance of resisting communism.

The president was not alone in his views. Although the antiwar protesters became a vocal group, they did not represent majority opinion on Vietnam. In a poll taken in early 1968, 53 percent of the respondents favored stronger military action in Vietnam, compared to only 24 percent who wanted an end to the war. Of those Americans who supported the policy in Vietnam, many openly criticized the protesters for a lack of patriotism.

By 1968 the nation seemed to be divided into two camps. Those who wanted the United States to withdraw from Vietnam were known as doves. Those who insisted that the United States stay and fight came to be known as hawks. As the two groups debated, the war took a dramatic turn for the worse, and the nation endured a year of shock and crisis.

✓ **Reading Check** **Explaining** What led to the passage of the Twenty-sixth Amendment?

1968: The Pivotal Year

The most turbulent year of the chaotic 1960s was 1968. The year saw a shocking political announcement, a pair of traumatic assassinations, and a violent political convention. First, however, the nation endured a surprise attack in Vietnam.

TURNING POINT

The Tet Offensive On January 30, 1968, during Tet, the Vietnamese New Year, the Vietcong and North Vietnamese launched a massive surprise attack. In this **Tet offensive,** the guerrilla fighters attacked virtually all American airbases in South Vietnam and most of the South's major cities and provincial capitals. Vietcong commandos even blasted their way into the American embassy in Saigon.

Militarily, Tet turned out to be a disaster for the Communist forces. After about a month of fighting, the American and South Vietnamese soldiers repelled the enemy troops, inflicting heavy losses on them. General Westmoreland boasted that the Communists' "well-laid plans went afoul," while President Johnson triumphantly added that the enemy's effort had ended in "complete failure."

In fact, the North Vietnamese had scored a major political victory. The American people were shocked that an enemy supposedly on the verge of defeat could launch such a large-scale attack. When General Westmoreland requested 209,000 troops in addition to the 500,000 already in Vietnam, it seemed to be an admission that the United States could not win the war.

To make matters worse, the mainstream media, which had tried to remain balanced in their war coverage, now openly criticized the effort. "The American people should be getting ready to accept, if they haven't already, the prospect that the whole Vietnam effort may be doomed," the *Wall Street Journal* declared. Walter Cronkite, then the nation's most respected television newscaster, announced after Tet that it seemed "more certain than ever that the bloody experience in Vietnam is to end in a stalemate."

Public opinion no longer favored the president. In the weeks following the Tet offensive, the president's approval rating plummeted to a dismal 35 percent, while support for his handling of the war fell even lower, to 26 percent. The administration's credibility gap now seemed too wide to repair.

Johnson Leaves the Presidential Race With the war growing increasingly unpopular and Johnson's credibility all but gone, some Democrats began looking for an alternative candidate to nominate for president in 1968. In November 1967, even before the Tet disaster, a little-known liberal senator from Minnesota, Eugene McCarthy, became the first dove to announce his candidacy against Johnson. In March 1968, McCarthy stunned the nation by winning more than 40 percent of the votes in the New Hampshire primary

| Fact | Fiction | Folklore |

The Peace Symbol This familiar symbol of the 1960s was originally designed to stand for the fight for nuclear disarmament. Created by British artist Gerald Holtom in 1958, the symbol was first used at a British demonstration against a research center for the development of nuclear weapons. It combined the semaphore for the letters "N" and "D," standing for nuclear disarmament. Semaphore is a system of visual signaling using two flags, one held in each hand. N is two flags held in an upside-down V, and D is one flag pointed straight up and the other pointed straight down.

WORK FOR PEACE

CHINA

NORTH VIETNAM
★ Hanoi

Gulf of Tonkin

LAOS

Demilitarized Zone

Khe Sanh
Hue
Da Nang
Hoi An
Chu Lai
Quang Ngai
Kontum
Qui Nhon
Tuy An
Tuy Hoa
Nha Trang
Da Lat
SOUTH VIETNAM
Phan Thiet

THAILAND

Places attacked during Tet offensive
Ho Chi Minh Trail

CAMBODIA

Ban Me Thuot

Bien Hoa
Xuan Loc

American embassy attacked, January 31, 1968

Gulf of Thailand

Saigon
My Tho
Tan An
Can Tho
Ben Tre
Vinh Long

Mekong Delta

South China Sea

0   200 miles
0   200 kilometers
Miller Cylindrical projection

20°N
10°N
110°E

Mekong R.

A view of the U.S. embassy in Saigon after it was bombed during the Tet offensive

Geography Skills

1. **Interpreting Maps** Most of the Ho Chi Minh Trail lies within which countries?
2. **Applying Geography Skills** How broad was the Tet offensive, and why did this shock Americans?

and almost defeating the president. Realizing that Johnson was vulnerable, Senator Robert Kennedy, who also opposed the war, quickly entered the race for the Democratic nomination.

With the division in the country and within his own party growing, Johnson addressed the public on television on March 31, 1968. He stunned viewers by stating, "I have concluded that I should not permit the presidency to become involved in the partisan divisions that are developing in this political year. Accordingly, I shall not seek, and I will not accept, the nomination of my party for another term as your President."

A Season of Violence Following Johnson's announcement, the nation endured even more shocking events. In April James Earl Ray was arrested for killing Dr. Martin Luther King, Jr., an event which led to riots in several major cities. Just two months later, another assassination rocked the country—that of Robert Kennedy. Kennedy, who appeared to be on his way to winning the Democratic nomination, was

gunned down on June 5 in a California hotel just after winning the state's Democratic primary. The assassin was Sirhan Sirhan, an Arab nationalist apparently angry over the candidate's pro-Israeli remarks a few nights before.

The violence that seemed to plague the country at every turn in 1968 culminated with a chaotic and well-publicized clash between protesters and police at the Democratic National Convention in Chicago. Thousands of protesters descended on the August convention, demanding that the Democrats adopt an antiwar platform.

On the third day of the convention, the delegates chose Hubert Humphrey, President Johnson's vice president, as their presidential nominee. Meanwhile, in a park not far from the convention hall, the protesters and police began fighting. A full-scale riot soon engulfed the streets of downtown Chicago. As officers tried to disperse demonstrators with tear gas and billy clubs, demonstrators taunted the authorities with the chant, "The whole world is watching!"

Nixon Wins the Presidency The violence and chaos now associated with the Democratic Party benefited the 1968 Republican presidential candidate, Richard Nixon. Although defeated in the 1960 election, Nixon had remained active in national politics. A third candidate, Governor George Wallace of Alabama, also decided to run in 1968 as an independent. Wallace, an outspoken segregationist, sought to attract those Americans who felt threatened by the civil rights movement and urban social unrest.

Public opinion polls gave Nixon a wide lead over Humphrey and Wallace. Nixon's campaign promise to unify the nation and restore law and order appealed to Americans who feared their country was spinning out of control. Nixon also declared that he had a plan for ending the war in Vietnam, although he did not specify how the plan would work.

At first Humphrey's support of President Johnson's Vietnam policies hurt his campaign. After Humphrey broke with the president and called for a complete end to the bombing of North Vietnam, he began to move up in the polls. A week before the election, President Johnson helped Humphrey by announcing that the bombing of North Vietnam had halted and that a cease-fire would follow.

Johnson's announcement had come too late. In the end, Nixon's promises to end the war and restore order at home were enough to sway the American people. On Election Day, Nixon defeated Humphrey by more than 100 electoral votes, although he won the popular vote by a slim margin of 43 percent to 42. Wallace helped account for the razor-thin margin by winning 46 electoral votes and more than 13 percent of the popular vote.

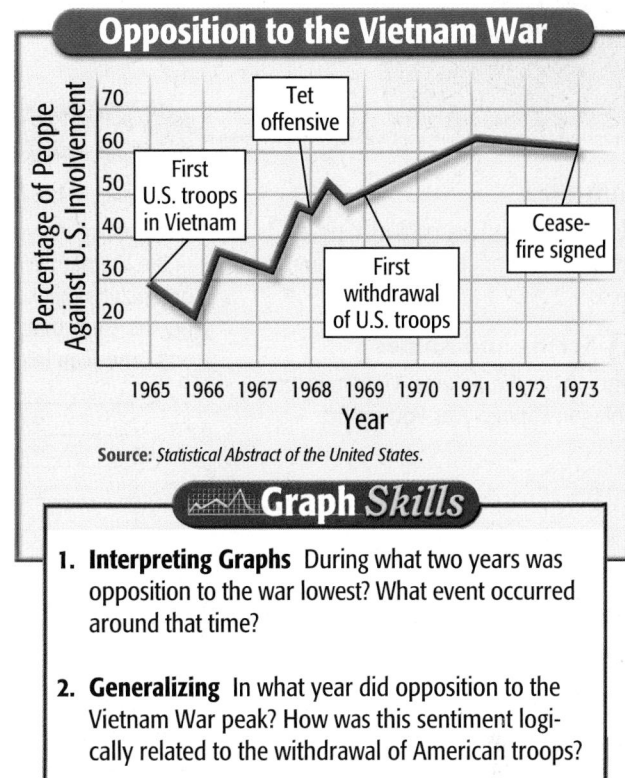

Opposition to the Vietnam War

Tet offensive

First U.S. troops in Vietnam

First withdrawal of U.S. troops

Cease-fire signed

Percentage of People Against U.S. Involvement

1965 1966 1967 1968 1969 1970 1971 1972 1973
Year

Source: *Statistical Abstract of the United States.*

Graph Skills

1. **Interpreting Graphs** During what two years was opposition to the war lowest? What event occurred around that time?

2. **Generalizing** In what year did opposition to the Vietnam War peak? How was this sentiment logically related to the withdrawal of American troops?

Speaking to reporters after his election, Nixon recalled seeing a young girl carrying a sign at one of his rallies that said: "Bring Us Together." This, he promised, would be his chief goal as president. Nixon also vowed to implement his plan to end the Vietnam War.

✓ **Reading Check** **Explaining** Why did President Johnson not run for re-election in 1968?

SECTION 3 ASSESSMENT

Checking for Understanding

1. **Define:** credibility gap, teach-in, dove, hawk.
2. **Identify:** William Westmoreland, Tet offensive.
3. **Summarize** three important events that occurred in 1968.

Reviewing Themes

4. **Civic Rights and Responsibilities** Why did many people believe that the Vietnam War reflected racial and economic injustices in the United States?

Critical Thinking

5. **Synthesizing** Why did support of the Vietnam War begin to dwindle by the late 1960s?
6. **Organizing** Use a graphic organizer similar to the one below to list the effects of the Tet offensive.

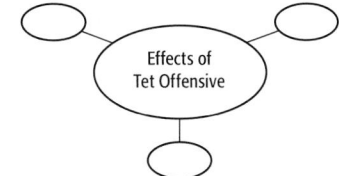

Effects of Tet Offensive

Analyzing Visuals

7. **Analyzing Photographs** Study the photograph on page 906. The phrase "flower power" was a slogan of the hippie movement. Explain what you think the phrase meant and how the slogan was used to express opposition to the war.

Writing About History

8. **Expository Writing** Imagine that you are living in 1968. Write a paragraph for the local newspaper in which you explain your reasons for either supporting or opposing the Vietnam War.

Main Idea

After nearly eight years of fighting in Vietnam, the United States withdrew its forces.

Key Terms and Names

Henry Kissinger, linkage, Vietnamization, Pentagon Papers, War Powers Act

Reading Strategy

Organizing As you read about the end of the Vietnam War, complete a graphic organizer similar to the one below by listing the steps that President Nixon took to end American involvement in Vietnam.

Steps Nixon Took

Reading Objectives

- **Explain** the events of Nixon's first administration that inspired more antiwar protests.
- **Summarize** the major lessons the United States learned from the Vietnam War experience.

Section Theme

Government and Democracy The Vietnam War led to changes in the way the U.S. military is deployed.

Preview of Events

♦1969   ♦1971   ♦1973   ♦1975

1969
Secret peace negotiations between the U.S. and North Vietnam begin

1972
Nixon initiates Christmas bombings

1973
Cease-fire signed

1975
Evacuation of the last Americans from Vietnam

★ An American Story ★

On the evening of April 29, 1975, Frank Snepp, a young CIA officer, scrambled up to the American embassy rooftop to catch one of the last helicopters out of Saigon. Throughout that day, Snepp had witnessed the desperation of the South Vietnamese people as they besieged the embassy grounds in an to effort escape the approaching Communist army. Now he was leaving. Later, he recalled the scene:

❝The roof of the Embassy was a vision out of a nightmare. In the center of the dimly lit helo-pad a CH-47 was already waiting for us, its engines setting up a roar like a primeval scream. The crew and controllers all wore what looked like oversized football helmets, and in the blinking under-light of the landing signals they reminded me of grotesque insects rearing on their hindquarters. Out beyond the edge of the building a Phantom jet streaked across the horizon as tracers darted up here and there into the night sky.❞

—quoted in *Decent Interval*

Nixon Moves to End the War

Frank Snepp was one of the last Americans to leave Vietnam. Shortly after taking office, President Nixon had taken steps to end the nation's involvement in the war, but the final years of the conflict would yield much more bloodshed and turmoil.

As a first step, Nixon appointed Harvard professor **Henry Kissinger** as special assistant for national security affairs and gave him wide authority to use diplomacy to end the conflict. Kissinger embarked upon a policy he called linkage, which meant improving relations with the Soviet Union and China—suppliers of aid to North Vietnam—so he could persuade them to cut back on their aid.

Kissinger also rekindled peace talks with the North Vietnamese. In August 1969, Kissinger entered into secret negotiations with North Vietnam's negotiator, Le Duc Tho. In their talks, which dragged on for four years, Kissinger and Le Duc Tho argued over a possible cease-fire, the return of American prisoners of war, and the ultimate fate of South Vietnam.

Meanwhile, Nixon cut back the number of American troops in Vietnam. Known as Vietnamization, this process involved the gradual withdrawal of U.S. troops while South Vietnam assumed more of the fighting. On June 8, 1969, Nixon announced the withdrawal of 25,000 soldiers. Nixon refused to view this troop withdrawal as a form of surrender. He was determined to maintain a strong American presence in Vietnam to ensure bargaining power during peace negotiations. In support of that goal, the president increased air strikes against North Vietnam and began bombing Vietcong sanctuaries in neighboring Cambodia.

✔ **Reading Check** **Identifying** When did secret negotiations with the North Vietnamese begin?

Turmoil at Home Continues

Even though the United States had begun scaling back its involvement in Vietnam, the American home front remained divided and volatile as Nixon's war policies stirred up new waves of protest.

Massacre at My Lai In November 1969, Americans learned of a horrifying event. That month, the media reported that in the spring of 1968, an American platoon under the command of Lieutenant William Calley had massacred possibly more than 200 unarmed South Vietnamese civilians in the hamlet of **My Lai.** Most of the victims were old men, women, and children. Calley eventually went to prison for his role in the killings.

Most American soldiers acted responsibly and honorably throughout the war. The actions of one soldier, however, increased the feeling among many citizens that this was a brutal and senseless conflict. Jan Barry, a founder of the Vietnam Veterans Against the War, viewed the massacre at My Lai as a symbol of the dilemma his generation faced in the conflict:

“To kill on military orders and be a criminal, or to refuse to kill and be a criminal is the moral agony of America's Vietnam war generation. It is what has forced upward of sixty thousand young Americans, draft resisters and deserters to Canada, and created one hundred thousand military deserters a year in this country and abroad.”

—quoted in *Who Spoke Up?*

The Invasion of Cambodia Sparks Protest

Americans heard more startling news when Nixon announced in April 1970 that American troops had invaded Cambodia. The troops wanted to destroy Vietcong military bases there.

Many viewed the Cambodian invasion as a widening of the war, and it set off many protests. At **Kent State University** on May 4, 1970, Ohio National Guard soldiers, armed with tear gas and rifles, fired on demonstrators without an order to do so. The soldiers killed four students and wounded at least nine others. Ten days later, police killed two African American students during a demonstration at Jackson State College in Mississippi.

Picturing **History**

National Trauma When members of the Ohio National Guard fired on Kent State University demonstrators, the event triggered a nationwide student strike that forced hundreds of colleges and universities to close. How does this image connect with the phrase "the war at home"?

The Pentagon Papers In addition to sparking violence on campuses, the invasion of Cambodia cost Nixon significant congressional support. Numerous legislators expressed outrage over the president's failure to notify them of the action. In December 1970, an angry Congress repealed the Gulf of Tonkin Resolution, which had given the president near complete power in directing the war in Vietnam.

Support for the war weakened further in 1971 when Daniel Ellsberg, a disillusioned former Defense Department worker, leaked what became known as the **Pentagon Papers** to the *New York Times*. The documents revealed that many government officials during the Johnson administration privately questioned the war while publicly defending it.

The documents contained details of decisions that were made by the presidents and their advisers without the consent of Congress. They also showed how the various administrations acted to deceive Congress, the press, and the public about the situation in Vietnam. The Pentagon Papers confirmed what many Americans had long believed: The government had not been honest with them.

✓ **Reading Check** **Evaluating** What did the Pentagon Papers confirm for many Americans?

The United States Pulls Out of Vietnam

By 1971 polls showed that nearly two-thirds of Americans wanted to end the Vietnam War as quickly as possible. In April 1972, President Nixon dropped his longtime insistence that North Vietnamese troops had to withdraw from South Vietnam before any peace treaty could be signed. In October, less than a month before the 1972 presidential election, Henry Kissinger emerged from his secret talks with Le Duc Tho to announce that "peace is at hand."

A month later, Americans went to the polls to decide on a president. Senator George McGovern, the Democratic candidate, was an outspoken critic of the war. He did not appeal to many middle-class Americans, however, who were tired of antiwar protesters. When the votes were cast, Nixon won re-election in a landslide.

The Two Sides Reach Peace Just weeks after the presidential election, the peace negotiations broke down. South Vietnam's president, **Nguyen Van Thieu,** refused to agree to any plan that left North Vietnamese troops in the South. Kissinger tried to win additional concessions from the Communists, but talks broke off on December 16, 1972.

The next day, to force North Vietnam to resume negotiations, the Nixon administration began the most destructive air raids of the entire war. In what became known as the "Christmas bombings," American B-52s dropped thousands of tons of bombs on North Vietnamese targets for 11 straight days, pausing only on Christmas day.

In the wake of the bombing campaign, the United States and North Vietnam returned to the bargaining table. Thieu finally gave in to American pressure and allowed North Vietnamese troops to remain in the South. On January 27, 1973, the warring sides signed an agreement "ending the war and restoring the peace in Vietnam."

The United States promised to withdraw the rest of its troops, and both sides agreed to an exchange of prisoners of war. The parties did not resolve the issue of South Vietnam's future, however. After almost eight years of war—the longest war in American history—the nation ended its direct involvement in Vietnam.

South Vietnam Falls The United States had barely pulled out its last troops from Vietnam when the peace agreement collapsed. In March 1975, the North Vietnamese army launched a full-scale invasion of the South. Thieu desperately appealed to Washington, D.C., for help.

President Nixon had assured Thieu during the peace negotiations that the United States "[would] respond with full force should the settlement be violated by North Vietnam." Nixon, however, had resigned under pressure following the Watergate scandal. The new president, Gerald Ford, asked for funds to aid the South Vietnamese, but Congress refused.

On April 30, the North Vietnamese captured Saigon, South Vietnam's capital, and united Vietnam under Communist rule. They then renamed Saigon Ho Chi Minh City.

Reading Check **Explaining** Why did the peace talks break down in December 1972?

The Legacy of Vietnam

"The lessons of the past in Vietnam," President Ford declared in 1975, "have already been learned—learned by Presidents, learned by Congress, learned by the American people—and we should have our focus on the future." Although Americans tried to put the war behind them, Vietnam left a deep and lasting impact on American society.

The War's Human Toll The United States paid a heavy price for its involvement in Vietnam. The war had cost the nation over $170 billion in direct costs and much more in indirect economic expenses. More significantly, it had resulted in the deaths of approximately 58,000 young Americans and the injury of more than 300,000. In Vietnam, around one million North and South Vietnamese soldiers died in the conflict, as did countless civilians.

Even after they returned home from fighting, some American veterans, as in other wars, found it hard to escape the war's psychological impact. Army Specialist Doug Johnson recalled the problems he faced on returning home:

66It took a while for me to recognize that I did suffer some psychological problems in trying to deal with my experience in Vietnam. The first recollection I have of the effect took place shortly after I arrived back in the States. One evening . . . I went to see a movie on post. I don't recall the name of the movie or what it was about, but I remember there was a sad part, and that I started crying uncontrollably. It hadn't dawned on me before this episode that I had . . . succeeded in burying my emotions. 99

—quoted in *Touched by the Dragon*

One reason it may have been harder for some Vietnam veterans to readjust to civilian life was that many considered the war a defeat. Many Americans wanted to forget the war. Thus, the sacrifices of many veterans often went unrecognized. There were relatively few welcome-home parades and celebrations after the war.

The war also lingered for the American families whose relatives and friends were classified as

Picturing **History**

Desperate Pleas When President Ford ordered all Americans to leave Vietnam immediately in April 1975, many Saigon residents stormed the U.S. embassy pleading for rescue. When did the North Vietnamese take control of Saigon?

prisoners of war (POWs) or missing in action (MIA). Despite many official investigations, these families were not convinced that the government had told the truth about POW/MIA policies in the last years of the war.

The nation finally began to come to terms with the war almost a decade later. In 1982 the nation dedicated the Vietnam Veterans Memorial in Washington, D.C., a large black stone wall inscribed with the names of those killed and missing in action in the war. "It's a first step to remind America of what we did," veteran Larry Cox of Virginia said at the dedication of the monument.

GOVERNMENT

The War's Impact on the Nation The war also left its mark on the nation as a whole. In 1973 Congress passed the **War Powers Act** as a way to reestablish some limits on executive power. The act required the president to inform Congress of any commitment of troops abroad within 48 hours and to withdraw them in 60 to 90 days unless Congress explicitly approved the troop commitment.

The legislation addresses the struggle between the executive and legislative branches over what checks and balances are proper in matters of war and foreign policy. No president has recognized this limitation,

Student Web Activity Visit the *American Vision* Web site at tav.glencoe.com and click on *Student Web Activities— Chapter 30* for an activity on the Vietnam War.

Analyzing Photographs Study the photograph on page 913 of South Vietnamese citizens attempting to enter the U.S. embassy.

World Geography Connection

The War's Refugees

Another of the Vietnam War's enduring legacies was the wave of human migration and resettlement it prompted. From the mid-1970s through the 1980s, between 1.5 and 2 million people fled the newly installed Communist regimes in Vietnam, Cambodia, and Laos. These men, women, and children became known as "boat people" because their main route of escape was by sea. More than half of these refugees came to the United States. Between 1980 and 1990, the Vietnamese population of the United States more than doubled from about 245,000 to almost 615,000. *Why do you think the United States was willing to accept so many refugees from the Vietnam War?*

and the courts have tended to avoid the issue as a strictly political question. In general, the war shook the nation's confidence and led some to embrace a new kind of isolationism. In the years after the war, many Americans became more reluctant to intervene in the affairs of other nations.

On the domestic front, the Vietnam War increased Americans' cynicism about their government. Many felt the nation's leaders had misled them. Together with Watergate, a scandal that broke as the war was winding down, Vietnam made Americans more wary of their leaders.

✓ **Reading Check** **Describing** How did the Vietnam War affect Americans' attitudes toward international conflicts?

SECTION 4 ASSESSMENT

Checking for Understanding

1. **Define:** linkage, Vietnamization.
2. **Identify:** Henry Kissinger, Pentagon Papers, War Powers Act.
3. **Describe** what happened in Vietnam in 1975 after the United States withdrew.

Reviewing Themes

4. **Government and Democracy** Why did Congress pass the War Powers Act? How did this act reflect a struggle between the legislative and executive branches?

Critical Thinking

5. **Analyzing** Why did the invasion of Cambodia cost President Nixon congressional support?
6. **Organizing** Use a graphic organizer similar to the one below to list the effects of the Vietnam War on the nation.

Effects of Vietnam War

Analyzing Visuals

7. **Analyzing Photographs** Study the photograph on page 913 of South Vietnamese citizens attempting to enter the U.S. embassy. How do you think this image affected American attitudes toward the war? Why do you think so?

Writing About History

8. **Descriptive Writing** Imagine that you are a college student in 1970. Write a journal entry expressing your feelings about the events at Kent State University and Jackson State College.

Social Studies SKILLBUILDER

Conducting an Interview

Why Learn This Skill?

Suppose that your friends went to see a concert, but you were unable to attend. How would you find out how the show was?

Learning the Skill

You probably would not normally think of asking your friends questions about a concert as conducting an interview, but that is exactly what you are doing. Interviews are an excellent way of collecting important facts and opinions from people. Interviews allow you to gather information from people who witnessed or participated in an event firsthand. For example, William Prochnau interviewed many different people and used the results to write his book *Once Upon a Distant War*, which examines the way the press covered the Vietnam War. To conduct an interview with someone, follow these steps.

- **Make an appointment.** Contact the person and explain why you want to conduct the interview, what kinds of things you hope to learn, and how you will use the information. Discuss where and when you will conduct the interview, and ask if you may use a tape recorder.

- **Gather background information.** Find out about the education, career, and other accomplishments of the person you want to interview. Research the topics you wish to discuss.

- **Prepare questions.** Group questions into subject categories. Begin each category with general questions and move toward more specific questions. Formulate each question carefully. If the answer could be simply yes or no, rephrase the question.

- **Conduct the interview.** Introduce yourself and restate the purpose of the interview. Ask questions and record responses accurately. Ask follow-up questions to fill gaps in information.

- **Transcribe the interview.** Convert your written or tape-recorded notes into a *transcript,* a written record of the interview presented in a question-and-answer format.

Practicing the Skill

Imagine you are assigned to interview someone who participated in or is old enough to remember the events that occurred during the Vietnam War.

❶ What kind of background information might you gather?

❷ What are some broad categories of questions you might ask based on what you know about the person you are interviewing and what you know about the war?

❸ What are some general questions you might want to ask within these broad categories? Consider the responses you might get to these general questions, and formulate follow-up questions for each.

Skills Assessment

Complete the Practicing Skills questions on page 917 and the Chapter 30 Skill Reinforcement Activity to assess your mastery of this skill.

Applying the Skill

Conducting an Interview The Vietnam War probably included some people you know—your parents, grandparents, aunts, uncles, or neighbors. Even if they were not directly involved with the conflict, they probably remember what the United States was like during the war. Use the questions you developed above to interview one or more of these people. Ask about their experiences regarding Vietnam, including their attitudes toward the war and its many related issues, past and present. Summarize your findings in a short report or in a comparison chart.

 GO TO

Glencoe's **Skillbuilder Interactive Workbook CD-ROM, Level 2,** provides instruction and practice in key social studies skills.

CHAPTER 30 ASSESSMENT and ACTIVITIES

Reviewing Key Terms

On a sheet of paper, use each of these terms in a sentence.

1. domino theory
2. guerrilla
3. Vietcong
4. napalm
5. credibility gap
6. teach-in
7. dove
8. hawk
9. linkage
10. Vietnamization

Chapter Summary

American Involvement in Vietnam

Roots of the Conflict

- Eisenhower financially supported French war against Vietnam
- Geneva Accords established North and South Vietnam
- U.S.-backed leader of South Vietnam refused national elections, fearing defeat by Communist opponent
- Kennedy sharply increased military aid and presence in South Vietnam
- Johnson escalated U.S. involvement and gained war powers after the incident in the Gulf of Tonkin

Full-Scale War

- President Johnson responded to a Vietcong attack with aggressive air strikes; American people applauded his actions
- U.S. committed over 380,000 ground troops to fighting in Vietnam by the end of 1966

Opposition to the War

- American people questioned the government's honesty about the war, creating the so-called "credibility gap"
- Wartime economy hurt domestic spending efforts
- President Nixon was elected largely on promises to end the war and unite the divided country

The End of the War

- Nixon withdrew troops but increased air strikes
- American troops pulled out after a 1973 peace agreement
- Congress passed the War Powers Act to limit the power of the president during times of war

Reviewing Key Facts

11. **Identify:** Ho Chi Minh, Tet offensive.
12. How did President Eisenhower defend American policy in Vietnam?
13. When did the number of American military personnel begin to increase in Vietnam?
14. How did Vietnamese peasants respond to the strategic hamlets program?
15. What actions made Ngo Dinh Diem an unpopular leader in South Vietnam?
16. What was the effect of the Tet offensive on Americans?
17. How did Richard Nixon benefit from the chaos in the nation in 1968?
18. What did the Pentagon Papers reveal?

Critical Thinking

19. **Analyzing Themes: Civic Rights and Responsibilities** How did Americans show their frustration with the direction the country was taking in 1968?
20. **Analyzing** How do you think the use of chemicals such as Agent Orange and napalm by the United States affected Vietnamese feelings toward Americans and the war?
21. **Organizing** Use a graphic organizer to list the reasons the United States became involved in Vietnam and the effects the war had on the nation.

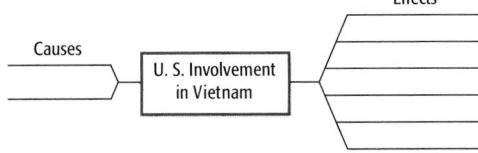

22. **Interpreting Primary Sources** In the 1960s many young Americans enlisted or were drafted for military service. Some believed they had a duty to serve their country. Many had no clear idea of what they were doing or why. In the following excerpt, a young man interviewed for Mark Baker's book *Nam* presents his thoughts about going to war.

❝I read a lot of pacifist literature to determine whether or not I was a conscientious objector. I finally concluded that I wasn't. . . .

The one clear decision I made in 1968 about me and the war was that if I was going to get out of it, I was going to get out in a legal way. I was not going to defraud the system in order to beat the system. I wasn't going to leave the country, because the odds of coming back looked real slim. . . .

> With all my terror of going into the Army . . . there was something seductive about it, too. I was seduced by World War II and John Wayne movies. . . . I had been, as we all were, victimized by a romantic, truly uninformed view of war. 99

—quoted in *Nam*

a. What options did the young man have regarding going to war?

b. Do you think World War II movies gave him a realistic view of what fighting in Vietnam would be like?

Practicing Skills

23. **Conducting an Interview** Review the material on page 915 about interviewing. Then follow these steps to prepare for an interview with President Johnson on his Vietnam policies.
   a. Study Section 2 of this chapter on the president's Vietnam policies and conduct library or Internet research on this subject.
   b. Prepare a list of 10 questions to ask the president.

Geography and History

24. The map on this page shows supply routes and troop movements during the Vietnam War. Study the map and answer the questions below.
   a. **Interpreting Maps** What nations besides North and South Vietnam were the sites of battles or invasions?
   b. **Analyzing** Why did the Ho Chi Minh Trail pass through Laos and Cambodia instead of South Vietnam?

Chapter Activity

25. **Evaluating Bias** A person's life experiences often influence his or her arguments one way or another, creating a biased opinion. Reread the speeches in Different Viewpoints on pages 898–899. What might have influenced the points of view of George Ball and George Kennan? Create a cause-and-effect chart showing possible reasons for their biases and effects their experiences have had on their political opinions.

Writing Activity

26. **Portfolio Writing** Many songs and pieces of literature have been written on the Vietnam War. Find examples, then write an original poem or song lyrics in which you present antiwar or pro-war sentiments about the Vietnam War. Include your work in your portfolio.

NATIONAL GEOGRAPHIC **The Vietnam War**

CHINA

Dien Bien Phu

Hanoi · Haiphong

LAOS

NORTH VIETNAM

Gulf of Tonkin

20°N

THAILAND

Khe Sanh

Invasion of Laos Feb. 8–March, 1971

Demilitarized Zone
17th Parallel

Quang Tri

·Hue

Da Nang · Da Nang

Tam Ky

Chu Lai

My Lai Massacre March 16, 1968

Ho Chi Minh Trail

Pleiku · Qui Nhon

SOUTH VIETNAM

CAMBODIA

Invasion of Cambodia May 1–June 29, 1970

Ban Me Thuot

· Nha Trang

Phnom Penh ⊛

Phoc Binh

Saigon
Long Binh

Gulf of Thailand

Can Tho

*Mekong — South — 10°N
Delta China
Sea*

Khanh Hung

Quan Long

| Major U.S. and South Vietnamese troop movements
| Major North Vietnamese supply lines
▪ U.S. bases

0   150 miles

0   150 kilometers
Miller Cylindrical projection

110°E

CHAPTER 31

The Politics of Protest 1960–1980

Why It Matters

Protest characterized the 1960s. Young people often led the civil rights and antiwar movements. Some of them wanted to change the entire society and urged more communal, less materialistic values. Young people were not the only protesters, however. Using the civil rights movement as a model, women, Hispanic Americans, and Native Americans also organized to gain greater recognition and equality.

The Impact Today

Changes of the 1960s still affect our lives today.
* *Women are visible in many more leadership roles in government and business.*
* *Hispanic political organizations represent a growing segment of the population.*
* *The cultural traditions of Native Americans receive greater recognition.*

 The American Vision *Video* *The Chapter 31 video, "Behind the Scenes with César," profiles the role that César Chávez played in the United Farm Workers organization.*

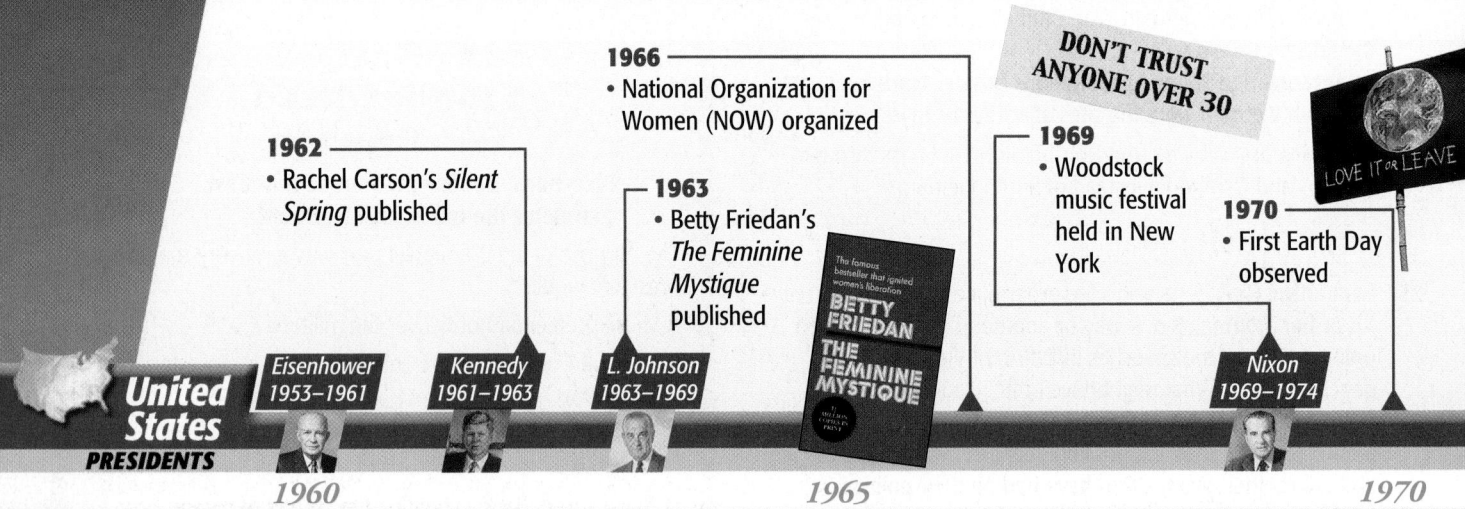

1962
* Rachel Carson's *Silent Spring* published

1966
* National Organization for Women (NOW) organized

1963
* Betty Friedan's *The Feminine Mystique* published

1969
* Woodstock music festival held in New York

DON'T TRUST ANYONE OVER 30

1970
* First Earth Day observed

LOVE IT OR LEAVE IT

United States PRESIDENTS

Eisenhower 1953–1961

Kennedy 1961–1963

L. Johnson 1963–1969

Nixon 1969–1974

1960

1965

1970

 World

1962
* China and Soviet Union have diplomatic disagreements

1964
* China becomes world's fifth nuclear power

1966
* Indira Gandhi becomes prime minister of India

1968
* Soviet Union halts democratic uprising in Czechoslovakia

Labor leader César Chávez meeting with farmworkers

1972
- Use of pesticide DDT banned

1973
- Supreme Court issues *Roe* v. *Wade* ruling
- AIM and government clash at Wounded Knee, South Dakota

1979
- Nuclear accident at Three Mile Island

Ford
1974–1977

Carter
1977–1981

1975

1980

1972
- Britain imposes direct rule on Northern Ireland

1975
- End of the Portuguese empires in Africa

1979
- Ayatollah Khomeini leads Islamic overthrow of Iran

HISTORY *Online*

Chapter Overview
Visit the *American Vision* Web site at tav.glencoe.com and click on *Chapter Overviews—Chapter 31* to preview chapter information.

SECTION 1 — The Student Movement and the Counterculture

Preview of Events

♦1961	♦1964	♦1967	♦1970

1962
Students for a Democratic Society deliver Port Huron Statement

1964
Free Speech Movement begins; the Beatles embark on their first U.S. tour

August, 1969
400,000 young people gather at Woodstock music festival

★ An American Story ★

On December 2, 1964, Mario Savio, a 20-year-old philosophy student at the University of California at Berkeley, stood before a supportive crowd at the school's administration building. The massive "sit-in" demonstration was the climax of a month-long battle between school officials and students over unpopular campus policies. Facing the crowd, Savio urged them to continue pressuring school officials. In his speech he called the university a cold and heartless "machine" that deserved to be shut down.

❝There's a time when the operation of the machine becomes so odious, makes you so sick at heart, that you . . . can't even tacitly take part," he declared. "And you've got to put your bodies upon the gears and upon the wheels . . . you've got to make it stop. And you've got to indicate to the people who run it, to the people who own it, that unless you're free the machine will be prevented from working at all.❞

—quoted in *Decade of Shocks*

The Growth of the Youth Movement

The 1960s was one of the most tumultuous and chaotic decades in United States history. The decade also gave birth to a conspicuous youth movement, which challenged the American political and social system and conventional middle-class values. Perhaps no other time in the nation's history witnessed such protest.

The Roots of the Movement The roots of the 1960s youth movement stretched back to the 1950s. In the decade after World War II, the nation's economy boomed, and much of the country enjoyed a time of peace and prosperity. Prosperity did not extend to all, however, and some, especially the artists and writers of the "beat" movement, had openly criticized American society. They believed it valued conformity over independence and financial gain over spiritual and social advancement. Meanwhile, such events as the growing nuclear arms race between the United States and the Soviet Union made many more of the nation's youth uneasy about their future. Writer Todd Gitlin, who was a senior at the Bronx High School of Science in 1959, recalls the warning that the editors of his student yearbook delivered.

> ❝In today's atomic age . . . the flames of war would write *finis* not only to our civilization, but to our very existence. Mankind may find itself unable to rise again should it be consumed in a nuclear pyre of its own making. In the years to come, members of this class will bear an ever-increasing responsibility for the preservation of the heritage given us.❞
> —from *The Sixties*

Concern about the future led many young people to become more active in social causes, from the civil rights movement to President Kennedy's Peace Corps. The emergence of the youth movement grew out of the huge numbers of people of the postwar "baby boom" generation. By 1970, 58.4 percent of the American population was 34 years old or younger. (By comparison, those 34 or younger in 2000 represented an estimated 48.9 percent.)

The early 1960s saw another phenomenon that fueled the youth movement—the rapid increase in enrollment at colleges throughout the nation. The economic boom of the 1950s led to a boom in higher education, since more families could afford to send their children to college. Between 1960 and 1966, enrollment in 4-year institutions rose from 3.1 million to almost 5 million

students. College life empowered young people with a newfound sense of freedom and independence. It also allowed them to meet and bond with others who shared their feelings about society and fears about the future. It was on college campuses across the nation where the protest movements would rage the loudest.

Students for a Democratic Society Some youths were concerned most about the injustices they saw in the country's political and social system. In their view, a few wealthy elites controlled politics, and wealth itself was unfairly divided. These young people formed what came to be known as the New Left. (The "new" left differed from the "old" left of the 1930s, which had advocated socialism and communism.) A prominent organization of this group was the **Students for a Democratic Society** (SDS). It defined its views in a 1962 declaration known as the **Port Huron Statement.** Written largely by **Tom Hayden,** editor of the University of Michigan's student newspaper, the declaration called for an end to apathy and urged citizens to stop accepting a country run by big corporations and big government.

SDS groups focused on protesting the Vietnam War, but they also addressed such issues as poverty, campus regulations, nuclear power, and racism.

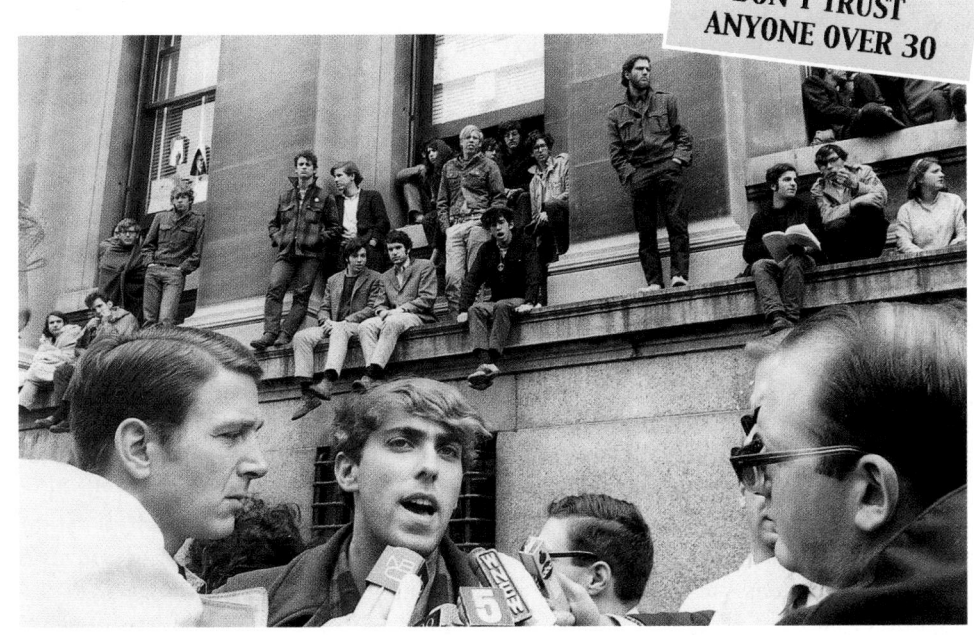

Picturing **History**

Youth Movement The Students for a Democratic Society (SDS) worked to address many of the problems they saw in the 1960s. Made up primarily of college students, the group was suspicious of the motives of adults. Where did the SDS begin its reform crusade?

The Counterculture Commonly known as "hippies," members of the counterculture separated themselves from society in the 1960s by trying to create their own culture of love and tolerance. *What western city was a focal point of the hippie culture?*

In 1968, for example, SDS leaders assisted in an eight-day occupation of several buildings at Columbia University in New York City to protest the administration's plan to build a new gym in an area that served as a neighborhood park near Harlem.

The Free Speech Movement Another group of protesters who captured the nation's attention were members of the Free Speech Movement, led by **Mario Savio** and others at the University of California at Berkeley. The issue that sparked the movement was the university's decision in the fall of 1964 to restrict students' rights to distribute literature and to recruit volunteers for political causes on campus. The protesters, however, quickly targeted more general campus matters and drew in more and more supporters.

Like many college students, those at Berkeley were disgruntled with the practices at their university. Officials divided huge classes into sections taught by graduate students, while many professors claimed they were too busy with research to meet with students. Faceless administrators made rules that were not always easy to obey and imposed punishments for violations. Isolated in this impersonal environment, many Berkeley students found a purpose in the Free Speech Movement.

The struggle between school administrators and students peaked on December 2, 1964, with the sit-in and Savio's famous speech at the administration

building. Early the next morning, California Governor Pat Brown sent in 600 police officers to break up the demonstration. Police arrested more than 700 protesters.

The arrests set off a new and even larger protest movement. Within a few days, thousands of Berkeley students participated in a campus-wide strike, stopping classes for two days. Much of the faculty also voiced its support for the Free Speech Movement. In the face of this growing opposition, the administration gave in to the students' demands shortly before the Christmas recess.

The following week, the Supreme Court validated the students' First Amendment rights to freedom of speech and assembly on campus. In a unanimous vote, the Court upheld the section of the Civil Rights Act assuring these rights in places offering public accommodations, which, by definition, included college campuses. The Berkeley revolt was one of the earliest outbursts in a decade of campus turmoil. The tactics the protesters used there—abandoning classes and occupying buildings—would serve as a model for college demonstrators across the country.

Reading Check **Synthesizing** What were three reasons for the growth of the youth movement of the 1960s?

The Counterculture

While a number of young Americans in the 1960s sought to challenge the system, others wanted to leave it and build their own society. Throughout the decade, thousands of mostly white youths turned away from their middle- and upper-class existence and created a new lifestyle—one that promoted the virtues of flamboyant dress, rock music, drug use, and free and independent living. With their alternative ways of life, these young men and women formed what became known as the counterculture and were commonly called "hippies."

Hippie Culture Originally, hippie culture represented a rebellion against the dominant culture in the United States. This included a rejection of Western civilization, of rationality, order, and the traditional values of the middle class. At its core, the counterculture held up a utopian ideal: the ideal of a society that was freer, closer to nature, and full of love, empathy, tolerance, and cooperation. Much of this was in reaction to the 1950s American stereotype of the man in the gray flannel suit who led a constricted and colorless life.

When the movement grew larger, many of the new-comers did not always understand these original ideas of the counterculture. For them, what mattered were the outward signs that defined the movement—long hair, Native American headbands, cowboy boots, long dresses, shabby jeans, and the use of drugs such as marijuana and LSD. Drug use, especially, came to be associated with the hippie culture.

Many hippies desired to literally drop out of society by leaving home and living together with other youths in communes—group living arrangements in which members shared everything and worked together. A number of hippies established communes in small and rural communities, while others lived together in parks or crowded apartments in the nation's large cities. One of the most popular hippie destinations became San Francisco's **Haight-Ashbury district.** By the mid-1960s, thousands of hippies had flocked there.

New Religious Movements

In their rejection of materialism, many members of the counterculture embraced spirituality. This included a broad range of beliefs, from astrology and magic to Eastern religions and new forms of Christianity.

Many of the religious groups centered around authoritarian leaders. In these groups, the leader dominated others and controlled their lives, sometimes to the point of arranging marriages between members. Religion became the central experience in the believer's life. The authoritarian figure was a sort of parent figure, and believers formed an extended family that took the place of the family into which a member had been born. This could lead to painful conflicts. Some parents accused religious sects of using mind-control methods; some attempted to recapture and "deprogram" their children.

Two new religious groups that attracted considerable attention beginning in the 1960s were the **Unification Church** and the **Hare Krishna** movement. Both were offshoots of established religions, and both came from abroad. Members of the Unification Church were popularly known as "Moonies," after their Korean-born founder, the Reverend Sun Myung Moon. He claimed to have had a vision in which Jesus told Moon that he was the next messiah and was charged with restoring the Kingdom of God on Earth. The Hare Krishnas traced their spiritual lineage to a Hindu sect that began in India in the 1400s and worshiped the god Krishna. In dress, diet, worship, and general style of living, Hare Krishnas tried to emulate these Hindu practitioners of another time and place.

The Counterculture Declines

After a few years, the counterculture movement began to deteriorate. Some hippie communities in the cities soon turned into seedy and dangerous places where muggings and other criminal activity became all too frequent. The glamour and excitement of drug use soon waned, especially as more and more young people became addicted or died from overdoses. In addition, a number of the people involved in the movement had gotten older and moved on in life. Upon witnessing the decline of Haight-Ashbury, one writer dismissed the one-time booming urban commune as "the desperate attempt of a handful of pathetically unequipped children to create a community out of a social vacuum." In the end, most of the young men and women of the counterculture, unable to establish an ideal community and unable to support themselves, gradually returned to mainstream society.

Reading Check **Summarizing** What were the core ideals of members of the counterculture?

Impact of the Counterculture

In the long run, the counterculture did change American life in some ways. Over time, mainstream America accepted many of these changes.

Fashion The counterculture generation, as one observer of the 1960s noted, dressed in costumes rather than in occupational or class uniforms. The colorful, beaded, braided, patched, and fringed garments that both men and women wore turned the fashion industry upside down. The international fashion world took its cues from young men and

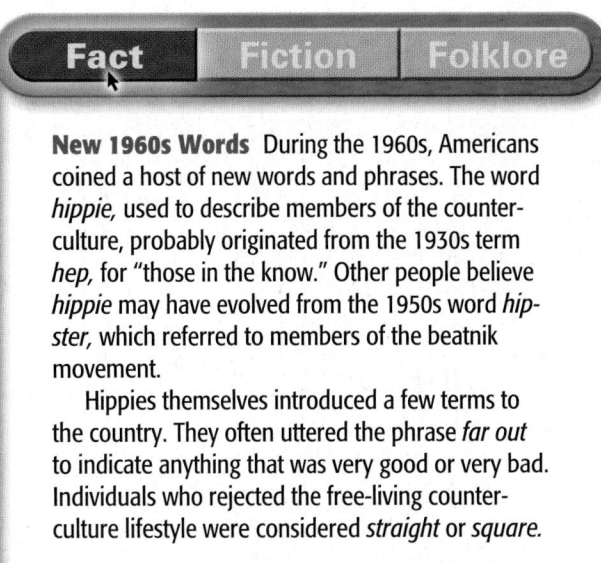

Fact | Fiction | Folklore

New 1960s Words During the 1960s, Americans coined a host of new words and phrases. The word *hippie*, used to describe members of the counterculture, probably originated from the 1930s term *hep*, for "those in the know." Other people believe *hippie* may have evolved from the 1950s word *hipster*, which referred to members of the beatnik movement.

Hippies themselves introduced a few terms to the country. They often uttered the phrase *far out* to indicate anything that was very good or very bad. Individuals who rejected the free-living counterculture lifestyle were considered *straight* or *square.*

women on the street. As a result, men's clothing became more colorful, and women's clothing became more comfortable.

Protesters often expressed themselves with their clothing. The counterculture adopted military surplus attire not only because it was inexpensive, but also because it expressed rejection of materialist values and blurred the lines of social class. For the same reasons, clothing of another age was recycled, and worn-out clothing was repaired with patches. Ethnic clothing was popular for similar reasons. Beads and fringes imitated Native American costumes, while tie-dyed shirts borrowed techniques from India and Africa.

Perhaps the most potent symbol of the era was hair. A popular 1967 musical about the period was titled, fittingly, *Hair.* Long hair on a young man was the ultimate symbol of defiance. Slogans appeared, such as "Make America beautiful—give a hippie a haircut." School officials debated the acceptable length of a student's hair—could it curl over the collar or not? Once the initial shock wore off, however,

longer hair on men and more individual clothing for both genders became generally accepted. What was once clothing of defiance was now mainstream.

Art During the 1960s, one art critic observed, the distinctions between traditional art and popular art, or **pop art,** dissolved. Pop art derived its subject matter from elements of popular culture, such as photographs, comic books, advertisements, and brand-name products. Artist **Andy Warhol,** for example, used images of famous people, such as Marilyn Monroe and Elizabeth Taylor, and repeated them over and over. Warhol also reproduced items such as cans of soup, making the pictures as realistic as possible. Roy Lichtenstein used frames from comic strips as his inspirations. He employed the bold primary colors of red, yellow, and black, and put words like *blam* and *pow* into his paintings in comic book fashion.

Pop artists expected these symbols of popular culture to carry some of the same meaning as they did in their original form. The artists sometimes referred to themselves as only the "agents" of the art and said it

NATIONAL GEOGRAPHIC

MOMENT in HISTORY

WOODSTOCK NATION

In August 1969, more than 400,000 young people descended on a 600-acre farm in upstate New York for what was billed as "three days of peace and music." Organizers of the Woodstock Music and Art Fair were overwhelmed by the turnout. Massive traffic jams, supply shortages, inadequate first aid and sanitation facilities, and torrential rainfall did not dampen the joyous spirit of the crowd. People shared their food and blankets, bathed in the rain, and listened to an amazing collection of some of the greatest musicians of the 1960s.

was up to the observer to give meaning to the work and thus become part of it.

Music and Dance Counterculture musicians hoped that their music, rock 'n' roll, would be the means of toppling the establishment and reforming society. This did not happen because rock music was absorbed into the mainstream, where it brought material success worth billions of dollars to performers, promoters, and record companies.

One of the most famous rock groups, the **Beatles,** took the country by storm in 1964. "Beatlemania" swept the country, inspiring hundreds of other rock 'n' roll groups both in Great Britain and the United States.

Many of the new groups combined rock 'n' roll rhythms with lyrics that expressed the fears and hopes of the new generation and the widening rift between them and their parents. **Bob Dylan** became a major voice of this movement. The spirited performances of artists like Janis Joplin also communicated this rebellious message.

The use of electrically amplified instruments also drastically changed the sound and feel of the new music. One master of this new sound was **Jimi Hendrix,** a guitarist from Seattle. Hendrix lived overseas and achieved stardom only after returning to the United States with the influx of musicians from Great Britain. His innovative guitar playing continues to influence musicians today.

History *Through Art*

Pop Art Artists like Roy Lichtenstein mocked certain aspects of American life by using common examples of commercial art, such as comics and advertisements. *What statement is this piece of art making?*

At festivals such as **Woodstock,** in upstate New York in August 1969, and Altamont, California, later that year, hundreds of thousands of people got together to celebrate the new music. Though the fast-paced, energetic beat of rock 'n' roll was made for dancing, the style of dancing had changed dramatically. Each person danced without a partner, surrounded by others who also danced alone—a perfect metaphor for the counterculture, which stressed individuality within the group.

Headline-grabbing events such as Woodstock made it difficult for the nation to ignore the youth movement. By this time, however, other groups in society were also raising their voices in protest. For example, many women began renewing their generations-old efforts for equality, hoping to expand upon the successes gained during the early 1900s.

Reading Check **Evaluating** What lasting impact did the counterculture have on the nation?

SECTION 1 ASSESSMENT

Checking for Understanding

1. **Define:** counterculture, commune.
2. **Identify:** Port Huron Statement, Tom Hayden, Haight-Ashbury district, Jimi Hendrix.
3. **Summarize** two legacies of the counterculture movement.

Reviewing Themes

4. **Government and Democracy** How did the U.S. Supreme Court validate the actions of the members of the Free Speech Movement?

Critical Thinking

5. **Contrasting** How were hippies different from members of the New Left?
6. **Analyzing** Why did the counterculture movement decline?
7. **Organizing** Use a graphic organizer similar to the one below to list the causes of the youth movement.

Causes

——————————→ Youth Movement

Analyzing Visuals

8. **Analyzing Photographs** Look closely at the photograph of a group of hippies and their bus on page 922. How does the bus itself represent values of the counterculture?

Writing About History

9. **Descriptive Writing** Imagine you are a journalist in the 1960s. Write an article in which you visit a commune and describe the hippie culture you see.

The Feminist Movement

Guide to Reading

Main Idea

During the 1960s and 1970s, a large number of American women organized to push for greater rights and opportunities in society.

Key Terms and Names

feminism, Equal Pay Act, Equal Employment Opportunity Commission, Betty Friedan, National Organization for Women, Title IX, Phyllis Schlafly

Reading Strategy

Categorizing As you read about the women's movement, use a graphic organizer similar to the one below to compare the ideas of the two organizations that formed when the women's movement split.

Organization	Ideas

Reading Objectives

• **Describe** the workplace concerns that fueled the growth of the women's movement.
• **Identify** major achievements of the women's movement.

Section Theme

Civic Rights and Responsibilities Women organized to claim their rights and responsibilities as citizens and employees.

Preview of Events

◆1963   ◆1970   ◆1977   ◆1984

1963
Betty Friedan's *The Feminine Mystique* published

1966
Women activists form NOW

1973
Roe v. *Wade* decision ensures abortion rights

1982
Equal Rights Amendment fails

★ *An American Story* ★

In 1960 the housewife-oriented magazine *Redbook* asked readers to send examples of "Why Young Mothers Feel Trapped." Some 24,000 women responded. One of them was Herma Snider, a housewife and mother of three in Nevada. Snider wrote that as a high school and college student, she had dreamed of a career in journalism. After getting married and having three children, that dream died.

"Cemented to my house by three young children," she wrote, "there were days in which I saw no adult human being except the milkman as he made his deliveries and spoke to no one from the time my husband left in the morning until he returned at night." She added, "Each night as I tucked my sons into bed, I thanked God that they would grow up to be *men,* that they would able to teach, write, heal, advise, travel, or do anything else they chose."

Desperate for greater fulfillment in her life, Snider eventually took a job as a part-time hotel clerk. About this decision, she said:

❝My cashier's job is not the glamorous career I once dreamed of. And I know that it can be said that my solution is not a solution at all, merely an escape. But it seems to me that when the demands of children and household threaten to suffocate you, an escape *is* a solution.❞

—**quoted in *The Female Experience: An American Documentary***

A Weakened Women's Movement

Herma Snider was not alone. Although many women were content to be homemakers, by the early 1960s scores of them had grown dissatisfied with their roles. At the same time, those who worked outside the home were recognizing their unequal status as reflected in lower pay and fewer opportunities. These developments led to the rise of a new feminist movement in the 1960s.

Feminism, the belief that men and women should be equal politically, economically, and socially, had been a weak and often embattled force since the adoption of the Nineteenth Amendment guaranteeing women's voting rights in 1920. Soon after the amendment's passage, the women's movement split into two camps. One group, the League of Women Voters, tended to promote laws to protect women and children, such as limiting the hours they could work. The National Woman's Party (NWP), on the other hand, opposed protective legislation for women. The NWP believed it reinforced workplace discrimination. In 1923 the NWP persuaded members of Congress to introduce the first Equal Rights Amendment aimed at forbidding federal, state, and local laws from discriminating on the basis of gender. Since the women's movement was divided, however, Congress could afford to ignore the amendment.

The onset of World War II provided women with greater opportunity, at least temporarily. With many men enlisted in the army, women became an integral part of the nation's workforce. When the war ended, however, many women lost their jobs to the returning men.

Despite having to return to their domestic work, many women gradually reentered the labor market. By 1960 they made up almost one-third of the nation's workforce. Yet many people continued to believe that women, even college-educated women, could better serve society by remaining in the home to influence the next generation of men.

✓ **Reading Check** **Examining** How did World War II affect women?

The Women's Movement Reawakens

By the early 1960s, many women were increasingly resentful of a world where newspaper ads separated jobs by gender, clubs refused them memberships, banks denied them credit, and, worst of all, they often were paid less for the same work. Generally, women found themselves shut out of higher-paying and prestigious professions such as law, medicine, and finance. Although about 47 percent of American women were in the workforce in the 1960s, three-fourths of them worked in lower paying and routine clerical, sales, or factory jobs, or

as cleaning women and hospital attendants. As more women entered the workforce, the protest against inequities grew louder.

Women had also gained a better understanding of their inequality in society from their experiences in the civil rights and antiwar movements. Often they were restricted to menial tasks and rarely had a say in any policy decisions. From the broader perspective, the women's movement was part of the 1960s quest for rights.

GOVERNMENT

Fighting for Workplace Rights Two forces helped bring the women's movement to life again. One was the mass protest of ordinary women. The second was a government initiative: the **President's Commission on the Status of Women,** established by President Kennedy and headed by Eleanor Roosevelt. The commission's report highlighted the problems of women in the workplace and helped create networks of feminist activists, who lobbied Congress for women's legislation. In 1963, with the support of labor, they won passage of the **Equal Pay Act,** which in most cases outlawed paying men more than women for the same job.

Congress gave women another boost by including them in the 1964 Civil Rights Act, a measure originally designed to fight racial bias. **Title VII** of the act outlawed job discrimination by private employers not only on the basis of race, color, religion, and

Picturing **History**

Perfect Home, Perfect Wife This image of a proud wife in her spotless kitchen reflects some of the traditional ideas of the 1950s and 1960s. What did the women's movement criticize about these ideas?

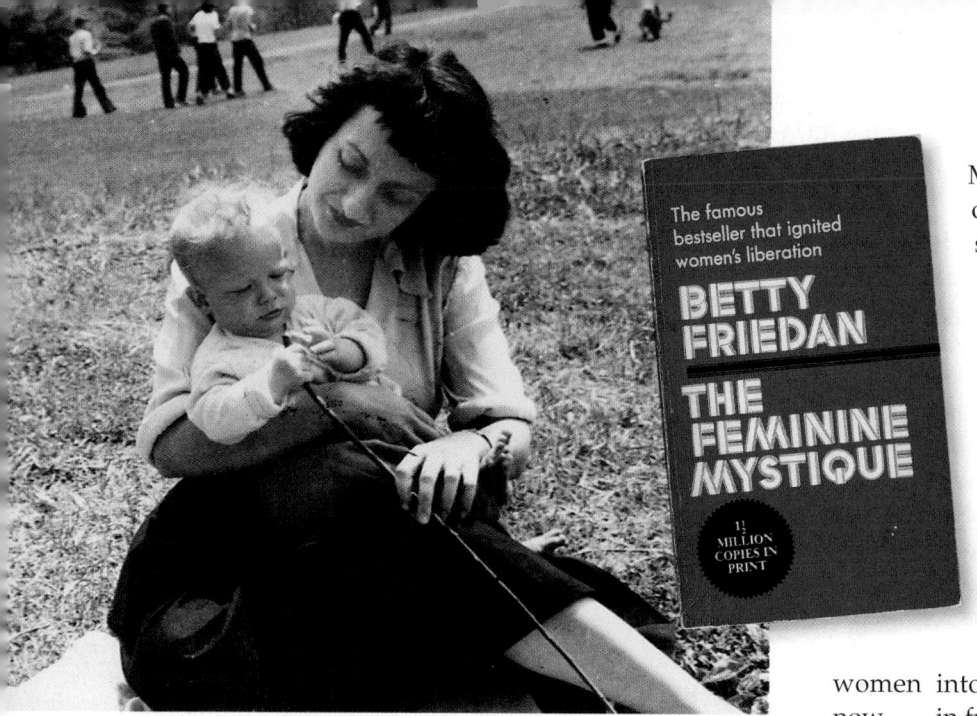

The Feminine Mystique Betty Friedan's best-selling book (right) exposed a sense of dissatisfaction that many women experienced but were reluctant to speak about openly. What political organization stemmed from women's growing sense of unfulfillment?

national origin, but also of gender. This measure became decisive legal basis for advances made by the women's movement.

Given prevailing attitudes about what kind of work was proper for women, change took time. Even the federal agency charged with administering the new law, the **Equal Employment Opportunity Commission** (EEOC), still held to the idea that jobs should be distinguished by gender. In August 1965, for example, the commission ruled that gender-segregated help-wanted ads were legal.

The Feminine Mystique Many date the women's movement from the publication of **Betty Friedan's** *The Feminine Mystique* in 1963. Friedan had traveled around the country interviewing the women who had graduated with her from Smith College in 1942. She found that while most of these women reported having everything they could want in life, they still felt unfulfilled. Friedan described these feelings in her book:

❝The problem lay buried, unspoken, for many years in the minds of American women. . . . Each suburban wife struggled with it alone. As she made the beds, shopped for groceries . . . chauffeured Cub Scouts and Brownies . . . she was afraid to ask even of herself the silent question—'Is this all?'❞

—from *The Feminine Mystique*

Friedan's book became a best-seller. Many women soon began reaching out to one another, pouring out their anger and sadness in what came to be known as consciousness-raising sessions. While they talked informally about their unhappiness, they were building the base for a nationwide movement.

The Time Is NOW In June 1966, Friedan returned to a thought that she and others had been considering, the need for women to form a national organization. On the back of a napkin, she scribbled down her intentions "to take the actions needed to bring women into the mainstream of American society, now . . . in fully equal partnership with men." Friedan and others then set out to form the **National Organization for Women** (NOW).

NOW soon leapt off the napkin and into the headlines. In October 1966, a group of about 300 women and men held the founding conference of NOW. "The time has come," its founders declared, "to confront with concrete action the conditions which now prevent women from enjoying the equality of opportunity and freedom of choice which is their right as individual Americans and as human beings."

The new organization responded to frustrated housewives by demanding greater educational opportunities for women. The group also focused much of its energy on aiding women in the workplace. NOW leaders denounced the exclusion of women from certain professions and from most levels of politics. They lashed out against the practice of paying women less than men for equal work, a practice the Equal Pay Act had not eliminated.

The efforts to pass the Equal Rights Amendment pushed the organization's membership over 200,000. By July 1972, the movement even had a magazine of its own, *Ms.,* which kept readers informed on women's issues. The editor of the new magazine was **Gloria Steinem,** an author and public figure who was one of the movement's leading figures.

☑ **Reading Check** **Identifying** What two forces helped bring the women's movement to life again?

Successes and Failures

During the late 1960s and early 1970s, the women's movement fought to enforce Title VII of the Civil Rights Act, lobbied to repeal laws against abortion, and worked for legislation against gender discrimination in employment, housing, and education. Along the way, it experienced success as well as failure.

Striving for Equality in Education One of the movement's notable achievements was in education. Kathy Striebel's story highlighted the discrimination female students often faced in the early 1970s. In 1971, Striebel, a high school junior in St. Paul, Minnesota, wanted to compete for her school's swim team, but the school did not allow girls to join. Kathy's mother, Charlotte, was a member of the local NOW chapter. Through it, she learned that St. Paul had recently passed an ordinance prohibiting gender discrimination in education. She filed a grievance with the city's human rights department, and officials required the school to allow Kathy to swim.

Shortly after joining the team, Kathy beat out one of the boys and earned a spot at a meet. As she stood on the block waiting to swim, the opposing coach declared that she was ineligible to compete because the meet was outside St. Paul and thus beyond the jurisdiction of its laws. "They pulled that little girl right off the block," Charlotte Striebel recalled angrily.

Recognizing the problem, leaders of the movement pushed lawmakers to enact federal legislation banning gender discrimination in education. In 1972 Congress responded by passing a law known collectively as the Educational Amendments. One section, Title IX, prohibited federally funded schools from discriminating against girls and young women in nearly all aspects of its operations, from admissions to athletics. Many schools implemented this new law slowly or not at all, but women now had federal law on their side.

Roe v. Wade One of the most important goals for many women activists was the repeal of laws against abortion. Until 1973, the right to regulate abortion was reserved to the states. This was in keeping with the original plan of the Constitution, which reserved all police power—the power to control people and property in the interest of safety, health, welfare, and morals—to the state. Early in the country's history, some abortion was permitted in the early stages of pregnancy, but after the middle of the 1800s, when states adopted statutory law, abortion was prohibited except to save the life of the mother. Women who chose to have an abortion faced criminal prosecution.

In the late 1960s, some states began adopting more liberal abortion laws. For example, several states allowed abortion if carrying a baby to term might endanger the woman's mental health or if she was a victim of rape or incest. The big change came with the 1973 Supreme Court decision in *Roe v. Wade.* The Supreme Court ruled that state governments could not regulate abortion during the first three months of pregnancy, a time that was interpreted as being within a woman's constitutional right to privacy. During the second three months of pregnancy, states could regulate abortions on the basis of the health of the mother. States could ban abortion in the final three months except in cases of a medical emergency.

Those in favor of protecting abortion rights cheered *Roe* v. *Wade* as a victory, but the issue was far

Profiles IN HISTORY

Shirley Chisholm
1924–2005

Shirley Chisholm once remarked, "Of my two 'handicaps,' being female put more obstacles in my path than being black." Her attempts to overcome these obstacles propelled the Brooklyn, New York, native into the national spotlight and provided encouragement for other women and African Americans attempting to overcome discrimination.

Chisholm first gained national prominence when she defeated two other candidates for Congress from New York's 12th District in 1968. Upon her swearing in, she became the first African American woman to serve in the United States Congress.

In Congress Chisholm became an ardent defender of several causes. An opponent of the seniority system, she protested the ways that party leaders assigned House members to committees and was instrumental in changing them. Chisholm was an early opponent of arms sales to South Africa's racist regime. She also worked on education issues and to increase day care

programs, and she cosponsored a bill to guarantee an annual income to families.

In 1972 Chisholm ran for the Democratic nomination for president. She campaigned extensively and entered primaries in 12 states, winning 28 delegates and receiving 152 first ballot votes at the convention.

She returned to Congress after the convention and continued her crusade to help women and minorities for several more terms. She declined to run for re-election in 1982, citing the difficulties of campaigning for liberal issues in an increasingly conservative political atmosphere.

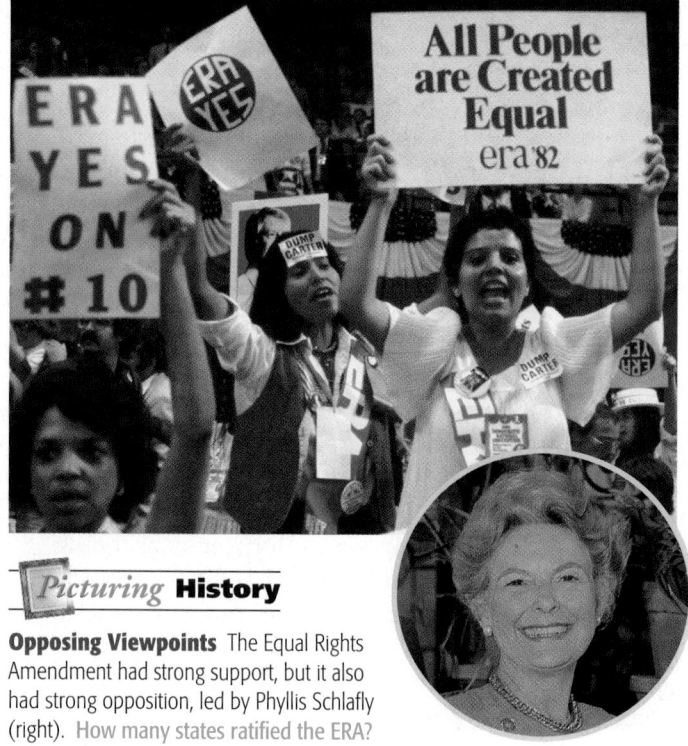

Picturing **History**

Opposing Viewpoints The Equal Rights Amendment had strong support, but it also had strong opposition, led by Phyllis Schlafly (right). How many states ratified the ERA?

some traditional rights, such as the right to alimony in divorce cases or the right to have single-gender colleges. One outspoken opponent was **Phyllis Schlafly,** who organized the Stop-ERA campaign. The Equal Rights Amendment finally failed in 1982.

The Impact of the Women's Movement Despite the failure of the ERA, the women's movement would ultimately bring about profound changes in society. Since the 1970s, many more women have pursued college degrees and careers outside of the home than did so in previous decades. Since the women's movement began, two-career families are much more common than they were in the 1950s and 1960s, although a need for greater family income may also be a factor. Employers began to offer employees options to help make work more compatible with family life, including flexible hours, on-site child care, and job-sharing.

Even though the women's movement helped change social attitudes toward women, a significant income gap between men and women still exists. A major reason for the income gap is that most working women still hold lower-paying jobs such as bank tellers, administrative assistants, cashiers, schoolteachers, and nurses. It is in professional jobs that women have made the most dramatic gains since the 1970s. By 2000 women made up over 40 percent of the nation's graduates receiving medical or law degrees.

from settled. The decision gave rise to the right-to-life movement, whose members consider abortion morally wrong and advocate its total ban. After the *Roe* v. *Wade* ruling, the two sides began an impassioned battle that continues today. 📖 *(For more information on* Roe v. Wade, *see page 1082.)*

The Equal Rights Amendment In 1972 Congress passed the Equal Rights Amendment (ERA). To become part of the Constitution, this amendment to protect women against discrimination had to be ratified by 38 states. Many states did so—35 by 1979—but there was significant opposition to the amendment as well. Some people feared the ERA would take away

✔ **Reading Check** **Summarizing** What successes and failures did the women's movement experience during the late 1960s and early 1970s?

SECTION 2 ASSESSMENT

Checking for Understanding
1. **Define:** feminism, Title IX.
2. **Identify:** Equal Pay Act, Equal Employment Opportunity Commission, Betty Friedan, National Organization for Women, Phyllis Schlafly.
3. **Summarize** Shirley Chisholm's political contributions.

Reviewing Themes
4. **Civic Rights and Responsibilities** How have women's rights improved since the 1960s?

Critical Thinking
5. **Synthesizing** What two events weakened the women's movement after 1920?
6. **Organizing** Use a graphic organizer similar to the one below to list the major achievements of the women's movement.

Achievements

Analyzing Visuals
7. **Analyzing Photographs** Study the photograph on page 927 of a housewife in her kitchen. Think about depictions of housewives in modern television or magazine advertisements. How would you compare the photograph on page 927 with today's images?

Writing About History
8. **Persuasive Writing** Take on the role of a supporter or opponent of the ERA. Write a letter to the editor of your local newspaper to persuade people to support your position.

American LITERATURE

Charlotte Perkins Gilman was a prominent American social critic and feminist writer in the late 1800s and early 1900s. In her most famous work, *The Yellow Wallpaper* (1899), she presents the story of a woman diagnosed with hysteria, for whom a doctor has prescribed total rest. Cut off from any intellectual activity, the woman is slowly driven mad by her "cure."

In this work, Gilman makes a statement against a common belief of the time—that women were generally unfit for scholarship. The story remained obscure for almost 50 years but was rediscovered in the 1970s. It has become a staple of many college literary courses.

Read to Discover
How does the narrator feel about her "illness"? How does her opinion differ from that of her physician and her family?

Reader's Dictionary
scoff: make fun of

phosphates: a carbonated drink, often used as medicine in the 1800s and early 1900s

congenial: agreeable; pleasant

from The Yellow Wallpaper
by Charlotte Perkins Gilman

In the following excerpt, the narrator of the story, writing in a secret journal, is describing her "illness" and how her husband John and others feel about it.

John is practical in the extreme. He has no patience with faith, an intense horror of superstition, and he scoffs openly at any talk of things not to be felt and seen and put down in figures.

John is a physician, and *perhaps*—(I would not say it to a living soul, of course, but this is dead paper and a great relief to my mind)—*perhaps* that is one reason I do not get well faster.

You see he does not believe I am sick!

And what can one do?

If a physician of high standing, and one's own husband, assures friends and relatives that there is really nothing the matter with one but temporary nervous depression—a slight hysterical tendency—what is one to do?

My brother is also a physician, and also of high standing, and he says the same thing.

So I take phosphates or phospites—whichever it is, and tonics, and journeys, and air, and exercise, and am absolutely forbidden to "work" until I am well again.

Personally, I disagree with their ideas.

Personally, I believe that congenial work, with excitement and change, would do me good.

But what is one to do?

I did write for a while in spite of them; but it *does* exhaust me a good deal—having to be so sly about it, or else meet with heavy opposition.

Analyzing Literature
1. What is the main idea in this passage? How does it support the author's point?
2. Does the narrator think this remedy will help her? Why or why not? What clues can you find about how the narrator feels about her illness?

Interdisciplinary Activity
Science Using the Internet and other resources, research some ways that diseases and illnesses were treated in the 1800s and 1900s. Do we still use these treatments today? Create a chart showing the progression of treatment for some of the illnesses you researched.

SECTION 3 New Approaches to Civil Rights

Guide to Reading

Main Idea

Throughout the 1960s and 1970s, minority groups developed new ways to improve their status in the United States.

Key Terms and Names

affirmative action, Allan Bakke, busing, Jesse Jackson, Congressional Black Caucus, César Chávez, *La Raza Unida*, bilingualism, American Indian Movement

Reading Strategy

Sequencing As you read about the civil rights movement's new approaches, complete a time line similar to the one below to record new groups and their actions.

Reading Objectives

- **Describe** the goal of affirmative action policies.
- **Analyze** the rise of Hispanic and Native American protests.

Section Theme

Civic Rights and Responsibilities African Americans, Hispanics, and Native Americans organized to fight discrimination and to gain access to better education and jobs.

Preview of Events

♦1965   ♦1969   ♦1973

1966
Hispanic Americans form United Farm Workers of America

1968
Kerner Commission reports on racism in the United States

1969
Hispanic leaders form *La Raza Unida*

1973
Native Americans and government clash in South Dakota

★ An American Story ★

In 1968 Vernon and Clyde Bellecourt, along with other Native Americans in Minneapolis, were struggling to earn a living. The Bellecourts decided to take a stand against their conditions. Spurred by the 1960s protest movements and by reawakened pride in their culture, the brothers helped organize the American Indian Movement (AIM). AIM's goal was to combat discrimination and brutality by the local police. Vernon recalled how AIM worked:

66They got a small grant from the Urban League of Minneapolis to put two-way radios in their cars and to get tape recorders and cameras. They would listen to the police calls, and when they heard . . . that police were being dispatched to a certain community or bar, they'd show up with cameras and take pictures of the police using more than normal restraint on people. . . . AIM would show up and have attorneys ready. Often they would beat the police back to the station. They would have a bondsman there, and they'd start filing lawsuits against the police department.99

—quoted in *Native American Testimony*

Fighting for Greater Opportunity

At a time of heightened protest in the United States, Native Americans began raising their voices for reform and change. Other groups did as well. During the 1960s and early 1970s, Hispanic Americans organized to improve their status in society. In the wake of the assassination of Dr. Martin Luther King, Jr., African Americans continued their fight for greater civil rights, now focusing more on access to jobs.

Affirmative Action By the end of the 1960s, many African American leaders expressed a growing sense of frustration. Although most legal forms of racial discrimination had been dismantled, many African Americans felt there had been little improvement in their daily lives. In the eyes of leading civil rights activists, the problems facing most African Americans lay in their lack of access to good jobs and adequate schooling. As a result, leaders of the civil rights movement began to focus their energies on these problems.

As part of their effort, civil rights leaders looked to an initiative known as affirmative action. Enforced through executive orders and federal policies, affirmative action called for companies and institutions doing business with the federal government to actively recruit African American employees with the hope that this would lead to improved social and economic status. Officials later expanded affirmative action to include other minority groups and women.

Supporters of the policy argued that because so few companies hired from these groups in the past, they had had little chance to develop necessary job skills. If businesses opened their doors wider to minorities, more of them could begin building better lives.

In one example of affirmative action's impact, Atlanta witnessed a significant increase in minority job opportunities shortly after **Maynard Jackson** became its first African American mayor in 1973. When Jackson took office, less than one percent of all city contracts went to African Americans, even

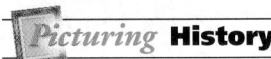

Equal Opportunity Allan Bakke graduated from medical school after the Supreme Court overturned the University of California's use of specific racial quotas. *How did the* Bakke *case affect affirmative action?*

though they made up about half of Atlanta's population. Jackson used the expansion of the city's airport to redress this imbalance by opening the bidding process for airport contracts more widely to minority firms. Through his efforts, small companies and minority firms took on 25 percent of all airport construction work, earning them some $125 million in contracts.

Challenges to Affirmative Action Affirmative action programs did not go unchallenged. Critics viewed them as a form of "reverse discrimination." They claimed that qualified white workers were kept from jobs, promotions, and a place in schools because a certain number of such positions had been set aside for minorities or women.

One of the more notable attacks on affirmative action came in 1974, after officials at the University of California Medical School at Davis turned down the admission of a white applicant named **Allan Bakke** for a second time. When Bakke learned that slots had been set aside for minorities, he sued the school. Bakke argued that by admitting minority applicants, some of whom had scored lower than Bakke on their exams, the school had discriminated against him due to his race.

In 1978, in *University of California Regents* v. *Bakke,* the Supreme Court, in a 5 to 4 ruling, declared that the university had indeed violated Bakke's rights. On the other hand, it ruled that schools could use racial criteria as part of their admissions process so long as they did not use "fixed quotas." While *Bakke* was not a strong and definitive ruling, the Court had nevertheless supported affirmative action programs as constitutional. 📖 *(See page 1082 for more information on* University of California Regents *v.* Bakke.*)*

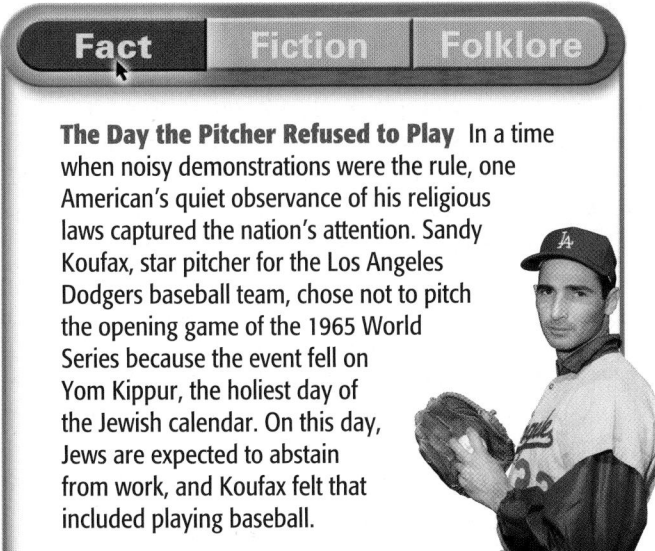

Fact | Fiction | Folklore

The Day the Pitcher Refused to Play In a time when noisy demonstrations were the rule, one American's quiet observance of his religious laws captured the nation's attention. Sandy Koufax, star pitcher for the Los Angeles Dodgers baseball team, chose not to pitch the opening game of the 1965 World Series because the event fell on Yom Kippur, the holiest day of the Jewish calendar. On this day, Jews are expected to abstain from work, and Koufax felt that included playing baseball.

Picturing History

New African American Leadership Andrew Young and Jesse Jackson both worked with Dr. Martin Luther King, Jr., in the civil rights movement. Young went on to become the first African American ambassador to the United Nations, while Jackson has become a prominent member of the Democratic Party. What group of African American members of Congress became influential in the 1970s?

Equal Access to Education By the early 1970s, African American leaders also had begun to push harder for educational improvements. In the 1954 case of *Brown* v. *Board of Education of Topeka, Kansas,* the Supreme Court had ordered an end to segregated public schools. In the 1960s, however, many schools remained segregated as local communities moved slowly to comply with the Court. Since children normally went to neighborhood public schools, segregation in schooling reflected the race segregation of neighborhoods. White schools were usually far superior to African American schools, as Ruth Baston of the NAACP noted in 1965 after visiting Boston schools:

66When we would go to white schools, we'd see these lovely classrooms with a small number of children in each class. The teachers were permanent. We'd see wonderful materials. When we'd go to our schools, we'd see overcrowded classrooms, children sitting out in the corridors. And so then we decided that where there were a large number of white students, that's where the care went. That's where the books went. That's where the money went.99

—quoted in *Freedom Bound*

To ensure desegregated schools, local governments resorted to a policy known as busing, transporting children to schools outside their neighborhoods to achieve greater racial balance. The Supreme Court upheld the constitutionality of busing in the 1971 case, *Swann* v. *Charlotte-Mecklenburg Board of Education.* (See page 1083 for more information on *Swann* v. *Charlotte-Mecklenburg Board of Education.*)

Many whites responded to busing by taking their children out of public schools. Nearly 20,000 white students left Boston's public system for parochial and private schools. By late 1976, African Americans, Hispanics, and other minorities made up the majority of Boston's public school students. This "white flight" also occurred in other cities.

New Political Leaders In their struggle for equal opportunity, African Americans found new political leaders in people such as **Jesse Jackson.** In 1971 Jackson founded People United to Save Humanity, or PUSH, a group aimed at registering voters, developing African American businesses, and broadening educational opportunities. In 1984 and 1988, Jackson sought the Democratic presidential nomination. Although both attempts were unsuccessful, Jackson did win over millions of voters.

African Americans also became more influential in Congress. In 1971 African American members of Congress reorganized an existing organization into the **Congressional Black Caucus** in order to more clearly represent the concerns of African Americans. Another leader who emerged was Louis Farrakhan of the Nation of Islam. In 1994 he helped organize the Million Man March, a gathering of African American men in Washington, D.C., to promote self-reliance and community responsibility.

✓ **Reading Check** **Examining** What were the goals of affirmative action policies?

Hispanic Americans Organize

Hispanic Americans also worked for greater rights in this period. In 1960 about 3 million Hispanics lived in the United States. By the late 1960s, that number had increased to 9 million.

Hispanics came to the United States from different places and for different reasons. Many Puerto Ricans migrated to eastern cities, particularly New York, to find jobs. Cubans often came to flee their country's Communist regime. The largest Hispanic group was Mexican Americans, many of whom arrived during and after World War II to work on huge farms in the South and West.

Hispanics often faced prejudice and limited access to adequate education, housing, and employment. Encouraged by the civil rights movement, they began to organize a protest movement.

César Chávez and the UFW One notable Hispanic American campaign was the effort to win rights for farmworkers. Most Mexican American farm laborers earned little pay, received few benefits, and had no job security. In the early 1960s, **César Chávez** and **Dolores Huerta** organized two groups that fought for farmworkers. In 1965 the groups cooperated in a strike against California growers to demand union recognition, increased wages, and better benefits.

When employers resisted, Chávez enlisted college students, churches, and civil rights groups to organize a national boycott of table grapes, one of California's largest agricultural products. An estimated 17 million citizens stopped buying them, and industry profits tumbled.

Under the sponsorship of the American Federation of Labor and Congress of Industrial Organization (AFL-CIO), in 1966 Chávez and Huerta merged their two organizations into one—the **United Farm Workers** (UFW). The union's combined strength ensured that the boycott would continue. The boycott ended in 1970, when the grape growers finally agreed to a contract to raise wages and improve working conditions.

Growing Political Activism

Hispanic Americans became more politically active during the 1960s and 1970s. In 1969 José Angel Gutiérrez organized a new political party in Texas called *La Raza Unida,* or "the United People." Working with similar organizations in Colorado and California, the group mobilized Mexican American voters with calls for job-training programs and greater access to financial institutions. In the 1970s, the party demonstrated significant strength at the polls.

During this period, a growing number of Hispanic youths became involved in civil rights. In March 1968, about 1,000 Mexican American students and their teachers at an East Los Angeles high school walked out of their classrooms to protest racism.

One issue both Hispanic students and political leaders promoted was bilingualism, the practice of teaching immigrant students in their own language

HISTORY Online

Student Web Activity Visit the *American Vision* Web site at tav.glencoe.com and click on *Student Web Activities—Chapter 31* for an activity on protest movements.

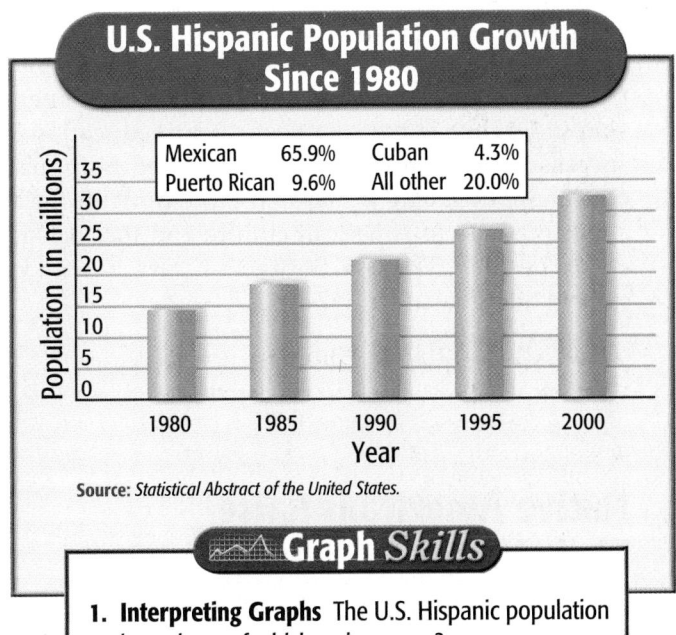

U.S. Hispanic Population Growth Since 1980

| Mexican | 65.9% | Cuban | 4.3% |
| Puerto Rican | 9.6% | All other | 20.0% |

Source: *Statistical Abstract of the United States.*

Graph Skills

1. **Interpreting Graphs** The U.S. Hispanic population is made up of which main groups?
2. **Drawing Conclusions** Why have Hispanic Americans experienced growing political influence in recent years?

Dolores Huerta
1930–

Dolores Huerta began her career as an elementary school teacher, but she soon left, believing that she could do more good for Mexican Americans outside the classroom. "I couldn't stand seeing kids come to class hungry and needing shoes," she said. "I thought I could do more by organizing farmworkers than by trying to teach their hungry children."

In the early 1950s, Huerta helped found the Stockton, California, chapter of the Community Service Organization (CSO). This grassroots group led voter registration drives, pushed for improved public services, and fought for legislation on behalf of low-income workers.

It was through her work with the CSO that Huerta met César Chávez. Together, they organized farmworkers into a union and fought for better wages and working conditions.

José Angel Gutiérrez
1944–

As a young social activist, José Angel Gutiérrez set out to organize Mexican Americans from Crystal City, Texas, into a political force. In 1970 his newly founded political party, *La Raza Unida,* participated in local elections. Over the next few years, Mexican Americans gained control of Crystal City's school system and government.

As *La Raza Unida* gained a more national following, Gutiérrez became a prominent figure. He eventually stepped away from the political scene, serving first as a judge and then as a college professor. Gutiérrez found it difficult to stay away from politics, however, and in 1993, he ran unsuccessfully for a U.S. Senate seat. After that, he established his own legal center. Looking upon Gutiérrez's career, one historian said, "He represents the new breed of Chicano professionals produced by the colleges and universities, but he is still a Chicano with the old dream of revolution."

while they also learned English. Many Hispanics argued they would be at a competitive disadvantage with native English speakers unless they had schooling in their native language. Congress supported their arguments, passing the **Bilingual Education Act** in 1968. This directed school districts to set up classes for immigrants in their own language as they were learning English.

In recent years there has been some movement away from bilingualism in states with large Hispanic populations. Some educators argue that total immersion in English is the soundest road to educational success. Some American voters opposed bilingual education, believing it makes it more difficult for a child to adjust to American culture and that it was costly besides. The U.S. Supreme Court, however, upheld bilingualism in 1974.

✓ **Reading Check** **Explaining** How did Hispanic Americans increase their economic opportunities in the 1960s?

Native Americans Raise Their Voices

Native Americans in 1970 were one of the nation's smallest minority groups, constituting less than one percent of the U.S. population. Few minority groups, however, had more justifiable grievances than the descendants of America's original inhabitants. The average annual family income of Native Americans

was $1,000 less than that of African Americans. The Native American unemployment rate was 10 times the national rate. Joblessness was particularly high on reservation lands, where nearly half of all Native Americans lived. Most urban Native Americans suffered from discrimination and from limited education and training. The bleakest statistic of all showed that life expectancy among Native Americans was almost seven years below the national average. To improve conditions, many Native Americans began organizing in the late 1960s and 1970s.

A Protest Movement Emerges In 1961 more than 400 members of 67 Native American groups gathered in Chicago to discuss ways to address their numerous problems. They issued a manifesto, known as the **Declaration of Indian Purpose,** calling for policies to create greater economic opportunities on reservations.

Unlike other groups demanding more assimilation into mainstream society, many Native Americans wanted greater independence from it. They took a step toward this goal in 1968 when Congress passed the Indian Civil Rights Act. It guaranteed reservation residents the protections of the Bill of Rights, but it also recognized the legitimacy of local reservation law.

Native Americans who viewed the government's reform efforts as too modest formed more militant groups, such as the **American Indian Movement** (AIM). Typically, such groups employed a more combative style. In 1969 AIM made a symbolic protest by occupying the abandoned federal prison on Alcatraz Island in San Francisco Bay for 19 months, claiming ownership "by right of discovery."

A more famous and violent protest occurred later at Wounded Knee, South Dakota, where federal troops had killed hundreds of Sioux in 1890. In February 1973, AIM members seized and occupied the town of Wounded Knee for 70 days. They demanded radical changes in the administration of reservations and that the government honor its long-forgotten treaty obligations to Native Americans. A brief clash between the occupiers and the FBI killed two Native Americans and wounded several on both sides. Shortly thereafter, the siege came to an end.

Native American high school student

Native Americans Make Notable Gains

The Native American movement fell short of achieving all its goals, but it did win some notable victories. In 1975 Congress passed the Indian Self-Determination and Educational Assistance Act, which increased funds for Native American education and expanded local control in administering federal programs. More Native Americans also moved into policy-making positions at the Bureau of Indian Affairs, and the agency pushed for more Native American self-determination.

Through the federal court system, Native Americans also won a number of the land and water rights they sought. The Pueblo of Taos, New Mexico, regained property rights to Blue Lake, a place sacred to their religion. In 1980, a federal court settled a claim of the Passamaquoddy and the Penobscot groups. The government paid the groups $81.5 million to relinquish their claim on land in the state of Maine. The two groups purchased 300,000 acres with the money and invested much of the remainder. Other court decisions gave Native American groups authority to impose taxes on businesses on their reservations and to perform other sovereign functions.

Since Native Americans first began to organize, many reservations have dramatically improved their economic conditions by actively developing businesses, such as electric plants, resorts, cattle ranches, and oil and gas wells. More recently, gambling casinos have become a successful enterprise. Because of rulings on sovereignty, Native Americans in some areas are allowed to operate gaming establishments under their own laws even though state laws prevent others from doing so. In these ways, Native Americans have tried to regain control of their economic future, just as other American minorities did in the 1960s and 1970s.

Reading Check **Analyzing** What conditions led Native Americans to organize in the 1960s?

SECTION 3 ASSESSMENT

Checking for Understanding

1. **Define:** affirmative action, busing, bilingualism.
2. **Identify:** Allan Bakke, Jesse Jackson, Congressional Black Caucus, César Chávez, *La Raza Unida,* American Indian Movement.
3. **Analyze** how the *Bakke* case, along with other cases, affected affirmative action.

Reviewing Themes

4. **Civic Rights and Responsibilities** How did the Supreme Court support civil rights during the 1970s? Cite two court cases and their decisions.

Critical Thinking

5. **Synthesizing** Why have African Americans become significantly more influential in the U.S. Congress since the early 1970s?
6. **Categorizing** Use a graphic organizer similar to the one below to identify civil rights leaders and their causes during the 1960s and 1970s.

Civil Rights Leaders	Causes

Analyzing Visuals

7. **Analyzing Graphs** Study the graph on page 935 of U.S. Hispanic population growth since 1980. The largest percentage of Hispanics is represented by Mexican Americans. What was the approximate percentage growth for Hispanic Americans from 1980 to 2000?

Writing About History

8. **Expository Writing** Write a magazine article about the conditions that gave rise to the Native American protest movement of the 1960s and 1970s. In your article, discuss the movement's goals and activities.

Critical Thinking
SKILLBUILDER

Analyzing Primary Sources

Why Learn This Skill?

To determine what happened in the past, historians do some detective work. They comb through bits of evidence from the past to reconstruct events. These bits of written and illustrated historical evidence are called *primary sources.*

Learning the Skill

Primary sources are records of events made by the people who witnessed them. They include letters, diaries, photographs, news articles, and legal documents.

Primary sources yield several important kinds of information. Often they give detailed accounts of events. However, the account reflects only one perspective. For this reason, you must examine as many perspectives as possible before drawing any conclusions. To analyze primary sources, follow these steps.

• Identify the author of the source.

• Identify when and where the document was written.

• Read the document for its content and try to answer the five "W" questions: Who is it about? What is it about? When did it happen? Where did it happen? Why did it happen?

• Determine what kind of information may be missing from the primary source.

Practicing the Skill

The primary source that follows is a small part of a United States legal document. Read the source, and then answer the questions.

Title IX, Education Amendments of 1972, Section 1684. Blindness or visual impairment; prohibition against discrimination

No person in the United States shall, on the grounds of blindness or severely impaired vision, be denied admission in any course of study by a recipient of Federal financial assistance for any education program or activity; but nothing herein shall be construed to require any such institution to provide any special services to such person because of his blindness or visual impairment.

❶ When was this document written?

❷ Who is affected by this legal document?

❸ What is the purpose of this legal requirement?

❹ Why do you think this document was written?

Skills Assessment

Complete the Practicing Skills questions on page 947 and the Chapter 31 Skill Reinforcement Activity to assess your mastery of this skill.

Applying the Skill

Analyzing Primary Sources Find a primary source from your past—a photo, a report card, an old newspaper clipping, or your first baseball card. Bring this source to class and explain what it shows about that time in your life.

 Glencoe's **Skillbuilder Interactive Workbook CD-ROM, Level 2,** provides instruction and practice in key social studies skills.

Guide to Reading

Main Idea

During the 1960s and 1970s, environmental issues became a significant concern for many Americans.

Key Terms and Names

Rachel Carson, smog, Environmental Protection Agency, fossil fuel, Three Mile Island, Ralph Nader

Reading Strategy

Organizing As you read about the nation's environmental problems in the 1960s and 1970s, complete a graphic organizer by including actions taken to combat these problems.

Actions Taken

Reading Objectives

- **Explain** the origins of the environmental movement.
- **Identify** the significant measures taken to combat environmental problems.

Section Theme

Groups and Institutions Increased awareness of environmental issues inspired a grassroots campaign to protect nature.

Preview of Events

♦1962   ♦1968   ♦1974   ♦1980

1962
Rachel Carson's *Silent Spring* published

1965
Ralph Nader's *Unsafe at Any Speed* published

1970
First Earth Day celebrated; EPA established

1972
U.S. bans use of pesticide DDT

1979
Nuclear accident at Three Mile Island

★ *An American Story* ★

In 1966 Carol Yannacone of Patchogue, a small community on Long Island, New York, learned that officials were using a powerful pesticide, DDT, as part of a mosquito control operation in a local lake. Alarmed that the pesticide would poison lakes and streams, Yannacone and her husband, Victor, an attorney, contacted several local scientists, who confirmed their suspicions. The Yannacones then successfully sued to halt the use of the pesticide.

The Yannacones had discovered a new strategy for addressing environmental concerns. The legal system, Victor Yannacone insisted, was the one place where facts and evidence, not politics and emotions, would decide the outcome:

❝A court . . . is the only forum in which a full inquiry into questions of environmental significance can be carried on. . . . Only on the witness stand, protected by the rules of evidence though subject to cross-examination, can a scientist be free of the harassment of legislators seeking re-election of higher political office; free from the glare of the controversy-seeking media; free from unsubstantiated attacks of self-styled experts representing vested economic interests and yet who are not subject to cross examination.❞

—quoted in *Since Silent Spring*

The Beginnings of Environmentalism

Shortly after the Yannacones' court victory, the scientists involved in the case established the Environmental Defense Fund and used its contributions for a series of legal actions across the country to halt DDT spraying. Their efforts led to a nationwide ban on the use of the pesticide in 1972.

The Power of One Rachel Carson, a marine biologist, sounded a warning note for the environment. Her concern over how humans affect the environment helped start a new reform movement. *What pesticide in particular worried Carson?*

The effort to ban DDT was only one aspect of a larger environmental movement that took shape in the 1960s and 1970s. During this period, a growing number of Americans began to examine more closely how their highly industrialized society was affecting the environment. Many were alarmed at what they discovered. It seemed to some that the nation had little regard for the environment. An increasing use of pesticides had damaged a wide range of wildlife. A rise in pollution had fouled both the air and the water. Potentially deadly nuclear energy was being used more and more. These developments prompted many citizens to address environmental problems more actively.

A wider realization that the nation's natural environment was threatened had begun to grow in the early 1960s. The person who sounded the loudest alarm bell was not a political leader or prominent academic, but a soft-spoken marine biologist, **Rachel Carson.** Carson's 1962 book *Silent Spring* assailed the increasing use of pesticides, particularly DDT. She contended that while pesticides curbed insect populations, they also killed birds, fish, and other creatures that might ingest them. Carson warned Americans of a "silent spring," in which there would be few birds

left to usher spring in with their songs. In her book, she imagined such a scene from a fictitious town:

> 66There was a strange stillness. The birds, for example—where had they gone? Many people spoke of them, puzzled and disturbed. The feeding stations in the backyards were deserted. The few birds seen anywhere were moribund; they trembled violently and could not fly. It was a spring without voices. On the mornings that had once throbbed with the dawn chorus of robins, catbirds, doves, jays, wrens, and scores of other bird voices there was now no sound; only silence lay over the fields and woods and marsh.99
>
> —from *Silent Spring*

Silent Spring became one of the most controversial and powerful books of the 1960s. It sold nearly half a million copies within six months of its publication and was widely discussed. The chemical industry was outraged and began an intense campaign to discredit Carson and her arguments. Nonetheless, many Americans took Carson's warnings to heart and began to focus on environmental issues.

✓ **Reading Check** **Identifying** What natural resources did environmental groups want to protect?

The Environmental Movement Blossoms

During the 1960s, Americans began to feel that environmental problems plagued every region of the nation. In the Northwest, timber companies were cutting down acres of forestland. Smog, or fog made heavier and darker by smoke and chemical fumes, was smothering major cities. In 1969 a major oil spill off Santa Barbara, California, ruined miles of beach and killed scores of birds and aquatic animals. A dike project in the Florida Everglades indirectly killed millions of birds and animals. Meanwhile, pollution and garbage had caused nearly all the fish to disappear from Lake Erie. By 1970 a growing number of citizens were convinced that the time had come to do something about protecting the environment.

A Grassroots Effort Begins Many observers point to April 1970 as the unofficial beginning of the environmental movement. That month, the nation held its first **Earth Day** celebration, a day devoted to addressing the country's environmental concerns. The national response was overwhelming. On 2,000 college campuses, in 10,000 secondary schools, and in hundreds of communities, millions of Americans participated in activities to show their environmental awareness. Senator Gaylord Nelson of Wisconsin, who had put forth the idea of an Earth Day celebration, commented on the event: "The people cared and Earth Day became the first opportunity they ever had to join in a nationwide demonstration to send a message to the politicians—a message to tell them to wake up and do something."

After Earth Day, the grassroots effort intensified. Citizens formed local environmental groups, while long-standing nonprofit organizations such as the Sierra Club, the Audubon Society, and the Wilderness Society gained prominence. These organizations worked to protect the environment and promote the conservation of natural resources. In 1970 activists started the Natural Resources Defense Council to coordinate a nationwide network of scientists, lawyers, and activists working on environmental problems.

Many communities and businesses have responded to the efforts of these organizations and have started including sustainable development in their planning. City planners try to reduce urban sprawl and expand green spaces, builders include energy efficiency in their designs, and the forestry industry has begun reforestation programs.

GOVERNMENT

The Government Steps In
With the environmental movement gaining public support, the federal government took action. In 1970 President Nixon signed the National Environmental Policy Act, which created the **Environmental Protection Agency** (EPA). The EPA took on the job of setting and enforcing pollution standards, promoting research, and coordinating anti-pollution activities with state and local governments. The agency also monitored other federal agencies with respect to their impact on the environment.

The **Clean Air Act** also became law in 1970 over President Nixon's veto. This act established emissions standards for factories and automobiles. It also ordered that all industries comply with such standards within five years.

In following years, Congress passed two more pieces of significant environmental legislation. The **Clean Water Act** (1972) restricted the discharge of pollutants into the nation's lakes and rivers, and the **Endangered Species Act** (1973) established measures for saving threatened animal species. Over time these laws produced a dramatic improvement in some areas. Smog in industrial cities was reduced, as was pollution in many lakes, streams, and rivers.

Love Canal
Despite the flurry of federal environmental legislation, Americans continued to mobilize on the community level throughout the 1970s. One of the most powerful displays of community activism occurred in a housing development near Niagara Falls, New York, known as Love Canal.

During the 1970s, residents of Love Canal began to notice increasingly high incidences of health problems in their community, including nerve damage, blood diseases, cancer, miscarriages, and birth defects. The residents soon learned that their community sat atop a decades-old toxic waste dump. Over time its hazardous contents had leaked into the ground.

Led by a local woman, **Lois Gibbs,** the residents joined together and demanded that the government take steps to address these health threats. Hindered at first by local and state officials, the residents refused to back down, and by 1978 they had made their struggle known to the entire nation. That year, in the face of mounting public pressure and evidence of the dangers posed by the dump, the state permanently relocated more than 200 families.

Picturing **History**

Environmental Awareness Numerous oil spills and events such as Earth Day have brought environmental concerns to the attention of Americans. What issues does the Sierra Club address?

Solar Energy

Concerns in the 1970s about the environment and safe energy led to a strong interest in solar energy. Sunlight is composed of photons, particles of solar energy. The use of photovoltaic (PV) cells allows solar energy to be used for a wide range of energy needs, from powering generators to running agricultural water pumps or simple calculators. *Why was solar power seen as an environmentally friendly power source?*

1 Solar arrays or panels are made up of thousands of PV cells and capture the sun's rays.

2 This magnification shows the composition of a **PV cell.**

3 This schematic shows a **cross-section of a cell** and how its electrons respond to sunlight to create a flow of electricity.

In 1980, after hearing protests from the families who still lived near the landfill, President Carter declared Love Canal a federal disaster area and moved over 600 remaining families to new locations. In 1983 Love Canal residents sued the company that had created the dump site and settled the case for $20 million. The site was cleaned up by sealing the waste within an underground bunker and burning homes located above the dumping ground.

Concerns Over Nuclear Energy During the 1970s, a number of citizens expressed concern over the growth of nuclear power. As nuclear power plants began to dot the nation's landscape, the debate over their use intensified. Supporters of nuclear energy hailed it as a cleaner and less expensive alternative to fossil fuels, such as coal, oil, and natural gas, which are in limited supply. Opponents warned of the risks nuclear energy posed, particularly the devastating consequences of an accidental radiation release into the air.

The debate moved to the nation's forefront in shocking fashion in 1979. In the early hours of March 28, one of the reactors at the **Three Mile Island** nuclear facility outside Harrisburg, Pennsylvania, overheated after its cooling system failed. Two days later, as plant officials scrambled to fix the problem, low levels of radiation escaped from the reactor.

Officials evacuated many nearby residents, while others fled on their own. Citizens and community groups expressed outrage in protest rallies. Officials closed down the reactor and sealed the leak. The Nuclear Regulatory Commission, the federal agency that regulates the nuclear power industry, eventually declared the plant safe. President Carter even visited the site to allay the public's concerns.

The accident at Three Mile Island had a powerful impact and left much of the public in great doubt about the safety of nuclear energy. Such doubts have continued. Since Three Mile Island, 60 nuclear power plants have been shut down or abandoned, and no new facilities have been built since 1973.

Reading Check **Summarizing** What is the environmental movement's main goal?

The Consumer Movement

During the 1960s and 1970s, a number of citizens also questioned the quality and safety of the many new "technologically advanced" products flooding the market. In an atmosphere of protest and overall distrust of authority, more and more buyers demanded product safety, accurate information, and a voice in government formulation of consumer policy.

Perhaps the most notable figure of this new consumer protection movement was **Ralph Nader,** a young lawyer from Connecticut. During the early 1960s, Nader began taking note of what he considered an alarmingly high number of automobile fatalities. He presented his findings in a 1965 book, *Unsafe at Any Speed.* Nader charged car designers and manufacturers with putting style, cost, and speed ahead of safety. He also challenged one of the auto industry's long-held claims that drivers were to blame for most auto accidents:

> 66The American automobile is produced exclusively to the standards which the manufacturer decides to establish. It comes into the marketplace unchecked. When a car becomes involved in an accident, the entire investigatory, enforcement and claims apparatus that makes up the post-accident response looks almost invariably to driver failure as the cause. . . . Should vehicle failure be obvious in some accidents, responsibility is seen in terms of inadequate maintenance by the motorist. Accommodated by superficial standards of accident investigation, the car manufacturers exude presumptions of engineering excellence and reliability, and this reputation is accepted by many unknowing motorists.99
>
> —from *Unsafe at Any Speed*

Nader's efforts received an accidental boost from an unlikely source: the auto industry. Shortly after his book came out, a car company hired private detectives to follow Nader in an attempt to uncover information that might discredit him. The detectives found nothing, and when this corporate spying incident came to light, the publicity pushed *Unsafe at Any Speed* up the bestseller list. As a result, the public became much more aware of auto safety issues. Nader sued the car company for invasion of privacy and used the settlement money to fund several consumer organizations.

Nader's efforts helped spur Congress to pass the **National Traffic and Motor Vehicle Safety Act** in 1966. The act set mandatory safety standards and established a procedure for notifying car owners about defects. For the first time, the automobile industry was subject to federal safety regulations. Carmakers had to incorporate safety standards into their car designs so that auto crashes would be less devastating. Requirements that called for the installation of seat belts, door locks, safer fuel tanks, and other improvements have since saved hundreds of thousands of lives and prevented millions of injuries.

Nader's success led to calls for a closer examination of numerous other consumer goods during the 1960s and 1970s. Organizations lobbied Congress and state legislatures to pass laws regulating such products as dangerous toys, flammable fabrics, and potentially unsafe meat and poultry. In the midst of so many protest movements during this period, the consumer protection effort may have appeared small. It made a substantial impact, however, on the daily lives of millions of Americans.

✓ **Reading Check** **Describing** What was the impact of the consumer protection movement?

SECTION 4 ASSESSMENT

Checking for Understanding
1. **Define:** smog, fossil fuel.
2. **Identify:** Rachel Carson, Environmental Protection Agency, Three Mile Island, Ralph Nader.
3. **List** three measures taken to combat environmental problems in the 1960s and 1970s.

Reviewing Themes
4. **Groups and Institutions** What groups lobbied for government legislation to protect the environment in the 1960s and 1970s?

Critical Thinking
5. **Evaluating** Which environmental issue do you think is the most pressing problem the environment faces today? Explain your response.
6. **Categorizing** Use a graphic organizer similar to the one below to list the environmental laws passed in the 1970s and explain their purposes.

Environmental Legislation	Purpose

Analyzing Visuals
7. **Analyzing Posters** Examine the "Love It or Leave It" poster on page 941. This phrase was first used by Vietnam War supporters, directed toward war critics and referring to the United States. How has the phrase been adapted here?

Writing About History
8. **Descriptive Writing** Take on the role of an investigative reporter and describe the environmental disaster at either Love Canal or Three Mile Island. Explain how community activism brought the issue to the nation's attention.

Engines are made in **Canada,** close to the automotive assembly centers of the United States.

GERMANY

CANADA

Transmissions are manufactured in **Mexico,** where labor costs are relatively low.

UNITED STATES
Bowling Green, KY

MEXICO

ECUADOR

Light and durable balsa wood **floor plates** are produced in **Ecuador**, because the wood is abundant there.

The production of a GM Chevrolet Corvette in Bowling Green, Kentucky, requires the assembly of components from around the world: an engine from Canada, a transmission from Mexico, balsa wood floor plates from Ecuador, switches from Germany, circuit boards from several Asian nations, and brakes from Australia.

Global Cars

A **German** factory produces very high quality **switches** that can easily be shipped to the United States.

JAPAN

Circuit boards are assembled with parts from **Japan, Thailand,** and **Singapore.**

THAILAND

SINGAPORE

AUSTRALIA

An **Australian** company with manufacturing facilities in the United States provides the premier **brake pads** needed in high-performance vehicles.

Cars are shipped all over the world. Here, Japanese cars are unloaded from a large container ship in Baltimore, Maryland.

The globalization of the world economy since the end of World War II has revolutionized the way in which industries and corporations operate. Tremendous advances in technology, communications, and the transport of goods have enabled corporations to turn more and more often to manufacturing facilities and resources around the world. The car industry is a good example of this trend.

For decades American automakers have operated assembly plants in foreign countries, including Brazil, Poland, India, and China. Car companies have also established plants abroad that manufacture particular components, which are then assembled in an American factory. As shown on the world map on the left, foreign manufacturers build major components of the Chevrolet Corvette and ship them to Bowling Green, Kentucky. There, workers assemble the parts—along with some 1,900 others manufactured by about 400 suppliers—into the finished car. The process of finding part suppliers outside of the company, known as "outsourcing," is one way multinational corporations try to gain a competitive advantage over their rivals. Companies contract with foreign suppliers that meet a combination of criteria, including cost, quality, and ease of delivery.

Computers and the Internet have made worldwide communication dramatically easier, faster, and cheaper.

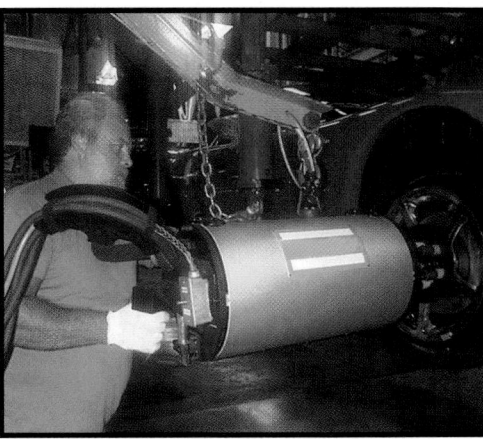

A worker assembles a Corvette at a plant in Bowling Green, Kentucky.

Technological advances have also made manufacturing more efficient. For example, automakers can keep track of parts and suppliers so that the essential components can be delivered to factories from anywhere in the world "just in time" to assemble the finished product.

Multinational corporations now account for about two-thirds of the world's trade in products. Global corporations have become enormous, and the largest ones are wealthier than entire countries. The income of General Motors, for instance, rivals gross national products of the mid-sized economies of nations such as South Africa, Turkey, and Saudi Arabia.

The auto industry has come a long way since Henry Ford perfected assembly line production techniques that made cars affordable for the mass market. Today's automakers have adopted global assembly lines, applying Ford's innovations—standardized job tasks and division of labor—across international boundaries.

LEARNING FROM GEOGRAPHY

1. What three criteria are considered in decisions about suppliers?

2. Why might geography no longer be as big a factor as it once was in the location of a production plant?

Reviewing Key Terms

On a sheet of paper, use each of these terms in a sentence.

1. counterculture
2. commune
3. feminism
4. Title IX
5. affirmative action
6. busing
7. bilingualism
8. smog
9. fossil fuel

Reviewing Key Facts

10. **Identify:** Tom Hayden, Haight-Ashbury district, Jimi Hendrix, Equal Employment Opportunity Commission, Betty Friedan, National Organization for Women, Allan Bakke, Jesse Jackson, Congressional Black Caucus, *La Raza Unida,* American Indian Movement, Rachel Carson, Environmental Protection Agency, Ralph Nader.

11. How did Title VII of the Civil Rights Act of 1964 promote women's equality?

12. How did Betty Friedan stimulate the feminist movement?

13. Why were some conservatives opposed to the Equal Rights Amendment?

14. How did Native Americans expand their political rights and economic opportunities in the 1960s and 1970s?

15. How did the environmental movement begin?

Critical Thinking

16. **Analyzing Themes: Civic Rights and Responsibilities** Choose a minority group discussed in this chapter, and explain how this group worked to gain civil rights and to improve its status in American society during the 1960s and 1970s.

17. **Organizing** Use a graphic organizer to list the protest movements of the 1960s and 1970s and their goals.

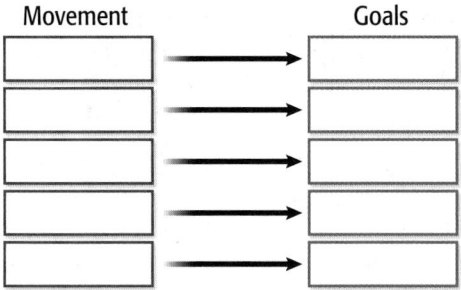

Movement   Goals

Chapter Summary

Speaking Out for Equality

Youth Movement	Women's Movement	Minority Groups	Environmental and Consumer Groups
Protests Status Quo	**Regains Momentum**	**Continue the Fight**	**New Concerns Emerge**
• Grows out of earlier "beat" movement	• Fights for equal economic rights in workplace and society	• Expand on earlier success and speed up access to previous gains	• First Earth Day sparks widespread awareness of environmental issues
• Becomes increasingly influential as "baby boom" generation matures	• Demands equal opportunities in education	• Affirmative Action advocates equality in work environment for minority and disadvantaged groups	• Federal government establishes pollution standards and begins monitoring environmental problems
• Protests injustices facing African Americans, the poor, and the disadvantaged	• *Roe* v. *Wade* expands access to abortion	• Native Americans gain more power on reservations and fight discrimination, unemployment, police brutality, and poverty	• State and federal legislatures pass laws regulating the safety standards for a wide variety of consumer products
• Free Speech Movement establishes tactics of boycotting college classes and occupying buildings		• Hispanic Americans lobby for better working conditions and job training	
• Hippie counterculture rebels against system, visualizes utopian ideals			

18. **Evaluating** In what ways did the counterculture movement change American society?

19. **Drawing Conclusions** Why do you think so many protest movements emerged in the United States during the 1960s and 1970s?

Practicing Skills

20. **Analyzing Primary Sources** Reread "An American Story" at the beginning of Section 2 on page 926. Then answer the questions below.
    a. Whose opinion is expressed in this letter?
    b. When was this letter written? In what publication did it appear?
    c. What role in society is the writer discussing? What is her opinion of this role?

Chapter Activities

21. **American History Primary Source Document Library CD-ROM** Under *Struggle for Civil Rights,* read "Delano Grape Workers, A Proclamation" by the Delano Grape Workers. Using information from the grape workers' proclamation, work with a few of your classmates to create a two-minute television advertisement to persuade all Americans to join the grape boycott. In your advertisement, you should use facts you learned about the grape boycott and also appeal to people's emotions.

22. **Creating a Database, Thematic Model, and Quiz** Use the Internet and other resources to research student protests in the 1960s and 1970s. Create a database of these protests that clearly depicts where, when, and why the protests took place. Then create a thematic model of this information by labeling the locations of the protests on a map of the United States. Finally, create a quiz for your classmates by writing five questions about the geographic distribution of the protests and the patterns this might suggest.

Writing Activity

23. **Persuasive Writing** Use library and Internet resources to learn about the predictions scientists are making on how future population growth and distribution will affect the physical environment. Pay special attention to the evidence that these scientists use and the types of predictions that each makes. Is there agreement or disagreement in the scientific community about population growth and its environmental effects? Present the findings of your research in a written report.

NATIONAL GEOGRAPHIC

ERA Ratification, 1972–1982

Date Ratified:
- 1972
- 1973
- 1974
- 1975
- 1977
- Did not ratify

Geography and History

24. The map above shows the states that ratified the Equal Rights Amendment between 1972 and 1982. Study the map and answer the questions below.
    a. **Interpreting Maps** How many states had ratified the Equal Rights Amendment by 1977?
    b. **Applying Geography Skills** What conclusion can you draw about the distribution of states that did not approve the ERA?

Standardized Test Practice

Directions: Choose the phrase that best completes the following sentence.

Women faced all of the following kinds of discrimination in the 1960s EXCEPT

F unequal pay for performing the same tasks as men.

G being prohibited from attending certain universities.

H being denied the right to vote.

J the inability to obtain loans and credit.

Test-Taking Tip: This question is looking for the *exception.* Three of the answer choices describe types of discrimination that women faced *in the 1960s.* Women gained the right to vote in 1920, when the Nineteenth Amendment was ratified by the states.

UNIT
10 A Changing Society

1968–Present

Why It Matters

A reassessment of postwar developments marked the last three decades of the twentieth century. The Cold War ended and political boundaries were redrawn. The United States remained a global force, but the role of the federal government was diminished in the wake of scandal and a renewed conservatism. As the United States entered a new century, the nation continued to redefine itself. The country's social diversity posed new challenges and provided new strength to the nation. Understanding the shifts of this period will help prepare you for your future. The following resources offer more information about this time in American history.

Primary Sources Library

See pages 1056–1057 for primary source readings to accompany Unit 10.

Use the **American History Primary Source Document Library CD-ROM** to find additional primary sources about the changes in recent years of American history.

Handheld computer and stylus

New Yorkers celebrate the millennium, January 1, 2000

CHAPTER 32 Politics and Economics *1971–1980*

Why It Matters

The protests of the 1960s were passionate and sometimes violent. The nation elected President Nixon on a promise to uphold the values of what Nixon called "Middle America." In foreign policy, Nixon charted a new path with a historic visit to China. At home he introduced "New Federalism." In 1974 the Watergate scandal forced Nixon to resign. Presidents Ford and Carter faced an economic downturn and a major energy crisis.

The Impact Today

Experiences of the 1970s have had an impact today.
- *The Watergate scandal has left many Americans less confident in political leaders.*
- *The Department of Energy, created by President Carter, still exists as a cabinet-level agency.*

The American Vision *Video* *The Chapter 32 video, "The Watergate Break-In," examines the circumstances surrounding this scandal.*

1973
- *Roe* v. *Wade* Supreme Court decision legalizes abortion
- Senate Watergate investigations begin
- OPEC oil embargo leads to fuel shortages

1974
- Nixon resigns
- Gerald Ford becomes president

1972
- Nixon visits China and the Soviet Union
- Watergate burglars arrested at Democratic National Committee headquarters

United States
PRESIDENTS

Nixon 1969–1974

Ford 1974–1977

1971

1974

World

1971
- People's Republic of China admitted to UN

1973
- Britain, Ireland, and Denmark join Common Market

1974
- India becomes world's sixth nuclear power

950

President Nixon with Chinese premier Zhou Enlai (on Nixon's right) during Nixon's historic visit to China in 1972

1975
• President Ford signs Helsinki Accords

1976
• Jimmy Carter elected president

plant a **WIN** garden
WHIP INFLATION NOW

NO GAS

1979
• Iranian revolutionaries seize U.S. embassy in Tehran

Carter 1977–1981

1977

1980

1976
• Mao Zedong dies

1977
• Human rights manifesto signed by 241 Czech activists and intellectuals

1979
• Sandinista guerrillas overthrow dictatorship of Somoza

• Margaret Thatcher becomes prime minister of Great Britain

HISTORY *Online*

Chapter Overview
Visit the *American Vision* Web site at tav.glencoe.com and click on **Chapter Overviews—Chapter 32** to preview chapter information.

The Nixon Administration

Guide to Reading

Main Idea
President Nixon sought to restore law and order and traditional values at home and to ease Cold War tensions abroad.

Key Terms and Names
Southern strategy, revenue sharing, impound, Henry Kissinger, détente, summit

Reading Strategy
Organizing As you read about President Nixon's administration, complete a graphic organizer by listing his domestic and foreign policies.

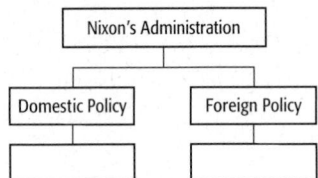

Reading Objectives
- **Describe** Nixon's domestic agenda.
- **Discuss** Nixon's foreign policy achievements.

Section Theme
Global Connections One of President Nixon's most dramatic accomplishments was changing the relationship between the United States, Communist China, and the Soviet Union.

Preview of Events

♦1968   ♦1970   ♦1972   ♦1974

1968
Nixon wins presidential election

1969
Nixon proposes Family Assistance Plan

February 1972
Nixon visits China

May 1972
Moscow hosts American-Soviet summit

★ An American Story ★

Millions of Americans saw police and demonstrators clash on the streets of Chicago at the Democratic National Convention in late August 1968. Many television viewers were outraged at the police tactics they saw. G.L. Halbert, however, was not one of them. To make his support of police efforts public, Halbert wrote a letter to *Newsweek* magazine:

❝Congratulations to Mayor Daley and the Chicago police on their tough handling of the yippies, Vietniks, and newsmen. If more mayors and police departments had the courage to crack down on those who carry only the flags of our enemies and newsmen who consistently slant their coverage of events in favor of those who would undermine and disrupt our country, there would be greater freedom for the majority of Americans rather than greater lawlessness for the few. It is a tragedy that such individuals are allowed to cringe behind our constitutional guarantees after they have wreaked destruction by their agitation.❞

—**quoted in *Newsweek*, September 16, 1968**

Appealing to Middle America

The views expressed by G.L. Halbert were not unusual. While they did not shout as loudly as the protesters, many Americans supported the government and longed for an end to the violence and turmoil that seemed to plague the nation in the 1960s. The presidential candidate in 1968 who appealed to many of these frustrated citizens was

Richard Nixon, a Republican. Nixon aimed many of his campaign messages at these Americans, whom he referred to as "Middle America" and the "silent majority." He promised them "peace with honor" in Vietnam, law and order, a streamlined government, and a return to more traditional values at home.

The Election of 1968

Nixon's principal opponent in the 1968 presidential election was Democrat **Hubert Humphrey,** who had served as vice president under Lyndon Johnson. Nixon also had to wage his campaign against a strong third-party candidate, **George Wallace,** an experienced Southern politician and avowed supporter of segregation. In a 1964 bid for the Democratic presidential nomination, the former Alabama governor had attracted considerable support.

On Election Day, Wallace captured an impressive 13.5 percent of the popular vote, the best showing of a third-party candidate since 1924. Nixon managed a victory, however, receiving 43.4 percent of the popular vote to Humphrey's 42.7 and 301 electoral votes to Humphrey's 191.

The Southern Strategy

One of the keys to Nixon's victory was his surprisingly strong showing in the South. Even though the South had long been a Democratic stronghold, Nixon had refused to concede the region. To gain Southern support, Nixon had met with powerful South Carolina senator Strom Thurmond and won his backing by promising several things: to appoint only conservatives to the federal courts, to name a Southerner to the Supreme Court, to oppose court-ordered busing, and to choose a vice presidential candidate acceptable to the South. (Nixon ultimately chose Spiro Agnew, governor of the border state of Maryland.)

Nixon's efforts paid off on Election Day. Large numbers of white Southerners deserted the Democratic Party, granting Humphrey only one victory in that region—in Lyndon Johnson's home state of Texas. While Wallace claimed most of the states in the Deep South, Nixon captured Virginia, Tennessee, Kentucky, and North Carolina. Senator Strom Thurmond's support delivered his state of South Carolina for the Republicans as well.

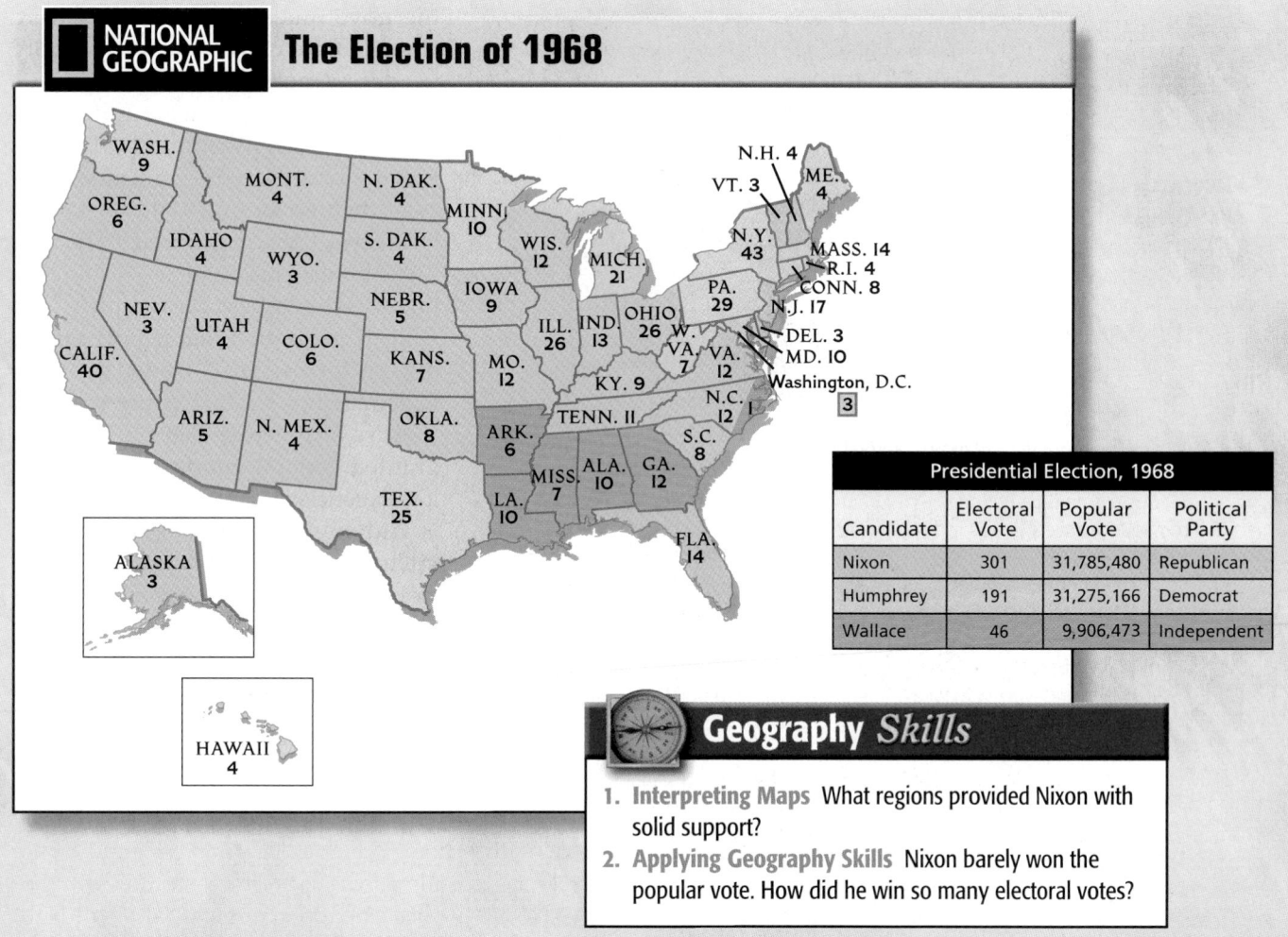

NATIONAL GEOGRAPHIC **The Election of 1968**

Presidential Election, 1968			
Candidate	Electoral Vote	Popular Vote	Political Party
Nixon	301	31,785,480	Republican
Humphrey	191	31,275,166	Democrat
Wallace	46	9,906,473	Independent

Geography *Skills*

1. **Interpreting Maps** What regions provided Nixon with solid support?
2. **Applying Geography Skills** Nixon barely won the popular vote. How did he win so many electoral votes?

Following his victory, Nixon set out to attract even more Southerners to the Republican Party, an effort that became known as the **Southern strategy.** Toward this end, the president fulfilled his agreements with Thurmond and took steps to slow desegregation. During his tenure, Nixon worked to overturn several civil rights policies. He reversed a Johnson administration policy, for example, that had cut off federal funds for racially segregated schools.

A Law-and-Order President

Having also won the presidency with a promise of law and order, Nixon immediately set out to battle crime in America. His administration specifically targeted the nation's antiwar protesters. Attorney General John Mitchell declared that he stood ready to prosecute "hard-line militants" who crossed state lines to stir up riots. Mitchell's deputy, Richard Kleindienst, went even further with the boast, "We're going to enforce the law against draft evaders, against radical students, against deserters, against civil disorders, against organized crime, and against street crime."

Nixon also went on the attack against the recent Supreme Court rulings that expanded the rights of accused criminals. Nixon openly criticized the Court and its chief justice, Earl Warren. The president promised to fill vacancies on the Supreme Court with judges who would support the rights of law enforcement over the rights of suspected criminals.

When Chief Justice Warren retired shortly after Nixon took office, the president replaced him with **Warren Burger,** a respected conservative judge. He also placed three other conservative justices on the Court, including one from the South. The Burger Court did not reverse Warren Court rulings on the rights of criminal suspects. It did, however, refuse to expand those rights further. For example, in *Stone* v. *Powell* (1976), it agreed to limits on the rights of defendants to appeal state convictions to the federal judiciary. The Court also continued to uphold capital punishment as constitutional. 📖 *(See page 1083 for more information on* Stone v. Powell.*)*

The New Federalism

President Nixon's Republican constituency also favored dismantling a number of federal programs and giving more control to state and local governments. Nixon called this **New Federalism.** He argued that it would provide the government agencies that were closest to the citizens the opportunity to address more of their issues.

"I reject the patronizing idea that government in Washington, D.C., is inevitably more wise and more efficient than government at the state or local level," Nixon declared. "The idea that a bureaucratic elite in Washington knows what's best for people . . . is really a contention that people cannot govern themselves." Under the New Federalism program, Congress passed a series of revenue-sharing bills that granted federal funds to state and local agencies to use.

Although **revenue sharing** was intended to give state and local agencies more power, over time it gave the federal government new power. As states came to depend on federal funds, the federal government could impose conditions on the states. Unless they met those conditions, their funds would be cut off.

While he worked to limit federal government responsibilities, Nixon also sought to increase the power of the executive branch. Nixon did not build many strong relationships in Congress. His lack of camaraderie with lawmakers and the fact that the Republican Party controlled neither house led to struggles with the legislative branch. Nixon often responded by trying to work around Congress and use greater executive authority. For instance, when Congress appropriated money for programs he opposed, Nixon impounded, or refused to release, the funds. The Supreme Court eventually declared the practice of impoundment unconstitutional.

The Family Assistance Plan One federal program Nixon sought to reform was the nation's welfare system—**Aid to Families with Dependent Children** (AFDC). The program had many critics, Republican and Democratic alike. They argued that AFDC was structured so that it was actually better for poor people to apply for benefits than to take a low-paying job. A mother who had such a job, for example, would then have to pay for child care, sometimes leaving her with less income than she had on welfare. There was also great inequity among states since each was allowed to develop its own guidelines.

In 1969 Nixon proposed replacing the AFDC with the Family Assistance Plan. The plan called for providing needy families a guaranteed yearly grant of $1,600, which could be supplemented by outside earnings. Many liberals applauded the plan as a significant step toward expanding federal responsibility for the poor. Nixon, however, presented the program in a conservative light, arguing it would reduce federal supervision and encourage welfare recipients to become more responsible.

Although the program won approval in the House in 1970, it soon came under harsh attack. Welfare recipients complained that the federal grant was too low, while conservatives, who disapproved of guaranteed income, also criticized the plan. Such opposition led to the program's defeat in the Senate.

Reading Check **Evaluating** What impact did third party candidate George Wallace have on the 1968 election?

Nixon's Foreign Policy

Despite Nixon's domestic initiatives, a State Department official later recalled that the president had a "monumental disinterest in domestic policies." Nixon once expressed his hope that a "competent cabinet" of advisers could run the country. This would allow him to focus his energies on the subject that truly fascinated him, foreign affairs. Embarking on an ambitious foreign policy agenda

Fact | Fiction | Folklore

"Ping-Pong Diplomacy" In April 1971, nearly a year before President Nixon made his historic trip there, Communist China welcomed a different kind of U.S. delegation—the American ping-pong team. When the team received their surprise invitation, *Time* magazine called it "the ping heard round the world." The nine players, four officials, and two spouses who arrived on the Chinese mainland were the first Americans to enter China since the Communist takeover in 1949.

that included historic encounters with both China and the Soviet Union, Nixon set out to leave his mark on the world stage.

Nixon and Kissinger In a move that would greatly influence his foreign policy, Nixon chose as his national security adviser **Henry Kissinger,** a former Harvard professor. As a teenager Kissinger had fled to the United States from Germany with his family in 1938 to escape Nazi persecution of Jews. He had served as a foreign policy consultant for Presidents Kennedy and Johnson. Though Secretary of State William Rogers technically outranked him, Kissinger soon took the lead in helping shape Nixon's foreign policy.

Nixon and Kissinger shared views on many issues. Both believed simply abandoning the war in Vietnam would damage the United States's position in the world. Thus they worked toward a gradual withdrawal. Nixon and Kissinger also believed in shaping a foreign policy rooted in practical approaches rather than ideologies. They felt the nation's decades-long anticommunist crusade had created a foreign policy that was too rigid and often worked against the nation's interests. While both leaders wanted to continue to contain communism, they believed that engagement and negotiation with Communists offered a better way for the United States to achieve its international goals. As a surprised nation watched, Nixon and Kissinger put their philosophy into practice by forging friendlier relations with the Soviet Union and China.

Analyzing *Political Cartoons*

Arms Buildup Anxiety The urgent need to negotiate a reduction in nuclear arms is demonstrated in this 1970 cartoon. When was the SALT I agreement finally signed?

play. This "multipolar" world of the future demanded a different approach to American foreign policy.

With Kissinger's help, Nixon fashioned an approach called **détente,** or relaxation of tensions, between the United States and its two major Communist rivals, the Soviet Union and China. In explaining détente to the American people, Nixon said that the United States had to build a better relationship with its main rivals in the interests of world peace:

> ❝We must understand that détente is not a love fest. It is an understanding between nations that have opposite purposes, but which share common interests, including the avoidance of a nuclear war. Such an understanding can work—that is, restrain aggression and deter war—only as long as the potential aggressor is made to recognize that neither aggression nor war will be profitable.❞
>
> —quoted in *The Limits of Power*

Nixon Visits China Détente began with an effort to improve American-Chinese relations. Since 1949, when a Communist government came to power in China, the United States had refused to recognize the Communists as the legitimate rulers. Instead, the American government recognized the exiled regime on the island of Taiwan as the Chinese government. Having long supported this policy, Nixon now set out to reverse it. He began by lifting trade and travel restrictions and withdrawing the Seventh Fleet from defending Taiwan.

After a series of highly secret negotiations between Kissinger and Chinese leaders, Nixon announced that he would visit China in February 1972. During the historic trip, the leaders of both nations agreed to establish "more normal" relations between their countries. In a statement that epitomized the notion of détente, Nixon told his Chinese hosts during a banquet toast, "Let us start a long march together, not in lockstep, but on different roads leading to the same goal, the goal of building a world structure of peace and justice."

In taking this trip, Nixon hoped not only to strengthen ties with the Chinese, but also to encourage the Soviets to more actively pursue diplomacy. Since the 1960s, a rift had developed between the Communist governments of the Soviet Union and China. Troops of the two nations occasionally clashed along their borders. Nixon believed détente with China would encourage Soviet premier Leonid Brezhnev to be more accommodating with the United States.

The Establishment of Détente The Soviet Union was not initially pleased when Nixon, a man with a history of outspoken anticommunist actions, became president. The Washington correspondent for the Soviet newspaper *Izvestia*, Yuri Barsukov, had called the election "unwelcome news for Moscow" and predicted that Soviet leaders "would have to deal with a very stubborn president."

Things did not turn out that way, however. Nixon was still a staunch anticommunist, but he came to reject the notion of a bipolar world in which the superpowers of the United States and the Soviet Union confronted one another. He believed the United States needed to understand the growing role that China, Japan, and Western Europe would soon

U.S.-Soviet Tensions Ease Nixon's feelings about the Soviets proved correct. Shortly after the public learned of U.S. negotiations with China, the Soviets proposed an American-Soviet summit, or high-level diplomatic meeting, to be held in May 1972. On May 22, President Nixon flew to Moscow for a weeklong summit. Thus, he became the first American president since World War II to visit the Soviet Union.

Before Nixon's visit, Secretary of Commerce Maurice Stans spent 11 days in the Soviet Union. In his visits to a tractor plant, a steel mill, and an oil field, Stans recalled, "It was as friendly a meeting as if I were representing California and negotiating with the state of Arizona." Before leaving, however, Stans requested a favor from his Soviet host, Alexei Kosygin:

66'There is one thing I hope you will take care of: on the highway into Moscow there is a great big billboard with the United States pictured as a vicious killer, with a sword in one hand and a gun in the other, killing people all over the world. I don't think that will be a good entrance for President Nixon, and the sign ought to come down.' He said, 'It will.'99

—quoted in *Nixon: An Oral History of His Presidency*

During the historic Moscow summit, the two superpowers signed the first **Strategic Arms Limitation Treaty,** or SALT I, a plan to limit nuclear arms the two nations had been working on for years. Nixon and Brezhnev also agreed to increase trade and the exchange of scientific information.

Détente profoundly eased tensions between the Soviet Union and the United States. By the end of Nixon's presidency, one Soviet official admitted that

Picturing **History**

Détente Discussion Soviet premier Leonid Brezhnev listens to President Nixon during Brezhnev's June 1973 visit to Washington, D.C. On June 22 the two signed an agreement on the prevention of nuclear war. *What does the word détente mean?*

"the United States and the Soviet Union had their best relationship of the whole Cold War period." President Nixon indeed had made his mark on the world stage. As he basked in the glow of his 1972 foreign policy triumphs, however, trouble was brewing on the home front. A scandal was about to engulf his presidency and plunge the nation into one of its greatest constitutional crises.

✓ **Reading Check** **Summarizing** What were the results of the 1972 American-Soviet summit?

SECTION 1 ASSESSMENT

Checking for Understanding
1. **Define:** impound, détente, summit.
2. **Identify:** Southern strategy, revenue sharing, Henry Kissinger.
3. **Describe** Nixon's New Federalism policy.

Reviewing Themes
4. **Global Connections** What were the results of Nixon's policy of détente?

Critical Thinking
5. **Evaluating** How did Nixon's China visit affect Soviet relations?
6. **Categorizing** Use a graphic organizer similar to the one below to describe how President Nixon established détente in the countries listed.

China	
Soviet Union	

Analyzing Visuals
7. **Analyzing Political Cartoons** Study the cartoon on page 956. What is its message about the impact of the arms buildup on average citizens in both the Soviet Union and the United States?

Writing About History
8. **Expository Writing** Take on the role of a member of President Nixon's staff. Write a press release explaining Nixon's domestic and foreign policies.

The Watergate Scandal

★ An American Story ★

As Bob Woodward, a young reporter for the *Washington Post,* sat in a Washington, D.C., courtroom on the morning of June 17, 1972, he was in a rather foul mood. His editor had ruined his Saturday by calling him in to cover a seemingly insignificant but bizarre incident. In the early hours of that morning, five men had broken into the Democratic National Committee (DNC) headquarters in the city's Watergate apartment-office complex.

Woodward sat toward the back of the courtroom listening to the bail proceedings for the five defendants. At one point, the judge asked each man his occupation. One of the men, James McCord, answered that he was retired from government service.

"Where in government?" asked the judge.

"CIA," McCord whispered.

Woodward sprang to attention. Why was a former member of the Central Intelligence Agency involved in what seemed to be nothing more than a burglary?

Over the next two years, Woodward and another reporter, Carl Bernstein, would investigate this question. In so doing they uncovered a scandal that helped bring about a grave constitutional crisis and eventually forced the president to resign.

—**adapted from *All the President's Men***

The Roots of Watergate

The scandal known as **Watergate** originated from the Nixon administration's attempts to cover up its involvement in the break-in at the Democratic National Committee (DNC) headquarters, along with other illegal actions committed during

Nixon's re-election campaign. While the affair began with the burglary at the Watergate complex, a number of scholars attribute the scandal in large part to the character of Richard Nixon and the atmosphere that he and his advisers created in the White House.

Nixon and His "Enemies" Richard Nixon had fought hard to become president. He had battled back from numerous political defeats, including a loss to John Kennedy in the 1960 presidential election, to win the presidency in 1968. Along the way, however, Nixon had grown defensive, secretive, and often resentful of his critics.

In addition, Nixon had become president during a time when the United States was still very much at war with itself. Race riots and protests over the Vietnam War continued to consume the country. In Nixon's view, these protesters and other "radicals" were out to bring down his administration. Nixon was so consumed with his opponents that he compiled an "enemies list" filled with people—from politicians to members of the media—whom he considered a threat to his presidency.

Mounting a Re-election Fight As Nixon's re-election campaign got underway in 1972, many in his administration expressed optimism about winning a second term. The president had just finished triumphant trips to China and the Soviet Union. In May, former Alabama governor George Wallace, who had mounted a strong third-party campaign in 1968, had dropped his bid for another run at the White House after an assassin's bullet paralyzed him. Meanwhile, Nixon's Democratic

opponent, South Dakota senator George McGovern, was viewed as too liberal on many issues.

At the same time, Nixon's hold on the presidency was uncertain. Despite the high approval ratings for the president's summit meetings in Beijing and Moscow, the unpopular Vietnam War still raged. Nixon staffers also remembered how close the margin of Nixon's 1968 victory had been. Seeking to gain an edge in every way they could, Nixon's team engaged in a host of subversive tactics, from spying on opposition rallies to spreading rumors and false reports.

These tactics included an effort to steal information from the Democratic Party's headquarters. In the early hours of June 17, 1972, five Nixon supporters broke into the party's office at the Watergate complex in Washington, D.C. They had intended to obtain any sensitive campaign information and to place wiretaps on the office telephones. While the burglars were at work, a security guard making his rounds spotted a piece of tape holding a door lock. The guard ripped off the tape, but when he passed the door later, he noticed that it had been replaced. He quickly called police, who arrived shortly and arrested the men.

The Cover-Up Begins In the wake of the Watergate break-in, the media discovered that one of the burglars, James McCord, was not only an ex-CIA official but also a member of the Committee for the Re-election of the President (CRP). Reports soon surfaced that the burglars had been paid to execute the break-in from a secret CRP fund controlled by the White House.

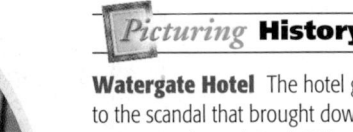

Picturing **History**

Watergate Hotel The hotel gave its name to the scandal that brought down President Nixon. Hotel guard Frank Willis, pictured here, reported to police the evidence of a break-in at the Democratic National Committee headquarters there. What was Nixon's response to the break-in?

As questions swirled about a possible White House connection to the burglary, the cover-up began. Administration officials destroyed incriminating documents and provided false testimony to investigators. Meanwhile, President Nixon stepped in. While the president may not have ordered the break-in, he did order a cover-up. With Nixon's consent, administration officials asked the CIA to intervene and stop the FBI from inquiring into the source of the money paid to the burglars. Their justification was that such an investigation would threaten national security.

All the while, the White House strongly denied any involvement in the break-in. Nixon's press secretary dismissed the incident as a "third-rate burglary attempt," while the president himself told the American public, "The White House has had no involvement whatever in this particular incident."

The strategy worked. Most Americans believed President Nixon. Despite efforts by the media, in particular the *Washington Post*, to keep the story alive, few people paid much attention to the Watergate affair during the 1972 presidential campaign. On Election Day, Nixon won re-election by one of the largest margins in history with nearly 61 percent of the popular vote compared to 37.5 percent for George McGovern. The electoral vote was 520 votes for Nixon and 17 for McGovern.

Reading Check **Examining** Why did members of the CRP break into the Democratic National Committee headquarters?

The Cover-Up Unravels

Shortly after his triumphant re-election, an exuberant and confident Nixon told his cabinet and staff that 1973 "can be and should be the best year ever." In a matter of months, however, the Watergate affair would erupt, and the coming year would be one of the president's worst.

The First Cracks Show In 1973 the Watergate burglars went on trial. Under relentless prodding from federal judge John J. Sirica, McCord agreed to cooperate with both a grand jury investigation and with the Senate's Select Committee on Presidential Campaign Activities, which had been recently established under Senator **Sam J. Ervin** of North Carolina. McCord's testimony opened a floodgate of confessions, and a parade of White House and campaign officials exposed one illegality after another over the next several months. Foremost among the officials was counsel to the president **John Dean,** a member of the inner circle of the White House who leveled allegations against Nixon himself.

A Summer of Shocking Testimony In June 1973, John Dean testified before Senator Ervin's committee that former Attorney General John Mitchell had ordered the Watergate break-in and that Nixon had played an active role in attempting to cover up any White House involvement. As a shocked nation absorbed Dean's testimony, the Nixon administration strongly denied the charges.

A standoff ensued for the next month, as the Senate committee attempted to determine who was telling the truth. Then, on July 16, the answer appeared unexpectedly. On that day, White House aide Alexander Butterfield testified that Nixon had ordered a taping system installed in the White House to record all conversations. The president had done so, Butterfield said, to help him write his memoirs after he left office. For members of the committee, however, the tapes would tell them exactly what the president knew and when he knew it.

Picturing **History**

Sitting in Judgment Representative Barbara Jordan from Texas was an outspoken member of the House Judiciary Committee. What was this committee's role in the impeachment process?

High Political Drama After resigning his office on August 9, 1974, President Nixon and his family say goodbye to aides and friends on the White House lawn. On the capital's streets, a reader takes in the news in the *Washington Post,* the newspaper that started the Watergate investigation. Who replaced Nixon as president?

The Case of the Tapes All the groups investigating the scandal sought access to the tapes. Nixon refused, pleading executive privilege—the principle that White House conversations should remain confidential to protect national security. A special prosecutor appointed by the president to handle the Watergate cases, Archibald Cox, took Nixon to court in October 1973 to force him to give up the recordings. Nixon, clearly growing desperate, ordered Attorney General Elliot Richardson, and then Richardson's deputy, to fire Cox. Both men refused and resigned in protest. Solicitor General Robert Bork finally fired Cox, but the incident, nicknamed the "Saturday Night Massacre" in the press, badly damaged Nixon's reputation with the public.

The fall of 1973 proved to be a disastrous time for Nixon for other reasons as well. His vice president, Spiro Agnew, was forced to resign in disgrace. Investigators had discovered that Agnew had taken bribes from state contractors while he was governor of Maryland and that he had continued to accept bribes while serving in Washington. Gerald Ford, the Republican leader of the House of Representatives, became the new vice president. Nixon then had to defend himself against allegations about his own past financial dealings.

GOVERNMENT

Nixon Resigns In an effort to quiet the growing outrage over his actions, President Nixon appointed a new special prosecutor, Texas lawyer Leon Jaworski, who proved no less determined than Cox to obtain the president's tapes. In April 1974, Nixon released edited transcripts of the tapes, claiming that they proved his innocence. Investigators felt otherwise and went to court again to force Nixon to turn over the unedited tapes. In July the Supreme Court ruled that the president had to turn over the tapes themselves, not just the transcripts. With nowhere else to appeal, Nixon handed over the tapes.

Several days later, the House Judiciary Committee voted to impeach Nixon, or officially charge him of presidential misconduct. The committee charged that Nixon had obstructed justice in the Watergate cover-up; misused federal agencies to violate the rights of citizens; and defied the authority of Congress by refusing to deliver tapes and other materials that the committee had requested. The next step was for the entire House of Representatives to vote whether or not to impeach the president.

As the nation held its collective breath in anticipation, investigators finally found indisputable evidence against the president. One of the unedited tapes revealed that on June 23, 1972, just six days after the Watergate burglary, Nixon had ordered the CIA to stop the FBI's investigation of the break-in. With this news, even the president's strongest supporters conceded that impeachment and conviction in the Senate now seemed inevitable. On August 9, 1974, Nixon resigned his office in disgrace. Gerald Ford took the oath of office and became the nation's 38th president.

Reading Check **Explaining** What was the significance of John Dean's testimony before the Senate committee?

The Impact of Watergate

Upon taking office, President Ford urged Americans to put the Watergate affair behind them and move on. "Our long national nightmare is over," he declared. The effects of the scandal, however, endured long after Richard Nixon's resignation.

The Watergate crisis prompted a series of new laws intended to limit the power of the executive branch. In the 1970s Congress passed a number of laws aimed at reestablishing a greater balance of power in government. The **Federal Campaign Act Amendments** limited campaign contributions and established an independent agency to administer stricter election laws. The Ethics in Government Act required financial disclosure by high government officials in all three branches of government. The FBI Domestic Security Investigation Guidelines restricted the bureau's political intelligence-gathering activities. After Watergate, Congress also established a

means for appointing an independent counsel to investigate and prosecute wrongdoing by high government officials.

Despite these efforts, Watergate left many Americans with a deep distrust of their public officials. Speaking some 20 years after the Watergate affair, Alexander Haig, a former high-level Nixon aide, said the scandal had produced, "a fundamental discrediting of respect for the presidency . . . [and] a new skepticism about politics, in general, which every American feels to this day." On the other hand, some Americans saw the Watergate affair as proof that in the United States, no person is above the law. As Bob Woodward observed:

Watergate was probably a good thing for the country; it was a good, sobering lesson. Accountability to the law applies to everyone. The problem with kings and prime ministers and presidents is that they think that they are above it, and there is no accountability, and that they have some special rights, and privileges, and status. And a process that says: No. We have our laws and believe them, and they apply to everyone, is a very good thing.

—quoted in *Nixon: An Oral History of His Presidency*

After the ordeal of Watergate, most Americans attempted to put the affair behind them. In the years ahead, however, the nation encountered a host of new troubles, from a stubborn economic recession to a heart-wrenching hostage crisis overseas.

Reading Check **Evaluating** Why did Congress pass new laws after the Watergate scandal?

Ford and Carter

Main Idea

During the 1970s, Presidents Gerald Ford and Jimmy Carter attempted to lead the United States through both domestic and foreign crises.

Key Terms and Names

inflation, embargo, stagflation, Helsinki Accords, Department of Energy

Reading Strategy

Organizing As you read about the administrations of Presidents Ford and Carter, complete a graphic organizer listing the causes of economic problems in the 1970s.

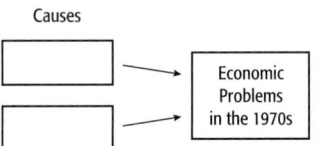

Causes

Economic Problems in the 1970s

Reading Objectives

• **Explain** the reasons for economic troubles in the United States during the 1970s.

• **Discuss** Jimmy Carter's domestic and foreign policies.

Section Theme

Economic Factors A weakening economy and growing energy crisis marred the terms of Ford and Carter.

Preview of Events

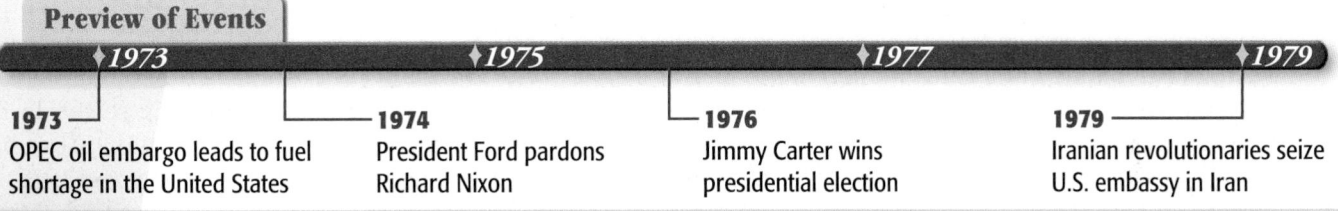

♦1973 ♦1975 ♦1977 ♦1979

1973
OPEC oil embargo leads to fuel shortage in the United States

1974
President Ford pardons Richard Nixon

1976
Jimmy Carter wins presidential election

1979
Iranian revolutionaries seize U.S. embassy in Iran

★ An American Story ★

On a sunny February day in 1977, Ellen Griffith and her fiancé, Roger Everson, both of Nashville, Tennessee, sat together in a place where neither of them dreamed they would be—the state unemployment office. Just a month before, Griffith, a 20-year-old salesclerk in a shopping center, and Everson, 21, had been excitedly making wedding plans. Now, with Everson laid off and Griffith on a reduced work schedule, the young couple had decided to put their future plans on hold. "It cost something to get married, you know," said Everson.

What had landed the two in this predicament was a one-two punch of a particularly bitter winter and an energy shortage that had gone on for much of the decade. The brutally cold weather in the Midwest and East had increased the demand for oil and fuel, already in short supply throughout the country. In response, the government had asked numerous companies and shops to conserve energy by cutting back on their business hours. As a result, Griffith saw her work schedule slashed from 40 hours per week to 20 hours.

As the couple sat stoically in the unemployment office waiting for their names to be called, Griffith wondered how she would pay her bills on her reduced salary and whatever she might be able to get from the state. "I just feel like we've been rained on," she said glumly.

—adapted from the *New York Times*, February 3, 1977

The Economic Crisis of the 1970s

Since the end of World War II, the American economy had been the envy of the world. During the 1950s and 1960s, many Americans enjoyed remarkable prosperity and had come to assume it was the norm. This prosperity rested in large part on easy access to raw materials around the world and a strong manufacturing industry at home. By the 1970s, however, the boom years gave way to a decade of hard times.

A Mighty Economic Machine Slows
The nation's economic troubles began in the mid-1960s. President Johnson significantly increased federal deficit spending when he attempted to fund both the Vietnam War and his ambitious Great Society program without raising taxes. This pumped large amounts of money into the economy, which spurred inflation, or a rise in the cost of goods.

Rising costs of raw materials due to greater competition for them was another cause of inflation. In particular, the rising cost of oil dealt a strong blow to the nation's economy. More than any other nation, the United States based its economy on the easy availability of cheap and plentiful fossil fuels. With the highest volume of oil consumption in the world, the nation had become heavily dependent on imports from the Middle East and Africa.

For years, the **Organization of Petroleum Exporting Countries** (OPEC) sold oil for its member countries. Prices remained low until the early 1970s, when OPEC decided to use oil as a political and economic weapon. In 1973 the Yom Kippur War was raging between Israel and its Arab neighbors. Tension had existed between Israel and the Arab world ever since the founding of modern Israel in 1948. Since most Arab states did not recognize Israel's right to exist, U.S. support of Israel made American relations with Arab states uneasy.

Picturing **History**

A Scarce Commodity Americans had to schedule their lives around the availability of gasoline during the OPEC oil embargo. Why did OPEC institute the embargo?

Now OPEC announced that its members would embargo, or stop shipping, petroleum to countries that supported Israel, namely the United States and some Western European nations. OPEC also raised the price of crude oil by 70 percent, and then by another 130 percent a few months later. As a result, the United States suffered its first fuel shortage since World War II.

Although the embargo ended a few months after it began, oil prices continued to rise. OPEC raised prices three more times in the 1970s and again in 1980. By that time, the price of a barrel of crude oil had risen from $3 in 1973 to $30 in 1980. The increase accelerated inflation. As prices rose for oil-based products, Americans had less money to spend on other goods, which helped cause a recession.

ECONOMICS

A Stagnant Economy
Another economic problem was the decline of the manufacturing sector. In the years following World War II, the United States had dominated international trade, but by the 1970s, it faced increased international competition. Many manufacturing plants were now decades old and less efficient than the newer plants that Japan and European industrial nations built after the war. In 1971, for the first time since 1889, the United States imported more goods than it exported. By 1985, Americans were also borrowing more money from foreigners than they were lending abroad.

These factors forced many factories to close, and millions of workers lost their jobs. Although new jobs were available in the growing information and service-oriented sector, many industrial workers were poorly equipped for them. The result was a growing pool of unemployed and underemployed workers.

Thus in the early 1970s President Nixon faced a new and puzzling economic dilemma that came to be known as "stagflation," a combination of rising prices and economic stagnation. Economists who emphasized the demand side of economic theory, including supporters of Keynesianism, did not think that inflation and recession could occur at the same time. They believed that demand drives prices and that inflation would only occur in a booming economy when

Analyzing *Political Cartoons*

Coping With Shortages Cartoonist Brant Parker reflected the public's frustration over the oil shortages of the 1970s. What message does the cartoonist convey with the statement "the figs are next"?

demand for goods was high. As a result, they did not know what fiscal policy the government should pursue. Increased spending might help end the recession, but it would increase inflation. Raising taxes might slow inflation, but it would also keep the economy in recession.

Nixon decided to focus on controlling inflation. The government moved first to cut spending and raise taxes. The president hoped that higher taxes would prompt Americans to spend less, which would ease the demand on goods and drive down prices. Congress and much of the public, however, protested the idea of a tax hike. Nixon then tried to reduce consumer spending by getting the Federal Reserve Board to raise interest rates. When this failed, the president tried to stop inflation by imposing a 90-day freeze on wages and prices and then issuing federal regulations limiting future wage and price increases. This too met with little success.

When Nixon resigned in 1974, the nation's inflation rate was still high, despite many efforts to reduce prices. Meanwhile, the unemployment rate was over five percent. It would now be up to Gerald Ford to confront stagflation.

Reading Check **Explaining** How did President Nixon attempt to stop stagflation?

Ford Takes Over

Most Americans considered Gerald Ford a decent and honest if not particularly dynamic leader. When he became vice president, Ford had readily acknowledged his bland personality. "I'm a Ford, not a Lincoln," he said. Still, the new president boasted excellent credentials, including a degree from Yale

Law School, naval service during World War II, and service in the House of Representatives since 1949. His fellow Republicans had elected him as minority leader in 1965. Ford would need to draw on all his experience during his time in office.

Ford Pardons Nixon Ford was in the White House just a month when his efforts to restore faith in the nation's leadership suffered a serious setback. On September 8, 1974, Ford announced that he would grant a "full, free, and absolute pardon" to Richard Nixon for any crimes he "committed or may have committed or taken part in" while president. "This is an American tragedy in which we all have played a part," he told the nation. "It could go on and on and on, or someone must write the end to it."

Ford insisted he was acting not out of sympathy for Nixon, but in the public interest. Ford's position was that he wanted to avoid the division that charges against Nixon and a public trial would create. Nonetheless, the pardon aroused fierce criticism. Ford's approval ratings soon plunged from 71 percent to 50 percent.

Ford Tries to "Whip" Inflation By 1975 the American economy was in its worst recession since the Great Depression, with unemployment at nearly nine percent. Rejecting the notion of mandatory wage and price controls to reduce inflation, Ford requested voluntary controls. Under a plan known as WIN—Whip Inflation Now—he urged Americans to cut back on their oil and gas consumption and to undertake other energy-conserving measures. The plan stirred up little enthusiasm and eventually failed. The president then turned to cutting government spending and advocating higher interest rates to curb inflation. This too failed.

Picturing History

Reassuring Presence After the turmoil of Watergate, President Gerald Ford, shown here with First Lady Betty Ford, was a comforting leader, but he was unable to solve the problem of inflation. *Through what methods did Ford try to "whip inflation now"?*

As Ford attempted to revive the economy, he also attempted to limit federal authority, balance the budget, and keep taxes low. Ford vetoed more than 50 bills that the Democratic-led Congress passed during the first two years of his administration.

Ford's Foreign Policy

In foreign policy, Ford continued Nixon's general strategy. Ford kept Kissinger on as secretary of state and continued to pursue détente with the Soviets and the Chinese. In August 1975 he met with leaders of NATO and the Warsaw Pact to sign the **Helsinki Accords.** Under the accords, the parties recognized the borders of Eastern Europe established at the end of World War II. The Soviets in return promised to uphold certain basic human rights, including the right to move across national borders. The subsequent Soviet failure to uphold these basic rights turned many Americans against détente.

Ford also encountered problems in Southeast Asia. In May 1975, Cambodia seized the *Mayaguez*, an American cargo ship traveling near its shores, claiming that it had been on an intelligence-gathering mission. Calling the ship's seizure an "act of piracy," Ford dispatched U.S. Marines to retrieve it. Cambodia released the crew before the marines arrived.

The Election of 1976 As the 1976 presidential election approached, Americans were pessimistic and unsure of the future. With rising inflation and unemployment, many citizens were undergoing an adverse change of lifestyle. There were equally serious problems in foreign affairs. Political turmoil in developing nations threatened world stability, while the Soviet Union was pursuing an aggressive foreign policy. Americans therefore looked to elect a man who could meet these challenges.

The presidential race pitted Gerald Ford against James Earl Carter, Jr., or Jimmy Carter, as he liked to be called. Carter was somewhat of a political outsider. A former governor of Georgia, Carter had no national political experience. Nonetheless, he had won the Democratic primary with an inspiring and well-organized campaign. Carter sought to take advantage of his outsider image, promising to restore morality and honesty to the federal government. He also promised new programs for energy development, tax reform, welfare reform, and national medical care.

More than the programs he proposed, it was Carter's image as a moral and upstanding individual that attracted most supporters. Ford meanwhile characterized Carter as a liberal whose social program spending would produce higher rates of inflation and require tax increases.

In the end, Carter edged Ford with 50.1 percent of the popular vote to Ford's 47.9 percent, while capturing 297 electoral votes to Ford's 240. On Inauguration Day, to demonstrate his man-of-the-people style, Carter declined the traditional limousine ride and walked from the Capitol to the White House.

✓ **Reading Check** **Examining** What steps did President Ford take to try to control inflation?

Carter Battles the Economic Crisis

Carter devoted much of his domestic agenda to trying to fix the economy. At first he tried to end the recession and reduce unemployment by increasing government spending and cutting taxes. When inflation surged in 1978, he changed his mind. He delayed the tax cuts and vetoed the spending programs he had himself proposed to Congress. He then tried to ease inflation by reducing the money supply and raising interest rates. His main focus, however, was on the energy crisis. In the end, none of his efforts succeeded.

A "War" Against Consumption Carter felt that the nation's most serious problem was its dependence on foreign oil. In one of his first national addresses, he tried to rally Americans to support what he termed a "war" against rising energy consumption. "Our decision about energy will test the character of the American people and the ability of the President and Congress to govern this nation," Carter stated.

Carter proposed a national energy program to conserve oil and to promote the use of coal and renewable energy sources such as solar power. He persuaded Congress to create a **Department of Energy** and also asked Americans to make personal sacrifices to reduce their energy consumption. Most of the public complied as best they could, although many ignored the president's suggestion.

At the same time, many business leaders and economists urged the president and Congress to deregulate the oil industry. The regulations, first imposed as part of President Nixon's price control plan, limited the ability of oil companies to pass on OPEC price increases to American consumers. As a result, oil companies found it difficult to make a profit, and they lacked the capital to invest in new domestic oil wells. These regulations, combined with OPEC price increases, helped create the energy crisis of the 1970s. Carter agreed to support deregulation but insisted on a "windfall profits tax" to prevent oil companies from overcharging consumers. The tax, however, conflicted with the basic idea of deregulation, which was to free up corporate capital for use in searching for new sources of oil. In the end, Carter's contradictory plan did not solve the country's energy crisis.

In the summer of 1979, instability in the Middle East produced a second major fuel shortage and deepened the nation's economic problems. Under increasing pressure to act, Carter made several proposals in a television address. The speech was notable for Carter's bleak assessment of the national condition. He complained about a "crisis of confidence" that had struck "at the very heart and soul of our national will." The address became known as the "malaise" speech, although Carter had not specifically used that word. Many Americans interpreted the speech not as a timely warning but as Carter blaming the people for his failures.

Carter's Leadership Problems In retrospect, President Carter's difficulties in solving the nation's economic problems lay in his inexperience and inability to work with Congress. Carter, who was proud of his outsider status, made little effort to reach out to Washington's legislative leaders. As a result, Congress blocked many of his energy proposals.

Carter also failed to translate his ideas into a concrete set of goals to inspire the nation. He offered no unifying theme for his administration, but instead followed a cautious middle course that left people confused. By 1979 public opinion polls showed that Carter's popularity had dropped lower than President Nixon's during Watergate.

 Reading Check **Summarizing** To what did President Carter devote much of his domestic agenda?

Carter's Foreign Policy

In contrast to his uncertain leadership at home, Carter's foreign policy was more clearly defined. A man of strong religious beliefs, Carter argued that the United States must try to be "right and honest and truthful and decent" in dealing with other nations. Yet it was on the international front that President Carter suffered one of his most devastating defeats.

Picturing **History**

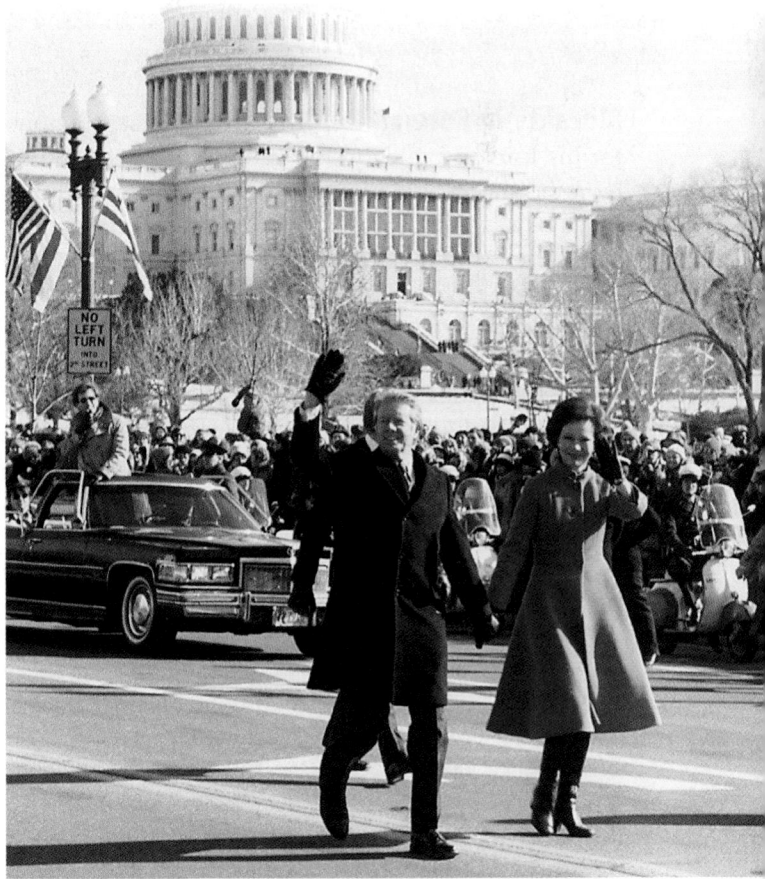

Change of Pace Jimmy Carter underscored his campaign image of being a new kind of politician by walking to the White House after his inauguration. What about Carter's image in 1976 might have been appealing to the public?

NATIONAL GEOGRAPHIC
MOMENT in HISTORY

HOSTAGE TO TERROR
Bound and blindfolded, American diplomat Jerry Miele is led out of the U.S. embassy in Tehran, Iran, after militants stormed the building on November 4, 1979. Ten months earlier, an Islamic fundamentalist revolution had overthrown the Shah of Iran, a staunch American ally. President Carter's decision to allow the ailing Shah to seek medical treatment in the United States led to the embassy takeover. Of the Americans taken captive, 52 were held for more than a year. The crisis contributed to Carter's defeat in the presidential election in 1980.

Morality in Foreign Policy Carter had set the tone for his foreign policy in his inaugural speech, when he announced, "Our commitment to human rights must be absolute. . . . The powerful must not persecute the weak, and human dignity must be enhanced." With the help of his foreign policy team—including **Andrew Young,** the first African American ambassador to the United Nations—Carter strove to achieve these goals.

The president put his principles into practice in Latin America. To remove a major symbol of U.S. interventionism in the region, he moved to give the Panamanians control of the Panama Canal. The United States had built and run the canal since 1903. In 1978 the president won Senate ratification of two Panama Canal treaties, which transferred control of the canal to Panama on December 31, 1999.

Most dramatically, Carter singled out the Soviet Union as a violator of human rights. He strongly condemned, for example, the Soviet practice of imprisoning people who protested against the government. Relations between the two superpowers suffered a further setback when Soviet troops invaded the Central

Asian nation of Afghanistan in December 1979. Carter responded by imposing an embargo on the sale of grain to the Soviet Union and boycotting the 1980 Summer Olympic Games in Moscow. Under the Carter administration, détente virtually collapsed.

Triumph and Failure in the Middle East It was in the volatile Middle East that President Carter met his greatest foreign policy triumph and his greatest failure. In 1978 Carter helped broker a historic peace treaty, known as the **Camp David Accords,** between Israel and Egypt, two nations that had been bitter enemies for decades. The treaty was formally signed in 1979. Most other Arab nations in the region opposed the treaty, but it marked a first step to achieving peace in the Middle East.

Just months after the Camp David Accords, Carter encountered a crisis in Iran. The United States had long supported Iran's monarch, the Shah, because Iran was a major oil supplier and a buffer against Soviet expansion in the Middle East. The Shah, however, had grown increasingly unpopular in Iran. He was a repressive ruler and had introduced Westernizing reforms to Iranian society. The Islamic clergy fiercely opposed the Shah's reforms. Opposition to the Shah grew, and in January 1979 protesters forced him to flee. An Islamic republic was then declared.

The new regime, headed by religious leader Ayatollah Khomeini, distrusted the United States because of its ties to the Shah. In November 1979, revolutionaries stormed the American embassy in Tehran and took 52 Americans hostage. The militants threatened to kill the hostages or try them as spies.

The Carter administration tried unsuccessfully to negotiate for the hostages' release. In April 1980, as pressure mounted, Carter approved a daring rescue attempt. To the nation's dismay, the rescue mission failed when several helicopters malfunctioned and one crashed in the desert. Eight servicemen died in the accident. Hamilton Jordan, President Carter's chief of staff, described the gloomy atmosphere in the White House the day after the crash:

66I arrived at the White House a few minutes before the President went on television to tell the nation about the catastrophe. He looked exhausted and careworn. . . . The mood at the senior staff meeting was somber and awkward. I sensed that we were all uncomfortable, like when a loved one dies and friends don't quite know what to say. . . . After the meeting, I wandered around the White House. . . . My thoughts kept returning to the bodies [of the servicemen] in the desert.99

—quoted in *Crisis: The Last Year of the Carter Presidency*

World Geography Connection

The Islamic State

In establishing an Islamic republic, the Ayatollah Khomeini created a state in which the codes and beliefs of Islam guide politics and thus direct nearly every aspect of life. Mullahs, or Islamic religious leaders, became political leaders as well, which allowed them to impose Islamic codes on Iranian citizens. In a religious state, religious practices are not a matter of choice but the law of the land. Politics and religion have joined forces in other parts of the Islamic world as well. In 1996 a group known as the Taliban transformed Afghanistan into an Islamic state. From insisting that men grow beards to forbidding women to work outside the home, Afghanistan's leaders enforced a social order based on an interpretation of Islam. ***What long-held American principle does the creation of a religious state violate?***

The crisis continued into the fall of 1980. Every night, news programs reminded viewers how many days the hostages had been held. The president's inability to free the hostages cost him support in the 1980 presidential election. Negotiations with Iran continued right up to Carter's last day in office. Ironically, on January 20, 1981, the day Carter left office, Iran released the Americans, ending their 444 days in captivity.

✓ **Reading Check** **Summarizing** What was President Carter's main foreign policy theme?

SECTION 3 ASSESSMENT

Checking for Understanding

1. **Define:** inflation, embargo, stagflation.
2. **Identify:** Helsinki Accords, Department of Energy.
3. **Identify** the achievement and failure President Carter experienced in the Middle East during his administration.

Reviewing Themes

4. **Economic Factors** How did President Carter attempt to deal with the nation's energy crisis?

Critical Thinking

5. **Evaluating** Do you think President Ford should have pardoned Richard Nixon? Why or why not?
6. **Organizing** Complete a graphic organizer similar to the one below by listing the ways that President Carter applied his human rights ideas to his foreign policy.

Carter's Human Rights Foreign Policy

Analyzing Visuals

7. **Analyzing Photographs** Study the photograph on page 968. What effect do you think images such as this one had on Americans who were living or traveling in other countries?

Writing About History

8. **Expository Writing** Write an essay identifying what you believe to be President Carter's most important foreign policy achievement. Explain your choice.

The "Me" Decade: Life in the 1970s

Main Idea

In the midst of widespread cynicism about their leaders and concerns about the economy, Americans sought fulfillment and escape during the 1970s.

Key Terms and Names

New Age movement, guru, transcendental meditation, *All in the Family*, disco

Reading Strategy

Categorizing As you read about life in the United States in the 1970s, complete a graphic organizer similar to the one below by listing the changes that occurred in family life during that time.

Changes in Family Life

Reading Objectives

- **Explain** the emergence of new spiritual movements and religions.
- **Discuss** social changes of the 1970s.

Section Theme

Culture and Traditions Even after the turbulent 1960s, American culture continued changing to reflect new trends and ideas.

Preview of Events

| ◆1970 | ◆1973 | ◆1976 | ◆1979 |

1971 — *All in the Family* debuts

1974 — *Good Times* debuts

1977 — Disco mania peaks with release of *Saturday Night Fever; The Complete Book of Running* published

★ An American Story ★

As the United States prepared to celebrate its bicentennial on July 4, 1976, a reporter asked Stoyan Christowe for his views on the state of the nation on the eve of its 200th birthday. The 77-year-old Vermont resident acknowledged that the United States was "in pretty bad shape," but added that the country would turn around—as it always had.

❝I believe in this country. I've always believed in it. There is a quotation by Benjamin Franklin, in a letter to George Washington during the Revolutionary War. Franklin talked of a cornfield during a drought, and how the cornstalks have shriveled and curled, and it was a sad sight. And then, he said a thunderstorm came along, spilling rain, and a day or two after, the sun came out, and the corn came to life, and it was a delight. . . . I know we're going through a kind of turmoil now, but the country is okay. . . . My faith in this country was never shaken. Like that cornfield—the sun will shine again, and the rains will come, and brother, those cornstalks will revive, and it will be a beautiful sight.❞

—**quoted in *Newsweek*, July 4, 1976**

The Search for Fulfillment

Like Stoyan Christowe, many Americans in the 1970s believed that the United States would eventually move beyond the Watergate scandal, the Vietnam War, and the country's nagging economic problems. In the meantime, some Americans sought ways to get on with their daily lives. As a way of coping with anxious times, they sought escape, laughter, and fulfillment in a wide range of fads, entertainment, and spiritual movements.

Writer Tom Wolfe labeled the 1970s the "me decade," referring to the idea that many Americans grew more self-obsessed in this decade as they strove for greater individual satisfaction. Indeed, the most popular books of the period included such titles as *I'm OK, You're OK; How to Be Your Own Best Friend;* and *Looking Out for Number One.* Journalist Richard Michael Levine argued that in light of the growing feelings of despair and cynicism about American society, it was little wonder that many people turned inward. "In the damp, late autumn of 1973, it did not take a religious fanatic in a tattered overcoat to sense that the real Kingdom lay within, things being as rotten as they were without," he wrote. In their quest for self-improvement, many Americans were willing to embrace new movements.

The New Age Movement

Disenchanted with the conventional religions of their parents, some young men and women sought fulfillment through the host of secular movements and activities that made up the **New Age movement.** New Age enthusiasts embraced the idea that people were responsible for and capable of everything from self-healing to creating the world. They believed spiritual enlightenment could be found in common practices, not just in traditional churchgoing. They tried activities such as yoga, martial arts, and chanting to achieve fuller spiritual awareness. Kathy Smith, a college student during the 1970s, recalled how she and others claimed to find "Zen," or enlightenment, in running and other physical activities:

> ❝They were beginning to understand how exercise affects your soul, how it affects your being. People started getting in the 'Zen' of things: the Zen of tennis, the Zen of working out, the Zen of motorcycle repair, the Zen of running. I, like many others, started connecting physical activity to the spiritual side. People also started looking at yoga and tai chi, and not only the stretching aspects of these disciplines but the mental aspects. Now they were working the body, the mind, and the spirit.❞

> —quoted in *The Century*

The New Age movement took many different paths to transform individuals and society. Some New Agers extolled the power of crystals and gemstones to improve life; others touted astrology. Some were inspired by the Eastern belief in reincarnation, which taught that people could be reborn many times until reaching perfection. Awareness of former lives was supposed to bring knowledge of the true inner self.

Transcendental Meditation

Many Americans who were dissatisfied with established religions sought new religions. A number of these new religions originated in Asia and centered on the teachings of gurus, or mystical leaders. One of the more well-known gurus was Maharishi Mahesh Yogi. A native of India, Maharishi moved to the United States in 1959, where he led a spiritual movement known as transcendental meditation. Maharishi worked in relative obscurity until 1967, when the wildly popular rock group the Beatles began to explore his teachings. Their attention brought an American following. Transcendental meditation suggested daily meditation and the silent repetition of spiritual mantras as a way of achieving peak intelligence, harmony, and health. If all the people on Earth practiced transcendental meditation, its advocates believed, the world would enjoy peace.

Changing Families

The search for fulfillment had an impact on many American families. The campaigns of the era, especially the women's movement, began to change how many women viewed their roles as wives and mothers. By 1970, 60 percent of women between the ages of 16 and 24 had joined the

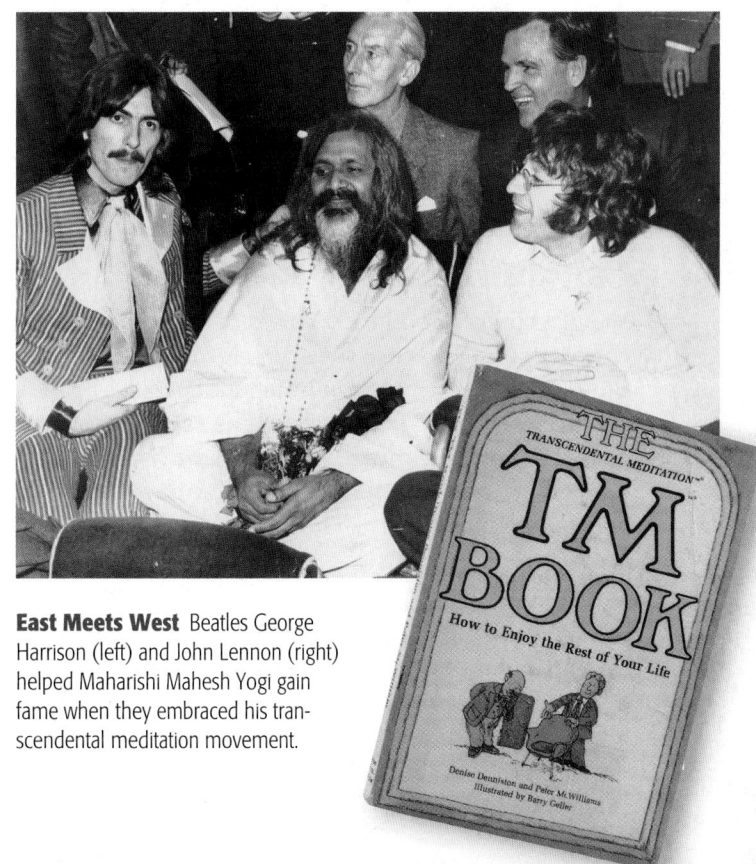

East Meets West Beatles George Harrison (left) and John Lennon (right) helped Maharishi Mahesh Yogi gain fame when they embraced his transcendental meditation movement.

What Life Was Like...

Bee Gees

Disco fans around the country and the world danced to the sounds of the Australian group the Bee Gees. The movie *Saturday Night Fever* featured their music and catapulted them into the limelight.

Disco

The counterculture of the 1960s provided music designed to raise people's consciousness of social issues. The disco music of the 1970s, with its simple lyrics and intense beats, was designed simply to entertain. By the end of the decade, millions of people throughout the nation and the world were dancing under flashing disco lights.

Fashion

New styles of clothing, first associated with disco patrons, became common for everyone. Men wore brightly patterned synthetic shirts, bell-bottom pants, and platform shoes or boots. Women wore wildly patterned dresses or jumpsuits with high heels or boots.

---

labor force. Between 1970 and 1980, women aged 25 to 34 had the largest annual percentage growth in the workforce.

These changes in turn led to changes in family life. With women increasingly active outside the home, smaller families became the norm. The birthrate fell to an all-time low in 1976, and parents and their children began spending less time together. A greater number of families also split apart, as the divorce rate doubled from 2.5 divorces per thousand people in 1966 to 5 per thousand 10 years later.

✓ **Reading Check** **Summarizing** What were the basic beliefs of the New Age movement?

Cultural Trends in the 1970s

Popular culture in the 1970s reflected many of the changes taking place in society. Television now sometimes portrayed women in independent roles or took on formerly taboo subjects such as racism, poverty, and abortion. Meanwhile, Americans listened and danced to new forms of music and sought fun and escape in a variety of new fads.

TURNING POINT

Television in the 1970s The decade opened with a revolutionary new situation comedy on Saturday nights. Unlike earlier sitcoms, *The Mary Tyler Moore Show* featured an unmarried woman with a meaningful career at its center. Actress Mary Tyler Moore played the main character, Mary Richards, who had left a small town for a big-city job as a television news producer. Mary sparred with her gruff but caring boss, despaired over the shallowness of the blow-dried news announcer, and had adventures with friends. Mary also went on dates but never got around to marrying.

The debut of the sitcom *All in the Family* in January 1971 marked an even bigger turning point in television programming. The show took risks by confronting potentially volatile social issues and by featuring a controversial hero, the blue-collar and bigoted Archie Bunker. Archie called his wife Edith "Dingbat" and his liberal son-in-law "Meathead." He also mocked his feminist daughter and various ethnic groups. Though Archie prided himself on being the man of the house, he never won any arguments with his liberal family or his African American neighbors.

By carefully mixing humor and sensitive issues and by not preaching to its audience, *All in the Family* provided viewers with a way to examine their own feelings about issues such as racism. Producer Norman Lear claimed that the show "holds a mirror up to our prejudices. . . . We laugh now, swallowing just the littlest bit of truth about ourselves. . . ."

Several years later, Archie Bunker's African American neighbors became the stars of another television series, *The Jeffersons*. George Jefferson, like Archie, was opinionated and prejudiced but

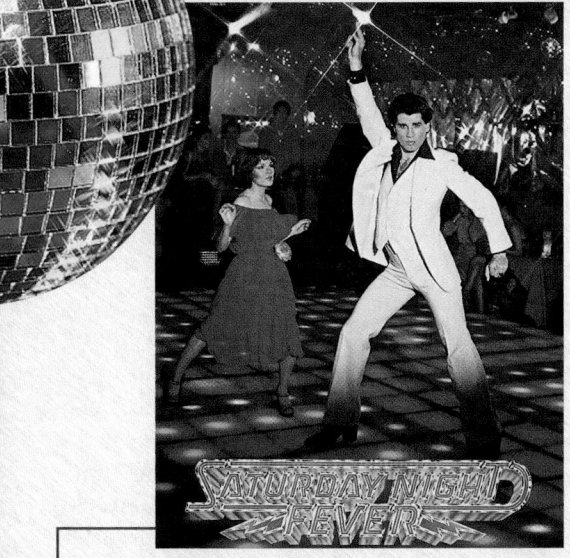

Saturday Night Fever
John Travolta played the role of Tony Manero in this 1977 film. By day Tony worked as a clerk in a Brooklyn store. At night, however, he transformed himself into a disco star. A popular success, the film showed Tony as a young working-class kid with a dream to escape his ordinary existence. Life at the disco provided a road to that escape.

ultimately likable. *The Jeffersons* portrayed African Americans in a new light: as successful and respected. *Maude,* another spin-off from *All in the Family,* featured Edith Bunker's feminist cousin, who had recently remarried after her third divorce. The strong-willed Maude did not need to depend on her new husband, Walter. This popular program drew intense controversy in 1972 when Maude made the difficult decision to have an abortion.

Maude's African American maid, Florida, generated another series in 1974. Starring Esther Rolle as Florida, *Good Times* portrayed an African American family struggling to raise three children in a low-income housing development in Chicago.

Music of the 1970s The music of this period reflected the end of the 1960s youth and protest movements. The hard-driving rock of the tumultuous 1960s gave way to softer sounds. "The fading out of ear-numbing, mind-blowing acid rock," *Time* commented in 1971, "is related to the softening of the youth revolution." The music became more reflective and less political, reflecting a desire to seek fulfillment from within. "These days, nobody wants to hear songs that have a message," said a member of the rock group Chicago. Popular entertainers in tune with the new meditative atmosphere included singers Barry Manilow and John Denver and the bands ABBA and the Eagles.

The 1970s also saw the rise of disco music. The disco craze of the later 1970s began in African

American and Latin nightclubs. There, disc jockeys played recorded dance music with a loud and persistent beat. The fast pace and easy rhythm attracted fans, but disco also seemed well suited for the "me generation." Unlike rock 'n' roll, disco allowed the people dancing to it to assume greater prominence than the music. As the co-owner of a popular discotheque in New York described the phenomena, "Everybody secretly likes to be on center stage and here we give them a huge space to do it all on."

Gus Rodriguez, who had moved with his family from Puerto Rico to Brooklyn 20 years earlier, recalled going to discos with his friends in the mid-1970s:

66We would go to the discos several times a week, but the weekends were always the best. Getting ready to go out was sort of a ritual, especially on Saturdays. During the day you would go buy that shirt, or that belt, or those platform shoes, all of which seemed incredibly important at the time. You had to have a particular type of look. And we all dressed the same way. We would call each other up to coordinate what color suits everybody was wearing—who's wearing the powder-blue suit, who's wearing the white suit, who's wearing this, who's wearing that. And then we would carefully iron everything so it was just so.99

—quoted in *The Century*

Disco mania reached its peak after the 1977 movie, *Saturday Night Fever.* In the film, a middle-class

All in the Family Many Americans saw a little of themselves in the characters of this popular sitcom.

Italian American teenager played by John Travolta transformed himself into a white-suited disco king each Saturday night. The movie's soundtrack sold millions of copies and spurred a wave of disco openings across the country and around the world.

Fads and Fashions In addition to disco, the nation embraced many other fads during the 1970s. Americans by the millions bought T-shirts that bore personalized messages, while teenagers flew down suburban and city streets on skateboards. Obsessed with self-discovery, a number of Americans slipped mood rings on their fingers to get in touch with their innermost feelings. Supposedly, the ring's color changed to match the wearer's ever-changing mood. Blue, for example, signaled happiness and bliss, while gray denoted nervousness and anxiety.

Meanwhile, millions of drivers bought citizens band ("CB") radios for their vehicles. This radio system allowed drivers to talk to each other over a two-way frequency within a range of a few miles. Many truck drivers installed the radios in an effort to warn each other of police and speed traps. Soon, however, average drivers had purchased them, mostly for entertainment purposes. Drivers adopted their own CB name, or "handle," and talked to each other using CB jargon and code words.

Fitness was another trend during the "me decade," as many Americans turned to exercise to improve the way they felt and looked. One popular type of exercise in the 1970s was aerobics. Physician Kenneth H. Cooper popularized the exercise concept in his 1968 book *Aerobics*. It was a way to achieve cardiovascular fitness without the drudgery and isolation that often accompanies physical exercise. This new way to stay fit while having fun and interacting socially with others quickly gained popularity. By the mid-1970s, men and women were dancing in gyms across the country. Running also attracted a wide following, as scores of Americans began pounding the pavement to stay fit and trim. In a testament to the popularity of running, athlete Jim Fixx's work *The Complete Book of Running* was a bestseller following its publication in 1977.

By the end of the 1970s, a number of these fads and trends began to fade. A decade in which Americans came to recognize their country's vulnerability and its limits had ended. As the new decade dawned, Americans looked forward to regaining confidence in their country and optimism in their own futures.

✓ **Reading Check** **Examining** What was the impact of disco music on American society?

SECTION 4 ASSESSMENT

Checking for Understanding

1. **Define:** guru, transcendental meditation, disco.
2. **Identify:** New Age movement, *All in the Family.*
3. **Summarize** the basic beliefs of followers of transcendental meditation.

Reviewing Themes

4. **Culture and Traditions** What new cultural trends affected American society in the 1970s?

Critical Thinking

5. **Analyzing** How did television in the 1970s reflect society at that time?
6. **Organizing** Complete a graphic organizer similar to the one below by listing the cultural trends of the 1970s.

Cultural Trends of the 1970s

Analyzing Visuals

7. **Analyzing Photographs** Study the photographs in the "What Life Was Like" feature on pages 972–973. How has popular music and fashion changed since the 1970s?

Writing About History

8. **Descriptive Writing** View a television program that was popular in the 1970s. Write a description of the program and explain how it reflected society at that time.

Critical Thinking
SKILLBUILDER

Analyzing Secondary Sources

Why Learn This Skill?

This textbook, like many other history books, is a secondary source. Secondary sources draw from primary sources to explain a topic. The value of a secondary source depends on how its author uses primary sources. Learning to analyze secondary sources will help you figure out whether those sources are presenting a complete and accurate picture of a topic or event.

Learning the Skill

To determine whether an author uses primary sources effectively, ask these questions:

- Are there references to primary sources in the text, footnotes, or acknowledgments?

- Who are the authors of the primary sources? What insights or biases might these people have?

- Is the information from the primary sources interwoven effectively to support or describe an event?

- Are different kinds of primary sources considered? Do they represent varied testimony?

- Is the interpretation of the primary sources sound and logical?

Practicing the Skill

In the following excerpt from *The Cold War, 1945–1987,* author Ralph B. Levering discusses President Carter's China policy. Carter sent his national security adviser, Zbigniew Brzezinski, to China to encourage better relations and thus put pressure on the Soviets. As you read, identify the primary sources Levering uses to make his argument.

During his trip to Peking, Brzezinski did everything he could to please the Chinese leaders. . . . He stressed repeatedly the evil nature of the Soviet Union. . . . Upon his return, Brzezinski told a New York Times *reporter that the trip was intended to "underline the long-term strategic nature of the United States' relationship to China."*

. . . Soviet leaders were deeply concerned. An editorial in Pravda *on May 30, 1978, stated that Brzezinski "stands before the world as an enemy of détente."*

President Nixon and First Lady Pat Nixon visiting the Great Wall of China during their historic 1972 trip.

Pravda *also blamed China, stating on June 17 that "Soviet-American confrontation . . . is the cherished dream of Peking." On the whole, U.S. officials were not displeased by the Kremlin's anger and concern: perhaps it would make Soviet leaders more anxious to conclude the SALT negotiations and more inclined to show restraint in the Third World.*

❶ What kind of primary source does Levering use twice in this passage?

❷ Do you think this kind of primary source has any possible weaknesses?

❸ Would the use of government documents strengthen the author's argument? Why or why not?

Skills Assessment

Complete the Practicing Skills questions on page 977 and the Chapter 32 Skill Reinforcement Activity to assess your mastery of this skill.

Applying the Skill

Analyzing Secondary Sources Find and read an in-depth article in a newspaper. Then list the primary sources the article uses and analyze how reliable you think they are.

Glencoe's **Skillbuilder Interactive Workbook CD-ROM, Level 2,** provides instruction and practice in key social studies skills.

Reviewing Key Terms

On a sheet of paper, use each of these terms in a sentence.

1. impound
2. détente
3. summit
4. executive privilege
5. impeach
6. inflation
7. embargo
8. stagflation
9. guru
10. transcendental meditation
11. disco

Reviewing Key Facts

12. **Identify:** Southern strategy, Sam J. Ervin, OPEC, New Age movement.

13. What were the main aspects of President Nixon's domestic and foreign policies?

14. What was the impact of the Watergate scandal on the American people?

15. Why did President Nixon freeze wages and prices in the early 1970s?

16. What factors caused economic problems in the United States in the 1970s?

17. What changes in family life occurred in the United States in the 1970s?

Critical Thinking

18. **Analyzing Themes: Government and Democracy** How did the Watergate scandal affect the relationship among the three branches of government?

19. **Evaluating** What impact did cultural phenomena such as disco music, the use of CB radios, and exercise trends have on the U.S. economy?

20. **Forming an Opinion** Alexander Haig stated that the Watergate scandal led to "a fundamental discrediting of respect for the presidency . . . [and] a new skepticism about politics, in general, which every American feels to this day." Do you agree with his statement? Why or why not?

21. **Interpreting Primary Sources** When the Arab-Israeli War of 1973 developed into a stalemate, the Arab nations imposed an oil embargo on the United States, the chief supporter of Israel. Because Arab countries supplied much of the oil used in the United States, the embargo created an energy crisis. The excerpt below is taken from an article in the December 3, 1973, issue of *U.S. News & World Report.* It details the growing energy problems that the United States was facing at that time. Read the excerpt and answer the questions that follow.

❝Evidence of the full dimensions of the energy crisis in this country is becoming more clear each day.

- Electric-power brownouts, even blackouts, are predicted for many parts of the U.S. before the end of the year.

- Voltage reduction of 5 percent from 4 P.M. to 8 P.M. each day was ordered starting November 26 in all six New England States, where fuel shortages threaten homes, schools, factories. . . .

- As a first step to cut gasoline use, President Nixon was reportedly ready to order closing of service stations nationwide from 9 P.M. Saturday to midnight Sunday on weekends. . . .

Chapter Summary

Uniting a Divided Country

- Nixon's conservative politics appeal to "Middle America."
- Nixon begins pulling ground troops out of Vietnam.
- Tensions with Soviet Union and China ease.
- Nixon signs treaty limiting nuclear arms.

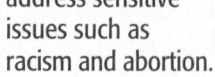

Scandal and Economic Turmoil

- Watergate scandal brings down Nixon.
- Congress enacts new laws to limit presidential power.
- Inflation, energy crisis, and foreign competition cause economic slowdown.
- Ford and Carter fail to revive economy.

Challenging Traditional Values

- New Age movement advocates self-fulfillment.
- More women join the workforce.
- Television shows prominently feature African Americans and independent women; address sensitive issues such as racism and abortion.

- Immediate rationing of gasoline and fuel oil is being urged on the President by top oil-industry executives. . . .

  One major piece of legislation . . . directs the President to take measures necessary to reduce the nation's energy demands by 25 percent within four weeks.

  Speed limits would be cut nationally; lighting and heating of public and commercial buildings would be curtailed; home-owners would be given tax deductions to winterize their homes. . . .

  Other pending measures would impose year-round daylight saving time and would open naval oil reserves for intensive exploration. . . .

  a. What proposals did the U.S. government make to deal with the energy crisis?

  b. What lessons do you think the United States might have learned from the crisis?

22. **Categorizing** Complete a chart similar to the one below by listing the attempts each president made to strengthen the nation's economy.

President	Attempts to Strengthen Economy
Nixon	
Ford	
Carter	

Practicing Skills

23. **Analyzing Secondary Sources** Examine the Bob Woodward quotation on Watergate's impact on page 962. Then use the steps you learned on the subject of analyzing secondary sources on page 975 to answer the following questions.
    a. Who is Bob Woodward, and how was he related to the Watergate scandal?
    b. How knowledgeable or reliable do you think Woodward is as a source? Why do you think so?

Chapter Activity

24. **Researching Artifacts** One useful way of learning about cultures of different periods is by examining artifacts from the era. Many of these artifacts can be found in museums and art galleries, while others may be found in your own home. What sorts of artifacts could you find about the 1970s? What would they tell you about the culture and lifestyle of that era? Create a chart listing possible artifacts and how they represent the 1970s.

Inflation, 1960–1992

Writing Activity

25. **Persuasive Writing** Imagine you are an aide to President Nixon during the early 1970s. Nixon has just returned from his historic mission to China to establish diplomatic relations with the Communist nation. Write a press release on the president's trip for reporters, explaining the reasons Nixon reversed American policy and the expected benefits from doing so.

Economics and History

26. The graph above shows inflation rates in the United States from 1960 to 1992. Study the graph and answer the questions below.
    a. **Interpreting Graphs** How did the nation's inflation rate change between 1965 and 1980?

    b. **Determining Cause and Effect** What factor was most important in causing this change?

Standardized Test Practice

Directions: Choose the phrase that best completes the following sentence.

As a political conservative, President Nixon wanted to

A increase federal spending on welfare programs.

B take more aggressive federal action to speed desegregation.

C return power to state governments.

D appoint activist-minded justices to the Supreme Court.

Test-Taking Tip: Think of the meaning of *political conservative:* someone who believes that the federal government's role in society should be limited. Choose the answer that best reflects this meaning.

CHAPTER 33 Resurgence of Conservatism

1980–1992

Why It Matters

The 1980s saw the rise of a new conservatism. President Reagan, standing for traditional values and smaller government, symbolized this movement. While tax cuts and new technologies fueled an economic boom, Reagan embarked on a massive military buildup and expanded efforts to contain communism. During President George Bush's term, the United States fought the Persian Gulf War, and the Cold War came to a dramatic end with the fall of the Soviet Union.

The Impact Today

Developments of the Reagan era are still visible today.
* *The struggle between conservative and liberal ideas often defines American politics.*
* *Foreign policy has greatly changed because of the fall of the Soviet Union.*
* *The Americans with Disabilities Act has opened up doors for disabled citizens.*

The American Vision *Video* *The Chapter 33 video, "Tear Down This Wall!" describes the history of the Berlin Wall, one of the Cold War's most powerful symbols.*

1979
* Jerry Falwell's "Moral Majority" movement begins

1981
* American hostages released in Iran
* Launch of *Columbia*, first space shuttle

1983
* U.S. Marine barracks bombed in Lebanon

United States
PRESIDENTS

Carter 1977–1981

Reagan 1981–1989

1979　　　　　　　　　　*1982*　　　　　　　　　　*1985*

World

1979
* Iranian revolution establishes Islamic republic
* Soviets invade Afghanistan

1980
* War begins between Iran and Iraq

1985
* Mikhail Gorbachev becomes leader of Soviet Union

President Reagan at the Berlin Wall in 1987

1986
- Iran-Contra scandal enters the news

1987
- INF Treaty between U.S. and USSR reduces land-based intermediate-range nuclear missiles

1988
- More than 35,000 cases of AIDS diagnosed for the year

G. Bush 1989–1993

1988

1991
- Persian Gulf War occurs between Iraq and UN coalition

1991

1986
- Dictatorship of Ferdinand Marcos overthrown in the Philippines

1989
- Tiananmen Square protests for democracy break out in China
- Several Communist governments in Eastern Europe collapse

1990
- Germany reunified into one nation

1991
- Soviet Union dissolves

HISTORY Online

Chapter Overview
Visit the *American Vision* Web site at tav.glencoe.com and click on **Chapter Overviews—Chapter 33** to preview chapter information.

Main Idea
In the 1980s, discontent with government and changes in society resulted in the rise of a new conservative coalition.

Key Terms and Names
liberal, conservative, William F. Buckley, Sunbelt, Billy Graham, televangelist, Moral Majority

Reading Strategy
Taking Notes As you read about the rise of a new conservative coalition in the United States, use the major headings of the section to create an outline similar to the one below.

The New Conservatism
I. Conservatism and Liberalism
    A.
    B.
II.
    A.

Reading Objectives
- **Explain** how discontent with government led to a conservative shift in Americans' political convictions.
- **Describe** how the nation's population shifts led to a change in voting patterns.

Section Theme
Economic Factors High taxes as well as economic and moral concerns led the country toward a new conservatism.

Preview of Events

♦1965   ♦1970   ♦1975   ♦1980

1964
Conservative Barry Goldwater is defeated for presidency

1972
Nixon wins re-election

1976
Reagan challenges Ford for nomination

1979
Jerry Falwell's "Moral Majority" movement begins

1980
Reagan wins presidential election

★ *An American Story* ★

Midge Decter, a New Yorker and a writer for the conservative publication *Commentary,* was appalled at the terror that hit her city on a hot July night in 1977. On the night of July 13, the power failed in New York City. Street lights went dark. Elevators, subways, and air conditioners stopped running. The blackout left millions of people in darkness, and looting and arson rocked the city.

City officials and the media blamed the lawlessness on the anger and despair of youth in neglected areas. "They were just waiting for something like this so they could go berserk," said Lydia Rivers, a Brooklyn resident. Decter, however, had other ideas about who was to blame for the terror in her city:

❝The answer is that all those young men went on their spree of looting because they had been given permission to do so. They had been given permission to do so by all the papers and magazines, movies and documentaries—all the outlets for the purveying of enlightened liberal attitude and progressive liberal policy—which had for years and years been proclaiming that race and poverty were sufficient excuses for lawlessness. . . .❞

—quoted in *Commentary,* September 1977

Conservatism and Liberalism

Midge Decter's article blaming liberalism for the riots in New York during the 1977 blackout exemplifies a debate in American politics that continues to the present day. On one side of the debate are people who call themselves liberals; on the other side are those who identify themselves as conservatives. Liberal ideas generally dominated American politics for much of the 1900s, but conservative ideas gained significant support among Americans in the 1970s. In 1980 Ronald Reagan, a strong conservative, was elected president.

Liberalism In American politics today, people who call themselves liberals believe several basic ideas. In general, liberals believe that the government should regulate the economy to protect people from the power of large corporations and wealthy elites. Liberals also believe that the government, particularly the federal government, should play an active role in helping disadvantaged Americans, partly through social programs and partly by putting more of society's tax burden on wealthier people.

Although liberals favor government intervention in the economy, they are suspicious of any attempt by the government to regulate social behavior. They are strong supporters of free speech and privacy, and they are opposed to the government supporting or endorsing religious beliefs, no matter how indirectly. They believe that a diverse society made up of many different races, cultures, and ethnic groups tends to be more creative and energetic.

Liberals often support high taxes on the wealthy, partly because they believe taxes weaken the power of the rich and partly because the government can transfer the wealth to other Americans to keep society more equal. They believe that most social problems have their roots in economic inequality.

Conservatism Unlike liberals, conservatives generally have a fundamental distrust of the power of government, particularly the federal government. They support the original intent of the Constitution and believe that governmental power should be divided into different branches and split between the state and federal levels to limit its ability to intrude into people's lives.

Conservatives believe that if the government regulates the economy, it makes the economy less efficient, resulting in less wealth and more poverty. They believe that the free enterprise system is the best way to organize society. They often argue that if people and businesses are free to make their own economic choices, there will be more wealth and a higher standard of living for everyone.

For this reason, conservatives generally oppose high taxes and government programs that transfer wealth from the rich to those who are less wealthy. They believe that taxes and government programs discourage investment, take away people's incentive to work hard, and reduce the amount of freedom in society.

The more the government regulates the economy, conservatives argue, the more it will have to regulate every aspect of people's behavior. Ultimately, conservatives fear, the government will so restrict people's economic freedom that Americans will no longer be able to improve their standard of living and get ahead in life.

Many conservatives believe that religious faith is vitally important in sustaining society. They believe most social problems result from issues of morality and character—issues, they argue, that are best addressed through commitment to a religious faith and through the private efforts of individuals and communities helping those in need. Despite this general belief, conservatives do support the use of the governmental police powers to regulate social behavior in some instances.

Reading Check **Contrasting** How do liberal and conservative opinions about government differ?

Conservatism Revives

During the New Deal era of the 1930s, conservative ideas had lost much of their influence in national politics. In the years following World War II, however, conservatism began to revive.

Conservatism and the Cold War Support for conservative ideas began to revive for two major reasons, both related to the Cold War. First, the struggle against communism revived the debate about the role of the government in the economy. Some Americans believed that liberal economic ideas were slowly leading the United States toward communism and became determined to stop this trend. They also thought the United States had failed to stop the spread of Soviet power because liberals did not fully understand the need for a strong anticommunist foreign policy.

At the same time, many Americans viewed the Cold War in religious terms. Communism rejected religion and emphasized the material side of life. To Americans with a deep religious faith, the struggle against communism was a struggle between good and evil. Liberalism, which emphasizes economic welfare, gradually lost the support of many religious Americans, who increasingly turned to conservatism.

Conservatives Organize In 1955 a young conservative named **William F. Buckley** founded a new conservative magazine called *National Review.* Buckley's magazine helped to revive conservative ideas in the United States. Buckley debated in front of college students and appeared on radio and television shows, spreading conservative ideas to an even wider audience.

Within the Republican Party, conservatives, particularly young conservatives, began to push their ideas and demand a greater role in party decision-making. In 1960 some 90 young conservative leaders met at Buckley's family estate and founded Young Americans for Freedom (YAF), an independent conservative group, to push their ideas and to support conservative candidates.

By 1964 the new conservative movement had achieved enough influence within the Republican Party to enable the conservative **Barry Goldwater** to win the nomination for president. To the dismay of the conservatives, however, President Johnson easily defeated Goldwater and won the election in a landslide.

William F. Buckley

✓ **Reading Check** **Explaining** Why did conservatism revive in the 1950s?

Conservatism Gains Support

Conservatism could not have become a mass movement if Americans had not responded to conservative ideas. The events of the late 1960s and 1970s played an important role in convincing Americans to support conservatism. After Goldwater's huge loss in 1964, American society moved decisively in a conservative direction.

GEOGRAPHY

The Rise of the Sunbelt One of the problems facing conservatives in the 1950s and early 1960s was that they generally split their votes between the Republicans and the Democrats. Two regions of the country, the South and the West, were more conservative than other areas. Southern conservatives, however, generally voted for the Democrats, while conservatives in the West voted Republican. This meant that the party that won the heavily populated Northeast would win the election. Since the Northeast strongly supported liberal ideas, both parties were pulled toward liberal policies.

This pattern began to change during World War II, when large numbers of Americans moved south and west to take jobs in the war factories. The movement to the South and West—together known as the **Sunbelt**—continued after the war. As the Sunbelt's economy expanded, Americans living in those regions began to view the federal government differently from people living in the Northeast.

Sunbelt Conservatism Industry in the Northeast was in decline, leading to the region's nickname—the **Rust Belt.** This region had more unemployed people than any other, and its cities were often congested and polluted. These problems prompted Americans in the Northeast to look to the federal government for programs and regulations that would help them solve their problems.

In contrast, Americans in the Sunbelt opposed high taxes and federal regulations that threatened to interfere with their region's growth. Many white Southerners were also angry with the Democrats for supporting civil rights, which they interpreted as an effort by the federal government to impose its policies on the South.

When Barry Goldwater argued in 1964 that the federal government was becoming too strong, many Southerners agreed. For the first time since Reconstruction, they began voting Republican in large numbers. Although Goldwater lost the election, his candidacy showed Republicans that the best way to attract Southern votes was to support conservative policies.

Americans living in the West also responded to conservative attacks on the size and power of the federal government. Westerners were proud of their frontier heritage and spirit of "rugged individualism." They resented federal environmental regulations that limited ranching, controlled water use, and restricted the development of the region's natural resources. Western anger over such policies inspired the "Sagebrush Rebellion" of the early 1970s—a widespread protest led by conservatives against federal laws hindering the region's development.

By 1980 the population of the Sunbelt had surpassed the Northeast. This gave the conservative regions of the country more electoral votes and therefore more influence in shaping party policies. With Southerners shifting their votes to the Republican Party, conservatives could now build a coalition to elect a president.

Suburban Conservatism As riots erupted and crime soared during the 1960s and 1970s, many Americans moved to suburbs to escape the chaos of the cities. Even there, however, they found the quiet middle-class lifestyle they desired to be in danger. The rapid inflation of the 1970s had caused the

WASH.
2,378,963
4,132,000

OREG.
1,521,341
2,633,000

IDAHO
588,637
944,000

MONT.

N. DAK.

MINN.

CANADA

ME.

VT.
N.H.

N.Y. MASS.
R.I.
CONN.

WYO.
290,529
470,000

S. DAK.

WIS.

MICH.

NEV.
106,083
800,000

UTAH
688,862
1,461,000

COLO.
1,325,089
2,890,000

NEBR.

IOWA

ILL. IND.

OHIO

PA.

N.J.

DEL.
MD.

CALIF.
10,586,223
23,668,000

MO.

KY.

W.
VA. VA.

ARIZ.
749,587
2,718,000

N. MEX.
681,187
1,303,000

KANS.

ARK.

TENN.

N.C.

S.C.

OKLA.

MISS. ALA.

GA.
3,444,578
5,463,000

TEX.
7,711,194
14,229,000

LA.

FLA.
2,771,305
9,746,000

PACIFIC
OCEAN

ATLANTIC
OCEAN

N
W E
S

Gulf of
Mexico

MEXICO

TROPIC OF CANCER

Legend

□ Sunbelt states

749,587 Population (1950)

944,000 Population (1980)

■ Percent growth
(1 bar equals 50% growth)

Population shown only for states
having 50% or more population
growth between 1950 and 1980

0 ——— 500 miles
0 ——— 500 kilometers
Lambert Azimuthal Equal-area projection

Geography *Skills*

1. **Interpreting Maps** What Sunbelt states have more than 8 million residents?
2. **Applying Geography Skills** Nevada has the highest percentage growth in population for the time period shown. Looking at its 1950 population, how would you explain this large percentage increase?

buying power of the average middle-class family to shrink while taxes remained high.

Many Americans resented the taxes they had to pay for New Deal and Great Society programs when they themselves were losing ground economically. By the late 1970s, Americans had begun to rebel against these high taxes. In 1978 Howard Jarvis, a conservative activist, launched the first successful tax revolt in California with **Proposition 13,** a referendum on the state ballot that greatly reduced property taxes.

Soon afterward anti-tax movements appeared in other states, and tax cuts quickly became a national issue. For many Americans, the conservative argument that the government had become too big meant simply that taxes were too high. As conservatives began to call for tax cuts, middle-class Americans flocked to their cause.

The Religious Right While many Americans turned to conservatism for economic reasons, others were drawn to it because they feared American society had lost touch with its traditional values. For many

Americans of deep religious faith, the events of the 1960s and 1970s were shocking. The Supreme Court decision in *Roe* v. *Wade,* which established abortion as a constitutional right, greatly concerned them. Other Supreme Court decisions that limited prayer in public schools and expanded the rights of people accused of crimes also drew criticism from religious groups. *(See page 1083 for more information on* Roe v. Wade.*)*

The feminist movement and the push for the Equal Rights Amendment (ERA) further alarmed religious Americans because it seemed to represent an assault on the traditional family. Many religious people were also shocked by the behavior of some university students in the 1960s, whose contempt for authority seemed to indicate a general breakdown in American values and morality. These concerns helped expand the conservative cause into a mass movement.

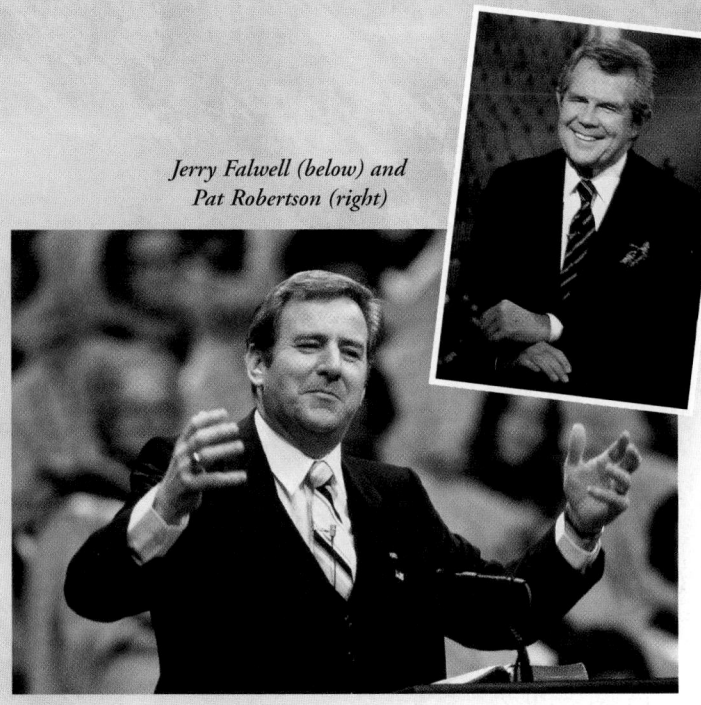

Jerry Falwell (below) and Pat Robertson (right)

"televangelists," as they were nicknamed, included Marion "Pat" Robertson, who founded the Christian Broadcasting Network, and Jerry Falwell, who used his television show *The Old-Time Gospel Hour* to found a movement that he called the **"Moral Majority."** Using television and mail campaigns, the Moral Majority built up a network of ministers to register new voters who backed conservative candidates and issues. Falwell later claimed to have brought in 2 million new voters by 1980.

A New Coalition By the end of the 1970s, the new conservative coalition of voters had begun to come together in the United States. Although the members of this coalition were concerned with many different issues, they were held together by a common belief that American society had somehow lost its way.

The Watergate scandal, high taxes, and special interest politics had undermined many Americans' faith in their government. Rising unemployment, rapid inflation, and the energy crisis had shaken their confidence in the economy. Riots, crime, and drug abuse suggested that society itself was falling apart. The retreat from Vietnam, the hostage crisis in Iran, and the Soviet invasion of Afghanistan made the nation look weak and helpless internationally. Many Americans were tired of change and upheaval. They wanted stability and a return to what they remembered as a better time. For some, the new conservatism and its most prominent spokesperson, Ronald Reagan, offered hope to a nation in distress.

Although religious conservatives included people of many different faiths, the largest group within the social conservative movement was evangelical Protestant Christians. Evangelicals believe they are saved from their sins through conversion (which they refer to as being "born again") and a personal commitment to follow Jesus Christ, whose death and resurrection reconciles them to God.

After World War II, a religious revival began in the United States. Protestant ministers such as **Billy Graham** and Oral Roberts built national followings. By the late 1970s, about 70 million Americans described themselves as "born again." Christian evangelicals owned their own newspapers, magazines, radio stations, and television networks.

Television in particular allowed evangelical ministers to reach a large nationwide audience. These

Reading Check **Summarizing** Why did many Americans begin to support the conservative movement?

SECTION 1 ASSESSMENT

Checking for Understanding

1. **Define:** liberal, conservative, televangelist.
2. **Identify:** William F. Buckley, Sunbelt, Billy Graham, Moral Majority.
3. **Explain** why evangelical Protestant Christians began to support conservative issues.

Reviewing Themes

4. **Economic Factors** What kind of economy did conservatives want?

Critical Thinking

5. **Analyzing** How did Christian evangelicals contribute to a growing conservative national identity?
6. **Organizing** Use a graphic organizer similar to the one below to list conservative beliefs.

Conservative Beliefs

Analyzing Visuals

7. **Analyzing Maps** Study the map of the Sunbelt on page 983. What impact would the migration patterns shown have on representation in the U.S. House of Representatives?

Writing About History

8. **Persuasive Writing** Many conservatives believe that "government that governs least, governs best." Write a paragraph supporting or opposing this statement.

The Reagan Years

Main Idea

The presidency of Ronald Reagan brought a new conservative attitude to government.

Key Terms and Names

supply-side economics, Reaganomics, budget deficit, Sandra Day O'Connor, William Rehnquist, Geraldine Ferraro, contra, Iran-Contra scandal, Oliver North, Mikhail Gorbachev

Reading Strategy

Organizing As you read about the Reagan presidency, complete the graphic organizer below by filling in the major points of the supply-side theory of economics.

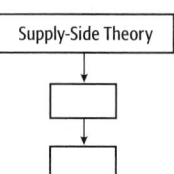

Reading Objectives

- **Explain** President Reagan's economic recovery plan.
- **Discuss** Reagan's policies toward the Soviet Union.

Section Theme

Global Connections President Reagan believed the United States should take strong action to resist Communist influence overseas.

Preview of Events

♦1980	♦1983	♦1986	♦1989

1980
Reagan elected president

1983
Terrorists bomb U.S. Marine barracks in Lebanon

1984
Reagan reelected

1986
Iran-Contra scandal breaks

1987
Reagan and Gorbachev sign INF Treaty

★ An American Story ★

In 1926 when he was 15 years old, Ronald Reagan earned $15 a week as a lifeguard at Lowell Park on the Rock River in Illinois. Being a lifeguard, Reagan later wrote, taught him quite a bit about human nature:

66Lifeguarding provides one of the best vantage points in the world to learn about people. During my career at the park, I saved seventy-seven people. I guarantee you they needed saving—no lifeguard gets wet without good reason. . . . Not many thanked me, much less gave me a reward, and being a little money-hungry, I'd done a little daydreaming about this. They felt insulted. I got to recognize that people hate to be saved. . . .99

—quoted in *Where's the Rest of Me?*

The belief that people did not really want to be saved by someone else was one of the ideas that Ronald Reagan took with him to the White House. It fit with his philosophy of self-reliance and independence.

The Road to the White House

Ronald Reagan grew up in Dixon, Illinois, the son of an Irish American shoe salesman. After graduating from Eureka College in 1932, Reagan worked as a sports broadcaster at an Iowa radio station. In 1937 he took a Hollywood screen test and won a contract from a movie studio. Over the next 25 years, he made over 50 movies. As a broadcaster and actor, Reagan learned how to speak publicly and how to project an image, skills that proved invaluable when he entered politics.

Different Viewpoints

Carter and Reagan on Government

As President Carter sought re-election in 1980, he had to deal with inflation, unemployment, and an energy crisis. He urged Americans to make sacrifices so that the government could solve these problems. His opponent, Ronald Reagan, disagreed. Reagan argued that Americans should trust themselves, not the government, to solve their problems.

President Jimmy Carter:

"[A] president cannot yield to the shortsighted demands, no matter how rich or powerful the special interests might be that make those demands. And that is why the president cannot bend to the passions of the moment, however popular they might be. And that is why the president must sometimes ask for sacrifice when his listeners would rather hear the promise of comfort.

. . . The only way to build a better future is to start with realities of the present. But while we Democrats grapple with the real challenges of a real world, others talk of a world of tinsel and make-believe.

. . . A world of good guys and bad guys, where some politicians shoot first and ask questions later.

No hard choices. No sacrifice. No tough decisions. It sounds too good to be true—and it is."

—from his acceptance speech at the Democratic National Convention, August 14, 1980

California governor Ronald Reagan:

"The American people, the most generous people on earth, who created the highest standard of living, are not going to accept the notion that we can only make a better world for others by moving backwards ourselves. Those who believe we *can* have no business leading the nation.

I will not stand by and watch this great country destroy itself under mediocre leadership that drifts from one crisis to the next, eroding our national will and purpose.

"Trust me" government asks that we concentrate our hopes and dreams on one man; that we trust him to do what's best for us. My view of government places trust not in one person or one party, but in those values that transcend persons and parties. The trust is where it belongs—in the people."

—from his acceptance speech at the Republican National Convention, July 17, 1980

Learning From History

1. **Recognizing Ideologies** How do the two candidates differ regarding the role of government in solving the nation's problems?
2. **Making Inferences** Ronald Reagan won the election of 1980. What part of his speech do you think may have had the most influence on voters? Why?

Moving to Conservatism In 1947 Reagan became president of the **Screen Actors Guild**—the actors' union. As head of the union, he testified about communism in Hollywood before the House Un-American Activities Committee. Reagan had been a staunch Democrat and supporter of the New Deal, but his experience in dealing with Communists in the union began shifting him toward conservative ideas.

In 1954 Reagan became the host of a television program called *General Electric Theater* and agreed to be a motivational speaker for the company. As he traveled around the country speaking to workers, secretaries, and managers, he became increasingly conservative. Over and over again, Reagan said later, he heard stories from average Americans about how high taxes and government regulations made it impossible for them to get ahead.

By 1964 Reagan had become such a popular national speaker that Barry Goldwater asked him to make a televised speech on behalf of Goldwater's presidential campaign. Reagan's speech greatly impressed several wealthy entrepreneurs in California. They convinced Reagan to run for governor of California in 1966 and helped finance his campaign. Reagan won the election and was reelected in 1970. Ten years later, he won the Republican presidential nomination.

The Election of 1980 Reagan's campaign appealed to Americans who were frustrated with the economy and worried that the United States had become weak internationally. Reagan promised to cut taxes and increase defense spending. He won the support of social conservatives by calling for a constitutional amendment banning abortion. During one debate with Carter, Reagan asked voters, "Are you better off than you were four years ago?" On Election Day, the voters answered "No." Reagan won nearly 51 percent of the popular vote and 489 electoral votes, easily defeating Carter in the Electoral College. For the first time since 1954, Republicans also gained control of the Senate.

✓ **Reading Check** **Describing** What event jump-started Ronald Reagan's political career as a conservative leader?

Reagan's Domestic Policies

Ronald Reagan believed the key to restoring the economy and overcoming problems in society was to get Americans to believe in themselves again. He expressed this idea in his Inaugural Address:

❝We have every right to dream heroic dreams. . . . You can see heroes every day going in and out of factory gates. Others, a handful in number, produce enough food to feed all of us. . . . You meet heroes across a counter. . . . There are entrepreneurs with faith in themselves and faith in an idea who create new jobs, new wealth and opportunity. . . . Their patriotism is quiet but deep. Their values sustain our national life.❞

—from Reagan's First Inaugural Address

Reagan also explained that Americans should not look to Washington for answers: "In this present crisis, government is not the solution to our problem. Government is the problem."

ECONOMICS

Reaganomics Reagan's first priority was the economy, which was suffering from stagflation—a combination of high unemployment and high inflation. According to most economists, the way to fight unemployment was to increase government spending. Increasing spending, however, made inflation worse. Stagflation puzzled many economists, who did not expect inflation and high unemployment to occur at the same time.

Conservative economists offered two competing ideas for fixing the economy. One group, known as **monetarists,** argued that inflation was caused by too much money in circulation. They believed the best solution was to raise interest rates. Another group supported supply-side economics. They argued that the economy was weak because taxes were too high.

Supply-side economists believed that high taxes took too much money away from investors. If taxes were cut, businesses and investors could use their extra capital to make new investments, and businesses could expand and create new jobs. The result would be a larger supply of goods for consumers, who would now have more money to spend because of the tax cuts.

Reagan combined monetarism and supply-side economics. He encouraged the Federal Reserve to keep interest rates high, and asked Congress to pass a massive tax cut. Critics called his approach **Reaganomics** or "trickle-down economics." They believed Reagan's policy would help corporations and wealthy Americans, while only a little bit of the wealth would "trickle down" to average Americans.

Reagan made deals with conservative Democrats in the House and moderate Republicans in the Senate. Eventually Congress passed a 25 percent tax rate cut.

Cutting Programs Cutting tax rates meant the government would receive less money. This would increase the budget deficit—the amount by which expenditures exceed income. To keep the deficit under control, Reagan proposed cuts to social programs. Welfare benefits, including the food stamp program and the school lunch program, were cut back. Medicare payments, student loans, housing subsidies, and unemployment compensation were also reduced.

After a struggle, Congress passed most of these cuts. The fight convinced Reagan that he would never get Congress to cut spending enough to balance the budget. He decided that cutting taxes and building up the military were more important than balancing the budget. He accepted the high deficit as the price of getting his other programs passed.

Deregulation Reagan believed that burdensome government regulations were another cause of the economy's problems. His first act as president was to sign an executive order eliminating price controls on oil and gasoline. Critics argued that getting rid of controls would

HISTORY Online

Student Web Activity Visit the *American Vision* Web site at tav.glencoe.com and click on **Student Web Activities—Chapter 33** for an activity on the 1980s.

drive prices up, but in fact, they began to fall. The falling energy prices freed up money for businesses and consumers to spend elsewhere, helping the economy to recover.

Other deregulation soon followed. The National Highway Traffic and Safety Administration reduced its demand for air bags and higher fuel efficiency for cars. The Federal Communications Commission abandoned efforts to regulate the new cable television industry. Carter had already begun deregulating the airline industry, and Reagan encouraged the process, which led to price wars, cheaper fares, and the founding of new airlines.

Reagan's Secretary of the Interior, **James Watt,** increased the amount of public land corporations could use for oil drilling, mining, and logging. Watt's decisions angered environmentalists, as did the Environmental Protection Agency's decisions to ease regulations on pollution control equipment and to reduce safety checks on chemicals and pesticides.

The Economy Booms
In 1983 the economy finally began to recover. By 1984 the United States had begun the biggest economic expansion in its history up to that time. The median income of American families climbed steadily, rising 15 percent by 1989. Sales of goods and services shot upward. Five million new businesses and 20 million new jobs were created. By 1988 unemployment had fallen to about 5.5 percent, the lowest in 14 years.

Shifting the Judicial Balance
Reagan did not apply his conservative ideas only to the economy. He also tried to bring a strict constructionist outlook to the federal judiciary. Reagan wanted judges who followed the original intent and wording of the Constitution rather than those who interpreted and expanded its meaning. He also changed the face of the Supreme Court by nominating **Sandra Day O'Connor** to be the first woman on the Supreme Court.

In 1986 Chief Justice Warren Burger retired. Reagan chose the most conservative associate justice, **William Rehnquist,** to succeed him. He then named **Antonin Scalia,** also a conservative, to fill the vacancy left by Rehnquist. In 1987 Reagan's nomination of Robert Bork to the Court led to a bitter confirmation fight in the Senate. Liberals argued that Bork's opinions on issues were too extreme, and they managed to block his confirmation. **Anthony Kennedy,** a moderate, ultimately became the new associate justice.

Reagan Wins Re-election
As the 1984 election approached, the growing economy made Reagan very popular. Democrats nominated Jimmy Carter's vice president, **Walter Mondale.** He chose as his running mate Representative **Geraldine Ferraro,** the first woman to run for vice president for a major party.

Instead of arguing issues with his opponent, Reagan emphasized the good economy. In an overwhelming landslide, he won about 59 percent of the popular vote and all the electoral votes except those from Mondale's home state of Minnesota and the District of Columbia.

☑ **Reading Check** **Explaining** What is supply-side economics?

Reagan Builds Up the Military

Reagan did not limit his reforms to the domestic scene. He adopted a new Cold War foreign policy that rejected both containment and détente. Reagan called the Soviet Union "the focus of evil in the modern world" and "an evil empire." In his view, the United States should not negotiate with or try to contain evil. It should try to defeat it.

The Attempt to Kill the President, March 30, 1981

Barely two months after the inauguration, on March 30, 1981, John Hinckley tried to kill President Reagan in a misguided attempt to impress actress Jodie Foster. Hinckley fired six shots as Reagan left a hotel in Washington, D.C. One bullet bounced off the president's rib and lodged near his heart. Another bullet seriously wounded press secretary Jim Brady. Reagan's recovery was long, but he stayed upbeat. His jaunty reply to his wife, "Honey, I forgot to duck," won the affection of many.

John Hinckley (center)

Peace Through Strength In Reagan's opinion, the only option open to the United States in dealing with the Soviet Union was "peace through strength"— a phrase he used during his campaign. The military buildup Reagan launched was the largest peacetime buildup in American history. It cost about $1.5 trillion over five years.

Reagan and many of his advisers believed that if the Soviets tried to match the American buildup, it might put so much pressure on their economy they would be forced to either reform their system or collapse. In 1982 Reagan told students at Eureka College that massive Soviet defense spending eventually would cause the Communist system to collapse:

> ❝The Soviet empire is faltering because rigid centralized control has destroyed incentives for innovation, efficiency, and individual achievement. But in the midst of social and economic problems, the Soviet dictatorship has forged the largest armed force in the world. It has done so by preempting the human needs of its people and in the end, this course will undermine the foundations of the Soviet system.❞

—quoted in *Ronald Reagan*

America also aimed its power at countries accused of supporting terrorism. After charging Libya with backing a terrorist bombing in Berlin, the United States launched an air attack on Libya on April 14, 1986. The raids killed 37 and injured 200.

A Growing Deficit Reagan's military buildup created new jobs in the defense industries. Supply-side economists had predicted that despite the spending, lower taxes combined with overall cuts in government programs would generate enough growth to increase tax revenues and balance the budget. Tax revenues did rise, but other programs were too popular for Reagan to cut as sharply as he wanted. As a result, the annual budget deficit went from $80 billion to over $200 billion.

✓ **Reading Check** **Describing** How did Reagan's Cold War military policy affect the nation's economy?

Profiles IN HISTORY

Justice Sandra Day O'Connor *1930–*

When a Supreme Court vacancy opened up in 1981, President Reagan decided to fulfill his campaign promise to name the first woman justice. He chose Sandra Day O'Connor, an Arizona appeals court judge.

When Reagan called O'Connor to ask to nominate her, she was surprised. "I was overwhelmed and, at first, speechless," O'Connor said. "After a moment I managed to tell him that I would be honored."

O'Connor grew up on the Day family's Lazy B Ranch in Arizona. Unlike most Supreme Court justices, she also had broad political experience. After earning a law degree in 1952, she found that most law firms would not hire a woman—except as a legal secretary. She went into public service, had three sons, and practiced law privately.

Appointed to a state senatorial vacancy in 1969, she successfully ran for the position and became its first woman majority leader in 1972. O'Connor won election as superior court judge in 1974 and was later appointed to the appeals court.

Her nomination to the Supreme Court had strong support from Justice William Rehnquist—a classmate at Stanford Law School—and Arizona senator Barry Goldwater. O'Connor's nomination was opposed by the Moral Majority because she had supported the Equal Rights Amendment (ERA) and refused to back an antiabortion amendment or criticize the *Roe* v. *Wade* decision. Others, however, praised her legal judgment and conservative approach to the law. As a moderate conservative, she quickly became an important swing-vote on the Court, between more liberal and more conservative justices.

The Reagan Doctrine

Building up the military was only part of Reagan's military strategy. He also believed the United States should support guerrilla groups who were fighting to overthrow Communist or pro-Soviet governments. This policy became known as the Reagan Doctrine.

Aid to the Afghan Rebels Perhaps the most visible example of the Reagan Doctrine was in Afghanistan. In late December 1979, the Soviet Union invaded Afghanistan to support a Soviet-backed government. The Soviets soon found themselves fighting Afghan guerrillas known as the *mujahadeen.*

President Carter sent about $30 million in military aid to the Afghan guerrillas, but Reagan sent $570 million more. The Soviets were soon trapped in a situation similar to the American experience in Vietnam. They could not defeat the Afghan guerrillas. As casualties mounted, the war put additional strain on the Soviet economy. In 1988 the Soviets agreed to withdraw.

Nicaragua and Grenada Reagan was also concerned about Soviet influence in Nicaragua. Rebels known as the **Sandinistas** had overthrown a

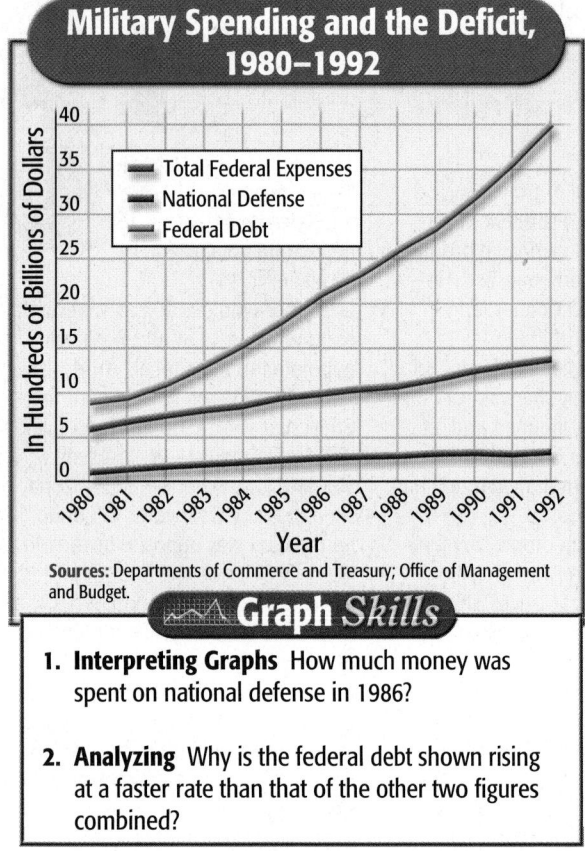

Military Spending and the Deficit, 1980–1992

In Hundreds of Billions of Dollars

- Total Federal Expenses
- National Defense
- Federal Debt

Year

Sources: Departments of Commerce and Treasury; Office of Management and Budget.

Graph Skills

1. **Interpreting Graphs** How much money was spent on national defense in 1986?

2. **Analyzing** Why is the federal debt shown rising at a faster rate than that of the other two figures combined?

pro-American dictator in Nicaragua in 1979. The Sandinistas set up a socialist government. They also accepted Cuban and Soviet aid and began supporting antigovernment rebels in nearby El Salvador.

In response, the Reagan administration began secretly arming an anti-Sandinista guerrilla force known as the contras, from the Spanish word for "counterrevolutionary." When Congress learned of this policy, it banned further aid to the contras.

Aiding the contras was not Reagan's only action in Latin America. In 1983 radical Marxists overthrew the left-wing government on the tiny Caribbean island of Grenada. In October, Reagan sent in American troops. The Cuban and Grenadian soldiers were quickly defeated and a new anticommunist government was put in place.

The Iran-Contra Scandal

Although Congress had prohibited aid to the Nicaraguan contras, individuals in Reagan's administration continued to illegally support the rebels. These officials secretly sold weapons to Iran in exchange for the release of American hostages being held in the Middle East. Profits from these sales were then sent to the contras.

News of the illegal operations broke in November 1986. One of the chief figures in the **Iran-Contra**

scandal was Marine Colonel **Oliver North,** an aide to the National Security Council (NSC). He and other senior NSC and CIA officials testified before Congress and admitted to covering up their actions, including shredding documents to destroy evidence.

President Reagan had approved the sale of arms to Iran, but the congressional investigation concluded that he had not been informed about the diversion of the money to the contras. To the end, Reagan insisted he had done nothing wrong, but the scandal tainted his second term in office.

Reading Check **Identifying** What was the Reagan Doctrine?

New Approaches to Arms Control

As part of the military buildup, Reagan decided to place nuclear missiles in Western Europe to counter Soviet missiles in Eastern Europe. This decision triggered a new peace movement. Tens of thousands of protesters pushed for a "nuclear freeze"—a halt to the deployment of new nuclear missiles.

Reagan offered to cancel the deployment of the new missiles if the Soviets removed their missiles from Eastern Europe. He also proposed Strategic Arms Reduction Talks (START) to cut the number of missiles on both sides in half. The Soviets refused and walked out of the arms control talks.

"Star Wars" Despite his decision to deploy missiles in Europe, Reagan generally disagreed with the military strategy known as nuclear deterrence, sometimes called "mutual assured destruction." This strategy assumed that as long as the United States and Soviet Union could destroy each other with nuclear weapons, they would be afraid to use them.

Reagan believed that mutual assured destruction was immoral because it depended on the threat to kill massive numbers of people. He also felt that if nuclear war did begin, there would be no way to defend the United States. In March 1983, Reagan proposed the **Strategic Defense Initiative** (SDI). This plan, nicknamed "Star Wars," called for the development of weapons that could intercept and destroy incoming missiles.

A New Soviet Leader In 1985 **Mikhail Gorbachev** became the leader of the Soviet Union and agreed to resume arms control talks. Gorbachev believed that the Soviet Union had to reform its economic system or it would soon collapse. It could not afford a new arms race with the United States.

Reagan and Gorbachev met in a series of summit meetings. The first of these were frustrating for both, as they disagreed on many issues. Gorbachev promised to cut back Soviet nuclear forces if Reagan would agree to give up SDI, but Reagan refused.

Reagan then challenged Gorbachev to make reforms. In West Berlin, Reagan stood at the Brandenburg Gate of the Berlin Wall, the symbol of divided Europe, and declared: "General Secretary Gorbachev, if you seek peace, if you seek prosperity for the Soviet Union and Eastern Europe . . . tear down this wall!"

Relations Improve By 1987 Reagan was convinced that Gorbachev did want to reform the Soviet Union and end the arms race. While some politicians distrusted the Soviets, most people welcomed the Cold War thaw and the reduction in the danger of nuclear war. In December 1987 the two leaders signed the Intermediate-Range Nuclear Forces (INF) Treaty. It was the first treaty to call for the destruction of nuclear weapons.

No one realized it at the time, but the treaty marked the beginning of the end of the Cold War. With an arms control deal in place, Gorbachev felt confident that Soviet military spending could be reduced. He pushed ahead with economic and political reforms that eventually led to the collapse of communism in Eastern Europe and in the Soviet Union.

With the economy booming, the American military strong, and relations with the Soviet Union rapidly improving, Ronald Reagan's second term came to an end. As he prepared to leave office,

Picturing **History**

Superpower Summits During the 1980s, President Reagan and Premier Gorbachev met several times to discuss nuclear arms reductions. *What Reagan defense proposal did Gorbachev want to eliminate before beginning arms reduction talks?*

Reagan assessed his presidency: "They called it the Reagan revolution. Well, I'll accept that, but for me it always seemed more like the great rediscovery, a rediscovery of our values and our common sense."

✓ **Reading Check** **Interpreting** What was the significance of the INF Treaty?

SECTION 2 ASSESSMENT

Checking for Understanding

1. **Define:** supply-side economics, budget deficit, contra.
2. **Identify:** Reaganomics, Sandra Day O'Connor, William Rehnquist, Geraldine Ferraro, Iran-Contra scandal, Oliver North, Mikhail Gorbachev.
3. **List** the groups that Ronald Reagan appealed to in the 1980 presidential election.

Reviewing Themes

4. **Global Connections** What was President Reagan's stance on foreign policy?

Critical Thinking

5. **Forming an Opinion** Do you think that SDI (Star Wars) is a good idea? Why or why not?
6. **Organizing** Use a graphic organizer similar to the one below to list the ways that the Reagan doctrine was implemented.

Analyzing Visuals

7. **Analyzing Graphs** Study the graph on page 990 detailing the amount of money spent by the federal government from 1980 to 1992. What relationship do you see between military spending and the national debt?

Writing About History

8. **Expository Writing** Take on the role of a newspaper editorial writer during the Reagan administration. Write an article in which you present your opinion of Reagan's plans for a military buildup.

Urban America on the Move

Since the end of World War II, millions of Americans have abandoned older cities to find better lives—safer neighborhoods, bigger homes, better schools, and better jobs. Many found what they were seeking in the suburbs. Cities have grown into metropolitan areas that have continued to expand farther and farther into formerly rural regions.

The map at right shows patterns of recent population growth in the United States. The yellow and red areas represent growth since 1993. Radiating out from the cities, suburban development has changed the face of the United States. A lot of growth has taken place in the Sunbelt states of the South. The Atlanta region, for example, has more than doubled its population to 3.3 million in the last 30 years. It is now so big—and congested—that residents drive an average of 34 miles (55 km) per day.

Such rapid urban growth, or "sprawl," has brought a variety of cultural, social, and economic problems. In central cities and older suburbs, it has resulted in deteriorating infrastructure and a shortage of affordable housing. In the newer suburbs, growth has increased traffic and taxes and has resulted in declining air quality and a loss of open space.

Many city planners have mixed emotions about continued growth, and some—like those of Austin, Texas—have tried to curb it. Such efforts have been dubbed "smart growth." Proponents of smart growth seek to improve conditions in existing communities and to limit the spread of urbanization in outlying and rural areas. Specifically, they encourage developers to build housing and businesses in city centers rather than in the suburbs. They promote the preservation of undeveloped areas and parks near metropolitan regions. Smart growth advocates endorse expanding public transportation, combining residential and commercial areas, and building pedestrian-friendly communities as ways to reduce reliance on the automobile.

With smarter growth, cities can channel development in ways that maintain quality of life and make existing communities more inviting. Faced with long commutes on congested highways, some suburban residents are now opting to return to the cities that were so readily abandoned after the Second World War.

Existing development as of 1993
- Intense
- Moderate

Development since 1993
- Intense
- Moderate

LEARNING FROM GEOGRAPHY

1. Why did many Americans move to the suburbs after World War II?

2. In what parts of the country are cities growing fastest?

Urban sprawl, traffic congestion, high ozone levels, and skyrocketing property taxes are part of the price Atlanta has paid for rapid growth.

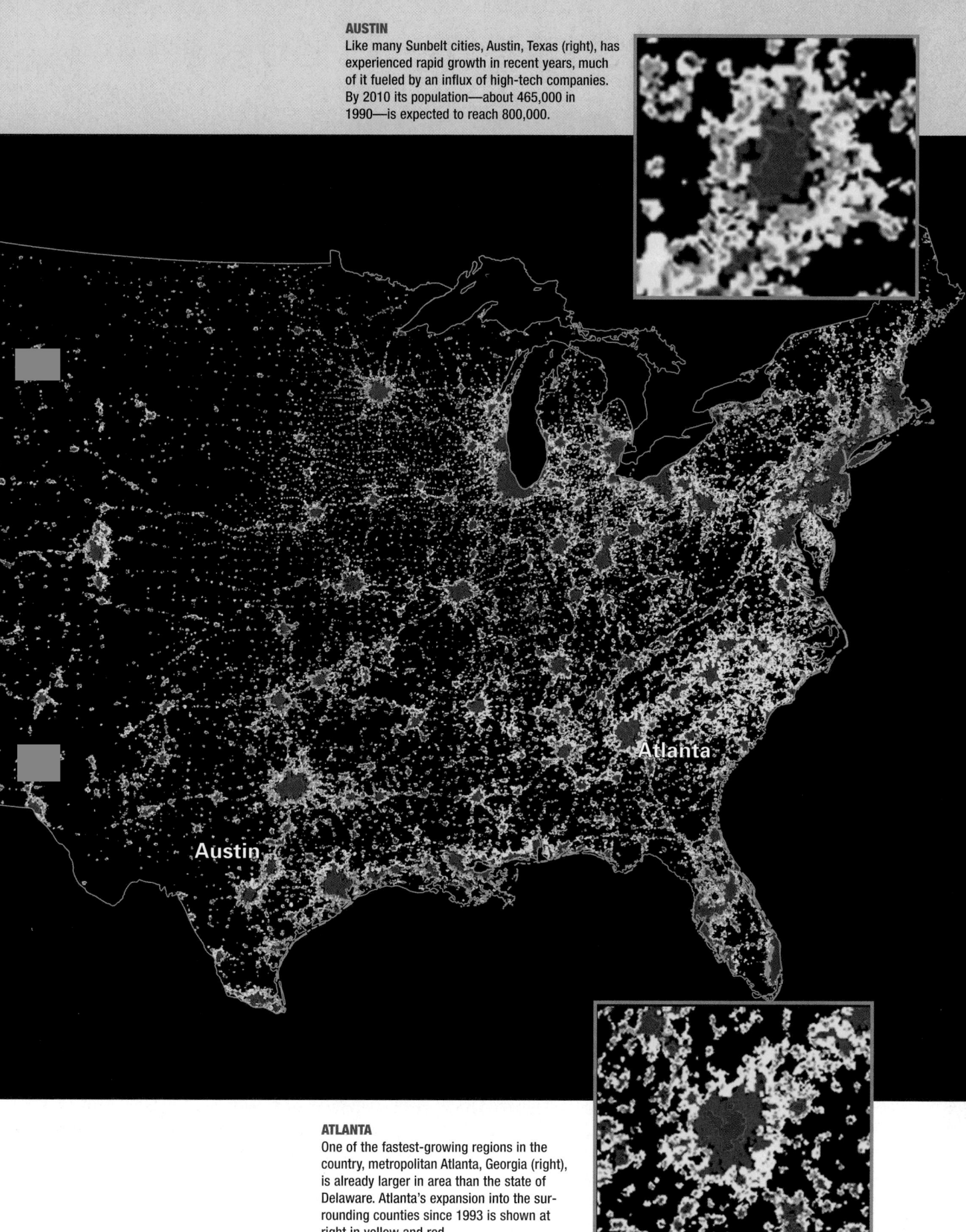

AUSTIN
Like many Sunbelt cities, Austin, Texas (right), has experienced rapid growth in recent years, much of it fueled by an influx of high-tech companies. By 2010 its population—about 465,000 in 1990—is expected to reach 800,000.

Atlanta

Austin

ATLANTA
One of the fastest-growing regions in the country, metropolitan Atlanta, Georgia (right), is already larger in area than the state of Delaware. Atlanta's expansion into the surrounding counties since 1993 is shown at right in yellow and red.

Main Idea
The 1980s was a decade characterized by wealth, but it was also a time of renewed activism.

Key Terms and Names
yuppie, AIDS, Sierra Club, American Association of Retired Persons, space shuttle, space station

Reading Strategy
Organizing As you read about life in the 1980s, complete a graphic organizer similar to the one below by listing the kinds of social issues that the United States faced in this decade.

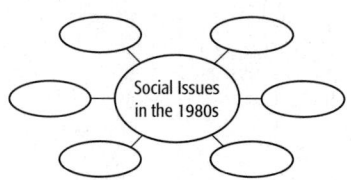

Social Issues in the 1980s

Reading Objectives
• **Discuss** the importance of money to the culture of the 1980s.
• **Explain** the growth in social activism during the decade.

Section Theme
Science and Technology Achievements in space and technology during the 1980s symbolized the optimism many associated with the Reagan era.

Preview of Events

◆1981	◆1984	◆1987	◆1990

1981
MTV goes on the air

1985
"Live Aid" rock concert benefit

1986
Space shuttle *Challenger* explodes

1988
More than 35,000 cases of AIDS diagnosed for the year

★ *An American Story* ★

In the 1980s many young, ambitious professionals entered the heady world of finance. Julie Katzman, in her twenties, was on the fast track:

❝I constantly spent my time at the firm. I mean, all the time. I worked probably eighty hours a week. At the end of the summer, that Labor Day weekend, I got involved in another huge acquisition. That weekend I worked two and a half days without sleeping, and from that point until early December I didn't work a single week less than a hundred hours. You spend all your time working. You're kind of wiped out, but there's a lot of fulfillment. There's an incredible adrenaline rush. This is what you live on. You live on the highs.❞

—from *Sleepwalking Through History*

A Decade of Indulgence

The inauguration of Ronald Reagan introduced a decade that celebrated wealth. Limousines and corporate jets brought guests wearing diamonds and designer gowns to the inaugural ball. Status symbols such as expensive watches and luxury cars became important. Popular television shows such as *Dallas* and *Dynasty* glamorized the lives of the very wealthy.

By late 1983, the economy had revived after the 1981 recession. Aggressive young stockbrokers, speculators, lawyers, and real estate developers made multimillion-dollar deals. They bought and sold hundreds of companies. Real estate and stock values soared. Developer Donald Trump said: "I don't do it for the money. I've got enough, much more than I'll ever need. I do it to do it. Deals are my art form. Other people paint beautifully on canvas or write wonderful poetry. I like making deals, preferably big deals."

The new moneymakers were young, ambitious, and hardworking. Journalists called them yuppies, from "young urban professionals." Many worked in law or finance. They rewarded themselves with expensive stereo systems and luxury cars. They bought designer clothes and ate in upscale restaurants.

The rapid economic growth and emphasis on accumulating wealth in the 1980s was partly caused by the baby boom. By the 1980s, many baby boomers had finished college, entered the job market, and begun building their careers. Young people entering the workforce often placed an emphasis on acquiring goods and getting ahead in their jobs. Because baby boomers were so numerous, their concerns tended to shape the culture.

The strong economic growth of the 1980s mostly benefited middle- and upper-class Americans. As a result, the emphasis on acquiring wealth had another effect on society. From 1967 to 1986, the amount of money earned by the top 5 percent of Americans fluctuated between 15.6 and 17.5 percent of the nation's total income. In the late 1980s, their share of the nation's income began to rise. By the mid-1990s, the top 5 percent of Americans earned well over 21 percent of the nation's income.

Reading Check **Identifying** Who were yuppies?

Technology and the Media

In the 1980s, technology began transforming broadcast news and entertainment. In the 1950s, '60s, and '70s, families had often listened to and watched

---

Fact | Fiction | Folklore

Food and Fashion A swing to the more conservative right in the 1980s, along with more high-powered jobs for women, marked an end to colorful hippie styles and casual, tie-dyed T-shirts. Instead, the 1980s introduced "power dressing" into offices and businesses. For women in business, design houses such as Chanel and Armani made well-cut "power suits" with tailored jackets and wide, padded shoulders.

Armani produced elegant business suits for men as well. Colorful vests were a popular male accessory. Designers also introduced expensive "power ties," often bright yellow or red.

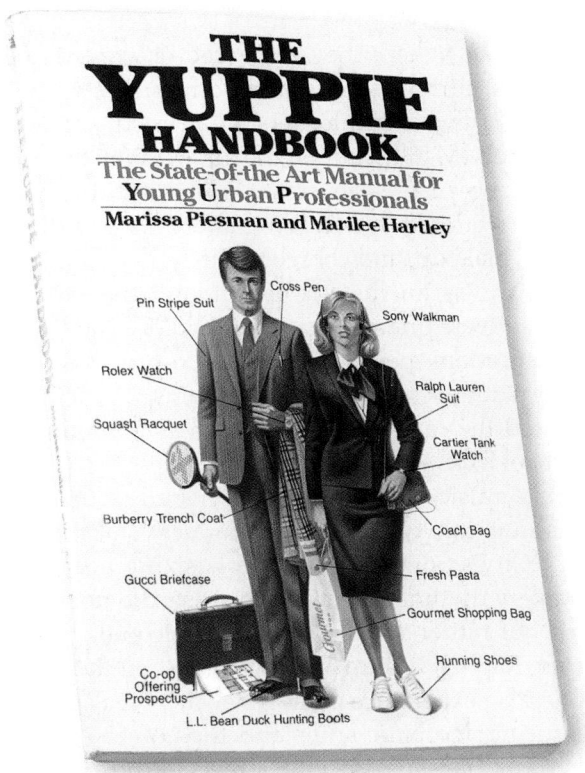

Picturing **History**

Yuppie Know-How This book poked fun at the new young urban professionals focused on wealth and personal gratification. What other attitudes do you think people may have had toward yuppies?

---

the same radio and television shows. Now new technology divided the broadcast media into smaller audience segments.

Cassette tapes and the Sony Walkman made music portable. By the end of the 1980s, many homes also had videocassette recorders (VCRs). People watched movies at home whenever they wanted.

Until the 1980s, television viewers had been limited to three commercial networks and public television. In the 1980s, cable and satellite television rapidly expanded. Dozens of channels offered programs for specialized audiences, including minorities, sports fans, shoppers, churchgoers, and others. The Cable News Network (CNN) became the first all-news television network. In 1987 the new Fox network challenged the older networks by scheduling programs aimed at a younger audience.

In 1985 CNN introduced the first phone-in television talk show, *Larry King Live*. Other talk shows employed different formats. Some hosts, like Phil Donahue, interacted with studio audiences and shared their feelings. Oprah Winfrey's highly successful show began in 1984 as a rival to Donahue.

The more traditional talk show format featured panels of journalists, politicians, and experts with different points of view. On shows like *Firing Line* or *Face the Nation,* they discussed or argued about business, current events, and politics.

In 1981 music and technology merged, and Music Television (MTV) went on the air. MTV mixed songs and video images to create music videos. Music videos were like fast-moving short films, with costumes, makeup, and choreography.

MTV was an instant hit, though the videos it showed were often criticized for violence and sexual content. Many performers began to produce videos along with each of their new albums. Music videos boosted the careers of artists such as Madonna and Michael Jackson.

Rap music was another new sound of the 1980s. This musical style originated in local clubs in New York City's South Bronx. Emphasizing heavy bass and very rhythmic sounds, rap artists did not usually sing but rather spoke over the music and rhythmic beats. Rap's lyrics frequently focused on the African American experience in the inner city. Break dancing, featuring acrobatic spins and flips on the ground, also got its start on city streets. While rap was initially popular among East Coast African Americans, it has grown in popularity, becoming a multimillion-dollar industry that appeals to music lovers across the country.

Picturing **History**

Homelessness During the 1980s, many people began living on the streets in makeshift shelters of boxes and rags. A lack of low-income housing and care for the mentally ill contributed to the problem. How do you think the country's general prosperity influenced people to think about this problem?

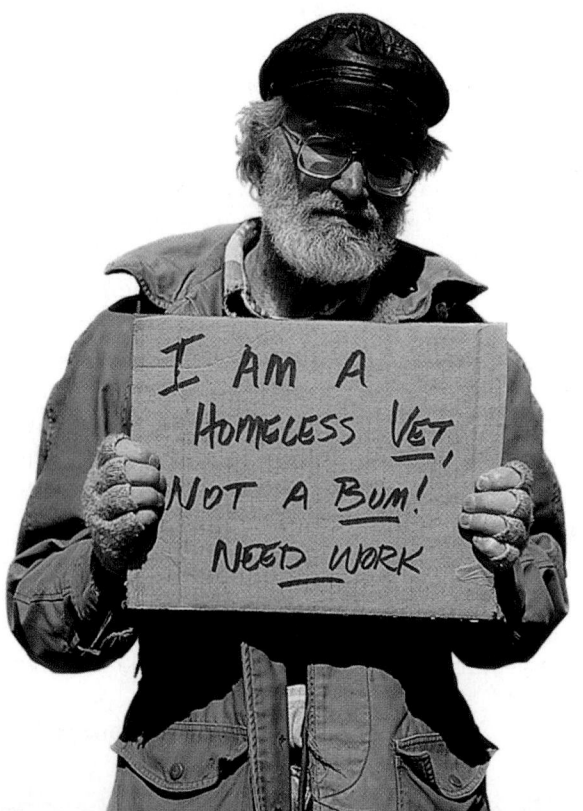

While the music industry was changing, new forms of entertainment also developed, including home video games. Early video games grew out of military computer technology. The first video arcade game was a game called *Pong,* released in 1972. Home video games developed quickly. In the early 1980s, sales reached about $3 billion with the sale of games such as *PacMan* and *Space Invaders.* Video arcades became the new spot for young people to meet.

By the mid-1980s, new technology allowed home video games to compete with arcade games in color and speed. The trend toward home video game sales continued through the 1990s.

✓ **Reading Check** **Describing** What forms of entertainment gained popularity in the 1980s?

A Society Under Stress

The 1980s was a decade of wealth and prosperity, but at the same time, many social problems continued to plague the nation.

Crime and Drugs Ongoing problems with drug abuse in the 1980s made many city neighborhoods dangerous. Drug users often committed crimes in order to get money for drugs, and dealers backed by street gangs fought to protect their territory. Cocaine use increased, especially a concentrated form, crack cocaine, which made users hostile and aggressive. First Lady Nancy Reagan tried to discourage teen drug use with her "Just Say No" campaign. Many young people, however, continued to use drugs, especially marijuana and amphetamines. Drug use spread from cities to small towns and rural areas.

Problems With Alcohol Abuse of alcohol was also a serious concern. Teenagers with fake identification cards could easily buy beer and other alcoholic beverages. Nonetheless, teen alcohol use actually declined during the 1980s, although thousands of alcohol-related auto accidents involved young people. In 1980 **Mothers Against Drunk Driving** (MADD), a grassroots organization, was founded to look for effective solutions to underage drinking problems and drunk driving. In 1984 Congress cut highway funds to any state that did not raise the legal drinking age to 21. All states quickly complied.

A Deadly Epidemic In 1981 researchers identified a disease which caused seemingly healthy young men to become sick and die. They named it "acquired immune deficiency syndrome," or **AIDS.** AIDS weakens the immune system, lowering resistance to illnesses such as pneumonia and several types of cancer. HIV, the virus that causes AIDS, is spread through bodily fluids.

In the United States, AIDS was first noticed among homosexual men. Soon AIDS began to spread among heterosexual men and women as well. A few people got the disease from blood transfusions. Other victims included drug users who shared needles and, through them, infected blood. Many people were infected by sexual partners. In 1987 alone, more than 28,000 cases of AIDS were diagnosed in the United States, and between 1981 and 1988, the **Centers for Disease Control** identified more than 100,000 cases.

✓ **Reading Check** **Evaluating** What social problems did Americans face in the 1980s?

Social Activism

AIDS increased the visibility of the country's gay and lesbian community, but some homosexuals had been engaged in efforts to defend their civil rights since the 1960s. On June 27, 1969, New York City police raided a Greenwich Village nightclub called the Stonewall Inn. The police had a history of raiding the nightclub and targeting its patrons because of their sexual orientation. Frustration among the gay and lesbian onlookers boiled over into a public disturbance. The **Stonewall riot** marked the beginning of a gay activist movement. Soon after, organizations such as the Gay Liberation Front tried to increase tolerance of homosexuality and media coverage of gays and lesbians.

Although the election of Ronald Reagan marked the rise of a powerful conservative movement in America, the social activism of the 1960s and 1970s did not end. Many Americans continued to organize and promote causes they believed were important, including the environment and world hunger.

Think Globally, Act Locally Trying to promote environmental protection during the Reagan years was frustrating for environmental activists. Secretary of the Interior James Watt encouraged development on public lands, saying, "We will mine more, drill more, cut more timber." Congress, under pressure from environmental groups, blocked many of Watt's plans. Worried about Watt's program, many new members joined groups such as the **Sierra Club.**

The environmental movement born in the 1970s continued to grow in the 1980s. Environmentalists were active in protesting nuclear power plants and protecting fragile wetlands. Communities started recycling programs. Activists became concerned about issues such as global warming and the destruction of the ozone layer and rain forests.

Rocking for Good Causes In the 1980s, ministers, politicians, and others targeted and criticized rock musicians as promoters of drug use and other negative behavior. Still, singers, actors, and other entertainers often helped those whom society ignored. In hits such as "Born in the USA," Bruce Springsteen sang about working-class Americans. A social activist, he gave concerts to benefit food banks and the homeless.

To help starving people in Ethiopia, Irish rocker Bob Geldof organized musicians in England to present "Band Aid" concerts in 1984. The next year, the event grew into "Live Aid." People in some 100 countries watched benefit concerts televised from London, Philadelphia, and Sydney, Australia. Musicians including Paul McCartney, Madonna, The Who, and Tina Turner participated in the musical benefits. Its theme song, "We Are the World," was a best-seller. The same year, country singer Willie Nelson organized "Farm Aid" to help American farmers going through hard times.

Other Groups Become Activists One noticeable political change in the 1980s was the stronger presence of senior citizens. Decades of improvements in medicine had resulted in more Americans surviving to an older age. In addition, the birthrate had declined, so younger people represented a comparatively smaller proportion of the population. The fact that more Americans were receiving Social Security payments created budget pressures for the government.

Older Americans became very vocal in the political arena, opposing cuts in Social Security or Medicare. Because they tended to vote in large numbers, senior citizens became an influential interest group. Their major lobbying organization was the **American Association of Retired Persons** (AARP), founded in 1958.

Reading Check **Summarizing** What issues did environmental activists focus on in the 1980s?

A New Era in Space

President Reagan, like many Americans, saw space as an exciting frontier. Improved technology and new exploration programs rekindled the nation's excitement for space exploration.

The Space Shuttle After the series of moon landings of the 1970s, the National Aeronautics and Space Administration (NASA) concentrated on the space shuttle. Though it looked like a huge airplane, the shuttle was rocketed into space, then glided back to Earth for another flight. Unlike earlier spacecraft, the shuttle was reusable. The shuttle *Columbia* made the first space shuttle flight in April 1981.

Earlier astronauts had been military pilots, but shuttle crews now included civilians. In 1983 **Sally Ride** became the first American woman in space. Female astronauts quickly grew more common. To involve the public, NASA recruited a teacher to travel into space. In January 1986, Christa McAuliffe, a teacher from New Hampshire, joined six others on the *Challenger*. As millions of Americans watched in anticipation, the shuttle lifted off the launchpad— and then suddenly exploded. All on board were killed.

Shocked Americans mourned the worst disaster in the country's history of space exploration. President Reagan made a speech praising the crew:

66 The crew of the space shuttle *Challenger* honored us by the manner in which they lived their lives. We will never forget them, nor the last time we saw them, this morning as they prepared for their journey and waved goodbye and 'slipped the surly bonds of earth to touch the face of God.' 99

—from *Speaking My Mind*

In June 1986, a presidential commission reported that defective seals in the solid rocket boosters allowed combustible gas to ignite.

Profiles IN HISTORY

Franklin R. Chang-Diaz
1950–

Born in Costa Rica, Franklin R. Chang-Diaz dates his fascination with space to hearing about the *Sputnik* launching in 1957. His mother told him that a new star, made by humans, had been placed in the heavens. This convinced him, he said later, to become "a space explorer."

Chang-Diaz managed to save enough money—$50—to immigrate to the United States at the age of 18. He went to Hartford, Connecticut, where he had relatives. After completing high school and college, he went on to earn a doctorate in applied plasma physics and fusion technology at MIT in 1977.

His goal of becoming an astronaut came true in 1980 when NASA selected him for the space shuttle program. In the following years, Chang-Diaz worked as part of the astronaut support crew and in early space station design studies.

His first spaceflight came in January 1986 on the space shuttle *Columbia*. In the late 1980s and 1990s, Chang-Diaz flew a number of shuttle missions.

First Female Astronaut Dr. Sally Ride (below) was accepted into the astronaut program in 1978. She became the first American woman to orbit the earth when she flew aboard the space shuttle *Challenger* in June 1983. The space shuttle *Discovery* is shown on the right.

A Home in Space By September 1988 engineers had fixed the problem with the booster seals, and new space shuttle missions began. Between September 1988 and December 2002, the shuttle completed 87 missions. It placed many satellites in orbit, including the Hubble Space Telescope.

One reason NASA built the shuttle was to provide transportation to space stations—manned orbiting platforms that served as a base of operations for space research. The United States had launched the space station *Skylab* in 1973, but it stayed in orbit only until 1979. In 1986 President Reagan announced that the United States would build a new space station.

In the years following Reagan's announcement, the space station became an international project, and 16 nations helped create the International Space Station. Shuttle astronauts began assembling the station in December 1998, and the station's first crew arrived in October 2000. By December 2002 the shuttle had completed 16 missions to the space station.

Seventeen years after the *Challenger* disaster, tragedy struck again. On Febuary 1, 2003, the shuttle *Columbia* came apart while reentering the earth's atmosphere. All seven crew members were killed. As people around the world mourned, NASA began investigating the accident. Speaking to the nation, President George W. Bush proclaimed, "Mankind is led into the darkness beyond our world by the inspiration of discovery and the longing to understand." The president then promised that American space exploration would continue.

✓ **Reading Check** **Describing** How was the space shuttle different from previous spacecraft?

SECTION 3 ASSESSMENT

Checking for Understanding

1. **Define:** yuppie, space shuttle, space station.
2. **Identify:** AIDS, Sierra Club, American Association of Retired Persons.
3. **Summarize** the causes for which several musicians held concert benefits in the 1980s.

Reviewing Themes

4. **Science and Technology** What new innovations occurred in the nation's space program in the 1980s?

Critical Thinking

5. **Comparing** How do the social problems the United States faces today compare with those the nation faced in the 1980s?
6. **Organizing** Use a graphic organizer similar to the one below to list the changes in entertainment in the 1980s.

Analyzing Visuals

7. **Examining Diagrams** Study the illustration on page 995. What elements of the diagram depict the concept of materialism?

Writing About History

8. **Persuasive Writing** Choose one of the social problems of the 1980s. Write a letter to members of your favorite band asking them to perform a concert to benefit your cause. Your letter should include reasons the cause is important.

SKILLBUILDER

Analyzing News Media

Why Learn This Skill?

Every citizen needs to be aware of current issues and events in order to make good decisions when exercising citizenship rights. To stay informed, people use a variety of news sources, including print media, broadcast media, and electronic media.

Learning the Skill

To get an accurate profile of current events, you must learn to think critically about the news. The steps below will help you think critically.

- First, think about the source of the news story. Reports that reveal sources are more reliable than those that do not. If you know the sources, you can evaluate them.

- Many news stories analyze and interpret events. Such analyses may be more detailed than other reports, but they also reflect a reporter's biases. Look for biases as you read or listen to news stories.

- Ask yourself whether the news is even-handed and thorough. Is it reported on the scene or secondhand? Does it represent both sides of the issue? How many sources are used? The more sources cited for a fact, the more reliable it usually is.

Practicing the Skill

Follow the steps below to analyze two types of print media.

❶ Find two articles, one in a current newspaper and the other in a newsmagazine, on a decision made by the president or Congress on a topic such as Social Security, education, or taxes.

❷ What points were the articles trying to make? Were the articles successful? Can the facts be verified?

❸ Did either of the articles reflect a bias toward one viewpoint or the other? List any unsupported statements.

❹ Was the news reported on the scene or secondhand? Do the articles seem to represent both sides fairly?

❺ How many sources can you identify in the articles? List them.

Skills Assessment

Complete the Practicing Skills questions on page 1009 and the Chapter 33 Skill Reinforcement Activity to assess your mastery of this skill.

Applying the Skill

Analyzing News Media Think of an issue in your community or in the nation on which public opinion is divided. Read newspaper features and editorials and monitor television reports about the issue. Can you identify any biases? Which reports more fairly represent the issue? Which reports are the most reliable?

Glencoe's **Skillbuilder Interactive Workbook CD-ROM, Level 2,** provides instruction and practice in key social studies skills.

The End of the Cold War

Guide to Reading

Main Idea
President George Bush's foreign policy commanded broad support, but his domestic agenda did not.

Key Terms and Names
perestroika, glasnost, Boris Yeltsin, Tiananmen Square, Saddam Hussein, downsizing, capital gains tax, H. Ross Perot, grassroots movement

Reading Strategy
Categorizing As you read about the administration of President Bush, complete a chart similar to the one below by describing U.S. foreign policy in each of the places listed on the chart.

Place	Foreign Policy
Soviet Union	
China	
Panama	
Middle East	

Reading Objectives
- **Identify** the events that brought an end to the Cold War.
- **Explain** the domestic challenges facing the Bush administration.

Section Theme
Economic Factors The deficit and an economic slowdown hurt George Bush's attempt to win re-election in 1992.

Preview of Events

| ♦1989 | ♦1990 | ♦1991 | ♦1992 |

May, 1989
Tiananmen Square protests begin

November, 1989
Berlin Wall falls

August, 1990
Iraq invades Kuwait

January, 1991
Persian Gulf War begins

December, 1991
Soviet Union collapses

★ *An American Story* ★

On October 31, 1990, General Colin Powell, who was the chairman of the Joint Chiefs of Staff, Secretary of Defense Dick Cheney, and other high-ranking officials met with President George Bush. In August the country of Iraq had invaded neighboring Kuwait. American troops had been rushed to the Middle East in response. Now the president had to decide whether to go to war.

General Brent Scrowcroft, a close adviser to Bush, began the meeting: "Mr. President, we are at a Y in the road. Down one branch we can continue sanctions. . . . Down the other branch we . . . go on the attack." Powell then presented the plan for attacking Iraq. Several advisers gasped at the numbers, which called for over 500,000 American troops. "Mr. President," Powell began, "I wish . . . that I could assure you that air power alone could do it but you can't take that chance. We've gotta take the initiative out of the enemy's hands if we're going to go to war." Cheney later recalled that Bush "never hesitated." He looked up from the plans and said simply, "Do it."

—adapted from *Triumph Without Victory* and *PBS Frontline Gulf War Interviews*

George Bush Takes Office

The war in the Persian Gulf was only one of many international crises that confronted President George Bush after his election in 1988. Fortunately, Bush's strength was in foreign policy. In the 1970s, he had served as ambassador to the UN and as the nation's first

Revolution in Eastern Europe, 1989–1993

NORWAY

SWEDEN

DENMARK

Reval ⊛

ESTONIA

❺ Baltic States became independent, 1991

LATVIA

Riga ⊛

LITHUANIA

Vilnius ⊛

RUSSIA

❹ Germany reunited, 1990

RUSSIA

⊛ Minsk

BELARUS

UNITED KINGDOM

NETH.

GERMANY ⊛ Berlin

POLAND

Warsaw ⊛

❶ Democratic elections, 1989

BELG.

❸ Berlin Wall torn down, Nov. 1989

⊛ Kiev

LUX.

Prague ⊛
CZECH REPUBLIC

❻ Czechoslovakia separated, 1993

UKRAINE

LIECH.

SLOVAKIA

Bratislava ⊛

FRANCE

SWITZ.

AUSTRIA

⊛ Budapest

HUNGARY

MOLDOVA

⊛ Chisinau

ROMANIA

❷ Non-Communist governments created, 1989

Ljubljana ⊛

SLOVENIA ⊛ Zagreb

CROATIA

SAN MARINO

BOSNIA & ⊛ Belgrade
HERZEGOVINA
⊛ Sarajevo

⊛ Bucharest

Danube R.

Black Sea

MONACO

Corsica
Fr.

ITALY

YUGOSLAVIA   BULGARIA
⊛ Sofia

Mediterranean Sea

Sardinia
It.

ALBANIA ⊛ Skopje
Tirana ⊛ MACEDONIA

30°E TURKEY

300 miles

GREECE

0   300 kilometers
Lambert Azimuthal Equal-Area projection

Geography Skills

1. **Interpreting Maps** Which Eastern European countries abandoned communism first?
2. **Applying Geography Skills** Why was the fall of communism in East Germany significant?

diplomatic envoy to the People's Republic of China. He then headed the CIA from 1976 to 1977 before becoming vice president in 1981.

When Ronald Reagan left office, few Americans were thinking about foreign policy. They generally wanted a continuation of Reagan's domestic policies—low taxes and less government action. When Bush accepted the Republican nomination in 1988, he tried to reassure Americans by making a promise: "Read my lips: No new taxes."

The Democrats hoped to regain the White House in 1988 by promising to help working-class Americans, minorities, and the poor. One candidate for the nomination, civil rights leader Jesse Jackson, tried to create a "rainbow coalition"—a broad group of minorities and the poor—by speaking about homelessness and unemployment. Jackson finished second in the primaries, the first African American to make a serious run for the nomination.

The Democrats' final choice was Massachusetts governor Michael Dukakis. The Bush campaign

portrayed him as too liberal, unpatriotic, and "soft on crime." The Democrats questioned Bush's leadership abilities, but Bush had Reagan's endorsement, and with the economy still doing well, few Americans wanted to switch parties. Bush won 54 percent of the popular vote and defeated Dukakis 426 to 111 in the Electoral College. Democrats, however, kept control of Congress.

✓ **Reading Check**

Describing What kind of strategy did the Bush campaign use in the 1988 election?

The Cold War Ends

Almost immediately after taking office, President Bush had to draw on his foreign policy experience. With the help of Secretary of State James Baker, the president steered the United States through an era of sweeping change that resulted from the sudden end of the Cold War.

Gorbachev's Reforms As president, Bush continued Reagan's policy of cooperation with Soviet leader Mikhail Gorbachev. By the late 1980s, the Soviet economy was suffering from years of inefficient central planning and huge expenditures on the arms race. To save the economy, Gorbachev instituted *perestroika,* or "restructuring," and allowed some private enterprise and profit-making.

The other principle of Gorbachev's plan was *glasnost,* or "openness." It allowed more freedom of religion and speech, allowing people to discuss politics openly.

Revolution in Eastern Europe With Gorbachev's support, *glasnost* spread to Eastern Europe. In 1989 peaceful revolutions replaced Communist rulers with democratic governments in Poland, Hungary, Czechoslovakia, Romania, and Bulgaria. The spreading revolution soon reached East Germany, and at midnight on November 9, 1989, guards at the Berlin Wall opened the gates. Within days, bulldozers leveled the hated symbol of Communist repression. Within a year, East and West Germany had reunited.

The Soviet Union Collapses As Eastern Europe abandoned communism, Gorbachev faced mounting criticism from opponents at home. In August 1991, a group of Communist officials and army officers staged a coup—an overthrow of the government. They arrested Gorbachev and sent troops into Moscow.

In Moscow, Russian president **Boris Yeltsin** defied the coup leaders from his offices in the Russian Parliament. About 50,000 people surrounded the Russian Parliament to protect it from troops. President Bush telephoned Yeltsin to express the support of the United States. Soon afterward, the coup collapsed, and Gorbachev returned to Moscow.

The defeat of the coup brought change swiftly. All 15 Soviet republics declared their independence from the Soviet Union. Yeltsin outlawed the Communist Party in Russia. In late December 1991, Gorbachev announced the end of the Soviet Union. Most of the former Soviet republics then joined in a federation called the Commonwealth of Independent States.

☑ **Reading Check** **Explaining** Why did Mikhail Gorbachev institute the policy of *perestroika?*

The "New World Order"

After the Cold War, the world became increasingly unpredictable. In a phrase made popular by President Bush, a "new world order" was developing. While trying to redefine American foreign policy, Bush faced crises in China, Panama, and the Middle East.

Tragedy in Tiananmen Square Despite the collapse of communism in Eastern Europe and the Soviet Union, China's Communist leaders were determined to stay in power. China's government had relaxed controls on the economy, but it continued to repress political speech and dissent. In May 1989, Chinese students and workers held demonstrations for democracy. In early June, government tanks and soldiers crushed their protests in **Tiananmen Square** in Beijing—China's capital. Many people were killed and hundreds of pro-democracy activists were arrested. Many were later sentenced to death.

These events shocked the world. The United States and several European countries halted arms sales and reduced their diplomatic contacts with China. The World Bank suspended loans. Some congressional

NATIONAL GEOGRAPHIC

MOMENT in HISTORY

A CITY REUNITED

Built in 1961, the Berlin Wall served to stem the mounting tide of immigration from Communist East Germany into the democratic western sector of the city. The wall also stood as a symbol of Cold War tensions between the world's superpowers. As reforms sparked by Mikhail Gorbachev swept through Eastern Europe, however, East German citizens began pressuring their government to open its borders. On November 9, 1989, the gates were thrown open, and East and West Berliners finally mingled freely. With great enthusiasm, they took hammers and chisels to the wall and tore down the hated symbol of division.

Why It Matters

Strait of Hormuz

The Strait of Hormuz is a narrow shipping lane between the Persian Gulf, the Gulf of Oman, and the Arabian Sea. Most of the crude oil produced in the Middle East passes through the Strait of Hormuz. In 1997 about 14 million barrels of crude oil passed through the Strait every day. Since the waterway is only about 40 miles (64 km) across at its widest point, it is possible that a country might block or hamper passage of ships. During the 1980s, the United States began escorting oil tankers through the Strait to protect them from Iranian attacks. If the passage were ever closed, oil would have to be shipped overland by pipeline—a much more expensive option.

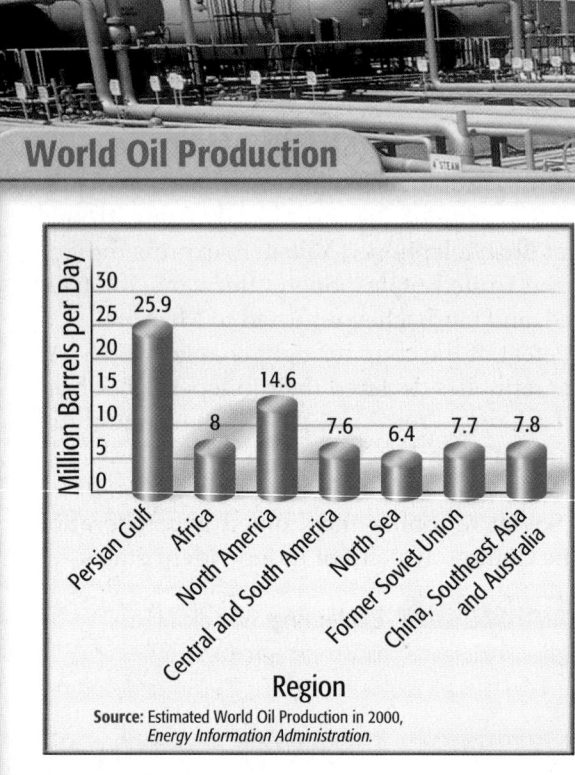

World Oil Production

Million Barrels per Day

- Persian Gulf: 25.9
- Africa: 8
- North America: 14.6
- Central and South America: 7.6
- North Sea: 6.4
- Former Soviet Union: 7.7
- China, Southeast Asia and Australia: 7.8

Region

Source: Estimated World Oil Production in 2000, Energy Information Administration.

The Persian Gulf countries consist of Saudi Arabia, Iran, Iraq, Kuwait, Qatar, and the United Arab Emirates. They may hold as much as 70 percent of the world's proven oil reserves.

leaders urged even stronger sanctions, but President Bush resisted these harsher measures, believing that trade and diplomacy would eventually moderate China's behavior.

Panama While President Bush struggled to deal with global events elsewhere, a crisis developed in Panama. In 1978 the United States had agreed to give Panama control over the Panama Canal by the year 2000. Because of the canal's importance, American officials wanted to make sure Panama's government was both stable and pro-American.

By 1989 Panama's dictator, General Manuel Noriega, had stopped cooperating with the United States. He also aided drug traffickers, cracked down on opponents, and harassed American military personnel defending the canal. In December 1989, Bush ordered American troops to invade Panama. The troops seized Noriega, who was sent to the United States to stand trial on drug charges. The troops then helped the Panamanians hold elections and organize a new government.

The Persian Gulf War President Bush faced perhaps his most serious crisis in the Middle East. In August 1990, Iraq's dictator, **Saddam Hussein,** sent his army to invade oil-rich Kuwait. American officials feared the invasion was only the first step and that Iraq's ultimate goal was to capture Saudi Arabia and its vast oil reserves.

President Bush persuaded other UN member countries to join a coalition to stop Iraq. Led by the United States, the United Nations first imposed economic sanctions on Iraq and demanded the Iraqis withdraw. The coalition forces included troops from the United States, Canada, Europe, and Arab nations. The UN set a deadline for the Iraqi withdrawal, or the coalition would use force to remove them. Congress also voted to authorize the use of force if Iraq did not withdraw.

Iraq refused to comply with the UN deadline, and on January 16, 1991, the coalition forces launched **Operation Desert Storm.** Dozens of cruise

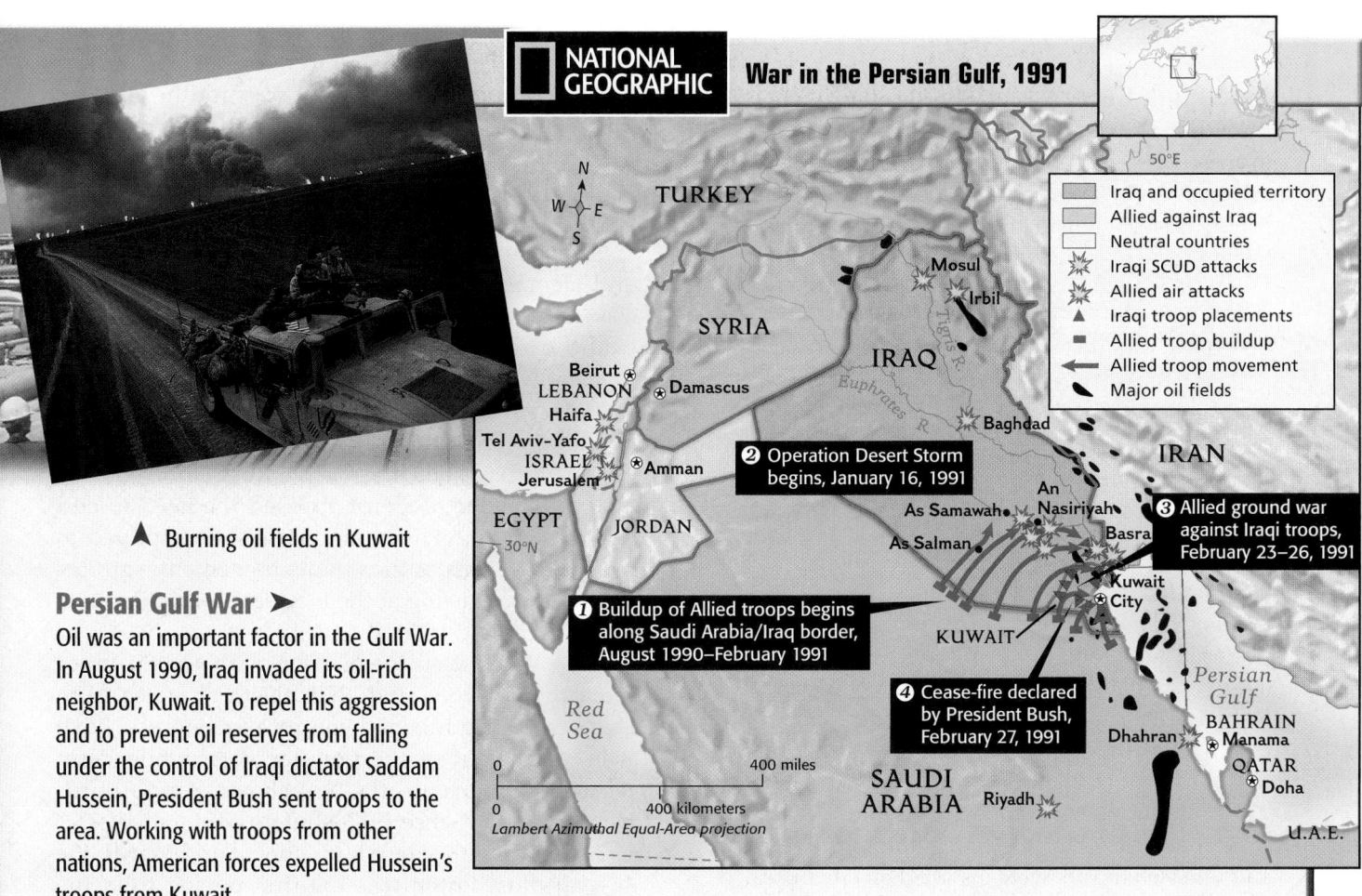

NATIONAL GEOGRAPHIC   **War in the Persian Gulf, 1991**

▲ Burning oil fields in Kuwait

Persian Gulf War ➤
Oil was an important factor in the Gulf War. In August 1990, Iraq invaded its oil-rich neighbor, Kuwait. To repel this aggression and to prevent oil reserves from falling under the control of Iraqi dictator Saddam Hussein, President Bush sent troops to the area. Working with troops from other nations, American forces expelled Hussein's troops from Kuwait.

Map legend:
- Iraq and occupied territory
- Allied against Iraq
- Neutral countries
- Iraqi SCUD attacks
- Allied air attacks
- ▲ Iraqi troop placements
- ■ Allied troop buildup
- ← Allied troop movement
- Major oil fields

❶ Buildup of Allied troops begins along Saudi Arabia/Iraq border, August 1990–February 1991

❷ Operation Desert Storm begins, January 16, 1991

❸ Allied ground war against Iraqi troops, February 23–26, 1991

❹ Cease-fire declared by President Bush, February 27, 1991

---

missiles and thousands of laser-guided bombs fell on Iraq, destroying its air defenses, bridges, artillery, and other military targets. After about six weeks of bombardment, the coalition launched a massive ground attack. Waves of tanks and troop carriers smashed through Iraqi lines and encircled the Iraqi forces defending Kuwait.

The attack killed thousands of Iraqi soldiers, and hundreds of thousands more surrendered. Fewer than 300 coalition troops were killed. Just 100 hours after the ground war began, President Bush declared Kuwait to be liberated. Iraq accepted the coalition's cease-fire terms, and American troops returned home to cheering crowds.

✓ **Reading Check** **Examining** Why did President Bush take action when Iraqi troops invaded Kuwait?

Domestic Challenges

President Bush spent much of his time dealing with foreign policy, but he could not ignore domestic issues. He inherited a growing deficit and a slowing economy. With the Persian Gulf crisis, the economy plunged into a recession and unemployment rose.

ECONOMICS

The Economy Slows The recession that began in 1990 was partly caused by the end of the Cold War. As the Soviet threat faded, the United States began reducing its armed forces and canceling orders for military equipment. Thousands of soldiers and defense industry workers were laid off.

Other companies also began downsizing—laying off workers and managers to become more efficient. The nation's high level of debt made the recession worse. Americans had borrowed heavily during the 1980s and now faced paying off large debts.

In addition, the huge deficit forced the government to borrow money to pay for its programs. This borrowing kept money from being available to businesses. The government also had to pay interest on its debt, money that might otherwise have been used to fund programs or boost the economy.

As the economy slowed, hundreds of savings and loans institutions collapsed. After they had been deregulated under President Reagan, many had made risky or even dishonest investments. When these investments failed, depositors collected on federal programs to insure deposits. The cost to the public may have reached $500 billion.

Gridlock in Government Shortly after taking office, Bush tried to improve the economy. He called for a cut in the capital gains tax—the tax paid by businesses and investors when they sell stocks or real estate for a profit. Bush believed the tax cut would encourage businesses to expand. Calling the idea a tax break for the rich, Democrats in Congress defeated it.

Aware that the growing federal deficit was hurting the economy, Bush broke his "no new taxes" campaign pledge. After meeting with congressional leaders, he agreed to a tax increase in exchange for cuts in spending. This decision turned many voters against Bush. They blamed him both for the tax increase and for trying to cut social programs.

Extending Rights Although President Bush and Democrats in Congress disagreed on economic issues, they cooperated on other legislation. One example was the Americans with Disabilities Act (ADA), signed by Bush in 1990. The legislation forbade discrimination in workplaces and public places against people who were physically or mentally challenged. The law had widespread effect. Access ramps were added to buildings, closed-captioned television became more commonplace, and wheelchair lifts were installed on city buses.

✔ **Reading Check** **Summarizing** Why did President Bush lose popularity as the 1992 election approached?

The 1992 Election

Although the recession had weakened his popularity, Bush won the Republican nomination. Bush promised to address voters' economic concerns, and he blamed congressional Democrats for the gridlock that seemingly paralyzed the nation's government.

The Democrats nominated Arkansas governor Bill Clinton, despite stories that questioned his character and his failure to serve in Vietnam. Calling himself a "New Democrat" to separate himself from more liberal Democrats, Clinton promised to cut middle-class taxes and spending and to reform the nation's health care and welfare programs. His campaign repeatedly blamed Bush for the recession.

Many Americans were not happy with either Bush or Clinton. This enabled an independent candidate, billionaire Texas businessman **H. Ross Perot,** to make a strong challenge. Perot stressed the need to end deficit spending. His no-nonsense style appealed to many Americans. A grassroots movement—groups of people organizing at the local level—put Perot on the ballot in all 50 states.

Bill Clinton won the election with 43 percent of the popular vote and 370 electoral votes. The Democrats also retained control of Congress. Bush won 37 percent of the popular vote, while Perot received 19 percent—the best showing for a third-party candidate since 1912—but no electoral votes.

As the first president born after World War II, the 46-year-old Clinton was the first person from the "baby boom" generation to enter the White House. It was his task to revive the economy and guide the United States in a rapidly changing and increasingly technological world.

✔ **Reading Check** **Evaluating** Why did some people vote for H. Ross Perot in 1992? How successful was his election campaign as a third-party candidate?

SECTION 4 ASSESSMENT

Checking for Understanding

1. **Define:** *perestroika, glasnost, downsizing, capital gains tax, grassroots movement.*

2. **Identify:** Boris Yeltsin, Tiananmen Square, Saddam Hussein, H. Ross Perot.

3. **Describe** how Mikhail Gorbachev tried to reform the Soviet government.

Reviewing Themes

4. **Economic Factors** How did the economy affect the 1992 election?

Critical Thinking

5. **Analyzing** How did the United States and its Western allies finally achieve victory in the Cold War?

6. **Organizing** Use a graphic organizer similar to the one below to list the causes of the recession of the early 1990s.

Budget Problems	Economic Problems	Foreign Developments

Analyzing Visuals

7. **Studying Maps** Examine the map on page 1005. Which nations have significant oil resources?

Writing About History

8. **Descriptive Writing** Imagine that you are traveling in West Germany in 1989 when the Berlin Wall is being torn down. Write a letter back home to describe the event and the feelings of the German people. Also include your reaction to the situation and how you think it will affect the United States.

American LITERATURE

Richard Rodriguez

Hispanic Americans are the fastest-growing minority in the United States. Hispanics cherish their heritage, and many speak only Spanish among their friends and family. Most of their children's teachers, however, speak only English. As a result, Hispanic students often find school confusing and humiliating. Hispanic American Richard Rodriguez describes his struggle to become educated in his autobiography, *Hunger of Memory*.

In this excerpt, Rodriguez describes the difficulties he encountered at home after he became comfortable speaking English at school.

Read to Discover

What is the reaction of Richard's relatives to his reluctance to speak Spanish to them?

Reader's Dictionary

reticent: reluctant

anglicized: made to sound English

diminutive: shorter or more affectionate version

from Hunger of Memory

by Richard Rodriguez

I grew up victim to a disabling confusion. As I grew fluent in English, I no longer could speak Spanish with confidence. I continued to understand spoken Spanish. And in high school, I learned how to read and write Spanish. But for many years I could not pronounce it. A powerful guilt blocked my spoken words; an essential glue was missing whenever I'd try to connect words to form sentences. . . .

When relatives and Spanish-speaking friends of my parents came to the house, my brother and sisters seemed reticent to use Spanish, but at least they managed to say a few necessary words before being excused. . . . I was cursed with guilt. Each time I'd hear myself addressed in Spanish, I would be unable to respond with any success. I'd know the words I wanted to say, but I couldn't manage to say them. I would try to speak, but everything I said seemed to me horribly anglicized. My mouth would not form the words right. . . .

It surprised my listeners to hear me. They'd lower their heads, better to grasp what I was trying to say. They would repeat their questions in gentle, affectionate voices. But by then I would answer in English. No, no, they would say, we want you to speak to us in Spanish. . . . But I couldn't do it. *Pocho* then they called me. Sometimes playfully, teasingly, using the tender diminutive—*mi pochito.* Sometimes not so playfully, mockingly, *Pocho.* (A Spanish dictionary defines that word as an adjective meaning "colorless" or "bland." But I heard it as a noun, naming the Mexican-American who, in becoming an American, forgets his native society. . . .)

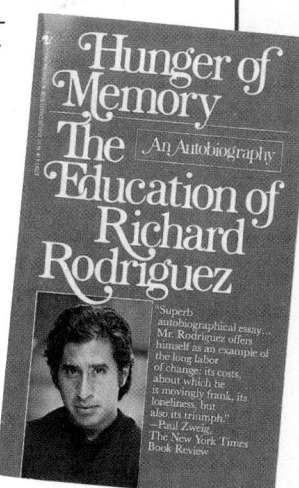

Analyzing Literature

1. **Recall and Interpret** What do you think Richard meant when he said that "an essential glue was missing" whenever he tried to speak Spanish?

2. **Evaluate and Connect** Why did Richard's relatives nickname him *Pocho?*

Interdisciplinary Activity

Journalism Interview a bilingual friend, relative, or classmate about when and where they use each of the languages they speak. Write a transcript of the interview.

Reviewing Key Terms

On a sheet of paper, use each of these terms in a sentence.

1. liberal
2. conservative
3. televangelist
4. supply-side economics
5. budget deficit
6. contra
7. yuppie
8. space shuttle
9. space station
10. *perestroika*
11. *glasnost*
12. downsizing
13. capital gains tax
14. grassroots movement

Reviewing Key Facts

15. **Identify:** William F. Buckley, William Rehnquist, Mikhail Gorbachev, AIDS, Boris Yeltsin, Saddam Hussein, H. Ross Perot.
16. Why did people in the Sunbelt tend to be conservative?
17. What three steps did President Reagan take to improve the economy?
18. What social issues did the United States face in the 1980s?
19. What event triggered the Persian Gulf War?
20. What economic problems did President George Bush face during his administration?

Critical Thinking

21. **Analyzing Themes: Global Connections** What event brought an end to the Cold War in the 1980s? What effect did that have on U.S. policies and on the U.S. economy?

22. **Synthesizing** How did conservatives gain political power in the 1980s?
23. **Forming an Opinion** On what part of the liberal-conservative spectrum would you place yourself? Why?
24. **Interpreting Primary Sources** President Ronald Reagan addressed the American people for the last time at the end of his presidency in 1988. The following is an excerpt from that address:

❝It's been quite a journey this decade, and we held together through some stormy seas. And at the end, together, we are reaching our destination. . . . The way I see it, there were two great triumphs, two things that I'm proudest of. One is the economic recovery, in which the people of America created—and filled—19 million new jobs. The other is the recovery of our morale. America is respected again in the world and looked to for leadership. . . .

Common sense told us that when you put a big tax on something, the people will produce less of it. So, we cut the people's tax rates, and the people produced more than ever before. The economy bloomed. . . . Common sense told us that to preserve the peace, we'd have to become strong again after years of weakness and confusion. So, we rebuilt our defenses, and this New Year we toasted the new peacefulness around the globe. . . .

Countries across the globe are turning to free markets and free speech and turning away from the ideologies of the past. . . .

Chapter Summary

Resurgence of Conservative Politics

- The Cold War promotes a strong foreign policy and an emphasis on minimal government intervention in economics.
- Cold War fears of communism encourage religious Americans to turn to conservative ideas.
- Barry Goldwater wins the 1964 Republican presidential nomination.
- The growth of the Sunbelt increases conservative support.

Reagan's Agenda

- Supply-side economics emphasizes large tax cuts.
- Reagan's administration takes a strong anti-Communist stance in Latin America, the Caribbean, and the Middle East.
- Reagan and Gorbachev begin new nuclear arms reductions.
- Military spending drives the growing budget deficit to record levels.

The Bush Years

- Communism collapses in Eastern Europe and the Soviet Union.
- The uncertainty of a "New World Order" replaces the dualism of the Cold War.
- The Persian Gulf War drives Bush's popularity to its highest level.
- A domestic economic recession weakens Bush's re-election campaign.

Self-Check Quiz

Visit the *American Vision* Web site at tav.glencoe.com and click on *Self-Check Quizzes—Chapter 33* to assess your knowledge of chapter content.

[O]ne of the things I'm proudest of in the past eight years [is] the resurgence of national pride that I called the new patriotism. This national feeling is good, but it won't count for much, and it won't last unless it's grounded in thoughtfulness and knowledge. . . .

An informed patriotism is what we want. . . . Let's start with some basics: more attention to American history and greater emphasis on civic ritual. . . .⁹⁹

—from *Speaking My Mind*

a. What did Reagan believe were his greatest accomplishments as president?

b. What did Reagan believe would promote patriotism in the nation? Do you agree with his belief? Why or why not?

25. Organizing Use a graphic organizer similar to the one below to list the domestic and foreign issues faced by the Reagan and Bush administrations.

Issues	Reagan Administration	Bush Administration
Domestic		
Foreign		

Practicing Skills

26. Analyzing News Media Choose one current issue or event and compare its coverage in two different media. Which medium supplies the most facts? Is the coverage that is provided by both media consistent? What are the advantages and disadvantages of each medium? Write a two-page analysis comparing the two media, including a conclusion about which one is better.

Writing Activity

27. Writing a Report Research the status today of the independent republics formed from the Soviet Union. Find out about their political, social, and economic situations. Present your findings in a written report.

Chapter Activity

28. Creating a Thematic Graph Using a scale of 1 to 10, evaluate how successful each president was in dealing with the issues you listed in question 25. Create a thematic graph depicting each president's success rate per issue.

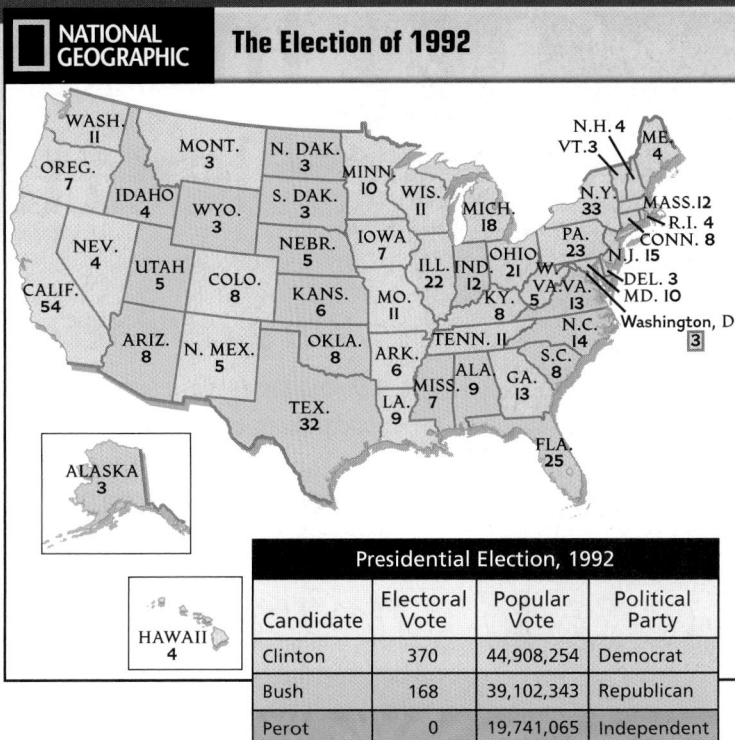

NATIONAL GEOGRAPHIC — **The Election of 1992**

Presidential Election, 1992			
Candidate	Electoral Vote	Popular Vote	Political Party
Clinton	370	44,908,254	Democrat
Bush	168	39,102,343	Republican
Perot	0	19,741,065	Independent

Geography and History

29. The map above shows the results of the 1992 presidential election. Study the map and answer the questions below.

a. Interpreting Maps How far short did President Bush fall in the race for Electoral College votes?

b. Applying Geography Skills Bill Clinton won his strongest support in which region of the nation?

Standardized Test Practice

Directions: Choose the phrase that best completes the following sentence.

The Strategic Defense Initiative (SDI) was proposed to strengthen the military by

A preventing the expansion of Communist countries.

B reemphasizing the use of infantry troops in future wars.

C developing weapons that would intercept and destroy incoming nuclear missiles.

D severely reducing the number of American troops stationed worldwide.

Test-Taking Tip: Eliminate answers that do not make sense. Reducing the number of American troops (answer D), for example, probably would not strengthen the military.

CHAPTER 34 Into a New Century

1992–present

Why It Matters

During the 1990s, a technological revolution transformed society. President Clinton pushed for budget cuts, health care and welfare reforms, and global trade. He also worked for peace in the Middle East and the Balkans. In 2000 George W. Bush won the presidency. He supported tax cuts, a new energy program, increased trade, and a missile defense system. After terrorists killed thousands of people in the United States, the new president launched a war on terrorism.

The Impact Today

Major developments of the era continue to influence modern society.
- *The use of the Internet is widespread in commerce, schools, and government.*
- *The North American Free Trade Agreement (NAFTA) continues to shape economic relations between the United States, Canada, and Mexico.*
- *The debate between conservatives and liberals continues in the United States.*

The American Vision Video The Chapter 34 video, "America's Response to Terrorism," examines how ordinary Americans responded to the terrorist attacks in New York City and Washington, D.C.

1996
- Bill Clinton reelected

1994
- U.S., Mexico, and Canada inaugurate NAFTA

1995
- Budget impasse shuts down federal government
- Oklahoma City bombing

1993
- Mosaic, the first popular Web browser is released

1991
- U.S. leads coalition of nations against Iraq in Operation Desert Storm

United States PRESIDENTS

G. Bush 1989–1993

Clinton 1993–2001

1990   *1993*   *1996*

World

1991
- Bosnia declares independence from Yugoslavia

1992
- Earth Day summit held in Rio de Janeiro, Brazil

1993
- Israeli-Palestinian peace accord signed
- European Union launched

1994
- Multiracial elections held in South Africa; Nelson Mandela elected president

1995
- Cease-fire signed in Bosnian war

January 20, 2001: George W. Bush is inaugurated as the nation's 43rd president.

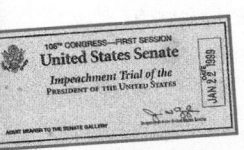

1998
- House of Representatives impeaches President Clinton

2000
- Electoral crisis delays naming of 43rd president

1999
- Senate acquits Clinton

2001
- First map of the human genome completed
- Terrorist attacks destroy World Trade Center and damage Pentagon

2002
- Winter Olympics held in Salt Lake City, Utah

G.W. Bush
2001–

1999

2002

1997
- Britain returns control of Hong Kong to China

2000
- Mexico's election of Vicente Fox ends 71 years of single-party rule

2001
- China chosen to be site of 2008 Olympic Games

HISTORY
Online

Chapter Overview
Visit the *American Vision* Web site at tav.glencoe.com and click on **Chapter Overviews—Chapter 34** to preview chapter information.

The Technological Revolution

Guide to Reading

Main Idea

The introduction of the first electronic digital computer in 1946 launched a technological revolution.

Key Terms and Names

ENIAC, integrated circuit, Silicon Valley, microprocessor, Bill Gates, software, telecommute, Internet, biotechnology, James Watson, Francis Crick, DNA

Reading Strategy

Categorizing As you read about the computer age, complete a chart similar to the one below to describe products that revolutionized the computer industry.

	How It Revolutionized Computer Industry
Microprocessors	
Apple II	
Macintosh	
Windows	

Reading Objectives

• **Describe** the evolution of the computer from scientific tool to household appliance.
• **Evaluate** how the computer has revolutionized science, medicine, and communications.

Section Theme

Economic Factors The computer has helped reshape the nation's economy.

Preview of Events

◆1993	◆1996	◆1999	◆2002

1993
Mosaic, the first popular Web browser, introduced

1996
Congress deregulates telephone companies

1999
Over 86 million Americans own cell phones

2001
Human Genome Project maps the human genome

★ *An American Story* ★

After years as a magazine editor and television news commentator, Michael Kinsley jumped into the new technology of the Internet in 1996, by agreeing to edit an online magazine called *Slate.* "I was determined," Kinsley said, "to be on the next train to pull out of the station no matter where it was going—provided that I was the engineer."

Soon newspaper and print magazines were also developing Web resources. Television stations also used the Internet to update news stories, allowing consumers to access news when and how they wanted. As Kinsley explained:

❝Web readers *surf.* They go quickly from site to site. If they really like a particular site, they may visit it often, but they are unlikely to devote a continuous half-hour or more to any one site. . . . This appears to be in the nature of the Web and not something that is likely to change.❞

—from "Slate Goes Free," Slate, February 13, 1999

The Rise of the Compact Computer

The development of a computer capable of supporting publications such as *Slate* began at the end of World War II. The world's first electronic digital computer, called **ENIAC** (Electronic Numerical Integrator and Computer), went into operation in

February 1946. ENIAC weighed over 30 tons and was the size of a small house. In early 1959, Robert Noyce designed the first **integrated circuit**—a complete electronic circuit on a single chip of silicon—which made circuits much smaller and very easy to manufacture. Noyce's company was located south of San Francisco. As new companies sprang up nearby to make products using integrated circuits, the region became known as **Silicon Valley.**

In 1968 Noyce and colleague Gordon Moore formed Intel, for "Integrated Electronics," a company that revolutionized computers by combining on a single chip several integrated circuits containing both memory and computing functions. Called micro-processors, these new chips further reduced the size of computers, increased their speed.

Computers for Everyone
Using microprocessor technology, Stephen Wozniak and his 20-year-old friend Steven Jobs set out to build a small computer suitable for personal use. In 1976 they founded Apple Computer and completed the Apple I. The following year they introduced the Apple II, the first practical and affordable home computer.

Apple's success sparked intense competition in the computer industry. In 1981 International Business

Picturing **History**

Apple Founders In 1984 Apple president John Sculley (center), along with Steve Jobs (left) and Steve Wozniak, show off their new briefcase-sized Apple IIc computer. On what basic technology do personal computers rely?

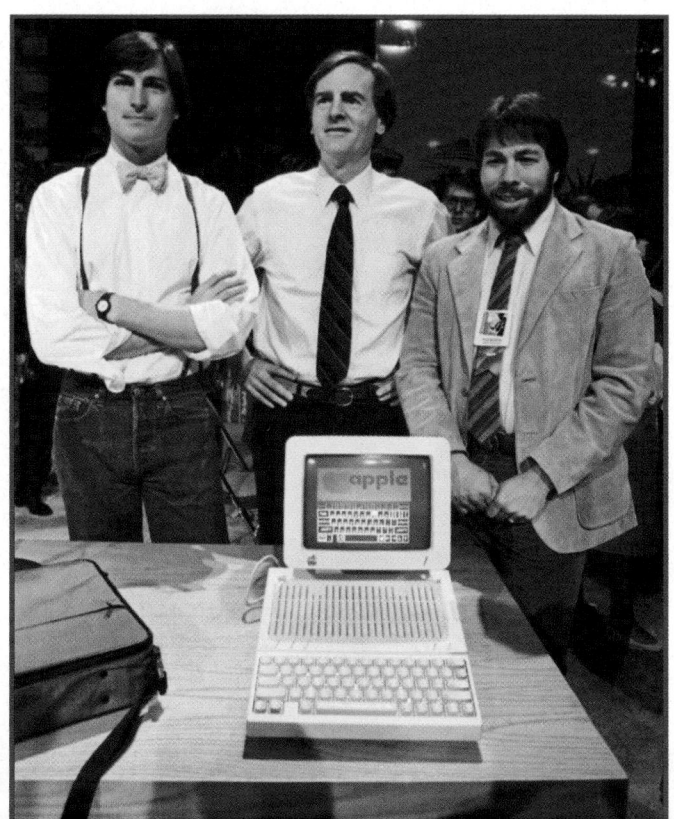

Machines (IBM) introduced its own compact machine, which it called the **"Personal Computer"** (PC). Apple responded in 1984 with the revolutionary **Macintosh,** a new model featuring a simplified operating system using on-screen graphic symbols called icons, which users could manipulate with a hand-operated device called a mouse.

Bill Gates and Microsoft As Jobs and Wozniak were creating Apple, 19-year-old Harvard dropout **Bill Gates** co-founded Microsoft to design PC software, the instructions used to program computers to perform desired tasks. In 1980 IBM hired Microsoft to develop an operating system for its new PC. Gates quickly paid a Seattle programmer $50,000 for the rights to his software, and with some refinements, it became MS-DOS (Microsoft Disk Operating System). In 1985 Microsoft introduced the "Windows" operating system, which enabled PCs to use mouse-activated, on-screen graphic icons.

Compact computers soon transformed the workplace, linking employees within an office or among office branches. They became essential tools in virtually every kind of business. By the late 1990s, many workers used home computers and electronic mail to "telecommute," or do their jobs from home via computer. Other electronic devices, such as programmable calculators and handheld computers, also found their way into American homes and offices.

Reading Check **Describing** How was Microsoft different from other computer companies?

The Telecommunications Revolution
A parallel revolution in communications coincided with the growing impact of computers. In the 1970s, 1980s, and 1990s, the government loosened telecommunications regulations, allowing more companies to compete in the telephone and television industries. In 1996 Congress passed the Telecommunications Act. This act allowed telephone companies to compete with each other and to send television signals, but it also permitted cable television companies to offer telephone service. Such developments spurred the creation of new

technologies such as Web-enabled cellular phones and other mixing of data-platforms.

✓ **Reading Check** **Explaining** How did deregulation affect the telecommunications industry?

The Rise of the Internet

Digital electronics also made possible a new worldwide communications system. The Internet let computer users post and receive information and communicate with each other. It had its roots in a computer networking system that the U.S. Defense Department's Advanced Research Project Agency established in 1969. Known as ARPANET, this system linked government agencies, defense contractors, and scientists at various universities, enabling them to communicate with each other by electronic mail. In 1985 the National Science Foundation funded several supercomputer centers across the country. This paved the way for the Internet, a global information system that operated commercially rather than through the government.

At first, Internet users employed different types of information. With the development of the hypertext transport protocol (http) and new software known as Web browsers, the Internet rapidly expanded. Users could now click on Internet links using their computer mouse and easily jump from Web site to Web site. Internet use expanded by almost 300 percent between 1997 and 2000.

The Internet also spawned a "dot-com" economy (from the common practice of using a business name as a World Wide Web address, followed by ".com"). Seemingly rich with promise, a wide variety of dot.com companies made millions of dollars for stock investors without ever earning actual profit from operations. Internet-related stocks helped fuel the prosperity of the 1990s but dropped dramatically in 2000, raising questions about the ultimate profitability of online companies.

✓ **Reading Check** **Explaining** How did the Internet expand business opportunities?

Breakthroughs in Biotechnology

Computers greatly assisted scientists engaged in **biotechnology**—the managing of biological systems to improve human life. Computers made it possible to study and manipulate genes and cells at the molecular level. Through biotechnology, researchers developed new medicines, animal growth hormones, genetically engineered plants, and industrial chemicals.

TECHNOLOGY & History

Magnetic Resonance Imaging

One extension of computer technology is magnetic resonance imaging (MRI). An MRI allows physicians to diagnose certain diseases, abnormalities, and injuries without resorting to x-rays or surgery. An MRI unit is made up of a large cylindrical magnet, devices for transmitting and receiving radio signals, and a computer. **Why do you think physicians prefer MRIs over x-rays and surgery?**

1 A large **cylindrical magnet** with a magnetic field 30,000 times stronger than the earth's magnetic field surrounds the patient.

2 **Radio signals** are transmitted within the machine and pass through the patient's body.

3 A **computer** converts the radio signals into precise images of the body's internal structure.

cylindrical magnet

computer

radio signals

Unraveling the Secrets of Life The first steps toward biotechnology came in 1953, when American molecular biologist **James Watson** and his British colleague, **Francis Crick,** deciphered the structure of deoxyribonucleic acid (DNA). DNA is the genetic material in cells that determine all forms of life.

Once scientists learned how to read the message of DNA, their new knowledge improved medical research and provided law enforcement with new methods of identification. Further research in biotechnology created artificial genes and assisted genetic engineering for plants, animals, and humans.

The Human Genome Project For years scientists talked of mapping out the human genome by recording the DNA sequence of the human species. With the development of supercomputers, the Human Genome Project began in earnest at the National Institutes of Health (NIH) in 1990. NIH decided to place all of the Human Genome Project's data on the Internet to make it available to scientists all over the world, free of charge. Researchers hoped to prevent any single nation or private laboratory from controlling the outcome and limiting the use of genome findings. In February 2001, the project completed its first map of

the human genome. Medical researchers expected that this information would help them determine which genes made people more susceptible to disease, thereby improving medical diagnoses and preventive medication and assisting in finding cures.

✓ **Reading Check** **Explaining** How did computers assist the development of biotechnology?

Profiles IN HISTORY

Jerry Yang
1968–

Jerry Yang was born in Taiwan in 1968 and immigrated with his family to San Jose, California, when he was 10 years old. Yang is a cofounder of Yahoo!, one of the world's best-known gateways to information and consumer goods on the Web. It is estimated that by the late 1990s, around 40 million people were visiting the Yahoo! Web site every month.

The company developed out of Yang's desire to be able to find good Web sites quickly. At Stanford University, he and cofounder David Filo were doctoral students sharing office space in a trailer. They also shared information on their favorite Web sites, and Yang began compiling a list of

them. He nicknamed the list "Jerry's Guide to the World Wide Web," and he posted it on the Internet.

Inquiries to the site boomed, and Yang and Filo concluded that they had found an untapped market. With the help of a loan from an imaginative venture capitalist, Yahoo! was born. Yang says they chose the name because it suggested the sort of "Wild West" character of the Internet. The mission for Yahoo! was not just to collect Web sites but to organize them into convenient categories, such as news, sports, games, and weather. Yahoo! became a popular gateway, or "portal," to the Web.

SECTION 1 ASSESSMENT

Checking for Understanding

1. **Define:** microprocessor, software, telecommute, Internet, DNA.
2. **Identify:** ENIAC, integrated circuit, Silicon Valley, Bill Gates, biotechnology, James Watson, Francis Crick.
3. **Explain** how scientific discoveries in biotechnology have improved people's lives.

Reviewing Themes

4. **Economic Factors** How have personal computers transformed the workplace?

Critical Thinking

5. **Analyzing** How have advances in telecommunications and the rise of the Internet affected the standard of living in the United States?
6. **Organizing** Complete a graphic organizer similar to the one below by listing developments that led to the technological revolution.

Technological Revolution

Analyzing Visuals

7. **Analyzing Photographs** Study the crowd in the photograph of George W. Bush's inauguration on page 1011. How would you describe the attitudes reflected in the faces of the people photographed?

Writing About History

8. **Descriptive Writing** Write two paragraphs describing the ways that you and your family use the Internet and how your way of life would be different without it.

Guide to Reading

Main Idea

Although President Clinton struggled with Republicans in Congress and faced impeachment, several major economic and social reforms were achieved during his presidency.

Key Terms and Names

AmeriCorps, Contract with America, Kenneth Starr, perjury, ethnic cleansing, Dayton Accords

Reading Strategy

Taking Notes As you read about the administration of President Clinton, use the major headings of the section to create an outline similar to the one below.

The Clinton Years
I. Clinton's Agenda
   A.
   B.
   C.
   D.
II.

Reading Objectives

- **Describe** the difficulties and successes of Bill Clinton's two terms as president.
- **Discuss** the nation's involvement in world affairs during the Clinton presidency.

Section Theme

Economic Factors The United States, along with much of the industrialized world, experienced economic prosperity in the 1990s.

Preview of Events

♦1993   ♦1995   ♦1997   ♦1999

1993
Israeli-Palestinian peace accord

1994
Republicans win both houses of Congress

1995
Federal government shuts down during budget impasse

1998
House impeaches Clinton

1999
Senate acquits Clinton; NATO aircraft bomb Serbia

★ *An American Story* ★

Bill Clinton was the third-youngest person ever to serve as president and the first of the "baby boom" generation to reach the Oval Office. Clinton brought with him a team of young energetic advisers. In the early weeks of the administration, Clinton's team spent many hours at the White House adjusting to their new life. In early 1993, they began discussing plans for Clinton's new economic strategy for paying down the deficit and reducing interest rates. George Stephanopoulos, an aide to the president, remembers their inexperienced beginnings:

❝The president presided over the rolling Roosevelt Room meetings in shirtsleeves, with glasses sliding down the end of his nose. . . . Clinton let everyone have a say, played us off against one another, asked pointed questions, and took indecipherable notes. But the reminders of who we were and what we were doing was never far away. Late one night, we ordered pizzas. When they arrived, the president grabbed a slice with the rest of us . . . [b]ut just before he took his first bite, [a secret service] agent placed a hand on his shoulder and told him to put it down. The pie hadn't been screened. . . .❞

—quoted in *All Too Human*

Clinton's Agenda

Clinton's first years in office were filled with grandiose plans and the difficult realities of politics. The new president put forth an ambitious domestic program focusing on five major areas: the economy, the family, education, crime, and health care.

Raising Taxes, Cutting Spending As he had promised in his election campaign, Clinton focused first on the economy. The problem, in the president's view, was the federal deficit. Under Reagan and Bush, the deficit had nearly quadrupled, adding billions of dollars annually to the national debt. High deficits forced the government to borrow large sums of money, which helped to drive up interest rates.

Clinton believed that the key to economic growth was to lower interest rates. Low interest rates would enable businesses to borrow more money to expand and create more jobs. Low rates would also make it easier for consumers to borrow money for mortgages, car loans, and other items, which in turn would promote economic growth.

One way to bring interest rates down was to reduce the federal deficit. In early 1993, Clinton sent Congress a deficit reduction plan. In trying to cut the deficit, however, Clinton faced a serious problem. About half of all government spending went to entitlement programs, such as Social Security, Medicare, and veterans' benefits. These programs are hard to cut because so many Americans depend on them.

Faced with these constraints, Clinton decided to raise taxes, even though he had promised to cut taxes during his campaign. Clinton's plan raised tax rates for middle- and upper-income Americans and placed new taxes on gasoline, heating oil, and natural gas. The tax increases were very unpopular, and Republicans in Congress refused to support them. Clinton pressured Democrats, and after many amendments, a modified version of Clinton's plan narrowly passed.

Stumbling on Health Care During his campaign, Clinton had promised to reform the U.S. health care system. An estimated 40 million Americans, or roughly 15 percent of the nation, did not have private health insurance. The president appointed a task force headed by his wife, **Hillary Rodham Clinton**—an unprecedented role for a first lady. The task force developed a plan that guaranteed health benefits for all Americans, but it put much of the burden of payment of these benefits on employers. Small-business owners feared they could not afford it. The insurance industry and doctors' organizations also opposed the plan.

Republicans opposed the plan as being complicated, costly, and reliant on government control. Congressional Democrats were divided. Some supported alternative plans, but no plan had enough support to pass. Faced with public opposition, Clinton's plan died without a vote.

Families and Education Clinton did manage to push several major pieces of legislation through Congress. During his campaign, he had stressed the need to help American families. His first success was the **Family Medical Leave Act.** This law gave workers up to 12 weeks per year of unpaid family leave for the birth or adoption of a child or for the illness of a family member.

Clinton also persuaded Congress to create the **AmeriCorps** program. This program put students to work improving low-income housing, teaching children to read, and cleaning up the environment. AmeriCorps volunteers earned a salary and were awarded a scholarship to continue their education.

In 2000 Clinton had better success on health care. Congress passed part of his proposals to cover 5 million uninsured people by expanding Medicaid, Medicare, and other programs.

Crime and Gun Control Clinton had also promised to get tough on crime during his campaign, and he strongly endorsed new gun-control laws. Despite strong opposition from many Republicans and the **National Rifle Association** (NRA), the Democrats in Congress passed a gun-control law known as the **Brady Bill.** The bill imposed a waiting period before people could buy handguns. It also required gun dealers to have police run a background check on a person's criminal record before selling them a handgun. The following year, Clinton introduced another crime bill. The bill provided states with extra funds to build new prisons and hire 100,000 police officers.

✓ **Reading Check** **Explaining** Why did President Clinton's proposed health care plan fail?

Picturing **History**

High Hopes The Clintons entered the White House in 1993 determined to change the United States for the better. It took time for them to adjust to life in Washington, and many of their ambitious plans were defeated in Congress. What legislative proposal was given to the First Lady to oversee?

The Republicans Gain Control of Congress

Despite his successes, Clinton was very unpopular by late 1994. Instead of cutting taxes, he had raised them, and he had not fixed health care. Although the economy was improving, many companies were still downsizing. Several personal issues involving President Clinton further weakened public confidence in him. These factors convinced many Americans to vote Republican in 1994.

The Contract With America As the 1994 midterm elections neared, congressional Republicans, led by Newt Gingrich of Georgia, created the **Contract with America.** This program proposed 10 major changes, including lower taxes, welfare reform, tougher anticrime laws, term limits for members of Congress, and a balanced budget amendment. Republicans won a stunning victory—for the first time in 40 years, they had a majority in both houses of Congress.

In their first 100 days in office, House Republicans passed almost the entire Contract with America, but they soon ran into trouble. The Senate defeated several proposals, including the balanced budget amendment, while the president vetoed others.

The Budget Battle In 1995 the Republicans lost more momentum when they clashed with the president over the new federal budget. Clinton vetoed several Republican budget proposals, claiming they cut into social programs too much. Gingrich believed that if Republicans stood firm, the president would back down and approve the budget. Otherwise, the entire federal government would shut down for lack of funds. Clinton, however, refused to budge, and allowed the federal government to close.

By standing firm against Republican budget proposals and allowing the government to shut down, Clinton regained much of the support he had lost in 1994. The Republicans in Congress realized they needed to work with the president to pass legislation. Soon afterward, they reached an agreement with Clinton to balance the budget.

In the months before the 1996 election, the president and the Republicans worked together to pass new legislation. In August Congress passed the Health Insurance Portability Act. This act improved coverage for people who changed jobs and reduced discrimination against people with preexisting illnesses.

Later that month, Congress passed the **Welfare Reform Act,** which limited people to no more than two consecutive years on welfare and required them to work to receive welfare benefits. The law also increased childcare spending and gave tax breaks to companies that hired new employees who had been on welfare.

✓ **Reading Check** **Identifying** What two reforms did Clinton and Congress agree to support?

The 1996 Election

As the 1996 campaign began, Clinton took credit for the economy. The economic boom of the 1990s was the longest sustained period of growth in American history. Unemployment and inflation fell to their lowest levels in 40 years. The stock market soared, wages rose, crime rates fell, and the number of people on welfare declined. With the economy booming, Clinton's popularity climbed rapidly.

The Republican Party nominated Senator **Bob Dole** of Kansas, the Republican leader in the Senate, to run against Clinton. Dole chose as his running mate Jack Kemp, a former member of Congress from New York. Dole promised a 15 percent tax cut and tried to portray Clinton as a tax-and-spend liberal.

H. Ross Perot also ran again as a candidate. This time he ran as the candidate of the Reform Party, which he had created. Once again Perot made the deficit the main campaign issue.

President Clinton won re-election, winning a little more than 49 percent of the popular vote and 379 electoral votes. Dole received almost 41 percent and 159 electoral votes, and Perot won about 8.4 percent of the vote. Despite Clinton's victory, Republicans retained control of Congress. They also kept control after the 1998 elections, although the Democrats gained 5 seats in the House of Representatives.

Reading Check **Explaining** Why do you think President Clinton won re-election in 1996?

Clinton's Second Term

During Clinton's second term, the economy continued its expansion. As people's incomes rose, so too did the amount of taxes they paid. At the same time, despite their differences, the president and Congress continued to shrink the deficit. In 1997, for the first time in 24 years, the president was able to submit a balanced budget to Congress. Beginning in 1998, the government began to run a surplus—that is, it collected more money than it spent.

Despite these achievements, Clinton's domestic agenda was less aggressive in his second term. Much of his time was spent on foreign policy and in struggling against a personal scandal.

Putting Children First During his second term, Clinton's domestic agenda shifted toward helping the nation's children. He began by asking Congress to pass a $500 per child tax credit. He also signed the Adoption and Safe Families Act and asked Congress to ban cigarette advertising aimed at children. In August 1997, Clinton signed the Children's Health Insurance Program—a plan to provide health insurance for children whose parents could not afford it.

Clinton also continued his efforts to help students. "I come from a family where nobody had ever gone to college before," Clinton said. "When I became president, I was determined to do what I could to give every student that chance." To help students, he asked for a tax credit, a large increase in student grants, and an expansion of the Head Start program for preschoolers.

Clinton Is Impeached The robust economy and his high standing in the polls allowed Clinton to regain the initiative in dealing with Congress. By 1998, however,

Impeaching the President

The Constitution gives Congress the power to remove a president from office "upon impeachment for and Conviction of, Treason, Bribery, or other High Crimes and Misdemeanors." The House of Representatives has the sole power over impeachment—the formal accusation of wrongdoing in office. If the majority of the House votes to impeach the president, the Senate conducts a trial. A two-thirds vote of those present is needed for conviction. When the impeachment proceeding involves a president, the chief justice of the United States presides.

Chief Justice William Rehnquist being sworn in for the impeachment trial in the Senate

A somber President and Mrs. Clinton after the decision for impeachment was reached

he had become entangled in a serious scandal that threatened to undermine his presidency.

The scandal began in Clinton's first term, when he was accused of arranging illegal loans for Whitewater Development—an Arkansas real estate company—while he was governor of that state. Attorney General **Janet Reno** decided that an independent counsel should investigate the president. A special three-judge panel appointed **Kenneth Starr,** a former federal judge, to this position.

In early 1998, a new scandal emerged involving a personal relationship between the president and a White House intern. Some evidence suggested that the president had committed perjury, or had lied under oath, about the relationship. The three-judge panel directed Starr to investigate this scandal as well. In September 1998, after examining the evidence, Starr sent his report to the Judiciary Committee of the House of Representatives. Starr argued that Clinton had obstructed justice, abused his power as president, and committed perjury.

After the 1998 elections, the House began impeachment hearings. Clinton's supporters charged that Starr's investigation was politically motivated. Clinton's accusers argued that the president was accountable if his actions were illegal.

On December 19, 1998, the House of Representatives passed two articles of impeachment, one for perjury and one for obstruction of justice. The vote split almost evenly along party lines, and the case moved to the Senate for trial. On February 12, 1999, the senators cast their votes. The vote was 55 to 45 that Clinton was not guilty of perjury, and 50–50 on the charge of obstruction of justice. Although both votes were well short of the two-thirds needed to remove the president from office, Clinton's reputation had suffered.

Reading Check **Examining** What events led to the impeachment of President Clinton?

Clinton's Foreign Policy

While attracting worldwide attention, the impeachment drama did not affect world affairs. The collapse of the Soviet Union virtually ended the struggle between communism and democracy, but small bloody wars continued to erupt around the world. On several occasions President Clinton used force to bring an end to regional conflicts.

The Haitian Intervention In 1991 military leaders in Haiti overthrew Jean-Bertrand Aristide, the country's first democratically elected president in many decades. Aristide sought refuge in the United States. The new rulers of Haiti used violence, even murder, to suppress the opposition. Seeking to restore democracy, the Clinton administration convinced the United Nations to impose a trade embargo on Haiti. The embargo created a severe economic crisis in that country. Thousands of Haitian refugees fled to the United States in small boats, and many died at sea.

Determined to put an end to the crisis, Clinton ordered an invasion of Haiti. Before the troops arrived, however, former president Jimmy Carter convinced Haiti's rulers to step aside.

Peacekeeping in Bosnia and Kosovo The United States also was concerned about mounting tensions in southeastern Europe. During the Cold War, Yugoslavia had been a single federated nation made up of many different ethnic groups under a strong Communist government. In 1991, after the collapse of communism, Yugoslavia split apart.

In Bosnia, one of the former Yugoslav republics, a vicious three-way civil war erupted between Orthodox Christian Serbs, Catholic Croatians, and Bosnian Muslims. Despite international pressure, the fighting continued until 1995. The Serbs began what they called ethnic cleansing—the brutal expulsion of an ethnic group from a geographic area. In some cases, Serbian troops slaughtered the Muslims instead of moving them.

The United States convinced its NATO allies that military action was necessary. NATO warplanes attacked the Serbs in Bosnia, forcing them to negotiate. The Clinton administration then arranged peace talks in Dayton, Ohio. The participants signed a peace plan known as the **Dayton Accords.** In 1996 some 60,000 NATO troops, including 20,000 Americans, entered Bosnia to enforce the plan.

In 1998 another war erupted, this time within the Serbian province of Kosovo. Kosovo has two major ethnic groups—Serbs and Albanians. Many of the Albanians wanted Kosovo to separate from Serbia. To keep Kosovo in Serbia, Serbian leader **Slobodan Milosevic** ordered a crackdown. The Albanians then organized their own army to fight back. Worried by reports of Serbian violence against Albanian civilians, President Clinton convinced European leaders that NATO should again use force to stop the fighting. In March 1999, NATO began bombing Serbia. The bombing convinced Serbia to pull its troops out of Kosovo.

Peacemaking in the Middle East Despite the overwhelming defeat Iraq suffered in the Persian Gulf War, Iraqi President Saddam Hussein remained in power and continued to make threats against Iraq's neighbors. In 1996 Iraq attacked the Kurds, an ethnic group whose homeland lies in northern Iraq. To stop the attacks, the United States fired cruise missiles at Iraqi military targets.

Relations between Israel and the Palestinians were even more volatile. In 1993 Israeli Prime Minister **Yitzhak Rabin** and Palestine Liberation Organization leader **Yasir Arafat** reached an agreement. The PLO recognized Israel's right to exist, and Israel recognized the PLO as the representative of the Palestinians. President Clinton then invited Arafat and Rabin to the White House, where they signed the Declaration of Principles—a plan for creating a Palestinian government.

Opposition to the peace plan emerged on both sides. Radical Palestinians exploded bombs in Israel and in 1995 a right-wing Israeli assassinated Prime Minister Rabin.

In 1998 Israeli and Palestinian leaders met with President Clinton at the Wye River plantation in Maryland to work out details of the withdrawal of Israeli troops from the West Bank and the Gaza Strip. This agreement, however, failed to settle the status of Jerusalem, which both sides claimed.

In July 2000, President Clinton invited Arafat and Israeli Prime Minister Ehud Barak to reach an agreement, but these talks failed. Beginning in October, violence started to break out between Palestinians and Israeli soldiers. The region was as far from peace as ever.

Middle East Conflict The struggle over control of the Israeli/Palestinian areas intensified in the 1990s. Although President Clinton directed many negotiations to attempt to resolve the conflict, the region remained a very dangerous place. Which leaders agreed to a framework for peace in 1993?

Clinton Leaves Office As he prepared to leave office, President Clinton's legacy was uncertain. He had balanced the budget and presided over the greatest period of economic growth in American history. Clinton's presidency was marred, however, by the impeachment trial, which had divided the nation and widened the divide between liberals and conservatives. In the election of 2000, that division would lead to the closest election in American history.

✓ **Reading Check** **Identifying** In what three regions of the world did Clinton use force to support his foreign policy?

SECTION 2 ASSESSMENT

Checking for Understanding
1. **Define:** perjury, ethnic cleansing.
2. **Identify:** AmeriCorps, Contract with America, Kenneth Starr, Dayton Accords.
3. **Explain** why the federal government shut down in 1995.

Reviewing Themes
4. **Economic Factors** What government policies helped create the U.S. prosperity of the 1990s?

Critical Thinking
5. **Analyzing** Why was President Clinton able to win re-election in 1996?
6. **Categorizing** Complete a chart similar to the one below by explaining the foreign policy issues facing President Clinton in each of the areas listed.

Region	Issue
Latin America	
Southeastern Europe	
Middle East	

Analyzing Visuals
7. **Analyzing Photographs** Study the photographs on page 1019 of Clinton's impeachment trial. What elements in the photograph reflect the seriousness of the occasion?

Writing About History
8. **Persuasive Writing** Take on the role of a member of Congress. Write a letter in which you attempt to persuade other lawmakers to vote either for or against the impeachment of President Clinton. Provide reasons for your position.

Guide to Reading

Main Idea

As the world adjusted to a new era, it faced the advantages and disadvantages of growing economic globalization and the end of the U.S.-Soviet rivalry.

Key Terms and Names

trade deficit, North American Free Trade Agreement, euro, nuclear proliferation, global warming, Kyoto Protocol

Reading Strategy

Organizing Complete a graphic organizer like the one below to chart the major political and economic problems facing the world at the turn of the century.

Global Concerns

Reading Objectives

• **Explain** the development of regional economic blocs around the world.
• **Assess** environmental issues that have become important internationally.

Section Theme

Global Connections Economic, health, and environmental developments in recent years have led to the world's nations becoming more interdependent.

Preview of Events

♦1992   ♦1995   ♦1998   ♦2001

1993
European Union launched

1994
United States, Mexico, and Canada inaugurate NAFTA

1995
Oklahoma City bombing

1998
Terrorist bombings in Kenya and Tanzania

2000
U.S. gives permanent trade status to China

★ *An American Story* ★

It was an important breakthrough when President Clinton appointed Madeleine Albright in 1996 to be the first woman to serve as secretary of state. Born in Czechoslovakia, Albright immigrated to the United States as a young girl. She earned a Ph.D. in Russian studies from Columbia University. Her tough-talking approach as U.S. ambassador to the United Nations earned her the nation's top foreign policy job.

As secretary of state, Albright dealt with everything from peace negotiations in the Middle East to improving trade relations with China. She also championed women's rights in developing countries. Here, she expresses her views on women's rights:

❝[Halting violence against women] is a goal of American foreign policy around the world, where abuses range from domestic violence . . . to forcing young girls into prostitution. Some say all this is cultural, and there's nothing we can do about it. I say it's criminal, and we each have a responsibility to stop it.❞

—**quoted in** *Madeleine Albright and the New American Diplomacy*

The New Global Economy

In the latter part of the 1900s, American leaders became more concerned with many global issues. Economies around the world had become much more interdependent. Computer technology and the Internet played a big role in forging a global economy.

Selling American-made goods abroad had long been important to American prosperity. By the 1970s, however, serious trade deficits had mounted—Americans purchased more from foreign nations than American industry and agriculture sold abroad. The United States found it necessary to compete harder in the global marketplace by streamlining industry, using new technology, and opening new markets.

From World War II to the present, Republican and Democratic administrations have both tried to lower barriers to international trade. They reasoned that the U.S. economy benefited from the sale of American exports, and that the purchase of imports would keep consumer prices, inflation, and interest rates low for Americans. Opponents warned that the global economy might cost the United States industrial jobs as manufacturing shifted to lesser-developed nations with few environmental regulations and cheap labor. By the 1990s, the debate between supporters of free trade and those who wanted to limit trade to protect industries had become an important part of American politics.

Regional Blocs One means of increasing international trade was to create regional trade pacts. In 1994 the **North American Free Trade Agreement** (NAFTA) joined Canada, the United States, and Mexico in a free-trade zone. With NAFTA in operation, exports of American goods to both Canada and Mexico rose dramatically. From 1993 to 2000, it is estimated that combined exports to those two countries rose from $142 to $290 billion, an increase of 104 percent.

One concern of many Americans was that industrial jobs would go to Mexico, where labor costs were lower. Although some jobs were lost to Mexico, unemployment rates in the United States fell during this period and wages rose. Many American businesses upgraded their technology, and workers shifted to more skilled jobs or to the service industry.

NAFTA faced competing regional trade blocs in Europe and Asia. In 1993 the **European Union** (EU) was created to promote economic and political cooperation among many European nations. The EU created a common bank and the euro, a common currency for member nations. The organization also removed trade barriers between its members and set policies on imports from nations outside the community.

EU rules tended to favor imports from the European nations' former colonies in Asia, Africa, and the Pacific over competing products from the United States. The EU also banned scientifically modified food, such as hormone-treated beef from the United States. American exporters argued that hormones were a safe way to accelerate livestock growth rates and produce leaner meat. They protested that European fears lacked a scientific basis.

The **Asia Pacific Economic Cooperation** (APEC) was an attempt to create a Pacific trade community to rival the European Union. APEC represented the fastest-growing region in the world and controlled 47 percent of global trade in 2001. APEC began as a

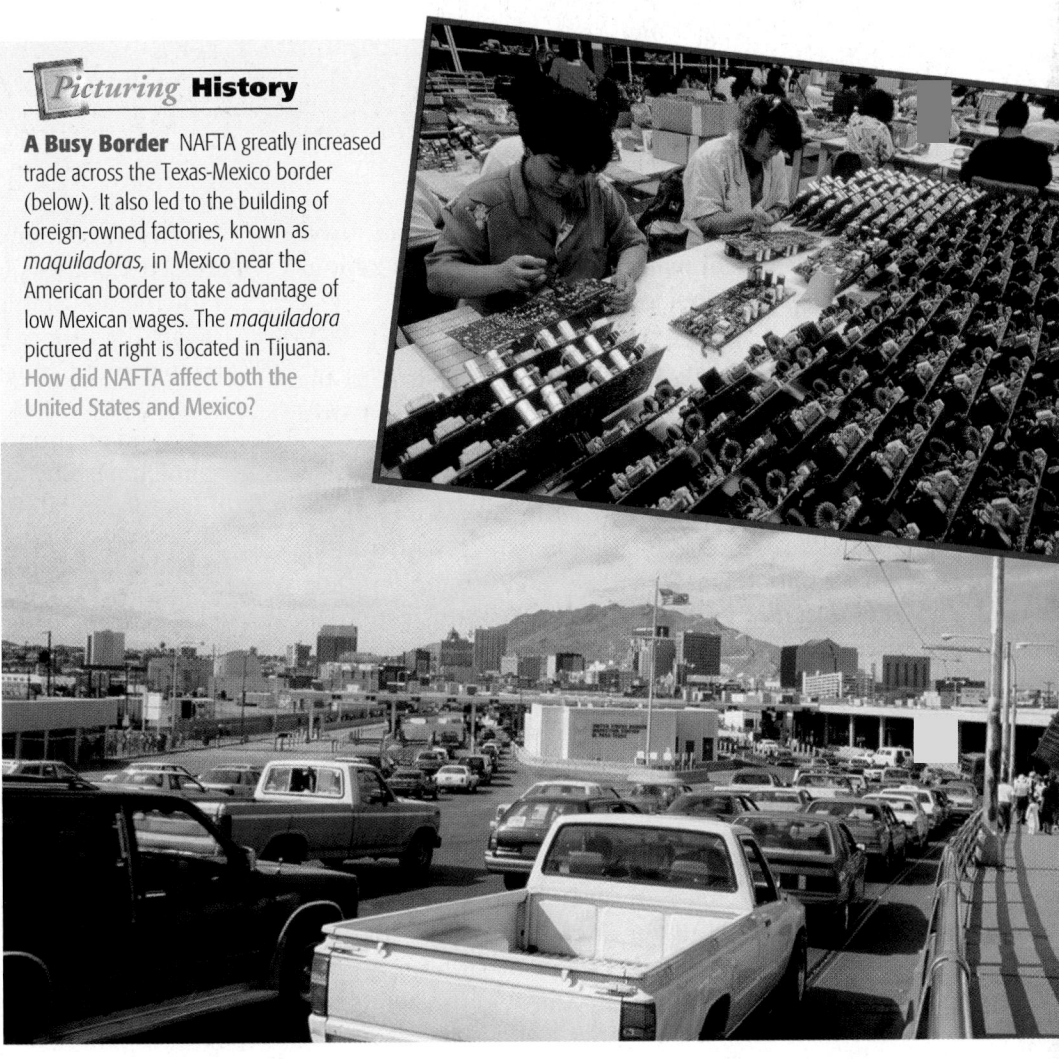

Picturing **History**

A Busy Border NAFTA greatly increased trade across the Texas-Mexico border (below). It also led to the building of foreign-owned factories, known as *maquiladoras,* in Mexico near the American border to take advantage of low Mexican wages. The *maquiladora* pictured at right is located in Tijuana. How did NAFTA affect both the United States and Mexico?

NATIONAL GEOGRAPHIC
MOMENT in HISTORY

TERRORISM IN THE HEARTLAND

A couple comforts each other after placing flowers on one of the 168 chairs that form part of the Oklahoma City National Memorial. The site was dedicated on April 19, 2000—five years to the day after Timothy McVeigh detonated a massive bomb outside the Alfred P. Murrah Federal Building in downtown Oklahoma City. Most of the 168 killed and hundreds injured were government employees, but 19 children attending a day-care facility in the building also died in the blast. A jury found McVeigh guilty, and he was executed in 2001.

forum to promote economic cooperation and lower trade barriers, but major political differences kept its members from acting together.

The World Trade Organization Central to the effort to promote a global economy was the **World Trade Organization** (WTO). The WTO administered international trade agreements and helped settle trade disputes. American supporters of the WTO cited benefits for U.S. consumers, including cheaper imports, new markets, and copyright protection for the American entertainment industry. On the other hand, the United States had no veto power in the WTO and poorer nations could outvote it.

Trade With China China played an increasingly important role in world trade. Its huge population offered vast potential as a market for American goods. Many Americans, however, had strong reservations about China's record on human rights, and they worried about its threats to invade Taiwan. Despite these concerns, President Clinton argued that regularizing trade with China would help bring it into the world community.

After negotiating a new trade agreement, Clinton pressed Congress to grant China permanent normal trade relation status. Those opposing the bill were an unusual coalition. Labor unions were concerned that inexpensive Chinese goods would flood U.S. markets; conservatives objected to China's military ambitions; and environmentalists worried about pollution from Chinese factories. Despite their opposition, the bill passed in late 2000.

✓ **Reading Check** **Explaining** Why was the European Union (EU) created in 1993?

Issues of Global Concern

Although the end of the Cold War had reduced the threat of nuclear war between the United States and the Soviet Union, it also increased fears that nuclear weapons might fall into the wrong hands. Equally worrisome were efforts by several nations, including Pakistan, North Korea, and Iraq, to acquire nuclear weapons and long-range missiles. Beginning in the 1980s, nations also began to be concerned about the environment.

TECHNOLOGY

Nuclear Proliferation

During the Cold War, only a few nations had possessed nuclear weapons, and they tried to restrict the spread of nuclear technology to other countries. When Russia agreed to reduce its nuclear arsenal, concerns arose that some of its nuclear weapons or radioactive material could be lost, stolen, or sold on the black market. In response, the United States provided funds to Russia to assist in the reduction of its nuclear stockpile.

Other measures followed to reduce the threat of nuclear proliferation, or the spread of nuclear weapons to new nations. Congress passed legislation that cut aid and imposed sanctions on nations seeking to acquire nuclear weapons. In 1996 President Clinton also signed the Comprehensive Nuclear Test Ban Treaty, but the U.S. Senate refused to ratify it fearing it would limit American nuclear research.

Concern About Ozone

In the 1980s, scientists discovered that chemicals called chlorofluorocarbons (CFCs) had the potential to deplete the earth's atmosphere of ozone. Ozone is a gas in the atmosphere that protects life on Earth from the cancer-causing ultraviolet rays of the sun. At that time, CFCs were widely used in air conditioners and refrigerators. Many environmental activists began to push for a ban on CFC production. In the late 1980s, public awareness of the ozone issue increased dramatically when stories appeared documenting a large ozone "hole" over Antarctica. In 1987 the United States and 22 other nations agreed to phase out the production of CFCs and other chemicals that might be weakening the ozone layer.

Global Warming

In the early 1990s, another global environmental issue developed when some scientists found evidence of global warming—an increase in average world temperatures over time. Such a rise in temperature could eventually lead to more droughts and other forms of extreme weather. A furious debate is now underway among scientists over how to measure changes in the earth's temperature and what the results mean.

Many experts believe carbon dioxide emissions from factories and power plants caused global warming, but others disagree. Some question whether global warming even exists. The issue is very controversial because the cost of controlling emissions would affect the global economy. Industries would have to pay the cost of further reducing emissions, and those costs would eventually be passed on to consumers. Developing nations trying to industrialize would be hurt the most, but economic growth in wealthier nations would be hurt, too.

Concern about global warming led to an international conference in Kyoto, Japan, in 1997. Thirty-eight nations and the EU signed the **Kyoto Protocol** promising to reduce emissions, but very few put it into effect. President Clinton did not submit the Kyoto Protocol to the Senate for ratification because most senators were opposed to it. In 2001 President George W. Bush withdrew the United States from the Kyoto Protocol, citing flaws in the treaty. As the 2000s began, Americans struggled to balance economic progress with environmental concerns.

Reading Check **Identifying** What is the ozone layer, and why is it important?

SECTION 3 ASSESSMENT

Checking for Understanding

1. **Define:** trade deficit, euro, nuclear proliferation, global warming.
2. **Identify:** North American Free Trade Agreement, Kyoto Protocol.
3. **Describe** the international response to concerns about global warming.

Reviewing Themes

4. **Global Connections** Why was China an important factor in world trade?

Critical Thinking

5. **Analyzing** Do you think the new global economy has helped or hurt the United States?
6. **Organizing** Complete a graphic organizer similar to the one below by listing and describing the regional trade blocs that formed in the 1990s.

Analyzing Visuals

7. **Analyzing Photographs** Study the photograph on page 1024 of the Oklahoma City National Memorial. What do the empty chairs represent? How has the memorial helped relatives of the victims?

Writing About History

8. **Expository Writing** Decide which issue of global concern today is the most serious. In an essay, explain why you think it is the most serious problem, and provide some possible solutions.

America Enters a New Century

Guide to Reading

Main Idea

The closest presidential election in American history served as the prelude to the new century. The new president initiated an ambitious program.

Key Terms and Names

Al Gore, George W. Bush, Ralph Nader, chad, strategic defense

Reading Strategy

Organizing As you read about the 2000 presidential election, complete a graphic organizer similar to the one below by charting the key post-election events culminating in George W. Bush's victory.

Reading Objectives

• **Describe** the unusual circumstances surrounding the outcome of the 2000 presidential election.
• **Evaluate** the programs President George W. Bush initiated.

Section Theme

Government and Democracy The 2000 presidential election was very close, and the outcome was controversial.

Preview of Events

♦Aug. 2000	♦Dec. 2000	♦Mar. 2001	♦June 2001

August 2000
Republicans nominate Bush; Democrats nominate Gore

November 2000
Election takes place; recounts begin in Florida

December 2000
Gore concedes election to Bush

January 2001
George W. Bush inaugurated as president

June 2001
Bush signs tax cut bill into law

★ *An American Story* ★

The 2000 presidential election was very close. Two candidates battled over the Electoral College votes of one state—Florida. The election remained undecided for more than a month. Though this election was a spectacle of demonstrations and detailed ballot evaluations, some people tried to put it all in perspective. May Akabogu-Collins, an American citizen originally from Nigeria, contrasted the "turmoil" and "chaos" of the election with the transfer of power in other parts of the world:

❝America should be grateful that this election was as wild as it gets. Some of us originally came from places where heads would have rolled during a similar crisis. So far, not a gunshot has been heard on account of the balloting, and you call this 'wild'? An election held in Nigeria in 1993 led to the President-elect's being thrown in jail for trying to assume office and ultimately to his mysterious death. Going to court to decide who won this contest is, in my opinion, as civilized as it gets.❞

—**quoted in *Time*, December 11, 2000**

A New President for a New Century

The close election of 2000 was, in some ways, another legacy of Bill Clinton's years in power. Clinton's presidency had left the country deeply divided. Many people were pleased with the economy but disappointed with the president's personal behavior. As the election approached, the Republicans and the Democrats both tried to find candidates who would appeal to a broad cross-section of society.

The Candidates Are Chosen

The Democrats nominated Vice President **Al Gore** for president in 2000. As his running mate, Gore chose Senator Joseph Lieberman from Connecticut, the first Jewish American ever to run for vice president on a major party ticket.

The Republican contest for the presidential nomination came down to two men: Governor **George W. Bush** of Texas, son of former president George Bush, and Senator John McCain of Arizona, a former navy pilot and prisoner of war in North Vietnam. Most Republican leaders endorsed Bush, who was also popular with conservative Republicans. He easily won the nomination, despite some early McCain victories in the primaries. Bush chose former defense secretary Richard Cheney as his vice presidential running mate.

The 2000 Campaign

The election campaign revolved around the question of what to do with surplus tax revenues. Both Bush and Gore agreed that Social Security needed reform, but they disagreed on the details. Both promised to cut taxes, although Bush proposed a much larger tax cut than Gore. Both men also promised to improve public education and to support plans to help seniors pay for prescription drugs.

The healthy economy helped Gore, who stressed that the Clinton-Gore administration had brought prosperity to the nation. Many voters, however, were concerned with what they perceived as a decline in moral values among the nation's leaders. Bush promised to restore dignity to the White House.

Frustrated by the similarities between Bush and Gore, well-known consumer advocate **Ralph Nader** entered the race as the nominee of the Green Party. Nader was known for his strong environmentalist views and his criticism of the power of large corporations. Nader argued that both Bush and Gore were

A controversial punch ballot from West Palm Beach, Florida

Picturing **History**

A Tense Wait During the unprecedented wait for a winner in the 2000 presidential election, candidate George W. Bush (right) waits with his father, the 41st president. The outcome of the election depended on the vote counts in which state?

The Florida Election, 2000

Bars represent the number of votes by which Bush led in Florida, in 15-minute intervals.

Gore has lead for 15 minutes. AP, networks call him winner of Florida.

Over next two hours, Bush lead builds to nearly 150,000 votes.

Florida called "undecided" around 10:30 P.M. Bush lead soon begins to shrink.

Networks call Bush winner in Florida— and president-elect— just after 2:15 A.M.

Bush's lead shrinks to **1,655 votes;** state again called a toss-up.

Gore declared winner
Winner undecided
Bush declared winner

160,000
140,000
120,000
100,000
80,000
60,000
40,000
20,000
0
-20,000

7 P.M. 8 P.M. 9 P.M. 10 P.M. 11 P.M. Midnight 1 A.M. 2 A.M. 3 A.M. 4 A.M. 5 A.M.

Source: *Associated Press.*

The Election of 2000

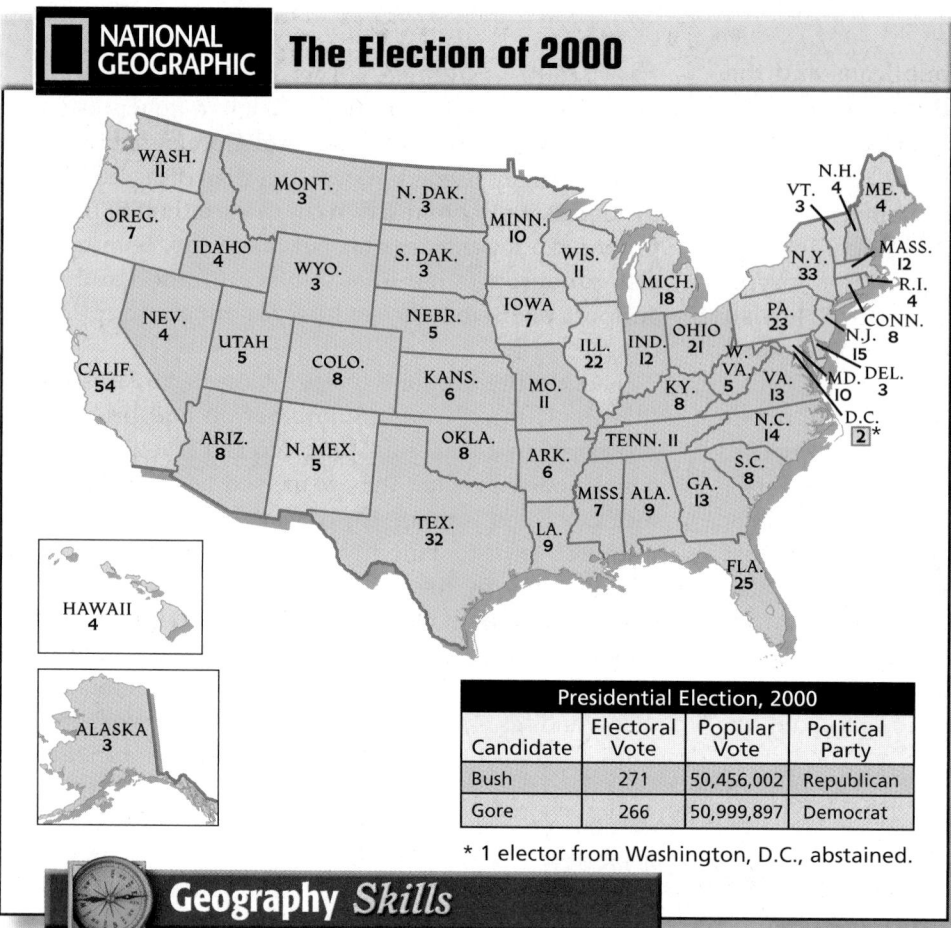

Presidential Election, 2000			
Candidate	Electoral Vote	Popular Vote	Political Party
Bush	271	50,456,002	Republican
Gore	266	50,999,897	Democrat

* 1 elector from Washington, D.C., abstained.

Geography Skills

1. **Interpreting Maps** Which single New England state did George W. Bush win in the election?
2. **Applying Geography Skills** Though Gore won less than half of the states, the election was extremely close. Why?

After the machine recount showed Bush still ahead, a battle began over the manual recounts. Most Florida ballots required voters to punch a hole. The little piece of cardboard punched out of the ballot is called a chad. The problem for vote counters was how to count a ballot when the chad was still partially attached. On some, the chad was still in place, and the voter had left only a dimple on the surface of the ballot. When looking at the ballots, vote counters had to determine what the voter intended—and different counties used different standards.

Under state law, Florida officials had to certify the results by a certain date. When it became clear that not all of the recounts could be finished in time, Gore went to court to overturn the deadline. The Florida Supreme Court agreed to set a new deadline. At Bush's request, the United States Supreme Court then intervened in the case to decide whether the Florida Supreme Court had acted unconstitutionally.

While lawyers for Bush and Gore prepared their arguments for the Supreme Court, the hand recounts continued. Despite having more time, not all of the counties where Gore wanted recounts were able to meet the new deadline. On November 26, Florida officials certified Bush the winner by 537 votes.

dependent on campaign funds from large companies and were unwilling to support policies that favored American workers and the environment.

A Close Vote The 2000 election was one of the closest in American history. Gore narrowly won the popular vote. He received 48.4 percent of the vote to 47.9 for Bush. To win the presidency, however, candidates have to win a majority of state electoral votes, not the overall popular vote.

Neither candidate had the 270 electoral votes needed to win. The election came down to the Florida vote—both men needed its 25 electoral votes.

The results in Florida were so close that state law required a recount of the ballots using vote-counting machines. There were, however, thousands of ballots that had been thrown out because the counting machines could not discern a vote for president. Gore immediately asked for a hand recount of ballots in several strongly Democratic counties.

Bush v. Gore Although Bush had been declared the winner in Florida, Gore's lawyers headed back to court arguing that thousands of ballots were still uncounted. The Florida Supreme Court ordered all Florida counties to begin a hand recount of ballots rejected by the counting machines. As counting began, the United States Supreme Court ordered the recount to stop until it had issued its ruling.

On December 12, in ***Bush v. Gore***, the United States Supreme Court ruled 7–2 that the hand recounts in Florida violated the equal protection clause of the Constitution. The Court argued that because different vote counters used different standards, the recount did not treat all voters equally. *(See page 1080 for more information on Bush v. Gore.)*

Both federal law and the Constitution require the electoral votes for president to be cast on a certain day. If Florida missed that deadline, its electoral votes would not count. The Court ruled 5–4 that there was not enough time left to conduct a manual recount that would pass constitutional standards. This ruling left Bush the certified winner in Florida. The next day, Gore conceded the election.

✓ **Reading Check** **Analyzing** Why did the U.S. Supreme Court stop the manual recounts in Florida?

Bush Becomes President

On January 20, 2001, George W. Bush became the 43rd president of the United States. In his inaugural address, Bush promised to improve the nation's public schools, to cut taxes, to reform Social Security and Medicare, and to build up the nation's defenses.

After taking office, the president's first priority was to cut taxes to try to boost the economy. During the election campaign, the economy had begun to slow. The stock market dropped sharply, and many new Internet-based companies went out of business. Many other businesses laid off thousands of workers. Despite opposition from some Democrats, Congress passed a large $1.35 trillion tax cut to be phased in over 10 years. In the summer of 2001, Americans began receiving tax rebate checks that put about $40 billion back into the economy in an effort to prevent a recession.

Soon after Congress passed the tax cut plan, President Bush proposed two major reforms in education. He wanted public schools to hold annual standardized tests, and he wanted to allow parents to use federal funds to pay for private schools if their public schools were doing a poor job. Although Congress refused to give federal funds to private schools, it did vote in favor of annual reading and math tests in public schools for grades 3–8.

President Bush also focused on Medicare reform. By the summer of 2002, Congress had introduced a bill adding prescription drug benefits to this health care program. The bill remained mired in controversy until it was finally passed in November 2003.

Congress also reacted to a rash of corporate scandals. For example, at one large energy trading company, Enron, corporate leaders cost investors and employees billions of dollars before the company went bankrupt. The federal government tightened accounting regulations and toughened penalties for dishonest executives.

Shortly after taking office, President Bush asked Secretary of Defense Donald Rumsfeld to conduct a comprehensive review of the nation's military. The president wanted to increase military spending, but he also wanted new military programs designed to meet the needs of the post–Cold War world.

One military program Bush strongly favored was strategic defense—the effort to develop missiles and other devices that could shoot down nuclear missiles. Bush argued that missile defense was needed because many unfriendly nations were developing the technology to build nuclear missiles.

As the debate about the nation's military programs continued in the summer of 2001, a horrific event changed everything. On September 11, 2001, terrorists crashed passenger jets into the World Trade Center and the Pentagon. A new war had begun.

✓ **Reading Check** **Explaining** What was President George W. Bush's first priority when he took office?

SECTION 4 ASSESSMENT

Checking for Understanding

1. **Define:** chad, strategic defense.
2. **Identify:** Al Gore, George W. Bush, Ralph Nader.
3. **Reviewing Facts** What did the Supreme Court decide in *Bush* v. *Gore?*

Reviewing Themes

4. **Government and Democracy** What caused the vote-count controversy in Florida in the 2000 election?

Critical Thinking

5. **Forming an Opinion** Do you think the 2000 presidential election was decided fairly? Why or why not?
6. **Organizing** Complete a graphic organizer similar to the one below by listing President Bush's goals when he took office.

Analyzing Visuals

7. **Interpreting Graphs** Study the graph on page 1027. By how many votes was Gore leading when news networks declared him the winner in Florida? What was Bush's lead when networks declared him to be the winner?

Writing About History

8. **Persuasive Writing** Take on the role of a Supreme Court justice. Write a statement explaining how you voted in *Bush* v. *Gore.*

Social Studies
SKILLBUILDER

Reading a Cartogram

Why Learn This Skill?

On most maps, land areas are drawn in proportion to their actual surface areas on the earth. On some maps, however, a small country may appear much larger than usual, and a large country may look much smaller. The shapes of the countries may also look different.

Learning the Skill

Maps that distort country size and shape are called **cartograms.** In a cartogram, country size reflects some value *other* than land area, such as population or gross national product. For example, on a conventional map, Canada appears much larger than India. In a cartogram showing world population, however, India would appear larger because it has a much larger population. The cartogram is a tool for making visual comparisons. At a glance, you can see how each country or region compares with another in a particular value.

To use a cartogram, first read the title and key to identify what value the cartogram illustrates. Then examine the cartogram to see which countries or regions appear. Find the largest and smallest countries. Compare the cartogram with a conventional land-area map to determine the degree of distortion of particular countries. Finally, draw conclusions about the topic.

Practicing the Skill

Study the cartogram shown on this page, and then answer these questions.

❶ What is the subject of the cartogram?

❷ Which region appears largest on the cartogram? Which appears smallest?

❸ Compare the cartogram to the map of the United States found in the Atlas. Which region is the most distorted in size compared to a land-area map?

❹ Provide a brief explanation for this distortion.

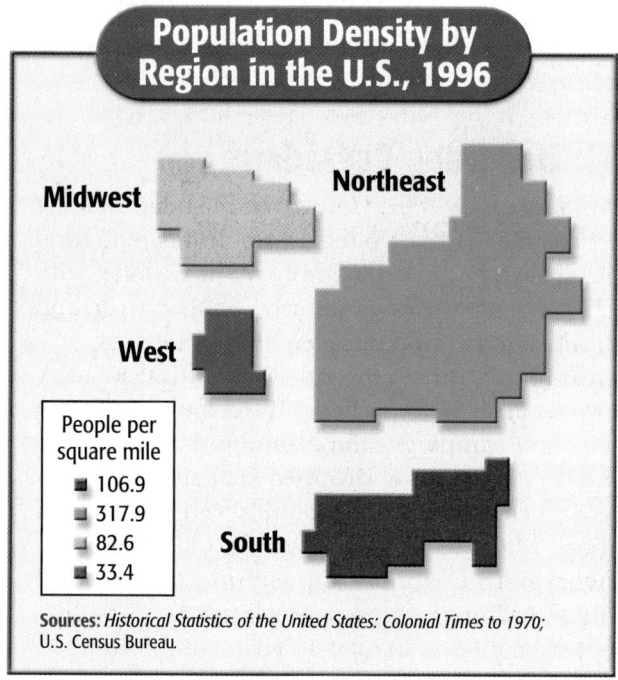

Population Density by Region in the U.S., 1996

Midwest Northeast

West

People per square mile
- 106.9
- 317.9
- 82.6
- 33.4

South

Sources: *Historical Statistics of the United States: Colonial Times to 1970;* U.S. Census Bureau.

Skills Assessment

Complete the Practicing Skills questions on page 1039 and the Chapter 34 Skill Reinforcement Activity to assess your mastery of this skill.

Applying the Skill

Reading a Cartogram Find statistics that compare some value for different states or countries. For example, you might compare the number of farms in each state or the annual oil consumption of countries on one continent. Be creative in your choice. Convert these statistics into a simple cartogram. Determine the relative size of each country or state according to the chosen value. For example, if the United States consumes five times more oil than Canada, then the United States should appear five times larger.

GO TO

Glencoe's **Skillbuilder Interactive Workbook CD-ROM, Level 2,** provides instruction and practice in key social studies skills.

The War on Terrorism

Main Idea

After suffering the worst terrorist attack in its history when airplanes crashed into the Pentagon and the World Trade Center, the United States launched a massive effort to end international terrorism.

Key Terms and Names

terrorism, state-sponsored terrorism, Osama bin Laden, al-Qaeda, anthrax

Reading Strategy

As you read about America's war on terrorism, complete a graphic organizer similar to the one below to show the different reasons terrorists attack Americans.

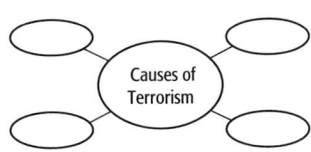

Causes of Terrorism

Reading Objectives

- **Describe** the development of Middle East terrorism.
- **Explain** the response of the United States to the terrorist attacks on the World Trade Center and the Pentagon.

Section Theme

Global Connections International terrorists targeted Americans in order to coerce the United States.

Preview of Events

◆1980	◆1990	◆2000

1979
Soviet Union invades Afghanistan

1988
Al-Qaeda is organized

1998
Bombs explode at U.S. embassies in Kenya and Tanzania

2001
Attacks on the Pentagon and World Trade Center

★ *An American Story* ★

At 8:45 A.M. Eastern Daylight Time on September 11, 2001, a Boeing 767 passenger jet slammed into the North Tower of the World Trade Center in New York City. As people below gazed in horror, a second plane collided with the South Tower. Soon afterward, a third plane crashed into the Pentagon in Washington, D.C. At 9:50 A.M., the South Tower collapsed in a billowing cloud of dust and debris. The North Tower fell about 40 minutes later. The falling towers killed thousands of people, burying them beneath a vast mound of rubble.

The airplanes did not crash accidentally. Hijackers deliberately crashed them into the buildings. Hijackers also seized a fourth airplane, United Airlines Flight 93, probably hoping to crash it into the White House or the Capitol. Many passengers on Flight 93 had cell phones. After hearing about the World Trade Center, four passengers—Todd Beamer, Thomas Burnett, Jeremy Glick, and Mark Bingham—decided to do something. An operator listening over a cell phone heard Todd Beamer's voice: "Are you ready, guys? Let's roll." Soon afterward, Flight 93 crashed in a field in Pennsylvania. At that moment, Vice President Dick Cheney was in a bunker under the White House. After hearing that Flight 93 had crashed, he said, "I think an act of heroism just took place on that plane."

—**adapted from** *Let's Roll: Ordinary People, Extraordinary Courage*

September 11, 2001

The terrorist attacks on September 11, 2001, killed all 266 passengers and crewmembers on the four hijacked planes. Another 125 people died in the Pentagon. In New York City, nearly 3,000 people died. More Americans were killed in the attacks than died at Pearl Harbor or on D-Day in World War II.

The attacks on the World Trade Center and the Pentagon were acts of terrorism. Terrorism is the use of violence by nongovernmental groups against civilians to achieve a political goal. Terrorist acts are intended to instill fear in people and to frighten their governments into changing their policies.

Middle East Terrorism Although there have been many acts of terrorism in American history, most terrorist attacks on Americans since World War II have been carried out by Middle Eastern groups. The reason Middle Eastern terrorists have targeted Americans can be traced back to events early in the twentieth century.

As oil became important to the American economy in the 1920s, the United States invested heavily in the Middle East oil industry. This industry brought great wealth to the ruling families in some Middle Eastern kingdoms, but most of the people remained poor. Some became angry at the United States for supporting the wealthy kingdoms and families.

The rise of the oil industry increased the Middle East's contact with Western society. As Western ideas spread through the region, many Muslims—followers of the region's dominant religion—feared that their traditional values and beliefs were being weakened. New movements arose calling for a strict interpretation of the Quran—the Muslim holy book—and a return to traditional Muslim religious laws.

These Muslim movements wanted to overthrow pro-Western governments in the Middle East and create a pure Islamic society. Muslims who support these movements are referred to as fundamentalist militants. Although the vast majority of Muslims believe terrorism is contrary to their faith, militants began using terrorism to achieve their goals.

American support of Israel also angered many in the Middle East. In 1947 the UN divided British-controlled Palestine into two territories to provide a home for Jews. One part became Israel. The other part was to become a Palestinian state, but fighting between Israel and the Arab states in 1948 left this territory under the control of Israel, Jordan, and Egypt.

The Palestinians wanted their own nation. In the 1950s, they began staging guerrilla raids and terrorist attacks against Israel. Since the United States gave military and economic aid to Israel, it became the target of Muslim hostility. In the 1970s, several Middle Eastern nations realized they could fight Israel and the United States by providing terrorist groups with money, weapons, and training. When a government secretly supports terrorism, this is called state-sponsored terrorism. The governments of Libya, Syria, Iraq, and Iran have all sponsored terrorism.

A New Terrorist Threat In 1979 the Soviet Union invaded Afghanistan. In response, Muslims from across the Middle East headed to Afghanistan to join the struggle against the Soviets. Among them was a 22-year-old Muslim named **Osama bin Laden.** Bin Laden came from one of Saudi Arabia's wealthiest families. He used his wealth to support the Afghan resistance. In 1988 he founded an organization called **al-Qaeda** (al KY·duh), or "the Base." Al-Qaeda recruited Muslims and channeled money and arms to the Afghan resistance.

Bin Laden's experience in Afghanistan convinced him that superpowers could be beaten. He also believed that Western ideas had contaminated Muslim society. He was outraged when Saudi Arabia allowed American troops on Saudi soil after Iraq invaded Kuwait.

Operating first from Sudan and then from Afghanistan—then under the control of Muslim fundamentalists known as the Taliban—bin Laden dedicated himself and al-Qaeda to driving Westerners, and especially Americans, out of the Middle East. In 1998 he called on Muslims to kill Americans. Soon afterward, bin Laden's followers set off bombs at the American embassies in Kenya and Tanzania. Over 200 people died in the attacks, including 12 Americans, and more than 5,400 were injured.

Shortly after these bombings, President Clinton ordered cruise missiles launched at terrorist facilities in Afghanistan and Sudan. The attacks did not deter bin Laden. In 1999 al-Qaeda terrorists were arrested while trying to smuggle explosives into the United States in an attempt to bomb Seattle. In October 2000, al-Qaeda terrorists crashed a boat loaded with explosives into the USS *Cole,* an American warship, while it was docked in the Middle Eastern country of Yemen.

✓ **Reading Check** **Explaining** What are the three main reasons certain Muslims became angry with the United States?

America Unites

The attack on the *Cole* and the attempted bombing of Seattle were overshadowed by the close presidential election of 2000 and the policies of President George W. Bush's new administration. Then, on September 11, 2001, terrorists struck again, hijacking four American passenger planes and executing the most devastating terrorist attack in history.

Citizens Respond to the Crisis The attacks on the World Trade Center and the Pentagon shocked Americans, but they responded rapidly to the crisis. Firefighters and medical workers from other cities headed to New York to help. Across the nation, Americans donated blood, raised money, and collected food, blankets, and other supplies. Within weeks, Americans had donated over one billion dollars. From around the world came sympathy. "We are all Americans!" wrote one French journalist.

Everywhere across the nation, Americans put up flags to show their unity and resolve. They held candlelight vigils and prayer services as they searched for ways to help. If the terrorists had hoped to divide Americans, they failed. As the Reverend Billy Graham noted at a memorial service: "A tragedy like this could have torn our country apart. But instead it has united us and we have become a family."

A National Emergency The American government also responded quickly. All civilian airliners were grounded. The armed forces were put on high alert. Americans in the National Guard left their civilian jobs and reported for duty. The Air National Guard began patrolling the skies over major cities, and

American Heroes

After two hijacked aircraft slammed into the twin towers of the World Trade Center on September 11, survivors in the building headed down smoky, dust-choked stairways to escape. Yet even as thousands of people streamed out of the buildings, hundreds more headed into the blazing structures, fully aware of the danger they faced.

The people climbing the staircases into the burning buildings were New York City firefighters and rescue workers. When the towers collapsed, over 300 firefighters died. The tragedy at the World Trade Center reminded everyone that these men and women who daily risk their lives to save others are true American heroes whose sacrifices must not be forgotten.

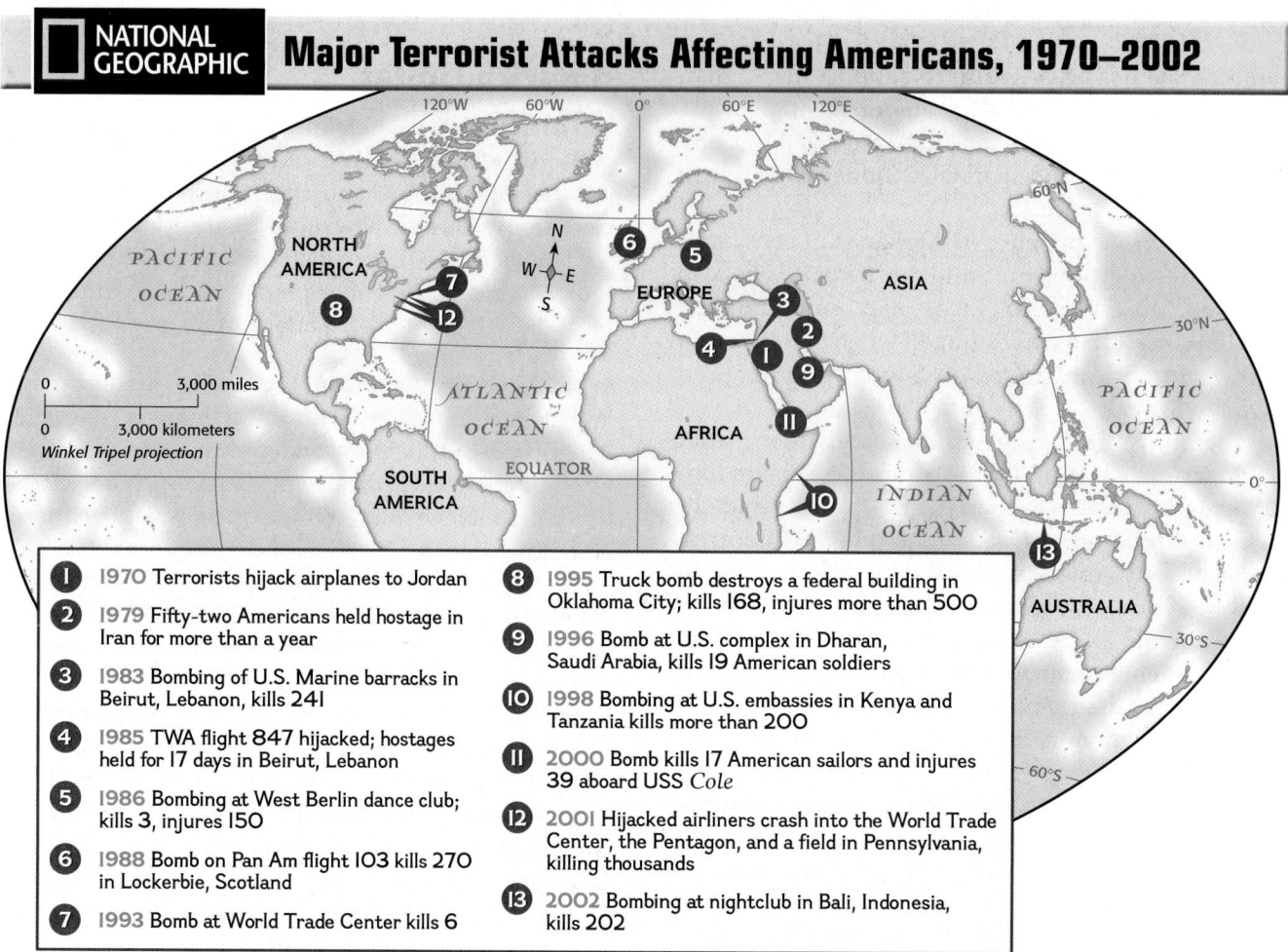

Major Terrorist Attacks Affecting Americans, 1970–2002

NATIONAL GEOGRAPHIC

① **1970** Terrorists hijack airplanes to Jordan

② **1979** Fifty-two Americans held hostage in Iran for more than a year

③ **1983** Bombing of U.S. Marine barracks in Beirut, Lebanon, kills 241

④ **1985** TWA flight 847 hijacked; hostages held for 17 days in Beirut, Lebanon

⑤ **1986** Bombing at West Berlin dance club; kills 3, injures 150

⑥ **1988** Bomb on Pan Am flight 103 kills 270 in Lockerbie, Scotland

⑦ **1993** Bomb at World Trade Center kills 6

⑧ **1995** Truck bomb destroys a federal building in Oklahoma City; kills 168, injures more than 500

⑨ **1996** Bomb at U.S. complex in Dharan, Saudi Arabia, kills 19 American soldiers

⑩ **1998** Bombing at U.S. embassies in Kenya and Tanzania kills more than 200

⑪ **2000** Bomb kills 17 American sailors and injures 39 aboard USS *Cole*

⑫ **2001** Hijacked airliners crash into the World Trade Center, the Pentagon, and a field in Pennsylvania, killing thousands

⑬ **2002** Bombing at nightclub in Bali, Indonesia, kills 202

Army National Guard troops headed to airports to strengthen security.

On September 14, President Bush declared a national emergency. Congress voted to authorize the use of force to fight the terrorists. Intelligence sources and the FBI quickly identified the attacks as the work of Osama bin Laden and the al-Qaeda network.

President Bush decided the time had come to end the threat of terrorism in the world. While Secretary of State Colin Powell began building an international coalition to support the United States, Secretary of Defense Donald Rumsfeld began deploying troops, aircraft, and warships to the Middle East.

The president then issued an ultimatum to the Taliban regime in Afghanistan, demanding they turn over bin Laden and his supporters and close all terrorist camps. He also declared that although the war on terrorism would start by targeting al-Qaeda, it would not stop there. "It will not end," he announced, "until every terrorist group of global reach has been found, stopped, and defeated."

The president also announced that the United States would no longer tolerate states that aided terrorists. "From this day forward," the president proclaimed, "any nation that continues to harbor or support terrorism will be regarded by the United States as a hostile regime." The war, President Bush warned, would not end quickly, but it was a war the nation had to fight:

> 66 Great harm has been done to us. We have suffered great loss. And in our grief and anger we have found our mission and our moment. . . . Our Nation—this generation—will lift a dark threat of violence from our people and our future. . . . 99
>
> —President George W. Bush, Address to Joint Session of Congress, September 20, 2001

✔ **Reading Check** **Explaining** How did American citizens respond to the terrorist attacks?

A New War Begins

In a letter to the *New York Times*, Secretary of Defense Rumsfeld warned Americans that "this will be a war like none other our nation has faced." The enemy, he explained, "is a global network of terrorist organizations and their state sponsors, committed to denying free people the opportunity to live as they choose." Military force would be used to fight terrorism, but other means would be used as well.

Cutting Terrorist Funding

One important way to fight terrorist organizations is to cut off their funding. On September 24, President Bush issued an executive order freezing the financial assets of several individuals and groups suspected of terrorism. The president also asked other nations to help, and within weeks, some 80 nations had issued orders freezing the assets of suspected terrorists.

Fighting Terrorism At Home

As part of his effort to protect the American people from further terrorist attacks, President Bush created the Office of Homeland Security to coordinate the dozens of federal agencies working to prevent terrorism. He then appointed Pennsylvania governor Tom Ridge to serve as the agency's director.

The president also asked Congress to pass legislation to help law enforcement agencies track down terrorist suspects. Drafting the legislation took time. Congress had to balance Americans' Fourth Amendment protections against unreasonable search and seizure with the need to increase security.

President Bush signed the new antiterrorist bill—known as the USA Patriot Act—into law in October 2001. The new law allowed secret searches to avoid tipping off suspects in terrorism cases. It also allowed authorities to obtain a single nationwide search warrant that could be used anywhere. The law also made it easier to wiretap suspects, and it allowed authorities to track e-mail and seize voice mail.

In the months following the attack, the Office of Homeland Security found it difficult to coordinate all of the federal agencies fighting terrorism. In June 2002, President Bush asked Congress to merge the agencies responsible for the public's safety into one department to be called the Department of Homeland Security.

The president's proposal led to an intense debate in Congress, but after the midterm elections in November 2002, the new department was created. It controls the Coast Guard, the Border Patrol, the Immigration and Naturalization Service, the Customs Service, the Federal Emergency Management Agency, and many other agencies.

Bioterrorism Strikes America

As the nation tried to cope with the events of September 11, a new terrorist attack began. On October 5, 2001, a Florida newspaper editor died from anthrax. **Anthrax** is a type of bacteria. Several nations, including the United States, Russia, and Iraq, have used it to create biological weapons. Antibiotics can cure anthrax, but if left untreated, it can kill quickly.

Soon after appearing in Florida, anthrax was found at several news organizations in New York City. In Washington, D.C., a letter filled with anthrax arrived at Senator Tom Daschle's office. It became clear that terrorists were using the mail to spread anthrax. Several postal workers contracted anthrax, and two died. The FBI investigated the anthrax attacks, but no suspects were publicly identified.

War in Afghanistan

On October 7, 2001, the United States began bombing targets in Afghanistan. In an

Airport Security Airline passengers, such as these at Denver International Airport, had to wait in long lines to go through checkpoints when American airports increased security measures after the terrorist attacks of 9/11.

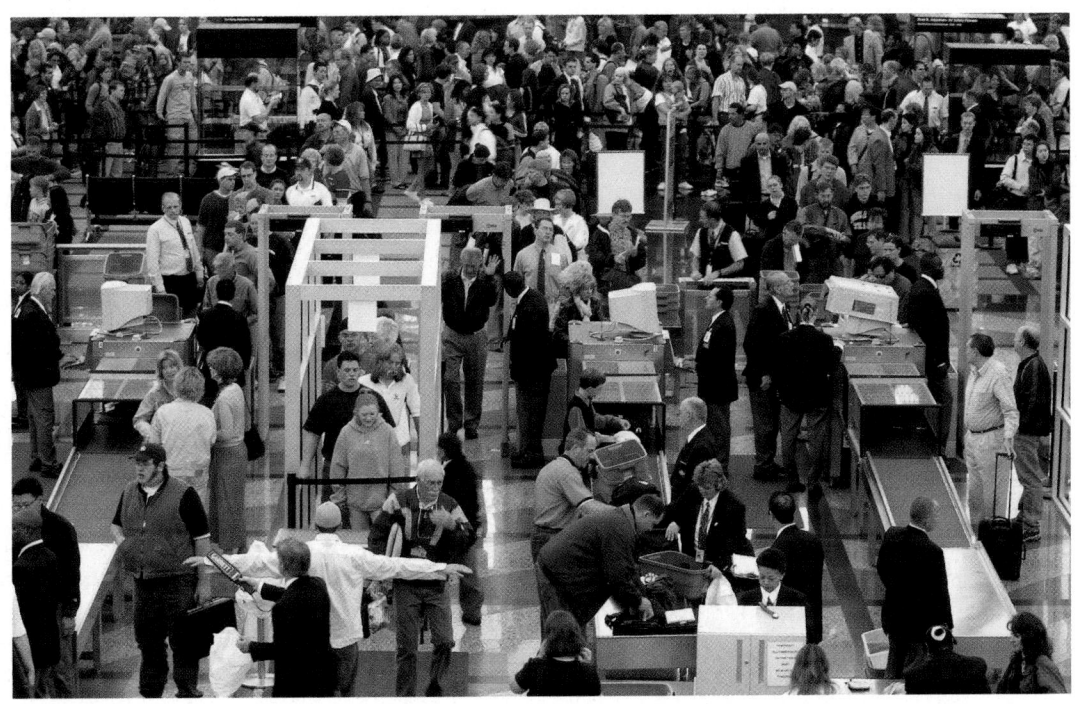

address to the nation, President Bush explained that he had ordered the military to attack al-Qaeda's camps and the Taliban's military forces. He explained that Islam and the Afghan people were not the enemy, and he announced that the United States would drop food, medicine, and other supplies by parachute to Afghan refugees. The president also explained that the attack on the Taliban was only the beginning:

> 66 Today we focus on Afghanistan, but the battle is broader. If any government sponsors the outlaws and killers of innocents, they have become outlaws and murderers, themselves. And they will take that lonely path at their own peril. . . . The battle is now joined on many fronts. We will not waver; we will not tire; we will not falter; and we will not fail. Peace and freedom will prevail. 99
>
> —President George W. Bush, Address to the Nation, October 7, 2001

While American warplanes bombed the Taliban's forces, the United States began sending aid to a coalition of Afghan groups, known as the Northern Alliance, that had been fighting the Taliban. The American bombing campaign quickly shattered the Taliban's defenses. The Northern Alliance then launched a massive attack on Taliban lines. By early December, the Taliban regime had collapsed. The United States and its allies then helped Afghan leaders create a new government, and they promised more than $4 billion in aid. Meanwhile, thousands of American and allied troops began arriving in Afghanistan to act as peacekeepers and to hunt for al-Qaeda terrorists.

By March 2002, Taliban and al-Qaeda forces had begun to regroup in the mountains near Pakistan's border. The United States responded by launching Operation Anaconda. Several Americans died during the difficult battle high in the mountains, but the al-Qaeda troops were defeated and forced to scatter. Throughout 2002, the United States and its allies continued their worldwide hunt for al-Qaeda members.

The Axis of Evil
The attacks of September 11, 2001, created fear that groups such as al-Qaeda might acquire nuclear, chemical, or biological weapons. These **weapons of mass destruction** could kill tens of thousands of people all at once.

In his state of the union speech in January 2002, President Bush warned that an "axis of evil," made up of Iraq, Iran, and North Korea, posed a grave threat to the world. Each of these countries had been known to sponsor terrorism and was suspected of trying to

develop weapons of mass destruction. The president promised to take strong action: "The United States of America will not permit the world's most dangerous regimes to threaten us with the world's most destructive weapons."

Danger From North Korea
In October 2002, North Korea announced that it had restarted its nuclear weapons program. The Bush administration tried to use diplomatic pressure to persuade the North Korean government to stop the program. The North Koreans, however, argued that they needed the weapons to protect themselves from a U.S. attack.

✓ **Reading Check** **Outlining** What steps did the president take in response to the terrorist attacks?

Confronting Iraq

President Bush considered Iraq a more immediate threat than North Korea in developing and distributing weapons of mass destruction. Iraq's dictator, Saddam Hussein, had already used chemical weapons twice, once in Iraq's war against Iran in the 1980s and again in 1988 against the Kurds, an ethnic minority in northern Iraq who had rebelled against Hussein's regime. After the Gulf War in 1991, UN inspectors found evidence that Iraq had developed biological weapons and was working on a nuclear bomb.

In the summer of 2002, President Bush increased pressure on Iraq, calling for a regime change in the country. At the urging of Secretary of State Colin Powell, Bush tried to gain UN support for a war against Iraq. On September 12, he asked for a new resolution demanding that Iraq give up weapons of mass destruction. He made it clear, though, that the United States would act with or without UN support.

The 2002 Election
While the UN Security Council began debating a new resolution on Iraq, President Bush asked Congress to authorize the use of force against Iraq. With the midterm elections only weeks away, many Democrats instead wanted to focus on the economy. The economy was growing very slowly, unemployment was high, and stock prices remained low. Democrats believed that the poor economy would enable them to pick up seats in Congress in the elections.

In mid-October, Congress voted to authorize the use of force against Iraq. The Democrats hoped that people would now turn to the economy. President Bush, however, successfully kept the focus on national security issues. In 2002 Republicans picked up seats in the House of Representatives and regained control of the Senate.

War and Its Aftermath Soon after the elections, the United Nations approved a new resolution that set a deadline for Iraq to readmit weapons inspectors. It required Iraq to declare all of its weapons of mass destruction, to stop supporting terrorism, and to stop oppressing its people. The resolution threatened "serious consequences" if Iraq did not comply.

Weapons inspectors returned to Iraq, but some Americans doubted their effectiveness. The Bush administration argued that the Iraqis were still hiding weapons of mass destruction that were ready or nearly ready to use. Others had more confidence in the inspection process and wanted to give the inspectors more time. In the UN Security Council, the Bush administration pushed for a resolution for war. France and Russia, two permanent members of the Council with veto power, refused to back such a resolution immediately. The United States and Great Britain, with the support of about 30 other countries, prepared for war as millions of people around the world participated in antiwar protests.

On March 20, 2003, the U.S.-led coalition forces attacked Iraq. Over the next six weeks, much of the

War in Iraq On April 9, 2003, just three weeks after the war in Iraq began, American troops reached the capital of Baghdad and helped Iraqis tear down a statue of former dictator Saddam Hussein.

Iraqi army dissolved as soldiers refused to risk their lives for Hussein. The coalition forces quickly seized control of the country, and on May 1, President Bush declared that the major combat was over. About 140 Americans, and several thousand Iraqis, had died. Saddam Hussein, though, was not captured until mid-December 2003.

The controversy over Iraq continued, however, as did the fighting. By December 2003, Americans had found no evidence that Iraq possessed weapons of mass destruction. While many Iraqis welcomed American troops, others did not. Bombings, sniper attacks, and sporadic battles plagued American soldiers. In fact, more Americans died after May 1 than had died in the six weeks of major combat. As American deaths and expenses mounted, President Bush began to seek support from the UN and other countries to help stabilize and rebuild Iraq. "Iraqi democracy will succeed," President Bush insisted, "and that success will send forth the news, from Damascus to Tehran, that freedom can be the future of every nation."

✓ **Reading Check** **Summarizing** Why did President Bush decide to confront Iraq?

SECTION 5 ASSESSMENT

Checking for Understanding

1. **Define:** terrorism, state-sponsored terrorism.
2. **Identify:** Osama bin Laden, al-Qaeda, anthrax.
3. **Explain** how the United States responded to the attacks on New York City and Washington, D.C.

Reviewing Themes

4. **Global Connections** Why does American foreign policy anger Islamic fundamentalists in the Middle East?

Critical Thinking

5. **Interpreting** What factors have contributed to the rise of Middle Eastern terrorist groups?
6. **Organizing** Use a graphic organizer similar to the one below to list the reasons why President Bush declared war on Iraq.

```
_____  \
_____   \
_____ ——— War on Iraq
_____   /
_____  /
```

Analyzing Visuals

7. **Examining Maps** Study the map on page 1034 of terrorist attacks. In what region of the world did most of the attacks take place?

Writing About History

8. **Persuasive Writing** The attacks on New York City and Washington, D.C., convinced many Americans that more security was needed, even if it meant giving up some freedoms. Write a letter to a newspaper explaining why you are for or against increased security.

Reviewing Key Terms

On a sheet of paper, use each of these terms in a sentence.

1. microprocessor
2. software
3. telecommute
4. Internet
5. perjury
6. ethnic cleansing
7. trade deficit
8. euro
9. nuclear proliferation
10. global warming
11. chad
12. strategic defense
13. terrorism
14. state-sponsored terrorism

Reviewing Key Facts

15. **Identify:** ENIAC, Silicon Valley, AmeriCorps, Contract with America, Kenneth Starr, NAFTA, Kyoto Protocol, Al Gore, George W. Bush, Ralph Nader, Osama bin Laden, al-Qaeda.

16. How did compact computers transform the workplace?

17. What advances in biotechnology occurred in the 1990s?

18. After his election in 1992, how did President Clinton propose to strengthen the nation's economy?

19. What regional trade blocs were formed in the 1990s to increase international trade?

20. Which state was significant in the 2000 presidential election?

Critical Thinking

21. **Analyzing Themes: Global Connections** What foreign-policy challenges did President Clinton face? Do you think he handled the situations effectively? Why or why not?

22. **Evaluating** What developments in the Middle East explain the rise of terrorist groups that want to attack Americans?

23. **Analyzing Points of View** Read the excerpt below about global warming, and then answer the questions that follow.

❝The world is getting warmer, and by the end of the 21st century could warm by another 6 degrees Celsius (10.8 degrees Fahrenheit). . . . And climate scientists at the heart of the research are now convinced that human action is to blame for some or most of this warming. . . .

Everywhere climatologists look—at tree-ring patterns, fossil successions in rock strata, ocean-floor corings . . . they see evidence of dramatic shifts from cold to hot to cold again. . . . None of these ancient shifts can be blamed on humans. . . . There is still room for argument about the precise role of the sun or other natural cycles in the contribution to global warming. . . . Richard S. Lindzen, a leading meteorologist at the Massachusetts Institute of Technology said . . . the picture of a consensus about global warming was 'misleading to the public and even to scientists. . . .' But most climate scientists . . . now believe that the climate is being influenced by human beings.❞

—from *World Press Review,* February 2001

a. According to the article, what two points of view exist about global warming?

b. Why is the debate on global warming important?

Chapter Summary

The Technological Revolution

- Personal computers grow faster and more powerful.
- Communications deregulation expands cellular phone usage.
- The Internet provides a worldwide network of information.
- Biotechnology research increases knowledge of human genetics.

The Clinton Years

- A new global economy emerges based on regional trade blocs.
- The ozone layer and global warming become major environmental issues.
- Clinton and Congress cut spending; reform welfare and health care.
- U.S. economy grows rapidly; federal budget is balanced.
- U.S. tries to end violence in Haiti, the Middle East, and the Balkans.
- Scandal and impeachment tarnish the Clinton administration.

Bush Takes Office

- 2000 election results disputed in Florida; Supreme Court resolves dispute; George W. Bush becomes president.
- Bush focuses on cutting taxes, reforming education, and working on energy problems.
- Terrorists destroy the World Trade Center and attack the Pentagon.
- Bush organizes a global coalition and launches a new war on terrorism.
- War in Iraq ends the regime of Saddam Hussein.

24. Categorizing Complete the graphic organizer below by listing changes in communications, politics, the economy, and population that occurred in the United States by the end of the 1900s.

	Change
Communications	
Politics	
Economy	
Population	

Practicing Skills

25. Reading a Cartogram Create a cartogram that reflects the importance of each state in the Electoral College. Research the number of votes held by each state, and alter the size of each state to roughly show that state's number of available votes. Create questions that refer to the information you present in your cartogram.

Chapter Activities

26. Applying Chronology Skills Absolute chronology refers to specific dates, while relative chronology looks at when something occurred with reference to when other things occurred. Practice relative chronology by listing the presidents of the twentieth century in the order they served as president. Then practice absolute chronology by giving the dates of their terms in office.

27. Researching Election Results Study the 2000 election map and chart on page 1028. Then use library or Internet resources to research statistics on the 1996 presidential election. Using the 2000 election map and chart as a guide, create a similar thematic map and chart of the 1996 election. Create questions about your map and chart that would help a classmate understand the data you have compiled.

Writing Activity

28. Informative Writing Research the changing roles of the federal and state governments as a result of recent legislative reforms, including gun control and welfare reforms. Based on your research, write a short paper predicting how the role of the federal government and the state governments might change in order to implement the legislative programs. Present your predictions to the class.

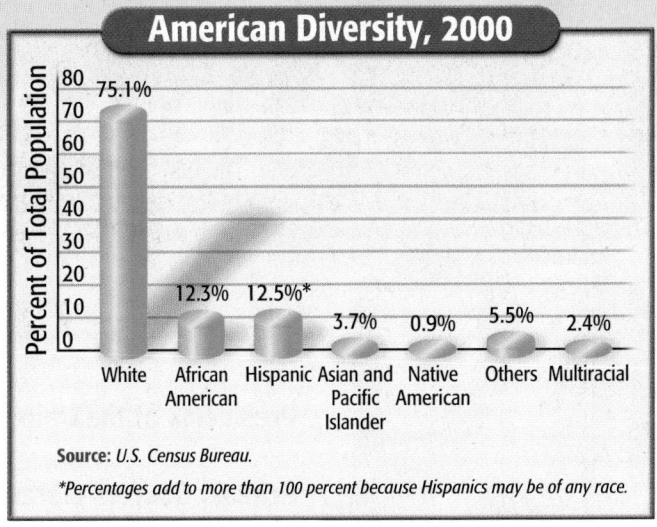

American Diversity, 2000

Percent of Total Population

White 75.1% · African American 12.3% · Hispanic 12.5%* · Asian and Pacific Islander 3.7% · Native American 0.9% · Others 5.5% · Multiracial 2.4%

Source: *U.S. Census Bureau.*

Percentages add to more than 100 percent because Hispanics may be of any race.

Geography and History

29. The graph above shows the diverse population of the United States at the beginning of the new century. Study the graph and answer the questions below.
   a. Interpreting Graphs Why is getting accurate data on the Hispanic population difficult?
   b. Making Generalizations How will population diversity affect government in the future?

Standardized Test Practice

Directions: Choose the phrase that best completes the following sentence.

The Contract with America involved

F a commitment by Russia to eliminate land-based nuclear weapons.

G a campaign promise by President Clinton to create a national health care system for all Americans.

H a legislative agenda promoted by the Republican Party in 1994.

J programs intended to increase the size and readiness of the military.

Test-Taking Tip: This question requires that you remember details of a specific program. Use the process of elimination if you are unsure. Does the Contract with America sound like a foreign policy agreement between two countries?

Appendix

Contents

Presidents of the United States 1041

Primary Sources Library 1046

Documents of American History 1058

Supreme Court Case Summaries 1080

Flag Etiquette 1084

Glossary 1085

Spanish Glossary 1095

Index 1107

Acknowledgments and Photo Credits 1135

Presidents of the United States

In this resource you will find portraits of the individuals who served as presidents of the United States, along with their occupations, political party affiliations, and other interesting facts.

**The Republican Party during this period developed into today's Democratic Party. Today's Republican Party originated in 1854.

1 George Washington

Presidential term: 1789–1797
Lived: 1732–1799
Born in: Virginia
Elected from: Virginia
Occupations: Soldier, Planter
Party: None
Vice President: John Adams

2 John Adams

Presidential term: 1797–1801
Lived: 1735–1826
Born in: Massachusetts
Elected from: Massachusetts
Occupations: Teacher, Lawyer
Party: Federalist
Vice President: Thomas Jefferson

3 Thomas Jefferson

Presidential term: 1801–1809
Lived: 1743–1826
Born in: Virginia
Elected from: Virginia
Occupations: Planter, Lawyer
Party: Republican**
Vice Presidents: Aaron Burr, George Clinton

4 James Madison

Presidential term: 1809–1817
Lived: 1751–1836
Born in: Virginia
Elected from: Virginia
Occupation: Planter
Party: Republican**
Vice Presidents: George Clinton, Elbridge Gerry

5 James Monroe

Presidential term: 1817–1825
Lived: 1758–1831
Born in: Virginia
Elected from: Virginia
Occupation: Lawyer
Party: Republican**
Vice President: Daniel D. Tompkins

6 John Quincy Adams

Presidential term: 1825–1829
Lived: 1767–1848
Born in: Massachusetts
Elected from: Massachusetts
Occupation: Lawyer
Party: Republican**
Vice President: John C. Calhoun

7 Andrew Jackson

Presidential term: 1829–1837
Lived: 1767–1845
Born in: South Carolina
Elected from: Tennessee
Occupations: Lawyer, Soldier
Party: Democratic
Vice Presidents: John C. Calhoun, Martin Van Buren

8 Martin Van Buren

Presidential term: 1837–1841
Lived: 1782–1862
Born in: New York
Elected from: New York
Occupation: Lawyer
Party: Democratic
Vice President: Richard M. Johnson

9 William H. Harrison

Presidential term: 1841
Lived: 1773–1841
Born in: Virginia
Elected from: Ohio
Occupations: Soldier, Planter
Party: Whig
Vice President: John Tyler

10 John Tyler

Presidential term: 1841–1845
Lived: 1790–1862
Born in: Virginia
Elected as V.P. from: Virginia
Succeeded Harrison
Occupation: Lawyer
Party: Whig
Vice President: None

11 James K. Polk

Presidential term: 1845–1849
Lived: 1795–1849
Born in: North Carolina
Elected from: Tennessee
Occupation: Lawyer
Party: Democratic
Vice President: George M. Dallas

12 Zachary Taylor

Presidential term: 1849–1850
Lived: 1784–1850
Born in: Virginia
Elected from: Louisiana
Occupation: Soldier
Party: Whig
Vice President: Millard Fillmore

13 Millard Fillmore

Presidential term: 1850–1853
Lived: 1800–1874
Born in: New York
Elected as V.P. from: New York
Succeeded Taylor
Occupation: Lawyer
Party: Whig
Vice President: None

14 Franklin Pierce

Presidential term: 1853–1857
Lived: 1804–1869
Born in: New Hampshire
Elected from: New Hampshire
Occupation: Lawyer
Party: Democratic
Vice President: William R. King

15 James Buchanan

Presidential term: 1857–1861
Lived: 1791–1868
Born in: Pennsylvania
Elected from: Pennsylvania
Occupation: Lawyer
Party: Democratic
Vice President: John C. Breckinridge

16 Abraham Lincoln

Presidential term: 1861–1865
Lived: 1809–1865
Born in: Kentucky
Elected from: Illinois
Occupation: Lawyer
Party: Republican
Vice Presidents: Hannibal Hamlin, Andrew Johnson

17 Andrew Johnson

Presidential term: 1865–1869
Lived: 1808–1875
Born in: North Carolina
Elected as V.P. from: Tennessee
Succeeded Lincoln
Occupation: Tailor
Party: Republican
Vice President: None

18 Ulysses S. Grant

Presidential term: 1869–1877
Lived: 1822–1885
Born in: Ohio
Elected from: Illinois
Occupations: Farmer, Soldier
Party: Republican
Vice Presidents: Schuyler Colfax,
Henry Wilson

19 Rutherford B. Hayes

Presidential term: 1877–1881
Lived: 1822–1893
Born in: Ohio
Elected from: Ohio
Occupation: Lawyer
Party: Republican
Vice President: William A.
Wheeler

20 James A. Garfield

Presidential term: 1881
Lived: 1831–1881
Born in: Ohio
Elected from: Ohio
Occupations: Laborer, Professor
Party: Republican
Vice President: Chester A.
Arthur

21 Chester A. Arthur

Presidential term: 1881–1885
Lived: 1830–1886
Born in: Vermont
Elected as V.P. from: New York
Succeeded Garfield
Occupations: Teacher, Lawyer
Party: Republican
Vice President: None

22 Grover Cleveland

Presidential term: 1885–1889
Lived: 1837–1908
Born in: New Jersey
Elected from: New York
Occupation: Lawyer
Party: Democratic
Vice President: Thomas A.
Hendricks

23 Benjamin Harrison

Presidential term: 1889–1893
Lived: 1833–1901
Born in: Ohio
Elected from: Indiana
Occupation: Lawyer
Party: Republican
Vice President: Levi P. Morton

24 Grover Cleveland

Presidential term: 1893–1897
Lived: 1837–1908
Born in: New Jersey
Elected from: New York
Occupation: Lawyer
Party: Democratic
Vice President: Adlai E.
Stevenson

25 William McKinley

Presidential term: 1897–1901
Lived: 1843–1901
Born in: Ohio
Elected from: Ohio
Occupations: Teacher, Lawyer
Party: Republican
Vice Presidents: Garret Hobart,
Theodore Roosevelt

26 Theodore Roosevelt

Presidential term: 1901–1909
Lived: 1858–1919
Born in: New York
Elected as V.P. from: New York
Succeeded McKinley
Occupations: Historian, Rancher
Party: Republican
Vice President: Charles W. Fairbanks

27 William H. Taft

Presidential term: 1909–1913
Lived: 1857–1930
Born in: Ohio
Elected from: Ohio
Occupation: Lawyer
Party: Republican
Vice President: James S. Sherman

28 Woodrow Wilson

Presidential term: 1913–1921
Lived: 1856–1924
Born in: Virginia
Elected from: New Jersey
Occupation: College Professor
Party: Democratic
Vice President: Thomas R. Marshall

29 Warren G. Harding

Presidential term: 1921–1923
Lived: 1865–1923
Born in: Ohio
Elected from: Ohio
Occupations: Newspaper Editor, Publisher
Party: Republican
Vice President: Calvin Coolidge

30 Calvin Coolidge

Presidential term: 1923–1929
Lived: 1872–1933
Born in: Vermont
Elected as V.P. from: Massachusetts
Succeeded Harding
Occupation: Lawyer
Party: Republican
Vice President: Charles G. Dawes

31 Herbert C. Hoover

Presidential term: 1929–1933
Lived: 1874–1964
Born in: Iowa
Elected from: California
Occupation: Engineer
Party: Republican
Vice President: Charles Curtis

32 Franklin D. Roosevelt

Presidential term: 1933–1945
Lived: 1882–1945
Born in: New York
Elected from: New York
Occupation: Lawyer
Party: Democratic
Vice Presidents: John N. Garner, Henry A. Wallace, Harry S Truman

33 Harry S Truman

Presidential term: 1945–1953
Lived: 1884–1972
Born in: Missouri
Elected as V.P. from: Missouri
Succeeded Roosevelt
Occupations: Clerk, Farmer
Party: Democratic
Vice President: Alben W. Barkley

34 Dwight D. Eisenhower

Presidential term: 1953–1961
Lived: 1890–1969
Born in: Texas
Elected from: New York
Occupation: Soldier
Party: Republican
Vice President: Richard M. Nixon

35 John F. Kennedy

Presidential term: 1961–1963
Lived: 1917–1963
Born in: Massachusetts
Elected from: Massachusetts
Occupations: Author, Reporter
Party: Democratic
Vice President: Lyndon B. Johnson

36 Lyndon B. Johnson

Presidential term: 1963–1969
Lived: 1908–1973
Born in: Texas
Elected as V.P. from: Texas
Succeeded Kennedy
Occupation: Teacher
Party: Democratic
Vice President: Hubert H. Humphrey

37 Richard M. Nixon

Presidential term: 1969–1974
Lived: 1913–1994
Born in: California
Elected from: New York
Occupation: Lawyer
Party: Republican
Vice Presidents: Spiro T. Agnew, Gerald R. Ford

38 Gerald R. Ford

Presidential term: 1974–1977
Lived: 1913–
Born in: Nebraska
Appointed as V.P. upon Agnew's resignation; succeeded Nixon
Occupation: Lawyer
Party: Republican
Vice President: Nelson A. Rockefeller

39 James E. Carter, Jr.

Presidential term: 1977–1981
Lived: 1924–
Born in: Georgia
Elected from: Georgia
Occupations: Business, Farmer
Party: Democratic
Vice President: Walter F. Mondale

40 Ronald W. Reagan

Presidential term: 1981–1989
Lived: 1911–2004
Born in: Illinois
Elected from: California
Occupations: Actor, Lecturer
Party: Republican
Vice President: George H.W. Bush

41 George H.W. Bush

Presidential term: 1989–1993
Lived: 1924–
Born in: Massachusetts
Elected from: Texas
Occupation: Business
Party: Republican
Vice President: J. Danforth Quayle

42 William J. Clinton

Presidential term: 1993–2001
Lived: 1946–
Born in: Arkansas
Elected from: Arkansas
Occupation: Lawyer
Party: Democratic
Vice President: Albert Gore, Jr.

43 George W. Bush

Presidential term: 2001–
Lived: 1946–
Born in: Connecticut
Elected from: Texas
Occupation: Business
Party: Republican
Vice President: Richard B. Cheney

U.S. Presidents

Primary Sources Library

TABLE OF CONTENTS

Letter of Don Antonio de Otermin
on Popé's Revolt in 1680 1048–1049

Patrick Henry's "Give Me Liberty
or Give Me Death" 1049

John O'Sullivan on Manifest Destiny 1050

"Battle Cry of Freedom" 1051

Willa Cather's *My Ántonia* 1052

Andrew Carnegie's "Gospel of Wealth" 1053

John Steinbeck's *The Grapes of Wrath* 1054

Georgia O'Keeffe's *Oriental Poppies* 1055

Audie Murphy's "Alone and Far Removed" . . .1055

"Letter from a Birmingham Jail"
by Martin Luther King, Jr. 1056–1057

Elva Trevino Hart's *Barefoot Heart* 1057

Using Primary Sources

Primary sources are written or artistic testimony to an era in history or to an important development. They can also be objects of daily life, reflecting how people lived and thought at a certain time. Perhaps a primary source represents the ideas of an industrial leader like Andrew Carnegie, who helped shape the American economy. Perhaps the source is a soldier's poem or the autobiography of a migrant worker.

Reading primary sources is important because it is an excellent way to understand how and why people believed and acted as they did in the past. While many people might have written down their stories or beliefs, the sources chosen here are from witnesses who were close to events or especially sensitive to them.

Opera glasses, late 1800s

Checking Your Sources

When you read primary or secondary sources, you should analyze them to figure out if they are dependable or reliable. Historians usually prefer primary sources to secondary sources, but both can be reliable or unreliable, depending on the following factors.

Time Span

With primary sources, it is important to consider how long after the event occurred the primary source was written. Generally, the longer the time span between the event and the account, the less reliable the account. As time passes, people often forget details and fill in gaps with events that never took place. Although we like to think we remember things exactly as they happened, the fact is we often remember them as we wanted them to occur.

Reliability

Another factor to consider when evaluating a primary source is the writer's background and reliability. First, try to determine how this person knows about what he or she is writing. How much does he or she know? Is the writer being truthful? Is the account convincing?

Opinions

When evaluating a primary source, you should also decide whether the account has been influenced by emotion, opinion, or exaggeration. Writers can have reasons to distort the truth to suit their personal purposes. Ask yourself: Why did the person write the account? Do any key words or expressions reveal the author's emotions or opinions? You may wish to compare the account with one written by another witness to the event. If the two accounts differ, ask yourself why.

Interpreting Primary Sources

To help you analyze a primary source, use the following steps:

- **Examine the origins of the document.**
  You need to determine if it is a primary source.

- **Find the main ideas.**
  Read the document and summarize the main ideas in your own words. These ideas may be fairly easy to identify in newspapers and journals, for example, but are much more difficult to find in poetry.

- **Reread the document.**
  Difficult ideas are not always easily understood on the first reading.

- **Use a variety of resources.**
  Form the habit of using dictionaries, encyclopedias, and maps. These resources are tools to help you discover new ideas and knowledge, and they can be used to check the validity of various sources.

Log book from Lewis and Clark expedition

Classifying Primary Sources

Primary sources fall into different categories:

Printed publications include books such as biographies and autobiographies. Printed publications also include newspapers and magazines.

Songs and poems include works that express personal thoughts and feelings or political or religious beliefs of the writer, often using rhyming and rhythmic language.

Visual materials include a wide range of forms: original paintings, drawings, and sculpture; photographs; film; and maps.

Oral history collects spoken memories and personal observations through recorded interviews. In contrast, oral tradition involves stories that people have passed along by word of mouth from generation to generation.

Personal records are accounts of events kept by an individual who is a participant in or witness to these events. Personal records include diaries, journals, and letters.

Artifacts are objects such as tools or ornaments. Artifacts present information about a particular culture or a stage of technological development.

From the Beginnings to American Nationhood

Europeans arriving in the Americas fought with Native Americans for control of the continent, just as British colonists later fought against the British government for their rights.

The first excerpt tells the story of the Pueblo people's revolt against their colonial Spanish rulers in what is today the American Southwest. Catholic missionaries had been trying to suppress the Pueblo religion. In 1680 a religious leader named Popé led a revolt which drove the Spanish from the region for a dozen years. The letter from the colonial governor asks for relief forces to be sent.

The second excerpt is from a speech of Patrick Henry (1736–1799). A lawyer by profession, Henry was already known for his eloquence from speeches in the Virginia House of Burgesses. He delivered this passionate plea at the second Virginia convention during a debate over whether to resist the British by force of arms.

Reader's Dictionary

don: honorary title for Spanish nobleman or gentleman

lamentable: sad; tragic

comport: to behave in a proper way

extenuate: to make excuses for or try to justify

Letter of Don Antonio de Otermin on Popé's revolt in 1680

My very reverend Father, Sir, and friend, most beloved Fray Francisco de Ayeta:

The time has come when, with tears in my eyes and deep sorrow in my heart, I commence to give an account of the lamentable tragedy, such as has never before happened in the world. . . .

On Tuesday, the 13th of the said month, at about nine o'clock in the morning, there came in sight of us in the suburb of Analco . . . all the Indians of the Tanos and Pecos nations and the Queres of San Marcos, armed and giving war whoops. As I learned that one of the Indians who was leading them was from the villa and had gone to join them shortly before, I sent some soldiers to summon him and tell him on my behalf that he could come to see me in entire safety, so that I might ascertain from him the purpose for which they were coming. Upon receiving this message he came to where I was, and . . . I asked him how it was that he had gone crazy too—being an Indian who spoke our language, was so intelligent, and had lived all his life in the villa among the Spaniards, where I had placed such confidence in him—and was now coming as a leader of the Indian rebels. He replied to me that they had elected him as their captain, and that they were carrying two banners, one white and the other red, and that the white one signified peace and the red one war. Thus if we wished to choose the white it must be upon our agreeing to leave the country, and if we chose the red, we must perish, because the rebels were numerous and we were very few;

Stone cross

Patrick Henry giving his speech in 1775

"Give Me Liberty or Give Me Death" by Patrick Henry (1775)

there was no alternative, inasmuch as they had killed so many religious and Spaniards.

On hearing this reply, I spoke to him very persuasively, to the effect that he and the rest of his followers were Catholic Christians, asking how they expected to live without the religious; and said that even though they had committed so many atrocities, still there was a remedy, for if they would return to obedience to his Majesty they would be pardoned; and that thus he should go back to this people and tell them in my name all that had been said to him, and persuade them to agree to it and to withdraw from where they were; and that he was to advise me of what they might reply. He came back . . . after a short time, saying that his people asked that all classes of Indians who were in our power be given up to them, both those in the service of the Spaniards and those of the Mexican nation of that suburb of Analco. He demanded also that his wife and children be given up to him, and likewise that all the Apache men and women whom the Spaniards had captured in war be turned over to them, inasmuch as some Apaches who were among them were asking for them. If these things were not done they would declare war immediately, and they were unwilling to leave the place where they were because they were awaiting the Taos, Percuries, and Teguas nations, with whose aid they would destroy us. . . .

The question before the House is one of awful moment to this country. For my own part, I consider it as nothing less than a question of freedom or slavery. . . . Mr. President, it is natural to man to indulge in the illusions of hope. We are apt to shut our eyes against a painful truth. . . .

I have but one lamp by which my feet are guided, and that is the lamp of experience. . . . And judging by the past, I wish to know what there has been in the conduct of the British ministry for the last ten years to justify those hopes with which gentlemen have been pleased to solace themselves and the House. . . . Ask yourselves how this gracious reception of our petition comports with those warlike preparations which cover our waters and darken our land. Are fleets and armies necessary to a work of love and reconciliation? . . . They are meant for us: they can be meant for no other. . . . And what have we to oppose to them? Shall we try argument? Sir, we have been trying that for the last ten years. . . . We must fight! . . .

They tell us, sir, that we are weak; unable to cope with so formidable an adversary. But when shall we be stronger? Will it be the next week, or the next year? Will it be when we are totally disarmed? . . . It is in vain, sir, to extenuate the matter. Gentlemen may cry, Peace, Peace—but there is no peace. . . . I know not what course others may take; but as for me, give me liberty or give me death!

Analyzing Primary Sources

1. What Spanish actions triggered Popé's revolt?
2. Why does Don Otermin write that Popé has "gone crazy"?
3. What does Patrick Henry use to judge British intentions?
4. Why does Henry say it is foolish to wait longer before resisting?

From Dynamic Nationalism to Civil War

During the first half of the 19th century, the United States expanded its population and its borders. At the same time, the North and the South were developing their own identities. Each viewed the growing power of the federal government differently. Many Southerners believed increased federal power posed a threat to slavery.

The first excerpt is by New York City journalist John L. O'Sullivan. In 1845, in an article on Texas annexation, O'Sullivan coined the phrase "Manifest Destiny" to sum up his feelings about territorial expansion.

Northerner George F. Root wrote the "Battle Cry of Freedom," but the tune was so popular a Confederate version was written, too. Both versions are shown against the background of an Augustus Saint-Gaudens sculpture. The sculpture honors the 54th regiment of African American soldiers under the command of Robert Gould Shaw. The memorial is in Boston, Massachusetts, Shaw's hometown. The regiment's story was the subject of the movie Glory.

Reader's Dictionary

intrude: to force in or upon something without permission

Anglo-Saxon: term loosely used for any native whites in English-speaking countries

Dixie: nickname for the South, popularized in Daniel Emmett's song, "Land of Dixie"; term may derive from the French *dix* for "ten," referring to Louisiana ten-dollar bank notes

bonnie: fine, attractive, or fair

"Annexation" by John L. O'Sullivan (1845)

Printed Publications

It is time now for opposition to the Annexation of Texas to cease. . . . Texas is now ours. . . . Why, were other reasoning wanting in favor of . . . the reception of Texas into the Union . . . , it surely is to be found . . . in the manner in which other nations have undertaken to intrude themselves into it . . . for the avowed object of . . . limiting our greatness and checking the fulfilment of our manifest destiny to overspread the continent allotted by Providence for the free development of our yearly multiplying millions.

. . . Texas has been absorbed into the Union in the inevitable fulfilment of the general law which is rolling our population westward; the connexion of which with that ratio of growth in population . . . is too evident to leave us in doubt of the manifest design of Providence in regard to the occupation of this continent.

. . . Already the advance guard of the irresistible army of Anglo-Saxon emigration has begun to pour down upon (California), armed with the plough and the rifle, and marking its trail with schools and colleges, courts and representative halls, mills and meeting-houses. . . . The day is not distant when the Empires of the Atlantic and Pacific would again flow together into one. . . . The day cannot be distant which shall witness the conveyance of the representatives from Oregon and California to Washington within less time than a few years ago was devoted to a similar journey by those from Ohio. . . .

"Battle Cry of Freedom"

BATTLE CRY OF FREEDOM

VERSE 3

Union: We will wel-come to our num-bers the loy-al, true and brave,
Confederate: They have laid down their — lives on the blood-y bat-tle field,

Shout-ing the bat-tle cry of Free-dom, And al-though he may be poor Not a
Shout, shout the bat-tle cry of Free-dom, Their_ mot-to is re-sis-tance, To

man shall be a slave, Shout-ing the bat-tle cry of Free - dom
ty-rants we'll not yield! Shout, shout the bat-tle cry of Free - dom

CHORUS

The Un-ion for-ev-er, Hur-rah, boys, Hur-rah!
Our Dix-ie for-ev-er, she's never at a loss

Down with the trai-tor, up with the star; While we ral-ly 'round the flag boys,
Down with the eag-le, up with the cross. We'll_ ral-ly 'round the bonnie flag,

ral-ly once a-gain Shout-ing the bat-tle cry of Free - dom.
we'll rally once a-gain Shout, shout the bat-tle cry of Free - dom.

Analyzing Primary Sources

1. What is O'Sullivan's main argument in favor of annexation?
2. How did white settlers justify their claim to the California territory?
3. What is the main theme of the Union lyrics to "Battle Cry"?
4. In the Confederate lyrics to "Battle Cry," how are Northerners portrayed?

From Settling the West to Becoming a World Power

In the latter part of the 19th century, immigrants flocked to the United States to settle on farms or to work in newly industrializing cities. The experience transformed both the immigrants and the still-youthful nation. Change created many political and social problems, and Progressivism tried to solve them. New challenges arose in foreign affairs as well, as the nation began to wield the influence that came with an expanding economy.

In the first excerpt, the 1918 novel My Ántonia *by Willa Cather provides us with a glimpse of the life of Easterners and immigrants who moved west. Cather drew on her own experiences to create her characters. Her fiction has a strong sense of place, as can be seen in this passage where Jim Burden gets his first sight of the Nebraska prairie.*

In the second excerpt, Andrew Carnegie presents his personal solution to the problem of a nation with both rich and poor citizens, a solution termed the "Gospel of Wealth." An immigrant himself, Carnegie became one the nation's wealthiest industrialists. His charitable donations of about $350 million supported more than 2,800 libraries and other institutions.

Reader's Dictionary

plush: a luxurious fabric

surplus wealth: in a capitalist system, the wealth remaining after labor and other costs are met

antidote: a remedy for a poison; something that prevents or relieves a problem

unostentatious: plain, not flashy or showy

My Ántonia by Willa Cather

 Printed Publications

I do not remember crossing the Missouri River, or anything about the long day's journey through Nebraska. Probably by that time I had crossed so many rivers that I was dull to them. The only thing very noticeable about Nebraska was that it was still, all day long, Nebraska.

I had been sleeping, curled up in a red plush seat, for a long while when we reached Black Hawk. . . . We stumbled down from the train to a wooden siding, where men were running about with lanterns. I couldn't see any town, or even distant lights; we were surrounded by utter darkness. . . .

Another lantern came along. A bantering voice called out: "Hello, are you Mr. Burden's folks? If you are, it's me you're looking for. I'm Otto Fuchs. I'm Mr.

Carnegie Library, Shelbyville, Ind.

Burden's hired man, and I'm to drive you out. Hello, Jimmy, ain't you scared to come so far west?"

. . . He told us we had a long night drive ahead of us, and had better be on the hike. He led us to a hitching-bar where two farm-wagons were tied. . . . I rode on the straw in the bottom of the wagon-box, covered up with a buffalo hide. . . .

I tried to go to sleep, but the jolting made me bite my tongue, and I soon began to ache all over. When the straw settled down, I had a hard bed. Cautiously I slipped from under the buffalo hide, got up on my knees and peered over the side of the wagon. There seemed to be nothing to see; no fences, no creeks or trees, no hills or fields. If there was a road, I could not make it out in the faint starlight. There was nothing but land: not a country at all, but the material out of which countries are made. . . . I had the feeling that the world was left behind, that we had got over the edge of it, and were outside man's jurisdiction. I had never before looked up at the sky when there was not a familiar mountain ridge against it. But this was the complete dome of heaven, all there was of it. I did not believe that my dead father and mother were watching me from up there; they would still be looking for me at the sheep-fold down by the creek, or along the white road that led to the mountain pastures. I had left even their spirits behind me. The wagon jolted on, carrying me I knew not whither. I don't think I was homesick. If we never arrived anywhere, it did not matter. Between that earth and that sky I felt erased, blotted out. I did not say my prayers that night: here, I felt, what would be would be.

"Gospel of Wealth" by Andrew Carnegie (1889)

Printed Publications

We start, then, with a condition of affairs under which the best interests of the race are promoted, but which inevitably gives wealth to the few. . . .

There are but three modes in which surplus wealth can be disposed of. It can be left to the families of the decedents; or it can be bequeathed for public purposes; or, finally, it can be administered during their lives by its possessors. . . .

The growing disposition to tax more and more heavily large estates left at death is a cheering indication of the growth of a salutary change in public opinion. . . . Of all forms of taxation, this seems the wisest. . . .

There remains, then, only one mode of using great fortunes: but in this way we have the true antidote for the temporary unequal distribution of wealth, the reconciliation of the rich and the poor. . . . Even the poorest can be made to . . . agree that great sums . . . gathered by some of their fellow-citizens and spent for public purposes, from which the masses reap the principal benefit, are more valuable to them than if scattered among them through the course of many years in trifling amounts.

This, then, is held to be the duty of the man of Wealth: First, to set an example of modest, unostentatious living, . . . ; to provide moderately for the legitimate wants of those dependent upon him; and . . . to consider all surplus revenues which come to him simply as trust funds . . . the man of wealth thus becoming the . . . trustee for his poorer brethren, . . . doing for them better than they would or could do for themselves.

Analyzing Primary Sources

1. Is Willa Cather giving an objective description of the landscape, or do her feelings color her description? Why do you think so?

2. How does Willa Cather convey a sense of endless space?

3. What does Carnegie believe wealthy people should do with their excess money?

4. How does Carnegie think wealthy people should live? What are their other responsibilities?

From Prosperity, through the Depression, to World War

Many artists and writers blossomed in the 1920s when the freer values of modern society took hold. Artists no longer tried to copy European models so much but instead created thoroughly American works. Art flourished during the Depression as well; at that time it often focused on the sorrows and hopes of the common people. Artists of the World War II era produced many works on themes of heroism and death.

Georgia O'Keeffe (1887–1986) created some of the most original images in the history of American art. A 1929 New Mexico trip powerfully influenced her style. Known for her strong sense of color, her most famous works are of single flowers.

John Steinbeck (1902–1968) is best known for his 1940 novel, The Grapes of Wrath. *It describes the Joad family's effort to find a new life in California after they have lost their Oklahoma farm. On the trip west, the Joads and thousands of others find solace at the makeshift camps they create along the way.*

The sacrifices that come with struggle are expressed in Audie Murphy's poetry on World War II. The son of a poor Texas sharecropper, Murphy is the most decorated U.S. combat soldier of that war.

Reader's Dictionary

scuttle: to run with short, shuffling steps

biomorphic: resembling or suggesting the forms of living organisms

The Grapes of Wrath
by John Steinbeck (1940)

 Printed Publications

The cars of the migrant people crawled out of the side roads onto the great cross-country highway, and they took the migrant way to the West. In the daylight they scuttled like bugs to the westward; and as the dark caught them, they clustered like bugs near to shelter and to water. And because they were lonely and perplexed, because they had all come from a place of sadness and worry and defeat, and because they were all going to a new mysterious place, they huddled together; they talked together; they shared their lives, their food, and the things they hoped for in the new country. Thus it might be that one family camped near a spring, and another camped for the spring and for company, and a third because two families had pioneered the place and found it good. And when the sun went down, perhaps twenty families and twenty cars were there.

In the evening a strange thing happened: the twenty families became one family, the children were the children of all. The loss of home became one loss, and the golden time in the West was one dream. And it might be that a sick child threw despair into the hearts of twenty families, of a hundred people; that a birth there in a tent kept a hundred people quiet and awestruck through the night and filled a hundred people with birth-joy in the morning. A family which the night before had been lost and fearful might search its goods to find a present for a new baby. In the evening, sitting about the fires, the twenty were one. They grew to be units of the camps, units of the evenings and the nights. A guitar unwrapped from a blanket and tuned— and the songs, which were all of the people, were sung in the nights. Men sang the words, and women hummed the tunes.

John Steinbeck

Georgia O'Keeffe's *Oriental Poppies* (1927)

 Visual Materials

Georgia O'Keeffe's paintings of biomorphic flowers, rocks, and skulls are *abstract* paintings, meaning that they symbolize things other than what they actually are. *Oriental Poppies*, for example, could be seen as representing a cave-like enclosure.

Georgia O'Keeffe

"Alone and Far Removed"
by Audie Murphy

 Songs & Poems

Alone and far removed from earthly care
The noble ruins of men lie buried here.
You were strong men, good men
Endowed with youth and much the will to live
I hear no protest from the mute lips of the dead.
They rest; there is no more to give.

So long my comrades,
Sleep ye where you fell upon the field.
But tread softly please
March o'er my heart with ease
March on and on,
But to God alone we kneel.

Audie Murphy

Analyzing Primary Sources

1. According to Steinbeck, what binds the families of migrant people together?
2. How do you think Steinbeck feels about the migrants?
3. What is an abstract painting? How is it different from other paintings?
4. What is the main mood of Murphy's poem?

From Divisiveness to Diversity

American society took a sharp turn in the 1960s as a new generation sought to change some American values. Change became the challenge throughout the century as many new immigrants came to the United States to make it their home. By the year 2000, the nation was much more diverse. Hispanic Americans alone made up 12.5 percent of the population, approximately the same percentage as African Americans.

The 1960s were a breakthrough time for African Americans. Martin Luther King, Jr., persuaded many white Americans to acknowledge the need for more just laws for minorities. His "Letter from a Birmingham Jail" of April 16, 1963, makes the case that nonviolent resistance is not only moral, but is as American as the Boston Tea Party.

Elva Trevino Hart, born in southern Texas to Mexican immigrants, has a story that mirrors that of many immigrants. A migrant worker as a child, Hart eventually earned a master's degree from Stanford University. In this excerpt, she describes her father and his reaction to her graduation from high school.

Reader's Dictionary

conversely: reversed in order or action

civil disobedience: peaceful refusal to obey government demands as a means of forcing government concessions or changes in the law

admonish: to warn or express disapproval

macho: a strong sense of masculine pride

Letter from a Birmingham Jail
by Martin Luther King, Jr.
(1963)

Personal Records

My dear fellow clergymen:
. . . Birmingham is probably the most thoroughly segregated city in the United States. On the basis of these conditions, Negro leaders sought to negotiate with the city fathers. . . . As in so many past experiences, our hopes had been blasted. . . . We had no alternative except to prepare for direct action, whereby we would present our very bodies as a means of laying our case before the conscience of the local and the national community. . . .

You may well ask: . . . Why sit-ins, marches and so forth? Isn't negotiation a better path?" . . . Indeed, this is the very purpose of direct action. Nonviolent direct action seeks to create such a crisis . . . that a community . . . is forced to confront the issue. . . .

. . . For years now I have heard the word "Wait!" It rings in the ear of every Negro with piercing familiarity. This "Wait" has almost always meant "Never." We must come to see, with one of our distinguished

Martin Luther King, Jr., (right) and Ralph Abernathy in Birmingham, Alabama

jurits, that "justice too long delayed is justice denied." . . . Perhaps it is easy for those who have never felt the stinging dark of segregation to say, "Wait." . . .

You express a great deal of anxiety over our willingness to break laws. . . . One may . . . ask: "How can you advocate breaking some laws and obeying others?" The answer lies in the fact that there are two types of laws: just and unjust. . . . One has not only a legal but a moral responsibility to obey just laws. Conversely, one has a moral responsibility to disobey unjust laws. . . .

Of course, there is nothing new about this kind of civil disobedience. . . . It was practiced superbly by the early Christians, who were willing to face hungry lions . . . rather than submit to certain unjust laws of the Roman Empire. . . . In our own nation, the Boston Tea Party represented a massive act of civil disobedience. . . .

. . . We will have to repent in this generation not merely for the hateful words and actions of the bad people but for the appalling silence of the good people. Human progress never rolls in on wheels of inevitability; it comes through the tireless efforts of men willing to be co-workers with God. . . .

I have heard numerous Southern religious leaders admonish their worshipers to comply with a desegregation decision because it is the law, but I have longed to hear white ministers declare: "Follow this decree because integration is morally right and because the Negro is your brother." . . . But even if the church does not come to the aid of justice, I have no despair about the future. . . . We will reach the goal of freedom . . . all over the nation, because the goal of America is freedom. . . . We will win our freedom because the sacred heritage of our nation and the eternal will of God are embodied in our echoing demands. . . .

Analyzing Primary Sources

1. Why does King say African Americans should not wait longer for change?
2. Who in ancient history practiced nonviolent resistance?
3. Why did Hart's father take his family so far to work in the summers?

Barefoot Heart
by Elva Trevino Hart

Printed Publications

"To get ahead, hijos (children). That's why we go a los trabajos (to work). When I first came from Mexico, I got paid dos reales al dia (two Spanish coins a day). I worked at building the railroad, . . . clearing land. . . . The only thing I would never do is strap on the contraption to burn brush with liquid fuel. Too dangerous. . . ."

I fingered the nickels in the pocket of my sun dress and tried to imagine Apa (Daddy) working for fifty cents a day. And I felt I understood why we had to go to Minnesota. Our family could make more money in the migrant fields than anywhere else. . . .

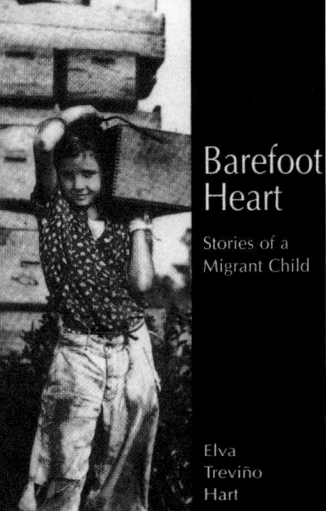

Barefoot Heart
Stories of a Migrant Child

Elva Treviño Hart

* * *

(My father) had only gone as far as the fourth grade in Mexico. . . . When I was in the fourth grade, I told my father that I wanted to go to college. . . .

On (high school) graduation night I delivered the valedictory speech, entitled "He Conquers who Conquers Himself." I wish now I had said "she," but it has remained the theme of my life nevertheless. Apa came up to me afterwards with big macho tears in his eyes. I had never seen him even close to crying before.

He pressed two thousand dollars in cash into my hand. "I have been saving this for you, mija (my daughter). It's your money to go to college." . . . I knew that this money would only be enough for about one semester, but I didn't tell him. Instead I hugged him, crying violently.

Documents of American History

TABLE OF CONTENTS

The Magna Carta, 1215 1060
The Mayflower Compact, 1620 1061
The Fundamental Orders of Connecticut, 1639 1062
The English Bill of Rights, 1689 1063
Second Treatise of Government, 1690 1064
The Virginia Statute for Religious
Freedom, 1786 1065
The Federalist No.10, 1787 1066
The Federalist No. 51, 1788 1067
The Federalist No. 59, 1788 1067
Washington's Farewell Address, 1796 1068
The Kentucky Resolution, 1799 1069
"The Star-Spangled Banner," 1814 1069
The Monroe Doctrine, 1823 1070

The Seneca Falls Declaration, 1848 1070
The Emancipation Proclamation, 1863 1071
The Gettysburg Address, 1863 1072
The Pledge of Allegiance, 1892 1072
President Harrison on Hawaiian Annexation, 1893 ...1073
The American's Creed, 1918 1073
The Fourteen Points, 1918 1074
The Four Freedoms, 1941 1075
The Truman Doctrine, 1947 1076
Brown v. Board of Education, 1954 1077
"I Have a Dream," 1963 1078
The Gulf of Tonkin Resolution, 1964 1079
President Bush's Address to Joint Session
of Congress, September 20, 2001 1079

*(above) Notes for Washington's
Farewell Address*

*(right) Lincoln's drafts of the
Gettysburg Address*

Magna Carta

Why They Matter

Documents are often public statements by a president or an official body, such as a legislature, on an important issue. They have become documents because they define a particular issue so well that Americans continue to refer to them. Many documents here address fundamental American beliefs, such as the rights of the individual and the proper limits of government. Other documents, such as the Monroe Doctrine or the Truman Doctrine, address the nation's position and responsibilities in the world.

Documents matter because they are guides to American government and values. Sometimes people study them to learn how Americans came to believe in certain principles. Other times people read documents simply because these writings express certain principles passionately.

Signing the Mayflower Compact

Founding Documents of the American Republic

The first seven documents in this collection represent some of the founding documents of American democracy. Each contributed an essential building block for American political principles. Ultimately these principles were embodied in the Declaration of Independence, the Bill of Rights, and the Constitution.

DOCUMENT	WHY IT MATTERS
The Magna Carta In signing this charter in 1215, King John of England granted his subjects certain permanent liberties or rights, such as the right to a fair trial by a jury of their peers.	Over the centuries, English people believed that the Magna Carta gave them certain rights. They took this idea with them when they settled the American colonies. Some provisions of the Bill of Rights reflect ancient Magna Carta liberties.
The Mayflower Compact In 1620 the Pilgrims signed a compact while still aboard the *Mayflower.* This document laid out a plan for self-government the Pilgrims would use once they landed in America.	This document is the first plan for self-government put into effect in the English colonies. It reflected the idea that government should be based on a consensus of the entire community.
The Fundamental Orders of Connecticut Connecticut settlers agreed they would be governed according to a certain set of laws and through certain institutions. All citizens, not only those of a certain religion, could vote.	This document, the first written constitution drawn up in America, strengthened the colonists' beliefs about governing themselves.
The English Bill of Rights In 1689, after the Glorious Revolution, Parliament forced the king to accept this Bill of Rights guaranteeing basic civil rights.	This document clearly established that English subjects had certain rights and that the king could be removed from power for violating those rights.
Second Treatise of Government English philosopher John Locke wrote this document during the 1680s. One of his basic arguments was that government should be based on a contract between a ruler and those who are ruled. Rebellion is justified if a ruler violates the contract.	During the American Revolution, the colonists drew from Locke's theories of government and especially his ideas about the right to rebel.
The Virginia Statute for Religious Freedom This 1786 statute declared that the state of Virginia should not support Anglicanism or any other religious denomination.	The religious clauses of the Bill of Rights protecting the free exercise of religion and prohibiting an official religion were based on this statute.
The Federalist No. 10 In 1787 James Madison wrote this paper, one of a series arguing for stronger central government as reflected in the new Constitution.	The framework for American government today— a representative government with a strong federal government—was laid out in the Federalist Papers.

Use the ***American History Primary Source Document Library CD-ROM*** *to find additional primary sources about American heritage.*

The Magna Carta

The Magna Carta, signed by King John of England in 1215, marked a decisive step forward in the development of English constitutional government. Later it served as a model for the colonists, who carried the Magna Carta's guarantees of political rights to America.

John, by the grace of God, king of England, lord of Ireland, duke of Normandy and Aquitaine, and count of Anjou: to the archbishops, bishops, abbots, earls, barons, justiciaries, foresters, sheriffs, reeves, ministers, and all bailiffs and others his faithful subjects, greeting. . . .

1. We have, in the first place, granted to God, and by this our present charter, confirmed for us and our heirs forever that the English church shall be free. . . .

9. Neither we nor our bailiffs shall seize any land or rent for any debt so long as the debtor's chattels are sufficient to discharge the same. . . .

12. No scutage [tax] or aid shall be imposed in our kingdom unless by the common counsel thereof. . . .

14. For obtaining the common counsel of the kingdom concerning the assessment of aids. . . or of scutage, we will cause to be summoned, severally by our letters, the archbishops, bishops, abbots, earls, and great barons; we will also cause to be summoned generally, by our sheriffs and bailiffs, all those who hold lands directly of us, to meet on a fixed day . . . and at a fixed place. . . .

20. A free man shall be amerced [punished] for a small fault only according to the measure thereof, and for a great crime according to its magnitude. . . . None of these amercements shall be imposed except by the oath of honest men of the neighborhood.

21. Earls and barons shall be amerced only by their peers, and only in proportion to the measure of the offense. . . .

38. In the future no bailiff shall upon his own unsupported accusation put any man to trial without producing credible witnesses to the truth of the accusation.

39. No free man shall be taken, imprisoned, disseised [seized], outlawed, banished, or in any way destroyed, nor will we proceed against or prosecute him, except by the lawful judgment of his peers and by the law of the land.

40. To no one will we sell, to none will we deny or delay, right or justice. . . .

42. In the future it shall be lawful . . . for anyone to leave and return to our kingdom safely and securely by land and water, saving his fealty to us. Excepted are those who have been imprisoned or outlawed according to the law of the land. . . .

61. Whereas we, for the honor of God and the amendment of our realm, and in order the better to allay the discord arisen between us and our barons, have granted all these things aforesaid. . . .

63. Wherefore we will, and firmly charge . . . that all men in our kingdom shall have and hold all the aforesaid liberties, rights, and concessions . . . fully, and wholly to them and their heirs . . . in all things and places forever. . . . It is moreover sworn, as well on our part as on the part of the barons, that all these matters aforesaid will be kept in good faith and without deceit. Witness the above named and many others. Given by our hand in the meadow which is called Runnymede. . . .

The Mayflower Compact

*On November 21, 1620, 41 colonists drafted the Mayflower Compact while still aboard the **Mayflower**. It was the first self-government plan ever put into effect in the English colonies. The compact was drawn up under these circumstances, as described by Governor William Bradford:*

"This day, before we came to harbor, observing some not well affected to unity and concord, but gave some appearance of faction, it was thought good there should be an association and agreement that we should combine together in one body, and to submit to such government and governors as we should by common consent agree to make and choose, and set our hands to this that follows word for word."

In the Name of God, Amen. We, whose names are underwritten, the Loyal Subjects of our dread Sovereign Lord King James, by the Grace of God, of Great Britain, France, and Ireland, King, Defender of the Faith, etc.

Having undertaken for the Glory of God, and Advancement of the Christian Faith, and the honor of our King and Country, a Voyage to plant the first Colony in the northern Parts of Virginia, Do by these Presents, solemnly and mutually, in the Presence of God and one another, covenant and combine ourselves together into a civil Body Politick, for our better Ordering and Preservation, and Furtherance of the Ends aforesaid; And by Virtue hereof do enact, constitute, and frame, such just and equal Laws, Ordinances, Acts, Constitutions, and Offices, from time to time, as shall be thought most meet and convenient for the general Good of the Colony; unto which we promise all due Submission and Obedience. In Witness whereof we have hereunder subscribed our names at Cape Cod the eleventh of November, in the Reign of our Sovereign Lord King James of England, France, and Ireland, the eighteenth and of Scotland, the fifty-fourth. Anno Domini, 1620.

Signing of the Mayflower Compact

The Fundamental Orders of Connecticut

In January 1639, settlers in Connecticut, led by Thomas Hooker, drew up the Fundamental Orders of Connecticut—America's first written constitution. It is essentially a body of laws and a compact among the settlers.

Forasmuch as it has pleased the Almighty God by the wise disposition of His Divine Providence so to order and dispose of things that we, the inhabitants and residents of Windsor, Hartford, and Wethersfield are now cohabiting and dwelling in and upon the river of Conectecotte and the lands thereunto adjoining; and well knowing where a people are gathered together the Word of God requires that, to maintain the peace and union of such a people, there should be an orderly and decent government established according to God, . . . do therefore associate and conjoin ourselves to be as one public state or commonwealth. . . . As also in our civil affairs to be guided and governed according to such laws, rules, orders, and decrees as shall be made, ordered, and decreed, as follows:

1. It is ordered . . . that there shall be yearly two general assemblies or courts; . . . The first shall be called the Court of Election, wherein shall be yearly chosen . . . so many magistrates and other public officers as shall be found requisite. Whereof one to be chosen governor . . . and no other magistrate to be chosen for more than one year; provided aways there be six chosen besides the governor . . . by all that are admitted freemen and have taken the oath of fidelity, and do cohabit within this jurisdiction. . . .

4. It is ordered . . . that no person be chosen governor above once in two years, and that the governor be always a member of some approved congregation, and formerly of the magistracy within this jurisdiction; and all the magistrates freemen of this Commonwealth. . . .

5. It is ordered . . . that to the aforesaid Court of Election the several towns shall send their deputies. . . . Also, the other General Court . . . shall be for making of laws, and any other public occasion which concerns the good of the Commonwealth. . . .

7. It is ordered . . . that . . . the constable or constables of each town shall forthwith give notice distinctly to the inhabitants of the same . . . that . . . they meet and assemble themselves together to elect and choose certain deputies to be at the General Court then following to [manage] the affairs of the Commonwealth; . . .

10. It is ordered . . . that every General Court . . . shall consist of the governor, or someone chosen to moderate the Court, and four other magistrates, at least, with the major part of the deputies of the several towns legally chosen. . . . In which said General Courts shall consist the supreme power of the Commonwealth, and they only shall have power to make laws or repeal them, to grant levies, to admit of freemen, dispose of lands undisposed of to several towns or person, and also shall have power to call either Court or magistrate or any other person whatsoever into question for any misdemeanor. . . .

Connecticut settlers on their way to Hartford

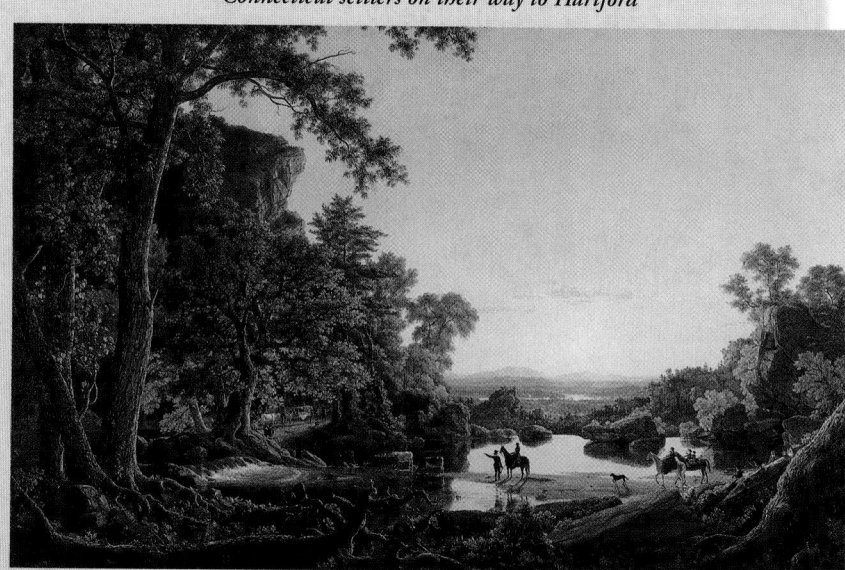

The English Bill of Rights

In 1689 William of Orange (pictured at right) and his wife Mary became joint rulers of England after accepting a list of conditions that later became known as the English Bill of Rights. This document assured the English people of certain basic civil rights and limited the power of the English monarchy.

An act declaring the rights and liberties of the subject and settling the succession of the crown. Whereas the lords spiritual and temporal and commons assembled at Westminster lawfully fully and freely representing all the estates of the people of this realm did upon the thirteenth day of February in the year of our Seal of William and Mary Lord one thousand six hundred eighty-eight [-nine] present unto their majesties . . . William and Mary prince and princess of Orange . . . a certain declaration in writing made by the said lords and commons in the words following viz [namely]

Whereas the late king James the second, by the assistance of divers evil counsellors, judges, and ministers employed by him did endeavor to subvert and extirpate the protestant religion and the laws and liberties of this kingdom.

By assuming and exercising a power of dispensing with and suspending of laws and the execution of laws without consent of parliament. . . .

By levying money for and to the use of the crown by pretence of prerogative for other time and in other manner than the same was granted by parliament.

By raising and keeping a standing army within this kingdom in time of peace without consent of parliament and quartering soldiers contrary to law. . . .

By violating the freedom of election of members to serve in parliament. . . .

And excessive bail hath been required of persons committed in criminal cases to elude the benefit of the laws made for the liberty of the subjects.

And excessive fines have been imposed.

And illegal and cruel punishments inflicted. . . .

And thereupon the said lords spiritual and temporal and commons . . . do . . . declare that the pretended power of suspending of laws or the execution of laws by regal authority without consent of parliament is illegal. . . .

That levying money for or to the use of the crown . . . without grant of parliament for longer time or in other manner than the same is or shall be granted is illegal.

That it is the right of the subjects to petition the king and all commitments and prosecutions for such petitioning are illegal.

That the raising or keeping a standing army within the kingdom in time of peace unless it be with consent of parliament is against law. . . .

That election of members of parliament ought to be free. . . .

That excessive bail ought not to be required nor excessive fines imposed nor cruel and unusual punishments inflicted. . . .

The said lords . . . do resolve that William and Mary, prince and princess of Orange, be declared king and queen of England, France, and Ireland. . . .

Second Treatise of Government

English philosopher John Locke (above) wrote "Two Treatises of Government" in the early 1680s. Published in 1690, the "Second Treatise of Government" argues that government should be based on an agreement between the people and their ruler, and that if the ruler violates the agreement, a rebellion by the people may be justified.

Of the State of Nature

To understand Political Power right, and to derive it from its Original, we must consider what State all Men are naturally in, and that is, a State of perfect Freedom to order their Actions, and dispose of their Possessions, and Persons as they think fit, within the bounds of the Law of Nature, without asking leave, or depending upon the Will of any other Man. . . .

Of the Beginning of Political Societies

Men being, as has been said, by Nature, all free, equal and independent, no one can be put out of this Estate, and subjected to the Political Power of another, without his own Consent.

The only way whereby any one divests himself of his Natural Liberty, and puts on the bonds of Civil Society is by agreeing with other Men to joyn and unite into a Community, for their comfortable, safe, and peaceable living one amongst another, in a secure Enjoyment of their properties, and a greater Security against any that are not of it. This any number of Men may do, because it injures not the Freedom of the rest; they are left as they were in the Liberty of the State of Nature. . . .

Whosoever therefore out of a state of Nature unite into a Community, must be understood to give up all the power, necessary to the ends for which they unite into Society, to the majority of the Community. . . .

Of the Dissolution of Government

Governments are dissolved from within . . . when the Legislative is altered. . . . First, that when such a single Person or Prince sets up his own Arbitrary Will in place of the Laws, which are the Will of the Society, declared by the Legislative, then the Legislative is changed. . . . Secondly, when the Prince hinders the legislative from . . . acting freely, pursuant to those ends, for which it was Constituted, the Legislative is altered. . . . Thirdly, When by the Arbitrary Power of the Prince, the Electors, or ways of Election are altered, without the Consent, and contrary to the common Interest of the People, there also the Legislative is altered. . . .

In these and the like Cases, when the Government is dissolved, the People are at liberty to provide for themselves, by erecting a new Legislative, differing from the other, by the change of Persons, or Form, or both as they shall find it most for their safety and good. For the Society can never, by the fault of another, lose the Native and Original Right it has to preserve itself. . . .

The Virginia Statute for Religious Freedom

This statute, excerpted below, was the basis for the religion clauses in the Bill of Rights. Thomas Jefferson drafted the statute, and James Madison guided it through the Virginia legislature in 1786. The issue it addresses arose when the new state considered whether citizens should continue to support the Anglican Church, as they had in colonial times, or whether they should support any or all other denominations.

Whereas Almighty God hath created the mind free; that all attempts to influence it by temporal punishments . . . tend only to beget habits of hypocrisy and meanness, and are a departure from the plan of the Holy author of our religion; . . . that the impious presumption of legislators and rulers, civil as well as ecclesiastical, who being themselves but fallible and uninspired men, have assumed dominion over the faith of others, setting up their own opinions and modes of thinking as the only true and infallible, and as such endeavouring to impose them on others, hath established and maintained false religions over the greatest part of the world, and through all time; . . . that to compel a man to furnish contributions of money for the propagation of opinions which he disbelieves, is sinful and tyrannical; . . . that our civil rights have no dependence on our religious opinions, any more than our opinions in physics or geometry; that therefore the proscribing any citizen as unworthy the public confidence by laying upon him an incapacity of being called to offices of trust . . . unless he profess or renounce this or that religious opinion, is depriving him injuriously of those privileges and advantages to which in common with his fellow-citizens he has a natural right; that it tends only to corrupt the principles of that religion it is meant to encourage, by bribing with a monopoly of worldly honours and emoluments, those who will externally profess and conform to it . . . :

Be it enacted by the General Assembly, That no man shall be compelled to frequent or support any religious worship, place, or ministry whatsoever, nor shall be enforced, restrained, molested, or burthened in his body or goods, nor shall otherwise suffer on account of his religious opinions or belief; but that all men shall be free to profess, and by argument to maintain, their opinion in matters of religion, and that the same shall in no wise diminish enlarge, or affect their civil capacities. . . .

Thomas Jefferson

The Federalist No. 10

James Madison (pictured at right) wrote several articles for a New York newspaper supporting ratification of the Constitution. In the excerpt below, he argues for the idea of a federal republic as a guard against factions, or overzealous parties, in governing the nation.

The latent causes of faction are thus sown in the nature of man; and we see them everywhere. . . . A zeal for different opinions concerning religion, concerning government, and many other points; . . . an attachment to different leaders ambitiously contending for pre-eminence and power . . . have, in turn, divided mankind into parties . . . disposed to vex and oppress each other than to cooperate for their common good. . . . But the most common and durable source of factions has been the various and unequal distribution of property. Those who hold and those who are without property have ever formed distinct interests in society. Those who are creditors, and those who are debtors, fall under a like discrimination. A landed interest, a manufacturing interest, a mercantile interest, a moneyed interest, with many lesser interests, grow up of necessity in civilized nations, and divide them into different classes, actuated by different sentiments and views. The regulation of these various and interfering interests forms the principal task of modern legislation and involves the spirit of party and faction in the necessary and ordinary operations of government. . . .

The inference to which we are brought is that the causes of faction cannot be removed and relief is only to be sought in the means of controlling its effects. . . .

By what means is this object attainable? Evidently by one of two only. Either the existence of the same passion or interest in a majority at the same time must be prevented, or the majority, having such coexistent passion or interest, must be rendered, by their number and local situation, unable to concert and carry into effect schemes of oppression. . . .

From this . . . it may be concluded that a pure democracy, by which I mean a society consisting of a small number of citizens, who assemble and administer the government in person, can admit of no cure for the mischiefs of faction. A common passion or interest will, in almost every case, be felt by a majority of the whole; a communication and concert results from the form of government itself; and there is nothing to check the inducements to sacrifice the weaker party or an obnoxious individual. Hence it is that such democracies have ever been spectacles of turbulence and contention. . . .

A republic, by which I mean a government in which the scheme of representation takes place, opens a different prospect and promises the cure for which we are seeking. . . .

The two great points of difference between a democracy and a republic are: first, the delegation of the government in the latter to a small number of citizens elected by the rest; secondly, the greater number of citizens and great sphere of country over which the latter may be extended.

The Federalist No. 51

The author of this Federalist paper is not known. It may have been either James Madison or Alexander Hamilton. The author argues that the Constitution's federal system and separation of powers will protect the rights of the people.

In order to lay a due foundation for that separate and distinct exercise of the different powers of government, which to a certain extent is admitted on all hands to be essential to the preservation of liberty, it is evident that. . . the great security against a gradual concentration of the several powers in the same department, consists in giving to those who administer each department the necessary constitutional means and personal motives to resist encroachments of the others. . . .

Ambition must be made to counteract ambition. . . . A dependence on the people is, no doubt, the primary control on the government; but experience has taught mankind the necessity of auxiliary precautions. . . . The constant aim is to divide and arrange the several offices in such a manner as that each may be a check on the other. . . . In the compound republic of America, the power surrendered by the people is first divided between two distinct governments, and then the portion allotted to each subdivided among distinct and separate departments. . . .

In a free government the security for civil rights must be the same as that for religious rights. It consists in the one case in the multiplicity of interests, and in the other in the multiplicity of sects. . . . In the extended republic of the United States, and among the great variety of interests, parties, and sects which it embraces, a coalition of a majority of the whole society could seldom take place on any other principles than those of justice and the general good. . . . It is no less certain than it is important . . . that the larger the society, provided it lie within a practical sphere, the more duly capable it will be of self-government.

The Federalist No. 59

In this Federalist paper, Alexander Hamilton explains why Congress, and not the states, should have the final say in how federal elections are conducted.

The natural order of the subject leads us to consider . . . that provision of the Constitution which authorizes the national legislature to regulate, in the last resort, the election of its own members. . . . Its propriety rests upon the evidence of this plain proposition, that every government ought to contain in itself the means of its own preservation. . . . Nothing can be more evident, than that an exclusive power of regulating elections for the national government, in the hands of the state legislatures, would leave the existence of the union entirely at their mercy. They could at any moment annihilate it, by neglecting to provide for the choice of persons to administer its affairs. . . .

It is certainly true that the state legislatures, by forbearing the appointment of senators, may destroy the national government. But it will not follow that, because they have a power to do this in one instance, they ought to have it in every other. . . . It is an evil; but it is an evil which could not have been avoided without excluding the states . . . from a place in the organization of the national government. If this had been done, it would doubtless have been interpreted into an entire dereliction of the federal principle; and would certainly have deprived the state governments of that absolute safeguard which they will enjoy under this provision. . . .

Washington's Farewell Address

Washington never orally delivered his Farewell Address. Instead, he arranged to have it printed in a Philadelphia newspaper on September 19, 1796. Designed in part to remove him from consideration for a third presidential term, the address also warned about dangers the new nation was facing, especially the dangers of political parties and sectionalism.

Washington preparing to leave office

Friends and Fellow Citizens:

The period for a new election of a citizen to administer the executive government of the United States being not far distant . . . I should now apprise you of the resolution I have formed to decline being considered. . . .

The unity of government which constitutes you one people is . . . a main pillar in the edifice of your real independence; the support of your tranquility at home, your peace abroad; of your safety; of your prosperity in every shape; of that very liberty which you so highly prize. But as it is easy to foresee that, from different causes and from different quarters, much pains will be taken, many artifices employed to weaken in your minds the conviction of this truth. . . .

The name of American, which belongs to you, in your national capacity, must always exalt the just pride of patriotism more than any appellation derived from local discriminations. . . .

In contemplating the causes which may disturb our Union, it occurs as matter of serious concern that any ground should have been furnished for characterizing parties by geographical discriminations: Northern and Southern; Atlantic and Western; whence designing men may endeavor to excite a belief that there is a real difference of local interests and views. . . .

Let me now take a more comprehensive view and warn you in the most solemn manner against the baneful effects of the spirit of party generally. . . .

The alternate domination of one faction over another, sharpened by the spirit of revenge natural to party dissension . . . is itself a frightful despotism. . . .

Of all the dispositions and habits which lead to political prosperity, religion and morality are indispensable supports. . . . A volume could not trace all their connections with private and public felicity. Let it simply be asked where is the security for property, for reputation, for life, if the sense of religious obligation desert the oaths, which are the instruments of investigation in courts of justice? And let us with caution indulge the supposition, that morality can be maintained without religion. Whatever may be conceded to the influence of refined education on minds of peculiar structure—reason and experience both forbid us to expect that national morality can prevail in exclusion of religious principle.

The great rule of conduct for us, in regard to foreign nations, is in extending our commercial relations to have with them as little political connection as possible. . . .

In offering you, my countrymen, these counsels of an old and affectionate friend, I dare not hope that they will make the strong and lasting impression I could wish. . . . But if I may even flatter myself that they may be productive of some partial benefit. . . .

The Kentucky Resolution

The Alien and Sedition Acts of 1798 made it easier for the government to suppress criticism and to arrest political enemies. This Federalist legislation inspired fierce opposition among Republicans, who looked to the state governments to reverse the acts. Two states, Kentucky and Virginia, passed resolutions stating their right to, in effect, disregard federal legislation. The resolutions laid the groundwork for the states' rights often cited during the Civil War. Thomas Jefferson wrote the Kentucky Resolution, excerpted below, which was adopted in 1799.

RESOLVED, . . . that if those who administer the general government be permitted to transgress the limits fixed by that compact, by a total disregard to the special delegations of power therein contained, annihilation of the state governments, and the erection upon their ruins, of a general consolidated government, will be the inevitable consequence; that the principle and construction contended for by sundry of the state legislatures, that the general government is the exclusive judge of the extent of the powers delegated to it, stop nothing short of despotism; . . . that the several states who formed that instrument, being sovereign and independent, have the unquestionable right to judge of its infraction; and that a nullification, by those sovereignties, of all unauthorized acts done under colour of that instrument, is the rightful remedy; . . .

"The Star-Spangled Banner"

Francis Scott Key

During the British bombardment of Fort McHenry during the War of 1812, a young Baltimore lawyer named Francis Scott Key was inspired to write the words to "The Star-Spangled Banner." Although it became popular immediately, it was not until 1931 that Congress officially declared "The Star-Spangled Banner" as the national anthem of the United States.

O! say can you see, by the dawn's early light,

What so proudly we hail'd at the twilight's last gleaming,

Whose broad stripes and bright stars through the perilous fight,

O'er the ramparts we watch'd, were so gallantly streaming?

And the Rockets' red glare, the Bombs bursting in air,

Gave proof through the night that our Flag was still there;

O! say, does that star-spangled Banner yet wave,

O'er the Land of the free, and the home of the brave!

Fort McHenry flag

The Monroe Doctrine

When Spain's power in South America began to weaken, other European nations seemed ready to step in. The United States was developing trade and diplomatic relations with South America, and it wanted to curb European influence there. The following is a statement President Monroe made on the subject in his annual message to Congress on December 2, 1823.

The occasion has been judged proper for asserting, as a principle in which the rights and interests of the United States are involved, that the American continents, by the free and independent condition which they have assumed and maintain, are henceforth not to be considered as subjects for future colonization by any European powers. . . .

. . . We owe it, therefore, to candor and to the amicable relations existing between the United States and those [European] powers to declare that we should consider any attempt on their part to extend their system to any portion of this hemisphere as dangerous to our peace and safety. With the existing colonies or dependencies of any European power we have not interfered and shall not interfere. But with the Governments who have declared their independence and maintain it, and whose independence we have, on great consideration and on just principles, acknowledged, we could not view any interposition for the purpose of oppressing them, or controlling in any other manner their destiny, by any European power in any other light than as the manifestation of an unfriendly disposition toward the United States. . . .

Our policy in regard to Europe, which was adopted at an early stage of the wars which have so long agitated that quarter of the globe, nevertheless remains the same, which is, not to interfere in the internal concerns of any of its powers; to consider the government de facto as the legitimate government for us; to cultivate friendly relations with it, and to preserve those relations by a frank, firm, and manly policy, meeting in all instances the just claims of every power, submitting to injuries from none.

The Seneca Falls Declaration

One of the first documents to call for equal rights for women was the Declaration of Sentiments and Resolutions, issued in 1848 at the Seneca Falls Convention in Seneca Falls, New York. Led by Lucretia Mott and Elizabeth Cady Stanton, the delegates at the convention used the language of the Bill of Rights to call for women's rights.

We hold these truths to be self-evident: that all men and women are created equal; that they are endowed by their Creator with certain inalienable rights; that among these are life, liberty, and the pursuit of happiness; that to secure these rights governments are instituted, deriving their just powers from the consent of the governed. Whenever any form of government becomes destructive of these ends, it is the right of those who suffer from it to refuse allegiance to it, and to insist upon the institution of a new government. . . .

The history of mankind is a history of repeated injuries and usurpations on the part of man toward woman, having in direct object the establishment of an absolute tyranny over her.

Now, in view of this entire disfranchisement . . . we insist that they have immediate admission to all the rights and privileges which belong to them as citizens of the United States. . . .

Lucretia Mott

The Emancipation Proclamation

On January 1, 1863, President Abraham Lincoln issued the Emancipation Proclamation, which freed all enslaved persons in states under Confederate control. The Proclamation was a significant step toward the passage of the Thirteenth Amendment (1865), which ended slavery in the United States.

Whereas, on the 22nd day of September, in the year of our Lord 1862, a proclamation was issued by the President of the United States, containing, among other things, the following, to wit:

That on the 1st day of January, in the year of our Lord 1863, all persons held as slaves within any state or designated part of a state, the people whereof shall then be in rebellion against the United States, shall be then, thenceforward, and forever free; and the executive government of the United States, including the military and naval authority thereof, will recognize and maintain the freedom of such persons and will do no act or acts to repress such persons, or any of them, in any efforts they may make for their actual freedom.

That the executive will, on the 1st day January aforesaid, by proclamation, designate the states and parts of states, if any, in which the people thereof, respectively, shall then be in rebellion against the United States; and the fact that any state or the people thereof shall on that day be in good faith represented in the Congress of the United States by members chosen thereto at elections wherein a majority of the qualified voters of such states shall have participated shall, in the absence of strong countervailing testimony, be deemed conclusive evidence that such state and the people thereof are not then in rebellion against the United States.

Now, therefore, I, Abraham Lincoln, President of the United States, by virtue of the power in me vested as commander in chief of the Army and Navy of the United States, in time of actual armed rebellion against the authority and government of the United States, and as a fit and necessary war measure for suppressing said rebellion, do, on this 1st day of January, in the year of our Lord 1863, and in accordance with my purpose so to do, publicly proclaimed for the full period of 100 days from the day first above mentioned, order, and designate as the states and parts of states wherein the people thereof, respectively, are this day in rebellion against the United States. . . .

And, by virtue of the power and for the purpose aforesaid, I do order and declare that all persons held as slaves within said designated states and parts of states are, and henceforward shall be, free; and that the executive government of the United States, including the military and naval authorities thereof, will recognize and maintain the freedom of said persons. . . .

And upon this act, sincerely believed to be an act of justice, warranted by the Constitution upon military necessity, I invoke the considerate judgment of mankind and the gracious favor of Almighty God. . . .

Abraham Lincoln

The Gettysburg Address

National monument at Gettysburg

President Abraham Lincoln delivered the Gettysburg Address on November 19, 1863, during the dedication of the Gettysburg National Cemetery. The dedication was in honor of the more than 7,000 Union and Confederate soldiers who died in the Battle of Gettysburg earlier that year. Lincoln's brief speech is often recognized as one of the finest speeches in the English language. It is also one of the most moving speeches in the nation's history.

There are five known manuscript copies of the address, two of which are in the Library of Congress. Scholars debate about which, if any, of the existing manuscripts comes closest to Lincoln's actual words that day.

Four score and seven years ago our fathers brought forth on this continent a new nation, conceived in liberty and dedicated to the proposition that all men are created equal.

Now we are engaged in a great civil war, testing whether that nation or any nation so conceived and so dedicated can long endure. We are met on a great battlefield of that war. We have come to dedicate a portion of that field as a final resting-place for those who here gave their lives that that nation might live. It is altogether fitting and proper that we should do this.

But in a larger sense, we cannot dedicate, we cannot consecrate, we cannot hallow this ground. The brave men, living and dead who struggled here have consecrated it far above our poor power to add or detract. The world will little note nor long remember what we say here, but it can never forget what they did here. It is for us the living rather to be dedicated here to the unfinished work which they who fought here have thus far so nobly advanced. It is rather for us to be here dedicated to the great task remaining before us— that from these honored dead we take increased devotion to that cause for which they gave the last full measure of devotion—that we here highly resolve that these dead shall not have died in vain, that this nation under God shall have a new birth of freedom, and that government of the people, by the people, for the people shall not perish from the earth.

The Pledge of Allegiance

In 1892 the nation celebrated the 400th anniversary of Columbus's landing in America. In connection with this celebration, Francis Bellamy, a magazine editor, wrote and published the Pledge of Allegiance. The words "under God" were added by Congress in 1954 at the urging of President Dwight D. Eisenhower.

I pledge allegiance to the Flag of the United States of America and to the Republic for which it stands, one Nation under God, indivisible, with liberty and justice for all.

Students in a New York City school reciting the Pledge of Allegiance

President Harrison on Hawaiian Annexation

An early expression of American imperialism came in the annexation of Hawaii. With the support of the American government, a small number of American troops overthrew the Hawaiian monarchy in January 1893. The excerpt below is from President Benjamin Harrison's written message to Congress. He sent the message along with the treaty for annexation to Congress on February 15, 1893.

I do not deem it necessary to discuss at any length the conditions which have resulted in this decisive action. It has been the policy of the administration not only to respect but to encourage the continuance of an independent government in the Hawaiian Islands so long as it afforded suitable guarantees for the protection of life and property and maintained a stability and strength that gave adequate security against the domination of any other power. . . .

The overthrow of the monarchy was not in any way promoted by this government, but had its origin in what seems to have been a reactionary and revolutionary policy on the part of Queen Liliuokalani, which put in serious peril not only the large and preponderating interests of the United States . . . but all foreign interests. . . . It is quite evident that the monarchy had become effete and the queen's government is weak and inadequate as to be the prey of designing and unscrupulous persons. The restoration of Queen Liliuokalani . . . is undesirable . . . and unless actively supported by the United States would be accompanied by serious disaster and the disorganization of all business interests. The influence and interest of the United States in the islands must be increased and not diminished.

Only two courses are now open—one the establishment of a protectorate by the United States, and the other annexation, full and complete. I think the latter course, which has been adopted in the treaty, will be highly promotive of the best interest of the Hawaiian people and is the only one that will adequately secure the interests of the United States. These interests are not wholly selfish. It is essential that none of the other great powers shall secure these islands. Such a possession would not consist with our safety and with the peace of the world. This view of the situation is so apparent and conclusive that no protest has been heard from any government against proceedings looking to annexation.

The American's Creed

In the patriotic fervor of World War I, national leaders sponsored a contest in which writers submitted ideas for a national creed that would be a brief summary of American beliefs. Of the 3,000 entries, the judges selected that of William Tyler Page as the winner. In a 1918 ceremony in the House of Representatives, the Speaker of the House accepted the creed for the United States.

I believe in the United States of America as a Government of the people, by the people, for the people, whose just powers are derived from the consent of the governed; a democracy in a republic; a sovereign Nation of many sovereign States; a perfect union, one and inseparable; established upon those principles of freedom, equality, justice, and humanity for which American patriots sacrificed their lives and fortunes.

I therefore believe it is my duty to my Country to love it; to support its Constitution; to obey its laws; to respect its flag, and to defend it against all enemies.

The Fourteen Points

On January 8, 1918, President Woodrow Wilson went before Congress to offer a statement of war aims called the Fourteen Points. They reflected Wilson's belief that if the international community accepted certain basic principles of conduct and set up institutions to carry them out, there would be peace in the world.

We entered this war because violations of right had occurred. . . . What we demand in this war, therefore, is . . . that the world be made fit and safe to live in. . . .

The only possible programme, as we see it, is this:

I. Open covenants of peace, openly arrived at, after which there shall be no private international understandings of any kind but diplomacy shall proceed always frankly and in the public view.

II. Absolute freedom of navigation upon the seas, outside territorial waters, alike in peace and in war. . . .

III. The removal, so far as possible, of all economic barriers and the establishment of an equality of trade conditions among all the nations. . . .

IV. Adequate guarantees given and taken that national armaments will be reduced to the lowest point consistent with domestic safety.

V. A free, open-minded, and absolutely impartial adjustment of all colonial claims, based upon a strict observance of the principle that in determining all such questions of sovereignty the interests of the populations concerned must have equal weight with the equitable claims of the government whose title is to be determined.

VI. The evacuation of all Russian territory and . . . opportunity for the independent determination of her own political development and national polity. . . .

VII. Belgium . . . must be evacuated and restored. . . .

VIII. All French territory should be freed and the invaded portions restored, and the wrong done to France by Prussia in 1871 in the matter of Alsace-Lorraine should be righted. . . .

IX. A readjustment of the frontiers of Italy should be effected along clearly recognizable lines of nationality.

X. The peoples of Austria-Hungary . . . should be accorded the freest opportunity of autonomous development.

XI. Rumania, Serbia, and Montenegro should be evacuated; occupied territories restored . . . the relations of the several Balkan states to one another determined by friendly counsel along historically established lines of allegiance and nationality. . . .

XII. The Turkish portions of the present Ottoman Empire should be assured a secure sovereignty. . . .

XIII. An independent Polish state should be erected which should include the territories inhabited by indisputably Polish populations. . . .

XIV. A general association of nations must be formed under specific covenants for the purpose of affording mutual guarantees of political independence and territorial integrity. . . .

Discussion of the Fourteen Points at the Versailles peace conference

The Four Freedoms

President Franklin D. Roosevelt delivered this address on January 6, 1941, in his annual message to Congress. In it, Roosevelt called for a world founded on "four essential human freedoms": freedom of speech and expression, freedom of worship, freedom from want, and freedom from fear.

Just as our national policy in internal affairs has been based upon a decent respect for the rights and dignity of all our fellow men within our gates, so our national policy in foreign affairs has been based on a decent respect for the rights and dignity of all nations, large and small. And the justice of morality must and will win in the end.

Our national policy is this:

First, by an impressive expression of the public will and without regard to partisanship, we are committed to all-inclusive national defense.

Second, by an impressive expression of the public will and without regard to partisanship, we are committed to full support of all those resolute peoples, everywhere, who are resisting aggression and are thereby keeping war away from our Hemisphere. . . .

Third . . . we are committed to the proposition that principles of morality and considerations for our own security will never permit us to acquiesce in a peace dictated by aggressors. . . .

Let us say to the democracies, "We Americans are vitally concerned in your defense of freedom. We are putting forth our energies, our resources, and our organizing powers to give you the strength to regain and maintain a free world. We shall send you, in ever increasing numbers, ships, planes, tanks, guns. This is our purpose and our pledge." In fulfillment of this purpose we will not be intimidated by the threats of dictators that they will regard as a breach of international

Caricature of President Roosevelt

law and as an act of war our aid to the democracies which dare to resist their aggression. . . .

In the future days, which we seek to make secure, we look forward to a world founded upon four essential human freedoms.

The first is freedom of speech and expression everywhere in the world.

The second is freedom of every person to worship God in his own way everywhere in the world.

The third is freedom from want, which, translated into world terms, means economic understandings which will secure to every nation a healthy peacetime life for its inhabitants everywhere in the world.

The fourth is freedom from fear—which, translated into world terms, means a worldwide reduction of armaments to such a point and in such a thorough fashion that no nation will be in a position to commit an act of physical aggression against any neighbor—anywhere in the world. . . .

The Truman Doctrine

President Harry S Truman addressed a joint session of Congress on March 12, 1947, to request aid to fight Communist influence in Greece and Turkey. His message that communism had to be contained represents the central idea of American foreign policy during the Cold War.

The United States has received from the Greek Government an urgent appeal for financial and economic assistance. . . .

When forces of liberation entered Greece they found that the retreating Germans had destroyed virtually all the railways, roads, port facilities, communications, and merchant marine. More than a thousand villages had been burned. Eighty-five percent of the children were tubercular. Livestock, poultry, and draft animals had almost disappeared. Inflation had wiped out practically all savings. As a result of these tragic conditions, a militant minority, exploiting human want and misery, was able to create political chaos which, until now, has made economic recovery impossible.

Greece is today without funds to finance the importation of those goods which are essential to bare subsistence. Under these circumstances the people of Greece cannot make progress in solving their problems of reconstruction. Greece is in desperate need of financial and economic assistance to enable it to resume purchases of food, clothing, fuel and seeds. These are indispensable for the subsistence of its people and are obtainable only from abroad. Greece must have help to import the goods necessary to restore internal order and security, so essential for economic and political recovery. . . .

Meanwhile, the Greek Government is unable to cope with the situation. The Greek army is small and poorly equipped. It needs supplies and equipment if it is to restore the authority of the government throughout Greek territory. Greece must have assistance if it is to become a self-supporting and self-respecting democracy.

The United States must supply that assistance. We have already extended to Greece certain types of relief and economic aid but these are inadequate. There is no other country to which democratic Greece can turn. . . .

No government is perfect. One of the chief virtues of a democracy, however, is that its defects are always visible and under democratic processes can be pointed out and corrected. The Government of Greece is not perfect. Nevertheless it represents eighty-five percent of the members of the Greek Parliament who were chosen in an election last year. . . .

Greece's neighbor, Turkey, also deserves our attention. The future of Turkey as an independent and economically sound state is clearly no less important to the freedom-loving peoples of the world than the future of Greece. The circumstances in which Turkey finds itself today are considerably different from those of Greece. Turkey has been spared the disasters that have beset Greece. And during the war, the United States and Great Britain furnished Turkey with material aid. Nevertheless, Turkey now needs our support.

. . . To ensure the peaceful development of nations, free from coercion, the United States has taken a leading part in establishing the United Nations. The United Nations is designed to make possible lasting freedom and independence for all its members. We shall not realize our objectives, however, unless we are willing to help free peoples to maintain their free institutions . . . against aggressive movements that seek to impose upon them totalitarian regimes. . . .

This is an investment in world freedom and world peace. . . . The seeds of totalitarian regimes are nurtured by misery and want. They spread and grow in the evil soil of poverty and strife. They reach their full growth when the hope of a people for a better life has died. We must keep that hope alive. . . . If we falter in our leadership, we may endanger the peace of the world—and we shall surely endanger the welfare of our own nation.

Brown v. Board of Education

On May 17, 1954, the Supreme Court ruled in **Brown** *v.* **Board of Education of Topeka, Kansas,** *that racial segregation in public schools was unconstitutional. This decision provided the legal basis for court challenges to segregation in every aspect of American life.*

These cases come to us from the States of Kansas, South Carolina, Virginia, and Delaware. They are premised on different facts and different local conditions, but a common legal question justifies their consideration together in this consolidated opinion.

In each of the cases, minors of the Negro race, through their legal representatives, seek the aid of the courts in obtaining admission to the public schools of their community on a nonsegregated basis. In each instance, they had been denied admission to schools attended by white children under laws requiring or permitting segregation according to race. This segregation was alleged to deprive the plaintiffs of the equal protection of the laws under the Fourteenth Amendment.

The plaintiffs contend that segregated public schools are not "equal" and cannot be made "equal," and that hence they are deprived of the equal protection of the laws. Because of the obvious importance of the question presented, the Court took jurisdiction. . . .

. . . Our decision . . . cannot turn on merely a comparison of these tangible factors in the Negro and white schools involved in each of the cases. We must look instead to the effect of segregation itself on public education.

In approaching this problem, we cannot turn the clock back to 1868 when the Amendment was adopted, or even to 1896 when *Plessy* v. *Ferguson* was written. We must consider public education in the light of its full development and its present place in American life throughout the nation. Only in this way can it be determined if segregation in public schools deprives these plaintiffs of the equal protection of the laws.

Today, education is perhaps the most important function of state and local governments. Compulsory school attendance laws and the great expenditures for education both demonstrate our recognition of the importance of education to our democratic society. . . . In these days, it is doubtful that any child may reasonably be expected to succeed in life if he is denied the opportunity of an education. Such an opportunity, where the state has undertaken to provide it, is a right which must be made available to all on equal terms.

We come then to the question presented: Does segregation of children in public schools solely on the basis of race, even though the physical facilities and other "tangible" factors may be equal, deprive the children of the minority group of equal educational opportunities? We believe that it does.

. . . We conclude that, in the field of public education, the doctrine of "separate but equal" has no place. Separate educational facilities are inherently unequal. Therefore, we hold that the plaintiff and others similarly situated for whom the actions have been brought are, by reason of the segregation complained of, deprived of the equal protection of the laws guaranteed by the Fourteenth Amendment. . . .

Linda Brown

"I Have a Dream"

On August 28, 1963, while Congress was debating broad civil rights legislation, Martin Luther King, Jr., led more than 200,000 people in a march on Washington, D.C. On the steps of the Lincoln Memorial, King gave a stirring speech in which he eloquently spoke of his dreams for African Americans and for the United States.

Martin Luther King, Jr., speaking at the march

Five score years ago, a great American, in whose symbolic shadow we stand, signed the Emancipation Proclamation. This momentous decree came as a great beacon light of hope to millions of Negro slaves who had been seared in the flames of withering injustice. It came as a joyous day-break to end the long night of captivity.

But one hundred years later, we must face the tragic fact that the Negro is still not free. One hundred years later, the life of the Negro is still sadly crippled by the manacles of seg-regation and the chains of discrimination. . . .

There are those who are asking the devotees of civil rights, "When will you be satisfied?"

We can never be satisfied as long as the Negro is the victim of the unspeakable horrors of police brutality.

We can never be satisfied as long as our bodies, heavy with the fatigue of travel, cannot gain lodging in the motels of the highways and the hotels of the cities.

We cannot be satisfied as long as the Negro's basic mobility is from a smaller ghetto to a larger one.

We can never be satisfied as long as a Negro in Mississippi cannot vote and a Negro in New York believes he has nothing for which to vote.

No, no, we are not satisfied, and we will not be satisfied until justice rolls down like waters and righteousness like a mighty stream. . . .

I say to you today, my friends, that in spite of the difficulties and frustrations of the moment I still have a dream. It is a dream deeply rooted in the American dream.

I have a dream that one day this nation will rise up and live out the true meaning of its creed: "We hold these truths to be self-evident; that all men are created equal. "

I have a dream that one day on the red hills of Georgia the sons of former slaves and the sons of former slaveowners will be able to sit down together at the table of brotherhood.

I have a dream that one day even the state of Mississippi, a desert state sweltering with the heat of injustice and oppression, will be transformed into an oasis of freedom and justice.

I have a dream that my four little children will one day live in a nation where they will not be judged by the color of their skin but by the content of their character. . . .

When we let freedom ring, when we let it ring from every village and every hamlet, from every state and every city, we will be able to speed up that day when all of God's children, black men and white men, Jews and Gentiles, Protestants and Catholics, will be able to join hands and sing in the words of the old Negro spiritual, "Free at last! Free at last! Thank God Almighty, we are free at last!"

Gulf of Tonkin Resolution

On August 7, 1964, Congress passed the Gulf of Tonkin Resolution, which stood as the legal basis for the Vietnam War.

Resolved by the Senate and House of Representatives of the United States of America in Congress assembled,

That the Congress approves and supports the determination of the President, as Commander in Chief, to take all necessary measures to repel any armed attack against the forces of the United States and to prevent further aggression.

Section 2. The United States regards as vital to its national interest and to world peace the maintenance of international peace and security in southeast Asia. Consonant with the Constitution of the United States and the Charter of the United Nations and in accordance with its obligations under the Southeast Asia Collective Defense Treaty, the United States is, therefore, prepared, as the President determines, to take all necessary steps, including the use of armed force, to assist any member or protocol state of the Southeast Asia Collective Defense Treaty requesting assistance in defense of its freedom.

President Bush's Address to Joint Session of Congress, September 20, 2001

On September 11, 2001, terrorists crashed airplanes into the World Trade Center in New York City and the Pentagon in Washington, D.C. Thousands of people were killed. In his address, President George W. Bush announced a new kind of war against terrorism.

. . . On September the eleventh, enemies of freedom committed an act of war against our country. . . . Americans have known surprise attacks—but never before on thousands of civilians. All of this was brought upon us in a single day—and night fell on a different world, a world where freedom itself is under attack. . . .

The evidence we have gathered all points to a collection of loosely affiliated terrorist organizations known as al-Qaeda. . . . Our war on terror begins with al-Qaeda, but it does not end there. It will not end until every terrorist group of global reach has been found, stopped, and defeated.

Americans are asking: Why do they hate us? They hate what we see right here in this chamber—a democratically elected government. Their leaders are self-appointed. They hate our freedoms. . . . By sacrificing human life to serve their radical visions—by abandoning every value except the will to power—they follow in the path of fascism, and Nazism, and totalitarianism. And they will follow that path all the way, to where it ends: in history's unmarked grave of discarded lies.

. . . We will direct every resource at our command—every means of diplomacy, every tool of intelligence, every instrument of law enforcement, every financial influence, and every necessary weapon of war—to the disruption and defeat of the global terror network. . . .

I know there are struggles ahead, and dangers to face. But this country will define our times, not be defined by them. . . . Great harm has been done to us. We have suffered great loss. And in our grief and anger we have found our mission and our moment. . . . Our Nation—this generation—will lift a dark threat of violence from our people and our future. We will rally the world to this cause, by our efforts and by our courage. We will not tire, we will not falter, and we will not fail.

Supreme Court Case Summaries

The following case summaries explain the significance of major Supreme Court cases mentioned in the text.

Abington School District v. Schempp (1963) struck down a Pennsylvania statute requiring public schools in the state to begin each school day with Bible readings and a recitation of the Lord's Prayer. The Court held that the Constitution's establishment clause leaves religious beliefs and religious practices to each individual's choice and expressly commands that government not intrude into this decision-making process.

Abrams v. United States (1919) upheld a conviction under the Sedition Act and Espionage Act of 1917. The Court ruled that freedom of speech could be limited if there was a threat to the country.

Baker v. Carr (1962) established that federal courts can hear suits seeking to force state authorities to redraw electoral districts. In this case, the plaintiff wanted the population of each district to be roughly equal to the population in all other districts. The plaintiff claimed that the votes of voters in the least populous districts counted as much as the votes of voters in the most populous districts.

Brown v. Board of Education (1954) overruled *Plessy v. Ferguson* (1896) and abandoned the separate-but-equal doctrine in the context of public schools. In deciding this case, the Supreme Court rejected the idea that equivalent but separate schools for African Americans and white students would be constitutional. The Court stated that the Fourteenth Amendment's command that all persons be accorded the equal protection of the law (U.S. Const. amend. XIV, sec. 1) is not satisfied by ensuring that African American and white schools "have been equalized, or are being equalized, with respect to buildings, curricula, qualifications, and salaries, and other tangible factors."

The Court then held that racial segregation in public schools violates the equal protection clause because it is inherently unequal. In other words, the separation of schools by race marks the separate race as inferior. The ruling in this case has been extended beyond public education to virtually all public accommodations and activities.

Bush v. Gore (2000) found that a manual recount of disputed presidential ballots in Florida lacked a uniform standard of judging a voter's intent, thus violating the equal protection clause of the Constitution. The Court also ruled that there was not enough time to conduct a new manual recount that would meet constitutional standards. The case arose when Republican candidate George W. Bush asked the Court to stop a hand recount. This decision ensured that Bush would receive Florida's electoral votes and win the election.

Chisholm v. Georgia (1793) stripped the immunity of the states to lawsuits in federal court. The Supreme Court held that a citizen of one state could sue another state in federal court without that state consenting to the suit. The Court's decision created a furor and led to the adoption of the Eleventh Amendment, which protects states from federal court suits by citizens of other states.

Dred Scott v. Sandford (1857) was decided before the Fourteenth Amendment. The Fourteenth Amendment provides that anyone born or naturalized in the United States is a citizen of the nation and of his or her state. In this case, the Supreme Court held that a slave was property, not a citizen, and thus had no rights under the Constitution. The decision was a prime factor leading to the Civil War.

Engel v. Vitale (1962) held that the establishment clause (U.S. Const. amend. I, cl. 1) was violated by a public school district's practice of starting each school day with a prayer which began, "Almighty God, we acknowledge our dependence upon Thee." The Supreme Court ruled that religion is a personal matter and that government should not align itself with a particular religion in order to prevent religious persecution.

Escobedo v. Illinois (1964) held that Danny Escobedo's right to counsel, as provided by the Sixth Amendment, had been violated. Throughout police questioning, Escobedo asked repeatedly, but unsuccessfully, to see his attorney. The Supreme Court reversed Escobedo's murder conviction, holding that an attorney could have assisted Escobedo in invoking his Fifth Amendment right against self-incrimination. This case served as a forerunner to *Miranda v. Arizona*.

Gibbons v. Ogden (1824) made it clear that the authority of Congress to regulate interstate commerce (U.S. Const. art. I, sec. 8, cl. 3) includes the authority to regulate intrastate commercial activity that relates to interstate commerce. Before this case, it was thought that the Constitution would allow a state to close its borders to interstate commercial activity. This ruling says that a state can only regulate internal commercial activity, but Congress can regulate commercial activity that has both intrastate and interstate dimensions.

Gideon v. Wainwright (1963) ruled that poor defendants in criminal cases have the right to a state-paid attorney under the Sixth Amendment. The ruling in this case has been refined to apply only when the defendant, if convicted, can be sentenced to more than six months in jail.

Griswold v. Connecticut (1965) overturned the conviction of two Planned Parenthood employees charged with violating an 1879 state law banning the use of contraceptives. In deciding this case, the Court went beyond the actual words of the Constitution to protect a right—the right to privacy—which is not listed in the Constitution. The case also served as a forerunner to the *Roe v. Wade* decision that legalized abortion on the same basis.

Heart of Atlanta Motel, Inc. v. United States (1964) upheld the Civil Rights Act of 1964, which prohibits racial discrimination by those who provide goods, services, and facilities to the public. The Georgia motel in the case drew its business from other states but refused to rent rooms to African Americans. The Supreme Court explained that Congress had the authority to prohibit such discrimination under both the equal protection clause (U.S. Const. amend. XIV, sec. 1) and the commerce clause (art. I, sec. 8, cl. 3). With respect to the commerce clause, the Court explained that Congress had ample evidence to conclude that racial discrimination by hotels and motels impedes interstate commerce.

Korematsu v. United States (1944) allowed the federal government's authority to exclude Japanese Americans, many of whom were citizens, from designated military areas that included almost the entire West Coast. The government defended the orders as a necessary response to Japan's attack on Pearl Harbor. Yet, in upholding the orders, the Court established that government actions that discriminate on the basis of race would be subject to strict scrutiny.

Loving v. Virginia (1967) ruled that state laws that outlaw interracial marriages are unconstitutional under the Fourteenth Amendment. The Court explained that such laws violated the equal protection clause and deprived "citizens of liberty without due process of law." The Court went on to say, "Marriage is one of the basic civil rights of man, fundamental to our very existence and survival."

Mapp v. Ohio (1961) established that evidence seized in violation of the Fourth Amendment could not be used by the prosecution as evidence of a defendant's guilt at the federal, state, or local level.

Marbury v. Madison (1803) established one of the most important principles of American constitutional law. The Supreme Court held that the Court itself has the final say on what the Constitution means. It is also the Supreme Court that has the final say whether or not an act of government—legislative or executive at the federal, state, or local level—violates the Constitution.

Martin v. Hunter's Lessee (1816) affirmed that the Supreme Court has the authority to review state court decisions and is the nation's final court of appeal. The Supreme Court ruled that section 25 of the Judiciary Act of 1789 was constitutional. This section granted the Supreme Court appellate jurisdiction over state courts in certain situations, such as a state court denying the authority of federal law.

McCulloch v. Maryland (1819) established the basis for the expansive authority of Congress. The Supreme Court held that the necessary and proper clause (U.S. Const. art. I, sec. 8, cl. 18) allows Congress to do more than the Constitution specifically authorizes it to do. This case holds that Congress can enact almost any law that will help it achieve the ends established by Article I, Section 8 of the Constitution. For example, Congress has the power to regulate interstate commerce; the necessary and proper clause permits Congress to do so in ways not specified in the Constitution.

Miranda v. Arizona (1966) held that a person in police custody may not be held unless reminded of his or her rights. These rights include: 1) the right to remain silent, 2) the right to an attorney (at government expense if the person is unable to pay), and 3) that anything the person says after acknowledging that he or she understands these rights can be used as evidence of guilt at a trial.

The Supreme Court explained that a person alone in police custody may not understand, even if told, that he or she can remain silent and thus might be misled into answering questions. The presence of an attorney is essential.

Morgan v. Virginia (1946) challenged racial segregation in the South. Irene Morgan was convicted for refusing to give up her seat on an interstate bus bound from Virginia to Maryland. The Court ruled that the Virginia law posed an undue burden on interstate commerce and struck down the statute. However, segregation on southern buses continued on an informal basis.

National Labor Relations Board v. Jones and Laughlin Steel Corp. (1937) upheld President Franklin Roosevelt's New Deal legislation, the National Labor Relations Act, which allowed workers to organize unions in businesses operating or affecting interstate commerce. Employers were prohibited from discriminating against their employees because of union membership. Prior to this case, the Supreme Court had ruled much New Deal legislation unconstitutional. This ruling came less than a week after Roosevelt's proposed court-packing plan. The president intended on "packing" the Supreme Court with additional justices in order to obtain a pro-New Deal majority on the Court.

New York Times Co. v. Sullivan (1964) extended the protections afforded to the press by the free press clause (U.S. Const. amend. I). In this case, the Supreme Court held that a public official or public figure suing a publisher for libel (i.e., defamation) must prove that the publisher published a story that he or she knew was false or published the story in "reckless disregard of its truth or falsity," which means that the publisher did not take professionally adequate steps to determine the story's truth or falsity.

Norris v. Alabama (1935) overturned the conviction of Clarence Norris, an African American sentenced to death for a crime in Alabama. The Supreme Court held that the grand jury and trial jury had systematically eliminated African American jurors. Thus, the Court reversed the conviction because it violated the equal protection clause of the Fourteenth Amendment.

Northern Securities Company v. United States (1904) dealt with the application of congressional antitrust legislation. The party involved held three-fourths of the stock in two parallel railroad lines. By a narrow 5–4 decision, the Court upheld the application of the Sherman Antitrust Act. The Court ruled that the holding company clearly intended to eliminate competition between the two railroads, violating the constitutional right of Congress to regulate interstate commerce.

Plessy v. Ferguson (1896) upheld the separate-but-equal doctrine used by Southern states to perpetuate segregation after the Civil War officially ended law-mandated segregation. The decision upheld a Louisiana law requiring passenger trains to have "equal but separated accommodations for the white and colored races." The Court held that the Fourteenth Amendment's equal protection clause required only equal public facilities for the two races, not equal access. This case was overruled by *Brown* v. *Board of Education* (1954).

Regents of the University of California v. Bakke (1978) was the first Supreme Court decision to suggest that an affirmative action program could be justified on the basis of diversity. The Court explained that racial quotas were not permissible under the equal protection clause of the Fourteenth Amendment. However, the justices ruled that the diversity rationale was a legitimate interest that would allow a state medical school to consider an applicant's race in evaluating his or her application for admission. (Recent Supreme Court cases suggest that the diversity rationale is no longer enough to defend an affirmative action program.)

Reynolds v. Sims (1964) extended the one-person, one-vote doctrine announced in *Wesberry* v. *Sanders* to state legislative elections. The Court held that the inequality of representation in the Alabama legislature violated the equal protection clause of the Fourteenth Amendment.

Roe v. Wade (1973) held that women have the right under various provisions of the Constitution—most notably, the due process clause of the Fourteenth Amendment—to decide whether or not to terminate a pregnancy. The Court's ruling in this case was the most significant in a long line of decisions over a period of 50 years that recognized a constitutional right of privacy, even though the word *privacy* is not found in the Constitution.

Schechter Poultry Corporation v. United States (1935) overturned the conviction of the employers, who were charged with violating the wage and hour limitations of a law adopted under the authority of the

National Industrial Recovery Act. The Court held that because the defendants did not sell poultry in interstate commerce, they were not subject to federal regulations on wages and hours.

Schenck v. United States (1919) upheld convictions under the Federal Espionage Act. The defendants were charged under the act with distributing leaflets aimed at inciting draft resistance during World War I; their defense was that antidraft speech was protected under the First Amendment.

The Supreme Court unanimously rejected the defense, explaining that whether or not speech is protected depends on the context in which it occurs. Because the defendants' antidraft rhetoric created a "clear and present danger" to the success of the war effort, it was not protected.

Stone v. Powell (1976) reversed a Court of Appeals decision that evidence was seized illegally and should therefore be excluded. The Court ruled that the defendant was provided a fair and legal opportunity to claim a Fourth Amendment violation before a trial jury. The trial jury found that the search was constitutional and the evidence should not be excluded. The Court stated, "Where the state has provided an opportunity for full and fair litigation of a Fourth Amendment claim, a state prisoner may not be granted federal habeas corpus relief."

Swann v. Charlotte-Mecklenburg Board of Education (1971) established a new plan to ensure that public schools were not segregated. Many school systems were slow to desegregate after *Brown v. Board of Education* and used various tactics to appear to be resolving the problem. This case ordered that busing students, reorganizing school boundaries, and racial ratios all be used as methods to obtain desegregated public school systems.

Sweatt v. Painter (1950) held that it was unconstitutional for African Americans to be denied admission to the University of Texas Law School based on race. An inferior law school established for African Americans did not give the state justification to deny admission to the main school. This act was a violation of the Fourteenth Amendment.

Wabash v. Illinois (1886) held that states have no authority to regulate railroad rates for interstate commerce. The Supreme Court held that the commerce clause (U.S. Const. art. I, sec. 8, cl. 3) allowed states to enforce "indirect" but not "direct" burdens on interstate commerce. State railroad rates were ruled "direct" burdens and therefore could not be enforced by states. The decision created a precedent by establishing rate regulation of interstate commerce as an exclusive federal power.

Wickard v. Filburn (1942) indicated how far the Supreme Court had come in complying with President Franklin Roosevelt's economic philosophies. The Court upheld specific parts of the Second Agricultural Adjustment Act. In its ruling, the Supreme Court held that marketing quotas could be applied to wheat that never left the farm. Using the commerce clause (U.S. Const. art. I, sec. 8, cl. 3) as the basis for its decision, the Court ruled that wheat that never left the farm still had an effect on interstate commerce. Farmers growing their own grain depressed the overall demand and market price of wheat. The decision further extended the power of the commerce clause.

Worcester v. Georgia (1832) overturned the conviction of Samuel A. Worcester, a missionary among the Cherokee. Worcester was imprisoned under a Georgia law forbidding whites to reside in Cherokee country without taking an oath of allegiance to the state and obtaining a permit. The Supreme Court voided the state law, ruling that the Cherokee were an independent nation based on a federal treaty and free from the jurisdiction of the state. Georgia ignored the decision, and President Jackson refused to enforce it, instead supporting the removal of the Cherokee to the Indian Territory.

Flag Etiquette

For Americans, the flag has always had a special meaning. It is a symbol of our nation's freedom and democracy.

Rules and Customs

Over the years, Americans have developed rules and customs concerning the use and display of the flag. One of the most important things every American should remember is to treat the flag with respect.

- The flag should be raised and lowered by hand and displayed only from sunrise to sunset. On special occasions, the flag may be displayed at night, but it should be illuminated.

- The flag may be displayed on all days, weather permitting, particularly on national and state holidays and on historic and special occasions.

- No flag may be flown above the American flag or to the right of it at the same height.

- The flag should never touch the ground or floor beneath it.

- The flag may be flown at half-staff by order of the president, usually to mourn the death of a public official.

- The flag may be flown upside down only to signal distress.

- When the flag becomes old and tattered, it should be destroyed by burning. According to an approved custom, the Union (stars on blue field) is first cut from the flag; then the two pieces, which no longer form a flag, are burned.

Continental Colors
1775-1777

First Stars and Stripes
1777-1795

Betsy Ross Flag
c. 1790

15-Star Flag
1795-1818

20-Star Flag
1818

Great Star Flag
1818

35-Star Flag
1863-1865

38-Star Flag
1877-1890

48-Star Flag
1912-1959

50-Star Flag
1960

Glossary

A

abolition the immediate ending of slavery (p. 285)

affirmative action an active effort to improve employment or educational opportunities for minorities (p. 933)

agrarianism philosophy that agriculture and owning land is the backbone of the economy (p. 214)

agricultural revolution period when early Americans learned how to plant and raise crops (p. 13)

alien a person living in a country who is not a citizen of that country (p. 219)

allotment a plot of land assigned to an individual or family for cultivation (p. 430)

amendment a change to the Constitution (p. 169)

Americanization causing someone to acquire American traits and characteristics (p. 485)

amnesty the act of granting a pardon to a large group of people (p. 387)

amphtrac an amphibious tractor used to move troops from ships to shore (p. 760)

anarchist person who believes that there should be no government (p. 611)

annexation incorporating a territory within the domain of a country (p. 304)

annuity money paid by contract on regular intervals (p. 426)

Antifederalist an opponent of the Constitution (p. 173)

appeasement accepting demands in order to avoid conflict (p. 714)

appropriate to allocate funds for spending (p. 183)

arbitration settling a dispute by agreeing to accept the decision of an impartial outsider (pp. 458, 557)

armistice a temporary agreement to end fighting (p. 596)

artisan a skilled worker who practices a trade or handicraft (p. 95)

assembly line a production system with machines and workers arranged so that each person performs an assigned task again and again as the item passes before him or her (p. 641)

assimilate to absorb a group into the culture of a larger population (p. 430)

astrolabe device used to determine direction, latitude, and local time (p. 36)

attrition the act of wearing down by constant harassment or attack (p. 355)

B

baby boom a marked rise in birthrate, such as occurred in the United States following World War II (p. 816)

bailiff minor officer of the courts (p. 662)

benevolent society an association focusing on spreading the word of God and combating social problems (p. 279)

bilingualism the practice of teaching immigrant students in their own language (p. 935)

bill a proposed law (p. 183)

bill of exchange credit slip given by English merchants to planters in exchange for sugar or other goods (p. 95)

binding arbitration process whereby a neutral party hears arguments from two opposing sides and makes a decision that both must accept (p. 692)

black codes laws passed in the South just after the Civil War aimed at controlling freedmen and enabling plantation owners to exploit African American workers (p. 393)

black power the mobilization of the political and economic power of African Americans, especially to compel respect for their rights and to improve their condition (p. 884)

blitzkrieg name given to sudden violent offensive attacks the Germans used during World War II; "lightning war" (p. 715)

blockade runner ship that runs through a blockade, usually to smuggle goods through a protected area (p. 359)

blue-collar jobs in the manual labor field, particularly those requiring protective clothing (p. 815)

blues style of music evolving from African American spirituals and noted for its melancholy sound (p. 628)

Bohemian a person (as an artist or writer) leading an unconventional lifestyle (p. 621)

bonanza farm a large, highly-profitable wheat farm (p. 422)

bond a note issued by the government which promises to pay off a loan with interest (p. 212)

bounty money given as a reward, as to encourage enlistment in the army (p. 358)

brinkmanship the willingness to go to the brink of war to force an opponent to back down (p. 799)

broker state role of the government to work out conflicts among competing interest groups (p. 700)

budget deficit the amount by which expenses exceed income (p. 987)

bull market a long period of rising stock prices (p. 657)

burgesses representatives to the general assembly of the Virginia colony (p. 64)

busing a policy of transporting children to schools outside their neighborhoods to achieve greater racial balance (p. 934)

C

cabinet a group of advisers to the president (pp. 184, 211)

capital gains tax a federal tax paid by businesses and investors when they sell stocks or real estate (p. 1006)

capitalist person who invests wealth, particularly money, in a business (p. 97)

Glossary

caravel sailing ship capable of long-distance exploration (p. 37)

carpetbagger name given to many Northerners who moved to the South after the Civil War and supported the Republicans (p. 399)

cash crop a crop grown primarily for profit (p. 85)

caucus system a system in which members of a political party meet to choose their party's candidate for president or decide policy (p. 268)

cede to give up by treaty (p. 311)

censure to express a formal disapproval of an action (p. 795)

chad a small piece of cardboard produced by punching a data card (p. 1028)

charter a constitution (p. 771)

checks and balances the system in which each branch of government has the ability to limit the power of the other branches to prevent any from becoming too powerful (p. 168)

circumnavigate to sail around (p. 43)

civilization a highly organized society marked by knowledge of trade, government, the arts, science, and, often, written language (p. 14)

closed shop an agreement in which a company agrees to hire only union members (pp. 458, 809)

cloture a motion which ends debate and calls for an immediate vote, possible in the U.S. Senate by a vote of 60 senators (p. 878)

Cold War the ideological and often confrontational conflict between the United States and the Soviet Union between 1946 and 1990 (p. 778)

Columbian Exchange series of complex societal and environmental interactions between Europe and the Americas begun with Columbus's first voyage (p. 43)

commission plan a plan in which a city's government is divided into different departments with different functions, each placed under the control of a commissioner (p. 548)

committee of correspondence committee organized in each colony to communicate with and unify the colonies (p. 127)

commune a group living arrangement in which members share everything and work together (p. 923)

concentration camp a camp where persons are detained or confined (p. 723)

concurrent powers those powers which the state and federal governments share (p. 181)

Confederacy nation declared to have been formed by the southern states that seceded from the Union in 1860–1861 (p. 343)

conference committee a special joint committee organized to help the House and Senate work on a compromise bill acceptable to both houses (p. 183)

conquistador Spanish for conqueror, the men who led the expeditions to conquer the Americas (p. 52)

conscription requiring people to enter military service (pp. 353, 585)

consensus general agreement (p. 856)

conservative a person who believes government power, particularly in the economy, should be limited in order to maximize individual freedom (p. 981)

constituent a resident of an electoral district (p. 183)

containment the policy or process of preventing the expansion of a hostile power (p. 784)

contra Spanish for counterrevolutionary, an anti-Sandinista guerrilla force in Nicaragua (p. 990)

contraband goods whose importation, exportation, or possession is illegal (p. 581)

convoy a group that travels with something, such as a ship, to protect it (p. 594)

convoy system a system in which merchant ships travel with naval vessels for protection (p. 746)

cooperative store where farmers bought products from each other; an enterprise owned and operated by those who use its services (p. 502)

cooperative individualism President Hoover's policy of encouraging manufacturers and distributors to form their own organizations and volunteer information to the federal government in an effort to stimulate the economy (p. 648)

corporation an organization that is authorized by law to carry on an activity but treated as though it were a single person (p. 448)

"corrupt bargain" an illegitimate agreement between politicians (p. 259)

cost of living the cost of purchasing goods and services essential for survival (p. 599)

cost-plus a government contract to pay a manufacturer the cost to produce an item plus a guaranteed percentage (p. 737)

cotton gin a machine that removed seeds from cotton fiber (p. 252)

counterculture a culture with values and beliefs different than the mainstream (p. 922)

coureur de bois French fur traders who lived among the Native Americans (p. 56)

covert not openly shown or engaged in (p. 801)

creationism the belief that God created the world and everything in it, usually in the way described in Genesis (p. 614)

credibility gap lack of trust or believability (p. 905)

crop lien obligation placed on a farmer to repay a debt with crops (p. 407)

customs duty a tax on imports and exports (p. 119)

de facto segregation segregation by custom and tradition (p. 867)

debt peonage condition of sharecroppers who could not pay off their debts and therefore could not leave the property they worked (p. 407)

deficit spending government practice of spending borrowed money rather than raising taxes, usually an attempt to boost the economy (p. 690)

deflation a decline in the volume of available money or credit that results in lower prices, and, therefore, increases the buying power of money (pp. 455, 501)

deport to expel individuals from the country (p. 602)

détente a policy which attempts to relax or ease tensions between nations (p. 956)

developing nation a nation whose economy is primarily agricultural (p. 801)

direct primary a vote held by all members of a political party to decide their candidate for public office (p. 549)

disco popular dance music characterized by hypnotic rhythm, repetitive lyrics, and electronically produced sounds (p. 973)

disfranchise to deprive of the right to vote (p. 740)

DNA the genetic material in cells that determines all forms of life (p. 1015)

dollar diplomacy a policy of joining the business interests of a country with its diplomatic interests abroad (p. 541)

domino theory the belief that if one nation in Asia fell to the Communists, neighboring countries would follow (p. 894)

dove a person in favor of the United States withdrawing from the Vietnam War (p. 907)

downsizing reducing a company in size by laying off workers and managers to become more efficient (p. 1005)

dry farming a way of farming dry land in which seeds are planted deep in the ground where there is some moisture (p. 422)

due process a judicial requirement that laws may not treat individuals unfairly, arbitrarily, or unreasonably, and that courts must follow proper procedures and rules when trying cases (pp. 186, 844)

Dust Bowl name given to the area of the southern Great Plains severely damaged by droughts and dust storms during the 1930s (p. 663)

duty a tax on imports (p. 159)

dynamic conservatism policy of balancing economic conservatism with some activism (p. 811)

E

economies of scale the reduction in the cost of a good brought about especially by increased production at a given facility (p. 448)

emancipation the act or process of freeing enslaved persons (pp. 150, 286)

embargo a government ban on trade with other countries (pp. 225, 964)

empresario a person who arranged for the settlement of Texas in the 1800s (p. 301)

encomienda system of rewarding conquistadors tracts of land, including the right to tax and exact labor from Native Americans (p. 54)

Enlightenment movement during the 1700s that promoted science, knowledge, and reason (p. 108)

entrepreneur one who organizes, manages, and assumes the risks of a business or enterprise (pp. 97, 438)

enumerated powers powers listed in the Constitution as belonging to the federal government (pp. 181, 213)

envoy a person delegated to represent one country to another (p. 309)

espionage spying, especially to gain government secrets (p. 588)

ethnic cleansing the expulsion, imprisonment, or killing of ethnic minorities by a dominant majority group (p. 1020)

eugenics a pseudo-science that deals with the improvement of hereditary qualities of a race or breed (p. 611)

euro the basic currency shared by the countries of the European Union since 1999 (p. 1023)

evolution the scientific theory that humans and other forms of life have evolved over time (p. 614)

executive branch branch of government that implements and enforces laws (p. 168)

executive privilege principle stating that communications of the executive branch should remain confidential to protect national security (p. 961)

extermination camp a camp where prisoners were sent to be executed (p. 723)

F

fallout radioactive particles dispersed by a nuclear explosion (p. 796)

fallout shelter a shelter built with the intent to house and protect people from nuclear fallout (p. 796)

fascism a political system headed by a dictator that calls for extreme nationalism and racism and no tolerance of opposition (p. 709)

"favorite son" men who enjoyed the support of leaders from their own state and region (p. 259)

featherbedding practice of limiting work output in order to create more jobs (p. 809)

federalism political system in which power is divided between the national and state governments (pp. 168, 181)

Federalist a supporter of the Constitution (p. 173)

feminism the belief that men and women should be equal politically, economically, and socially (p. 927)

Glossary

feudalism political system in which powerful leaders gave land to nobles in exchange for pledges of loyalty and service (p. 33)

filibuster an attempt to kill a bill by having a group of senators take turns speaking continuously so that a vote cannot take place (p. 878)

fireside chats radio broadcasts made by FDR to the American people to explain his initiatives (p. 684)

fixed costs costs a company must pay regardless of whether or not it is operating (p. 448)

flapper a young woman of the 1920s who showed freedom from convention, especially in dress (p. 613)

flexible response the buildup of conventional troops and weapons to allow a nation to fight a limited war without using nuclear weapons (p. 847)

forage to search or raid for food (p. 370)

foreclose to take possession of a property from a mortgagor because of defaults on payments (p. 671)

fossil fuel a fuel formed in the earth from decayed plant or animal remains (p. 942)

franchise the right or license to market a company's goods or services in an area, such as a store of a chain operation (p. 815)

freedmen persons freed from slavery (p. 389)

Freedom Riders name given to a group of people who traveled to the South in 1961 to protest the South's refusal to integrate bus terminals (p. 875)

fundamentalist a Protestant evangelical Christian who believes in being saved from sins by being born again and making a personal commitment to follow Jesus Christ (p. 614)

furnishing merchant merchant who provides sharecroppers with supplies on credit at high interest rates (p. 407)

general strike a strike involving all the workers in a particular geographic location (p. 600)

generation gap a cultural separation between parents and their children (p. 824)

gentry wealthy landowners in the South, also called the planter elite (p. 86)

glacier a huge ice sheet (p. 13)

glasnost a Soviet policy permitting open discussion of political and social issues and freer dissemination of news and information (p. 1002)

global warming an increase in average world temperatures over time (p. 1025)

gold standard a monetary standard in which one ounce of gold equaled a set number of dollars (p. 681)

goldbug a person who believes that American currency should be based on a gold standard (p. 506)

gradualism theory that slavery should be ended gradually (p. 285)

graduated income tax tax based on the net income of an individual or business and which taxes different income levels at different rates (p. 504)

graft the acquisition of money in dishonest ways, as in bribing a politician (pp. 400, 473)

grandfather clause a clause that allowed individuals who did not pass the literacy test to vote if their fathers or grandfathers had voted before Reconstruction began; an exception to a law based on preexisting circumstances (p. 510)

grassroots movement a group of people organizing at the local or community level, away from political or cultural centers (p. 1006)

Great Awakening movement during the 1700s that stressed dependence on God (p. 108)

greenback a piece of U.S. paper money first issued by the North during the Civil War (pp. 352, 501)

gross national product the total value of goods and services produced by a country during a year (p. 436)

guerrilla member of an armed band that carries out surprise attacks and sabotage rather than open warfare (pp. 577, 894)

guerrilla warfare a hit-and-run technique used in fighting a war; fighting by small bands of warriors using tactics such as sudden ambushes (p. 139)

guru a person with knowledge or expertise, especially a religious teacher and spiritual guide in Hinduism (p. 971)

habeas corpus a legal order for an inquiry to determine whether a person has been lawfully imprisoned (p. 353)

hacienda a huge ranch (p. 55)

hardtack a hard biscuit made of wheat flour (p. 366)

hawk someone who believed the United States should continue its military efforts in Vietnam (p. 907)

headright system in which settlers were granted land in exchange for settling in Virginia (p. 64)

hedgerow row of shrubs or trees surrounding a field, often on a dirt wall (p. 765)

hemispheric defense zone national policy during World War II that declared the Western Hemisphere to be neutral and that the United States would patrol this region against German submarines (p. 727)

heretic a dissenter from established church beliefs (p. 69)

hidalgo low-ranking nobles who came to America as conquistadors (p. 54)

hobo a homeless and usually penniless wanderer (p. 662)

holding company a company whose primary business is owning a controlling share of stock in other companies (p. 450)

Holocaust name given to the mass slaughter of Jews and other groups by the Nazis during World War II (p. 719)

homestead method of acquiring a piece of U.S. public land by living on and cultivating it (p. 421)

Hooverville nickname given to shantytowns in the United States during the Depression (p. 662)

horizontal integration the combining of competing firms into one corporation (p. 449)

I

Ice Age a period of extremely cold temperatures when part of the planet's surface was covered with massive ice sheets (p. 13)

immunity freedom from prosecution (p. 638)

impeach to formally charge a public official with misconduct in office (pp. 169, 182, 394, 961)

imperialism the actions used by one nation to exercise political or economic control over a smaller or weaker nation (p. 521)

implied powers powers not specifically listed in the Constitution but claimed by the federal government (p. 213)

impound to take possession of (p. 955)

impressment a kind of legalized kidnapping in which people are forced into military service (p. 225)

income tax a tax based on the net income of a person or business (p. 568)

indentured servant an individual who contracts to work for a colonist for a specified number of years in exchange for transportation to the colonies, food, clothing, and shelter (p. 86)

industrial union an organization of common laborers and craft workers in a particular industry (p. 455)

inflation the loss of value of money (pp. 120, 501, 844)

initiative the right of citizens to place a measure or issue before the voters or the legislature for approval (p. 549)

installment buying an item on credit with a monthly plan to pay off the value of the good (p. 662)

insubordination disobedience (p. 565)

insurrection an act of rebellion against the established government (p. 337)

interchangeable parts uniform pieces that can be made in large quantities to replace other identical pieces (p. 248)

internationalism a national policy of actively trading with foreign countries to foster peace and prosperity (p. 712)

Internet an electronic communications network that connects computer networks and organizational computer facilities around the world (p. 1014)

interposition theory that a state should be able to intervene between the federal government and the people to stop an illegal action (p. 220)

iron curtain the political and military barrier that isolated Soviet-controlled countries of Eastern Europe after World War II (p. 782)

isolationism a national policy of avoiding involvement in world affairs (pp. 649, 711)

J

jazz American style of music that developed from ragtime and blues and which uses syncopated rhythms and melodies (p. 627)

Jim Crow laws statutes or laws created to enforce segregation (p. 510)

jingoism extreme nationalism marked by aggressive foreign policy (p. 529)

joint committee a committee organized with members from both the House and Senate to work on specific issues (p. 183)

joint-stock company form of business organization in which many investors pool funds to raise large amounts of money for large projects (p. 61)

judicial branch branch of government that interprets laws and renders judgment in cases involving those laws (p. 168)

judicial review power of the Supreme Court to determine whether laws of Congress are constitutional and to strike down those that are not (pp. 185, 223)

juvenile delinquency antisocial or criminal behavior of young people (p. 831)

K

kachina a good spirit that the Pueblo people believed brought messages from the gods to their town each year (p. 21)

kamikaze during World War II, a Japanese suicide pilot whose mission was to crash into his target (p. 761)

kinship group large group of extended families (p. 23)

kiva circular ceremonial room built by the Anasazi (p. 16)

L

labor union an organization of workers formed for the purpose of advancing its members' interests (p. 249)

laissez-faire policy that government should interfere as little as possible in the nation's economy (p. 438)

land grant a grant of land by the federal government especially for roads, railroads, or agricultural colleges (p. 445)

legislative branch a branch of government that makes the nation's laws (p. 168)

letters of marque licenses issued by Congress to private ship owners authorizing them to attack British merchant ships (p. 143)

liberal a person who generally believes the government should take an active role in the economy and in social programs but should not dictate social behavior (p. 981)

Liberty ship basic cargo ship used by the United States during World War II (p. 738)

limited war a war fought with limited commitment of resources to achieve a limited objective, such as containing communism (p. 789)

line of demarcation north-south line of longitude through the Atlantic Ocean dividing lands in the Americas claimed by Spain and Portugal (p. 42)

linkage policy of improving relations with the Soviet Union and China in hopes of persuading them to cut back their aid to North Vietnam (p. 910)

lockout a company tool to fight union demands by refusing to allow employees to enter its facilities to work (p. 456)

longhouse large, rectangular building with barrel-shaped roofs covered in bark, used by some Native Americans (p. 23)

long drive driving cattle long distances to a railroad depot for fast transport and great profit (p. 417)

Loyalist American colonists who supported Britain and opposed the War for Independence (p. 129)

lynching an execution performed without lawful approval (p. 511)

M

maize one of the first crops grown by early Americans, known today as corn (p. 14)

mandate authorization to act given to a representative (p. 378)

Manifest Destiny idea popular in the United States during the 1800s that the country must expand its boundaries to the Pacific Ocean (p. 295)

manorialism economic system in which peasants provide services to a feudal lord in exchange for protection (p. 33)

manumission the voluntary freeing of enslaved persons (p. 151)

margin buying a stock by paying only a fraction of the stock price and borrowing the rest (p. 657)

margin call demand by a broker that investors pay back loans made for stocks purchased on margin (p. 657)

martial law the law administered by military forces that is invoked by a government in an emergency (p. 345)

Marxism theory of socialism in which a class struggle would exist until the workers were finally victorious, creating a classless society (p. 456)

mass media a medium of communication (as in television and radio) intended to reach a wide audience (p. 623)

mass production the production of large quantities of goods using machinery and often an assembly line (p. 641)

massive retaliation a policy of threatening a massive response, including the use of nuclear weapons, against a Communist state trying to seize a peaceful state by force (p. 798)

matrilineal relating to, based on, or tracing descent through the maternal line (p. 30)

maverick a stray calf with no identifying symbol (p. 418)

mercantilism the theory that a state's power depends on its wealth (p. 98)

microprocessor a computer processor containing both memory and computing functions on a single chip (p. 1013)

Middle Passage the difficult journey slaves endured in crossing the Atlantic Ocean to the Americas (p. 89)

military-industrial complex an informal relationship that some people believe exists between the military and the defense industry to promote greater military spending and influence government policy (p. 802)

minutemen companies of civilian soldiers who boasted they were ready to fight on a minute's notice (p. 129)

missile gap belief that the Soviet Union had more nuclear weapons than the United States (p. 841)

monopoly total control of a type of industry by one person or one company (p. 449)

moratorium a suspension of activity (p. 650)

mosque Muslim place of worship (p. 28)

most-favored nation a policy between countries ensuring fair trading practices (p. 216)

muckraker a journalist who uncovers abuses and corruption in a society (p. 547)

mudslinging attempt to ruin an opponent's reputation with insults (p. 260)

multinational corporation large corporations with overseas investments (p. 815)

N

napalm a jellied gasoline used for bombs (pp. 768, 900)

nationalism loyalty and devotion to a nation (pp. 232, 578)

nativism hostility toward immigrants (pp. 274, 468)

natural rights fundamental rights all people are born possessing, including the right to life, liberty, and property (p. 102)

naturalism a philosophy and approach to art and literature based on the belief that nature can be understood through scientific observation and that society functions best with some governmental regulation (p. 483)

nomad a person who continually moves from place to place, usually in search of food (pp. 13, 425)

nonimportation agreement a pledge by merchants not to buy imported goods from a particular source (p. 121)

normalcy the state or fact of being normal (p. 637)

Northwest Passage the mythical northern water route through North America to the Pacific Ocean (p. 55)

nuclear proliferation the spread of nuclear weapons to new nations (p. 1025)

nullification theory that states have the right to declare a federal law invalid (pp. 220, 268)

obsidian a dark glass formed by the cooling of molten lava (p. 14)

Open Door policy a policy that allowed each foreign nation in China to trade freely in the other nations' spheres of influence (p. 538)

open range vast areas of grassland owned by the federal government (p. 416)

open shop a workplace where workers are not required to join a union (p. 645)

operating costs costs that occur while running a company (p. 448)

overlander someone who travels overland to the West (p. 296)

override ability of Congress to reverse a presidential veto by a two-thirds majority vote (p. 182)

pacifism opposition to war or violence as a means of settling disputes (p. 75)

party boss the person in control of a political machine (p. 473)

Patriot American colonist who supported the War for Independence (p. 129)

patronage another name for the spoils system, in which government jobs or favors are given out to political allies and friends (p. 492)

penitentiary prison whose purpose is to reform prisoners (p. 280)

perestroika a policy of economic and government restructuring instituted by Mikhail Gorbachev in the Soviet Union in the 1980s (p. 1002)

periphery the outer boundary of something (p. 745)

perjury lying when one has sworn under oath to tell the truth (pp. 792, 1020)

philanthropy providing money to support humanitarian or social goals (p. 478)

pietism movement in the 1700s that stressed an individual's piety and an emotional union with God (p. 108)

Pilgrim a Separatist who journeyed to the American colonies in the 1600s for religious freedom (p. 67)

pillage to loot or plunder (p. 379)

placer mining method of extracting mineral ore by hand using simple tools like picks, shovels, and pans (p. 415)

plantation a large, commercial, agricultural estate (p. 85)

planter plantation owners who held 20 or more enslaved people (p. 253)

pocket veto indirectly vetoing a bill by letting a session of Congress expire without signing the bill (p. 388)

police powers a government's power to control people and property in the interest of public safety, health, welfare, and morals (p. 615)

political machine an organization linked to a political party that often controlled local government (p. 473)

poll tax a tax of a fixed amount per person that had to be paid before the person could vote (pp. 510, 879)

pool a group sharing in some activity; for example, among railroad owners who made secret agreements and set rates among themselves (p. 448)

popular sovereignty government subject to the will of the people (p. 168); before the Civil War, the idea that people living in a territory had the right to decide by voting if slavery would be allowed there (pp. 180, 321)

populism political movement founded in the 1890s representing mainly farmers, favoring free coinage of silver and government control of railroads and other large industries (p. 500)

poverty line a level of personal or family income below which one is classified as poor by the federal government (p. 828)

presidio fort built by the Spanish in the Americas (p. 54)

privateer privately owned ship licensed by the government to attack ships of other countries (p. 61)

progressivism a political movement that crossed party lines which believed that industrialism and urbanization had created many social problems and that government should take a more active role in dealing with these problems (p. 547)

prohibition laws banning the manufacture, transportation, and sale of alcoholic beverages (p. 553)

propaganda the spreading of ideas about an institution or individual for the purpose of influencing opinion (p. 581)

proprietary colony a colony owned by an individual (p. 64)

protective tariff tax on imports designed to protect American manufacturers (p. 241)

protectorate a country that is technically independent but is actually under the control of another country (p. 521)

public works projects such as highways, parks, and libraries built with public funds for public use (p. 669)

pueblo Spanish for village, term used by early Spanish explorers to denote large housing structures built by the Anasazi (p. 16)

Puritan someone who wanted to purify the Anglican Church during the 1500s and 1600s (p. 60)

quartz mining method of extracting minerals involving digging beneath the surface (p. 415)

Glossary

racism prejudice or discrimination against someone because of his or her race (p. 882)

radiocarbon dating method of determining how old biological objects are by measuring the radioactivity left in a special type of carbon (p. 13)

ragtime a type of music with a strong rhythm and a lively melody with accented notes (p. 480)

rationalism philosophy that emphasizes the role of logic and reason in gaining knowledge (p. 108)

rationing the giving out of scarce items on a limited basis (p. 753)

realism an approach to literature, art, and theater that attempts to accurately portray things as they really are and holds that society will function best if left to itself (p. 478)

reapportionment the method states use to draw up political districts based on changes in population (p. 843)

rebate a partial refund to lower the rate of a good or commodity (p. 495)

recall the right that enables voters to remove unsatisfactory elected officials from office (p. 549)

recession an economic slowdown (p. 160)

Reconstruction the reorganization and rebuilding of the former Confederate states after the Civil War (p. 387)

referendum the practice of letting voters accept or reject measures proposed by the legislature (pp. 335, 549)

relief aid for the needy, welfare (p. 670)

Renaissance French for rebirth, a period in Europe from 1350 to 1600 during which a rebirth of interest in the culture of ancient Greece and Rome occurred (p. 36)

reparations payment by the losing country in a war to the winner for the damages caused by the war (p. 596)

republic form of government in which power resides in a body of citizens entitled to vote (p. 147)

reserved powers those powers which, according to the Constitution, are retained by the states (p. 181)

Restoration term used to describe when the English Parliament decided to put the monarchy back into place in 1660 (p. 73)

revenue tariff tax on imports for the purpose of raising money (p. 241)

revival large public meeting for preaching and prayer (p. 108)

right-to-work law a law making it illegal to require employees to join a union (p. 809)

romanticism a literary, artistic, and philosophical movement in the 1700s emphasizing the imagination and the emotions, advocating feeling over reason, inner spirituality over external rules, the individual above society, and nature over environments created by humans (p. 276)

safety net something that provides security against misfortune; specifically, government relief programs intended to protect against economic disaster (p. 700)

savannah a rolling grassland (p. 27)

scalawag name given to Southerners who supported Republican Reconstruction of the South (p. 399)

secede to leave or withdraw (p. 268)

secession withdrawal from the Union (p. 323)

sedition incitement to rebellion (p. 219)

segregation the separation or isolation of a race, class, or group (p. 510)

select committee a committee organized in the House or Senate to complete a specific task (p. 183)

selectmen men chosen to manage a town's affairs (p. 94)

self-determination belief that people in a territory should have the ability to choose their own government (p. 578)

separate-but-equal doctrine established by the 1896 Supreme Court case *Plessy* v. *Ferguson* that permitted laws segregating African Americans as long as equal facilities were provided (p. 867)

separation of powers government principle in which power is divided among different branches (p. 168)

Separatist a Puritan who broke away from the Anglican Church (p. 66)

serf person bound to a manor (p. 33)

settlement house institution located in a poor neighborhood that provided numerous community services such as medical care, child care, libraries, and classes in English (p. 485)

shantytown an economically depressed section of town consisting of crudely built dwellings usually made of wood (p. 662)

sharecropper farmer who works land for an owner who provides equipment and seed and receives a share of the crop (pp. 407, 509)

siege a military blockade of a city or fortified place to force it to surrender (p. 370)

silverite person who believes that coining silver currency in unlimited quantities will eliminate economic crisis (p. 506)

sin tax federal tax on alcohol and tobacco (p. 404)

sit-down strike method of boycotting work by sitting down at work and refusing to leave the establishment (p. 693)

sit-in a form of protest involving occupying seats or sitting down on the floor of an establishment (p. 868)

skyscraper a very tall building (p. 470)

slash-and-burn agriculture farming technique in which land is cleared and made fertile by cutting down and burning forests (p. 23)

slave code a set of laws that formally regulated slavery and defined the relationship between enslaved Africans and free people (pp. 90, 254)

smog fog made heavier and darker by smoke and chemical fumes (p. 940)

soap opera a serial drama on television or radio using melodramatic situations (p. 664)

Social Security Act a law requiring workers and employers to pay a tax; the money provides a monthly stipend for retired people (p. 694)

socialism belief that business should be publicly owned and run by the government (p. 553)

sodbuster a name given to Great Plains farmers (p. 422)

software a computer program (p. 1013)

space race refers to the Cold War competition over dominance of space exploration capability (p. 847)

space shuttle a reusable spacecraft designed to transport people and cargo between Earth and space (p. 998)

space station a large satellite designed to be occupied for long periods and to serve as a base for operations in space (p. 999)

speakeasy a place where alcoholic beverages are sold illegally (p. 615)

speculation act of buying stocks at great risk with the anticipation that the price will rise (p. 657)

speculator person who risks money in hopes of a financial profit (p. 212)

sphere of influence section of a country where one foreign nation enjoys special rights and powers (p. 538)

spoils system practice of handing out government jobs to supporters; replacing government employees with the winning candidate's supporters (p. 267)

Square Deal Theodore Roosevelt's promise of fair and equal treatment for all (p. 556)

squatter someone who settles on public land under government regulation with the hopes of acquiring the title to the land (p. 295)

stagflation persistent inflation combined with stagnant consumer demand and relatively high unemployment (p. 964)

standing committee a permanent committee in the House or Senate organized for a specific area of focus (p. 183)

state-sponsored terrorism violent acts against civilians that are secretly supported by a government in order to attack other nations without going to war (p. 1032)

steerage cramped quarters on a ship's lower decks for passengers paying the lowest fares (p. 465)

stock market a system for buying and selling stocks in corporations (p. 657)

strategic defense a plan to develop missiles and other devices that can shoot down nuclear missiles before they hit the United States (p. 1029)

strategic materials materials needed for fighting a war (p. 729)

strike work stoppage by workers to force an employer to meet demands (p. 249)

subsistence farming farming only enough food to feed one's family (p. 87)

subversion a systematic attempt to overthrow a government by using persons working secretly from within (p. 791)

suffrage the right to vote (p. 549)

summit a meeting of heads of government (p. 957)

Sunbelt a new industrial region in southern California and the Deep South developing during World War II (p. 751)

supply-side economics economic theory that lower taxes will boost the economy as businesses and individuals invest their money, thereby creating higher tax revenue (pp. 648, 987)

syndicate a business group (p. 564)

teach-in an extended meeting or class held to discuss a social or political issue (p. 905)

Tejano Spanish-speaking inhabitants of Texas (p. 300)

telecommute to work at home by means of an electronic linkup with a central office (p. 1013)

televangelist an evangelist who conducts regularly televised religious programs (p. 984)

temperance moderation in or abstinence from alcohol (pp. 279, 553)

tenant farmer farmer who works land owned by another and pays rent either in cash or crops (p. 407)

tenement multi-family apartments, usually dark, crowded, and barely meeting minimum living standards (p. 471)

termination policy a government policy to bring Native Americans into mainstream society by withdrawing recognition of Native American groups as legal entities (p. 830)

terrorism the use of violence by non-governmental groups against civilians to achieve a political goal by instilling fear and frightening governments into changing policies (p. 1032)

time zone a geographical region in which the same standard time is kept (p. 444)

Title IX section of the 1972 Educational Amendments prohibiting federally funded schools from discriminating against girls and young women in nearly all aspects of their operations (p. 929)

town meeting a gathering of free men in a New England town to elect leaders which developed into the local town government (p. 94)

trade deficit the difference between the value of a country's imports versus its exports (p. 1023)

trade union an organization of workers with the same trade or skill (p. 455)

Glossary

transcendental meditation a technique of meditation in which a mantra is chanted as a way of achieving peak intelligence, harmony, and health (p. 971)

transcendentalism a philosophy stressing the relationship between human beings and nature, spiritual things over material things, and the importance of the individual conscience (p. 276)

transcontinental railroad a railway system extending across the continent (p. 328)

triangular trade a three-way trade route that exchanged goods between the American colonies and two other trading partners (p. 95)

trust a combination of firms or corporations formed by a legal agreement, especially to reduce competition (p. 450)

U-boat German submarine, term means *Unterseeboot* (undersea boat) (p. 581)

Underground Railroad a system that helped enslaved African Americans follow a network of escape routes out of the South to freedom in the North (p. 327)

unfair trade practices trading practices which derive a gain at the expense of the competition (p. 569)

union shop a business that requires employees to join a union (p. 809)

urban renewal government programs that attempt to eliminate poverty and revitalize urban areas (p. 829)

utopia community based on a vision of a perfect society sought by reformers (p. 277)

vaquero men who herded cattle on haciendas (p. 55)

vaudeville stage entertainment made up of various acts, such as dancing, singing, comedy, and magic shows (p. 480)

vertical integration the combining of companies that supply equipment and services needed for a particular industry (p. 449)

veto power of the chief executive to reject laws passed by the legislature (p. 169)

victory garden gardens planted by American citizens during war to raise vegetables for home use, leaving more for the troops (pp. 586, 754)

Vietcong the guerrilla soldiers of the Communist faction in Vietnam, also known as the National Liberation Front (p. 897)

Vietnamization the process of making South Vietnam assume more of the war effort by slowly withdrawing American troops from Vietnam (p. 911)

War Hawks members of Congress during Madison's presidency who pressed for war with Britain (p. 229)

war on poverty antipoverty program under President Lyndon Johnson (p. 856)

welfare capitalism system in which companies enable employees to buy stock, participate in profit sharing, and receive benefits such as medical care common in the 1920s (p. 645)

white-collar jobs in fields not requiring work clothes or protective clothing, such as sales (p. 815)

wigwam conical or dome-shaped dwelling built by Native Americans using bent poles covered with hides or bark (p. 23)

writ of assistance a search warrant enabling customs officers to enter any location to look for evidence of smuggling (p. 122)

yellow journalism type of sensational, biased, and often false reporting for the sake of attracting readers (p. 528)

yeoman farmer owner of a small farm with four or fewer enslaved persons, and usually none (p. 253)

yuppie a young college-educated adult who is employed in a well-paying profession and who lives and works in or near a large city (p. 995)

Glossary

Spanish Glossary

A

abolition/abolición el final inmediato de la esclavitud (p. 285)

affirmative action/acción afirmativa un esfuerzo activo para mejorar las oportunidades educacionales y de empleo para las minorías (p. 933)

agrarianism/agrarismo filosofía de que la agricultura y la propiedad de tierras son los elementos principales de la economía (p. 214)

agricultural revolution/revolución agrícola período cuando los primeros americanos aprendieron plantar y cultivar la cosecha (p. 13)

alien/extranjero una persona que vive en un país del cual no es ciudadano (p. 219)

allotment/parcela un terreno asignado a un individuo o familia para su cultivación (p. 430)

amendment/enmienda un cambio a la Constitución (p.169)

Americanization/americanización causar que una persona adquiera características y rasgos americanos (p. 485)

amnesty/amnistía el acto de otorgar perdón a un número grande de personas (p. 387)

amphtrac/*amphtrac* un tractor anfibio utilizado para mover tropas desde barcos a la orilla del mar (p. 760)

anarchist/anarquista una persona que cree que no debe haber ningún gobierno (p. 611)

annexation/anexión incorporar un territorio dentro del dominio de un país (p. 304)

annuity/anualidad dinero pagado por contrato en intervalos regulares (p. 426)

Antifederalist/antifederalista oponente a la Constitución (p. 173)

appeasement/apaciguamiento demandas aceptadas a fin de evitar conflictos (p. 714)

appropriate/asignar apartar fondos para gastos (p. 183)

arbitration/arbitraje arreglar una disputa acordando aceptar la decisión de una persona imparcial (pp. 458, 557)

armistice/armisticio acuerdo temporal de paz para terminar con una lucha (p. 596)

artisan/artesano trabajador diestro que practica las artesanías y habilidades manuales (p. 95)

assembly line/línea de montaje sistema de producción con máquinas y trabajadores arreglados para que cada persona haga su trabajo designado una y otra vez mientras el artículo pasa frente a ellos (p. 641)

assimilate/asimilar incorporar a un grupo dentro de la cultura de una población más grande (p. 430)

astrolabe/astrolabio instrumento usado para determinar la dirección, latitud y la hora de una localidad (p. 36)

attrition/atrición acto de desalentar por constantes ataques o acoso (p. 355)

B

baby boom/auge de nacimientos aumento marcado en la taza de natalidad, tal como ocurrió en Estados Unidos después de la Segunda Guerra Mundial (p. 816)

bailiff/alguacil oficial en rango menor de las Cortes (p. 662)

benevolent society/sociedad de beneficencia una asociación enfocada en llevar la palabra de Dios y combatir problemas sociales (p. 279)

bilingualism/bilingualismo la práctica de enseñar a estudiantes inmigrantes en su propio lenguaje (p. 935)

bill/proyecto de ley una ley propuesta (p. 183)

bill of exchange/letra de cambio crédito en papel dado por mercaderes ingleses a colonos a cambio de azúcar (p. 95)

binding arbitration/arbitraje obligatorio proceso por el cual un partido neutral escucha argumentos de dos partidos opositores y toma una decisión que ambos deben aceptar (p. 692)

black codes/códigos negros leyes aprobadas en el Sur al terminar la Guerra Civil para controlar a los libertos y permitir a los dueños de plantaciones la explotación de los trabajadores afroamericanos (p. 393)

black power/poder negro mobilización del poder económico y político de afroamericanos especialmente para imponer respeto por sus derechos y para mejorar su condiciones (p. 884)

blitzkrieg/guerra relámpago nombre dado a los ataques repentinos ofensivos violentos que los alemanes usaron durante la Segunda Guerra Mundial (p. 715)

blockade runner/forzador de bloqueo un barco que navega a través de un bloqueo, usualmente para pasar contrabando a través de un área protegida (p. 359)

blue-collar/collar azul trabajos de mano de obra, particularmente aquellos que requieren ropa protectora (p. 815)

blues/*blues* estilo de música que evolucionó de la música espiritual de los afroamericanos, distinguida por su sonido melancólico (p. 626)

Bohemian/bohemio una persona (como artista o escritor) que lleva un estilo de vida poco convencional (p. 621)

bonanza farm/granja en bonanza extensa granja de trigo que produce muchas ganancias (p. 422)

bond/bono una obligación emitida por el gobierno que promete pagar un préstamo con interés (p. 212)

bounty/recompensa dinero dado para animar el alistamiento en el ejército (p. 358)

brinkmanship/política arriesgada la buena voluntad para ir al borde de guerra para forzar a un oponente a que se retracte (p. 799)

broker state/estado intermediario el papel del gobierno para resolver conflictos entre grupos con intereses competitivos (p. 700)

budget deficit/déficit del presupuesto la cantidad por la cual los gastos exceden los ingresos (p. 987)

bull market/bolsa al alza largo período durante el cual los precios de acciones en la bolsa se incrementan (p. 657)

burgesses/burgueses representantes elegidos para la asamblea general de la colonia de Virginia (p. 64)

busing/traslado obligatorio la política de transportar estudiantes a escuelas fuera de sus vecindarios para alcanzar un balance racial (p. 934)

cabinet/gabinete grupo de consejeros al presidente (p. 184, 211)

capital gains tax/impuestos a las ganancias del capital impuesto federal pagado por inversionistas y negocios cuando ellos venden acciones y bienes raíces (p. 1006)

capitalist/capitalista persona que invierte riqueza, particularmente dinero, en un negocio (p. 97)

caravel/carabela buque capaz de explorar largas distancias (p. 37)

carpetbagger/*carpetbagger* nombre dado a muchos norteños que se mudaron al Sur después de la Guerra Civil y apoyaron a los republicanos (p. 399)

cash crop/cultivo comercial cosecha cultivada para ganancia (p. 85)

caucus system/sistema de junta electoral sistema en el cual los miembros de un partido político se reúnen para escoger el candidato a la presidencia de su partido o para decidir políticas (p. 268)

cede/ceder darse por vencido por un tratado (p. 311)

censure/censura expresar la desaprobación formal sobre una acción (p. 795)

chad/agujereado pedazo pequeño de cartón producido taladrando una tarjeta de computadora (p. 1028)

charter/carta de privilegio una constitución (p. 771)

checks and balances/control y balances sistema en el cual cada ramo de gobierno tiene la habilidad para limitar el poder a los otros ramos para que ninguno vuelva a ser demasiado poderoso (p. 168)

circumnavigate/circunnavegar navegar alrededor de (p. 43)

civilization/civilización cultura sumamente desarrollada distinguida por un conocimiento de comercio, gobierno, las artes, las ciencias, y frecuentemente lenguaje escrito (p. 14)

closed shop/taller cerrado acuerdo en el que una compañía contrata solamente a miembros del sindicato (pp. 458, 809)

cloture/clausura una moción que termina con el debate y requiere un voto inmediato, posible en el Senado de EEUU por un voto de 60 senadores (p. 878)

Cold War/Guerra Fría conflicto ideológico caracterizado por frecuentes confrontaciones entre Estados Unidos y la Unión Soviética entre los años 1946 y 1990 (p. 778)

Columbian Exchange/Intercambio Colombiano una serie de interacciones complejas sociales y del medio ambiente entre Europa y las Américas que empezó con el primer viaje de Colón (p. 43)

commission plan/gobierno por comisión plan en el cual el gobierno municipal está dividido dentro de diferentes departamentos con diferentes funciones, cada uno bajo la dirección de un comisionado (p. 548)

committee of correspondence/comité de correspondencia comité organizado en cada colonia para comunicar entre las colonias y unificarlas (p. 127)

commune/comuna un arreglo de vivienda en el cual los miembros de un grupo trabajan juntos y comparten todo (p. 923)

concentration camp/campo de concentración un campamento donde personas están detenidas o encerradas (p. 723)

concurrent powers/poderes concurrentes poderes compartidos por los estados y el gobierno federal (p. 181)

Confederacy/Confederación nación formada por los estados sureños que se separaron de la Unión en 1860-1861 (p. 343)

conference committee/comité de conferencia una comisión paritaria especial organizada para ayudar a la Cámara y al Senado a forjar un compromiso de ley aceptable para ambas cámaras (p. 183)

conquistador/conquistador los hombres que condujeron las expediciones para conquistar las Américas (p. 52)

conscription/reclutamiento requerir que personas ingresen en el servicio militar (pp. 353, 585)

consensus/consenso acuerdo general (p. 856)

conservative/conservador una persona que cree que el poder del gobierno, particularmente en la economía, debe estar limitado para llevar al máximo la libertad individual (p. 981)

constituent/elector residente de un distrito electoral (p. 183)

containment/contención la política o proceso de prevenir la expansión de un poder hostil (p. 784)

contra/contra contrarevolucionario, la fuerza guerilla anti-Sandinista en Nicaragua (p. 990)

contraband/contrabando artículos de los que la importación, exportación o posesión es ilegal (pp. 581)

Spanish Glossary

convoy/convoy un grupo que viaja junto con algo, tal como un barco, para protegerlo (p. 594)

convoy system/sistema de convoy un sistema en el cual barcos mercantes viajan con buques navales para protección (p. 746)

cooperative/cooperativa tienda donde los granjeros compraban productos el uno del otro; empresa poseída y operada por los que usan sus servicios (p. 502)

cooperative individualism/individualismo cooperativo política del Presidente Hoover para alentar a los manufactureros y distribuidores a formar sus propias organizaciones y pasar información voluntariamente al gobierno federal en un esfuerzo para estimular la economía (p. 648)

corporation/sociedad anónima organización autorizada por ley a montar una actividad, tratada como si fuera una sola persona (p. 448, 686)

"corrupt bargain"/trato corrupto un acuerdo ilegítimo entre políticos (p. 259)

cost of living/costo de vida el costo de comprar artículos y servicios esenciales para la supervivencia (p. 599)

cost-plus/costo más beneficio contrato del gobierno para pagar el costo de fabricación para producir un artículo más un porcentaje garantizado (p. 737)

cotton gin/despepitadora de algodón máquina que sacaba las semillas de las fibras de algodón (p. 252)

counterculture/contracultura una cultura con valores y creencias diferentes de los de la cultura principal (p. 922)

coureur de bois/*coureur de bois* franceses que comerciaban con pieles y vivían entre los Nativos Americanos (p. 56)

covert/secreto no hecho o mostrado abiertamente (p. 801)

creationism/creacionismo la creencia que Dios creó al mundo y todo lo que hay en él, usualmente como se describe en Génesis (p. 614)

credibility gap/barrera de credibilidad falta de confianza (p. 905)

crop lien/derecho de cultivo obligación impuesta a un agricultor para cubrir la deuda por medio de cosecha (p. 407)

customs duty/derecho de aduana impuesto sobre importaciones y exportaciones (p.119)

D

de facto segregation/segregación de facto segregación por costumbre y tradición (p. 867)

debt peonage/esclavitud deudora condición de aparceros que no podían pagar sus deudas y por lo tanto no podían abandonar la propiedad que trabajaban (p. 407)

deficit spending/gastos déficits práctica del gobierno de gastar dinero prestado en vez de aumentar impuestos, usualmente una tentativa para levantar la economía (p. 690)

deflation/deflación un decremento de la cantidad de dinero o crédito disponible el cual resulta en precios reducidos y por lo tanto aumenta el poder adquisitivo de la moneda (pp. 455, 501)

deport/deportar expulsar del país a individuos (p. 602)

détente/*détente* una política que intenta relajar o borrar la tensión entre naciones (p. 956)

developing nation/nación en desarrollo nación en donde la economía es principalmente agrícola (p. 801)

direct primary/elección primaria voto tomado por todos los miembros de un partido político para elegir a su candidato para un puesto público (p. 549)

disco/música disco música popular para danza caracterizada por ritmo hipnótico, cantos repetitivos y sonidos producidos electrónicamente (p. 973)

disfranchise/privación civil privar el derecho al voto (p. 740)

DNA/ADN material genético de las células que determina toda forma de vida (p. 1015)

dollar diplomacy/diplomacia del dólar política de juntar los intereses comerciales de un país con sus intereses diplomáticos en el extranjero (p. 541)

domino theory/teoría dominó la creencia que si una nación en Asia se derrumbara ante los comunistas, sus países vecinos hubieran caído en seguida (p. 894)

dove/paloma persona a favor de que Estados Unidos se retirara de la guerra en Vietnam (p. 907)

dry farming/cultivo seco manera de cultivar tierra seca plantando las semillas en la profundidad de la tierra donde hay algo de humedad (p. 422)

due process/proceso justo requerimiento judicial de que las leyes no deben tratar individuos injusta, arbitraria, o irracionalmente y que las cortes deben de seguir procesos y reglamentos justos al jurar casos (pp. 186, 844)

Dust Bowl/Cuenca Polvada nombre dado al área sureña de las Grandes Planicies severamente dañada por sequías y tormentas de polvo durante los años 1930 (p. 663)

duty/impuesto un impuesto sobre importaciones (p.159)

dynamic conservatism/conservatismo dinámico política de alcanzar un balance entre el conservatismo económico y algún activismo (p. 811)

E

economies of scale/economía a gran escala reducción del costo de un producto a causa de la producción aumentada en una fábrica de producción (p. 448)

emancipation/emancipación el proceso de liberar a personas esclavizadas (p. 150, 286)

Spanish Glossary

embargo/embargo prohibición gubernamental contra el comercio con otros países (pp. 225, 964)

empresario/**empresario** persona que arreglaba el asentamiento de tierras en Texas durante los años 1800 (p. 301)

encomienda/**encomienda** sistema de recompensar a los conquistadores con extensiones de tierra y el derecho de recaudar impuestos y exigir mano de obra a los indígenas americanos (p. 54)

Enlightenment/Siglo Ilustrado movimiento durante los años 1700 que promovió el conocimiento, la razón, y las ciencias (p. 108)

entrepreneur/empresario persona que organiza, dirige y asume el riesgo de un negocio o empresa (pp. 97, 438)

enumerated powers/poderes enumerados poderes nombrados en la Constitución que pertenecen solamente al gobierno federal (pp. 181, 213)

espionage/espionaje espiar, especialmente para obtener secretos gubernamentales (p. 588)

ethnic cleansing/purificación étnica expulsión, encarcelamiento o asesinato de minorías étnicas por un grupo mayoritario dominante (p. 1020)

eugenics/eugenesia seudociencia que trata con el perfeccionamiento de las cualidades hereditarias de una raza o especie (p. 611)

euro/eurodólar moneda básica compartida por los países de la Unión Europea desde 1999 (p. 1023)

evolution/evolución teoría científica que los humanos y otras formas de vida se han evolucionado tras el tiempo (p. 614)

executive branch/ramo ejecutivo ramo de gobierno que implementa y refuerza las leyes (p. 168)

executive privilege/privilegio ejecutivo el principio de que las comunicaciones del ramo ejecutivo deben de permanecer confidenciales para proteger la seguridad nacional (p. 961)

extermination camp/campo de exterminación campo donde los prisioneros eran enviados para ser ejecutados (p. 723)

fallout/caída radioactiva partículas radioactivas dispersadas por una explosión nuclear (p. 796)

fallout shelter/refugio atómico un refugio construido para proteger a las personas de la caída radioactiva (p. 796)

fascism/fascismo un sistema político encabezado por un dictador que pide por nacionalismo y racismo extremo y poca tolerancia de la oposición (p. 709)

favorite son/hijo favorito hombres que disfrutaban del apoyo de los líderes de su estado y región natales (p. 259)

featherbedding/paro técnico práctica de limitar la producción con el fin de crear más trabajos (p. 809)

federalism/federalismo sistema político en el cual el poder está dividido entre los estados y el gobierno federal (pp. 168, 181)

Federalist/federalista persona que apoya la Constitución (p. 173)

feminism/feminismo la creencia que los hombres y las mujeres deben ser iguales política, económica y socialmente (p. 927)

feudalism/feudalismo un sistema político en el cual los líderes poderosos dieron tierra a los nobles a cambio de compromisos de lealtad y servicio (p. 33)

filibuster/filibustero un atentado para acabar con un proyecto de ley hablando continuamente a turnos un grupo de senadores para que no pueda haber un voto (p. 878)

fireside chats/pláticas hogareñas emisiones de radio transmitidas por FDR al pueblo americano para explicar sus iniciativas (p. 684)

fixed costs/costos fijos costos que una compañía debe pagar si está operando o no (p. 448)

flapper/*flapper* mujer jóven de los años 1920 que demostró libertad de las costumbres tradicionales especialmente en vestido (p. 613)

flexible response/respuesta flexible formación de tropas y armas convencionales para permitir que un país entre en una guerra limitada sin usar armas nucleares (p. 847)

forage/forrajear buscar alimento (p. 370)

foreclose/ejecutar una hipoteca tomar posesión de una propiedad por falta de pagos hipotecarios (p. 671)

fossil fuel/combustible fósil un combustible formado en la tierra de los restos descompuestos de plantas o animales (p. 942)

franchise/concesión derecho o licencia para vender los bienes o servicios de una compañía en un área tal como una cadena de tiendas (p. 815)

freedman/liberto persona liberada de la esclavitud (p. 389)

Freedom Riders/Jinetes de la Libertad nombre dado a un grupo de personas que viajaron al Sur en 1961 para protestar la negativa del Sur para integrar las terminales de autobuses (p. 755)

fundamentalist/fundamentalista un cristiano protestante evangélico que cree en ser salvado de pecados volviendo a nacer otra vez y haciendo un compromiso personal para seguir a Cristo Jesus (p. 614)

furnishing merchant/mercader usurero comerciante que proporciona abastos a los aparceros a crédito con un interés muy alto (p. 407)

G

general strike/huelga general una huelga por todos los trabajadores de un lugar geográfico (p. 600)

generation gap/barrera generacional una separación cultural entre padres e hijos (p. 824)

gentry/pequeña nobleza ricos terratenientes del Sur, también llamados plantadores de la élite (p. 86)

glacier/glaciar trozo enorme de hielo (p. 13)

glasnost/glasnost política soviética que permitía discusión abierta de temas políticos y sociales y diseminación más libre de noticias e información (p. 1002)

global warming/calentamiento global aumento en la temperatura promedio mundial tras un período (p. 1025)

gold standard/patrón oro norma monetaria en la cual una onza de oro igualaba a un número fijo de dólares (p. 681)

goldbug/goldbug persona que cree que la moneda americana debe de estar basada en un patrón oro (p. 506)

gradualism/gradualismo teoría de que la esclavitud debería terminarse gradualmente (p. 285)

graduated income tax/impuesto graduado de utilidades impuesto basado en los ingresos netos de un individuo o empresa en el cual la taza del impuesto se diferencia de acuerdo a diferentes niveles de salario (p. 504)

graft/soborno adquisición de dinero de manera deshonesta tal como el sobornar a un político (pp. 400, 473)

grandfather clause/cláusula de abuelo cláusula que permitió votar a los que no aprobaron el examen de leer si sus padres o sus abuelos habían votado antes de que empezara la Reconstrucción; excepción a una ley basada en circunstancias preexistentes (p. 510)

grassroots movement/movimiento local grupo de personas que se organiza a nivel local y popular lejos de centros políticos o culturales (p. 1006)

Great Awakening/Gran Despertar movimiento durante los años 1700 que enfatizó la dependencia en Dios (p. 108)

greenback/billete dorso verde billete de papel moneda de EEUU expedido por primera vez por el Norte durante la Guerra Civil (pp. 352, 501)

gross national product/producto nacional bruto valor total de bienes y servicios producidos por un país durante un año (p. 436)

guerrilla/guerrilla banda armada que usa ataques sorpresas o sabotaje en vez de la guerra organizada (pp. 577, 894)

guerrilla warfare/guerra de guerrillas técnica de tirar y darse a la huida usada en combates de guerra; peleas por pequeñas bandas de guerreros usando tácticas tales como emboscadas repentinas (p. 139)

guru/gurú persona con conocimiento y experiencia, dicho especialmente de un maestro religioso y guía espiritual en el indoísmo (p. 971)

H

habeas corpus/hábeas corpus orden legal para una encuesta para determinar si una persona ha sido encarcelada legalmente (p. 353)

hacienda/hacienda un rancho extenso (p. 55)

hardtack/hardtack galleta dura hecha de harina de trigo (p. 366)

hawk/halcón persona que creía que Estados Unidos debía continuar sus esfuerzos militares en Vietnam (p. 907)

headright/derecho de terreno sistema en el cual los colonizadores recibían tierra a cambio de establecerse en Virginia (p. 64)

hedgerow/seto fila de arbustos o árboles cercando un campo a menudo sobre un muro de tierra (p. 765)

hemispheric defense zone/zona de defensa hemisférica política nacional durante la Segunda Guerra Mundial que declaró que el Hemisferio Oeste fue neutral y que Estados Unidos patrullaría esta región en contra de submarinos alemanes (p. 727)

heretic/hereje disidente de creencias establecidas por la iglesia (p. 69)

hidalgo/hidalgo noble de bajo rango que vino a América como conquistador (p. 54)

hobo/vagabundo persona errante sin hogar y usualmente sin dinero (p. 662)

holding company/compañía de valores compañía de la cual el negocio principal es poseer el control de acciones en otras compañías (p. 450)

Holocaust/Holocausto nombre dado a la exterminación masiva de judíos y otros grupos hecha por los nazis durante la Segunda Guerra Mundial (p. 719)

homestead/posesionar método de adquirir una extensión de tierra pública de EEUU viviendo en ella y cultivándola (p. 421)

Hooverville/Hooverville apodo dado a los barrios en Estados Unidos durante la Depresión (p. 662)

horizontal integration/integración horizontal asociación de firmas competitivas en una sociedad anónima (p. 449)

I

Ice Age/Época Glacial período de temperaturas extremadamente frías cuando parte de la superficie del planeta estaba cubierta de capas masivas de hielo (p. 13)

immunity/inmunidad libertad de prosecusión (p. 638)

impeach/acusar acusar formalmente a un oficial público de mala conducta en la oficina (pp. 169, 182, 394, 961)

imperialism/imperialismo acciones usadas por una nación para ejercer el control político o económico sobre naciones más pequeñas o débiles (p. 521)

implied powers/poderes implícitos poderes no nombrados específicamente en la Constitución pero reclamados por el gobierno federal (p. 213)

impound/confiscar tomar posesión de (p. 955)

impressment/requisición un tipo de secuestro legalizado en el cual personas son forzadas a servir en el servicio militar (p. 225)

income tax/impuesto de utilidades impuesto basado en el ingreso neto de una persona o empresa (p. 568)

indentured servant/sirviente contratado individuo contratado para trabajar para un colono durante cierto número de años a cambio de transportación a las colonias, alimento, ropa y refugio (p. 86)

industrial union/sindicato industrial organización de trabajadores comunes y obreros calificados en una industria (p. 455)

inflation/inflación pérdida del valor del dinero (pp. 120, 501, 844)

initiative/iniciativa derecho de los ciudadanos de poner una propuesta o tema ante los votantes o la legislatura para su aprobación (p. 549)

installment/pago a plazos compra de un artículo a crédito con un plan de pago mensual para pagar el valor del artículo (p. 662)

insubordination/insubordinación desobediencia (p. 565)

insurrection/insurrección un acto de rebelión en contra del gobierno establecido (p. 337)

interchangeable parts/partes intercambiables piezas uniformes que pueden ser hechas en grandes cantidades para reemplazar otras piezas idénticas (p. 248)

internationalism/internacionalismo política nacional de intercambio comercial activo con países extranjeros para promover la paz y la prosperidad (p. 712)

Internet/*Internet* red de comunicaciones electrónicas que conecta redes de computación y facilidades de computación de organizaciones alrededor del mundo (p. 1014)

interposition/interposición teoría que un estado debiera poder intervenir entre el gobierno federal y la gente para detener una acción ilegal (p. 220)

iron curtain/cortina de hierro barrera política y militar que aisló a los países de Europa Oriental controlados por los soviéticos después de la Segunda Guerra Mundial (p. 782)

isolationism/aislacionismo política nacional de evitar el involucramiento en asuntos mundiales (pp. 649, 711)

jazz/*jazz* estilo de música americana que se desarrolló de *ragtime* y *blues* y que usa melodías y ritmos sincopados (p. 627)

Jim Crow Laws/Leyes de Jim Crow leyes creadas para reforzar la segregación (p. 510)

jingoism/patriotismo extremo nacionalismo marcado por la agresiva política extranjera (p. 529)

joint committee/comité paritaria comité organizado con miembros de la Cámara y el Senado para trabajar en temas específicos (p. 183)

joint-stock company/compañía por acciones forma de organización de negocios en la cual muchos inversionistas compran acciones para juntar grandes cantidades de dinero para grandes proyectos (p. 61)

judicial branch/ramo judicial ramo del gobierno que interpreta las leyes dando juicios de los casos involucrando esas leyes (p. 168)

judicial review/revisión judicial derecho de la Suprema Corte para determinar si las leyes del Congreso son constitucionales y para derribar aquellas que no lo son (pp. 185, 223)

juvenile delinquency/delincuencia juvenil comportamiento antisocial o criminal de los jóvenes (p. 831)

kachina/kachina espíritu bueno que la gente Pueblo creyó traía mensajes de los dioses a su pueblo cada año (p. 21)

kamikaze/kamikase durante la Segunda Guerra Mundial un piloto suicida japonés de quien la misión fue chocar en su objetivo (p. 761)

kinship group/grupo de parentesco grupo grande de familias (p. 23)

kiva/kiva cuarto circular ceremonial construido por los Anasazi (p. 16)

L

labor union/sindicato organización de trabajadores formada con el propósito de promover los intereses de sus miembros (p. 249)

laissez-faire/*laissez-faire* política que el gobierno debe interferir tan poco como sea posible en la economía del país (p. 438)

land-grant/concesión de tierras una concesión de terrenos por el gobierno federal especialmente para carreteras, vías de ferrocarril y colegios agrícolas (p. 445)

legislative branch/ramo legislativo ramo del gobierno que hace las leyes de una nación (p. 168)

letters of marque/patente de corso cédula autorizada por el Congreso para propietarios de naves privadas autorizándoles a atacar barcos mercantes británicos (p. 143)

liberal/liberal persona que generalmente cree que el gobierno debe desempeñar un papel active en la economía y programas sociales pero que el gobierno no debe dictar el comportamiento social (p. 981)

Liberty ship/barco de Libertad barco de carga básico utilizado por Estados Unidos durante la Segunda Guerra Mundial (p. 738)

limited war/guerra limitada guerra peleada con compromisos limitados de recursos para alcanzar un objetivo limitado, tal como la contención del comunismo (p. 789)

line of demarcation/línea de demarcación línea de longitud de norte a sur a través del Océano Atlántico que dividía las tierras en las Américas reclamadas por España y Portugal (p. 42)

linkage/enlace política de mejorar relaciones con la Unión Soviética y China con la esperanza de persuadirlas a que redujeran su ayuda a Vietnam del Norte (p. 910)

lockout/cierre patronal práctica de una empresa para rechazar las demandas sindicales negándose a permitir a los empleados a entrar al área de trabajo (p. 456)

long drive/manejo largo conducción de ganado por largas distancias a estaciones de ferrocarril para la transportación rápida y grandes ganancias (p. 417)

longhouse/casa comunal edificio grande rectangular con techo en forma de barril cubierto de corteza de árbol utilizado por unos indígenas americanos (p. 23)

Loyalist/lealista colono americano que apoyó a la Gran Bretaña y se opuso a la guerra para la independencia (p. 129)

lynching/linchamiento ejecución hecha sin aprobación legal (p. 511)

M

maize/maíz una de las primeras cosechas cultivadas por los antiguos americanos, conocido hoy en día como elote (p. 14)

mandate/mandato autorización dado a un representante (p. 379)

Manifest Destiny/Destino Manifiesto idea popular en Estados Unidos durante los años 1800 de que el país debía extender sus fronteras hasta el Océano Pacífico (p. 295)

manorialism/señorialismo sistema económico en el cual los campesinos proporcionan sus servicios a un lord feudal a cambio de protección (p. 33)

manumission/manumisión liberación voluntaria de personas esclavizadas (p. 151)

margin/margen comprar acciones pagando solamente una fracción del precio y pidiendo prestado el resto (p. 657)

margin call/llamada de reserva demanda de un accionista a que los inversionistas paguen los préstamos hechos para la compra de acciones al margen (p. 657)

martial law/derecho marcial derecho administrado por fuerzas militares que es invocado por un gobierno en una emergencia (p. 345)

Marxism/marxismo teoría de socialismo en la cual una lucha de clases sociales existiría hasta que los trabajadores salieran finalmente victoriosos, creando una sociedad sin distinción de clases (p. 456)

mass media/medios informativos medios de comunicación (como televisión y radio) con la intención de llegar a la audiencia extensa (p. 623)

mass production/fabricación en serie producción de grandes cantidades de productos usando máquinas y a menudo una línea de montaje (p. 641)

massive retaliation/represalia masiva una política que amenaza una respuesta masiva, incluyendo el uso de armas nucleares, contra un estado comunista que trata de captar un país pacífico por la fuerza (p. 798)

matrilineal/por línea materna relacionado o basado en la línea materna (p. 30)

maverick/*maverick* un res descarriado sin ningún símbolo de identificación (p. 418)

mercantilism/mercantilismo teoría que el poder de una estado depende de su riqueza (p. 98)

microprocessor/microprocesador procesador de computadora que contiene memoria y funciones de computación en un solo chip (p. 1013)

military-industrial complex/compejo militar industrial relación informal que algunas personas creen que existe entre lo militar y la industria de defensa para promover mayores gastos militares y para influenciar la política gubernamental (p. 802)

minutemen/*minutemen* compañías de soldados civiles que se jactaban de que podrían estar listos para tomar armas en sólo un minuto (p. 129)

missile gap/diferencia de proyectiles creencia que la Unión Soviética tenía más armas nucleares que Estados Unidos (p. 841)

monopoly/monopolio control total de una industria por una persona o una compañía (p. 449)

moratorium/moratoria suspensión de actividad (p. 650)

most-favored nation/nación más favorecida política entre países asegurando prácticas de tratado de comercio justo (p. 216)

muckraker/*muckraker* periodista que revela abusos y corrupción en una sociedad (p. 547)

Spanish Glossary

mudslinging/*mudslinging* intentar arruinar la reputación de un adversario con insultos (p. 260)

multinational corporation/corporación multinacional grandes corporaciones de inversión extranjera (p. 815)

napalm/*napalm* gasolina gelatinosa utilizada para bombas incendiarias (pp. 768, 900)

nationalism/nacionalismo lealtad y devoción a una nación (p. 232, 578)

nativism/nativismo sentimientos de hostilidad hacia imigrantes (pp. 274, 468)

natural rights/derechos naturales derechos fundamentales de las personas que nacen con ellos, incluyendo el derecho a vivir, de libertad y propiedad (p. 102)

naturalism/naturalismo filosofía y perspectiva en arte y literatura en la cual la naturaleza es tratada realísticamente, puede ser entendida a través de observación científica y que la sociedad funcionará mejor con algunas regulaciones gubernamentales (p. 483)

nomad/nómada persona que se mueve de un lugar a otro, generalmente en busca de alimentos o pastos (pp. 13, 425)

nonimportation agreement/acuerdo de no importación compromiso por mercaderes de no comprar artículos importados de una fuente indicada (p. 121)

normalcy/normalidad estado de ser normal (p. 637)

Northwest Passage/Pasaje del Noroeste ruta acuática mítica del norte a través de América del Norte al Océano Pacífico (p. 55)

nuclear proliferation/proliferación nuclear distribución de armas nucleares a nuevas naciones (p. 1025)

nullification/anulación teoría que los estados tienen el derecho de declarar inválida una ley federal (p. 220, 268)

obsidian/obsidiana vidrio obscuro formado por el enfriamiento de la lava líquida (p. 14)

Open Door policy/política de Puertas Abiertas política que permitió a cada nación extranjera en China intercambiar libremente en las esferas de influencia de otras naciones (p. 538)

open range/terreno abierto gran extensión de pastos propiedad del gobierno federal (p. 416)

open shop/taller abierto lugar de trabajo donde los trabajadores no son requeridos de ser miembros del sindicato (p. 645)

operating cost/costos de operación costos que ocurren operando una compañía (p. 448)

overlander/viajero persona que viaja al oeste por tierra (p. 296)

override/anular habilidad del Congreso de rechazar un veto presidencial por el voto de una mayoría de dos tercios (p. 182)

pacifism/pacifismo oposición a la guerra o violencia como un medio para arreglar disputas (p. 75)

party boss/jefe de partido persona que lleva el control de la maquinaria política (p. 473)

Patriot/Patriota colono americano que apoyó la guerra para independencia (p. 129)

patronage/patronazgo otro nombre para el sistema de despojos política en el cual puestos y favores gubernamentales son dados a aliados políticos y amigos (p. 492)

penitentiary/penitenciaría prisión cuyo propósito es de reformar prisioneros (p. 280)

perestroika/*perestroika* política de reestructuración económica y gubernamental instituida por Mikhail Gorbachev en la Unión Soviética en los años 1980 (p. 1002)

periphery/periferia frontera externa de algo (p. 745)

perjury/perjurio mentir cuando uno ha jurado decir la verdad (p. 1020)

philanthropy/filantropía proporcionar dinero para apoyar metas humanitarias o sociales (p. 478)

pietism/piedad movimiento en los años 1700 que enfatizó la piedad individual y la unión emocional con Dios (p. 108)

Pilgrim/peregrino Separatista que viajó a las colonias americanas durante los años 1600 para libertad religiosa (p. 67)

pillage/saquear botín y robo (p. 379)

placer mining/explotación de placeres método para extraer mineral a mano utilizando simples herramientas manuales como picos, palas y bateas (p. 415)

plantation/plantación hacienda comercial y agrícola muy grande (p. 85)

planter/plantador dueño de plantación que tenía 20 ó más esclavos (p. 253)

pocket veto/veto indirecto vetar indirectamente un proyecto de ley permitiendo que una sesión del Congreso expire sin firmar el proyecto (p. 388)

police power/fuerza policiaca poder gubernamental para controlar a personas y propiedades para la seguridad, salud, bienestar, y moral pública (p. 615)

political machine/maquinaria política organización aliada con un partido político que a menudo controlaba el gobierno local (p. 473)

poll tax/impuesto de capitación impuesto de cantidad fija por cada persona, el cual tenía que ser pagado antes de que una persona pudiera votar (pp. 510, 879)

pool/consorcio grupo compartiendo una actividad; por ejemplo, dueños de ferrocarril que tomaban acuerdos secretos y fijaban tipos entre ellos mismos (p. 448)

popular sovereignty/soberanía popular teoría política de que el gobierno está sujeto a la voluntad del pueblo; antes de la Guerra Civil, la idea de que la gente que vivía en un territorio tenía el derecho de decidir votando si ahí sería permitida la esclavitud (pp. 180, 321)

populism/populismo movimiento político fundado en los años 1890 representando principalmente a los granjeros que favoreció libre acuñación de plata y el control gubernamental de ferrocarriles y otras industrias grandes (p. 500)

poverty line/línea de pobreza nivel de ingreso individual o familiar bajo del cual uno es clasificado por el gobierno federal como pobre (p. 828)

presidio/presidio fuerte construido por los españoles en las Américas (p. 54)

privateer/buque corsario buque de propiedad privada autorizado por el gobierno para atacar a buques de otros países (p. 61)

progressivism/progresivismo movimiento político que cruzó las líneas partidarias que creyó que la industria y la urbanización habían creados muchos problemas sociales y que el gobierno debía tomar un papel más activo para resolver estos problemas (p. 547)

prohibition/prohibición leyes que prohibían la manufactura, transportación y venta de bebidas alcohólicas (p. 553)

propaganda/propaganda diseminación de ideas sobre una institución o individuo con el propósito de influenciar la opinión (p. 581)

proprietary colony/colonia propietaria colonia propiedad de un individuo (p. 64)

protective tariff/arancel protectora impuesto en importaciones diseñado para proteger a los manufactureros americanos (p. 241)

protectorate/protectorado país que es técnicamente independiente pero que en realidad queda bajo el control de otro país (p. 521)

public works/obras públicas proyectos como carreteras, parques y bibliotecas construidos con fondos públicos para uso público (p. 669)

pueblo/pueblo término usado por los primeros exploradores españoles para denotar grandes estructuras habitacionales construidas por los Anasazi (p. 16)

Puritan/puritano persona que quería purificar la Iglesia Anglicana en los años 1500 y 1600 (p. 60)

quartz mining/minería de cuarzo método para extraer minerales excavando debajo de la superficie (p. 415)

racism/racismo prejuicio o discriminación en contra de alguien por su raza (p. 882)

radiocarbon dating/datar con carbó radioactivo método para determinar la edad de objetos biológicos midiendo la radioactividad en una clase especial de carbón (p. 13)

ragtime/*ragtime* tipo de música con un ritmo fuerte y una melodía animada con notas acentuadas (p. 480)

rationalism/racionalismo filosofía que enfatiza el papel de la lógica y la razón para obtener el conocimiento (p. 108)

rationing/racionamiento proporcionar escasos artículos de manera limitada (p. 753)

realism/realismo perspectiva de literatura, arte, y teatro que intenta representar las cosas tal como son y que la sociedad funcionará mejor si la dejan en paz (p. 478)

reapportionment/nueva repartición método usado por los estados para formar distritos políticos basados en los cambios de población (p. 843)

rebate/descuento devolución parcial para reducir el costo de un producto o bien (p. 495)

recall/elección de revocación derecho que permite a los votantes quitar del cargo a los oficiales elegidos que son inadecuados (p. 549)

recession/recesión retraso económico (p. 160)

Reconstruction/Reconstrucción reorganización y reconstrucción de los estados de la ex-Confederación después de la Guerra Civil (p. 387)

referendum/referéndum práctica de permitir a los votantes aceptar o rechazar medidas propuestas por la legislatura (pp. 335, 549)

relief/asistencia pública ayuda para los necesitados; beneficencia (p. 670)

Renaissance/Renacimiento período en Europa desde 1350 hasta 1600 durante el cual ocurrió el renacimiento de interés en la cultura de la antigua Grecia y Roma (p. 36)

reparations/indemnización pago hecho por el país perdedor de una guerra al país ganador por los daños causados por la guerra (pp. 596, 649)

republic/república forma de gobierno en el cual el poder reside en un cuerpo de ciudadanos con derecho al voto (p. 147)

reserved powers/poderes reservados los poderes nombrados en la Constitución que son retenidos por los estados (p. 181)

Spanish Glossary

Restoration/Restauración término usado para describir cuando el Parlamento Inglés decidió reponer a la monarquía en el año 1660 (p. 73)

revenue tariff/arancel de ingresos impuesto en las importaciones con el propósito de recaudar dinero (p. 241)

revival/asamblea evangelista reunión pública grande para predicar y rezar (p. 108)

right-to-work law/derecho a trabajar ley que hace ilegal la demanda que los trabajadores se unan a un sindicato (p. 809)

romanticism/romanticismo movimiento literario, artístico, y filosófico del siglo XVIII que enfatizó la imaginación y las emociones, promoviendo el sentido en lugar de la razón, la espiritualidad interior en lugar de reglas externas, el individuo en lugar de la sociedad, y la naturaleza en lugar de medios ambientes credos por los humanos (p. 276)

safety net/red de seguridad algo que proporciona seguridad en contra de desgracias, específicamente, programas de beneficencia gubernamentales para proteger en contra del desastre económico (p.700)

savannah/sabana pasto ondulante (p. 27)

scalawag/*scalawag* nombre dado a los sureños que apoyaron la Reconstrucción republicana del Sur (p. 399)

secede/separarse abandonar o retirar (p. 268)

secession/secesión retiro de la Unión (p. 323)

sedition/sedición incitación a la rebelión (p. 219)

segregation/segregación separación o aislamiento de una raza, clase o grupo (p. 510)

select committee/comité selecto comité organizado en la Cámara o el Senado para hacer una tarea específica (p. 183)

selectmen/concejales hombres escogidos para manejar los asuntos de un pueblo (p. 94)

self-determination/autodeterminación creencia que las personas en un territorio deberían tener la habilidad para escoger su propio gobierno (p. 578)

separate-but-equal/separados pero iguales doctrina establecida por la Suprema Corte en el caso *Plessy contra Ferguson* en 1896 que las leyes que segregaron a los afroamericanos fueron permitidas si facilidades iguales fueron proporcionadas (p. 867)

separation of powers/separación de poderes principio de gobierno en el cual el poder está dividido entre diferentes ramos (p. 168)

Separatist/separatista puritano que dejó la Iglesia Anglicana (p. 66)

serf/siervo persona atada a un señorío (p. 33)

settlement house/casa de beneficencia institución establecida en una vecindad pobre que proveía numerosos servicios comunitarios tal como cuidado médico, cuidado de niños, bibliotecas, e instrucción en inglés (p. 485)

shantytown/villa miseria barrio pobre de un pueblo que consiste de viviendas mal construidas, normalmente hechas de madera (p. 662)

sharecropper/aparcero agricultor que labra la tierra para un dueño que proporciona equipo y semillas y recibe una porción de la cosecha (pp. 407, 509)

siege/sitio bloqueo militar de una ciudad o un recinto fortificado para forzarlo a rendirse (p. 370)

silverite/defensor de plata persona que cree que la acuñación de monedas de plata en cantidades sin límite eliminará la crisis económica (p. 506)

sin tax/impuesto pecadero impuesto federal sobre el alcohol y tabaco (p. 404)

sit-down strike/huelga de brazos caídos método de boicotear el trabajo por medio de sentarse en el lugar de trabajo y de rehusar a abandonar el establecimiento (p. 693)

sit-in/plantón forma de protesta ocupando las sillas o sentándose en el piso de un establecimiento (p. 868)

skyscraper/rascacielos edificio de gran altura (p. 470)

slash-and-burn agriculture/agrícola de tala y quema técnica agrícola en la cual la tierra es preparada y fertilizada derrumbando los bosques y quemándolos (p. 23)

slave code/código de esclavos leyes aprobadas que regularon formalmente la esclavitud y definieron la relación entre los africanos esclavizados y la gente libre (p. 90, 254)

smog/*smog* niebla hecha más pesada y oscura por el humo y vapores químicos (p. 940)

soap opera/novela drama en serie de radio o televisión utilizando situaciones melodramáticas (p. 664)

Social Security Act/Acta de Seguro Social ley que requiere que los trabajadores y empleados paguen un impuesto; el dinero proporciona un ingreso mensual para la gente jubilada (p. 694)

socialism/socialismo creencia que los negocios deben ser propiedad del gobierno y dirigidos por él (p. 553)

sodbuster/rompeterrón nombre dado a los granjeros de las Grandes Planicies (p. 422)

software/*software* programa de computadora (p. 1013)

space race/carrera espacial se refiere a la competencia durante la Guerra Fría sobre el dominio de la exploración espacial (p. 847)

space shuttle/puente espacial nave espacial diseñada para transportar personas y carga entre la tierra y el espacio la cual puede ser usada una y otra vez (p. 998)

space station/estación espacial satélite grande diseñado para ser ocupado por largos períodos y para servir como base para operaciones en el espacio (p. 999)

speakeasy/*speakeasy* lugar donde son vendidas clandestinamente bebidas alcohólicas (p. 615)

speculation/especulación acciones compradas con alto riesgo con la anticipación que los precios subirán (p. 657)

speculator/especulador persona que arriesga dinero con la esperanza de obtener una ganancia financiera (p. 212)

sphere of influence/esfera de influencia sección de un país donde una nación extranjera tiene derechos y poderes especiales (p. 538)

spoils system/sistema de despojos práctica de dar puestos gubernamentales a los partidarios; reemplazando a los empleados del gobierno con los partidarios del candidato victorioso (p. 267)

Square Deal/Trato Justo promesa de Theodore Roosevelt para un trato justo e igual para todos (p. 556)

squatter/colono usurpador persona que se establece en tierras públicas bajo reglamento gubernamental con la esperanza de adquirir el título de propiedad (p. 295)

stagflation/*stagflación* inflación persistente combinado con la demanda estancada y una taza de desempleo alta (p. 964)

standing committee/comité permanente comité permanente en la Cámara o el Senado organizado para enfocarse en un área específica (p. 183)

state-sponsored terrorism/terrorismo patrocinado por el estado actos violentos en contra de civiles que son secretamente apoyados por un gobierno con el motivo de atacar a otras naciones sin entrar en la guerra (p. 1032)

steerage/tercera clase cuarteles apretados de las cubiertas bajas de un barco para los pasajeros que pagan los pasajes más bajos (p. 465)

stock market/bolsa de valores sistema para comprar y vender acciones de corporaciones (p. 657)

strategic defense/defensa estratégica plan para desarrollar proyectiles y otras armas que pueden derribar proyectiles nucleares antes de que estos golpeen en Estados Unidos (p. 1029)

strategic materials/materiales estratégicos materiales necesarios para una guerra (p. 729)

strike/huelga paro de trabajo por los trabajadores para forzar al empresario a satisfacer sus demandas (p. 249)

subsistence farming/agricultura de subsistencia labranza que sólo produce la cosecha que se necesita para alimentar a la familia de uno (p. 87)

subversion/subversión intento sistemático para derrocar un gobierno utilizando personas que trabajan secretamente desde adentro (p. 791)

suffrage/sufragio derecho al voto (p. 549)

summit/cumbre junta de jefes de gobiernos (p. 957)

Sunbelt/Región Solada nueva región industrial en el sur de California y el Bajo Sur que se desarrolló durante la Segunda Guerra Mundial (p. 751)

supply-side economics/economía de oferta teoría económica de que los impuestos bajos levantarían la economía invirtiendo su dinero los negocios y los individuos, así creando un alto ingreso del impuesto (pp. 648, 987)

syndicate/sindicato grupo de negocios (p. 564)

teach-in/plantón educacional junta o clase extendida para discutir un asunto político o social (p. 905)

***Tejano*/tejano** habitante de Texas de habla española (p. 300)

telecommute/viajar electrónicamente trabajar en casa por medio de conexión electrónica con una oficina central (p. 1013)

televangelist/televangelista evangelista que transmite regularmente programas evangélicos por televisión (p. 984)

temperance/templanza moderación o abstinencia del uso del alcohol (pp. 279, 553)

tenant farmer/granjero arrendatario granjero que labra la tierra de un terrateniente y paga la renta ya sea con dinero efectivo o cosecha (p. 407)

tenement/casa de vecindad apartamentos para varias familias, normalmente obscuros, apretados que apenas cumplen con los estándares mínimos de viviendas (p. 471)

termination policy/política de terminación política gubernamental para traer a los Nativos Americanos dentro de la sociedad principal retirando el reconocimiento de los grupos Nativos Americanos como entidades legales (p. 830)

terrorism/terrorismo el uso de violencia por grupos no del gobierno en contra de civiles para alcanzar una meta política impartiendo miedo y amenazando gobiernos para que cambien su política (p. 1032)

time zone/huso horario región geográfica en la cual la misma norma horaria es mantenida (p. 444)

Title IX/Título IX sección de las Enmiendas Educacionales de 1972 prohibiendo que las escuelas que recibían fondos federales discriminaran contra niñas y mujeres jóvenes en casi todo aspecto de su operación (p. 929)

town meeting/junta municipal asamblea de hombres libres de un pueblo de Nueva Inglaterra para elegir líderes la cual desarrolló en gobierno local (p. 94)

trade deficit/déficit de intercambio diferencia entre el valor de las importaciones de un país y las exportaciones (p. 1023)

trade union/gremio organización de trabajadores con el mismo oficio o destreza (p. 455)

Spanish Glossary

transcendental meditation/meditación transcendental técnica de meditación en la cual una persona repite una palabra una y otra vez como manera de alcanzar la máxima inteligencia, armonía y salud (p. 971)

transcendentalism/transcendentalismo filosofía que acentúa la relación entre los seres humanos y la naturaleza, cosas espirituales sobre las materiales y la importancia de la conciencia del individuo (p. 276)

transcontinental railroad/ferrocarril transcontinental sistema de ferrocarril que se extiende a través del continente (p. 328)

triangular trade/comercio triangular una ruta comercial de tres ramas para intercambiar productos entre las colonias americanas y otros dos asociados comerciales (p. 95)

trust/cártel combinación de empresas o sociedades anónimas formada por acuerdo legal, especialmente para reducir la competición (p. 450)

U-boat/nave-U apodo inglés para submarino alemán, de *Unterseeboot*, término que significa barco submarino (p. 581)

Underground Railroad/Ferrocarril Clandestino sistema que ayudó a los afroamericanos esclavizados a seguir una red de rutas de escape fuera del Sur hacia la libertad en el Norte (p. 327)

unfair trade practices/prácticas comerciales injustas prácticas comerciales que ganan el beneficio perjudicando a la competencia (p. 569)

union shop/taller sindicalizado comercio que requiere que los trabajadores se unan al sindicato (p. 809)

urban renewal/renovación urbana programas gubernamentales que intentan eliminar la pobreza y revitalizar las áreas urbanas (p. 829)

utopia/utopía comunidad basada en una visión de la sociedad perfecta buscada por los reformistas (p. 277)

vaquero/vaquero hombres que conducían el ganado en las haciendas (p. 55)

vaudeville/vodevil entretenimiento compuesto de varios actos, tal como baile, canción, comedia, y espectáculos de magia (p. 480)

vertical integration/integración vertical asociación de compañías que abastecen equipo y servicios necesarios a una industria particular (p. 449)

veto/veto poder del jefe del ejecutivo de rechazar leyes aprobadas por la legislatura (p. 169)

victory garden/huerto de victoria huertos plantados por ciudadanos americanos durante la guerra para cultivar vegetales para usar en casa así dejando más para las tropas (pp. 586, 754)

Vietcong/*Vietcong* soldados guerrilleros de la facción comunista en Vietnam, también conocidos como Frente Nacional de Liberación (p. 897)

Vietnamization/vietnamización el proceso de hacer que el Vietnam del Sur asumiera más de los esfuerzos de la guerra sacando poco a poco a las tropas americanas de Vietnam (p. 911)

War Hawks/halcones de guerra miembros del Congreso durante la presidencia de Madison que insistían en la guerra contra la Gran Bretaña (p. 229)

war on poverty/guerra contra la pobreza programa antipobreza bajo el Presidente Lyndon Johnson (p. 856)

welfare capitalism/capitalismo de beneficencia sistema en el cual las compañías permiten a los trabajadores comprar acciones, compartir las ganancias, y recibir beneficios tal como atención médica, común en los años 1920 (p. 645)

white-collar/collar blanco trabajos que no requieren ropa de protección o de trabajo, asi como los vendedores (p. 815)

wigwam/*wigwam* vivienda en forma de cono o domo construida por Nativos Americanos utilizando palos curvados cubiertos con piel o corteza de árbol (p. 23)

writ of assistance/escrito de asistencia documento legal que permitió a los oficiales aduanales entrar cualquier lugar en busca de evidencia de contrabando (p. 122)

yellow journalism/periodismo amarillista tipo de reportaje sensacional, tendencioso, y a menudo falso con el propósito de atraer a los lectores (p. 528)

yeoman farmer/terrateniente menor dueño de una granja pequeña con cuatro o menos esclavos, normalmente ninguno (p. 253)

yuppie/*yuppie* adulto joven educado en la universidad empleado en una profesión de buen salario y que vive y trabaja en o cerca de una ciudad grande (p. 995)

Italicized page numbers refer to illustrations. The following abbreviations are used in the index:
m = map; c = chart; p = photograph or picture; g = graph; crt = cartoon; ptg = painting; q = quote

A

ABBA, 973

Abernathy, Ralph, 886

Abingdon School District v. Schempp, c844, 845

abolitionists, 284–88, 326–28, 363; American Colonization Society, 285; Underground Railroad, 327–28

Abrams v. United States, 588

Acheson, Dean, 785, 793

Adams, Henry, *q498*

Adams, John, 120, *q120,* 132–33, 140, 145, 146, 148, 165, 218–19; as President, 218–19; Declaration of Independence, 132–33; defense lawyer, 120; political ideology, 148; Quasi-War, 218; XYZ Affair, 218

Adams, John Quincy, 244, 259, *p259,* 260

Adams, Samuel, *q113,* 122, *p122,* 173, 175

Adamson Act, 570

Adams-Onís Treaty, 244

Addams, Jane, 459, 475, *q475,* 532

Adena, the, *c14,* 16, *p17*

Adoption and Safe Families Act, 1019

Advanced Research Project Agency (ARPANET), 1014

advertising, 451, *p644,* 645, 816, 821, 841; mass, 644; politics and, 841; television, 821, 841

aerobics, 974

affirmative action, 933

Afghanistan, 968, 969, 989, 1032–33, 1034, 1035–36; Reagan Doctrine and, 989; terrorists and, 1033, 1034, 1035–36

Africa. *See* African cultures.

African Americans: abolitionist movement, 284–88, 326–28; activism, 511–12, 570, 869–70, 873–74; affirmative action and, 933; African Colored Farmers' National Alliance, 509; American Antislavery Society, 286; American Colonization Society, 285; American Revolution, and, 132, 150–51; assassination of Martin Luther King Jr., 885–86; Atlanta Compromise, 510; black codes, 392–93, 400; black nationalism, 629–30; Black Panthers, 885; black power, 884; Bloody Sunday, 880; *Brown v. Board of Education,* 844, *c844,* 868–69, 871, 934; Chicago race riots, 601; civil rights legislation, 867, 872, 877–79; civil rights movement, 511, 810, 864–86; Colored Farmers' National Alliance, 509; conditions in rural South, 509–10; constitutional amendments and, 510–11, 550, 844, 868; cowboys, 418; cultural assimilation, 884; culture of, 106–07; 150–51, 626–30, 823–25, 972–73; de facto segregation, 867, 883; discrimination against, 486, 511, 750, 751, 822, 824, 829; during wartimes, 585–87, 749–51; economic disparity and, *p829,* 829–30; economic rights of, 883–85; education, 275, 388, 400, *p400,* 871, 876; Eisenhower and, 871–72; emancipated, *p388;* Emancipation Proclamation, 363; 54th Massachusetts, 366; Exodusters, 509; Fourteenth Amendment, 392, 511, 550, 844, 868; free, 254–55; freedmen, 389; Freedom Riders, 874–75; Great Migration of, 587, 626–27, 629, 751, *m751;* Harlem Renaissance, 627–28; impact of Supreme Court rulings, 844, 867; in Colonial America, 89–91, 106–07; integration, 740, 871, 876; inventors, 397; Johnson and, 859, 872, 879–80, 883; Kennedy and, 875–76; Ku Klux Klan, 398, *p398,* 402, *p402, crt611,* 611–12, 875; Liberian settlement, 285; lynching, 511, 629, 810; mass migration to Kansas, 509; Montgomery bus boycott, 869–70; political "firsts," 399, 929, 933, 934, 968; politics and, 629–30, 695–96, *p810,* 868; racial pride, 627–30; racial purity and separation, 629–30; Reconstruction, 387–89, 391–93, 395, 398–407; role of religion and, 151, 870–71; segregation, 508–12, 739–40, 867–69, 873–80; "separate-but-equal" doctrine, 867; sharecropping, 407, 509; sit-in movement, 873–74; unemployment and, 882; urban problems of, 881–83; violence against, 393, 395, 402, 511, 611, 629, 871–72, 874, 879–80; voting rights, 629, 857; wartime contributions of, 366, *p366,* 531, 585, 600, *p600,* 740, *p740,* 905–06; workplace and, 601, 749–51, 882. *See also* slavery.

African cultures, 26–31, 88; art, 29; artifacts of, *p27, p28;* Central Africa, 30; empires of, *m30;* forest kingdoms of Guinea, 20–30; geography and, 27; Ghana, 26, 27–28; Mali, 26; matrilineal society in, 30; music of, 285; slavery and, 30–31, 89; song, 88; Songhai, 26; Southern Africa, 30; trade in, 27–31; West Africa, 27–29, *p29*

African Methodist Episcopal (AME) Church, 151

Agent Orange, 900

Agnew, Spiro, 953, 961

agrarianism, 214

Agricultural Adjustment Administration (AAA), 685, 686, 697

agriculture: backcountry farming, 87; bonanza farms, 422; cash crops, 85, 86, 96, 251, 352; colonial, 84–86, 96–97, 422; commercial, 84–85; dry farming, 422; early crop cultivation, 21; economic crises, 160–61, 501–04, *g645,* 645–46, *p646;* Farmers' Alliance, 502–03; furnishing merchants, 407; government and, 421, 422, 685, 687, 697, 699; Grange, 502; grape boycott, 935; Great Depression and, 685; Great Plains, 421–23; Mesoamerican revo-

lution in, 13–14, 15, 17; Native American, 21, 23, 24; political issues, 500–04; private cultivation, 63; Resettlement Act, 692, *c692;* sharecropping, 407, 509; slash-and-burn, 23; subsidies in, 810–11; subsistence farming, 87, 810–11; technological innovations in, 14, 33, 295, *p421,* 421–22; tenant farming, 86–88, 407; U.S. Department of, 558–59; *Wabash v. Illinois,* 496; yeoman farmers, 253

AIDS, 996–97; AIDS quilt, *p997*

Aid to Families with Dependent Children (AFDC), 955

airline industry, 643, 988; deregulation of, 988

Akabogu-Collins, May, 1026, *q1026*

Alabama, 53, 252, 342, 359, 394, 407, 875–77, 879–80

Alamo, Battle of the, 302, 303

Alamogordo, New Mexico, 769

Alaska, 22, 244, 395, 507

Albania, 1020

Albany Conference, 117

Albany Plan of Union, 117

Albright, Madeleine, 1022, *q1022*

alcohol, 279, 552–53, 615–16, 625, 657, 996

Aleutian Islands, 23

Alfred P. Murrah Federal Building, 1024

Alger, Horatio, 477, *p477*

Alger, Philip R., *q534*

Algonquian people, the, 23

al-Idrisi, 39

Alien and Sedition Acts, 219

aliens, 219

Ali, Muhammad, 853

Ali, Sonni, 28–29

Allen, Gracie, 664

Alliance for Progress, 847

Allied Forces, 744–47

Allies, 580, 581, 593, 594, 595–96

All in the Family, 972, *p973*

allotments, 430

al-Qaeda, 1033, 1034, 1036

amendments, 169, 199–207; amendment process, 169, 198

America: affluence of, 814–19, 994–95; anti-war movement, 904–06, 911–12; automobile society, 813; beginnings of modern, 410–31; civil rights movement, 510–12, 696, 740, 750, 809–11, 843, 857, 864–86, p871, p877, 922, 932–37; communism in, 602, 610, 709, 791–96; conformity in, 815; conservatism in, 978–1006; consumer society, 644–46, 815–16; corporate, 447–51, 495–96, 553, 645, 648, crt815; counterculture, 922–25; crime in, 882, 996; cultural movements in, 478, 480, 622, 624, 627, 628, 630, 631, 665, 824, 825, 926–30, 972–74; cultures of, 273–77, 622–23, 820–25, 920–25, 970–73, p973, 974, 994–99; during wartimes, 364–68, 584–89, 749–54, 904–06; education in, 388, 400, 832, 858, 871, 876, 921, 928–29, 933–34, 937; environmentalism in, 939–43; family life in, 771, 817, 851–52; first civilization in, 13–15; heroes in, p1032; inequality in, 828–32, 854–60; isolationism, 711–12, 726; Jazz Age, 608–30; juvenile delinquency, 831–32, p832; life in the 1920s, p614; literary renaissance, 276–77; media in, 820–22; migration in, 469–70, 751, m751, 816; migration to, 12–19; modernism in, 621–22; mourning in, p1033; nativism, 456, 468, 610–11, 632; neutrality in, 580, 581; postwar, p807, 808–32; Progressivism in, 544–70; Prohibition, 553, 615–16, 625, 657; Red Scare, 601–02, 790–96; reform in, 278–82, 499, 550; rights in, 843–45; spread of American democracy, 148; suburbs in, 816; theater opening night, ptg635; treatment of minorities, 828–32, 873–80; unity in, 1033–34, p1037; urbanization of, 462–86, 498, 829–30, 859; women in, 585–87, 741, 817, 926–30; youth culture in, 823–25, 920–22. See also United States.

America First Committee, 726, 727

American Antislavery Society, 286

American Association of Retired Persons (AARP), 998

American Civil Liberties Union (ACLU), 615

American Colonization Society (ACS), 285

American Communist Party, 671

American Crisis, 140–41, 153

American Federation of Labor, 458–59, 504, 569, 935

American Federation of Labor and Congress of Industrial Organizations (AFL-CIO), 935

American Indian Movement (AIM), 932, 936

Americanization, 468, 485

American Liberty League, 690

American Party, 275, 333, c333, 334

American Protective Association, 468

American Railway Union, 458

American Revolution, 116–25, 126–27, 128–29, 132–33, 141–43; advantages and disadvantages of each side, c139; Battle at Bunker Hill, 131; Battle of Concord and Battle of Lexington, 130, m130; beginning of, 126–33; Burgoyne's surrender to Washington, ptg142; causes and effects of, 116–25, crt123, 126–28, crt127, c129; end of, 144–45; France and, 142; French and Indian War and, 116–19; impact on American society, 147–52; militias, 129, 131, 139, 143, 144; loyalists and patriots, 129–30; Northern campaigns, 139–40; Olive Branch Petition, 131; Proclamation of 1763, 119; Southern campaigns, 143–44; Treaty of Paris, 532; turning points, 141–42; Valley Forge, 138, 141; war at sea, 142–43; war for independence, m140, m144; war in the west, 142; women in, 150

American's Creed, 1073

American Socialist Party, 553; candidacy of Eugene V. Debs, 553

American Sugar Refining Company, 497

Americans with Disabilities Act (ADA), 1006

American System, 259

American Temperance Union, 279

Americorps, 1017

amnesty, 387

amphtracs, 759–60

Anaconda Plan, 356

anarchism, 456, 458, 611

Anasazi, the, 15–16, p16

Andersonville, Georgia, 368

Andros, Sir Edmund, 100

Angel Island, 467, p467

Anglican Church, 60, 64, 66, 67, 69, 100, 149

Anglo-Saxonism, 521–22, 524, 537

An Indian Teacher Among Indians, 431

annexation, 304, 307, 308, 523

annuities, 426

Anschluss, 714

Anthony, Susan B., 499, p499, 550, p550

anthrax, 1035

Anti-Comintern Pact, 711

Antietam, Battle of (Battle of Sharpsburg), 362–63

Antifederalists, 173–75, 182

anti-Semitism, 720, 722

antiterrorist bill, 1035

antitrust actions, 497, 557, 565, 568–69

antiwar movement, 904–06, 911–12

Anzio, 757

Apollo Theater, 628

Appalachia, 831, p831

Appalachian Mountains, 143, 159, 219, 294

Appeal to the Colored Citizens of the World, 285

appeasement, 714, p714

appellate courts, 184–85

Apple computer, 1013, p1013

Appomattox Courthouse, 380

apportionment, 202–03

appropriations, 181, 182

Aquinaldo, Emilio, 530, 532, p532

Arab nations, the, 800–01, 964, 1004–05

Arafat, Yasir, 1021

Arawak, the, 40

arbitration, 458, 557

Area Redevelopment Act, 843

Argentina, 419

Argonne Forest, Battle of, 596

Aristide, Jean-Bertrand, 1020

Arizona, 311, 329, 550

Arkansas, 53, 270, 344, 394

armistice, 596

arms control, 990–91

arms race, 850, 921, crt956, 991

arms reduction, 850

arms sales, 711–12, 726, crt726

Armstrong, Louis Daniel, 624, p624, 626, q626, 627, 628

Armstrong, Neil, 848

Army-McCarthy hearings, 795

Army Nursing Corps, 585, p585

Arnaz, Desi, 820

Arnold, Benedict, 141, 144–45

ARPANET, 1014

art and architecture: Andy Warhol, 924; counterculture, 924–25; Depression-era, 664–65; Hohokam, 15; Hopewell, p17; impact of American Revolution on, 152; Middle Ages, 33; modern Americana, 621; Native American, 15, p17, 21; New Deal and, 691–92; Olmec, 14; photography, 662, p662, 665; pop, 924; Puritan, 94; realism in, 478–79; social values and, 478–79; Toltec, 15; West African, 29

Arthur, Chester A., 493

Articles of Confederation and Perpetual Union, 158–59; weaknesses of, c162

artificial genes, 1015

artisans, 94, 95, 159, 214, 247, 254

Asia, 12–13, 786–89; migration to America, 12–13; spread of Cold War to, 786–89; trade route to, 35–37, 59, 61; trade with Europe, 35. See also China, Japan.

Asian Americans: immigration, 467–68; internment of, 752, p752; treatment of, 752

Asia Pacific Economic Cooperation (APEC), 1023

assembly line, 641, p641

assimilation, policy of, 430, 830

Associated Press, 248–49

astrolabe, 36

astronauts, 998, p998, 999, p999

Atahualpa, 53

Atchison, David, 330

Atkinson, Edward, 477, q477

Atlanta Compromise, 512

Atlanta, Georgia, 378–79, 406, ptg406

Atlantic, Battle of the, 746–47

Atlantic Charter, 727, 728

Atlantic Monthly, 277

atomic bomb, 720, 769–70, p770, 771, 787, 789, 795, 797–98, 1024–25

Attlee, Clement, p781

attorney general, 875–76

attrition, 355, 901

Attucks, Crispus, 123, p125

audiencia, 55

Audubon Society, 941

Auschwitz, 719, 723–24

Austin, Stephen F., 300, q300, 301, 302

Austria, 244, 578, 714, 721

Austro-Hungarian Empire, 578–80, 596

automobile, 640–42, p642, 737–38, g738, p738, 813, 943, 944–45, p944, p945; federal safety regulations, 943; global production of, 944–45; production of, 641–42, g738, p738, 944–45; social impact of, 641–42; society, 812–13

auto workers strike, 693, p693

Avondale Mine, 454

Axis Powers, 711, 712–13, 715, m715, 742–47, 755–61, m767; rise and fall of, m767

Aztec, the, 14–15, c15, 50, q50, 51–52, q52, q53

B

baby boom, g816, 816–17

backcountry farmers, 87, 88–89

Bacon, Nathaniel, p87, 88–89

Bacon's Rebellion, 88–89

bailiffs, 662

Baker, Ella, 874

Baker, James, 1002

Baker, Josephine, 628

Baker v. Carr, 843, c844

Bakke, Allan, 933, p933

balanced budget, 690, 697, 1018, 1019

balance of power, 581, 962; impact of Watergate on, 962

Balkans, 578–80

Ball, George W., 898, q898, 899

Ball, Lucille, 820

Ballinger, Richard, 564, p564, 565

Baltimore, Lord (George Calvert), 64, 73

bank holidays, 681, 683

bank notes, 212, 241, 270

Bank of North America, 139

Bank of the United States, 212–13, 219, 241, 270, 271

bank runs, 656, 681

banks: closings, 404; commercial, 684; Emergency Banking Relief Act, 683, g692; failures of, 656, p656, 659, 661; government insurance deposits, 684–85; holidays, 681, 683; lending policies, 271; reforming, 568–69; regulations of, 684–85; runs on, 656, p656, 681, 683

Banneker, Benjamin, 222

Bañuelos, Romana Acosta, 954, p954

Baptists, 109, 149, 150, 275, 285

Barak, Ehud, 1021

barbed wire, 419

bar graph, reading, 103, 111

Barksdale, Ethelbert, 403, q403

Barnett, Ross, 876

barnstormers, 622, p622

barrios, 587

bayonets, 355

Barry, Marion, 874

Barsukov, Yuri, 956

Barton, Clara, 367, 527, q527

Baruch, Bernard, 586

baseball, 478, p622, 623, p478

basic freedoms, 186. *See also* rights.

Bass, Leon, q723

Bataan Death March, 743, m748

Bataan Peninsula, 743

Bayard, James, 220

Bay of Pigs, 848–49

Beamer, Todd, 1031

Bear Flag Republic, 310

Beatles, the, 925, p971

beat movement, 824, 921

beats, the, 824

Beauregard, P.G.T., 357, 361

Beck, Leon, 743, q743

Beecher, Catherine, 282

Beecher, Lyman, 279

Bee Gees, the, 972, p972

Belgium, 580, 596, 649, 716, 720, 722, 765

Belknap, William, 404

Bell, Alexander Graham, 439–40

Bell, John, 341

Bellamy, Edward, 483

Bellecourt, Clyde, 932

Bellecourt, Vernon, 932, p932, q932

Benavidez, Roy P., 912, p912

benevolent societies, 279

Benny, Jack, 664

Benton, Thomas Hart, 665

Beringia, 13

Bering Strait, 13, m18, m19

Berkeley, Lord John, 74

Berkeley, Sir William, 87–88

Berlin airlift, 786, p786

Berlin Wall, 849, p979, 1002

Bermuda, 726

Bernstein, Carl, 958

Berry, Chuck, 823, 824

Bessemer process, 435, 449; "The Big Blow: the Bessemer Process," ptg435

Bethlehem, Pennsylvania, 97, p97

Bethune, Mary McLeod, 696, p696

Better Homes and Gardens, 817

Bevin, Ernest, 784

bibliography, preparing, 887, 889

big business, 418–19, 447–51, 496–97, 501, 506, 521, 522, 523, 525, 552, 553, 556, crt556, 557, 565, 568–69, 585–86, 683, 685–86, 749–51, 843, 1005; advertising in, 451; consolidation of industry, 448–51; cooperation with government, 683, 685; corporations, 448–51; downsizing, 1005; fair competition codes, 685; farmers and, 501; holding companies, 450; Kennedy and, 843; monopolies, 449; politics and, 496–97, 506, 521, 522, 523, 525, 553, 556, 565, 568; price-fixing, 685–86; Progressivism and, 553; ranching as, 418–19; recruitment of minorities to, 749–51; reforming, 568–69; regulations, 450, 497, 553; rise of, 447–48, 450;

Roosevelt and, 556–57; Sherman Anti-Trust Act, 497; socialism and, 553; stock battles, 556, crt556; taxes on, 586; trusts, 449

Big Three, 757, p757

Bilingual Education Act, 936

bilingualism, 935–36

bill, 183, c183

bill of rights, 173–75

Bill of Rights, English, 101, 102, 1063

Bill of Rights, U.S., c182, 199–200, 211, 844

bills of exchange, 95

binding arbitration, 692

bin Laden, Osama, 1032–33, 1034

biological weapons, 1036

biotechnology, 1014–15

bioterrorism, 1036

Birmingham, Alabama, 876–77; civil rights protests, 876–77, p877; "Letter from a Birmingham Jail," 876

Bitterroot Range, 227

Black Cabinet, 696

black codes, 392–93, 400

Black Kettle, Chief, 427

blacklists, 456

Black Muslims, 884–85

black nationalism, 629–30

Black Panthers, 885

black power, 884; black power salute, p885

Blackshirts, 709

Black Thursday, 658, 668

Black Tuesday, 659, crt659

Blackwell, Elizabeth, 281, 367

Blaine, James G., 494–95, 523–24

Blair Jr., Ezell, 873, p873

"Bleeding Kansas," m330, 330–31

blitzkrieg, 715–16, 737

Bliven, Bruce, 693, q693

blockade runners, 359

Bloody Sunday, 880

blue-collar workers, 815

Blue Jacket, Chief, 217

Blues, the, 627

Board of Governors, 568

Bohemian lifestyle, 621

Bolsheviks, 595, 601, 709

bonanza farms, 422

Bonaparte, Napoleon, 223, 224, 229

bonds, 212

Bonhomme Richard, 143

Bonnin, Gertrude Simmons, 431, *p431*

Bonus Army, 671

boomtowns, 415–16

Booth, John Wilkes, 380

bootlegging, 616, *p616*

border ruffians, 330–31

Bork, Robert, 961, 988

Bosnia, 578, 1020

Boston, Massachusetts, 69, 123, 126, 128, 130

Boston Manufacturing Company, 248

Boston Massacre, 123, *p123*, 124–25

Boston Police Strike, 600–01

Boston Tea Party, 126, 127, *p127*

Boulder City, Nebraska, 667

bounty, 358

Bourke-White, Margaret, 665

Boxer Rebellion, 538–39

boycotts, 121, 122–23, 335, 935

Bozeman Trail, 427

Bracero program, 750–51, 830

Braddock, General Edward, 117

Bradford, William, 67

Bradley, General Omar, 758–59

Bradstreet, Anne, 101, *q101*

Brady Bill, 1017

Brady, Jim, 988, *p988*

Bragg, Braxton, 361, 372

Brant, Chief Joseph, 142, *ptg151*

bread lines, 662, *p670*

Breckenridge, John C., 341–42

Brezhnev, Leonid, *p956*, 957

Bridger, Jim, 295

Briggs, Laura, 749, *q749*

brinkmanship, 799, 801

Britain, Battle of, 717, *p717*, 718, *p718*

British East India Company, 127

broker state, 699

Brook Farm, 277

Brooklyn Bridge, 470

Brooks, Preston, 331, *crt331*

Brotherhood of Sleeping Car Porters, 750

Brown, John, 336–37, *p337*, *q337*

Brown, Linda, *p392*, 868, *p868*

Brown v. Board of Education of Topeka, Kansas, 392, 844, *c844*, 868–69, 871, 934, 1077

Bryan, William Jennings, 506, *p506*, *q506*, 507, 537, 581, 615

Buchanan, James, 334–35

Buchenwald, 723, 764

Buckley, William F., *p981*, 981–82

budget deficit, 648, 669, 690, 842, 964, 987, 989, *g990*

Buell, Don Carolos, 361

Buffalo Bill's Wild West Show, 427

Bulgaria, 1002

Bulge, Battle of the, 765

bull markets, 657

Bull Run, Battle of, (Battle of Manassas), 357–58, *m358*, 362

Bundy, McGeorge, 899

Bunker Hill, Battle of, 131, *ptg131*

Bureau of Corporations, 557, 559, 565

Bureau of Indian Affairs, 428, 937

Bureau of Mines, 565

Bureau of Standards, 648

Burger, Warren, 954

burgesses. *See* House of Burgesses.

Burgoyne, John, 141–42

Burns, George, 664

Burnside, Ambrose, 370

Burr, Aaron, 219, 224; duel with Alexander Hamilton, 224

Bush, George H.W., 1001–06, *p1027*; domestic challenges, 1005–06; end of Cold War, 1002–03; "New World Order," 1003–05; Persian Gulf War, 1001, 1004–05; Tiananmen Square, 1003–04

Bush, George W., *p949*, *q949*, *p1011*, 1025, *p1027*, 1027–29, *q1029*, 1034, 1037, *q1037*; address to Congress, 1079; *Bush v. Gore*, 392, 1028–29; domestic agenda, 1029; election of 2000, 1028–29; response to terrorism, 1034–37

Bush v. Gore, 392, 1028–29

busing, 934

Butler Act, 615

Butler, Andrew P., 331, *crt331*

Butterfield, Alexander, 960

"button craze," 974, *p974*

Byrd, Harry F., 868–69

Byrd, William II, 84, *q84*, 87

Byrnes, James, 784

Cabeza de Vaca, Alvar Nuñez, 53

cabinet, 184, 195, 211; Washington's, 211, *p211*

Cable News Network (CNN), 995

cables, 470

cable television, 995

Cabot, John, 58–59

Cahokia, 17

Calhoun, John C., 229, 241, *p241*, 243, 268–69, 321, 323, *p323*, 324

California, 54, 295, 310, 311, 322, 323, 416, 550, *p662*, 663, 666, *m666*, 667, 983; application for statehood, 323; Bear Flag Republic, 310; California Gold Rush, 322–23; cattle ranching in, 416; tax revolt, 983

California Trail, 295

Calley, Lieutenant William, 911

Calvin, John, 60

Cambodia, 895, 911, 966

Camelot, 843

Camp David Accords, 968–69

Canada, 230–31, 1023

canals, 236, 237, 245, 247

Cannon, Joseph G., 564

Cape Canaveral (Cape Kennedy), Florida, 818–19

Cape Cod, Massachusetts, 67

capital gains tax, 1006

capitalists, 97

Capone, Al, 616

caravels, 36, *p36*, 40

Carmichael, Stokely, 884

Carnegie, Andrew, 448–49, *q449*, 478, *q478*, 486, 532

carpetbaggers, 399, 401, 402

Carroll, Lieutenant John Bentz, 755, *p755*, *q755*

Carson, Kit, 295

Carson, Rachel, 940, *p940*, *q940*

Carter, Jr., Jimmy 942, 966–67, *p967*, *p968*, 968–69, 986, *p986*, *q986*, 989, 1020; Camp David Accords, 968–69; domestic agenda, 966–67; economic crisis, 966–67; foreign policy, 966–68; Iran hostage crisis, *p968*, 968–69; Panama Canal, 968

Carteret, Sir George, 74

Cartier, Jacques, 55

cartogram, reading, 1030, 1039

Carver, George Washington, 485, *p485*

Casablanca Conference, 756

cash crops, 85, 86, 96, 251, 352

Cass, Lewis, 321

Cassino, 757

Castile and Leon, banner of, 44

Castle Garden, 274, *p274*

Castro, Fidel, 841, 848–49

Catherine of Aragon, 60

Catholic Croatians, 1020

Catt, Carrie Chapman, 551

cattle ranching, 416, *m417*, 417–19, *ptg418*; *Breaking Camp*, *p418*; cattle drives, 416–18

caucus system, 268

cause and effect, understanding, 146, 155

Cavada, Frederico, 361, *p361*

cease and desist orders, 693

cede, 311

cellular phones, 1019

censure, 795

Centers for Disease Control, 997

Central America, 536, 538, *p538*, 539, *crt539*, *m539*, 968, 1004

Central Intelligence Agency (CIA), 801, 848, 958, 1002

Central Pacific Railroad Company, 442, 443, *p443*, 444, 445, 467

Central Powers, 580, 581, 594, 595, 596

Century of Dishonor, A, 430

Chaco Canyon, 15–16

chad, 1028

chain store, 451

Challenger, 999, *p999*

Chamberlain, Neville, 714

Chambers, Whittaker, 791

Champlain, Samuel de, 56

Chang-Diaz, Franklin R., 998, *p998*

Charles, Ray, 824

Charles I, King of England, 64, 73

Charles II, King of England, 73, 74, 75, 76, 99

Charleston, South Carolina, 76, 255, 256, 341

Charles Town, South Carolina, 76, 95, 132, 143

charter, 771

Chattanooga, Battle of, 372–73

Chattanooga, Tennessee, 372–73

chattel slavery, 90

Chavez, César, 853, *p919*, 935, *q935*

checks and balances, 108, 148, 168–69, 181–82, 222. *See also* constitution, U.S.

Cheney, Dick, 1001, 1027, 1031

Cherokee, *ptg8–9*, 142, 270

Chesapeake, 225

Chesapeake Bay region, 85

Chestnut, Mary, 340, *q340*

Chicago, Illinois, 470–71, *p474*, 475, *p475*, 561, 601, 854, *p854*, *q854*, 883, *p883*, 908–09; civil rights movement, *p883*; race riots, 601

Chicago Movement, 883, *p883*

Chichén Itzá, 14

Chichimec, the, 15

Chickamauga, 372, 373

Chiffons, the, 825

child labor, 551–52, *p552*, 565, 569, 699

Child Nutrition Act, 858, *c858*

Children's Bureau, 565

Children's Health Insurance Program, 1019

China, 522–23, 537–39, 649, 712, 729, 786–87, 789, 800, 901, 951, *p951*, 955–56, 1003–04, 1024; Boxer Rebellion, 538–39; communism, 786–87, 1003–04; human rights and, 1003–04; Korean War, 789; Nixon and, 955–56; revolution in, 786–87; trade with, 537, 1024; war with Japan, 538

Chinese Exclusion Act, 468

Chisholm, Shirley, 929, *p929*

Chisholm Trail, 417

Chivington, Colonel John, 427–28

chlorofluorocarbons (CFCs), 1025

Christianity: Anglo-Saxonism and, 521; colonies and, 54, 56, 64, 66–71, 74–75, 94–95; Crusades and, 34–35; evangelism, 984; fundamentalism, 984; Great Awakening, 108–09, 275; Prohibition and, 553; Protestantism, 614–15; religious right, 983–84; social reform, 484; Spanish and, 51–53; views on Darwinism, 478; women's movement and, 281–82

Christowe, Stoyan, 970, *q970*

chronological thinking, 45

Chrysler, 642

church covenants, 93

Churchill, Winston, 717, *q717*, 718, *p718*, 726, 728, 736–37, 745, 756, 757, *p757*, 779–80, 782, *q782*; Atlantic Charter, 728; Casablanca Conference, 756; Destroyers-for-Bases Deal, 726; Yalta Conference, 779–80

Church of Jesus Christ of Latter-Day Saints, 276, 297

Cinemascope, 822

CIO, 792

circuit court of appeals, 184–85, *c185*

circular letter, 122

circumnavigation, 43

citizenship: naturalization, 192; rights and responsibilities of, 185–87

Civilian Conservation Corps (CCC), 686, 687, *c687*, *p688*

civilizations, early, 12–19

civil liberties, 588–89, 603

Civil Rights Acts, 393, 510, 857, 872, 877–79, 886, 927, 928; **of 1875,** 510; **of 1957,** 872; **of 1964,** 857, 877–79, 927, 928; **of 1968,** 886; U.S. Supreme Court overturns, 510

civil rights movement, 499, 508–12, 550–51, 570, 601, 603, 611, 629–30, 696, 740, 749–50, 753, 809–11, 830, 843, 844–45, 853, 857, *p865*, 864–71, *p871*, 872–73, *p873*, 873–74, *p874*, 875–77, *p877*, *p878*, 878–86, 888–89, 900, 922, 927, 928, 930, 932–37, 946, 947; beginning of, 868–70; boycotts of, 866; *Brown* v. *Board of Education,* 392, 844, *c844*, 868–69, 871, 934, 1077; car pool during Montgomery bus boycott, *p869*; Congress of Racial Equality, 868; court challenges, 867; crisis in Little Rock, *p871*, 871–72; Fair Employment Practices Commission, 750; Fifteenth Amendment, 510; Fourteenth Amendment, 511; Freedom Riders, 875–76; Greensboro sit-in, 873, *p873*, 874, *p874*; legislation, 510, 857, 872, 877–79, 886, 927, 928; legislative opposition to, 811; Montgomery bus boycott, 869–70; National Council of Negro Women, 696; nonviolent resistance, 870, 873, 874, 877–78; origins of, 866–68; presidential policies, 809–10, 872, 879–80, 883; protests, 873–74, 876–80; role of religion, 870–71; Selma to Montgomery march, *p865*; sit-ins, 868, 873–74, *p874*, 922; Student Nonviolent Coordinating Committee, 874; violence during, 871–72, 874–75, *p877*, 880, 882, 885–86; voting and, 872, 879, 880; Washington March, 877–78, *p878*

Civil Service Commission, 493

Civil War, 318–24, 326–31, 332–38, 340–45, *c345*, 350–56, 357–63, 364–68, 369–73, 376–80; advantages and disadvantages of each side, 351–52; African Americans during, 366; battlefield medicine, 366–67; cannon, *p357*; casualties of, *g378*; causes and effects of, 318–24, 326–31, 332–38, 340–45, *c345*; choosing sides in, 350–51; conscription, 353, 358; diplomatic challenges, 353–54; dissolution of Union, 340–45; domestic and foreign affairs, *c383*; early stages of, 357–63; end of, 376–80; economics of, 351–52; end of, 376–80; final campaigns, 376–78, *g378*, *p378*, 379–86; financing and resources, 352, *g354*; in the East, 361–63; in the West, *m360*, 360–61; life during, 364–68; military campaigns, *c383*; military technology, tactics, 354–55; naval war, 358–60; prisoners of war, 368; sectional conflicts, 318–24, 326–38, 340–45; strategies, 355–56; surrender, 380; suspension of writs of habeas corpus, 353; telegraph, 365; troop mobilization, 357–58; turning points, 369–73; wartime economies, 364–65; women during, 367–68

Civil Works Administration (CWA), *c687*, 688

Clark, George Rogers, 142

Clark, Jim, 880

Clark, William, 223, 227; map by, *m227*

Clarke, John H., 588, *q588*

Clay, Henry, 229, 241, *p241*, 258, 259, 285, 307, 323, *p323*, 324, 327

Clayton Antitrust Act, 569

Clean Air Act, *c858*, 941

Clean Water Act, 941

Cleaver, Eldridge, 885

Clemenceau, Georges, 596

Clermont, 247, 249

Cleveland, Grover, 458, 494–95, *q495*, 496, *p496*, 505, 528

Clinton, George, 173, 175

Clinton, Hillary Rodham, 1017, *p1017*

Clinton, Sir Henry, 143

Clinton, William Jefferson, 1016–21, *p1017*, *p1019*, 1026, 1033; domestic agenda, 1016–17; economic policies, 1017, 1019; foreign policy, 1020–21; impeachment of, 1019–20, *p1019*, *p1020*; Republican control of Congress and, 1018; second term, 1019–20

closed shops, 458, 809

cloture, 878–79

Clurman, Harold, 680, *q680*

Coal Strike of 1902, 556–57, *p557*

code breakers, 744

code names, 755, 758

Coercive Acts, 127–28

Coffin, Levi, 328, *q328*

Cold War: American society and, 790–96; Bay of Pigs, 848–49; beginning of, 776–802; Berlin crisis, 785–86; Berlin Wall, 849; causes and effects of, 784, *c784*; conservatism and, 981; construction of missile sites in Cuba, 849–50, *p850*; early years of, 783; end of, 1002; impact in America, 791–96, 798, 812, 842, 843, 989, 991; in Asia, 786–87; origins of, 778–82; presidential policies and, 796, 797–802, 846–51, 988–89; space race, 847–48;

spread of, 786–89; Western victory in, 955–57, 966, 968, 976–77, 988–89, 990, 991, 1002–04, 1006

Cole, Nat King, 824

Coleman, Bessie, 643, *p643*

collective bargaining, 686, 692

colonies: Africans in, 106–07; cities of, *c107; Colonial Wedding, ptg83;* comparing European, *c77;* economies of, 84–86, 91–93, *c110;* English, 58–77; ethnic diversity, 105–106, *m107;* family life, 104–05; first written constitution, 70; geography of, *c110;* government of, 63, 64, 68, 70, 75, 76, 94, 100, 101; health conditions, 105; impact of the Enlightenment and Great Awakening on, 108–09; Imperial system and, 98–102; laws of, 68–69, 75, 99–100; life in, 82–102, 104–109; Middle, 72–76, 96–97; New England, 66–71, 91–95; population, *g103,* 105, *c110;* proprietary, 64; relationship with Native Americans, 51–56, 62, 64, 67, 69, 70–71, 75; religion in, 64, 66–71, 74–75, 94–95; royal, 64, 71, 76, 101; slavery in, 89–91, 106–07; society of, 86–87, 93–97, *c110;* Southern, 76–77, 84–90; taxation and, 64, 68, 75, 88, 100; trade, *m96;* voting, 70, 75, 88, 94; ways of life, 82–102, 103–09; women in, 105. *See also* American Revolution.

Colorado, 224, 311, 416

Colorado River, 666–67

Colored Farmers' National Alliance, 509

Columbia, 998

Columbia Broadcasting System, 644

Columbian Exchange, *c43,* 43–44

Columbia River, 224

Columbus Christopher, 38, *q38,* 39, 40, *q40,* 41, *p41; The Landing of Christopher Columbus in San Salvador, ptg11*

Command of the Army Act, 394

Commerce, Illinois, 276

Commercial Bureau of the American Republics, 524

commission plan, 548, 549, *c549*

Committee for Industrial Organization (CIO), 693

Committee on Equal Employment Opportunity (CEEO), 875

Committee on Public Information, 588

committees of correspondence, 127

Committee to Defend America by Aiding the Allies, 726

common house, 93

common laborers, 455

Common Sense, 133

Commonwealth v. Hunt, 250

communes, 923

communications, 439–40, 1013–14. *See also* technological innovations.

Communism: collapse of in Eastern Europe, 991; containing, 783–85; domino theory, 894; fighting covertly, 801–02; in America, 602, 610, 709, 791–96; in Asia, 786–87; in Eastern Europe, 782; in Greece, 785; in USSR, 709–10, 727, 1002–03; Korean War and, 788–89; McCarran Act, 794; Project Venona, 792; Reagan and, 988–89; Red Scare, 601–02, 791–96; Vietnam and, 894, 897, 898

comparisons, making, 163, 177

compass, 37, *p37*

competition: business, 248, 249, 443, 448, 450, 502, 523, 524–25, 567, 568, 683, 684; military, 524–25

Comprehensive Nuclear Test Ban Treaty, 1025

Compromise of 1850, 324, *c324,* 326

Compromise of 1877, 406

computers, 817, *p817,* 819, 931, 1012–13; chips, 1013; compact, *p817;* early technology, 819; ENIAC, *p817,* 1012–13; home, 1013; integrated circuits, 1013; microprocessors, 1013; operating systems, 1013; software, 1013

Comstock Boomtown, 416, *p416*

Comstock, Henry, 415

Comstock Lode, 414

concentration camps, 723, 764, *m724, m733*

Concord, Battle of, 130, *m130*

concurrent powers, 180–81

"conductors," 327

Coney Island, 479

Confederacy, 343–45, 350–80. *See also* Civil War.

Confederate States of America, 343. *See also* Civil War.

Confederation Congress, 159–60

conference committees, 183

Congregationalists, 109

Congressional Black Caucus, 935

Congress of Industrial Organizations, 694

Congress of Racial Equality (CORE), 830, 868, 874, 876, 884

Congress, U.S., 211–13, 216, 219, 222, 229, 230, 241, 243, 246, 253, 257, 258, 268, 269, 271, 295, 321, 323, 324, 329–31, 333, 335, 342, 352, 392, 394, 395, 402, 404, 557–58, 730, 1013, 1018, 1020, 1025, 1034, 1035, 1036–37. *See also* legislative branch of government.

Connecticut, 70–71, 121, 165, 167, 286

Connecticut Compromise, 167

Connor, Theophilus Eugene, 875, 876–77

conoidal bullets, 355, *p355*

conquistadors, 53, 54

Conscience Whigs, 322

conscription, 353, 358, 585

consensus, 856

consequences, predicting, 325, 347

conservatism, 978–1006, *m983;* George H. Bush administration, 1001–06; new, 980–84; organization of, 981–82; Reagan administration, 985–91; religious right, 983–84; Sagebrush rebellion, 982; social, 983–94; suburban, 982–83; Sunbelt, 982; support of, 982–84; versus liberalism, 980–81

constituents, 183

Constitutional Convention, 164–69; Connecticut Compromise, 167; compromises in, 167–68; framework for limited government, 168–69; ratification celebration, *ptg157;* Three-Fifths Compromise, 167; Virginia and New Jersey Plans, 166. *See also* constitution, U.S.

constitutional conventions, state, 388, 392, 394, 399

constitutional republic, 148

Constitutional Union Party, 341

Constitution of the Five Nations, The, 24–25

Constitution, U.S., 164–69, 178–207, 549, 568, 867, 868, 870, 872, 981, 988; amendments, *c181,* 182, *c184,* 198, 199–207; bicentennial of, 179; Bill of Rights, *c182,* 199–200, 211, 844; checks and balances, 108, 148, 168–69, 181–82, 222; concurrent powers, *c180,* 181; Connecticut Compromise and, 167; delegated powers, *c180;* enumerated powers, 181; executive branch of government, 168–69, 181, *c181,* 183–84, 194–96; federalism, 180–81; framework for limited government, 180; framing of, 164–69; judicial branch of government, 168–69, 181, *c181,* 184–85, 196–97; legislative branch of government, 168–69, 181, *c181,* 182–83, 189–94; national supremacy, 196; New Jersey Plan, 166; popular sovereignty, 168, 180, 321, 336; preamble to, 189; principles of, 180–82; ratification, 172–77, *crt173;* relations among states, 197–98; representative democracy, 180; republicanism, 180; reserved powers, *c180,* 181; rights and freedoms, 182, 185–86; separation of powers, 181; shared power, 180; two-thirds vote, 169; Virginia Plan, 165–66. *See also* executive branch of government, judicial branch of government, legislative branch of government.

constructionism, 988

consumer credit, 644

consumer demand, 437

consumer goods, 642, 643, 644; advertisements of, *p644*

consumerism, 815–16

consumer movement, 942–43

consumer protection, 558, 942–43

consumer society, 644–46, 815–16; attitudes toward debt, 644

containment, 784, 801

Continental Army, 130, 139. *See also* militias.

Index

Continental Congress, 128–29, 133–33, 141, 158

Continental Navy, 131

contraband, 581

Contract with America, 1018

contras, 990

convoys, 594

convoy system, 746

Coolidge, Calvin, 600–01, *q600–01,* 636, *q636,* 638, 639, *p639, q639;* alignment with big business, 639; philosophy of government, 639

cooperative individualism, 648

cooperatives, 502, 509

Cooper, James Fenimore, 276

Cooper, Peter, 247

copperheads, 353, *crt353*

Coral Sea, Battle of the, 744

Cornwallis, General Charles, 143–45

Coronado, Francisco Vásques de, 53

corporations, 447–51, 495–96, 553, 645, 648, 815, *crt815. See also* big business.

Corps of Discovery, 224, 226, 227

Corregidor, 743, *m748*

corrupt bargain, 259, 260

Cortés, Hernán, 50–52, *q52,* 53

cost of living, 599, 809

cost-plus contracts, 737

cotton, 248, 252–53, 352

Cotton Club, 627, *p628*

cotton gin, 252, *p252*

Cotton Whigs, 322

Coughlin, Father Charles, 690, *p690,* 696

Council of the Indies, 55

counterculture, 922, *p922,* 923–25; art, 924–25; decline of, 923; hippie movement, 922–23; impact of, 923–25; Woodstock, 924, *p924,* 925

coureurs de bois, 56

court-packing plan, 697, 698

courts of appeal, *c185,* 184–85, 211

covenants, 93

covert operations, 801

Cox, Archibald, 961

Cox, James M., 603

craft workers, 455

Crandall, Prudence, 286, *p286*

Crawford, William, 259

Crazy Horse, Chief, 427

creationism, 614–15

credibility gap, 904–05, *crt905*

Crédit Mobilier, 446, 495

Creel, George, 586, 588, *p589*

Crick, Francis, 1015

crime, 882, 996

"The Crime of '73," 502

criollos, 54

Crittenden, John J., 343

Crittenden's Compromise, 343

Cromwell, Oliver, 73, *p73*

Cronkite, Walter, 907

crop liens, 407

Crusades, 32, 34–35

Crystals, the, 824

Cuba, 51, 118–19, 361, *ptg528,* 528–34, 722, 841, 846–50; *p850;* American support of, 528–29; Bay of Pigs, 848–49; construction of missile sites in, *p850;* missile crisis, 846, 849–50; Platt Amendment, 533; rebellion in, 528, *ptg528;* Spanish–American War and, 528–34; U.S. military government of, 533

Cullen, Countee, 627

cultural assimilation, 884

cultures: African, 26–31; African American, 106–07, 151, 626–30, 823–25, 972–73; colonial, 86–87, 93–97; converging, 10–17, 18–19, 20–24, 26–31, 32–37, 38–44; counter, 922–25; European, 32–37; Gilded Age, 476–80; Mesoamerican, 13–15; Native American, 12–13, *m13, c14,* 14–15, *c15, p16,* 16–17, *p17, p20,* 20–22, *m22, p23,* 23–24, 25, 485; popular, 622–23, 820–25, 920–25, 970–73, *p973,* 974, 994–99; North American, 12–13, *m13, c14,* 14–15, *c15, p16,* 16–17, *p17, p20,* 20–22, *m22, p23,* 23–24

Cummings, Kate, 367, *q368*

Curran, Henry, 612, *q612*

currency, 35, 160–61, 212, 352, 501, 505, 507, 1023

Currency Act of 1764, 120

Cushing, William, *q147*

Custer, Colonel George A., 429

customs duty, 119

customs union, 524

Czechoslovakia, 714, *p714,* 1002

Czolgosz, Leon, 537

D

da Gama, Vasco 37

Dakota Territory, 416, 427

Daley, Richard, 883

Danzig, 714

Darrow, Clarence, 615

Darwin, Charles, 477–78, 614

Darwinism. *See* Social Darwinism.

database, building, 673, 675

Daugherty, Harry, 638, 647

Daughters of Liberty, 123

Davis, Benjamin O., 740, *p740*

Davis, Jefferson, 328, 343, *p343, q343,* 355–56

Dawes, Charles G., 649

Dawes, William, 130

Dawes Act, 430, 649

daylight savings time, 586

Dayton Accords, 1020

D-Day, 755, 757–59, 762, *m762,* 763, 1031

DDT, 939–40, 942

de Aguilar, Jeronimo, 51

Dean, James, 826, *p826*

Dean, John, 960

Deane, Silas, 142

death camps, 723, *p723*

de Balboa, Vasco, 43

debates, political, 336–37, *ptg336–37,* 840, *p840*

Debs, Eugene V., 458, 553, 584, *q584*

debt peonage, 407

debt relief, 686–87

decision making, 803, 805

Declaration of Independence, 132–37; preamble to, 134; slavery and, 132

Declaration of Indian Purpose, 936

Declaration of Liberated Europe, 780–81, 782

Declaration of Principles, 1021

Declaration of Rights and Grievances, 129

Declaratory Act, 122

Decter, Midge, 980, *q980*

Deere, John, 295

de facto segregation, 867, 883

defense plants, 750

deficit reduction, 1017

deficit spending, 648, 690, 842, 964, 987, 989, *g990*

deflation, 455, 501–02, 504

de Grasse, Admiral Francois, 145

Dekanawidah, 24, 25, *q25*

Delaware, 96–97, 351

Delaware River, 23

delegated powers, *c180*

de Lôme, Enrique Dupuy, 529

demarcation, 42

demilitarized zone (DMZ), 799

democracy, 148

Democratic National Committee (DNC), 958

Democratic Party, 213, 259, 271, *c272,* 321, 330, 332, *c333,* 335, 336, 341–42, 352–53, 379, 391, 393, 395, 399, 404–06, 493–97, 503, 504–06, 509, 514, 529, 564, 565, 566, 567, 568, 569, *crt638,* 639, 657, 678, 679, 680, 690, 695, 697, 699, 793, 809, 810, 811, 841, 842, 868, 874, 875, 908–09, 929, 934, 952, 953, 982, 1002, 1006, 1017, 1027–28

Democratic-Republican Party, 213, 214, *c214,* 216, 218, 219, 220, 222, 225, 228, 240, 258, 259, *c272*

Demonstration Cities and Metropolitan Development Act, *c858*

Dempsey, Jack, 622

Denver, Colorado, 416

Denver, John, 973

Department of Commerce and Labor, 557

Department of Energy, 950, 967; impact, 950

Department of Homeland Security, 1035, 1037

Department of Housing and Urban Development (HUD), 860

Department of State, 211

Department of the Treasury, 211

Department of Transportation, 860

Department of War, 211

deportation, 602

DePriest, Oscar, 629

deregulation, 967, 987–88

desegregation, 843, 867, 870, 871, 872, 879, 880, 934

de Soto, Hernando, 53

détente, 956, 966, 988

deterrence, 1036

Detroit, Michigan, 882–83

developing nations, 801

Dewey, Commodore George, 530

Index

Dewey, Thomas, 810

Dias, Bartolomeu, 37

d'Iberville, Lord, 57

Dickinson, Emily, 277

dictatorships, 709–10

Dien Bien Phu, 894

Dietrich, Marlene, 664

digital electronics, 1014

direct elections, 203, 549

direct primary, 549

Dirksen, Everett, 842

disarmament, 649

disco, 972, 973

discrimination, 150–51, 274–75, 425–26, 428–29, 468, 508, 585, 587, 600, 601, 611, 612, 629, 696, 786, 829, 830, 864–71, 879, 883

disease, impact of: AIDS, 996–97; Centers for Disease Control, 997; Columbian Exchange, 43–44; in Civil War, 367; on building of the Panama canal, 536; on colonization, 62, 67; on Native Americans, 43–44, 51–52

disenfranchisement, 740

Disney, Walt, 664

district courts, 184, 211

District of Columbia, 206, 212, 222–23, p223, 323, 343

divorce rates, 832

Dix, Dorothea, 278

Dixiecrat Party, 810

DNA (deoxyribonucleic acid), 13, 1015

Dodge, Grenville, 442, q442, 443, q443

Dole, Bob, 1018–19

dollar diplomacy, 541

Dominion of New England, 100, 101

Domino Fats, 825, p825

domino theory, 894

Donahue, Phil, 995

Donner Party, 296

"Do Nothing Congress," 810

Doolittle, Lieutenant Colonel James, 743, p743; Doolittle raid, 743, p743

dot-coms, 1014

"Double V" campaign, 740

doughboys, 591, 594, p601

Douglass, Frederick, 254, q254, p255, q255, 286–87, p288, 299, p299, 327, 366, q366

Douglas, Stephen, A., 324, 329, 330, 335, 336–37, 341–42, q366

"doves," 907

downsizing, 1005

Doyle, H.S., 508, q508

draft, 585, 905–06

Drake, Edwin, 437

Dred Scott v. Sandford, 334–35, 341; newspaper headline, p335

Drifters, the, 824

driver, slave, 254

dry farming, 422

Du Bois, W.E.B., 149, 512, p512, 570, q590, 629

"duck and cover," 796

due process, 120, 186, 199, 792, 844

Dukakis, Michael, 1002

DUKW, 756

Dulles, Allen, 801, p801

Dulles, John Foster, 799, q799, 800, 801, p801, 802

Dunkirk, Battle of, 716, q716

Dunkirk, France, 716–17

Dunmore, Lord, 131–32

Duquesne, Marquis, 117

Dust Bowl, 663, m663

Dutch, 72–74

duty, 159

Dylan, Bob, 925

dynamic conservatism, 811–12

E

Eagles, the, 973

Eakins, Thomas, 478; Baseball Players Practicing, ptg478

Earhart, Amelia, 643, p643

Earth Day, 940

Eastern Europe, m1002, 1002–03

Eastern Woodlands, 23–24; Native American deer hunting, ptg23

East Germany, 849

Eastland, James, 876

E bonds, 754

ecclesiastical tyranny, 149

Eckford, Elizabeth, 871, p871

economic nationalism, 241–42

Economic Opportunity Act, 857

economics: as key to world peace, 779; balancing with the environment, 1025; boom and bust, 415, 416; competition and, 248; cycles, 415–16; debt and, 686; deflation, 455, 501–02, 504; depressions, 505, 654–73, 712; downsizing in, 1005; European, 33–34, 785; expansionist policies, 521, c521; Federal Reserve System, 568, m569; global economy, 944–45, 1022–24; gold standard, 681; Imperialism, 521–22; importance of natural resources in, 437; Keynesian, 698, 964; laissez-faire, 438–39; mercantilism, 98–99; monetarism, 987; overproduction and, 659–60; recessions, 523, 610, 965–66, 1005; stagflation, 964–65, 987; supply-side, 648, 842, 987, 989

economies of scale, 448

economy, U.S.: anti-immigration sentiment and, 611–12; anti-trust actions and, 497, 514, 553, 556, 559, 565; Area Redevelopment Act, 843; bank failures, 656, p656, 659, 661; bank reform, 568; businesses and, 415–17, 447–51, 496–97, 506, 521, 522, 523, 525, 553, 556, 565, 568, 585–86, 749–51; colonial 84–86, 91–93, c110; consumer society, 644–46; crises in, 500–04, 963–65; decline of inner city and, 829–30; deficit spending and, 241, 648, 690, 842, 964, 987, 989, g990, 1017; diplomacy and, 538, 539, 648, 649, 650; dollar diplomacy, 541; domination of world economy, 648–49; E bonds, 754; Economic Opportunity Act, 857; economic prosperity, 640–50, 657, 808–09, 812–23, 826–29, 832, 834–35, 921, 963, 988; global economy and, 944–45, 1022–24; Great Depression, 654–74; growth of labor unions, 692–94; impact of Cold War on, 798, 812, 842, 843, 989, 991; impact of New Deal measures, 682–88, 699–700; industrialization and, 248; inflation, 501, 568, 599, 600, 753, 809, 964, 965, 966, g977, 983, 987; interest rates, 241, 271, 660, 965, 966, 987, 1017; Interstate Commerce Commission and, 496, 514, 541, 542, 553, 557, 558, 559, 565, 567; Kennedy's theories, 842–43; links to WWI allies, 581; money supply, 271, 501; national banks, 139, 212–13, 241, 270–71; national debt, 648, 690, 842, 964, 987, 989, g990; Northwest Ordinance impact on, 161; oil and, 964; Open Door Policy and, 538–39; opposition to government regulation of business, 647–48; overseas investments and, 528; Panic of 1873, 271; Panic of 1893, 505; popular culture and, 623, 664–65, 820–23, 825, 925, 976, 996; postwar turmoil, 599–602, 808–09, 815–16; private property rights and, 416–22, 432; Reaganomics, 987; recessions, 697–98; stock markets, 404, 505, 645, 656–59, crt659, 684, 1014, 1018, 1029; Supreme Court decisions and, 699–700; tariffs, 211–12, 496, 497, 501, 504, 564, 646, 649; tax cuts and, 648; unemployment, 662, 680, 687–88, 689, 697, 964–65; wage and price controls, 497, 646, 753–54; wartime effects, 351–52, 386–407; 581, 586, 587, 599, 600, 601, 616, 669, 737–39, 858–61

ecosystems, 43–44

Ederle, Gertrude, 623

Edison, Thomas Alva, 436, q436, 440

Edo, the, 29–30

education, 152, 280–81, 400, 485, 486, 858, c858, 871, 876, 921–22, 928–29, 933–34, 936–37; affirmative action and, 933; African Americans and, 275, 388, 400, p400, 871, 876; Americorps, 1017; bilingual, 936; busing, 934; compulsory education laws, 557; desegregation of, 843, 867, 870, 871, 872, 879, 880, 934; discrimination in, 928; equal access to, 934; Freedmen's Bureau and, 400; higher, 152, 400, 858, 876, 921, 922; impact of the American Revolution on, 152; impact of youth movement, 921; Native American, 936–37; New England School, ptg280; Project Head Start, 858, c858, 860; public, 152, 280–81, 485; reform, 280–81; segregation in, 934; Title IX, 929; women and, 276, 281, 926–29

Educational Amendments, 929

Edwards, Jonathan, 108

Egypt, 745–46, 800, 968, 1032

Eighteenth Amendment, 203–04, 615, 616; repeal of, 616

Eighth Amendment, *c182,* 200

Einstein, Albert, 720, *p720,* 769, *q826*

Eisenhower, General Dwight D., 746, 756, 757–59, *p759,* 765–66, 798–802, *p802, q802,* 811–13, *m812,* 843, 848, 871–72, 894, 897; civil rights and, 871–72; domestic policies, 811–13; dynamic conservatism, 811–12; foreign policies, 798–802, 848, 894, 897; interstate highway system, 812, *m812;* massive retaliation policy, 798; "middle of the road," 811; Warren appointment, 843; with troops, *p759,* 765–66

elastic clause, 193, 571

El Camino Real, 54

elections: certification of results, 1028; direct, 203, 549; *Election Day in Philadelphia, ptg239; Electioneering in a Country Town, ptg491;* of 1794, 213; of 1796, 218; of 1800, 219–20, *m220;* of 1824, 258–59; of 1828, 260, 267, 268, *g268, m269;* of 1840, 271–72; of 1844, 307; of 1848, 322; of 1856, 334; of 1860, 340–42, *m341, crt342;* of 1864, 379–80; of 1868, 395; of 1876, 405, *m405;* of 1884, *m494,* 494–95; of 1896, 506–07; of 1900, 537; of 1912, 566–67; of 1924, 639; of 1928, 656–57; of 1936, 696–97; of 1940, 726–27; of 1948, 810, *m811;* of 1956, 811; of 1960, 840–41; of 1964, 857; of 1968, 953, *m953;* of 1976, 966; of 1980, 987; of 1984, 988; of 1992, 1006; of 1996, 1018–19; of 2000, 1026–29, *g1027, m1028;* recounts in, 1028

electoral changes, 549

Electoral College, 219, 259, 982, 1026

electoral votes, 219, 259, 405, 982, 1019, 1026, 1028. *See also* elections.

electors, 219

electricity, 436, 440, 471, 666, *m666*

electronic spreadsheet, using, 526, 543

electronic mail, 1013–14

Elementary and Secondary Education Act, 858, *c858*

Eleventh Amendment, 200

Eliot, T.S., 621

Elizabeth, Queen of England, 60, 61

Ellington, Duke, 627

Ellis Island, 466, 612

Elmire Castle, *p89*

emancipation, 150, 286, 363

Emancipation Proclamation, 363, 1071

Embargo Act of 1807, 225

embargoes, 225, 964, 969

embassy bombings, 1033

Emergency Banking Relief Act, 683

Emergency Quota Act, 612

Emergency Relief and Construction Act, 670

Emerson, Ralph Waldo, 276

Emmanuel, Victor, King of Italy, 756

empresarios, 301

enclosure movement, 61, 86

encomenderos, 54

encomienda, 54

Endangered Species Act, 941

energy conservation, 964–67

Enforcement Acts, 402

Engel v. Vitale, c844, 845

England. *See* English Empire, Great Britain.

English Civil War, 72–73

English Empire: alliance with Spain, 59; colonies, 58–77; early explorations, 58–59; French-Indian War, 118; Glorious Revolution, 100–01; Imperial system, 98–102; Reformation, 60. *See also* American Revolution, Great Britain.

ENIAC (Electronic Numerical Integrator and Computer), *p817,* 1012–13

Enlightenment, the, 108

Enola Gay, 770

Enron, 1029

entertainment industry: 623, 664–65, 995–96

entrepreneurs, 97, 248, 438, 448, 477

enumerated powers, 181, 192, 213

enumeration, 189

environmental conservation, 558–59, 565

Environmental Defense Fund, 939

environmentalism: beginnings of, 939–40; environmental movement, 939–43; global concerns, 1025; government efforts, 941, 982, 988; grassroots efforts, 940–41; legal system and, 939; Reagan and, 988

Environmental Protection Agency (EPA), 941, 982, 988

envoys, 308

Equal Employment Opportunity Commission (EEOC), 879, 928

Equal Pay Act, 843, 927

equal protection clause, 186, 202–03, 392, 511, 550, 844, 868

Equal Rights Amendment, 927, 928, *p930,* 983; support of and opposition to, *p930*

Equiano, Olaudah, 89, *q89*

Era of Good Feelings, 240

Ericsson, Leif, 39

Erie Canal, *p236–37,* 245, 247

Ervin, Sam J., 960

Escobedo v. Illinois, c844, 844–45

espionage, 588

Essay on Human Understanding, 108

Essex Junto, 224

Estéban, 53

Ethics in Government Act, 962

ethnic cleansing, 1020

Eubanks, Robert, 808, *p808*

eugenics, 611

euro, 1023

European cultures, 32–44, *c77;* age of exploration, *m34;* causes and effects of European exploration, *c35;* colonization by, *c77;* Columbian Exchange and, 43–44; Crusades, 34–35; exploration of America, 38–44; explorations and settlements, *m59;* religion and, 32, 34–35; Renaissance, 36

European Union (EU), 1023

evolution, theory of, 614–15

Ewuare, Oba, 29

exchanges, 502–03

executive branch of government, *c181,* 183–84; 954–55, 960, 962; at work, 184; chief executive and chief diplomat, 184; chief of state, 184; commander in chief, 184;

departments of, 184; legislative leader, 184; roles of the president, 184

executive privilege, 961

Exodusters, 509, *p509*

Expedition Act, 557

Export Control Act, 729

extermination camps, *p723,* 723–24

Face the Nation, 996

fact from opinion, distinguishing, 651, 653

Fair Deal, 810

Fair Employment Practices Commission, 750

Fair Labor Standards Act, 699

Fair Packaging and Labeling Act, 858, *c858*

Fall, Albert B., 638

Fallen Timbers, Battle of, 217; monument to, *p217*

fall line, 93

fallout, 796

fallout shelter, *p795,* 826, *p826,* 827

Falwell, Jerry, 984, *p984*

Family Medical Leave Act, 1017

Fannin, James W., 303

Farewell To Manzanar, 773

Farm Credit Administration, 687

Farmer, James, 868, 874, 876

Farmers' Alliance, *p502,* 502–03

farmers' revolt, 671, *p671, m675*

farming. *See* agriculture.

Farm Security Administration, 699

Farragut, David G., 359–60, 378

fascism, 709, 711; anti–fascism poster, *p711*

Faubus, Orval, 871–72

Faulkner, William, 665

favorite sons, 258

featherbedding, 809

Federal Bureau of Investigation, 602, 791

Federal Campaign Act Amendments, 962

Federal Communications Commission (FCC), 988

federal court system, 184–85, *c185;* claims courts, *c185;* court of veteran's appeals, c185; federal regulatory agencies, c185; international trade courts, c185; military courts, c185; tax courts, c185; territorial courts, c185

federal deficit, 222, 648, 690, 842, 964, 987, 989, g990, 1017, 1019

Federal Deposit Insurance Corporation (FDIC), 684–85, 687, c687

Federal Emergency Relief Agency, c687, 687–89

Federal Farm Loan Act, 570

Federal Hall, 212, p212

Federal Highway Act, 812

federal income tax, 203, 352, 568, 586

federalism, 180–81

Federalist Party, 173–74, 213–20, 222, 224, 225, 232, 240, c272

Federalists, 173–75. *See also* constitution, U.S.

Federalist, The, 174, 1066–1067

Federal Land Banks, 570

Federal Mobilization Agencies, c587

Federal Number One, 691–92

Federal Radio Commission, 644

Federal Reserve Act, 568

Federal Reserve Board, 660, 670

Federal Reserve System, 568, m569, 648

federal revenue agents, 615–16, p616

Federal Theater Project, 692

Federal Trade Commission, 569

Feminine Mystique, The, 928; book cover, p928

feminism, 927

feminist movement, 926–30, 983

Ferdinand, Archduke Franz, p578, 578–79

Ferdinand, King of Spain, 40–41

Ferraro, Geraldine, 988

Fetterman, Captain William, 427

Fetterman's Massacre, 427, 428

feudalism, 33, 35

Fifteenth Amendment, 203, 395, 499, 510, 550

Fifteenth Regiment, 629

Fifth Amendment, c182, 186, 199

"**Fifty-four Forty or Fight,**" 308

54th Massachusetts Regiment, 366

Fight for Freedom Committee, 726

filibuster, 877–80

film industry, 664, 822

Filmore, Millard, 324, 334

"**final solution,**" 722, p722, 723

Finney, Charles Grandison, 275

fireside chats, 684

Firing Line, 995–96

First Amendment, c182, 186, 199, 588, 589, 922

First Continental Congress, 128–29

first New Deal, 682–86, c687, 687–88

First Virginia Militia, p344

fishing industry, 91–92

Fiske, John, 521, q521

Fitzgerald, F. Scott, q620, 622, q624

Five Nations Confederate Council, 24, 25

Five Power Naval Limitation Treaty, 649–50, c649

fixed costs, 448

flags: America's, 145, p145, 229, p229; English, 108, p108; French, 57, p57

flappers, 613, 614, p614, p615

Fletcher, Captain Luther, 764, p764

flexible response, 847

Flint, Michigan, 693

Florida, 43, 53, 107, 270, 394, 1026–29, c1028

Florida, 359

Florida Supreme Court, 1028

flowchart, reading, 233, 235

Foch, Ferdinand, 596

Folsom, New Mexico, 12

Food and Drug Administration, 586

foraging, 370, 371

Force Bill, 289

Ford, Gerald, 961, p961, 965–66, p966; foreign policy, 966; Helsinki Accords, 966; Nixon pardon, 965; WIN plan, 965

Ford, Henry, 640, q640, 641, p641, q641, 642, p642, 738, 945; assembly line, 641, p641

Fordney-McCumber Act, 646

Ford's Theater, 380

foreclosures, 671

Fort Detroit, 57

Fort Duquesne, 117, 118

Forten, James, 255

Fort McHenry, 228, 229, 231

Fort Necessity, 117

Fort Pickens, 342

Fort Pitt, 118

Fort St. Louis, 57

Fort Sumter, 340, 342–44

Forty-Niners, 322, p322

fossil fuels, 942

442nd Regimental Combat Team, 753

Founding Fathers, 165–66

Four Freedoms, 727, 1075

Four-Minute Men, 588

Four Power Treaty, 649–50, c650

Fourteen Points, 596, 1074

Fourteenth Amendment, 186, 202–03, 392, 499, 511, 550, 844, 868

Fourth Amendment, c182, 185, 199, 1036

France, 55–57, 216, 218, 223–25, 229, 538, 578, 580, 596, 649, 714–18, 722, 800–01, 849, 893–94; American Revolution and, 142; Battle of Dunkirk, 716–17; control of Vietnam, 893–94; Louisiana Purchase, 223–24; mapping of North America, 55; New France, 56–57, 117–18; war with Britain, 216, 225; WWI, 596; WWII, 714–18, 757–59, 764. *See also* French Empire, World War I, World War II.

franchises, 814

Franco, Francis, 711

Frank, Anne, 721

Franklin, Benjamin, q98, 104, q104, 117, 132–33, 140, 142, 145, 164, q164, 165, 167, q170

Fredericksburg, Virginia, 364, 370–71, p371

Fredonia, 301

Freed, Alan, 823

freedmen, 389

Freedmen's Bureau, 389, 400

freedom of assembly, 186, 199

freedom of religion, 148–49, 186, 199

freedom of speech, 148, 186, 199

freedom of the press, 186, 199

freedom of worship, 101, 199

Freedom Riders, 874–75, p875, 876

free enterprise system, 248, 438, 439

Freeman, Elizabeth (Mumbet), 149, p149

freemen, 68

Freeport Doctrine, 336

free soil, 322, 335

Free-Soil Party, 322, 330, c333

free speech movement, 922

free states, 257–68, 322, 329, 330

free trade, 439. *See also* trade.

Fremont, John C., 310, 334

French-Indian War, 118

French Revolution, 215–16

Friedan, Betty, 928, p927, p928, q928

Frobisher, Martin, 61

Frontenac, Count, 57

Fuel Administration, 586

Fugitive Slave Act, 325, 327

Fuller, Margaret, 276, p276, 282

Fulton, Robert, 247

fundamentalism, 614–15

fundamentalists, 614

Fundamental Orders of Connecticut, 70, 1062

furnishing merchants, 407

fur trade, 56–57, 71, 73, 74

G

Gable, Clark, 664

Gadsden, James, 328–29

Gadsden Purchase, 329

Gage, Thomas, 128, 129, 130, 131

Galbraith, John Kenneth, 814

Gallatin, Albert, 222

Galloway, Joseph, 128

Galveston, Texas, 548, p548, 549

Gálvez, Bernardo de, 143, p143

Gandhi, Mohandas, 870

gang system, of slavery, 254

Garbo, Greta, 664

Garfield, James A., 446, 492–93; assassination, 492, 493, p493; scandal investigation, 446

Garrison, William Lloyd, 284, 285, q286, 286–88

Garvey, Marcus, 629–30, p630, 884

Index

Gary, Elbert H., 601

gas chambers, 719, 723, 724

Gaspee, 127

Gates, Bill, 1013

Gates, General Horatio, 142, *q142,* 143

gauchos, 419

Gay Liberation Movement, 997

Geer, Elizabeth, *q296*

General Accounting Office, 648

General Court, 68, 69, 70, 93, 94

General Electric Theater, 986

generalizations, making, 731, 733

General Motors, 642, 693

general strike, 600

generation gap, 824

genetic engineering, 1015

Geneva Accords, 895

Genius of Universal Emancipation, 285

"gentlemen's agreement," 557

geographers, 39

Geography, 39

geography: Civil War border states, 344–45; Dust Bowl, 663; global cars, 944–45; Hoover Dam, *p666,* 666–67, *p667;* immigration and, 466, *m474,* 474–75, *m475, p475;* invading the North and, *m374,* 375; island hopping in the Pacific, 759–60, *m760;* land bridge to America, *m18,* 19, *m19;* Lewis and Clark expeditions, 226, *m226,* 227; links to war, 730, 759–60, 762, *p762;* nightmare at Omaha, 762, *m762,* 763, *m763;* rise of the Sunbelt, 982, *m983;* Spanish missions, 312–13; trails west, 295; urban America on the move, 992–93, *p992–93;* Yosemite, 560, *m560,* 561, *m561, p561*

geography skills, 1–5; dictionary, 6–7; elements of geography, 4–5; environment and society, 5; globes, 1; human systems, 5; location, 4; maps, 1–3; physical systems, 5; regions, 4; uses of geography, 5. *See also* maps, interpreting.

George, David Lloyd, *q590,* 596

George, Henry, 482, *q482*

George II, King of England, 76

George III, King of England, 127–28, 131, 141

Georgia, 76, 243, 251, 252, 259, 270, 341, 342, 378–79

Germany, 538, 540, 578, 580, 592–95, 596, 601, 649, 707, *p707,* 708–18, 730, 737, 755–61, 764–65, *p779,* 780–81, 1002; Afrika Korps, 746; Anti-Comintern Pact, 711; devastation of, *p779;* division of after WWII, 780; Holocaust, 713–18; Nazi-Soviet Non-Aggression Pact, 715, 727; reunification of, 1002; rise of Nazi Party, 710; warfare used by, 593–95, 715–16, 718; WWI, 592–97; WWII, 707, 708–18, 742–47, 755–61, 764–65

Gerry, Elbridge, 215, 218

Gestapo, 721

Gettysburg, Pennsylvania, 369, 371–72, *m374,* 375

Gettysburg Address, 371, 1072

Ghana, 22, 27–28

Ghost Dance, 430

Gibbons v. *Ogden,* c242, 243

Gibbs, Lois, 941

GI Bill, 808, 809, *p809,* 816

Gibson, Annetta, 656, *q656*

Gideon v. *Wainwright,* 392, 844, *c844*

Gilded Age, 476–80

Gingrich, Newt, 1018, *p1018*

Ginsburg, Allen, 824

"G.I.s," 739

glaciers, 13

Gladden, Washington, 484

glasnost, 1002

Glasser, Robert J., 900, *q900*

Glass–Skagall Banking Act, 684

Glenn, John, *q852, p853*

global economy, 944–45, 1022–24

global warming, 1025

Glorious Revolution, 100–01

Godey, Louis A., 277; *Godey's Lady Book,* 277

Goebbels, Joseph, 720, 722

Goering, Herman, 716

gold, 35, 40–41, 98–99, 322–23, 415–16, 501, 505, 507, 681; California Gold Rush, 322–23; gold reserves, 505; gold standard, 681; mercantilism, 98–99; mining, 415–16; search for, 40–41

Goldberg, Ruth, 790

goldbugs, 505–06

gold spike, 443

gold standard, 681

Gold Standard Act, 507

Goldwater, Barry, 857, *p857,* 982, 986

Gompers, Samuel, 458, *p458,* 532, 569

Gone With the Wind, 664

Gorbachev, Mikail, 990–91, *p991,* 1002

Gore, Al, 1027–29

Gorgas, Dr. William, 536

Gorges, Sir Fernando, 71

Gospel of Wealth, 478

Gould, Jay, 446, 458

government, foreign: central, 36; dictatorships, 709–10; early European, 33–34; emergence of strong European states, 35–36; Taliban, 969

government, U.S.: Albany Plan of Union, 117; Americans with Disabilities Act, 1006; anti-poverty programs, 856–57; antitrust actions, 557, 565, 568–69; articles of confederation, 158–59; as a safety net, 700; business and, 438–39, 553, 557, 683, 809, 842–43; campaign amendments, 962; colonial, 63, 64, 68, 70, 75, 76, 94, 100, 101; commission form, *c549;* conservatism and, 981, 987; contracts, 737, 868; contract theory of, 102, 108; cost-plus contracts, 737; council-manager form, 549, *c549;* credibility gap of, 905; curtailment of civil liberties, 344, 353, 588; deceptions, 912; development of, 14; efficiency of, 548; efforts to find communists, 791–94; Fair Deal, 810; financing, 211; Fundamental Orders of Connecticut, 70; gender bias in, 928; General Courts, 68–70, 93–94; Great Binding Law, 24; gridlock in, 1006; immigration laws, 468, 612; impact of Progressivism on, 554–59, 565, 568–70, 585–89; institutions of power, 211; issuance of war bonds, 754; Kerner Commission, 883; legacy of John Locke, 101–02, 108; liberal ideas of, 981; limiting role of, 812; Mayflower Compact, 67; National Housing Act, 698–99, 810; Native American, 21, 23–24, 25, 426; "One Man, One Vote," 843; Pendleton Act, 493; police power in, 615; public housing, 751; railroads and, 443; reforms in, 565, 566–67, 568, 570, 843; religion and, 845, 983; resolution, 898–99, 912; role of, 438–39, 482–83, 495–96, 504, 555–59, 669–72, 680, 683, 690, 856, 986; shaping public opinion, *c587,* 587–88; Social Security system, 810; state opposition to federal, 872; territorial, 323; urban renewal and, 829; use of propaganda, 588; use of public opinion, 685–86; Wilmot Proviso, 321. *See also* Constitution, U.S.

gradualism, 285

graduated income tax, 504

graft, 400, 473

Graham, Billy, 1034

Grand Banks, 92

grandfather clause, 510

Grange, Red, 623

Grange, the (Patrons of Husbandry), 502

Grant, Ulysses S., 360–61, 369–70, 372, *p372,* 373, 376–77, 380, 394, 395, *p402,* 403–05; administration of, 403–05; Civil War and, 373, 376–77, 380; economic crisis, 404–05; General-in-chief, 373; scandals of administration, 404

Grapes of Wrath, The, 665

grassroots movements, 940–41, 1006

Great American Desert, 421

Great Awakening, 108–09

Great Binding Law, 24

Great Britain, 229, 244, 248, 295, 308, 354, 359, 362–63, 538, 540, 578, 580, 581–82, 593–94, 649, 713–18, *p718,* 726–28, 755–61, 800–01, 849, 1037; blockade by, 581–82; bombing raids by Germany, *p717, p718;* Lend-Lease Act and, 727; World War I, 580, 581, 593–94; World War II, 715–18, 742–47, 755–61. *See also* English Empire.

Great Compromise, 167

Great Depression, 650–72, 679, 682–94, 695–700, 749; bank failures, 659, 661; bread lines, 662, *p670;* building of the Hoover Dam, 666, *m666,* 667, *p667;* causes of, 650–60, *g658,* 661, 673; cyclical effect of, *g658*; decline in world-wide trade, 660; effects of on economy, 657–60; effects of on government, 668–72; entertainment during, 663–65, *p698*; Hoover's response to, 668–72; housing during, 662–65; hunger marches, 670–71; image of an era, *p662*, *p671*; impact on farmers, 685; life during, 661–65, *p662*; New Deal and, 679, 682–88, 689, 690, 691–94; overproduction and, 659–60; stock market crash, *g658*, 658–59; unemployment, 660, 661–62; uneven distribution of wealth and, 659–60

Great Migration, 68, *m69*, 587, 626–27, 629, 751, *m751*

Great Plains, 224, 295, 327, 416–19, 420–23, 432, 499, 502, *p505*, 663; agriculture of, 421–23, 499; cattle ranching, 416–19; challenges to settlement of, 420–21; climate and geography of, 420–21; Dust Bowl, 663, *m663*; homesteading, 421; impact of railroads on, 421; life on, *p505*; private property rights and settlement of, 416–22, 432

Great Railroad Strike of 1877, 457

Great Salt Lake, 297, 299

Great Society, 857–60; legacy of, 859–60; programs of, *c858*

"Great White Fleet," 539

Greeley, Horace, 404, *q498*

Greenback Party, 502, 504

greenbacks, 352, 501

Greene, General Nathaniel, 143–44

Green Party, 1027

Greensboro sit-in, 873, *p873*, 874, *p874*

Greenwich Village, 621

Grenada, 990

Grenville, George, 119–20

Grierson, Benjamin, 370

Grimke, Sarah and Angelina, 286

Griswold v. *Connecticut*, 845

gross national product (GNP), 436–37, 842

group doctrine, 815

Grundy, Felix, 229

Grynszpan, Herschel, 720

Guadalcanal, 760

Guam, 530, 532

Guatemala, 801

guerrilla warfare, 139, 528–29, 530, 532, 577, 785, 847, 894, 989, 1032

Guinea, 29–30

Guiteau, Charles, 492, *q492*

Gulf of Tonkin, 902–03

Gulf of Tonkin Resolution, 898–99, 1079

Gullah, 106

gunpowder, 373

gurus, 971, *p971*

Gutiérrez, José Angel, 936, *p936*

habeas corpus, 353

haciendas, 55

Haig, Alexander, 962

Haight-Ashbury district, 923

Haiti, 1020

Halbert, G.I., 952, *p952*

Hale, Nathan, 140

Hale, Sarah Buell, 249

Halfbreeds, 493

Halvorsen, Lieutenant Gail, 783

Hamer, Fannie Lou, 874

Hamilton, Alexander, 145, 165, 174, 211, *p211*, *q212*, 212–14, *c214*, 224; duel with Aaron Burr, 224; Federalist national visions, 213–14, *c214*; financial program, 212–13

Hamilton, Andrew, 106

Hancock, John, 120, 129, 173

Hansberry, Lorraine, 828, *q828*, 830

Harding, Warren G., 603, *q603*, 612, 623, *q624*, 636–37, *p637*, *q637*, 638, *crt638*, 648, *p648*; cabinet, 637, 648, *p648*; political philosophy, 637; scandals of the administration, 637–38, *crt638*

hardtack, 366

Hare Krishna, 923

Hari, Mata, 591

Harlem, 627, 629, 630

Harlem Renaissance, 626–28; artists of, *p628*

Harpers Ferry, *ptg319*, 337

Harper's Weekly, 277

Harriman, Florence, *q590*

Harrington, Michael, 829, *q829*, 830, *q852*, 854–55

Harrisburg, Pennsylvania, 942

Harris, Essic, 398

Harrison, Benjamin, 496–97, 505

Harrison, William Henry, 229, 271, 272

Hartford, Connecticut, 232

Hartford Convention, 232

Hawaii, 520, 523

"hawks," 907

Hawley-Smoot Tariff, 660

Hawthorne, Nathaniel, 276

Hayden, Tom, 921

Hayes, Rutherford B., 405, *q406*, 493

Hay, John, 538, 540

Haymarket Riot, 458

Haymarket Square, 495

Hayne, Robert, 269

Hay-Pauncefote Treaty, 540

hazmet, 1036

headrights, 64, 86

Head Start, 858

Health Insurance Portability Act, 1018

Hearst, William Randolph, 528

Heart of Atlanta Motel v. *United States*, *c844*

hedgerow, 765

Hefferman, Joseph, 668

Helsinki Accords, 966

Hemingway, Ernest, 621

hemisphere defense zone, 727

Hendrix, Jimi, 925

Henry, Patrick, 172, *q172*, 173, 175

Henry IV, King of France, 56

Henry VII, King of England, 58–59

Henry VIII, King of England, 60

Henry Street Settlement, 481

Henry the Navigator (Prince Henry of Portugal), 37

Hepburn Act, 557

hereditary system, of slavery, 90

heretics, 69

Herrera, José Joaquín, 308

Hiawatha, 24

hidalgos, 54

Higginson, Francis, *q91*

Higher Education Act, 858, *c858*

highjackings, 1031–32

high society, 471

Highway Safety Act, 858, *c858*

Hill, A.P., 371

Hill, James H., 446

Hinckley, John, 988, *p988*

hippies, 922, *p922*, 923

Hiroshima, 770, *p770*

Hispanic Americans, 752, 830, 932–33, *g935*, 935–36, 954, *p954*; Bracero program and, 830; civil rights, 935–36; La Raza Unida, 935; migrant labor conditions, 830; political activism of, 935–36; population growth of, *g935*; poverty and, 830

Hispaniola, 40–41, 43

Hiss, Alger, 791–92

Hitler, Adolf, *p707*, 709–10, *p710*, 711, 713–14, 716–17, 720, 747, 765, 766; decision at Dunkirk, 716–17; European response to, 714; racial policies of, 710, 720; review of Nazi troops, *p707*

Hitler youth camp, 708

Hobby, Oveta Culp, 741

hobos, 662, *c664*

Ho Chi Minh, 892, 893, *p894*, 895, 897

Ho Chi Minh City, 913, *p913*

Ho Chi Minh Trail, 901

Hohokam, the, 15

holding companies, 450, 553, 556, 557

Holmes, Oliver Wendell, 588, *q588*

Holocaust, the, 719–24

homelessness, 996, *p996*

Home Owner's Loan Corporation (HOLC), 686–87, 699

Homestead Act, 421

homesteading, 421–23

Hooker, Joseph, 370

Hoover, Herbert, 586, *p607*, *q607*, 637, 648, 656, 657, *p657*, 668, 669, *p669*, 670, 672, *p672*, 678, 726; philosophy of government, 668; public perception of, 672

Hoover, J. Edgar, 602, *p603*, 791

Hoover Dam, 666, *m666*, 667, *m667*, *p667*

Hoovervilles, 662, 671

Hopewell, the, 16; artifact, *p17*

Hopkins, Harry, 687–88, 689, 691

Index

Hopper, Edward, 621, *ptg621*

horizontal integration, 449, *g449*, 450

House of Burgesses, 58, 63, 73, 88, 121, 123, 128

House of Representatives, 494, 496

Houser, George, 868

House Un-American Activities Committee (HUAC), 791–92; film industry hearing, 792, *p792*, *p793*

Housing and Urban Development Act, 858, *c858*

Houston, Sam, 302, *p302*, 303–04

Houston, Texas, 303

Howdy Doody, *p821*

Howe, General William, 131, 138, 139, 140, 143

Howe, Julia Ward, 550

Howells, William Dean, 479

Huckleberry Finn, 479

Hudson, Henry, 73

Huerta, Dolores, 935, 936, *p936*

Huerta, General Victoriano, 577

Hughes, Charles Evans, 650

Hughes, Langston, 627, 631, *p631*

Huguenots, 56

Hull House, 475, 485

Human Genome Project, 1015

Humphrey, Hubert, 908–09, 953

Hundred Days, 682

Hungary, 578, 802, 1002

hunger marches, 670–71

Hunger of Memory, 1007

Hurston, Zora Neale, 627, *p627*

Hussein, Saddam, 1004, 1021, 1036–37

Hutchinson, Anne, 69–70

hydrogen bomb, 798, *p798*

hypertext transport protocol (http), 1014

hypothesizing, 487, 489

I

Ice Age, 13, 19

Ickes, Harold, 698

"I Have a Dream," 1078

Il Duce, 709

Illinois, 217, 258, 324

Illinois Exchange, 503

immigration: Angel Island, 467–68; Asian immigrants, 465–66; Atlantic voyage, 465–66; attitudes toward, *crt466*, 468, 603; changes in, *g633*; colonies, 62, 63, 64, 75, 76, 97, 105, 106; controlling, *crt611*, 612; detention and deportation, 602–03; Ellis Island, *p463*, 466; European immigrants, 464–66, 612–13, *m613*; Germans, 274; Hispanic, 612; Huguenots, 56; impact of legislation on, 612; industrialization and, 437; Irish, 274; Jewish, 56, 106; living conditions of immigrants, 467, 471, 472, 475, *p475*; Mennonites, 105; mid-1850s, 273–74; nativism, 274–75, 468; Pacific voyage, 467; Palmer raids, 602–03; Pennsylvania Dutch, 106; problems of immigrants, 465–66, 467–68, 475, 610–12; reasons for 465, 467; restrictions of Jews in WWII, 722; Scotch Irish, 106; U.S. *g633*

Immigration Reform Act, 859

immunity, 638

impeachment, 181–82, 189–90, 222, 394–95, 961, 1019–20

Imperialism, 518–41; American diplomacy, 536–41; anti-, 532; building support for, 520–22; expansion and annexation, 522–23, 532; foreign relations, 523–24, 537–39; Roosevelt Corollary, 540–41; willingness to risk war and, 523–24

Imperial system, 98–102

implied powers, 213

impoundment, 955

impressment, 225, 232

Inca, the, 53

income tax, 203, 352, 568, 586

incorporation laws, 248

indentured servants, 86–87, 88, 255

Independence Hall, 168, *p168*

Independent National Party, 502

Indiana, 217, 229, 328, 336

Indian Civil Rights Act, 936

Indian Peace Commission, 428

Indian Removal Act, 270

Indian Self-Determination and Educational Assistance Act, 937

indigo, 86, 95

individualism, 477

individual rights. *See* rights.

industrialization, 436–40, 442–51, 454–59, 471, 477–82, 547, 641–45, 859; assembly line production, 641–42; big business and, 447–51; consumer society, 644–45; critics of, 481–82; government's role in, 438–39; impact of, 455, 477–82, 642, 644–45; Progressive views of, 547; railroad expansion and, 442–46; restrictions on, 859; social changes brought on by 481–82; society and, 471, 477, 644–45; unions, 454–59

Industrial Revolution, 247–49, 436; beginnings, 247; British industrial techniques, 248; entrepreneurial investment in, 248; impact of technology on, 248; labor, 248–49; urban growth during, 249; women during, 248

industry: airline, 643–44; automobile, 640–42; consumer goods, 642–43; entertainment, 623, 664–65; managerial revolution in, 645; manufacturing, 241, 248, *p248*; percentage of national income generated by, *g645*; socialism and, 553; wartime, 736–38; welfare capitalism, 645

inferences, making, 441, 461

inflation, 160, 271, 352, 501, 569, 600, 723, 753, 809, 964, 965, 966, *g977*, 983, 987, 1018, 1023

information, analyzing, 598, 605

information, synthesizing, 617, 633

initiative, 549

inner-city poverty, 829, *p829*

inoculation, 105

Inouye, Daniel, 725, *g725*

insider trading, 446

installments, 660

insubordination, 565

insurrection, 337

integrated circuit, 1013

Intel, 1013

interchangeable parts, 248

interdependent world, 1022–25

interest rates, 271, 407, 965, 966, 987, 1017, 1023

Intermediate-Range Nuclear Forces (INF) Treaty, 991

Internal Security Act, 794

International Business Machines (IBM), 1013

internationalism, 712

International Military Tribunal (IMT), 772

Internet, 1012, 1014–15, 1022

Internet research, 931, 1014–15, 1022

internment camps, 752, *p752*

interposition, 219

interstate commerce, 243

Interstate Commerce Act, 496

Interstate Commerce Commission, 495–96, 553, 557, 559, 565, 876

interstate highway system, *m812*, 812–13, *m813*, *p813*

interview, conducting, 915, 917

Intolerable Acts, 128

Iowa, 328

Iran, 784–85, 801, 968, 969, 1036

Iran-Contra scandal, 990

Iraq, 1001, 1004–05, 1021, 1033, 1036–37

iron curtain, 782

iron lung, 818, *p818*

Iroquois, the, 23–24, 25, 117, 141, 142

Iroquois League, 24, 25, 79

irrigation, 15

Isabella, Queen of Spain, 40–41

Islam, 26, 969, 1032; society, 1032; Islamic state, 969

isolationism, 648–49, 711–12, 726

Israel, 964, 968, 1021, 1032

Italy, 35, 649, *c649*, 709, 711, 756; early trade in, 35; fascism in, 709; surrender to Allies, 756

"I, Too," 631

Iwo Jima, 767–68; raising the flag on, *p768*

Izvestia, 956

J

Jackson, Andrew, 232, 243, 259–60, 261, 266, 267, *p267*, *p268*, 268–71, *crt271*, 304; economic policies, 270–71; nullification crisis, 268–69; political cartoon of, *crt271*; spoils system, 267

Jackson, Helen Hunt, 430

Jackson, Jesse, 874, 934, *p934*, 1002

Jackson, Maynard, 933

Jackson, Thomas J. (Stonewall), 358

James, Henry, 479

James, Jesse, 499, *p499*

Index

James I, King of England, 60, 62, 63, 64, 66

James II, King of England, 100–01

Jamestown settlement, 58, 62, 63, *p63*, 64

Japan, 522–23, 538–39, 710, 711, 712, 728–30, 742–45, *m744*, 759–61, 766–71, 787; American embargoes and, 728–29; attack at Pearl Harbor, 729–30; Bataan Death March, 743; Battle of Midway, *m744*, 745; bombing of, 743–44; defeat of, 766–71; post-WWI economy, 710; Roosevelt and, 539; trade with, 522–23; use of Kamikaze attacks, 761; World War II, 742–45, 759–61, 766–71

Japanese American Citizens League, 752–53

Japanese Americans, *p752*, 752–53; internment of, *p752*, 752–53; service in WWII, 753

Jarvis, Howard, 983

Jaworski, Leon, 961

Jay, John, 145, 174

Jay's Treaty, 216, *crt216*, 218, 219

Jazz Age, 608–30, *p609*; African American culture during, 626–30; cultural innovations of, 620–23; entertainment in, 622–23; values of, 610–17

Jazz Singer, The, 623

Jefferson, Thomas, 132, *q132*, 149, *q174*, 211, *p211*, 212, 213, 214, *c214*, 218, 219, 221–25, 227, 234, *p257*, *q257*, 333; as Secretary of State, 211, *q257*, 333; Declaration of Independence, 132–33; Democratic-Republicans' vision, 214, *c214*; economic ideals, 221–22; foreign affairs, 224–25; Lewis and Clark Expedition, 224, 227; Louisiana Purchase, 223–24; westward expansion, 223–24

Jeffersons, The, 972

Jews, 56, 74, 79, 106, 710, 719–24, *p721*, *p722*, *m724*, 764, 933; concentration camps, 723; early colonization by, 74; extermination camps, 723–24; families, *p721*; first synagogue, 79; Hitler's final solution, 722, *p722*, 723; Holocaust, 719–24, *m724*; immigration

to America, 56; Nuremberg Laws, 720; refugees, 721–23

Jezer, Martin, 904, *p904*

Jim Crow Laws, 392, 510–11

jingoism, 529

Job Corps, 857

Jobs, Steven, 1013, *p1013*

Johnson, Andrew, 391–96, *p396*; Alaska purchase, 395; impeachment, 394–95; reconstruction, 392

Johnson, Hugh, 685

Johnson, Lady Bird, 855

Johnson, Lyndon B., *p835*, *q837*, *p838*, 850, 851, 852, *p852*, *p855*, *q855*, 855–60, 872, 879, 880, 883, 898–99, *p902*, 902–03, 907–08, 964; approval rating, 907; Cabinet appointments, 859; civil rights and, 872, 879; domestic policies, 855–59, 872, 879; Gulf of Tonkin Resolution, 898–99, 902–03; Kerner Commission, 883; leadership style, 855–56; political ideals, 855–60; Vietnam policy, 898–99; voting rights and, 880

Johnston, Joseph E., 361–62

Joint Chiefs of Staff, 810

joint-stock company, 61

Joliet, Louis, 56

Jones, Bobby, 623

Jones, John Paul, 143

Jones, Mary Harris "Mother," 456, *p456*, 599, *q599*

Joplin, Scott, 480

Jordan, 1032

Jordan, Barbara, 960, *p960*

Joseph, Chief, 298, *p298*, 428, 429, *q429*

journalists, 662, 665, 708, 726, 759, 843, 958, *p958*

journal writing, 833, 835

judicial branch of government, 108, 148, 166, 181, *c181*, 184–85, *c185*, 196–97, 697–98; apellate courts, 184–85; apellate jurisdiction, 196; circuit courts of appeal, *c185*; court-packing plan, 697–98; district courts, 184, *c185*; federal courts, 184–85, *c185*, 196; original jurisdiction, 196; ruling on the constitutionality of the executive and legislative branches, *c181*; shift in, 988; state courts, *c185*; Supreme Court, *c181*, 185, *c185*, 196

judicial nationalism, 242–43

judicial review, 186, 223

Judiciary Act of 1789, 211, 223

Judiciary Act of 1801, 222

Julian, George, *q363*

The Jungle, 558, *q558*, 571

Justice Department, 875–76

juvenile delinquency, 831–32

kachinas, 21

Kaiser, Henry, 738

Kamikaze attacks, 761, *p769*

Kansas, 53, *m330*, 330–31, 334, 336, 337, 418, 422, 500, 503, 504, 1018

Kansas-Nebraska Act, 330–33

Kasserine Pass, Battle of, 746

Katzman, Julie, 994, *p994*, *q994*

Kearny, Colonel Stephen W., 310

Keating-Owen Child Labor Act, 569

Kellogg-Briand Pact, 650

Kelly, Oliver H., 502

Kelly Act, 643

Kennan, George F., 784, 898, 899, *q899*, 905

Kennedy, Anthony, 988

Kennedy, Jacqueline, 841–42, *p842*, 843, *p851*, 855

Kennedy, John F., *p839*, 840, 841–42, *p842*, 843–45, 846–51, *p851*, *q852*, 861, *p861*, 875–76, *q877*, 897, 927; assassination of, 850–51; Bay of Pigs, 848–49; civil rights and, 875–76; Cold War, 846–51; Cuban missile crisis, 846, 849–50; domestic agenda, 842–43; economic theories, 842–43; foreign policies, 846–51; inauguration of, *p839*; New Frontier, 842–43; space race, 847; state funeral of, 851, *p851*, *p859*; struggles with Congress, 842, 861; Test Ban Treaty, 850; use of media, 840–42; Vietnam policy, 897; women's rights and, 843, 927

Kennedy, Robert F., 875, 876, 908; assassination of, 908

Kent State University, *p911*, 912; protest at, *p911*, 912

Kentucky, 217, 241, 251, 275, 320, 326, 328, 336, 345, 361

Kentucky Resolution, 219, 1069

Kenya, 1033

Kerouac, Jack, 824, *p824*

Key, Francis Scott, 228, *q228*

Keynes, John Maynard, 698

Khomeini, Ayatollah, 969

Khrushchev, Nikita, 675, 801–02, 848–49

Kinache, 243, *q243*

King, Coretta Scott, 883, 886, *p886*

King Jr., Martin Luther, *q852*, *p865*, 869–70, 875, 876–78, *p878*, *q878*, 879–80, 883–86, *p886*, 905–06, *q906*; assassination of, 886; Birmingham demonstrations, 876–77; critics of, 883–86; jailing of, 876–77; March on Washington, 877–78, *p878*; Montgomery Improvement Association, 869–70; mourning, 886, *p886*; Selma March, 879–80

Kings Mountain, Battle of, 143

kinship groups, 23

Kinsley, Michael, 1012, *q1012*

Kissinger, Henry, 910–11, 912, 955–56, 966

kivas, 16

Kiyoshi, Nozaki, *q770*

Knapp, Isaac, 285

Knights of Labor, 457–58, 504

Know-Nothings, 275, 333, *c333*, 334

Knox, General Henry, 211, *p211*

Korea, *m787*, 788–89, 799, 1036

Korematsu v. the United States, 753

Kosovo, 1020

Kosygin, Alexei, 957, *q957*

Koufax, Sandy, 933, *p933*

Kramel, Marlene, 896

Kristallnacht, 721, *p721*

Ku Klux Klan, 398, 402, *p402*, 611–12, 875

Ku Klux Klan Act, 402

Kurds, 1021

Kuwait, 1001, 1004–05, 1033

Kyoto Protocol, 1025

labor: African American, 601, 749–51, 882; blue-collar, 815; child, 248, 249, 459, 551–52,

565; *Commonwealth v. Hunt*, 250; court rulings on, 249, 250, 692; during industrialization, 458–59; fair competition codes, 685; government regulations of, 569, 692–94, 792, 809; Mexican American laborers, 935; minimum wage, 685–86; mobilization of workforce during WWI, 587; National War Labor Board, 587; negotiations, 693–94; organization of, 249, 685, 692–93, *g693*, 694, 935; political positions on, 504–05; protests about, *p552*; reduced work day, 250; strikes, 495, 505, 557, 600–01, 693, *p693*, 809, 935; unemployment, 842–43, 936, 963, 987, 988; unemployment compensation, 813; unrest, 495; wages, 248–49, 642; white-collar, 815; women in workforce, 248–49, 457, 459, 927–28, 930; work day, 250; working conditions, 443, 452, 454–55, *p455*, 456, 470, 569, 641, 642, 692–94, *g694*, 699. *See also* unions.

La Brigada, 848

Lafayette, Marquis de, 141

LaFollette, Robert M., 549, 639

LaFollette Jr., Robert M., 793

laissez-faire economic policy, 438–39, 478, 482–83, 547, 559

Lake Champlain, Battle of, 232

Lake Erie, 231

"lame duck," 204

Lampasas County, Texas, 502, *p502*

Land-Grant colleges, 422

land grants, 149, 445

Landon, Alfred, 696

Lange, Dorothea, 665, *p665*; photographs of, *p662*

La Raza, Unida, 935

Larcom, Lucy, 249, *q249*

Larry King Live, 995

Larsen, Nella, 627

La Salle, 56–57

Las Casas, Bartolome de, *q9*, 55, *q78*

Last of the Mohicans, The, 276

lateen sails, 36, *p36*, 37

Latin America, 148, 244, 541, 847

latitude and longitude, understanding, 305, 315

Lawrence, Kansas, 330–31

Leadville, Colorado, 416

League of Nations, 596, 648–49

League of Women Voters, 927

Leahy, Admiral William, 769–70

Lease, Mary Ellen, 504, *p504*

Leatherstocking Tales, 276

Leaves of Grass, 276

Lecompton Constitution, 335

Le Duc Fo, 911, 912

Lee, Arthur, 142

Lee, Richard Henry, 173, 175

Lee, Robert E., 337, 350, *q350*, 355, *p355*, 362, 370–71, 372, *p372*, 373, 376–77, 380

Legal Tender Act, 352

legislative branch of government, 181, *c181*, 182–83, *c183*, 189–94; appropriations, 182; bills, 183, 191; conference committees, 183; Congress at work, 183; impeachment, 190; joint committees, 183; powers granted to, 192; role of Congress, 182–83; select committees, 183; standing committees, 183; veto overrides, 181, 183

Leigh, Vivien, 664

LeMay, Curtis, 768

Lend-Lease Act, 727, 729

L'Enfant, Pierre Charles, 222; medallion honoring, *p223*

Lenin, Vladmir Illyich, 591, *p591*, 595, 601, 709, *p709*

Letter from a Birmingham Jail, 876

Letters from a Pennsylvania Farmer, 122

letters of marque, 143

Levitt, Alfred, 610, *q610*

Levitt, Bill, 816

Levittown, New York, 816

Lewis, John L., 693–94

Lewis, Meriwether, 224, 227, *p227*

Lewis, Sinclair, 622

Lewis and Clark Expedition, 224, 227

Lexington, Battle of, 130, *m130*

Leyte Gulf, Battle of, 761

liberalism, 980–81

liberals, 980–81

Liberator, 285, 288

Liberia, 285

Liberty Bonds, 586

Liberty Party, 308, 322, *c333*

Liberty ships, 738

Libya, 1033

Lichtenstein, Roy, 924

Lieberman, Joseph, 1027

Life magazine, 665

Liliuokalani, Queen of Hawaii, 520, 523, *p523*

limited liability, 248

limited war, 789

Lincoln, Abraham, *p317*, *q317*, *q332*, 336, *p336*, *q336*, 337, *q337*, 341–43, *q343*, 344–45, 353, 357, 363, 364, 370, 371, *q372*, 379, 386–88, 443; assassination, 380; debates with Douglas, 336–37; Emancipation Proclamation, 363; Gettysburg Address, 371; martial law and, 344–45; suspension of writs of habeas corpus, 353. *See also* Civil War.

Lindbergh, Charles, 620, *p625*, 643–44, *q733*

line graph, reading, 261, 263

line of demarcation, 42

linkage, 910

literature: analyzing, 25, 283, 339, 571, 773, 931, 1007; Depression era, 665; naturalism in, 483; realism in, 479; renaissance in, 276–77; transcendentalism in, 276

Little Bighorn, Battle of, 429

Little Crow, Chief, 426–27

Little Richard, 824, 825, *p825*

Little Rock, Arkansas, 871–72

Little Turtle, Chief, 217

Livingston, Colonel Henry Beckman, 138, *q138*

Livingston, Robert, 132–33, 223, 247

Locke, Alain, 627

Locke, John, 101–02, *p102*, 108

lockout, 456

Lodge, Henry Cabot, 524, 611, 897

Lonely Crowd, The, 815

Lone Ranger and Tonto, 821, *p821*

Long, Henry, 327

Long, Huey, 690, *p690*

Long, Stephen, 421, *q421*

longboats, 39

long drives, 417–18, *p418*

longhouses, 23

longitude, 39, 305, 315

Long Telegram, 784

Longworth, Alice Roosevelt, 637, *q637*

Los Alamos, New Mexico, 769

Lost Colony, 61

Louis XIV, King of France, 56–57

Louisiana, 57, 117, 223–24, 251, 252, 342, 394, 510, 511

Louisiana Purchase, 223–24

Love, Nat, 418, *q418*

Love Canal, 941–42

Lovejoy, Elijah, 288

Loving v. *Virginia*, *c844*

Lowell, Amy, 621

Lowell, Francis C., 248

Lowell, James Russell, 277

Lowell Mills, 248–49

Loyalists, 129, 131, 132, 143, 151

loyalty review program, 791

Luce, Henry, 665

Luftwaffe, 718

lumber industry, 93

Lundy, Benjamin, 285

Lusitania, 582, *p582*

Luther, Martin, 60

LVT, 759

lynching, 511, 629, 810

Lyon, Mary, 281

MacArthur, General Douglas, 532, 672, 729, 743, 759–61, *p761*, 787, 788–89

Macintosh, 1013

Macon, Nathaniel, 229

Macune, Charles W., 502–03

Madison, James, 165, *p165*, 166, *q174*, 175, 211, 212, 213, 219, 228–32, *q230*, 232, 234, *q237*, 285; Bill of Rights, 211; Federalist debate, 165, 175; Presidency, 228–32

Magellan, Ferdinand, 43

Maginot Line, 716

Magna Carta, 102, 569, 1060

magnetic resonance imaging (MRI), 1014; device for, *p1014*

Mahan, Alfred T., 525

Maine, 71, 258, 279, 326

Makkah (Mecca), 26

Malcolm X, *q852*, 884, *p884*, 885

Mali, 26, 28

Malinche, (Doña Marina), 51

Malinke, the, 28

managerial revolution, 637, 645, 647, *p647,* 648

Manassas, Battle of, (Battle of Bull Run), 358, 362

Manchuria, 538, 710, 712

mandate, 379

Manhattan Island, 73, 140

Manhattan Project, 769

Manifest Destiny, 295–97, 300–04, 306–11, 521, 525

Mann, Horace, 280, *q280*

Mann-Elkins Act, 565

manorialism, 33

mansa, 28

manumission, 151

Mao Zedong, 786–87

"Map of New England," 67

Mapp v. *Ohio,* 844, *c844*

maps: cartographers, 2; general-purpose, 1; interpreting, *m13, m22, m30, m47, mm59, m69, m70, m76, m86, m92, m96, m107, m140, m144, m220, m258, m270, m287, m296, m303, m310, m329, m330, m341, m358, m360, m362, m379, m394, m417, m428, m437, m457, m465, m579, m595, m605, m633, m653, m663, m666, m667, m715, m724, m730, m733, m751, m760, m762, m763, m767, m774, m775, m789, m811, m863, m893, m908, m917, m953, m977, m983, m992–93, m1002, m1009, m1028;* LANDSAT, 1; mapmaking, 39–40, 55; parts of, 81; physical, 1; political, 1; projections, 2–3; special-purpose 1, 748, *m748;* thematic, 748; tools of, 2; types of, 1

maquiladoras, 1023

Marbury, Chief Justice William, 223

Marbury v. *Madison,* 223

March of Dimes, 680, *p680*

March to the Sea, 379

margin, buying on, 657

margin call, 657

Mariana Islands, 760

Marin, John, 621

Marine Corps, 131

Marion, Francis ("Swamp Fox"), 144

Marm, Joe, 772, *p772*

Marquette, Jacques, 56

Marshall, General George C., 738, *q738,* 785, *p785, q785,* 793

Marshall, James, 322

Marshall, John, 215, *q215,* 218, 242, 270, 285

Marshall, Thurgood, 868, 870, *p870,* 875, 876

Marshall Islands, 760

Marshall Plan, 785

Martha and the Vandellas, 825

martial law, 344, 353

Marti, José, 528

Martin v. *Hunter's Lessee,* *c242*

Marx, Arthur, *q658–59*

Marx, Groucho, 658–59, 664

Marx, Karl, 456

Marxism, 456

Maryland, 64, 73, 86, 90, 154, 165, 175, 242, 243, 247, 251

Maryland Toleration Act of 1649, 73

Mary, Queen of England, 101

Mary Tyler Moore Show, 972

Mason, George, 173

Mason, James, 354

Mason, John, 70–71

Massachusetts, 66–69, 99–100, 101, 123, 125–27, 128, 130, 141, 148, 151, 166, 174, 175, 241, 248, 258, 269, 280, 331, 387, 388

Massachusetts Bay Company, 67–69

Massachusetts Provincial Congress, 129, 130

mass advertising, 645

massive retaliation, 798

mass media, 623, 820–22

mass production, 248, 641

mass transit, 470–71

Mather, Cotton, 105, *q105*

matrilineal society, 23, 30

mavericks, 418

Mayaguez, 966

Maya, the, 14–15, *c15*

Mayflower, 66, 67

Mayflower Compact, 67, 1061; signing of, *ptg67*

Mayhew, Johnathan, *q102*

McAuliffe, Christa, 998

McCain, Franklin, 873, *p873*

McCain, John, 1027

McCarran Act, 794

McCarthy, Joseph R., 793–94, *p794,* 795

McCarthyism, 794, *p794*

McCarty, Cecee, 255

McClellan, George B., 361–62, 379

McClure's Magazine, 547, *p547*

McCord, James, 958, 959

McCormick, Cyrus, 295

McCulloch v. *Maryland,* 193, 271

McDowell, Irwin, 358, 366, *q366*

McGovern, George, 959, 960

McGuffey, William, 281

McGuffey's Readers, 281, p281

McJunkin, George, 12

McKay, Claude, 627, *p627*

McKinley, William, 497, 507, 529–30, 532, *q532,* 533, 537, 538, 555

McKinley Tariff, 497, *p506,* 507, 523, 555

McNamara, Robert, 899, 902–03

McNeil, Joseph, 873, *p873*

McPherson, Aimee Semple, 614

McVeigh, Timothy, 1024

Mead, Margaret, 614

Meade, George, 371

Meat Inspection Act, 558

media, 820–22, 905, 995–96, 1000

Medicaid, 838, 858, *c858,* 860

Medicare, 838, 858, *c858,* 860, 998, 1029

Medicine Crow, Chief, 426, *p426*

meditation, 971

meetinghouse, 94

Mellon, Andrew, 637, 647, 648

Melville, Herman, 276

Memphis, Tennessee, 393, 885–86

mercantilism, 98–99

mercenaries, 132

Meredith, James, 853, 876

Merrimack, 359

Mesoamerica, *m13,* 13–14, *c14,* 15

mestizos, 54

Metacomet, 71

Methodists, 109, 150, 271, 275

Mexican Americans, 587, 750–52, *m751;* farm workers, 750–51; migration of, 587, 751, *m751;* prejudice against, 751–52; wartime contributions, 750–52, *m751*

Mexico, 50–55, 295, 301, *p307,* 307–09, *m310,* 311, 323, 416, 577, 1023; cedes territory to U.S., *m310,* 311; colonization laws, 301; NAFTA, 1023; revolution, 577; Spanish conquest of, 50–52; war

with U.S., *p307,* 307–11; Wilson sends troops to, 577

Michigan, 320, 321, 333

microprocessors, 1013

Microsoft, 1013

Middle Ages, 33; artifacts of, *p33*

middle class, 471

Middle Colonies: 72–76, 96–97; economy of, 96–97; society in, 96–97

Middle East, 1021, 1032–33

Middle Passage, 89

midnight judges, 222

Midway, Battle of, *m744,* 745

Miele, Jerry, 968, *p968*

military: American Revolution, 129, 130, 131, 132, 139–44; build-up of, 540–41, 584–85, 988–89; Civil War, 354–55, 358–60; districts, 394, *m394;* draft, 584–85, 905–06; Korean War, *m787,* 788–89; Persian Gulf War, 1004–05; reduction of, 798, 1005; Spanish-American War, 529–30, 536–37; spending, 990, *g990;* Vietnam War, 896, *g901,* 907–08; World War I, 587–88; World War II, 736–41

military industrial complex, 802

Military Reconstruction Act, 394

militias, 129, 131, 139, 143, 144, 230, 231

Milosevic, Slobodan, 1020

mineral strike, 415–16

minimum wage, 459, 809–10, 813, 843

mining, 414–15, *p415,* 416, *p557,* 809; conditions, *p557;* mining sluice, 415, *p415*

Minnesota, 422, 503

minutemen, 129, 130

Mir, 999

Miranda rights, 845

Miranda v. *Arizona,* *c844,* 845

missile gap, 841

missions, 54, *p54*

Mississippi, 57, 252, 342, 361, 369, 370, 510, 876, 879

Mississippi Freedom Democratic Party, 874

Mississippi River, 217, 224

Missouri, 258, 328, 330, 345

Missouri Compromise, 258, *m258,* 323–25, 332

Missouri River, 224, 227

Mitchell, John, 954, 960

Mobile, Alabama, 378

Model T, 641

modernism: in art, 621–22; in literature, 621

molasses, 120

Molotov, Vyacheslav, 778

Mondale, Walter, 988

monetarists, 987

money supply, 501–02, 504, 966

Mongol Empire, 35

monopolies, 243, 270, 449, 452–53, 497, 567, 568

Monroe, James, 240, *q240,* 244, 285; Era of Good Feelings, 240; Monroe Doctrine, 244

Monroe Doctrine, 244, 523, 541, 1070

Montana, 418, 429, 580

Montesquieu, Baron, 108

Montezuma, 50, 51, 53, *q78*

Montgomery, Alabama, 343, 869–70; bus boycott, *p869,* 869–70

Montgomery, General Bernard, 876

Montgomery Improvement Association, 869

Montreal, Canada, 141

Moody, Dwight L., 484–85

Moore, Gordon, 1013

Moral Majority, 984

Moran, Mary, 88, *p88*

moratorium, 649

Morgan, J.P., 556

Morgan v. Virginia, 867

Morgenthau, Henry, 697

Mormons, 276, 297, 299

Morrill Land Grant Act, 486

Morrill Tariff, 438–39

Morris, Robert, 139, 165

Morse, Samuel F.B., 248

Morse code, 248

Morton, Frederick, *q721*

Moscow Summit, 957, *p957*

Moses, Robert, 874

mosques, 28

most favored nation status, 216

Mothers Against Drunk Driving (MADD), 996

Mott, Lucretia, 282, 286, 549

mound-building cultures, 16, *p17*

movie industry, 664, 822

Moyers, Bill, 587

Ms., 928

MS-DOS (Microsoft Disk Operating System), 1013

muckrakers, 547, 549, 552

mudslinging, 260

mugwumps, 495

Muhammad, Askiya, 29

Muhammed Ali, 873

mujahadeen, 989

multimedia presentation, developing, 289, 290

multinational corporations, 815

Munich Conference, 714, *p714*

Musa, Mansa, 26, 28

music: disco, 973; Harlem Renaissance, 627–28; Jazz Age, 622–23; of the 1970s, 973–74; rap, 996; technology and, 996

Music Television (MTV), 996

Muslims, 27–29, 31, 35, 1020, 1032–33

Mussolini, Benito, 709, *p710,* 711, *p711,* 713, 756

Myrick, Andrew, 426, *q426–27*

Nader, Ralph, 943, *q943,* 1027

Nagasaki, 771

napalm, 768, 900

Narrative of the Life of Frederick Douglass, 287, 339

Natchez, the, 20

National Advisory Commission on Civil Disorders, 876, 879, 883; racial violence in, 876, 879

National Aeronautics and Space Administration (NASA), 799, 848, 849, *p849,* 998–99; technological innovations of, 849, *p849*

National Association for the Advancement of Colored People (NAACP), 149, 569, 570, 629, 830, 866, 867, 868, 870, 874, 876, 934

National Broadcasting Company, 644

National Child Labor Committee, 552

National Colonization Act, 301

National Council of Negro Women, 696

National Credit Corporation, 670

National Defense Education Act (NDEA), 799

National Environmental Policy Act, 941

national health insurance, 809–10

National Highway Traffic and Safety Administration, 988

National Housing Act, 699, 810

National Industrial Recovery Act (NIRA), 685, 692

National Institutes of Health (NIH), 1015

nationalism, 232, 241–43, 483, 578, 893, 895; black, 884; economic, 241–42; fascism as, 709; Hitler's, 710; in Europe, 578; Japan, 710; judicial, 242–43; nationalist diplomacy, 243–44; Vietnamese, 893, 895

nationalists, 164–65

National Labor Relations Act, 692, 699; *NLRB v. Jones and Laughlin Steel,* 699

national nominating committee, 268

National Organization for Women (NOW), 928, 929

National Origins Act, 612

National Prohibition Act, 615

National Recovery Administration, 685–86, *c686*

National Republicans, 259, 271, *c272*

National Resources Defense Council, 941

National Review, 981

National Rifle Association (NRA), 1017

National Security Council, (NSC), 990

National Socialist German Worker's Party (Nazi Party), 709

National Traffic and Motor Vehicle Safety Act, 943

National Union for Social Justice, 690

National Urban League, 740

National War Labor Board, 587

National Woman's Party, 551, 927

National Woman Suffrage Association, 550, *p550*

National Youth Administration (NYA), 696

Nation of Islam, 884–85

Native Americans: Adena, 16; agriculture of, 15, 21, 23, 24; Aleut, 22; Algonquian, 23; alliance with British, 216, 229 American Indian Movement, 936–37; Anasazi, 15–16; Apache, 21, 300; Arapaho, 297, 427; architecture, 14–17, 21, 23; assimilation, 830; attempts to convert, 294–95, 312; Battle of Fallen Timbers, 217; Battle of Little Bighorn, 429; battle sites, *m428;* Bureau of Indian Affairs, 428; Cayuga, 23–24; Cherokee, 24; Cheyenne, 297, 427, 429; Chickasaw, 24; Chief Osceola, 243; Chief Pontiac, 119; Chief Powhatan, 62; Chinook, 21; Chippewa, 216; Choctaw, 24; cities, 16, 17, civil rights movement, 936–37; Columbian Exchange, 43–44; Comanche, 300; constitution, 24; Creek, 24; cultures of, 425–30; Dakota Sioux, 426–27; Dawes Act, 430; Declaration of Indian Purpose, 936; Dekanawidah, 24, 25; Delaware, 23, 119, 142, 217; disease and, 43–44, 51, 52, 312; Eastern woodlands, 23–24; economics, 936–37; education, 936; *encomienda* system, 54; Erie, 23; exile of, 427; Far North, 22; federal government and, 426–27; Fetterman's Massacre, 427, 428; Fourteenth Amendment, 392; fur traders and, 56; gender roles, 21, 23, 426; government of, 21, 23–24, 25, 426; Great Binding Law, 24; Great Plains, 21–22; Haida, 21; Hiawatha, 24; Hohokam, 15; Hopewell, 15, 16; Hopi, 21; horses and, 21; housing of, 15, 21, 23, 24; Huron, 23; Indian Peace Commission, 428; Indian Removal Act, 270, *m270;* Inuit, 22; Iowa, 21; Iroquois, 23–24; Iroquois League, 23–24; Jackson's policies toward, 269–70; job training, 830, *p830;* kachina cult, 21; Kansas, 21; King Philip's War, 71; kinship groups, 24; Kwakiutls, 21; Lakota Sioux, 429, 430; languages of, 23; last wars of, 429–30; Lenni Lenape, 75; life expectancy of, 936; longhouses, 23; mining

Index

Index

labor, 55; Mississippians, 16–17; Mohawk, 16, 23, 24, 142; Mohegan, 70–71; mound builders, 16; Narragansett, 23, 69, 71; Natchez, 24; Navajo, 21, 54; negative impact of western settlement, 425–30; Neutral, 23; Nez Perce, 21, 429; nomads, 21, 425, 427; Nootkas, 21; Northeast, 23; Northwest Passage and, 217; Northwest Territory and, 217; Oneida, 23–24; Onondaga, 23–24; Ottawa, 119, 217; Pacific Coast, 21; Pawnee, 21; Peace Towns, 24; Pequot, 23, 70–71; Pequot War, 70; Plains Indians, 425–26; policy of assimilation, 430; Pomo, 21; Potowatomi, 217; Powhatan Confederacy, 23, 62; protest movement, 936–37; protests by, 932; Pueblo people, 21, 54; railroads impact population, 424; relationship with settlers, 51–56, 62, 64, 67, 69, 70–71, 75, 296–97, 426–27; relocation of, 270, *m270*; reservations in 1890, 428, *m428*, 429; Sacagawea, 224, 227; Salish, 21; Sand Creek Massacre, 427–28; Seminoles, 243, 270; Seneca, 380; Shawnee, 23, 142, 217, 229; Shoshone, 21, 224, 227; Sioux, 21–22, 297, 426–27; slaughter of buffalo, 429; slavery of, 76; Southeast, 24; Southwest, 21; Spanish and, 51–54; spiritual beliefs of, 15, 21, 40, 54, 426; Squanto, 67; Susquehannock, 88; Tecumseh, 229; termination policy, 830–31; Tippecanoe, 229; Tlingit, 21; Trail of Tears, 270; treaties with, 75, 425–30; unemployment, 936; uprisings, 427; Ute, 21; Wampanoag, 23, 67, 71; wampum, 23; War Towns, 24; Western cultures, 20–22; wigwams, 23; *Worcester* v. *Georgia*, 271; Wyandot, 119; Yakima, 21; Zuni, 21

nativism, 274–75, 333, 456, 468, 610–11, 632

NATO, 786, 800, *m800*, 1020

Nat Turner Rebellion, 256

naturalism, 483

naturalization, 192

natural resources, 437, *m437*

natural rights, 102, 108, 134

natural selection, 477

Navajo Code Talkers, 750, *p750*

Navigation Act, 99, 100, *c100*

navigational instruments, 36–37

Nazis: 709, 713–14, 720–24, 764, 772; atrocities of, 720, 723–24, 764; European response to, 714; ideology, 720; Nuremberg trials, 772; propaganda of, 720–22; Wannese Conference, 723

Nazi-Soviet Non-Aggression Pact, 715, 727

Nebraska, 329, 330, 422, 443, 501, *p501*, 502, 503, 504, 506

"necessary and proper" clause, 193, 213, 242, 243

"Negro Speaks of Rivers, The," 631

Neighborhood Youth Corps, 857

Ness, Elliot, 616

Neutrality Acts, 711, 726

neutral rights, 232

Nevada, 311, 415, 667

New Age Movement, 971, *p971*

New Amsterdam, 72, 73

New Deal, 679, 682–89, 691–94, *g692*, 695–700; as cause of political realignment, 695–97; coalition, 695–700; end of era, 699–700; impact and legacy of, 699–700

New England Colonies, 66–71, *m70*, 91–96, *m92*; economy, 91–93, *m92*; life in, 93–96; society of, 93–96

New Federalism, 954–55

Newfoundland, 726

New France, 56–57, 117–18

New Freedom, 567, 569, 683

New Frontier, 840–45

New Hampshire, 71, 175

New Imperialism, 521

New Jersey, 74, 75, 96–97, 166

New Jersey Plan, 166

Newlands Reclamation Act, 556–57, 612

New Lights, 108

New Mexico, 54, 311, 323, 329, 416–19

new morality, 612–14, 632

New Nationalism, 567, 683

New Netherland, 73, 74

New Orleans, 118–19, 223

New Orleans, Battle of, 232, 359–60

New Republic, 693

news media, analyzing, 1000, 1009

New Spain, 52–55

Newton, Huey, 885

New York, 72, 74, 96–97, 128, 151, 166, 174, 175, *p236–37*, 258, 467, 469, 470, 473, *p474*, 1029, 1031–32

New York City, 140, 141, 145, *p274*, 467, 469, 470, 473, *p474*, 1029, 1031–32; harbor, *p274*

New York Stock Exchange, 451

New York Times v. *Sullivan*, *c844*

Ngo Dinh Diem, 895, 896, *p897*, 897–98

Nguyen Van Thieu, 912, 913

Niagara Movement, 570

Nicaragua, 541, 989–90

Nicodemus, Kansas, 397

Nimitz, Admiral Chester, 742–43, 744–45, 746, *p746*, 759, 768

Nine-Power Treaty, 649–50, *c650*

Nineteenth Amendment, 204, 551, 927

Nineteen Twenties, the: Coolidge administration, 638–39; economics of, 640–45, 648; Harding administration, 636–38; Jazz Age, 627–29; normalcy, 636–38; policies of, 647–50; prosperity of, 647–50

Ninth Amendment, *c182*, 186, 200

Nixon, Richard, *p777*, 791, 811, 840, 841, *p897*, 909, 911–13, 941, *p951*, 953–56, *q956*, 957, *p957*, 958–62, 965; domestic policies, 955; election of 1968, 953, 959–60; foreign policy, 955–57; "law and order" president, 954; New Federalism, 954–55; pardon of, 965; relationship with Congress, 955; resignation, *p961*, 961–62; Southern strategy, 953–54; Watergate scandal, 958–62

NLRB v. *Jones and Laughlin Steel*, 699

Nobel Peace Prize, 539, 720

Noche triste, 52

nomads, 13, 27, 30, 54, 425, 427

"no-man's land," 593

nonimportation agreement, 122, 123

nonimportation association, 129

Non-Intercourse Act, 229

nonviolent resistance, 870, 873–74

Noriega, Manuel, 1004

normalcy, 637

normal schools, 257

normal trade relations, 1024

Normandy, France, 758–59

Norris v. *Alabama*, 867

note-taking, 554, 573

North, Oliver, 990

North, the: Civil War, 343–45, 350–54, *g354*; 355–80; industrialization of, 248; politics of, 214

North Africa, 745–56

North American Free Trade Agreement (NAFTA), 1023

North Atlantic Treaty Organization (NATO), 786, 800, *m800*, 1020

North Carolina, 24, 53, 55, 61, 76, 132, 142, 151, 152, 174, 229, 281, 285, 344, 392, 394

North Dakota, 502

Northern Alliance, 1036

Northern Securities v. *United States*, 556

North Korea, 788–89, 1024, 1036

Northrup, Solomon, 251, *q251*

North Star, 287

North Vietnam, 895, 898–901, 907, 911

Northwest Ordinance, 159, 160, *m161*

Northwest Passage, 55, 61, 227

Northwest Territory, 217

Norway, 716

nuclear: energy, 942; freeze, 990; holocaust, 795; missiles, 799, 990; power, 942; radiation, 796; reduction, 957; SALT I, 957; weapons, *p795*, 798, 1024–25

nuclear proliferation, 1025

Nuclear Regulatory Commission, 942

nullification, 219, 268–69

Nuremberg Laws, 720

Nuremberg trials, 772

Nye, Gerald P., 711, 726

Nye Committee, 711

O

Oakley, Annie, 427, *p427*, *q499*

Oberlin College, Ohio, 275

obiter dictum, 335

Ocala Demands, 503–04

O'Connor, Sandra Day, 988–89, *p989*

Office of Attorney General, 211

Office of Economic Opportunity (OEO), 857, *c858*

Office of Economic Stabilization (OES), 753

Office of Homeland Security, 1035

Office of Price Administration (OPA), 753

Office of War Mobilization (OWM), 739

Oglethorpe, James, 76

Ohio, 217, 328

Ohio Gang, 637

Ohio National Guard, *p911*

Ohio River Valley, 23, 117

oil: embargoes, 964; production, 437, 964, *c964, m964*; shortages, 964, *p964*, 965, *crt965*; spills, 940, *p941*; terrorism and, 1032

Oklahoma, 270, 429, 663, *p663*

Oklahoma City bombing, *p1024*

Oklahoma City National Memorial, 1024, *p1024*

Old lights, 108

Olive Branch Petition, 131

Olmec, the, 14, *c14*

Omaha Beach, *p735*, 758–59, *m762*, 763, *m763, p763*

O'Neill, Eugene, 621, 628

On the Road, 824, *p824*

Open Door Policy, 538–39

open range, 416–17

operating costs, 448

operating systems, 1013

Operation Desert Storm, 1004–05

Operation Overlord, 757–59

Operation Rolling Thunder, 899

Oppenheimer, J. Robert, 769

Oregon, 295, 308

Oregon Territory, 244, 307, 308

Oregon Trail, 294, 295

O'Reilly, Lenore, 459

Organization Man, The, 815, *crt815*

Organization of American States, 524

Organization of Petroleum Exporting Countries (OPEC), 964; oil embargo, *p964*

Orlando, Vittorio, 596

Orthodox Christian Serbs, 1020

Osceola, Chief, 243, *p243*

O'Shaughnessy, Edith, 576, *p576, q576*

O'Sullivan, John Louis, 295

O'Sullivan, Mary Kenney, 459

Oswald, Lee Harvey, 851

Other America, The, 829, 854–55

Otis, James, 120

outlining, 701, 703

overlanders, 296

overmountain men, 143

overproduction, 659, 660

override, Congressional, 181, 183

ozone, 1025

Ozzie and Harriet, 821, *p821*

P

Pacific Fleet, 759

Pacific Northwest, 295

Pacific Ocean, 224, 227, 295

Pacific Railway Act, 443

pacifism, 720

Paine, Thomas, 132–33, *q133*, 140–41, *q141*, 153

Pakistan, 1024

Palestine, 1021, 1032

Palestine Liberation Organization (PLO), 1021

Palmer, A. Mitchell, 602, *p603*

Palmer raids, 602–03, *p603*

Panama Canal, 536, 538, *p538*, 539, *m539*, 540, *crt636*, 968, 1004; Carter and, 968; negotiations with Britain over, 540; revolt in Panama, 540; Roosevelt's involvement in, 540

Pan-Americanism, 524

Panic of 1837, 271

Panic of 1893, 505

pardons, 181, 392

Parker, John J., 629

Parks, Rosa, 866, 869–70

Paterson, Wiliam, 166

party boss, 473, 549, 678

Patriots, 129, 132–33

patronage, 492–93

Patton, General George, 746, 756, 765

Paul, Alice, 546, 550–51

Payne-Aldrich Tariff, 564, 565

Peace Commission, 428

Peace Corps, 847, 921; legacy of, 847

peace symbol, 907

peacetime draft, 739

Peale, Charles Willson, 152

Pearl Harbor, 523, 725, 728, *m728, p729*, 729–30, 736, 742, 745

peasants, 33

Pendleton Act, 493

penitentiaries, 280

Pennsylvania, *ptg74*, 74–75, 96–97, 141, 165, 387, 1031, *c1034, m1034*

Pennsylvania Dutch, 106

Penn, William, 74–75

penny papers, 277

Pentagon, bombing of, 1031–32, *p1032, c1034, m1034*

Pentagon Papers, 912

People's Party, 503–04, 506, 509

People's Republic of China, 787

People United to Save Humanity (PUSH), 934–35

Pequot War, 70

perestroika, 1002

periphery, 745

perjury, 792, 1020

Perkins, Frances, 694, 696, *p696*

Perot, H. Ross, 1006, 1019

Perry, Commodore Matthew C., 522, *p522*

Perry, Commodore Oliver, 231

Pershing, General John J., 577, 585, 592, *q592*, 596

Persian Gulf War, 1001, 1004–05, *m1005*,

"Personal Computer," 1013

Peru, 53

pesticides, 939–40

Petain, Marshal Philippe, 717

Petersburg, Virginia, 377–78; siege of, *g377*

Peterson, Esther, 843, 860, *p860*

petroleum. *See* oil.

Philadelphia, Pennsylvania, 75, 95, 128, 140, 141, 165, 255

Philadelphia Federal Hall, 212, *p212*

philanthropy, 478

Philippines, 118–19, 529, 530, *p530*, 532, *p532*, 729, 743, 760–61

Phillips, Wendell, 286

photojournalism, 662, 665

Pickett, George E., 371

Pickett's Charge, 371

Pierce, Franklin, 522

pietism, 108

Pike, Zebulon, 224, *p224*

Pike's Peak, 224

Pilgrims, 66–67

pillaging, 379

Pinchot, Gifford, 559, *q559*, 564, *q564*, 565

Pinckney, Charles, 215, 218, 228

Pinckney, Thomas, 216

Pinckney's Treaty, 216–17

ping pong diplomacy, 955

pioneers, 293–97; *The Emigrant Train Bedding Down for the Night, ptg293*; land rights, 295; Native Americans and, 295–97; Pre-emption Act, 295; settling the Pacific, 295; squatters, 295; wagon train life, 295–96, *p296*

Pitcher, Molly (Mary Ludwig Hays), 150

Pizarro, Francisco, 53

placer mining, 415

plantations, *p84*, 85, 86, *p86*, 87, 253, 254; life in, *ptg254*

planter elite, 86–87

Platt, Senator Orville, 533

Platt Amendment, 533

Plessy, Homer, 511

Plessy v. Ferguson, 511, 867, 868

Plunkitt, George, 473, *q473*

Plymouth Colony, 66–67

Pocahontas, 62, *p62*

pocket veto, 388

Poe, Edgar Allen, 276, 299

point of view, analyzing, 513, 515

Poitier, Sidney, 822, *q822*

Poland, 713–16, 779, 781, 799–800, 1002

police powers, 615, 929

polio, 680, *p680*, 691, 817–18

political cartoons, interpreting, 390, 452, 495, 538, 541, 556, 611, 638, 659, 700, 726, 754, 815, 965

political machine, 473, 549, 637, 690

politics: areas of party control, 493–94; baseball and, *crt342;* "born in a log cabin," 334; caucus, 268; conservatism, 980–86; Contract with America, 1018; corruption in, 473; debates, 336–37, *ptg336–37,* 777, *p777,* 840, *p840;* direct primaries, 549; farmers and, 500–04; first parties, 213, 215–20; geography and, 982–83; grassroots movements, 940–41, 1006; harmony in, 240–44; impact of third-party and independent candidacies, 500, 503, 504, 505, 506, 507, 508, 510, 553, 567, 584, 629, 639, 810, 909, 953, 1006; issues in, 473; money in, 496–97; morals and, 494–95; mudslinging, 260; of protest, 918–30, 932–37, 939–43; partisan, 215–20; Pendleton Act, 493; political bosses, 493; political machines, 494; political parties of the 1850s, *c303;* political platforms, 504; political reform, 549; populism, 500–04, 509; public opinion about, 493; reapportionment and, 843; reform of, 266–68, 490–94; religion and, 495, 506, 841; rise of political parties, 213–14; South, the, 229–30, 868–69; spoils system, 492–93; strategies, 503–04; Supreme Court and, 392, 843–44, 1028–29; symbols in, 638, *crt638;* Tammany Hall, 473, 494; television and, 840–41; two-party system, 492–97; 2000 election in Florida, 1026–29; urban, 472–73, 507; war between the parties, *crt219;* West, 229–30; women and, 696, 928, 988, 998. *See also* elections, sectional conflicts.

Polk, James K., 307, 309, 321, 323

Polk, Leonidas L., 500, *p500*

poll tax, 206, 510, 879

pollution, 472, 940

Ponce de Leon, Juan, 42–43

Pontiac, Chief, 119

pools, 448

Poor People's Campaign, 885–86

pop art, 924

Popé, 54

popular culture: after industrialization, 479–80; counterculture, 922–23; entertainment in, 479–80; fads and fashions, 974; hippie culture, 922–23; music, 480, 973–74; of the 1970s, 972–73; religious movements, 923; symbols of, 972, *p972,* 974, *p974;* television, 972–73

popular sovereignty, 168, 180, 321, 336

popular vote, 259, 1028

population: baby boom, 816–17, *g816;* boomtowns, 415; California, 295; density by region, *m1030;* Hispanic, 612, *g935;* immigrant, 464–66, 612–13, 724, *g935;* impact on industrialization of U.S., 437; loss of in Dust Bowl, *m663;* of New York City, 397; suburban, *g835;* Sunbelt, 982–83, *m983;* urban, 474–75, 992–93

populism, 500–07, 509, 510

Populists, *p501,* 500–07, 509, 510, 514

Port Huron Statement, 921

Portsmouth, Rhode Island, 70

Portugal, 36–37, 41, 42

Potsdam, 781

Pound, Ezra, 621

poverty: African American, *p829,* 829–30; Hispanic, 830; in Appalachia, 831; Native American, 830–31; rural, 856, *p856;* urban, 829, *p829,* 830; war on, 856–57

poverty line, 828

Powell, General Colin, 1001, 1037

power dressing, 995

Powers, Francis Gary, 797, 802, 1035

Powhatan, Chief, 62

Preamble: Declaration of Independence, 134; U.S. Constitution, 189

Pre-emption Act, 295

Presbyterians, 109, 275

Prescott, Dr. Samuel, 130

Prescott, William, 131

Presidential Commission on the Status of Women, 843, 927

presidios, 54

Presley, Elvis, 823, *p823,* 824

Preston, Thomas, 123, 124, *q124,* 125

primary sources, 938, 947, 1046–57

Principles of Scientific Management, The, 548

prisoners of war, 368

privateering, 61, 131, 255

private property: fascism and, 709; rights, 248, 779; settlement of Great Plains and, 416–22, 432

probable cause, 199

problem solving, 861, 863

Proclamation of Amnesty and Reconstruction, 387, 392

Proclamation of 1763, 119, *m119*

profit motive, 438

Progressive Party, 547, 567; new, 639, 810

Progressivism, 544–70, 581, 584–87, 603, 683, 810; as a reaction against free market system, 547; child labor, 551–52; coordination of business and labor, 553, 556, 581, 586–87; efficiency, 548; end to, 603; failures of, 570; legacy of, 569–70; political reform, 549; Prohibition movement, 553; rise of, 546–48; Roosevelt and, 555–59, 567; selective service, 584–85; Seventeenth Amendment, 549; social welfare, 551; suffrage movement, 550–51; Taft years, 562–65; use of scientific principles, 547–48; views on government, 548–49; Wilson years, 566–70; workers' compensation laws, 552; zoning laws, 552

Prohibition, 203, 205, 279, 552–53, 615–16, *p616,* 625, 657

Project Head Start, 858, *c858,* 860

Project Venona, 792

Promontory Summit, Utah, 442, *p443*

propaganda, 581

Prophetstown, 229

Proposition 13, 983

proprietary colonies, 64

protective tariff, 241

protectorate, 521

Protestant Reformation, 60

protests, 121, 876–80, 918–43; antiwar, 921; civil rights, 876–80; colonial, 121, *p121;* environmental, 941–42; free speech, 922; politics of, 918–43; World Trade, 121, *p121*

Providence, Rhode Island, 69

provisional government, 520, 595

Prussia, 578

Ptolemy, Claudius, 39

public debt, 202

public education, 485. *See also* education.

public housing, 751, 809–10, 829, 842

public libraries, 485

public schools, 280–81

Public Utility Holding Company Act, *g692*

public works, 669

Public Works Administration (PWA), 686, *c686,* 688, 698

publishing industry, 249

Pueblo peoples, the, 21

pueblos, 16

Puerto Rico, 532–33

Pulitzer, Joseph, 528

Pullman Strike, 458

Pure Food and Drug Act, 558

Puritans, 60, 64, 66–68, *p68,* 70–73, 94

Purvis, Robert, 335, *q335*

pyramids, 14, 15, *p20*

Quadruple Alliance, 244

Quakers, 75, 149, 150, 271, 285, 320, 328, 676

Quartering Act, 121

quartz mining, 415

Quasi-War, 218

Quebec, 56, 128, 131

Quebec, Battle of, 118, *ptg118*

Quebec Act, 128

Quetzalcóatl, 51

Quran, 1032

Rabin, Yitzhak, 1021

racism, 285, 425–30, 456, 466–68, 471, 508–09, 510, 511–12, 585, 587, 597, 600, 601, 610–11, 627, 629, 751–52, 753, 824, 864–72, 882–83, 885; theory of eugenics, 611

Radical Republicans, 387–88, 393

radio industry, 644, 664, 822–23

ragtime, 480, *p480*

railroads, 247, 328–29, 407, 417, 437, 439, 442–46, *m445*, 467, 502–04, 505, 557; American Association of Railroads, 444; bankruptcies of, 505; "Big Four," 443; building of, 443–44; Central Pacific, 442, 443; creation of time zones, 444; Credit Mobilizer scandal, 446; economic impact of, 417, 437, 502–04; entrepreneurs, 443–44, 445–46; expansion of, 442–43; government's role, 439, 443, 445; Great Northern Railroad, 446; impact on Interstate Commerce Commission, 557; land-grant system, 445; *Northern Securities* v. *United States*, 556; Pacific Railway Act, 443; Promontory Summit, Utah, 442, *p443*; public opinion of, 495; rail lines, *m445*; rates and, 495, 496, 502, 557; regulating, 496, 502; Union Pacific, 442, 443, 445; *Wabash v. Illinois*, 496, 502, 529, 556, 569

Rainbow Coalition, 1002

Rainey, Joseph, 399, *p399*

Rainey, Ma, 628

Raisin in the Sun, A, 828, 830

Raleigh, Walter, 61–62

ranching, 416–19, *m417*, 445; business of, 418–19; cattle, 416–19; cattle trails, *m417*; long drive, 417–18; open range, 416–18; range wars, 419

Randolph, A. Philip, 750, 877

Randolph, Edmund, 166, 173, 211, *p211*, 213

Rankin, Jeannette, 580, *p580*, 591, *p591*

ratification, 198, 172–73, crt173, 174–77

rationalism, 108, 275

rationing, 753

Rauschenbusch, Walter, 356

Reagan, Nancy, 996

Reagan, Ronald, *p979*, 981, *q985*, *p986*, *q986*, 986–88, *p988*, *q989*, 989–91, *p991*, *q998*, 1002; assassination attempt, 988, *p988*; build up of military, 988–89; deficit spending, 987; deregulation, 987–88; domestic policies,

987–88; economy, 989; foreign policy, 989–91; Gorbachev and, 991, *p991*; Iran–Contra scandal, 989; Reagan Doctrine, 989–90

Reaganomics, 987, *q987*

realism, 478–79

reapportionment, 843

rebate, 495

recall, 549

recession, 697–98

reconcentration camps, 529, 532

Reconstruction, 386–89, 391–95, 398–402, 403–07, 418; collapse of, 403–07; Congressional, 391–95; Jackson's plan for, 392; Lincoln's plan for, 387; Republican rule and, 398–402

Reconstruction Finance Corporation, 670, 737, 812

Red Cloud, Chief, 427

Redding, Saunders, 740

Red Scare, 601–02, 791–96

referendum, 335, 549

Reformation, the, 60

Reform Darwinism, 482–83

Reform Party, 1019

reforms: abolitionist movement, 284–88; benevolent societies, 279; cultural, 273–77; political, 266–68, 490–94; religious, 275–76; societal, 278–82

Rehnquist, William, 988, 1019, *p1019*

Reichstag, 710

relief, economic, 670

religion: Aztec, 15; freedom of, 149, 186, 199; Great Awakening,108–09, 275; in the colonies, 64, 66–71, 74–75, 94–95; intolerance for, 274–76, 333; politics and, 981, 983–84; reforms, 275–76; *Religious Camp Meeting, ptg275*; religious movements, 923; religious right, 983–84; revivalism, 275; Second Great Awakening; separation of church and state, 70, 845; slavery and, 106–07, 255; tolerance of, 69, 75

Renaissance, the, 36–37

Reno, Janet, 1020

reparations, 596, 649

representative democracy, 180

republic, 147–48, 180

republicanism, 147–48, 180

Republican Party, *c272*, 333, *c333*, 334, 335, 336, 337, 341–42, 352–53, 363, 379, 387, 393, 394, 395, 404–06, 493–97, 504, 506, 514, 529, 550, 564, 565, 567, 569, 601, 629, 638, 639, 657, 670, 678, 679, 696, 697, 699, 794, 809, 810–11, 841, 857, 982, 1002, 1006, 1017–19, 1027–28; birth of, 332–34

reservations, 270

reserved powers, 180–81

Resettlement Act, *g692*

resolutions, 192

Restoration, the, 73

Reuben, James, 728

Revels, Hiram, 399, *p399*

Revenue Act of 1767, 122

revenue bill, 191

revenue sharing, 954

revenue tariffs, 241

Revere, Paul, 130

reverse discrimination, 933

revivalism, 275, *ptg275*, 279

revivals, 275

Reynolds v. *Sims,* 844, *c844*

Rhode Island, 70, 128, 165, 174, 248

rice, 86, 95, 251, 253

Rice, George, *q453*

Richardson, Elliot, 961

Richmond, David, 873, *p873*

Richmond, Virginia, 344, 351, 361, *p387*

Ride, Sally, 998

Ridge, Tom, 1035

Riesman, David, 815

rights: absolute, 199; basic freedoms, 186; equal treatment, 186; individual, 182, 199; limits on, 186; natural, 102, 108, 134; of citizens, 202; of judicial review, 186, 223; of the accused, 200; to assemble peaceably, 186, 199; to bear arms, 199; to legal representation, 200, 844–45; to petition, 186, 199; to privacy, 845; to a speedy trial, 200; to trial by jury, 182, 197, 200; voting, 203, 204, 843–44

right-to-work laws, 809–10

Riis, Jacob, 467, *q467*, 472, 498, 547

Rio Grande, 224

Ripley, George, 277

Roanoke, 61–62

robber barons, 446

Robertson, Pat, 984, *p984*

Robeson, Paul, 628

Robinson, Jo Ann, 869

Rochambeau, Jean Baptist, 145

Rockefeller, John D., 447, *crt447*, 449, 452, *p452*, 478

"rock 'n' roll," 823–24, 925

Rocky Mountains, 224, 295

Rodriguez, Gus, *q973*

Rodriquez, Richard, 1007, *p1007*

Roebling, John A., 470

Roe v. *Wade,* 929–30, 983

Rogers, Will, 682, *q682*

Rolfe, John, 63

Roman Catholic Church, 32, 34, 54, 60, 64, 100, 301, 709, 792; anti–Catholic sentiment, 274–75

Roman Empire, 33

Romania, 780–81, 1002

romanticism, 276

Rome-Berlin Axis, 711

Rommel, General Erwin, 746–47

Ronettes, the, 825

Roosevelt, Eleanor, 679, *p679*, 680, 696, 699, 736, 927

Roosevelt, Franklin Delano, *q669*, 678, 679, *p679*, 680, 681, *ptg681*, *q681*, 682–83, *p683*, 684–88, 689–91, *p691*, 692–94, 695–97, *p697*, 698–700, *q698*, crt698, crt700, *q705*, 711–12, *q712*, 725–30, 736, 737–54, 756, 757, *p757*, 764–66, 769, 779–80, 809; cabinet appointments, 683, 696; Casablanca Conference, 756; consideration of minorities, 696, 740; critics of New Deal programs, 690–91; death of, 766; Destroyers-for-Bases deal, 726; domestic wartime policies, 737–54; early political career, 679–80; economic theory, 779; end of New Deal era, 699; end to banking crisis, 683–84; fireside chats, 684, 727; first New Deal, 682–88, *c687*; foreign policies, 726–28, 764–65; impact of court-packing plan, 697; public opinion of 697, 700, crt700; radio addresses, 683, *p683*, 684, 727; recession of 1937, 697–98; second hundred days, 692; second inaugural address, 698, *q698*; second New Deal, 689–94; third term, 726–27;

Yalta Conference and,
779–80

Roosevelt, Theodore, *q517*,
p517, *p519*, 525, 529, 531,
p531, 536–37, *crt538*, 539,
540, 541, *crt541*, *q541*, 547,
q547, 553, 555, 556, *crt556*,
q556, 557, 558–59, *p559*, 561,
p561, 562, *q562–63*, 567,
q567, *q590*, 679, 682, 683;
acquisition of Panama
Canal Zone, 540; conser-
vation and, 558–59; involvement in Spanish-American
War, 529, 531; legacy of, 559;
Nobel Peace Prize, 539;
peace negotiations, 539;
political ideals, 537, 540,
crt541, 555; rise to power,
536–37; Roosevelt Corollary,
540–41; social welfare in,
558; trusts and, 556, *crt556*

Roosevelt Corollary, 540–41

Rosecrans, William, 361, 372

Rosenberg, Ethel and Julius,
p791, 792

"Rosie the Riveter," 750

Royal African Company, 89

royal colonies, 64, 71, 76, 101

Royal Proclamation of 1763,
119

Ruby, Jack, 851

Rumsfeld, Donald, 1035, 1037

Rush, Benjamin, *q170*

Rusk, Dean, 902–03, 905

Russia, 244, 395, 538, 578, 580,
594–95, 596, 601, 709, 1025.
See also Soviet Union.

Rust Belt, 982

Ruth, Babe, 622, *p623*

Rutledge, Edward, 140

Ryczke, Mira, 719, *q719*, 724

Sabin, Florence, 614

Sacagawea, 224, 227

Sacco-Vanzetti case, 611, *p618*,
618–19, *p619*

safety net, 700

Sahara, the, 27

Saigon, *p908*, 913, *p913*

Salem, Massachusetts, 94

Salem Witchcraft Trials, 94, *p94*

Salinger, Pierre, *q842*

Salk, Jonas, 680, *p680*, 818,
p819

saloons, 479

Salvation Army, 483–84

Sandburgh, Carl, 621

Sand Creek Massacre, 427, 428,
430

Sandinistas, 990

San Francisco, California, 322,
416, 467, 470, 475

Sanger, Margaret, 614

San Jacinto, Battle of, 303,
ptg304

San Salvador Island, 40

Santa Anna, Antonio López
de, 300–04, 309, 329

Santa Fe, New Mexico, 54, 309

Santa Fe Trail, 295

Santa Maria, 41

Santanta, Chief, *q431*

Santo Domingo, 41

Saratoga, New York, 141

Sassacus, Chief, 70

satellite nations, 782, 785

Saturday Night Fever, 973,
973–74

"Saturday Night Massacre,"
961

savannah, 27

Savannah, Georgia, 143

Savio, Mario, 920, *q920*, 922

scalawags, 399

Scalia, Antonin, 988

Scarlet Letter, 276

Schecter v. *United States*, 692

Scheeler, Charles, 621

Schlafly, Phyllis, 930, *p930*

scientific discoveries. *See*
technological innovations.

scientific management, 548

Scopes, John T., 615

Scotch-Irish, 106

Scott, Dred, 334–35, *p335*

Scott, General Winfield, *p310*,
311, 355–56; *General Scott's
Entrance Into Mexico*, *ptg311*

scrap drives, 754

Screen Actors Guild, 986

Scrowcroft, General Brent,
1001

Sculley, John, 1013, *p1013*

Seals, Bobby, 885

Seattle General Strike, 600

Seattle, Washington, 600

secession, 224, 268, 323, 342

Second Amendment, *c182*, 199

secondary sources, analyzing,
975, 977

Second Bank of the United
States, 241, 270

Second Continental Congress,
130, 131–33, 141, 158

Second front, 745

Second Great Awakening, 275,
285

second hundred days, 692

Second New Deal, 691–92,
c692, 693–94

Second Treatise of
Government, 1064

Second U.S. Colored Light
Artillery, 366, *p366*

Secretary of State: Colin
Powell, 1037; Dean
Acheson, 793; Dean Rusk,
905; Henry Clay, 259;
Henry Kissinger, 955,
966; James Baker, 1002;
James G. Blaine, 523; John
Foster Dulles, 799; John
Hay, 538; John Quincy
Adams, 243; Madeleine
Albright, 1022; Thomas
Jefferson, 211

sectional conflicts, 318–24,
326–31, 332–38, 340–45

sectionalism, 217–18, 241,
258–60

Securities and Exchange
Commission (SEC), 684,
686, *c686*

sedition, 219

Sedition Act of 1918, 588

segregation, 151, 508–12, 697,
739–40, 844, *c844*, 867–69,
871, 873–80, 934; *Brown* v.
Board of Education, 844,
c844, 868–69, 871, 934;
challenging, 873–80;
Freedom Riders and,
874–75; interstate travel,
867, 875–76; legalizing, 510;
military, 739–40; rise of,
508–12; segregated facilities,
p867; Southern Manifesto,
869

select committees, 183

Selective Service, 584–85, 739

selectmen, 94

self-determination, 578, 596

Selma March, 879–80

Seminoles, the, 271

Senate's Select Committee on
Presidential Campaign
Activities, 960

Senate, U.S., 494, 496, 549, 961.
See also legislative branch of
government.

Seneca Falls Convention, 282

Seneca Falls Declaration, 1070

"separate but equal," 511, 867

separation of church and state,
70, 845

separation of powers, 108, 148,
166, 697

Separatists, 66–67, 69

Serapis, 143

Serbians, 578–80, 1020

serfs, 33

Serra, Junipero, 54

settlement houses, 485

Seven Days Battle, 362

Seven Golden Cities of Cibola,
53

Seventeenth Amendment, 203,
549

Seventeenth Parallel, 895

Seventh Amendment, 200

Seward, William, 395

Shah of Iran, 968–69

Shakers, 277

shanty towns, 662

sharecroppers, 407, 509

Shays's Rebellion, 161–62, 165

Sheridan, Philip, 377, 380

Sherman, General William
Tecumseh, 378, 425, *q425*,
430

Sherman, Roger, 132–33, 165,
p167, 167

Sherman Antitrust Act, 497,
553, 556, 565

"Sherman neckties," 378

Sherman Silver Purchase Act,
504; repeal of, 505

Sherrod, Robert, 759, *q759*

Shiloh, Battle of, 361

shipbuilding, 93

Shirelles, the, 825

Shoah, 720

siege, 370, 377

Sierra Club, 941, 997

Sigsbee, Charles D., 534, *p534*,
q534

Silent Spring, 940

silicon, 1013

Silicon Valley, 1013

silver, 55, 98–99, 415–16,
501–02, 504, 505, 506; mercantilism, 98–99; mining, 55,
415–16

silverite, 505–06

Sims, Admiral William S., 594

Sinclair, Upton, 558, 571, *p571*

Index

Singletary, Amos, *q173*

sin tax, 404

Sirica, John J., 960

sit-down strike, 693

sit-ins, 868, 873–74, 922

Sitting Bull, Chief, 427, 429, *p429,* 430

Sixteenth Amendment, 474, 568

Sixth Amendment, *c182,* 200

Skylab, 999

skyscrapers, 470

slash-and-burn, agriculture, 23

Slater, Samuel, 248

slave codes, 90, 254, 341

slave labor, 724

slavery: abolitionists, 284–88, 326–28; agriculture and, 252–53; American Colonization Society, 285; American Revolution and, 150–51; antislavery meeting poster, *p321;* chattel, 90; Compromise of 1850, 324, *c324;* Constitution and, 167–68; coping with, 255–56; culture of, 106–107, 255–56; drivers, 254; English policies, 89; Fugitive Slave Act, 326–27; gang system, 254; hereditary system of, 90; holding area for, *p89;* in African society, 30; in the colonies, 89–91, 106–07; John Brown's raid, 336–37; Kansas-Nebraska Act, 330–31; legal rights, 254; Missouri Compromise, 258, *m258;* opposition to, 150; religion and, 106–07; resistance and rebellions against, 256; rice cultivation and, 86; Royal African Company, 89; sectional conflicts and, 318–24, 326–31, 332–38, 340–45; slave codes, 90; slave states and free states, 257–58, 322, 329, 330; slave voyage to America, 89; steps to end, 150; Stono Rebellion, 107; task system, 254; trade, 89–90; Underground Railroad, 327–28; westward expansion and, 320–24; Wilmot Proviso, 321

Slavic people, the, 578, 720

Slidell, John, 308, 354

smallpox, 105, 312

Smith, Alfred E., 657

Smith, Bessie, 628, *p628*

Smith, Captain John, 62, 63, *p63,* 67

Smith, Joseph, 276

Smith, Margaret, Bayard, *q266*

smog, 940

Snepp, Frank, 910

soap operas, 664

social activism, 997–98

social conditions, *c482*

Social Darwinism, 477–78, 482–83, 485, 521, 555

Social Gospel Movement, 483–84, 485

Socialism, 553, 584

social reforms, 547–48, 551–52, 997–98

Social Security, *c692,* 809–10, 812–13, 998, 1029

Social Security Act, *g692,* 694

social welfare Progressivism, 551–52

sodbusters, 422

software, 1013–14

Songhai, 28–29

Soninke people, the, 27–28

Sons of Liberty, 121

Sorko, the, 28–29

Sound and the Fury, The, 665

soup kitchens, 662

South, the: agriculture of, 84–85, 251–53; Civil War, 318–24, 326–31, 332–38, 340–45, *c345,* 350–56, 357–63, 364–68, 369–73, 376–80; Farm Security Administration, 699; industrialization, 253; needs of postwar, *c408;* "New South," 406; politics of, 214, 502, 503, 504, 505, 696, 810, 953, 982; populism, 503, 504, 505, 506; poverty, 699; Reconstruction, 368–89, 391–95, 398–407; rural, 502, 503, 504, 506; secession, 268, 323, 342; segregation in, 510–11, 868–72, 873–75; society of, 86–87, 253; voting, 510, *m551. See also* Civil War, sectional conflicts.

South Carolina, 76, 86, 106, 107, 132, 175, 241, 251, 268–69, 321, 342, 379, 342, 344

South Dakota, 502, 503

Southern Christian Leadership Conference (SCLC), 870–71, 872, 874, 879, 880, 883, 885

Southern Colonies, 76–77, 84–90; agriculture of, 84–85, *m85,* 86–89; Bacon's Rebellion, 87–89; economy of, 84–86; founding of, 76–77; slavery in, 86–89; society in, 86–87

Southern gentry, 86–87, 254, *p254*

Southern Manifesto, 869

Southern strategy, 953–54

South Vietnam, 895, 896–901, 905, 907, 911, 912, 913, *p913*

Southwest, the, 21

Soviet Union, 709, *p709,* 714, 715, 727, 765, *p765,* 772, 778–82, 783–89, 790–91, 799, 800–02, 841, 846, 847, 849, 850, 955–57, 968, 988–99, 1002–03, 1038; allied arms buildup, 850; arms reduction and, 990; Berlin Crisis, 785–86; Carter and, 968; collapse of, 1003; Cuban missile crisis, 846, 849–50; death of Stalin, 801; defection of Igor Gouzenko, 791; invasion of Afghanistan, 989; Khrushchev and, 801–02; launch of Sputnik, 799; Mikail Gorbachev, 990–91, 1002–03; Moscow summit, 957; Nixon and, 955–57, *p957;* Non-Aggression Pact, 715, 727; Reagan and, 989; Red Scare, 601–02; soldiers with American forces, *p765;* space race, 847; space station, 999; Suez crisis, 800–01; tests of atomic and H-bombs, 787, 789, 795; violation of Declaration of Liberated Europe, 780–81; Warsaw Pact, 786

space program, 848, *p848,* 998–99

space race, 847, 853, *p853*

space shuttle, 998–99

space station, 999

Spain, 243, 244, 527–33, 711; Adams-Onís Treaty 244; armor and weaponry of, *p51;* conquest of Mexico, 50–53; explorations by, 40–43; Florida, 243; rivalry with France, 57; Spanish American society of, 54–55; Spanish-American War, 527–33; Spanish armada, *p60;* Spanish Civil War, 711; Treaty of Tordesillas, 42; viceroyalties, 55

Spanish-American War: 527–28, *p528,* 529–33, *c530, m530, p531,* 711; Cuban rebellion, *p528,* 528–29; mobilization of military, 529–31; peace treaty, 531–32;

Rough Riders, 531, *p531;* U.S. casualties, *c530;* USS *Maine,* 527

speakeasies, 615–16

Special Forces, 847

speculation, 657

speculators, 212

Spencer, Herbert, 477, *p477*

sphere of influence, 538

Spirit of the Laws, 108

spoils system, 267, 492–93

Sprague, Frank J., 471

Sputnik, 796, 798–99, *crt799,* 818

Squanto, 67

Square Deal, 556

squatters, 295

SS St. Louis, 722

"stagflation," 964, 987

Stalingrad, Battle of, 747, *p747*

Stalin, Joseph, 709, *p709,* 715, 727, 745, 757, *p757,* 779–82, *p781,* 782, 784–85

stalwarts, 493

Stamp Act, 120, 123, *crt123*

Stamp Act Congress, 121

standard of living, 470, 471, 632, 640, 641, 643, 644, 646, 815, 819, 995, 999, 1013–14; impact of automobile, 641; impact of telecommunication advances, 1013–14

Standard Oil, 447, 449, 450, 452, 478, 495

standard time, 444, 499

standing committees, 183

Stanford, Leland, 443–44

Stans, Maurice, 957, *q957*

Stanton, Edwin M., 394

Stanton, Elizabeth Cady, 282, *q396,* 549, 550

Staple Act, 99

Starr, Kenneth, 1020

Stars and Stripes, 145, 229

Star-Spangled Banner, 228–29, 1069

state government, 180–81

state powers, 211

state-sponsored terrorism, 1032, 1036

states' rights, 241, 242, 243, 259

statistics, interpreting, 424

St. Augustine, Florida, 57

steamboats, 247

steel, 415, 448–49, 470, 843; Andrew Carnegie and, 448–49, *q449;* placer mining, 415; production of, 415, 449, 470

steerage, 465

Steffens, Lincoln, 547

Stein, Gertrude, 621

Steinbeck, John, 665

Steinem, Gloria, 928

Steiner, Edward, 465, *q465*

Stephanopoulos, George, 1016, *q1016*

Stephens, Alexander, 353, 392

Stevens, John L., 520, *q520*

Stevens, Thaddeus, 387, *p387, q396*

Stevenson, Adlai, 811

St. Lawrence River, 55

stock, 248, 448, 450, 451, 452, 1014

stockholder, 448, 450

stock market, 404, 505, 645, 656–59, *crt659,* 684, 1014, 1018, 1029; bull markets, 657; crashes, 656, 658–59; dot.com investment, 1014, 1029; regulation of, 684; speculation in, 657–58

Stone, Lucy, 550

Stone v. Powell, 954

Stonewall riot, 997

Stono Rebellion, 107

storm troopers, 710, 721

Stowe, Harriet Beecher, 326, *q326*

Strait of Hormuz, 1004

Strategic Arms Limitation Treaty (SALT 1), 957

strategic defense, 1029

Strategic Defense Initiative (SDI), "Star Wars," 990

strategic hamlets, 897

strategic materials, 729

Strategic Arms Reduction Talks (START), 990

stream-of-consciousness technique, 665

Striebel, Kathy, 929

strikebreakers, 456

strikes, 249, 600–01, 809

Strong, Josiah, *q411,* 521–22, *q522*

Student Nonviolent Coordinating Committee (SNCC), 874

Students for a Democratic Society (SDS), 921–22

Stuyvesant, Peter, 72

St. Vincent Millay, Edna, 621

submarine warfare, 581–83, 594, 727

subsistence farming, 87, 92

subtreasuries, 503–04

suburbanization, 813, 816

subversion, 791

Sudbury, Massachusetts, 93, *c93, m93*

Suez Canal, 540, *m540,* 746, 800–01; crisis, 800–01

suffrage, 545, 546, 549–51, *m551*

suffragists, 546, *p546, q546,* 549–51, *m551;* National American Woman Suffrage Association, 550–51; political power of, 551

sugar, 31, 95, 86, 251, 520, 523, 528

Sugar Act, 120

Sullivan, Ed, 821

Sullivan, Louis, 470, *q470*

summits, 956–57, 991

Sumner, Charles, 331, *crt331,* 387, 391, *q391*

Sumner, William Graham, 476, *q476,* 477

Sunbelt, 751, 982–83, *m983*

Sunday, Billy, 614

supply and demand, 61, 85, 97, 241, 438

supply-side economics, 648, 987

supremacy clause, 198

Supreme Court, 211, 502, 529, 556, 569, 588–89, 699, 843–45, *p845,* 867, 868, 954, 961, 988, 989; *Abingdon School District v. Schempp, c844,* 845; *Abrams v. United States,* 588; activism of, 843–45; appellate jurisdiction, 185, 196; appointment of justices, 185; as nation's court of final appeal, 185, *c185,* 241–42, *c242; Baker v. Carr,* 843, *c844; Brown v. Board of Education,* 392, 844, *c844,* 868–69, 871, 934; Burger Court, 954; *Bush v. Gore,* 392, 1028–29; *Cohens v. Virginia, c242; Commonwealth v. Hunt,* xx; court-packing plan, 697; *Dred Scott v. Sandford,* 334–35, 341; *Engel v. Vitale, c844,* 845; *Escobedo v. Illinois, c844,* 844–45; first African American on, 868, 870, *p870,* 875, 876; first woman appointment to, 988, *p989; Fletcher v. Peck, c242; Gibbons v. Ogden, c242,* 243; *Gideon v.*

Wainwright, 392, 844, *c844; Griswold v. Connecticut,* 845; *Heart of Atlanta Motel v. United States, c844;* impact of decisions on politics, 983; impact on state courts, 844–45; impeachment, 222–23; independence of, 185; judicial nationalism, 242–43; judicial review, 186, 223; *Korematsu v. the United States,* 753; limitations on free speech, 589; *Loving v. Virginia, c844; Mapp v. Ohio,* 844, *c844; Marbury v. Madison,* 23, *c242; Martin v. Hunter's Lessee, c242; McCulloch v. Maryland,* 193, 242, *c242; Miranda v. Arizona, c844,* 844, 845; *Morgan v. Virginia,* 867; *New York Times v. Sullivan, c844; NLRB v. Jones and Laughlin Steel,* 699; *Norris v. Alabama,* 867; *Northern Securities v. United States,* 556; overturn of Civil Rights Act of 1875, 510; *Plessy v. Ferguson,* 392, 511, 868; *Reynolds v. Sims,* 844, *c844,* 862; rise of, 222–23; *Roe v. Wade,* 929–30, 983; ruling on bilingualism, 936; ruling on Nixon tapes, 961; *Schecter v. United States,* 589, 692; shift of judicial balance, 988; *Stone v. Powell,* 954; *Swann v. Charlotte- Mecklenberg Board of Education,* 934; *Sweatt v. Painter,* 867; *University of California Regents v. Bakke,* 933; validation of free speech, 922; *Wabash v. Illinois,* 496, 502, 569; Warren court, 843–45, *p845; Wickard v. Filburn,* 699–700, 753; William Rehnquist, 988; *Worcester v. Georgia,* 271

Supreme Order of the Star Spangled Banner, 275

Supremes, the, 825

Sussex Pledge, 582

Sutter, John, 295

Swann v. Charlotte-Mecklenberg Board of Education, 934

Sweatt v. Painter, 867

Sweden, 716

Sylvis, William, 456, *q456–57*

syndicate, 564

Syria, 1033

Szilard, Leo, 769

Taft, William Howard, 532, 541, 562, 563, *p563, q563,* 564, 565, 567, 587

Taft-Hartley Act, 792, 809

Taiwan, 787, 800

Taliban, 969, 1033, 1036

Talmadge Jr., James, 258

Tammany Hall, 473, 494

Taney, Roger B., 334–35, *p335, q335*

Tappan, Arthur and Lewis, 286

Tarbell, Ida, 547

Tariff of 1789, 211–12

Tariff of 1816, 241

Tariff of Abominations, 268

tariffs, 496, 497, 501, 504, 564, 646, 649

task system of slavery, 254

taxation, 35, 64, 68, 119–23, 206, 211, 213, 222, 438–39, 510, 568, 648, 669–70, 754, 810, 843, 879, 982–83, 987, 1006; Bush and, 1006; capital gains taxes, 983, 1006; concept of laissez-faire and, 438–39; during colonial times, 64, 68, 75, 88, 119–23; during WWII, 754; Great Depression and, 669–70; lowering taxes, 987, 1002, 1006, 1018; poll taxes, 206, 510, 810, 879; Proposition 13, 983; protective tariffs, 241; public opinion on, 982–83; Reagan and, 987; revenue bills, 191; Sixteenth Amendment, 568; tax revolt, 983; trade and, 35, 119–123, 211; Whiskey Tax, 213, 222

Taylor, General Zachary, 309, *p309,* 310, 322, 323, 324

Tea Act, 127

teach-in, 905

Teapot Dome Scandal, 638, *crt638*

technological innovations: agricultural, 14, 33, 295, 420–23, 645; airline industry, 643–44; artificial satellites, 799; automobile, 613, 640–41; aviation, 798–99, 819; biotechnology, 1014–15; communications, 848, *p848;* computers, 817, *p817,* 819; consumer goods industry, 643; cotton gin, 252; depth charges, 747; electricity, 440; electronics, 817; exploration and, 36–37; hydrogen bomb,

795–96, *p798*; impact on communication, 439–40; impact on entertainment industry, 664–65, 815, 996; impact on medicine, 105, 817–18; impact on trade, 522; impact on transportation, 439–40, 444; impact on urbanization, 470–71; in manufacturing, 247, 248, 440; in space, 818–19; interchangeable parts as, 248; intercontinental ballistic missiles as, 799; in warfare, 51, 361, 592, 799, 593–94, 718, 737–38, 747, 756, 759–60, 798–99, 1004; Japanese adoption of, 538; NASA and, 849, *p849*; Native American, 16, 22; navigational tools, 36–37; radar, 718, 747; radio industry, 644; revolution in, 1012–15; sonar, 747; steel production, 449; submarines, 799; telecommunications, 1013–14; telegraph, 248–49; telephone, 439–40; television and, 995, 996; transportation, 471; turn-of-the-century products 450, *p450*

Tecumseh, 229, *p230*

Tejanos, 300, 301

telecommunications, 1013–14

Telecommunications Act of 1996, 1013

telecommuting, 1013

telegraph, 248–49

telephone, 439–40

televangelists, 984

television, 820, *p821*, 821–22, 840, 972–73, 984, 995–96

temperance movement, 279, 553; innkeeper's temperance sign, *p279*

tenant farmers, 86–88, 407

Ten Bears, Chief, 425, *q425*

tenements, 471, *p472*, *p474*, 475, 481, 498

Tennessee, 53, 217, 251, 259, 307, 341, 344, 361, 372–73, 391, 394

Tennessee Coal and Iron Company, 565

Tennessee Valley Authority (TVA), 684, *m684*, 685, *p685*, 686, *c686*, 812; power facility, *p685*

Tenochitlán, 15, 50, 51, 52

Tenskwatawa, 229

Tenth Amendment, *c182*, 200

Tenure of Office Act, 394

Teotihuacán, 14

termination policy, 830–31

term limits, 205

Terrell, Mary Church, 510, *p510*

terrorism, 1031–37; antiterrorism bill, 1035; attempted Seattle bombing, 1033; bioterrorism, 1035; bombing of the Pentagon, 1031–34, *p1032*; bombing of the USS *Cole*, 1033; bombing of the World Trade Centers, 1029, 1031–34; citizen response to, 1033; cutting terrorist funding, 1035; embassy bombings, 1033; Middle East and, 1032–33; national emergency, 1033–34; new war against, 1034–36; oil and, 1032; Oklahoma City bombing, 1024; state-sponsored, 1032; terrorist attacks, *c1034*, *m1034*

Terry, General Alfred H., 429

Test Ban Treaty, 850

Tet offensive, 907, *m908*, *p908*

Texas, 53, 57, 224, 251, 252, 301–03, *m303*, 304, 323, 342, 416–19, 502, 935

Texas Exchange, 503

Texas longhorn, 416

Thatch, James S., 742, *q742*

Third Amendment, 199

Thirteenth Amendment, 201, 379–80

Thompson, Dorothy, *q700*, 708, *q708*

Thoreau, Henry David, *q247*, 276, 283, 299, *q327*, 338

Three-Fifths Compromise, 167

Three Mile Island, 942

Thurmond, J. Strom, 810, 953

Tiananmen Square, 1003–04

Tidewater, the, 88

Tilden, Bill, 623

Tilden, Samuel, 405

Timbuktu, 26, 27, 29

time line reading, 45, 47

time zones, 444, 499

Tippecanoe, Battle of, 229

Title VII, 927, 928

Title IX, 929

tobacco, *c85*, 76, 85–86, 251

Toleration Act of 1649, 101

Toltec, the, 14–15, *c15*

Tomb of the Unknown Soldier, 649, *p649*

Tom Thumb, 247, *p247*

tonnage, 211

Toombs, Robert, 338, 341

torpedo, 378

town meetings, 94

town proprietors, 94

Townsend, Dr. Francis, 690–91; Townsend Plan, 690

Townshend, Charles, 122

Townshend Acts, 122

trade: agreements, 1024; associations, 648; barriers, 1023; blocs, 1023; camels and, 27; colonial, *m96*; deficits, 1023; disputes, 1024; early African cultures, 27–31; early Mesoamerican, 14; embargoes, 1020; free, 1023–24; international, 964, 1022–24; normal trade relations, 1024; restrictions, 229; routes, 27, 28, 35; salt, 26, 27, 29; slavery and, 31; tobacco, *c85*; treaties, 522–23; triangular, 95; unfair trade practices, 568; unions, 455; wheat, 97; World Trade Organization (WTO), 121, 1024

trade agreements, 1023

Trail of Tears, 270

trains. *See* railroads.

transcendentalism, 276

transcendental meditation, 971

transcontinental railroad, 328–39

transistor, 817

transportation, 243–42, 245–47, 249; advances in, 249; air travel, 643, 988; Erie Canal, 245; hovercraft, 249, *p249*; National Road, 246; revolution, 245–47, *g246*; roads, canals, railroads, 242, *m246*, 247; steamboats, 247, 249, *p249*. *See also* railroads.

Trans-Siberian Railroad, 444

Travis, William B., 302, *q302*

Travolta, John, *p973*, 974

treason, 197

Treatise on Domestic Economy, A, 282

Treaty of Brest-Litovsk, 595

Treaty of Fort Laramie, 297

Treaty of Ghent, 232

Treaty of Greenville, 217, 229

Treaty of Guadalupe Hidalgo, 311

Treaty of Paris, 118, 145, 532

Treaty of Shackamaxon, 75

Treaty of Tordesillas, 41–42

Treaty of Versailles, 596, 709

Tredegar Iron Works, 351

trench warfare, 593, *p593*

Trent Affair, 354

trial by jury, 182, 200

Triangle Shirtwaist Company, 552

triangular trade, 95

tribute, 15, 28, 51

Triple Alliance, 578, 580

Triple Entente, 578, 580

Truman, Harry S., 765–66, 769, 770, 778, 781, *p781–82*, 784–86, 788–89, 791, *q809*, 809–10, *p810*, *q810*, *p811*, 894; Berlin crisis, 785–86; domestic programs, 809–10; election of 1948, 810, *p811*; fair deal, 810; Korean War, 788–89; limited war policy, 789; loyalty review program, 791; MacArthur, firing of, 789; Potsdam Conference, 781; support from laborers, African Americans and farmers, 810; Truman Doctrine, 785, 810; Vietnam policy, 894

Truman Doctrine, 785, 810, 1076

Trumbull, John, 152

trustbuster, 556, 565

trust busting, 683, 684

trustee, 450

trusts, 450, 497, 549, 553, 556, 565, 683

Truth, Sojourner, 287

Tubman, Harriet, 328, *p328*

Turner, Nat, 256, *p256*, 288

Tuskegee Airmen, 740, *p740*

T.V. dinners, *p822*

Twain, Mark (Samuel Clemens), *q253*, *q396*, 476–77, 479, 484, *p484*, *q484*, 532

Tweed, William M. "Boss," 473

Twelfth Amendment, 201

Twentieth Amendment, 204

Twenty-First Amendment, 205, 616

Twenty-Second Amendment, 205–06

Twenty-Third Amendment, 206

Twenty-Fourth Amendment, 206, 879

Index

Twenty-Fifth Amendment, 206–07

Twenty-Sixth Amendment, 207, 906

Twenty-Seventh Amendment, 207

Two Treatises of Government, 101–02, 1064

tying agreements, 568

Tyler, John, 272, 307

U-boats, 581–83

Uncle Tom's Cabin, 326–27

Underground Railroad, 327–28, *m329*

Underwood Tariff Act, 568

unemployment, 842–43, 936, 963, 987, 988; line at unemployment office, *p963*

unfair trade practices, 568

Unification Church, 923

Union, the, 318–24, 326–31, 330–38, 340–45, 350–56, 357–63, 364–68, 369–73, 376–80. *See also* Civil War.

Union of Soviet Socialist Republics (USSR). *See* Soviet Union.

Union Pacific, 442, 443, *p443*, 445, 446

Union Party, 697

unions: American Federation of Labor, 458–59; boycotts, 457–58; decline of, 648; early, 455–56; impact of Knights of Labor, 457–58; industrial, 455–56; injunctions against, 458; Iron Molders Union, 456; labor organizers, 456–57; membership, 693, *g693*; National Labor Union, 456; opposition to organizing, 455–56; strikes, *m457*, 457–58, 809; trade, 455; working conditions, 457–59

union shops, 809

union strikes, *m457*, 457–58, 809

Unitarianism, 275

United Auto Workers (UAW), 694

United Farm Workers, 935

United Mine Workers, 456, 556–57, 693

United Nations, 771, 787, 788, 1036–1037

United States: acquisition of Panama Canal Zone, 540; acquisition of Philippines, 530, 532; annexation of Hawaii, 523; anti-Imperialism, 532; as industrial power, 434–59; as world power, 518–41; big business in, 418–19, 447–51, 496–97, 501, 506, 521, 522, 523, 525, 552, 553, 556, *crt556*, 557, 565, 568–69, 585–86, 683, 685–86, 749–51, 843, 1005; 276–77; first permanent town, 57; foreign investments, *g521*; 438–39; role in Latin American affairs, 523–24, 540–41; Soviet aggression and, 778–86, 789, 791, 792, 804, 805, 849–50; Spanish–American War, 527–33; Treaty of Paris, 532; urbanization of, 462–86, 498, *p498*, *q498*, 547, 829–30, *crt882*, 882–83, 992, *m992–93*, *p992*; *See also* America, American Revolution; Civil War; constitution, U.S.; economy, U.S.; government, U.S; industrialization.

United States Army, 738–41

United States Commission on Civil Rights, 872

United States Constitution. *See* Constitution, U.S.

United States Department of Agriculture, 558–59

United States Housing Authority, 699

United States Industrial Commission, 452

United States Navy, *p524*, 524–25, 529, 537

United States Sanitary Commission, 367

United States Steel Corporation, 694

United States Treasury, 501, 504, 505

United Steelworkers, 694

Universalism, 275

Universal Negro Improvement Association (UNIA), 629–30

University of California Regents v. *Bakke,* 933

Unsafe at Any Speed, 943

Upson, Theodore, 350

Urban II, Pope, 32, 34

urbanization: 249, 462–86, 498, *p498*, *q498*, 547, 829–30, *crt882*, 882–83, 992, *m992–93*, *p992*; class separations, 471; crime, 472; impact on individual and societal values, 477–80; impact on public education, 485–86; Industrial Revolution and, 249; living conditions, 470, 471–72, 498, *p498*; mass transit, 470–71; minorities and, 882, *crt882*, 883; politics and, 472–73; problems of, 472; progressive view of, 547; technology of, 470, *p470*, *p992*; urban poor, 483, *p483*, 829–30; urban society, 253, 471, 547

urban renewal, 829

urban sprawl, 992

USA Patriot Act, 1035

USS *Cole,* 1033, *crt1034*

USS *Maine,* *p524*, 527, 528, 529, *p534*, 534–35, *crt535*, *p535*

USS *Missouri,* 784–85

U.S. Steel, 601

U.S. Treasury, 615

Utah, 297

Utah Territory, 276

utopia, 277

utopian communities, 277

Valley Forge, Pennsylvania, 138, 141; march to Valley Forge, *ptg141*

Van Buren, Martin, 250, 270, 271, 272, 307, 322

Vanderbilt, Cornelius, 444

Van Doren, Charles, 822

vaqueros, 35

vaudeville, 480

V-E Day, 765, *p765*, 766

Velazquez, 51

Vermont, 281

Verrazano, Giovanni da, 55

vertical integration, 449, *g449*

Vesey, Denmark, 256

Vespucci, Amerigo, 42

veto, 787

viceadmiralty courts, 119–20, 122

viceroy, 55

viceroyalties, 55

Vicksburg, Mississippi, 369–70, *p370*

Victory Bonds, 586

victory gardens, 586, 753–54

video cassette recorders (VCRs), 995

Vietcong, 897, 900–01, 907

Vietminh, 893–95

Vietnam, 892–93, *m893*, *p893*, 894–95, *p895*, 896–906, *p906*, 907–14; Declaration of Independence, 893; division of, 895; French control of, 893–94; Geneva Accords, 895; Japanese control of, 892–93; nationalism, 893, 895; rural economy of, *p893*; strategic hamlets, 897

Vietnamization, 911

Vietnam War, 890–900, *p895*, *p898*, *p900*, *g901*, 901–05, *crt905*, *p905*, 906–09, *q909*, 910–13, *p913*, 914, *m917*; Americans in combat, 899, *p900*, 900–01, 907; antiwar movement, 904–06, 911–12; attrition, 901; credibility gap about, 905, *crt905*; deaths in, *g901*; deception about, 912; end of, 911–12; fall of Saigon, 913, *p913*; full-scale war, 896–914; Gulf of Tonkin incident, 902–03; Gulf of Tonkin Resolution, 898–99; Henry Cabot Lodge and, 897; Johnson and, 898–99, 902, *p902*, 903, 907–08; Kent State, *p911*, 912–13, *q962*; legacy of, 913–14; memorial dedication, *p891*, 914; MIAs, 914; Nixon and, 909, 911–13; Pentagon Papers, 912; prisoners of war (POWs), 914; refugees of, 914; roots of, 892–901; "television war," 905; Tet offensive, 907, *m908*, *p908*

vigilance committees, 415

Vikings, 38–39; artifacts of, *p39*

Villa, Pancho, 577, *p577*

Virginia, 62–64, 73, 85–86, 89, 90, 107, 128, 132, 142, 144, 148, 165, 166, 174, 175, 217, 251, 254, 256, 285, 343, 344, 350, 359, 361. *See also* House of Burgesses.

Virginia City, Nevada, 416, *p416*

Virginia Company, 62, 64, 67

Virginia Declaration of Rights, 148, 211

Virginia Plan, 165, 166

Virginia Resolutions, 219

Virginia Resolves, 123

Virginia Statute for Religious Freedom, 149, 211, 1065

Index

VISTA (Volunteers in Service to America), 857, *p859*

V-J Day, 771, *p772*

Volstead Act, 615

von Richthofen, Manfred (Red Baron), 591

Voter Education Project, 874

voting: African Americans and, 151, 629, 695–96; after the American Revolution, 148–49; age, 906, 907; certification of results in, 1028; disenfranchisement of, 510–12; Fifteenth Amendment, 510, 550; Fourteenth Amendment, 550; literacy tests, 510; Nineteenth Amendment, 551; poll taxes, 206, 510, 879; recounts, 1028; responsibilites of, 185–86; rights, 180, 203, 549–50, 844, 857, 872, 879–80; SCLC and, 872; suffragists, *p545*, 546, *q546*, 549–51, *m551*; women and, 150, 549–50, 696. *See also* elections.

Voting Rights Act of 1965, 857, 880

Wabash v. Illinois, 496, 502

Wade-Davis Bill, 388

Wagner, Robert, 692

Wagner Act, 692, *g692*, 693

wage and price controls, 753, 965

wagon trains, 295–96, *p297*

Wald, Lillian, 459, 481, *q481*, 485

Walden, 283

Waldorf, Jacob, 414

Walker, David, 285

Walker, Mary Richardson, 294, *q294*

Walker, Quock, 147

Wallace, George, 877, 909, 953, 959

Wallace, Henry, 685

Wall Street, 504, 505

Wannese Conference, 723

War Democrats, 352–53

Ward, Lester Frank, 482–83

Ward, Samuel Ringgold, 255, *q255*

War Hawks, 229–30, 241

Warhol, Andy, 924

War Industries Board, 586, 683

War Labor Board (WLB), 753

Warm Springs, Georgia, 680, 766

Warner, Charles, 476–77

War of 1812, 228–32, *m231*; Baltimore raid, 231; financing, 230; invasion of Canada, 230; strategy, 230–31; Treaty of Ghent, 232; War Hawks, 229–30; Washington raid, 231

War on Poverty, *p856*, 856–57

War Powers Act, 914

War Production Board (WPB), 738–39

warrant, 148, 199

Warren, Earl, 843, *p845*, 868, 954

Warren Commission, 851

Warren court, 843–45, *c844*, *p845*

Warsaw Pact, 786, *m800*

War with Mexico, 307–09, *m310*, 310–11, 320–21; beginning of fighting, 309–10; *General Scott's Entrance Into Mexico, ptg311*; impact of 320–21; military strategy, 309; Treaty of Guadalupe Hidalgo, 311

Washington, Booker T., 485, *p485*, 486, 511–12, 629

Washington, D.C., 222–23, *p223*

Washington, George, 112–13, *ptg115*, 117, 118, 130, 132, 140, 141, 145, 158, 165, *q176*, 209, *ptg209*, 210, *q210*, 211–17, 234; commander of Continental Army, 130, 132, 140, 141, 145; farewell address, 217–18; foreign policy, 215–17; inauguration of, *ptg112–13*; *Painter and the President, ptg209*; reviews the troops, *p213*; *Washington Crossing the Delaware, ptg115*

Washington Conference, 649–50, *c650*

Washington-on-the-Brazos, 301

"Washington's Farewell Address," 217–18, 1068

Washington (state), 294

Watergate, 958–62; break-in, 958–59; cover-up, 959–60; hotel, *p959*; impact of, 962

Water Quality Act, 858, *c858*

Watson, James, 1015

Watson, Tom, 508, *q508*, 509

Watt, James, 988, 997

Watts Riot, 882

Wayne, General Anthony, 145, 217

weapons of mass destruction, 1036–37

Weaver, James B., 504, 505

Weaver, Robert, 859

Web browsers, 1014

Web site, evaluating, 381, 383

Web sites, 1014

Webster, Daniel, 241, 252, *p252*, 269, *q269*, 285, *p323*, 324, *q324*

Webster-Ashburton Treaty, 272

Weld, Theodore, 286

welfare capitalism, 645

welfare reform, 1018

Welfare Reform Act, 1018

Welles, Sumner, 713, *q713*

Wells, Ida B., 499, 511, *p511*

West Africa, 27–29, *p29*

West, Dorothy, 627

West, the, 292–97; 412–24, 436–37, 502–04, 509, 558–59; farming, 420–23, 502, 503, 504; Great Plains, 420–23; impact of demographic changes in, 415–16, 423–24, 436–37; land development in, 558–59; Lewis and Clark Expedition, 224, 227; Manifest Destiny, 292–97, 300–11; mining industry, 414, 416; Oregon Territory, 244, 307, 308; Oregon Trail, 294, 295; pioneers, 294–97, 307; politics of, 214, 502, 504; ranching, 416–19; settlement of, 294–97, 412–19, 421–23; trails west, 295, *m296*

West, Thomas (Lord De La Warr), 62, 63

West Berlin, 785–86, 849

Western Front, 593, 595, *m595*

West Germany, 785–86

Westmoreland, General William, 905, 907

West Virginia, 197, 246

Weyler, General Valeriano, 529

Wharton, Edith, 479, 614

wheat, 96–97, 422–23; boom, 96–97, 422–23

Wheat Belt, 421–22

Whigs, 129, 241, 271, 272, *c272*, 307, 308, 309, 321, 322, 329, 330, 332, 333, 336, 341, 399

Whip Inflation Now (WIN), 965

Whiskey Rebellion, 213

White, H. Theodore, 843

White, John, 61, *q78*

White, William Allen, 726

white-collar workers, 815, *crt815*

Whitefield, George, 108, *p109*

"whites-only," 511

white supremacy, 872, 875. *See also* Ku Klux Klan.

Whitman, Walt, 276, 397

Whitney, Eli, 248, 252

Whittier, John Greenleaf, 286

Whyte Jr., William H., 815

Wickard v. Filburn, 699–700

wigwam, 23

Wilderness Society, 941

Wiley, Calvin, 281

Wiley, Dr. W.H., 558

Wilkes, Charles, 354

Wilkeson, Samuel, 369, *q369*

Willard, Emma, 281

William, King of England, 101

Williams, Dessie Mae, 881, *p881*

Williams, Roger, 69, *q78*

Williams, William Carlos, 621

Willis, Frank, 959, *p959*

Wills, Helen, 623

Wilmot, David, 321

Wilmot Proviso, 321

Wilson, Henry, 388, *q388*

Wilson, Kemmons, 814, *q814*

Wilson, Woodrow, 551, 566, *q566*, 567, *ptg567*, *q567*, 568, 576–77, 580–83, *q583*, *q590*, 596, 597, 611, *q624*, 679, 683, 708; antitrust actions, 568; diplomacy, 576–77; election poster, *p566*; foreign policy, 577; Fourteen Points, 596; political ideals, 576–77; regulation of the economy, 567–68; Senate rejection of Treaty of Versailles, 597; views of world peace, 596–97; WWI, 580–83

"windfall" profits tax, 967

Windows operating system, 1013

Winfrey, Oprah, 995

Winslow, Rose, 546, *q546*

Winthrop, John, 67, *q68*, 69, *p69*, *q69*

Wirz, Harry, 368

Wisconsin, 549

Wizard of Oz, 664

Wolfe, Tom, 971

women: abolitionists, 286; activists, 927–28; African American entertainers, 824–25; changing role of, 926–30, 971–72; education of, 276, 281 926–29; feminist movement, 281–82, 926–30; first in space, 998, *p999*; gender discrimination, 927, 928–29; in the fifties, 817; in the military, 585, 741; in the 1920s, 613–14, 617, *g617*; in the workplace, 457, 459, 587, 613–14, 750, 817, 927–28; in WWI, 585, *p585*, 587; in WWII, 741, 750; labor organizers, 456, 459; National Organization for Women, 928; political appointments of, 696, 860, 988, 998; reforms and, 278–79; rights of, 696, 817, 843, 927–29; *Roe v. Wade*, 929; role of, 822, 927, *p927*; suffrage, 204, *p545*, 546, *p546*, 549–51, *m551*; Title IX, 929; trade and, 30; violence against, 1022; voting, 696; wages for 457, 459; wartime and, 276, 585–87, 741, 749–51

Women Airforce Service Pilots (WASPS), 741, *p741*

Women's Army Corps (WAC), 741

Women's Christian Temperance Union, 553

Women's Political Council, 869

Women's Trade Union League, 459

Wood, Colonel Leonard, 531

Wood, Grant, 665

Wood, Jeghro, 295

Wooden, William H., 683

Woodstock, 924, *p924,* 925

Woodward, Bob, 958, 962, *q962*

Worcester v. *Georgia,* 270

workforce, 437, 443–59

working class, 471

Workingman's Party of California, 468

Works Progress Administration (WPA), 691–92, *g692,* 698

World Oil Production, 1004, *g1004, p1004*

World Trade Center, al-Qaeda attack on, 1029, 1031–34, *p1032*; mourning, *p1033, c1034, m1034*

World Trade Organization (WTO), 121, 1024

World War I: Alliance system, 578; Allies, 580, 581, 592–97; American artillery, *p596*; American neutrality, 580–81; American soldiers in Argonne Forest, *p575*; Balkan Crisis, 578; battles of, 592–97, *m594, m595*; Central Powers, 580; combat in, 592–94; declarations of war, 582, 583, *p583*; draft in, 584–85; European alliances, *m579*; federal mobilization agencies, 586–87, *c587*; financing for, 586; "firsts" in, 590; global war, 597; impact of, 599–603; industry during, 587–88; liberties, 588; life in America during, 584–89; military deaths, *c595*; propaganda in, 581, *p586*; sinking of the *Lusitania*, 582, *p582*; submarine warfare, 581–83; Sussex Pledge, 582; Treaty of Versailles, 596–97; Triple Entente, 578, 580; United States curtailment of civil dissolutions of Austro-Hungarian, German Ottoman, Russia Empires, 596–97; Wilson's "Fourteen Points," 596

World War II: African Americans during, *p749,* 750; Allied bombing campaigns, 756, 767–71; Allied force operations, *p735,* 742–47, 755–61, *m760,* 761, 763, *m763, p763;* 767–71; Allied forces land at Omaha Beach, *p735;* America enters, 725–30; American homefront during, 749–54; America mobilization, 736–41; attack on Pearl Harbor, 725, 729; Bataan Death March, 743, *m748;* Battle of Britain, 718; Battle of Midway, *m744,* 745; Battle of Stalingrad, 747, *p747;* Battle of the Atlantic, 746–47; blitzkrieg, 715; bombing of Japan, 743, *p743,* 744; Casablanca Conference, 756; causes of, 708–12, 725–26; collapse of Third Reich, 764–66; creation of International Military Tribune, 772; defeat of Japan, 766–71; Destroyers-for-Bases Deal, 726; domestic effects of, 737, 738, 741, 749, 750, 751, 753, 921, 927, 963; Doolittle Raid, 743, *p743;* friendship of American and Soviet forces, *p765;* German submarine warfare in, 746–47; Germany in ruins, *p779;* Holocaust, 719–24; importance of code breakers, 744; invasion of Guadalcanal, 760, *m760;* invasion of Normandy, 757–59; invasion of Okinawa, 769; invasion of Poland, 713, 714–16; island hopping in the Pacific, 759, *m760;* Italian Campaign, 756–57; Iwo Jima, 767–68; Maginot Line, 716; major issues and events of, 737–74; Mexicans in, 750–51; military and civilian deaths in, *c767, m767;* "Miracle at Dunkirk," 716–17; Navajo Code Talkers, 750–51; Operation Overlord, 757–59, *m762;* propaganda, *p737;* rationing, 753, *p753;* reasons for U.S. involvement in, 708–12, 720–21, 725, 728–30, 900, 901; rebuilding Europe after, 785–86; refugees, *p780;* reparations, 780–82; segregated army, 739; softening the Gustav line, *p756;* soldier of, *p705;* Soviet assault of Stalingrad, *p747;* Tuskeegee Airmen, 740, *p740;* two-front war, 736–37; V-E Day, 766; V-J Day, 771, *p772;* wartime production, *g738, p738, g739, g861;* women and, *p741,* 741, 750

World Wide Web (www), 1014

Wounded Knee, South Dakota, 430, 937

Wozniak, Stephen, 1013, *p1013*

Wright, Frank Lloyd, 469, *q469*

Wright, Wilbur and Orville, 441

Wrigley, William, *q498*

writs, 122, 353; of assistance, 122; of habeas corpus, 353xz

Wyoming, 317, 418, 427, 638

XYZ Affair, 215, 218, *crt218*

Yahoo!, 1015

Yalta Conference, 779–80

Yamamoto, Admiral Isoroku, 744–45, 746, *p746*

Yang, Jerry, 1015, *p1015*

Yannacome, Carol, 939, *p939*

Yeardley, Sir George, 58

yellow journalism, 528

Yeltsin, Boris, 1003

yeoman farmer, 253

yeomen, 87

Yoffeh, Aalmen, *q471*

Yokohama, Japan, *p522*

Yom Kippur, 933

Yom Kippur War, 964

York, Corporal Alvin, 593, *p593*

Yorktown, Battle of, 145

Yoruba, the, 29–30

Young, Andrew, 934, *p934,* 968

Young, Brigham, 276, 297, 299

Young, Jesse Bowman, *q371*

Young Americans for Freedom, 982

Young Men's Christian Association (YMCA), 483–84

youth movement, 920–22, *p921,* 946; roots of, 921; Students for a Democratic Society, 921–22; Supreme Court rulings, 922

Yucatan Peninsula, 51

Yugoslavia, 1020

yuppies, 995, *p995*

Zavala, Lorenzo de, 302, *p302*

Zen, 971, *q971*

Zenger, John Peter, 106

Zhou Enlai, *p951*

Zimmerman telegram, 582

Zionism, 720

zoot suits, 751

Index

Acknowledgments and Photo Credits

Acknowledgments

631 "The Negro Speaks of Rivers" and "I, Too," from *The Collected Poems of Langston Hughes* by Langston Hughes. Copyright © 1994 by the Estate of Langston Hughes. Used by permission of Alfred A. Knopf, a division of Random House, Inc.

773 From *Farewell to Manzanar* by Jeanne Wakatsuki Houston and James D. Houston. Copyright © 1973 by James D. Houston. Reprinted by permission of Houghton Mifflin Company.

1007 From *Hunger of Memory* by Richard Rodriguez (Boston: David R. Godine, Publisher, 1981). Copyright © 1981 by Richard Rodriguez. Reprinted by permission of Georges Borchardt, Inc., for the author.

1054 From *The Grapes of Wrath* by John Steinbeck. Copyright © 1939, renewed 1967 by John Steinbeck. Used by permission of Viking Penguin, a division of Penguin Putnam, Inc.

1055 "Alone and Far Removed" by Audie Murphy. Reprinted by permission of the Estate of Audie Murphy.

1056 "Letter from Birmingham Jail" reprinted by arrangement with the Estate of Martin Luther King, Jr., c/o Writers House, Inc. as agent for the proprietor. Copyright Martin Luther King 1963, copyright renewed 1991 by Coretta Scott King.

1057 From *Barefoot Heart: Stories of a Migrant Child* by Elva Trevino Hart. Reprinted by permission of Bilingual Press.

1078 From "I Have a Dream," reprinted by arrangement with the Estate of Martin Luther King, Jr., c/o Writers House, Inc. as agent for the proprietor. Copyright Martin Luther King 1968, copyright renewed 1996 by Coretta Scott King.

Glencoe would like to acknowledge the artists and agencies that participated in illustrating this program: Morgan Cain & Associates; Ortelius Design, Inc.; and QA Digital.

Photo Credits

Cover: (left to right) (steamboat)Sean Sexton/CORBIS, (covered wagon)David Muench/CORBIS, (Ellis Island)CORBIS, (assembling Model T automobiles) Bettmann/CORBIS, (Asian American holding flag)Catherine Karnow/CORBIS, (express train)Reuters NewMedia Inc./CORBIS, (firemen raising flag)Thomas E. Franklin/Bergen Record/CORBIS Saba, (naturalization ceremony)CORBIS/Bettmann, (child worker)Lewis Hine/CORBIS, (Air Force jet)CORBIS, (Thomas Edison & son)CORBIS/Bettmann, (Martin Luther King Jr.)Robert Mills/CORBIS, (Roberto Clemente, Mulberry Street)CORBIS/Bettmann, (Condoleeza Rice)AFP/CORBIS, (others)PhotoDisc CORBIS; **iv** (tr)Lee Boltin Picture Library; (bl)CORBIS/Bettmann, (br)J. McGrail/H. Armstrong Roberts; **v** (t)Panhandle-Plains Historical Museum, (b)The Library of Congress; **vi** (tl)Michael J. Howell/Stock Boston, (tr)National Air and Space Museum, Smithsonian Institution, (cl)courtesy Baylor University/Wings Across America, (bl)Air Force Museum Foundation, Inc.; **vii** (tr)Picture Research Consultants, (bl bc)Collection of Janice L. and David J. Frent, (br)Collection of Chester Stott/Picture Research Consultants; **viii** CORBIS; **xxii–xxiii** PhotoDisc; **xxiv** CORBIS/Bettmann; **xxv** Courtesy Ford Motor Company; **RA20** PhotoDisc; **1** NASA; **4** (t)PhotoDisc, (b)Mark Newman/Folio, Inc.; **5** (tl)Ron Jautz/Folio, Inc., (tr)PhotoDisc, (inset)David R. Frazier Photolibrary/ Folio, Inc., (bl)Grant Heilman, (br)Picture Research Consultants, (inset)US Geological Survey; **8** CORBIS; **8–9** Courtesy Schwarz Gallery, Philadelphia; **9** Archivo de Indias, Seville, Spain/Mithra-Index/Bridgeman Art Library; **10** (l)Boltin Picture Library, (r)Richard A. Cooke III; **10–11** The City of Plainfield, NJ; **11** (tl)Field Museum of Natural History, Chicago, (tr)The Detroit Institute of Art, Dirk Bakker, (bl)The British Museum, (br)National Maritime Museum; **14** (l)Lee Boltin Picture Library, (r)Runk/Schoenberger from Grant Heilman; **15** Lee Boltin Picture Library; **16** (l)MarkFiennes/ Chequers/Buckinghamshire, UK/Bridgeman Art Library, (r)Richard A. Cooke III; **17** (t)Richard A. Cooke III, (b)Ohio Historical Society; **18** Jacques Cinq-Mars/CMC; **21** Werner Forman Archive/Art Resource, NY; **22** Richard A. Cooke III; **23** The Library of Congress; **24** Picture Research Consultants; **25** (l)CORBIS/Bettmann, (r)Hulton Archive; **27** Smithsonian Institution;

28 (l)Bonhams, London, UK/Bridgeman Art Library, (r)private collection/ Heini Schneebeli/ Bridgeman Art Library; **29** James L. Stanfield; **33** (t)Scala/Art Resource, NY, (b)Bridgeman Art Library; **37** CORBIS; **39** (t)Werner Forman/CORBIS, (b)Canadian Museum of Civilization; **40** (l)National Maritime Museum, London, (r)The British Library; **41** Scala/Art Resource, NY; **42** (l)PhotoDisc, (r)The Thomas Gilcrease Institute of American History and Art, Tulsa OK; **43** Picture Research Consultants; **48** (t)private collection, (b)American Numismatic Society; **48–49** J.D. Bangs/Leiden American Pilgrim Museum; **49** Pilgrim Society; **51** The Oakland Museum; **52** (l)Picture Research Consultants, (r)Higgins Armory Museum; **53** American Museum of Natural History; **54** Chris Corrie Photography; **55** Biblioteca Colombina, Sevilla, Spain; **56** (l)Bushnell-Soifer/Getty Images, (r)Historical Society of Pennsylvania; **60–61** National Maritime Museum, London; **62** National Portrait Gallery, Washington DC; **63** (t)Association for the Preservation of Virginia Antiquities, (b)Virginia State Library, Photographic Collection; **67** Private collection; **68** Berry-Hill Galleries; **69** American Antiquarian Society; **73** Art Resource, NY; **74** (l)file photo, (r)courtesy Jonathan Horne; **82** (l)Association for the Preservation of Virginia Antiquities, Bacon's Castle, Library of Virginia, (r)Philadelphia Museum of Art/photo by Graydon Wood; **82–83** The Warner Collection of Gulf States Paper Corporation, Tuscaloosa, AL; **83** (l)William Gladstone, (r)Josh Nefslay; **86** Picture Research Consultants; **87** The Newberry Library; **88** (l)Inko Production; **88–89** Maggie Steber/CORBIS Saba; **89** National Maritime Museum, London; **90** Exeter City Museum & Art Gallery; **94** (t)The Folger Shakespeare Library, (b)Peabody Essex Museum/photo by Mark Sexton; **97** Miriam & Ira D. Wallach Division of Art, Prints and Photographs, The New York Public Library, Astor Lenox and Tilden Foundation; **99** Miriam & Ira D. Wallach Division of Art, Prints and Photographs, The New York Public Library, Astor Lenox and Tilden Foundation; **101** Courtesy The Massachusetts Historical Society; **102** CORBIS/Bettmann; **103** Museum of Fine Arts, Boston; **105** Philadelphia Museum of Art/photo by Graydon Wood; **106** Josh Nefslay; **109** National Portrait Gallery, London; **112** Charles H. Phillips/Smithsonian Institution; **112–113** Lora Robins Collection of Virginia Art, Virginia Historical Society; **113** Museum of Fine Arts, Boston; **114** Colonial Williamsburg; **114–115** CORBIS; **115** (l)Gwynn M. Kibbe/Stock Boston, (c)The Library of Congress, (r)National Archives; **117** file photo; **118** The Library of Congress; **120** American Antiquarian Society; **121** (t)Picture Research Consultants, (b)Karie Hamilton/CORBIS Sygma; **122** National Portrait Gallery/ Smithsonian Institution/Art Resource, NY; **123** John Carter Brown Library; **124** The Library of Congress; **124–125** PhotoDisc; **125** (l)Kevin Fleming, (r)The Library of Congress; **127** North Wind Picture Archives; **128** CORBIS; **129** J. McGrail/H. Armstrong Roberts; **131** Chicago Historical Society; **132** The Library of Congress; **135** Yale University Art Gallery; **137** CORBIS; **141** The Valley Forge Historical Society; **142** (l)Yale University Art Gallery/ Trumbull Collection, (r)National Portrait Gallery, Washington DC/Art Resource, NY; **143** Archives Division, Texas State Library; **146** The British Library; **149** Courtesy The Massachusetts Historical Society; **151** New York State Historical Association, Cooperstown NY; **152** Collection of The New York Historical Society; **156** All presidential paintings courtesy The White House Historical Association; **156** (l)Picture Research Consultants, (r)National Postal Museum; **156–157** The Library of Congress/American Antiquarian Society; **157** (t)Picture Research Consultants, (b)The New York Historical Society; **160–161** Don Hamerman/Folio, Inc; **161** Joseph Sohm, ChromoSohm, Inc./CORBIS; **165** The Library of Congress; **166** (t)Independence National Historic Park Collection, (b)Fraunces Tavern Museum, New York; **167** Yale University Art Gallery. Gift of Roger Sherman White, BA1859; **168** Library of Philadelphia, Rare Books Room; **173** American Antiquarian Society; **174** (l)The Thomas Gilcrease Museum, Tulsa OK, (r)courtesy Independence National Historic Park Collection; **208** (l)Christie's Images, NY, (c)Smithsonian Institution, (r)Missouri Historical Society; **208–209** CORBIS/Bettmann; **209** Field Museum of Natural History; **211** North Wind Picture Archives; **212 213** Winterthur Museum; **216** The Library of Congress; **217** (l)Independence National Historical Park, (r)Doug Martin; **218** The Library of Congress; **219** Boston Public Library; **222** Courtesy Monticello, photo by Colonial Williamsburg Foundation; **222–223** Maryland

Historical Society; **223** (t)Picture Research Consultants, (b)The Historical Society of Washington, DC; **224** Colorado Historical Society; **227** The Thomas Gilcrease Museum, Tulsa, OK; **229** Smithsonian Institution; **230** Field Museum of Natural History; **232** Anne S.K. Brown, Brown Military Collection/Brown University Library; **234** (tl tr br)National Portrait Gallery, Smithsonian Institution/Art Resource, NY, (bl)Yale University Art Gallery/Trumbull Collection; **236** The New York Historical Society; **236–237** Canajoharie Library & Art Gallery; **237** Gilbert Stuart, 1907. Bowdoin College Museum of Art, Brunswick ME; **238** (l)National Portrait Gallery/Smithsonian Institution/Art Resource, NY, (r)private collection; **238–239** Winterthur Museum; **239** (l)The New York Historical Society, (r)Jack Naylor Collection; **241** (l)New York Historical Society, (r)Greenville County Museum of Art; **242** Washington and Lee University, Lexington VA; **243** The Library of Congress; **246** The Library of Congress; **247** B&O Railroad Museum; **248** Courtesy Jack Naylor; **249** (t)The Metropolitan Museum of Art. Gift of I.N. Phelps Stokes, Edward S. Hawes, Alice Mary Hawes, Marion Augusta Hawes, 1937, (b)Bob Rowan/Progressive Image/CORBIS; **250** The Bicycle Museum of America; **254** (l)The Library of Congress, (r)Fitchburg Art Museum; **255** CORBIS/Bettmann; **256** Picture Research Consultants; **259** The Metropolitan Museum of Art. Gift of I.N. Phelps Stokes, Edward S. Hawes, Alice Mary Hawes, Marion Augusta Hawes, 1937. (37.14.34); **264** (l)David R. Barker/Ohio Historical Society, (r)Concord Museum, Concord MA; **264–265** The Saint Louis Art Museum from the art collections of Bank of America; **265** (l) Collection of Janice L. and David J. Frent, (r)New York Historical Society; **267** (t)Private Collection/National Portrait Gallery, (b)Frank & Marie-Therese Wood/The Picture Bank; **268** CORBIS; **271** The New-York Historical Society; **274** (t)Museum of The City of New York, (b)The Bostonian Society, photo by Mark Sexton; **275** Old Dartmouth Historical Society/New Bedford Whaling Museum; **276** Collection of Constance Fuller Threinen; **279** (l) Museum of the City of New York, Harry T. Peters Collection, (r)The Connecticut Historical Society, Hartford; **280** (t)Massachusetts Historical Society, (bl)Mercer Museum/Bucks County Historical Society, (br)Picture Research Consultants; **281** (t)Ron Huntley, (b)National Museum of American History/Smithsonian Institution; **283** (l)The Connecticut Historical Society, Hartford, (tr)The New York Public Library, Rare Book Department, Astor, Lenox and Tilden Foundations, (br)Aronson/Stock Boston; **285** Massachusetts Historical Society/Picture Research Consultants; **286** CORBIS; **288** Collection of J. Paul Getty Museum; **289** Aaron Haupt; **292** Texas Department of Highways and Public Transportation; **292–293** The Corcoran Gallery of Art, Washington DC. Gift of Mr. and Mrs. Lansdell K. Christie; **293** (l)Lake County Museum/CORBIS, (c)Texas State Library/Archives Division, (r)California State Capitol; **297** (t)National Archives, (b)courtesy Museum of Art, Brigham Young University; **298** (l)Edwards S. Curtis/CORBIS, (r)O. Pierre Havens/CORBIS; **299** (l)The Library of Congress/CORBIS, (r)CORBIS/Bettmann; **301** Center for American History/Barker Collection/University of Texas, Austin; **302** (l)Texas State Library & Archive Commission, photo by Eric Beggs, (r)Texas State Library & Archives Commision #1983/74-1; **303** Texas Department of Transportation; **304** (l)Texas State Library & Archive Commission, photo by Eric Beggs, (r)San Jacinto Museum History Association; **307** Henry Groskinsky; **308** The Library of Congress; **310** Courtesy American Antiquarian Society; **311** The Library of Congress; **313** George H.H. Huey; **316** First Image; **316–317** National Park Service; **317** McLellan Lincoln Collection. Gift of John D. Rockefeller Jr., Class of 1897; **318** Courtesy Wells Fargo Bank; **318–319** Courtesy Robert M. Hicklin Jr., Inc.; **319** (l c) Chicago Historical Society, (r)Fort Sumter National Monument; **321** American Antiquarian Society; **322** California State Library, Sacramento; **323** New York Public Library Print Division; **328** The Library of Congress; **329** Raymond Bial; **330** The Kansas State Historical Society, Topeka; **331** (l)McKissick Museum, (r)CORBIS; **334** Illinois State Historical Library, Old State Capitol; **335** (l)The Supreme Court of the United States Office of the Curator, #1991.402.2, (r)The Library of Congress; **336–337** Henry Horner Lincoln Collection; **338** Boston Athenaeum; **339** (l)CORBIS/Bettmann, (r)The Library Company of Philadelphia; **342** (l)Museum of American Political Life/photo by Steve Laschever, (r)Museum of American Political Life; **343** The Library of Congress; **344** The "Richmond Grays" Valentine Museum/Richmond History Center, VA; **348** (l)Museum of the Confederacy, (r)The Library of Congress; **348–349** Don Troiani, courtesy Historical Art Prints Inc., Southbury CT; **349** Illinois State Historical Library; **351** Kean E. Wilcox Collection; **352** (t)American Numismatic Association, (b)CORBIS; **353** The Library of Congress; **355** (t)Collection of David & Kevin Kyl, (b)Washington & Lee University, VA; **359** (t)The Library of Congress, (b)Chicago Historical Society; **360** The Cincinnati Historical Society; **361** file

photo; **366** Chicago Historical Society; **367** (l)Burns Archive, (r)US Army Military History Institute; **368** National Archives/Picture Research Consultants; **370** The Library of Congress; **371** Al Freni; **372** (l)The Library of Congress, (r)CORBIS; **374** Courtesy Atlanta History Center, Dubose Collection; **375** Steen Cannons, Ashland, KY; (b)Kunstler Enterprises, Ltd. *It's My Fault,* National Geographic Society; **377** The Library of Congress; **378–379** National Archives; **381** Bob Daemmrich; **384** (l)American Museum of Political Life, (r)Collection of Janice L. and David J. Frent; **384–385** Los Angeles County Museum; **385** The Library of Congress; **387** (t)Thaddeus Stevens by Edward Dalton, The Library of the Union League of Philadelphia, photo by Rick Echelmeyer, (b)The Library of Congress; **388** Photographic History Collection, National Museum of American History, Smithsonian Institution; **390** The Library of Congress; **392** (t)Carl Iwasaki/TimePix, (b)CORBIS/ Bettmann; **393** (t)Flip Schulke/Black Star, (b)Reuters NewMedia Inc./CORBIS; **399** (l)Herbert F. Johnson Museum of Art, Cornell University, (r)The Library of Congress; **400** Cook Collection/Valentine Museum; **402** CORBIS; **404** The Library of Congress; **406** Southern Light/Hinklin; **407** CORBIS; **410** Picture Research Consultants; **410–411** Curt Teich Postcard Archives; **411** Mark Steinmetz; **412** (tl)Oakland Museum History Department, (tr)Fenimore House Museum, Cooperstown NY; **412–413** Wyoming Division of Cultural Resources; **413** (tl)CORBIS, (tr)Trustees of the Boston Public Library; **416** (t)Nevada Historical Society, (b)Roy Bishop/Stock Boston; **417** (l)Thomas Gilcrease Museum, Tulsa OK, (r)Montana Historical Society, Helena; **418** (t)Amon Carter Museum, Fort Worth TX, (b)Robert Holmes/CORBIS; **419** Panhandle-Plains Historical Museum; **421** State Historical Society of Wisconsin; **422** (tl)Frank Siteman/Stock Boston, (bl)Doug Martin, (r)Bob Daemmrich/Stock Boston; **426** National Anthropological Archives, Smithsonian Institution; **427** The Library of Congress; **429** Picture Research Consultants; **431** (l)National Portrait Gallery, Smithsonian Institution/Art Resource, NY, (r)Chick Harrity; **434** (l)The New York Historical Society, (r)Chicago Historical Society; **434–435** Private collection; **435** Picture Research Consultants; **437** CORBIS/Bettman; **438** (l)CORBIS/Bettmann, (tr)Smithsonian Institution, (br)Culver Pictures; **439** (l)US Department of the Interior/National Park Service/Edison National Historic Site, (c)Smithsonian Institution, (r)CORBIS/Bettmann; **441** Library of Congress; **443** Union Pacific Railroad Museum; **450** Brown Brothers; **451** New York Stock Exchange; **452** (l)CORBIS, (tr)courtesy Rockefeller Archive Center, (br)CORBIS/Bettmann; **453** (tl)E.O. Hoppe/CORBIS, (bl)PhotoDisc, (tr)file photo; **455** The Library of Congress; **456** CORBIS/ Bettmann; **458** George Meany Memorial Archives; **459** Chicago Historical Society; **462** The Library of Congress; **462–463** Brown Brothers; **463** (l)Doug Martin, (r)CORBIS; **466** Picture Research Consultants; **467** National Archives; **470** (l)The Museum of the City of New York. Gift of Mr. Shirley C. Burden, (r)The Library of Congress; **471** Berry-Hill Galleries; **475** Mark Seider/ National Geographic Society; **477** (t)Brown Brothers, (b)Frank & Marie Wood/The Picture Bank; **478** Museum of Art, Rhode Island School of Design; Jesse Metcalf and Walter H. Kimball Funds; **479** Baseball Hall of Fame Library, Cooperstown NY; **480** Frank Driggs Collection; **483** United Charities Collection/Chicago Historical Society; **485** (l)Brown Brothers, (r)The Library of Congress; **486** Lake County Museum/CORBIS; **487** Bob Daemmrich; **488** (l)Michael J. Howell/Stock Boston, (r)Collection of Janice L. and David J. Frent; **490** (tl)East Carolina University, (tc)Collection of Janice L. and David J. Frent, (tr)Picture Research Consultants; **490–491** E.L. Henry; **491** (l)Amistad Foundation/Wadsworth Athenaeum, (r)Collection of Janice L. and David J. Frent; **493** The Library of Congress; **494** Picture Research Consultants; **495** University of California at Berkeley, Bancroft Library; **496** CORBIS; **497** Picture Research Consultants; **498 499** Brown Brothers; **501** Nebraska State Historical Society; **502** Private collection; **503** (l)Picture Research Consultants, (r)Photograph by Krueger, State Historical Society of Wisconsin; **504** Kansas State Historical Society; **505** Nebraska State Historical Society, Solomon D. Butcher Collection; **506** (l)Nebraska State Historical Society, (r)Ohio Historical Society; **509** Kansas State Historical Society; **510** (t)The Library of Congress, (b)Amistad Foundation/ Wadsworth Athenaeum; **511** Courtesy University of Chicago, Department of Special Collections; **512** Brown Brothers; **513** CORBIS; **516** Collection of Colonel Stuart S. Corning/photo by Rob Huntley/Lightstream; **516–517** West Point Museum/Joshua Nefsky; **517** The Library of Congress; **518** Courtesy US Naval Academy Museum; **518–519** The Library of Congress; **519** (l)Hawaii State Archives, (tr)Picture Research Consultants, (br)The Library of Congress; **522** (t)National Portrait Gallery, Smithsonian Institution/Art Resource, NY, (b)The Library of

Congress; **523** Hawaii State Archives; **526** Bob Rowan, Progressive Image/CORBIS; **528** Picture Research Consultants; **531** Culver Pictures; **532** (t)California Museum of Photography, (b)The Library of Congress; **534** (l)The Library of Congress, (tr)Picture Research Consultants, (br)The Library of Congress; **534–535** CORBIS/Bettmann; **535** (l)The Library of Congress, (r)Michael Ventura/Folio; **538** CORBIS; **538–539** The Mariner's Museum, Newport News VA; **539** Picture Research Consultants; **541** CORBIS; **544** (l)Museum of the City of New York Print Archives, (r)Pelletier Library, Allegheny College, Meadville PA/photo by Bill Owen; **544–545** CORBIS/Bettmann; **545** Sagamore Hill National Historic Site; **547** Picture Research Consultants; **548** CORBIS/Bettmann; **550** Susan B. Anthony House; **551** CORBIS/Bettmann; **552** The Library of Congress; **554** Bob Daemmrich; **556** The Library of Congress; **557** CORBIS; **558** Christie's Images; **559** Collection of the New York Historical Society; **561** (t)CORBIS/Bettmann, (b)The Library of Congress; **563** The Library of Congress; **564** (l)The Library of Congress, (c)Picture Research Consultants, (r)USDA Forest Service, Grey Towers, NHL, Milford PA; **567** National Portrait Gallery, Smithsonian Institution/Art Resource, NY; **568** John Skowronski/Folio; **569** (t)courtesy NAACP; (b)AP/Wide World Photos; **571** (l)Hulton-Deutsch Collection/ CORBIS, (tr br)Chicago Historical Society; **574** (l)Museum of the City of New York. Gift of John Campbell, (r)courtesy Special Collections, Ellis Library, University of Missouri—Columbia; **574–575** CORBIS/ Bettmann; **575** National Archives; **577 578** CORBIS/Bettmann; **580** CORBIS; **582** (t)Picture Research Consultants, (b)The Library of Congress; **583** Picture Research Consultants; **585** National Archives; **586** (l r cl)The Library of Congress, (cr)courtesy Special Collections, Ellis Library, University of Missouri—Columbia; **589** CORBIS/Bettmann; **593** (l)CORBIS/Bettmann, (r)Imperial War Museum; **596** CORBIS; **598** National Portrait Gallery, Smithsonian Institution/Art Resource, NY. Gift of the Hon. Henry Cabot Lodge; **600** CORBIS/Bettmann; **602** Brown Brothers; **603** (l)The Library of Congress, (r)Culver Pictures; **604** CORBIS/Bettmann; **606** Picture Research Consultants; **606–607** Whitney Museum of American Art, New York/photo by Sheldan C. Collins, NJ; **607** National Portrait Gallery, Smithsonian Institution/Art Resource, NY; **608** CORBIS/Bettmann; **608–609** CORBIS; **609** (l)Picture Research Consultants, (c)Langston Hughes National Portrait Gallery, (r)National Air and Space Museum, Smithsonian Institution; **611** The Library of Congress; **614** (l)Smithsonian Institution, (r)Picture Research Consultants, (b)CORBIS; **615** (r)CORBIS/Bettmann; **616** Culver Pictures; **618** Collection of Janice L. and David J. Frent; **618–619** Picture Research Consultants; **619** (t)Picture Research Consultants, (b)CORBIS; **621** Art Institute of Chicago, Friends of American Art Collection; **622** CORBIS/Bettmann; **623** National Archives; **627** Yale Collection of American Literature, Beinecke Rare Book Room and Manuscript Library, Yale University; **628** Frank Driggs Collection; **628–629** Donna Mussenden Van Der Zee. All rights reserved; **629** Brown Brothers; **630** CORBIS/Bettmann; **631** (l)Langston Hughes National Portrait Gallery, (r)Frank Driggs Collection; **634** (l)Collection of Janice L. and David J. Frent, (r)Culver Pictures; **634–635** Museum of the City of New York; **635** (l)CORBIS, (c)Picture Research Consultants; **637** (t c)Collection of Janice L. and David J. Frent, (b)Bettman/CORBIS; **638 639** Culver Pictures; **642** The Library of Congress; **643** (l)CORBIS, (r)Schlesinger Library; **644** Courtesy Frank & Marie-Therese Wood; **646** CORBIS/ Bettmann; **648** CORBIS; **650** Rob Crandall/ Folio; **652** (l)Stanford University Museum of Art; **654** (l)Picture Research Consultants, (r)Museum of American Financial History; **654–655** AP/Wide World Photos; **655** Chicago Historical Society; **657** National Portrait Gallery, Smithsonian Institution/Art Resource, NY; **658** CORBIS/Bettmann; **659** Collection of John P. Axelrod; **660** CORBIS/Bettmann; **662 663 665** The Library of Congress; **667** (l)Robert Cameron/Getty Images, (r)US Department of the Interior/Bureau of Reclamation; **669** Picture Research Consultants; **670** Dorothea Lange Collection, The Oakland Museum of California. The City of Oakland. Gift of Paul S. Taylor; **671** (l)*St. Paul Daily News*/Minnesota Historical Society, (r)AP/Wide World Photos; **672** National Archives and Records Administration/AP/Wide World Photos; **673** Bob Daemmrich; **676** (l)CORBIS/Bettmann, (r)The Library of Congress; **676–677** Courtesy Roosevelt Arts Project/photo by Josh Nefsky; **677** The Equitable Life Assurance Society of the United States; **679** Franklin D. Roosevelt Library; **680** (l)CORBIS/Bettmann, (r)Picture Research Consultants; **681** CORBIS; **683** CORBIS/Bettmann; **684** Picture Research Consultants; **684–685** Tennessee Valley Authority; **685** PhotoDisc; **686** Franklin D. Roosevelt Library; **688** US Forest Service; **690** CORBIS/Bettmann; **691** Franklin D. Roosevelt Library; **693** CORBIS; **696** (l)Franklin D. Roosevelt Library, (r)CORBIS/Bettmann; **697** (l)Franklin D. Roosevelt

Library, (r)Collection of Janice L. and David J. Frent; **698** Peter Arno, 1936, *The New Yorker;* **699** (l)San Diego Historical Society, (r)Brown Brothers; **699–700** Parker Brothers/ National Geographic Society; **700** CORBIS/Bettmann; **704** Collection of Chester Stott/Picture Research Consultants & Archives; **704–705** CORBIS; **705** National Portrait Gallery, Smithsonian Institution/Art Resource, NY; **706** (t)Herbert Hoover Library, (b)Picture Research Consultants; **706–707** TimePix; **707** (l)private collection, (c)National Archives, (r)The Library of Congress; **709** Hulton-Deutsch/Corbis; **710** Archive Photos/Getty Images; **711** Archivo Iconografico, S.A./CORBIS; **712** CORBIS; **714** CORBIS; **717** Hulton/ Archive/Getty Images; **718** The Library of Congress; **720** The Library of Congress; **721** (l)George Fogelson, courtesy US Holocaust Memorial Museum, (r)National Archives, courtesy US Holocaust Memorial Museum; **721 through 723** (background)Mark E. Gibson/CORBIS; **722** Yivo Institute for Jewish Research; **722–723** Yad Vashem Photo Archives, courtesy US Holocaust Memorial Museum; **723** National Archives: Suitland, courtesy US Holocaust Memorial Museum; **726** Chicago Historical Society; **727** (t)Herbert Hoover Library, (b)Thomas McAvoy/*Life*/Time Warner; **729** Picture Research Consultants; **731** CORBIS; **734** (l)private collection, (r)CORBIS/Bettmann; **734–735** Digital Stock; **735** (l c)CORBIS, (r)John Launois/Black Star; **737** Courtesy Smithsonian Institution; **738–739 740** CORBIS/Bettmann; **741** (l)Air Force Museum Foundation, (r)courtesy Baylor University/Wings Across America; **743** Digital Stock, (inset)Norm Avery; **746** (l)Oscar White/CORBIS, (r)CORBIS; **747** Hulton/Archive/Getty Images; **750** National Archives; **752** Toyo Miyatake; **753** (l)Stock Montage, (r)CORBIS/Bettmann; **754** Dr. Seuss Collection/Mandeville Special Collections Library/University of California, San Diego; **756** Texas Military Forces Museum, 36th Infantry Division Gallery, Austin TX; **756–75** CORBIS/Bettmann; **758–759 761** Digital Stock; **763** (l)Robert E. Pratt, (c)Cornelius Ryan Collection of World War II Papers, Alden Library, Ohio University, Athens, (r)CORBIS; **765** CORBIS; **768** Digital Stock; **769** Digital Stock, (inset)Hulton/Archive/Getty Images; **770** National Geographic Society; **770–771** National Geographic Society; **771** Kari Haavisto; **772** Alfred Eisenstaedt/TimePix; **773** (l)Robert Scheer, (r)Digital Stock; **776** National Portrait Gallery, Smithsonian Institution/Art Resource, NY. Gift of Frances O. Tames; **776–777** AP/Wide World Photos; **777** Smithsonian Institution; **779** John Florea/TimePix; **780** American Red Cross; **781** Picture Research Consultants; **785** National Portrait Gallery, Smithsonian Institution. Transfer from National Gallery of Art. Gift of Ailsa Mellon Bruce, 1951; **786** CORBIS/Bettmann; **788** National Archives; **791** CORBIS; **792** CORBIS/Bettmann; **793** (l)Collection of Michael Barson; **794** Robert Phillips/*Life*/Time Warner; **794–795** Getty Images; **799** Ross Lewis Milwaukee Public Library; **801** CORBIS/Bettmann; **803** Courtesy Truman Library; **806** (l)Picture Research Consultants, (r)CORBIS/Bettmann; **806–807** SuperStock; **807** (l)Getty Images, (r)Natural Museum of American History/Smithsonian Instutution; **809** CORBIS; **811** CORBIS/Bettmann; **812** (l)CORBIS, (r)PhotoDisc; **813** (l)TimePix, (tr)courtesy Wig Wam Motel, (br)CORBIS; **815** B. Wiseman/from *Hey, Can't You Forget Business?* by Charles Preston, 1953, E.P. Dutton & Co., Inc.; **817** (t)Computer Museum History Center, (b)Christopher Thomas/Getty Images; **818** CORBIS/ Bettmann; **819** CORBIS; **821** (l br) PhotoFest, (tr)The Kobal Collection; **822** Tom Kelley/Getty Images; **823** Globe Photos; **824** (l)Elliot Erwitt/Magnum Photos, (r)Picture Research Consultants; **825** (l)PhotoFest, (c)National Museum of American History/Smithsonian Institution, (r)Michael Ochs Archives; **829** Chicago Historical Society; **831** National Archives; **832** Danny Lyon/Magnum Photos, Inc.; **833** Private collection; **836** Picture Research Consultants; **836–837** John Eastcott/Yva Momatiuk/Stock Boston; **837** CORBIS/Bettmann; **838** (l)Ohio Historical Society, (r)AP/Wide World Photos; **838–839** Paul Schultzer/ *Life*/TimePix; **839** Collection of Janice L. and David J. Frent; **841** Ohio Historical Society; **842** JFK Library/CORBIS/Sygma; **845** The Supreme Court of the United States Office of the Curator; **848** (l tr)NASA, (br)Picture Research Consultants; **849** (l r)Bill Ingalls/NASA, (c)Lockheed Martin Global Communication; **850** AP/Wide World Photos; **851** John S. Boyer/National Geographic Society; **855 856** AP/Wide World Photos; **857** (l)CORBIS/Bettmann, (t b)Collection of Janice L. and David J. Frent, **860** AP/Wide World Photos; **861** John F. Kennedy Library; **864** CORBIS/ Bettmann; **864–865** Steve Schapiro/TimePix; **865** (l)New York Public Library, (c)CORBIS, (r)Collection of Janice L. and David J. Frent; **867** The Library of Congress; **868** Carl Iwaski/TimePix; **869** Dan Weiner/courtesy Sandra Weiner; **870** CORBIS; **871** Picture Research Consultants; **874** Vic Colley/*Nashville Banner;* **875** CORBIS; **877** Charles Moore 1963/Black Star; **878** (t)Francis Miller/TimePix, (b)Steve Schapiro/

This textbook contains one-stop Internet resources for teachers, students, and parents. Log on to <u>tav.glencoe.com</u> for more information. Online study tools include Chapter Overviews, Self-Check Quizzes, an Interactive Tutor, and E-Flashcards. Online research tools include Student Web Activities, Beyond the Textbook Features, Current Events, Web Resources, and State Resources. The interactive online student edition includes the complete Interactive Student Edition along with textbook updates. Especially for teachers, Glencoe offers an online Teacher Forum, Web Activity Lesson Plans, and Literature Connections.

TIME

PRESIDENT
GEORGE W. BUSH

NOVEMBER 3, 2004

FOUR MORE YEARS

ELECTION ★ NOTEBOOK

BREAKING DOWN THE NATIONAL VOTE

POPULAR VOTE

Kerry 48.5%
Bush 51%

Nader, others: .5%

ELECTORAL VOTE

Kerry 251
Bush 286

Edwards: 1

★ WHERE BUSH HAD THE EDGE ★

White males
Kerry 38%
Bush 61%

Married women
Kerry 45%
Bush 54%

Veterans
Kerry 42%
Bush 57%

Once-a-week churchgoers
Kerry 41%
Bush 58%

★ WHERE KERRY HAD THE EDGE ★

African Americans
Kerry 89%
Bush 11%

Hispanics
Kerry 55%
Bush 42%

First-time voters
Kerry 54%
Bush 45%

Not married
Kerry 59%
Bush 40%

THOSE FOR WHOM TERRORISM WAS THE MOST IMPORTANT ISSUE

Bush 86%
Kerry 14%

THOSE FOR WHOM MORAL VALUES WAS THE MOST IMPORTANT ISSUE

Bush 79%
Kerry 18%

THOSE WHO DISAPPROVE OF THE U.S. DECISION TO GO TO WAR WITH IRAQ

Bush 11%
Kerry 87%

THOSE FOR WHOM THE ECONOMY/JOBS WAS MOST IMPORTANT

Bush 18%
Kerry 80%

Source: National Election Pool exit poll conducted by Edison/Mitofsky. Margin of error is ±3 percentage points for national data and ±4 percentage points for state data.

★ NUMBERS ★

34 Number of states visited by George W. Bush during the presidential campaign

41 Number of states visited by Senator John Kerry

36 Number of visits made by Kerry to Ohio, the most by any candidate to one state

630,000 Total number of TV campaign commercials aired this election season

5,480 Number of campaign ads aired in Florida's Miami-Fort Lauderdale market during October

$1.45 billion Total spent at all levels on campaign advertising this year

$140 million Amount raised during the campaign by liberal 527 groups (non-profit organizations whose goal is to influence elections)

$75 million Amount raised by conservative 527 groups

2,256 Number of lawyers the Democrats sent to Ohio to monitor voting

8 Number of U.N. electoral assistance workers in Iraq

Samantha Appleton/Aurora

Gregory Heisler/Time Life Pictures/Getty Images

"My fellow Americans, this is the most important election of our lifetime."

JOHN KERRY,
Massachusetts Senator, accepting the Democratic nomination for President

"Trying to challenge the two-party dictatorship is like trying to climb a cliff with a slippery rope."

RALPH NADER,
independent candidate, who won less than 1% of national vote

"Jenna and I aren't very political, but we love our Dad too much to watch from the sidelines."

AP Photo/Susan Walsh

BARBARA BUSH,
23, on why she and her twin sister decided to campaign

"We promised ... that every vote would count and that every vote would be counted."

JOHN EDWARDS,
Democratic vice-presidential candidate, at 2:30 a.m. on Nov. 3, 2004, on why Kerry was holding back his concession

"I'll reach out to everyone who shares our goals."

GEORGE W. BUSH,
at his first post-election press conference, Nov. 5, 2004

★ A LOOK AT VOTER TURNOUT ★

More Americans voted for—and against—George W. Bush than for any other presidential candidate in U.S. history, and turnout was higher than in any election since 1968. Among 18- to 24-year-olds, turnout rose by 5.8 percentage points, with nearly 2 million more members of this age group voting than in 2000.

Turnout of Young Voters in Presidential Elections, 1972–2004

1972	1976	1980	1984	1988	1992
52% / 68%	45% / 66%	43% / 66%	44% / 67%	39% / 64%	46% / 67%

■ % of 18- to 24-year-olds who voted
■ % of adults 25 and over who voted

1996	2000	2004
36% / 61%	36.5% / 64%	42.3% / 70%

Source: The Center for Information and Research on Civic Learning and Engagement; 2004 figures are preliminary estimates based on exit polls

★ WHAT HAPPENED IN THE SWING STATES ★

Three of the most intense battles between Kerry and Bush came in Pennsylvania, Ohio, and Florida, key swing states with a total of 68 electoral votes among them. While Kerry won in Pennsylvania, Bush carried Florida and Ohio. A Kerry win in either Florida or Ohio would have given him the White House.

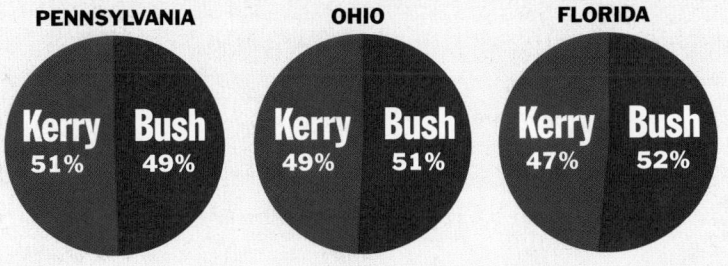

PENNSYLVANIA
Kerry 51% — Bush 49%

OHIO
Kerry 49% — Bush 51%

FLORIDA
Kerry 47% — Bush 52%

ELECTION 2004: THE PRESIDENCY

FOUR MORE YEARS

How the Bush team orchestrated its nail-biting win

By NANCY GIBBS

IN THE END, AN ELECTION that was supposed to be about all the ways the country is divided at least brought Americans together at 193,000 polling places in democracy's messy leap of faith. Turnout was huge even in states where the result was assured. In Ohio the polls closed at 7:30, but the lines were so long that people were still voting at midnight. Some people admitted they just did not want to face their neighbors or their children at the end of the day and say they had not bothered to show up. Others said if you don't vote, you can't complain and did not want to be silent at a time like this.

About 120 million Americans voted, 15 million more than in 2000. When the electoral votes were tallied, Republican George W. Bush had won 286 to Democrat John Kerry's 251. Of the three most hotly contested swing states, Kerry took Pennsylvania, while

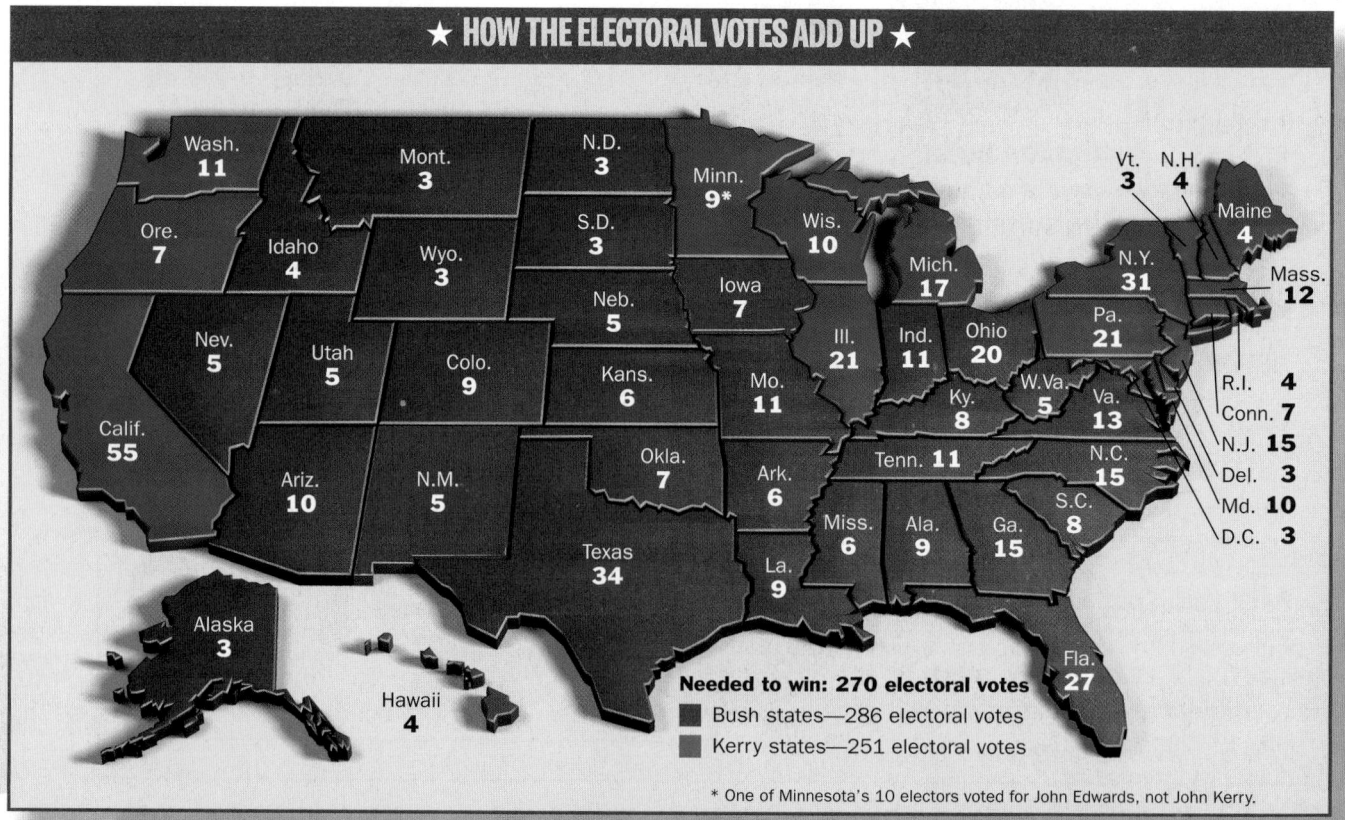

★ HOW THE ELECTORAL VOTES ADD UP ★

Needed to win: 270 electoral votes
Bush states—286 electoral votes
Kerry states—251 electoral votes

* One of Minnesota's 10 electors voted for John Edwards, not John Kerry.

Wash. 11; Ore. 7; Idaho 4; Mont. 3; Wyo. 3; N.D. 3; S.D. 3; Minn. 9*; Wis. 10; Mich. 17; Vt. 3; N.H. 4; Maine 4; N.Y. 31; Mass. 12; Nev. 5; Utah 5; Colo. 9; Neb. 5; Iowa 7; Ill. 21; Ind. 11; Ohio 20; Pa. 21; R.I. 4; Conn. 7; N.J. 15; Del. 3; Md. 10; D.C. 3; Calif. 55; Ariz. 10; N.M. 5; Kans. 6; Mo. 11; Ky. 8; W.Va. 5; Va. 13; N.C. 15; Okla. 7; Ark. 6; Tenn. 11; S.C. 8; Texas 34; La. 9; Miss. 6; Ala. 9; Ga. 15; Alaska 3; Hawaii 4; Fla. 27

Bush snagged Florida and Ohio. Bush also became the first president since 1988 to win a majority of the popular vote, with about 51% to 48.5% for Kerry.

So consider the obstacles Bush overcame to win the hotly contested election. Since the country previously

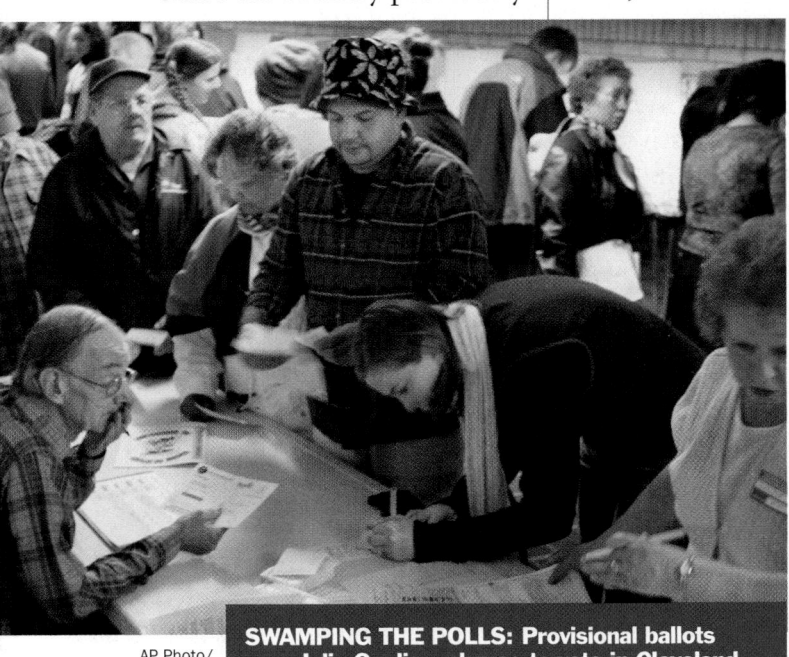

AP Photo/
David Anderson

SWAMPING THE POLLS: Provisional ballots gave Julie Goulis a chance to vote in Cleveland.

met at the polls, voters have encountered a record deficit, job losses, airport shoe searches, rising bankruptcies, and bruising battles over stem-cell research and the definition of marriage. On the eve of Election Day, fully 55% of voters said the country was moving in the wrong direction. Only 49% approved of the job the president was doing, and anything below 50% is supposed to be fatal to an incumbent. A war that Bush promised would cost no more than $50 billion a year

is running at nearly three times that. His character and values were attacked by well-organized detractors throughout the campaign. And he faced an opponent with a long record of public service, decorations from his service during the Vietnam War, and a Democratic base that had never been so united.

Bush says the war on terrorism is not a clash of civilizations, but this campaign was, by his careful design. He never really pretended to have much to say to Democrats beyond I will keep you safe. He relied largely instead on inspiring those who agreed with him already, who want to protect marriage as an institution, think stem-cell research has been oversold, and believe abortion is a sin. Even Republicans who disagreed with him on one or more issues—like the civil libertarians who would like the Patriot Act changed or the fiscal conservatives who worry about the massive national debt—are still willing to side with him.

His 97% approval rate within his party surpassed even Ronald Reagan's. Bush plainly understood that his best weapon against Kerry was less what Bush did than who he was. You may disagree with me, he said at every stop, but you know where I stand.

Overall, Bush succeeded in making Kerry appear an elitist defending moderation at a time when nothing less than passion would do. In Boston at their convention, the Democrats held a somber remembrance of 9/11. A month later in New York City, the Republicans unleashed a battle cry, and the contrast was plain: the party of victims vs. the party of warriors.

For Kerry supporters, there is some consolation that Bush will have to take responsibility for finishing what he started in Iraq. For Bush supporters, there is an obligation to recognize that the intense effort of the other side was as much an expression of love of country as any pledge, hymn, or flag. For people on both sides, there is relief that the day affirmed the sustaining virtue of American democracy. However fierce the battle and however high the stakes, on Election Day citizens go to the polls, close a curtain, and cast their vote—and then go home to honor the outcome because we have only one president at a time.

REPUBLICANS EXTEND CONTROL OF CONGRESS

G.O.P. Strengthens Its Decade-Long Grip on the House, Adds Senate Seats

REPUBLICANS PICKED up seats in both chambers of Congress on Election Day, leaving Speaker Dennis Hastert (R-IL) and Majority Leader Tom DeLay (R-TX) in charge of the House and toppling Tom Daschle (D-SD) from his post as Senate Minority Leader. The key to strengthening G.O.P. control of the House lay in Texas, where four incumbent Democrats lost their seats as a result of a controversial redistricting plan backed by DeLay. This is the sixth consecutive election since 1994 in which Republicans have held a majority in the House.

Democrats had hoped to regain control of the Senate this year but wound up losing ground. They were defeated in several pivotal races, including those in Georgia, South Carolina, North Carolina, Alaska, and Florida. Despite these losses, Senate Democrats will retain enough votes to make it hard for Republicans to pass legislation without opposition. That's because it takes 60 votes to end debate on a bill.

Given the makeup of the new Congress, Republicans say they'll push for approval of measures that have been stalled—including oil exploration in the Arctic National Wildlife Refuge and limits on lawsuits.

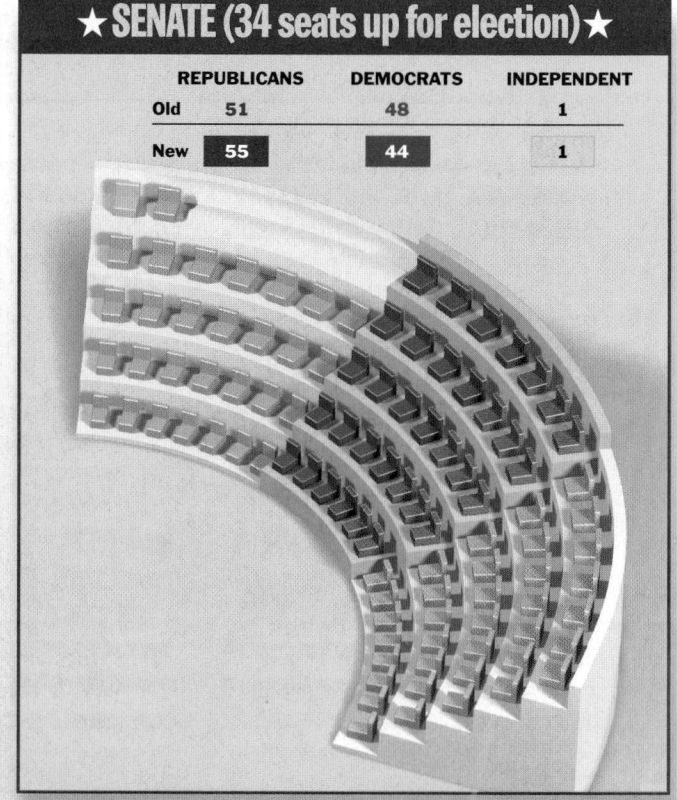

★ HOUSE (All seats up for election) ★

	REPUBLICANS	DEMOCRATS	INDEPENDENT
Old	227	205	1 (2 vacancies)
New	232	202	1

★ SENATE (34 seats up for election) ★

	REPUBLICANS	DEMOCRATS	INDEPENDENT
Old	51	48	1
New	55	44	1

Faces to watch in the 109th Congress

AP Photo/Doug Dreyer

The Giant Killer

Elections are not just about votes. They're also about symbols. And for Senate Republicans, minority leader Tom Daschle has long been Moby Dick. Here was a Democrat from a solidly Republican state, South Dakota, who not only couldn't be defeated but also seemed to emerge from each electoral and legislative battle bigger and more powerful. So when John Thune arrives in Washington, he will not be just another freshman senator. He will be a conquering hero—the man who fulfilled the G.O.P.'s 18-year quest to unseat Daschle.

Thune, a former congressman, ran a profoundly focused race, taking every opportunity to remind voters that Daschle's positions on gun control and abortion set him at odds with "South Dakota values." But he did not bag his big game alone. Majority leader Bill Frist broke with Senate etiquette by visiting South Dakota to campaign for Daschle's ouster. In fact, the last time a Senate leader visited his opposite's state to rail against him was in 1900.

"We're All Connected"

In the past year, Barack Obama, 43, has been compared, in all seriousness, to Abraham Lincoln, Martin Luther King Jr., and Bill Clinton. Democrats debate whether he should run for President in 2012 or 2016. Following a landslide victory on Election Day, Obama became the only African American in the U.S. Senate— and just the third in the past 100 years.

AP Photo/Stephan Savoia

The turning point in Obama's career came in Boston on July 27, 2004, when he delivered one of the best speeches ever heard at a political convention. Facing thousands of Democrats, he spoke of a country not pock-marked by racism or fear— a place in which an African immigrant could marry a Midwestern white woman and their middle-class son could go to Harvard Law School. And he told the cheering crowd that "we're all connected as one people. If there is a child on the South Side of Chicago who can't read, that matters to me . . . If there's an Arab American family being rounded up without benefit of an attorney or due process, that threatens my civil liberties."

The Tough-Talking Cuban

When Cuban parents launched Operation Pedro Pan in 1960, they were trying to get their children safely out of Cuba and into the U.S. Nobody knew then that one of those children—Mel Martinez— would go on to become the first Cuban American elected to the U.S. Senate. Martinez, now 58, served as Secretary of Housing and Urban Development from 2001 to 2003 and received strong support from the White House and Florida Governor Jeb Bush.

AP Photo/Chris Omeara

An Advocate for Children

As a state senator, Allyson Schwartz was called the "Mother of Pennsylvania Children's Health Insurance" for devising an insurance plan that many states later copied. Now she hopes to pass similar legislation on the federal level. Schwartz is one of 65 women who will serve in the House—a gain of five from the 108th Congress. Among the new faces are Melissa Bean (D-IL), who unseated Philip Crane, the longest-serving Republican in the House; and Gwen Moore (D-WI), the first African American to represent Wisconsin.

Courtesy Allyson Schwartz